May 31–June 4, 2015
Melbourne, Victoria, Australia

Association for
Computing Machinery

Advancing Computing as a Science & Profession

SIGMOD'15

Proceedings of the 2015 ACM SIGMOD International Conference on Management of Data

Sponsored by:

ACM SIGMOD

Supported by:

Microsoft, Oracle, Facebook, Google, IBM, SAP, Tableau, Twitter, Intel, RMIT University, NEC, Morgan & Claypool, and Elsevier

Association for
Computing Machinery

Advancing Computing as a Science & Profession

The Association for Computing Machinery
2 Penn Plaza, Suite 701
New York, New York 10121-0701

ISBN: 978-1-4503-2758-9 (Digital)

ISBN: 978-1-4503-3863-9 (Print)

Additional copies may be ordered prepaid from:

ACM Order Department
PO Box 30777
New York, NY 10087-0777, USA

Phone: 1-800-342-6626 (USA and Canada)
+1-212-626-0500 (Global)
Fax: +1-212-944-1318
E-mail: acmhelp@acm.org
Hours of Operation: 8:30 am – 4:30 pm ET

Printed in the USA

Welcome Message from the SIGMOD Chairs

Welcome to SIGMOD 2015 – officially, the 2015 ACM SIGMOD International Conference on the Management of Data! This year's conference is being held in the beautiful cultural capital of Australia, Melbourne. During the Gold Rush period of the 19th Century, Melbourne was the richest city in the world, and as a result it is filled with many unique neighborhoods and distinctive buildings. In addition to wonderful neighborhoods to explore, the city has great museums and other cultural attractions, as well as a fine multi-cultural atmosphere. For those who would like to explore the outdoors, popular highlights are the Phillip Island Nature Park (90 minutes away), which features wild penguins who return in a parade each day at sunset, and the Great Ocean Road, one of the world's most scenic coastal drives, including the famous towering 12 Apostles.

SIGMOD 2015's exciting technical program reflects not only traditional topics, but the database community's role in broader data science and data analytics. The keynote from Laura Haas, "The Power Behind the Throne: Information Integration in the Age of Data-Driven Discovery" highlights the role of database and data integration techniques in the growing field of data science. Jignesh Patel's talk, "From Data to Insights @ Bare Metal Speed," explains how hardware and software need to be co-evolved to support the needs of scalable data analytics. Jennifer Widom, winner of the 2015 ACM-W Athena Lecturer Award for fundamental contributions to computer science, will give her award talk, "Three Favorite Results," on Tuesday. Christopher Ré will lead a panel on "Machine Learning and Databases: The Sound of Things to Come or a Cacophony of Hype?," with participants Divyakant Agrawal, Magdalena Balazinska, Michael Cafarella, Michael Jordan, Tim Kraska, and Raghu Ramakrishnan. Of course, there are also 106 research paper presentations, 4 tutorials, 30 demonstrations, and 18 industrial papers. Papers will be presented both as talks during the research sessions, and as part of plenary Poster Sessions.

SIGMOD 2015 is preceded by the PhD Workshop, as well as workshops on leading-edge topics like data analytics (DanaC), databases and the Web (WebDB), exploratory search (ExploreDB), managing and mining spatial data (GeoRich), and graph data (GRADES); the New Researcher Symposium will take place on Wednesday. The banquet will be held in a Melbourne landmark, the Town Hall.

We are grateful to the many researchers who have shaped the conference program. Specific thanks go to the keynotes chair, Renée Miller; the panel chairs, Michael Franklin and Tova Milo; the tutorial chair, Wenfei Fan; the industrial program chairs, Sihem Amer-Yahia and Christopher Olston, as well as the industrial program committee members; the demonstrations chairs, Vanessa Braganholo and Juliana Freire, as well as the demonstration program committee members; the workshops chairs, Anastasia Ailamaki and Yi Chen; the undergraduate research chairs, Anisoara Nica and Anastasios Kementsietsidis; and the New Researcher Symposium chairs, Julia Stoyanovich and Alexandria Meliou. We would also like to express our immense gratitude to the members of the SIGMOD 2015 program committee and especially the "Group Leaders" who helped oversee the review process: Alin Deutsch, Yanlei Diao, Jens Dittrich, Luna Dong, Hank Korth, Alexandros Labrinidis, Feifei Li, Dan Olteanu, Jignesh Patel, Sunita Sarawagi, Pierre Senellart, Wang-Chiew Tan, Jun Yang, and Xiaofang Zhou.

As in recent years, we had two submission deadlines for SIGMOD this year, one in August and one in November. The review process was journal-style, with multiple rounds of reviews coordinated by the Group Leaders. We accepted 34 of 137 papers from the first deadline and 72 of 278 from the second deadline. The total acceptance rate was about 25.5%, and we believe that the revision process has improved the quality of the technical program.

We thank the members of the SIGMOD 2015 organizing committee, as well as the SIGMOD Executive Committee, for their invaluable help and guidance throughout the process leading up to the conference. The team includes the finance chair Xiuzhen Jenny Zhang, the publicity and social media chairs Egemen Tanin and Jagan Sankaranarayanan, the sponsorship chairs Nick Koudas and Mohamed Mokbel, the local arrangements chair Yanchun Zhang, the registration chair Arkady Zaslavsky, the demonstration and workshop local arrangements chair Benjamin Rubinstein, the web/information chair Kai (Kevin) Zheng, the travel award committee chairs Alexandra Meliou and Eugene Wu, the programming contest chair Thomas Neumann, and the wonderful team of ICE Australia who supported the whole organization. We also extend our appreciation to the student volunteers – the success of this conference is impossible without their hard work and dedication. Finally, we benefited from a great deal of advice and help from Tamer Ozsu, as a former Program Chair, and K. Selçuk Candan, as both a liaison to the SIGMOD Executive and as a former SIGMOD General Chair. We are also grateful to the Microsoft Research Conference Management Toolkit (CMT) team for their extremely prompt and helpful support throughout the complex conference reviewing process.

We thank the many SIGMOD 2015 supporters, whose contributions helped to keep the conference registration fees manageable, particularly for student attendees. Sponsors include: Platinum Level – Microsoft and Oracle; Gold Level – Facebook, Google, IBM Research, SAP, Tableau, and Twitter; and Silver Level – Intel and RMIT University. NEC has also supported SIGMOD 2015. Finally, Microsoft, Google, the National Science Foundation and the SIGMOD Executive Committee have generously financially the SIGMOD 2015 student travel award program.

Welcome to Melbourne, and we hope you enjoy the conference!

Timos Sellis
General Chair

Susan Davidson & Zachary Ives
Program Co-Chairs

Huiping Cao & Xiang Lian
Proceedings Co-Chairs

Table of Contents

Research Session 5 – Keyword Search and Text

Research Session 6 – Graph Primitives

Research Session 7 – Data Mining

Research Session 8 – Uncertainty and Linking

Research Session 10 – Privacy

Research Session 11 – Streams

Session: Demo A

Session: Demo B

Research Session 14 – Indexing & Performance

Research Session 15 – Data Cleaning

Session: Demo C

Research Session 17 – Hardware-Aware Query Processing

Research Session 18 – Graph Propagation, Influence, Mining

Research Session 19 – Social Networks

Industry Session 4 – Performance

Tutorial 3

Research Session 20 – Information Extraction and Record Linking

Research Session 21 – RDF and SPARQL

Research Session 22 – Time Series & Graph Processing

Industry Session 5 – Usability

Research Session 23 – Advanced Query Processing

Research Session 24 – New Models

Tutorial 4

Undergraduate Abstracts

SIGMOD 2015 Conference Organization

General Chair:	Timos Sellis (RMIT University, Australia)
Program Chairs:	Susan B. Davidson (University of Pennsylvania, USA) Zack Ives (University of Pennsylvania, USA)
Proceedings Chairs:	Huiping Cao (New Mexico State University, USA) Xiang Lian (University of Texas - Pan American, USA)
Tutorial Chair:	Wenfei Fan (University of Edinburgh, UK)
Keynotes Chair:	Renée Miller (University of Toronto, Canada)
Panels Chairs:	Michael Franklin (University of California, Berkeley, USA) Tova Milo (Tel Aviv University, Israel)
Industrial Program Chairs:	Sihem Amer-Yahia (CNRS, Grenoble, France) Christopher Olston (Google, USA)
Demonstration Chairs:	Vanessa Braganholo (Universidade Federal Fluminense, Brazil) Juliana Freire (New York University, USA)
Workshops Chairs:	Anastasia Ailamaki (Ecole Polytechnique Federale de Lausanne, Switzerland) Yi Chen (New Jersey Institute of Technology, USA)
Undergraduate Research Chairs:	Anisoara Nica (SAP) Anastasios Kementsietsidis (Google)
New Researcher Symposium Chairs:	Julia Stoyanovich (Drexel University, USA) Alexandra Meliou (University of Massachusetts Amherst, USA)
Finance Chair:	Xiuzhen Jenny Zhang (RMIT University, Australia)
Publicity and Social Media Chairs:	Egemen Tanin (University of Melbourne, Australia) Jagan Sankaranarayanan (NEC Labs America, USA)
Sponsorship Chairs:	Nick Koudas (University of Toronto, Canada) Mohamed Mokbel (University of Minnesota, USA)
Programming Contest Chair:	Thomas Neumann (Technische Universität München, Germany)
Local Arrangements Chair:	Yanchun Zhang (Victoria University, Australia)

Registration Chair: Arkady Zaslavsky (CSIRO, Australia)

Demonstration and Workshop Local Arrangements Chair: Benjamin Rubinstein (University of Melbourne, Australia)

Travel Award Selection Committee Chairs: Alexandra Meliou (University of Massachusetts Amherst, USA)
Eugene Wu (Massachusetts Institute of Technology, USA)

Web/Information Chair: Kai (Kevin) Zheng (The University of Queensland, Australia)

Program Committee Group Leaders: Alin Deutsch (University of California, San Diego, USA)
Yanlei Diao (University of Massachusetts, Amherst, USA)
Jens Dittrich (Saarland University, Germany)
Luna Dong (Google, USA)
Hank Korth (Lehigh University, USA)
Alex Labrinidis (University of Pittsburgh, USA)
Feifei Li (University of Utah, USA)
Dan Olteanu (University of Oxford, UK)
Jignesh Patel (University of Wisconsin, USA)
Sunita Sarawagi (Indian Institute of Technology, Bombay, India)
Pierre Senellart (Telecom ParisTech, France)
Wang-Chiew Tan (University of California, Santa Cruz, USA)
Jun Yang (Duke University, USA)
Xiaofang Zhou (University of Queensland, Australia)

Program Committee Members: Yanif Ahmad (Johns Hopkins University, USA)
Reza Akbarinia (INRIA Sophia Antipolis, France)
Magda Balazinska (University of Washington, USA)
Zhuowei Bao (Facebook, USA)
Pablo Barcelo (Universidad de Chile, Chile)
Srikanta Bedathur (Indraprastha Institute of Information Technology, Delhi, India)
Spyros Blanas (Ohio State University, USA)
Philip Bohannon (Facebook, USA)
Stephane Bressan (National University of Singapore, Singapore)
Michael Cafarella (University of Michigan, USA)
K. Selçuk Candan (Arizona State University, USA)
Badrish Chandramouli (Microsoft Research, USA)
Shimin Chen (Chinese Academy of Science, China)
Lei Chen (The Hong Kong University of Science & Technology, China)
James Cheng (The Chinese University of Hong Kong, China)
Alvin Cheung (Massachusetts Institute of Technology, USA)

Program Committee Members (continued):

Fei Chiang (McMaster University, Canada)
Rada Chirkova (North Carolina State University, USA)
John Cieslewicz (Google, USA)
Sarah Cohen-Boulakia (LRI Université Paris Sud, France)
Dario Colazzo (Université Paris-Dauphine, France)
Tyson Condie (University of California, Los Angeles, USA)
Bin Cui (Peking University, China)
Antonios Deligiannakis (Technical University of Crete, Greece)
Amol Deshpande (University of Maryland, USA)
Daniel Deutch (Tel Aviv University, Israel)
Eduard Dragut (Temple University, USA)
Alan Fekete (University of Sydney, Australia)
Avrilia Floratou (IBM Almaden, USA)
Tim Furche (University of Oxford, UK)
Minos Garofalakis (Technical University of Crete, Greece)
Wolfgang Gatterbauer (Carnegie Mellon University, USA)
Tingjian Ge (University of Massachusetts, Lowell, USA)
Boris Glavic (Illinois Institute of Technology, Chicago, USA)
TJ Green (LogicBlox, USA)
Torsten Grust (University of Tübingen, Germany)
Carmem Hara (Universidade Federal do Parana, Brazil)
Michael Hay (Colgate University, USA)
Melanie Herschel (University Paris-Sud 11, France)
Vagelis Hristidis (University of California, Irvine, USA)
Panos Ipeirotis (New York University, USA)
Chris Jermaine (Rice University, USA)
Alekh Jindal (Massachusetts Institute of Technology, USA)
Panagiotis Karras (Skoltech, Russia)
Gjergji Kasneci (Hasso-Plattner-Institute, Germany)
Tasos Kementsietsidis (IBM Research, USA)
Oliver Kennedy (University at Buffalo, USA)
Martin Kersten (Centrum Wiskunde & Informatica, Netherlands)
Daniel Kifer (Pennsylvania State University, USA)
George Kollios (Boston University, USA)
Tim Kraska (Brown University, USA)
Wolfgang Lehner (Technische Universität Dresden, Germany)
Chengkai Li (University of Texas, Arlington, USA)
Guoliang Li (Tsinghua University, China)
Lipyeow Lim (University of Hawaii at Manoa, USA)
Xuemin Lin (University of New South Wales, Australia)
Chengfei Liu (Swinburne University of Technology, Australia)
Jiaheng Lu (Renmin University of China, China)
Qiong Luo (The Hong Kong University of Science and Technology, China)
Ashwin Machanavajjhala (Duke University, USA)

Program Committee Members (continued):

Nikos Mamoulis (University of Hong Kong, China)
Silviu Maniu (University of Hong Kong, China)
Amelie Marian (RutgersUniversity, USA)
Davide Martinenghi (Politecnico di Milano, Italy)
Sharad Mehrotra (University of California, Irvine, USA)
Alexandra Meliou (University of Massachusetts, USA)
Xiaofeng Meng (Renmin University of China, China)
Ahmed Metwally (Google, USA)
Sebastian Michel (Saarland University, Germany)
Arnab Nandi (Ohio State University, USA)
Thomas Neumann (Technische Universität München, Germany)
Fatma Özcan (IBM research, USA)
Olga Papaemmanouil (Brandeis University, USA)
Stelios Paparizos (Microsoft Research, USA)
Aditya Parameswaran (University of Illinois at Urbana-Champaign, USA)
Srinivasan Parasarathy (Ohio State University, USA)
Andy Pavlo (Carnegie Mellon University, USA)
Rachel Pottinger (University of British Columbia, Canada)
Nicoleta Preda (University of Versailles, France)
Li Qian (Facebook)
Jorge Quiané-Ruiz (Qatar Computing Research Institute, Qatar)
Rajeev Rastogi (Amazon, USA)
Chris Ré (Stanford University, USA)
Juan Reutter (Pontificia Universidad Católica de Chile, Chile)
Sudeepa Roy (University of Washington, USA)
Senjuti B Roy (University of Washington Tacoma, USA)
Elke A Rundensteiner (Worcester Polytechnic Institute, USA)
Florin Rusu (University of California, Merced, USA)
Cyrus Shahabi (University of Southern California, USA)
Mohamed A Sharaf (University of Queensland, Australia)
Dennis Shasha (New York University, USA)
Michael Spear (Lehigh University, USA)
Julia Stoyanovich (Drexel University, USA)
Kian-Lee Tan (National University of Singapore, Singapore)
Nan Tang (Qatar Computing Research Institute, Qatar)
Yufei Tao (The Chinese University of Hong Kong, China)
Nesime Tatbul (Massachusetts Institute of Technology, USA)
Evimaria Terzi (Boston University, USA)
Martin Theobald (University of Antwerp, Belgium)
Dimitrios Theodoratos (New Jersey Institute of Technology, USA)
Dimitrios Tsoumakos (National Technical University of Athens, Greece)
Vasilis Vassalos (Athens University of Economics and Business, Greece)
Marcos Vaz Salles (University of Copenhagen - DIKU, Denmark)

Program Committee Members (continued):

Stratis Viglas (University of Edinburgh, UK)
Haixun Wang (Google Inc., USA)
Steven E Whang (Google Inc., USA)
Sai Wu (Zhejiang University, China)
Yinghui Wu (University of California, Santa Barbara, USA)
Melanie Y Wu (Indiana University, USA)
Kuixiao Xiao (Nanyang Technological University, Singapore)
Jianliang Xu (Hong Kong Baptist University, China)
Ke Yi (The Hong Kong University of Science & Technology, China)
Cong Yu (Google, USA)
Wenyuan Yu (Facebook, USA)
Jeffrey Xu Yu (The Chinese University of Hong Kong, China)
Carlo Zaniolo (University of California, Los Angeles, USA)
Demetris Zeinalipour (University Cyprus, Cyprus)
Rui Zhang (University Melbourne, Australia)
Baihua Zheng (Singapore Management University, Singapore)
Kai Zheng (The University of Queensland, Australia)

Tutorial Program Committee Members:

Philip Bohannon (Facebook, USA)
Floris Geerts (University of Antwerp, Belgium)
Felix Naumann (Hasso Plattner Institut, Germany)
Meral Ozsoyoglu (Case Western Reserve University, USA)
Tamer Özsu (University of Waterloo, Canada)
Jignesh Patel (University of Wisconsin, USA)
Divesh Srivastava (AT&T Labs, USA)
Haixun Wang (Google, USA)

Demonstration Program Committee Members:

Amr El Abbadi (University of California Santa Barbara, USA)
Serge Abiteboul (INRIA, France)
Medha Atre (University of Pennsylvania, USA)
Luciano Barbosa (IBM Research, Brazil)
Yi Chen (New Jersey Institute of Technology, USA)
Sara Cohen (The Hebrew University of Jerusalem, Israel)
Eli Cortez (Microsoft Research, USA)
Lois Delcambre (Portland State, USA)
Boris Glavic (IIT Chicago, USA)
Todd Green (LogicBlox, USA)
Carmem Hara (Universidade Federal do Paraná, Brazil)
Thomas Heinis (Imperial College, UK)
Stratos Idreos (Harvard, USA)
Dmitri V. Kalashnikov (University of California Irvine, USA)
Verena Kantere (University of Geneva, Switzerland)

Demonstration Program Committee Members (cont'd):
Yannis Katsis (University of California San Diego, USA)
David Koop (UMass-Dartmouth, USA)
Flip Korn (Google Research)
Georgia Koutrika (HP Labs, USA)
Chao Li (Google Inc., USA)
Ashwin Machanavajjhala (Duke University, USA)
Ioana Manolescu (INRIA, France)
Yannis Manolopoulos (Aristotle University of Thessaloniki, Greece)
Paolo Merialdo (Universita Roma Tre, Italy)
Mirella Moro (Universidade Federal de Minas Gerais, Brazil)
Mario Nascimento (University of Alberta, Canada)
Eduardo Ogasawara (CEFET/RJ, Brazil)
Daniel Oliveira (Universidade Federal Fluminense, Brazil)
Andy Pavlo (Carnegie Mellon University, USA)
Lucian Popa (IBM Research, USA)
Maya Ramanath (IIT Delhi, India)
Sudeepa Roy (University of Washington, USA)
Yasin N. Silva (Arizona State University, USA)
Emad Soroush (GraphLab Inc, USA)
Valéria Times (Universidade Federal de Pernambuco, Brazil)
Ricardo Torres (UNICAMP, Brazil)
Pinar Tozun (EPFL, Switzerland)
Huy Vo (New York University, USA)
Xiaochun Yang (Northeastern University, China)
Wenchao Zhou (Georgetown University, USA)

Industrial Program Committee Members:
Jose Blakeley (Microsoft)
Paul Brown (Paradigm 4)
Ed H. Chi (Google, USA)
Carlo Curino (Microsoft)
Shel Finkelstein (University of California Santa Cruz)
Stratos Idreos (Harvard University, USA)
Mohsen Jamali (WalmartLabs)
Grigoris Karvounarakis (LogicBlox, Greece)
Donald Kossmann (ETH Zurich)
Benjamin Reed (Facebook)
Jean-Michel Renders (Xerox Labs, France)
Philippe Rigaux (Internet Memory, France)
Mehul Shah (Amiato)
Eric Simon (SAP, France)
Theo Vassilakis (Metanautix)
Todd Walter (Teradata)
Ken Yocum (Illumina)

Additional reviewers

(In alphabetical order by Last Name):

Afsin Akdogan
Cem Aksoy
Peter Alvaro
Panayiotis Andreou
Vaibhav Arora
Joy Arulraj
Mohammad Asghari
Ramoza Ashan
Andreas Behrend
Souvik Bhattacherjee
Panagiotis Bouros
Matteo Brucato
Francesca Bugiotti
Damian Bursztyn
Lei Cao
Bogdan Cautis
Aniket Chakrabarty
Lijun Chang
Georgios Chatzimilioudis
Amit Chavan
Muhammad Aamir Cheema
Rui Chen
Yan Chen
Shiwen Cheng
Yu Cheng
Shumo Chu
Eleonora Ciceri
Andrew Crotty
Mahashweta Das
Ananya Dass
Dingxiong Deng
Dong Deng
Aggeliki Dimitriou
Katerina Doka
S.M. Faisal
Liyue Fan
Ioannis Flouris
David Fuhry
Alexander Galakatos
Yihan Gao
Theodore Georgiou
Nikos Giatrakos
Anastasios Gounaris
Eric Gribkoff
Sairam Gurajada
Samuel Haney
Sona Hasani
Naeemul Hassan
Xi He
Zhenying He
Haibo Hu
Huiqi Hu
Silu Huang
Weihuang Huang
Xin Huang
Yuzheng Huang
Zengfeng Huang
Sergey Ivanov
Srini Iyer
Ayush Jain
Nandish Jayaram
Lilong Jiang
Niranjan Kamat
Zoi Kaoudi
Konstantinos Karanasos
Ashwin Kayyoor
Udayan Khurana
Albert Kim
Georgios Kollias
Ios Kotsogiannis
Christos Laoudias
Chuan Lei
Jianxin Li
Jinfeng Li
Yafei Li
Yaguang Li
Xiang Lian
Xika Lin
Miguel Liroz Gistau
Yi Lu
Ying Lu
Gerasimos Marketos
Thomas Marshall
Julian McAuley
Rui Meng
Xianrui Meng
Umar Farooq Minhas
Prasenjit Mitra

Additional reviewers (continued):

Jayanta Mondal
Tobias Müller
Faisal Nawab
Apostolos Papadopoulos
Nikolaos Papailiou
Huy Pham
Yann Ponty
Olga Poppe
Mohiuddin Abdul Qader
Li Qian
Chengjie Qin
Lu Qin
Teng Qin
Abdul Quamar
Nisarg Raval
Medhabi Ray
Alexandra Roatis
Yiye Ruan
Shouq Sadah
Cetin Sahin
Zechao Sang
Carlo Sartiani
Rebeca Schroeder
Vivek Shah
Moloud Shahbazi
Anil Shanbhag
Yingxia Shao
Jieming Shi
Juwei Shi
Yanchen Shi
Lefteris Sidirourgos
Afroza Sultana
Youze Tang
Yu Tang
Hien To
Yongxin Tong
Tassos Venetis
Domagoj Vrgoc
Chi Wang
Jingjing Wang
Sibo Wang
Wei Wang
Xiang Wang
Xiaolan Wang
Xiaoyang Wang
Zhengkui Wang
Mingrui Wei
Zhewei Wei
Zeyi Wen
Matthew Wiley
Huanhuan Wu
Xiaoying Wu
Yingjun Wu
Qin Xiao
Jie Xu
Da Yan
Fan Yang
Shiyu Yang
Erfan Zamanian
Stamatis Zampetakis
Gensheng Zhang
Jun Zhang
Xiaofei Zhang
Yang Zhang
Ying Zhang
Rui Zhou
Haohan Zhu
Linhong Zhu
Honglei Zhuang
Zhongfang Zhuang
George Zois
Zainab Zolaktaf
Andreas Zuefle

SIGMOD 2015 Sponsor & Supporters

Sponsor:

Platinum Supporters:

Gold Supporters:

Silver Supporters:

Other Supporters:

Platinum Publisher:

MORGAN & CLAYPOOL PUBLISHERS

Gold Publisher:

ELSEVIER

Private Release of Graph Statistics using Ladder Functions

Jun Zhang[1] Graham Cormode[2] Cecilia M. Procopiuc[3*] Divesh Srivastava[4] Xiaokui Xiao[1]

[1]Nanyang Technological University
{jzhang027, xkxiao}@ntu.edu.sg

[2]University of Warwick
g.cormode@warwick.ac.uk

[3]Google Inc.
mpro@google.com

[4]AT&T Labs – Research
divesh@research.att.com

ABSTRACT

Protecting the privacy of individuals in graph structured data while making accurate versions of the data available is one of the most challenging problems in data privacy. Most efforts to date to perform this data release end up mired in complexity, overwhelm the signal with noise, and are not effective for use in practice. In this paper, we introduce a new method which guarantees differential privacy. It specifies a probability distribution over possible outputs that is carefully defined to maximize the utility for the given input, while still providing the required privacy level. The distribution is designed to form a 'ladder', so that each output achieves the highest 'rung' (maximum probability) compared to less preferable outputs. We show how our ladder framework can be applied to problems of counting the number of occurrences of subgraphs, a vital objective in graph analysis, and give algorithms whose cost is comparable to that of computing the count exactly. Our experimental study confirms that our method outperforms existing methods for counting triangles and stars in terms of accuracy, and provides solutions for some problems for which no effective method was previously known. The results of our algorithms can be used to estimate the parameters of suitable graph models, allowing synthetic graphs to be sampled.

Categories and Subject Descriptors

H.2.7 [**Database Administration**]: Security, integrity & protection

Keywords

Differential privacy; subgraph counting; local sensitivity

1. INTRODUCTION

A large amount of private data can be well-represented by graphs. Social network activities, communication patterns, disease transmission, and movie preferences have all been encoded as graphs, and studied using the tools of graph theory. Given the private nature of the information stored in graphs, and the increasing pressure to allow controlled release of private data, there has been much interest in ways to do so with some guarantee of anonymity.

The current locus of privacy work is around differential privacy. The model is popular, since it offers both provable properties on the results and practical algorithms to provide them. It is a statistical model of privacy which ensures that the output of the process undergoes sufficient perturbation to mask the presence or absence of any individual in the input. This model is very effective for releasing data in the form of histograms or counts, since the magnitude of the statistical noise is often dominated by random variation in the data. Applying this model to graph data has proven much more fraught. The main technical roadblock is that direct application of standard methods seems to require such a large scale of random modification of the graph input as to completely lose all its properties. Concretely, any method which tries to directly output a modified version of the input graph under differential privacy is indistinguishable from random noise.

Instead, progress has been made by focusing on releasing properties of the input graph under differential privacy, rather than the graph itself. For example, it is straightforward to release the number of nodes and edges with this guarantee, by appealing to standard techniques. It is valuable to find statistical properties of the graph, since there are many random graph models which take these as parameters (e.g., Kronecker graph models [26] and Exponential Random Graph Models [17]), and allow us to sample graphs from this family, which should have similar properties to the input graph. The properties of the graph are also important in their own right, determining, for instance, measures of how much clustering there is in the graph, and other characteristics of group behavior. See the discussion in [17], and references therein.

The problem then becomes one of providing effective ways to release statistics on the input graph privately. The most important statistics are *subgraph counts*: the number of occurrences of particular small subgraphs within the input graph. This remains a challenging problem, since standard differential privacy techniques still add a large amount of noise to the result. Take as a canonical problem the question of counting the number of triangles within a graph. The presence or absence of one relationship (represented by an edge) in the graph can contribute to a large number of potential triangles, and so the noise added to the count has to be scaled up by this amount. There have been numerous prior attempts to privately release statistics on graphs via more complex methods, but these still suffer from high noise, and high running time.

In this paper, we introduce a new technique for producing differentially private output, which is applied to the problem of producing subgraph counts. The technique builds upon ideas from differential privacy, specifically notions of the "sensitivity" of a function, and sampling possible output values using the exponential mecha-

*Author worked on this result while she was at AT&T Labs.

SIGMOD'15, May 31–June 4, 2015, Melbourne, Victoria, Australia.

http://dx.doi.org/10.1145/2723372.2737785

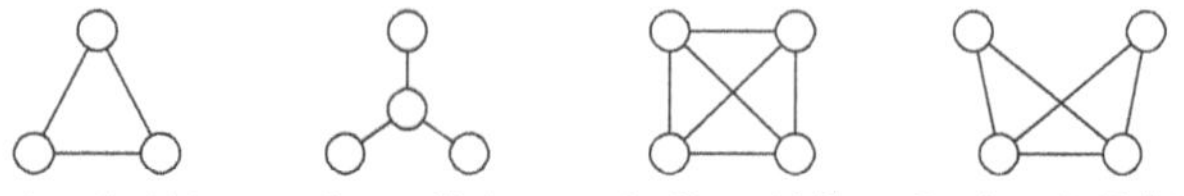

Figure 1: Examples of subgraphs

nism and a carefully tuned quality function. We combine these in a new way to define a class of "ladder functions", which provide the optimal sampling distribution for outputs. When applied to subgraph counting queries, the results are efficient to compute, and improve substantially over prior work on these problems, where applicable.

1.1 Our Contributions

We show how to answer subgraph counting queries in a differentially private manner [7]. Given a subgraph H, e.g., a triangle, we aim to release the number of isomorphic copies of H in the sensitive graph, while protecting individual privacy in the meantime. We write $f_H(g)$ to denote the function that computes the number of copies of subgraph H in graph g. We focus on a number of important classes of H. The function $f_\triangle$ counts the number of triangles in the graph: this is the most heavily studied subgraph counting query, as the triangle is the smallest non-trivial subgraph of interest. Other important subgraph counting functions include: $f_{k\star}$, for counting k-stars (one node of degree k connected to k nodes of degree 1); $f_{k\mathbb{C}}$, for counting k-cliques; and $f_{k\triangle}$ for counting k-triangles (a pair of adjacent nodes i, j that have k common neighbors). Figure 1 shows the smallest non-trivial example of each of these classes: note that the 3-clique and the 1-triangle are simply the standard triangle.

We draw up the following list of criteria that our desired solution for differentially private subgraph counting should satisfy:

1. The solution should achieve pure differential privacy;
2. It should be applicable to a wide range of queries, e.g., triangle counting, k-star counting, k-triangle counting and k-clique counting for a constant k;
3. Its time complexity should be no larger than that of computing the true query answer for the queries of interest;
4. It should have high accuracy on its output, bettering that of any previous applicable solution.

Outline of Ladder Framework Development. Our ladder framework achieves all the above criteria. It relies on the careful design of a probability distribution for outputting answers to count queries that tries to maximize the probability of outputting the true answer, or one that is near to it, and minimize the probability of outputting answers that are far from the true answer. The framework of differential privacy places constraints on how these probabilities should behave: the probability of providing output x for input graph g should be "close" (as determined by the parameter ε) to that for input graph g', if g and g' are close (differ by one edge). Rather than go right back to first principles to design these probability distributions, we make use of the exponential mechanism [25], since this approach is general: any differentially private mechanism can be expressed as an exponential mechanism.

Instantiating the exponential mechanism still takes some careful design. We arrive at the design of a symmetric "ladder function" specific to the input graph g, so-called because it is formed from a series of rungs. The first rung groups together a number of outputs that are close to the true answer to $f_H(g)$ (i.e. $f_H(g) \pm 1, f_H(g) \pm 2 \ldots$). The second rung groups together outputs that are a little further away, and so on (see Figure 3). The height of each rung determines the probability of outputting the corresponding values, while the width is the number of output values sharing the same height. Ideally, we would make each rung as narrow as possible, to maximize the dropoff in probabilities away from f_H. However, to guarantee differential privacy, we need to make the rungs wide enough so that the ith rung of the ladder for g overlaps with the $i-1$st, ith or $i+1$st rung of the ladder for all neighboring g' (in the language of the exponential mechanism, we seek bounded 'sensitivity' of the derived quality function). We call this the "small leap property".

It turns out that we can design such ladder functions which have rungs that are not too wide but which satisfy the small leap property. Moreover, these can be computed efficiently from the input graph g and used to perform the required output sampling. Our development of these objects takes multiple steps. First, we fill in the necessary details of differential privacy (Section 2). Then we show how the use of ladder functions can lead to a practical differentially private solution, if we assume the small leap property, and that the functions converge to a constant rung width (Section 3). We still have to show that we can create such functions, and this is the focus of Section 4, where we show that the concept of "local sensitivity at distance t" can be used to create a ladder function with the required properties. This provides a general solution which satisfies privacy; however, some of the quantities required can be time consuming to compute for certain subgraph counting queries. Hence, Section 5 considers how to instantiate our framework for specific queries, and provides alternate ladder functions for some queries to enable efficient computation. Our experimental evaluation of this approach, and comparison with previous works (where applicable) is detailed in Section 6.

1.2 Previous Work on Subgraph Counting

An obvious first attempt to differentially private subgraph counting is to apply the Laplace mechanism [11]. The Laplace mechanism answers a (numeric) query f by adding Laplace noise to the true answer, where the scale of noise is proportional to the *global sensitivity* of f. The global sensitivity is defined as the maximum possible change of query answer if one tuple is added to/deleted from an arbitrary database. This method fails since the global sensitivity of subgraph counting queries is very large, making the noise large enough to overwhelm the true answer. In the case of triangles, for example, adding or deleting an edge can affect a number of triangles proportional to the number of nodes, and hence the global sensitivity is very high.

Nissim et al. [29] and Karwa et al. [17] present an idea of utilizing a local version of global sensitivity, called *local sensitivity*, to build the noise distribution. The local sensitivity is a function of the input database, which is equal to the maximum change of query answer if one tuple is added in/deleted from the input database. The local sensitivity can be dramatically smaller than its global counterpart, but cannot be used directly to guarantee privacy. Instead, an upper bound on local sensitivity called *smooth sensitivity* is computed as a part of the noise scale. In [17], the authors give algorithms for computing smooth sensitivity of $f_\triangle$ and $f_{k\star}$. However, their idea fails when the smooth sensitivity of a query is hard to compute, e.g., $f_{k\triangle}$. In recompense, they propose an approach tailored specifically for $f_{k\triangle}$, which only achieves a restricted version of differential privacy.

Instead of answering the subgraph counting query directly, Chen et al. [5] release a lower bound on the result, whose global sensitivity is relatively low. This method suffers from a bias between the true query answer and the lower bound, in exchange for less noise. The authors claim that their method can be extended to a variety of subgraph counting queries, but it involves solving a linear program

Table 1: Table of notation

Notation	Description
f, g	the graph query and its sensitive input
$\mathcal{G}_n$	the set of simple graphs with n nodes
$d(g, g')$	minimum edit distance between two graphs
GS	global sensitivity of f
$LS(g)$	local sensitivity of f, given g
$LS(g, t)$	local sensitivity of f at distance t, given g
$q(g, k)$	quality of output k, given input g
Δ_q	sensitivity of quality function q
$I_t(g)$	the ladder function

with $O(L)$ variables where L equals the number of subgraphs H in the input times the number of edges in H. So the time complexity is super-quadratic in the answer value, making this method infeasible even for an input graph of moderate size (see details in Section 6).

Finally, Hay et al. [15] give a differentially private algorithm for publishing degree sequence of a sensitive graph. Since the number of k-stars is a function of the degree sequence, this approach implicitly allows k-star counting. It first utilizes the Laplace mechanism to generate a private version of the degree sequence, then applies a postprocessing step to enforce consistency of the sequence in order to reduce noise. Though better than the naive Laplace mechanism, it is reported to be less accurate than the solutions in [17] on k-star counting (see Section 6.3 of [17]). We note that this method was not designed for k-star counting; also it does *not* support other counting queries discussed in this paper.

2. PRELIMINARIES

In this section, we review the definition of differential privacy, two conventional mechanisms to achieve differential privacy, and some basic concepts of local sensitivity. The notational conventions of this paper are summarized in Table 1.

2.1 Differential Privacy

Let $g \in \mathcal{G}_n$ be a sensitive simple graph with n nodes, and f be the subgraph counting query of interest. Differential privacy requires that, prior to $f(g)$'s release, it should be modified using a randomized algorithm $\mathcal{A}$, such that the output of $\mathcal{A}$ does not reveal much information about any edge in g. The definition of differential privacy that we adopt in the context of graphs is as follows:

DEFINITION 2.1 (ε-DIFFERENTIAL PRIVACY [11, 15]). *A randomized algorithm $\mathcal{A}$ satisfies ε-differential privacy, if for any two graphs g and g' that differ by at most one edge, and for any possible output O of $\mathcal{A}$, we have*

$$\Pr[\mathcal{A}(g) = O] \le e^{\varepsilon} \cdot \Pr[\mathcal{A}(g') = O], \qquad (1)$$

where $\Pr[\cdot]$ denotes the probability of an event.

In what follows, we say that two graphs g, g' which differ by at most one edge are *neighboring*, i.e., their minimum edit distance [4] $d(g, g') \le 1$. While there are many approaches to achieving differential privacy, the best known and most-widely used two for this purpose are the *Laplace mechanism* [11] and the *exponential mechanism* [25].

The Laplace mechanism releases the result of a function f that takes as input a dataset and outputs a vector of numeric values. Given f, the Laplace mechanism transforms f into a differentially private algorithm by adding i.i.d. noise (denoted as η) into each output value of f. The noise η is sampled from a *Laplace distribution* $\text{Lap}(\lambda)$ with the following pdf: $\Pr[\eta = x] = \frac{1}{2\lambda} e^{-|x|/\lambda}$. Dwork et al. [11] show that the Laplace mechanism achieves ε-differential privacy if $\lambda \ge GS^f/\varepsilon$, where GS^f is the *global sensitivity* of f. In our problem setting (i.e., f is a subgraph counting query), GS^f is defined as follows:

DEFINITION 2.2 (GLOBAL SENSITIVITY [11]). *Let f be a function that maps a graph into a real number. The global sensitivity of f is defined as*

$$GS^f = \max_{g, g' \mid d(g, g') \le 1} \left| f(g) - f(g') \right|, \qquad (2)$$

where g and g' are any two neighboring graphs.

Intuitively, GS^f measures the maximum possible change in f's output when we modify one arbitrary edge in f's input.

For an analysis task f with a categorical output (e.g., a zipcode), injecting random noise no longer yields meaningful results, but the exponential mechanism [25] can be used instead. The exponential mechanism releases a differentially private version of f, by sampling from f's output domain Ω. The sampling probability for each $k \in \Omega$ is determined based on a user-specified *quality function* q, which takes as input any dataset g and any element $k \in \Omega$, and outputs a numeric score $q(g, k)$ that measures the quality of k: a larger score indicates that k is a better output with respect to g. More specifically, given a graph g, the exponential mechanism samples $k \in \Omega$ with probability:

$$\Pr[k \text{ is selected}] \propto \exp\left(\frac{\varepsilon}{2\Delta_q} \cdot q(g, k)\right), \qquad (3)$$

where Δ_q is the sensitivity of the quality function, i.e.,

$$\Delta_q = \max_{g, g', k \in \Omega} \left| q(g, k) - q(g', k) \right| \text{ for } g, g' \text{ s.t. } d(g, g') \le 1.$$

McSherry and Talwar [25] prove that the exponential mechanism ensures ε-differential privacy.

Both mechanisms can be applied quite generally; however, to be effective we seek to ensure that (i) the noise introduced does not outweigh the signal in the data, and (ii) it is computationally efficient to apply the mechanism. This requires a careful design of the functions to use in the mechanisms.

2.2 Local Sensitivity

The scale of noise added by the Laplace mechanism is proportional to GS^f of the query, when the privacy budget ε is fixed. For all queries discussed in this paper, this approach is not effective since they all have large GS^f relative to the size of the query answer. In [29], the authors seek to address this problem by presenting a local measurement of sensitivity, as in Definition 2.3:

DEFINITION 2.3 (LOCAL SENSITIVITY [29]). *Let f be a function that maps a graph into a real number. The local sensitivity of f is defined as*

$$LS^f(g) = \max_{g' \mid d(g, g') \le 1} \left| f(g) - f(g') \right|, \qquad (4)$$

where g' is any neighboring graph of g.

Note that global sensitivity can be understood as the maximum of local sensitivity over the input domain, i.e., $GS^f = \max_g LS^f(g)$. For simplicity, we write GS and $LS(g)$ instead in the remainder of the paper, if there is no ambiguity about the subgraph counting query of interest in context.

We refine the definition of local sensitivity, by defining the sensitivity for a particular pair of nodes (i, j), denoted by $LS_{ij}(g)$, to

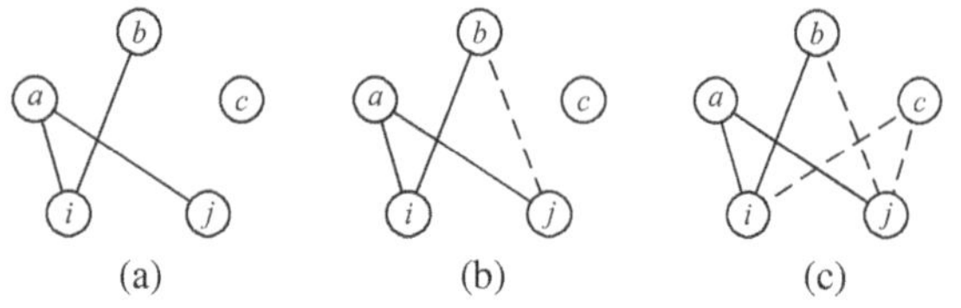

Figure 2: Examples of local sensitivity at distance t

indicate the magnitude of change of f when the connection between i and j is modified (added if absent; deleted if present) in the input graph. This then satisfies $LS(g) = \max_{i,j} LS_{ij}(g)$.

Although tempting, it is not correct to simply substitute $LS(g)$ for GS in the Laplace mechanism. This is because $LS(g)$ itself conveys information from the sensitive data. To address this problem, Nissim et al. [29] introduce *smooth sensitivity*, an upper bound of $LS(g)$, and show that differential privacy can be achieved by injecting Cauchy noise (instead of Laplace noise) calibrated to smooth sensitivity. As we show in Section 6, however, the adoption of Cauchy noise considerably degrades the quality of the output from a differentially private algorithm. This issue could be alleviated by combining smooth sensitivity with Laplace noise, but the resulting solution would only achieve a weakened version of ε-differential privacy (referred to as (ε, δ)-differential privacy [10]).

In this paper, we do not use smooth sensitivity, but adopt an intermediate notion of *local sensitivity at distance t* as a crucial part of our solution.

DEFINITION 2.4 (LOCAL SENSITIVITY AT DISTANCE t [29]). *The local sensitivity of f at distance t is the largest local sensitivity attained on graphs at distance at most t from g. The formal definition is:*

$$LS(g,t) = \max_{g^* | d(g,g^*) \leq t} LS(g^*). \tag{5}$$

Note that $LS(g,t)$ is a monotonically increasing function of t.

By analogy with $LS(g,t)$ and $LS(g)$, we further define $LS_{ij}(g,t)$ as the largest $LS_{ij}(\cdot)$ attained on graphs at distance at most t from g. Then $LS(g,t) = \max_{i,j} LS_{ij}(g,t)$.

Figure 2 gives an example of local sensitivity at distance t for triangle counting. The initial graph g in Figure 2(a) contains five nodes, three edges and no triangle. Its local sensitivity equals 1, achieved by adding edge (i, j) to the graph, i.e., $LS(g) = LS_{ij}(g) = 1$. Thereafter, $LS(g,1)$ allows one extra modification before calculating LS. In Figure 2(b), we show how the dashed edge (b, j) affects $LS_{ij}(\cdot)$, making $LS(g,1) = LS_{ij}(g,1) = 2$. Furthermore, we find that LS could never rise to 3 within 2 steps of modifications, and Figure 2(c) illustrates one example achieving $LS(g,3) = 3$.

3. OVERVIEW OF SOLUTION

This section presents the steps for using our ladder framework for answering subgraph counting queries under ε-differential privacy, given an appropriate function with some assumed properties (these functions are instantiated and proved to possess these properties in subsequent sections). Like the Laplace mechanism, we add a certain amount of noise to the true answer to prevent inference of sensitive information. However, to achieve better results, we aim to exploit the fact that most realistic graphs can tolerate a lower amount of noise while still providing the needed privacy. Towards this end, we need to tailor the noise to the given input, without revealing anything about the input by our choice of noise distribution. We introduce how to build such a distribution through the exponential mechanism in Section 3.1, then give an algorithm for efficient sampling in Section 3.2.

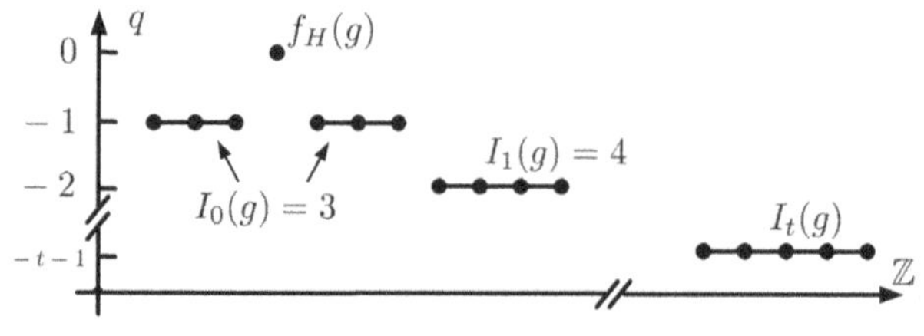

Figure 3: An example of a ladder quality

3.1 Building a Solution Distribution

Assume that we are given a query $f_H(g)$ that counts the number of subgraphs H in g. Let η be the distribution of the solution that we return as a private version of $f_H(g)$. In a nutshell, η is a discrete distribution defined over the integer domain, such that $\eta(k)$ increases with $q(g,k)$, where $q(g,k) \leq 0$ is a non-positive integer that quantifies the loss of data utility when we publish k instead of $f_H(g)$. We refer to q as a *quality function*, since we will use it as a quality function in the exponential mechanism. The expression of $\eta(k)$ as a function of $q(g,k)$ is given in equation (3) of Section 2.1.

Our choice of q is determined by a function $I_t(g)$, which defines how q varies. Figure 3 gives a working example of the q and $I_t(g)$. In particular, q is a symmetric function over the entire integer domain, centered at $f_H(g)$. We define the quality function to take its maximum value at $f_H(g)$. Without loss of generality, we set $q(g, f_H(g)) = 0$. For other possible answers, the quality decreases as the distance to the true answer increases. The decreasing speed is controlled by function $I_t(g)$. We refer to each quality level $(0, -1, -2, \ldots)$ as a *rung* of the ladder. In the figure, the first rung, corresponding to a quality level of -1, consists of the $I_0(g)$ integers on each side of $f_H(g)$, whose distances to $f_H(g)$ are no larger than $I_0(g)$. The next rung is formed of the next $I_1(g)$ integers on each side with quality -2, and so on. We say that I_t gives the "width" of the $t+1$st rung.

DEFINITION 3.1 (LADDER QUALITY). *Formally, given function $I_t(g)$ we define the ladder quality function $q(g,k)$ by*

(i) $q(g, f_H(g)) = 0$;

(ii) $\forall k \in f_H(g) \pm \left(\sum_{t=0}^{u-1} I_t(g), \sum_{t=0}^{u} I_t(g)\right]$, *set* $q(g,k) = -u-1$.

After assigning each integer a quality score, we need to determine the sensitivity of the quality function,

$$\Delta_q = \max_{k,g,g' | d(g,g') \leq 1} |q(g,k) - q(g',k)|,$$

in order to apply the exponential mechanism. For arbitrary query class f_H and function $I_t(g)$, there is no simple answer: it can be the case that Δ_q is unbounded. Consequently, we restrict our attention to a class of well-behaved functions $I_t(g)$ that we will refer to as *ladder functions*. By analogy, we require that if we place two ladders corresponding to neighboring graphs g, g' next to each other and stand on the t'th rung of g's ladder, we can easily "leap across" to g''s ladder, since the rung at the corresponding position is at almost the same height. Formally,

PROPERTY 3.1 (SMALL LEAP PROPERTY). *The ladder quality $q(g,k)$ defined by $I_t(g)$ has bounded Δ_q.*

In Section 4, we give a class of functions that meet this property since they have a constant $\Delta_q = 1$. For now, we simply assume that Δ_q is bounded and known to us, therefore, we can build the solution distribution using the exponential mechanism.

Algorithm 1 NoiseSample (f_H, g, ε, I_t): returns f^*

1: Compute true answer $f_H(g)$;
2: $range[0] = \{f_H(g)\}$; $weight[0] = 1 \cdot \exp\left(\frac{\varepsilon}{2\Delta_q} \cdot 0\right)$;
3: Initialize $dst = 0$;
4: **for** $t = 1$ to M **do**
5:     $range[t] = f_H(g) \pm (dst, dst + I_{t-1}(g)]$;
6:     $weight[t] = 2I_{t-1}(g) \cdot \exp\left(\frac{\varepsilon}{2\Delta_q} \cdot -t\right)$;
7:     $dst = dst + I_{t-1}(g)$;
8: **end for**
9: $weight[M+1] = \dfrac{2C \cdot \exp\left(\frac{\varepsilon}{2\Delta_q} \cdot -(M+1)\right)}{1 - \exp\left(-\frac{\varepsilon}{2\Delta_q}\right)}$;
10: Sample an integer $t \in [0, M+1]$ with a probability $weight[t]$ over sum of weights;
11: **if** $t \leq M$ **then**
12:     **return** a uniformly distributed random integer in $range[t]$;
13: **else**
14:     Sample an integer i from the geometric distribution with parameter $p = 1 - \exp\left(-\frac{\varepsilon}{2\Delta_q}\right)$;
15:     **return** a uniformly distributed random integer in $f_H(g) \pm \{dst + i \cdot C + (0, C]\}$;
16: **end if**

3.2 Efficient Sampling from the Distribution

Our solution proceeds by using the ladder quality function to instantiate the exponential mechanism. This results in a solution which is guaranteed to provide differential privacy. However, the output of the mechanism can range over a very large, if not unbounded, number of possibilities, which we must sample from. The naive approach of computing the probability associated with each output value is not feasible: there are too many to calculate. Instead, we need a way to perform sampling in a tractable way. To reduce the time complexity of working with this infinite distribution, we assume a convergence property of $I_t(g)$, that there is a "bottom rung" of our ladder below which all rungs are the same width.

PROPERTY 3.2 (REGULAR STEP PROPERTY). *$I_t(g)$ converges to a constant C within M steps, i.e., $I_t(g) = C$ for any $t \geq M$.*

With these two properties, we can more effectively use the exponential mechanism, since there is a bounded number of sampling probabilities. Algorithm 1 gives pseudocode for the sampling process under these assumptions, which we now explain. Our algorithm aggregates all integers with the same quality, say $-t$, as t'th rung. The range function (Line 5) describes the domain of each rung, and the weight function (Line 6) gives the sum of weights within the domain. We illustrate how to calculate the range and weight for the first few rungs, e.g., rung 0 (the center) to rung M (Lines 2-8). For other rungs with indices $t > M$, we observe that their weights $2C \cdot \exp(\varepsilon/2\Delta_q \cdot -t)$ form a geometric sequence of t with common ratio $\exp(-\varepsilon/2\Delta_q)$. Therefore, we can write down a closed form sum of weights for all remaining rungs, as in Line 9, considered as one large rung indexed by $M+1$.

Lines 10-16 perform the random sampling. First, one rung is sampled with a probability proportional to its weight. If it is rung $M+1$, then we need to further specify the rung index by sampling from a geometric distribution (Line 14). At the end, we return a random integer within the range of the sampled rung as the final result. The time complexity of Algorithm 1 except Line 1 is $O(M)$.

Privacy guarantee. The correctness of Algorithm 1 follows from the correctness of the exponential mechanism [25]. Therefore, we have the following theorem (proof in Appendix B).

THEOREM 3.1. *Algorithm 1 satisfies ε-differential privacy, provided I_t has Properties 3.1 and 3.2.*

4. LADDER FUNCTIONS

The previous section explains how to build and sample a solution distribution with Algorithm 1, given a suitable function $I_t(g)$. In what follows, we consider how best to define such functions in general; we then apply this insight for the functions of interest that count various types of subgraph in the next section.

Some requirements for a good function are as follows. $I_t(g)$ should be a function of input graph g and step t, such that (i) $I_t(g)$ satisfies Properties 3.1 and 3.2, to guarantee the correctness of Algorithm 1; (ii) $I_t(g)$ is small. The rationale is that $I_t(g)$ controls the shape of the ladder. The smaller $I_t(g)$ the faster the quality decreases away from the true answer, and hence, the exponential mechanism tends to generate a distribution with higher probabilities for outputs closer to the true answer (smaller noise). In what follows, we first introduce a class of *ladder functions*, and give several examples. Then we prove that ladder functions always achieve a constant value for Δ_q, the sensitivity of the quality function (providing Property 3.1). Last, we construct a convergent ladder function for subgraph counting queries which always converges to the global sensitivity within $\binom{n}{2}$ steps (meeting Property 3.2).

We now formalize our notion of a ladder function.

DEFINITION 4.1 (LADDER FUNCTION). *$I_t(g)$ is said to be a* ladder function *of query f if and only if*

(a) $LS^f(g) \leq I_0(g)$, for any g;

(b) $I_t(g') \leq I_{t+1}(g)$, for any pair of neighboring graphs g, g', and any nonnegative integer t.

A straightforward example of a ladder function is the constant function $I_t(g) = GS$, since $LS(g) \leq GS$ for any g, and a constant always satisfies the second requirement. However, as discussed in Section 2.2, GS can be extremely large for subgraph counting, which does not adapt to typical graphs, which may not require so much noise. The local sensitivity $I_t(g) = LS(g)$ could be much smaller than GS, but unfortunately is not a ladder function because $LS(g') \leq LS(g)$ does *not* hold for all pairs of neighboring graphs. Our insight for designing good ladder functions is that we can use a relaxation of local sensitivity instead. Specifically, we adopt the notion of local sensitivity at distance t, i.e., $LS(g,t)$. We now prove that this choice is optimal within our framework: local sensitivity at distance t is the *minimum ladder function*, i.e. it is the lower envelope of all possible ladder functions.

THEOREM 4.1. *$LS(g,t)$ is the minimum ladder function that satisfies $LS(g,t) \leq I_t(g)$ for any ladder function $I_t(g)$.*

PROOF. We first prove that $LS(g,t)$ is a ladder function.

(i) $LS(g) = LS(g,0)$ (meeting Definition 4.1(a));

(ii) $\{g^* \mid d(g', g^*) \leq t\}$ is a subset of $\{g^* \mid d(g, g^*) \leq t+1\}$, given a pair of neighboring graphs g, g' such that $d(g,g') \leq 1$. Therefore, it meets Definition 4.1(b), since:

$$\begin{aligned} LS(g',t) &= \max_{g^* \mid d(g',g^*) \leq t} LS(g^*) \\ &\leq \max_{g^* \mid d(g,g^*) \leq t+1} LS(g^*) = LS(g,t+1). \end{aligned}$$

Next we prove $LS(g,t)$ is no larger than any ladder function $I_t(g)$ by induction on t.

Basis: when $t = 0$, $LS(g,0) = LS(g) \le I_0(g)$ for all g;

Inductive step: suppose that $LS(g,t) \le I_t(g)$ holds for all g. It must be shown that $LS(g,t+1) \le I_{t+1}(g)$ holds for all g. For any pair of neighboring graphs g, g', we have $I_{t+1}(g) \ge I_t(g')$ given $I_t(g)$ is a ladder function. Thus, $I_{t+1}(g) \ge \max_{g'|d(g,g')\le 1} I_t(g')$ holds for all g. Then given the assumption that $LS(g,t) \le I_t(g)$ holds for all g,

$$\begin{aligned} I_{t+1}(g) &\ge \max_{g'|d(g,g')\le 1} I_t(g') \ge \max_{g'|d(g,g')\le 1} LS(g',t) \quad \text{by hypothesis} \\ &= \max_{g'|d(g,g')\le 1} \max_{g^*|d(g',g^*)\le t} LS(g^*) \\ &= \max_{g^*|d(g,g^*)\le t+1} LS(g^*) = LS(g,t+1) \end{aligned}$$

thus showing that indeed $LS(g,t+1) \le I_{t+1}(g)$ holds for all g. By induction, $LS(g,t) \le I_t(g)$ holds for all g and all nonnegative t. □

$LS(g,t)$ plays an important role in our framework. For certain subgraph counting queries, e.g., $f_\triangle, f_{k\star}$, it is the best ladder function that we can ever find. However, it is not always the preferred choice: as shown in Section 5, $LS(g,t)$ can be very hard to compute for some queries. To tackle this problem, we will present how to construct an alternate ladder function (basically, a relaxation of $LS(g,t)$) which is (i) computationally efficient and (ii) still much smaller than GS.

4.1 Bounded Δ_q

This subsection proves the most important property of ladder functions, that they satisfy Property 3.1.

THEOREM 4.2. *If $I_t(g)$ is a ladder function then the resulting quality function q has $\Delta_q = 1$.*

PROOF. To prove this theorem, we must show that for any pair of neighboring graphs g, g', and any integer $k \in \mathbb{Z}$, $|q(g,k) - q(g',k)| \le 1$ always holds. That is, the quality ascribed to providing k as an output differs by at most 1 for neighboring graphs. In what follows, we discuss three different cases based on how close the value of k is to the top of the ladder.

Special case 1, the center: $k = f_H(g) \Rightarrow q(g,k) = 0$. Given the properties of local sensitivity and ladder function (Definition 4.1(a)) $|k - f_H(g')| \le LS(g')$ and $LS(g') \le I_0(g')$, we have

$$f_H(g') - I_0(g') \le f_H(g) \le f_H(g') + I_0(g'). \tag{6}$$

That is, since k is the query answer for a neighboring graph of g', it must fall within the local sensitivity of the query answer for g'. From Definition 3.1(i) and (ii) with $u = 0$ we have $q(g',k) \in \{0, -1\}$. Thus, the difference of quality is bounded by 1.

Special case 2, first rung: If $k \in f_H(g) + (0, I_0(g)]$, then $q(g,k) = -1$: k is on the first rung. By the construction of the ladder function, $q(g',k)$ should be on the center, the first or the second rung, and so the quality changes by at most 1. Formally, the lower bound of k as a function of g' is

$$k > f_H(g) \ge f_H(g') - I_0(g') \qquad \text{(from (6))};$$

and the upper bound is

$$k \le f_H(g) + I_0(g) \le f_H(g') + I_0(g') + I_1(g'),$$

using Definition 4.1(b) to show $I_0(g) \le I_1(g')$, combined with (6). Applying Definition 3.1, the value of the quality function satisfies $q(g',k) \in \{0, -1, -2\}$, and so the bound holds.

General case: Consider $k \in f_H(g) + (\sum_{t=0}^{u-1} I_t(g), \sum_{t=0}^{u} I_t(g)]$ so $q(g,k) = -u-1$, where $u > 0$—we are on the $u+1$st rung on the ladder for g. We argue that we can only climb or descend a single rung when we move to the ladder for g'. The lower bound on k as a function of g' can be obtained using similar steps to case 2 above, from (6) and $u-1$ invocations of Definition 4.1(b):

$$\begin{aligned} k > f_H(g) + \sum_{t=0}^{u-1} I_t(g) &= f_H(g) + I_0(g) + \sum_{t=1}^{u-1} I_t(g) \\ &\ge f_H(g') + \sum_{t=0}^{u-2} I_t(g'). \end{aligned}$$

The upper bound uses a similar argument:

$$\begin{aligned} k &\le f_H(g) + \sum_{t=0}^{u} I_t(g) \\ &\le f_H(g') + I_0(g') + \sum_{t=1}^{u+1} I_t(g') \;=\; f_H(g') + \sum_{t=0}^{u+1} I_t(g'). \end{aligned}$$

Therefore, $q(g',k)$ is close to $q(g,k) = u-1$:

$$\begin{aligned} k \in f_H(g') + &\left(\sum_{t=0}^{u-2} I_t(g'), \sum_{t=0}^{u+1} I_t(g') \right] \\ &\Rightarrow q(g',k) \in \{-u, -u-1, -u-2\}. \end{aligned}$$

The analysis above proves the result for all $k \ge f_H(g)$. For integers $k < f_H(g)$, the proofs of special case 2 and the general case are symmetric, and yield the required result. □

4.2 Convergence

This subsection shows how to design a *convergent* ladder function for subgraph counting queries that meets Property 3.2. First, we state a useful lemma for our subsequent analysis. The proof is immediate given the definition of ladder functions, so we omit it.

LEMMA 4.1. *If $f(g,t)$ and $h(g,t)$ are ladder functions, $\min(f(g,t), h(g,t))$ is a ladder function.*

Using this result, one can easily design a convergent ladder function, e.g., $\min(I_t(g), GS)$, if the original function $I_t(g)$ is unbounded. This is critical since Algorithm 1 requires a convergent function. Unlike $LS(g,t)$ which converges to GS naturally, some ladder functions may need to be explicitly bounded by GS.

THEOREM 4.3. *For any subgraph counting query f_H, $\min(I_t(g), GS)$ is a ladder function of f_H that converges to GS within $\binom{n}{2}$ steps, given $I_t(g)$ is a ladder function of f_H.*

PROOF. $\min(I_t(g), GS)$ is a ladder function: since $I_t(g)$ and GS are both ladder functions we can invoke Lemma 4.1.

As the distance between any two graphs in $\mathcal{G}_n$ is no larger than $\binom{n}{2}$, we have that $\{g^* \mid d(g,g^*) \le \binom{n}{2}\} = \mathcal{G}_n$ holds for any graph $g \in \mathcal{G}_n$. Thus, the local sensitivity at distance $\binom{n}{2}$ equals GS, i.e.,

$$LS\left(g, \tbinom{n}{2}\right) = \max_{g^*|d(g,g^*)\le\binom{n}{2}} LS(g^*) = \max_{g^*\in\mathcal{G}_n} LS(g^*) = GS.$$

Given $LS(g,t)$ is the minimum ladder function and is monotonically increasing in t, it follows $I_t(g) \ge LS(g,t) \ge LS\left(g, \binom{n}{2}\right) = GS$ for any $t \ge \binom{n}{2}$. Hence, $\min(I_t(g), GS) = GS$ for any $t \ge \binom{n}{2}$. □

Recall that the time complexity of Algorithm 1 (except Line 1) is linear in M. Therefore we can conclude that the algorithm terminates in $O(n^2)$ time for any subgraph counting query, if a ladder function $I_t(g)$ is given in advance. Quadratic time can still be large, so in the next section, we find ladder functions for classes of subgraphs which converge in $O(n)$ steps.

5. APPLICATIONS

In this section, we show how to apply our framework for a variety of subgraph counting queries, including $f_\triangle, f_{k\star}, f_{k\mathbb{C}}$ and $f_{k\triangle}$. $LS(g,t)$ of the functions $f_\triangle$ and $f_{k\star}$ are carefully studied in [17,29], which can serve as ladder functions for these two queries directly. However, as we will show in this section, computing $LS(g,t)$ can be hard for some queries, e.g., $f_{k\mathbb{C}}$ and $f_{k\triangle}$. Instead of using $LS(g,t)$, we present an efficient method to build a convergent upper bound of $LS(g,t)$, which is shown to satisfy the requirements in Definition 4.1. Such an upper bound could be used as the ladder function for $f_{k\mathbb{C}}$ and $f_{k\triangle}$.

Graph statistics. Our detailed analysis of global sensitivity, local sensitivity and its upper bound rely on some simple graph statistics related to the (common) neighborhood of nodes.

DEFINITION 5.1 (GRAPH STATISTICS). *Let $(x_{ij})_{n\times n}$ be the adjacency matrix of an undirected, simple graph on n nodes. $x_{ij} = 1$ when there exists an edge between nodes i and j, 0 otherwise. Let d_i denote the degree of node i, and $d_m = \max_i d_i$ be the maximum degree of the graph.*

Let A_{ij} be the set of common neighbors of i and j. Node l belongs to A_{ij} if and only if $x_{il}x_{lj} = 1$. Let $a_{ij} = |A_{ij}|$ be the number of common neighbors of i, j, and $a_m = \max_{i,j} a_{ij}$ be the maximum number of common neighbors of a pair of nodes in the graph. Let $b_{ij} = d_i + d_j - 2a_{ij} - 2x_{ij}$ denote the the number of nodes connected to exactly one of the two nodes i, j.

5.1 $LS(g,t)$ as Ladder Function

Triangle counting. In Lemma 5.1, we give the global sensitivity and local sensitivity at distance t of triangle counting.

LEMMA 5.1 (CLAIM 3.13 OF FULL VERSION OF [29]). *The global sensitivity of $f_\triangle$ is $GS = n-2$; The local sensitivity at distance t of $f_\triangle$ is $LS(g,t) = \max_{i,j} LS_{ij}(g,t)$, where*

$$LS_{ij}(g,t) = \min\left(a_{ij} + \left\lfloor \frac{t+\min(t,b_{ij})}{2} \right\rfloor, n-2\right).$$

It is easy to prove that $LS(g,t)$ converges to GS when $t \geq 2n$. The time complexity of computing $LS(g,t)$ for $t \in [0,2n]$ is $O(M(n))$, where $M(n)$ is the time needed to multiply two $n \times n$ matrices.

***k*-star counting.** Another important problem of subgraph counting studied in [5, 17] is k-star counting. Lemma 5.2 shows its global sensitivity and local sensitivity at distance t.

LEMMA 5.2 (LEMMA 3.4 OF [17]). *The global sensitivity of $f_{k\star}$ is $GS = 2\binom{n-2}{k-1}$; The local sensitivity at distance t of $f_{k\star}$ is $LS(g,t) = \max_{i,j} LS_{ij}(g,t)$, where*

$$LS_{ij}(g,t) = \begin{cases} \binom{\bar{d}_i+t}{k-1} + \binom{\bar{d}_j}{k-1}, & \text{if } t \leq B_i; \\ \binom{n-2}{k-1} + \binom{\bar{d}_j+t-B_i}{k-1}, & \text{if } B_i < t \leq B_i + B_j; \\ 2\binom{n-2}{k-1}, & \text{if } B_i + B_j < t. \end{cases}$$

Here $\bar{d}_i = d_i - x_{ij}$ and $B_i = n-2-\bar{d}_i$. $\bar{d}_j$ and B_j are defined analogously. Without loss of generality, assume that $d_i \geq d_j$.

As with $f_\triangle$, $LS(g,t)$ of $f_{k\star}$ converges to GS when $t \geq 2n$. It takes $O(n\log n + m)$ time to compute $LS(g,t)$ for $t \in [0,2n]$.

5.2 Customized Ladder Function

Although $LS(g,t)$ works well for triangle and k-star counting, it cannot be extended to the class of queries whose $LS(g,t)$ are NP-complete to compute, e.g., k-clique counting for a constant $k > 3$ (the reduction is shown for completeness in Appendix A) and k-triangle counting for $k > 1$ (proved in [17]). To address this problem, the authors of [17] propose to use a *differentially private* version of local sensitivity, to replace the inefficient $LS(g,t)$. However, this method is quite restricted because (i) it is specifically for k-triangle counting; (ii) it achieves (ε,δ)-differential privacy only, and ε is limited to $(0, \frac{3}{2}\ln\frac{3}{2} \approx 0.6]$. In this section, we illustrate how to avoid using $LS(g,t)$ by designing a new customized ladder function.

5.2.1 *k-clique counting*

We first emphasize that we are only interested in a small constant k here, otherwise the counting query $f_{k\mathbb{C}}$ itself is hard to compute. 1- and 2-clique counting are trivial in our setting, and 3-clique (triangle) counting is already well addressed in Lemma 5.1. For other constant $k > 3$, we aim to design a function $I_t(g)$ which satisfies all the requirements in Definition 4.1.

First of all, we introduce some building blocks of $I_t(g)$, i.e., a_m (see Definition 5.1), and the global and local sensitivity of $f_{k\mathbb{C}}$ in the next lemma

LEMMA 5.3. *The global sensitivity of $f_{k\mathbb{C}}$ is $GS = \binom{n-2}{k-2}$; the local sensitivity of $f_{k\mathbb{C}}$ is*

$$LS(g) = \max_{i,j} \mathbb{C}(g(A_{ij}), k-2),$$

where $g(S)$ denotes the subgraph induced on g by the node subset S, and $\mathbb{C}(g,k)$ is the number of k-cliques in graph g.

The global sensitivity is achieved when deleting one edge from a complete graph with n nodes. The local sensitivity at (i,j), i.e., $\mathbb{C}(g(A_{ij}), k-2)$, indicates the number of k-cliques that contain nodes i and j when edge (i,j) is added.

Next we give our ladder function for k-clique counting in Theorem 5.1 and explain the intuition of this design in the proof.

THEOREM 5.1.

$$I_t(g) = \min\left(LS(g) + \binom{a_m+t}{k-2} - \binom{a_m}{k-2}, GS\right)$$

is a ladder function for $f_{k\mathbb{C}}$.

PROOF. By Lemma 4.1, we learn that proving $LS(g) + \binom{a_m+t}{k-2} - \binom{a_m}{k-2}$ is a ladder function is sufficient to prove this theorem. The proof contains the following three steps.

(1) $LS(g) \leq I_0(g)$, for any g. This step is trivial since $I_0(g) = LS(g)$;

(2) $I_0(g') \leq I_1(g)$, for any pair of neighboring graphs g, g'. Let A_{ij} (A'_{ij}) be the set of common neighbors of nodes i, j in g (g'). Let a_m (a'_m) be maximum number of common neighbors in g (g'). Note that the size of A_{ij} is bounded by a_m.

$$\begin{aligned} LS(g') - LS(g) &= \max_{i,j} \mathbb{C}(g'(A'_{ij}), k-2) - \max_{i,j} \mathbb{C}(g(A_{ij}), k-2) \\ &\leq \max_{i,j} \left(\mathbb{C}(g'(A'_{ij}), k-2) - \mathbb{C}(g(A_{ij}), k-2)\right). \end{aligned}$$

Recall that there is only one edge difference between g and g'. To increase the number of $(k-2)$-cliques in $g(A_{ij})$ by editing one edge, one can either (i) add one edge within $g(A_{ij})$ while keeping the set A_{ij} unchanged, or (ii) expand A_{ij} by one new node. The maximum increase, i.e., $\binom{a_m}{k-3}$ is achieved in the case that $g(A_{ij})$ is a complete graph of size a_m and $g'(A'_{ij})$ is a complete graph of size $a_m + 1$. However, observe that since

$$\binom{a_m}{k-3} = \binom{a_m+1}{k-2} - \binom{a_m}{k-2}$$

we have

$$LS(g') \le LS(g) + \binom{a_m+1}{k-2} - \binom{a_m}{k-2} \quad \Leftrightarrow \quad I_0(g') \le I_1(g).$$

(3) $I_t(g') \le I_{t+1}(g)$, for any neighboring graphs g, g' and integer $t > 0$. We make use of the combinatorial identity $\sum_{k=0}^{n} \binom{k}{m} = \binom{n+1}{m+1}$ and obtain

$$LS(g') + \binom{a'_m+t}{k-2} - \binom{a'_m}{k-2} = LS(g') + \sum_{i=0}^{t-1} \binom{a'_m+i}{k-3}$$

$$\le LS(g) + \binom{a_m}{k-3} + \sum_{i=0}^{t-1} \binom{a_m+i+1}{k-3}$$

$$= LS(g) + \sum_{i=0}^{t} \binom{a_m+i}{k-3} = LS(g) + \binom{a_m+t+1}{k-2} - \binom{a_m}{k-2},$$

which is equivalent to $I_t(g') \le I_{t+1}(g)$. The central step of the proof relies on an important property of the maximum number of common neighbors: its global sensitivity equals 1. So it holds that $a'_m - a_m \le 1$, and so $\binom{a'_m+i}{k-3} \le \binom{a_m+i+1}{k-3}$. □

This ladder function converges to GS when $t \ge n$. The major computational overhead of $I_t(g)$ for $t \in [0, n]$ is $LS(g)$, which can be computed within $O(n^k)$ time via exhaustive search. In our experiment, we implement a sophisticated algorithm which utilizes the sparsity of the input to improve efficiency. It returns $LS(g)$ within a few seconds for all graphs tested in the next section.

5.2.2 *k-triangle counting*

Besides k-clique counting, we also present k-triangle counting as another example of using customized ladder function. We state the currently known results about k-triangle counting as Lemma 5.4.

LEMMA 5.4 (LEMMA 4.1 AND 4.2 OF [17]). *The global sensitivity of $f_{k\triangle}$ is $GS = \binom{n-2}{k} + 2(n-2)\binom{n-3}{k-1}$. The local sensitivity of $f_{k\triangle}$ is*

$$LS(g) = \max_{i,j} \left(\binom{a_{ij}}{k} + \sum_{l \in A_{ij}} \binom{a_{il} - x_{ij}}{k-1} + \binom{a_{lj} - x_{ij}}{k-1} \right);$$

We also have $LS(g') \le LS(g) + 3\binom{a_m}{k-1} + a_m\binom{a_m}{k-2}$, given a pair of neighboring graphs g and g'.

Similarly, one can design a ladder function for k-triangle counting, as shown in Theorem 5.2. The proof follows the same lines as that of Theorem 5.1.

THEOREM 5.2.

$$I_t(g) = \min \left(LS(g) + \sum_{i=0}^{t-1} U(a_m+i), GS \right)$$

is a ladder function for $f_{k\triangle}$, where $U(a) = 3\binom{a}{k-1} + a\binom{a}{k-2}$.

It takes $t \ge 3n$ steps for this ladder function to converge to GS, and the time complexity of computing $I_t(g)$ for $t \in [0, 3n]$ would be $O(n^3)$ using a naive method.

To summarize, we observe some similarities between k-clique and k-triangle counting. First, their $LS(g,t)$ functions are both NP-complete to compute, which motivates our customized ladder functions. Second, there exist efficient ways to compute the local sensitivities $LS(g)$, and $LS(g') - LS(g)$ is bounded by a function of a variable whose global sensitivity is constant, e.g., a_m or d_m. Any subgraph counting query with these two properties could be processed by our framework with a customized ladder function as in Theorems 5.1 and 5.2.

6. EXPERIMENTS

6.1 Experimental Settings

Datasets. We make use of six real-world graph datasets in our experiments: AstroPh, HepPh, HepTh, CondMat and GrQc are collaboration networks from the e-print arXiv, which cover scientific collaborations between authors who submitted papers to Astro Physics, High Energy Physics, High Energy Physics Theory, Condensed Matter and General Relativity categories, respectively. In particular, if a paper is co-authored by k authors, the network generates a completed connected subgraph (k-clique) on k nodes representing these authors. Enron is an email network obtained from a dataset of around half a million emails. Nodes of the network are email addresses and if an address i sent at least one email to address j, the graph contains an undirected edge from i to j. Tabel 2 illustrates the properties of the datasets and their results to four subgraph counting queries. All datasets can be downloaded from Stanford Large Network Dataset Collection [21].

Baselines. To justify the performance of our algorithm (denoted as Ladder) in answering subgraph counting queries, we compare it with other four approaches: (i) Laplace [11], which directly injects Laplace noise with scale GS/ε to the true subgraph counts. (ii) Smooth [17, 29], which first computes a smooth upper bound SS of the local sensitivity, then adds Cauchy noise scaled up by a factor of $6SS/\varepsilon$ to the answer. It is only evaluated on two queries $f_\triangle$ and $f_{k\star}$ due to the hardness of computing SS for $f_{k\mathbb{C}}$ and $f_{k\triangle}$. (iii) NoisyLS [17], which achieves differential privacy by adding noise proportional to a *differentially private* upper bound on local sensitivity (instead of the smooth upper bound used in Smooth). This approach is designed for $f_{k\triangle}$, and is the only (ε, δ)-differentially private baseline algorithm. The parameter ε is restricted to $(0, \frac{3}{2}\ln\frac{2}{3}]$ while δ is set to a fixed value 0.01 in our experiments. (iv) Recursive [5], which answers the query by releasing a differentially private lower bound (which has low-sensitivity) of the counting result. The time complexity of this algorithm is super-quadratic to the number of subgraphs. All experiments using the Recursive mechanism failed to complete within 4 days except for two cases: HepTh-△ and GrQc-△ since their counting results are relatively small. In contrast, all local sensitivity based solutions (i.e., Ladder, Smooth, NoisyLS) are rather efficient, and in fact share the same time complexity.

Evaluation. We evaluate the performance of Ladder and four baselines on four subgraph counting queries over all six datasets. We measure the accuracy of each method by the *median relative error* [17], i.e., the median of the random variable $|\mathcal{A}(g) - f(g)|/f(g)$ where $\mathcal{A}(g)$ is the differentially private output and $f(g)$ is the true answer. The reason of choosing this measurement is that the mean of Cauchy noise (used in Smooth) is undefined. In other words, the mean error of the Smooth method is never stable, no matter how large the sampling set is. Therefore, in accordance with prior works [5, 17], we choose to report median error. We also include a bold line to indicate a relative error of 1. Any result above this line is of no practical value. For each result reported, we repeat each experiment 10,000 times to get the median, except for Recursive (where we perform 100 repetitions).

6.2 Counting Queries

Figures 4-7 show all experimental results on counting queries, varying the privacy budget ε from 0.05 to 1.6. The title of each subfigure (e.g., AstroPh) indicates the reported dataset.

Table 2: Datasets properties

datasets	nodes	edges	avg. deg.	density	$\triangle$	$3\star$	$4\mathbb{C}$	$2\triangle$
AstroPh	18,772	198,050	21.101	0.1124%	1,351,440	545,677,550	9,580,415	72,355,715
HepPh	12,008	118,491	19.735	0.1644%	3,358,499	1,276,967,000	150,281,372	936,890,335
HepTh	9,877	25,975	5.260	0.0533%	28,339	2,098,336	65,592	429,013
CondMat	23,133	93,439	8.078	0.0349%	173,361	37,115,060	294,008	2,349,650
Enron	36,692	183,831	10.020	0.0273%	727,044	4,909,606,844	2,341,639	36,528,276
GrQc	5,242	14,485	5.527	0.1054%	48,260	2,482,748	329,297	2,041,499

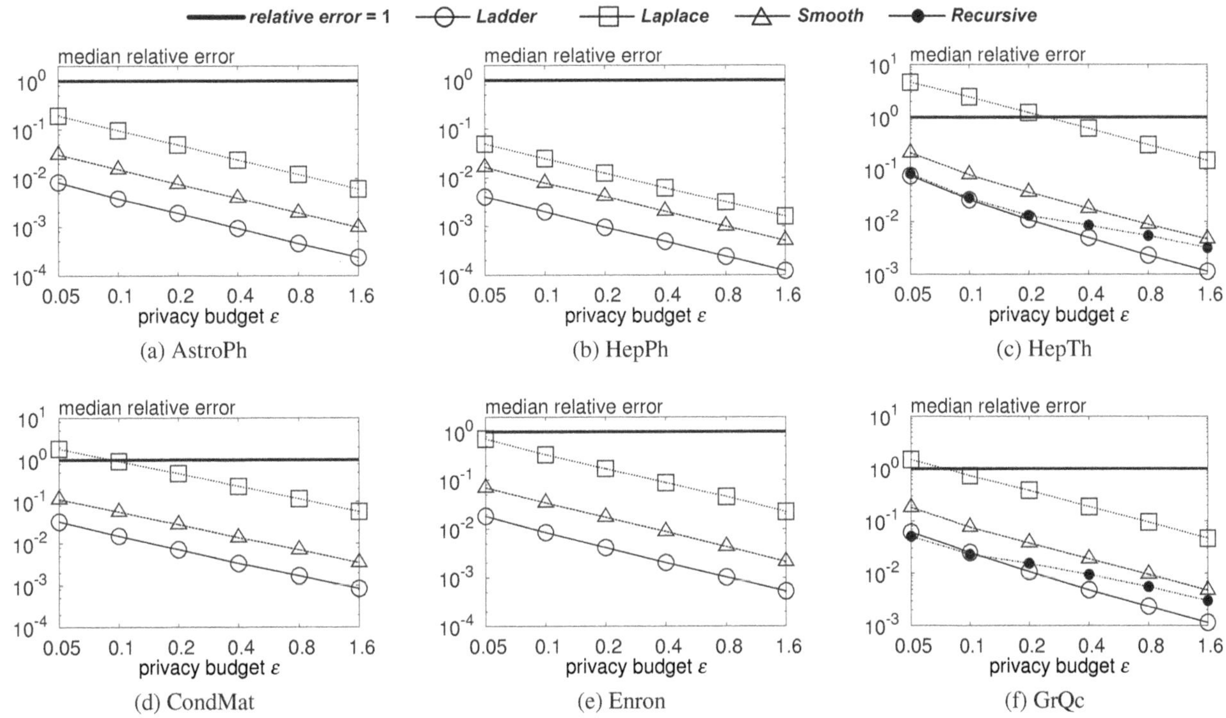

(a) AstroPh (b) HepPh (c) HepTh (d) CondMat (e) Enron (f) GrQc

Figure 4: Triangle counting

Triangle counting. The first query that we evaluate is the triangle counting $f_\triangle$ (see Figure 4). In summary, Ladder achieves good accuracy on $f_\triangle$ over all datasets. When privacy budget is relatively large, e.g., $\varepsilon = 1.6$, its median relative error always stays below or close to 0.1%. With the decrease of ε, the accuracy drops but it is still smaller than 10% even when $\varepsilon = 0.05$. Compared with other differentially private methods, Ladder clearly outperforms Laplace and Smooth in all cases, simply because it injects less noise to the true results. The improvement is significant since the y-axis in shown on a log scale. As for Recursive, it is rather competitive when ε is small, say $\varepsilon \leq 0.1$. However, the gap between Recursive and Ladder begins to grow when ε increases. To explain, recall that the error of Recursive comes from two parts: bias of the lower bound and noise injected to the lower bound. As ε increases, the scale of noise reduces, while the bias is less sensitive to the change of ε then becomes the dominating factor of the error.

***k*-star counting.** Next we evaluate different methods for 3-star counting $f_{3\star}$ in Figure 5. Ladder keeps returning extremely accurate results for large ε, and reasonably good results for small ε. Meanwhile, it is still the best solution with an ε-differential privacy guarantee in all settings. In contrast to the case of triangle counting, the performance of Laplace degrades significantly compared to other two local sensitivity based solutions. The main reason is that *GS* of triangle counting is linear to n while that of 3-star counting is quadratic. On the other hand, the counting results do not increase so dramatically due to the locality of inputs. Therefore the relative error of Laplace increases. Local sensitivity, however, can capture the locality of inputs, leading to a stable relative error when the query is changed.

***k*-clique counting.** Figure 6 presents the results of 4-clique counting ($f_{4\mathbb{C}}$). Ladder is the only private solution besides the naive Laplace, and the former is orders of magnitude better than the latter in terms of accuracy. The lines of Ladder always stay below the bold lines except for two points where ε is extremely small, and the gaps increase markedly with ε. In contrast, the quality of results from Laplace tends to be rather poor, if it is usable at all. Thus we conclude that Ladder is the only effective and efficient algorithm for releasing private k-clique counting.

***k*-triangle counting.** The last query of interest in our experiment is 2-triangle counting $f_{2\triangle}$. We have a new baseline NoisyLS for this query and compare it with Ladder in Figure 7. The superiority of Ladder is three-fold: (i) it is always more accurate than NoisyLS when ε varies from 0.05 to 0.4; (ii) it has no extra constraint on privacy budget ε; (iii) it provides stronger privacy protection than

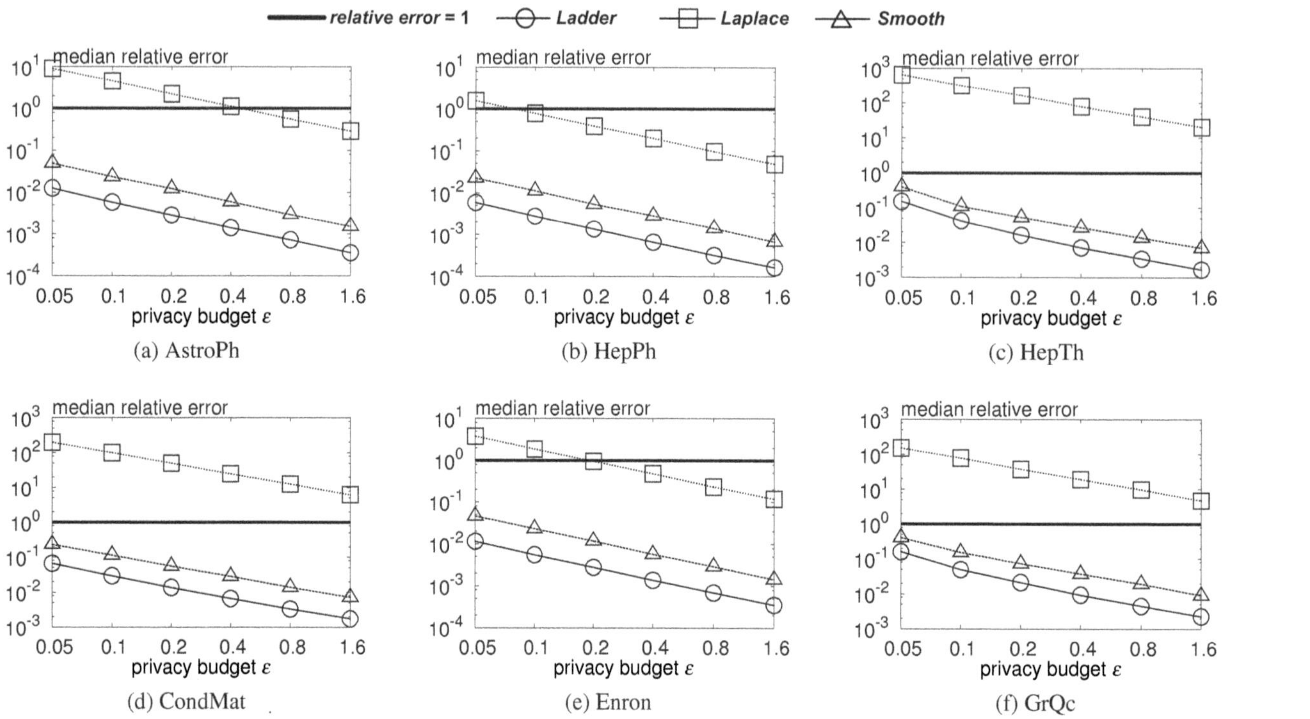

(a) AstroPh (b) HepPh (c) HepTh

(d) CondMat (e) Enron (f) GrQc

Figure 5: 3-**star counting**

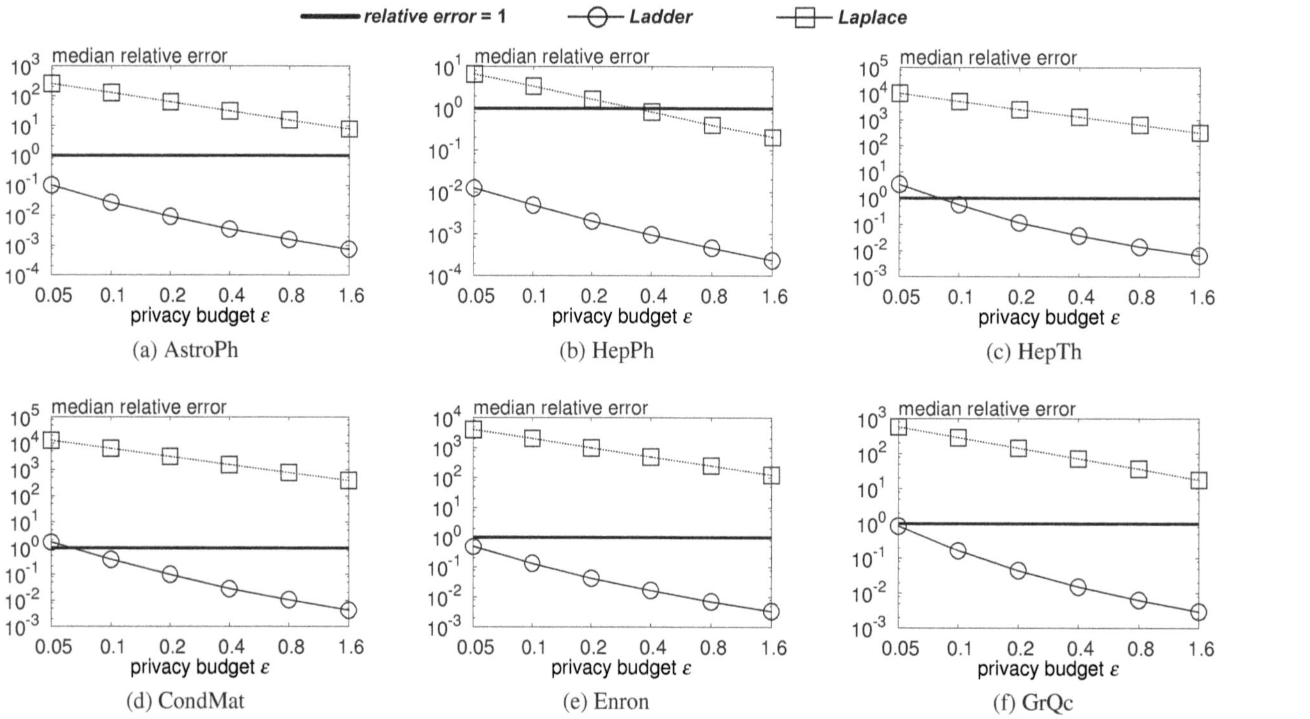

(a) AstroPh (b) HepPh (c) HepTh

(d) CondMat (e) Enron (f) GrQc

Figure 6: 4-**clique counting**

NoisyLS. In summary, Ladder is a more preferable solution for private k-triangle counting.

Average degree and density. Besides the comparison among private algorithms, we are also interested in the impact of input graphs to the private counting results. Intuitively, a graph with more edges (assuming a fixed number of nodes) is likely to have more copies of subgraphs and a larger local sensitivity, but the global sensitivity is never a function of number of edges. Thus, we can expect relatively good performance of Laplace on denser graphs. Nevertheless, the impact of graph density to local sensitivity is still unclear. From Table 2, we can learn that AstroPh and HepPh are denser graphs with higher average degree, on which Laplace does

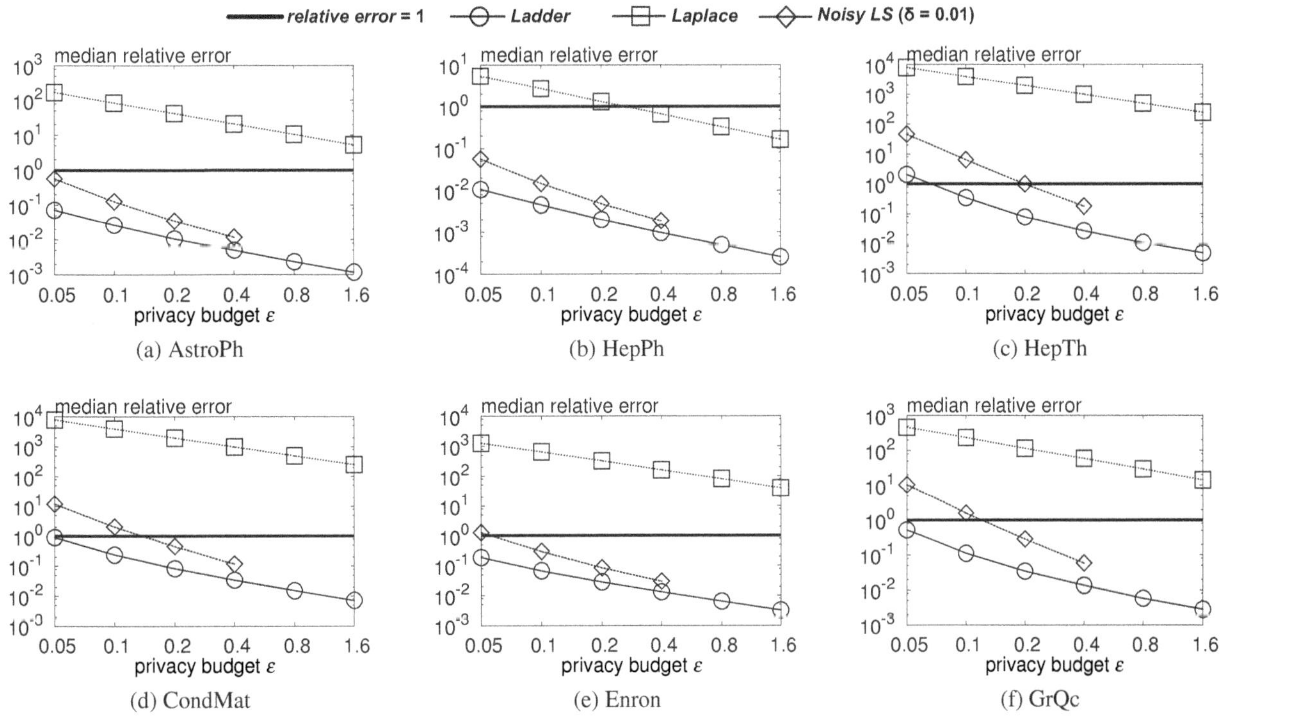

Figure 7: 2-triangle counting

have better overall accuracy. Interestingly, local sensitivity based algorithms like Ladder and Smooth also benefit notably from high density inputs, implying that local sensitivity does not increase as drastically as the counting results as the graph gets denser.

6.3 Stochastic Kronecker Models

To further justify the importance of subgraph counts, we show how accurate counts lead to accurate graph models. Here we adopt the stochastic Kronecker model [20], a sophisticated method which can simulate large real-world graphs with only a few parameters. The algorithm in [13, 26] provides a way to estimate parameters of the simplest Kronecker model from a small set of subgraph counts: f_e (the number of edges), $f_\triangle$, $f_{2\star}$ and $f_{3\star}$. Therefore, one can easily build a Kronecker model then generate synthetic Kronecker graphs with differential privacy guarantees, if provided four *private* counts in advance. We aim to evaluate how the noise in private counts affects the accuracy of Kronecker models. In this set of experiments, we build three types of Kronecker models: (i) Kron-True is a non-private model, and tuned from the true subgraph counts of the graph; (ii) Kron-Ladder satisfies ε-differential privacy. The privacy budget ε is split into four parts equally, and each is used to generate a private subgraph count. The Laplace mechanism is effective enough to release f_e since it has a constant $GS = 1$. For $f_\triangle$, $f_{2\star}$ and $f_{3\star}$, we employ Ladder. (iii) Kron-Smooth is identical to Kron-Ladder except that $f_\triangle$, $f_{2\star}$ and $f_{3\star}$ are released by the Smooth mechanism.

To measure the distortion of Kron-Ladder from Kron-True, we look into the difference of their synthetic graphs. For Kron-True, we simply sample 100 synthetic graphs from the model. However, given that Ladder is a stochastic process, we first generate 100 independent Kron-Ladder models, and from each we sample 100 graphs. Therefore, Kron-Ladder is represented by a set of 10,000 graphs. Then the error between each pair of graphs from these two sets is measured, and an aggregate value is reported as the final result. The evaluation of Kron-Smooth follows the same procedures. We report the error of five graph queries including median relative error of f_e, $f_\triangle$, $f_{2\star}$, $f_{3\star}$ and average Euclidian error of the sorted degree sequence (as in [15]).

Table 3 shows the empirical results with two datasets (Enron and GrQc) and two privacy budgets ($\varepsilon = 0.2$ and 1.6). Kron-Ladder outperforms Kron-Smooth by considerable margins in all settings, which implies that Kron-Ladder generates more accurate Kronecker models. It is interesting to observe that the synthetic graphs of Kron-Ladder perform better in answering f_e (recall that both methods use Laplace mechanism for f_e). Note that the parameter estimation algorithm [13, 26] is designed to find a Kronecker model that fits *all* counts well. Hence the noise in any count could affect the choice of Kronecker model, then introduce bias to other properties of the synthetic graphs. This explains how the large scale of noise in $f_\triangle$, $f_{2\star}$ and $f_{3\star}$ propagates to f_e in Kron-Smooth.

7. RELATED WORK

The question of being able to release information on graphs in a privacy-preserving way has been of interest for a number of years, driven by recent efforts around privacy-preserving data publishing. It is interesting to note that within the computer science community, the recent slew of interest in graph anonymization began with publications that emphasized the difficulty of this problem. Backstrom *et al.* [2] showed that an adversary could easily learn neighborhood information of targeted nodes from a "deidentified" (unlabeled) released graph, if they could insert a small number of edges. Hay *et al.* [16] showed that the neighborhood around a node in an unlabeled graph is often sufficiently distinctive to identify it. Narayanan and Shmatikov [27, 28] "weaponized" these observations into effective attacks able to extract sensitive link information from deidentified and lightly perturbed graphs—most famously, by linking individuals from the Netflix prize data set to public IMDB profiles.

Table 3: Accuracy of Kronecker models tuned from noisy counts

datasets	methods	$\varepsilon = 0.2$					$\varepsilon = 1.6$				
		f_e	$f_\triangle$	$f_{2\star}$	$f_{3\star}$	deg. seq.	f_e	$f_\triangle$	$f_{2\star}$	$f_{3\star}$	deg. seq.
Enron	Kron_Ladder	0.306%	0.595%	0.511%	0.691%	0.4628	0.043%	0.083%	0.071%	0.096%	0.4388
	Kron_Smooth	1.347%	2.791%	2.394%	3.247%	1.2383	0.171%	0.331%	0.285%	0.385%	0.6027
GrQc	Kron_Ladder	2.195%	9.849%	4.490%	14.52%	0.9048	0.187%	0.728%	0.298%	1.061%	0.3993
	Kron_Smooth	5.908%	24.32%	11.56%	31.70%	1.5223	0.854%	3.088%	1.620%	4.469%	0.5744

The response of the research community to these demonstrations of the weakness of deidentification was the design of numerous methods which aimed to be more robust to attack. Drawing inspiration from concurrent efforts on k-anonymity for tabular data, several approaches aimed to modify the input graph structure to produce an output graph that was not susceptible to the techniques used to defeat deidentification. Of particular note was the work of Liu and Terzi [23] which aimed to make graphs *k-degree anonymous*, so that an adversary possessed of the knowledge of the degree of a target node would find at least k nodes in the released graph sharing that degree. Many subsequent works built on this foundation by proposing stronger structural requirements on the released graph. Zhou and Pei [37] considered graphs with nodes of certain types, and sought to ensure that for every set of neighborhood links around a target node, there are multiple possible matches in the released graph. Zou *et al.* [38] proposed *k-automorphism*, requiring that every node in the released graph has at least $k-1$ structurally indistinguishable counterparts (i.e. have the same pattern of links between neighbors, and neighbors-of-neighbors, etc.). A parallel set of works were based on "clustering" within graphs, where groups of nodes are replaced by a "cluster" in the output graph, and only aggregate statistics of the cluster are revealed [6, 16, 34].

A survey of the state of the art in 2008 provides a snapshot of several dozen contributions in this area; in the intervening years that have been many more efforts in this direction. Nevertheless, a number of criticisms of this philosophy towards data anonymization have emerged. Principal amongst these is that methods which seek to prevent a specific attack by an adversary with a certain type of information and an assumed approach to reasoning are not robust against "real-world" adversaries, who can bring unanticipated knowledge and inference techniques to circumvent these. Secondarily, there is the perception that these methods provide only ad hoc rather than principled guarantees, and do not adequately preserve utility for their inputs. Instead, there has been growing interest in ways to provide a more formal guarantee of privacy. The main such model is Differential Privacy, which is not without its critics or identified limitations, but which nevertheless represents the current focus of efforts to provide workable privacy solutions.

Differential privacy [7] is rigorously formulated based on statistics and offers an extremely strong privacy protection. A plethora of efforts has been made to apply differential privacy to a broad range of problems. It is beyond the scope of this paper to give full coverage of all differential privacy methods; instead, see recent surveys [8,9,12,30] and references therein. A brief survey of differentially private algorithms for releasing subgraph counts is given in Section 1.2. In what follows, we review some other related efforts to realize privacy protection for graph data.

Hay et al. [15] translated the language of differential privacy to the graph context, and give the formal definitions of edge and node differential privacy. This paper and subsequent related approaches [18,22] provide effective solutions to releasing the degree sequence of a sensitive graph, and use some sophisticated post-processing techniques to reduce noise. Proserpio et al. [31] and Sala et al. [33] further extend the problem to higher-order joint degree sequences, which model more detailed information within the sensitive graph. A later work by Wang and Wu [35] improves Sala's solution by calibrating noise based on smooth sensitivity, rather than the large global sensitivity. Moreover, the authors illustrate that synthetic graphs generated from the noisy joint degree sequence have a series of appealing properties. In addition, Mir and Wright [26] show how to bridge differentially private subgraph counts with Kronecker graph models, providing another method to generate synthetic graphs with privacy guarantees. In a different vein, [1, 14, 36] investigate differentially private spectral analysis (e.g., singular value decomposition and random projection) for graph data. Their results imply a great potential to process/release large scale sensitive graphs like the Facebook friendship graph and call/SMS/email networks. Recently, Lu and Miklau [24] describe the use of a chain mechanism to release alternating k-star and k-triangle counting with an (ε, δ)-differentially private guarantee. They also show how the published counts can be used to estimate the parameters of exponential random graph models.

The above discussion principally focuses on methods that provide edge differential privacy, where two graphs are considered neighbors if they differ only in the presence of a single edge. There is also a branch of work studying other variants of graph differential privacy. For example, [3, 5, 19] are the first few methods to provide *node* differential privacy with non-trivial utility guarantees. Node differential privacy is a qualitatively stronger privacy guarantee than edge differential privacy, where two graphs are considered neighbors if they differ in the presence of a node and all its incident edges. As a consequence, it generally requires substantially more noise to protect the released information. Meanwhile, Rastogi et al. [32] consider a relaxed version of edge differential privacy, called edge *adversarial* privacy, which relies on some assumptions about prior knowledge of the malicious user. As those assumptions might plausibly be violated in practice, this new definition actually provide less privacy assurance, compared to the conventional edge differential privacy.

8. CONCLUDING REMARKS

The problem of releasing information about private data is a timely one, and there continues to be pressures to make relevant information available in a privacy-respecting fashion. We have shown that the widely-respected differential privacy guarantee can be obtained for graph statistics, specifically subgraph counts, in a way that is efficient and accurate. Future work includes extending the solution to a large scale graph like Facebook. Moreover, the ladder method developed, although tailored for subgraph counts, can be applied more generally, to functions outside the domain of graphs. The main challenge in lifting the notion to other domains is to ensure that concepts such as local sensitivity at distance t are well-defined. It will be natural to study the usefulness of the ladder framework for other structured mathematical objects, such as matrix representations of data, as well as special cases of graphs, such as trees or directed acyclic graphs.

Acknowledgments

This work was supported in part by European Commission Marie Curie Integration Grant PCIG13-GA-2013-618202, by Nanyang Technological University under SUG Grant M4080094.020, by Microsoft Research Asia under a gift grant, by the Ministry of Education (Singapore) under an AcRF Tier-2 grant, and by AT&T under an unrestricted gift grant.

9. REFERENCES

[1] F. Ahmed, R. Jin, and A. X. Liu. A random matrix approach to differential privacy and structure preserved social network graph publishing. *CoRR*, abs/1307.0475, 2013.

[2] L. Backstrom, C. Dwork, and J. M. Kleinberg. Wherefore art thou r3579x?: anonymized social networks, hidden patterns, and structural steganography. In *WWW*, pages 181–190, 2007.

[3] J. Blocki, A. Blum, A. Datta, and O. Sheffet. Differentially private data analysis of social networks via restricted sensitivity. In *Proceedings of the 4th conference on Innovations in Theoretical Computer Science*, pages 87–96. ACM, 2013.

[4] H. Bunke. On a relation between graph edit distance and maximum common subgraph. *Pattern Recogn. Lett.*, 18(9):689–694, Aug. 1997.

[5] S. Chen and S. Zhou. Recursive mechanism: Towards node differential privacy and unrestricted joins. In *SIGMOD*, pages 653–664, 2013.

[6] G. Cormode, D. Srivastava, T. Yu, and Q. Zhang. Anonymizing bipartite graph data using safe groupings. *VLDB J.*, pages 115–139, 2010.

[7] C. Dwork. Differential privacy. In *ICALP*, pages 1–12, 2006.

[8] C. Dwork. Differential privacy: A survey of results. In *TAMC*, pages 1–19, 2008.

[9] C. Dwork. The differential privacy frontier (extended abstract). In *TCC*, pages 496–502, 2009.

[10] C. Dwork, K. Kenthapadi, F. McSherry, I. Mironov, and M. Naor. Our data, ourselves: Privacy via distributed noise generation. In *Advances in Cryptology-EUROCRYPT 2006*, pages 486–503. Springer, 2006.

[11] C. Dwork, F. McSherry, K. Nissim, and A. Smith. Calibrating noise to sensitivity in private data analysis. In *TCC*, pages 265–284, 2006.

[12] C. Dwork and A. Smith. Differential privacy for statistics: What we know and what we want to learn. *Journal of Privacy and Confidentiality*, 1(2):2, 2010.

[13] D. F. Gleich and A. B. Owen. Moment-based estimation of stochastic kronecker graph parameters. *Internet Mathematics*, 8(3):232–256, 2012.

[14] M. Hardt and A. Roth. Beyond worst-case analysis in private singular vector computation. In *STOC*, 2013.

[15] M. Hay, C. Li, G. Miklau, and D. Jensen. Accurate estimation of the degree distribution of private networks. In *ICDM*, pages 169–178, 2009.

[16] M. Hay, G. Miklau, D. Jensen, D. F. Towsley, and C. Li. Resisting structural re-identification in anonymized social networks. *VLDB J.*, pages 797–823, 2010.

[17] V. Karwa, S. Raskhodnikova, A. Smith, and G. Yaroslavtsev. Private analysis of graph structure. *TODS*, 39(3):22, 2014.

[18] V. Karwa and A. B. Slavković. Differentially private graphical degree sequences and synthetic graphs. In *Privacy in Statistical Databases*, pages 273–285. Springer, 2012.

[19] S. P. Kasiviswanathan, K. Nissim, S. Raskhodnikova, and A. Smith. Analyzing graphs with node differential privacy. In *Theory of Cryptography*, pages 457–476. Springer, 2013.

[20] J. Leskovec, D. Chakrabarti, J. Kleinberg, C. Faloutsos, and Z. Ghahramani. Kronecker graphs: An approach to modeling networks. *The Journal of Machine Learning Research*, 11:985–1042, 2010.

[21] J. Leskovec and A. Krevl. SNAP Datasets: Stanford large network dataset collection. http://snap.stanford.edu/data, June 2014.

[22] B.-R. Lin and D. Kifer. Information preservation in statistical privacy and bayesian estimation of unattributed histograms. In *SIGMOD*, pages 677–688, 2013.

[23] K. Liu and E. Terzi. Towards identity anonymization on graphs. In *SIGMOD*, pages 93–106, 2008.

[24] W. Lu and G. Miklau. Exponential random graph estimation under differential privacy. In *KDD*, pages 921–930, 2014.

[25] F. McSherry and K. Talwar. Mechanism design via differential privacy. In *FOCS*, pages 94–103, 2007.

[26] D. Mir and R. N. Wright. A differentially private estimator for the stochastic kronecker graph model. In *Proceedings of the 2012 Joint EDBT/ICDT Workshops*, pages 167–176. ACM, 2012.

[27] A. Narayanan and V. Shmatikov. Robust de-anonymization of large sparse datasets. In *IEEE Symposium on Security and Privacy*, pages 111–125, 2008.

[28] A. Narayanan and V. Shmatikov. De-anonymizing social networks. In *IEEE Symposium on Security and Privacy*, pages 173–187, 2009.

[29] K. Nissim, S. Raskhodnikova, and A. Smith. Smooth sensitivity and sampling in private data analysis. In *STOC*, pages 75–84, 2007.

[30] M. M. Pai and A. Roth. Privacy and mechanism design. *ACM SIGecom Exchanges*, 12(1):8–29, 2013.

[31] D. Proserpio, S. Goldberg, and F. McSherry. Calibrating data to sensitivity in private data analysis. *PVLDB*, 7(8), 2014.

[32] V. Rastogi, M. Hay, G. Miklau, and D. Suciu. Relationship privacy: output perturbation for queries with joins. In *PODS*, pages 107–116, 2009.

[33] A. Sala, X. Zhao, C. Wilson, H. Zheng, and B. Y. Zhao. Sharing graphs using differentially private graph models. In *IMC*, pages 81–98. ACM, 2011.

[34] T. Tassa and D. Cohen. Anonymization of centralized and distributed social networks by sequential clustering. *TKDE*, 25(2), 2013.

[35] Y. Wang and X. Wu. Preserving differential privacy in degree-correlation based graph generation. *Trans. Data Privacy*, 6(2):127–145, Aug. 2013.

[36] Y. Wang, X. Wu, and L. Wu. Differential privacy preserving spectral graph analysis. In *Advances in Knowledge Discovery and Data Mining*, pages 329–340. 2013.

[37] B. Zhou and J. Pei. Preserving privacy in social networks against neighborhood attacks. In *ICDE*, pages 506 –515, 2008.

[38] L. Zou, L. Chen, and M. T. Özsu. K-automorphism: A general framework for privacy preserving network publication. In *PVLDB*, pages 946–957, 2009.

APPENDIX

A. NP-COMPLETENESS

THEOREM A.1. *Computing $LS(g,t)$ of $f_{k\mathbb{C}}$ for a constant $k > 3$ is NP-complete.*

PROOF. We first prove that it is NP-complete to compute $LS_{ij}(g,t)$ given a particular pair of nodes (i,j), to which the well-known Clique Problem is polynomial-time reducible.

Given an instance of Clique Problem $\langle g,t\rangle$ (i.e., whether a given graph g has a clique of at least size t), we extend g to g^+ by adding two extra nodes i and j. Then we make i connected to all other nodes in g^+ while keeping j isolated (except i). This construction can be done in time that is polynomial in the size of Clique Problem instance. Next, we prove that

$$LS_{ij}(g^+,t) = \binom{t}{k-2} \Leftrightarrow g \text{ contains a } t\text{-clique},$$

where k can be set to any *constant* integer within $(3,t)$.

Recall from Lemma 5.3 that local sensitivity of $f_{k\mathbb{C}}$ over (i,j) is the number of $(k-2)$-cliques in the subgraph induced by their common neighbors A_{ij}. In g^+, A_{ij} is empty since j is isolated from g. After t modification steps on the graph, the size of A_{ij} could reach t if we connect j to t nodes in g (i is already connected to all nodes in g); and the maximum number of $(k-2)$-cliques, i.e., $\binom{t}{k-2}$, is achieved if and only if new neighbors of i and j form a t-clique. Therefore, it implies the existence of a t-clique in g.

We remark that this proof does not apply in the case of $k = 3$ (triangle counting), since the t-clique is not the only subgraph of size t that maximizes the number of 1-cliques (nodes). Indeed, computing $LS_{ij}(g,t)$ of triangle counting is polynomial-time solvable as shown by Lemma 5.1.

Last, we extend the result to $LS(g,t)$ through a reduction from the same NP-complete problem, Clique Problem. For any instance $\langle g,t\rangle$ where g has n nodes, we construct g^+ from g by adding a n-clique and a hub node i which is connected to all other nodes in g^+. Then we show that

$$LS(g^+,t) = \binom{n-1}{k-2} + \binom{t}{k-2} \Leftrightarrow g \text{ contains a } t\text{-clique}.$$

Let j be an arbitrary node in the n-clique. It is easy to prove that $LS(g^+,t) = LS_{ij}(g^+,t)$. Therefore, $LS(g^+,t)$ equals the number of $(k-2)$-cliques in the subgraph of A_{ij}. At the beginning, subgraph of A_{ij} is a $(n-1)$-clique. To extend it, one can use one modification to either (i) add a node of g to A_{ij} by connecting it to j, or (ii) add an edge into the subgraph of A_{ij}. The optimum is only attained by adding t nodes of g to A_{ij}, who form a t-clique in g. Thus, the new subgraph of A_{ij} contains two separated components: a $(n-1)$-clique and a t-clique, and it has $\binom{n-1}{k-2} + \binom{t}{k-2}$ different $(k-2)$-cliques. □

B. PROOF OF THEOREM 3.1

In what follows, we rewrite the proof of Theorem 6 of [25] using the concepts and notations developed in this paper.

PROOF. The first step is to observe that Algorithm 1 draws from a probability distribution over the integers where the probability associated with output k is proportional to $\exp\left(\varepsilon q(g,k)/2\Delta_q\right)$, normalized by the sum of this quantity over all integers. Note that we do not compute this probability directly; instead, for the sake of efficiency, we group together all integers which share the same probability (in our terminology, which are on the same rung) for the rungs 0 to M. Additionally, we compute the aggregate probability for all outputs on rungs below M as a single value captured by $M+1$, as described after the description of the algorithm. It is straightforward to check that the actions of Algorithm 1 in the creation of the *weight* array give these sums of (unnormalized) probabilities. The action of the algorithm can then be seen as following two steps: first, we select a rung of the ladder (where rung $M+1$ is considered as a special case) according to the relative value of the *weight* of the rung. Then, we pick an integer from the corresponding rung. For rungs 0 to M, this is simple: all integers on the rung have the same probability, so we just pick one uniformly. For rung $M+1$, which corresponds to an unbounded tail of possible outputs, we take advantage of the structure to first pick how many further rungs down the ladder to go, and then to again pick uniformly from these. This gives the desired probability distribution of producing each possible value.

Hence as argued above, the output probability distribution of Algorithm 1 at integer k is equal to

$$\Pr[k] = \frac{\exp\left(\frac{\varepsilon}{2\Delta_q}\cdot q(g,k)\right)}{\sum_{k\in\mathbb{Z}}\exp\left(\frac{\varepsilon}{2\Delta_q}\cdot q(g,k)\right)}. \quad (7)$$

Now if the input g is replaced by its neighboring graph g', the quality of k will be changed by at most Δ_q, i.e., $|q(g,k) - q(g',k)| \le \Delta_q$. Therefore, the numerator of (7) can change at most by a factor of $\exp(\varepsilon\Delta_q/2\Delta_q) = \exp(\varepsilon/2)$ and the denominator minimum by a factor of $\exp(-\varepsilon/2)$. Thus the ratio of the new probability of k (with g') and the original one is at most $\exp(\varepsilon)$. □

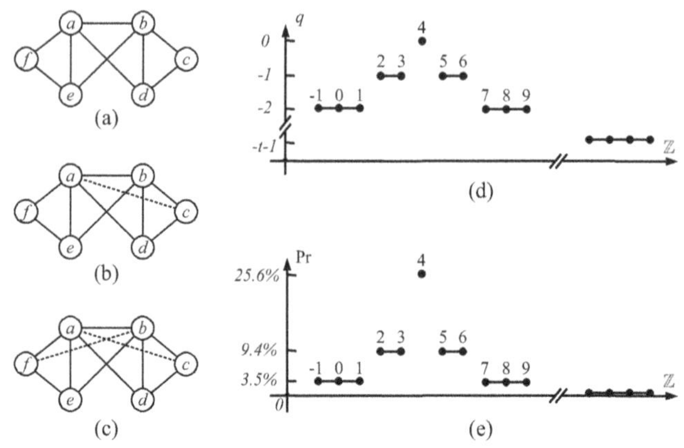

Figure 8: An end-to-end example

C. AN END-TO-END EXAMPLE

In this section, we review the end-to-end workflow of our algorithm with an example input in Figure 8(a). The query in use is the triangle counting $f_\triangle$. Our algorithm consists of the following steps:

1. Compute the number of triangles $f_\triangle(g) = 4$, i.e., $\triangle_{abd}$, $\triangle_{abe}$, $\triangle_{bcd}$ and $\triangle_{aef}$.

2. Generate the ladder function of query $f_\triangle$, input g and step t, i.e., $I_t(g)$, for each $t \in [0,M]$. We describe the definition and key properties of ladder functions in Section 4, then illustrate how to compute ladder functions for specific queries in Section 5. For triangle counting query, we use its local sensitivity at distance t as the ladder function. $I_0(g) = LS(g,0) = 2$ achieved by removing edge

(a,b) from the graph. $LS(g,1)$ allows one extra change before calculating LS. In Figure 8(b), we show how the dashed edge (a,c) affects LS_{ab}, making $LS(g,1) = LS_{ab}(g,1) = 3$. Then Figure 8(c) shows an example achieving $LS(g,2) = 4$, where the value converges to the global sensitivity. Therefore, this step terminates with $M = 2$.

3. Build the ladder quality function $q(g,k)$ for $k \in \mathbb{Z}$, by combining the true answer $f_{\triangle}(g)$ and ladder functions $I_t(g)$; see Definition 3.1 of Section 3.1. Figure 8(d) gives a part of the quality function q over the integer domain. The true answer $k = 4$ takes the maximum value 0, which is the center of the function. Next to it are two first rungs, each consisting of $I_0(g) = 2$ integers on one side of the center. All integers on first rungs are assigned quality score -1. The next rung is formed of the next $I_1(g) = 3$ integers on each side with quality -2 and so on. Note that every integer will be given a quality score.

4. Generate the output distribution from the exponential mechanism that takes $q(g,k)$ as quality function; see equation (3) of Section 2.1. As the distribution changes with the privacy budget ε, we fix ε to 2 in the following discussion. Now the sampling probability for $k = 4$ is proportional to $\exp\left(\varepsilon q(g,4)/2\Delta_q\right) = e^0$, given $\Delta_q = 1$ (see Theorem 4.2) and $q(g,4) = 0$. Similarly, the probability for $k = 5$ is proportional to e^{-1}. After normalization, we have $\Pr[k = 4] = 25.6\%$ and $\Pr[k = 5] = 9.4\%$, as shown in Figure 8(e).

5. Sample the distribution and return. Algorithm 1 and Section 3.2 are dedicated to detailing the efficient sampling technique.

Bayesian Differential Privacy on Correlated Data

Bin Yang
Rakuten Institute of Technology, Rakuten Inc.
Tokyo, Japan
yangbin64@gmail.com

Issei Sato
Information Technology Center
The University of Tokyo, Japan
sato@r.dl.itc.u-tokyo.ac.jp

Hiroshi Nakagawa
Information Technology Center
The University of Tokyo, Japan
nakagawa@dl.itc.u-tokyo.ac.jp

ABSTRACT

Differential privacy provides a rigorous standard for evaluating the privacy of perturbation algorithms. It has widely been regarded that differential privacy is a universal definition that deals with both independent and correlated data and a differentially private algorithm can protect privacy against arbitrary adversaries. However, recent research indicates that differential privacy may not guarantee privacy against arbitrary adversaries if the data are correlated.

In this paper, we focus on the private perturbation algorithms on correlated data. We investigate the following three problems: (1) the influence of data correlations on privacy; (2) the influence of adversary prior knowledge on privacy; and (3) a general perturbation algorithm that is private for prior knowledge of any subset of tuples in the data when the data are correlated. We propose a Pufferfish definition of privacy, called Bayesian differential privacy, by which the privacy level of a probabilistic perturbation algorithm can be evaluated even when the data are correlated and when the prior knowledge is incomplete. We present a Gaussian correlation model to accurately describe the structure of data correlations and analyze the Bayesian differential privacy of the perturbation algorithm on the basis of this model. Our results show that privacy is poorest for an adversary who has the least prior knowledge. We further extend this model to a more general one that considers uncertain prior knowledge.

Categories and Subject Descriptors

K.4.1 [**Computers and Society**]: Privacy

General Terms

Theory, Privacy, Optimization

Keywords

Private data analysis; Differential privacy; Output perturbation; Gaussian Markov random field; Optimization

SIGMOD'15, May 31–June 4, 2015, Melbourne, Victoria, Australia.

http://dx.doi.org/10.1145/2723372.2747643.

1. INTRODUCTION

Privacy-preserving data publishing has received increasing attention because of its huge social benefits. Trusted databases collect data from individuals and release the results of queries on it to data consumers, such as research organizations, interested in the statistical properties of the published data. However, because the original data may contain sensitive information about individuals, publishing it without any changes may compromise privacy. Since the provider of such databases is obligated to ensure the privacy of individuals, the results of the queries must be perturbed before being published. The use of probabilistic output perturbation ensures data consumers to learn useful information while at the same time ensuring that sensitive information about individuals cannot be inferred from the output.

Many privacy definitions have been proposed to limit leakage of private information about individuals that could be inferred from query results. The current state-of-the-art standard notion of privacy is differential privacy [4]. Intuitively, differential privacy requires that what can be learned from the published data is not significantly affected by the presence or absence of an individual. Differential privacy offers a strong privacy guarantee without any limit on the power of the adversary's background knowledge.

1.1 Correlated Data

Although differential privacy has been widely considered to be a robust standard, previous studies [16] have shown that the privacy of individuals may be compromised when data are correlated. Example 1 is similar to one in [16]:

EXAMPLE 1. *Consider a social network including ten people and their relationships, such as family, friends, and colleagues. Suppose an "attacker" knows all the information about the relationships in the network, but does not know who has caught influenza. This attacker may ask "how many persons in this social network have had influenza during the last month?". In order to protect each individual's health information, a Laplacian noise* $Lap(1/\epsilon)$ *is added to the true query and the noisy query is answered. Previous research tells us that the noisy query result satisfies* ϵ*-differential privacy. (1) If these ten persons have no relationship with each other, it is difficult to infer the health of any one of them, since the output distributions are very similar whether or not this person is in the network; (2) If these persons have a strong relationship with each other, for example, their data are a family living together, the true query result can be assumed to be either* 0 *or* 10*, since they are highly correlated. Accordingly, a change in the health of one person may cause* *a ten fold increase in the variety of the query result. To guarantee privacy of the same level, it is necessary to add Laplacian noise* $Lap(1/10\epsilon)$ *to the true result; (3) The intermediate case is one in which the persons are friends who, for example, hold weekly parties. Here, although someone's catching influenza will pose a higher risk to the other members, the true result is not a certain value; hence, there is no appropriate way to calibrate the noise. So, the question is what kind of noise should we add to the true result?*

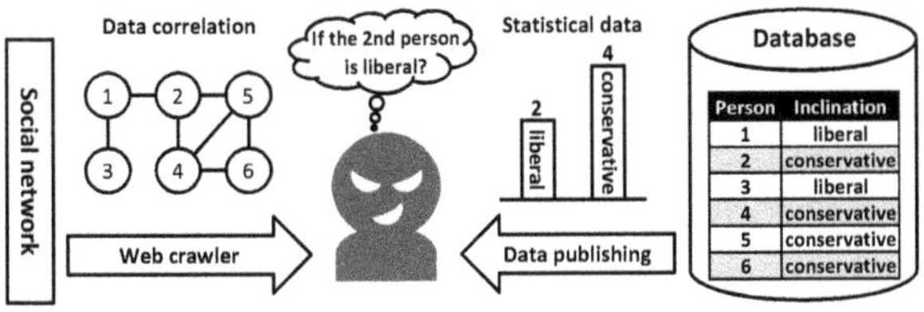

Figure 1: Attack Sensitive Information Using Data Correlation.

In practice, data correlations are quite easy to obtain from social networks, etc. For example, an adversary could ascertain the social network structure by using a web crawler algorithm and learn the correlations between persons from this structure. Given query results, such as "the numbers of persons whose political inclinations are liberal and conservative", he/she may attempt to infer the political inclinations of a specific person from the fact that highly correlated persons are likely to have the same political inclination (Figure 1). As a result, it is important to carefully study the effect of data correlations on privacy.

It is worth emphasizing that the adversaries might have different correlation structures, since they could collect information from different sources. This would result in different mechanisms. For example, a strong correlation structure in which all tuples are nearly equal requires a mechanism with a large noise, and vice versa. In this paper, we only consider a mechanism with respect to a single correlation structure specified by the data publisher. Consequently, protections can only be enabled for this correlation structure and there are unknown protections against adversaries who do not use this correlation structure.

1.2 Prior Knowledge of the Adversary

Differential privacy is designed to preserve the privacy in the face of intrusions by the strongest adversary who exactly knows everything about all individual entities except the object of its attack. The underlying assumption is that the strongest adversary is better able to learn more sensitive information from the query output. In fact, as we will show in Section 3, differential privacy does guarantee privacy against intrusion by any adversary when all the entities in the database are independent. Furthermore, we show that it is valid when the data are probabilistically correlated and all adversaries have full knowledge. However, it may have privacy vulnerabilities when the data are correlated and the adversary does not have full knowledge (see Table 1).

1.3 Our Contribution

This paper focuses on how data correlations and prior knowledge affect privacy. We ascertain reasons for the phenomena in Table 1 by analyzing some examples (Section 3).

We propose a new Pufferfish privacy definition - Bayesian differential privacy - to rationally represent the leakage of

Table 1: Validity of Differential Privacy.

Data \ Adversary	Strong	Arbitrary
Independent	Valid	Valid
Correlated	Valid	Invalid

private information from a probabilistic output perturbation mechanism. Bayesian differential privacy is equivalent to differential privacy when the tuples in the database are independent or when all adversaries have full background knowledge. It also guarantees privacy against correlated data and partial background knowledge; that is, it is more rigorous than differential privacy (Section 4).

We propose a Gaussian correlation model to describe complex data correlations and use it to analyze the privacy of the output of the perturbation mechanism. Our results show that, under the assumption that the data are correlated according to a Gaussian correlation model, the adversary with the least prior knowledge poses the highest risk of information leakage. Moreover, we develop an efficient algorithm to find a general Bayesian differentially private mechanism for outputting a sum query on these data (Section 5).

It is shown that the utility will be too low if the adversary is extremely weak. We extend the Gaussian correlation model by introducing uncertain prior knowledge, so that the adversary does not become not too weak. The extended model is more general than the Gaussian correlation model. The theoretical analysis illustrates that this extended model can be used to enhance the utility of the output (Section 6).

A binary correlation model is also proposed on the basis of the Gaussian correlation model. With this model, a Bayesian differentially private mechanism for the counting query and the histogram can be derived (Section 7).

Finally, Section 8 shows several experimental results on artificial and real data.

2. RELATED WORK

Adversarial privacy is a probabilistic privacy definition that is explicitly expressed in terms of prior and posterior probabilities of the entity to be attacked. Suppose x and r are random variables. x is sensitive, and r is the output of the database in response to a query. Miklau and Suciu [20] declared x to be perfectly private given r if and only if $\Pr(x|r) \equiv \Pr(x)$. Intuitively, this implies the posterior of x given r has not changed from its prior. Unfortunately, if there is no constraint on the distribution, no pair (x, r) of non-trivial properties will have perfect privacy. Much of the related work has focused on how to relax this constraint [7, 1, 3, 5, 6, 14, 24, 13]. Differential privacy [4] is a definition of indistinguishability. It is widely considered to be a rigorous privacy guarantee. A number of variations on differential privacy have been proposed [2, 15, 21, 22].

Kifer and Machanavajjhala [16] have raised an important issue that differential privacy may not guarantee the privacy of correlated data against arbitrary adversaries, because the strong correlations make the sensitive data easier to be distinguished from output. They [16] also modified the definition of differential privacy to adapt it to databases with deterministic constraints by redefining neighboring. Gehrke et al. [9, 8] also focused on privacy in relation to correlated data and proposed a zero-knowledge privacy relying on the

Table 2: Notation

Symbol	Description
$\mathbf{x}$	A database instance $\{x_1, x_2, \cdots, x_n\}$.
$[n]$	The tuple set $\{1, 2, \cdots, n\}$.
i	The tuple one attempts to attack.
$\mathcal{K},\mathcal{U}$	The set of known/unknown tuples.
$\mathcal{C}$	The attack tuple and known tuples $\{i\} \cup \mathcal{K}$.
x_i, x_i'	Two different values of tuple $i \in [n]$.
$\mathbf{x}_{-i}$	The database $\mathbf{x}$ with x_i eliminated.
$\mathbf{x}'$	The database $\mathbf{x}$ with x_i replaced with x_i'.
$\mathbf{x}_\mathcal{K}, \mathbf{x}_\mathcal{U}$	The instances of known/unknown tuples.
$\mathcal{A}(i, \mathcal{K})$	An adversary with knowledge $\mathcal{K}$ to attack x_i.
f	A query function on database $\mathbf{x}$.
$\mathcal{M}$	A randomized mechanism over $\mathbf{x}$.
r	The random request generated by $\mathcal{M}$.

same notion from cryptography. A perturbation mechanism satisfying this criterion was proposed to protect the privacy of correlated data, in which the aggregate function set needs to be carefully selected. A Bayesian framework for defining privacy - Pufferfish - was proposed [17]. It can be regarded as the framework of our new privacy definition. Blowfish [12] is a special privacy definition inspired by the Pufferfish framework. It increases utility by specifying necessary secrets and constraints. Another Bayesian definition of privacy [25] is one, in which the attributes of each tuple form a Bayesian network. Rastogi et al. [23] considered correlated data and gave an adversarial definition weaker than that of differential privacy that would improve utility against specific adversaries. In [23], a query over a network structure is published and this structure is unknown to adversaries. The problem setting is different from that in this paper, in which the published query is not over the data correlation (network) and the correlation structure is assumed to be exactly known to adversaries. Other differentially private mechanisms have been proposed for social networks [11].

3. PRIVACY AND CORRELATED DATA

We will now formulate the probabilistic privacy model.

3.1 Notations and Assumptions

A trusted database with n tuples, denoted as the set of indices $[n] = \{1, 2, \cdots, n\}$, releases the results of a query function $q = f(\mathbf{x})$ on an instance of the dataset, $\mathbf{x} = \{x_1, x_2, \cdots, x_n\}$. To protect the privacy of individual tuples, it only releases a perturbed version of the query result $r = \mathcal{M}(\mathbf{x})$ generated by a randomized perturbation mechanism $\mathcal{M}$. Since $\mathcal{M}$ is a randomized function, it can be described as a probability distribution $\Pr(\mathcal{M}(\mathbf{x}) \in S)$, or equivalently a conditional distribution, $\Pr(r \in S|\mathbf{x})$, where $S \subseteq \mathit{Range}(\mathcal{M})$. In most cases, $\mathcal{M}$ is designated to be a randomized function on the query result q; hence, the probability becomes $\Pr(r \in S|q)$. The main notations are listed in Table 2. The next sections describe the assumptions underlying our problem.

3.1.1 Data Correlation

By treating all tuples as random variables, we can generally express their probabilistic correlations as a joint distribution $\Pr(x_1, x_2, \cdots, x_n)$. A Markov random field [18] can efficiently express this joint distribution as a graph.

Definition 1. (Markov Random Field) Let V be a set of random variables. An undirected graph, $G = (V, E)$, forms a Markov random field if, $\forall X, Y \in V$,

$$X \perp\!\!\!\perp Y|V \setminus \{X, Y\} \quad \text{if and only if } \{X, Y\} \notin E,$$

where $X \perp\!\!\!\perp Y|V \setminus \{X, Y\}$ denotes that X and Y are conditionally independent given all values of $V \setminus \{X, Y\}$.

Assumption 1. Tuples in the database may be probabilistically correlated or independent, and their correlations are known to everyone.

3.1.2 Adversary

We define each adversary by exactly specifying the target of the attack, the known and unknown tuple sets.

Definition 2. (Adversary) Let $i \in [n]$ be a tuple in the database and $\mathcal{K} \subseteq [n] \setminus \{i\}$ be a tuple set. We denote an adversary as $\mathcal{A}(i, \mathcal{K})$ (or $\mathcal{A}(i, \mathbf{x}_\mathcal{K})$), if he/she exactly knows the values of all tuples in $\mathcal{K}$ (with value $\mathbf{x}_\mathcal{K}$) and attempts to attack the value of tuple i. We denote the set of unknown tuples as $\mathcal{U} = [n] \setminus \{i\} \setminus \mathcal{K}$.

Particularly, we say that adversary $\mathcal{A}(i, \mathcal{K})$ is the strongest adversary if $\mathcal{K} = [n] \setminus \{i\}$ and say that it is the weakest adversary if $\mathcal{K} = \phi$. Note that there are n strongest adversaries and n weakest adversaries.

Assumption 2. The background knowledge $\mathcal{K}$ of adversary $\mathcal{A}(i, \mathcal{K})$ who attempts to attack tuple i could be any subset of the database except tuple i, i.e., $\mathcal{K} \subseteq [n] \setminus \{i\}$.

3.1.3 Mechanism

Like most cryptography algorithms in modern security theory, the mechanism is supposed to be published.

Definition 3. (Mechanism) Let $\mathbf{x}$ be a database. We call a randomized function $\mathcal{M}(\mathbf{x})$ a (randomized) perturbation mechanism on $\mathbf{x}$, if the output $r = \mathcal{M}(\mathbf{x})$ follows a conditional distribution $\Pr(r \in S|\mathbf{x})$, or $p(r|\mathbf{x})$.

Assumption 3. $\mathcal{M}$ and the randomized output r are published to everyone. In other words, everyone knows the randomized output r and how it was generated.

In summary, data correlation, perturbation mechanism, and output are assumed to be known to all. As the information consumer may act as an adversary and attempt to attack individual tuples, the attack model is the problem of an adversary inferring individual tuples from data correlation, mechanism $\mathcal{M}$, output r, and its background knowledge.

3.2 Differential Privacy

We will express differential privacy [4] using our notation.

Definition 4. (Differential Privacy) A randomized mechanism $\mathcal{M}$ satisfies ϵ-*differential privacy*, or ϵ-DP, if

$$DP(\mathcal{M}) := \sup_{i, \mathbf{x}_{-i}, x_i, x_i', S} \log \frac{\Pr(r \in S|x_i, \mathbf{x}_{-i})}{\Pr(r \in S|x_i', \mathbf{x}_{-i})} \leq \epsilon. \quad (1)$$

The Laplacian mechanism [4] is a mechanism satisfying ϵ-DP that answers a query $f(\cdot)$ by adding noise from a Laplace distribution with a density $p(z) \sim \mathit{Lap}(\lambda)$ ($\lambda = S(f)/\epsilon$)), where $S(f) = \sup \|f(\mathbf{x}) - f(\mathbf{x}')\|_1$ is the sensitivity of the function f. Since $r = f(\mathbf{x}) + z$, the densities of the output are $p(r|\mathbf{x}) = \frac{1}{2\lambda} e^{-\frac{1}{\lambda}|r - f(\mathbf{x})|}$ and $p(r|\mathbf{x}') = \frac{1}{2\lambda} e^{-\frac{1}{\lambda}|r - f(\mathbf{x}')|}$ (Figure 2). Since ϵ is small, ϵ-DP can be intuitively understood to mean that it ensures $p(r|\mathbf{x}) \approx p(r|\mathbf{x}')$ $(\forall r, \mathbf{x}_{-i}, x_i, x_i')$.

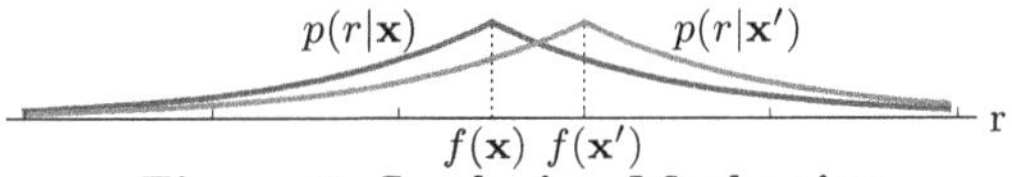

Figure 2: Laplacian Mechanism.

Table 3: Joint Distributions ($\Pr(x_1, x_2)$)

	$x_1 = 0$	$x_1 = 1$
$x_2 = 0$	0.1	0.15
$x_2 = 1$	0.3	0.45

(a) Independent

	$x_1 = 0$	$x_1 = 1$
$x_2 = 0$	0.49	0.01
$x_2 = 1$	0.01	0.49

(b) Positively correlated

	$x_1 = 0$	$x_1 = 1$
$x_2 = 0$	0.01	0.49
$x_2 = 1$	0.49	0.01

(c) Negatively correlated

3.3 Validity of Differential Privacy

Now, let us discuss the validity of differential privacy for the cases in Table 1. The differential privacy limits the distinguishability, $\mathfrak{R} = \frac{p(r|x_i, \mathbf{x}_{-i})}{p(r|x'_i, \mathbf{x}_{-i})}$, to be within a narrow range, i.e., $e^{-\epsilon} \le \mathfrak{R} \le e^{\epsilon}$ $(\forall x_i, x'_i, \mathbf{x}_{-i}, r)$. It assumes that the adversaries are the strongest, i.e., $\mathcal{K} = [n] \setminus \{i\}$. For arbitrary adversaries, on the other hand, we replace $\mathbf{x}_{-i}$ with $\mathbf{x}_{\mathcal{K}}$ and analyze the extended distinguishability $\mathfrak{R} = \frac{p(r|x_i, \mathbf{x}_{\mathcal{K}})}{p(r|x'_i, \mathbf{x}_{\mathcal{K}})}$ $(\mathcal{K} \subseteq [n] \setminus \{i\})$ instead. Let us investigate whether $\mathfrak{R}$ is still bounded in $[e^{-\epsilon}, e^{\epsilon}]$ when the data are correlated.

3.3.1 Independent Data

If all tuples are independent, the distinguishability $\mathfrak{R}$ is bounded in $[e^{-\epsilon}, e^{\epsilon}]$ for both strong and weak adversaries.

EXAMPLE 2. *Suppose the database, $\mathbf{x} = \{x_1, x_2\}$ $(x_1, x_2 \in \{0,1\})$, with the probability in Table 3(a). Consider a query function, $f(x_1, x_2) = x_1 + x_2$. The Laplacian mechanism, $\mathcal{M}$, adds Laplacian noise, $Lap(1/\epsilon)$, to the query result.*

For a strong adversary $\mathcal{A}(1, \{2\})$ with knowledge x_2 who attempts to attack tuple 1, as Figure 3(a) and (b) show, the distinguishability is bounded, i.e., $e^{-\epsilon} \le \frac{p(r|x_1=0, x_2)}{p(r|x_1=1, x_2)} \le e^{\epsilon}$, since $\mathcal{M}$ satisfies ϵ-DP.

On the other hand, for a weak adversary $\mathcal{A}(1, \phi)$, x_2 is unknown. From Bayes' theorem, $p(r|x_1) = \sum_{x_2} p(r|\mathbf{x}) \Pr(x_2|x_1)$. Hence, $p(r|x_1)$ becomes the weighted sum of those distributions in Figure 3-(a) and (b). Since x_1 and x_2 are independent, we have $\Pr(x_2|x_1) \equiv \Pr(x_2)$. For $\mathcal{M}$ satisfying ϵ-DP, we have $e^{-\epsilon} \le \frac{p(r|x_1=0)}{p(r|x_1=1)} \le e^{\epsilon}$ (Figure 3(c)).

3.3.2 Correlated Data

If the tuples are probabilistically correlated. The distinguishability is still bounded for strong adversary, but it may not be bounded for weak adversaries.

EXAMPLE 3. *The assumptions are the same as those in Example 2, with the exception that x_1 and x_2 are correlated, for instance, with the probabilities in Table 3(b).*

As in Example 2 (Figures 3(a) and (b)), the distinguishability is bounded, if the adversary is the strongest.

For a weak adversary $\mathcal{A}(i, \phi)$, $p(r|x_1) = \sum_{x_2} p(r|x_1, x_2) \cdot p(x_2|x_1)$. Since $x_1 = x_2$ with high probability, $p(r|x_1 = 0) \approx p(r|x_1 = 0, x_2 = 0)$ and $p(r|x_1 = 1) \approx p(r|x_1 = 1, x_2 = 1)$ (Figure 3(d)). As the curves $p(r|x_1 = 0)$ and $p(r|x_1 = 1)$ separate, the distinguishability is no longer bounded in $[e^{-\epsilon}, e^{\epsilon}]$, although mechanism $\mathcal{M}$ still satisfies ϵ-DP.

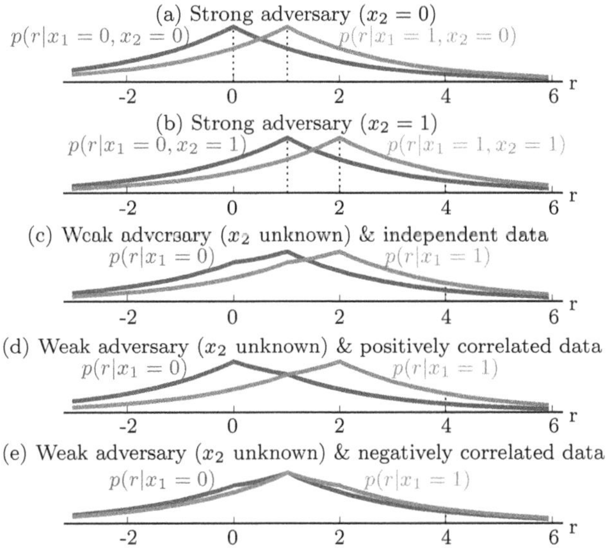

Figure 3: Laplacian Noise with Correlated Data.

We can learn from Example 3 that an adversary with less knowledge may obtain more information about a private individual because the missed tuples and the high correlation enhance the variation of the query results with respect to different values of the private individual. Consequently, distinguishability is enhanced. Note, however, that this is not always true. The following is a counterexample.

EXAMPLE 4. *The assumptions are the same as those in Example 3, with the exception that x_1 and x_2 are distributed according to the probabilities in Table 3(c).*

For a weak adversary $\mathcal{A}(i, \phi)$, $p(r|x_1) = \sum_{x_2} p(r|\mathbf{x}) \Pr(x_2|x_1)$. Here, $x_1 = x_2$ with low probability, $p(r|x_1 = 0) \approx p(r|x_1 = 0, x_2 = 1)$ and $p(r|x_1 = 1) \approx p(r|x_1 = 1, x_2 = 0)$ (Figure 3-(e)). In this case, the two curves are very close to each other; hence, $x_1 = 0$ and $x_1 = 1$ are very difficult to distinguish. In this example, $Lap(1/\epsilon)$ is private for all adversaries.

In summary, a stricter definition is necessary for rationally evaluating privacy versus all adversaries.

4. BAYESIAN DIFFERENTIAL PRIVACY

The above examples indicate that differential privacy may be vulnerable when data are correlated. The reason is that the expected change in the output is enhanced by missed tuples and data correlations. In this section, we will extend the definition of differential privacy in a Bayesian way and propose a new Pufferfish privacy definition so that the level of private information leakage is rationally expressed.

4.1 Definitions

The essence of differential privacy is to find a perturbation mechanism such that the output distribution is not significantly changed by adding, removing, or modifying the value of one tuple. Similarly, we propose a new privacy definition in which weak adversaries are described by their background knowledge being incomplete. The main idea is to connect the uncertain query answer with the given tuples in a Bayesian way, in which the unknown tuples are marginalized using the data correlations.

Definition 5. (Bayesian Differential Privacy) Let $\mathcal{A} = \mathcal{A}(i, \mathcal{K})$ be an adversary ($\mathcal{K} \subseteq [n] \setminus \{i\}$) and $\mathcal{M}(\mathbf{x}) = \Pr(r \in S|\mathbf{x})$ be a randomized perturbation mechanism on database $\mathbf{x}$. The *Bayesian differential privacy leakage* of $\mathcal{M}$ w.r.t. $\mathcal{A}$ is

$$BDPL_{\mathcal{A}}(\mathcal{M}) := \sup_{x_i, x_i', \mathbf{x}_{\mathcal{K}}, S} \log \frac{\Pr(r \in S|x_i, \mathbf{x}_{\mathcal{K}})}{\Pr(r \in S|x_i', \mathbf{x}_{\mathcal{K}})}, \quad (2)$$

in which, if $\mathbf{x}$ is continuous-valued,

$$\Pr(r \in S|x_i, \mathbf{x}_{\mathcal{K}}) = \int \Pr(r \in S|\mathbf{x}) p(\mathbf{x}_{\mathcal{U}}|x_i, \mathbf{x}_{\mathcal{K}}) d\mathbf{x}_{\mathcal{U}}; \quad (3)$$

and, if $\mathbf{x}$ is discrete-valued,

$$\Pr(r \in S|x_i, \mathbf{x}_{\mathcal{K}}) = \sum_{\mathbf{x}_{\mathcal{U}}} \Pr(r \in S|\mathbf{x}) \Pr(\mathbf{x}_{\mathcal{U}}|x_i, \mathbf{x}_{\mathcal{K}}). \quad (4)$$

We say $\mathcal{M}$ satisfies ϵ-*Bayesian differential privacy*, or ϵ-BDP, if

$$\sup_{\mathcal{A}} BDPL_{\mathcal{A}}(\mathcal{M}) \leq \epsilon. \quad (5)$$

If r is continuous-valued and its density is continuous, the Bayesian differential privacy leakage is equivalent to

$$BDPL_{\mathcal{A}}(\mathcal{M}) = \sup_{x_i, x_i', \mathbf{x}_{\mathcal{K}}, t} \log \frac{p(r = t|x_i, \mathbf{x}_{\mathcal{K}})}{p(r = t|x_i', \mathbf{x}_{\mathcal{K}})}; \quad (6)$$

and if r is discrete-valued, it is equivalent to

$$BDPL_{\mathcal{A}}(\mathcal{M}) = \sup_{x_i, x_i', \mathbf{x}_{\mathcal{K}}, t} \log \frac{\Pr(r = t|x_i, \mathbf{x}_{\mathcal{K}})}{\Pr(r = t|x_i', \mathbf{x}_{\mathcal{K}})}. \quad (7)$$

The only difference from differential privacy is that the prior knowledge is $\mathbf{x}_{\mathcal{K}}$ ($\forall \mathcal{K}$), instead of $\mathbf{x}_{-i}$. The unknown tuples are estimated using Bayes' theorem on the data correlation. In (3) and (4), $\Pr(r \in S|x_i, \mathbf{x}_{\mathcal{K}})$ is separated into two parts. $\Pr(r \in S|\mathbf{x})$ corresponds to perturbation mechanism $\mathcal{M}$, while $p(\mathbf{x}_{\mathcal{U}}|x_i, \mathbf{x}_{\mathcal{K}})$ corresponds to the data correlations. In this definition, $BDPL_{\mathcal{A}}$ expresses the largest difference between $\Pr(r \in S|x_i, \mathbf{x}_{\mathcal{K}})$ and $\Pr(r \in S|x_i', \mathbf{x}_{\mathcal{K}})$. This is the worst case in which one can distinguish x_i and x_i'. If the leakage is bounded by ϵ, the perturbation mechanism is considered to be private at the level of ϵ, i.e., ϵ-BDP.

4.2 BDP vs. DP

BDP is actually an extension of DP and is strictly stronger than DP. Using (3), BDP can be expressed as a probabilistic representation of $\mathcal{M}$ and data correlations:

$$BDPL_{\mathcal{A}}(\mathcal{M}) = \sup_{x_i, x_i', \mathbf{x}_{\mathcal{K}}, S} \log \frac{\int \Pr(r \in S|\mathbf{x}) p(\mathbf{x}_{\mathcal{U}}|x_i, \mathbf{x}_{\mathcal{K}}) d\mathbf{x}_{\mathcal{U}}}{\int \Pr(r \in S|\mathbf{x}') p(\mathbf{x}_{\mathcal{U}}|x_i', \mathbf{x}_{\mathcal{K}}) d\mathbf{x}_{\mathcal{U}}}. \quad (8)$$

The essential relationship between BDP and DP is that the unknown tuples set $\mathbf{x}_{\mathcal{U}}$ is marginalized.

4.2.1 Independent Data

Suppose all tuples in the database are mutually independent; hence, $p(\mathbf{x}_{\mathcal{U}}|x_i, \mathbf{x}_{\mathcal{K}}) \equiv p(\mathbf{x}_{\mathcal{U}})$ for $\forall \mathcal{K} \subset [n]$ (the upper row in Table 1).

THEOREM 1. *(Independent Data) ϵ-BDP is completely equivalent to ϵ-DP, if all tuples in the database are independent.*

PROOF. (DP $\Rightarrow$ BDP). From Definition 4, ϵ-DP implies

$$\Pr(r|x_i, \mathbf{x}_{-i}) \leq e^{\epsilon} \Pr(r|x_i', \mathbf{x}_{-i}),$$

$p(\mathbf{x}_{\mathcal{U}}|x_i, \mathbf{x}_{\mathcal{K}}) \equiv p(\mathbf{x}_{\mathcal{U}}|x_i', \mathbf{x}_{\mathcal{K}}) \equiv p(\mathbf{x}_{\mathcal{U}})$. Multiplying both sides by $p(\mathbf{x}_{\mathcal{U}})$ and summing them up w.r.t. $\mathbf{x}_{\mathcal{U}}$, we obtain $BDPL_{\mathcal{A}}(\mathcal{M}) \leq \epsilon$, as in (8), which implies ϵ-BDP.

(BDP $\Rightarrow$ DP). Suppose a perturbation mechanism satisfies ϵ-BDP (2). Then it is also satisfied for the strongest adversary ($\mathcal{K} = [n] \setminus \{i\}$), which implies ϵ-DP. □

4.2.2 Correlated Data and Strong Adversaries

Let us consider correlated data with adversaries limited to those who are the strongest (the lower left item in Table 1).

THEOREM 2. *(Correlated Data and Strong Adversaries) Suppose each adversary knows all tuples in the database other than the one it is attempting to infer. Then, ϵ-BDP is completely equivalent to ϵ-DP.*

PROOF. Consider the strongest adversary, $\mathcal{A}(i, [n] \setminus \{i\})$, who knows all tuples other than x_i and is attempting to infer x_i. Here, ϵ-BDP (5) becomes $BDPL_{\mathcal{A}(i,[n]\setminus\{i\})}(\mathcal{M}) \leq \epsilon$; thus, it reduces to (1), which is actually ϵ-DP. □

4.2.3 Correlated Data and Arbitrary Adversaries

The above discussion indicates that BDP is nothing more than DP when the tuples are independent or all adversaries are the strongest. However, in real applications, the tuples are always correlated and adversaries do not know all of the tuples. We therefore need to consider the privacy of correlated data and arbitrary adversaries (the lower right item in Table 1).

EXAMPLE 5. *Database $\mathbf{x} = \{x_1, x_2\}$ only contains two tuples, and their joint distribution is summarized in Table 3(b). Consider a query function, $f(\mathbf{x}) = x_1 + x_2$.*

Let $\mathcal{A}(1, \{2\})$ be a strong adversary with knowledge $\{x_2\}$ who wants to attack x_1 ($i = 1, \mathcal{K} = \{2\}, \mathcal{U} = \phi$). Moreover, let $\mathcal{A}(1, \phi)$ be a weak adversary, who knows nothing, but wants to attack x_1 ($i = 1, \mathcal{K} = \phi, \mathcal{U} = \{2\}$). Consider a Laplacian mechanism $\mathcal{M}$ that adds noise, $Lap(1/\epsilon)$ ($\epsilon = 0.1$), to the query result r. From Theorem 2, the privacy leakage of $\mathcal{A}(1, \{2\})$ is $BDPL_{\mathcal{A}(1,\{2\})}(\mathcal{M}) = \epsilon$. However, the privacy leakage of $\mathcal{A}(1, \phi)$ is

$$\begin{aligned} & BDPL_{\mathcal{A}(1,\phi)}(\mathcal{M}) \\ = & \sup_r \left| \log \frac{\sum_{x_2} \Pr(r|x_1 = 0, x_2) \Pr(x_2|x_1 = 0)}{\sum_{x_2} \Pr(r|x_1 = 1, x_2) \Pr(x_2|x_1 = 1)} \right| \\ = & \left| \log \frac{0.98 + 0.02e^{-\epsilon}}{0.02e^{-\epsilon} + 0.98e^{-2\epsilon}} \right| \approx 0.196 \approx 2\epsilon. \end{aligned}$$

Since $BDPL_{\mathcal{A}(1,\phi)}(\mathcal{M}) > \epsilon$, it does not satisfy ϵ-BDP.

If $x_1 = 0$, then $x_2 = 0$ with a high degree of probability; hence, $f = 0$ with a high degree of probability. In the same way, if $x_1 = 1$, then $f = 2$ with a high degree of probability. In other words, different values of x_1 cause large changes in the output. Therefore, it is easier to infer the original x_1 from the output r generated by $\mathcal{M}$. Thus, the privacy leakage is large, or in other words, the privacy level is low. In this sense, BDP rationally expresses the privacy level.

In the above example, the Laplacian mechanism $Lap(1/\epsilon)$ does not bind distinguishability against a weak adversary. Hence, we need find an $\epsilon'(\geq \epsilon)$, such that $Lap(1/\epsilon')$ ensures distinguishability to be bounded in $[e^{-\epsilon}, e^{\epsilon}]$ against the weak adversary. Note that $Lap(1/\epsilon')$ ensures privacy against the strong adversary. So, it ensures privacy against all adversaries. As a result, the weakest adversary poses the biggest threat to privacy, so it essentially determines whether the mechanism is private or not. However, is this situation always true? Let us consider the following example.

EXAMPLE 6. *Let us modify the joint distribution as in Table 3(c), and keep all other assumptions in Example 5. The privacy leakage to a weak adversary $\mathcal{A}(1,\phi)$ is*

$$\begin{aligned} & BDPL_{\mathcal{A}(1,\phi)}(\mathcal{M}) \\ = & \max_r \left| \log \frac{\sum_{d_2} \Pr(r|d_1=0,d_2)\Pr(d_2|d_1=0)}{\sum_{d_2} \Pr(r|d_1=1,d_2)\Pr(d_2|d_1=1)} \right| \\ = & \left| \log \frac{0.02+0.98e^{-\epsilon}}{0.98e^{-\epsilon}+0.02e^{-2\epsilon}} \right| \approx 0.004 \ll \epsilon. \end{aligned}$$

Therefore, $BDPL_{\mathcal{A}}(\mathcal{M}) \le \epsilon$ for $\forall \mathcal{A}$; hence, it is ϵ-BDP.

f is likely to be 1, regardless of whether $x_1 = 0$ or 1. In other words, different values of x_1 do not cause large changes in the output. Therefore, the privacy level should be high; hence, the value of $BDPL_{\mathcal{A}(1,\phi)}(\mathcal{M})$ should be less than ϵ. Nevertheless, since the privacy of strong adversaries is ϵ, the total privacy leakage to arbitrary adversaries is still ϵ.

To summarize, the weakest adversary poses a bigger threat in Example 5, whereas the strongest adversary poses the biggest threat in Example 6. This indicates that it is necessary to consider all adversaries when computing BDP. Moreover, since ϵ-DP is equivalent to $BDPL_{\mathcal{A}(i,[n]\setminus\{i\})}(\mathcal{M}) \le \epsilon$ and ϵ-BDP is equivalent to $BDPL_{\mathcal{A}(i,\mathcal{K})}(\mathcal{M}) \le \epsilon$, BDP is actually more rigorous than DP.

4.3 BDP vs. Pufferfish Privacy

Pufferfish privacy [17] is a privacy framework presented in a Bayesian way. This framework requires a privacy definition clearly specifying potential secrets, discriminative pairs and evolution scenarios, in which the set of potential secrets is an explicit declaration of targets that should be protected; the set of discriminative pairs specifies secret pairs, each of which should be prevented from being distinguished by attackers; and the evolution scenarios are a set of assumptions that indicate how the data were generated, how the data are correlated, and what knowledge a potential attacker has.

As we have clearly defined data correlation, adversary, and mechanism, our Bayesian differential privacy can be treated as a special case of the Pufferfish privacy. That is, Pufferfish privacy becomes Bayesian differential privacy if we designate the potential secrets to be the set of all possible values of tuples, discriminative pairs to be the set of all pairs of potential secrets, and evolution scenarios to be the data correlation which is described by a random field.

4.4 Discussion

Intuitively, a strong adversary has more background knowledge; hence, it should pose a greater risk to privacy. If so, then why is the weak adversary in Example 5 a greater risk in our definition of privacy?

From the discussion in [17], the Bayesian differential privacy leakage can be expressed as the difference between the prior and posterior odds

$$BDPL_{\mathcal{A}}(\mathcal{M}) = \sup \left(\log \frac{\Pr(x_i|r,\mathbf{x}_{\mathcal{K}})}{\Pr(x_i'|r,\mathbf{x}_{\mathcal{K}})} - \log \frac{\Pr(x_i|\mathbf{x}_{\mathcal{K}})}{\Pr(x_i'|\mathbf{x}_{\mathcal{K}})} \right).$$

For a strong adversary $\mathcal{A}(1,\{2\})$, the prior distribution $\Pr(x_1| x_2 = 1)$ is $\{0.02, 0.98\}$, while after the output (e.g. $r = 2$) is published, the posterior distribution $\Pr(x_1|r = 2, x_2 = 1)$ becomes $\{0.018, 0.982\}$. For weak adversary $\mathcal{A}(1,\phi)$, on the other hand, the prior and posterior distributions are $\{0.5, 0.5\}$ and $\{0.45, 0.55\}$, respectively. Since the variation in certainty between the prior and posterior distributions in this example are larger for the weak adversary than for the strong adversary, the BDPL of weak adversary is larger.

The data correlations and the unknown tuples may cause a larger change in the query result, hence cause additional information leakage of individual tuples. Bayesian differential privacy can capture this additional leakage, since it deals with the unknown tuples and the prior distribution in it explicitly describes the data correlation.

4.5 Continuous-valued Attributes

A continuous-valued model can be used to analyze attributes such as salary, blood pressure, etc. Some of them, e.g., salary, may be unbounded. Similar to the solution presented in [17], we limit the difference between x_i and x_i' to be less than a positive value M in the privacy definition. Therefore, the BDPL (2) becomes

$$BDPL_{\mathcal{A}}(\mathcal{M}; M) := \sup_{|x_i - x_i'| \le M, \mathbf{x}_{\mathcal{K}}, S} \log \frac{\Pr(r \in S|x_i, \mathbf{x}_{\mathcal{K}})}{\Pr(r \in S|x_i', \mathbf{x}_{\mathcal{K}})}. \tag{9}$$

For $\forall x_i, x_i'$ such that $|x_i - x_i'| \le M$, if ϵ-BDP guarantees that the privacy leakage (9) is bounded in $[-\epsilon, \epsilon]$; thus, x_i and x_i' are difficult to distinguish. For example, let us suppose that an attacker wants to determine whether the salary of a person is higher than that of another person in the same office of a company. This information is very sensitive. However, if the difference between the salaries is small, the information can be protected with an ϵ-BDP mechanism. On the other hand, for x_i, x_i' such that $|x_i - x_i'| = 100M$, an ϵ-BDP mechanism can only ensure distinguishability to be bounded in $[e^{-100\epsilon}, e^{100\epsilon}]$; thus, x_i and x_i' may be easy to distinguish. However, the ability to distinguish two significantly different values is trivial in many cases. For example, an adversary should be able to determine whether a person has a very low salary or is a millionaire. Since the distinguishability is not bounded in $[e^{-\epsilon}, e^{\epsilon}]$, the information can be clearly distinguished. Nevertheless, we do not care about this distinction, as such information would be obvious under the circumstances.

5. GAUSSIAN CORRELATION MODEL

We will mainly deal with the sum query in what follows, since it is widely used in data publishing. Moreover, many other queries, such as the counting query and histogram, can be derived from the sum query.

5.1 Model

An arbitrary Markov random field is actually an arbitrary multivariate distribution. Our purpose here is to construct a correlation model that can express complex data correlations and whose Bayesian differential privacy leakage can be efficiently computed. To compute Bayesian differential privacy, we need to take into account at least $n \cdot 2^{n-1}$ different adversaries. This computation is generally intractable.

We employ a special Markov random field, Gaussian Markov random field, because of the following characteristics.

First, any two tuples in the real data could be correlated or not, and the correlation level between them could be arbitrary. Such a correlation can be described by a weighted network with an arbitrary topology structure, in which strong correlations correspond to the linkage with large weights. The Gaussian Markov random field can directly translate this network into a probability distribution (Definition 6).

Second, to evaluate the BDPL, we need to compute the conditional distribution of some of the tuples given other tuples. The Gaussian Markov random field assumes that the joint distribution of all tuples is Gaussian, so all of these conditional distributions have the same form - Gaussian. Hence, it is possible to derive our main result (Theorem 4).

Third, the Gaussian distribution is easy to compute, meaning that we can derive an efficient algorithm (Algorithm 1).

Finally, although the Gaussian correlation model is for infinite continuous data, it can be easily extended to a model for discrete data, by modeling the parameters of their distributions into a Gaussian correlation model (Section 7).

We treat the dataset $\mathbf{x}$ and the correlations as a weighted undirected graph $G(\mathbf{x}, W)$, in which each vertex $x_i \in \mathbf{x}$ corresponds to a tuple i in $\mathbf{x}$ and each weight $w_{ij} \in W (w_{ij} \geq 0)$ denotes the correlation between tuples i and j. Here, we assume that the network is connective; i.e., for any tuples i and j, there exists at lease one path from i to j. The larger the value of w_{ij}, the more likely that x_i is near to x_j. This kind of data correlation can be described by a Gaussian Markov random field. Informally, a Gaussian Markov random field with respect to a graph is a multivariate Gaussian distribution with a precision matrix, whose i, j item is equal to 0 if and only if vertices i and j are not adjacent.

Definition 6. (Gaussian Correlation Model) Let $G(\mathbf{x}, W)$ be a weighted undirected graph, in which each vertex $x_i \in \mathbf{x}$ denotes a tuple i in the dataset, while each edge with weight $w_{ij} \in W (w_{ij} \geq 0)$ denotes the correlation between tuples i and j. Let $\mathbf{W} = (w_{ij})$ be the weighted adjacent matrix, $\mathbf{D} = diag(w_1, w_2, \cdots, w_n)$ be the weighted degree matrix of $G(\mathbf{x}, W)$ where $w_i = \sum_{j \neq i} w_{ij}$, and $\mathbf{L}$ be the Laplacian matrix of $G(\mathbf{x}, W)$, i.e.,

$$\mathbf{L} = \mathbf{D} - \mathbf{W} = \begin{pmatrix} w_1 & -w_{12} & \cdots & -w_{1,n} \\ -w_{12} & w_2 & \cdots & -w_{2,n} \\ \vdots & \vdots & \ddots & \vdots \\ -w_{1,n} & -w_{2,n} & \cdots & w_n \end{pmatrix}.$$

We call the pair $(\mathbf{x}, \mathbf{L})$ a Gaussian correlation model, denoted as $G(\mathbf{x}, \mathbf{L})$, and call the matrix $\mathbf{L}$ the Gaussian correlation matrix of $G(\mathbf{x}, \mathbf{L})$, if $\forall i \in [n]$, the conditional joint probability of $\mathbf{x}_{-i} = \mathbf{x}_{[n]\setminus\{i\}}$ is

$$p(\mathbf{x}_{-i}|x_i) \propto \exp\left(-\frac{\mathbf{x}^{\mathrm{T}}\mathbf{L}\mathbf{x}}{2}\right). \tag{10}$$

Note that the Gaussian correlation model could be more general if it also contains a linear term, like $e^{-\frac{(\mathbf{x}-\boldsymbol{\mu})^{\mathrm{T}}\mathbf{L}(\mathbf{x}-\boldsymbol{\mu})}{2}}$. We can eliminate the linear term by introducing an auxiliary variable $\mathbf{z} = \mathbf{x} - \boldsymbol{\mu}$ and then considering $\mathbf{z}$ instead of $\mathbf{x}$.

Although (10) seems to be a Gaussian distribution, it is worth emphasizing that, if all $x_i \in \mathbf{x}$ are regarded as random variables, they do not form a Gaussian joint distribution, because $\mathbf{L}$ is singular. Nevertheless, in order to analyze the Bayesian differential privacy (3), it is only necessary to consider a conditional probability $p(\mathbf{x}_{\mathcal{U}}|x_i, \mathbf{x}_{\mathcal{K}})$ whose condition contains at least one tuple i. Let $\mathcal{C} = \{i\} \cup \mathcal{K}$. From the definition of the adversary, we have $\mathcal{U} \cup \mathcal{C} = [n]$ and $\mathcal{U} \cap \mathcal{C} = \phi$. Hence, $\mathbf{x} = \begin{pmatrix} \mathbf{x}_{\mathcal{U}} \\ \mathbf{x}_{\mathcal{C}} \end{pmatrix}$ and $\mathbf{L} = \begin{pmatrix} \mathbf{L}_{\mathcal{U}} & \tilde{\mathbf{L}} \\ \tilde{\mathbf{L}}^{\mathrm{T}} & \mathbf{L}_{\mathcal{C}} \end{pmatrix}$. Then, we have

$$\mathbf{x}^{\mathrm{T}}\mathbf{L}\mathbf{x} = (\mathbf{x}_{\mathcal{U}}{}^{\mathrm{T}}, \mathbf{x}_{\mathcal{C}}{}^{\mathrm{T}}) \begin{pmatrix} \mathbf{L}_{\mathcal{U}} & \tilde{\mathbf{L}} \\ \tilde{\mathbf{L}}^{\mathrm{T}} & \mathbf{L}_{\mathcal{C}} \end{pmatrix} \begin{pmatrix} \mathbf{x}_{\mathcal{U}} \\ \mathbf{x}_{\mathcal{C}} \end{pmatrix}. \tag{11}$$

For any adversary $\mathcal{A}(i, \mathcal{K})$, $p(\mathbf{x}_{\mathcal{U}}|x_i, \mathbf{x}_{\mathcal{K}})$ can be expressed as the following form, regardless what i, $\mathcal{K}$ and $\mathcal{U}$ are.

$$p(\mathbf{x}_{\mathcal{U}}|\mathbf{x}_{\mathcal{C}}) \propto p(\mathbf{x}_{\mathcal{U}}, \mathbf{x}_{\mathcal{K}}|x_i) \propto \exp\left(-\frac{\mathbf{x}^{\mathrm{T}}\mathbf{L}\mathbf{x}}{2}\right). \tag{12}$$

The conditional distribution $p(\mathbf{x}_{\mathcal{U}}|x_i, \mathbf{x}_{\mathcal{K}})$ for any adversary is given by a unique formula. Substituting (11) into (12) and omitting the constants, it becomes

$$p(\mathbf{x}_{\mathcal{U}}|\mathbf{x}_{\mathcal{C}}) \propto \exp\left(-\frac{\mathbf{x}_{\mathcal{U}}{}^{\mathrm{T}}\mathbf{L}_{\mathcal{U}}\mathbf{x}_{\mathcal{U}} + 2\mathbf{x}_{\mathcal{C}}{}^{\mathrm{T}}\tilde{\mathbf{L}}^{T}\mathbf{x}_{\mathcal{U}}}{2}\right). \tag{13}$$

PROPOSITION 1. *Let $\mathbf{L}$ be a Gaussian correlation matrix of a correlated data set, $\mathcal{U} \subset [n]$ be a subset of $[n]$, where $0 < |\mathcal{U}| < n$. Suppose that $\mathbf{L}_{\mathcal{U}}$ is the sub-matrix of $\mathbf{L}$ with respect to the index set $\mathcal{U}$. Then, $\mathbf{L}_{\mathcal{U}}$ is positive-definite.*

PROOF. See Appendix A.1. □

Proposition 1 guarantees that (13) is actually a multivariate Gaussian distribution over $\mathbf{x}_{\mathcal{U}}$, since Gaussian distribution requires a positive-definite covariance matrix. In Section 6, we will extend the Gaussian correlation model to a more general one by adding a prior distribution to each tuple, so that it forms a Gaussian joint distribution on all tuples. We will show that the Gaussian correlation model in this section is actually an extreme case of that one.

In particular, if $\mathcal{U}$ contains only one tuple, e.g., $\mathcal{U} = \{u\}$, (13) becomes the conditional probability of x_u given all other tuples $\mathbf{x}_{-u} = \mathbf{x} \setminus \{x_u\}$, $(\mathcal{C} = [n] \setminus \{u\})$ i.e.,

$$p(x_u|\mathbf{x}_{-u}) \propto \exp\left(-\frac{w_u x_u^2 + 2\mathbf{x}_{-u}^{\mathrm{T}}\tilde{\mathbf{L}}^{\mathrm{T}}x_u}{2}\right) \tag{14}$$

where

$$\mathbf{x}_{-u} = (x_1, \cdots, x_{u-1}, x_{u+1}, \cdots, x_n)^{\mathrm{T}},$$

$$\tilde{\mathbf{L}} = (-w_{1u}, \cdots, -w_{u-1,u}, -w_{u,u+1}, \cdots, -w_{un}).$$

Therefore, (14) is a Gaussian distribution

$$p(x_u|\mathbf{x}_{-u}) \propto \exp\left(-\frac{w_u}{2}(x_u - \sum_{j \neq u}\frac{w_{uj}}{w_u}x_j)^2\right).$$

The mean of this distribution $\sum_{j \neq u} \frac{w_{uj}}{w_u} x_j$ is the weighted average of all neighbors of x_u. A large correlation w_{uj} means that x_j has a large affect on the mean of x_u. The precision $w_u = \sum_{j \neq u} w_{uj}$ is the sum of the correlations between x_u and all its neighbors. This property fits many cases in practice. Moreover, although the Gaussian correlation model is a continuous-valued model, we can extend it to a discrete-valued model (Section 7).

In many cases, it might be necessary to answer a sum query over a subset of the data. We just need to construct a subnetwork by choosing the vertices in the subset and the edges between them from the entire network. Hence, $\mathbf{W}$ and $\mathbf{L}$ for this subnetwork can be formed in the same way.

5.2 Correlation Analysis

Now, let us sketch the analysis of Bayesian differential privacy. We will consider a sum query over the tuples in a Gaussian correlation model and the privacy of the Laplacian mechanism. More specifically, let $s = sum(\mathbf{x})$ be the sum query on tuples $\mathbf{x}$ and $r = s + Lap(1/\epsilon)$ be its randomized output. In order to compute the Bayesian differential privacy leakage, we need to evaluate $p(r|x_i, \mathbf{x}_\mathcal{K})$ for any $\mathcal{A}(i, \mathcal{K})$. From the marginalization rule, we have

$$p(r|x_i, \mathbf{x}_\mathcal{K}) \propto \int p(r|s)p(s|x_i, \mathbf{x}_\mathcal{K})ds. \tag{15}$$

Here, $p(s|x_i, \mathbf{x}_\mathcal{K})$ is the correlation between the tuples and the true query result, and $p(r|s)$ is the Laplacian mechanism. We will analyze the correlation $p(s|x_i, \mathbf{x}_\mathcal{K})$ in this section and the Laplacian mechanism $p(r|s)$ in the next section.

Then, let us evaluate $p(s|x_i, \mathbf{x}_\mathcal{K})$ for each adversary $\mathcal{A}(i, \mathcal{K})$. Since there are 2^{n-1} different instances of $\mathcal{K}$ for each tuple $i \in [n]$, the problem is intractable when n is big. Our idea is to find a subset of adversaries, say the most *dangerous* adversary set that contains the adversary with the highest privacy leakage. Hence, we only need to find the adversary with the highest privacy leakage among them. To find the most dangerous adversary set, we define a hierarchical structure based on the inclusion relation between $\mathcal{K}$s, by which the relationship between different adversaries can be investigated. For any adversary $\mathcal{A} = \mathcal{A}(i, \mathcal{K})$, $\mathcal{A}' = \mathcal{A}(i, \mathcal{K}')$ is said to be weaker than $\mathcal{A}$ if $\mathcal{K}' \subset \mathcal{K}$. $\mathcal{A}$ is said to be stronger than $\mathcal{A}'$. In addition, if $|\mathcal{K}| - |\mathcal{K}'| = 1$, $\mathcal{A}'$ is said to be an ancestor of $\mathcal{A}$, and $\mathcal{A}$ is a descendant of $\mathcal{A}'$. For example, Figure 4 shows the hierarchical structure for each $i \in [n]$ in a dataset with four tuples ($n = 4$).

In general, $\forall \mathcal{A}(i, \mathcal{K})$, we have

$$\begin{aligned} p(s|x_i, \mathbf{x}_\mathcal{K}) &= p(s_\mathcal{U} = s - s_\mathcal{K} - x_i | x_i, \mathbf{x}_\mathcal{K}) \\ &\propto p(s_\mathcal{U}, \mathbf{x}_\mathcal{K} | x_i) \end{aligned} \tag{16}$$

where $s_\mathcal{U} = \sum_{i \in \mathcal{U}} x_i$. Since $\mathbf{x}_\mathcal{U}$ is unknown, $s_\mathcal{U}$ can be treated as a random variable. Consider an ancestor $\mathcal{A}(i, \mathcal{K}')$; i.e., there exists $j \in \mathcal{K}$, such that $\mathcal{K}' = \mathcal{K} \setminus \{j\}$. Then, we have $\mathcal{U}' = \mathcal{U} \cup \{j\}$. Thus $s_{\mathcal{U}'} = s_\mathcal{U} + x_j$, and we have

$$p(s_{\mathcal{U}'}, \mathbf{x}_{\mathcal{K}'} | x_i) = p(s_\mathcal{U} + x_j, \mathbf{x}_{\mathcal{K}'} | x_i). \tag{17}$$

On the other hand,

$$p(s_\mathcal{U}, \mathbf{x}_\mathcal{K} | x_i) = p(s_\mathcal{U}, x_j, \mathbf{x}_{\mathcal{K}'} | x_i). \tag{18}$$

Here, (17) can be derived from (18) by combining $s_\mathcal{U}$ and x_j into one variable, $s_{\mathcal{U}'}$. This transformation is done by marginalization.

When $\mathcal{K} = [n] \setminus \{i\}$, i.e., all tuples appear in the condition of the probability, s is a fixed value; hence, the probability density function $p(s|x_i, \mathbf{x}_\mathcal{K})$ is a Dirac delta distribution $\delta(s)$ with an argument equal to $s = x_i + \sum_{j \in \mathcal{K}} x_j$. When $\mathcal{K} \subset [n] \setminus \{i\}$, s becomes a probabilistic variable; hence, the dataset $\{s\} \cup \mathbf{x}_\mathcal{K}$ forms a new correlation model. For convenience, we consider the average of tuples $\mathbf{x}_\mathcal{U}$, $x_0 = \frac{\sum_{j \in \mathcal{U}} x_j}{|\mathcal{U}|}$, instead of s. We denote this average as tuple 0. It is obvious that each adversary $\mathcal{A}$ corresponds to a variable set $\mathbf{x}_\mathcal{A} := \{x_0, x_i\} \cup \mathbf{x}_\mathcal{K}$. Proposition 2 states that $\mathbf{x}_\mathcal{A}$ is a Gaussian correlation model, denoted by $G(\mathbf{x}_\mathcal{A}, \mathbf{L}_\mathcal{A})$, and provides the relation between Gaussian correlation matrices of different adversaries. It is a central rule for analyzing Bayesian differential privacy in Gaussian correlation model.

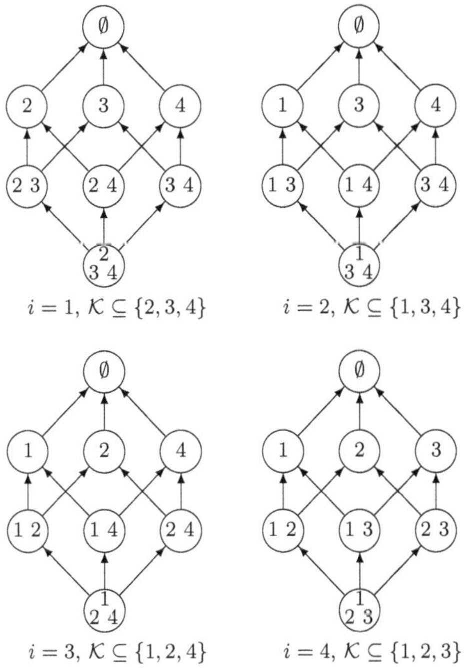

Figure 4: Hierarchical structure for $\mathcal{K}$.

PROPOSITION 2. *(Combination) Let $G(\mathbf{x}, \mathbf{L})$ be a Gaussian correlation model. For any adversary $\mathcal{A} = \mathcal{A}(i, \mathcal{K})$, let $\mathcal{C} = \{i\} \cup \mathcal{K}$, $\mathcal{U} = [n] \setminus \mathcal{C}$ and $m = |\mathcal{U}|$ be the size of $\mathcal{U}$. Suppose $x_0 = \frac{\sum_{u \in \mathcal{U}} x_u}{m}$ is a random variable and $\mathbf{x}_\mathcal{A} = \{x_0, x_i\} \cup \mathbf{x}_\mathcal{K} = \{x_0\} \cup \mathbf{x}_\mathcal{C}$. Then, $G(\mathbf{x}_\mathcal{A}, \mathbf{L}_\mathcal{A})$ is also a Gaussian correlation model. Furthermore, suppose adversary $\mathcal{A}' = \mathcal{A}(i, \mathcal{K}')$ is an ancestor of $\mathcal{A}$, i.e., $\exists j \in \mathcal{K}$, such that $\mathcal{K}' = \mathcal{K} \setminus \{j\}$. Let $\mathcal{U}' = \mathcal{U} \cup \{j\}$ and $\mathcal{C}' = \mathcal{K}' \cup \{i\}$. If the Gaussian correlation matrix of $\mathcal{A}$ is*

$$\mathbf{L}_\mathcal{A} = \begin{pmatrix} w_0 & -\mathbf{w}_{0\mathcal{C}}^{\mathrm{T}} \\ -\mathbf{w}_{0\mathcal{C}} & \mathbf{W}_\mathcal{C} \end{pmatrix} = \begin{pmatrix} w_0 & -w_{0j} & -\mathbf{w}_{0\mathcal{C}'}^{\mathrm{T}} \\ -w_{0j} & w_j & -\mathbf{w}_{j\mathcal{C}'}^{\mathrm{T}} \\ -\mathbf{w}_{0\mathcal{C}'} & -\mathbf{w}_{j\mathcal{C}'} & \mathbf{W}_{\mathcal{C}'} \end{pmatrix}, \tag{19}$$

then the Gaussian correlation matrix of $\mathcal{A}'$ is

$$\mathbf{L}_{\mathcal{A}'} = \begin{pmatrix} w_0' & -\mathbf{w}_{0\mathcal{C}'}^{\prime\mathrm{T}} \\ -\mathbf{w}_{0\mathcal{C}'}' & \mathbf{W}_{\mathcal{C}'}' \end{pmatrix}, \tag{20}$$

where

$$\begin{aligned} w_0' &= \frac{(m+1)^2(w_0 w_j - w_{0j}^2)}{m^2 w_j + 2m w_{0j} + w_0} \\ \mathbf{w}_{0\mathcal{C}'}' &= (m+1)\frac{(w_{0j} + m w_j)\mathbf{w}_{0\mathcal{C}'} + (w_0 + m w_{0j})\mathbf{w}_{j\mathcal{C}'}}{m^2 w_j + 2m w_{0j} + w_0} \\ \mathbf{W}_{\mathcal{C}'}' &= \mathbf{W}_{\mathcal{C}'} - \frac{(\mathbf{w}_{0\mathcal{C}'} - m\mathbf{w}_{j\mathcal{C}'})(\mathbf{w}_{0\mathcal{C}'}^{\mathrm{T}} - m\mathbf{w}_{j\mathcal{C}'}^{\mathrm{T}})}{m^2 w_j + 2m w_{0j} + w_0}. \end{aligned}$$

PROOF. See Appendix A.2. □

5.3 Output Perturbation

We have obtained from (15) that the conditional distribution $p(r|x_i, \mathbf{x}_\mathcal{K})$ is composed of the perturbation mechanism $p(r|s)$ and the data correlation $p(s|x_i, \mathbf{x}_\mathcal{K})$. Furthermore, we have analyzed the data correlation in the previous section.

In this section, we take into account the perturbation mechanism $p(r|s)$. We will choose a suitable Laplacian mechanism, so that the Bayesian differential privacy is guaranteed. Suppose noise z is drawn from a Laplacian distribution with scale λ and location 0.

$$z \sim Lap(\lambda) = \frac{1}{2\lambda} e^{-\frac{|z|}{\lambda}}.$$

This noise is added to the true result of the query s, and $r = s+z$ is published. A large λ corresponds a large variance of the noise and thus causes low utility. In the following, we will find the smallest λ that satisfies Bayesian differential privacy. The following lemma is necessary for our analyses.

LEMMA 1. *Let $G(x;b)$ be a function on $x \in \mathbb{R}$, with parameter $b > 0$*

$$G(x;b) = e^{x}\left(1 - \Phi(\frac{x}{b} + b)\right) + e^{-x}\Phi(\frac{x}{b} - b) \quad (21)$$

where $\Phi(x)$ is the cumulative distribution function of a standard Gaussian distribution. Then, $\frac{\partial \log G(x;b)}{\partial x}$ is monotonically decreasing with respect to x and

$$\lim_{x \to -\infty} \frac{\partial \log G(x;b)}{\partial x} = 1; \quad \lim_{x \to +\infty} \frac{\partial \log G(x;b)}{\partial x} = -1.$$

PROOF. See Appendix A.3. □

Now, let us analyze $p(r|x_i, \mathbf{x}_{\mathcal{K}})$ by combining the perturbation mechanism $p(r|s)$ and the data correlation $p(s|x_i, \mathbf{x}_{\mathcal{K}})$, and then evaluating the Bayesian differential privacy leakage. Theorem 3 states that the change in the probability can be bounded in an interval determined by the correlation matrix. We will use this theorem to derive our main result.

THEOREM 3. *Suppose $G(\mathbf{x}, \mathbf{L})$ is a Gaussian correlation model and $s = sum(\mathbf{x}) = \sum_{i \in [n]} x_i$ is a sum query on $\mathbf{x}$. Let $\mathcal{M}$ be a Laplacian mechanism whose perturbed output is $r = \mathcal{M}(\mathbf{x}) = sum(\mathbf{x}) + z$ where $z \sim Lap(\lambda)$. Given an adversary $\mathcal{A} = \mathcal{A}(i, \mathcal{K})$, let $x_0 = \frac{\sum_{u \in \mathcal{U}} x_u}{|\mathcal{U}|}$ be the average of unknown tuples and $\mathbf{x}_{\mathcal{A}} = \begin{pmatrix} x_0 \\ \mathbf{x}_{\mathcal{C}} \end{pmatrix} = \begin{pmatrix} x_0 \\ x_i \\ \mathbf{x}_{\mathcal{K}} \end{pmatrix}$. Suppose the corresponding Gaussian correlation matrix is*

$$\mathbf{L}_{\mathcal{A}} = \begin{pmatrix} w_0 & -w_{0i} & -\mathbf{w}_{0\mathcal{K}}^{\mathrm{T}} \\ -w_{0i} & w_i & -\mathbf{w}_{i\mathcal{K}}^{\mathrm{T}} \\ -\mathbf{w}_{0\mathcal{K}} & -\mathbf{w}_{i\mathcal{K}'} & \mathbf{W}_{\mathcal{K}} \end{pmatrix}.$$

Let $M > 0$ and $m = |\mathcal{U}|$. Then, the Bayesian differential privacy leakage of $\mathcal{M}$ with respect to $\mathcal{A}$ is

$$BDPL_{\mathcal{A}}(\mathcal{M}; M) = \frac{M}{\lambda}\left(1 + \frac{m w_{01}}{w_0}\right).$$

PROOF. See Appendix A.4. □

We can find from the proof that the BDPL is not related the linear term, so we only need to consider the correlation matrix. In the rest of this paper, we call $\ell_{\mathcal{A}} = \frac{m w_{0i}}{w_0}$ the *leakage coefficient* of the correlation model with respect to adversary $\mathcal{A}$. Hence, $BDPL_{\mathcal{A}}(\mathcal{M}; M) = (1 + \ell_{\mathcal{A}})\frac{M}{\lambda}$.

5.4 Mechanism

Theorem 3 evaluates the Bayesian differential privacy leakage with respect to an adversary $\mathcal{A}$, $BDPL_{\mathcal{A}}$. In this section, we will find an adversary whose BDPL is the largest. Hence, a Laplacian mechanism satisfying ϵ-BDP for all adversaries can be constructed based on this adversary.

THEOREM 4. *Suppose $G(\mathbf{x}, \mathbf{L})$ is a Gaussian correlation model and $s = sum(\mathbf{x}) = \sum_{i \in [n]} x_i$ is a summation query on $\mathbf{x}$. Let $\mathcal{M}$ be a Laplacian mechanism whose perturbed output is $r = \mathcal{M}(\mathbf{x}) = sum(\mathbf{x}) + z$, where $z \sim Lap(\lambda)$. Given an adversary $\mathcal{A} = \mathcal{A}(i, \mathcal{K})$ and any ancestor adversary $\mathcal{A}' = \mathcal{A}(i, \mathcal{K}')$, the following inequality holds.*

$$\ell_{\mathcal{A}} \leq \ell_{\mathcal{A}'}.$$

Straightforwardly, for any $M > 0$,

$$BDPL_{\mathcal{A}}(\mathcal{M}; M) \leq BDPL_{\mathcal{A}'}(\mathcal{M}; M).$$

PROOF. See Appendix A.5. □

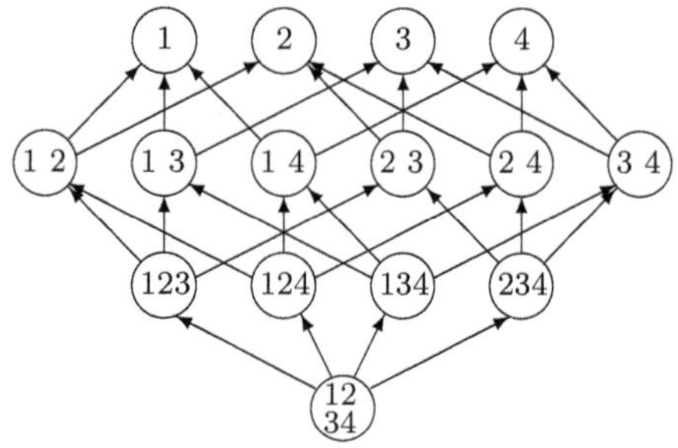

$\mathcal{C} \subseteq \{1, 2, 3, 4\}$

Figure 5: Hierarchical structure for $\mathcal{C}$.

Theorem 4 tells us that, given $Lap(\lambda)$, the BDPL with respect to an adversary is always smaller than that with respect to his/her ancestor. Hence, the weakest adversary has the largest privacy leakage. In contrast, to satisfy ϵ-BDP for all adversaries, the variance λ should satisfy $\lambda \geq (1+\ell_{\mathcal{A}})\frac{M}{\epsilon}$ ($\forall \mathcal{A}$). Thus, λ should be at least $\lambda_0 = \frac{M}{\epsilon}(1 + \max_{\mathcal{A}} \ell_{\mathcal{A}})$. The problem thus becomes one of finding the adversary with the largest BDPL. There are n weakest adversaries $\mathcal{A}(i, \phi)$, and the adversary with the largest BDPL must exist among them. As we are given the Gaussian correlation matrix for the entire database, we need to combine the tuples by using Proposition 2 via the path in Figure 4 in order to obtain the correlation matrix for each of the weakest adversaries, and then find the largest BDPL among them. From Proposition 2, on the other hand, we found that the Gaussian correlation matrix for adversary $\mathcal{A}(i, \mathcal{K})$ is only related to $\mathcal{C} = \{i\} \cup \mathcal{K}$. For example, for a tuple $i' \in \mathcal{K}$, $\mathcal{A}(i, \mathcal{K})$ and $\mathcal{A}(i', \mathcal{K} \cup \{i\} \setminus \{i'\})$ are different adversaries. However, since their correlation matrices are the same, we only need to perform the computation one time. On the basis of the inclusion relation between $\mathcal{C}$, we can construct a hierarchical structure on $\mathcal{C}$. Figure 5 shows a hierarchical structure for a dataset with four tuples. We only need to compute the leakage coefficient for the top 4 adversaries and select the largest one from them to generate the Laplacian mechanism.

Algorithm 1 computes the leakage coefficient for each weak adversary $\mathcal{A}(i, \phi)$ ($\forall i \in [n]$). Since this entails combining the tuples one by one, the computation for each weak adversary corresponds to a path from the bottom node (e.g., $\{1, 2, 3, 4\}$) to each of the top nodes (e.g., $\{1\}, \{2\}, \{3\}, \{4\}$) in Figure 5. Lines 9 and 15 in Algorithm 1 calls the Combine operator in Theorem 2, by which i^{th} tuple is combined to the average x_0, i.e., $x_0 \leftarrow (m x_0 + x_i)/(m+1)$. The computational time of this operation is $O(n^2)$; hence, the computational time for a weakest adversary should be $O(n^3)$. Therefore, the time for all n weakest adversaries will be $O(n^4)$. However, some computations can be omitted. For

Algorithm 1 Calculate the leakage coefficient

```
input: L - the Gaussian correlation matrix
input: m - |U| (the number of tuples in x_U)
output: ℓ - the leakage coefficient
function CalcLeakageCoefficient(L, m = 1)
    n ← SizeOf(L)
    if n ≤ 2 then
        return w0 / w01
    end if
    k ← ⌈(n+1)/2⌉
    L1 ← L
    for i = k → 2 step −1 do
        L1 ← Combine(L1, i, m)          ▷ (Proposition 2)
        m ← m + 1
    end for
    ℓ1 ← CalcLeakageCoefficient(L1, m)
    L2 ← L
    for i = n → k + 1 step −1 do
        L2 ← Combine(L2, i, m)          ▷ (Proposition 2)
        m ← m + 1
    end for
    ℓ2 ← CalcLeakageCoefficient(L2, m)
    return max(ℓ1, ℓ2)
end function
```

example, suppose that we have computed $\{1\}$ via the path $\{1,2,3,4\} \to \{1,2,3\} \to \{1,2\} \to \{1\}$. When we compute $\{2\}$, the intermediate result $\{1,2\}$ in the previous can be reused; i.e., it is not necessary to compute $\{1,2\}$ again.

THEOREM 5. *The time and space complexities of the algorithm of calibrating noise are $O(n^3)$ and $O(n^2)$, respectively.*

PROOF. See Appendix A.6. ☐

The weakest adversary $\mathcal{A}(i,\phi)$ poses the largest privacy leakage and the corresponding Gaussian correlation matrix is a 2×2 matrix $\begin{pmatrix} w_0 & -w_{0i} \\ -w_{0i} & w_0 \end{pmatrix}$ and $m = n-1$. From the definition of the Gaussian correlation matrix, we have $w_0 = w_{0i}$. In combination with Theorem 3, we have

$$BDPL_{\mathcal{A}(i,\phi)}(\mathcal{M}; M) \equiv \frac{nM}{\lambda}.$$

Hence, we need to add Laplacian noise with n times variance to ensure Bayesian differential privacy. Obviously, the utility is too low. To achieve a more useful query answer, we will extend our model in Section 6 to guard against an adversary that is reasonably weak but not extremely weak.

5.5 Positive and Negative Correlations

In Definition 6, tuples in a Gaussian correlation model are positively correlated. More specifically, if one of the tuples becomes larger, other unknown tuples are expected to be larger. Therefore, the final result will increase more significantly. Moreover, a larger number of unknown tuples will cause a larger increment in the result. Consequently, the weakest adversary has the largest sensitivity; and hence, he/she has the largest privacy leakage. However, correlations in real data may not always be positive. For example, the correlation "the sum of two tuples is equal to 100" implies, once a tuple becomes larger, the other will become smaller. In such a case, the weakest adversary may not correspond to the largest privacy leakage (Example 4).

6. GAUSSIAN CORRELATION MODEL WITH PRIORS

In the previous discussion, we assumed that an adversary exactly knows everything about some of the tuples, but nothing about the others. However, it will be more general in practice that an adversary does not know exactly what the sensitive information about an individual is, but rather knows something about it. For example, one may know what range the salary of a person is likely to be in. In this section, we define a smoother prior distribution for each adversary, and use this model to analyze the privacy leakage.

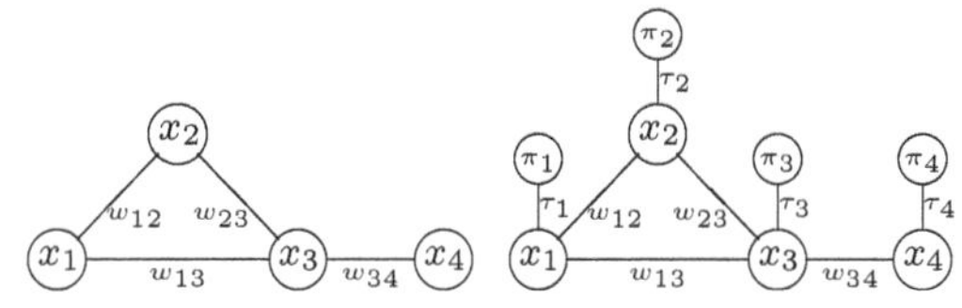

(a). Gaussian correlation model without prior. (b). Gaussian correlation model with prior.

Figure 6: Gaussian correlation models without and with prior knowledge.

6.1 Model

Let $\mathcal{P}$ be the set of tuples with uncertain prior knowledge. We define a Gaussian prior distribution for each such tuple,

$$p(x_i) \sim \mathcal{N}(\mu_i, \tau_i^{-1}) \propto e^{-\frac{\tau_i(x_i-\mu_i)^2}{2})} \quad (\forall i \in \mathcal{P}), \tag{22}$$

in which τ_i is the precision of tuple i, i.e., $\tau_i = \frac{1}{\sigma_i^2}$.

Let us denote the adversary with prior knowledge as $\mathcal{A}(i, \mathcal{K}, \mathcal{P}, \boldsymbol{\tau}_\mathcal{P})$, in which i and $\mathcal{K}$ denote the attack target tuple and exact known tuples, respectively. Moreover, $\mathcal{P} \subseteq [n] \setminus \{i\} \setminus \mathcal{K}$ denotes the tuples with uncertain prior knowledge, and $\boldsymbol{\tau}_\mathcal{P}$ denotes the precisions of tuple set $\mathcal{P}$. The same as before, $\mathcal{U} = [n] \setminus \{i\} \setminus \mathcal{K} \setminus \mathcal{P}$ denotes unknown tuples.

Using these prior distributions, we can extend the Gaussian correlation model to a Gaussian Markov random field by defining the joint distribution of $\mathbf{x}$ as $p(\mathbf{x}) = \prod_{i \in \mathcal{P}} p(x_i) \cdot \exp\left(-\frac{1}{2}\mathbf{x}^\mathrm{T}\mathbf{L}\mathbf{x}\right)$. Substituting (22) into $p(\mathbf{x})$, we get

$$p(\mathbf{x}) = e^{-\frac{1}{2}\mathbf{x}^\mathrm{T}\hat{\mathbf{L}}\mathbf{x}}.$$

where $\hat{\mathbf{L}} = \mathbf{L} + \mathbf{T}$ and $\mathbf{T} = diag(\boldsymbol{\tau}) = diag(\tau_1, \tau_2, \cdots, \tau_n)$. Here, $\tau_i = 0$ if $i \notin \mathcal{P}$.

This model can be derived more formally, as follows. Suppose that $G(\mathbf{x}, \mathbf{L})$ is a Gaussian correlation model (Figure 6(a)). We add an auxiliary variable, denoted by π_i, to each tuple i, expressing the prior distribution of tuple i. Each π_i has only one edge connected to tuple i with weight τ_i, as Figure 6(b) shows. Let $\boldsymbol{\pi} = \{\pi_i : i \in [n]\}$ be the set of all auxiliary variables. We construct a Gaussian correlation model for all tuples and auxiliary variables, i.e., $G(\mathbf{x} \cup \boldsymbol{\pi}, \mathbf{L}_{\boldsymbol{\pi}})$, where

$$\mathbf{L}_{\boldsymbol{\pi}} = \begin{pmatrix} \hat{w}_1 & \cdots & -w_{1n} & -\tau_1 & \cdots & 0 \\ \vdots & \ddots & \vdots & \vdots & \ddots & \vdots \\ -w_{1n} & \cdots & \hat{w}_n & 0 & \cdots & -\tau_n \\ -\tau_1 & \cdots & 0 & \hat{\tau}_1 & \cdots & 0 \\ \vdots & \ddots & \vdots & \vdots & \ddots & \vdots \\ 0 & \cdots & -\tau_n & 0 & \cdots & \hat{\tau}_n \end{pmatrix}.$$

From Definition 6, we have $\hat{\tau}_i = \tau_i$ and $\hat{w}_i = w_i + \tau_i$ where $w_i = \sum_{j \neq i} w_{ij}$ $(i \in [n])$. Hence, $\mathbf{L}_\pi = \begin{pmatrix} \mathbf{L}+\mathbf{T} & -\mathbf{T} \\ -\mathbf{T} & \mathbf{T} \end{pmatrix}$. Then, the Gaussian correlation model of $G(\mathbf{x} \cup \boldsymbol{\pi}, \mathbf{L}_\pi)$ is

$$p(\mathbf{x}, \boldsymbol{\pi}_{-i}|\pi_i) \propto \exp\{-\frac{1}{2}(\mathbf{x}^{\mathrm{T}}, \boldsymbol{\pi}^{\mathrm{T}}) \begin{pmatrix} \hat{\mathbf{L}} & -\mathbf{T} \\ -\mathbf{T} & \mathbf{T} \end{pmatrix} \begin{pmatrix} \mathbf{x} \\ \boldsymbol{\pi} \end{pmatrix}\}$$

Note that $\boldsymbol{\pi}$ is always given, so it becomes

$$p(\mathbf{x}|\boldsymbol{\pi}) \propto p(\mathbf{x}, \boldsymbol{\pi}_{-i}|\pi_i) \propto e^{-\frac{1}{2}(\mathbf{x}^{\mathrm{T}}\hat{\mathbf{L}}\mathbf{x} - 2\boldsymbol{\pi}^{\mathrm{T}}\mathbf{T}\mathbf{x})}$$

As long as $\mathbf{T} \neq \mathbf{0}$, $\hat{\mathbf{L}} = \mathbf{L} + \mathbf{T}$ is positive-definite. Consequently, $p(\mathbf{x}|\boldsymbol{\pi})$ is a multivariate Gaussian distribution. Hence, $\mathbf{x}$ is a Gaussian Markov random field. As the linear term can be absorbed into the second order term, it is no longer necessary to consider the linear term.

τ_i shows how much prior knowledge the adversary has. Intuitively, the larger τ_i is, the higher certainty of tuple i becomes, and hence, the more prior knowledge there is about x_i. Particularly, when $\tau_i \to \infty$, the prior distribution of v_i becomes a Dirac delta function. It is equivalent to that v_i is given. In contrast, when $\tau_i \to 0$, the prior distribution of v_i has a very large variance; hence, there is no prior knowledge about v_i. If $\tau_i \to 0$ for all $i \in [n]$, the model becomes the Gaussian correlation model; i.e., $\exp\left(-\frac{1}{2}\mathbf{x}^{\mathrm{T}}\mathbf{L}\mathbf{x}\right)$.

6.2 Prior vs. Privacy

We will now discuss the influence of the prior knowledge on privacy leakage. Note that the computation for this model is the same as that for the Gaussian correlation model (Algorithm 1). The tuples in $\mathcal{P}$ should be marginalized out.

THEOREM 6. *Let $G(\mathbf{x}, \mathbf{L})$ be a Gaussian correlation model and $\mathcal{M}$ be a Laplacian mechanism for a sum query. Suppose that $\mathcal{A} = \mathcal{A}(i, \mathcal{K}, \mathcal{P}, \boldsymbol{\tau}_\mathcal{P})$ is an extended adversary, with prior knowledge $\boldsymbol{\tau}_\mathcal{P}$. For $\forall j \in \mathcal{P}$, let $\boldsymbol{\tau}'_\mathcal{P}$ be prior knowledge that is equal to $\boldsymbol{\tau}_\mathcal{P}$ with an exception that $\tau'_j \geq \tau_j$. Let*

$$\begin{aligned} \mathcal{A}' &= \mathcal{A}(i, \mathcal{K}, \mathcal{P}, \boldsymbol{\tau}'_\mathcal{P}); \\ \mathcal{A}'' &= \mathcal{A}(i, \mathcal{K}, \mathcal{P} \setminus \{j\}, \boldsymbol{\tau}_{\mathcal{P}\setminus\{j\}}); \\ \mathcal{A}''' &= \mathcal{A}(i, \mathcal{K} \cup \{j\}, \mathcal{P} \setminus \{j\}, \boldsymbol{\tau}_{\mathcal{P}\setminus\{j\}}). \end{aligned}$$

Then, the following inequalities hold for $M > 0$.

$$\begin{aligned} BDPL_\mathcal{A}(\mathcal{M}; M) &\geq BDPL_{\mathcal{A}'}(\mathcal{M}; M); \quad (23) \\ \lim_{\tau_j \to 0} BDPL_\mathcal{A}(\mathcal{M}; M) &= BDPL_{\mathcal{A}''}(\mathcal{M}; M); \\ \lim_{\tau_j \to +\infty} BDPL_\mathcal{A}(\mathcal{M}; M) &= BDPL_{\mathcal{A}'''}(\mathcal{M}; M). \end{aligned}$$

PROOF. See Appendix A.7 □

Theorem 6 shows that each tuple in $\mathcal{P}$ is just an intermediate case between $\mathcal{K}$ and $\mathcal{U}$. From monotonicity (23), the larger the value of τ_j, the more private a mechanism will be. If all priors are limited to $+\infty$, i.e., all tuples are known, the case is one of differential privacy; hence, we only need use $Lap(1/\epsilon)$ to satisfy ϵ-BDP. If all priors are limited to zero, i.e., all tuples are unknown, we need $Lap(n/\epsilon)$ to satisfy ϵ-BDP. This mechanism has very low utility. However, the general priors $(0 < \tau_j < \infty)$ correspond to intermediate cases. As a result, $\mathcal{K}$, $\mathcal{U}$, and $\mathcal{P}$ can be integrated into $\boldsymbol{\tau}$ $(0 \leq \tau_j \leq +\infty)$, in which $\tau_j = +\infty$ corresponds to $\mathcal{K}$, $\tau_j = 0$ corresponds to $\mathcal{U}$, and others corresponds to $\mathcal{P}$.

7. MODELS FOR DISCRETE ATTRIBUTES

Although the Gaussian correlation model has a rich representation for describing data correlations, it can only deal with continuous attributes. However, data in the real world are not always continuous. For example, to publish the number of persons who has influenza, one should designate each person as a binary attribute, denoting whether he/she has influenza, and then publish the sum of these attributes.

In the following, we will construct a binary correlation model based on the Gaussian correlation model. Suppose that each tuple has a binary attribute y_i, which is generated from a Bernoulli distribution with a hyper parameter $p_i = sigmoid(\alpha x_i)$ $(x_i \in \mathbb{R}, \alpha > 0)$. Since a larger α makes p_i easier to be near to zero or one, it can be used to adjust the certainty of y_is. We assume that all x_is are correlated according to the Gaussian correlation model, as shown in Figure 7. Our goal is to publish $s = \sum_i y_i$.

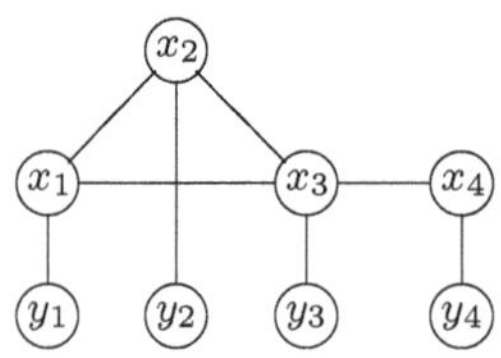

x_1, x_2, x_3, x_4
$\sim$ Gaussian correlation;
$p_i = sigmoid(\alpha x_i) = \frac{1}{1+e^{-\alpha x_i}}$;
$y_i \sim Bernoulli(p_i)$.

Figure 7: Binary correlation models.

In order to protect the privacy of each tuple y_i, we add noise z to the true result s and output $r = s + z$, so that the Bayesian differential privacy is satisfied. Since s is an integer, we employ the geometric mechanism [10], a discrete version of Laplacian noise, i.e., $z \sim Geo(\lambda) = \frac{1-e^{-\frac{1}{\lambda}}}{1+e^{-\frac{1}{\lambda}}} e^{-\frac{|z|}{\lambda}}$ $(z \in \mathbb{Z})$. The following theorem guarantees that the geometric mechanism satisfies Bayesian differential privacy.

THEOREM 7. *Suppose $G(\mathbf{x}, \mathbf{L})$ is a Gaussian correlation model, $y_i \sim Bernoulli(sigmoid(\alpha x_i))$ is a binary attribute for tuple i, and $s = sum(\mathbf{y}) = \sum_{i \in [n]} y_i$ is a sum query on $\mathbf{y}$. Let $\mathcal{M}$ be a geometric mechanism whose perturbed output is $r = \mathcal{M}(\mathbf{y}) = sum(\mathbf{y}) + z$ where $z \sim Geo(\lambda)$. Given an adversary $\mathcal{A} = \mathcal{A}(i, \mathcal{K})$, let $\ell_\mathcal{A}$ be the leakage coefficient of the correlation model $G(\mathbf{x}, \mathbf{L})$ with respect to adversary $\mathcal{A}$. Then, the Bayesian differential privacy leakage of $\mathcal{M}$ with respect to $\mathcal{A}$ satisfies*

$$BDPL_\mathcal{A}(\mathcal{M}) \leq \frac{1}{\lambda}\left(1 + \frac{\alpha}{2}\ell_\mathcal{A}\right).$$

PROOF. See Appendix A.8. □

Given $\epsilon > 0$, if we add noise $z \sim Geo(\frac{1}{\epsilon}\left(1 + \frac{\alpha}{2}\ell_\mathcal{A}\right))$ to the query result, then $BDPL_\mathcal{A}(\mathcal{M}) \leq \epsilon$. Hence, ϵ-BDP is satisfied. This algorithm allows us to publish the counting query and the histogram satisfying BDP, as shown in [4].

8. EXPERIMENTS

We present some experimental results in this section.

8.1 Artificial Network Data

We randomly generated networks with different vertex numbers and different degrees. For a given vertex number n, we constructed an $n \times n$ weight adjacent matrix $\mathbf{W}$ with all its items equal to zero. Note that $\mathbf{W}$ is a symmetric matrix $(w_{ij} \equiv w_{ji})$. Given the average degree, d, we uniformly

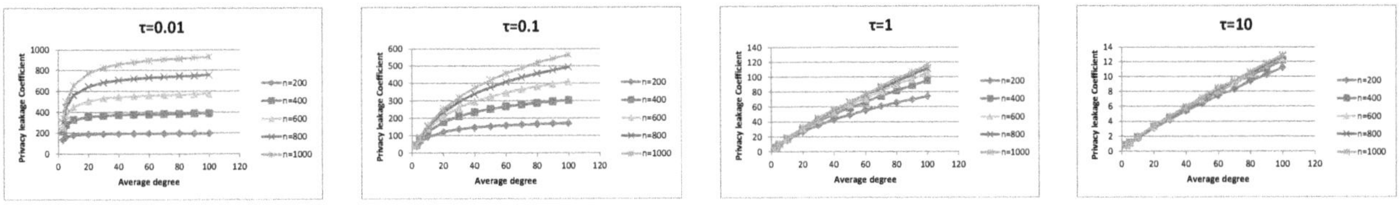

Figure 8: Experimental Result of Artificial Network Data.

drew $\frac{nd}{2}$ weights from the $\frac{n(n-1)}{2}$ weights in the upper triangle of the matrix (w_{ij} such that $i < j$) and set these weights and their symmetric entries (w_{ji}) to be one. Therefore, the average degree was d. We generated such data for different vertex numbers and different average degrees. We then computed the Laplacian matrix $\mathbf{L} = \mathbf{D} - \mathbf{W}$ for each simulated network data. Finally, we added the prior to the matrix. More specifically, for different real numbers τ, we added $\mathbf{T} = \tau \cdot \mathbf{I}$ to $\mathbf{L}$, i.e., $\hat{\mathbf{L}} = \mathbf{L} + \tau \cdot \mathbf{I}$.

As the Bayesian differential privacy is determined by the leakage coefficient, we computed the leakage coefficient for network data with respect to different vertex numbers, different average degrees, and different prior τ using Algorithm 1. We ran each case twenty times. The average leakage coefficients are shown in Figure 8. The horizontal axis denotes the average degree of the network, while the vertical axis denotes the largest leakage coefficient $\max_{\mathcal{A}} \ell_{\mathcal{A}}$ of the network. n and τ denote the number of tuples and the prior, respectively. We found that the larger the average degree of the network, the larger the privacy leakage. This is because greater degrees mean stronger correlations between tuples. Figure 8 also shows that, when τ is very small, the leakage coefficient is nearly n; thus, the necessary variance of the Laplacian noise is nearly n times larger than that of differential privacy. This query answer has extremely less utility. However, as the prior τ increases, the leakage coefficient becomes smaller. Hence, utility can be significantly enhanced.

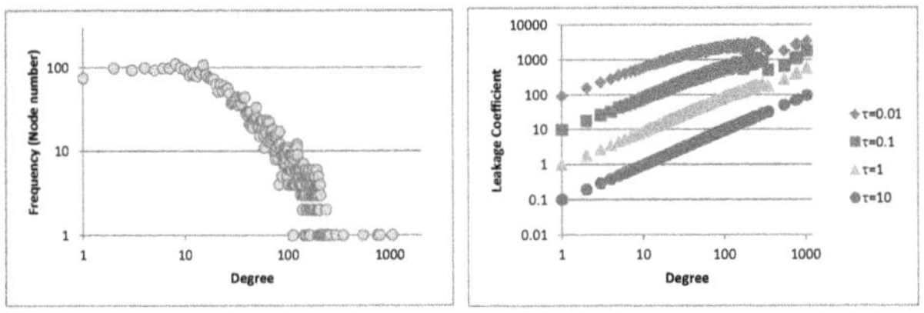

(a). Degree Distribution. (b). Leakage vs. Degree.

Figure 9: Experimental Results of Real Data.

8.2 Real Social Network Data

We used a dataset in *Stanford Large Network Dataset Collection* [19] which was collected from survey participants in Facebook. This dataset contains 4039 nodes and 88234 edges. Figure 9(a) shows the degree distribution of this network. The largest degree in this network is 1045. We constructed matrix $\mathbf{W}$ by setting w_{ij} (and w_{ji}) to be one if node i is adjacent to j and zero otherwise; and then, added a prior to its Laplacian matrix, i.e., $\hat{\mathbf{L}} = \mathbf{D} - \mathbf{W} + \tau \cdot \mathbf{I}$. We evaluated the average leakage coefficients for different degrees of vertices with respect to different priors and showed the result in Figure 9(b). For each prior τ, we compared the vertex degree and the average leakage coefficient ℓ in Figure 9(b). We found that the vertex with the largest degree (1045) has the largest leakage coefficient for each prior τ, since this vertex has the largest correlation to other vertices in the network. Figure 9(b) also shows that the leakage coefficient is decreased with the increment of the prior.

9. CONCLUSIONS

We investigated differential privacy against arbitrary adversaries when the data may be correlated. We found that a differentially private mechanism may be especially vulnerable when the data are correlated and the adversary does not have full knowledge. We proposed a new Pufferfish privacy definition, called Bayesian differential privacy, to overcome this problem. We then constructed a Gaussian correlation model to describe correlated data with a complex correlation structure. As the computation of Bayesian differential privacy is generally intractable, we presented an efficient algorithm to design a Bayesian differentially private mechanism. Finally, we extended the Gaussian correlation model by introducing a smooth prior distribution, and showed that this extended model can be used to describe the uncertain prior knowledge and to enhance the utility of the output.

10. REFERENCES

[1] A. Blum, C. Dwork, F. McSherry, and K. Nissim. Practical privacy: the sulq framework. In *PODS*, pages 128–138, New York, NY, USA, 2005. ACM.

[2] A. Blum, K. Ligett, and A. Roth. A learning theory approach to non-interactive database privacy. In *STOC*, pages 609–617, 2008.

[3] I. Dinur and K. Nissim. Revealing information while preserving privacy. In *PODS*, pages 202–210, 2003.

[4] C. Dwork, F. Mcsherry, K. Nissim, and A. Smith. Calibrating noise to sensitivity in private data analysis. In *TCC*, pages 265–284. Springer, 2006.

[5] C. Dwork and K. Nissim. Privacy-preserving datamining on vertically partitioned databases. In *CRYPTO*, pages 528–544. Springer, 2004.

[6] A. Evfimievski, R. Fagin, and D. P. Woodruff. Epistemic privacy. In *PODS*, pages 171–180, 2008.

[7] A. Evfimievski, J. Gehrke, and R. Srikant. Limiting privacy breaches in privacy preserving data mining. In *PODS*, pages 211–222, 2003.

[8] J. Gehrke, M. Hay, E. Lui, and R. Pass. Crowd-blending privacy. In *ECRYPTO*, pages 479–496. 2012.

[9] J. Gehrke, E. Lui, and R. Pass. Towards privacy for social networks: A zero-knowledge based definition of privacy. In *TCC*, pages 432–449, 2011.
[10] A. Ghosh, T. Roughgarden, and M. Sundararajan. Universally utility-maximizing privacy mechanisms. In *STOC*, pages 351–360, 2009.
[11] M. Hay, C. Li, G. Miklau, and D. Jensen. Accurate estimation of the degree distribution of private networks. In *ICDM*, pages 169–178, 2009.
[12] X. He, A. Machanavajjhala, and B. Ding. Blowfish privacy: Tuning privacy-utility trade-offs using policies. In *SIGMOD*, pages 1447–1458, 2014.
[13] K. Kenthapadi, N. Mishra, and K. Nissim. Simulatable auditing. In *PODS*, pages 118–127, 2005.
[14] D. Kifer. Attacks on privacy and definetti's theorem. In *SIGMOD*, pages 127–138, 2009.
[15] D. Kifer and B.-R. Lin. Towards an axiomatization of statistical privacy and utility. In *PODS*, pages 147–158, 2010.
[16] D. Kifer and A. Machanavajjhala. No free lunch in data privacy. In *SIGMOD*, pages 193–204, 2011.
[17] D. Kifer and A. Machanavajjhala. Pufferfish: A framework for mathematical privacy definitions. *ACM Trans. Database Syst.*, 39(1):3:1–3:36, Jan. 2014.
[18] R. Kindermann and J. L. Snell. *Markov Random Fields and Their Applications.* American Mathematical Society, 1980.
[19] J. Leskovec and A. Krevl. SNAP Datasets: Stanford large network dataset collection. http://snap.stanford.edu/data, June 2014.
[20] G. Miklau and D. Suciu. A formal analysis of information disclosure in data exchange. In *SIGMOD*, pages 575–586, 2004.
[21] I. Mironov, O. Pandey, O. Reingold, and S. Vadhan. Computational differential privacy. In *CRYPTO*, 2009.
[22] K. Nissim, S. Raskhodnikova, and A. Smith. Smooth sensitivity and sampling in private data analysis. In *STOC*, pages 75–84, 2007.
[23] V. Rastogi, M. Hay, G. Miklau, and D. Suciu. Relationship privacy: output perturbation for queries with joins. In *PODS*, pages 107–116, 2009.
[24] V. Rastogi, D. Suciu, and S. Hong. The boundary between privacy and utility in data publishing. In *VLDB*, pages 531–542, 2007.
[25] J. Zhang, G. Cormode, C. M. Procopiuc, D. Srivastava, and X. Xiao. Privbayes: Private data release via bayesian networks. In *SIGMOD*, pages 1423–1434, 2014.

APPENDIX

A. PROOFS

A.1 Proof of Proposition 1

PROOF. $\forall \mathcal{U} \subset [n]$, let $u = |\mathcal{U}|$. Without loss of generality, we set $\mathcal{U} = \{1, 2, \cdots, u\}$, i.e.,

$$\mathbf{L} = \begin{pmatrix} \mathbf{L}_{\mathcal{U}} & \tilde{\mathbf{L}} \\ \tilde{\mathbf{L}}^{\mathrm{T}} & \mathbf{L}_{\mathcal{C}} \end{pmatrix}, \textit{ where } \mathbf{L}_{\mathcal{U}} = \begin{pmatrix} w_1 & \cdots & -w_{1u} \\ \vdots & \ddots & \vdots \\ -w_{1u} & \cdots & w_u \end{pmatrix}.$$

If $u = 1$, $\mathbf{L}_{\mathcal{U}} = (w_i)$. Since $w_i > 0$, $\mathbf{L}_{\mathcal{U}}$ is positive-definite. Let $2 \le u \le n-1$. Suppose that, $\forall \mathcal{U}' \in \{\mathcal{U}' : |\mathcal{U}'| = u-1\}$, $\mathbf{L}_{\mathcal{U}'}$ is positive-definite. Now, let us consider $\mathcal{U} \in \{\mathcal{U} : |\mathcal{U}| = u\}$. $\forall i \in [u]$, let $w_i^{(u)} = \sum_{j=1}^{u} w_{ij}$ and $w_i^{(c)} = \sum_{j=u+1}^{n} w_{ij}$. Accordingly, $w_i = w_i^{(u)} + w_i^{(c)}$, i.e., $\mathbf{L}_{\mathcal{U}} = \mathbf{L}_{\mathcal{U}}^{(u)} + \mathbf{L}_{\mathcal{U}}^{(c)}$ where

$$\mathbf{L}_{\mathcal{U}}^{(u)} = \begin{pmatrix} w_1^{(u)} & \cdots & -w_{1u} \\ \vdots & \ddots & \vdots \\ -w_{1u} & \cdots & w_u^{(u)} \end{pmatrix}; \mathbf{L}_{\mathcal{U}}^{(c)} = \begin{pmatrix} w_1^{(c)} & \cdots & 0 \\ \vdots & \ddots & \vdots \\ 0 & \cdots & w_u^{(c)} \end{pmatrix}.$$

$\mathbf{L}_{\mathcal{U}}^{(u)}$ is a Laplacian matrix and $\mathbf{L}_{\mathcal{U}}^{(c)}$ is a diagonal matrix. Note that a Laplacian matrix must be positive-semidefinite. In addition, from the connectivity of the network, $\exists i \in [u]$, such that $w_i^{(c)} > 0$. Without loss of generality, we assume $w_u > 0$. $\forall \mathbf{v} = (v_1, v_2, \cdots, v_u)^{\mathrm{T}}$, let us consider $\mathbf{v}^{\mathrm{T}}\mathbf{L}_{\mathcal{U}}\mathbf{v}$.
(i). If $v_u \neq 0$, then $\mathbf{v}^{\mathrm{T}}\mathbf{L}_{\mathcal{U}}^{(c)}\mathbf{v} \ge v_u w_u^{(c)} v_u > 0$. Hence, $\mathbf{v}^{\mathrm{T}}\mathbf{L}_{\mathcal{U}}\mathbf{v} = \mathbf{v}^{\mathrm{T}}\mathbf{L}_{\mathcal{U}}^{(u)}\mathbf{v} + \mathbf{v}^{\mathrm{T}}\mathbf{L}_{\mathcal{U}}^{(c)}\mathbf{v} > 0$.
(ii). If $v_u = 0$, then $\mathbf{v}^{\mathrm{T}}\mathbf{L}_{\mathcal{U}}\mathbf{v} = \mathbf{v}'^{\mathrm{T}}\mathbf{L}_{\mathcal{U}'}\mathbf{v}'$, where

$$\mathbf{v}' = \begin{pmatrix} v_1 \\ \vdots \\ v_{u-1} \end{pmatrix} \text{ and } \mathbf{L}_{\mathcal{U}'} = \begin{pmatrix} w_1 & \cdots & -w_{1,u-1} \\ \vdots & \ddots & \vdots \\ -w_{1,u-1} & \cdots & w_{u-1} \end{pmatrix}.$$

From the assumption, $\mathbf{v}'^{\mathrm{T}}\mathbf{L}_{\mathcal{U}'}\mathbf{v}' > 0$. So, $\mathbf{v}^{\mathrm{T}}\mathbf{L}_{\mathcal{U}}\mathbf{v} > 0$. □

A.2 Proof of Proposition 2

PROOF. (Proposition 2) We have obtained from (16) that each adversary $\mathcal{A} = \mathcal{A}(i, \mathcal{K})$ corresponds to a tuple set $\mathbf{x}_{\mathcal{A}} = \{x_0\} \cup \mathbf{x}_{\mathcal{C}}$, where $\mathcal{C} = \mathcal{K} \cup \{i\}$ and $x_0 = \frac{\sum_{u \in \mathcal{U}} x_u}{|\mathcal{U}|}$ denotes the average of the unknown tuples.

When $|\mathcal{U}| = 1$, e.g., $\mathcal{U} = \{u\}$, we have $x_0 = x_u$ and $\mathcal{C} = [n] \setminus \{u\}$ ($\mathcal{K} = [n] \setminus \{u, i\}$). Thus, the corresponding adversary is $\mathcal{A} = \mathcal{A}(i, [n] \setminus \{u, i\})$, hence $\mathbf{x}_{\mathcal{A}} = \mathbf{x}$. Since $\mathbf{x}$ is a Gaussian correlation model, $\mathbf{x}_{\mathcal{A}}$ is a Gaussian correlation model. Now, we only need to prove that $\mathbf{x}_{\mathcal{A}'}$ must be a Gaussian correlation model if $\mathbf{x}_{\mathcal{A}}$ is a Gaussian correlation model and if $\mathcal{A}' = \mathcal{A}(i, \mathcal{K}')$ is an ancestor of $\mathcal{A} = \mathcal{A}(i, \mathcal{K})$. In the following, we denote a column vector as $\mathbf{x}_{\mathcal{A}}$.

Suppose that $\mathbf{x}_{\mathcal{A}} = \begin{pmatrix} x_0 \\ \mathbf{x}_{\mathcal{C}} \end{pmatrix}$ is a Gaussian correlation model with a Gaussian correlation matrix $\mathbf{L}_{\mathcal{A}}$ (19), i.e.,

$$p(x_0, \mathbf{x}_{\mathcal{C}} | x_i) \propto e^{-\frac{1}{2}\mathbf{x}_{\mathcal{A}}^{\mathrm{T}}\mathbf{L}_{\mathcal{A}}\mathbf{x}_{\mathcal{A}}}.$$

Since $\mathcal{A}'$ is an ancestor of $\mathcal{A}$, $\exists j \in \mathcal{K}$, such that $\mathcal{K}' = \mathcal{K} \setminus \{j\}$; hence, $\mathcal{C}' = \mathcal{C} \setminus \{j\}$, i.e., $\mathcal{C} = \mathcal{C}' \cup \{j\}$. Therefore,

$$p(x_0, x_j, \mathbf{x}_{\mathcal{K}'} | x_i) \propto e^{-\frac{1}{2}\mathbf{x}_{\mathcal{A}}^{\mathrm{T}}\mathbf{L}_{\mathcal{A}}\mathbf{x}_{\mathcal{A}}}.$$

Now, let us consider the tuple set $\mathbf{x}_{\mathcal{A}'} = \begin{pmatrix} x_0' \\ \mathbf{x}_{\mathcal{C}'} \end{pmatrix}$ where $\mathcal{C}' = \mathcal{K}' \cup \{i\} = \mathcal{C} \setminus \{j\}$ and $x_0' = \frac{\sum_{i \in \mathcal{U}'} x_i}{|\mathcal{U}'|} = \frac{m x_0 + x_j}{m+1}$. Let $\tilde{\mathbf{x}}_{\mathcal{A}'} = \begin{pmatrix} x_0' \\ x_j \\ \mathbf{x}_{\mathcal{C}'} \end{pmatrix}$. Note that $\mathbf{x}_{\mathcal{A}} = \begin{pmatrix} x_0 \\ x_j \\ \mathbf{x}_{\mathcal{C}'} \end{pmatrix}$. Thus, we have

$$\tilde{\mathbf{x}}_{\mathcal{A}'} = \mathbf{T}\mathbf{x}_{\mathcal{A}}, \quad \mathbf{x}_{\mathcal{A}} = \mathbf{T}^{-1}\tilde{\mathbf{x}}_{\mathcal{A}'}$$

where

$$\mathbf{T} = \begin{pmatrix} \frac{m}{m+1} & \frac{1}{m+1} & \mathbf{0}^{\mathrm{T}} \\ 0 & 1 & \mathbf{0}^{\mathrm{T}} \\ \mathbf{0} & \mathbf{0} & \mathbf{I} \end{pmatrix}, \quad \mathbf{T}^{-1} = \begin{pmatrix} \frac{m+1}{m} & \frac{-1}{m} & \mathbf{0}^{\mathrm{T}} \\ 0 & 1 & \mathbf{0}^{\mathrm{T}} \\ \mathbf{0} & \mathbf{0} & \mathbf{I} \end{pmatrix}.$$

Using above transformation formula, we can obtain the density of $\mathbf{x}_{\mathcal{A}'}$. Note that $|\mathbf{T}|$ is a constant.

$$p(x_0', x_j, \mathbf{x}_{\mathcal{K}'}|x_i) \propto e^{-\frac{1}{2}\tilde{\mathbf{x}}_{\mathcal{A}'}^{\mathrm{T}}\tilde{\mathbf{L}}\tilde{\mathbf{x}}_{\mathcal{A}'}}.$$

where

$$\begin{aligned}
\tilde{\mathbf{L}} &= \mathbf{T}^{-1\mathrm{T}}\mathbf{L}_{\mathcal{A}}\mathbf{T}^{-1} = \begin{pmatrix} a & -b & -\mathbf{e}^{\mathrm{T}} \\ -b & d & -\mathbf{f}^{\mathrm{T}} \\ -\mathbf{e} & -\mathbf{f} & \mathbf{W}_{\mathcal{C}'} \end{pmatrix}; \\
a &= \frac{(m+1)^2}{m^2}w_0; \quad b = \frac{m+1}{m}\left(\frac{1}{m}w_0 + w_{0j}\right); \\
d &= \frac{w_0 + 2mw_{0j} + m^2 w_j}{m^2}; \\
\mathbf{e} &= \frac{m+1}{m}\mathbf{w}_{0\mathcal{C}'}; \quad \mathbf{f} = \mathbf{w}_{j\mathcal{C}'} - \frac{1}{m}\mathbf{w}_{0\mathcal{C}'}.
\end{aligned}$$

Marginalizing x_j, we obtain the density,

$$p(x_0', \mathbf{x}_{\mathcal{K}'}|x_i) \propto e^{-\frac{1}{2}\mathbf{x}_{\mathcal{A}'}^{\mathrm{T}}\mathbf{L}_{\mathcal{A}'}\mathbf{x}_{\mathcal{A}'}}$$

where $\mathbf{L}_{\mathcal{A}'} = \begin{pmatrix} a - \frac{b^2}{d} & -\mathbf{e}^{\mathrm{T}} - \frac{b}{d}\mathbf{f}^{\mathrm{T}} \\ -\mathbf{e} - \frac{b}{d}\mathbf{f} & \mathbf{W}_{\mathcal{C}'} - \frac{1}{d}\mathbf{f}\mathbf{f}^{\mathrm{T}} \end{pmatrix}$, which is equal to (20). We also need to prove that $\mathbf{L}_{\mathcal{A}'}$ is a Gaussian correlation matrix. Note that, $\forall k \in \mathcal{K}'$, $w_{0k}, w_{jk} \geq 0$. From the description of $\mathbf{L}_{\mathcal{A}'}$, we have $w_{0k}' \geq 0$. Let $\mathbf{1}_m = (1, 1, \cdots, 1)^{\mathrm{T}}$ and $\mathbf{0}_m = (0, 0, \cdots, 0)^{\mathrm{T}}$ be m-dimensional vectors with all m elements being 1 and 0, respectively. In the following, we will prove that $\mathbf{L}_{\mathcal{A}'}$ is a Gaussian correlation matrix, i.e., $\mathbf{L}_{\mathcal{A}'} \cdot \mathbf{1}_{|\mathcal{C}'|+1} = \mathbf{0}_{|\mathcal{C}'|+1}$. Since $\mathbf{L}_{\mathcal{A}}$ is a Gaussian correlation matrix, $\mathbf{L}_{\mathcal{A}} \cdot \mathbf{1}_{|\mathcal{C}'|+2} = \mathbf{0}_{|\mathcal{C}'|+2}$, i.e.,

$$\begin{aligned}
w_0 - w_{0j} - \mathbf{w}_{0\mathcal{C}'}^{\mathrm{T}} \cdot \mathbf{1}_{|\mathcal{C}'|} &= 0 \\
-w_{0j} + w_j - \mathbf{w}_{j\mathcal{C}'}^{\mathrm{T}} \cdot \mathbf{1}_{|\mathcal{C}'|} &= 0 \\
-\mathbf{w}_{0\mathcal{C}'} - \mathbf{w}_{j\mathcal{C}'} + \mathbf{W}_{\mathcal{C}'} \cdot \mathbf{1}_{|\mathcal{C}'|} &= \mathbf{0}_{|\mathcal{C}'|}.
\end{aligned}$$

Using the above equations and (20), we can confirm (24) and (25) are always true.

$$w_0' - \mathbf{w}_{0\mathcal{C}'}^{\prime\mathrm{T}} \cdot \mathbf{1}_{|\mathcal{C}'|} = 0, \tag{24}$$
$$-\mathbf{w}_{0\mathcal{C}'}' + \mathbf{W}_{\mathcal{C}'}' \cdot \mathbf{1}_{|\mathcal{C}'|} = \mathbf{0}_{|\mathcal{C}'|}. \tag{25}$$

Thus, $\mathbf{L}_{\mathcal{A}'}$ is a Gaussian correlation matrix. □

A.3 Proof of Lemma 1

PROOF. (Lemma 1) For convenience, let

$$H(x) = e^{-x}\Phi\left(\frac{x}{b} - b\right).$$

Hence,

$$G(x; b) = H(-x) + H(x).$$

This implies that $G(x; b)$ is an even function with respect to x. Moreover, let $\phi(x)$ be the probability density function of standard Gaussian distribution, i.e.,

$$\phi\left(\frac{x}{b} + b\right) \propto e^{-\frac{1}{2}\left(\frac{x^2}{b^2} + 2x + b^2\right)}.$$

Then, it is easy to obtain that

$$\begin{aligned}
\frac{\partial G(x; b)}{\partial x} &= H(-x) - H(x), \\
\frac{\partial \log G(x; b)}{\partial x} &= \frac{H(-x) - H(x)}{H(-x) + H(x)}, \\
\frac{\partial^2 \log G(x; b)}{\partial x^2} &= 2 \cdot \frac{H'(-x)H(x) - H'(x)H(-x)}{(H(-x) + H(x))^2}.
\end{aligned}$$

In the following, we will prove that

$$H'(-x)H(x) - H'(x)H(-x) < 0. \tag{26}$$

which is equivalent to

$$\frac{\partial \log H(-x)}{\partial x} < \frac{\partial \log H(x)}{\partial x}. \tag{27}$$

It is easy to confirm the following equation.

$$y\Phi(y) + \phi(y) = \int_{-\infty}^{y} \Phi(t)dt > 0 \quad (\forall y \in \mathbb{R}). \tag{28}$$

Substituting $y = \frac{x}{b} - b$ and $y = -\frac{x}{b} - b$ into (28), we get

$$\begin{aligned}
\frac{\partial \log H(-x)}{\partial x} &= \frac{-\phi(-\frac{x}{b} - b)}{b\Phi(-\frac{x}{b} - b)} + 1 < -\frac{x}{b^2} \\
&< \frac{\phi(\frac{x}{b} - b)}{b\Phi(\frac{x}{b} - b)} - 1 = \frac{\partial \log H(x)}{\partial x}.
\end{aligned}$$

In summary, (26) and (27) are satisfied, hence

$$\frac{\partial^2 \log G(x; b)}{\partial x^2} < 0.$$

This implies $\frac{\partial \log G(x;b)}{\partial x}$ is a monotonically decreasing function. On the other hand,

$$\frac{H(-x)}{H(x)} = e^{2x}\frac{\Phi(\frac{-x}{b} - b)}{\Phi(\frac{x}{b} - b)}.$$

When $x \to +\infty$, $t < \frac{-x}{b} - b$, i.e., $x < -bt - b^2$. Hence,

$$\begin{aligned}
e^{2x}\Phi\left(\frac{-x}{b} - b\right) &= \int_{-\infty}^{\frac{-x}{b} - b} e^{2x}e^{-\frac{t^2}{2}}dt \\
&< \int_{-\infty}^{\frac{-x}{b} - b} e^{2(-bt - b^2)}e^{-\frac{t^2}{2}}dt \to 0.
\end{aligned}$$

Since $\Phi(\frac{x}{b} - b) \to 1$ $(x \to \infty)$, we have $\lim_{x\to+\infty} \frac{H(-x)}{H(x)} = 0$. Therefore,

$$\lim_{x\to+\infty} \frac{\partial \log G(x; b)}{\partial x} = \lim_{x\to+\infty} \frac{\frac{H(-x)}{H(x)} - 1}{\frac{H(-x)}{H(x)} + 1} = -1.$$

Since $\frac{\partial \log G(x;b)}{\partial x}$ is odd, $\lim_{x\to-\infty} \frac{\partial \log G(x;b)}{\partial x} = 1$. With the monotonicity, we have

$$-1 \leq \frac{\partial \log G(x; b)}{\partial x} \leq 1.$$

□

A.4 Proof of Theorem 3

PROOF. (Theorem 3) The conditional density of x_0 is

$$\begin{aligned}
p(x_0|x_i, \mathbf{x}_{\mathcal{K}}) &\propto e^{-\frac{1}{2}\mathbf{x}_{\mathcal{A}}^{\mathrm{T}}\mathbf{L}_{\mathcal{A}}\mathbf{x}_{\mathcal{A}} + \mathbf{a}^{\mathrm{T}}\mathbf{x}_{\mathcal{A}}} (\exists \mathbf{a}) \\
&\propto e^{-\frac{1}{2}w_0(x_0 - \frac{w_{0i}}{w_0}x_i - \frac{\mathbf{w}_{0\mathcal{K}}^{\mathrm{T}}\mathbf{x}_{\mathcal{K}}}{w_0} - \frac{a_0}{w_0})^2}.
\end{aligned}$$

Since $s = mx_0 + x_i + s_{\mathcal{K}}$; i.e., $x_0 = \frac{s - x_i - s_{\mathcal{K}}}{m}$, we have

$$p(s|x_i, \mathbf{x}_{\mathcal{K}}) \propto e^{-\frac{1}{2}\frac{w_0}{m^2}(s - x_i - \frac{mw_{0i}}{w_0}x_i - s_{\mathcal{K}} - \frac{m\mathbf{w}_{0\mathcal{K}}^{\mathrm{T}}\mathbf{x}_{\mathcal{K}}}{w_0} - \frac{ma_0}{w_0})^2}.$$

Note that $r = s + z$ and s and z are independent, so

$$p(r|x_i, \mathbf{x}_{\mathcal{K}}) = \int_{-\infty}^{\infty} p(r - z|x_i, \mathbf{x}_{\mathcal{K}})Lap(\lambda)dz$$

Let $t = r-(1+\frac{mw_{0i}}{w_0})x_i - s_\mathcal{K} - \frac{m\mathbf{w}_{0\mathcal{K}}^T\mathbf{x}_\mathcal{K}}{w_0} - \frac{ma_0}{w_0}$ and $\tilde{w}_0 = \frac{w_0}{m^2}$. Using $G(x;b)$ defined in (21), we have

$$\begin{aligned} p(r|x_i, \mathbf{x}_\mathcal{K}) &\propto \int_{-\infty}^{\infty} e^{-\frac{\tilde{w}_0}{2}(t-z)^2 - \frac{|z|}{\lambda}} dy \\ &= \int_{-\infty}^{0} e^{-\frac{\tilde{w}_0}{2}(t-z)^2 + \frac{z}{\lambda}} dz + \int_{0}^{\infty} e^{-\frac{\tilde{w}_0}{2}(t-z)^2 - \frac{z}{\lambda}} dz \\ &= \sqrt{2\pi}\tilde{w}_0^{-\frac{1}{2}} e^{\frac{1}{2\tilde{w}_0\lambda^2}} \cdot G(\frac{t}{\lambda}; \sqrt{\tilde{w}_0}\lambda). \end{aligned} \quad (29)$$

Let $t' = r - (1+\frac{mw_{0i}}{w_0})x'_i - s_\mathcal{U} - \frac{m\mathbf{w}_{0\mathcal{K}}^T\mathbf{x}_\mathcal{K}}{w_0} - \frac{ma_0}{w_0}$. In the same way, we have

$$p(r|x'_i, \mathbf{x}_\mathcal{K}) = \sqrt{2\pi}\tilde{w}_0^{-\frac{1}{2}} e^{\frac{1}{2\tilde{w}_0\lambda^2}} \cdot G(\frac{t'}{\lambda}; \sqrt{\tilde{w}_0}\lambda).$$

Therefore,

$$\log\frac{p(r|x_i,\mathbf{x}_\mathcal{K})}{p(r|x'_i,\mathbf{x}_\mathcal{K})} = \log G(\frac{t}{\lambda}; \sqrt{\tilde{w}_0}\lambda) - \log G(\frac{t'}{\lambda}; \sqrt{\tilde{w}_0}\lambda).$$

From Lemma 1, we have

$$\left|\log\frac{p(r|x_i,\mathbf{x}_\mathcal{K})}{p(r|x'_i,\mathbf{x}_\mathcal{K})}\right| \le \left|\frac{t}{\lambda} - \frac{t'}{\lambda}\right| = \frac{1}{\lambda}\left(1+\frac{mw_{01}}{\lambda w_0}\right)|x - x'|.$$

On the other hand, the equality is true when $x, x' \to +\infty$. So, we have

$$BDPL_\mathcal{A} = \sup_{|x_i - x'_i|\le M}\left|\log\frac{p(r|x_i,\mathbf{x}_\mathcal{K})}{p(r|x'_i,\mathbf{x}_\mathcal{K})}\right| = \frac{M}{\lambda}\left(1+\frac{mw_{01}}{w_0}\right).$$

□

A.5 Proof of Theorem 4

PROOF. (Theorem 4) Since $\mathcal{A}'$ is an ancestor of $\mathcal{A}$, there exists $j \in \mathcal{K}$, such that $\mathcal{K}' = \mathcal{K}\setminus\{j\}$ and $\mathcal{U}' = \mathcal{U}\cup\{j\}$. Let us consider Gaussian correlation models for adversaries $\mathcal{A}$ and $\mathcal{A}'$, respectively. We denote their Gaussian correlation matrices as $\mathbf{L}_\mathcal{A}$ and $\mathbf{L}_{\mathcal{A}'}$, respectively. Let them be

$$\mathbf{L}_\mathcal{A} = \begin{pmatrix} w_0 & -w_{0j} & -w_{0i} & -\mathbf{w}_{0\mathcal{K}'}^T \\ -w_{0j} & w_j & -w_{ji} & -\mathbf{w}_{j\mathcal{K}'}^T \\ -w_{0i} & -w_{ji} & w_i & -\mathbf{w}_{i\mathcal{K}'}^T \\ -\mathbf{w}_{0\mathcal{K}'} & -\mathbf{w}_{j\mathcal{K}'} & -\mathbf{w}_{i\mathcal{K}'} & \mathbf{W}_{\mathcal{K}'} \end{pmatrix}$$

and

$$\mathbf{L}_{\mathcal{A}'} = \begin{pmatrix} w'_0 & -w'_{0i} & -\mathbf{w}'^T_{0\mathcal{K}'} \\ -w'_{0i} & w'_i & -\mathbf{w}'^T_{i\mathcal{K}'} \\ -\mathbf{w}'_{0\mathcal{K}'} & -\mathbf{w}'_{i\mathcal{K}'} & \mathbf{W}'_{\mathcal{K}'} \end{pmatrix}.$$

From Proposition 2, we have

$$\begin{aligned} w'_0 &= \frac{(m+1)^2(w_0 w_j - w_{0j}^2)}{m^2 w_j + 2m w_{0j} + w_0} \\ w'_{0i} &= (m+1)\frac{(w_{0j} + m w_j)w_{0i} + (w_0 + m w_{0j})w_{ji}}{m^2 w_j + 2m w_{0j} + w_0}. \end{aligned}$$

Therefore,

$$\ell_{\mathcal{A}'} = \frac{(m+1)w'_{0i}}{w'_0} = \frac{(w_{0j} + m w_j)w_{0i} + (w_0 + m w_{0j})w_{ji}}{(w_0 w_j - w_{0j}^2)}.$$

Since $w_{0j}w_{0i} + w_0 w_{ji} \ge 0$, we have

$$\ell_{\mathcal{A}'} = \frac{(m+1)w'_{0i}}{w'_0} \ge \frac{m w_{0i}}{w_0} = \ell_\mathcal{A}.$$

Therefore, $\ell_{\mathcal{A}'} \ge \ell_\mathcal{A}$. □

A.6 Proof of Theorem 5

PROOF. (Theorem 5) Suppose there exists a $k > 1$ such that $\mathbf{L}$ is 2^k. Let $\mathbf{L}(k)$ denote a correlation matrix with size 2^k and $C(k)$ denote the computation cost of the function CalcLeakageCoefficient$(\mathbf{L}(k), \cdot)$. In the beginning, the function CalcLeakageCoefficient$(\mathbf{L}(k), 0)$ combines 2^k tuples into 2^{k-1} tuples and calls CalcLeakageCoefficient$(\mathbf{L}(k-1), \cdot)$ two times. The cost of the combination is

$$2^{2k} + (2^k-1)^2 + \cdots + (2^{k-1}+1)^2 = \frac{1}{24}(2^k+1)(7\cdot 2^{2k} + 2\cdot 2^k),$$

while the cost of calling CalcLeakageCoefficient$(\mathbf{L}(k-1), \cdot)$ is $2C(k-1)$. So, we obtain the recursion of $C(k)$

$$C(k) = 2C(k-1) + a2^{3k} + b2^{2k} + c2^k + d,$$

where a, b, c, d are constant real values. For all $2 \le i \le k$,

$$2^{k-i}C(i) = 2^{k-i+1}C(i-1) + 2^{k-i}(a2^{3i} + b2^{2i} + c2^i + d).$$

Summing them up, we have

$$\sum_{i=2}^{k} 2^{k-i}C(i) = \sum_{i=1}^{k-1} 2^{k-i}C(i) + \sum_{i=2}^{k} 2^{k-i}(a2^{3i} + b2^{2i} + c2^i + d).$$

Note that $C(1) = 0$, so we have $C(k) = 2^k\sum_{i=2}^{k}(a2^{2i} + b2^i + c + d2^{-i})$. Since $\sum_{i=2}^{k} 2^{2i} \sim O(2^{2k}) = O(n^2)$, $C(k) \sim O(n^3)$.

As for space complexity, the amount of storage for the matrix is at least n^2. After separating the tuples into two parts and combining them, we only need save two matrices of size $\frac{n}{2}$. The necessary space is $\frac{n^2}{2}$. As a result, the space complexity is at most $C(n^2)$. □

A.7 Proof of Theorem 6

PROOF. (Theorem 6) Let $\mathcal{P}_{-j} = \mathcal{P}\setminus\{j\}$, i.e., $\mathcal{P} = \mathcal{P}_{-j}\cup\{j\}$. Let us permute the tuple in the order $\mathcal{U}, \mathcal{P}_{-j}, \{j, i\}, \mathcal{K}$. Let $\mathbf{T}$ and $\mathbf{T}'$ be the prior matrices of $\mathcal{A}$ and $\mathcal{A}'$, respectively. First, we consider $\mathcal{A}$. We combine $\mathcal{U}$ and $\mathcal{P}_{-j}$ into one variable $x_0 = \frac{\sum_{u\in\mathcal{U}\cup\mathcal{P}\setminus\{j\}} x_u}{|\mathcal{U}|+|\mathcal{P}|-1}$ and call it tuple 0. Let the Gaussian correlation matrix for $\mathcal{A}$ which is corresponding to tuples $\{0, j, i\}\cup\mathcal{K}$ be

$$\hat{\mathbf{L}}_\mathcal{A} = \begin{pmatrix} w_0 & -w_{0j} & -w_{0i} & -\mathbf{w}_{0\mathcal{K}}^T \\ -w_{0j} & w_j & -w_{ji} & -\mathbf{w}_{j\mathcal{K}}^T \\ -w_{0i} & -w_{ji} & w_i & -\mathbf{w}_{i\mathcal{K}}^T \\ -\mathbf{w}_{0\mathcal{K}} & -\mathbf{w}_{j\mathcal{K}} & -\mathbf{w}_{i\mathcal{K}} & \mathbf{W}_\mathcal{K} \end{pmatrix}.$$

Let $\Delta\tau = \tau'_j - \tau_j \ge 0$. From Proposition 2, all elements in the Gaussian correlation matrix $\hat{\mathbf{L}}_{\mathcal{A}'}$ for $\mathcal{A}'$ which is corresponding to $\{0, j, i\}\cup\mathcal{K}$ are the same as $\hat{\mathbf{L}}_\mathcal{A}$ except w_j, i.e.,

$$\hat{\mathbf{L}}_{\mathcal{A}'} = \begin{pmatrix} w_0 & -w_{0j} & -w_{0i} & -\mathbf{w}_{0\mathcal{K}}^T \\ -w_{0j} & w_j + \Delta\tau & -w_{ji} & -\mathbf{w}_{j\mathcal{K}}^T \\ -w_{0i} & -w_{ji} & w_i & -\mathbf{w}_{i\mathcal{K}}^T \\ -\mathbf{w}_{0\mathcal{K}} & -\mathbf{w}_{j\mathcal{K}} & -\mathbf{w}_{i\mathcal{K}} & \mathbf{W}_\mathcal{K} \end{pmatrix}.$$

Combining x_0 with x_j, the Gaussian correlation matrix for $\mathcal{A}$ which is corresponding to $\{0, i\}\cup\mathcal{K}$ becomes

$$\hat{\hat{\mathbf{L}}}_\mathcal{A} = \begin{pmatrix} w'_0 & -w'_{0i} & -\mathbf{w}'^T_{0\mathcal{K}} \\ -w'_{0i} & w'_i & -\mathbf{w}'^T_{i\mathcal{K}} \\ -\mathbf{w}'_{0\mathcal{K}} & -\mathbf{w}'_{i\mathcal{K}} & \mathbf{W}'_\mathcal{K} \end{pmatrix}$$

where $w'_{0i} = (m+1)\frac{(w_{0j}+mw_j)w_{0i}+(w_0+mw_{0j})w_{ji}}{m^2w_j+2mw_{0j}+w_0}$ and $w'_0 = \frac{(m+1)^2(w_0w_j-w_{0j}^2)}{m^2w_j+2mw_{0j}+w_0}$. Therefore,

$$\ell_{\mathcal{A}} = \frac{(m+1)w'_{0i}}{w'_0} = \frac{(w_{0j}+mw_j)w_{0i}+(w_0+mw_{0j})w_{ji}}{w_0w_j - w_{0j}^2}.$$

On the other hand, $\ell_{\mathcal{A}'}$ can be derived from $\ell_{\mathcal{A}}$ by replacing w_j with $w_j + \Delta\tau$. It is easy to confirm that $\ell_{\mathcal{A}} \geq \ell_{\mathcal{A}'}$.

When $\tau_j \to 0$, we have $\hat{w}_j - w_j$. Accordingly, it is straightforward to prove that $\ell_{\mathcal{A}} \to \ell_{\mathcal{A}''}$ when $\tau_j \to 0$.

When $\tau_j \to \infty$, $w_j \to \infty$, we have

$$\ell_{\mathcal{A}} = \frac{(\frac{w_{0j}}{w_j}+m)w_{0i}+(w_0+mw_{0j})\frac{w_{ji}}{w_j}}{w_0 - \frac{w_{0j}^2}{w_j}}.$$

Therefore, $\ell_{\mathcal{A}} \to \frac{mw_{0i}}{w_0} = \ell_{\mathcal{A}'''}$. □

A.8 Proof of Theorem 7

PROOF. (Theorem 7) Let $\mathcal{A} = \mathcal{A}(i, \mathbf{y}_\mathcal{K})$ be an arbitrary adversary. From Definition 5, we have

$$BDPL_{\mathcal{A}} = \sup_{\mathbf{y}_\mathcal{K}, r} \left| \log \frac{\Pr(r|y_i = 1, \mathbf{y}_\mathcal{K})}{\Pr(r|y_i = 0, \mathbf{y}_\mathcal{K})} \right|.$$

Since $y_i, \mathbf{y}_\mathcal{K}$ are given, we assume that x_i approximates -1 (if $y_i = 0$) or 1 (if $y_i = 1$), and so does $\mathbf{x}_\mathcal{K}$. Then,

$$BDPL_{\mathcal{A}} \approx \sup_{\mathbf{x}_\mathcal{K}, r} \left| \log \frac{\Pr(r|x_i = 1, \mathbf{x}_\mathcal{K}, y_i = 1, \mathbf{y}_\mathcal{K})}{\Pr(r|x_i = -1, \mathbf{x}_\mathcal{K}, y_i = 0, \mathbf{y}_\mathcal{K})} \right|,$$

where $r = s + z$, $s = \sum_i y_i$ and $z \sim Geo(\lambda)$.

Let us consider $\Pr(\mathbf{x}_\mathcal{U}|x_i = -1, \mathbf{x}_\mathcal{K})$ and $\Pr(\mathbf{x}_\mathcal{U}|x_i = 1, \mathbf{x}_\mathcal{K})$. From the definition of the Gaussian correlation model, they have the same covariance matrix. Let $\boldsymbol{\mu}^{(0)}$ and $\boldsymbol{\mu}^{(1)}$ be their mean vectors. Suppose $\boldsymbol{\delta} = \boldsymbol{\mu}^{(1)} - \boldsymbol{\mu}^{(0)}$. We know that $\delta_u > 0$ ($\forall u \in \mathcal{U}$) and $\sum_{u\in\mathcal{U}} \delta_u = 2\ell_{\mathcal{A}}$. Thus,

$$\Pr(\mathbf{x}_\mathcal{U} = \boldsymbol{\chi}|x_i = -1, \mathbf{x}_\mathcal{K}) \equiv \Pr(\mathbf{x}_\mathcal{U} = \boldsymbol{\chi} + \boldsymbol{\delta}|x_i = 1, \mathbf{x}_\mathcal{K}). \tag{26}$$

Let $\mathcal{U}_1 \subseteq \mathcal{U}$, $r_\phi = s_\mathcal{K} + y_i + z$ and $r_{\mathcal{U}_1} = r_\phi + s_{\mathcal{U}_1} = r_\phi + \sum_{u\in\mathcal{U}_1} y_u$, then $r = r_\phi + s_\mathcal{U}$. We will now prove that

$$\xi(\mathcal{U}_1, t) := \left| \log \frac{f_{\mathcal{U}_1}(t,1)}{f_{\mathcal{U}_1}(t,0)} \right| \leq \frac{1}{\lambda}\left(1 + \frac{\alpha}{4}\sum_{u\in\mathcal{U}_1} \delta_u\right) \tag{27}$$

$$\zeta(\mathcal{U}_1, t) := \left| \log \frac{f_{\mathcal{U}_1}(t,y)}{f_{\mathcal{U}_1}(t-1,y)} \right| \leq \frac{1}{\lambda} \tag{28}$$

hold for $\forall \mathcal{U}_1 \subseteq \mathcal{U}$, $\forall t \in \mathbb{Z}$ and $\forall y \in \{0, 1\}$, where

$$f_{\mathcal{U}_1}(t,0) := \Pr(r_{\mathcal{U}_1} = t|x_i = -1, \mathbf{x}_\mathcal{U} = \boldsymbol{\chi}, y_i = 0, \mathbf{y}_\mathcal{K}),$$
$$f_{\mathcal{U}_1}(t,1) := \Pr(r_{\mathcal{U}_1} = t|x_i = 1, , \mathbf{x}_\mathcal{U} = \boldsymbol{\chi} + \boldsymbol{\delta}, y_i = 1, \mathbf{y}_\mathcal{K}).$$

When $\mathcal{U}_1 = \phi$, given $s_\mathcal{K} = \sum_{k\in\mathcal{K}} y_k$ and y_i, we have

$$f_\phi(t,y) = \Pr(r_\phi = t|x_i, y_i = y, \mathbf{y}_\mathcal{K}) \propto e^{-\left|\frac{t-s_\mathcal{K}-y}{\lambda}\right|}.$$

Hence, (27) and (28) are true.

Suppose that $\mathcal{U}_1 \subset \mathcal{U}$ ($\mathcal{U}_1 \neq \mathcal{U}$), such that (27) holds. Then, for $j \in \mathcal{U} \setminus \mathcal{U}_1$, let $\mathcal{U}_2 = \mathcal{U}_1 \cup \{j\}$. We have

$$f_{\mathcal{U}_2}(t,y) = f_{\mathcal{U}_1}(t,y)(1-p_y) + f_{\mathcal{U}_1}(t-1,y)p_y,$$

where

$$p_0 = \Pr(y_j = 1|x_j = \chi_j) = \frac{1}{1+e^{-\alpha\chi_j}},$$
$$p_1 = \Pr(y_j = 1|x_j = \chi_j + \delta_j) = \frac{1}{1+e^{-\alpha(\chi_j+\delta_j)}}.$$

Hence,

$$\xi(\mathcal{U}_2, t) = \left| \log \frac{f_{\mathcal{U}_1}(t,1)(1-p_1) + f_{\mathcal{U}_1}(t-1,1)p_1}{f_{\mathcal{U}_1}(t,0)(1-p_0) + f_{\mathcal{U}_1}(t-1,0)p_0} \right|.$$

Let $u = \log\frac{f_{\mathcal{U}_1}(t,1)}{f_{\mathcal{U}_1}(t-1,1)}$, $v = \log\frac{f_{\mathcal{U}_1}(t,0)}{f_{\mathcal{U}_1}(t-1,0)}$ and $w = \log\frac{f_{\mathcal{U}_1}(t-1,1)}{f_{\mathcal{U}_1}(t-1,0)}$. From the assumption, we have $|u| \leq \frac{1}{\lambda}$, $|v| \leq \frac{1}{\lambda}$, $|w| \leq A$ and $|u-v+w| \leq A$, where $A = \frac{1}{\lambda}\left(1 + \frac{\alpha}{4}\sum_{u\in\mathcal{U}_1}\delta_u\right)$. Thus,

$$\begin{aligned} g(\delta_j) &:= A + \frac{\alpha\delta_j}{4\lambda} - \log\frac{f_{\mathcal{U}_1}(t,1)(1-p_1) + f_{\mathcal{U}_1}(t-1,1)p_1}{f_{\mathcal{U}_1}(t,0)(1-p_0) + f_{\mathcal{U}_1}(t-1,0)p_0} \\ &= A + \frac{\alpha\delta_j}{4\lambda} - \log e^w \frac{e^u(1-p_1)+p_1}{e^v(1-p_0)+p_0} \\ &= A + \frac{\alpha\delta_j}{4\lambda} - w - \log\frac{1+e^{-\alpha\chi_j}}{1+e^{-\alpha(\chi_j+\delta_j)}}\frac{e^u e^{-\alpha(\chi_j+\delta_j)}+1}{e^v e^{-\alpha\chi_j}+1}. \end{aligned}$$

Using the previous conditions, we have

$$g(0) = A - w - \log\frac{e^u e^{-\alpha\chi_j}+1}{e^v e^{-\alpha\chi_j}+1} \geq 0.$$

On the other hand,

$$\begin{aligned} g'(\delta_j) &= \frac{\alpha}{4\lambda} + \frac{\alpha}{1+e^{-\alpha(\chi_j+\delta_j)}} - \frac{\alpha}{e^u e^{-\alpha(\chi_j+\delta_j)}+1} \\ &\geq \frac{\alpha}{4\lambda} + \frac{\alpha}{1+m} - \frac{\alpha}{e^{-1/\lambda}m+1} \\ &\quad (m := e^{-\alpha(\chi_j+\delta_j)} > 0) \\ &= \alpha\int_0^{\frac{1}{\lambda}} \left(\frac{1}{4} - \frac{me^{-x}}{(1+me^{-x})^2}\right)dx \\ &= \alpha\int_0^{\frac{1}{\lambda}} \frac{(1-me^{-x})^2}{4(1+me^{-x})^2}dx > 0. \end{aligned}$$

So, we have $g(\delta_j) > 0$. In the same way, we can prove

$$\begin{aligned} h(\delta_j) &:= A + \frac{\alpha\delta_j}{4\lambda} + \log\frac{f_{\mathcal{U}_1}(t,1)(1-p_1) + f_{\mathcal{U}_1}(t-1,1)p_1}{f_{\mathcal{U}_1}(t,0)(1-p_0) + f_{\mathcal{U}_1}(t-1,0)p_0} \\ &> 0. \end{aligned}$$

This implies (27) holds for $\mathcal{U}_2$; i.e.,

$$\xi(\mathcal{U}_2, t) \leq A + \frac{\alpha\delta_j}{4\lambda} = \frac{1}{\lambda}\left(1 + \frac{\alpha}{4}\sum_{u\in\mathcal{U}_2}\delta_u\right).$$

Since $f_{\mathcal{U}_2}$ is composed of $f_{\mathcal{U}_1}$, with (28), we have

$$\zeta(\mathcal{U}_2, t) = \left| \log\frac{f_{\mathcal{U}_1}(t,y)(1-p_y) + f_{\mathcal{U}_1}(t-1,y)p_y}{f_{\mathcal{U}_1}(t-1,y)(1-p_y) + f_{\mathcal{U}_1}(t-2,y)p_y} \right| \leq \frac{1}{\lambda}.$$

Accordingly, let $\mathcal{U}_1 = \mathcal{U}$, we have

$$\sup \xi(\mathcal{U}, t) \leq \frac{1}{\lambda}\left(1 + \frac{\alpha}{4}\sum_{u\in\mathcal{U}}\delta_u\right) = \frac{1}{\lambda}\left(1 + \frac{\alpha\ell_{\mathcal{A}}}{2}\right). \tag{29}$$

On the other hand, combining (26) with (29) yields

$$\begin{aligned} &BDPL_{\mathcal{A}} \\ &\approx \sup_{\mathbf{x}_\mathcal{K}, r} \left| \log\frac{\Pr(r|x_i = 1, \mathbf{x}_\mathcal{K}, y_i = 1, \mathbf{y}_\mathcal{K})}{\Pr(r|x_i = -1, \mathbf{x}_\mathcal{K}, y_i = 0, \mathbf{y}_\mathcal{K})} \right| \\ &= \sup_{\mathbf{x}_\mathcal{K}, r} \left| \log\frac{\int f_{\mathcal{U}_1}(t,1)\Pr(\mathbf{x}_\mathcal{U} = \boldsymbol{\chi} + \boldsymbol{\delta}|x_i = 1, \mathbf{x}_\mathcal{K})d\boldsymbol{\chi}}{\int f_{\mathcal{U}_1}(t,0)\Pr(\mathbf{x}_\mathcal{U} = \boldsymbol{\chi}|x_i = -1, \mathbf{x}_\mathcal{K})d\boldsymbol{\chi}} \right| \\ &\leq \frac{1}{\lambda}\left(1 + \frac{\alpha\ell_{\mathcal{A}}}{2}\right). \end{aligned}$$

□

Modular Order-Preserving Encryption, Revisited

Charalampos Mavroforakis
Boston University
cmav@cs.bu.edu

Nathan Chenette
Rose-Hulman Institute of Technology
chenett1@rose-hulman.edu

Adam O'Neill
Georgetown University and NIST
adam@cs.georgetown.edu

George Kollios
Boston University
gkollios@cs.bu.edu

Ran Canetti
Boston University
canetti@bu.edu

ABSTRACT

Order-preserving encryption (OPE) schemes, whose ciphertexts preserve the natural ordering of the plaintexts, allow efficient range query processing over outsourced encrypted databases without giving the server access to the decryption key. Such schemes have recently received increased interest in both the database and the cryptographic communities. In particular, *modular* order-preserving encryption (MOPE), due to Boldyreva *et al.* [8], is a promising extension that increases the security of the basic OPE by introducing a secret modular *offset* to each data value prior to encrypting it. However, executing range queries via MOPE in a naïve way allows the adversary to learn this offset, negating any potential security gains of this approach.

In this paper, we systematically address this vulnerability and show that MOPE can be used to build a practical system for executing range queries on encrypted data while providing a significant security improvement over the basic OPE. We introduce two new query execution algorithms for MOPE: our first algorithm is efficient if the user's query distribution is well-spread, while the second scheme is efficient even for skewed query distributions. Interestingly, our second algorithm achieves this efficiency by leaking the *least-important* bits of the data, whereas OPE is known to leak the *most-important* bits of the data. We also show that our algorithms can be extended to the case where the query distribution is adaptively learned online. We present new, appropriate security models for MOPE and use them to rigorously analyze the security of our proposed schemes. Finally, we design a system prototype that integrates our schemes on top of an existing database system and apply query optimization methods to execute SQL queries with range predicates efficiently. We provide a performance evaluation of our prototype under a number of different database and query distributions, using both synthetic and real datasets.

SIGMOD'15, May 31–June 4, 2015, Melbourne, Victoria, Australia.

http://dx.doi.org/10.1145/2723372.2749455 .

Categories and Subject Descriptors

E.3 [**Data**]: Data Encryption

Keywords

order preserving encryption; range queries; database encryption; database security model

1. INTRODUCTION

Cloud computing and modern networking and virtualization infrastructures have made the idea of database outsourcing to a third party not only a possibility, but sometimes a necessity. Following the seminal papers on database outsourcing [20, 19], a number of systems have been proposed [4, 26, 18, 11, 1, 10, 12] that use cloud services for this task. However, despite the enormous benefits of this approach, it has been recognized that there are a number of important issues that need to be addressed for it to be viable, the most critical of which is security. There have been three main issues related to security in this context: confidentiality, integrity (verifiability), and availability [2].

In this paper, we focus on the confidentiality problem, i.e., how a client can keep the database contents private from the third party. A typical approach is that the client encrypts each record before sending it to the third party. Ideally, one would like to use an encryption scheme that provides very strong security guarantees, such as semantic security [17], while maintaining the ability to execute queries. Remarkable recent work on fully homomorphic encryption has shown that, in theory, we can in fact build such encryption schemes with polynomial-time overhead [14]. However, while this is an active area of research, such schemes remain far from practical and are not expected to be anywhere close to being used in real systems in the near future.

To this end, new encryption schemes have been proposed that, although providing weaker security guarantees, allow for much more efficient query processing. In this paper we consider one of the most important such schemes, order-preserving encryption (OPE) [3, 7, 8, 27]. In an OPE scheme, any two values x and y with a natural order, e.g., $x < y$, get encrypted as $Enc(x) < Enc(y)$. In other words, the encryption scheme preserves the original order of the plaintexts. This is a very useful primitive because it allows the database system to make comparisons between the ciphertexts and still get the same results as if it had operated on the plaintexts. Therefore, the database system can still build index structures, like B+-trees, on the encrypted attributes to efficiently answer exact match and range queries, the same way as with un-encrypted data.

We focus on a promising extension to OPE introduced by Boldyreva *et al.* [8] called *modular* OPE (MOPE). The idea behind MOPE is simple: a secret *modular offset* j is included in the secret key and the encryption of x becomes $MOPE(x) = OPE(x + j)$, where OPE is the underlying OPE scheme. At a first glance, this seems to provide a substantial improvement in security — given just the encrypted database, the adversary cannot deduce any information about the locations of the underlying plaintexts. In constrast, basic OPE leaks about half of the most-important bits of the locations [8]. We want to point out this is in fact crucial for applications where a database table contains a column that takes consecutive values, e.g., a date. In this case, the plaintexts might cover the complete domain and if their order is revealed, so are their values. (This is actually the case for some of the attributes in the TPC-H benchmark that we used in the experiments.)

However, there is a catch: As Boldyreva *et al.* [8] note, if the adversary, i.e., the third party database server, observes the user's queries, they can divulge the secret offset j and negate any security gain. This is because the queries will never intersect the interval in the ciphertext-space between the encryptions of the last and the first plaintext value. This gap (see Figure 1) allows the adversary to orient the space and get a better estimate of j.

1.1 Contributions

In this paper, we revisit *modular* OPE and investigate the security and efficiency of systems that use it to execute range queries on encrypted data. The goal of our schemes is to hide the user's query distribution by *mixing* it with another distribution. Our main contributions are summarized below.

Uniform Query Algorithm: In our first scheme, the perceived query distribution from the server's point of view is uniform across all possible queries, including "wrap around" queries. Specifically each time the user makes a query, our scheme will repeatedly flip a biased coin to decide whether to execute it or sample a fake query from an appropriate *completion* distribution, repeating until the former happens. The coin's bias and the completion distribution are carefully chosen so that the expected number of fake queries is minimized, while at the same time ensuring that the perceived query distribution is uniform. As a result, we perform about μM additional fake queries for every real query, where μ is the maximum probability of any particular query and M is the domain size.

For better efficiency, our scheme also transforms every range query to a set of one or more queries with some fixed size $k \leq M$. In this case, the space requirement for storing the query distribution is M values instead of M^2. As shown by our security analysis, the scheme completely hides the *location* of the plaintext values, however still reveals the $\log(M + qk)/2$ most-significant bits of the distance between any two plaintexts, where q bounds the total number of queries executed by the system.

Periodic Query Algorithm: Our first scheme becomes inefficient if the user's query distribution is highly skewed. For example, if μ is a large constant, the system performs roughly M fake queries for every user query, which is obviously prohibitive. Our second scheme addresses this inefficiency by mixing the user's query distribution with a different completion distribution, such that the perceived query distribution is *ρ-periodic* instead of uniform. In a ρ-periodic distribution the probability of a query depends only on its congruence class modulo ρ — recall that we transform queries into a set of queries with fixed size k, so in effect each query is represented by a single domain element —, where ρ is a parameter of the system. Again, by carefully choosing the coin's bias and the ρ-periodic completion distribution, we minimize the expected number of fake queries. Namely, the expected number of fake queries is $\mu_\rho M$, where μ_ρ is the average over the congruence classes modulo ρ of the maximum probability of a query in each class. As $\mu_\rho \leq 1/\rho$, this quantity can be small even when μ is high, resulting in much better efficiency than our first scheme in such a case. As shown by our security analysis, the scheme achieves this efficiency by revealing $\log \rho$ least-significant bits of the data. Tuning ρ balances between security and efficiency.

Learning the Query Distribution: A drawback of the above schemes is that, in order to calculate the appropriate coin bias and completion distribution, they both assume that the system knows the user's query distribution *a priori*. We show that they can be extended to learn this distribution *adaptively online*.

The key idea is to maintain a buffer of the user's queries and, at each step, use it to estimate their query distribution based on the queries seen so far. Then, each time a query is to be executed, the coin's bias and completion distribution are updated to reflect this estimate. As the user makes more queries, this estimate improves and so does the performance of the system. While the efficiency will be low in the beginning (for example, after the user makes the first query, the system estimates that the query distribution is entirely concentrated on this point and, almost always, runs a fake query), it improves over time and converges to the performance of the schemes discussed above. Remarkably, our experiments show that, for many real world datasets, convergence happens very quickly.

System Prototype and Evaluation: We develop a simple system prototype that implements the proposed schemes. In our system architecture, we have three parties: the client (it could be more than one), the proxy, and the server, as show in Figure 4. The client issues queries to the proxy, which processes them (and buffers them, in the online adaptive case) and issues real and fake queries to the server according to one of our schemes. The responses that are relevant to the client's queries are forwarded by the proxy to the client and the rest are dropped. We use a PostgreSQL system as a back-end database system. Furthermore, an important advantage of our approach (similar to CryptDB [31]) is that the underlying database server does not need to be modified and we can use any existing DBMS to execute the actual queries. Therefore, we can take advantage of query optimization techniques at the back-end to process many fake queries together very efficiently.

We provide a comprehensive evaluation, where we study experimentally how our prototype performs under a number of different database and query distributions. The experiments use datasets and SQL queries from the TPC-H benchmark. The results show that the proposed approaches are quite practical.

Security Analysis: In order to analyze the security of our schemes, we propose new security definitions that allow the adversary to see both the encrypted database *and* the user's encrypted queries. Previous security models for OPE did not make this distinction and essentially just allowed the adversary to see the encrypted database. Our security definitions extend those of [8] to capture both the *location privacy* (how much about the plaintext location is revealed) and *distance privacy* (how much about the pairwise distances between the plaintexts is revealed).

Under our new definitions, we show that MOPE with our uniform query algorithm achieves perfect location security, while in the worst case leaking the $\log(M+qk)/2$ high-order bits of the plaintext distances. Despite the fact that the perceived distribution of the queries is uniform, the analysis here is non-trivial because, as explained above, we transform the queries to have a fixed size k. This means that the adversary gets to see encryptions of plaintexts that it knows are distance k apart, a situation not considered in prior analyses of OPE. We also show that MOPE with our periodic query algorithm leaks at most the $\log \rho$ least-important bits of the data. These results also hold in the case where the user's query distribution is learned adaptively online. This means that learning the query distribution affects only the efficiency and not the security of the system.

These security results should be contrasted with the basic OPE, which was shown to leak half of the most-important bits of both the plaintext values and their pairwise distances [8]. In particular, we want to draw the reader's attention to the fact that using MOPE with our periodic query algorithm only leaks the *least-important* bits of the data, which seems much more desirable.

2. BACKGROUND ON (MODULAR) OPE

For a randomized algorithm A, we denote by $y \leftarrow\$ A(x)$ that y is the output of running A on input x and a fresh random tape. When A is deterministic, we denote this by $y \leftarrow A(x)$ instead. All algorithms in the paper are required to be efficient unless otherwise mentioned. For a number n we denote by $[n]$ the set $\{1, \ldots, n\}$.

2.1 Order-Preserving Encryption

An *order-preserving symmetric encryption* (OPE) scheme with plaintext-space $[M]$ and ciphertext space $[N]$ is a tuple of algorithms $\mathsf{OPE} = (\mathsf{Kg}, \mathsf{Enc}, \mathsf{Dec})$ where:

- The randomized key-generation algorithm Kg outputs a key K.
- The deterministic encryption algorithm Enc on inputs a key K and a plaintext m outputs a ciphertext c.
- The deterministic decryption algorithm Dec on inputs a key K and a ciphertext c outputs a plaintext m.

In addition to the usual correctness requirement that

$$\mathsf{Dec}(\mathsf{Enc}(K, m)) = m$$

for every plaintext m and key K, we require that

$$m_1 \leq m_2 \text{ if and only if } \mathsf{Enc}(K, m_1) \leq \mathsf{Enc}(K, m_2)$$

for all plaintexts m_1, m_2 and every key K.

For notational convenience, we extend encryption notation to sets. That is, if X is a set then $\mathsf{Enc}(K, X)$ denotes the set $\{\mathsf{Enc}(K, x) \mid x \in X\}$.

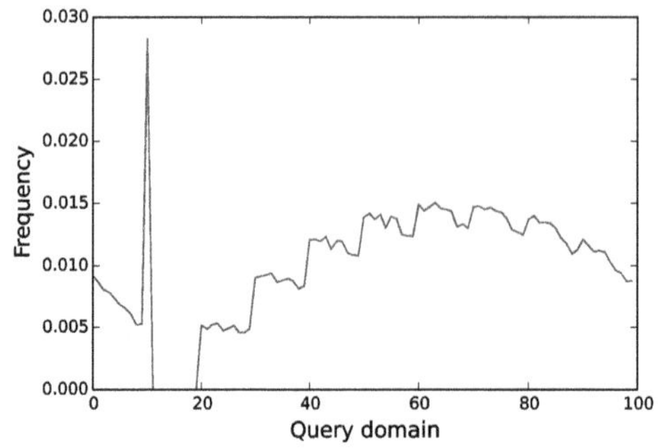

Figure 1: The gap in the query distribution reveals the displacement.

2.2 Modular Order-Preserving Encryption

A *modular order-preserving encryption* (MOPE) scheme is an extension to OPE that increases its security. Instead of defining such a scheme in general, we define a transformation to obtain it from a given OPE scheme.

THE TRANSFORMATION. Let $\mathsf{OPE} = (\mathsf{Kg}', \mathsf{Enc}', \mathsf{Dec}')$ be an OPE scheme. We define the associated *modular OPE scheme* $\mathsf{MOPE}[\mathsf{OPE}] = (\mathsf{Kg}, \mathsf{Enc}, \mathsf{Dec})$ where

- Kg generates $K \leftarrow\$ \mathsf{Kg}'$ and $j \leftarrow\$ [M]$; it outputs (K, j).
- Enc on inputs a key K and a plaintext m outputs $\mathsf{Enc}'(K, m + j \bmod M)$.
- Dec on inputs a key K and a ciphertext c outputs $\mathsf{Dec}(K, c) - j \bmod M$.

Above, the value j in the secret key of $\mathsf{MOPE}[\mathsf{OPE}]$ is called the *secret offset* or *displacement.*

3. NEW QUERY ALGORITHMS FOR MOPE

The Problem: With MOPE, as is also the case for OPE, it is very easy for the client to execute range queries: to make a range query $[m_L, m_R]$ for which $1 \leq m_L \leq m_R \leq M$, the client computes the pair $(c_L, c_R) = (\mathsf{Enc}(K, m_L), \mathsf{Enc}(K, m_R))$ and sends it to the server. The server then returns all database ciphertexts found in the range $[c_L, c_R]$. Note that in an MOPE scheme, this ciphertext interval could "wrap around" the space, i.e., if $c_R < c_L$ then the server returns database ciphertexts found in $[c_L, N] \cup [1, c_R]$. For simplicity, we will use the notation $[c_L, c_R]$ independent of whether or not the interval wraps around.

However, as pointed out by [8], there is a security vulnerability introduced by making range queries with MOPE. Note that all valid range queries, i.e., those $[m_L, m_R]$ for which $1 \leq m_L \leq m_R \leq M$, when encrypted may "cover" every value in the ciphertext-space $[N]$ *except* from those ciphertexts lying between $\mathsf{Enc}(K, M)$ and $\mathsf{Enc}(K, 1)$. Therefore, after observing enough queries, the adversary can get a better idea of where this gap lies, increasing its probability to predict j. In Figure 1 we show the histogram of the start values of a set of range queries for a small domain and displacement $j = 20$. In particular, we assume that the domain (and the range) is $[0, 100]$ and that all possible valid range queries with length 10 ($k = 10$) are generated and executed. In that case, the adversary will observe that there are no queries that start between the values 10 and 20, which correspond to the end of the domain before the displacement. Therefore, it can easily infer that the displacement is 20.

One natural step toward avoiding this attack is to introduce *wrap-around* queries [8]. A wrap-around range query corresponds to a pair m_L, m_R for which $m_R < m_L$. The desired interval of values wraps around the space, and is $[m_R, M] \cup [1, m_L]$. MOPE schemes naturally support wrap-around range queries in the same manner as standard range queries. These queries are not practically useful, but can be used as "dummy queries" in fooling the gap attack. However, [8] did not rigorously analyze the attack or explain how to implement dummy queries. Moreover, the one-wayness bounds of [8] did not consider the effect of observed range queries. A formal security model, constructions, and analysis are needed to address this scenario, and we take this as the starting point of our work.

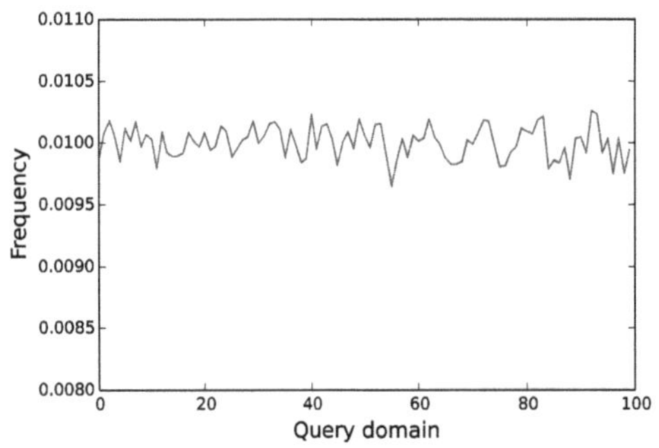

Figure 2: The query distribution after we add the fake queries. The real queries are obfuscated and the displacement gap is hidden.

3.1 Uniform Query Algorithm

The idea behind our basic query algorithm is as follows. We suppose that the user's queries come from some distribution $\mathcal{Q}$. Each time we need to make a query, we flip an α-biased coin, which returns heads with probability α, to decide whether to make a query from $\mathcal{Q}$ or from some other distribution $\tilde{\mathcal{Q}}$. We will choose α and $\tilde{Q}$ such that the convex combination $\alpha\mathcal{Q} + (1-\alpha)\tilde{\mathcal{Q}} = \mathcal{U}$, where $\mathcal{U}$ is the uniform distribution on the *entire* query space considered, including wrap-around queries in the case of MOPE). This solves two problems: (1) $\mathcal{Q}$ may not be uniform, even on standard (non-wrap-around) queries, invalidating the techniques for the security analysis developed in [8], and (2) $\mathcal{Q}$ depends on the secret offset, while $\mathcal{U}$ clearly does not, and consequently hides all information about it.

Completion of a distribution: To define our algorithm formally, we start with notation and a definition. Let $\mathcal{D}$ be a probability distribution on a finite set S. Define $\mu_{\mathcal{D}} = \max_{i \in S} \mathcal{D}(i)$, and define the *completion* of $\mathcal{D}$, denoted $\tilde{\mathcal{D}}$, as

$$\tilde{\mathcal{D}}(i) = \frac{\mu_{\mathcal{D}} - \mathcal{D}(i)}{\mu_{\mathcal{D}}|S| - 1}$$

for all $i \in S$.

Representation of the query distribution: To represent the query distribution we use a histogram on the query domain. However, since each query can have different start location and length, to represent all possible queries, we need to keep $O(M^2)$ values. In order to address this problem, we pick a fixed query length $k \geq 1$ and we decompose every query into a set of queries with length k. So, if an original user query has length smaller than k, we use a single fixed query that starts at the same location as the original query. On the other hand, if the original user query is larger than k, we split the query into a set of range queries of size k, where again the first fixed query starts from the start location of the original query. This approach guarantees that we need only $O(M)$ values to represent the query histogram. Notice that if a user's query q is decomposed into multiple fixed length queries, the results of all the decomposed queries should be returned to the user.

The query algorithm: Now we are ready to describe the algorithm, which we call QueryU ("U" for uniform), which processes a new query q. The algorithm is initialized with the completion distribution $\tilde{\mathcal{Q}}$, the maximum query probability $\mu_{\mathcal{Q}}$, and a fixed length query k. We denote by $\mathsf{Bern}(\alpha)$ the Bernoulli distribution with parameter α, i.e., $\mathsf{Bern}(\alpha) = 1$ with probability α. Note that the input to the algorithm is just the start location of the query, since the query has a fixed length.

Algorithm $\mathsf{QueryU}(q)$:
Until q is executed do:
  $\mathsf{coin} \leftarrow_{\$} \mathsf{Bern}\,(1/(\mu_{\mathcal{Q}}M))$
  If $\mathsf{coin} = 1$ then execute q
  Else ($\mathsf{coin} = 0$)
    $q_f \leftarrow_{\$} \tilde{\mathcal{Q}}$; Execute q_f

Above, "executing" a query q means that the ciphertexts $\mathsf{Enc}(K, q), \mathsf{Enc}(K, q + k)$ are issued, where Enc is the encryption algorithm for the MOPE scheme and K is the encryption key. To sample from the completion distribution $\tilde{\mathcal{Q}}$ we use the inversion method, i.e., inversion sampling [13]. Again, we just have to sample the start location of the query. In Figure 2 we show the perceived query distribution after we add the fake queries. In Section 7 we formally analyze the security of our scheme.

3.2 Periodic Query Algorithm

Note that the uniform query algorithm can be very inefficient when the user's distribution $\mathcal{Q}$ is highly skewed. In particular, on expectation $\mu_{\mathcal{Q}}M \in \Omega(M)$ fake queries are needed for every user query, which is no longer sub-linear to the size of plaintext domain.

We now present a periodic query algorithm that avoids this inefficiency, at the cost of leaking the least-significant bits of the secret offset in the MOPE scheme. In fact, it is a generalization of both QueryU and the straightforward algorithm that forwards all user queries directly; it offers any level of security vs. functionality trade-off, lying between these two extremes. Furthermore, we reduce the size of the histogram that is used to generate the fake queries from M to the size of the period.

Let $\mathcal{Q}$, as before, be the user's query distribution. Our periodic algorithm works like that of Section 3 with one exception: the distribution $\tilde{\mathcal{Q}}$ is chosen so that $\alpha\mathcal{Q} + (1-\alpha)\tilde{\mathcal{Q}} = \mathcal{P}_\rho$, where $\mathcal{P}_\rho$ is a periodic distribution on the query space with period ρ, an integer that divides M. That is, $\mathcal{P}_\rho(x) = \mathcal{P}_\rho(x+\rho)$ for all $x \in [M]$, where the addition is modular, i.e. it "wraps around" the query space. In partic-

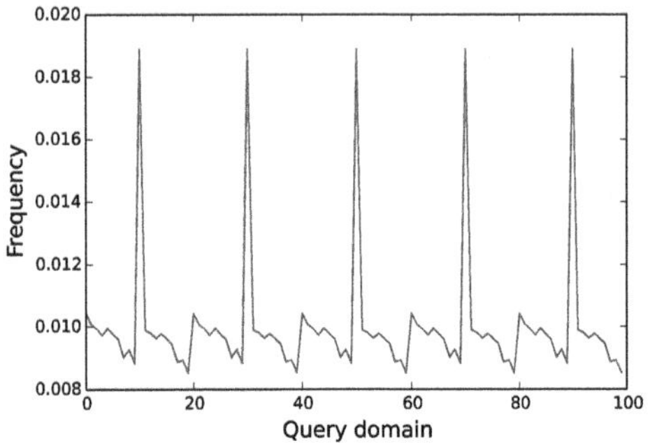

Figure 3: The periodic query distribution after we add the fake queries.

ular, we pick the appropriate $\tilde{\mathcal{Q}}$ to maximize α, which we formalize below.

ρ-periodic completion of a distribution: Let $\mathcal{D}$ be a probability distribution on a finite set $S = [M]$. Let ρ be an integer dividing M. Let sets $S_1, \ldots, S_\rho$ partition S into congruency classes modulo ρ. Define $\eta_j = \max_{i \in S_j} \mathcal{D}(i)$ for $j = 1, \ldots, \rho$ and $\eta_\mathcal{D} = \frac{1}{\rho}\sum_{j=1}^{\rho} \eta_j$. The *$\rho$-periodic completion* of $\mathcal{D}$, denoted $\tilde{\mathcal{D}}_\rho$, is

$$\tilde{\mathcal{D}}_\rho(i) = \frac{\eta_j - \mathcal{D}(i)}{\eta_\mathcal{D} M - 1}$$

for all $i \in S$.

The periodic query algorithm: The periodic query algorithm, QueryP[ρ], is the same as the one presented in Section 3 except that the coin is taken from Bern $(1/(\eta_\mathcal{Q} M))$ and the ρ-periodic completion $\tilde{\mathcal{Q}}_\rho$ is used in place of $\tilde{\mathcal{Q}}$. In Figure 3 we show the query distribution histogram for the example that we used before using a period of size $\rho = 20$.

Choosing ρ to balance efficiency and security: Using QueryU, we expect to see $\mu_\mathcal{Q} M$ fake queries for every real query, where $\mu_\mathcal{Q}$ is the maximum probability in $\mathcal{Q}$. Using QueryP instead, we expect $\eta_\mathcal{Q} M$ where $\eta_\mathcal{Q}$ is the average of the maximum probabilities of the congruency classes of $\mathcal{Q}$ modulo ρ. As $\eta_\mathcal{Q} \leq 1/\rho$, the ratio of fake to real queries is at most M/ρ, so even for skewed distributions we can achieve sublinear (in M) number of fake queries per real query by taking, e.g., $\rho = \sqrt{M}$.

On the other hand, notice that the ρ-periodic algorithm cannot protect the least-significant-bit information of the secret offset, as the cumulative distribution of real and fake queries is non-uniform. An adversary that knows the user's distribution can easily construct the cumulative distribution and match this to the perceived distribution of query ciphertexts. However, the adversary cannot determine which of the ρ possible shifts of this match is correct; i.e. the adversary can guess the least-significant bits of the encryption's secret offset, but cannot guess the most-significant bits. For example, if $\rho = \sqrt{M}$ then the most-significant half of the bits of the secret offset are hidden.

Thus, ρ is a parameter that enables us to fine-tune the efficiency-security trade-off: a larger ρ results in fewer fake queries but leaks more bits of the secret shift; a smaller ρ has the opposite effects. Notice that when $\rho = 1$, there is only one congruence class and the "periodic" algorithm is just the standard algorithm. When $\rho = M$, each value has its own congruence class and no fake queries are generated, so the user's distribution is exposed. In Section 7 we formally analyze the security of this scheme.

4. LEARNING THE QUERY DISTRIBUTION

In our schemes above, we assume that the user's query distribution is known *a priori*. Now we consider whether it can be learned adaptively online. The main idea is at each point to use the queries seen so far as the estimate of the user's query distribution. A naïve algorithm for this setting would then run the QueryU (or QueryP) algorithm to process each query with the updated histogram. However, this would result in extremely inefficient performance — we would need to execute roughly all possible range queries before the first real query is even executed. Instead, we maintain a buffer of the queries seen so far, which we use to represent the histogram, and issue only a single query before updating the buffer with the next query. For example, here is our adaptive online version of QueryU, which we call AdaptiveQueryU, to process a query q.

Algorithm AdaptiveQueryU(q):
  buffer.add(q)
  Compute $\mu_\mathcal{Q}$ and $\tilde{\mathcal{Q}}$ from buffer
  coin $\leftarrow_\$$ Bern $(1/(\mu_\mathcal{Q} M))$
  If coin $= 0$ then
    $q_f \leftarrow_\$ \tilde{\mathcal{Q}}$; Execute q_f
  Else (coin $= 1$)
    $q_r \leftarrow_\$$ buffer ; Execute q

The above algorithm should be repeated until all of the user's queries have been executed. Note that the second line regards the buffer as a histogram, in the obvious way. Furthermore, the last line randomly selects an item from the buffer, but leaves the buffer itself unmodified. An analogous adaptive version of QueryP, call it AdaptiveQueryP, can be obtained from the above.

In Section 7, we show that the adaptive online version of our algorithms achieve the same security guarantees as their counterparts in the basic model. For example, in the case of AdaptiveQueryU, the idea is that each individual query executed is uniformly distributed. To see this, note that in every execution of the while loop, sampling randomly from the buffer is identical to sampling randomly from the current $\mathcal{Q}$. Ensuring this identity is why we sample randomly from the buffer (rather than taking an arbitrary element from it).

Note that at some point the algorithm could declare the user's query distribution "learned" and delete any executed queries from the buffer (without changing a separate histogram $\mathcal{Q}$) until the buffer is empty, then switching to the basic QueryU or QueryP algorithms. We leave determining such a "cross-over" point for future work.

5. SYSTEM ARCHITECTURE

We now turn to developing a concrete system for executing queries on encrypted data using our algorithms. We consider a typical architecture used in database outsourcing systems [19], including CryptDB [31]. The system consists of a set of clients, a proxy server, and a (database) server as shown in Figure 4. The database server is an un-modified DBMS (in our experiments with TPC-H described later, we used a PostgreSQL server). The proxy is a trusted party

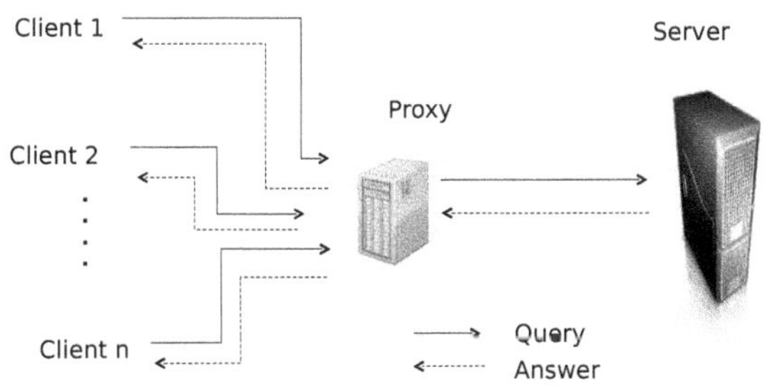

Figure 4: The architecture of the system.

and holds both the basic and the periodic completion distributions $\tilde{\mathcal{Q}}$ and $\tilde{\mathcal{Q}}_\rho$ respectively, as well as the encryption key for the MOPE scheme.

Initially, the data owner encrypts the database, using MOPE to encrypt attributes that support range query predicates and outsources the encrypted database to the untrusted database server. After that, the proxy starts sending queries (which are a mix of real and fake queries) to the server, which are executed using the DBMS, and the encrypted results are sent back to the proxy. We assume that the server executes queries correctly and returns the correct results. The proxy gets the results back, filters out the fake queries, and returns the requested results to each client. Next, we discuss how the proxy generates the fake queries and the query mix.

As we discussed before, our algorithms assume that all the queries have the same length k. However, an incoming query may have arbitrary length. Therefore, the proxy decomposes an original query q into a set of queries of size k that cover completely q. Assume that the set of these queries is $\tau_k(q)$. According to the previous algorithms we need to use a set of Bernoulli trials to generate a set of queries for each query in $\tau_k(q)$. However, we can directly compute the number of fake queries that we need each time, using the geometric distribution Geom. In particular, for each query in $\tau_k(q)$, we generate a value $\ell = \mathsf{Geom}\left(1/(\mu_{\mathcal{Q}} M)\right)$ and sample ℓ fake queries from $\tilde{\mathcal{Q}}$ using inversion sampling. Let the union of all the fake queries be $F(q)$. Finally, the proxy permutes all the queries in $F(q) \cup \tau_k(q)$ and sends them to the server.

Of course, the server may be able to detect the real queries if the number of fake queries is small and the real queries arrive in non-regular time intervals. We thus have the proxy issue queries to the server at fixed regular time intervals. This is a standard approach to hide real from fake queries that has been used in other systems, like in a practical ORAM implementation [25].

5.1 Multiple Range Query Execution

An advantage of our MOPE schemes compared to another recently proposed scheme that offers increased security over basic OPE [30] is that we do not need to modify the underlying DBMS when we execute the range queries. Thus, any optimization that the server can use for a regular database workload can also be used here. In particular, the fake queries are just some additional queries of the same form. Therefore, a simple and very efficient optimization is to consider multiple range predicates and execute them in a single query. For example, we can have many range query predicates connected with ORs in the WHERE clause of a single SQL query statement. This is an example of multiple query optimization [32] that allows sharing index and data access across multiple range queries. We can therefore execute multiple range queries at once and return the results to the proxy. This means of course that the proxy has to filter the query results and compute the tuples that satisfy the real queries. However, this slight extra work at the proxy can be justified if the performance at the server and the communication overhead (since the same record can be shared by multiple queries) improves significantly.

5.2 Other Practical Considerations

The completion distribution $\tilde{\mathcal{Q}}$ needs $O(M)$ space to be stored. If M is not very large, this is not a problem. On the other hand, it can be a non-negligible overhead if M is large. However, notice that M is actually the effective domain of the possible values of the encrypted attribute and not the domain of the attribute *per se*. In many applications, this can be much smaller than the potential complete value of M. For the periodic query algorithm the space is not a problem since the histogram needs only $O(\rho)$ space, where ρ is the period that we use in this approach.

Furthermore, another interesting point is that the proxy does not really execute any queries; it just creates the fake queries and keeps track of the state of the actual queries. Therefore, it is possible to implement the proxy using secure hardware, for example secure co-processors [6, 5]. This has a number of benefits. The operations executed from the proxy can be easily executed inside a secure hardware platform. Moreover, the proxy can be placed very close to the server and the communication overhead between the server and the proxy can be minimized.

6. EXPERIMENTS

In this section, we experimentally evaluate the uniform and periodic query algorithms, as well as their extensions that learn the user's query distribution adaptively online. We aim to (i) clearly illustrate the cost of these algorithms in different settings, (ii) measure the gain in performance when using the QueryP algorithm, (iii) explore the performance of an end-to-end system that runs range queries using MOPE, (iv) showcase the ability to deploy query optimization methods, and (v) evaluate the algorithm for learning the user's query distribution.

Query distributions: As we discussed in the previous sections, the performance of a query algorithm is determined by the user's behavior, i.e., the query distribution $\mathcal{Q}$. In order to evaluate our proposed algorithms with practical workloads, we simulate a user's query distribution in the following way: (i) We use a combination of real and synthetic datasets to define a distribution over the range of values in the database. This distribution will determine the position of each query, implicitly assuming that a user is more interested in querying records that are densely represented in the dataset. (ii) In order to account for variable query lengths, we sample the length of each range query from the normal distribution $N(0, \sigma^2)$ for different values of σ.

By combining the query's center and length, we generate the query distribution against which we will evaluate our algorithms.

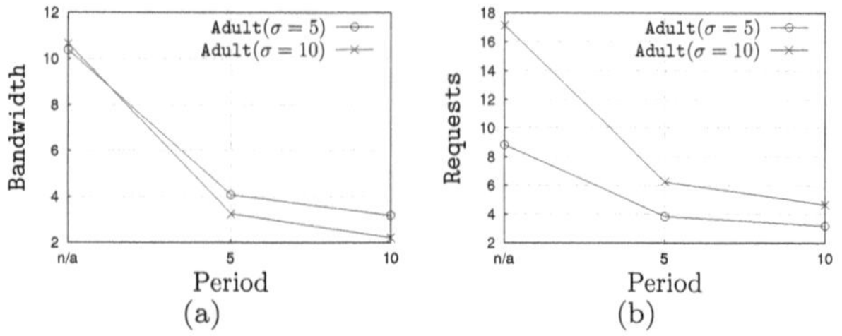

Figure 5: **Bandwidth**(5a) and **Requests**(5b) costs for the **Adult** query distribution with $\sigma = 5$ and 10.

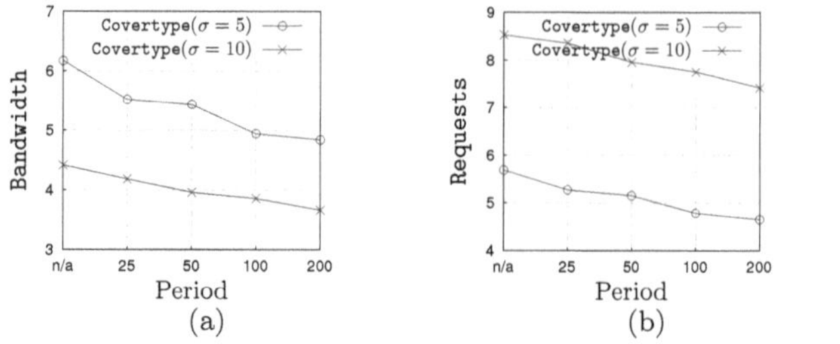

Figure 6: **Bandwidth**(6a) and **Requests**(6b) costs for the **Covertype** query distribution with $\sigma = 5$ and 10.

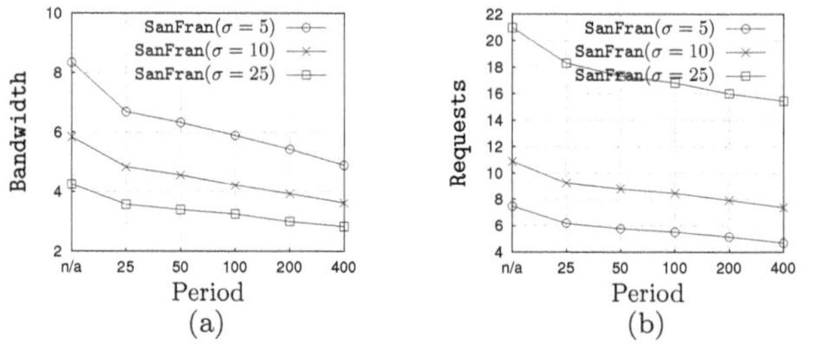

Figure 7: **Bandwidth**(7a) and **Requests**(6b) costs for the **SanFran** query distribution with $\sigma = 5$, 10 and 25.

The datasets that we used for step (i) above are: **Uniform**, **Zipf**, **Adult**, **Covertype**, **SanFran**. Details about these datasets can be found in the Appendix.

Each of the resulting query distributions is defined on a different domain. As such, we treat them differently during the experiments, by picking values for the period size and the query length that make sense.

In Section 6.3, we test our system against the popular TPC-H benchmark. Instead of generating simulated user queries, we use the ones that the benchmark provides. Specifically, we chose queries **Q4**, **Q6** and **Q14**, since they are the only ones to query ranges.

Notation: We denote by $\mathcal{R}$ the set of the user's real queries. The first step of both our algorithms is to break each query $q \in \mathcal{R}$ into a set of transformed queries $\tau_k(q)$, all of which are of length k and cover at least the same range of values as q. We define $\mathcal{T}$ to be the multi-set $\bigcup_{q \in \mathcal{R}} \tau_k(q)$. Finally, $\mathcal{F}$ will denote the set of fake queries.

Cost evaluation: In practice, cloud-service providers have different pricing schemes for the number of requests and the bandwidth that is being used. To reflect this, we introduce two different cost functions.

The first one captures the *overhead* in the number of records that we need to retrieve from the database and we formally define it as

$$\texttt{Bandwidth}(\mathcal{R}, \mathcal{F}) = \frac{\sum_{q \in \mathcal{F}} |q| + \sum_{q \in \mathcal{R}} (|q| \mod k)}{\sum_{q \in \mathcal{R}} |q|}$$

where $|q|$ denotes the size of the answer to query q (number of records returned). This cost depends on the number of fake records that are queried and the number of excess records requested due to the transformation of the original queries.

The second measure captures the *relative increase* in the number of requests to the service provider. We define it as

$$\texttt{Requests}(\mathcal{R}, \mathcal{T}, \mathcal{F}) = \frac{|\mathcal{T}| + |\mathcal{F}|}{|\mathcal{R}|}$$

6.1 The Cost of Security

In our first experiment, we aim to measure the cost of using each query algorithm, both in terms of **Bandwidth** and **Requests**. For each of the query distributions that we introduced above, we generate queries to simulate a user's behavior. We try different values for σ that make sense for the underlying database. Then, each query is handed over to the proxy, who runs one of the two algorithms, either QueryU or QueryP, with a fixed value $k = 10$. We let the proxy execute the queries and observe the sets $\mathcal{T}$ and $\mathcal{F}$. We report the results in Figures 5, 6 and 7. We got similar results for the **Uniform** and **Zipf** distributions, but we do not report them for brevity. We also repeated this experiment for multiple values of k; however the trend was similar.

6.1.1 *The Uniform Query Algorithm*

First, we consider QueryU. The results for QueryU correspond to the value of each of the cost functions for Period=**n/a**. As expected, for a constant k, the **Bandwidth** when the queries in $\mathcal{R}$ are short ($\sigma = 5$) is bigger than when they are longer. This can be attributed to the fact that the denominator, $\sum_{q \in \mathcal{R}} |q|$, becomes smaller as σ decreases.

On the other hand, **Requests** behaves oppositely. Longer queries in $\mathcal{R}$ mean that, for a fixed k, the set $\mathcal{T}$ will be strictly bigger and it will dominate the cost function.

6.1.2 *The Periodic Query Algorithm*

Next, we use the QueryP algorithm with different choices for the period size. It is clear that the cost functions decrease as we increase the size of the period. However, this comes with a price — larger periods leak more bits of information. The aim of this experiment is to measure the trade-off between the security and the performance of our scheme. Notice that the behavior of QueryP depends strongly on the user's query distribution. We observe that the cost for query distributions similar to **Adult** and **SanFran** is greatly decreased, even with just a small sacrifice in the security. On the other hand, the cost for query distributions such as **Covertype** seems to be much harder to change.

6.2 Choosing the Query Length

One important parameter of both QueryU and QueryP is the fixed length k of the transformed queries in $\mathcal{T}$. The reason of its importance is the fact that larger values for k lead to increased **Bandwidth** costs, but also tend to decrease the **Requests**. In this experiment, we explore how this choice affects the cost for the different query patterns that we use,

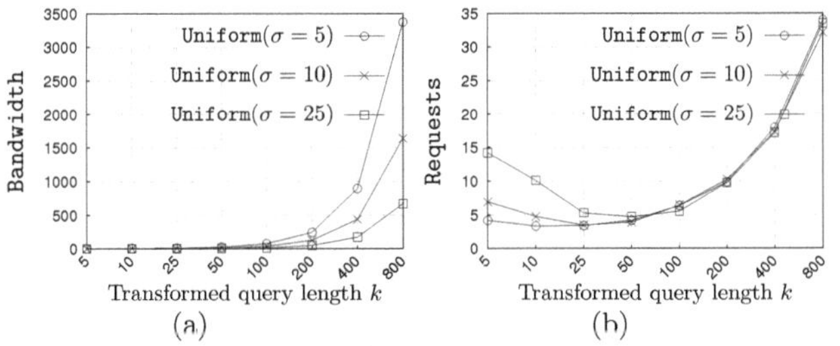

Figure 8: **Bandwidth**(8b) and **Requests**(8b) costs for **Uniform** query pattern and different k.

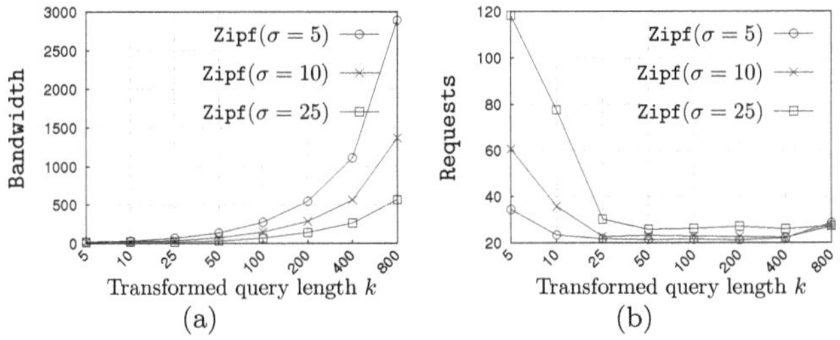

Figure 9: **Bandwidth**(9a) and **Requests**(9b) costs for **Zipf** query pattern and different k.

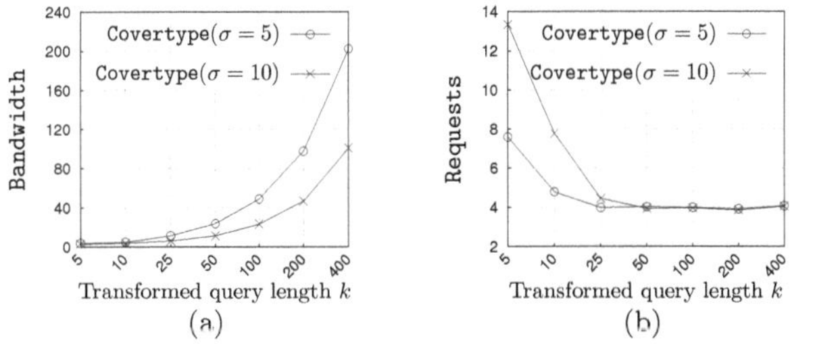

Figure 11: **Bandwidth**(6a) and **Requests**(6b) costs for **Covertype** query pattern and different k.

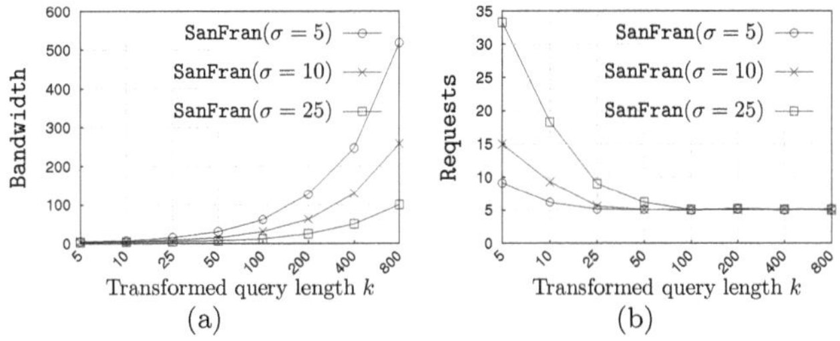

Figure 12: **Bandwidth**(7a) and **Requests**(6b) costs for **SanFran** query pattern and different k.

for the case of the QueryP algorithm with period size $\rho = 25$. However, the trend of the cost functions is similar for other period sizes, as well as for QueryU. We report the results of this experiment in Figures 8, 9, 10, 11 and 12.

We observe that, in order to minimize both costs, one should pick k to be above the median length of the queries in $\mathcal{R}$.

6.3 The TPC-H Benchmark

As part of this work, we built a prototype proxy that connects to a PostgreSQL database server and implements both QueryU and QueryP algorithms. We chose to test these algorithms against the TPC-H benchmark, a widely-used database performance benchmark. There are only a handful query templates in TPC-H that execute range queries. Specifically, **Q1**, **Q4**, **Q6** and **Q14** generate range queries on a date attribute of the database. This attribute represents the full range of dates between the years 1992 and 1998, inclusive. Apart from **Q1**, all of the queries are of fixed length (3 months, 1 year and 1 month for each query type respectively) and only cover the range of dates between 1993 and 1997. **Q1** runs range queries that retrieves almost the whole database, so we chose not to include it in the experiments. We used a Scale Factor (SF) equal to 1 for generating the

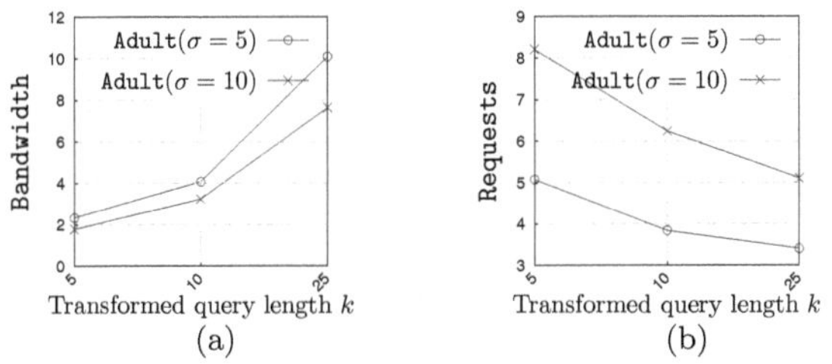

Figure 10: **Bandwidth**(5a) and **Requests**(5b) costs for **Adult** query pattern and different k.

TPC-H workload. Thus, the LINEITEM table contains 6M tuples, ORDERS 1.5M tuples, and PART 200K tuples.

We start by creating an encrypted version of the tables that these queries are executed on, i.e. we encrypt the date values using MOPE. Then, for each query that TPC-H generates, the proxy encrypts it and runs it on the encrypted tables of the database. We pick k equal to the fixed (original) query size and measure the performance of the algorithms for different period sizes. The times we report are for 1000 client queries. The baseline we are comparing against is the time it took the client to execute those 1000 queries, without using any encryption or requesting the help of the proxy's algorithms. Conveniently enough, this time is almost the same for both **Q6** and **Q14** (1.3 and 1.1 seconds respectively), so, for ease of presentation, we consider them to be equal. The results of this experiment for **Q6** and **Q14** are summarized in Figure 13. We observe that, if we allow the adversary to know where within a quarter the client's query is located, the time it takes to run 1000 queries drops to under 20 seconds (or about 20 msec for each query). We also need to add here that the naïve approach to return the whole database every time – a strategy that would result in perfect hiding – would require 8 hours 20 minutes and 14 hours, for **Q14** and **Q6** respectively, in order to execute all 1000 queries. This means that for **Q14** even the QueryU algorithm is more than 660 times faster than the naïve approach and for **Q6** the QueryP with period 1 month is more than 800 times faster.

We consider the case of **Q4** separately. A single, unencrypted, query of this type takes almost 4 seconds to run. This makes it a little bit more expensive to handle it the same way as **Q1** and **Q14**. So, instead of reporting the running time, we skip the execution of the queries and just measure the **Requests** cost for the proxy. The results of this experiment are summarized in Figure 14.

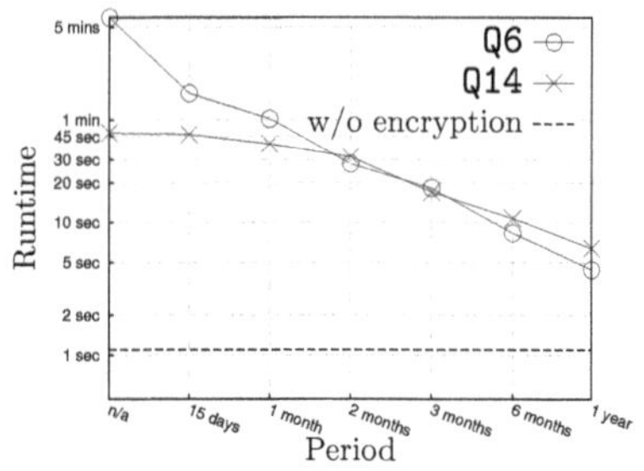

Figure 13: The time required to run 1000 queries generated by the Q6 and Q14 query templates using different period sizes.

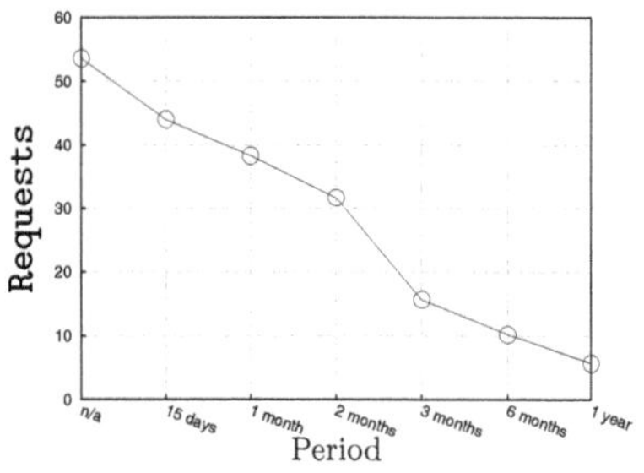

Figure 14: The **Bandwidth** cost when trying to hide the query pattern for Q4. A single query takes around 4 seconds to execute, so we can predict the actual running time.

6.4 Multiple Range Query Execution

As we discussed in Section 5, a big advantage of our MOPE schemes is that there is no need to modify the underlying DBMS in order to use it. As a result, practical query optimization methods are still applicable. To showcase this advantage, we do the following experiment: instead of executing the range queries one at a time, we combine a number of them into a disjunctive query (the WHERE clause is the logical disjunction of multiple ranges) and execute this instead. The setting is the same as in the previous section: the client executes 1000 encrypted queries of type Q6 and Q14 to the TPC-H database using the proxy's QueryU algorithm. Figure 15 shows that, as we combine more ranges, the time required for the proxy to execute all these queries is dramatically decreased. Notice that for the case of Q14, executing queries of 250 ranges at a time makes QueryU run in time comparable with the non-encrypted execution!

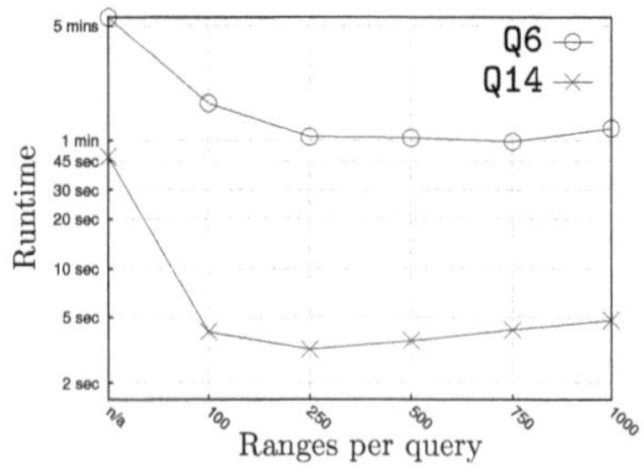

Figure 15: Combining multiple ranges into a single query results in dramatic speedups of the QueryU algorithm. The times reported are for 1000 queries.

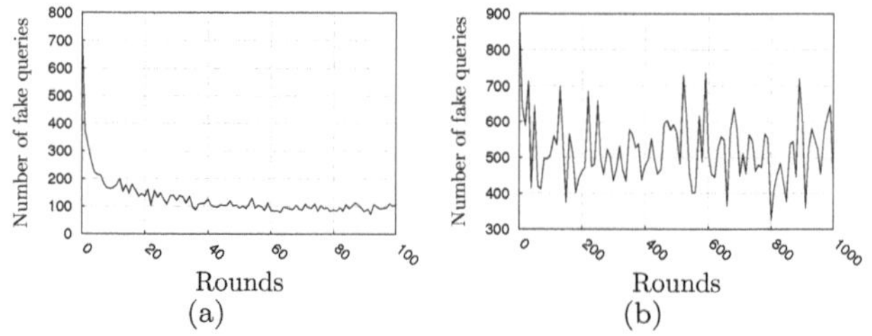

Figure 16: The number of fake queries executed for round of 10 real queries in SanFran10(16a) and Q14 of TPC-H(16b). The AdaptiveQueryU converges really fast, especially for Q14.

6.5 Learning the Query Distribution

For AdaptiveQueryU, we experimented with both a query distribution, i.e. SanFran, as well as the benchmark TPC-H (Q14). We measure the number of fake queries that need to be executed for each set of 10 unique real queries. Notice that because the sampling from the buffer is done with replacement, we may sample again a real query that has been executed before. In that case, we do not count this query as part of the unique queries but we count it as a fake query. In the beginning, when we do not know anything about the clients's query distribution, this number is expected to be large. However, as we observe more real queries, AdaptiveQueryU converges close to the performance of QueryU. Figure 16 summarizes these results. Indeed, each unique real query executed takes on average about 10 fake queries in the SanFran query pattern. For the case of Q14, what we observe is that the algorithm converges rapidly, since the distribution is practically over only 84 elements (one per month, for 7 years). The deviations we observe are due to randomness. We obtained similar results for all the other datasets.

7. SECURITY ANALYSIS

We follow the paradigm of *provable security*, the standard in modern cryptography. The first step is to capture the security of a scheme via a precise definition that specifies what an adversary is allowed to do when attacking the scheme and what its goals are. Such definitions are formulated via a probabilistic *experiment* that the adversary runs on some inputs, which is itself a randomized algorithm. For example, in a simple experiment the adversary may be given the encryptions of some messages and then tries to guess one of these messages. The adversary's *advantage* is defined to capture the probability that an adversary is able to violate the security according to the definition.

We can then analyze our candidate schemes under these definitions in order to assess their security, i.e., bound any efficient adversary's advantage against the scheme (usually under some well-accepted computational assumptions). It is important, especially in our context, to realize that the security of a scheme is not an all-or-nothing property, meaning that a scheme should not really be viewed as "either secure or not." Our schemes are such that some information about the data intentionally leaks in order to allow efficient query processing, and we strive to minimize information leakage beyond that. The provable security paradigm allows us to precisely capture and measure such a leakage.

7.1 Background on (M)OPE Security

We recall the security models for OPE and MOPE introduced in [7, 8]. Below, we fix a symmetric encryption scheme $\mathsf{SE} = (\mathsf{Kg}, \mathsf{Enc}, \mathsf{Dec})$. The definitions that follow do not assume that the scheme is (modular) order-preserving, but this is an important special case.

POPF security: We first define the notion of *pseudorandom order-preserving function* (POPF) security introduced in [7]. Intuitively, this notion asks that oracle access to the encryption algorithm of the scheme is indistinguishable from that to a truly random order-preserving function with the same domain and range (the "ideal object"). Let $\mathsf{OPF}[M, N]$ denote the set of all monotonically-increasing functions from $[M]$ to $[N]$. For every adversary A define its *POPF-advantage* as

$$\mathbf{Adv}^{\mathrm{popf}}_{\mathsf{SE}}(A) = \Pr[A^{\mathsf{Enc}(K,\cdot)} \text{ outputs } 1 : K \leftarrow\!\!\$\, \mathsf{Kg}] - \Pr[A^{f(\cdot)} \text{ outputs } 1 : f \leftarrow\!\!\$\, \mathsf{OPF}[M, N]] .$$

The work of [7] provides a POPF-secure OPE construction based on any standard blockcipher such as AES.

The related notion of *pseudorandom modular order preserving function* (PMOPF) security was introduced in [8]. Now, the "ideal object" is a random *modular* order-preserving function with the same domain and range. Let $\mathsf{MOPF}[M, N]$ denote the set of all modular order-preserving functions from $[M]$ to $[N]$ (that is, all order-preserving functions appended with all possible modular shifts). For every adversary A define its *PMOPF-advantage* as

$$\mathbf{Adv}^{\mathrm{pmopf}}_{\mathsf{SE}}(A) = \Pr[A^{\mathsf{Enc}(K,\cdot)} \text{ outputs } 1 : K \leftarrow\!\!\$\, \mathsf{Kg}] - \Pr[A^{f(\cdot)} \text{ outputs } 1 : f \leftarrow\!\!\$\, \mathsf{MOPF}[M, N]] .$$

[8] showed that one can easily extend a POPF-secure OPE (like that of [7]) to a MPOPF-secure MOPE by introducing a secret (pseudo)random shift to encryption and decryption.

WOW-L and WOW-D security: Next, we characterize the data privacy provided by a POPF-secure OPE scheme. Fix a parameter n, which is the number of ciphertexts in the database, and w, which is the "window size." For a set S let $\mathcal{S}_k(S)$ denote the set of all k-element subsets of S, for any $1 \leq k \leq |S|$.

We consider security experiments in which a database is sampled randomly and then the encrypted database is given to the adversary, who in turn tries to infer something about the plaintexts. Specifically, we use the notions of *window one-way wayness for location* (WOW-L) and *window one-way wayness for distance* (WOW-D) from [8]. Intuitively, WOW-L asks that it should be hard to specify a consecutive interval (i.e., a "window") of at most a certain length in which the decryption of some ciphertext lies. Analogously, WOW-D asks that it should be hard to specify a window of at most a certain length in which the distance between the decryption of some two ciphertexts lies. For more details we refer to [8].

Note that if OPE met the standard notion of semantic security, then the WOW-L and WOW-D advantage of any adversary would be upper-bounded by nw/M, since the adversary would get no useful information about the plaintexts and should just guess at random. (In general we could allow the adversary to choose a non-consecutive window in which a plaintext or distance could lie, but then in the case of OPE it is to the adversary's advantage to choose a consecutive one anyway.) Roughly, for OPE we get a $\sqrt{M}$ in the denominator instead. This means that roughly the *upper-half* of the bits of each plaintext, as well as the *upper-half* of the bits of the distance between each pair of plaintexts, are leaked by POPF-secure OPE.

Security bounds for POPF-secure MOPE: We now give the bounds from [8] for MOPE.

THEOREM 1. *Let* $\mathsf{OPE} = (\mathsf{Kg}, \mathsf{Enc}, \mathsf{Dec})$ *be a POPF-secure OPE scheme with* $N \geq 8M$ *and let* MOPE *be the associated MOPE scheme. Then for every adversary* A *there is an adversary* A' *such that*

$$\mathbf{Adv}^{\mathrm{wow}\text{-}\ell}_{\mathsf{MOPE},n,w}(A) \leq \mathbf{Adv}^{\mathrm{pmopf}}_{\mathsf{MOPE},n}(A') + \frac{nw}{M} .$$

The running-time of A' *is that of* A.

THEOREM 2. *Let* $\mathsf{OPE} = (\mathsf{Kg}, \mathsf{Enc}, \mathsf{Dec})$ *be a POPF-secure OPE scheme with* $N \geq 8M$ *and let* MOPE *be the associated MOPE scheme. Then for every adversary* A *there is an adversary* A' *such that*

$$\mathbf{Adv}^{\mathrm{wow}\text{-}\mathrm{d}}_{\mathsf{MOPE},n,w}(A) \leq \mathbf{Adv}^{\mathrm{pmopf}}_{\mathsf{MOPE},n}(A') + \frac{4n(n-1)w}{\sqrt{M-n+1}} .$$

The running-time of A' *is that of* A.

Intuitively, the above says that in the case of one-wayness for location, the security of MOPE is the same as for semantic security, i.e., no information about the location is revealed at all. However, in the case of distance, it is the same as for OPE.

7.2 New Security Models with Queries

As shown by the gap attack, in an appropriate security model for MOPE we need to take into account the queries seen by the adversary. Accordingly, we will now denote a MOPE scheme by $\mathsf{MOPE} = (\mathsf{Kg}, \mathsf{Enc}, \mathsf{Dec}, \mathsf{Query})$. Here the stateful and randomized algorithm Query on input a key K, an un-encrypted (standard or wrap-around) query (m_L, m_R), and state St outputs an encrypted query (c_L, c_R) and updated state St'. The un-encrypted query may also be the empty string ε, which indicates that there is no new query to process but that the next query in the encrypted query sequence should be returned. Note that in our general model the Query algorithm is otherwise arbitrary; in our analyses in Sections 7.3 and 7.4, it will be replaced by (appropriate modifications of) the algorithms from Sections 3 and 4.

For any choice of Query, it will be useful to define the following algorithm that takes as input a key K and an un-encrypted query sequence $Q = (m^1_L, m^1_R), \ldots, (m^q_L, m^q_R)$, and outputs a corresponding encrypted query sequence that contains the real encrypted queries embedded in it:

Algorithm $\mathsf{MakeQueries}(K, Q)$:
  $St \leftarrow \varepsilon$
  For $i = 1$ to q do: // process queries in Q
    $(c^i_L, c^i_R, St) \leftarrow\!\!\$\, \mathsf{Query}(K, (m^i_L, m^i_R), St)$
  While $St \neq \varepsilon$ do: // output remaining encrypted queries
    $i \leftarrow i + 1$; $(c^i_L, c^i_R) \leftarrow\!\!\$\, \mathsf{Query}(K, \varepsilon, St)$
  $C_Q \leftarrow ((c^1_L, c^1_R), \ldots, (c^i_L, c^i_R))$
  Return C_Q

Experiment $\mathbf{Exp}^{\text{wow}^*\text{-}\ell}_{\mathsf{SE},n,w,q,\mathcal{Q}}(A)$:
/* Sample encrypted database */
$K \leftarrow\$ \mathsf{Kg}$
$D \leftarrow\$ \mathcal{S}_n([M])$; $C_D \leftarrow\$ \mathsf{Enc}(K, D)$
$m \leftarrow\$ D$; $c \leftarrow\$ \mathsf{Enc}(K, m)$
$Count \leftarrow 0$
/* Now adversary can ask for queries */
$x \leftarrow\$ A^{\mathsf{NextQuery}(q, Count)}(C_D, c)$
If $m \in [x, x+w]$
Then return 1
Else return 0

Experiment $\mathbf{Exp}^{\text{wow}^*\text{-d}}_{\mathsf{SE},n,w,q,\mathcal{Q}}(A)$:
/* Sample encrypted database */
$K \leftarrow\$ \mathsf{Kg}$
$D \leftarrow\$ \mathcal{S}_n([M])$; $C_D \leftarrow\$ \mathsf{Enc}(K, D)$
$\{m_1, m_2\} \leftarrow\$ \mathcal{S}_2(D)$
$\{c_1, c_2\} \leftarrow\$ \mathsf{Enc}(K, \{m_1, m_2\})$
$Count \leftarrow 0$
/* Now adversary can ask for queries */
$x \leftarrow\$ A^{\mathsf{NextQuery}(q, Count)}(C_D, c_1, c_2)$
If $|m_1 - m_2| \in [x, x+w]$
Then return 1
Else return 0

Oracle $\mathsf{NextQuery}(q, Count)$:
If $Count \geq q$
Return $\perp$
$(m_L, m_R) \leftarrow\$ \mathcal{Q}$
$(c_L, c_R, St) \leftarrow\$ \mathsf{Query}(K, m_L, m_R, St)$
$Count \leftarrow Count + 1$
Return (c_L, c_R)

Figure 17: The security experiments (left and middle) give the adversary access to an oracle (right).

We require that for any Q, MakeQueries(K, Q) terminates with overwhelming probability over $K \leftarrow\$ \mathsf{Kg}$ and the coins of the algorithm itself.

WOW-L and WOW-D with queries: As before, let n be the database size and w be the window size. Let $\mathcal{Q}$ denote a distribution on queries; i.e., $\mathcal{Q}$ is a distribution on the set

$$\{(m_L, m_R) \mid 1 \leq m_L \leq m_R \leq M\} .$$

Intuitively, we want to consider window one-wayness when the adversary also sees queries. We want to protect privacy of both the data and the queries. The basic set-up is as follows: We give the adversary the encrypted database but also give it the ability to *request the next query* via an oracle that samples a query from an appropriate distribution. It can query this oracle (which takes no input) as much as it likes to receive more queries, up to some query limit q (which will play a role in our security bounds). Formally, we consider the experiments given in Figure 17. For an adversary A define its *WOW*-L advantage* (one-wayness for location with queries) as

$$\mathbf{Adv}^{\text{wow}^*\text{-}\ell}_{\mathsf{SE},n,w,q,\mathcal{Q}}(A) = \Pr\left[\mathbf{Exp}^{\text{wow}^*\text{-}\ell}_{\mathsf{SE},n,w,q,\mathcal{Q}}(A) \text{ outputs } 1\right] .$$

Similarly, for an adversary A define its *WOW*-D advantage* (one-wayness for distance with queries) as

$$\mathbf{Adv}^{\text{wow}^*\text{-d}}_{\mathsf{SE},n,w,q,\mathcal{Q}}(A) = \Pr\left[\mathbf{Exp}^{\text{wow}^*\text{-d}}_{\mathsf{SE},n,w,q,\mathcal{Q}}(A) \text{ outputs } 1\right] .$$

Note that we do *not* require the plaintext distances in the encrypted queries to be hidden; that is, we allow the adversary to learn the length of the requested plaintext ranges. This admits a much more practical solution.

Notice also a further change in the experiments $\mathbf{Exp}^{\text{wow}^*\text{-}\ell}$, $\mathbf{Exp}^{\text{wow}^*\text{-d}}$ from their non-query counterparts: we require that the adversary invert a *specific* plaintext or distance between two plaintexts (chosen at random). This change in definition allows us to consider applications where the database size n is large, and one is concerned with the ability of an adversary to uncover a specific message or distance—a more practical scenario. And while this weakens the security notions themselves, our later security results lose none of their potency from a practical standpoint.

7.3 The Uniform Query Algorithm

We can easily fit QueryU and AdaptiveQueryU into our general model above. For example, we can modify QueryU to maintain a buffer as in AdaptiveQueryU and return the next query to be executed instead of executing many queries until the input is executed. We slightly abuse notation and use the same names for the appropriately modified algorithms. Below we prove results about QueryU; analogous results hold for AdaptiveQueryU. The first result says that when using this algorithm to make range queries (regardless of the fixed query length) with MOPE, one-wayness for location is the best possible (no information is revealed at all).

THEOREM 3. *Let* OPE *be a POPF-secure OPE scheme on domain* $[M]$, *range* $[N]$. *Let* $\mathsf{MOPE} = (\mathsf{Kg}, \mathsf{Enc}, \mathsf{Dec}, \mathsf{QueryU})$ *be the associated MOPE scheme using the* QueryU *algorithm obtained from Section 3.1. Let* $\mathcal{Q}$ *be a distribution on* $[M]$. *Then for any query limit* q, *for every adversary* A *there is an adversary* A' *such that*

$$\mathbf{Adv}^{\text{wow}^*\text{-}\ell}_{\mathsf{MOPE},n,w,q,\mathcal{Q}}(A) \leq \mathbf{Adv}^{\text{pmopf}}_{\mathsf{MOPE},n}(A') + \frac{w}{M} .$$

The running-time of A' *is that of* A.

The next result is the most technically challenging to prove, and says that for distance one-wayness, using QueryU to make range queries with MOPE and fixing the query length to k leaks roughly at most the $\log(M+qk)/2$ most-significant bits of the distance between any two plaintexts.

THEOREM 4. *Let* $\mathsf{OPE} = (\mathsf{Kg}, \mathsf{Enc}, \mathsf{Dec})$ *be an OPE scheme on domain* $[M]$, *range* $[N]$, *with* $N \geq 16M$. *Let* $\mathsf{MOPE} = (\mathsf{Kg}, \mathsf{Enc}, \mathsf{Dec}, \mathsf{QueryU})$ *be the associated MOPE scheme using the* QueryU *algorithm obtained from Section 3.1. Let* $k \geq 1$ *be the fixed query length, with* $k \ll M$, q *be the query limit. Then for any adversary* A *there is an adversary* A' *such that*

$$\mathbf{Adv}^{\text{wow}^*\text{-d}}_{\mathsf{MOPE},n,w,q,\mathcal{Q}}(A) \leq \mathbf{Adv}^{\text{pmopf}}_{\mathsf{MOPE},n}(A') + \frac{8w}{\sqrt{M-qk-1}} .$$

The running-time of A' *is that of* A.

The proofs for the Theorems 3 and 4 appear in the Appendix.

7.4 The Periodic Query Algorithm

Again, we can easily fit QueryP and AdaptiveQueryP into our model above. We present our results for QueryP, but analogous results hold for AdaptiveQueryP. Below we show that using this algorithm to make range queries with MOPE leaks roughly at most the $\log \rho$ *least-significant* bits of the plaintexts.

THEOREM 5. *Let* $\mathcal{Q}$ *be a distribution on* $[M]$ *and let* ρ *be an integer that divides* M. *Let* OPE *be a POPF-secure OPE scheme on domain* $[M]$, *range* $[N]$, *and let* $\mathsf{MOPE}(\rho) =$

(Kg, Enc, Dec, Query) *be the associated MOPE scheme, with* Query(ρ) *defined as the periodic algorithm above. Then for any query limit q, for every adversary A there is an adversary A′ such that*

$$\mathbf{Adv}^{\text{wow}^*\text{-}\ell}_{\mathsf{MOPE}(\rho),n,w,q,\mathcal{Q}}(A) \leq \mathbf{Adv}^{\text{pmopf}}_{\mathsf{MOPE}(\rho),n}(A') + \frac{\rho w}{M}.$$

The running-time of A' is that of A.

The proof of Theorem 5 is also in the Appendix.

Notice that, in general, the periodic scheme has poor one-wayness for distance. In fact, depending on how the period ρ relates to the input distribution $\mathcal{Q}$, it may be quite easy for an adversary to guess distances based on knowledge of these parameters alone. For instance, suppose $\mathcal{Q}$ has equal spikes at a certain set of messages spaced ρ apart and is zero elsewhere. Then only distances $k\rho$ for integers k are possible, and thus low-order-bit information is leaked about distance (in addition to high-order-bit information about distance, which is always leaked by an RMOPF) resulting in poor distance one-wayness.

8. RELATED WORK

The idea of OPE was proposed by Agrawal et al. in [3] were they formally defined the problem and they provided a scheme to address it. Interestingly, this idea had already appeared before in [27, 19]. However, none of these works defined a formal security model as the one that we discuss here and no formal cryptographic security guarantees were discussed. The first to present a more formal security study of the problem was Boldyreva et al [7, 8].

A stronger notion of security for OPE would be that *only* order (or modular order, in the case of MOPE) among the plaintext is revealed. Unfortunately, [7] show such a definition is impossible to achieve. However, [30] (and an improvement by [23]) shows that this can be achieved by an "interactive" scheme that modifies existing encryptions in the database depending on the insertion of new values, and where encryption and decryption requires the interaction between the server and the client. However, here we work in the standard "non-interactive" setting. Remarkably, it has recently been shown that such security can even be achieved in the non-interactive setting by a "generalized" form of OPE that allows an arbitrary comparison operation on ciphertexts [16, 9], but such schemes are far from practical.

There are a number of works that use bucketization to store encrypted records for answering range queries, where each bucket corresponds to a given partition of the domain and each record is associated with a given partition. Given a range query, the buckets that intersect with the query must be identified by the client and an exact match query is issued at the server that retrieves all the records in these buckets. The records themselves are encrypted with a semantic security scheme. This idea has been used for both one dimensional [19, 22] and multidimensional range queries [21]. However, these works have weaker security models than ours and are susceptible to query pattern attacks.

Another work, that is related to our approach to obfuscate real queries using fake queries, is the work by Pang et al. [28], where they try to hide the terms in text search queries by introducing decoy terms. In a subsequent work [29], the same authors enhance a text query with a set of fake queries that can obfuscate the real query.

Some notable recent works on building database systems that run queries over encrypted data are CryptDB [31] and Monomi [34]. Both of them use an OPE scheme as one of their main encryption strategies that allows to execute database queries efficiently. Furthermore, two systems that use secure hardware and provide stronger security and better functionality are TrustedDB [6] and Cipherbase [5].

9. DISCUSSION AND FUTURE WORK

Relation to oblivious RAM: Oblivious RAM (ORAM), introduced by Goldreich and Ostrovsky [15] (see [33] and references therein for more recent work) is a technique that hides all information about what positions in an outsourced database are accessed by the client, by continually shuffling around and re-encrypting the data. In principle ORAM could be used generically to solve the problem of hiding the user's access pattern in our modular OPE setting. However, ORAM is less efficient than our solution and is actually an overkill: We need to hide the *distribution* of access locations by the client, not the locations themselves.

Thus, we achieve efficiency by taking in account the *actual distribution* of the user's queries, whereas in the ORAM model the access pattern of the client is arbitrary and fixed. It is an interesting future direction whether such an approach can be beneficial in the ORAM setting as well.

A note on the security model: We note that obtaining the security benefits of modular OPE over basic OPE crucially relies on the fact that we only allow the adversary a so-called "ciphertext-only" attack. In particular, the adversary in our security models is not allowed to see known plaintext-ciphertext pairs; if it could, it would be able to orient the dataset despite the use of the modular offset.

We envision that in many applications such an attack is unlikely — in any case, security will degrade back only the case of basic OPE (it cannot be *worse* than using basic OPE), so in some sense there is no reason not to use modular OPE anyway. However, it is interesting question for future research whether something can be done to mitigate the effect of plaintext-ciphertext pair exposure, such as re-encrypting portions of the data at regular intervals.

Acknowledgements

We thank Raluca Ada Popa, Kobbi Nissim, and Nickolai Zeldovich for discussions. Part of this work was done while Adam O'Neill was at Boston University, supported by NSF grants CNS-1012910 and CNS-0546614. George Kollios and Ran Canetti were supported by an NSF SaTC Frontier Award CNS-1414119.

10. REFERENCES

[1] D. Agrawal, A. El Abbadi, B. C. Ooi, S. Das, and A. J. Elmore. The evolving landscape of data management in the cloud. *IJCSE*, 7(1):2–16, 2012.

[2] D. Agrawal, A. El Abbadi, and S. Wang. Secure data management in the cloud. In *DNIS*, pages 1–15, 2011.

[3] R. Agrawal, J. Kiernan, R. Srikant, and Y. Xu. Order-preserving encryption for numeric data. In *SIGMOD Conference*, pages 563–574, 2004.

[4] Amazon. Amazon RDS. http://aws.amazon.com/rds/.

[5] A. Arasu, K. Eguro, M. Joglekar, R. Kaushik, D. Kossmann, and R. Ramamurthy. Transaction processing on confidential data using cipherbase. In *ICDE Conference*, 2015.

[6] S. Bajaj and R. Sion. Trusteddb: A trusted hardware based outsourced database engine. *PVLDB*, 4(12):1359–1362, 2011.

[7] A. Boldyreva, N. Chenette, Y. Lee, and A. O'Neill. Order-preserving symmetric encryption. In *EUROCRYPT*, pages 224–241, 2009.

[8] A. Boldyreva, N. Chenette, and A. O'Neill. Order-preserving encryption revisited: Improved security analysis and alternative solutions. In *CRYPTO*, pages 578–595, 2011.

[9] D. Boneh, K. Lewi, M. Raykova, A. Sahai, M. Zhandry, and J. Zimmerman. Semantically secure order-revealing encryption: Multi-input functional encryption without obfuscation. In *Advances in Cryptology - EUROCRYPT*, 2015.

[10] M. Brantner, D. Florescu, D. A. Graf, D. Kossmann, and T. Kraska. Building a database on s3. In *SIGMOD Conference*, pages 251–264, 2008.

[11] C. Curino, E. P. C. Jones, R. A. Popa, N. Malviya, E. Wu, S. Madden, H. Balakrishnan, and N. Zeldovich. Relational cloud: a database service for the cloud. In *CIDR*, pages 235–240, 2011.

[12] S. Das, D. Agrawal, and A. El Abbadi. Elastras: An elastic, scalable, and self-managing transactional database for the cloud. *ACM Trans. Database Syst.*, 38(1):5:1–5:45, Apr. 2013.

[13] L. Devroye. *Non-Uniform Random Variate Generation*. Springer-Verlag New York, 1986.

[14] C. Gentry. Fully homomorphic encryption using ideal lattices. In *STOC*, pages 169–178, 2009.

[15] O. Goldreich and R. Ostrovsky. Software protection and simulation on oblivious rams. *J. ACM*, 43(3):431–473, 1996.

[16] S. Goldwasser, S. D. Gordon, V. Goyal, A. Jain, J. Katz, F. Liu, A. Sahai, E. Shi, and H. Zhou. Multi-input functional encryption. In *Advances in Cryptology - EUROCRYPT*, pages 578–602, 2014.

[17] S. Goldwasser and S. Micali. Probabilistic encryption. *J. Comput. Syst. Sci.*, 28(2):270–299, 1984.

[18] Google. Google Cloud SQL. https://cloud.google.com/products/cloud-sql.

[19] H. Hacigümüs, B. R. Iyer, C. Li, and S. Mehrotra. Executing sql over encrypted data in the database-service-provider model. In *SIGMOD Conference*, pages 216–227, 2002.

[20] H. Hacigümüs, S. Mehrotra, and B. R. Iyer. Providing database as a service. In *ICDE Conference*, pages 29–38, 2002.

[21] B. Hore, S. Mehrotra, M. Canim, and M. Kantarcioglu. Secure multidimensional range queries over outsourced data. *VLDB J.*, 21(3):333–358, 2012.

[22] B. Hore, S. Mehrotra, and G. Tsudik. A privacy-preserving index for range queries. In *VLDB*, pages 720–731, 2004.

[23] F. Kerschbaum and A. Schropfer. Optimal average-complexity ideal-security order-preserving encryption. In *ACM SIGSAC Conference on Computer and Communications Security, CCS'14*, pages 1–12, 2014.

[24] F. Li, D. Cheng, M. Hadjieleftheriou, G. Kollios, and S. Teng. On trip planning queries in spatial databases. In *Advances in Spatial and Temporal Databases, 9th International Symposium, SSTD, Proceedings*, pages 273–290, 2005.

[25] M. Maas, E. Love, E. Stefanov, M. Tiwari, E. Shi, K. Asanovic, J. Kubiatowicz, and D. Song. PHANTOM: practical oblivious computation in a secure processor. In *ACM SIGSAC Conference on Computer and Communications Security, CCS'13*, pages 311–324, 2013.

[26] Microsoft. SQL Azure. http://www.windowsazure.com/en-us/develop/net/fundamentals/cloud-storage/.

[27] G. Özsoyoglu, D. A. Singer, and S. S. Chung. Anti-tamper databases: Querying encrypted databases. In *DBSec*, pages 133–146, 2003.

[28] H. Pang, X. Ding, and X. Xiao. Embellishing text search queries to protect user privacy. *Proc. VLDB Endow.*, 3(1-2):598–607, Sept. 2010.

[29] H. Pang, X. Xiao, and J. Shen. Obfuscating the topical intention in enterprise text search. In *ICDE Conference*, pages 1168–1179, 2012.

[30] R. A. Popa, F. H. Li, and N. Zeldovich. An ideal-security protocol for order-preserving encoding. In *2013 IEEE Symposium on Security and Privacy, SP*, pages 463–477, 2013.

[31] R. A. Popa, C. M. S. Redfield, N. Zeldovich, and H. Balakrishnan. Cryptdb: protecting confidentiality with encrypted query processing. In *SOSP*, pages 85–100, 2011.

[32] T. K. Sellis. Global query optimization. In *Proceedings of the 1986 ACM SIGMOD International Conference on Management of Data*, pages 191–205, 1986.

[33] E. Stefanov, M. van Dijk, E. Shi, C. W. Fletcher, L. Ren, X. Yu, and S. Devadas. Path oram: an extremely simple oblivious ram protocol. In *ACM Conference on Computer and Communications Security*, pages 299–310, 2013.

[34] S. Tu, M. F. Kaashoek, S. Madden, and N. Zeldovich. Processing analytical queries over encrypted data. *PVLDB*, 6(5), 2013.

APPENDIX

A. SECURITY PROOFS

First, we prove a short lemma. Let RMOPF be the "ideal" (inefficient) MOPE scheme that selects a random element from $\mathsf{MOPF}[M, N]$ as its key, and samples this function and its inverse for encryption and decryption.

LEMMA 1. *Given an adversary A to experiment WOW* (can be WOW*-L or WOW*-D) on scheme* MOPE*, there exists PMOPF adversary A' with the same running time such that*

$$\mathbf{Adv}^{\mathsf{wow}^*}_{\mathsf{MOPE},n,w}(A) - \mathbf{Adv}^{\mathsf{wow}^*}_{\mathsf{RMOPF},n,w}(A) = \mathbf{Adv}^{\mathsf{pmopf}}_{\mathsf{MOPE},n}(A').$$

(where wow^* *is either* wow^*-ℓ *or* wow^*-d.*)*

PROOF. Let A' be an algorithm for the PMOPF experiment that simulates experiment $\mathrm{WOW}^*_{\mathsf{SE},n,w}$ for adversary

A, using its oracle access to either MOPE's actual encryption function or a truly random MOPF on the same domain and range as "encryption" for SE, and outputs the result of the experiment. The PMOPF advantage of A' is equal to the difference in success probabilities for WOW* between using MOPE's actual encryption function versus a truly random MOPF. The former success probability is $\mathbf{Adv}^{\text{wow}^*}_{\text{MOPE},n,w}(A)$ and since a truly random MOPF is equivalent to the encryption function of RMOPF, the latter success probability is $\mathbf{Adv}^{\text{wow}^*}_{\text{RMOPF},n,w}(A)$. The result follows. □

PROOF OF THEOREM 3. By Lemma 1, it is enough to prove that

$$\mathbf{Adv}^{\text{wow}^*\text{-}\ell}_{\text{RMOPF},n,w}(A) \le \frac{w}{M}\,.$$

Recall that a random MOPF can be viewed as a random shift on the message space, followed by a random OPF. Notice then that even given the entire set of ciphertexts seen by the adversary, each ciphertext equally likely came from any element of the message space (because of the random shift.) Furthermore, all the adversary sees is ciphertexts. Thus, when the adversary guesses a window of size w, each ciphertext's likelihood to have come from a message in the window is simply w/M. □

PROOF OF THEOREM 4. In this proof, consider addition, subtraction, and "betweenness" of plaintexts and ciphertexts to be modular, i.e., they wrap around the plaintext and ciphertext spaces. Also, recall from [8] the definitions of *most likely plaintext* (m.l.p.) and *most likely plaintext distance* (m.l.d.): informally, the m.l.p. of a given ciphertext c is the plaintext m_c that most likely (over all keys and given knowledge) produced ciphertext c; the m.l.d. of given ciphertext pair c, c' is the plaintext distance $d_{c,c'}$ that most likely separates the plaintexts whose encryptions produced c_1 and c_2.

Invoking Lemma 1 and the trivial fact $\mathbf{Adv}^{\text{wow}^*\text{-d}}_{\text{RMOPF},n,w}(A) \le w \cdot \mathbf{Adv}^{\text{wow}^*\text{-d}}_{\text{RMOPF},n,1}(A)$, it is left to prove that

$$\mathbf{Adv}^{\text{wow}^*\text{-d}}_{\text{RMOPF},n,1}(A) \le \frac{8}{\sqrt{M}}\,.$$

$\mathbf{Adv}^{\text{wow}^*\text{-d}}_{\text{RMOPF},n,1}(A)$ is bounded by the probability of the most likely plaintext distance (m.l.d.) between random messages m_1, m_2 when c_1, c_2 are known to the adversary as well as ciphertexts (c^i_L, c^i_R) for $i \in [q]$, each pair of which comes from some uniformly random query m^i_L, $m^i_R = m^i_L + k - 1$.

This task is equivalent to the following experiment: given N balls, numbered 1 through N (the ciphertext space), we are told that a random M of them are black (representing which are actual ciphertexts under the key) and the rest are white. Also, balls c_1 and c_2 are black (as they are valid ciphertexts.) Furthermore, for $i \in [q]$, the balls c^i_L and c^i_R are black and there are precisely k total black balls between c^i_L and c^i_R, inclusive. The goal is to guess how many black balls lie between c_1 and c_2. (Notice that the MOPE scheme's secret shift is irrelevant in determining plaintext distance.)

We prove the bound by showing a more powerful adversary's advantage is bounded by the quantity desired. The more powerful adversary is given slightly more information in addition to the above:

- When two range queries overlap, i.e. $c^i_L < c^j_L < c^i_R$ for some $i, j \in [q]$, the adversary knows how many black balls lie in each subinterval. That is, the adversary is given the number of black balls between c^i_L and c^j_L, between c^j_L and c^i_R, and between c^i_R and c^j_R.
- When a challenge ciphertext lies in a range query, i.e. $c^i_L < c_1 < c^i_R$ (or analogously, $c^i_L < c_2 < c^i_R$), the adversary knows how many black balls lie in each subinterval. That is, the adversary is given the number of black balls between c^i_L and c_1, and between c_1 and c^i_R.

Let $\mathcal{C}$ be the set of ciphertexts within a range query, but not including c_1 or c_2.

All told, the adversary knows that some number $r \le kq$ of black balls lie within $\mathcal{C}$. Of these, say r_{in} lie strictly in between c_1 and c_2 and r_{out} lie outside, so that $r_{in} + r_{out} = r$. Of the remaining $M - r$ black balls, the adversary knows there are black balls at c_1 and c_2 but knows nothing of the others, other than that they are uniformly distributed among the other balls in $\mathcal{R}' = [N] \setminus \mathcal{C}$. Thus, the adversary's advantage is bounded by its ability to guess how many of these remaining balls between c_1 and c_2 are black. (This guess would be combined with r_{in} to find the adversary's best guess.) Let $N' = |\mathcal{R}'|$. Then this is equivalent to guessing the m.l.d. between two random ciphertexts on a domain of size $M - r$ and range of size N'. Notice that $|\mathcal{C}| \approx \frac{N}{M} r = \frac{N}{M} kq \ll N$. Thus $N' \ge N/2 \ge 8M \ge 8(M - r)$ and the bound of Theorem 2 applies, giving

$$\mathbf{Adv}^{\text{wow}^*\text{-d}}_{\text{RMOPF},n,1}(A) \le \frac{8}{\sqrt{M - r - 1}} \le \frac{8}{\sqrt{M - kq - 1}}.$$

Combining with the initial reductions, we achieve the result. □

PROOF OF THEOREM 5. Lemma 1 applies here, so it is enough to prove that

$$\mathbf{Adv}^{\text{wow}^*\text{-}\ell}_{\text{RMOPF}(\rho),n,w}(A) \le \frac{\rho w}{M}$$

where RMOPF(ρ) is the scheme that uses a completely random MOPF as encryption function and Query(ρ) as a query algorithm. Notice that the query algorithm samples messages from the ρ-periodic distribution $\mathcal{P}_\rho$, and in the random MOPF a random shift is applied in encryption. Thus, the set of ciphertexts seen by the adversary has equal probability of coming from one of M/ρ different shifts of a certain set of messages. Hence, when the adversary guesses a window of size w, each ciphertext's likelihood to have come from a message in the window is simply $\rho w/M$. □

B. DATASETS

Here we describe in more details that datasets that we used in the experimental evaluation:

- `Uniform`: The most basic distribution of queries is when every record has equal chance of being the center of a query. We use a domain size of 10000.
- `Zipf`: Often, user behavior resembles a power law. Certain ranges in the database are accessed far more frequently than the rest. Again, the domain size is 10000.
- `Adult`: We generate the distribution of the query center based on the *age* attribute of the `Adult`[1] dataset. The range of values of *age* is between 17 and 90. The probability of each record in the database is equal to the frequency with which that record appears in the dataset.

[1] `https://archive.ics.uci.edu/ml/datasets/Adult`

- `Covertype`: This is a real dataset based on the *elevation* attribute of the `Covertype`[2]. The range of values here is between 1859 and 3858.
- `SanFran`: This is a spatial dataset[3] of the California Road Network's nodes[24]. We use the *longitude* information of the nodes, after binning the dataset in 10000 bins. The probability of each record then is equal to the probability of picking the corresponding bin at random.

[2]`https://archive.ics.uci.edu/ml/datasets/Covertype`
[3]`http://www.cs.utah.edu/~lifeifei/SpatialDataset.htm`

Chiaroscuro: Transparency and Privacy for Massive Personal Time-Series Clustering

Tristan Allard[†] Georges Hébrail[*] Florent Masseglia[#] Esther Pacitti[+]
[†] IRISA & Univ. Rennes 1, France
[*] EDF R&D, Clamart, France
[#,+] Inria & Lirmm, Univ. Montpellier, France
first.last@{[†]irisa.fr, [*]edf.fr, [#]inria.fr, [+]lirmm.fr}

ABSTRACT

The advent of on-body/at-home sensors connected to personal devices leads to the generation of fine grain highly sensitive personal data at an unprecendent rate. However, despite the promises of large scale analytics there are obvious privacy concerns that prevent individuals to share their personnal data. In this paper, we propose *Chiaroscuro*, a complete solution for clustering personal data with strong privacy guarantees. The execution sequence produced by Chiaroscuro is massively distributed on personal devices, coping with arbitrary connections and disconnections. Chiaroscuro builds on our novel data structure, called *Diptych*, which allows the participating devices to collaborate privately by combining encryption with differential privacy. Our solution yields a high clustering quality while minimizing the impact of the differentially private perturbation. Chiaroscuro is both correct and secure. Finally, we provide an experimental validation of our approach on both real and synthetic sets of time-series.

Categories and Subject Descriptors: H.2.8 Database Management: Data Mining; K.4.1 Computers and Society: Privacy; H.2.4 Database Management: Distributed Databases;

Keywords: differential privacy; secure multi-party computation; clustering; k-means; time-series; gossip; sensors.

1. INTRODUCTION

Nowadays, individuals are able to monitor various biometric indicators (through, *e.g.,* heart-rate or blood-flow sensors, accelerometers, connected scales) for health, sports, or well-being reasons, as well as various consumption indicators (through, *e.g.,* smart-meters or smart-plugs for electricity or water consumption). This results in the production of *big personal data* in the form of sequences of time-stamped real values, called *time-series*, stored in the personal devices of the individuals.

Such wealth of personal time-series opens up exciting opportunities to learn valuable knowledge. Cluster analysis, also called *clustering*, aims at forming groups of data (or *clusters*) such that similar data appear in the same group and dissimilar data appear in different groups. Clustering is widely used in various application domains, *e.g.*, medicine, genetics, marketing, or social sciences. Clustering could, for example, allow a household to discover that its electrical price plan is not suited to its usage, compared to the price plan usually chosen by those having similar electrical consumption habits.

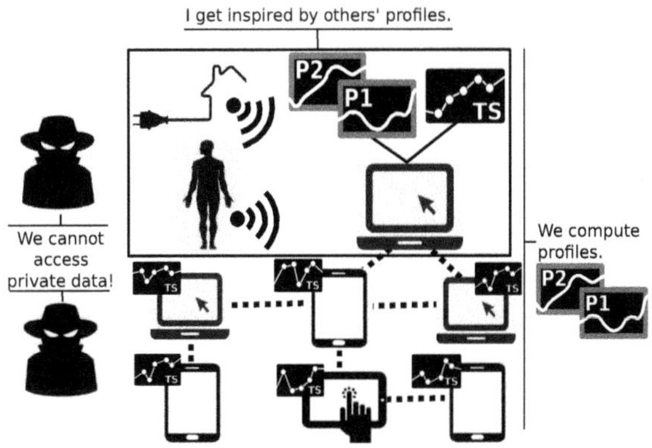

Figure 1: Collaborative Clustering of Massive Personal Time-Series with Privacy Guarantees

However, the quantity of information about individuals that fine grain personal time-series convey becomes worrying. Indeed, a personal time-series may disclose a wide and arbitrary variety of personal information, potentially leading to the identification and exposure of sensitive data. For example, a time-series containing the electrical consumption of a household recorded at the typical sampling rate of one measure every minute is a precise dissection of the in-home activities. At such fine grain, domestic appliances exhibit almost-unique electrical signatures that can then be identified accurately within the time-series [31, 32]. Demographic information, such as number or ages of individuals, may be inferred based on the volumes of electricity consumed and the times of consumption; For instance, a health status may be revealed by the presence of a clinic bed; even a religious orientation may become highly probable when observing regular electrical patterns (*e.g.*, the Jewish Shabbat involves a reduced electrical activity between Friday and Saturday sunsets). Similar conclusions are drawn when time-series come from different application domains (*e.g.*, physiological measures).

The usual approach for clustering time-series is centralized; it consists in copying the time-series from personal devices to a central server, assumed to be trustworthy, which is then in charge of performing clustering. However, although entrusting a single entity with this wealth of data is practical, it is hazardous in

SIGMOD'15, May 31–June 4, 2015, Melbourne, Victoria, Australia.

http://dx.doi.org/10.1145/2723372.2749453 .

an untrusted world. Millions of personal records are getting exposed each year due to outsider attacks, insider attacks, or basic negligence (*e.g.*, stolen laptop, lost post mail). Such cases feed the news on a daily basis (see, *e.g.*, `http://datalossdb.org`). According to recent reports (*e.g.*, [3, 34]), this trend is growing rapidly, backed up by the ever-increasing amount of personal data that is centralized. Thus, individuals are more and more concerned by the systematic collection and centralization of their personal data[1]. As a result, the centralized approach not only introduces an additional risk to data privacy but also an additional obstacle to large-scale personal data analysis.

In this paper, we address the problem of clustering personal time-series that are massively distributed on personal devices without jeopardizing their privacy (see Figure 1). This problem is not addressed satisfactorily by related work. First, the common use of random parts or of generic secure multi-party computation techniques [5, 17, 18, 19, 20] severely questions their ability to scale with the number of participating devices and cope with arbitrary connections/disconnections. Second, the straightforward disclosure of data-dependent information proposed in some work, *e.g.*, [22, 35], jeopardizes their privacy guarantees. When addressing this problem, we set the following requirements for the clustering solution:

R1 Transparent execution: clustering must be performed by the set of participating devices in a collaborative manner;

R2 Private execution: no information threatening the privacy of individuals must leak from the collaborative execution of clustering;

R3 Quality: the quality of clustering must be comparable to that of a centralized clustering;

R4 Practicality: the performance of clustering must be acceptable in contexts where the number of participating devices is in the order of several millions;

We propose *Chiaroscuro*[2], a complete solution for cluster analysis over personal time-series with strong privacy guarantees. Chiaroscuro comes with a privacy-preserving clustering algorithm fully decentralized on collaborating personal devices (also called *participants* in the following) that fulfills altogether the above requirements. Through requirement R2, Chiaroscuro relaxes the traditional *desideratum* that usually rules the security of distributed algorithms, allowing *differentially private* intermediate results to be revealed during the execution. The use of complex secure multi-party computation protocols is thus avoided by operating on cleartext data, while their privacy remains guaranteed by satisfying differential privacy.

We make the following contributions:

1. A massive distribution of the execution sequence on the set of participating personal devices based on gossip aggregation algorithms, thus fulfilling R1;
2. A data structure, called *Diptych*, which allows honest-but-curious participants to collaborate while never exporting any personal time-series out of any host device in a form that is neither homomorphically encrypted nor differentially private, thus fulfilling R2;
3. A set of heuristics designed to minimize the impact of differential privacy on the clustering quality, thus fulfilling R3;
4. A thorough experimental evaluation on both real and synthetic sets of time-series, which shows that R3 and R4 are fulfilled;

[1]Flagship examples include the Google Health, Google PowerMeter, and Microsoft Hohm products, abandoned because of insufficient adoption.

[2]Chiaroscuro is named after the conjunction of clarity - due to R1 - with obscurity - due to R2.

The paper is organized as follows. Section 2 defines more precisely the problem we tackle. Section 3 introduces necessary concepts and techniques. Section 4 describes Chiaroscuro with its data structure and the execution sequence, and shows its correctness and security. Section 5 deals with the quality of the clustering obtained. Section 6 experimentally validates the quality and practicality of Chiaroscuro. Section 7 discusses related work and Section 8 concludes.

2. PROBLEM DEFINITION

2.1 Time-Series and Clustering

Chiaroscuro aims at clustering time-series. A time-series is a sequence of real-valued variables. A usual representation of a time-series s having length n is given as an ordered set of real numbers: $s =< s[1]\ s[2]\ ...\ s[n] >$. Let S be a set of t times series, where each time-series s in S has length n, then S can be represented as a matrix, as follows:

$$S=\begin{bmatrix} s_1=< s_1[1] & \cdots & s_1[n]> \\ \vdots & \vdots & \vdots \\ s_t=< s_t[1] & \cdots & s_t[n]> \end{bmatrix} \tag{1}$$

Clustering is an unsupervised learning task that aims at building a disjoint set of clusters on a dataset. Let k be a parameter given by the end-user $(1<k<t)$ standing for the number of clusters to build. A disjoint set of clusters $\varsigma=\{\varsigma[1],\cdots,\varsigma[k]\}$ is obtained by a horizontal partitioning of S (*i.e.*, $\cup_{i=1}^{k}\varsigma[i]=S$ and $\forall i,j/i\neq j, \varsigma[i]\cap\varsigma[j]=\emptyset$). The goal of time-series clustering is to build such a partitioning, where similar series are grouped together, while dissimilar series are separated in different clusters. The result of clustering might be described by extension (enumerating the content of each cluster) or by intension with descriptors (*e.g.*, for each cluster, statistics, or a centroid such as a mean value).

2.2 Participants

Individuals participate in Chiaroscuro through their personal devices (*e.g.*, tablets, smartphones, laptops). In the rest of this paper, we call *participant* a computing node that participates in Chiaroscuro's execution sequence. We abstract participants by a set of assumptions about the resources they provide and the attack model they follow.

Resources. We expect a personal device to provide average resources: a multi-core CPU clocked at several GHz, a GB-sized RAM, and a GB-sized non-volatile memory (at least). It is also able to connect to the Internet at a high rate (*e.g.*, 1-10 Mb/s). However, since it is controlled by its owner, it does not provide any guarantee of availability: its connections and disconnections are arbitrary.

Attack model. A participant is called *honest-but-curious* when it follows strictly the execution sequence but exploits in any computationally-feasible way the information made available during the execution for inferring personal data. Moreover participants may collude together up to a reasonable bound initially fixed denoted by τ in the following.

2.3 Correctness and Security

Correctness. Chiaroscuro is *correct* iff (1) it terminates, and (2) outputs at least one centroid.

Secrets. The privacy guarantees of modern encryption/perturbation schemes rely on the secrecy of a small set of infor-

k-means Algorithm	
k	Initial number of centroids.
$\mathcal{C}_{init}$	Initial set of centroids.
θ	Convergence threshold.
Epidemic Aggregation Algorithm	
Λ	Initial local view.
n_e	Number of exchanges.
Cryptographic/Privacy Schemes	
χ	Public encryption key.
κ_i	Private i^{th} key-share.
τ	Key-shares threshold.
ϵ	Differential privacy level.
δ	Minimum probability to guarantee differential privacy.
n_ν	Number of noise-shares to be summed up together.

Table 1: Building Blocks' Initialization Parameters

mation such as the decryption key. We call them *secrets* and denote by Ξ the set of secrets. We present them in details in the next section.

Security.[3] Chiaroscuro is *secure* against honest-but-curious participants iff (1) no participant learns anything about the input time-series that has not been perturbed by a differentially-private mechanism (2) the uncertainty of a colluding participant over the set of secrets decreases gracefully with the number of collusions (which is bounded by the threshold τ).

3. PRELIMINARIES

In this section, we introduce basic concepts from clustering, distribution, and privacy-preserving techniques that are necessary in this work. Table 1 gives the initial parameters[4].

3.1 k-means Algorithm

The goal of k-means [28] is to propose k clusters that minimize an objective function. Usually, the objective function is the *intra-cluster inertia* (Definition 1), which measures the homogeneity of the set of time-series within clusters based on their average values, also called *centroids*. Let $\mathcal{C}$ denote the set of centroids. The centroid $\mathcal{C}[i]\in\mathcal{C}$ of the cluster $\zeta[i]\in\zeta$ is computed as follows: $\mathcal{C}[i]=<\mathcal{C}[i,1]\cdots\mathcal{C}[i,n]>$ where $\mathcal{C}[i,j]=\frac{1}{|\zeta[i]|}\sum_{\forall s\in\zeta[i]}s[j]$. Each centroid stands for the description by intension of its corresponding cluster.

Definition 1 (Inertia). *The* intra-cluster inertia *of a cluster $\zeta[i]$ is the weighted sum of the squared euclidean distances between the time-series in $\zeta[i]$ and the centroid $\mathcal{C}[i]$. The intra-cluster inertia of a set of clusters ζ, denoted by q^{ζ}_{intra}, is the sum of the intra-cluster inertia of $\zeta_i\in\zeta$: $q^{\zeta}_{intra}=\frac{1}{t}\cdot\sum_{i=1}^{k}\sum_{\forall s\in\zeta[i]}||\mathcal{C}[i]-s||^2$. The* inter-cluster inertia *of a set of clusters ζ measures their heterogeneity. It is the weighted sum of the squared euclidean distances between the clusters' centroids and the centroid of the complete set of time-series. We denote it by q^{ζ}_{inter} and compute it as : $q^{\zeta}_{inter}=\sum_{i=1}^{k}\frac{|\zeta[i]|}{t}\cdot||\mathcal{C}[i]-g||^2$, where g is the centroid of the complete set of time-series. The* full inertia *of the dataset is the addition of the intra-cluster inertia to the inter-cluster inertia : $q^{\zeta}=q^{\zeta}_{intra}+q^{\zeta}_{inter}$. It is a constant value.*

[3]The formal statement of our security model is in the Appendix.
[4]Participating devices can get the set of initial parameters, *e.g.*, as usual by downloading it at initialization time from a bootstrap server (which does not participate any further in the execution sequence), possibly after an authentication step.

Given k ($1<k<t$, with t the number of time-series), k-means initially sets the k initial centroids $\mathcal{C}_{init}$ to arbitrary values and the k clusters $\zeta[i]\in\zeta$ to empty sets. Then, it proceeds as follows:

1. **Assignment step:** For each $s\in S$, get its closest centroid $\mathcal{C}[i]\in\mathcal{C}$ and assign it to the corresponding cluster $\zeta[i]\in\zeta$.
2. **Computation step:** For each cluster $\zeta[i]\in\zeta$, compute $\mathcal{M}[i]\in\mathcal{M}$, its corresponding candidate centroid (also called its *mean* below).
3. **Convergence step:** If the distance between the centroids $\mathcal{C}$ and the means $\mathcal{M}$ is greater than θ, then set $\mathcal{C}\leftarrow\mathcal{M}$ and loop to the assignment step (Step 1), otherwise return $\mathcal{M}$.

3.2 Epidemic Aggregation Algorithms

Gossip protocols are lightweight fully decentralized protocols executed within large sets of participants. They simply consist in periodical point-to-point exchanges of information between participants. An initial list of IP addresses of some random participants, called the *local view*, and denoted by Λ in the following, bootstraps the exchanges. This simplicity makes gossip-based protocols easy to implement and highly scalable. Moreover, high levels of robustness and resistance to failures can be achieved by merging the local views at each exchange between participants [25]. *Epidemic aggregation algorithms* follow the gossip principles for computing approximations of global aggregates, such as sums or averages, over massively distributed data [23, 21]. Each participant holds its own approximation of the global aggregate, called *the local state*, and updates it, at each exchange, with the local state of the other participant through *the local update rule*. The approximation error depends on the number of gossip exchanges per participant and is guaranteed to converge to zero exponentially fast [21, 23]. Moreover, since the number of exchanges per participant is a parameter (denoted by n_e), it can be set so that the approximation error is as small as desired (*i.e.*, typically several orders of magnitude lower than the exact aggregate value [21], as illustrated in our experiments and shown in Appendix B).

Chiaroscuro is based on the epidemic computation of sums. In a context where the data is not sensitive, the epidemic sum algorithm proceeds as follows [23]. The local state of a participant i is made of a *sum*, denoted by σ_i, and a *weight*, denoted by ω_i. Each participant initializes σ_i to its local data and ω_i to zero[5] and starts its exchanges, updating σ_i and ω_i at each exchange. The local update rule simply consists in adding half of the local σ_i value (resp. ω_i) to half of the other participant's σ_j value (resp. ω_j). The local estimate of the global sum is σ_i/ω_i.

3.3 Encryption and Perturbation Schemes

3.3.1 Additively-Homomorphic Encryption Scheme

Chiaroscuro is independent of any specific encryption scheme provided that it satisfies the following properties:

1. **Semantic security**[14]: Stated informally, semantic security implies that, given a ciphertext, the public encryption key, and, some information about the plaintext, no probabilistic polynomial-time algorithm is able to gain additional knowledge on the plaintext. In particular, semantically secure schemes are not deterministic ;
2. **Additively-homomorphic:** Two encrypted integers can be added together to yield a correct encryption of their addition. Let a and b be two integers, χ be the encryption key and κ the decryption key, and $+_h$ be the homomorphic addition operator, then: $\mathtt{D}_\kappa(\mathtt{E}_\chi(a)+_h\mathtt{E}_\chi(b))==a+b$;

[5]One participant, no matter which one, must initialize ω_i to one. This is easily done in practice, *e.g.*, through a dedicated machine acting as a participant.

3. **Non-interactive threshold decryption:** The decryption key is a set of n_κ *key-shares* $\{\kappa_i\}$ so that decrypting a message requires to decrypt it partially by at least $\tau \leq n_\kappa$ distinct key-shares. Each partial decryption can be performed independently of the others;

The Damgard-Jurik encryption scheme [8] is an instance of such schemes:

1. **Encryption key:** The public encryption key is $\chi=(n,g)$, where n is an RSA modulus (the product of two large prime numbers) and g an element of the computation space, *i.e.*, the finite field $\mathbb{Z}^*_{n^{s+1}}$ (with $s>0$ a positive integer);
2. **Decryption key-shares:** Each decryption key-share κ_i is a point of a polynom of degree τ (so that τ points are necessary for knowing the polynom), where $\tau \leq n_\kappa$ is the key-shares threshold. The polynom is part of the set of secrets Ξ;
3. **Encryption:** The encryption of an integer a is $\mathtt{E}_\chi(a) = g^a \cdot r^{n^s} \mod n^{s+1}$ where $r \in \mathbb{Z}^*_{n^{s+1}}$ is a random number;
4. **Homomorphic addition:** The additively-homomorphic addition operator is simply the product between the two encrypted values: $\mathtt{E}_\chi(a) +_h \mathtt{E}_\chi(b) = \mathtt{E}_\chi(a) \times \mathtt{E}_\chi(b)$;
5. **Decryption:** Decryption is essentially performed by decrypting partially the encrypted value by at least $\tau \leq n_\kappa$ distinct key-shares, and by computing the product of the τ partial decryptions. A partial decryption consists basically in raising the encrypted value to a power that is a multiple of κ_i;

3.3.2 Differential Privacy and Laplace Perturbation

The ϵ-differential privacy model [10] (see Definition 2) requires that whatever the output of a (differentially-private) aggregation function, the probability that any given individual's data d was in the input is indistinguishable from the probability that d was not in the input. In our context, the aggregation function is the (time-series) sum, denoted by `Sum` in the following. It inputs a set of time-series, each of length n, and outputs their dimension-wise sum, *i.e.*, a single time-series of length n too where the variable at the ith dimension is the sum of the variables at the ith dimension of all the time-series input.

Definition 2 (ϵ-differential privacy from [10]). `Sum` *satisfies ϵ-differential privacy if, given the privacy parameter $\epsilon > 0$: $\mathtt{Pr}(\mathtt{Sum}(S_1) \in \mathcal{I}) \leq e^\epsilon \cdot \mathtt{Pr}(\mathtt{Sum}(S_2) \in \mathcal{I})$ for any set $\mathcal{I}$ and any set of time-series S_1 and S_2 such that S_2 can be obtained from S_1 by inserting or deleting one individual's time-series.*

In Chiaroscuro, the massive distribution of the differential privacy mechanism is based on approximate epidemic aggregation algorithms (see Section 3.2). In order to cope with the inherent approximation error, we relax the ϵ-differential privacy to a probabilistic variant, namely the (ϵ,δ)-probabilistic differential privacy[6] (Definition 3). The (ϵ,δ)-probabilistic differential privacy introduces a tradeoff between privacy and latency: together with other parameters, the value of δ determines the number of exchanges of the epidemic aggregation algorithms (see Appendix B).

Definition 3 (Probabilistic Differential Privacy). `Sum` *satisfies (ϵ, δ)-probabilistic differential privacy if, given the privacy parameters $\epsilon > 0$ and $\delta \in]0,1]$,* `Sum` *satisfies ϵ-differential privacy with a probability greater than or equal to δ.*

[6] A probabilistic relaxation of differential privacy, similar in spirit to our variant, was also proposed in [29].

A crucial property of the (ϵ, δ)-probabilistic differential privacy model is its *composability*: a set of n independent aggregates, each satisfying (ϵ, δ)-probabilistic differential privacy, satisfies $(\sum_{i=1}^{n} \epsilon_i,\ \delta^n)$-probabilistic differential privacy. Hence, the ϵ privacy level initially fixed can be seen as *a privacy budget* to be distributed across the various aggregates to perturb.

The ϵ-differential privacy model can be satisfied by perturbing the true results of the aggregation function through the *Laplace mechanism* so that the impact of any individual on the result is overwhelmed by the perturbation introduced [12]. The perturbation, called *noise* in the rest of the paper, is chosen at random in a Laplace distribution centered at 0 with a scale factor that depends on the privacy parameter ϵ and on the *sensitivity* of the sum function, *i.e.*, the maximum impact that an insertion/deletion of an individual's time-series can incur on its output. The exact value of the noise is part of the set of secrets Ξ.

Definition 4 (Laplace mechanism from [12]). *Let $\mathcal{L}(\lambda)$ denote a random variable which has a Laplace distribution with probability density function $f(x, \lambda) = \frac{1}{2\lambda} \cdot e^{-|x|/\lambda}$. Let S_1 and S_2 be any two sets of time-series such that S_2 can be obtained from S_1 by inserting or deleting one individual's time-series, and $[d_{min}, d_{max}]$ be the possible range of each variable in a time-series. The Laplace mechanism consists in adding $\mathcal{L}(\max \|\mathtt{Sum}(S_1) - \mathtt{Sum}(S_2)\|_1/\epsilon) = \mathcal{L}(n * \max(|d_{min}|, |d_{max}|)/\epsilon)$ to each variable of the time-series output by* `Sum`.

Lemma 1 states that a Laplace random variable can be generated by summing together an arbitrary number of independently identically distributed random variables formally defined in Definition 5 and called *noise-shares*[7].

Lemma 1 (Divisibility of Laplace from [24]). *Let $\mathcal{L}(\lambda)$ denote a random variable that has a Laplace distribution with probability density function $f(x,\lambda) = \frac{1}{2\lambda} \cdot e^{-|x|/\lambda}$. Then the distribution of $\mathcal{L}(\lambda)$ is infinitely divisible. Furthermore, for every integer $n_\nu \geq 1$, $\mathcal{L}(\lambda) = \sum_{i=1}^{n_\nu} (\nu_i)$ where each ν_i is a noise-share independently generated as defined in Definition 5 .*

Definition 5 (Noise-Share). *A noise share ν_i is a random variable computed as follows: $\nu_i = \mathcal{G}_1(n_\nu,\lambda) - \mathcal{G}_2(n_\nu,\lambda))$, where n_ν is the total number of noise-shares to be summed up together, and $\mathcal{G}_1(n_\nu,\lambda)$ and $\mathcal{G}_2(n_\nu,\lambda)$ are i.i.d. random variables having gamma distribution with PDF $g(x,n_\nu,\lambda) = \frac{(1/\lambda)^{1/n_\nu}}{\gamma(1/n_\nu)} \cdot x^{\frac{1}{n_\nu}-1} \cdot e^{-x/\lambda}$ where $x \geq 0$.*

4. CHIAROSCURO

In designing Chiaroscuro, we must cope with highly constrained challenges related to clustering, distribution and privacy. In this section, we propose our solutions for each of these challenges and show that the complete resulting execution sequence is both correct and secure. For simplifying the presentation, we defer to Section 5 the issues related to quality, including the management of the privacy budget.

4.1 Diptych Data Structure

Parallelizability is a crucial property in our massively distributed context, making a clustering algorithm such as *k-means* [28] especially relevant. However, exploiting it without any security safeguard would jeopardize privacy irremediably. A strong rethinking of its execution is thus essential. A traditional

[7] This well-known mathematical property is also used in [1]. However, the fault-tolerance needed in our context and the absence of central entity yields a significantly different noise generation algorithm (see Sections 4 and 7).

centralized k-means iteration consists in (1) partitioning the dataset according to the k centroids input by assigning each time-series to the closest centroid, and (2) computing the centers of mass of the resulting partitions, *i.e.*, the k means. The k-means algorithm is thus essentially based on a twofold data structure made of the centroids on one side and the means on the other side.

Our approach fundamentally stems from a major recast of this data structure and, consequently, of the execution sequence that manipulates it. We design Chiaroscuro so that participants perform (1) the assignment step on *differentially private cleartext centroids* and (2) the computation step on *additively-homomorphic encrypted means*. The resulting data structure, consisting in the differentially private centroids and the encrypted means, is called *Diptych*. The means part of the Diptych structure must be designed carefully because it must support the epidemic sum algorithm, which relies on a specific weighted data representation (see Section 3), and cope with the fact that data is additively-homomorphic encrypted, which excludes performing any division before decryption. The Diptych data structure is detailed in Definition 6.

DEFINITION 6 (DIPTYCH DATA STRUCTURE). *A Diptych follows the form* $(\mathcal{C},\mathfrak{M})$ *where any* $\mathcal{C}[i]\in\mathcal{C}$ *is a cleartext perturbed centroid, and any* $\mathfrak{M}[i]\in\mathfrak{M}$ *is an encrypted mean.* $\mathfrak{M}[i]$ *is represented by* $(\mathfrak{s}=\mathtt{E}_\chi(\sigma_{\text{sum}}),\mathfrak{c}=\mathtt{E}_\chi(\sigma_{\text{count}}),\omega)$, *where* $\mathtt{E}$ *is the additively-homomorphic encryption scheme,* χ *the encryption key,* $\mathtt{E}_\chi(\sigma_{\text{sum}})$ *and* $\mathtt{E}_\chi(\sigma_{\text{count}})$ *denote the encrypted epidemic representations of the mean's sum (a time-series) and its count (a real value), respectively, with* ω *their complementary weight.*

We emphasize that any information that depends on the participant's data is either encrypted (the sum and count parts of the epidemic representation) or perturbed by a differentially private mechanism (the centroids). We let the weight appear harmlessly in the clear because it is independent of the data.

4.2 Execution Sequence

The Diptych data structure is key for Chiaroscuro's execution sequence. This sequence is iterative, fully distributed on each participant, and proceeds without any global synchronization (the late participants simply synchronize on the latest iteration during their gossip exchanges). Basically, each iteration computes the set of means in an encrypted manner, perturbs them by a differentially private mechanism without decrypting them, and finally decrypts them. It consists of the following steps performed in loop until the centroids converge (see Algorithm 1 for the full execution sequence):

1. **Assignment step:** the local participant assigns its data to the closest centroid in $\mathcal{C}$ and initializes (1) the corresponding encrypted mean in $\mathfrak{M}$ with its local time-series (dimension-wise) encrypted and (2) the other means with $k-1$ zero-valued time-series (dimension-wise) encrypted;
2. **Computation step:** Compute $\mathcal{M}$, the set of *perturbed* means of the new clusters:
   (a) Epidemic computation of the encrypted means;
   (b) Epidemic perturbation of the encrypted means;
   (c) Epidemic decryption of the perturbed encrypted means;
3. **Convergence step:** if the distance between $\mathcal{C}$ and $\mathcal{M}$ is greater than θ, then $\mathcal{C}\leftarrow\mathcal{M}$ and loop to the assignment step (Step 1), otherwise return $\mathcal{M}$.

The assignment and convergence steps are both performed on cleartext data, so they do not present strong challenges. This is

Algorithm 1: Full execution sequence run by each participant

Req.: **The local data:** a time-series s.
The security parameters: the public encryption key χ, a private decryption key-share κ_i, the differential privacy level ϵ, the number of noise-shares n_ν.
The epidemic parameters: an initial local view Λ, the required number of exchanges n_e.
The k-means parameters: the initial vector of k centroids $\mathcal{C}_{init}$ and the maximum number of iterations n_{it}^{max}.

Let $\mathcal{C}$ denote the vector of centroids, $\mathcal{M}$ denote the vector of intermediate perturbed decrypted means, $\mathfrak{M}.s$ the vector of the encrypted sums of means, and $\mathfrak{M}.c$ the vector of the encrypted counts of means: $\mathcal{C}=\mathcal{C}_{init}$, $\mathcal{M}=\{\varnothing\}$.
Let $cv=$ **false** and $n_{it}=0$.
while $cv==$ *false and* $n_{it}\leq n_{it}^{max}$ **do**
  begin *Assignment step:*
    Compute the centroid that is the closest to s, $\mathcal{C}[j]$.
    Initialize the encrypted means: $\mathfrak{M}[j].\mathfrak{s}=\{\mathtt{E}_\chi(s_i)\}_{\forall s_i\in s}$, $\mathfrak{M}[j].\mathfrak{c}=\mathtt{E}_\chi(1)$; and $\forall i\neq j:\mathfrak{M}[i].s=\{\mathtt{E}_\chi(0)\}$, $\mathfrak{M}[l].c=\mathtt{E}_\chi(0)$; and $\omega=0$ for all means.
  begin *Computation step:*
    $\mathcal{M}=$ComputationStep($\mathfrak{M}$, χ, κ_i, ϵ, n_ν, Λ, n_e).
    (See Alg. 3 for details.)
  begin *Convergence step:*
    if HasConverged($\mathcal{C}$, $\mathcal{M}$)$==$*true* **then** $cv=true$;
    else $\mathcal{C}=\mathcal{M}$;
  Increment the number of iterations : $n_{it}{+}{+}$ (see Sec. 5).
Return $\mathcal{M}$

the computation step, detailed in Algorithm 3, that concentrates the three unsolved points of the execution sequence: the computation of the encrypted means (Section 4.2.1), their differentially private perturbation (Section 4.2.2), and finally their decryption (Section 4.2.3)[8].

4.2.1 Epidemic Computation of the Encrypted Means

The epidemic algorithm for computing the encrypted means, called `EESum` in the following, consists in performing repeated point-to-point exchanges of the encrypted means of the current Diptych data structure. Each participant picks at random a contact in its local view with which it exchanges its own encrypted means. Both update their respective Diptych and can then start another exchange if the number of exchanges sufficient for the epidemic sum to converge (fixed beforehand) has not been reached. The local update rule is specifically designed to cope with additively-homomorphic encrypted data: any division of encrypted data is delayed until its decryption so that only additions and scalar multiplications are performed. Algorithm 2 gives the local update rule of the `EESum` algorithm.

4.2.2 Epidemic Noise Generation

The perturbation function consists in adding a controlled amount of noise to each encrypted mean before its decryption. It must necessarily be performed in a collaborative manner so that no single participant knows the exact value of noise (which

[8]Note that when a cluster is small, the perturbation of its (low) mean shall give an irrelevant value. As a side-effect, such an outlying mean will simply be ignored *de facto* in the next iterations (no time series will correspond to it). Thus, our experiments show the number of clusters varying according to these "lost" means (Section 6).

Algorithm 2: Local update rule over encrypted data

Input: The public encryption key χ, the encrypted current local value $E_\chi(v_l)$, the current local weight ω_l, the current local number of exchanges performed so far n_l, the encrypted current remote value $E_\chi(v_r)$, the current remote weight ω_r, the current remote number of exchanges performed so far n_r.

if $n_r \neq n_l$ **then** *One value has to be scaled to be added*
  if $n_r > n_l$; **then** *Local value that must be scaled*
    $E_\chi(v_l) = E_\chi(v_l) \times_h 2^{n_r - n_l}$; $\omega_l = \omega_l \times 2^{n_r - n_l}$;
  else *Remote value must be scaled*
    $E_\chi(v_r) = E_\chi(v_r) \times_h 2^{n_l - n_r}$; $\omega_r = \omega_r \times 2^{n_l - n_r}$;
$E_\chi(v_l) = E_\chi(v_l) +_h E_\chi(v_r)$; $n_l = \text{MAX}(n_l, n_r) + 1$;

could otherwise be subtracted from the decrypted mean). In our context, the two parts of each encrypted mean must be perturbed, *i.e.*, its sum (a time-series) and its count (a real value). The epidemic perturbation function essentially amounts to the epidemic generation of $k*(n+1)$ Laplace random variables. It relies on two keystones: the Divisibility of Laplace lemma (see Lemma 1 in Section 3) and the `EESum` algorithm. Roughly, participants generate the noise-shares independently, as defined in Definition 5, and sum them up together through the `EESum` algorithm.

More precisely, each generated Laplace noise must satisfy two properties:

- **Correctness:** the noise must result from the sum of exactly n_ν distinct noise-shares (where n_ν is a parameter fixed beforehand);
- **Unicity:** the noise must be unique among the set of participants;

A straightforward value for the number of noise-shares is the size of the population, provided it is known beforehand. The noise generation is similar to the encrypted means computation: each participant generates a noise-share, encrypts it, and participates to the epidemic encrypted sum for approximating the global sum of the noise shares. However, the population size may not be known exactly in practice. The noise generation algorithm must be slightly adapted for this. First, the number of noise shares n_ν is set to an under-estimation of the population size, *e.g.*, to the estimated maximal lower bound. Thus, the epidemic noise generation will thus involve more noise shares than necessary: it can be corrected to involve the exact number of noise shares. Second, a cleartext counter, counting the number of nodes having actually participated in the noise generation, comes with the encrypted sum. A count being simply a sum of 1's, it follows the usual epidemic representation. The surplus of noise shares can now be estimated by subtracting n_ν to the actual value of the counter. Third, in order to guarantee the unicity property, *i.e.*, that all participants apply the same correction, each participant disseminates its locally generated correction, together with a random identifier. When participants disseminate their corrections, each one always keeps the correction associated to the smallest identifier. The probability of an incomplete dissemination is easily made negligible by standard dissemination protocols [23].

The two executions of the `EESum` algorithm - one for the encrypted means and one for their respective noise vectors - run in parallel. Their stopping criterion is the number of epidemic exchanges to perform for guaranteeing their convergence on the set of participants. After the sums, participants generate the noise corrections with their identifiers, and disseminate them,

Algorithm 3: Computation step

Input: The encrypted means $\mathfrak{M}$, the public encryption key χ, the private decryption key-share κ_i, the differential privacy level ϵ, the number of noise-shares n_ν, the local view Λ, the number of epidemic exchanges n_e necessary for the epidemic sum to converge (see Appendix B for fixing n_e).

begin *Epidemic computation of encrypted means*
  Background epidemic sums: Launch in background the encrypted epidemic algorithms for computing the encrypted means: $\mathfrak{M}$=EESum($\mathfrak{M}$, Λ, n_e, χ).
begin *Epidemic noise generation*
  Local noise-shares generation: Generate the vectors of noise-shares: $\mathcal{N}.\mathfrak{f}$ and $\mathcal{N}.\mathfrak{c}$ where each noise-share ν_i= GenNoise(ϵ, n_ν). Set the epidemic counter `ctr` to 1.
  Epidemic noise computation: Launch in background the encrypted epidemic sum algorithms dedicated to noise-shares: $\mathcal{N}$=EESum($\mathcal{N}$, Λ, n_e, χ), and the epidemic count algorithm: `ctr`=EpiSum(Λ, n_e).
  Epidemic noise correction: If `ctr`$>n_\nu$ generate a correction vector `cor`$=\sum_1^{\texttt{ctr}-n_\nu}$GenNoise($\epsilon$, n_ν) and a random identifier *idcor* for each of the noise vectors. Disseminate each epidemically `cor`=EpiDis(*cor*,*idcor*), and subtract each final correction vector to its respective noise vector.
  Encrypted perturbation: Add the vector of encrypted sums (resp. counts) to its vector of encrypted noises: $\mathfrak{M}.\mathfrak{f}=\mathfrak{M}.\mathfrak{f}+_h\mathcal{N}.\mathfrak{f}$ and $\mathfrak{M}.\mathfrak{c}=\mathfrak{M}.\mathfrak{c}+_h\mathcal{N}.\mathfrak{c}$.
begin *Epidemic decryption*
  Local partial decryption: Choose a random local key-share identifier *idk* and decrypt partially $\mathfrak{M}.\mathfrak{f}$ and $\mathfrak{M}.\mathfrak{c}$ with the local key-share: $\mathcal{S}=D_{\kappa_i}(\mathfrak{M}.\mathfrak{f})$ and $\mathcal{K}=D_{\kappa_i}(\mathfrak{M}.\mathfrak{c})$.
  Epidemic decryption: Launch the epidemic decryption: $\mathcal{S}$=EEDec($\mathfrak{M}.\mathfrak{f}$, $\mathcal{S}$, *idk*, Λ, κ_i)/$\mathfrak{M}.\omega$ and $\mathcal{K}$=EEDec($\mathfrak{M}.\mathfrak{c}$, $\mathcal{K}$, *idk*, Λ, κ_i)/$\mathfrak{M}.\omega$.
Compute the vector of perturbed means: $\mathcal{M}=\mathcal{S}/\mathcal{K}$.
Smooth the vector of perturbed means: $\mathcal{M}$=Smooth($\mathcal{M}$) (see Sec. 5).
Return $\mathcal{M}$.

keeping the one with the smallest identifier at each exchange. The stopping criterion for the epidemic dissemination is also the number of exchanges necessary for convergence. Finally, when the dissemination terminates, each participant adds the corrected converged encrypted noises to the converged encrypted means to obtain the perturbed encrypted means and is now ready to launch their epidemic decryption.

4.2.3 Epidemic Decryption

Similarly to the epidemic noise generation algorithm, epidemic decryption must be performed collaboratively, and be both correct and unique. First, collaboration is achieved based on the threshold decryption feature of the Damgard-Jurik encryption scheme (1) by assigning one key-share to each participant (*e.g.*, when it acquires the parameters) and (2) by decrypting partially the means at each epidemic decryption exchange. Second, unicity is trivially enforced through the convergence properties of the epidemic sum algorithm. Indeed, both the encrypted means and the encrypted noise vectors are guaranteed to be unique among the set of participants. Participants can decrypt them concurrently without threatening the unicity property. Third, correctness requires to apply exactly t distinct key-shares to the encrypted means of each participant. To this end, each participant is equipped with (1) a random *key-share identifier* and (2) a set storing the identifiers of the key-shares that have partially decrypted its current means. During an epidemic decryption exchange, both participants check that their respective set of identifiers does not already contain that of the other. Additionally, decryption latency can be reduced by erasing and replacing the partially decrypted means of the less advanced participant with that of the more advanced participant. The stopping criterion of the epidemic decryption algorithm is the equality between the cardinality of the set of key-shares applied and the required number of key-shares.

4.2.4 Termination

The traditional centralized termination criterion of k-means is centroids convergence. However, the convergence threshold is an arbitrary parameter that fixes a limit on the distance between two consecutive sets of centroids. Convergence becomes hard to guarantee when centroids are perturbed to satisfy differential privacy. In order to still guarantee termination (and to avoid exceeding the privacy parameters ϵ and δ), we simply limit the number of iterations to be executed. The termination criterion is thus the disjunction between the convergence of centroids and a limit on the number of iterations (denoted by n_{it}^{max} in the following). Section 5 discusses strategies dedicated to the production of high-quality centroids in a reduced number of iterations as well as the use of a smarter termination criterion that depends on the evolution of the centroids quality along iterations.

4.3 Correctness and Security

Theorem 1 states the correctness of Chiaroscuro and Theorem 2 states its security. We refer the interested reader to the Appendix for the proofs.

THEOREM 1. *Any instance π of Chiaroscuro (Algorithm 1) executed on a set of honest-but-curious participants is correct.*

THEOREM 2. *Any instance π of Chiaroscuro (Algorithm 1) executed on a set of honest-but-curious participants is secure.*

4.4 Extensions to Malicious Attackers

Chiaroscuro can be extended to cope with *malicious* attackers that deviate from the execution sequence. First, the security of participants can be increased by benefiting from the current rise of highly secure *trusted execution environments* embedded into personal devices (such as, *e.g.,* in [2]) so that tampering the execution sequence, which amounts to tampering the code executed, becomes prohibitively costly. Note that data integrity can also be enforced by these environments, hence countering "lying" malicious participants. Second, the population of participants can be strengthened by restricting the access to the execution sequence to the set of authorized devices through usual authentication techniques. Finally, the collaborative nature of the execution sequence (transparency requirement R1) is a sound basis for detecting malicious attacks thanks to the systematic dissemination of malicious behaviors (*e.g.,* checking that decrypted values are all equal across participants (epidemic dissemination)).

5. CLUSTERING QUALITY

Chiaroscuro discloses the centroids produced by each k-means iteration in order to achieve both scalability and fault-tolerance, and protects them through an appropriate, differentially private, perturbation scheme. However, the injection of noise in each intermediate result of the k-means algorithm has an impact on the quality of the final centroids. Naive strategies may even totally thwart the algorithm by injecting an overwhelming amount of noise. This section is dedicated to maintaining the quality of the clustering with perturbation, to a level comparable to the level reached by clustering with no perturbation, which corresponds to requirement R3. Two levels can be delved into for reducing the impact of the perturbation: the quality of the sequence of centroids (Section 5.1) and the quality of each centroid (Section 5.2).

5.1 Budget Concentration Strategies

A naive privacy budget distribution strategy could consist roughly in estimating the number n_{it} of iterations needed for a centralized k-means to converge, setting the maximum number of iterations to n_{it}, and assigning a budget equal to ϵ/n_{it} to each iteration. However, the estimated number of iterations may be high depending on the dataset, the k-means convergence threshold, and the initial centroids. Hence, a relevant solution is to concentrate the budget on the first iterations. The k-means algorithm is well-known for its logarithmic error loss rate [4]: the highest gains in quality are obtained during the first iterations.

We propose three proofs-of-concept budget concentration strategies that strive to preserve the quality of the centroids produced during the first iterations:

- **GREEDY (G):** The GREEDY strategy (G for short) favors the first iterations through an *exponential decrease* in the budget assignment: $1/2^i$ of the budget is assigned to the ith iteration. Since $\sum 1/2^i$ is bounded by 1, the privacy budget finally spent never exceeds ϵ;
- **GREEDY_FLOOR (GF):** The GREEDY_FLOOR strategy (GF for short) spreads each GREEDY assignment on a floor of f iterations. Each of the first f iterations is assigned $1/(2f)$ of the budget, each of the second f, $1/(2^2 f)$, and so forth. The budget assignment is thus *exponential by floor*;
- **UNIFORM_FAST (UF):** The UNIFORM_FAST strategy (UF for short) bounds the number of iterations to a strong limit (e.g., $n_{it} = 5$) and distributes the budget uniformly among them. The budget assignment is thus *constant* but limited to a reduced number of iterations;

The magnitude of the noise added by G and GF strategies increases with the number of iterations, possibly leading to a noise overwhelming the centroids before termination, and consequently to their non-convergence. Nevertheless, termination is still guaranteed by the limit on the number of iterations. (It is easy to make the termination criterion smarter by identifying the moment at which the noise becomes intractable and stop at that moment[9]. For simplicity, this work focuses on the criterion described above.) Other strategies can be designed, experimented, and finally plugged into Chiaroscuro if they lead to better results.

5.2 Smoothing the Means

After being perturbed, a mean $\mathcal{M}[i]$ might be far from its value prior to perturbation. In this case, data assigned to $\zeta[i]$ will probably be re-assigned to $\zeta[j]$ where $j \neq i$, which is against the convergence criterion of k-means. However, the noise added to each

[9]Participants can monitor the centroids quality through the inter-cluster inertia (Definition 1): (1) the cardinality of each cluster is already computed during the means computation and (2) the center of mass of the full dataset and its cardinality can be easily computed based on the encrypted gossip sum algorithm and the distributed noise generation, once and for all, before launching Chiaroscuro. Chiaroscuro would then stop when the quality starts to drop.

Dataset	
Number of time-series	3M (CER), 1.2M (NUMED)
Size of time-series	24 (CER), 20 (NUMED)
Privacy	
Key size	1024 bits
Key-shares threshold	$\tau \in [0.001\%, 10\%]$
Privacy budget	$\epsilon = 0.69$
Nb of noise-shares	$n_\nu = 100\%$
***k*-means**	
Initial nb of centroids	$k = 50$
GOSSIP	
Size of the local view	30
Churn	From 10% to 50%
Quality	
Floor size (G)	4
Max nb of iterations	$n_{it}^{max} = 5$ (UF only), $n_{it}^{max} = 10$
Moving average (SMA)	20%

Table 2: Experimental Parameters

measure is a Laplace random variable: it can be positive or negative with equal probability. Therefore, given a sliding window of size $w+1$, we can smooth the values of the sum part of $\mathcal{M}[i]$, *i.e.*, $\mathcal{S}[i]$, by averaging them as follows. Let $\mathcal{S}[i] = <\mathcal{S}[i,1]...\mathcal{S}[i,n]>$ be the sum part after perturbation and $\overline{\mathcal{S}[i,j]}$ be the smoothed value of $\mathcal{S}[i,j]$. Let $\mathtt{m}(\mathcal{S}[i,j])$ be the jth (modulo n) value in $\mathcal{S}[i]$, then $\overline{\mathcal{S}[i,j]} = (\mathtt{m}(\mathcal{S}[i,j-w/2]) + ... + \mathtt{m}(\mathcal{S}[i,j+w/2]))/(w+1)$. After having been smoothed by this *simple moving average* technique (denoted by SMA hereafter), the new mean is ready for the next iteration, guaranteeing both privacy (the output of a function performed on a differentially private input is differentially private too) and a better stability of *k*-means.

6. EXPERIMENTAL VALIDATION

6.1 Settings

We have implemented Chiaroscuro's execution sequence and integrated it into *Peersim* [30], a well-known distributed computing simulator. This implementation is a strong proof of concept and allows us to run experiments over medium-sized populations (*e.g.,* tenths of thousands of participants) on a single machine. However, experiments involving very large scale populations (*e.g.,* several millions of participants) would need a testing platform deployable over a number of nodes sufficient for coping with the load. To the best of our knowledge, such a platform is not available today. As a result, in order to launch experiments on very large scale populations, we evaluate: (1) the local costs (*i.e.,* CPU times and bandwidth consumption) by performing encryptions, decryptions, and encrypted additions on a typical participant, (2) the quality (*i.e.,* intra-cluster inertia) by running a *perturbed* centralized *k*-means implementation embedding our budget concentration strategies and means smoothing technique, and (3) the latency (*i.e.,* average number of messages per participant) by simulating the epidemic sum, dissemination, and decryption algorithms. Moreover, because of their arbitrary connection patterns, participants may join or leave an ongoing run of Chiaroscuro at any moment of its execution. The resulting churn impacts the quality of centroids (1) by making unavailable a random fraction of the population at each gossip exchange and (2) by dynamically changing the input set of time-series at each *k*-means iteration. We also evaluate these two aspects below with a fixed latency. The parameters values we used are synthesized in Table 2. They consist in typical values met in practical contexts.

6.1.1 Experimental Platform

In real-life, Chiaroscuro would be executed on a variety of desktops, tablets, smartphones, or laptops. All are equipped today with GB RAM and multi-core CPU. The experiments have been run on such hardware: a laptop containing an eight-core 2.6 GHz CPU with 8 GB RAM. The programming language was Java 7.

We evaluate Chiaroscuro with respect to a real dataset and a synthetic one, each related to a targeted application domain:

- **CER** The CER dataset [16] contains the electricity consumption time-series of thousands of Irish homes and businesses collected between 2009 and 2010 at the rate of one sample every half hour. In our experiments, we use three millions daily time-series randomly sampled from the dataset and reduced to twenty-four measures each (electricity consumption per hour). The range of each measure is [0,80] (sum sensitivity thus equals to 1920).
- **NUMED** The NUMED dataset is a set of 1.2 million time-series representing the tumor growth of cancer suffering patients. It was synthetically generated based on mathematical models of typical profiles [7] (at this scale, real health-related time-series are hard to access), at the rate of one sample every week, and for twenty weeks per patient. Each time-series contains one measure per week taking its value in [0,50] (sum sensitivity thus equal to 1000).

6.1.2 Settings: Local Costs

Three parameters fully determine the bandwidth consumption and the computation times of a participant. First, the number of clusters, initially set to $k=50$. Second, the size of a mean, equal to the size of a time-series (*i.e.,* twenty-four measures for the CER dataset and twenty measures for the NUMED dataset). Third, the length (in bits) of an encrypted value in a mean. It is similar to the size of the cryptographic key, which we set to 1024 bits in our experiments (average security). The linear relationship between these parameters and the local costs is simple, making easy to estimate the costs corresponding to other values for these parameters.

6.1.3 Settings: Quality

The perturbed centralized *k*-means satisfies (ϵ, δ)-probabilistic differential privacy where ϵ is set to a common value [11]: $\epsilon = \ln 2 = 0.69$. Since the value of δ has no impact on the centroids quality, we can simply ignore it here[10]. The floor-size of the GREEDY_FLOOR strategy was set to 4. We set the initial number of clusters to $k=50$. For the synthetic NUMED dataset, the initial centroids are chosen uniformly at random within the set of (synthetic) time-series. For the CER dataset, they are generated by CourboGen [9], the EDF bigdata generator (obvious privacy reasons preclude raw real-life time-series to be used as initial centroids).

6.1.4 Settings : Latency

The execution sequence of Chiaroscuro is made of two epidemic encrypted sums and one epidemic decryption. We evaluate experimentally the average number of messages per participant (1) to compute local approximations of the global sum, and (2) to decrypt the encrypted perturbed means. In order to exhibit the tendency of each curve, we vary the size of the

[10]In practice the δ parameter is set to a value close to 1. The larger the value of δ, the larger the number of gossip exchanges. Theorem 3 (from [25] - see Appendix B) shows that with the current connectivity layer of Chiaroscuro, high δ values (*e.g.,* $\delta=0.995$) can be reached with a reasonable number of gossip exchanges (*e.g.,* $n_e=47$).

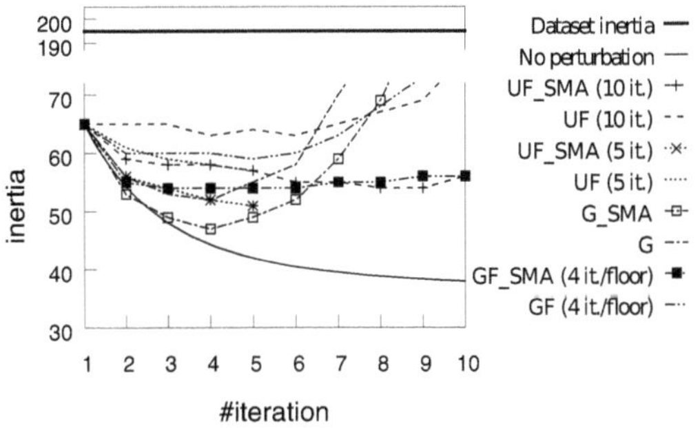

(a) CER: Evolution of the Pre-Perturbation Intra-Cluster Inertia

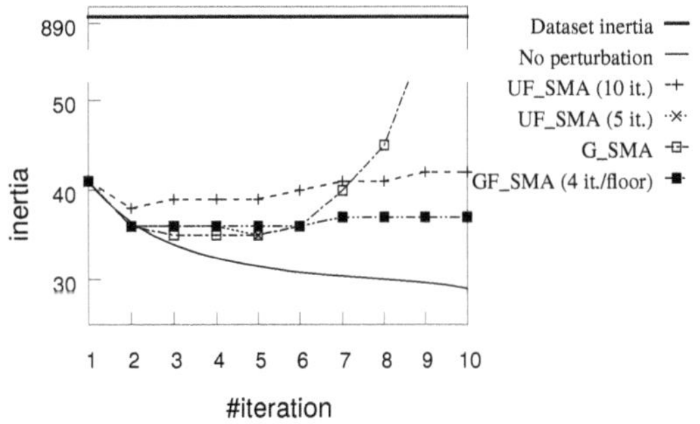

(b) NUMED: Evolution of the Pre-Perturbation Intra-Cluster Inertia

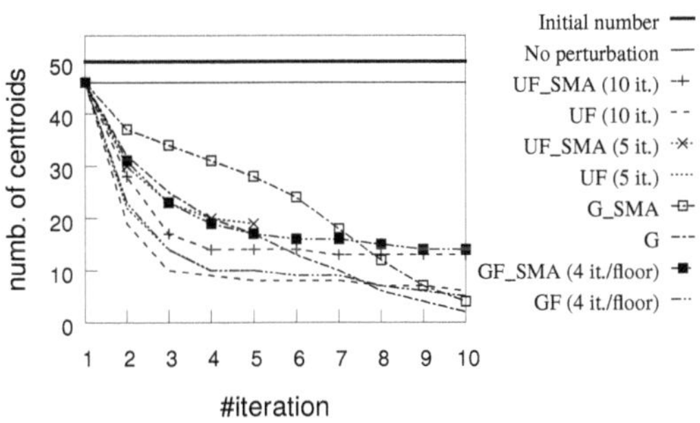

(c) CER: Evolution of the Number of Centroids

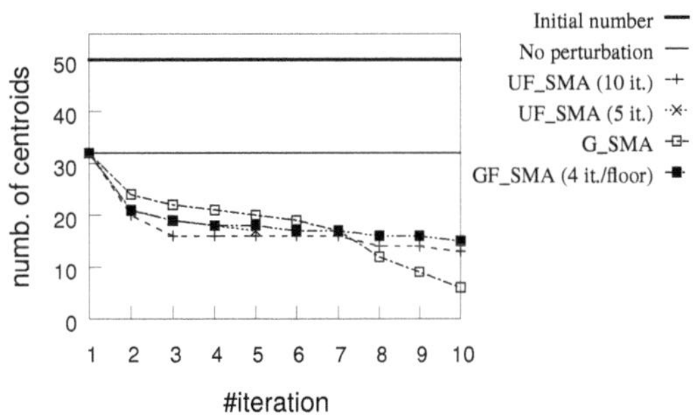

(d) NUMED: Evolution of the Number of Centroids

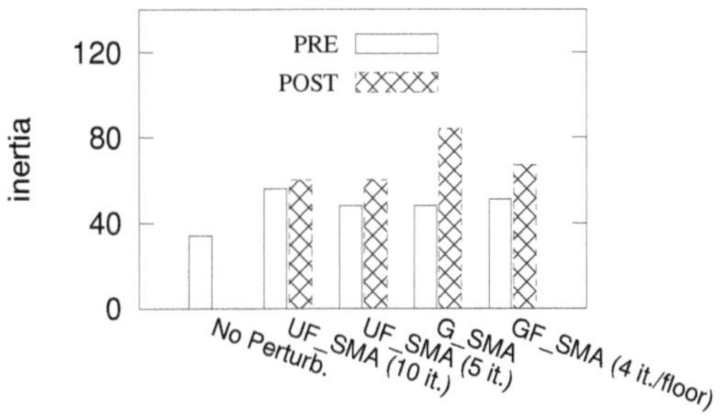

(e) CER: (1) Lowest Pre-Perturbation Inertia (PRE) and (2) Corresponding Post-Perturbation Inertia without Re-Assignment (POST)

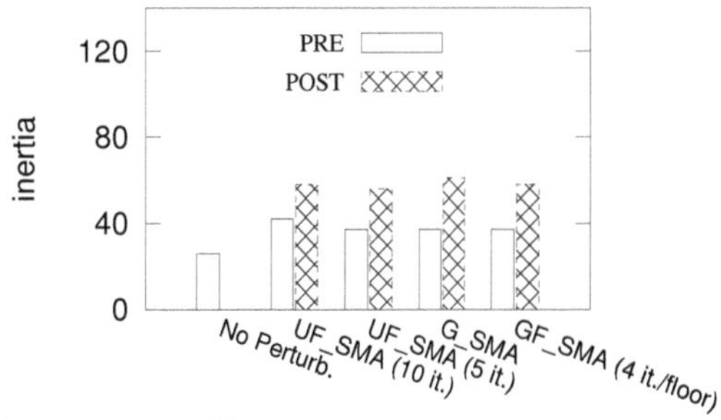

(f) NUMED: (1) Lowest Pre-Perturbation Inertia (PRE), (2) Corresponding Post-Perturbation Inertia without Re-Assignment (POST)

Figure 2: Quality of the Perturbed Clustering - CER: $3M$ time-series and NUMED : $1.2M$ time-series

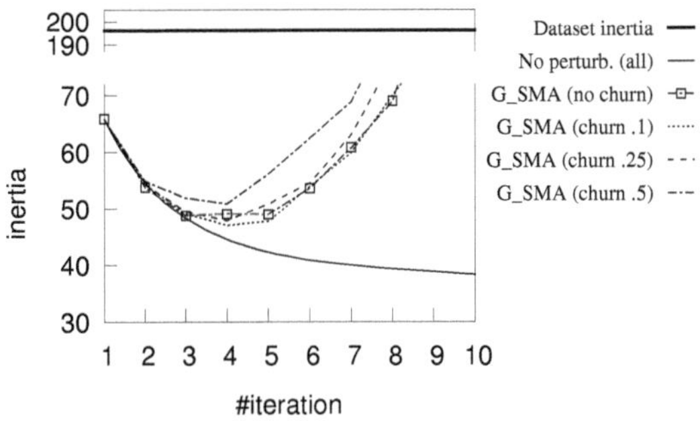

(a) *Churn-Enabled:* Evolution of the Pre-Perturbation Intra-Cluster Inertia (CER ($3M$ time-series))

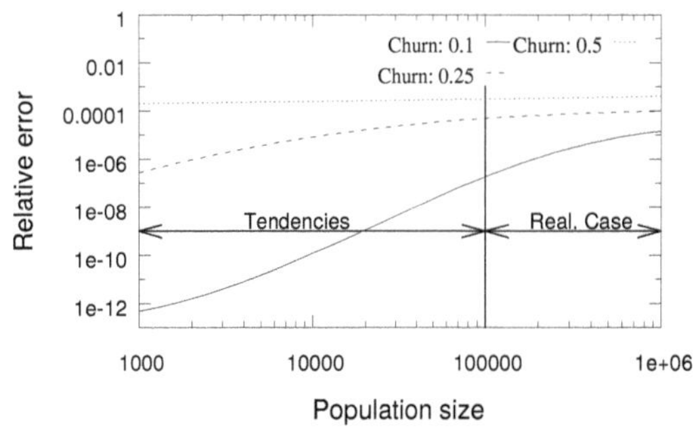

(b) *Churn-Enabled:* Relative Error between the Result of the Epidemic Encrypted Sum and the Exact Value of the Sum (100 Messages per Participant on Average)

Figure 3: Impact of Churn

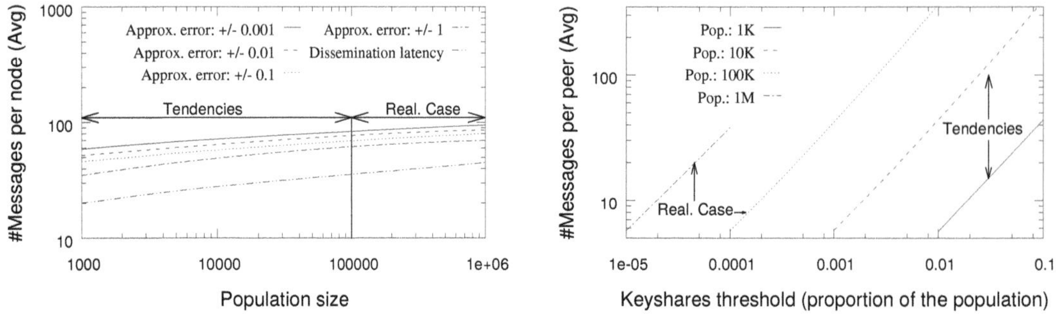

(a) Epidemic Encrypted Sum (Means Computation and Noise Generation) and Epidemic Dissemination (Noise Correction)

(b) Epidemic Decryption

Figure 4: Internal Latencies of the Computation Step

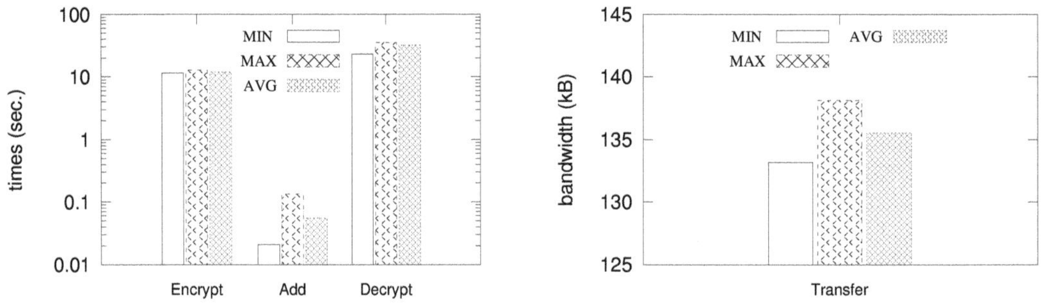

(a) Times Consumption for Encrypting or Decrypting One set of Means, or Adding Together Two Sets of Means (seconds)

(b) Bandwidth Consumption for Transferring One Set of Means (kilo-bytes)

Figure 5: Unitary Local Costs for a Set of 50 **Means,** 20 **Measures per Mean, and a** 1024 **Bits Encryption Key**

population from $n_p = 1K$ participants to $n_p = 1M$. We set the size of the local view per participant to $n_\Lambda = 30$ participants (an average case [21]). For the encrypted epidemic sum, we set the local data of any participant to a single integer value equal to 1, and launch the experiments for several absolute approximation errors targeted, *i.e.*, from 0.001 to 1. Concerning the epidemic decryption, this is the number of key-shares needed for decryption that we vary, expressed as a fraction of the population size, *i.e.*, from $\tau = 0.001\%$ to $\tau = 10\%$.

6.1.5 Settings : Impact of Churn on Quality

We model the churn as the uniform probability for each participant to be disconnected (1) at each gossip exchange of the epidemic encrypted sum and (2) at each perturbed k-means iteration. For the former, we measure the relative error of the encrypted epidemic sum for a number of participants varying from $n_p = 1K$ to $n_p = 1M$, a number of messages per participant equal to 100 on average, all participants having as local data a single integer equal to 1, and for three disconnection probabilities (at each gossip exchange) of 10%, 25%, and 50%. For the later, we measure the evolution of the intra-cluster inertia during the perturbed k-means clustering of the CER dataset in the same setting with no-churn one and with the above three disconnection probabilities (at each iteration).

6.2 Clustering Quality

We evaluate the impact of the perturbation on the clustering quality by monitoring the evolutions along the iterations of the k-means algorithm of (1) the intra-cluster inertia (both prior to perturbation and after) (2) the number of centroids. We run each experiment ten times and plot the average values. For keeping the figures readable, we do not plot the confidence intervals but give them in the corresponding paragraph.

Figure 2(a) shows the evolution of the intra-cluster inertia along the first ten iterations of the k-means algorithm executed over the CER dataset. We plot (1) the full inertia of the dataset (a constant, the *worstcase upper bound* of the intra-cluster inertia), (2) the evolution of the intra-cluster inertia in the traditional unperturbed k-means (a decreasing logarithm, the *best-case lower bound*), and (3) the evolution of the intra-cluster inertia in the perturbed k-means before perturbing the centroids. Each budget concentration strategy is shown, both with the means smoothing and without. Globally, the inertia in the perturbed cases stay close to the lower bound, especially during the first iterations where the k-means error loss rate is at its highest. The strategy that reaches the best inertia level is GREEDY (third to fifth iteration). For all strategies, the SMA smoothing positively impacts inertia. Figure 2(c) also shows that GREEDY with SMA smoothing preserves the highest number of centroids. This high number of centroids further explains partially the difference between its pre-perturbation inertia and its post-perturbation inertia shown in Figure 2(e) (where aberrant centroids unable to cope with the noise, as explained in Section 4.2, have been removed). Similar conclusions can be drawn with the NUMED dataset (Figures 2(b), 2(d), and 2(f)). We do not plot the inertia reached without smoothing because they are very close to the inertia reached with it. This can be explained by the distribution of data: the NUMED time-series are equally distributed across the clusters (contrary to the strongly concentrated CER time-series), keeping low the number of small clusters, *i.e.*, those that benefit the most from smoothing because of their high sensitivity to noise. Whatever the dataset and budget distribution strategy, the confidence intervals of the evolution of the inertia and number of centroids are similar, small, and stable during the first iterations (*i.e.*, ±2.5 points (resp. 1) for the CER (resp. NUMED) inertia, and ±2 points (resp. 1) for the CER (resp. NUMED) number of centroids) but they diverge when the noise starts to overwhelm centroids.

6.3 Performance

6.3.1 Local Bandwidth and Time Consumption

Figure 5 shows the minimum, maximum, and average time and bandwidth consumption per participant for a Peersim execution of Chiaroscuro with 20 measures per mean. Figure 5(a) shows the time required for encrypting a set of means, decrypting it, and adding together two sets of encrypted means. The decryption time represents the highest cost. However, being executed only once during an iteration and staying below a few seconds in our experiments, it remains affordable when executed in background by the participant. The addition of two sets of encrypted means is the most frequent operation. The time it consumes is below 0.1 second, *i.e.*, two orders of magnitude lower than the decryption times. Figure 5(b) shows the bandwidth consumption, in kilo-bytes, for transferring a set of encrypted means. A hundredth of kilo-bytes per transfer are necessary, which amounts to around 1 second for a humble 1 Mb/s connection speed. The epidemic sum algorithm requires two encrypted means transfers and the *once per iteration* epidemic decryption algorithm transfers both the encrypted means and their partially decrypted version - the equivalent of four encrypted means. Both algorithms thus transfer a few hundredth of kilo-bytes per epidemic exchange, which is clearly affordable given today's bandwidths.

6.3.2 Global Latency

Figure 4(a) depicts the number of messages for performing an encrypted epidemic sum given absolute approximation errors varying from ±0.001 to ±1. The number of messages remains very low, *i.e.*, under the hundred, even for a million participants population with the tightest absolute approximation error of ±0.001 (*i.e.*, equal to 10^{-9} the exact sum value)[11]. Moreover, the figure clearly shows that the number of messages grows logarithmically depending on the population size. On the same figure, we plot the dissemination latency of the smallest identifier noise correction. It remains in the same order of magnitude, and depends logarithmically too on the population size. Figure 4(b) shows the average number of messages per participant for performing epidemic decryption with respect to the key-shares threshold expressed as a fraction of the population size. The decryption latency exhibits a linear behavior depending on the size of the threshold. For one million participants, our experiments reach the limit of the experimental platform at a threshold size greater than 0.01% the population size. However, the linearity of the curves lets forecast a number of messages on the order of magnitude of the hundred for a realistic threshold size of 0.01% (*i.e.*, 100 distinct participants to contact for decryption). Finally, the total latency of an iteration is the latency of two epidemic encrypted sums, one epidemic dissemination, and one epidemic decryption. Given the practical settings discussed above (*i.e.*, one million participants, an approximation error in the sum of ±0.001, and a threshold size of 0.01%), the total latency of an iteration is on the order of a few hundreds of messages, dominated by the epidemic encrypted sums. Injecting the local costs observed above (NUMED dataset, G_SMA strategy) results in a first iteration completing after around 26 mins and a fifth one after around 10 mins (the effect of the noise made aberrant 60% of the initial number of centroids between the first and the fifth iteration). These times fit the context targeted by Chiaroscuro, where the users are the individuals and the results do not suffer from severe time constraints (*e.g.*, background analysis).

[11]With $n_e = 100$ gossip exchanges and a maximal approximation error $e_{max} = 10^{-9}$ (the other parameters reamining the same as above) and according to Theorem 3 (from [25] - see Appendix B), $\delta = (1 - 2 \cdot 10^{-51})^{480}$, which is very close to 1.

6.4 Impact of Churn on Quality

The churn-enabled experiments (Figures 3(a) and 3(b)) show a low sensitivity to churn. First, the churn-enabled intra-cluster inertia follow closely those without churn. Indeed, the exclusion of a random fraction of the highly redundant CER time-series at each iteration does not incur strong skews. The increasing divergence of the last iterations suggests that the reduction of the cardinalities of clusters is of higher importance : the higher the churn, the smaller the clusters and consequently the less robust to a high-magnitude noise. Second, the relative error of the encrypted epidemic sum due to the churn (Figure 3(b)) represents a negligible fraction of the exact sum for the three levels of churn (at most a bit less than 0.1% for the highest disconnection rate of 50% at each gossip exchange).

7. RELATED WORK

Generic secure multi-party computation (SMC) techniques [15, 37] are able to produce a distributed and secure version of any centralized polynomial-time algorithm. However these techniques cannot be used in practice for non-trivial algorithms and non-tiny input data because of the prohibitive cost of the distributed versions produced.

Specific SMC algorithms address the problem of clustering horizontally partitioned datasets [5, 17, 18, 19, 20, 22, 26, 27, 35]. Most of them consider only two participants, choose k-means or a similar algorithm for performing the clustering, and all tackle the honest-but-curious attack model. In [22], the algorithm is made of a local phase computing the local means, and a global phase averaging the two local sets of means. The computation of the means taking place at each iteration is protected through an homomorphic encryption scheme. However, the means are disclosed at the end of each iteration, a breach that can lead to uncontrolled data leaks. The authors of [20] distribute the k-means algorithm by splitting each centroid in two complementary random parts, one per participant. A sequence of SMC algorithms implements the usual k-means steps, guaranteeing a strong security level. However, the use of generic SMC techniques raises strong concerns about fault-tolerance and scalability. The solution proposed in [5] is also based on random parts and SMC algorithms, but it avoids generic SMC techniques through a smart use of homomorphic encryption and of a secure scalar product algorithm [13]. However, the achievements of scalability and fault-tolerance are still uncertain (transfer of the full database of a participant, encrypted, to the other participant, and use of random parts and SMC algorithms). The authors of [19] (which extends [17] and [18]) use similar SMC algorithms as well as random parts, and inherit from their drawbacks. The authors of [35] consider many more participants but (1) organize them in a rigid tree-like structure and use random parts and generic SMC techniques, which questions fault-tolerance and scalability, and (2) disclose the raw means, which raises security concerns. Other work has considered the adaptation of other clustering algorithms (*e.g.*, EM in [26], DBSCAN in [27]).

However, they use similar building blocks (random parts and SMC algorithms) and thus suffer from similar drawbacks.

Finally, the problem of computing differentially-private aggregates in a distributed manner has attracted attention in the last decade (*e.g.,* [1, 6, 33, 36]). This line of work usually (1) assumes the presence of at least one central entity, notably for driving the execution of (2) simple aggregate queries over (3) thousands of participants. On the contrary, our work (1) considers a full iterative k-means execution sequence (both specific and complex) and (2) fully distributes it (high parallelism, no central bottleneck, no unnecessary additional security/resource assumption) over (3) millions of participants.

8. CONCLUSION

We proposed Chiaroscuro, the first solution to address the problem of clustering massively distributed personal data with sound privacy guarantees. Our original Diptych data structure allows adapting k-means to a computing environment made of autonomous personal computing devices. Our gossip-based *modus operandi* provides scalability and fault-tolerance, while a novel combination of homomorphic encryption with differential privacy shields it against colluding dishonest nodes. We showed through an extensive experimental validation that Chiaroscuro achieves a quality comparable to centralized k-means executions at an affordable cost. Exciting research perspectives include characterizing the algorithms that Chiaroscuro can support. The class of iterative analytical algorithms (*e.g.,* expectation-maximization or probabilistic matrix factorization) especially fits the foundations laid down by Chiaroscuro.

9. REFERENCES

[1] G. Ács and C. Castelluccia. I have a dream!: Differentially private smart metering. In *IH*, pages 118–132, 2011.

[2] T. Allard, N. Anciaux, L. Bouganim, Y. Guo, L. Le Folgoc, B. Nguyen, P. Pucheral, I. Ray, I. Ray, and S. Yin. Secure personal data servers: A vision paper. *VLDB*, 3(1-2):25–35, 2010.

[3] O. T. Alliance. *Data Protection & Breach*, 2014.

[4] L. Bottou and Y. Bengio. Convergence properties of the kmeans algorithm. In *ANIPS*, volume 7. Denver, 1995.

[5] P. Bunn and R. Ostrovsky. Secure two-party k-means clustering. In *CCS*, pages 486–497, 2007.

[6] R. Chen, A. Reznichenko, P. Francis, and J. Gehrke. Towards statistical queries over distributed private user data. In *NSDI*, pages 169–182, 2012.

[7] L. Claret, M. Gupta, K. Han, A. Joshi, N. Sarapa, J. He, B. Powell, and R. Bruno. Evaluation of tumor-size response metrics to predict overall survival in western and chinese patients with first-line metastatic colorectal cancer. *J. Clin. Onc.*, 31(17):2110–2114, 2013.

[8] I. Damgård and M. Jurik. A generalisation, a simplification and some applications of paillier's probabilistic public-key system. In *PKC*, pages 119–136, 2001.

[9] L. D. P. dos Santos, A. G. da Silva, B. Jacquin, M.-L. Picard, D. Worms, and C. Bernard. Massive smart meter data storage and processing on top of hadoop. In *Int. Work. on End-to-end Man. of Big Data, VLDB*, 2012.

[10] C. Dwork. Differential privacy. In *ICALP*, pages 1–12, 2006.

[11] C. Dwork. A firm foundation for private data analysis. *CACM*, 54(1):86–95, 2011.

[12] C. Dwork, F. McSherry, K. Nissim, and A. Smith. Calibrating noise to sensitivity in private data analysis. In *TCC*, pages 265–284, 2006.

[13] B. Goethals, S. Laur, H. Lipmaa, and T. Mielikäinen. On private scalar product computation for privacy-preserving data mining. In *ICISC*, pages 104–120, 2004.

[14] O. Goldreich. Foundations of cryptography: a primer. *Found. Trends in Theoretical Computer Science*, 1(1):1–116, April 2005.

[15] O. Goldreich, S. Micali, and A. Wigderson. How to play ANY mental game. In *STOC*, pages 218–229, 1987.

[16] ISSDA. *The Commission for Energy Regulation, Electricity Customer Behaviour Trial*, 2012. http://www.ucd.ie/issda.

[17] G. Jagannathan, K. Pillaipakkamnatt, and D. Umano. A secure clustering algorithm for distributed data streams. In *ICDM Work.*, pages 705–710, 2007.

[18] G. Jagannathan, K. Pillaipakkamnatt, and R. N. Wright. A new privacy-preserving distributed k-clustering algorithm. In *SDM*, pages 494–498, 2006.

[19] G. Jagannathan, K. Pillaipakkamnatt, R. N. Wright, and D. Umano. Communication-efficient privacy-preserving clustering. *Trans. Data Privacy*, 3(1):1–25, 2010.

[20] G. Jagannathan and R. N. Wright. Privacy-preserving distributed k-means clustering over arbitrarily partitioned data. In *SIGKDD*, pages 593–599, 2005.

[21] M. Jelasity, A. Montresor, and O. Babaoglu. Gossip-based aggregation in large dynamic networks. *Trans. Comp. Sys.*, 23(3):219–252, Aug. 2005.

[22] S. Jha, L. Kruger, and P. McDaniel. Privacy preserving clustering. In *ESORICS*, pages 397–417, 2005.

[23] D. Kempe, A. Dobra, and J. Gehrke. Gossip-based computation of aggregate information. In *FOCS*, pages 482–491, 2003.

[24] S. Kotz, T. J. Kozubowski, and K. Podgorski. *The Laplace Distribution and Generalizations.* 2001.

[25] W. Kowalczyk and N. A. Vlassis. Newscast EM. In *NIPS*, pages 713–720, 2004.

[26] X. Lin, C. Clifton, and M. Zhu. Privacy-preserving clustering with distributed EM mixture modeling. *Know. Inf. Sys.*, 8(1):68–81, 2005.

[27] J. Liu, J. Z. Huang, J. Luo, and L. Xiong. Privacy preserving distributed DBSCAN clustering. In *EDBT-ICDT Work.*, pages 177–185, 2012.

[28] S. Lloyd. Least squares quantization in PCM. *Trans. Inf. Theor.*, 28(2):129–137, 1982.

[29] A. Machanavajjhala, D. Kifer, J. Abowd, J. Gehrke, and L. Vilhuber. Privacy: Theory meets practice on the map. In *ICDE*, pages 277–286, 2008.

[30] A. Montresor and M. Jelasity. PeerSim: A scalable P2P simulator. In *P2P*, pages 99–100, 2009.

[31] M. Newborough and P. Augood. Demand-side management opportunities for the uk domestic sector. *Gen., Trans. and Dist.*, 146(3):283–293, 1999.

[32] A. Prudenzi. A neuron nets based procedure for identifying domestic appliances pattern-of-use from energy recordings at meter panel. In *PESW*, volume 2, pages 941–946, 2002.

[33] V. Rastogi and S. Nath. Differentially private aggregation of distributed time-series with transformation and encryption. In *SIGMOD*, pages 735–746, 2010.

[34] I. Risk Based Security. *Data Breach QuickView*, 2014.

[35] J. Sakuma and S. Kobayashi. Large-scale k-means clustering with user-centric privacy preservation. In *PAKDD*, pages 320–332, 2008.

[36] E. Shi, T.-H. H. Chan, E. G. Rieffel, R. Chow, and D. Song. Privacy-preserving aggregation of time-series data. In *NDSS*, 2011.

[37] A. C. Yao. Protocols for secure computations. In *FOCS*, pages 160–164, 1982.

APPENDIX

A. ACKNOWLEDGEMENTS

The authors warmly thank Patrick Valduriez for his thorough proofreadings as well as the anonymous reviewers for their detailed feedback.

B. SECURITY

B.1 Differential Privacy of the Perturbation Mechanism

The encrypted sum and count vectors of the means must be perturbed by vectors of random variables that are sampled in the appropriate Laplace distribution in order to satisfy differential privacy. In Chiaroscuro, the Laplace noises are computed based on the **EESum** algorithm and the infinite divisibility of the Laplace distribution (Lemma 1): the **EESum** algorithm simply performs the homomorphically-encrypted sum of noise-shares (Definition 5) generated locally by each participant. Such gossip-based noise computation differs from a standard centralized noise generation algorithm in two ways. First, gossip aggregation algorithms are approximate in nature; the resulting noise thus contains an approximation error. Second, due to the massive distribution of gossip algorithms, the number of noise-shares involved in the noise computation may be hard to know and to fix beforehand. This may result in an additional error in the noise generated. We show below that probabilistic differential privacy is satisfied.

B.1.1 Approximate Sum

Although gossip aggregation algorithms are inherently approximate, their approximation errors can be made arbitrarily small in practice. Indeed, the gossip approximation error depends essentially on the number of gossip exchanges per participant. First, it is guaranteed to converge to zero exponentially fast [21, 23] (see Theorem 3 below). Second, since the number of exchanges per participant is a parameter, it can be set so that the approximation error is as small as desired - *i.e.*, typically several orders of magnitude lower than the exact aggregate value. We show below how the approximation error due to the **EESum** algorithm is taken into account in the achievement of the (ϵ, δ)-probabilistic differential privacy model. First, Lemma 2 shows how to compensate the approximation error. Then, Theorem 3 (from [25]) shows how to compute the minimum number of gossip exchanges per participant required for reaching the desired (ϵ, δ) privacy level.

LEMMA 2. *Let S denote the gossip approximate sum of values, i.e., $S = (1+e_S)\cdot\sum_i x_i$ where $x_i \in [d_{min}, d_{max}]$ and e_S denote the relative gossip approximation error. The approximation error is such that $0 < |e_S| \leq e_{max}$ with probability at least $1-\iota$ [23]. Let $\lambda = (1+e_{max})\cdot\max(|d_{min}|, |d_{max}|)/\epsilon$. Let N denote the gossip approximate sum of noise-shares, i.e., $N = (1+e_N)\cdot\sum_i^{n_\nu}\nu_i = (1+e_N)\cdot\mathcal{L}(\lambda)$ where n_ν is the number of noise-shares, each ν_i is a noise-share (Definition 5), and e_N denote the relative gossip approximation error. Similarly to e_S, e_N is such that $0<|e_N|\leq e_{max}$ with probability at least $1-\iota$. Then, $S'=S+\overline{N}$ satisfies (ϵ, δ)-probabilistic differential privacy, where $\overline{N}=(1+e_{max}/(1-e_{max}))\cdot N$ and $\delta=(1-\iota)^2$.*

PROOF. The sensitivity of S is equal to : $(1+e_{max})\cdot\max(|d_{min}|, |d_{max}|)$ with probability at least $1-\iota$. Adding to S a perturbation sampled in $\mathcal{L}(\lambda)$, where $\lambda = (1+e_{max})\cdot\max(|d_{min}|,|d_{max}|)/\epsilon$, would thus satisfy ϵ-probabilistic differential privacy with probability at least $1-\iota$ by definition. However, the gossip sum of noise-shares does not yield the exact perturbation because of its approximation error : $N=(1+e_N)\cdot\mathcal{L}(\lambda)$ where $0<|e_N|\leq e_{max}$ with probability at least $1-\iota$. Since e_N may be negative, the magnitude of the perturbation may be reduced, which may question the privacy guarantees. The maximum loss occurs when e_N is minimum, *i.e.*, when $e_N=-e_{max}$. It can be compensated by slightly increasing the perturbation. Let c denote the relative compensation. The objective is to have $(1+c)\cdot N \geq \mathcal{L}(\lambda)$, so $(1+c)\cdot(1+e_N)\cdot\mathcal{L}(\lambda) \geq \mathcal{L}(\lambda)$. At worst, $e_N = -e_{max}$, so we have $(1+c)\cdot(1+e_N)\cdot\mathcal{L}(\lambda) \geq (1+c)\cdot(1-e_{max})\cdot\mathcal{L}(\lambda)$. As a result, after the straightforward development of $(1+c)\cdot(1-e_{max})\cdot\mathcal{L}(\lambda)\geq\mathcal{L}(\lambda)$, we must have $c\geq e_{max}/(1-e_{max})$. So the approximation error of the gossip sum of noise-shares can be compensated by increasing the perturbation by a factor equal to $c=e_{max}/(1-e_{max})$. Consequently, $S'=S+(1+e_{max}/(1-e_{max}))\cdot(1+e_N)\cdot\mathcal{L}(\lambda)$ satisfies (ϵ, δ)-probabilistic differential privacy, where $\lambda=(1+e_{max})\cdot\max(|d_{min}|,|d_{max}|)/\epsilon$ and $\delta=(1-\iota)^2$. □

Next, we show how to compute the minimum number of gossip exchanges required. The exact convergence speed depends on the underlying network topology. The current version of Chiaroscuro relies on Newscast [25] for managing the connectivity between participants. The convergence speed of aggregate computation in Newscast is given by Theorem 3 [25], which allows to compute the minimum number of gossip exchanges required for reaching the desired approximation error with the desired probability. If Chiaroscuro changes its connectivity layer, the same computation would apply based on a different formula. For simplicity, Theorem 3 considers a synchronous setting where each participant performs a gossip exchange one after the other.

THEOREM 3 (FROM [25]). *With probability $1-\iota$, after $n_e = \lceil 0.581(\log n_p + 2\log s + 2\log\frac{1}{e_{max}} + \log\frac{1}{\iota})\rceil$ exchanges per participant, we have $\max_i|\sigma_i - \sigma| \leq e_{max}$, where σ_i is the estimate of the sum component of individual i's local state and σ is its exact global value, n_p is the cardinality of the population, $e_{max}>0$ is an upper bound on the approximation error, and s^2 is the data variance.*

As a result, given the targeted privacy parameter δ and the maximum number of iterations n_{it}^{max}, the differential privacy probability assigned to each perturbed value is computed : $\delta_{atom} = \sqrt[(n_{it}^{max}*2n)]{\delta}$. Then, given δ_{atom}, the maximal error e_{max}, and the expected data variance s^2 (if unknown, it can be set to, *e.g.*, an estimated upper bound), the minimum required number of gossip exchanges n_e per execution of the **EESum** algorithm is computed (Theorem 3). For example, with $\delta=0.995$, $e_{max}=10^{-12}$, $s^2=1$, and values from Section 6 (*i.e.*, $n_{it}^{max}=10$, $n_p=10^6$, and $n=24$), we have $\delta_{atom} = \sqrt[480]{0.995}\approx 1-10^{-5}$. Then, according to Theorem 3, $n_e=47$ exchanges. This formula can be adapted to a churn-enabled context by modeling the churn and taking into account the evolving Newscast network topology.

B.1.2 Approximate Number of Noise-Shares

The noise-share generation algorithm is parameterized by n_ν, the expected total number of noise-shares that will be summed up. Ideally, this parameter shall be set to the number of participants involved in the sum. When the latter is predictable (*e.g.*, when there is no churn), n_ν can be set to the exact number of noise-shares that will be actually summed up. Otherwise, n_ν is not exact. In order to guarantee differential privacy, n_ν is set to the expected maximal lower bound on the number of noise-shares to be actually summed up. The actual sum thus involves more noise-shares than necessary. We show below that this surplus does not threaten the differential privacy guarantees.

LEMMA 3. *Let S denote the gossip approximate sum of values and $\widetilde{N}$ denote the gossip approximate sum of noise-shares.*

$\widetilde{N}$ *results from summing up more noise-shares than necessary, i.e.,* $\widetilde{N} = (1+e_{max}/(1-e_{max}))\cdot(1+e_N)\cdot(\sum_i^{n_\nu}\nu_i+\sum_i^{n_\nu^+}\nu_i)$ *where* n_ν *is the lower bound of noise-shares and* n_ν^+ *is the number of additional noise-shares. Then,* $S' = S+\widetilde{N}$ *satisfies* (ϵ, δ)*-probabilistic differential privacy, where* $\delta=(1-\iota)^2$.

PROOF. We have $\widetilde{N} = (1+e_{max}/(1-e_{max}))\cdot(1+e_N)\cdot(\sum_i^{n_\nu}\nu_i+\sum_i^{n_\nu^+}\nu_i)$. Let a denote the noise-independent factors due to the gossip approximation, *i.e.*, $a=(1+e_{max}/(1-e_{max}))\cdot(1+e_N)$. Then $\widetilde{N}=a\cdot(\sum_i^{n_\nu}\nu_i+\sum_i^{n_\nu^+}\nu_i)$, and consequently $\widetilde{N}=a\cdot\mathcal{L}(\lambda)+a\cdot\sum_i^{n_\nu^+}\nu_i$. By adding $\widetilde{N}$ to S we have $S'=S+\widetilde{N}=S+\overline{N}+a\cdot\sum_i^{n_\nu^+}\nu_i$. Since (1) $S+\overline{N}$ satisfies (ϵ, δ)-probabilistic differential privacy where $\delta=(1-\iota)^2$ (Lemma 2), and (2) $a\cdot\sum_i^{n_\nu^+}\nu_i$ is independent from S and $\overline{N}$, then $S'=S+\widetilde{N}$ satisfies (ϵ, δ)-probabilistic differential privacy too. □

Additionally, participants can correct the sum of noise-shares $\widetilde{N}$ by subtracting a quantity equivalent in expectation to the non-necessary noise-shares included in the sum. Similarly to the additional noise-shares summed up in $\widetilde{N}$, the correction is independent from S and $\overline{N}$. Thus, its subtraction does not threaten differential privacy.

B.2 Security Against Inferences

We assess formally the security of Chiaroscuro against inferences according to the usual secure multi-party computation (SMC) methodology [14]. Informally speaking, it consists in comparing the information about the input dataset that leaks from the distributed algorithm instantiated on the distributed architecture (*real setting*), to the information that leaks from a centralized version of the algorithm run by an *ideally* trusted third party (*ideal setting*). If the difference between the two is negligible, then the distributed algorithm is said to be secure. The comparison is usually done based on the notion of *computational indistinguishability* [14], which states roughly that two distribution ensembles are computationally indistinguishable (denoted by $\overset{c}{\equiv}$) if no probabilistic polynomial-time algorithm is able to draw a significant difference between them.

We first formalize the security model of Chiaroscuro against inferences from honest-but-curious participants, which was informally stated in Section 2.3. Based on this model, we then give the full-length proof of security against inferences of Theorem 2 (stated in Section 4.3).

In the real setting, the adversary is (within) a participant. We follow the standard practical assumption that the adversary is computationally-bounded and model it as a probabilistic polynomial-time algorithm. The real-setting adversary has thus access to the participant's local data and parameters, to local transient information used or generated during the execution, and to the output of the algorithm. He exploits all this in any computationally-feasible way in order to gain additional knowledge about the other input time-series. In the ideal setting, the adversary has only access to the output of the centralized k-means algorithm perturbed by a differentially-private mechanism.

Loosely speaking, our security model (Definition 7) states that Chiaroscuro securely computes k-means if the side-effect information disclosed during the execution of an instance of Chiaroscuro (1) is perturbed by a differentially-private mechanism, (2) is independent from the input time-series and with the noise, or (3) does not increase significantly the adversarial knowledge (as defined by computational indistinguishability).

DEFINITION 7. *Let* π *be an instance of Chiaroscuro executed on a set of participants and* Δ *be the union of (1) the set of all perturbed means (either disclosed during* π *or output by the ideal-setting k-means) and (2) the set of all the information independent from the input time-series and noise. Given an input set of time-series* S*, an attacker* $\mathtt{A}$*, and an arbitrary background knowledge* $\chi\in\{0,1\}^*$*, we denote* $\mathbf{REAL}_{\pi,\mathtt{A}(\chi,\Delta)}(S)$ *the distribution representing the adversarial knowledge over the input dataset in the real setting - with a full knowledge of* Δ*, and* $\mathbf{IDEAL}_{kMeans,\mathtt{A}(\chi,\Delta)}(S)$ *the distribution representing the adversarial knowledge in the ideal setting - with a full knowledge of* Δ *too. We say that* π securely computes k-means *iff for every adversary* $\mathtt{A}_r$ *attacking* π*, there exists an adversary* $\mathtt{A}_i$ *for the ideal model so that for every* $\chi\in\{0,1\}^*$*:*

$$\{\mathbf{REAL}_{\pi,\mathtt{A}_r(\chi,\Delta)}(S)\}_S \overset{c}{\equiv} \{\mathbf{IDEAL}_{kMeans,\mathtt{A}_i(\chi,\Delta)}(S)\}_S$$

PROOF. The security of π against honest-but-curious participants can be shown through a thorough and exhaustive examination of the data structures that are communicated among participants along the execution sequence in the real setting. We focus on the computation step because the assignment step and the convergence step at each iteration are performed locally, by each participant, without any data transfer.

1. Epidemic computation of the encrypted means: the semantically-secure encryptions $\mathfrak{M}.\mathfrak{f}$ and $\mathfrak{M}.\mathfrak{c}$, and the data-independent $\mathfrak{M}.\omega$ and n;
2. Epidemic noise generation: *idem*, and the data-independent `ctr` and `cor`;
3. Epidemic decryption: the partially encrypted $\mathfrak{M}.\mathfrak{f}$ and $\mathfrak{M}.\mathfrak{c}$, the perturbed $\mathcal{M}$, and the data-independent *idk*;

We can easily observe that (1) any information depending on the personal time-series is communicated either after having been encrypted by a semantically-secure encryption scheme (step 1) or after having been perturbed by a differentially-private mechanism (step 3), and (2) *idem* for the information depending on the value of the noise generated (step 2). The remaining data structures depend neither on the time-series nor on the noise. In other words, by denoting by $\mathcal{E}$ the set of information encrypted by a semantically-secure encryption scheme (which output is computationally-indistinguishable from the output of a pseudo-random bitstring generator) : $\mathcal{E}=\{\mathfrak{M}.\mathfrak{f},\mathfrak{M}.\mathfrak{c}\}$ and $\{\mathfrak{M}.\omega$, n, `ctr`, `cor`, *idk*,$\mathcal{M}\}\in\Delta$.

As a result :

$$\{\mathbf{REAL}_{\pi,\mathtt{A}_r(\chi,\Delta)}(S)\}_S \overset{c}{\equiv} \{\mathbf{IDEAL}_{kMeans,\mathtt{A}_i(\chi,\Delta,\mathcal{E})}(S)\}_S$$

Moreover, since the ideal-setting adversary can simulate $\mathcal{E}$ through a pseudo-random bistring generator, then :

$$\{\mathbf{IDEAL}_{kMeans,\mathtt{A}_i(\chi,\Delta,\mathcal{E})}(S)\}_S \overset{c}{\equiv} \{\mathbf{IDEAL}_{kMeans,\mathtt{A}_i(\chi,\Delta)}(S)\}_S$$

Consequently :

$$\{\mathbf{REAL}_{\pi,\mathtt{A}_r(\chi,\Delta)}(S)\}_S \overset{c}{\equiv} \{\mathbf{IDEAL}_{kMeans,\mathtt{A}_i(\chi,\Delta)}(S)\}_S$$

□

B.3 Collusions

The degree of resistance to collusions is defined by the number of key-shares and noise-shares used. Compromising a participant results essentially in disclosing its key-share and its noise-share. First, the disclosure of a key-share leaks nothing about the secret polynom in Ξ if the attacker has not $\tau-1$ other key-shares. Second, the disclosure of a noise-share leaks the smallest possible fraction of noise (the number of noise-shares is maximal because noise-shares are distributed on the complete population). For example, with one million participants, and a participant colluding with $c-1$ others, there remains 10^6-c unknown other noise-shares used for generating the noise. As a result, the fraction of the secret noise in Ξ unknown to a colluding participant p decreases linearly with the number of collusions from p (bounded by the given threshold τ).

C. CORRECTNESS

Chiaroscuro follows an iterative execution sequence. Each iteration has three steps : the assignment step, the computation step, and the convergence step. We start by showing the correctness of both the assignment step and the convergence step. Then we concentrate on the correctness of the computation step.

C.1 Assignment Step, Convergence Step, and Termination

During the assignment step, each participant computes the distance between its time-series and each of the centroids output by the previous iteration (they appear in the clear, their privacy being guaranteed by differential privacy) to identify the closest centroid. During the convergence step, each participant computes the distance between the new set of centroids (resulting from the previous computation step) and the old ones (output by the previous iteration) and compares it to the given convergence threshold. These two steps (1) involve local computations only (2) based on cleartext data. They are consequently trivially correct.

The k-means iterations stop either when centroids have converged or when a fixed number of iterations has been reached. This disjunctive termination criterion is easy to check locally and guarantees that the k-means algorithm terminates.

C.2 Computation Step

C.2.1 Epidemic Computation of the Encrypted Means

First, the encrypted sum and count vectors of the means (*i.e.*, $\mathfrak{M}.s$ and $\mathfrak{M}.c$) are computed by the `EESum` algorithm, our gossip-based algorithm dedicated to computing homomorphically-encrypted sums. While the local update rule of the standard non-encrypted gossip-based sum algorithm [23] performs a division by two at each exchange, the local update rule of the `EESum` algorithm (Algorithm 2) simply delays it to the end of the algorithm (homomorphic encryptions do not support divisions). It is easy to see that both update rules are arithmetically equivalent.

PROOF. With the standard non-encrypted local update rule, a given variable will have been divided by 2^i after its ith average. This is the same with our homomorphically-encrypted update rule. Indeed, we keep track (1) of the encrypted sum of variables and (2) of the divisor. First, by definition, the divisor is always equal to 2^{n_l}, where n_l is the current number of exchanges. Second, all variables having been averaged less than n_l times, say i times, are multiplied by 2^{n_l-i} during the exchange (*i.e.*, the scaling operation in the update rule). As a result, their actual divisor at exchange n_l is equal to $2^{n_l}/2^{n_l-i}=2^i$ where i is the current number of times they have been averaged. This is arithmetically equivalent to performing directly the average on values. The local update rule of the `EESum` algorithm is thus correct. □

The `EESum` algorithm terminates after a maximum number of exchanges fixed beforehand to a value sufficient for the sum to converge. Since the actual number of exchanges performed by each participant increases monotonically, the termination criterion is guaranteed to be satisfied eventually. Since it can be trivially enforced locally by each participant, the `EESum` algorithm is thus guaranteed to terminate.

C.2.2 Epidemic Noise Generation

The epidemic noise generation step computes the sum of noise-shares based on the `EESum` algorithm and corrects it if necessary by disseminating the correction vector associated to the lowest identifier. The `EESum` algorithm has been shown above to be correct; we focus on the correctness of the dissemination algorithm. First, each participant having contributed to the sum of noise-shares independently computes a correction proposal and assigns it a random identifier. Next, participants disseminate it based on standard epidemic dissemination algorithms, keeping at each exchange the correction proposal with the lowest identifier. Because the set of corrections (and identifiers) is fixed (only the participants involved in the sum can propose a correction vector), the standard diffusion speed results of epidemic dissemination algorithms apply [23]. Similarly to gossip aggregation algorithms, the probability that the disseminated correction vector does not reach a part of the population (1) depends on the number of gossip exchanges and (2) converges to zero exponentially fast (*e.g.*, in our experiments, a value was disseminated to one million participants with less than 50 messages per participant). We consider it as negligible in practice.

C.2.3 Epidemic Decryption

Finally, the correctness of the epidemic decryption is easy to state. First, a given key-share is applied at most once to a given encrypted value. Indeed, each participant keeps the identifiers of the key-shares having been applied to his local encrypted value. Second, at most n_κ key-shares are applied to each encrypted value. By counting the number of key-shares identifiers kept locally, any participant knows when n_κ is reached. Finally, the local sets of key-shares grow monotonically, guaranteeing the termination of the epidemic decryption. Indeed, by definition, no key-share is removed from a local set.

D. ILLUSTRATION ON 2D POINTS

In order to further illustrate the results of Chiaroscuro, we have used a $750K$ two-dimensional points dataset. These points are distributed into a set of 50 clusters[12]. We have executed both the standard k-means algorithm and Chiaroscuro (GREEDY strategy) over it with the parameters used in the evaluation section (Section 6). Our version of this dataset was generated by duplicating 100 times each of the $7.5K$ points contained in the A3 dataset and adding to each copy a uniform random value small enough to preserve the clusters. Two-dimensional points differ from time-series in the absence of temporal relationship between dimensions (though they are similar to time-series of size 2 for the privacy part). Therefore, the quality-enhancing smoothing techniques presented in Section 5.2 cannot apply.

Figures 6(a) and 6(b) represent the set of two-dimensional points (*i.e.*, small green points) (1) with the centroids obtained by the non-private standard k-means algorithm for the former figure, and (2) with the centroids obtained by the perturbed k-means algorithm (GREEDY strategy) for the latter figure. Both centroids were produced at the iteration #6, *i.e.*, the highest-quality iteration for the perturbed k-means. Although the perturbed centroids are less accurate, they appear mostly within an actual cluster, close to it, or between several clusters, which is similar to the usual behaviour of the non-perturbed version of k-means.

[12] I. Kärkkäinen and P. Fränti, "Dynamic local search algorithm for the clustering problem", Research Report A-2002-6, available at `https://cs.joensuu.fi/sipu/datasets/`

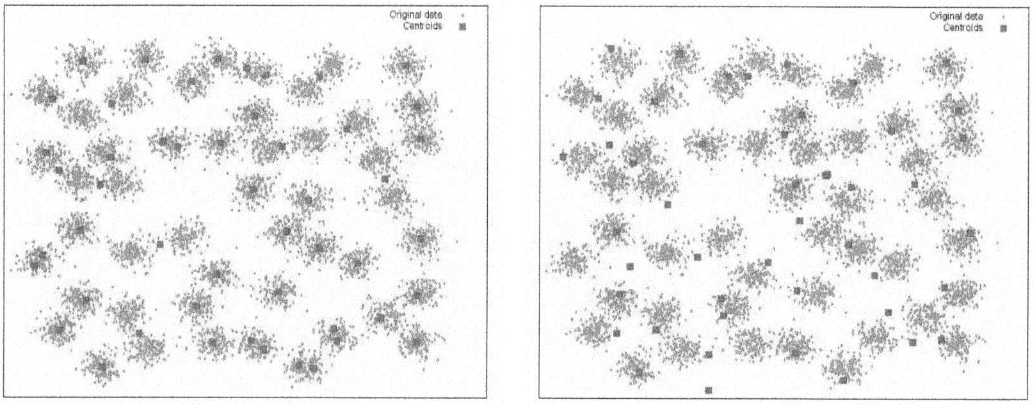

(a) In the Clear

(b) Chiaroscuro (GREEDY, no smoothing)

Figure 6: Centroids Resulting from k-means Executions over the $750K$ Two-Dimensional Points (6th iteration)

Persistent Data Sketching

Zhewei Wei*
School of Information, Renmin University of China
Key Laboratory of Data Engineering and Knowledge Engineering, MOE
zhewei@ruc.edu.cn

Ge Luo†
The Hong Kong University of Science and Technology
luoge@cse.ust.hk

Ke Yi
The Hong Kong University of Science and Technology
yike@cse.ust.hk

Xiaoyong Du‡
School of Information, Renmin University of China
and Key Laboratory of Data Engineering and Knowledge Engineering, MOE
duyong@ruc.edu.cn

Ji-Rong Wen
School of Information, Renmin University of China
and Key Laboratory of Data Engineering and Knowledge Engineering, MOE
jrwen@ruc.edu.cn

ABSTRACT

A *persistent data structure*, also known as a *multiversion data structure* in the database literature, is a data structure that preserves all its previous versions as it is updated over time. Every update (inserting, deleting, or changing a data record) to the data structure creates a new version, while all the versions are kept in the data structure so that any previous version can still be queried.

Persistent data structures aim at recording all versions accurately, which results in a space requirement that is at least linear to the number of updates. In many of today's big data applications, in particular for high-speed streaming data, the volume and velocity of the data are so high that we cannot afford to store everything. Therefore, streaming algorithms have received a lot of attention in the research community, which use only sublinear space by sacrificing slightly on accuracy.

All streaming algorithms work by maintaining a small data structure in memory, which is usually called a *sketch*, *summary*, or *synopsis*. The sketch is updated upon the arrival of every element in the stream, thus is *ephemeral*, meaning that it can only answer queries about the current status of the stream. In this paper, we aim at designing persistent sketches, thereby giving streaming algorithms the ability to answer queries about the stream at any prior time.

*This work was partially supported by the National Key Basic Research Program (973 Program) of China under grant No. 2014CB340403 and the Fundamental Research Funds for the Central Universities, the Research Funds of Renmin University of China.

†Ge Luo and Ke Yi are supported by HKRGC under grants GRF-621413 and GRF-16211614, and by a Microsoft grant MRA14EG05.

‡Partially supported by 973 Program of China (Project No. 2012CB316205)

SIGMOD'15, May 31–June 4, 2015, Melbourne, Victoria, Australia.

http://dx.doi.org/10.1145/2723372.2749443.

1. INTRODUCTION

History is a lens on the future. As our ability to collect, store, and process data increases at an unprecedented rate, so is our desire to ask questions about our data at any prior time instance, instead of only on its current status. The study on managing historical data has a long history itself. After some earlier not-so-successful attempts, a breakthrough was made in 1989 in a landmark paper by Driscoll, Sarnak, Sleator, and Tarjan [15], in which general techniques for building *persistent data structures* were introduced. These techniques allow us to store all versions of a data structure, one after each update (insertion or deletion of a data record), into a single data structure whose size is linear in the total amount of differences between every two consecutive versions, so that each version can still be efficiently queried. After more years of theoretical and experimental work, persistent data structures have become a mature technique that is now being incorporated into commercial multiversion database systems such as Microsoft Immortal DB [18]. Search engines, such as Google, also have adopted similar ideas, but tailored to their specific needs and environment, to support queries about the web at any prior time instance or interval.

Most past research on persistent data structures has focused on supporting historical queries accurately. This means that we have to store all the updates, and a persistent data structure essentially attains this inherent limit. However, due to the high volume and high velocity of data in the "big data" era, even this linear space cost, which used to be good enough, is now often considered prohibitive. The area of streaming algorithms is exactly devoted to solving this problem. A streaming algorithm works by storing a small data structure, often called a *sketch*, *summary*, or *synopsis*, in memory, and updates it with every element in the stream. Since the sketch size is only sublinear in the amount of data it has processed, exact query results are not possible, but the error can be bounded by some small ε, which can be decided by the user in advance. The sketch size is then inversely related to ε, yielding a tradeoff between space and accuracy.

However, all the sketches used by streaming algorithms are *ephemeral*, i.e., every update creates a new version while past versions are forgot. In this paper, we aim at making the sketches persistent, thus giving streaming algorithms the ability to answer queries at any prior time in history, still with a small ε error. More generally, we present sketching techniques that support *historical window queries*, which are asked on all elements in the stream that arrived in a given time interval $(s, t]$. It is clear that a traditional historical query supported by persistent data structures is a special case where $s = 0$. Our techniques are fairly general, and applicable to any sketch that consists of a set of counters. In particular, we show how to make the Count-Min Sketch [11] and the AMS/Count Sketch [2, 9] persistent, which are two of the most widely used sketches. They support some of the most fundamental queries in data analytics, such as point query, heavy hitters, and join size estimation. We show how the persistent versions of the Count-Min Sketch and the AMS/Count Sketch can be used to support these queries within any given time window $(s, t]$, with provably error guarantees. Meanwhile, the size of the persistent sketch remains sublinear, which is an essential property of streaming algorithms.

We envision many applications where persistent sketches could be useful. First, in any application that currently deploys persistent data structures, replacing them with persistent sketches will result in significant space savings, as long as a small error can be tolerated. At the same time, as the sketch is much smaller in size than a full data structure, it is possible to keep the sketch completely in main memory. This will greatly improve update and query efficiency, leading to better system scalability. Secondly, in scientific research where one experiment may run for days or even months while generating high-speed streams of numerical readings, it will be very useful to use persistent sketches to keep track of the progress over time. Since numerical readings in scientific experiments usually already have errors due to equipment inaccuracy and rounding, it is often acceptable to have some small and bounded error in the sketches in return for reduced space/time costs. Third, even for nonnumerical data streams such as network traffic (e.g., streams of IP packets), streaming algorithms have been widely deployed to monitor some statistical properties of the stream (e.g., the most frequent IP addresses). Using persistent sketches in these algorithms will enable statistical tracking of the entire history, rather than just the current status. Eventually, this line of work may lead to multiversion data stream systems, just like how persistent data structures have made multiversion database systems possible.

1.1 Related Work

This work lies in the intersection between persistent data structures and streaming algorithms, but these two areas have so far evolved separately with little interaction. Below we briefly review each area and point out where the gap is.

Persistent data structures.

Early approaches for managing historical data include: (1) store all the updates in a "changelog", and "replay" the history when a historical query is issued; and (2) create and keep a version of the data structure after every update. These approaches will result in either a long query time or a huge storage cost. In a landmark paper by Driscoll, Sarnak, Sleator, and Tarjan [15], the concept of persistent data structures was formally introduced, together with a suite of techniques for making an ordinary (i.e., ephemeral) data structure persistent. The persistence (or multiversion) model used in the database community is actually called *partial persistence* in [15], in which queries can be asked on any previous version, but updates can only be applied to the current version. There are two other types of persistence, namely *full persistence* and *confluent persistence*, which allow more complicated history models. They are more relevant to version control in software development, so we will not discuss them further in this paper.

Driscoll et al. [15] have introduced general techniques for turning any pointer-based ephemeral data structure into a persistent one with optimal overhead. Since then, there has been considerable development of persistent data structures, both in theory and practice. In particular, their techniques have been extended to the Multiversion B-tree [5, 7, 31], Time-Split B-tree [19], which has enabled the application of persistence techniques in database systems, and eventually led to the development of multiversion database systems and techniques such as Microsoft Immortal DB [18, 20], SNAP [29], Ganymed [25], Skippy [28] and LIVE[27].

However, the existing persistence techniques are not readily applicable to the persistent sketch problem. First, they only work on a pointer-based data structure (i.e., lists, binary trees, graphs), but the majority of sketches are not pointer-based. More seriously, these techniques aim at preserving every change to the data structure, thus directly applying them to a sketch would result in a persistent sketch whose size is at least linear in the stream length, which completely violates the first requirement of streaming algorithms. On the other hand, since a sketch is already an approximate data structure, it does not make sense to preserve all the versions accurately. Therefore, the key question in making a sketch persistent is to decide when and how to preserve the changes as long as the error guarantee is maintained, which has never been an issue for persistent data structures.

Streaming algorithms.

Streaming algorithms have been an area of active research in the past 20 years, with both rich theories and many practical data stream systems developed. Several streaming models have been considered in the literature [22]: In the *cash register model*, each record in the stream inserts an element, and queries are asked on the set of all the elements in the stream so far. In the *turnstile model*, the stream consists of both insertions and deletions, where a deletion removes an element previously inserted. These models only look at the current status of the stream.

Another streaming model that has a bit of "historical" flavor is the *sliding window* model [3, 6, 13], where we are only interested in the last k elements in the stream (a *count-based window*), or all elements that have arrived in the past (say) 24 hours (a *time-based window*). However, as more elements arrive in the stream and the window slides forward, past windows are lost. Note that this is actually a special case of historical window query where $t = now$ and $s = t - w$ for some fixed window length w.

Finally, the closest work to ours is that of Tao et al. [30], who designed a quantile summary for historical data. However, it is still far from a real persistent sketch because it does not work on streaming data. All the updates must be given in advance. Once the summary is built, it supports historical queries but no more new changes can be made. Moreover, their quantile summary is pointer-based so it is easy to use the techniques from [15], but the majority of the sketches in the streaming literature are not.

1.2 Preliminaries

We adopt the standard streaming model [4, 22] (a.k.a. the *cash register model*), defined as follows. Let $S = (e_1, e_2, \dots, e_m)$ be a data stream, where the e_j's are elements from the universe $[n] = \{1, \dots n\}$. The *frequency vector* of S is $\mathbf{f} = (f_1, f_2, \dots, f_n)$, where frequency $f_i = \sum_{j:e_j=i} 1$ is the number of times that element i appears. We use a discrete time model and assume that e_t arrives at time t, for $t = 1, \ldots, m$. If nothing arrives at time t, then $e_t = null$. In the more complex situation where the tuples in the stream have multiple attributes, we can view each attribute as a stream, and build sketches on each attribute stream. Since we use the standard streaming model, our sketches can be plugged into any architecture that adopts the standard streaming model. Please see the survey paper [4] for more discussion. For a distributed streaming system such as S4 [23] and D-Streams [32], our technique can be deployed to each single node.

Another commonly used streaming model is the *turnstile model*, which generalizes the standard streaming model by allowing deletions. In this model, the data stream $S = ((e_1, c_1), (e_2, c_2), \ldots, (e_m, c_m))$, where e_j's are the elements and c_i's denote the frequency change of element e_j, which can be $1, 0$, or -1. The frequency of item i is $f_i = \sum_{j:e_j=i} c_j$. Note that by restricting c_i to be 1 or 0, the turnstile model becomes the standard streaming model. The turnstile model allows deletions and may result in negative frequency, so we will focus on the standard streaming model in this paper. We only point out that all our persistent sketches work for the turnstile model as well, and present the corresponding space and query time bounds. These bounds may be of theoretical interest, as the Count-Min Sketch and AMS Sketch work for the turnstile model as well.

The Count-Min Sketch and the AMS Sketch are two widely used sketches, and we briefly describe them here. Let $h_j : [n] \rightarrow [w], j = 1, \ldots, d$ be a set of d pairwise-independent hash functions. The Count-Min Sketch maintains a $d \times w$ array of counters. Let $C[j][k]$ be the counter in the j-th row and k-th column. To process a new element i, the Count-Min Sketch performs $C[j][h_j(i)] \leftarrow C[j][h_j(i)] + 1$ for $j = 1, \ldots, d$. The Count-Min Sketch supports two fundamental queries: point query and heavy hitters. A point query asks for how many times an item i appears in the stream, and is estimated as $\text{median}_{j\in[d]}\{C[j][h_j(i)]\}$ by the sketch. Point queries are a building block for more complex queries, such as wavelet [16], range query [11]. Heavy hitters, also known as frequent items, are the items with frequencies above a given threshold. This problem has been extensively studied in the database literature [12, 21], but existing data structures are not persistent.

The (fast) AMS Sketch is similar to the Count-Min Sketch. It maintains a $d \times w$ array of counters and uses d hash functions $h_j : [n] \rightarrow [w]$ to map the elements in the universe to a counter in each row. The only difference is that, upon an update i, the AMS Sketch does $C[j][h_j(i)] \leftarrow C[j][h_j(i)] + \xi_j(i)$, where $\xi_j : [n] \rightarrow \{-1, +1\}$ is an 4-wise independent hash function, for $j \in [d]$. A important class of query supported by the AMS Sketch is the join size query, which asks for the join size of two streams. The join size query is useful for estimating query result sizes and measuring the skewness of the data [1, 26]. Meanwhile, join size query is the building block of more complex queries, such as binary joins, wavelets, and l_p differencing [14].

1.3 Problem Formulation

We now formally define the problem we are trying to address in this paper. Given a time interval $(s, t] = \{s + 1, s + 2, \ldots, t\}$, define $\mathbf{f}_{s,t}$ to be the frequency vector of all the elements having arrived within $(s, t]$, i.e., $\mathbf{f}_{s,t} = (f_1(s, t), f_2(s, t), \ldots, f_n(s, t))$, where $f_i(s, t) = \sum_{j:e_j=i, s<j\leq t} 1$ is the number of appearance of element i in time window $(s, t]$, for $i = 1, \ldots, n$. For historical queries, we have $s = 0$, and we simplify the notation as $\mathbf{f}_{0,t} = \mathbf{f}_t$. With a slight abuse of notation, we also use the frequency vectors $\mathbf{f}$, $\mathbf{f}_t$ and $\mathbf{f}_{s,t}$ to denote that part of the stream that defines these frequency vectors, respectively.

In this paper, we focus on four types of queries: 1) Historical window point query: Given an index i and a time range $(s, t]$, return $f_i(s, t)$. 2) Historical window heavy hitters query: Given an threshold ϕ, and a time range $(s, t]$, return elements with frequency $f_i(s, t) \geq \phi\|\mathbf{f}_{s,t}\|_1$. Here $\|\mathbf{f}_{s,t}\|_1 = \sum_{i=1}^{n} |f_i(s, t)|$ is the L_1 norm of $\mathbf{f}_{s,t}$. 3) Historical window join size: For two streams $\mathbf{f}$ and $\mathbf{g}$, given a time range $(s, t]$, return $I(\mathbf{f}_{s,t}, \mathbf{g}_{s,t}) = \sum_{i=1}^{n} f_i(s, t)g_i(s, t)$. 4) Historical window self-join size: Given a time range $(s, t]$, return $\|\mathbf{f}_{s,t}\|_2^2 = \sum_{i=1}^{n} f_i(s, t)^2$.

1.4 Our Results

We observe that most known sketches in the turnstile model are *linear sketches* of the following form. One or more hash functions are used to map the elements in the universe $[n]$ to an array of counters, and the value of each counter is a linear combination of the frequencies of the elements mapped to that counter. Upon the arrival of each update in the stream for a particular element, all counters that the element is mapped to are then updated accordingly. We present two general persistence techniques that, practically speaking, can be applied to any linear sketch of this form. However, in order to provide provable error guarantees, each technique is more suitable for a particular class of sketches. Specifically, we obtain the following results.

PLA-based persistent sketch.

We first present a persistence technique that uses *piecewise-linear functions* to approximate each counter of the sketch over time. This technique introduces an error that depends on the L_1-norm of the frequency vector, so it is more suitable for sketches that also provide such an error guarantee. In particular, we apply this technique to the Count-Min Sketch [11], and show that a persistent Count-Min Sketch can be used to answer historical window point queries and heavy hitters queries with error $\varepsilon\|\mathbf{f}_{s,t}\|_1 + \Delta$, with an arbitrarily high constant probability. The error consists of a relative term $\varepsilon\|\mathbf{f}_{s,t}\|_1$, which inherits from the Count-Min Sketch itself, as well as an additive term Δ, which is due to persistence. Note that, however, an additive term is unavoidable because the window can be arbitrarily small and it may contain each single element in the stream. If we did not have an additive error term, the persistent sketch would have to store all the data accurately. On the other hand, if we only consider historical queries (i.e., $s = 0$), then we can avoid this term (see later).

The size of a persistent Count-Min Sketch depends on the data distribution. It can be large on adversarial inputs, but our experimental results show that on many real-world and non-adversarial synthetic data sets, its size is actually very small. We back up this empirical observation with a theoretical justification: Under a reasonable random streaming model (random turnstile model and random stream model defined in Section 3), the persistent Count-Min Sketch has size $O(\frac{1}{\varepsilon} + \frac{m}{\Delta^2})$ in expectation, which is a factor of Δ smaller than a baseline solution.

The persistent Count-Min Sketch cannot handle join size queries (or rather, cannot provide a meaningful error bound), which are addressed by our second persistence technique.

Sampling based persistent sketch.

Next, we present a sampling based persistence technique that works well with sketches with error guarantees in terms of the L_2-

norm. We show how this can be applied to the AMS Sketch [2][1] to answer historical window self-join size queries with error $\varepsilon\|\mathbf{f}_{s,t}\|_2^2+\frac{\Delta^2}{\varepsilon}$, and join size queries between two streams $\mathbf{f}$ and $\mathbf{g}$ with error

$$\mathcal{E}=\varepsilon\sqrt{\left(\|\mathbf{f}_{s,t}\|_2^2+(\frac{\Delta_{\mathbf{f}}}{\varepsilon})^2\right)\left(\|\mathbf{g}_{s,t}\|_2^2+(\frac{\Delta_{\mathbf{g}}}{\varepsilon})^2\right)}.$$

Similarly, these errors all have an additive term, for the same reason as argued above. For join size queries between two streams $\mathbf{f}$ and $\mathbf{g}$, we allow them to use different additive error parameters $\Delta_{\mathbf{f}}$ and $\Delta_{\mathbf{g}}$. The size of a persistent AMS Sketch is $O(\frac{1}{\varepsilon^2}+\frac{m}{\Delta})$ in expectation regardless of the input, in both the turnstile model and the standard streaming model.

Historical queries.
Finally, we show how these persistent sketches can be specialized to solve historical queries for which s is fixed at 0. In this case, we can avoid the additive error term, and provide an error bound identical to that of the ephemeral sketch at time t. More precisely, the persistent Count-Min Sketch answers historical point queries and heavy hitters queries with error $\varepsilon\|\mathbf{f}_t\|_1$, and the persistent AMS Sketch answers historical self-join size queries with error $\varepsilon\|\mathbf{f}_t\|_2^2$ and join size queries with error $\varepsilon\|\mathbf{f}_t\|_2\|\mathbf{g}_t\|_2$.

Under this setting, the size of the persistent Count-Min Sketch is $O(\frac{1}{\varepsilon^2})$ under the random stream model and $O\left(\sum_{t=1}^{m}\frac{1}{\varepsilon^2\|\mathbf{f}_t\|_1^2}\right)$ under the random turnstile model. The size of the persistent AMS Sketch becomes $O(\frac{1}{\varepsilon^2}+\frac{\sqrt{m}}{\varepsilon})$ in the standard streaming model, and $O\left(\frac{1}{\varepsilon^2}+\sum_{t=1}^{m}\frac{1}{\varepsilon\|\mathbf{f}_t\|_2}\right)$ in the turnstile model, regardless of the input.

Finally, another appealing feature of our persistent sketches is that they are very easy to implement, with minimal modifications to the original, ephemeral sketches. However, the analyses, including both error analysis and space complexity, are nontrivial and quite involved for a general audience. Thus, we only present the results and some high-level ideas of the proofs in the main text, while deferring all details to the appendix.

1.5 An Illustrating Example

Consider the following example: a website receives an enormous number of visits every day, and one is interested in the most frequently requested URLs, and more importantly, how the frequencies of these URLs change over time. One could build a persistent data structure that supports top-k queries for any arbitrary past time window. However, as the update speed is very fast and data size is huge, such a persistent data structure must reside on disk or distributed system, which is costly. In this case, we can build a persistent sketch which supports historical window heavy hitters queries and hence top-k queries [9]. Since the size of a persistent sketch is sub-linear, it can fit in main memory. This will greatly improve update and query efficiency, leading to better system scalability.

We used the 1998 World Cup web site access log[2], which consists of all requests made to the 1998 World Cup web site between April 30 and July 26, 1998. Each request is a tuple that consists of 8 attributes: 1) timestamp: time of the request; 2) clientID, an anonymized integer of the IP address of the request ; 3) objectID, an anonymized integer of the requested URL; 4) size: number of bytes in the response; 5) method: method contained in the client's request; 6) status: response status code; 7) type: type of file requested 8) server: indicates which server handled the request.

[1]The version we are using is the improved version known as the "fast AMS Sketch", which is similar to the Count Sketch [9].
[2]http://ita.ee.lbl.gov/traces/WorldCup/WorldCup.html

URL	actual count	estimation
/	1138896	1138970
/images/space.gif	1117634	1120050
/images/dot.gif	880322	880765
/images/hm_nbg.jpg	818126	818586
/images/home_intro.anim.gif	799697	800323

Table 1: Top-5 most frequently requested URLs and their estimated frequencies at the end of the stream .

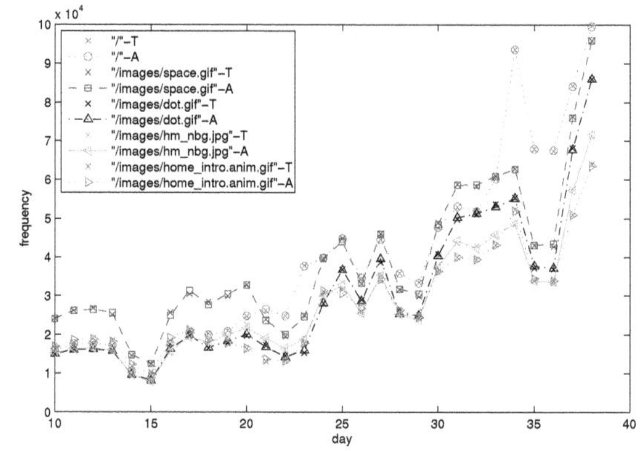

Figure 1: A illustration of the frequency change of top-5 most requested URLs over the days. Here legends with"T" denote the true frequencies, and legends with"A" denote the approximated frequencies.

Suppose we are interested in the most frequently requested URLs, and how their frequencies change over time. Then we can view the objectID attribute as a stream of elements, each arriving at the respective timestamp. If we build an ephemeral Count-Min Sketch on this objectID stream, we could only get the top-k URLs at the end of the stream (Table 1). However, if we had built a persistent Count-Min Sketch, we would be able to query the sketch and see how the frequencies of these URLs change over time (Figure 1). Note that all this information is extracted from the persistent sketch only, *without* accessing the raw data stream, which may have been dumped to slow secondary storage or even discarded.

2. A BASELINE SOLUTION

A baseline solution can be designed using properties of *linear sketches*. Recall that each counter in a linear sketch is a linear function of the frequency vector $\mathbf{f}$. Let C_t be the set of counters at time t. If we record C_t for every t, then given a historical window $(s,t]$, we can compute $C_{s,t}=C_t-C_s$. By linearity, this is exactly the set of counters for $\mathbf{f}_{s,t}$, i.e., the partial stream within that window, which can be used to answer various queries on $\mathbf{f}_{s,t}$.

The above approach would result in a persistent sketch with linear space. To achieve sub-linear space, we keep track of each counter in the sketch over time, but record a value only when it has deviated from the last recorded value by more than Δ. To answer a historical window query with time range $(s,t]$, for each counter we find the recorded value with timestamp closest to s (resp. t) to form $\hat{C}_s$ (resp. $\hat{C}_t$) as an approximation of C_s (resp. C_t), and uses $\hat{C}_{s,t}=\hat{C}_t-\hat{C}_s$ as an approximation of $C_{s,t}$ to answer queries on $\mathbf{f}_{s,t}$. Note that each counter in $\hat{C}_{s,t}$ might deviate from that in $C_{s,t}$ by up to 2Δ; but by scaling Δ down by a factor of 2, this is not an issue.

However, the baseline solution suffers from two drawbacks: (1) The space complexity is still high. Given an additive error parameter Δ, the space usage is proportional to $\frac{m}{\Delta}$, where m is the length of the stream. (2) This approach can only handle queries that depend on one (or a small number of) counters in the sketch, which is the case for point and heavy hitters queries. For join size and self-join queries, the answer depends non-linearly on *all* the counters in the sketch. Thus the total error would be amplified significantly. We present our two persistence techniques in the next two sections, which will exactly address these drawbacks.

3. PLA-BASED PERSISTENT SKETCH

In this section, we present our first persistence technique, which is based on the idea of using piecewise-linear approximations (PLA) to keep track of the counters over time. For concreteness, we show how it is applied to the Count-Min Sketch, resulting in a persistent Count-Min Sketch that answers historical window point and heavy hitter queries with error depending on the L_1-norm.

3.1 Piecewise Linear Approximation

We first briefly review the PLA technique. Here, the aim is to approximate a function $v(\cdot)$ with a piecewise-linear function $f(\cdot)$ with bounded error having a small number of segments. Note that the segments in f may not be connected. In our setting, $v(\cdot)$ will be the value of a counter over time, and we want $|f(t) - v(t)| \leq \Delta$ for all t for some error parameter Δ.

There is a greedy algorithm that can construct such an f having the minimum number of segments [24]. The algorithm is very simple and we describe it here for completeness. We view each counter value at time t as a point $(t, v(t))$ in the plane. Let P be the set of points we have processed so far. The algorithm maintains the invariant that all points in P can be approximated with a single line within error Δ. Let p be the next point. We check if $P \cup \{p\}$ can still be approximated with a single line. If yes, we add p to P and continue onto the next point; otherwise, we output a line segment that approximates P, set $P \leftarrow \{p\}$, and continue. The optimality of the algorithm is trivial; O'Rourke [24] in addition showed how this algorithm can be implemented in $O(1)$ space and amortized $O(1)$ time per point.

3.2 Persistent Count-Min Sketch

Our basic idea is to keep track of each counter in the Count-Min Sketch using a PLA. Recall that the Count-Min Sketch maintains a $d \times w$ array of counters. Let $C[j][k]$ be the counter in the j-th row and k-th column. Let $h_j : [n] \to [w], j = 1, \ldots, d$ be a set of d pairwise-independent hash functions. To make the Count-Min Sketch persistent, we run an instance of the above PLA algorithm for each counter $C[j][k]$, which generates a piecewise-linear function that approximates this counter over time with additive error Δ. We store this function together with $C[j][k]$, and denote it as $\mathsf{PLA}[j][k]$. Below, we provide detailed procedures for updating and querying this persistent Count-Min Sketch.

Update. Consider an update i arriving at time t, meaning that the frequency f_i is updated as $f_i \leftarrow f_i + 1$. For $j = 1, \ldots, d$, we first update the counter in the ephemeral sketch as

$$C[j][h_j(i)] \leftarrow C[j][h_j(i)] + 1.$$

Then, we feed the point $(t, C[j][h_j(i)])$ to the PLA algorithm running for $C[j][h_j(i)]$. If this algorithm outputs a segment, we append it to $\mathsf{PLA}[j][h_j(i)]$.

Historical window point query. Recall that in a historical window point query, we are given an element i and a time interval $(s, t]$, and the goal is to estimate $f_i(s, t)$, the frequency of element i in time range $(s, t]$. For each $j = 1, \ldots, d$, we retrieve an approximation of $C[j][h_j(i)]$ at time s, denoted as $\hat{C}^s[j][h_j(i)]$, from $\mathsf{PLA}[j][h_j(i)]$. This is done by a binary search on $\mathsf{PLA}[j][h_j(i)]$. Similarly we retrieve $\hat{C}^t[j][h_j(i)]$. Finally we return

$$\hat{f}_i(s, t) = \text{median}_{j \in [d]}\{\hat{C}^t[j][h_j(i)] - \hat{C}^s[j][h_j(i)]\}$$

as the estimator for $f_i(s, t)$.

Note that here we do not take the minimum as in the original Count-Min Sketch, since $\hat{C}^t[j][h_j(i)] - \hat{C}^s[j][h_j(i)]$ may be either an overestimate or an underestimate of $f_i(s, t)$.

Historical window heavy hitters queries. Recall that in a historical window heavy hitters query, we are given a time range $(s, t]$ and a parameter ϕ, and the goal is to return all the elements i with frequency $f_i(s, t) \geq \phi \|\mathbf{f}\|_1$. To be able to efficiently identify the heavy hitters, we use the dyadic range sum technique in [12] to decompose the universe $[n]$. More precisely, a dyadic range at level ℓ is an interval of the form $[j2^\ell + 1, (j+1)2^\ell)$, for $\ell = 0, \ldots, \log n$ and $j = 0, \ldots, \frac{n}{2^\ell} - 1$. For a particular level ℓ, we divide the universe into $\frac{n}{2^\ell}$ dyadic ranges, each of size 2^ℓ, and use a persistent Count-Min Sketch to track total frequency of elements in every dyadic range. Thus we maintain $\log n + 1$ persistent Count-Min Sketches in total. When an update (i, c) arrives, in each level, we find the dyadic interval that contains i, and update the corresponding counters.

In order to find all heavy hitters, we ask point queries on the $\log n + 1$ levels recursively. More precisely, suppose at level ℓ we have identified at most $\frac{1}{\phi}$ heavy dyadic ranges (a dyadic range is *heavy* if the estimated total frequency of all elements in that range is more than $\phi \|\mathbf{f}_{s,t}\|_1$). These ranges are split into $\frac{2}{\phi}$ dyadic ranges in level $\ell + 1$. Then at level $\ell + 1$, we ask point queries on these $\frac{2}{\phi}$ heavy dyadic ranges to identify again at most $\frac{1}{\phi}$ heavy dyadic ranges. We repeat this process until we find all heavy hitters at level 0, which are returned as the estimated heavy hitters.

3.3 Analysis

In this section, we give the error guarantees of the persistent Count-Min Sketch, as well as the analysis of its space and time complexity. We set the parameters as $w = O(1/\varepsilon)$, $d = O(\log \frac{1}{\delta})$ where δ is the failure probability, and PLA error $O(\Delta)$.

Error guarantees. For historical window point queries, the persistent Count-Min Sketch can provide the following error bound:

THEOREM 3.1. *Given a time interval $(s, t]$ and an element i, the persistent Count-Min Sketch provides an estimate $\hat{f}_i(s, t)$ for $f_i(s, t)$ such that*

$$\Pr\left[\left|\hat{f}_i(s, t) - f_i(s, t)\right| \leq \varepsilon \|\mathbf{f}_{s,t}\|_1 + \Delta\right] \geq 1 - \delta.$$

Theorem 3.1 follows from the linearity of the Count-Min Sketch, its own ε-guarantee, and the fact that the PLA introduces an additional additive Δ error. The detailed proof can be found in the appendix.

Similarly, we have the following error guarantee for historical window heavy hitters queries:

THEOREM 3.2. *Given a time interval $(s, t]$, for any element i with $f_i(s, t) \geq (\phi + \varepsilon)\|\mathbf{f}_{s,t}\|_1 + \Delta$, the persistent Count-Min Sketch returns it with probability as least $1 - \delta$; for any element i with $f_i(s, t) < \phi \|\mathbf{f}_{s,t}\|_1$, the persistent Count-Min Sketch returns it with probability at most δ.*

Space complexity. For space complexity analysis, we only focus on point queries; if heavy hitters queries are to be supported, the space usage simply grows by a $\log n$ factor due to the dyadic range sum technique.

In the worst case, every Δ updates might trigger the PLA algorithm to generate a segment, resulting in a total space of $O((\frac{m}{\Delta} + \frac{1}{\varepsilon}) \log \frac{1}{\delta})$ (the $\frac{1}{\varepsilon}$ part is for the ephemeral sketch). This is as bad as the baseline solution. However, our empirical results in Section 6 show that the persistent Count-Min Sketch achieves much better space usage in practice. To provide some theoretical justification behind this phenomenon, we analyze its space complexity under the following *random stream model*, and prove a much better space bound under this model.

DEFINITION 3.1 (RANDOM STREAM MODEL). *Let $\mathcal{P}$ be an unknown but fixed distribution over the set of all possible elements $[n] = \{1, 2, \dots, n\}$. Each update in the stream is drawn independently and uniformly at random from $[n]$ according to $\mathcal{P}$.*

This model is also known as the *random order model* [17]. As argued in [17], there is often a lot of randomness in real-world data streams. Although they may not be as fully random as required in the model above, the model is actually a better approximation of reality than assuming worst-case, adversarial inputs. Note that we do not have any assumption on $\mathcal{P}$ (such as uniform or Gaussian); it can be any any distribution (unknown to the algorithm) so that the our results will apply to a variety of scenarios.

Note that the random stream model can also be generalized to *random turnstile model*, in which each update is drawn independently and uniformly at random from $U = \{(i, c) \mid i \in [n], c \in \{-1, 0, +1\}\}$ following some unknown but fixed distribution $\mathcal{P}$. To generalize our technique, we will prove the following space bound for the persistent Count-Min Sketch under the random turnstile model:

THEOREM 3.3. *In the random turnstile model, the persistent Count-Min Sketch uses $O((\frac{m}{\Delta^2} + \frac{1}{\varepsilon}) \log \frac{1}{\delta})$ space in expectation.*

Note that Theorem 3.3 directly implies the same space for the random stream model. This bound is roughly a Δ-factor improvement from the baseline solution, which can be significant, since Δ is an additive error, and is usually set to be on the same order as $\varepsilon \|\mathbf{f}_{s,t}\|_1$. The key insight in the proof of this bound is that the value of each counter over time can be viewed as a random walk that vibrates around a line, which is being constructed by the PLA algorithm. A single line segment of the PLA fails to approximate the counter only when the random walk "escapes" from a region of width 2Δ centered at the line. Then using some random walk theory, we are able to show that it takes a quadratic number of steps to escape from this region. The rigorous proof, however, is quite involved and is provided in the appendix.

Query time. The analysis on query time is straightforward. For point queries, since we retrieve $O(d)$ estimates from the PLA, and each involves a binary search, the total query cost is $O(d \log m) = O(\log \frac{1}{\delta} \log m)$. By the standard technique of fractional cascading [10], this can be improved to $O(\log \frac{1}{\delta} + \log m)$.

For heavy hitters queries, observe that we make $O(\frac{1}{\phi})$ point queries to $O(\log n)$ persistent Count-Min Sketches. Thus the query cost is $O(\frac{1}{\phi} \log m \log n \log \frac{\log n}{\phi\delta})$, which can again be improved to $O(\log m + \frac{1}{\phi} \log n \log \frac{\log n}{\phi\delta})$ by fractional cascading. We omit the details as the focus of the paper is on the error-space tradeoff.

4. SAMPLING BASED PERSISTENT SKETCH

In this section, we present our second persistence technique based on random sampling. When applied with the AMS Sketch, this yields a persistent sketch answers historical window point queries and join size queries with provable error bounds.

4.1 Persistent AMS Sketch

In order to apply the sampling technique, we need each counter to be monotonically increasing (for reasons that will become clear later). Thus, we decompose each counter $C[j][k]$ into two components $C[j][k][1]$ and $C[j][k][0]$, such that both components monotonically increase. Specifically, to process an update i, if $\xi_j(i) = 1$, we increment $C[j][h_j(j)][1]$ by 1; if $\xi_j(i) = -1$, we increment $C[j][h_j(j)][0]$ by 1. It is clear that the correct value as in the original AMS Sketch, $C[j][k]$, is equal to $C[j][k][1] - C[j][k][0]$.

To make the AMS Sketch persistent, for each counter $C[j][k][b]$, we associate it with $L[j][k][b]$, a list that we call a *history list*. This list stores the values of the counter sampled over time, together with a timestamp indicating when each value is sampled.

Update. Consider an update i arriving at time t, meaning that frequency f_i is updated as $f_i \leftarrow f_i + 1$. For each $j = 1, \dots, d$, we first update $C[j][h_j(i)][b]$ as described above where $b = 1$ or 0 depending on $\xi_j(i)$. Then we update the history list $L[j][h_j(i)][b]$ as follows. With probability $p = 1/\Delta$, we sample the new value of the counter and append the pair $(C[j][h_j(i)][b], t)$ at the end of $L[j][h_j(i)][b]$.

Historical window point query. The primary functionality of the AMS Sketch is to support join size estimation. Nevertheless, it also supports point queries as noted in [9], with an error depending on the L_2-norm of the frequency vector. As point queries are simpler to describe, below we first show how our persistent AMS Sketch supports historical window point queries, and then move on to join size estimation.

Consider a historical window point query for element i in a time range $(s, t]$, which asks for an estimate of $f_i(s, t)$. For each $j = 1, \dots, d$ and each $b = 0, 1$, we do a binary search in $L[j][h_j(i)][b]$ to find the *predecessor* of t, i.e., the record with the largest timestamp before t (including t). Let $\bar{C}^t[j][h_j(i)][b]$ be the counter value of the predecessor of t in $L[j][h_j(i)][b]$. Intuitively, $\bar{C}^t[j][h_j(i)][b]$ is a good approximation of the counter value at time t, but we may have missed some increments since $\bar{C}^t[j][h_j(i)][b]$ was sampled. We thus compensate our estimate as

$$\hat{C}^t[j][h_j(i)][b] = \begin{cases} \bar{C}^t[j][h_j(i)][b] + \Delta - 1, \\ \qquad \text{if } t \text{ has a predecessor in } L[j][h_j(i)][b]; \\ 0, \quad \text{otherwise.} \end{cases} \tag{1}$$

Then we compute

$$\hat{D}^t[j][h_j(i)] = \xi_j(i) \cdot \left(\hat{C}^t[j][h_j(i)][1] - \hat{C}^t[j][h_j(i)][0] \right),$$

which is an estimate of f_i at time t. We compute $\hat{D}^s[j][h_j(i)]$, an estimate of f_i at time s in the same manner. We then compute $\hat{D}^{s,t}[j][h_j(i)] = \hat{D}^t[j][h_j(i)] - \hat{D}^s[j][h_j(i)]$ as an estimate of $f_i(s, t)$. Finally, across all rows j, we return the median as the final estimate $\hat{f}_i(s, t) = \text{median}_{i \in [d]} \hat{D}^{s,t}[j][h_j(i)]$.

Historical window join size estimation. To support join size estimation between two streams $\mathbf{f}$ and $\mathbf{g}$, the two persistent AMS Sketches on the two streams, denoted as $C_{\mathbf{f}}$ and $C_{\mathbf{g}}$, need to use the same set of hash functions h_j and ξ_j, $j = 1, \dots, d$. As they are just pairwise and 4-wise independent hash functions, each can be described in $O(1)$ space, and can be shared between the two streams with $O(1)$ communication.

Recall that for a given a time interval $(s, t]$, the join size between the two streams is $I(\mathbf{f}_{s,t}, \mathbf{g}_{s,t}) = \sum_i f_i(s, t) g_i(s, t)$. For each $j = 1, \dots, d$, we first compute $\hat{D}_{\mathbf{f}}^{s,t}[j][k]$ and $\hat{D}_{\mathbf{g}}^{s,t}[j][k]$ in as we did for point queries above, the only difference being that for point queries, we only care about a single $k = h_j(i)$, but now we need to compute $\hat{D}_{\mathbf{f}}^{s,t}[j][k]$ and $\hat{D}_{\mathbf{g}}^{s,t}[j][k]$ for all $k \in [w]$.

After we have computed $\hat{D}_{\mathbf{f}}^{s,t}[j][k]$ and $\hat{D}_{\mathbf{g}}^{s,t}[j][k]$ for all j and k from the two persistent sketches, we can estimate the join size between $\mathbf{f}_{s,t}$ and $\mathbf{g}_{s,t}$ as in the original AMS Sketch, i.e.,

$$\hat{I}(\mathbf{f}_{s,t}, \mathbf{g}_{s,t}) = \text{median}_{j\in[d]} \left\{ \sum_{k=1}^{w} \hat{D}_{\mathbf{f}}^{s,t}[j][k] \cdot \hat{D}_{\mathbf{g}}^{s,t}[j][k] \right\}.$$

Historical window self-join size estimation. A self join query on stream $\mathbf{f}$ can be processed as a join between $\mathbf{f}$ and itself. One technical issue, however, is that our analysis on join size estimation requires the history lists from two streams to be independent. This is not true if we use one set of history lists for the same stream. We can solve this issue by storing two independent history lists for each counter. This modification will increase the size of the persistent sketch by a factor of 2.

4.2 Analysis

In this section, we first explain on an intuitive level why the sampling based persistence technique can provide provable error guarantees for join size estimation, while the baseline method and the PLA based technique cannot. Then we formalize our results and give rigorous proofs (in the appendix). To ensure the error guarantee, we set the parameters as $w = O(1/\varepsilon)$, and $d = O(\log \frac{1}{\delta})$ where δ is the failure probability.

The fundamental difference between a point query and join size estimation is that the former depends only one the value of one counter per row, while the latter is a *holistic* query that depends on all counters. With the baseline method and the PLA based technique, the bias of estimating a counter is as large as $\Omega(\Delta)$. As the algorithm is deterministic, there is no way to correct the bias. For self-join size estimation, we need to compute the *sum of squares* of all counters, so the bias from each counter will be significantly amplified (by a factor of the L_1 norm in the worst case). On the other hand, we show that the sampling technique can provide *unbiased* estimators for the counters, which is the key behind a much better error bound in the final estimate for join and self-join queries.

Error guarantees. For historical window point queries, the persistent AMS Sketch can provide the following error bound:

THEOREM 4.1. *Given a time interval $(s, t]$ and an index i, the persistent AMS Sketch provides an estimate $\hat{f}_i(s,t)$ for $f_i(s,t)$ such that*

$$\Pr\left[\left|\hat{f}_i(s,t) - f_i(s,t)\right| \le \varepsilon\|\mathbf{f}_{s,t}\|_2 + \Delta\right] \ge 1-\delta.$$

The $\|\mathbf{f}_{s,t}\|_2$ term inherits from the original AMS Sketch (or rather, the Count Sketch analysis [9]), while the Δ term is the error introduced by the sampling based persistence technique.

For join size queries involving two streams $\mathbf{f}$ and $\mathbf{g}$, we allow them to use different error parameters $\Delta_{\mathbf{f}}$ and $\Delta_{\mathbf{g}}$ for the persistence part, but for the ephemeral sketch, the parameters (i.e., w and d) have to be the same, together with the same set of hash functions. With this setup, we have the following error bound for historical window join size queries:

THEOREM 4.2. *Given a historical window join size query with a time interval $(s, t]$, the persistent AMS Sketches provides an estimate $\hat{I}(\mathbf{f}_{s,t}, \mathbf{g}_{s,t})$ for $I(\mathbf{f}_{s,t}, \mathbf{g}_{s,t})$ such that*

$$\Pr\left[\left|\hat{I}(\mathbf{f}_{s,t}, \mathbf{g}_{s,t}) - I(\mathbf{f}_{s,t}, \mathbf{g}_{s,t})\right| \le \mathcal{E}\right] \ge 1-\delta,$$

where $\mathcal{E} = \varepsilon\sqrt{\left(\|\mathbf{f}_{s,t}\|_2^2 + (\frac{\Delta_{\mathbf{f}}}{\varepsilon})^2\right)\left(\|\mathbf{g}_{s,t}\|_2^2 + (\frac{\Delta_{\mathbf{g}}}{\varepsilon})^2\right)}$.

Self-join size estimation is a special case, and the above theorem holds by setting $\|\mathbf{f}_{s,t}\|_2 = \|\mathbf{g}_{s,t}\|_2$ and $\Delta_{\mathbf{f}} = \Delta_{\mathbf{g}}$.

Space and query time. The space complexity analysis is straightforward for the persistent AMS Sketch. The ephemeral sketch has $O(\frac{1}{\varepsilon^2}\log\frac{1}{\delta})$ counters. Each update goes to $O(\log\frac{1}{\delta})$ counters, and in expectation, a fraction of $1/\Delta$ of the updates are sampled. So the total space used is $O((\frac{m}{\Delta}+\frac{1}{\varepsilon^2})\log\frac{1}{\delta})$. This is the same as the baseline method, but remember that the baseline method cannot handle join size queries.

For point queries, since we retrieve $O(d)$ estimates from $O(d)$ history lists, and each involves a binary search, the total query cost is $O(d\log m) = O(\log\frac{1}{\delta}\log m)$. By fractional cascading, this can be improved to $O(\log\frac{1}{\delta} + \log m)$.

For join size queries, we retrieve $O(wd)$ estimates from $O(wd)$ history lists, and each involves a binary search. The total query cost is $O(wd\log m) = O(\frac{1}{\varepsilon^2}\log\frac{1}{\delta}\log m)$ which again can be improved to $O(\frac{1}{\varepsilon^2}\log\frac{1}{\delta} + \log m)$ using fractional cascading.

5. SKETCHES FOR HISTORICAL QUERIES

Our persistent sketches for general historical windows all have an additive error term that does not exist for the respective ephemeral sketch. But we argued earlier that this is necessary because we allow arbitrary historical windows. Nevertheless, if the starting time of the window is fixed at $s = 0$, the persistent sketches described above can be easily modified so as to eliminate the additive error, therefore yielding the same error guarantee as in the ephemeral sketch.

5.1 Persistent Count-Min Sketch for Historical Queries

Recall that a historical query is a historical window query with time interval $(0, t]$. We now show how to modify the persistent Count-Min Sketch to answer historical point queries and heavy hitter queries with additive error $\varepsilon\|\mathbf{f}_t\|_1$. The idea is to adaptively change the PLA error Δ in a way such that it is always within a constant factor of $\varepsilon\|\mathbf{f}_t\|$, so that the error bound translates to $\varepsilon\|\mathbf{f}_t\|_1 + \Delta = O(\varepsilon\|\mathbf{f}_t\|_1)$.

More precisely, we divide the stream into *epochs*, such that $\|\mathbf{f}_t\|_1$ fluctuates within a constant factor (say, 2) in an epoch. Note that $\|\mathbf{f}_t\|_1$ is simply the total number of insertions minus the total number of deletions so far, so we can track it easily using a single counter. Whenever $\|\mathbf{f}_t\|_1$ doubles or halves, we declare end for the current epoch and starts a new one. Let $[t_i, t_{i+1})$ be the time period for the i-th epoch. In the i-th epoch, we set $\Delta = \varepsilon\|\mathbf{f}_{t_i}\|_1$ as the PLA error and construct a persistent Count-Min Sketch until time t_{i+1}.

To answer a historical query with time instance t, we simply find the epoch that contains t, and handle the query with the persistent sketch in that epoch.

Error guarantees. As before, we set $w = O(1/\varepsilon)$ and $d = O(\log\frac{1}{\delta})$. For historical point and heavy hitters queries, the modified persistent Count-Min Sketch provides the following error bounds:

THEOREM 5.1. *Given a time instance t and an element i, the modified persistent Count-Min Sketch provides $\hat{f}_i(t)$ as an estimate for $f_i(t)$ such that*

$$\Pr\left[\left|\hat{f}_i(t) - f_i(t)\right| \le \varepsilon\|\mathbf{f}_t\|_1\right] \ge 1-\delta.$$

THEOREM 5.2. *Given a time instance t, for any element i with $f_i(t) \ge (\phi+\varepsilon)\|\mathbf{f}_t\|_1$, the modified persistent Count-Min a sketch returns it with probability as least $1-\delta$; for any element i with $f_i(t) < \phi\|\mathbf{f}_t\|_1$, the persistent Count-Min Sketch returns it with probability at most δ.*

Theorem 5.1 and Theorem 5.2 follow directly by setting $s = 0$ and $\Delta = \Theta(\varepsilon \|\mathbf{f}_t\|_1)$ in Theorem 3.1 and Theorem 3.2, respectively.

Space complexity. For space complexity analysis, we only focus on point queries; the bound for heavy hitters queries grows by a $\log n$ factor. We are able to prove the following result under the random stream model:

THEOREM 5.3. *In the random stream model, the modified persistent Count-Min Sketch uses $O(\frac{1}{\varepsilon^2} \log \frac{1}{\delta})$ space in expectation.*

In fact, we will prove that in the random turnstile model, the modified persistent sketch uses $O((\sum_{t=1}^{m} \frac{1}{\varepsilon^2 \|\mathbf{f}_t\|_1^2} + \frac{1}{\varepsilon}) \log \frac{1}{\delta})$ space in expectation. In the standard streaming model, $\|\mathbf{f}_t\|_1 = t$, so the size of the sketch becomes $O(\frac{1}{\varepsilon^2} \log \frac{1}{\delta})$. A more rigorous proof is given in the appendix.

Query time. Comparing to the query time analysis in Section 3, the only additional cost is to search for the epoch that contains the time instance t, which takes $\log m$ time. Therefore the query time remains the same as before (asymptotically).

5.2 Persistent AMS Sketch for Historical Queries

Next, we show how to modify the persistent AMS Sketch to support historical queries with error only related to the L_2 norm.

The basic idea is the same as in the Count-Min Sketch, that is, we will adaptively change Δ so that it is always within a constant factor of $\varepsilon \|\mathbf{f}_t\|_2$. However, unlike the L_1-norm, the L_2-norm cannot be tracked with a single counter. We will use an additional AMS Sketch of width $w = O(1)$ and depth $d = O(\log \frac{m}{\delta})$, which can approximate $\|\mathbf{f}_t\|_2$ within a constant factor with probability at least $1 - \delta$, *for all* time instances. This way we always have a constant approximation of $\|\mathbf{f}_t\|_2$. Then we can divide the stream into epochs, such that the L_2 norm of the frequency vector fluctuates within a constant factor in each epoch. Let $[t_i, t_{i+1})$ denote the i-th epoch. Within the i-th epoch, we set $\Delta = \varepsilon \|\mathbf{f}_i\|_2$ and construct the sampling-based persistent AMS Sketch until time t_{i+1}.

To answer a historical query with time t, we first find the epoch that contains t. Let $[t_{i-1}, t_i)$ be that epoch. Then we simply invoke the same algorithm as in Section 4. One small technical issue is that in Section 4, if we cannot find any predecessor for time t in a history list, we simply set the estimate as 0 (as in Equation (1)). Here we have multiple epochs, and a counter in an epoch may not start from 0, thus we need to record the starting value of each counter in each epoch. When we cannot find a predecessor in a counter's history list, we set the estimate to its starting value in this epoch.

Error guarantees. We set $w = O(1/\varepsilon^2)$ and $d = O(\log \frac{1}{\delta})$. For historical point and join size queries, the modified persistent AMS Sketch can provide the following error bounds:

THEOREM 5.4. *Given a time instance t and an element i, the modified persistent AMS Sketch provides an estimate $\hat{f}_i(t)$ for $f_i(t)$ such that*

$$\Pr\left[\left|\hat{f}_i(t) - f_i(t)\right| \le \varepsilon \|\mathbf{f}_t\|_2\right] \ge 1 - \delta.$$

THEOREM 5.5. *Given a time instance t, the modified persistent AMS Sketches provide an estimate $\hat{I}(\mathbf{f}_t, \mathbf{g}_t)$ for $I(\mathbf{f}_t, \mathbf{g}_t)$ such that*

$$\Pr\left[\left|\hat{I}(\mathbf{f}_t, \mathbf{g}_t) - I(\mathbf{f}_t, \mathbf{g}_t)\right| \le \varepsilon \|\mathbf{f}_t\|_2 \|\mathbf{g}_t\|_2\right] \ge 1 - \delta.$$

These two theorems follow by setting $s = 0$ and $\Delta_{\mathbf{f}} = \Theta(\varepsilon \|\mathbf{f}_t\|_2)$, $\Delta_{\mathbf{g}} = \Theta(\varepsilon \|\mathbf{g}_t\|_2)$ in Theorem 4.1 and Theorem 4.2, respectively.

Space complexity We have the following result on the space complexity of the modified persistent AMS Sketch.

THEOREM 5.6. *In the standard streaming model, the modified persistent AMS Sketch uses expected space $O((\frac{\sqrt{m}}{\varepsilon} + \frac{1}{\varepsilon^2}) \log \frac{1}{\delta})$.*

We will prove the space usage is $O((\sum_{t=1}^{m} \frac{1}{\varepsilon \|\mathbf{f}_t\|_2} + \frac{1}{\varepsilon^2}) \log \frac{1}{\delta})$ in the turnstile model. In the standard streaming model, we have $\|\mathbf{f}_t\|_2 = \sqrt{t}$, so the size of the sketch becomes $O((\frac{\sqrt{m}}{\varepsilon} + \frac{1}{\varepsilon^2}) \log \frac{1}{\delta})$. As with the modified Count-Min Sketch, there is no change in the query time for the modified persistent AMS Sketch.

6. EXPERIMENTS

6.1 Experimental setup

We conducted an experimental study on synthetic and real-world data sets to evaluate the goodness of the proposed persistent sketches. They are evaluated primarily on two measures: the space used by the sketch, and the accuracy of the query results.

Data sets. For synthetic data, we generated a data set called Zipf_3, which consists of 1 million items randomly drawn from a universe $[2^{24}]$ with Zipf distribution of coefficient 3. This is a highly skewed data set. For real-world data, we used the 1998 World Cup web site access log. We selected 7,000,000 requests from Day 46, and insert each request as an update according to the timestamp attribute. We are interested in two attributes: 1) objectID, an anonymized integer of the requested URL, and 2) clientID, an anonymized integer of the IP address of the requests. Each timestamp, clientID, and objectID can fit into a 32-bit integer. We denote the set of (timestamp, clientID) tuples as ClientID, and the set of the (timestamp, objectID) tuples as ObjectID. We note that ClientID is a very uniform data set, with maximum frequency being 14645, while ObjectID is more skewed, with most frequencies concentrating on around 500 items. The two data sets exhibit different characteristics in terms of join size and heavy hitters.

Competitors and parameters. In the following, we refer to the two persistent sketches by their persistence technique, i.e., we use the name PLA for the persistent Count-Min Sketch , and Sample for the persistent AMS Sketch. We compare PLA and Sample to the two baseline solutions: PWC_CountMin and PWC_AMS. Recall that in these two sketched, we record the value of a counter when it has deviated from the last recorded value by more than Δ, so it is essentially using a piecewise-constant function to approximate each counter, hence the names.

We set the width and depth of all ephemeral sketches to be $w = 20000$ and $d = 7$, regardless of the type of the sketches. Note that this corresponds to $\varepsilon = 0.000005$ for the persistent Count-Min Sketch, and $\varepsilon = 0.01$ for the persistent AMS Sketch. The hash functions used by the sketches are pairwise and 4-wise independent functions constructed with the polynomial universal hashing method by Carter and Wegman [8]. All experiments are conducted on a machine with 16G RAM and a 3.00GHz processor.

6.2 Space usage

We measure the *extra space* needed to make an ephemeral sketch persistent, that is, the space used by the sketch excluding the size of the ephemeral sketch. As each sketch uses different approaches to store information, we will measure the actual space in terms of the number of machine words used. For Sample, PWC_CountMin and PWC_AMS, we need an integer to store the recorded value, and another integer to store the timestamp, so the space usage is the number of recorded values multiplied by 2. On the other hand, each segment in PLA needs 3 parameters: the slope a, the offset b and the starting timestamp t. Therefore the space usage for PLA is the number of segments multiplied by 3.

The tradeoffs between the space usage and the error parameter Δ are shown in Figure 3. Note that we use log scale on both axes. Our first observation from the results is that the space used by PLA is indeed smaller than the worst-case space bound $O(dm/\Delta)$. In

Zipf_3 where each update is drawn from a Zipf distribution independently, the space usage of PLA is up to 500 times smaller than the worst-case bound. This concurs with the inverse quadratic relation between space and Δ in Theorem 3.3. We also notice that the space usage for Sample is always $O(dm/\Delta)$ in all three data sets. This is because on average we exactly sample one out of every Δ tuples, regardless of the data distribution.

Finally, we observe that while PWC_CountMin and PWC_AMS use almost the same space as the theoretical bound on Zipf_3 and ObjectID, they do exhibit an accelerated space drop in ClientID after $\Delta \geq 300$, and almost match the space usage of PLA. This phenomenon can be explained as follow. By the construction of PWC_CountMin and PWC_AMS, they do not record any value (or generate a PLA segment) for counters less than Δ. So on a "long tail" data distribution, the additional space usage for most counters will be 0 once Δ exceeds some threshold. Note that this does not make PWC_CountMin and PWC_AMS superior to Sample since (1) the space drop will hurt the quality of the approximation, which we shall see later; and (2) the space drop makes it very hard to get desired space by controlling Δ, unless we know the data distribution beforehand. On the other hand, in Sample, we can precisely control the space usage by adjusting the error parameter Δ.

6.3 Query accuracy

To evaluate the qualities of the approximation provided by the persistent sketches, we fix a historical window $(s, t]$ with $s = 0.2 * m$ and $t = 0.6 * m$, and measure the actual errors for various historical window queries with time interval $(s, t]$.

Point Query. We measure the absolute error between the estimators and the actual frequencies. More precisely, if f_i is the actual frequency and $\hat{f}_i$ is the estimator, then the absolute error of the approximation is equal to $\left|\hat{f}_i - f_i\right|$. We used the top 1000 most frequent elements in the time interval $(s, t]$ from each data sets, and queried about them with each sketch over $(s, t]$. We then took the average absolute error of the 1000 point queries. We constructed the persistent sketches for various values of Δ, and measured the average error for each Δ. Note that we do not evaluate point queries for Sample, since answering queries only involve 1 counter per row is not the strong point for Sample, as we suggested in Section 4.

Figure 4 shows how the average measured errors varies according to the error parameter Δ, and Figure 5 shows the tradeoffs between the measured error and the actual space usage, for each sketch on the 3 data sets. From Figure 5a and Figure 5c we observe that PLA provides a better accuracy-space tradeoffs on Zipf_3 and ObjectID. This is as expected, since PLA uses smaller space on these two data sets, and provides the same error guarantee as the baseline solution. Moreover, Figure 4a and Figure 4c suggest that on these two data sets, even for a fixed Δ, the measured error of PLA is smaller than that of PWC_CountMin and PWC_AMS. We conjecture that this is due to the fact that these two data sets exhibit more randomness than ClientID, which may reduce bias for a linear approximation.

From Figure 5b, we do not see a major difference between PLA and PWC_CountMin or PWC_AMS, with PLA and PWC_AMS performing slightly better. The main reason is that the sketch sizes of PWC_CountMin and PWC_AMS are also much smaller than $O(dm/\Delta)$ on ClientID, which offsets the space advantage of PLA. Meanwhile, Figure 4b suggests there is no significant difference PLA and PWC_CountMin or PWC_AMS in terms of actual error, as all the curves rise rapidly to 500. This is due to the fact that ClientID is a very uniform data set, so the frequencies are hard to approximate for any method.

Heavy Hitters. Recall that a historical window heavy hitters query with time interval $(s, t]$ should return elements with frequency $\geq \phi\|\mathbf{f}_{s,t}\|$. We set $\phi = 0.0002$, and issue a historical window heavy hitters query with $(s, t]$ on PLA and PWC_CountMin. The quality of heavy hitters query is evaluated by *precision* and *recall*, where precision is the fraction of heavy hitters returned by the sketch that are actual heavy hitters, and recall is the fraction of actual heavy hitters that are returned by the sketch.

Figure 6 shows how the space usage varies according to the error parameter Δ. These tradeoffs concur with Figure 3 as they are simply scaled by a factor $\log n$ according to the construction in Section 3. Figure 7 shows how the measured error varies according to the error parameter Δ, and Figure 8 shows the tradeoffs between the measured error and space usage. Note that we use log scale on the x-axes for both figures. We first observe that both PLA and PWC_CountMin achieve better precision than recall, which reveal that they tend to return a subset of real heavy hitters. Figure 7 shows that for a fixed Δ, PWC_CountMin provides a slightly better precision, while PLA provides a significantly better recall. For data sets Zipf_3 and ObjectID, Figure 8a and 8c show that the recall of PWC_CountMin quickly becomes unusable as the sketch size drops to 10^4, while PLA retains both a high recall and a high precision for smaller sketch size. Finally, Figure 8b suggests that there is no clear winner between PLA and PWC_CountMin on ClientID, which concurs with our observation in the point query experiments.

Self-Join Size Estimation. The quality of join size approximations has been evaluated by issuing a historical window self-join size query with the same time interval $(s, t]$ as above. We measured the relative error between the estimators and the actual self-join size. More precisely, let $I_{s,t}(\mathbf{f}, \mathbf{f})$ denote the actual self-join size, and $\hat{I}_{s,t}(\mathbf{f}, \mathbf{f})$ denote the estimator, then the relative error is equal to $\frac{|\hat{I}_{s,t}(\mathbf{f},\mathbf{f}) - I_{s,t}(\mathbf{f},\mathbf{f})|}{I_{s,t}(\mathbf{f},\mathbf{f})}$. We constructed the persistent sketches for various values of Δ, and issued self-join size queries with $(s, t]$ and computed the relative error. We repeated the process 10 times and took the average relative error.

Figure 9 shows how the measured error varies according to the error parameter Δ, and Figure 10 shows the tradeoffs between the measured error and the space usage, for self-join size queries on the 3 data sets. Note that we use log scale on the y-axes for Figure 9 and log scale on both axes for Figure 10. As expected, Sample gives better accuracy in general. However, the performance gap varies on different data sets. Figure 9c shows that on ObjectID, both Sample and PWC_AMS perform well for large sketch size ($\geq$ 50000). However, once the sketch size drops down to 1000 to 5000, the errors of Sample are 5 to 10 times smaller than that of PWC_CountMin or PWC_AMS on average. This translates to a gap of around 5 to 10 on the error-space tradeoff in Figure 10. For data set ClientID, Figure 10b shows that Sample provides significantly better error-space tradeoffs. For reasonable error range (0.0001 to 0.1), the space usage of Sample is 10 to 100 times smaller than that of PWC_AMS or PWC_CountMin. Figure 9b also suggests that the errors of PWC_CountMin and PWC_AMS grow rapidly to close to 1, for $\Delta \leq 1000$. This makes it difficult to choose Δ in practice. On the other hand, Sample provides a much less skewed tradeoffs between error and Δ, which enable us to achieve desired error-space tradeoff by manipulating Δ.

Figure 9a and Figure 10a indicate that on the synthetic data set Zipf_3, the advantage of Sample over the baseline solutions becomes less clear. The accuracy of Sample is 2-5 times better than that of PWC_AMS or PWC_CountMin on average for a fixed sketch size. This can be explained theoretically by observing that each update from the synthetic data set is independently generated,

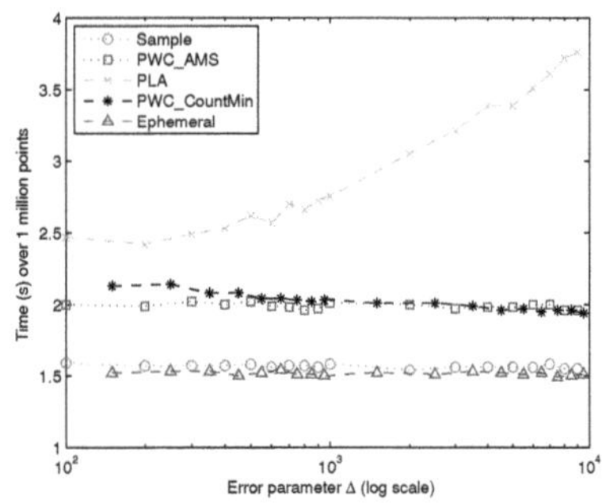

Figure 2: The processing time over 1 million updates

and thus the estimators provided by the baseline sketches can be viewed as a random sample without compensation.

6.4 Update time

Finally, Figure 2 shows the processing time over 1 million updates. We see that Sample is the fastest, followed up by PWC_CountMin and PWC_AMS. PLA has the highest update cost, which scales roughly with $\log \Delta$. However, all running times are within a small constant factor of the running time for ephemeral sketch, meaning that we do not pay a large time overhead in making the sketches persistent.

7. CONCLUSION

In this paper, we present sketching techniques that support historical window queries and historical queries, which give the Count-Min Sketch and the AMS Sketch the ability to do statistical tracking of the entire history, rather than just the current status. We have shown that our persistent sketches are theoretically sound by proving various space and error bounds. We also have evaluated the persistent sketches on synthetic and real-world data, showing that they provide satisfying performance in practice.

8. REFERENCES

[1] N. Alon, P. B. Gibbons, Y. Matias, and M. Szegedy. Tracking join and self-join sizes in limited storage. In *Proc. ACM Symposium on Principles of Database Systems*, pages 10–20, 1999.

[2] N. Alon, Y. Matias, and M. Szegedy. The space complexity of approximating the frequency moments. *Journal of Computer and System Sciences*, 58(1):137–147, 1999.

[3] A. Arasu and G. S. Manku. Approximate counts and quantiles over sliding windows. In *Proc. ACM Symposium on Principles of Database Systems*, pages 286–296, 2004.

[4] B. Babcock, S. Babu, M. Datar, R. Motwani, and J. Widom. Models and issues in data stream systems. In *Proc. ACM Symposium on Principles of Database Systems*, 2002.

[5] B. Becker, S. Gschwind, T. Ohler, B. Seeger, and P. Widmayer. An asymptotically optimal multiversion B-tree. *The VLDB Journal*, 5(4):264–275, 1996.

[6] V. Braverman, R. Ostrovsky, and C. Zaniolo. Optimal sampling from sliding windows. In *Proc. ACM Symposium on Principles of Database Systems*, pages 147–156, 2009.

[7] G. S. Brodal, S. Sioutas, K. Tsakalidis, and K. Tsichlas. Fully persistent B-trees. In *Proc. ACM-SIAM Symposium on Discrete Algorithms*, 2012.

[8] J. L. Carter and M. N. Wegman. Universal classes of hash functions. In *Proc. ACM Symposium on Theory of Computing*, pages 106–112, 1977.

[9] M. Charikar, K. Chen, and M. Farach-Colton. Finding frequent items in data streams. In *Proc. International Colloquium on Automata, Languages, and Programming*, pages 693–703. Springer, 2002.

[10] B. Chazelle and L. Guibas. Fractional cascading: I. A data structuring technique. *Algorithmica*, 1(1), 1986.

[11] G. Cormode and S. Muthukrishnan. An improved data stream summary: the count-min sketch and its applications. *Journal of Algorithms*, 55(1):58–75, 2005.

[12] G. Cormode and S. Muthukrishnan. What's hot and what's not: tracking most frequent items dynamically. *ACM Transactions on Database Systems*, 30(1):249–278, 2005.

[13] M. Datar, A. Gionis, P. Indyk, and R. Motwani. Maintaining stream statistics over sliding windows. *SIAM Journal on Computing*, 31(6):1794–1813, 2002.

[14] A. Dobra, M. Garofalakis, J. Gehrke, and R. Rastogi. Processing complex aggregate queries over data streams. In *Proc. ACM SIGMOD International Conference on Management of Data*, pages 61–72, 2002.

[15] J. R. Driscoll, N. Sarnak, D. D. Sleator, and R. Tarjan. Making data structures persistent. *Journal of Computer and System Sciences*, 38:86–124, 1989.

[16] A. C. Gilbert, Y. Kotidis, S. Muthukrishnan, and M. Strauss. Surfing wavelets on streams: One-pass summaries for approximate aggregate queries. In *Proc. International Conference on Very Large Data Bases*, volume 1, pages 79–88, 2001.

[17] S. Guha and A. McGregor. Stream order and order statistics: Quantile estimation in random-order streams. *SIAM Journal on Computing*, 38(5), 2009.

[18] D. Lomet, R. Barga, M. F. Mokbel, G. Shegalov, R. Wang, and Y. Zhu. Immortal DB: transaction time support for SQL server. In *Proc. ACM SIGMOD International Conference on Management of Data*, pages 939–941, 2005.

[19] D. Lomet and B. Salzberg. Access methods for multiversion data. In *Proc. ACM SIGMOD International Conference on Management of Data*, pages 315–324, 1989.

[20] D. B. Lomet and F. Li. Improving transaction-time dbms performance and functionality. In *Proc. IEEE International Conference on Data Engineering*, pages 581–591, 2009.

[21] A. Metwally, D. Agrawal, and A. E. Abbadi. An integrated efficient solution for computing frequent and top-k elements in data streams. *ACM Transactions on Database Systems*, 31(3):1095–1133, 2006.

[22] S. Muthukrishnan. *Data streams: algorithms and applications.* Foundations and trends in theoretical computer science. Now Publishers, 2005.

[23] L. Neumeyer, B. Robbins, A. Nair, and A. Kesari. S4: Distributed stream computing platform. In *Pro. IEEE International Conference on Data Mining Workshops*, pages 170–177, 2010.

[24] J. O'Rourke. An on-line algorithm for fitting straight lines between data ranges. *Communications of the ACM*, 24(9):574–578, 1981.

[25] C. Plattner, A. Wapf, and G. Alonso. Searching in time. In *Proc. ACM SIGMOD International Conference on Management of Data*, pages 754–756, 2006.

[26] F. Rusu and A. Dobra. Statistical analysis of sketch estimators. In *Proc. ACM SIGMOD International Conference on Management of Data*, pages 187–198, 2007.

[27] A. D. Sarma, M. Theobald, and J. Widom. Live: a lineage-supported versioned dbms. In *Scientific and Statistical Database Management*, pages 416–433. Springer, 2010.

[28] R. Shaull, L. Shrira, and H. Xu. Skippy: a new snapshot indexing method for time travel in the storage manager. In *Proc. ACM SIGMOD International Conference on Management of Data*, pages 637–648, 2008.

[29] L. Shrira and H. Xu. Snap: Efficient snapshots for back-in-time execution. In *Proc. IEEE International Conference on Data Engineering*, pages 434–445, 2005.

[30] Y. Tao, K. Yi, C. Sheng, J. Pei, and F. Li. Logging every footstep: Quantile summaries for the entire history. In *Proc. ACM SIGMOD International Conference on Management of Data*, pages 639–650, 2010.

[31] P. J. Varman and R. M. Verma. An efficient multiversion access structure. *IEEE Transactions on Knowledge and Data Engineering*, 9(3):391–409, 1997.

[32] M. Zaharia, T. Das, H. Li, T. Hunter, S. Shenker, and I. Stoica. Discretized streams: Fault-tolerant streaming computation at scale. In *Proc.ACM Symposium on Operating Systems Principles*, pages 423–438, 2013.

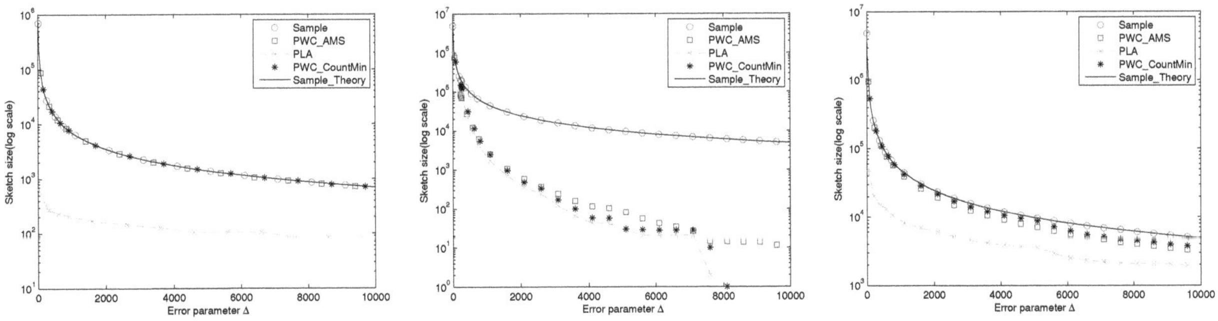

(a) Zipf_3 (b) ClientID (c) ObjectID

Figure 3: Tradeoffs between sketch size and error parameter Δ.

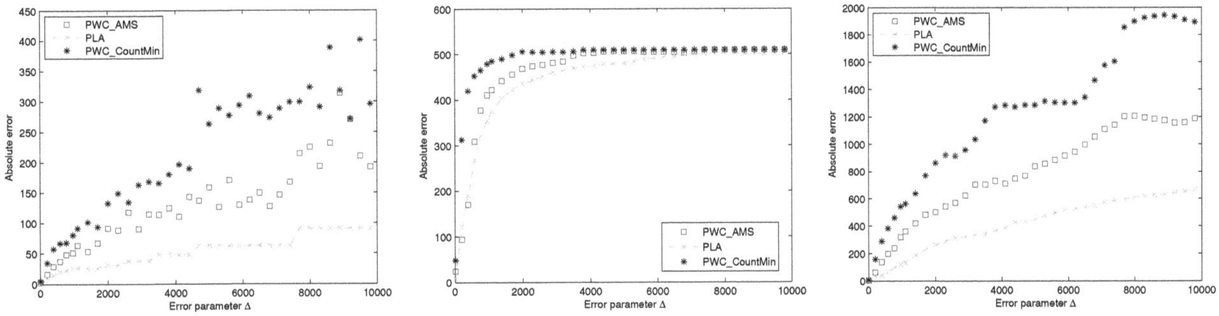

(a) Zipf_3 (b) ClientID (c) ObjectID

Figure 4: Tradeoffs between actual error and Δ for point queries.

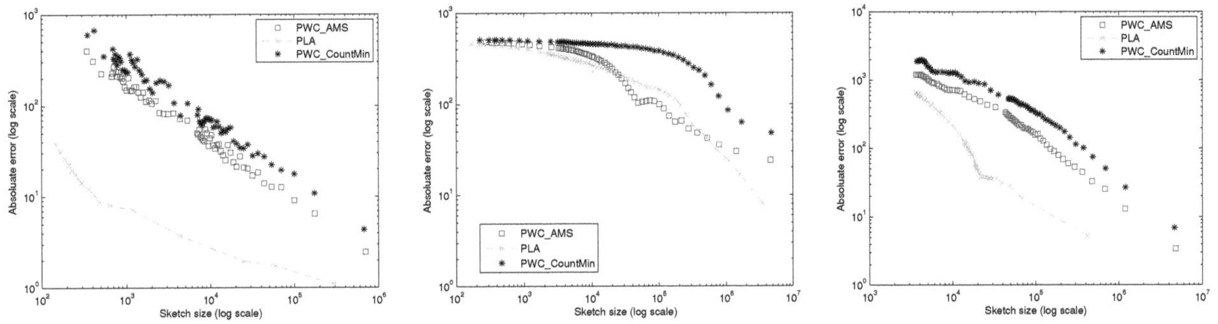

(a) Zipf_3 (b) ClientID (c) ObjectID

Figure 5: Tradeoffs between actual error and actual sketch size for point queries.

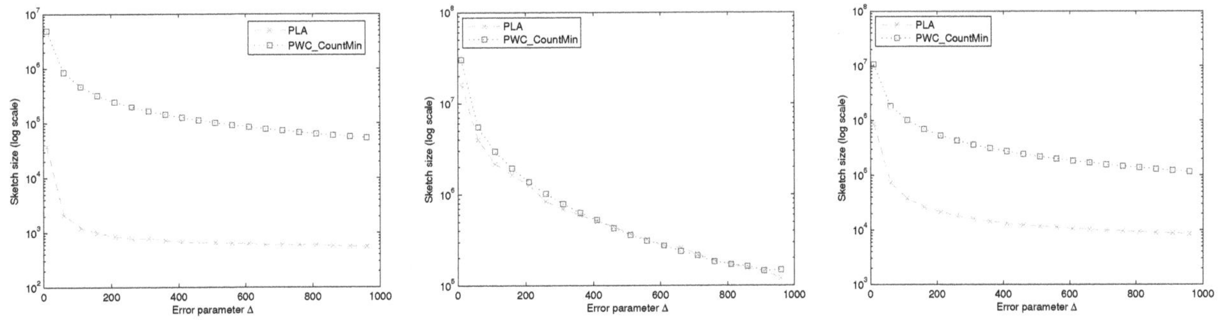

(a) Zipf_3 (b) ClientID (c) ObjectID

Figure 6: Tradeoffs between sketch size and Δ for heavy hitters queries.

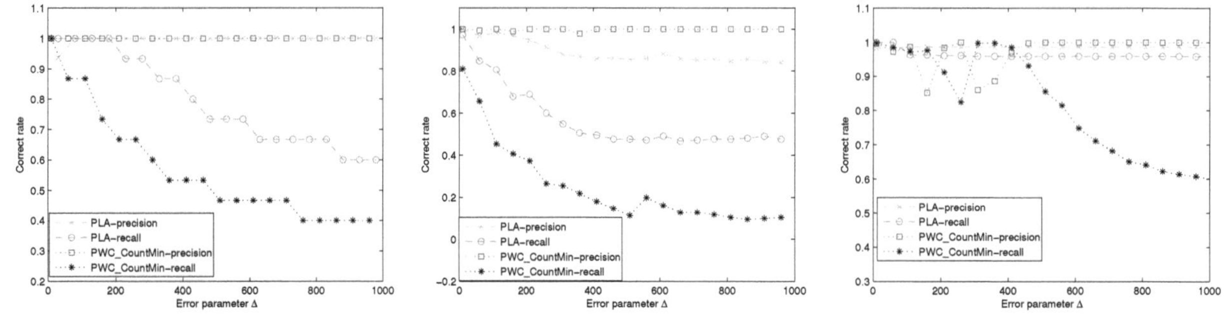

(a) Zipf_3 (b) ClientID (c) ObjectID

Figure 7: Tradeoffs between the precision and Δ for heavy hitters queries.

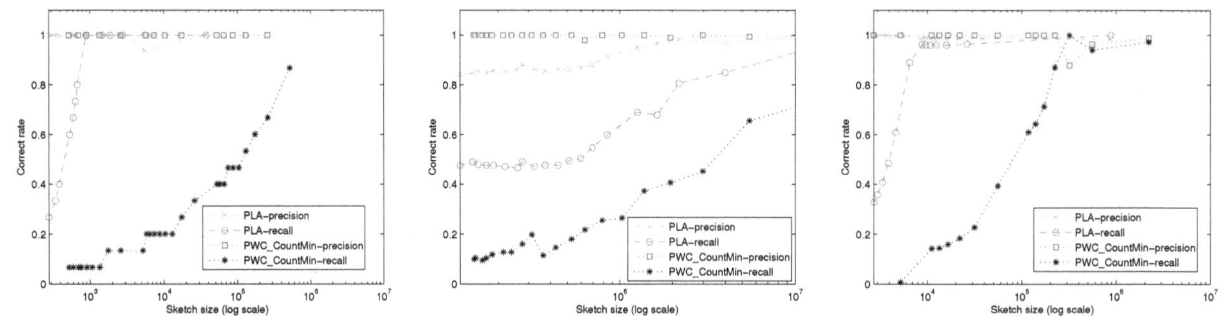

(a) Zipf_3 (b) ClientID (c) ObjectID

Figure 8: Tradeoffs between precision and actual sketch size for heavy hitters queries.

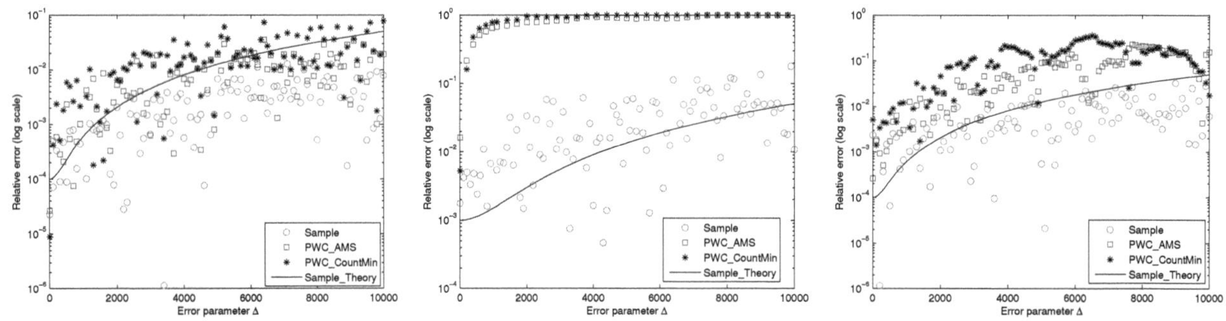

(a) Zipf_3 (b) ClientID (c) ObjectID

Figure 9: Tradeoffs between actual error and Δ for self-join size queries.

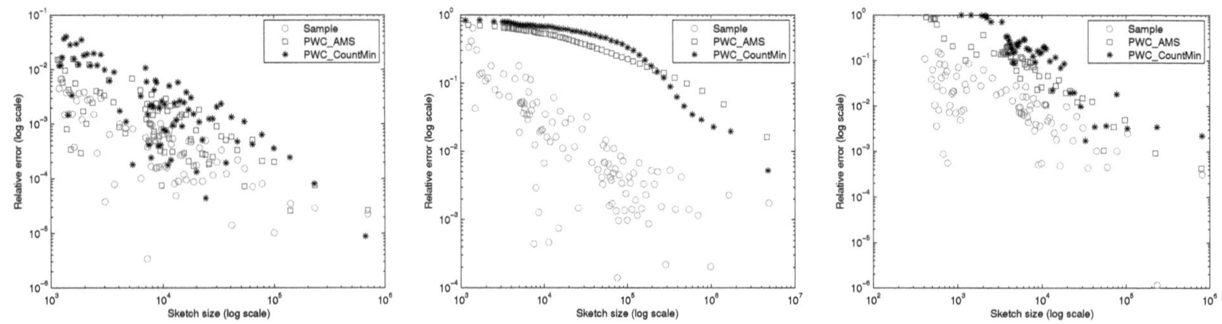

(a) Zipf_3 (b) ClientID (c) ObjectID

Figure 10: Tradeoffs between actual error and actual space for self-join size queries.

APPENDIX

A. DETAILED PROOFS

A.1 Proof of Theorem 3.1

PROOF. Consider a single row C. For the ease of presentation, we ignore the row index j and use $C[k]$ to denote the k-th counter. Let h denote the hash function. We define $C^l[k]$ to be the value of counter $C[k]$ at time l, and correspondingly $D^{s,t}[k] = C^t[k] - C^s[k]$ for $k \in [w]$. Since Count-Min Sketch is a linear sketch, $D^{s,t} = \{D^{s,t}[k] \mid k \in [w]\}$ is a Count-Min Sketch on stream $\mathbf{f}_{s,t}$. We call $D^{s,t}$ the *ephemeral Count-Min Sketch* on stream $\mathbf{f}_{s,t}$. By the property of the Count-Min Sketch, $D^{s,t}$ provides $D^{s,t}[h(i)]$ as an estimate for $f_i(s,t)$ such that

$$\Pr\left[\left|D^{s,t}[h(i)] - f_i(s,t)\right| \le \varepsilon \|\mathbf{f}_{s,t}\|_1\right] \ge 1/2.$$

Let $\hat{D}^{s,t}[h(i)]$ denote the estimator provided by the PLA generator for $D^{s,t}[h(i)]$, it follows that $\|\hat{D}^{s,t}[h(i)] - D^{s,t}[h(i)]\| \le 2\Delta$. Shrinking Δ by a factor of 2 follows that

$$\Pr\left[\left|\hat{D}^{s,t}[h(i)] - f_i(s,t)\right| \le \varepsilon \|\mathbf{f}_{s,t}\|_1 + \Delta\right] \ge 1/2.$$

Standard Chernoff bound shows that by taking the median of $O(\log \frac{1}{\delta})$ independent estimates, we can boost the successful probability to $1 - \delta$, and the Theorem follows. □

A.2 Proof of Theorem 3.2

PROOF. We note that we need to perform $\frac{2\log n}{\Phi}$ point queries to identify all heavy hitters at level 0. It is sufficient to prove all these point queries succeed with probability $1-\delta$. Since we set the depth of each sketch to be $d = \Theta(\log \frac{\log n}{\Phi\delta})$, a single query succeeds with probability $1 - \frac{\Phi\delta}{2\log n}$. By union bound, all $\frac{\log n}{\Phi\delta}$ queries succeed with probability $1 - \delta$, and the theorem follows. □

A.3 Proof of Theorem 3.3

Consider a single row in a persistent Count-Min Sketch. If we can prove that the expected total number of segments used by the piece-wise linear functions in this row is $O(\frac{m}{\Delta^2})$, the Theorem will follow. Consider a fixed counter, since each update is drawn independently from a probability distribution, we can assume that at each time instance, with probability p_1, p_2 and $1 - p_1 - p_2$, each update increases by 1, decreases by 1, and remains unchanged, respectively. Since at each time instance at most one of the counter will be updated, so the summation of p_1 and p_2 over all counters in this row is less or equal to 1. Thus it is sufficient to prove the expected number of segments used for this counter is $O(\frac{(p_1+p_2)m}{\Delta^2})$.

We use $v(t)$ to denote the value of the counter at time t. Let S denote the number of segments used by the PLA generator to cover all m data points, and H_i denote the number of data points covered by the i-th segment. Notice that S and H_i's are all random variables. Our goal is to prove $\mathrm{E}[S] \le \frac{2(p_1-p_2)m}{\Delta^2}$.

Random Walk and Escaping Time.

Consider the following random walk process: starting from the origin, at each timestamp a player moves 1 step forward with probability p_1, and move 1 step backward with probability p_2, and stays at current position with probability $1 - p_1 - p_2$. It is easy to see that the player will vibrate along the line $y = (p_1 - p_2)x$. Let τ denote the *escaping time*, that is, the first time the player escapes from the line $y = (p_1 - p_2)x$ by deviation Δ. It is easy to see that τ is the time before linear function $y = (p_1 - p_2)x$ fails to serve as a valid linear approximation, and thus is a lower bound on the number of points covered by a segment. To prove Theorem 3.3, we need the following lemma on the expectation and variance of τ.

LEMMA A.1. *For $\Delta > 10$, the escaping time τ satisfies $\mathrm{E}[\tau] = \Delta^2/\alpha$ and $\mathrm{Var}[\tau^2] \le 5\Delta^4/6\alpha^2$.*

Here α is defined as follow. Let $X_1, \ldots, X_m$ be m independently and identically distributed random variables. Each X_i takes value $1-(p_1-p_2)$ with probability p_1, $-1-(p_1-p_2)$ with probability p_2, and value $-(p_1-p_2)$ with probability $1 - p_1 - p_2$. Let $S_l = \sum_{i=1}^{k} X_i$, then S_k is the deviation from the line $y = (p_1 - p_2)x$ at time k. The random walk stops at time τ where $S_\tau = \Delta$ or $-\Delta$. We notice that $\mathrm{E}[X_i] = 0$. Let $\alpha = \mathrm{E}[X_i^2]$, $\beta = \mathrm{E}[X_i^3]$, $\gamma = \mathrm{E}[X_i^4]$ denote the second, third and fourth moments of X_i.

Martingales and Optional Stopping Theorem.

To prove Lemma A.1, we will make use of the fact that the escaping time τ is a type of stopping time on certain martingales. Formally, we define four martingale sequences.

LEMMA A.2. *For $k \in [m]$, the following four sequences are martingales: $Z_1 = \{S_k\}$, $Z_2 = \{S_k^2 - \alpha k\}$, $Z_3 = \{S_k^3 - 3\alpha k S_k - \beta k\}$, $Z_4 = \{S_k^4 - 6\alpha k S_k^2 - 4\beta k S_k + 3\alpha^2 k^2 + (3\alpha^2 - \gamma)k\}$.*

PROOF. We call Z_1, Z_2, Z_3 and Z_4 the first, second, third and fourth martingale sequence of S, respectively. To prove they are indeed martingales, we verify using the definition of martingale. More precisely, we will prove $E[Z_j[k] \mid Z_j[k-1]] = Z_j[k-1]$ for any k and $j \in [4]$.

For the first martingale list, we have $\mathrm{E}[Z_1[k] \mid Z_1[k-1]] = \mathrm{E}[S_k \mid S_{k-1}] = Z_1[k-1]$. For the second martingale list, we verify $\mathrm{E}[Z_2[k] \mid Z_2[k-1]] = Z_2[k-1]$ by

$$\mathrm{E}[S_k^2 - \alpha k \mid S_{k-1}] = S_{k-1}^2 + \alpha - \alpha k = S_{k-1}^2 - \alpha(k-1).$$

For the third martingale list, we verify $\mathrm{E}[Z_3[k] \mid Z_3[k-1]] = Z_3[k-1]$ as follow

$$\begin{aligned}\mathrm{E}[S_k^3 - 3\alpha k S_k - \beta k \mid S_{k-1}] &= S_{k-1}^3 + 3\alpha S_{k-1} + \beta - 3\alpha k S_{k-1} - \beta k \\ &= S_{k-1}^3 - 3\alpha(k-1)S_{k-1} - \beta(k-1).\end{aligned}$$

Finally, we verify $\mathrm{E}[Z_4[k] \mid Z_4[k-1]] = Z_2[k-1]$ as follow:

$$\begin{aligned}&\mathrm{E}[S_k^4 - 6\alpha k S_k^2 - 4\beta k S_k + 3\alpha^2 k^2 + (3\alpha^2 - \gamma)k \mid S_{k-1}] \\ &= S_{k-1}^4 - 6\alpha(k-1)S_{k-1}^2 - 4\beta(k-1)S_{k-1} + 3\alpha^2(k-1)^2 \\ &\quad + (3\alpha^2 - \gamma)(k-1).\end{aligned}$$

Thus the lemma follows. □

We also need the well-known *optional stopping theorem*:

LEMMA A.3 (OPTIONAL STOPPING THEOREM). *Let $Z[k]$ be a martingale and T be a stopping time with respect to a filter $(\mathcal{F}_k)$. Then $\mathrm{E}[Z[T]] = \mathrm{E}[Z[0]]$ provided: 1. $E[T] < \infty$; 2. $E[|Z[k] - Z[k-1]| \mid \mathcal{F}_k)] \le c$ for some c.*

It is easy to see that all four martingale sequences in Lemma A.2 have bounded stopping time expectations. We also note that the difference $|Z_i[k] - Z_i[k-1]|$ is bounded by $O(\Delta^4)$ for $i \in [4]$, so the optional stopping theorem applies to all four martingales.

PROOF OF LEMMA A.1. For the expectation of τ, we first notice that S_τ takes value from $\{\Delta, -\Delta\}$. Suppose $\Pr[S_\tau = \Delta] = p^*$, and $\Pr[S_\tau = -\Delta] = 1 - p^*$. Applying optional stopping theorem to the first martingale list $Z_1 = \{S_k\}$, we have $\mathrm{E}[S_\tau] =$

$\mathrm{E}[S_0] = 0$, which implies $p^* = 1/2$. Applying the optional stopping theorem to the second martingale list $Z_2 = \{S_k^2 - \alpha k\}$ follows that $\mathrm{E}[S_\tau^2 - \alpha\tau] = \mathrm{E}[S_0^2 - 0] = 0$. This implies

$$\mathrm{E}[\alpha\tau] = \mathrm{E}[S_\tau^2] = p^*\Delta^2 + (1-p^*)\Delta^2 = \Delta^2,$$

and thus we have $\mathrm{E}[\tau] = \Delta^2/\alpha$. This gives the expectation of τ.

To bound the variance of τ, we first compute $\mathrm{E}[\tau S_\tau]$ as an immediate step. Apply optional stopping theorem to the third martingale list $Z_3 = \{S_k^3 - 3\alpha k S_k - \beta k\}$, and we have $\mathrm{E}[S_\tau^3 - 3\alpha k S_\tau - \beta k] = \mathrm{E}[S_0^3 - 0 - 0] = 0$. It follows that

$$\mathrm{E}[3\alpha\tau S_\tau] = \mathrm{E}[S_\tau^3 - \beta\tau] = \mathrm{E}[S_\tau^3] + \beta\mathrm{E}[\tau] = \frac{\beta\Delta^2}{\alpha},$$

and thus $\mathrm{E}[\tau S_\tau] = \beta\Delta^2/3\alpha^2$. Finally, we consider the fourth matingale sequence $Z_4 = \{S_k^4 - 6\alpha k S_k^2 - 4\beta k S_k + 3\alpha^2 k^2 + (3\alpha^2 - \gamma)k\}$. By optional stopping theorem, we have

$$\mathrm{E}[S_\tau^4 - 6\alpha\tau S_\tau^2 - 4\beta\tau S_\tau + 3\alpha^2\tau^2 + (3\alpha^2 - \gamma)\tau] = 0. \quad (2)$$

Plugging $S_\tau^4 = \Delta^4$, $S_\tau^2 = \Delta^2$, $\mathrm{E}[\tau] = \Delta^2/\alpha$ and $\mathrm{E}[\tau S_\tau] = \beta\Delta^2/3\alpha^2$ in(2), it follows that

$$\begin{aligned}\mathrm{E}[3\alpha^2\tau^2] &= -\Delta^4 + 6\alpha\frac{\Delta^4}{\alpha} + \frac{4\beta^2\Delta^2}{3\alpha^2} - \frac{(3\alpha^2-\gamma)\Delta^2}{\alpha}\\ &= 5\Delta^4 + \left(\frac{4\beta^2}{3\alpha^2} - \frac{(3\alpha^2-\gamma)}{\alpha}\right)\Delta^2.\end{aligned}$$

Notice that since X_i takes value in $[-2,2]$, we have $\mathrm{E}[X_i^4] \le 2\left|\mathrm{E}[X_i^3]\right| \le 4\mathrm{E}[X_i^2]$, therefore $\gamma \le 2|\beta| \le 4\alpha$, so

$$\mathrm{E}[3\alpha^2\tau^2] \le 5\Delta^4 + (\frac{16}{3} + 4)\Delta^2 \le 5\Delta^4 + \frac{1}{6}\Delta^4 = \frac{11}{3}\Delta^2,$$

Here we use $\Delta^2 \ge 56$. This implies $\mathrm{E}[\tau^2] \le 11\Delta^4/6\alpha^2$, and thus

$$\mathrm{Var}[\tau] = \mathrm{E}[\tau^2] - \mathrm{E}[\tau]^2 = \frac{11\Delta^4}{6\alpha^2} - \frac{\Delta^4}{\alpha^2} = \frac{5\Delta^4}{6\alpha^2}.$$

This completes the proof of Lemma A.1. □

Bernoulli Trials and Negative Binomial distribution.

Withe the help of Lemma A.1, we are able to prove Theorem 3.3.

PROOF OF THEOREM 3.3. By Lemma A.1, we can bound the probability of τ being too small using Chebyshev's inequality:

$$\Pr\left[\tau \le \frac{\Delta^2}{12\alpha}\right] = \Pr\left[\tau - \frac{\Delta^2}{\alpha} \le -\frac{11\Delta^2}{12\alpha}\right] \le 120/121.$$

It follows $\Pr[\tau \ge \Delta^2/12\alpha] \ge 1/121$. Combining with $\alpha = \mathrm{E}[X_i^2] \le p_1 + p_2$, we have

$$\Pr[\tau \ge \frac{\Delta^2}{12(p_1+p_2)}] \ge \frac{1}{121}, \quad (3)$$

for any $1 \le i \le S$.

We notice that the H_i's, the number of points covered by each segment, are identically and independently distributed (i.i.d.). Equation (3) implies that each H_i covers at least $\frac{\Delta^2}{12(p_1+p_2)}$ points with some constant probability $c = 1/121$. We work with the worst case where H_i covers exactly $\frac{\Delta^2}{12(p_1+p_2)}$ points with probability d, and 0 points with probability $1-c$. Note that this modification will not reduce the expected number of segments $\mathrm{E}[S]$. We consider a sequence of independent Bernoulli trials, in which the i-th trial succeeds if H_i covers exactly $\frac{\Delta^2}{12(p_1+p_2)}$ points , and fails if H_i covers 0 points. Observe that if we have $\frac{12(p_1+p_2)m}{\Delta^2}$ successful trials, all m points will be covered. Therefore, S is the number of trials until we see $\frac{12(p_1+p_2)m}{\Delta^2}$ successful trials. This immediate implies that the number of fail trials, denoted $S - \frac{12(p_1+p_2)m}{\Delta^2}$, follows the *negative binomial distribution* with successful trial number $\frac{12(p_1+p_2)m}{\Delta^2}$ and probability c, and thus has expectation equals to $\frac{12c(p_1+p_2)m}{(1-c)\Delta^2}$. This proves that $\mathrm{E}[S] = O(\frac{(p_1+p_2)m}{\Delta^2})$, and Theorem 3.3 follows. □

A.4 Proof of Theorem 4.1

Consider one row of counters. To simplify notation, we omit the row index j and use $C[k][b]$ to denote the counters in this row, and use h to denote the hash function for that row. For any $k \in [w]$, let $C^l[k][b]$ be the value of counter $C[k][b]$ at time l. We further define $D^l[k] = C^l[k][1] - C^l[k][0]$. By the construction of the persistent AMS Sketch, $D^l[k]$ is the value of the corresponding counter in the ephemeral sketch at time l. By the linearity of the AMS Sketch, $D^{s,t}[k] = D^t[k] - D^s[k]$ is the value of the counter if we built an AMS Sketch on $\mathbf{f}_{s,t}$.

Unbiasedness of the Estimator.

We first show that $\hat{D}^{s,t}[k]$ is an unbiased estimator of $D^{s,t}[k]$ with a bounded variance. Define $x_k = \hat{D}^{s,t}[k] - D^{s,t}[k]$ to be the deviation between our estimate from the persistent sketch from the counter value in the AMS Sketch built on $\mathbf{f}_{s,t}$.

LEMMA A.4. *For any $k \in [w]$, $E[x_k] = 0$ and $\mathrm{E}[x_k^2] \le 24\Delta^2$.*

For any time r, define $X^r[k] = \hat{C}^r[k][1] - C^r[k][1]$ and $Y^r[k] = \hat{C}^r[k][0] - C^r[k][0]$. Recall $x_i = \hat{D}^{s,t}[k] - D^{s,t}[k]$ is the deviation between the final estimator and ephemeral estimator. It follows that

$$\begin{aligned}\hat{D}^t[k] &= \hat{C}^t[k][1] - \hat{C}^t[k][0] = C^t[k][1] + X^t[k] - (C^t[k][0] + Y^t[k])\\ &= D^t[k] + X^t[k] - Y^t[k].\end{aligned}$$

Similarly , we have $\hat{D}^s[k] = D^s[k] + X^s[k] - Y^s[k]$ for s. Thus

$$\begin{aligned}x_i &= \hat{D}^{s,t}[k] - D^{s,t}[k] = \left(\hat{D}^t[k] - \hat{D}^s[k]\right) - \left(D^t[k] - D^s[k]\right)\\ &= \left(\hat{D}^t[k] - D^t[k]\right) - \left(\hat{D}^s[k] - D^s[k]\right)\\ &= X^t[k] - Y^t[k] - (X^s[k] - Y^s[k]). \quad (4)\end{aligned}$$

Set $p = 1/\Delta$, we have the following lemma that bounds the expectation and variance of $X^r[k]$ and $Y^r[k]$:

LEMMA A.5. *For any time instances $r, q \in [m]$ and $i \in [4w]$, $X^r[k]$ and $Y^q[k]$ are independent, and satisfy (1) $E[X^r[k]] = E[Y^q[k]] = 0$; (2) $\mathrm{E}[X^r[k]^2] \le 1/p^2$ and $\mathrm{E}[Y^q[k]^2] \le 1/p^2$.*

PROOF. Since $\bar{C}^r[k][1]$ and $\bar{C}^r[k][0]$ are independently sampled, it is easy to verify that $X^r[k]$ and $Y^r[k]$ are independent.

By the definitions of $X^r[k]$ and $\hat{C}^r[k][1]$, we have

$$X^r[k] = \begin{cases}\bar{C}^r[k][1] - C^r[k][1] - 1 + \frac{1}{p}, & 0 < \bar{C}^r[k][1] \le C^r[k][1];\\ \bar{C}^r[k][1] - C^r[k][1], & \bar{C}^r[k][1] = 0.\end{cases} \quad (5)$$

Recall that $\bar{C}^r[k][1]$ is the last sampled predecessor of $C^r[k][1]$, and here we set $\bar{C}^r[k][1] = 0$ is there is no such predecessor $L[j][h_j(i)][1]$. If we review the sample process backwards from $C^r[k][1]$ to $\bar{C}^r[k][1]$, then $\bar{C}^r[k][1]$ is the first successful trial as we keep flipping a coin with success probability p, with $C^r[k][1]$ being the upper bound of the number of trials. It follows that

$$\Pr[\bar{C}^r[k] = C^r[k][1] - l] = \begin{cases}(1-p)^l p, & \text{for } 0 \le l < C^r[k][1];\\ (1-p)^{C^r[k][1]}, & \text{for } l = C^r[k][1].\end{cases} \quad (6)$$

Combing (5) and (6), we have

$$\Pr\left[X^r[k] = \frac{1}{p} - l - 1\right] = \begin{cases}(1-p)^l p, & 0 \le l < C^r[k][1];\\ (1-p)^{C^r[k][1]}, & l = C^r[k][1] + 1 + \frac{1}{p}.\end{cases}$$

We can compute the expectation of $X^r[k][1]$ as follows:

$$\begin{aligned}\mathrm{E}[X^r[k]] &= \sum_{l=0}^{C^r[k][1]-1}(-l-1+\frac{1}{p})(1-p)^l p - C^r[k][1](1-p)^{C^r[k][1]}\\ &= C^r[k][1](1-p)^{C^r[k][1]} - C^r[k][1](1-p)^{C^r[k][1]} = 0.\end{aligned}$$

We can bound the expectation of $X^r[k]^2$ as follow:

$$\begin{aligned}\mathrm{E}[X^r[k]^2] &= \sum_{l=1}^{C^r[k][1]}(-l+\frac{1}{p})^2(1-p)^{l-1}p + C^r[k][1]^2(1-p)^{C^r[k][1]}\\ &= \frac{(1-p)(1-(1-p)^{C^r[k][1]})}{p^2} \le \frac{1}{p^2}.\end{aligned}$$

The same analysis holds for $Y^q[k]$, and thus the lemma follows. □

Now we are ready to prove Lemma A.4.

PROOF OF LEMMA A.4. By equation (4), we have

$$\begin{aligned}\mathrm{E}[x_k] &= \mathrm{E}\left[X^t[k] - Y^t[k] - (X^s[k] - Y^s[k])\right]\\ &= \mathrm{E}[X^t[k]] - \mathrm{E}[Y^t[k]] - (\mathrm{E}[X^s[k]] - \mathrm{E}[Y^s[k]]) = 0.\end{aligned}$$

For the second moment x_k^2, we have

$$\begin{aligned}\mathrm{E}[x_k^2] &= \mathrm{E}\left[\left(X^t[k] - Y^t[k] - (X^s[k] - Y^s[k])\right)^2\right]\\ &= \mathrm{E}[X^t[k]^2] + \mathrm{E}[Y^t[k]^2] + \mathrm{E}[X^s[k]^2] + \mathrm{E}[Y^s[k]^2]\\ &\quad - 2\mathrm{E}[X^t[k]X^s[k]] - 2\mathrm{E}[Y^t[k]Y^s[k]]. \qquad (7)\end{aligned}$$

The second equation follows by the fact that any cross term of form $X^t[k]Y^t[k]$, $X^t[k]Y^s[k]$, $X^s[k]Y^t[k]$, and $X^s[k]Y^s[k]$ are products of two independent and unbiased random variables, and thus have 0 expectation. By Lemma A.4, we can upper bound the expectation of each square term with $\frac{1}{p^2}$. We also notice that the expectation of a cross term $-2\mathrm{E}[X^t[k]X^s[k]]$ satisfies

$$-2\mathrm{E}[X^t[k]X^s[k]] \le \left(\mathrm{E}[X^t[k]^2] + \mathrm{E}[X^s[k]^2]\right) \le \frac{2}{p^2},$$

Similarly, we have $-2\mathrm{E}[Y^t[k]Y^s[k]] \le \frac{2}{p^2}$. Plugging into (7) follows that $\mathrm{E}[x_k^2] \le \frac{4}{p^2} + \frac{2}{p^2} + \frac{2}{p^2} = \frac{8}{p^2}$. □

Proof of Theorem 4.1.

PROOF. The following lemma follows from the key properties of the AMS Sketch.

LEMMA A.6 ([9]). *For any $j \in [d]$,*

1. $\mathrm{E}[\xi(i)\cdot D^{s,t}[h(i)]] = f_i(s,t)$ *and* $\mathrm{Var}[\xi(i)\cdot D^{s,t}[h(i)]] \le \varepsilon^2\|\mathbf{f}_{s,t}\|_2^2$;
2. $\mathrm{E}\left[\sum_{k=1}^{w} D_{\mathbf{f}}^{s,t}[k]^2\right] = \|\mathbf{f}_{s,t}\|_2^2$ *and* $\mathrm{E}[\sum_{k=1}^{w} D_{\mathbf{f}}^{s,t}[k]D_{\mathbf{g}}^{s,t}[k]] = I(\mathbf{f}_{s,t}, \mathbf{g}_{s,t})$;
3. $\mathrm{Var}\left[\sum_{k=1}^{w} D_{\mathbf{f}}^{s,t}[k]D_{\mathbf{g}}^{s,t}[k]\right] \le \frac{1}{w}\|\mathbf{f}_{s,t}\|_2\|\mathbf{g}_{s,t}\|_2$.

The space bound follows by the fact that we sample each of the m updates with probability $p = \Theta(1/\Delta)$ in a row, and thus the expected number of samples is $O(\frac{m}{\Delta})$.

Now we turn to the error bound. For a single row C with hash function h, recall that the persistent AMS Sketch uses $\xi(i)\cdot\hat{D}^{s,t}[h(i)]$ as an estimator for $f_i(s,t)$. Thus

$$\mathrm{E}[\xi(i)\hat{D}^{s,t}[h(i)]] = \mathrm{E}\left[\xi(i)D^{s,t}[h(i)] + \xi(i)x_{h(i)}\right] = f_i(s,t).$$

The last equation follows from $\mathrm{E}[D^{s,t}[h(i)]] = f_i(s,t)$ by Lemma A.6, and $\mathrm{E}[x_{h(i)}] = 0$ by Lemma A.4. To utilize Chebyshev's inequality, we consider the variance of $\xi(i)\cdot\hat{D}^{s,t}[h(i)]$:

$$\mathrm{Var}[\xi(i)\cdot\hat{D}^{s,t}[h(i)]] = \mathrm{Var}\left[D^{s,t}[h(i)] + x_{h(i)}\right].$$

Since $D^{s,t}[h(i)]$ and $x_{h(i)}$ are independent, we have

$$\mathrm{Var}[\xi\cdot\hat{D}^{s,t}[h(i)]] = \mathrm{Var}\left[D^{s,t}[h(i)]\right] + \mathrm{Var}\left[x_{h(i)}\right],$$

We know that $\mathrm{Var}[D^{s,t}[h(i)]] \le \varepsilon^2\|\mathbf{f}_{s,t}\|_2^2$ by Lemma A.6, and $\mathrm{Var}[x_{h(i)}] \le \mathrm{E}[x_{h(i)}^2] \le 8\Delta^2$ by Lemma A.4, it follows that

$$\mathrm{Var}[\xi\cdot\hat{D}^{s,t}[h(i)]] \le \varepsilon^2\|\mathbf{f}_{s,t}\|_2^2 + 8\Delta^2 \le 8\cdot(\varepsilon\|\mathbf{f}_{s,t}\|_2 + \Delta)^2.$$

By Chebyshev's inequality, we have

$$\Pr[|D^{s,t}[h(i)] - f^{s,t}(i)| \ge 4(\varepsilon\|\mathbf{f}_{s,t}\|_2 + \Delta)] \le \frac{1}{2}.$$

Since the final estimator $\hat{f}_i(s,t)$ is the median of $d = O(\log\frac{1}{\delta})$ independent copies of $D^{s,t}[h(i)]$, standard chernoff bound implies

$$\Pr\left[\left|\hat{f}_i(s,t) - f_i(s,t)\right| \ge 4(\varepsilon\|\mathbf{f}_{s,t}\|_2 + \Delta)\right] \ge 1-\delta.$$

Scaling down ε and Δ by a constant factor, Theorem 4.1 follows. □

A.5 Proof of Theorem 4.2

With the help of Lemma A.6 and Lemma A.4, we compute the expectations and variances of our estimators, and then use Chebyshev's inequality to bound the error probability.

Consider a single row from each sketch. Let $C_{\mathbf{f}}$ and $C_{\mathbf{g}}$ denote the rows, respectively, and h denote the common hash function used by the two rows. We assume the two rows use sample probabilities $p_{\mathbf{f}} = 3/\Delta_{\mathbf{f}}$ and $p_{\mathbf{g}} = 3/\Delta_{\mathbf{g}}$, respectively. Given a window join size query with time range $[s,t]$, recall that we extract $\hat{D}_{\mathbf{f}}^{s,t}[k] = D_{\mathbf{f}}^{s,t}[k] + x_k$ from $C_{\mathbf{f}}$ and $\hat{D}_{\mathbf{g}}^{s,t}[k] = D_{\mathbf{g}}^{s,t}[k] + y_k$ from $C_{\mathbf{g}}$ for all $k \in [w]$, and use

$$\sum_{k=1}^{w}\hat{D}_{\mathbf{f}}^{s,t}[k]\hat{D}_{\mathbf{g}}^{s,t}[k] = \sum_{k=1}^{w}(D_{\mathbf{f}}^{s,t}[k] + x_k)(D_{\mathbf{g}}^{s,t}[k] + y_k).$$

to estimate $I(\mathbf{f}_t, \mathbf{g}_t)$. Lemma A.4 gives a probabilistic bound on x_k and y_k. We also note x_k and y_k are independent. To simplify the representation, we define *singular cross term* to be a term with one of the following forms: (1) $x_k\cdot r(x_{i_1}, y_{i_2}, D_{\mathbf{f}}^{s,t}[i_3], D_{\mathbf{g}}^{s,t}[i_4])$, for $i \ne i_1$; (2) $y_k\cdot r(x_{i_1}, y_{i_2}, D_{\mathbf{f}}^{s,t}[i_3], D_{\mathbf{g}}^{s,t}[i_4])$, for $i \ne i_2$. Here r denotes an arbitrary function. We claim that all singular cross terms are unbiased.

LEMMA A.7. *The expectation of a singular cross term is* 0.

PROOF. Without loss of generality, assume the singular term $T = x_k r(x_{i_1}, y_{i_2}, D_{\mathbf{f}}^{s,t}[i_3], D_{\mathbf{g}}^{s,t}[i_4])$ where $i \ne i_1$. Observe that x_k is unbiased and independent from x_{i_1}, y_{i_2}, $D_{\mathbf{f}}^{s,t}[i_3]$ and $D_{\mathbf{g}}^{s,t}[i_4]$, so we have

$$\mathrm{E}[T] = \mathrm{E}[x_k]\,\mathrm{E}\left[r(x_{i_1}, y_{i_2}, D_{\mathbf{f}}^{s,t}[i_3], D_{\mathbf{g}}^{s,t}[i_4])\right] = 0,$$

and the lemma follows. □

PROOF OF THEOREM 4.2. Now we can compute the expectation of the estimation.

$$\mathrm{E}\left[\sum_{k=1}^{w} \hat{D}_{\mathbf{f}}^{s,t}[k]\hat{D}_{\mathbf{g}}^{s,t}[k]\right] = \mathrm{E}\left[\sum_{k=1}^{w} D_{\mathbf{f}}^{s,t}[k]D_{\mathbf{g}}^{s,t}[k]\right] + \sum_{k=1}^{w}\mathrm{E}\left[x_k D_{\mathbf{g}}^{s,t}[k]\right] + \sum_{k=1}^{w} E\left[y_k D_{\mathbf{f}}^{s,t}[i]\right] + \sum_{k=1}^{w}\mathrm{E}\left[x_k y_k\right].$$

By Lemma A.6, the first term $\mathrm{E}\left[\sum_{k=1}^{w} D_{\mathbf{f}}^{s,t}[k]D_{\mathbf{g}}^{s,t}[k]\right] = I(\mathbf{f}_{s,t}, \mathbf{g}_{s,t})$. We also observe that the rest terms are summations of singular cross terms, and thus have expectations 0. It follows that

$$E[\hat{I}(\mathbf{f}_{s,t}, \mathbf{g}_{s,t})] = \mathrm{E}\left[\sum_{k=1}^{w} D_{\mathbf{f}}^{s,t}[k]D_{\mathbf{g}}^{s,t}[k]\right] = I(\mathbf{f}_{s,t}, \mathbf{g}_{s,t}).$$

This proves the unbiasedness of our estimator.

We now bound the variance of our estimation.

$$\mathrm{Var}\left[\hat{I}(\mathbf{f}_{s,t}, \mathbf{g}_{s,t})\right] = \mathrm{E}\left[\hat{I}(\mathbf{f}_{s,t}, \mathbf{g}_{s,t})^2\right] - \mathrm{E}\left[\hat{I}(\mathbf{f}_{s,t}, \mathbf{g}_{s,t})\right]^2. \tag{8}$$

Note that $\mathrm{E}[(\sum_{k=1}^{w} \hat{D}_{\mathbf{f}}^{s,t}[k]\hat{D}_{\mathbf{g}}^{s,t}[k])^2]$ can be expanded as

$$\mathrm{E}\left[\hat{I}(\mathbf{f}_{s,t}, \mathbf{g}_{s,t})^2\right] = \mathrm{E}\left[\left(\sum_{k=1}^{w}(D_{\mathbf{f}}^{s,t}[k] + x_k)(D_{\mathbf{g}}^{s,t}[k] + y_k)\right)^2\right]$$

$$= \mathrm{E}\left[\left(\sum_{k=1}^{w}\left(D_{\mathbf{f}}^{s,t}[k]D_{\mathbf{g}}^{s,t}[k] + x_k D_{\mathbf{g}}^{s,t}[k] + y_k D_{\mathbf{f}}^{s,t}[k] + x_k y_k\right)\right)^2\right].$$

Note that the right hand of above equation can be expanded as sum of square terms and cross terms. We observe that any cross term that contains x_k or y_k, for $k \in [w]$, is a singular cross terms. It follows that

$$\mathrm{E}\left[\hat{I}(\mathbf{f}_{s,t}, \mathbf{g}_{s,t})^2\right] = \mathrm{E}\left[\left(\sum_{k=1}^{w} D_{\mathbf{f}}^{s,t}[k]D_{\mathbf{g}}^{s,t}[k]\right)^2\right] + E\left[\sum_{k=1}^{w} x_k^2 D_{\mathbf{g}}^{s,t}[k]^2\right] + E\left[\sum_{k=1}^{w} y_k^2 D_{\mathbf{f}}^{s,t}[k]^2\right] + E\left[\sum_{k=1}^{w} x_k^2 y_k^2\right]. \tag{9}$$

Using the fact that $\mathrm{E}[x_k^2] \le 8/p_{\mathbf{f}}^2 \le \Delta_{\mathbf{f}}^2$ from Lemma A.4, and $\mathrm{E}[\sum_{k=1}^{w} D_{\mathbf{g}}^{s,t}[k]^2] = \|\mathbf{g}_{s,t}\|_2^2$ from Lemma A.6, and the fact that x_k^2 and $D_{\mathbf{g}}^{s,t}[k]^2$ are independent, we can bound the second term in (9) as follow:

$$\mathrm{E}\left[\sum_{k=1}^{w} x_k^2 D_{\mathbf{g}}^{s,t}[k]^2\right] \le \Delta_{\mathbf{f}}^2 \mathrm{E}\left[\sum_{k=1}^{w} D_{\mathbf{g}}^{s,t}[k]^2\right] \le \Delta_{\mathbf{f}}^2 \|\mathbf{g}_{s,t}\|_2^2. \tag{10}$$

Similarly, we have the following inequality for the third term in (9):

$$\mathrm{E}\left[\sum_{k=1}^{w} y_k^2 D_{\mathbf{f}}^{s,t}[k]^2\right] \le \Delta_{\mathbf{g}}^2 \|\mathbf{f}_{s,t}\|_2^2. \tag{11}$$

Using $\mathrm{E}[x_k^2] \le 8/p_{\mathbf{f}}^2 \le \Delta_{\mathbf{f}}^2$ and Using $\mathrm{E}[y_k^2] \le 8/p_{\mathbf{g}}^2 \le \Delta_{\mathbf{g}}^2$ from Lemma A.4 and the fact that x_k^2 and y_k^2 are independent, we have

$$E\left[\sum_{k=1}^{w} x_k^2 y_k^2\right] = \sum_{k=1}^{w} E\left[x_k^2 y_k^2\right] \le \sum_{k=1}^{w} \Delta_{\mathbf{f}}^2 \cdot \Delta_{\mathbf{g}}^2 = w\Delta_{\mathbf{f}}^2\Delta_{\mathbf{g}}^2. \tag{12}$$

Finally, by Lemma A.6, it follows that

$$\mathrm{E}\left[(\sum_{k=1}^{w} D_{\mathbf{f}}^{s,t}[k]D_{\mathbf{g}}^{s,t}[k])^2\right] - \mathrm{E}\left[\sum_{k=1}^{w} D_{\mathbf{f}}^{s,t}[k]D_{\mathbf{g}}^{s,t}[k]^2\right]$$

$$= \mathrm{Var}[\sum_{k=1}^{w} D_{\mathbf{f}}^{s,t}[k]D_{\mathbf{g}}^{s,t}[k])^2] \le \frac{1}{w}\|\mathbf{f}_t\|_2\|\mathbf{g}_t\|_2. \tag{13}$$

Plugging (10), (11), (12) and (13) into (8) follows that

$$\mathrm{Var}[\hat{I}(\mathbf{f}_t, \mathbf{g}_t)] \le \frac{1}{w}\|\mathbf{f}_t\|_2^2\|\mathbf{g}_t\|_2^2 + \Delta_{\mathbf{f}}^2\|\mathbf{g}\|_2^2 + \Delta_{\mathbf{g}}^2\|\mathbf{f}\|_2^2 + w\Delta_{\mathbf{f}}^2\Delta_{\mathbf{g}}^2$$
$$\le \frac{1}{w}\left(\|\mathbf{f}_t\|_2^2 + w\Delta_{\mathbf{f}}^2\right)\left(\|\mathbf{g}\|_2^2 + w\Delta_{\mathbf{g}}^2\right).$$

Using Chebyshev's inequality, it follows that

$$\Pr\left[\left|\hat{I}(\mathbf{f}_t, \mathbf{g}_t) - I(\mathbf{f}_t, \mathbf{g}_t)\right| \ge 2\sqrt{\frac{1}{w}\left(\|\mathbf{f}_t\|_2^2 + w\Delta_{\mathbf{f}}^2\right)\left(\|\mathbf{g}\|_2^2 + w\Delta_{\mathbf{g}}^2\right)}\right]$$

$$\le \mathrm{Var}[\hat{I}(\mathbf{f}_t, \mathbf{g}_t)]\Big/4\left(\frac{1}{w}\left(\|\mathbf{f}_t\|_2^2 + w\Delta_{\mathbf{f}}^2\right)\left(\|\mathbf{g}\|_2^2 + w\Delta_{\mathbf{g}}^2\right)\right) \le 1/4.$$

By setting $w \ge 4/\varepsilon^2$, we have

$$\Pr\left[\left|\hat{I}(\mathbf{f}_{s,t}, \mathbf{g}_{s,t}) - I(\mathbf{f}_{s,t}, \mathbf{g}_{s,t})\right| \le \mathcal{E}\right] \le 1/4,$$

where $\mathcal{E} = \varepsilon\sqrt{\left(\|\mathbf{f}_t\|_2^2 + (\frac{\Delta_{\mathbf{f}}}{\varepsilon})^2\right)\left(\|\mathbf{g}\|_2^2 + (\frac{\Delta_{\mathbf{g}}}{\varepsilon})^2\right)}$. Finally, recall that we have $d = O(\log 1/\delta)$ estimators $\hat{I}_j(\mathbf{f}_t, \mathbf{g}_t)$ for $j = 1, \ldots, d$, and we take the median $\hat{I}(\mathbf{f}_t, \mathbf{g}_t) = \mathrm{median}_{j\in[d]}\{\hat{I}_j(\mathbf{f}_t, \mathbf{g}_t)\}$ as the final estimator. By standard Chernoff bound, we have

$$\Pr\left[\left|\hat{I}(\mathbf{f}_t, \mathbf{g}_t) - I(\mathbf{f}_t, \mathbf{g}_t)\right| \ge \mathcal{E}\right] \ge 1 - \delta.$$

This complete the proof of Theorem 4.2. □

A.6 Proof of Theorem 5.3

PROOF. By the proof of Theorem 3.3, the number of segment for a single row in epoch $[t_{i-1}, t_i)$ is $O(\frac{t_i - t_{i-1}}{\Delta_{t_{i-1}}^2})$,thus the total size of the historical lists for this row is $O(\sum_{k=1}^{s} \frac{t_i - t_{i-1}}{\Delta_{t_{i-1}}^2})$. Since $\varepsilon\|\mathbf{f}_t\|_1 = \Theta(\Delta_{t_{i-1}})$ for $t_{i-1} \le t < t_i$, for $k = 1, \ldots, s$. It follows that the total size of the historical lists for this row is

$$O\left(\sum_{k=1}^{s} \frac{t_i - t_{i-1}}{\Delta_{t_{i-1}}^2}\right) = O\left(\sum_{k=1}^{s}\sum_{j=t_{i-1}}^{t_i - 1} \frac{1}{\Delta_{t_{i-1}}^2}\right) = O\left(\sum_{k=1}^{m} \frac{1}{\varepsilon^2\|\mathbf{f}_t\|_1^2}\right).$$

In the random streaming model, we have $\|\mathbf{f}_t\|_1^2 = t^2$, and thus the number of segments becomes $O\left(\sum_{k=1}^{m} \frac{1}{\varepsilon^2 t^2}\right) = O(1/\varepsilon^2)$. Summing up all $d = O(\log \frac{1}{\delta})$ rows, and the Theorem follows. □

A.7 Proof of Theorem 5.6

PROOF. By the proof of Theorem 4.1, the size of the historical lists for this row in epoch $[t_{i-1}, t_i)$ is $O(\frac{t_i - t_{i-1}}{\Delta_{t_{i-1}}})$, thus the total size of the historical lists for this row is $O(\sum_{k=1}^{s} \frac{t_i - t_{i-1}}{\Delta_{t_{i-1}}})$. Since $\varepsilon\|\mathbf{f}_t\|_2 = \Theta(\Delta_{t_{i-1}})$ for $t_{i-1} \le t < t_i$, for $k = 1, \ldots, s$. It follows that the total size of the historical lists for this row is $O\left(\sum_{k=1}^{s}\sum_{j=t_{i-1}}^{t_i - 1} \frac{1}{\varepsilon\|\mathbf{f}_t\|_2}\right) = O\left(\sum_{k=1}^{m} \frac{1}{\varepsilon\|\mathbf{f}_t\|_2}\right)$.

In the standard streaming model, we have $\|\mathbf{f}_t\|_2 \ge \sqrt{\|\mathbf{f}_t\|_1} = \sqrt{t}$, thus the size of historical lists becomes $O\left(\sum_{k=1}^{m} \frac{1}{\varepsilon\sqrt{t}}\right) = O\left(\frac{\sqrt{m}}{\varepsilon}\right)$. Summing up all $d = O(\log \frac{1}{\delta})$ rows, and the Theorem follows. □

Scalable Distributed Stream Join Processing

Qian Lin† Beng Chin Ooi† Zhengkui Wang† Cui Yu§

†School of Computing, National University of Singapore
§Department of Computer Science and Software Engineering, Monmouth University
†{linqian, ooibc, wangzhengkui}@comp.nus.edu.sg, §cyu@monmouth.edu

ABSTRACT

Efficient and scalable stream joins play an important role in performing real-time analytics for many cloud applications. However, like in conventional database processing, online theta-joins over data streams are computationally expensive and moreover, being memory-based processing, they impose high memory requirement on the system. In this paper, we propose a novel stream join model, called *join-biclique*, which organizes a large cluster as a complete bipartite graph. Join-biclique has several strengths over state-of-the-art techniques, including *memory-efficiency*, *elasticity* and *scalability*. These features are essential for building efficient and scalable streaming systems. Based on join-biclique, we develop a scalable distributed stream join system, *BiStream*, over a large-scale commodity cluster. Specifically, BiStream is designed to support efficient full-history joins, window-based joins and online data aggregation. BiStream also supports adaptive resource management to dynamically scale out and down the system according to its application workloads. We provide both theoretical cost analysis and extensive experimental evaluations to evaluate the efficiency, elasticity and scalability of BiStream.

1. INTRODUCTION

In recent years, data have been rapidly generated in many applications as data streams, such as stock trading, mobile and networked information management systems. It is increasingly challenging and critical to provide efficient real-time analytics for such applications. Data aggregation is one of the most important and widely used operations in analytics, e.g., online analytical processing in relational databases, as it provides a high level view by summarizing the data using group-by and aggregate functions such as `count`, `sum` and `avg`. Most data aggregations are applied over the join results of two data streams with respect to a given join predicate; hence, efficient progressive stream join processing [15, 6] is essential and important to data stream systems.

There has been a lot of research on data stream join processing. Existing centralized algorithms [39, 18, 17] that were originally designed for a single server are not capable of handling the massive data stream workload. On the other hand, existing distributed and parallel stream join processing algorithms are mainly tailored for equi-join, which would not be efficient for high-selectivity joins such as the theta-join. Further, these methods mostly adopt various hash techniques for workload partitioning, which is sensitive to load distribution and inflexible to scaling out the system due to maintenance complexity.

In order to design an efficient distributed stream theta-join processing system, the following two requirements must be considered. First, in-memory processing is essential to provide efficient stream join and real-time analytics. Second, scalable stream processing is critical to support large-scale data stream applications. That is, a distributed stream join system has to be both memory-efficient and scalable. Among many of the related work, Join-matrix model [34] which was studied a decade ago has recently been revisited for supporting distributed join processing such as in MapReduce-like systems [28] and also stream applications [12]. Intuitively, it models a join operation between two input relations as a matrix, where each side of which corresponds to a relation as shown in Figure 1.a. Each processing unit (i.e., matrix cell) represents a potential join output result. However, the join-matrix model has three inherent weaknesses. First, it has high memory usage as the data need to be replicated and stored in an entire row or column. Second, it is not flexible to scale out/down since it has to add/release one entire row or column each time. Third, it does not scale well, because when a new processing unit to one row/column is added, the data in other units within the same column/row have to be replicated to the new unit. These weaknesses limit the memory-efficiency, elasticity and scalability of the systems that employ the join-matrix model.

In this paper, we propose *join-biclique*, a novel stream join model that is scalable and elastic with respect to the network size, and efficient and effective in terms of memory requirement and resource utilization. The core abstraction of join-biclique is to organize all the processing units in a cluster as a complete bipartite graph (a.k.a. biclique), where each side corresponds to a relation. Suppose R and S are the two input stream relations. Given $m + n$ processing units, m units on one side of the bipartite graph are for R and the other n units are for S. Figure 1.b shows one join-biclique example where m and n are 2 and 3, respectively. The result of $R \bowtie_\theta S$ can be obtained by evaluating each $R_i \bowtie_\theta S_j$ where R_i is the ith partition of R with $i \in \{1, ..., m\}$, and S_j is the jth partition of S with $j \in \{1, ..., n\}$. The

SIGMOD'15, May 31–June 4, 2015, Melbourne, Victoria, Australia.

http://dx.doi.org/10.1145/2723372.2746485.

join-biclique model has two important features. First, each relation is stored in its corresponding units without data replicas, which enables the model to be memory-efficient. Second, the processing units are independent of each other, which facilitates scalability and elasticity.

We next propose a distributed stream join system, *BiStream*, based on the join-biclique model. BiStream adopts a two-level architecture, including *router* and *joiner*. The router involves multiple shufflers and dispatchers that are in charge of ingesting the input streams and routing them to the corresponding processing units. The joiner consists of all the processing units which are responsible for data storing and join processing. BiStream adopts a simplified topological design of join-biclique where each processing unit only communicates with the router instead of among themselves to reduce the degree of inter-unit connectivity. Based on this design principle, the basic stream join processing flow works as follows: when one input tuple $r \in R$ (resp. $s \in S$) arrives at the router, it is routed to one of the processing units in R (resp. S) to store, and meanwhile it is sent to join the tuples stored in all the processing units in S (resp. R). As a consequence, r (resp. s) can be directly discarded from the units of S (resp. R) after join processing. This greatly lowers the memory requirement and hence improves the system capacity to efficiently support in-memory real-time analytics.

In summary, we make the following contributions:

- We propose a novel memory-efficient stream join model, *join-biclique*, for joining big data streams.
- Based on join-biclique, we design and develop a scalable stream join system, *BiStream*, for a large-scale commodity cluster. We also discuss how to efficiently support full-history and window-based stream joins, and online data aggregation.
- We propose an adaptive resource management for BiStream to dynamically scale out or down the system based on workload. The adaptive resource management allows the system to automatically increase and release the computation resources to minimize the system running cost.
- We theoretically analyze the proposed techniques and also conduct extensive experimental evaluation over a cluster of 40 nodes. The evaluation results confirm that BiStream is memory-efficient, elastic and scalable.

The remainder of this paper is organized as follows. We summarize the related work of stream join processing in Section 2. We define the join-biclique model and introduce BiStream in Section 3, following which we analyze BiStream in Section 4. Section 5 presents how BiStream supports adaptive stream join processing in the cloud. Evaluation of BiStream is demonstrated in Section 6 and finally, we conclude the paper in Section 7.

2. RELATED WORK

A great deal of research on distributed join processing has been conducted. However, the works [8, 35] have been proposed mainly for non-streaming scenarios. They cannot be directly applied to the streaming systems. For stream join processing, much research has also been devoted mainly for a stand-alone environment [39, 18, 17]. To name a few, symmetric hash join [39] is the earliest proposal for joining finite data streams. While reading in tuples of each relation in turn, it progressively constructs two hash tables (one for

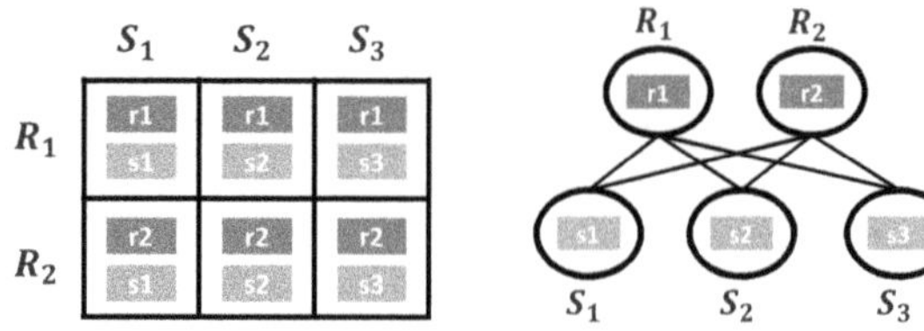

(a) Join-matrix (b) Join-biclique

Figure 1: Stream join models.

each relation) in memory and produces join results by probing them mutually. Online nested-loops join [18] is the first non-blocking join algorithm to progressively report the estimates of the join-based aggregate query results in real-time. Ripple join [17] and its variants [27, 20, 10] further generalize such processing towards online aggregation. However, all these algorithms rely on a centralized maintenance of the entire join states and hence, they are not easy to scale.

Further, several stream join algorithms have been proposed for the multi-core and main-memory environment [36, 14, 21, 29]. For instance, CellJoin [14] parallelizes the execution of stream joins on multi-core Cell processors, but its efficiency highly relies on the hardware parallelism of Cell processors. Handshake join [36, 31] organizes the processing units as a doubly linked list. The two joining streams are fed into the system in the opposite directions, and the join condition for each pair of joining tuples is evaluated once they meet in some unit. However, this model is susceptible to node failure and message loss if it is extended to the distributed environment.

Recently, much research has been devoted to stream join processing in a distributed environment with a cluster of commodity machines. Photon [4] was specifically designed for joining data streams of web search queries and user clicks on advertisements in Google. It relies on a centralized coordinator to search for the join tuples through key-value matching, but it is not designed to support general theta-join predicates. D-Streams [41] breaks continuous streams into discrete units and processes them as ordered batch jobs on Spark [40]. Such batch processing for stream joins can only provide approximate results, as a few target tuple pairs in separated batches may miss each other for join operation. TimeStream [30] exploits the dependencies of tuples to perform the joins. PSP [38] transforms a macro join operator into a series of smaller sub-operators by time-slicing of the join states, and the join processing is distributed to these sub-operators in a ring architecture. However, both TimeStream and PSP incur high communication overhead to maintain the dependencies or synchronize the distributed join states. For design and optimization of distributed and in-memory data processing, please refer to [26, 42].

The join-matrix model was adopted in a recently proposed distributed join processing [12]. It organizes the processing units as a matrix, each side of which corresponds to the partitions of one relation. Each matrix cell represents a potential join output result. Figure 1.a shows an example of join-matrix model with 2 and 3 partitions for relations R and S respectively. For instance, when $r1 \in R$ arrives, it is shuffled to one partition of R (e.g., R_1) and replicated to all units in the row R_1; meanwhile, it joins with the tuples of S stored in these units. This model is able to handle theta-join in a parallel and decentralized manner. However, it suffers from high memory consumption as it has to replicate each

Table 1: List of notations.

Notations	Description
R, S	Stream relation
r, s	Stream tuple
R_i, S_j	i-th and j-th partition of R and S
G_R, G_S	Universal set of partitions of R (S)
m, n	Number of partitions of R (S)
$G_{R,k}$, $G_{S,l}$	Subgroup of partitions of R (S)
d, e	Number of subgroups of R (S)
ω	Size of the sliding window
$\mathcal{P}$	Archive period of the chained in-memory index
$\mathcal{D}$	Maximum network latency

input tuple to multiple units. Moreover, it is not easy to scale out or down as it has to maintain the matrix structure. To address these issues, our join-biclique model is designed to be memory-efficient and amenable to scaling.

In addition, prior work on stream partitioning [13, 7] was focused on designing approaches to partition a large amount of skewed input streams into different units in order to achieve a balanced load in the unit or a minimized stream redirection cost. They are mainly designed for unary operations such as selection, projection and aggregate functions, not trivially applicable to binary stateful operators like join. Differently, our work is primarily focused on designing a scalable stream join processing model that is effective in both stream partitioning and join operation.

3. THE JOIN-BICLIQUE MODEL

3.1 Definition

Table 1 lists the notations used throughout the rest of the paper. Join-biclique model is developed with the main objectives of reducing memory consumption and facilitating scalability. The formal definition of join-biclique is presented as follows:

Definition 1 (Join-Biclique Model). Given a cluster with $m+n$ processing units (or units when there is no ambiguity), join-biclique organizes all of these units as a complete bipartite graph (a.k.a. biclique). Suppose there are two relations R and S. Each side of the bipartite graph corresponds to one relation for storage. Specifically, data of relation R are partitioned and stored into one side of the bipartite graph with m units without replicas (i.e., $G_R = \{R_1, ..., R_m\}$). Similarly, data of relation S is partitioned into the other side with n units (i.e., $G_S = \{S_1, ..., S_n\}$). In the bipartite graph, there exists an edge (R_i, S_j) between units R_i and S_j where $i \in \{1, ..., m\}$ and $j \in \{1, ..., n\}$. Each edge (R_i, S_j) represents a potential join result produced by $R_i \bowtie_\theta S_j$.

Each edge in the join-biclique represents the join operation between two units of the opposite relations and the join-biclique is able to generate the Cartesian product of the join participants. As a result, the join-biclique model can support any join predicate. In a typical real deployment, one physical machine may host multiple processing units according to the machine configuration. That is, the units of R and S may only be logically separated.

3.2 BiStream System Design

Next, we present a distributed stream join system, *BiStream*, based on the join-biclique model. For the ease of explanation, we focus on the full-history joins (i.e., joining all tuples entered so far) to illustrate how the system works. Discussion on supporting the window-based joins is deferred to Section 3.3.

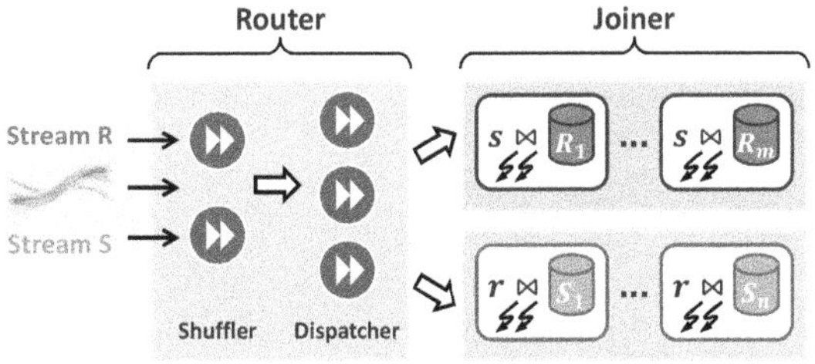

Figure 2: Overall architecture of BiStream.

3.2.1 System Architecture

BiStream is built on top of Storm [1], a distributed real-time computation platform. In order to appreciate BiStream, we shall first briefly introduce Storm terminologies. A Storm topology is a graph of *spouts* and *bolts*. Each spout acts as a stream source adapter, and each bolt consumes the input streams and possibly emits new streams. Spouts and bolts are connected with various *stream groupings* which define how streams' tuples are distributed among bolt tasks. Towards data stream system development on Storm, the system logic is decomposed into functionalities which are further implemented as spouts and bolts, and the dataflows are defined through stream grouping.

Figure 2 depicts the architecture of BiStream. BiStream consists of two functional components: *router* and *joiner*. The router is designed to ingest and route the input streams to the corresponding units for further processing, and the joiner is in charge of data storing and join processing for the data received from the router.

The BiStream topology follows the join-biclique model but reduces the degree of inter-unit connectivity. Conceptually, in a join-biclique, each unit needs to connect with all units of the other relation. Fortunately, this is not necessary, and BiStream avoids the communication among the units by separating the router and the joiner since the data routing is independent from the data store and join processing. That is, each unit only communicates with the router to receive the data to store or join without communicating among each other. Specifically, an incoming tuple (e.g., $r \in R$) is sent to one of the units R_i to store, and at the same time it is sent to all the units of S for join processing. After the join processing, r can be discarded from the units in S.

Router. Figure 2 illustrates a two-tier architecture of the router, consisting of *shuffler* and *dispatcher*. The shuffler, implemented as a spout, ingests the input streams and forwards every incoming tuple to the dispatcher. The dispatcher, implemented as a bolt, forwards every received tuple from the shuffler to the corresponding units in the joiner to store and join. Meanwhile, the dispatcher is in charge of maintaining the statistics about how the data is stored among the units.

The main aim of separating shuffler and dispatcher in the router topology is to isolate the ingestion of incoming tuples and the maintenance of storage statistics. To trace the order and time of each incoming event, BiStream assigns one timestamp to each stream input event. This enables the system to always process and join the input events in the right order, especially for the time-based sliding-window joins (i.e.,

Algorithm 1: Control of ContRand routing.

```
Input: tuple t
Procedure Route(t):
    group ← GetSubgroup(key(t), t.rel)
    p ← a unit randomly chosen from group
    forward(t, p)                                /* to store */
    group ← GetSubgroup(key(t), opposite(t.rel))
    foreach unit q ∈ group do
        forward(t, q)                            /* to join */

Input: value v, relation rel
Function GetSubgroup(v, rel):                    /* for equi-join */
    rel match
        R: return G_{R,i} s.t. v ∈ ValueRangeOf(G_{R,i})
        S: return G_{S,j} s.t. v ∈ ValueRangeOf(G_{S,j})
```

joining the tuples with a time constraint). A timestamp is assigned to each tuple based on the time when the tuple arrives at the shuffler in the system. It is important that the tuples arriving at the same time get the same timestamp. To guarantee that, we need to synchronize the timers in the router which is a costly process since the number of timers may be large. There is however a clear demarcation of roles and tasks; the shuffler is in charge of timestamp assignment while the dispatcher handling statistics collection and other routing decision tasks. With this design, the number of shuffler tasks can be greatly reduced, and it will effectively ease the synchronization among the timers.

Joiner. The joiner component consists of all the processing units. It is designed to process the streams from the router. Each unit runs a stateful bolt task that consumes the tuples from the router. Each task has two execution branches – data storing and join processing, whose runtime depends on whether the tuple belongs to the corresponding relation of the unit or from the other joining relation. To be specific, the data storing operation is triggered when one input tuple $r \in R$ arrives at its corresponding unit $R_i \in G_R$, where r will be stored. If one unit $R_i \in G_R$ receives a tuple $s \in S$ from the other relation, the join processing is conducted by joining s with all the tuples stored in R_i.

To support efficient join processing, BiStream adopts a variety of in-memory indexes to index the data, such as hash maps for equi-joins and balanced binary search trees for non equi-joins. More details of the indexing and join processing are described in Section 3.3.

3.2.2 Dataflow Control

The main objective of dataflow control is to balance the load in the system to improve the degree of processing parallelism. To facilitate load balancing, we design BiStream dataflow, which is illustrated in Figure 2. It is a two-stage process: (1) from the shuffler to the dispatcher, and (2) from the dispatcher to the joiner. For dataflow control in the first stage (1), BiStream adopts a random routing strategy, where tuples emitted by the shuffler are randomly distributed across dispatcher tasks such that each dispatcher task receives an equal number of tuples. The stream for random routing is implemented using the *shuffle stream grouping* in Storm. Being content-insensitive, the random routing strategy should be effective in automatically balancing the workload among the dispatcher tasks.

The second stage (2) involves two streams: the store stream and the join stream. The store stream is for routing each tuple to a unit for storing, and the join stream is for sending the tuples to the proper units for join processing. Different routing strategies in these two streams can be implemented for different joins based on join selectivity.

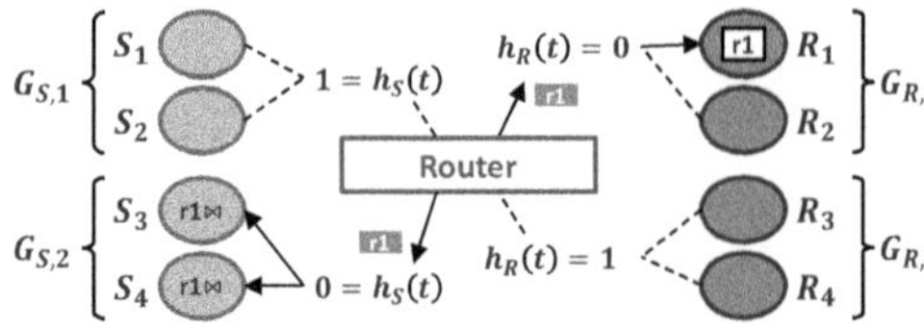

Figure 3: An example of ContRand routing.

For *high-selectivity* joins such as inequality joins, the random routing strategy should be adopted. High-selectivity joins may generate a large number of join results in most, if not all, of the units, while the random routing strategy helps to automatically balance the load among all the units of a relation and makes the system resilient to data skew. With the random routing strategy, $r \in R$ (resp. $s \in S$) is randomly shuffled to one unit R_i (resp. S_j) to store in a content-insensitive manner (i.e., regardless of the content of tuples) via the store stream. Meanwhile, it is sent to all the units belonging to S (resp. R) for join operation via the join stream. We note that r (resp. s) will be only stored in one R (resp. S) unit whereas it can be discarded after the join operation in each S (resp. R) unit.

For *low-selectivity* joins such as equi-join, a content-sensitive routing strategy may be preferred, e.g. hash-partitioning. Hash-partitioning is able to partition the tuples with the same hash values into the same unit. It guarantees the data locality which facilities efficient join processing. However, hash-partitioning may incur load imbalance when the data is skew. The load imbalance of hashing can be alleviated by pre-computing the data distribution (e.g., histogram) as in traditional DBMS. However, this approach does not work well in the stream system, since it is difficult to obtain such information in advance.

To tackle the problem of load imbalance in content-sensitive routing, we adopt a hybrid routing strategy, *ContRand*, to make use of both the content-sensitive and random routing strategies. Algorithm 1 shows the control flow of ContRand routing, whose basic idea is as follows:

1) Suppose there are m units for relation R (i.e., $G_R = \{R_1, ..., R_m\}$) and n units for relation S (i.e., $G_S = \{S_1, ..., S_n\}$). G_R is logically divided into d disjoint subgroups (i.e., $\{G_{R,1}, ..., G_{R,d}\}$) where each $G_{R,i}$ includes one or more units and $\bigcup_{k=1}^{d} G_{R,k} = G_R$. Similarly, G_S is divided into e subgroups (i.e., $\{G_{S,1}, ..., G_{S,e}\}$). For instance, Figure 3 indicates four units of relation R which are logically divided into two subgroups $G_{R,1} = \{R_1, R_2\}$ and $G_{R,2} = \{R_3, R_4\}$.

2) Based on the partition above, ContRand decides which unit to store a tuple r by hashing r to a subgroup (content-sensitive manner) and randomly choosing a unit in that subgroup (content-insensitive manner). A composite function over r is used, such as $(rand \circ h_R)(r)$, where $rand$ and h_R are random and hashing functions for relation R, respectively. For the example given in Figure 3, according to the hashing value of $r1$, $r1$ is assigned to a unit in the first subgroup $G_{R,1}$. Similarly, ContRand uses $(rand \circ h_S)(s)$ to store tuple s in G_S. This approach is expected to work better than the pure content-sensitive routing strategy, especially when the data is skewed.

3) For join processing, ContRand routes r to all the units

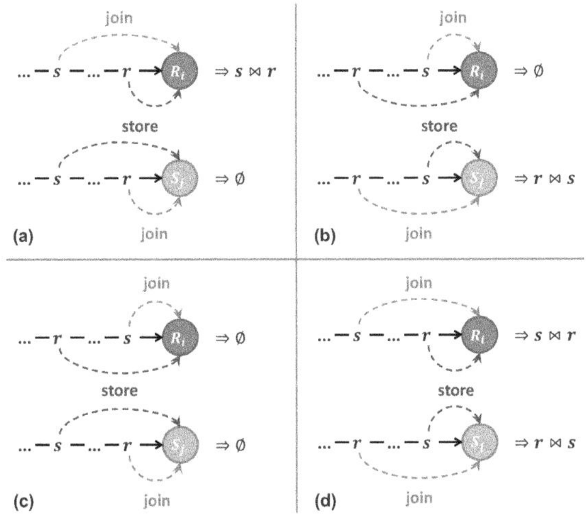

Figure 4: All cases of store-and-join processing.

in a subgroup calculated using $h_S(r)$. This guarantees that r is sent to all the units in one subgroup storing s which has the same hash value as r.

In the implementation of ContRand, we have two extreme cases to handle. First, when each group has only one unit (i.e., $d = m$ and $e = n$), ContRand becomes pure content-sensitive. Second, when there is only one group in each relation (i.e., $d = e = 1$), ContRand falls back to the content-insensitive one. The corresponding quantitative analysis will be presented in Section 4. In the implementation of ContRand, we extend the *field stream grouping* in Storm to support local random routing inside a hash-defined subgroup for the store stream and adopt the *direct stream grouping* for the join stream.

3.2.3 Protocol Design

To ensure the completeness of join results, the join protocol must be carefully designed to handle the situation that the tuples may arrive at the processing unit in different orders. Recall that BiStream does not store the tuples that are sent to the units of the other joining relation for join processing. However, the timing of discarding these tuples needs to be carefully considered. Naively discarding each tuple immediately after the join operation would lead to anomalies due to the out-of-order issue of tuples in the streams.

Suppose there are two input tuples $r \in R$ and $s \in S$ that satisfy the join condition of $R \bowtie S$. Figure 4 illustrates all the possible orders in which they may reach the two units R_i and S_j, where the closer a tuple is drawn to a unit, the earlier it arrives at the unit. Among all the possible cases, Figure 4.a and Figure 4.b work well to generate exactly one join result. For instance, in Figure 4.a, for the R_i side, r arrives earlier than s and is stored into R_i; the later arriving s joins with the stored r and produces the join result. For the S_j side, r which arrives earlier does not join with the later arriving s and is discarded before the arrival of s. As a consequence, only one join result is produced between r and s in Figure 4.a. The symmetric situation is applied to Figure 4.b as well. These two cases share the property that r and s arrive at R_i and S_j in consistent orders. Unfortunately, anomalies arise when the order of arriving r and s conflicts with the order that R_i and S_j are supposed to maintain during the join operation. In Figure 4.c, no join result is produced in the R_i side because s which arrives earlier is discarded before the arrival of r. Similarly, no join result is produced in the S_j side because r is discarded before the arrival of s. As a result, no join result is produced between r and s though they satisfy the join condition. We term this as a *missed-join* problem. On the other hand, in Figure 4.d, the result of $r \bowtie s$ is produced twice because the later arriving s joins with the stored r in R_i and the later arriving r joins with the stored s in S_j. We call this a *duplicated-join* problem.

To avoid the aforementioned anomalies, one solution is to perform a temporal-relational join processing based on the application timestamps [11]. For instance, by assigning each tuple one timestamp based on the application time, we can define constraints on the timestamp ordering of the joining tuples. Let T_r and T_s be the timestamps for r and s respectively. Each unit R_i (resp. S_j) does not evaluate the relational join condition on two joining tuples r and s unless they satisfy the temporal constraint $T_r \leq T_s$ (resp. $T_s < T_r$). By doing so, the expected join behavior can be enforced regardless of the physical timing of tuple arrival. The straightforward implementation of this approach, however, requires each unit to keep the tuples from both relations in memory, which incurs high memory consumption. Hence, we further design a protocol to discard the tuples in a proper way to reduce the memory usage, yet guarantee the correctness of the join results.

As mentioned earlier, if two tuples are processed at the units with a consistent order, the join result is produced correctly. To guarantee such a consistent order, we introduce a protocol to ensure that the relative order for any two joining tuples r and s only depends on one global order, and is consistent over all the units.

Definition 2 (Order-Consistent Protocol). Given a set of dispatcher tasks Y and a set of processing units U, each task $y_i \in Y$ sends a set of tuples $X_i = \{x_{i_1}, ..., x_{i_k}, ...\}$ as a stream. Each tuple is broadcast to a set of processing units. A network protocol is called *order-consistent* if and only if: There exists a global tuple sequence $Z = (x_{z_1}, x_{z_2}, ...)$, where Z contains each tuple exactly once. For each unit $u_j \in U$, it receives all the tuples assigned to it (i.e., no loss in the network), and the sequence of tuples it processes is a subsequence of the global tuple sequence Z.

First, we need the message passing and processing between every pair of dispatcher task and processing unit is first-in-first-out (FIFO). Otherwise, the unit cannot determine whether a received tuple is delayed in the network. For example, suppose r and s are sent by the same dispatcher task. R_i receives r and then s, however, r is delayed in S_j. It is impossible to determine how long S_j should wait for r before processing the early arriving s, unless there exists some kind of communication between R_i and S_j. To this end, we design a *pairwise FIFO protocol* to guarantee that for every pair of dispatcher task and processing unit, the in-between message passing and processing is FIFO.

Definition 3 (Pairwise FIFO Protocol). Given a dispatcher task y and a processing unit u, y sends a set of tuples $X = \{x_1, ..., x_k, ...\}$ to u as a stream. A network protocol is called *pairwise FIFO* if and only if: For any two tuples x_a and x_b, if x_a is sent by y before x_b, then x_a is processed at u before x_b.

This protocol is widely used in the design of communication networks [24]. The basic idea is to give each tuple an id which is incremented by one after every sent tuple (dispatcher side) or received tuple (processing unit side). The receiver u only processes those tuples with the correct tuple id. Thus, when a tuple is delayed or lost, the tuple id to be received will be held and other tuples cannot be received. However, they can be buffered to make the overhead of this protocol lightweight, and this depends on the implementation of this protocol.

Now we can design the order-consistent protocol based on the above pairwise FIFO protocol. The key component of the protocol is the logical clock [25]. Each dispatcher task maintains a logical clock (i.e., a monotonically increasing counter) which is incremented by one per tuple from the shuffler. Every time before emitting a tuple, the dispatcher task appends a logical timestamp to the tuple. Each processing unit sorts the received tuples based on the timestamp. In this case, the global sequence is just based on the order of timestamp. However, in the context of stream processing, we cannot wait till the last tuple before sorting tuples and output. For this reason, the protocol must know the current status of each dispatcher task, and which part of tuples can be to sort and process (i.e., no more incoming tuples containing such timestamp). Here, we use an idea similar to stream punctuation [37] to solve it. For each dispatcher task, it broadcasts a signal tuple with timestamp to all the units periodically (e.g., every 10ms). Since message passing and processing within every pair of dispatcher task and processing unit are FIFO, such a signal indicates that all tuples (from this dispatcher task) before this timestamp have been received by the units. Each processing unit maintains a table of the latest signal timestamp from each dispatcher task. If all the dispatcher tasks' logical clocks reach a certain timestamp, the processing unit must have received all the tuples before this timestamp. Thus, we use a priority queue in each processing unit to buffer every receive tuple, and process (i.e., store or join) those tuples that have a smaller timestamp than the smallest current latest signal timestamp.

For this protocol, each dispatcher task needs to generate timestamp for its tuple based on its own knowledge. An ideal case is that all the dispatchers have a same global time, which is usually not easy to obtain. However, if we can relax the constraint of timer synchronization among different dispatcher tasks (e.g., within 100ms difference), it would become easier to achieve. Such time difference will not affect the correctness of the protocol. Instead, we only need to buffer more since the difference of the latest signals timestamp from dispatchers may become larger.

By using the order-consistent protocol to send tuples from multiple dispatcher tasks to multiple processing units, the order of tuple processing will be consistent in all processing units. Therefore, the missed-join and duplicated-join problems due to the inconsistent processing order can be definitely avoided.

3.3 Window-Based Stream Joins

Unlike a full-history stream join, a window-based stream join evaluates the join condition only for tuples within the designated window [6]. The most widely used window-based stream join is to apply the time-based sliding window [16, 33]. Typically, given a time window size ϖ, for any input stream tuple $r \in R$ (resp. $s \in S$), it is joined only with the

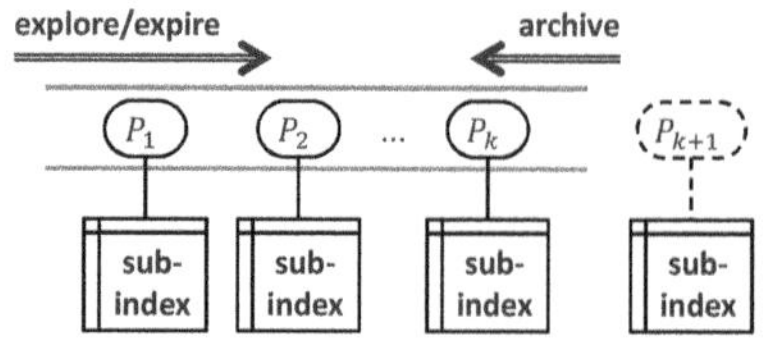

Figure 5: Chained in-memory index.

tuple $s \in S$ (resp. $r \in R$) such that $0 \leq r.time - s.time \leq \varpi$ (resp. $0 \leq s.time - r.time \leq \varpi$).

Two operations are essential for the maintenance of a sliding window. One operation is to verify the window constraint, which determines the tuples that should participate in the join operation. To do this, it requires the system to assign a synchronized timestamp to each incoming tuple. In BiStream, the timestamp is assigned at the shuffler. The other essential operation is to invalidate and discard the expired tuples from memory. This operation is important for releasing the memory and performing efficient join. Theorem 1 provides the criterion when a tuple can be safely removed from memory.

Theorem 1. *Given the maximum network delay $\mathcal{D}$, the stored tuples $r \in R_i$ can be safely discarded from memory, when R_i receives an incoming tuple $s \in S$ iff $s.time - r.time > \varpi + \mathcal{D}$. Likewise, $s \in S$ can be discarded from S_j once S_j receives one tuple such that $r.time - s.time > \varpi + \mathcal{D}$.*

Proof. Given a tuple $r \in R_i$, it needs to join $s \in S$ whose timestamp is within $[r.time, r.time + \varpi]$. With $\mathcal{D}$, the last tuple s' within r's window arrives at R_i at the moment of $r.time + \varpi + \mathcal{D}$ such that $s'.time = r.time + \varpi$. Thus, if $s \in S$ arrives later than s', then $s.time > r.time + \varpi$ which is outside $[r.time, r.time + \varpi]$. In other words, r will not be in any window of s after s' and thus can be safely discarded from memory. □

Indexes are required to support efficient stream join processing. However, the existing approaches of organizing the entire stream data with one single index incur high overhead for re-adjusting the index when expired tuples are discarded. To facilitate low-overhead data discarding and index exploration, we propose the *chained in-memory index* to overcome the high overhead incurred in using a single index.

Figure 5 illustrates the structure of the chained in-memory index. The basic idea is to partition the streaming tuples with respect to the discrete time intervals and construct a subindex per interval. The span of the time interval is referred as the *archive period* $\mathcal{P}$. Each subindex is associated with the minimum and maximum timestamps of the tuples it contains. All subindexes are chained as a linked list by the order of their construction time. According to the window constraint, expired data are discarded from memory in the granularity of subindex-level rather than tuple-level. This reduces the overhead of data discarding since the valid subindexes are not affected when the obsolete subindexes are discarded. We summarize the main procedures of indexing data, discarding data, and join processing in the chained in-memory index as follows.

Data Indexing: When each input tuple (say $r \in R_i$) is inserted into an active subindex, it first updates the minimum and maximum timestamps. It then calculates whether the difference between the minimum and maximum timestamps has exceeded $\mathcal{P}$. If this is true, the active subindex becomes inactive and is archived into the chain, and a new empty active subindex is created. Otherwise, the current active subindex remains active. Only one active subindex is used to index an input tuple.

Data Discarding: An expired subindex can be safely removed from memory. Checking for the expired subindexes is triggered when a tuple reaches the unit belonging to the other relation (e.g., s reaches R_i where $s \in S$). The criterion to discard one subindex from the chain is the difference between the timestamp of s and the maximum timestamp of the subindex being large than $\varpi + \mathcal{D}$ according to Theorem 1. Theorem 1 ensures that the removal of the subindex from memory does not affect the integrity of join results. This coarse-grained level data discarding improves the discarding efficiency by avoiding pairwise comparisons inside each subindex.

Join Processing: After data discarding, s needs to join with all the tuples in the remaining in-memory subindexes. Recall that, for sliding-window joins, the window verification is necessary to identify whether each tuple falls in the window. One optimization we adopted to speed up this window verification is to identify which subindex is partially or completely expired in the window, by comparing the difference between $s.time$ and the minimum timestamp of the subindex. If the minimum timestamp is in the window that s may interact with, then the entire subindex does not need to conduct the window verification and can directly perform join processing. Otherwise, the pairwise window verification is needed during join processing in the partially expired subindex.

3.4 Supporting Other Operators

Besides the join operator, a typical stream query may also involve other operations such as selection, projection and aggregation. Such a query is typically referred to as a stream select-project-join-aggregation (SPJA) query [3]. An example stream SPJA query is shown below.

```
SELECT ONLINE R.a2, sum(S.b2)
FROM R, S
WHERE R.a1 > S.b1 WITHIN 10 minutes
GROUP BY R.a2;
```

where the `WITHIN` clause indicates that it is a sliding-window query. If the `WITHIN` clause is omitted, the aggregation of the query would be based on the full-history join results.

A complex stream SPJA query may need to join more than two streams. For such a complex query, a binary tree-like (e.g., right-deep tree [9]) execution plan is constructed accordingly, which comprises a sequence of binary stream join operators. All the join operators are executed in a pipeline manner: each operator joins two streams, each of which is either an input stream or from another join operation, and produces the join result that is potentially fed to another operator implemented using *shuffle stream grouping* in storm. Focusing on the join processing, we further describe how selection, projection and aggregation are supported for stream SPJA queries in BiStream.

3.4.1 Selection and Projection

The selection and projection operations could be either duplicate-preserving or duplicate-eliminating. Duplicate-preserving selection and projection allow the existence of duplicated results. They are stateless and thus can be easily conducted by filtering the streams in a tuple-at-a-time manner without using any extra memory for storing the intermediate state [5]. BiStream can naturally support these operations at the router side over the input streams and at the joiner side over the stream join results according to the query plan.

However, duplicate-eliminating selection and projection need to remove the duplicated results, which typically requires the stream system to add an additional bolt (referred as the *deduplicator*) to filter out the duplicates. Many existing duplicate-eliminating techniques (such as hash probing [22]) can be used in the implementation of the deduplicator. Due to the potentially unbound memory usage for keeping track of the distinct values over the full-history data [5], in practice, these operators are always applied with windowed constraints. In BiStream, they can be supported by integrating the deduplicator into either the router or the joiner to enable duplicate elimination.

3.4.2 Online Data Aggregation

In order to facilitate real-time decision making, BiStream also supports online data aggregation over the stream join outputs. Performing online data aggregation comprises two tasks: join and aggregation. The join processing can be performed by directly exploiting the proposed join approach (e.g., using the join predicate $R \bowtie_{R.a1>S.b1} S$). The aggregation computation is to aggregate the join results based on group-by and aggregate functions (e.g., in the example query, group by $R.a2$ and perform `sum` over $S.b2$). To support efficient distributed aggregation processing, we adopt a two-phase approach [32]. The first phase is to pre-aggregate a partial local view in each unit in the joiner. As each unit contains part of the join outputs independently, the local view computation can be directly performed. The second phase is to shuffle the local views to a coordinating component (referred as the *merger*) and merge them into a global view from time to time. The merger is implemented as a bolt receiving the data stream from the joiner. The merger may involve multiple processing units to parallelize the processing of constructing the global view.

In a stream environment, frequent view updates may incur high communication and computation overhead between the joiner and the merger. One improvement is to adopt the lazy-update or batch-update strategy. Instead of pushing the local aggregation results to the merger immediately when every tuple arrives, we compute the updated views by batching the updated tuples based on a time period. In this way, multiple local aggregate updates can be batched together so that the overhead can be reduced.

3.5 Fault Tolerance

Two types of failures that typically occur in a stream system are *data loss* and *message loss*. Data loss happens when there is power failure or node corruption, which results in the loss of data stored in memory, and hence, loss of the join states. Message loss is often due to network partition or hiccup, which results in the loss of on-the-fly data during message passing, and hence, incomplete dataflow processing.

To handle data loss, BiStream adopts data replication to prevent data loss for the unit failure in the joiner. BiStream maintains one in-memory data as the primary copy and several other copies as backups for failure recovery purposes. As we have discussed above, during the join processing, every tuple r of R (resp. s of S) is stored into one unit of R (resp. S) that is considered as the primary copy to support the join processing. The other copies are stored in the units of S (resp. R) where r (resp. s) is sent for join processing. Intuitively, when r is sent to the units of S for join, BiStream enforces some units to store r into their persistent storage (e.g., hard disk) as replicas after the join operation. When the system detects a unit failure, the failed partition can be restored from other archived replicas in the system.

To handle message loss, since the topology of the router and joiner is a directed acyclic graph (DAG), BiStream adopts the upstream backup technique [19]. Specifically, the upstream nodes act as backups for their downstream neighbors by preserving tuples in their output queues while their downstream neighbors process them. If the message in the downstream fails, its upstream nodes replay the logged tuples on the recovery node.

4. COMPARATIVE ANALYSIS

In this section we provide the comparative analysis between join-biclique and join-matrix models in terms of memory consumption, scalability and communication cost. Table 2 lists the notations used throughout this section. In addition, we use the subscripts *bi* and *mat* to distinguish join-biclique and join-matrix.

Assume that there are m and n partitions for relations R and S respectively, and the join keys over $R \bowtie_\theta S$ are of uniform distribution. With this setup, join-biclique requires $m + n$ units while join-matrix requires $m \times n$ units. In addition, as the random routing strategy is an extreme case of the ContRand routing strategy, our discussion will be based on ContRand routing for join-biclique where m and n partitions are divided into d ($\leq m$) and e ($\leq n$) subgroups, respectively.

4.1 Memory Consumption

We quantify the memory consumption for the full-history join. As the full-history join can be viewed as an extreme case of the window-based join where the size of window is infinite, the following analysis also applies to the window-based join in the context of the worst case analysis.

The data stored in join-biclique consist of the stored tuples of both joining relations and the buffered tuples within a time window (say $\mathcal{D}$) required by the join protocol. Thus, the total amount of memory consumption is as follows:

$$W_{bi} = \chi_R \cdot (|R| + n \cdot \frac{\varphi_R}{e} \cdot \mathcal{D}) + \chi_S \cdot (|S| + m \cdot \frac{\varphi_S}{d} \cdot \mathcal{D})$$

where $|R|$ and $|S|$ quantify the stored tuples, and $n \cdot \frac{\varphi_R}{e} \cdot \mathcal{D}$ and $m \cdot \frac{\varphi_S}{d} \cdot \mathcal{D}$ quantify the buffered tuples. Typically, the number of stored tuples is much larger than the temporarily buffered ones, inferring $n \cdot \frac{\varphi_R}{e} \cdot \mathcal{D} \ll |R|$ and $m \cdot \frac{\varphi_S}{d} \cdot \mathcal{D} \ll |S|$. By ignoring the memory usage of buffering tuples, the memory consumption of join-biclique can be approximated as

$$W_{bi} \approx \chi_R \cdot |R| + \chi_S \cdot |S| \quad (1)$$

Different from join-biclique, join-matrix replicates each input tuple over an entire row or column. As a consequence, the memory consumption of join-matrix is as follows:

$$W_{mat} = \chi_R \cdot n \cdot |R| + \chi_S \cdot m \cdot |S| \quad (2)$$

Equation 2 shows the memory consumption for join-matrix is sensitive to the matrix configuration. This infers that join-matrix suffers from high memory consumption when m and n are large. Differently, Equation 1 shows the memory consumption of join-biclique is independent on the partitioning scheme and only proportional to the amount of inputs. This indicates that join-biclique is much more memory-efficient.

Table 2: Terms used in the analytical model.

Terms	Description
$R_{k,i}$	The i-th partition of the k-th subgroup of R
$S_{l,j}$	The j-th partition of the l-th subgroup of S
m_k	Number of partitions in the k-th subgroup of R
n_l	Number of partitions in the l-th subgroup of S
$\lvert R\rvert$, $\lvert S\rvert$	Number of arrived tuples of relation R (S)
χ_R, χ_S	Size of a tuple of relation R (S)
W	Cluster memory consumption
φ_R, φ_S	Average incoming rate of stream R (S)
$In(\cdot)$	Input bandwidth of a node
B	Intermediate stream bandwidth

4.2 Scalability

We consider two important properties with respect to system scalability. The first is on the *flexibility* of adding or removing the units into or from the system. This can be measured by the system scaling granularity in terms of the number of units being added or removed. The second is on the *effectiveness* of utilizing the memory of newly added units. This can be measured by the scaling gain ratio (SGR).

Definition 4 (Scaling Gain Ratio). In system scaling, the scaling gain ratio (SGR) is the percentage of newly added memory that can be used for processing new inputs. Higher SGR indicates better scalability.

In the join-matrix model, since the system needs to maintain the matrix structure, it can only add or remove one entire row or column during system scaling out or down. It does not support single unit increment per scaling operation, as this violates the matrix structure. Especially, when there is a big matrix, adding one row or column may increase many more machines which may not be actually needed. This therefore limits the flexibility of the system. On the contrary, join-biclique does not need to maintain a rigid partitioning scheme, enabling it to be more flexible in scaling. In join-biclique, each unit is independent to each other, and any number of units (even single unit) can be easily added or removed from the system for either relation. In other words, join-biclique supports a more fine-grained units change which provides the flexibility in scaling.

For the effectiveness of resource utilization, in join-matrix, when a new unit is added (corresponding either a row or column increases), part of its memory is used to store the replicas of the in-memory data in other units and only the remainders can be used to increase the system storage capacity. As shown in Figure 1.a, when a row is added for R, tuples of relation S have to be replicated to the new unit in the same column to guarantee the correctness of join processing. The space required for storing the replicas is therefore $\chi_S \cdot (|S|/n)$, where n is the number of columns. Thus, the SGR of adding a new partition for relation R is

$$SGR_{mat,R} = \frac{\mathcal{C} - \chi_S \cdot (|S|/n)}{\mathcal{C}} = 1 - \frac{\chi_S}{\mathcal{C}} \cdot \frac{|S|}{n} \quad (3)$$

where $\mathcal{C}$ is the memory capacity of a unit. Similarly, when adding a partition for relation S, we can calculate SGR as

$$SGR_{mat,S} = \frac{\mathcal{C} - \chi_R \cdot (|R|/m)}{\mathcal{C}} = 1 - \frac{\chi_R}{\mathcal{C}} \cdot \frac{|R|}{m} \quad (4)$$

As can be seen from Equation 3 and Equation 4, for join-matrix, the SGR of expanding relation R (resp. S) is affected by the number of tuples stored in S (resp. R) and the number of partitions of S (resp. R). Consequently, the SGR will be very small when the number of stored tuples becomes large. This indicates the effectiveness of system scaling out tends to be marginal with the growth of system storage capacity.

For join-biclique, as no data replication is needed, the whole memory of the new unit can be utilized to increase the capacity of system storage. For instance, when one unit is added to relation R, no data from other units are replicated to the new unit. In this case, the SGR remains 1 whenever the system scales out, as 100% of the memory can be utilized to share the workload.

4.3 Communication Cost

We further provide the comparative analysis on the communication cost of intermediate streams in different models.

In join-biclique, the bandwidth usage for each unit $R_{k,i}$ or $S_{l,j}$ is provided as follows:

$$In(R_{k,i}) = \chi_R \cdot \frac{\varphi_R}{d} \cdot \frac{1}{m_k} + \chi_S \cdot \frac{\varphi_S}{d}$$

$$In(S_{l,j}) = \chi_S \cdot \frac{\varphi_S}{e} \cdot \frac{1}{n_l} + \chi_R \cdot \frac{\varphi_R}{e}$$

Let $\Sigma_R = \chi_R \cdot \varphi_R$ and $\Sigma_S = \chi_S \cdot \varphi_S$. Then the bandwidth of intermediate streams required by join-biclique is:

$$\begin{aligned} B_{bi} &= \sum_{k=1}^{d}\sum_{i=1}^{m_k} In(R_{k,i}) + \sum_{l=1}^{e}\sum_{j=1}^{n_l} In(S_{l,j}) \\ &= (\frac{n}{e}+1)\cdot\Sigma_R + (\frac{m}{d}+1)\cdot\Sigma_S \end{aligned} \quad (5)$$

In join-matrix, the bandwidth of intermediate streams is:

$$B_{mat} = n \cdot \Sigma_R + m \cdot \Sigma_S \quad (6)$$

As can be seen from Equation 5 and Equation 6, join-biclique is superior to join-matrix in bandwidth usage to support the same number of partitions in most cases. Only when a random routing is adopted (i.e., $d = e = 1$), it is inferior to join-matrix with an extra $\Sigma_R + \Sigma_S$ for the entire cluster.

5. ADAPTIVE RESOURCE MANAGEMENT

The goal of adaptive resource management is to achieve dynamic recalibration, reacting to frequent changes in data and statistics. Adaptive solutions can supplement regular execution with an adaptive resource manager that monitors the unit load and triggers changes. Considering the ContRand routing strategy, each subgroup is independent to each other. In BiStream, the resource manager monitors the load situation of the units in each subgroup and performs scaling out/down operations within each subgroup. We use the *memory load volume* (MLV) as a metric to calculate the memory consumption in each unit.

BiStream adopts a two-phase scaling (2PS) protocol – a *requesting* phase and a *scaling* phase – to adaptively adjust the resource management. For the ease of illustration, we assume all the units are homogeneous with the same memory capacity $\mathcal{C}$. However, the protocol can be easily extended to the heterogeneous scenarios. Next we introduce the basic idea of 2PS protocol. The detailed algorithm is omitted here due to space constraint.

1.) In the requesting phase, the resource manager broadcasts a request to all the units to collect the load status. Each unit acknowledges the request by reporting its MLV to the resource manager. After receiving all the responses, the resource manager summarizes the load status and determines whether a scaling operation is necessary. Once a scaling decision of either scaling out or down is made, the system goes to the scaling phase.

2.) In the scaling phase, the resource manager conducts the scaling operation based on the decision. For scaling out operation, the resource manager allocates new units and performs necessary data migration to rebalance the load among the units in the current subgroup. For scaling down operation, the resource manager first distributes the data in the units that will be removed to other units in the same current subgroup, and then releases these units.

Since BiStream conducts the adjustment in each subgroup independently, we illustrate the control flow based on one subgroup (e.g., subgroup G with k units). The resource manager periodically sends the request messages $q_1, ..., q_k$ to all the k units in G. Every i-th unit acknowledges the request q_i through a response message p_i with its current MLV, denoted as $MLV(p_i)$, where $i \in \{1, 2, ..., k\}$.

After the resource manager has received all the responses $\{p_1, ..., p_k\}$, it calculates the percentage τ of the memory usage in the subgroup as

$$\tau = \frac{\Sigma_{i=1}^{k} MLV(p_i)}{k \cdot \mathcal{C}}$$

τ is used as an indicator to make the decision. Intuitively, if τ exceeds a stated threshold $\mathcal{T}_h$, the system is considered to be overloaded. In contrast, if τ is below a stated threshold $\mathcal{T}_l$, the system is considered to be underloaded. There are two important issues we need to address during the system adjustment. The first one is how to avoid false positive scaling due to the fluctuation of inputs; the second one is how to determine the number of units to adjust.

To address the first issue, the resource manager periodically collects the load status of units and justifies the demand of system adjustment. The adjustment is confirmed only when the resource manager makes the same adjustment decisions for consecutive iterations. This is implemented by maintaining a counter. The counter is incremented by one if the decision is the same as in the precious iteration. Otherwise, the counter is reset to zero. Once the counter reaches the stated threshold, the adjustment is confirmed. In this way, the protocol can tolerate the fluctuation of instant load and avoid making the false positive scaling decision.

The number of units required for adjustment of resources can be quantified as follows:

$$\Delta = \frac{\Sigma_{i=1}^{k} MLV(p_i)}{\Psi \cdot \mathcal{C}} - k = (\frac{\tau}{\Psi} - 1) \cdot k \quad (7)$$

where Ψ ($\Psi \in (\mathcal{T}_l, \mathcal{T}_h)$) is the expected value that indicates the overall load status after adjustment. Equation 7 is applicable to both scaling out and down operations. When Δ is positive, it indicates the system should add units to the subgroup. When Δ is negative, $|\Delta|$ units should be removed from the subgroup.

6. EVALUATION

BiStream is built on Storm [1] and uses Kafka [23] as the input stream adapter. The ripple join is used as the local join algorithm at each joiner task. We compare BiStream with the stream join system developed over join-matrix [1].

6.1 Experimental Setup

Environment. We conduct all the experiments on a cluster of 40 servers, each of which is equipped with an Intel Xeon X3430 @ 2.4GHz CPU and runs CentOS 5.11. Each server is logically partitioned into two processing units, each of which has 2GB RAM. Overall, there are 80 processing units available exclusively for our experiments.

Data sets. We focus on our study using the existing benchmark TPC-H [2]. We generate the TPC-H data sets using the `dbgen` tool shipped with TPC-H benchmark. All the input data sets are pre-generated before feeding to the stream system. In addition, the benchmark tables are projected before feeding into the join system with the attributes only needed in the queries. Different numbers of data are generated to support different data volume requirement during the evaluation. We run all the experiments with asymmetric input rates of two join streams in which case the data volume per second in each stream remains almost the same.

Queries. We consider three join queries including two equi-joins from the TPC-H benchmark and one synthetic band-join which are also used in [12]. The two equi-joins, namely $Q5$ and $Q7$, represent the most expensive join operations in the queries Q5 and Q7 from the benchmark. The synthetic band-join (*Band*) is as follows:

```
SELECT * FROM LINEITEM L1, LINEITEM L2
WHERE ABS(L1.orderkey-L2.orderkey) <=1
AND (L1.shipmode='TRUCK' AND L2.shipinstruct='NONE')
AND L1.Quantity > 48
```

We have also evaluated the performance with online aggregation queries. Due to space constraint, please refer to Appendix B for the results.

Settings. For both join-biclique (JB) and join-matrix (JM), we use the static partitioning schemes that are optimal to the input streams. Specially, to offer the best performance for JM, we consider the square matrix data partitioning scheme for joining equivalent volume streams [12]. For JB, we also assign the same number of units to each relation. Throughout the discussion, we use three different types of join processing settings under JM and JB: `JMx`, `JBx` and `JBx-CRy`. The details of these settings are listed in Table 3.

In addition, we define the *processing volume* as the number of input tuples processed by the system. The *maximum processing volume* is the point when the unit reaches its memory saturation threshold (i.e., the capacity of in-memory processing). Meanwhile, we use the memory load volume (MLV) to measure the memory consumption in each unit.

6.2 Memory Consumption

We first show the memory consumption comparison between JB and JM. Figure 6.a provides the average MLV changes of these two models when the processing volume varies from 1M (million) to 19M. It is conducted over the full-history joins for queries $Q5$, $Q7$ and *Band*. In this experiment, both JB and JM use 16 units, i.e., JB16 and JM16. The memory saturation threshold for each unit is set to 1.5GB. As expected, we can see that JM always consumes memory faster than JB for all the three queries. For example, for query $Q7$, JM reaches the maximum processing volume at 5.8M tuples, whereas JB is at 19M tuples. Similarly, JM reaches the maximum processing volume much earlier than JB for $Q5$ and *Band*. This is because JM needs to store many replications in the joining model, while JB does not. The experimental result confirms that JB is much more memory-efficient and can benefit more in-memory processing than JM over a fixed size of cluster.

Unlike full-history joins, sliding-window joins can bound the memory usage to the size of the workload within the time window, since expired tuples can be discarded from memory. To illustrate the effectiveness of the chained in-memory index, Figure 6.b shows the memory consumption of JB16 for query $Q5$ with sliding windows of 3, 5 and 8 minutes. In this experiment, the average input rate is set to 15K tuples per second and the archive period $\mathcal{P}$ of the chained in-memory index is set to one-tenth of the window size. The experiment results show that after one window time, the memory usage is bounded via data discarding. The ripples in the MLV curve indicates the memory consuming decreases quickly when the data is discarded. This benefits from the data discarding strategy in JB because the discarding is based on the granularity of subindex other than individual tuple.

Furthermore, Figure 6.b also indicates that a longer window (or a bigger processing volume) causes a higher MLV. For example, the 8-minute window uses more memory than the 3-minute and 5-minute windows. In other words, the maximum size of processing volume that a system can support reflects the size of the time window it can achieve for in-memory join processing. As shown in Figure 6.a, JB can support a much bigger processing volume than JM. This provides us another insight: given a cluster, JB is able to support a much bigger window size in supporting in-memory sliding-window joins than JM. More experimental evaluations about the derived maximum sizes of sliding windows with respect to different settings can be found in Appendix C.

Table 3: List of model settings.

Name	Description
JMx	The join-matrix over $\sqrt{x} \times \sqrt{x}$ matrix, where each partition corresponds to $\sqrt{x}$ units.
JBx	The join-biclique over $x/2 + x/2$ units with random routing, where each relation corresponds to $x/2$ units.
JBx-CRy	The join-biclique over $x/2 + x/2$ units with ContRand routing, where each relation has $x/2$ units partitioned into y subgroups.

6.3 Throughput and Latency

Next, we study the throughput comparison among the different models. To provide a comprehensive study, we test five different settings, where JB8 has the same number of partitions (4 partitions for each relation) with JM16, and the remaining three settings with JB16 use the same number of units (16 units in total) as JM16. Figure 8 presents the throughput comparisons for queries $Q5$, $Q7$ and *Band* when the system is fed in 10GB, 80GB and 320GB data sets.

As shown in Figure 8.a, for $Q5$, all different settings provide comparative throughput when the system is fed with 10GB data. This is because the memory is sufficient to hold all the 10GB data in memory in all settings. We observe that the throughput of JB16 (with random routing) is smaller than JM16 in the 10GB case. This is because, under random routing, all the units of one relation are involved in the join processing of every input tuple of the other

[1]`https://github.com/epfldata/squall`

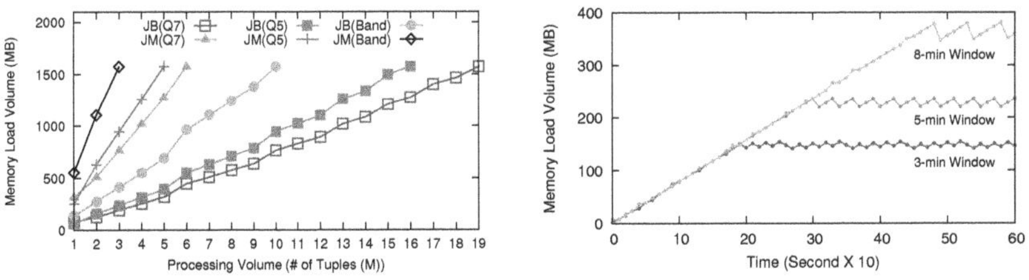

(a) Full-history joins. (b) Sliding-window joins.

Figure 6: Memory usage.

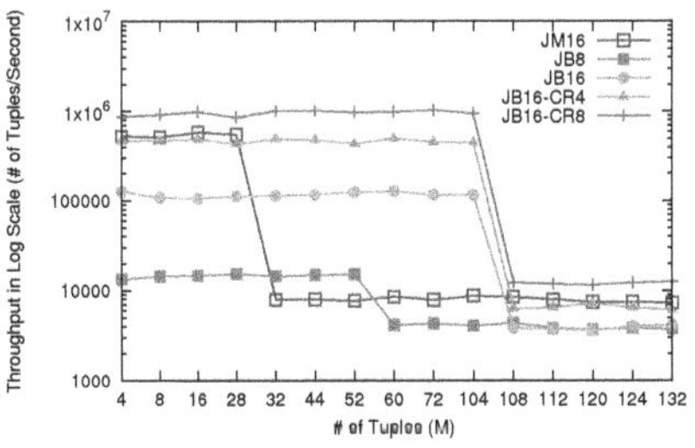

Figure 7: Real-time throughput.

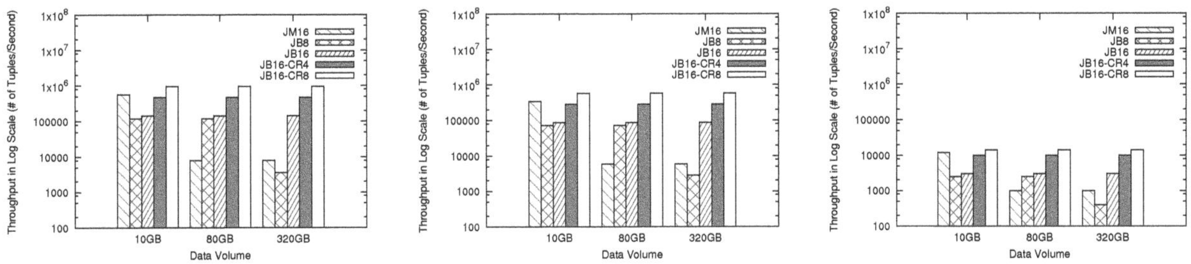

(a) Throughput for query $Q5$. (b) Throughput for query $Q7$. (c) Throughput for query *Band*.

Figure 8: Average throughput with different processing volume.

relation. This causes each unit to process more tuples in JB16 than in JM16, resulting in the throughput decrease of JB16. As shown in the 10GB case, once JB adopts the ContRand routing strategy, its throughput becomes similar or even higher than JM. When the system is fed with 80GB data, the throughput of JM16 decreases sharply and performs far behind JB. For example, JB16-CR8 performs better than JM16 for almost two orders of magnitude. Interestingly, JM16 with 16 units performs even worse than JB8 with 8 units for one order of magnitude. This is because 80GB has exceeded the maximum processing volume of JM16, resulting in frequent disk I/Os, thereby reducing the throughput. With 80GB data, the processing in other JB settings remains in-memory. As shown in Figure 8.a, the throughput of JB8 decreases as well after JB8 reaching its maximum processing volume for 320GB. This further confirms that in-memory processing is the key to efficient stream join processing.

For queries $Q7$ and *Band*, we observe similar trends of throughput change with different settings as query $Q5$. Note that the throughput of $Q5$ is around 1.5X bigger than $Q7$ on average where the difference is unclear after using the log scale in the results. Figure 8 shows that the throughput of processing $Q5$ and $Q7$ is much higher than that of processing *Band*. This is within expectation, as query *Band* involves inequality join and incurs higher computation overhead than equi-join queries $Q5$ and $Q7$.

Figure 7 illustrates the throughput change along the increase of tuples ingested for query $Q5$. Consistently, JB16-CR8 provides the highest throughput than all the other settings. In addition, JM is the first one to reach its system memory capacity when 28M tuples are fed. Interestingly, the maximum processing volume of JB8 is around 52M tuples, which is much larger than that of JM16. Furthermore, the JB settings with 16 units yield high throughput and provide much larger memory capacity than JM for efficient in-memory join processing. Another insight we obtain is that the content-sensitive routing strategy can increase the throughput of JB. Figure 8 and Figure 7 confirm that JB16-CR8 (resp. JB16-CR4) outperforms JB16-CR4 (resp. JB16) in terms of the throughput. This is because the content-sensitive routing strategy renders each input tuple sent to some specific units instead of all units for join processing.

We also examine the latency of different models. The latency is measured by capturing the difference between the time producing a join result and the time of a more recent tuple participated in the join entering the join system. Figure 9 provides the latency of JM and JB under different settings for queries $Q5$, $Q7$ and *Band*. The box in each series encloses the 25/75 percentile of the distribution with median shown as a horizontal line within each box. The top and bottom horizontal lines outside the box show the worst and best cases respectively. The statistical results are collected after the system is running at maximum throughput with in-memory processing. The results indicate that JB and JM achieve a similar average latency (within 10ms difference) within each query. We observe that the latency is dominated by the network transfer (due to the routing architecture) and the queuing of massive tuple processing in each unit. It is not surprising that JB16 setting generates a slightly larger latency than the others due to more data shuffling and join processing. It also shows that the latency of JB decreases when the ContRand routing strategy is adopted. For instance, the JB16-CR8 achieves a lower latency than JM for all the queries. This further confirms that the content-sensitive routing is able to prune the unrelated join tuples and further reduce latency.

6.4 Scalability and Elasticity

We further study the scalability by observing how the maximum processing volume changes when the system scales out. Figure 10 shows the results of processing query $Q7$ on the number of units varying from 4 to 64. As studied in [12], a square matrix is able to achieve a good performance for JM-based processing. So, we only show the results on the perfect squares of units for JB and JM. Interested readers

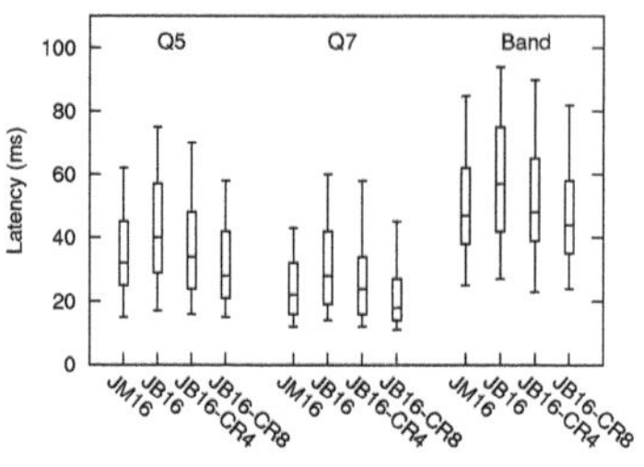

Figure 9: Latency.

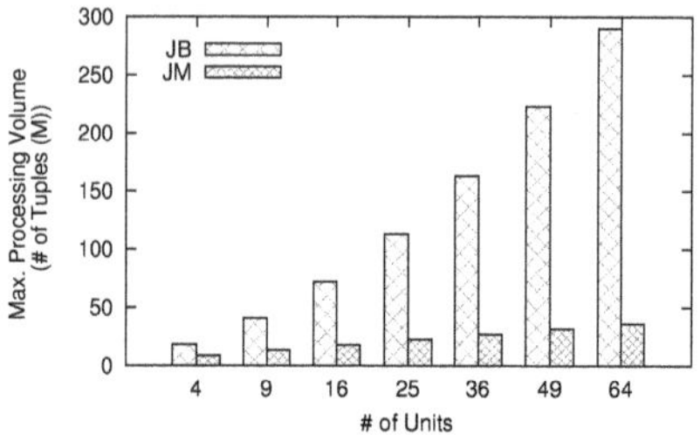

Figure 10: Scalability.

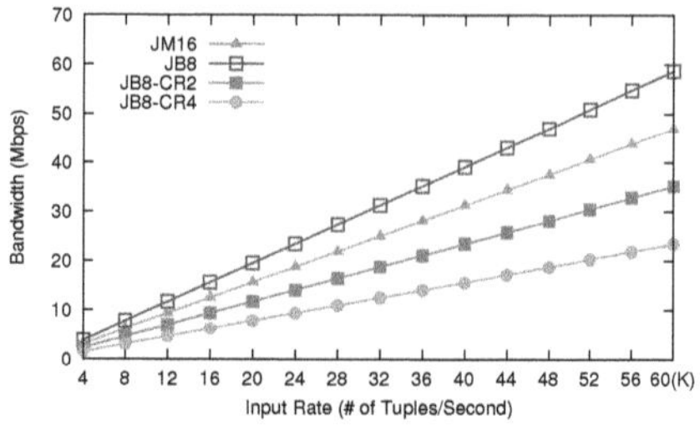

Figure 11: Bandwidth consumption.

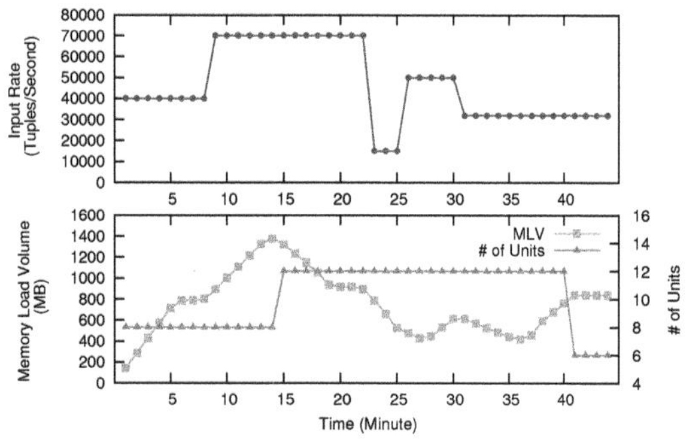

Figure 12: Dynamic resource management.

may refer to Appendix D for more results on other combinations of units. Experimental results indicate that JM does not scale well as the number of units increases. For example, it supports 19M and 37M tuples over 16 and 64 units, respectively. This is reasonable as JM has to store more data replicas with the increased size of matrix. This thereby limits the scalability of JM. As expected, we observe that JB achieves almost linear scalability. The maximum processing volume of JB increases in double when the number of units doubles. For example, JB supports 76M tuples of maximum processing volume with 16 units, while the tuples number increases to 290M with 64 units. This benefits from the unit independence such that the newly added units do not replicate any data from other units.

We next evaluate the capability of BiStream to dynamically adjust the number of resources according to the stream input rate changes. The experiment is conducted using $Q7$ for a 5-minute window join with JB8 as the initial setting. The top of Figure 12 presents the varying stream input rates during the 50 minutes of evaluation. As the input stream rate changes, the MLV changes as well. The overload and underload thresholds are set as $\mathcal{T}_h = 0.8$ and $\mathcal{T}_l = 0.3$ respectively, and the target load status after adjustment is set as $\Psi = 0.6$. In this experiment, we allow the resource manager to check the MLV in each processing unit with a 1-minute period. The scaling out/down operation is triggered once it receives the same scaling requests for 3 consecutive times. The bottom of Figure 12 shows how the processing units are dynamically added/released from the system while the MLV changes. From the result, we can see that the system is able to dynamically add/release the processing units once the memory is over/under loaded. For instance, 4 and 6 processing units are effectively added and removed from the system when the MLV reaches above 1.2GB and falls below 450MB respectively. During the system scaling, for sliding-window join, data migration is avoided since the system discards the expired tuples and controls the storage distribution of the new incoming tuples to equivalently achieve load balancing among the units. This favors no system downtime and no impact on the average latency. Another observation is that BiStream is able to handle the fluctuation of the workload to avoid the false adjustment. BiStream does not trigger any scaling out/down operation when the input stream is shortly increased and deceased between the 22nd and 31st minutes.

6.5 Communication Cost

Finally, we evaluate the network bandwidth usage within the join processing. Figure 11 provides the bandwidth consumption for processing query $Q5$, when the input rate varies from 4K to 60K tuples per second. For the ease of comparison, we measure the bandwidth usage for JM16, JB8, JB8-CR2 and JB8-CR4, where each relation has 4 partitions. Note that under this setting, JB can support double storage capacity than JM. The results of JB8 and JM16 in Figure 11 indicate that JB consumes higher bandwidth than JM, which is due to random routing. Once ContRand routing is adopted, JB8-CR2 and JB8-CR4 consume less bandwidth than JB8. From the experimental results, we can draw two insights: First, ContRand routing strategy can greatly reduce the bandwidth consumption in JB; Second, JB has competitive bandwidth requirement as JM but offers a larger maximum processing volume. Appendix E provides more experimental results on the bandwidth consumption over different settings.

In summary, our experiments show that JB is superior to JM in terms of memory-efficiency, elasticity and scalability, and is comparable in terms of latency. Integration of the content-sensitive routing strategy enables the system to further achieve a lower network consumption and latency.

7. CONCLUSION

In this paper, we proposed a novel stream join model, called join-biclique, for online stream joins with general predicates. Join-biclique logically models all the processing units as a bipartite graph for stream joins with no data replication, flexible partition scheme and processing units independence designs. On the basis of join-biclique, we designed and developed a distributed stream join processing system, *BiStream* with a large-scale commodity cluster. Specifically, it is designed to support efficient full-history joins, window-based joins and other operations including selection, projection and online data aggregation. BiStream also supports an adaptive resource management where the system can dynamically scale out or down. We theoretically analyzed the proposed techniques and also conducted extensive experimental evaluation. The evaluation results demonstrate that BiStream is memory-efficient, elastic and scalable.

Acknowledgments

This research is funded by the National Research Foundation (NRF), Prime Minister's Office, Singapore under its Campus for Research Excellence and Technological Enterprise (CREATE) programme ("SP-2: Database Support for Research on Megacities" R-252-000-496-281), and the A*STAR project 1321202073. We would like to thank the anonymous reviewers for their insightful feedback.

APPENDIX

A. REFERENCES

[1] Apache storm. `http://storm.apache.org`.

[2] The tpc-h benchmark. `http://www.tpc.org/tpch`.

[3] S. Agarwal, A. P. Iyer, A. Panda, S. Madden, B. Mozafari, and I. Stoica. Blink and it's done: Interactive queries on very large data. *Proceedings of the VLDB Endowment*, 5(12):1902–1905, 2012.

[4] R. Ananthanarayanan, V. Basker, S. Das, A. Gupta, H. Jiang, T. Qiu, A. Reznichenko, D. Ryabkov, M. Singh, and S. Venkataraman. Photon: fault-tolerant and scalable joining of continuous data streams. In *Proc. of SIGMOD*, pages 577–588, 2013.

[5] A. Arasu, B. Babcock, S. Babu, J. McAlister, and J. Widom. Characterizing memory requirements for queries over continuous data streams. *ACM Transactions on Database Systems*, 29(1):162–194, 2004.

[6] B. Babcock, S. Babu, M. Datar, R. Motwani, and J. Widom. Models and issues in data stream systems. In *Proc. of PODS*, pages 1–16, 2002.

[7] C. Balkesen, N. Tatbul, and M. T. Özsu. Adaptive input admission and management for parallel stream processing. In *Proc. of DEBS*, pages 15–26, 2013.

[8] S. Blanas, Y. Li, and J. M. Patel. Design and evaluation of main memory hash join algorithms for multi-core cpus. In *Proc. of SIGMOD*, pages 37–48, 2011.

[9] M.-S. Chen, M.-L. Lo, P. S. Yu, and H. C. Young. Using segmented right-deep trees for the execution of pipelined hash joins. In *Proc. of VLDB*, pages 15–26, 1992.

[10] S. Chen, P. B. Gibbons, and S. Nath. Pr-join: a non-blocking join achieving higher early result rate with statistical guarantees. In *Proc. of SIGMOD*, pages 147–158, 2010.

[11] D. Dey, T. M. Barron, and V. C. Storey. A complete temporal relational algebra. *The VLDB Journal*, 5(3):167–180, 1996.

[12] M. Elseidy, A. Elguindy, A. Vitorovic, and C. Koch. Scalable and adaptive online joins. In *Proc. of VLDB*, pages 441–452, 2014.

[13] B. Gedik. Partitioning functions for stateful data parallelism in stream processing. *The VLDB Journal*, 23(4):517–539, 2014.

[14] B. Gedik, P. S. Yu, and R. R. Bordawekar. Executing stream joins on the cell processor. In *Proc. of VLDB*, pages 363–374, 2007.

[15] J. Gehrke, F. Korn, and D. Srivastava. On computing correlated aggregates over continual data streams. In *Proc. of SIGMOD*, pages 13–24, 2001.

[16] L. Golab and M. T. Özsu. Processing sliding window multi-joins in continuous queries over data streams. In *Proc. of VLDB*, pages 500–511, 2003.

[17] P. J. Haas and J. M. Hellerstein. Ripple joins for online aggregation. In *Proc. of SIGMOD*, pages 287–298, 1999.

[18] J. M. Hellerstein, P. J. Haas, and H. J. Wang. Online aggregation. In *Proc. of SIGMOD*, pages 171–182, 1997.

[19] J.-H. Hwang, M. Balazinska, A. Rasin, U. Cetintemel, M. Stonebraker, and S. Zdonik. High-availability algorithms for distributed stream processing. In *Proc. of ICDE*, pages 779–790, 2005.

[20] C. Jermaine, A. Dobra, S. Arumugam, S. Joshi, and A. Pol. The sort-merge-shrink join. *ACM Transactions on Database Systems*, 31(4):1382–1416, 2006.

[21] T. Karnagel, D. Habich, B. Schlegel, and W. Lehner. The hells-join: A heterogeneous stream join for extremely large windows. In *Proc. of DaMoN*, 2013.

[22] M. Kitsuregawa, H. Tanaka, and T. Moto-Oka. Application of hash to data base machine and its architecture. *New Generation Computing*, 1(1):63 74, 1983.

[23] J. Kreps, N. Narkhede, and J. Rao. Kafka: A distributed messaging system for log processing. In *Proc. of NetDB*, 2011.

[24] J. F. Kurose and K. W. Ross. *Computer networking: a top-down approach (6th edition)*. Pearson Education, 2012.

[25] L. Lamport. Time, clocks, and the ordering of events in a distributed system. *Communications of the ACM*, 21(7):558–565, 1978.

[26] F. Li, B. C. Ooi, M. T. Özsu, and S. Wu. Distributed data management using mapreduce. *ACM Computing Surveys*, 46(3):31:1–31:42, 2014.

[27] G. Luo, C. J. Ellmann, P. J. Haas, and J. F. Naughton. A scalable hash ripple join algorithm. In *Proc. of SIGMOD*, pages 252–262, 2002.

[28] A. Okcan and M. Riedewald. Processing theta-joins using mapreduce. In *Proc. of SIGMOD*, pages 949–960, 2011.

[29] J. Qian, Y. Li, Y. Wang, H. Chen, and Y. Dong. An embedded co-processor for accelerating window joins over uncertain data streams. *Microprocessors and Microsystems*, 36(6):489–504, 2012.

[30] Z. Qian, Y. He, C. Su, Z. Wu, H. Zhu, T. Zhang, L. Zhou, Y. Yu, and Z. Zhang. Timestream: reliable stream computation in the cloud. In *Proc. of EuroSys*, pages 1–14, 2013.

[31] P. Roy, J. Teubner, and R. Gemulla. Low-latency handshake join. In *Proc. of VLDB*, pages 709–720, 2014.

[32] A. Shatdal and J. F. Naughton. Adaptive parallel aggregation algorithms. In *Proc. of SIGMOD*, pages 104–114, 1995.

[33] U. Srivastava and J. Widom. Memory-limited execution of windowed stream joins. In *Proc. of VLDB*, pages 324–335, 2004.

[34] J. W. Stamos and H. C. Young. A symmetric fragment and replicate algorithm for distributed joins.

IEEE Transactions on Parallel and Distributed Systems, 4(12):1345–1354, 1993.
[35] J. Teubner, G. Alonso, C. Balkesen, and M. T. Ozsu. Main-memory hash joins on multi-core cpus: Tuning to the underlying hardware. In *Proc. of ICDE*, pages 362–373, 2013.
[36] J. Teubner and R. Mueller. How soccer players would do stream joins. In *Proc. of SIGMOD*, pages 625–636, 2011.
[37] P. A. Tucker, D. Maier, T. Sheard, and L. Fegaras. Exploiting punctuation semantics in continuous data streams. *IEEE Transactions on Knowledge and Data Engineering*, 15(3):555–568, 2003.
[38] S. Wang and E. Rundensteiner. Scalable stream join processing with expensive predicates: workload distribution and adaptation by time-slicing. In *Proc. of EDBT*, pages 299–310, 2009.
[39] A. Wilschut and P. M. G. Apers. Dataflow query execution in a parallel main-memory environment. In *Proc. of PDIS*, pages 68–77, 1991.
[40] M. Zaharia, M. Chowdhury, T. Das, A. Dave, J. Ma, M. McCauley, M. J. Franklin, S. Shenker, and I. Stoica. Resilient distributed datasets: A fault-tolerant abstraction for in-memory cluster computing. In *Proc. of NSDI*, pages 2–2, 2012.
[41] M. Zaharia, T. Das, H. Li, T. Hunter, S. Shenker, and I. Stoica. Discretized streams: fault-tolerant streaming computation at scale. In *Proc. of SOSP*, pages 423–438, 2013.
[42] H. Zhang, G. Chen, B. C. Ooi, K.-L. Tan, and M. Zhang. In-memory big data management and processing: A survey. *IEEE Transactions on Knowledge and Data Engineering*, 2015.

B. EVALUATION FOR ONLINE DATA AGGREGATION

We modify the three queries used in Section 6 to add aggregation functions for the online aggregation evaluation. For queries $Q5$ and $Q7$, we apply the `sum` aggregate function to the join results with the corresponding group-by operations as defined in the TPC-H specification [2]. For query *Band*, we add three different aggregate functions `count`, `min` and `max` simultaneously based on the group-by attribute of nation name *n_name*. BiStream adopts the two-phase aggregation approach as described in Section 3.4.2 to support online data aggregation. Figure 13 shows the throughput comparison between the three queries with and without the aggregation functions over the JB16 and JB16-CR4 settings. It can be seen that the aggregation operation exerts negligible impact on the throughput. This is reasonable, as each joiner task directly aggregates its join results in a pipeline fashion and thus is efficient.

Figure 14 shows the network bandwidth usage, when different aggregation strategies are adopted. Recall that BiStream adopts one batch optimization to pre-aggregate the join results in each joiner before generating the global view. This experiment is conducted over a JB16-CR4 setting using queries $Q5$, $Q7$ and *Band* with the input rates of 450K, 270K and 9K tuples per second respectively. From the results, we can see that the batch local view update approach greatly reduces the bandwidth usage for aggregation operation.

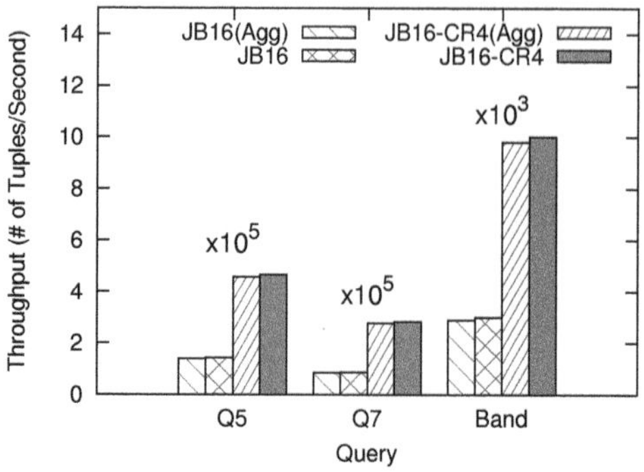

Figure 13: Throughput with and without aggregation.

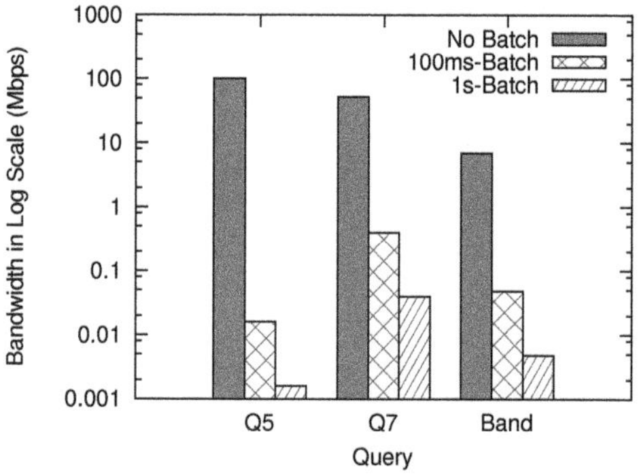

Figure 14: Bandwidth usage with aggregation.

C. MAXIMUM SIZE OF SLIDING WINDOW

Table 4 demonstrates the maximum window size that join-biclique and join-matrix can support in-memory sliding-window join processing. It includes the results for both queries $Q5$ and $Q7$ running on five different settings JB8, JB16, JB36, JM16 and JM36. For query $Q5$, all settings are evaluated under two different input rates of 50K and 80K tuples per second. For query $Q7$, all settings are evaluated with the input rates of 30K and 50K tuples per second. The results confirm that JB can support a larger window for in-memory processing than JM.

Table 4: Maximum size of sliding window.

Query	Rate	JB8	JB16	JB36	JM16	JM36
$Q5$	50K/s	278	549	1262	140	207
	80K/s	171	351	785	88	136
$Q7$	30K/s	572	1167	2636	292	439
	50K/s	341	697	1543	173	262

(Unit: Second)

D. RESULTS ON SCALABILITY

Figure 15 and Figure 16 provide maximum processing volume comparison between join-biclique and join-matrix when the number of units varies from 4 to 64 for queries $Q5$ and *Band* respectively. Similarly to the result for query $Q7$ provided in Section 6, JB shows better scalability than JM for $Q5$ and *Band*.

Figure 17 illustrates the maximum processing volume changes when the number of units varies from 4 to 64 with more partitioning schemes. As shown in the results, the maximum processing volume exhibits linear increment with the increasing number of units in JB.

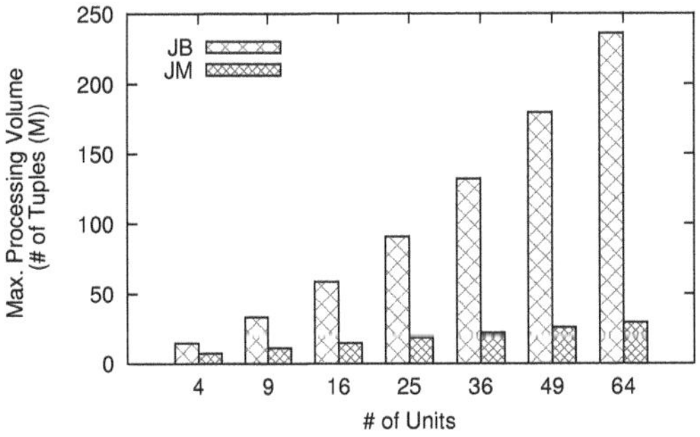

Figure 15: Scalability comparison on query $Q5$.

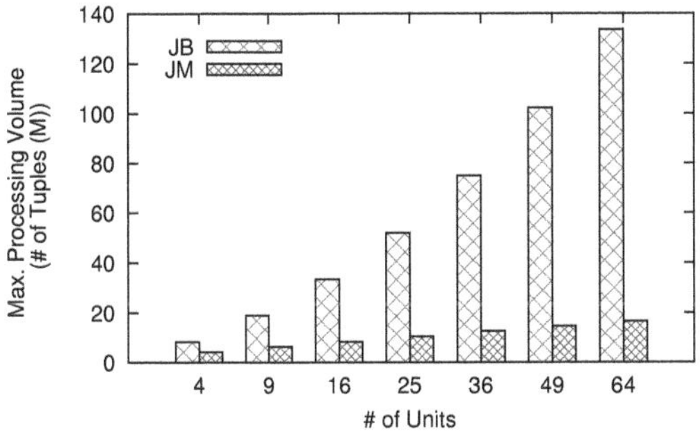

Figure 16: Scalability comparison on query *Band*.

E. RESULTS ON COMMUNICATION COST

Figure 18 and Figure 19 provide more experimental results of bandwidth usage for queries $Q7$ and *Band* respectively. For query $Q7$, the bandwidth usage is evaluated by changing the input rates from 10K to 50K tuples per second. For query *Band*, the bandwidth usage is evaluated when the input rates vary from 200 to 1600 tuples per second. The results confirm that the ContRand routing strategy is able to reduce the bandwidth usage in JB, and JB offers a larger maximum processing volume while using competitive bandwidth as JM.

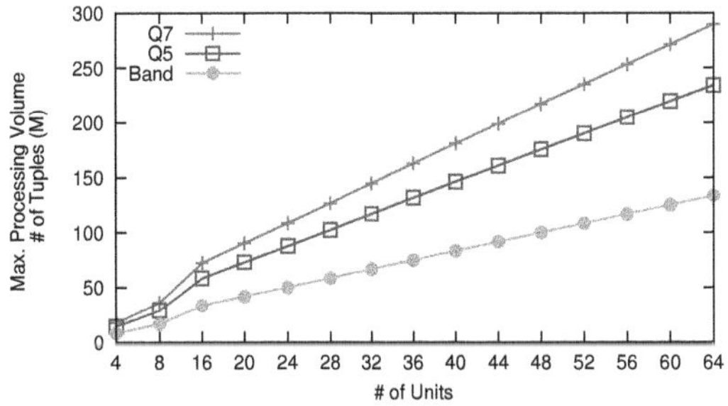

Figure 17: Scalability of join-biclique.

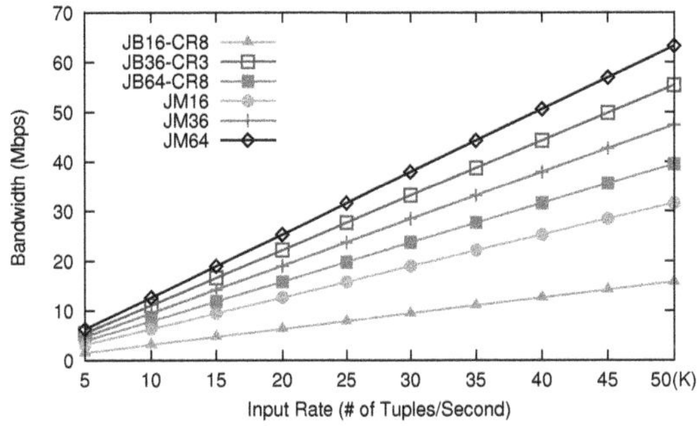

Figure 18: Bandwidth on query $Q7$.

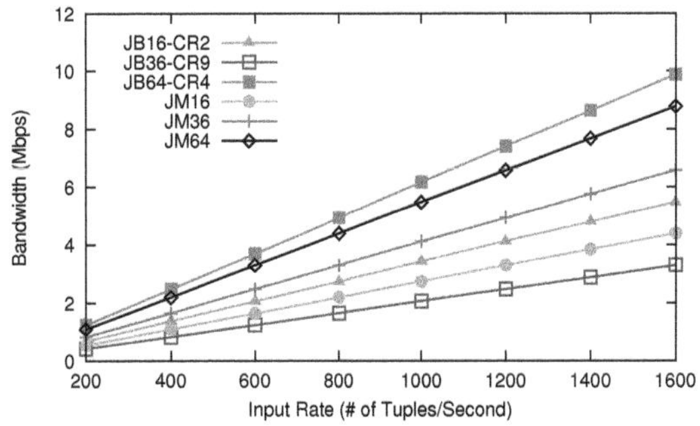

Figure 19: Bandwidth on query *Band*.

SCREEN: Stream Data Cleaning under Speed Constraints

Shaoxu Song[§] Aoqian Zhang[§] Jianmin Wang[§] Philip S. Yu[‡]

[§]KLiss, MoE; TNList; School of Software, Tsinghua University, China
{sxsong, jimwang}@tsinghua.edu.cn zaq13@mails.tsinghua.edu.cn

[‡]Department of Computer Science, University of Illinois at Chicago, USA &
Institute for Data Science, Tsinghua University, China psyu@cs.uic.edu

ABSTRACT

Stream data are often dirty, for example, owing to unreliable sensor reading, or erroneous extraction of stock prices. Most stream data cleaning approaches employ a smoothing filter, which may seriously alter the data without preserving the original information. We argue that the cleaning should avoid changing those originally correct/clean data, a.k.a. the *minimum change principle* in data cleaning. To capture the knowledge about *what is clean*, we consider the (widely existing) constraints on the speed of data changes, such as fuel consumption per hour, or daily limit of stock prices. Guided by these semantic constraints, in this paper, we propose SCREEN, the first constraint-based approach for cleaning stream data. It is notable that existing data repair techniques clean (a sequence of) data *as a whole* and fail to support stream computation. To this end, we have to relax the global optimum over the entire sequence to the local optimum in a window. Rather than the commonly observed NP-hardness of general data repairing problems, our major contributions include (1) polynomial time algorithm for global optimum, (2) linear time algorithm towards local optimum under an efficient *Median Principle*, (3) support on out-of-order arrivals of data points, and (4) adaptive window size for balancing repair accuracy and efficiency. Experiments on real datasets demonstrate that SCREEN can show significantly higher repair accuracy than the existing approaches such as smoothing.

Categories and Subject Descriptors

H.2.0 [**Database Management**]: General

Keywords

Data repairing; speed constraints

1. INTRODUCTION

Dirty values commonly exist in data streams, e.g., in traditional sensor data due to the unreliable readers [10]. Even in the domains of Stock and Flight where people believed data are reliable, a large amount of inconsistent data are surprisingly observed [15]. According to the study, the accuracy of Stock in *Yahoo! Finance* is 0.93, and the Flight data accuracy in *Travelocity* is 0.95. Reasons for imprecise values include ambiguity in information extraction, unit error or pure mistake. For instance, the price of SALVEPAR (SY) is misused as the price of SYBASE, which is denoted by SY as well in some sources. (See more examples of data errors below.) Such inaccurate values, e.g., taken as the 52-week low price, may seriously mislead business investment.

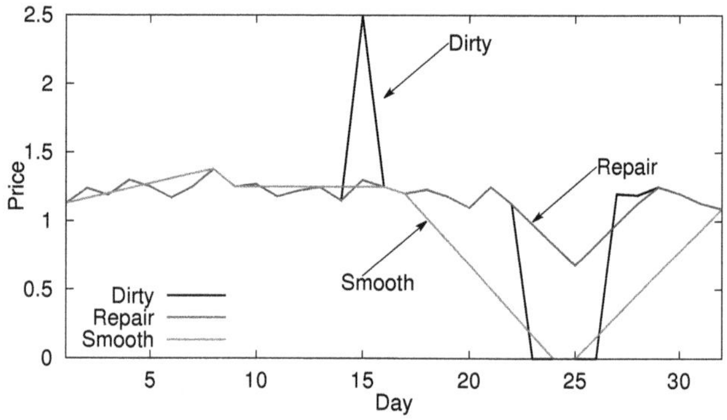

Figure 1: Smoothing filter seriously alters the original correct data, while the minimum repair under speed constraints aim to preserve the original information as much as possible

A temporal smoothing filter, e.g., via segmentation in sliding windows [13], may modify almost all the data values, most of which are originally correct/clean. It thus seriously damages the precision of individual data points (such as daily stock prices). Indeed, in order to preserve the original clean information as much as possible, the *minimum change principle* is widely considered in improving data quality [1].

To capture the knowledge about *what is clean*, we notice that the "jump" of values in a stream is often constrained, so called *speed constraints*. In financial and commodity markets, prices are only permitted to rise or fall by a certain number of ticks per trading session. In environment monitoring, the temperature difference of any two days in a week should not be greater than 20 degrees. The fuel consumption of a crane should not be negative and not exceed 40 liters per hour. We believe that with these meaningful constraints on value change speed, cleaning could be more accurate.

Example 1. *Consider the prices of a stock in 32 trading days, in Figure 1. As illustrated, large spikes appear in the*

SIGMOD'15, May 31–June 4, 2015, Melbourne, Victoria, Australia.
Copyright © 2015 ACM 978-1-4503-2758-9/15/05 ...$15.00.
http://dx.doi.org/10.1145/2723372.2723730.

dirty data (in black), e.g., in day 15, owing to ambiguity in information extraction as discussed or pure mistake. It may also be raised by temporary loss of data (days from 23 to 26) and the subsequent coding of these missing values as zero by the data collection system.

The smoothing method (in red) modifies almost all the price values, most of which are indeed accurate. Without preserving the original clean price of each day, the modified data values become useless. It is obviously not the best way for cleaning the stream data.

The speed constraints derived from price limit[1] *state that the price difference of two consecutive trading days should not be greater than 0.5. The maximum speed* $s_{\max} = 0.5$ *specifies that the increase amount is no larger than 0.5 in a single trading day from the previous day's settlement price. The minimum speed* $s_{\min} = -0.5$ *indicates that the decrease should be within 0.5.*

With speed constraints, the imprecise value of day 15 can be detected. It obviously increases too much from the price of the previous day 14. As shown, the speed constraint-based repair (proposed in this study) preserves more originally clean price values (in blue).

Challenges. Unlike the existing techniques on smoothing time series [13], we propose to minimally modify the data values such that the declared speed constraints are satisfied. This constraint-based cleaning, however, is non-trivial and challenging especially in the following aspects:

(1) *Soundness.* Owing to the inherent hardness of general data repair problems, a greedy strategy is employed in the existing repair [4]. It modifies values to eliminate currently observed violations (w.r.t. the given constraints) in each round which may introduce new violations to other data points, and thus evokes another round of repairing. In particular, the greedy repair could be trapped in local optima, and thus cannot eliminate all the violations. In other words, the soundness w.r.t. satisfaction of (speed) constraints is not guaranteed. According to our empirical study (see details in Section 6), 40-80% values in the greedily repaired results may still be in violation w.r.t. the speed constraints.

(2) *Online Computing.* Typically, data repair techniques consider a global optimization function on modifying the entire data [1]. It has to first collect all the data, and then repair them as a whole. Online cleaning on the streaming data is not supported. To enable streaming computation, we have to decompose the global optimum into a list of local optimum on each data point, respectively. Integral cleaning can thus be applied by incrementally computing the local optimal repair on every data point of the sequence in turn.

(3) *Out-of-order Arrival.* Network latencies or device failures may cause data to arrive out-of-order [16]. To avoid output blocking, it is necessary to carry on the cleaning with the absence of some data, and update the results later when the delayed data come. The repair on a data point depends not only on the previous data points, but also on the future data points. That is, the arrival of each delayed data point may cause some of the previous data points to be repaired again. How to efficiently determine the data points affected and the amount to be adjusted is the main challenge.

(4) *Throughput.* The speed constraint is often meaningful in a period with certain lengths. For instance, it is meaningless to consider the constraint on temperature of two days in different years. Such a large window size requires to compare more data points w.r.t. speed constraints, and thus may result in huge system latencies and memory resource overflow. On the other hand, with a small window size, while the time efficiency is improved, the power of speed constraints could be limited in repairing (as illustrated in Example 2). Even worse, such trade-off on window sizes may vary with the evolving of the arrival rate (the number of data points arrived in a period). To increase system throughput, it is promising to devise adaptive window sizes that can automatically balance the cleaning accuracy and efficiency.

Contributions. To the best of our knowledge, this is the first study on constraint-based stream data cleaning. The proposed SCREEN (Speed Constraint-based stREam data clEaNing) is a linear time, constant space cleaning approach. Our main contributions are summarized as follows.

(1) We formalize the repair problem under speed constraints (in Section 2). By considering the entire sequence as a whole, the monolithic cleaning finds a repaired sequence that minimally differs from the input. Unlike NP-hardness of general data repair problems [17, 14], we show that stream data cleaning under speed constraints can be modeled as a linear programming problem, i.e., polynomial time solvable.

(2) We devise an online cleaning algorithm (in Section 3). To support integral cleaning (i.e., incrementally repair one data point a time in the sequence rather than monolithic cleaning as a whole), we relax the global optimum over the entire sequence to the local optimum in a window. The main idea is to locally compute a data point repair, which is minimal w.r.t. the upcoming data points in a window and also compatible with the previously repaired data points. In particular, to efficiently compute the local optimum, we propose a novel *Median Principle*, following the intuition that a solution with the minimum distance (i.e., as close as possible to each point) probably lies in the middle of the data points. It is notable that soundness w.r.t. speed constraint satisfaction is guaranteed in the devised algorithm.

(3) We extend the algorithm for out-of-order data arrival (in Section 4). An update of previously repaired results is performed when the delayed data comes. We further reduce the latency by heuristically applying the updates.

(4) We propose a sampling-based, adaptive window (in Section 5). By modeling data points as random samples of approaching the speed constraints, the criteria in distribution approximation can be employed to suggest increasing or reducing the window sizes for acquiring more or less samples.

Finally, experiments on real data demonstrate that our proposed SCREEN achieves significantly higher repair accuracy than the smoothing method [13]. Moreover, compared to the state-of-the-art data repair method [4], SCREEN with local optimum shows up to 4 orders of magnitude improvement in time costs without losing much accuracy.

Table 2 in the Appendix lists the frequently used notations. Proofs of major results can be found in the long version technique report [6].

2. MONOLITHIC CLEANING

First, considering a sequence as a whole, we perform monolithic repair towards the globally minimum repair distance.

[1]In some markets, the price limit is specified by a certain percentage. See Section 6.4 for obtaining max/min speed from such price limit.

2.1 Preliminary

Consider a sequence $x = x[1], x[2], \ldots$, where each $x[i]$ is the value of the i-th data point. Each $x[i]$ has a timestamp $t[i]$. For brevity, we write $x[i]$ as x_i, and $t[i]$ as t_i.

A *speed constraint* $s = (s_{\min}, s_{\max})$ with window size w is a pair of minimum speed $s_{\min}$ and maximum speed $s_{\max}$ over the sequence x. We say that a sequence x *satisfies* the speed constraint s, denoted by $x \models s$, if for any x_i, x_j in a window, i.e., $0 < t_j - t_i \leq w$, it has $s_{\min} \leq \frac{x_j - x_i}{t_j - t_i} \leq s_{\max}$.

The window w denotes a period of time. In real settings, speed constraints are often meaningful within a certain period. For example, it is reasonable to consider the maximum walking speed in hours (rather than the speed between two arbitrary observations in different years), since a person usually cannot keep on walking in his/her maximum speed for several years without a break. In other words, it is sufficient to validate the speed w.r.t. two points x_i, x_j in a window $w =$ 24 hours, i.e., whether $s_{\min} \leq \frac{x_j - x_i}{t_j - t_i} \leq s_{\max}, 0 < t_j - t_i \leq w$. In contrast, considering the speed w.r.t. two points in an extremely large period (e.g., two observation points in different years) is meaningless and unnecessary. Similar examples include the speed constraints on stock price whose daily limit is directly determined by the price of the *last* trading day, i.e., with window size 1.

The speed constraint s can be either positive (restricting value increase) or negative (on decrease). In most scenarios, the speed constraint is natural, e.g., the fuel consumption of a crane should not be negative and not exceed 40 liters per hour, while some others could be derived. (See Section 6.4 for a discussion on obtaining speed constraints.)

A *repair* x' of x is a modification of the values x_i to x'_i where $t'_i = t_i$. Referring to the minimum change principle in data repairing [1], the repair distance is evaluated by the difference between the original x and the repaired x',

$$\Delta(x, x') = \sum_{x_i \in x} |x_i - x'_i|. \tag{1}$$

Example 2 (Speed constraints, violations, and repairs). *Consider a sequence* $x = \{12, 12.5, 13, 10, 15, 15.5\}$ *of six data points, with timestamps* $t = \{1, 2, 3, 5, 7, 8\}$. *Figure 2(a) illustrates the data points (in black). Suppose that the speed constraints are* $s_{\max} = 0.5$ *and* $s_{\min} = -0.5$.

For a window size $w = 2$ *in the speed constraints, data points* x_3 *and* x_4*, with timestamp distance* $5 - 3 \leq 2$ *in a window, are identified as violations to* $s_{\min} = -0.5$*, since the speed is* $\frac{10-13}{5-3} = -1.5 < -0.5$. *Similarly,* x_4 *and* x_5 *with speed* $\frac{15-10}{7-5} = 2.5 > 0.5$ *are violations to* $s_{\max} = 0.5$.

To remedy the violations (denoted by red lines), a repair on x_4 *can be performed, i.e.,* $x'_4 = 14$ *(the white data point). As illustrated in Figure 2(a), the repaired sequence satisfies both the maximum and minimum speed constraints. The repair distance is* $\Delta(x, x') = |10 - 14| = 4$.

Note that if the window size is too small such as $w = 1$*, the violations between* x_3 *and* x_4 *(as well as* x_4 *and* x_5*) could not be detected, since their timestamp distance is* $2 > 1$. *On the other hand, if the window size is too large, say* $w = 10$*, then all the pairs of data points in* x *have to be compared. Although the same repair* x' *is obtained, the computation overhead is obviously higher (and unnecessary). Nevertheless, we propose to determine an adaptive window size (in Section 5) for balancing accuracy and efficiency.*

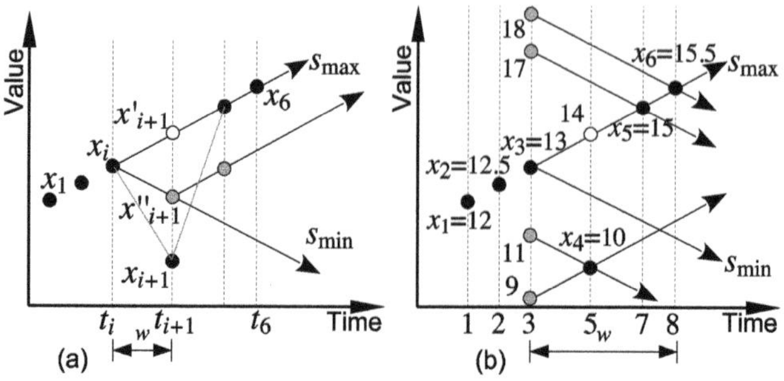

Figure 2: Possible repairs under speed constraints

2.2 Global Optimum

The cleaning problem is to find a repaired sequence that satisfies the speed constraints and minimally differs from the original sequence, called *global optimum*.

Problem 1. *Given a finite sequence* x *of* n *data points and a speed constraint* s*, the* global optimal repair *problem is to find a repair* x' *such that* $x' \models s$ *and* $\Delta(x, x')$ *is minimized.*

A broad class of repair problems have been found to be NP-hard, for instance, repairing under functional dependencies for categorized data [14], or repairing under denial constraints that supports numeric data [17]. It is not the case for repairing under speed constraints.

We write the global optimal repair problem as

$$\min \sum_{i=1}^{n} |x_i - x'_i| \tag{2}$$

$$\text{s.t.} \quad \frac{x'_j - x'_i}{t_j - t_i} \leq s_{\max}, \quad t_i < t_j \leq t_i + w, \quad 1 \leq i \leq n, 1 \leq j \leq n \tag{3}$$

$$\frac{x'_j - x'_i}{t_j - t_i} \geq s_{\min}, \quad t_i < t_j \leq t_i + w, \quad 1 \leq i \leq n, 1 \leq j \leq n \tag{4}$$

where $x'_i, 1 \leq i \leq n$, are variables in problem solving.

The correctness of result x' in the aforesaid problem is obvious. Formula (2) is exactly the repair distance in formula (1) to minimize. The speed constraints are ensured in formulas (3) and (4), by considering all the t_j in the window starting from t_i, for each data point i in the sequence.

By transforming the problem to a linear programming (LP) problem, existing solvers can directly be employed. (See Appendix A for transformation details.)

3. INTEGRAL CLEANING

The global optimum considers the entire sequence as a whole, and does not support online cleaning over streaming data. To support integral repair w.r.t. the current short period in a stream, we study the local optimum, which concerns only the constraints locally in a window. By sliding windows in the sequence, the result of local optimum x_{local} guarantees to satisfy the speed constraints in the entire sequence, i.e., also a feasible solution to the constraints in formulas (3) and (4) of global optimum. Since the global optimum returns a minimum distance repair x_{global} that satisfies all the constraints, we always have $\Delta(x, x_{\text{local}}) \geq \Delta(x, x_{\text{global}})$. (For the upper bound, unfortunately, we don't find any constant factor.) Referring to the minimum change principle [1] that a repair with lower repair distance is more likely to be the truth, the repair accuracy of local optimum may not be as high as that of global optimum. Although we don't have a theoretical upper bound of local repair distance compared to the global one, in practice, the repair distances of local and global repairs are very close (as shown in Figures 10(b) and 11(b)). Compared to the global optimum, the local optimal approach can show significant improvement in time costs (about 2 order of magnitude improvement in Figure 11(a)) but without losing much repair accuracy (only a small decrease of 0.01 in Figure 11(d)).

3.1 Local Optimum

We say a data point x_k *locally satisfies* the speed constraint s, denoted by $x_k \vDash s$, if for any x_i in the window starting form x_k, i.e., $t_k < t_i \leq t_k+w$, it has $s_{\min} \leq \frac{x_i - x_k}{t_i - t_k} \leq s_{\max}$.

Problem 2. *Given a data point x_k in a sequence x and a speed constraint s, the* local optimal repair *problem is to find a repair x' such that $x'_k \vDash s$ and $\Delta(x, x')$ is minimized.*

Similar to the global optimum, we write the local optimal repair problem as

$$\min \sum_{i=1}^{n} |x_i - x'_i| \tag{5}$$

$$\text{s.t.} \quad \frac{x'_k - x'_i}{t_k - t_i} \leq s_{\max}, \qquad t_k < t_i \leq t_k + w, 1 \leq i \leq n$$

$$\frac{x'_k - x'_i}{t_k - t_i} \geq s_{\min}, \qquad t_k < t_i \leq t_k + w, 1 \leq i \leq n$$

where $x'_i, 1 \leq i \leq n$ are variables in problem solving.

The local optimal repair in formula (5) modifies only the data points i with $t_k \leq t_i \leq t_k + w$ in the window of the current x_k, i.e., much fewer variables. The constraints (in the window) are not sacrificed.

Example 3 (Local optimum). *Consider again the sequence $x = \{12, 12.5, 13, 10, 15, 15.5\}$ in Example 2 and the speed constraints $s_{\max} = 0.5$ and $s_{\min} = -0.5$ with window size $w = 5$, as illustrated in Figure 2(b).*

Let $k = 3$ be the currently considered data point. Referring to formula (5), the constraint predicates for the local optimum on $k = 3$ are:

$$\frac{x'_4 - x'_3}{5-3} \leq 0.5, \quad \frac{x'_5 - x'_3}{7-3} \leq 0.5, \quad \frac{x'_6 - x'_3}{8-3} \leq 0.5,$$

$$\frac{x'_4 - x'_3}{5-3} \geq -0.5, \quad \frac{x'_5 - x'_3}{7-3} \geq -0.5, \quad \frac{x'_6 - x'_3}{8-3} \geq -0.5.$$

The local optimal solution with the minimum distance is $x'_3 = 13, x'_4 = 14, x'_5 = 15, x'_6 = 15.5$. That is, $x'_3 = x_3 = 13$ is not necessary to be modified w.r.t. the local optimum on $k = 3$.

3.2 The Median Principle

Intuitively, a solution with the minimum distance (i.e., as close as possible to each point) probably lies in the *middle* of the data points. We propose to efficiently search the local optimum in the scope of such middle data points, namely the **Median Principle** (in Proposition 3). Following this median principle, we devise a linear time algorithm for computing the local optimal repair, instead of $O(n^{3.5}L)$ by LP.

Before presenting the median principle, let us first show that computing the local optimum w.r.t. x_k is indeed equivalent to determine an optimal repair x'_k, where the solution of other x'_i (in formula (5)) can be naturally derived.

3.2.1 Reformulating the Local Optimum Problem

We transform the local optimal repair problem in formula (5) to a new form w.r.t. only one variable x'_k. The idea is to illustrate that there always exists an optimal solution x', whose x'_i can be derived from x'_k.

Proposition 1. *Let x^* be a local optimal solution w.r.t. x_k. The following $x'$is also local optimal, with $x'_k = x^*_k$ and*

$$x'_i = \begin{cases} x'_k + s_{\max}(t_i - t_k) & \text{if } \frac{x'_k - x_i}{t_k - t_i} > s_{\max} \\ x'_k + s_{\min}(t_i - t_k) & \text{if } \frac{x'_k - x_i}{t_k - t_i} < s_{\min} \\ x_i & \text{otherwise} \end{cases} \tag{6}$$

where $t_k < t_i \leq t_k + w, 1 \leq i \leq n$.

Formula (6) constructs an optimal solution x' upon x^*_k, where either no change or border change w.r.t. $s_{\max}$ and $s_{\min}$ needs to be made. By border changes, we mean $\frac{x'_k - x'_i}{t_k - t_i} = s_{\max}$ or $\frac{x'_k - x'_i}{t_k - t_i} = s_{\min}$. Intuitively, as illustrated in Figure 3, all the values in the range of $[x'_k + s_{\min}(t_i - t_k), x'_k + s_{\max}(t_i - t_k)]$ are valid repair candidate for x'_i. If the speed exceeds $s_{\max}$, a repair on the "border" drawn by $s_{\max}$ is obviously the closest to x_i, i.e., with the minimum repair distance.

We denote $g(x_i, x'_k) = |x_i - x'_i| =$

$$\begin{cases} x'_k - x_i - s_{\max}(t_k - t_i) & \text{if } \frac{x'_k - x_i}{t_k - t_i} > s_{\max} \\ x_i - x'_k - s_{\min}(t_k - t_i) & \text{if } \frac{x'_k - x_i}{t_k - t_i} < s_{\min} \\ 0 & \text{otherwise} \end{cases}$$

for $t_k < t_i \leq t_k + w, 1 \leq i \leq n$. The local optimal repair problem in formula (5) can be rewritten as

$$\min_{x'_k} \sum_{i=1}^{n} g(x_i, x'_k), \tag{7}$$

where x'_k is the only variable in problem solving.

3.2.2 Median Solution in a Finite Set of Candidates

According to Proposition 1, the local optimal repair problem is equivalent to find a x'_k that can minimize formula (7). To this end, we first capture a finite set of candidates for x'_k, where the optimal solution can always be found. Let

$$X_k^{\min} = \{x_i + s_{\min}(t_k - t_i) \mid t_k < t_i \leq t_k + w, 1 \leq i \leq n\},$$
$$X_k^{\max} = \{x_i + s_{\max}(t_k - t_i) \mid t_k < t_i \leq t_k + w, 1 \leq i \leq n\}.$$

Intuitively, as shown in Figure 4, each candidate in $X_k^{\max}$ corresponds to a possible x'_k such that x_i serves as a border repair w.r.t. x'_k (as presented in Figure 3). Referring to the aforesaid discussion on minimum distances of border repairs, it is not surprising to have the following conclusion.

Lemma 2. *We can always find a local optimal solution x^* w.r.t. x_k such that $x^*_k \in X_k^{\min} \cup X_k^{\max} \cup \{x_k\}$.*

Let $m = |\{i \mid t_k < t_i \leq t_k + w, 1 \leq i \leq n\}|$ be the number of data points in the window starting from k. It is easy to see $2m + 1$ candidates in $X_k^{\min} \cup X_k^{\max} \cup \{x_k\}$.

For any x'_k, the construction of solution x' is indeed to "shrink" data points in violations to the border. **Intuitively,**

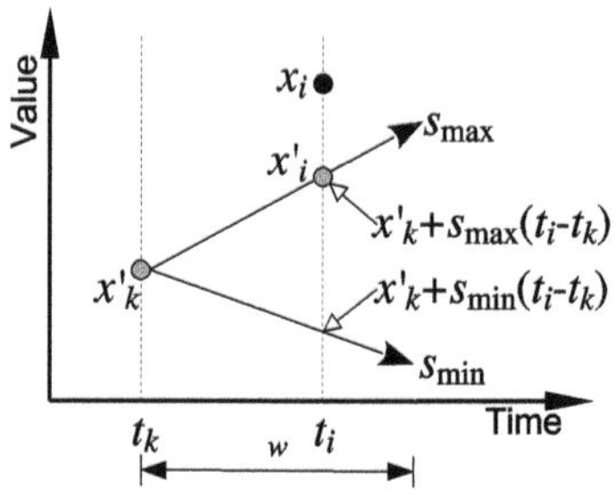

Figure 3: Build solution from x'_k

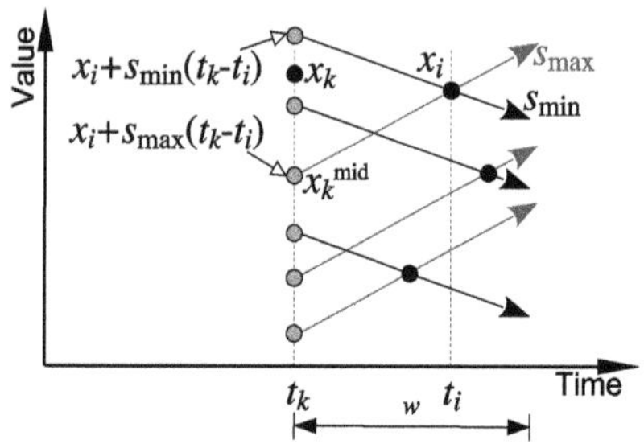

Figure 4: Capture candidates for x'_k

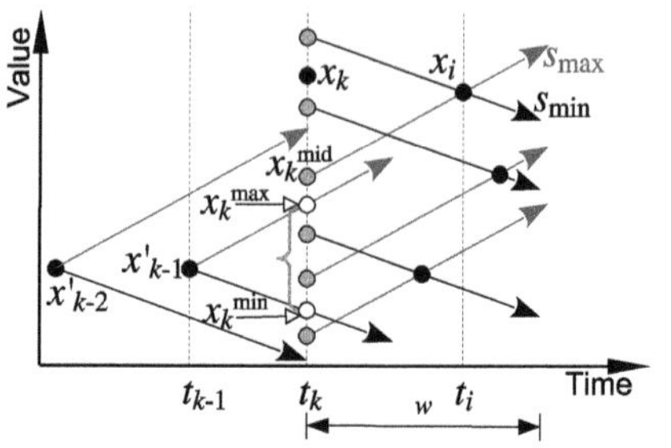

Figure 5: Compute x'_k in integral repair

a candidate in the middle of all data points x_i probably has less shrink distances.

Let x_k^{mid} denote the median of all candidates,

$$x_k^{\text{mid}} = \text{median}(X_k^{\min} \cup X_k^{\max} \cup \{x_k\}). \tag{8}$$

The following shows that the median x_k^{mid} is exactly the optimal solution to the problem in formula (7), and can be used to build the local optimal solution by Proposition 1.

Proposition 3 (The Median Principle). *A solution x' with x'_i determined by formula (6) and $x'_k = x_k^{\text{mid}}$ is local optimal.*

Example 4 (Candidates and local optimum, Example 3 continued). *Consider data points 4, 5 and 6, in Figure 2(b), whose timestamps are within t_3+w, w.r.t. the current $k=3$. Each data point suggests two candidates w.r.t. $s_{\min}$ and $s_{\max}$ for $X_3^{\min}$ and $X_3^{\max}$, respectively. For instance, $x_4 = 10$ contributes $10-0.5(5-3) = 9$ in $X_3^{\max}$ and $10+0.5(5-3) = 11$ in $X_3^{\min}$. Finally, the candidate sets are*

$$X_3^{\min} = \{11, 17, 18\}, \qquad X_3^{\max} = \{9, 13, 13\}.$$

According to formula (8), we have $x_3^{\text{mid}} = 13$.

Referring to Proposition 3, by $x'_3 = x_3^{\text{mid}}$ and formula (6), we build a solution $x'_3 = 13, x'_4 = 14, x'_5 = 15, x'_6 = 15.5$. It is exactly the local optimal solution in Example 3.

3.3 Streaming Computation

The integral cleaning algorithm is to iteratively determine the local optimal x'_k, for $k = 1, 2, \ldots$. Let us first assume that data points come in-order, i.e., $t_j < t_i$ for any $j < i$. (The handling of out-of-order arrival will be introduced in the next section.)

3.3.1 Candidate Range

Consider x_k, where $x'_1, \ldots, x'_{k-1}$ have been determined in the previous steps. Referring to the speed constraints, each fixed $x'_j, t_k - w \le t_j < t_k, 1 \le j < k$, indicates a range of candidates for x'_k, i.e., $[x'_j + s_{\min}(t_k - t_j), x'_j + s_{\max}(t_k - t_j)]$.

The following proposition states that considering the last x'_{k-1} is sufficient to determine the range of possible repairs for x'_k. The rationale is that for any $1 \le j < i < k$, x'_i should be in the range specified by x'_j as well. In other words, the candidate range of x'_k specified by x'_i is subsumed in the range by x'_j.

Proposition 4. *For any $1 \le j < i < k, t_k - w \le t_j < t_i < t_k$, we have $x'_j + s_{\min}(t_k - t_j) \le x'_i + s_{\min}(t_k - t_i)$, and $x'_i + s_{\max}(t_k - t_i) \le x'_j + s_{\max}(t_k - t_j)$.*

For instance, as illustrated in Figure 5, the candidate range of x'_k specified by x'_{k-2} subsumes that by x'_{k-1}. Consequently, we can obtain a tight range of candidates for x'_k by x'_{k-1}, i.e., $[x_k^{\min}, x_k^{\max}]$ as presented in Figure 5, where

$$\begin{aligned} x_k^{\min} &= x'_{k-1} + s_{\min}(t_k - t_{k-1}), \\ x_k^{\max} &= x'_{k-1} + s_{\max}(t_k - t_{k-1}). \end{aligned} \tag{9}$$

The repair problem thus becomes to finding the local optimum x'_k in the range of $[x_k^{\min}, x_k^{\max}]$.

3.3.2 Optimal Solution in Candidate Range

Formula (8) gives a repair candidate x_k^{mid} suggested by x_i after x_k $(t_k < t_i)$, while formula (9) indicates a candidate range $[x_k^{\min}, x_k^{\max}]$ specified by x_{k-1} before x_k.

If the suggested local optimal solution x_k^{mid} in formula (8) drops into the range of $[x_k^{\min}, x_k^{\max}]$ in formula (9), the optimal solution is directly obtained, i.e., $x'_k = x_k^{\text{mid}}$. Otherwise, we need to re-calculate the local optimum w.r.t. the range $[x_k^{\min}, x_k^{\max}]$.

Fortunately, we have the following monotonicity of the function in formula (7).

Proposition 5. *For any $u_1, u_2, v_1, v_2 \in X_k^{\min} \cup X_k^{\max} \cup \{x_k\}$ such that $u_1 \le u_2 \le x_k^{\text{mid}} \le v_1 \le v_2$, we have*

$$\sum_{i=1}^{n} g(x_i, u_1) \ge \sum_{i=1}^{n} g(x_i, u_2) \ge \sum_{i=1}^{n} g(x_i, x_k^{\text{mid}}),$$

$$\sum_{i=1}^{n} g(x_i, x_k^{\text{mid}}) \le \sum_{i=1}^{n} g(x_i, v_1) \le \sum_{i=1}^{n} g(x_i, v_2).$$

That is, for any candidate $u < x_k^{\max} < x_k^{\text{mid}}$, it always has $\sum_{i=1}^{n} g(x_i, u) \ge \sum_{i=1}^{n} g(x_i, x_k^{\max})$. $x_k^{\max}$ is thus the optimal solution in the range of $[x_k^{\min}, x_k^{\max}]$. Similar conclusion can also be made for $v > x_k^{\min} > x_k^{\text{mid}}$.

Consequently, according to Proposition 5, the local optimal solution is directed computed by

$$x'_k = \begin{cases} x_k^{\max} & \text{if } x_k^{\max} < x_k^{\text{mid}} \\ x_k^{\min} & \text{if } x_k^{\min} > x_k^{\text{mid}} \\ x_k^{\text{mid}} & \text{otherwise} \end{cases} \tag{10}$$

Algorithm 1 presents the integral repair of a sequence x w.r.t. local optimum under the speed constraint s. For each data point k in the sequence, $k = 1, 2, \ldots, n$, Lines 3 and 4 computes the candidate range in formula (9). By considering all the succeeding data points i in the window of k, Line 10 calculates x_k^{mid} in formula (8). Finally, x'_k is obtained following the computation in formula (10).

It is easy to see that the number of distinct data points in a window is at most w. The median in the window can be trivially found in $O(w)$, i.e., the average complexity of quickselect [9]. Considering all the n data points in the sequence, Algorithm 1 runs in $O(nw)$ time. For a fixed w, it is

Algorithm 1: Local(x, s)

Data: an ordered sequence x and speed constraints s
Result: a repair x' of x w.r.t. local optimum
1 **for** $k \leftarrow 1$ **to** n **do**
2 $\quad X_k^{\min} \leftarrow \emptyset$; $X_k^{\max} \leftarrow \emptyset$;
3 $\quad x_k^{\min} \leftarrow x'_{k-1} + s_{\min}(t_k - t_{k-1})$, or $-\infty$ for $k = 1$;
4 $\quad x_k^{\max} \leftarrow x'_{k-1} + s_{\max}(t_k - t_{k-1})$, or $+\infty$ for $k = 1$;
5 $\quad$ **for** $i \leftarrow k + 1$ **to** n **do** // compute x_k^{mid}
6 $\quad\quad$ **if** $t_i > t_k + w$ **then**
7 $\quad\quad\quad$ break;
8 $\quad\quad X_k^{\min} \leftarrow X_k^{\min} \cup \{x_i + s_{\min}(t_k - t_i)\}$;
9 $\quad\quad X_k^{\max} \leftarrow X_k^{\max} \cup \{x_i + s_{\max}(t_k - t_i)\}$;
10 $\quad x_k^{\text{mid}} \leftarrow \text{median}(X_k^{\min} \cup X_k^{\max} \cup \{x_k\})$;
11 $\quad$ **if** $x_k^{\max} < x_k^{\text{mid}}$ **then** // compute x'_k
12 $\quad\quad x'_k \leftarrow x_k^{\max}$;
13 $\quad$ **else if** $x_k^{\min} > x_k^{\text{mid}}$ **then**
14 $\quad\quad x'_k \leftarrow x_k^{\min}$;
15 $\quad$ **else**
16 $\quad\quad x'_k \leftarrow x_k^{\text{mid}}$;
17 **return** x'

a linear time, constant space algorithm. In practice, to minimize the changes, we may heuristically skip the repairing on those points x_k that satisfy the speed constraints with its neighbors, i.e., $x_k^{\min} \le x_k \le x_k^{\max}$ and $x_{k+1}^{\min} \le x_{k+1} \le x_{k+1}^{\max}$.

Example 5 (Example 4 continued). *Consider the next data point $k = 4$ in the current sequence $\{12, 12.5, 13, 10, 15, 15.5\}$, in Figure 2(b). According to formula (9), a candidate range $[x_k^{\min}, x_k^{\max}] = [12, 14]$ is given by $x'_3 = 13$ (which is determined in the previous step in Example 4).*

Following the same line of Example 4, we compute $X_4^{\min} = \{16, 17\}$ and $X_4^{\max} = \{14, 14\}$ by points 5 and 6 that are in the window of point 4. It follows $x_4^{\text{mid}} = 14$, which is in the candidate range $[12, 14]$. According to formula (10), the local optimal repair on $k = 4$ is $x'_4 = 14$.

The integral repair moves on to the next $k = 5$ and terminates when reaching the end of the sequence. A repaired sequence $\{12, 12.5, 13, 14, 15, 15.5\}$ is finally returned.

4. OUT-OF-ORDER CLEANING

When a delayed data point comes, the straightforward approach is to insert the data point into the right position of the sequence according to timestamps, and recompute all the results for data points near (and after) the inserted position. However, complete re-computation is not necessary. Instead, we can efficiently update the repairs over the previously computed results. To further reduce the computation, we propose a heuristic strategy that updates the results only when the previous results are known to be invalid for sure.

4.1 Updating Local Optimum

Consider an out-of-order arrival x_k, $t_k < t_{k-1}$. We reorder the sequence by timestamps, i.e., removing x_k and inserting it as a new x_ℓ where $x_\ell = x_k$, $t_{\ell-1} < t_\ell < t_{\ell+1}$, $\ell < k$.

The updates introduced by x_ℓ include two aspects: (1) for $x_j, j < \ell$, where x_ℓ suggests candidates for determine x_j^{mid}; and (2) for $x_i, i > \ell$, whose candidate range $[x_i^{\min}, x_i^{\max}]$ is influenced (directly or indirectly) by x'_ℓ.

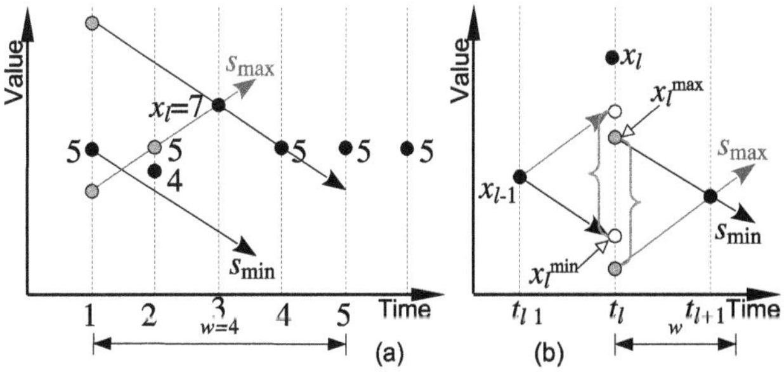

Figure 6: Update x'_ℓ and compute x'_ℓ in heuristic

First, for any x_j with $t_\ell - w \le t_j < t_\ell, 1 \le j < \ell$, we update its median by adding the candidates w.r.t. the new x_ℓ in $X_j^{\min}$ and $X_j^{\max}$ (in Lines 6 and 7 in Algorithm 2). It is worth noting that x_j^{mid} may remain unchanged after introducing two new candidates by x_ℓ. If one of the candidate is greater than x_j^{mid} and the other is less than x_j^{mid}, obviously, x_j^{mid} is still the median in the new set $X_j^{\min} \cup X_j^{\max} \cup \{x_j\}$.

Proposition 6. *For any x_j with $t_\ell - w \le t_j < t_\ell$, if $s_{\min} \le \frac{x_j^{\text{mid}} - x_\ell}{t_j - t_\ell} \le s_{\max}$ for the new arrived x_ℓ, x_j^{mid} is not changed.*

Once the medians are updated, we recalculate the repairs w.r.t. the new medians. It further leads to the updates on succeeding ones (including $i > \ell$, with candidate range $[x_i^{\min}, x_i^{\max}]$ determined by previous repairs).

Algorithm 2 presents the update of x' when a delayed x_ℓ is newly observed. The algorithm is called before Line 2 of Algorithm 1, when an out-of-order data point comes and is placed in the position ℓ after reordering the sequence.

Algorithm 2: Update(x', s, ℓ, k)

Data: a repair x' with the first k data points ordered by timestamps and a newly observed x_ℓ, $\ell < k$
Result: an updated repair x' of x w.r.t. local optimum
1 compute x_ℓ^{mid} by formula (8);
2 **for** $i \leftarrow \ell - 1$ **to** 1 **do**
3 $\quad$ **if** $t_i < t_\ell - w$ **then**
4 $\quad\quad$ break;
5 $\quad$ **if** $\frac{x_j^{\text{mid}} - x_\ell}{t_j - t_\ell} < s_{\min}$ *or* $\frac{x_j^{\text{mid}} - x_\ell}{t_j - t_\ell} > s_{\max}$ **then**
6 $\quad\quad X_j^{\min} \leftarrow X_j^{\min} \cup \{x_\ell + s_{\min}(t_j - t_\ell)\}$;
7 $\quad\quad X_j^{\max} \leftarrow X_j^{\max} \cup \{x_\ell + s_{\max}(t_j - t_\ell)\}$;
8 $\quad\quad$ update x_j^{mid} by formula (8);
9 **for** $j \leftarrow i + 1$ **to** k **do**
10 $\quad$ update $x_i^{\min}, x_i^{\max}$ by formula (9);
11 $\quad$ update x'_i by formula (10);
12 $\quad$ **if** *x'_i is unchanged, $i > \ell$* **then**
13 $\quad\quad$ break;
14 **return** x'

Example 6 (Out-of-order update). *Let $x = \{5, 4, 5, 5, 5\}$ be the currently processed sequence, with timestamps $t = \{1, 2, 4, 5, 6\}$, as illustrated in Figure 6(a). The speed constraints are $s_{\max} = 2$ and $s_{\min} = -2$ with window size $w = 4$.*

Suppose that the next data point is $x_6 = 7$ with timestamp $t_6 = 3 < t_5 = 6$, i.e., an out-of-order arrival. We first reorder the sequence by timestamps, $x = \{5, 4, 7, 5, 5, 5\}$ and $t = \{1, 2, 3, 4, 5, 6\}$, where the new data point locates in $\ell =$

3. *Referring to the window size $w = 4$, data points 1 and 2 are influenced by the new point.*

For x_1, suppose that $x_1^{\text{mid}} = 5$ before the new point ℓ is inserted. We compute $\frac{x_1^{\text{mid}} - x_\ell}{t_1 - t_\ell} = \frac{5-7}{1-3} = 1$, which is in the range $[s_{\min}, s_{\max}]$. According to Proposition 6, $x_1^{\text{mid}} = 5$ will not be changed after inserting ℓ. For x_2, we have $x_2^{\text{mid}} = 4$ before inserting ℓ and $\frac{4-7}{2-3} = 3 > s_{\max}$. That is, x_2^{mid} should be updated after inserting ℓ, having $x_2^{mid} = 5$. And $x_3^{\text{mid}} = 7$ for $\ell = 3$ can also be computed by formula (8). Since x_2^{mid} is updated and x_3^{mid} is newly introduced, the repair should be refreshed following formula (10), i.e., $x' = \{5, 5, 7, 5, 5, 5\}$.

4.2 Heuristic

Although exact result w.r.t. local optimum is guaranteed, the update (possibly on all the data points near and after x_ℓ) is costly. If a data point is delayed at the very beginning of the sequence, almost the entire sequence may be updated.

Heuristically, we could choose to update only when the existing repairs are found to be invalid for sure. That is, after inserting the data point on position ℓ, the existing x' violates speed constraints (no matter what the value x'_ℓ is).

Such invalid scenario occurs, because of the disagreement on the possible values for x'_ℓ. The existing repair $x'_{\ell-1}$ specifies a range of possible repairs for x'_ℓ, as presented in formula (9). Symmetrically, $x'_{\ell+1}$ as an existing repair also indicates another range for x'_ℓ. Contradiction between two ranges may occur (if $x'_{\ell+1}$ is not in the window of $x'_{\ell-1}$).

We capture the minimum and maximum candidates for x'_ℓ that are specified by $x'_{\ell-1}$ and $x'_{\ell+1}$ together,

$$\begin{aligned} x_\ell^{\min} &= \max(x'_{\ell-1} + s_{\min}(t_\ell - t_{\ell-1}), x'_{\ell+1} + s_{\max}(t_\ell - t_{\ell+1})), \\ x_\ell^{\max} &= \min(x'_{\ell-1} + s_{\max}(t_\ell - t_{\ell-1}), x'_{\ell+1} + s_{\min}(t_\ell - t_{\ell+1})), \end{aligned} \tag{11}$$

where $t_{\ell+1} - t_{\ell-1} \leq 2 \cdot w$. Here, $x_\ell^{\min}$ takes the maximum of bounds (in formula (9)) determined by $\ell - 1$ and $\ell + 1$, as illustrated in Figure 6(b), and similarly $x_\ell^{\max}$ takes the lower one of the bounds given by $\ell - 1$ and $\ell + 1$. In other words, a x'_ℓ within the range $[x'_{\ell-1}, x'_{\ell+1}]$ will satisfy the speed constraints w.r.t. both $\ell - 1$ and $\ell + 1$.

Obviously, if $x_\ell^{\min} > x_\ell^{\max}$, contradiction occurs. That is, the current repair x' is invalid, and the update by Algorithm 2 should be performed.

On the other hand, if valid candidates exist, i.e., $x_\ell^{\min} \leq x_\ell^{\max}$, we can heuristically select a repair x'_ℓ in $[x_\ell^{\min}, x_\ell^{\max}]$ without updating the others. As shown in Lines 3 and 4 in Algorithm 3, x_ℓ is taken as x_ℓ^{mid} in heuristic. According to formula (10), x'_ℓ leaves unchanged if x_ℓ is in $[x_\ell^{\min}, x_\ell^{\max}]$. Otherwise, the border $x_\ell^{\min}$ or $x_\ell^{\max}$, which is closer to x_ℓ, is assigned as the repair x'_ℓ.

A natural concern is how often the full Update in Line 7 in Algorithm 3 occurs. We show in the following conclusion that Update would never be performed if the time interval $t_{\ell+1} - t_{\ell-1}$ is within w.

Proposition 7. *For any $x_\ell^{\min} > x_\ell^{\max}$ computed by formula (11), it always has $w < t_{\ell+1} - t_{\ell-1} \leq 2 \cdot w$.*

In other words, the Update may occur only when $t_{\ell-1}$ and $t_{\ell+1}$ are far away ($> w$). In practice, such large "breaks" appear rarely especially in continuous monitoring streams. By greatly avoiding Update, the Heuristic approach can significantly reduce the repair time costs (in the experiments).

Algorithm 3: Heuristic(x', s, ℓ, k)

Data: a repair x' with the first k dat points ordered by timestamps and a newly observed x_ℓ, $\ell < k$, and speed constraints s

Result: an updated repair x' of x w.r.t. local optimum

```
1 compute x_ℓ^min, x_ℓ^max by formula (11);
2 if x_ℓ^min ≤ x_ℓ^max then
3 |   x_ℓ^mid ← x_ℓ;
4 |   compute x'_ℓ by formula (10);
5 |   return x'
6 else
7 |   return Update(x', s, ℓ, k)
```

Example 7 (Heuristic, Example 6 continued)**.** *Consider again the reordered sequence, $x = \{5, 4, 7, 5, 5, 5\}$ with timestamps $t = \{1, 2, 3, 4, 5, 6\}$, where $\ell = 3$ is the newly inserted data point, as illustrated in Figure 6(a).*

Referring to formula (9), data point $\ell - 1$ gives a candidate range $[2, 6]$ for x'_ℓ w.r.t. the speed constraints $s_{\max} = 2$ and $s_{\min} = -2$. Symmetrically, another candidate range $[3, 7]$ for x'_ℓ is also determined by $\ell + 1$. By taking the intersection of two candidate ranges, we have $[x_\ell^{\min}, x_\ell^{\max}] = [3, 6]$ as defined in formula (11). Since $x_\ell^{\min} \leq x_\ell^{\max}$, we heuristically determine the repair $x'_3 = 6$ without update the other repair results, having $x' = \{5, 4, 6, 5, 5, 5\}$.

5. ADAPTIVE WINDOWS

The trade-off in setting window size w for speed constraints is: small windows fail to capture the minimum repair (e.g., if w=1 in Figure 2(b) of Example 2), while large windows obviously increase the computation overhead (as more constrained data pairs need to be specified in formulas (3) for global optimum or (5) for local optimum). It is nontrivial to predefine an appropriate window size. Even worse, the arrival rate (the number of data points in a period) may vary. Rather than a fixed window size, we propose to automatically determine the adaptive window size w online.

To tackle the aforesaid trade-off in choosing window sizes, we introduce a statistical sampling-based method. The idea is to model data points as *random samples* of approaching the speed constraints. The adaption of windows, extending or shrinking, is thus performed based on the closeness to the extreme speeds ($s_{\max}$ or $s_{\min}$) of the samples, grounded in statistical sampling theory.

Sampling Model. Consider a window starting from i with length w, $W_i = \{j \mid 0 < t_j - t_i \leq w\}$. Assume that the (repaired) data points in the window satisfy speed constraint s.

Intuitively, the speed constraint (say $s_{\max}$) takes strong effect, if a x_j in the window approaches $x_i + s_{\max}(t_j - t_i)$, i.e., the speed $\frac{x_j - x_i}{t_j - t_i}$ approaches the constraint $s_{\max}$. On the other hand, the speed constraints are useless, if the speed $\frac{x_j - x_i}{t_j - t_i}$ is far away from $s_{\min}$ or $s_{\max}$. Let

$$p_{i,j} = \frac{\frac{x_i - x_j}{t_i - t_j} - s_{\min}}{s_{\max} - s_{\min}} \tag{12}$$

denote the degree of x_j approaching the (maximum) speed constraints, having $0 \leq p_{i,j} \leq 1$. When the speed $\frac{x_j - x_i}{t_j - t_i} = s_{\max}$, we have $p_{i,j} = 1$. And $p_{i,j} = 0$ corresponds to the

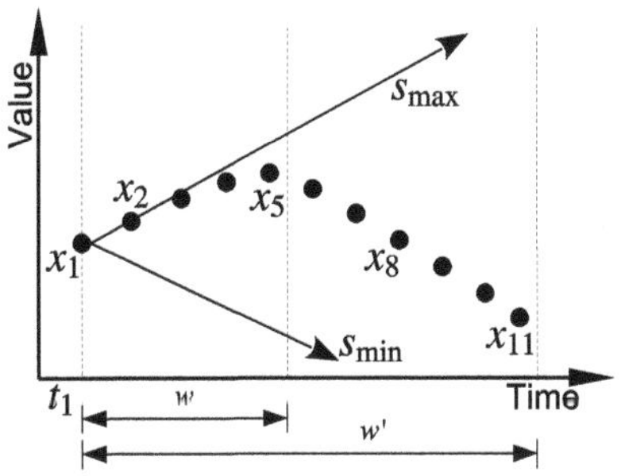

Figure 7: Adjust w based on closeness to speed constraints

speed equal to $s_{\min}$. In contrast, if the speed is far away from the speed constraints, e.g., in the middle of $\frac{1}{2}(s_{\max}+s_{\min})$ with $p_{i,j}=0.5$, the speed constraint is useless.

Assume that each data point in the window has the same probability p of approaching the maximum speed constraint w.r.t. x_i. The probability p can be estimated by the average degree of data points approaching the maximum speed constraints, $p_i=\frac{\sum_{j\in W_i} p_{i,j}}{|W_i|}$.

We view each data point as a random sample of approaching the maximum speed constraint. The total number of data points that reach $s_{\max}$, denoted by S, is thus a random variable that follows *binomial distribution*, i.e., $S\sim B(|W_i|,p_i)$. Referring to the standard probability theory, the expectation and variance can be expressed as $\mathrm{E}(S)=|W_i|\cdot p_i$ and $\mathrm{Var}[S]=|W_i|\cdot p_i\cdot(1-p_i)$.

Adaptive Window. Next, we introduce how to use the aforesaid binomial sampling model to adjust the window sizes. Intuitively, the closer the speeds of data points to the constraints $s_{\min}$ and $s_{\max}$, the more necessary the constraints are to guard the correctness of data points. That is, the window could be enlarged to involve more data points. On the other hand, if the observed speeds are far from the border $s_{\min}$ and $s_{\max}$, the constraints are useless. The windows may shrink for computation efficiency.

In normal approximation [2], a reasonable approximation to $B(n,p)$ is given by the normal distribution $\mathcal{N}(np,np(1-p))$. This approximation generally improves as n increases and is better when p is not near to 0 or 1. Rules are designed to decide whether n is large enough, and p is far enough from the extremes of zero or one. A commonly used rule states that the normal approximation is appropriate only if everything within 3 standard deviations of its mean is within the range of possible values, i.e., $np\pm 3\sqrt{np(1-p)}\in[0,n]$.

In this sense, we can use the evaluation of normal approximation (whether the samples are not enough) to infer whether the window size is not large enough, or (whether the probability is far enough from 0 or 1) to infer whether the window size is too large such that speed constraints are useless (with data points far from the speed constraints $s_{\min}$ and $s_{\max}$). Referring to the rule for normal approximation, if $\mathrm{E}(S)\pm 3\sqrt{\mathrm{Var}[S]}\in[0,|W_i|]$, the samples are large enough and the probability p_i is far enough from the extremes of zero or one, i.e., far away from the speed constraints (which are useless). Thereby, we reduce the window size, e.g., according to w' in Figure 7 in the following Example 8. On the other hand, if $\mathrm{E}(S)\pm 3\sqrt{\mathrm{Var}[S]}\notin[0,|W_i|]$, more samples are needed by increasing the window size (e.g., as suggested by w in Figure 7). (Please refer to Appendix C for more details on normal approximation and adjusting window sizes.)

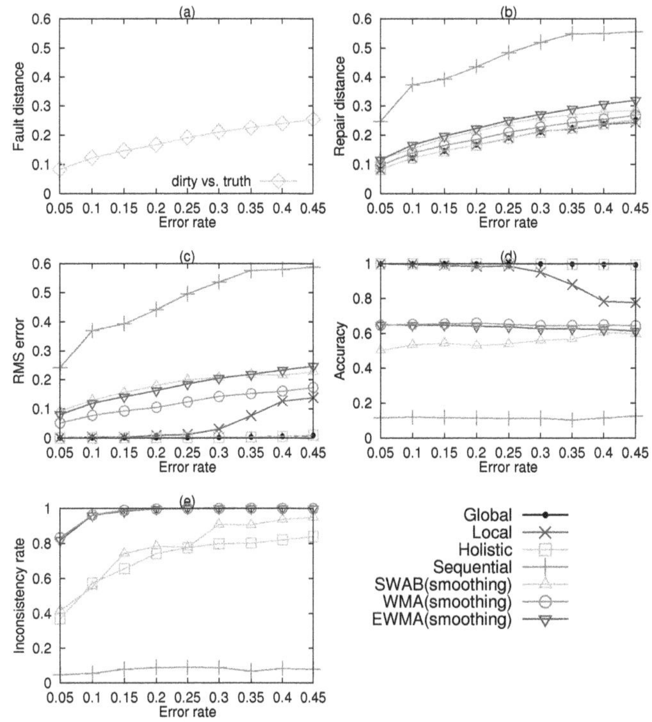

Figure 8: Varying error rates (FUEL)

Example 8. *Consider two windows $W_1=\{2,3,4,5\}$ with size w and $W_1'=\{2,3,4,5,6,7,8,9,10,11\}$ with size w' in Figure 7. By formula (12), we compute $p_{1,2}=1$, since x_2 exactly reaches the maximum speed w.r.t. x_1. Similar $p_{1,j}$ can be computed for $j=3,\ldots,11$, e.g., $p_{1,8}=0.5$ which is neither close to $s_{\max}$ nor $s_{\min}$.*

For W_1, the probability $p_1=0.91$ is computed by the average of $p_{1,2},\ldots,p_{1,5}$. The $\mathrm{E}(S)\pm 3\sqrt{\mathrm{Var}[S]}$ values corresponding to the 4 samples in W_1 are $4{\cdot}0.91{\pm}3\sqrt{4\cdot 0.91\cdot 0.09}$, i.e., 1.92 or 5.35. The later one does not belong to [0,4]. The window W_1 suggests to extend the window size.

For W_1' with 10 samples, the computed probability is $p_1'=0.52$. The $\mathrm{E}(S)\pm 3\sqrt{\mathrm{Var}[S]}$ values are 0.46 and 9.93, in the range of [0,10]. That is, the window W_1' could shrink.

Finally, for each data point i, it makes a decision on enlarging or shrinking the window sizes (for the succeeding windows). Such decision making may also be conducted periodically, e.g., in every 10 minutes.

6. EXPERIMENT

In the experimental evaluation, we employ 3 real datasets, FUEL, STOCK and GPS. (Please refer to Appendix D.1 for dataset preparation.) The evaluation criteria includes: 1) the fault distance between dirty and truth data, 2) the repair distance between dirty input and repair result, 3) the RMS error [10] between the repair result and truth data, 4) the repair accuracy relative to the dirty data, 5) the rate of inconsistent data retained in the repair result. (See Appendix D.2 for the relationships among the measures.)

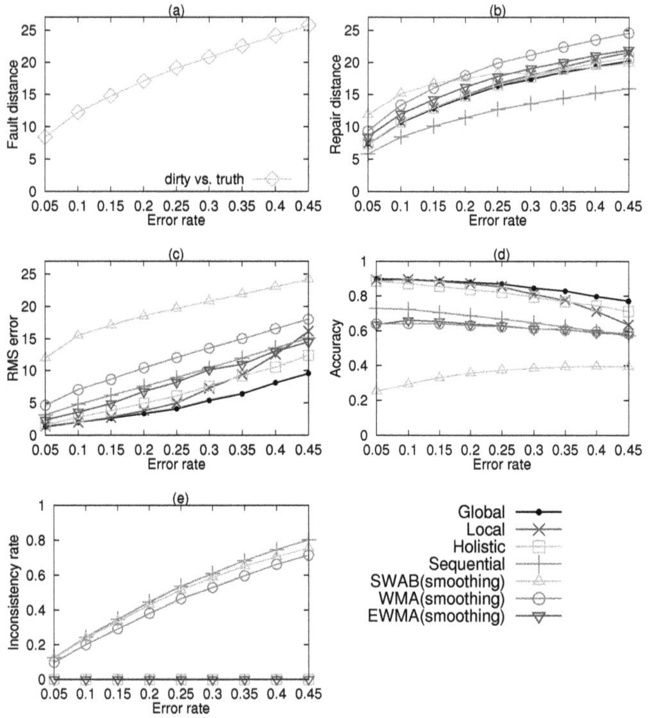

Figure 9: Varying error rates (STOCK)

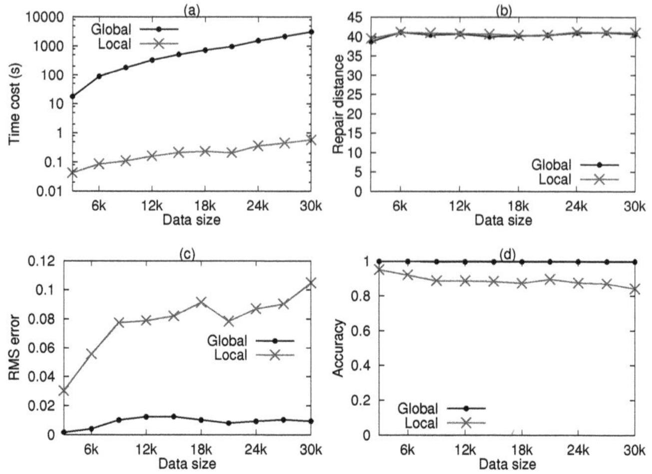

Figure 10: Global vs. Local (FUEL)

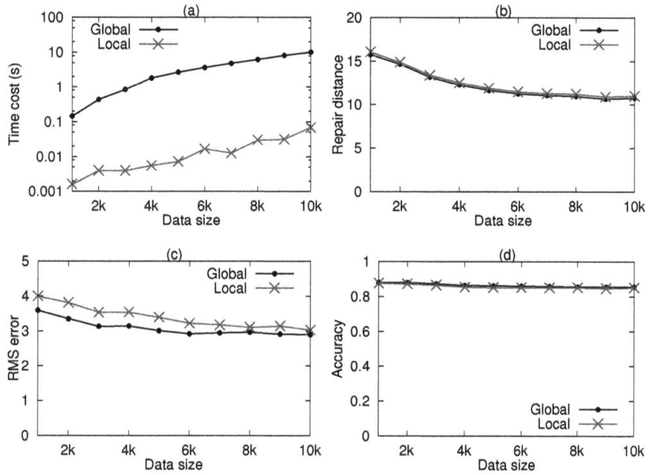

Figure 11: Global vs. Local (STOCK)

Table 1: GPS data with manually labeled ground truth

Method	Repair distance	RMS error	Accuracy	Inconsistency
Global	0.1198	0.0658	0.6881	–
Local	0.1311	0.0682	0.6886	–
Holistic	0.1197	0.0653	0.6842	0.0403
Sequential	0.9589	0.9646	0.0001	0.1285
SWAB	0.6368	0.6372	0.0649	0.0639
WMA	1.5700	1.5627	0.0184	0.1492
EWMA	1.7054	1.6993	0.0166	0.0556

6.1 Comparison with Existing Approaches

In the first experiment, we compare our proposed SCREEN with Global and Local optimum to the following approaches in two categories: 1) smoothing-based, SWAB [13], WMA and EWMA [7], and 2) constraint-based, Holistic repair [4] and repair with Sequential Dependency [8].

Figures 8 and 9 consider various error rates (denoting the amount of injected errors) with data sizes (the number of data points/the length of the sequence) 3k and 2k, in FUEL and STOCK, respectively. Figures 10 and 11 study the scalability by varying data sizes (with error rate 0.3 and 0.2). The full results of all compared methods are in Figures 18 and 19. Table 1 presents the results over the GPS dataset with manually labeled ground truth.

First, it is not surprising that RMS error of all the smoothing methods is high, while their accuracy is lower, compared with our proposed Global or Local (e.g., in Table 1). As illustrated in Figure 8(b), the repair distances of SWAB, WMA and EWMA smoothing are very similar. These smoothing methods show similar RMS error and accuracy as well in Figures 8(c)(d). It is notable that the inconsistency rates of smoothing are very high in Figure 8(e). That is, a large number of data points are still in violation w.r.t. speed constraints. The corresponding accuracy of smoothing is thus significantly lower than our proposal in Figure 8(d).

Holistic repair, the approximation of our Global as introduced in Appendix B, show similar accuracy as Global. However, its time cost is close to the exact approach Global as well. Even worse, as shown in Figures 8(e), the inconsistency rate of Holistic is high. An inconsistency rate 0.4 denotes that about 40% data points are still involved in violation to speed constraints, after Holistic repair. For STOCK with window size $w = 1$, there are fewer constraint predicates declared between data points. Therefore, inconsistencies remained after Holistic repair are fewer as well, i.e., lower inconsistency rate in Figures 9(e).

Sequential dependencies (SDs) consider the constraints on value difference (e.g., ≤ 5) of two consecutive data points. When the time interval of any two consecutive data points is the same, for instance, in every trading day or in every 5 minutes, SDs denote exactly the speed constraints. There-

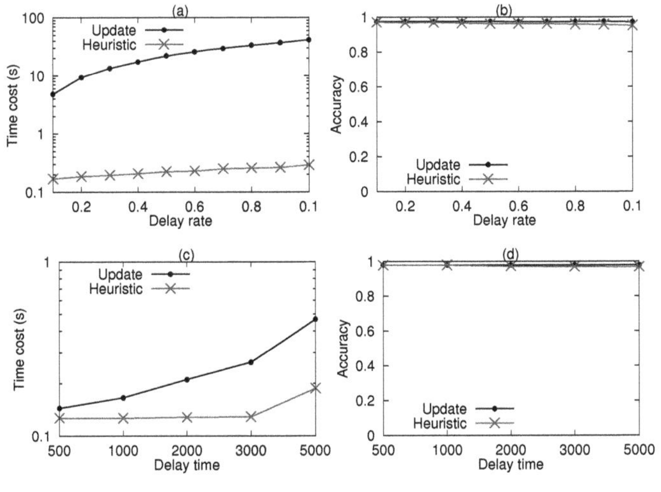

Figure 12: Evaluation on out-of-order (FUEL)

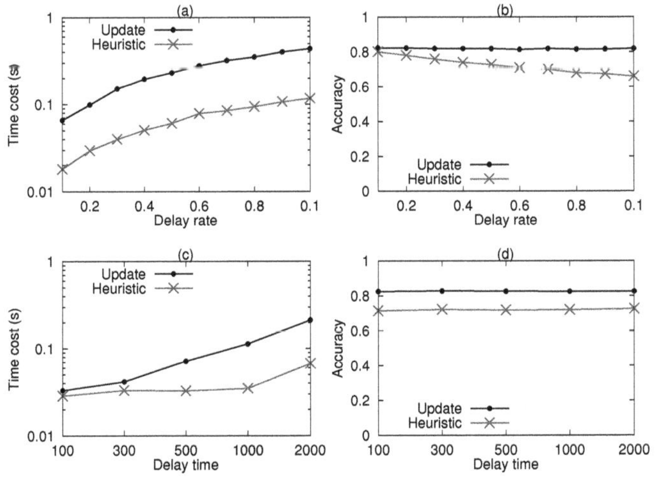

Figure 13: Evaluation on out-of-order (STOCK)

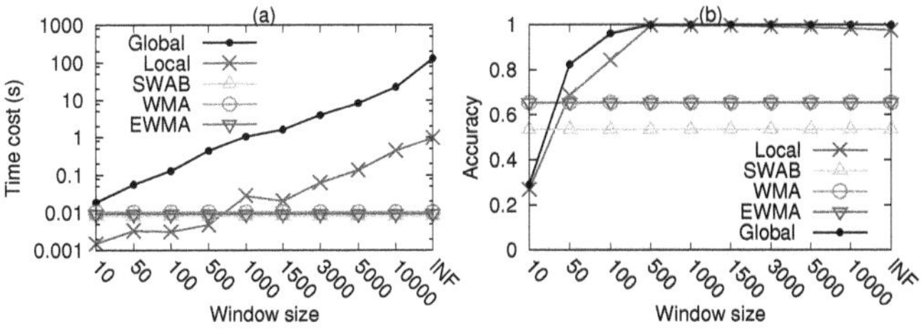

Figure 14: Evaluation on various window sizes

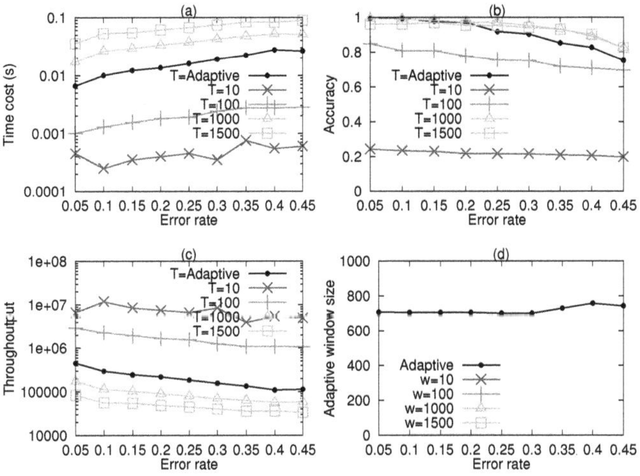

Figure 15: Evaluation on adaptive window sizes

fore, in STOCK, the accuracy of Sequential is relatively high, while its RMS error is low (compared with SWAB). However, if the data point arrival is dynamic without a fixed time interval, such as FUEL, SDs can no longer denote the speed semantics. Consequently, the performance of Sequential is low in Figures 8(c)(d), even worse than SWAB.

The repair distance of Global is always lower than that of Local, in Figures 10(b) and 11(b). The corresponding RMS error of Global is lower in Figures 10(c) and 11(c) and the repair accuracy of Global is higher in Figures 10(d) and 11(d). Nevertheless, the Local method have very similar repair distance and accuracy to Global, especially compared with the other baseline approaches in Figures 18 and 19. The results verify our analysis (e.g., $\Delta(x, x_{\text{local}}) \geq \Delta(x, x_{\text{global}})$ at the beginning of Section 3), and demonstrate the time and accuracy performance of Local optimum compared to Global in practice.

6.2 Evaluation over Streaming Data

Next, we evaluate the online cleaning over streaming data. Since none of the existing methods support out-of-order arrivals, we mainly compare the proposed Update technique in Algorithm 2 and Heuristic in Algorithm 3 for handling delayed data points. Figures 12 and 13 report the out-of-order evaluation, by varying delay rate (e.g., 0.1 denotes that 10% of data points are delayed in arrival) and delay time (referring to the average distance between the actual timestamp and the arrival time). Settings of delay time for Figures 12(a)(b) and 13(a)(b) are 5000 and 1000, respectively, and the delay rate in Figures 12(c)(d) and 13(c)(d) is 0.05.

Generally, the larger the delay rate or delay time is, the higher the time costs are. For Heuristic, since the full update occurs only when the previously repaired results are found to be wrong for sure, its time cost is significantly lower. As shown in Figures 12 and 13, Heuristic method has comparable accuracy with Update, while the former one can show 1-2 orders of magnitude improvement in time costs.

6.3 Evaluation on Adaptive Windows

This experiment evaluates the cleaning performance under various window sizes of speed constraints. Since the window size is fixed to 1 for STOCK, we focus on the FUEL dataset (with data size 3k, and error rate 0.05 for Figure 14).

As shown in Figure 14, the Local method requires a bit larger window size (e.g., 100) to achieve the same accuracy of Global (at 50). For a window larger than 500, both Global and Local have considerably high accuracy. The time cost of an infinite window (INF, throughout the lifetime of the data stream) is extremely high, while a smaller window size (e.g., 500) that has much lower time cost can achieve an accuracy as high as INF. The results verify that, in a real setting, it is not necessary to consider extremely large windows, since a small window size is sufficient to achieve the same accuracy with significantly lower time cost. On the other hand, if the window size is too small, e.g., $w = 10$ in Figure 14, many

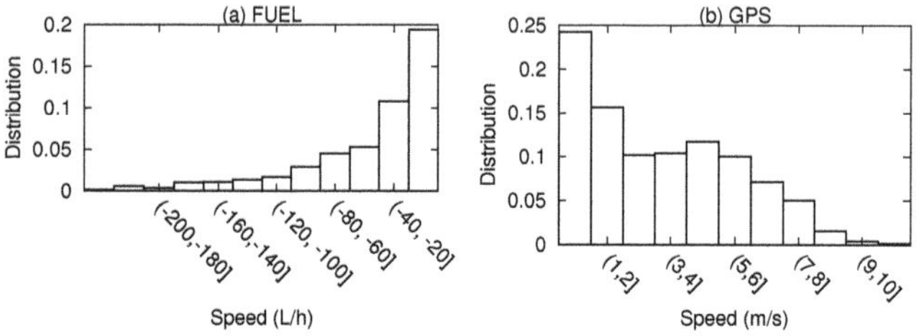

Figure 16: Statistical distribution on speeds

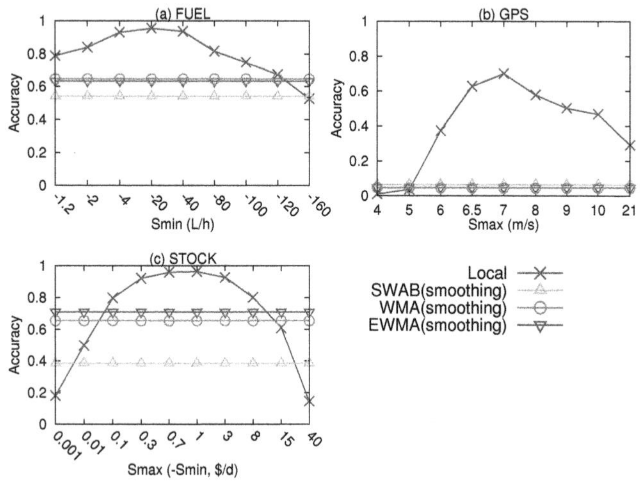

Figure 17: Evaluation on various speed constraints

data points will be out of control by the speed constraints, and fewer repairs are performed. The repair accuracy is thus lower (even lower than the smoothing baselines).

Nevertheless, as illustrated in Figure 15, our adaptive window technique can determine an appropriate window size (around 700), which shows relatively low time cost and high throughput without losing much accuracy. These results verify our trade-off analysis between cleaning accuracy and efficiency in Section 5. In other words, our proposed adaptive windows can balance the effectiveness and efficiency.

6.4 Capturing Speed Constraints

We note that in most scenarios, the speed constraint is natural, e.g., the fuel consumption of a crane should not be negative ($s_{\max} = 0$ for FUEL), while some others could be derived. According to our consultation with experts of the equipment, the fuel consumption does not exceed 40 liters per hour ($s_{\min} = -40$). For STOCK, the speed constraints are naturally derived by the business semantics. The price limit in the market declares that the increase or decrease of daily price should not exceed $l \cdot r$ where l is the price of the last trading day and $r = 10\%$ is a percentage. We consider the highest price $h = 60$ in the dataset, having $l \leq h$ for any day in the period. The maximum speed $s_{\max}$ (with $w = 1$) in the period is thus $h \cdot r = 6$, while $s_{\min} = -h \cdot r = -6$. The GPS dataset is collected by a person carrying a smartphone and walking around at campus. We require 7 meters per second as the maximum walking speed of the person.

Nevertheless, for a particular domain where speed knowledge is not available, the speed constraints can be extracted from data. We consider the statistical distribution of speeds by sampling data pairs over FUEL and GPS in Figure 16.

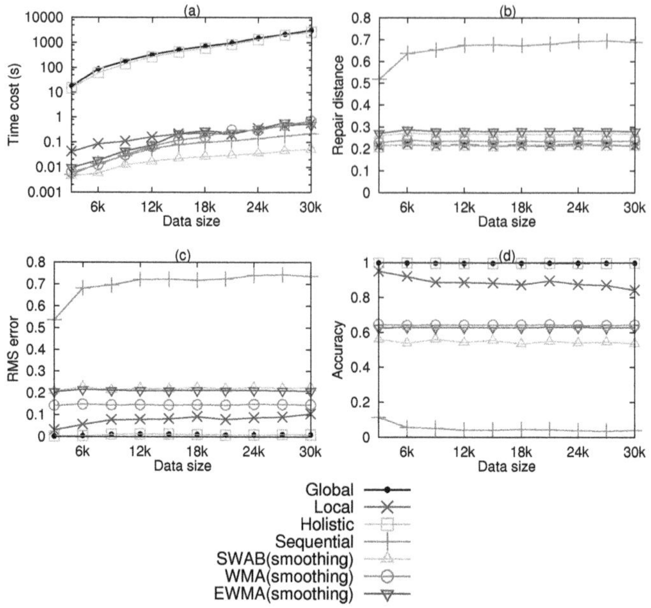

Figure 18: Scalability (FUEL)

As mentioned, the FUEL meter change is non-increasing ($s_{\max} = 0$) during consumption, while the walking speed for GPS is non-negative ($s_{\min} = 0$). Thereby, we mainly observe the speeds for determining $s_{\min}$ for FUEL and $s_{\max}$ for GPS. Referring to statistics, it is to determine a confidence interval that acts as a good estimate of the unknown population parameter $s_{\min}$ ($s_{\max}$). In applied practice, confidence intervals are typically stated at the 95% confidence level [11]. In other words, 95% of the speeds are regarded as accurate (within $s_{\min}$ or $s_{\max}$). It suggests $s_{\max} = 7$ for GPS and $s_{\min} = -80$ for FUEL (although the expert's suggestion is -40 in the experiments). As illustrated in Figure 17, given such speed constraints (either -80 or -40 for FUEL), the accuracies are much higher than the smoothing baselines.

Generally, if the speed constraints are set too loose, e.g., $s_{\min} = -160$ in Figure 17(a) or $s_{\max} = 40$ in Figure 17(c), almost everything will pass the examination of speed constraints without repairing and thus the repair accuracy (of Local) is low. On the other hand, if the speed constraints are too tight, say $s_{\max} = 0.001$ in Figure 17(c), most values would be regarded as violations to such tight constraints. With over-repairing, the corresponding repair accuracy is low too. Nevertheless, the accuracy of the constraint-based method (Local) is higher than that of the constraint-oblivious baselines, in a wide range of speed constraints, e.g., either the expert suggested -40 or the aforesaid statistical suggestion -80 in Figure 17(a). For GPS data in Figure 17(b), there is also a wide range, from 6 to 21, where the constraint-aware Local clearly outperforms the constraint-oblivious baselines. Indeed, in common sense, it is irrational for a person walking with a speed greater than 21 meters per second.

6.5 Summary of Experiments

We summarize the experimental results as follows: 1) The accuracy is significantly improved by our proposal (Global and Local) compared to the existing SWAB, WMA and EWMA smoothing; 2) Without considering the precise speed constraints, the existing SD-based repair has much lower ac-

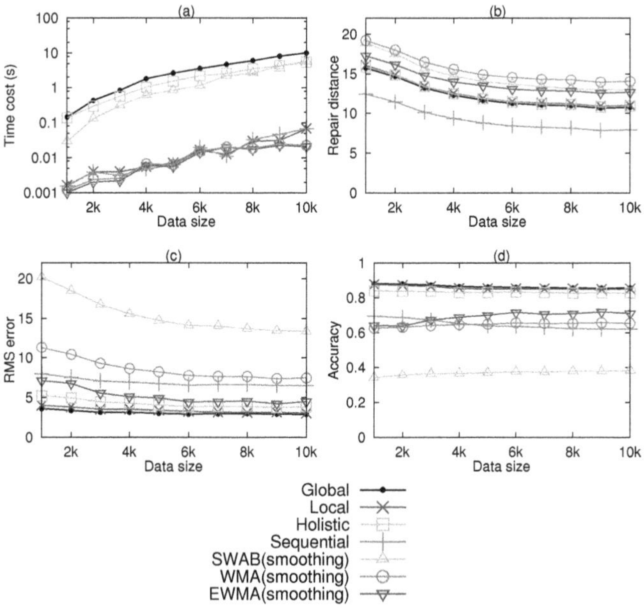

Figure 19: Scalability (STOCK)

curacy than our Global and Local; 3) The proposed Local approach with online cleaning supports shows orders of magnitude improvement in time costs compared to the Holistic method; 4) The heuristic update strategy significantly reduces the time costs in handling out-of-order arrival; 5) The adaptive window technique can automatically suggests an appropriate window size (around 700), which shows relatively low time costs without losing much accuracy.

7. RELATED WORK

Smoothing-based Data Cleaning. The SWAB smoothing [13] is a linear interpolation/regression-based, online smoothing method of stream data. With a sliding window, SWAB uses linear interpolation or linear regression to find the approximating line of a time series. Besides, the moving average [3] is also commonly used to smooth time series data and make forecasts. A simple moving average (SMA) is the unweighted mean of the last k data. This average is used for forecasting the next value of the time series. Whereas in the simple moving average the past observations are weighted equally, a weighted moving average (WMA) multiplies factors to give different weights to data at different positions in the sample window, e.g., using the inverse value of time interval as the weight. Moreover, the exponentially weighted moving average (EWMA) [7] assigns exponentially decreasing weights over time. It is obvious to see that all these smoothing methods will modify a large number of data points. Therefore, as the example illustrated in Figure 1, the major issue of smoothing is the serious damage of the originally correct data points. One of our major contributions in this paper is the employment of speed constraints to supervise the more accurate cleaning. Following the minimum change principle in constraint-based repairing, the original precise values are maximally preserved. Consequently, the accuracy of our proposed method is much higher than that of smoothing, as observed in our experimental evaluation.

Constraint-based Data Repairing. To the best knowledge of our knowledge, Holistic cleaning [4] is the only existing constraint-based technique that can support speed constraints (expressed by denial constraints). Since the approach is proposed for repairing the general (tableau) data, it cannot support the online/integral cleaning over sliding windows in streaming data. In this sense, one of our contributions in this study is the SCREEN with local optimum, which supports not only online cleaning but also out-of-order data arrival. Consequently, as illustrated in the experiments, our proposal can show up to 4 orders of magnitude improvement in time costs compared with Holistic cleaning.

Moreover, Sequential Dependency (SD) [8] cannot express precisely the speed constraints. SDs concern the difference of two consecutive data points in a sequence. As discussed, data streams often deliver data points in various time intervals. Given different timestamp distances, the value difference of two consecutive points does not exactly denote the speed semantics. Owing to such imprecise constraint knowledge, as presented in the experiments, the accuracy of SD (Sequential) based repair could be much lower compared to our speed constraint-based proposal. Our another contribution is the employment of the more accurate speed rather than the simple value distance in repairing streaming data.

Besides our studied speed constraints, Fischer et al. [5] propose a nice notation, Stream Schema, for representing structural and semantic constraints on data streams. The Stream Schema concerns general constraints with various semantics such as orderings between attribute values, while our study focuses only on the specific speed constraints over numeric values. As a promising future direction, it is interesting to extend the stream data cleaning w.r.t. the more general Stream Schema constraints.

8. CONCLUSIONS

In this study, we first indicate the inappropriateness of the smoothing-based stream data cleaning. It could not repair the dirty data such as large spikes, and even worse may seriously damage the originally accurate values. Following the same line of employing integrity constraints for relational data cleaning, in this paper, we propose SCREEN, the first constraint-based stream data cleaning approach. The repairing of imprecise data is guided by the innovative constraints on speed. The speed constraint semantics could be easily captured, such as daily price limit in financial markets, or fuel consumption limit of devices. With speed constraints, SCREEN supports online streaming cleaning in linear time, out-of-order arrival of data points, and high throughput via adaptive window sizes. In particular, the novel *Median Principle* can fast identify the local optimum, following the intuition that a solution with the minimum distance (i.e., as close as possible to each point) probably lies in the middle of the data points. Experiments on real datasets demonstrate that our SCREEN can show significantly higher repair accuracy than the smoothing-based approach, and up to 4 orders of magnitude improvement in time performance compared to the state-of-the-art data cleaning methods.

Acknowledgement

This work is supported in part by China NSFC under Grants 61325008, 61202008 and 61370055; US NSF through grants CNS-1115234, and OISE-1129076.

9. REFERENCES

[1] P. Bohannon, M. Flaster, W. Fan, and R. Rastogi. A cost-based model and effective heuristic for repairing constraints by value modification. In *SIGMOD Conference*, pages 143–154, 2005.

[2] G. E. P. Box. Statistics for experimenters: an introduction to design, data analysis, and model building. 1978.

[3] D. R. Brillinger. *Time series: data analysis and theory*, volume 36. Siam, 2001.

[4] X. Chu, I. F. Ilyas, and P. Papotti. Holistic data cleaning: Putting violations into context. In *ICDE*, pages 458–469, 2013.

[5] P. M. Fischer, K. S. Esmaili, and R. J. Miller. Stream schema: providing and exploiting static metadata for data stream processing. In *EDBT*, pages 207–218, 2010.

[6] Full Version. http://ise.thss.tsinghua.edu.cn/sxsong/doc/screen.pdf.

[7] E. S. Gardner Jr. Exponential smoothing: The state of the art–part ii. *International Journal of Forecasting*, 22(4):637–666, 2006.

[8] L. Golab, H. J. Karloff, F. Korn, A. Saha, and D. Srivastava. Sequential dependencies. *PVLDB*, 2(1):574–585, 2009.

[9] C. A. R. Hoare. Quicksort. *Comput. J.*, 5(1):10–15, 1962.

[10] S. R. Jeffery, M. N. Garofalakis, and M. J. Franklin. Adaptive cleaning for rfid data streams. In *VLDB*, pages 163–174, 2006.

[11] H. Z. Jerrold. Biostatistical analysis. *Biostatistical analysis*, 1999.

[12] N. Karmarkar. A new polynomial-time algorithm for linear programming. In *STOC*, pages 302–311, 1984.

[13] E. J. Keogh, S. Chu, D. M. Hart, and M. J. Pazzani. An online algorithm for segmenting time series. In *ICDM*, pages 289–296, 2001.

[14] S. Kolahi and L. V. S. Lakshmanan. On approximating optimum repairs for functional dependency violations. In *ICDT*, pages 53–62, 2009.

[15] X. Li, X. L. Dong, K. Lyons, W. Meng, and D. Srivastava. Truth finding on the deep web: Is the problem solved? *PVLDB*, 6(2):97–108, 2012.

[16] M. Liu, M. Li, D. Golovnya, E. A. Rundensteiner, and K. T. Claypool. Sequence pattern query processing over out-of-order event streams. In *ICDE*, pages 784–795, 2009.

[17] A. Lopatenko and L. Bravo. Efficient approximation algorithms for repairing inconsistent databases. In *ICDE*, pages 216–225, 2007.

APPENDIX

A. TRANSFORMATION TO LP

We transform the global optimal repair problem in formula (2) to a standard linear programming (LP) problem, so that existing solvers can directly be employed.

Table 2: Notations

Symbol	Description
x	sequence
$x[i]$ or x_i	value of i-th data point in x
t	timestamp
s	speed constraint
w	window size of speed constraint
n	length of a finite sequence
x'	repair of sequence x
$x_i^{\min}, x_i^{\max}$	the lower, upper bound of a valid repair x_i'

Let $u_i = \frac{|x_i'-x_i|+(x_i'-x_i)}{2}$ and $v_i = \frac{|x_i'-x_i|-(x_i'-x_i)}{2}$. We have $|x_i' - x_i| = u_i + v_i$ and $x_i' - x_i = u_i - v_i$. It follows

$$\begin{aligned}
\min \quad & \sum_{i=1}^{n} u_i + v_i \\
\text{s.t.} \quad & \frac{u_j - v_j + v_i - u_i - x_i + x_j}{t_j - t_i} \le s_{\max}, \quad t_i < t_j \le t_i + w, \\
& \qquad 1 \le i \le n, 1 \le j \le n \\
& \frac{u_j - v_j + v_i - u_i - x_i + x_j}{t_j - t_i} \ge s_{\min}, \quad t_i < t_j \le t_i + w, \\
& \qquad 1 \le i \le n, 1 \le j \le n \\
& u_i \ge 0, v_i \ge 0, \qquad 1 \le i \le n
\end{aligned}$$

where u_i, v_i are the variables in problem solving.

Example 9 (Global optimum, Example 2 continued). *Consider again the sequence x and the speed constraints $s_{\max} = 0.5$ and $s_{\min} = -0.5$ with window size $w = 2$ in Example 2.*

According to formulas (3) and (4), the constraint predicates declared w.r.t. $s_{\max}$ and $s_{\min}$ are:

$$\frac{x_2' - x_1'}{2-1} \le 0.5, \frac{x_4' - x_3'}{5-3} \le 0.5, \frac{x_2' - x_1'}{2-1} \ge -0.5, \frac{x_4' - x_3'}{5-3} \ge -0.5,$$
$$\frac{x_3' - x_1'}{3-1} \le 0.5, \frac{x_5' - x_4'}{7-5} \le 0.5, \frac{x_3' - x_1'}{3-1} \ge -0.5, \frac{x_5' - x_4'}{7-5} \ge -0.5,$$
$$\frac{x_3' - x_2'}{3-2} \le 0.5, \frac{x_6' - x_5'}{8-7} \le 0.5, \frac{x_3' - x_2'}{3-2} \ge -0.5, \frac{x_6' - x_5'}{8-7} \ge -0.5.$$

The corresponding transformation is as follows,

$$\frac{u_2 - v_2 + v_1 - u_1 - 12 + 12.5}{2-1} \le 0.5 \qquad \ldots$$
$$\frac{u_3 - v_3 + v_2 - u_2 - 12.5 + 13}{3-2} \le 0.5 \qquad \ldots$$
$$\frac{u_3 - v_3 + v_1 - u_1 - 12 + 13}{3-1} \le 0.5 \qquad \ldots$$

where $u_1 = \frac{|x_1'-x_1|+(x_1'-x_1)}{2}$, $v_1 = \frac{|x_1'-x_1|-(x_1'-x_1)}{2}, \ldots$.

By solving the problem with these constraint predicate (using LP solvers), the global optimal solution is exactly the repair x' in Example 2, with $x_4' = 14$ and the minimum repair distance 4.

Referring to Karmarkar's algorithm [12], it is sufficient to conclude that the global optimal repair problem is polynomial time solvable.

Corollary 8. *The global optimal repair can be computed in $O(n^{3.5}L)$ time, where n is the size of sequence, and L is the number of bits of input.*

B. GLOBAL OPTIMUM APPROXIMATION

As presented in Corollary 8, solving the global optimal repair problem in formula (2) by existing LP solvers is still costly, owing to the large number of speed constraint predicates in formulas (3) and (4). Rather than considering all the constraint relationships over the entire data set and eliminating all the violations at one time, existing approximate repair approaches [4, 14] often greedily repair the data (pairs) involved in violations, in multiple rounds.

In light of the greedy strategy in data repairing [4], we consider only the pairs x_i, x_j that violates the speed constraints, i.e., either $\frac{x_j - x_i}{t_j - t_i} > s_{\max}$ or $\frac{x_j - x_i}{t_j - t_i} < s_{\min}$.

$$\min \sum_{i=1}^{n} |x_i - x_i'| \tag{13}$$

$$\text{s.t.} \quad \frac{x_j' - x_i'}{t_j - t_i} \le s_{\max}, \quad \frac{x_j - x_i}{t_j - t_i} > s_{\max}, t_i < t_j \le t_i + w, \quad 1 \le i \le n, 1 \le j \le n \tag{14}$$

$$\frac{x_j' - x_i'}{t_j - t_i} \ge s_{\min}, \quad \frac{x_j - x_i}{t_j - t_i} < s_{\min}, t_i < t_j \le t_i + w, \quad 1 \le i \le n, 1 \le j \le n \tag{15}$$

Its solution x' eliminates the violation between the aforesaid data points i and j. Since less constraint predicates are specified, the problem solving could be more efficient.

However, new violations may be introduced between the modified x_i' and x_k' in x', where x_i, x_k are not in violation before repairing (i.e., the constraint between x_i and x_k is not previously considered in formulas (14) and (15)). It needs to iteratively repair the violations introduced in the previous round of problem solving. As presented in [4], the iteration terminates till no new x_i' is modified in the last round.

The major issue of this approximation is the soundness of repairing w.r.t. speed constraints, i.e., not all the violations are guaranteed to be eliminated. The reason is that the greedy repair could be trapped in local optima, and the number of violations cannot be further reduced. In other words, as also observed in the experiments in Section 6, a large number of data are still in violation to the speed constraints in the returned approximate repair results.

Example 10 (Approximation, Example 9 continued). *Rather than enumerating all the constraint predicates in Example 9 for global optimum, the approximation considers only the pairs of data points in violations, i.e., (x_3, x_4) and (x_4, x_5) as indicated in Example 2 (red lines in Figure 2(a)).*

According to formulas (14) and (15), the constraint predicates for approximation method are

$$\frac{x_4' - x_3'}{5-3} \ge -0.5, \frac{x_5' - x_4'}{7-5} \le 0.5,$$

which is exactly a subset of the constraint predicates in Example 9 for global optimum.

Let $x' = \{12, 12.5, 13, 12, 13, 15.5\}$ be the solution w.r.t. the aforesaid constraint predicates. The modified data points are $x_4' = 12$ and $x_5' = 13$ denoted by gray points in Figure 2(a). Note that the modification $x_5' = 13$ introduces a new violation between data points 5 and 6.

Therefore, another round of problem solving is evoked, with the following constraint predicate:

$$\frac{x_6' - x_5'}{8-7} \le 0.5.$$

Let the result be $x'' = \{12, 12.5, 13, 12, 15, 15.5\}$, where the modified data point is $x_5'' = 15$. That is, the value is changed back to the original x_5, and the computation is trapped in local optima. According to [4], since data point 5 has been repaired in the previous step and no new data point is modified in this iteration, the program terminates and leaves the violation unsolved between $x_4'' = 12$ and $x_5'' = 15$.

C. NORMAL APPROXIMATION FOR ADAPTIVE WINDOWS

Consider two window sizes w and w' in Figure 7 in Example 8. We show the Binomial probability mass function for $B(n, p)$ and normal probability density function approximation for $\mathcal{N}(np, np(1-p))$ in Figure 20. For w with $n = 4$ data points and $p = 0.91$, we plot $B(4, 0.91)$ and $\mathcal{N}(3.64, 0.3276)$ in Figure 20(a). For w' with $n = 10$ and $p = 0.52$, Figure 20(b) illustrates $B(10, 0.52)$ and $\mathcal{N}(5.2, 2.496)$.

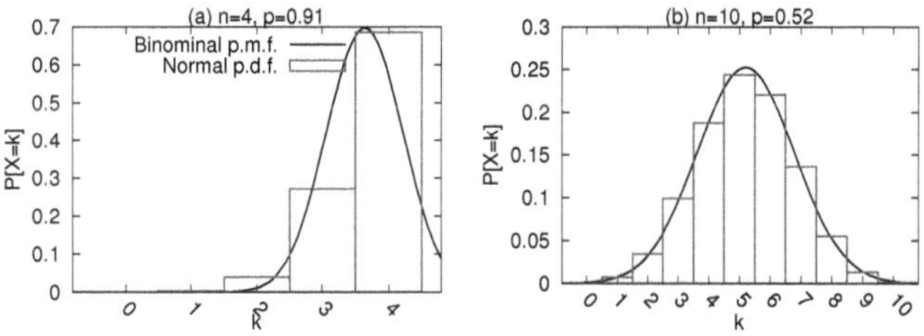

Figure 20: Distribution approximation

In normal approximation [2], if $np \pm 3\sqrt{np(1-p)} \in [0, n]$, then n is large enough, and p is far enough from the extremes of zero or one. That is, the normal approximation is appropriate for binomial distribution, e.g., in Figure 20(b). It is the case for w' as presented in Example 8. As shown in Figure 7, a large number of data points within w' are far from the speed constraints $s_{\min}$ and $s_{\max}$. In other words, the number of data points n is large enough, and p is far enough from the extremes of 0 or 1 referring to the modeling of $p_{i,j}$ in formula (12). Since speed constraints are useless in a large window, according to the intuition of adapting windows, the window may shrink for computation efficiency.

On the other hand, for w with $np \pm 3\sqrt{np(1-p)} \notin [0, n]$, the rule for evaluating normal approximation indicates that n is *not* large enough, and p is *not* far enough from the extremes of zero or one (i.e., the normal approximation is inappropriate as illustrated in Figure 20(a)). By enlarging w, more data points may be involved under the guard of speed constraints to ensure their correctness.

D. MORE DETAILS IN EXPERIMENTS

All programs are implemented in Java. Experiments were performed on a PC with 3.4 GHz CPU and 16 GB RAM.

D.1 Real Dataset Preparation

The STOCK[2] dataset records the daily prices of a stock from 1984-09 to 2010-02, with 12826 data points in total. Since the STOCK data is originally clean, following the same line of precisely evaluating the repair effectiveness [1], errors are injected by randomly replacing the values of some data

[2]http://finance.yahoo.com/q/hp?s=AIP.L+Historical+Prices

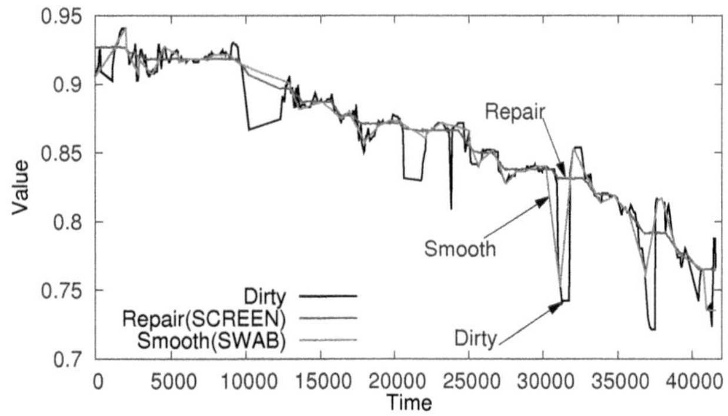

Figure 21: Example of real data FUEL

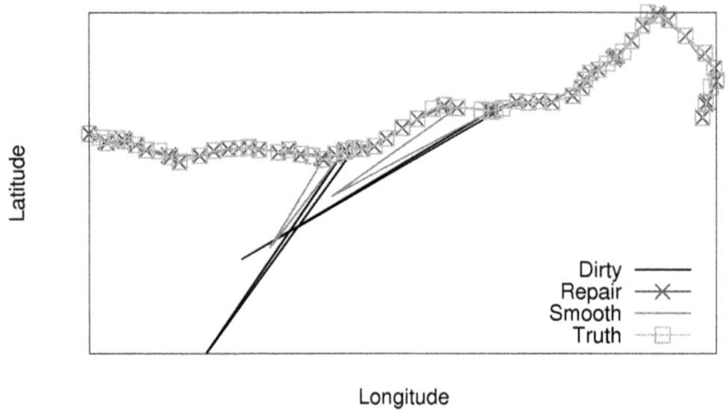

Figure 22: Example of real data GPS

points. For example, an error rate 0.1 denotes that 10% data point values are replaced. For each replaced data point, it takes a random value between the minimum and maximum values in the dataset.

The FUEL dataset gathers readings of fuel gauge of a crane, in every 20-40 seconds when the device is working. There are total 29750 data points collected in a period of 32 days. The entire sequence is divided into several segments by refueling, so that the speed constraint on fuel consumption does not apply across two segments separated by refueling. For the originally dirty FUEL, since the ground truth of each data point is unknown, we first filter out the dirty data points by speed constraints. The remaining data points that are clean w.r.t. speed constraints perform the aforesaid error injection (as done in STOCK).

In order to evaluate over a real dataset with *true errors* (instead of synthetically injected errors), a real GPS dataset is collected by a person carrying a smartphone and walking around at campus. Since we know exactly the path of walking, a number of 368 dirty points are manually identified (among total 3441 points in the trajectory). True locations of dirty points are also manually labeled, as ground truth.

Figures 21 and 22 present two segments of FUEL and GPS data, respectively, with the original dirty points, the truth points and the repairs. Similar to the STOCK example in Figure 1, large spikes (where a data point suddenly jumps far away from the path and the following one comes back soon) also appear in Figures 21 and 22. As shown, the smooth (SWAB) method is not able to correct such mistakes. Our proposed SCREEN repair can successfully address all the spikes, while preserve the original data largely. Consequently, as the results reported in Table 1, the accuracy of our constraint-based Global and Local repairing is significantly higher than that of smoothing methods.

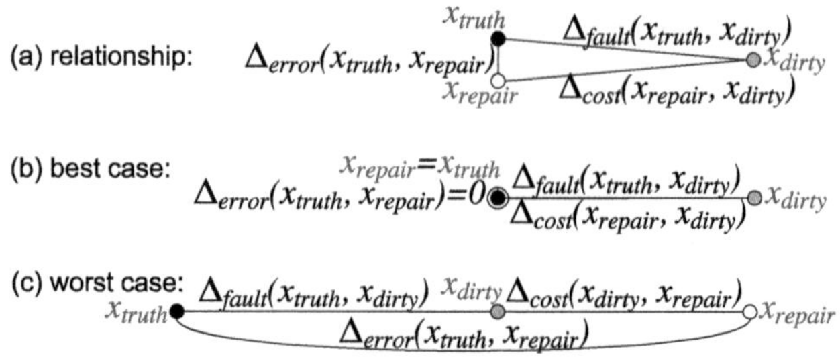

Figure 23: Accuracy measure

D.2 Evaluation Criteria

Let x_{truth} be the ground truth of clean sequence, x_{dirty} be the error sequence with faults embedded, and x_{repair} be the repaired sequence. We denote $\Delta_{dist}(x_{repair}, x_{dirty})$ the distance paid in repairing, i.e., *the minimum change metric* in formula (2) in the optimization problem formulation.

The rationale of the minimum change metric [1] is built upon the discipline that people or systems always try to minimize mistakes in practice, i.e., minimizing the fault distance $\Delta_{fault}(x_{truth}, x_{dirty})$ between the ground truth and the dirty data. Following this discipline, it finds a repair that is closest to the input, i.e., minimizing the repair distance $\Delta_{dist}(x_{repair}, x_{dirty})$, as an *estimate* of the truth.

To study the relationship between $\Delta_{fault}(x_{truth}, x_{dirty})$ and $\Delta_{dist}(x_{repair}, x_{dirty})$, Figures 8(a) and 9(a) observe the fault distance $\Delta_{fault}(x_{truth}, x_{dirty})$ between the ground truth and the dirty sequence. As illustrated, e.g., in Figures 8(a) and (b), the fault distance is roughly *proportional* to the repair distance (for those approaches with accurate repairs such as Global and Local). The results verify the rationale of using the minimum distance repair to estimate the ground truth.

However, it is obvious to see that x_{repair} may not always be an *accurate estimate* of x_{truth}, even though both of them are minimized w.r.t. their distances to the input x_{dirty}. In Figure 23(c), although $\Delta_{dist}(x_{repair}, x_{dirty})$ is proportional to $\Delta_{fault}(x_{truth}, x_{dirty})$, x_{repair} may be far away from x_{truth}.

The *repair accuracy measures* evaluate how close the minimum distance x_{repair} estimates x_{truth}, e.g., by root-mean-square error (RMS) [10], which denotes the error distance $\Delta_{error}(x_{truth}, x_{repair})$ between the ground truth x_{truth} and the repaired sequence x_{repair}. The lower the RMS error $\Delta_{error}(x_{truth}, x_{repair})$ is, the closer (more accurate) the repair is to the ground truth.

It is notable that RMS error is not normalized (e.g., into a range of [0,1] for easy interpretation), and considers only the x_{truth} and x_{repair} but not their distances to the dirty data x_{dirty}. To this end, we further observe the normalized accuracy relative to x_{dirty} by

$$1 - \frac{\Delta_{error}(x_{truth}, x_{repair})}{\Delta_{dist}(x_{repair}, x_{dirty}) + \Delta_{fault}(x_{truth}, x_{dirty})},$$

According to triangle inequality on distances, in the worst case, we have $\Delta_{error}(x_{truth}, x_{repair}) = \Delta_{dist}(x_{repair}, x_{dirty}) + \Delta_{fault}(x_{truth}, x_{dirty})$ with *accuracy*=0. For the best repair results, $\Delta_{error}(x_{truth}, x_{repair}) = 0$, we have *accuracy*=1.

Location-Aware Pub/Sub System: When Continuous Moving Queries Meet Dynamic Event Streams

Long Guo #1, Dongxiang Zhang #2, Guoliang Li †3, Kian-Lee Tan #4, Zhifeng Bao *5

#School of Computing, National University of Singapore, Singapore

†Department of Computer Science, Tsinghua University, Beijing, China

*School of Computer Science & Information Technology, RMIT University, Melbourne, Australia

{[1]guolong,[2]zhangdo,[4]tankl}@comp.nus.edu.sg, [3]liguoliang@tsinghua.edu.cn, [5]zhifeng.bao@rmit.edu.au

ABSTRACT

In this paper, we propose a new location-aware pub/sub system, Elaps, that continuously monitors moving users subscribing to dynamic event streams from social media and E-commerce applications. Users are notified instantly when there is a matching event nearby. To the best of our knowledge, Elaps is the first to take into account continuous moving queries against dynamic event streams. Like existing works on continuous moving query processing, Elaps employs the concept of safe region to reduce communication overhead. However, unlike existing works which assume data from publishers are static, updates to safe regions may be triggered by newly arrived events. In Elaps, we develop a concept called *impact region* that allows us to identify whether a safe region is affected by newly arrived events. Moreover, we propose a novel cost model to optimize the safe region size to keep the communication overhead low. Based on the cost model, we design two incremental methods, iGM and idGM, for safe region construction. In addition, Elaps uses boolean expression, which is more expressive than keywords, to model user intent and we propose a novel index, BEQ-Tree, to handle spatial boolean expression matching. In our experiments, we use geo-tweets from Twitter and venues from Foursquare to simulate publishers and boolean expressions generated from AOL search log to represent users intentions. We test user movement in both synthetic trajectories and real taxi trajectories. The results show that Elaps can significantly reduce the communication overhead and disseminate events to users in real-time.

Categories and Subject Descriptors

H.2 [**Database Management**]: Database applications;
H.2.8 [**Database applications**]: Spatial database and GIS

Keywords

pub/sub; continuous moving queries; dynamic event streams

1. INTRODUCTION

The prevalence of social networks and mobile devices has facilitated the real-time dissemination of local events such as sales, shows and exhibitions. To avoid missing interesting events in the neighborhood, various location-aware pub/sub systems have been proposed. These fall into two categories: they either focused on how to handle incoming event streams efficiently by assuming users' locations are static [1, 2, 3, 4]; or they attempted to process continuous moving subscriptions against a static event dataset [5, 6, 7, 8, 9, 10]. None of them can really support subscriptions from mobile users moving all the time against spatial events that are continuously published by local businesses.

In this paper, we propose a new location-aware pub/sub system, Elaps, that continuously monitors moving users subscribing to dynamic event streams from social media and E-commerce applications. Users are notified instantly when there is a matching event nearby. Unlike existing pub/sub systems, Elaps uses boolean expressions, which are more expressive than keywords, to model user intent. This means users can subscribe to structured, semi-structured and unstructured data.

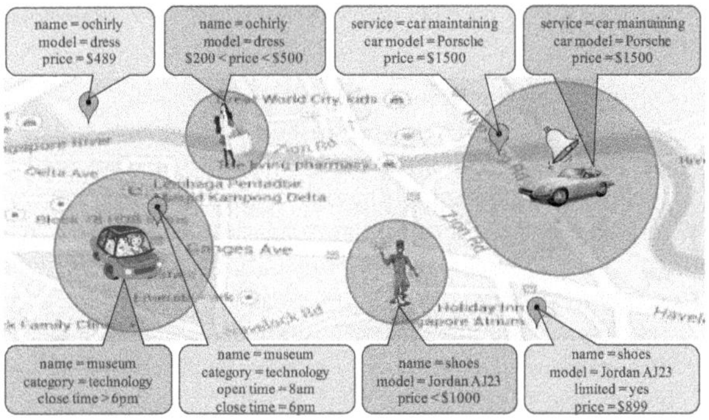

Figure 1: A working scenario of Elaps

Fig. 1 illustrates a working scenario of such a system. Here, the subscribers with mobile devices are the moving objects, and a subscription is represented in the form of a boolean expression. For example, if a user is interested in Jordan basketball shoes, he can use a boolean expression to model the interest: (name=shoes $\wedge$ model=Jordan AJ23 $\wedge$ price $<$ \$1000). Note that pub/sub systems based on keyword subscription cannot support numeric attribute matching such as price $<$ \$1000. To specify the locational matching constraint, a subscriber can set a notification radius so that events lying inside the circle are considered as candidates. For example, the circles in Fig. 1 represent the notification regions of different users. When a user moves, the notification region moves along. On the publisher side, an event is published at a location. If a shoe shop is on sale, then the location of the shop is the event location. Our system continuously monitors the moving subscribers and notify them once there is a matching event in their circles.

SIGMOD'15, May 31–June 4, 2015, Melbourne, Victoria, Australia.

http://dx.doi.org/10.1145/2723372.2746481.

	Location-aware news feed		Location-aware pub/sub			Continuous spatial queries		
	GeoFeed[1]	MobiFeed[11]	R^t-tree[2]	IQ-tree[3]	CLCB[4]	KNN/Range	Spatial keyword	Elaps
continuous moving queries	✗	✗	✗	✗	✗	✓	✓	✓
dynamic event streams	✓	✓	✓	✓	✓	✗	✗	✓
matching semantic	-	-	keyword	keyword	BE	-	keyword	BE

Table 1: Comparison of existing location-aware pub/sub system

To meet the above desiderata, our system is designed to tackle the two main challenges:

a) how to effectively process continuous moving subscriptions against dynamic event streams. Safe region has been widely used to reduce communication cost for continuous moving query processing [5, 6, 7, 8, 9, 10]. The intuition behind the notion of safe region is that if there are no matching events nearby, the users are safe to disconnect from the server and do not need to periodically update their locations. However, we observed that the safe region techniques used in [5, 6, 7, 8, 9, 10] fail to work effectively when dynamic events are considered. This is because newly arrived events can trigger new communication needed to update the safe regions, besides the communication incurred by location updates. Moreover, these two types of communication have conflicting requirements on the size of safe regions. Therefore, there is a need to reconsider how best to exploit safe regions.

b) how to support symmetric boolean expression matching with spatial constraints between subscribers and publishers. In other words, when a subscriber arrives, we need to search in the event database for matching events within the specified notification radius; when a new event arrives, we need to search in the subscriber database to find matching subscribers and notify them.

More specifically, our technical contributions are summarized as follows:

- We optimize the design and processing of safe regions in several ways. First, given a safe region, we derive its *impact region*. The impact region is a novel concept used to identify if its corresponding safe region is affected by newly arrived events. Second, we propose a cost-based approach to determine the optimal safe region size to keep the communication overhead low. Our cost model considers the communication cost incurred by location updates as well as that incurred by event arrival. Third, based on the cost model, we design two new schemes, iGM and idGM, to incrementally construct safe regions.

- We propose a new index named BEQ-Tree which integrates Quadtree [12] with boolean expressions seamlessly to support spatial boolean expression matching and safe region construction efficiently.

Moreover, we conduct comprehensive experiments using real datasets to evaluate the system performance. We use geo-tweets from Twitter and venues from Foursquare to simulate publishers and boolean expressions generated from AOL search log to represent users intentions. We test user movement in both synthetic trajectories and real taxi trajectories. The results show that our proposed iGM and idGM can reduce the communication overhead by 10 times. Also, our proposed index handles spatial boolean expression matching significantly faster than the competing methods.

The rest of this paper is organized as follows. We first review various location-based pub/sub systems and boolean expression matching and give a problem statement in Section 2. We then propose how to handle continuous moving queries against dynamic event streams in Section 3. We further introduce how to handle spatial boolean expression matching in Section 4. Based on the techniques proposed in Section 3 and Section 4, we present the system framework of Elaps in Section 5. Finally, we evaluate our system performance in Section 6 and conclude the paper in Section 7.

2. RELATED WORK

In Elaps, our primary goal is to build a pub/sub system that caters for both continuous moving subscribers and dynamic event streams from publishers, and our secondary goal is to support a more expressive event matching semantic than pure keywords. Thus, in this section, we first highlight the novelty of Elaps as compared with existing location-aware pub/sub systems and then present the related work about boolean expression matching. Finally we give a problem statement.

2.1 Location-aware Pub/sub

To clearly distinguish Elaps from other works in the literature, we first present a taxonomy of the existing location-aware pub/sub systems and our proposed Elaps in three aspects: support for continuous moving queries, support for dynamic event streams and event matching semantic (see Table 1).

Location-aware pub/sub system. A location-aware pub/sub system sends matching geo-tagged events to the corresponding subscribers. Compared to existing location-aware pub/sub systems [2, 3, 4], Elaps has two distinguishing features, as shown in Table 1. First, it continuously monitors users' locations and sends nearby notifications in real time, while [2, 3, 4] assume users' locations are static. Second, it allows users to specify their interests with boolean expressions, which provides better flexibility and expressiveness in shaping an interest than keyword subscription in [2, 3].

Continuous spatial queries. Another problem that is closely related to our research is the processing of continuous spatial queries such as continuous KNN/range queries [5, 6, 7] and continuous spatial keyword queries [8, 9, 10]. Given a moving query, existing works have developed techniques to continuously return a set of objects satisfying the spatial constraint [5, 6, 7] or the combined spatial and textual constraints [8, 9, 10]. To reduce the communication overhead, these methods typically require users to update their locations only when they move out of their safe regions. Moreover, users within the safe regions can safely disconnect from the server as long as there is no matching event in their neighborhood. Since we focus on range query, the safe region construction methods for spatial keyword query in [8, 9, 10] cannot be applied. Besides, those proposed for continuous knn/range queries [5, 6, 7] assume the publisher events are static, so they fail to solve our problem either (Please refer to Section 3 for a detailed justification). Lastly, these methods allow users to search for relevant events by keyword subscriptions while Elaps uses a more expressive boolean expression to model user intent.

Location-aware news feed system. We also note that location-aware news feed systems enable mobile users to share geo-tagged user-generated messages. In GeoFeed [1], users retrieve geo-related message updates from either their social friends or social media. It differs from Elaps in that: (1) GeoFeed is pull-based, which poses a high chance of missing interesting events, (2) users are static objects, (3) users cannot customize the messages they are interested in explicitly. MobiFeed [11] extends GeoFeed to support mobile users. Instead of monitoring the location of moving users from time to time like Elaps, it predicts the potential next locations for a moving user in advance and pushes the messages around these locations to the user. Thus, it cannot support continuous moving queries; moreover, there is no guarantee that users will not miss any matching event.

Therefore, to our knowledge, Elaps is the first location-aware pub/sub system that takes into account continuous moving queries as well as dynamic event streams.

2.2 Boolean expression matching

There have been several studies on efficient *event matching* over a large quantity of subscriptions [13, 14, 15]. Whang et al. [14] proposed k-index which partitions the subscriptions into inverted lists, whose key is a triple of subscription size, attribute name and attribute value. To further improve efficiency and expressiveness, Sadoghi and Jacobsen proposed the BE-Tree [15] and developed a two-stage partition mechanism to facilitate pruning. Zhang et al. [16] proposed a scalable and extensible index named OpIndex to support high-dimensional and sparse database effectively. OpIndex adopts a two-layer partition scheme and can be extended to support more expressive subscriptions.

In Elaps, we require not only *event matching* but also *subscription matching* over a large quantity of events. Among the above methods, only k-index and OpIndex can be extended to support *subscription matching*. Both indexes adopt a two-layer partitioning scheme and use the inverted list to group the attributes in the second layer. Their difference is the way they partition the events in the first layer. k-index partitions the events based on the event size, while OpIndex partitions the events based on the pivot attribute selected for each event. However, both partitioning schemes are not efficient in supporting subscription matching, especially when the spatial matching is taken into consideration. In this paper, we propose a more efficient index BEQ-Tree to support spatial subscription matching.

2.3 Problem Statement

In this paper, we study the efficient processing of continuous moving range queries against dynamic event streams. Given a set of continuous arriving events, for a moving subscriber with a boolean expression subscription associated with a notification region, the subscriber is notified once there is a matching event located within his notification region. We aim for a solution that (i) optimizes the client/server communication cost and (ii) guarantees that the matching events are disseminated to subscribers in real-time.

3. CONTINUOUS MOVING QUERIES OVER DYNAMIC EVENT STREAMS

Compared to existing location-based pub/sub systems, Elaps is the first to consider continuous moving queries against dynamic event streams from publishers. The main challenge is to reduce communication overhead because users have to periodically report their current locations to the server to guarantee that no matching events in their neighborhood are missed. Existing pub/sub systems that can handle moving users mainly use safe region techniques to reduce communication cost. The intuition behind the notion of safe region is that if there are no matching events nearby, the users are safe to disconnect from the server and do not need to periodically update their locations. In this way, the communication cost can be significantly reduced and there would be no matching events missed. In this section, we first propose how to apply these techniques into our pub/sub application. Then, we explain why the safe regions constructed in these systems fail to work well when dynamic event streams are considered. Finally, we propose our solutions based on a concept named *impact region* as well as a new cost model for safe region construction.

3.1 Safe Region against Static Event Datasets

Safe region has been widely used to reduce communication cost for continuous spatial query processing [5, 6, 7]. In these work, a common assumption is that the continuous query is issued against a static dataset and the goal is to determine an area in which there is no matching events or the matching events remain the same. Since the publisher dataset is static, there would be no new event matching in the safe region. For our application, we define a region is safe if its minimum distance to any matching event is larger than the user's notification radius, denoted by r [1].

DEFINITION 1 (SAFE REGION). *The safe region $\mathcal{R}$ for a subscriber s is a region such that $s \in \mathcal{R}$ and for any matching event e, we have $d(p, e) > r$ for any $p \in \mathcal{R}$.*

In the following, we examine existing safe region techniques and show how to apply them for continuous proximity detection between subscribers and their matching events.

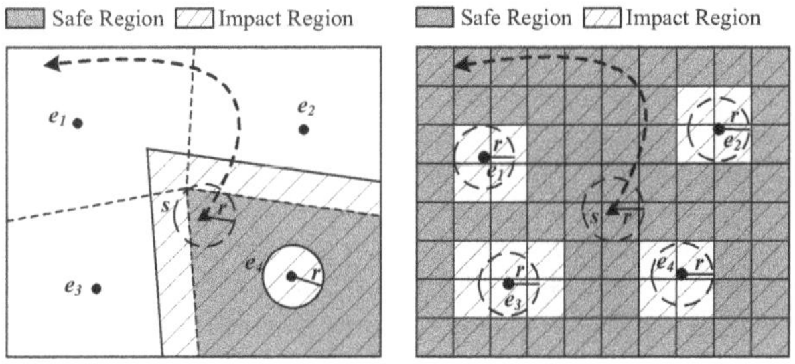

(a) VM (b) GM

Figure 2: Applying existing methods for safe region construction

Voronoi-based Method (VM). Voronoi diagram is often used in processing continuous kNN queries in continuous spatial query applications [5, 6]. Since the publisher dataset is static, the space is partitioned into voronoi cells based on the locations of publishers. Each voronoi cell indicates a region dominated by a publisher such that as long as a subscriber moves in that cell, the publisher is assured to be the nearest neighbor. To apply voronoi diagram in our application, we first find all the matching events outside of the notification region [2] and construct voronoi cells based on the matching events. Each cell contains one matching event. The safe region is the voronoi cell containing the user, excluding the circle centered at the matching event with notification radius.

Figure 2(a) shows an example of safe region based on voronoi diagram. There are four matching events that partition the space into four voronoi cells. Since the subscriber is located in e_4, the safe region is the voronoi cell for e_4 excluding the circle and marked in the shaded area. As long as the user moves in the safe region, we can guarantee that there is no matching event nearby and the

[1] A notation table consisting of symbols and their meanings is provided in Table 3(Appendix A)

[2] If a matching event appears in the notification region, we notify the subscriber immediately about the matching. Then, the event will not be considered again for this user in the future.

user only need to check his distance with e_4 and can temporarily disconnect from the server.

Grid-based Method (GM). In [7], safe region based on grid cells was proposed to handle spatial alarm applications. By partitioning the space into cells, a safe region is represented by a set of cells whose distance to any matching events is larger than the notification radius. An example of grid-based safe region is shown in Figure 2(b). The safe region for the subscriber contains the whole space except the cells close to the matching events. Compared to the voronoi diagram method, the grid based safe region is easier to construct and contains a larger region than VM.

When the event dataset is static, GM generates a larger safe region and achieves better performance in terms of communication I/O. However, when we consider dynamic event streams, the results can be totally different. In this case, a larger safe region does not necessarily mean a better solution. When a new matching event arrives close or inside the safe region, the region may not be "safe" any more. Then the whole safe region has to be re-constructed, leading to additional communication I/O. This observation motivates us to first develop a new concept named impact region to identify whether a safe region is "safe" or not when a new event arrives, and then propose a novel cost model based on the safe region and impact region to guide the construction of the safe region .

3.2 Impact Region

We first define the *impact region* for a certain safe region $\mathcal{R}$, and use it to determine whether $\mathcal{R}$ will be affected by the arrival of a new event. Intuitively, if a new matching event arrives in the impact region, the safe region $\mathcal{R}$ is not "safe" any more and needs to be updated. Otherwise, the safe region remains the same. With the help of the impact region, we do not need to update the safe region each time a new matching event arrives. Thus, the impact region can help reduce the communication cost incurred by event arrival. The concept of impact region will also be needed in our proposed cost model to estimate the expected time before the next matching event affects its corresponding safe region.

DEFINITION 2 (IMPACT REGION). *Given a safe region $\mathcal{R}$, the impact region $\mathcal{I}$ for $\mathcal{R}$ is defined as*

$$\{p \mid p \in U \text{ and } \exists\, p' \in \mathcal{R}\,(d(p,p') < r)\}$$

where U is the whole space and r is the notification radius.

Based on the definition, we know that if a point is located outside the impact region, its minimum distance to safe region $\mathcal{R}$ must be larger than r. Hence, we can consider impact region as an expansion of the safe region by the length of notification radius. Note that the impact region is uniquely determined by the safe region and should always be used together with the safe region. In the following, we briefly introduce how to construct impact regions from the safe regions in Figure 2.

EXAMPLE 1. *In VM, the impact region is constructed by expanding the Voroni cell of the nearest event with distance r. As shown in Figure 2, the impact region covers the notification region of the subscriber after the expansion. We can guarantee that when a new event arrives outside the impact region, its minimum distance to the impact region is larger than the notification radius. This new event will not fall inside the notification region as long as the user moves within the safe region. Hence, we only need to update the safe regions whose impact region contains this new event.*

In GM, the impact region is constructed by expanding the safe region with r to see which cells are contained in or intersected with the expanded region, which is the whole space in this example. When a new matching event arrives in the impact region, we need users to report their location to guarantee that the current safe region is "safe" and no matching notification is missed. Since the impact region contains the whole space, new communication overhead is incurred each time when a new matching event arrives.

Up till now, we have introduced the three types of regions maintained for each moving user: notification region $\mathcal{O}$, safe region $\mathcal{R}$ and impact region $\mathcal{I}$. The notification region is set by the subscribers and move with them. It is a circle centered at the subscriber's current location with radius r. For each subscriber, the system constructs a safe region and an impact region for him. The safe region is sent to the subscriber to monitor the location update and the impact region is stored at the server side to monitor the event arrival. Their relationships are summarized as follows:

LEMMA 1. *$\mathcal{O}$ is contained in $\mathcal{I}$, denoted by $\mathcal{O} \subseteq \mathcal{I}$.*

PROOF. Suppose we can find a point $p \in \mathcal{O}$ but $p \notin \mathcal{I}$. Since $p \notin \mathcal{I}$, based on the definition of the impact region, for any point p' in the safe region $\mathcal{R}$, we have $d(p,p') > r$. Since the safe region is required to cover the user's current location s, i.e, $s \in \mathcal{R}$, we have $d(p,s) > r$. However, since p is located in the notification region, for any points $p \in \mathcal{O}$, we have $d(p,s) < r$. This leads to a contradiction. □

LEMMA 2. *$\mathcal{R}$ is contained in $\mathcal{I}$, denoted by $\mathcal{R} \subseteq \mathcal{I}$.*

PROOF. Based on the definition of impact region, for any point $p \in \mathcal{R}$, if we can find a point $p' \in \mathcal{R}$ such that $d(p,p') < r$, we know p is also a point in the impact region. Let $p = p'$ and we finish the proof. □

Note that the safe region $\mathcal{R}$ does not necessarily contain the notification region $\mathcal{O}$. In fact, when a user increases his notification radius r, the safe region shrinks such that the minimum distance of the new safe region to any matching event is guaranteed to be larger than r. In addition, we can prove that the area of impact region grows when the safe region expands.

LEMMA 3. *Given $\mathcal{I}_1$ derived from $\mathcal{R}_1$ and $\mathcal{I}_2$ derived from $\mathcal{R}_2$, if $\mathcal{R}_1 \subseteq \mathcal{R}_2$, we have $\mathcal{I}_1 \subseteq \mathcal{I}_2$.*

PROOF. Suppose we can find a point $p \in \mathcal{I}_1$ but $p \notin \mathcal{I}_2$. Since $p \notin \mathcal{I}_2$, based on the definition of the impact region, for any point $p' \in \mathcal{R}_2$, we have $d(p,p') > r$. Since $\mathcal{R}_1 \subseteq \mathcal{R}_2$, this conclusion also applied in the sub-region, i.e., for any point $p' \in \mathcal{R}_1$, we have $d(p,p') > r$. This leads to a contradiction with $p \in \mathcal{I}_1$. Hence, if $p \in \mathcal{I}_1$, we have $p \in \mathcal{I}_2$. a new matching event e with p as its location will influence $\mathcal{R}_1$ because e is located within $\mathcal{I}_1$. Since $\mathcal{R}_1 \subseteq \mathcal{R}_2$, e will also influence $\mathcal{R}_2$. However, since e is located outside $\mathcal{I}_2$, this contradicts with the definition of impact region that any matching event located outside the impact region will not influence the safe region. Hence, if $p \in \mathcal{I}_1$, we have $p \in \mathcal{I}_2$. □

In the following, we show that there is no matching event in the impact region.

LEMMA 4. *Suppose $\mathcal{I}$ is an impact region constructed for subscriber s, for any event e matching s, e is located outside $\mathcal{I}$.*

PROOF. If there is a matching event $e \in \mathcal{I}$, based on the definition of the impact region, we can find a point p in the safe region such that $d(p,e) < r$. Then, by following the definition of safe region, since $p \in \mathcal{R}$, we have $d(p,e) > r$. This leads to a contradiction. Hence, e must be located outside $\mathcal{I}$. □

From Lemma 4, we can ensure that if a matching event expires, it is located outside the impact region and has no effect on the current safe region.

3.3 Cost Model for Safe Region Construction

Since we consider continuous query processing against dynamic event streams, we first identify all the possible cases in which new communication can be triggered for an existing subscriber.

1. The subscriber moves out of his current safe region. He needs to report his new precise location to the server. At the server side, a new safe region is calculated and sent back to the user.
2. A new matching event arrives in the system. Whether a communication is triggered depends on the location of the new event. If the event is located outside the impact region, the safe region is not affected based on the definition. Otherwise, the safe region has to be updated. This triggers a new communication. First, the server notifies the subscriber to update the location. Then, the precise location is reported by the client. When the server receives the accurate location, it calculates the distance from the event to the subscriber. If the distance is smaller than the user's notification radius, a matching notification is sent to the user. Otherwise, the server needs to calculate and sends a new safe region to the client. In the meanwhile, the impact region is updated, but stored at the server side.
3. An existing matching event is expired and removed from the system. Based on Lemma 4, the matching event is located outside the impact region. We can guarantee that the current safe region is still "safe". As long as the subscriber is in the current safe region, he can disconnect from the server and no matching event will be missed.

Therefore, there are two types of communication incurred when handling a continuous query over dynamic event streams: I) The subscriber moves out of the safe region. II) A new matching event arrives in the impact region. These two types of communication have conflicting requirements on the size of safe region. The first type prefers larger safe region so that it takes longer time for the subscriber to move out of the safe region. However, the second type prefers smaller safe region. This is because a smaller safe region results in a smaller impact region according to Lemma 3 and it becomes less likely for a matching event to occur in the impact region. Existing safe region techniques do not work well for dynamic event streams because they neglect the second type of communication. Therefore, we propose a new cost model for safe region construction taking into account all these two types of communication.

The goal of our cost model is to minimize the communication overhead which is measured by the number of the two types of communication I/O for a subscriber s. Hence, we construct a safe region $\mathcal{R}$ for s such that the expected elapsed time before the next communication I/O is maximized. The expected elapsed time is denoted by $f_{obj}(\mathcal{R},\mathcal{I})$ and used as the objective function to maximize. Let $t_s(\mathcal{R})$ denote the expected time to move out of the current safe region $\mathcal{R}$ and $t_i(\mathcal{I})$ denote the expected time before the next matching event occurs in the impact region $\mathcal{I}$ constructed from $\mathcal{R}$. Since there are only two circumstances in which communication I/O is triggered, we have

$$f_{obj}(\mathcal{R},\mathcal{I}) = \min(t_s(\mathcal{R}), t_i(\mathcal{I})) \quad (1)$$

Next, we define b_m to measure the tradeoff between the two types of communication.

$$b_m(\mathcal{R},\mathcal{I}) = \frac{t_s(\mathcal{R})}{t_i(\mathcal{I})} \quad (2)$$

We can prove that $b_m(\mathcal{R},\mathcal{I})$ has a positive correlation with the area of $\mathcal{R}$:

LEMMA 5. *Given two safe regions $\mathcal{R}$ and $\mathcal{R}'$ with $\mathcal{R} \subseteq \mathcal{R}'$, we have $b_m(\mathcal{R},\mathcal{I}) \leq b_m(\mathcal{R}',\mathcal{I}')$.*

PROOF. Since $\mathcal{R} \subseteq \mathcal{R}'$, we know that $t_s(\mathcal{R}) \leq t_s(\mathcal{R}')$ and $t_i(\mathcal{I}) \geq t_i(\mathcal{I}')$ based on Lemma 3 and the definition of t_s and t_i. Hence, $b_m(\mathcal{R},\mathcal{I}) = \frac{t_s(\mathcal{R})}{t_i(\mathcal{I})} \leq \frac{t_s(\mathcal{R}')}{t_i(\mathcal{I}')} = b_m(\mathcal{R}',\mathcal{I}')$. □

If $b_m(\mathcal{R},\mathcal{I}) \leq 1$, we have $t_s(\mathcal{R}) \leq t_i(\mathcal{I})$ and $f_{obj} = t_s(\mathcal{R})$. In this case, we need to maximize $t_s(\mathcal{R})$ and we prefer a larger safe region for $\mathcal{R}$. If $b_m(\mathcal{R},\mathcal{I}) > 1$, we have $f_{obj} = t_i(\mathcal{I})$ and we prefer a smaller safe region for $\mathcal{R}$. The relationship between $f_{obj}(\mathcal{R},\mathcal{I})$ and $b_m(\mathcal{R},\mathcal{I})$ are stated in the following two lemmas:

LEMMA 6. *Given two safe regions $\mathcal{R}$ and $\mathcal{R}'$ with $\mathcal{R} \subseteq \mathcal{R}'$, suppose $b_m(\mathcal{R}',\mathcal{I}') \leq 1$, we have $f_{obj}(\mathcal{R},\mathcal{I}) \leq f_{obj}(\mathcal{R}',\mathcal{I}')$.*

PROOF. Based on Lemma 5, $b_m(\mathcal{R},\mathcal{I}) \leq b_m(\mathcal{R}',\mathcal{I}') \leq 1$ because $\mathcal{R} \subseteq \mathcal{R}'$. For $\mathcal{R}$, since $b_m(\mathcal{R},\mathcal{I}) \leq 1$, we have $t_s(\mathcal{R}) \leq t_i(\mathcal{I})$ and thus $f_{obj}(\mathcal{R},\mathcal{I}) = t_s(\mathcal{R})$. Similarly, $f_{obj}(\mathcal{R}',\mathcal{I}') = t_s(\mathcal{R}')$. Since $\mathcal{R}$ is contained in $\mathcal{R}'$, we have $t_s(\mathcal{R}) \leq t_s(\mathcal{R}')$. Therefore, $f_{obj}(\mathcal{R},\mathcal{I}) = t_s(\mathcal{R}) \leq t_s(\mathcal{R}') = f_{obj}(\mathcal{R}',\mathcal{I}')$. □

LEMMA 7. *Given two safe regions $\mathcal{R}$ and $\mathcal{R}'$ with $\mathcal{R} \subseteq \mathcal{R}'$, suppose $b_m(\mathcal{R},\mathcal{I}) \geq 1$, we have $f_{obj}(\mathcal{R},\mathcal{I}) \geq f_{obj}(\mathcal{R}',\mathcal{I}')$.*

PROOF. Based on Lemma 5, $b_m(\mathcal{R}',\mathcal{I}') \geq b_m(\mathcal{R},\mathcal{I}) \geq 1$ because $\mathcal{R} \subseteq \mathcal{R}'$. For $\mathcal{R}$, since $b_m(\mathcal{R},\mathcal{I}) \geq 1$, we have $t_s(\mathcal{R}) \geq t_i(\mathcal{I})$ and thus $f_{obj}(\mathcal{R},\mathcal{I}) = t_i(\mathcal{I})$. Similarly, $f_{obj}(\mathcal{R}',\mathcal{I}') = t_i(\mathcal{I}')$. Since $\mathcal{R}'$ is contained in $\mathcal{R}$, we have $t_i(\mathcal{I}) \geq t_i(\mathcal{I}')$. Therefore, $f_{obj}(\mathcal{R},\mathcal{I}) = t_i(\mathcal{I}) \geq t_i(\mathcal{I}') = f_{obj}(\mathcal{R}',\mathcal{I}')$. □

Our safe region construction method relies on the above lemmas. The idea is to start from the user's current location and incrementally expand the area towards an "optimal" safe region (i.e., f_{obj} is maximized). Initially, $\mathcal{R}$ contains only a point. Thus, t_s can be seen as 0 and $b_m(\mathcal{R},\mathcal{I}) \leq 1$. When we expand $\mathcal{R}$, $b_m(\mathcal{R},\mathcal{I})$ and $f_{obj}(\mathcal{R},\mathcal{I})$ also increase (Lemma 5 and 6). In this case, it encourages us to expand the safe region until any further expansion would cause $b_m(\mathcal{R},\mathcal{I}) \geq 1$ or the region not "safe". This is because $f_{obj}(\mathcal{R},\mathcal{I})$ decreases when $b_m(\mathcal{R},\mathcal{I}) \geq 1$ if we continue to expand $\mathcal{R}$ based on Lemma 7.

Note that there are many possible ways to expand a safe region, resulting in lots of candidate safe regions. For each of these candidate safe regions, we have $b_m \leq 1$ and thus $f_{obj} = t_s$. Hence, the "optimal" safe region is the candidate safe region with the largest t_s. Based on this observation, we should expand the safe region in such a way that the corresponding t_s can be maximized.

3.4 Incremental Grid-based Method

We are now ready to present our incremental method, named iGM (incremental Grid-based Method), towards optimal safe region construction. Since we need a flexible way to represent safe region in arbitrary shape, we partition the space into $N \times N$ cells and a safe region is represented by the set of cells that it covers. Our algorithm starts from the cell containing the user's current location and iteratively expands it to cover nearby cells. In each expansion, a "good" cell based on certain criteria is added to the current safe region. When a cell is added into the current safe region, we also need to expand the corresponding impact region to calculate $b_m(\mathcal{R},\mathcal{I})$. The algorithm terminates when any further expansion would cause $b_m(\mathcal{R},\mathcal{I}) > 1$ or there is no more valid adjacent cells to expand. In the following, we introduce the estimation of $b_m(\mathcal{R},\mathcal{I})$ for a candidate safe region $\mathcal{R}$ as well as the selection criteria for the next cell to expand.

Algorithm 1: ConstructSafeRegion

input: Subscription s
output: Safe region $\mathcal{R}$ and impact region $\mathcal{I}$

1 $b_m \leftarrow 0$
2 $n_e \leftarrow 0$
3 $\mathtt{d}(s,\mathcal{R}) \leftarrow 0$
4 $\mathcal{H} \leftarrow \emptyset$
5 $c \leftarrow$ the cell that contains s
6 HEntry $h \leftarrow$ tuple$(c, d(s,c))$
7 insert h into $\mathcal{H}$, mark c as visited
8 **while** $\mathcal{H} \neq \emptyset$ **do**
9   HEntry $(c', d(s,c')) \leftarrow \mathcal{H}.pop()$
10   **if** $\beta[c'] \neq false$ **then**
11     $\mathtt{d}(s,\mathcal{R}) \leftarrow min\{\mathcal{H}.top().dist, min\{d(s,c'')\}\}$
12     $\mathcal{I}_c \leftarrow getImpactCells(c')$
13   **foreach** $c_n \in \mathcal{I}_c$ **do**
14       $n_e = n_e + \phi[c_n]$
15     $b_m = \frac{f \cdot n_e \cdot \mathtt{d}(s,\mathcal{R})}{n \cdot v_s}$
16   **if** $b_m \leq 1$ **then**
17       $\mathcal{R} \leftarrow \mathcal{R} \cup c'$
18       $\mathcal{I} \leftarrow \mathcal{I} \cup \mathcal{I}_c$
19   **foreach** non-visited adjacent unit cell c'' **do**
20   HEntry $h \leftarrow$ tuple $(c'', \mathtt{d}(s,c''))$
21   insert h into $\mathcal{H}$, mark c'' as visited
22 return $\mathcal{R}$ and $\mathcal{I}$

Assume that subscribers are moving with linear motion functions. The expected time $t_s(\mathcal{R})$ to move out of $\mathcal{R}$ can be calculated by

$$t_s(\mathcal{R}) = \frac{\mathtt{d}(s,\mathcal{R})}{v_s} \tag{3}$$

where $\mathtt{d}(s,\mathcal{R})$ is the minimum distance from a subscriber's location to the boundary of a candidate safe region $\mathcal{R}$ and v_s is the current moving speed.

The expected time $t_i(\mathcal{I})$ before the next matching event occurs in the impact region $\mathcal{I}$ for $\mathcal{R}$, is estimated by

$$t_i(\mathcal{I}) = \frac{t_e}{p(e,\mathcal{I})} \tag{4}$$

where t_e is the average time interval between two new events arriving at the system and $p(e,\mathcal{I})$ is the probability for a new event to match subscriber s and occur in his impact region $\mathcal{I}$.

We can estimate t_e from the average arrival speed in the event streams. We denote the average arriving rate of the new events by f and we have $t_e = \frac{1}{f}$. The probability $p(e,\mathcal{I})$ can also be estimated from the distributions of the existing events in the system. Let n_e be the number of matching events located in the impact region $\mathcal{I}$. n_e can be estimated by $n_e = \sum_{c \in \mathcal{I}} n_c$ where n_c is the number of existing matching events located within cell c. Let n be the total number of events in the system. We can estimate $p(e,\mathcal{I}) = \frac{n_e}{n}$. Then t_i can be calculated as follows.

$$t_i(\mathcal{I}) = \frac{n}{f \cdot n_e} \tag{5}$$

Based on Equation 3 and Equation 5, we have

$$b_m(\mathcal{R},\mathcal{I}) = \frac{t_s(\mathcal{R})}{t_i(\mathcal{I})} = \frac{f \cdot n_e \cdot \mathtt{d}(s,\mathcal{R})}{n \cdot v_s} \tag{6}$$

Note that among the parameters, v_s, f and n are system statistics and are independent of the safe region and impact region. $\mathtt{d}(s,\mathcal{R})$ and n_e are dependent on the areas of the candidate safe region and impact region respectively.

Next, we introduce our expansion criteria. Suppose the current safe region is $\mathcal{R}$. We mark all the cells covered by or intersected

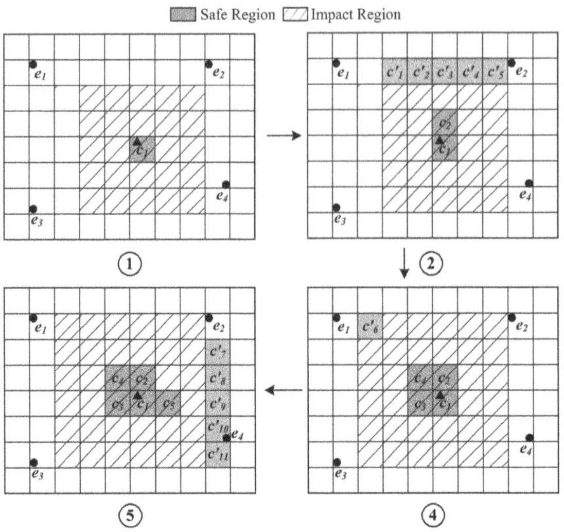

Figure 3: Safe region and impact region expansion

with $\mathcal{R}$ as visited. The candidate cells to expand include all the adjacent cells of $\mathcal{R}$ that are unvisited. Our expansion criteria is to pick the cell c with the minimum distance to the subscriber. In other words, we expand the area circularly. This is because we expand the safe region until any expansion would cause $b_m(\mathcal{R},\mathcal{I}) \geq 1$. In this process, we have $b_m(\mathcal{R},\mathcal{I})$ always smaller than 1 and our goal is to maximize t_s. Since the moving pattern of the subscriber is not available, we expand the cells in every direction uniformly so as to improve the performance in the worst case.

Our iGM algorithm for safe region construction is shown in Algorithm 1. The input is a subscription s with notification radius r and speed v_s. We first initialize the parameters b_m, n_e and $\mathtt{d}(s,\mathcal{R})$ (lines 1-3) and build a min-heap $\mathcal{H}$ whose root stores the cell candidate with the minimum distance to s. The heap is initialized to contain the cell c where the subscriber is located (lines 4-7). After the initialization steps, we expand the safe region in a breadth-first fashion (lines 8-21). The candidate cell c' with the minimum distance to s is popped in each iteration (line 9). A boolean array $\mathcal{B}$ is used to indicate whether a grid cell is *safe* or not. A cell in the array is set to *safe* if its distance to the nearest matching event is larger than the notification radius of s. If c' is not *safe*, we simply ignore it and continue to examine the next cell in the heap. Otherwise, we calculate $\mathtt{d}(s,\mathcal{R})$ and n_e for the enlarged safe region $R \cup c'$ and impact region $\mathcal{I} \cup \mathcal{I}_c$ to evaluate b_m (lines 10-18), where $\mathcal{I}_c$ is the set of candidate cells that need to be added to $\mathcal{I}$ if c' is added to $\mathcal{R}$. The calculation of $\mathtt{d}(s,\mathcal{R})$ follows the equation:

$$\mathtt{d}(s,\mathcal{R} \cup c') = min\{\mathcal{H}.top().dist, min\{d(s,c'')\}\} \tag{7}$$

where c'' is an unvisited adjacent cell of c'(line 11). The procedure $getImpactCells$ is used to get $\mathcal{I}_c$(line 12). Then we update $n_e(\mathcal{I} \cup \mathcal{I}_c)$ (lines 13-14) and calculate $b_m(\mathcal{R} \cup c', \mathcal{I} \cup \mathcal{I}_c)$ (line 15). If $b_m(\mathcal{R} \cup c', \mathcal{I} \cup \mathcal{I}_c) \leq 1$, we enlarge $\mathcal{R}$ to contain cell c' and $\mathcal{I}$ to contain the cells in $\mathcal{I}_c$ (lines 16-18). We then insert the adjacent cells of c' which are not visited to $\mathcal{H}$ (lines 19-21). The whole algorithm terminates when $\mathcal{H}$ becomes empty and we return the safe region and impact region. Note that the two types of regions are constructed together in the expansion.

When a cell is added into the current safe region, we expand the impact region in the meanwhile. A naive solution is to scan all the cells within the notification radius and add them into current impact region. However, this incurs many redundant operations because a candidate cell will be added into impact region multiple times. To avoid scanning so many cells in each expansion, we propose an incremental solution that is able to add only the unvisited cells into the impact region. We use an example to illustrate our idea.

EXAMPLE 2. *Illustrating examples of safe region expansion in multiple steps are shown in Figure 3. In the first step, the safe region $\mathcal{R}$ is initialized to the cell containing s, i.e., $\mathcal{R} = c_1$ and the impact region is an enlarged area of $\mathcal{R}$ by notification radius r. In the second step, a neighboring cell c_2 with the minimum distance is selected. Since c_2 has a neighboring cell c_1 included in the safe region, we know that the cells within distance to c_1 has been added in the impact region. Thus, we can directly add cells c'_1, c'_2, c'_3, c'_4 and c'_5 into the impact region without scanning all the cells. In the third step, c_3 is selected into the safe region. The expansion of impact region is similar to the second step and we do not show this step in the figure. In the fourth step, the nearest unvisited cell c_4 is selected. This time, the cell has two adjacent cells included in the safe region. We only need to add one cell c'_6 to the impact region. As the expansion process continues, the safe region and impact region become larger, resulting in a larger b_m. Suppose c_5 is the last cell to cause $b_m \leq 1$ during the expansion, we can terminate the algorithm after we expand the safe region to include c_5 and update the impact region accordingly.*

Next, we propose a direction-aware version of iGM when the direction information of the moving objects is available.

3.5 Incremental Direction-aware GM

Since most smartphones are equipped with sensors for direction detection, we propose a direction-aware iGM, named idGM, that takes into account user moving direction to better maximize $t_s(\mathcal{R})$, the expected time to leave a safe region.

To make iGM direction-aware, we should take into account the direction information when expanding the safe region. In other words, the original expansion mechanism relies on the distance between $d(s, \mathcal{R} \cup c)$ and each time the cell with the minimum distance is selected. We extend the idea to propose a more general scoring function in determining the next cell to expand. The ranking function takes into account of the user moving direction as well as the cell distance and is defined as follows:

$$\tau(s,c) = \alpha \cdot \mathcal{A}(s,c) + (1-\alpha) \cdot \mathcal{D}(s,c) \tag{8}$$

The direction preference $\mathcal{A}(s,c)$ is the cosine value of the angle θ between the moving direction $\vec{v_s}$ and the vector $\vec{sc}$ from s to c.

$$\mathcal{A}(s,c) = cos\theta = \frac{\vec{v_s} \cdot \vec{sc}}{||\vec{v_s}||\,||\vec{sc}||} \tag{9}$$

The distance preference $\mathcal{D}(s,c)$ is the normalized distance from c to s, which is defined as

$$\mathcal{D}(s,c) = \frac{d(s,c)}{d_{max}} \tag{10}$$

where d_{max} is a normalization parameter which can be set to the maximum distance between any two points in the space.

Note that our goal is to maximize t_s in the safe region construction until the condition $b_m \leq 1$ is not satisfied. If the user moving pattern is predictable and we have high confidence that the user will continue to move along the direction, we can set α to a value close to 1. Then, the cells within the user's moving direction have higher priority to be added to the safe region. As long as the direction does not change, the user can stay in the safe region for a long time. If the user moving pattern is not clear and there are many uncertainties, we can set α to be a small value and uniformly expand the safe region in all directions.

With the new scoring function τ, we can modify Algorithm 1 to be direction-aware. The entry of $\mathcal{H}$ is modified as a tuple $(c, d(s,c), \tau)$ (line 7). And the entries in $\mathcal{H}$ are sorted in increasing order of τ. Now the algorithm expands the safe region by taking both the distance preference and direction preference into consideration. The grid cell with the minimum τ will be accessed firstly. Compared to iGM, idGM constructs a direction-aware safe region which takes a longer period before the next communication occurs. In Appendix B, we present how to reduce the bytes transferred in the communication between the server and the subscribers.

4. SPATIAL BE-MATCHING

In Section 3, we have introduced how to optimize the communication cost between the server and the client. In this section, we present how to disseminate the matching events to the subscribers in real-time. We observe that existing pub/sub systems using boolean expression matching [13, 14, 15, 16] rarely pay attention to index construction for the event stream. However, in the location-based service scenario, a subscriber wants to be notified when there is a matching event near him, even though this event has already been published before his subscription. This motivates us to build an index to cater for continuously arriving subscriptions' matching, namely BEQ-Tree (Boolean Expression Quad-Tree). In addition, we can utilize BEQ-Tree to improve the efficiency of construcing the safe region in iGM and idGM.

First of all, we describe the problem setting. In Elaps, a subscriber expresses his interest in the form of spatial subscription and is modeled as a moving object, while a publisher is associated with a geo-location and publishes spatial events.

Spatial Subscription. A spatial subscription extends a boolean expression with a notification region $\mathcal{O}$. In this paper, we model a boolean expression as a conjunction of predicates. Each predicate is determined by three elements: an attribute A, an operator f_{op} and an operand $\overline{o}$. It accepts an input value x and the output is a boolean value indicating whether the operator constraint is satisfied or not: $P^{(A,f_{op},\overline{o})}(x) \rightarrow \{0,1\}$. Elaps can support relational operators $<, \leq, =, >, \geq, [\,]$ [3] and set operators $\in, \notin$. As mentioned, the notification region $\mathcal{O}$ is a circle centered at user's current location with radius r. Formally, a spatial subscription s is defined over $|s|$ predicates and an notification region $\mathcal{O}$:

$$s : P_1^{A,f_{op},\overline{o}}(x) \wedge P_2^{A,f_{op},\overline{o}}(x) \wedge ... \wedge P_{|s|}^{A,f_{op},\overline{o}}(x) \wedge \mathcal{O}$$

For example, a user interested in Samsung TQ can submit a subscription like *(brand=samsung ∧ size>50)∧ r=1km ∧ lat=1.28 ∧ lng=103.8)*. Note that the location is detected automatically. Hereafter, we use spatial subscription and subscription interchangeably.

Spatial Event. A spatial event e contains $|e|$ tuples and a location loc: $e : (A_1 = \overline{o}_1) \wedge (A_2 = \overline{o}_2) \wedge ... \wedge (A_{|e|} = \overline{o_{|e|}}) \wedge loc$, where A_i is the attribute and $\overline{o}_i$ is the associated value or operand. For example, a Samsung TQ promotion event can be represented by *(brand=samsung ∧ size=55 ∧ 3D=yes ∧ lat=1.28 ∧ lng=103.8)*.

Spatial Subscription Match. The match between a spatial boolean expression s and an event e consists of two aspects: boolean expression match and spatial match, as defined below.

DEFINITION 3 (BOOLEAN EXPRESSION MATCH). *A boolean expression match is satisfied if for each predicate P in s, P is satisfied by a tuple $A_i = \overline{o}_i$ in e. We use $s \sim_b e$ to denote a boolean expression match and say S be-matches E.*

[3] In this case, the operand $\overline{o}$ contains two values: $\overline{o}.l$ and $\overline{o}.r$

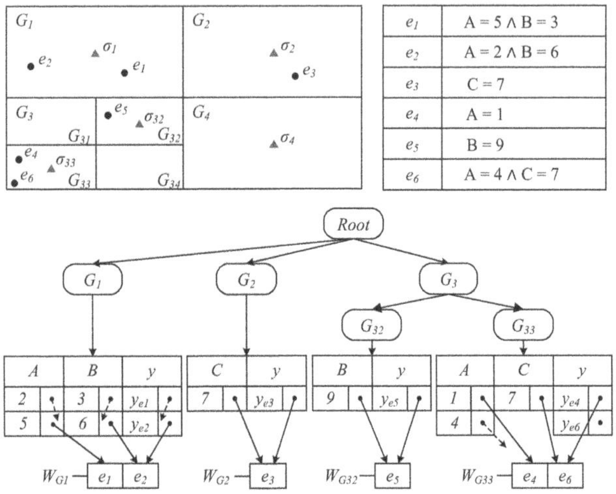

Figure 4: An example for BEQ-Tree

DEFINITION 4 (SPATIAL MATCH). *We say there is a spatial match between* s *and* e*, denoted by* $s \sim_s e$*, if the location* loc *of* e *is inside the notification region* $\mathcal{O}$ *of* s*.*

DEFINITION 5 (MATCH). *We say a subscription* s *matches an event* e*, denoted by* $s \sim e$*, if* $s \sim_b e$ *and* $s \sim_s e$*.*

4.1 Spatial Event Index

BEQ-Tree is designed to be efficient in both query processing and event update. It adopts a two-layer partitioning mechanism, one for the spatial attribute and the other for the predicates in the boolean expression.

In the first layer, we partition the events based on the spatial attribute. Since Quadtree [12] can answer spatial range query quickly and support efficient update operations, we adopt it to partition the space such that each cell in the leaf level contains at most E_{max} events, where E_{max} is a moderately large number. In each cell, we select a reference point and adopt the idea of *iDistance* [17] to calculate and index the distance from each event to the reference point. The reference point is denoted as σ and selected as the center of a tree cell in this paper.

In the second layer, we further partition the events in each cell based on the attributes in the predicates. The predicates with the same attribute and appear in the same tree cell are organized in the same inverted list, denoted by $L_{\langle G_i, A \rangle}$ where G_i is the tree cell and A is the attribute. The location of an event e in G_i is converted to a single dimensional value $y = dist(e, \sigma_i)$, where $dist(e, \sigma_i)$ represents the Euclidean distance between e and σ_i. We then build an inverted list for attribute y for each cell. Each inverted list is sorted by the operand value. For each cell, we also maintain a counter array for all the events in this cell.

EXAMPLE 3. *Fig. 4 shows an example for the BEQ-Tree, where we set* $E_{max} = 2$ *for a Quadtree cell. The space is first hierarchically partitioned into cells. Each cell* G_i *is associated with a set of inverted lists to store predicates with the same attribute. All tuple lists are sorted in ascending order of their tuple values. There is an extended attribute* y *to store the distance from the event to the reference point in a cell. Each predicate has a pointer to a counting array for the corresponding Quadtree cell, which will be used in subscription matching.*

Algorithm 2: BESpatialMatch(Subscription s, Cell partition G)

1 $R_e \leftarrow \emptyset$
2 **for** each predicate $(A\ f_{op}\ \bar{o}) \in s$ **do**
3 　**if** G does not contain A **then**
4 　　return R_e
5 $W_G \leftarrow$ counter array associated with G
6 **for** each predicate $(A\ f_{op}\ \bar{o}) \in s$ **do**
7 　**for** each operator $f_{op} \in \{=, \neq, \leq, \geq, [\,]\}$ **do**
8 　　determine the range R_a in $L_{\langle G,A \rangle}$
9 　　**for** each matching entry $t \in R_a$ **do**
10 　　　++$W_G[t.e]$
11 $y \leftarrow dist(s, \sigma)$
12 **if** *s is located within G* **then**
13 　$d_{min} \leftarrow y - r$, $d_{max} \leftarrow y + r$
14 **else**
15 　$d_{min} \leftarrow y - r$
16 　determine d_{max} accordingly
17 **for** each $t \in L_{\langle G,y \rangle}$ and $t.\bar{o} \in [d_{min}, d_{max}]$ **do**
18 　**if** $W_G[t.e] == |s|$ **then**
19 　　**if** $dist(s.l, t.l) \leq r$ **then**
20 　　　add the corresponding event into R_e
21 **return** R_e

4.2 Subscription Matching

In the following, we show how to find the matching events given a subscription s with an notification region $\mathcal{O}$. We first find all the leaf cells that intersect with $\mathcal{O}$ using the Quadtree, and then examine the events in each candidate leaf cell G by calling Algorithm 2.

In Algorithm 2, we first check whether a cell partition G in the BEQ-Tree contains all the attributes that appear in s. If we find an attribute of s not appearing in G, we can prune the search space and examine other cells (lines 2-4). Otherwise, we copy the counter array associated with G and set the initial values of the entries to be 0 (line 5). Next, we introduce how to find the matching events by performing boolean expression match (lines 6-10) and spatial range match (lines 11-20).

The boolean expression match algorithm adopts the idea of the classic counting algorithm in [18, 13, 14]. Given a predicate A f_{op} $\bar{o}$, we use different accessing strategy for different operators in s (lines 6-8). If f_{op} is '=', we can check whether $\bar{o}$ appears in the sorted tuple list $L_{\langle G,A \rangle}$ using binary search. If f_{op} is '$\neq$', all the values in the tuple list except $\bar{o}$ are visited. If f_{op} is '$\leq$' ('$<$'), all the tuple entries whose value is no larger (smaller) than $\bar{o}$ match A f_{op} $\bar{o}$. The case is similar for '$\geq$' (or '$>$') and '[ ]'. For each list entry visited, we increase the corresponding counter value by 1 (lines 9-10). If the value increases to the size of s, the corresponding event be-matches s (see Definition 3).

We use Fig. 5 to explain how to perform spatial range match. Similar to boolean expression match, we need to locate the interval in the spatial list within which the corresponding event may fit in the notification region $\mathcal{O}$. There are two cases to consider. First, s is located within G (lines 11-13). In this case, the interval is $[y - r, y + r]$, where y is the one-dimensional distance value of s. Second, s lies out of G (lines 14-16). In this case, the lower bound of the interval is $y - r$. If the notification range contains a vertex of G, we have $d_{max} = \infty$, which means that we start from d_{min} and traverse to the end of the spatial list. Otherwise, $d_{max} = max\{dist(\sigma, p_i)\}$, where p_i is one of the intersection points between G and $\mathcal{O}$. As shown in Fig. 5, the notification region crosses two grid cells and we need to conduct spatial range search in these two partitions. The shaded areas indicate the search interval using the indexed distance. The interval for G_1 is $[y-r, y+r]$, because s is located within G_1. The interval for G_2 is $[y-r, d_{max}]$,

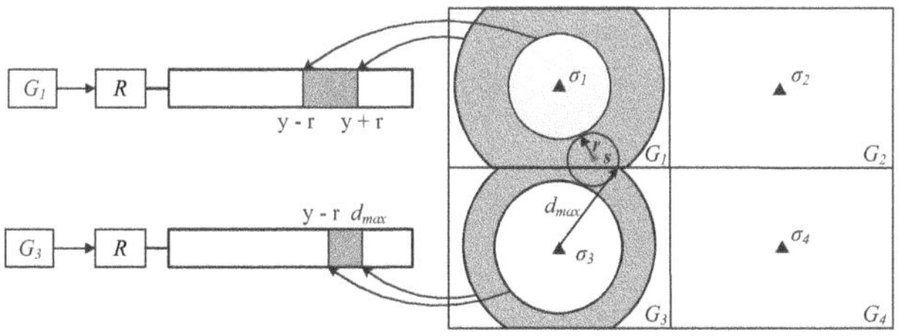

Figure 5: Spatial range match

because s is located outside G_2 and $\mathcal{O}$ does not contain the vertex. For each tuple in the interval, if its corresponding event be-matches s, we check whether the event is located within $\mathcal{O}$. If yes, we find a match (lines 17-20). Since subscribers tend to specify a small notification range, the spatial range match would be very efficient, because only a few entries in the spatial list are traversed.

By performing the boolean expression match and spatial match, we only need to traverse a small part of entries in a list, which can further improve the matching performance besides the spatial pruning of the first layer.

BEQ-Tree used in iGM and idGM. To construct the safe region in iGM and idGM, the set of be-matching events should be found first. A naive method is to find all the be-matching events in the whole space. However, one property of iGM and idGM is that these two algorithms usually do not expand to the whole space with the constraint of $b_m(\mathcal{R}, \mathcal{I}) \leq 1$. Based on this property, we use BEQ-Tree in an incremental manner to get the be-matching events on demand. To construct the safe region for a subscriber s, we start from the cell c containing s and search the BEQ-Tree to get the set of be-matching events in c. In the meantime, if the leaf Qudatree cells intersected with c contains other cells around c, we also get the be-matching events in these cells. When iGM or idGM expands to a cell whose be-matching events have not been found, we check the surrounding Quadtree cells to get the be-matching events. In this way, we only need to find the set of be-matching events on demand and traverse only a part of the space.

5. SYSTEM FRAMEWORK

So far, we have introduced the techniques of safe region and impact region to reduce communication I/O and the BEQ-Tree to reduce the response time. In this section, we present the system framework in Fig. 6 as a whole picture to see how different function components are connected. In particular, we introduce how to process subscription arrival/expiration, event arrival/expiration and user location update.

Subscription arrival/expiration. In Elaps, users can submit new subscriptions and an existing subscription expires if the user is no longer interested in receiving matching events. Such kind of messages are handled by the *Subscription Processor*. When a new subscription arrives, we need to find if there exist any matching events in the event database. Since this is an extension of boolean expression matching with spatial constraints, we propose a new index named BEQ-Tree to solve the problem in Section 4. For each new subscriber, we also call Algorithm 1 in Section 3 to construct a new safe region and impact region for the user. The safe region is sent to the user and the impact region is maintained at the server side. The impact region is inserted into an inverted index with cell id as the key and the elements are impact regions covering the cell. When a subscription expires, we remove it from the subscription index and impact region index.

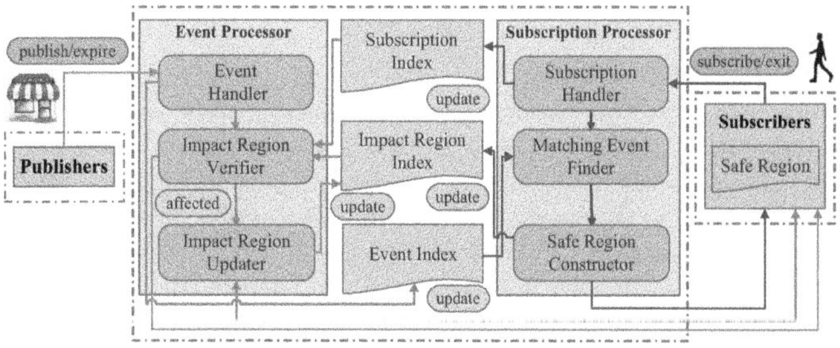

Figure 6: The workflow in Elaps framework

Event arrival and expiration. When a new event e arrives, we need to identify from the subscriber database the users whose interests match the new event (e is contained in the notification region) and those users whose safe regions are affected (e is contained in the impact region). Since we use safe region to reduce the communication overhead, the subscriber's precise location is not maintained at the server side. We only know the user is currently in the safe region but the precise location is not available. Thus, we build separate indexes to handle boolean expression matching and spatial constraint verification. For the boolean expression matching, we can simply adopt existing subscription index such as OpIndex [16] and BE-Tree [15]. For the spatial attribute, we store the impact region for subscribers in the impact region index maintained as a hash table. When e arrives, we find the matching users U from the subscription index. For each subscriber $u \in U$, we check whether e locates within his impact region. If yes, the server send e to u. If the distance from u to e is smaller than the notification radius, the user is notified. Otherwise, we calculate a new safe region and impact region. The new safe region is sent to the subscriber and the impact region index is also updated.

User location update. Each time a subscriber moves out of the safe region, he reports the new location to the server. Once the server receives the new location, it calls Algorithm 1 to construct a new safe region and impact region for the user. Again, the safe region is sent to the subscriber and the inverted index for impact regions is updated.

6. EXPERIMENTAL STUDY

In this section, we present a comprehensive evaluation of the performance for Elaps. In particular, we are interested in evaluating (1) the communication overhead caused by continuous moving query processing against dynamic event streams and (2) the matching efficiency of our proposed BEQ-Tree. For safe region techniques, we compare our proposed iGM and idGM based on the new cost model against existing methods VM and GM. In all these methods, we calculate and store the impact regions at the server side for performance evaluation. For spatial boolean expression matching, we compare BEQ-Tree with three baseline algorithms: (i) Quad-tree, which first filters events outside the notification region using the spatial index Quad-tree [19] and then verifies the boolean expression matching; (ii) extension of k-index [14], which finds matching events for a given subscription. The be-matching events are further verified for spatial matching; (iii) OpIndex, which first filters the events not matching the boolean expressions using a variant of OpIndex [16] and then verifies the spatial matching. Note that all the indexes are memory resident and all the approaches produce the same and complete results. We implemented all the methods in C++ and conducted the experiments on a server with 48GB memory running Centos 5.6.

6.1 Experimental Setup

Event and Subscription Datasets. We use geo-tweets from Twitter and venues from Foursquare to simulate the event streams. In Twitter, each geo-tweet is considered as a spatial event. We treat each keyword as an attribute and the value is the frequency of the keyword in the tweet. This converts a geo-tweet into a list of attribute-value pairs. In the following experiments, we use 50 million geo-tweets as the event database and another 10 million to simulate a dynamic event stream. To generate subscriptions on the Twitter dataset, we adopt the same technique in [16] to convert a keyword query in AOL search log [4] into a boolean expression. For example, a query "SIGMOD Melbourne" can be transformed to (SIGMOD=1 ∧ Melbourne=1) to support equal operator or (SIGMOD∈[5,20] ∧ MelBourne∈[2,8]) to support interval operator. The dataset description and experimental results of Foursquare is presented in Appendix D.2 due to space limitations.

User Trajectory Datasets. We use both synthetic trajectories and real trajectories to simulate user moving patterns. For the synthetic trajectories, we generate $10,000$ trajectories using Brinkoff's generator [20]. The average travel period of each trajectory is 1000 timestamps. In our experiments, timestamp is used to capture the periodicity of location update. We set each timestamp to be 5 seconds in the following experiments, which means the GPS location of a user is sampled every 5 seconds. For the real trajectories, we use the GPS probing records of taxies in Singapore as the real trajectories [21]. We extract 10,000 trajectories from different taxies and each trajectory contains 1000 sequential points.

Communication Overhead	
Event arrival rate f $(/tm)$	10, 50, **100**, 500
Moving speed v_s (m/tm)	20, 40, **60**, 80, 100
Notification radius r (km)	1, **2**, 3, 4, 5
Number of events $\mathbb{E}$	10M, **20M**, 30M, 40M, 50M
Matching Performance	
Number of events $\mathbb{E}$	10M, **20M**, 30M, 40M, 50M
Avg. sub size δ	1, 2, 3, **4**, 5
Notification radius r (km)	1, **2**, 3, 4, 5

Table 2: Parameters evaluated in the experiments

Evaluation Parameters. Table 2 shows the main parameters and values used throughout the experiments (default values are in bold). To evaluate continuous moving query processing, we examine the scalability with respect to increasing event arrival rate f, user moving speed v_s, notification radius r and event corpus size $\mathbb{E}$. To evaluate the matching performance of spatial boolean expressions, we examine increasing event corpus size $\mathbb{E}$, average subscription size δ and notification radius r. The system performance can be measured by the average communication I/O and event matching time for a subscriber. Note that we do not need to examine the performance w.r.t. increasing number of subscribers. This is because the subscribers will not affect each other in terms of communication overhead and event matching efficiency. In our system, the number of subscribers directly influences the scalability of the subscription index (see Fig. 6). However, in this work, we adopt an existing index (OpIndex [16]) which has been shown to be scalable even for a large number of subscribers. Moreover, the focus of this work is not on the subscription index. Thus, we did not look into this any further. Pease refer to [15] for details.

Parameter Tuning. There are two parameters that require tuning for iGM and idGM: N (the whole space is partitioned into $N \times N$ cells) and α (the tuining parameter of the preference score τ), and one parameter that requires tuning for BEQ-Tree: E_{max} (the maximum number of events in a Qudatree cell). We conduct several experiments to tune the parameters and the results are shown in Appendix D.1. Based on the results, we set N to be 600, α to be 0.5 and E_{max} to be 60K.

[4]http://www.gregsadetsky.com/aol-data/

6.2 Continuous Moving Query Processing

In this part, we evaluate the communication overhead caused by continuous moving query processing against dynamic event streams.

6.2.1 *Synthetic Trajectories*

The first set of experiments on continuous moving query processing are conducted on the synthetic trajectories using the Twitter and Foursquare events.

Effect of the event arrival rate f. Fig. 7(a) presents the impact of the event arrival rate f on the performance. We report the communication overhead incurred when users move out of the safe region (location update) and when a new matching event occurs in the impact region (event arrival) respectively. We have the following observations. (1) As f increases, all the methods scale in varying degrees. Because there would be more matching events that fall within the impact region, which increases the cost incurred by event arrival. (2) in terms of the total communication cost, iGM and idGM can outperform the other baseline methods by one order of magnitude. Such performance gain increases when f increases, especially on the cost incurred by event arrival. This is because iGM and idGM can adjust the size of the safe region dynamically according to several parameters of the system to balance the cost incurred by location update and the cost incurred by event arrival. (3) Regarding the cost incurred by location update alone, GM has the smallest one, because it constructs the largest safe region. VM performs much worse than the other methods, because it constructs a safe region around the nearest matching event regardless of the user's location. idGM performs better than iGM, because idGM can construct a safe region with a larger t_s which is the expected time before the subscriber leaves the safe region by considering the user's moving direction. (4) Regarding the cost incurred by event arrival alone, GM is the highest, because it constructs a rather large impact region even though f is very high. Although VM can construct a smaller impact region compared to GM, the impact region of VM always contains some highly skewed area (around the nearest matching event). Therefore, the cost incurred by event arrival of VM is also high. When f is larger, iGM and idGM would construct a smaller safe region and impact region based on the cost model. Thus, the cost incurred by event arrival can be controlled very well.

Effect of the speed v_s. Fig. 7(b) depicts the effect of another key factor, the moving speed v, on the communication overhead. When v increases, the subscriber would leave the safe region more frequently, resulting in an increased cost incurred by location update. Therefore, the total communication cost increases for all methods except GM. GM is not sensitive to v for Foursquare and Twitter, because it constructs a rather large safe region. As shown, iGM and idGM still outperform the rest, since they can dynamically increase the size of the safe region as v increases. We can also observe that the superiority of idGM compared with iGM is more significant with a larger v.

Effect of the notification radius r. Next, we evaluate the effect of the notification radius r. The results are shown in Fig. 7(c). A larger r results in a smaller safe region, which increases the cost incurred by location update for all the methods. For VM, the cost incurred by event arrival increases. This is because we expand the safe region for VM by the length of r and thus a larger r results

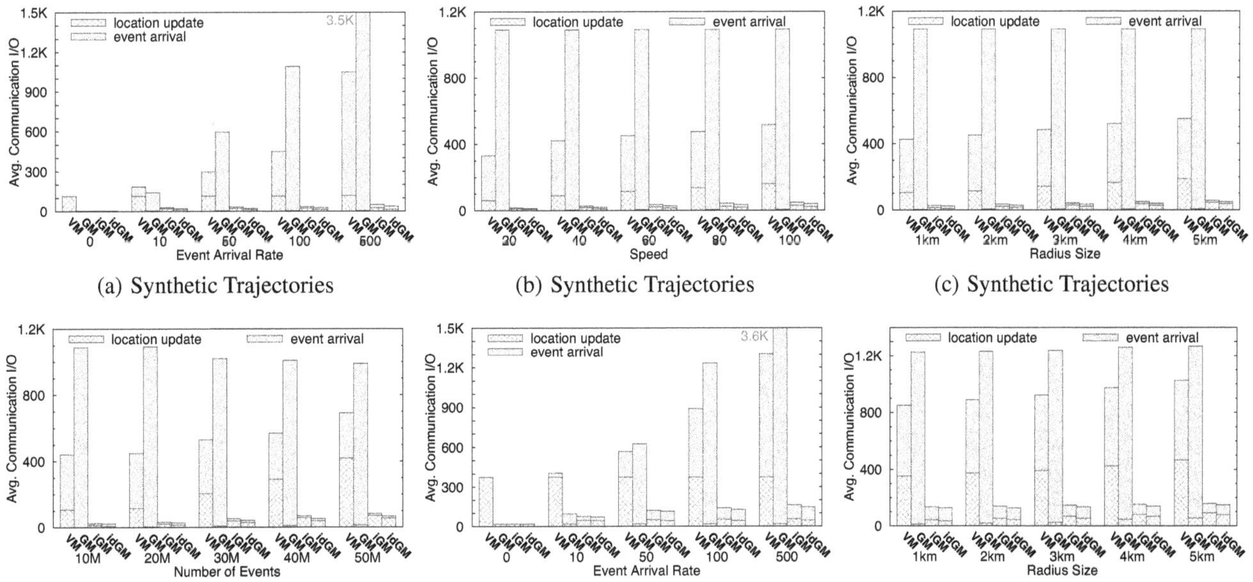

(a) Synthetic Trajectories (b) Synthetic Trajectories (c) Synthetic Trajectories

(d) Synthetic Trajectories (e) Taxi Trajectories (f) Taxi Trajectories

Figure 7: Communication I/O on Twitter.

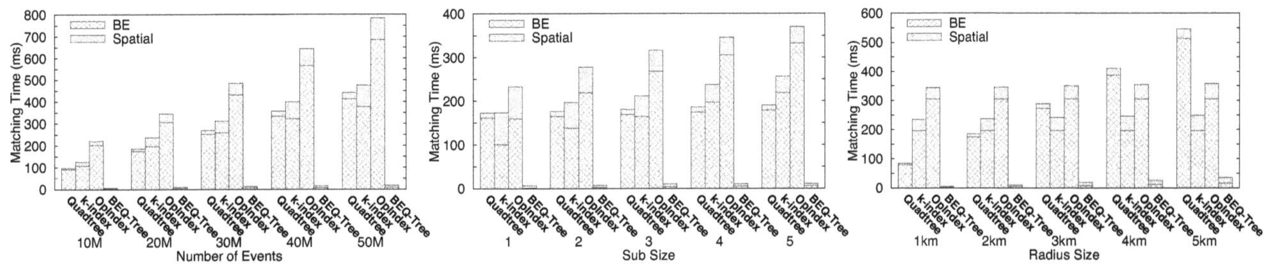

(a) Varing number of events (b) Varing sub size (c) Varing radius

Figure 8: Experiments on the event index.

in a larger impact region. In contrast, iGM and idGM can adjust the size of the impact region dynamically even though r increases. Thus, iGM and idGM show 10X better performance than the other baseline methods.

Effect of the number of events $\mathbb{E}$. Lastly, we study the communication overhead when increasing the size of the Twitter events from 10M to 50M. The results are shown in Fig. 7(d). More events (i.e., more matching events) in the system result in a smaller safe region and impact region. A smaller safe region leads to more cost incurred by location update, while a smaller impact region leads to less cost incurred by event arrival. For VM, the overall communication overhead increases because the increase in the cost incurred by location update surpasses that in the cost incurred by event arrival. On the other hand, for GM, the overall communication overhead decreases, because the performance of GM relies more on the impact region. Compared with VM and GM, our two methods can adjust the area of the safe region and impact region better when the system environment changes and thus scale very well when the event size increases.

6.2.2 *Taxi Trajectories*

The second set of experiments are conducted on the real taxi trajectories in Singapore. Since the trajectories are only located within Singapore, we extract those geo-tweets located within Singapore from the Twitter dataset. In total, we extract 906,977 geo-tweets. We use 0.5 million of them as the event database and the remaining to simulate the event stream. We evaluate the communication overhead with respect to the event arrival rate f and the notification radius r. The results are shown in Fig. 7(e) and Fig. 7(f). Compared with the synthetic trajectories where the speed is constant, the taxi trajectories contain all kinds of taxies with different moving status. Besides, the moving speed of a taxi is influenced by the road traffic greatly. Therefore, it is more difficult to predict the moving behavior for the taxi trajectories. However, as can be seen, our two methods can still achieve a much better performance compared with the other baseline methods. As compared to the counterpart GM, our iGM and idGM have a comparable performance in terms of the cost incurred by location update and reduce the cost incurred by event arrival significantly by more than 1 order of magnitude.

6.2.3 *Cost Model Evaluation*

In this part, we study the optimality and robustness of our cost model.

Optimality Evaluation. When constructing a safe region for a subscriber, we start from his location and incrementally expand. In this process, the value of $b_m(\mathcal{R}, \mathcal{I})$ increases and our cost model indicates that the best safe region occurs when $b_m(\mathcal{R}, \mathcal{I}) = 1$. To test the optimality, we terminate the expansion at different values

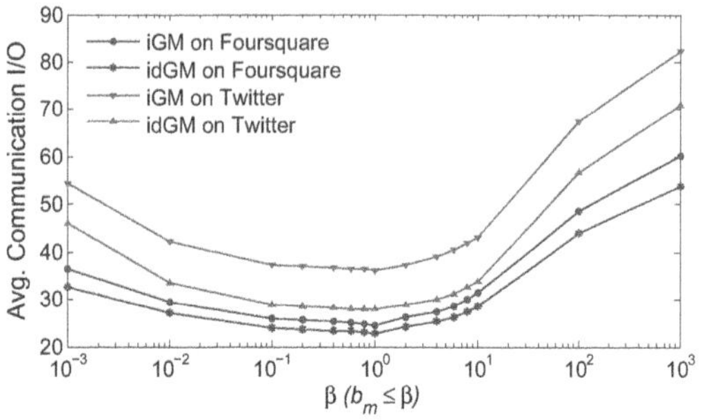

Figure 9: Optimality evaluation.

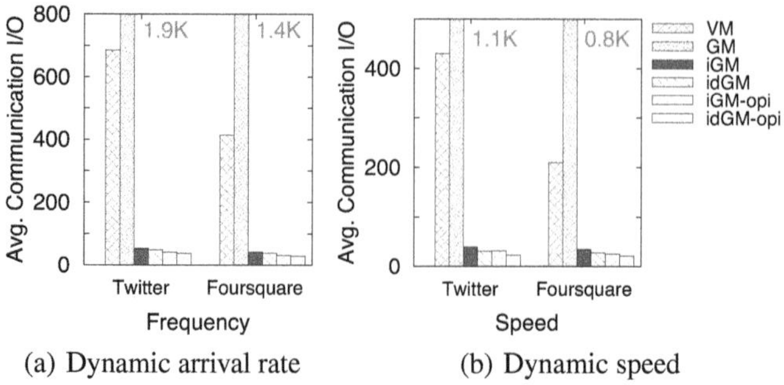

Figure 10: Adaptability evaluation.

of $b_m(\mathcal{R}, \mathcal{I})$ and this value is denoted by β. As shown in Fig. 9, we can see that when terminating too early ($\beta < 1$) or too late ($\beta > 1$), the performance is inferior to the case when $\beta = 1$.

Adaptability Evaluation. To evaluate the robustness of our cost model, we look into two parameters that may change frequently in reality: the event arrival rate f and the speed v_s (The other parameters are dependent on the area of safe region and impact region). We set up a dynamic environment in which f or v_s varies all the time. For comparison, we designed two optimal methods, iGM-opi and idGM-opi with the knowledge of future pattern update in advance. When f or v varies, the optimal methods would construct a new safe region accordingly using the new parameters and such safe region update is not counted as a new communication I/O in the experiments. Fig. 10(a) and Fig. 10(b) show the experimental results with dynamic f and v_s respectively. We gradually increase the event arrival rate f from $0/tm$ to $500/tm$ and then reduce it back to $0/tm$. This process is repeated 10 times. The dynamic moving speed v_s is set in a similar way ($0 \to 100m/tm \to 0m/tm$). As shown in Figure 15, iGM and idGM can achieve a comparable performance as iGM-opt and idGM-opt due to the good adaptability, because they can adapt to the update of f and v_s when the update causes a communication. This shows that our methods are robust to different user motion and event arrival patterns.

6.3 Spatial Boolean Expression Matching

In this section, we study the efficiency in spatial boolean expression matching, which can be further categorized into the elapsed time on the boolean expression match and that on the spatial match, namely BE and Spatial respectively. In particular, we use the Twitter dataset to compare our proposed BEQ-Tree with several baseline indexes as described at the beginning of Section 6.

Effect of the number of events $\mathbb{E}$. We evaluate the average matching time when increasing the number of events. From the results presented in Fig. 8(a), we have the following findings: (1) Quadtree can do the spatial match quickly, but it needs much time to filter candidate events. (2) k-index and OpIndex need more time for spatial match compared to Quadtree. (3) BEQ-Tree outperforms the other methods, and exhibits a 97% better matching time as compared to the next best algorithm. This is because it utilizes a Quadtree-like structure in the first layer that exhibits good pruning power, and maintains a sorted inverted list in the second layer, with which fewer events are examined. As shown, BEQ-Tree can answer the subscription matching within a few microseconds for a 20 million dataset, which is highly favored in real applications.

Effect of the subscription size δ. Fig. 8(b) presents the elapsed time w.r.t the varying subscription size δ. We make three observations. (1) Overall, BEQ-Tree achieves a speedup of 20 times w.r.t. Quadtree, k-index and OpIndex respectively. (2) Regarding the boolean expression match (BE) time, more attributes are involved in the match as δ increases, resulting in a higher computation time. (3) Regarding the spatial match time, k-index and OpIndex are sensitive to the subscription size, because they generate fewer candidate events as δ increases.

Effect of the notification radius r. The matching performance w.r.t. varying notification radius r is presented in Fig. 8(c). Only Quadtree is sensitive to r, because more candidate events are generated in the first step. In contrast, the performance of BEQ-Tree is stable and scales very well with r.

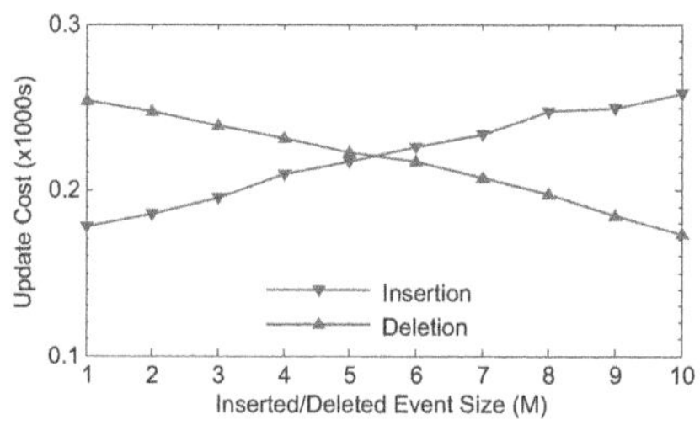

Figure 11: Update cost for BEQ-Tree.

BEQ-Tree Update Cost. At last, Fig. 11 shows the update cost for BEQ-Tree. To test the insertion cost, we start from a BEQ-Tree with 20 million events and incrementally insert 10 million events. The total time of inserting every 1 million tuples is plotted in Figure 11. We can see that as the size BEQ-Tree increases, it takes more time to insert the same number of tuples because the tree height also increases. The deletion process starts from a BEQ-Tree with 30 million events and the cost for deleting every 1 million records is reported in Figure 11 as well. We can see that as more records are deleted, the tree becomes smaller and the deletion operation becomes faster. In both cases, it takes less than 300 seconds to delete or insert 1 million events, which means our BEQ-Tree is efficient in update.

7. CONCLUSION

In this paper, we build a novel location-aware pub/sub system, Elaps, which takes into account continuous moving queries over dynamic event streams. To reduce communication overhead, we propose a concept named impact region and a novel cost model. Based on the cost model, we propose two incremental methods to construct the safe region and impact region. To reduce the response time of Elaps, we propose a novel index BEQ-Tree which can support efficient spatial subscription matching over a collection of events in the dynamic event environment. Experimental results on real datasets show that Elaps can greatly reduce the communication overhead and disseminate events to users in real-time.

8. ACKNOWLEDGMENT

This work is funded by the NExT Search Centre (grant R-252-300-001-490), which is supported by the Singapore National Research Foundation under its International Research Centre @ Singapore Funding Initiative and administered by the IDM Program Office. Guoliang Li is partly supported by the Chinese Special Project of Science and Technology (2013zx01039-002-002), the NSFC project (61422205, 61472198) and the 973 Program of China (2015CB358700).

9. REFERENCES

[1] J. Bao, M. Mokbel, and C.-Y. Chow, "Geofeed: A location aware news feed system," in *ICDE*, 2012, pp. 54–65.

[2] G. Li, Y. Wang, T. Wang, and J. Feng, "Location-aware publish/subscribe," in *KDD*, 2013, pp. 802–810.

[3] L. Chen, G. Cong, and X. Cao, "An efficient query indexing mechanism for filtering geo-textual data," in *SIGMOD*, 2013, pp. 749–760.

[4] G. Cugola and A. Margara, "High-performance location-aware publish-subscribe on gpus," in *Middleware*, 2012, pp. 312–331.

[5] J. Zhang, M. Zhu, D. Papadias, Y. Tao, and D. L. Lee, "Location-based spatial queries," in *SIGMOD*, 2003, pp. 443–454.

[6] M. Hasan, M. A. Cheema, X. Lin, and Y. Zhang, "Efficient construction of safe regions for moving knn queries over dynamic datasets," in *SSTD*, 2009, pp. 373–379.

[7] B. Bamba, L. Liu, A. Iyengar, and P. S. Yu, "Safe region techniques for fast spatial alarm evaluation," *Georgia Institute of Technology*, 2008.

[8] D. Wu, M. L. Yiu, C. S. Jensen, and G. Cong, "Efficient continuously moving top-k spatial keyword query processing," in *ICDE*, 2011, pp. 541–552.

[9] W. Huang, G. Li, K.-L. Tan, and J. Feng, "Efficient safe-region construction for moving top-k spatial keyword queries," in *CIKM*, 2012, pp. 932–941.

[10] L. Guo, J. Shao, H. Aung, and K.-L. Tan, "Efficient continuous top-k spatial keyword queries on road networks," *GeoInformatica*, pp. 1–32, 2014.

[11] W. Xu, C.-Y. Chow, M. L. Yiu, Q. Li, and C. K. Poon, "Mobifeed: A location-aware news feed system for mobile users," in *SIGSPATIAL '12*, 2012, pp. 538–541.

[12] R. Finkel and J. Bentley, "Quad trees a data structure for retrieval on composite keys," *Acta Informatica*, vol. 4, no. 1, pp. 1–9, 1974.

[13] F. Fabret, H. A. Jacobsen, F. Llirbat, J. Pereira, K. A. Ross, and D. Shasha, "Filtering algorithms and implementation for very fast publish/subscribe systems," in *SIGMOD*, 2001, pp. 115–126.

[14] S. E. Whang, H. Garcia-Molina, C. Brower, J. Shanmugasundaram, S. Vassilvitskii, E. Vee, and R. Yerneni, "Indexing boolean expressions," *PVLDB*, vol. 2, no. 1, pp. 37–48, 2009.

[15] M. Sadoghi and H.-A. Jacobsen, "Be-tree: An index structure to efficiently match boolean expressions over high-dimensional discrete space," in *SIGMOD*, 2011, pp. 637–648.

[16] D. Zhang, C.-Y. Chan, and K.-L. Tan, "An efficient publish/subscribe index for ecommerce databases," *PVLDB*, vol. 7, no. 8, pp. 613–624, 2014.

[17] H. V. Jagadish, B. C. Ooi, K.-L. Tan, C. Yu, and R. Zhang, "idistance: An adaptive b+-tree based indexing method for nearest neighbor search," *TODS*, vol. 30, no. 2, pp. 364–397, 2005.

[18] T. W. Yan and H. García-Molina, "Index structures for selective dissemination of information under the boolean model," *TODS*, vol. 19, no. 2, pp. 332–364, 1994.

[19] A. Guttman, "R-trees: A dynamic index structure for spatial searching," in *SIGMOD*, 1984, pp. 47–57.

[20] T. Brinkhoff, "A framework for generating network-based moving objects," *Geoinformatica*, vol. 6, no. 2, pp. 153–180, 2002.

[21] J. Zhou, A. K. Tung, W. Wu, and W. S. Ng, "A “semi-lazy” approach to probabilistic path prediction in dynamic environments," in *KDD '13*, 2013, pp. 748–756.

[22] G. Antoshenkov and M. Ziauddin, "Query processing and optimization in oracle rdb," *The VLDB Journal*, vol. 5, no. 4, pp. 229–237, 1996.

[23] K. Wu, E. J. Otoo, and A. Shoshani, "Optimizing bitmap indices with efficient compression," *ACM Trans. Database Syst.*, vol. 31, no. 1, pp. 1–38, Mar. 2006.

[24] F. Ramsak, V. Markl, R. Fenk, M. Zirkel, K. Elhardt, and R. Bayer, "Integrating the ub-tree into a database system kernel," in *VLDB '00*, 2000, pp. 263–272.

APPENDIX

A. LIST OF SYMBOLS

Symbol	Description
s	a moving subscriber
e	a spatial event
$\mathcal{O}$	notification region specified by a subscriber
r	notification radius
$\mathcal{R}$	safe region of a subscriber
$\mathcal{I}$	impact region of a subscriber
f	event arrival rate
v_s	user moving speed
n	total number of events in the system
n_e	total number of matching events in $\mathcal{I}$
$\mathtt{d}(s, \mathcal{R})$	the minimum distance from s to the boundary of $\mathcal{R}$
c	a grid cell in iGM and idGM
G	a cell partition in BEQ-Tree
σ	a reference point in G
y	the spatial attribute for distance indexing
W	counter array in each cell partition in BEQ-Tree

Table 3: Summary of Notations

B. REPRESENTATION OF THE SAFE REGION

To reduce the bytes transferred in the communication between servers and subscribers, we use Bitmap as a more compact representation of safe region. We allocate a Bitmap whose length is the number of cells. If a cell is in the safe region, we set the corresponding element of the Bitmap to be 1. During the communication, we adopt the run-length encoding compression method (e.g., BBC [22] and WAH [23]) to further reduce the size of the Bitmap.

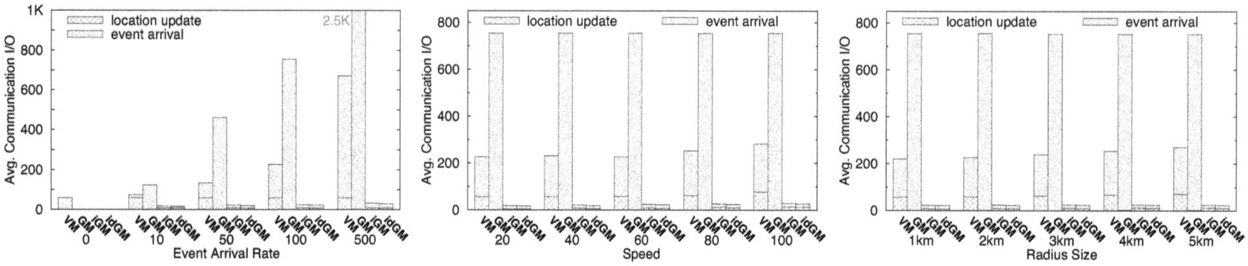

(a) Varing event arrival rate (b) Varing speed (c) Varing radius

Figure 12: Communication I/O on Foursquare.

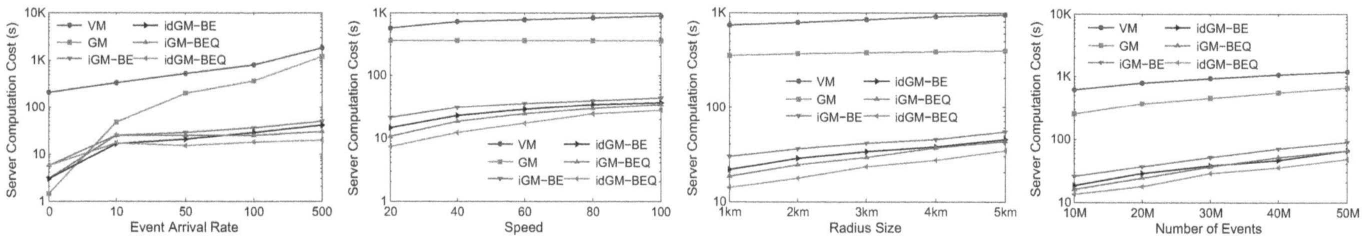

(a) Varing event arrival rate (b) Varing speed (c) Varing radius (d) Varing number of events

Figure 13: Server computation cost for safe region construction.

In this way, we achieve a very compact representation of the safe region. When subscribers receive the message, they first decode it into the original Bitmap and can easily detect whether the cell they are located in is in the safe region or not.

In our implementation, we assign each cell a value derived from the z-ordering of the cells [24]. Based on the z-order, the cells close to each other will be assigned similar ids. Then, we use the classic WHC [23] to compress the list of ids. Our experimental results show that the size of compressed ids is around $5\% - 10\%$ of the original size.

C. INDEX MAINTENANCE OF BEQ-TREE

In our system, new events will be continually published by the publishers. Each event has a valid period and will expire after this period. Thus, BEQ-Tree should be efficient in terms of the maintenance cost.

We first consider how a new event is inserted into the BEQ-Tree index. Given an event E, we first find the cell with the lowest level that contains E. If the number of events within that cell is smaller than max_{event}, we append a new entry e in the associated counter array V_{G_i} and set its value to the location of E. For each non-spatial attribute, we insert its value and the key pointing to e into the corresponding tuple list. For the spatial attribute, we convert it to the one-dimensional distance y and insert y to the spatial list. If the cell is full, we need to partition it into four child cells and insert the event into the corresponding child cell.

The delete operation is processed as follows. We first find the cell with the lowest level that contains E. Then, we traverse the inverted lists whose attribute is contained in E and delete the tuple. The deletion is fast because the list is sorted and we can use binary search to quickly identify the tuple to delete. If the cell becomes empty after deletion, we check whether its sibling nodes are also empty. If yes, we merge them to the parent node.

Memory Cost. Let E denote the set of spatial events published to Elaps, $\mathbb{E}$ denote the size of E, $|T|$ denote the total number of tuples in E and $|t|$ denote the memory space cost by an entry in the list. The event index contains two components: the tuple lists and the counter arrays. Each tuple corresponds to a unique entry in the tuple lists. Thus, the tuple lists occupy $O(|T||t|)$ memory space. In addition, each event corresponds to a unique entry in the counter arrays. Since the size of an entry in the counter arrays is much smaller than the size of an entry in the tuple list, the total memory cost for the index is $O(|T||t|)$. As can be seen, our index takes linear space cost. The index maintenance of BEQ-Tree is presented in Appendix C due to space limitations.

Update Complexity. Let $\mathbb{N}$ denote the maximum level of the BEQ-Tree, $|L|$ denote the maximum length of the tuple lists and $\mathbb{P}$ denote the maximum number of conjunctions in a subscription. The cost of Quadtree cell identification is $O(\mathbb{N})$. The insertion or deletion cost of a conjunction into a sorted list is $log(|L|)$. Thus, the total insertion or deletion complexity is $O(N) + O(\mathbb{P}log|L|) = O(\mathbb{P}log|L|)$, because usually $N \ll L$ in our BEQ-Tree. Note that with the help of the hierarchical structure in our index, $|L|$ will not be too large, making the index maintenance very efficient.

D. ADDITIONAL EXPERIMENTAL RESULTS

D.1 Parameter Tuning

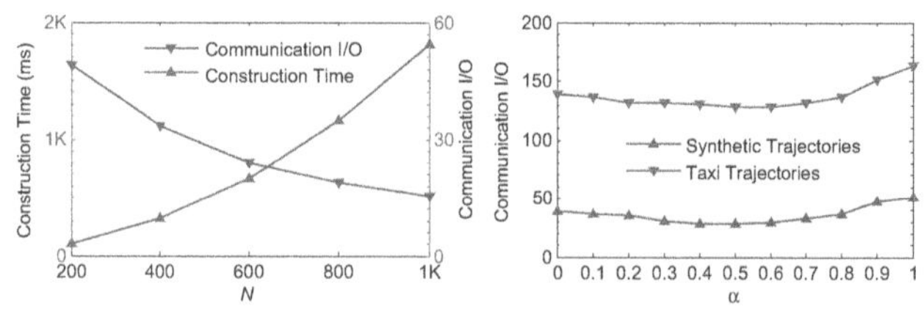

(a) Varying N (b) Varying α

Figure 14: Parameter tuning for iGM and idGM.

In continuous moving query processing, our proposed iGM and idGM use small cells to approximate the safe region and impact region. Suppose the whole space is split into $N \times N$ cells and we increase N from 200 to 1000 to test how the performance varies when the cell size becomes smaller. As shown in Fig. 14(a), when N increases, we can represent the cell in a more precise fashion and the optimal safe region is better approximated. Thus, it can reduce communication I/O. However, it requires more construction time since we need more iterations to expand the safe region until the termination condition is satisfied. For the following experiments, we set N to be 600 as a tradeoff between communication I/O and CPU cost in safe region construction[5]

Another parameter in $idGM$ is α which reflects the confidence level of user moving pattern. In the synthetic trajectories, we increase α from 0 to 1.0. If $\alpha = 0$, idGM degrades to iGM. We can see that direction is a factor that can improve system performance. The optimal performance occurs when $\alpha = 0.5$. If α is set very high, the performance is bad because the system assumes that the subscriber always moves along the original direction and is likely to construct a safe region along the direction. Then, it is easy for the subscriber to move out of the safe region when he changes the moving direction.

For BEQ-Tree, we tune the parameter E_{max} which is the maximum number of events in a cell. Fig. 15(a) and Fig. 15(b) illustrate the matching time and construction time of BEQ-Tree when varying E_{max}. When E_{max} increases, the cell becomes larger and the effect of spatial pruning degrades. Thus, it takes more matching time (Fig. 15(a)). However, a smaller E_{max} results in more levels in the BEQ-Tree, which increases the update cost (Fig. 15(b)). Therefor, we set E_{max} to be 60K as a good tradeoff between subscription matching time and event update cost.

D.2 Experiments on Foursquare

Foursquare Dataset. In Foursquare, each venue is considered as one spatial event. We extract structured information, i.e., attribute-value pairs, from the venues. Each venue has around 50 attributes and we harvest 1,832,418 venues. Among them, we use 1.5 million venues as the event database and the remaining to simulate the event stream. To generate the subscriptions over the Foursquare venue stream, we let the subscriptions follow the same distribution as the venues. In other words, if an attribute is frequent in the venues, it is also frequent in the subscriptions. The operators and operands in the predicates are synthetically attached.

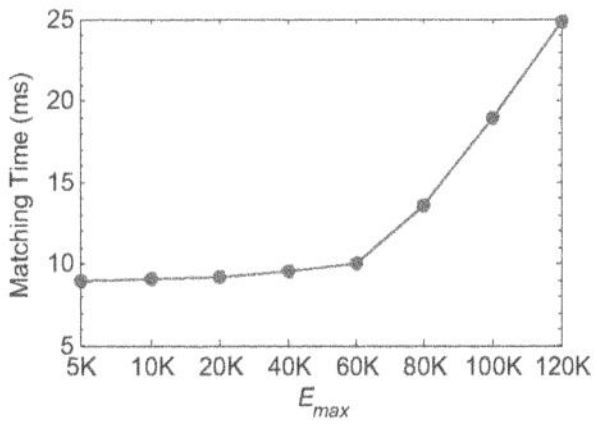

(a) Matching Time

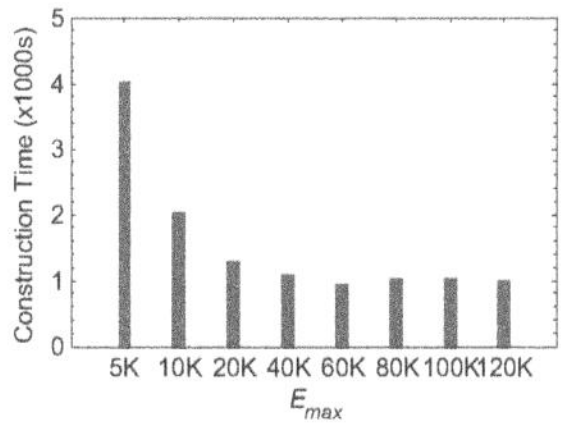

(b) Index Construction Time

Figure 15: Parameter tuning for BEQ-Tree.

Fig. 12 shows the average communication I/O on Foursquare dataset. As shown, the performance is similar with that tested on the Twitter dataset. iGM and idGM can reduce the communication cost incurred by event arrival significantly, and achieve a comparable performance as GM to constrol the communication cost incurred by location update.

D.3 Server Computation Cost

In the following, we report the average server computation cost for safe region and impact region construction during the experiment period (i.e., 1000 timestamps), which have not been included into the main experimental section due to space limitations. For VM, GM, iGM-BE, idGM-BE, we use k-index to find all the matching events first and then construct the safe region and impact region. For iGM-BEQ and idGM-BEQ, we use BEQ-Tree to find the set of matching events on demand, as described in Section 4.2. The results are shown in Fig. 13. We have the following observations. (1) VM performs worse than GM in terms of computation cost although VM incurs less communication cost than GM, because VM needs more time to construct the safe region and impact region. (2) iGM and idGM can outperform VM and GM by one order of magnitude, because each communication would trigger an update for the safe region and impact region while the communication cost of iGM and idGM can be reduced significantly with the guide of the cost model. (3) iGM-BEQ and idGM-BEQ show superior performance than iGM-BE and idGM-BE, because our safe region construction methods usually do not expand to the whole space and we can use BEQ-Tree to traverse only a part of the whole space. In addition, the advantage is more obvious when the event arrival rate is higher or the number of events is larger, making our system more scalable.

[5]The parameter tuning in this section hold for all the data set and experiments.

CE-Storm: Confidential Elastic Processing of Data Streams

Nick R. Katsipoulakis, Cory Thoma, Eric A. Gratta,
Alexandros Labrinidis, Adam J. Lee, Panos K. Chrysanthis

Department of Computer Science, University of Pittsburgh, Pittsburgh, PA 15260, USA
{katsip, corythoma, eag55, labrinid, adamlee, panos}@cs.pitt.edu

ABSTRACT

Data Stream Management Systems (DSMS) are crucial for modern high-volume/high-velocity data-driven applications, necessitating a distributed approach to processing them. In addition, data providers often require certain levels of confidentiality for their data, especially in cases of user-generated data, such as those coming out of physical activity/health tracking devices (i.e., our motivating application). This demonstration will showcase Synefo, an infrastructure that enables elastic scaling of DSMS operators, and CryptStream, a framework that provides confidentiality and access controls for data streams while allowing computation on untrusted servers, fused as *CE-Storm*. We will demonstrate both systems working in tandem and also visualize their behavior over time under different scenarios.

Categories and Subject Descriptors

H.2.4 [**Database Management**]: Systems—*Query processing; Distributed Databases*

Keywords

Distributed Data Stream Management System; Continuous Queries; Confidentiality; Elasticity

1. INTRODUCTION

The convergence of computing / sensing / mobile devices is generating a plethora of diverse data streams and is one critical aspect of the *Big Data* landscape [12], often referred to as the *Velocity* dimension. Modern data stream management systems (*DSMSs*) have been proposed to address the needs of monitoring applications over incoming data streams. *DSMSs* have been around for many years, as academic prototypes [4, 5, 7, 23] and commercially [1, 2]. A lot of the systems research work in *DSMSs* has dealt with *scheduling* in single-server environments [8, 18, 13], *load shedding* in single-server environments [20, 19, 16, 15], and *fault tolerance* in distributed environments [9].

SIGMOD '15 May 31 - June 4, 2015, Melbourne, Victoria, Australia

ACM 978-1-4503-2758-9/15/05 ...$15.00.
http://dx.doi.org/10.1145/2723372.2735357

The system that we will demonstrate, *CE-Storm*, has two distinct components that are working in tandem. First of all, we have *Synefo*, which provides a data/control routing infrastructure on top of the Storm engine [21], in order to enable scale-out and scale-in of Continuous Query (*CQ*) operators. Secondly, we have *CryptStream*, which provides confidentiality and access controls for streaming data, according to policies established by the data providers.

Motivating Application We assume an environment where personal health data (e.g., heart beats per minute) and physical activity data (e.g., number of steps walked, number of miles ran) of individuals, along with location and environmental data (e.g., barometric pressure), are being generated by monitoring devices such as Fitbit, Microsoft Band, Apple iWatch, etc. This data serves as input to a set of monitoring applications, which are implemented as *CQs*. Such applications can be running:

- on behalf of the user (e.g., notify me when I reach 10,000 steps in a day),
- on behalf of the user's primary care physician (who has been previously given full access by the user),
- by health insurance companies (to which the user may have provided only aggregate-level permissions in order to get a "healthy-living" discount),
- by scientists running experiments with micro-climate data (to which the user has previously provided only barometer reading access), and
- by the city (to which the user may have provided only aggregate-level permissions on location data), in order to help identify walk-friendly/bicycle-friendly areas.

Demonstration Overview This demonstration will visualize what is happening "under the hood" for CE-Storm and its components Storm, Synefo, and CryptStream. At first, we will showcase the different confidentiality levels that CryptStream supports, implementing access control policies for data providers, compute servers, or data consumers, for a workload where there is no need for scale-out / scale-in. Our demonstration will show which data tuples are transmitted encrypted (color-coded for the different encryption schemes), which tuples are special punctuation tuples, the load at each compute node, the underlying topology, the access control policies of each data provider, etc. Then, we will demonstrate CryptStream running over Synefo with a workload that requires scale-out, in order to avoid overload.

Over-time, the workload will return to normal levels and will showcase the scale-in operation.

Next, we present the CE-Storm System Model (Sec. 2), followed by a short introduction to *Synefo* (Sec. 3) and to CryptStream (Sec. 4). We conclude with a detailed description of the demonstration setup and scenarios (Sec. 5).

2. SYSTEM MODEL

Fig. 1 depicts the stack of CE-Storm. On the bottom layer, Storm's [21] engine is used. We preferred Storm over other systems, like Spark Streaming [23], mainly because the former is designed for per-tuple granularity during processing. Above Storm, *Synefo* is our proposed elastic shared–nothing approach for online scale–out/in stream processing. On top of that, *CryptStream* is responsible for ensuring confidentiality and access control of streaming data, according to data provider, server, or data consumer policies.

Synefo assumes a generic *data-flow oriented* computation model. This means that input is typically in the form of *data streams* and different *data processing tasks* can be executed at each processing node (or component, c_i). We assume a distributed system, so the processing nodes are part of a *topology*[1]. Each data processing task will receive input from one or more nodes; its output will be "fed" to another node in the topology, in a pipeline fashion.

Our generic model allows for different styles of computation. In particular, it can support *DSMS*-style computation: predefined *CQs*, consisting of multiple operators executing at one or more components, continuously processing the incoming streaming input and producing streaming output. This generic model can also support multi-stage computation that is typical with Map/Reduce and other modern analytics frameworks: each job j is broken down into a set of tasks $t \in T$, representing the consecutive stages of a data transformation process. Tasks are connected to form an execution tree (or a topology). A task is executed by one or more components c_i in parallel, and either disseminates data in the topology, or processes incoming data.

3. SYNEFO OVERVIEW

Load management in *DSMSs* has previously been addressed in stand-alone and distributed environments, primarily through *load shedding*, i.e., by dropping some of the tuples when there is an overload, in order to guarantee an acceptable Quality of Service (*QoS*). Such QoS is usually described in the form of the maximum acceptable response time or *delay target* [20, 19]. Load shedding is typically able to maintain latency and throughput at acceptable levels, however, this usually happens at the expense of the Quality of Data (*QoD*) produced. Load balancing becomes even more challenging when transaction processing or decision-making workloads are involved. Previously demonstrated work has shown how in–memory relational database management systems handle streaming data for the aforementioned types of workloads [11].

Unfortunately, most (if not all) of the previous approaches

[1]We make the distinction between physical and active topology; this is explained in the next section.

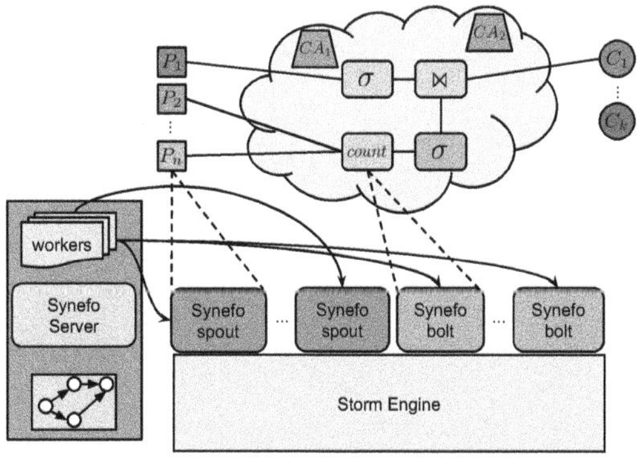

Figure 1: The proposed system stack.

assume that available processing components are known before the start of the computation and all of them remain active all the time during the computation, irrespective of whether they are used in the computation or not [21, 3, 23]. This requirement can impact a system's efficiency, in terms of cost, energy consumption and performance. On the one hand, if fewer components are provisioned, the system will soon reach its maximum capacity, and performance will deteriorate. On the other hand, if more components have been provisioned but are under–utilized, there will clearly be wasted resources, which would translate in extra energy costs, extra wear on computing nodes, etc.

Synefo[2] aims to provide an elastic execution environment for data–flow oriented computation, which can change the number of active processing components during runtime. Additional processing nodes can be included in the execution, if some of the active nodes are struggling, and under–utilized ones can be combined in order to keep the energy consumption of the cluster low. Our proposed system initiates execution by dividing the available components into *active* (i.e., components participating in processing) and *inactive* (i.e., components which are part of the cluster, but are not processing tuples). *Synefo*'s main role is to manage the activity status of available processing components, and route tuples to components accordingly. Our implementation works with Storm and it consists of (a) a Storm component API (*Synefo* bolt and spout), and (b) a coordinating entity for orchestrating the scale–out/in actions (*Synefo* server) (Fig. 1). Our design choice to have *active* and *inactive* operational components emanates from Storm's design limitations and our initial goal to have *Synefo* work with vanilla Storm clusters.

Online scale–out with shared state among processing components has been previously proposed in the work of Fernandez et al. [10]. Their prototype used virtual machine (*VM*) backups of upstream operators, which were responsible for disseminating state when operators were scaled out. However, the backup upstream operators will be a bottleneck in congested environments. Also, maintaining shared state among operators can become "painful" in a *DSMS*, where hundreds of operators exist. Our approach aims to eliminate shared state costs and achieve better scalability by following the share–nothing paradigm. Recent work from Wu

[2]*Synefo* comes from the Greek word συννεφο which means cloud.

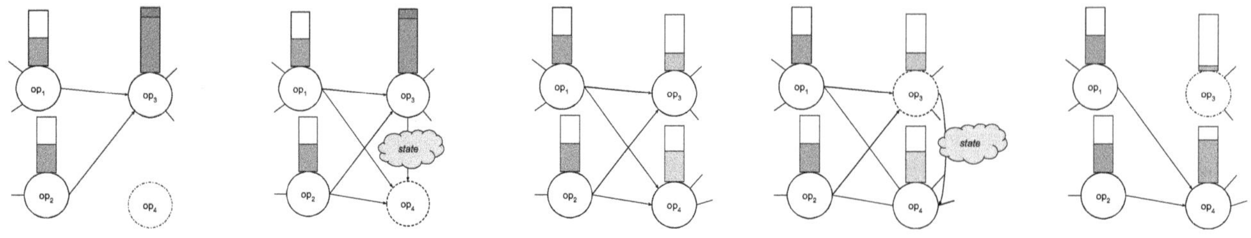

(a) op_3 is over–utilized and op_4 is inactive (b) op_3's state is replicated to op_4 (c) Both operators are active (d) *Synefo* triggers a scale–in (e) op_3 is inactive and op_4 is processing tuples

Figure 2: *Synefo*'s scale–out and scale–in scenario

et al. [22] has demonstrated ChronoStream, an elastic distributed stream processing engine. *Synefo* provides similar functionality, in terms of elasticity, but in a shared–nothing manner and is designed to work on top of Storm.

Every time a data processing task is given to the *DSMS*, an execution topology is created. There are two types of topologies in *Synefo*: the physical topology of components available in the distributed network of components, and the active topology of components participating in the data processing. Every time a scale–out/in command is given, components are added to (or removed from) the active topology.

Next, we give a brief overview of *Synefo*'s main parts: (i) *Synefo* server, (ii) *Synefo* spout, and (iii) *Synefo* bolt.

3.1 Synefo Server

The *Synefo* server monitors resource utilization levels in the cluster and has an active role during the initiation of a data processing task in the *DSMS*. The server awaits for incoming connections of *Synefo* Storm components. A Coordinator thread is launched so that it synchronizes the execution of all worker threads, which are responsible for accumulating resource usage statistics from each component. By the time all components have connected and registered to the server, topology information is gathered and the execution of the topology initiates.

Our prototype follows a centralized management approach for the *Synefo* server. This can potentially lead to the server being the single point of failure of the application. We will consider fault tolerance as part of our future work.

3.2 Synefo Spout

The component responsible for disseminating data into the topology is the *Synefo* spout. This is just a sub–class of Storm's BaseRichSpout, having been extended to: (i) initiate operation by registering to the *Synefo* server, and (ii) perform scale–out/in operations. In addition, during execution the *Synefo* spout reports resource usage data periodically and is able to execute scale–out/in commands directed by the *Synefo* server. A downstream component of a *Synefo* spout is assumed to always be a *Synefo* bolt, because a spout represents a stream of incoming data in Storm. Every time a scale-out/in command is received by a *Synefo* spout, it updates its routing information accordingly. For instance, if a *Synefo* spout is directed to scale–out by adding a bolt in its active downstream tasks list, the following happens:

- Sends command tuples to all downstream bolts notifying them about the scale–out operation
- Updates routing table information, to include the newly added bolt in the active downstream components.

At this point we have to mention that as in the *Synefo* server, the *Synefo* spout has to maintain an active connection with its worker counterpart in the server.

3.3 Synefo Bolt

The *Synefo* bolt is the last part of our *Synefo* system and is similar to a *Synefo* spout. The main difference between bolts and spouts is that the former are extended to handle incoming command tuples for scaling out/in and exchanging state with other bolts.

Bolts are required to maintain operator state, such as intermediate results or join window data. When a *Synefo* bolt receives a command tuple for scaling–out/in, this state needs to be transferred. If an additional *Synefo* bolt is added to that stage of the computation, the new bolt has to receive the current state of the already active bolt. Similarly, when a bolt is scaled–in (meaning that is not going to be active any more) its state should be sent to all operating bolts performing a part of the same computation. *Synefo* bolts transfer state transparently from the operation which is currently executed in a component. It is the operator's implementation responsibility to utilize the received state accordingly.

Fig. 2 illustrates a scale–out and scale–in operation in *Synefo*. The circles represent active components executing data processing tasks and the bars indicate the load on each one. Components op_1 and op_2 are sending their output to op_3, which has exceeded its operational capacity (Fig. 2a). Therefore, *Synefo* decides that op_3 should be scaled–out and identifies op_4 as an inactive component available. Components op_1 and op_2 are directed to involve op_4 as their downstream component, and op_3 transfers its state to op_4 (Fig. 2b). After the scale–out finishes, we can see that the load has been balanced among components and, in fact, op_3 is underutilized (Fig. 2c). Hence, *Synefo* initiates a scale–in procedure (remaining state in op_3 is sent to op_4) and components op_1 and op_2 are directed to exclude op_3 from their active components (Fig. 2d). Finally, the components carry on with the execution and component op_3 is inactive (Fig. 2e).

Our prototype has been implemented as a general extension to the current Storm API. We decided to maintain the separation of data routing from computation as is the case for

Scheme	Type of Queries	Supported operators	Information Gained by Adversary
RND	None	None	Nothing
DET	Equality	Select, Project, Equi-Join, Count, Group By, Order by	Equality of attributes
OPE	Range	Select, Join, Count	A partial to full order of tuples
HOM	Summations	Aggregates over summations	Nothing

Table 1: Summary of what types of queries and operators are supported by each encryption scheme, as well as what each scheme could reveal to a potential adversary.

Storm. Therefore, it is the operators' responsibility to keep state consistent at a time of an imminent scale–out, so that a *Synefo* bolt transfers it to its peer bolts correctly.

4. CRYPTSTREAM OVERVIEW

Traditional database systems rely on login and user authentication to maintain access controls over their data. When these systems are outsourced, simple user authentication may not be enough since a third party now has access to the data, and is in control of the physical location of data storage. A malicious third party may wish to gain knowledge of their clients by snooping on their data. Systems like CryptDB [17] aim at allowing third party storage without leaking plaintext values through the use of encryption. While this helps ensure confidentiality for traditional database models, the techniques used by CryptDB do not extend to the data streaming paradigm. The main issue is that streaming data often does not have the data consumer controlling or owning any part of the data provider, and therefore cannot control how to encrypt data entering the system. To help alleviate this problem, we developed *CryptStream*.

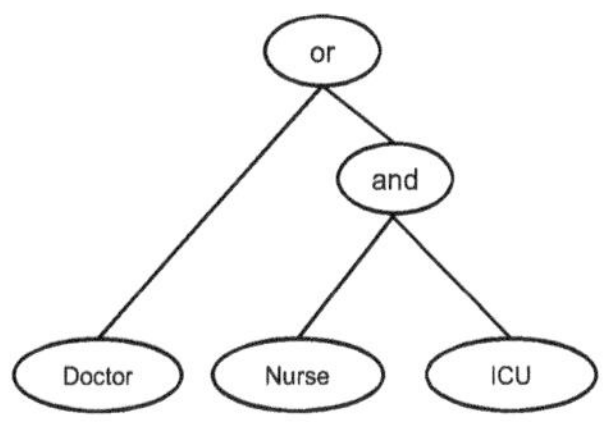

Figure 3: Simple ABAC policy stating that the Client be either a doctor or a nurse in the ICU.

CryptStream aims at enforcing access controls in *DSMSs* via cryptographic protocols which prevent unauthorized parties from accessing data. Working under the assumption of an honest-but-curious adversary, *CryptStream* protects a data provider's data from third party cloud service providers or other untrusted computing platforms. Access control is enforced through the union of Security Punctuations [14] and Attribute Based Access Controls (ABAC). ABAC policies grant or deny access based on what attributes the querier possesses. ABAC policies form a tree where each leaf node is an attribute and internal nodes are the "and" or "or" of the child nodes. An example is given in Fig. 3. This example illustrates a scenario where a data provider wants the data consumer to be a doctor or a nurse in the ICU ($doctor \vee (nurse \wedge ICU)$). ABAC policies are transmitted via a Security Punctuation (SP). A SP is a tuple emitted into a data stream wherein a data provider includes information on which data is being protected, how the data is being protected (i.e. what access control policy is being enforced) along with timestamps, ids, and other information.

Since *CryptStream* assumes an untrusted server, ABAC policies are enforced via Attribute Based Encryption (ABE). Both the security policy and data remain hidden to the server since only an encrypted string passes through the server. Work done prior to *CryptStream* utilized ABE for all data transmissions, which lead to prohibitively large performance overheads given the costly nature of ABE [6]. To improve upon this method, ABE is only used to encrypt cryptographic keys from faster protocols which allow computation to be preformed on the server without large overheads. *CryptStream* will only pay the cost of ABE whenever an access control policy is updated by data providers.

Similar to CryptDB, there are four encryption techniques used by *CryptStream*: *random* (RND), *deterministic* (DET), *order preserving* (OPE), and *Homomorphic* (HOM). Each encryption type enables some sort of computation on the server, but also may reveal some information to the server about each tuple. RND provides the strongest guarantee by leaking no information, but does so at the sacrifice of computation, since none can be done server-side. DET allows the server to decide if two values are the same, which enables equality selection and join queries, but will leak tuple equality. OPE provides more functionality than RND and DET since it holds the property that if $x < y$ then $OPE(x) < OPE(y)$. This allows the server to run range selections and joins, but it does provide the server with orderings amongst tuples. Finally, HOM allows the server to compute summations and does so without sacrifice in confidentiality since no information is leaked. Table 1 summarizes these techniques. It is important to note that the Data Provider chooses which level to encrypt their data based what they are willing to reveal to the server.

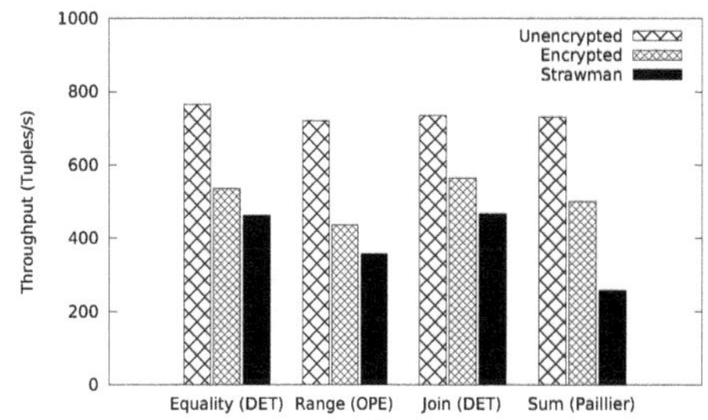

Figure 4: Throughput for each of the different operations supported for both unencrypted and encrypted streams. Join includes both equality and range oriented joins.

CryptStream allows for both data consumers and servers to provide security policies in addition to those from the data providers. Data consumer policies utilize Security Punctuations, but are not limited to ABAC policies as long as the server can support the intended policy. Server policies can be of any variety that is supported. *CryptStream* will first check the server policy to make sure a data consumer is allowed access by their internal policy. The data consumer policy is then verified, and if both return true, the tuple is sent. ABAC and ABE enforce the data provider access control policies, so if the data consumer was not given permission via their attributes, the tuple is useless to them. *CryptStream* provides the above listed contributions with modest overheads. Fig. 4 shows the overheads of each encryption type above. Tests were run on a cluster of 10 Mac Minis running with 2 GB of ram and a 1.83 GHz Intel CPU 1400 processor. All components were programmed in Java and packaged in Jar files for distribution. The system accepted simulated twitter-like data from a workload generator which provided control over distribution and frequency of keywords. Throughput is not greatly affected by the increase in computation, and confidentiality remains preserved.

5. DEMONSTRATION OVERVIEW

Our demonstration will focus on showing: (i) *CryptStream*'s ability to enforce confidentiality policies on streaming data, (ii) *Synefo*'s scale–out and scale–in abilities, and (iii) our visualization tool for Storm/*Synefo*/*CryptStream*.

We will be using the Motivating Application described in Section 1 for our demonstration, where the input data streams are physical activity and health data of individuals, which come with different levels of confidentiality, depending on the type of data consumers.

The audience will be able to see *CryptStream*'s confidentiality enforcement and the way sensitive data can be protected from possible adversaries in a cloud infrastructure. Also, it will be made clear how *Synefo* makes elasticity feasible in a widely accepted stream processing framework like Storm.

5.1 Storm User Survey

The motivation behind the development of a visualization framework for Storm came from a user study we performed in the Fall of 2014. A survey about Storm's usability was presented to members of the Storm users mailing list in order to gauge the difficulty of using Storm. After one week, we have gathered 10 responses from a variety of end users, ranging from academic researchers to data analysts. We present some of those results, in aggregate form here. Table 2a shows that more than 30% of the users mentioned that debugging is the most disruptive task in Storm, followed by logging and monitoring an application. In addition, we wanted to get users' opinions on features of Storm that need to be improved (Table 2b). Most participants replied that the visualization techniques of Storm are poor and need to be enhanced with extra features.

5.2 Visualizing CE-Storm

The purpose of the visualization component of our demonstration is to show what is happening "under the hood" for Storm, Synefo, and CryptStream. In particular, we will employ the familiar visual paradigm of a network of connected nodes to illustrate the topology of the underlying system. We will provide both topology "views": the physical topology, where each node of the network is a compute node, and the logical topology, where each node of the network is a data processing task or *CQ* operator.

Operation	Percent
debug	30.43
log	26.08
monitor	26.08
docs	13.04
deploy	4.34

(a) Operation that users found most disruptive in Storm

Feature	Percent
visuals	35.71
docs	21.42
new features	21.42
support	21.42

(b) Storm features that need improvement.

Table 2: Storm User Study Results

For each node, we will primarily show the current load information and give the option to drill down to get more detailed information. This would be other useful statistics such as a breakdown of the different types of tuples going through the system (e.g., punctuation vs regular, unencrypted/RND/DET/OPE/SUM), amount of state stored, etc. Within each node we will be able to see a sample of tuples going through the system. Tuples will be coded according to their type, as well as an indication as to the encryption used for a given attribute in the tuple. We will provide aggregate statistics for each edge of the network. Our visualization will include a panel with summary information about the overall status of the system, including input and output rates. We will be able to make changes to the input workload using this panel.

We aim to make the demonstration fairly interactive. Towards that end we will have video-playback type functionality. In particular, we will also provide a *pause* button, that will then allow us to slow down the speed of the visualization, *reverse*, *fast-forward*, or skip to live mode. It should be noted that execution at Storm/*Synefo*/*CryptStream* will not be affected; we will only be able to see the outcome of the execution at our own pace. Another interactive feature will be the ability to drill down and get more information about different parts of the system (e.g., for nodes/edges, as mentioned above or the different access control policies). Finally, we will show changes to the system (e.g., changing policies, forcing scale-out/in, etc) through the user-interface.

5.3 Demonstration Setup

The testbed of our demonstration is going to be a cluster of EC2 instances, forming a distributed network of stream operators. The entire stack of Fig. 1 will be setup in each EC2 instance. For data input, we are going to use synthetic data produced by our own custom stream generator, which produces data that follow user–defined (i) frequency distributions, (ii) vocabulary, and (iii) word sampling methods.

5.4 Demonstration Scenarios

Our live demonstration will have four distinct phases:
(i) Simple: A simple demonstration of *CryptStream*, with two different policies, meant to familiarize the audience with the visualization interface; **(ii) Complex**: A demonstration of *CryptStream*, with a more complex scenario, having policies from data providers and from data consumers;
(iii) Scale–out: A demonstration of *Synefo*'s scale–out mechanism, by utilizing a workload where the incoming rate is too high for an operator to be handled by a single node;
(iv) Scale–in: A demonstration of *Synefo*'s scale-in mechanism, using a workload where a high input rate is reduced,

so that fewer nodes are needed for the processing of the operator that was previously scaled–out. We provide more details for the four different phases next.

Simple Scenario We will demonstrate different access control policies, as explained in the Motivating example. *CryptStream* will enforce different levels of access by deploying its set of encryption techniques (Section 4). This will illustrate the ability of *CryptStream* to provide different levels of access to different data consumers depending on the trust level for that data consumer.

Complex Scenario We will demonstrate a more complicated scenario, where access control policies come from data providers, data consumers, and compute servers. We will show detailed access control policies information and update the policies to see how *CryptStream* handles the changes.

Scale–out Scenario The third scenario is going to focus on the elastic ability provided by *Synefo* and the trade–off between elasticity and confidentiality experienced in complex scenarios of CE-Storm. We will extend the *Simple Scenario*, but have an increased data input rate above the system's capacity. This increase in the volume of incoming data might be caused by a "health scare" that requires more data to be accumulated to better monitor changes in personal well being, or by New Year's resolutions which prompt more people to join a gym and try to get fit. In order to avoid dropping tuples, *Synefo* will take action by scaling–out the congested operators. This scale–out will be triggered automatically by following user–defined usage thresholds (provided to *Synefo* at start–up). Our system will act proactively and if an operator reaches a usage percentage equal or above the user–defined threshold, it will be scaled–out. An important part of this scenario will be to demonstrate the cost of scaling–out, in terms of confidentiality. For instance, some operators with strict confidentiality policies might have to scale–out to machines that are not trusted. Therefore, we will demonstrate a number of trade–offs in terms of performance gain compared to confidentiality constraints relaxation.

Scale–in Scenario The last scenario will demonstrate a scale–in situation, where the data input rate falls below a certain limit, resulting in computing nodes being underutilized. This could happen because, for example, the health scare went away, or with the arrival of March (for those trying to stick to their New Year's resolutions).

Acknowledgments

This material is based on work supported by the National Science Foundation under grants CNS-1253204, IIS-0746696, and OIA-1028162.

6. REFERENCES

[1] IBM System S. `http://researcher.watson.ibm.com/researcher/view_group_subpage.php?id=2534`.

[2] SQLstream. `http://www.sqlstream.com/`.

[3] Summingbird. `http://github.com/twitter/summingbird`.

[4] D. J. Abadi et al. Aurora: A new model and architecture for data stream management. *The VLDB Journal*, 12(2):120–139, Aug. 2003.

[5] Y. Ahmad et al. Distributed operation in the borealis stream processing engine. In *Proc. of ACM SIGMOD*, pages 882–884, 2005.

[6] D. T. T. Anh and A. Datta. Streamforce: outsourcing access control enforcement for stream data to the clouds. In *CODASPY*, pages 13–24. ACM, 2014.

[7] A. Arasu et al. Stream: The stanford data stream management system. Technical Report 2004-20, Stanford InfoLab, 2004.

[8] B. Babcock, S. Babu, R. Motwani, and M. Datar. Chain: Operator scheduling for memory minimization in data stream systems. In *Proc. of ACM SIGMOD*, pages 253–264, 2003.

[9] M. Balazinska et al. Fault-tolerance in the borealis distributed stream processing system. *ACM Trans. Database Syst.*, 33(1):3:1–3:44, Mar. 2008.

[10] R. Castro Fernandez et al. Integrating scale out and fault tolerance in stream processing using operator state management. In *Proc. of ACM SIGMOD*, pages 725–736, 2013.

[11] U. Çetintemel et al. S-store: A streaming newsql system for big velocity applications. *PVLDB*, 7(13):1633–1636, 2014.

[12] H. V. Jagadish et al. Big data and its technical challenges. *Comm. of the ACM*, 57(7):86–94, Jul 2014.

[13] L. A. Moakar, A. Labrinidis, and P. K. Chrysanthis. Adaptive class-based scheduling of continuous queries. In *Proc. of IEEE SMDB Workshop*, pages 1–6, 2012.

[14] R. Nehme, E. A. Rundensteiner, and E. Bertino. A security punctuation framework for enforcing access control on streaming data. In *Proc. of IEEE ICDE Conference*, pages 406–415, 2008.

[15] T. N. Pham, P. K. Chrysanthis, and A. Labrinidis. Self-managing load shedding for data stream management systems. In *Proc. of SMDB Workshop*, pages 1–7, 2013.

[16] T. N. Pham, L. A. Moakar, P. K. Chrysanthis, and A. Labrinidis. Dilos: A dynamic integrated load manager and scheduler for continuous queries. In *Proc. of SMDB Workshop*, pages 10–15, 2011.

[17] R. A. Popa et al. CryptDB: protecting confidentiality with encrypted query processing. In *Proc. of ACM SOSP*, pages 85–100, 2011.

[18] M. A. Sharaf et al. Algorithms and metrics for processing multiple heterogeneous continuous queries. *ACM Trans. Database Syst.*, 33(2):5.1–5.44, 2008.

[19] N. Tatbul, U. Çetintemel, and S. Zdonik. Staying fit: Efficient load shedding techniques for distributed stream processing. In *Proc. of VLDB*, pages 159–170, 2007.

[20] N. Tatbul et al. Load shedding in a data stream manager. In *Proc. of VLDB*, pages 309–320, 2003.

[21] A. Toshniwal et al. Storm@twitter. In *Proc. of ACM SIGMOD Conference*, pages 147–156, 2014.

[22] W. Yingjun and T. Kian-Lee. Chronostream: Elastic stateful stream computation in the cloud. In *Proc. of IEEE ICDE Conference*, 2015.

[23] M. Zaharia, T. Das, H. Li, S. Shenker, and I. Stoica. Discretized streams: An efficient and fault-tolerant model for stream processing on large clusters. In *Proc. of HotCloud Conference*, pages 423–438, 2012.

A SQL Debugger Built from Spare Parts

Turning a SQL:1999 Database System into Its Own Debugger

Benjamin Dietrich Torsten Grust

Universität Tübingen
Tübingen, Germany

[b.dietrich, torsten.grust]@uni-tuebingen.de

ABSTRACT

We demonstrate a new incarnation of Habitat, an **observational debugger for SQL**. In observational debugging, users highlight parts of a—presumably faulty—query to observe the evaluation of SQL subexpressions and learn about the query's actual runtime behavior. The present version of Habitat has been redesigned from scratch and employs a query instrumentation technique that exclusively relies on the SQL facilities of the underlying RDBMS. We particularly shed light on new features like (1) the debugging of recursive SQL queries and (2) the observation of row groups (before and after aggregation). Habitat can turn any reasonably modern SQL:1999 RDBMS into its own language-level SQL debugger.

Categories and Subject Descriptors: H.2.3 [**Database Management**]: Languages—*Query languages*; D.2.5 [**Software Engineering**]: Testing and Debugging—*Debugging aids*

General Terms: Algorithms, Languages

Keywords: SQL; debuggers; observational debugging

1. AN OBSERVATIONAL SQL DEBUGGER

We demonstrate a completely rethought and redesigned version of Habitat, an **observational debugger for SQL**. Given the text of a—presumably buggy—SQL query, users mark subexpressions of arbitrary size and position for runtime observation. Much like the judicious placement of `printf()` calls in the debugging of procedural code, Habitat's observations help to gain detailed insight into the query evaluation process. Habitat uses the user's markings to transform and re-evaluate the instrumented query, collects the desired observations on the way, and finally prepares a tabular display of these observations and the context in which they occurred.

The logic and functional programming language communities pioneered this observational style of debugging [7, 9] which proves to be a good fit for the declarative SQL language as well. With Habitat, the debugging of logical (*not*: performance) SQL bugs happens on the level of the user-facing query language and its tabular data model. Users are not exposed to engine internals or query plans (they do not need to: the plans are okay—it is the query logic that needs fixing). The RDBMS host itself produces and collects the observations while it evaluates the instrumented query against the original database instance, *i.e.*, in the presence of built-in or user-defined functions, views, and types (the query is observed in "its own habitat".) Habitat's debugging model is orthogonal to those of existing SQL stored procedure debuggers [6] in which the evaluation of a query constitutes a monolithic and opaque action.

SIGMOD'15, May 31–June 4, 2015, Melbourne, Victoria, Australia.

ACM 978-1-4503-2758-9/15/05 ...$15.00.
http://dx.doi.org/10.1145/2723372.2735358.

A new Habitat, assembled from the spare parts around you. Earlier, we have described an implementation of the Habitat idea that relied on a rather complex and non-standard translation of SQL into an intermediate table algebra [3, 4]. With it came the requirement of an external code generator that would turn instrumented algebraic queries back into executable SQL text. Users were constrained in what kind of subexpressions could be observed and where markings could be placed.

The present work demonstrates a new incarnation of Habitat that has been *exclusively built using the host DBMS's own SQL facilities.* We focus on PostgreSQL [8] for this demonstration but the design immediately applies to other SQL:1999 database systems. The new Habitat debugger

- admits the free placement of markings and can observe subexpressions including atomic values, arithmetic and Boolean expressions, groups of rows before and after aggregation, (correlated) subqueries as well as recursive SQL queries,
- places a set of observations into a common context to illustrate the runtime interplay of individual query pieces,
- supports "*what if?*"-style debugging that allows to tinker with (sub)query results before a final fix is committed to,
- collects observations in relational tables as a side-effect during regular query evaluation, and
- comes with a visual browser-based frontend that supports subexpression marking, an interactive observation display, and allows to establish and keep focus on key observations.

The demonstration will feature a fully functional and live version of the new Habitat debugger running atop a PostgreSQL 9.3 backend. Here, we continue to briefly explore two SQL debugging scenarios. Our aim is to provide a flavor of the methodology of observational SQL debugging and to give an impression of what the demo audience can experience on-site.

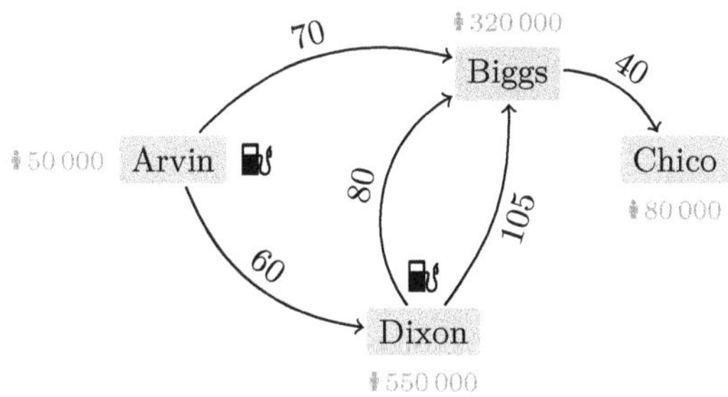

(a) Road network with travel distances between cities, locations of fueling stations (⛽) and population size (🚹).

cities

	city	population	fuel
c_1	Arvin	50 000	1
c_2	Biggs	320 000	0
c_3	Chico	80 000	0
c_4	Dixon	550 000	1

roads

	here	dist	there
r_1	Arvin	70	Biggs
r_2	Arvin	60	Dixon
r_3	Biggs	40	Chico
r_4	Dixon	80	Biggs
r_5	Dixon	105	Biggs

(b) Tables cities and roads.

Figure 1: Simplified relational model of cities and their connecting road network.

```
 1 WITH RECURSIVE hops(city, gauge) AS (
 2     VALUES ('Arvin', 0)
 3   UNION ALL
 4     SELECT r.there AS city,
 5            h.gauge + c.fuel * 100 - r.dist AS gauge
 6     FROM   cities AS c, roads AS r, hops AS h
 7     WHERE  h.city = c.city
 8     AND    h.city = r.here
 9     AND    h.gauge + c.fuel * 100 >= r.dist
10 )
11 SELECT *
12 FROM   hops;
```

Figure 2: Which cities can be reached from Arvin? (Buggy.)

```
 1 WITH RECURSIVE hops(city, gauge) AS (
 2     VALUES ('Arvin', 0)
 3   UNION ALL
 4     SELECT r.there AS city,
 5            h.gauge + c.fuel * 100 ④ - r.dist ③ AS gauge
 6     FROM   cities AS c, roads AS r, hops AS h
 7     WHERE  h.city = c.city                   ②
 8     AND    h.city = r.here
 9     AND    h.gauge + c.fuel * 100 >= r.dist
10 )                                          ①
11 SELECT *
12 FROM   hops;
```

Figure 4: Habitat allows the placement of markings (▭) to observe the evaluation of selected SQL subexpressions.

2. UNRAVELING AND FIXING SQL BUGS

Let us focus on two debugging showcases that go beyond the capabilities of the initial Habitat version: (1) a recursive (or iterative) road network exploration, formulated using SQL's `WITH RECURSIVE` construct, and (2) a SQL query that revolves around the grouping and subsequent aggregation of rows. In both cases we obtain unexpected (read: incorrect) results and we will use Habitat to unravel the queries and then fix their SQL bugs.

The simple two-table database of Figure 1 serves as the scenario for both showcases. We model an acyclic network of unidirectional roads that connects four cities. In selected cities, marked with a ⛽ symbol in Figure 1(a), drivers have the opportunity to refuel their cars (tank volume: 100 ℓ). Traveling along a road $\xrightarrow{d}$ costs d liters of fuel. Figure 1(b) shows how this road network is represented in terms of relational tables. Table roads encodes the network itself while table cities holds city details: the presence of a gas station (0/1 in column fuel) as well as the current population size. (Ignore the c_i and r_j row identifiers for now.)

2.1 Recursion in SQL

Road network exploration. Start in Arvin with an empty tank, refill, then travel along any road requiring no more than 100 ℓ of fuel. Upon arrival, take note of the destination reached (city) as well as the fuel that remains (gauge). Refill at the destination if possible, then continue the journey. Which cities can we reach from Arvin?

The recursive SQL query reproduced in Figure 2 computes table hops(city, gauge) to answer this question. The base case starts us off in Arvin with an empty tank (line 2). In the recursive case, the hop(s) we reached last are available in row variable `h`. We join with tables cities and roads to learn about the destination city `c` and the roads `r` that leave from `c` (lines 6 to 8). Should the remaining fuel `h.gauge` plus a possible refill in `c`—if there is no gas station in `c`, `c.fuel * 100` = 0—bridge the distance `r.dist` (line 9), we have established `r.there` as a possible next hop. To complete this step of the recursion, we enter `r.there` along with the then remaining fuel into the hops table (lines 4 and 5).

Evaluating this recursive query against the database of Figure 1(b) yields the hops table of Figure 3. The result looks suspicious. Row ⟨`Chico`, `20`⟩, in particular, is unexpected: there is no option to reach Biggs—where we cannot refill—with the residual 40 ℓ of fuel needed to bridge the distance to Chico. Row ⟨`Biggs`, `60`⟩ thus is questionable as well.

city	gauge
Arvin	0
Biggs	30
Dixon	40
Biggs	35
Biggs	60
Chico	20

Figure 3: Final hops table. (Incorrect.)

Debugging a recursive query. Since we are not sure where the problem with the query might lie, we start by *marking* the entire body of the `WITH RECURSIVE` clause. For reference, Figure 4 depicts the markings that we place during this debugging session (we have just placed Marking ①; Markings ② to ④ will be added in the process). Habitat instruments the SQL query according to Marking ①, runs the modified query, and responds with a tabular display of *observations* made at runtime (Figure 5).

Each cell in a Habitat observation reflects one evaluation (of many, in general) of a marked SQL subexpression. The observation of Figure 5 shows that the base case of the `WITH RECURSIVE` clause ran once while the recursive part was evaluated an additional three times (cf. the rows numbered 0 to 3). A cell marked ▨ indicates that an observed

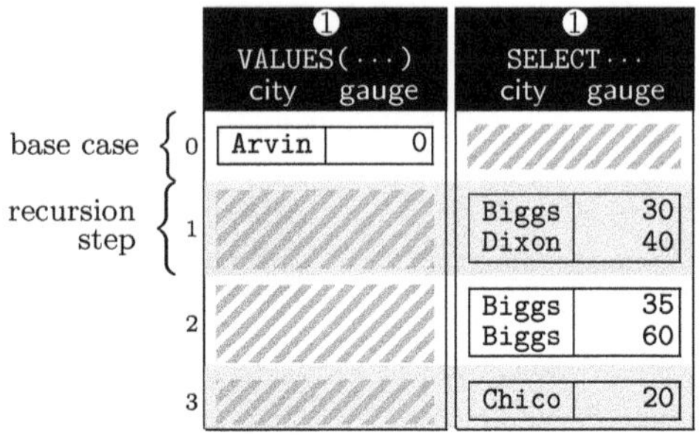

Figure 5: Observation for Marking ①. Left column relates to the `VALUES(···)` expression, right column shows the evaluations of the recursive `SELECT` clause (after `UNION ALL`).

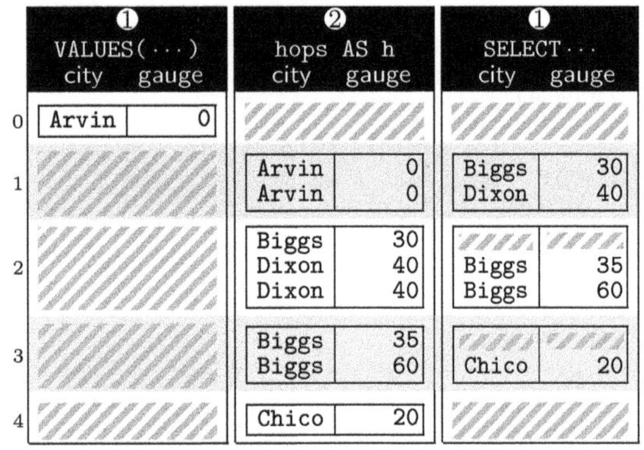

Figure 6: Observations for Markings ① and ② in context.

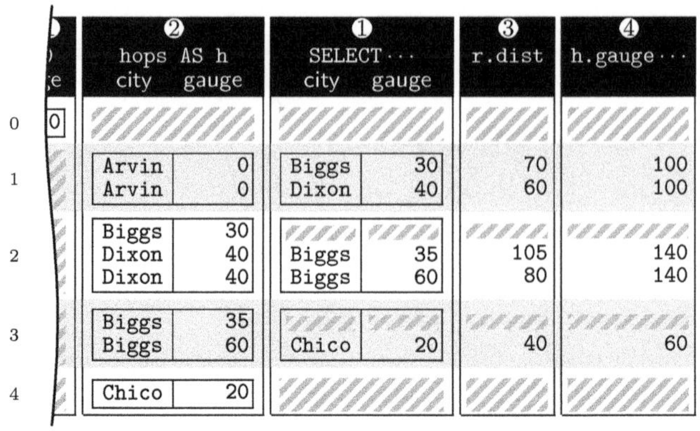

Figure 7: Display of observations for Markings ① to ④.

```
WITH RECURSIVE hops(city, gauge) AS (
   VALUES ('Arvin', 0)
  UNION ALL
   SELECT r.there AS city,
          LEAST(100, h.gauge + c.fuel * 100) - r.dist AS gauge
   FROM   cities AS c, roads AS r, hops AS h
   WHERE  h.city = c.city
   AND    h.city = r.here
   AND    LEAST(100, h.gauge + c.fuel * 100) >= r.dist
)
SELECT *
FROM   hops;
```

Figure 8: Repaired road network exploration query (fixes).

expression has not been evaluated in that particular recursive step (or iteration). Note that both, the `VALUES` expression as well as the recursive `SELECT`, yield *tables* of rows on each evaluation—Habitat renders such tabular values inside boxes ▭ for clarity. We see that Chico has been reached in the third (final) step of the recursion—as is expected since the city is located at the fringe of the road network.

To understand how we (erroneously) got to Chico, we place Marking ② which brings the hops themselves into context. Habitat now prepares the merged display of Figure 6 which relates the observations for Markings ① and ②. In recursion step 1 we reach both Biggs and Dixon coming from Arvin. In step 2, we do not get anywhere from Biggs with a tank of 30 ℓ. However, we can refill in Dixon to reach Biggs on two different roads. The remaining fuel levels in Biggs of 35 ℓ and 60 ℓ look suspiciously high, though. In fact, the residual 60 ℓ allows us to reach Chico in step 3. (Note that step 4 indicates that we get nowhere from Chico: row ⟨**Chico**, 20⟩ does not find any join partner such that the `SELECT` clause of Marking ① is never evaluated; this indicates the end of the recursion according to the semantics of `WITH RECURSIVE` [1].)

Do we take the proper travel distances into account? We place Marking ③ to observe the atomic subexpression `r.dist`. Habitat grows the display once more (refer to the column labeled ③ in Figure 7). Checking with table roads, the distances look as expected. Does the fuel level calculation work correctly? We highlight expression `h.gauge + c.fuel * 100` to obtain Marking ④ and its associated observation (Figure 7). Here is the bug! Apparently, a refill may exceed the tank volume of 100 ℓ (in Dixon we fill up from 40 to 140 ℓ).

One obvious fix is to properly cap the fuel level on a refill. The SQL query of Figure 8 uses `LEAST(·,·)` to implement this. (Section 3 illustrates how Habitat allows to experiment with a capped fuel level *before* such a concrete query fix is applied.) Table hops of Figure 9 holds the correct result of the road network exploration.

city	gauge
Arvin	0
Dixon	40
Biggs	30
Biggs	20

Figure 9: Table hops. (Corrected.)

2.2 Observing Groups Before Aggregation

The `GROUP BY` construct and the groups of rows it produces are, in a sense, second-class concepts in SQL: queries can compute aggregates of a group but may not return the *group itself* (a restriction due to the flat 1NF nature of the relational data model). Nevertheless, a look at such groups of rows can be insightful during the debugging of queries featuring `GROUP BY`.[1] It can also help learners to understand the otherwise opaque behavior of `GROUP BY`. This second debugging session illustrates how the new Habitat treats groups as being first-class.

[1]Queries can be rewritten to reveal group contents but this manual process is error-prone [2, 5] and does not preserve the original query intent.

```
SELECT   r.there AS city, SUM(c.population) AS belt
FROM     cities AS c, roads AS r
WHERE    c.city = r.here
GROUP BY r.there;
```

Figure 10: Computing commuter belt sizes. (Buggy.)

```
1 SELECT    r.there AS city, SUM(c.population) AS belt
2 FROM      cities AS c, roads AS r
3 WHERE     c.city = r.here
4 GROUP BY  r.there;
```

Figure 12: Markings placed to debug the query of Figure 10.

	⑤ SELECT ··· city	belt	⑥ c.population
1	Biggs	1 150 000	50 000 550 000 550 000
2	Chico	320 000	320 000
3	Dixon	50 000	50 000

Figure 13: Observations made for Markings ⑤ and ⑥. Nested boxes in column ⑥ represent groups.

	⑤ SELECT ··· city	belt	⑥ c.population	⑦ roads AS r here	dist	there
1	Biggs	1 150 000	50 000 550 000 550 000	Arvin Dixon Dixon	70 80 105	Biggs Biggs Biggs
2	Chico	320 000	320 000	Biggs	40	Chico
3	Dixon	50 000	50 000	Arvin	60	Dixon

Figure 14: Complete display of observations for Markings ⑤ to ⑦. The double Dixon in iteration 1 hints at the bug.

```
SELECT    r.there AS city, SUM(c.population) AS belt
FROM      cities AS c,
          (SELECT DISTINCT here, there FROM roads) AS r
WHERE     c.city = r.here
GROUP BY  r.there;
```

Figure 15: Patched commuter belt query (fix).

Commuter belt size. For each city with incoming roads, compute the sum of the population sizes of the city's direct neighbors. The result serves as a measure for the expected commuter traffic (useful input in road planning).

The query of Figure 10 uses tables `cities` and `roads` (Figure 1(b)) to implement this commuter belt computation in SQL. For each `city` with incoming roads—found in column `there` in table `roads`—we find all neighboring cities `c` (lines 2 and 3), collect them in a common group (line 4), and finally sum the neighbors' populations (line 1) to find the belt size (`belt`). The resulting two-column table is shown in Figure 11 but its contents look dubious: the commuter belt size of Biggs alone exceeds the overall population (1 000 000) of the entire region.

city	belt
Biggs	1 150 000
Chico	320 000
Dixon	50 000

Figure 11: Commuter belts. (Incorrect.)

Debugging with first-class groups. Once more we start the session by highlighting the entire SQL query text (Marking ⑤ in Figure 12). The resulting observation merely mirrors the query's result. It would be more insightful to know which cities' population sizes contribute to the obviously incorrect belt size aggregates. We thus place the Marking ⑥. Note that we highlight the subexpression `c.population` but omit the enclosing `SUM` aggregate function. Habitat instruments and re-runs the SQL query, then renders the observation display of Figure 13. In each of the three iterations of the query's `SELECT` clause, marked subexpression `c.population` evaluates to a *group of rows*: column ⑥ thus uses nested boxes ▭ to visualize the group contents.

The group associated with Biggs (iteration 1) indicates incoming traffic of 550 000 twice. Is that okay? Marking ⑦ on **`roads as r`** lets us observe the associated roads `r` that carry the traffic. The augmented display of Figure 14 indicates that we counted the population of Dixon twice when we explored the neighborhood of Biggs (two roads lead from Dixon to Biggs).

city	belt
Biggs	600 000
Chico	320 000
Dixon	50 000

Figure 16: Corrected commuter belts.

The `DISTINCT` fix of Figure 15 makes the SQL query disregard such multi-road connections between cities and establishes the intended notion of neighborhood. Figure 16 shows the corrected commuter belt sizes.

3. BEHIND THE SCENES

Instrumentation. Habitat's operation is based on the *instrumentation* of the SQL query under debugging. In a nutshell, a marked subexpression e is replaced by a function call $\mathtt{h}_i(\ldots, e)$. SQL function $\mathtt{h}_i$ inserts the value of e into Habitat-created table $\mathtt{obs}_i$ and otherwise acts as the identity by returning e, allowing the evaluation of the instrumented query to proceed normally.

Figure 17 shows the fully instrumented variant of the recursive road exploration query. The four markings of Figure 4 turn into calls to functions $\mathtt{h}_{1,\ldots,8}$ (if e is table-valued, the columns of e are instrumented separately). Function $\mathtt{h}_6$ and its associated observation table $\mathtt{obs}_6$ are shown in Figures 18 and 19, respectively (in these $\mathtt{obs}_i$ tables, the observed value of e is found in column `observation`). Note that $\mathtt{h}_i$ is declared as a `VOLATILE` SQL function to announce its side effect on the $\mathtt{obs}_i$ table, forcing the RDBMS to re-evaluate $\mathtt{h}_i$ on every invocation.

Observations in context. Once the evaluation of the instrumented query is complete, Habitat's frontend reads from the observation tables $\mathtt{obs}_i$ to prepare the displays discussed in Section 2. Recall that these displays relate multiple observations by merging them into a coherent whole—a requirement of the observational debugging paradigm in which markings are added over time to establish a chain of cause and effects, eventually leading to the detection of the bug [7]. Along with the observed value of e, Habitat thus collects information that identifies the *context* in which e was evaluated. A display relates observations that share the same context.

Habitat derives context information from three sources (as required and applicable):

- for any SQL row variable v in scope, the identifier $\mathrm{TID}(v)$ of the row v is currently bound to,
- the values of the criteria $c_1, \ldots, c_n$ ($n \geqslant 1$) that uniquely identify each group built by a `GROUP BY` $c_1, \ldots, c_n$ clause (*e.g.*, $c_1 \equiv$ `r.there` in the query of Figure 12), and
- the depth $\mathrm{DEPTH}()$ of the current recursion ($\mathrm{DEPTH}() \in \{0, \ldots, 4\}$ for the example of Figures 6 and 7).

```
1  WITH RECURSIVE hops(city, gauge) AS (
2    SELECT  hops.city, hops.gauge
3    FROM    (VALUES (DEPTH())) AS _(rec),                                    ①
4    LATERAL (SELECT h1(rec, TID(v), v.city) AS city, h2(rec, TID(v), v.gauge) AS gauge
5            FROM    (VALUES ('Arvin', 0)) AS v(city, gauge)
6            ) AS hops
7  UNION ALL
8    SELECT  hops.city, hops.gauge
9    FROM    (VALUES (DEPTH())) AS _(rec),
10   LATERAL (SELECT h7(rec, TID(c), TID(r), h.id, r.there) AS city,
11                   h8(rec, TID(c), TID(r), h.id,                ④                           ③
12                     h6(rec, TID(c), TID(r), h.id, h.gauge + c.fuel * 100) - h5(rec, TID(c), TID(r), h.id, r.dist)) AS gauge,
13           FROM    cities AS c, roads AS r,                                                     ② ①
14                   (SELECT TID(h) AS id, h3(rec, TID(h), h.city) AS city, h4(rec, TID(h), h.gauge) AS gauge
15                    FROM   hops AS h) AS h
16           WHERE   h.city = c.city
17           AND     h.city = r.here
18           AND     h.gauge + c.fuel * 100 >= r.dist
19           ) AS hops
20 )
21 SELECT hops.*
22 FROM   hops;
```

Figure 17: Full instrumentation of the recursive SQL query of Figure 4.

```
1 CREATE FUNCTION h6(rec BIGINT, c TID, r TID, h BIGINT,
2                   observation INT) RETURNS INT AS
3 $$
4   INSERT INTO obs6 VALUES (rec, c, r, h, observation);
5   SELECT observation; -- return value of e (act as identity)
6 $$
7 LANGUAGE SQL VOLATILE;
```

Figure 18: Function h_6 implements Marking ④, observing expression $e \equiv$ `h.gauge + c.fuel * 100` of type `INT`.

obs6

rec	TID(c)	TID(r)	TID(h)	observation
1	c_1	r_1	1	100
1	c_1	r_2	1	100
2	c_4	r_4	1	140
2	c_4	r_5	1	140
3	c_2	r_3	2	60

Figure 19: Observation table obs6. Populated by function h_6 when the instrumented query of Figure 17 is evaluated.

Contemporary SQL RDBMSs provide a variety of options to obtain these bits of context:

TID(v): If v ranges over a base table, identify rows by their system-provided row ids[2] (with PostgreSQL TID(v) $\equiv$ v.`ctid` and Oracle TID(v) $\equiv$ v.`rowid`, for example). Otherwise (v ranges over an intermediate subquery result), generate surrogate row ids via a SQL:1999 row number generator: TID(v) $\equiv$ `ROW_NUMBER() OVER ()`.

DEPTH(): Create a temporary SQL sequence generator s and draw successive numbers $0, 1, \dots$ from s: DEPTH() $\equiv$ `NEXT VALUE FOR` s (for PostgreSQL: `nextval('`s`')`).

To illustrate, function h_6 receives the current recursion depth as well as the identifiers of the rows bound to variables `c`, `r`, and `h` as context. Observation table obs6 holds the recorded context along with the result of the observed expression: value `60` was observed in the third recursion step when variables `c`, `r`, and `h` were bound to the rows with ids c_2, r_3, and 2, respectively (the row ids c_i, r_j are found in Figure 1(b); `h` ranges over `hops`, an intermediate result table—Habitat implements TID(h) (line 14 in Figure 17) in terms of surrogate row identifiers of type `BIGINT`).

[2]It suffices that these row ids are stable while the instrumented query is evaluated.

```
5 SELECT CASE WHEN (rec, c, r, h) IN ((2,c4,r4,1), (2,c4,r5,1))
             THEN 100
             ELSE observation
        END;
```

Figure 20: "What if?" debugging: replacement for line 5 in function h_6 (Figure 18).

Instrumentation and (non-)interference. Instrumentation involves the risk of interfering with the evaluation of the debugged subject query. Habitat's query instrumentation diligently avoids such interference:

- If possible, context information is generated inside separate `LATERAL` subqueries: in `FROM` … e_c, `LATERAL` e, expression e_c can compute context information which Habitat may use to instrument expressions in subquery e (see lines 3 and 9 in Figure 17 where the current recursion depth is made available in column `rec`).
- If Habitat needs to introduce additional columns to hold context information (cf. column `id` in line 14), care is taken to not interfere with query evaluation: this relates to the expansion of `SELECT *`, duplicate elimination via `DISTINCT`, or the semantics of set operations (*e.g.*, `UNION`), for example.

"*What if?*" debugging. The presence of evaluation context information enables Habitat to offer a "*what if?*"-approach to debugging in which users can tentatively alter the behavior of the subject query before a corresponding fix needs to be implemented. Reconsider the road exploration query where we have found the fuel gauge expression marked ④ to erroneously exceed the tank volume. *Would the query work if these values had not exceeded 100 ℓ?* To explore this hypothesis, users select the two values `140` in the display of Figure 7 and instead provide the desired value of `100`. When the subject query is re-evaluated, the marked subexpression will yield `100` for the two highlighted instances (but otherwise evaluate as before).

Under the hood, the frontend passes the context information associated with the selected occurrences of `140` to Habitat which then alters the definition of h_6 (see Figure 20). Based on the evaluation context, the new (non-identity) function h_6 will return `100` instead of the original observation made, effectively creating the desired "*what if?*" scenario.

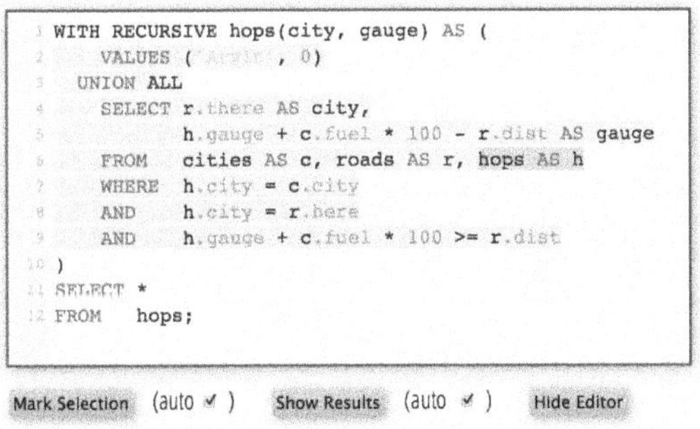

(a) Markings ① ( ) and ② ( ) placed in the road exploration query (refer to Figure 4).

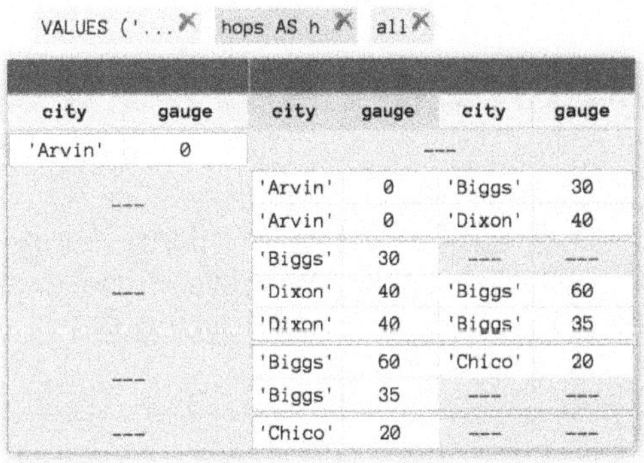

(b) Debugger display with observations ① and ②. Dashes (---) indicate non-evaluated expressions (in Figure 6).

Figure 21: Screenshots of the interactive browser-based (HTML5, JavaScript) frontend to Habitat.

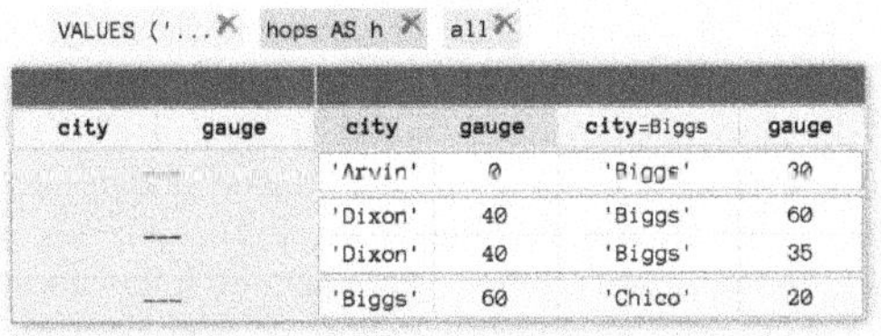

Figure 22: Debugger display with all non-Biggs rows filtered. Interesting rows ( ) remain in focus.

4. DEMONSTRATION SETUP

The on-site demo is based on a full-featured implementation of the new Habitat SQL debugger, talking to a PostgreSQL (version 9.3) backend. Habitat comes with a browser-based frontend that comprises a syntax-highlighting SQL editor as well as tabular displays that grow or shrink as debugging sessions progress. Markings can be placed and observation displays manipulated with minimal user interaction to encourage an exploratory (or playful) style of debugging: a single mouse drag suffices to place a marking and instantly update the display, for example. Figure 21 provides impressions of the debugger's new frontend. Not shown is Habitat's scenario archive which collects earlier debugging sessions.

Some markings may yield a potentially large number of rows. The debugger thus aims to help users to gain and retain focus during a session. *Column filters* may be used to hide all observations that fail to contain a given value. (Again, to promote rapid interaction, drop-down menus already provide the values in the column's active domain.) In addition, specific observations (*i.e.*, rows or groups of rows in a display) may be highlighted as *interesting*. Filters and highlights persist even if the debugger display changes dynamically—to implement this behavior, the frontend uses the observation contexts discussed in Section 3.

Figure 22 shows a snapshot of our first debugging session in which we have (1) identified the observation of `Chico` as interesting (*how did we get there?*) and, subsequently, (2) filtered all non-`Biggs` rows once we found that city was the last hop before we reached `Chico`.

Debugging scenarios. Based on audience interest and available time, we can offer a variety of scenarios that showcase the debugger and its implementation:

- *Quick demo:* uses a variant of the road network scenario in the present paper—simple queries and compact data set that still allow to explore interesting bugs.
- *Query understanding:* propose your own queries, then observe how (selected clauses of) these queries are evaluated—much like in a possible classroom use of Habitat.
- *SQL bug puzzle:* use Habitat to guide your hunt for particularly tricky bugs in SQL queries—based on canned queries held in Habitat's scenario archive.

The demonstration will be live: ad hoc SQL queries can be formulated and debugged at will. A log of instrumented queries along with their supporting functions $\mathtt{h}_i$ provides a peek under Habitat's hood.

Acknowledgments. Philipp Moers implemented the browser-based frontend for the new Habitat debugger.

5. REFERENCES

[1] ANSI/ISO. *Database Language SQL—Part 2: Foundation (SQL/Foundation).* IEC 9075.

[2] R. Ganski and H. Wong. Optimization of Nested SQL Queries Revisited. *SIGMOD Record*, 16(3), 1987.

[3] T. Grust, F. Kliebhan, J. Rittinger, and T. Schreiber. True Language-Level SQL Debugging. In *Proceedings of the 14th International Conference on Extending Database Technology (EDBT)*, Uppsala, Sweden, 2011.

[4] T. Grust and J. Rittinger. Observing SQL Queries in their Natural Habitat. *ACM TODS*, 38(1), 2013.

[5] W. Kim. On Optimizing an SQL-like Nested Query. *ACM TODS*, 7(3), 1982.

[6] Microsoft Corporation. *Transact-SQL (T-SQL) Debugger in Microsoft SQL Server 2008.* `http://msdn.microsoft.com/en-us/library/cc645997.aspx`.

[7] B. Pope and L. Naish. Practical Aspects of Declarative Debugging in Haskell 98. In *Proceedings of the 5th ACM SIGPLAN International Conference on Principles and Practice of Declarative Programming (PPDP)*, Uppsala, Sweden, 2003.

[8] *The PostgreSQL Relational Database System.* `postgresql.org`.

[9] E. Shapiro. *Algorithmic Program Debugging.* MIT Press, Cambridge, MA, USA, 1983.

Exploratory Keyword Search with Interactive Input

Zhifeng Bao [+] Yong Zeng [*] H.V. Jagadish [#] Tok Wang Ling [*]
[+]RMIT University, Australia [*]National University of Singapore [#]University of Michigan
zhifeng.bao@rmit.edu.au zengyong@nus.edu.sg jag@umich.edu lingtw@comp.nus.edu.sg

ABSTRACT

Due to the intrinsic ambiguity of keyword queries, users usually need to reformulate their queries multiple times to get the desired information. Even worse, users either have no way to precisely specify their search intention, or have limited domain knowledge on the data to precisely express their search intention. Moreover, they may just have a general interest to explore the data by keyword query. Therefore, our goal is to design an exploratory search paradigm that is able to bring humans more actively into the search process, in order to meet various user information needs, ranging from simple lookup to learning and understanding of the data.

Besides, keyword queries against data with structure, such as XML, can run into multiple difficulties: how to identify the search target; more types of ambiguity arise as a keyword can be part of the structure as well as content of data, etc. Effectively addressing these requires solutions to multiple challenges. While some have been addressed to some extent individually, there is no previous effort to develop a comprehensive system to meet these important user needs and meet all of these challenges.

Therefore, we propose a framework called ClearMap [1] that natively supports visualized exploratory search paradigm on XML data. In particular, we offer an interactive and visualized mechanism to present the outcome of the query, enable user to explore and manipulate the underlying data to either quickly find desired information or learn the relationship among data items, as well as provide interactive suggestions when their expected results do not exist in the data. A preliminary version of ClearMap and its source code are available for try at http://xmlclearmap.comp.nus.edu.sg.

1. INTRODUCTION

The primary interaction between users and databases starts from the traditional structured query, which assumes that users are to some extent familiar with the content and structure of the database and also have a clear understanding of their information needs. As databases get larger and accessible to a more diverse and less technically oriented audience, new forms of data exploration become increasingly more attractive [3]. Since keyword search paradigm frees users from the hindrance of learning query syntax and database schema, it is widely adopted as an entry to building the exploratory search engine.

SIGMOD'15, May 31–June 4, 2015, Melbourne, Victoria, Australia.

http://dx.doi.org/10.1145/2723372.2735361.

Regarding keyword search over databases, we also observed an evolution on the granularity of users' information needs when more and more (semi-)structured data become available for search. They are not merely content to simply retrieving the basic facts from database (like most users do in web search), but desire for advanced information needs, such as learning and understanding the results as well as the underlying data [6]. Such advanced needs are substantial in practice for at least two reasons: (1) Users do not have enough background knowledge on either the structure or the content of the underlying data; so a typical search cycle is actually a process of examining and comparing results and possibly reformulating queries until user's desired information needs are met [8]. (2) Users usually assume the thing they are looking for is out there, but users may be stuck if the desired information does not even exist in the database, regardless how they reformulate their queries.

Our goal is to design an exploratory search paradigm that is able to bring humans more actively into the search process, in order to meet various user information needs, ranging from simple lookup to learning and understanding of the data. Specifically, we aim to support human users' navigational browsing and exploration of semi-structured data, and ultimately they may not need to reformulate their query for resubmission many a time.

Doing so requires addressing challenges in multiple spheres, including index design, result retrieval and result visualization. So before we design our exploration model, it is worth having an overview of the challenges brought by keyword search over semi-structured data and the past endeavors made in addressing them. Compared to web search, search over semi-structured data brings extra challenges: (1) how to identify the search target of a user query (while in web search web page is the target); (2) more types of ambiguity may occur, because a keyword can be part of the structure as well as the content of data, and users may also have limited or wrong knowledge of the schema and value of the underlying database [7]; (3) semi-structured data is usually modeled as a tree or a graph, and the search result is a subtree or a subgraph, and two issues remain open problems: (a) how to present the results in a human-interpretable way and convey the relationship between data items [4]; (b) how to find subtrees (or subgraphs) of appropriate size, including relevant yet non-overwhelming information [2].

Over the years, we have made continuous efforts to address every individual challenge above. E.g. we tried to identify and rank the search targets and constraints to address the keyword ambiguity [2], proposed visualization methods to display results at different granularity [13], and provided suggestions (and explanations deriving such suggestions) to cater for the mismatch between user's information needs and the returned results [12]. But without interaction with user, these challenges cannot be addressed thoroughly [4]. Taking search target identification as an example, even though [2] tried to find the promising search targets for a single query, we may not be able to guarantee that the target found fits to each individual user's search context. More importantly, those individual works employ individual indexing and retrieval methods to work. Therefore, it is demanding to build a comprehensive search engine that meets the above challenges systematically, in terms of index design, result retrieval and result visualization.

To achieve our goal, we build a keyword search engine called ClearMap [1], which helps users get beyond finding to understanding and learning of the information resources in the database, and ClearMap is comprehensive in that it meets all of the above challenges. In particular, we make the following contributions.

- We define a center search concept, called Visualized Search Object (VSO), around which both structure and content of the database can be indexed and organized by search engine, and results in form of VSO can be manipulated by users.
- We utilize the inter-connectivity of the data in semi-structured databases to design a novel exploration model, to allow users to expand their manipulation from results to the whole database.
- We natively support the exploratory search paradigm with interaction and visualization enabled by making a seamless integration of VSO and our previous experiences [13, 2, 12].
- We design a multi-level index on VSO which can maximize the reuse of index information by different components, as well as providing support to visualization of huge subtree.

As a result, ClearMap has the following central characteristics:

- Interactive - It allows users to use the visual output as a visual interface for specifying additional operations on either the underlying data or the search results.
- Exploratory - For users who do not find their desired information by their initial query, they can explore the visualized data directly without reformulating their query; it also benefits users who simply want to explore what is inside the database.
- Context sensitive - It provides ways for users to specify or choose their context (i.e. search target and constraint) when creating the visual output that they desire.
- Diversified - It diversifies the results and groups the results of same structure, which can satisfy different users' search intentions.

In the rest of this paper, we firstly introduce VSO and then illustrate how users can operate on VSOs to explore the database, and how such exploratory search paradigm helps address each unique challenge of XML search as compared to web search (in Sec. 2). Then we present our system architecture to support different users' information needs in terms of index design and information retrieval methods (in Sec. 3). Lastly, we showcase how ClearMap helps address each of the aforementioned challenges (in Sec. 4).

2. ADDRESSING VARIOUS USER INFORMATION NEEDS

In this section, we present typical scenarios that represent different user information needs, and show how a combination of our interactive exploratory search paradigm with our previous work can help address each of them. In ClearMap, we focus on three critical yet commonly encountered scenarios: what users search for is available in the data, users have a general interest (but no specific knowledge) to explore and learn from the database by keyword query, and what users search for is unavailable in the data. These three scenarios are also a snapshot of the three facets of exploratory search: lookup, learning and understanding [9]. Accordingly, we will showcase our solution to each problem in Sec. 4.

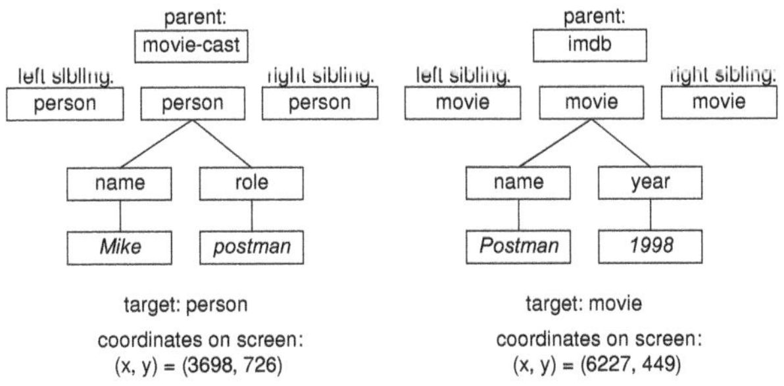

(a) VSO 1 (b) VSO 2

Figure 1: Two Sample Visualized Search Objects (VSOs)

2.1 Visualized Search Object

Before introducing various information needs and challenges, we present a central concept called Visualized Search Object (VSO), around which we organize, retrieve, visualize and manipulate the results of a keyword query, and further enable an interactive exploration of the database by exploiting the inter-connectivity of all query results in a database.

DEFINITION 1. *Given a keyword query Q, a matching VSO of Q is in form of a hierarchical tree, which includes*

- *an associated search target node st,*
- *a hierarchical subtree with structure context and the content of each node encapsulated,*
- *the index information of the siblings and parent of st in the XML data,*
- *the associated coordinates used for display on screen.*

Note that, the search target is essentially a node type T as later discussed in "*Search Target Identification*" of this section. A search target node st is a node of type T in the XML data, and the query result is a subtree rooted at the search target node st.

VSO forms a basic representation of the result, and possess the following properties:

- *Mergeable*: VSOs with the same search target and compatible structure [13] can be merged as one single VSO.
- *Diversified*: for any two VSOs with different structures but matching a certain keyword query, the differences are highlighted for easy distinction.
- *Navigational*: users can do a navigational browsing to another VSO which is a sibling, child or parent of the current VSO visited. As a result, users can navigate any part of the data due to the inter-connectivity of nodes in XML data.

EXAMPLE 1. *Fig. 1 shows two sample VSOs for the keyword query "postman" on IMDB dataset[1]. Fig. 1(a) and Fig. 1(b) correspond to two different search targets even though they both contain "postman"; such difference is used to diversify the search results.*

[1]IMDB is a database containing movies' information like title, rating, director, actor, actress, etc. http://www.imdb.com/interfaces

Note that they do not have the same target or compatible structure, so they cannot be merged in this case. The VSO in Fig. 1(a) corresponds to a subtree rooted at the search target which is a person *node. Besides the target, a VSO records the subtree as well as the index to its two sibling nodes and parent node. Such information supports the navigational property, where users can navigate from one VSO to another.*

Since all query results are interconnected in a tree structure [13], the structure context serves as a link among query results. More importantly, each VSO not only visualizes a particular result subtree, but also provides a mechanism for users to manipulate and interact with that result, to further explore all related information (in the database) connected with that result, and finally to find their desired information without reformulating the current query. This is achieved by maintaining for each VSO the index information of its siblings and parent, which we will discuss in 3.1.

2.2 Scenario 1: What Users Search For is Available in the Data

First, let us look at how traditional XML keyword search handles users' queries. XML data is usually modeled as a rooted tree. Existing works mainly focus on defining the matching semantics, i.e. what should be returned as results, and designing efficient retrieval methods for a particular matching semantic. A basic one is to find the subtree whose root node is the lowest common ancestor (LCA) of all query keywords, upon which various semantics such as Smallest LCA (SLCA) [5], Exclusive LCA (ELCA) [11] and object-oriented LCA [10] are proposed. We will present how our proposed interactive and exploratory search paradigm enhances the search in the following four aspects, while users do not need to reformulate their queries.

2.2.1 Search Target Identification

The first and foremost challenge in database keyword search is the identification of search target, while in web search it is simply the web document. Without figuring out the search target of a user query, the matching results associated with different search targets are messed up together, which badly annoys users in result consumption. Since XML data contains both structural and content information, queries usually contain various ambiguities [2]:

1. A keyword can appear both as an XML tag name and as a text value of some other nodes.
2. A keyword can appear as the text values of different types of XML nodes and carry different meanings.
3. A keyword can appear as an XML tag name in different contexts and carry different meanings.

The keyword ambiguity problem may lead to various interpretations of the search target and constraint. Therefore, we first distinguish the type of a node in XML data by its prefix path from root node, and the search target is referred as node type. Next, we propose guidelines to capture human intuitions in measuring the confidence of a certain node type T as the desired search target of a query Q. A desired target node should be related to every query keyword and contain enough relevant yet non-overwhelming information (details can be found in [2]). As a result, we provide a list of promising targets T for user to choose, after which we proceed to retrieve the result as a subtree rooted at T.

2.2.2 Result Diversification

The ambiguity may cause not only various search targets, but also various 'search constraints' (implicitly expressed in a keyword query). However, existing works do not distinguish such constraints in result retrieval or ranking stage. Again, much user time has to be spent on consuming results, especially when the desired results are ranked far behind. Therefore, instead of driving users to reformulate their queries, we can achieve better user experience by grouping the query results by different search constraints. Since results are of hierarchical structure, we classify and quantify different search constraints by capturing the confidence of a node n to be searched via (as a constraint) and the structural relationship of nodes, as illustrated in our earlier work [2]. Then the query results can be grouped, and users can see a high-level result group (in form of VSOs) before they choose to zoom in to see all results matching a certain search intention.

2.2.3 Result Visualization

We also find that existing search methods all return a list of independent subtrees as query results. However, all the data in an XML tree are *interconnected* by the hierarchical structure. Each query result thus is a part of the XML tree, and many of them may have sibling or containment relationship in the global context of the whole XML database. Without showing such relationship, the results alone could be misleading or less comprehensible. For example, suppose there is a subtree containing the information of a pencil, such a subtree may not contain all the important information of the pencil, like category, because category node could appear as a parent node of that subtree in the XML database. Simply showing subtrees as independent subtrees could be misleading, say a pencil in *make-up* category is very different from a pencil in *stationary* category. Therefore, how to visualize the query results for XML keyword search properly is a crucial part in enhancing the search experience. In particular, how to support zoom in/out for users to view results at various granularity of details and how to dynamically load the data in user's device window are two challenges.

In order to maximize the usefulness of visualization, we combine the VSO defined in this paper with our map-styled visualization of the XML data [13], in order to visualize the query results within the global context of the whole XML database. In such a manner, users can easily tell the difference and see the relationship among the query results. Furthermore, when visualizing all results of a query in the screen, we merge those visualized search objects (VSO) that are compatible (i.e. having the same search target and structure context), by utilizing the *mergeable* characteristic of VSO.

2.3 Scenario 2: Interactive Result Exploration & Data Navigation

Besides complementing the traditional lookup task in scenario 1, another important type of information need from user is to learn from the data or the result for a better understanding of the data they are playing with. Learning is an iterative process that requires a search-refine paradigm, but with exploratory search facility provided, users can get rid of such reformulating process.

In particular, there are at least two cases to consider.

Case (i): Users have a general interest but no specific knowledge on the data, and intend to explore and learn through keyword query. For instance, they may try to learn the schema or structure of the database from the results of their keyword query.

Case (ii): When users finish one round of search, it is also common that users may want to further explore more information of a particular query result. For example, users who finished searching for a particular laptop may also want to further search for the shops selling such a laptop or other items sold by this shop.

Unfortunately, such interactive exploration is more or less ignored by existing XML keyword search techniques, which usually handle one round of "lookup" search. If users need to further explore a particular query result in the previous round of search, they have to reformulate the original query and re-submit the new query (at least once). In contrast, recall Definition 1 the VSO stores the reference to its parent and siblings, which facilitates the exploration from one result to another (for case (i)); meanwhile, the inter-connectivity of the VSOs and the aforementioned result visualization module enable a natural navigation of the underlying data (for case (ii)). For instance, the information related to a particular result subtree appears right above it, connected by the hierarchical tree structure of the XML data, and a simple upward navigation operator serves the purpose.

2.4 Scenario 3: What Users Search For is Unavailable in The Data

In this scenario, a search engine may return an empty result or even worse, return erroneous mismatch results because what users search for is unavailable in the data. E.g., a list of mismatch results are returned when what users search for is unavailable [12]. We proposed to take user interaction to improve the user experience by providing the following three categories of information to guide users based on our earlier work [12].

(1) Notification. It is necessary to give a notification "what you search for is unavailable" to users. Otherwise, users have to wade through the mismatch results even to realize that what they search for is unavailable. Existing XML keyword search semantics are all based on LCA, which is trying to find the subtree whose root node is the lowest common ancestor of all query keywords. As long as all the query keywords appear in the XML data, it can always find some subtrees as results according to the LCA semantics. Even what users search for is unavailable in the XML data, some mismatch results will be returned. E.g., if users want to search for a particular laptop model *Vaio W* with red color by issuing a query "Vaio W red", and somehow red color is unavailable for that laptop model in the data. Mismatch results will be returned with "Vaio W" matches one laptop and "red" match another laptop. We proposed a detection approach in [12] by verifying the query results at schema level for detecting the mismatch results.

(2) Explanation. An explanation on which keyword(s) lead to empty result or mismatch result can greatly help users understand how the problem occurred. E.g., if a user wants to find a laptop model *Vaio W* with red color by issuing a query "Vaio W red", and somehow red color is unavailable for that model in the data, then it is natural to let the user know which keyword(s) lead the whole query to empty or mismatch result, say the keyword "red". We try to find such explanation by searching for approximate results in the XML data [12]. Then we can discover which keyword(s) is not satisfied in the approximate results and leads to the mismatch results.

(3) Suggestion. Another crucial part is suggested queries, which should be generated based on the availability of the data and should not lead to empty result or mismatch results. E.g., if red color is unavailable for a product, some suggested queries by replacing red color to some other available color will be a great help to users. Such suggestion can be found in the approximate results discovered in the previous step.

Following the above framework on how interactive input can help improve XML keyword search, we built ClearMap with source codes public for access at [1]. To the best of our knowledge, it is the first XML keyword search system which can fulfill all the above interaction mechanisms to improve the user experience and overcome the major challenges of keyword search over XML databases.

3. SYSTEM ARCHITECTURE

The architecture of ClearMap is shown in Fig. 2. The input of the system is a keyword query issued by users, and the output is a set of results in the form of Visualized Search Objects (VSOs), which provide users the visualized content as well as the structure context of the results (see Definition 1).

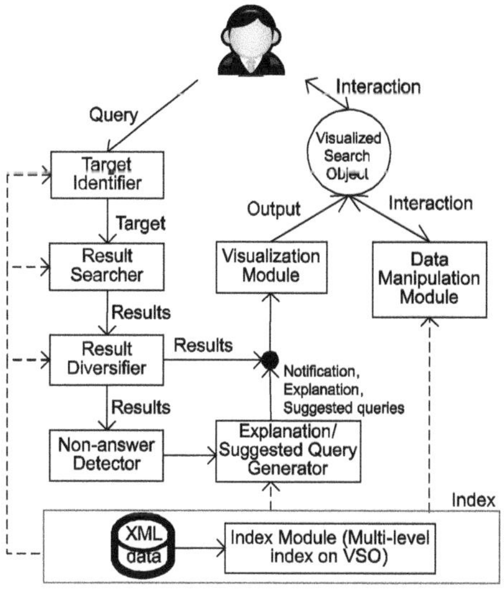

Figure 2: Architecture of ClearMap

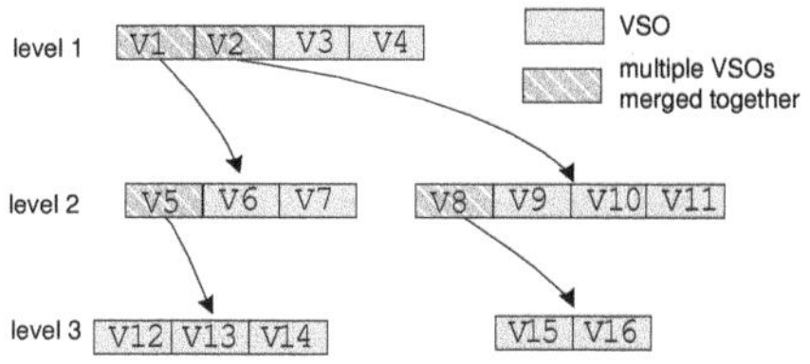

Figure 3: Multi-level VSO index

ClearMap comprises several components, each of which is in charge of a particular task in one of the three scenarios aforementioned. The workflow of ClearMap is as follows. First, user's query will be passed to *Target Identifier*, once the possible targets are identified, it interacts with the user to decide the search target that fits to his/her context. Then, it proceeds to *Result Searcher*, which will generate the query results (by any existing XML keyword search method) in the form of VSOs. Next, the query results will be passed to *Result Diversifier* which will cluster the results by different search constraints (at structure level). When results are returned to user, they will be fed to *Non-answer Detector* simultaneously to check whether any mismatch problem occurs. If so, it means there is no desired answer for users' query and it will inform the *Explanation/Suggested Query Generator* to generate notification, explanation as well as suggested queries. After that, both the suggestions and the results of the original query are passed to *Visualization Module*, which is in charge of (VSO) result presentation to users in a precise, interactive and user-friendly way. When users interact with the VSOs to either further explore the query results or navigate the databases, the interaction is captured and sent to *Exploration Module*, which will retrieve the necessary data dynamically from the data and index at server side.

3.1 Challenges in Index Building

Since ClearMap integrates many different solutions, each of which works on standalone indexes, it poses the first challenge, i.e. how to build a one-size-fits-all *Index Module* such that relevant information requested by different components of the system architecture can be efficiently retrieved. To tackle the fist challenge, we analyze each component and extract the common index information shared

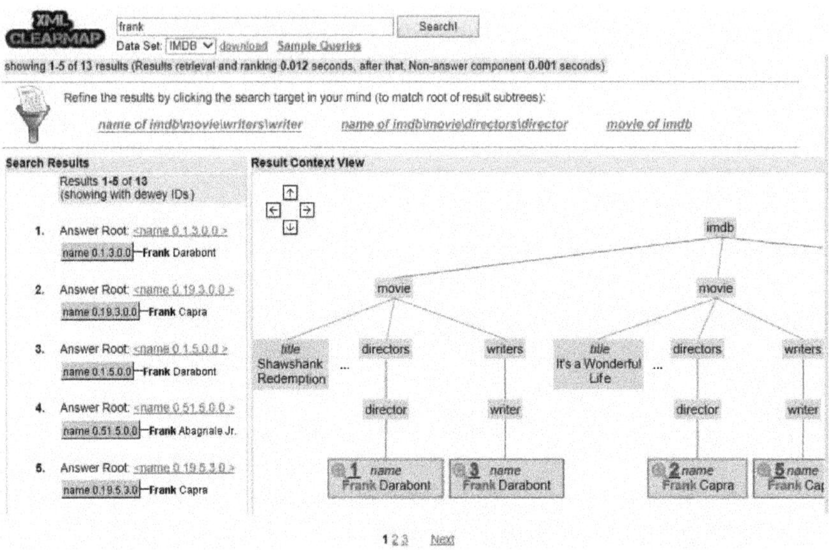

Figure 4: Interactive Exploratory Search Paradigm for Scenario 1, i.e. what users search for is *available*

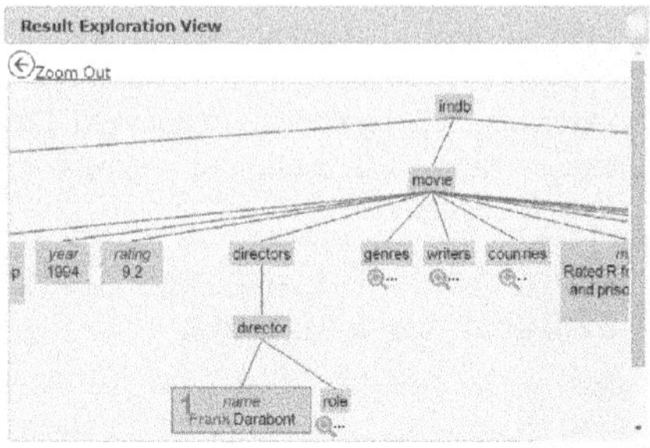

Figure 5: Interactive Exploratory Search Paradigm for Scenario 2, i.e. interactive result exploration and data navigation

by more than one component. As a result, the *Index Module* consists of three different indexes: inverted list index, statistics index and visualization index. To further improve the performance, we also build a buffer pool in the *Index Module* to buffer the retrieved information for subsequent reuse. E.g., given a query, *Target Identifier* and *Result Searcher* may both access the inverted list index for the same set of keywords. Therefore, we buffer the inverted lists retrieved by *Target Identifier* for later reuse by *Result Searcher.*

The second challenge is how to visualize a VSO when a VSO is a huge subtree. For instance, for a VSO corresponding to a movie subtree (in IMDB dataset), it may contain hundreds of VSOs corresponding to actor/actress information. Thus it is inappropriate to show such overwhelming information under this subtree to user. To properly visualize the movie VSO, we can merge all the actor/actress VSOs in order to hide those similar information, by exploiting the mergeable property of VSO. Merged VSOs will be expanded in an interactive way according to user's navigation operator (e.g. click-through to see details, drag down, up, left, right, etc.). In order to index the VSOs and the merged VSOs for efficient retrieval, we build a multi-level VSO index which is similar to an R-tree index. Fig. 3 shows a sample of the multi-level VSO index, where merged VSO $V1$ contains VSO $V6$, $V7$ and another merged VSO $V5$. When users navigate to expand a merged VSO, hidden information can be retrieved following the index from level to level. This idea originates from our previous work [13] in presenting the same results at different granularity, but differs with [13] in that all the output are organized, indexed and operated around VSOs instead of nodes of XML data tree.

4. DEMONSTRATION

It is challenging in itself to define what constitutes an exploratory search, and determine whether an exploratory search system is effective. In this section we will demonstrate how exploratory search with user's interactive input helps address the specific challenges raised in XML keyword search (illustrated in Sec. 2). Since users will undoubtedly be able to tell what works well for them, we very welcome the audience to try our demo and provide their evaluation and feedback (online or offline), for us to further improve the usability of our exploration search paradigm.

In particular, we demonstrate the interaction and visualization of ClearMap in three scenarios, as shown in Figures 4, 5 and 6. Currently two datasets are available, i.e. DBLP and IMDB.

Scenario 1: what users search for is available in the data
Fig. 4 is a screenshot of the system for a query "frank" issued over IMDB. Traditional methods will find some subtrees containing all query keywords as results. E.g., the left pane of Fig. 4 shows a list of direct results found by the XML search techniques adopted by *Result Searcher.* They are just some *name* nodes containing the keyword "frank". As we can see, simply displaying them is far from enough to meet users' information needs. On the right pane in Fig. 4, the query results are shown in the form of VSO. The relationship among the VSOs are clearly shown to users. This is critical because the query results are actually interconnected in the XML data. Without showing the relationship users could have difficulty in consuming the results. E.g., from the right pane users can know that result 1 and result 2 refer to the name of directors, while result 3 and result 5 refer to the name of writers. Besides, users can also tell that result 1 (director) and result 3 (writer) are actually working for the same movie. These information is critical for users to properly understand the query results.

Right under the search box at the top of Fig. 4, the *Target Identifier* helps identify the promising search targets for user to choose, to further refine the results. E.g. in Fig. 4 we find three promising search targets for query "frank", i.e. writer, director and movie. Since they have different targets, they are highlighted by rectangles with different colors. User can designate the desired one and the visualization will be updated to show only those results under the designated target, otherwise we will keep all promising targets in mind by default. Then *Result Diversifier* will analyze possible search constraints and cluster the results with same constraints in the left pane, highlighted in different colors. All in all, it comes to how to visualize the above targets, constraints, results and even the data itself (for exploration purpose) in an efficient and interactive way. Our visualization has two features: (1) Similar to any Geo-map, we generate several copies of the same XML data with different degrees of detail, allowing users to zoom in/out to check the result/data. Most XML data store many similar-structured data at the same hierarchical level, and keep growing along the horizon-

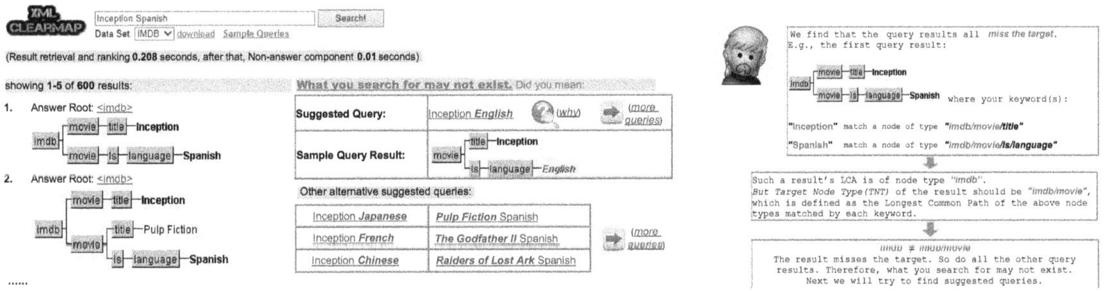

(a) Non-answer Notification, Explanation and Suggested Queries (b) Explanation after clicking "why" button

Figure 6: Interactive Exploratory Search Paradigm for Scenario 3, i.e. what users search for is *unavailable*

tal axis. E.g., right below the *imdb* node, the movie items keep growing, leading to a wide XML data tree. In order to provide proper granularity of detail, we propose to merge/expand compatible VSOs to hide/show different level of details, by utilizing the mergeable characteristic of VSO.

Scenario 2: Interactive Result Exploration & Data Navigation Users can explore a particular query result by clicking the result ID in the right pane of Fig. 4. An exploration window will be popped up, as shown in Fig. 5. Within the exploration window the whole XML data is available for exploration with that result at the center. The whole exploration process is formed by navigating (by dragging down, up, left and right) and zooming in/out (by clicking the suspension points to zoom in an area for hidden information). E.g., in Fig. 5, users can dragging the display to explore the structure information of result 1, i.e. director Frank Darabont. Users can easily get the structure information, like Frank is a director of a movie, what information is available for the movie, above the movie node is the imdb database root node, etc. Besides, hidden information is represented as suspension points in the display. Users can click the suspension points to zoom in to that subtree, like genres, writers and countries information of that movie. Such an operation will lead the system to load more VSOs dynamically from the server, supported by a R-tree liked index [13].

Besides, a dragging pad is provided for users to move left/right/up/down, to further explore the relationship between query results and XML data. In this way, users with different search intentions can easily adjust the query results to meet their needs without reformulating a new keyword query.

Scenario 3: what users search for is unavailable in the data Fig. 6 is a screenshot of the system for a query "Inception Spanish" issued over IMDB dataset. As we can see at the left pane of Fig. 6(a), for all results being returned, "Inception" matches movie title and "Spanish" matches movie language. The search target is very likely to be a movie. However, the movie *Inception* has no Spanish version in our dataset. All results being returned are mismatch results, i.e., the subtrees rooted at *imdb* node, because what users search for is unavailable in the data. To detect mismatch results for XML keyword search is not an easy task, we use the MisMatch solution in [12] for detecting mismatch results, generating notification, explanation and suggested queries. All these helpful information are shown to users, as shown at the right-hand side of Fig. 6(a). Here, one suggested query is "Inception English" that provides an English version of the same movie. Furthermore, users can click the "why" button to seek detailed explanations deriving the suggestions, as shown in Fig. 6(b). Users can also find more suggested queries by clicking the "more queries" button. All the suggested queries are derived from the XML data and guaranteed to have reasonable query results.

The main idea in [12] works as follows. We first infer users' possible search targets for a query Q based on its results R; then it will investigate each result r in R, to check whether it matches one possible search target. If none of them can match a possible target, we claim that Q has no available result in the data. Hereafter, to generate suggested queries, we propose a TF*IDF-inspired scoring measure to help find "important" keywords in the original query. Then based on each query result r, we try to find some "approximate" query results which contain these "important" query keywords and are structurally consistent with r, while having reasonable replacement for the "less-important" query keywords. Finally, the suggested queries can be inferred from the approximate results.

Acknowledgement. H.V. Jagadish is supported in part by NSF IIS-1250880 and IIS-1017296.

5. REFERENCES

[1] *XML ClearMap*. http://xclearmap.comp.nus.edu.sg.

[2] Z. Bao, T. W. Ling, B. Chen, and J. Lu. Effective XML keyword search with relevance oriented ranking. In *ICDE*, pages 517–528, 2009.

[3] G. Koutrika, L. V. S. Lakshmanan, M. Riedewald, and K. Stefanidis. Exploratory search in databases and the web. In *Workshops of the EDBT/ICDT*, pages 158–159, 2014.

[4] F. Li and H. V. Jagadish. Usability, databases, and HCI. *IEEE Data Eng. Bull.*, 35(3):37–45, 2012.

[5] Z. Liu and Y. Chen. Identifying meaningful return information for XML keyword search. In *SIGMOD*, pages 329–340, 2007.

[6] G. Marchionini. Exploratory search: From finding to understanding. *Commun. ACM*, 49(4):41–46, Apr. 2006.

[7] A. Nandi and H. V. Jagadish. Guided interaction: Rethinking the query-result paradigm. *PVLDB*, 4(12):1466–1469, 2011.

[8] A. Spink, B. J. Jansen, D. Wolfram, T. Saracevic, and T. Saracevic. From e-sex to e-commerce: Web search changes. *IEEE Computer*, pages 107–109, 2002.

[9] R. W. White and R. A. Roth. Exploratory search: Beyond the query-response paradigm. *Synthesis Lectures on Information Concepts, Retrieval, and Services*, 1(1):1–98, 2009.

[10] H. Wu and Z. Bao. Object-oriented XML keyword search. In *ER*, pages 402–410, 2011.

[11] Y. Xu and Y. Papakonstantinou. Efficient LCA based keyword search in XML data. In *EDBT*, pages 535–546, 2008.

[12] Y. Zeng, Z. Bao, T. W. Ling, H. V. Jagadish, and G. Li. Breaking out of the mismatch trap. In *ICDE*, pages 940–951, 2014.

[13] Y. Zeng, Z. Bao, T. W. Ling, and L. Li. Malex: a map-like exploration model on xml database. In *KEYS*, pages 32–38, 2012.

QE3D: Interactive Visualization and Exploration of Complex, Distributed Query Plans

Daniel Scheibli Christian Dinse Alexander Boehm
SAP SE, Walldorf, Germany
firstname.lastname@sap.com

ABSTRACT

QE3D is a novel query plan visualization tool that aims at providing an intuitive and holistic view of distributed query plans executed by the SAP HANA database management system. In this demonstration, we show how its interactive, three-dimensional plan representation helps to understand and quickly identify hotspots in complex, real-world scenarios.

Categories and Subject Descriptors

H.2.m [**Database Management**]: Miscellaneous

Keywords

SQL; SQL query analysis; parallel database; visualization

1. INTRODUCTION

The task of analyzing and tuning the performance of database queries is very common for any database management system. Consequentially, all major DBMS offer corresponding facilities that assist users and administrators in this process. Typically, the SQL-based textual `EXPLAIN PLAN` functionality is complemented by graphical tools that visualize the logical and/or physical query execution plans as an operator tree [4, 5, 6, 11]. These tools allow to reason about important aspects of the execution plan, such as the access paths and physical operators being used.

In the context of the SAP HANA in-memory database management system [2], we frequently face the limitations of these state-of-the-art tools, basically for two reasons:

First, business users (e.g. using SAP's business suite) have an increasing demand of running complex, analytical queries on their transactional data to get real-time insights without previous data extraction, transformation, or pre-aggregation [7]. As data is usually distributed across a large number of tables, the corresponding analytical queries quickly span dozens or even hundreds of tables [1, 10]. As a consequence, the query plans become very complex and easily include thousands of operators.

A second source of complexity is distribution: As the main memory capacity of a single host system is rather limited (with a capacity of a few terabytes only) compared to the size of most Business Warehouse (BW) installations [9], the HANA database management system is frequently deployed on a cluster of machines. In such a setup, individual tables are deployed to corresponding nodes, and large tables (e.g. the fact tables in BW) are horizontally partitioned over some or even all the available nodes.

Consequentially, the state-of-the-art tools suffer from the high number of tables and operators involved. Moreover, the support for the specific aspects of distributed query execution such as temporal interleaving of individual host activity, communication patterns, data volumes transferred and landscape-global parameters such as network utilization is usually very limited.

There are several attempts to improve on the state of the art, e.g. by combining multiple different analysis views such as plan graphs and (textual) profiler output into a single tool and allowing users to dynamically navigate query plans and switch between these perspectives. An example for this approach is the Stethoscope [3] tool. Interesting contributions were also made by the Vertica Query Analyzer team [13] who combined multiple different views (e.g. pie charts for cardinality estimates, Gantt charts for temporal operator interleaving) in the context of a single analysis tool, and added key performance indicators (such as intra-operator parallelism) to the tree-based operator view itself.

Even with this multitude of visualization options and improvements in place, the process of performance analysis for complex, distributed queries involves looking at various different diagram types in parallel, each of them focusing on a different aspect of the distributed query plan (e.g. network communication, physical operator interleaving, host utilization, temporal operator interleaving). Specifically, there is no holistic view to the entire query plan, that combines these aspects into a comprehensible visualization that enables the user to get an overview of the general structure and performance characteristics of a query.

2. QE3D

The goal of *Query Execution 3D* (*QE3D*) is to overcome the limitations of the state of the art of distributed query performance analysis tools outlined above. Specifically, it aims at providing the user with a high-level, intuitive understanding of key performance aspects of complex queries

SIGMOD'15, May 31–June 4, 2015, Melbourne, Victoria, Australia.

ACM 978-1-4503-2758-9/15/05 ...$15.00.
http://dx.doi.org/10.1145/2723372.2735364.

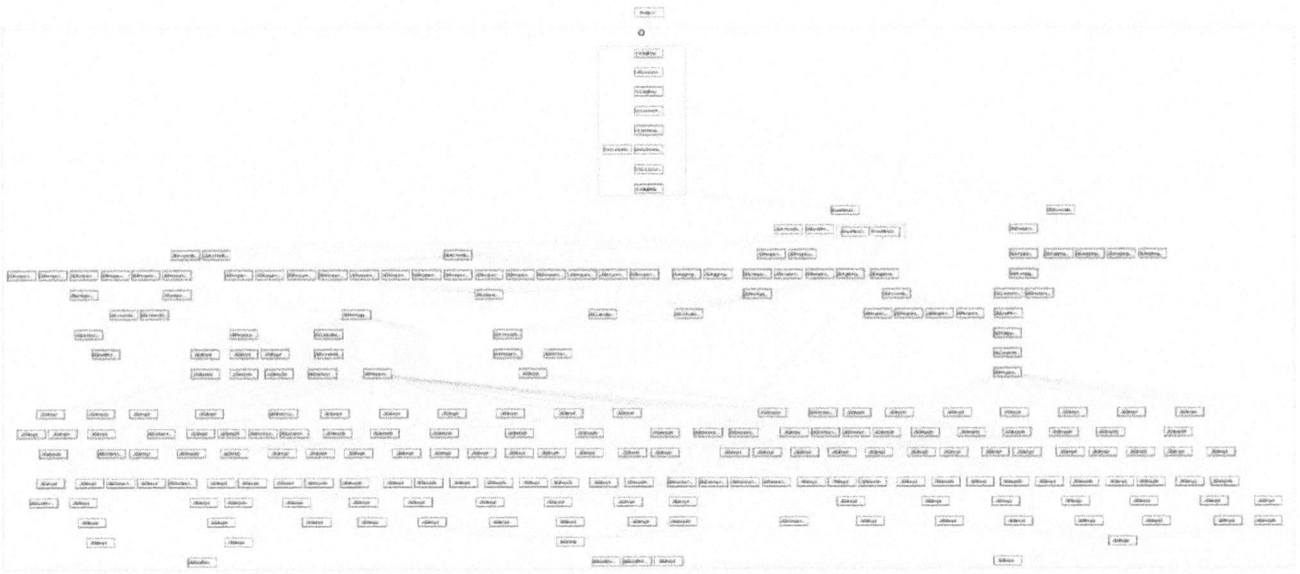

Figure 1: PlanViz visualizing a plan in graph view

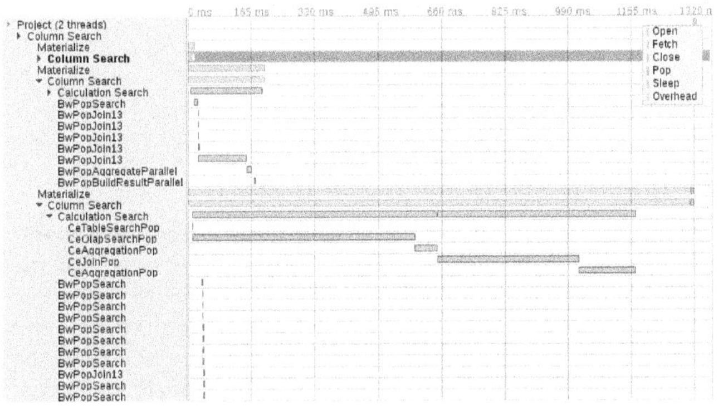

Figure 2: PlanViz visualizing a plan in timeline view

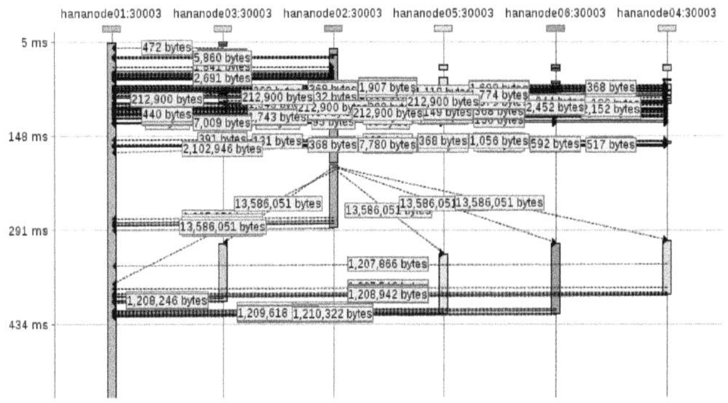

Figure 3: PlanViz visualizing the network traffic of a BW query running on 6 hosts

in order to identify specific starting points for a more detailed query analysis in the traditional tools.

QE3D is a Java application that is based on a stand-alone architecture. It is installed on a client machine and uses Processing [8] for implementing the interactive visualizations.

Users start by opening a XML encoded trace file that contains the collected details about the query execution. The data are parsed and the initial overview (see Figure 4) is shown. Now the user can navigate and explore the visualization using mouse and keyboard. Interactions include zooming, turning and rotating the visualization, accessing plan operator details or switching between different rendering alternatives.

Visualizing query plans, our central approach has been to come up with visualization approaches that *scale*. The graph like representations of plans (see Figure 1) are, as an example, very powerful in outlining data flows and the relation between operators. However displaying hundreds or even thousands of operators, as we see in complex queries, shows this approach to be less effective because graph structure and wealth of detail become overwhelming. By raising the level of abstraction and for instance visualizing the activity during query processing as a basic line plot, we gain a visualization that works equally well across the before mentioned range of operators.

QE3D is built on this principle. In the following we will discuss the different components and aspects that comprise the visualization as shown in Figure 4.

2.1 Visualizing Host Interaction

QE3D is designed for the interactive visualization of distributed query plans. We assume that there are a number of database nodes $N_1, \ldots, N_n$ that are spread across a number of hosts. During the execution of a distributed query, the database nodes interact with each other over the network in order to coordinate and to ship intermediate results. While there are typical communication patterns like the ones between the coordinating node and the other database nodes, it is possible that any node N_i is communicating with any other node N_j. In state-of-the-art tools, such as HANA's Plan Visualizer (PlanViz) [11], these communications are typically shown in Sequence Diagram like

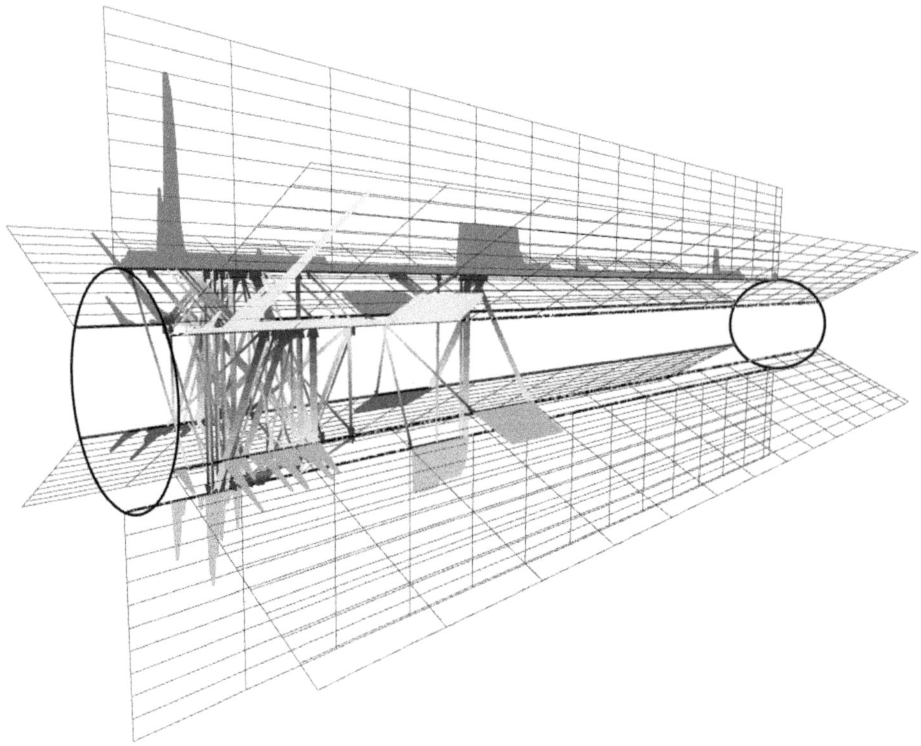

Figure 4: QE3D Visualizing a BW query running on 6 hosts

structures as shown in Figure 3. However this visualization is limited, because it is prone to overlapping information, e.g. when node N_1 transfers data to node N_3 and at the same time node N_2 is sending data to N_4. As a result transfers will intersect and otherwise recognized communication patterns might be missed.

To overcome this, we start with a *ring* on which all the involved database nodes are evenly placed in a circular manner. If there is an interaction between any two nodes, a connecting line segment is drawn between them. This visualization is known in the network monitoring domain, where tools like Etherman [12] provide similar representations. Unlike them, we know the time interval of interest, namely the total execution time of the query. As a result we extended the ring to a *cylinder* where the cylinder height represents time. We place the cylinder horizontally, such that the query starts on the left at time 0 and ends on the right hand side at time t_{total}. Now data transfers are drawn at the time when they take place. Here we provide three different modes of visualization. As an example, let us assume that node N_{source} is transferring data to N_{dest} and that the transfer starts at time t_{start} and ends at t_{end}. Let us further define that a point in the cylinder can be represented by the tuple (N, t).

- In the first mode, we draw an arrow from (N_{source}, t_{start}) to (N_{dest}, t_{start}).
- In the second mode, we draw an arrow from (N_{source}, t_{start}) to (N_{dest}, t_{end}).
- In the third mode, we draw a rectangular plane where (N_{source}, t_{start}) and (N_{dest}, t_{end}) define two opposing corners of the plane.

Given the duration of a transfer can typically be used as a proxy for the transferred data volume, we can use the third mode to easily spot where in the query large data transfers are taking place. The disadvantage however is that the planes might overlap and even hide each other. Therefore the second mode is a good compromise as it comes with less overlap, but still provides visual feedback on the duration of the data transfer. Here short duration transfers are near perpendicular to the time axis (similar to the first mode), while long duration transfers show a more acute angle.

To further improve readability, we indicate the direction of the transfer by adding a gradient to the line or rectangle. Furher, we ensure that the coordinating node, where the client connects and where the query starts and ends, is placed at the cylinders 12 o'clock position.

2.2 Visualizing Host Activity

In addition to visualizing the data traffic between database nodes, QE3D is also visualizing the activity on each node. This is done by providing a plot area per individual node and placing it next to the nodes location on the cylinder. In case of node N_i, the baseline of the plot area is defined by $(N_i, 0)$ and (N_i, t_{total}). Consequently the X axis of the plot area and the timeline of the cylinder are aligned. The Y axis of the plot area is facing outward and represents the KPI data.

Each of the plot areas only show activities for their respective database node. The default KPI shown is the number of active operators, which is defined as the number of operators that are running at a given time. Even though the number of active operators is a good initial indicator to understand host activity, the visualization is not limited to this. It is also possible to add one or multiple additional system level KPIs like the CPU utilization, memory consumption or similar.

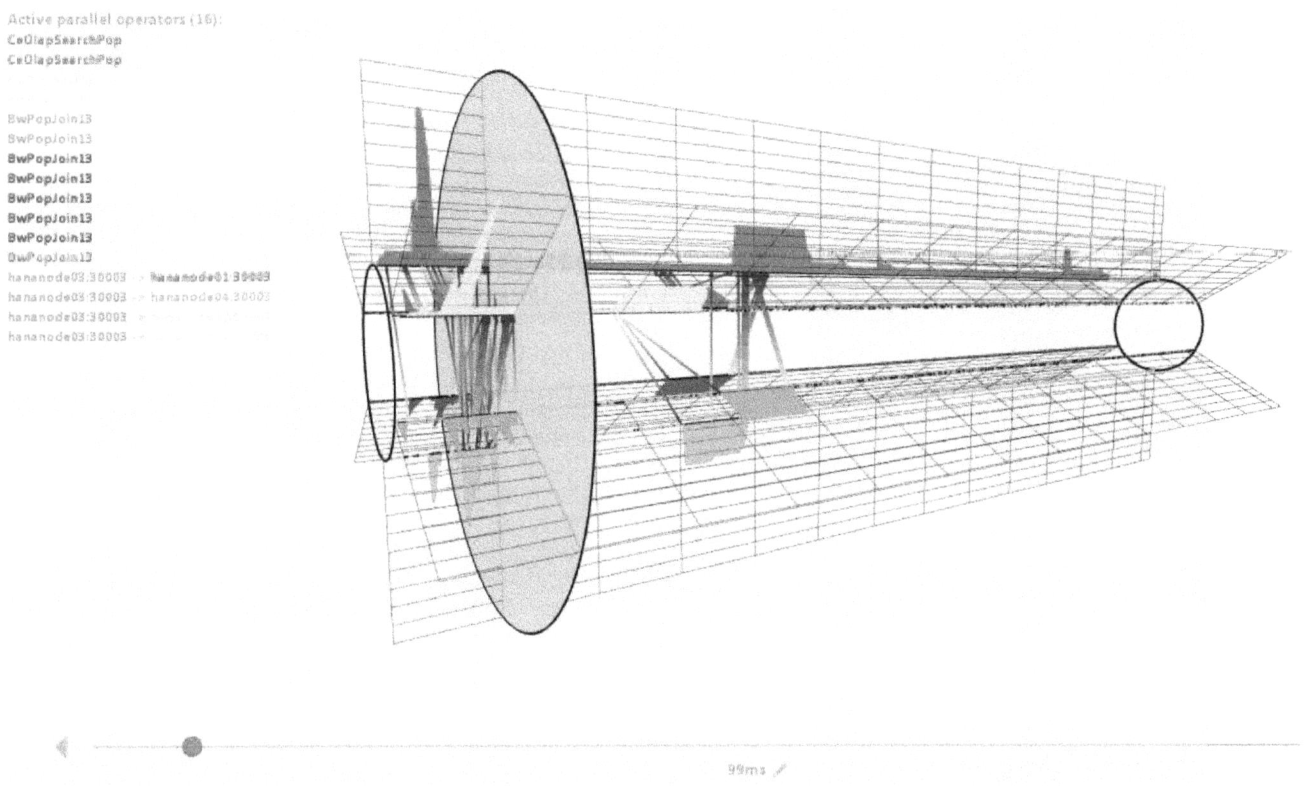

Figure 5: QE3D with selector

As an optimization, we segmented the query runtime into a configurable number of evenly spaced time intervals. For each time interval the KPI is calculated and the result is shown. Given the limits in screen resolution this is possible and it helps us to ensures similar frame rates for visualizing query plans of different complexities.

2.3 Detail Selection

Once an interesting aspect of the plan has been identified, it is important to learn more about that particular part. In some cases it is enough to further zoom into the plan, but at some point additional operator details are needed.

For this we introduced the *selector* which is shows as a disk that can be moved along the time axis (see Figure 5). Moving the selector is done by dragging a slider at the bottom of the screen. If dragging is done close to the slider at the bottom of the screen, the movement in time is fast. The further away the dragging is done, the slower the movement in time will be. With this interaction pattern it is possible to do effective millisecond level positioning inside a query that might run for minutes.

Once a specific point in time has been selected with the selector, the then active operators are listed with their names on the left hand side of the screen. To further improve the mapping of operators to database nodes, they share the same color with the nodes they are executed on.

Selecting a single operator is done by moving the mouse over it. This will open the operator details window shown in Figure 6 that contains information like start and stop times, resource consumption, payloads, the name of the processed database objects and other information.

3. DEMONSTRATION

Our demonstration is built on a number of complex, distributed database queries that we collected from both internal testing systems and production scenarios deployed by our customers running the HANA database management system. First, we quickly recap the state of the art of query analysis and visualization by showing the query structure in the existing visual explain facilities that HANA provides [11]. These include a tree-based plan graph (Figure 1) and Gantt-charts for temporal operator interleaving (Figure 2) and network communication (Figure 3). Already for a rather small cluster with only six active machines, the high complexity of the query plans make these visualization techniques impractical. As a result plan analysis is very tedious.

As a next step, we load the same query plans into the QE3D tool. We explain the various dimensions that are visualized by the tool (as discussed in Section 2 in detail) and show how the individual parts of complex plans (e.g. semi-join reduction and result assembly) translate into interaction patterns between the hosts that are part of the ring-based visualization. Next, we explain how both CPU and network bottlenecks can be easily identified using the various visualization modes of network communication, and the node-specific display of parallelism and workload characteristics.

Additionally, we demonstrate the replay functionality that animates the progression of the query plans in a given speed (with the original total execution time as default).

The last step of our demonstration is to introduce the selector feature discussed in Section 2.3. We show how it can be used to retrieve very fine-granular information from the

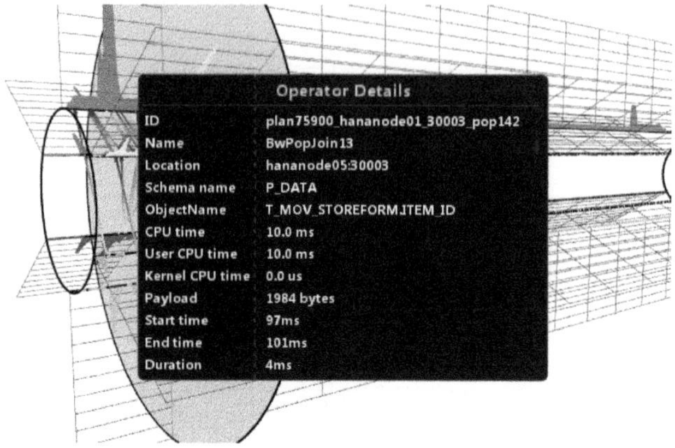

Figure 6: QE3D with selector and operator details overlay

complex query plans, such as operator-specific cardinality information or CPU consumption.

We conclude our demonstration by handing over the control of the notebooks running the tool to our audience: As Q3ED provides a very intuitive interface that allows mouse-based navigation, rotation and zooming within the plan visualization, the attendees can directly try the tool hands-on and use it for interactive analysis of complex query plans. Using this, to the best of our knowledge, never before shown visualization approach, we are hopeful, that attendees will be able to identify hotspots and bottlenecks in complex query plans, they have never seen before, in a matter of just a few seconds.

4. CONCLUSION

Our demonstration shows QE3D, a novel tool for the visualization and interactive exploration of complex, distributed query plans executed by the SAP HANA database management system. In contrast to state-of-the-art tools that are based on two-dimensional visualization such as operator trees and Gantt charts, QE3D provides a three-dimensional view of complex query plans in a distributed environment. QE3D allows users to get a quick and intuitive understanding of the query-specific aspects of distributed query execution (such as network communication, plan parallelism and operator interleaving) and to easily identify bottlenecks.

As the visualization and techniques demonstrated in this paper are not specific to SAP HANA, we are confident that similar techniques can also help to improve performance analysis and supportability for other database management systems that need to handle complex query workloads.

5. ACKNOWLEDGMENTS

We are grateful to our Business Warehouse and HANA Performance Analyzer colleagues for their input and feedback on the QE3D visualization.

6. REFERENCES

[1] N. Dieu, A. Dragusanu, F. Fabret, F. Llirbat, and E. Simon. 1,000 tables inside the from. *PVLDB*, 2(2):1450–1461, 2009.

[2] F. Färber, S. K. Cha, J. Primsch, C. Bornhövd, S. Sigg, and W. Lehner. SAP HANA database: data management for modern business applications. *SIGMOD Rec.*, 40(4):45–51, Jan. 2012.

[3] M. Gawade and M. L. Kersten. Stethoscope: A platform for interactive visual analysis of query execution plans. *PVLDB*, 5(12):1926–1929, 2012.

[4] IBM Corporation. DB2 Version 9 for Linux, UNIX, and Windows: Visual Explain overview. http://publib.boulder.ibm.com/infocenter/db2luw/v9/topic/com.ibm.db2.udb.admin.doc/doc/c0005135.htm. Retrieved November 16, 2014.

[5] Microsoft. Displaying Graphical Execution Plans (SQL Server Management Studio). http://msdn.microsoft.com/en-us/library/ms178071.aspx. Retrieved November 16, 2014.

[6] Oracle Corporation. MySQL Workbench Performance Tools: Visual Explain Plan. http://dev.mysql.com/doc/workbench/en//wb-performance-explain.html. Retrieved November 16, 2014.

[7] H. Plattner. A Common Database Approach for OLTP and OLAP Using an In-Memory Column Database. In *Proc. SIGMOD*, pages 1–2, 2009.

[8] C. Reas and B. Fry. *Processing: A Programming Handbook for Visual Designers and Artists.* The MIT Press, 2007.

[9] SAP SE. SAP EHP1 for SAP NetWeaver Business Warehouse 7.3, powered by SAP HANA. http://help.sap.com/nw731bwhana. Retrieved November 16, 2014.

[10] SAP SE. SAP Fiori for SAP Business Suite. http://help.sap.com/fiori. Retrieved November 16, 2014.

[11] SAP SE. SAP HANA Troubleshooting and Performance Analysis Guide: Analyzing SQL Execution with the Plan Visualizer. http://help.sap.com/hana/SAP_HANA_Troubleshooting_and_Performance_Analysis_Guide_en.pdf. Retrieved November 16, 2014.

[12] M. Schulze, G. Benko, and C. Farrell. Homebrew network monitoring: A prelude to network management. Technical report, Curtin University of Technology, Perth, West Australia, 1993.

[13] A. Simitsis, K. Wilkinson, J. Blais, and J. Walsh. VQA: vertica query analyzer. In C. E. Dyreson, F. Li, and M. T. Özsu, editors, *International Conference on Management of Data, SIGMOD 2014, Snowbird, UT, USA, June 22-27, 2014*, pages 701–704. ACM, 2014.

DataXFormer: An Interactive Data Transformation Tool

John Morcos[1] Ziawasch Abedjan[2] Ihab F. Ilyas[1]
Mourad Ouzzani[3] Paolo Papotti[3] Michael Stonebraker[2]
[1] University of Waterloo [2] MIT CSAIL [3] Qatar Computing Research Institute
{jmorcos,ilyas}@uwaterloo.ca {abedjan,stonebraker}@csail.mit.edu {mouzzani,ppapotti}@qf.org.qa

ABSTRACT

While syntactic transformations require the application of a formula on the input values, such as unit conversion or date format conversions, semantic transformations, such as *zip code to city*, require a look-up in some reference data. We recently presented **DataXFormer**, a system that leverages Web tables, Web forms, and expert sourcing to cover a wide range of transformations. In this demonstration, we present the user-interaction with **DataXFormer** and show scenarios on how it can be used to transform data and explore the effectiveness and efficiency of several approaches for transformation discovery, leveraging about 112 million tables and online sources.

Categories and Subject Descriptors

H.2.5 [**Database Management**]: Heterogeneous Databases

Keywords

data integration, data enrichment, data transformation, web tables, web forms, wrapper, deep web

1. INTRODUCTION

Several data analytics tasks require integrating various heterogeneous data sources, where the same or highly related information might be expressed in different forms. While there has been a considerable amount of research on schema matching and schema mapping, the related task of transforming the actual values from one representation to the target representation has been neglected. Examples of data transformation tasks include mapping stock symbols to company names, changing date format from `MM-DD to DD-MM` and replacing cities by their countries. While some transformations such as *liters to gallons* can be performed by applying a formula or a program on the input values, others, such as *company name to stock symbol* and *event to date*, require finding the mappings between the input and output values in a repository of reference data. We refer to the former type of transformations as "syntactic transformations" and to the latter as "semantic transformations".

Syntactic transformations are supported by many tools, including the popular MS-Excel, Google Spreadsheets and the more recent Wrangler [7]. However, to the best of our knowledge, no automatic system or tool is available that significantly covers the class of semantic transformations, Semantic transformations are prevalent in many real-world integration tasks, as witnessed in workloads of the data curation tool Tamr [9] and other data vendor companies.

When companies need to explore or aggregate their data, they create dynamic views that join multiple databases. Here, it is desirable to dynamically discover the desired transformations that allows them to join multiple sources on a unified attribute. Furthermore, useful mappings, such as *US Dollars to EUR*, *genome to coordinates*, *location to temperature*, change over time and requires users to look-up in a continuously updated repository, making previously acquired reference datasets obsolete.

The main reason of why semantic transformations have been neglected so far is that they cannot be computed by solely considering the input values and applying a formula or a string operation on them. Rather, the required transformations can often be found in a mapping table that is either explicitly available to the application (e.g., as a dimension table in a data warehouse) or hidden behind a transformation service or a Web form.

While collecting the adequate reference data for one specific transformation task is doable, it requires tedious crawling and curation exercises. This process cannot easily scale for a large number of transformation tasks covering the long tail of domains and topics. Usually, the subject matter expert in a company who is interested in converting its data does not have the skills to obtain the reference data or to code the transformation formula. Considering that the Web provides a large repository of resources, it is useful to have a service that can leverage these resources for on-demand transformation tasks.

At CIDR 2015, we presented **DataXFormer** [1], a system that leverages Web tables and Web forms to perform syntactic and semantic transformations. **DataXFormer** expects a transformation task specified as a variable-sized collection of examples, giving the entire input X and some examples of the desired output Y. The following are examples for the *airport code to city name* transformation: $\{(LHR, London), (ORD, Chicago), (CDG, Paris)\}$. In most cases, the user provides the column labels of the

SIGMOD'15, May 31–June 4, 2015, Melbourne, Victoria, Australia.

http://dx.doi.org/10.1145/2723372.2735366.

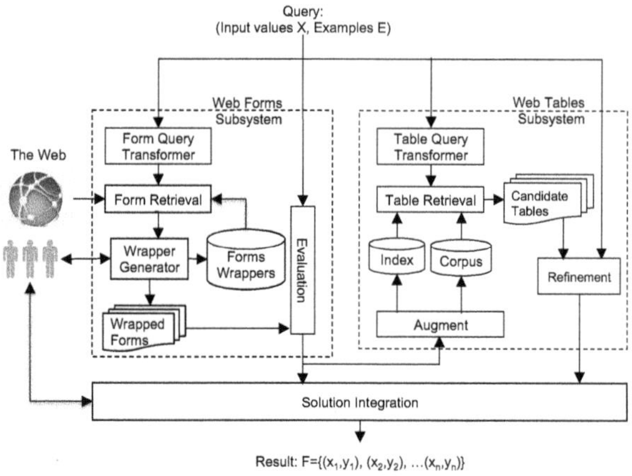

Figure 1: DataXFormer architecture

input and output values for the desired transformation, which we denote by I_X and I_Y, e.g., I_X = *airportcode* and I_Y = *city*.

In this demonstration, we show the various features of DataXFormer and how it finds transformation answers in Web tables and Web forms. We also show how DataXFormer interacts with the user to enrich its corpora, provide better answers and unlock previously unusable Web forms. In particular, we trace the intermediate steps of DataXFormer to find and wrap Web forms in an interactive manner. An initial version of DataXFormer is already available at http://dataxformer.org.

2. DataXFormer OVERVIEW

DataXFormer (see Figure 1) consists of two complementary transformation engines: one based on locally-stored static Web tables and another based on dynamically discovered Web forms. The user starts by submitting a query, such as the query that transforms airport codes to city names. DataXFormer converts the user query into the corresponding internal forms for each of the retrieval components, which in turn return candidate Web tables and Web forms.

DataXFormer dispatches the transformation query simultaneously to both transformation engines. While the two engines differ in their retrieval interface, response time and coverage, we are currently taking the straightforward approach of engaging both systems simultaneously. In a final step, the *solution integration* component presents the best effort results from both sources for a given query. Here, the user can intervene to choose among different transformation discovery approaches and results. We present and rank the results of each subsystem separately because of the significant difference in response time. Note that the Web forms subsystem has a higher response time than the local Web tables subsystem because it has to submit a request to a remote server to transform each value. Having an automatic mechanism for merging the results of both sources is a future effort, considering that they are good at different transformation tasks.

2.1 Web tables subsystem

The task of the tables subsystem is to identify all the tables that contain a minimum number of the user examples in one of their column projections. We refer to this minimum threshold as τ. Our experiments showed that $\tau = 2$ is a reasonable threshold for filtering irrelevant tables while maintaining very high recall [1].

A major challenge is to maintain the interactivity of the system through fast response times while being able to sift through 112 million tables in the corpus to find matches for the given examples. Thus, we maintain an inverted index that points to the columns and tables that contain the X or Y values. Since Web tables are heterogeneous and differ in schema and size and some even lack column labels, we store the tables within a universal main table (relation *Cells* as in Figure 2); every cell of a Web table is represented by a tuple that records the table, column and row IDs, along with the tokenized, stemmed form of its value (*tokenized*). Using this schema, we can simulate an inverted index by having an index on the *tokenized* column. The relation is ordered by *tableid*, *columnid*, *rowid*, simultaneously achieving two advantages: (i) every column from a web table is stored contiguously, and (ii) the space requirement of this schema is alleviated by compression, which is provided by most modern column-stores.

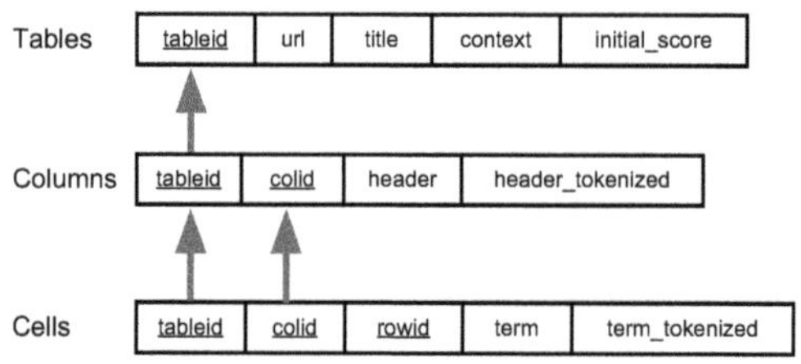

Figure 2: Schema for storing Web tables in a column-store

In the current prototype, we store the Web tables in a multi-node Vertica instance. Vertica employs projections on tables in place of an inverted index. A projection is a specialized materialized view that is efficient to maintain and load. We use a projection on *Cells* that is sorted on the tokenized values. Additionally, DataXFormer includes a similarity index to retrieve all existing similar representations of given X and Y values within a given edit distance threshold. Using a projection, the *table retrieval* component retrieves a set of relevant candidate tables for the given user query and verifies the coverage of the candidate tables with respect to the query examples. If the coverage is above the user-defined threshold, DataXFormer extracts the rest of the required transformation values.

We now proceed to describe the transformation discovery approaches that use DataXFormer's Web table repository.

Direct matching The fastest and simplest way to find the required transformation in the tables is to find tables that contain the required minimum number of given examples, as evidence for the two columns that encode the transformation. While the look-up operation is very fast, it is very sensitive to the choice of the initial examples. In Figure 3, we refer to the direct matching as *iteration 1* of the look-up operation, which matches Tables 1 and 2, with transformations for the airport codes *FRA*, *LAX*, and *BOS*.

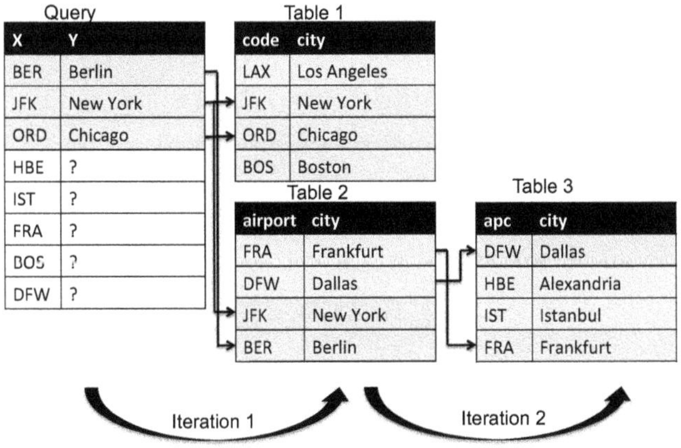

Figure 3: Iterations for transformation discovery for $\tau = 2$

Iterative matching The direct matching approach is fast and simple. However, the transformation entries may sometimes be fragmented over several tables (Figure 3). Most Web tables were designed for human consumption, and thus, large tables are usually fragmented over separate tables on different Web pages in a given Web site. Since the input examples are very few, only a small fraction of all the tables that encode the transformation might match the transformation query. In Figure 3, our query examples only match tables that focus on airports in the USA, and cannot find the transformation for *IST* and *HBE* in those tables.

To increase the recall, the iterative matching looks for indirect matches by using newly found results as examples for the next iteration. As illustrated in Figure 3, the new iteration uses the transformation results for *FRA* and *DFW* in Table 2 as new examples, which enables `DataXFormer` to reach Table 3 and find the transformations for *HBE* and *IST*. Iterative matching increases the recall at the cost of a longer execution time. There might also be a reduction in precision as non-evaluated transformation results are used as examples. We solve this issue in the reconciliation phase where different results are ranked based on their redundancy and the authoritativeness of their sources.

Fuzzy matching To further increase recall, the user might decide to relax the matching of values, accounting for typos and slight changes in representation. Our basic approach already tolerates some fuzziness by considering tokenization and stemming of transformation values. However, variations such as typos or abbreviations of a term cannot be captured by stemming and tokenization. For example, "Washington DC" and "Washington D.C." can only be matched by tolerating a certain degree of edit distance, since most tokenization techniques would assume that "DC" is a token by itself, while "D.C." consists of two tokens. We apply the popular Levenshtein similarity measure to capture some of these fuzzy matches. Fuzzy matching takes a step further towards increasing recall, at the expense of the execution time.

Reconciling different transformation results Our transformation results may stem from multiple different tables. Hence, for some X values, multiple Y may be retrieved. To reconcile these contradicting results, `DataXFormer` applies an expectation-maximization approach [5] that assigns scores to transformation results, which in turn affect the perceived authoritativeness of the tables providing them. Initially, the model takes into account the prevalence of the number of correct examples in a table. Furthermore, the model takes into account how authoritative a table is, based on its initial score. The initial score of a table changes based on user-feedback. Over time, we capture whether users accept or reject transformation results and use their evaluation to enhance or decrease initial scores of the corresponding tables. Also it is possible to manually add authoritative tables to the repository. More details on the reconciliation process of `DataXFormer` and how it converges can be found in our previous paper [1].

2.2 Web forms subsystem

A Web form allows user-interaction through different fields and buttons. The input values given by a user are either processed directly on the client side through `JavaScript` or are sent as an HTTP request (GET or POST) to a back-end server for further processing. Figure 4a illustrates a Web form for discovering location attributes of a given airport code. Putting *ORD* into the search field on Web page (a) retrieves the result Web page (b) that contains the corresponding city name *Chicago*.

As with Web tables, we assume a Web form is relevant if it covers at least τ of the example transformations. There are two main challenges in using Web forms: (1) as there is no common repository of Web forms, we have to look for them through crawling billions of Web pages; and (2) a new Web form appears as a black box. This means that an invocation strategy (i.e., wrapper) has to be developed to use the form for producing the desired transformations. It has been shown [4] that both tasks are very hard, even with human intervention. `DataXFormer` tackles both challenges using search engines and a Web browser simulator that allows to analyze the HTML code of a Web form. Additionally, the user is involved whenever any of the tasks fail.

Web form retrieval `DataXFormer` maintains a local repository of previously used Web forms. The repository is organized as a document store where each document represents one wrapper. Using the document store is suitable for this task because we also store and index the textual content of Websites that contain the specific Web form. If `DataXFormer` fails to find a relevant form in the repository, it uses a search engine to find forms online. In our preliminary experimental results [1], we noticed that the keyword query "I_X `to` I_Y" has a high success rate for finding a page containing a transformation form in its top results. By examining the search engine results, `DataXFormer` identifies candidate forms. Then, for each candidate form, we generate a "wrapper" to be able to query the form and to obtain the transformation values. In case `DataXFormer` fails to generate a wrapper or to find a relevant Web form, the user is asked for help. The wrapped forms are invoked using the input examples and are evaluated based on their coverage in the *evaluation* step. Candidate Web forms are then queried using the examples from the user query.

Wrapping Web forms To wrap Web forms, we have to simulate a Web browser and probe the forms using the given examples to identify the relevant input field to fill in the X values, the output field that contains the desired transformation result Y, and the request method for invoking the

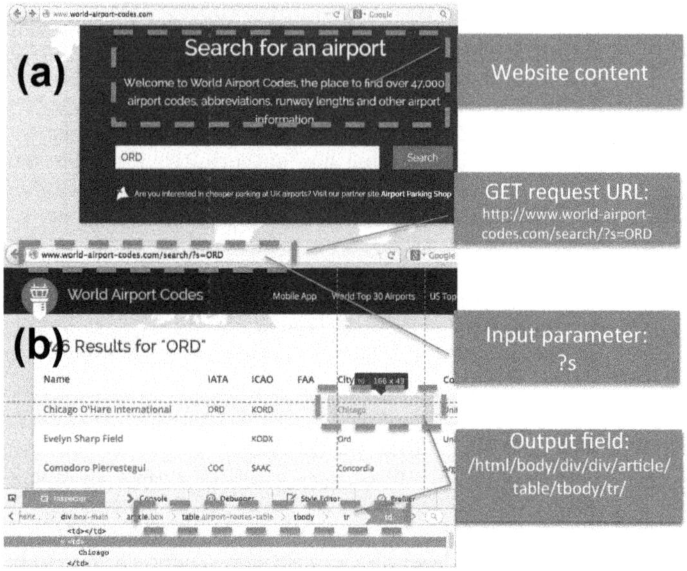

(a) Web form components that need to be stored

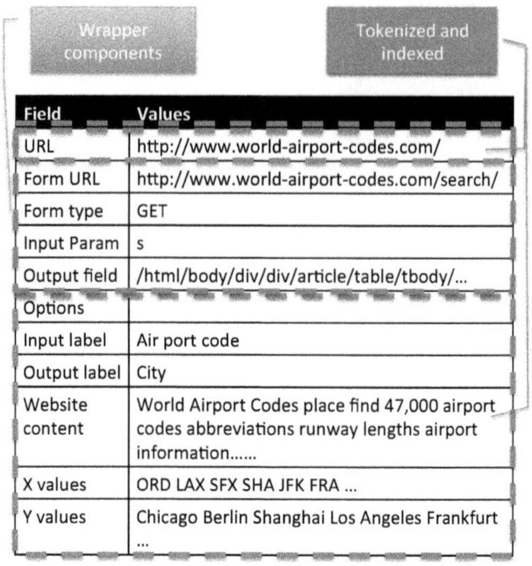

Field	Values
URL	http://www.world-airport-codes.com/
Form URL	http://www.world-airport-codes.com/search/
Form type	GET
Input Param	s
Output field	/html/body/div/div/article/table/tbody/...
Options	
Input label	Air port code
Output label	City
Website content	World Airport Codes place find 47,000 airport codes abbreviations runway lengths airport information......
X values	ORD LAX SFX SHA JFK FRA ...
Y values	Chicago Berlin Shanghai Los Angeles Frankfurt ...

(b) Web form wrapper as a document in the repository

Figure 4: Web form wrapper components

form. Current wrapper generation approaches [4, 8] invoke the form using all possible combinations of input fields, select fields, and radio buttons, and use the results to identify the semantics of the various components of the form. In the current prototype, we apply some heuristics to reduce the number of combinations; for example, we only consider text and text area fields as input fields for our X values, and we choose radio button options that resemble our attribute labels or denote the transformation direction. In Figure 4a, we highlight the visible relevant components such as the Website content, the GET request URL, the input parameter s, and the XPath for the output value.

Once the XPath to our given example is discovered on the output result page, `DataXFormer` invokes the wrapped form using the remaining input examples and evaluates its coverage in the *evaluation* step. If the user is satisfied with the Web form results, she can trigger the *Augment* component to store the Web form results as a new table in the table repository. Finally, `DataXFormer` stores all components of a successfully wrapped Web form as illustrated in Figure 4b.

Some of the stored fields (framed red in Figure 4b) contain meta-data that is indexed to effectively retrieve the wrapper for a given transformation query. For example, *Website content* and example X values are tokenized and indexed. Other fields that are framed in blue in Figure 4b store the configuration parameters of the wrapper, such as the *Form URL* and *Input Param*.

2.3 Datasets and Implementation Setup

`DataXFormer` uses a Vertica column-store to store the Web tables and a Lucene index that indexes successfully wrapped Web forms. Initially, the Web tables corpus was filled with the Dresden Web Table Corpus [1], a collection of about 112 million data tables extracted from the Common Crawl [2]. We further cleaned the dataset by removing cells that contained comments or other long text content which does not serve our purpose. The disk usage of the Vertica storage comprises about 350 GB on 4 nodes.

The Web forms are stored as documents, where each document contains the URI of a Web form and all its relevant fields, to allow reconstructing the generated wrapper of the Web form. Furthermore, we store some meta-data, such as the textual content of the Website that provides the Web form, as well as a limited set of previously performed example transformations. Some of the wrappers refer to the same Web form with a different configuration, e.g., both directions for *km to/from miles*.

3. DEMONSTRATION

An initial version of `DataXFormer`, which is already at `http://dataxformer.org`, answers transformation queries through direct and iterative matching on Web tables and through indexed Web forms.

The demonstration's audience can come up with its own transformation queries for `DataXFormer`. For example a user might be interested in discovering transformations of her favourite *athlete to associated club*. Additionally, we will provide and describe some prepared transformation queries from our previous benchmark [1], such as *airport code to city*, *company ticker to company name*, and *EUR to USD*.

3.1 Using DataXFormer

A user can submit a query either by uploading a CSV file containing the two columns X and Y or by filling in the examples through a simple table form (see Figure 5).

Then, the user can start the transformation engine, which will initiate the selected transformation discovery algorithm (direct, indirect, or fuzzy matching) over the Web tables and the Web form retrieval. `DataXFormer` dispatches both subsystems in parallel. Figure 6 presents the retrieved indirect match results for the query. The selected values in the

[1] `https://wwwdb.inf.tu-dresden.de/misc/dwtc/`
[2] `http://commoncrawl.org/`

Figure 5: Our transformation query aims at transforming airport code to the city location. Here, we provided the corresponding cities for three of the airport codes.

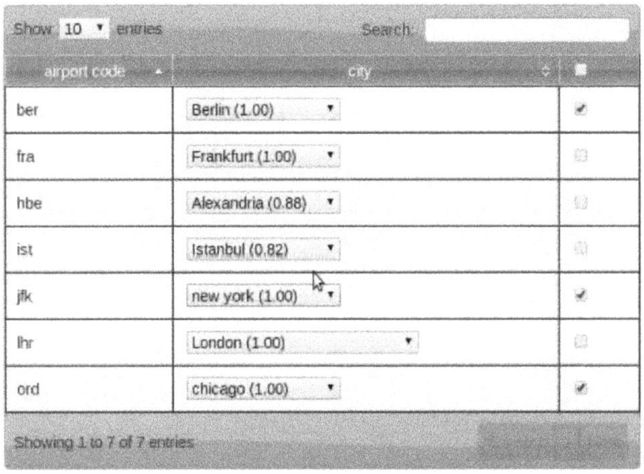

Figure 6: Tranformation results of the iterative matching approach

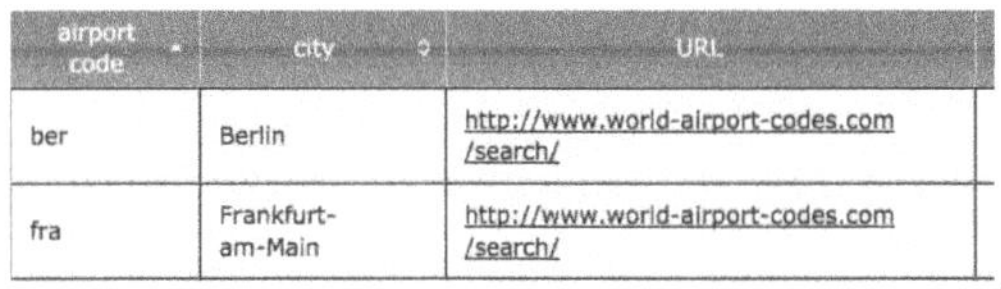

Figure 7: `DataXFormer` found a Webform that can find the desired cities.

city column are the transformation results with the highest scores, which are displayed in brackets. At the same time, `DataXFormer` also presents the results that were produced by a Web form (Figure 7).

If the user is not satisfied with the results, she might use the drop down boxes to choose from alternative transformations, if available (see Figure 8). Note that the results are ranked according to their confidence score assigned by `DataXFormer`'s expectation-maximization approach [1]. Upon choosing an option, pop-up widgets provide further background information, such as the number of tables that agreed on this specific transformation. Furthermore, the user can display the actual content of a table to understand the provenance of a transformation result (see Figure 9).

Alternatively, the user can resend the transformation query with a subset of successfully performed transformations. Depending on the initial matching algorithm, the user can also choose to enhance the transformation results by changing the matching algorithm on the Web tables.

If the user is satisfied, she can save the complete result set or a subset of the results by checking the corresponding check boxes and add it to the corpus. A table that is stored by a user has a higher initial score. We will demonstrate the evolution of the corpus by resubmitting the initial query and showing that the results and scores have been changed.

3.2 Tracing Web form discovery and user-based wrapper induction

Our demonstration also includes a walkthrough of the Web form subsystem by showing the intermediate steps and results. We will show how `DataXFormer` leverages the search engine, and which aspects of a Website matter for the automatic wrapper induction. Furthermore, we show a scenario where the user can intervene in the wrapper induction without having any background in Web programming. `DataXFormer` analyzes a given website, extracts its HTML elements, and simulates its Web forms within `DataXFormer`'s own framework. In Figure 10 `DataXFormer` identifies two Web forms on `http://world-airport-codes.com`, and renders an interactive wrapper induction interface. Note, that `DataXFormer` identifies human-readable descriptions. Pop-ups will show the corresponding original HTML code. The user can then continue to configure the selected form, by choosing the correct input field and form options. `DataXFormer` captures the user's interaction with the simulated form and uses the selected parameters to wrap the original Web form for the transformation task.

4. RELATED WORK

The closest tool to `DataXFormer` is Google Spreadsheets [3]. The autofill feature uses machine learning to predict the transformation values of a column given a few examples. In contrast, `DataXFormer` does not try to explicitly define the transformation, but rather finds the necessary look-up tables in a corpus of Web tables and Web forms. Since Google Spreasheets tries to interpolate the transformation solely from the input, it cannot provide semantic transformations, such as *"airport code to city"*, while `DataXFormer` can since it uses external knowledge.

InfoGather [10] uses Web tables for attribute discovery and entity augmentation. While the two approaches are quite similar, InfoGather relies on pre-computing the full semantic-match graph for the whole corpus, while `DataXFormer`

[3] `http://spreadsheets.google.com`

Figure 8: The user can choose between different transformation results, which are ranked according to their confidence score

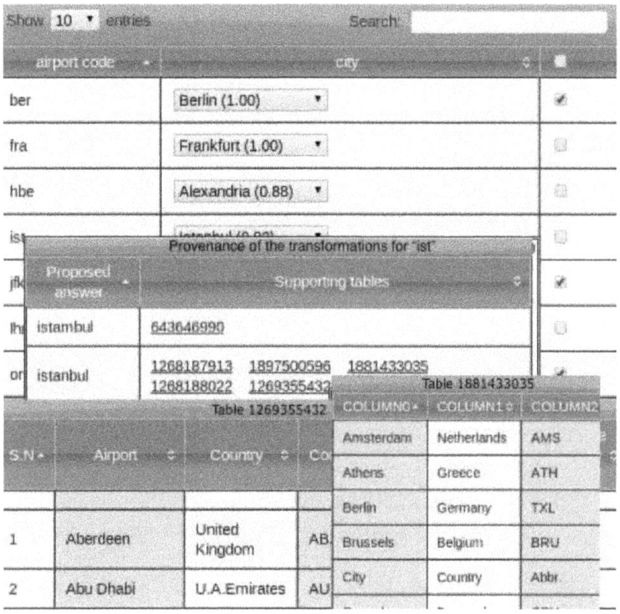

Figure 9: **DataXFormer** shows the provenance of a transformation result. Note that some tables do not have column headers.

Former finds the required tables on the fly, and leverages Web forms as well.

Wrangler [7] provides an easy interface to specify scripts of data transformation. It supports the concept of semantic roles as well, providing additional functions to be included in the scripts. **DataXFormer** requires minimal user interaction, as it locates Web tables and forms automatically. Similarly to Google Spreadsheets, Wrangler cannot provide transformations that rely on external knowledge.

Many proposed systems focus on answering keyword queries over relational tables by efficiently generating candidate networks of joined tuples to form answers, with search terms from the query spanning multiple records across multiple tables [2,3,6]. **DataXFormer** differs from these systems in that it tries to find tables that provide a transformation given a few examples for the transformation, rather than building candidate tuple networks.

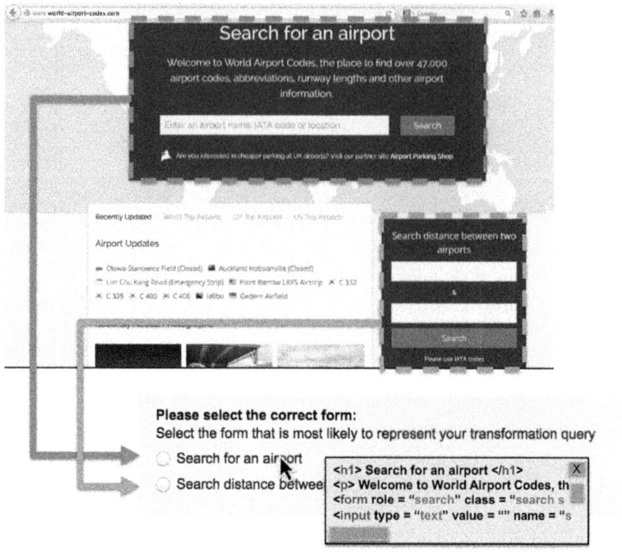

Figure 10: **DataXFormer** identifies the forms on a web page and presents them as radio options.

5. REFERENCES

[1] Z. Abedjan, J. Morcos, M. Gubanov, I. Ilyas, M. Stonebraker, P. Papotti, and M. Ouzzani. Dataxformer: Leveraging the web for semantic data transformations. In *CIDR*, 2015.

[2] B. Aditya, G. Bhalotia, S. Chakrabarti, A. Hulgeri, C. Nakhe, P. Parag, and S. Sudarshan. Banks: Browsing and keyword searching in relational databases. In *VLDB*, pages 1083–1086, 2002.

[3] S. Agrawal, S. Chaudhuri, and G. Das. Dbxplorer: A system for keyword-based search over relational databases. In *ICDE*, pages 5–16, 2002.

[4] L. Barbosa and J. Freire. An adaptive crawler for locating hidden-web entry points. In *WWW*, pages 441–450, New York, NY, USA, 2007.

[5] A. P. Dawid and A. M. Skene. Maximum likelihood estimation of observer error-rates using the em algorithm. *Applied statistics*, pages 20–28, 1979.

[6] V. Hristidis and Y. Papakonstantinou. Discover: Keyword search in relational databases. In *VLDB*, pages 670–681, 2002.

[7] S. Kandel, A. Paepcke, J. Hellerstein, and J. Heer. Wrangler: Interactive visual specification of data transformation scripts. In *CHI*, pages 3363–3372, New York, NY, USA, 2011.

[8] J. Madhavan, D. Ko, L. Kot, V. Ganapathy, A. Rasmussen, and A. Halevy. Google's deep web crawl. *PVLDB*, 1(2):1241–1252, Aug. 2008.

[9] M. Stonebraker, D. Bruckner, I. F. Ilyas, G. Beskales, M. Cherniack, S. B. Zdonik, A. Pagan, and S. Xu. Data curation at scale: The data tamer system. In *CIDR*, 2013.

[10] M. Yakout, K. Ganjam, K. Chakrabarti, and S. Chaudhuri. Infogather: Entity augmentation and attribute discovery by holistic matching with web tables. In *SIGMOD*, pages 97–108, New York, NY, USA, 2012.

Quality-Driven Continuous Query Execution over Out-of-Order Data Streams

Yuanzhen Ji[1], Hongjin Zhou[1], Zbigniew Jerzak[1], Anisoara Nica[2], Gregor Hackenbroich[1], Christof Fetzer[3]
[1]SAP SE, Germany [2]SAP SE, Canada
[3]Systems Engineering Group, Technische Universität Dresden, Germany
[1,2]firstname.lastname@sap.com [3]christof.fetzer@tu-dresden.de

ABSTRACT

Executing continuous queries over out-of-order data streams, where tuples are not ordered according to timestamps, is challenging; because high result accuracy and low result latency are two conflicting performance metrics. Although many applications allow trading exact query results for lower latency, they still expect the produced results to meet a certain quality requirement. However, none of existing disorder handling approaches have considered minimizing the result latency while meeting user-specified requirements on the quality of query results.

In this demonstration, we showcase *AQ-K-slack*, an adaptive, buffer-based disorder handling approach, which supports executing sliding window aggregate queries over out-of-order data streams in a quality-driven manner. By adapting techniques from the field of sampling-based approximate query processing and control theory, *AQ-K-slack* dynamically adjusts the input buffer size at query runtime to minimize the result latency, while respecting a user-specified threshold on relative errors in produced query results.

We demonstrate a prototype stream processing system, which extends SAP Event Stream Processor with the implementation of *AQ-K-slack*. Through an interactive interface, the audience will learn the effect of different factors, such as the aggregate function, the window specification, the result error threshold, and stream properties, on the latency and the accuracy of query results. Moreover, they can experience the effectiveness of *AQ-K-slack* in obtaining user-desired latency vs. result accuracy trade-offs, compared to naive disorder handling approaches that make extreme trade-offs. For instance, by scarifying 1% result accuracy, our system can reduce the result latency by 80% when compared to the state of the art.

Categories and Subject Descriptors

H.2.4 [**Database Management**]: Systems

Keywords

Out-of-order data streams; Disorder handling; Data stream processing; Continuous queries;

SIGMOD'15, May 31–June 4, 2015, Melbourne, Victoria, Australia.

ACM 978-1-4503-2758-9/15/05 ...$15.00.
http://dx.doi.org/10.1145/2723372.2735371.

1. INTRODUCTION

Data streams in the form of potentially unbounded sequences of tuples arise naturally in many domains, such as sensor networks [21], network monitoring [9], and financial markets [7]. Analyzing data streams involves *continuous queries*. A continuous query is issued once and returns results to users continuously as new tuples arrive. The *sliding window aggregate* query is at the heart of many continuous analytics applications. A sliding window aggregate query continuously constructs time-based or count-based windows over a data stream, and evaluates a certain aggregate function (e.g., SUM, AVG, QUANTILE) on each window.

Stream tuples are normally tagged with timestamps as they are generated. Timestamps naturally define a temporal order among all tuples within a stream. A stream where tuples are not ordered according to their timestamps are referred to as an *out-of-order stream*. Out-of-order streams occur in many distributed data computing scenarios because of the inherent network asynchrony. For instance, in a sensor network, tuples sent from different sensors to a "sink" node may experience various delays, and therefore, the stream observed by the sink node is out of order. Another typical cause of stream disorder is MapReduce-style data-parallel processing, where data are partitioned and processed by several parallel instances of a query operator. Results from parallel operator instances may arrive out of order at the merger because of different processing speeds of instances [11]. Even individual query operators, such as join [25] and union, may produce out-of-order data streams.

Dealing with disorder within data streams is one of the basic requirements for stream processing systems [24]. However, executing sliding window queries over out-of-order data streams is challenging; because out-of-order tuple arrival makes it difficult to determine the content of a window, and can lead to inaccurate query results or high result latency. Indeed, there is an inevitable trade-off between the result latency and the result accuracy in out-of-order stream processing, which we illustrate with the example in Figure 1.

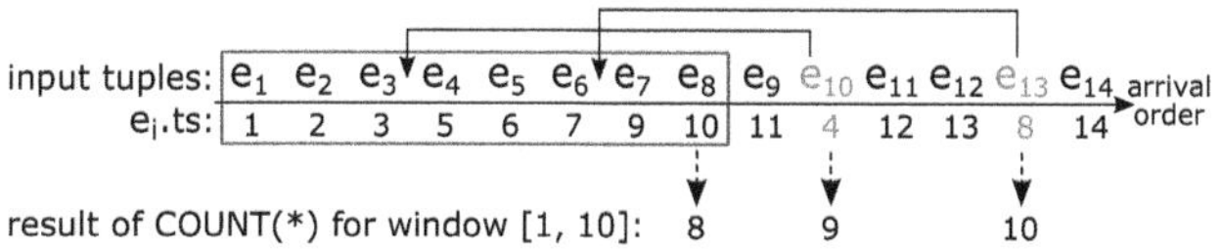

Figure 1: Trade-off between the latency and the accuracy of query results in out-of-order stream processing.

We denote a stream tuple by e_i, where i represents the arrival order of the tuple. We refer to the timestamp of a tuple e by $e.ts$. The tuples e_{10} and e_{13} in this example, whose timestamps are 4 and 8 respectively, are two *late arrivals*; because for each of them, tuples with larger timestamps have arrived earlier. Assume that a sliding window COUNT(*) query is executed over this stream and the window size is ten time units. Consider the window ranged from timestamp one to ten. The lowest result latency can be obtained if we return the COUNT(*) result for this window immediately when the window is closed at the arrival of e_8 ($e_8.ts = 10$). However, the returned result is inaccurate since the tuples e_{10} and e_{13} also fall into the window scope $[1, 10]$ but are not counted. We can obtain a more accurate result if we delay the return of the result until the arrival of e_{10}. To obtain the exact query result, we must further delay the return of the result until the arrival of e_{13}.

Many stream processing applications, e.g., network traffic monitoring and environment monitoring, do not demand exact query results. These applications accept trading result accuracy for lower latency to support timely data analytics. However, significantly inaccurate results may cause severe consequences if further actions are based on these results. Hence, low quality results are unacceptable either.

Various disorder handling approaches have been proposed: using buffers to reorder [1, 3, 19], using punctuations to explicitly indicate that no more late arrivals to a window are expected [12, 15–17, 23], or producing results speculatively with [4, 5, 20] or without [6, 8, 10] applying a compensation technique to correct early emitted inaccurate query results when late arrivals are detected. Most of these approaches make extreme trade-offs; namely, they either try to maximize the result accuracy [3, 15–17, 19, 23] or try to minimize the result latency [6, 8, 10]. Approaches that attempt to balance these two metrics have shortcomings including unguaranteed result accuracy [1] and increased complexity in operator implementation and application logic [4, 5, 20].

Most applications care about both the latency and the quality of query results when processing out-of-order streams. Based on this observation, in this demonstration, we present *AQ-K-slack*, an adaptive, quality-driven, buffer-based disorder handling approach for executing sliding window aggregate queries. *AQ-K-slack* dynamically adjusts the size of the input buffer to minimize the result latency caused by the time to wait for late arrivals, while honoring a user-specified threshold for relative errors in produced query results. The error threshold is in the form of (ϵ_{thr}, δ), stating that the relative error in query results exceeds ϵ_{thr} with probability at most δ. *AQ-K-slack* enables flexible and user-controllable latency vs. result accuracy trade-off by exploiting techniques from the field of sampling-based query processing [13, 18] and control theory [14], with adaptations to cope with the unique characteristic of late arrivals—that is, late arrivals that have missed contributing to a query result are observed only after the result has been produced.

We implemented *AQ-K-slack* in the SAP Event Stream Processor (ESP) [22] stream processing system. For demonstration purpose, we built an interactive web-based interface, which connects to an instance of the prototypical version of ESP. The interface allows the audience to observe visually the user-controllable latency vs. result accuracy trade-offs that *AQ-K-slack* can provide for various aggregate functions, window specifications, result relative error thresholds, and out-of-order data streams, comparing to naive disorder handling approaches that make extreme trade-offs.

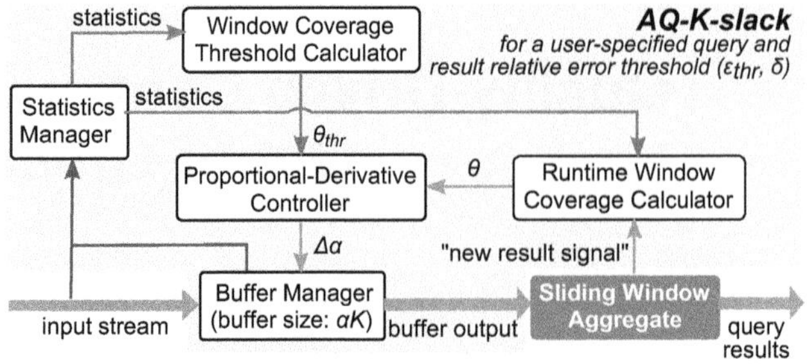

Figure 2: Overview of *AQ-K-slack* implemented in our stream processing system.

2. DESIGN OF AQ-K-SLACK

Figure 2 illustrates the design of *AQ-K-slack*, which consists of several logical components. For each sliding window aggregate query annotated with a result relative error threshold, we create an instance of *AQ-K-slack* according to the aggregate function, the window specification (size w and slide β), and the error threshold. In this section, we explain how *AQ-K-slack* performs quality-driven disorder handling by describing its logical components and interactions between these components. Without loss of generality, in the remainder of this paper, we focus on discussing queries with time-based sliding windows.

2.1 Buffer Manager

AQ-K-slack is a buffer-based disorder handling approach. It extends the *K-slack* approach presented in [19]. Tuples from the input stream are first sorted in a buffer in ascending timestamp order before being presented to the sliding window aggregate operator. Buffering and sorting delay the processing of input tuples by the query operator, thus adding latency to query results.

The size of the buffer is maintained by the Buffer Manager component in Figure 2. Originally in [19], the buffer size is K time units. An input tuple e is kept in the buffer until $e.ts \le t_{curr} - K$, where t_{curr} represents the greatest timestamp among all previously received tuples. The value of K is initialized to zero, and is updated dynamically at runtime to always capture the maximum *delay* of late arrivals in the stream history. The delay of a late arrival e is defined as the difference between the timestamp of the first in-order tuple received after e and the timestamp of e. For instance, the delay of e_{10} in Figure 1 is $e_{11}.ts - e_{10}.ts = 8$ time units; and the delay of e_{13} is $e_{14}.ts - e_{13}.ts = 6$ time units.

In summary, the K-slack approach in [19] dynamically adjusts the buffer size to a big-enough value to accommodate all late arrivals, aiming to provide near exact query results. To trade result accuracy for lower latency in a quality-driven manner, *AQ-K-slack* extends this approach by introducing a parameter α ($\alpha \in [0, 1]$) on top of K. The parameter α is initialized to one; after a predefined *warm-up period*, it is dynamically adapted to meet the user-specified result relative error threshold. The adaptation of α is triggered by each newly produced query result. We explain details of α adaptation in the following sections. Note that the introduction of α changes the effective buffer size to αK, and the condition for releasing an input tuple e from the buffer to $e.ts \le t_{curr} - \alpha K$. When $\alpha < 1$, a smaller than necessary buffer is applied for sorting input tuples. Consequently, late arrivals whose delays are larger than the applied buffer size cannot be handled successfully. Our strategy for dealing with an unsuccessfully handled late arrival is as follows: if the late arrival can still contribute to results of future windows, it is retained and presented to the aggregate operator; otherwise, it is discarded.

2.2 Window Coverage Threshold Calculator

Each unsuccessfully handled late arrival—either a retained one or a discarded one—may cause inaccurate results of some previous windows closed at the aggregate operator(cf. Figure 1). Our ultimate goal is to meet the user specified threshold for relative errors in query results; however, using relative errors to guide the buffer size adaptation is expensive. The reason is that computing the relative error of a result requires the corresponding exact result, which we cannot produce before we have received all late arrivals that fall into the corresponding window. Moreover, the way to compute an exact result is aggregate-function dependent. For instance, for the COUNT function, we can maintain previously produced inaccurate results and correct them incrementally, whereas for the QUANTILE function, we must maintain original input tuples within each window.

To enable efficient buffer-size adaptation, we introduce an intermediate metric for measuring the quality of aggregate results—the *window coverage* θ. Formally, we define the window coverage of a result as *the ratio between the number of tuples that contribute to the result and the total number of tuples that fall into the corresponding window of the result.* The window coverage metric is aggregation-function independent, and is easier to obtain than the relative error.

We introduce the window coverage metric to exploit proven techniques in sampling-based query processing. Sampling-based query processing refers to the technique of evaluating queries approximately over a random sample of original input tuples. Existing work in this field [2, 13, 18] has shown that one can use statistical inequalities and the *central limit theorem* to build an error model for results of an aggregate query produced under sampling. The error model relates the sampling rate p to the relative error ϵ in a produced query result. Hence, given an error threshold, one can derive the minimum sampling rate required to meet the threshold. For each window over the data stream, the sampling rate determines the proportion of tuples within the window to be retained for processing; thus, there is a direct semantics mapping between the sampling rate and the window coverage. This observation inspires us to build the error model for query results produced after disorder handling in a similar way as for results produced after sampling, and then derive the minimum window coverage required to meet the user-specified error threshold. We refer to this minimum window coverage value as the *window coverage threshold* θ_{thr}.

Window Coverage Threshold Calculator in Figure 2 is responsible for computing the window coverage threshold for the user-specified query and result error threshold. The calculation is aggregate-function-specific. Take the SUM function as an example. Denote the set of tuples belonging to a window in the absence of tuple disorder as V, the number of tuples in V (denoted as $|V|$) as N, the values of the tuples to be summed up as v_1, v_2, $\ldots$, v_N, and the exact SUM result over V as $A = \sum_{i=1}^{N} v_i$. Now assume that tuple disorder presents. Let us denote the set of tuples that actually get included into the window after disorder handling by the time the window is closed as V'. Obviously, V' is a subset of V. Without knowing which tuples in V are absent in V', we assume that the probability that a tuple in V gets included in V' is P, i.e., $|V'| = N \times P$. Hence, the window coverage is $\theta = \frac{|V'|}{|V|} = \frac{N \times P}{N} = P$. Namely, the value of P equals the value of θ. Based on this value-equivalence between P and θ, we can define N random variables X_1, X_2, $\ldots$, X_N, such that $X_i = v_i$ ($i \in [1, N]$) with probability θ and $X_i = 0$ with probability $1-\theta$. The sum of these random variables is $\hat{A} = \sum_{i=1}^{N} X_i$, which is also the SUM result over V'. Assume that the mean and the variance of tuples in V are $\mu = \sum_{i=1}^{N} v_i/N$ and $\sigma^2 = \sum_{i=1}^{N}(v_i - \mu)^2/N$, respectively. We can derive the mean and variance of the random variable $\hat{A}$ as follows:

$$
\begin{aligned}
E[\hat{A}] &= \sum_{i=1}^{N} E[X_i] = \sum_{i=1}^{N} (v_i \times \theta + 0 \times (1-\theta)) = \theta A, \\
Var[\hat{A}] &= E[\hat{A}^2] - E[\hat{A}]^2 = E[\hat{A}^2] - (\theta A)^2 \\
&= \sum_{i=1}^{N} E[X_i^2] + \sum_{1 \le i \ne j \le N} E[X_i]E[X_j] - (\theta A)^2 \\
&= \sum_{i=1}^{N} \theta v_i^2 + \sum_{1 \le i \ne j \le N} \theta^2 v_i v_j - (\theta A)^2 \\
&= (\theta - \theta^2) \sum_{i=1}^{N} v_i^2 = (\theta - \theta^2) \frac{\sigma^2 + \mu^2}{N\mu^2} A^2.
\end{aligned}
$$

By the central limit theorem, we can assume that $\hat{A}$ is normally distributed with mean θA and variance $(\theta - \theta^2)\frac{\sigma^2+\mu^2}{N\mu^2}A^2$. Further, we can derive that, to guarantee that the relative error of $\hat{A}$ exceeds ϵ_{thr} with probability at most δ, the value of θ must satisfy the condition

$$
(1-\theta) + z_c(\delta)\sqrt{(\theta - \theta^2) \times \frac{\sigma^2 + \mu^2}{N\mu^2}} \le \epsilon_{thr}, \qquad (1)
$$

where $z_c(\delta)$ is the *critical value* corresponding to the confidence level δ based on the error function of a normal distribution. The minimum θ satisfying condition (1) is the *window coverage threshold* θ_{thr} for the given relative error threshold (ϵ_{thr}, δ). The value of N can be calculated from the window size and the tuple arrival rate estimated by Statistics Manager in our system (cf. Section 2.5). The values of μ and σ are estimated by Statistics Manager as well based on tuples seen so far.

At query runtime, θ_{thr} is first calculated at the end of a predefined *warm-up period.* The warm-up phase is set to allow Statistics Manager to collect enough statistics that are required by the calculation. To adapt to changes in the tuple arrival rate and data characteristics, we re-calculate θ_{thr} periodically during the lifetime of the query.

Note that in sampling-based query processing [13, 18], the random variable X_i is defined to take the value v_i/p with probability p and the value zero otherwise. Hence, the produced SUM result is the sum of tuples in V', scaled by the inverse of the sampling rate p. The goal is to compensate values of sample-excluded tuples. In contrast, we do not scale up the SUM result computed over V' by the inverse of θ to compensate values of late arrivals. We explain the reason for this decision in Section 2.3.

2.3 Window Coverage Runtime Calculator

AQ-K-slack determines whether the buffer size should be increased or decreased by comparing window coverages of produced query results against the calculated window coverage threshold. Note that in sampling-based query processing, the amount of tuples excluded from a window is determined only by the applied sampling rate. In contrast, in disorder handling, the amount of unsuccessfully handled late arrivals of a window is not directly controllable, but is determined by both the applied buffer size and the disorder situation among tuples within the window. The Window Coverage Runtime Calculator component in Figure 2 is responsible for measuring window coverages of produced results. Specifically, denoting the total number of received tuples in a window as N_{rcv}, and the number of unsuccessfully handled late arrivals for this window as N_{late}, we can compute the window coverage θ for the result of the window as $\theta = \frac{N_{rcv}}{N_{rcv}+N_{late}}$. Values of N_{late} and N_{rcv} are maintained by Statistics Manager, which we explain in Section 2.5.

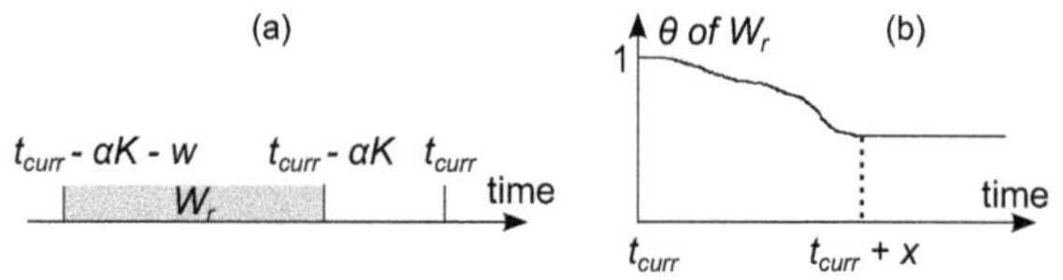

Figure 3: (a) Relationships between W_r, t_{curr}, and the input buffer size at the time W_r is closed; (b) Runtime behavior of the measured window coverage θ for W_r.

The sliding window aggregate operator produces the result of a window as soon as the window is closed. Denoting the most recent window closed at the aggregate operator as W_r, we can depict the relationship between W_r, t_{curr}, and the input buffer size at the time W_r is closed with Figure 3a.

Intuitively, one would expect to adjust the buffer size based on the window coverage of the most recent result, namely the result of W_r. However, at the time when W_r is constructed, any previously received late arrival either does not belong to W_r, and hence is irrelevant to the result of W_r; or belongs to W_r, and has been correctly sorted by the buffer to contribute to the result of W_r. Namely, at the time when W_r is closed, all previously received late arrivals belonging to W_r have been successfully handled. Therefore, the calculated window coverage of W_r at this moment is 1. Although there might still be late arrivals belonging to W_r in the input stream, they can be detected only at later points of time. Only then, we know that the actual window coverage for this window is not 1. We schematically depict the variance of the measured window coverage of a window over time in Figure 3b; starting from the point in time when a window is closed, its measured window coverage gradually decreases—from 1—as more and more late arrivals belonging to the window are observed, and reaches a stable value when all late arrivals belonging to the window are received. Because the measured window coverage of the most recent window is always 1, it is meaningless to scale up a SUM result by the inverse of the measured window coverage at the time the result is produced.

Figure 3b suggests that the measured window coverage of a result gets more and more accurate over time. In other words, window coverages of old results are more accurate than those of recent results. Adjusting the buffer size based on inaccurate window coverages may lead to wrong adjustment decisions. To avoid such wrong decisions, we decide to use the window coverage of an old result to drive the buffer size adaptation. One question that arises immediately is which result to choose. In theory, without knowing the exact upper bound of delays of late arrivals within the input stream, we can never be certain when the window coverage of a result is stable. In our work, we estimate this upper bound as the maximum delay among previously received late arrivals, which is captured by the parameter K in *AQ-K-slack* (cf. Section 2.1). Thus, denoting the upper endpoint of the corresponding window of a result as t_{up}, we assume that the window coverage of the result becomes stable when $t_{up} < t_{curr} - K$. In other words, we assume that window coverages of results produced before $t_{curr} - K$ are stable.

Adapting the buffer size based on window coverages of old results means that the adaptation is delayed. On the one hand, we want to drive the adaptation with accurate window coverages; on the other hand, we also want to minimize the adaptation delay by using window coverages of recent results. Note that K represents the worst case tuple delay, which may occur rarely. To reduce the effect of uncommon delay spikes on the responsiveness of the adaptation, and to take skews in the distribution of late arrivals within the input stream into account, we choose to use the window coverage of the result which is produced L time units earlier than t_{curr}, where L equals the q-quantile ($0 < q < 1$) of delays of previously received late arrivals. In our implementation, we empirically set $q = 0.99$. However, q is a system parameter and can be adjusted to trade off accuracy of measured window coverages against the adaptation responsiveness.

2.4 Proportional-Derivative Controller

Recall that the adaptation of the buffer size in *AQ-K-slack* is essentially the adaptation of the parameter α, which is triggered by each new query result produced after the warm-up period (cf. Section 2.1). Taking window coverages θ of produced results from Window Coverage Runtime Calculator (cf. Section 2.3), and the window coverage threshold θ_{thr} from Window Coverage Threshold Calculator (cf. Section 2.2), we use a *proportional-derivative (PD) controller*—a variant of the well-known *proportional-integral-derivative (PID) controller* [14]—to perform runtime α adaptation.

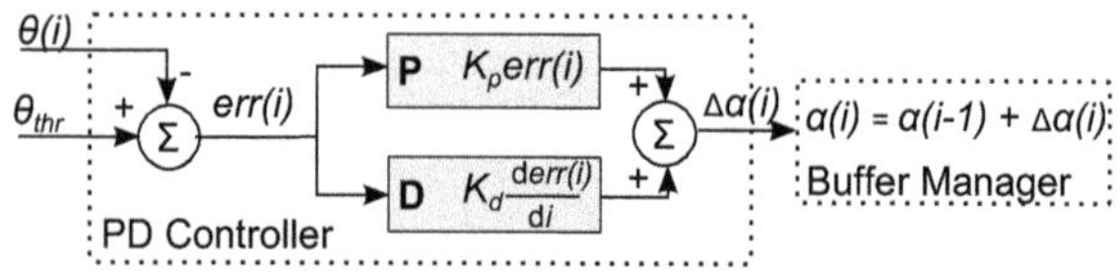

Figure 4: Adaptation of α using a PD controller.

Figure 4 illustrates our α adaptation solution. The output of the controller is the adjustment—that is, the increase or the decrease—of α, denoted by $\Delta\alpha$. For the i-th measured window coverage $\theta(i)$ sent to the controller, the controller determines $\Delta\alpha(i)$ based on the *control error* $err(i)$; $err(i)$ is defined as the deviation between the measured window coverage $\theta(i)$ and the calculated window coverage threshold θ_{thr}, i.e., $err(i) = \theta_{thr} - \theta(i)$. The value of $\Delta\alpha(i)$ is determined by two components of the control error: a proportional component (P), which corresponds to the present error; and a derivative component (D), which corresponds to a prediction of future errors. The value of $\Delta\alpha(i)$ is a weighted sum of the two components, where the weights are configured by parameters K_p and K_d. Presently, we apply manual tuning on top of the Ziegler-Nichols method [26] to configure the parameters K_p and K_d.

Note that in contrast to a typical PID controller, a PD controller does not consider the *integral component* of the control error. We decide to apply a PD controller because the integral component accumulates past errors, and can cause the so-called *integral windup* problem, if window coverages of produced results keep above the window coverage threshold for an extended period. This problem can easily occur during periods when the data stream is only slightly out of order. During these periods, the window coverages of produced results may stay well above the threshold, even though the buffer size is reduced to zero.

2.5 Statistics Manager

The Statistics Manager component in Figure 2 constantly monitors the input stream and estimates statistics, such as the data arrival rate, the mean and the variance of tuples within a window, that are required for calculating the window coverage threshold θ_{thr} (cf. Section 2.2). Currently, we re-calculate θ_{thr} periodically; however, we can extend Statistics Manager with more sophisticated mechanisms to trigger the re-calculation of θ_{thr}, e.g., based on monitoring changes of data characteristics in the stream. In addition, to calculate window coverages of produced results (cf. Section 2.3), Statistics Manager uses a histogram $\mathcal{H}$ to maintain the distribution of delays of history late arrivals, and a data structure $\mathcal{M}$ to maintain *late-tuple counters* N_{late} as well as *received-tuple counters* N_{rcv} for closed windows (i.e., produced results). For each later arrival e that is not handled successfully by the input buffer, previous windows that e belongs to are identified based on $e.ts$ and the window specification (w, β). The N_{late} counters of those windows are then increased. For each in-order tuple and each successfully handled late arrival, windows that the tuple belongs to are identified in the same way, and their N_{rcv} counters are increased. We periodically purge $\mathcal{M}$ to remove entries of very old results, e.g., results produced before $t_{curr} - K$, to minimize the space consumption of $\mathcal{M}$.

3. DEMONSTRATION DESCRIPTION

This demonstration showcases the effectiveness of *AQ-K-slack* in obtaining user-desired latency vs. result accuracy trade-offs using both real-world and synthetic out-of-order data streams. Our demo system consists of an interactive web interface and a prototypical version of the SAP ESP [22] engine running on a remote Linux machine with 24 cores (1.2 GHz per core) and 96 GB RAM. We arrange the demonstration into three parts. In the first part, we introduce the technical background of *AQ-K-slack* using a poster. In the second part, we execute a number of predefined scenarios on our system to show the quality-driven latency-minimization behavior of *AQ-K-slack* compared to the state of the art, using queries with different aggregate functions, window specifications, and error thresholds, and data streams with different data and disorder characteristics. In the final part, we invite the audience to create custom scenarios via the *Query Addition* page (cf. Figure 5a), to get more insights on the effect of different dimensions, such as the window size, the aggregate function, on the behavior of *AQ-K-slack*.

Scenario I. *AQ-K-slack for a predefined combination of query, out-of-order data stream, and error threshold.* The aim of this scenario is to demonstrate the runtime behavior of *AQ-K-slack*, and to compare *AQ-K-slack* with naive disorder handling approaches that make extreme latency vs. result accuracy trade-offs. We use the real-world soccer game data collected from sensors put on soccer players [21]. The stream contains about 50% out-of-order tuples. To show the runtime behavior of *AQ-K-slack*, we provide a *Query*

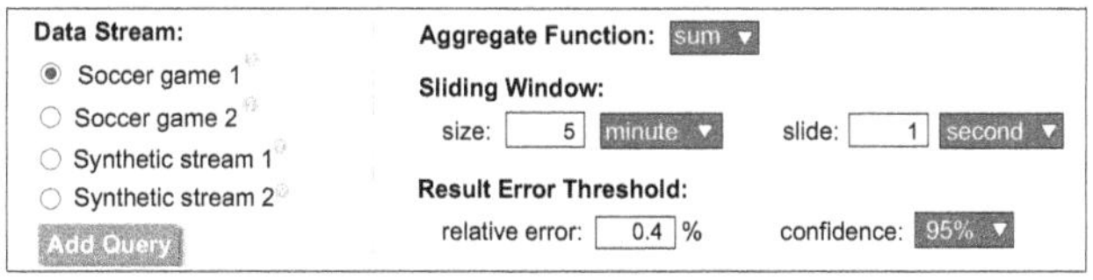

(a) Query Addition page.

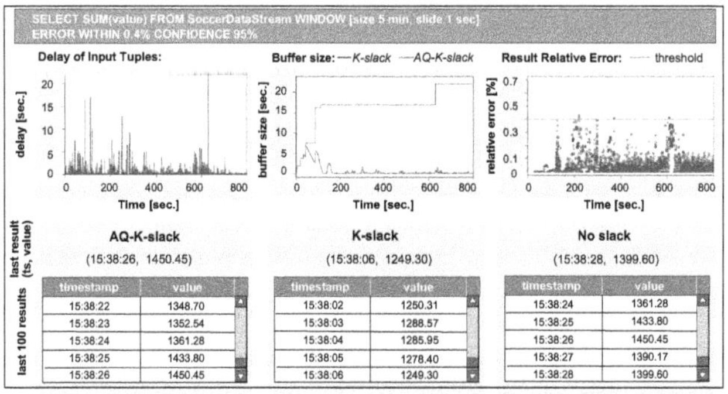

(b) Query Monitor page.

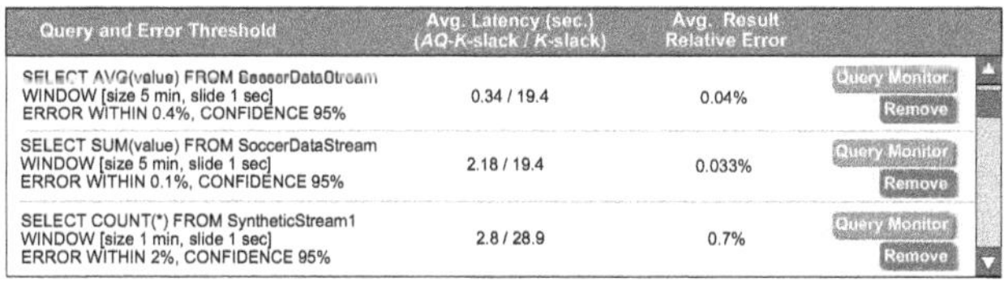

(c) Overview page.

Figure 5: Web interface of the demo system.

Monitor page (cf. Figure 5b) for each running query. On that page, we visualize—in a live manner—delays of input tuples, the variance of the buffer size, and produced query results. Although *AQ-K-slack* adjusts the buffer size based on window coverages, rather than relative errors of query results, we visualize relative errors of results as well, so that the audience can observe the trade-off between the latency and the accuracy of query results directly. In addition to the query executed with *AQ-K-slack*, we execute two additional copies of the same query using disorder handling approaches that make extreme trade-offs. Specifically, the first query copy is executed with the *K-slack* algorithm described in [19], which trades the result latency for maximum result accuracy; the second query copy is executed without applying any buffer, to trade result accuracy for minimum result latency[1]. All three query copies are executed in parallel, consuming broadcast tuples from the same soccer game stream. For each query copy, we show the last 100 query results and highlight the last result on the *Query Monitor* page. Each query result is tagged with a timestamp indicating the upper endpoint of the result's corresponding window. Hence, the audience can observe the differences between result latencies of different disorder handling approaches by comparing the result timestamps. The audience can compare the resulting latency vs. result accuracy trade-offs for the three query copies. For instance, for a SUM query with window specification ($w = 0.5$ *sec*, $\beta = 0.1$ *sec*), by scarifying 1% result accuracy, *AQ-K-slack* can reduce the latency by 80% compared to the approach proposed in [19].

[1]However, we still guarantee that late arrivals that can still contribute to results of future windows are retained.

Scenario II. *AQ-K-slack for different error thresholds.* In this scenario, we use the same query and data stream as in *Scenario I*, but change the specification of the error threshold (ϵ_{thr}, δ). The goal is to show the effect of different error thresholds on the latency vs. result accuracy trade-offs, and the capability of *AQ-K-slack* in fulfilling different user-specified quality requirements. For lower ϵ_{thr} and higher δ values, *AQ-K-slack* tends to use bigger buffer sizes to meet the quality requirement; whereas for higher ϵ_{thr} and lower δ values, *AQ-K-slack* tends to use smaller buffer sizes.

Scenario III. *AQ-K-slack for streams with different disorder characteristics.* We use this scenario to show that *AQ-K-slack* can make user-desired latency vs. result accuracy trade-offs dynamically for streams with different disorder characteristics, without requiring a priori knowledge of the stream disorder characteristics. We run the same query with the same error threshold over two synthetic out-of-order data streams. Both streams are created from a common in-order data stream by introducing a random delay to each tuple. All introduced delays are taken from the same range. However, the introduced delays follow a Zipfian distribution in one stream and a Uniform distribution in the other stream. Here we show that the bigger the number of late arrivals with large delays in the stream, the bigger the buffer is needed to meet the same result accuracy requirement. The query used in this scenario is different from that used in previous scenarios, to showcase the capability of *AQ-K-slack* for different aggregate functions and window specifications.

In addition to predefined scenarios, the audience can create custom scenarios via the *Query Addition* page, to test different combinations of all dimensions. We provide an *Overview* page (cf. Figure 5c). It lists all queries running in the system, along with long-term performance statistics, such as the average result latency and the average relative error in query results. This page is to facilitate the comparison of trade-offs that *AQ-K-slack* makes for different queries, error thresholds, and out-of-order data streams.

4. CONCLUSION

This paper introduces a prototype stream processing system that extends SAP Event Stream Processor with *AQ-K-slack*—an adaptive, quality-driven, buffer-based disorder handling approach for processing sliding window aggregate queries over out-of-order data streams. By exploiting techniques from sampling-based approximate query processing and control theory, *AQ-K-slack* can provide user-desired trade-offs between the latency and the accuracy of query results on the fly, which has not been provided by existing disorder handling approaches. *AQ-K-slack* achieves this merit without requiring any a priori knowledge of disorder characteristics of the data stream. The demonstration highlights the effectiveness of *AQ-K-slack* in obtaining user-desired latency vs. result accuracy trade-offs, compared to naive disorder handling approaches that make extreme trade-offs.

5. REFERENCES

[1] D. J. Abadi, D. Carney, U. Çetintemel, M. Cherniack, C. Convey, S. Lee, M. Stonebraker, N. Tatbul, and S. Zdonik. Aurora: A new model and architecture for data stream management. *VLDB*, 12(2):120–139, 2003.

[2] S. Agarwal, B. Mozafari, A. Panda, H. Milner, S. Madden, and I. Stoica. BlinkDB: Queries with bounded errors and bounded response times on very large data. EuroSys, pages 29–42, 2013.

[3] S. Babu, U. Srivastava, and J. Widom. Exploiting k-constraints to reduce memory overhead in continuous queries over data streams. *ACM Trans. Database Syst.*, 29(3):545–580, 2004.

[4] R. S. Barga, J. Goldstein, M. H. Ali, and M. Hong. Consistent streaming through time: A vision for event stream processing. CIDR, pages 363–374, 2007.

[5] A. Brito, C. Fetzer, H. Sturzrehm, and P. Felber. Speculative out-of-order event processing with software transaction memory. DEBS, pages 265–275, 2008.

[6] C. Busch and S. Tirthapura. A deterministic algorithm for summarizing asynchronous streams over a sliding window. STACS, pages 465–476, 2007.

[7] S. Chaudhuri, U. Dayal, and V. Narasayya. An overview of business intelligence technology. *ACM Commun.*, 54(8):88–98, 2011.

[8] G. Cormode, F. Korn, and S. Tirthapura. Time-decaying aggregates in out-of-order streams. PODS, pages 89–98, 2008.

[9] C. D. Cranor, Y. Gao, T. Johnson, V. Shkapenyuk, and O. Spatscheck. Gigascope: high performance network monitoring with an SQL interface. SIGMOD, page 623, 2002.

[10] S. Gandhi, L. Foschini, and S. Suri. Space-efficient online approximation of time series data: Streams, amnesia, and out-of-order. ICDE, pages 924–935, 2010.

[11] M. Hirzel, R. Soulé, S. Schneider, B. Gedik, and R. Grimm. A catalog of stream processing optimizations. *ACM Comput. Surv.*, 46(4):46:1–46:34, 2014.

[12] S. Krishnamurthy, M. J. Franklin, J. Davis, D. Farina, P. Golovko, A. Li, and N. Thombre. Continuous analytics over discontinuous streams. SIGMOD, pages 1081–1092, 2010.

[13] Y. Law and C. Zaniolo. Improving the accuracy of continuous aggregates and mining queries on data streams under load shedding. *Int. J. Bus. Intell. Data Min.*, 3(1):99–117, 2008.

[14] W. S. Levine. *The control handbook, Second Edition.* CRC Press New York, 2011.

[15] J. Li, D. Maier, K. Tufte, V. Papadimos, and P. A. Tucker. Semantics and evaluation techniques for window aggregates in data streams. SIGMOD, pages 311–322, 2005.

[16] J. Li, K. Tufte, V. Shkapenyuk, V. Papadimos, T. Johnson, and D. Maier. Out-of-order processing: A new architecture for high-performance stream systems. *VLDB*, 1(1):274–288, 2008.

[17] M. Liu, M. Li, D. Golovnya, E. Rundensteiner, and K. Claypool. Sequence pattern query processing over out-of-order event streams. ICDE, pages 784–795, 2009.

[18] B. Mozafari and C. Zaniolo. Optimal load shedding with aggregates and mining queries. ICDE, pages 76–88, 2010.

[19] C. Mutschler and M. Philippsen. Distributed low-latency out-of-order event processing for high data rate sensor streams. IPDPS, pages 1133–1144, 2013.

[20] C. Mutschler and M. Philippsen. Reliable speculative processing of out-of-order event streams in generic publish/ subscribe middlewares. DEBS, pages 147–158, 2013.

[21] C. Mutschler, H. Ziekow, and Z. Jerzak. The DEBS 2013 grand challenge. DEBS, pages 289–294, 2013.

[22] SAP Event Stream Processor. `http://www.sap.com/pc/tech/database/software/sybase-complex-event-processing/index.html`.

[23] U. Srivastava and J. Widom. Flexible time management in data stream systems. PODS, pages 263–274, 2004.

[24] M. Stonebraker, U. Çetintemel, and S. Zdonik. The 8 requirements of real-time stream processing. *SIGMOD Rec.*, 34(4):42–47, 2005.

[25] J. Teubner and R. Mueller. How soccer players would do stream joins. SIGMOD, pages 625–636, 2011.

[26] J. G. Ziegler and N. B. Nichols. Optimum settings for automatic controllers. *Trans. of ASME*, 64:759–768, 1942.

MoDisSENSE: A Distributed Spatio-Temporal and Textual Processing Platform for Social Networking Services

Ioannis Mytilinis * Ioannis Giannakopoulos * Ioannis Konstantinou *
Katerina Doka * Dimitrios Tsitsigkos ◊ Manolis Terrovitis ◊ Lampros Giampouras ‡
Nectarios Koziris *

*CSLAB, NTUA
{gmytil,ggian,ikons,katerina, nkoziris}@cslab.ece.ntua.gr

◊IMIS, RC Athena
{tsitsigkosdim,mter}@imis.athena-innovation.gr

‡Athens Technology Center S.A., Athens, Greece
l.giampouras@atc.gr

ABSTRACT

The amount of social networking data that is being produced and consumed daily is huge and it is constantly increasing. A user's digital footprint coming from social networks or mobile devices, such as comments and check-ins contains valuable information about his preferences. The collection and analysis of such footprints using also information about the users' friends and their footprints offers many opportunities in areas such as personalized search, recommendations, etc. When the size of the collected data or the complexity of the applied methods increases, traditional storage and processing systems are not enough and distributed approaches are employed. In this work, we present MoDisSENSE, an open-source distributed platform that provides personalized search for points of interest and trending events based on the user's social graph by combining spatio-textual user generated data. The system is designed with scalability in mind, it is built using a combination of latest state-of-the art big data frameworks and its functionality is offered through easy to use mobile and web clients which support the most popular social networks. We give an overview of its architectural components and technologies and we evaluate its performance and scalability using different query types over various cluster sizes. Using the web or mobile clients, users are allowed to register themselves with their own social network credentials, perform socially enhanced queries for POIs, browse the results and explore the automatic blog creation functionality that is extracted by analyzing already collected GPS traces.

1. INTRODUCTION

The advent of Web 2.0 has brought an unprecedented data explosion on the web. The wide adoption of social networks has concluded in terabytes of produced data every day. In June 2014 for example, Facebook had on average 654 million mobile active users [1] on a daily basis. Tweets, Facebook "likes", Foursquare check-ins and Instagram pictures are just a part of the social-media data deluge.

SIGMOD'15, May 31–June 4, 2015, Melbourne, Victoria, Australia.
Copyright 2015ACM 978-1-4503-2758-9/15/05 ...$15.00
http://dx.doi.org/10.1145/2723372.2735375.

As this data is mostly a product of human communication, it is susceptible to reveal relationships between different entities. This linkage of data provides tremendous opportunities for data analytics [3], predictions [12] and smart recommendation systems [11]. Taking advantage of the data access that social network APIs provide, developers launch their own third-party social applications to offer smart services and leverage user experience.

Personalization is undoubtedly the newest trend in social networks. Indeed, the most prevalent social networks launch everyday new services that exploit the social graph in order to provide personalized experience. A very recent such example is the new Foursquare and Swarm services that enable users to search for restaurants or other venues based on tastes and friend recommendations.

To this end, we offer a more detailed architectural overview and a comprehensive demonstration of MoDisSENSE [9] a social, geo-location system built on top of a distributed big-data enabled platform. MoDisSENSE combines heterogeneous data from various data sources, such as user GPS traces from cell phones, profile information and comments from existing friends in various social networks connected with the platform (MoDisSENSE currently supports Facebook, Twitter and Foursquare, but it can be extended to more platforms with the appropriate plugin implementation). Through distributed spatio-temporal and textual analysis, our system provides the following functionalities:

- Socially enhanced search of Points of Interest (*POIs*) based on criteria such as user location, automatic sentiment extraction of a user's social media friends preferences or a combination of the above.
- Automatic discovery of new POIs and trending events, i.e., spontaneous gatherings of people in a specific location, such as concerts, traffic jams etc.
- Inference of the user's semantic trajectory through the combination of her GPS traces with background information such as maps, check-ins, user comments, etc.
- Semi-Automatic extraction of a user's daily activities in the form of a blog.

A user can search for POIs on a bounding box on the map posing both simple as well as more advanced criteria. Simple criteria include commonly used features such as keywords characterizing the POI or a time frame of interest. Advanced criteria refer to socially charged information such as the *interest* of a POI, i.e., the opinion of one's friends of it or its *hotness*, i.e., the crowd concentration over time in it. Thus, MoDisSENSE is capable of answering queries such as "Show me the top ten restaurants in Melbourne that (a specific subset, or all) of my Facebook friends prefer for dinner during summer" or "Show me the five hottest (i.e., most visited) places in town yesterday night".

The latter query is a *trending events* query. Tripadvisor already offers a trending events capability. However, MoDisSENSE adds a personalized flavor, making feasible personalized trending events queries with configurable time granularity. So MoDisSENSE can resolve the query "Show me the three hottest places in Melbourne visited by my x specific Foursquare friends the last y hours".

One additional feature of MoDisSENSE is the automatic POIs detection. A distributed version [7] of DBSCAN, a well-known clustering algorithm, is applied to MoDisSENSE users' GPS traces. A dense concentration of traces signifies a POI existence. Furthermore, the correlation of spatio-temporal information provided by the GPS traces with POI related texts automatically produces a daily blog with the user's activity. The produced blog can be manually updated by the user and can be shared in Facebook or Twitter.

The contribution of this work is manyfold:

- We devise a highly scalable architecture that efficiently handles data from heterogeneous sources and is able to deal with big data scenarios.
- We provide an Apache License-2.0 open-source [2] implementation of a social network based application which leverages the capabilities of other existing applications.
- We adapt and finely-tune well-known classification and clustering algorithms in a Hadoop-based environment.
- We experiment with datasets in the order of tens of GB, from Tripadvisor, Facebook, Foursquare and Twitter.
- We validate the efficiency, accuracy and scalability of the proposed architecture and algorithms.

The remainder of this paper is organized as follows: Section 2 presents the MoDisSENSE architecture, Section 3 provides an experimental evaluation of the platform, Section 4 describes the features to be presented to the demo attendees and Section 5 presents the related work.

2. ARCHITECTURE

MoDisSENSE features an architecture that is illustrated in Figure 1. In favor of flexibility and ease of maintenance, the system follows a completely modular design. Among system modules a fundamental distinction is applied: each module is classified as a frontend or a backend module.

The frontend consists of the web and two mobile (Android and iOS) applications. The web, Android and iOS clients are developed using DotNetNuke, Java Android SDK and Objective-C technologies respectively and can be downloaded from the github repository [2].

The frontend applications communicate with the backend through a REST API. A specific JSON format has been defined in order to send requests to the backend and return results to the user. This feature enables the seamless integration of more client applications with the platform.

As Figure 1 shows, the backend contains a set of processing and storage modules. For the processing modules, a web server farm and a Hadoop cluster are established. The

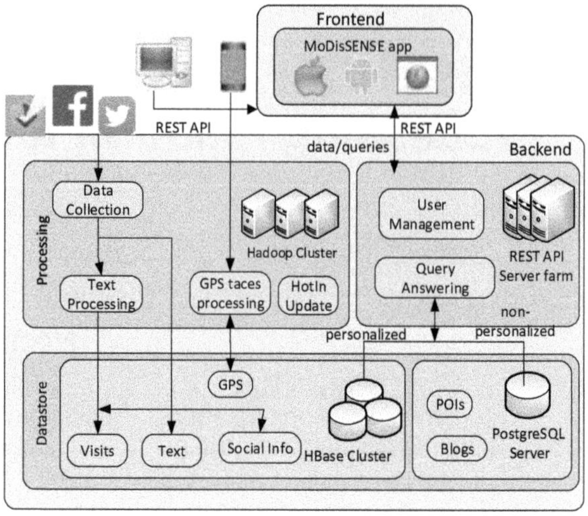

Figure 1: MoDisSENSE platform architecture.

widespread use of social networks has lead to an environment where huge amounts of data are created on high and unpredictable rates. Thus, the volume of data, needed to be processed, demands a distributed approach. Since the Hadoop framework emerges for large-scale analytics, we design and deploy the following Hadoop-based processing modules:

- Data Collection Module
- HotInt Update Module
- Text Processing Module
- Event detection module

Apart from the processing subsystem, a storage system is employed to the backend, in order to store the collected and derived data. We refer to the components of the storage subsystem as repositories. Repositories are conceptually classified to primitive and non-primitive data repositories. We consider primitive data to be the one have not been processed. Primitive data are collected from external data sources such as social networks(Facebook, Foursquare, Twitter) and GPS traces and are directly stored to the platform. Non-primitive data repositories, which are the ones serving answers to queries, hold information extracted from primitive data through spatio-textual algorithms.

When multiple concurrent users issue queries to the platform, system design should meet demand. Thus, there is a need for a scalable approach. To this end, the Apache HBase NoSQL datastore is used. However, there are queries which require either complex indexing schemes or extended random access to the underlying data. These queries cannot be efficiently executed in HBase. For this reason, we devise a hybrid architecture that uses HBase for batch queries that can be efficiently executed in parallel and PostgreSQL for online random-access queries that cannot. In addition to the already mentioned modules, we deploy the User Management and the Query Answering Module on the web server farm that acts as a gateway to the platform. Both modules are implemented as lightweight web services which put load to the datastore without stressing the web servers.

In the following subsections, we describe with further details the repositories and the processing modules of the MoDisSENSE platform.

2.1 Datastore Repositories

POI Repository. It contains all the information MoDisSENSE needs to know about POIs. The name of a POI, its geographical location, the keywords characterizing it and the hotness/interest metrics are all stored in this repository. A new entry to the repository can be inserted either explicitly by the user through the frontend GUI or automatically by the Event Detection Module. While POI repository has to deal with low insert/update rates, it should be able to handle heavy, random access read loads. The indexing capabilities PostgreSQL offers make it an ideal infrastructure for hosting POI repository.

Social Info Repository. This is a HBase-resident table where social graph information is held. For each MoDisSENSE user and for each connected social network, the list of friends is persisted. More specifically, we store a compressed list with the unique social network id, the name and the profile picture of each friend.

Text Repository. The textual data is the most demanding part, in terms of utilized disk space, in the MoDisSENSE ecosystem. For this reason , it is stored in the NoSQL cluster and is spread across all available cluster nodes. The Text repository holds all the collected comments and reviews about POIs. Texts are indexed by user, POI and time. For any given POI, we are able to retrieve the comments that a specified user made at any given time interval.

Visits Repository. Visits Repository is also persisted as an HBase table. In order to make POI recommendations based on social friends' preferences, we need to keep track of all visits of a user's friends. Each visit is represented by a struct with the complete POI information (name, latitude, longitude, etc). Moreover, this struct is enriched with the *interest* and *hotness* metrics. Every time a MoDisSENSE user or a user's social friend visits a POI, a visit struct indexed by user and time is added to the repository. Thus, for any given time interval, we know the places that all of a user's friends have been and a score indicating each friend's opinion.

Since the visit struct, that we persist each time someone visits a POI, contains the whole POI information, there is high replicated data. The alternative schema design strategy would be joining POI information with visit information at query time. However, our experiments suggest data replication to be more efficient. Our schema in combination with HBase coprocessors and a fully parallel query mechanism, it seems to offer more scalability and achieve lower latency numbers even when many concurrent users with many friends each stress the system.

GPS Traces Repository. The mobile devices, that have MoDisSENSE application installed, can push their GPS traces to the platform. Since the platform may continuously receive GPS traces, this repository is expected to deal with a high update rate. Furthermore, as GPS traces are not queried directly by the users but are periodically processed in bulk, there is no need to build indices on them. The volume of data, the opportunities for parallel bulk processing and the absence of indices are the main reasons why we choose to put GPS repository in HBase.

Blogs Repository. We define a semantic trajectory to be a timestamped sequence of POIs summarizing user's activity during the day. As POIs, blogs are frequently queried by users but they do not have to deal with heavy updates and thus are stored as a PostgreSQL resident table.

2.2 Processing Modules

User Management Module. The User Management module is responsible for the user authentication to the platform. The user is registered either through the mobile applications or the website. MoDisSENSE does not require a username or password. The signing-in process is carried out only with the use of the social network credentials. The registration workflow follows the OAuth protocol. The OAuth authorization framework enables a third-party application to obtain access to an HTTP service on behalf of a resource owner. When the authentication is successful, the user logs in and an access token is returned to the MoDisSENSE platform. With this token, MoDisSENSE can interact with the connected social networks on behalf of the end user. It can monitor user's activity, user's friends activity, make posts etc. Being an authorized member of the platform, the user can connect to the MoDisSENSE account more social networks. When more than one social networks are connected to the platform, MoDisSENSE joins the acquired data and enriches the information that is indexed and stored.

Data Collection Module. The functionality of this module is to collect data from external data sources. Periodically, the Data Collection Module scans in parallel all the authorized users of MoDisSENSE; each worker scans a different set of users. For each user and for all connected social networks, it downloads all the interesting updates from the user's social profile. Since MoDisSENSE provides social geo-location services, interesting updates are considered to be user check-ins and the accompanying comments as well as status updates. From this information, MoDisSENSE is able to gain knowledge about the existence of POIs and people's opinion about them. Once data is streamed to the platform, it is in-memory processed and then indexed and stored to the appropriate repositories.

Text Processing Module. The Text Processing Module performs sentiment analysis to all textual information the platform collects through the Data Collection Module. Comments from check-ins and POI reviews are classified, real-time and in-memory, as positive or negative. The score which results from the sentiment analysis is persisted to the datastore along with the text itself.

As a classification algorithm, we choose the Naive Bayes classifier that the Apache Mahout framework provides. Naive Bayes is a supervised learning algorithm and thus it needs a pre-annotated dataset for its training. For the training, data from Tripadvisor, containing reviews for hotels, restaurants and attractions, is used. The chosen dataset offers two key advantages: First, it is semantically close to our application data and thus results in a high quality training and second, Tripadvisor comments are annotated with a rank from 1 to 5 that can be used as a classification score. After an extensive experimental study and a fine-tuning of the algorithm parameters, we managed to create a highly accurate classifier that achieves an accuracy ratio of 94% towards unseen data.

Event Detection Module. New events and POIs detection constitute a core functionality of MoDisSENSE. A distributed, Hadoop-based implementation of the DBSCAN clustering algorithm [7] is employed for this reason. The module is called periodically and processes in parallel the updates of GPS Traces Repository in order to find traces of high density; high density traces imply the existence of a new POI. In order to avoid detecting already known POIs to MoDisSENSE, traces falling near to existing POIs in POI Repository are filtered out and are not taken into consideration for clustering.

HotIn Update Module. POI Repository contains all the non-personalized information about POIs. Two attributes of the information stored for each POI are: *hotness* and *interest*. Hotness and interest are inferred by an aggregation over all visits persisted in Visits Repository within a configurable time frame T. In order to aggregate hotness and interest, a MapReduce job configured with a scanner over all visits in T, is instantiated. HotIn Update Module is called periodically in order to update the hotness/interest information of the POI repository in PostgreSQL.

Query Answering Module. The Query Answering is the module used for answering search queries. A search query can take as input the following parameters:

- a bounding box on the map
- a list of keywords
- a list of social network friends
- a time window
- results sorting criteria
- the number of results to be returned

If a list of friends is provided, the query is considered to be personalized. As Figure 1 shows, non-personalized queries are answered by PostgreSQL while personalized ones by the NoSQL cluster. A non-personalized query is a *select* SQL query in PostgreSQL, since POI repository contains all the demanded information.

In the case where some selected friends' opinion should be taken into account, MoDisSENSE should know whether the selected friends have visited any place in the area of interest and what score has been extracted by their visit. In order to efficiently obtain this information, HBase coprocessors are used. Each coprocessor is responsible for a region of the Visit Repository table and performs HBase *get* requests to the users under its authority. Since different friends are located with high probability in different regions, a different coprocessor is in charge of serving their visits and multiple get requests are issued in parallel. Increasing the regions number leads to increase in coprocessors number and thus achieves higher degree of parallelism within a single query.

3. EXPERIMENTS

In this section we provide experiments and validate both our architectural design and the selected optimizations for the training of the Naive Bayes classifier.

3.1 Performance Evaluation

We first present some experiments for the scalability and performance of the query answering module. Using a synthetic dataset, we test the ability of the platform to respond to personalized queries issued by its users for various loads and different cluster sizes. Each personalized query involves a set of friends; the opinion expressed by them for POIs they have visited will determine the score of each POI for a platform user. The platform user can set a number of other parameters as well: the POI type, as expressed by the keywords that accompany it, its geographical location, its name, the time period of the visits, etc. In our experiments, we identified that the dominant factor in the execution time of the query is the number of social network friends that the platform users define.

For the synthetic dataset generation, we collected information from OpenStreetMap about 8500 POIs located in Greece. Based on those POIs, we emulated the activity of 150k different social network users, each of whom has visited a number of POIs and assigned a grade to it; this grade corresponds to the classification grade of the comment of the user for this visit. The number of visits for each social network friend follows the Normal Distribution with $\mu = 170$ and $\sigma = 10$[1]. The dataset is deployed into an HBase cluster consisting of 16 dual-core VMs with 2 GB of RAM each, running Linux (Ubuntu 14.04). The VMs are hosted in a private Openstack cluster.

At first, we are going to study the impact of the number of social network friends into the execution time of a single query. At this point we will also examine how the cluster size affects the execution time of a query. Secondarily, we are going to extend our study to multiple concurrent queries where we will also examine the behavior of the platform for different number of concurrent queries and different cluster configurations.

For the first point, we evaluate the execution time of a query for different numbers of friends. In Figure 2 we provide our findings. In this experiment, we executed one query at a time involving from 500 to 10k SN friends for three different cluster setups consisting of 4, 8 and 16 nodes. The friends for each query are picked randomly in a uniform manner. We repeated each query ten times and we provide the average of those runs.

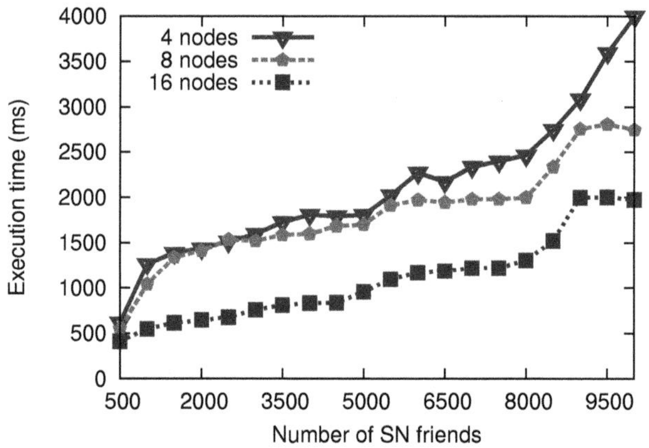

Figure 2: Query latency vs number of users

The number of friends affects the execution time in an almost linear manner. Furthermore, an increase in the cluster size leads to a latency decrease, since the execution is happening in parallel to multiple nodes. By utilizing HBase coprocessors, we managed to exploit the locality of the computations into specific portions of the data: each coprocessor operates into a specific HBase region (holding a specific portion of the data), eliminates the visits that do not satisfy the user defined criteria, aggregates multiple visits referring to the same POI and sorts the candidate POIs according to the aggregated scores. Finally, each coprocessor returns to the Web Server the sorted list of POIs which, in turn, merges the results and returns the final list of POIs to the end user.

Using the previously described technique, we achieved to get latencies lower than 1 second for more than 5000 users.

[1]The vast majority of the users has performed between 140 and 200 visits in different pois.

Bearing into consideration that social networks like Facebook, retain a limit on the maximum number of connections (5000 friends per user), we can guarantee that the latency for each query remains in an acceptable level for a real time application.

We now extend our analysis for the cases where multiple queries are issued concurrently to the platform. For our experiments we create a number of concurrent queries involving 6000 social network friends each and we measure their execution time for different cluster sizes. In Figure 3, we provide our results. The execution time in the vertical axis represents the average execution time for each case.

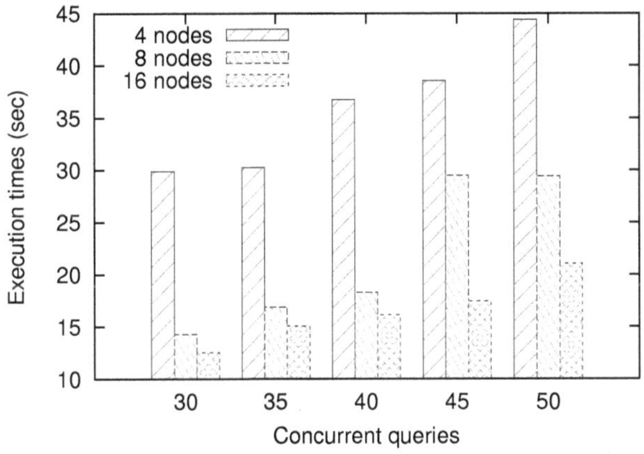

Figure 3: Average execution time for concurrent queries

As Figure 3 demonstrates, an increase in the number of concurrent queries leads to worse performance (larger execution time). However, for larger cluster sizes we can make the following observations: (a) even for the lowest number of concurrent queries the 16 cluster case is approximately 2.5 times better than the 4 cluster case, indicative of the proper utilization of more resources and (b) larger cluster sizes do not allow execution time to rise fast as the number of concurrent queries increases. Specifically, when the cluster consists of 4 nodes, the execution time is high even for the lowest number of concurrent queries and it continues to rise rapidly while the number of queries is increased. In the 8 nodes case, although at first the achieved execution times are relatively low, the increase becomes rapid for more concurrent queries, whereas in the 16 nodes case we see that the increase is held in a minimum level. This is indicative of the scalability of the platform, since more resources are properly utilized and the platform becomes resistant to concurrency.

Finally, since greater number of concurrent queries leads to more threads in the Web Server which, in turn, hits the cluster, we can avoid any potential bottlenecks by replicating the Web Servers while simultaneously, we use a load balancer to route the traffic to the web servers accordingly. In our experimental setup, we identified that two 4-cores web servers with 4 GB of RAM each are more than enough to avoid such bottlenecks.

3.2 Accuracy Evaluation

In this section we evaluate the tuning of the Naive Bayes classifier we use for sentiment analysis. As we have already mentioned, for the training of the classifier, we crawl and use data from Tripadvisor. We consider a Tripadvisor review about a place to be a classification document. We divide training documents into two sets: positive and negative opinion documents. Both sets should have almost the same cardinality. Before feed the training set to the classifier, a preprocessing step is applied which involves stemming, turning all letters to lowercase and removing all words belonging to a list of stopwords. When the preprocessing step is finished, Naive Bayes is applied to the data. Let this procedure be the baseline training process. As a next step, we experiment with the following optimizations: use of the *tf* metric, *2-grams*, *Bi-Normal Separation* and deletion of words with less than x occurrences. These optimizations can be given as parameters to the classification algorithm. Experiments with different combinations for the algorithm parameters were also conducted but are omitted due to space constraints.

Figure 4 shows the classification accuracy for various training set sizes, when the baseline and the optimized classification are used. We observe that when optimizations are applied, classification results are more accurate for any training size. Especially, for a training set of 500k documents, we achieve an accuracy of 93.8%. As we can see, the 500k documents form a threshold for the classifier. For both versions of the algorithm after this point accuracy degrades. This is because there is an overfit of data, which is a classic problem in Machine Learning approaches.

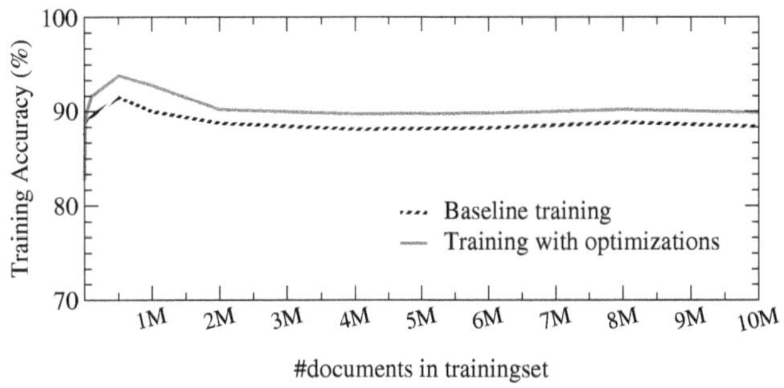

Figure 4: Classification accuracy for different training sizes

4. DEMO DESCRIPTION

The demonstration will allow attendees to interact with MoDisSENSE web and mobile clients and explore their functionality. In Figure 5 we present screenshots from the iOS client, nevertheless the Android and web clients share the same functionality and will also be available for demonstration. Attendees will be able to register themselves using their social network credentials and browse the respective clients. Due to lack of historical data and social context for the attendee accounts, we will utilize a set of demo accounts to showcase the personalized search functionality. In a nutshell, users will be able to perform the following: (a) Login and link their social network accounts with MoDisSENSE (Figure 5a), (b) Perform personalized or not keyword search for POIs between a map bounding box for a time window and sorted by hotness or interest and (c) Explore the semi-automated blog creation, editing and publishing functionality.

In the first case the users will be able to join the MoDisSENSE platform by linking one or more of their Facebook, Twitter or Foursquare accounts. When the linkage is done, the social networking context (i.e., user and friend lists avatar icons, etc) will be available at the respective client.

In the second scenario, we will showcase the personalized search functionality. Two MoDisSENSE users with com-

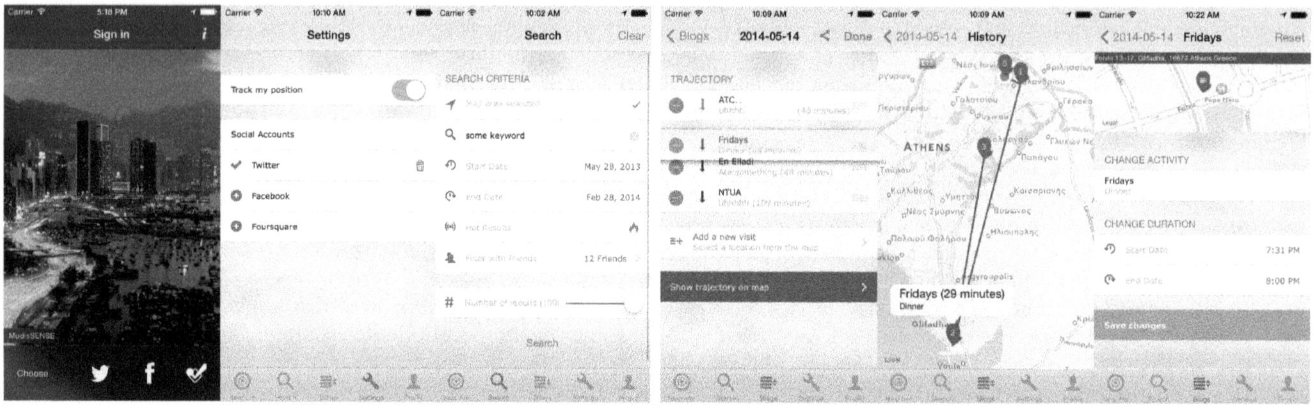

(a) Login and search GUI. (b) Blog GUI functionalities.

Figure 5: Screenshots from the iOS mobile application.

pletely different social profiles are going to perform the same search query on the same geographical area. The returned POIs are expected to be different depending on the user executing the query. For example, we assume that the first user's friends love fast food while the other's prefer luxurious restaurants. A personalized query with the keyword "restaurant" is expected to return fast food places in the case of the first user whereas luxurious expensive restaurants in the case of the second user.

For the third scenario, users will be able to create, edit and post their own blog entries, or examine the extracted blogs of the test accounts. The attendees will have the chance to see the inferred semantic trajectories and also edit the respective blog entries. Screenshots from the blog GUI are presented in Figure 5b. In the first two screenshots the semantic trajectory of the user is presented. The leftmost screenshot permits the user to edit the order the POIs were visited while the one in the middle presents the trajectory on the map. Finally the rightmost screenshot allows the editing of visit information such as arrival and departure time.

5. RELATED WORK

This work is not the first that proposes a social network based geo-location service. In [13, 4] two POI recommendation systems are presented. However, recommendations are based only on historical location data from GPS traces and check-ins, whereas MoDisSENSE combines spatio-textual data in order to produce more accurate recommendations. Furthermore, MoDisSENSE proves to be scalable while no implementation and performance information is provided for the other systems. In [5] a collaborative filtering based system is presented. The presented system collects check-in data from Gowalla, a location-based social network, and makes a POI recommendation. And in this system, recommendation is solely based on check-ins and not on the combination of heterogeneous data. The importance of the textual content of social networks as a mean of expressing opinion is already recognized. Many works such as [8, 10, 6] perform sentiment analysis on Twitter data in order to extract user sentiment. Nevertheless, none of these works combines the inferred knowledge with geo-location information for POI recommendation.

6. ACKNOWLEDGMENTS

This work has been partially funded by the Hellenic (GSRT) "COOPERATION 2009" National Action "09SYN-72-881" MoDisSense Project and the European Commission in terms of the ASAP FP7 ICT Project under grant agreement no 619706. Dr. Terrovitis and Mr. Tsitsigkos were partly supported by the GSRT in terms of the EU/Greece funded KRIPIS Action: MEDA Project.

7. REFERENCES

[1] Facebook Stats. http://newsroom.fb.com/company-info/.
[2] MoDiSSENSE Code. https://github.com/modissense.
[3] C. C. Aggarwal. *An introduction to social network data analytics*. Springer, 2011.
[4] J. Bao, Y. Zheng, and M. F. Mokbel. Location-based and preference-aware recommendation using sparse geo-social networking data. In *SIGSPATIAL*, 2012.
[5] B. Berjani and T. Strufe. A recommendation system for spots in location-based online social networks. In *SNS*, 2011.
[6] A. Go, R. Bhayani, and L. Huang. Twitter sentiment classification using distant supervision. *CS224N Project Report, Stanford*, 2009.
[7] Y. He, H. Tan, W. Luo, H. Mao, D. Ma, S. Feng, and J. Fan. Mr-dbscan: An efficient parallel density-based clustering algorithm using mapreduce. *ICPADS*, 2011.
[8] E. Kouloumpis, T. Wilson, and J. Moore. Twitter sentiment analysis: The good the bad and the omg! *ICWSM*, 2011.
[9] I. Mytilinis, I. Giannakopoulos, I. Konstantinou, K. Doka, and N. Koziris. MoDisSENSE: A Distributed Platform for Social Networking Services over Mobile Devices. *IEEE Big Data*, 2014.
[10] A. Pak and P. Paroubek. Twitter as a corpus for sentiment analysis and opinion mining. In *LREC*, 2010.
[11] O. Phelan, K. McCarthy, and B. Smyth. Using twitter to recommend real-time topical news. In *RecSys*, 2009.
[12] A. Tumasjan, T. O. Sprenger, P. G. Sandner, and I. M. Welpe. Predicting elections with twitter: What 140 characters reveal about political sentiment. *ICWSM*, 2010.
[13] Y. Zheng, Y. Chen, X. Xie, and W.-Y. Ma. GeoLife2. 0: a location-based social networking service. In *MDM*, 2009.

DocRicher: An Automatic Annotation System for Text Documents Using Social Media

Qiang Hu *1, Qi Liu #2, Xiaoli Wang *1, Anthony K.H. Tung #2, Shubham Goyal *1, and Jisong Yang *1
*SeSaMe Centre, #School of Computing, National University of Singapore
1 {qiang.hu, dcswxl, idmsg, idmyj}@nus.edu.sg, 2 {qiliu, atung}@comp.nus.edu.sg

ABSTRACT

We demonstrate a system, *DocRicher*, to enrich a text document with social media, that implicitly reference certain passages of it. The aim is to provide an automatic annotation interface to satisfy users' information need, without cumbersome queries to traditional search engines. The system consists of four components: text analysis, query construction, data assignment, and user feedback. Through text analysis, the system decomposes a text document into appropriate topical passages, of which each is represented using detected key phrases. By submitting combinations of these phrases as queries to social media systems, the relevant results are used to suggest new annotations, that are linked to the corresponding passages. We have built a user-friendly visualization tool for users to browse automatically recommended annotations on their reading documents. Users are either allowed to rate a recommended annotation by accepting it or not; or add a new annotation by manually highlighting texts and adding personal comments. Both these annotations are regarded as the ground truth to derive new queries for retrieving more relevant contents. We also apply data fusion to merge the query results from various contexts and retain most relevant ones.

Categories and Subject Descriptors

H.3.3 [**Information Search and Retrieval**]: Retrieval models, Relevance feedback, Clustering

General Terms

Theory and design

Keywords

Document enrichment, Social media, Ranking

1. INTRODUCTION

The popularity of e-reader applications for desktops, tablets and mobile devices, gives rise to implicit information need of readers. To enhance users' reading experience, existing systems attempt to augment text documents with supplementary materials mined from the web (e.g., [1, 6, 10, 12]). Though making much progress on linking web contents to words, phrases, and sections, they either require the document to have explicit section structure, or assume that items (words or phrases) are really important for readers. Such assumptions, however, are indeed unpractical. First, many text documents like web pages do not have obvious section structure. Second, no technique can guarantee that all readers are interested in the selected items based on their respective requirements. Others attempt to link social media to a short article (e.g., [10]). It is hard to adapt such work to support lengthy documents, as they completely ignore the reference between social media and the detailed contents.

In this paper, we focus on a new task: *given a text document, we find social media contents, which implicitly reference certain passages of it.* We use social media as the augmentation materials, instead of other web contents for two reasons. First, social media often reflects an individual's interests [11]. This presents the opportunity to amplify a document with additional information following users' interests. Second, social media often contains rich information, such as images and videos, that can enhance the text contents. This avoids the complex steps in previous work, to identify media data like images, from the results of search engines [1]. We focus on attaching social media to relevant passages of the document, instead of specific terms or the whole article. We believe that this is a better way to direct users to better understand the detailed reference between them. It poses three challenging problems to address the task: 1) How to segment the document into appropriate granularity of passages? 2) How to generate effective keyword queries to retrieve relevant social media? 3) How to efficiently assign the query results into correct passages?

We develop an automatic annotation system, denoted by *DocRicher*, by proposing techniques to solve the aforementioned problems. The main idea follows three steps in Figure 1 from (a) to (c). In Step 1, we detect the topic hierarchy of a document, to decompose it into an appropriate number of textual units. Although several topic hierarchy generation techniques have been proposed (e.g., [2, 14]), they either have no guarantee of obtaining high quality of segmentation [3], or are difficult to construct the topical tree. Consequently, we define the problem as finding a best clustering among consecutive text segments, and adapt the idea of finding the V-optimal histogram [8], to solve it. We employ a dynamic programming algorithm to find best boundaries among clus-

SIGMOD'15, May 31–June 4, 2015, Melbourne, Victoria, Australia.

http://dx.doi.org/10.1145/2723372.2735379.

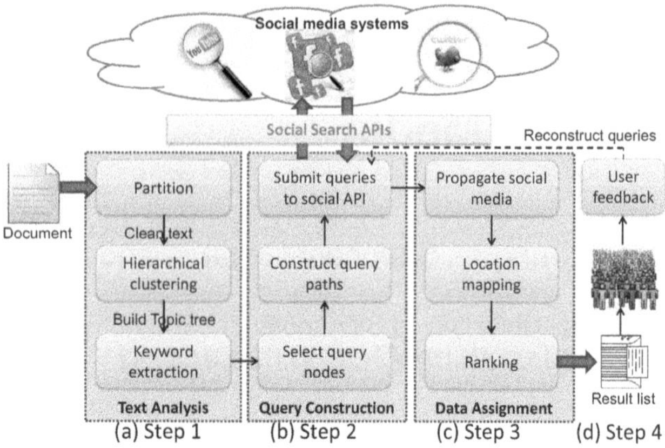

Figure 1: System workflow

ters, and use the clustering results in each iteration to build each level of topic hierarchy. Step 2 uses the topic hierarchy to generate a limited number of keyword queries. Each query is constructed from a subtree in the hierarchy, containing combinations of selective phrases in the tree nodes within the subtree. The number of queries can be flexibly controlled by the rate limit in social media systems[1]. In Step 3, the returned results are only propagated to the leaf nodes in the corresponding subtree. We assign each result in a greedy way, by computing its Overlap to each tree node. Within a leaf node, we map most relevant results into the location of a segment based on the cosine similarity.

Based on the above methodology, the system automatically crawls social media systems, and assigns the query results to relevant passages in a document. For each passage, the assigned results are used to generate annotations for recommendation. As shown in Figure 1 (d), the system also implements a user-friendly interface to visualize the suggested annotations, allowing users to make feedback by accepting them or not. Moreover, users are allowed to add manual annotations by attaching personal comments into highlighted texts. We take the accepted results of highest ranks and the manual annotations of most popular as new contexts to build new keyword queries, and use effective data analytics and fusion tools to refine the query results.

Compared to existing systems, we provide a more elegant platform to augment a document with social media. First, social contents present the opportunity to amplify a document with information following the user's interests. Second, displaying annotations by highlighting the corresponding passages are more user-friendly for users to understand a document. This avoids the complex term selection techniques required by existing work, and overcomes the limitations on previous work that can be only applied to documents with explicit section structures.

2. TECHNICAL FOUNDATION

2.1 Text Analysis

Given a document, we analyze its text contents to construct a topic hierarchy, aiming to decompose it into an appropriate number of textual units. This paper defines the problem as finding a best clustering among consecutive text segments based on the term vector model [4].

[1]http://en.wikipedia.org/wiki/Rate_limiting

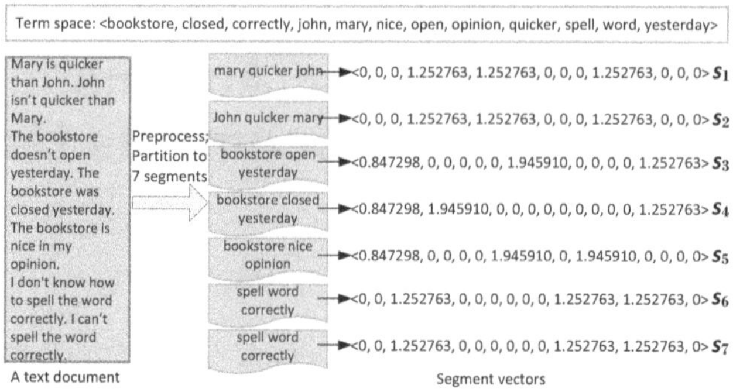

Figure 2: Segment vectors from a text document

Let d be a text document, t be a term representing a word, and $|d| = M$ be the total number of unique terms in a document. Suppose that a document is partitioned into N segments and each segment is represented as a weight vector in the term space. Let $\{\boldsymbol{s_1}, \ldots, \boldsymbol{s_N}\}$ be the set of N segment vectors, where each $\boldsymbol{s_i} \in R^M$ for $1 \leq i \leq N$, i.e., $\boldsymbol{s_i} = (w_{1,i}, \ldots, w_{M,i})$. For $1 \leq j \leq M$, we have

$$w_{j,i} = tf(t_j, \boldsymbol{s_i}) \times isf(t_j) = tf(t_j, \boldsymbol{s_i}) \times \ln \frac{N}{sf(t_j)},$$

where $tf(t_j, \boldsymbol{s_i})$ is the frequency of t_j in $\boldsymbol{s_i}$, and $sf(t_j)$ is the number of segments containing t_j. The weight evaluates a term based on its frequency within a segment and its distribution across all segments. We have $isf(t_j) = 0$ if t_j appears in every segment. This helps to avoid terms that may not be useful for identifying segment boundaries.

EXAMPLE 1. *In Figure 2, a text document is preprocessed and partitioned into 7 segments, i.e., $N = 7$. The term space has totally 12 unique terms, i.e., $M = 12$. For each segment vector $\boldsymbol{s_i}$ with $1 \leq i \leq 7$, we compute its weight value from $w_{1,i}$ to $w_{12,i}$. For example, $\boldsymbol{s_3}$ is computed as* $<0.847298, 0, 0, 0, 0, 1.945910, 0, 0, 0, 0, 1.252763>$. *The weight value of $w_{1,3} = tf_{1,3} \times isf_3 = 1 \times \ln \frac{7}{3} = 0.847298$, as there are three segments containing the term of "bookstore".*

We preprocess the text document before using the term vector model. There are typically three steps for document preprocessing: sentence boundary identification, top-word elimination, and stemming [7]. In general, the punctuation of dot is used as the sentence boundary, and words without any semantic information are eliminated. For the purpose of stemming, we use a popular open source tool [9].

As segments may have different lengths, we normalize a segment vector $\boldsymbol{s_i}$ to a unit segment vector $\hat{\boldsymbol{s_i}}$, i.e.,

$$\hat{\boldsymbol{s_i}} = \frac{\boldsymbol{s_i}}{\|\boldsymbol{s_i}\|},$$

where $\|\boldsymbol{s_i}\|$ is the L^2 norm of $\boldsymbol{s_i}$. It can be computed as $\sqrt{w_{1,i}^2 + w_{2,i}^2 + \ldots + w_{M,i}^2}$. Intuitively, this normalization helps to identify similar segments that have different lengths but deal with the same topic. A normalized segment vector $\hat{\boldsymbol{s}}$ lies on the unit sphere in R^M. For example, the segment vector $\boldsymbol{s_3}$ in Figure 2 can be normalized into a unit vector $\hat{\boldsymbol{s_3}}$ of $<0.343797, 0, 0, 0, 0, 0.789567, 0, 0, 0, 0, 0.508318>$ as shown in Figure 4. Given two such unit vectors $\hat{\boldsymbol{s_1}}$ and $\hat{\boldsymbol{s_2}}$, let $\theta(\hat{\boldsymbol{s_1}}, \hat{\boldsymbol{s_2}})$ denote the angle between them. The cosine similarity is computed as the inner product, i.e.,

$$cos(\theta(\hat{\boldsymbol{s_1}}, \hat{\boldsymbol{s_2}})) = \hat{\boldsymbol{s_1}}^T \hat{\boldsymbol{s_2}}.$$

In this paper, we use the cosine similarity to evaluate the similarity between two segments. Intuitively, two segments with higher cosine value are more similar. That means that they may have more similar term distributions, and may follow the same subtopic. Accordingly, we formulate the problem of finding a best clustering among consecutive text segments as follows.

PROBLEM 1. *Given a text document with its normalized segment vectors, a limit k on the number of clusters, and an objective function called "MaxQuality", find a clustering that maximizes the objective function and follows the constraint that each cluster contains continuous segments.*

The objective function, is the sum of cosine similarities between all segment centres and their neighborhoods in the same cluster. In each cluster denoted by $\boldsymbol{I_i}$, the segment centre is defined as $\boldsymbol{c_i} = \frac{1}{|\boldsymbol{I_i}|}\sum_{\hat{\boldsymbol{s}}\in \boldsymbol{I_i}} \hat{\boldsymbol{s}}$, where $|\boldsymbol{I_i}|$ is the number of segments in the cluster $\boldsymbol{I_i}$. We normalize it as $\hat{\boldsymbol{c_i}} = \frac{\boldsymbol{c_i}}{\|\boldsymbol{c_i}\|}$. Then the *MaxQuality* of $\boldsymbol{I_i}$ is computed as

$$\sum_{\hat{\boldsymbol{s}}\in \boldsymbol{I_i}} \hat{\boldsymbol{s}}^T \hat{\boldsymbol{c_i}} = \|\sum_{\hat{\boldsymbol{s}}\in \boldsymbol{I_i}} \hat{\boldsymbol{s}}\|.$$

We develop an optimal algorithm to solve problem 1. The solution is similar to finding the V-optimal histogram using dynamic programming [8], that attempts to find the best boundaries among k clusters by maximizing the objective function. The optimal algorithm uses a systematic search to solve the problem. In Figure 3, the optimal clustering of k clusters can be reduced to the optimal clustering of k-1 clusters by enumerating all possible boundaries for the last k^{th} cluster. Therefore, the *MaxQuality* of the optimal clustering can be computed using dynamic programming.

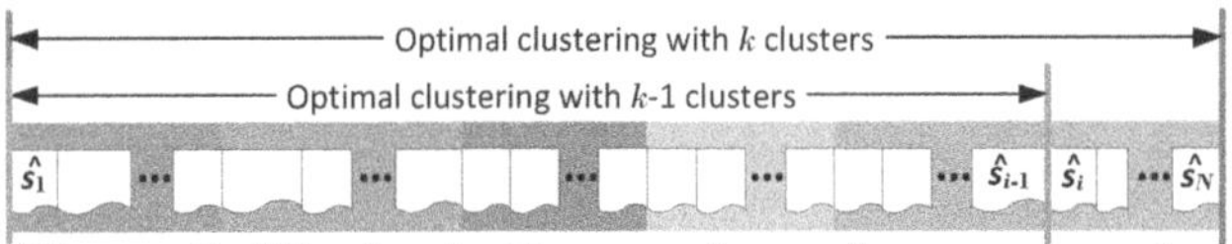

Figure 3: The basic idea on dynamic programming

Continuing with Example 1, suppose we normalized the 7 obtained segment vectors into unit vectors. We then present how to build a V-optimal histogram with $k = 3$ clusters on these unit vectors using dynamic programming.

EXAMPLE 2. *Consider the input of 7 unit segment vectors in Figure 4 (a). Figure 4 (b) shows three iterations to run the optimal algorithm. Iteration 1 first constructs the V-optimal histogram with 1 cluster. The MaxQuality is computed for every possible interval. For example, MaxQuality[1..3] is computed as the MaxQuality in the interval of "1..3" (=* $\{\hat{\boldsymbol{s_1}}, \hat{\boldsymbol{s_2}}, \hat{\boldsymbol{s_3}}\}$*), i.e., MaxQuality[1..3] = 2.23. Iteration 2 constructs the histogram of 2 clusters using the results from Iteration 1. Figure 4 (b) shows an example to calculate MaxQuality[1..7]. There are six possible clustering. By computing the MaxQuality for each clustering, the second or fifth one is the best one that has a maximum value. Our algorithm randomly pick the fifth one as the best clustering. Thus, we have MaxQuality[1..7] = 4.86. Similarly, Iteration 3 computes the histogram of 3 clusters. Finally, the optimal clustering for 7 given vectors is found with MaxQuality[1..7] = 6.04.*

We use the output of the optimal algorithm to produce the topic hierarchy in a top-down approach. See the running example in Figure 4. We output the best clustering in each iteration of the optimal algorithm and retain the hierarchical relationships between clusters as shown in Figure 4 (c). Then, the topic hierarchy can be naturally generated by representing each node using the selective keywords or phrases from the segment centre in each cluster as shown in Figure 4 (d). The only problem is how to extract informative keywords to label the tree nodes. We use a new ranking score, denoted by *ctf-dtf*, for selecting the keywords based on the term frequency. Given a cluster $\boldsymbol{I_i}$ and a term t. The $ctf(t, \boldsymbol{I_i})$ is the number of occurrences of t in $\boldsymbol{I_i}$. The $dtf(t)$ is the number of occurrences of t in the whole document d.

$$\text{ctf-dtf}(t, \boldsymbol{I_i}) = \alpha \times \frac{ctf(t, \boldsymbol{I_i})}{|\boldsymbol{I_i}|} + (1-\alpha) \times \frac{dtf(t)}{|d|}$$

Here, α is a predefined weight with $0 \leq \alpha \leq 1$. In our implementation, we use $\alpha = 0.5$. A term occurring both frequently in the cluster and in the whole document will have a high ranking score. Consequently, it will be a strong candidate for being a representative keyword. Consider the cluster in the first level in Figure 4 (c). Terms "bookstore, ..., word" of higher scores are selected, and used as labelled keywords for the root tree node as shown in Figure 4 (d). To detect key phrases containing more useful context information, we use an adjacency list to index each item, storing all its adjacent words in the document. For any two keywords, we use the adjacency list to check whether they are adjacency or not, and return the count they appear together in a passage. If the count exceeds a given threshold, we combine them into one phrase. In Figure 4 (d), two keywords "closed" and "yesterday" are combined into one phrase.

In our optimal algorithm, the parameter k is flexible to control the granularity of segmentation, i.e., the node number: how many textual units are to be identified at each level. With dynamic programming, we can expand the level number by incrementally computation from its parent level, with guarantee on the quality of clustering, i.e., the quality of segmentation in each level. As far as we know, no previous technique can satisfy all these requirements.

2.2 Query Construction

The topic hierarchy can represent a text document in a top-down fashion. That is to say, the lower-level nodes can summarize topical passages more specifically than the upper-level ones, by reserving the context. Based on the hierarchy, it is easy to derive multiple queries for retrieving relevant social media contents. The naive approach is to construct one query for each root-to-leaf path, using the combination of selective phrases in the leaf node. As shown in Figure 4 (e), three queries are generated using all the root-to-leaf paths of the topic tree in Figure 4 (d). For each query path, the selected keywords or phrases are submitted to the API of social media systems like Twitter Search API using the OR search[2]. Clearly, the query count is equal to the leaf node number. Note that a phrase including multiple keywords is regarded as AND operators in the search.

In practice, the naive solution sometimes fails to satisfy our requirements, as the social media system like Twitter

[2]https://dev.twitter.com/rest/public/search

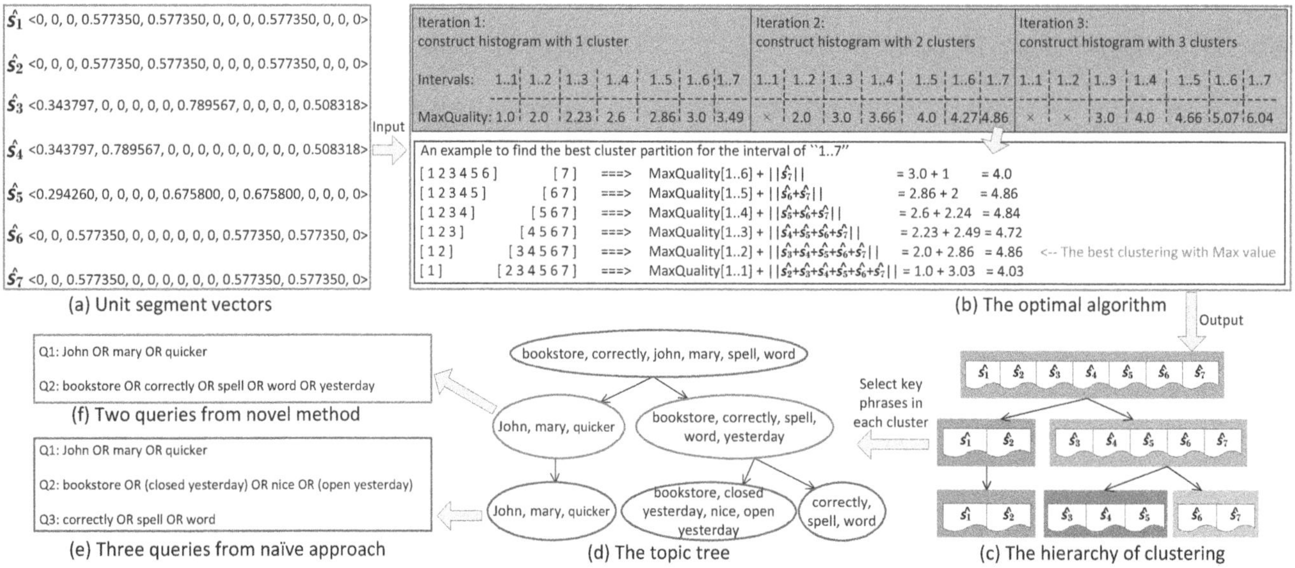

Figure 4: A running example

has the rate limit problem[3]. The need arises to construct a limited number of queries, especially when the allowed request number is less than the leaf node number. So far, no work takes this need into account.

We propose a bottom-up aggregation method to reduce the query number. The intuition is to group some query paths together if their leaf nodes contain the lowest common ancestor[4] (LCA). Based on the property of topic tree, each level only has one pair of nodes derived from a LCA in one step higher level. If we aggregate two query paths containing this pair of nodes into one subtree from the bottom level, we can reduce the query number one by one until the cardinality of query set obeys the rate limit. For each query subtree, we can construct one query using the selected phrases of its LCA, as an OR search to retrieve social media systems. For a query subtree having only one branch, we can use any descendant as the selected LCA. Continuing with the example in Figure 4 (e), Q2 and Q3 are grouped into one query using their LCA in Figure 4 (f). The LCAs are presented in the red circles in Figure 4 (d).

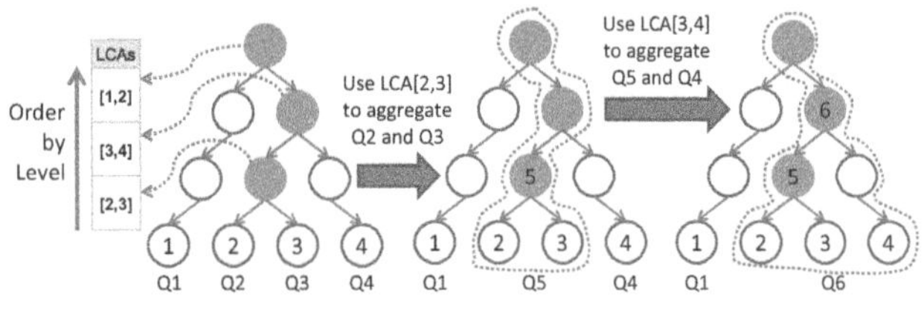

Figure 5: An example to store LCAs

To efficiently support query aggregation, the need arises to pre-compute LCAs for each pair of consecutive nodes in the topic tree. We adapt Tarjan's off-line lowest common ancestors algorithm [5], to store LCAs in each level of the tree. See Figure 5. Given a four-level topic tree, we find LCAs for each pair of consecutive leaf nodes, which are indexed in a list. For example, the LCA of leaf nodes 2 and 3 is denoted by "[2,3]" in the list of LCAs. Clearly, each level contains only one LCA, and the LCA list is ordered by level number from bottom to top. With this index, it is easy for us to apply the bottom-up query aggregation. Suppose the limit only allows us to submit two queries. Given four root-to-leaf paths, we have four queries of Q1, Q2, Q3, and Q4, which are constructed using the combination of phrases from four leaf nodes. We show how to reduce the query number using the LCA index. We scan the list to first access the LCA of "[2,3]". Then, the query paths containing leaf nodes of 2 and 3 are aggregated into one query subtree, as shown in the red dotted region in the second three in the figure. Then a new query Q5 is generated by using the LCA of node 5. Similarly, we can further integrate two queries of Q5 and Q4 into one query of Q6 by using the LCA of "[3,4]". Thus, the two queries of Q1 and Q6 are finally constructed and submitted to the social search API.

2.3 Data Assignment

While obtaining relevant social media contents, we employ a propagation based method to assign the query results to relevant passages in two phases.

1. For each query, we propagate the returned results down to the descendant nodes of the query subtree using a greedy algorithm. For each result, we compute its Overlap to all the descendant nodes, and assign it to the one with the highest Overlap value. All results are finally assigned into the leaf nodes of the topic tree.

2. For each leaf node, we use the cosine similarity to rank the results and map each result into the appropriate segment (passage). For each segment, we only retain most relevant results and discard those of very low ranking scores. Moreover, if there is no result in a segment, we submit the selected phrases of it as an AND search to retrieve its relevant contents.

We use the Overlap to evaluate the similarity between a result and a tree node, that is defined as the size of the intersection between two term vectors. To finally rank the assigned results for a passage, we use cosine similarity as it is a most common measure [4].

[3]https://dev.twitter.com/rest/public/rate-limiting

[4]http://en.wikipedia.org/wiki/Lowest_common_ancestor

2.4 User Feedback

As described above, the query results are used to automatically suggest annotations that are attached to appropriate passages. We further improve the quality of enrichment by adopting the idea of crowdsourcing[5]. That is, we implement a visualization tool that allows users to browse social media annotations for a document and make feedback. Users can either rate the relevance of a suggested annotation by accept or reject it, or manually add an annotation with personal comments by highlighting texts. For a suggested annotation, we assume that it is more relevant if more users accept it and vice versa; while for a manual annotation, we consider it is more popular with more likes and replies (users can like or comment a manual annotation). According to user feedback, we use the most relevant or popular annotations as the ground truth, to generate new queries for retrieving social media. See Figure 6. The crowdsourcing results from users are re-used as the new contexts for constructing queries. We also apply standard data fusion approaches [13], to merge query results from various contexts and retain most relevant social contents.

2.5 Technical Advantages

The topic hierarchy generation algorithm is the main techniques in our *DocRicher* system. It contains obvious benefits that are three-fold: 1) we propose a global optimal solution with guarantee on the quality of clustering in each level of the topic hierarchy; 2) we provide a flexible way to generate a given number of keyword queries using the hierarchical relationship, overcoming the rate limit problem of social APIs; 3) we use the propagate strategy to assign the query results to avoid unnecessary cross-passage similarity computations.

3. DEMONSTRATION

We demonstrate the *DocRicher* system, with all characteristics described above, such that users can have better understanding of how *DocRicher* employs social media contents like Tweets to augment a document.

Figure 7 presents a snapshot of the ebook reader interface after automatic enrichment on a guide book[6]. The right column exhibits the ebook reading panel; while the left panel marked as (A) presents the "Top Related Tweets", which are suggested annotations automatically returned from our *DocRicher* system. Users can conveniently browse new incoming tweets by clicking the "Enrich" button on the top. When users move the mouse cursor to a specific tweet, such as the one marked as (B), the ebook reading panel automatically show up the highlighted texts of the corresponding passage, marked as (C), that is associated with the tweet. Meanwhile, users can interact with the system to judge that whether a suggested tweet is relevant to the highlighting passage or not, by clicking the "Accept" or "Reject" button inside the tweet. Users are also allowed to do a manual annotation by highlighting a passage and writing the comment. The region marked as (D) lists such manual annotations.

DocRicher is equipped with an automatic recommendation system based on knowledge discovery on a text document and its annotations. We run a periodical task on the background to process each text document. Given a page of "Tourist Guide Sydney" as an example, we first analyze its text contents to generate a three-level topic tree, as shown in the region marked as (E), with each node consisting of extracted phrases. For example, the second leaf node has phrases of *tourist*, *Sydney Opera House* and *Opera*, which are summarized from the passage marked as (C). We construct a query with combinations of these phrases to search the Twitter API, and visualize most relevant results for users to understand the underlying discoveries in an interactive manner. For example, the first three tweets in the region marked as (A) are the top-3 results. If the suggested annotation marked as (B) is accepted as a relevant result by many users, then we save this as a permanent annotation, that will be late displayed in the region marked as (D). We further adopt those permanent annotations with highest relevant scores to construct new queries for retrieving social media, and do data fusion for both old and new results. The top results for each passage are updated, and will be displayed in the region marked as (A) when users refresh current "Tourist Guide Sydney" page or click the "Enrich" button.

[5]http://en.wikipedia.org/wiki/Crowdsourcing

[6]The book is from http://www.australiatourism.com.

Acknowledgment

This work was supported by the Singapore NRF under its IRC@SG Funding Initiative and administered by the IDMPO, at the SeSaMe Centre, under the project of Readpeer.

4. REFERENCES

[1] R. Agrawal, S. Gollapudi, A. Kannan, and K. Kenthapadi. Similarity search using concept graphs. In *CIKM*. ACM Association for Computing Machinery, November 2014.

[2] R. Angheluta, R. D. Busser, and M.-F. Moens. The use of topic segmentation for automatic summarization. In *Workshop on Text Summarization in Conjunction with the ACL*, pages 11–12, 2002.

[3] L. Carroll. Evaluating hierarchical discourse segmentation. *ACL*, 2010.

[4] I. S. Dhillon, Y. Guan, and J. Kogan. Refining clusters in high dimensional text data. In *SIAM*, pages 71–82, 2002.

[5] H. N. Gabow and R. E. Tarjan. A linear-time algorithm for a special case of disjoint set union. In *STOC*, pages 246–251, 1983.

[6] N. Gandhi, V. Gaikwad, P. Kasat, N. Garg, A. Doke, V. Kumar, S. Karande, V. Banahatti, and N. Pedanekar. Pustack: Towards an augmented, scalable and personalized interface for paper textbooks. In *APCHI*, pages 174–177, 2013.

[7] V. Gupta and G. S. Lehal. A survey of text summarization extractive techniques. *JETWI*, 2(3):258–268, 2010.

[8] H. V. Jagadish, N. Koudas, S. Muthukrishnan, V. Poosala, K. C. Sevcik, and T. Suel. Optimal histograms with quality guarantees. In *VLDB*, pages 275–286, 1998.

[9] A. G. Jivani. A comparative study of stemming algorithms. *Int. J. Comp. Tech. Appl*, 2(6):1930–1938, 2011.

[10] W. Kang, A. K. H. Tung, W. Chen, X. Li, S. Qiyue, C. Zhang, F. Zhao, and X. Zhou. Trendspedia: An internet observatory for analyzing and visualizing the evolving web. In *ICDE*, 2014.

[11] M. Michelson and S. A. Macskassy. Discovering users' topics of interest on twitter: A first look. In *AND*, pages 73–80, 2010.

[12] R. Mihalcea and A. Csomai. Wikify!: Linking documents to encyclopedic knowledge. In *CIKM*, CIKM '07, pages 233–242, 2007.

[13] J. A. Shaw, E. A. Fox, J. A. Shaw, and E. A. Fox. Combination of multiple searches. In *TREC*, pages 243–252, 1994.

[14] Y. Yaari. Segmentation of expository texts by hierarchical agglomerative clustering. *RANLP*, 1997.

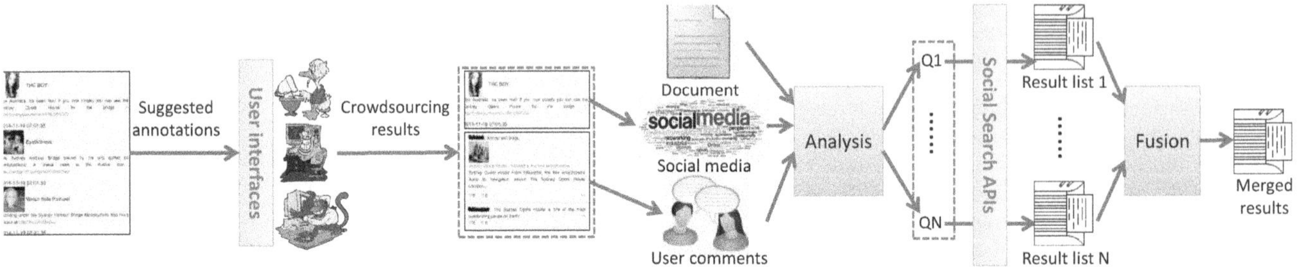

Figure 6: The architectural implementation of user feedback

Figure 7: Current ebook reader with enriched tweet annotations

A Demonstration of Rubato DB: A Highly Scalable NewSQL Database System for OLTP and Big Data Applications

Li-Yan Yuan
Department of Computing Science
University of Alberta
yuan@cs.ualberta.ca

Lengdong Wu
Department of Computing Science
University of Alberta
lengdong@cs.ualberta.ca

Jia-Huai You
Department of Computing Science
University of Alberta
you@cs.ualberta.ca

Yan Chi
Shanghai Shifang Software
chiyan@rubatodb.com

ABSTRACT

We propose to demonstrate Rubato DB, a highly scalable NewSQL system, supporting various consistency levels from ACID to BASE for OLTP and big data applications. Rubato DB employs the staged grid architecture with a novel formula based protocol for distributed concurrency control. Our demonstration will present Rubato DB as one NewSQL database management system running on a collection of commodity servers against two of benchmark sets.

The demo attendees can modify the configuration of system size, fine-tune the query workload, and visualize the performance on the fly by the graphical user interface. Attendees can experiment with various system scales, and thus grasp the potential scalability of Rubato DB, whose performance, with the increase of the number of servers used, can achieve a linear growth for both OLTP application with the strong consistency properties and key-value storage applications with the weak consistency properties.

Categories and Subject Descriptors

H.2.4 [**Database Management**]: Systems—*Concurrency, Transaction processing*; H.3.4 [**Information Storage and Retrieval**]: Systems and Software—*Distributed systems*

Keywords

Scalability; Architecture; Concurrency Control; ACID; BASE

1. INTRODUCTION

Today, data is flowing into organizations at an unprecedented scale in the world. The ability to scale out for processing an enhanced workload has become an important factor for the proliferation and popularization of data management system. The pursuit for tackling the big data challenges has given rise to a plethora of data management systems characterized by high scalability. Diverse systems for processing big data explore various possibilities in the infrastructure design space [17]. The trend of using lower-end, commodity servers to scale out configurations has become popular, due to the drop in prices for the hardware and the improvement in performance and reliability.

A notable phenomena is the NoSQL movement that began in early 2009 and is growing rapidly. NoSQL systems are characterized as simplified highly scalable systems addressing properties of schema-free, simple-API, horizontal scalability and relaxed consistency [2, 5, 8].

The recently proposed NewSQL systems (relative to NoSQL) aim to achieve the high scalability and availability same as NoSQL, while preserving the ACID properties for transactions and complex functionality of relational databases [11]. NewSQL database systems are appropriate in applications where traditional RDBMS have been used, but requiring additional scalability and performance enhancement.

According to the core requirement differences between NoSQL systems and NewSQL systems, there are challenges in the design and implementation of NewSQL systems in the following aspects:

- **Data model.** NoSQL systems usually merely support non-relational data model such as key-value stores [5] and Bigtable-like stores [1]. NoSQL systems represent a recent evolution by making trade-off between scalability and complexity of the data model. Thus the implementation of NewSQL systems faces with the first issue:

  Is the complex relational data model an obstacle of scalability?

- **Consistency model.** NoSQL systems represent an evolution in building scalable infrastructure by sacrificing strong consistency and opting for weak consistency [2, 5, 8]. However, strong consistency levels such as ACID properties are essential for NewSQL systems to manage critical data which requires both liveness and safety guarantees. The implementation of NewSQL systems meets the second challenge:

  Is it possible to achieve high scalability with ACID?

SIGMOD'15, May 31–June 4, 2015, Melbourne, Victoria, Australia.

http://dx.doi.org/10.1145/2723372.2735380.

- **Architecture.** Traditional database vendors employ new techniques to explore the scalability of the symmetric multiple processing (SMP) architecture and the massively parallel processing (MPP) architecture. However, because of the inherent deficiencies due to the resources contention, the scalability of such architectures is not comparable with NoSQL systems. Some NoSQL systems based on the Bigtable [1] and MapReduce framework [4] utilize the shared-nothing infrastructure to provide high scalability. A set of systems with high-level declarative languages, including Yahoo! Pig [9] and Facebook Hive [13], are realized to compile queries into the MapReduce framework on the Hadoop platform.

  To achieve high performance and scalability, innovative software architecture should be applied to NewSQL systems, then we need to consider:

  Is it possible to scale out commonly used single server database system design?

We have developed a highly scalable NewSQL system, called Rubato DB [19] with satisfactory solutions for the challenges as mentioned above, by applying the principles as following:

- Exploring the close integration of data partitioning and relational data model to eschew data skew for transactions.
- Obtaining high scalability with the MapReduce [4] sevice-oriented architecture.
- Scaling out the concurrency control protocol for ACID based on timestamps rather than any locking mechanism.
- Overcoming the weakness of BASE through stronger consistency models such as BASIC [16].

The implementation of Rubato DB combines and extends the ideas from:

> hybrid data partitioning, staged-event driven architecture (SEDA) [15], data-intensive MapReduce framework [4], and distributed timestamp-based concurrency control;

and using innovative technologies such as

> formula based protocol, software instruction, lazy loading, dynamic timestamp ordering, multiple communication protocols.

Rubato DB[1] is a highly scalable NewSQL database system running on a collection of commodity servers that supports various consistency guarantees including the traditional ACID and BASE, and a novel consistency level in between, i.e., BASIC [16]; and conforms with the SQL2003; and has been used in some commercial applications.

The proposed demo is to demonstrate and verify the performance and scalability of Rubato DB under both TPC-C benchmark [14] and YCSB benchmark [3]. More specifically, the demonstration will allow demo attendees to try out Rubato DB for the following objectives:

1. **Feasible Configuration**. To deploy Rubato DB on a collection of commodity servers, ranging from 1 to 16.
2. **Data Loading**. To load large size of data distributed across numbers of nodes automatically according to pre-defined data partitioning schema.
3. **High Scalability**. To demonstrate the linear scalability of Rubato DB for typical OLTP applications requiring the ACID properties under TPC-C benchmark.
4. **Various Consistency Levels**. To compare performances of Rubato DB with either BASE or BASIC properties and other NoSQL systems with BASE properties under YCSB benchmark.

A friendly Graphical User Interface will be provided in the proposed demo to enable demo attendees to choose different experiments and deployment configurations, and to display performance results and internal working loads.

The rest of the paper is organized as follows. Section 2 describes the architecture of Rubato DB and some of its key features; and Section 3 outlines the experiment setup and the demonstration we plan to show. The conclusion is in Section 4.

2. OVERVIEW OF RUBATO DB

Rubato DB is a scalable NewSQL database system supporting relational data model for data-centric applications. The main architectural components of Rubato DB are depicted in Figure 1 [19]. We firstly give a brief overview of the several essential Rubato DB components as below, before describing the contents of our demonstration.

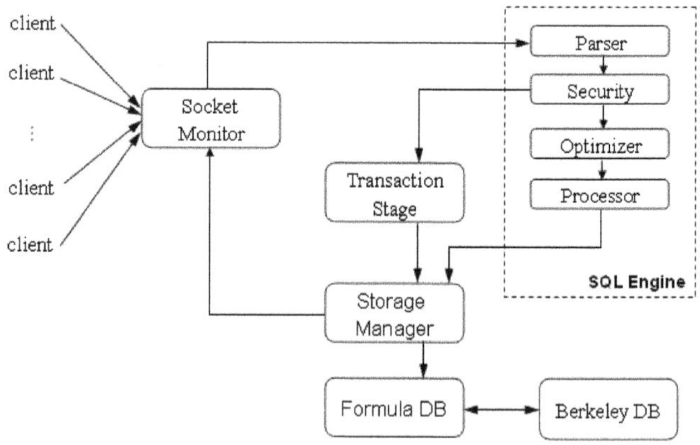

Figure 1: RubatoDB system architecture

2.1 Socket Monitor

Rubato DB runs on a collection of servers as one database management system, with a single socket monitor to establish and record the connection states for all client requests.

The socket monitor adopts a loading control schema, called *lazy loading*, to reduce data contention and to minimize unnecessary rollbacks. The socket monitor maintains two lists of clients: a list of active clients with active transactions, and a list of requesting clients whose requests are waiting to be evaluated. The socket monitor will guarantee that the

[1]The name Rubato, (from Italian rubare), in music, means subtle rhythmic manipulation and nuance in performance. It describes the practice of Rubato DB for supporting various consistencies with freedom.

waiting transaction is among the oldest 20% ones base on the following practical principle: if all the current requests have higher potential to conflict with other requests, the system should rather wait awhile for new requests with lower conflict potential to arrive.

2.2 SQL Engine

Rubato DB's SQL engine is used to process all the SQL queries, including aggregate functions and nested queries, updates, and all other requests according to SQL2003 [18].

The SQL engine is composed as a set of staged grid modules, each of which is a self-contained software module consisting of an incoming request queue, as illustrated in Figure 2. Threads within each staged grid module operate by pulling a sequence of requests, one at a time, off the input queue, invoking the application-supplied event handler (e.g. parser, optimizer, query, update, etc) to process requests, and dispatching outgoing results by enqueuing them on the request queues of outgoing staged grid module, located either in the same server or another server within LAN. Each request to the system will be processed in a relay-style by being passed from one staged grid module to the next one until it is completed. Both parallelism and pipeline execution are supported by the engine.

A set of software instructions are employed to carry the operation's backpack with its private state and data. The instruction with a uniform format is the only packet flowing through different staged grid modules. To improve the performance, multiple communication protocols are utilized depending on the source and destination locations of stages and/or system resources.

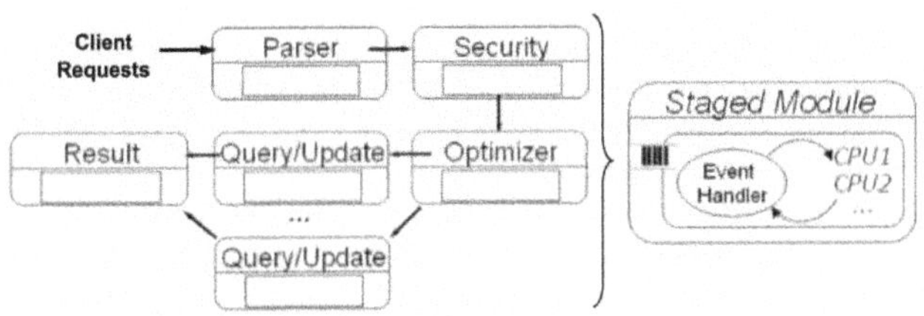

Figure 2: Staged Modules of SQL Engine

2.3 Transaction Manager

The transaction manager, consisting of *Transaction stage* and *Formula DB*, is responsible for coordinating data access on multiple nodes based on a novel formula protocol for concurrency (FPC) to ensure serializability. It is the transaction manager that performs all the transactional operations, including pre-commit (necessary for distributed concurrency), commit, and rollback.

The FPC is a novel implementation of the classical Multiversion Timestamp Concurrency Control Protocol [12], with two distinct features:

1. Instead of using multiple versions of updated data items, FPC uses formulas stored in memory (associated with the updated data items) to represent the multiple values of updated data items, which will reduce overhead of storing multiple versions of data replicas.

2. The timestamp ordering of transactions may be altered to allow a transaction with older timestamp to read the data item updated by a later transaction, as long as the serializability is respected, which will increase the degree of concurrency.

The two parts of the transaction manager perform their respective responsibilities:

(a) *Transaction stage.* A dedicated stage grid module that is located in every grid server and is responsible for all the basic transactional operations including *pre_commit*, *commit* and *rollback* of the transaction manager.

(b) *Formula DB.* A thread-free layer on the top of the Berkeley DB such that all disk accesses in Rubato DB are through Formula DB.

Three consistency levels are supported by Rubato DB:

1. **ACID.** The strongest end of the consistency spectrum for the transactional functionalities.

2. **BASE.** The most notable weak consistency model used by NoSQL systems [2, 5, 8]. The BASE can be summarized as: the system responses basically all the time (Basically Available), is not necessary to be always consistent (Soft-state), but has to come to a consistent state eventually (Eventual consistency) [10].

3. **BASIC.** Rubato DB is not limited to merely ACID that is too strong and BASE that is too weak, but rather supports BASIC, a spectrum between these two extreme. BASIC stands for Basic Availability, Scalability, and Instant Consistency [16]. BASE and BASIC provide different choices between the model that is faster but requiring extra efforts to deal with inconsistent results and the model that delivers consistent results but is relatively slower with higher latency.

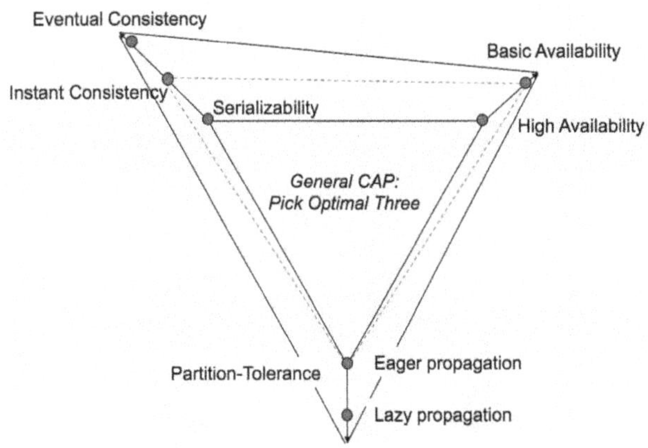

Figure 3: Generalized CAP Theorem [16]

Figure 3 illustrates the various consistency levels supported by Rubato DB together with different tolerance for fault or network partition.

Serializability enforces a serial execution order of all operations on partitions. *Instant Consistency* guarantees that all partitioned data seen by each read operation reflects a consistent snapshot. *Eventual consistency* ensures that if no new updates are made to the data, eventually all accesses will return the last updated value.

High availability enforces that all writes will successfully commit as long as the client does not explicitly abort it. *Basic availability* is relatively relaxed comparing with high availability. An internal abort for write can occur to guarantee continuous response. Read can return an out-of-date version in both high availability and basic availability.

Partition tolerance depends on the policy of update manipulation consisting of eager propagation or lazy propagation. We can have that a system achievable in BASIC (i.e., the inner dashed line triangle) provides stricter consistency level than a system providing BASE (i.e., the outer solid line triangle).

2.4 Storage Manager

Rubato DB uses a hybrid data storage partition solution to allow a table to be partitioned vertically and horizontally and stored separately over different grid nodes.

Storage manager uses Berkeley DB for all disk accesses to direct attached storages (DAS). All tables and their partitions if any are stored on local disk as a Berkeley DB file. To obtain maximum performance, when a table is created according to the schema, the storage manager provides facilities for users to specify fine-grained hybrid storage partitioning based on application semantics and query workload.

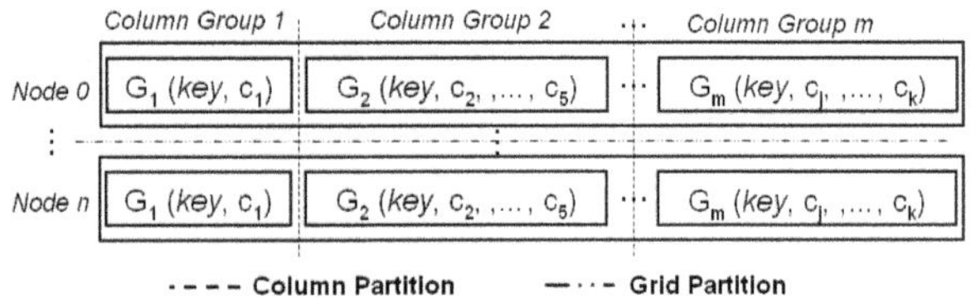

Figure 4: Hybrid partition of Storage Manager

As depicted in Figure 4, the column partition enables users to store a single relation as a collection of disjoint (none-key columns) vertical partitions of different groups. Columns frequently accessed together are clustered into the same frequent column group, while columns seldom accessed are categorized into static column groups. Compression can be applied to take the benefits of column-oriented layout.

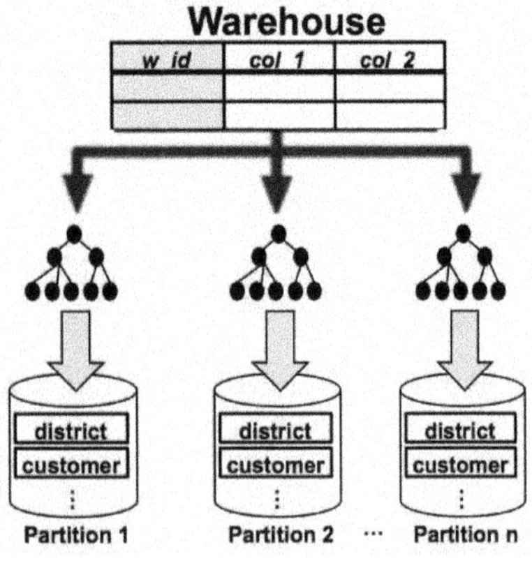

Figure 5: Grid partition illustration

The grid partition is used to deploy data on multiple nodes and thus provides scale-out capability. Rubato DB applies a tree-based schema for grid partitioning, as demonstrated in Figure 5. Tuples in every descendent table are partitioned according to the ancestor that they descend from. As a consequence, data accessed within a transaction will be located in the same data node [6, 7]. This tree structure implies that, there are a group of related rows in the descendant tables corresponding to every row in the root table. All rows inherent from the same root are guaranteed to be co-located.

3. DEMONSTRATION

The proposed demo is to demonstrate and verify the performance of Rubato DB under both TPC-C [14] and YCSB benchmark tests [3]. The demonstration will allow demo attendees to try out Rubato DB for the following objectives:

1. **Feasible Configuration**. How to deploy Rubato DB on a collection of commodity servers?
2. **Data Loading**. How to load large size of data distributed across numbers of nodes automatically according to the predefined data partitioning schema?
3. **High Scalability**. What is the scalability of Rubato DB for the typical OLTP applications requiring the ACID properties?
4. **Various Consistency Levels**. What are performance comparisons between Rubato DB with either BASE or BASIC properties and other NoSQL systems with BASE property for big data applications?

A graphical user interface for Rubato DB will be provided to facilitate users to explore Rubato DB.

3.1 Setup Details

All the demo will be conducted on a collection of four (4) commodity servers with 4 quad-core Intel Xeon CPUs, 64 GB of main memory, SATA disks configured in RAID0, running Linux Ubuntu 12.04 LTS.

For simplicity, each server may be used as 1 to 4 nodes, that is, Rubato DB may be configured and then deployed on all four servers as 16 nodes such that all nodes will be connected only through the TCP/IP protocol.

Our demo is based on two well-known representative benchmarks. We use the TPC-C [14] benchmark's set of transactions, database schema, and pre-generated data as our target domain for demo about OLTP workloads. All the demos conducted are according to the TPC-C specification. In addition, demo attendees can also take the Yahoo! Cloud Serving Benchmark (YCSB) [3] on Rubato DB. The number of operations per second will be reported with varying distribution of read/write operations.

In order to demonstrate most important features of Rubato DB within a limited time, we have pre-load all the initial databases as per the benchmark specifications.

For the TPC-C benchmark, we have populated 2000 warehouses, and all TPC-C tables are column-partitioned in to frequent and static column groups; and then grid-partitioned across different nodes according to a schema structure. The number of warehouses deployed is proportional to the system size chosen by the attendee.

For YCSB which is relatively simple, we define a multi-column structure for each record, which consists of one key column of integer type and 20 data columns of text type. We pre-load 100 million 1KB records on each node, resulting 120GB of raw data per node.

3.2 Demonstration Details

The proposed demonstration will perform both TPC-C and YCSB benchmarks on various configurations, including the number of nodes (scalability), the number of warehouses (the work load for TPC-C), and weights in read/write (the workload for YCSB). The following table summarizes the results displayed for various tasks and/or configurations.

Task	Nodes	Work load	Display
TPC-C	1-16	100-2000 (warehouses)	tmpC CPU/Memory Usage
YCSB	1-12	0% - 10% (write operations)	Throughput Latency

3.3 User Interaction

To facilitate interaction with Rubato DB during the demonstration, a friendly graphical user interface is provided, as shown in the mock-up in Figure 6.

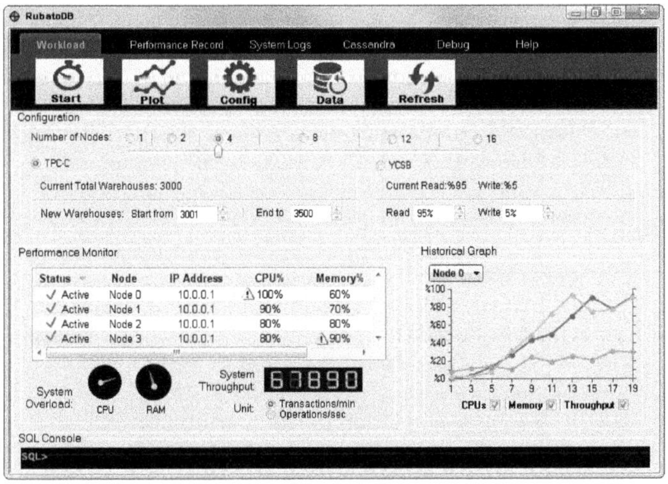

Figure 6: Graphical User Interface of Rubato DB

The interface consists of the following panels.

1. Configuration Panel:

   This panel enable users to choose

   (a) the demo tasks: TPC-C or YCSB tests;

   (b) the number of nodes, from 1 to 16 nodes;

   (c) the workload: the number of warehouses for TPC-C and the read/write weight for YCSB;

   (d) various consistency levels: ACID, BASIC, BASE.

2. Performance Monitor Panel:

   This panel displays the demo performance, including the number of transactions/minute (TPC-C) or the number of operations/second (YCSB), the CPU time and the memory usage, and the status of each node.

3. Historical Graph Panel:

   It is used to visualize the change curve of throughput as well as the CPU time and memory usage of each node, as specified by the user.

4. SQL Panel:

   An SQL console is provided for users to query the Rubato DB as well to manipulate workload control.

3.4 Performance Expectation

Demo attendees can obtain the performance of Rubato DB using the GUI. Here we provide the expected performance results so that attendees can make the comparison and verify the features of Rubato DB.

Figure 7 demonstrates that the performance (tpmC)[2] of the TPC-C benchmark test of Rubato DB increases from 5000 concurrent clients (500 warehouses) running on a system instance with 1-node, to 67,000 concurrent clients (6700 warehouses) running on a system instance with 16 nodes[3]. The result under the TPC-C benchmark test clearly shows that: (1) the performance of Rubato DB scales up linearly with the increase of the number of nodes deployed in the system; and (2) the rollback ratio is stable at a low level no matter to what size the system increases.

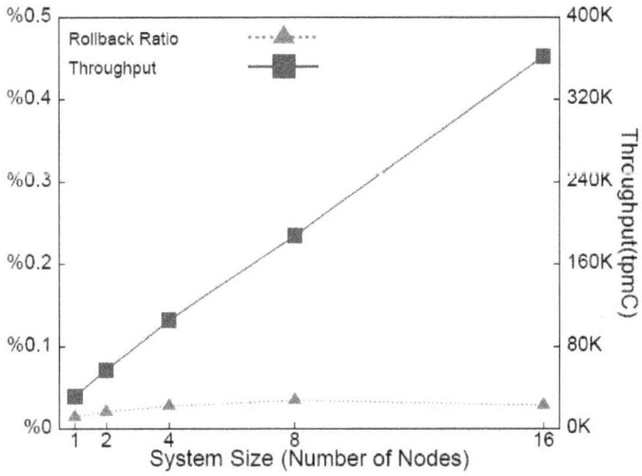

Figure 7: Expected Results of TPC-C Benchmark

For the results of YCSB, though users can set any proportion for read/write operation, we present the performance for a typical read-intensive workloads: read intensive (90% read and 10% write operations).

Also, we present the comparison with Cassandra[4] [8]: an open-source key-value store clone of Dynamo [5], HBase[5]: an open-source bigtable-like system [1]. The experiments are conducted with the number of nodes as 1, 2, 4, 8 and 12. Results shown in Figure 8, 9 can clearly demonstrate that: the performance and scalability of Rubato DB is comparable with that of other popular scalable NoSQL system.

By demonstrating the performance of Rubato DB with BASIC properties in Figure 8, 9, we can also show that Rubato DB with BASIC properties still preserves near-linear scalability with increasing throughput and flat latency, same as systems with BASE. We can conclude that: the cost induced by BASIC is acceptable comparing with the extra efforts needed to manipulate the inconsistent soft states for BASE. BASIC pays a reasonable price for a higher consistency than BASE.

---

[2]tpmC is defined as the number of New-Order transactions per minute a system generates while executing other transactions (Payment, Order-Status, Delivery, Stock-Level).

[3]As the demo will be carried out in 16 nodes running on 4 servers, the performance results of Rubato DB represented in the figures is not necessarily that of the demo.

[4]http://cassandra.apache.org/

[5]http://hbase.apache.org/

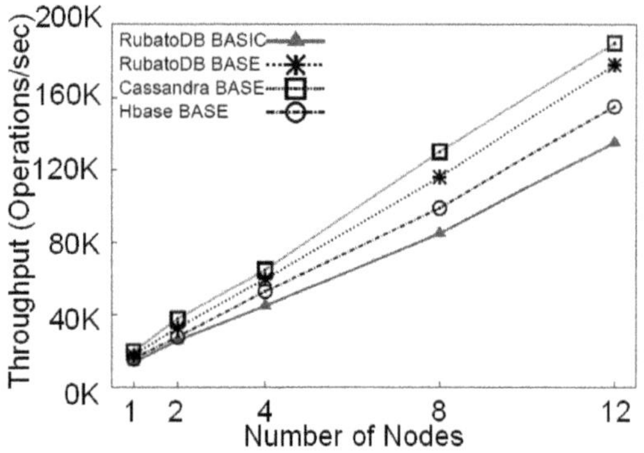

Figure 8: Expected Throughout Comparison of YCSB

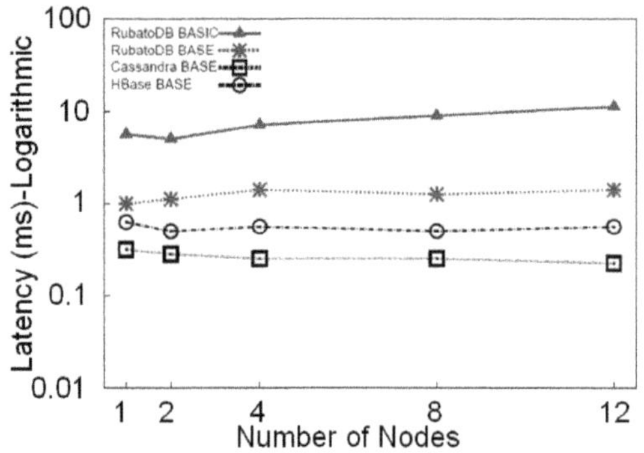

Figure 9: Expected Latency Comparison of YCSB

4. CONCLUSION

The development of NewSQL database systems is a topic with strong interest over recent years and with a great potential impact on data management, especially in the face of big data challenges. We present a demonstration of Rubato DB, a scalable NewSQL system, showcasing the main feature of scalability with various consistency properties from ACID to BASE, which provides a positive answer to the question on the design and implementation of the new generation of database systems.

5. ACKNOWLEDGEMENTS

Rubato DB is partially supported by the Natural Sciences and Engineering Research Council of Canada (NSERC) under Grant No.RES0001375, and Shanghai Shifang Company under Grant No.RES0012485. We also sincerely thank Cybera's Rapid Access Cloud for providing experimental server resources for Rubato DB.

6. REFERENCES

[1] F. Chang, J. Dean, S. Ghemawat, and etc. Bigtable: A distributed storage system for structured data. *ACM Transactions on Computer Systems*, 26(2):4, 2008.

[2] B. F. Cooper, R. Ramakrishnan, U. Srivastava, A. Silberstein, P. Bohannon, H.-A. Jacobsen, N. Puz, D. Weaver, and R. Yerneni. Pnuts: Yahoo!'s hosted data serving platform. *Proceedings of the VLDB Endowment*, 1(2):1277–1288, 2008.

[3] B. F. Cooper, A. Silberstein, E. Tam, R. Ramakrishnan, and R. Sears. Benchmarking cloud serving systems with ycsb. In *Proc. the 1st ACM Symposium on Cloud computing*, pages 143–154. ACM, 2010.

[4] J. Dean and S. Ghemawat. Mapreduce: simplified data processing on large clusters. *Communications of the ACM*, 51(1):107–113, 2008.

[5] G. DeCandia, D. Hastorun, M. Jampani, G. Kakulapati, A. Lakshman, A. Pilchin, S. Sivasubramanian, P. Vosshall, and W. Vogels. Dynamo: Amazon's highly available key-value store. *ACM SIGOPS Operating Systems Review*, 41(6):205–220, 2007.

[6] M. Grund, J. Krüger, H. Plattner, A. Zeier, P. Cudre-Mauroux, and S. Madden. Hyrise: a main memory hybrid storage engine. *Proc. the VLDB Endowment*, 4(2):105–116, 2010.

[7] E. P. Jones, D. J. Abadi, and S. Madden. Low overhead concurrency control for partitioned main memory databases. In *Proc. the 2010 ACM SIGMOD International Conference on Management of Data*, pages 603–614. ACM, 2010.

[8] A. Lakshman and P. Malik. Cassandra: a decentralized structured storage system. *ACM SIGOPS Operating Systems Review*, 44(2):35–40, 2010.

[9] C. Olston, B. Reed, U. Srivastava, R. Kumar, and A. Tomkins. Pig latin: a not-so-foreign language for data processing. In *Proc. the 2008 ACM SIGMOD International Conference on Management of Data*, pages 1099–1110. ACM, 2008.

[10] D. Pritchett. Base: An acid alternative. *Queue*, 6(3):48–55, 2008.

[11] M. Stonebraker. New opportunities for new sql. *Communications of the ACM*, 55(11):10–11, 2012.

[12] R. Thomas. A solution to the concurrency control problem for multiple copy databases. In *Digest of papers IEEE COMPCON spring*, pages 56–62, 1984.

[13] A. Thusoo, J. S. Sarma, N. Jain, Z. Shao, P. Chakka, S. Anthony, H. Liu, P. Wyckoff, and R. Murthy. Hive: a warehousing solution over a map-reduce framework. *Proc. the VLDB Endowment*, 2(2):1626–1629, 2009.

[14] TPC-C. http://www.tpc.org/tpcc/. 2010.

[15] M. Welsh, D. Culler, and E. Brewer. Seda: an architecture for well-conditioned, scalable internet services. *ACM SIGOPS Operating Systems Review*, 35(5):230–243, 2001.

[16] L. Wu, L. Yuan, and J. You. Basic, an alternative to base for large-scale data management system. In *2014 IEEE International Conference on Big Data*, 2014.

[17] L. Wu, L. Yuan, and J. You. Survey of large-scale data management systems for big data applications. *Journal of Computer Science and Technology*, 30(1):163–183, 2015.

[18] L. Yuan. Correlated tables for nested query evaluation. In *Proc. the International Conference on Internet Studies*, 2014.

[19] L. Yuan, L. Wu, J. You, and Y. Chi. Rubato db: a highly scalable staged grid database system for oltp and big data applications. In *Proc. the 23rd ACM International Conference on Conference on Information and Knowledge Management*, pages 1–10. ACM, 2014.

G-OLA: Generalized On-Line Aggregation for Interactive Analysis on Big Data

Kai Zeng[†] Sameer Agarwal[‡] Ankur Dave[†] Michael Armbrust[‡] Ion Stoica[†]
[†]University of California, Berkeley [‡]Databricks Inc.
[†]{kaizeng, ankurd, istoica}@cs.berkeley.edu [‡]{sameer, michael}@databricks.com

ABSTRACT

Nearly 15 years ago, Hellerstein, Haas and Wang proposed online aggregation (OLA), a technique that allows users to (1) observe the progress of a query by showing iteratively refined approximate answers, and (2) stop the query execution once its result achieves the desired accuracy. In this demonstration, we present `G-OLA`, a novel mini-batch execution model that generalizes OLA to support general OLAP queries with arbitrarily nested aggregates using efficient delta maintenance techniques. We have implemented `G-OLA` in `FluoDB`, a parallel online query execution framework that is built on top of the Spark cluster computing framework that can scale to massive data sets. We will demonstrate `FluoDB` on a cluster of 100 machines processing roughly 10TB of real-world session logs from a video-sharing website. Using an ad optimization and an A/B testing based scenario, we will enable users to perform real-time data analysis via web-based query consoles and dashboards.

1. INTRODUCTION

More and more organizations are increasingly turning towards extracting value from huge amounts of data. In many cases, such value primarily comes from data-driven decisions. Hundreds of thousands of servers, in data centers owned by corporations and businesses, log millions of records every second. These records contain a variety of information—highly confidential financial or medical transactions, visitor information or even web content—and require analysts to run exploratory queries on huge volumes of data. For example, continuously analyzing large volumes of system logs can reveal critical performance bottlenecks in large-scale systems or analyzing user access patterns can give useful insights about what content is popular, which in turn can affect the ad placement strategies. While the individual use cases can be wide and varied, many such scenarios value timeliness of query results over perfect accuracy. Furthermore, in many such cases, the analysis is a human-driven interactive process, and the accuracy needs or the time constraints are usually not known a priori for they can dynamically change based on unquantifiable human factors and the insights gained during the analysis.

SIGMOD'15, May 31–June 4, 2015, Melbourne, Victoria, Australia.

http://dx.doi.org/10.1145/2723372.2735381.

A natural solution to support such interactive exploratory analysis on large volumes of data is online aggregation [17] (OLA). With OLA, given an aggregate query, the system presents the user with some *approximate* but *meaningful* result with an associated error estimate (e.g., confidence intervals), as soon as it has processed a small portion of the whole dataset. The approximate result will be continuously refined, at a speed comfortable to the user, while the system is crunching a larger and larger fraction of the whole dataset. This process continues until either the user is satisfied with the accuracy of the query result and stops the query, or the system has processed all the data. This way, OLA gives the user a smooth observation and control over processing, allowing her to make the accuracy-time trade-off on the fly, based on dynamic and unquantifiable factors including accuracy needs and time constraints.

While being incredibly useful, existing OLA techniques are limited to simple SPJA (Select-Project-Join-Aggregation) queries.[1] In particular, existing OLA only works well for queries that are (practically) monotonic, i.e., whose result can be updated by only looking at the new input tuples. Unfortunately, many aggregate queries, such as the ones in popular OLAP workloads, are *not* monotonic. As an example, consider a simplified `Sessions` log, storing the web sessions of users accessing a video-sharing website, with three columns: `session_id`, `buffer_time`, `play_time`. The "Slow Buffering Impact" (`SBI`) query (Example 1) can be used to find out how a longer (than average) buffering time impacts user retention on the website. While `SBI` is a fairly straightforward nested aggregate query, note that it is non-monotonic as any refinement of the inner aggregate `AVG(buffer_time)` could cause to recompute the whole query. This makes it extremely costly for online processing.

EXAMPLE 1 (SLOW BUFFERING IMPACT).

```
SELECT AVG(play_time)
FROM Sessions
WHERE buffer_time >
   (SELECT AVG(buffer_time)
    FROM Sessions)
```

In this demonstration, we introduce the `G-OLA` (Generalized On-Line Aggregation) execution model for interactive exploratory analysis on large volumes of data. `G-OLA` supports the OLA interface on general OLAP queries—nested aggregate queries with arbitrary nesting and user-defined functions and aggregates. `G-OLA` accomplishes this by efficient delta maintenance techniques that exploit the convergence property of nested aggregate subqueries.

In addition to generalizing OLA, we argue that `G-OLA` can significantly simplify the design of Sampling-based Approximate Query Processing (S-AQP) systems, by addressing one of the main chal-

[1]SPJA queries are those that consist of any combinations of select, project and join operators followed by an aggregation operator.

lenges of these systems—that of predicting the optimal sample size given a user-specified accuracy or time constraint. Specifically, due to the limitations of error estimation techniques, it is very hard for existing S-AQP systems to accurately predict the smallest sample size that could satisfy an accuracy criterion. On one hand, closed-form error estimation techniques, such as the ones based on Central Limit Theorem (CLT) or deviation inequalities (e.g., Hoeffding Bounds) can only predict sample size for simple SPJA queries. On the other hand, resampling methods such as bootstrap [14], although can estimate errors for complex SQL queries, lack the ability to predict the sample size. One workaround proposed in BlinkDB [3, 4] is to bootstrap the query on different sample sizes, and fit a profile curve of error vs. sample size based on an extrapolated cost model. However, there are several limitations with this technique. First, it complicates the system design making it harder to tune and manage. Second, it wastes valuable resources and increases the response time which goes against the very purpose of AQP. Finally, the hypothetical model may not hold for complex queries. Similarly, figuring out the optimal sample size given a time constraint requires building an error-latency profile, which is both challenging and error-prone for complex OLAP queries. On the contrary, `G-OLA` gives the user a smooth observation and control of query processing, which does not need to predict the sample size at all.

`G-OLA` is a mini-batch execution model for online processing which randomly partitions the dataset into smaller batches of uniform size, and processes them one by one. `G-OLA` iteratively refines the query results by computing a delta update on each mini-batch of data. The batch granularity is determined by how frequently the user wants the query result to be updated. To avoid recomputing the whole query during delta updates for non-monotonic queries (as shown in Example 1), `G-OLA` carefully partitions the intermediate output of each subquery into two parts — the *uncertain* and *deterministic* sets. The tuples in the deterministic set will not change across mini-batches, while those in the uncertain set may change. Therefore, during delta updates, we only need to consider the tuples in the uncertain set and the new incoming mini-batch. This partitioning is based on the observation that *during online processing, the running results produced by any aggregate subquery should converge to the corresponding final result computed on the whole dataset, and thus their variation decreases with the increase in data size.* Since the uncertain sets are very small in practice (as shown in Section 5), `G-OLA` can achieve continuous and smooth feedback to the user.

We have implemented `G-OLA` in `FluoDB`, an online query execution framework running on Spark[2]. `FluoDB` extends SparkSQL[3] and BlinkDB[4], and is backward compatible with Apache Hive[5]. In this demo, we will demonstrate `FluoDB` running on 100 Amazon EC2 nodes, providing interactive analysis over 10TB session logs from a video-sharing website. The audience will be able to interact with the system through query consoles and dashboards in order to diagnose issues related to ad revenue and user retention in real time. We will also run a traditional SparkSQL engine in batch mode side by side to show `FluoDB`'s superior performance and great user experience.

2. THE G-OLA EXECUTION MODEL

`G-OLA` is designed to support interactive aggregate OLAP queries over massive sets of data. In particular, this new execution model can enable any query processing framework to present the users with meaningful approximate results (with error bars) that are continuously refined and updated during query execution. This not only completely alleviates the need for sampling the data in advance, but also enables the user to observe the progress of a query and control its execution on the fly. `G-OLA` is capable of handling a wide variety of SQL queries including the core relational algebra, standard aggregates (such as `COUNT, SUM, AVG, STDEV` and `QUANTILES`), user-defined functions (`UDFs` and `UDAFs`), subqueries and nested aggregates.

In order to provide statistically unbiased approximate answers to queries on an arbitrary granularity of data, we iteratively execute the query on its input dataset in random order. Furthermore, `G-OLA` also gives precise control to users in specifying only a subset of input relations that needs to be processed in an online fashion. For example, if the `SBI` query were to contain more than one input relations, the user could explicitly specify to stream through a large *fact* table like `Sessions` while reading smaller dimension tables in entirety. By default, `G-OLA` supports partition-wise randomness by randomly picking data partitions to process. This works well when the attributes needed in the query are not correlated with the partitions. However, if this assumption does not hold, `G-OLA` also provides data pre-processing tools to randomly shuffle the entire input dataset, so that any subset of the shuffled data is a uniform sample of the original dataset. Similar to the `POSTGRES-OLA` implementation [17], the users can stop the execution at any time when the result meets their desired accuracy criterion.

2.1 Mini-Batch Execution Model

`G-OLA` uses a mini-batch execution model for online processing. Specifically, we randomly partition the dataset into multiple mini-batches of uniform size, and process through the data by taking a single mini-batch at a time. The batch granularity is determined by how frequently the user wants the query result to be updated. At any point during query processing, `G-OLA` presents the user with the approximate query result and its associated error estimate (e.g., confidence interval) as if the query was computed on all the mini-batches seen so far.

When processing each mini-batch of data, `G-OLA` incrementally maintains the query result previously obtained by computing a delta update on the incoming data. To compute this delta update efficiently, we carefully partition the intermediate output at each operator in the query plan into two parts — the *uncertain* and the *deterministic* sets. With very high probability, tuples in the deterministic set are unlikely to change as we refine the query result. In contrast, the uncertain set of tuples are likely to change when we recompute the query on more data. Therefore, when we process the next mini-batch, we only need to consider the tuples in the uncertain set and the ones in the new mini-batch to compute a delta update. We will explain our delta maintenance techniques in detail in Section 3.

2.2 Query Semantics

This subsection gives a brief overview of the query execution semantics in `G-OLA`. Consider that the user submits a query Q on a dataset D. During query processing, the system first randomly partitions D into k parts $\Delta D_1, \cdots, \Delta D_k$, where $|\Delta D_1| = \cdots = |\Delta D_k|$. At the i-th iteration, $1 \leq i \leq k$, it processes partition ΔD_i, and returns $Q(D_i, \frac{k}{i})$ as an approximation to the final result $Q(D)$, along with the error estimation (*e.g.*, a confidence interval) of $Q(D_i, \frac{k}{i})$, where D_i is the dataset $\Delta D_1 \cup \cdots \cup \Delta D_i$; $Q(D_i, \frac{k}{i})$ is simply evaluating Q on enhanced D_i where each tuple is annotated with a multiplicity $m = \frac{k}{i}$. This annotated multiplicity means that seeing a tuple in $\Delta D_1 \cup \cdots \cup \Delta D_i$ is roughly equivalent to it being seen m times in D (as $\Delta D_1 \cup \cdots \cup \Delta D_i$ is a random sample from D). Computing $Q(D_i, \frac{k}{i})$ follows the standard multiset semantics that are exposed

[2]https://spark.apache.org/
[3]https://spark.apache.org/sql/
[4]http://blinkdb.org
[5]https://hive.apache.org/

in many commercial databases. For the sake of simplicity, we will use $Q(D_i)$ and $Q(D_i, \frac{k}{i})$ interchangeably throughout the paper.

In G-OLA, we use the *bootstrap* [14] to estimate the confidence interval of $Q(D_i)$ with respect to $Q(D)$, that consists of a simple Monte-Carlo procedure—it repeatedly carries out a sub-routine called a *trial*. Each trial generates a simulated database, say $\hat{D}_{i,j}$, which is of the same size as D_i (by sampling $|D_i|$ tuples i.i.d. from D_i *with* replacement), and then computes query Q on $\hat{D}_{i,j}$. The collection $\{Q(\hat{D}_{i,j})\}$ from all the bootstrap trials forms an empirical distribution, based on which a confidence interval can be computed.

3. DELTA MAINTENANCE IN G-OLA

In this section, we describe G-OLA's delta maintenance techniques in detail. As an illustration, consider answering the SBI query (Example 1) on the dataset shown in Figure 1(b). Figure 1(a) depicts the query plan of the SBI query.

To process the SBI query, G-OLA partitions the Sessions relation into k mini-batches $\{\Delta D_1, \cdots, \Delta D_k\}$ where each ΔD_i is of size n, e.g., $\Delta D_1 = \{t_1, \cdots t_n\}$ and $\Delta D_2 = \{t_{n+1}, \cdots t_{2n}\}$ and so on. G-OLA processes through these chunks incrementally, delivering an approximate result of the SBI query (denoted by Q) at the i-th mini-batch as if Q is computed on $D_i = \Delta D_1 \cup \cdots \cup \Delta D_i$ (See Section 2.2). However, instead of computing $Q(D_i)$ directly, we treat D_i as D_{i-1} updated by inserting new tuples ΔD_i (i.e., $D_i = D_{i-1} \cup \Delta D_i$), and compute $Q(D_i)$ by applying a delta query to the result obtained in the $(i-1)$-th iteration (i.e., $Q(D_i) = Q(D_{i-1}) + \Delta Q(D_{i-1}, \Delta D_i)$)[6]. The intuition is that computing $\Delta Q(D_{i-1}, \Delta D_i)$, and using the result to update $Q(D_{i-1})$, would be much faster than recomputing $Q(D_i)$ from scratch, enabling quicker feedback to the user. Similar intuition is shared by online aggregation [17] and the work on incremental view maintenance [5, 16, 19].

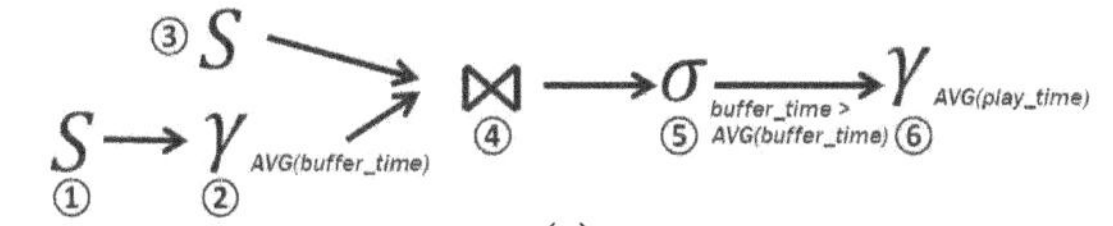

(a)

	session_id	buffer_time (s)	play_time (s)
t_1	s_1	36	238
t_2	s_2	58	135
...	...	...	...
t_n	s_n	17	617
t_{n+1}	s_{n+1}	56	194
t_{n+2}	s_{n+2}	19	308
...	...	...	...
t_{2n}	s_{2n}	26	319
...	...	...	...

(b) *Sessions*

Figure 1: (a) The query plan of the SBI query in Example 1, and (b) an example of the Sessions relation.

3.1 Issues with Classical Delta Maintenance

Unfortunately, the above intuition does not always hold: for complex OLAP queries involving nested aggregates, e.g., the SBI query, computing $\Delta_i Q(D_{i-1}, \Delta D_i)$ using classical delta maintenance is no better than computing $Q(D_i)$.

This is due to the non-monotonicity of some relational operators. In particular, the aggregation operator, which is of extreme importance in OLAP, is blocking in nature [7], i.e., aggregation will not produce an accurate answer until it sees all the input. This blocking nature of aggregation makes delta maintenance of OLAP queries very challenging—as more and more data comes in, the query engine may flip its previous decision, resulting in completely recomputing the query on all the data that was seen previously.

For instance, consider the first two mini-batches of the SBI query. In the first batch, computing the inner aggregate query AVG(buffer_time) on D_1 results in 37. As a consequence, tuple t_1 is filtered out as its buffer_time is lower than the running average buffering time. However, in the second batch, after taking ΔD_2 into account, AVG(buffer_time) is updated to 35.3, which in turn requires t_1 to be selected. Unfortunately, since t_1 is already dropped in the first batch, the query engine has to read through D_1 again in order to compute the correct answer for the second batch. Even worse, such wasteful re-computation may recur at each batch. In general, at the i-th batch, we need to compute the query on all the tuples seen previously (i.e., D_{i-1}) alongside the new data ΔD_i. Therefore, the update cost increases linearly with batches, hindering continuous update. Roughly, processing through all the k mini-batches will process $O(k^2) \cdot n$ of data in total, which could be much larger than the original dataset (of size kn).

3.2 Discovering Certainty in Uncertainty

We have seen that due to their blocking nature, the running results of aggregates that are computed on samples, are approximate and uncertain. This makes complex OLAP queries with nested aggregates non-monotonic, making simple delta maintenance techniques extremely inefficient. However, there is a key principle behind all S-AQP techniques—running aggregate results will eventually converge to the ground truth (i.e., the aggregate result computed on the full dataset) as the sample size increases. Therefore, as the query engine processes through the mini-batches, the intermediate aggregate results will concentrate in a relatively small range around the ground truth, and this range will shrink as more and more batches are processed.

G-OLA utilizes this important property in developing an efficient delta maintenance technique. As an example, assume that all the intermediate results of AVG(buffer_time) throughout its online processing are within the range of 37 ± 8.1. This implies that across all mini-batches, tuple t_2 will be selected, while tuple t_n will be filtered out. For these tuples, the decisions made by the query engine will never change across all mini-batches. Thus, if we know this fact a priori, we can prune these non-uncertain tuples during online processing. Formally, for an uncertain[7] attribute u in an intermediate tuple, we define its *variation range* as the set of all the possible values that u may take during the online execution, denoted by $\mathfrak{R}(u)$. For simplicity, we uniformly define the variation range of a deterministic value d as itself, i.e., $\mathfrak{R}(d) = \{d\}$.

Next, for simplicity, we will explain G-OLA's delta-maintenance algorithm by first assuming that these variation ranges are given, and then explain how these variation ranges can be approximated in practice. In the i-th mini-batch, at any predicate $x \ \theta \ y$ involving uncertain values,[8] G-OLA classifies the input tuples into two sets: the *uncertain* set U_i in which tuples satisfy $\mathfrak{R}(x) \cap \mathfrak{R}(y) \neq \emptyset$, and the *deterministic* set C_i in which tuples satisfy $\mathfrak{R}(x) \cap \mathfrak{R}(y) = \emptyset$. For instance, if $\mathfrak{R}(\texttt{AVG(buffer\_time)}) = [28.9, 45.1]$, then $t_2, t_n \in C_1$, while $t_1 \in U_1$. Clearly, for the tuples in U_i, the predicate may evaluate to different answers in different batches, while for the tuples in C_i, the predicate will evaluate to the same answer across all batches. Therefore, in batch $(i-1)$, we cache U_{i-1}; and in batch i, instead

[6] Here, + is a way of combining a relation with a change to it. This could include inserting new tuples, deleting old tuples, or updating an existing tuple with new attribute values.

[7] An attribute is uncertain if it is computed by a nested aggregate subquery.

[8] θ is some comparison operator.

of computing $Q(D_i)$ from scratch, G-OLA only needs to compute a delta update based on U_{i-1} and ΔD_i.

Of course, the variation ranges cannot be known until we have finished the query. In practice, G-OLA approximates the variation ranges using running estimates. Recall that we use bootstrap to estimate the accuracy of the running query results. As a by-product of this process, we can obtain a set of bootstrap outputs $\hat{u}$ for each uncertain value u, where $\hat{u}$ is shown to be an accurate approximation of the true distribution of u[9]. In practice, we use the range defined by $\hat{\mathfrak{R}}(u) = [min(\hat{u}) - \varepsilon, max(\hat{u}) + \varepsilon]$ to approximate $\mathfrak{R}(u)$, where ε is a slack variable which can controlled by the user. $\hat{\mathfrak{R}}(u)$ may fail in the sense that some running value of u or a bootstrap output in $\hat{u}$ exceed the variation range in some batch, which will result in incorrect query answers. However, the system can detect this *failure*, and can correct the answer by recomputing the query on the data seen since the last mini-batch with the correct variation ranges. The user can also decrease the chance of recomputation by setting a larger ε (at the cost of increasing the size of the uncertain sets). In practice, setting ε to the standard deviation of $\hat{u}$ achieves a good balance in controlling the probability of recomputation and reducing the size of the uncertain sets.

3.3 Lineage and Lazy Evaluation

In order to correctly compute the delta update in batch i, U_{i-1} cached in batch $i-1$ has to be updated with the latest values. For instance, consider the above example where tuple t_1 is classified in U_1. In batch 2, t_1 has to be updated with the latest AVG(buffer_time) in order to evaluate the predicate correctly.

To efficiently support this update and avoid regenerating the uncertain tuples from scratch, G-OLA keeps track of all the values used to compute the uncertain attributes in a tuple, i.e., its *lineage*, and propagates the lineage with each tuple. During delta maintenance, we update the uncertain set by re-evaluating the operation on the lineage carried with each uncertain tuple, and this evaluation is done lazily when the corresponding values are accessed.

However, since aggregates are computed from a set of values, propagating the lineage of aggregates will cause an explosion in the storage and networking overhead. We optimize the lineage propagation by dividing a query into multiple *lineage blocks*. A lineage block is a maximal subtree of the query plan that is an SPJA (Select-Project-Join-Aggregation) block, i.e., a subtree consisting of any combinations of select, project and join operators followed by an aggregation operator. It is maximal in the sense that extending the subtree with any node in the query plan will violate this requirement. As an example, the query plan shown in Figure 1(a) can be divided into two lineage blocks: {①, ②}, {③, ④, ⑤, ⑥}. G-OLA propagates lineage within each lineage block, while simply broadcasts the latest aggregate results between lineage blocks, thus bounding the overall cost of lineage propagation.

4. SYSTEM ARCHITECTURE

We have implemented G-OLA in FluoDB. FluoDB is a parallel online query execution framework that is build on top of SparkSQL and BlinkDB, and enables us to be backwards compatible with Apache Hive in terms of both storage and query language. Underneath, it runs on Spark, a distributed computing framework that supports efficient in-memory computation. Figure 2 depicts the system architecture of FluoDB. FluoDB extends the optimization framework of SparkSQL, poissonized resampling based error estimation techniques of BlinkDB and the computation infrastructure of Spark, by adding three major components to empower online execution:

[9]We refer interested readers to [3] for the implementation details of bootstrap.

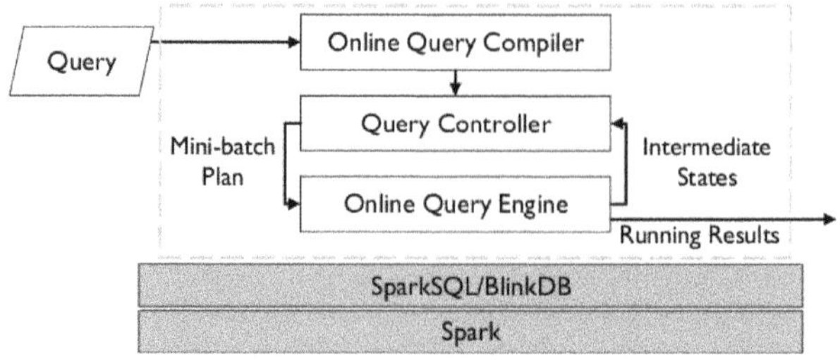

Figure 2: The system architecture of FluoDB.

1. **Online Query Compiler.** The online query compiler compiles the query into a meta query plan, which when plugged with different mini-batches of data, turns into a series of mini-batch queries. In this series, each mini-batch query depends on the state computed in the previous iteration, and computes delta-updates on the results of its predecessor.

2. **Query Controller.** The query controller is in charge of partitioning the input data into mini-batches, and generating/scheduling the series of mini-batch queries given a meta query plan. It also manages, caches and distributes the intermediary uncertain sets during each iteration. Since our delta-maintenance algorithm (see Section 3) relies on the correctness of the running approximate variation ranges, the controller monitors the correctness of all the variation ranges as well, and schedules recomputing jobs to correct the query results when a failure is detected.

3. **Online Query Engine.** The online query engine implements a set of online relational algebra operators on Spark.

5. PERFORMANCE

In this section, we briefly discuss the performance of G-OLA. Our experiments are based on a synthetic 100GB dataset from the TPC-H benchmark[10], and a 100GB subset of a 10TB anonymized real-world video content distribution workload from Conviva Inc.[11] To simplify random partitioning during mini-batch execution, we denormalize the TPC-H data into a single fact table. The Conviva dataset contains a single de-normalized fact table. Our queries are based on a subset of the TPC-H benchmark queries and the original Conviva query trace.

We compare the performance of G-OLA with existing online processing techniques in OLA [17] and incremental view maintenance work [5, 16, 19] by processing a set of illustrative queries in mini-batches of 1GB each. To clearly demonstrate the expressiveness and effectiveness of G-OLA, we focus only on complex OLAP queries with nested aggregates. Queries C1, C2, C3 are based on the Conviva query trace and compute statistics (such as histograms of play_time and join_failure_rate) of sessions with abnormal behaviors (e.g., those with a longer than average buffering time). Queries Q11, Q17, Q18, Q20 are from the TPC-H benchmark.[12]

Figure 3(a) demonstrates a typical query process in G-OLA using TPC-H Q17. As one can see, any traditional query engine will only

[10]http://www.tpc.org/tpch/

[11]http://www.conviva.com/

[12] Please note that while we retained the original structure of the TPC-H queries, we had to modify some very selective WHERE and GROUP BY clauses in the original queries to avoid undesirably sparse results for small samples of data.

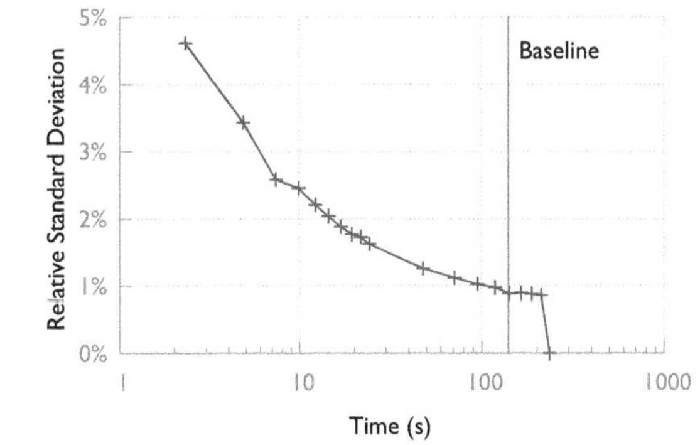

(a)

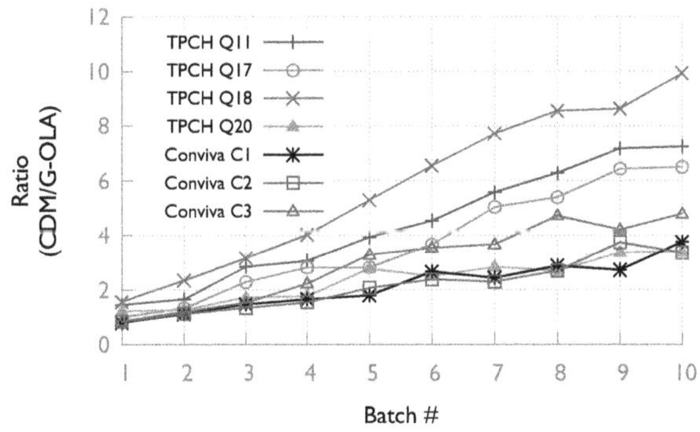

(b)

Figure 3: (a) The relative standard deviation vs. query time curve delivered by G-OLA on TPC-H Q17. We plot the values for the first 10 mini-batches, and then for brevity, the 20th, 30th mini-batch and so on. (b) The ratio of query times of the first 10 batches of G-OLA and classical delta maintenance (CDM) techniques. Note that the ratio of query times for each iteration grows linearly with the number of iterations.

be able to deliver an answer after processing the entire dataset, which in this case, would incur 2.34 minutes latency (marked by the vertical bar). On the other hand, G-OLA can deliver an approximate answer in 2.3 secs (i.e., only in about 1.6% of the whole query time). Furthermore, G-OLA continuously refines the answer at a very user-friendly pace of roughly every 2.5 seconds. It is worth noting that while G-OLA incurs an additional 60% overhead in processing the whole dataset as compared to the baseline (primarily due to the error estimation overheads), it enables the user to make a smooth trade-off between error and latency by allowing her to stop the query execution at any time. For instance, if the user is satisfied with an accuracy of say, 2% relative standard deviation, she can stop the query at 16 seconds, which is almost 10× faster than a batched execution.

We also compare the delta maintenance techniques in G-OLA with the classical delta maintenance techniques. The results for the query response time for the first 10 mini-batches (of size 1GB each) are shown in Figure 3(b). We plot the ratio of the query times spent by classical delta maintenance algorithms (CDM) and G-OLA for each batch. While these queries and datasets cannot necessarily form a representative sample of the incredibly wide range of real-world OLAP queries and datasets, we observe that G-OLA significantly outperforms the classical delta-maintenance algorithms. In the classical algorithms, every update on an inner aggregate subquery causes the engine to recompute the query on the entire data that was previously processed, while G-OLA could effectively limit the size of the

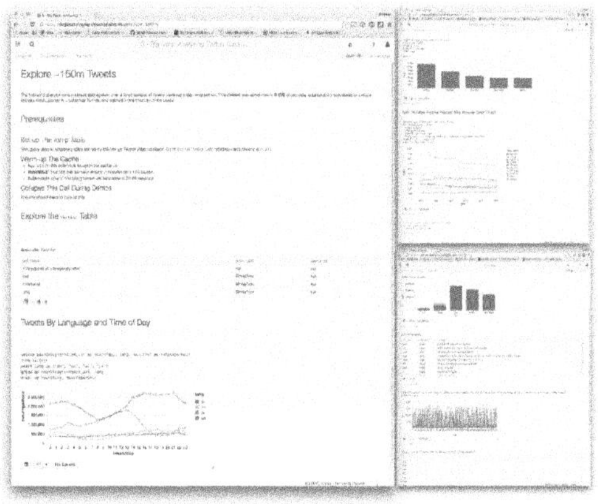

Figure 4: Sample screenshots of an interactive web-based console that will allow attendees to launch custom online SQL queries on the underlying data.

uncertain set of tuples in each iteration, achieving almost constant query time for each iteration.

6. DEMONSTRATION DETAILS

Our demonstration scenario places the attendees in the shoes of a Data Scientist at *MyTube Inc.*, a popular (and imaginary) video-sharing website that wants to adapt its policies and decisions in near real time to maximize ad revenue and improve user retention. *MyTube* collects a variety of user metrics (ranging from sessions IDs, content IDs, video start/stop times or geographical locations) that it aggregates across multiple dimensions to continuously derive insights about its viewers.

As part of this demo, the attendees will be able to interact with a web-based dashboard that will compute and plot a number of ad popularity and user retention metrics while cycling through various user groups and/or geographical regions. Since each of these metrics are computed by fairly complex queries on massive amounts of data, the dashboard will feature approximate answers with error bars that will get progressively refined with time. As shown in Fig. 4, we will also feature a powerful web-based console that would allow the attendees to launch arbitrary SQL aggregate queries on the underlying data. For a side-by-side comparison of performance and user experience, we will also demonstrate a traditional SparkSQL engine running in batched execution mode on the same dataset.

6.1 Data Characteristics

Our 10 TB workload trace would comprise of a de-normalized fact table of session logs from a video-sharing website. This table will consist of billions of rows and hundreds of columns (ranging from sessionIDs, contentIDs, adIDs, and video or ad start/end times), and will be stored in HDFS (or partially cached in memory) across 100 Amazon EC2 machines. Each tuple in the table will correspond to a session log entry, such as a video or an ad being played.

6.2 Demonstration Scenarios

To demonstrate the power and expressiveness of G-OLA in terms of the types of queries it can support, we will feature two real-time data analysis scenarios that are closely modeled after real-world use-cases:

Real-time Ad Optimization. In this scenario, *MyTube Inc.* wants to adapt its policies and decisions in near real time to maximize its ad revenue. This involves aggregating over a number of user metrics across multiple dimensions to understand how an ad performs for a particular group of users or content at a particular time of day.

Performing such analysis quickly is essential, especially when there is a change in the environment, *e.g.*, new ads, or a new page layout. The ability to re-optimize the ad placement every minute as opposed to every day or week often leads to a material difference in revenue.

A/B Testing. In this scenario, *MyTube Inc.* aims to optimize its business by improving user retention, or by increasing their user engagement. Often this is done by using A/B testing to experiment with anything from new content to slight changes in the number and/or the duration of ads that are shown. While the number of combinations and changes that one can test is daunting, the ability to quickly understand the impact of various tests and identify important trends is critical to rapidly improving the business.

In these and many other scenarios, the queries are unpredictable (because the exact problem, or the query is not known in advance) and quick response time is essential as data is changing quickly, and the potential profit is inversely proportional to the response time. In this demo, we will specifically focus on these scenarios.

7. RELATED WORK

Online Aggregation. Online aggregation [17] and its successors [13, 20] proposed the idea of allowing users to observe the progress of aggregation queries and control the execution on the fly. The users can trade accuracy for time in a smooth manner. However, online aggregation is limited to simple SPJA queries without any support for nested aggregation subqueries.

Sampling-based Approximate Query Processing. There has been substantial work on using sampling to provide approximate query answers, many of which [2, 4, 8, 11, 21] focus on constructing the optimal samples to improve query accuracy. STRAT [11], SciBORQ [21], Babcock et al. [8] and AQUA [2] construct and/or pick the optimal stratified samples given a fixed time budget, but do not allow users to specify an error bound for a query. BlinkDB [4] supports sample selection given user-specified time or accuracy constraints. Such selection relies on an error-latency profile, which is built for a query by repeatedly trying out the query on smaller sample sizes and extrapolating the points.

Incremental View Maintenance. Incremental view maintenance (IVM) is a very important topic in database view management, and has been studied for over three decades. IVM focuses on a similar problem—computing a *delta update* query when the input data is updated. Maintaining SQL query answers have been studied in both the *set* [9, 10] and *bag* [12, 16] semantics. Computing the delta update query has been studied for query with aggregates [16, 19] and temporal aggregates [24]. However, majority of work in this area only focuses on simple SPJA queries without nested and correlated aggregation subqueries. More recently, DBToaster [5] has investigated higher-order IVM and support for nested queries. However, for queries with nested aggregates, the *delta update* query obtained by higher-order IVM is often no simpler than the original query. G-OLA's delta-maintenance technique doesn't have this limitation.

Data Stream Processing. Data stream processing [1, 15, 18, 22] combines (1) incremental processing (e.g., sliding windows) and (2) sublinear space algorithms for handling updates. These techniques mainly rely on manual programming and composing, and thus have limited adoption and generalization. There has also been work on one-pass streaming algorithms [6, 23] for single layer of nested aggregate queries that rely on building correlated aggregate summaries on streams of data. However, it is non-trivial to automatically build these summaries for queries with arbitrary levels of nesting and/or user defined aggregates. G-OLA on the other hand provides automatic incremental processing to general SQL queries, including those with multiple levels of nesting and arbitrary aggregates.

Acknowledgments

This research is supported in part by NSF CISE Expeditions Award CCF-1139158, LBNL Award 7076018, and DARPA XData Award FA8750-12-2-0331, and gifts from Amazon Web Services, Google, SAP, The Thomas and Stacey Siebel Foundation, Adatao, Adobe, Apple, Inc., Blue Goji, Bosch, C3Energy, Cisco, Cray, Cloudera, EMC, Ericsson, Facebook, Guavus, Huawei, Informatica, Intel, Microsoft, NetApp, Pivotal, Samsung, Splunk, Virdata and VMware.

8. REFERENCES

[1] D. J. Abadi, Y. Ahmad, M. Balazinska, U. Cetintemel, M. Cherniack, J.-H. Hwang, W. Lindner, A. Maskey, A. Rasin, E. Ryvkina, et al. The design of the borealis stream processing engine. In *CIDR*, volume 5, pages 277–289, 2005.

[2] S. Acharya, P. B. Gibbons, V. Poosala, and S. Ramaswamy. The aqua approximate query answering system. In *SIGMOD Record*, volume 28, pages 574–576, 1999.

[3] S. Agarwal, H. Milner, A. Kleiner, A. Talwalkar, M. I. Jordan, S. Madden, B. Mozafari, and I. Stoica. Knowing when you're wrong: building fast and reliable approximate query processing systems. In *SIGMOD*, pages 481–492, 2014.

[4] S. Agarwal, B. Mozafari, A. Panda, H. Milner, S. Madden, and I. Stoica. Blinkdb: queries with bounded errors and bounded response times on very large data. In *EuroSys*, pages 29–42, 2013.

[5] Y. Ahmad, O. Kennedy, C. Koch, and M. Nikolic. Dbtoaster: Higher-order delta processing for dynamic, frequently fresh views. *PVLDB*, 5(10):968–979, 2012.

[6] R. Ananthakrishna, A. Das, J. Gehrke, F. Korn, S. Muthukrishnan, and D. Srivastava. Efficient approximation of correlated sums on data streams. *IEEE Trans. Knowl. Data Eng.*, 15(3):569–572, 2003.

[7] B. Babcock, S. Babu, M. Datar, R. Motwani, and J. Widom. Models and issues in data stream systems. In *PODS*, pages 1–16, 2002.

[8] B. Babcock, S. Chaudhuri, and G. Das. Dynamic sample selection for approximate query processing. In *SIGMOD*, pages 539–550, 2003.

[9] J. A. Blakeley, P.-A. Larson, and F. W. Tompa. Efficiently updating materialized views. In *SIGMOD*, volume 15, pages 61–71, 1986.

[10] O. P. Buneman and E. K. Clemons. Efficiently monitoring relational databases. *TODS*, 4(3):368–382, 1979.

[11] S. Chaudhuri, G. Das, and V. Narasayya. Optimized stratified sampling for approximate query processing. *TODS*, 32(2):9, 2007.

[12] S. Chaudhuri, R. Krishnamurthy, S. Potamianos, and K. Shim. Optimizing queries with materialized views. In *ICDE*, pages 190–190, 1995.

[13] T. Condie, N. Conway, P. Alvaro, J. M. Hellerstein, J. Gerth, J. Talbot, K. Elmeleegy, and R. Sears. Online aggregation and continuous query support in mapreduce. In *SIGMOD*, pages 1115–1118, 2010.

[14] B. Efron and R. J. Tibshirani. *An Introduction to the Bootstrap*. Chapman & Hall, New York, 1993.

[15] T. M. Ghanem, A. K. Elmagarmid, P.-Å. Larson, and W. G. Aref. Supporting views in data stream management systems. *TODS*, 35(1):1, 2010.

[16] T. Griffin and L. Libkin. Incremental maintenance of views with duplicates. In *ACM SIGMOD Record*, volume 24, pages 328–339, 1995.

[17] J. M. Hellerstein, P. J. Haas, and H. J. Wang. Online aggregation. In *SIGMOD*, pages 171–182, 1997.

[18] R. Motwani, J. Widom, A. Arasu, B. Babcock, S. Babu, M. Datar, G. Manku, C. Olston, J. Rosenstein, and R. Varma. Query processing, approximation, and resource management in a data stream management system, 2002.

[19] T. Palpanas, R. Sidle, R. Cochrane, and H. Pirahesh. Incremental maintenance for non-distributive aggregate functions. In *PVLDB*, pages 802–813, 2002.

[20] N. Pansare, V. R. Borkar, C. Jermaine, and T. Condie. Online aggregation for large mapreduce jobs. volume 4, pages 1135–1145, 2011.

[21] L. Sidirourgos, M. L. Kersten, and P. A. Boncz. Sciborq: Scientific data management with bounds on runtime and quality. In *CIDR*, volume 11, pages 296–301, 2011.

[22] H. Thakkar, N. Laptev, H. Mousavi, B. Mozafari, V. Russo, and C. Zaniolo. SMM: A data stream management system for knowledge discovery. In *ICDE*, pages 757–768, 2011.

[23] S. Tirthapura and D. P. Woodruff. A general method for estimating correlated aggregates over a data stream. In *ICDE*, pages 162–173, 2012.

[24] J. Yang and J. Widom. Incremental computation and maintenance of temporal aggregates. In *ICDE*, pages 51–60, 2001.

Mining and Forecasting of Big Time-series Data

Yasushi Sakurai
Kumamoto University
yasushi@cs.kumamoto-u.ac.jp

Yasuko Matsubara
Kumamoto University
yasuko@cs.kumamoto-u.ac.jp

Christos Faloutsos
Carnegie Mellon University
christos@cs.cmu.edu

ABSTRACT

Given a large collection of time series, such as web-click logs, electric medical records and motion capture sensors, how can we efficiently and effectively find typical patterns? How can we statistically summarize all the sequences, and achieve a meaningful segmentation? What are the major tools for forecasting and outlier detection? Time-series data analysis is becoming of increasingly high importance, thanks to the decreasing cost of hardware and the increasing on-line processing capability.

The objective of this tutorial is to provide a concise and intuitive overview of the most important tools that can help us find patterns in large-scale time-series sequences. We review the state of the art in four related fields: (1) similarity search and pattern discovery, (2) linear modeling and summarization, (3) non-linear modeling and forecasting, and (4) the extension of time-series mining and tensor analysis. The emphasis of the tutorial is to provide the intuition behind these powerful tools, which is usually lost in the technical literature, as well as to introduce case studies that illustrate their practical use.

Categories and Subject Descriptors

H.2.8 [**Database management**]: Database applications—*Data mining*

General Terms

Algorithms, Experimentation, Theory

Keywords

Time-series; Tensors; Pattern discovery; Forecasting;

1. INTRODUCTION

Time series data occur naturally in countless domains including medical analysis [17, 33], financial analysis [56], online text [14], sensor network monitoring [22, 41] and social activity mining [26, 31, 32]. The increasing volume of online, time-stamped activity represents a vital new opportunity for data scientists and analysts to measure the collective behavior of social, economic, and other important evolutions [21, 13]. In many applications the logging rate has increased greatly with the progress made on hardware and storage technology. In such a situation, the most fundamental requirements are the efficient and effective mining of "big" time-series sequences.

Time-series data analysis is a well-known topic that has attracted huge interest in various research communities (e.g., theory, databases, data mining, networking) for a few decades. However, recent studies has revealed some new directions for research on time-series analysis, which include:

- **Large-scale tensor analysis:** Many time-series data can be modeled as tensors, and tensor analysis is an important data mining tool that has various applications including sensor streams, hyperlinks, medical records and social networks over time.
- **Non-linear modeling:** Non-linear models are widely used in a variety of areas, such as epidemiology, biology, physics and economics. In the database and mining fields, analyses of social media and online user behavior have attracted considerable interest, and recent studies have focused on non-linear time-series analysis to understand the dynamics of social networks.
- **Automatic mining:** We also emphasize the importance of fully-automatic mining. Most of the existing time-series tools require parameter tuning, and they are very sensitive to these parameters. In fact, faced with "big data", fully automatic mining is even more important: otherwise, the user would have to try several parameter tuning steps, each of which would take too long (e.g., hours, or days).

This tutorial provides a concise and intuitive overview of the most important tools that we can use to help us understand and find patterns in large-scale time evolving sequences. We will provide a comprehensive overview and the above new directions for time-series analysis, and deal specifically with the following key topics: (1) similarity search and pattern discovery, (2) linear modeling and summarization, (3) non-linear modeling and forecasting, and (4) the extension of time-series mining and tensor analysis.

Who should attend. The target audience is data mining and data management researchers who wish to get up to speed with the major tools used in time sequence analysis. Also, practitioners who want a concise, intuitive overview of the state of the art.

Prerequisites. None. The emphasis is on the intuition behind all these mathematical tools.

Related tutorials. Related tutorials have been presented, e.g., (a) Indexing and Mining Streams, by Christos Faloutsos, SIGMOD 2004, (b) Indexing and Mining Time Sequences, by Christos Faloutsos and Lei Li, SIGKDD 2010, and (c) Mining Shape and Time Series Databases with Symbolic Representations, by Eamonn Keogh,

SIGMOD'15, May 31–June 4, 2015, Melbourne, Victoria, Australia.

http://dx.doi.org/10.1145/2723372.2731081.

SIGKDD 2007. However, these tutorials look at different approaches and tools. Moreover, they do not focus on large-scale evolving tensors, or non-linear dynamical systems.

2. CONTENT AND OUTLINE

Our tutorial is structured as follows:

1. Similarity search and pattern discovery (60 minutes)
   (a) Why we need similarity search
      i. Indexing
      ii. Fast searching
   (b) Distance function and similarity measure
      i. Euclidean distance
      ii. Dynamic time warping
      iii. Correlation
   (c) Feature extraction
      i. Discrete Fourier transform, wavelets
      ii. Singular value decomposition, independent component analysis
      iii. Multi-dimensional scaling
   (d) Streaming pattern discovery
      i. Component analysis
      ii. Correlation monitoring
      iii. Time warping over streams
2. Linear modeling and summarization (30 minutes)
   (a) Linear modeling and forecasting
      i. Main idea behind linear forecasting
      ii. AR methodology and multivariate regression
      iii. Recursive least square
      iv. Streaming algorithms
   (b) Sequence summarization
      i. Linear dynamic systems
      ii. Probabilistic models
      iii. Automatic mining of co-evolving sequences
3. Non-linear modeling and forecasting (30 minutes)
   (a) Non-linear forecasting
      i. Lag-plots
      ii. Fractal dimension and power-law
   (b) Non-linear dynamical systems
      i. Main idea: non-linear equations
      ii. Non-linear epidemic models
      iii. Gray-box non-linear mining
      iv. Non-linear dynamical systems for online activities
      v. Information diffusion in social networks
4. Extension of time-series mining - tensor analysis (60 minutes)
   (a) Tensor decomposition
      i. Basic approaches
      ii. Decompositions of higher-order tensors
   (b) Mining of complex time-stamped tensors
      i. Complex time-stamped events and big sparse tensors
      ii. Feature extraction from sparse tensors
      iii. Forecasting of complex time-stamped events
   (c) New directions of tensor analysis
      i. Non-linear modeling for tensors
      ii. Automatic non-linear analysis

1. Similarity search and pattern discovery. In this first part of the tutorial, we explain the most common and fundamental tools of time series data mining. More specifically, we demonstrate some traditional approaches applied to time series data mining including similarity search e.g., euclidean distance, dynamic time warping and correlation [43, 46, 42, 34]; feature extraction including singular value decomposition (SVD), independent component analysis (ICA) [38, 44], segmentation [17]; multi-dimensional scaling [10]. We also answer the following important question: What can we do in the highly likely case that the users need real-time, online data processing while in practice they require high accuracy? Specifically, we introduce several mining algorithms for online data streams, including component analysis [40, 41], correlation monitoring [56, 45] and time warping over streams [45, 49].

2. Linear modeling and summarization. In this part, we explain the main ideas behind linear modeling and forecasting. For example, auto regression and moving averaging models have been studied for many years in statistics and finance [4], and have been applied to time-series data mining [6, 16, 23]. We introduce AR methodology and several important tools including MUSCLES [55] and AWSOM [39]. We also introduce linear dynamical systems (LDS), Kalman filters (KF) and their variants [15, 25, 24, 48]. As regards probabilistic time-series analysis, hidden Markov models (HMMs) have been used in various applications including speech recognition [52], and sensor monitoring [22, 32, 12]. For example, Wang et al. [51] presented a pattern-based hidden Markov model (pHMM) for time-series segmentation and clustering, while [28] developed AutoPlait, a fully-automatic mining algorithm for co-evolving time sequences. Given a large collection of co-evolving multiple sequences, which contains an unknown number of patterns of different durations, AutoPlait automatically identifies all distinct patterns and spots the time position of each variation.

3. Non-linear modeling and forecasting. In this part, we introduce several advanced techniques, and focus specifically on non-linear time series analysis. We start by explaining non-linear forecasting e.g., lag-plots [7], which is based on nearest-neighbor search. We also explain some fundamental concepts such as fractal dimension and power law [36, 2, 27]. We then review the most common non-linear equations, including the logistic function (LF) [5], the susceptible-infected (SI) model [1], the independent cascade (IC) model [9], the so-called "Bass" model [3], the Lotka-Volterra (LV) model [35] and other non-linear equations [37]. We explain the importance of non-linear equations and the concept of gray-box non-linear mining. In this part, we also review recent work on understanding the non-linear time evolution of online user activities. Analyses of epidemics, blogs, social media, propagation and the cascades they create have attracted much interest. We answer several important topics such as how popularity of "memes" changes over time [21]; how to find temporal patterns in information diffusion process through online media, e.g., blogs, hashtags [54, 53], and YouTube [8, 11]; how to describe rising and falling patterns of information propagation (e.g., memes, hashtags and keyword search volume) using non-linear dynamical systems [31, 29].

4. Extension of time-series mining - tensor analysis. The goal in this part is to present large-scale studies of complex time-stamped events and big sparse tensors. We first introduce some basic approaches including Tucker, PARAFAC, and higher-order SVD (HOSVD) [18, 19, 47, 20]. Complex time-stamped events can be represented as a tensor with several dimensions. For example, given a set of time-stamped event entries of the form { object, actor, timestamp} (e.g., web-clicks: {URL, userID, timestamp}), we can treat them as a 3rd order tensor. Here, one subtle, but important issue is that the complex time-stamped tensor is *very sparse*, which derails all typical time-series mining and forecasting tools. We introduce a scalable algorithm, TriMine [30] to deal with this issue. TriMine has the ability to find meaningful patterns in complex time-stamped tensors, and forecast future events, e.g., estimate the number of clicks from user "Smith" to URL "CNN.com" for the next 30 days.

Finally, we show new directions for tensor analysis, namely, automatic and non-linear analysis for big time-series tensors. Specifically, we introduce a unifying analytical model, FUNNEL [33], for mining and forecasting large-scale epidemiological data (e.g., the Project Tycho [50]) as well as an efficient fitting algorithm, which solves the problem. We also discuss the importance of fully-automatic mining for time-series tensor analysis. There are many fascinating and useful tools for time-series analysis. However, most existing methods require parameter settings and fine tuning, such as the number of coefficients, and the reconstruction error thresholds, and they are very sensitive to these parameters. The ideal method should look for arbitrary patterns and require no initial human intervention to guide it.

3. PRESENTERS - BIOS

Yasushi Sakurai is a Professor at Kumamoto University. He obtained his B.E. degree from Doshisha University in 1991, and his M.E. and Ph.D. degrees from Nara Institute of Science and Technology in 1996 and 1999, respectively. In 1998, he joined NTT Laboratories, and became a Senior Research Scientist in 2005. He was a Visiting Researcher at Carnegie Mellon University during 2004-2005. He received two KDD best paper awards in 2008 and 2010. His research interests include time-series analysis, web mining, and sensor data processing.

Yasuko Matsubara is an Assistant Professor in the Department of Computer Science and Electrical Engineering at Kumamoto University, Japan. She obtained her BS and MS degrees from Ochanomizu University in 2007 and 2009 respectively, and her PhD from Kyoto University in 2012. She was a Visiting Researcher at Carnegie Mellon University during 2011-2012 and 2013-2014. Her research interests include time-series data mining and non-linear dynamic systems.

Christos Faloutsos is a Professor at Carnegie Mellon University. He has received the Presidential Young Investigator Award by the National Science Foundation (1989), the Research Contributions Award in ICDM 2006, the SIGKDD Innovations Award (2010), twenty "best paper" awards (including two "test of time" awards), and four teaching awards. Five of his advisees have attracted KDD or SCS dissertation awards. He is an ACM Fellow, he has served as a member of the executive committee of SIGKDD; he has published over 300 refereed articles, 17 book chapters and two monographs. He holds eight patents and he has given over 35 tutorials and over 15 invited distinguished lectures. His research interests include data mining for graphs and streams, fractals, database performance, and indexing for multimedia and bio-informatics data.

Acknowledgement

This work was supported by JSPS KAKENHI Grant-in-Aid for Scientific Research Number 26730060, 24500138, 26280112, 25·7946. This material is based upon work supported by the National Science Foundation under Grants No. CNS-1314632 and IIS-1408924; and by the Army Research Laboratory (ARL) under Cooperative Agreement Number W911NF-09-2-0053; and by a Google Focused Research Award. Any opinions, findings, and conclusions or recommendations expressed in this material are those of the author(s) and do not necessarily reflect the views of the National Science Foundation, ARL, or other funding parties. The U.S. Government is authorized to reproduce and distribute reprints for Government purposes notwithstanding any copyright notation here on.

4. REFERENCES

[1] R. M. Anderson and R. M. May. *Infectious Diseases of Humans Dynamics and Control*. Oxford University Press, 1992.

[2] A. L. Barabasi. The origin of bursts and heavy tails in human dynamics. *Nature*, 435, 2005.

[3] F. M. Bass. A new product growth for model consumer durables. *Management Science*, 15(5):215–227, 1969.

[4] G. E. Box, G. M. Jenkins, and G. C. Reinsel. *Time Series Analysis: Forecasting and Control*. Forecasting and Control Series. Prentice Hall, Englewood Cliffs, NJ, 3rd edition, 1994.

[5] F. Brauer and C. Castillo-Chavez. *Mathematical models in population biology and epidemiology*, volume 40. Springer Verlag, New York, 2001.

[6] P. J. Brockwell and R. A. Davis. *Time Series: Theory and Methods*. Springer-Verlag New York, Inc., New York, NY, USA, 1987.

[7] D. Chakrabarti and C. Faloutsos. F4: large-scale automated forecasting using fractals. In *CIKM*, pages 2–9, 2002.

[8] R. Crane and D. Sornette. Robust dynamic classes revealed by measuring the response function of a social system. In *PNAS*, 2008.

[9] D. Easley and J. Kleinberg. *Networks, Crowds, and Markets: Reasoning About a Highly Connected World*. Cambridge University Press, 2010.

[10] C. Faloutsos and K.-I. Lin. Fastmap: A fast algorithm for indexing, data-mining and visualization of traditional and multimedia datasets. In *SIGMOD*, pages 163–174, 1995.

[11] F. Figueiredo, J. M. Almeida, Y. Matsubara, B. Ribeiro, and C. Faloutsos. Revisit behavior in social media: The phoenix-r model and discoveries. In *PKDD*, pages 386–401, 2014.

[12] Y. Fujiwara, Y. Sakurai, and M. Yamamuro. Spiral: efficient and exact model identification for hidden markov models. In *KDD*, pages 247–255, 2008.

[13] J. Ginsberg, M. Mohebbi, R. Patel, L. Brammer, M. Smolinski, and L. Brilliant. Detecting influenza epidemics using search engine query data. *Nature*, 457:1012–1014, 2009.

[14] M. D. Hoffman, D. M. Blei, and F. R. Bach. Online learning for latent dirichlet allocation. In *NIPS*, pages 856–864, 2010.

[15] A. Jain, E. Y. Chang, and Y.-F. Wang. Adaptive stream resource management using kalman filters. In *SIGMOD*, pages 11–22, 2004.

[16] K. Kalpakis, D. Gada, and V. Puttagunta. Distance measures for effective clustering of arima time-series. In *ICDM 2001: Proceeding of 2001 IEEE International Conference on Data Mining*, pages 273–280, 2001.

[17] E. J. Keogh, S. Chu, D. Hart, and M. J. Pazzani. An online algorithm for segmenting time series. In *ICDM*, pages 289–296, 2001.

[18] T. G. Kolda and B. W. Bader. Tensor decompositions and applications. *SIAM Review*, 51(3):455–500, 2009.

[19] T. G. Kolda, B. W. Bader, and J. P. Kenny. Higher-order web link analysis using multilinear algebra. In *ICDM*, pages 242–249, 2005.

[20] L. D. Lathauwer, B. D. Moor, and J. Vandewalle. A multilinear singular value decomposition. *SIAM J. Matrix Anal. Appl.*, 21(4):1253–1278, 2000.

[21] J. Leskovec, L. Backstrom, and J. M. Kleinberg. Meme-tracking and the dynamics of the news cycle. In *KDD*, pages 497–506, 2009.

[22] J. Letchner, C. Ré, M. Balazinska, and M. Philipose. Access methods for markovian streams. In *ICDE*, pages 246–257, 2009.

[23] L. Li, C.-J. M. Liang, J. Liu, S. Nath, A. Terzis, and C. Faloutsos. Thermocast: A cyber-physical forecasting model for data centers. In *KDD*, 2011.

[24] L. Li, J. McCann, N. Pollard, and C. Faloutsos. Dynammo: Mining and summarization of coevolving sequences with missing values. In *KDD*, 2009.

[25] L. Li, B. A. Prakash, and C. Faloutsos. Parsimonious linear fingerprinting for time series. *PVLDB*, 3(1):385–396, 2010.

[26] M. Mathioudakis, N. Koudas, and P. Marbach. Early online identification of attention gathering items in social media. In *WSDM*, pages 301–310, 2010.

[27] Y. Matsubara, L. Li, E. E. Papalexakis, D. Lo, Y. Sakurai, and C. Faloutsos. F-trail: Finding patterns in taxi trajectories. In *PAKDD*, pages 86–98, 2013.

[28] Y. Matsubara, Y. Sakurai, and C. Faloutsos. Autoplait: automatic mining of co-evolving time sequences. In *SIGMOD*, pages 193–204, 2014.

[29] Y. Matsubara, Y. Sakurai, and C. Faloutsos. The web as a jungle: Non-linear dynamical systems for co-evolving online activities. In *WWW*, 2015.

[30] Y. Matsubara, Y. Sakurai, C. Faloutsos, T. Iwata, and M. Yoshikawa. Fast mining and forecasting of complex time-stamped events. In *KDD*, pages 271–279, 2012.

[31] Y. Matsubara, Y. Sakurai, B. A. Prakash, L. Li, and C. Faloutsos. Rise and fall patterns of information diffusion: model and implications. In *KDD*, pages 6–14, 2012.

[32] Y. Matsubara, Y. Sakurai, N. Ueda, and M. Yoshikawa. Fast and exact monitoring of co-evolving data streams. In *ICDM*, 2014.

[33] Y. Matsubara, Y. Sakurai, W. G. van Panhuis, and C. Faloutsos. FUNNEL: automatic mining of spatially coevolving epidemics. In *KDD*, pages 105–114, 2014.

[34] Y. Matsubara, Y. Sakurai, and M. Yoshikawa. Scalable algorithms for distribution search. In *ICDM*, pages 347–356, 2009.

[35] R. M. May. Qualitative stability in model ecosystems. *Ecology*, 54(3):638–641, 1973.

[36] M. McGlohon, J. Leskovec, C. Faloutsos, M. Hurst, and N. Glance. Finding patterns in blog shapes and blog evolution. In *International Conference on Weblogs and Social Media*, Boulder, Colo., March 2007.

[37] M. Nowak. *Evolutionary Dynamics*. Harvard University Press, 2006.

[38] J.-Y. Pan, H. Kitagawa, C. Faloutsos, and M. Hamamoto. Autosplit: Fast and scalable discovery of hidden variables in stream and multimedia databases. In *PAKDD*, May 26-28 2004.

[39] S. Papadimitriou, A. Brockwell, and C. Faloutsos. Adaptive, hands-off stream mining. In *VLDB*, pages 560–571, 2003.

[40] S. Papadimitriou, J. Sun, and C. Faloutsos. Streaming pattern discovery in multiple time-series. In *VLDB*, pages 697–708, 2005.

[41] S. Papadimitriou and P. S. Yu. Optimal multi-scale patterns in time series streams. In *SIGMOD*, pages 647–658, 2006.

[42] T. Rakthanmanon, B. J. L. Campana, A. Mueen, G. E. A. P. A. Batista, M. B. Westover, Q. Zhu, J. Zakaria, and E. J. Keogh. Searching and mining trillions of time series subsequences under dynamic time warping. In *KDD*, pages 262–270, 2012.

[43] Y. Sakurai, C. Faloutsos, and M. Yamamuro. Stream monitoring under the time warping distance. In *Proceedings of the 23rd International Conference on Data Engineering, ICDE 2007, April 15-20, 2007, The Marmara Hotel, Istanbul, Turkey*, pages 1046–1055, 2007.

[44] Y. Sakurai, L. Li, Y. Matsubara, and C. Faloutsos. Windmine: Fast and effective mining of web-click sequences. In *SDM*, pages 759–770, 2011.

[45] Y. Sakurai, S. Papadimitriou, and C. Faloutsos. Braid: Stream mining through group lag correlations. In *SIGMOD*, pages 599–610, 2005.

[46] Y. Sakurai, M. Yoshikawa, and C. Faloutsos. Ftw: Fast similarity search under the time warping distance. In *PODS*, pages 326–337, Baltimore, Maryland, June 2005.

[47] J. Sun, D. Tao, and C. Faloutsos. Beyond streams and graphs: dynamic tensor analysis. In *KDD*, pages 374–383, 2006.

[48] Y. Tao, C. Faloutsos, D. Papadias, and B. Liu. Prediction and indexing of moving objects with unknown motion patterns. In *SIGMOD*, pages 611–622, 2004.

[49] M. Toyoda, Y. Sakurai, and Y. Ishikawa. Pattern discovery in data streams under the time warping distance. *VLDB J.*, 22(3):295–318, 2013.

[50] W. G. van Panhuis, J. Grefenstette, S. Y. Jung, N. S. Chok, A. Cross, H. Eng, B. Y. Lee, V. Zadorozhny, S. Brown, D. Cummings, and D. S. Burke. Contagious diseases in the united states from 1888 to the present. *NEJM*, 369(22):2152–2158, 2013.

[51] P. Wang, H. Wang, and W. Wang. Finding semantics in time series. In *SIGMOD Conference*, pages 385–396, 2011.

[52] J. G. Wilpon, L. R. Rabiner, C. H. Lee, and E. R. Goldman. Automatic recognition of keywords in unconstrained speech using hidden Markov models. *IEEE Transactions on Acoustics, Speech, and Signal Processing*, 38(11):1870–1878, 1990.

[53] J. Yang and J. Leskovec. Modeling information diffusion in implicit networks. In *ICDM*, pages 599–608, 2010.

[54] J. Yang and J. Leskovec. Patterns of temporal variation in online media. In *WSDM*, pages 177–186, 2011.

[55] B.-K. Yi, N. Sidiropoulos, T. Johnson, H. Jagadish, C. Faloutsos, and A. Biliris. Online data mining for co-evolving time sequences. *ICDE*, pages 13–22, 2000.

[56] Y. Zhu and D. Shasha. Statstream: Statistical monitoring of thousands of data streams in real time. In *VLDB*, pages 358–369, 2002.

Optimal Spatial Dominance: An Effective Search of Nearest Neighbor Candidates

Xiaoyang Wang†, Ying Zhang‡, Wenjie Zhang†
Xuemin Lin†, Muhammad Aamir Cheema♮
†The University of New South Wales, Australia ‡University of Technology, Sydney, Australia
♮Monash University, Australia
xiaoyangw@cse.unsw.edu.au, Ying.Zhang@uts.edu.au
{zhangw, lxue}@cse.unsw.edu.au, aamir.cheema@monash.edu

ABSTRACT

In many domains such as computational geometry and database management, an object may be described by multiple instances (points). Then the distance (or similarity) between two objects is captured by the pair-wise distances among their instances. In the past, numerous *nearest neighbor* (NN) functions have been proposed to define the distance between objects with multiple instances and to identify the NN object. Nevertheless, considering that a user may not have a specific NN function in mind, it is desirable to provide her with a set of NN candidates. Ideally, the set of NN candidates must include every object that is NN for at least one of the NN functions and must exclude every non-promising object. However, no one has studied the problem of NN candidates computation from this perspective. Although some of the existing works aim at returning a set of candidate objects, they do not focus on the NN functions while computing the candidate objects. As a result, they either fail to include an NN object w.r.t. some NN functions or include a large number of unnecessary objects that have no potential to be the NN regardless of the NN functions.

Motivated by this, we classify the existing NN functions for objects with multiple instances into three families by characterizing their key features. Then, we advocate three spatial dominance operators to compute NN candidates where each operator is *optimal* w.r.t. different coverage of NN functions. Efficient algorithms are proposed for the dominance check and corresponding NN candidates computation. Extensive empirical study on real and synthetic datasets shows that our proposed operators can significantly reduce the number of NN candidates. The comprehensive performance evaluation demonstrates the efficiency of our computation techniques.

Categories and Subject Descriptors

H.3.3 [**Information Storage and Retrieval**]: Information Search and Retrieval

Keywords

Spatial dominance; NN candidates; NN functions

SIGMOD'15, May 31–June 4, 2015, Melbourne, Victoria, Australia.
Copyright © 2015 ACM 978-1-4503-2758-9/15/05 ...$15.00.
http://dx.doi.org/10.1145/2723372.2749442.

1. INTRODUCTION

Nearest neighbor (NN) search identifies the closest (or most similar) object to a given query object. It is a classical problem with applications in many domains such as computational geometry, multi-media database, information retrieval and machine learning, to name a few. In many real-world applications, an object may be described by a set of points (i.e., instances). Each point is associated with a value (e.g., weight and probability). For example, in multi-media database, an object (e.g., an image) may be mapped onto a set of feature vectors (i.e., points) [19, 28, 35]. The performance of an NBA player can be evaluated by his historical game records [26, 25, 42, 37]. Suppose the number of points, assistants and rebounds are kept for each game record, a player can be described by a set of points in a three dimensional space. Due to the limitations of measuring equipment, the location of an object (e.g., a person or a mobile device) may be uncertain [40] and hence be represented by a set of possible locations. Each location is associated with an *occurrence probability*.

In traditional NN search problem, each object (and query) is modeled as a single point in a multi-dimensional space. The distance between the object and the query is computed using the given distance metric (e.g., Euclidean distance) and the object with the smallest distance value is returned. However, it is non-trivial to extend the NN semantics for objects with multiple instances because the similarity between two objects is described by their distance distribution (i.e., pair-wise distances). Consequently, a large body of NN functions are proposed in the literature. In this paper, we propose three models to characterize the intrinsic nature of these NN functions (details are introduced in Section 3).

- ($\mathcal{N}_1$) **All pairs** based NN functions (e.g., *min*, *max*, *expected*, and *quantile* distances [17, 37]).
- ($\mathcal{N}_2$) **Possible world** based NN functions (e.g., NN probability [21, 7], expected rank [40], and parameterized rank [23]).
- ($\mathcal{N}_3$) **Selected pairs** based NN functions (e.g., Hausdorff distance [27], Earth Mover's distance [10, 28, 35] and Netflow distance [27]).

These three types of NN functions cover the popular NN functions for both discrete uncertain/probabilistic objects (e.g.,[12, 4, 22, 3]) and traditional multi-valued/multi-instance objects (e.g.,[37, 42, 20, 34]). These two object models have different semantics [37]. Specifically, a *discrete uncertain object* is a discrete random variable where each instance is associated with a probability value. The uncertain object model enforces the exclusive property when the possible world based NN functions ($\mathcal{N}_2$) are used because two instances of an uncertain object (e.g., two possible locations of an object) cannot occur in the same possible world. Uncertain object model has also been used by some NN functions in $\mathcal{N}_1$ (e.g., expected distance [12]) and $\mathcal{N}_3$ (e.g., Earth Mover's distance [28, 35]). *A multi-valued object* consists of a set of points (instances), and each instance carries a weight to reflect its significance. Note that the instances of a multi-valued object will co-exist and hence the multi-valued object model is not suitable to the possible world semantics (i.e., NN functions in $\mathcal{N}_2$). Functions in $\mathcal{N}_1$ (e.g., expected distance and quantile distance [37]) and $\mathcal{N}_3$ (e.g., Earth Mover's distance [10]) are used for multi-valued objects.

While the scope of this paper covers both discrete uncertain objects and multi-valued objects, we observe that the stochastic order [29] and its variants are effective tools to derive the candidates for various NN functions. To this end, despite of the different semantics, we may treat a multi-valued object as a random variable if the weights of its instances can be normalized. In particular, we say the multi-valued objects can be normalized w.r.t. an NN function f if their NN ranks remain the same after the instance weights normalization. It can be immediately verified that the multi-valued objects can be normalized for NN functions investigated in this paper, if the total weight mass of each object is the same, which is common in practice. In this way, we can generate *correct* NN candidates w.r.t. corresponding NN functions. Thereafter, we may use a discrete uncertain object (i.e., a discrete random variable) to denote an object with multiple instances.

Nearest Neighbor Candidates (NNC) Search. In practice, users often do not have a specific NN function in mind. One solution is that the system explains different NN functions before a user performs NN search, so she can choose one or a few desirable NN functions. Considering that it might be difficult for an inexperienced user to choose some complicated NN functions as well as the settings of the parameters, as a valuable complement, system may provide the user a small set of "good" NN candidates. Then she can browse the NN candidates and make her decision, e.g., by using visualization tools. Such an approach is also useful when an inexperienced or "greedy" user wants to make personal trade-off among the results of many different NN functions, which rank objects from various perspectives. To the best of our knowledge, there are two existing approaches which can provide the nearest neighbor candidates (NNC).

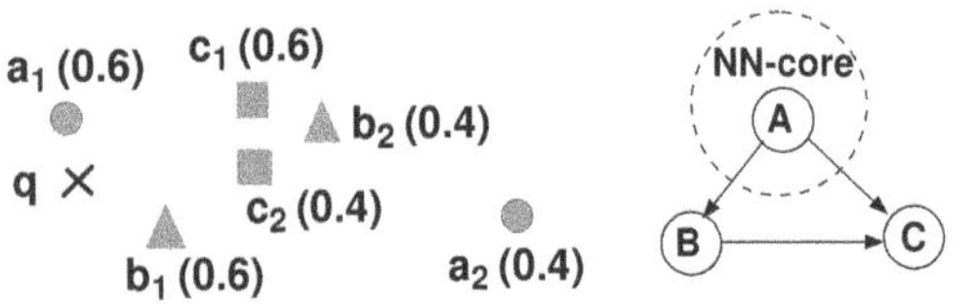

Figure 1: Example of NN-core

In [36], NN candidates (namely *NN-core*) are derived based on the pair-wise competition among the objects where an object U is said to supersede another object V if U is more likely to be closer to the query than V. Then, NN-core is the minimal set of objects such that each object in NN-core supersedes every object not in the NN-core. Figure 1 illustrates an example of the NN-core of three objects $\{A, B, C\}$ where the query object has a single instance q and each of the objects consists of two instances with probability 0.6 and 0.4, respectively. In this example, A is closer to q than B with probability 0.6, and hence A supersedes B (denoted by $A \rightarrow B$ in Figure 1). Similarly, we have A supersedes C and B supersedes C, and hence the NN-core is $\{A\}$.

(a) F-SD(A,B,Q) (b) ¬F-SD(A,C,Q)

Figure 2: Examples of F-$\mathcal{SD}$

The *full spatial dominance* (**F-SD**) operator has been used recently to prune non-promising NN candidates where each object is approximated by a rectangle [16] or a hypersphere [25]. Given two objects U and V, and a query Q, we say U fully spatially dominates V w.r.t. Q, denoted by F-$\mathcal{SD}(U,V,Q)$, if and only if for every instance $q \in Q$, U is closer to q than V; that is, $\delta(u, q) \leq \delta(v, q)$ for every $u \in U$ and every $v \in V$ where $\delta(x, y)$ denotes the distance between two points (instances) x and y. Then, NN candidates are the objects which are not fully spatially dominated by any other object. Figure 2 shows examples of F-$\mathcal{SD}$ where instances of each object are bounded by a circle. Then we have F-$\mathcal{SD}(A,B,Q)$ in Figure 2(a) as $\delta(a, q) < \delta(b, q)$ for *every* $q \in Q$, $a \in A$, and $b \in B$. Figure 2(b) shows that F-$\mathcal{SD}(A,C,Q)$ does not hold, denoted by $\neg$F-$\mathcal{SD}(A,C,Q)$, since we have $\delta(c, q) < \delta(a, q)$ for the given $q \in Q$, $a \in A$, and $c \in C$.

Motivation and Challenges. As discussed earlier, there are many possible NN functions that can be used to retrieve the NN objects. Intuitively, the computation of NN candidates should consider these functions and, ideally, the NN candidates must include every object that can be the NN object for at least one NN function and must not contain any object that can never be the NN object regardless of which function is used. Unfortunately, none of the existing works investigates the problem from this perspective. Specifically, NN-core [36] is too aggressive in the sense that NN object may be missed from NN-core for some popular NN functions. For instance, in Figure 1, C is the NN object if function *max* is used while B becomes the NN object if the *expected distance* is considered. Unlike NN-core that is too aggressive, F-$\mathcal{SD}$ is overly pessimistic and may return a large number of objects which can never be the NN of Q.

Motivated by the above facts, we devise spatial dominance (SD) operators that compute NN candidates by carefully considering various NN functions. Let $f(X)$ denote the distance between X and Q computed using an NN function f. We say that a spatial dominance operator $\mathcal{SD}$ is **optimal** w.r.t. a family $\mathcal{N}$ of NN functions if it satisfies the following two properties.

- **Correctness.** $\mathcal{SD}(U,V,Q)$ implies that $f(U) \leq f(V)$ for every $f \in \mathcal{N}$, i.e., V is not closer to Q than U for every function $f \in \mathcal{N}$. In this paper, we say that $\mathcal{SD}$ *covers* the functions in $\mathcal{N}$ if it is *correct* w.r.t. $\mathcal{N}$.
- **Completeness.** $\neg\mathcal{SD}(U,V,Q)$ implies that there exists a function $f \in \mathcal{N}$ such that $f(V) < f(U)$, i.e., V is closer to Q than U w.r.t. f.

The *correctness* property of the $\mathcal{SD}$ guarantees that it is safe to exclude the object V from NN candidates w.r.t. $\mathcal{N}$. The *completeness* property indicates that $\mathcal{SD}$ is the *tightest* dominance operator w.r.t. $\mathcal{N}$ in the sense that U cannot exclude V from NN candidates if and only if there exists a function $f \in \mathcal{N}$ for which V is ranked better than U.

Given a family of NN functions, a straightforward way to compute NN candidates is to retrieve NN objects for all possible NN functions. However, this is infeasible not only due to the unnecessary computations involved but also because the number of NN functions is infinite, e.g., ϕ-quantile distance depends on the input parameter ϕ that may take every value between 0 to 1 [37].

Next, we give an informal but intuitive explanation of three *optimal* spatial dominance (SD) operators to obtain NN candidates, which are *optimal* w.r.t. different coverage of the NN functions.

Stochastic SD (S-$\mathcal{SD}$, opt. w.r.t. $\mathcal{N}_1$). A function $f \in \mathcal{N}_1$ is an aggregate function on the *distance distributions* of the two objects, i.e., all pair-wise distances. We apply the widely employed *usual stochastic order* [29] to model the S-$\mathcal{SD}$ operator which is optimal w.r.t. $\mathcal{N}_1$. Given two random variables X and Y, we say X *is smaller than* (or dominates) Y in usual stochastic order, denoted by $X \preceq_{st} Y$, if $Pr(X \leq \lambda) \geq Pr(Y \leq \lambda)$ for every $\lambda \in R$. Note that smaller value is preferred in this paper. Thus, we have S-$\mathcal{SD}(U,V,Q)$ if $U_Q \preceq_{st} V_Q$ where U_Q (V_Q) denotes the distance distribution of U (V) w.r.t. Q. Intuitively, S-$\mathcal{SD}(U,V,Q)$ implies that, for every λ, the probability that the distance between U and Q is at most λ is not smaller than that of V.

Figure 3(a) shows an example where each object (query) has two instances with the same probability (0.5), and Figure 3(b) depicts the distance distributions of three objects regarding the query. In each distance distribution (e.g., A_Q), each pair of instances between the query and the object (e.g., q_1a_1) carries probability 0.25, and they are sorted based on their distance values. Clearly, we have S-$\mathcal{SD}(A,B,Q)$, S-$\mathcal{SD}(A,C,Q)$, and $\neg$S-$\mathcal{SD}(B, C, Q)$.

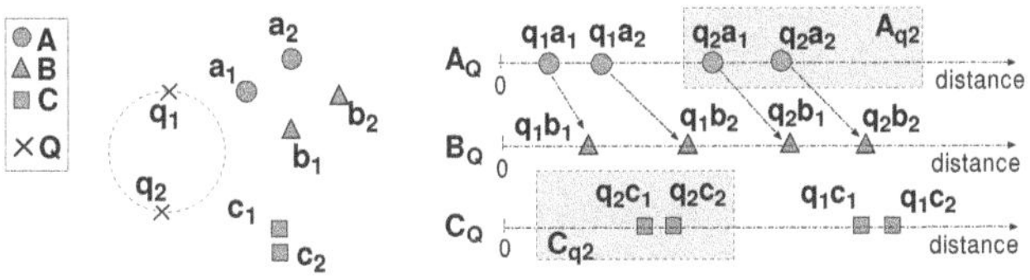

(a) NN search (b) Distance Distributions

Figure 3: Examples of S-$\mathcal{SD}$ and SS-$\mathcal{SD}$

Strict Stochastic SD (SS-$\mathcal{SD}$, opt. w.r.t. $\mathcal{N}_{1,2}$). NN functions in $\mathcal{N}_2$ apply the possible world semantics. Generally, each possible world contains one instance from each object and the query. Then, the rank of an object in a possible world can be calculated following the traditional NN semantics. The final score can be derived for each object based on their performance in all possible worlds.

Since each possible world contains exactly one instance from each object and the query, two instance pairs q_1a_1 and q_2c_1 in Figure 3(b) will never be evaluated in the same possible world because q_1 and q_2 cannot appear in the same possible world. This may lead to the case in which an object C is an NN object while C is stochastically dominated by another object A w.r.t. Q. In Figure 3, we have S-$\mathcal{SD}(A,C,Q)$. However, note that C is always closer to q_2 than A and B (i.e., C beats A and B in half of all 16 possible worlds) and hence the NN probability of the object C is 0.5, which is larger than that of A and B (0.375 and 0.125 respectively). Therefore, C is the NN object if the NN probability based NN function is used, which indicates that S-$\mathcal{SD}$ does not cover the possible world based NN functions (i.e., $\mathcal{N}_2$). This motivates us to propose Strict Stochastic SD (SS-$\mathcal{SD}$) operator that covers all functions in $\mathcal{N}_1 \cup \mathcal{N}_2$ (denoted as $\mathcal{N}_{1,2}$).

SS-$\mathcal{SD}$ enforces the stochastic order for each individual query instance $q \in Q$; that is, SS-$\mathcal{SD}(U,V,Q)$ holds if and only if $U_q \preceq_{st} V_q$ for every $q \in Q$ where U_q (V_q) is the distance distribution of U (V) w.r.t. q. In Section 4.2, we show that SS-$\mathcal{SD}$ is optimal w.r.t. $\mathcal{N}_{1,2}$. In the example of Figure 3, we have SS-$\mathcal{SD}(A,B,Q)$, and $\neg$SS-$\mathcal{SD}(A,C,Q)$.

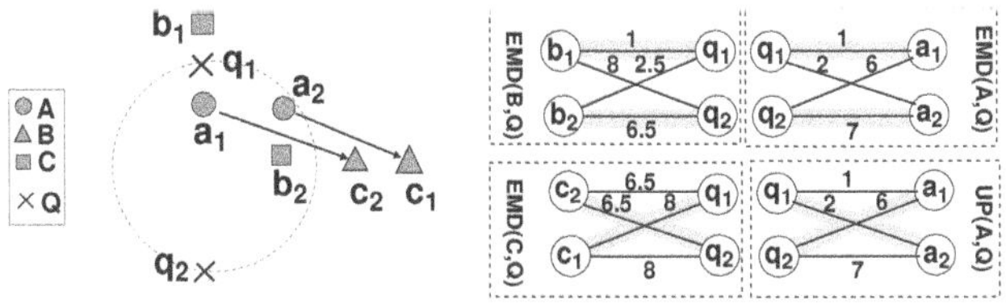

(a) NN search (b) Bipartite graphs

Figure 4: Examples of P-$\mathcal{SD}$

Peer SD (P-$\mathcal{SD}$, opt. w.r.t. $\mathcal{N}_{1,2,3}$). A function in $\mathcal{N}_3$ selects a *subset* of pair-wise distances for computation. Earth Movers Distance (EMD) [10] is an example of such functions. In Figure 4, we assume each object (query) has two instances with probability 0.5, and a distance distribution can be regarded as a fully connected bipartite graph where the label of an edge represents the distance between two vertexes (instances). In this example, EMD(A,Q) corresponds to the minimal weighted sum of any two *disjoint* edges in the bipartite graph of A and Q, where the weight of each edge is 0.5. For instance, two shaded edges in EMD(A,Q) (i.e., $\langle a_1, q_1\rangle$ and $\langle a_2, q_2\rangle$) represent the subset of pairs chosen for the computation. Thus, we have EMD$(A,Q)= 0.5 \times 1 + 0.5 \times 7 = 4$ and EMD$(B,Q) = 0.5 \times 1 + 0.5 \times 6.5 = 3.75$. Although both S-$\mathcal{SD}(A,B,Q)$ and SS-$\mathcal{SD}(A,B,Q)$ hold in Figure 4, we have EMD$(A,Q)>$EMD(B,Q). This implies that both S-$\mathcal{SD}$ and SS-$\mathcal{SD}$ do not cover $\mathcal{N}_3$.

To accommodate the functions in $\mathcal{N}_3$, we propose the *peer spatial dominance* (P-$\mathcal{SD}$) operator. We say P-$\mathcal{SD}(U,V,Q)$ holds if there exists a one-to-one mapping between two objects U and V such that, for every $u \in U$, u is not further than v w.r.t. all query instances, denoted by $u \preceq_Q v$, where v is the *peer* instance of u (i.e., u is mapped to v). As shown in Figure 4, there is a mapping: $a_1 \to c_2$ and $a_2 \to c_1$ such that $a_1 \preceq_Q c_2$ and $a_2 \preceq_Q c_1$. Thus, P-$\mathcal{SD}(A,C,Q)$ holds. Meanwhile, we have $\neg$P-$\mathcal{SD}(A,B,Q)$. Section 4.2 shows that P-$\mathcal{SD}$ is *optimal* w.r.t. $\mathcal{N}_{1,2,3}$.

Comparison of SD operators. Section 4.1 shows that the four spatial dominance operators are closely related in the sense that we have F-$\mathcal{SD} \subset$ P-$\mathcal{SD} \subset$ SS-$\mathcal{SD} \subset$ S-$\mathcal{SD}$. Here, $\mathcal{SD}_1 \subset \mathcal{SD}_2$ denotes that $\mathcal{SD}_1$ is *covered* by $\mathcal{SD}_2$; that is, $\mathcal{SD}_1$ has stronger dominance condition which may result in more NN candidates as well as larger coverage of NN functions. Figure 5 illustrates the NN candidates and their coverage on different dominance operators, which suggests that: (*i*) F-$\mathcal{SD}$ includes redundant objects (i.e., is not *complete*) regarding the NN function families studied in this paper since P-$\mathcal{SD}$ has the same coverage but smaller candidate size, and (*ii*) users may make a trade-off between the NN candidate size and coverage among P-$\mathcal{SD}$, SS-$\mathcal{SD}$, and S-$\mathcal{SD}$. Particularly, as shown in Section 4, the P-$\mathcal{SD}$ can be applied to current popular NN ranking mechanisms on objects with multiple instances ($\mathcal{N}_{1,2,3}$). If users are only interested in NN functions in $\mathcal{N}_{1,2}$, SS-$\mathcal{SD}$ can be used to reduce the number of candidate objects. The candidate size can be further reduced if only the simple NN functions in $\mathcal{N}_1$ are considered, where S-$\mathcal{SD}$ will be applied. Moreover, Section 4.1 shows that P-$\mathcal{SD}$, SS-$\mathcal{SD}$, and S-$\mathcal{SD}$ are equivalent to each other when the query has only one instance.

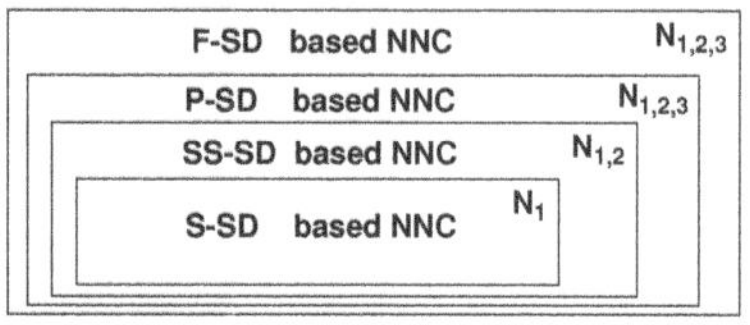

Figure 5: NN Candidates w.r.t. Different SDs

NN Candidates (NNC) Computation. Given a spatial dominance operator $\mathcal{SD}$, the NN candidates are the objects which are not dominated by any other objects. Regarding S-$\mathcal{SD}$ operator, NNC in the example of Figure 3 is $\{A\}$ whereas NNC is $\{A, C\}$ if SS-$\mathcal{SD}$ is employed. Similarly, NNC is $\{A\}$ and $\{A, B\}$ if SS-$\mathcal{SD}$ and P-$\mathcal{SD}$ are employed in Figure 4, respectively.

In addition to the semantics and theoretical properties of the spatial dominance operators, it is imperative to develop efficient dominance check algorithms as well as the NN candidate computation algorithms. In particular, we show that the dominance check of S-$\mathcal{SD}$ and SS-$\mathcal{SD}$ can be finished with one single scan of the pair-wise distances if they are already sorted. Moreover, efficient statistic-based and cover-based filtering techniques are proposed to enhance the performance. Regarding the dominance check of P-$\mathcal{SD}$, the problem can be reduced to the well known max-flow problem [11]. Besides the effective pruning and verification rules, we further improve the performance by utilizing some interesting geometric properties. We also propose a general framework for the computation of NN candidates regarding four spatial dominance operators.

Contributions. Our principle contributions in this paper can be summarized as follows.

- This is the first work to systematically investigate the problem of NN candidate search for objects with multiple instances with careful consideration of NN functions.
- Three families of NN functions are formalized, including all pairs based NN functions ($\mathcal{N}_1$), possible world based NN functions ($\mathcal{N}_2$), and selected pairs based NN functions ($\mathcal{N}_3$). We show that they cover popular NN ranking mechanisms.
- We advocate three *spatial dominance* (SD) operators, namely *stochastic* SD (S-$\mathcal{SD}$), *strict stochastic* SD (SS-$\mathcal{SD}$), and *peer* SD (P-$\mathcal{SD}$). We show that S-$\mathcal{SD}$, SS-$\mathcal{SD}$ and P-$\mathcal{SD}$ are *optimal* dominance operators w.r.t. $\mathcal{N}_1$, $\mathcal{N}_{1,2}$, and $\mathcal{N}_{1,2,3}$, respectively.
- Efficient dominance testing algorithms are proposed for three spatial dominance operators. Novel pruning and validation rules are developed to significantly speed up the computation. Then a general framework is proposed to efficiently calculate the NN candidates.
- Comprehensive experiments demonstrate the effectiveness and efficiency of our NN candidate search techniques.

Roadmap. The rest of the paper is organized as follows. Section 2 introduces the problem studied in this paper. Section 3 provides three general models to summarize the existing NN functions. Section 4 studies important properties of the spatial dominance operators proposed in this paper. Efficient dominance check algorithms as well as NN candidate computation algorithms are proposed in Section 5. The experimental results are reported in Section 6. We conclude the paper in Section 7. In the appendix of the paper, we introduce the details of some NN functions (Section A), details of the proof (Section B), additional experiments and analysis (Section C) and related works (Section D).

2. BACKGROUND

In this section, we provide formal definitions of the spatial dominance operators as well as some important notations. Table 1 summarizes the notations frequently used throughout the paper.

Notation	Meaning
U, V, A, B	objects with multiple instances
u, v, a, b	instances (points)
$Q(q)$	query object (instance)
$\lvert U\rvert(\lvert Q\rvert)$	number of instances in U (Q)
$p(u)$	probability of an instance u
$\Upsilon(U)$	ranking score of U
$M_{U,V}$	a match between U and V
$\mathcal{M}_{U,V}$	all possible matches between U and V
$u \preceq_Q v$	u is not further than v w.r.t. every $q \in Q$
U_Q	distance distribution of U w.r.t. Q
U_q	distance distribution of U w.r.t. q
X, Y	univariate random variables
$X \preceq_{st} Y$	X is smaller than Y in stochastic order
$X \preceq_M Y$	X is smaller than Y in match order
$W, \mathcal{W}$	a possible world, all possible worlds
$\mathcal{W}_q$	possible worlds in which q occurs
$\mathcal{SD}$	spatial dominance (SD) operator
$\mathcal{SD}_1 \subset \mathcal{SD}_2$	$\mathcal{SD}_1$ is *covered* by $\mathcal{SD}_2$
$\mathcal{SD}(U,V,Q)$	*U spatially dominates V* regarding Q
$\neg\mathcal{SD}(U,V,Q)$	$\mathcal{SD}(U,V,Q)$ does not hold

Table 1: The summary of notations.

2.1 Problem Definition

A point (instance) p is in a d-dimensional space and the i-th dimensional coordinate value of p is denoted by $p[i]$. $\delta(u, v)$ denotes the distance between two instances u and v. Although we assume that $\delta(u, v)$ represents Euclidean distance between u and v, our techniques can be trivially extended to other metric distances. We use $\delta_{min}(x, S)$ to denote the minimal distance between a point x and a set S of points, i.e., $\delta_{min}(x, S) = min_{y \in S}\, \delta(x, y)$.

Modeling object with multiple instances. In this paper, we model an object with multiple instances as a **discrete random variable** (i.e., discrete uncertain object). Particularly, an object U consists of a set $\{u_1, u_2, \ldots, u_m\}$ of instances (points), and a *discrete probability mass function* assigns each instance u_i a probability value, denoted by $p(u_i)$. In this paper, we assume $\sum_{i=1}^{m} p(u_i) = 1$, and objects are independent to each other. Moreover, we assume the weights of the multi-valued objects can be normalized to probabilities where $p(u_i) = \frac{w(u_i)}{\sum_{j=1}^{m} w(u_j)}$ and $w(u_j)$ is the weight of the instance u_j so that a multi-valued object is also treated as a discrete random variable. We remark that the transformation from multi-valued objects to discrete uncertain objects is only for the dominance check purpose (i.e., NN candidates computation), and will not introduce any new NN semantics (i.e., new NN functions). We use the term *object* to refer to the object with multiple instances whenever clear by context.

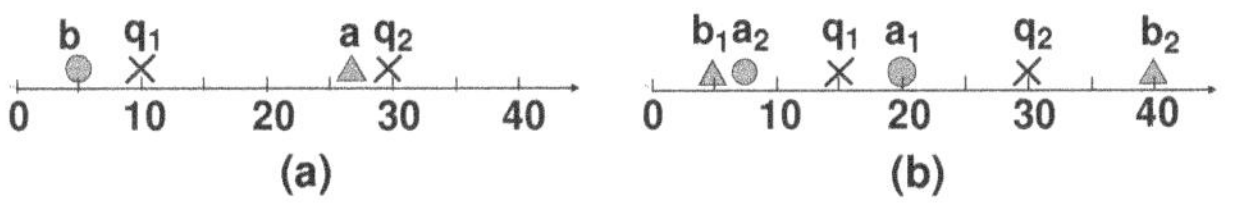

Figure 6: Examples for S-$\mathcal{SD}$ and SS-$\mathcal{SD}$

Distance distribution. Given an object U and a query Q, the distance distribution between U and Q, denoted by U_Q, is a discrete random variable consisting of all pair-wise distances. Specifically, U_Q consists of every instance pair (q,u) for every $q \in Q$ and every $u \in U$, where each instance pair (q,u) is assigned two values: $\delta(q,u)$ denotes the distance and $p(q) \times p(u)$ denotes the probability of the instance pair. For a query instance $q \in Q$, the distance distribution between U and q, denoted by U_q, consists of only the instance pairs where q is involved; that is, U_q contains every (q,u) for all $u \in U$ where each pair (q,u) is associated with $\delta(q,u)$ denoting the distance and $p(u)$ denoting the probability of the instance pair.

EXAMPLE 1. *In Figure 6(b), both the query Q and the object A have two instances with the same probability 0.5. Then the distance distribution A_Q is $\{(\delta(q_1,a_1),0.25), (\delta(q_1,a_2), 0.25), (\delta(q_2,a_1), 0.25), (\delta(q_2,a_2),0.25)\} = \{(5, 0.25), (8, 0.25), (10, 0.25), (23, 0.25)\}$. Meanwhile, the distance distribution between the query instance q_1 and the object A, A_{q_1}, is $\{(\delta(q_1,a_1),0.5), (\delta(q_1,a_2),0.5)\} = \{(5,0.5), (8, 0.5)\}$.*

Our first two spatial dominance operators are proposed based on the **stochastic order** [29] which has been widely used in various domains to compare the "goodness" of two random variables (distributions).

DEFINITION 1. ***Stochastic Order.*** *Given two independent random variables X and Y, we say X is smaller than Y in usual stochastic order, denoted by $X \preceq_{st} Y$, if $Pr(X \leq \lambda) \geq Pr(Y \leq \lambda)$ for every $\lambda \in R$.*

Then we immediately have the definitions of two stochastic order based dominance operators.

DEFINITION 2. ***Stochastic SD(S-$\mathcal{SD}$).*** *Given two objects U and V, and the query Q, we have S-$\mathcal{SD}$(U,V,Q) if and only if $U_Q \preceq_{st} V_Q$ and $U_Q \neq V_Q$.*

DEFINITION 3. ***Strict Stochastic SD (SS-$\mathcal{SD}$).*** *Given two objects U and V, and the query Q, we have SS-$\mathcal{SD}$(U,V,Q) if and only if $U_q \preceq_{st} V_q$ for every $q \in Q$ and $U_Q \neq V_Q$.*

Note that the condition $U_Q \neq V_Q$ is used to avoid the scenario that two objects dominate each other.

EXAMPLE 2. *We assume all instances of the same object (query) has the same probability value. In Figure 6(a), each of objects A and B have one instance and the query Q has two instances q_1 and q_2. Since A_Q=$\{(3, 0.5), (17,0.5)\}$ and $B_Q = \{(5,0.5), (25,0.5)\}$ we have S-$\mathcal{SD}$(A,B,Q). Nevertheless, since $A_{q_1} = \{(17, 1.0)\}$ and $B_{q_1} = \{(5, 1.0)\}$, we have $\neg$SS-$\mathcal{SD}$(A,B,Q). In Figure 6(b), since $A_{q_1} = \{(5,0.5), (8, 0.5)\}$, $A_{q_2} = \{(10,0.5), (23, 0.5)\}$, $B_{q_1} = \{(10,0.5), (25, 0.5)\}$, $B_{q_2} = \{(10,0.5), (25, 0.5)\}$, we have $A_{q_1} \preceq_{st} B_{q_1}$ and $A_{q_2} \preceq_{st} B_{q_2}$, and hence SS-$\mathcal{SD}$(A,B,Q) holds.*

Before we formally define the third dominance operator, Peer SD (P-$\mathcal{SD}$), we first extend the semantics of *one-to-one mapping* for the general case where different objects may have different number of instances and instance probabilities. We formally define a *match* between two discrete random variables (e.g., objects and distance distributions), which can actually be regarded as a one-to-one mapping by splitting some instances.

DEFINITION 4. ***Match*** *($M_{U,V}$). Given two discrete random variables U and V, a match between U and V, denoted by $M_{U,V}$, consists of a set of tuples $\{t\langle u,v,p\rangle\}$ where $t.u \in U$, $t.v \in V$ and $t.p$ is the probability associated with t. Moreover, we have $\sum_{t \in M_{U,V} \wedge t.u=u} t.p = p(u)$ and $\sum_{t \in M_{U,V} \wedge t.v=v} t.p = p(v)$.*

In this paper, we use $\mathcal{M}_{U,V}$ to denote all possible matches between U and V. Figure 7 shows two objects A=$\{(a_1,0.5), (a_2,0.3), (a_3,0.2)\}$ and B=$\{(b_1,0.5), (b_2,0.5)\}$. Each shadowed edge corresponds to one tuple in the match with probability labeled, e.g., Figure 7(a) and Figure 7(b) show two matches $\{\langle a_1,b_1,0.5\rangle, \langle a_2,b_2,0.3\rangle, \langle a_3,b_2,0.2\rangle\}$ and $\{\langle a_1,b_1,0.2\rangle, \langle a_1,b_2,0.3\rangle, \langle a_2,b_1,0.3\rangle, \langle a_3,b_2,0.2\rangle\}$, respectively. According to Definition 4, the assignment in Figure 7(c) is not a match.

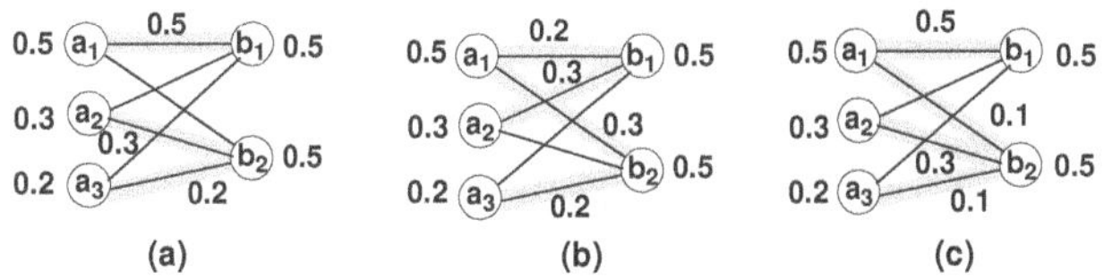

Figure 7: Example of Matches

We say that a point u is *closer* to the query Q than v, denoted by $u \preceq_Q v$, if we have $\delta(u,q) \leq \delta(v,q)$ for every $q \in Q$. Following is a formal definition of P-$\mathcal{SD}$.

DEFINITION 5. ***Peer SD (P-$\mathcal{SD}$).*** *Given two objects U and V, and query Q, we have P-$\mathcal{SD}$(U,V,Q) if and only if there is a match $M_{U,V}$ such that $t.u \preceq_Q t.v$ for every $t \in M_{U,V}$, and $U_Q \neq V_Q$.*

EXAMPLE 3. *In Figure 8, given the match between A and B $M_{A,B}$= $\{(a_1, b_1, 0.5), (a_2, b_2, 0.5)\}$, we have $a_1 \preceq_Q b_1$ and $a_2 \preceq_Q b_2$ since $\delta(a_1,q_1) = 5 < 10 = \delta(b_1,q_1)$, $\delta(a_1,q_2) = 15 < 20 = \delta(b_1,q_2)$, $\delta(a_2,q_1) = 20 < 25 = \delta(b_2,q_1)$, $\delta(a_2,q_2) = 10 < 15 = \delta(b_2,q_2)$. Consequently, P-$\mathcal{SD}$(A,B,Q) holds.*

Next, we formally define NN candidates and the *cover* relationship among spatial dominance operators.

DEFINITION 6. ***NN Candidates (NNC).*** *Given a set $\mathcal{O}$ of objects, a query Q and a spatial dominance operator SD, the nearest neighbor candidates, denoted by NNC($\mathcal{O}$,Q,SD), consist of every object that is not dominated by any other object w.r.t. SD.*

DEFINITION 7. ***Cover.*** *Given two spatial dominance operators $\mathcal{SD}_1$ and $\mathcal{SD}_2$, we say $\mathcal{SD}_2$ **covers** $\mathcal{SD}_1$, denoted by $\mathcal{SD}_1 \subset \mathcal{SD}_2$, if $\mathcal{SD}_1$(U,V,Q) implies $\mathcal{SD}_2$(U,V,Q) but the converse does not hold.*

Note that $\mathcal{SD}_1 \subset \mathcal{SD}_2$ implies that the dominance condition of $\mathcal{SD}_1$ is *stronger* than that of $\mathcal{SD}_2$, and hence NNC($\mathcal{O}$,Q,$\mathcal{SD}_2$) $\subseteq$ NNC($\mathcal{O}$,Q,$\mathcal{SD}_1$). In Section 4.1, we show that F-$\mathcal{SD}$ $\subset$ P-$\mathcal{SD}$ $\subset$ SS-$\mathcal{SD}$ $\subset$ S-$\mathcal{SD}$. Based on the relations among four dominance operators and the definition of NNC, as shown in Figure 5, we have NNC($\mathcal{O}$,Q,S-$\mathcal{SD}$) $\subseteq$ NNC($\mathcal{O}$,Q,SS-$\mathcal{SD}$) $\subseteq$ NNC($\mathcal{O}$,Q,P-$\mathcal{SD}$) $\subseteq$ NNC(Q,$\mathcal{O}$,F-$\mathcal{SD}$). As shown in Section 4.1, P-$\mathcal{SD}$, SS-$\mathcal{SD}$ and S-$\mathcal{SD}$ are equivalent to each other when the query has only one instance.

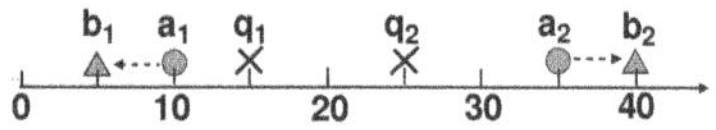

Figure 8: Examples for P-$\mathcal{SD}$

3. MODELING NN FUNCTIONS

In this section, we first discuss the *stable* property of aggregate functions. Then we propose three general models for three representative families of NN ranking functions (denoted by $\mathcal{N}_1$, $\mathcal{N}_2$ and $\mathcal{N}_3$), which well capture the existing NN ranking mechanisms.

3.1 Stable Aggregate Function

Similar to [12], we argue that the aggregate functions used by NN ranking mechanism should satisfy the *stable* property.

DEFINITION 8. ***Stable Aggregate Function.*** *Let g denote an aggregate function on a random variable, we say g is a stable aggregate function if and only if for any two random variables X and Y, $X \preceq_{st} Y$ implies that $g(X) \leq g(Y)$.*

We also introduce the *match order* which is essentially another interpretation of *usual stochastic order.* We remark that both orders are frequently used in our theoretical analysis since they interpret the dominance relationship from different perspectives.

DEFINITION 9. ***Match Order.*** *Given two independent random variables X and Y, we say X is smaller than Y in match order, denoted by $X \preceq_M Y$, if there is a match $M_{X,Y}$ between X and Y with $t.x \leq t.y$ for every $t \in M_{X,Y}$.*

Following theorem indicates that the two orders are equivalent to each other.

THEOREM 1. *The match order is equivalent to the usual stochastic order.*

PROOF. See Appendix B.1 □

According to Definition 9, given two random variables X and X^* with $X^* \preceq_M X$ (i.e., $X^* \preceq_{st} X$), X^* can be regarded as an enhancement of X by, roughly speaking, pushing some of the probability mass of X to the left (assuming left represents smaller values). It is rather intuitive that we should have $g(X^*) \leq g(X)$ for any reasonable aggregate function used in NN search.

3.2 All pairs based NN ($\mathcal{N}_1$)

Model. A simple and intuitive way to identify the nearest neighbor is to apply an aggregation function on the distance distribution (i.e., all pair-wise distances) of each object. The NN function family $\mathcal{N}_1$ is defined as follows,

$$\mathcal{N}_1 := \{f \mid f(U) = g(U_Q), g \in \mathcal{G}\} \tag{1}$$

where $\mathcal{G}$ represents the family of stable aggregate functions.
Instantiations. In the literature, the aggregate functions such as *min*, *max*, *mean* (a.k.a., *expected*), and *quantile* distances (e.g., [29, 37]) have been widely employed to identify the NN objects. It is immediate that both *min* and *max* are stable aggregate functions. Given $X \preceq_M Y$, there is a match $M_{X,Y}$ with $t.x \leq t.y$ for every $t \in M_{X,Y}$. Since we have $mean(X) = \sum_{t \in M_{X,Y}} t.x \times t.p$, it is immediate that *mean* function is a stable. Below, we can show that *quantile* function also has the stable property.

DEFINITION 10. **ϕ-quantile** *($quan_\phi$). Given a random variable X, and we assume its instances are sorted in non-decreasing order. The ϕ-quantile ($0 < \phi \leq 1$) of X, denoted by $quan_\phi(X)$, is the value of x_i where i is the first instance such that $\sum_{1 \leq j \leq i} p(x_j) \geq \phi$.*

According to the above definition, *ϕ-quantile* is a stable aggregate function since we have $Pr(X \leq quan_\phi(Y)) \geq Pr(Y \leq quan_\phi(Y))$ for any ϕ ($0 < \phi \leq 1$) if $X \preceq_{st} Y$.

Besides the above premier NN functions, we may easily come up with various stable NN functions based on their combinations or some linear weighted functions on distance distribution. Note that the expected distance is an example of the linear weighted function.

3.3 Possible world based NN ($\mathcal{N}_2$)

In recent years, a large body of work have addressed the problem of NN search on uncertain objects following the possible world semantics.
Possible world semantics. Given a set $\mathcal{O} \cup Q$ of objects and the query, a possible world W is a set of instances with one instance from each object in $\mathcal{O} \cup Q$. Let $\mathcal{W}$ denote the set of all possible worlds. Then, $\sum_{W \in \mathcal{W}} Pr(W) = 1$ where $Pr(W)$ is the occurrence probability of the possible world W. Moreover, we use $\delta(U, W)$ to denote the distance between U and Q in the possible world W. By $r(U, W)$ we mean U is ranked at $r(U, W)$-th position according to its distance to the query point in W.
Model. In each possible world W, a score $s(U, W)$ is assigned to each object U which is either determined by $r(U, W)$ or by $\delta(U, W)$. Particularly, we assume that $s(U, W) \leq s(V, W)$ if $\delta(U, W) < \delta(V, W)$ because we are in favor of the object closer to the query in each possible world W. The *score distribution* of U is denoted by $U_\mathcal{W}$ = $\{s(U, W), Pr(W)\}$ for all $W \in \mathcal{W}$. Then the set of possible world based NN functions, denoted by $\mathcal{N}_2$, is defined as follows.

$$\mathcal{N}_2 := \{f \mid f(U) = g(U_\mathcal{W}), g \in \mathcal{G}\} \tag{2}$$

Instantiations. Jian et al. [23] show that the existing popular ranking methods for uncertain data can be unified by the parameterized ranking model. We use $\Upsilon(U)$ to denote the NN score of an object U,

$$\Upsilon(U) = \sum_i \omega(i) \times Pr(r(U) = i) \tag{3}$$

where $Pr(r(U) = i)$ denotes the probability that U is ranked as the i-th closest object and $\omega(i)$ is the weight of the position i. In practice, we have $\omega(i) \leq \omega(j)$ for any two ranking positions i and j with $i < j$ because the higher position is usually at least as desirable as those behind it and thus should be given a smaller weight. As shown in [23], other popular ranking methods can be unified by setting the value of $\omega(i)$ appropriately. In the context of NN search, we have $\omega(i) = -1$ and $\omega(i) = i$ in U-top-k rank model [32] and expected rank model [12], respectively. For global top k model [39], $\omega(i) = -1$ for $i \leq k$, and $\omega(i) = 0$ otherwise. Note that the NN probability function is its special case with $k = 1$.

Now we show that NN functions based on parameterized ranking model belong to $\mathcal{N}_2$. By setting $s(U,W) = \omega(r(U,W))$ and g as the *mean* function on $U_\mathcal{W}$, we have $f(U) = \sum_{W \in \mathcal{W}} s(U,W) \times Pr(W) = \sum_i \omega(i) \times Pr(r(U) = i) = \Upsilon(U)$. Clearly, there are infinite number of possible NN functions in $\mathcal{N}_2$ due to various settings of ω values.

We remark that the multi-valued object model should not be applied to the possible world semantics due to the co-exists of the instances from the same object.

3.4 Selected pairs based NN ($\mathcal{N}_3$)

Model. A function $f \in \mathcal{N}_3$ computes the score of an object U based on a *subset of distance distribution* U_Q which is denoted by $\sigma_U(U_Q) = \{t\langle\delta(u,q),p\rangle\}$ where $t.u \in U$, $t.q \in Q$ and $t.p$ is the probability value associated with the pair tuple t. Remark that $t.p$ here is not necessarily $p(t.u) \times p(t.q)$ and may take a different value depending on the function $f \in \mathcal{N}_3$. $\sigma_V(U_Q)$ is the counterpart of V w.r.t. U, which will be explained later. Then we have $f(U) = g(\sigma_U(U_Q))$ where g is a stable aggregate function.

The key property of the selected pairs based NN function f is that it must be *counterpart computable*. First, we introduce the concept of *counterpart* and then explain counterpart computable. Given $\sigma_V(V_Q)$ and a match $M_{U,V}$, $\sigma_V(U_Q)$ contains a subset of pairs from U_Q that are selected using $\sigma_V(V_Q)$ and $M_{U,V}$. Informally, if v_i matches to u_j in $M_{U,V}$ and (v_i, q_k) is a pair in $\sigma_V(V_Q)$, then the pair (u_j, q_k) will be inserted in $\sigma_V(U_Q)$. Formally, the tuples in $\sigma_V(U_Q)$ are selected as follows: for each tuple $m\ \langle\delta(v,q),p\rangle \in \sigma_V(V_Q)$, we find every tuple $t \in M_{U,V}$ for which $t.v = m.v$. Then, for each such t, we create a tuple $m'\langle\ \delta(t.u, m.q),\ \frac{t.p \times m.p}{p(v)}\rangle$ and insert m' in $\sigma_V(U_Q)$.

EXAMPLE 4. *Figure 4(b) illustrates a simple example of counterpart of A w.r.t. C, i.e.,* $\sigma_C(A_Q)$. *We have* $\sigma_C(C_Q) = \{\langle\delta(c_1,q_1),0.5\rangle, \langle\delta(c_2,q_2),0.5\rangle\}$. *Regarding the match* $M_{A,C} = \{\langle a_1, c_2, 0.5\rangle, \langle a_2, c_1, 0.5\rangle\}$ *in Figure 4(a),* $\sigma_C(A_Q)$ *corresponds to shadowed edges in UP(A,Q) where* $\sigma_C(A_Q) = \{\langle\delta(a_2,q_1),0.5\rangle, \langle\delta(a_1,q_2),0.5\rangle\}$.

We say that a function is *counterpart computable* if, for every match $M_{U,V}$ between U and V, $g(\sigma_V(U_Q)) \geq g(\sigma_U(U_Q))$, i.e., the score of an object U (i.e., $f(U) = g(\sigma_U(U_Q))$) is no larger than the score of the counterpart of U w.r.t. V. In the example of Figure 4, $\sigma_A(A_Q) = \{\langle\delta(a_1,q_1),0.5\rangle, \langle\delta(a_2,q_2),0.5\rangle\}$. It can be verified that $g(\sigma_C(A_Q)) > g(\sigma_A(A_Q))$, i.e., EMD is counterpart computable.

Following is a formal definition of NN functions in $\mathcal{N}_3$.

$$\mathcal{N}_3 := \{f \mid f(U) = g(\sigma_U(U_Q)), g \in \mathcal{G}\} \qquad (4)$$

where f is a counterpart computable function.

Instantiations. We show that three popular NN ranking functions belong to $\mathcal{N}_3$ (the detailed definitions are given in Appendix A) . In *Hausdorff distance* [27], an instance $u \in U$ will pick its closest instance in Q to form an instance-pair. Let q' denote the instance picked for u in the counterpart of U, clearly we have $\delta_{min}(u,Q) \leq \delta(u,q')$. Same observation holds for the instances $q \in Q$. Consequently, both distances are counterpart computable. As their aggregate functions are stable, *Hausdorff distance* belongs to $\mathcal{N}_3$.

Under our problem settings where each object has a probability mass 1, the definitions of Earth Mover's distance [10] and Netflow distance [27] are equivalent to each other. Taking the Earth Mover's distance EMD(U,Q) as an example, a *feasible* solution corresponds to a *match* between U and Q with cost $\sum_{t \in M_{U,Q}} \delta(t.u, t.q) \times t.p$. Given the pair-wise distances chosen in EMD(V,Q) (i.e.,$\sigma_V(V_Q)$) and a match $M_{V,U}$, it is easy to see that the counterpart in U_Q, i.e., $\sigma_V(U_Q)$, corresponds to a feasible solution with cost not less than EMD(U,Q), because EMD(U,Q) represents the minimal cost of all feasible solutions. Consequently, Earth Mover's distance and Netflow distance are both *counterpart computable.*

4. PROPERTIES OF SD OPERATORS

In this section, we investigate important properties of the four spatial dominance operators and their relationships.

4.1 Comparison of SD Operators

This subsection investigates the "cover" relationships among four spatial dominance operators.

THEOREM 2. *F-$\mathcal{SD}$ ⊂ P-$\mathcal{SD}$ ⊂ SS-$\mathcal{SD}$ ⊂ S-$\mathcal{SD}$.*

PROOF. See Appendix B.2. □

Theorem 2 is not only of theoretical interest but it also enables effective pruning and validation rules to speed up the dominance check, as shown in Section 5. Particularly, given $\mathcal{SD}_1 \subset \mathcal{SD}_2$, we can safely claim $\mathcal{SD}_2(U,V,Q)$ holds (i.e., **validation**) if $\mathcal{SD}_1(U,V,Q)$ is verified. Similarly, we have $\neg\mathcal{SD}_1(U,V,Q)$ if $\neg\mathcal{SD}_2(U,V,Q)$ (i.e.,**pruning**).

The following theorem suggests that P-$\mathcal{SD}$, SS-$\mathcal{SD}$ and S-$\mathcal{SD}$ are equivalent to each other for the special case when the query has only one instance, which is not uncommon in practice. However, F-$\mathcal{SD}$ still has stronger dominance check condition even for this special case.

THEOREM 3. *When $|Q| = 1$, we have F-$\mathcal{SD}$ ⊂ P-$\mathcal{SD}$ = SS-$\mathcal{SD}$ = S-$\mathcal{SD}$.*

PROOF. See Appendix B.3. □

In [16], efficient filtering technique is proposed to check F-$\mathcal{SD}$ against the minimal bounding rectangles (MBR) of the objects in $O(d)$ time, where d is the dimensionality. The following theorem suggests that we can directly apply the technique in [16] for validation purpose. The correctness is immediate based on the definition of F-$\mathcal{SD}$ and Theorem 2.

THEOREM 4. *F-$\mathcal{SD}(U_{mbr},V_{mbr},Q_{mbr})$ implies that we have F-$\mathcal{SD}(U,V,Q)$, P-$\mathcal{SD}(U,V,Q)$, SS-$\mathcal{SD}(U,V,Q)$, and S-$\mathcal{SD}(U,V,Q)$.*

Clearly, filtering technique in [25] may also be applied if objects are approximated by hyperspheres.

4.2 Optimality Property

In this subsection, we show that three spatial dominance operators proposed in this paper are optimal w.r.t. $\mathcal{N}_1$, $\mathcal{N}_{1,2}$ and $\mathcal{N}_{1,2,3}$ respectively.

THEOREM 5. *S-$\mathcal{SD}$ is optimal w.r.t. $\mathcal{N}_1$, and S-$\mathcal{SD}$ does not cover $\mathcal{N}_{2,3}$.*

PROOF. See Appendix B.4. □

THEOREM 6. *SS-$\mathcal{SD}$ is optimal w.r.t. $\mathcal{N}_{1,2}$, and SS-$\mathcal{SD}$ does not cover $\mathcal{N}_3$.*

PROOF. See Appendix B.5. □

THEOREM 7. *P-$\mathcal{SD}$ is optimal w.r.t. $\mathcal{N}_{1,2,3}$.*

PROOF. See Appendix B.6. □

The following theorem indicates that although both P-$\mathcal{SD}$ and F-$\mathcal{SD}$ cover functions in $\mathcal{N}_{1,2,3}$, F-$\mathcal{SD}$ is not as tight as P-$\mathcal{SD}$ since it does not have the completeness property. This results in redundant NN candidate objects w.r.t. functions in $\mathcal{N}_{1,2,3}$.

THEOREM 8. *F-$\mathcal{SD}$ is correct w.r.t. $\mathcal{N}_{1,2,3}$, but does not satisfy the completeness property w.r.t. $\mathcal{N}_{1,2,3}$.*

PROOF. See Appendix B.7 □

4.3 Transitivity Property

Given three objects $\{U,V,Z\}$ and the query Q, we say that a dominance operator $\mathcal{SD}$ has the transitivity property if $\mathcal{SD}(U,V,Q)$ and $\mathcal{SD}(V,Z,Q)$ imply $\mathcal{SD}(U,Z,Q)$. The following theorem shows that all four spatial dominance operators have the transitivity property, which is critical in the computation of NN candidates in Section 5.

THEOREM 9. *S-$\mathcal{SD}$, SS-$\mathcal{SD}$, P-$\mathcal{SD}$ and F-$\mathcal{SD}$ have the transitivity property.*

PROOF. See Appendix B.8 □

5. NN CANDIDATES COMPUTATION

In this Section, we develop efficient spatial dominance based NN candidate computation algorithms.

5.1 Spatial Dominance Check

In this subsection, we present dominance check algorithms for three spatial dominance operators, S-$\mathcal{SD}$, SS-$\mathcal{SD}$ and P-$\mathcal{SD}$ as well as effective filtering techniques.

5.1.1 S-$\mathcal{SD}$ and SS-$\mathcal{SD}$

The dominance check algorithms for S-$\mathcal{SD}$ and SS-$\mathcal{SD}$ are very efficient if pair-wise distances are sorted in non-decreasing order. By recording the differentiation of the accumulated instance probabilities of two objects, denoted by $F(x) = Pr(U_Q \leq x) - Pr(V_Q \leq x)$, we terminate the search and claim $\neg$S-$\mathcal{SD}(U,V,Q)$ if there exists an x such that $F(x) < 0$, otherwise we have S-$\mathcal{SD}(U,V,Q)$. Similarly, we maintain $|Q|$ indicators for the distance distributions of the query instances, and claim $\neg$SS-$\mathcal{SD}$ (U,V,Q) if any of them becomes negative. Suppose instances of each object are organized by an R-tree, we may easily extend the above algorithms to conduct dominance check in a level-by-level fashion.

Time Complexity of the dominance check is $O(m \times |Q| \log(m \times |Q|))$ for both S-$\mathcal{SD}$ and SS-$\mathcal{SD}$ where m ($|Q|$) is the average number of instances in the object (query). Following theorem implies that our dominance check algorithms for S-$\mathcal{SD}$ and SS-$\mathcal{SD}$ are optimal in the worst case where the distance distribution has $m \times |Q|$ instances.

THEOREM 10. *Given two random variables X and Y with n instances each, any algorithm to determine whether $X \preceq_{st} Y$ must have complexity of at least $\Omega(n \log(n))$ if the algorithm is based only on comparisons between elements from X and Y.*

PROOF. See Appendix B.9 □

Below we introduce efficient and effective pruning and validation techniques, which avoid exploring all pair-wise distances.

Pruning. Theorem below indicates that we may claim that the dominance relation does not hold (i.e., *pruning*) based on some simple statistic values of two distance distributions.

THEOREM 11. *Given two random variables X and Y, $X \preceq_{st} Y$ implies that $min(X) \leq min(Y)$, $mean(X) \leq mean(Y)$ and $max(X) \leq max(Y)$.*

PROOF. Since three functions (min, max and $mean$) are *stable* functions as shown in Section 3.2. The correctness of is immediate according to Definition 8. □

Then we have the following statistic-based pruning rule.

Statistic-based Pruning. If $min(U_Q) > min(V_Q)$, $mean(U_Q) > mean(V_Q)$, or $max(U_Q) > max(V_Q)$, we have $\neg$S-$\mathcal{SD}(U,V,Q)$.

Similar pruning rule goes to SS-$\mathcal{SD}$ with the same rationale where statistics are kept for every query instance.

On the other hand, as shown in Definition 7, we have $\neg\mathcal{SD}_1$ implies $\neg\mathcal{SD}_2$ if $\mathcal{SD}_2$ covers $\mathcal{SD}_1$. The following pruning rule is immediate based on Theorem 5.

Cover-based Pruning. We have $\neg$SS-$\mathcal{SD}(U, V, Q)$ if $\neg$S-$\mathcal{SD}(U, V, Q)$.

Validation. According to Theorem 4, we may utilize the efficient filtering technique in [16] to validate the dominance based on the minimal bounding rectangles of the objects and the query.

Cover-based Validation. We have S-$\mathcal{SD}(U, V, Q)$ and SS-$\mathcal{SD}(U, V, Q)$ if F-$\mathcal{SD}(U_{mbr}, V_{mbr}, Q_{mbr})$ holds.

5.1.2 P-$\mathcal{SD}$

Given two objects U and V, a straightforward way to determine P-$\mathcal{SD}(U,V,Q)$ need to consider all possible matches between U and V which is cost-prohibitive because we may have to verify up to $m!$ possible matches. In this paper, we first show that P-$\mathcal{SD}$ check can be reduced to the max-flow problem [11], then a set of techniques are proposed to enhance the performance.

Let N (E) denote a set of vertices (edges) and C records the capacities of the edges, G=$<N,E,C>$ is a network with s , $t \in N$ being *source* and *sink* respectively. A feasible flow f of the network G maps each edge $e \in E$ a non-negative value $f(e)$ following the capacity constraint and conservation of flows constraint [11]. The value $|f|$ of the flow is defined as $|f| = \sum_{\langle s,x \rangle \in E} f(\langle s,x \rangle)$. Then the network for two objects U and V w.r.t. a query Q, denoted by $G_{U,V}$, can be constructed as follows.

- Vertices s and t for source and sink respectively.
- Each instance $u \in U$ contributes a vertex u and an edge $<s,u>$ with $c(s,u) = p(u)$.
- Each instance $v \in V$ contributes a vertex v and an edge $<u,t>$ with $c(v,t) = p(v)$.
- For any two instances $u \in U$ and $v \in V$, there is an edge $\langle u,v \rangle$ with $c(u,v) = \infty$ if $u \preceq_Q v$.

The following theorem indicates that we can apply the max-flow algorithm to check Peer spatial dominance.

THEOREM 12. *Let $G_{U,V}$ be the network constructed based on two objects U, V and the query Q, we have P-$\mathcal{SD}(U,V,Q)$ if and only if $|f^*| = 1$ where f^* is a max-flow of $G_{U,V}$.*

PROOF. See Appendix B.10 □

EXAMPLE 5. *Figure 9 illustrates an example of P-$\mathcal{SD}$ check, which is reduced to max-flow problem. In Figure 9(a),*

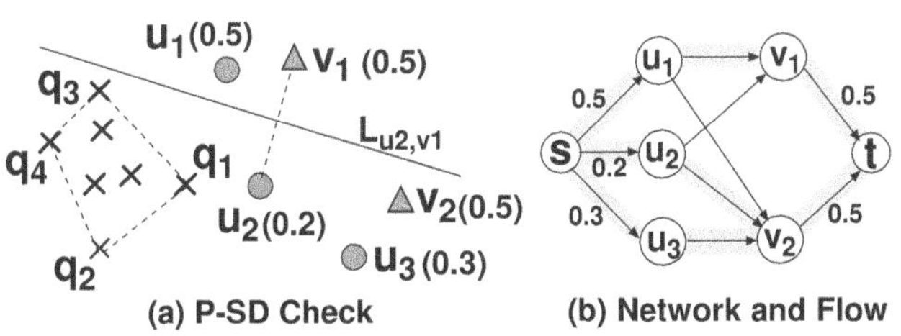

Figure 9: Example of P-$\mathcal{SD}$ Check

the object U (V) consists of 3 (2) instances and the probability of each instance is labeled. Since we have $u_1 \preceq_Q v_1$, $u_1 \preceq_Q v_2$, $u_2 \preceq_Q v_1$, $u_2 \preceq_Q v_2$, *and* $u_3 \preceq_Q v_2$, *the corresponding network* $G_{U,V}$ *is depicted in Figure 9(b) where the capacities of the edges are labeled. Note that the edges unlabeled have capacity* ∞. *There is a match* $M_{U,V} = \{\langle u_1, v_1, 0.5\rangle, \langle u_2, v_2, 0.2\rangle, \langle u_3, v_2, 0.3\rangle\}$, *which justifies that P-*$\mathcal{SD}(U,V,Q)$. *The corresponding flow will go through the shaded edges in Figure 9(b).*

Time Complexity. It takes $O(d|Q|)$ time to check if an instance $u \in U$ can be assigned to $v \in V$. So the network construction time is $O(d|Q|m^2)$ where m is the average number of instances per object. Let $|E|$ denote the number of edges in the network, the max-flow computation takes $O(m|E|\log(|E|))$ time [11].

Pruning. Since P-$\mathcal{SD}$ is covered by S-$\mathcal{SD}$ and SS-$\mathcal{SD}$, we have the following cover-based pruning rule.

Cover-based Pruning. We have $\neg$F-$\mathcal{SD}(U,V,Q)$ if $\neg$S-$\mathcal{SD}(U,V,Q)$ or $\neg$SS-$\mathcal{SD}(U,V,Q)$.

Validation. According to Theorem 4, we have the following cover-based validation rule.

Cover-based Validation. We have P-$\mathcal{SD}(U,V,Q)$ if F-$\mathcal{SD}(U_{mbr},V_{mbr},Q_{mbr})$ holds.

Utilizing Geometrical Properties. As observed in some recent work (e.g., [30, 15]) $u \preceq_Q v$ implies that all query instances fall on the left side (i.e., the same side with u) of the half-space divided by the bisector between u and v. In Figure 9(a), we have $u_2 \preceq_Q v_1$ since all query instances reside on the left side of the bisector line L_{u_2,v_1}. Consequently, we only need to consider query points on the convex hull of the query, denoted by $\mathcal{CH}(Q)$. In the example of Figure 9(a), only 4 query points need to be involved in the dominance check. Moreover, it is immediate that P-$\mathcal{SD}(U,V,Q)$ does not hold for any object U if an instance of V falls in the convex hull of the query Q.

Suppose there are k query points in $\mathcal{CH}(Q)$, then each instance u can be mapped to a point u' in a k-dimensional space with $u[i] = \delta(u, q_i)$. For each instance $v \in V$, we may issue a rectangular range query with lower corner $(0,\dots,0)$ and upper corner v', and we have $u \preceq v$ if u' is contained by the range search. By taking advantage of the efficient range search in spatial indexing techniques (e.g., R-Tree), we can efficiently improve the network construction time.

Level-by-level Pruning/Validation. Instead of directly testing P-$\mathcal{SD}(U,V,Q)$ against the instances of U and V, we may conduct the testing in a top down manner such that the computation may terminate at a high level, and hence significantly reduce the computational costs.

Let U^i denote a set of instances of U with minimal bounding rectangle U^i_{mbr}, and $p(U^i)$ represents the total probability mass of the instances in U^i. We assume U consists of k disjoint sets $U^1, \dots, U^k$. Similarly we have $V = \{V^1, \dots, V^k\}$. By regarding each set U^i (V^i) as a virtual instance, we may conduct dominance check on these virtual instances for *validation* purpose. In particular, since F-$\mathcal{SD}(U^i_{mbr}, V^j_{mbr}, Q_{mbr})$ implies that for every $q \in Q$, we have $u \preceq_Q v$ for every $u \in U^i$ and $v \in V^j$. There is an edge from U^i to V^j if F-$\mathcal{SD}(U^i_{mbr}, V^j_{mbr}, Q_{mbr})$ holds. Let $G^-_{U,V}$ denote the corresponding network, we have $|f^-| \le |f|$ where $|f^-|$ and $|f|$ are max-flow of $G^-_{U,V}$ and $G_{U,V}$, respectively. Consequently, we can claim P-$\mathcal{SD}(U,V,Q)$ if $|f^-| = 1$. Regarding the *pruning*, an edge is assigned from U^i to V^j if $\neg$F-$\mathcal{SD}(V^j_{mbr},U^i_{mbr},Q_{mbr})$. This is because $\neg$F-$\mathcal{SD}(V^j_{mbr},U^i_{mbr},Q_{mbr})$ indicates that we have chance to find $u \in U^i$ and $v \in V^j$ such that $u \preceq_Q v$. Let $G^+_{U,V}$ denote the corresponding network, we have $|f^+| \ge |f|$ where $|f^+|$ and $|f|$ are max-flow of $G^+_{U,V}$ and $G_{U,V}$, respectively. Thus, we have $\neg$P-$\mathcal{SD}(U,V,Q)$ if $|f^+| < 1$.

Suppose instances of U and V are organized by hierarchical structure (e.g., R-Tree), we can iteratively conduct the above pruning and validation procedures in a level-by-level fashion until the algorithm is terminated at high level or instances of the objects are reached.

5.2 NN candidate computation

In this subsection, we introduce the NN candidates (NNC) computation algorithm for a given spatial dominance operator $\mathcal{SD}$.

Suppose MBRs of the objects are organized by a *global* R-Tree $R_{\mathcal{O}}$, Algorithm 1 outlines our NNC computation algorithm. By maintaining a min heap H, entries and objects are visited in a non-decreasing ordering based on their minimal distance to the query Q. In Line 5-9, each visited object V will be evaluated against existing NNC objects based on the dominance checking algorithms proposed in Section 5.1. Then V becomes an NN candidate if it survives the dominance check (Line 10-11). According to the cover-based verification rules, an entry e (i.e., objects associated with e) is discarded if F-$\mathcal{SD}(U_{mbr},e_{mbr},Q_{mbr})$ holds (Line 13-16). Otherwise, its child entries or associated objects will be pushed into H for further processing (Line 17-21). The algorithm terminates when H becomes empty. The objects in $\mathcal{NCC}$ are NN candidates of $\mathcal{O}$ for the given query Q.

Correctness. According to Theorem 4, F-$\mathcal{SD}(U_{mbr},V_{mbr},Q_{mbr})$ implies that we have F-$\mathcal{SD}(U,V,Q)$, P-$\mathcal{SD}(U,V,Q)$, SS-$\mathcal{SD}(U,V,Q)$, and S-$\mathcal{SD}(U,V,Q)$. Since V_{mbr} is contained by e_{mbr} for every object V in the entry e, it is safe to exclude an entry e in Algorithm 1 if F-$\mathcal{SD}(U_{mbr},e_{mbr},Q_{mbr})$ holds at Line 15. Moreover, V is not an NNC object if $\mathcal{SD}(U,V,Q)$ holds at Line 8. Consequently, all objects excluded in Algorithm 1 are not NNC objects. Now we show every non-candidate object will be discarded. Since objects are accessed based on their minimal distance to Q, an object V cannot be dominated by any object accessed after V according to the statistic-based pruning rules and cover-based pruning rules. Together with the fact that all four spatial dominance operators have the *transitivity* property, we only need to conduct dominance check against NNC objects seen so far to guarantee that all non-candidate objects will be excluded.

Progressive property of Algorithm 1. As stated in the above proof, we can safely claim that an object is an NN candidate object if it is not dominated by any objects seen as far. This implies that Algorithm 1 is a progressive

Algorithm 1: NNC($\mathcal{O}$,Q,$\mathcal{SD}$)

Input : $\mathcal{O}$: a set of objects $\mathcal{O}$
Q : query, $\mathcal{SD}$: SD operator
Output: $\mathcal{NNC}(\mathcal{O}, Q, \mathcal{SD})$

1 $\mathcal{NNC} := \emptyset$;
2 push root of $R_{\mathcal{O}}$ into a heap H;
3 **while** $H \neq \emptyset$ **do**
4     $e := H.deheap()$;
5   **if** e is an object V **then**
6         $F := false$;
7   **for** each object $U \in \mathcal{NNC}$ **do**
8   **if** $\mathcal{SD}(U, V, Q)$ **then**
9                 $F := true$; break;
10   **if** $F = false$ **then**
11             $\mathcal{NNC} := \mathcal{NNC} \cup V$;
12   **else**
13         $F := false$;
14   **for** each object $U \in \mathcal{NNC}$ **do**
15   **if** F-SD(U_{mbr}, e_{mbr}, Q_{mbr}) **then**
16                 $F := true$; break;
17   **if** $F = false$ **then**
18   **if** e is a data entry associated with object U **then**
19   push U into H;
20   **else**
21   Push all child entries of e into H;
22 **return** $\mathcal{NNC}$

algorithm in the sense that an object can be output before exploring all objects.

6. PERFORMANCE EVALUATION

In this section, we present the results of a comprehensive performance study to evaluate the effectiveness and efficiency of the proposed techniques in this paper.

Algorithms. We implement **SSD**, **SSSD**, **PSD**, **FSD** and **F$^+$SD** which are NN candidate search methods based on Algorithm 1 by replacing $\mathcal{SD}$ at Line 8 with S-$\mathcal{SD}$, SS-$\mathcal{SD}$, P-$\mathcal{SD}$, F-$\mathcal{SD}$ and F$^+$-$\mathcal{SD}$ respectively. Here, F$^+$-$\mathcal{SD}$ (U,V,Q) is F-$\mathcal{SD}$(U_{mbr},V_{mbr},Q_{mbr}) where MBRs of objects are organized by an R-Tree, and the implementation is from [16]. In addition, pruning and validation rules, level by level searching mechanism and geometrical properties introduced in Section 5.1 are also included for the corresponding dominance operators.

Note that the dominance check of F-$\mathcal{SD}$(U,V,Q) on instance level is not investigated in [16, 25]. Thus, we propose an efficient dominance check algorithm for performance evaluation. Similar to P-$\mathcal{SD}$, we observe that only the query points on the convex hull need to be considered for F-$\mathcal{SD}$. In particular, for each $q \in \mathcal{CH}(Q)$, we issue an NN search and a furthest neighbor search against the instances of V and U, respectively. We may immediately claim $\neg$F-$\mathcal{SD}$(U,V,Q) if there is a query instance q with $\delta_{max}(q, U) > \delta_{min}(q, V)$, otherwise F-$\mathcal{SD}$($U$,$V$,$Q$) holds. The dominance check is rather efficient because instances of each object are organized by a local R-Tree in the experiment.

REMARK 1. *As shown in Section 1, NN-core approach [36] may miss important NN objects, and cannot even cover popular NN functions in $\mathcal{N}_1$. Therefore, we do not evaluate the NN-core approach in our experiment.*

Datasets. Two real datasets, **NBA**[1] and **GW**[2], are deployed in the experiments. NBA dataset is extracted from NBA players' game statistics, of 1,313 players with 298,051 records, each of which consists of the number of points, assistances and rebounds for a player in a game. Thus, each player is an object and each record is treated as a 3-dimensional instance (point). GW is obtained from GoWalla check-in dataset, consisting of 107,092 users with 6,442,890 check-ins. In GW, each user is regarded as an object and its check-ins are 2-dimensional instances (points). Instances in the same object have the same occurrence probability in this experiment.

Also, three real datasets, **HOUSE**[3], **CA**[4] and **USA**[5] are employed to represent the centers of objects as semi-real data. HOUSE is a 3-dimensional dataset with 127,932 records, each of which represents the percentage of an American family's annual income on 3 types of expenditures. CA is a 2-dimensional spatial dataset of 62k locations in California. USA dataset is obtained from the U.S. Geological Survey (USGS) with 1 million locations. USA dataset is used to evaluate the scalability of the proposed methods. By using methodologies in [8], we also generate synthetic centers for objects following the *anti-correlated* (A) or *independent* (E) distribution, where anti-correlated is the default distribution for synthetic data. The dimensionality (d) varies from 2 to 5, with default value 3. The number of objects (n) we used in synthetic dataset is kept as 100k. To generate instances for object centers, the expected edge length (h_d) of minimal bounding box (MBB) for objects varies from 100 to 500 with default value 400. Given a h_d, the lengths of objects are randomly chosen between 0 and $2 \times h_d$. Each object has m_d instances on average which follows *Normal* (N) distribution, with standard deviation $\frac{h_d}{2}$. m_d varies from 20 to 100 with default value 40. All dimensions are normalized to domain [0, 10000]. Note that, the total number of instances in the default synthetic dataset is 100k×40 =**4 million**, and for the largest dataset USA, the instance number reaches **40 million**. The experiment parameters are list in Table 2, where the default value is in bold font.

Evaluation parameter	Values
dimensionality d	2, **3**, 4, 5
# of objects n	**100k**, 200k, 400k, 600k, 1M
# of object instances m_d	20, **40**, 60, 80, 100
edge length of object h_d	100, 200, 300, **400**, 500
object center distribution	**anti (A)**, indep (E)
# of query instances m_q	10, 20, **30**, 40, 50
edge length of query h_q	100, **200**, 300, 400, 500

Table 2: The summary of experiment parameter.

Workload. The query workload for NN candidates search consists of 100 randomly selected objects or centers from the underlying dataset. For the semi-real and synthetic data, the instance distribution of each query is the same as the objects. Moreover, the edge length of query (h_q) varies from

[1] http://www.nba.com
[2] http://snap.stanford.edu/data/loc-gowalla.html
[3] http://www.ipums.org
[4] http://www.census.gov/geo/www/tiger
[5] http://www.usgs.gov/

100 to 500 with 200 as default. The number of instances (m_q) varies from 10 to 50 with default value 30.

All algorithms are implemented in C++ with GNU GCC 4.8.2. Experiments are conducted on a PC with Intel Xeon 3.4GHz CPU and 32G memory using Ubuntu Linux. Similar to existing works (e.g., [26, 21, 37]), we employ $n+1$ R-trees to organize the n objects. Particularly, we use a global R-Tree to organize MBRs of the uncertain objects, and the page size is 4096 bytes. For each individual object, its instances are kept in a local R-Tree with fan-out 4, and we load the whole local R-tree into the main memory if it could not be pruned based on its MBR. The code for convex hull related computation is obtained from `www.qhull.org`.

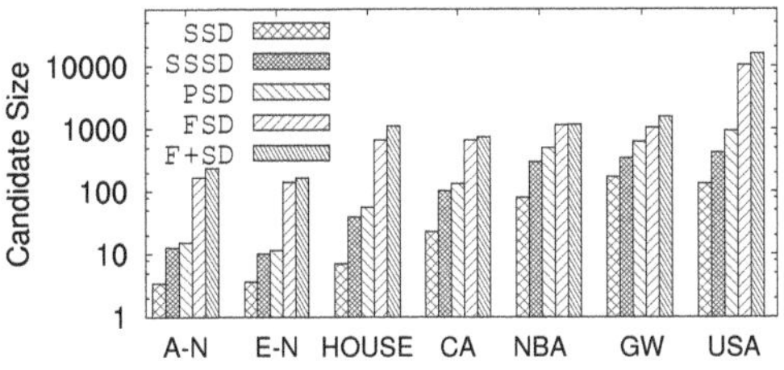

Figure 10: Candidate Size of Different Datasets

6.1 Effectiveness Evaluation

In this subsection, we evaluate the effectiveness of the algorithms through the average number of NN candidates.

In the first set of experiments, Figure 10 reports effectiveness of SSD, SSSD, PSD, FSD and F$^+$SD against all the datasets A-N, E-N, HOUSE, CA, NBA, GW and USA under the default setting. Particularly, A-N denotes the 3 dimensional synthetic data whose centers and instances follow the *anti-correlated* and *Normal* distribution, respectively. Similar definition goes to E-N. As expected, the candidate size of SSD, SSSD, PSD, FSD and F$^+$SD increase level by level in all datasets due to the NN candidates inclusion relationship illustrated in Figure 5. Moreover, we observe that the candidate size of PSD is much smaller than that of FSD and F$^+$SD, given that the three operators have the same coverage of NN functions. SSD and SSSD can further significantly reduce the NN candidates size with smaller coverage of NN functions. For instance, in HOUSE dataset, SSD, SSSD and PSD have 7, 38, and 55.8 candidates respectively, while FSD and F$^+$SD have reached 657 and 1100, respectively. The gap becomes more significant in A-N, E-N and USA. Particularly, in USA dataset, the candidate size of FSD and F$^+$SD have reached 10415 and 15580.4 respectively, while the candidate size of SSD, SSSD and PSD are quite stable, with 133.2, 422.5 and 933 respectively. In NBA and GW datasets, the instances of objects are highly overlapped, which renders an increase in the candidate size for all algorithms. Nevertheless, the performance of SSD, SSSD and PSD still outperforms that of FSD and F$^+$SD by a large margin.

We also evaluate the impact of different parameters against the NN candidate size on synthetic dataset and USA dataset. Figure 11(a) and Figure 11(b) depict the candidate size as a function of the number of object instances (m_d) and the edge length (h_d) on A-N dataset, respectively. It is shown that SSD, SSSD and PSD are well scalable to the growth of m_d and h_d. However, the performance of FSD and F$^+$SD is rather sensitive to the growth of h_d. This is because the full spatial dominance heavily relies on the boundaries (i.e., $\delta_{min}(q,U)$ and $\delta_{max}(q,U)$) of the objects, while S-$\mathcal{SD}$, SS-$\mathcal{SD}$ and P-$\mathcal{SD}$ are much less sensitive, since the distance distributions are considered. Similar observation is reported in Figure 11(c) and Figure 11(d) where the number of instances and the edge length grow regarding the queries on A-N dataset.

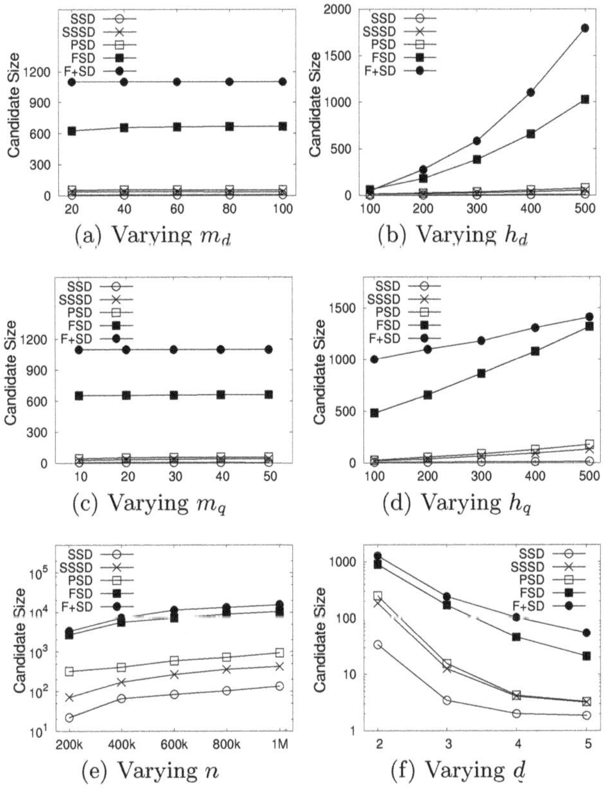

Figure 11: Impact of Diff. Parameters on Effectiveness

To evaluate the scalability of proposed operator on the number of object (n), we conduct experiment on USA dataset by using 200k, 400k, 600k, 800k and 1M data. It is reported that the performance of FSD and F$^+$SD deteriorates with the growth of n, while SSD, SSSD and PSD are less sensitive. In Figure 13(f), we evaluate the impact of dimension (d) on A-N dataset. It shows that the number of candidates drops dramatically when the dimensionality varies from 2 to 5. This is because when the dimensionality d grows, the volume of minimal bound box of the objects becomes relatively smaller, which results in less overlapping among objects.

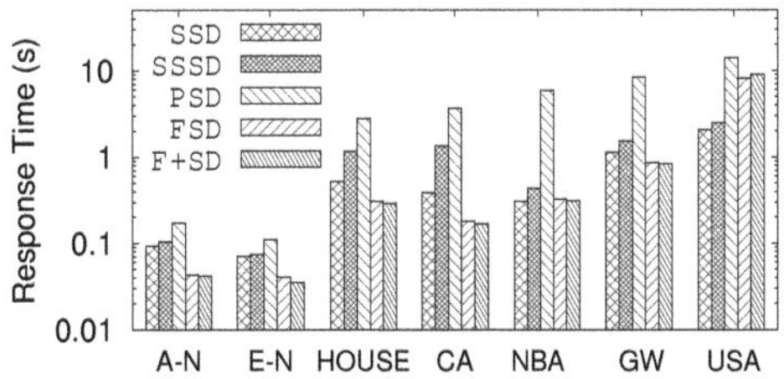

Figure 12: Response Time of Different Datasets

6.2 Efficiency Evaluation

In this subsection, we demonstrate the efficiency of the algorithms by reporting the average query response time.

Figure 12 reports the performance of 5 algorithms against A-N, E-N, HOUSE, CA, NBA, GW and USA datasets un-

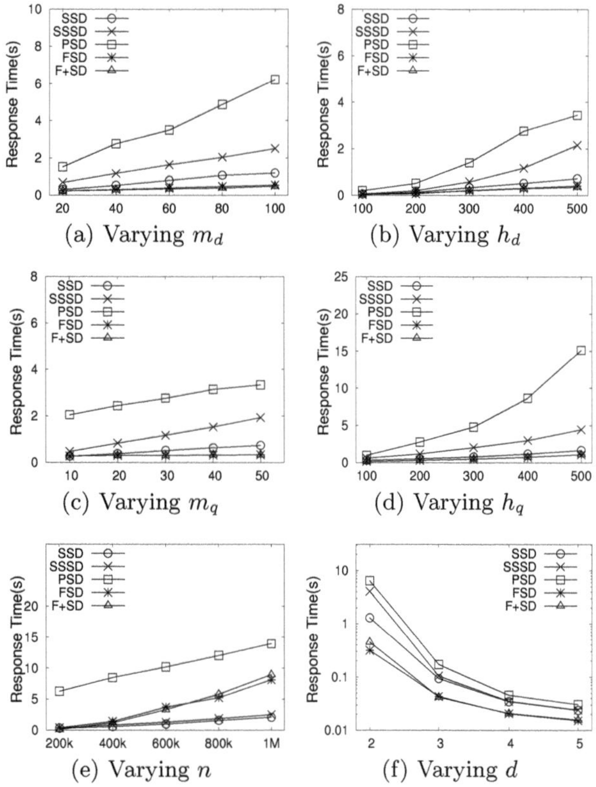

(a) Varying m_d (b) Varying h_d

(c) Varying m_q (d) Varying h_q

(e) Varying n (f) Varying d

Figure 13: Impact of Diff. Parameters on Efficiency

der the default setting. Due to the simplicity of dominance check, FSD and F$^+$SD demonstrate superior performance in all datasets except USA. This is because, in USA dataset, the candidate size of both operators is too large (up to 15000), which renders plenty of verification cost in the search of candidates. Moreover, it is not surprising that PSD has the worst performance among 5 algorithms due to the expensive dominance checking costs. Nevertheless, considering that PSD keeps the same coverage of NN functions compared to FSD and F$^+$SD, but provides much smaller candidate set, the gain of PSD is significant. This is because a smaller candidate size is more crucial in our problem settings, e.g., the user may need to manually check the candidates and choose the object of her choice. As expected, SSD and SSSD outperform PSD because of the smaller candidate size and the cheaper dominance checking cost. Moreover, it is noticed that the performance of SSD and SSSD is even comparable to that of FSD and F$^+$SD on the hard datasets (e.g., NBA and GW) and outperforms FSD and F$^+$SD on USA dataset, due to the large number of candidates obtained by FSD and F$^+$SD. This suggests that when users are only interested in the ranking functions in $\mathcal{N}_{1,2}$ [1, 23], which actually already covers the majority of the NN functions, SSSD can provide NN candidates with much smaller size than that of PSD with a faster query response time. The performance can be further improved in terms of both candidate size and query delay if users only consider stable aggregation functions ($\mathcal{N}_1$) [2, 37], which have been widely used in many applications.

Figure 13 demonstrates the impact of various parameters on 5 algorithms on synthetic dataset and USA dataset. It is observed that FSD and F$^+$SD outperform other competitors when the number of object instances (m_d) , the edge length of object (h_d), the number of object instances (m_q) and the edge length of object (h_q) increases. However, in Figure 13(e), SSD and SSSD outperform FSD and F$^+$SD towards the number of object (n), when the dataset size increases from 200k to 1M. As explained before, this is because the significant growth in candidate size of FSD and F$^+$SD leading to lots of verification cost. Nevertheless, SSD and SSSD also perform reasonably well and are less sensitive to the change in m_d, h_d, m_q, h_q and n. As reported in Figure 11(f), the number of candidates is significantly reduced towards the dimensionality. Consequently, the same trend is observed for the time efficiency in Figure 13(f).

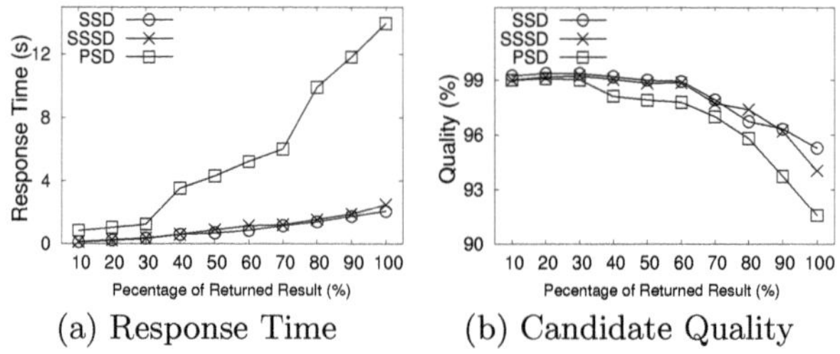

(a) Response Time (b) Candidate Quality

Figure 14: Performance of Progressive Property

Next we demonstrate the progressive property of the algorithm on USA dataset. As shown in Figure 14, x-axis is the candidate return progress, i.e., the percentage of candidate returned, and the corresponding response time and candidate quality (avg. number of objects dominated by returned candidates) are reported. As shown in Figure 14(a), for PSD, 20 percentage candidates are returned in less than 1s and 70 percentage candidates are return in half time, since as the number of returned candidates grows the verification cost also increases. In Figure 14(b), we can observe that higher quality candidates are often tendered to be returned first. Thus, the progressive property of the algorithm is well suited for users to explore the candidates in a progressive way without waiting until all candidates are returned, like web search engine. Due to the space limitation, we defer the experimental results of the effectiveness of different filtering techniques and experiment summary to the Appendix C.

7. CONCLUSION

To address new challenges arising in the NN search on objects with multiple instances, we studied the problem of NN candidates search which can effectively provide users a small set of candidates for a given query object. By modeling various existing NN ranking functions as three representative families, we devised three spatial dominance operators which are *optimal* w.r.t. different coverage of NN functions with theoretical underpinnings. Effective and efficient filtering and verification techniques have been proposed for the dominance check and NN candidates computations. Our comprehensive experiments justified the effectiveness of the new spatial dominance operators, which confirmed that users can make a good trade-off among the NN candidates size and the coverage of NN functions. Moreover, our extensive performance evaluation demonstrated the efficiency of our techniques proposed in this paper.

Acknowledgments. Ying Zhang is supported by ARC DE140100679 and DP130103245. Wenjie Zhang is supported by ARC DP150103071 and DP150102728. Xuemin Lin is supported by ARC DP150102728, DP140103578, and DP120104168. Muhammad Aamir Cheema is supported by ARC DE130101002 and DP130103405.

8. REFERENCES

[1] P. K. Agarwal, B. Aronov, S. Har-Peled, J. M. Phillips, K. Yi, and W. Zhang. Nearest neighbor searching under uncertainty II. In *PODS*, pages 115–126, 2013.

[2] P. K. Agarwal, A. Efrat, S. Sankararaman, and W. Zhang. Nearest-neighbor searching under uncertainty. In *PODS*, pages 225–236, 2012.

[3] L. Antova, T. Jansen, C. Koch, and D. Olteanu. Fast and simple relational processing of uncertain data. In *ICDE*, pages 983–992, 2008.

[4] D. Barbará, H. Garcia-Molina, and D. Porter. The management of probabilistic data. *TKDE*, 4(5):487–502, 1992.

[5] I. Bartolini, P. Ciaccia, and M. Patella. The skyline of a probabilistic relation. *TKDE*, 2012.

[6] M. Ben-Or. Lower bounds for algebraic computation trees (preliminary report). In *STOC*, pages 80–86, 1983.

[7] G. Beskales, M. A. Soliman, and I. F. Ilyas. Efficient search for the top-k probable nearest neighbors in uncertain databases. *PVLDB*, 1(1), 2008.

[8] S. Börzsönyi, D. Kossmann, and K. Stocker. The skyline operator. In *ICDE 2001*.

[9] R. Cheng, J. Chen, M. F. Mokbel, and C.-Y. Chow. Probabilistic verifiers: Evaluating constrained nearest-neighbor queries over uncertain data. In *ICDE*, 2008.

[10] S. D. Cohen and L. J. Guibas. The earth mover's distance under transformation sets. In *ICCV*, pages 1076–1083, 1999.

[11] T. H. Cormen, C. E. Leiserson, R. L. Rivest, and C. Stein. *Introduction to Algorithms (second edition)*. 2001.

[12] G. Cormode, F. Li, and K. Yi. Semantics of ranking queries for probabilistic data and expected ranks. In *ICDE*, 2009.

[13] N. N. Dalvi and D. Suciu. Efficient query evaluation on probabilistic databases. In *VLDB*, pages 864–875, 2004.

[14] T. Eiter and H. Mannila. Distance measures for point sets and their computation. *Acta Inf.*, 34(2):109–133, 1997.

[15] T. Emrich, H. Kriegel, P. Kröger, M. Renz, and A. Züfle. Constrained reverse nearest neighbor search on mobile objects. In *ACM SIGSPATIAL*, 2009.

[16] T. Emrich, H. Kriegel, P. Kröger, M. Renz, and A. Züfle. Boosting spatial pruning: on optimal pruning of mbrs. In *SIGMOD*, pages 39–50, 2010.

[17] B. Fitzenberger, R. Koenker, and J. A. Machado. *Economic Applications of Quantile Regression (Studies in Empirical Economics)*. 2002.

[18] M. Hua, J. Pei, W. Zhang, and X. Lin. Ranking queries on uncertain data: A probabilistic threshold approach. In *SIGMOD*, 2008.

[19] H. Kriegel, S. Brecheisen, P. Kröger, M. Pfeifle, and M. Schubert. Using sets of feature vectors for similarity search on voxelized CAD objects. In *SIGMOD*, pages 587–598, 2003.

[20] H. Kriegel, A. Pryakhin, M. Schubert, and A. Zimek. COSMIC: conceptually specified multi-instance clusters. In *ICDM*.

[21] H.-P. Kriegel, P. Kunath, and M. Renz. Probabilistic nearest-neighbor query on uncertain objects. In *DASFAA*, pages 337–348, 2007.

[22] L. V. S. Lakshmanan, N. Leone, R. B. Ross, and V. S. Subrahmanian. Probview: A flexible probabilistic database system. *ACM Trans. Database Syst.*, 22(3):419–469, 1997.

[23] J. Li, B. Saha, and A. Deshpande. A unified approach to ranking in probabilistic databases. *VLDB J.*, 20(2), 2011.

[24] X. Lin, Y. Zhang, W. Zhang, and M. A. Cheema. Stochastic skyline operator. In *ICDE*, pages 721–732, 2011.

[25] C. Long, R. C. Wong, B. Zhang, and M. Xie. Hypersphere dominance: an optimal approach. In *SIGMOD*, pages 111–122, 2014.

[26] J. Pei, B. Jiang, X. Lin, and Y. Yuan. Probabilistic skylines on uncertain data. In *VLDB*, 2007.

[27] J. Ramon and M. Bruynooghe. A polynomial time computable metric between point sets. *Acta Inf.*, 37(10):765–780, 2001.

[28] B. E. Ruttenberg and A. K. Singh. Indexing the earth mover's distance using normal distributions. *PVLDB*, 5(3):205–216, 2011.

[29] M. Shaked and J. G. Shanthikumar. *Stochastic Orders and Their Applications*. Academic Press, 2007.

[30] M. Sharifzadeh and C. Shahabi. The spatial skyline queries. In *VLDB*, pages 751–762, 2006.

[31] S. Singh, C. Mayfield, S. Mittal, S. Prabhakar, S. E. Hambrusch, and R. Shah. Orion 2.0: native support for uncertain data. In *SIGMOD Conference*, 2008.

[32] M. A. Soliman, I. F. Ilyas, and K. C. Chang. Top-k query processing in uncertain databases. In *ICDE 2007*.

[33] W. Son, M. Lee, H. Ahn, and S. Hwang. Spatial skyline queries: An efficient geometric algorithm. In *SSTD*, pages 247–264, 2009.

[34] H. Wang, F. Nie, and H. Huang. Learning instance specific distance for multi-instance classification. In *AAAI*, 2011.

[35] J. Xu, Z. Zhang, A. K. H. Tung, and G. Yu. Efficient and effective similarity search over probabilistic data based on earth mover's distance. *VLDB J.*, 21(4):535–559, 2012.

[36] S. M. Yuen, Y. Tao, X. Xiao, J. Pei, and D. Zhang. Superseding nearest neighbor search on uncertain spatial databases. *IEEE Trans. Knowl. Data Eng.*, 22(7):1041–1055, 2010.

[37] W. Zhang, X. Lin, M. A. Cheema, Y. Zhang, and W. Wang. Quantile-based knn over multi-valued objects. In *ICDE*, 2010.

[38] W. Zhang, X. Lin, Y. Zhang, M. A. Cheema, and Q. Zhang. Stochastic skylines. *TODS*, 37(2), 2012.

[39] X. Zhang and J. Chomicki. On the semantics and evaluation of top-k queries in probabilistic databases. In *DBRank*, 2008.

[40] Y. Zhang, X. Lin, G. Zhu, W. Zhang, and Q. Lin. Efficient rank based knn query processing over uncertain data. In *ICDE*, 2010.

[41] Y. Zhang, W. Zhang, X. Lin, M. A. Cheema, and C. Zhang. Matching dominance: capture the semantics of dominance for multi-dimensional uncertain objects. In *SSDBM*, 2014.

[42] Y. Zhang, W. Zhang, J. Pei, X. Lin, Q. Lin, and A. Li. Consensus-based ranking of multi-valued objects: A generalized borda count approach. *TKDE*, 26(1):83–96, 2014.

APPENDIX

A. SOME NN FUNCTIONS

In this section, we introduce three popular NN functions that belong to $\mathcal{N}_3$, which derive the NN score based on a subset of pair-wise distances.

Informally, two sets of points are close in the Hausdorff distance [14, 27] if every point of either set is close to some points of the other set. Given two objects U and Q, following is a formal definition of their Hausdorff distance.

Definition 11. ***Hausdorff distance.***

$$D_h(U,Q) = max\{\max_{u \in U} \delta_{min}(u,Q), \max_{q \in Q} \delta_{min}(q,U)\} \quad (5)$$

Under our problem settings where each object has multiple instances with total probability mass 1, the definitions of **Earth Mover's distance** [10] and **Netflow distance** [27] are equivalent to each other. Below we formally introduce the Netflow distance [27].

Distance Network. Let N (E) denote a set of vertices (edges) and W (C) records the weights (capacities) of the edges. G=<N,E,C,W> is a network with s, $t \in N$ being *source* and *sink*, respectively. A feasible flow f of the network G maps each edge $e \in E$ a non-negative value $f(e)$ following the capacity constraint and conservation of flow constraint [11]. The value $|f|$ of the flow is defined as $|f| = \sum_{\langle s,x\rangle \in E} f(\langle s,x\rangle)$, and the cost $c(f)$ of the flow is defined as $c(f) = \sum_{e \in E} w(e)f(e)$.

In this paper, we assume that the total probability (weight) of the instances for each object is 1. Then the distance network between the object U and the query Q, denoted by $G_{U,Q}$, can be constructed as follows.

- Vertices s and t for source and sink respectively.
- Each instance $q \in Q$ contributes a vertex q and an edge $<s,q>$ with $c_{s,q} = p(q)$ and $w_{s,q} = 0$.
- Each instance $u \in U$ contributes a vertex u and an edge $<u,t>$ with $c_{u,t} = p(u)$ and $w_{u,t} = 0$.
- For any two instances $q \in Q$ and $u \in U$, there is an edge $<u,q>$ with $c_{u,q} = \infty$ and $w(\langle u,q\rangle) = \delta(u,q)$.

DEFINITION 12. ***Netflow distance.*** *Given the distance network $G_{U,Q}$ of the object U and query Q, the netflow distance between U and Q, denoted by $M_{nd}(U,Q)$, is the minimal cost of the maximal flow $c(f)$ of $G_{U,Q}$ with $|f| = 1$.*

B. PROOFS

B.1 Proof of Theorem 1

THEOREM 1. *Match order is equivalent to the usual stochastic order.*

PROOF. "$\Rightarrow$": Given $X \preceq_M Y$, there is a match $M_{X,Y}$ where $t.x \leq t.y$ for every $t \in M_{X,Y}$. Then we have $X \preceq_{st} Y$ because for every $t \in M_{X,Y}$, $t.y \leq \lambda$ implies that $t.x \leq \lambda$ for every $\lambda \in R$.

"$\Leftarrow$": Given $X \preceq_{st} Y$, we show how to iteratively find a feasible match $M_{X,Y}$ such that $t.x \leq t.y$ for every $t \in M_{X,Y}$. We visit the instances of Y (X) in non-decreasing order. Let x_i and y denote the smallest unvisited instance of X and Y, respectively. Since $Pr(X \leq y) \geq Pr(Y \leq y)$ and the same amount of probability mass has been consumed in previous instance matches, there is a set of instance $\{x_i, \ldots, x_k\}$ where x_k is the smallest instance such that $\sum_{i \leq j \leq k} p(x_j) \geq p(y)$. If $\sum_{i \leq j \leq k} p(x_j) > p(y)$, we may split the instance x_k such that $\sum_{i \leq j \leq k} p(x_j) = p(y)$. For every $x_j \in \{x_i, \ldots, x_k\}$, we generate a tuple $t\langle x_j, y, p(x_j)\rangle$. Figure 3(b) illustrates a simple example of the match between A_Q and B_Q. In this way, we generate a feasible match $M_{X,Y}$ and $X \preceq_M Y$ follows. □

B.2 Proof of Theorem 2

THEOREM 2. *F-$\mathcal{SD}$ $\subset$ P-$\mathcal{SD}$ $\subset$ SS-$\mathcal{SD}$ $\subset$ S-$\mathcal{SD}$.*

PROOF. <u>SS-$\mathcal{SD}$ $\subset$ S-$\mathcal{SD}$</u>: Given two objects U and V, and the query Q, we show that SS-$\mathcal{SD}$(U,V,Q) implies S-$\mathcal{SD}$(U,V,Q) but not vice versa. Given SS-$\mathcal{SD}$(U,V,Q), we have $\Pr(U_q \leq \lambda) \geq \Pr(V_q \leq \lambda)$ for every $\lambda \in R$ regarding every $q \in Q$. Since we have $\Pr(U_Q \leq \lambda) = \sum_{q \in Q} Pr(U_q \leq \lambda) \times p(q)$ and $\Pr(V_Q \leq \lambda) = \sum_{q \in Q} Pr(V_q \leq \lambda) \times p(q)$, it is immediate that we have $\Pr(U_Q \leq \lambda) \geq \Pr(V_Q \leq \lambda)$, and hence $U_Q \preceq_{st} V_Q$. Thus, S-$\mathcal{SD}$(U,V,Q) holds. On the other hand, Figure 3 illustrates an example where we have S-$\mathcal{SD}$(A,C,Q) and $\neg$SS-$\mathcal{SD}$(A,C,Q). Therefore, SS-$\mathcal{SD}$ $\subset$ S-$\mathcal{SD}$ follows.

<u>P-$\mathcal{SD}$ $\subset$ SS-$\mathcal{SD}$</u>: P-$\mathcal{SD}$(U,V,Q) implies that there is a match $M_{U,V}$ such that $t.u \preceq_Q t.v$ for each $t \in M_{U,V}$. Therefore, for each $q \in Q$, we have $\delta(t.u,q) \leq \delta(t.v,q)$, and hence $U_q \preceq_M V_q$. Then we have $U_q \preceq_{st} V_q$ according to Theorem 1. Thus, SS-$\mathcal{SD}$(U,V,Q) holds. Figure 4 gives an example where SS-$\mathcal{SD}$(A,B,Q) but $\neg$P-$\mathcal{SD}$(A,B,Q).

<u>F-$\mathcal{SD}$ $\subset$ P-$\mathcal{SD}$</u>: F-$\mathcal{SD}$(U,V,Q) implies that for every $q \in Q$, $\delta_{max}(q,U) \leq \delta_{min}(q,V)$. Thus, for every match $M_{U,V}$, we have $\delta(t.u,q) \leq \delta(t.v,q)$ for every $t \in M_{U,V}$ and $q \in Q$. Thus, P-$\mathcal{SD}$(U,V,Q) holds. In the example of Figure 4, we have P-$\mathcal{SD}$(A,C,Q) but $\neg$F-$\mathcal{SD}$(A,C,Q). □

B.3 Proof of Theorem 3

THEOREM 3. *When $|Q| = 1$, we have F-$\mathcal{SD}$ $\subset$ P-$\mathcal{SD}$ = SS-$\mathcal{SD}$ = S-$\mathcal{SD}$.*

PROOF. Since $|Q| = 1$, it is immediate that SS-$\mathcal{SD}$ is equivalent to S-$\mathcal{SD}$. Moreover, according to Theorem 1, we have P-$\mathcal{SD}$ = SS-$\mathcal{SD}$ = S-$\mathcal{SD}$. Figure 15 illustrates an example where we have P-$\mathcal{SD}$(A,B,Q), SS-$\mathcal{SD}$(A,B,Q), S-$\mathcal{SD}$(A,B,Q) but $\neg$F-$\mathcal{SD}$(A,B,Q). Together with Theorem 2, we have F-$\mathcal{SD}$ $\subset$ P-$\mathcal{SD}$. □

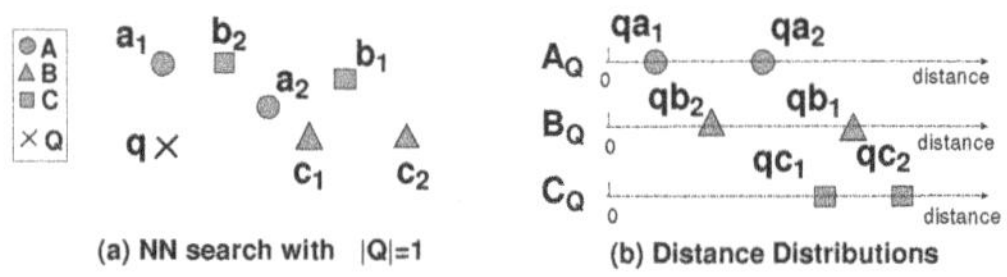

Figure 15: Example of Theorem 3

B.4 Proof of Theorem 5

THEOREM 5. *S-$\mathcal{SD}$ is optimal w.r.t. $\mathcal{N}_1$, and S-$\mathcal{SD}$ does not cover $\mathcal{N}_{2,3}$.*

PROOF. <u>Correctness.</u> Given two independent objects U and V, and query Q, U_Q and V_Q are two independent random variables and S-$\mathcal{SD}$(U,V,Q) implies that $U_Q \preceq_{st} V_Q$. Since a *stable* aggregate function will be used against all pair-wise distances for a function $f \in \mathcal{N}_1$, it is immediate that we have $f(U) \leq f(V)$ according to Definition 8.

<u>*Completeness.*</u> $\neg$S-$\mathcal{SD}$(U,V,Q) implies that there is a $\lambda \in R$ such that $\Pr(U_Q \leq \lambda) < \Pr(V_Q \leq \lambda)$. Let $\phi = \Pr(V_Q \leq \lambda)$, we have $quan_\phi(U_Q) > quan_\phi(V_Q)$ according to Definition 10 where *quantile* is a function in $\mathcal{N}_1$.

<u>*Not cover $\mathcal{N}_{2,3}$.*</u> In the example of Figure 3, we have S-$\mathcal{SD}$(A,C,Q) but C is NN object if NN probability is used, which is a function in $\mathcal{N}_2$. Moreover, the example in Figure 4 shows that S-$\mathcal{SD}$(A,C,Q) but EMD(A,Q)>EMD(C,Q) where EMD is a function in $\mathcal{N}_3$. Consequently, S-$\mathcal{SD}$ does not cover $\mathcal{N}_{2,3}$. □

B.5 Proof of Theorem 6

THEOREM 6. *SS-$\mathcal{SD}$ is optimal w.r.t. $\mathcal{N}_{1,2}$, and SS-$\mathcal{SD}$ does not cover $\mathcal{N}_3$.*

PROOF. <u>Correctness.</u> The correctness is immediate regarding $\mathcal{N}_1$ since SS-$\mathcal{SD}$ $\subset$ S-$\mathcal{SD}$ and S-$\mathcal{SD}$ is optimal w.r.t. $\mathcal{N}_1$. Now we only consider $\mathcal{N}_2$. Given objects U and V, and the query Q, SS-$\mathcal{SD}$(U,V,Q) indicates that for every $q \in Q$ we have $U_q \preceq_{st} V_q$. So for every $\lambda \in R$, we have $\Pr(U_q \leq \lambda) \geq \Pr(V_q \leq \lambda)$ regarding a given query instance q since U_q and V_q are independent. Recall that $\delta(U,W)$ and $s(U,W)$ denote the distance and score of the object U in the possible world W, respectively, and we have $s(U,W) \leq s(V,W)$ if $\delta(U,W) < \delta(V,W)$ for every function in $\mathcal{N}_2$. Let $\mathcal{W}_q$ denote the possible worlds in which q occurs, we have $\Pr(U_q \leq \lambda) \geq \Pr(V_q \leq \lambda)$ for every $\lambda \in R$. This implies that $\sum_{W \in \mathcal{W}_q \wedge s(U,W) \leq \xi} Pr(W) \geq \sum_{W \in \mathcal{W}_q \wedge s(V,W) \leq \xi} Pr(W)$ for every possible score ξ. Consequently, we have $U_{\mathcal{W}} \preceq_{st} V_{\mathcal{W}}$ as $U_q \preceq_{st} V_q$ held for every $q \in Q$. Since the stable aggregate function is used to derive the NN score, we have $f(U) \leq f(V)$ for every $f \in \mathcal{N}_{1,2}$.

Completeness. Given $\neg$SS-$\mathcal{SD}(U,V,Q)$, there is at least one query instance $q_1 \in Q$ such that $U_{q_1} \not\preceq_{st} V_{q_1}$; that is, there exists a $\lambda_1 \in R$ where $\Pr(U_{q_1} \leq \lambda_1) < \Pr(V_{q_1} \leq \lambda_1)$, i.e., $\Pr(U_{q_1} > \lambda_1) > \Pr(V_{q_1} > \lambda_1)$. Then we can construct a function f as follows. Let the aggregate function g be the weighted sum of scores where the weight of a score $s(U,W)$ is set to $Pr(W)$ if $W \in \mathcal{W}_{q_1}$, and it is set to 0 otherwise. Clearly, g is a stable function. Moreover, we set $s(U,W)$ to 1 if $\delta(U,W) > \lambda_1$, and 0 otherwise. In this way, we have $f(U) = \Pr(U_q > \lambda_1) \times p(q_1)$ and $f(V) = \Pr(V_q > \lambda_1) \times p(q_1)$. Thus, we have $f(U) > f(V)$.

Not cover $\mathcal{N}_3$. In the example of Figure 4, we have SS-$\mathcal{SD}(A,C,Q)$ and EMD(A,Q) > EMD(C,Q) where EMD is a function in $\mathcal{N}_3$. □

B.6 Proof of Theorem 7

THEOREM 7. *P-$\mathcal{SD}$is optimal w.r.t. $\mathcal{N}_{1,2,3}$.*

PROOF. Correctness. The correctness is immediate regarding $\mathcal{N}_{1,2}$ since P-$\mathcal{SD}$ ⊂ SS-$\mathcal{SD}$ and SS-$\mathcal{SD}$ is optimal w.r.t. $\mathcal{N}_{1,2}$. Now we only consider $\mathcal{N}_3$. Given objects U and V, and the query Q, P-$\mathcal{SD}(U,V,Q)$ implies that there is a match $M_{U,V}$ such that $t.u \preceq_Q t.v$ for every $t \in M_{U,V}$. For every function $f \in \mathcal{N}_3$ with aggregate stable function g, $\sigma_V(V_Q)$ denotes the corresponding selected pair-wise distances from V_Q during the computation of $f(V)$. Based on the match $M_{U,V}$, we can construct the counterpart $\sigma_V(U_Q)$ for object U. For every pair $\langle \delta(v,q), p \rangle$ in $\sigma_V(V_Q)$, its counterpart in U_Q is $\langle \delta(u,q), p \rangle$ with $\delta(u,q) \leq \delta(v,q)$ since v is assigned to u in $M_{U,V}$. Consequently, we have $\sigma_V(U_Q) \preceq_{st} \sigma_V(V_Q)$, and hence $g(\sigma_V(U_Q)) \leq g(\sigma_V(V_Q))$. Since f is a counterpart computable function, we have $f(U) \leq g(\sigma_V(U_Q))$, and then $f(U) \leq f(V)$ holds.

Completeness. $\neg$P-$\mathcal{SD}(U,V,Q)$ implies that for every possible match $M_{V,U}$, we can find a pair $\langle \delta(v,q), p \rangle$ from V_Q such that $\delta(v,q)$ is always smaller than its counterpart in U_Q. By simply selecting the pair $\langle \delta(v,q), p \rangle$ in V_Q and its counterpart pair in U_Q regarding a match $M_{U,V}$, we have $f(U) > f(V)$. □

B.7 Proof of Theorem 8

THEOREM 8. *F-$\mathcal{SD}$ is correct w.r.t. $\mathcal{N}_{1,2,3}$, but does not have completeness property w.r.t. $\mathcal{N}_{1,2,3}$.*

PROOF. Since we have F-$\mathcal{SD}$ ⊂ P-$\mathcal{SD}$, the correctness of F-$\mathcal{SD}$ is immediate. In Figure 4, we have $\neg$F-$\mathcal{SD}$ (A,C,Q) because $\delta(a_2, q_2) > \delta(c_2, q_2)$. Nevertheless, we have $f(A) \leq f(C)$ for every $f \in \mathcal{N}_{1,2,3}$ because P-$\mathcal{SD}$ (A,C,Q) holds. Consequently, F-$\mathcal{SD}$ is not complete w.r.t. $\mathcal{N}_{1,2,3}$. □

B.8 Proof of Theorem 9

THEOREM 9. *S-$\mathcal{SD}$, SS-$\mathcal{SD}$, P-$\mathcal{SD}$ and F-$\mathcal{SD}$ have the transitivity property.*

PROOF. Given S-$\mathcal{SD}(U,V,Q)$ and S-$\mathcal{SD}(V,Z,Q)$, we have $\Pr(U_Q \leq \lambda) \geq (V_Q \leq \lambda)$ and $\Pr(V_Q \leq \lambda) \geq (Z_Q \leq \lambda)$ for every $\lambda \in R$. This immediately implies that $\Pr(U_Q \leq \lambda) \geq \Pr(Z_Q \leq \lambda)$. Thus, S-$\mathcal{SD}(U,Z,Q)$ holds. We show that SS-$\mathcal{SD}$ also satisfies this property with similar rationale.

Given F-$\mathcal{SD}(U,V,Q)$ and F-$\mathcal{SD}(V,Z,Q)$, for every $q \in Q$, we have $\delta_{max}(q,U) \leq \delta_{min}(q,V)$ and $\delta_{max}(q,V) \leq \delta_{min}(q,Z)$. Then we have $\delta_{max}(q,U) \leq \delta_{min}(q,Z)$, and hence F-$\mathcal{SD}(U,Z,Q)$ holds.

Given P-$\mathcal{SD}(U,V,Q)$ and P-$\mathcal{SD}(V,Z,Q)$ we have two matches $M_{U,V}$ and $M_{V,Z}$ with $t.u \preceq_Q t.v$ and $m.v \preceq_Q m.z$ for every $t \in M_{U,V}$ and $m \in M_{V,Z}$. By splitting instances, we can come up with two new matches with the same number of tuples, denoted by $M^*_{U,V}$ and $M^*_{V,Z}$. For every tuple $t \in M^*_{U,V}$ and its counterpart tuple $m \in M^*_{V,Z}$, we generate a tuple $t^*\langle t.u, m.z, t.p \rangle$ for the new match $M_{U,Z}$. With similar rationale to F-$\mathcal{SD}$, $u \preceq_Q v$ and $v \preceq_Q z$ implies that $u \preceq_Q z$. Therefore, P-$\mathcal{SD}$ satisfies the transitivity property because P-$\mathcal{SD}(U,Z,Q)$ holds. □

B.9 Proof of Theorem 10

THEOREM 10. *Given two random variables X and Y with n instances each, any algorithm to determine whether $X \preceq_{st} Y$ must have complexity of at least $\Omega(n \log(n))$ if the algorithm is based only on comparisons between elements from X and Y.*

PROOF. Given two random variables X and Y, it is immediate that $X = Y$ if $X \preceq_{st} Y$ and $Y \preceq_{st} X$ since for any value λ, $P(X \leq \lambda) = P(Y \leq \lambda)$. Since a set can be regarded as a random variable in which each element has the same probability, we can determine whether two sets are equal by conducting two stochastic dominance checks. As shown in [6], for any computation tree solving the problem of set equality, its lower bound time complexity must be $\Omega(n \log n)$ where n is the size of the set. This implies that any comparison based algorithm to determine whether $X \preceq_{st} Y$ must have complexity of $\Omega(n \log(n))$. □

B.10 Proof of Theorem 12

THEOREM 12. *Let $G_{U,V}$ be the network constructed based on two objects U, V and the query Q, we have P-$\mathcal{SD}(U,V,Q)$ if and only if $|f^*| = 1$ where f^* is a max-flow of $G_{U,V}$.*

PROOF. P-$\mathcal{SD}(U,V,Q)$ implies that there is a match $M_{U,V}$ between U and V where $t.u \preceq_Q t.v$ for every $t \in M_{U,V}$. Then we can construct a flow f of $G_{U,V}$ as follows. For every tuple $t \in M_{U,V}$, we set $f(\langle t.u, t.v \rangle) = t.p$. Moreover, for every $u \in U$ and $v \in V$, we set $f(s,u) = p(u)$ and $f(v,t) = p(v)$. Clearly this flow f is feasible (i.e., satisfying capacity and conservation constraints) with $|f| = 1$. which is a max-flow since $\sum_{u \in U} c(s,u) = 1$. With similar rationale, given $|f^*| = 1$ we can construct a match $M_{U,V}$ to verify that P-$\mathcal{SD}(U, V, Q)$ holds. □

C. EXPERIMENTS AND ANALYSIS

C.1 Additional Experiments

In this experiments, Figure 16 demonstrates the effectiveness of different filtering techniques proposed in Section 5.1 on SSD, SSSD and PSD. The number of data instance (m_d) varies from 20 to 100 on HOUSE dataset and the number of average instance comparison is reported. We explore the effectiveness of filtering strategies by adding them to the

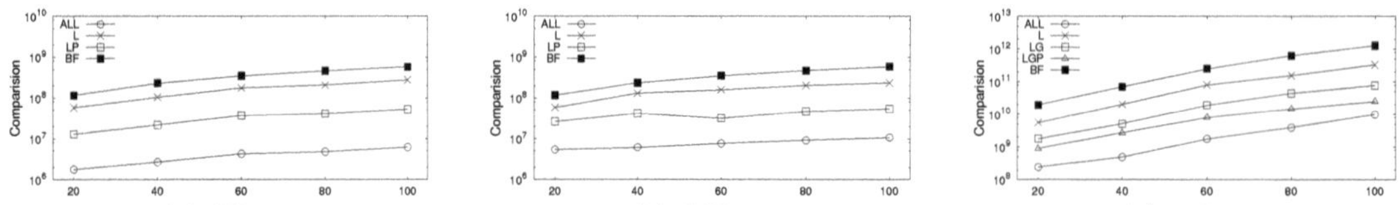

(a) SSD (b) SSSD (c) PSD

Figure 16: Effectiveness of Diff. Filtering Techniques

brute force method one by one. In particular, **All** is the algorithm with all filtering techniques; **BF** is method without any filtering techniques, i.e., the brute force method; **L** is the algorithm that adds level by level searching mechanism to BF; **LP** stands for the method adding pruning rules to L; **LG** stands for the method adding geometrical strategy on L; **LGP** stands for the method adding pruning rules on LG. It is reported that all four techniques make remarkable contribution in improving the efficiency of the NN candidates searching. Given the filtering strategies, SSD and PSD save up to 2 order of magnitude of cost and SSSD saves 60 times of cost comparing with the brute force method respectively.

C.2 Summary

In the experiment, we evaluate the NN candidates computation algorithms based on five spatial dominance operators. Following are some important observations.

- Experiments confirm that F+SD [16, 25] and FSD algorithms always lead to a much larger number of NN candidates compared with SSD, SSSD and PSD. Thus, they are not suitable to provide NN candidates for users.
- It is observed that three spatial dominance operators (S-$\mathcal{SD}$, SS-$\mathcal{SD}$ and P-$\mathcal{SD}$) proposed in this paper can significantly reduce the number of candidate objects, which is crucial in our problem since users need to make decision among the NN candidates. Moreover, experiments shows that users may make a good trade-off between the candidate size (time efficiency) and the coverage of NN functions.
- Experiments demonstrate that our algorithms can instantly output a large portion of high quality NN candidates. This can enhance the users' satisfaction since they can immediately start to browse the promising results once the query is issued.

D. RELATED WORK

In this section, we review the existing works on objects with multiple instances which are closely related to this paper.

D.1 NN Search

NN candidate search on objects with multiple instances has been studied in different contexts. As discussed in Section 3, given the distance measure of two points (instances), there are three representative families of NN ranking mechanisms including all pairs based NN search ($\mathcal{N}_1$), possible world based NN search ($\mathcal{N}_2$), and selected pairs based NN search ($\mathcal{N}_3$).

There is a long history of study for NN functions in $\mathcal{N}_1$ and $\mathcal{N}_3$. In many applications such as economics and social study, distance between two objects is derived based on an aggregation function against the pair-wise distances. Typical examples include *min*, *max*, *mean*, and *quantile* distances (e.g., [29, 37]). To describe the closeness of two set of points or distributions, various distances such as Hausdorff distance [27], Earth Mover's distance [10], and Netflow distance [27] have been proposed based on a subset of the pair-wise distances.

In recent years, the inherent uncertainty of data in many applications lead to the emergence of many uncertain database models (e.g., [13, 31]). A variety of ranking methods have been proposed in the literature for uncertain data processing such as U-top k[32], global top k [39, 18], *expected rank* [12], and *parameterized ranking* [23], which have been employed in nearest neighbor search on uncertain objects (e.g., [21, 7, 9, 40, 2, 1]). Besides the possible world semantics based approaches, Earth Mover's distance has also been applied to retrieve NN object on uncertain data (e.g., [35, 28]).

D.2 NN Candidate Search

The *spatial dominance* operator is first introduced by Sharifzadeh et al. in [30]. Informally, we say a point x spatially dominates another point y w.r.t. a set of query points if x is closer to every query point than y. Efficient algorithms [30, 33] have been developed to compute spatial skyline. Nevertheless, the problem studied in this paper is inherently different, since the work in [30, 33] focuses on the case where each object has only one instance. The full spatial dominance (F-$\mathcal{SD}$) operator in [16, 25] can be regarded as its natural extension in the context of NN search on multi-instance objects. Various efficient algorithms (e.g., [16, 25, 15]) have been proposed to check the spatial dominance in the context of NN search, all NN search, and reverse NN search on both certain and uncertain data. We remark that these works focus on how to efficiently prune the non-promising objects at high level, based on the approximations (e.g., rectangles and hyperspheres) of the objects to speed up the computation, instead of providing the end-user with a set of NN candidates with consideration of popular NN ranking functions. In [36], Yuen *et al.* introduce the concept of NN-core to retrieve NN candidates based on the pair-wise competitions among the objects. However, as discussed in Section 1, NN objects regarding some popular NN ranking functions may be missed by NN-core.

D.3 Skyline Computation

The problem of skyline computation has been investigated in the context of uncertain data. Probabilistic skyline on uncertain data is first tackled in [26]. Efficient techniques are proposed following the bounding-pruning-refining framework. P-*domination* is proposed by Bartolini *et al.* [5] to capture the dominance among uncertain objects based on the tuple-level uncertain object model. The stochastic order based skyline computation for multi-dimensional uncertain objects is investigated in [24, 38]. Recently, Zhang et al. [41] propose a layer based indexing technique for multi-dimensional uncertain objects based on the match based dominance operator. Our problem can be regarded as the skyline computation based on new spatial dominance operators. Nevertheless, the problem is inherently different from previous studies since a query object with multiple instances is involved.

THERMAL-JOIN: A Scalable Spatial Join for Dynamic Workloads

Farhan Tauheed*
Oracle Labs Zurich,
Switzerland.

Thomas Heinis*
Imperial College London,
United Kingdom.

Anastasia Ailamaki
École Polytechnique Fédérale
de Lausanne, Switzerland.

ABSTRACT

Simulations have become ubiquitous in many domains of science. Today scientists study natural phenomena by first building massive three-dimensional spatial models and then by simulating the models at discrete intervals of time to mimic the behavior of natural phenomena. One frequently occurring challenge during simulations is the repeated computation of spatial self-joins of the model at each simulation time step. The join is performed to access a group of neighboring spatial objects (groups of particles, molecules or cosmological objects) so that scientists can calculate the cumulative effect (like gravitational force) on an object.

Computing a self-join even in memory, soon becomes a performance bottleneck in simulation applications. The problem becomes even worse as scientists continue to improve the precision of simulations by increasing the number as well as the size (3D extent) of the objects. This leads to an exponential increase in join selectivity that challenges the performance and scalability of state-of-the-art approaches.

We propose THERMAL-JOIN, a novel spatial self-join algorithm for dynamic memory-resident workloads. The algorithm groups objects in spatial proximity together into *hot spots*. Hot spots minimize the cost of computing join as objects assigned to a hot spot are guaranteed to overlap with each other. Using a nested spatial grid, THERMAL-JOIN partitions and indexes the dataset to locate hot spots. With experiments we show that our approach provides a speedup between 8 to 12× compared to the state of the art and also scales as scientists improve the precision of their simulations.

1. INTRODUCTION

Scientists no longer solely depend on studying a phenomena in their laboratory or in nature. They nowadays improve their understanding by first building three-dimensional spatial models and then by simulating the models at discrete intervals of time steps to gather key insight of the underlying principals that govern the phenomena. This enables scientists to make discoveries and even predict the behavior of phenomena, for example in cosmology [21] or seismology [1].

Computing the interaction between spatial objects that make up the model is crucial for many simulations. Doing so requires that the simulation identify at runtime all pairs of objects whose three-dimensional extents overlap. Identifying overlapping pairs of objects essentially translates into a spatial self-join that is performed repeatedly at each time step of the simulation. For example, to compute the gravitational force on a particular planet in n-body cosmological simulations [21], all other cosmological objects in proximity are retrieved using a spatial self-join.

During the simulation, the location of all spatial objects is changed at each time step to mimic the behavior of the phenomena studied, i.e., the locations of objects is read from main memory, manipulated and then updated in-place to reflect the latest state of the object. Two aspects of this problem introduce new challenges that limit the applicability of known approaches. First, all objects move together, i.e., the location of all objects is updated at every time step. All objects moving together is in stark contrast to use cases and applications, studied extensively in the literature, where only a subset of objects move at any instance in time. In case all objects move using an incremental join by re-using old results becomes unfeasible and executing a full join from scratch is more efficient. Second, unlike vehicular objects, the assumption that objects move in predictable trajectories for short distances does not hold and techniques involving trajectories or motion approximation thus cannot be used.

Recent analyses [34, 37] have demonstrated the limitations of existing join techniques for the problem of moving objects. Furthermore, known approaches do not scale in case scientists increase the precision of the simulation application. Increasing simulation precision is accomplished by increasing the number of objects in the dataset to reduce approximation errors due to spatial discretization and by increasing the threshold spatial region around the object to consider the effect of more objects in a wider spatial region. The consequence of both, i.e., increasing the number as well as spatial extent of the objects leads to an increasing join selectivity, which challenges known join techniques.

In this paper we present THERMAL-JOIN, an in-memory spatial self-join algorithm for moving objects. The approach is designed to address both the spatial aspect (high join selectivity) and the temporal aspect of the problem (massive and unpredictable updates). The key contributions are:

- THERMAL-JOIN leverages the dataset density to minimize the cost of joining. We introduce the concept of *hot spots*, i.e., regions with high spatial density, where all objects are guaranteed to overlap with each other. Hot spots

* This work was done while the author was at EPFL.

SIGMOD'15, May 31–June 4, 2015, Melbourne, VIC, Australia.

ACM 978-1-4503-2758-9/15/05 ...$15.00.
http://dx.doi.org/10.1145/2723372.2749434.

avoid the costly evaluation of overlap predicates. The benefits increase as the join selectivity increases, thus making the approach scalable.

- We use a novel linked-hash table to build, join and maintain a nested uniform grid. The rationale behind using a uniform grid is to index hot spots rather than to index spatial objects as is done in known grid-based approaches.
- The algorithm adapts and self-tunes the indexing structures used to account for the dynamic nature of the workload. We use a hill-climbing based approach that quickly converges without incurring an undue performance penalty.

Unlike previous studies we analyze the performance of competing approaches using three-dimensional datasets for both real (neuroscience) and synthetic benchmarks. We show that THERMAL-JOIN outperforms existing approaches while remaining competitive in terms of memory footprint. Most importantly, we demonstrate that THERMAL-JOIN scales with dataset size and object extent, two characteristics that are crucial to improve the simulation precision.

The remainder of the paper is structured as follows. In Section 2 we discuss related work and in Section 3 we motivate our work. In Section 4 we present our approach THERMAL-JOIN and discuss optimizations. We compare THERMAL-JOIN to related approaches in Section 5, analyze its performance in Section 6 and finally draw conclusions in Section 7.

2. RELATED WORK

Using our motivating application we review related work discussing how suited it is for workloads where the position of nearly all objects changes rapidly. We classify existing work based on whether it primarily serves for joining static spatial datasets (rebuilding and updating index structures at every time step) or if it has been designed for dynamic datasets, i.e., for joining moving objects. We do not distinguish whether approaches have initially been developed for main memory or disk as the ones developed for the latter can also be used in the former.

2.1 Iterative Static Spatial Join

One strategy is to use known static spatial join techniques [16] and update or rebuild their data structures from scratch at each time step before the join. Rebuilding the complete index or updating nearly all the objects at every simulation step is a considerable time investment that substantially slows down the simulation and is difficult to amortize over a join operation [36]. Both the nested loop join and the plane sweep join [29] thus do not maintain auxiliary data structures but at the same time their join process is prohibitively slow.

To improve the slow join process many join techniques use indexes. Updating the index, however, is very costly and it is typically cheaper to rebuild the index from scratch at every iteration (and to throw away the index after leading to short lived throw-away indexes [8]). Space-oriented partitioning indexes are particularly efficient in building an index as they use spatial grids or hierarchical space decomposition to index the objects. For example, PBSM [27] uses a uniform grid to partition the data and replicates objects based on how many partitions the object intersects with. Each partition is locally joined using a plane-sweep approach. Because objects are replicated, the same pair of objects may be tested multiple times, resulting in a substantial increase of intersection tests.

Hierarchical decomposition can be used to avoid replication as the widely used Octree [3] shows. The Octree and the MX-CIF Octree [15] are based on a uniform grid and split a cell uniformly if the number of objects in it exceeds a defined threshold. The objects in the split cell are assigned to the cells in which they do not intersect with a boundary (ideally to the children of the split cell). Similar to the Octree, S3 [19] uses a hierarchy of grids to index objects based on the smallest grid cell that fully encloses the object. The performance of both, S3 and Octree, suffers when objects are mapped to the root (or cells close to the root) of the hierarchical structure as they then have to be compared with all objects on lower levels, resulting in unnecessary intersection tests. The loose Octree [30] allows for a degree of imprecision so that objects can be assigned to lower levels when they intersect only slightly with a cell. The idea of using grids to parallelize the join has also been optimized for GPUs [33] as well as on a larger scale on the MapReduce framework[12, 23].THERMAL-JOIN as presented here is single threaded but can be parallelized like the aforementioned approaches.

THERMAL-JOIN also uses the idea of throw-away indexes based on space-oriented partitioning (grids) but attempts to reuse parts of the index whenever possible. The fundamental difference is that we do not use the grid to index the objects but rather to find the densely populated regions. Doing so enables us to avoid the problem of replication (every object is assigned to one grid cell only) and unnecessary intersections (objects are assigned based on the cells enclosing the center rather than the full object).

Data-oriented partitioning techniques avoid replication by dividing the space based on the distribution of objects (and assigning each object to one node only). The indexed nested-loop join [9] builds an R-Tree on one dataset and executes a range query on it for each object in the other dataset to find intersecting objects. The synchronous R-Tree traversal [5] joins two spatial datasets by traversing two R-Tree indexes built for each dataset from the roots to the leaf levels. While recursively traversing the trees, nodes on the same level are tested for intersection. The CR-Tree [18] optimizes the R-Tree for memory and targets at reducing cache misses and at reducing the index size (mainly through quantization). The optimizations generally improve performance by a constant factor over the regular R-Tree but do little to address the fundamental problem of overlap. In fact, quantization can also degrade performance as the approximated MBRs lead to more overlap. A further index based on the R-Tree and optimized for memory is TOUCH [26]. It reduces the number of overlap tests considerably and thus the join time but it is not designed for iterative changes to the dataset and the index has to be rebuilt in every iteration from scratch.

Data-oriented approaches like the R-Tree in general are prone to the problem of overlap and dead space [13], both of which severely degrade join performance. For our problem of datasets changing over discrete intervals of time, recent findings indicate that rebuilding the R-Tree and using the synchronous R-Tree traversal is the most efficient approach [34].

Several approaches based on a single grid level have also been developed for high-dimensional data (similarity join) and can be equally used for low dimensions. The Epsilon Grid Order [4] uses a high-dimensional grid of ϵ width and chooses the order to join grid cells I/O-efficient, i.e., avoiding thrashing. The same ideas also helps in main memory to avoid cache pollution. Based on multiple grids and inspired by the quicksort algorithm, QuickJoin [17] uses a recursive partitioning technique and a nested loop join to join the results within each partition. DBSimJoin [32] builds on the QuickJoin technique and implements it as a non-blocking operator using an iterator interface.

For distributed map-reduce workloads, ClusterJoin [31] provides a framework for scalable similarity joins on skewed datasets. SSJOIN [2] addresses the set similarity join challenge by using locality sensitive hashing to compute the joins. Adopting similarity join techniques for spatial joins is feasible but they are not competitive compared to techniques designed for three-dimensional euclidean spaces as we show with experiments.

2.2 Joining Moving Objects

Instead of joining the dataset at each time step from scratch, spatio-temporal join methods [25] that are optimized for moving objects can be used. These methods join incrementally, i.e., reuse data structures built and used in previous time steps. Similar to static spatial indexes, joins can be performed using moving object indexes by querying the index for each object in the dataset. The ST2B-Tree [7] maps all objects on a uniform grid and indexes each object along with its identifier in a B+-Tree (cell identifiers are assigned based on a space-filling curve). OCTOPUS [36] on the other hand avoids an index and the associated maintenance cost when the data changes over time. It is, however, only applicable for mesh spatial datasets as it relies on the mesh connectivity to retrieve query results. The parallel implementation of a recently proposed moving object join [38] also uses a uniform spatial grid to index the locations of objects. The separation of the grid cells is exploited to use multiple threads to either update or join the data simultaneously.

To reduce the overhead of frequent maintenance proposed approaches [28, 35, 14] exploit the predictability in movement of the objects by approximating them with trajectories. The data structure used in the join therefore only has to be updated when the trajectory of the moving objects changes. Similarly, the adaptive two-level hashing approach [20] classifies objects according to their speed of movement. Slow moving objects are indexed with a fine-grained grid while fast objects are indexed with a coarse-grained grid. With our driving application, however, we cannot assume any predictability of the object movement and these techniques thus cannot be used.

3. MOTIVATION

Scientists no longer only rely on the study of a phenomena in their laboratory or in nature. Instead, they complement their understanding of the phenomena by building spatial models of it and by simulating the resulting models. In doing so they face considerable challenges in dealing with the data involved in simulations. One challenge they face is executing queries on fast changing spatial models used in simulations. Spatial simulations are used across many different scientific disciplines, from cosmology, medicine to material sciences. The development of THERMAL-JOIN is consequently driven by the needs of scientists who are facing performance bottleneck in simulating changes in massive spatial datasets.

In the following we first describe the scientific use cases and the problem in detail. We conclude this section by describing the novel data management challenges in the context of this problem.

3.1 Use Cases

The application motivating the development of THERMAL-JOIN originates from a collaboration with the neuroscientists in the Human Brain Project [24]. In the collaboration we study the performance bottlenecks and scalability of neural simulations. These simulations use part of the brain tissue represented by a collection of three-dimensional cylindrical spatial objects as shown in Figure 1(a). The simulations mimic the process of neural plasticity where the structure and connectivity of the cells change over time. In the first step of the simulation a distance join with the distance predicate d is executed to find pairs of objects within distance d of each other. The distance join is essentially performed by enlarging the spatial object by d in all dimensions and testing the enlarged extent for overlap. In the next step the electrical attraction and repulsion forces between pairs of objects are calculated to determine how the shape and connectivity of the neuron cells changes in subsequent simulation time steps.

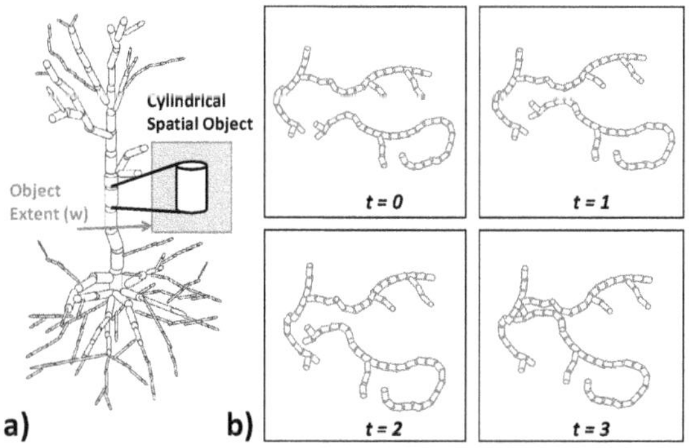

Figure 1: Cylindrical object representation of neurons with the spatial extent defined by the rectangle (a). Neural structure simulation at time t (b).

Finding pairs of overlapping objects efficiently is a challenge in simulation in general, as overlap or proximity between objects (representing parts of neurons, molecules or cosmological objects) usually defines how different spatial objects interact with each other. There are several interaction frameworks used by simulation applications that define how the models should be built and how the simulation can be discretized in space and time. The most widely used methods are smoothed particle hydrodynamics (SPH) [11] which are extensively used in computational fluid dynamics, N-Body simulations [3] used in particle and cosmology simulations and the Lennard-Jones pair potential method [10] used in molecular simulations. In all of these interaction frameworks the basic but also most crucial task is to access all pairs of overlapping objects which in the case of neural simulation takes 66% of the total time (using an octree based join technique). This task is performed several times during the simulation as the objects change their location over time and the problem thus translates into an iterative spatial self-join in main memory.

3.2 Iterative Spatial Self-Join

We first discuss the static (spatial) aspect of the iterative spatial self-join challenge and then describe the dynamic (temporal) aspect. Consider a spatial dataset D with N three-dimensional spatial objects. As is standard practice in related work [16], we use the minimum bounding rectangle (MBR) as the spatial extent w_i for each spatial object

$s_i \in D$. The problem of a spatial self-join is to find all pairs of spatial objects $(s_i, s_j) \in D \times D$, such that the spatial object pair satisfies the predicate of spatial overlap, i.e., $overlap(w_i, w_j) > 0$. The self-join result does not allow reflexive object pairs (s_i, s_i) and counts commutative object pairs $[(s_i, s_j), (s_j, s_i)]$ as one join result. In scientific simulations the spatial extent w_i (also known as cut-off radius or ϵ) is the same for each object in the dataset and represents a region where an object might interact with another object, e.g., a gravitation field.

During the simulation the location of each spatial object is changed (updated in-place) by the simulation application to mimic the behavior of the phenomena studied, making the problem of a spatial (self-) join more challenging. The spatial extent w_i and number of objects remain constant for a during simulation (but can change for different simulation runs) because each object represents a physical entity (planets or stars) that remains the same during the course of the simulation (as shown in Figure 1(b)). The changes are applied iteratively at discrete intervals that affect every object in the dataset. This is different from previous work [28, 14] where only a subset of objects change location or velocity.

Our goal is to design a general solution, not limited to a particular simulation application. We therefore treat the simulation application as a black box and do not rely on the update mechanism of the spatial objects to optimize the approach. The changes to location of the objects are therefore treated as unpredictable. This means known approaches based on time parametrization and predictable trajectories [28, 35] are ill-suited.

3.3 Data Management Challenge

Even for reasonably small dataset sizes (a few gigabytes in main memory) an iterative spatial self-join can take hours to complete and it therefore creates a substantial bottleneck in simulation applications. To make matters worse scientists want to increase the precision of their simulations by first, increasing the spatial dataset size (to increase the spatial resolution of the models) and then increasing the three-dimensional objects' extent (to consider more surrounding objects to compute the interaction). Both, increase in dataset size and object extent, make simulations more realistic but at the same time they also increase join selectivity resulting in poor scalability of known approaches for self joins.

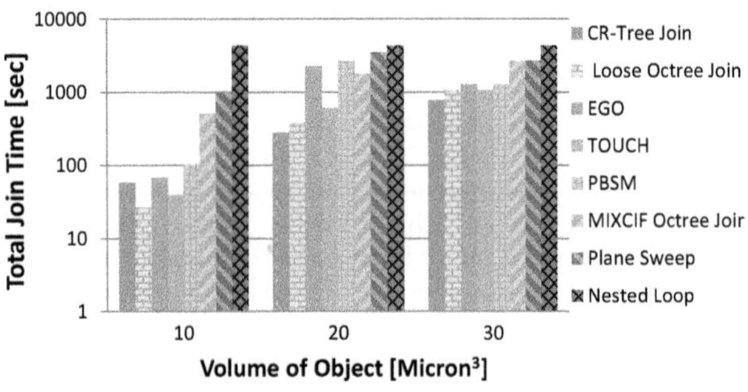

Figure 2: Effect of join selectivity on self-join time.

To demonstrate the effect of join selectivity we perform an experiment using a small neural dataset consisting of one million objects. Figure 2 shows the results of a self-join for one time step of the simulation by comparing existing in-memory join techniques. We change only the volume of the objects extent w from $10\mu m^3$ to $30\mu m^3$ to increase the join selectivity. As the experiment shows, the join time increases by one order of magnitude and the performance of known methods approaches the prohibitively slow nested-loop join.

Existing approaches reduce the join time by minimizing the unnecessary overlap tests between objects that are far apart in space. If, however, the join selectivity increases, the "necessary" overlap tests between objects that satisfy the join predicate increase quadratically, making known approaches inefficient for datasets with high join selectivity.

4. THE THERMAL-JOIN APPROACH

THERMAL-JOIN, the approach we develop, addresses the problem of high join selectivity by organizing the dataset into *hot spots*, i.e., regions of very high spatial density. The intuition behind THERMAL-JOIN is to process a self-join within each hot spot as efficiently as possible while minimizing the overhead of joining objects of a hot spot with objects in its surrounding spatial region. A hot spot is a region in which all objects are guaranteed to overlap with each other and it thus makes pair-wise overlap tests among objects that are in the hot spot unnecessary. The proposed join strategy used in THERMAL-JOIN is therefore fundamentally different to existing join approaches where the focus has been to provide better join performance by minimizing the unnecessary overlap tests between objects far apart in space.

Finding hot spots in spatial datasets in simulations can become expensive as the dataset changes unpredictably at every time step of the simulation. We use a two-level nested spatial grid to do so efficiently. In contrast to existing grid-based solutions, the primary purpose of using the grid in THERMAL-JOIN is to provide efficient access to hot spots instead of using the index structure to query the dataset and to locate objects in spatial proximity of each other. The choice of using a spatial grid further favors efficient rebuilding and maintenance as the dataset changes during the simulation.

In the following we describe the THERMAL-JOIN approach in detail and highlight the key insights it uses for self-joining dynamic spatial datasets. We divide the approach into three phases:

1. **Index Building:** In Section 4.1 we describe how to build the spatial grid structure using a linked-hash table data structure that provides efficient access to the hot spots and also to the neighboring regions while keeping the memory footprint low.
2. **Joining:** In Section 4.2 we describe the join algorithm that uses the grid index. We divide the joining phase into two parts, first joining objects within each grid cell (internal Join) and then each grid cell with adjacent cells (external Join).
3. **Index Maintenance:** As the dataset changes during simulation we tune the grid index to provide better join performance. In Section 4.3 we describe how to find an efficient configuration for the grid index and also a mechanism to recycle grid cells to further minimize the index building/maintenance time and memory footprint.

4.1 Index Building

The index building of THERMAL-JOIN requires efficient means to build and maintain spatial grids. In the following we describe in detail the spatial grid indexes used along with the linked-hash data structure that we use to implement the grid index and to avoid both the problem of overlap and that of empty grid cells.

Join algorithms based on data-oriented partitioning like variants of the R-Tree [5, 26] suffer from the overhead of overlapping nodes in the tree structure and high index building cost. To avoid the issue of overlap we partition the datasets using space-oriented partitioning or, more precisely, by using a uniform spatial grid. The spatial objects of the model dataset are mapped to the grid based on their center and therefore are not replicated unlike space-oriented join techniques like PBSM [27]. Avoiding replication is pivotal as it makes the technique scale with the increasing spatial density of the dataset joined.

Real simulation datasets have a skewed data distribution that cause the majority of the grid cells to remain empty. Managing empty cells is crucial because it can be a substantial overhead in terms of storage space required. For example, just using a null pointer to indicate an empty cell for a rather coarse resolution 3D grid with (1000 × 1000 × 1000) cells requires 7.5GB of space in memory. Our approach uses a hash table that only keeps cells that have at least one object assigned to it. This reduces the memory consumption significantly but the cost of accessing (spatially) neighboring cells during the join phase increases as hash lookups are required which cause a significant overhead due to collisions (particularly in the case of fine grained grids).

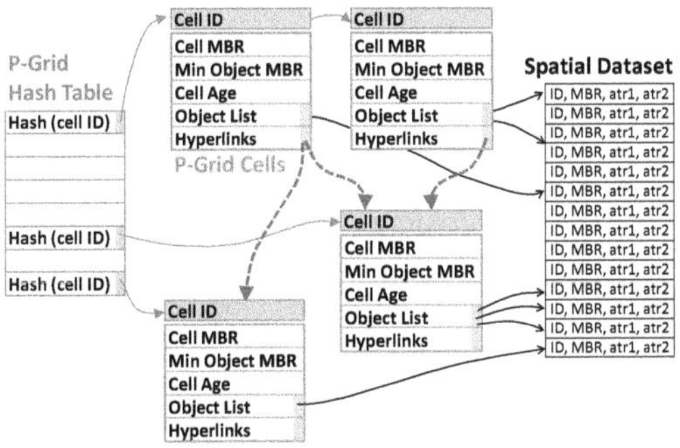

Figure 3: Linked-hash table data structure.

THERMAL-JOIN addresses the problem by using a linked-hash table that provides direct access to neighboring cells through pointers (hyperlinks) introduced in the index building phase as shown in Figure 3. This means we can use the same hash table for both index building and join phase. During index building hash lookups are used to map objects to their respective cells while in the more costly join phase the hyperlinks are used to avoid hash lookups when accessing neighboring cells.

THERMAL-JOIN uses a two-level nested grid. The primary (permanent) grid, or simply P-Grid, is built and maintained to reflect the most recent location of each object for the last time step. For each cell of the P-Grid it is possible to further divide the space using a temporary throw away grid T-Grid to enhance join performance. Crucially, as opposed to many hierarchical grid [19] or tree based techniques [30], the resolution of each T-Grid built for each cell of P-Grid can be different and in many cases a T-Grid is not even required to further organize a cell of the P-Grid.

The P-Grid is built by calculating the cell each object belongs to. The assignment is based on the information of what cell the center of an object falls into. Once the unique identifier of the cell containing the object is obtained, the identifier is used to perform a hash lookup to determine if a new cell is needed or if the object pointer can be assigned

Algorithm 1 THERMAL-JOIN: Index Building Phase

```
Input: Dataset: Spatial model dataset
Data: PGrid: Empty hash table of cells
Output: PGrid: Hash table with objects assigned
foreach object ∈ Dataset do
    center ← object.MBR
    cellID ← calculateCellID(center)
    targetCell ← PGrid.hashlookup(cellID)
    if targetCell.found() then
        targetCell.objectlist.insert(&object)
    else
        cell ← newCell()
        cell.objectlist.insert(&object)
        PGrid.insert(cellID, &cell)
    end
end
foreach cell ∈ PGrid do
    cell.objectlist.sortX()
    neighborsList ← getNeighbors(cell)
    foreach n ∈ neighborList do
        neighborCell ← PGrid.hashlookup(n)
        cell.Hyperlinks.insert(&neighborCell)
    end
end
return PGrid
```

to an existing cell's object list. Once all the objects are assigned to their grid cells, the object lists are sorted along the x-dimension to facilitate the join phase. Furthermore, for each cell we find all the neighboring adjacent cells and add their pointers to the hyperlink list to provide efficient access to neighboring cells. The algorithm used to build a P-Grid is described in pseudocode in Algorithm 1. The temporary T-Grid is built during the join phase for each cell. We will discuss this process in Section 4.2.

The algorithm described terminates by returning a P-Grid hash table with all objects assigned based on their centers and each cell linked to neighboring cells. This algorithm is used for building the P-Grid from scratch. Its performance can be further improved by re-using cell structures during index maintenance, described in Section 4.3.

4.2 Joining

Once the P-Grid is constructed the join phase can start. It works by processing each P-Grid cell from the hash table in no particular order. The algorithm works in two parts; first, joining objects in each cell with its adjacent P-Grid cells (external join) and then joining all objects within each P-Grid cell (internal join).

4.2.1 External Join

Assigning objects based on the center has the advantage that every object is assigned to only one P-Grid cell, thereby avoiding object replication. In order to retrieve accurate join results, however, the objects assigned to each cell need to be joined with the objects assigned to adjacent grid cells as well. To avoid any pair of cells being considered for external join more than once we only consider half of the adjacent cells. The number of adjacent cells taken into account for the external join depends on the P-Grid cell width and the width of largest object in the dataset. For example, if the P-Grid resolution is set such that the width of the cell is equal to the width of the largest object then we only need to consider half of the immediate adjacent cells, e.g., only the cells located in northwest, north, northeast, east direction as shown in Figure 4(a) (as a two-dimensional illustration). For three-dimensional datasets the number of adjacent cells is 13. In case the P-Grid resolution is set such that the width of the cell is less than the width of the largest object in the dataset then multiple layers of adjacent cells need to be considered for the external join as shown in Figure 4(b). The number of layers of adjacent cells can be calculated by dividing the P-Grid cell by the width of the largest object.

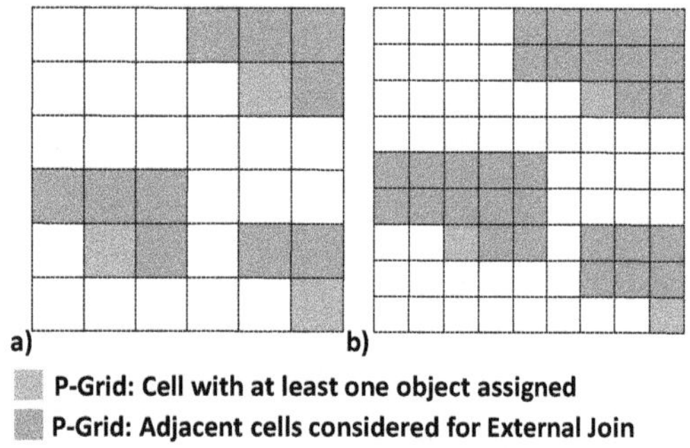

Figure 4: Adjacent cells used in the external join, (a) when P-Grid cell width = largest object width, (b) when P-Grid cell width ≤ largest object width.

The $getNeighbors(x)$ function in Algorithm 1 computes the cell identifiers of half of the adjacent cells in order to introduce hyperlinks that provide efficient access to these adjacent cells. THERMAL-JOIN determines the size of the largest object in the dataset while loading the dataset.

Once the index is built and the hyperlinks are created, we join each object a_i assigned to every cell A in the P-Grid with all the objects b_{jk} in each adjacent cells B_k of A. The join is performed using the plane-sweep approach which explains why we sorted the object list of each cell on the x-dimension during building as described in Algorithm 1. We use an optimized variant of plane-sweep approach, i.e., if the MBR of any object a_i encloses the entire MBR of cell B_k then we can avoid expensive overlap tests for this object during the external join and directly report that all $b_{jk} \in B_k$ overlap with a_i. This is because the MBR of cell B_k encloses the center of all objects assigned to it and therefore every object in B_k is guaranteed to overlap with a_i.

4.2.2 *Internal Join*

The concept of *hot spots* is central to THERMAL-JOIN. We define a hot spot as a grid cell, whose width in dimension k is equal to or less than the width of the smallest object assigned to that cell in dimension k (smallest object with respect to dimension k). By choosing the width of the cell less than or equal to the width of the smallest object we can ensure that irrespective of where the centers of the objects are located inside the cell, all objects will overlap with each other and therefore expensive pair-wise overlap tests can be avoided, thereby substantially accelerating the internal join.

Naturally, designing the P-Grid such that each cell is equal to the width of the smallest object in the entire dataset means that all cells are hot spots. However, if the dataset contains only a few very small objects this strategy forces the grid to have a very fine resolution. Doing so speeds up the internal join but will also increase the overhead for the external join because smaller cells mean that more adjacent cells need to be considered as shown in Figure 4. Making the P-Grid cell larger than the smallest object, on the other hand, requires fewer adjacent cells to be considered but not

Algorithm 2 THERMAL-JOIN: Joining Phase

```
Data: PGrid: Hash table with objects assigned,
      TGrid: Empty array of cells
Output: results: List of object pairs (result of the join)
foreach cellA ∈ PGrid do
    foreach cellB ∈ cellA.Hyperlinks do
        results ← PlaneSweep(cellA, cellB)
    end
    if cellA.MBR ≤ cellA.minObjectMBR then
        results ← allCombinations(cellA.objectlist)
    else
        TGrid.initialize(cellA.minObjectMBR)
        foreach o ∈ cellA.objectlist do
            center ← o.MBR
            id ← calculateCellID(center)
            TGrid.cellArray[id].objectlist.insert(&o)
        end
        foreach subCell ∈ TGrid do
            results ← allCombinations(subCell.objectlist)
            neighborSubCells ← getNeighbors(subCell)
            foreach neighbor ∈ neighborSubCells do
                results ← PlaneSweep(subCell, neighbor)
            end
        end
        TGrid.clear()
    end
end
return results
```

all P-Grid cells satisfy the condition of a hot spot and the internal join may thus take longer. Setting the P-Grid resolution introduces an interesting trade-off that we will discuss in Section 4.3.

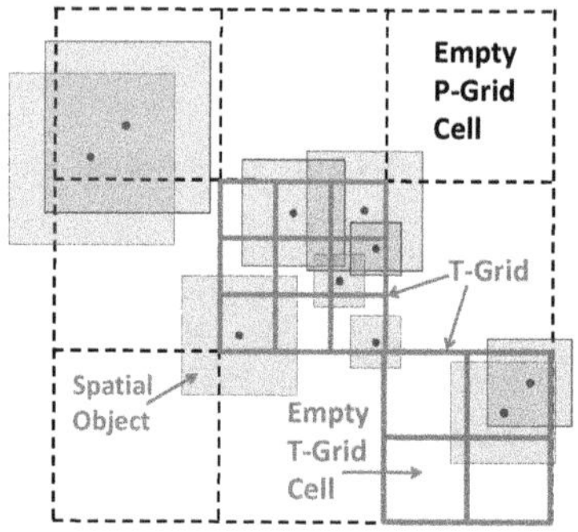

Figure 5: Nested T-Grid built for each P-Grid cell.

If any P-Grid cell is a hot spot then the join results can be directly reported by generating all possible pair-wise combinations (without overlap test) for objects assigned to that grid cell. The case where a P-Grid cell is a hot spot is shown in Figure 5 (top left cell).

Joining the objects in a P-Grid cells that are not hot spots is more challenging. The objects assigned to the same P-Grid cell are densely packed together with a considerable chance (but no certainty) that all of the objects will overlap with each other. Using a plane-sweep approach to join inside the P-Grid cell, as we use for the external join, is not efficient anymore, because the plane-sweep join degenerates into a nested-loop join given the high object density.

We repeat the process of creating hot spots within P-Grid cells that do not satisfy the condition of hot spots themselves. Objects assigned to the same P-Grid cell are likely to have a smaller variation in terms of object width compared to the entire dataset and we can thus design the nested grid T-Grid such that the width of each cell in T-Grid is exactly equal to the width of the smallest object assigned to the P-Grid cell. Each P-Grid cell that is not a hot spot can therefore have a different resolution for the sub grid (T-Grid) as is shown in Figure 5.

The resulting cells in the T-Grid are certain to be hot spots and consequently no further recursive subdivision is necessary. Similar to joining the P-Grid we join objects assigned to the T-Grid in two phases, i.e., first joining objects between two different T-Grid cells using an optimized variant of the plane-sweep approach described in Section 4.2.1, followed by a quick internal T-Grid cell join by simply reporting all pair-wise combinations of objects assigned to the cell as join results. The implementation we use for the T-Grid is different from the P-Grid. We use an array to manage the grid cells instead of a linked-hash table because the T-Grid in practice has only a few cells and therefore the space overhead of representing empty cells is insignificant. Moreover, using an array implementation makes building the T-Grid very fast. This means we can now build the grid on demand and throw it away after we have processed the internal join for a P-Grid cell as described in Algorithm 2.

4.3 Index Maintenance

The discussion of THERMAL-JOIN so far has focused on a static scenario. To make use of THERMAL-JOIN for dynamic, i.e., changing datasets, the grid needs to be updated at runtime, e.g., of a simulation application. We first discuss an incremental index maintenance strategy and then describe a mechanism to adaptively tune the index resolution at each time step of the simulation.

4.3.1 Incremental Index Maintenance

Performing the spatial self-join iteratively requires that the index reflects the recent location of the objects at every time step. A straightforward approach like building the index from scratch for each time step using the method described in Section 4.1 introduces considerable overhead. Using an incremental approach instead is likely to yield substantially better results. Existing strategies like join techniques based on predictable trajectories or techniques that assume that only a small subset of objects change their location, will not work as we cannot assume to be able to predict trajectory or location of all objects during simulation.

In THERMAL-JOIN we implement the idea of incremental maintenance by re-using parts of the P-Grid index. At each time step every object's location is inspected and the object is assigned to a new P-Grid cell (if needed). Time in this process can be saved by recycling data structures: for objects assigned to the same P-Grid cell or to a non-empty neighboring cell no new cells and hyperlinks need to be created. The performance benefits of recycling data structures increase considerably for fine resolution grids where many cells need to be created.

In order to implement the incremental maintenance approach Algorithm 1 only needs to be changed so that for each time step the P-Grid is not deleted but only the *objectlist* of a cell is cleared before assigning objects based on the last time step.

This means that if all the objects in a cell migrate away from it, the vacant cell will still exist in the P-Grid hash table. This becomes useful in case any object in the future moves and tries to reuse the vacant cell. In the long run, however, the memory footprint of the P-Grid will increase and keeping empty cells will become unsustainable. To address this issue we use a garbage collection approach to prune out the vacant cells. A garbage collection does not need to run at every time step instead it can be triggered using a simple policy, e.g., garbage collection is performed if the number of vacant cell exceeds a defined threshold, e.g., the number of vacant cells exceeds 35% of the total number of cells of the P-Grid.

4.3.2 Index Tuning

Grid-based join techniques are challenging to configure (i.e., to set the grid resolution) for optimal performance. One approach is to develop and use an analytical model based on the workload and the compute resources to configure the grid. Doing so requires sampling the workload to capture the data distribution and also requires in-depth knowledge about the hardware. THERMAL-JOIN, on the other hand, uses a more pragmatic method and iteratively tunes the grid resolution during the simulation.

The idea of iterative tuning makes the assumption that during the simulation the spatial distribution (not the individual location of objects) of the workload does not change drastically between subsequent time steps. In other words, once tuned, the THERMAL-JOIN configuration can be used for several simulation time steps efficiently and the overhead of tuning can thus be amortized over several time steps. This assumption works for real world workloads, for example, in cosmological simulation even though the objects (stars) change their location the distribution (clustering in galaxies) does not drastically change between two time steps.

In THERMAL-JOIN we use two grids. The resolution of the T-Grid is always fixed such that the width of the cells is equal to the width of the smallest object in the dataset. The resolution of the P-Grid can vary and the performance of THERMAL-JOIN depends on configuring this grid properly. We discuss the P-Grid resolution using a normalized metric r, where $r = 1$ means that the grid resolution is fixed (cell width is equal to the width of largest object in the dataset).

To understand the trade-off associated with the P-Grid resolution, let us assume that all objects are of equal size. If we set the resolution of the P-Grid such that $r > 1$ then the cost of performing the internal join increases because the P-Grid cell no longer is a hot spot. Using a fine resolution grid with $r \leq 1$, on the other hand, means that the cost of internal join is reduced but at the same time the number of cells required in the external join of the P-Grid increases drastically, thereby increasing the cost of external join and of building the index. The discussion implies that the function modeling the performance of THERMAL-JOIN at time step t is a convex function $F_t(r)$ of resolution r with a single global minima at the optimal resolution r_{opt}.

The sweet spot r_{opt}, however, is different for different workloads. Figure 6 shows the trade-off by experimenting with THERMAL-JOIN on four synthetic (uniform random distribution) datasets containing 10 million objects each. The join selectivity is increased by increasing the object width in each dataset. The experiment shows the result of performing self-join for one time step (static) to highlight the convex performance function with different r_{opt}.

Our goal for tuning THERMAL-JOIN is not to find the optimal r_{opt} but to find r' with reasonable overhead such that $F_t(r') \approx F_t(r_{opt})$. We thus use a hill climbing approach to iteratively search for r' starting with $r_1 = 1$ and define the convergence based on Equation 1.

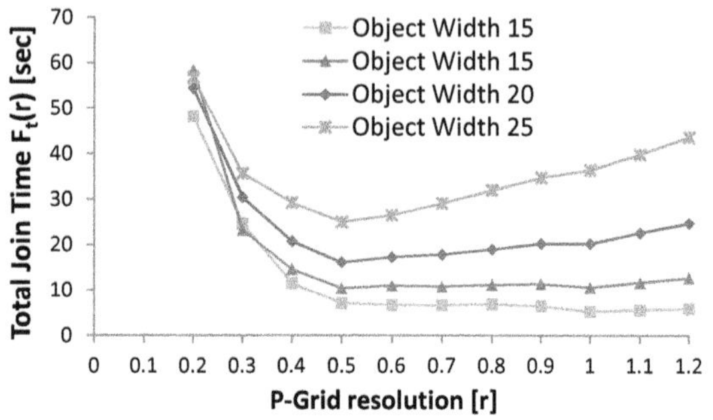

Figure 6: Impact of resolution r on join $F_t(r)$.

$$|F_{n-1}(r_{n-1}) - F_n(r_n)| \leq threshold \qquad (1)$$

Each time we use a different r_n we need to rebuild the P-Grid from scratch leading to a substantial overhead in terms of building time. During the iterative hill climbing we may encounter r_n such that $F_n(r_n)$ is very high causing additional overhead. In practice, however, we experience that the performance spikes only appear in the first few iterations of hill climbing when the algorithm is trying to explore the performance function F.

Already with a threshold of 10% we see that the tuning process converges quickly, i.e., typically in 6-8 time steps. Once the convergence is achieved we use r' for subsequent time steps by turning off the iterative tuning. In case the distribution of the workload changes during the simulation, we need to re-tune P-Grid by turning the tuning on again. THERMAL-JOIN does so in case of significant performance change during simulation as described by Equation 2.

$$|F_{n-1}(r') - F_n(r')| > threshold \qquad (2)$$

5. EXPERIMENTAL EVALUATION

In this section we first describe the experimental setup and demonstrate the benefits of THERMAL-JOIN by using real neural simulation workload. Furthermore, we perform a sensitivity analysis using a synthetic moving object benchmark to understand the performance by changing one workload variable at a time. Before we conclude we also analyze the THERMAL-JOIN algorithm in depth by discussing a breakdown of the performance and the impact of index tuning.

5.1 Setup and Methodology

The experiments are run on a Linux Ubuntu 2.6 machine equipped with 2x Intel Xeon Processors each with 6 cores running at 2.8GHz, with 64kb L1, 256KB L2 and 12MB L3 cache and 48GB RAM at 1333MHz. The storage consists of 2 SAS disks of 300GB capacity each. In the following we discuss the software setup as well as the configuration details for the competing approaches.

5.1.1 Software Setup

Each join algorithm implemented uses a single CPU core to ensure a fair comparison. We do not use the available implementations provided in [34] because the code assumes two-dimensional spatial datasets and extending it to support the three-dimensional dataset we use is not trivial [37]. The implementations are all written in C++.

The simulation datasets are loaded in memory and organized as a list of spatial objects that includes the minimum bounding rectangle (MBR) of each object, identifiers as well as attributes related to the properties of the object (e.g., electrical conductivity, mass, etc.). The simulation software processes the list at each iteration, i.e., it reads the objects, changes their location and then it writes the new location of each object in-place.

None of the join algorithms rearranges the list of spatial objects because the simulation application assumes the object to be in a particular order. Every approach therefore uses pointers to objects in the list to inspect the current location of the object (similar to Figure 3). The self-join is performed (atomically) at every time step only after the simulation application has completed modifying the list of spatial objects. The dataset in main memory is therefore always in a consistent state when the self-join is executed.

5.1.2 Competing Approaches

We use the fastest in-memory self-join approaches to compare against THERMAL-JOIN based on the results we obtained in Figure 3. First we use the synchronous R-Tree traversal which has recently been identified as the fastest in-memory join approach [34]. Second, we use a grid based join technique Epsilon Grid Order (EGO) [4] proposed for n-dimensional similarity joins and finally, we also include two recent approaches, the in-memory join algorithm TOUCH [26] and the join algorithm based on the space-oriented loose Octree [30]. In the following we discuss the configuration of each approach:

- CR-Tree: We implement the synchronous R-Tree join using a cache conscious variant of the R-Tree. Using the CR-Tree [18] not only improves performance but also reduces the memory footprint by using quantized tree nodes. To perform a self-join the tree is built only once using the STR R-Tree [22] bulkloading technique, while two pointer based synchronized breadth-first-search traversals are used to implement the algorithm. We perform a parameter sweep to determine the best tree fan-out (i.e., 11) for our workloads.
- TOUCH: Similar to the CR-Tree join, we use a parameter sweep to find the best fan-out (i.e., 2) for our workloads.
- Loose Octree: We build an indexed nested-loop variant of the join algorithm over a Loose Octree index that promises fast index building. After building the index the same dataset of spatial objects is used as range queries to find all overlapping object pairs by taking care not to report reflexive and commutative pairs. By performing a parameter sweep we found that the looseness factor of $p = 0.1$ yields the best join performance.
- EGO: We implement the epsilon grid order join for three-dimensional in-memory workload. The grid resolution (epsilon) is based on the object size used in the dataset.
- THERMAL-JOIN: we do not need a parameter sweep to configure the resolution of the P-Grid as the algorithm self-tunes at runtime. We use 10% as the convergence threshold to terminate the hill-climbing approach. Garbage collection is triggered if the vacant cells exceed more than 35% of the total cells.

5.2 Neural Simulation

We use a real neural simulation workload as described in Section 3.1 for comparing the performance of THERMAL-JOIN with existing approaches. The dataset represents a

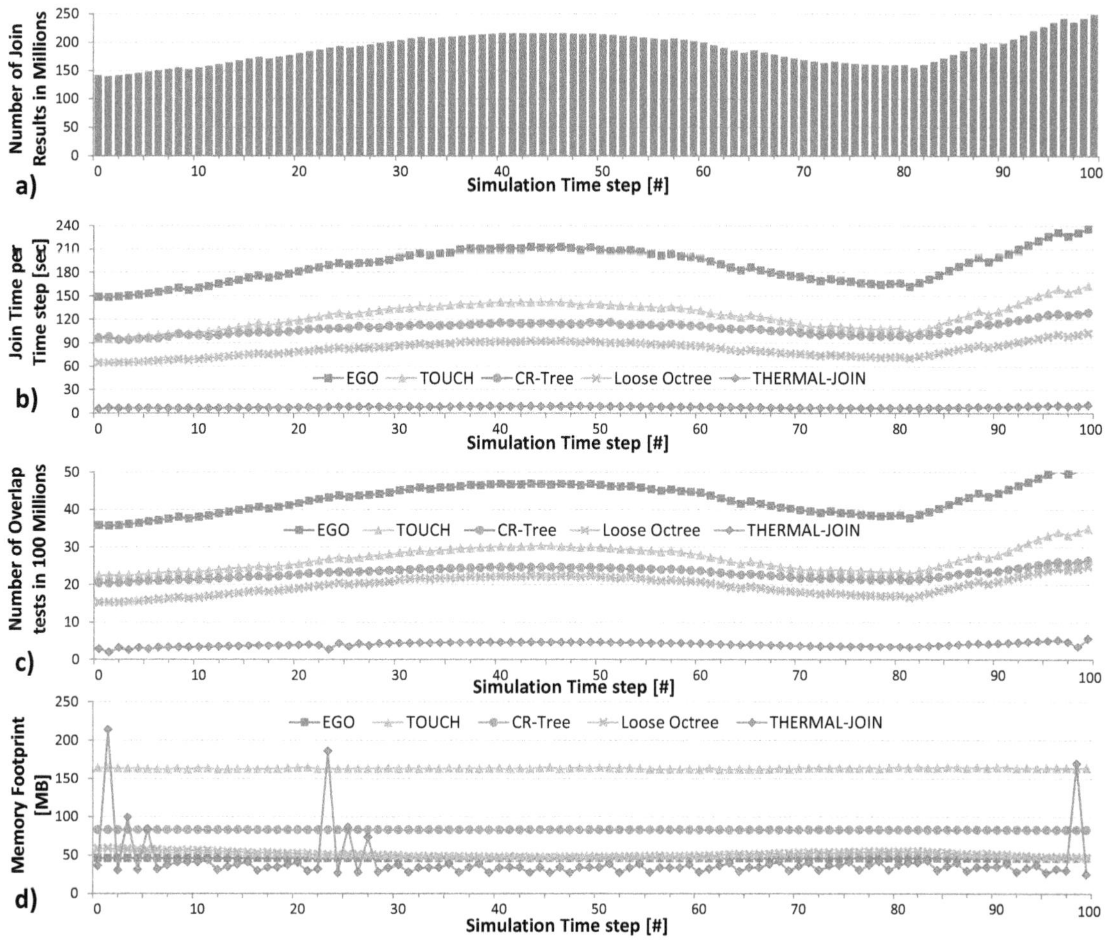

Figure 7: Neural simulation for 100 time steps. (a) Join selectivity in terms of number of join results, (b) total join time per time step, (c) total overlap tests per time step and (d) memory footprint per time step.

small part of the rat brain tissue containing 1692 neurons. The full dataset contains the branches of the neurons (as illustrated in Figure 1) modelled with 4 million cylindrical objects amounting to 160 MB on disk. Already with a small dataset like this the self-join can take several hours as we show with experiments. We fix the object extent to $15micron^3$ and present the results for the full 100 time step simulation. Subsequently we study the scalability of the competing approaches by increasing the dataset size as well as object extent.

5.2.1 *Full Simulation*

During the simulation the objects change their location which can also lead to a change of the distribution of the spatial objects. This affects the join selectivity: if, for example, the spatial density of a region increases, the number of join results for a time step increases as well as is shown in Figure 7(a). In Figure 7(b) we can see how existing approaches are very sensitive to the join selectivity because the number of overlap tests required dominates the join time (takes more than 95% of the join time and increases with the selectivity).

The join based on the loose Octree provides the second best performance for this dataset. THERMAL-JOIN on the other hand provides a further speedup from 9.4× to 11.1× when compared to the loose Octree. Crucially, THERMAL-JOIN is the least sensitive to the join selectivity thanks to the concept of hot spots that reduce the number of overlap tests as corroborated by Figure 7(c).

In terms of memory footprint, EGO, CR-Tree and TOUCH remain unaffected by the join selectivity as shown in Figure 7(d). Both CR-Tree and TOUCH approaches use variants of the R-Tree algorithm where the number of nodes in the tree depends on the dataset size rather than the distribution. The CR-Tree, however, uses quantized MBRs that reduce the space required for each node and it is thus more space efficient than TOUCH. EGO simply builds a spatial grid where objects are assigned to at most one grid cell similar to Octree techniques but no hierarchical structure is used, making it memory efficient. The nodes of the loose Octree [30] do not have a fixed number of objects assigned to them and as the distribution of the dataset becomes denser in certain areas, more objects can be assigned to the same node, thereby decreasing the number of nodes and the memory footprint when the join selectivity increases.

For THERMAL-JOIN we observe considerable spikes of memory consumption which is due to the index being tuned during at certain time steps. This tuning is not done once because the dataset changes distribution considerably during the simulation, triggering the tuning process three times in 100 time steps. The hill-climbing method used for tuning the P-Grid often explores the option of using very fine grid resolutions that increase the number of cells required and therefore increase the memory footprint. Apart from the spikes, it appears that the memory footprint measurement resembles a saw-tooth function. This is because of incremental building of the P-Grid and then periodic garbage collection to deallocate vacant cells.

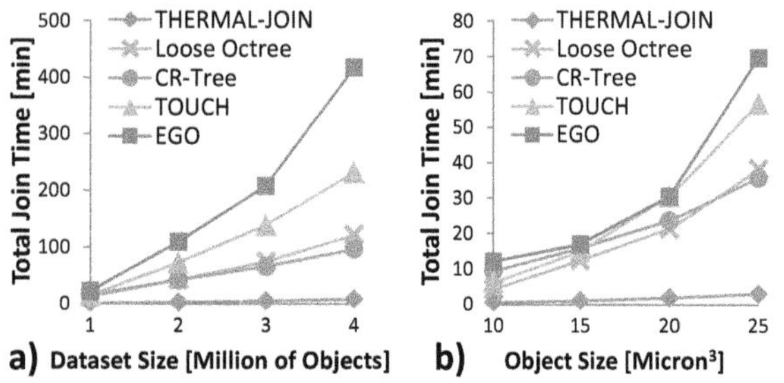

Figure 8: Scaling-up neural simulations in terms of (a) dataset size, (b) object width.

5.2.2 Scalability

We study the scalability with shorter duration simulations, i.e., only until the first 10 time steps to measure the join time for larger and more selective neural datasets. In Figure 8(a) we increase the dataset size based on the neural samples provided by the neuroscientists where the larger neural datasets are built by increasing the number of neurons (roughly 420 neurons resulting in approximately 1 million objects) considered for each experiment. In this experiment the object extent (or object width) is fixed to $15 micron^3$. Increasing the number of spatial objects used in the neural simulation in the same space increases the density of the dataset and thus also increases the join selectivity.

In this experiment THERMAL-JOIN outperforms competing approaches by a factor of 11.4× to 12×. Interestingly, although the loose Octree performs better for the dataset with one million objects, it scales poorly compared to the CR-Tree. This is because the join using the loose Octree uses a simple indexed nested-loop while the CR-Tree benefits from the synchronized traversal method as the dataset size grows. Although EGO uses a very efficient grid-based index, the join uses a nested loop join and therefore does not scale as the number of objects increase in each grid cell.

In Figure 8(b) we increase the object extent and keep the number of objects fixed to one million objects. In this experiment the CR-Tree again scales better than the loose Octree as the join selectivity increases. For THERMAL-JOIN the speedup increases from 8× to 12× suggesting that its benefit will further increase with increasing join selectivity.

5.3 Synthetic Benchmark

Experimenting with real workloads is essential to assess how approaches behave in real world scenarios. When doing so, however, understanding the impact of each individual workload characteristic on the performance is difficult. We therefore use a synthetic benchmark to isolate each characteristic and perform a sensitivity analysis by changing six different workload characteristics.

We use the benchmark described for moving object datasets [6] to calculate iterative self-joins. Unless stated, we use the following default workload characteristics of the benchmark. We use a uniform random distributed benchmark with 10 million three-dimensional spatial objects (with a size of 400MB) inside a boundary defined by (0,0,0) and (1000,1000,1000). Each object has a fixed object width of 15 units and the simulation lasts for 10 time steps. During the simulation each object is assigned a uniform random motion vector that is used to translate the object by 10 units at each time step. If the objects intersect with the boundary of the spatial extent the motion vector is inverted to ensure that the spatial boundaries remain the same.

Similarly, a second benchmark is created representing a skewed workload with 10 million objects and 15 units of object width. The skewed distribution is created using a normal distribution with the center of the cluster chosen randomly (uniform) and a spread defined by the standard deviation $sd = 1$. All objects within the skewed cluster have the same motion vector so that during simulation the distribution is preserved.

In the following experiments we use the uniform benchmark to understand the impact and benefits of THERMAL-JOIN by changing only one characteristic at a time, i.e., dataset size, object width, variation in object width and translation distance. We exclude the performance measurement when changing the aspect ratio of each object (while keeping the volume of the object constant). As expected we found no significant difference in terms of performance for THERMAL-JOIN and the competing approaches because none of the techniques depend on the aspect ratio of the spatial objects used. Similarly, for the skewed benchmark, we change the spread of the cluster, i.e., the standard deviation of the normal distribution and the number of clusters.

5.3.1 Dataset Size

In a first experiment we study the impact of the dataset size by increasing the dataset size of a uniform benchmark from 10 million objects (400MB) to 50 million objects (2GB). As the results in Figure 9(a) show, using more objects in the dataset degrades the performance of the loose Octree further compared to TOUCH and the CR-Tree. In this experiment the THERMAL-JOIN outperforms competing approaches and yields a speedup of 7.1× when compared to the second best technique, the CR-Tree. Some results for TOUCH, the loose Octree and EGO are missing as they did not finish execution within the 72 hour time limit we set.

5.3.2 Object Size

We next increase the width of the objects from 5 to 25 units uniformly so that all objects have the same extent in all dimensions. This increases the volume of the objects cubically and therefore increases the selectivity of the join. As Figure 9(b) shows THERMAL-JOIN provides a speedup of 7.2× compared to the CR-Tree.

5.3.3 Variation in Object Size

Although the objects in scientific simulations have the same size, in Figure 9(c) we also experiment with different object sizes (widths) of the smallest and largest object to further study the behavior of THERMAL-JOIN. The object width difference of zero in Figure 9(c) denotes that all objects have the same width of 15 units, while the difference of 4 units means the smallest object has a width of 13 units and the largest object 17 units (in all dimensions). Crucially, although the width changes linearly on the x-axis the difference in terms of volume of the objects increases cubically, e.g., in case of a width difference of 16 units, the volume of the largest object is 35 times larger than the smallest object.

Objects are chosen uniform randomly between the two extreme object sizes. In the best case, when all objects have the same size (difference zero), THERMAL-JOIN achieves a speedup of 13.7×. For the worst case the performance of

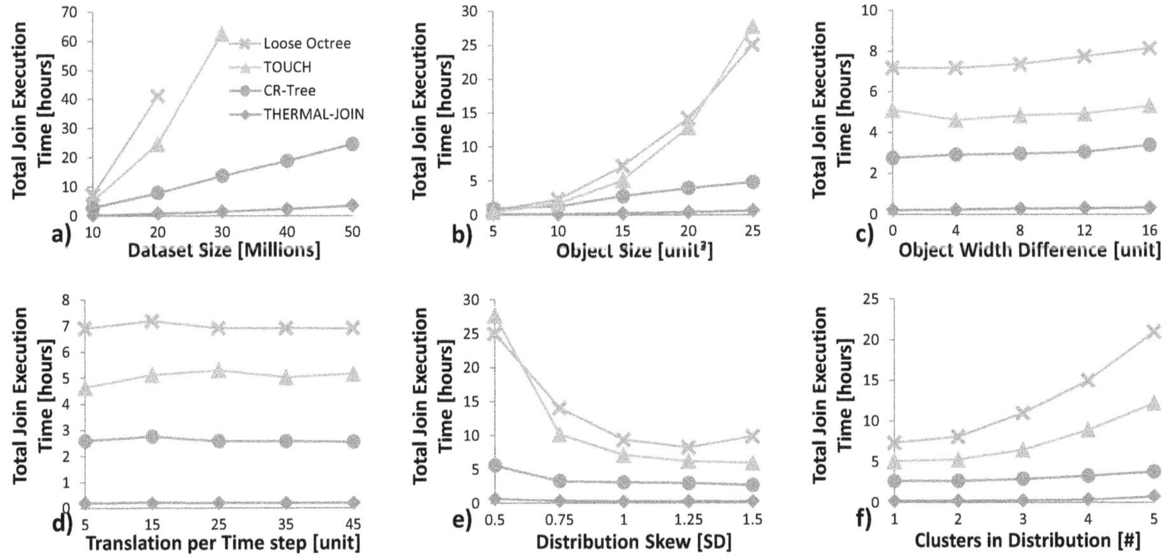

Figure 9: Sensitivity analysis using a synthetic benchmark.

THERMAL-JOIN decreases but it still achieves a speedup of 10.4× over related work. The performance drops because in the worst case the T-Grid needs to be built for each P-Grid as it does not satisfy the condition of a hot spot.

5.3.4 Temporal Resolution

In this experiment we change the temporal resolution of the simulation by increasing the distance each object is allowed to move between any two time steps. Doing so does not affect the distribution of the dataset.

The results shown in Figure 9(d) confirm the results expected, i.e., none of the techniques depend on the dynamics of the simulation. While TOUCH, CR-Tree and the loose Octree are rebuilt from scratch at every time step, THERMAL-JOIN uses incremental building and garbage collection to keep the overhead of building the index low, both in terms of space and performance. In the extreme case where an object always changes its P-Grid cell (making big jumps), the overhead is equal to rebuilding the P-Grid index from scratch. This effect is visible when we move the objects by 45 units (and the speedup is reduced by a small fraction from 13.3× to 13.0×). Similarly, the garbage collection strategy loses its effectiveness and the memory footprint increases by 27%.

5.3.5 Distribution Skew

To test sensitivity to distribution skew, we use a skewed benchmark and change the spread of the normal distribution to measure the impact on the performance. Using the standard deviation <1, reduces the spread and increases the join selectivity. Figure 9(e) shows higher join selectivity favors THERMAL-JOIN and therefore it outperforms competing approaches and achieves a speedup of 8.8×.

5.3.6 Clustering

Another way to vary the spread of the skewed distribution is to create several small clusters rather than just one. Keeping the standard deviation constant at one, we divide the same number of objects among many clusters. The density around the smaller clusters is relatively lower than the density of a single cluster. Although THERMAL-JOIN outperforms competing approaches, the speedup drops from 12× to 5× because the join is no longer as selective as with a single cluster as Figure 9(f) shows.

6. THERMAL-JOIN ANALYSIS

In this section we present experiments that highlight the internal working of THERMAL-JOIN, i.e., how do the join phases and the memory footprint change when we change the P-Grid resolution. We conclude by briefly discussing the applicability of THERMAL-JOIN based on the design choices we made along with limitations of the approach.

6.1 P-Grid resolution

In the following experiment we analyze and break down the performance of THERMAL-JOIN and describe how it changes as we change the grid resolution. In Figure 10(a) we vary the grid resolution r from 0.5 to 2 and then observe the cost of building and performing the self-join. For the experiment we use a real neural workload with one million objects with object width equal to $15 micron^3$. As we increase the resolution from $r > 1$ the cost of internal join starts to become substantial. This is because the P-Grid cells are no longer hot spots. As we decrease the resolution, i.e., $r < 1$ we increase the building and join time substantially because there is a considerable number of cells that require a long time to build and then to perform the external join despite all the objects are in hot spots.

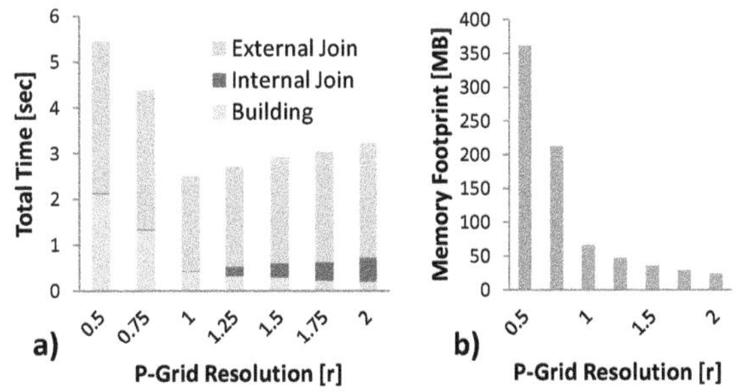

Figure 10: Effect of changing grid resolution r on (a) join time, (b) footprint of THERMAL-JOIN.

The memory required on the other hand only depends on the number of grid cells instantiated and as we increase r

so that $r > 1$, fewer cells are needed and thus the footprint becomes insignificant as shown in Figure 10(b).

6.2 Applicability

We do not make any particular assumption regarding the semantics of the simulation application and THERMAL-JOIN thus is applicable to many different problems that require iterative spatial self-join. Obvious non-scientific use cases for the approach are video games. Similar to the problem of scientific simulations, in multi-player games a cut-off radius (region of visibility) is defined for all characters that are changing their location at discrete intervals of time.

Furthermore, the assumption that the number and the shape of objects should remain constant during the simulation does not limit applicability as no part of the THERMAL-JOIN algorithm relies on this assumption.

6.3 Limitations

THERMAL-JOIN is designed to address the challenges of joining highly selective datasets that change unpredictably during the simulation. This means for cases where such extreme access pattern are not observed, simpler solutions can be used. For example, if the join selectivity is very low a straightforward approach may be to use an iterative plane-sweep join. In case the objects are changed over time predictably, trajectory based techniques may be more suitable.

The design choices for THERMAL-JOIN prioritize runtime performance and scalability. In terms of memory footprint, however, spikes are observed due to the iterative tuning. This can be improved by avoiding a very fine resolution grid that would exceed a memory quota given by the user.

7. CONCLUSIONS

In this paper we present the THERMAL-JOIN approach, a high performance and scalable solution for executing spatial self-joins iteratively in main memory. The algorithm is practical to use, i.e., it does not require tuning elaborate configuration parameters and it is resilient to different workload characteristics as we show in Section 5.3. The approach uses the novel concept of spatial hot spots that improve the performance for workloads with high join selectivity such as scientific simulations. Using real neural workloads we show that the approach achieves speedup of 8 to 12× when compared to the state-of-the-art and remains competitive in terms of memory footprint.

Acknowledgements

This work is supported by the Hasler Foundation (Smart World - Databasing the Brain, No 11031) and the EU Framework Programme (FP7/2007-2013) under grant 604102 (HBP).

8. REFERENCES

[1] V. Akcelik et al. High Resolution Forward and Inverse Earthquake Modeling on Terascale Computers. In *Supercomputing '03*.

[2] A. Arasu, V. Ganti, and R. Kaushik. Efficient Exact Set-Similarity Joins. In *VLDB '06*.

[3] G. Blelloch and G. Narlikar. A Practical Comparison of N-Body Algorithms. In *Parallel Algorithms '97*.

[4] C. Böhm, B. Braunmüller, F. Krebs, and H.-p. Kriegel. Epsilon Grid Order: An Algorithm for the Similarity Join on Massive High-Dimensional Data. *SIGMOD Record*, 30, 2001.

[5] T. Brinkhoff, H.-P. Kriegel, and B. Seeger. Efficient Processing of Spatial Joins Using R-Trees. In *SIGMOD '93*.

[6] S. Chen, C. S. Jensen, and D. Lin. A Benchmark for Evaluating Moving Object Indexes. In *VLDB '08*.

[7] S. Chen, B. C. Ooi, K.-L. Tan, and M. A. Nascimento. ST2B-tree: A Self-tunable Spatio-temporal B+-tree Index for Moving Objects. In *SIGMOD '08*.

[8] J. Dittrich, L. Blunschi, and M. A. Vaz Salles. Indexing moving objects using short-lived throwaway indexes. In *SSTD '09*.

[9] R. Elmasri and S. B. Navathe. *Fundamentals of Database Systems*. Addison Wesley, 3rd edition, 2000.

[10] D. Frenkel and B. Smit. *Understanding Molecular Simulation*, volume 1. Academic Press, 2001.

[11] R. A. Gingold and J. J. Monaghan. Smoothed Particle Hydrodynamics-theory and Application to Non-spherical Stars. *Astrophysical journal*, 181:375–389, 1977.

[12] H. Gupta, B. Chawda, S. Negi, T. A. Faruquie, L. V. Subramaniam, and M. Mohania. Processing Multi-way Spatial Joins on Map-reduce. EDBT '13.

[13] A. Guttman. R-Trees: A Dynamic Index Structure for Spatial Searching. In *SIGMOD '84*.

[14] G. S. Iwerks, H. Samet, and K. P. Smith. Maintenance of K-nn and Spatial Join Queries on Continuously Moving Points. *ACM TODS*, 31(2), 2006.

[15] C. L. Jackins and S. L. Tanimoto. Oct-trees and Their Use in Representing Three-dimensional Objects. *Computer Graphics and Image Processing*, 14(3), 1980.

[16] E. H. Jacox and H. Samet. Spatial Join Techniques. *ACM TODS*, 32(1), 2007.

[17] E. H. Jacox and H. Samet. Metric Space Similarity Joins. *ACM TODS*, 33(2), 2008.

[18] K. Kim, S. K. Cha, and K. Kwon. Optimizing Multidimensional Index Trees for Main Memory Access. In *SIGMOD '01*.

[19] N. Koudas and K. Sevcik. Size Separation Spatial Join. In *SIGMOD '97*.

[20] D. Kwon et al. An Adaptive Hashing Technique for Indexing Moving Objects. *TKDE*, 56(3):287–303, 2006.

[21] Y. Kwon, D. Nunley, J. Gardner, M. Balazinska, B. Howe, and S. Loebman. Scalable Clustering Algorithm for N-Body Simulations in a Shared-Nothing Cluster. In *SSDBM '10*.

[22] S. Leutenegger et al. STR: a Simple and Efficient Algorithm for R-Tree Packing. In *ICDE '97*.

[23] W. Lu, Y. Shen, S. Chen, and B. C. Ooi. Efficient Processing of K Nearest Neighbor Joins Using MapReduce. In *VLDB '12*.

[24] H. Markram et al. Introducing the Human Brain Project. In *European Future Technologies '11*.

[25] M. F. Mokbel, T. M. Ghanem, and W. G. Aref. Spatio-temporal Access Methods. *IEEE Data Engineering Bulletin*, 26:40–49, 2003.

[26] S. Nobari, F. Tauheed, T. Heinis, P. Karras, S. Bressan, and A. Ailamaki. TOUCH: In-Memory Spatial Join by Hierarchical Data-Oriented Partitioning. In *SIGMOD '13*.

[27] J. M. Patel and D. J. DeWitt. Partition Based Spatial-Merge Join. In *SIGMOD '96*.

[28] J. M. Patel et al. STRIPES: an Efficient Index for Predicted Trajectories. In *SIGMOD '04*.

[29] F. Preparata and M. Shamos. *Computational Geometry: An Introduction*. Springer, 1993.

[30] H. Samet, J. Sankara, and M. Auerbach. Indexing Methods for Moving Object Databases: Games and Other Applications. In *SIGMOD '13*.

[31] A. D. Sarma, Y. He, and S. Chaudhuri. ClusterJoin: A Similarity Joins Framework using Map-Reduce. In *VLDB '14*.

[32] Y. Silva, S. Pearson, and J. Cheney. Database Similarity Join for Metric Spaces. In *Similarity Search and Applications*. 2013.

[33] C. Silvestri et al. GPU-Based Computing of Repeated Range Queries over Moving Objects. In *International Conference on Parallel, Distributed and Network-Based Processing*, 2014.

[34] B. Sowell, M. V. Salles, T. Cao, A. Demers, and J. Gehrke. An Experimental Analysis of Iterated Spatial Joins in Main Memory. In *VLDB '14*.

[35] Y. Tao, D. Papadias, and J. Sun. The TPR*-tree: an Optimized Spatio-temporal Access Method for Predictive Queries. In *VLDB '03*.

[36] F. Tauheed, T. Heinis, F. Schürmann, H. Markram, and A. Ailamaki. OCTOPUS: Efficient Query Execution on Dynamic Mesh Datasets. In *ICDE '14*.

[37] D. Šidlauskas and C. S. Jensen. Spatial Joins in Main Memory: Implementation Matters! In *VLDB '15*.

[38] D. Šidlauskas, S. Šaltenis, and C. S. Jensen. Processing of Extreme Moving-object Update and Query Workloads in Main Memory. *VLDB '14*.

Indexing Metric Uncertain Data for Range Queries

Lu Chen†, Yunjun Gao†,*, Xinhan Li†, Christian S. Jensen‡, Gang Chen†, Baihua Zheng§

†College of Computer Science, Zhejiang University, Hangzhou, China
*Innovation Joint Research Center for Cyber-Physical-Society System, Zhejiang University, China
‡Department of Computer Science, Aalborg University, Aalborg, Denmark
§School of Information Systems, Singapore Management University, Singapore

†{luchen, gaoyj, xhli, cg}@zju.edu.cn ‡csj@cs.aau.dk §bhzheng@smu.edu.sg

ABSTRACT

Range queries in metric spaces have applications in many areas such as multimedia retrieval, computational biology, and location-based services, where *metric uncertain data* exists in different forms, resulting from equipment limitations, high-throughput sequencing technologies, privacy preservation, or others. In this paper, we represent metric uncertain data by using an object-level model and a bi-level model, respectively. Two novel indexes, the *uncertain pivot B^+-tree* (UPB-tree) and the *uncertain pivot B^+-forest* (UPB-forest), are proposed accordingly in order to support probabilistic range queries w.r.t. a wide range of uncertain data types and similarity metrics. Both index structures use a *small* set of *effective* pivots chosen based on a newly defined criterion, and employ the B^+-tree(s) as the underlying index. By design, they are easy to be integrated into any existing DBMS. In addition, we present efficient metric probabilistic range query algorithms, which utilize the validation and pruning techniques based on our derived probability lower and upper bounds. Extensive experiments with both real and synthetic data sets demonstrate that, compared against existing state-of-the-art indexes for metric uncertain data, the UPB-tree and UPB-forest incur much *lower* construction costs, consume *smaller* storage spaces, and can support *more efficient* metric probabilistic range queries.

Categories and Subject Descriptors

H.2 [**Information Systems**]: Database Management

Keywords

Range query; Uncertain data; Metric space; Index structure

1. INTRODUCTION

Given a query object q and a distance threshold R, a range query returns the objects that are located in the circle centered at q and with radius R. This operation is common in many areas of computer science, such as multimedia retrieval, computational biology, location based services, to name but a few. Therein, *uncertainty* arises in different forms, resulting from the limitations of equipment and measurements, high-throughput sequencing technologies, privacy preservation, and so forth, which makes range queries inaccurate. Motivated by this, in this paper, we study probabilistic range queries over uncertain data, with two representative examples given as follows.

Application 1 (*Multimedia Retrieval*). In an image retrieval system, the similarity between images can be measured by the L_p-*norm* distance, cosine similarity, or other distance metrics between feature vectors. Since the limitations of extraction methods and accuracy measurements may result in uncertainty [8], probabilistic range queries can help to find similar figures for a specified image.

Application 2 (*Computational Biology*). In a protein-protein interaction network, the distance between two proteins, which represents how well proteins interact with each other, can be measured by the shortest path, maximum flow, or other measures. However, the protein data is uncertain due to a number of factors in the high-throughput sequencing techniques [20]. Therefore, probabilistic range queries can help to find the proteins that are more likely to interact with a given query protein.

Considering a wide range of data types in the aforementioned application scenarios, e.g., images, strings, and protein sequences, a generic model is desirable that is capable of accommodating not just a single type, but a wide spectrum. In addition, distance metrics for comparing the similarity between objects, such as edit distance used for strings and Jaccard coefficient used for sets, are not restricted to the Euclidean distance (i.e., L_2-norm) any more. To accommodate a wide range of similarity notions, we investigate *probabilistic range queries on metric uncertain data*, where *no* detailed representations of uncertain objects are required and any similarity notion satisfying the *triangle inequality* can be used.

Although there are many previous efforts on indexing uncertain data to accelerate probabilistic range queries [27, 40, 42, 46, 47], they mainly aim at the Euclidean space or, more generally, at the vector space. To be more specific, existing work models uncertain data as a multi-dimensional uncertain region with an associated probabilistic density function (PDF), and performs probabilistic range queries by exploiting various geometric properties (such as minimum bounding box (MBB) [40] and grid technique [47]). Unfortunately, these uncertain models and geometric properties are restricted to the vector space, rendering them inapplicable to more complex data (e.g., DNA sequences, sets) that cannot be fit into Euclidean models. Hence, Angiulli and Fassetti [4] first study the indexing on metric uncertain data, and present the UP-Index. However, this index can be improved in several ways because (i) it processes metric uncertain data using the vector space uncertain model, which limits its applicability to complex metric uncertain data such as uncertain sets and uncertain graphs; (ii) it stores *unnecessary* information which leads to *redundancy*; (iii) it has to scan the *entire* index, for any range query, in order to prune away objects using the probability upper bounds; and (iv) it cannot validate objects due to *no probability lower bounds*. These observations suggest that there is still room for improvement on indexing metric uncertain data.

SIGMOD'15, May 31–June 4, 2015, Melbourne, Victoria, Australia.

http://dx.doi.org/10.1145/2723372.2723728.

In order to design efficient external-memory indexes on metric uncertain data, three challenging issues have to be addressed. First, *how shall we model metric uncertain data instead of using the vector space uncertain model?* In this paper, we propose two metric uncertain data models to represent the uncertainty in metric spaces. Second, *how can we support efficient probabilistic range queries?* Here, efficiency is measured by both the number of distance computations (i.e., CPU cost) and the number of page accesses (i.e., I/O cost). We tackle this by identifying a small set of effective pivots to map uncertain objects from the metric space to the vector space, based on which the probability lower and upper bounds are derived to validate and prune uncertain objects. Moreover, MBBs and a space-filling curve (e.g., Hilbert curve) are utilized to cluster uncertain data to further reduce I/O cost. Third, *how do we achieve low cost of index storage, construction, and manipulation?* To save storage cost, our solution only stores necessary information and makes use of a space-filling curve dimensionality reduction. To support efficient index construction and manipulation, we use the B^+-tree(s) as the underlying index.

The resulting proposals are so-called *uncertain pivot B^+-tree* (UPB-tree) and *uncertain pivot B^+-forest* (UPB-forest) based on two proposed metric uncertain data models. They do not depend on the detailed representations of objects, and can support all the distance metrics that satisfy the triangle inequality. To sum up, the key contributions of this paper are as follows:

- We develop two metric uncertain data models and their corresponding disk-based indexing structures, i.e., the UPB-tree and the UPB-forest, which map uncertain objects from a metric space to a vector space using a set of pivots, utilize a space-filling curve for dimensionality reduction, and employ the B^+-tree(s) as the underlying index.
- We propose efficient algorithms for metric probabilistic range queries that use the validation and pruning techniques based on new lower and upper bounds of the probabilities, and we explore an interesting MPRQ variant, i.e., M*k*PRQ.
- We present an efficient pivot selection algorithm based on a novel criterion to choose a small set of effective pivots.
- We conduct extensive experiments using both real and synthetic data sets to demonstrate that, the UPB-tree and the UPB-forest are several orders of magnitude better than the state-of-the-art competitors on metric uncertain data, owing to their much smaller construction and storage costs, and more efficient and scalable query processing power.

The rest of this paper is organized as follows. Section 2 reviews related work. Section 3 formalizes the problem. Section 4 and Section 5 elaborate the indexing structures and their corresponding metric probabilistic range query algorithms. Section 6 presents the pivot selection algorithm. Experimental results and our findings are reported in Section 7. Finally, Section 8 concludes the paper with some directions for future work.

2. Related Work

In this section, we review briefly the related work on indexing techniques for probabilistic range queries and metric range queries.

2.1 Probabilistic Range Queries

Given a set U of uncertain data, a range region RR, and a probabilistic threshold θ, a probabilistic range query in a vector space returns uncertain data u ($\in U$) with $Pr(u \in RR) \geq \theta$. Cheng et al. [13] first address probabilistic range queries on one-dimensional uncertain data. Then, R-Tree based approaches [29, 30, 40] are proposed, in which the MBB of an object serves as the summary of its PDF. Tao et al. [42] introduces a U-tree, as the PDF summary of an object is a finite set of probabilistically constrained regions. Next, range queries with constraints where PDFs of uncertain data follow Gaussian or Uniform distributions are studied [8, 12, 18]. Aggarwal and Yu [3] show how to construct an effective index structure in order to handle uncertain range queries in high dimensionality. Assuming that PDFs of objects are histograms, Agarwal et al. [2] provide a thorough theoretical analysis of various indexing schemes with linear or near-linear space and logarithmic query time. Recently, Zhang et al. [46] present the UI-tree, considering every uncertain object is a set of groups that are disjointed partitions of its PDF. Kimura et al. [27] propose a primary indexing technique named UPI to speed up query processing on uncertain data by clustering heap files. More recently, Zhang et al. [47] develop a U-Quardtree, which employs a Quardtree to organize multi-dimensional uncertain objects. Zhu et al. [48] propose MRST and R-MRST to capture approximately the PDF of an uncertain object, with strong pruning power and lower space cost. The indexing techniques over one-dimensional uncertain data are explored [15, 28], which divide the interval of an uncertain object into several disjoint sub-intervals. As pointed out in Section 1, all the above approaches are *unsuitable* for range queries on metric uncertain data for two reasons. First, uncertain models used are restricted to the vector space, rendering them inapplicable to complex data (e.g., sets, DNA sequences, etc.). Second, to accelerate query processing, they utilize some *geometric properties* (e.g., MBB [29, 30, 40], grid [47]) that are *unavailable* in the metric space.

To the best of our knowledge, only Angiulli and Fassetti [4] study the indexing of metric uncertain data, and propose a pivot-based index UP-Index. The UP-Index stores pre-computed histograms of the probability distribution for every uncertain object w.r.t. a set of pivots, and it prunes uncertain objects during search using the upper bound of the probability derived by reverse triangle inequality. Although the UP-Index supports flexible distance metrics satisfying the triangle inequality, it is still based on the vector space uncertain model, i.e., it has to transform non-vector uncertain data into vectors before building the index. Since metric uncertain data (e.g., uncertain sets, uncertain graphs, etc.) cannot be efficiently transformed into multi-dimensional vectors, the UP-Index has restricted applicability. Furthermore, as demonstrated in Section 7, the performance of the UP-Index is not competitive. This is because: (i) it needs to store the pre-computed histograms w.r.t. the whole distance range, resulting in *larger* storage cost; (ii) as pointed out in [47], it has to scan the *whole* index, for any probabilistic range query, to prune uncertain objects using the probability upper bounds without any early termination condition or batch pruning technique; and (iii) it cannot validate objects because it has *no probability lower bounds*.

In addition, some efforts have been devoted to probabilistic range queries [16, 24], similarity queries [19], *k* nearest neighbor (*k*NN) search [17, 37], similarity joins [23, 31], and reverse *k*NN (R*k*NN) retrieval [7] for specific metric uncertain data (e.g., sets, data series, graphs, etc.). Nevertheless, all these works utilize uncertain models and design special algorithms for the particularly metric uncertain data they aim at. Thus, they are not applicable to support probabilistic range queries over metric uncertain data efficiently. Further, *k*NN and R*k*NN queries on uncertain data try to reduce the cost for computing the probability of an uncertain object being a real answer object (e.g., distance partitioning [17], probabilistic pruning [7]). Since their probability computation is substantially different from that of range retrieval, the techniques developed cannot also be extended to solve our problem.

Table 1. Symbols and description

Notation	Description
U or u	a set of uncertain objects or an uncertain object
u_{ij}	an instance object of an uncertain object u_i
$\mathcal{G}_{p,i}$	the *PDF* of the distance between u_i and a pivot p
$MPRQ(q, R, \theta)$	a metric probabilistic range query w.r.t. query object q, search radius R, probability threshold θ
$MkPRQ(q, R, \theta)$	the top-k $MPRQ(q, R, \theta)$
P	a set of pivots p_t
$d()$	the distance function in a metric space
$D()$	the L_∞-norm metric in a mapped vector space
d^+	the maximum distance in a metric space
n or s	the number of slots or the intervals of each slot
R_q	a range search region in the metric space
$\phi_{pt}(R_q)$ or $\phi(R_q)$	R_q in the mapped vector space using p_t ($\in P$) or P
$\phi(q)$ or $\phi(u)$	q or u in the mapped vector space
$\pi(u, R_q)$	the probability of u contained in R_q
$l\pi(u, R_q)$ or $u\pi(u, R_q)$	the lower bound or the upper bound of $\pi(u, R_q)$
LB_k or UB_k	the k-th maximum $l\pi(u, R_q)$ or $u\pi(u, R_q)$ ($u \in U$)

2.2 Metric Range Queries

Given an object set O, a query object q, and a search radius R in a metric space, a metric range query retrieves the objects in O with their distances to q bounded by R. To accelerate metric range queries, a large number of metric indexing structures are proposed, which can be generally classified into two categories, namely, compact partitioning methods [14, 26] and pivot-based methods [25, 36, 41, 44]. For two objects q and o, the distance $d(q, o)$ cannot be smaller than $|d(q, p) - d(o, p)|$ for any pivot p, due to the triangle inequality. Hence, it may be possible to prune away an object o as a match for q using the lower bound value $|d(q, p) - d(o, p)|$ instead of calculating $d(q, o)$. This capability makes pivot-based approaches outperform compact partitioning methods in terms of the number of distance computations, one of key performance criteria in metric spaces. In this paper, we also adopt the pivot techniques, and therefore, we focus mostly on pivot-based methods.

Pivot-based methods store pre-computed distances from every object in the database to a set of pivots, and then utilize these distances and the triangle inequality to prune objects during search. AESA [44] and its variants LAESA [34], EP [38], and Clustered Pivot-table [35] use a pivot table to preserve pre-computed distances. BKT [10] and FQT [5] are tree structures designed for discrete distance functions, while VPT [45] and MVPT [9] are designed for continuous distance functions. The Omni-family [25] employs existing structures (e.g., the R-tree) to index pre-computed distances. Recently, PM-tree [41] uses the cut-regions defined by pivots to boost the efficiency of similarity queries on the M-tree [14]. In particular, the concept of cut-regions could be used to improve the performance of metric indexes with simple ball-regions [32]. M-Index [36] compacts the objects with pre-computed distances to their closest pivots.

In addition, other spatial queries (e.g., kNN queries [6, 14, 36], similarity joins [22, 39], and RkNN retrieval [1, 43]) in metric spaces are also well-studied in the literature.

None of the aforementioned works consider uncertainty, and therefore, they cannot be applied to tackle the problem we study in this paper.

3. Problem Statement

In this section, we review properties of the metric space, present metric uncertain data models, and formulate the probabilistic

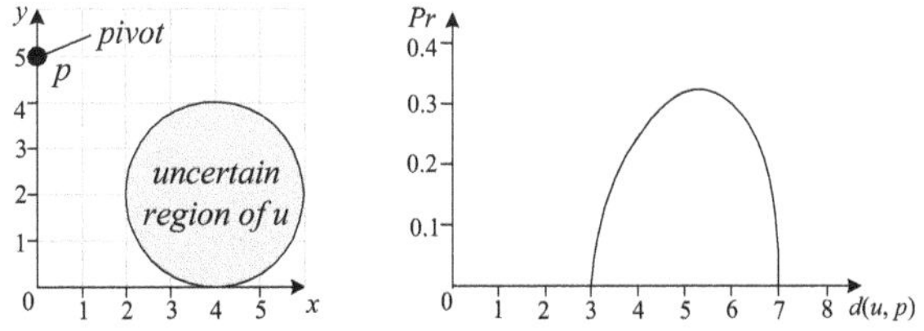

(a) Uncertain object u (b) Continuous PDF of $d(u, p)$

Figure 1: Example of the bi-level model

range query in the metric space. Table 1 summarizes the symbols frequently used throughout the paper.

3.1 Metric Space

A metric space is denoted by a tuple (M, d), in which M is an object domain and d is a distance function to measure "similarity" between objects in M. In particular, the distance function d has four properties: (1) *symmetry*: $d(q, o) = d(o, q)$; (2) *non-negativity*: $d(q, o) \geq 0$; (3) *identity*: $d(q, o) = 0$ iff $q = o$; and (4) *triangle inequality*: $d(q, o) \leq d(q, p) + d(p, o)$.

3.2 Metric Uncertain Data Models

Usually, an uncertain object can be represented in two ways: (1) using all possible instances with each assigned a probability, and (2) using a probability density function (PDF). Consequently, we develop two metric uncertain data models as follows.

Object-level model. Every uncertain object u_i can be modeled by all the multiple possible instances and their corresponding non-negative probabilities $\{\langle u_{i1}, Pr(u_{i1})\rangle, \langle u_{i2}, Pr(u_{i2})\rangle, \ldots, \langle u_{im}, Pr(u_{im})\rangle\}$ with $\sum_{j=1}^{m} Pr(u_{ij}) = 1$, in which $Pr(u_{ij})$ denotes the non-negative probability of u_i being u_{ij}.

For example, an uncertain English word u can be modeled as {⟨ "defoliation", 0.2⟩, ⟨"defoliated", 0.1⟩, ⟨"defoliating", 0.4⟩, ⟨ "defoliates", 0.3⟩}, using the object-level model.

Bi-level model. Each uncertain object u_i can utilize any other uncertainty model as the underlying model, based on which it can be further represented by using the PDF $\mathcal{G}_{p,i}$ of its distance to a pivot p, satisfying that $\int_0^{d^+} \mathcal{G}_{p,i}(x)dx = 1$ or $\sum_0^{d^+} \mathcal{G}_{p,i}(x) = 1$ for *continuous* or *discrete* PDFs, respectively. Here, x is the distance $d(u_i, p)$ from u_i to p, and d^+ is the maximum distance of $d(u_i, p)$.

To support query processing for a wide range of uncertain data types, the bi-level model can take any specific uncertain model (e.g., vector space uncertain model [13, 18, 47], p-set model [19] for uncertain set) as its underlying model, based on which an upper model is built to represent its distance uncertainty. Consider the example of the bi-level model built on the vector space uncertain model shown in Figure 1. The uncertain object u locates uniformly within the uncertain region, as illustrated in Figure 1(a), and the PDF of the distance $d(u, p)$ is shown in Figure 1(b).

For the bi-level model, although a PDF can be both discrete and continuous, we concentrate on the continuous case for simplicity. Notice that, all the proposed techniques can be adapted easily to work with discrete PDFs. However, for the object-level model, we aim at the discrete case according to its definition.

3.3 Metric Probabilistic Range Queries

Given a query object q and a search radius R in a metric space, a *metric range query* finds the objects with their distances to q within R, i.e., finding the objects located into a circular search

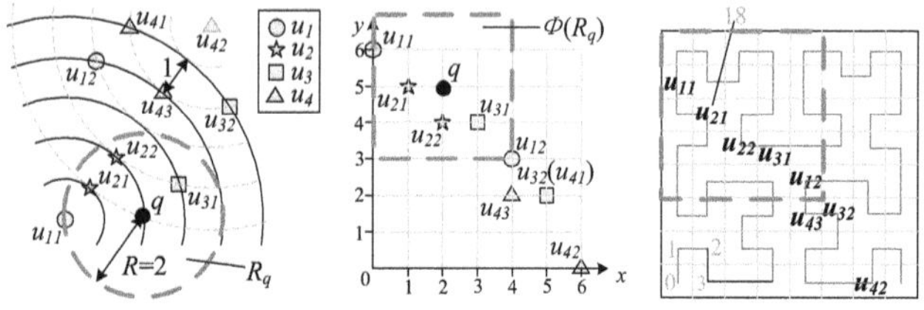

(a) Metric space (b) Vector space (c) Hilbert curve

Figure 2: Example of the MPRQ using UPB-tree

region R_q. Taking into account uncertainty, let $\pi(u, R_q)$ be the probability of a metric uncertain object u contained in R_q, i.e., $\pi(u, R_q) = Pr(d(q, u) \leq R)$, we formally define the probabilistic range query on metric uncertain data below.

DEFINITION 1 (Metric Probabilistic RANGE QUERY). *Given a set U of uncertain objects, a query object q, a search radius R, and a probabilistic threshold* θ $(0 < \theta \leq 1)$ *in a metric space, a* metric probabilistic range query (MPRQ) *is to find the uncertain objects in U whose probabilities of being contained in* R_q *are no smaller than* θ, *i.e.,* $MPRQ(q, R, \theta) = \{u \mid u \in U \wedge \pi(u, R_q) \geq \theta\}$.

In the sequel, we propose two novel indexes in Sections 4 and 5 based on the object-level and bi-level models respectively, and show how they can be employed to speed up MPRQ processing.

4. The UPB-tree

In this section, we propose a novel index structure, i.e., *UPB-tree*, to index uncertain objects based on the object-level model, and then present corresponding MPRQ algorithm and its cost analysis. In the rest of the section, we employ a running example to facilitate the understanding of the UPB-tree and the MPRQ processing. Specifically, consider an uncertain object set $U = \{u_1, u_2, u_3, u_4\}$ illustrated in Figure 2(a), with $u_1 = \{(u_{11}, 0.6), (u_{12}, 0.4)\}$, $u_2 = \{(u_{21}, 0.5), (u_{22}, 0.5)\}$, $u_3 = \{(u_{31}, 0.4), (u_{32}, 0.6)\}$, $u_4 = \{(u_{41}, 0.2), (u_{42}, 0.3), (u_{43}, 0.5)\}$. The corresponding UPB-tree is shown in Figure 3 using a pivot set $P = \{u_{11}, u_{42}\}$. Assume that the L_2-*norm* is used as the similarity measurement, the result of a $MPRQ(q, 2, 0.5)$ is uncertain objects u_1 and u_2.

4.1 UPB-tree Structure

The UPB-tree construction is based on a two-stage mapping. In the first stage, we map all instances of metric uncertain objects into the data points in a vector space, using selected pivots. We prefer the vector space than the metric space when designing search approaches, because it has nice geometric and coordinate information that is not available in the metric space. In the second stage, we utilize the *space-filling curve* (SFC) to map the data points in vector space into the integers in a one-dimensional space, since SFC preserves spatial proximity when performing the dimensionality reduction. Finally, we utilize a B$^+$-tree with MBB information to index metric uncertain objects.

Pivot mapping. Given a pivot set $P = \{p_1, p_2, \ldots, p_{|P|}\}$, a metric space (M, d) can be mapped into a vector space $(R^{|P|}, L_\infty)$. Specifically, for any instance object u_{ij} in the metric space, it can be represented as a point $\phi(u_{ij}) = \langle d(u_{ij}, p_1), d(u_{ij}, p_2), \ldots, d(u_{ij}, p_{|P|})\rangle$ in the vector space. Consider, for instance, Figure 2, in which $U = \{u_1, u_2, u_3, u_4\}$. If $P = \{u_{11}, u_{42}\}$, U can be mapped to a two-dimensional vector space as depicted in Figure 2(b), where x-axis denotes $d(u_{ij}, u_{11})$ and y-axis represents $d(u_{ij}, u_{42})$.

As mentioned in Section 2.2, given a pivot set P, $d(u_{ij}, u_{ij}') \geq \max\{|d(u_{ij}, p) - d(u_{ij}', p)| \mid p \in P\} = D(\phi(u_{ij}), \phi(u_{ij}'))$ according to

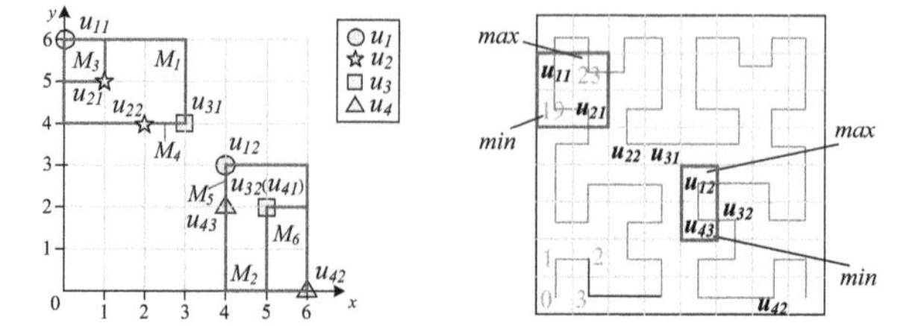

(a) MBBs of UPB-tree (b) MBB representation

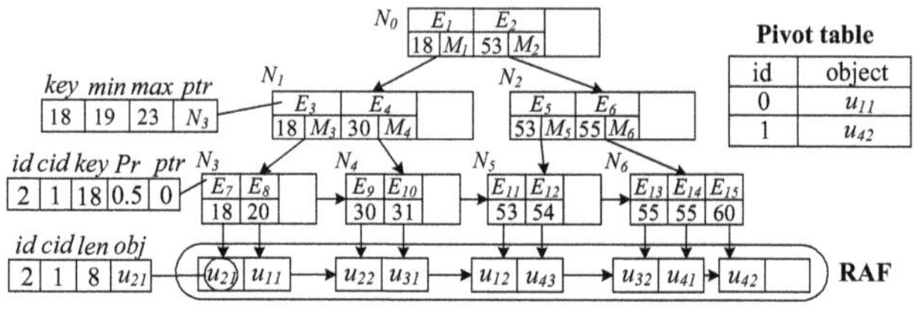

(c) The UPB-tree

Figure 3: Example of the UPB-tree for the dataset in Figure 2

the triangle inequality, in which $D(\,)$ is a L_∞-norm metric. Clearly, the distance in the mapped vector space is the *lower bound* of that in the original metric space. Consider the example shown in Figure 2 again, $d(u_{43}, u_{32}) > D(\phi(u_{43}), \phi(u_{32})) = 1$.

Space-filling curve mapping. Given a vector $\phi(u_{ij})$ after the pivot mapping, SFC can map $\phi(u_{ij})$ to an integer $SFC(\phi(u_{ij}))$. Consider the SFC mapping example illustrated in Figure 2(c), where $SFC(\phi(u_{21})) = 18$. Although we employ the Hilbert curve in this paper, any SFC is applicable to the UPB-tree.

A UPB-tree used to index a metric uncertain object set based on the object-level model contains three parts, i.e., a pivot table, a *random access file* (RAF), and a B$^+$-tree. Figure 3 depicts a UPB-tree example to index $U = \{u_1, u_2, u_3, u_4\}$. The pivot table stores selected pivots (e.g., u_{11} and u_{42} in this case) to map a metric space into a vector space. The RAF is sorted to store instance objects in ascending order of SFC values as they appear in the B$^+$-tree, to enhance the efficiency of managing complex uncertain objects. Each RAF entry records (1) an uncertain object identifier *id*, (2) an instance identifier *cid*, (3) the storage overhead *len* (in bytes) of the instance object, and (4) the real instance object *obj*. As shown in Figure 3(c), the RAF entry associated with the object u_{21} records the uncertain object identifier 2, the instance identifier 1, the storage overhead 8, and the real instance object u_{21}.

A B$^+$-tree is employed to index the SFC values of instance objects. The structure of every node entry varies, dependent on whether it is an entry in a leaf node or an entry in a non-leaf node. Each leaf entry in the leaf node (e.g., N_3, N_4, N_5, and N_6) of the B$^+$-tree records (1) an uncertain object identifier *id*, (2) an instance identifier *cid*, (3) a SFC value *key*, (4) a probability *Pr*, and (5) the pointer *ptr* to the real instance object, which is the address of the instance object kept in the RAF. As an example depicted in Figure 3(c), the leaf entry E_7 associated with u_{21} records the uncertain object identifier 2, the instance identifier 1, the Hilbert value 18, the probability 0.5, and the storage address 0 of u_{21} in RAF. Every non-leaf entry in the root or intermediate node (e.g., N_0, N_1, and N_2) of the B$^+$-tree records (1) the minimum SFC value *key* in its subtree, (2) the pointer *ptr* to the root node of its subtree, and (3) the SFC values *min* and *max* for $\langle a_1, a_2, \ldots, a_{|P|}\rangle$ and $\langle b_1, b_2, \ldots, b_{|P|}\rangle$, to represent the MBB M_i (= $\{[a_t, b_t] \mid t \in [1, |P|]\}$) of the root node N_i of its subtree. For instance, the non-leaf entry E_3 uses *min* (= 19) and *max* (= 23) to denote the M_3 of N_3.

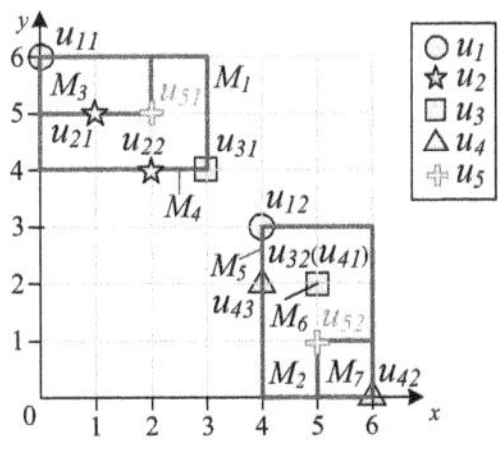

(a) MBBs of UPB-tree

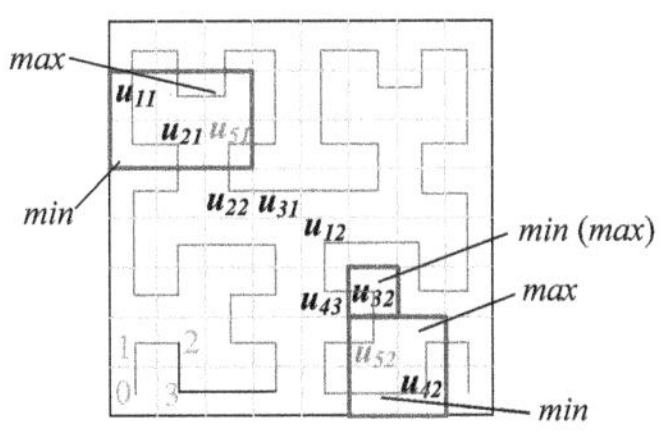

(b) MBB representation

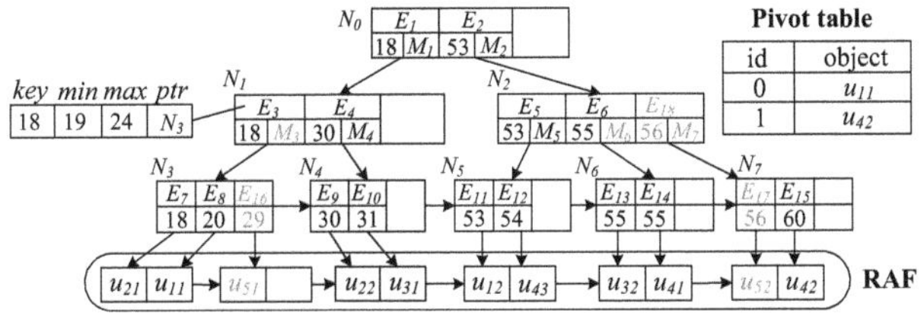

(c) The UPB-tree after inserting u_5 in Figure 3

Figure 4: Example of the insertion operation on UPB-tree

Insertion/Deletion operation. For a new uncertain object u_i to be inserted or deleted, we insert or delete all its instance objects u_{ij}. For every u_{ij}, we first compute $\phi(u_{ij})$ using P and then $SFC(\phi(u_{ij}))$. Thereafter, leaf entry e (= $\langle i, j, SFC(\phi(u_{ij})), pr(u_{ij}), ptr(u_{ij})\rangle$) and u_{ij} are inserted into or deleted from the B^+-tree and the RAF, respectively. Finally, the MBBs for e's ancestor entries are updated accordingly if necessary. Note that, the insertion or deletion may lead to page splits or merges of B^+-tree or/and the RAF. When that happens, the corresponding MBBs are updated if necessary. Figure 4 depicts the UPB-tree after inserting u_5 in Figure 3.

Update operation. For an uncertain object u_i to be updated, if only $pr(u_{ij})$ of its uncertain instance objects u_{ij} needs to be updated, we traverse B^+-tree to find out the corresponding leaf entries e and update $e.pr$; otherwise, we remove all the original uncertain instance objects u_{ij} and then insert the new ones.

Note that, although some existing index structures (e.g., R-tree) can also be used to index the mapped vector space, UPB-tree uses a B^+-tree to index the SFC values of instance objects after the pivot mapping. This is attractive because (i) the use of an SFC can cluster objects into compact regions, reducing the amount of storage needed for pre-computed distances; and (ii) update operations on the UPB-tree are simple and effective as they rely on the manipulation of the B^+-tree.

4.2 UPB-tree based MPRQ Algorithm

Given a set U of uncertain objects, MPRQ finds the uncertain objects u_i in U with their probabilities of being contained in R_q no smaller than θ, i.e., $\pi(u_i, R_q) \geq \theta$. Since an uncertain object u_i can be represented by all instance objects u_{ij} with associated non-negative probabilities based on the object-level model, $\pi(u_i, R_q)$ can be calculated by summarizing all the probabilities of its instance objects u_{ij} ($\in R_q$). Thus, to derive $\pi(u_i, R_q)$ of an uncertain object u_i, a naive solution is checking every instance objects u_{ij} to determine whether u_{ij} is contained in R_q. However, as stated in Lemma 1 below, we only need to verify the instance objects u_{ij} with $\phi(u_{ij}) \in \phi(R_q)$, in which $\phi(R_q)$ denotes the *mapped search region* in the vector space using a pivot set P. For example, the dashed line circle in Figure 2(a) represents R_q, and the dashed line rectangle in Figure 2(b) denotes $\phi(R_q)$ using $P = \{u_{11}, u_{42}\}$.

LEMMA 1. *Given a pivot set P, if an instance object u_{ij} is enclosed in R_q, then $\phi(u_{ij})$ is certainly contained in the mapped range region $\phi(R_q)$, where $\phi(R_q) = \{\langle x_1, x_2, \ldots, x_{|P|}\rangle \mid 1 \leq t \leq |P| \wedge x_t \geq 0 \wedge x_t \in [d(q, p_t) - R, d(q, p_t) + R]\}$.*

PROOF. Please refer to Appendix A. □

Based on Lemma 1, if the MBB of a node N does not overlap $\phi(R_q)$, we can prune N because the instance objects u_{ij} contained in N cannot contribute to the value of $\pi(u_i, R_q)$. Here, MBB can be obtained easily by using SFC values *min* and *max* stored in the UPB-tree. Consider the MPRQ example depicted in Figure 2 and Figure 3, N_6 can be discarded due to $M_6 \cap \phi(R_q) = \varnothing$.

When computing $\pi(u_i, R_q)$, Lemma 1 is used to avoid distance computations for the instance objects u_{ij} having $\phi(u_{ij}) \notin \phi(R_q)$. Nonetheless, we still have to verify the instance objects u_{ij} with $\phi(u_{ij})$ enclosed in $\phi(R_q)$. Therefore, we develop Lemma 2 to further avoid unnecessary distance computations.

LEMMA 2. *Given a pivot set P, for an instance object u_{ij}, if there exists a pivot p_t ($\in P$) satisfying $d(u_{ij}, p_t) \leq R - d(q, p_t)$, then u_{ij} is certainly included in R_q.*

PROOF. Please refer to Appendix B. □

Consider the MPRQ example shown in Figure 2. Suppose $R = 3$, then for an object u_{21}, there exists a pivot u_{11} satisfying $d(u_{21}, u_{11}) = R - d(q, u_{11}) = 3 - 2 = 1$. Hence, u_{21} is certainly contained in R_q without incurring any further distance computation of $d(q, u_{21})$.

To speed up MPRQ processing, we can also validate or prune away uncertain objects u_i using the upper and lower bounds of $\pi(u_i, R_q)$ without any further verification for computing $\pi(u_i, R_q)$, as stated in Theorem 1 below.

THEOREM 1. *Given a MPRQ(q, R, θ), let $u\pi(u_i, R_q)$ and $l\pi(u_i, R_q)$ be the upper bound and lower bound of $\pi(u_i, R_q)$ respectively, then (1) u_i can be safely pruned if $u\pi(u_i, R_q) < \theta$, and (2) u_i can be validated if $l\pi(u_i, R_q) \geq \theta$.*

The proof of Theorem 1 is straightforward and thus omitted. To use Theorem 1, we have to derive *tight* upper bound $u\pi(u_i, R_q)$ and lower bound $l\pi(u_i, R_q)$. According to Lemma 1, by summarizing all the probabilities of instances u_{ij} of an uncertain object u_i with $\phi(u_{ij}) \in \phi(R_q)$, we can get the upper bound of $\pi(u_i, R_q)$ as follows.

LEMMA 3. *Given a MPRQ(q, R, θ) and a pivot set P, $u\pi(u_i, R_q) = \sum_{\phi(u_{ij}) \in \phi(R_q)} Pr(u_{ij})$.*

PROOF. Please refer to Appendix C. □

Consider the *MPRQ*(q, 2, 0.5) example depicted in Figure 2. We have $u\pi(u_1, R_q) = Pr(u_{11}) + Pr(u_{12}) = 1$ and $u\pi(u_3, R_q) = Pr(u_{31}) = 0.4$, since $\phi(u_{11})$, $\phi(u_{12})$, and $\phi(u_{31})$ are inside $\phi(R_q)$. Hence, u_3 can be pruned by Theorem 1 due to $u\pi(u_3, R_q) < \theta$. It is worth noting that, for u_i that cannot be filtered out, when computing accurate $\pi(u_i, R_q)$ during the verification phase, we can further tighten $u\pi(u_i, R_q)$ to achieve stronger pruning power. Specifically, if $\phi(u_{ik}) \in \phi(R_q)$ but $d(q, u_{ik}) > R$, then $u\pi(u_i, R_q)$ can be tightened to $\sum_{\phi(u_{ij}) \in \phi(R_q)} Pr(u_{ij}) - Pr(u_{ik})$. As an example, in Figure 2, $u\pi(u_1, R_q)$ can be reduced to 0.6 as $\phi(u_{12}) \in \phi(R_q)$ but $d(q, u_{12}) > 2$.

Next, we derive the lower bound of $\pi(u_i, R_q)$ using Lemma 2, by accumulating all the probabilities of the instance objects stratifying the condition of Lemma 2.

LEMMA 4. *Given a MPRQ(q, R, θ) and a pivot set P, $l\pi(u_i, R_q) = \sum_{\exists p_t \in P \text{ st. } d(u_{ij}, p_t) \leq R - d(q, p_t)} Pr(u_{ij})$.*

PROOF. Please refer to Appendix D. □

Algorithm 1 UPB-tree based MPRQ Algorithm (UtMA)

Input: q, R, θ, an uncertain object set U indexed by a UPB-tree
Output: the result set S_r of a $MPRQ(q, R, \theta)$
/* S_c: a set of candidate uncertain objects; IS_c: a candidate instance set. */
1: compute $\phi(q)$ and $\phi(R_q)$ using a pivot table P // $\phi(q) = \langle d(q, p_i) \mid p_i \in P\rangle$
2: push the root node of B^+-tree into a heap H
3: **while** $H \neq \emptyset$ **do**
4: de-heap the top node N from H
5: **if** N is non-leaf node **then**
6: **for** each entry e in N **do**
7: **if** $MBB(e.ptr) \cap \phi(R_q) \neq \emptyset$ **then**
8: push $e.ptr$ into H
9: **else** // N is leaf node
10: **if** $MBB(N) \subseteq \phi(R_q)$ **then**
11: **for** each entry e in N **do**
12: **if** $e.id \notin S_c$ **then** insert $e.id$ into S_c
13: update $u\pi(e.id, R_q)$ using Lemma 3
14: update $l\pi(e.id, R_q)$ or insert $e.ptr$ into IS_c using Lemma 4
15: **else**
16: **for** each entry e in N **do**
17: **if** $\phi(e.ptr) \in \phi(R_q)$ **then** // $\phi(e.ptr)$ is obtained by $e.key$
18-20: these lines are identical to the above lines 12-14
21: **for** each u_i in S_c **do**
22: **if** $l\pi(u_i, R_q) \geq \theta$ **then** // Theorem 1
23: insert u_i into S_r and remove all u_{ik} from IS_c
24: **else if** $u\pi(u_i, R_q) < \theta$ **then** remove all u_{ik} form IS_c // Theorem 1
25: **for** each u_{ij} in IS_c **do**
26: **if** $d(q, u_{ij}) \leq R$ **then** update $l\pi(u_i, R_q)$
27: **else** update $u\pi(u_i, R_q)$
28: **if** $l\pi(u_i, R_q) \geq \theta$ **then**
29: insert u_i into S_r and remove all u_{ik} from IS_c
30: **else if** $u\pi(u_i, R_q) < \theta$ **then** remove all u_{ik} from IS_c
31: **return** S_r

Consider the $MPRQ(q, 2, 0.5)$ example shown in Figure 2 again. We have $l\pi(u_1, R_q) = Pr(u_{11}) = 0.6$, as there exists a pivot u_{11} satisfying $d(u_{11}, u_{11}) \leq 2 - d(q, u_{11})$. Also, we can tighten $l\pi(u_i, R_q)$ during the verification phase. To be more specific, if u_{ik} does not satisfy the condition of Lemma 2 but $u_{ik} \in R_q$, then $l\pi(u_i, R_q)$ can also be tighten to $\sum_{\exists p_t \in P \text{ st. } d(u_{ij},p_t)\leq R-d(q,p_t)} Pr(u_{ij}) + Pr(u_{ik})$.

Based on the aforementioned Theorem 1 and Lemmas 1 to 4, we develop *UPB-tree based MPRQ Algorithm* (UtMA), which follows a filtering-refinement framework. The pseudo-code of UtMA is presented in Algorithm 1, which takes as inputs q, R, θ, and an uncertain object set U indexed by a UPB-tree, and outputs the result set S_r. In the filtering phase, UtMA first computes $\phi(q)$ and $\phi(R_q)$ using a pivot table P (line 1). Then, it traverses B^+-tree in a depth-first manner (lines 2-20), to find candidate uncertain objects (maintained in a set S_c) and the uncertain instance objects needed further verification (preserved in a set IS_c) by Lemma 1 and Lemma 2, and to update $u\pi(u_i, R_q)$ and $l\pi(u_i, R_q)$ for uncertain objects u_i in S_c via Lemma 3 and Lemma 4. Thereafter, UtMA validates or filters out the uncertain objects u_i in S_c by Theorem 1, and removes corresponding uncertain instance objects u_{ik} from IS_c (lines 21-24). After that, during the refinement phase, UtMA first verifies every uncertain instance object u_{ij} in IS_c in order to tighten $u\pi(u_i, R_q)$ and $l\pi(u_i, R_q)$ for the corresponding uncertain object u_i (lines 26-27), and then, it validates or prunes u_i based on Theorem 1, and removes corresponding uncertain instance objects u_{ik} from IS_c (lines 28-30). Finally, S_r is returned (line 31).

EXAMPLE 1. *We illustrate UtMA using the $MPRQ(q, 2, 0.5)$ depicted in Figure 2 with the UPB-tree in Figure 3. In the filtering phase, UtMA computes $\phi(q) = (2, 5)$ using $P = \{u_{11}, u_{42}\}$ and gets $\phi(R_q)$. Then, it traverses B^+-tree to obtain candidate uncertain objects ($S_c = \{u_1, u_2, u_3\}$) and uncertain instance objects ($IS_c = \{u_{21}, u_{22}, u_{31}, u_{12}\}$) by Lemmas 1 and 2. Meanwhile, $l\pi(u_i, R_q)$ and $u\pi(u_i, R_q)$ ($u_i \in S_c$) are updated by Lemmas 3 and 4. After that, the algorithm validates or prunes away the uncertain objects in S_c. Specifically, u_1 is inserted into S_r due to $l\pi(u_1, R_q) = 0.6 > 0.5$, and u_{12} is removed from IS_c; u_3 is filtered out as $u\pi(u_3, R_q) = 0.4 < 0.5$, and u_{31} is removed from IS_c. Thereafter, the algorithm has $S_c = \{u_2\}$, $IS_c = \{u_{21}, u_{22}\}$, and $S_r = \{u_1\}$. Next, in the refinement phase, for u_{21} in IS_c, $l\pi(u_2, R_q)$ is tightened to 0.5 due to $d(q, u_{21}) < 2$, and thus, u_2 is validated. Finally, the result set $S_r = \{u_1, u_2\}$ of the $MPRQ(q, 2, 0.5)$ is returned.* □

4.3 Discussion

During the SFC mapping, if the range of $d(\ )$ in an original metric space is *discrete* integers (e.g., edit distance), SFC can directly map $\phi(u_{ij})$ to an integer $SFC(\phi(u_{ij}))$. On the other hand, if the range of $d(\ )$ (e.g., L_∞-*norm*) in a metric space covers *continuous* real numbers, the whole real numeric range can be portioned into n slots, namely, slot 0, slot 1, …, slot n with corresponding intervals $[0, s)$, $[s, 2\times s)$, …, $[(n-1)\times s, d^+)$, in which $s = d^+/n$. Thus, the entire mapped vector space can be divided into $n^{|P|}$ cells. Then, $\phi(u_{ij})$ can be approximated as $\langle \lfloor d(u_{ij}, p_1)/s \rfloor, \lfloor d(u_{ij}, p_2)/s \rfloor, \ldots, \lfloor d(u_{ij}, p_{|P|})/s \rfloor \rangle$. As to be verified in Section 7, the value of n might affect query efficiency. If n is too small, the collision probability $\mathbf{Pr}(collision) = |U|/n^{|P|}$ that different instance objects share the same vector representation increases, resulting in more distance computations during search. Instead, if n is very large, the transformed vector space becomes too sparse, i.e., the vast majority of the cells must be empty, incurring large search space.

CPU cost. The cost of distance computations is the dominant component of the CPU cost for a search in the metric space, since the distance computation is usually expensive (e.g., edit distance, Jaccard coefficient, etc.). Hence, the CPU cost of UtMA can be estimated based on the number of distance computations, which includes the number of distance computations for computing $\phi(q)$ and that for verifying whether an instance object u_{ij} is contained in R_q. In worst case, UtMA needs to verify all instance objects u_{ij} with $\phi(u_{ij}) \in \phi(R_q)$ according to Lemma 1. Thus, the CPU cost of UtMA in terms of distance computations can be calculated as:

$$UtMA_{CPU} = |P| + \sum_{u_{ij}\in U} I(u_{ij}, \phi(R_q)) \quad (1)$$

where $I(u_{ij}, \phi(R_q)) = \begin{cases} 1 & \phi(u_{ij}) \in \phi(R_q) \\ 0 & \text{otherwise} \end{cases}$.

I/O cost. The I/O cost of UtMA on a UPB-tree includes two parts, i.e., B^+-tree and RAF page accesses. To obtain the number of B^+-tree page accesses, it is sufficient to sum all the nodes whose MBBs are intersected with the search region $\phi(R_q)$. In addition, the number of RAF page accesses can be estimated as $UtMA_{CPU}/f$. Here, $UtMA_{CPU}$ is used to estimate the total number of instance objects visited, and f represents the average number of instance objects per RAF page because, the instance objects accessed in RAF are supposed to be stored close to each other. Hence, the I/O cost of UtMA in terms of page accesses can be calculated as:

$$UtMA_{I/O} = \sum_{M_i \text{ for } N_i \in B^+\text{-tree}} I(M_i, \phi(R_q)) + \frac{UtMA_{CPU}}{f} \quad (2)$$

where $I(M_i, \phi(R_q)) = \begin{cases} 1 & M_i \text{ intersects with } \phi(R_q) \\ 0 & \text{otherwise} \end{cases}$.

MkPRQ. In order to further improve the efficiency of MPRQ, we also study an interesting variant, termed as MkPRQ, which only returns top k qualified uncertain objects with the largest

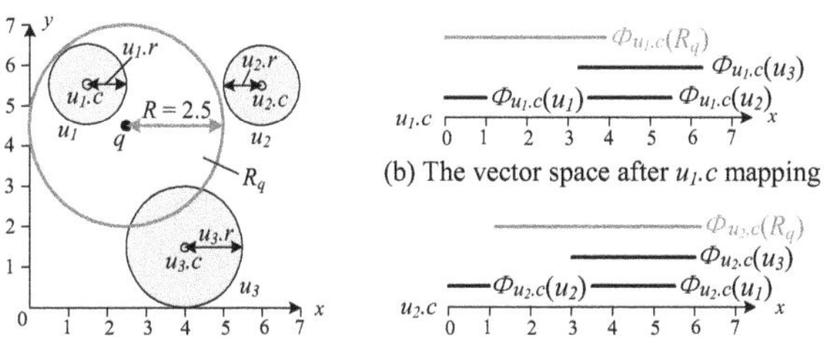

(b) The vector space after $u_1.c$ mapping

(a) Metric space (c) The vector space after $u_2.c$ mapping

Figure 5: Example of the MPRQ using UPB-forest

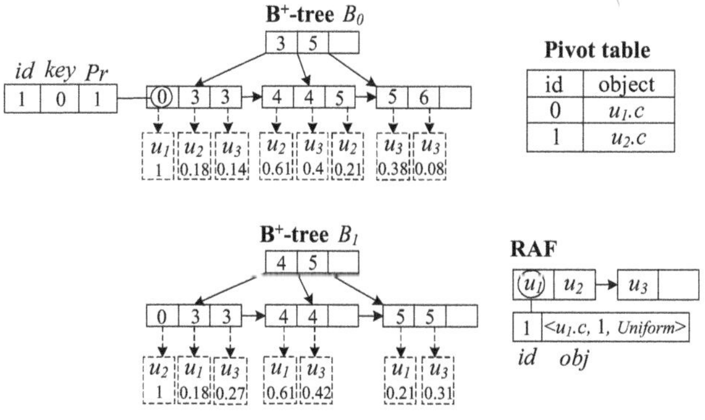

Figure 6: Example of the UPB-forest for the dataset in Figure 5

probabilities. Although UtMA can support M*k*PRQ naturally by sorting answer objects in descending order of their probabilities and returning the top *k* objects, it is very inefficient due to the unnecessary verifications. In light of this, we develop the following theorem by utilizing the characteristics of M*k*PRQ, to speed up M*k*PRQ processing.

THEOREM 2. *Given a MkPRQ(q, R, θ), let* LB_k (UB_k) *be the k-th largest value of* $l\pi(u, R_q)$ ($u\pi(u, R_q)$) *for* $u \in U$, *then* (1) u_i *can be safely pruned if* $u\pi(u_i, R_q) < LB_k$, *and* (2) u_i *can be validated if* $l\pi(u_i, R_q) \geq UB_k$.

PROOF. Please refer to Appendix E. □

Based on Theorem 2, we propose the algorithm *k*UtMA (see Appendix F), which follows the framework of UtMA. The main difference is that, when verifying each uncertain instance u_{ij} in IS_c, *k*UtMA uses Theorem 2 to further avoid unqualified verifications. In particular, if $u\pi(u_i, R_q) < LB_k$, *k*UtMA can remove all u_{ik} from IS_c; and if $l\pi(u_i, R_q) \geq UB_k$, it inserts u_i into S_r and removes all u_{ik} from IS_c accordingly.

5. The UPB-forest

In this section, we first present a UPB-forest structure based on the bi-level model (only considering the continuous case as stated in Section 3.2), and then elaborate corresponding MPRQ algorithm and cost analysis. In what follows, we employ another running example to facilitate the understanding of the UPB-forest and the MPRQ processing. Specifically, consider an uncertain object set $U = \{u_1, u_2, u_3\}$ illustrated in Figure 5, with $u_1 = \langle u_1.c, 1, Uniform\rangle$ (indicating that u_1 is located uniformly within the uncertain region centered at $u_1.c$ having radius 1), $u_2 = \langle u_2.c, 1, Uniform\rangle$, and $u_3 = \langle u_3.c, 1.5, Uniform\rangle$. The corresponding UPB-forest is depicted in Figure 6 using a pivot set $P = \{u_1.c, u_2.c\}$. Assume that L_2-*norm* is used to measure the similarity, the final result of a *MPRQ*(*q*, 2.5, 0.15) is the uncertain object u_1.

5.1 UPB-forest Structure

Similar as UPB-tree, UPB-forest first maps a metric space into multiple vector spaces using a pivot set *P*, and then utilizes B$^+$-trees to index mapped vector spaces. However, unlike the UPB-tree which only uses a single B$^+$-tree, UPB-forest utilizes in total $|P|$ B$^+$-trees to index intervals (for continuous PDF) or points (for discrete PDF) in the mapped one-dimensional vector space. i.e., one B$^+$-tree is needed for every $p \in P$. This is because, as discussed in Section 3.2, a metric uncertain object can be denoted as $|P|$ PDFs w.r.t. each pivot in *P* based on the bi-level model, and it is difficult for a metric uncertain object represented as a multivariate PDF w.r.t the whole pivot set *P*.

Given a pivot set $P = \{p_1, p_2, \ldots, p_{|P|}\}$, a metric space (*M*, *d*) can be mapped into $|P|$ one-dimensional vector spaces (R, L_∞). To be more specific, for any uncertain object u_i (denoted as an uncertain region centered at $u_i.c$ with radius $u_i.r$) in the metric space, it can be represented as $|P|$ intervals $\phi_{pt}(u_i) = [d(u_i.c, p_t) - u_i.r, d(u_i.c, p_t) + u_i.r]$ ($p_t \in P$) with associated continuous PDFs in the one-dimensional vector space. As an example, Figure 5(b) and Figure 5(c) illustrate the mapped one-dimensional vector spaces using pivots $u_1.c$ and $u_2.c$, respectively. According to the triangle inequality, given a query object *q* and a pivot p_t, $d(q, u_i) \geq |d(q, p_t) - d(u_i, p_t)| = D(\phi_{pt}(q), \phi_{pt}(u_i))$. Obviously, we can conclude that the distance in the mapped vector space is the *lower bound* of that in the original metric space.

In order to index the intervals with continuous PDFs after the pivot mapping, the whole real numeric range is partitioned into *n* slots, i.e., slot 0, slot 1, …, slot *n*, with corresponding intervals [0, *s*), [*s*, 2×*s*), …, [(*n*−1)×*s*, d^+), and $s = d^+/n$. Thus, $\phi_{pt}(u_i)$ can be partitioned in several sub-intervals, and every continuous $\mathcal{G}_{p_t,i}$ ($p_t \in P$) can be approximated as discrete $g_{p_t,i}$, in which $g_{p_t,i}(j)$ denotes the probability integration of $\mathcal{G}_{p_t,i}$ on the slot *j* (i.e., the interval [*j*×*s*, (*j*+1)×*s*)). Take Figure 5 as an example. Suppose *n* = 10 and *s* = 1, $\phi_{u_1.c}(u_3)$ can be partitioned into four slots (i.e., slot 3, slot 4, slot 5, and slot 6), and thus, $\mathcal{G}_{u_1.c,3}$ can be approximated as $g_{u_1.c}$, with $g_{u_1.c,3}(3) = \int_3^4 \mathcal{G}_{u_1.c,3}(x)dx = 0.14$, $g_{u_1.c,3}(4) = \int_4^5 \mathcal{G}_{u_1.c,3}(x)dx = 0.4$, $g_{u_1.c,3}(5) = 0.38$, and $g_{u_1.c,3}(6) = 0.08$.

A UPB-forest used to index a metric uncertain object set based on the bi-level model contains three parts, viz., a pivot table, a RAF, and $|P|$ B$^+$-trees. Figure 6 shows a UPB-forest example to index an uncertain object set $U = \{u_1, u_2, u_3\}$ depicted in Figure 5. The pivot table stores selected pivots *P* (e.g., $u_1.c$ and $u_2.c$ in this case) to map a metric space into $|P|$ one-dimensional vector spaces. The RAF is utilized to keep uncertain objects in ascending order of their identifiers, which achieves the efficiency of managing complex uncertain objects. Every RAF entry records (1) an uncertain object identifier *id*, and (2) the real uncertain object *obj*. Continue the above example, in Figure 6(c), the RAF entry associated with an uncertain object u_1 records its uncertain object identifier 1, and its real uncertain object $\langle u_1.c, 1, Uniform\rangle$.

B$^+$-trees B_t ($0 \leq t < |P|$) w.r.t. each pivot p_t in the pivot table are employed to index the intervals $\phi_{pt}(u_i)$ after the pivot mapping. Every leaf entry in the leaf node of B_t ($0 \leq t < |P|$) records (1) an uncertain object identifier *id*, (2) the slot number *key* ($0 \leq key < n$), and (3) the probability integration *Pr* of $\mathcal{G}_{p_t,id}$ on the corresponding slot (i.e., $g_{p_t,id}(key)$). As an example, in Figure 6, the first leaf entry of B_0 records the uncertain object identifier *id* = 1, the slot number *key* = 0, and the probability integration *Pr* = 1 equivalent to the numeric integration of $\mathcal{G}_{u_1.c,1}$ on slot 0.

Algorithm 2 UPB-forest based MPRQ Algorithm (UfMA)

Input: q, R, θ, an uncertain object set U indexed by a UPB-forest
Output: the result set S_r of a $MPRQ(q, R, \theta)$
1: compute $S_{pt} = \{x \mid x \in [\lfloor (d(q, p_t) - R)/s \rfloor, \lceil (d(q, p_t) + R)/s \rceil - 1]\}$ and $S'_{pt} = \{x \mid x \in [0, \lfloor (R - d(q, p_t))/s \rfloor - 1]\}$ for every $p_t \in P$ // $s = d^+/n$, and S_{pt} is a set of slots x ($\in \phi_{pt}(R_q) = [d(q, p_t) - R, d(q, p_t) + R]$)
2: **for** each B$^+$-tree B_t ($0 \le t < |P|$) of the UPB-forest **do**
3: **for** each leaf entry $\langle u_i, key, pr \rangle$ in B_t with the $key \in S_{pt}$ or $key \in S'_{pt}$ **do**
4: update $u\pi(u_i, R_q)$ or $l\pi(u_i, R_q)$ using Lemma 5 or Lemma 6
5: **if** $u\pi(u_i, R_q) \ge \theta$ and $u_i \notin S_c$ **then** // Theorem 1
6: insert u_i into S_c
7: **for** every $u_i \in S_c$ **do**
8: **if** $l\pi(u_i, R_q) \ge \theta$ **then** // Theorem 1
9: insert u_i into S_r
10: **else if** $u\pi(u_i, R_q) < \theta$ **then** // Theorem 1
11: prune u_i
12: **else if** $\pi(u_i, R_q) \ge \theta$ **then**
13: insert u_i into S_r
14: **return** S_r

Insertion/Deletion operation. For a new uncertain object u_i to be inserted or deleted, we first compute the intervals $\phi_{pt}(u_i)$ ($0 \le t < |P|$) using P. Then, for each slot *key* contained in $\phi_{pt}(u_i)$, we get $g_{p_t,i}(key)$, after which leaf entries e ($\langle i, key, g_{p_t,i}(key) \rangle$) are inserted into or deleted from the corresponding B$^+$-tree B_t. Finally, u_i is inserted into or deleted from the RAF according to its identifier, because uncertain objects are stored in ascending order of their identifiers.

Update operation. For an uncertain object u_i to be updated, we delete the original u_i and then insert the new one.

Note that, unlike UP-Index [4], which needs to store the pre-computed histograms w.r.t. the *whole* distance range for every uncertain object u_i, UPB-forest only stores *necessary* information. To be more specific, for each u_i, UPB-forest only records non-zero $g_{p_t,i}(j)$ values on slot j, instead of the entire slot set. In addition, B$^+$-trees of UPB-forest preserve entries in ascending order of their corresponding slot values, which achieves high I/O efficiency as the entries to be visited are stored close to each other.

5.2 UPB-forest based MPRQ Algorithm

To accelerate the MPRQ processing, we first derive the upper bound $u\pi(u_i, R_q)$ and lower bound $l\pi(u_i, R_q)$ of $\pi(u_i, R_q)$ based on the UPB-forest, in order to filter out and validate uncertain objects according to Theorem 1, without any further verification.

LEMMA 5. *Given a pivot set P and a query object q, for an uncertain object u_i, $u\pi(u_i, R_q) = \boldsymbol{min}_{p_t \in P} \int_{d(q,p_t)-R}^{d(q,p_t)+R} \mathcal{G}_{p_t,i}(x)dx$.*

PROOF. Please refer to Appendix G. □

Take a $MPRQ(q, 2.5, 0.15)$ depicted in Figure 5 as an example. Given $P = \{u_1.c, u_2.c\}$, $u\pi(u_3, R_q) = \int_{d(q,u_1.c)-R}^{d(q,u_1.c)+R} \mathcal{G}_{u_1.c,3}(x)dx \approx 0.14 < \theta$, and thus, u_3 can be pruned away.

As mentioned in Section 5.1, $\mathcal{G}_{p_t,i}$ is approximated as $g_{p_t,i}$ to build the UPB-forest. Hence, to utilize Lemma 5, $u\pi(u_i, R_q)$ can be calculated as $\boldsymbol{min}_{p_t \in P} \sum_{\lfloor (d(q,p_t)-R)/s \rfloor}^{\lceil (d(q,p_t)+R)/s \rceil - 1} g_{p_t,i}(x)$. Again taking Figure 5 as an example, $u\pi(u_3, R_q) = g_{u_1.c,3}(3) = 0.14$.

Note that, according to Lemma 5, if $\phi_{pt}(u)$ does not intersect with $\phi_{pt}(R_q)$ ($p_t \in P$), then u_i can be safely pruned by Theorem 1 as $u\pi(u_i, R_q) = 0 < \theta$. Thus, we only need to verify uncertain objects u_i with $\phi_{pt}(u_i)$ crossing $\phi_{pt}(R_q)$ for every $p_t \in P$, i.e., $\phi(u_i) \cap \phi(R_q) \ne \varnothing$, since $\phi(u_i)$ and $\phi(R_q)$ represent the hypercubes in the mapped multi-dimensional vector space using the whole pivot set P.

LEMMA 6. *Given a pivot set P and a query object q, for an uncertain object u_i, $l\pi(u_i, R_q) = \boldsymbol{max}_{p_t \in P} \int_0^{R-d(q,p_t)} \mathcal{G}_{p_t,i}(x)dx$.*

PROOF. Please refer to Appendix H. □

Consider $MPRQ(q, 2.5, 0.15)$ depicted in Figure 5 again, where $l\pi(u_1, R_q) = \int_0^{R-d(q,u_1.c)} \mathcal{G}_{u_1.c,1}(x)dx = 1 > \theta$. Therefore, u_1 can be validated without further verification. Similarly, to utilize Lemma 6, $l\pi(u_i, R_q)$ can be calculated as $\boldsymbol{max}_{p_t \in P} \sum_0^{\lfloor (R-d(q,p_t))/s \rfloor - 1} g_{p_t,i}(x)$. For instance, in Figure 5, $l\pi(u_3, R_q) = g_{u_1.c,1}(0) = 1$.

Based on the derived upper and lower bounds above, we present *UPB-forest based MPRQ Algorithm* (UfMA), which follows a filtering-refinement framework. The pseudo-code of UfMA is shown in Algorithm 2. It takes as inputs q, R, θ, and an uncertain object set U indexed by a UPB-forest, and outputs the result set S_r of a $MPRQ(q, R, \theta)$. In the filtering phase, UfMA first computes the set S_{pt} of slots contained in the mapped search region $\phi_{pt}(R_q)$ and the set S'_{pt} for each $p_t \in P$ (line 1). It then traverses each B$^+$-tree B_t of the UPB-forest to search leaf entries $\langle u_i, key, pr \rangle$ of B_t with their *keys* $\in S_{pt}$ or *keys* $\in S'_{pt}$ (line 3), updates $u\pi(u_i, R_q)$ or $l\pi(u_i, R_q)$ based on Lemma 5 or Lemma 6 (line 4), and inserts all the qualified candidates u_i (i.e., $u\pi(u_i, R_q) \ge \theta$ and $u_i \notin S_c$) into S_c (lines 5-6). In the refinement phase, for every $u_i \in S_c$, the algorithm adds u_i to S_r if $l\pi(u_i, R_q) \ge \theta$ (lines 8-9), and filters out u_i if $u\pi(u_i, R_q) < \theta$ (lines 10-11). Otherwise, it computes $\pi(u_i, R_q)$ using the numerical integration and inserts u_i into S_r if $\pi(u_i, R_q) \ge \theta$ (lines 12-13). Note that, $\pi(u_i, R_q)$ is derived by using GNU Scientific Library with the error bound set to 10^{-5}. Finally, the final result set S_r of the $MPRQ(q, R, \theta)$ is returned (line 14).

EXAMPLE 2. *We illustrate UfMA using the $MPRQ(q, 2.5, 0.15)$ example depicted in Figure 5 with the UPB-forest shown in Figure 6, and suppose $n = 10$ and $s = 1$. UfMA computes $S_{u1.c} = \{x \mid x \in [-2, 3]\}$, $S_{u2.c} = \{x \mid x \in [1, 6]\}$, $S'_{u1.c} = \{x \mid x = 0\}$ and $S'_{u2.c} = \varnothing$. Then, it traverses the B$^+$-tree B_0 to find the leaf entries with their keys contained in S_{pt} or S'_{pt},* i.e., $\langle u_1, 0, 1 \rangle$, $\langle u_2, 3, 0.18 \rangle$, *and* $\langle u_3, 3, 0.14 \rangle$; *updates* $l\pi(u_1, R_q) = u\pi(u_1, R_q) = 1$, $u\pi(u_2, R_q) = 0.18$, *and* $u\pi(u_3, R_q) = 0.14$ *based on Lemmas 5 and 6; and adds u_1 and u_2 to S_c. Next, similarly, B_1 is traversed, after which $u\pi(u_2, R_q)$ is updated to* 0. *In the sequel, UfMA checks every uncertain object in S_c. It inserts u_1 into S_r due to $l\pi(u_1, R_q) > \theta$, and prunes u_2 by Theorem 1 as $u\pi(u_2, R_q) < \theta$ holds. Finally, the result set $S_r = \{u_1\}$ of the* $MPRQ(q, 2.5, 0.15)$ *is returned.* □

5.3 Discussion

CPU cost. Like UtMA, the CPU cost of UfMA can be estimated by using the number of distance computations, which includes distance computations for computing $\phi_{pt}(R_q)$ for each $p_t \in P$ and that for verifying whether an uncertain object u_i is a real answer object. According to Lemma 5, in worst case, UfMA needs to verify all uncertain objects u_i with $\phi_{pt}(u_i) \cap \phi_{pt}(R_q) \ne \varnothing$ for every $p_t \in P$, i.e., $\phi(u_i) \cap \phi(R_q) \ne \varnothing$. Hence, the CPU cost of UfMA in terms of distance computations can be calculated as:

$$UtMA_{CPU} = |P| + \sum_{u_i \in U} I(u_i, \phi(R_q)) \quad (3)$$

where $I(u_i, \phi(R_q)) = \begin{cases} 1 & \phi(u_i) \text{ intersects with } \phi(R_q) \\ 0 & \text{otherwise} \end{cases}$.

I/O cost. The I/O cost of UfMA on the UPB-forest includes two parts, i.e., B$^+$-tree and RAF page accesses. To obtain the number of B$^+$-tree page accesses, it is sufficient to sum all the B$^+$-tree B_t ($0 \le t < |P|$) nodes whose MBBs are intersected with the search region $\phi_{pt}(R_q)$. In addition, the number of RAF page accesses can be estimated as $UfMA_{CPU}/f$, in which $UfMA_{CPU}$ is used to estimate the total number of uncertain objects accessed, and f represents the average number of uncertain objects per RAF page because, the uncertain objects visited in RAF are supposed to be stored close to each other. Thus, to sum up, the I/O cost of UfMA in terms of pace accesses can be calculated as:

$$UfMA_{I/O} = \sum_{M_i \text{ for } N_i \in B_t(0 \le t < |P|)} I(M_i, \phi_{p_t}(R_q)) + \frac{UfMA_{CPU}}{f} \quad (4)$$

where $I(M_i, \phi_{p_t}(R_q)) = \begin{cases} 1 & M_i \text{ intersects with } \phi_{p_t}(R_q) \\ 0 & \text{otherwise} \end{cases}$.

M*k*PRQ. We also investigate M*k*PRQ processing using the UPB-forest. First, Theorem 2 (presented in Section 4.3) can also be integrated into UfMA to improve query efficiency. Second, since UfMA verifies candidate uncertain objects in order, a new top-*k* query processing technique can be developed as follows.

THEOREM 3. *Given a MkPRQ(q, R, θ), let PB_k be the k-th largest value of $\pi(u, R_q)$ found so far, then u_i can be safely pruned if $u\pi(u_i, R_q) \le PB_k$.*

The proof of Theorem 3 is obvious and thus omitted. Based on Theorems 2 and 3, we present *k*UfMA algorithm (see Appendix I), which follows the framework of UfMA. The main difference is that, when verifying each candidate uncertain object u_i, if $u\pi(u_i, R_q) < \max\{\theta, LB_k, PB_k\}$, *k*UfMA prunes u_i; and if $l\pi(u_i, R_q) \ge UB_k$, *k*UfMA inserts u_i into S_r according to Theorems 1, 2, and 3.

6. Pivot Selection

In this section, we first introduce a criterion to qualify a pivot set, and then, we propose an efficient pivot selection algorithm to obtain a high-quality pivot set based on the criterion defined.

According to the cost analysis in Section 4.3 and Section 5.3, the cost of MPRQ using UPB-tree or UPB-forest highly depends on the pivot set P. Hence, it makes sense to define a criterion to measure the quality of the pivots. Since our MPRQ algorithms follow the filtering-refinement framework, they prune the uncertain object u using its probability upper bound $Pr(D(\phi(q), \phi(u)) \le R)$, to avoid unnecessary computation of $Pr(d(q, u) \le R)$, as $D(\ )$ is the lower bound of $d(\ )$. In order to achieve high performance, i.e., fewer computations of $Pr(d(q, u) \le R)$, the lower bound distances should be close to the actual distances, i.e., the mapping to vector space should preserve the proximity in metric space.

Let $\epsilon(x,y)$ $(x, y \in U)$ denote the random variable defined as $\epsilon(x,y) = D(\phi(x), \phi(y))/d(x,y)$. Note that, $0 \le \epsilon(x,y) \le 1$. Then, the expected value of $\epsilon(x,y)$ can be calculated as:

$$E[\epsilon(x,y)] = \int_0^1 z \times Pr(D(\phi(x), \phi(y))/d(x,y) = z)dz \quad (5)$$

To obtain an optimal pivot set P, we need to pick up pivots to maximize $E[\epsilon(x,y)]$. Nevertheless, it is costly to obtain the distribution of $\epsilon(x,y)$ for every uncertain object pair. Therefore, random sampling is exploited to estimate the value of $E[\epsilon(x,y)]$, denoted as $\underline{E}[\epsilon(x,y)]$, for achieving the goal that

$$Pr(|E[\epsilon(x,y)] - \underline{E}[\epsilon(x,y)]| < \xi) > 1 - \delta \quad (6)$$

According to the Hoeffding's inequality [21],

$$Pr(|E[\epsilon(x,y)] - \underline{E}[\epsilon(x,y)]| < \xi) > 1 - 2 \cdot exp(-2T\xi^2) \quad (7)$$

Here, T represents the sampled size. Hence, to reach the target stated in equation (6), $T \ge \frac{1}{2\xi^2}log(\frac{2}{\delta})$.

Given a set U_S ($|U_S| \ge \frac{1}{2\xi^2}log(\frac{2}{\delta})$) of uncertain instance pairs sampled from an uncertain object set U, the uncertain instance object u_{ij} with higher probability $Pr(u_{ij})$ contributes more to derive constrictive upper bound of $u\pi(u_i, R_q)$, according to Lemma 3. Thus, taking the probability of the uncertain instance object into consideration, we offer a criterion to measure the quality of a pivot set P based on the sampled metric uncertain data.

DEFINITION 2(ϵ_P). *Given a set U_S of sampled instance object pairs on the metric uncertain data, the* quality *of a pivot set P is evaluated as,*

$$\epsilon_P = \frac{1}{|U_S|} \sum_{<u_{ij}, u_{mn}> \in U_S} \frac{D(\phi(u_{ij}), \phi(u_{mn}))}{d(u_{ij}, u_{mn})} \cdot Pr(u_{ij}) \cdot Pr(u_{mn}) \quad (8)$$

The more the pivots, the better the pruning capability but the higher the cost of utilizing transformed objects, as to be confirmed in Section 7. In particular, if P contains more pivots, we can expect a larger $D(\phi(u_{ij}), \phi(u_{mn}))$; then $D(\phi(u_{ij}), \phi(u_{mn}))$ approaches $d(u_{ij}, u_{mn})$, and hence, ϵ_P approaches 1. Therefore, we can prune more uncertain objects using a larger pivot set. On the other hand, the cost (e.g., $D(\phi(u_{ij}), \phi(u_{mn}))$ computation cost) to prune away unqualified uncertain objects increases as well.

As proved in [4], the problem, to determine whether there exists a pivot set P ($|P| \ge 1$) which makes the penalty function Q of a defined criterion no larger than a nonnegative real number, is *NP-hard.* Thus, a greedy pivot selection algorithm can be employed here, to pick a high-quality pivot set P (from U) of a fixed size to maximize ϵ_P. Nonetheless, the time complexity $O(|P| \times |U|)$ is still very high, especially for a large uncertain object set. Note that, since pivots are certain objects, to select P ($\subseteq U$), we need to replace the uncertain objects in U with a set of representative certain objects, denoted as *cert*(U). To further reduce the time complexity, we present the *incremental pivot selection algorithm* (IPS) (see Appendix J). It first employs HF algorithm [25] to obtain outliers as candidate pivots P_c, and then selects incrementally effective pivots from P_c. The reason behind is that, as pointed out in [11], good pivots are usually outliers, but outliers are not always good pivots. Consequently, the time complexity of IPS is reduced to $O(|P| \times |P_c|)$, in which the cardinality of P_c is very small, and is only related with the distribution of the object set. In this paper, we fix $|P_c|$ to 40 (as in [33]), which is enough to find all the outliers in our experiments.

7. Experiments

In this section, we experimentally evaluate the performance of UPB-tree and UPB-forest. First, we study the effectiveness of our pivot selection algorithm. Then, we compare the UPB-tree and the UPB-forest with state-of-the-art indexes. Finally, the scalability of our indexing structures and the M*k*PRQ performance are explored. We implemented the UPB-tree, the UPB-forest, the MPRQ, and the M*k*PRQ algorithms in C++. All experiments were conducted on an Intel Core 2 Duo 2.93GHz PC with 8GB RAM.

We employ four real datasets *English*, *Color*, *SF*, and *DNA*, as depicted in Table 2. Please refer to Appendix K for detailed descriptions. In our experimental settings, *English* and *Color* use the *object-level model* to represent the uncertainty. Specifically, every uncertain object is represented using m ($100 \le m \le 300$) instances with their distances to the word or image feature in *English* or *Color* bounded by Υ, resulting in a total of 12M instances for the default *English* and 11.2M instances for the default *Color*. The associated instance probability follows two popular distributions *Normal* and *Arbitrary* for *English* and *Color*, respectively. *SF* and *DNA* utilize the *bi-level model* to represent the uncertainty. For *SF*, the uncertain object u is denoted as an uncertain region centered at every location in *SF* with the radius

Table 2. Statistics of datasets used

Dataset	Cardinality	Dim.	Ins. Dim.	Measurement
English	60K	1~22	4.75	*Edit distance*
Color	56K	8	2.9	L_5-norm
SF	176K	2	4.7	L_2-norm
DNA	200K	108	7.12	*Hamming distance*
Synthetic (set)	[50K, 250K]	30~60	24.5	*Jaccard coefficient*

Table 3. Parameter settings

Parameter	Setting	Default
the number $\|P\|$ of pivots	1, 3, 5, 7, 9	5
uncertain region size Υ (% of d^+)	4, 6, 8, 10, 12	8
the number m of instances	100, 150, 200, 250, 300	200
the number n of slots	200, 400, 600, 800, 1000	1000
search radius R (% of d^+)	2, 4, 8, 16, 32	8
probabilistic threshold θ	0.1, 0.3, 0.5, 0.7, 0.9	0.5
cardinality	50K, 100K, 150K, 200K, 250K	150K
the number k required	1, 2, 4, 8, 16	4

bounded by Υ, and the probability for u located in the uncertain region follows *Uniform* distribution. For *DNA*, each uncertain string uses the character-element model [23] as the underlying uncertain model. Synthetic (*set*) datasets based on both the object-level and bi-level models are also generated, in which every set in *Synthetic* has [30, 60] elements, and Jaccard coefficient is utilized to measure the similarity. Note that, for the bi-level model, the uncertain *set* uses the *p*-set model [19] as its underlying uncertain model. Table 2 lists the statistics of the datasets used in our experiments. All indexing structures to index the datasets are configured to use a fixed disk page size of 4KB.

We investigate the efficiency of MPRQ and M*k*PRQ algorithms using the UPB-tree and the UPB-forest under various parameters, as shown in Table 3. In each experiment, we vary one factor, and fix the others to their default values. The main performance metrics include the number of page accesses (*PA*), the number of distance computations (*compdists*), and the total query time (i.e., the sum of the I/O time and CPU time). Each measurement we report is the average of 50 random queries.

7.1 Effectiveness of Pivot Selection Algorithm

The first set of experiments compares the effectiveness of our pivot selection algorithm IPS against the existing pivot selection algorithm PSA [4]. We utilize the MPRQ performance on UPB-tree and UPB-forest to demonstrate the effectiveness of the pivot selection algorithms. Figure 7 depicts the experimental results using real datasets *English* and *DNA*, where abbreviations of pivot selection algorithms (**IP** for IPS, **PS** for PSA) are shown at the bottom of each column, and the I/O percentage is listed at the top of every column. The first observation is that, IPS performs better than PSA. The reason is that, MPRQ performance is highly related with ϵ_P as defined in Definition 2, and IPS tries to maximize ϵ_P. The second observation is that, the number of distance computations decreases as the number of pivots grows. This is because, using more pivots, the query efficiency improves as ϵ_P becomes larger, incurring fewer distance computations. The total query time first drops and then stays stable or increases when the number of pivots ascends. The reason is that the cost of filtering out unqualified uncertain objects grows as the number of pivots increases. Hence, MPRQ achieves better performance in all performance metrics, when the number of pivots approaches the *instinct dimensionality* (i.e., Ins. Dim. for short in Table 2) of the dataset [25].

Table 4. Construction costs of UP-Index and UPB-tree

	UP-Index		*UPB-tree*	
	English	*Color*	*English*	*Color*
PA	127,696	704,279	523,830	564,418
compdists	68,105,000	56,000,000	68,105,000	56,000,000
Time (sec)	2,226.702	1,701.898	1,621.668	1,683.104
Storage (KB)	510,784	2,817,116	489,669	707,909

Table 5. Construction costs of UP-Index and UPB-forest

	UP-Index		*UPB-forest*	
	SF	*DNA*	*SF*	*DNA*
PA	1,709,708	280,702	454,293	179,700
compdists	874,780	1,000,000	874,780	1,000,000
Time (sec)	4,928.816	667.344	1,703.991	693.23
Storage (KB)	6,838,832	1,122,808	608,037	506,306

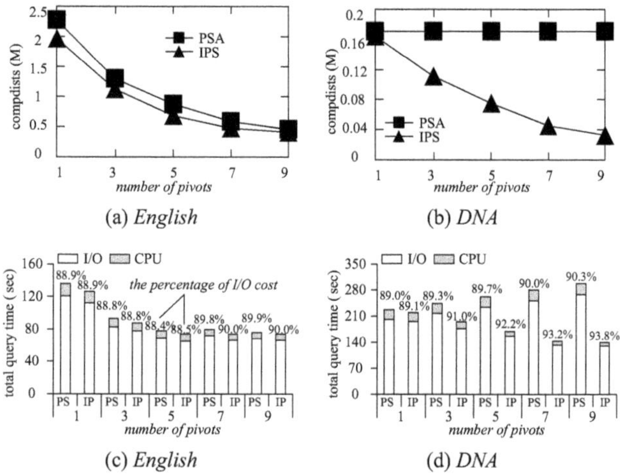

Figure 7: Efficiency of pivot selection algorithms vs. $|P|$

7.2 Comparisons with UP-index

The second set of experiments compares the efficiency of the UPB-tree and the UPB-forest with state-of-the-art UP-Index [4].

Construction cost. First, Tables 4 and 5 show the construction costs and storage sizes for the UP-Index, UPB-tree, and UPB-forest, using real datasets. Clearly, the UPB-tree and the UPB-forest have much lower construction costs, in terms of the number of page accesses (i.e., *PA*) and the construction time (denoted by *Time*) in most cases. The reason is that, our two indexes utilize the B^+-tree(s) as the underlying index in order to achieve construction efficiency. In addition, the storage sizes (denoted by *Storage*) of the two indexes are also much smaller than those of the UP-Index in most cases, because the two indexes only store necessary information, while the UP-Index needs to preserve the histograms w.r.t. the whole distance range for each uncertain object. Notice that, on *English*, the UP-Index has smaller *PA* than the UPB-tree, due to the small distance range (i.e., [0, 22]) of the dataset.

Update cost. Further, we evaluate the update efficiency of the UPB-tree and the UPB-forest based on real datasets. In particular, we simulate uncertain objects updates, by removing 50 randomly chosen uncertain objects and inserting 50 new ones, with the average update cost depicted in Table 6. As expected, the UPB-tree and the UPB-forest achieve update efficiency, since this operation relies on the manipulation of B^+-tree(s). Note that, the UPB-forest update cost on *DNA* is much smaller than that on *SF*. This is because the distance domain (i.e., [0, 108]) of *DNA* is much smaller, resulting in fewer entry insertions.

Table 6. Update costs of UPB-tree and UPB-forest

	UPB-tree		*UPB-forest*	
	English	*Color*	*SF*	*DNA*
PA	1,841.01	1,510.22	1,820.44	304.8
compdists	1,000	1,000	5	5
Time (sec)	3.801	3.084	3.716	0.6316

Table 7. Comparisons with U-Quadtree and CSQ

	Color		*Synthetic (set)*		
	U-Quadtree	*UPB-tree*	*CSQ*	*UPB-forest*	*CSQ+UPB*
PA	166,879	12,638	—	33,824	33,769
compdists	—	52,098	28,746	43,757	19,260
Time (sec)	334.658	27.794	111.35	73.293	71.994

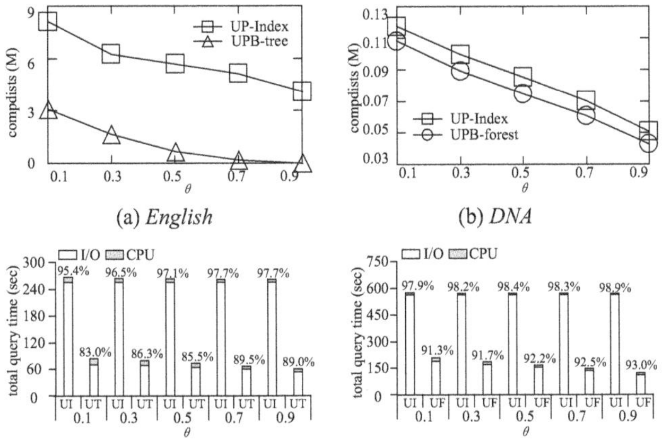

(a) *English* (b) *DNA* (c) *English* (d) *DNA*

Figure 8: MPRQ performance vs. θ

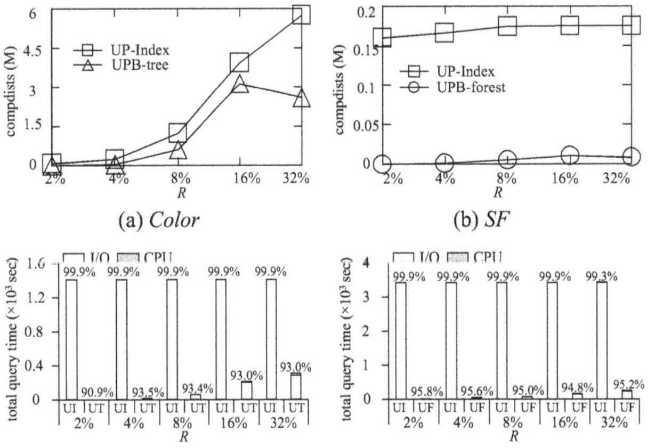

(a) *Color* (b) *SF* (c) *Color* (d) *SF*

Figure 9: MPRQ performance vs. *R*

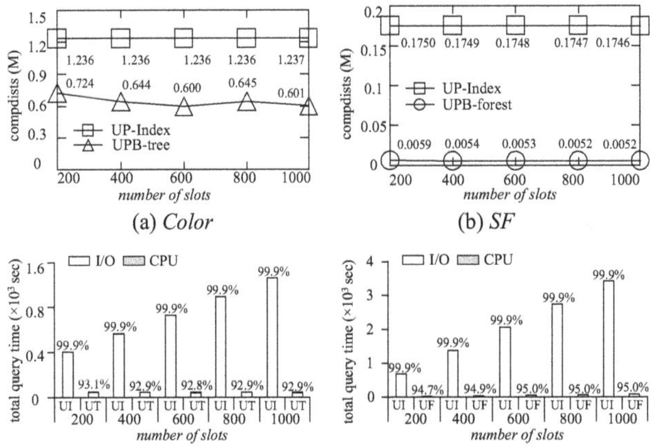

(a) *Color* (b) *SF* (c) *Color* (d) *SF*

Figure 10: MPRQ performance vs. *n*

Effect of *θ*. Figure 8 illustrates the influence of θ on the efficiency of MPRQ algorithms using *English* and *DNA* datasets. Abbreviations of indexes (**UI** for UP-Index, **UT** for UPB-tree, **UF** for UPB-forest) are shown at the bottom of each column. The first observation is that, the UPB-tree and the UPB-forest based MPRQ algorithms are better in terms of *compdists*. The reason is that, our pivot selection algorithm selects effective pivots to avoid a large number of distance computations, and the MPRQ algorithms can avoid unnecessary distance computations by validating or pruning uncertain objects based on the probability lower and upper bounds. However, the UP-Index cannot validate uncertain objects due to no probability lower bounds. As observed, the UPB-tree and the UPB-forest based MPRQ algorithms are I/O bound, and they perform much better in terms of total query time. This is because, the UP-Index has to scan the entire index to prune uncertain objects, incurring high query cost. Nevertheless, for UPB-tree and UPB-forest, they achieve I/O efficiency since only qualified B^+-tree entries and uncertain objects are visited based on Lemmas 1 to 6 and Theorem 1. In addition, the MPRQ cost drops with the growth of θ since the pruning power increases with θ.

Effect of *R*. Figure 9 depicts the performance of MPRQ under various R values, using *Color* and *SF* datasets. As expected, UPB-tree and UPB-forest based MPRQ algorithms perform better in terms of *compdists* and total query time. The query cost increases with R, because the search space grows with R. Notice that, the *compdists* drops when R reaches 32% on *Color*. This is because, according to Lemma 4, the validation power of the UPB-tree increases with R, resulting in fewer distance computations.

Effect of *n*. In order to inspect the impact of the number of slots n on the efficiency of indexes, we employ *Color* and *SF* datasets since the range of their distance functions is real numeric. Figure 10 plots the experimental results with respect to various n values. As observed, *compdists* drops with the growth of n. The reason is that, as n increases, the discrete case approaches to the continuous case, which helps tighten the probability upper and lower bounds calculations, hence reduce distance computations. However, for the UP-Index and the UPB-forest, the total query time increases with n, because their storage costs grow with n in order to preserve the pre-computed histogram or approximated discrete PDF for every uncertain object, resulting in higher I/O cost.

Effect of *ϒ* and *m*. Figures 11 and 12 show the performance of MPRQ when varying Υ and m, using real datasets. As observed, the query costs including *compdists* and the total query time increase with the growth of m. The reason is that, the search space grows with m. Notice that, query costs are not sensitive to Υ, and they drop slightly when Υ reaches 12%. This is because, for the uncertain objects with larger uncertain regions, the total number of qualifying answer objects drops with fixed search radius.

7.3 Comparisons with U-Quadtree and CSQ

To further explore the efficiency of UPB-tree and UP-forest, we also compare them with the state-of-the-art U-Quadtree [47] and CSQ [19] in specific uncertain metric spaces. Table 7 depicts all the experimental results on *Color* and *Synthetic* datasets. Here,

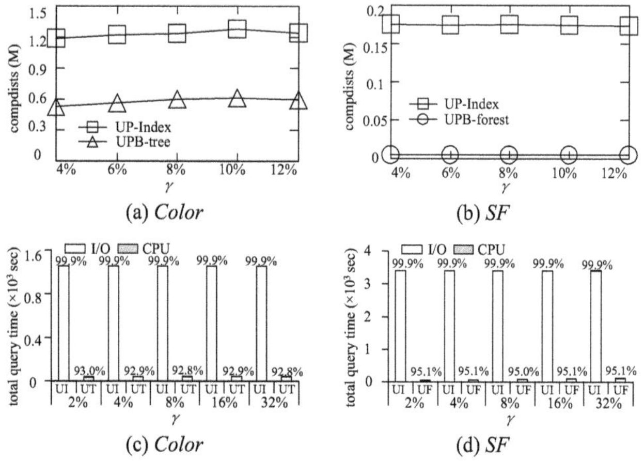

(a) *Color* (b) *SF*

(c) *Color* (d) *SF*

Figure 11: MPRQ performance vs. γ

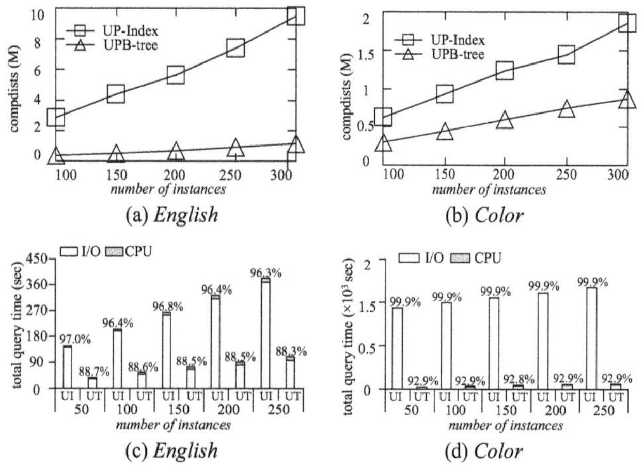

(a) *English* (b) *Color*

(c) *English* (d) *Color*

Figure 12: MPRQ performance vs. *m*

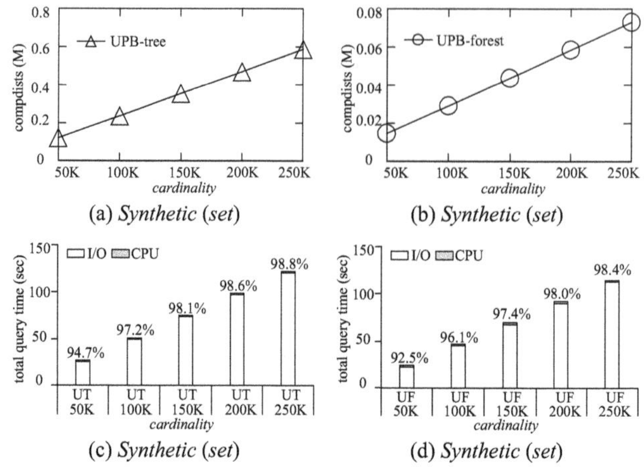

(a) *Synthetic* (*set*) (b) *Synthetic* (*set*)

(c) *Synthetic* (*set*) (d) *Synthetic* (*set*)

Figure 13: Scalability of UPB-tree and UPB-forest

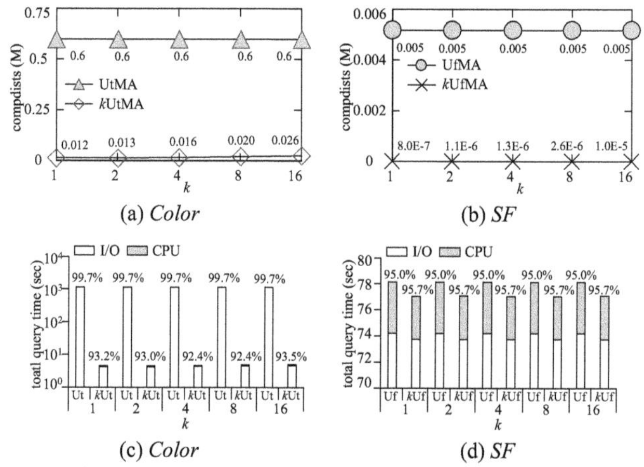

(a) *Color* (b) *SF*

(c) *Color* (d) *SF*

Figure 14: M*k*PRQ performance on UPB-tree and UPB-forest

"—" denotes the missing value of *PA* for CSQ or *compdists* for U-Quadtree, since CSQ is an in-memory method without any I/O cost, and since the verification of the U-Quadtree does not need any distance computation. As observed, our indexing structures outperform U-Quadtree and CSQ in most cases, but CSQ is more efficient in terms of the number of distance computations. This is because CSQ utilizes the characteristics of set data to prune away uncertain sets. Nonetheless, the individual and batch pruning techniques used by CSQ can be easily integrated into our algorithm (denoted as *CSQ + UPB*), to further improve the query efficiency on uncertain set data, as shown in Table 7.

7.4 Scalability of UPB-tree and UPB-forest

Figure 13 plots the MPRQ performance as a function of cardinality, using *Synthetic* (*set*) datasets. Evidently, the query costs, including the number of distance computations and the total query time, grow linearly with the cardinality, because the search space grows as the dataset cardinality increases.

7.5 Performance of M*k*PRQ

Figure 14 shows the M*k*PRQ performance w.r.t. *k*, using *Color* and *SF*, where abbreviations (**Ut** for UtMA, ***k*Ut** for *k*UtMA, **Uf** for UfMA, ***k*Uf** for *k*UfMA) are depicted at the bottom of each column. Notice that, *k*UtMA and *k*UfMA are several orders of magnitude better than UtMA and UfMA, since Theorems 2 and 3 are utilized to avoid unnecessary uncertain object verifications.

8. Conclusions

To address the uncertainty in various applications, we consider object-level model and bi-level model, and propose corresponding indexing structures, i.e., the UPB-tree and the UPB-forest, to support a wide range of data types and similarity metrics. Our indexes use a few effective pivots to map metric space to vector space, and employ the B^+-tree(s) as the underlying index, which can be integrated easily into any (existing) DBMS. Also, we present efficient metric probabilistic range query algorithms using these indexes that utilize the validation and pruning techniques based on new probability lower and upper bounds. Extensive experiments on both real and synthetic data show that, compared against state-of-the-art methods, our indexes have much *lower* construction costs and *smaller* storage sizes, and can support *more efficient* and *scalable* MPRQ processing. In the future, we plan to extend our indexes to distributed environments.

9. Acknowledgements

This work was supported in part by the National Key Basic Research Development Program (i.e., 973 Program) No. 2015CB352502 and 2015CB352503, NSFC Grants No. 61379033 and 61472348, the Fundamental Research Funds for the Central Universities, and the Key Project of Zhejiang University Excellent Young Teacher Fund (Zijin Plan). We would like to express our gratitude to the anonymous reviewers for their valuable and helpful comments.

10. REFERENCES

[1] E. Achtert, C. Böhm, P. Kröger, P. Kunath, A. Pryakhin, and M. Renz. Efficient reverse *k*-nearest neighbor search in arbitrary metric spaces. In *SIGMOD*, pages 515–526, 2006.

[2] P. K. Agarwal, S.-W. Cheng, Y. Tao, and K. Yi. Indexing uncertain data. In *PODS*, pages 137–146, 2009.

[3] C. Aggarwal and P. Yu. On high dimensional indexing of uncertain data. In *ICDE*, pages 1460–1461, 2008.

[4] F. Angiulli and F. Fassetti. Indexing uncertain data in general metric space. *IEEE Trans. Knowl. Data Eng.*, 24(9):1640–1657, 2012.

[5] R. Baeza-Yates, W. Cunto, U. Manber, and S. Wu. Proximity matching using fixed-queries trees. In *CPM*, pages 198–212, 1994.

[6] T. Bernecker, T. Emrich, F. Graf, H.-P. Kriegel, P. Kröger, M. Renz, E. Schubert, and A. Zimek. Subspace similarity search: efficient *k*-NN queries in arbitrary subspaces. In *SSDBM*, pages 555–564, 2010.

[7] T. Bernecker, T. Emrich, H.-P. Kriegel, M. Renz, S. Zankl, and A. Züfl. Efficient probabilistic reverse nearest neighbor query processing on uncertain data. *PVLDB*, 4(10):669–680, 2011.

[8] C. Bohm, P. Kunath, and M. Schubert. The Gauss-Tree: Efficient object identification of probabilistic feature vectors. In *ICDE*, article 9, 2006.

[9] T. Bozkaya and M. Ozsoyoglu. Distance-based indexing for high-dimensional metric spaces. In *SIGMOD*, pages 357–368, 1997.

[10] W. Burkhard and R. Keller. Some approaches to best-match file searching. *Commun. ACM*, 16(4):230–236, 1973.

[11] B. Bustos, G. Navarro, and E. Chavez. Pivot selection techniques for proximity searching in metric spaces. *Pattern Recognition Letters*, 24(14):2357–2366, 2003.

[12] J. Chen and R. Cheng. Efficient evaluation of imprecise location-dependent queries. In *ICDE*, pages 586–595, 2007.

[13] R. Cheng, Y. Xia, S. Prabhakar, R. Shah, and J. S. Vitter. Efficient indexing methods for probabilistic threshold queries over uncertain data. In *VLDB*, pages 876–887, 2004.

[14] P. Ciaccia, M. Patella, and P. Zezula. M-tree: An efficient access method for similarity search in metric spaces. In *VLDB*, pages 426–435, 1997.

[15] C.-W. Chung, C.-H. Pan, and C.-M. Liu. An effective index for uncertain data. In *IS3C*, pages 482–485, 2014.

[16] D. Dai, J. Xie, H. Zhang, and J. Dong. Efficient range queries over uncertain strings. In *SSDBM*, pages 75–95, 2012.

[17] M. Dallachiesa, T. Palpanas, and I. F. Ilyas. Top-*k* nearest neighbor search in uncertain data series. *PVLDB*, 8(1):13–24, 2014.

[18] E. Frentzos, K. Gratsias, and Y. Theodoridis. On the effect of location uncertainty in spatial querying. *IEEE Trans. Knowl. Data Eng.*, 21(3): 366–383, 2009.

[19] M. Gao, C. Jin, W. Wang, X. Lin, and A. Zhou. Similarity query processing for probabilistic sets. In *ICDE*, pages 913–924, 2013.

[20] T. Ge and Z. Li. Approximate substring matching over uncertain strings. *PVLDB*, 4(11): 772–782, 2011.

[21] W. Hoeffding. Probability inequalities for sums of bounded random variables. *J. American Statistical Association*, 58(301):13–30, 1963.

[22] E. H. Jacox and H. Samet. Metric space similarity joins. *ACM Trans. Database Syst.*, 33(2):article 7, 2008.

[23] J. Jestes, F. Li, Z. Yan, and K. Yi. Probabilistic string similarity joins. In *SIGMOD*, pages 327–338, 2010.

[24] R. Jin, L. Liu, B. Ding, and H. Wang. Distance constraint reachability computation in uncertain graphs. *PVLDB*, 4(9):511–562, 2011.

[25] C. T. Jr., R. F. S. Filho, A. J. M. Traina, M. R. Vieira, and C. Faloutsos. The Omni-family of all-purpose access methods: A simple and effective way to make similarity search more efficient. *VLDB J.*, 16(4):483–505, 2007.

[26] C. T. Jr., A. Traina, B. Seeger, and C. Faloutsos. Slim-trees: High performance metric trees minimizing overlap between nodes. In *ICDE*, pages 51–65, 2000.

[27] H. Kimura, S. Madden, and S. B. Zdonik. UPI: A primary index for uncertain databases. *PVLDB*, 3(1):630–637, 2010.

[28] A. Knight, Q. Yu, and M. Rege. Efficient range query processing on complicated uncertain data. *Information Reuse and Integration in Academia and Industry*, pages 51–72, 2013.

[29] H.-P. Kriegel, P. Kunath, M. Pfeifle, and M. Renz. Probabilistic similarity join on uncertain data. In *DASFAA*, pages 295–309, 2006.

[30] X. Lian and L. Chen. A generic framework for handling uncertain data with local correlations. *PVLDB*, 4(1):12–21, 2010.

[31] X. Lian and L. Chen. Set similarity join on probabilistic data. *PVLDB*, 3(1):650–659, 2010.

[32] J. Lokoc, J. Mosko, P. Cech, and T. Skopal. On indexing metric spaces using cut-regions. *Inf. Syst.*, 43:1–19, 2014.

[33] R. Mao, W. L. Mirankerb, and D. P. Mirankerc. Pivot selection: Dimension reduction for distance-based indexing. *J. Discrete Algorithms*, 13:32–46, 2012.

[34] L. Mico, J. Oncina, and R. C. Carrasco. A fast branch & bound nearest neighbour classifier in metric spaces. *Pattern Recognition Letters*, 17(7):731–739, 1996.

[35] J. Mosko, J. Lokoc, and T. Skopal. Clustered pivot tables for I/O-optimized similarity search. In *SISAP*, pages 17–24, 2011.

[36] D. Novak, M. Batko, and P. Zezula. Metric Index: An efficient and scalable solution for precise and approximate similarity search. *Inf. Syst.*, 36(4):721–733, 2011.

[37] M. Potamias, F. Bonchi, A. Gionis, and G. Kollios. K-nearest neighbors in uncertain graphs. *PVLDB*, 3(1): 997–1008, 2010.

[38] G. Ruiz, F. Santoyo, E. Chavez, K. Figueroa, and E. S. Tellez. Extreme pivots for faster metric indexes. In *SISAP*, pages 115–126, 2013.

[39] Y. N. Silva, S. Pearson, and J. A. Cheney. Database similarity join for metric spaces. In *SISAP*, pages 266–279, 2013.

[40] S. Singh, C. Mayfield, S. Prabhakar, R. Shah, and S. E. Hambrusch. Indexing uncertain categorical data. In *ICDE*, pages 616–625, 2007.

[41] T. Skopal, J. Pokorny, and V. Snasel. PM-tree: Pivoting metric tree for similarity search in multimedia databases. In *ADBIS*, pages 803–815, 2004.

[42] Y. Tao, X. Xiao, and R. Cheng. Range search on multidimensional uncertain data. *ACM Trans. Database Syst.*, 32(3), article 15, 2007.

[43] Y. Tao, M. L. Yiu, and N. Mamoulis. Reverse nearest neighbor search in metric spaces. *TKDE*, 18(9):1239–1252, 2006.

[44] E. Vidal. An algorithm for finding nearest neighbors in (approximately) constant average time. *Pattern Recognition Letters*, 4(3):145–157, 1986.

[45] P. N. Yianilos. Data structures and algorithms for nearest neighbor search in general metric spaces. In *SODA*, pages 311–321, 1993.

[46] Y. Zhang, X. Lin, W. Zhang, J. Wang, and Q. Lin. Effectively indexing the uncertain space. *IEEE Trans. Knowl. Data Eng.*, 22(9): 1247–1261, 2010.

[47] Y. Zhang, W. Zhang, Q. Lin, and X. Lin. Effectively indexing the multi-dimensional uncertain objects for range searching. In *EDBT*, pages 504–515, 2012.

[48] R. Zhu, B. Wang, and G. Wang. Indexing uncertain data for supporting range queries. In *WAIM*, pages 72–83, 2014.

APPENDIX

A. PROOF OF LEMMA 1

LEMMA 1. *Given a pivot set P, if an instance object u_{ij} is enclosed in R_q, then $\phi(u_{ij})$ is certainly contained in the mapped range region $\phi(R_q)$, where $\phi(R_q) = \{\langle x_1, x_2, \ldots, x_{|P|}\rangle \mid 1 \le t \le |P| \wedge x_t \ge 0 \wedge x_t \in [d(q, p_t) - R, d(q, p_t) + R]\}$.*

PROOF. Assume, to the contrary, that there exists an instance object $u_{ij} \in R_q$ but $\phi(u_{ij}) \notin \phi(R_q)$, i.e., $\exists\, p_t \in P$, $d(u_{ij}, p_t) > d(q, p_t) + R$ or $d(u_{ij}, p_t) < d(q, p_t) - R$. If $d(u_{ij}, p_t) > d(q, p_t) + R$ or $d(u_{ij}, p_t) < d(q, p_t) - R$, then $d(q, u_{ij}) \ge |d(u_{ij}, p_t) - d(q, p_t)| > R$ according to the triangle inequality, which contradicts with our assumption. Consequently, the proof completes. □

B. PROOF OF LEMMA 2

LEMMA 2. *Given a pivot set P, for an instance object u_{ij}, if there exists a pivot p_t ($\in P$) satisfying $d(u_{ij}, p_t) \le R - d(q, p_t)$, then u_{ij} is certainly included in R_q.*

PROOF. Given a query object q, an instance object u_{ij}, and a pivot p_t, we have $d(q, u_{ij}) \le d(u_{ij}, p_t) + d(q, p_t)$ because of the triangle inequality. If $d(u_{ij}, p_t) \le R - d(q, p_t)$, then $d(q, u_{ij}) \le R - d(q, p_t) + d(q, p_t) = R$. Thus, u_{ij} is for sure contained in R_q, which completes the proof. □

C. PROOF OF LEMMA 3

LEMMA 3. *Given a MPRQ(q, R, θ) and a pivot set P,* $u\pi(u_i, R_q) = \sum_{\phi(u_{ij}) \in \phi(R_q)} Pr(u_{ij})$.

PROOF. Let $S_{ui} = \{u_{ij} \mid u_{ij} \in R_q\}$ and $S_{\phi(ui)} = \{u_{ij} \mid \phi(u_{ij}) \in \phi(R_q)\}$. We have $S_{ui} \subseteq S_{\phi(ui)}$ according to Lemma 1. Consequently, $\pi(u_i, R_q) = \sum_{u_{ij} \in S_{ui}} Pr(u_{ij}) \le \sum_{u_{ij} \in S_{\phi(ui)}} Pr(u_{ij}) = \sum_{\phi(u_{ij}) \in \phi(R_q)} Pr(u_{ij})$. Hence, $u\pi(u_i, R_q)$ can be set as $\sum_{\phi(u_{ij}) \in \phi(R_q)} Pr(u_{ij})$. The proof completes.□

D. PROOF OF LEMMA 4

LEMMA 4. *Given a MPRQ(q, R, θ) and a pivot set P,* $l\pi(u_i, R_q) = \sum_{\exists p_t \in P \text{ st. } d(u_{ij}, p_t) \le R - d(q, p_t)} Pr(u_{ij})$.

PROOF. Let $S_{ui} = \{u_{ij} \mid u_{ij} \in R_q\}$ and $S_P = \{u_{ij} \mid \exists\, p_t\ (\in P) \text{ s.t. } d(u_{ij}, p_t) \le R - d(q, p_t)\}$. According to Lemma 2, we can get that $S_{ui} \supseteq S_P$. Consequently, $\pi(u_i, R_q) = \sum_{u_{ij} \in S_{ui}} Pr(u_{ij}) \ge \sum_{u_{ij} \in S_P} Pr(u_{ij}) = \sum_{\exists p_t \in P \text{ st. } d(u_{ij}, p_t) \le R - d(q, p_t)} Pr(u_{ij})$. Therefore, $l\pi(u_i, R_q)$ can be set as $\sum_{\exists p_t \in P \text{ st. } d(u_{ij}, p_t) \le R - d(q, p_t)} Pr(u_{ij})$, which completes the proof. □

E. PROOF OF THEOREM 2

THEOREM 2. *Given a MkPRQ(q, R, θ), let* LB_k (UB_k) *be the k-th largest value of* $l\pi(u, R_q)$ ($u\pi(u, R_q)$) *for* $u \in U$, *then (1)* u_i *can be safely pruned if* $u\pi(u_i, R_q) < LB_k$, *and (2)* u_i *can be validated if* $l\pi(u_i, R_q) \ge UB_k$.

PROOF. According to the definitions of $l\pi(u, R_q)$ and $u\pi(u, R_q)$, $l\pi(u, R_q) \le \pi(u, R_q) \le u\pi(u, R_q)$. First, if $u\pi(u_i, R_q) < LB_k$, there exists k uncertain objects u_j $(1 \le j \le k)$ with $\pi(u_i, R_q) \le u\pi(u_i, R_q) < LB_k \le l\pi(u_j, R_q) \le \pi(u_j, R_q)$. Thus, u_i can not be a real answer object, and can be discarded safely. Second, assume, to the contrary, that an uncertain object u_i cannot be an actual answer object if $l\pi(u_i, R_q) > UB_k$. In other words, there exists k uncertain objects u_j $(1 \le j \le k)$, with $\pi(u_j, R_q) > \pi(u_i, R_q)$. Since $\pi(u_i, R_q) \ge l\pi(u_i, R_q) \ge UB_k$, there exists k uncertain objects u_j $(1 \le j \le k)$ with $u\pi(u_j, R_q) \ge \pi(u_j, R_q) > \pi(u_i, R_q) \ge UB_k$, which contradicts with the definition of UB_k. Consequently, u_i can be validated if $l\pi(u_i, R_q) \ge UB_k$. The proof completes. □

F. PSEUDO-CODE OF *k*UtMA

Algorithm 3 depicts the pseudo-code of *UPB-tree based MkPRQ Algorithm* (*k*UtMA), which follows a filtering-refinement framework. It takes as inputs q, R, θ, and an uncertain object set U indexed by a UPB-tree, and outputs the result set S_r of the *MkPRQ(q, R, θ)*. In the filtering phase, *k*UtMA first computes $\phi(q)$ and $\phi(R_q)$ using a pivot table P (line 1). Then, it traverses B$^+$-tree in a depth-first manner (lines 2-20). During the traversal, it finds the candidate uncertain objects (maintained in a set S_c) and the uncertain instance objects needed further verification (preserved in a set IS_c) based on Lemma 1 and Lemma 2, and updates $u\pi(u_i, R_q)$ and $l\pi(u_i, R_q)$ for the uncertain objects u_i in S_c via Lemma 3 and Lemma 4. Next, LB_k and UB_k are updated using S_c according to their definitions (line 21). Thereafter, the algorithm validates or filters out the uncertain objects u_i in S_c according to Theorems 1 and 2, and removes corresponding uncertain instance objects u_{ik} from IS_c (lines 22-26). After that, during the refinement phase, *k*UtMA first verifies every uncertain instance object u_{ij} in IS_c in order to tighten $u\pi(u_i, R_q)$, $l\pi(u_i, R_q)$, LB_k, and UB_k (lines 28-29), and then, it validates or prunes u_i according to Theorems 1 and 2, and removes corresponding uncertain instance objects u_{ik} from IS_c (lines 30-33). Finally, the result set S_r of the *MkPRQ(q, R, θ)* is retrieved to complete the process (line 34).

Algorithm 3 UPB-tree based M*k*PRQ Algorithm (*k*UtMA)

Input: q, R, θ, an uncertain object set U indexed by a UPB-tree
Output: the result set S_r of a *MkPRQ(q, R, θ)*
/* S_c: a set of candidate uncertain objects; IS_c: a candidate instance set. */
1: compute $\phi(q)$ and $\phi(R_q)$ using a pivot table P // $\phi(q) = \langle d(q, p_t) \mid p_t \in P \rangle$
2: push the root node of B$^+$-tree into a heap H
3: **while** $H \ne \varnothing$ **do**
4: de-heap the top node N from H
5: **if** N is non-leaf node **then**
6: **for** each entry e in N **do**
7: **if** $MBB(e.ptr) \cap \phi(R_q) \ne \varnothing$ **then**
8: push $e.ptr$ into H
9: **else** // N is leaf node
10: **if** $MBB(N) \subseteq \phi(R_q)$ **then**
11: **for** each entry e in N **do**
12: **if** $e.id \notin S_c$ **then** insert $e.id$ into S_c
13: update $u\pi(e.id, R_q)$ using Lemma 3
14: update $l\pi(e.id, R_q)$ or insert $e.ptr$ into IS_c using Lemma 4
15: **else**
16: **for** each entry e in N **do**
17: **if** $\phi(e.ptr) \in \phi(R_q)$ **then** // $\phi(e.ptr)$ is obtained by $e.key$
18-20: these lines are identical to the above lines 12-14
21: update LB_k and UB_k using S_c
22: **for** each u_i in S_c **do**
23: **if** $l\pi(u_i, R_q) \ge UB_k$ **then** // Theorem 2
24: insert u_i into S_r and remove all u_{ik} from IS_c
25: **else if** $u\pi(u_i, R_q) < \max\{\theta, LB_k\}$ **then** // Theorems 1-2
26: remove all u_{ik} form IS_c
27: **for** each u_{ij} in IS_c **do**
28: **if** $d(q, u_{ij}) \le R$ **then** update $l\pi(u_i, R_q)$ and LB_k
29: **else** update $u\pi(u_i, R_q)$ and UB_k
30: **if** $l\pi(u_i, R_q) \ge UB_k$ **then** // Theorem 2
31: insert u_i into S_r and remove all u_{ik} from IS_c
32: **else if** $u\pi(u_i, R_q) < \max\{\theta, LB_k\}$ **then** // Theorems 1-2
33: remove all u_{ik} from IS_c
34: **return** S_r

G. PROOF OF LEMMA 5

LEMMA 5. *Given a pivot set P and a query object q, for an uncertain object* u_i, $u\pi(u_i, R_q) = \min_{p_t \in P} \int_{d(q,p_t)-R}^{d(q,p_t)+R} \mathcal{G}_{p_t,i}(x)dx$.

PROOF. Based on the triangle inequality, given *a* pivot p_t, we have $d(q, p_t) - R \le d(u_i, p) \le d(q, p_t) + R$ if $d(q, u_i) \le R$, but the reverse is not true. Hence, $\pi(u_i, R_q) = Pr(d(q, u_i) \le R) \le Pr(d(q, p_t) - R \le d(u_i, p) \le d(q, p_t) + R) = \int_{d(q,p_t)-R}^{d(q,p_t)+R} \mathcal{G}_{p_t,i}(x)dx$, and $u\pi(u_i, R_q)$ can be set as $\min_{p_t \in P} \int_{d(q,p_t)-R}^{d(q,p_t)+R} \mathcal{G}_{p_t,i}(x)dx$. The proof completes. □

H. RPOOF OF LEMMA 6

LEMMA 6. *Given a pivot set P and a query object q, for an uncertain object* u_i, $l\pi(u_i, R_q) = \max_{p_t \in P} \int_{0}^{R-d(q,p_t)} \mathcal{G}_{p_t,i}(x)dx$.

PROOF. According to the triangle inequality, given *a* pivot p_t, if $d(u_i, p_t) \ge R - d(q, p_t)$, then $d(q, u_i) \le R$. Hence, $\pi(u_i, R_q) = Pr(d(q, u) \le R) \ge Pr(d(u_i, p_t) \ge R - d(q, p_t)) = \int_{0}^{R-d(q,p_t)} \mathcal{G}_{p_t,i}(x)dx$, and thus, $l\pi(u_i, R_q)$ can be set as $\max_{p_t \in P} \int_{0}^{R-d(q,p_t)} \mathcal{G}_{p_t,i}(x)dx$, which completes the proof. □

Algorithm 4 UPB-forest based M*k*PRQ Algorithm (*k*UfMA)

```
Input: q, R, θ, an uncertain object set U indexed by a UPB-forest
Output: the result set S_r of a MkPRQ(q, R, θ)
1: PB_k = 0 and compute S_pt = {x | x ∈ [⌊(d(q, p_t) − R)/s⌋, ⌈(d(q, p_t) + R)/s⌉ −
   1]} and S′_pt = {x | x ∈ [0, ⌊(R − d(q, p_t))/s⌋ − 1]} for every p_t ∈ P  // s =
   d⁺/n, and S_pt is a set of slots x (∈ φ_pt(R_q) = [d(q, p_t) − R, d(q, p_t) + R])
2: for each B⁺-tree B_t (0 ≤ t < |P|) of the UPB-forest do
3:   for each leaf entry ⟨u_i, key, pr⟩ in B_t with the key ∈ S_pt or key ∈ S′_pt do
4:     update uπ(u_i, R_q) or lπ(u_i, R_q) using Lemma 5 or Lemma 6
5:     if uπ(u_i, R_q) ≥ θ and u_i ∉ S_c then  // Theorem 1
6:       insert u_i into S_c
7: update LB_k and UB_k using S_c
8: for every u_i ∈ S_c do
9:   if lπ(u_i, R_q) ≥ UB_k then  // Theorem 2
10:    insert u_i into S_r
11:  else if uπ(u_i, R_q) < max{θ, LB_k, PB_k} then  // Theorems 1-3
12:    prune u_i
13:  else if π(u_i, R_q) ≥ max{θ, PB_k} then  // Theorems 1 and 3
14:    update S_r and PB_k
15: return S_r
```

I. PSEUDO-CODE OF *k*UfMA

Algorithm 4 presents the pseudo-code of *UPB-forest based MkPRQ Algorithm* (*k*UfMA), which follows a filtering-refinement framework. It takes as inputs q, R, θ, and an uncertain object set U indexed by a UPB-forest, and outputs the result set S_r of the *MkPRQ*(q, R, θ). In the filtering phase, *k*UfMA first initializes PB_k to 0, and computes the set S_{pt} of the slots contained in the mapped search region $\phi_{pt}(R_q)$ and the set S'_{pt} for each $p_t \in P$ (line 1). It then traverses each B$^+$-tree B_t of UPB-forest to search leaf entries $\langle u_i, key, pr\rangle$ of B_t with their $keys \in S_{pt}$ or $keys \in S'_{pt}$ (line 3), updates $u\pi(u_i, R_q)$ or $l\pi(u_i, R_q)$ based on Lemma 5 or Lemma 6 (line 4), and inserts all the qualified candidates u_i (i.e., $u\pi(u_i, R_q) \geq \theta$ and $u_i \notin S_c$) into S_c (lines 5-6).Next, LB_k and UB_k are updated using S_c according to their definitions (line 7). In the refinement phase, for every $u_i \in S_c$, the algorithm adds u_i to S_r if $l\pi(u_i, R_q) \geq UB_k$ (lines 9-10), and filters out u_i if $u\pi(u_i, R_q) < \max\{\theta, LB_k, PB_k\}$ according to Theorems 1-3 (lines 11-12). Otherwise, it computes $\pi(u_i, R_q)$ using the numerical integration, which is derived by calling GNU Scientific Library with the error bound set to 10^{-5} and then updates S_r and PB_k using u_i based on Theorems 1 and 3 (lines 13-14). Finally, the final result set S_r of the *MkPRQ*(q, R, θ) is returned to complete the process (line 15).

Algorithm 5 Incremental Pivot Selection Algorithm (IPS)

```
Input: a set U of uncertain objects, the number t of pivots requested
Output: a set P of t pivots (i.e., |P| = t)
1: P_c = HF(cert(U), cp_scale)  // get a candidate pivot set P_c with
                                    |P_c| = cp_scale
2: P = ∅
3: while |P| < t do
4:   select p from P_c with the maximum ϵ_{P∪{p}}
5:   P = P ∪ {p} and P_c = P_c − {p}
6: return P
```

J. PSEUDO-CODE OF IPS

Algorithm 5 depicts the pseudo-code of IPS. First, IPS invokes HF algorithm to get a candidate pivot set P_c from *cert*(U) (line 1), as *cert*(U) contains representative certain objects for the uncertain objects in U. Thereafter, it picks incrementally the pivots from P_c to maximize ϵ_P (lines 3-5). Initially, a pivot set P is empty. Then, IPS performs a *while-loop* until $|P| = t$, i.e., t pivots are selected. Each time, the algorithm chooses a pivot p from P_c to maximize $\epsilon_{P\cup\{p\}}$ (line 4), and updates P to $P \cup \{p\}$ and P_c to $P_c - \{p\}$ (line 5). Finally, the set P of t selected pivots is returned (line 6).

K. DESCRIPTION OF DATA

English (available at *http://www.sisap.org/Metric_Space _Library.html*) contains the words extracted from the English language dictionary, and edit distance is employed to compute the distance between two words. *Color* (available at *http://www.sisap.org/Metric_Space_Library.html*) denotes the first eight dimensions of color histograms extracted from an image database, and L_5-norm is utilized to compare the color image features. *SF* (available at *http://www.dbs.informatik.uni-muenchen.de/~seidl*) consists of the locations in San Francisco, and L_2-norm is used to measure their similarity. *DNA* (available at *http://www.ncbi.nlm.nih.gov/genome*) includes DNA data, and hamming distance is utilized to measure the similarity.

Efficient Route Planning on Public Transportation Networks: A Labelling Approach

Sibo Wang[1] Wenqing Lin[2] Yi Yang[3] Xiaokui Xiao[1] Shuigeng Zhou[3]

[1]Nanyang Technological University
{wang0759, xkxiao}@ntu.edu.sg

[2] Institute for Infocomm Research, Singapore
linw@i2r.a-star.edu.sg

[3]Fudan University
{yyang1, sgzhou}@fudan.edu.cn

ABSTRACT

A public transportation network can often be modeled as a *timetable graph* where (i) each node represents a station; and (ii) each directed edge $\langle u, v \rangle$ is associated with a *timetable* that records the departure (resp. arrival) time of each vehicle at station u (resp. v). Several techniques have been proposed for various types of route planning on timetable graphs, e.g., retrieving the route from a node to another with the shortest travel time. These techniques, however, either provide insufficient query efficiency or incur significant space overheads.

This paper presents *Timetable Labelling (TTL)*, an efficient indexing technique for route planning on timetable graphs. The basic idea of *TTL* is to associate each node u with a set of *labels*, each of which records the shortest travel time from u to some other node v given a certain departure time from u; such labels would then be used during query processing to improve efficiency. In addition, we propose query algorithms that enable *TTL* to support three popular types of route planning queries, and investigate how we reduce the space consumption of *TTL* with advanced preprocessing and label compression methods. By conducting an extensive set of experiments on real world datasets, we demonstrate that *TTL* significantly outperforms the states of the art in terms of query efficiency, while incurring moderate preprocessing and space overheads.

Categories and Subject Descriptors

H.2.8 [**Database Applications**]: Spatial Databases and GIS

Keywords

Transportation Network; Path Queries; Algorithm

1. INTRODUCTION

Identifying fast routes in transportation networks is an important problem with applications in map services and navigation systems. This problem has been extensively studied in the past decades, yielding a plethora of indexing techniques that aim to improve query efficiency at reasonable costs of pre-computation and space.

SIGMOD'15, May 31–June 4, 2015, Melbourne, Victoria, Australia.

ACM 978-1-4503-2758-9/15/05 ...$15.00.
http://dx.doi.org/10.1145/2723372.2749456 .

Most of the existing techniques, however, consider *private transportation*, i.e., they assume that the traversal from one network location to another is carried out with a private vehicle without any service time constraint. In contrast, relatively less effort has been made for the (equally important) case of *public transportation*, where any traversal between different network locations relies on transportation services (e.g., buses, subways, ferries, etc.) that run on fixed routes with pre-defined schedules.

Route planning for public transportation drastically differs from that for private transportation, as the former needs to take into account additional spatiotemporal constraints that do not apply to the latter, such as the time required to wait for a bus at a station, or the feasibility of transferring from one bus to another given their respective schedules. Towards addressing the problem, a common approach is to model a public transportation network as a *timetable graph* [32], where (i) each node represents a station; and (ii) each directed edge $\langle u, v \rangle$ is associated with a timetable that records the departure (resp. arrival) time of each vehicle at station u (resp. v). Three types of route planning queries on timetable graphs have been extensively studied:

1. *Earliest Arrival Path (EAP):* If we are at station A at time t_d, what is the earliest time that we can arrive at station B, and which is the corresponding route?

2. *Latest Departure Path (LDP):* If we plan to arrive at station B no later than time t_a, what is the latest time that we should depart from station A, and which route should we take?

3. *Shortest Duration Path (SDP):* If we are to depart from station A no sooner than time t_d and arrive at station B no later than time t_a, which is the route that would minimize the duration of our trip from A to B?

As shown by Cooke et al. in [10], each of the above three types of queries can be solved with a modified version of the Dijkstra's algorithm [17] that exploits the temporal information in the timetable graph G. Cooke et al.'s method, however, is inefficient for the large transportation networks (with millions of temporal edges) commonly seen in practice. Therefore, numerous techniques (e.g., [7, 12, 16, 21]) are proposed to improve over Cooke et al.'s solution in terms of query efficiency. In particular, the state-of-the-art techniques either pre-arrange the temporal edges in G in a certain order [16] or augment G with information about certain important routes [21], and they accelerate query processing by utilizing the edge arrangement or the pre-computed information. Nevertheless, as we will show in our experiments, these techniques [16, 21] still incur considerable query overheads on sizable timetable graphs G, since they require traversing a substantial portion of the temporal

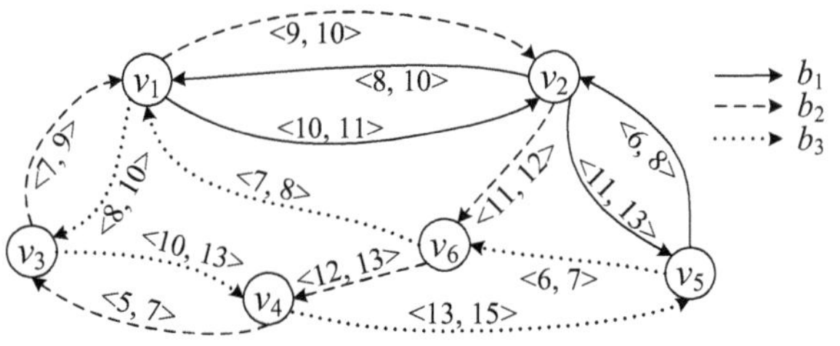

Figure 1: A timetable graph G.

edges in G (or its augmented version). This motivates us to develop a more efficient route planning schema on transportation networks.

Contributions. This paper presents *Timetable Labelling (TTL)*, an efficient indexing technique for route planning on timetable networks. The basic idea of *TTL* is to associate each node u with a set of *labels*, each of which records the shortest travel time from u to some other node v given a certain departure time from u. The labels are constructed in such a way that, for any EAP, LDP, or SDP query from a node u to another node v, we can efficient retrieve a tiny summary of the query result by inspecting the label sets of u and v (without inspecting G), and we can easily convert the summary into the corresponding path in $O(k)$ time, where k is the number of nodes in the path. Compared with the existing techniques [10, 16, 21], *TTL* incurs lower query overheads as it completely avoids traversing G during query processing. In particular, in our experiments on 11 real transportation networks, *TTL* is shown to outperform the state of the art by up to 3 orders of magnitude in terms of query efficiency.

TTL is similar in spirit to *hierarchical hub labelling (HHL)* [3] (i.e., the state-of-the-art approach for shortest path queries on simple graphs), as both of them rely on pre-computed label sets for query processing. Nevertheless, *TTL* is not a straightforward extension of *HHL* that simply augments each label set with timetable information. Instead, *TTL* incorporates a set of non-trivial optimization techniques in its preprocessing and query algorithms, which exploit the characteristics of timetable graphs to achieve significant improvements in terms of both query performance and space consumptions. More specifically, we make the following contributions.

- We propose *TTL*, an indexing approach for timetable graphs that assigns two label sets for each node. We devise an advanced query processing algorithm for *TTL*, such that each EAP, LDP, or SDP query from a node u to another node v can be answered with a linear scan of u and v's label sets, followed by an $O(k)$-time process to retrieve the query result P, where k is the number of nodes in P. In contrast, a straightforward query algorithm would require quadratic (instead of linear) time in inspecting the label sets of u and v. (Sections 3 and 4)
- We study the preprocessing algorithm for *TTL* from both theoretical and practical perspectives. On the theoretical side, we show that there is a polynomial time algorithm that returns a *TTL* whose space consumption is $O(\sqrt{m})$ times larger than the optimal solution, where m is the number of edges in the timetable graph. On the practical side, we present a preprocessing algorithm motivated by our theoretical results, and show that it strikes a good balance between pre-computation cost and index quality. (Sections 5 and 6)
- We improve the performance of *TTL* by devising several efficient techniques: (i) novel techniques for compressing the label sets of *TTL*, which significantly reduce space consumption without substantial effects on query performance, and (ii) a simple and intuitive method to concisely represent the results of route planning queries on transportation networks, which not only is user friendly but also leads to higher query efficiency in *TTL*. (Sections 7 and 8)
- We experimentally evaluate *TTL* against the states of the art, using 11 real transportation networks with up to 4 million edges. Our results demonstrate that *TTL* significantly outperforms competitors in terms of query efficiency, while incurring moderate preprocessing and space overheads. (Section 10)

2. PROBLEM DEFINITION

Let G be a multigraph with n nodes, such that (i) each node represents a station in a public transportation network, and (ii) each edge e from a node u to another node v is associated with a vehicle b and two timestamps t_d and t_a, which indicate that there is a vehicle b that departs from u at t_d and arrives at v at t_a, without any stops in between. (Note that there may exist multiple edges from u to v.) For convenience, we represent e as a tuple $\langle u, v, t_d, t_a, b\rangle$. We refer to b, t_d, and t_a as the vehicle, departure time, and arrival time of e, respectively, and we define the *duration* of e as $t_a - t_d$. In addition, we say that e is an *outgoing edge* of u and an *incoming edge* of v. We define the *out-degree* (resp. *in-degree*) of v as the number of its outgoing (reps. incoming) edges, denoted by $d_{out}(v)$ (resp. $d_{in}(v)$). We define the paths in G as follows:

DEFINITION 1 (PATHS). *A* ***path*** *P in G is a sequence $\langle e_1, e_2, \dots, e_k\rangle$ of edges in G, such that for any $i \in [1, k-1]$, the starting node of e_{i+1} equals the ending node of e_i, and the departure time of e_{i+1} is after the arrival time of e_i.* □

We define the starting node (resp. departure time) of P as that of e_1, the ending node (resp. arrival time) of P as that of e_k, and the duration of P as the difference between P's starting and arrival time. In addition, if all edges on P have the same vehicle b (i.e., P does not contain a transfer), then we refer to b as the vehicle of P; otherwise, we define the vehicle of P as $null$.

We consider three types of route planning queries on G, as defined in the following.

DEFINITION 2 (EARLIEST ARRIVAL PATH QUERY). *Given two nodes u and v in G and a starting timestamp t, an* ***earliest arrival path (EAP)*** *query asks for the path with the earliest arrival time among those that (i) start from u no sooner than t and (ii) end at v.* □

DEFINITION 3 (LATEST DEPARTURE PATH QUERY). *Given two nodes u and v in G and an ending timestamp t', a* ***latest departure path (LDP)*** *query asks for the path with the latest departure time among those that (i) start from u and (ii) end at v no later than t'.* □

DEFINITION 4 (SHORTEST DURATION PATH QUERY). *Given two nodes u and v in G, a starting timestamp t, and an ending timestamp t', a* ***shortest duration path (SDP)*** *query asks for the path with the shortest duration those that (i) start from u no sooner than t and (ii) end at v no latter than t'.* □

For simplicity, we use the term *path queries* to refer to EAP, LDP, and SDP queries. We illustrate Definitions 2-4 with an example.

EXAMPLE 1. Figure 1 shows a timetable graph G containing 6 nodes $v_1, v_2, \dots, v_6$, and 14 edges. The ordered pair $\langle t_d, t_a\rangle$ on each edge e indicates that the departure (resp. arrival) time of the edge equals t_d (resp. t_a). We use solid, dashed, and dotted lines to represent the edges correspond to vehicles b_1, b_2, and b_3, respectively. Suppose that we are at v_5 at time $t = 5$, and plan to travel to v_1. In that case, the earliest time that we can arrive at v_1 is

Notation	Description
G	a timetable graph
n	the number of nodes in G
$\langle v, u, t_d, t_a, b\rangle$	an edge in E
$P = \langle e_1, \ldots, e_k\rangle$	a path in G (see Section 2)
$o(v)$	the rank of v in the node order o (see Section 3)
$\mathcal{L}$	the TTL on G (see Definition 7)
$\langle v, t_d, t_a, b, p\rangle$	a label in $\mathcal{L}$ (see Definition 7)
$L_{in}(v)$	the in-label set of v (see Definition 7)
$L_{out}(v)$	the out-label set of v (see Definition 7)
$\cdot$	a placeholder that denotes irrelevant information in the context

Table 1: Table of notations.

$t' = 8$, for which we need to take vehicle b_3 from v_5 at time 6, and stay on the vehicle until it arrives at v_1. In other words, if we have an EAP query from v_5 to v_1 with a starting timestamp $t = 5$, then the answer to the query is a path via vehicle b_3 that starts from v_5 at time 6 and ends at v_1 at time 8. On the other hand, for an LDP query from v_1 to v_4 with an ending timestamp $t' = 13$, then the answer is a path that (i) starts from v_1 at time 10 via vehicle b_1, (ii) transfers to vehicle b_2 at v_2, and then (iii) arrives at v_4 at time 13 on b_2. Finally, for an SDP query from v_5 to v_1 with starting time $t = 6$ and ending time $t' = 10$, the query result is identical to the EAP query mentioned above. □

Given G, our objective is to construct an index structure on G that can efficiently answer path queries. Table 1 lists the notations that we will frequently use in the paper. In particular, we will use "$\cdot$" as a placeholder to denote some information that is irrelevant to the discussions in the context.

3. TIMETABLE LABELLING

This section presents *timetable labelling (TTL)*, our index structure for route planning on timetable graphs. At a high level, a *TTL* index pre-computes two sets of *labels*, $L_{in}(v)$ and $L_{out}(v)$, for each node v in G, such that each label in $L_{in}(v)$ (resp. $L_{out}(v)$) is a tuple concerning a "fast" path that ends at (starts from) v. The construction of the label sets is governed by a strict total order o on the nodes in G, which, intuitively, defines the relative importance of each node with respect to the others. We refer to o as the *node order*, and use $o(v)$ to denote the rank of a node v in o. Without loss of generality, we assume that $o(v)$ is an integer in $[1, n]$, and say that v ranks lower than another node u if $o(v) > o(u)$. Given a timetable graph G and a node order o, the *TTL* index can be uniquely constructed. Specifically, *TTL* is defined based on the concepts of *canonical paths*.

DEFINITION 5 (CANONICAL PATHS). *Given a node order o and two nodes u and v in G, a path P from u to v is a* **canonical path**, *if it satisfies the following constraints:*

1. ***Dominance Constraint:*** *There does not exist a path from u to v with (i) departure time later than P's and arrival time no later than that of P, or (ii) departure time no earlier than P's and arrival time earlier than that of P.*
2. ***Rank Constraint:*** *Among all nodes on P, either u or v has the highest rank.* □

Intuitively, the dominance constraint in Definition 5 requires that a canonical path to be both the earliest arrival path and the latest departure path from u to v at a certain timestamp. Meanwhile, the rank constraint is crucial in proving the correctness of *TTL*'s query algorithm, which will be discussed in Section 4. We illustrate Definition 5 with an example.

v	$L_{in}(v)$	$L_{out}(v)$
v_2	$\langle v_1, 9, 10, b_2, null\rangle$ $\langle v_1, 10, 11, b_1, null\rangle$	$\langle v_1, 8, 10, b_1, null\rangle$
v_4	$\langle v_1, 10, 13, null, v_2\rangle$ $\langle v_2, 11, 13, b_2, v_6\rangle$ $\langle v_3, 10, 13, b_3, null\rangle$	$\langle v_1, 5, 9, b_2, v_3\rangle$ $\langle v_3, 5, 7, b_2, null\rangle$

Table 2: The label sets of v_2 and v_4 in a *TTL* index for Figure 1, with a node order $o(v_i) = i$ for $i \in [1, 6]$.

EXAMPLE 2. Consider the timetable graph in Figure 1. Assume that we use a node order $o(v_1) < o(v_2) < \ldots < o(v_6)$. The path P from v_5 to v_1 taking vehicle b_3 at time $t = 6$ is a canonical path, since (i) no path from v_5 to v_1 after time $t = 6$ can arrive at v_1 earlier than P does or arrive v_1 before time $t = 8$ with departure time later than P's, and (ii) the rank of v_1 is the highest among all nodes on P. In contrast, the path from v_6 to v_3 taking b_3 via v_1 at time $t = 7$ is not a canonical path, since the rank of v_1 is higher than those of v_3 and v_6. □

In relation to canonical paths, we also introduce the concepts of *intermediate nodes* and *pivots*.

DEFINITION 6 (PIVOTS). *An* ***intermediate node*** *of a path P refers to any node on P, except for P's starting and ending nodes. The* ***pivot*** *of a canonical path is null if the path contains only two nodes; otherwise, it is the intermediate node of the path with the highest rank.* □

Given Definition 5 and 6, a *TTL* index on G is *uniquely* determined by a node order o as follows:

DEFINITION 7 (TIMETABLE LABELLING). *Given a node order o, let $\mathcal{C}$ be the set of all canonical paths on G. For each $P \in \mathcal{C}$, let u, v, t_d, t_a, b, and p be P's starting node, ending node, departure time, arrival time, vehicle, and pivot, respectively. A* ***Timetable Labelling (TTL)*** *consists of label sets where P is mapped to a label $l = \langle x, t_d, t_a, b, p\rangle$ in either $L_{out}(u)$ or $L_{in}(v)$ as follows:*

1. *If $o(u) > o(v)$ (i.e., u ranks lower than v), then $x = v$ and $l \in L_{out}(u)$.*
2. *If $o(u) < o(v)$, then $x = u$ and $l \in L_{in}(v)$.* □

In short, in a *TTL* index, the label sets $L_{in}(v)$ and $L_{out}(v)$ for a node v only contain the information about the canonical paths between v and the nodes that rank higher than v. For convenience, we refer to $L_{in}(v)$ (resp. $L_{out}(v)$) as the *in-label set* (resp. *out-label set*) of v, and each label in $L_{in}(v)$ (resp. $L_{out}(v)$) as an *in-label* (resp. *out-label*) of v. As an example, Table 2 shows the label sets of v_2 and v_4 in Figure 1, assuming a node order $o(v_1) < o(v_2) < \ldots < o(v_6)$.

The label sets of a *TTL* index have an important property: for any path query from a node u to another node v, we can retrieve essential information about the query result from the label sets of u and v, as shown in the following lemma.

LEMMA 1. *Let q be a path query from a node u to another v, and P be the result of q. Then, $L_{out}(u)$ contains a label $\langle w, t_d, t_a, b, p\rangle$, and $L_{in}(v)$ contains a label $\langle w', t'_d, t'_a, b', p'\rangle$, such that one of the following conditions holds:*

1. *$w = v$, and t_d, t_a, b, p equal P's departure time, arrival time, vehicle, and pivot, respectively. That is, $L_{out}(u)$ contains a label pertinent to P.*

2. $w' = u$, and t'_d, t'_a, b', p' equal P's departure time, arrival time, vehicle, and pivot, respectively. That is, $L_{in}(v)$ contains a label pertinent to P.

3. $w = w'$, $t_a \leq t'_d$, and t_d (resp. t'_a) equals P's departure (resp. arrival) time. That is, P contains a node w, such that $L_{out}(u)$ (resp. $L_{in}(v)$) contains a label pertinent to the sub-path of P from u to w (resp. from w to v). □

We demonstrate Lemma 1 with the following example.

EXAMPLE 3. Consider the label sets shown in Table 2 for the timetable graph in Figure 1. For an EAP query that from v_4 to v_2 with a starting timestamp $t = 4$, the result is a path P via vehicle b_2 that starts from v_4 at time 5, passes through v_3 and v_1, and ends at v_2 at time 10. Observe that the out-label set $L_{out}(v_4)$ of v_4 contains a label $\langle v_1, 5, 9, b_2, v_3 \rangle$, which captures the sub-path of P from v_4 to v_1. Meanwhile, the in-label set $L_{in}(v_2)$ of v_2 contains a label $\langle v_1, 9, 10, b_2, null \rangle$, which captures the sub-path of P from v_1 to v_2. □

Lemma 1 is the basis of the query algorithms for *TTL*, we clarify in Section 4. Meanwhile, the following lemma shows that the label sets of a *TTL* index is *minimal*, in the sense that if we remove any label from the label sets, we can no longer answer queries based on Lemma 2.

LEMMA 2. *For any node v, if we remove any label from $L_{in}(v)$ or $L_{out}(v)$, then Lemma 1 no longer holds.* □

In subsequent sections, we first introduce *TTL*'s query processing procedure (in Section 4), followed by its preprocessing algorithm (in Section 5) and several optimizations in terms of query time and index space (in Section 6 and 7). This is for the ease of exposition, since the preprocessing method of *TTL* is considerably more sophisticated than its query algorithm.

Remark. *TTL* can be regarded as a non-trivial extension of *Hierarchical Hub Labelling (HHL)* [3], which is the state-of-the-art indexing approach for answering shortest path queries on simple graphs. In particular, *HHL* also constructs label sets based on a total order of nodes, and it utilizes the label sets for query processing; nevertheless, the label sets of *HHL* do not contain any temporal information. Compared with *HHL*, *TTL*'s preprocessing and query algorithms are much more sophisticated, due to the complexity induced by the spatiotemporal constraints in timetable graphs. Furthermore, *TTL* features several novel optimization methods (for reducing space consumption and improving query efficiency) that are unique to timetable graphs, as we clarify in Sections 7 and 8.

4. QUERY PROCESSING

This section presents the query algorithm for *TTL*. In a nutshell, *TTL*'s query algorithm consists of three phases:

1. *Candidate Generation:* This phase inspects the label sets of *TTL* to retrieve a set of *path sketches*, each of which corresponds to a *candidate* path that could be the answer for the given query.
2. *Refinement:* This phase inspects the path sketches produced by the candidate generation phase, and then pinpoints the sketch s_{ans} corresponds to the query answer.
3. *Path Reconstruction:* This phase converts the sketch s_{ans} back to a path on G, and returns the path as the query result.

In what follows, we elaborate each phase of *TTL*'s query algorithm, assuming that we are given an SDP query from a node u to another node v, with a starting timestamp t and an ending timestamp t'. We will clarify how the algorithm can be modified to handle EAP and LDP queries in Section 4.3.

4.1 Candidate Generation and Refinement

Consider the out-label set $L_{out}(u)$ of u and the in-label set $L_{in}(v)$ of v. By Definition 7, the labels in $L_{out}(u)$ and $L_{in}(v)$ capture the information about a set $\mathcal{P}_{uv}$ of paths from u to v as follows. First, if $L_{out}(u)$ contains a label $l_1 = \langle v, t_d, t_a, \cdot, \cdot \rangle$, then there exists a path P_1 from u to v with departure time t_d and arrival time t_a. In this case, we define the ordered pair $\langle l_1, null \rangle$ as a *sketch* of P_1. Second, if $L_{in}(v)$ contains a label $l_2 = \langle u, t'_d, t'_a, \cdot, \cdot \rangle$, then there is a path P_2 from u to v with departure time t'_d and arrival time t'_a. Accordingly, we refer to $\langle null, l_2 \rangle$ as a sketch of P_2. Third, if $L_{out}(u)$ and $L_{in}(v)$ contains labels $l_3 = \langle w, t^*_d, t^*_a, \cdot, \cdot \rangle$ and $l_4 = \langle w, t^\circ_d, t^\circ_a, \cdot, \cdot \rangle$, respectively, such that $t^*_a \leq t^\circ_d$, then there exists a path P_3 from u to v with departure time t^*_d and t°_a. In that case, we say that $\langle l_3, l_4 \rangle$ is a sketch of P_3. In summary, based on $L_{out}(u)$ and $L_{in}(v)$, we can construct the sketches for a set $\mathcal{P}_{uv}$ of paths from u to v, and each sketch records the departure and arrival time of the corresponding path.

By Lemma 1, $\mathcal{P}_{uv}$ must contain the answer P_{ans} to an SDP query from u to v with a starting timestamp t and an ending timestamp t'. If we are given the sketches of all paths in S_{uv}, then we can easily identify one corresponding to P_{ans}, by searching for the sketch with the shortest duration among those with departure time no sooner than t and arrival time no later than t'. However, constructing sketches for all paths in $\mathcal{P}_{uv}$ is costly, since $|\mathcal{P}_{uv}| = |L_{out}(u)| \cdot |L_{in}(v)|$ in the worst case. (This worst case occurs when each label in $L_{out}(u)$ can be combined with any label in $L_{in}(v)$ to form a path sketch.) Nevertheless, many of the sketches could have been omitted without affecting the correctness of the query result. For example, consider the label sets $L_{out}(v_4)$ and $L_{in}(v_2)$. Observe that $L_{out}(v_4)$ contains a label $l_1 = \langle v_1, 5, 9, b_2, v_3 \rangle$, which can form two path sketches when combined with the labels $l_2 = \langle v_1, 9, 10, b_2, null \rangle$ and $l_3 = \langle v_1, 10, 11, b_1, null \rangle$ in $L_{in}(v_2)$. However, the sketch $\langle l_1, l_3 \rangle$ is *dominated* by the sketch $\langle l_1, l_2 \rangle$, in the sense that $\langle l_1, l_2 \rangle$ corresponds to a path that departs from u at time 5 and arrives at v at time 10, which is strictly better than the path corresponding to $\langle l_1, l_3 \rangle$, as the latter has departure time 5 and arrival time 11. In other words, the path pertinent to $\langle l_1, l_3 \rangle$ can never be the result for any path query, and hence, we can omit $\langle l_1, l_3 \rangle$ during query processing.

In general, when *TTL* inspects label sets in its candidate generation phase, it only constructs path sketches that are not dominated by others, so as to improve query efficiency. To facilitate this, the preprocessing algorithm of *TTL* sorts the labels l in each label set in ascending order of $f(l)$, where $f(l)$ is a total order of labels as follows: for any two labels $l_1 = \langle v, t_d, t_a, \cdot, \cdot \rangle$ and $l_2 = \langle v', t'_d, t'_a, \cdot, \cdot \rangle$ in the same label set, we have $f(l_1) < f(l_2)$ if and only if

1. $o(v) < o(v')$ (i.e., v ranks higher than v'), or
2. $o(v) = o(v')$ and $t_d < t'_d$, or
3. $o(v) = o(v')$, $t_d = t'_d$, and $t_a < t'_a$.

With the above ordering of labels, *TTL* generates path sketches in $O(|L_{out}(u)| + |L_{in}(v)|)$ time using the *SketchGen* method in Algorithm 1. The input to the algorithm includes $L_{out}(u)$ and $L_{in}(v)$, as well as the SDP query's starting timestamp t and ending timestmp t'; its output is a set S_{uv} of path sketches corresponding to the candidate answers for the query. The basic idea of the algorithm is to generate path sketches with two concurrent linear scans on $L_{out}(u)$ and $L_{in}(v)$, respectively.

Algorithm 1: *SketchGen*

input : $L_{out}(u)$, $L_{in}(v)$, t, t'
output: a set S_{uv} of path sketches

1 initialize $i = 1$, $j = 1$, and $C = \emptyset$;
2 **while** $i \le |L_{out}(u)|$ *or* $j \le |L_{in}(v)|$ **do**
3   let $l_u = \langle w, t_d, t_a, \cdot, \cdot \rangle$ be the i-th label of $L_{out}(v)$;
4   **if** $[t_d, t_a] \not\subseteq [t, t']$ **then**
5   increase i by one, and then goto Line 4;
6   **else if** $w = v$ **then**
7   insert $\langle l_u, null \rangle$ into S_{uv};
8   increase i by one, and then goto Line 4;
9   let $l_v = \langle w', t'_d, t'_a, \cdot, \cdot \rangle$ be the j-th tuple of $L_{in}(u)$;
10   **if** $[t'_d, t'_a] \not\subseteq [t, t']$ **then**
11   increase j by one, and then goto Line 4;
12   **else if** $w' = u$ **then**
13   insert $\langle null, l_v \rangle$ into S_{uv};
14   increase j by one, and then goto Line 4;
15   **if** $w = w'$ **then**
16   **if** $t_a \le t'_d$ **then**
17   add $\langle l_u, l_v \rangle$ into S_{uv};
18   increase i by one;
19   **else**
20   increase j by one;
21   **else**
22   **if** $o(w) < o(w')$ **then**
23   increase i by one;
24   **else**
25   increase j by one;
26 **return** S_{uv};

Specifically, *SketchGen* first scans the labels in $L_{out}(u)$, until it finds a label $l_u = \langle w, t_d, t_a, \cdot, \cdot \rangle$ with $t_d \ge t$ and $t_a \le t'$ (Lines 1-5). If $w = v$, then *SketchGen* inserts l_u into S_{uv} as a path sketch, since l_u captures a candidate path from u to v with departure time t_d and arrival time t_a; after that, *SketchGen* moves on to the next label in $L_{out}(u)$ (Lines 6-8).

On the other hand, if $w \ne v$, then *SketchGen* turns its attention to $L_{in}(v)$, and scans the labels in $L_{in}(v)$ until it counters a label $l_v = \langle w', t'_d, t'_a, \cdot, \cdot \rangle$ with $t'_d \ge t$ and $t'_a \le t'$ (Lines 9-11). If $w' = u$, then *SketchGen* adds l_v into S_{uv} as a path sketch, and moves on to the next label in $L_{in}(v)$ (Lines 12-14).

Meanwhile, if $w' \ne u$, then *SketchGen* considers whether l_u and l_v can be combined to form a path sketch $\langle l_u, l_v \rangle$. In particular, if $w = w'$ and $t_a \le t'_d$, then *SketchGen* inserts $\langle l_u, l_v \rangle$ into S_{uv}, and move on to the next label in $L_{out}(u)$ (Lines 15-18). However, if $w \ne w'$ or $t_a > t'_d$, then *SketchGen* would move on to the next label in either $L_{out}(u)$ or $L_{in}(v)$ to continue the construction of path sketches. Here, *SketchGen* differentiates two cases.

Case 1: $w = w'$ but $t_a > t'_d$. In this case, *SketchGen* proceeds to the next label in $L_{in}(v)$ (Lines 19-20). The rationale is that, due to the way that we sort the labels in $L_{in}(v)$, the next label in $L_{in}(v)$ could be $l^*_v = \langle w, t^*_d, \cdot, \cdot, \cdot \rangle$ with $t_a \le t^*_d$, in which case l_u and l^*_v may form a path sketch.

Case 2: $w \ne w'$. In this case, *SketchGen* checks whether $o(w) < o(w')$. If $o(w) < o(w')$ holds, then *SketchGen* moves on to the next label in $L_{out}(u)$ (Lines 21-23), since the label could be $l^*_u = \langle w', \cdot, t^*_a, \cdot, \cdot \rangle$, in which case l^*_u and l_v may form a path sketch. On the other hand, if $o(w) > o(w')$, then the next label in $L_{out}(u)$ cannot be combined with l_v as a path sketch, and hence, *SketchGen* would proceed to the next label in $L_{in}(v)$ instead.

In general, our discussions above are applicable for any pair of labels $l_u \in L_{out}(u)$ and $l_v \in L_{in}(v)$ encountered by *SketchGen* during its linear scans of $L_{out}(u)$ and $L_{in}(v)$. In particular, any labels with starting time before t or ending time after t' are omitted (Lines 4-5 and 10-11), while any remaining $l_u \in L_{out}(u)$ that concerns v and any remaining $l_v \in L_{in}(u)$ that concerns u are inserted into S_{uv} as path sketches (Lines 6-8 and 12-14). For the other labels, *SketchGen* carefully decides (i) whether a pair of labels can form a path sketch, and (ii) whether it should proceed to the next label in $L_{out}(v)$ or $L_{in}(v)$ (Lines 15-25).

It can be verified that *SketchGen* runs in $O(|L_{out}(u)| + |L_{out}(v)|)$ time and generates at most $O(|L_{out}(u)| + |L_{out}(v)|)$ path sketches in S_{uv}, since it linearly scans $L_{out}(u)$ and $L_{out}(v)$. In addition, S_{uv} always contains a sketch that corresponds to the answer of the given SDP query, as shown in Lemma 3. The rationale is that, due to the order in which *TTL* sorts the labels in each label set, the linear scans employed by *SketchGen* only omit the label pairs that either (i) cannot form path sketches or (ii) correspond to paths that are dominated by others.

LEMMA 3. *Let S_{uv} be the set of sketches that SketchGen returns for an SDP query, and P_{ans} be the answer of the query. Then, one of the sketches in S_{uv} corresponds to P_{ans}.* □

Once S_{uv} is obtained, it is straightforward to identify the sketch in S_{uv} that is pertinent to the SDP query result P_{ans}. In particular, for each sketch in S_{uv}, we can calculate the duration of the corresponding path based on the departure and arrival time recorded in the sketch; based on that, we can pinpoint the sketch with the shortest duration. In Section 4.2, we will explain how we can convert this sketch back into P_{ans}.

4.2 Path Reconstruction

Let s_{ans} be the sketch in S_{uv} that corresponds to the result P_{ans} of the given SDP query. Then, $s_{ans} = \langle l_u, l_v \rangle$, where l_u (resp. l_v) is either $null$ or a label in $L_{out}(u)$ (resp. $L_{in}(v)$). To transform s_{ans} back to P_{ans}, it suffices to convert $l_u \ne null$ (resp. $l_v \ne null$) to the canonical path P_u (resp. P_v) in G that correspond to l_u (res. l_v). Such conversions can be performed by exploiting the pivot of P_u (resp. P_v), which is recorded in l_u (resp. l_v). To explain, we first present a lemma about pivots.

LEMMA 4. *Let P be a canonical path from u to v, and p be the pivot of P. Then, the sub-path of P from u to p (resp. from p to v) is also a canonical path.* □

Suppose that the pivot of P_u is a node p, and $l_u = \langle w, \cdot, \cdot, \cdot, p \rangle$. Let P_1 (resp. P_2) be the sub-path of P from u to p (resp. from p to w). By Lemma 4, both P_1 and P_2 are canonical paths. Then, by Definition 7, there should exists two labels l_1 and l_2 (in *TTL*) that correspond to P_1 and P_2, respectively. In other words, we can "unfold" l_u into a sequence of labels $S = \langle l_1, l_2 \rangle$, such that the canonical path pertinent to l_u equals a concatenation of the canonical paths corresponding to l_1 and l_2. We refer to l_1 (resp. l_2) as the left (resp. right) child of l_u.

In general, the above unfolding method can be applied on any label $\langle \cdot, \cdot, \cdot, \cdot, p \rangle$ where $p \ne null$ (i.e., the label corresponds to a canonical path that contains at least two edges). Therefore, given the label sequence $S = \langle l_1, l_2 \rangle$ mentioned above, we can recursively modify S by replacing each label with its children, until every label in S has a $null$ pivot. In that case, each label in S represents an edge in G. Then, by replacing each label in S with its corresponding edge, we can transform S into the canonical path P_u pertinent to l_u. Using the same method, we can unfold l_v into its corresponding canonical path P_v, after which we can concatenate P_u and P_v to obtain the answer P_{ans} of the given SDP query.

Algorithm 2: *PathUnfold*

input : a label $l = \langle \cdot, \cdot, \cdot, \cdot, p \rangle$ in *TTL*
output: the canonical path corresponding to l

if $p = null$ **then**
  return a path that only contains the edge in G corresponding to l;
else
  l_1 = the left child of l;
  l_2 = the right child of l;
  P_1 = *PathUnfold*(l_1);
  P_2 = *PathUnfold*(l_2);
  set P = a concatenation of P_1 and P_2, with P_1 proceeding P_2;
  return P;

Algorithm 2 shows the pseudo-code of the above unfolding approach, which takes as input a label l and returns the canonical path P corresponding to l. The most crucial step of the algorithm is the identification of l's children. To ensure the efficiency of this step, *TTL* pre-computes two pointers from each label to its left and right children, respectively, so that its takes $O(1)$ time to pinpoint the children of any label. As such, the running time of Algorithm 2 is linear to the number of nodes on P.

EXAMPLE 4. Consider an SDP query from v_2 to v_4 in Figure 1, with starting time $t = 8$ and ending time $t' = 13$. By a linear scan of the labels in $L_{out}(v_2)$ and $L_{in}(v_4)$ (in Table 2), we obtain two path sketches: (i) $\langle l_1, l_2 \rangle$, with $l_1 = \langle v_1, 8, 10, b_1, null \rangle$ in $L_{out}(v_2)$ and the label $l_2 = \langle v_1, 10, 13, null, v_2 \rangle$ in $L_{in}(v_4)$, (ii) $\langle null, l_3 \rangle$, with $l_3 = \langle v_2, 11, 13, b_2, v_6 \rangle$ in $L_{in}(v_4)$. Then, we set $s_{ans} = \langle null, l_3 \rangle$, since $\langle null, l_3 \rangle$ has a shorter duration than $\langle l_1, l_2 \rangle$. After that, we unfold l_3 by recursively reconstructing the SDPs from v_2 to v_6 and v_6 to v_4. In the end, we obtain the path $P_{ans} = \langle \langle v_2, v_6, 11, 12, b_2 \rangle, \langle v_6, v_4, 12, 13, b_2 \rangle \rangle$. □

The following corollary shows the correctness of Algorithm 2.

COROLLARY 1. *Given a label l in TTL, Algorithm 2 returns the canonical path corresponding to l.* □

4.3 Summary and Query Extensions

Summing up the discussions in Sections 4.1 and 4.2, *TTL* answers any SDP query from u to v in $O(|L_{out}(u)| + |L_{in}(v)| + k)$ time, where k is the number of nodes on the query result. Furthermore, *TTL*'s query algorithm for SDP queries can be easily extended to support EAP and LDP queries. In particular, the extension is based on the following lemma about *SketchGen*.

LEMMA 5. *Let $L_{out}(u)$, $L_{in}(v)$, t, and t' be the input to SketchGen (as in Algorithm 1), and S_{uv} be its output. When $t' = +\infty$, one of the sketches in S_{uv} corresponds to the answer of an EAP query from u to v with starting time t. On the other hand, if $t = -\infty$, then S_{uv} contains a sketch corresponding to the answer of an LDP query from u to v with ending time t'.* □

By Lemma 5, if we are to answer an EAP query from u to v with starting time t, we can first invoke *SketchGen*, setting $t' = +\infty$. Then, we examine the path sketches returned by *SketchGen* to identify the one s_{ans} with the earliest arrival time. After that, we unfold s_{ans} into a path using Algorithm 2, and return the path as the query result.

On the other hand, if we are given an LDP query from u to v with ending time t, we can apply *SketchGen* with $t = -\infty$, and obtain a set of sketches S_{uv}. After that, we inspect S_{uv} to pinpoint the sketch s_{ans} with the latest departure time. Finally, we use Algorithm 2 to convert s_{ans} into the query answer. It can be verified that the above query algorithms for EAP and LDP queries have the same time complexity as the one for SDP queries.

5. INDEX CONSTRUCTION

This section presents the algorithms for constructing *TTL* indices, assuming that the node order o is given. (We will discuss the choice of node order in Section 6.) By Definition 7, each label in *TTL* corresponds to a canonical path in G, and vice versa. Therefore, if we are to build a *TTL* index $\mathcal{L}$ based on a node order o, then conceptually, we should identify all canonical paths in G, and convert each of them into a label in $\mathcal{L}$. But how can we derive all canonical paths in G? A straightforward approach is to run the temporal Dijkstra's algorithm to retrieve all temporal shortest paths in G, and then examine the paths obtained to identify the canonical paths. This approach, however, incurs prohibitive preprocessing costs due to the large number of temporal shortest paths that it retrieves. To address this issue, we will first present an algorithm for computing paths in G that satisfy the Dominance Constraint (referred to as the *non-dominated* paths) in Section 5.1. Then, we explain how the algorithm can be used to avoid computing the paths that violate Rank Constraint, which allows us to construct a *TTL* index $\mathcal{L}$ in a more efficient manner. Note that, even though our index construction algorithm has the same worst-case complexity as the straightforward approach, the former's practical efficiency is significantly higher than that of the latter, as we show in Appendix D.2.

5.1 Computing Non-Dominated Paths

Let u be a node in G, and T_d be a set that contains the departure timestamps of all outgoing edges of u. Suppose that we are to compute all non-dominated paths that start from a node u in G. We first make an interesting observation as follows.

OBSERVATION 1. *Let $t_{\dashv}$ be the largest timestamp in T_d. Then, any earliest arrival path (EAP) P from u to a node v with departure time $t_{\dashv}$ is a non-dominated path.* □

Based on Observation 1, we can compute all non-dominated paths that start from u at time $t_{\dashv}$, by deriving all EAPs from u at time $t_{\dashv}$. This derivation can be performed with a modified version of Dijkstra's algorithm [10], referred to as *temporal Dijkstra's algorithm*. First, we create a hash table A that maps each node v to the earliest arrival time (EAT) t_v from u to v. We initialize $t_v = +\infty$ for any $v \neq u$, and $t_v = 0$ otherwise. Then, we collect all outgoing edges of u with departure time $t_{\dashv}$, and insert them into a min-heap H that sorts edges in ascending order of their arrival timestamps. After that, we iteratively remove the top edge $e = \langle x, y, t_d, t_a, \cdot \rangle$ in H, and process it as follows. We first retrieve the current EAT of x and y (denoted as t_x and t_y, respectively) from the hash table A. If $t_d \geq t_x$ and $t_a < t_y$, we set $t_y = t_a$, and insert into H all outgoing edges of y with departure time no sooner than t_a. Finally, we proceed to pop the next edge in H. When H becomes empty, we terminate the algorithm. Then, by Observation 1, each final EAT t_v recorded in H corresponds to a non-dominated path (from u to v with starting time $t_{\dashv}$).

Now suppose that we apply the temporal Dijkstra's algorithm to compute all EAPs that start from u at time $t^*_{\dashv}$, where $t^*_{\dashv}$ denotes the second largest timestamp in T_d. We have another observation as follows.

OBSERVATION 2. *Then, any EAP P from u with departure time $t^*_{\dashv}$ is a non-dominated path, if it is not dominated by any EAP from u with departure time $t_{\dashv}$.* □

Given any EAP from u to v with departure time $t^*_{\dashv}$, we can decide whether it is a non-dominated path, by comparing its arrival time with that of the EAP from u to v with departure time $t_{\dashv}$. In general, an EAP from u with departure time t is a non-dominated path, if it is not dominated by any EAP from u with departure time $t^* > t$. Therefore, if we are to compute all non-dominated paths from u, we can examine the timestamps in T_d in descending order, and apply the modified Dijkstra's algorithm once for each timestamp $t \in T_d$, to identify the non-dominated EAPs from u with departure t. The following lemma shows that our approach does not miss any non-dominated path that starts from u.

LEMMA 6. *For any non-dominated path P starting from u, there exists a timestamp $t \in T_d$, such that P is an EAP starting from u at time t.* □

Finally, let us consider a "backward" version of the temporal Dijkstra's algorithm, such that (i) the min-heap H sorts edges based on arrival time, (ii) the hash table A records the latest departure time of each node, and (iii) we start by inserting into H all incoming edges of u with a given arrival time t'. It can be verified that such an algorithm computes the latest departure paths (LDP) that arrive at u at time t'. In addition, we can observe that an LDP to v with arrival time t' is non-dominated, if it is not dominated by any LDP to v with arrival time $t < t'$. Furthermore, we have the following lemma.

LEMMA 7. *Let T_a be a set that contains the arrival timestamps of all incoming edges of u. For any non-dominated path P ending at u, there exists a timestamp $t' \in T_a$, such that P is an LDP ending at u at time t'.* □

Therefore, we can compute all non-dominated paths ending at u, by enumerating the timestamps in T_a in ascending order, and by applying the reverse version of our Dijkstra's algorithm once for each timestamp. In Section 5.2, we will utilize our modified version of the Dijkstra's algorithm to identify canonical paths and construct label sets.

5.2 Construction of Label Sets

Algorithm 3 shows the preprocessing method of *TTL*, referred to as *IndexBuild*. Given G and a node order o, *IndexBuild* first identifies the node u_1 with the highest rank, as well as the latest departure time t_d among the outgoing edges of u_1 (Lines 1-4). After that, it invokes the temporal Dijkstra's algorithm to compute the EAPs from u starting at t_d (Lines 5-28), with some simple bookkeeping to keep track of the vehicle b of each EAP P (Lines 17-20 and 23-24), as well as the intermediate node p on P with the highest rank (Lines 25-28). For each EAP P ending at a node v at time t_a, *IndexBuild* inserts a label $\langle u_1, t_d, t_a, b, p\rangle$ into $L_{in}(v)$ (Lines 30-34). The reason is as follows. First, based on our discussions in Section 5.1, P satisfies the Dominance Constraint in Definition 5. Second, given that u has a higher rank than all other nodes, P also satisfies the Rank Constraint in Definition 5. Therefore, P is a canonical path, and hence, we add into $L_{in}(v)$ a label corresponding to P (see Definition 7).

After that, *IndexBuild* examines the other departure time of u_1's outgoing edges in descending order (Line 5). For each departure time t_d, *IndexBuild* derives the EAPs starting from u_1 at time t_d, using the temporal Dijkstra's algorithm (6-8). For each of the EAP P derived, if P ends at a node v at time t_v, then *IndexBuild* examines whether the current $L_{in}(v)$ contains a label $l = \langle u_1, \cdot, t_a, \cdot, \cdot\rangle$ with $t_a \le t_v$ (Line 31). If such a label exists, then P is dominated by an EAP that *IndexBuild* previously derived, in which case P will be omitted; otherwise, P must be a canonical path, and hence, *IndexBuild* inserts into $L_{in}(v)$ a label corresponding to P.

Once all departure timestamps from u_1 are enumerated, *IndexBuild* employs the reverse version of the temporal Dijkstra's algorithm to derive all canonical paths ending at u_1 (Line 34). In particular, *IndexBuild* examines the arrival timestamps at v in ascending order and, for each timestamp t_a, uses the backward Dijkstra's algorithm to compute the LDPs that end at u_1 at time t_a.

Algorithm 3: *IndexBuild*

input : G and a node order o
output: a *TTL* index $\mathcal{L}$

1 let $G_1 = G$;
2 **for** $i = 1, 2, \ldots, n$ **do**
3 let u_i be the node with $o(u_i) = i$;
4 let T_d be a set containing the departure timestamps of all outgoing edges of u in G_i;
5 **for each** $t_d \in T_d$ *in descending order* **do**
6 create a hash table A that maps each node v to a tuple $\langle t_v, b_v, p_v\rangle$, where t_v is the earliest arrival time at v from u (initialized as $+\infty$), b_v is a vehicle (initialized as a placeholder $\star$), and p_v is a pivot node (initialized as $null$);
7 create a min-heap H that (i) accepts entries of the form $\langle e, p\rangle$, where e is an edge, and p is a node, and (ii) sorts entries in ascending order of the arrival time of their edges;
8 **for each** *outgoing edge e' of u with departure time t_d* **do**
9 insert an entry $\langle e', null\rangle$ into H;
10 **while** *H is not empty* **do**
11 remove the top entry $\langle e, p\rangle$ from H;
12 let $\langle x, y, t_d, t_a, b\rangle$ denote e;
13 retrieve the tuple $\langle t_x, b_x, p_x\rangle$ associated with x in A;
14 retrieve the tuple $\langle t_y, b_y, p_y\rangle$ associated with y in A;
15 **if** $t_x = +\infty$ *or* $t_d \ge t_x$ *and* $t_a < t_y$ **then**
16 set $t_y = t_a$ and $p_y = p$;
17 **if** $b_y = \star$ **then**
18 set $b_y = b$;
19 **else if** $b_y \ne b$ **then**
20 set $b_y = null$;
21 **for each** *outgoing edge e^* of y* **do**
22 let $\langle \cdot, \cdot, \cdot, \cdot, b^*\rangle$ denote e^*;
23 **if** $b^* \ne b$ **then**
24 set $b^* = null$;
25 **if** $p = null$ *or* $o(p) < o(y)$ **then**
26 insert $\langle e^*, p\rangle$ into H;
27 **else**
28 insert $\langle e^*, y\rangle$ into H;
29 **for each** *node v in G_i* **do**
30 let $\langle t_v, b_v, p_v\rangle$ be the tuple in A corresponding to v;
31 **if** *there is no $\langle u, \cdot, t_a, \cdot, \cdot\rangle \in L_{in}(v)$ with $t_a \le t_v$* **then**
32 **if** *there does not exist $\langle u_j, t'_d, t'_a, \cdot, \cdot\rangle \in L_{out}(u_i)$ and $\langle u_j, t^*_d, t^*_a, \cdot, \cdot\rangle \in L_{in}(v)$, such that $t'_a < t^*_d$ and $[t'_d, t^*_a] \subset [t_d, t_v]$* **then**
33 insert into $L_{in}(v)$ a label $\langle u_i, t_d, t_v, b_v, p_v\rangle$;
34 repeat Lines 4-33 to construct labels in the out-label set of each node, using the reverse version of temporal Dijkstra's algorithm;
35 remove v from G_i, and let G_{i+1} denote the resulting graph;
36 **return** the collection of all label sets as a *TTL* index $\mathcal{L}$;

Based on the LDPs computed, *IndexBuild* identifies all canonical paths ending at u_1, and constructs labels in other nodes' out-label sets, in a manner similar to the processing of canonical paths starting from u. After that, *IndexBuild* removes u_1 from G (Line 35), and proceeds to process the remaining nodes.

Let u_i denote the node with $o(u_i) = i$ ($i \in [2, n]$). The subsequent execution of *IndexBuild* inspects u_i in ascending order of i. For each u_i, *IndexBuild* examines a modified version of G (denoted as G_i) where all nodes with higher rank than u_i are removed. In particular, *IndexBuild* computes the all non-dominated paths in G_i that start from u_i, using the same approach as in the case of u_1 (Lines 5-28). The set $\mathcal{S}$ of non-dominated paths thus derived would satisfy the Rank Constraint in Definition 5, since they do not contain any node that ranks higher than u_i. However, as they are derived on G_i instead of G, they may not all be non-dominated paths in G. To identify the paths in $\mathcal{S}$ that are non-dominated in G, *IndexBuild* processes each path $P \in \mathcal{S}$ as follows. Assume that P starts from u_i at time t_d and ends at a node v at time t_a. If $L_{out}(u_i)$ contains a label $l_1 = \langle u_j, t'_d, t'_a, \cdot, \cdot \rangle$ and $L_{in}(v)$ has a label $l_2 = \langle u_j, t^*_d, t^*_a, \cdot, \cdot \rangle$, such that $t'_a < t^*_d$ and $[t'_d, t^*_a] \subset [t_d, t_a]$, then P is dominated by a path in G that goes from u_i to v via u_j. (Note that $j < i$ always holds, due to the order in which *IndexBuild* processes nodes.) In that case, *IndexBuild* omits P (Line 32). On the other hand, if such labels l_1 and l_2 do not exist, then P is not dominated by any path in G that passes through a node u_k with $k < i$. In that case, P must be a non-dominated path in G. Then, given that P satisfies the Rank Constraint in Definition 5, it is a canonical path on G; as such, *IndexBuild* would insert into $L_{in}(v)$ a label pertinent to P (Line 33). In a similar fashion, *IndexBuild* would also apply the backward Dijkstra's algorithm to compute all canonical paths that ends at u_i, and create labels in the out-label sets accordingly. Interested readers are referred to Appendix C for an example that demonstrates the execution of *IndexBuild*.

Once all u_i are processed, *IndexBuild* returns the collection of all label sets constructed as a *TTL* index $\mathcal{L}$. The following Lemma 8 shows the correctness and time complexity of *IndexBuild*.

LEMMA 8. *Given G and a node order o, IndexBuild returns a TTL index in $O(n \cdot m + n^2 \cdot \log n)$ time, where m is the number of edges in G.* □

6. NODE ORDERING

As shown in Sections 2 and 5, a *TTL* index $\mathcal{L}$ on G is uniquely decided by the given node ordering o. As such, the choice of o has a profound effect on the *size* of $\mathcal{L}$, defined as

$$|\mathcal{L}| = \sum_{v \in V} \Big(|L_{in}(v)| + |L_{out}(v)| \Big). \quad (1)$$

The following example illustrates how o may affect $|\mathcal{L}|$:

EXAMPLE 5. Consider a graph G that contains n nodes $v_1, v_2, \ldots, v_n$, and contains a path P representing a vehicle route that traverses v_i in ascending order of i. For simplicity, assume that G contains no other edges except for those in P, and that n is a power of 2. Suppose that $o(v_i) = i$ for $1 \le i \le n$. Then, the size of the corresponding $\mathcal{L}$ is $O(n^2)$, since each v_i would be added into the label set $L_{in}(v_j)$ for all v_j with $j > i$.

Now consider that we construct the index with a different node order o, in n iterations as follows. In the first iteration, we set $o(v_{n/2}) = 1$, and then remove $v_{n/2}$ from P, obtaining two sub-paths of P. After that, in the j-th iteration ($j > 1$), we select the longest sub-path of P in our collection, and identify the node v' exactly in the middle of the sub-path; then, we set $o(v') = j$ and remove v' from the sub-path, which breaks the sub-path into two smaller sub-paths. With such an ordering, each node v' is added only into the label sets of the nodes on the sub-path from which v' is removed, and hence, the resulting $\mathcal{L}$ has a size of $O(n \log n)$. □

In what follows, we investigate the choice of o, aiming to reduce $|\mathcal{L}|$. In particular, we first present an approximation algorithm for the minimization of $\mathcal{L}$ (in Section 6.1), and then introduce a heuristic method that runs well in practice (in Section 6.2).

6.1 Approximation Algorithm

Let $\mathcal{N}$ be the set of all non-dominated paths on G. Intuitively, if a node v appears on a large number of non-dominated paths, then v is likely to be an *important* node, in which case it should be given a high rank in a node order. Our approximation algorithm exploits this intuition in selecting the node order o. To explain, we first introduce a few notations. We say that a node v *covers* a non-dominated path $P \in \mathcal{N}$, if v is on P. We use $\mathcal{N}(v)$ to denote the set of non-dominated paths in $\mathcal{N}$ that are covered by v, and we refer to $|\mathcal{N}(v)|$ as the *coverage* of v.

Let u_i ($i \in [1, n]$) denote the node with the i-th highest rank in our node order o. We first choose u_1 to be the node with the maximum coverage. After that, for $i \in [2, n]$, we decide u_i in ascending order of i, and we set u_i to the node that covers the largest number of non-dominated paths that have not been covered by $u_1, u_2, \ldots, u_{i-1}$, i.e.,

$$u_i = \arg\max_v |R_i(v)|,$$

$$\text{where } R_i(v) = \left| \mathcal{N}(v) \setminus \cup_{j=1}^{i-1} \mathcal{N}(u_j) \right|.$$

For example, in Figure 2a, $R_1(v_1) = 6, R_1(v_2) = 9$, and $R_1(v_3) = 6$; accordingly, $u_1 = v_2$. That is, in our choice of u_i, we take into account the nodes that are selected before u_i, and aim to maximize u_i's *residual* coverage with respect to the previously selected nodes. Note that this ordering method runs in polynomial time, since (i) $\mathcal{N}$ can be constructed in polynomial time using our algorithm in Section 5.1, and (ii) the total number of nodes in the paths in $\mathcal{N}$ is polynomial to the number of edges in G.

To analyze the theoretical guarantee of our method, we first define the *influence set* of u_i (denoted as $I(u_i)$) as the set of non-dominated paths in $R_i(u_i)$ that either start from u_i or end at u_i. Observe that each path P in $I(u_i)$ is a canonical path with respect to our node order. Furthermore, if we construct a *TTL* based on our node order, then P would be mapped into a label $\langle u_i, \cdot, \cdot, \cdot, \cdot \rangle$. In other words, $|I(u_i)|$ equals the number of labels that are due to u_i, and we have $|\mathcal{L}| = \sum_{i=1}^{n} |I(u_i)|$. Intuitively, $|I(u_i)|$ captures the space overhead incurred by u_i in the *TTL* index.

For any node v in G, let $T_d(v)$ (resp. $T_a(v)$) be the set that contains the departure (resp. arrival) timestamps of all outgoing (resp. incoming) edges of v, and

$$\alpha = \sum_{v \text{ in } G} (|T_d(v)| + |T_a(v)|). \quad (2)$$

The following lemma shows an upper-bound of $|I(u_i)|$ based on $|R_i(u_i)|$ and α.

LEMMA 9. $|I(u_i)| \le \sqrt{\alpha} \cdot \sqrt{|R_i(u_i)|}$.

Let $v_1, v_2, \ldots, v_n$ be the node ordering minimizing $|\mathcal{L}|$. We define

$$R'_i(v) = \left| \mathcal{N}(v) \setminus \cup_{j=1}^{i-1} \mathcal{N}(v_j) \right|.$$

The influence set $I(v_i)$ of v_i can be similarly defined as the set of non-dominated paths in $R'_i(v_i)$ that either start from v_i or end at v_i. The following lemma shows a lower-bound of $|I(v_i)|$ based on $|R'_i(v_i)|$.

LEMMA 10. $\sqrt{|R'_i(v_i)|} \le |I(v_i)|$.

The following lemma shows the connection between $|R_i(u_i)|$ and $|R'_i(v_i)|$:

LEMMA 11. $\sum_{i=1}^{n} \sqrt{|R_i(u_i)|} \le 2 \cdot \sum_{i=1}^{n} \sqrt{|R'_i(v_i)|}$.

Based on Lemmas 9, 10 and 11, we show in Theorem 1 the approximation ratio of our ordering method.

THEOREM 1. *A TTL index based on a node order $u_1, u_2, \ldots, u_n$ has a size that is at most $2\sqrt{\alpha}$ times of that with the optimal node ordering. To derive such a node order, it takes $O(n^2 \cdot m)$ time and $O(n \cdot m)$ space, where m is the number of edges in the timetable graph.* □

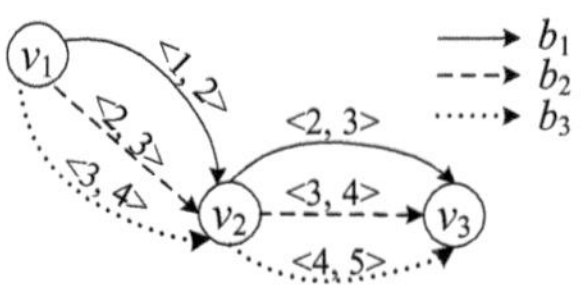

(a) Timetable graph G'.

$\langle v_1, 1, 3, b_1, v_2\rangle$
$\langle v_1, 2, 4, b_2, v_2\rangle$
$\langle v_1, 3, 5, b_3, v_2\rangle$
$\langle v_2, 2, 3, b_1, null\rangle$
$\langle v_2, 3, 4, b_2, null\rangle$
$\langle v_2, 4, 5, b_3, null\rangle$

(b) $L_{in}(v_3)$.

$\langle v_1, null, null, r_1, v_2\rangle$
$\langle v_2, null, null, r_1, null\rangle$

(c) $L_{in}(v_3)$ compressed.

route	vehicle	v_1		v_2		v_3	
		t_a	t_d	t_a	t_d	t_a	t_d
r_1	b_1	-	1	2	2	3	-
	b_2	-	2	3	3	4	-
	b_3	-	3	4	4	5	-

(d) Timetable for r_1.

Figure 2: An example of route-based compression.

6.2 Heuristic Approach

As shown in Theorem 1, the approximation algorithm in Section 6.1 incurs tremendous overheads, which renders it inapplicable in sizable graphs. To remedy this issue, we devise a heuristic approach that has the same spirit of the approximation algorithm, but entails much smaller computation costs. First, we randomly sample a number of edges from G. After that, for each edge $e = \langle u, \cdot, t_d, \cdot, \cdot\rangle$, we employ the temporal Dijkstra's algorithm to identify all EAPs starting from u at time t_d. Notice that all these EAPs form a tree T rooted at u, such that the directed path from the root to any leave is an EAP from u. Furthermore, for any node v in T, the number of nodes in the subtree under v (including v itself) equals the number of EAPs from u that are covered by v. We refer to this number as the *coverage* of v in T, and refer to T as the *EAP tree* from u at time t_d. Note that the coverage of all nodes in T can be computed in $O(n)$ time using a bottom-up scan of T.

Let $\mathcal{T}$ denote the set of all EAP trees that we have sampled, and $u_1, u_2, \ldots, u_n$ denote the node order that we chose. To decide our node order, we maintain an array that records, for each node v, the sum of the coverage of v in all trees in $\mathcal{T}$. We refer to this sum as the *coverage sum* of v. We first identify u_1 as the node with the maximum coverage sum, i.e., u_1 covers the largest number of EAPs that we constructed. Then, we remove, from each EAP tree $T \in \mathcal{T}$, the subtree under u_1 (including u_1), and we update the coverage sum of each node accordingly. Subsequently, for each $i \in [2, n]$ in ascending order, we select u_i to be the node with the maximum coverage sum in the modified $\mathcal{T}$ with the subtrees under $u_1, \ldots, u_{i-1}$ removed.

The above heuristic approach runs in $O(n^2 \cdot |\mathcal{T}|)$ time, where $|\mathcal{T}|$ denotes the number of EAP trees in $\mathcal{T}$. To explain, observe that for any $i \in [1, n]$, we take $O(n \cdot |\mathcal{T}|)$ time to identify u_i, remove it and its subtrees from all EAP trees, and update the remaining nodes' coverage sums. Therefore, the total running time of the heuristic approach equals $O(n^2 \cdot |\mathcal{T}|)$. Apparently, a larger $|\mathcal{T}|$ leads to a better node ordering but a larger computation overheads. In our implementation of *TTL*, we start from $\mathcal{T} = \emptyset$, then iteratively sample EAP trees from G, until the total number of edges in the EAP trees reaches $x \cdot m$, where x is a constant and m is the number of edges in G. That is, we restrict the total size of the EAP trees. Our experiments show that $x = 8$ strikes a good tradeoff between index size and preprocessing time.

7. LABEL COMPRESSION

Even with a good node order o, a *TTL* index $\mathcal{L}$ may still have a sizable number of labels and incur considerable space overheads. To reduce the space consumption of $\mathcal{L}$, we propose to *compress* the labels in $\mathcal{L}$ by exploiting their similarities. In particular, we present a *route-based* compression approach in Section 7.1, followed by a *pivot-based* compression method in Section 7.2.

7.1 Route-Based Compression

Consider the example in Figure 2a, where we have three vehicles b_1, b_2, and b_3 serving the same *route* $r_1 = \langle v_1, v_2, v_3\rangle$, i.e., they all start from node v_1, pass by v_2, and then arrive at v_3. Figure 2b shows the label sets of v_3, assuming that $o(v_1) < o(v_2) < o(v_3)$. Observe that the labels in $L_{in}(v_3)$ are rather redundant, as they repeatedly record the arrival time of b_1, b_2, and b_3. To eliminate such redundancy, we propose to replace the labels in $L_{in}(v_3)$ with two labels $\langle v_1, null, null, r_1, v_2\rangle$ and $\langle v_2, null, null, r_1, null\rangle$, as shown in Figure 2c. That is, we *combine* the labels in $L_{in}(v_3)$ that share the same starting node, ending node, and pivot. To ensure lossless decompression, we create a time table that records, for v_1, v_2, and v_3, the departure and arrival time of each bus serving route r_1, as shown in Figure 2d. During query processing, if we encounter the label $\langle v_1, null, null, r_1, v_2\rangle$ in $L_{in}(v_3)$, then we inspect the timetable entries associated with v_1 and v_3 to reconstruct three original labels concerning b_1, b_2, and b_3. The label $\langle v_2, null, null, r_1, null\rangle$ can be decompressed in the same way.

In general, in the in-label set $L_{in}(v)$ of a node v, if all labels from a node u are associated with vehicles serving the same route r (hence the same pivot p), then we compress the labels into a single label $\langle u, null, null, r, p\rangle$, and create the timetables of r associated with u and v. The out-label sets in $\mathcal{L}$ can be compressed in the same manner. We observe that this *route-based* compression approach is particularly effective on a path that is only served by buses from one route, as in the case of Figure 2a.

7.2 Pivot-Based Compression

The route-based compression approach is applicable on a label l, only if the vehicle of l is not $null$, i.e., the canonical path corresponding to l is carried out by one vehicle without transfer. Nonetheless, we may still compress labels pertinent to paths with vehicle transfers, by exploiting the pivots recorded in the labels. For example, consider an in-label set $L_{in}(v)$ of a node v, where there are three labels from a node u: $l_1 = \langle u, t_d, t_a, null, p\rangle$, $l_2 = \langle u, t'_d, t'_a, null, p\rangle$, and $l_3 = \langle u, t^*_d, t^*_a, null, p\rangle$. Although the vehicles of l_1, l_2, and l_3 equal $null$, they all have the same pivot p, i.e., the canonical paths corresponding to l_1, l_2, and l_3 all pass through p. In that case, we compress l_1, l_2, and l_3 into a single label $l_c = \langle u, null, null, null, p\rangle$.

After that, whenever we encounter l_c during query processing, we decompress it by reconstructing l_1, l_2, and l_3 using their children (see Section 4.2). For instance, suppose that $o(u) < o(p) < o(v)$. Then, $L_{in}(p)$ must contain three labels $\langle u, t_d, \cdot, \cdot, \cdot\rangle$, $\langle u, t'_d, \cdot, \cdot, \cdot\rangle$, $\langle u, t^*_d, \cdot, \cdot, \cdot\rangle$, which are the left children of l_1, l_2, and l_3, respectively. In addition, $L_{in}(v)$ should have three labels $\langle p, \cdot, t_a, \cdot, \cdot\rangle$, $\langle p, \cdot, t'_a, \cdot, \cdot\rangle$, $\langle p, \cdot, t^*_a, \cdot, \cdot\rangle$ that are the right children of l_1, l_2, and l_3, respectively. Therefore, we can easily reconstruct l_1, l_2, and l_3, by inspecting $L_{in}(p)$ and $L_{in}(v)$, based on the pivot information in l_c.

In general, in an in-label (resp. out-label) set, if all in-labels from (resp. out-labels to) a node u' have the same pivot p', then we may replace them with a compressed label $\langle u', null, null, null, p'\rangle$. There is one caveat, though: if a label l and its left (resp. right) child are both compressed, then the reconstruction of l would also require reconstruction of its left (resp. right) child. Such recursive reconstruction incurs considerable overheads, which degrades query efficiency on compressed label sets. To avoid such recursions, we impose a constraint in label compression: if a label is compressed, then neither of its children should be compressed. An immediate question is, how should we choose the labels to compress, so as to minimize space consumption without violating the compression constraint?

To answer the above question, we construct a *dependency graph* as follows. First, in the in-label set $L_{in}(v)$ (resp. out-label set $L_{out}(v)$) of a node v, if we may generate a compressed label $\langle u, null, null, null, p\rangle$, then we create a tuple $\langle u, v, p\rangle$ (resp. $\langle v, u, p\rangle$). After that, we map each tuple into a node, and draw an undirected edge between any two nodes with a parent-child relationship, e.g., $\langle u, v, p\rangle$ and $\langle u, p, \cdot\rangle$. In addition, we assign to each node $\langle u, v, p\rangle$ a weight that equals $c-1$, where c equals the number of labels compressed into $\langle u, v, p\rangle$. In other words, c captures the reduction of space due to $\langle u, v, p\rangle$. We refer to the resulting graph as a dependency graph D.

Observe that, if we are to create a set S of compressed labels under our compression constraints, then the labels in S correspond to an independent set on D. Accordingly, we can maximize the effect of compression by identifying the maximum-weight independent set on D, which is NP-hard. We address the problem by adopting an approximation algorithm [29] for maximum-weight independent set, which runs in $O(n' \log n' + m')$ time, where n' and m' are the numbers of nodes and edges in D, respectively.

Finally, we note that the above *pivot-based* compression method can be combined with the route-based compression approach in Section 7.1. Specifically, we first apply route-based compression on the label sets, and then, employ pivot-based compression but exclude those labels that have been compressed using the route-based approach. As such, we benefit from both types of compression. We refer readers to Appendix B for a more detailed description of *TTL*'s query algorithm under a compressed index structure.

8. EXTENSIONS

Concise Representation of Query Results. Recall that our query algorithms always return a path P represented as a sequence of edges $\langle e_1, e_2, ..., e_k\rangle$ in G. Although such an edge sequence provides very detailed information about P, users in practice may prefer a more concise representation of P as the query result. For example, suppose that $e_1, e_2, \ldots, e_j$ ($j < k$) have the same vehicle b_1, while $e_{j+1}, \ldots, e_k$ all concern the same vehicle b_2. In other words, the path P requires the user to (i) take vehicle b_1 from node u at time t_d (where u and t_d are the starting node and departure time of e_1, respectively), and then (ii) get off b_1 at node w and transfer to vehicle b_2 at time t'_d (where t'_d is the departure time of e_{j+1}), and stay on b_2 until she reaches her destination. In that case, instead of presenting P to the user, we could provide her with a concise description of P_c, which is a sequence of two tuples: $\langle u, b_1, t_d\rangle$, $\langle w, b_2, t'_d\rangle$. Such a *concise path* is more user-friendly as it is easier to comprehend and remember than P. Moreover, the concise representation of query results is favorable to the compression techniques in Section 7, since it reduces the amount of label decompression required during query processing.

To generate a concise path P_c for a query, a straightforward approach is to first derive the corresponding path P, and then convert P into P_c by identifying the edges on P where there are changes of vehicles. Interestingly, our query algorithm can be easily modified to return P_c without even deriving P. In particular, given a path query q, we first invoke our candidate generation and refinement algorithms (in Section 4.1) to identify the path sketch $s_{ans} = \langle l_u, l_v\rangle$ of the query result. After that, we invoke the *PathUnfold* algorithm to unfold the labels in s_{ans}, with one slight modification: during the unfolding process, whenever we encounter a label l whose vehicle does not equal $null$ (i.e., the path corresponding to l does not involve a transfer), then we do not unfold l. The output of modified algorithm would then be a *partially unfolded* path, which is a sequence where each element is either an edge in G or a label whose corresponding path is carried out by one vehicle. After that, it is straightforward to construct P_c from the partially unfolded paths. This partial unfolding approach leads to higher query efficiency since it not only reduces the number of paths to unfold, but also accelerates the construction of P_c.

Extended Timetables. So far we have assumed that we are given a timetable graph G with a finite set E of temporal edges. For example, E corresponds to the predefined vehicles routes on a weekday. However, if we construct a *TTL* index on such a timetable graph G, then the index can only return paths whose starting and ending time are within the same day, e.g., we will miss paths that start on late Monday night and ends on early Tuesday morning. To address this issue, we can extend E to include the timetables of two consecutive weekdays, and construct a *TTL* index accordingly. Then, the index could return any path whose total duration does not exceed 24 hours. In case that the weekend timetable is different from that of a weekday, we can create three additional *TTL* indices, each of which incorporates the timetables of two consecutive days from Friday to Monday. We note that such *indexing partitioning* approach is widely adopted in spatial-temporal indexing (e.g., [25]).

9. RELATED WORK

A plethora of techniques [7,8,10,12,16,21–23,27,28,32,35,37] have been proposed for processing EAP, LAP, and SDP queries on timetable graphs. Among them, the states of the art include the *Connection Scan Algorithm (CSA)* [16,38], the *Contraction Hierarchies for Timetables (CHT)* [21], and *T.Patterns* [5]. In particular, *CSA* represents the timetable graph G as two sequences of edges, such that the first (resp. second) sequence sorts edges in ascending order of their departure timestamps (resp. in descending order of their arrival timestamps). For any path query, *CSA* derives the query answer using one linear scan of one of the edge sequences. This technique incurs very small preprocessing overheads, and is shown to outperform the temporal Dijkstra's algorithm [10] in terms of query time.

Meanwhile, *CHT* [21], preprocesses G by constructing *shortcuts* (i.e., artificial edges) among the nodes in G, such that each shortcut captures a fastest route between the two nodes that it connects. During query processing, *CHT* employs a bidirectional Dijkstra-like search from the source and destination nodes simultaneously, and it utilizes the pre-computed shortcuts to reduce the number of nodes that need to be traversed. *T.Patterns* [5] exploits a similar idea to *CHT*, but instead of maintaining shortcuts, it pre-computes a set of fastest paths in G and record them in a set S. Then, when processing queries, *T.Patterns* utilizes the pre-computed paths to construct the major parts of the query results, which improves query performance. Nevertheless, *T.Patterns* does not guarantee exact query results, e.g., its answer for an EAP query might not be an actual EAP. In other words, *T.Pattern* trades query accuracy for efficiency. In our experiments, we compare *TTL* with *CSA* and *CHT* instead of *T.Patterns*, since we aim to provide exact answers for path queries.

Apart from *CSA*, *CHT*, and *T.Patterns*, other techniques for timetable graphs can be divided into two categories. Techniques in the first category [22,23,27,28,37] convert G into a *time-expanded graph* G', such that each spatiotemporal event in G (e.g., arrival of a vehicle b at a station u) is mapped to a node in G', and two consecutive events (e.g., arrival of b at u, followed by its departure) is mapped to a directed edge in G'. Based on G', various techniques [22, 23, 27, 28, 37] have been proposed to accelerate path queries. However, as pointed out in [6,8], such techniques are generally not incomparable to the state-of-the-art methods that process queries on G instead of G'. On the other hand, techniques in the second category [11,13,15,18,30,31,33,36] considers query types that are more sophisticated than EAP, LDP, SDP, in that they take into account advanced query constraints, such as the cost of making a transfer, the fare of a ride, etc.

In addition, there is a line of research [10,12,14,19,20,24,26–28,34] on route planning on *time-dependent graphs*, i.e., simple graphs where the length of each edge is a function of time. Such graphs are typically used to model road networks where the traveling time of an edge is a certain pre-defined function of time. Techniques developed for time-dependent graphs can also be applied on timetable graphs (via a sophisticated mapping from timetables to time-dependent functions), but as shown in [7,12,21], they are inferior to *CHT* in terms of query performance on timetable graphs.

Finally, there exists a large body of literature on processing shortest path and distance queries on simple graphs without temporal information (see [6] for a recent survey). The classic approach for this problem is Cohen et al.'s *2-hop labelling (2HL)* [9] for distance queries. Cohen et al. present a preprocessing algorithm for *2HL* that achieves an $O(\log n)$ approximation in terms of index size, but the algorithm has $O(n^5)$ complexity and does not scale to large graphs. To address this issue, the state-of-the-art approach is to construct *2HL* based on a total order on the nodes. The resulting indexing method is referred to as *Hierarchical Hub Labelling (HHL)* [3,4]. Compared with Cohen et al's method, *HHL* provides higher query efficiency and smaller pre-computation cost. However, approximation algorithms for *HHL* (in terms of index size) remain an open problem.

10. EXPERIMENTS

This section experimentally evaluates *TTL* on a machine with an Intel E5-2650V2 2.60GHz CPU and 64GB RAM, running Ubuntu 14.04.1. All methods tested are implemented in C++ and compiled with GCC 4.8.2. In each experiment, we repeat each method 5 times, and report the average measurement.

Datasets. We use 11 publicly available datasets from [1] as our datasets. Each dataset records the timetable of the public transportation network of a major city or country on a weekday. Table 3 shows the characteristics of the data.

Query Sets. For each dataset, we generate 10^5 queries for EAP, LDP, and SDP, respectively, and we report the average query time of each method for each query set. Each query is generated by selecting source and destination node uniformly at random. In addition, the starting and ending timestamps of each query are also randomly generated, except that the starting (resp. ending) timestamp of an LDP (resp. EAP) query is always set to $-\infty$ (resp. $+\infty$).

Methods. We evaluate two versions of *TTL*: one with the compression methods in Section 7 applied (referred to as *C-TTL*), and one without (referred to as *TTL*). For each version, we test its query performance under two scenarios: when it returns a complete path in answering a query, and when it returns a concise representation of the path. We compare all versions of *TTL* with the state-of-the-art indexing methods on timetable graphs, namely, *CHT* [21] and *CSA* [16]. Unless otherwise specified, we use heuristic algorithm in Section 6.2 to decide the node ordering used in *TTL* and *C-TTL*.

10.1 Performance of Query Processing

In the first set of experiments, we evaluate the query efficiency of all methods. Figure 3 shows the average query time of each method for SDP queries in log-scale. Observe that, *TTL* and *C-TTL* significantly outperform *CSA* and *CHT* in all cases. In particular, the average query time of *TTL* is always below $30\mu s$, and is at least three (resp. two) orders lower than that of *CSA* (resp. *CHT*) in almost all cases. *C-TTL* is slightly slower than *TTL* (as it needs to decompress labels during query processing), but is still orders of magnitude faster than *CSA* and *CHT*. Meanwhile, *CHT* is superior to *CSA*, as it adopts a more advanced index structure than the latter.

dataset	$\|V\|$	$\|E\|$	avg degree
Austin	2.7K	317.5K	118.7
Madrid	4.6K	1912.2K	412.5
Budapest	5.5K	1375.2K	251.5
Salt Lake City	6.3K	329.0K	52.6
Rome	8.8K	2267.7K	258.3
Denver	9.5K	708.7K	74.5
Houston	9.8K	1111.8K	112.9
Toronto	10.8K	3295.1K	305.4
Berlin	12.8K	1965.8K	153.0
Los Angeles	15.0K	1903.2K	126.6
Sweden	51.4K	3926.5K	76.4

Table 3: Public transportation networks (K=10^3).

Interestingly, the query time of *TTL* and *C-TTL* does not always increase with the size of the input dataset. To explain, observe that the average query cost of *TTL* and *C-TTL* is decided by two factors: (i) the average number of labels in each label set, denoted as l_{avg}, and (ii) the average number of path unfolding operations required during path reconstructions, which is roughly comparable to the average number of nodes on the query result path (denoted as n_{avg}). We observe that neither l_{avg} nor n_{avg} necessarily increases with the dataset size. For example, on the *Austin* dataset, $l_{avg} \approx 1600$, and $n_{avg} \approx 39$ for SDP queries; in contrast, on *Sweden*, we have $l_{avg} \approx 775$ and $n_{avg} \approx 19$ for SDP queries, even though *Sweden* is more than ten times larger than *Austin*. In addition, we note that a similar phenomenon is also demonstrated in previous work [3,4] on labelling indices for conventional graphs, i.e., the query cost of a labelling approach depends more on the input data's topology than its size.

The above results concern the case when we return a detailed path for each SDP query. In addition to that, Figure 3 also plots the performance of *TTL* and *C-TTL* when they return concise paths as query results. Observe that the query efficiency of both *TTL* and *C-TTL* improves noticeably when concise paths are adopted. This is because when *TTL* and *C-TTL* return concise paths instead of complete paths, their costs of path reconstruction during query processing are significantly reduced, due to the decreased amount of path unfolding operations, as mentioned in Section 8. In addition, the performance gap between *TTL* and *C-TTL* is reduced in the case of concise paths, because *C-TTL* performs a smaller number of label decompressions when constructing concise paths.

Apart from SDP queries, we also evaluate the average query time of each method for EAP and LDP queries, respectively, and we observe that *TTL* and *C-TTL* consistently outperform *CSA* and *CHT* by large margins. Interested readers are referred to Appendix D for these experimental results.

10.2 Preprocessing and Space Overheads

Our second set of experiments evaluates the space overheads of each method. Figure 4 shows the results in log-scale. The index size of *CSA* is rather small, since it only requires storing two copies of G (in the form of sorted edge sequences). The space consumption of *CHT* is comparable to that of *CSA*, which indicates that the shortcuts that it creates take roughly the same space as the input graph G. On the other hand, the space costs of *TTL* and *C-TTL* are considerably larger than those of *CSA* and *CHT*. However, the relatively large space overhead of *TTL* and *C-TTL* is justified by their superior query performance against *CSA* and *CHT*. Furthermore, even on the country-scale transportation network *Sweden*, the in-

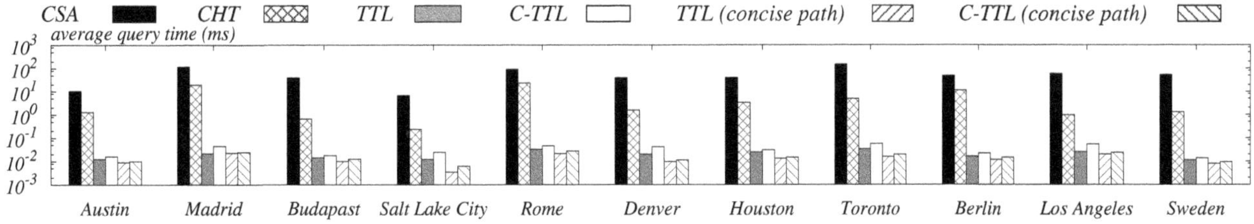

Figure 3: Average query time for SDP queries.

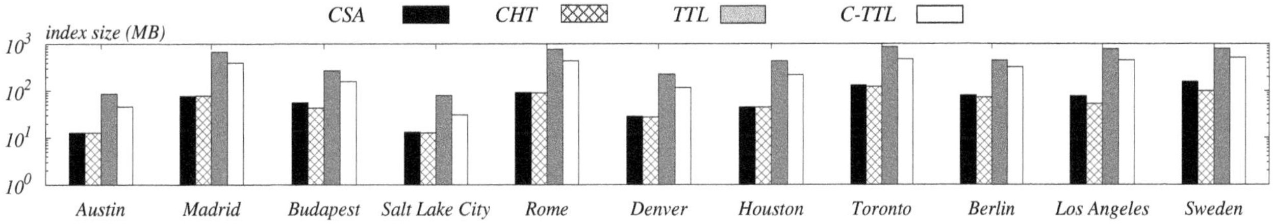

Figure 4: Index size.

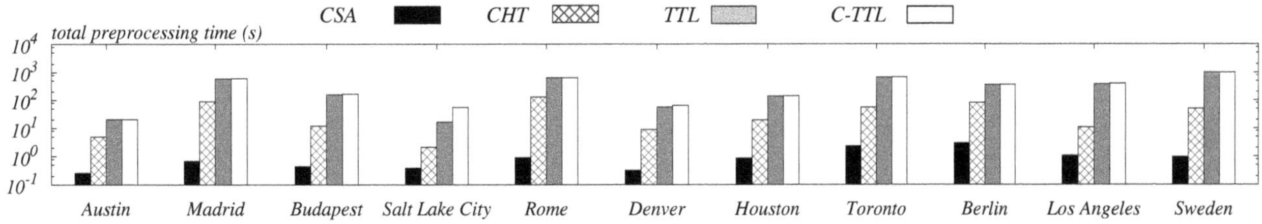

Figure 5: Total preprocessing time.

dex size of *TTL* (resp. *C-TTL*) is only a few hundred MB, which can easily fit in the main memory of a commodity machine. In other words, the space overheads of *TTL* and *C-TTL* are still acceptable for practical applications.

In the next set of experiments, we evaluate the effectiveness of label compression schemes. In particular, on each dataset, we construct four *TTL* indices: (i) one without compression, denoted as $\mathcal{L}$; (ii) one with route-based compression, denoted as $\mathcal{L}_1$; (iii) one with pivot-based compression, denoted as $\mathcal{L}_2$, and (iv) one with both route-based and pivot-based compressions, denoted as $\mathcal{L}_3$. We define $\Delta_i = |\mathcal{L}| - |\mathcal{L}_i|$ $(i = 1, 2, 3)$. Table 4 shows the values of $\Delta_1/|\mathcal{L}|$, $\Delta_2/|\mathcal{L}|$, and $\Delta_3/|\mathcal{L}|$ on each dataset. Observe that, by using route-based compression and pivot-based compression separately, our index size can be reduced by up to 38.00% and 38.78%, respectively. When both compression techniques are applied, the size of our *TTL* indices can be reduced by up to 61.43%.

This reduction in space consumption comes at a moderate cost of query efficiency, though. For instance, on the *Budapest* dataset, our compression techniques reduce the size of *C-TTL* by 41.71%, but increase the query time (when returning concise paths) from $10\mu s$ to $12\mu s$. Nonetheless, even with compression applied, the query performance of *C-TTL* is still significantly better than that of *CSA* and *CHT*, as shown in Figure 3. As such, *C-TTL* is a competitive method compared to *TTL*, especially when the index size is a concern (e.g., when the index is to be loaded in a mobile devise).

Finally, Figure 5 shows the preprocessing time of all methods. *CSA* incurs the smallest pre-computation overheads as it only requires sorting the edges in G twice. *CHT* has a much larger preprocessing cost, since it needs to construct a sizable number of shortcuts on G. The pre-computation time of *TTL* and *C-TTL* are larger than that of *CSA* and *CHT*, but is still below 17 minutes even on the largest dataset *Sweden*. Furthermore, *TTL* and *C-TTL* have similar pre-processing overheads, which indicates that the compression algorithms adopted by *C-TTL* entail negligible additional costs. We also refer interested readers to Appendix D for additional experiments on the effectiveness of *TTL*'s preprocessing algorithm.

dataset	$\Delta_1/\lvert\mathcal{L}\rvert$	$\Delta_2/\lvert\mathcal{L}\rvert$	$\Delta_3/\lvert\mathcal{L}\rvert$
Austin	20.25%	33.66%	46.20%
Madrid	16.52%	30.23%	45.61%
Budapest	10.41%	35.45%	41.71%
Salt Lake City	38.00%	38.78%	61.43%
Rome	14.42%	31.85%	43.87%
Denver	23.84%	34.92%	49.23%
Houston	28.77%	32.62%	49.54%
Toronto	19.95%	32.77%	44.78%
Berlin	6.70%	23.51%	27.58%
Los Angeles	16.78%	31.68%	41.66%
Sweden	12.74%	28.52%	35.92%

Table 4: Compression ratio.

11. CONCLUSIONS

This paper presents *Timetable Labelling (TTL)*, an efficient indexing technique for route planning on public transportation networks. We investigate various aspects in the design of *TTL* indices, and propose advanced algorithms for query processing, index construction, and label compression. With extensive experiments on real datasets, we show that *TTL* significantly outperforms the state-the-art in terms of query efficiency.

12. ACKNOWLEDGMENTS

This work was supported by AcRF Tier 2 Grant ARC19/14 from the Ministry of Education, Singapore, an SUG Grant from Nanyang Technological University, Grant No.14JC1400300 from Shanghai Municipal Commission of Science and Technology, and a gift from Microsoft Research Asia.

13. REFERENCES

[1] https://code.google.com/p/googletransitdatafeed/wiki/PublicFeeds.

[2] https://sites.google.com/site/timetablelabelling/.

[3] I. Abraham, D. Delling, A. V. Goldberg, and R. F. F. Werneck. Hierarchical hub labelings for shortest paths. In *ESA*, pages 24–35, 2012.

[4] T. Akiba, Y. Iwata, and Y. Yoshida. Fast exact shortest-path distance queries on large networks by pruned landmark labeling. In *SIGMOD Conference*, pages 349–360, 2013.

[5] H. Bast, E. Carlsson, A. Eigenwillig, R. Geisberger, C. Harrelson, V. Raychev, and F. Viger. Fast routing in very large public transportation networks using transfer patterns. In *ESA*, pages 290–301, 2010.

[6] H. Bast, D. Delling, A. Goldberg, M. Müller-Hannemann, T. Pajor, P. Sanders, D. Wagner, and R. Werneck. Route planning in transportation networks. *MSR Technical Report*, 2014.

[7] G. V. Batz, D. Delling, P. Sanders, and C. Vetter. Time-dependent contraction hierarchies. In *ALENEX*, volume 9, 2009.

[8] R. Bauer, D. Delling, and D. Wagner. Experimental study of speed up techniques for timetable information systems. *Networks*, 57(1):38–52, 2011.

[9] E. Cohen, E. Halperin, H. Kaplan, and U. Zwick. Reachability and distance queries via 2-hop labels. In *SODA*, pages 937–946, 2002.

[10] K. L. Cooke and E. Halsey. The shortest route through a network with time-dependent internodal transit times. *Journal of mathematical analysis and applications*, 14(3):493–498, 1966.

[11] B. C. Dean. *Continuous-time dynamic shortest path algorithms*. PhD thesis, Massachusetts Institute of Technology, 1999.

[12] D. Delling. Time-dependent sharc-routing. *Algorithmica*, 60(1):60–94, 2011.

[13] D. Delling, B. Katz, and T. Pajor. Parallel computation of best connections in public transportation networks. *Journal of Experimental Algorithmics (JEA)*, 17:4–4, 2012.

[14] D. Delling and G. Nannicini. Bidirectional core-based routing in dynamic time-dependent road networks. In *Algorithms and Computation*, pages 812–823, 2008.

[15] D. Delling, T. Pajor, and R. F. F. Werneck. Round-based public transit routing. In *ALENEX*, pages 130–140, 2012.

[16] J. Dibbelt, T. Pajor, B. Strasser, and D. Wagner. Intriguingly simple and fast transit routing. *SEA*, 7933:43–54, 2013.

[17] E. W. Dijkstra. A note on two problems in connexion with graphs. *Numerische Mathematik*, 1(1):269–271, 1959.

[18] Y. Disser, M. Müller-Hannemann, and M. Schnee. Multi-criteria shortest paths in time-dependent train networks. In *SEA*, pages 347–361, 2008.

[19] S. E. Dreyfus. An appraisal of some shortest-path algorithms. *Operations research*, 17(3):395–412, 1969.

[20] L. Foschini, J. Hershberger, and S. Suri. On the complexity of time-dependent shortest paths. *Algorithmica*, 68(4):1075–1097, 2014.

[21] R. Geisberger. Contraction of timetable networks with realistic transfers. In *SEA*, pages 71–82, 2010.

[22] A. V. Goldberg and C. Harrelson. Computing the shortest path: *A* search meets graph theory. In *SODA*, pages 156–165, 2005.

[23] A. V. Goldberg, H. Kaplan, and R. F. Werneck. Reach for a*: Efficient point-to-point shortest path algorithms. In *ALENEX*, pages 129–143, 2006.

[24] M. Hilger, E. Köhler, R. H. Möhring, and H. Schilling. Fast point-to-point shortest path computations with arc-flags. *The Shortest Path Problem: Ninth DIMACS Implementation Challenge*, 74:41–72, 2009.

[25] C. S. Jensen, D. Lin, and B. C. Ooi. Query and update efficient b+-tree based indexing of moving objects. In *PVLDB*, pages 768–779, 2004.

[26] E. Kanoulas, Y. Du, T. Xia, and D. Zhang. Finding fastest paths on a road network with speed patterns. In *ICDE*, page 10, 2006.

[27] U. Lauther. An extremely fast, exact algorithm for finding shortest paths in static networks with geographical background. *Geoinformation*, 22:219–230, 2004.

[28] R. H. Möhring, H. Schilling, B. Schütz, D. Wagner, and T. Willhalm. Partitioning graphs to speed up dijkstra's algorithm. In *WEA*, pages 189–202, 2005.

[29] J. Monnot. A simple approximation algorithm for WIS based on the approximability in k. *European Journal of Operational Research*, 171(1):346–348, 2006.

[30] M. Müller-Hannemann and M. Schnee. Paying less for train connections with MOTIS. In *ATMOS*, 2005.

[31] M. Müller-Hannemann and M. Schnee. Efficient timetable information in the presence of delays. In *Robust and Online Large-Scale Optimization*, pages 249–272. Springer, 2009.

[32] M. Müller-Hannemann, F. Schulz, D. Wagner, and C. Zaroliagis. Timetable information: Models and algorithms. In *Algorithmic Methods for Railway Optimization*, pages 67–90, 2007.

[33] K. Nachtigall. Time depending shortest-path problems with applications to railway networks. *European Journal of Operational Research*, 83(1):154–166, 1995.

[34] G. Nannicini, D. Delling, L. Liberti, and D. Schultes. Bidirectional a^* search for time-dependent fast paths. In *SEA*, pages 334–346, 2008.

[35] G. Nannicini, D. Delling, D. Schultes, and L. Liberti. Bidirectional a* search on time-dependent road networks. *Networks*, 59(2):240–251, 2012.

[36] E. Pyrga, F. Schulz, D. Wagner, and C. Zaroliagis. Efficient models for timetable information in public transportation systems. *Journal of Experimental Algorithmics*, 12:2–4, 2008.

[37] P. Sanders and D. Schultes. Engineering highway hierarchies. In *ESA*, pages 804–816, 2006.

[38] H. Wu, J. Cheng, S. Huang, Y. Ke, Y. Lu, and Y. Xu. Path problems in temporal graphs. *PVLDB*, 7(9):721–732, 2014.

APPENDIX

A. PROOFS

We omit the proofs of Lemma 8-10 due to the space constraint. A technical report that includes all proofs is available from [2].

Proof of Lemma 1. We prove the lemma by contradiction: Assume that there does not exist a label $\langle w, t_d, t_a, b, p\rangle$ in $L_{out}(u)$ or a label $\langle w', t'_d, t'_a, b', p'\rangle$ in $L_{in}(v)$ such that either of them satisfies any one of the conditions in the lemma. In other words, there are two cases, stated as follows.

Case 1: There does not exist a canonical path from u to v.

Case 2: There does not exist a node w^* such that both the paths from u to w^* and from w^* to v contain a canonical path respectively.

Given that P is the result of the path query q from u to v, we have that P is not dominated by the other paths that answer q by Definitions 2, 3, and 4. Besides, any sub-path of P is also not dominated by the other paths. If not, we can replace the sub-path with the dominated one.

Let w^o be the node with highest rank among nodes in P. If w^o equals u or v, then P is a canonical path (by Definition 5), which contradicts *Case 1*. On the other hand, if w^o does not equal u or v, let P_1 be the sub-path from u to w^o, and P_2 be the sub-path from w^o to v. As such, we have P_1 and P_2 as canonical paths (by Definition 5), which contradicts *Case 2*. Thus, the lemma is proved. □

Proof of Lemma 2. Let $l = \langle u, t_d, t_a, b, p\rangle$ be an in-label in $L_{in}(v)$, and $l' = \langle u', t'_d, t'_a, b', p'\rangle$ be an out-label in $L_{out}(v)$. The lemma says that if we remove l or l', there exists a path query q whose result P does not satisfy the constraints in Lemma 1.

Consider l. Given that $\langle u, t_d, t_a, b, p\rangle \in L_{in}(v)$, we have $o(u) < o(v)$ and l is pertinent to a canonical path P from u to

v. Let q be a path query from u to v with starting timestamp t_d and ending timestamp t_a, and P be the result of q. By contradiction, assume that after removing l from $L_{in}(v)$, P still satisfies Lemma 1. Since $o(u) < o(v)$, by Definition 7, v cannot appear in any label of $L_{out}(u)$. Then, there must exist a node w, such that $\langle w, t_d, t_a^*, \cdot, \cdot\rangle \in L_{out}(u)$, $\langle w, t_d^*, t_a, \cdot, \cdot\rangle \in L_{in}(v)$, and $t_a^* \leq t_d^*$. That is, the path P from u to v passes w, and w has a higher rank than both u and v, which contradicts the Rank Constraint in Definition 5. The case for l' can be proved in a similar manner. □

Proof of Lemma 3. Consider a path query q from u to v with a starting timestamp t and an ending timestamp t'. Let P_{ans} be the result of q, $l = \langle w, t_d, t_a, \cdot, \cdot\rangle$ be an out-label of u, and $l' = \langle w', t_d', t_a', \cdot, \cdot\rangle$ be an in-label of v. If l is pertinent to P_{ans} or the sub-path of P_{ans}, we have $t \leq t_d$ and $t_a \leq t'$, which is checked by Line 4 of Algorithm 1. Similarly, the timestamps of l' are checked by Line 10 of Algorithm 1. By Lemma 1, there are three cases:

Case 1: If $w = v$, we have P_{ans}, which is pertinent to l.

Case 2: If $w' = u$, we have P_{ans}, which is pertinent to l'.

Case 3: If $w \neq v$, $w' \neq u$, $t_a \leq t_d'$ and $w = w'$, we have l and l' each of which is pertinent to a sub-path of P_{ans}.

Obviously, *Case 1* and *Case 2* can be correctly handled by Lines 6-8 and Lines 12-14 respectively. Now, we focus on the discussion of *Case 3*. By contradiction, assume that Lines 15-20 cannot find a sketch corresponding to P_{ans}. Since labels in $L_{out}(u)$ and $L_{in}(v)$ are sorted, we have $t_a > t_d'$ for all pairs of l and l' where $w = w'$. This contradicts *Case 3*, which completes the proof. □

Proof of Lemma 4. Without loss of generality, let $o(u) < o(v)$, i.e., the rank of u is higher than that of v. Let P_1 denote the sub-path of P from u to p, and P_2 the sub-path of P from p to u. By Definition 6, the rank of p is higher than all nodes in P, except u and v. As such, both P_1 and P_2 satisfy the Rank Constraint in Definition 5.

Assume on the contrary that either P_1 or P_2 is not a canonical path. Consider that P_1 is not a canonical path. Since P_1 satisfies the Rank Constraint, there must exist another path P^o from u to p dominating P_1. This contradicts that P is a canonical path. The case for P_2 can be similarly established. □

Proof of Lemma 5. By Lemma 1 and Lemma 3, given a starting timestamp t and an ending timestamp t', we can find the sketches pertinent to all paths from u to v, each of which is an SDP regarding its departure time $t_d \geq t$ and arrival time $t_a \leq t'$. Denote these paths by $SDP(u, v, t, t')$. As such, when $t' = +\infty$, we can obtain the sketches pertinent to paths in $SDP(u, v, t, +\infty)$. Hence, we are able to find the EAP whose arrival time is the minimum in $SDP(u, v, t, +\infty)$. The similar analysis can be applied to the extension of LDP queries. □

Proof of Lemmas 6 and 7. Consider Lemma 6. Given the non-dominated path P starting from u at time $t \in T_d$ and ending at v at time t', assume that P is not an EAP. In other words, there exists another path P' such that P' also starts from u at time t but ends at v at time t^*, which is earlier than t', i.e., $t^* < t'$. However, this violates that P is a non-dominated path, which completes the proof of Lemma 6. The proof of Lemma 7 can be established in the similar manner. □

Proof of Theorem 1. Let $|\mathcal{L}_{apx}|$ be the index size with the node ordering given by the approximation algorithm, and $|\mathcal{L}_{opt}|$ be the index size with the optimal node ordering. Then, we have

$$
\begin{aligned}
|\mathcal{L}_{apx}| &= \textstyle\sum_{i=1}^{n} |I(u_i)| \\
&\leq \sqrt{\alpha} \cdot \textstyle\sum_{i=1}^{n} \sqrt{|R_i(u_i)|} && \text{(By Lemma 9)} \\
&\leq 2\sqrt{\alpha} \cdot \textstyle\sum_{i=1}^{n} \sqrt{|R_i'(v_i)|} && \text{(By Lemma 11)} \\
&\leq 2\sqrt{\alpha} \cdot \textstyle\sum_{i=1}^{n} |I(v_i)| && \text{(By Lemma 10)} \\
&= 2\sqrt{\alpha} \cdot |\mathcal{L}_{opt}|.
\end{aligned}
$$

In other words, the approximation algorithm yields a $2\sqrt{\alpha}$ approximation in terms of index size.

To obtain the node order with the above approximation guarantee, the main challenges are to (i) compute the number of the non-dominated paths covered by each node, and (ii) update the number when another node is ordered. We address these challenges by maintaining three hash tables, T_1, T_2, and T_3. In particular, for each item in T_1 (resp. T_2), its key is a triple $\langle u, v, t_d\rangle$ (resp. $\langle u, v, t_a\rangle$), and its value is the arrival time t_a (resp. departure time t_d) of the canonical path that is from u to v with departure time t_d (resp. arrival time t_a). As such, t_a (resp. t_d) of a non-dominated path can be retrieved from T_1 (resp. T_2) in constant time given $\langle u, v, t_d\rangle$ (resp. $\langle u, v, t_a\rangle$). Besides, for each item in T_3, its key is a quadruple $\langle u, v, t_d, t_a\rangle$, and its value is $True$ if the non-dominated path from u to v with departure time t_d and arrival time t_a has been covered, otherwise $False$. Furthermore, a counter $r(v)$ for a node v is maintained to record the number of non-dominated paths covered by v but not covered by any node u with $o(u) < o(v)$. Since the number of non-dominated paths starting from a node v is at most $O(n \cdot d_{out}(v))$, the space complexity of three hash tables is $O(n \cdot m)$.

Specifically, we first compute $r(v)$ for each node v and construct the hash tables using the temporal Dijkstra's algorithm, which can be finished in $O(n^2 \cdot m)$ time. Then, in each iteration, we choose the node v' with the highest $r(v')$ score, after which we identify the non-dominated paths covered by node v', and update $r(v)$ of the other nodes v accordingly. Consider the total cost of retrieving the non-dominated paths in all n iterations. To retrieve the non-dominated paths covered by node v', we need to examine all possible non-dominated paths that start from a node u, end at a node w, and pass through v'. To compute such paths, we first examine all incoming edges e of v', and identify the arrival timestamp t_a of e; after that, we search T_2 for an entry with a key $\langle u, v', t_a\rangle$, and obtain the corresponding departure time t_1. Then, we inspect all outgoing edges e' of v', and obtain the departure timestamp t_d of e'; after that, we search T_1 for an entry with the key $\langle v', w, t_d\rangle$, and obtain the corresponding arrival time t_2. Finally, we search T_3 for an entry with a key $\langle u, w, t_1, t_2\rangle$, to see if the path is a non-dominated path that has not been covered. Note that the checking for all paths from u to w can be done in $d_{in}(v') + d_{out}(v')$ time. As there are $O(n^2)$ combinations of u and w, the cost to compute the non-dominated paths covered by v' is $O(n^2 \cdot (d_{in}(v') + d_{out}(v')))$. Summing up the costs in n iterations, the total cost of computing all non-dominated paths is $O(n^2 \cdot m)$.

Next, consider the cost of updating $r(v)$ of an unordered node v, after we obtain all non-dominated paths covered by v'. Let P be a non-dominated path covered by v'. If v also covers P, we decrease $r(v)$ by one. Let u (resp. w) be the starting (resp. ending) node of P, and t_d (resp. t_a) be the departure (resp. arrival) time of P. To check whether P is covered by v, we first search T_1 for an entry with a key $\langle u, v, t_d\rangle$, and obtain the corresponding arrival time t_1; then, we search T_2 for an entry with a key $\langle v, w, t_a\rangle$, and obtain the corresponding departure time t_2. If t_1 is no larger than t_2, then P is covered by v, and we decrease $r(v)$ by one. Such a check takes constant time. As we needs to perform such check for each node on each of the $O(n \cdot m)$ non-dominated path covered by v', the total

Algorithm 4: *CPathUnfold*

```
   input : a label l = ⟨·, ·, ·, ·, p⟩ in TTL
   output: the canonical path corresponding to l
1  if p = null then
2      return a path that only contains the edge in G corresponding to l;
3  else
4      l1 = the left child of l;
5      l2 = the right child of l;
6      let l1' be the original label of l1 to be computed;
7      if l1 is a label with route-based compression then
8          obtain l1' by inspecting the timetable of the route associated
           with l1;
9      else if l1 is a label with pivot-based compression then
10         obtain l1' by inspecting the left and right children of l1;
11     P1 = CPathUnfold( l1' );
12     repeat Lines 7-14 by replacing l1 with l2, l1' with l2', and P1 with
       P2;
13     set P = a concatenation of P1 and P2, with P1 proceeding P2;
14     return P;
```

cost of the checks is $O(n^2 \cdot m)$. In summary, the approximation algorithm runs in $O(n^2 \cdot m)$ time and $O(n \cdot m)$ space. □

B. QUERY WITH COMPRESSED LABELS

In Section 7, we have explained how we can reconstruct original labels from the ones generated by our compression methods. In what follows, we clarify how we can process queries on the compressed index. In particular, we first explain the candidate generation and refinement process on compressed labels, and then introduce the algorithm for path reconstruction. For ease of exposition, we focus on SDP queries, but our solution can be easily extended to EAP and LDP queries.

Candidate Generation and Refinement. Given a query asking for the SDP from u to v with a starting timestamp t and an ending timestamp t', we generate the set S_{uv} of path sketches by linearly scanning $L_{out}(u)$ and $L_{in}(v)$ using Algorithm 1, with one modification: whenever we encounter a compressed label l, we decompress it based on the compression technique used. In particular, if l is produced by the route-based compression, then l should be in the form of $\langle \cdot, null, null, r, \cdot \rangle$, i.e., the route information r of l is available. Then, as explained in Section 7.1, the original labels associated with l can be easily retrieved from the timetable associated with r. Next, consider that l is generated by the pivot-based compression. In that case, l should be in the form of $\langle \cdot, null, null, null, p \rangle$. Let $l_1, l_2, \ldots, l_j$ ($j \geq 1$) be the original labels associated with l. Without loss of generality, assume that $o(u) < o(p) < o(v)$. Then, as explained in Section 7.2, the left (resp. right) children of $l_1, l_2, \ldots, l_j$ are stored in $L_{in}(p)$ (resp. $L_{in}(v)$). As such, we can recover $l_1, l_2, \ldots, l_j$ by inspecting the labels in $L_{in}(p)$ and $L_{in}(v)$ based on the pivot information of l. After that, we can replace l with $l_1, l_2, \cdots, l_j$ in the linear scan.

After the linear scan, the set S_{uv} of all the path sketches with respect to the SDP query can be obtained. Then, we identify the sketch s_{ans} in S_{uv} that is pertinent to the SDP query result, using the same approach as described in Section 4.1. Note that all labels in s_{ans} are not compressed, due to the decompression operations performed during the linear scan.

Path Reconstruction. Once s_{ans} is identified, we proceed to reconstruct the path corresponding to s_{ans}. Algorithm 4 presents the pseudo-code of *CPathUnfold*, namely, the method for path reconstruction with the compressed index. *CPathUnfold* takes as input a label l (in s_{ans}), which, as mentioned, is guaranteed to be uncompressed due to the way s_{ans} is generated. Without loss of generality, assume that the left child l' of l is compressed. Then, the departure timestamp of l' is the same as that of l, and the starting node and ending node of l' can be learnt from l. Therefore, to decompress l', it suffices to identify the arrival timestamp and vehicle of l'. If l' is produced from the route-based compression, then we can pinpoint the arrival timestamp and vehicle of l' by inspecting the timetable of the route associated with l'. Meanwhile, if l' is generated by the pivot-based compression, then l' can be reconstructed by inspecting the children of l' and the pivot information in l' (as explained in Section 7.2). The case that the right child of l is compressed can be addressed in a similar manner.

v	$L_{in}(v)$	$L_{out}(v)$
v_2	$\emptyset$	$\emptyset$
v_1	$\emptyset$	$\langle v_2, 1, 2, b_1, null \rangle$ $\langle v_2, 2, 3, b_2, null \rangle$ $\langle v_2, 3, 4, b_3, null \rangle$
v_3	$\langle v_2, 2, 3, b_1, null \rangle$ $\langle v_2, 3, 4, b_2, null \rangle$ $\langle v_2, 4, 5, b_3, null \rangle$	$\emptyset$

Table 5: The label sets of v_1, v_2, and v_3 in a *TTL* index of G' in Figure 2a, with a node order $o(v_2) = 1, o(v_1) = 2$, and $o(v_3) = 3$.

C. ADDITIONAL EXAMPLE

EXAMPLE 6. Consider the timetable graph G' in Figure 2a with a node order $o(v_2) = 1$, $o(v_1) = 2$, and $o(v_3) = 3$. The index construction algorithm first selects v_2, and performs a temporal Dijkstra traversal from v_2 with the largest departure timestamp, i.e., 4. Then it obtains one EAP, based on which *IndexBuild* inserts a label $\langle v_2, 4, 5, b_3, null \rangle$ into $L_{in}(v_3)$. Next, it performs a temporal Dijkstra traversal from v_2 at timestamp 3 and timestamp 2 in sequence. These two traversals lead to two additional labels. After that, a backward Dijkstra is performed from v_2 with the smallest arrival timestamp, i.e., 2. Then it obtains one LDP, and *IndexBuild* inserts a label $\langle v_2, 1, 2, b_1, null \rangle$ into $L_{out}(v_1)$ corresponding to this LDP. Afterwards, two more backward Dijkstra traversals are performed from v_2 at timestamp 3 and 4 in a row, resulting in two more labels. This finishes the traversal from v_2, and v_2 is removed from the graph. Then v_1 and v_3 have no incoming and outgoing edges, and both incur no label cost during the traversal. This finishes the index construction, ending up with 6 labels as shown in Table 5. □

D. ADDITIONAL EXPERIMENTS

D.1 EAP and LDP queries

Figure 6 and Figure 7 report the average query time for EAP and LDP queries, respectively. Observe that the performance of each method for EAP and LDP queries on each dataset is generally similar. However, *CSA* and *CHT* incur several times less query time for EAP and LDP queries than for SDP queries. This is because, to answer EAP (resp. LDP) queries, they only maintain the earliest arrival time to (resp. latest departure time from) each node that is traversed. However, to answer an SDP query, they both need to maintain a list to record the departure time and arrival time of each non-dominated path that ends at a certain traversed node, which can be excessively large. Overall, *TTL* and *C-TTL* still outperform *CSA* and *CHT* by a large margin.

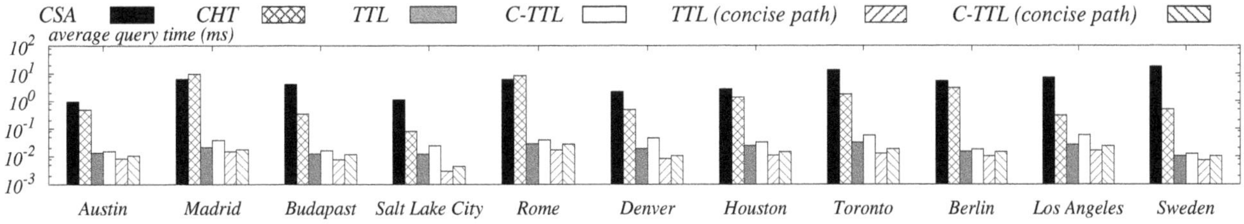

Figure 6: Average query time for EAP queries.

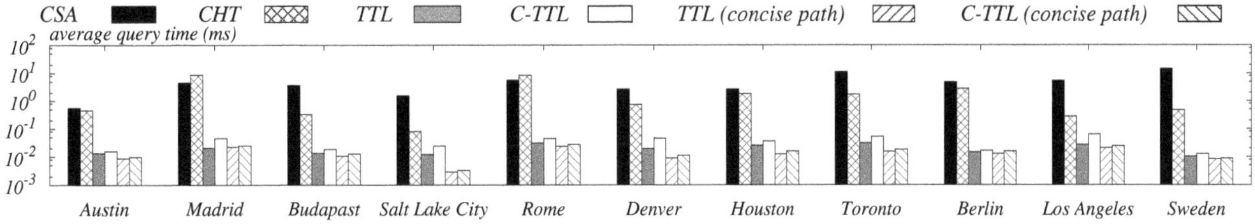

Figure 7: Average query time for LDP queries.

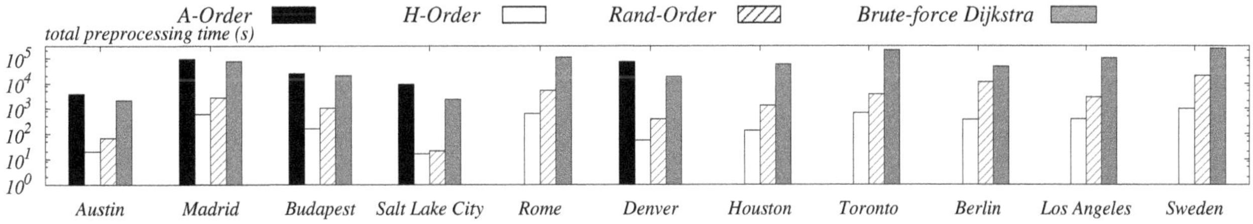

Figure 8: Total preprocessing time.

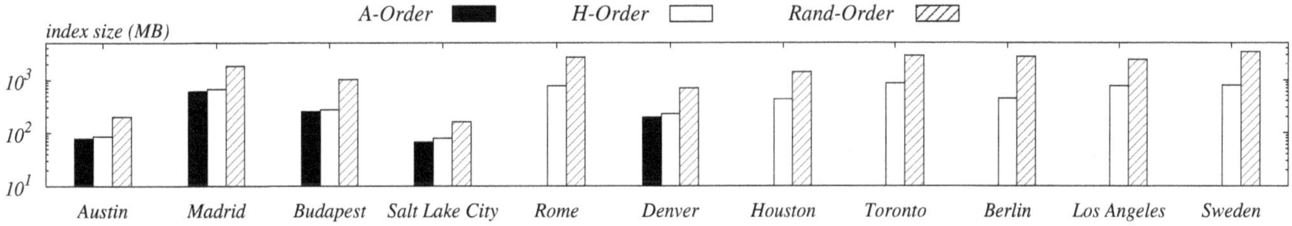

Figure 9: Index size.

D.2 Index Construction and Node Orders

In this set of experiments, we evaluate the efficiency of our index construction algorithm and the effectiveness of our ordering algorithms. In particular, we first compare our index construction algorithm with a baseline approach that (i) runs the temporal Dijkstra's algorithm $O(n)$ times to compute all temporal shortest paths in G, and then (ii) examines the paths obtained to identify the canonical paths. We denote the baseline approach as *brute-force Dijkstra*. Figure 8 reports the index construction time of Algorithm 3 (referred to as *H-Order*) and *brute-force Dijkstra*, both of which adopt *H-Order* as the ordering methods. Observe that Algorithm 3 is at least two orders of magnitude faster than *brute-force Dijkstra*, even though both algorithms have the same worst-case time complexity. The main reason is that Algorithm 3 performs a more advanced version of the Dijkstra's search from v_i, with various heuristics adopted to prune the search space (see Section 5). For instance, whenever it encounters a node v_j with $o(v_j) < o(v_i)$ during the search, it would omit all edges pertinent to v_j, since any path that contains those edges would violate the Rank Constraint in Definition 5 (and hence, cannot be canonical). This demonstrates that our index construction algorithm is highly superior to the *brute-force Dijkstra* approach in terms of practical efficiency.

Next, we compare our heuristic ordering algorithm (referred to as *H-Order*) and our approximate ordering algorithm (referred to as *A-Order*), with a baseline approach that orders nodes randomly (denoted by *Rand-Order*). Figure 9 reports the index size of *TTL* (in log-scale) for each of the three node ordering methods. The results of *A-Order* are omitted on some datasets due to its prohibitive memory consumption ($> 64GB$). Observe that, both *A-Order* and *H-Order* outperform the baseline approach by large margins, which demonstrates the importance of node ordering in index construction and the superiority of our approaches. In particular, the index size of *H-Order* is more than one order of magnitude smaller than that of *Rand-Order* on *Berlin* dataset. Besides, the index size of *H-Order* is comparable to that of *A-Order*, which shows the effectiveness of our heuristic ordering approach.

Figure 8 presents the total processing time of *TTL* for each ordering methods. The total processing time of *A-Order* is at least 2 orders of magnitude larger than that of *H-Order*, since *A-Order* incurs significant overheads in computing all non-dominated paths and updating the marginal coverage of each node. In addition, *Rand-Order* has a total processing time several times larger than that of *H-Order* , since the former generates an enormous number of labels (see Figure 9). In summary, our heuristic ordering method yields similar index size as the approximation algorithm, but incurs much less preprocessing cost.

The Importance of Being Expert: Efficient Max-Finding in Crowdsourcing*

Aris Anagnostopoulos
Sapienza University
Rome, Italy
aris@dis.uniroma1.it

Luca Becchetti
Sapienza University
Rome, Italy
becchetti@dis.uniroma1.it

Adriano Fazzone
Sapienza University
Rome, Italy
fazzone@dis.uniroma1.it

Ida Mele
Max Planck Institute for Informatics
Saarbrücken, Germany
imele@mpi-inf.mpg.de

Matteo Riondato†
Stanford University
Stanford, CA, USA
rionda@cs.stanford.edu

Οὐ πάνυ ἡμῖν οὕτω φροντιστέον τί ἐροῦσιν οἱ πολλοὶ ἡμᾶς, ἀλλ᾽ ὅτι ὁ ἐπαΐων περὶ τῶν δικαίων καὶ ἀδίκων. [Σωκράτης, Πλάτωνος "Κρίτων"]

We should not care so much about what the many say about us, but about what says whoever is expert on what is right and wrong. [Socrates in Plato's "Crito"]

ABSTRACT

Crowdsourcing is a computational paradigm whose distinctive feature is the involvement of human workers in key steps of the computation. It is used successfully to address problems that would be hard or impossible to solve for machines. As we highlight in this work, the exclusive use of nonexpert individuals may prove ineffective in some cases, especially when the task at hand or the need for accurate solutions demand some degree of specialization to avoid excessive uncertainty and inconsistency in the answers. We address this limitation by proposing an approach that combines the wisdom of the crowd with the educated opinion of experts. We present a computational model for crowdsourcing that envisions two classes of workers with different expertise levels. One of its distinctive features is the adoption of the threshold error model, whose roots are in psychometrics and which we extend from previous theoretical work. Our computational model allows to evaluate the performance of crowdsourcing algorithms with respect to accuracy and cost. We use our model to develop and analyze an algorithm for approximating the best, in a broad sense, of a set of elements. The algorithm uses *naïve* and *expert* workers to find an element that is a constant-factor approximation to the best. We prove upper and lower bounds on the number of comparisons needed to solve this problem, showing that our algorithm uses expert and naïve workers optimally up to a constant factor. Finally, we evaluate our algorithm on real and synthetic datasets using the CrowdFlower crowdsourcing platform, showing that our approach is also effective in practice.

†Part of the work performed while visiting Sapienza University of Rome.

*This research was partially supported by the Google Focused Research Award "Algorithms for Large-Scale Data Analysis," the EU FET projects MULTIPLEX 317532 and SIMPOL 610704, the Italian MIUR PRIN project "ARS TechnoMedia," and by the NSF award IIS-1247581.

SIGMOD'15, May 31–June 4, 2015, Melbourne, Victoria, Australia.

ACM 978-1-4503-2758-9/15/05 ...$15.00.
http://dx.doi.org/10.1145/2723372.2723722.

Categories and Subject Descriptors

F.2.0 [**Analysis of Algorithms and Problem Complexity**]: General; H.3.3 [**Information Storage and Retrieval**]: Information Filtering; H.1.2 [**Models and Principles**]: User/Machine Factors—*Human information processing*

Keywords

Crowdsourcing; human computation; max algorithm; worker models

1. INTRODUCTION

Crowdsourcing is a computational paradigm that enables outsourcing pieces of the computation to humans, who perform them under monetary compensation. The main rationale for the involvement of humans is the existence of tasks that are easy to perform for a person but very difficult or impossible to accomplish for a machine. Crowdsourcing-based systems [14] and algorithms have been developed to answer important queries for which relational DBMSs have traditionally been used, such as selectivity estimation, counting, ranking, and filtering [7, 24, 25, 32]. Crowdsourcing has applications in various areas, including machine learning, visualization, recommendation systems, computational photography, and data analytics.

One of the main reasons for bringing humans into the computational loop is that the task is underspecified or cannot be specified sufficiently in details for a machine to perform it, whereas humans can use intuition and their background knowledge to understand what is requested from them. Even when the job is well specified, humans may perform the task much better than a machine.

Despite the fact that humans can carry out some operations better or more easily than machines, they do not always perform them correctly. Indeed, it has been observed that the output of crowdsourcing systems can be extremely noisy [16, 37]. There are two main sources of error. The first is *incompleteness of information*: tasks may be underspecified in many respects, so that individual factors come into play when humans perform them. In this case, although a ground truth may exist (e.g., cars come with factory prices), humans may err because they possess only partial information and/or their judgment may be clouded by personal biases. The second source of error, or actually set of sources, includes mistakes due to input errors, misunderstanding of the requirements, and malicious behavior (*crowdsourcing spamming*).

To motivate the topic of this work, assume that we ask you which of the two pictures of Figure 1(a) has *fewer* dots; which one would you select? (Try, if you want, before proceeding!) The correct answer is the first one (180 vs. 200). Most humans can answer questions like this thanks to abilities that are either hard-wired or naturally learnt in the course of time. Thus, if we ask several individuals the same question, we expect that the majority will answer correctly, and the more people we ask, the higher is our confidence that the preferred answer is correct. In cases like this we can successfully apply the paradigm of the *wisdom of crowds* [30]. Indeed, it is for this reason that crowdsourcing platforms offer the possibility to ask the same question to several human workers.

Consider now Figure 1(b) and the question "Which car has a *higher* price?" (Try to guess again!), and similarly for Figure 1(c). In both cases the correct answer is the second car. Yet, unless one is an expert on car pricing or has access to accurate information about the cars, she probably cannot figure out why the Mercedes ($114K) is more expensive than the BMW ($100K), yet cheaper than the Audi ($120K)[1]. In this case the wisdom of crowds will not work: it is hard to guess the correct answer when the price difference is small, unless one is a real expert on U.S. car prices or is able to retrieve accurate information about the prices. For this reason, crowdsourcing platforms have started introducing the concept of *experts*. Amazon mechanical Turk now has *masters* and CrowdFlower allows to employ *skilled workers*. Although the concept of an expert is broad, there are three characteristics that expert workers possess in contrast with *naïve* (i.e., nonexpert) workers: (1) they obtain training or pass tests to certify that they produce higher-quality results for specific application domains with respect to regular workers; (2) they are a much scarcer resource than regular workers; (3) they offer their services at a much higher price.

The design and analysis of algorithms that employ human workers on crowdsourcing platforms require computational and cost models that are flexible enough to allow performance analysis and that are realistic enough to reflect the actual runtime and costs of the algorithms. In this respect, two crucial aspects make crowdsourcing different from most other computational paradigms: *human error* and *monetary cost*. The computational and cost models must allow the expression and analysis of these aspects in a realistic way. In addition, as already mentioned, the recent trend in crowdsourcing platforms to organize the available workforce into different classes with different skills demands a suitable modeling of the expert workers, who allow to achieve higher quality results, which cannot be attained by naïve workers but which come at a higher cost.

1.1 Contributions and Roadmap

In this paper we introduce a computational model that captures important aspects of crowdsourcing and present and analyze a max-finding algorithm on top of this model. We introduce the concept of *expert worker*, who can add qualitatively more power to the computations that we are able to perform. We show how expert workers can help in a practical case by presenting an algorithm that leverages on experts to find the maximum among a set of elements. This is a problem often encountered in practice in crowdsourcing scenarios (e.g., ranking of search results, evaluation of web-page relevance to a query, selection of the best labeling for a picture [6]). Whereas this problem is simple enough in the standard computational model, it becomes nontrivial in more complex scenarios as the one we present here. For these reasons, it is one of the most studied problems in the context of crowdsourcing [34, 35] (without considering experts). Our algorithm can be used inside systems like CrowdDB [14] to answer a wider range of queries using the crowd. To summarize our contributions:

- By performing experiments on the CrowdFlower crowdsourcing platform, we identify key characteristics of workers' performance in diverse scenarios (Section 3.1).
- Building on the findings we present models that can capture the behavior in the diverse settings (Section 3.2).
- We introduce the concept of crowdsourcing experts and we incorporate them in our model (Section 3.3).
- Building on our models, we formally define the problem of finding the maximum element. We provide lower bounds on the number of expert and nonexpert comparisons required to solve it. We provide an algorithm for this problem that computes a constant-factor approximation to the maximum ele-

[1]Prices are from August 2013.

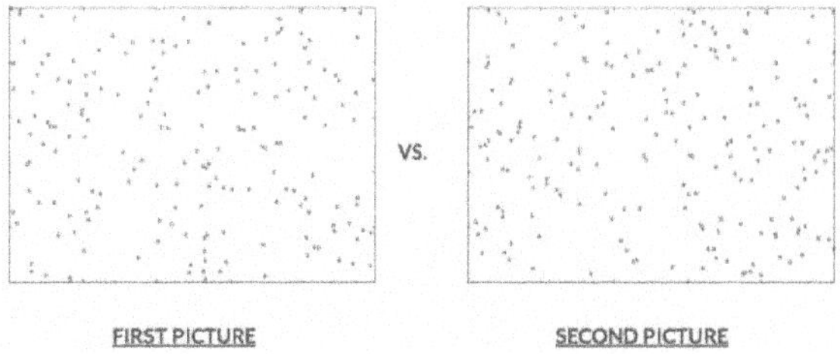

(a) Task: select the picture with fewer dots.

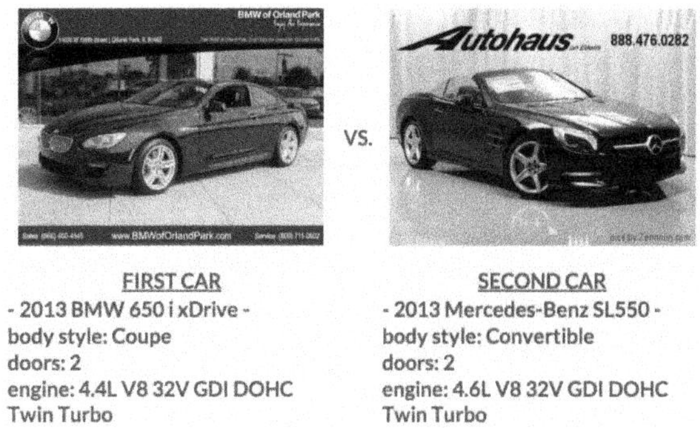

(b) Task: select the most expensive car.

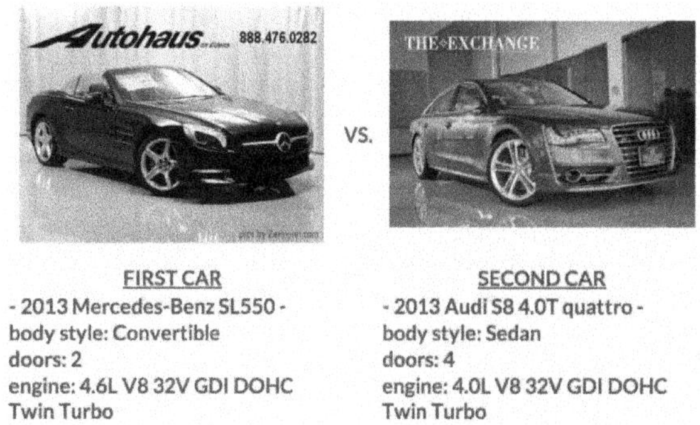

(c) Task: select the most expensive car.

Figure 1: Examples of crowdsourcing tasks.

ment and makes an optimal (modulo constant factors) use of the workers (Section 4).

- We perform a series of simulations for evaluating the efficiency of our algorithm in practice complementing our theoretical analysis, and we perform a set of experiments on CrowdFlower to show its effectiveness in finding the maximum (Section 5). Among others, we apply our approach on the problem of evaluation of search results to show the applicability of our approach in a real-life scenario.

2. RELATED WORK

Many works in the algorithmic literature have dealt with the problem of sorting or computing the maximum of a set of elements using comparators some of which may be faulty [28, 36], even without considering the crowdsourcing settings. Various different models and solutions have been proposed. A number of works considered the idea that the comparator errs with some probability at each comparison, independently from other comparisons [3, 8, 11, 15, 17, 18, 35]. They presented algorithms to compute the maximum element, studying numerous variants of this purely probabilistic error model. In the simplest variant, each comparator has a fixed probability associated to it, and this remains constant over all comparisons, independently of the values of the elements. This is for example the case for the basic models considered by Feige et al. [11] and Davidson et al. [8] (in both works, more sophisticated probabilistic models are also considered, but they do not incorporate the concept of experts, crucial in our work). An important consequence of this probabilistic modeling of the error is the following: *If the error probabilities are independent and less than* $1/2$ *then, given two items to compare, independently of their mutual distance, it is possible to identify the element with higher value with arbitrarily high probability by performing the same comparison multiple times, and taking the element that won the majority of the comparisons (or an arbitrary element in case of a tie).* In our work, we consider a different model (the *threshold* model) where such conclusion is not possible: an expert has more capabilities than a naïve worker and her answers *cannot* be simulated by aggregating the answers of multiple naïve workers. Another model is presented by Aigner [1], where at each step of the computation a fraction p of the answers returned so far could be wrong. This setting is in part related to past work on comparisons with faulty memories [12, 13] and more generally to computational tasks involving communication across noisy channels. Pelc [26] presents a survey of this broader area of research. Other works considered a threshold model, where the comparator may err if the elements have values very close to each other [2]. We extend and adapt some of the results from these previous contributions to the crowdsourcing model of computation. None of these consider the main idea of the present work, namely that comparators may belong to different classes with different error parameters and different costs, and one cannot be used to simulate the other.

In the crowdsourcing environment, Marcus et al. [20] looked at how to select the maximal element and sort a sequence of elements by splitting the input into nonoverlapping sets with the same size and sort these sets recursively. No guarantee is given on the running time and accuracy of the algorithms.

Venetis and Garcia-Molina [34] and Venetis et al. [35] present algorithms for finding the maximum in crowdsourcing environments based on static and dynamic tournaments. They consider error models taken from the psychometrics literature and, given a specific error model and a budget of computational resources, they compute the optimal parameters for the algorithms using simulated annealing. They do not discuss, though, about the possibility of having experts and the tradeoffs between accuracy and costs that this possibility would allow.

The need for experts is pointed out by Sun et al. [29]: a single majority vote from all the workers is only accurate for low difficulty tasks, but it is insufficient as the difficulty of tasks increases.

Some works [14, 21, 25] took into account the probability of mistakes and different cost measure to optimize various filtering tasks using crowdsourcing, but without analyzing their effect in a formal framework. We present a different model and algorithm, giving precise guarantees on the performances.

Karger et al. [17] presented an algorithm for crowdsourcing that learns the reliability of each worker and assigns tasks to workers according to their reliability, using this piece of information to minimize the number of questions asked to the workers. Other works [4, 5, 9, 19, 27, 33] presented methods to identify sets of well performing workers or to detect badly performing workers and rule them out, whereas we assume to know precisely who the experts are, as they may reside outside a classical crowdsourcing system. As an example, consider the case where the task requires to select the best picture representing the Colosseum. A professional photographer would be an expert in this case, to whom we ask to solve the task offline. She is hired for the precise reason that she is an expert, hence her status is known in advance. Alternatively, it is possible to apply the algorithms presented in those works to detect a set of experts and then use our algorithm to leverage their additional expertise. In this sense, our work is orthogonal and complementary to that from [4, 5, 9, 19, 27, 33].

Mason and Watts [22] investigated the effect of increasing the financial incentives for workers on the quality of the performed work. They found out that there is no improvement in quality as the incentive grows. This implies that one cannot just pay some workers more than others and use them as experts. Instead, in our model we pay experts more than others for the only reason that they are experts and are going to perform the work with higher precision.

Mo et al. [23] proposed algorithms to compute the number of workers whom to ask the same question such as to achieve the best accuracy with a fixed available budget. The workers all belong to the same class and they perform a task correctly or incorrectly with a probability that depends on the task but not on the workers.

Davidson et al. [8] introduced algorithms inspired by Feige et al. [11] to solve max, top-k, and group-by queries under a new error model where the probability of error when comparing two elements depends on the distance between the elements. The probability of error is the same for all workers, so there is no concept of experts and nonexperts.

3. MODELING CROWDSOURCING

In this section we formalize crowdsourcing computation for computing the maximum (or best) among a set of elements. We perform some crowdsourcing experiments and we use the findings to justify a class of models that we introduce.

Finding the maximum over a set of elements. Let $\mathcal{U}$ be a universe of elements and let $\mathsf{v}(\cdot)$ be a function from $\mathcal{U}$ to the reals: $\mathsf{v}: \mathcal{U} \to \mathbb{R}$. For an element $e \in \mathcal{U}$ we call $\mathsf{v}(e)$ the *value of* e. The function v establishes a partial[2] order over the elements of $\mathcal{U}$. We define the *distance between two elements* $u, v \in \mathcal{U}$ as $\mathsf{d}(u,v) = |\mathsf{v}(u) - \mathsf{v}(v)|$. Given a set L of n elements from $\mathcal{U}$, let $V_L = \max_{e \in L} \mathsf{v}(e)$. We denote with M_L any of the elements from L with value V_L, so that, $\mathsf{v}(M_L) = V_L$ by definition, and we refer to it as the *maximum element of* L. The set L will often be clear from

[2]The order is partial because it is possible to have $\mathsf{v}(e_1) = \mathsf{v}(e_2)$ for $e_1 \neq e_2$.

the context and we will drop it from the notation of M_L and only use M. The problem of interest in this work is the selection of an element $e \in L$ whose value $\mathsf{v}(e)$ is equal to or closely approximates V_L, as formally defined in Section 4.

Human workers and crowdsourcing algorithms. Both the universe $\mathcal{U}$ and the value function v are arbitrary. In particular, v may be very difficult or time consuming to evaluate or even approximate for computers but very easy to evaluate or approximate for humans. In this work we develop a crowdsourcing algorithm to compute an element from L whose value is close to that of the maximum element M, using a set of human *workers* W. We assume that a worker can only compare two elements at a time (this assumption is often present also in prior works as it simplifies the formalization) and returns the one that she believes has the maximum value. Following Venetis et al. [35], the algorithms we consider are organized in *logical time steps*. In the s-th logical step, a batch B_s of pairwise comparisons is sent to the crowdsourcing platform, which, after some time, returns the corresponding answers from the human workers. Depending on these answers, the algorithm selects the next batch B_{s+1} of comparisons, and so on, until the algorithm terminates. Depending on the size of W, each logical step s in general corresponds to a sequence $\mathsf{F}(s)$ of consecutive *physical time steps*. In particular, in the generic physical time step $t \in \mathsf{F}(s)$, a subset $W_t \subseteq W$ of the workers is active. Each active worker $w \in W_t$ receives a pair (k, j) of *distinct*[3] elements from $L \times L$. Worker w then "computes" a *comparison function* $\mathsf{m}_w(k, j)$, which returns the element from k, j that she *believes* has the maximum value. We say that the returned element *wins* the comparison.

Remark. Venetis et al. [35] simply call *steps* what we call *logical steps* here. The reason is that they consider the number of logical time steps (according to our terminology) a reasonable measure of the time complexity.

Given the generality of the function v and of the universe $\mathcal{U}$, the worker w may not be able to compute v exactly, but only to somehow approximate it. Hence, the element returned by the function m_w may not be the one with maximum value. To delve more into this question, we start by performing a set of crowdsourcing experiments, which allow us to observe how humans err in different max-finding tasks and how we can use their collective knowledge.

3.1 Workers' Accuracy in Crowdsourcing

To find the properties required for our models, we performed a series of experiments on the CrowdFlower crowdsourcing platform.[4] We describe first the two main datasets that we created and then we provide some details about the CrowdFlower setup. The task at hand is to ask workers to compare two items. The main question that we want to address with our experiment is: *is it always possible to improve accuracy by asking multiple workers to answer the same question independently, or is there a* cognitive barrier, *at least for certain types of questions, that does not allow to achieve arbitrarily high precision?*

Datasets. We created two main datasets:

- DOTS (inspired by [33]): It consists of a collection of images containing randomly placed dots. The number of dots in each picture ranges from 100 to 1500, with steps of 20.
- CARS: This dataset contains descriptions of cars. We downloaded a set of approximately 5000 new cars from the `cars.com` web site. For each car we collected a *photo*, the *make*, *model*, *body style* (e.g., SUV, sedan, coupe, etc.), *engine informations*, *number of doors*, and its *price* (in August 2013). We cleaned the dataset and created a set of 110 cars with price between 14K and 130K. For every pair of cars the difference in price is at least $500.

  CARS is a very noisy dataset. For instance we found several sets of cars of the same make and model that varied significantly in the price, often in the order of several thousands dollars. Most of the times this difference is a result of the differences in equipment, but sometimes different dealers also sell the same car at different prices. Showing the entire equipment to workers is impractical and would lead to higher error rate, so we decided to show only limited information about each car. We ensured that for the same brand and year the car models are not repeated, by selecting a representative that was in the middle of the price range.

Measuring Workers' Accuracy. We used the CrowdFlower platform, a paid crowdsourcing service, available since 2009. It offers quality-ensured results at massive scale, good APIs, and multiple channels.

For each dataset we used 50 elements for comparisons, and some additional ones for *gold* comparisons, which are comparisons for which the ground-truth value is provided and which are used by CrowdFlower to evaluate the performance of workers and reduce the effect of spam (responses of workers whose performance on gold comparisons has accuracy less than 70% are ignored). In total, 15% of the queries that we performed are gold queries. We selected pairs covering the overall range of values and differences. We submitted 105 pairs from DOTS and 154 from CARS (we found that for the latter we needed more data points). For each pair to be compared we requested at least 21 answers. Figure 1 shows snapshots of the pairs presented to the workers.

Our goal is twofold. First, we want to measure the accuracy of workers as the difference of the value of the two items under comparison varies. Second, we want to study to what extent we can improve the accuracy by increasing the number of workers.

We summarize our findings in Figure 2. In Figure 2(a), which refers to DOTS, each line corresponds to responses obtained for a given range of difference between the actual number of dots. For example, the red (lowest) line accumulates the responses of queries where the relative difference between the number of dots ranged from 0 to 10% (these are the hardest questions), whereas the green (second lowest) corresponds to the range 10–20%. On the x-axis we vary the number of workers whose (independent) responses we observe (we consider the votes of 1 worker to 21 workers, ordered by time of response) and on the y-axis we report the aggregate accuracy of the workers when we take a *majority vote*. Note that the accuracy is generally quite low when considering a single worker but it improves as we ask more workers, arriving very close to 1. Figure 2(b) shows the same plot for CARS. When the relative difference between the price of the two cars is relatively large, the accuracy approaches 1 as the number of workers increases. However, for smaller differences (up to 20%) the accuracy of the workers plateaus: it does not surpass 0.6 or 0.7, depending on the difference.

The results allow us to draw two conclusions. First, we need different error models to capture the different behaviors that we observed. For the behavior in DOTS we need a model in which the accuracy increases with the number of workers. Instead, for CARS we need a model where, for small values of the difference, an increase to the number of workers is not sufficient to increase the accuracy. This is the topic of the next section.

[3]By distinct we just mean that a worker does not receive two copies of the same element, not that $\mathsf{d}(k, j) \neq 0$.

[4]`http://crowdflower.com`

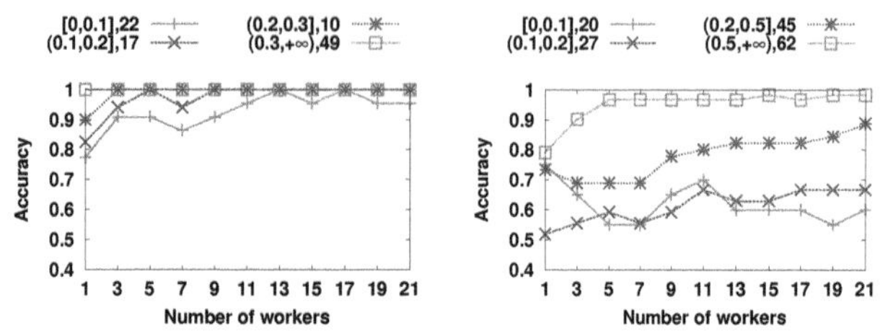

(a) DOTS dataset (b) CARS dataset

Figure 2: Relative accuracy of responses varying the number of workers for different deltas.

Second, these results show a key difference in the tasks: one of them allows to leverage on innate expertise and collective wisdom (counting dots), whereas the other seems to require acquired knowledge at some point (must know car prices). This observation led us to the introduction and modeling of *experts*, skilled workers who are able to rank elements with close values correctly, but who require a higher monetary compensation. Higher compensation can either reflect an immediate cost, or it can model scenarios in which experts are a scarce resource and thus their time is more valuable. This is the topic of Section 3.3.

3.2 Simple Error Models

There are a number of reasons and scenarios in which a worker may commit a mistake as we mentioned in the introduction, and in the previous section we saw that in different settings these can lead to qualitatively different behavior. We next present the probabilistic model, common in prior works, which can model the behavior in DOTS, but not the one in CARS. Then we present a threshold-based model, which captures the behavior in the CARS experiment.

Probabilistic Error Model. A common approach is to assume that an error occurs with some probability, not necessarily fixed: when a worker is given two elements to compare, she chooses the one with highest value with some probability, and the one with lower value with the residual probability, independently of any other comparison she or other workers might perform [3, 8, 11, 15, 17, 18, 35]. The error probability may depend on the difference of the values of the elements to compare, and grows as the difference shrinks, even though for purposes of analysis a common assumption is that it is fixed and independent from the difference.

Assume that for a given question, the probability of error is $p < 0.5$. Then one can show that if we ask the same question to k workers, the probability that the element with *lower* value receives the *majority* of votes is bounded by $e^{-\frac{(1-2p)^2}{8(1-p)}k}$. It decreases exponentially fast to 0 as k grows, implying that we can get arbitrarily good precision by increasing the number of workers; this is qualitatively the behavior that we observed in Figure 2(a). Of course, one can create instances for DOTS on which we cannot aim to reach accuracy equal to 1: e.g., we can create one image with n dots (for large n) and another with $n+1$ dots. In this case, the probability p of error is essentially 0.5 and it will not decrease no matter how many workers we use.

The CARS experiment exemplifies situations in which the comparison tasks may require an expertise not possessed by unskilled (*naïve* in the following) workers. Hence, it is not possible to achieve arbitrary precision and confidence levels by just aggregating the answers from a suitable number of naïve workers. To capture such scenarios, we developed a generalization of the probabilistic model, which we present next.

Threshold Model. To capture scenarios like those mentioned at the end of the previous section, we consider the *threshold model* $\mathcal{T}(\delta, \varepsilon)$, an extension of the model introduced by Ajtai et al. [2] to formalize the concept of *Just Noticeable Difference* by Weber and Fechner (then generalized by Thurstone [31]). Here, whenever a worker is presented with two elements k, j to compare, she chooses the less valuable one (i.e., errs) with a probability that depends on their distance $\mathsf{d}(k, j)$ as follows: let δ be a nonnegative parameter, which models the *discernment ability* of the workers, and let $\varepsilon \in [0, 1)$ be a *residual error probability*. If $\mathsf{d}(k, j) > \delta$ and (without loss of generality) $\mathsf{v}(k) > \mathsf{v}(j)$, the worker returns k with probability $1 - \varepsilon$ and j with probability ε.[5] Instead, if the two elements have values close to each other ($\mathsf{d}(k, j) \leq \delta$) the worker returns either k or j *completely arbitrarily*. In particular, if asked multiple times to compare k and j, the worker may return k on some occasions and j in others, or always k or j. As a result, when the question is hard, asking a lot of workers does not help to increase the accuracy, which is the behavior observed in CARS.

The parameter δ acts as a distance *threshold*, hence the name of the model. In other words, if $\mathsf{d}(k, j) > \delta$, the worker is able to discriminate between the two elements k and j, but for a number of reasons she may still, with low probability, return the one with the lower value. Modeling this uncertainty when the elements are farther apart than δ allows us to take into account workers input errors, malicious workers, or prior bias that the workers may have.

We say that two elements u, v with $\mathsf{d}(u, v) \leq \delta$ are *indistinguishable*. A set of indistinguishable elements is a set of elements such that each two of them are indistinguishable. Note that, assuming the comparison model we just described, it is impossible to exactly compute the element M of L with maximum value if there is another element $e \in L$ indistinguishable from M.

For simplicity, we assume that if the difference is above the threshold then the probability of error is the fixed value ε. This can be generalized to an error probability that depends on the difference, as in the probabilistic model. In addition, δ can be 0, so the threshold model is a generalization of the probabilistic model.

3.3 Threshold Model with Experts

The experimental findings of Section 3.1 demonstrate that there are types of questions that typically require knowledge or skills that are neither innate nor naturally learnt; these questions exhibit an accuracy barrier which cannot be overcome without involving skilled workers with the required expertise. Here, a skilled worker (*expert* in the following) should be seen as an abstraction. In some scenarios, an expert is an actual skilled worker, with the necessary expertise to perform the required comparison tasks with an accuracy that is not achievable by naïve workers. In other settings, an expert models the extra effort needed to perform a comparison task with higher accuracy, for example, by accessing authoritative, external information sources on the topic of the comparison. Yet another setting is where the naïve worker corresponds, for example, to a machine-learning algorithm and an expert to a human. The main characteristic is that the presence of an actual expert or the acquisition of authoritative information about the topic of a comparison *cannot be simulated by simply increasing the number of naïve workers*. Crowdsourcing platforms have become aware of this necessity and they have introduced the concept of experts.

The extension of the threshold model to capture experts is natural. The workers from W are split into two classes, one of *naïve* workers and one of *expert* workers. Naïve workers follow the threshold model $\mathcal{T}(\delta_n, \varepsilon_n)$, whereas experts follow $\mathcal{T}(\delta_e, \varepsilon_e)$, with $\delta_n \gg$

[5] The probabilistic error model is a special case of the threshold model when $\delta = 0$.

δ_e and $\varepsilon_e \leq \varepsilon_n$ (possibly $\varepsilon_e = 0$). Given that there are now two thresholds, we talk of *naïve-indistinguishable* elements for elements u, v with $\mathsf{d}(u, v) \leq \delta_n$, and of *expert-indistinguishable* if $\mathsf{d}(u, v) \leq \delta_e$. Indeed, under our model, two elements that are expert-indistinguishable are also naïve-indistinguishable.

Remarks. We assume to know in advance whether a worker is an expert or not. This is orthogonal and complementary to the approach taken in previous related works that tackle the problem of finding the experts [4, 5, 9, 19, 27, 33]. Our assumption is intuitive given the definition of an expert worker, which is someone who is hired for the specific reason that she is an expert in the task at hand. As we mention in Section 2, an example of this could be a photographer hired to select the best picture of a monument. We may have thousands of pictures to choose from and given the much higher cost of the professional photographer we want to use the cheap naïve workers to filter out the least interesting ones, so that the photographer only has to look at few of them. Alternatively, one can use the aforementioned algorithms to find a group of experts and then use our algorithm to exploit their additional skills and computational power.

In our model we consider two classes of workers, but a natural extension models multiple classes of workers with different expertise levels, or even a continuous measure of expertise for ranking workers. We leave these extensions as future work.

3.4 Cost Model

We analyze our algorithms with respect to monetary cost. We express the cost of the algorithm as a function of the size of the input $n = |L|$.

The main measure of resource consumption that is usually of interest in crowdsourcing applications is the number of operations performed by workers, as they correspond directly to monetary costs, given that workers are paid for each operation they perform. In the presence of experts, we assume that naïve and expert workers have different costs: experts have an associated cost c_e per operation that is much greater than the cost c_n per operation associated to naïve workers ($c_e \gg c_n$). Therefore, if an algorithm performs $x_e(n)$ expert comparisons and $x_n(n)$ naïve comparisons, the total *monetary cost* of the algorithm is

$$\mathsf{C}(n) = x_e(n) \cdot c_e + x_n(n) \cdot c_n.$$

4. FINDING THE MAXIMUM ELEMENT

In this section we delve into the problem of finding the maximum among a set of elements. Apart from the foundational nature of the problem, we study it for the following reasons: (1) many common crowdsourcing tasks are essentially problems of finding the maximum according to some criterion (e.g., finding the best result to a query, the most relevant ad to a page or query, or the best design among a set of candidates [6]); (2) indeed many past works on crowdsourcing algorithms studied the problem of finding the maximum [20, 34, 35]; (3) it is well specified and amenable to (albeit nontrivial) theoretical analysis. Furthermore, we hope that this work will stimulate the rigorous and analytical study of yet more complicated crowdsourcing problems (e.g., evaluation of classification or other machine-learning algorithms).

Given a multiset L of $|L| = n$ elements from a universe $\mathcal{U}$, our algorithm selects an element $e \in L$ whose value is close to the maximum value among the elements in L. We consider the threshold comparison model with experts. Recall that $M \in L$ is an element with maximum value among those in L. The algorithm finds an element $e \in L$ such that $\mathsf{d}(M, e) \leq 3\delta_e$. Its cost depends on the value $\mathsf{u}_n(n)$, which represents the number of elements in L that are naïve-indistinguishable from M: $\mathsf{u}_n(n) = |\{e : \mathsf{d}(M, e) \leq \delta_n\}|$. We assume that $\mathsf{u}_n(n) = o(n)$, giving power to naïve users to discriminate a large part of the input from the maximum element; this assumption is reasonable for typical crowdsourcing datasets and tasks.

Remark. For the sake of presentation we assume that both residual errors ε_n and ε_e (see Section 3.3). are equal to 0 Our results can be extended to any value less than $1/2$.

4.1 An Expert-Aware Max-Finding Algorithm

The algorithm consists of two phases, summed up in Algorithm 1. In the first phase, it uses naïve workers to filter out the majority of the elements that cannot possibly be the maximum, leaving a small set S of candidate elements containing M. In more detail, in the first phase we solve the following problem:

PROBLEM 1. *Given an initial set L of n elements, return a subset $S \subset L$ of size $O(\mathsf{u}_n(n))$ that contains M, using only naïve workers to perform comparisons.*[6]

Algorithm 1: Find an element close to the maximum M

Input : A set L of n elements, a function $\mathsf{u}_n(n) = o(n)$.
Output: An approximation of the maximum element M in L.
Obtain a set $S \subset L$ using Algorithm 2 with naïve workers
Return the output of Algorithm 3 with expert workers on input S

In the second phase, we apply a max-finding algorithm to the set S found in the first phase, using only experts to perform the comparisons. More precisely, we solve the following problem:

PROBLEM 2. *Given an input set S of size $O(\mathsf{u}_n(n))$ containing M, return an element e, such that $\mathsf{d}(M, e) = O(\delta_e)$, using only experts and performing as few comparisons as possible.*[7]

One could solve this problem with $\Theta(|S|^2)$ experts comparisons by performing a simple *all-play-all tournament*[8] among the elements in S. To reduce the number of comparisons performed by experts, we instead use one of the algorithms proposed in [2, Section 3] and return the element found by this algorithm. More details about the second phase are given in Section 4.1.2.

4.1.1 First phase

In the first phase we want to solve Problem 1 using only naïve workers and requesting as few comparisons as possible to minimize monetary cost. We outline our algorithmic approach in Algorithm 2. It relies on some combinatorial properties of all-play-all tournaments, which we prove below. In particular, Lemma 1 shows a key property of the maximum element M in all-play-all tournaments.

LEMMA 1. *In an all-play-all tournament among the elements of L, the maximum element M wins at least $n - \mathsf{u}_n(n)$ comparisons.*

[6]The exact value of $|S|$ and the reason for such a choice are motivated in Section 4.1.1. In a nutshell, this choice allows to achieve an asymptotically optimal number of (naïve) comparisons, as shown in Section 4.3.

[7]In practice, $\mathsf{d}(M, e) \leq 3\delta_e$ or $\mathsf{d}(M, e) \leq 2\delta_e$, according to the algorithm used to solve Problem 2; see Section 4.1.2.

[8]In an all-play-all tournament, each element is compared against every other element. This is also sometimes known as a round-robin tournament.

PROOF. By definition of $u_n(n)$, there are at most $u_n(n)$ elements e such that $d(e, M) \leq \delta_n$, whereas M wins every element e such that $d(e, M) > \delta_n$. $\square$

The previous lemma suggests a way (described below) to filter out elements that are certainly *not* the maximum and eventually obtain a set of candidates for further processing by expert workers. In the following lemma (whose proof is deferred to Appendix B) we prove that the size of this set is small. Actually, we prove a slightly more general result that holds for any set of elements playing an all-play-all tournament and any minimum number of wins, and does not depend on the error model.

LEMMA 2. *Let A be a set of elements and let $r < |A|$. In an all-play-all tournament among the elements of A, there are at most $2r - 1$ elements that win at least $|A| - r$ comparisons each.*

Lemmas 1 and 2 combined lead to an efficient algorithm to solve Problem 1, that is, to compute a set $S \subsetneq L$ of size at most $O(u_n(n))$, such that $M \in S$. In particular, Lemma 1 suggests that we should make sure that S contains all the elements that would win at least $n - u_n(n)$ comparisons in an all-play-all tournament, otherwise we may miss M. We could easily find S by performing an all-play-all tournament among all elements in L and then picking those that win at least $n - u_n(n)$ times; this would require $\binom{n}{2} = \Theta(n^2)$ comparisons. With the help of Lemma 2 we can find S more efficiently (i.e., with fewer comparisons) as follows: We partition L into small subsets of size $g = 4u_n(n)$ (except for one subset, which may have fewer), and then perform an all-play-all tournament within each subset. We discard elements that lose at least $u_n(n)$ comparisons in the all-play-all tournament of their subset and we keep those that win at least $g - u_n(n)$ comparisons. In the next level, we partition the set of all surviving elements into subsets of size g and perform all-play-all tournaments within each of the subsets, and so on, until the set of survivors contains fewer than $2u_n(n)$ elements. The pseudocode of the algorithm is presented as Algorithm 2. In Lemma 3 (proof in Appendix B) we prove its correctness and we show that it requires only $O(nu_n(n))$ comparisons. Later, in Section 4.3 we prove that this bound is optimal, within constant factors.

LEMMA 3. *Algorithm 2 computes a set S such that $M \in S$ and $|S| \leq 2u_n(n) - 1$ by performing at most $4nu_n(n)$ comparisons.*

4.1.2 Second phase

The outcome of the first phase is a set S of size at most $2u_n(n) - 1$ containing M; the second phase is devoted to solving Problem 2, that is, retrieving M (or a nearby element) from S, using experts to perform comparisons. We have three options to solve Problem 2:

1. Perform an all-play-all tournament on the set S and pick the element e with the most wins; it is guaranteed that $d(M, e) \leq 2\delta_e$. This method requires $\Theta(u_n(n)^2)$ expert comparisons.
2. Use the deterministic algorithm 2-MaxFind [2, Section 3.1] (pseudocode in Algorithm 3); it performs $O(u_n(n)^{3/2})$ expert comparisons to return an element e such that $d(M, e) \leq 2\delta_e$.
3. Use the randomized algorithm from [2, Section 3.2] (pseudocode in Algorithm 5 in Appendix B); this performs $\Theta(u_n(n))$ expert comparisons and it returns an element e with the guarantee that $d(M, e) \leq 3\delta_e$ whp.

Clearly, we do not consider the first option as it is dominated by the second one (assuming that we memorize results and we do not repeat comparisons that we have already performed). For the theoretical analysis we assume that we use the third one. This allows us to obtain asymptotically optimal results in terms of expert comparisons, with the downside that the value returned can be up to $3\delta_e$ far from the maximum, whp. In practice though it turns out that the second option is superior to the third one for the values of n (and $u_n(n)$) that we consider: even though the third option is a linear algorithm, the constants are so high that for the values of n of our interest they lead to a much higher cost. The second option has also the advantage that it guarantees to return an element that is closer to the maximum (only $2\delta_e$ far, the best possible for the model [2]). For this reason we use the 2-MaxFind algorithm for the simulations in Section 5.

For the sake of completeness, we now outline the algorithm and present its pseudocode in Algorithm 3 (see also [2, Section 3.1]). Consider the candidate set S returned by Algorithm 2 and let $s = |S| \leq 2u_n(n) - 1$. Algorithm 2-MaxFind works by iteratively selecting an arbitrary subset of $\sqrt{s}$ elements and then performing an all-play-all tournament among them. All the elements are then compared to the winner of the tournament (i.e., one of the elements with the highest number of wins). Those that lose against the winner are removed. This process is iterated on the remaining elements until only $\sqrt{s}$ elements are left. A final all-play-all tournament among these elements determines the winner.

Algorithm 2: Find a set of candidates containing the maximum element M

Input : A set L of n elements, a function $u_n(n) = o(n)$.
Output: A set of size at most $2u_n(n) - 1$ containing the maximum element M of L.

$g \leftarrow 4u_n(n)$
$i \leftarrow 0$
$L_i \leftarrow L$
while $|L_i| \geq 2u_n(n)$ **do**
  $L_{i+1} \leftarrow \emptyset$
  Partition L_i into subsets $G_1, \ldots, G_\ell$ of size g (the last one may be smaller)
  forall the $G_j, 1 \leq j \leq \ell - 1$ **do**
    Perform an all-play-all tournament among the elements of G_j
    Let W_j be the set of the elements of G_j that win at least $g - u_n(n)$ comparisons in the all-play-all tournament.
    $L_{i+1} \leftarrow L_{i+1} \cup W_j$
  end
  if $|G_\ell| \leq u_n(n)$ **then**
    $L_{i+1} \leftarrow L_{i+1} \cup G_\ell$
  else
    Let W_ℓ be the set of the elements of G_j that win at least $|G_\ell| - u_n(n)$ comparisons in the all-play-all tournament
    $L_{i+1} \leftarrow L_{i+1} \cup W_\ell$
  end
  $i \leftarrow i + 1$
end
return L_i

4.2 Analysis of the Algorithm

In this section we analyze the correctness and efficiency of the algorithm presented in the previous section. As we mentioned previously, for the purpose of the analysis, we assume that, in the second phase, Algorithm 3 is replaced by its randomized counterpart from [2, Section 3.2] (pseudocode in Algorithm 5 in Appendix B).

Algorithm 3: 2MaxFind: find (approximation of) maximum element M

Input : A set S of s elements.
Output: An estimate of the maximum element M in S.

```
Label all items as candidates
while more than ⌈√s⌉ candidates do
    Pick an arbitrary set of ⌈√s⌉ candidate elements and play
    them in an all-play-all tournament. Let x have the most
    number of wins
    Compare x against all candidate elements and eliminate all
    elements that lose to x
end
Play a final all-play-all tournament among the at most ⌈√s⌉
elements survived and return the element with the most wins
```

Correctness. The following lemma shows the correctness of our algorithm, assuming that we use the randomized algorithm from [2, Section 3.2][9] (i.e., option 3 from the discussion in the previous section).

LEMMA 4. *With probability at least* $1-|S|^{-c}$, *for any constant* c *and* S *large enough, our algorithm returns an element* e *such that* $\mathsf{d}(M, e) \leq 3\delta_e$.

PROOF. Immediate from the fact that S contains M and [2, Theorem 4]. □

Cost analysis. The following lemma quantifies the cost of our algorithm assuming, as we mentioned, that in the second phase we apply the randomized algorithm in [2, Section 3.2].

LEMMA 5. *Our algorithm performs* $O(n\mathsf{u}_n(n))$ *naïve and* $O((\mathsf{u}_n(n))^{1.7} + (\mathsf{u}_n(n))^{0.6} \log^2 \mathsf{u}_n(n))$ *expert comparisons. Accordingly, its monetary cost* $\mathsf{C}(n)$ *is*

$$\mathsf{C}(n) = O(c_n n\mathsf{u}_n(n) + c_e((\mathsf{u}_n(n))^{1.7} + (\mathsf{u}_n(n))^{0.6} \log^2 \mathsf{u}_n(n))) \ .$$

If we use algorithm 2-MaxFind to perform the second phase, the following theorem follows from Lemma 3 and from [2, Lemma 1]:

THEOREM 1. *There exists an algorithm that computes an element* e *such that* $\mathsf{d}(e, M) \leq 2\delta_e$ *and that performs at most* $4n\mathsf{u}_n(n)$ *naïve comparisons and* $2\mathsf{u}_n(n)^{3/2}$ *expert ones.*

4.3 Lower Bounds

In this section, we study the inherent complexity of Problems 1 and 2, into which we have divided the task of the maximum element of a set: (1) identifying a small candidate set containing the maximum using cheap, naïve workers and (2) selecting the maximum or a nearby element out of S, using experts to perform comparisons.

We start with Problem 2, which is easier to analyze. It is simple to conceive instances of the problem for which $\mathsf{u}_n(n)$ elements are naïve indistinguishable from the maximum. This implies that the number of expert comparisons required are in the worst case $\Omega(\mathsf{u}_n(n))$. Actually, it is possible to prove stronger results. The following theorem follows from [2].

LEMMA 6. *Any deterministic algorithm that computes an element* e *such that* $\mathsf{d}(e, M) \leq 2\delta_e$ *must perform at least* $\Omega(\mathsf{u}_n(n)^{4/3})$ *expert comparisons.*

[9] An analogous result holds deterministically if we use the 2-MaxFind algorithm.

Next, we turn our attention to Problem 1. Here, we prove in Corollary 1 below that the number of comparisons performed by Algorithm 2 in Phase 1 is optimal. To prove this corollary, we first show the key fact that, if we want to identify a subset of elements containing the maximum out of the initial set L of size n using naïve workers, we need to identify all elements that win at least $n - \mathsf{u}_n(n)$ comparisons in an all-play-all tournament among the elements of L, because any of them could be the maximum.

LEMMA 7. *Let* C *be any set of comparisons by naïve workers. If there exists an element* e *that takes part in at most* $\mathsf{u}_n(n)$ *comparisons in* C, *then there exists an assignment of values to the elements such that (1) the assignment of values is compatible with the outcomes of* C *and (2)* e *is the element with maximum value.*

PROOF. Let element e have the maximum value, and let E_1 be the set of (at least $n - \mathsf{u}_n(n)$, by Lemma 1) elements that the maximum wins and E_2 the other (at most $\mathsf{u}_n(n)$) elements. We construct the following instance (see Figure 8 in the appendix). We arrange the elements in E_1 at distance about $1.5\delta_n$ from e such that they are distinct (say, we arrange them evenly in an interval of length $0.1\delta_n$, centered at distance $1.5\delta_n$ from element e). We arrange the elements in E_2 in a similar way at distance $0.8\delta_n$ from element e. This is a valid instance for the model because there are at most $\mathsf{u}_n(n)$ elements with distance at most δ_n from the maximum, and the maximum wins against all the elements at distance more than δ_n. With the exception of e, all the other elements are at a distance δ_n from each other, so any comparison result among them is compatible with the results in C. □

As a corollary, we obtain the fact that if we want to return a small set of candidates for the maximum, then we must make at least $\Omega(n\mathsf{u}_n(n))$ comparisons. This number of comparisons is required even if the algorithm returns a large (up to a constant fraction) set.

COROLLARY 1. *Any algorithm that uses only comparisons by naïve workers, and that returns a set* S *that is guaranteed to contain the maximum and such that* $|S| \leq n/2$, *must perform at least* $n\mathsf{u}_n(n)/4$ *comparisons.*

PROOF. The algorithm returns the set S with candidates for the maximum, so it deduces that no element in the set $L \setminus S$ is the maximum. By Lemma 7, each of the elements in $L \setminus S$ must take part in at least $\mathsf{u}_n(n)$ comparisons (otherwise it is impossible to deduce for sure that it is not the maximum). We have $|S| \leq n/2$, therefore $|L \setminus S| \geq n/2$. Each comparison involves two elements, so the required number of comparisons is at least $n\mathsf{u}_n(n)/4$. □

4.4 Estimation of $\mathsf{u}_n(n)$

A nice feature of the algorithm is that it only requires one parameter, namely $\mathsf{u}_n(n)$, which we assume to be $o(n)$. Overestimating this parameter can only harm in cost but not in accuracy. We next show how we can estimate an upper bound to $\mathsf{u}_n(n)$ using a *training set*, that is, a set of $\hat{n}$ elements of which we know the one with highest value (we denote this element with $\hat{M}$). Training data like this (or even richer; for example, assuming that the results of all pairwise comparisons are known) are typically used in crowdsourcing platforms to evaluate the workers and are sometimes referred to as *gold data*.

First, we note that without additional assumptions on the model it is impossible to estimate the value of $\mathsf{u}_n(n)$. Indeed, the model allows for the workers to reply correctly when the difference in the values of the elements presented to them is under the threshold δ_n, thus providing no information about δ_n. Therefore we are required to perform some additional assumptions:

Assumption 1. We assume that the training set reflects the statistical properties of the actual dataset we will work with. In particular, we assume that the number of items within distance δ_n from M is distributed like the number of items within distance δ_n from $\hat{M}$, the element with maximum value in the training set, so that $\frac{n}{\hat{n}} \mathsf{u}_n(\hat{n})$ is a reasonable estimator of $\mathsf{u}_n(n)$.

Assumption 2. We assume that, for comparisons between elements whose difference in value is below the (naïve) threshold, workers err with some probability $p_{err} > 0$. We assume that the empirical error rate in the training set (i.e., the fraction of times that the workers select the wrong element in a comparison) is a good estimator for p_{err}.

For example, if we look at Figure 2(b), we might assume $p_{err} \approx 0.4$ for accuracies up to 20%. We further assume that comparisons performed by different workers or involving different item pairs are statistically independent. This assumption, except for being required as we noted previously, seems to be reasonable. Indeed, if a worker is being tested and he never errs then we can consider him an expert!

We remark that the assumptions are only needed to estimate $\mathsf{u}_n(n)$; the algorithms discussed in Section 4 are completely oblivious to these assumptions. We also stress once more that overestimating $\mathsf{u}_n(n)$ has no impact on the correctness of the algorithm or on the quality guarantees, only on the cost.

Below we describe the procedure to estimate $\mathsf{u}_n(n)$ as Algorithm 4. Note that this algorithm does not assume any knowledge of the naïve threshold δ_n. In this algorithm, c is a suitable constant that is used to tune the level of confidence with which we return an upper bound on $\mathsf{u}_n(n)$.

Algorithm 4: Estimating $\mathsf{u}_n(n)$ from training data.

```
Input  : Training set containing n̂ elements.
Output: An estimate of u_n(n).
#errors ← 0
forall the x in training set do
    Ask a worker to compare pair (x, M̂).
    if the worker made an error then
        #errors ← #errors + 1
    end
end
return (n/n̂) max{ c ln n, 2(#errors)/p_err }
```

Next we show that, under Assumption 2, we have

$$\mathsf{u}_n(\hat{n}) \leq \max\left\{c \ln n, \frac{2(\#\, errors)}{p_{err}}\right\}$$

whp, which, using Assumption 1, implies that the above procedure returns an upper bound for $\mathsf{u}_n(n)$.

If $\mathsf{u}_n(\hat{n}) < c \ln n$ we are done, so in the following we assume that $\mathsf{u}_n(\hat{n}) \geq c \ln n$. Because there exist $\mathsf{u}_n(\hat{n})$ elements in the training set that workers can confuse with the maximum, we have

$$\mathbf{E}\left[\#\, errors\right] = p_{err} \mathsf{u}_n(\hat{n}).$$

Then, under Assumption 2 above, an application of a Chernoff bound [10, Section 1.6] implies that:

$$\mathbf{P}\left(\#\, errors < \frac{p_{err}}{2} \mathsf{u}_n(\hat{n})\right) < e^{-\frac{p_{err}}{8} \mathsf{u}_n(\hat{n})} \leq n^{-\frac{c p_{err}}{8}},$$

which implies that whp we have that $\mathsf{u}_n(\hat{n}) \leq \frac{2(\#\, errors)}{p_{err}}$, and proves our claim.

Notice that we now need to estimate the value p_{err}. We next discuss how this value is much easier to estimate than $\mathsf{u}_n(n)$ if we assume our model reflects workers' behavior. To this purpose, we consider a subset of element pairs from our training set and we compare them using naïve workers, assigning each pair to multiple workers for comparison. For a given pair, if there is consensus among the workers it was assigned to, we take this as an indication that the difference in the values between the two elements of the pair is at least δ_n, up to a residual probability that decreases exponentially in the number of workers, following the same arguments as in Section 3.2. On the other hand, for pairs in which the values of the two elements to compare differ by less than δ_n, the error probability on these pairs is exactly p_{err}, and a simple application of a Chernoff bound shows that, with high probability, we can achieve an accurate estimate of p_{err} with a small number of workers. For issues concerning the estimation of the value p_{err} in real life and for a more general discussion, we refer the reader to Appendix A.

5. EXPERIMENTS

To evaluate the efficiency of our algorithm we performed a series of simulations, which we present next. In Section 5.1 we perform experiments to compare the accuracy of our algorithm with simpler ones. In Section 5.2 we measure the loss in accuracy and cost if we err in the estimation of $\mathsf{u}_n(n)$. Finally, in Section 5.3 we show how our algorithm performs when using real workers from the CrowdFlower platform, first in two controlled applications and then on the more realistic problem of evaluating search results.

We study the performance of the algorithms both on randomly and on adversarially generated inputs. For the former, we selected n random values independently and uniformly at random from a range. We experimented with various values for the parameters n, δ_n, and δ_e; the last two, in particular, define the values of $\mathsf{u}_n(n)$ and $\mathsf{u}_e(n)$, respectively. When a worker is asked to rank a pair of elements whose value difference is below her threshold (δ_n or δ_e), each element is chosen as the answer with probability 1/2.

The adversarial data were created so as to maximize the number of comparisons of 2-MaxFind algorithm. Specifically, in all the comparisons of step 4 of Algorithm 3, whenever the difference is below the threshold, we make element x lose, such as to maximize the number of elements that go to the next round. Furthermore, whenever the algorithm compares two elements whose values have a difference smaller than the threshold, the response is such that it maximizes the number of comparisons of the algorithm. For our algorithm we considered the upper bound predicted by the theory, even though the actual bound may be lower.

5.1 Comparison of Accuracy and Cost

Our algorithm is optimal asymptotically in the sense that it minimizes both naïve and expert comparisons (see Section 4). In this section, we compare our algorithm against two other approaches, (1) 2-MaxFind [2] (see also Section 4.1.2) when it uses only naïve users and (2) 2-MaxFind when it uses only expert users. We will refer to the former approach as 2-MaxFind-naïve and to the latter as 2-MaxFind-expert. In particular, we compare the three approaches with respect to their cost and accuracy. By *accuracy* we mean the rank of the element returned. If the rank is 1 then we have perfect accuracy, and the higher is the rank the lower is the accuracy.

We start by comparing the accuracy of the three approaches. In Figure 3 we depict the true rank of the element returned for each of them. As expected, we can observe that the best approach is 2-MaxFind-expert, with our Algorithm following closely, whereas 2-MaxFind-naïve returns an element with a much lower rank, which worsens as $\mathsf{u}_n(n)$ increases.

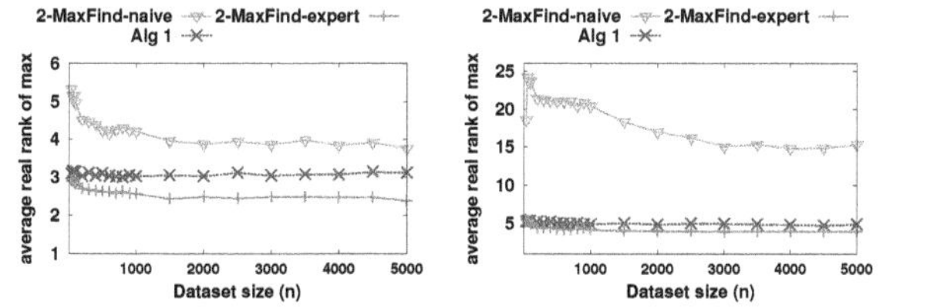

(a) $u_n(n) = 10, u_e(n) = 5$ (b) $u_n(n) = 50, u_e(n) = 10$

Figure 3: Accuracy as a function of n for different values of $u_n(n)$ and $u_e(n)$. We compare our approach (Alg 1) with the 2-MaxFind algorithm that uses either only expert or only naïve users.

Thus, unless $u_n(n)$ is very small, which would mean that the naïve users perform very well or that the dataset is small, if we require high accuracy we need to resort either to our algorithm or to 2-MaxFind-expert. Which one is preferable depends also on the cost, which we explore next.

We next compare the number of naïve and expert comparisons of the three approaches in Figure 4, on average and in the worst case. First note how much smaller is the number of expert comparisons for our algorithm; it only depends on the leftover set, and is expected to stay constant as n grows. On the other hand, this comes at a price. We now perform a high number of naïve comparisons, actually higher than the number of expert comparisons that 2-MaxFind-expert performs, in the average case. If the cost of an expert and of a naïve worker is comparable (obviously the exact values will depend on the platform and on the application), then the cost of our algorithm will be higher than 2-MaxFind-expert, and it is better to simply use the latter. On the other hand, in settings where expert comparisons have a much higher cost than naïve comparisons, our algorithm leads to a significantly lower cost. In particular, in the case where naïve comparisons are performed by machines and expert ones by humans, the cost savings can be tremendous. Similarly, in cases where experts are a limited resource, as is often the case when the experts are hired outside of the crowdsourcing platform, it may be a necessity to use cheaper naïve users to prefilter the items before eventually resorting to experts.

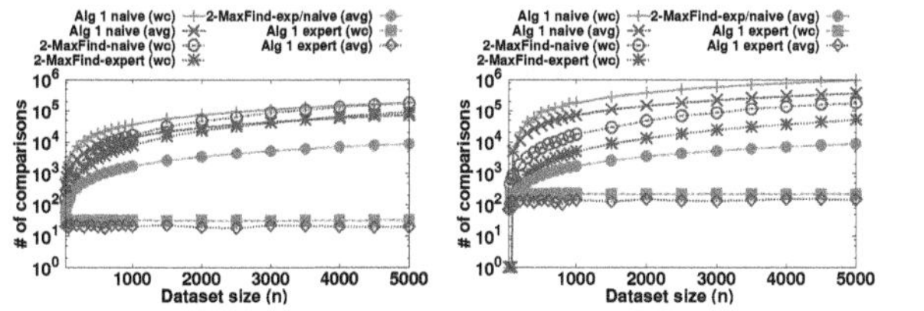

(a) $u_n(n) = 10, u_e(n) = 5$ (b) $u_n(n) = 50, u_e(n) = 10$

Figure 4: Number of comparisons as a function of n for two values of $u_n(n)$ and $u_e(n)$. Note that the y-axis is on a log scale. We depict the number of expert and naïve comparisons for our algorithms, the number of expert comparisons of 2-MaxFind-expert and the number of naïve comparisons of 2-MaxFind-naïve. In each, we present the number of comparisons in both the average-case and the worst-case scenario. The average number of expert comparisons of 2-MaxFind-expert and the average number of naïve comparisons of 2-MaxFind-naïve are very close to each other, and we depict them with a single curve.

To quantify the savings in cost, we apply the model of Section 3.4, with unit cost for c_n and various values for c_e. In Figure 5 we observe how the average cost increases in the input size, for various parameters. Figure 9 contains the same information for the worst-case cost, calculated as we mentioned previously. We

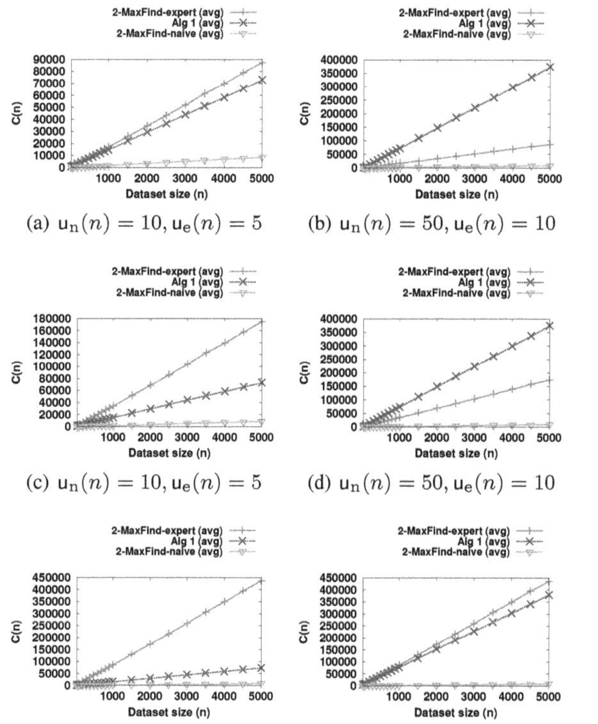

(a) $u_n(n) = 10, u_e(n) = 5$ (b) $u_n(n) = 50, u_e(n) = 10$

(c) $u_n(n) = 10, u_e(n) = 5$ (d) $u_n(n) = 50, u_e(n) = 10$

(e) $u_n(n) = 10, u_e(n) = 5$ (f) $u_n(n) = 50, u_e(n) = 10$

Figure 5: Average cost as a function of n with $c_n = 1$ and different values of c_e, $u_n(n)$ and $u_e(n)$. We have $c_e = 10$ (row 1), 20 (row 2), 50 (row 3). We compare our approach (Alg 1) with the 2-MaxFind algorithm that uses either only expert or only naïve users.

can observe that the savings of our two-phase algorithm become higher as the the ratio c_e/c_n of the expert cost over the naïve cost becomes higher. Notice that the average cost of 2-MaxFind-expert is lower in cases in which the ratio c_e/c_n is relatively small (but the worst-case cost is still comparable or higher). In such cases, it is probably beneficial to use the 2-MaxFind-expert—the exact scenarios depend on the values of $u_n(n)$, $u_e(n)$, and the aforementioned ratio. In particular, we found that if the ratio is less than 10, then our algorithm has a higher cost in the average case. As the cost of an expert worker becomes much higher than the cost of a naïve one, the savings can become tremendous. A typical case for these scenarios is when we would use a crowdsourcing service as a provider for naïve workers, and use external professionals as experts, as we expect to be the case in the application of evaluation of search results that we describe in Section 5.3. The ratio can be even higher when a naïve worker corresponds to a machine-learning algorithm, whereas the expert is a human professional.

The overall conclusion of this set of experiments is that unless the cost of an expert is comparable to the cost of a naïve worker (less than 10 times more expensive), we can achieve great cost savings by our approach taking advantage of both naïve and expert users.

5.2 Under/Over Estimation of $u_n(n)$

In this section we analyze the effects of inaccurate estimation of parameter $u_n(n)$ on the accuracy and cost of our algorithm.

To this end, we vary the input size and we measure the accuracy as the average real rank of the maximum element returned by the algorithms we consider, where the average is taken over a set of randomly generated instance of the given size, for the three approaches that we considered in the previous section: our algorithm (Alg 1), 2-MaxFind-expert, and 2-MaxFind-naïve. We describe the inaccuracy in the estimation of $u_n(n)$ by the *estimation factor*, defined as the ratio between the estimated and the true value of $u_n(n)$. We consider the values $\{0.2, 0.5, 0.8, 1, 1.2, 2\}$ for the estimation factor.

The effects of inaccurate estimation of $u_n(n)$ on the accuracy are summarized in Figure 6. As expected, when $u_n(n)$ is overestimated the results do not worsen w.r.t. the case that we have the exact value of $u_n(n)$ because in the end of the first phase of the algorithm we end up with a larger set (though this comes at a higher cost). When $u_n(n)$ is underestimated, the accuracy of our algorithm potentially decreases, because it could return an empty set of elements or a set of elements that does not contain the real max. In practice, we find that the results are not much worse compared to the case that the underestimation is not very large. For instance, if the estimation factor is 0.8 then the set returned in the first round contains the real max in 99% of the times, whereas for an estimation factor of 0.5 results start to worsen with the max appearing in 82% of the sets. When the estimation factor drops to 0.2 the number of times the maximum arrives in the second round is only 38%. Yet the element recovered is not very bad, as we see in Figure 6.

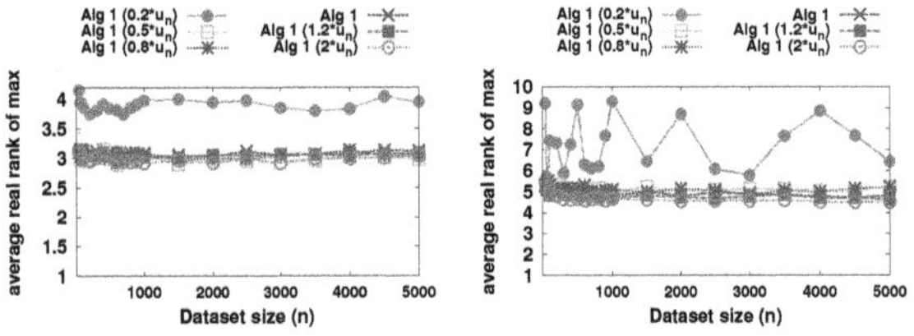

(a) $u_n(n) = 10, u_e(n) = 5$ (b) $u_n(n) = 50, u_e(n) = 10$

Figure 6: Accuracy as a function of n for different values of $u_n(n)$ and $u_e(n)$. We compare the accuracy of our 2-phase algorithm for various values of the estimation factor.

Next we examine the effect on the cost. figures 7 and 10 depict the change of the cost for different estimation factors as we vary the dataset size. As in the Section 5.1 we consider both the average and the worst-case datasets. Figure 7 shows that the cost has a smooth linear behavior; for instance, an estimation factor of 2 doubles the cost both in the average and the worst case.

As a general conclusion, a small overestimate or underestimate of the value $u_n(n)$ does not affect radically, neither the accuracy, nor the cost of our algorithm, at least for the datasets that we considered, indicating a robust behavior of our algorithm.

5.3 Experiments on CrowdFlower

We finally conducted a series of experiments on CrowdFlower, whose goal was twofold: (1) Assessing the ability of our algorithm to compute a value close to the maximum; (2) investigating the accuracy of a naïve-only approach based on 2-MaxFind on real problem instances. The first two problems are somewhat artificial, but were chosen as they admit objective, numerical answers, which allow the evaluation of our approach. The third problem we considered is representative of a class of potential applications in which the presence of experts may make a difference.

Settings. We used the datasets DOTS and CARS described in Section 3.1. For each dataset we conducted two identical experiments, namely, they have equal configuration and receive the same input data. From each dataset we downsampled a set of $n = 50$ elements. This volume of data allows to draw conclusions on the performance of the algorithm on real data at reasonable cost. The real data we

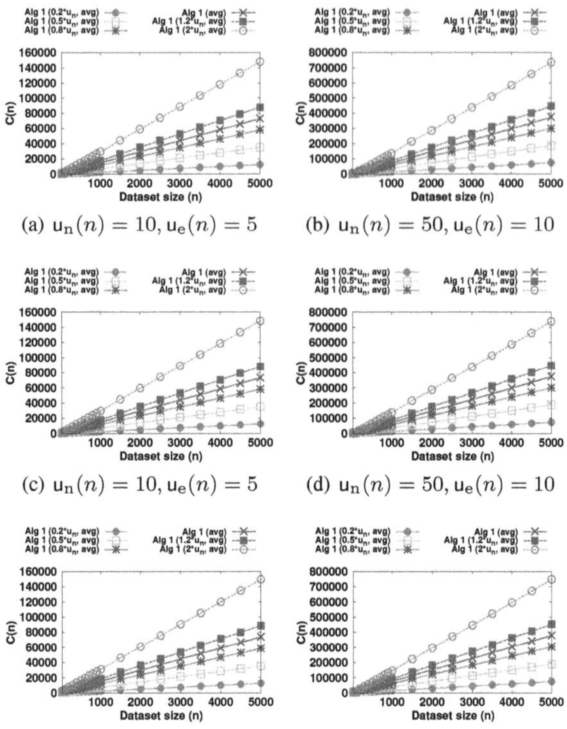

(a) $u_n(n) = 10, u_e(n) = 5$ (b) $u_n(n) = 50, u_e(n) = 10$

(c) $u_n(n) = 10, u_e(n) = 5$ (d) $u_n(n) = 50, u_e(n) = 10$

(e) $u_n(n) = 10, u_e(n) = 5$ (f) $u_n(n) = 50, u_e(n) = 10$

Figure 7: Average cost as a function of n with $c_n = 1$ and different values of c_e, $u_n(n)$ and $u_e(n)$. We have $c_e = 10$ (row 1), 20 (row 2), 50 (row 3). We compare the cost of our 2-phase algorithm for various values of the estimation factor.

used suggested choosing a value $u_n(n) = 5$ for Algorithm 2. We used the CrowdFlower workers to perform the naïve comparisons.

CrowdFlower does not provide a service of experts for the problem that we address, so we leveraged the wisdom-of-crowd effect [30], simulating each expert query by 7 naïve queries and selecting the answer that received most votes, just as we did in Section 3.1. As we saw there, this approach is effective in the DOTS experiment but not in the CARS one. This points to the dependency of the crowd's performance on the type of expertise required for the task at hand. We report the results for this latter experiment (CARS) as well, as they provide further evidence for the findings of Section 3.1.

Experiments on DOTS. This experiment was inspired from previous work [33]. We used images of random dots extracted from DOTS. In particular, we used 80 images of random dots (50 images are used for building the dataset and 30 for the golden set, used for gold comparisons). The golden set associated to this dataset is formed by images with a number of dots from 200 to 800 with step 20. The two sets have no elements in common. We performed two experiments asking the users to select the image with the minimum number of random dots.

The final results were almost perfect. In both experiments, nine elements passed to the second phase, and in both they were the real top-9 elements.

From the discussion in Section 3.1 about the findings presented in Figure 2(a), for the DOTS experiment we can simulate expert workers by using several naïve ones. Indeed, that is what we did for the second phase of our algorithm. Since CrowdFlower does not provide a service of experts for the problem that we address, we leveraged the wisdom-of-crowd effect [30], simulating each expert query by 7 naïve queries and selecting the answer that received most votes, just as we did in Section 3.1. As we saw there, this approach is effective in the DOTS experiment.

In Table 1 we can see a summary of the results of the second phase, which confirm the conclusions of Section 3.1: The second-phase (simulated) experts were able to always find the minimum, and, further, the output correctly orders the top-9 elements, except in one case for one of the experiments, in which the top-6 and top-7 elements are swapped. This verifies that this is an example of a question where using expert users is clearly not recommended.

# dots	Exp. 1	Exp. 2
100	1	1
120	2	2
140	3	3
160	4	4
180	5	5
200	7	6
220	6	7
240	8	8
260	9	9

Table 1: The ranking of the last round of the two DOTS experiments.

Indeed, performing the two-level approach for this problem is an overkill. The results of the 2-MaxFind algorithm with CrowdFlower workers are almost equally as good. We repeated the algorithm 14 times in which in all but one case the correct instance was returned.

Experiments on CARS. In this experiment we wanted to study the quality of the results when the data are much more fuzzy. The goal is to perform queries to find the car that is most highly priced.

Again we conducted two experiments. The results here are also very good. Again nine cars passed to the second round and in both cases the most expensive car passed to the second round even though in this case some of the top-ranked cars did not pass to the second round. As with the DOTS experiment, we attempted to simulate an expert by performing 7 naïve queries. The conclusions of Section 3.1 about Figure 2(b) suggest that in this case this approach will not work, and here we want to check this hypothesis.

We can see the ranking of the last round in Table 2 in Appendix C. Note that, as we mentioned, the top car always reaches the last round. However, in contrast with DOTS, the simulated experts are not able to identify it, indicating the need for real experts for this task. Furthermore, note that because of the fuzziness of the data some cars far from the top-10 arrive at the second phase.

We obtained the results for 14 executions of 2-MaxFind for this problem as well, but the algorithm performed poorly. In none of the executions was the real minimum returned. Instead most of the times the fourth-ranked car was given as a solution, and sometimes even cars not in the top-10. Clearly a truly informed expert opinion is required in this case.

Evaluation of Search Results. In the paragraphs above, we considered two rather artificial application examples that admit objectively correct answers, allowing us to test accurately the model and our algorithm with real workers. One though would expect that if we are interested in applying our approach to real life, we should assume that in many cases an objective answer might not exist (otherwise we would probably not resort to humans), yet it might still be possible to apply the same technique.

In the third set of experiments we considered a more realistic scenario, addressed often by search-engine companies, namely, comparing query results. Typically this is performed by human judges, who are experts in identifying the most relevant result for a given query and in a given context (e.g., user profile)—but even using this approach the inter-agreement among the judges is not perfect.

The objective evaluation of such a problem is far from trivial, as results depend on the particular user, context, and history. To alleviate this problem we considered two specific queries from the area of approximation algorithms: "asymmetric tsp best approximation" and "steiner tree best approximation." The reason for selecting such queries is twofold: (1) We believe that there is a clear best result for the majority of the searches—the paper or a link that contains the current (recently published) best result; (2) We can find real human experts (researchers in the area of algorithms) who can evaluate the results.

For each of the queries we obtained 50 results from Google, distributed uniformly among the top-100 results; this allowed us to have results that are relevant to the queries in different extents. We applied our two-phase algorithm considering workers from CrowdFlower as naïve and researchers in the area of algorithms as experts, who informed us about the best (and recent—within 5 year) approximation algorithms for the two problems. We experimented with values of $\mathsf{u_n}(50) = 6, 8, 10$. In both queries and for all these values of $\mathsf{u_n}(50)$ the maximum was promoted to the second round (and the experts identified it, of course).

Finally, we applied the 2-MaxFind algorithm, using only naïve users. In detail, for each query we executed two runs of 2-MaxFind on CrowdFlower, for a total of four independent runs. Results show that the naïve-only approach was not satisfying: naïve users were able to identify the best result only in one of the four cases (one run over the asymmetric TSP instance). This suggests that a naïve-only approach may not be sufficiently reliable for this type problem.

6. CONCLUSIONS

In this paper we defined computational and cost models for crowdsourcing, formalizing the idea of using workers with different expertise levels. Our main conclusion is that there are two types of tasks, tasks in which the wisdom-of-crowds paradigm holds, in which case we can simulate an expert by the use of several nonexpert users, and tasks in which it does not hold and in which there is a necessity for real expertise. To model these two types of applications we considered different error models. A novelty of our work is the definition of the *threshold error model with experts* and it is applicable precisely when we need workers with different expertise levels. We used these models to develop and analyze an algorithm for approximate max-finding in these settings. The algorithm uses naïve workers to filter out the majority of the elements, and then asks the expert workers to focus on a restricted set. We also provide lower bounds to the number of comparisons required to perform the task. Our experimental evaluation of the models and the algorithm on synthetic and real-world problems using the CrowdFlower platform shows that the former are realistic and the latter performs well in practice. In particular, it shows that for some applications simple crowdsourcing approaches can lead to erroneous results, and in these cases the use of real experts is of paramount importance.

7. ACKNOWLEDGEMENTS

We would like to thank CrowdFlower for granting us an academic license, allowing us to perform experiments with a reduced cost. We also want to thank Evgeniy Gabrilovich for useful feedback on the experiments. Finally, the anonymous reviewers have provided us with a lot of constructive comments, which have improved the paper with respect to both content and presentation.

8. REFERENCES

[1] M. Aigner. Finding the maximum and minimum. *Discrete Applied Mathematics*, 74(1):1 – 12, 1997.

[2] M. Ajtai, V. Feldman, A. Hassidim, and J. Nelson. Sorting and selection with imprecise comparisons. In *Automata, Languages and Programming*, volume 5555 of *Lecture Notes in Computer Science*, pages 37–48, 2009.

[3] S. Assaf and E. Upfal. Fault tolerant sorting networks. *SIAM Journal on Discrete Mathematics*, 4(4):472–480, 1991.

[4] A. Bozzon, M. Brambilla, S. Ceri, M. Silvestri, and G. Vesci. Choosing the right crowd: Expert finding in social networks. In *Proceedings of the 16th International Conference on Extending Database Technology*, EDBT '13, pages 637–648, New York, NY, USA, 2013. ACM.

[5] C. C. Cao, J. She, Y. Tong, and L. Chen. Whom to ask?: Jury selection for decision making tasks on micro-blog services. *Proc. VLDB Endow.*, 5(11):1495–1506, July 2012.

[6] CSE 2010. *Proceedings of the 1st SIGIR Workshop on Crowdsourcing for Information Retrieval (CSE 2010)*, 2010.

[7] A. Das Sarma, A. Parameswaran, H. Garcia-Molina, and A. Halevy. Crowd-powered find algorithms. In *Data Engineering (ICDE), 2014 IEEE 30th International Conference on*, pages 964–975, March 2014.

[8] S. B. Davidson, S. Khanna, T. Milo, and S. Roy. Using the crowd for top-k and group-by queries. In *Proceedings of the 16th International Conference on Database Theory*, ICDT '13, pages 225–236, New York, NY, USA, 2013. ACM.

[9] D. E. Difallah, G. Demartini, and P. Cudré-Mauroux. Pick-a-crowd: Tell me what you like, and i'll tell you what to do. In *Proceedings of the 22nd International Conference on World Wide Web*, WWW '13, pages 367–374, Republic and Canton of Geneva, Switzerland, 2013. International World Wide Web Conferences Steering Committee.

[10] D. P. Dubhashi and A. Panconesi. *Concentration of measure for the analysis of randomized algorithms*. Cambridge University Press, 2009.

[11] U. Feige, P. Raghavan, D. Peleg, and E. Upfal. Computing with noisy information. *SIAM Journal on Computing*, 23(5): 1001–1018, 1994.

[12] I. Finocchi and G. F. Italiano. Sorting and searching in the presence of memory faults (without redundancy). In *Proceedings of the thirty-sixth annual ACM symposium on Theory of computing*, pages 101–110. ACM, 2004.

[13] I. Finocchi, F. Grandoni, and G. F. Italiano. Designing reliable algorithms in unreliable memories. *Computer Science Review*, 1(2):77 – 87, 2007.

[14] M. J. Franklin, D. Kossmann, T. Kraska, S. Ramesh, and R. Xin. Crowddb: Answering queries with crowdsourcing. In *Proceedings of the 2011 ACM SIGMOD International Conference on Management of Data*, SIGMOD '11, pages 61–72, New York, NY, USA, 2011. ACM.

[15] S. Guo, A. Parameswaran, and H. Garcia-Molina. So who won?: dynamic max discovery with the crowd. In *Proceedings of the 2012 ACM SIGMOD International Conference on Management of Data*, SIGMOD '12, pages 385–396, New York, NY, USA, 2012. ACM.

[16] P.-Y. Hsueh, P. Melville, and V. Sindhwani. Data quality from crowdsourcing: a study of annotation selection criteria. In *Proceedings of the NAACL HLT 2009 workshop on active learning for natural language processing*, pages 27–35. Association for Computational Linguistics, 2009.

[17] D. R. Karger, S. Oh, and D. Shah. Iterative learning for reliable crowdsourcing systems. In J. Shawe-Taylor, R. S. Zemel, P. L. Bartlett, F. C. N. Pereira, and K. Q. Weinberger, editors, *NIPS*, pages 1953–1961, 2011.

[18] D. R. Karger, S. Oh, and D. Shah. Budget-optimal crowdsourcing using low-rank matrix approximations. In *Communication, Control, and Computing (Allerton), 2011 49th Annual Allerton Conference on*, pages 284–291. IEEE, 2011.

[19] H. Li, B. Zhao, and A. Fuxman. The wisdom of minority: Discovering and targeting the right group of workers for crowdsourcing. In *Proceedings of the 23rd International Conference on World Wide Web*, WWW '14, pages 165–176, Republic and Canton of Geneva, Switzerland, 2014. International World Wide Web Conferences Steering Committee.

[20] A. Marcus, E. Wu, D. Karger, S. Madden, and R. Miller. Human-powered sorts and joins. *Proc. VLDB Endow.*, 5(1): 13–24, Sept. 2011.

[21] A. Marcus, E. Wu, D. R. Karger, S. Madden, and R. C. Miller. Crowdsourced databases: Query processing with people. In *CIDR*, 2011.

[22] W. Mason and D. J. Watts. Financial incentives and the "performance of crowds". *SIGKDD Explor. Newsl.*, 11(2): 100–108, May 2010.

[23] L. Mo, R. Cheng, X. S. Yang, C. Ren, S. Lei, E. Lo, B. Kao, and D. W. Cheung. Optimizing task assignment for crowdsourcing environments. Technical Report HKU CS TR-2013-01, University of Hong Kong, 2013.

[24] A. Parameswaran, S. Boyd, H. Garcia-Molina, A. Gupta, N. Polyzotis, and J. Widom. Optimal crowd-powered rating and filtering algorithms. Technical report, Stanford University, 2014. URL `http://ilpubs.stanford.edu:8090/1078/`.

[25] A. G. Parameswaran, H. Garcia-Molina, H. Park, N. Polyzotis, A. Ramesh, and J. Widom. Crowdscreen: Algorithms for filtering data with humans. In *Proceedings of the 2012 ACM SIGMOD International Conference on Management of Data*, SIGMOD '12, pages 361–372, New York, NY, USA, 2012. ACM.

[26] A. Pelc. Searching games with errors – fifty years of coping with liars. *Theoretical Computer Science*, 270(1):71–109, 2002.

[27] A. Ramesh, A. Parameswaran, H. Garcia-Molina, and N. Polyzotis. Identifying reliable workers swiftly. Technical report, Stanford University, 2012. URL `http://ilpubs.stanford.edu:8090/1043/`.

[28] B. Ravikumar, K. Ganesan, and K. B. Lakshmanan. On selecting the largest element in spite of erroneous information. In *STACS 87*, volume 247 of *Lecture Notes in Computer Science*, pages 88–99, 1987.

[29] Y.-A. Sun, S. Roy, and G. Little. Beyond independent agreement: A tournament selection approach for quality assurance of human computation tasks. In *Human Computation*, volume WS-11-11 of *AAAI Workshops*. AAAI, 2011.

[30] J. Surowiecki. *The wisdom of crowds*. Random House LLC, 2005.

[31] L. L. Thurstone. A law of comparative judgment. *Psychological review*, 34(4):273, 1927.

[32] B. Trushkowsky, T. Kraska, M. J. Franklin, and P. Sarkar. Crowdsourced enumeration queries. *2013 IEEE 29th International Conference on Data Engineering (ICDE)*,

pages 673–684, 2013.
[33] P. Venetis and H. Garcia-Molina. Quality control for comparison microtasks. In *CrowdKDD 2012*. Stanford InfoLab, August 2012. URL http://ilpubs.stanford.edu:8090/1044/.
[34] P. Venetis and H. Garcia-Molina. Dynamic max algorithms in crowdsourcing environments. Technical report, Stanford University, August 2012. URL http://ilpubs.stanford.edu:8090/1050/.
[35] P. Venetis, H. Garcia-Molina, K. Huang, and N. Polyzotis. Max algorithms in crowdsourcing environments. In *Proceedings of the 21st international conference on World Wide Web*, WWW '12, pages 989–998, New York, NY, USA, 2012. ACM.
[36] A. Yao and F. Yao. On fault-tolerant networks for sorting. *SIAM Journal on Computing*, 14(1):120–128, 1985. doi: 10.1137/0214009.
[37] L. Zhao, G. Sukthankar, and R. Sukthankar. Robust active learning using crowdsourced annotations for activity recognition. In *Human Computation*, 2011.

APPENDIX

A. DISCUSSION ON THE MODEL AND ALGORITHM

Algorithm optimizations. It is possible to optimize the implementation of the algorithm to reduce the time and monetary costs by reducing the number of comparisons it performs in practice. Firstly, we can avoid repeating the comparison of two elements multiple times by the same type of workers. This can happen both in the first phase (naïve workers) or in the second phase (experts). In particular, in the first phase we may have that two elements belongs to the same group at different iterations of the loop on line 4: there is no need to compare them again after the first time. The algorithm will keep an $n \times n$ table containing in cell (i, j) the result of the first comparison between element e_i and element e_j. A second optimization allows to filter out more elements at the end of each iteration of the loop. This would have the net result of having a smaller L_w at the end of iteration w, and therefore terminating earlier. To understand this optimization one should realize that what the algorithm is doing in the first phase is trying to identify all the elements that would win at least $n - \mathsf{u}_\mathrm{n}(n)$ comparisons in an all-play-all tournament among all the n elements. Now, an element may never lose more than $\mathsf{u}_\mathrm{n}(n)$ comparisons in a single iteration of the loop, but it may lose more than that (against different elements) in multiple iterations. This would imply that in a global all-play-all tournament, the element would lose more than $\mathsf{u}_\mathrm{n}(n)$ comparisons so, according to Lemma 1, it cannot be the maximum. We can therefore keep, for each element, a counter of the number of losses against different elements across all the iterations. At the end of each iteration we check these counters for all the elements and remove from L_{i+1} the elements for which the counter is greater than $\mathsf{u}_\mathrm{n}(n)$.

Model vs. real life. Clearly, the model we considered (as is the case with several ones proposed in previous work) makes some simplifying but unrealistic assumptions, such as the existence of a partial order and of a unique error threshold common to all naïve users, and that responses are independent. This is part of the price we pay for a framework that can capture settings in which experts are beneficial or even necessary to achieve satisfactory results and that at the same time allows the design and rigorous analysis of algorithms.

Although the algorithms we propose apply directly to real settings as long as we can define suitable values for the parameters they require, generalizations of our model could reflect scenarios of practical interest more faithfully. For instance, for a more realistic model, we should assume that even if the difference between the values of two elements is above δ_n a worker may err, albeit with a smaller probability than p_err, that the error probability depends on the distance and the worker, and so on.

Extensive experimental work along the lines of the previous paragraph is of great interest but it may require considerable economic resources. Although it is in the scope of the present paper, our attention in this work is more shifted towards the definition of a model that captures naturally the concept of experts and is amenable to analysis. We leave the extensions mentioned above for future work; yet in Section 5 we apply our model in some controlled, albeit rather small, examples for which we possess a ground truth, showing its applicability in real-life scenarios.

B. MISSING PROOFS

In this section we include the proofs missing from the main body of the paper.

B.1 Proof of Lemma 2

PROOF. Let $S \subset A$ be the set of elements with at least $|A| - r$ wins. If $|S| \leq r$ the lemma follows immediately. So, assume that $|S| > r$. Each element in S can win against at most $|A| - |S|$ elements from $A \setminus S$. Then each element from S must also win against at least $|S| - r$ other elements from S so as to have at least $|A| - r$ wins. Indeed, for a given element $e \in S$, let x be the number of elements that e wins among the elements in $A \setminus S$ and y the number of elements that it wins among the elements in S. We will now show that $y \geq |S| - r$. Because $e \in S$, we have that $x + y \geq |A| - r$. In addition, $x \leq |A \setminus S| = |A| - |S|$. Combining these two equations we obtain $y \geq |A| - r - (|A| - |S|) = |S| - r$. Each element in S wins against at least $|S| - r$ other elements in S, so there must be at least $|S|(|S| - r)$ wins of elements in S against other elements in S. Within S one can play at most $\binom{|S|}{2}$ comparisons, so we have that

$$|S|(|S| - r) \leq \binom{|S|}{2},$$

which is true if and only if $|S| \leq 2r - 1$. □

B.2 Proof of Lemma 3

PROOF. The fact that $|S| \leq 2\mathsf{u}_\mathrm{n}(n) - 1$ follows trivially from the condition of the **while** block on line 4 of Algorithm 2. After each all-play-all tournament, we discard only elements that lose more than $\mathsf{u}_\mathrm{n}(n)$ comparisons so all elements that never lose more than $\mathsf{u}_\mathrm{n}(n)$ comparisons are never discarded and therefore are in S. This means that in particular S contains all elements that, in an all-play-all tournament among all elements of L, would lose at most $\mathsf{u}_\mathrm{n}(n)$ comparisons or, equivalently, that would win at least $n - \mathsf{u}_\mathrm{n}(n)$ comparisons. From Lemma 1 we know that the maximum $M \in L$ is in this latter set, so $M \in S$.

Suppose now that we are at iteration i and consider the elements in a subset G_j of L_i. (To simplify the presentation, we assume that also the last set G_ℓ contains g elements.) After the all-play-all tournament among the elements of G_j, it follows from Lemma 2 applied to G_j that there cannot be more than $2\mathsf{u}_\mathrm{n}(n) - 1$ elements with at least $g - \mathsf{u}_\mathrm{n}(n)$ wins. Then at most $2\mathsf{u}_\mathrm{n}(n) - 1$ elements from each set G_j belong to L_{i+1}. This means that (ignoring ceilings, for clarity of the presentation) as long as $|L_i| \geq 4\mathsf{u}_\mathrm{n}(n)$, we have

$$|L_{i+1}| \leq \frac{|L_i|}{g}(2\mathsf{u}_\mathrm{n}(n) - 1) = |L_i|\,\frac{2\mathsf{u}_\mathrm{n}(n) - 1}{4\mathsf{u}_\mathrm{n}(n)} \leq \frac{|L_i|}{2}.$$

When $|L_i|$ drops below $4\mathsf{u}_\mathrm{n}(n)$, then, by Lemma 2, by the end of the iteration we will obtain that $|L_{i+1}| < 2\mathsf{u}_\mathrm{n}(n)$ and in the next iteration the algorithm will terminate. Therefore the algorithm stops after at most i^* iterations, with

$$i^* = \log_2 n - \log_2 4\mathsf{u}_\mathrm{n}(n) + 1 \leq \log_2 n.$$

Furthermore, we have that $L_0 = n$, so $\sum_{i=0}^{i^*} |L_i| \leq 2n$.

At each iteration of the loop on line 4, the algorithm performs at most $\binom{g}{2}$ comparisons for the all-play-all tournament of a group G_i. In total, over all iterations and all groups, the number of comparisons that the algorithm performs is at most

$$\sum_{i=0}^{i^*} \frac{|L_i|}{g}\binom{g}{2} = \sum_{i=0}^{i^*} \frac{|L_i|\,(g-1)}{2} \leq \frac{g}{2}\sum_{i=0}^{i^*} |L_i| \leq gn \leq 4n\mathsf{u}_\mathrm{n}(n).$$

□

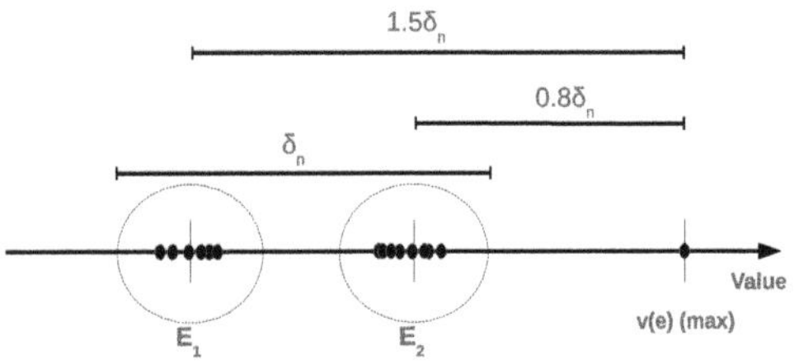

Figure 8: Instance considered in the proof of Lemma 7.

B.3 Randomized Algorithm for the Second phase

For completeness, we present as Algorithm 5 the randomized algorithm for the second phase by Ajtai et al. [2].

Algorithm 5: Randomized Algorithm for finding (approximation of) maximum element M

Input : A set S of s elements.
Output: An estimate of the maximum element M in S, whp.

$N_0 \leftarrow S$, $W \leftarrow \emptyset$, $i \leftarrow 0$
while $|N_i| \geq s^{0.3}$ **do**
  Sample from W $n^{0.3}$ elements at random and insert them into W
  Randomly partition the elements in N_i into sets of size $80(c+2)$, for some constant c
  In each set, perform an all-play-all tournament between the elements of each set to find the minimal element (the element with the fewest wins, with ties broken arbitrarily)
  Let N_{i+1} contain all of N_i except for the minimal elements found in the previous step
  $i \leftarrow i + 1$;
end
$W \leftarrow W \cup N_i$
Play all-play-all tournament between elements of W and return element with highest number of wins, ties broken arbitrarily

---

C. MISSING MATERIAL FROM SECT. 5

Model	Price	Exp. 1	Exp. 2
2013 BMW M6 Base -	$123985	2	2
2013 Audi S8 4.0T quattro -	$120375	5	-
2013 Mercedes-Benz ML63 AMG -	$114730	-	-
2013 Mercedes-Benz SL550 -	$114145	2	1
2012 Mercedes-Benz SL550 -	$111675	-	3
2013 Porsche Cayenne GTS -	$97162	7	5
2013 BMW 750 Li xDrive -	$95028	-	-
2012 Audi A8 L 4.2 quattro -	$88991	9	-
2013 Lexus LS 460 Base -	$88110	-	-
2013 Jaguar XJ XJL Portfolio -	$84970	-	-
2013 Chevrolet Corvette 427 -	$83999	1	-
2013 Land Rover Range Rover Sport -	$81151	-	6
2013 Cadillac Escalade Premium -	$75945	-	-
2013 BMW 550 i xDrive -	$72895	5	4
2013 Infiniti QX56 Base -	$71585	-	-
2013 Audi A7 3.0T quattro Premium -	$70020	-	-
2013 Cadillac Escalade EXT Luxury -	$68395	-	-
2013 Porsche Cayenne Diesel -	$67890	7	7
2013 Chevrolet Corvette Grand Sport -	$66510	2	-

Table 2: Ranking at last round of the top-19 cars in the two experiments.

Section 5.1: Plot on worst-case dataset.

In Figure 9 we can see the comparison of the three approaches of Section 5.1 and in Figure 10 the comparison of the cost for different values of the estimation factor (Section 5.2).

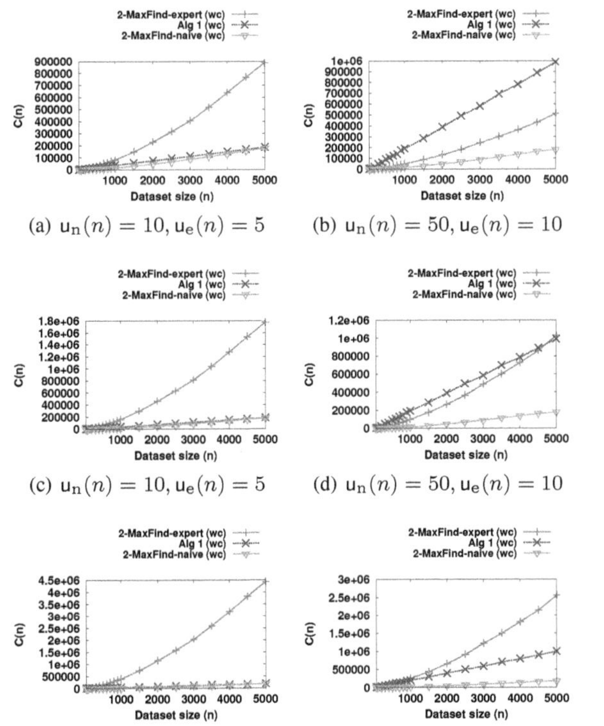

(a) $u_n(n) = 10, u_e(n) = 5$ (b) $u_n(n) = 50, u_e(n) = 10$

(c) $u_n(n) = 10, u_e(n) = 5$ (d) $u_n(n) = 50, u_e(n) = 10$

(e) $u_n(n) = 10, u_e(n) = 5$ (f) $u_n(n) = 50, u_e(n) = 10$

Figure 9: Worst-case cost as a function of n with $c_n = 1$ and different values of c_e, $u_n(n)$ and $u_e(n)$. We have $c_e =$ 10 (row 1), 20 (row 2), 50 (row 3). We compare our approach (Alg 1) with the 2-MaxFind algorithm that uses either only expert or only naïve users.

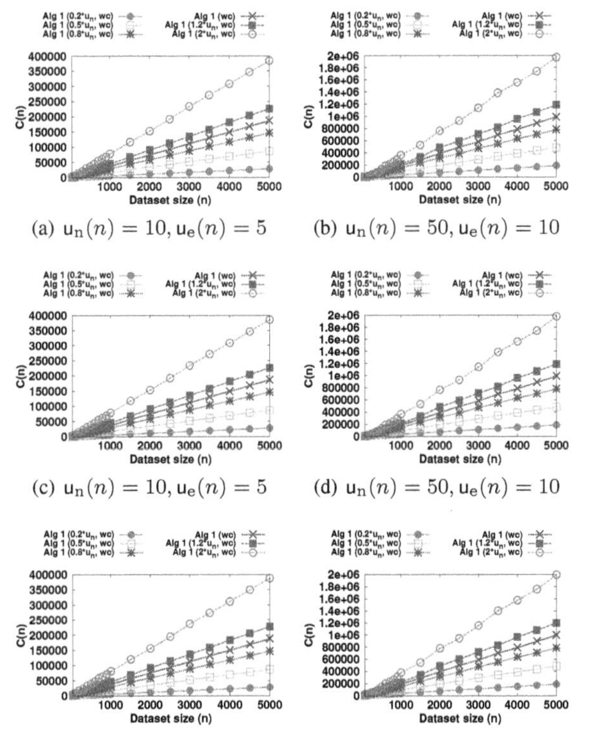

(a) $u_n(n) = 10, u_e(n) = 5$ (b) $u_n(n) = 50, u_e(n) = 10$

(c) $u_n(n) = 10, u_e(n) = 5$ (d) $u_n(n) = 50, u_e(n) = 10$

(e) $u_n(n) = 10, u_e(n) = 5$ (f) $u_n(n) = 50, u_e(n) = 10$

Figure 10: Worst-case cost as a function of n with $c_n = 1$ and different values of c_e, $u_n(n)$ and $u_e(n)$. We have $c_e =$ 10 (row 1), 20 (row 2), 50 (row 3). We compare the cost of our 2-phase algorithm for various values of the estimation factor.

Minimizing Efforts in Validating Crowd Answers

Nguyen Quoc Viet Hung, Duong Chi Thang, Matthias Weidlich[†], Karl Aberer
École Polytechnique Fédérale de Lausanne and [†]Imperial College London

ABSTRACT

In recent years, crowdsourcing has become essential in a wide range of Web applications. One of the biggest challenges of crowdsourcing is the quality of crowd answers as workers have wide-ranging levels of expertise and the worker community may contain faulty workers. Although various techniques for quality control have been proposed, a post-processing phase in which crowd answers are validated is still required. Validation is typically conducted by experts, whose availability is limited and who incur high costs. Therefore, we develop a probabilistic model that helps to identify the most beneficial validation questions in terms of both, improvement of result correctness and detection of faulty workers. Our approach allows us to guide the expert's work by collecting input on the most problematic cases, thereby achieving a set of high quality answers even if the expert does not validate the complete answer set. Our comprehensive evaluation using both real-world and synthetic datasets demonstrates that our techniques save up to 50% of expert efforts compared to baseline methods when striving for perfect result correctness. In absolute terms, for most cases, we achieve close to perfect correctness after expert input has been sought for only 20% of the questions.

Categories and Subject Descriptors: H.1.2 [User/Machine Systems]: Human information processing
Keywords: crowdsourcing; validation; guiding user feedback; expectation maximization

1. INTRODUCTION

Crowdsourcing has attracted much attention from both academia and industry, due to the high availability of ordinary Internet users (a.k.a. crowd workers) [37]. It has proved to be an efficient and scalable approach to overcome problems that are computationally expensive or unsolvable for machines, but rather trivial for humans. The number of crowdsourcing applications is tremendous, ranging from data acquisition [4], data integration [51], data mining [44], information extraction [17], to information retrieval [50]. To facilitate the development of crowdsourcing applications, more than 70 crowdsourcing platforms such as Amazon Mechanical Turk (AMT) and CrowdFlower have been developed in recent years.

SIGMOD'15, May 31–June 4, 2015, Melbourne, Victoria, Australia.

ACM 978-1-4503-2758-9/15/05 ...$15.00.
http://dx.doi.org/10.1145/2723372.2723731 .

Quality of crowd answers. A common crowdsourcing setup features users that post tasks in the form of questions, which are answered by crowd workers for financial rewards. Here quality control is a major obstacle. Workers have different backgrounds and wide-ranging levels of expertise and motivation [29], so that the collected answers are not always correct. To overcome this issue, tasks are often assigned to multiple workers to aggregate the results. In the presence of faulty workers giving random answers, however, the aggregated answer is not guaranteed to be correct.

The answer validation problem. To increase the trustworthiness of the obtained crowd answers (referred to as an *answer set*), crowdsourcing platforms such as AMT include a validation phase. Crowd answers are validated against the supposedly correct answers given by a human validator (henceforth called *expert*).

Validation of answer by an expert leads to a trade-off between the verified result correctness and the invested effort. The more effort the expert puts into providing answers that can be used to judge correctness of answers from crowd workers, the higher is the quality of the final answer set. Seeking expert input incurs high costs, so that, given the sheer amount of questions to be answered, only a fraction of the answer set can be validated based on the expert's answers. In fact, validating a large part of the crowd answers would negate the benefits of crowdsourcing in the first place.

Contributions. This paper targets the effective utilization of expert efforts in the validation of crowd answers. By (I) *aggregating answers* of crowd workers and (II) *guiding an expert* in the validation process, we go beyond the aforementioned trade-off and reduce the amount of expert efforts needed to achieve the same level of result correctness. Both steps, answer aggregation and expert guidance, are interrelated. On the one hand, answer aggregation exploits the reliability of workers, which is assessed based on the feedback given by an expert as part of the answer validation. On the other hand, an expert is guided based on the potential effect that the validation of a certain answer has for the aggregation of answers.

Answer aggregation.. To aggregate answers from crowd workers, we develop a probabilistic model estimating whether a certain answer is correct. Unlike traditional likelihood estimators which only take into account the answer set, see [23], our estimator is able to achieve higher accuracy by also considering expert input. In particular, the expert input is used to assess the reliability of a worker, formalized as a confusion matrix over the possible answers. The reliability of workers is then exploited to calculate the probability that a certain answer is correct. Moreover, a decision-theoretic measure allows us to conclude on the uncertainty related to an answer set based on the reliability of workers.

Since expert input is sought continuously, it is important to realize answer aggregation as pay-as-you-go process. In our approach, this is achieved by updating the model for worker reliability incrementally upon the arrival of new expert input.

Expert guidance.. To guide the validation of crowd answers by an expert, we formally define the problem of effort minimization to reach a validation goal in terms of result correctness. The problem can only be solved when assuming that workers are truthful. Even in that case, which is not realistic, however, the problem is intractable since even a restricted variant of the problem is NP-hard. Hence, we introduce two guidance strategies that cater for complementary aspects of the problem.

The first strategy aims at a maximal improvement of the result correctness. This strategy is motivated by the observation that some answer validations are more beneficial than others. Since workers and tasks are not independent, but connected by the workers' answers, a certain expert input may have a positive effect on the evaluation of the worker reliability and, thus, on the estimated result correctness. We show how a measure for the expected benefit of a validation question can be used to guide an expert.

The second strategy focuses on the detection of faulty workers (e.g. spammers), which can account for up to 40% of the worker community [29]. Faulty workers increase the cost of acquiring correct answers and contaminate the answer set by adding uncertainty. We address these issues by estimating the likelihood of a worker to be a spammer based on answer validations and show how an expert can be guided to detect faulty workers.

Both strategies have different strengths, so that we also present a hybrid approach that combines the two strategies dynamically.

We evaluated the developed approach with multiple real-world and synthetic datasets. Our techniques save up to 50% of expert efforts compared to a baseline method when striving for perfect result correctness. For most cases, we achieve close to perfect correctness with expert input on only 20% of the questions. Also, the explicit integration of answer validations as realized by our techniques is twice as effective in increasing result correctness compared to the traditional approach of integrating expert input as crowd answers. Moreover, we demonstrate robustness of the approach against erroneous expert input and show that, by distributing a cost budget between crowd workers and experts, it achieves high correctness while satisfying completion time and budget constraints.

The rest of the paper is organized as follows. Next we discuss characteristics of crowd workers and motivate the need to have their answers validated by an expert. §3 defines a formal model for crowdsourcing and gives an overview of our approach. The details on the proposed techniques are given subsequently: §4 introduces our method for probabilistic answer aggregation; §5 defines the problem of expert efforts minimization and presents heuristics to approximate a solution. Evaluation results are presented in §6, before we summarize related work in §7 and conclude in §8.

2. BACKGROUND

Crowdsourcing. Crowdsourcing is an efficient and scalable methodology that enables human computation for micro tasks [37]. Such tasks are broadly classified based on the function that is applied by crowd workers to some objects: In *discrete* tasks each object is assigned to a label [23]; *continuous* tasks require objects to be assigned to real values [48]; *partial-function* tasks define objects as rules [4]; in *similarity* tasks, each object is a pair of matches [19].

In this paper, we focus on discrete tasks, also known as *classification* tasks. They are the core of many applications such as training classifiers [44], entity extraction [10], sentiment analysis [33], and credibility evaluation [21]. As an example, we consider a classification task in which workers need to assign a label to an object, as it is done for tagging images, categorizing websites, or answering multiple-choice questions. Table 1 illustrates an exemplary crowdsourcing result, in which five workers (W_1 - W_5) assigned one out of four labels (1 - 4) to four objects (o_1 - o_4). The correct label assignments are shown in a separate column.

Table 1: Labels provided by 5 workers for 4 objects

	W_1	W_2	W_3	W_4	W_5	Correct	Majority Voting
o_1	2	3	2	2	3	2	2
o_2	3	2	3	2	3	3	3
o_3	1	4	1	4	3	1	1 or 4
o_4	4	1	2	1	3	2	1

Crowd workers. The quality of the result of a crowdsourcing task highly depends on the performance of the crowd workers. Previous studies [29] characterized different types of crowd workers to reflect their expertise: (1) Reliable workers have deep knowledge about specific domains and answer questions with very high reliability; (2) Normal workers have general knowledge to give correct answers, but make mistakes occasionally; (3) Sloppy workers have very little knowledge and thus often give wrong answers, but unintentionally; (4) Uniform spammers intentionally give the same answer for all questions; (5) Random spammers carelessly give random answers for all questions. Figure 1 illustrates the relation between worker types and the quality of crowdsourcing results for the simple case of binary classification tasks. Here, result quality is measured in terms of sensitivity (the proportion of positives that are correctly classified) and specificity (the proportion of negatives that are correctly classified). Sloppy workers, uniform and random spammers are problematic, as they increase the cost of obtaining a correct classification result.

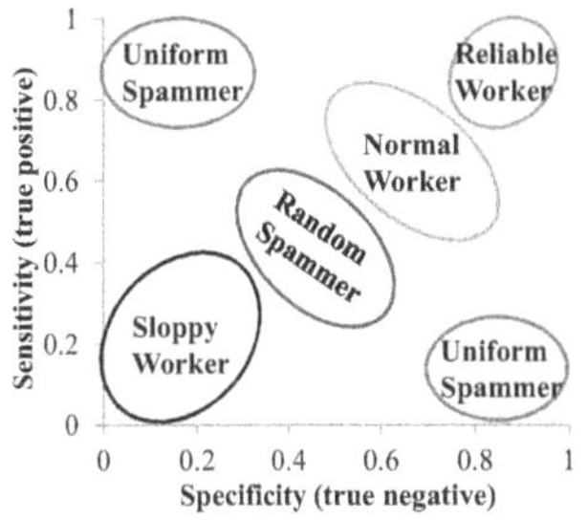

Figure 1: Characterization of worker types

For the above example given in Table 1, for instance, worker W_1 would be considered a normal worker (three out of four answers are correct), W_3 is a reliable worker (all answers are correct), whereas W_5 is a uniform spammer (same answer to all questions).

The need for answer validation. In practice, submitters of crowdsourcing tasks have limited control over the selection of crowd workers and little insights into the level of expertise and reliability of the workers that provided answers. Hence, tasks are often assigned to multiple workers to aggregate the results. Various methods for answer aggregation and estimation of worker reliability have been proposed in the literature. However, the results of automatic methods are inherently uncertain, since they are heuristic-based and no technique performs well in the general case [22].

The example in Table 1 illustrates an inconsistent label assignment due to different levels of expertise of workers. For instance, three out of four possible labels are assigned for object o_3, whereas all four possible labels are provided for object o_4. Yet, the popular approach of aggregating results by 'Majority Voting' would return only a partially correct result for the example.

State-of-the-art answer validation. To overcome the inherent uncertainty of crowdsourcing results, many crowdsourcing platforms

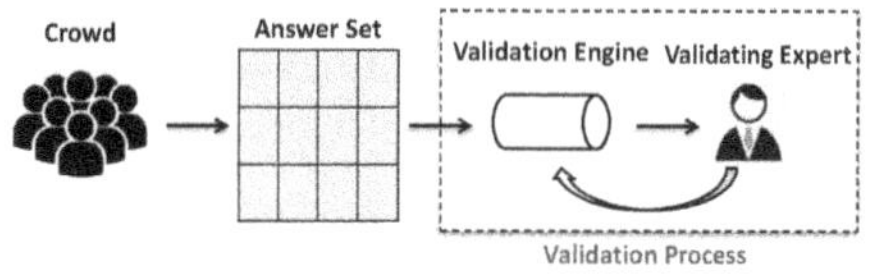

Figure 2: A simple answer validation process

such as AMT include a validation phase as depicted in Figure 2. This process features a validator (also referred to as a validating *expert*) that provides trustworthy answers. The integration of trustworthy input from experts is, in many cases, more efficient than simply enlarging the number of considered crowd workers. In fact, our evaluation in §6 shows that the inclusion of expert input, even though it is more expensive then additional input by crowd workers, is preferable in all but extreme cases (e.g., when the expert is more than 100 times more expensive than crowd workers).

Expert input is commonly considered to be correct, not only in crowdsourcing, but also in related fields, such as correction of errors in databases [49] or in active learning [5]. Then, expert input provides a ground truth for the assessment of the crowd answers. As part of our evaluation in §6, we empirically show that it is indeed reasonable to assume that experts provide correct answers. Yet, we later also investigate cases where expert input may include a certain amount of incorrect answers.

Although most crowdsourcing platforms acknowledge the need for validation, they only provide rudimentary support for the validation phase. The state-of-the-art in answer validation confronts the validating expert with the raw answer set data, complemented by simple statistics of the distribution of answer values [3, 2]. As such, the process of aggregating and validating answers from crowd workers is largely *unguided*. This is an issue given that the effort budget for validation is limited and, without guidance, validation effort is likely to be wasted on answers that have a limited potential for increasing the correctness of the overall result.

For the example in Table 1, the validation of 2 being the correct label for object o_1, for instance, would allow for assessing workers W_1, W_3 and W_4 as reliable. Feedback on object o_4 would be more beneficial, though, as it helps to identify W_3 as a reliable worker, who indeed labeled all objects correctly.

Against this background, our work is the first to propose a method for answer validation that combines crowd answers with expert feedback for pay-as-you-go quality control. With the goal to minimize validation efforts, we get the best of both worlds: the cost of crowdsourcing is lower than having an expert answering all questions, whereas answer validation increases the result correctness.

3. MODEL AND APPROACH

This section presents a crowdsourcing model and, based thereon, gives an overview of our overall approach to answer validation.

3.1 Model

We model the setting of crowdsourcing by a set of k workers $W = \{w_1, w_2, ..., w_k\}$ that provide answers for a set of n objects $O = \{o_1, o_2, ..., o_n\}$. Let $L = \{l_1, l_2, ..., l_m\}$ be a set of labels. Then, crowd answers are modeled as an $n \times k$ *answer matrix*:

$$\mathcal{M} = \begin{pmatrix} x_{11} & \dots & x_{1k} \\ \dots & \dots & \dots \\ x_{n1} & \dots & x_{nk} \end{pmatrix}$$

where $x_{ij} \in (L \cup \{\ominus\})$ for $1 \leq i \leq n$, $1 \leq j \leq k$. Here, the special label $\ominus$ denotes that a worker did not assign a label to an object. We write $\mathcal{M}(o, w)$ to denote the answer of worker w for object o.

Based on the above notions, we define an *answer set* as a quadruple $N = \langle O, W, L, \mathcal{M} \rangle$ where O is a set of objects, W a set of workers, L a set of labels, and $\mathcal{M}$ an answer matrix.

Expert input is modeled by an *answer validation function* $e : O \rightarrow (L \cup \{\ominus\})$ that assigns labels to objects. Again, the label $\ominus$ denotes that the expert has not yet assigned a label to an object.

Our model includes the reliability of workers by means of a *confusion matrix* over labels. For a worker $w \in W$ and a set of labels $L = \{l_1, l_2, ..., l_m\}$, there is an $m \times m$ confusion matrix $\mathcal{F}_w$, such that $\mathcal{F}_w(l, l') \in [0, 1]$ denotes the probability that the worker w assigns the label l' to an object for which the correct label is l.

Further, our work employs a probabilistic aggregation of crowd answers. For each combination of a label and an object, our model includes an assignment probability. For $O = \{o_1, o_2, ..., o_n\}$ as the set of objects and $L = \{l_1, l_2, ..., l_m\}$ as the set of labels, a probabilistic assignment is captured by an $n \times m$ *assignment matrix* $\mathcal{U}$. Here, $\mathcal{U}(o, l) \in [0, 1]$ denotes the probability that $l \in L$ is the correct label for object $o \in O$ and we require that the matrix defines a probability distribution for each object, i.e., $\sum_{l \in L} \mathcal{U}(o, l) = 1$.

Combining the above notions, a *probabilistic answer set* is a quadruple $P = \langle N, e, \mathcal{U}, C \rangle$ where $N = \langle O, W, L, \mathcal{M} \rangle$ is an answer set, e is an answer validation function, $\mathcal{U}$ is an assignment matrix, and $C = \bigcup_{w \in W} \{\mathcal{F}_w\}$ is a set of confusion matrices.

The actual result of the crowdsourcing process is a *deterministic assignment*, a function $d : O \rightarrow L$ assigning labels to objects.

3.2 The overall approach to answer validation

Validation process. Validation happens iteratively, such that in each step, an expert asserts the correct label for an object. This process halts either when reaching a *validation goal* or upon consumption of an *expert efforts budget*. The former relates to the desired quality of the result assignment, e.g., a threshold on the estimated correctness of the deterministic assignment. Since expert input is a scarce resource, the latter defines an upper bound for the number of validations and, thus, iterations of the validation process.

Starting with an answer set $N = \langle O, W, L, \mathcal{M} \rangle$, the validation process continuously updates a deterministic assignment that is considered to be correct. Each iteration of the validation process comprises the following steps:

(1) *select* an object o for which expert feedback shall be sought;
(2) *elicit* expert input on the label of object o and update $e(o)$,
(3) *conclude* the consequences of the expert input on the probabilistic answer set P;
(4) *filter* the deterministic assignment d assumed to be correct based on the probabilistic answer set P.

Instantiations of the general validation process differ in their implementation of steps (1), (3), and (4). For instance, a simple manual validation process is emulated as follows: an object is randomly *selected*; as part of the *conclusions*, the probability of the object for which feedback has been sought is updated; *filtering* selects, for all objects, the labels with highest assignment probability.

Validation framework. Using the notions introduced above, Figure 3 presents an overview of our overall approach. An initial answer set is built from the workers' responses, which is then used to construct a probabilistic answer set by means of *Answer Aggregation* under consideration of the worker reliability. Based on a probabilistic answer set and the input sought from the validating expert, we can automatically derive a deterministic assignment to be used by crowdsourcing applications, which is referred to as *Instantiation*. The quality of the deterministic assignment depends on the degree of uncertainty in the probabilistic answer set. This uncertainty stems from the decision whether to trust certain workers and select their answers when computing the assignment. *Expert*

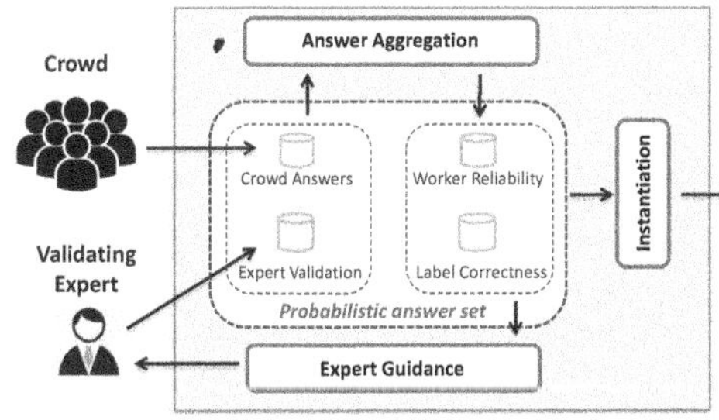

Figure 3: Framework for guided answer validation

Guidance helps to resolve the uncertainty by selecting and ranking candidate objects to seek expert input. This closes the cycle since the answer validation leads to a new assessment of the worker reliability and, thus, a new probabilistic answer set. Hence, the probabilistic answer set is updated in a pay-as-you-go process, where a deterministic assignment can be instantiated at any time.

There is the following relation between the components of the framework in Figure 3 and the validation process:

Answer Aggregation. This component assesses the reliability of workers and, based thereon, computes a probabilistic assignment of labels to objects. As such, it corresponds to step *conclude* in the validation process and creates the probabilistic answer set. The realization of this component is detailed in §4.

Expert Guidance. To guide the uncertainty reduction step, this component selects and ranks objects for which expert feedback should be sought. Hence, this component realizes step *select* in the validation process, for which the details are given in §5.

Instantiation. This component creates the deterministic assignment from the probabilistic answer set, realizing step *filter* in the validation process. It is implemented as the selection of the label with the highest probability in the assignment matrix for each object.

4. PROBABILISTIC ANSWER AGGREGATION

Given the answer set provided by the workers, a probabilistic answer set is constructed by assessing the worker reliability and computing the probabilistic assignment of labels to objects. We first describe the construction of a probabilistic answer set (§4.1) and then turn to a measure for the answer set uncertainty (§4.2).

4.1 Construction of a probabilistic answer set

In the construction of a probabilistic answer set, we consider the following aspects:

Expert validations. The expert input provides the supposedly correct labels for some of the objects. It helps not only to ensure correctness of the final deterministic assignment, but also allows for identifying reliable workers.

Worker Reliability. We expect label assignments done by reliable workers to be mostly correct, whereas unreliable workers provide mostly incorrect assignments. Yet, the level of reliability varies between workers and is not known apriori.

Assignment correctness. For each combination of labels and objects, we have to consider the possibility that the respective assignment is correct. Clearly, the correctness of such an assignment is not known except for those that have been obtained from the expert, but we can expect reliable workers to provide mostly correct assignments.

There is a mutually reinforcing relationship between workers and objects: one worker can label multiple objects and one object can be labeled by multiple workers. Aiding this relationship, expert validations provide a means to judge both, the reliability of workers and the correctness of label assignments. Therefore, we approach the construction of a probabilistic answer set using the Expectation-Maximization methodology [9], which allows for concurrent estimation of worker reliability and assignment correctness.

Requirements for Expectation-Maximization (EM). To be useful in our setting, an EM algorithm must meet two requirements. First, expert validations should be first class citizens to fully leverage their benefits. By assessing the worker reliability based on expert validations, the computation of the assignment probabilities is not limited to the objects for which expert input has been received.

Second, each iteration of the validation process changes the reliability of workers (via the confusion matrices) and the probabilistic assignment matrix only marginally. Hence, EM should proceed incrementally and avoid expensive re-computation of the worker reliability and the assignment probabilities in each iteration.

Existing Expectation-Maximization (EM) algorithms. Various EM algorithms have been proposed in the literature. Yet, none of the existing algorithms meets the aforementioned requirements. Traditional EM [23] operates in batch mode. Hence, the confusion matrices that capture worker reliability and the probabilistic assignment matrix would be re-computed starting from a random probability estimation every time new expert input arrives.

Algorithms for online EM [6], in turn, do not support the integration of a ground truth, i.e., the expert validations. They target incremental updates when the answer matrix changes (a new answer arrives), whereas our setting requires incremental updates over an unchanged answer matrix whenever the ground truth is extended (a new expert validation arrives). One may argue that expert validations may be modeled as new answers. However, this does not circumvent the issue since answers representing expert validations could be dominated by incorrect answers (e.g., due to Majority Voting). We later show experimentally that the explicit integration of expert validations, rather than considering them as ordinary answers, indeed yields more effective answer aggregation.

The *i*-EM algorithm. Against this background, we propose an incremental EM algorithm, called *i*-EM algorithm, that follows the view maintenance principle [7]. Estimation of worker reliability and assignment correctness is grounded in the results of the previous iteration of the validation process, which avoids re-computing them in each iteration. This does not only increase efficiency of the approach, but, as will be illustrated in our evaluation, also yields a better approximation compared to a random probability estimation.

The *i*-EM algorithm implements the *conclude* function of the validation process. In the s-th iteration of the expert validation process, the input of this function is given by the answer set N and the expert validation function e_s as it has been updated with the expert input received in the s-th iteration. However, the *i*-EM algorithm works incrementally, so that, in each iteration, we also maintain the state of the previous iteration in terms of the probabilistic answer set. That is, in the s-th iteration of the expert validation process, the probabilistic answer set $P_{s-1} = \langle N, e_{s-1}, \mathcal{U}_{s-1}, C_{s-1} \rangle$ of the previous iteration is also part of the input to the algorithm. The algorithm then returns a new probabilistic answer set $P_s = \langle N, e_s, \mathcal{U}_s, C_s \rangle$.

The actual Expectation-Maximization done in the s-th iteration of the expert validation step is also iterative, alternating between two steps, the Expectation step (E-step) and the Maximization step (M-step), until convergence. As part of EM iterations, the probabilistic assignment as well as the worker confusion matrices of the probabilistic answer set are updated. That is, in the s-th iteration of the expert validation process, the EM iterations create a sequence $\mathcal{U}_s^0, \mathcal{U}_s^1, \ldots, \mathcal{U}_s^z$ of assignment matrices and a sequence $C_s^0, C_s^1, \ldots, C_s^z$ of sets of confusion matrices.

E-step. In an E-step, we estimate the assignment probabilities based on the worker confusion matrices. The first E-step of the s-th iteration of the expert validation process is based on the worker confusion matrices $C_s^0 = \{\mathcal{F}_{w_1,s}^0, \mathcal{F}_{w_2,s}^0, \ldots, \mathcal{F}_{w_k,s}^0\}$, which are given as input from the previous iteration of the validation process, i.e., $C_s^0 = C_{s-1}^q = \{\mathcal{F}_{w_1,s-1}^q, \mathcal{F}_{w_2,s-1}^q, \ldots, \mathcal{F}_{w_k,s-1}^q\}$ with q being the number of EM iterations in the $(s-1)$-th iteration of the validation process. In the τ-th E-step of the s-th step of the validation process, for each object o for which no expert input has been received ($e_s(o) = \ominus$), the assignment probability of label l is estimated as:

$$\mathcal{U}_s^\tau(o,l) = \frac{p_s^{\tau-1}(l)\prod_{w\in W}\prod_{l'\in L}\left(\mathcal{F}_{w,s}^{\tau-1}(l,l')\right)^{d_w(o,l')}}{\sum_{l''\in L} p_s^{\tau-1}(l'')\prod_{w\in W}\prod_{l'\in L}\left(\mathcal{F}_{w,s}^{\tau-1}(l'',l')\right)^{d_w(o,l')}} \quad (1)$$

where d_w is a function encoding the existence of the respective label assignment by a worker $w \in W$ in the answer matrix $\mathcal{M}$,

$$d_w(o,l) = \begin{cases} 1 & \text{if } \mathcal{M}(o,w) = l \\ 0 & \text{otherwise} \end{cases} \quad (2)$$

and $p_s^{\tau-1}(l)$ is the prior probability of label l, given as

$$p_s^{\tau-1}(l) = \frac{\sum_{o\in O}\mathcal{U}_s^{\tau-1}(o,l)}{|O|}. \quad (3)$$

For objects for which an expert validation has been received already ($e_s(o) \neq \ominus$), assignment probabilities are trivially given as:

$$\mathcal{U}_s^\tau(o,l) = \begin{cases} 1 & \text{if } e_s(o) = l \\ 0 & \text{otherwise.} \end{cases} \quad (4)$$

M-step. In an M-step, we estimate the confusion matrices of the workers using the assignment probabilities. That is, in the τ-th M-step of the s-th step of the validation process, the probability $\mathcal{F}_{w,s}^\tau(l',l)$, which captures that worker w assigns the label l when the correct label is l', is computed as follows:

$$\mathcal{F}_{w,s}^\tau(l',l) = \frac{\sum_{o\in O}\mathcal{U}_s^\tau(o,l')d_w(o,l)}{\sum_{l''\in L}\sum_{o\in O}\mathcal{U}_s^\tau(o,l')d_w(o,l'')} \quad (5)$$

4.2 The uncertainty of answer aggregation

The heterogeneity among the workers renders it likely that many objects, which are supposed to have a single correct label, are assigned to different labels by the workers. The model of a probabilistic answer set, as constructed by the i-EM algorithm introduced above, provides us with a truthful representation of the uncertainty related to the aggregation of the answers. To guide an expert in the validation process, the uncertainty needs to be quantified.

Let $P = \langle N, e, \mathcal{U}, C\rangle$ be a probabilistic answer set constructed for answer set $N = \langle O, W, L, \mathcal{M}\rangle$. Recall that P defines an assignment $\mathcal{U}(o,l)$ for each label $l \in L$ and object $o \in O$, which represents the likelihood of l to be the correct label for o. Since the probabilities of the labels form a distribution, i.e., $\sum_{l\in L}\mathcal{U}(o,l) = 1$, we can model each object o as a random variable. Then, the overall uncertainty of the probabilistic answer set is computed by the Shannon entropy [43] over a set of random variables. More precisely, the entropy of an object o is measured as follows:

$$H(o) = -\sum_{l\in L}\mathcal{U}(o,l)\times\log(\mathcal{U}(o,l)) \quad (6)$$

The entropy of an object is the basis for the computation of the uncertainty of the probabilistic answer set P. It is defined as the sum of the entropies of all objects:

$$H(P) = \sum_{o\in O} H(o) \quad (7)$$

The entropy of an object and, thus, also of the probabilistic answer set, can only be 0, if all assignment probabilities are equal to 1 or 0. If so, there is a clear separation of correct and incorrect assignments for an object or all objects, respectively.

5. EXPERT VALIDATION GUIDANCE

This section presents techniques to guide an expert in the validation process that reduces the uncertainty of a probabilistic answer set. We first formalize the problem of effort minimization (§5.1). As the problem can be solved only under further assumptions on crowd workers and is computational hard, we present two heuristic solutions aiming at a maximal uncertainty reduction (§5.2) or the detection of faulty workers (§5.3), respectively. Then, we combine both heuristics (§5.4) and also elaborate on how to handle potentially erroneous expert input (§5.5).

5.1 The effort minimization problem

Instantiation of the generic answer validation process described in §3.2 requires the definition of a validation goal. For the answer aggregation introduced above, a reasonable validation goal is grounded in the uncertainty measure defined in §4.2.

Given the iterative nature of the validation process, we would like to minimize the number of necessary expert interaction steps for a given goal. For an answer set $N = \langle O, W, L, \mathcal{M}\rangle$, executing the answer validation process leads to a sequence of deterministic assignments $\langle d_0, d_1, \ldots, d_n\rangle$, termed a *validation sequence*, where d_i represents the assignment obtained after the i-th iteration. Given an expert efforts budget b and a validation goal Δ, we refer to sequence $\langle d_0, d_1, \ldots, d_n\rangle$ as being *valid*, if $n \leq b$ and d_n satisfies Δ. Let $\mathcal{R}(\Delta, b)$ denote a finite set of valid validation sequences that can be created by instantiations of the validation process. Then, a validation sequence $\langle d_0, d_1, \ldots, d_n\rangle \in \mathcal{R}(\Delta, b)$ is *minimal*, if for any validation sequence $\langle d'_0, d'_1, \ldots, d'_m\rangle \in \mathcal{R}(\Delta, b)$ it holds that $n \leq m$.

PROBLEM 1 (EXPERT EFFORTS MINIMIZATION). *Let $\langle O, W, L, \mathcal{M}\rangle$ be an answer set and $\mathcal{R}(\Delta, b)$ a set of valid validation sequences for an expert efforts budget b and a goal Δ. The problem of* expert efforts minimization *is the identification of a minimal sequence $\langle d_0, d_1, ..., d_n\rangle \in \mathcal{R}(\Delta, b)$.*

Assuming that the validation goal is defined in terms of the uncertainty of the probabilistic answer set, solving Problem 1 is challenging. First, the objects are not independent, due to the mutual reinforcing relationship between workers and objects. Validating one object can affect the uncertainty of label assignment of other objects. Second, the presence of malicious workers can alter the uncertainty of the answer set, as incorrect labels can be mistreated as correct labels and vice-versa. Further, even in the absence of faulty workers, finding an optimal solution requires investigation of all permutations of all subsets (with size $\leq b$) of objects, which is intractable. Appendix E outlines that even for a restricted version of the problem, finding an optimal solution is NP-hard.

5.2 Uncertainty-driven expert guidance

Our first heuristic to guide the selection of objects for validation aims at the maximal uncertainty reduction under the assumption of ethical workers. It exploits the contribution of a single validation using the notion of information gain from information theory [42].

First, we define a conditional variant of the entropy measure introduced earlier. It refers to the entropy of the probabilistic answer set $P = \langle N, e, \mathcal{U}, C\rangle$, $N = \langle O, W, L, \mathcal{M}\rangle$, conditioned on the expert input on object o. Informally, it measures the expected entropy of P under a certain expert assignment.

$$H(P \mid o) = \sum_{l\in L}\mathcal{U}(o,l)\times H(P_l) \quad (8)$$

where $P_l = conclude(N, e')$ is constructed by the i-EM algorithm with $e'(o) = l$ and $e'(o') = e(o')$ for $o' \in (O \setminus \{o\})$.

To take a decision on which object to select, we assess the expected difference in uncertainty before and after the expert input for an object. The respective change in entropy is the information gain that quantifies the potential benefit of knowing the true value of an unknown variable [42], i.e., the correct label in our case:

$$IG(o) = H(P) - H(P \mid o). \quad (9)$$

The information gain allows for selection of the object that is expected to maximally reduce the uncertainty of the probabilistic answer set in one iteration of the validation process. This is formalized by a selection function for uncertainty-driven expert guidance:

$$select_u(O') = \arg\max_{o \in O'} IG(o) \quad (10)$$

5.3 Worker-driven expert guidance

Uncertainty-driven expert guidance as introduced above assumes that workers are ethical, an assumption that is often violated in practice. Recent studies found that up to 40% of the workers in a worker community may be faulty (e.g. spammers) [29]. This section thus presents a technique for expert guidance that aims at the detection of the three problematic worker types discussed in §2, i.e., uniform spammers, random spammers, and sloppy workers.

Detecting uniform and random spammers. To assess the likelihood of a worker being a uniform or random spammer, we leverage the fact that the labels provided by random spammers tend to be uniformly distributed across the correct labels, whereas the labels provided by uniform spammers are all the same. These tendencies are directly visible in the confusion matrix.

Consider two workers $\mathcal{A}$ and $\mathcal{A}'$, who provide answers for six objects from a set of two labels $\{T, F\}$, as listed in Table 2. For worker $\mathcal{A}$, the numbers of T labels and F labels are equal for objects for which the correct label is T (or F, respectively). Consequently, rows in the confusion matrix tend to have equivalent values across columns, which indicates that $\mathcal{A}$ is a random spammer. For worker $\mathcal{A}'$, the confusion matrix has only a single column with values larger than 0. Thus, $\mathcal{A}'$ is likely to be a uniform spammer.

Table 2: Answers and confusion matrices for workers $\mathcal{A}$ and $\mathcal{A}'$

	o_1	o_2	o_3	o_4	o_5	o_6	o_7	o_8
Correct	T	T	F	F	T	F	T	F
$\mathcal{A}$	T	F	T	F	T	F	F	T
$\mathcal{A}'$	F	F	F	F	F	F	F	F

Worker $\mathcal{A}$	T	F
T	0.5	0.5
F	0.5	0.5

Worker $\mathcal{A}'$	T	F
T	0	1
F	0	1

Based on this observation, we rely on a variant of the *spammer score* proposed in [38] to estimate the probability that a worker is a uniform or random spammer. In [38], the confusion matrices are constructed from the labels that are estimated to be correct, which introduces a bias if this estimation is incorrect. Therefore, we construct the confusion matrices only based on the answer validations.

Confusion matrices that have rows with equivalent values across columns (random spammers) or a single column with values larger than 0 (uniform spammers) have similar characteristics as a rank-one matrix. Therefore, we calculate the spammer score $s(w)$ of a worker w as the distance of the confusion matrix to its closest rank-one approximation, using the Frobenius norm:

$$s(w) = \min_{\hat{\mathcal{F}}_w} \| \mathcal{F}_w - \hat{\mathcal{F}}_w \|_F \quad (11)$$

where $\mathcal{F}_w$ is the confusion matrix of worker w and $\hat{\mathcal{F}}_w$ is a matrix with rank one. This low-rank approximation problem can be solved using singular value decomposition [14]. We then set a threshold τ_s to filter uniform and random spammers from the population.

Detecting sloppy workers. Sloppy workers tend to provide labels incorrectly, which is also detected based on the confusion matrix. Following the above approach for uniform and random spammers, we construct a confusion matrix using the answer validations. As the labels provided by the sloppy workers are mostly incorrect, we can calculate the error rate of the worker. The error rate of a worker (denoted as e_w) is the sum of all values not on the main diagonal of the confusion matrix weighted by the priors of the labels. If this error rate e_w is larger than a threshold τ_p, the worker is considered as a sloppy worker.

Expert guidance. We exploit the detection techniques to guide the answer validation by selecting objects that will contribute to the identification of faulty workers. To this end, we measure the benefit of expert input on an object by the expected number of detected faulty workers. Formally, by $R(W \mid o = l)$, we denote the expected number of detected faulty workers, if the answer validation indicates that l is the correct label for object o.

$$R(W \mid o = l) = \mid \{w \mid s(w) < \tau_s\} \cup \{w \mid e_w > \tau_p\} \mid \quad (12)$$

Then, the total expected number of detected faulty workers for input on o is

$$R(W \mid o) = \sum_{l \in L} \mathcal{U}(o, l) \times R(W \mid o = l) \quad (13)$$

Hence, in each iteration of the answer validation process, the worker-driven expert guidance heuristic will select the object o with the highest total expected number of detected faulty workers, formalized by the following selection function:

$$select_w(O') = \arg\max_{o \in O'} R(W \mid o) \quad (14)$$

Handling faulty workers. A naive way to handle faulty workers is to define a threshold and exclude any worker with a spammer score higher than the threshold. However, this approach may mistakenly remove truthful workers, as illustrated by the example given in Table 3. Assuming that answer validations have been obtained only for $o_1, \ldots, o_4$, the confusion matrix would indicate that worker $\mathcal{B}$ is a random spammer, even though 4 out of 6 questions have been answered correctly. Hence, workers may be excluded too early if only a few of their answers are considered in the spammer score due to a small number of answer validations.

Table 3: Answer and confusion matrix of worker $\mathcal{B}$

	o_1	o_2	o_3	o_4	o_5	o_6
Correct	T	T	F	F	T	T
$\mathcal{B}$	T	F	T	F	T	T

	T	F
T	0.5	0.5
F	0.5	0.5

We overcome this issue by only excluding the answers of suspected faulty workers from the answer set, while continuing to collect their answers. Then, as more expert input becomes available, these answers are included again once the spammer score is higher than a threshold. In other words, any of the worker answers will be eventually be included if they are truly reliable.

5.4 A combined approach to expert guidance

There is a trade-off between the application of the uncertainty-driven and the worker-driven expert guidance. Focusing solely on uncertainty reduction may lead to contamination of the truthful workers' responses by faulty workers. On the other hand, an excessively worker-driven approach is undesirable as it may increase the overall expert efforts significantly. Therefore, we propose a dynamic weighting procedure that, in each iteration of the answer validation process, helps to choose among the two strategies.

Weighting procedure. Intuitively, there are two factors which affect the choice between the strategies:

Ratio of spammers. If a high number of faulty workers is detected, the worker-driven strategy is preferred. However, as this strategy depends on expert input, it may not be effective in the beginning when the number of answer validations is small. In this case, the uncertainty-driven strategy is favored.

Error rate. The deterministic assignment d_i captures the assignments considered to be correct in the i-th iteration of the answer validation process. If d_i turns out to be mostly incorrect, we have evidence of faulty workers in the community and, thus, favor the worker-driven strategy.

We balance both factors by combining the two strategies dynamically. In the beginning, with a low number of answer validations, it is mainly the error rate of the deterministic assignment that determines which strategy to use. At later stages, the number of detected faulty workers becomes the dominant factor.

To formalize this intuition, we denote the ratio of detected faulty workers in the i-th iteration of the answer validation process by r_i. The error rate of the deterministic assignment is computed by comparing the expert input for object o in the i-th iteration with the label l that has been assigned to o in d_{i-1}, i.e., in the previous iteration. Here, we leverage the probability $\mathcal{U}_{i-1}(o,l)$ of the probabilistic answer set $P_{i-1} = \langle N, e_{i-1}, \mathcal{U}_{i-1}, C_{i-1} \rangle$, $N = \langle O, W, L, \mathcal{M} \rangle$, of the $(i-1)$-th iteration of the answer validation process. Given the answer validation that assigns l to o in the i-th iteration, the error rate is computed as:

$$\varepsilon_i = 1 - \mathcal{U}_{i-1}(o,l)$$

Using the ratio of detected faulty workers r_i and the error rate ε_i, we compute a normalized score ($\in [0,1]$) for choosing the worker-driven strategy:

$$z_i = 1 - e^{-(\varepsilon_i(1-f_i)+r_i f_i)} \tag{15}$$

where $f_i = \frac{i}{|O|} \in [0,1]$ is the ratio of answer validations. This score mediates the trade-off between the error rate ε_i and the ratio of spammers r_i by the ratio of answer validations f_i. When the ratio f_i is small, the ratio of spammers has less influence and the error rate is the dominant factor. When the ratio f_i is large, the ratio of spammers becomes a more dominant factor.

Hybrid answer validation procedure. Instantiating the general answer validation process described in §3.2, the answer validation process that incorporates both uncertainty-driven and worker-driven expert guidance is defined in Algorithm 1.

Algorithm 1: The hybrid answer validation process

input : an answer set $N = \langle O, W, L, \mathcal{M} \rangle$,
a validation goal Δ,
an expert efforts budget b.
output: the result assignment d.

// Initialization
1 $e_0 \leftarrow (o \mapsto \ominus, o \in O)$;
2 $P_0 \leftarrow conclude(N, e_0)$;
3 $d_0 \leftarrow filter(P_0)$;
4 $i, z_0 \leftarrow 0$;
5 **while** *not* $\Delta \wedge i \leq b$ **do**
  // (1) Select an object
6   $x \leftarrow random(0,1)$;
7   **if** $x < z_i$ **then** $o \leftarrow select_w(\{o' \in O \mid e_i(o') = \ominus\})$;
8   **else** $o \leftarrow select_u(\{o' \in O \mid e_i(o') = \ominus\})$;
  // (2) Elicit expert input
9   Elicit expert input $l \in L$ on o;
10   Calculate error rate ε_i;
  // (3) Handle spammers
11   Detect spammers;
12   **if** $x < z_i$ **then** Handle detected spammers ;
13   Calculate ratio of spammers r_i;
14   $z_{i+1} = 1 - e^{-\left(\varepsilon_i\left(1-\frac{i}{|O|}\right)+r_i\frac{i}{|O|}\right)}$;
  // (4) Integrate the answer validation
15   $e_{i+1} \leftarrow (o \mapsto l \wedge o' \mapsto e_i(o'), o' \in O, o' \neq o)$;
16   $P_{i+1} \leftarrow conclude(N, e_{i+1})$;
17   $d_{i+1} \leftarrow (o' \mapsto filter(P_{i+1}), o' \in O, e_{i+1}(o') = \ominus \wedge o' \mapsto e_{i+1}(o'), o' \in O, e_{i+1}(o') \neq \ominus)$;
18   $i \leftarrow i+1$;
19 return d_i;

Selection of an object for which expert feedback shall be sought is done either by the worker-driven or the uncertainty-driven selection strategy ($select_w$ or $select_u$). The actual choice is realized by comparing factor z_i to a random number, thereby implementing a roulette wheel selection [18]. Thus, even if factor z_i assumes a large value, there is a chance that the uncertainty driven strategy is chosen. Once expert feedback has been elicited (line 9), the error rate is computed (line 10). Then, we run the method for detecting faulty workers (line 11). The workers detected in this step are handled if the worker-driven strategy had been selected (line 12). Further, the ratio of unethical workers r_i is calculated to compute score z_{i+1} (lines 13-14), used in the next iteration to choose between the selection strategies. Finally, we integrate the feedback by updating the answer validation function e_{i+1} (line 15), computing the probabilistic answer set P_{i+1} with the function *conclude* that implements probabilistic answer aggregation as defined in §4 (line 16), and updating the deterministic assignment set function d_{i+1} (line 17). For objects for which no expert input has been received, the correct assignment is estimated based on the probabilistic answer set using the function *filter*, as discussed in §3.2. The filtered assignments, together with the answer validations, define the deterministic assignment assumed to be correct at this validation step.

Implementation. A practical implementation of the hybrid answer validation process must cope with the complexity of the computation of the information gain and the expected spammer score for each object (as part of step (1)). Therefore, to achieve an efficient implementation, we consider two techniques:

Parallelization The computations of the information gain and the expected spammer score for different objects are independent and, therefore, can be executed in parallel for all objects.

Sparse matrix partitioning Due to the implied cognitive load, workers answer a limited amount of questions. Hence, the answer matrix is sparse when having a large number of objects [25]. Therefore, we use sparse matrix partitioning [28] to divide a large answer matrix into smaller dense ones that fit for human interactions and can be handled more efficiently.

5.5 Erroneous answer validations

As detailed in §2, it is commonly assumed that the answers provided by the validating expert are correct. Yet, in practice, expert input may contain mistakes, caused not by the lack of knowledge of the expert, but stemming from the interaction as part of the validation [39]. In other words, if such erroneous answer validations are detected, they can be fixed by the expert themselves.

There are two types of erroneous answer validations: (1) the crowd is right, i.e., the aggregated answer is correct, whereas the expert validation is wrong; (2) the crowd is wrong, but the answer validation is also wrong. As illustrated later in our evaluation, case (1) is unlikely to happen since a validating expert is confronted with statistics about crowd answers, so that a decision to deviate from the aggregated answer is typically taken well-motivated. Case (2), however, is more likely to happen since an expert is more likely to confirm the aggregated answer than to deliberately deviate from it.

We cater for erroneous answer validations as in case (2) by augmenting the answer validation process with a lightweight confirmation check. This check is triggered after a fixed number of iterations of the validation process and proceeds as follows:

(I) For every object o for which expert input has been sought, a deterministic assignment $d_{\sim o}$ is constructed based on the answer set N and the expert validations e from which the expert feedback for o has been excluded.

(II) The label for object o in $d_{\sim o}$ is compared with the respective expert feedback $e(o)$. If $d_{\sim o}(o) \neq e(o)$, then $e(o)$ is identified as an erroneous answer validation as in case (2).

Later, our evaluation will demonstrate that this simple check is highly effective, which makes the answer validation process robust against erroneous expert input.

6. EVALUATION

This section presents an empirical evaluation of the proposed approach using both real-world and synthetic datasets. We first discuss the experimental setup (§6.1), before turning to an evaluation of the following aspects of our solution:

- The runtime performance of the presented approach (§6.2).
- The benefits of integrating expert input as a first class citizen in the answer aggregation (§6.3).
- The performance of the proposed *i*-EM algorithm (§6.4).
- The effectiveness of the detection of faulty workers (§6.5).
- The effectiveness of hybrid expert guidance (§6.6).
- The robustness of the approach when experts provide erroneous answer validations (§6.7).
- The cost-effectiveness of expert-based answer validation (§6.8).

6.1 Experimental setup

Datasets. Our experiments have been conducted on five real-world datasets and synthetic datasets. The real-world data provides us with a realistic crowdsourcing setup by means of five classification problems that span different application domains, such as image tagging (dataset *bluebird (bb)*) or sentiment analysis (*twt* and *art* datasets). Statistics on the sizes of the real-world datasets are given in Table 4. We further employed synthetic datasets to explore parameter spaces and understand the influence of data characteristics on the performance of the algorithms. More details on both real-world and synthetic datasets are given in Appendix A.

Metrics. In addition to the uncertainty of the probabilistic answer set defined in Equation 7, we relied on the following measures:

Relative expert efforts (E_i) is the number of expert feedbacks i relative to the number of objects n in the dataset, i.e., $E = i/n$.

Precision (P_i) measures the correctness of the deterministic assignment at each validation step. Let $g : O \rightarrow L$ be the correct assignment of labels for all objects. Then, the precision of the deterministic assignment d_i at the i-th validation step is

$$P_i = \frac{|\{o \in O \mid d_i(o) = g(o)\}|}{|O|}.$$

Percentage of precision improvement (R_i) is a normalized version of precision as it measures the relative improvement. If the precision at the i-th validation step is P_i and the initial precision is P_0, then the percentage of precision improvement is

$$R_i = \frac{P_i - P_0}{1 - P_0}.$$

Experimental environment. All experimental results have been obtained on an Intel Core i7 system (3.4GHz, 12GB RAM).

6.2 Runtime performance

Since answer validation entails interactions with the expert, it should show a good runtime performance. In this experiment, we

Table 4: Statistics for real-world datasets

Dataset	Domain	# Objects	# Workers	# Labels
bb	Image tagging	108	39	2
rte	Semantic analysis	800	164	2
val	Sentiment analysis	100	38	2
twt	Sentiment analysis	300	58	2
art	Sentiment analysis	200	49	2

studied the effects of the number of objects on the runtime performance. The reported time is the response time of the system during one iteration of Algorithm 1, i.e., the time the expert has to wait for the selection of the next object after providing input.

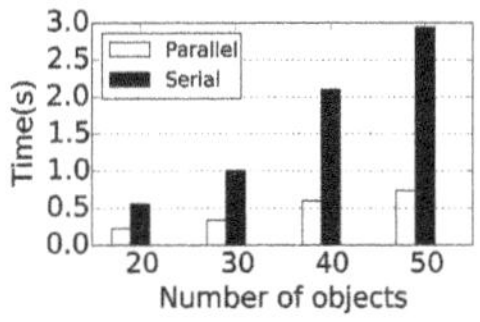

Figure 4: Response time

#questions per worker	Time (s)
10	3.1
20	4.3
40	7.5
60	9.8

Table 5: Computation time for matrix ordering

Figure 4 shows the results obtained as an average of 100 runs when using matrix partitioning (see §5.4) and the plain algorithm (*Serial*) or its parallel version (*Parallel*). Increasing the number of objects from 20 to 50, which are typically found in crowdsourcing platforms [22], increases the response time. However, even for 50 objects, the response time is less than 1 second when using parallelization, which enables immediate interactions with humans.

Further, we evaluate the start-up time required due to matrix partitioning *before* running the actual answer validation process (which does not affect the response time for the expert). We conducted an experiment with synthetic data, 16000 questions posted randomly to 1000 workers. The sparsity of the matrix is simulated by the maximal number of questions per worker which varies from 10, 20, 40, 60. Table 5 shows that the start-up time is a few seconds.

6.3 Expert validation as first-class citizen

To study the benefits of integrating expert input as a first class citizen instead of considering it as ordinary crowd answers, we compare two ways of using expert feedback. First, each expert input is a common crowd answer in the answer aggregation (*Combined*). Second, each expert input is used to validate crowd answers as proposed in our approach (*Separate*).

Figure 5 shows the results in terms of expert effort and precision improvement for the *val* dataset (results for other datasets are omitted as they exhibit similar characteristics). The *Separate* strategy outperforms the *Combined* strategy regardless of the expert efforts. This is expected—event though both approaches leverage the expert feedback, the precision of the *Combined* strategy is lower since expert answers are seen as equally important as those of the workers. Using the *Separate* strategy, expert input is deemed most important, overruling incorrect worker answers. As such, the results highlight the benefits of our method to integrate expert input as a first class citizen when aggregating crowd answers.

6.4 i-EM for answer aggregation

The *i*-EM algorithm (1) explicitly integrates answer validation from an expert as a ground truth and (2) works incrementally. Here, we evaluate the benefits of these two properties of the algorithm.

Benefits of answer validation. We evaluate the *i*-EM algorithm w.r.t the estimated assignment probability of the correct labels. For each object, a good answer aggregation would assign a higher probability to correct label than to incorrect ones. In the experiment, we keep track of the correct labels for objects and their associated

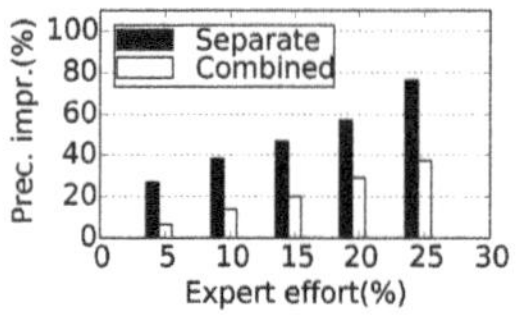

Figure 5: Ways of integrating expert input

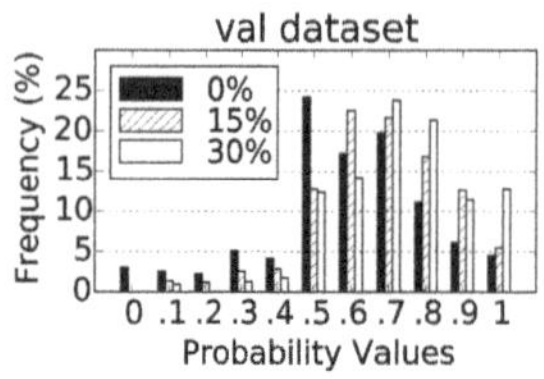

Figure 6: Benefits of answer validation

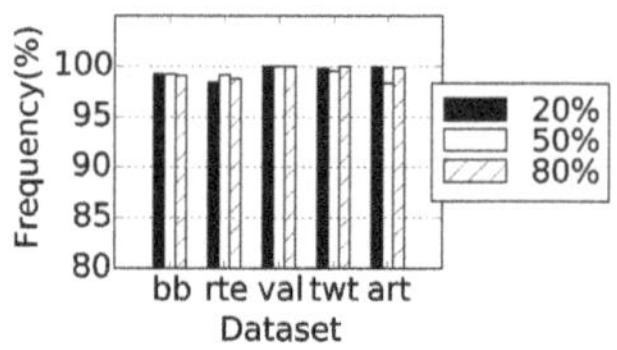

Figure 7: *i*-EM on guiding

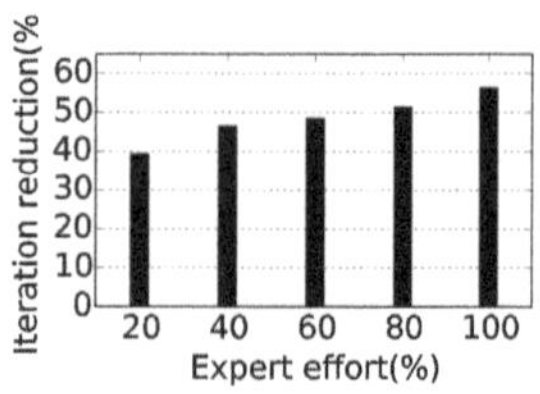

Figure 8: Efficiency of *i*-EM

probabilities while varying the expert efforts (0%, 15%, 30%). Figure 6 presents a histogram of the probability distribution in the *val* dataset (similar results, omitted for brevity, have been obtained for the other datasets). For each object o, we measure the assignment probability $\mathcal{U}(o,l)$ of its correct label l assigned by *i*-EM . If the assignment probability of the label for object o is in a probability bin, the count for that bin is increased.

We note that the number of correct labels which have a probability less than 0.5 is overall small. Still, around 3% of correct labels have a probability less than 0.1 when no expert input has been integrated (expert effort 0%), meaning that answer aggregation without validation (traditional EM) may assign a very low probability for some of the correct labels. Increasing the amount of expert input, the probability range covering most of the correct labels shifts from the 0.5 bin to higher probability bins. Hence, answer aggregation with more expert input (our *i*-EM algorithm) is able to assess the assignment probabilities of the correct labels better than without expert input (traditional EM algorithm).

Benefits of incrementality. Most EM-like algorithms are sensitive to initialization [22]. We study robustness of our *i*-EM algorithm by comparing two strategies: (i) *incremental* – upon new expert input, an iteration is initialized using the previous state of the probabilistic answer set (the *i*-EM algorithm), and (ii) *non-incremental* – each iteration is initialized with random values (traditional EM).

As different initializations lead to different estimations of probabilities, the selection of objects for validation of our guiding strategy may be affected. Therefore, we first analyze whether the two strategies suggest the same object. We compare the two strategies at different levels of expert efforts by running them to get the assignment probabilities and the confusion matrices, calculate the information gain for each object, and assess whether the same object has the highest information gain for both strategies. Figure 7 shows the results relative to the expert effort as the percentage of cases (averaged over 100 runs) where the two strategies select the same object. Indeed, both strategies select the same objects in virtually all cases, indicating initialization robustness of the *i*-EM algorithm.

Further, the idea of the *i*-EM algorithm is that by incrementalizing answer aggregation without affecting the validation guidance, we reduce the convergence ratio of expectation maximization. We verify this hypothesis by comparing the runtime performance of the two strategies in terms of convergence. For a synthetic dataset with 50 objects and 20 workers, for which the worker population is simulated as outlined in Appendix A with a reliability of 0.65 for normal workers, the obtained results are shown in Figure 8 (average over 100 runs). It depicts the percentage of expert input relative to the percentage of iterations saved by using the *incremental* strategy.

We note that the *i*-EM algorithm converges faster and saves more than 30% of the iterations, with the iteration reduction becoming larger with an increased number of answer validations. This is explained by the fact that the more expert input is available, the more the estimation of label correctness and worker reliability converges to the exact values. Since the *i*-EM algorithm estimates label correctness and worker reliability based on the values of the previous iteration, it requires less iterations over time.

6.5 Effectiveness of the spammer detection

Since our guiding technique includes the detection of faulty workers (e.g. spammers, sloppy workers), it is necessary to analyze the technique with different detection thresholds. Since real datasets do not have information about who is spammer, we resort to using synthetic data with 20 workers that assign one of two labels to 50 objects. We then vary the threshold τ_s to detect uniform and random spammers from 0.1 to 0.3 while keeping the threshold τ_p for sloppy workers at 0.8. We also vary the validation effort from 20% to 100%. We measured the precision (ratio of correctly identified spammers over all identified spammers) and recall (ratio of correctly identified spammers over all spammers) of the detection.

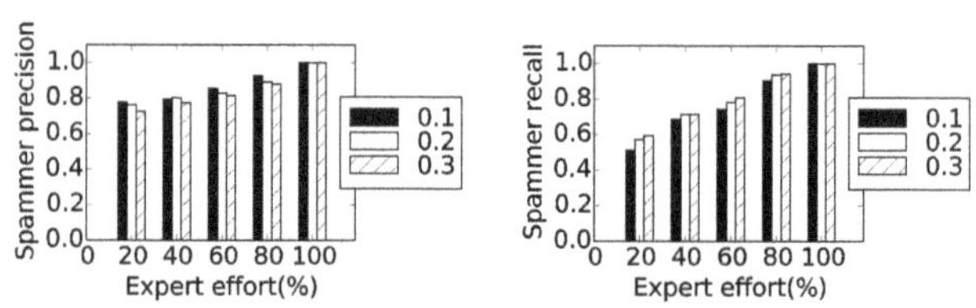

Figure 9: Efficiency of the spammer detection technique

Figure 9 (average of 100 runs) illustrates that, as the number of validations increases, both precision and recall of spammer detection increase. The confusion matrices used to detect spammers are built based on the answer validations. Hence, with more expert input, the confusion matrices better reflect the reliability of the workers. Also, we observe the trade-off between precision and recall as we increase the spammer score threshold. An increased threshold yields lower precision, but higher recall. Striving at a balance, we set the detection threshold to 0.2 in the remaining experiments.

6.6 Effectiveness of expert guidance

Next, we evaluate the effectiveness of our guiding approach for reducing expert efforts on real-world datasets. To this end, we first verified the underlying assumption of our techniques to expert guidance, i.e., that the uncertainty of a probabilistic answer set, quantified as introduced in §4.2, is correlated to the actual precision of the deterministic assignment. Our results, presented in detail in Appendix B, show that this is indeed the case and that there is a strong correlation between the measures (supported by Pearson's correlation coefficient value of −0.9461). Hence, the measured uncertainty is a truthful indicator of the result correctness.

Turning to the guidance strategies, we mimic the validating expert by using the ground-truth provided in the datasets until precision reaches 1.0. We compare the proposed approach (*hybrid*) with a method that implements the function *select* in the validation process by selecting the most 'problematic' object (*baseline*). Intuitively, we measure how 'problematic' an object is by the entropy of its probability (see Appendix C for a formal definition). This baseline method is better than random selection since it strives for the objects that are on the edge of being considered right or wrong, which are the major sources of uncertainty in the answer set.

Figure 10 shows the results for the first three real-world datasets (*bb*, *rte*, and *val*), the remaining datasets (*twt* and *art*) are discussed

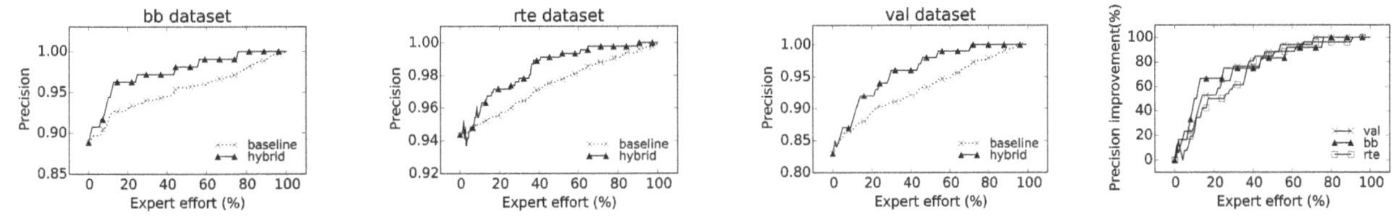

Figure 10: Effectiveness of guiding

Appendix C. The approach developed in this paper (*hybrid*) clearly outperforms the *baseline* method. For example, in the *bb* dataset, our approach leads to a precision above 0.95 with expert input on only 10% of the objects. The baseline method requires expert validation of around 50% to reach the same level of precision.

The relative improvement of precision for different expert effort levels is illustrated in the last plot in Figure 10. For instance, for 20% expert efforts, we achieve an improvement of precision of at least 50% for all datasets. Also, precision improvement is larger for smaller amounts of expert efforts, which emphasizes the effectiveness of our guidance strategy in particular for scenarios with a limited effort budget for the validation.

We further explored the effectiveness of our approach in relation to different aspects of a crowdsourcing setup using synthetic data. While the detailed results of these experiments are available in Appendix C, we summarize the main findings as follows. The presented approach outperforms the baseline method in terms of effectiveness (precision vs. expert effort) independent of (1) the number of possible labels, (2) the size of the crowd, (3) the worker reliability, (4) the difficulty of the questions, and (5) the presence of spammers. This indicates that the improvements obtained with the presented approach are not specific to particular crowdsourcing setups, but generalize to a wide range of applications.

6.7 Robustness against expert mistakes

In §5.5, we discussed two types of erroneous answer validations, the expert wrongly deviates from the aggregation of crowd answers or wrongly confirms it, along with a simple confirmation check to detect mistakes of the second type.

Types of erroneous answer validations. To analyze which of the two erroneous validations is more likely to occur, we developed a validation tool [1] that enables an expert to give feedback on crowd answers and shows the aggregated crowd answer for an object during validation. We conducted an experiment with five experts that used the tool for the two datasets *twt* and *art*, which comprised the actual questions posted to the crowd. Their input was verified against the ground truth.

In general, the number of erroneous answer validations is small. For the *twt* dataset, all experts provide correct input. For the *art* dataset, 8% of the expert input is erroneous. For these cases, we find that, throughout, the respective answer from the crowd workers is also incorrect. This indicates that indeed, the wrong confirmation of an aggregated answer is the more likely type of mistake.

Detecting erroneous answer validations. Next, we evaluate the effectiveness of the confirmation check to detect erroneous answer validations by simulating expert mistakes. For a given probability p, we change the expert input from a correct validation to an incorrect validation. The experiment is conducted on all real-world datasets with the *hybrid* selection strategy and when triggering the confirmation check after each 1% number of total validations.

Table 6 shows the percentage of detected mistakes when increasing the probability of an expert mistake. Across all datasets, the vast majority of artificially inserted mistakes is detected. For example, even with a relatively high probability for erroneous answer validations (p=15%), all mistakes in expert input are detected.

Expert guidance and erroneous answer validations. Finally, we study the relation between expert effort and precision in the presence of expert mistakes. The confirmation check is run after each 1% number of total validations. Upon each detected mistake, we allow the expert to reconsider the respective input; i.e increment the expert effort by 1. The experiment is conducted using the real-world dataset *art*, for which the experts indeed made mistakes. To aim for the worst-case scenario, we use the validations from the expert with the most mistakes.

As illustrated in Figure 11, the precision obtained with the *hybrid* strategy is still much better than the baseline method. Moreover, the actual obtained precision values are close to those obtained without erroneous answer validations (see Figure 16 in Appendix C). This result indicates that our approach is robust against potential mistakes in expert input.

6.8 Cost trade-off: Experts vs crowd workers

In the previous experiments, we have evaluated different aspects of our guiding approach for reducing expert efforts. In this final set of experiments, we aim to show that our approach is able to achieve high precision within a reasonable cost for different crowdsourcing setups. Technically, we compare two strategies: (i) *EV*, our approach that uses an expert to validate crowd answers, and (ii) *WO*, we use only the crowd and add more crowd answers with the assumption that this will increase the correctness of the answer set (i.e. aggregated results are computed by using the traditional EM).

Cost model. Our cost model for this experiment covers monetary cost and completion time.

Monetary cost: We assume that the cost of an expert input is θ-times more expensive than an answer by a worker. To estimate θ, we first consider the answer cost of a crowd worker via the average wage on AMT, which is just under 2.00$/h [40]. For the cost of an answer by an expert, we consider salary standards of traditional workers and select the most expensive case, i.e., 25$/h, the average wage in Luxembourg [46]. Then, the ratio θ between the cost per answer of an expert and a worker is about $(25\$/h)/(2\$/h) = 12.5$.

Completion Time: Crowdsourcing in practice is often subject to a time constraint (e.g., 1 hour for simple tasks on AMT). In our setting, the completion time involves (1) *crowd time*, time for the crowd workers to answer and (2) *expert time*, time for the experts to provide input for all the questions that can be covered by the budget. Crowd time is often considered to be constant, since workers work concurrently [50]. Hence, the completion time is primarily determined by the expert time, which is derived from the number of expert inputs (assuming constant validation time for all questions).

Below, we consider a setting where m workers have been hired to answer n questions. With ϕ_0 as the average cost of asking crowd workers per object, the initial cost for deriving the answers is $n \times \phi_0$. To improve the quality of the answer set, two strategies may be followed. First, an expert can be asked to validate i answers (the EV approach), which incurs an additional cost of $\theta \times i$ or in

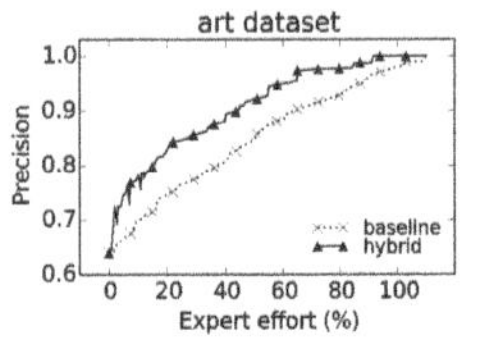

Figure 11: Guiding with expert mistakes

Dataset	p: probability of mistake			
	0.15	0.20	0.25	0.30
bb	100	100	94	82
rte	100	100	96	88
val	100	94	89	79
twt	100	100	92	87
art	100	92	88	81

Table 6: Percentage of detecting mistakes in expert validation

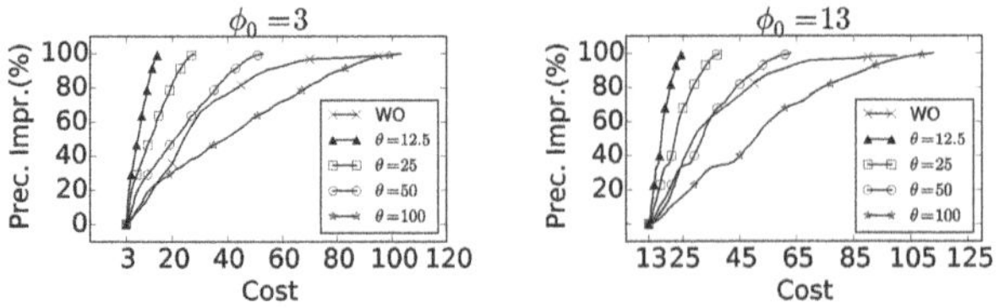

Figure 12: Collect more crowd answers vs. validate more

total $P_{EV} = \theta \times i + n \times \phi_0$. Second, the workers can be asked to answer more questions, which increases the average cost per object to $\phi > \phi_0$. Then, the total cost of the WO approach is $P_{WO} = n \times \phi$.

Trade-off with undefined budget. In general, there is a trade-off between the cost incurred by a crowdsourcing task and the result correctness. Higher cost, spent on answer validation by an expert or additional crowd answers, yields higher correctness of the aggregated answers. We analyze this trade-off to determine under which conditions hiring only additional crowd workers (*WO* approach) is less beneficial than hiring a validating expert (*EV* approach). Figure 12 illustrates the relation between the invested cost, normalized over the number of objects ($P_{WO}/n = \phi$ and $P_{EV}/n = \phi_0 + \theta \times i/n$), and the obtained improvement in precision for different expert-crowd cost ratios $\theta = 12.5, 25, 50, 100$ and initial costs $\phi_0 = 3, 13$.

The *EV* approach yields higher precision improvements for the same costs compared to the *WO* approach with different values of ϕ_0 and for $\theta = 12.5, 25, 50$. With $\phi_0 = 3$ and $\theta = 25$, for instance, to improve the precision by 80%, the EV approach requires a cost of 20 per object, while the cost of the WO approach is 40. Also, the WO approach does not achieve 100% precision even under high costs, due to faulty workers. Having more answers from these types of workers only increases the uncertainty in the answer set.

In sum, if high precision is desired, the EV approach yields better overall results. For instance, for a realistic setup with $\phi_0 = 13$ and $\theta = 12.5$, to achieve 100% precision improvement, our approach has a cost per object of 15. The WO approach, in turn, has a cost of 100, but is still not able to achieve 100% precision improvement. When expert input is very expensive ($\theta = 100$), increasing only the number of crowd workers yields better results. However, we consider an expert-crowd cost ratio of 100 to be unlikely in practice.

Trade-off with budget constraint. The results above indicate that, without budget constraints, the *EV* approach achieves higher precision with lower cost compared to the *WO* approach regardless of ϕ_0. However, using a fixed cost, the precision obtained with the *EV* approach depends on the value of the initial cost ϕ_0. We therefore analyze how to achieve the highest precision under a fixed budget b using the EV approach. That requires deciding how much of an overall budget should be spent on retrieving crowd answers. Finding an optimal value of ϕ_0 thereby determines the best budget allocation between the expert and the crowd workers. In practice, the budget b is bounded by the cost of using only an expert, i.e., $n \leq b \leq \theta \times n$. To parameterize the budget spent on expert feedback, we formulate it as $b = \rho \times \theta \times n$, where $\rho \in [1/\theta, 1]$.

Figure 13 illustrates the result correctness in terms of precision for different allocations of the budget to crowd workers ($\phi_0/(\rho \times \theta)$), when varying the ratio ρ and setting $\theta = 25$. As a reference, the figure also includes the result for the WO approach (crowd cost is 100%), which is a special case of the EV approach where all the budget is spent on crowd workers, i.e., $\theta \times i = 0$ and $\phi_0 = b/n$.

We observe that for each ratio ρ, there is an allocation point (ϕ_0) that maximizes precision. For instance, for $\rho = 0.4$, maximal precision is obtained with 75% of the budget being spent on crowd workers and 25% of the budget used for validation by an expert. Based on this analysis, we can therefore select the optimal allocation for a specific setup. Further, except for the case with little budget ($\rho = 0.3$), a distribution of the budget between the crowd workers and the validating expert leads to maximal precision, which highlights the benefits of integrating answer validation in a crowdsourcing setup.

Trade-off with budget and time constraints. Next, we consider a setup where the best budget allocation should be determined under both, budget and time constraints. Figure 14 extends the plot of the relation between the result precision and the budget allocation with the completion time captured by the amount of expert input (y2-axis). In this figure, point B denotes the intersection between the lines representing the time constraint (green dashed line) and the completion time (orange solid line). Based on point B, a region in which the time constraint is satisfied is identified, which, in Figure 14 is bounded by the range $[C, 100]$ in terms of the allocation of the budget to crowd workers. For this region, the maximum precision is denoted by point A. As a result, we have determined the budget allocation (x-value at point A) that yields the highest precision when satisfying both the time and budget constraint.

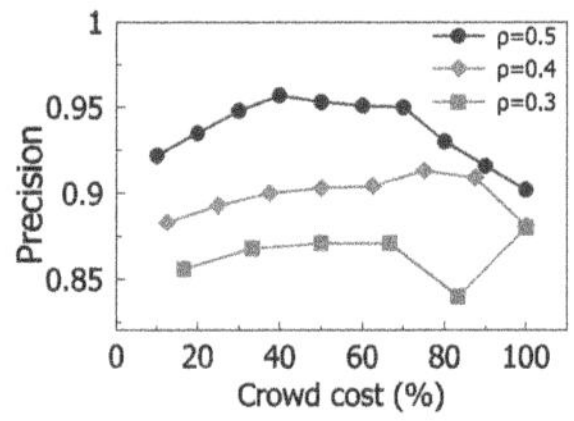

Figure 13: Allocation of fixed budget

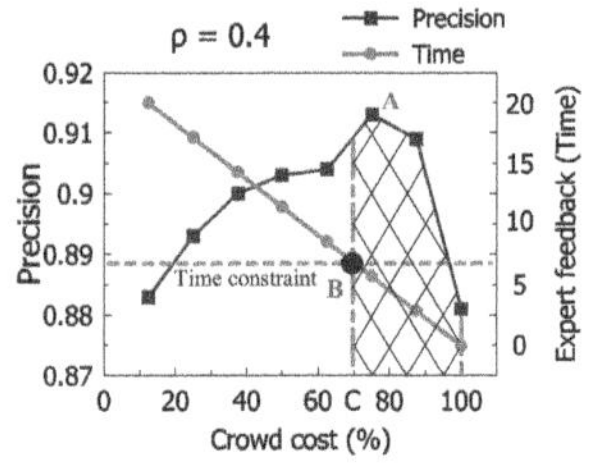

Figure 14: Balance with time and budget constraints

Finally, we analyzed the effects of faulty workers, worker reliability, and question difficulty, on the cost model and the handling of the trade-off. The details of these experiments are provided in Appendix D. We found that the presented approach of using an expert to validate crowd answers, in most cases, outperforms an approach that relies solely on crowd workers. Exceptions to this trend are observed only in borderline cases, e.g., if the budget is extremely small (meaning that only a small number of crowd workers can be hired in the first place) and experts are much more costly than crowd workers i.e $\theta \geq 100$ (which is very unlikely in practice as this means the tasks are overpaid or too difficult even for crowdsourcing). Hence, we conclude that the integration of an expert allows for more efficient crowdsourcing for a wide range of applications.

7. RELATED WORK

Crowdsourcing. Having discussed applications and types of crowdsourcing tasks already in §2, we turn to a discussion of the cost in crowdsourcing, including monetary costs and completion time. Several studies focused on minimizing cost when posting tasks [8, 50]. In this paper, we leverage existing works on task-posting mechanism as a black-box; i.e. all of the worker answers are collected in advance before being considered by our approach. The focus of our work is the guidance for minimizing a different aspect of crowdsourcing, i.e., the cost of validating crowd answers. As a side-effect, given a limited budget constraint, our approach can predict the optimal strategy of distributing the cost for the validation and for the crowd to achieve the highest output quality (see §6.8).

Regarding quality control in crowdsourcing, there is a plethora of automatic approaches that target an assessment of the worker quality, including expertise characterization [29] and spammer detection [32]. Complemented with a worker assessment mechanisms, answer aggregation tries to find the hidden ground truth from the answer set given by crowd workers. Answer aggregation methods can be classified into two categories: *non-iterative* and *iterative* approaches. Non-iterative approaches [32] use heuristic methods to compute a single aggregated value of each object separately. Iterative approaches [23] perform a series of convergent iterations by considering the answer set as a whole. Despite the above efforts, the results of automatic quality control are inherently uncertain, since they are heuristic-based and there is no technique that performs well in the general case [22]. To address this dilemma, the semi-automatic solution presented in this paper is to employ an expert to validate crowd answers.

Our approach aims at *guiding* an expert when *validating* input from crowd workers, which is different to other approaches for crowdsourcing that include experts, such as [20, 26, 27]. In particular, Karger et al. [27] rely on experts that know the reliability of crowd workers, a premise that is not realistic in the general setting for crowdsourcing explored in this work, to prove the optimality of their approach. Other work focuses on a related, but fundamentally different problem. The techniques presented in [20, 26] target the identification of correct labels for *new* objects based on the labels for known objects, whereas we aim at validation, i.e., finding the correct labels for known objects.

Truth Finding. Given a set of data items claimed by multiple sources, the truth finding (a.k.a. truth discovery) problem is to determine the true values of each claimed item, with various usages in information corroboration [15], and data fusion [13]. Similar to our crowdsourcing setting, existing work on truth finding also models the mutual reinforcing relationship between sources and data items, e.g., by a Bayesian model [52], maximum likelihood estimation [47], and latent credibility analysis [36]. In contrast to our setting, these techniques incorporate prior knowledge about various aspects of the source and the data, such as the dependence between sources [11] and the temporal dimension in evolving data [12]. As such, these techniques cannot be directly applied to our solution (workers perform the tasks individually, objects do not evolve over time). To the best of our knowledge, there is no work on employing answer validation by experts to check the results of automatic techniques. Therefore, our work on guiding validation effort can be tailored to the truth finding settings as well.

Recommendation systems. Close to our work is research on recommendation systems. Here, the core problem is, given an existing set of user ratings for particular items, to recommend one of these items that best fit a particular user in terms of information content [16]. This problem is similar to ours in the sense that we also select the objects with best information content (i.e., that yield the maximal uncertainty reduction) for answer validation. However, the underlying models of the two settings are completely different. In recommendation systems, the information of an item is measured by the notion of similarity: similar users would have similar preferences on similar items and vice-versa [41]. Whereas, this similarity assumption does not exist for workers and objects in crowdsourcing. Moreover, there is a also large body of work on recommendation systems studying malicious users [31], who provide untruthful ratings or reviews to manipulate the recommendation output. Although many detection techniques have been proposed, they cannot be applied in our context since they depend on the application domains and contextual features [35]. Most importantly, there is no method making use of validation input for identifying malicious users. As a result, our work on using a validating expert to handle spammers in crowdsourcing can be tailored for recommendation systems.

Guiding user feedback. Guiding user or expert feedback has been studied in different contexts. In the field of data integration, Jeffery et al. [24] proposed a decision theoretic framework to rank candidate matches for answer validation in order to improve the quality of a dataspace. Focusing on matching of data schemas in a network setting, Nguyen et al. [34] presented a reconciliation algorithm that leverages expert input. Yakout et al. [49], in turn, proposed an active-learning based process that requests expert input to help training classifiers in order to detect and repair erroneous data. Similar to these works, we rely on models from the fields of Decision Theory and Active Learning [42]. Despite the similarities in the applied models, there are two main differences between the aforementioned approaches to user guidance and the method presented here. First, in the above domains (data integration, schema matching), input stems from automatic tools, which renders it deterministic and traceable. In contrast, our methods have to cope with human input, which is unreliable, potentially non-deterministic or even malicious. Second, existing guidance methods aim at a different goal, which means that measures for the benefit of expert input are highly domain dependent (e.g., the approach in [24] is purely driven by the size of query results and independent of the source of user input). Our method, in turn, is tailored to the specific characteristics of crowdsourcing scenarios.

8. CONCLUSIONS AND FUTURE WORK

This paper proposed techniques to support an expert in validating crowd answers obtained for a crowdsourcing task. Based on the requirements identified for such techniques, we presented an answer validation process that features two steps: *answer aggregation* and *expert guidance*. The former relates to the creation of a probabilistic model that assesses the reliability of workers and the correctness of the crowd answers. The latter features different strategies for guiding an expert in the validation: worker-driven, uncertainty-driven, and a hybrid approach. The worker-driven method aims at detecting and removing faulty workers from the community, whereas the uncertainty-driven strives for a maximal improvement of the answer correctness under the assumption of truthful workers. Since both goals help to improve the overall result, our hybrid approach combines both methods with a dynamic weighting scheme.

Our evaluation showed that our techniques outperform respective baselines methods significantly and save up to 50% of expert efforts. Also, in most cases, close to perfect result correctness is reached with expert input for only 20% of the considered objects.

In future work, we aim to explore dynamic selection of the answer aggregation method. Since these methods have different strengths and shortcomings [22], expert input may be used to dynamically choose the most appropriate aggregation strategy. We also intend to lift our approach to other types of crowdsourcing tasks such as *continuous*, *partial-function*, and *similarity* tasks. For example, *continuous* tasks map to *discrete* tasks by changing probability mass functions to probability density functions and sums to integrals.

Acknowledgment. The research has received funding from the EU-FP7 EINS project (grant 288021) and the ScienceWise project.

9. REFERENCES

[1] https://code.google.com/p/crowdvalidator/.

[2] http://www.crowdflower.com/.

[3] http://www.mturk.com/.

[4] Y. Amsterdamer, Y. Grossman, T. Milo, and P. Senellart. Crowd mining. In *SIGMOD*, pages 241–252, 2013.

[5] A. Arasu, M. Götz, and R. Kaushik. On active learning of record matching packages. In *SIGMOD*, pages 783–794, 2010.

[6] A. Artikis, M. Weidlich, F. Schnitzler, I. Boutsis, T. Liebig, N. Piatkowski, C. Bockermann, K. Morik, V. Kalogeraki, J. Marecek, et al. Heterogeneous stream processing and crowdsourcing for urban traffic management. In *EDBT*, pages 712–723, 2014.

[7] J. A. Blakeley, P.-A. Larson, and F. W. Tompa. Efficiently updating materialized views. In *SIGMOD*, pages 61–71, 1986.

[8] C. C. Cao, J. She, Y. Tong, and L. Chen. Whom to ask?: jury selection for decision making tasks on micro-blog services. In *VLDB*, pages 1495–1506, 2012.

[9] A. P. Dawid and A. M. Skene. Maximum likelihood estimation of observer error-rates using the EM algorithm. *J. R. Stat. Soc.*, pages 20–28, 1979.

[10] G. Demartini, D. E. Difallah, and P. Cudré-Mauroux. Zencrowd: Leveraging probabilistic reasoning and crowdsourcing techniques for large-scale entity linking. In *WWW*, pages 469–478, 2012.

[11] X. L. Dong, L. Berti-Equille, Y. Hu, and D. Srivastava. Solomon: Seeking the truth via copying detection. In *VLDB*, pages 1617–1620, 2010.

[12] X. L. Dong, L. Berti-Equille, and D. Srivastava. Truth discovery and copying detection in a dynamic world. In *VLDB*, pages 562–573, 2009.

[13] X. L. Dong and F. Naumann. Data fusion: resolving data conflicts for integration. In *VLDB*, pages 1654–1655, 2009.

[14] C. Eckart and G. Young. The approximation of one matrix by another of lower rank. *Psychometrika*, pages 211–218, 1936.

[15] A. Galland, S. Abiteboul, A. Marian, and P. Senellart. Corroborating information from disagreeing views. In *WSDM*, pages 131–140, 2010.

[16] F. Garcin, B. Faltings, R. Jurca, and N. Joswig. Rating aggregation in collaborative filtering systems. In *RecSys*, pages 349–352, 2009.

[17] C. Gokhale, S. Das, A. Doan, J. F. Naughton, N. Rampalli, J. Shavlik, and X. Zhu. Corleone: Hands-off crowdsourcing for entity matching. In *SIGMOD*, pages 601–612, 2014.

[18] D. E. Goldberg. *Genetic Algorithms in Search, Optimization and Machine Learning*. Addison-Wesley Longman, 1989.

[19] R. G. Gomes, P. Welinder, A. Krause, and P. Perona. Crowdclustering. In *NIPS*, pages 558–566, 2011.

[20] Q. Hu, Q. He, H. Huang, K. Chiew, and Z. Liu. Learning from crowds under experts supervision. In *PAKDD*, pages 200–211. 2014.

[21] Z. Huang, A. Olteanu, and K. Aberer. Credibleweb: a platform for web credibility evaluation. In *CHI*, pages 1887–1892, 2013.

[22] N. Q. V. Hung, N. T. Tam, L. N. Tran, and K. Aberer. An evaluation of aggregation techniques in crowdsourcing. In *WISE*, pages 1–15, 2013.

[23] P. G. Ipeirotis, F. Provost, and J. Wang. Quality management on amazon mechanical turk. HCOMP, pages 64–67, 2010.

[24] S. R. Jeffery, M. J. Franklin, and A. Y. Halevy. Pay-as-you-go user feedback for dataspace systems. In *SIGMOD*, pages 847–860, 2008.

[25] H. J. Jung and M. Lease. Improving quality of crowdsourced labels via probabilistic matrix factorization. In *HCOMP*, pages 101–106, 2012.

[26] H. Kajino, Y. Tsuboi, I. Sato, and H. Kashima. Learning from crowds and experts. In *HCOMP*, pages 107–113, 2012.

[27] D. R. Karger, S. Oh, and D. Shah. Iterative learning for reliable crowdsourcing systems. In *NIPS*, pages 1953–1961, 2011.

[28] G. Karypis and V. Kumar. Metis-unstructured graph partitioning and sparse matrix ordering system, version 2.0. 1995.

[29] G. Kazai, J. Kamps, and N. Milic-Frayling. Worker types and personality traits in crowdsourcing relevance labels. In *CIKM*, pages 1941–1944, 2011.

[30] C.-W. Ko, J. Lee, and M. Queyranne. An exact algorithm for maximum entropy sampling. *Operations Research*, pages 684–691, 1995.

[31] S. K. Lam and J. Riedl. Shilling recommender systems for fun and profit. In *WWW*, pages 393–402, 2004.

[32] K. Lee, J. Caverlee, and S. Webb. The social honeypot project: protecting online communities from spammers. In *WWW*, pages 1139–1140, 2010.

[33] X. Liu, M. Lu, B. C. Ooi, Y. Shen, S. Wu, and M. Zhang. Cdas: a crowdsourcing data analytics system. In *VLDB*, pages 1040–1051, 2012.

[34] Q. V. H. Nguyen, T. T. Nguyen, Z. Miklós, K. Aberer, A. Gal, and M. Weidlich. Pay-as-you-go reconciliation in schema matching networks. In *ICDE*, pages 220–231, 2014.

[35] M. O'Mahony, N. Hurley, N. Kushmerick, and G. Silvestre. Collaborative recommendation: A robustness analysis. *TOIT*, pages 344–377, 2004.

[36] J. Pasternack and D. Roth. Latent credibility analysis. In *WWW*, pages 1009–1020, 2013.

[37] A. J. Quinn and B. B. Bederson. Human computation: a survey and taxonomy of a growing field. In *CHI*, pages 1403–1412, 2011.

[38] V. C. Raykar and S. Yu. Ranking annotators for crowdsourced labeling tasks. In *NIPS*, pages 1809–1817, 2011.

[39] J. Reason. *Human error*. Cambridge university press, 1990.

[40] J. Ross, L. Irani, M. Silberman, A. Zaldivar, and B. Tomlinson. Who are the crowdworkers?: shifting demographics in mechanical turk. In *CHI*, pages 2863–2872, 2010.

[41] N. Rubens, D. Kaplan, and M. Sugiyama. Active learning in recommender systems. In *Recommender Systems Handbook*, pages 735–767. Springer, 2011.

[42] S. J. Russell and P. Norvig. *Artificial Intelligence: A Modern Approach*. Pearson Education, 2003.

[43] C. E. Shannon. A mathematical theory of communication. *SIGMOBILE*, pages 3–55, 2001.

[44] C. Sun, N. Rampalli, F. Yang, and A. Doan. Chimera: Large-scale classification using machine learning, rules, and crowdsourcing. In *VLDB*, pages 1529–1540, 2014.

[45] J. Surowiecki. The wisdom of crowds: Why the many are smarter than the few and how collective wisdom shapes business, economies. *Economies, Societies and Nations*, 2004.

[46] TRAVAIL. Global wage report 2012-13. International Labour Organization (ILO), 2012.

[47] D. Wang, L. Kaplan, H. Le, and T. Abdelzaher. On truth discovery in social sensing: A maximum likelihood estimation approach. In *IPSN*, pages 233–244, 2012.

[48] P. Welinder and P. Perona. Online crowdsourcing: rating annotators and obtaining cost-effective labels. In *CVPRW*, pages 25–32, 2010.

[49] M. Yakout, A. K. Elmagarmid, J. Neville, M. Ouzzani, and I. F. Ilyas. Guided data repair. In *VLDB*, pages 279–289, 2011.

[50] T. Yan, V. Kumar, and D. Ganesan. Crowdsearch: Exploiting crowds for accurate real-time image search on mobile phones. In *MobiSys*, pages 77–90, 2010.

[51] C. J. Zhang, L. Chen, H. V. Jagadish, and C. C. Cao. Reducing uncertainty of schema matching via crowdsourcing. In *VLDB*, pages 757–768, 2013.

[52] B. Zhao, B. I. Rubinstein, J. Gemmell, and J. Han. A bayesian approach to discovering truth from conflicting sources for data integration. In *VLDB*, pages 550–561, 2012.

APPENDIX

A. FURTHER DETAILS ON DATASETS

Real-world data. We have used real-world datasets from different domains, namely *bluebird (bb)*, *rte*, *valence (val)*, *tweet (twt)*, and *article (art)*. In the *bb* dataset, workers have to identify one of two types of birds in an image. The crowdsourcing tasks of the *rte* dataset comprise two sentences and workers need to assert whether one sentence can be inferred from the other one. In the *val* dataset, workers are asked to annotate whether a headline expresses positive or negative meaning. The tasks for the *twt* and *art* datasets are both about sentiment analysis in which the workers need to evaluate the sentiment of a tweet or a scientific article. However, the questions of the *art* dataset are more difficult than the questions of the *twt* dataset as the sentiment of scientific articles are harder to analyze. All datasets are publicly available including the ground truth which is provided by the dataset owners.

Synthetic data:. We used several generated datasets. Since this data should exhibit similar characteristics as real-world data, we considered several parameters for the data generation, in particular: (i) n – the number of objects, (ii) k – the number of workers, (iii) m – the number of labels, (iv) r – the reliability of normal workers, reflecting the probability of their answers being correct and (v) σ – the percentage of spammers in the worker population. For the synthetic dataset, we also simulated the ground truth (the correct labels) for the objects. However, it is not known by the simulated workers and only used to simulate the answer validations.

An important part of our synthetic data is the crowd simulation. We follow a practical guideline [22] to simulate the different worker characteristics of the crowd. Specially, we distribute the worker population into α% reliable workers, β% sloppy workers and γ% spammers. According to a study on crowd population at real-world crowdsourcing services [29], we assign the default values of these parameters as follows: $\alpha = 43$, $\beta = 32$ and $\gamma = 25$. In the experiments, the distribution of the worker types is the same as discussed unless stated otherwise.

B. RELATION BETWEEN UNCERTAINTY AND PRECISION

In this experiment, we study the relation between the uncertainty of the probabilistic answer set and the precision of the deterministic assignment. To this end, we perform the uncertainty-driven expert guidance on a synthetic dataset, in which we vary the number of workers from 20 to 40, the percentage of spammers from 15% to 35%, and the reliability of the workers from 0.65 to 0.75. For each combination setting of the parameters, we guide the answer validation until precision reaches 1.0 and report the uncertainty of answer aggregation along the way.

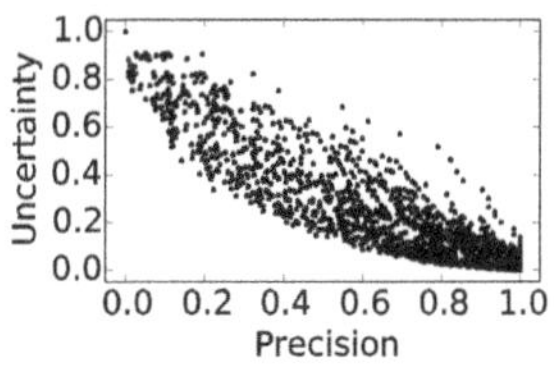

Figure 15: Relationship – uncertainty vs. precision

Figure 15 depicts the results in terms of the relation between precision and normalized uncertainty (i.e., dividing the uncertainty values by the maximum uncertainty obtained in the run). We observe a strong correlation between both measures, which is further supported by the Pearson's correlation coefficient of -0.9461. Hence, as the uncertainty decreases, the precision of the deterministic assignment increases. Also, there is a concentration of data points for precision values in $[0.8, 1.0]$ and normalized uncertainty values in $[0, 0.2]$. Hence, our approach helps to achieve near-perfect precision even when the uncertainty is not reduced to 0.

C. EVALUATIONS OF EXPERT GUIDANCE (CONT'D)

In the following experiments, we analyze the effects of the guiding strategy with different crowdsourcing setup, including the number of labels, the number of workers, worker reliability, question difficulty, and the presence of spammers. Since these experiments (except the experiment on question difficulty) require changing the workers' characteristics (which is not known for the real-world datasets), they are conducted using synthetic data.

We compare the results obtained with our guiding approach (*hybrid*) to a baseline guiding method that selects the object with the highest uncertainty to seek feedback (*baseline*):

$$select(O) = \arg\max_{o \in O} H(o)$$

Our *hybrid* approach is different from the baseline as it further considers the consequences of validation in addition to the mutually reinforcing relations between the reliability of workers and assignment correctness.

Effects of the number of labels. Many crowdsourcing applications are designed with multiple-choice questions, i.e., applications show different numbers of possible assignment labels. To evaluate the effect of the number of labels on the performance of our approach, we rely on a synthetic dataset containing 50 objects and 20 workers. The worker reliability is set to 0.65 for non-spammers and the spammers are simulated to follow the distribution discussed in Appendix A. We report the precision while varying the expert efforts (until precision reaches 1.0) and the number of labels ($m = 2$ and $m = 4$).

Figure 17 shows that our approach consistently outperforms the baseline method. Interestingly, the difference between the two approaches is very large in the setup with 4 assignment labels. For example, our approach (*hybrid*) increases precision to 1.0 using only 40% of expert input. However, the precision of 0.99 is already achieved using 10% of expert feedbacks. We can explain this observation as follows: with a higher number of labels, crowd workers are less likely to choose the correct answer by chance. Hence, our approach is able to detect reliable workers faster, which leads to a better overall performance. To test for the most challenging case, we fix the number of labels to 2 in the remaining experiments.

Effect of the number of workers. The idea behind crowdsourcing is that individual crowd answers complement each other. Thus, the aggregation of answers should be closer to the truth as more workers participate [45]. To verify this hypothesis, we vary the number of workers k from 20 to 40 that assign one of two labels to 50 objects. Figure 18 illustrates an important finding that our approach leads to better results for any number of workers. Taking a fixed amount of expert input, precision increases if more workers are employed. The reason is the widely quoted 'wisdom of the crowd' [45], which eventually leads to better precision. Another finding is that the precision improvement with the same amount of

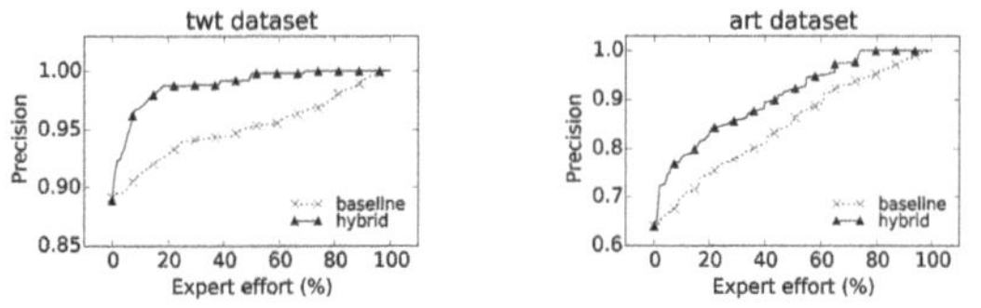

Figure 16: Effects of question difficulty

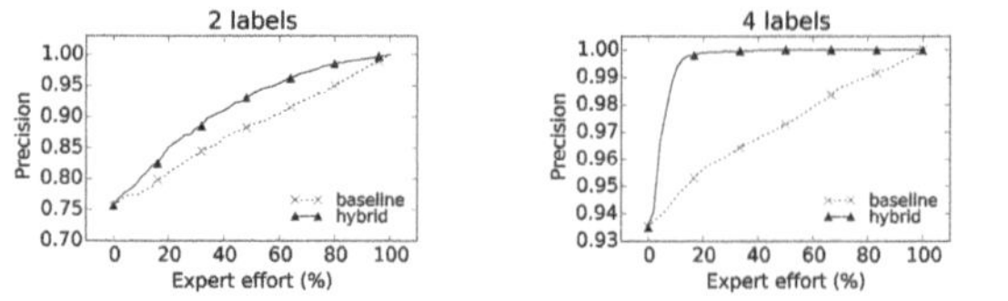

Figure 17: Effect of number of labels

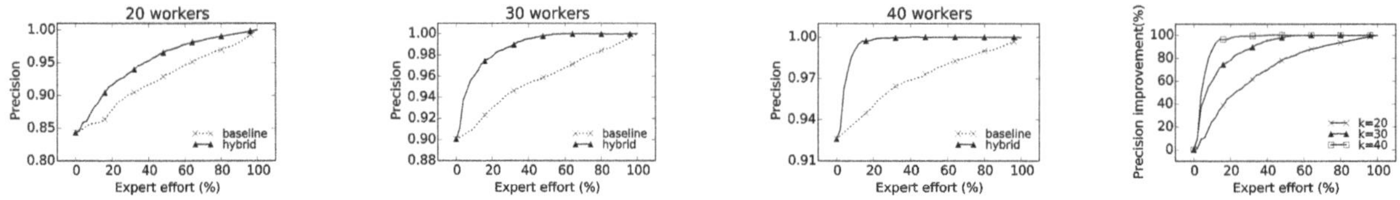

Figure 18: Effect of number of workers

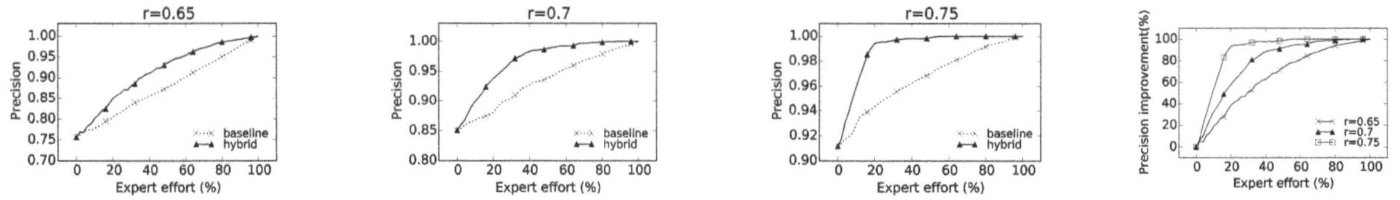

Figure 19: Effect of worker reliability

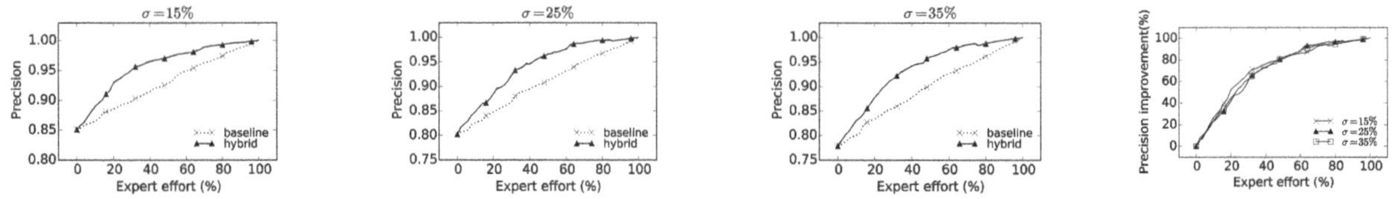

Figure 20: Effect of spammers

expert input is higher if we have more workers (most right plot in Figure 18). This is expected since, by having more workers, we acquire more answers for the same question, which results in better estimates of assignment probabilities and worker reliabilities. Our approach, thus, has a higher chance to select the objects that lead to a large gain in correctness.

In sum, the two findings suggest that increasing the number of workers is beneficial not only for computing assignment probabilities, but also for guiding answer validation. For the remaining experiments, we fix the number of workers to be the smallest tested value ($k = 20$), which is the most challenging scenario.

Effect of worker reliability. We further explored the effects of the worker reliability r on the effectiveness of our approach. As above, we used a dataset of 20 workers assigning one out of two labels to 50 objects. We then varied the reliability of the non-spammer workers from 0.65 to 0.75.

Figure 19 illustrates a significant improvement in precision using our approach (*hybrid*) compared to the *baseline* method. For instance, if the average worker reliability is 0.7, to achieve a precision of 0.93, our approach requires expert input for 20% of the objects, whereas the baseline method requires input for 40% of the objects. In other words, the amount of efforts the baseline method requires is twice that of our approach. Also, with the same amount of feedback, precision is increased if the average reliability of the workers is higher (most right plot in Figure 19). This is because an answer set provided by reliable workers requires less validation than an answer set coming from unreliable workers.

Effect of spammers. In this experiment, we studied the robustness of our guiding approach to spammers using the same dataset as in the previous experiment (20 workers, two labels, 50 objects). We varied the percentage of spammers σ in the worker population from 15% to 35% to analyze the effect of these spammers.

Independent of the percentage of spammers, our approach (*hybrid*) outperforms the *baseline* method, see Figure 20. The largest difference between the two approaches is observed when the percentage of spammers is 15%. In that case, to achieve a precision of 0.95, our approach needs 35% of expert input, while the baseline method requires 70%. Regarding the precision improvement (right most plot in Figure 20), the results are relatively similar across different percentages of spammers. For instance, using 40% of expert input, we are able to increase the precision of the deterministic assignment by 70%, independent of the percentage of spammers. Hence, our approach is indeed robust to the presence of spammers.

Effects of question difficulty. Beside worker reliability, another factor that can affect the performance of our method is the question difficulty. For hard questions, even reliable workers may give incorrect answers. As a result, there is a need to analyze the effects of question difficulty on the performance of our approach. We compared our approach with the baseline approach using two datasets: *twt* and *art*, where the questions in the *art* dataset is harder than the other. The experimental results are shown in Figure 16, where the x-axis depicts the expert efforts while the y-axis illustrates the precision of the deterministic assignment.

We observe that our approach is able to outperform the baseline approach for both datasets, meaning that the approach is robust against question difficulty. For instance, for the *twt* dataset with easy question, our approach needs only 15% of expert effort to achieve a precision of 0.95 while the baseline approach needs over 50% of expert efforts. Also, the performance of our approach when the questions are easy is better than in the setup with hard questions. This is expected and can be explained as follows. In the dataset with easy questions, most of the workers are able to give the correct answers, which makes the uncertainty in the dataset low. As

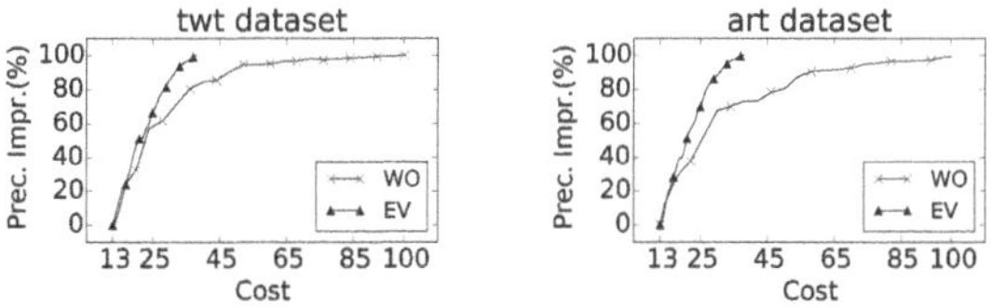

Figure 21: Effect of question difficulty on cost

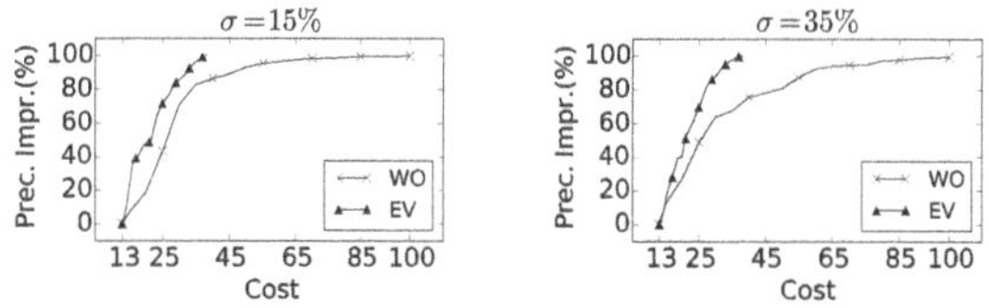

Figure 22: Effects of spammers on cost

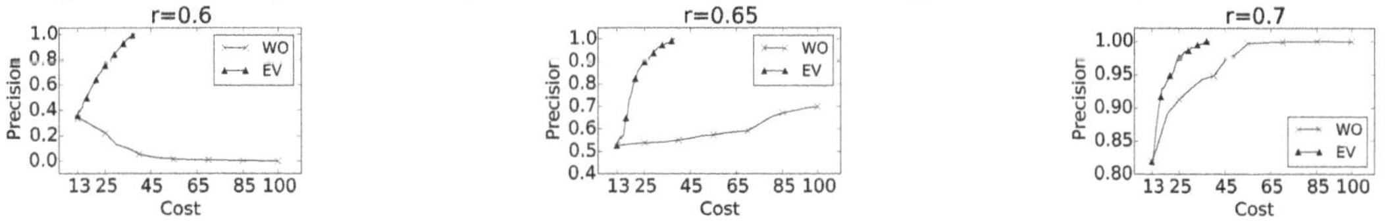

Figure 23: Effects of worker reliability on cost

a result, with the same amount of feedbacks, we can improve the precision higher than when the questions are hard.

D. COST TRADE-OFFS (CONT'D)

We complement the experiments reported in §6.8 by studying the effects of question difficulty, spammers, and worker reliability when comparing the *EV* approach with the *WO* approach.

Effects of question difficulty. In this experiment, we compare our EV approach with the WO approach with respect to the difficulty of the questions. We remove the answers from the answer matrix randomly such that 13 answers remain per question ($\phi_0 = 13$). Then, to simulate the addition of answers for the WO approach, we add the answers back to the questions. We fix the expert-crowd cost ratio to $\theta = 25$ and average the results over 100 experiment runs.

The experimental results are shown in Figure 21 where the X-axis depicts the normalized cost and the Y-axis measures the precision improvement of the deterministic assignment. The precision improvement of the EV approach is always higher than that of the WO approach, indicating that our EV approach is robust against the effects of question difficulty.

Effects of spammers. In this experiment, we analyze the effects of spammers by varying the percentage of spammers in the dataset from 15% to 35%. The experiment is conducted on the synthetic dataset with $\phi_0 = 13, \theta = 25$.

The results illustrated in Figure 22 show the benefits of using our approach with different percentages of spammers. The EV approach is able to achieve high precision improvement with a small amount of cost. For instance, when $\sigma = 35\%$, to improve the precision by 90%, a cost of 30 is required for the EV approach while the WO approach needs twice the amount. Also, the more spammers are part of the population, the better becomes the performance of the EV approach regarding the WO approach. For example, the difference in cost to achieve 90% precision improvement is about 10 when the percentage of spammers is 15%, but this increases three times to 30 as the percentage of spammers increases to 35%. Again, the reason is that as the percentage of spammer increases, the WO suffers from adding more answers as they are more likely to come from unreliable workers.

Effects of worker reliability. Worker reliability can affect the quality of crowd answers, thus also affects the cost model. If the worker reliability is high, the expert can spend less effort to give feedbacks as most of the answers are already correct. On the other hand, when the worker reliability is low, more feedbacks from the expert is required to achieve the same amount of precision. In this experiment, we analyze the effects of worker reliability on the cost of validating the crowd answers by varying the reliability of the normal workers from 0.6 to 0.7. Similar to the above experiment, we fix the following parameter: $\phi_0 = 13$, $\theta = 25$ and the workers population is simulated as discussed in §6.1.

The obtained results are illustrated in Figure 23, which highlights the relation between the cost normalized over each question and the precision of the deterministic assignment. Interestingly, when the reliability of the workers is 0.6, the precision of the deterministic assignment using the WO approach converges to 0 as we add more answers. The reason is that as we decrease the worker reliability, the average worker reliability becomes less than 0.5, which makes the precision converge to 0. This shows that adding more answers to the answer set may not improve but reduce the quality due to unreliable workers. When the reliability of the workers is 0.65, the precision of the deterministic assignment using the WO approach improves very slowly as the average reliability of the whole population is about 0.5. On the other hand, when the reliability of the workers is 0.7, the precision of the WO approach converges to 1. Yet, it requires higher cost to reach the same amount of precision as the EV approach. In summary, this experiment shows that our approach is robust against the reliability of the workers.

E. HARDNESS OF THE EFFORT MINIMIZATION PROBLEM

Now we consider a restricted version of Problem 1 in which we narrow down some problem conditions. First, instead of finding the minimal sequence, we consider the effort minimization as the identification of a minimal set $D = \{d_0, d_1, \ldots, d_n\} \in \mathcal{R}(\Delta, b)$. In other words, different sets of validation inputs will lead to different uncertainty values of the output. Second, we consider the reconciliation goal Δ as a thresholding condition defined on the joint entropy of the validated objects; i.e. $H(D) \geq \delta$. In other words, we select for validation the objects that lie on the edge of right and wrong, which is the key point to the effort minimization, rather than treating every object equally. As such, the effort minimization problem can be reformulated as:

$$\underset{D \subseteq O, |D| \leq k}{\arg\max}\ H(D) \tag{16}$$

This formulation can be interpreted as follows. We find a set of objects (with size as small as possible) for validation such that their joint entropy is maximal. In general, this problem is known to be NP-hard when the random variables of D are not independent [30], which is the case of our objects. Consequently, Problem 1 is harder than Equation16, given that finding the minimal sequence is difficult than finding the minimal set. Moreover, the goal Δ could be defined more complex. Due to the dependency between the objects via the crowd answers, satisfying Δ might need to look-ahead not only possible validation inputs of the objects but also the consequences of different orders of the validation.

iCrowd: An Adaptive Crowdsourcing Framework

Ju Fan[‡] Guoliang Li[†] Beng Chin Ooi[‡] Kian-lee Tan[‡] Jianhua Feng[†]

[‡]School of Computing, National University of Singapore, Singapore.
[†]Department of Computer Science, TNList, Tsinghua University, Beijing, China.
{fanj, ooibc, tankl}@comp.nus.edu.sg; {liguoliang,fengjh}@tsinghua.edu.cn

ABSTRACT

Crowdsourcing is widely accepted as a means for resolving tasks that machines are not good at. Unfortunately, Crowdsourcing may yield relatively low-quality results if there is no proper quality control. Although previous studies attempt to eliminate "bad" workers by using qualification tests, the accuracies estimated from qualifications may not be accurate, because workers have diverse accuracies across tasks. Thus, the quality of the results could be further improved by selectively assigning tasks to the workers who are well acquainted with the tasks. To this end, we propose an adaptive crowdsourcing framework, called *iCrowd*. *iCrowd* on-the-fly estimates accuracies of a worker by evaluating her performance on the completed tasks, and predicts which tasks the worker is well acquainted with. When a worker requests for a task, *iCrowd* assigns her a task, to which the worker has the highest estimated accuracy among all online workers. Once a worker submits an answer to a task, *iCrowd* analyzes her answer and adjusts estimation of her accuracies to improve subsequent task assignments. This paper studies the challenges that arise in *iCrowd*. The first is how to estimate diverse accuracies of a worker based on her completed tasks. The second is instant task assignment. We deploy *iCrowd* on Amazon Mechanical Turk, and conduct extensive experiments on real datasets. Experimental results show that *iCrowd* achieves higher quality than existing approaches.

Categories and Subject Descriptors

H.3.3 [**Information Storage and Retrieval**]: Information Search and Retrieval—*Information filtering*

Keywords

Crowdsourcing; Quality control; Adaptive task assignment

1. INTRODUCTION

Crowdsourcing outsources tasks for solutions from an unknown group of people (aka workers), which is indeed useful to many real-world applications, e.g., image search, entity resolution, answering database-hard queries [24, 23, 27, 28, 12, 32]. Due to its openness, crowdsourcing yields relatively low-quality results, or even noise, which attracts great interest in devising good quality control methods [17]. Existing methods [32, 18, 30] employ a *redundancy*-based strategy which publishes a crowdsourcing task to multiple workers and derives the result by aggregating worker answers. A naïve aggregation approach is majority voting that chooses the answer that the majority of the workers yield as the result. Recently, more sophisticated approaches have been proposed and they can be broadly classified into two categories. The *gold-injected* approaches [22] leverage small amounts of tasks with ground truth to estimate workers' quality, while the *EM*-based approaches [31, 8] simultaneously estimate worker quality and predict aggregated results using an Expectation-Maximization (EM) strategy. Moreover, existing approaches further improve the quality by eliminating "bad" workers. A well-known way is to use *qualification tests* to distinguish bad and good workers, and stop assigning tasks to workers that cannot give good answers to the qualification tasks.

Although existing methods perform well in simple crowdsourcing tasks, such as image labeling, they may have limitations on more complicated crowdsourcing tasks that require domain knowledge. In these tasks, workers may have diverse accuracies across tasks, as they are usually good at tasks in domains they are familiar with but may provide low-quality answers in unfamiliar domains. Take crowdsourced entity resolution [32] as an example. A worker acquainted with Samsung stands a better chance to correctly differentiate the models "Note4" and "S4", while she may not be good at tasks about iPad and cannot identify that "iPad with Retina display" is colloquially referred to as "iPad 4". Workers with different backgrounds may be good at different topics: a basketball fan stands a better chance to correctly annotate tables related to NBA, while a film enthusiast is more reliable for tables involving Hollywood films. Similar observations can be found in other tasks. We have conducted empirical investigation on two complicated crowdsourcing tasks, evaluating quality of Yahoo Answers and comparing items (e.g., which car is more fuel efficient), and report empirical observations of accuracy diversity in Figure 6.

The accuracy diversity in crowdsourcing engenders many challenges, making existing solutions inadequate for producing high-quality result. On the one hand, a worker, who gives good answers to qualification tests, may not provide promising answers to other assigned tasks. As such, the existing approaches may over- or under-estimate workers' ac-

SIGMOD'15, May 31 – June 4, 2015, Melbourne, Victoria, Australia.

http://dx.doi.org/10.1145/2723372.2750550.

Table 1: Microtasks for verifying whether two entities are matched.

Microtask	Verifying two entities	Tokens
t_1	(iphone 4 WiFi 32GB, iphone four 3G black)	{iphone 4 WiFi 32GB four 3G black}
t_2	(ipod touch 32GB WiFi, ipod touch headphone)	{ipod touch 32GB WiFi headphone}
t_3	(ipad 3 WiFi 32GB black, new ipad cover white)	{ipad 3 WiFi 32GB black new cover white}
t_4	(iphone four WiFi 16GB, iphone four 3G 16GB)	{iphone four WiFi 16GB 3G}
t_5	(iphone 4 case black, iphone 4 WiFi 32GB)	{iphone 4 case black WiFi 32GB}
t_6	(iphone 4 WiFi 32GB, iphone four WiFi 32GB)	{iphone 4 WiFi 32GB four}
t_7	(ipod touch 32GB WiFi, ipod touch case black)	{ipod touch 32GB WiFi case black}
t_8	(ipod touch headphone, ipod nano headphone)	{ipod touch nano headphone}
t_9	(ipod touch WiFi, ipod nano headphone)	{ipod touch WiFi nano headphone}
t_{10}	(ipad 3 WiFi 32GB black, iphone 4 cover white)	{ipad 3 WiFi 32GB black iphone 4 cover white}
t_{11}	(ipad 4 WiFi 16GB, ipad retina display WiFi 16GB)	{ipad 4 WiFi 16GB retina display}
t_{12}	(ipad 3 cover white, new ipad cover white)	{ipad 3 cover white new}

curacies and thus result in unreliable aggregated results. On the other hand, existing approaches neglect a fact that we can *adaptively* assign tasks to workers who have expertise on the tasks to further improve the quality, instead of random task assignment without considering workers' expertise.

To address the limitations of existing approaches, we propose an adaptive crowdsourcing framework, called *iCrowd*. *iCrowd* on-the-fly estimates accuracies of a worker by evaluating her performance on the completed tasks, and infers worker's accuracies on similar tasks. When a worker requests for a task, the framework assigns the worker a task, to which the worker has the highest estimated accuracy among all online workers. Once a worker submits her answer to a task, *iCrowd* analyzes her answer and adaptively adjusts the accuracy estimation to improve any subsequent task assignments. In this way, *iCrowd* can effectively predict which workers are more appropriate for a task, and adaptively assigns the task to these high-quality workers.

We address two main research challenges that arise in adaptive crowdsourcing. The first one is how to estimate the *diverse* accuracies of workers based on their completed tasks. To address this challenge, we propose an accuracy estimation method by considering the "similarity" of tasks: a worker may have comparable accuracies on tasks in similar domains. We first construct a graph to model similarity of tasks and evaluate worker accuracies on her completed tasks. The second one is instant task assignment based on the estimated accuracies. As workers are generally impatient to wait for too long for a task assignment, we need to efficiently assign tasks to the workers. We develop efficient algorithms to support instant task assignment. Since existing platforms, such as Amazon Mechanical Turk (AMT) [2], have no functionality to support assigning tasks to workers, we develop an *iCrowd* system which iteratively communicates with the platforms to receive task requests from workers, assign tasks to them, and obtain answers from the workers.

To summarize, we make the following contributions.

(1) We formulate the problem of adaptive crowdsourcing and develop a framework *iCrowd* to support adaptive crowdsourcing in existing crowdsourcing platforms (see Section 2).

(2) We propose a graph-based estimation model to estimate the accuracies of a worker based on her completed tasks, which can tackle the diverse accuracies of workers across tasks and provide accurate estimation (see Section 3).

(3) We devise an adaptive assignment framework, prove that the optimal task assignment problem is NP-hard, and develop a greedy algorithm to enable instant task assignments (see Section 4).

(4) We deploy *iCrowd* on AMT and conduct extensive experiments on two real datasets. Experimental results show that *iCrowd* achieves 10% - 20% improvement on accuracy compared with state-of-the-art approaches (see Section 6).

2. AN OVERVIEW OF ADAPTIVE CROWDSOURCING

2.1 Problem Statement

Microtasks. Consider a requester who publishes a set of microtasks $\mathcal{T} = \{t_1, t_2, \ldots t_m\}$. For ease of presentation, each microtask is a binary microtask with YES/NO choices. Note that our techniques can be extended to microtasks with more than two choices. Table 1 provides twelve microtasks for *entity resolution*. Each microtask wants workers to verify whether two records (in the second column) are matched as a same product model. For example, t_1 requires workers to verify whether "iphone 4 WiFi 32GB" and "iphone four 3G black" are duplicated models. The worker, who has been assigned with t_1, would answer YES if she agrees that they are the same product, or NO otherwise.

Workers. A set of workers $\mathcal{W} = \{w_1, w_2, \ldots, w_n\}$ will work on microtasks in $\mathcal{T}$. Note that worker set in crowdsourcing is *dynamic*: any existing worker may become *inactive* by stopping work on $\mathcal{T}$ while new workers may become *active*. Moreover, since workers are prone to errors [22], answers provided by them may not be always correct. To predict whether a worker can correctly answer a microtask, we introduce *accuracy* defined as below.

DEFINITION 1 (ACCURACY). *The accuracy of a worker $w \in \mathcal{W}$ on a microtask $t_i \in \mathcal{T}$, denoted by p_i^w, is the probability $p_i^w = Pr\{w$ correctly answers $t_i\}$.*

For simplicity, we use vector $\mathbf{p}^w = \{p_1^w, p_2^w, \ldots, p_{|\mathcal{T}|}^w\}$ to represent the accuracies of w on microtasks in $\mathcal{T}$.

Microtask Assignment. In crowdsourcing, to improve the quality, a microtask is usually assigned to multiple workers and its result is obtained via a voting scheme. Under this scheme, we assign a microtask t_i to a worker set $\mathcal{W}_{t_i} \subset \mathcal{W}$ with size k, where k is an *assignment size* to represent the number of workers that can be assigned with t_i. k is usually provided by the crowdsourcing requester. Given worker set $\mathcal{W}_{t_i}$, we utilize (weighted) majority voting, which is well accepted in many crowdsourcing approaches [11, 32, 7]. For ease of presentation, this paper considers the simple majority voting where k is an odd number. If more than or equal

Table 2: Notations.

$\mathcal{T}$	a set of microtasks for crowdsourcing
$\mathcal{W}$	a set of active workers working on $\mathcal{T}$
$\langle t_i, w \rangle$	assignment of microtask t_i and worker w
$\mathcal{W}_{t_i}$	a set of workers completing microtask t_i
$\mathbf{p}^w = \{p_i^w\}$	estimated accuracies of w
$\mathbf{q}^w = \{q_i^w\}$	observed accuracies of w
k	assignment size per microtask

to $\frac{k+1}{2}$ workers vote for a same answer (e.g., YES), then we take this consensus answer as the result of t_i, and consider t_i is *globally* completed. We can compute the accuracy of worker set $\mathcal{W}_{t_i}$, denoted by $Pr(\mathcal{W}_{t_i})$, based on the accuracy of each individual in $\mathcal{W}_{t_i}$. Specifically, this accuracy is the probability that more than half of the workers in $\mathcal{W}_{t_i}$ can provide the correct answer. Assuming the accuracies across workers are independent, we compute $Pr(\mathcal{W}_{t_i})$ as below.

$$Pr(\mathcal{W}_{t_i}) = \sum_{x=\frac{k+1}{2}}^{k} \sum_{\mathcal{W}_{t_i}^x} \Big(\prod_{w \in \mathcal{W}_{t_i}^x} p_i^w \prod_{w \in \mathcal{W}_{t_i} - \mathcal{W}_{t_i}^x} (1 - p_i^w) \Big) \quad (1)$$

where $\mathcal{W}_{t_i}^x$ is any x-size subsets of $\mathcal{W}_{t_i}$.

Based on worker set accuracy, an *optimal microtask assignment* problem assigns each microtask $t_i \in \mathcal{T}$ to a subset of workers $\mathcal{W}_{t_i}$ to maximize the sum of the probabilities that microtasks are correctly answered, i.e., $\max \sum_{t_i \in \mathcal{T}} Pr(\mathcal{W}_{t_i})$.

However, crowdsourcing has brought the following two great challenges that make microtask assignment much more difficult. First, due to the openness of crowdsourcing, we have limited, if not none, knowledge of workers. Thus, we cannot obtain the accuracy p_i^w upfront, which makes the computation of $Pr(\mathcal{W}_{t_i})$ in Equation (1) rather difficult. Second, the worker set $\mathcal{W}$ is dynamic: any existing worker may become inactive and new workers may become active. These challenges engender us to study the problem of *adaptive crowdsourcing*, which is described as follows.

Adaptive Crowdsourcing. This problem adaptively assigns microtasks to a dynamic set $\mathcal{W}$ of workers with unknown accuracy p_i^w to optimize the overall accuracy of crowdsourcing, i.e., $\max \sum_{t_i \in \mathcal{T}} Pr(\mathcal{W}_{t_i})$. Specifically, it on-the-fly estimates worker accuracy p_i^w based on the globally completed microtasks $\mathcal{T}^d \subseteq \mathcal{T}$. Then, based on the estimation, it adaptively assigns uncompleted microtasks in $\mathcal{T} - \mathcal{T}^d$ in iterations until all microtasks in $\mathcal{T}$ are globally completed, where each iteration is triggered by a request from an *active* worker w from a dynamic worker set $\mathcal{W}$.

For example, consider the microtasks in Table 1 and a worker set $\mathcal{W} = \{w_1, w_2, \ldots, w_5\}$. Adaptive crowdsourcing interacts with the workers in $\mathcal{W}$ for microtask assignment, where each assignment is triggered by a request from an active worker, say w_1. In the assignment, it considers the globally completed microtasks of w_1 to estimate the accuracy vector $\mathbf{p}^{w_1}$ of w_1, and assigns to w_1 a microtask with higher accuracy. After w_1 submits its answer to the assigned microtask, it adjusts the estimation of accuracies $\mathbf{p}^{w_1}$ based on the new $\mathcal{T}^d$, and continues to assign more microtasks.

For ease of presentation, we summarize the notations in this paper in Table 2, where some will be introduced later.

2.2 *i*Crowd Framework

Our *i*Crowd framework is illustrated in Figure 1. We develop *i*Crowd as an adaptive crowdsourcing component within the CDAS (Crowdsourcing Data Analytics System) project, along the lines of [22, 10]. The framework takes as input a set $\mathcal{T}$ of microtasks, and on-the-fly communicates with

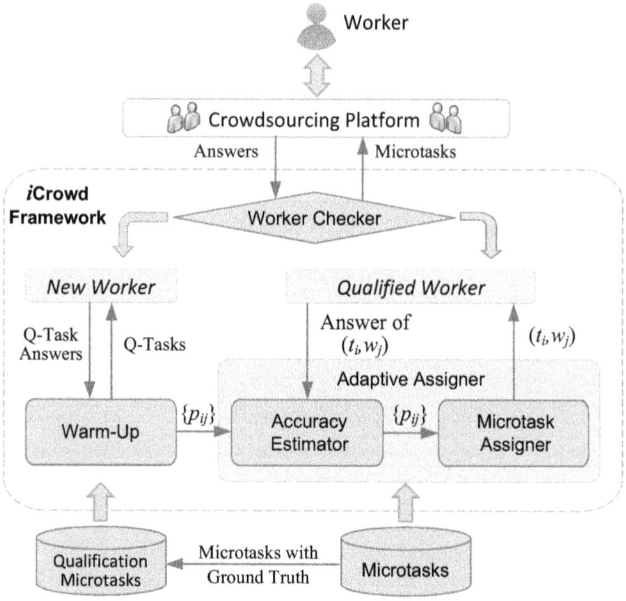

Figure 1: Framework of *i*Crowd.

a crowdsourcing platform (e.g., Amazon Mechanical Turk) for assigning microtasks to workers[1]. It adaptively assigns microtasks to workers by using the following components.

Adaptive Assigner. This component interacts with a requesting worker, and employs two modules, namely ACCURACY ESTIMATOR and MICROTASK ASSIGNER for adaptive microtask assignment.

ACCURACY ESTIMATOR takes as input the globally completed microtasks $\mathcal{T}^d$ and estimates accuracies $\mathbf{p}^w$ for each worker w. Compared with existing approaches [22, 18, 30] that employ some qualification tasks with ground truth to compute an average accuracy for all the microtasks, the highlight of our estimation is to consider accuracy diversity across microtasks. The basic idea is to infer the accuracy of a worker's answer on a microtask based on her performance on the globally completed microtasks which are similar to the microtask. Specifically, as illustrated in Figure 2, suppose worker w has provided correct answer to t_1 about iPhone, and incorrect answer to t_2 about iPod. Then, ACCURACY ESTIMATOR would have higher confidence on w's answers of other microtasks about iPhone (similar to t_1), while it would doubt her answers about iPod. To formulate this intuition, we introduce probabilistic models to evaluate the performance of w on globally completed microtasks $\mathcal{T}^d$, and employ a graph-based approach to infer accuracies $\mathbf{p}^w$ of w on the unassigned microtasks (see Section 3 for details).

MICROTASK ASSIGNER takes as input the active workers with their accuracies estimated by ACCURACY ESTIMATOR, and assigns a microtask to a requesting worker. It considers the dynamically estimated accuracies, and adaptively assigns a microtask to the top workers of the microtask with highest accuracies based on the current estimation. It also considers assigning the microtasks that would be more beneficial to improve the estimation of worker accuracies. Moreover, it devises effective indexes and develops efficient algorithms for supporting real-time microtask assignment. More details of microtask assigner can be found in Section 4.

[1]Note that the implementation details of the *online* communication between *i*Crowd and the crowdsourcing platform can be referred to Appendix A.

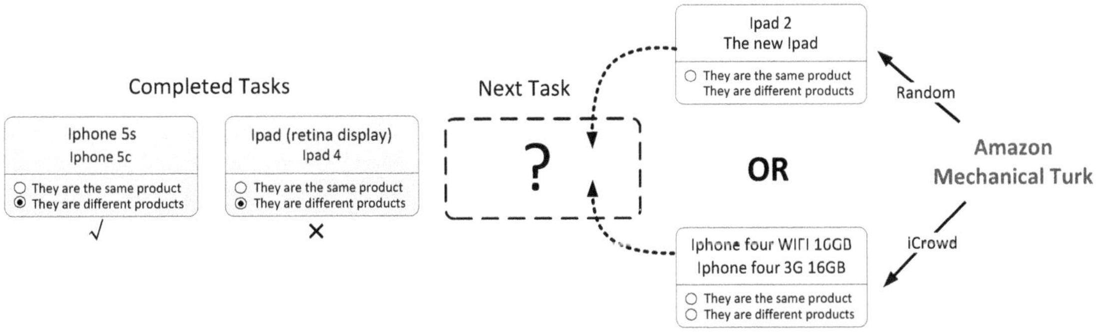

Figure 2: An Example of Using *iCrowd* to Assign Microtasks to Workers on Amazon Mechanical Turk.

Warm-Up. This component is used to address the cold-start problem: for a new worker w who does not vote for any globally completed microtask, *iCrowd* cannot estimate the worker accuracies $\mathbf{p}^w$. The component addresses the problem by leveraging some microtasks with ground truth, called qualification microtasks, for initial accuracy estimation. In the pre-processing step, it selects a small amount of "representative" microtasks from $\mathcal{T}$ and asks the requester to label ground truth for them. Then, when a new worker w requests for microtasks, it assigns some qualification microtasks to her (note that worker w is not aware that she is working on qualification microtasks). After w submits answers of the microtasks, the component compares her answers with the ground truth to estimate accuracies. Besides, it also seeks to eliminate "bad" workers based on qualification microtasks: if the average accuracy is lower than a given threshold, it rejects worker w as she is not qualified in working on the microtasks. For instance, given a threshold 0.6, if worker w correctly answers less than 3 qualification microtasks when completing 5 qualification microtasks, *iCrowd* rejects the worker (see Section 5 for more details).

3. ACCURACY ESTIMATION

This section introduces our accuracy estimation method that tackles accuracy diversity of workers on different microtasks. The basic idea of our method is to consider the "similarity" of microtasks: as observed from our empirical investigation in Section 6, the accuracies of a worker, although may vary in different domains, tend to be comparable on the microtasks in similar domains. As such, if we have observed that a worker w correctly completes some microtasks, we can infer that she would also perform well on microtasks in similar domains. Consider our example microtasks in Table 1: as t_1 and t_4 are similar (both of them are about "iPhone"), if we have observed that worker w correctly answers t_1, we can conjecture that w stands a better chance to correctly answer t_4 compared with other microtasks.

We formulate the aforementioned similarities of microtasks as a graph model, called *microtask similarity graph* (or similarity graph for simplicity). Formally, a similarity graph is a weighted undirected graph $\mathcal{G} = (\mathcal{T}, \mathcal{E})$ where $\mathcal{T}$ is a set of microtasks, and an edge e_{ij} between microtasks t_i and t_j represents that t_i and t_j are similar and their similarity is denoted by s_{ij}. Figure 3 illustrates a similarity graph of our example microtasks, where the number in an edge represents the similarity score of the connected microtasks (we will explain how the number is computed in Section 3.3).

Based on the similarity graph, we estimate the accuracy vector $\mathbf{p}^w = \{p_1^w, p_2^w, \ldots, p_{|\mathcal{T}|}^w\}$ of worker w on the set $\mathcal{T}$ of

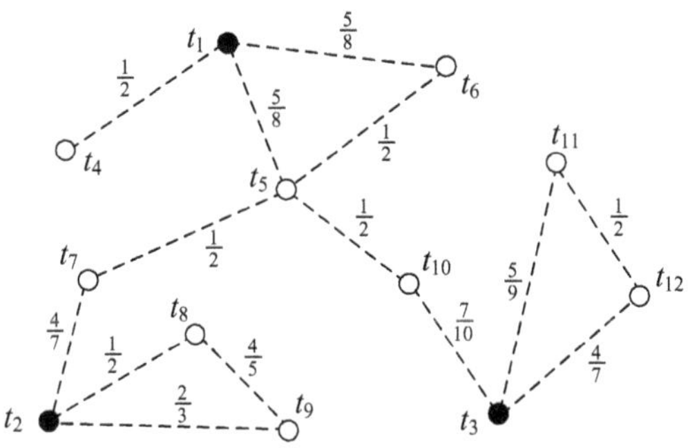

Figure 3: Similarity Graph of Example Microtasks.

Worker	Qualification	Completed Microtasks
w_1	$t_1^{\checkmark}$ $t_2^{\times}$ $t_3^{\times}$	(t_6, *YES*), (t_5, *NO*)
w_2	$t_1^{\times}$ $t_2^{\checkmark}$ $t_3^{\times}$	(t_6, *NO*), (t_7, *NO*)
w_3	$t_1^{\times}$ $t_2^{\times}$ $t_3^{\checkmark}$	(t_7, *YES*), (t_{11}, *YES*)
w_4	$t_1^{\checkmark}$ $t_2^{\checkmark}$ $t_3^{\times}$	(t_7, *NO*), (t_5, *YES*)
w_5	$t_1^{\checkmark}$ $t_2^{\times}$ $t_3^{\checkmark}$	(t_6, *YES*), (t_{11}, *NO*)

Figure 4: Completed Microtasks of Workers.

microtasks from the globally completed microtasks $\mathcal{T}^d \subseteq \mathcal{T}$. More formally, we introduce *observed accuracy*, denoted by q_i^w, to represent the probability that the answer of w on a globally completed microtask $t_i \in \mathcal{T}^d$ is correct. Similar to $\mathbf{p}^w$, for ease of presentation, we use a vector $\mathbf{q}^w$ to denote the observed accuracies of w on the microtask set $\mathcal{T}$. We will explain how to derive $\mathbf{q}^w$ from $\mathcal{T}^d$ in Section 3.2.

Now we are ready to formalize the problem of similarity-based accuracy estimation, which is defined as below.

DEFINITION 2 (SIMILARITY-BASED ACCURACY ESTIMATION). *Given a similarity graph $\mathcal{G} = (\mathcal{T}, \mathcal{E})$ and observed accuracy vector $\mathbf{q}^w$ of worker w, it estimates accuracies $\mathbf{p}^w = \{p_1^w, p_2^w, \ldots, p_{|\mathcal{T}|}^w\}$ for unassigned microtasks in $\mathcal{T} - \mathcal{T}^d$.*

Consider our example similarity graph mentioned above and five workers shown in Figure 4. Given a set of globally completed microtasks, including the qualification microtasks (t_1, t_2 and t_3 in Figure 4) and the microtasks that reach consensus (e.g., t_6 given assignment size $k = 3$), and a worker w_1, the accuracy estimation problem wants to compute the accuracies of w_1 on the microtasks which are not assigned to w_1 yet, e.g., t_4, t_7, etc.

In the remaining part, we first introduce our model for similarity-based accuracy estimation in Section 3.1. Then, we discuss how to derive $\mathbf{q}^w$ from $\mathcal{T}^d$ in Section 3.2 and how to construct the similarity graph in Section 3.3.

3.1 Graph-Based Estimation Model

The basic idea of our graph-based estimation model is to estimate accuracies based on similarity between microtasks in the graph: if the observed accuracies in $\mathbf{q}^w$ are known on some globally completed microtasks, we can conjecture similar accuracies of the unassigned microtasks which are connected to the completed ones in the graph. Take the similarity graph in Figure 3 as an example. Given previous performance of worker w, say correctly answering t_2 and providing incorrect answer to t_3, our method would conjecture that w would have higher accuracies on the microtasks closely connected to t_2 (e.g., t_7, t_8 and t_9), while may not be accurate on those connected to t_3 (e.g., t_{10}, t_{11} and t_{12}).

However, it is non-trivial to exploit the similarity graph for accuracy estimation, as the estimated accuracies $\mathbf{p}^w$ need to satisfy not only the *local* similarity that each pair of connected microtasks have similar accuracies, but also the *global* similarity that microtasks in coherent sub-graphs have similar accuracies. Moreover, $\mathbf{p}^w$ also needs to be consistent with the observed accuracies in $\mathbf{q}^w$: estimated accuracies should not largely deviate from the observed accuracies. We formalize these two objectives as follows. For ease of presentation, we respectively use $\mathbf{p}$, $\mathbf{q}$, p_i and q_i to represent $\mathbf{p}^w$, $\mathbf{q}^w$, p_i^w and q_i^w in the remaining part, if there is no ambiguity.

1) We want to minimize accuracy differences between similar microtasks. Formally, recall that $S = \{s_{ij}\}$ denotes the similarity matrix, where s_{ij} is the similarity between two microtasks t_i and t_j. We introduce $(p_i - p_j)^2$ to measure the difference between the estimated accuracies of worker w on t_i and t_j. We choose this quadratic expression due to the following reasons. First, the lower the difference of the accuracies on t_i and t_j is, the smaller $(p_i - p_j)^2$ is, and vice versa. Thus, we can minimize accuracy differences between similar microtasks by minimizing $(p_i - p_j)^2$. Second, it will enable us to easily obtain the optimal solution of our optimization problem, which will be elaborated later in Lemma 1. Given the difference expression, this objective aims to minimize $(p_i - p_j)^2$ for the pair of microtasks with large similarity s_{ij}. We further consider to normalize the similarities. Let $S' = D^{-\frac{1}{2}} S D^{-\frac{1}{2}}$, where D denotes the diagonal matrix with the (i,i) element equal to the sum of i-th row of S, i.e., $D_{ii} = \sum_{j=1}^{n} s_{ij}$, where n is the number of microtasks in $\mathcal{G}$. Then, we formalize the overall accuracy difference between similar microtasks as $\frac{1}{2}\sum_{i,j}(\frac{s_{ij}}{\sqrt{D_{ii}}}p_i - \frac{s_{ij}}{\sqrt{D_{jj}}}p_j)^2$, which is the summation of accuracy differences between microtask pairs weighted by the normalized similarity.

2) We want to minimize accuracy difference between $\mathbf{p}$ and $\mathbf{q}$, as we do not want the estimate to deviate too much from the observed accuracies. We utilize $\frac{1}{2}\sum_{i=1}^{n}(p_i - q_i)^2$ to model the differences between $\mathbf{p}$ and $\mathbf{q}$. Note that we will discuss how to compute q_i in Section 3.2.

By considering the above factors, we compute accuracy vector $\mathbf{p}^*$ by solving the following optimization problem.

$$\mathbf{p}^* = \arg\min_{\mathbf{p}} \frac{1}{2}\Big(\sum_{i,j} s_{ij}\big(\frac{p_i}{\sqrt{D_{ii}}} - \frac{p_j}{\sqrt{D_{jj}}}\big)^2 + \alpha \sum_{i}^{n} (p_i - q_i)^2\Big), \tag{2}$$

where α is a parameter balancing the two factors: a larger α indicates that we prefer $\mathbf{p}$ will be more similar to $\mathbf{q}$, while a smaller α indicates that we are more concerned that the estimated accuracies should be closer on similar microtasks.

Take our example similarity graph in Figure 3 as an example. Suppose that a worker w has correctly answered t_1 and provided wrong answers to t_2 and t_3. Then, we have a vector $\mathbf{q}$ of observed accuracies containing $q_1 = 1$, $q_2 = 0$ and $q_3 = 0$ (we will explain the details of computing these observed accuracies in Section 3.2). Then, our optimization objective in Equation (2) aims to predict estimated accuracy p_i for microtask t_i such that the microtasks, which are closely connected in the similarity graph (e.g., the subgraph containing t_2 in the bottom right), have similar values in p_i, and these values are also similar to $\mathbf{q}$. For instance, given the above $\mathbf{q}$, the predicted $\mathbf{p}$ should be that the microtasks in the subgroup around t_1 have larger estimated accuracies than those in the subgraphs around t_2 and t_3.

The optimization problem can be analytically solved, as illustrated in the following lemma.

LEMMA 1. *The solution of Equation (2) is*

$$\mathbf{p}^* = \frac{\alpha}{1+\alpha} \cdot (I - \frac{1}{1+\alpha}S')^{-1}\mathbf{q}. \tag{3}$$

PROOF. We prove the lemma by differentiating the Equation (2) with respect to $\mathbf{p}$ and then compute $\mathbf{p}^*$ by taking the first-order derivative equal to zero. □

As it is challenging to directly compute the inverse matrix $(I - \frac{1}{1+\alpha}S')^{-1}$, we employ the personalized pagerank algorithm [14] to iteratively compute $\mathbf{p}$. Specifically, we set vector $\mathbf{p}$ as the observed one $\mathbf{q}$ initially, and then update $\mathbf{p}$ by using the following equation.

$$\mathbf{p} = \frac{1}{1+\alpha} \cdot \mathbf{p}S' + \frac{\alpha}{1+\alpha} \cdot \mathbf{q}. \tag{4}$$

As illustrated in Equation (4), in each iteration, each element $p_i \in \mathbf{p}$ is computed by the sum of it nearby accuracies with similarity as weight at probability $\frac{1}{1+\alpha}$, or set to its observed accuracy q_i at probability $\frac{\alpha}{1+\alpha}$.

LEMMA 2. *The iterative algorithm based on Equation (4) can compute the optimal solution* $\mathbf{p}^*$ *in Equation (3).*

PROOF. This lemma is proved in [35]. □

The iterative algorithm based on Equation (4) is also very expensive, and it is not applicable for online accuracy estimation. To address this problem, we propose an efficient algorithm by utilizing a nice *linearity* property of personalized pagerank. Specifically, let $\mathbf{q}_{t_i}$ denote the observed accuracy vector that only q_i for microtask t_i is 1 and others are 0. Let $\mathbf{p}_{t_i}$ denote the converged result of Equation (4) given $\mathbf{q}_{t_i}$. There is a good property that we can compute $\mathbf{p}^*$ by a weighted summation of $\mathbf{p}_{t_i}$, as shown below.

LEMMA 3 (LINEARITY [14]). *Given* $\mathbf{p}_{t_i}$ *for each microtask* t_i *and* $\mathbf{q}$, *the optimal estimated accuracy vector* $\mathbf{p}^*$ *can be computed as* $\mathbf{p}^* = \sum_{q_i \in \mathbf{q}} q_i \cdot \mathbf{p}_{t_i}$.

Based on Lemma 3, we develop an efficient online estimation algorithm as shown in Algorithm 1. The algorithm takes as input a worker w, microtask set $\mathcal{T}$, and the set of globally completed microtasks $\mathcal{T}^d$. In particular, we also consider the qualification microtasks with ground truth as globally completed. The algorithm estimates accuracy vector $\mathbf{p}$ of worker w through the following steps. In the

Algorithm 1: EstimateAccuracy (w, $\mathcal{T}$, $\mathcal{T}^d$)

Input: w: A worker; $\mathcal{T}$: A microtask set ;
$\mathcal{T}^d$: A set of globally completed microtasks
Output: $\mathbf{p}^w$: Estimated accuracies of w

begin
  `/* Offline Computation */`
  Generate a similarity graph $\mathcal{G}$ on $\mathcal{T}$;
  for *Each microtask t_i in $\mathcal{G}$* **do**
    Compute $\mathbf{p}_{t_i}$ iteratively via Equation (4) ;
  `/* Online Estimation */`
  $\mathbf{q}^w \leftarrow$ ComputeObserved ($\mathcal{T}^d$) ;
  $\mathbf{p}^w \leftarrow \sum_{q_i^w \in \mathbf{q}^w} q_i^w \cdot \mathbf{p}_{t_i}$;
  return $\mathbf{p}^w$;
end

offline component, it generates a similarity graph $\mathcal{G}$ by computing microtask similarities, and pre-computes a vector $\mathbf{p}_{t_i}$ for each microtask t_i in $\mathcal{G}$ via Equation (4). For online estimation, it first computes observed accuracies $\mathbf{q}$ based on completed microtasks $\mathcal{T}^d$ by calling function ComputeObserved (see Section 3.2), and then employs the linearity property to compute $\mathbf{p}$. Thanks to the linearity property, the algorithm is efficient with time complexity $\mathcal{O}(|\mathcal{T}|)$.

For example, consider estimating accuracies for worker w_1 in Figure 4. In offline, the algorithm computes $\mathbf{p}_{t_i}$ for each t_i based on the graph in Figure 3. For instance, to compute $\mathbf{p}_{t_1}$, it initially sets $\mathbf{p}_{t_1} = \mathbf{q}_{t_1} = [1, 0, \ldots, 0]$, and then updates $\mathbf{p}_{t_1}$ via Equation (4) to obtain a converged vector. In the online component, after computing $\mathbf{q}^{w_1}$, it computes accuracies of w_1 as $\mathbf{p}^{w_1} = \sum_{q_i^{w_1} \in \mathbf{q}^{w_1}} q_i^{w_1} \cdot \mathbf{p}_{t_i}$.

3.2 Observed Accuracy Estimation

In this section, we discuss how to estimate the observed accuracies $\mathbf{q}^w$ that model worker w's previous performance on the globally completed microtasks.

The estimation is trivial if t_i is a qualification microtask with ground truth. In this case, we compare the answer from w with the ground truth of t_i, and set $q_i^w = 1$ if they are the same, or $q_i^w = 0$ otherwise. The non-trivial case is when t_i does not have ground truth. In this case, we estimate q_i^w by comparing w's answer with the consensus answer of microtask t_i. The basic idea is that, if the two answers are the same, we can use the probability that the consensus answer is correct to estimate q_i^w. Otherwise, we consider the probability of the complement event, i.e., the consensus answer is incorrect. Formally, we respectively use $\mathcal{W}_1$ and $\mathcal{W}_2$ to denote the workers of t_i having the answer equal to and not equal to the consensus answer. Then, the observed accuracy of worker w can be computed as

$$q_i^w = \begin{cases} \frac{P_1 \overline{P}_2}{P_1 \overline{P}_2 + \overline{P}_1 P_2}, & if\ \mathtt{ans}_i^w = \mathtt{ans}_i^* \\ \frac{\overline{P}_1 P_2}{P_1 \overline{P}_2 + \overline{P}_1 P_2}, & if\ \mathtt{ans}_i^w \neq \mathtt{ans}_i^* \end{cases} \quad (5)$$

where $\mathtt{ans}_i^w$ is w's answer, $\mathtt{ans}_i^*$ is the consensus answer, $P_1 = \prod_{w' \in \mathcal{W}_1} p_i^{w'}$, $\overline{P}_1 = \prod_{w' \in \mathcal{W}_1} 1 - p_i^{w'}$, $P_2 = \prod_{w' \in \mathcal{W}_2} p_i^{w'}$ and $\overline{P}_2 = \prod_{w' \in \mathcal{W}_2} 1 - p_i^{w'}$. Note that the above $p_i^{w'}$ can be estimated by the previously estimated accuracy of w'. When estimating $\mathbf{q}^w$ for the first time, we use the average accuracy returned by the Warm-Up component as an estimate.

Figure 4 provides some completed microtasks of the five workers where $t^{\checkmark}$ ($t^{\times}$) represents qualification t is correctly (incorrectly) answered. For worker w_1, we obtain $q_1^{w_1} = 1$, $q_2^{w_1} = q_3^{w_1} = 0$ based on the qualification. We compute $q_6^{w_1}$ for a globally completed microtask t_6 (assignment size $k = 3$). We consider the workers of t_6, $\{w_1, w_2, w_5\}$, and find w_1's answer being equal to the consensus answer. Thus, we compute $q_6^{w_1} = \frac{p_6^{w_1} p_6^{w_5} (1 - p_6^{w_2})}{p_6^{w_1} p_6^{w_5} (1 - p_6^{w_2}) + (1 - p_6^{w_1})(1 - p_6^{w_5}) p_6^{w_2}}$.

3.3 Discussion on Microtask Similarity

In this section, we discuss how to derive microtask similarities for generating the similarity graph. We utilize the well-known similarity techniques and examine the effect of these techniques in the experiments (see Appendix D.1). Note that this paper focuses on leveraging similarity for better accuracy estimation, and leaves a thorough study on similarity metrics as future work.

1) For textual microtasks, e.g., our example in Table 1, we can employ existing similarity metrics, e.g., Jaccard similarity, Edit distance, etc, to compute the similarity between microtasks. For instance, we derive our example similarity graph shown in Figure 3 by using Jaccard similarity. We first take each of microtasks as a set of tokens, and compute Jaccard similarity as the ratio of their intersection size to their union size, and consider that two microtasks are similar if their Jaccard similarity is not smaller than a given threshold. For example, the edge between microtasks t_2 and t_7 represents their similarity is 4/7, which is computed by Jaccard similarity between their token sets in Table 1. We also set a similarity threshold 0.5 to neglect the microtask pairs with similarity lower than 0.5. We can employ the techniques in [33] to select appropriate similarity metrics and thresholds. In addition, we can also exploit existing topic models, e.g., Latent Dirichlet Allocation (LDA) [6] to obtain a topic distribution for each microtask, and compute microtask similarity based on the topic distributions. In our experiment, we utilized the LDA-based similarity and achieved good performance.

2) For microtasks that can be represented as multiple-dimension features, e.g., images, spatial objects, etc, we can use the Euclidean similarity to quantify their similarity. For instance, consider microtasks for verifying place names for points-of-interest (POIs) in the map. Given two microtasks t_i and t_j, we consider their corresponding POIs (x_1, x_2) and (y_1, y_2). Then, we compute their Euclidean distance $\mathtt{dist}(t_i, t_j) = \sqrt{\sum_{d=1}^{2} (x_d - y_d)^2}$, and use $1 - \frac{\mathtt{dist}(t_i, t_j)}{\tau_d}$ to normalize their similarity between 0 and 1, where τ_d is the maximum distance between POIs in the microtasks.

3) For some more complicated microtasks, e.g. verifying translations of a paragraph of text, we can use classification-based methods to derive their similarity. We can train a classifier based on a training set. Then for each pair of microtasks, if we classify them as a similar pair, their similarity is 1, and 0 otherwise. We may use existing classification algorithms, e.g. SVM, to find similar microtasks.

4. ADAPTIVE TASK ASSIGNMENT

This section presents our adaptive approach for microtask assignments based on estimated accuracies. We introduce an adaptive assignment framework in Section 4.1 and discuss the *optimal microtask assignment* problem in Section 4.2.

4.1 Adaptive Assignment Framework

The basic idea of our microtask assignment framework is to adaptively "seek" for the *top workers* with higher accuracies to complete microtasks, as the estimated accuracies are continuously updated. A high-level overview of our framework is illustrated in Figure 5. At each time, the framework aims to assign the microtasks, which are not globally completed, to the current set of active workers. It first adaptively finds the top workers having the highest estimated accuracy p_i^w to complete each unassigned microtask t_i based on the up-to-date accuracy estimation, as illustrated by the dotted arrow in the figure. As worker w may be taken as top workers by multiple microtasks, the framework then determines a microtask to which w can contribute the most and assigns this microtask to w (solid arrows). Moreover, when a worker submits her answer to the assigned microtask, the framework adaptively updates the assignment scheme based on the new accuracy estimation.

For example, consider the five workers $w_1, w_2, \ldots, w_5$ in Figure 5. The framework considers the up-to-date accuracies $p_1^{w_1}, p_2^{w_2}, \ldots$ estimated by ACCURACY ESTIMATOR and selects top workers, e.g., the top workers of t_2 are w_1, w_3 and w_4. As some worker (e.g., w_3) may be selected as top worker for multiple microtasks (e.g., t_1 and t_2), the framework then determines assigning which microtask is more "beneficial" (will be explained later). Finally, our framework generates a scheme that assigns t_1 to workers w_2 and w_5, and t_2 to workers w_1, w_3 and w_4.

To formalize the above idea, our framework utilizes the following three steps for adaptive microtasks assignment.

Step 1 - Top worker set computation. This step first identifies *active* workers which are ready to work on our microtasks. We can use different methods for identifying active workers. One way is to use a time window (e.g., 30 minutes): if the span from the last time when worker w requests microtasks to the current time is smaller than the window, we consider w is active. Otherwise, w is inactive. Another method is to examine if or not a worker is still holding Human Intelligence Tasks (HITs) containing the microtasks (see Appendix A for more details): if w is holding a HIT, we consider w is active; otherwise, w is inactive.

Taking the set of active workers as candidates, the framework then computes for each microtask the top workers. Formally, let $\mathcal{W}^d(t_i)$ denote the set of workers who have been assigned to t_i, i.e., the workers either have completed or those are still working on t_i. Let $\mathcal{W}^u(t_i) = \mathcal{W} - \mathcal{W}^d(t_i)$ denote the workers to which t_i can be assigned. Recall that each microtask has an assignment size k that it could be assigned to k workers. We define the top workers as below.

DEFINITION 3 (TOP WORKER SET). *Top worker set of a microtask t_i, denoted by $\widehat{\mathcal{W}}(t_i)$, is a set of top $k' = k - |\mathcal{W}^d(t_i)|$ workers with the highest accuracies on t_i, i.e., $\forall w \in \widehat{\mathcal{W}}(t_i), \forall w' \in \mathcal{W}^u(t_i) - \widehat{\mathcal{W}}(t_i), p_i^w \geq p_i^{w'}$.*

Table 3 provides some example top worker sets ($k = 3$). For instance, microtask t_4 has no assigned set $\mathcal{W}^d(t_i)$ and its top worker set consists of $\{w_5, w_4, w_1\}$ with the highest accuracies (the numbers in parentheses). In addition, as t_{11} has been assigned to worker w_2 in previous interaction, its top worker set only contains two workers, w_5 and w_3.

Step 2 - Optimal microtask assignment. This step takes the microtasks and their top worker sets as input and generates an assignment scheme that satisfies the following two properties: 1) each worker w could be assigned with at most *one* microtask at each time, and 2) the number of workers that a microtask t_i can be assigned to is not greater than the available assignment size of t_i, i.e., the $k' = k - |\mathcal{W}^d(t_i)|$ in Definition 3. Consider our example in Table 3: both t_4 and t_{11} take w_5 as one of their top workers. However, w_5 can only work on one microtask from $\{t_4, t_{11}\}$ before w_5 submits her answer to the assigned microtasks and continues to request more microtasks. Under the above constraints, we want to find an *optimal* assignment scheme that achieves the highest overall accuracy. We formalize the problem of optimal microtask assignment and develop an efficient algorithm to solve the problem, which will be described in Section 4.2.

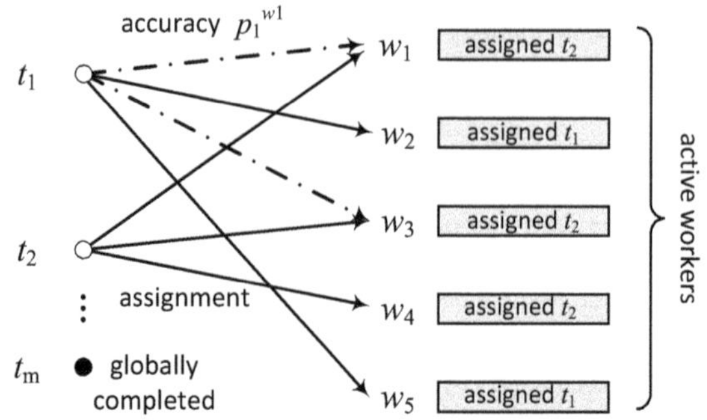

Figure 5: Overview of Microtask Assignment.

Table 3: An Example of Microtask Assignment.

Task	Top Worker Set $\widehat{\mathcal{W}}(t_i)$	Assigned $\mathcal{W}^d(t_i)$
t_4	$(w_5, 0.75), (w_4, 0.7), (w_1, 0.6)$	$\emptyset$
t_{11}	$(w_5, 0.85), (w_3, 0.8)$	$(w_2, 0.7)$
t_9	$(w_4, 0.85), (w_2, 0.75), (w_1, 0.7)$	$\emptyset$
t_{10}	$(w_3, 0.7), (w_1, 0.6)$	$(w_5, 0.8)$

Step 3 - Worker performance testing. After the previous step, some workers may still not be assigned with microtasks, as they are *currently* not taken as top workers of any microtask. This may be attributed to our limited knowledge about these workers. For example, suppose that a worker w has completed all the microtasks she is good at according to our accuracy estimation, say the microtasks in the subgraph near t_1 shown in Figure 3. Then, our ACCURACY ESTIMATOR is not sure if w can perform well in the other two subgraphs near t_2 and t_3, as w only completed a limited number of microtasks in these subgraphs.

In this case, our assignment framework *actively* tests the performance of w by considering the following two factors. The first factor is the uncertainty of the estimated accuracy of w on the microtask: we prefer to test a microtask, on which ACCURACY ESTIMATOR is not certain if w can perform well. We use the *estimation variance* to model the uncertainty. Suppose that w has completed N microtasks that are similar to t' (e.g., some microtasks in the left-bottom subgraph similar to t_2 in Figure 3), and N_1 microtasks are correctly answered (based on our estimation model in Section 3.2) while N_0 microtasks are incorrect. We estimate the estimation variance by assuming N_1 and N_0 follow a beta distribution (which is a commonly-used assumption in estimation) $\beta(N_1 + 1, N_0 + 1)$, and estimate the uncertainty by the variance of the beta distribution, i.e., $\frac{(N_1+1)\cdot(N_0+1)}{(N_1+N_0+2)^2\cdot(N_1+N_0+3)}$. Then, we prefer to select the microtask with larger variance. The second factor is the accuracies of existing workers which have been assigned to t': we prefer the microtask with high accuracies to make the performance

Algorithm 2: AssignTask $(\mathcal{W}, \mathcal{T}, \mathcal{T}^d, \{\mathbf{p}^w\})$

Input: $\mathcal{W}$: Active workers; $\mathcal{T}$: microtask set;
$\mathcal{T}$: globally completed microtask set;
$\{\mathbf{p}^w\}$: Estimated accuracies of workers
Output: Asg $= \{\langle w_j, t_i\rangle\}$: Assignments
begin
  // Step 1: Generating top worker sets ;
  for *each microtask* $t_i \in \mathcal{T} - \mathcal{T}^d$ **do**
    $\widehat{\mathcal{W}}(t_i) \leftarrow$ GenTopWorkers $(t_i, \{\mathbf{p}^w\})$;
  // Step 2: Compute optimal microtask assignment ;
  $\mathcal{A}^* \leftarrow$ OptAssign $(\mathcal{T} - \mathcal{T}^d, \mathcal{W}, \{\widehat{\mathcal{W}}(t_i)\})$;
  for *each* $\langle t, \mathcal{W}_t\rangle \in \mathcal{A}^*$ **do**
    Insert $\langle w, t\rangle$ into Asg for any $w \in \mathcal{W}_t$;
  // Step 3: Test performance for workers ;
  for *each* w *in* $\mathcal{W}$ *without assignment* **do**
    $t' \leftarrow$ ComputeTestAssignment (w) ;
    Insert $\langle w, t'\rangle$ into Asg ;
  Return Asg ;
end

Algorithm 3: GreedyAssign $(\mathcal{T} - \mathcal{T}^d, \mathcal{W}, \{\widehat{\mathcal{W}}(t_i)\})$

Input: $\mathcal{T} - \mathcal{T}^d$: uncompleted tasks; $\mathcal{W}$: Active workers;
$\{\widehat{\mathcal{W}}(t_i)\}$: Top worker set of each task t_i;
Output: $\mathcal{A}^* = \{\langle t_i, \widehat{\mathcal{W}}(t_i)\rangle\}$: assignment results
begin
  $\mathcal{A}^c \leftarrow \emptyset$;
  for $t_i \in \mathcal{T} - \mathcal{T}^d$ **do** $\mathcal{A}^c \leftarrow \mathcal{A}^c \cup \{\langle t_i, \widehat{\mathcal{W}}(t_i)\rangle\}$;
  $\mathcal{A}^* \leftarrow \emptyset$;
  while $\mathcal{A}^c$ *is not empty* **do**
    Choose a $\langle t, \widehat{\mathcal{W}}(t)\rangle \in \mathcal{A}^c$ with the maximum $\frac{\sum_{w \in \widehat{\mathcal{W}}(t)} p_t^w}{|\widehat{\mathcal{W}}(t)|}$;
    $\mathcal{A}^* \leftarrow \mathcal{A}^* \cup \{\langle t, \widehat{\mathcal{W}}(t)\rangle\}$;
    for *Each* $\langle t', \mathcal{W}_{t'}\rangle \in \mathcal{A}^c$ **do**
      if $\widehat{\mathcal{W}}(t') \cap \widehat{\mathcal{W}}(t) \neq \emptyset$ **then**
        Remove $\langle t', \mathcal{W}_{t'}\rangle$ from $\mathcal{A}^c$;
  return $\mathcal{A}^*$;
end

test more reliable. We use the estimated accuracies to measure quality of the existing worker set.

Algorithm 2 summarizes the pseudo-code of our adaptive assignment framework. It first generates top worker sets for the microtasks that are not globally completed. Then, it employs the top worker sets to compute an optimal assignment scheme. For the workers who are not assigned with microtasks, it further tests their accuracies by assigning microtasks that have been assigned to other workers. We next analyze the time complexity. The complexity of the first step is $\mathcal{O}(|\mathcal{T}| \cdot |\mathcal{W}|)$, as it computes top workers for each microtask. We will prove optimal microtask assignment OptAssign in the second step is NP-hard and devise a greedy approximate algorithm with complexity $\mathcal{O}(|\mathcal{T}|^2)$ in Section 4.2. The complexity of the third step is $\mathcal{O}(|\mathcal{W}| \cdot |\mathcal{T}|)$.

4.2 Optimal Microtask Assignment

This section formalizes the *optimal microtask assignment* problem mentioned in Section 4.1 and provides an algorithm to solve the problem. The basic idea is to find an assignment scheme to make as many microtasks to be globally completed as possible, so as to immediately obtain the consensus result of these microtasks and improve accuracy estimation. Note that, to globally complete a microtask t_i, we can assign the top worker set $\widehat{\mathcal{W}}(t_i)$ to t_i (see Definition 3). For example, consider the microtasks shown in Table 3. Suppose that we assign t_{11} to its top worker set $\widehat{\mathcal{W}}(t_{11}) = \{w_5, w_3\}$. This microtask can be globally completed after the workers submit their answers and we can then employ Algorithm 1 to improve accuracy estimation of these workers. However, if two microtasks t_i and t_j have common top worker sets, these two microtasks cannot be completed at the same time, as a worker can only complete one microtask at a time. For instance, if we assign t_4 to its top worker set $\widehat{\mathcal{W}}(t_4) = \{w_5, w_4, w_1\}$, w_5 and w_1 cannot respectively be assigned with t_{11} and t_9 until they submit answers to t_4. Under this constraint, we prefer to find a scheme that assigns workers to the microtasks with higher overall accuracy and make these microtasks globally completed. To formalize this intuition, we introduce the optimal microtask assignment problem as follows.

Definition 4 (Optimal Task Assignment). *Given a set of uncompleted microtasks $\mathcal{T} - \mathcal{T}^d$, a set of active workers $\mathcal{W}$, and top worker set $\widehat{\mathcal{W}}(t_i)$ for each microtask t_i, it finds an optimal assignment scheme $\mathcal{A}^* = \{\langle t_i, \widehat{\mathcal{W}}(t_i)\rangle\}$ to maximize the summation of the overall worker accuracy of each microtask in the scheme, i.e.,*

$$\mathcal{A}^* = \arg\max_{\mathcal{A}} \sum_{\langle t_i, \widehat{\mathcal{W}}(t_i)\rangle \in \mathcal{A}} \Big(\sum_{w \in \widehat{\mathcal{W}}(t_i)} p_i^w \Big)$$
$$\texttt{s.t.}\ \forall t_i, t_j, \widehat{\mathcal{W}}(t_i) \cap \widehat{\mathcal{W}}(t_j) = \emptyset.$$

where $\sum_{w \in \widehat{\mathcal{W}}(t_i)} p_i^w$ is the overall accuracy of workers that globally complete t_i. Summing such overall accuracy of each microtask in $\mathcal{A}$[2], $\sum_{\langle t_i, \widehat{\mathcal{W}}(t_i)\rangle \in \mathcal{A}} \big(\sum_{w \in \widehat{\mathcal{W}}(t_i)} p_i^w\big)$ can measure the accuracy of all globally completed microtasks: maximizing this formula can make as many microtasks to be globally completed with high-accuracy workers as possible.

For example, an assignment scheme in Table 3 is $\mathcal{A} = \{\langle t_9, \widehat{\mathcal{W}}(t_9)\rangle, \langle t_{11}, \widehat{\mathcal{W}}(t_{11})\rangle\}$, which makes t_9 and t_{11} to be globally completed by respectively assigning top worker sets $\widehat{\mathcal{W}}(t_9)$ and $\widehat{\mathcal{W}}(t_{11})$. The overall accuracy of this assignment scheme is $\sum_{w \in \widehat{\mathcal{W}}(t_{11})} p_{11}^w + \sum_{w \in \widehat{\mathcal{W}}(t_9)} p_9^w$.

Next, we show the optimal microtask assignment problem is NP-hard, as shown in the following lemma (see Appendix B for the proof).

Lemma 4. *The problem of optimal microtask assignment is NP-hard.*

A Greedy approximation algorithm. As the problem of microtask selection is NP-hard, we develop a greedy-based approximation algorithm to efficiently solve it, as shown in Algorithm 3. It takes as input the microtasks $\mathcal{T} - \mathcal{T}^d$ that are not globally completed, a set $\mathcal{W}$ of active workers and top worker set $\widehat{\mathcal{W}}(t_i)$ of each microtask, and produces an assignment scheme $\mathcal{A}^* = \{\langle t_i, \widehat{\mathcal{W}}(t_i)\rangle\}$. To this end, it first computes candidate assignments $\mathcal{A}^c$ by considering each $t_i \in \mathcal{T} - \mathcal{T}^d$ as well as its $\widehat{\mathcal{W}}(t_i)$, and then chooses assignments from $\mathcal{A}^c$ iteratively. In each iteration, it chooses the assignment $\langle t, \widehat{\mathcal{W}}(t)\rangle$ with the maximum average worker accuracy $\sum_{w \in \widehat{\mathcal{W}}(t)} p_t^w / |\widehat{\mathcal{W}}(t)|$. After inserting $\langle t, \widehat{\mathcal{W}}(t)\rangle$ into $\mathcal{A}^*$, it eliminates the assignment $\langle t', \widehat{\mathcal{W}}(t')\rangle \in \mathcal{A}^c$ overlapping with $\widehat{\mathcal{W}}(t)$. Finally, if there is no more candidate in

[2]In some special cases, $\mathcal{A}$ may be possibly empty.

$\mathcal{A}^c$, it terminates and outputs the scheme $\mathcal{A}^*$. The time complexity of the greedy algorithm is $\mathcal{O}(|\mathcal{T}|^2)$.

Take the microtasks in Table 3 as an example. The greedy algorithm produces $\mathcal{A}^*$ for the microtasks as follows. In the first iteration, it computes $\frac{\sum_{w \in \widehat{\mathcal{W}}(t_i)} p_i^w}{|\widehat{\mathcal{W}}(t_i)|}$ for each microtask and chooses t_{11} with the highest score. Then, it inserts $\langle t_{11}, \{w_5, w_3\}\rangle$ into $\mathcal{A}^*$ and removes $\langle t_4, \widehat{\mathcal{W}}(t_4)\rangle$, $\langle t_{10}, \widehat{\mathcal{W}}(t_{10})\rangle$ from $\mathcal{A}^c$. Similarly, in the second iteration, the algorithm chooses $\langle t_9, \{w_4, w_2, w_1\}\rangle$ and inserts it into $\mathcal{A}^*$. Then, given an empty $\mathcal{A}^c$, the algorithm terminates and outputs $\mathcal{A}^*$.

5. QUALIFICATION TASK ASSIGNMENT

Our framework in Algorithm 2 may not dispatch microtask to a worker w if w is not contained in any top worker set. This will occur if 1) w is a new worker, or 2) w performs worse than others on all microtasks. In both cases, our framework needs to further test the quality of worker w by assigning her microtasks. We propose to assign qualification microtasks with ground truth to this end. Intuitively, in the former case, these microtasks are used to test which microtask w is good at. In the latter case, we have known that w is less competitive on the microtask similar to what she has completed. Thus, we need to test whether or not w is good at other microtasks, as mentioned before.

It is worth noting that the requester can only label ground truth to a limited number of qualification microtasks. Thus, we need to determine what microtasks have larger "benefit" to be qualification microtasks. We introduce a method for selecting qualification microtasks. The basic idea is to select the microtasks that have the maximum "influence" to other microtasks in the similarity graph. Intuitively, the influence captures how many microtasks we can infer that a worker has potential to provide correct answer if she correctly answers qualification microtasks. Take the similarity graph in Figure 3 as an example. If we can only select 3 microtasks, a good choice is $\{t_1, t_2, t_3\}$ as they can influence more microtasks related to iPhone, iPad and iPod. On the other hand, the microtasks $\{t_1, t_4, t_5\}$ only have strong influence on microtasks about iPhone and weak influence on other microtasks, and thus they can only help us test whether workers are good at this topic.

Based on the above intuition, consider qualification microtasks $\mathcal{T}^{\mathtt{Q}} \subseteq \mathcal{T}$. We model the influence of $\mathcal{T}^{\mathtt{Q}}$ as the number of non-zero values in the estimated accuracy vector inferred from the qualification microtasks in $\mathcal{T}^{\mathtt{Q}}$. Formally, based on the linearity property introduced in Lemma 3, the estimated accuracy vector can be computed by $\sum_{t_i \in \mathcal{T}^{\mathtt{Q}}} \mathbf{p}_{t_i}$ where $\mathbf{p}_{t_i}$ is the converged result of Equation (4) under the condition that the observed accuracies satisfy that only q_i for microtask t_i is 1 and others are 0. The influence is then computed by $\mathtt{INF}(\mathcal{T}^{\mathtt{Q}}) = \sum_{p_i \in \sum_{t_i \in \mathcal{T}^{\mathtt{Q}}} \mathbf{p}_{t_i}} \mathcal{I}(p_i \neq 0)$ where $\mathcal{I}(\cdot)$ is an indicator function (i.e., $\mathcal{I}(p_i \neq 0) = 1$ if $p_i \neq 0$, and $\mathcal{I}(p_i \neq 0) = 0$ otherwise). Now, we are ready to introduce the problem of qualification selection.

DEFINITION 5 (QUALIFICATION MICROTASK SELECTION). *Given a similarity graph $\mathcal{G}$ and a number $\mathtt{Q}$, it selects a subset of microtasks $\mathcal{T}^{\mathtt{Q}} \subseteq \mathcal{T}$ satisfying: 1) the size $|\mathcal{T}^{\mathtt{Q}}| \leq \mathtt{Q}$, and 2) the influence of $\mathcal{T}^{\mathtt{Q}}$, $\mathtt{INF}(\mathcal{T}^{\mathtt{Q}})$ is maximized.*

LEMMA 5. *Qualification microtask selection is NP-hard.*

PROOF. See Appendix C for the proof. □

Algorithm 4: SELECTQUALIFICATION $(\mathcal{G}, \mathcal{T}, \mathtt{Q})$

Input: $\mathcal{G}$: A similarity graph; $\mathcal{T}$: microtask set; $\mathtt{Q}$: Number of qualification microtasks
Output: $\mathcal{T}^{\mathtt{Q}}$: Selected qualification microtasks

begin
  for *Each microtask t_i in $\mathcal{T}$* **do**
    Compute $\mathbf{p}_{t_i}$ iteratively on $\mathcal{G}$ via Equation (4) ;
  $\mathcal{T}^{\mathtt{Q}} \leftarrow \emptyset$;
  for $i = 1 \ldots \mathtt{Q}$ **do**
    Find a microtask t^* satisfying:

$$t^* = \arg\max_{t \in \mathcal{T} - \mathcal{T}^{\mathtt{Q}}} \{\mathtt{INF}(\mathcal{T}^{\mathtt{Q}} \cup \{t\}) - \mathtt{INF}(\mathcal{T}^{\mathtt{Q}})\},$$

    where $\mathtt{INF}(\mathcal{T}^{\mathtt{Q}}) = \sum_{p_i \in \sum_{t_i \in \mathcal{T}^{\mathtt{Q}}} \mathbf{p}_{t_i}} \mathcal{I}(p_i \neq 0)$;
    $\mathcal{T}^{\mathtt{Q}} \leftarrow \mathcal{T}^{\mathtt{Q}} \cup \{t^*\}$;
  Return $\mathcal{T}^{\mathtt{Q}}$;
end

We can devise a greedy algorithm for qualification microtask selection, as shown in Algorithm 4. The algorithm first computes $\mathbf{p}_{t_i}$ iteratively on the similarity graph $\mathcal{G}$ via Equation (4). Then, it selects qualification in $\mathtt{Q}$ iterations. In each iteration, it selects a task t^* that maximizes the marginal influence, i.e., $t^* = \arg\max_{t \in \mathcal{T} - \mathcal{T}^{\mathtt{Q}}} \{\mathtt{INF}(\mathcal{T}^{\mathtt{Q}} \cup \{t\}) - \mathtt{INF}(\mathcal{T}^{\mathtt{Q}})\}$.

We can prove that the approximation ratio of this greedy algorithm is $1 - \frac{1}{e}$ where e is the base of natural logarithm. Next, we analyze its time complexity. It has $\mathtt{Q}$ iterations, and, in each iteration, it computes $\mathtt{INF}(\mathcal{T}^{\mathtt{Q}} \cup \{t\})$ for each microtask $t \in \mathcal{T}$, which needs to scan all microtask in $\mathbf{p}_{t_i}$. Overall, the complexity of Algorithm 4 is $\mathcal{O}(\mathtt{Q} \cdot |\mathcal{T}|^2)$.

6. EXPERIMENTS

6.1 Experiment Setup

Datasets: We conducted experiments on real-world crowdsourcing platform Amazon Mechanical Turk (AMT) and evaluated the approaches on two real datasets.

1) `YahooQA` dataset: Evaluating quality of Question-Answers. The first dataset contained a set of microtasks that asked workers to evaluate whether a user-generated answer from *Yahoo Answers* can appropriately address its corresponding question. An example question and one of its answers were "*Who first proposed Heliocentrism?*" and "*Nicolaus Copernicus, a Renaissance mathematician and astronomer.*". A worker was required to do a Yes/No selection, i.e., whether the answer can appropriately address the question. We generated the ground truth of each task based on the ratings from Yahoo Answers: if an answer was rated as the "Best Answer" by the asker and attracted many more "Thumbs Up" than "Thumbs Down", the answer was labeled with 1. On the other hand, if the answer was not selected by the asker and had many more "Thumbs Down", it was labeled with 0. We selected 110 question-answer pairs as tasks in six domains, 2006 FIFA World Cup (`FF`), Books & Authors (`BA`), Diet & Fitness (`DF`), Home Schooling (`HS`), Hunting (`HT`) and Philosophy (`PH`). Table 4 shows statistics of `YahooQA`.

2) `ItemCompare` dataset: This dataset contained a set of microtasks that ask workers to compare two items based on a specified comparison criteria. We used four domains, `Food`, `NBA`, `Auto` and `Country`. In the `Food` domain, a microtask asked workers to compare two food items, say Chocolate and Honey, and identified which one had more calories. In the

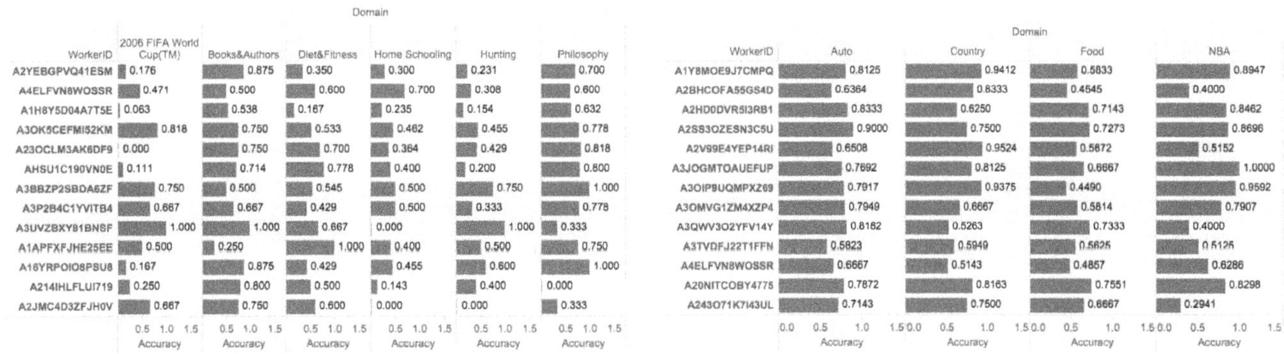

(a) YahooQA dataset. (b) ItemCompare dataset.

Figure 6: Diverse Workers' Accuracies Across Different Domains (Here, we only list workers that completed more than 20 microtasks).

Table 4: Dataset Statistics.

Dataset	YahooQA	ItemCompare
# of microtasks	110	360
# of domains	6	4
# of workers	25	53

NBA domain, workers compared two NBA teams, say Los Angeles Lakers and Milwaukee Bucks, and verified which team won more NBA champions. In the Auto domain, workers compared two cars, say 2014 Toyota Camry and 2014 Lexus ES, and verified which one was more fuel efficient. In the Country domain, workers compared two countries, say Brazil and Canada, and verified which one had larger total area. We generated 360 microtasks where each domain had 90 microtasks, and manually labelled the ground truth.

We published all the microtasks on AMT and evaluated different approaches. We put 10 microtasks as a batch in a Human Intelligence Task (HIT), and set the price of each assignment as $0.1. To ensure that all the approaches were compared on the same set of workers, we set the "Number of Assignments per HIT" to a large number (10 in our experiments) to collect enough answers. Based on the collected answers, we ran different approaches for task assignment and compared their performance. Table 4 shows statistics of the datasets and answers collected from AMT.

Baseline approaches: We implemented our methods and compared with baseline approaches. Note that we compared both task assignment and aggregation: Given an approach, we used its task assignment strategy to obtain answers from workers and employed its aggregation strategy to derive the final results for microtasks. We considered three baselines: 1) RandomMV: This approach used a random strategy for task assignment and aggregated workers' answers to generate the result by using majority voting. 2) RandomEM: The approach also used the random strategy for task assignment, but an Expectation-Maximization (EM) algorithm [31, 8] was used to aggregate the answers. The EM algorithm iteratively estimated worker's accuracy (called *confusion matrix* in [31, 8]) and exploited the estimated accuracy to compute the aggregated result. 3) AvgAccPV: This approach estimated an average accuracy for each worker by injecting some "gold" microtasks with ground truth, assigned microtasks to workers with higher accuracies, and aggregated the answers using the probabilistic verification model introduced in [22].

Evaluation metrics: We evaluated approaches on accuracy and efficiency. Accuracy was computed as the ratio of the microtasks with correctly predicted results, and the efficiency was measured by the elapsed time of task assignment.

Experiment settings: All approaches were evaluated under assignment size for each microtask $k = 3$. In addition, all the programs were implemented in JAVA and all the experiments were run on a Ubuntu machine with an Intel Core 2 Quad X5450 3.00GHz processor and 4 GB memory.

6.2 Diverse Accuracies across Domains

We first investigated the diversity of workers' accuracies across different domains by analyzing the collected answers in each dataset. For each worker, we computed the number of her completed microtasks and the accuracy (the ratio of correct answers to all of her completed microtasks) in each domain. Figure 6 shows the results on the two datasets, where the length of a bar represents the accuracy (the actual value of the accuracy is also labelled beside the bar).

We had the following observations of diversity. On the one hand, accuracies of each individual worker might be rather diverse across domains: workers could be very good in some domains, while performing badly in others. For example, as shown in Figure 6(a), the first worker A2YEBGPVQ41ESM had good accuracies in domains Books&Authors (0.875) and Philosophy (0.70) but had rather bad accuracies in Diet&Fitness (0.35), Home Schooling (0.30), Hunting (0.231), and FIFA (0.176). On the other hand, top workers w.r.t accuracy in different domains might also be diverse. As shown in Figure 6(b), the best worker in the Country domain was A2V99E4YEP14RI with accuracy 0.95. However, she was low-ranked in the NBA domain (due to the low accuracy 0.52), while the best worker in the NBA domain was worker A3JOGMTOAUEFUP. These observations have verified our claim in Section 1 that workers may have diverse accuracies across different tasks, and an average accuracy would be limited in reflecting worker's performance. These results also implied the necessity of our microtask assignment that took accuracy diversity into consideration, because some good workers (e.g., worker A2V99E4YEP14RI) in one domain (e.g., Country) could be a spammer in another domain (e.g., NBA).

6.3 Evaluation on Adaptive Crowdsourcing

Next, we evaluated our adaptive crowdsourcing approach on accuracy in this section. We first examined the effect of the parameters used in our approach, i.e., microtask similarity measures, parameter α in Equation (2) and assignment size k, and then evaluated the approximation error of our greedy algorithm for adaptive assignment. Due to the space

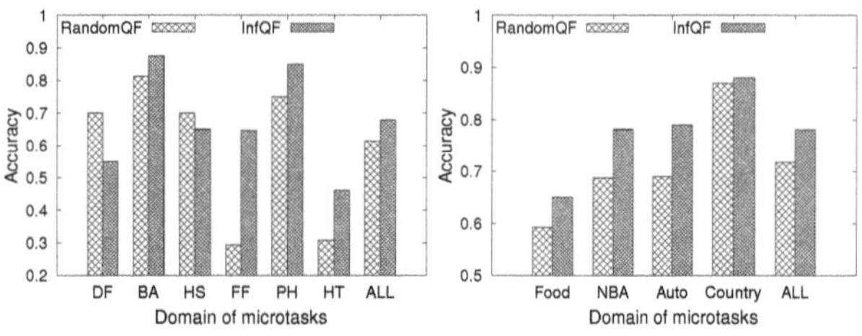

(a) YahooQA dataset. (b) ItemCompare dataset.

Figure 7: Effect of Qualification.

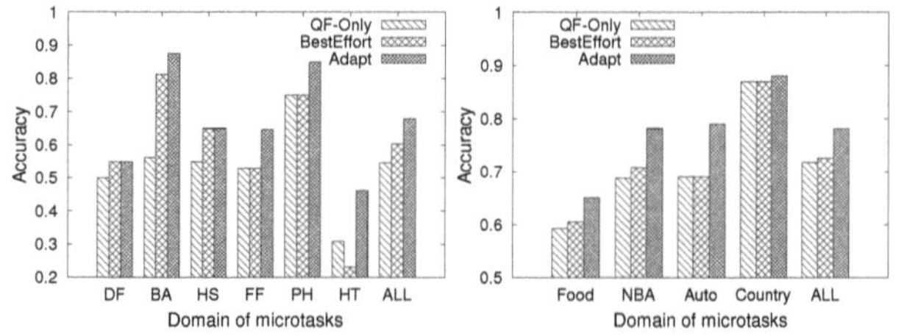

(a) YahooQA dataset. (b) ItemCompare dataset.

Figure 8: Effect of The Adaptive Strategy.

limitations, we put these results in Appendix D. Here we evaluated the effect of qualification and adaptive assignment.

6.3.1 *Effect of Qualification*

We evaluated the effect of qualification and compared two qualification strategies. The first one, denoted by `RamdomQF`, randomly selected a set of `Q` qualification microtasks, while the second one, denoted by `InfQF`, utilized the techniques introduced in Section 5 for qualification selection. In the experiments, we set the number `Q` as 10.

Figure 7 provides the experimental results. We can see that `InfQF` outperformed `RamdomQF` in most of the domains and the overall cases. For example, as shown in Figure 7(a), the accuracy of `InfQF` was higher than that of `RamdomQF` in four out of six domains (`Books&Authors`, `FIFA`, `Philosophy` and `Hunting`), and 8% higher in the overall case (`ALL`). In addition, `InfQF` outperformed `RamdomQF` in all the domains and the overall case on the `ItemCompare` dataset (Figure 7(b)). The main reason is that the qualification microtasks selected by `RamdomQF` might be scattered in different domains, and the number of qualification microtasks in each individual domain would thus be limited. This resulted in overestimation or underestimation of workers' accuracies in the individual domains. In contrast, the `InfQF` method was more "focused", as it would select more qualification microtasks that had large influence to individual domains. These more focused qualification microtasks were helpful to reduce estimation errors and eliminate "bad" workers in the early qualification phase. For instance, on the `YahooQA` dataset, `InfQF` identified and eliminated workers with limited accuracies in the `FIFA` domain, e.g., workers `A2YEBGPVQ41ESM` and `A1H8Y5D04A7T5E` shown in Figure 6(a), and achieved more than 30% improvement on accuracy compared with `RamdomQF` in the domain. In addition, we also observed that `RamdomQF` might select good workers via qualification in some special cases (e.g., `Diet&Fitness` and `Home Schooling` in Figure 6(a)), as it might select some qualification microtasks, which were good for these domains, by chance. However, the method had unsatisfactory performance in most of the cases and achieved low overall performance.

In the remaining part of this section, we use `InfQF` as the default method for qualification selection.

6.3.2 *Effect of Adaptive Assignment*

Then, we evaluated the effect of our adaptive microtask assignment strategy. We studied the following two alternative strategies: 1) `QF-Only`: this strategy utilizes the accuracy which is estimated by qualification microtasks for assignment and does not adaptively update accuracy estimation. 2) `BestEffort`: the strategy, although adaptively updates accuracy estimation, adopts a best effort method for microtask assignment: given a request from a worker, it compares the estimated accuracies of the microtasks the worker could work on and assigns the one with the highest accuracy. 3) `Adapt`: this strategy not only adaptively updates accuracy estimation using our graph-based estimation techniques introduced in Section 3, but also assigns microtasks based on our adaptive method proposed in Section 4.

Figure 8 shows the experimental results. We can see that `QF-Only` achieved the worst performance in most of the cases. This is due to the estimation error in qualification: as qualification microtasks only took a small portion of the dataset, estimation from these microtasks might not be very accurate. `BestEffort` improved the accuracy compared with `QF-Only` in many domains, because it adaptively updated accuracy estimation as workers completed microtasks. However, the improvement was not significant. This is mainly due to its microtask assignment strategy. The best microtask (with the highest accuracy) of a worker might not take the worker as the best candidate to complete the task, because there might be other better workers. As such, this assignment strategy introduced workers with relatively low accuracy and thus affected the majority voting result, which would also have negative influence on the following accuracy estimation. `Adapt` achieved the best accuracy on both datasets. The improvement was attributed to not only our adaptive accuracy estimation but also the assignment strategy that took optimal microtask assignment and worker accuracy testing. In the remainder of this section, we utilize `Adapt` as the default strategy of *i*`Crowd`.

6.4 Comparison with Existing Approaches

We compared *i*`Crowd` with the three baseline approaches mentioned in Section 6.1, `RandomMV`, `RandomEM` and `AvgAccPV`. We used the same set of microtasks for qualification.

Figure 9 shows the performance of these approaches on accuracy. We can see that the performance of random assignment strategies `RandomMV` and `RandomEM` largely depended on the quality of the worker set in a domain: if a domain contained many more good workers, the accuracy would be high; otherwise, the accuracy would be low. For example, as shown in Figure 6(a), the average worker quality of the `FIFA` domain was much lower than that of the `Philosophy` domain, and thus the random strategies achieved much worse result in `FIFA` (only about 0.4 on accuracy). We also had an interesting observation that the EM algorithm for worker answer aggregation might not always be helpful. For instance, the accuracy of `RandomEM` was lower than that of `RandomMV` in the domains `Auto` and `Country` in Figure 9(b). This was mainly attributed to the accuracy estimation mechanism of EM. The algorithm estimated worker accuracies without considering the inherent accuracy diversity over domains, and thus might overestimate some workers with limited accuracies. The iterative mechanism of EM might further propagate and aggravate the overestimation.

Moreover, `AvgAccPV` achieved limited performance on the two datasets, which verified our claim that the average accu-

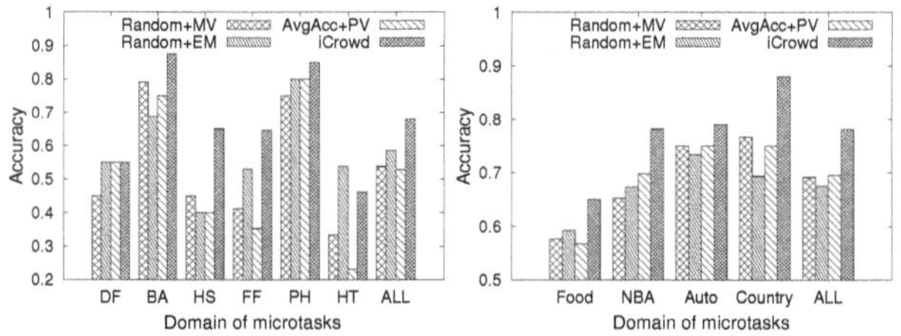

(a) YahooQA dataset. (b) ItemCompare dataset.

Figure 9: Approach Comparison.

racy without considering domain diversity may not be effective for microtask assignment. For example, AvgAccPV would incorrectly estimate that the first worker A2YEBGPVQ41ESM in Figure 6(a) with high average accuracy also had good performance in the Hunting domain, while the worker was bad in Hunting. This resulted in unsatisfactory accuracy of AvgAccPV in this domain (only 25% as shown in Figure 9(a)).

Our approach *i*Crowd outperformed the baseline approaches. As shown in Figure 9, it gained about 10% improvement in the average case (the ALL domain), and even more than 20% improvement in some domains (e.g., Home Schooling). The main reason was that *i*Crowd utilized the graph-based estimation model for capturing accuracy diversity in different domains, which was very helpful to identify the workers with expertise in each individual domain. Furthermore, the assignment strategy of *i*Crowd could effectively assign microtasks to high-quality workers and progressively improved accuracy estimation based on worker answers. We also observed that *i*Crowd had limited improvement in the Auto domain on the ItemCompare dataset. This is mainly because there was no very good workers in this domain: as shown in Figure 6(b), the best worker in Auto only had an accuracy of 0.76, while accuracies of the best workers in other three domain were more than 0.9. As a result, *i*Crowd might not have much space for choosing high-quality assignments.

6.5 Evaluation on Efficiency

We evaluated efficiency of our assignment algorithm using simulation. Initially, the entire microtask set was empty. We inserted 0.2 million microtasks at each time and ran *i*Crowd to evaluate the efficiency. We also considered the maximal number of "neighbors", which can be influenced by a microtask in our accuracy inference. Given a maximal neighbor number, say 40, and a microtask, we randomly selected 40 microtasks as neighbors of the microtask. Figure 10 shows the experimental results. We can see that our method was efficient and scaled very well: with the increase of the numbers of microtasks, the elapsed time increased sub-linearly. The good performance on efficiency was mainly because we devised effective index structures and developed efficient algorithms for microtask assignment.

7. RELATED WORK

The studies most related to our work are quality-control techniques in crowdsourcing. The existing approaches can be broadly classified into two categories. The *gold-injected* approaches [22, 1] leveraged a small amount of tasks with ground truth to estimate workers' reliability and aggregated their answers based on the reliability. The *EM*-based approaches [31, 8, 18, 21] simultaneously estimated worker accuracy and predicted aggregated results using an Expectation-Maximization (EM) strategy. Moreover, Ipeirotis et al. [17] studied how to evaluate the quality of workers to reject or

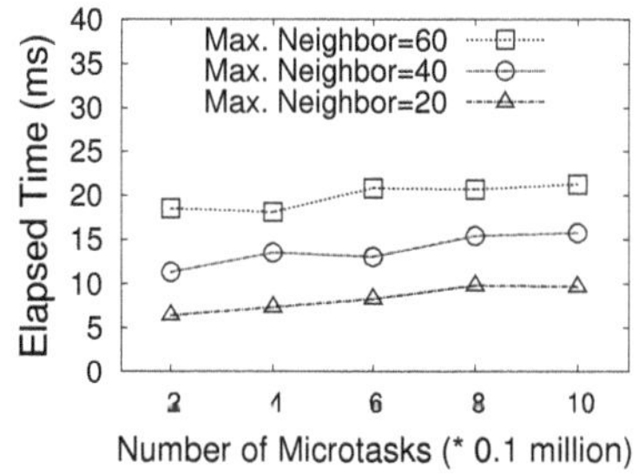

Figure 10: Evaluating Scalability with Simulation.

block low-quality workers. Parameswaran et al. [26] assumed the false positive and false negative rates of each worker, and studied the number of assignments that are required for a task. Our study is different from these quality-control techniques in that we tackle the accuracy diversity in more complicated crowdsourcing tasks for better accuracy estimation and *adaptively* assign tasks to workers, instead of random task assignment without considering workers' expertise.

Recently, some approaches for task assignment [15, 16, 19, 20] and recommendation [3] have been proposed. Although they also considered how to recommend and assign tasks to appropriate workers, they neglected the fact that different works had accuracy diversity across different tasks. Thus different from these studies, we attempted to address two new challenges. First, we studied how to effectively estimate the diverse accuracy of workers based on their completed tasks. Second, we proposed efficient algorithms to support instant task assignment based on workers' divserse accuracy.

There are some crowd-powered systems developed in the human-computer interaction community. Solyent [5] is a word processor that employs the *Find-Fix-Verify* interaction method. Adrenaline [4] is a crowd-powered camera that supports realtime crowdsourcing by using the interaction method called *rapid refinement*. Recent studies in the database community aim to leverage crowdsourcing to build database systems, which can support some queries that cannot be processed by machine-only methods (e.g. entity resolution and graph search) [25, 29, 12, 23, 27, 28, 32, 9, 34, 13, 10]. Nevertheless, *i*Crowd has a different goal from these studies: *i*Crowd focuses on adaptively assigning tasks to appropriate workers to improve the crowdsourcing quality.

8. CONCLUSION

We proposed *i*Crowd, an adaptive crowdsourcing framework to adaptively assign microtasks to appropriate workers who have high probabilities to correctly complete microtasks. We devised a graph-based estimation model to capture the diverse accuracies of workers across different tasks in order to provide more effective task assignment. We proved that the optimal task assignment is NP-hard and devised a greedy algorithm to enable instant task assignments. We deployed *i*Crowd on AMT and experimental results on two real datasets show that *i*Crowd achieved much higher quality than state-of-the-art methods.

Acknowledgement: This work was partly supported by the 973 Program of China (2015CB358700), a Singapore Ministry of Education AcRF Tier 1 Grant No. R-252-000-513-112, the "NExT Research Center" (WBS: R-252-300-001-490), the NSFC project (61422205, 61472198), the Chinese Special Project of Science and Technology (2013zx01039-002-002), Tencent, Huawei, SAP, YETP0105, and the FDCT/106/2012/A3.

9. REFERENCES

[1] http://crowdflower.com/.

[2] Amazon Mechanical Turk. https://www.mturk.com.

[3] G. Adomavicius and A. Tuzhilin. Toward the next generation of recommender systems: A survey of the state-of-the-art and possible extensions. *IEEE Trans. Knowl. Data Eng.*, 17(6):734–749, 2005.

[4] M. S. Bernstein, J. Brandt, R. C. Miller, and D. R. Karger. Crowds in two seconds: enabling realtime crowd-powered interfaces. In *UIST*, pages 33–42, 2011.

[5] M. S. Bernstein, G. Little, R. C. Miller, B. Hartmann, M. S. Ackerman, D. R. Karger, D. Crowell, and K. Panovich. Soylent: a word processor with a crowd inside. In *UIST*, pages 313–322, 2010.

[6] D. M. Blei, A. Y. Ng, and M. I. Jordan. Latent dirichlet allocation. In *NIPS*, pages 601–608, 2001.

[7] C. C. Cao, J. She, Y. Tong, and L. Chen. Whom to ask? jury selection for decision making tasks on micro-blog services. *PVLDB*, 5(11):1495–1506, 2012.

[8] A. P. Dawid and A. M. Skene. Maximum likelihood estimation of observer error-rates using the em algorithm. *Applied Statistics*, 28(1):20–28, 1979.

[9] G. Demartini, D. E. Difallah, and P. Cudré-Mauroux. ZenCrowd: leveraging probabilistic reasoning and crowdsourcing techniques for large-scale entity linking. In *WWW*, pages 469–478, 2012.

[10] J. Fan, M. Lu, B. C. Ooi, W. Tan, and M. Zhang. A hybrid machine-crowdsourcing system for matching web tables. In *IEEE 30th International Conference on Data Engineering, Chicago, ICDE 2014, IL, USA, March 31 - April 4, 2014*, pages 976–987, 2014.

[11] A. Feng, M. J. Franklin, D. Kossmann, T. Kraska, S. Madden, S. Ramesh, A. Wang, and R. Xin. Crowddb: Query processing with the vldb crowd. *PVLDB*, 4(12):1387–1390, 2011.

[12] M. J. Franklin, D. Kossmann, T. Kraska, S. Ramesh, and R. Xin. Crowddb: answering queries with crowdsourcing. In *SIGMOD*, pages 61–72, 2011.

[13] S. Guo, A. G. Parameswaran, and H. Garcia-Molina. So who won?: dynamic max discovery with the crowd. In *SIGMOD*, pages 385–396, 2012.

[14] T. H. Haveliwala. Topic-sensitive pagerank. In *WWW*, pages 517–526, 2002.

[15] C. Ho, S. Jabbari, and J. W. Vaughan. Adaptive task assignment for crowdsourced classification. In *ICML*, pages 534–542, 2013.

[16] C. Ho and J. W. Vaughan. Online task assignment in crowdsourcing markets. In *AAAI*, 2012.

[17] P. G. Ipeirotis, F. Provost, and J. Wang. Quality management on amazon mechanical turk. In *SIGKDD Workshop on Human Computation*, pages 64–67, 2010.

[18] D. R. Karger, S. Oh, and D. Shah. Iterative learning for reliable crowdsourcing systems. In *NIPS*, pages 1953–1961, 2011.

[19] D. R. Karger, S. Oh, and D. Shah. Budget-optimal task allocation for reliable crowdsourcing systems. *Operations Research*, 62(1):1–24, 2014.

[20] H. W. Kuhn. The hungarian method for the assignment problem. In *50 Years of Integer Programming 1958-2008 - From the Early Years to the State-of-the-Art*, pages 29–47. 2010.

[21] Q. Liu, J. Peng, and A. T. Ihler. Variational inference for crowdsourcing. In *NIPS*, pages 701–709, 2012.

[22] X. Liu, M. Lu, B. C. Ooi, Y. Shen, S. Wu, and M. Zhang. Cdas: A crowdsourcing data analytics system. *PVLDB*, 5(10):1040–1051, 2012.

[23] A. Marcus, E. Wu, D. R. Karger, S. Madden, and R. C. Miller. Human-powered sorts and joins. *PVLDB*, 5(1):13–24, 2011.

[24] A. Marcus, E. Wu, S. Madden, and R. C. Miller. Crowdsourced databases: Query processing with people. In *CIDR*, pages 211–214, 2011.

[25] A. G. Parameswaran, S. Boyd, H. Garcia-Molina, A. Gupta, N. Polyzotis, and J. Widom. Optimal crowd-powered rating and filtering algorithms. *PVLDB*, 7(9):685–696, 2014.

[26] A. G. Parameswaran, H. Garcia-Molina, H. Park, N. Polyzotis, A. Ramesh, and J. Widom. Crowdscreen: algorithms for filtering data with humans. In *SIGMOD*, pages 361–372, 2012.

[27] A. G. Parameswaran and N. Polyzotis. Answering queries using humans, algorithms and databases. In *CIDR*, pages 160–166, 2011.

[28] A. G. Parameswaran, A. D. Sarma, H. Garcia-Molina, N. Polyzotis, and J. Widom. Human-assisted graph search: it's okay to ask questions. *PVLDB*, 4(5):267–278, 2011.

[29] H. Park and J. Widom. Crowdfill: collecting structured data from the crowd. In *SIGMOD*, pages 577–588, 2014.

[30] V. C. Raykar and S. Yu. Ranking annotators for crowdsourced labeling tasks. In *NIPS*, pages 1809–1817, 2011.

[31] V. S. Sheng, F. J. Provost, and P. G. Ipeirotis. Get another label? improving data quality and data mining using multiple, noisy labelers. In *SIGKDD*, pages 614–622, 2008.

[32] J. Wang, T. Kraska, M. J. Franklin, and J. Feng. Crowder: Crowdsoucing entity resolution. *PVLDB*, 5(10), 2012.

[33] J. Wang, G. Li, J. X. Yu, and J. Feng. Entity matching: How similar is similar. *PVLDB*, 4(10):622–633, 2011.

[34] S. E. Whang, P. Lofgren, and H. Garcia-Molina. Question selection for crowd entity resolution. Technical report, Stanford University.

[35] D. Zhou, O. Bousquet, T. N. Lal, J. Weston, and B. Schölkopf. Learning with local and global consistency. In *NIPS*, 2003.

APPENDIX

A. IMPLEMENTATION OF ICROWD ON AMAZON MECHANICAL TURK

We developed a system to support adaptive crowdsourcing on Amazon Mechanical Turk (AMT), as shown in Figure 11. As AMT does not support advanced HIT assignment (it only randomly assigns HITs to workers), the system utilized the *ExternalQuestion* mechanism[3] to manage microtasks on our own Web server and take full control of microtask as-

[3] More information can be found in AMT Documentation at http://aws.amazon.com/documentation/mturk/

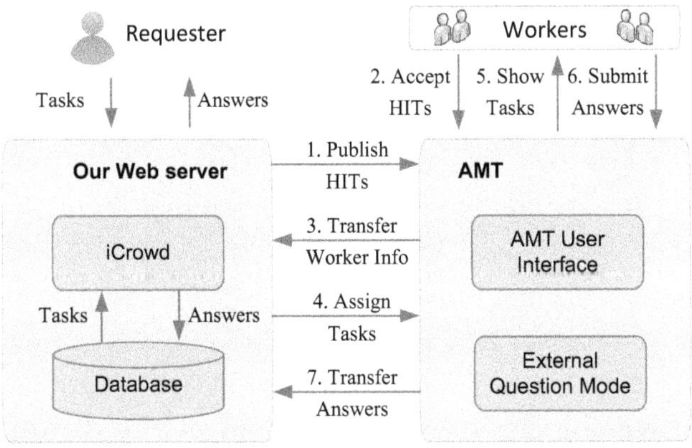

Figure 11: Implementation of *iCrowd* on AMT

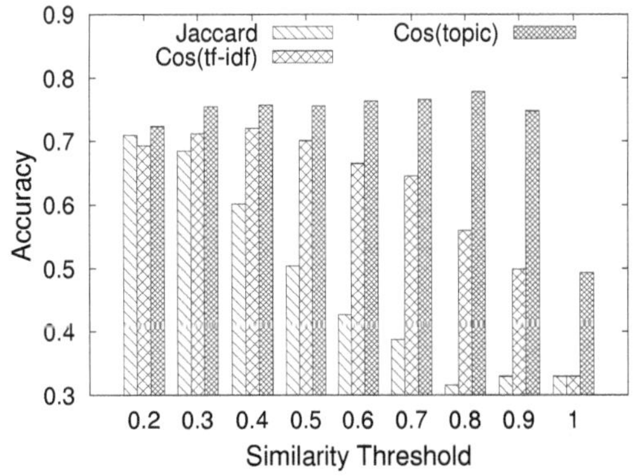

Figure 12: Evaluating Different Similarity Measures and Thresholds on The ItemCompare Dataset.

signments. Specifically, the system generates HITs with the ExternalQuestion mode, which are different from the ordinary HITs in that each of such HITs only contains a URL of our Web server, instead of the actual microtasks. Then, when a worker accepts a published HIT and requests for microtasks[4], AMT will send a request containing worker information to our server. Given the worker information, `iCrowd` in our server assigns microtasks to the worker and sends them back to AMT. Next, AMT embeds the assigned microtasks as an *HTML iframe* in its user interface to present the microtasks to the worker. After a worker submits her answers, AMT transfers the answers to our server and our server calls back some APIs of AMT to process payment. Finally, after collecting answers for all the microtasks, `iCrowd` aggregates the answers and stores the obtained result. Briefly speaking, when a worker requests a microtask, our system decides how to assign microtasks to the worker; when a worker submits an answer, it collects the answer, aggregates the answers, and computes which domains each worker is skilled in. Iteratively, our system can assign all tasks to appropriate workers.

B. PROOF OF LEMMA 4

We can prove the lemma by a reduction from the k-set packing problem, which is known to be NP-hard.

Recall that an instance of k-set packing problem $(\mathcal{U}, \mathcal{C}, k)$ consists of a universe of elements $\mathcal{U} = \{e_1, e_2, \ldots, e_{|\mathcal{U}|}\}$, a collection of subsets $\mathcal{C} = \{C_1, C_2, \ldots, C_{|\mathcal{C}|}\}$ where $C_i \subseteq \mathcal{U}$, and a number k. Each subset C_i contains less than k elements, i.e., $|C_i| \le k$, and it is associated with a weight $w(C_i)$. The problem aims to select some subsets $\mathcal{C}^* \subseteq \mathcal{C}$ satisfying $\forall C_i, C_j \in \mathcal{C}^*$ are disjoint, to maximize $\sum_{C_i \in \mathcal{C}^*} w(C_i)$.

Given any instance $(\mathcal{U}, \mathcal{C}, k)$ of the k-set packing problem, we create an instance of the microtask selection problem as follows. We first create a set of active workers $\mathcal{W}$, each of which corresponds to an element in $\mathcal{U}$. Then, we create a set of microtasks $\mathcal{T}$, each of which corresponds to a subset in $\mathcal{C}$, and let the number of assignments for each microtask be equal to k. Then, it is easy to prove that the optimization objectives of the problems are identical. The problem of microtask selection can be solved, only if the k-set packing problem is solved. Thus, we prove the lemma.

[4]Usually a HIT contains mutiple microtasks. For each HIT, we only need to tell the worker how many microtasks in the HIT and show the first microtask in the HIT. When the worker finishes the microtask and clicks the "Next" link, we assigns the next microtask to the worker.

C. PROOF OF LEMMA 5

We can prove the lemma by a reduction from the maximum coverage problem, which is known to be NP-hard.

Recall that an instance of maximum coverage problem $(\mathcal{U}, \mathcal{C}, k)$ consists of a set of elements $\mathcal{U} = \{u_1, u_2, \ldots, u_{|\mathcal{U}|}\}$, a collection of subsets $\mathcal{C} = \{C_1, C_2, \ldots, C_{|\mathcal{C}|}\}$ where $C_i \subseteq \mathcal{U}$, and a number k. The problem aims to select k subsets $\mathcal{C}^* \subseteq \mathcal{C}$ to maximize the number of covered elements, $|\bigcup_{C \in \mathcal{C}^*} C|$.

Given any instance $(\mathcal{U}, \mathcal{C}, k)$ of the maximum coverage problem, we create an instance of the qualification microtask selection problem as follows. We first create a set of microtask $\mathcal{T}$, each of which corresponds to an element in $\mathcal{U}$. Then, we create accuracy vector $\mathbf{p}_{t_i}$ corresponding to each set $C \in \mathcal{C}$: for any $u_i \in C$, we set the $p_i = 1$; otherwise $p_i = 0$. Next, we let the number of qualification microtasks be equal to k. Then, it is easy to prove that the problem of qualification microtask selection can be solved, only if the maximum coverage problem is solved. Thus, we prove the lemma.

D. ADDITIONAL EXPERIMENTS

D.1 Evaluation on Similarity Measures

We investigated the methods for measuring microtask similarity, which were essential to generate the similarity graph for accuracy estimation. To compute microtask similarity, we tokenized the text of microtasks and removed the stopwords. Then, given two microtasks, we considered the following three similarity measures: 1) `Jaccard`: this method took each microtask as a set of words and computed similarity of two microtasks as the their overlap size divided by their union size; 2) `Cos(tf-idf)`: this method took each microtask as a vector of words associated with TF-IDF weights, then it computed the similarity as the cosine similarity of the vectors; 3) `Cos(topic)`: this method first conducted *topic analysis* by using Latent Dirichlet Allocation (LDA) [6] to obtain a topic distribution for each microtask, and then computed microtask similarity via the cosine similarity of the two distributions. We also set a similarity threshold and only utilized the microtask pairs with similarity larger than the threshold.

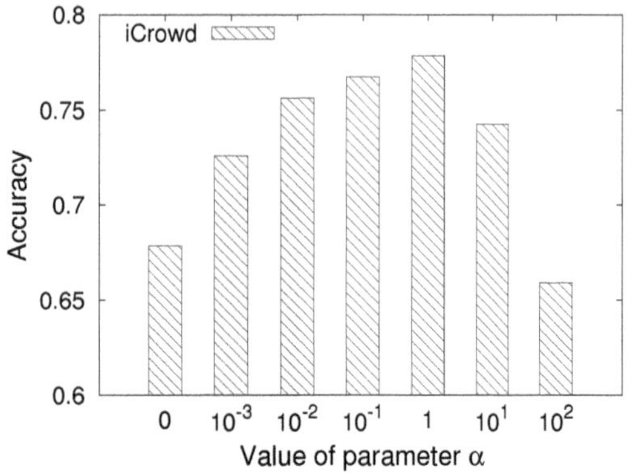

Figure 13: Evaluating Parameter α on The ItemCompare Dataset.

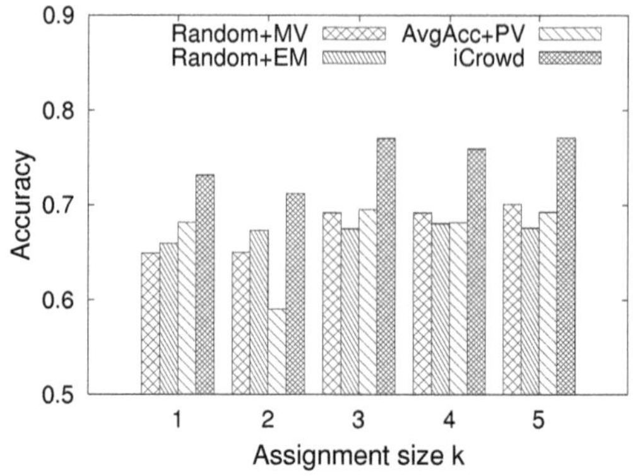

Figure 14: Evaluating Assignment Size k on The ItemCompare Dataset.

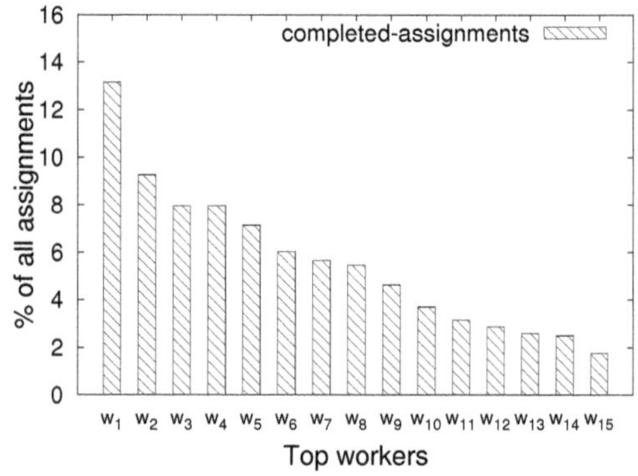

Figure 15: Distribution of Microtasks Completions for Top Workers on The ItemCompare Dataset.

The experimental result is shown in Figure 12. We have the following observations. First, different similarity measures did not significantly affect the performance. For example, for a small similarity threshold, the three methods achieved similar performance. Second, the similarity thresholds had effect on the performance. A small threshold involved some weak microtask connections and a large threshold eliminated many strong microtask connections. Thus an appropriate threshold could be helpful to achieve high performance. Third, `Cos(topic)` achieved better performance, because the topic analysis from the LDA model could discover the inherent topical relevance between microtasks in the same domain while differentiate microtasks in different domains.

We used `Cos(topic)` with threshold 0.8 as the default similarity measure and threshold for all of our experiments.

D.2 Evaluation on Parameter α

We evaluated the effect of α introduced in Equation (2). This parameter was used to leverage the two objectives in accuracy estimation: 1) minimizing accuracy difference between similar microtasks, and 2) minimizing the difference between estimated accuracies and observed accuracies. We varied α and examined the accuracy of our approach.

As shown in Figure 13, depending solely on one objective could not achieve satisfactory accuracy: On the one hand, only depending on the first objective ($\alpha = 0$) would lead to all connected microtasks having the same estimated accuracies, which failed to capture accuracy diversity. On the other hand, only depending on the second objective (α is a large number, say 100) would make estimated accuracies very close to the observed ones, which means the estimation could not benefit from the graph-based inference. In contrast, reconciling these two objectives (i.e., finding an appropriate α) produced much better accuracy.

W set $\alpha = 1.0$ as the default value for all of our experiments.

D.3 Evaluation on Assignment Size k

We evaluated the approaches, `RandomMV`, `RandomEM`, `AvgAccPV`, and *i*`Crowd`, by varying the assignment size k. As mentioned in Section 2.1, this parameter is used to set the number of workers which are assigned with each microtask.

Figure 14 shows the experimental result. We can see that our proposed approach *i*`Crowd` achieved the highest accuracy at every assignment size k, and outperformed the three baselines. This is because *i*`Crowd` could effectively estimate workers' diverse accuracies and, given each k, assign top-k workers with higher accuracies to each microtask. Besides, we observe that increasing k would generally improve the overall accuracy. For example, accuracy of *i*`Crowd` was improved by 5 percent from $k = 1$ to $k = 3$. This illustrates that voting among more workers could increase the accuracy. Nevertheless, the improvement might become insignificant given a larger assignment size. This is because the newly assigned workers have relatively lower estimated accuracies and thus have lower weights in the voting to affect the final result.

D.4 Approximation Error of Greedy Algorithm for Microtask Assignment

We evaluated our greedy algorithm (Algorithm 3) and examined its approximation error on the larger dataset `ItemCompare`. Specifically, we implemented an enumeration-based algorithm to find the optimal solution with the maximum overall accuracy, denoted by OPT: it enumerated all feasible assignment schemes and returned the one with the maximum overall accuracy. Meanwhile, we ran our greedy algorithm to produce a solution with overall accuracy denoted by APP. Then, we measured the approximation error using the equation

$$Error = \frac{OPT - APP}{OPT} \times 100\%. \tag{6}$$

Table 5 shows the result where we varied the number of active workers to be assigned (i.e., $\mathcal{W}$ in Algorithm 3). Notice that the enumeration-based algorithm took very long

Table 5: Approximation Errors of Algorithm 2 on The ItemCompare Dataset.

# active workers	3	4	5	6	7
Approx. Error (%)	1.9	0.6	0.5	1.3	1.5

computation time when the number of active workers was larger than 7 (we waited 30 minutes and did not get the result). This is because, in this case, there were 337 microtasks having non-empty top worker sets ($\{\widehat{\mathcal{W}}(t_i)\}$). The optimal algorithm had to enumerate all possible subsets of 337 microtasks such that the top worker sets in each of such subsets were disjoint, which was rather time-consuming. As such, we only reported the results for the number of active workers up to 7. As shown in Table 5, the approximation errors of our greedy algorithm were less than 2%.

This illustrated that the performance of the greedy algorithm was very close to that of the optimal task assignment.

D.5 Assignment Distribution w.r.t Workers

In this section, we examined the distribution of the number of microtask assignments to workers on the larger ItemCompare dataset. This dataset had 360 microtasks and the assignment size for each microtask was $k = 3$. Thus the number of total assignments was 1080.

Figure 15 shows the result for the top-15 workers. We can see that each of these worker completed a fair number of assignments, e.g., the first worker w_1 completed more than 13% of all the assignments, and these top-15 workers completed 84% of all the assignments. This observation supports our claim that the worker set that completed a crowdsourcing job was relatively stable.

QASCA: A Quality-Aware Task Assignment System for Crowdsourcing Applications

Yudian Zheng[†], Jiannan Wang[$], Guoliang Li[#], Reynold Cheng[†], Jianhua Feng[#]
[#]Tsinghua University, [†]The University of Hong Kong, [$]UC Berkeley
ydzheng2@cs.hku.hk, jnwang@berkeley.edu, liguoliang@tsinghua.edu.cn
ckcheng@cs.hku.hk, fengjh@tsinghua.edu.cn

ABSTRACT

A crowdsourcing system, such as the Amazon Mechanical Turk (AMT), provides a platform for a large number of questions to be answered by Internet workers. Such systems have been shown to be useful to solve problems that are difficult for computers, including entity resolution, sentiment analysis, and image recognition. In this paper, we investigate the *online task assignment problem*: Given a pool of n questions, which of the k questions should be assigned to a worker? A poor assignment may not only waste time and money, but may also hurt the quality of a crowdsourcing application that depends on the workers' answers. We propose to consider quality measures (also known as evaluation metrics) that are relevant to an application during the task assignment process. Particularly, we explore how Accuracy and F-score, two widely-used evaluation metrics for crowdsourcing applications, can facilitate task assignment. Since these two metrics assume that the ground truth of a question is known, we study their variants that make use of the probability distributions derived from workers' answers. We further investigate *online assignment strategies*, which enables optimal task assignments. Since these algorithms are expensive, we propose solutions that attain high quality in linear time. We develop a system called the Quality-Aware Task Assignment System for Crowdsourcing Applications (QASCA) on top of AMT. We evaluate our approaches on five real crowdsourcing applications. We find that QASCA is efficient, and attains better result quality (of more than 8% improvement) compared with existing methods.

Categories and Subject Descriptors

H.4.m [**Information Systems Applications**]: Miscellaneous

Keywords

Crowdsourcing; Quality Control; Online Task Assignment

1. INTRODUCTION

Crowdsourcing solutions have been proposed to solve problems that are often considered to be hard for computers (e.g., entity resolution [56,60] and sentiment analysis [30]). Consider the entity resolution problem, where objects in a database referring to the same real-world entity are to be identified. For instance, in a product review database, it is useful to collect all the users' comments about a particular product, which may be named differently by various users (e.g., *iPad Two* and *iPad 2*). To perform this task, crowdsourcing techniques have been developed to generate human understandable questions (e.g., Are *iPad Two* and *iPad 2* the same or not?) for the database owner (or *requester*) [56]. These questions, packed into *Human Intelligent Tasks* (HITs), are posted on a crowdsourcing platform (e.g., Amazon Mechanical Turk (AMT)). Internet users (or *workers*) are then invited to answer these questions, based on which the final result is returned to the requester.

In AMT, every HIT contains a certain number (k) of questions. Because a worker may give an incorrect answer, a HIT is assigned to a number (z) of workers. The result of each question is then derived based on voting strategies (e.g., Majority Vote). Upon completion of a HIT, the requester may pay a certain amount of money to the worker. A fundamental issue, which we call *task assignment*, is: Given a pool of n questions, which of the k questions should be selected and put to the HIT for the coming worker? In AMT, this issue is usually addressed in an *offline* manner: the questions assigned to all HITs were decided before they are shown to the workers. As pointed out in [3,30], the main drawback of this approach is that the difficulty level of a question is not considered: for an "easy" question, its final result can be determined even if the current number of answers received from workers is less than z, whereas a more difficult or controversial question may require answers from more than z workers. Notice that a requester may only have a limited amount of budget to pay the workers. It is thus important to decide the question(s) to be included in a HIT, in order to obtain the best answers under the limited budget. Recent solutions, such as CDAS [30] and AskIt! [3], address this problem through *online assignment strategies* – the HIT is generated *dynamically* when requested by a worker, i.e., the k questions are chosen for the HIT "on the fly". The statistical confidence of the answers obtained so far for each question is tracked, and questions whose answers are the least confident are put to the HIT. Thus, the number of times each question is asked can be different. These methods were shown to perform better than the AMT's approach.

However, existing online assignment strategies overlook an important factor – the applications that use the crowdsourced data. Depending on the application semantics, the metric used to gauge the quality of crowdsourced data can be different. In Twitter Sentiment Analysis, for instance, workers are invited to give their sentiments (e.g., "positive", "neutral" or "negative") for each crawled tweet [30]. The Accuracy metric, which is the fraction of returned tweets correctly classified, is often used to measure the quality of the sentiment labels [18,22,30,44]. As for entity resolution [56,60], which asks a worker to judge whether a pair of objects is "equal" or "non-equal", F-score [25,31,32,56,59] is often adopted to measure the quality of the entity-resolution results. As our experiments

SIGMOD'15, May 31–June 4, 2015, Melbourne, Victoria, Australia.

ACM 978-1-4503-2758-9/15/05 ...$15.00.
http://dx.doi.org/10.1145/2723372.2749430.

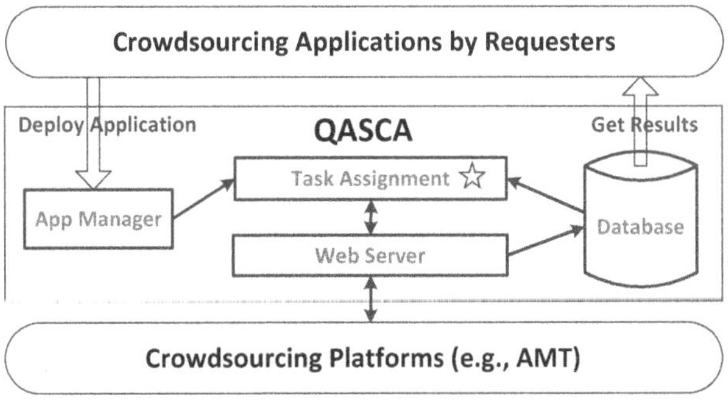

Figure 1: The QASCA Architecture.

show, considering evaluation metrics in the task assignment process can significantly improve the quality of the crowdsourced results.

Our solutions. In this paper, we propose a novel online task assignment framework, which takes application-driven evaluation metrics into account. We investigate two popular evaluation metrics, i.e., Accuracy and F-score, that are widely used by various crowdsourcing applications [18,22,30,44,56,59]. Conceptually, our algorithm enumerates all sets of k questions. For every set of k questions, our solution estimates the improvement in the quality of the answers, *if* these questions are really sent to the coming worker. The set of k questions that maximizes the quality improvement will constitute the new HIT. To realize this, we have to address two key issues:

• **Lack of ground truth.** Evaluation metrics, such as Accuracy and F-score, assume that each question's *ground truth* (or true answer) is known. However, during the task assignment process, it may not be possible to know the ground truth of a question. Thus, existing evaluation metrics are not readily used to solve the task assignment problem. We represent the possible true answer of a question by the *distribution matrix*, which captures the probability distributions of true answers. We study how to populate this matrix with two models, namely Worker Probability (WP) [16,26,30,62] and Confusion Matrix (CM) [1,22,61] that are commonly used to describe the performance of workers. We further incorporate the distribution matrix into Accuracy and F-score, resulting correspondingly in the proposed two functions: Accuracy* and F-score*.

• **Expensive evaluation.** Finding the best solution for the task assignment problem can be extremely expensive. Given a pool of n questions, there are $\binom{n}{k}$ sets of candidate questions for a HIT. Moreover, due to the incorporation of the distribution matrix, measuring the quality of the distribution matrix under Accuracy* or F-score* can be expensive. We explore efficient algorithms for quality measurement. We also propose two respective linear-time algorithms to find the best set of questions for assignment.

We have developed a system called QASCA. As shown in Figure 1, QASCA is run on top of a crowdsourcing platform (e.g., AMT). The *App Manager* stores the n questions and other information (e.g., budget) needed by the strategies. The *Task Assignment* runs the strategies and decides the k questions to be included in the HIT. The *Web Server* then sends the HIT to the workers. The workers' answers are then stored in the *Database* through the *Web Server*, and the derived results are sent back to the requester. The details of QASCA and how an entity resolution application can use QASCA are described in Appendix A.

To summarize, we make the following contributions:

(1) We propose a novel task assignment framework by incorporating evaluation metrics into assignment strategies, and formalize the *online task assignment problem* under the proposed framework;

(2) We generalize the definition of evaluation metrics to be able to quantify the result quality w.r.t a distribution matrix, and devise efficient algorithms to identify the optimal result of each question that can maximize the overall quality;

(3) We propose two respective linear online assignment algorithms that can efficiently select the best k questions for a coming worker;

(4) We develop a system called QASCA[1], which enables a popular crowdsourcing platform (i.e., AMT) to support our task assignment framework. We evaluate the performance of QASCA on five real applications. Experimental results indicate that QASCA can achieve much better (of more than 8% improvement) result quality compared with five state-of-the-art systems.

The remainder of this paper is organized as follows. Section 2 defines the task assignment problem. We define Accuracy* and F-score*, and explain how to evaluate them in Section 3. Efficient online assignment algorithms are devised in Section 4. Section 5 addresses how to compute distribution matrices. We present our experimental results in Section 6. Section 7 discusses related works. Finally, we present conclusions and future work in Section 8.

2. THE TASK ASSIGNMENT PROBLEM

We first discuss the question model in Section 2.1, and then formally define the task assignment problem in Section 2.2. Finally we explain the workflow of QASCA in Section 2.3.

2.1 Question Model

Let $S = \{q_1, q_2, \ldots, q_n\}$ denote the set of questions provided by a requester and each question has the same ℓ possible labels (or answers), denoted by $\{L_1, L_2, \ldots, L_\ell\}$. For example, the two labels for all generated questions in an entity resolution application [59] are $\{L_1$="equal", L_2="non-equal"$\}$. Let $D = \{D_1, D_2, \ldots, D_n\}$ denote the answer set for all questions. Each D_i contains a set of tuples where each tuple (w, j) denotes that question q_i has been answered by worker w with label L_j. For example, $D_2 = \{(w_1, 1), (w_3, 2)\}$ means that question q_2 is answered twice: worker w_1 has answered question q_2 with label L_1 and worker w_3 has answered question q_2 with label L_2.

When worker w completes a HIT, for each question q_i ($1 \le i \le n$), we can compute the probability distribution of question q_i's true label. The probability distributions of all questions form the question model, called *current distribution matrix*, denoted by Q^c, which is an $n \times \ell$ matrix. The i-th ($1 \le i \le n$) row $Q^c_i = [\, Q^c_{i,1}, Q^c_{i,2}, \ldots, Q^c_{i,\ell} \,]$ represents the probability distribution for question q_i's true label, and each cell $Q^c_{i,j}$ ($1 \le i \le n, 1 \le j \le \ell$) denotes the probability that question q_i's true label is L_j. We will discuss how to compute Q^c in Section 5.1.

Remarks: For ease of presentation, we assume that (1) the labels are pre-defined, and are the same for all questions; (2) each question's ground truth is a single label. These assumptions can be relaxed. First, if labels are not pre-defined, [50] addresses how to enumerate possible labels for questions. Second, if each question has multiple true labels, we can follow [40] to decompose each question into ℓ filter questions, where each filter question is to decide whether the original question satisfies a corresponding label or not. To handle a domain with continuous values, we can adopt the *bucketing* method [29], which discretizes the domain into different buckets, where each bucket indicates a label.

2.2 Task Assignment

Note that a worker may request multiple HITs, so we keep track of the history of previously assigned questions. Let S^w denote the candidate set of questions for worker w, i.e., the set of questions that have not been assigned to worker w (each worker has her unique S^w). QASCA will not assign duplicated questions to the same worker. When worker w requests a HIT, it selects k questions in S^w and assigns them to her. To select questions for worker

[1] http://i.cs.hku.hk/~ydzheng2/QASCA

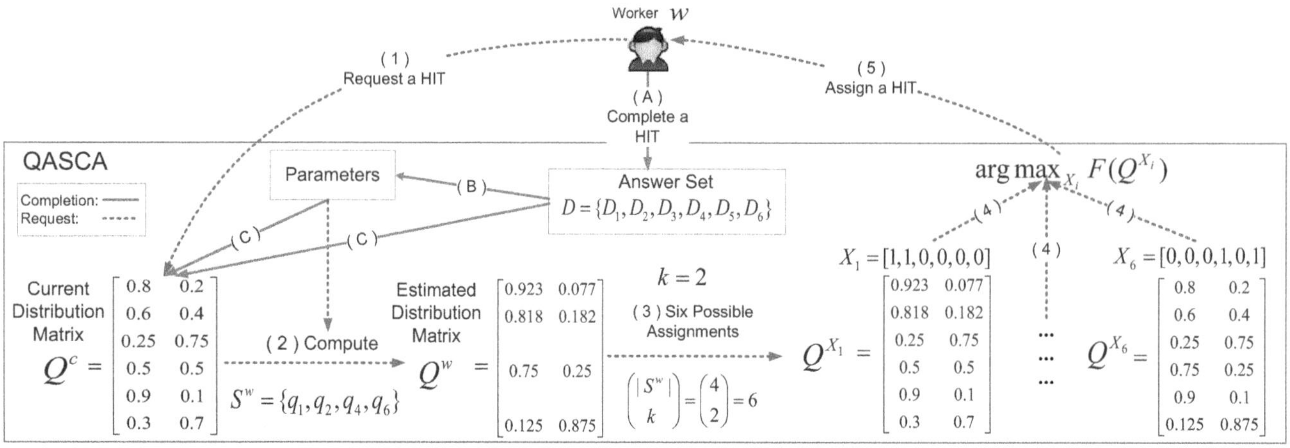

Figure 2: Workflow of QASCA.

w, QASCA first estimates the probability distribution of each question q_i's ($q_i \in S^w$) true label *if* worker w answers it. The estimated probability distributions of all questions in S^w form an $n \times \ell$ matrix Q^w, called *estimated distribution matrix for worker* w. The i-th ($q_i \in S^w$) row $Q^w_i = [\, Q^w_{i,1}, Q^w_{i,2}, \ldots, Q^w_{i,\ell} \,]$ represents the estimated probability distribution for question q_i's true label if it is answered by worker w. Each cell $Q^w_{i,j}$ ($q_i \in S^w, 1 \le j \le \ell$) denotes the estimated probability that question q_i's true label is L_j if it is answered by worker w. Note that row i (or Q^w_i) is empty when $q_i \notin S^w$. We will discuss how to compute Q^w in Section 5.3.

Let the vector $X = [x_1, x_2, \ldots, x_n]$ denote an assignment of HIT, where each element $x_i = 1$ (0) indicates that the question q_i will (not) be chosen to assign for the coming worker. When worker w comes, based on S^w, we define X as a *feasible assignment* if it satisfies (1) $\sum_{i=1}^{n} x_i = k$, and (2) if $x_i = 1$, then $q_i \in S^w$. There are k questions in a HIT and we can only assign questions in S^w to worker w. Thus the number of feasible X is $\binom{|S^w|}{k} \le \binom{n}{k}$.

Given Q^c, Q^w, and a feasible X, we construct a matrix Q^X called *assignment distribution matrix for X*. The i-th row, Q^X_i, is the (estimated) probability distribution of question q_i if worker w answers all the assigned questions in X. We can construct Q^X using Q^c and Q^w: for an unassigned question q_i in X (or $x_i = 0$), its distribution (Q^X_i) remains to be Q^c_i; for an assigned question q_i in X (or $x_i = 1$), its distribution (Q^X_i) is estimated to be Q^w_i, thus

$$Q^X_i = \begin{cases} Q^c_i & \text{if } x_i = 0, \\ Q^w_i & \text{if } x_i = 1. \end{cases} \tag{1}$$

Let $F(\cdot)$ be an evaluation metric, which is used to evaluate the quality of a distribution matrix. When worker w requests a HIT, there are $\binom{|S^w|}{k}$ feasible X, and the problem is to choose the optimal feasible X^* that maximizes $F(Q^X)$. We formally define the **(online) task assignment problem** in Definition 1.

DEFINITION 1. *When a worker w requests a HIT, given the current distribution matrix (Q^c), the estimated distribution matrix for the worker w (Q^w), and the function $F(\cdot)$, the problem of task assignment for the worker w is to find the optimal feasible assignment vector X^* such that $X^* = argmax_X \; F(Q^X)$.*

2.3 Workflow of QASCA

To deploy an application, a requester needs to set n questions with ℓ labels and she should also indicate the number of questions in each HIT (k), the amount of money paid for each HIT (b), the total invested budget (B) and the evaluation metric. In [20,23], the issues of setting appropriate values of k and b are discussed. The evaluation metric (e.g., Accuracy and F-score), which depends on the application semantics, will be addressed in Section 3.

There are two events from workers that QASCA should process: the event when a worker completes a HIT (called "HIT completion") and the event when a worker requests a HIT (called "HIT request"). Based on the workflow in Figure 2, we give an example (Example 1) to show how QASCA processes these two events.

EXAMPLE 1. *The solid (red) lines and the dotted (blue) lines in Figure 2 represent how QASCA processes a HIT completion event and a HIT request event, respectively:*
(1) when a worker w completes a HIT (HIT completion process), QASCA does several updates in the database: it first updates the answer set D [2] (step A), and then based on the new D, it updates some parameters such as workers' qualities (step B). Finally it uses these new parameters to update Q^c (step C);
(2) when a worker w requests a HIT (HIT request process), suppose $S = \{q_1, q_2, q_3, q_4, q_5, q_6\}$, and each HIT contains $k = 2$ questions. QASCA first extracts Q^c (step 1) and parameters from database to compute Q^w for worker w (step 2). Assume worker w has answered q_3 and q_5 previously, now the candidate set of questions for her is $S^w = \{q_1, q_2, q_4, q_6\}$. Since $|S^w| = 4$ and $k = 2$, there are $\binom{4}{2} = 6$ feasible assignments for worker w (step 3). Consider the first feasible assignment $X_1 = [1, 1, 0, 0, 0, 0]$, which assigns q_1 and q_2 to worker w. We construct Q^{X_1} by Equation 1, so $Q^{X_1}_i = Q^w_i$ for $i = 1, 2$ and $Q^{X_1}_i = Q^c_i$ for $i = 3, 4, 5, 6$. Similarly, we can construct Q^{X_2}, Q^{X_3}, Q^{X_4}, Q^{X_5}, Q^{X_6} for other feasible assignments. Based on the chosen function $F(\cdot)$ (Accuracy or F-score), assume that $F(Q^{X_i})$ ($1 \le i \le 6$) is maximized on Q^{X_6} (step 4) and since $X_6 = [0, 0, 0, 1, 0, 1]$, QASCA batches questions $\{q_4, q_6\}$ in a HIT and assigns it to worker w (step 5).

To help readers better understand our paper, we summarize notations in Appendix B. There are three challenges in Figure 2. Firstly, how can we define $F(\cdot)$ for different evaluation metrics; secondly, given Q^c, Q^w and $F(\cdot)$, how can we efficiently compute the optimal assignment in Definition 1 (step 4); thirdly, how can we compute Q^c when a HIT is completed (step C) and estimate Q^w for worker w when a HIT is requested (step 2). We respectively address these challenges in the following three sections.

3. EVALUATING QUALITY METRICS

In this section, we study the two popular evaluation metrics (Accuracy and F-score) in Sections 3.1 and 3.2, respectively. For each evaluation metric, we first introduce its original definition assuming the known ground truth, then we study its variants by incorporating a distribution matrix Q. Finally we define $F(\cdot)$ by discussing how to evaluate the quality of Q w.r.t. an evaluation metric.

We first clarify some notations. We denote the result vector by $R = [r_1, r_2, \ldots, r_n]$, where $1 \le r_i \le \ell$ and L_{r_i} is the returned

[2] Note that the answer set D is continuously updated. That is, in the HIT request process, the current D is used to decide which questions should be assigned; while in the HIT completion process, QASCA updates D based on worker's answers.

label (or result) for q_i. We also denote the ground truth vector by $T = [t_1, t_2, \ldots, t_n]$, where $1 \le t_i \le \ell$ and L_{t_i} is the ground truth label for q_i. The formal definition of function Accuracy or F-score is $F(T, R)$, which evaluates the quality of R based on known T. In task assignment scenarios, the ground truth vector T is unknown, but we can obtain a distribution matrix Q based on the crowd's answers. Thus, we generalize the evaluation metrics to be able to quantify the quality of result vector R (called "result quality") w.r.t the distribution matrix Q, i.e., $F^*(Q, R)$. Since given a distribution matrix Q, the requesters want the best results $R^* = \arg\max_R F^*(Q, R)$ to be returned. So in order to evaluate the quality of Q, we consider the choice of R^* and use the best quality that Q can reach to evaluate the quality of Q, i.e., $F(Q) = \max_R F^*(Q, R) = F^*(Q, R^*)$.

3.1 Accuracy

Accuracy is an evaluation metric used by many crowdsourcing applications [8,21,22,30,44]. It aims to measure the overall classification quality among all labels. For example, in a sentiment analysis application, if a requester focuses on the overall quality among all three labels (i.e., "positive", "neutral" and "negative"), Accuracy can be used as the evaluation metric. It is defined as the fraction of returned labels that are correct. Let $\mathbb{1}_{\{\cdot\}}$ denote an indicator function which returns 1 if its argument is true; 0, otherwise. For example, $\mathbb{1}_{\{5=2\}} = 0$ and $\mathbb{1}_{\{5=5\}} = 1$. Then we derive

$$\text{Accuracy}(T, R) = \frac{\sum_{i=1}^{n} \mathbb{1}_{\{t_i = r_i\}}}{n}. \tag{2}$$

Consider an example where $n = 4$, $\ell = 3$, $T = [2, 1, 3, 2]$ and $R = [2, 1, 3, 1]$. Since it correctly identifies the labels of the 1st, 2nd, and 3rd questions, we have $\text{Accuracy}(T, R) = \frac{3}{4} = 0.75$.

3.1.1 Accuracy*

As shown above, the definition of $\text{Accuracy}(T, R)$ requires to know the ground truth T. In practice, however, we only have the distribution matrix Q, which records the probability distribution of each question's true label. Therefore, we use the expected accuracy to measure the result quality. Since Q_i (the i-th row of Q) represents the probability distribution of question q_i's true label, then we have $P(t_i = j) = Q_{i,j}$ and $\mathbb{E}[\mathbb{1}_{\{t_i=j\}}] = P(t_i = j) \cdot 1 + P(t_i \neq j) \cdot 0 = Q_{i,j}$. Thus $\text{Accuracy}^*(Q, R)$ is defined as

$$\text{Accuracy}^*(Q, R) = \mathbb{E}[\ \text{Accuracy}(T, R)\ ] = \frac{\sum_{i=1}^{n} Q_{i,r_i}}{n}. \tag{3}$$

Specifically, $\text{Accuracy}^*(Q, R)$ represents the *expected* number of correctly answered questions out of all questions. For example, consider the distribution matrix Q^c in Figure 2. Given a result vector of $R = [1, 2, 2, 1, 1, 1]$, its accuracy (w.r.t Q^c) is defined as $\text{Accuracy}^*(Q^c, R) = \frac{0.8+0.4+0.75+0.5+0.9+0.3}{6} = 60.83\%$.

3.1.2 Identify the Optimal Result for Accuracy*

In order to measure the quality of a distribution matrix Q, we need to determine the optimal result vector R^* that maximizes $\text{Accuracy}^*(Q, R)$, i.e., $R^* = \text{argmax}_R\ \text{Accuracy}^*(Q, R)$. To compute R^*, an intuitive idea is to return the most likely label for each question, i.e., $R^* = [r_1^*, r_2^*, \ldots, r_n^*]$ where $r_i^* = \text{argmax}_j\ Q_{i,j}$. We next prove that the idea is correct in Theorem 1.

THEOREM 1. *For Accuracy*, the optimal result r_i^* ($1 \le i \le n$) of a question q_i is the label with the highest probability, i.e., $r_i^* = \arg\max_j Q_{i,j}$.*

Due to the space limits, we move all the proofs in our paper to the Appendix. Based on Theorem 1, we know that for Accuracy*, the optimal result of a question q_i only depends on its own distribution Q_i. Take Q^c in Figure 2 as an example. Consider the first question. Since $Q^c_{1,1}$ (0.8) $> Q^c_{1,2}$ (0.2), the optimal result for q_1 is $r_1^* = 1$. Similarly we can derive the optimal result vector R^* for all questions, i.e., $R^* = [1, 1, 2, 1, 1, 2]$ (or $[1, 1, 2, 2, 1, 2]$ as $Q^c_{4,1} = Q^c_{4,2}$). Thus the quality of Q^c for the metric Accuracy, is measured as $F(Q^c) = \text{Accuracy}^*(Q^c, R^*) = 70.83\%$

For Accuracy, the definition (Equation 3) and the optimal result selection (Theorem 1) are not very difficult. But for F-score, these problems become more challenging.

3.2 F-score

In applications such as text classification [7], sentiment analysis [31,32], entity resolution [56,59,60] and fact finding [42,63], a requester may only be interested in a particular label (which we call *target label*). In this situation, a question can be simplified as a two-label question (i.e., $\ell = 2$) where the two labels are the "target label" and "non-target label", denoted by L_1 and L_2, respectively. For example, in an sentiment analysis application, if the requester wants to pick out the "positive" sentiment tweets with a high confidence, then each question is to identify whether a sentence's sentiment is L_1="positive" or L_2="non-positive".

The F-score, introduced in [51], can be used to capture the quality of answers to the two-label questions above. This measure (F-score) is formally defined as the weighted harmonic mean of two commonly known metrics, namely Precision and Recall:

$$\text{F-score} = \frac{1}{\alpha \cdot \frac{1}{\text{Precision}} + (1 - \alpha) \cdot \frac{1}{\text{Recall}}}, \tag{4}$$

where
(1) **Precision** is the faction of questions with returned results L_1 that are actually correct, i.e.,

$$\text{Precision}(T, R) = \frac{\sum_{i=1}^{n} \mathbb{1}_{\{t_i=1\}} \cdot \mathbb{1}_{\{r_i=1\}}}{\sum_{i=1}^{n} \mathbb{1}_{\{r_i=1\}}}; \tag{5}$$

(2) **Recall** is the fraction of questions with ground truth L_1 that are actually returned with results L_1, i.e.,

$$\text{Recall}(T, R) = \frac{\sum_{i=1}^{n} \mathbb{1}_{\{t_i=1\}} \cdot \mathbb{1}_{\{r_i=1\}}}{\sum_{i=1}^{n} \mathbb{1}_{\{t_i=1\}}}; \tag{6}$$

(3) $\alpha \in (0, 1)$ is a parameter that controls the degree of emphasis: $\alpha \in (\frac{1}{2}, 1)$ emphasizes Precision; $\alpha \in (0, \frac{1}{2})$ emphasizes Recall; and we call the *balanced F-score* if $\alpha = \frac{1}{2}$.

By plugging Equations 5 and 6 into Equation 7, we obtain:

$$\text{F-score}(T, R, \alpha) = \frac{\sum_{i=1}^{n} \mathbb{1}_{\{t_i=1\}} \cdot \mathbb{1}_{\{r_i=1\}}}{\sum_{i=1}^{n} [\ \alpha \cdot \mathbb{1}_{\{r_i=1\}} + (1 - \alpha) \cdot \mathbb{1}_{\{t_i=1\}}]}. \tag{7}$$

For the parameter α, if a requester wants to select "positive" sentiment sentences with a high confidence, she can set α to a large value (e.g., 0.75) which emphasizes Precision more. On the other hand, if a company manager wants to collect as many "positive" comments for their products as possible, she can give more attention to Recall by setting α to a lower value (e.g., 0.25).

3.2.1 Challenges

As the numerator and denominator of $\text{F-score}(T, R, \alpha)$ both have the random variable $\mathbb{1}_{\{t_i=1\}}$, its expectation cannot be computed as easily as for Accuracy (Equation 3), so we resort to another way of computing its expectation. We denote τ as the set of all possible ground truth vectors, i.e., $\tau = \{1, 2\}^n$ and $|\tau| = 2^n$. Given Q, the probability that $T' = [t_1', t_2', \ldots, t_n'] \in \tau$ is the ground truth vector is $\prod_{i=1}^{n} Q_{i,t_i'}$. Then, we have

$$\mathbb{E}[\ \text{F-score}(T, R, \alpha)\ ] = \sum_{T' \in \tau} \text{F-score}(T', R, \alpha) \cdot \prod_{i=1}^{n} Q_{i,t_i'}. \tag{8}$$

There are two challenges related to this equation:

One is how to efficiently compute or estimate Equation 8. It is computationally expensive to enumerate all 2^n possible T'. But given α and R, for different $T' \in \tau$, the numerator and denominator of F-score(T', R, α) can only take at most $n+1$ possible values respectively, thus F-score(T', R, α) can only have at most $(n+1)^2$ possible values. Based on this observation, for a given Q and α, Equation 8 can be accurately calculated in $\mathcal{O}(n^3)$ time [24]. Nevertheless, this complexity is still very high to a task assignment system as it is a key step in task assignment. Thus it is better to find an accurate approximation that is efficient to compute.

Another challenge is that if we directly apply Equation 8 to derive the optimal result for each question, we observe two interesting facts that are different from Accuracy:

Observation 1: Returning the label with the highest probability in each question may not be optimal (even for $\alpha = 0.5$);

Observation 2: Deriving the optimal result of a question q_i does not only depend on the question's distribution (or Q_i) itself.

In order to verify these two observations, we next give two counter-examples in Example 2.

EXAMPLE 2. *Consider* $\alpha = 0.5$ *and* $Q = \begin{bmatrix} 0.35 & 0.65 \\ 0.55 & 0.45 \end{bmatrix}$. *If we return the label with the highest probability for each question, then we obtain a result vector* $\widetilde{R} = [2, 1]$ *and the corresponding* $\mathbb{E}[\text{ F-score}(T, \widetilde{R}, \alpha)\ ] = \frac{1}{0.5 \cdot 1 + 0.5 \cdot 2} \cdot 0.35 \cdot 0.55 + 0 \cdot 0.35 \cdot 0.45 + \frac{1}{0.5 \cdot 1 + 0.5 \cdot 1} \cdot 0.65 \cdot 0.55 + 0 \cdot 0.65 \cdot 0.45 = 48.58\%$ *(Equation 8). However, by enumerating all possible* $R \in \{1, 2\}^2$, *we can derive the optimal* $R^* = [1, 1]$ *and* $\mathbb{E}[\text{ F-score}(T, R^*, \alpha)\ ] = 53.58\%$. *This example verifies our first observation.*

Consider $\widehat{\alpha} = 0.5$ *and* $\widehat{Q} = \begin{bmatrix} 0.35 & 0.65 \\ 0.9 & 0.1 \end{bmatrix}$. *Using the same method as above, we can obtain the optimal* $\widehat{R}^* = [2, 1]$. *Compared with the above example, we can see that for the same* $\alpha = \widehat{\alpha} = 0.5$ *in F-score, even if* Q_1 *and* $\widehat{Q}_1$ *are the same (i.e.,* $[0.35, 0.65]$*), the computed* $r_1^* = 1$ *and* $\widehat{r}_1^* = 2$ *are different. This example shows that the optimal result for each question is not only dependent on the question's distribution itself.*

To address the above two challenges, we first give an approximation for $\mathbb{E}[\text{ F-score}(T, R, \alpha)\ ]$ in Section 3.2.2 and then discuss how to compute R^* for the approximated function in Section 3.2.3.

3.2.2 F-score*

Following Equation 7, we approximate $\mathbb{E}[\text{ F-score}(T, R, \alpha)\ ]$ as $\frac{\mathbb{E}[\ \sum_{i=1}^{n} \mathbb{1}_{\{t_i=1\}} \cdot \mathbb{1}_{\{r_i=1\}}\ ]}{\mathbb{E}[\ \sum_{i=1}^{n} [\ \alpha \cdot \mathbb{1}_{\{r_i=1\}} + (1-\alpha) \cdot \mathbb{1}_{\{t_i=1\}}]\ ]}$ to boost efficiency, which is the ratio of the expectation of numerator and denominator of F-score(T, R, α). By plugging Q inside, we can formally define F-score$^*(Q, R, \alpha)$ as:

$$\text{F-score}^*(Q, R, \alpha) = \frac{\sum_{i=1}^{n} Q_{i,1} \cdot \mathbb{1}_{\{r_i=1\}}}{\sum_{i=1}^{n} [\ \alpha \cdot \mathbb{1}_{\{r_i=1\}} + (1-\alpha) \cdot Q_{i,1}\ ]}. \quad (9)$$

For example, consider the values of $\widehat{\alpha}$, $\widehat{Q}$ and $\widehat{R}^*$ in Example 2. Based on Equations 8 and 9, we can obtain $\mathbb{E}[\text{ F-score}(T, \widehat{R}^*, \widehat{\alpha})\ ] = 79.5\%$ and F-score$^*(\widehat{Q}, \widehat{R}^*, \widehat{\alpha}) = \frac{0.9}{0.5 \cdot 1 + 0.5 \cdot (0.35 + 0.9)} = 80\%$, respectively. The error in the example is 0.5%.

Approximation Error. Let A and B denote two random variables. The same approximation ($\mathbb{E}\big[\frac{A}{B}\big] \approx \frac{\mathbb{E}[A]}{\mathbb{E}[B]}$) has also been used by other works [4,28,39,45] for efficiency's sake. Furthermore, [45] gives a general formula by expanding Taylor series: $\mathbb{E}\big[\frac{A}{B}\big] = \frac{\mathbb{E}[A]}{\mathbb{E}[B]} + \sum_{v=1}^{\infty} \phi_v$, where $\phi_v = (-1)^v \cdot \frac{\mathbb{E}[A] \cdot <^v B> + <A,^v B>}{(\mathbb{E}[B])^{v+1}}$, $<^v B> = \mathbb{E}[\ (B - \mathbb{E}[B])^v\ ]$, and $<A,^v B> = \mathbb{E}[\ (A - \mathbb{E}[A]) \cdot (B - \mathbb{E}[B])^v\ ]$. The standard approximation formula (derived by delta method) used in [4,39] is $\mathbb{E}\big[\frac{A}{B}\big] = \frac{\mathbb{E}[A]}{\mathbb{E}[B]} + \mathcal{O}(n^{-1})$ for $n \to \infty$. By setting A and B as the numerator and denominator of F-score(T, R, α), we can generally derive $\mathbb{E}[\text{ F-score}(T, R, \alpha)\ ] =$ F-score$^*(Q, R, \alpha) + \mathcal{O}(n^{-1})$. We also verify this in experiments (Section 6.1.2) and show that the error is small ($\leq 0.01\%$) when $n \geq 10^3$, which means that our approximation is reasonable.

3.2.3 Identify the Optimal Result for F-score*

Unlike Accuracy*, to identify the optimal result for F-score*, the method that chooses the most possible label of each question is not correct anymore. However, the intuition that it is preferable to return a label with a large probability value may still hold. Based on this idea, we conjecture that there exists a threshold w.r.t each question that can determine whether a target label should be returned or not. That is, a target label should be returned only when its probability is not lower than the threshold; otherwise the non-target label is returned. More formally, let θ_i be the threshold w.r.t a question q_i. If $Q_{i,1} \geq \theta_i$, we return the target label (i.e., $r_i^* = 1$); otherwise, the non-target label is returned (i.e., $r_i^* = 2$). We prove the correctness of the conjecture in Theorem 2. An interesting observation from the theorem is that every question has the same threshold, which is equal to $\lambda^* \cdot \alpha$, where λ^* represents the optimal value for F-score* (or the quality evaluation of Q), i.e., $\lambda^* = \max_R$ F-score$^*(Q, R, \alpha)$.

THEOREM 2. *Given* Q *and* α*, for F-score**, *the optimal result* r_i^* $(1 \leq i \leq n)$ *of a question* q_i *can be derived by comparing* $Q_{i,1}$ *with the threshold* $\theta = \lambda^* \cdot \alpha$, *i.e.,* $r_i^* = 1$ *if* $Q_{i,1} \geq \theta$ *and* $r_i^* = 2$ *if* $Q_{i,1} < \theta$.

As $\lambda^* = \max_R$ F-score$^*(Q, R, \alpha)$, Theorem 2 shows that for F-score*, a question's optimal result is related to the optimal value for F-score* w.r.t. Q, which takes all the questions' distributions into consideration. This explains that why the claim for Accuracy* (Theorem 1), i.e., "a question's optimal result is only dependent on its own distribution" does not hold. Next we focus on the problem of how to efficiently derive λ^*.

We first show that this problem can be reduced to a 0-1 fractional programming (FP) problem, and then present an iterative algorithm to identify the optimal value (λ^*). Let $B = [b_1, b_2, \ldots, b_n]$, $D = [d_1, d_2, \ldots, d_n]$ denote two coefficient vectors, and β, γ denote two scalars. The 0-1 FP problem is defined as:

$$\max \quad f(\mathbf{z}) = \frac{\sum_{i=1}^{n}(z_i \cdot b_i) + \beta}{\sum_{i=1}^{n}(z_i \cdot d_i) + \gamma} \quad s.t. \ \ \mathbf{z} \in \Omega \subseteq \{0,1\}^n$$

Comparing F-score* (Equation 9) with $f(\mathbf{z})$, we find that F-score* can actually be rewritten in the form of $f(\mathbf{z})$ as follows:

$$\begin{cases} z_i = \mathbb{1}_{\{r_i=1\}},\ b_i = Q_{i,1},\ d_i = \alpha \ \text{ for } 1 \leq i \leq n; \\ \beta = 0,\ \gamma = \sum_{i=1}^{n}(1-\alpha) \cdot Q_{i,1},\ \ \Omega = \{0,1\}^n. \end{cases} \quad (10)$$

Thus the problem of computing λ^* can be reduced to a 0-1 FP problem. The 0-1 FP problem can be efficiently solved based on the Dinkelbach framework [12]. We apply it to our problem, which consists of the following three steps:

<u>Initialization:</u> It first constructs a new function $g(\mathbf{z}, \lambda) = \sum_{i=1}^{n}(b_i - \lambda \cdot d_i) \cdot z_i$. Then it will iteratively update λ.

In our case, b_i, d_i and z_i $(1 \leq i \leq n)$ can be represented following Equation 10 and $g(\mathbf{z}, \lambda) = \sum_{i=1}^{n}(Q_{i,1} - \lambda \cdot \alpha) \cdot \mathbb{1}_{\{r_i=1\}}$.

<u>Iteration:</u> Let λ_t denote the λ for the t-th iteration. For the first iteration, the algorithm initializes λ as a constant value λ_{init} (for example, 0): $\lambda_1 = \lambda_{init}$, and then computes $\mathbf{z}' = \arg\max_{\mathbf{z}} g(\mathbf{z}, \lambda_1)$. By plugging the newly computed $\mathbf{z}'$ into $f(\mathbf{z})$, the algorithm updates λ_1 to $\lambda_2 = f(\mathbf{z}')$. Then it repeats the above iteration with the updated λ (i.e., λ_2).

In our case, in the first iteration, with initial $\lambda_1 = \lambda_{init}$, we have to compute $R' = \arg\max_R \sum_{i=1}^{n}(Q_{i,1} - \lambda_1 \cdot \alpha) \cdot \mathbb{1}_{\{r_i=1\}}$, and $R' = [r_1', r_2', \ldots, r_n']$ can be derived by setting

$$\mathbb{1}_{\{r_i'=1\}} = \begin{cases} 1 \ \ \text{(i.e., } r_i' = 1\text{) if } Q_{i,1} \geq \lambda_1 \cdot \alpha, \\ 0 \ \ \text{(i.e., } r_i' = 2\text{) if } Q_{i,1} < \lambda_1 \cdot \alpha. \end{cases}$$

Then λ_1 is updated as $\lambda_2 = \text{F-score}^*(Q, R', \alpha)$, and we repeat the above iteration with the updated λ_2.

Termination: The algorithm terminates at the c-th iteration when λ converges (or it is unchanged), i.e., $\lambda_{c+1} = \lambda_c$, and it returns λ_{c+1} which is computed for the c-th iteration.

The Dinkelbach framework guarantees that the iterative process will finally converge to the optimal objective value [12]. Thus our algorithm can return the optimal value for F-score*, i.e., $\lambda^* = \lambda_{c+1}$. The detailed algorithm is in Appendix E (Algorithm 1). We next run the two counter-examples demonstrated in Example 2, and analyze the time complexity in the end.

EXAMPLE 3. *Consider $\widehat{\alpha}$ and $\widehat{Q}$ in Example 2. In the 1st iteration, suppose $\lambda_1 = \lambda_{init} = 0$. As $\widehat{Q}_{1,1}$ and $\widehat{Q}_{2,1}$ are both $\geq \lambda_1 \cdot \widehat{\alpha} = 0$, then $R' = [1,1]$ and λ_1 is updated to $\lambda_2 = \text{F-score}(\widehat{Q}, R', \widehat{\alpha}) = \frac{0.35+0.9}{0.5\cdot 2+0.5\cdot(0.35+0.9)} = 0.77$. As $\lambda_2 \neq \lambda_1$, we continue. In the 2nd iteration, by comparing $\widehat{Q}_{1,1}$ and $\widehat{Q}_{2,1}$ with $\lambda_2 \cdot \widehat{\alpha} = 0.385$, we can construct $R' = [2,1]$, and $\lambda_3 = \text{F-score}(\widehat{Q}, R', \widehat{\alpha}) = \frac{0.9}{0.5\cdot 1+0.5\cdot(0.35+0.9)} = 0.8 \neq \lambda_2$. In the 3rd iteration, as the updated $\lambda_3 \cdot \widehat{\alpha} = 0.4$, we can construct $R' = [2,1]$. Since $\lambda_4 = \lambda_3 = 0.8$, it converges and $\widehat{\lambda}^* = 0.8$ is returned. Following Theorem 2, we can obtain the threshold $\widehat{\theta} = \widehat{\lambda}^* \cdot \widehat{\alpha} = 0.4$. Since $\widehat{Q}_{1,1} < \theta$ and $\widehat{Q}_{2,1} \geq \theta$, we have $\widehat{R}^* = [2,1]$.*

If we consider α and Q in Example 2, then similarly we derive $\lambda^* = 0.62$, $\theta = \lambda^* \cdot \alpha = 0.31$, and $R^* = [1,1]$. The above two examples show that the approximation function F-score$(\cdot)$ also conforms to the two observations verified in Example 2. Moreover, F-score*$(\cdot)$ gives us an intuitive explanation of why two observations occur: in the two examples, the optimal values of F-score* (λ^* and $\widehat{\lambda}^*$) affect the individual threshold (θ and $\widehat{\theta}$), and thus affecting the optimal result vectors (especially r_1^* and $\hat{r}_1^*$).*

Time Complexity. As each iteration requires $\mathcal{O}(n)$ time and there are c iterations in total, the time complexity is $\mathcal{O}(c \cdot n)$. To evaluate the time complexity in practice, we conduct extensive simulated experiments by randomly generating Q and $\alpha \in [0,1]$, which shows that the time complexity of the algorithm linearly increases w.r.t. n. It converges very fast, and $c \leq 15$ when $n = 2000$ (Section 6.1.2).

4. ONLINE ASSIGNMENT ALGORITHMS

Recall Definition 1, the quality of a given distribution matrix Q is measured as its maximal quality (or quality w.r.t R^*), i.e., $F(Q) = \max_R F^*(Q, R) = F^*(Q, R^*)$, where F can be Accuracy or F-score. To address the task assignment problem, one simple solution is to enumerate all feasible assignment vectors. For each one (X), Q^X can be constructed via Equation 1, and we compute the optimal result vector for Q^X, denoted as $R^X = \arg\max_R F^*(Q^X, R)$. Finally $X^* = \arg\max_X F(Q^X, R^X)$.

Obviously, this simple method is very expensive. To avoid enumerating $\binom{|S^w|}{k}$ feasible assignments, we propose two efficient algorithms: a Top-k Benefit Algorithm for Accuracy* (Section 4.1) and an Online Assignment Algorithm for F-score* (Section 4.2).

4.1 Accuracy*: Top-K Benefit Algorithm

Given Q^c and Q^w, let $R^c = [r_1^c, r_2^c, \ldots, r_n^c]$ and $R^w = [r_1^w, r_2^w, \ldots, r_n^w]$ denote their respective optimal result vectors, i.e., $r_i^c = \arg\max_j Q_{i,j}^c$ for $1 \leq i \leq n$ and $r_i^w = \arg\max_j Q_{i,j}^w$ for $q_i \in S^w$. As shown in Theorem 1, the choice of respective optimal result r_i^c (r_i^w) only depends on Q_i^c (Q_i^w). Therefore, based on the definition of Q^X (Equation 1), the optimal result vector for Q^X, denoted by $R^X = [r_1^X, r_2^X, \ldots, r_n^X]$, can be represented using R^c and R^w as follows:

$$r_i^X = \begin{cases} r_i^c & \text{if } x_i = 0, \\ r_i^w & \text{if } x_i = 1. \end{cases} \tag{11}$$

According to Definition 1, we aim to find the optimal feasible assignment X such that $\text{Accuracy}^*(Q^X, R^X) = \sum_{i=1}^n Q_{i,r_i^X}/n = \sum_{i=1}^n [\,(Q_{i,r_i^c}/n)\cdot \mathbb{1}_{\{x_i=0\}} + (Q_{i,r_i^w}/n)\cdot \mathbb{1}_{\{x_i=1\}}\,]$ is maximized. We can further derive $\text{Accuracy}^*(Q^X, R^X) =$

$$\sum_{i=1}^{n} \frac{Q_{i,r_i^c}^c}{n} + \sum_{i=1}^{n} \frac{Q_{i,r_i^w}^w - Q_{i,r_i^c}^c}{n} \cdot \mathbb{1}_{\{x_i=1\}}. \tag{12}$$

As for each X, the value $\sum_{i=1}^n Q_{i,r_i^c}^c/n$ is fixed. Then for each question q_i, we can define the benefit of assigning it to worker w as *Benefit*$(q_i) = Q_{i,r_i^w}^w - Q_{i,r_i^c}^c$, which indicates that the function Accuracy* will be increased by *Benefit*$(q_i)/n$ if q_i is assigned to worker w. Therefore, the optimal assignment consists of k questions with the largest benefits, and selecting them needs $\mathcal{O}(|S^w|) = \mathcal{O}(n)$ time[3]. Example 4 illustrates how to apply the *Top-k Benefit Algorithm* to assign questions in Figure 2 when the function is set as Accuracy*.

EXAMPLE 4. *Consider Q^c and Q^w in Figure 2. We can obtain $R^c = [1,1,2,1,1,2]$ (or $[1,1,2,2,1,2]$) and $R^w = [1,1,0,1,0,2]$.[4] For each $q_i \in S^w$, we compute its benefit as follows: Benefit$(q_1) = Q_{1,r_1^w}^w - Q_{1,r_1^c}^c = 0.123$, Benefit$(q_2) = 0.212$, Benefit$(q_4) = 0.25$ and Benefit$(q_6) = 0.175$. So q_2 and q_4 which have the highest benefits will be assigned to worker w.*

4.2 F-score*: Online Assignment Algorithm

Compared with Accuracy*, the online assignment for F-score* is more challenging. The main reason is that as shown in Section 3.2.3, based on F-score*, the optimal result for each question is not only dependent on its own distribution. Given a feasible X (Q^X can be constructed), deriving the optimal result vector R^X for Q^X is not as straightforward as Equation 11 for Accuracy*.

Next we show how to efficiently solve the task assignment problem for F-score*. Recall that X^* denotes the optimal assignment and let δ^* denote the optimal objective value, i.e.,

$$\delta^* = \max_R \text{F-score}^*(Q^{X^*}, R, \alpha). \tag{13}$$

The basic idea of our solution is to first initialize $\delta_{init} \leq \delta^*$ (say $\delta_{init} = 0$), and then iteratively update the initial δ_{init} to δ^* until convergence. Since δ^* is unknown, the main problem is how to ensure that δ_{init} is always *increasing* until it reaches δ^*. More formally, let δ_t denote the δ at the t-th iteration. Given δ_t, the updated δ_{t+1} should satisfy the following two properties:

Property 1: if $\delta_t < \delta^*$, then the updated δ_{t+1} should satisfy $\delta_t < \delta_{t+1} \leq \delta^*$;

Property 2: if $\delta_t = \delta^*$, then the updated δ_{t+1} should satisfy $\delta_t = \delta_{t+1} = \delta^*$.

Intuitively, Property 1 guarantees that starting from $\delta_{init} < \delta^*$, δ_{init} will be iteratively increased until δ^*. Property 2 guarantees that at convergence ($\delta_t = \delta_{t+1}$), we can get $\delta_{t+1} = \delta^*$. There are two challenges in solving the problem:

(1) Given δ_t, how can we construct δ_{t+1} such that the above two properties hold?

(2) The update should be solved efficiently to satisfy the performance requirement for task assignment.

To address the first challenge, we present our designed update in Definition 2 as follows:

DEFINITION 2 (UPDATE). *Given δ_t, Q^c, Q^w, α, and S^w, the update from δ_t to δ_{t+1} is defined as*

$$\delta_{t+1} = \max_X \textit{F-score}^*(Q^X, \widehat{R}^X, \alpha), \tag{14}$$

[3] The problem that finds the top k elements in an array can be solved linearly using the PICK algorithm [2].

[4] Note that for $q_i \notin S^w$, Q_i^w does not need to be computed, so we set $r_i^w = 0$ for $q_i \notin S^w$ and it will never be used.

where for each feasible X (Q^X can be constructed via Equation 1), $\widehat{R}^X = [\widehat{r}_1^X, \widehat{r}_2^X, \ldots, \widehat{r}_n^X]$ is constructed based on δ_t, i.e.,

$$\widehat{r}_i^X = \begin{cases} 1 & \text{if } Q_{i,1}^X \geq \delta_t \cdot \alpha, \\ 2 & \text{if } Q_{i,1}^X < \delta_t \cdot \alpha. \end{cases} \tag{15}$$

To help understand the meaning of δ_{t+1} in Definition 2, we will present a brute-force method to obtain δ_{t+1}. This method enumerates all possible feasible assignment vectors. For each feasible X, as Q^X and $\widehat{R}^X$ can be constructed following Equation 1 and 15 respectively, then F-score*$(Q^X, \widehat{R}^X, \alpha)$ can be computed. By comparing the computed values for all assignment vectors, we can obtain the maximum value, i.e., δ_{t+1}. Theorem 3 formally proves that the updated δ_{t+1} following Definition 2 satisfies the two properties.

THEOREM 3. *The defined δ_{t+1} (in Definition 2) satisfies Property 1 and Property 2.*

To address the second challenge above, as shown in Theorem 4, we find that this problem (computing δ_{t+1} in Definition 2) can actually be reduced to a 0-1 FP problem and efficiently solved by leveraging the Dinkelbach framework (similar to Section 3.2.3).

THEOREM 4. *The problem of computing δ_{t+1} (Definition 2) can be reduced to a 0-1 FP problem.*

Our designed algorithm, called *F-score Online Assignment Algorithm*, computes the optimal assignment. In each iteration, it calls the *Update Algorithm*, which leverages the Dinkelbach framework to compute the updated δ_{t+1}. Note that the Dinkelbach framework not only returns the updated δ_{t+1}, but also derives the corresponding assignment X' such that δ_{t+1} = F-score*$(Q^{X'}, \widehat{R}^{X'}, \alpha)$. Thus, at the time that δ converges, the δ^* and its corresponding optimal assignment X^* are both returned by the *Update Algorithm*. Appendix H gives the pseudo-codes of *F-score Online Assignment Algorithm* (Algorithm 2) and *Update Algorithm* (Algorithm 3).

Time Complexity: We analyze the time complexity of *F-score Online Assignment Algorithm*. It is an iterative algorithm, where it runs *Update Algorithm* in each iteration. Following Dinkelbach framework, *Update Algorithm* adopts an iterative approach and takes $\mathcal{O}(n)$ in each iteration. Suppose *F-score Online Assignment Algorithm* requires u iterations to converge and *Update Algorithm* requires v iterations to converge, then the total time complexity is $\mathcal{O}(u \cdot v \cdot n)$. We conduct extensive simulated experiments by randomly generating Q^c and Q^w ($n = 2000$), and varying $\alpha \in [0, 1]$, which shows that the bound $u \cdot v <= 10$ in practice (Section 6.1.3).

EXAMPLE 5. *Given S^w, k, Q^c and Q^w in Figure 2, if the evaluation metric is set as F-score* with $\alpha = 0.75$, we next derive the optimal assignment for worker w. With an initial $\delta_1 = \delta_{init} = 0$, we need to get δ_2. The brute-force way[5] is to enumerate all 6 feasible assignments, where for the first $X = [1, 1, 0, 0, 0, 0]$, we construct Q^X. As $Q_{i,1}^X \geq \delta_1 \cdot \alpha = 0$ for all $1 \leq i \leq n$, thus $\widehat{R}^X = [1, 1, 1, 1, 1]$ and F-score*$(Q^X, \widehat{R}^X, \alpha) = 0.68$. By considering all 6 feasible X, we derive the maximal F-score* value, i.e., 0.7, which corresponds to $X = [0, 1, 0, 1, 0, 0]$. Then $\delta_2 = 0.7$ and as $\delta_2 \neq \delta_1$, we continue with δ_2. Again consider $X = [1, 1, 0, 0, 0, 0]$, as $\delta_2 \cdot \alpha = 0.525$, by comparing each $Q_{i,1}^X$ ($1 \leq i \leq n$) with 0.525, we derive $\widehat{R}^X = [1, 1, 0, 0, 1, 0]$ and F-score*$(Q^X, \widehat{R}^X, \alpha) = 0.832$. By considering all 6 feasible X, the assignment $X = [1, 1, 0, 0, 0, 0]$ corresponds to the maximal F-score*, and $\delta_3 = 0.832 \neq \delta_2$. In the third iteration, similarly the assignment $X = [1, 1, 0, 0, 0, 0]$ corresponds to the $\delta_4 = 0.832$. As $\delta_4 = \delta_3$, we have $\delta^* = 0.832$ and return $X^* = [1, 1, 0, 0, 0, 0]$.*

Compared with Accuracy in Example 4, which assigns q_2 and q_4 with the highest benefits, here the optimal assignment is q_1 and q_2 if the evaluation metric is F-score* with $\alpha = 0.75$. The reason is that $\alpha = 0.75$ focuses on Precision, and it tries to assign questions such that the estimated probability for the target label L_1 is of high confidence (or $Q_{i,1}$ is high). Thus it is more beneficial to assign q_1 compared with q_4, as $Q_{1,1}^w$ (0.818) $\geq Q_{4,1}^w$ (0.75).*

[5] Here we present the brute-force way for illustration purpose.

5. COMPUTING CURRENT AND ESTIMATED DISTRIBUTION MATRICES

In this section, we examine how to compute Q^c and Q^w in Section 5.1 and 5.3 respectively. Since computing these two matrices requires some parameters, Section 5.2 discusses the parameters and the existing heuristics to compute them.

5.1 Current Distribution Matrix

When a worker completes a HIT, based on $D = \{D_1, D_2, \ldots, D_n\}$, we compute the parameters (including prior probability and worker model) and Q^c. As $Q_{i,j}^c$ represents the probability that question q_i's true label is L_j, we compute $Q_{i,j}^c$ based on the answer set of q_i, i.e., D_i. From Bayes' theorem we get

$$Q_{i,j}^c = P(t_i = j \mid D_i) = \frac{P(D_i \mid t_i = j) \cdot P(t_i = j)}{P(D_i)}. \tag{16}$$

Thus $Q_{i,j}^c \propto P(D_i \mid t_i = j) \cdot P(t_i = j)$. It means that if we derive $P(D_i \mid t_i = j) \cdot P(t_i = j)$ for each label L_j ($1 \leq j \leq \ell$), then we can normalize and finally get $Q_{i,j}^c$ for $1 \leq j \leq \ell$. We next discuss how to compute $P(t_i = j)$ and $P(D_i \mid t_i = j)$:

(1) $P(t_i = j)$ is the prior probability which represents that a question's true label is L_j, and it is commonly regarded as the proportion of questions whose true label is L_j, which is the same among different questions, so w.l.o.g., we denote $p_j = P(t_i = j)$. Existing works [1,21,22,56] usually estimated the prior as the expected fraction of questions whose ground truth is label L_j, i.e., $p_j = \mathbb{E}[\frac{\sum_{i=1}^n \mathbb{1}_{\{t_i = j\}}}{n}] = \frac{\sum_{i=1}^n Q_{i,j}^c}{n}$;

(2) $P(D_i \mid t_i = j)$ is the probability that the answer set for question q_i is D_i given that the question q_i's true label is L_j. Assume that the answers in D_i are independently answered by different workers (which was also adopted in [10,16,22,30,62]). Let a_i^w denote the index of answered label for q_i by worker w, then

$$P(D_i \mid t_i = j) = \prod_{(w, j') \in D_i} P(a_i^w = j' \mid t_i = j),$$

where $P(a_i^w = j' \mid t_i = j)$ is the probability that worker w answers label $L_{j'}$ given the true label is L_j, which can be expressed by worker model (Section 5.2). Initially, Q^c is set as uniform distribution for each question q_i, i.e., $Q_{i,j}^c = \frac{1}{\ell}$ for $1 \leq j \leq \ell$.

5.2 Parameters

For the issue about how to model a worker's quality, several works [16,26,30,62] define a worker w's quality as a single value $m^w \in [0, 1]$ called Worker Probability (WP) and

$$P(a_i^w = j' \mid t_i = j) = \begin{cases} m^w, & \text{for } j = j' \\ \frac{1 - m^w}{\ell - 1}, & \text{for } j \neq j' \end{cases}.$$

Some other works [1,22,61] define a worker w's quality as a $\ell \times \ell$ matrix M^w called Confusion Matrix (CM) and

$$P(a_i^w = j' \mid t_i = j) = M_{j,j'}^w \quad \text{for } 1 \leq j, j' \leq \ell.$$

For example, if an application has two labels, an example of WP for worker w is $m^w = 0.6$ and an example of CM for worker w is $M^w = \begin{bmatrix} 0.6 & 0.4 \\ 0.3 & 0.7 \end{bmatrix}$. In experiments (Section 6.2.2) we study the properties of different worker models on real datasets. For the initialization of WP and CM, each worker can be assumed as a perfect worker in the beginning (the assumption made by some prior work, e.g., Ipeirotis et al. [22]). Then for WP, $m^w = 1$; while for CM, $M^w_{j,j} = 1$ for $1 \le j \le \ell$ and $M^w_{j,j'} = 0$ for $j \neq j'$. Next Example 6 shows how to compute Q^c based on WP and prior.

EXAMPLE 6. *Suppose a question q_2 with three labels ($\ell = 3$) has been answered by two workers: $D_2 = \{(w_1, L_3), (w_2, L_1)\}$, where the worker models are $m^{w_1} = 0.7$, $m^{w_2} = 0.6$ and the priors are $p_1 = p_2 = p_3 = \frac{1}{3}$. In order to compute Q^c_2, based on Equation 16, we get $Q^c_{2,1} = P(t_2 = 1 \mid D_2) \propto P(a_2^{w_1} = 3 \mid t_2 = 1) \cdot P(a_2^{w_2} - 1 \mid t_2 - 1) \cdot P(t_2 - 1) - \frac{1-m^{w_1}}{\ell-1} \cdot m^{w_2} \cdot p_1 - 0.03$ and similarly $Q^c_{2,2} \propto 0.01$, $Q^c_{2,3} \propto 0.0467$. By normalization, we get $Q^c_2 = [0.346, 0.115, 0.539]$.*

To compute the worker model and prior parameters, we leverage the EM [10] algorithm, which uses the answer set as input, and adopts an iterative approach (in each iteration, E-step and M-step are applied) to update all parameters until convergence. The EM algorithm has been widely used [1,21,22,56] to infer the parameters and has a fast convergence rate. There are some other works [21,22,48,52,53,61] studying how to derive worker model and prior parameters, and they can be easily adapted to our system.

5.3 Estimated Distribution Matrix

We next discuss how to compute Q^w based on Q^c and w's worker model. For each $q_i \in S^w$, the computation of Q^w_i consists of two steps: in the first step, we estimate l^w_i, which is denoted as the index of the label that worker w will answer for q_i; in the second step, we construct an estimated answer set (denoted as D^w_i) for q_i by adding a tuple containing l^w_i into D_i, i.e., $D^w_i = D_i \cup \{(w, l^w_i)\}$, and then Q^w_i can be computed based on D^w_i. We next talk about the details.

First Step: In order to estimate l^w_i, we first compute the label distribution that worker w will answer q_i. We can derive $P(a^w_i = j' \mid D_i)$ by considering all possible true labels of question q_i:

$$P(a^w_i = j' \,|D_i) = \sum\nolimits_{j=1}^{\ell} P(a^w_i = j' \mid t_i = j, D_i) \cdot P(t_i = j \,|D_i). \quad (17)$$

(1) Given $t_i = j$ is known, $a^w_i = j'$ is independent of D_i, so $P(a^w_i = j' \mid t_i = j, D_i) = P(a^w_i = j' \mid t_i = j)$, which can be derived by w's worker model. (2) We have $Q^c_{i,j} = P(t_i = j \mid D_i)$. So we can compute $P(a^w_i = j' \mid D_i)$ for $1 \le j' \le \ell$.

Next, we predict l^w_i by capturing the label distribution, and the weighted random sampling method [13] is leveraged to select a label index $l^w_i \in \{1, 2, \ldots, \ell\}$, where the label index j has probability $P(a^w_i = j \mid D_i)$ to be sampled.

Second Step: To derive Q^w_i, we first construct $D^w_i = D_i \cup \{(w, l^w_i)\}$, then $Q^w_{i,j} = P(t_i = j \mid D^w_i) \propto P(D^w_i \mid t_i = j) \cdot p_j$. Similar to Section 5.1, we get $P(D^w_i \mid t_i = j) = P(a^w_i = l^w_i \mid t_i = j) \cdot \prod_{(w,j') \in D_i} P(a^w_i = j' \mid t_i = j)$. Take a further step, by considering Equation 16, we get

$$Q^w_{i,j} \propto Q^c_{i,j} \cdot P(a^w_i = l^w_i \mid t_i = j), \quad (18)$$

thus Q^w_i can be computed by normalization if we get $Q^c_{i,j} \cdot P(a^w_i = l^w_i \mid t_i = j)$ for $1 \le j \le \ell$. We next give an example (Example 7) to show how to compute Q^w based on Q^c in Figure 2.

EXAMPLE 7. *Given Q^c in Figure 2, suppose worker w with $m^w = 0.75$ requests a HIT. To compute Q^w, we take Q^w_1 as an example. In the first step we derive the label distribution to predict ℓ^w_1. Following Equation 17, $P(a^w_1 = 1 \,|D_1) = \sum_{j=1}^{2} P(a^w_1 = 1 \mid t_1 = j) \cdot P(t_1 = j \,|D_1) = 0.75 \cdot 0.8 + 0.25 \cdot 0.2 = 0.65$ and $P(a^w_1 = 2 \,|D_1) = 0.35$, thus the label distribution is $[0.65, 0.35]$. After weighted random sampling, suppose we get $\ell^w_1 = 1$. In the second step, following Equation 18, the proportion can be derived by multiplying $P(a^w_1 = 1 \mid t_1 = j)$ to $Q^c_{1,j}$ ($1 \le j \le 2$), which is $(0.8 \cdot 0.75) : (0.2 \cdot 0.25)$. To normalize the proportion, we get $Q^w_2 = [0.923, 0.077]$. Similarly other Q^w_i for $q_i \in S^w$ can be computed and Q^w can be constructed in Figure 2.*

6. EXPERIMENTS

We have conducted experiments on both simulated datasets (Section 6.1) and real datasets (Section 6.2).

6.1 Experiments on Simulated Data

We first describe the experimental settings (Section 6.1.1), then evaluate the performance of F-score* (Section 6.1.2), and finally examine the online assignment algorithms (Section 6.1.3)

6.1.1 Settings for Simulated Data

We show how to generate distribution matrices in simulated experiments. For F-score, as it focuses on a target label (L_1), to generate an $n \times 2$ distribution matrix Q, each question q_i's ($1 \le i \le n$) distribution is generated as follows: first the probability for target label is randomly generated as $Q_{i,1} \in [0, 1]$, then $Q_{i,2} = 1 - Q_{i,1}$. For Accuracy, to generate an $n \times \ell$ distribution matrix Q, for each question q_i ($1 \le i \le n$), we randomly generate $Q_{i,j} \in [0, 1]$ for $1 \le j \le \ell$, and then normalize Q_i to get a distribution. To achieve statistical significance, we perform each experiment for 1000 times and record its average value. Experiments are implemented in Python on a 16GB memory Ubuntu server.

6.1.2 Evaluating Our Techniques for F-Score*

As directly computing $\mathbb{E}[$ F-score(T, R, α) $]$ is inefficient, an approximation function F-score*(Q, R, α) is proposed in Section 3.2.2. In this section, we evaluate this approximation on randomly generated distribution matrices. We first evaluate the approximation error, and then show the performance of its optimal result vector selection algorithm.

Approximation Error. We study how the proposed function F-score*(Q, R, α) is approximate to $\mathbb{E}[$ F-score(T, R, α) $]$ from Figure 3(a)-(c). In Figure 3(a), we vary $\alpha \in [0, 1]$ and $n \in [20, 50]$ to observe the approximation error. For a fixed α and n, we randomly generate Q and result vector R, and record the approximation error $\epsilon = |$ F-score*$(Q, R, \alpha) - \mathbb{E}[$ F-score(T, R, α) $]$ $|$ in the figure (note that the error is averaged over 1000 repeated trials). It shows that as n varies in $[20, 50]$, the approximation error decreases, and when $n = 20$, the errors for different α are smaller than 0.5%. As α varies in $[0, 1]$, the average error reaches the highest at around $\alpha = 0.5$. Moreover, an interesting observation is that the curve is not symmetric, especially when $\alpha = 1$ (which is Precision) and $\alpha = 0$ (which is Recall). The reason is that (1) $\mathbb{E}[$ Precision(T, R) $] = \mathbb{E}[\frac{\sum_{i=1}^n \mathbb{1}_{\{t_i=1\}} \cdot \mathbb{1}_{\{r_i=1\}}}{\sum_{i=1}^n \mathbb{1}_{\{r_i=1\}}}] = \frac{\sum_{i=1}^n Q_{i,1} \cdot \mathbb{1}_{\{r_i=1\}}}{\sum_{i=1}^n \mathbb{1}_{\{r_i=1\}}} =$ F-score*$(Q, R, 1)$, so $\epsilon = 0$ as $\alpha = 1$; (2) $\mathbb{E}[$ Recall(T, R) $] = \mathbb{E}[\frac{\sum_{i=1}^n \mathbb{1}_{\{t_i=1\}} \cdot \mathbb{1}_{\{r_i=1\}}}{\sum_{i=1}^n \mathbb{1}_{\{t_i=1\}}}] \approx \frac{\sum_{i=1}^n Q_{i,1} \cdot \mathbb{1}_{\{r_i=1\}}}{\sum_{i=1}^n Q_{i,1}} =$ F-score*$(Q, R, 0)$, so $\epsilon \neq 0$ as $\alpha = 0$.

Furthermore, to observe the distribution of ϵ, in Figure 3(b), we set $n = 50$ and $\alpha = 0.5$, and record the frequency of ϵ over 1000 trials. We observe that the error is centered around the mean 0.19%, and ranges from 0% to 0.31%, which is small and stable. To observe how ϵ changes for a larger n, in Figure 3(c) we fix $\alpha = 0.5$ and record ϵ by varying $n \in [0, 10^3]$. The curve shows that ϵ consistently decreases and it conforms to the error bound (i.e., $\epsilon = \mathcal{O}(n^{-1})$) as derived in Section 3.2.2. Especially when $n = 1000$, the average $\epsilon \le 0.01\%$, which is fairly small.

To summarize, the proposed function F-score*(Q, R, α) (Equation 9) is a good approximation of $\mathbb{E}[$ F-score(T, R, α) $]$ in practice.

Optimal Result Vector Selection. In Figure 3(d)-(f), we study the result vector selection. Existing works [17,46,56] evaluate F-score by choosing the result of each question as the label with the highest probability. We first study the quality improvement by using our optimal returned result vector algorithm. Let R^* denote the optimal result vector, i.e., $R^* = \text{argmax}_R$ F-score*(Q, R, α). Let

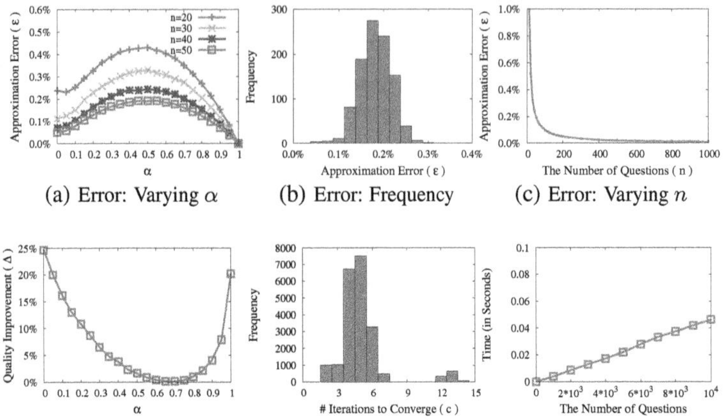

(a) Error: Varying α (b) Error: Frequency (c) Error: Varying n

(d) Improvement: Varying α (e) Efficiency: Convergence (f) Efficiency: Varying n

Figure 3: Evaluating F-Score* (Simulation)

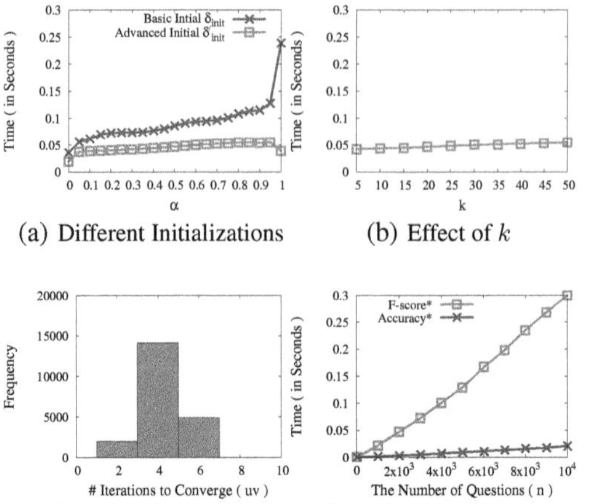

(a) Different Initializations (b) Effect of k

(c) Bounds of $u \cdot v$ (d) Assignment Efficiency

Figure 4: Efficiency of Assignments (Simulation)

$\widetilde{R} = [\widetilde{r}_1, \widetilde{r}_2, \ldots, \widetilde{r}_n]$ denote the result vector chosen by the existing works [17,46,56], i.e., $\widetilde{r}_i = 1$ if $Q_{i,1} \geq Q_{i,2}$ (or $Q_{i,1} \geq 0.5$) and $\widetilde{r}_i = 2$ if otherwise. We set $n = 2000$ and vary $\alpha \in [0,1]$, where for a fixed α, we randomly generate Q, and respectively compute R^* and $\widetilde{R}$ based on Q. Then we define the quality improvement as

$$\Delta = \mathbb{E}[\text{ F-score}(T, R^*, \alpha)\ ] - \mathbb{E}[\text{ F-score}(T, \widetilde{R}, \alpha)\ ], \qquad (19)$$

and we record Δ in Figure 3(d). It can be observed that R^* improves the quality of $\widetilde{R}$ a lot. As α varies in $[0,1]$, about 25% of the values of α result in an improvement of over 10%. We also observe that the curve is asymmetric bowl-shaped, especially when α is around 0.65, Δ becomes zero. Next we apply the approximated function F-score* to verify this interesting phenomenon in theory. For some unknown α', if $\widetilde{R}$ is equal to R^* (or $\widetilde{R} = R^*$),
(1) as $\widetilde{R}$ is constructed by comparing with the threshold 0.5, thus from Theorem 2 we know the threshold $\theta = \lambda^* \cdot \alpha' = 0.5$ and
(2) as $\lambda^* = \text{F-score}^*(Q, R^*, \alpha')$, and $R^* = \widetilde{R}$, we have $\lambda^* = \frac{\sum_{i=1}^{n} \mathbb{1}_{\{Q_{i,1} \geq 0.5\}} \cdot Q_{i,1}}{\alpha' \cdot \sum_{i=1}^{n} \mathbb{1}_{\{Q_{i,1} \geq 0.5\}} + (1-\alpha') \cdot \sum_{i=1}^{n} Q_{i,1}}$. Taking $\lambda^* \cdot \alpha' = 0.5$ inside, we can obtain $\sum_{i=1}^{n} Q_{i,1} \cdot \mathbb{1}_{\{Q_{i,1} \geq 0.5\}} = 0.5 \cdot [\sum_{i=1}^{n} \mathbb{1}_{\{Q_{i,1} \geq 0.5\}} + (\frac{1}{\alpha'} - 1) \cdot \sum_{i=1}^{n} Q_{i,1}]$. Note that as we randomly generate $Q_{i,1}$ $(1 \leq i \leq n)$ for all questions, it makes $Q_{i,1}$ $(1 \leq i \leq n)$ uniformly distributed in $[0,1]$. Thus if we take the expectation on both sides of the obtained formula, and apply the properties of uniform distribution, we can derive $0.75 \cdot \frac{n}{2} = 0.5 \cdot [\ \frac{n}{2} + (\frac{1}{\alpha'} - 1) \cdot 0.5 \cdot n\ ]$, and then get $\alpha' = 0.667$, which verifies our observation (around 0.65).

As the time complexity of optimal vector selection algorithm (Section 3.2.3) is $\mathcal{O}(c \cdot n)$, we next evaluate the bound of c (#iterations to converge) in Figure 3(e). For a fixed $n = 2000$, we vary α from 0 to 1 with a step of 0.1, and for each α, we randomly generate Q and record c by running our algorithm. Figure 3(e) illustrates the frequency of c for all α. It can be seen that $c \leq 15$ in general (for different α). To evaluate the efficiency with a larger n, we vary $n \in [0, 10^4]$ and record the running time in Figure 3(f), which shows that the time linearly increases with n, and our algorithm finishes within 0.05s even when n is large ($n = 10^4$).

6.1.3 Evaluating Online Assignment's Efficiency

We evaluate the online assignment algorithm's efficiency in Figure 4(a)-(d). First we compare different ways of initialization in our algorithm. A basic way is to initialize $\delta_{init} = 0$. By considering that the optimal F-score* for Q^{X^*} may not be far away from the optimal F-score* for Q^c (as they are only different in k questions' distributions), we propose another way of initialization: $\delta'_{init} = \max_R \text{ F-score}^*(Q^c, R, \alpha)$, which can be computed using the optimal result vector selection algorithm (Section 3.2.3). To compare their efficiency, in Figure 4(a) we set $n = 2000$, $k = 20$, and vary $\alpha \in [0,1]$. For a fixed α, we randomly generate Q^c and a confusion matrix, then Q^w can be computed (Equation 18). We run our algorithm with respective δ_{init} and δ'_{init}, and record the time in Figure 4(a). It can be seen that both initializations are efficient ($\leq$ 0.3s), but there is a sudden increase as $\alpha \geq 0.95$ for δ_{init} (mainly due to the fact that big α focuses on Precision, that is, only confident questions for L_1 will be returned, which leads to a big δ^*, and $\delta_{init} = 0$ is far away from δ^*). For δ'_{init}, it is steady with different α, as the initialization is computed by considering both Q^c and α. So we use δ'_{init} to initialize in later experiments.

We next evaluate the performance of different k in Figure 4(b). We set $n = 2000$ and vary $k \in [5, 50]$ to observe the assignment's efficiency, which shows that it is invariant with k. The main reason is that our algorithm iteratively updates δ, and the update solves a 0-1 FP problem via Dinkelbach framework, which is invariant of the size k. To evaluate the bound for $u \cdot v$, in Figure 4(c), we set $n = 2000$ and vary α from 0 to 1 with a step of 0.1. For each α, we generate Q^c and Q^w, and record the frequency of $u \cdot v$ in Figure 4(c). It showed that generally $u \cdot v \leq 10$ for different α.

We then evaluate the assignment's efficiency for Accuracy* and F-score* with a larger n. We set $k = 20$, $\alpha = 0.5$, and vary $n \in [0, 10^4]$ in Figure 4(d), which shows that both algorithms are efficient. For example, both of them finish within 0.3s when $n = 10^4$. As reported in [23], the number of HITs for a certain task is usually $\leq$ 5000, even for the top invested requesters. Therefore, our assignment algorithms can work well in a real crowdsourcing platform. Moreover, the assignment time both linearly increases for Accuracy* and F-score*, but with a larger factor in F-score*, as it has to deal with the converging complexity (i.e., $u \cdot v$).

To summarize, the assignment algorithms are both efficient for Accuracy* and F-score*, and they work well even for a large number of tasks (e.g., $n = 10^4$).

6.2 Experiments for Real Datasets

We first discuss the experimental setup (Section 6.2.1), then evaluate the properties of different worker models (Section 6.2.2), and finally compare with existing systems (Section 6.2.3).

6.2.1 Settings for Real Datasets

We generate five applications from real-world datasets (their ground truth is known for evaluation purposes). The result quality for the first two applications are evaluated in Accuracy, which is introduced as follows:

Films Poster (FS): *FS* uses the top 500 films (with posters) with the highest ratings from IMDB[6]. We generate 1,000 questions, where

[6] http://www.imdb.com/

Table 1: Application Properties (Per System)

Data	Labels	n	k	m	B	Evaluation Metric
FS	L_1 ="<", L_2 ="≥"	1000	4	750	\$15	Accuracy
SA	L_1 ="positive", L_2 ="neutral", L_3 ="negative"	1000	4	750	\$15	Accuracy
ER	L_1 ="equal", L_2 ="non-equal"	2000	4	1500	\$30	F-score for L_1 ($\alpha = 0.5$)
PSA	L_1 ="positive", L_2 ="non-positive"	1000	4	750	\$15	F-score for L_1 ($\alpha = 0.75$)
NSA	L_1 ="negative", L_2 ="non-negative"	1000	4	750	\$15	F-score for L_1 ($\alpha = 0.25$)

each question asks the crowd to compare two different films and the coming worker should decide whether one film is published earlier (<) or later (≥) than the other.

Sentiment Analysis (SA): *SA* uses the Twitter[7] dataset to label the sentiments of tweets w.r.t. different companies. It contains 5,152 hand-classified tweets. We select 1,000 tweets from them and each question asks the crowd to label the sentiment ("positive", "neutral" or "negative") of a tweet w.r.t. the related company.

The result quality for the other three applications is evaluated in F-score (with different α), which is introduced as follows:

Entity Resolution (ER): *ER* uses Product[8] dataset to evaluate whether the descriptions of two products refer to the same product or not. It contains 1,180,452 product pairs. For each pair (r_1,r_2), we compute the Jaccard similarity ($\frac{r_1 \cap r_2}{r_1 \cup r_2}$) and select 2,000 pairs with similarity ≥ 0.7 as our questions. Each question contains a product pair and the coming worker should decide whether they are "equal" or "non-equal". It is evaluated using balanced F-score for the "equal" label ($\alpha = 0.5$).

Positive Sentiment Analysis (PSA): Based on the demand that a company manager may want to select positive sentiment comments for their products with high confidence (emphasizing Precision), we generate *PSA* by selecting 1,000 tweets related to Apple company from the Twitter[7] dataset. Each question is to ask the crowd about whether the sentiment of a tweet related to Apple is "positive" or "non-positive". As it emphasizes Precision, we set the evaluation metric as F-score for "positive" where $\alpha = 0.75$.

Negative Sentiment Analysis (NSA): From another perspective, a company manager may want to collect as many negative sentiment comments as possible for their products (emphasizing Recall), then *NSA* is generated by selecting 1,000 tweets related to Apple company from the Twitter[7] dataset. Each question is to ask the crowd about whether the sentiment of a tweet related to Apple is "negative" or "non-negative". It is evaluated using F-score for "negative" where $\alpha = 0.25$ (emphasizing Recall).

We compare QASCA with other five systems, i.e., Baseline, CDAS [30], AskIt! [3], MaxMargin and ExpLoss:

(1) Baseline: It randomly assigns k questions to a coming worker.

(2) CDAS [30]: It adopts a quality-sensitive answering model to measure the confidence of questions' current results, and terminates assigning the questions which have already got confident results. It assigns k non-terminated questions.

(3) AskIt! [3]: It uses an entropy-like method to define the uncertainty of each question, and assigns k most uncertain questions.

(4) MaxMargin: It selects the next question with the highest expected marginal improvement, disregarding the characteristics of the worker, and it assigns k selected questions.

(5) ExpLoss: It selects the next question by considering the expected loss, defined as $\min_j \sum_{j'=1}^{\ell} p_{j'} \cdot \mathbb{1}_{\{j \neq j'\}}$ $(1 \leq j \leq \ell)$, and it assigns k selected questions.

[7] http://www.sananalytics.com/lab/twitter-sentiment/

[8] http://dbs.uni-leipzig.de/file/Abt-Buy.zip

Table 2: Comparison between Worker Models

	FS	*SA*	*ER*	*PSA*	*NSA*
CM	93.33%	87.09%	82.02%	91.73%	88.43%
WP	93.33%	78.64%	72.80%	92.61%	87.01%

Table 3: The average quality improvement ($\widehat{\Delta}$) of each system by using our optimal result selection algorithm (Section 3.2.3)

	Baseline	CDAS	AskIt!	MaxMargin	ExpLoss
ER ($\alpha = 0.5$)	2.59%	2.69%	4.56%	5.49%	4.32%
PSA ($\alpha = 0.75$)	4.14%	2.96%	1.26%	2.08%	1.66%
NSA ($\alpha = 0.25$)	14.12%	10.45%	12.44%	14.26%	9.98%

As workers may vary in quality for different rounds, we need to use the same set of workers in the comparison of all six systems. To achieve this, when worker w comes, we use each system to assign $k = 4$ questions, then $k \times 6 = 24$ questions are batched into a HIT in a random order and the HIT will be assigned to worker w. Following this way, we can evaluate six systems in a "parallel" way with the same set of workers. We pay each worker \$0.12 for doing a HIT, and assign each question to $z = 3$ workers on average, which are typical experimental settings in AMT [56,59]. The detailed settings are listed in Table 1. Take *FS* application as an example: there are $n = 1000$ generated questions, and the "parallel" way assigns $m = \frac{n \times z}{k} = \frac{1000 \times 3}{4} = 750$ HITs in total for all six systems, where each system corresponds to $k = 4$ questions in a HIT and each system takes $B = \frac{m \times \$0.12}{6} = \$15$ for *FS*. When HITs are finished, we compute the result quality w.r.t. the corresponding evaluation metric based on the questions' ground truth and report their comparison results. All the HITs are published during 5:00 pm $\sim$ 10:00 pm (PDT) on weekdays, and all the crowdsourcing applications are finished within 24 hours. The number of workers participated in five applications *FS*, *SA*, *ER*, *PSA* and *NSA* are respectively 97, 101, 193, 104, and 101.

We implement QASCA in Python using the Django web framework, and deploy it on a 16GB memory Ubuntu server. We conduct experiments on a widely-used crowdsourcing platform: AMT. We use the "external-HIT" way provided by AMT which embeds the generated HTML pages (by our server) into its frame and workers directly interact with our server through the frame. When a worker comes, we can identify the worker from the individual worker-id provided by AMT. Then we can dynamically batch the selected questions (from different systems) in a HIT for the coming worker.

6.2.2 Evaluating Worker Models

In this section, we especially study the selection of worker models in computing the distribution matrix. Recall that Section 5.2 reviews two typical worker models used in existing works: Worker Probability (WP) and Confusion Matrix (CM). Intuitively CM is better than WP as it is more complex. Even though what we observe from real datasets validates the intuition, we try to explain some interesting observations. We first collect the crowd's answers from the five published applications on AMT.

In Table 2, we compare WP and CM on five applications by leveraging the ground truth (t_i) of each question. Based on the collected answer set $D = \{D_1, D_2, \ldots, D_n\}$, for each worker w we compute the real WP and CM as follows

$$\begin{cases} \widetilde{m}^w = \dfrac{\sum_{i=1}^{n} \mathbb{1}_{\{(w,t_i) \in D_i\}}}{\sum_{i=1}^{n} \sum_{j=1}^{\ell} \mathbb{1}_{\{(w,j) \in D_i\}}}, \\ \widetilde{M}^w_{j,j'} = \dfrac{\sum_{i=1}^{n} \mathbb{1}_{\{t_i = j\}} \cdot \mathbb{1}_{\{(w,j') \in D_i\}}}{\sum_{i=1}^{n} (\mathbb{1}_{\{t_i = j\}} \cdot \sum_{z=1}^{\ell} \mathbb{1}_{\{(w,z) \in D_i\}})}. \end{cases} \quad (20)$$

We leverage the real priors (computed as $\widetilde{p}_j = \frac{\sum_{i=1}^{n} \mathbb{1}_{\{t_i = j\}}}{n}$ for $1 \leq j \leq \ell$) and two respective real worker models to derive the distribution matrix based on Equation 16, and then the optimal result vector R^* w.r.t. corresponding evaluation metric can be computed. Finally we evaluate the quality of R^* using the ground truths. To avoid overfitting, we randomly select 80% of the ques-

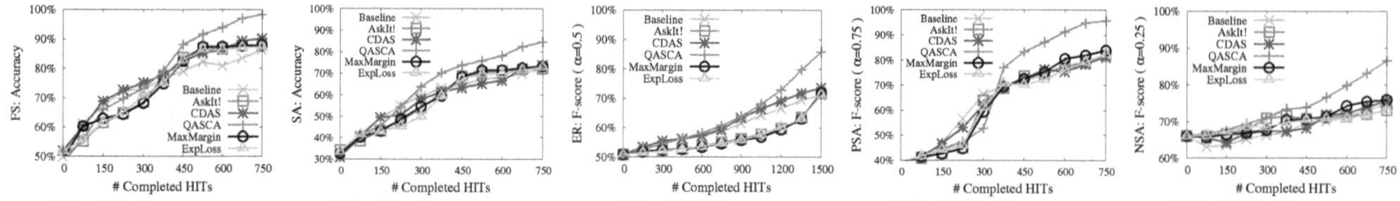

(a) *FS*: Accuracy (b) *SA*: Accuracy (c) *ER*: F-score (d) *PSA*: F-score (e) *NSA*: F-score

Figure 5: End-to-End Experiments (Comparison on Real Result Quality by Varying # Completed HITs)

tions answered by each worker to compute WP and CM, respectively. The random process is repeated over 1000 trails and we record the average quality of the results in Table 2. We observe that CM performs better than WP for *SA* and *ER* applications, while they perform approximately the same for other three applications.

To explain this, we know that $\widetilde{m}^w$ performs equally with $\widetilde{M}^w$ only if the following requirements hold: (1) $\widetilde{M}^w_{j,j'} = \widetilde{M}^w_{j,j''}$ for $j' \neq j \neq j''$ (non-triangular elements in $\widetilde{M}^w$, which expresses the relations between pairwise labels); (2) $\widetilde{M}^w_{j,j} = \widetilde{M}^w_{j',j'}$ (triangular elements in $\widetilde{M}^w$, which expresses the difficulty of individual label).

CM is better than WP on *SA* and *ER*, as they do not satisfy the above requirements: for *SA*, if a question's true label is "positive", a worker is more likely to answer "neutral" compared with "negative", i.e., $\widetilde{M}^w_{1,2} > \widetilde{M}^w_{1,3}$, which violates the first requirement, as there exists relations between pairwise labels; for *ER*, two product descriptions are "equal" only if all features (brand, color, etc.) are the same, while they are "non-equal" once a different feature is spotted, which implies that identifying a "non-equal" pair is easier than correctly identifying an "equal" pair, i.e., $\widetilde{M}^w_{1,1} < \widetilde{M}^w_{2,2}$ (*easier* means a higher probability), which violates the second requirement, as different labels have different difficulties.

To summarize, the above observations among labels in the two applications (*SA* and *ER*) can only be captured by CM other than WP. However, the labels in the other three applications (*FS*, *PSA* and *NSA*) do not have explicit relations or difficulties, which perform similarly for WP and CM. As CM performs at least as good as WP, we use the CM worker model in later experiments.

6.2.3 End-to-End Experiments

We compare QASCA with five other systems on five crowdsourcing applications in AMT.

Improvement of Optimal Result Selection. As we have validated the improvement in Section 6.1.2 on simulated datasets, here we further explore its benefit on real datasets. Recall the definition of R^* and $\widetilde{R}$ in Section 6.1.2. As the ground truth vector T is known on real datasets, we define the real quality improvement w.r.t. different result vectors (R^* and $\widetilde{R}$) as

$$\widehat{\Delta} = \text{F-score}(T, R^*, \alpha) - \text{F-score}(T, \widetilde{R}, \alpha). \quad (21)$$

As HITs are completed, we compute R^* and $\widetilde{R}$ based on Q by time, and record $\widehat{\Delta}$ at each time-stamp. Finally after all HITs are completed, we report the average $\widehat{\Delta}$ for three applications (i.e., *ER*, *PSA* and *NSA*)[9] with the evaluation metric F-score in Table 3. Recall that the three applications *ER*, *PSA* and *NSA* have different α (i.e., 0.5, 0.75 and 0.25), and their corresponding Δ in simulated experiments (Figure 3(d)) are around 2%, 1% and 9%, respectively. In Table 3, we observe that the average $\widehat{\Delta}$ are larger than zero on all applications, which means that all systems can benefit from choosing the optimal result vector R^*. We also observe that *NSA* ($\alpha = 0.25$) has a bigger improvement compared with *ER* and *PSA*, which conforms to the observation in simulated experiments. Note that the main reason that $\widehat{\Delta}$ may have some differences from Δ is that in our simulated experiments, the $Q_{i,1}$ for $1 \leq i \leq n$ is uniformly distributed. While in reality, as a question q_i gets more answers, the computed distribution Q_i may become more confident (either $Q_{i,1}$ is close to 1 or 0). To summarize, for F-score, all systems can benefit from choosing the optimal result vector R^* rather than returning a label with the highest probability ($\widetilde{R}$).

[9] In Theorem 1 we have proved that $R^* = \widetilde{R}$ for Accuracy*, so we did not include the applications with the evaluation metric Accuracy (i.e., *FS* and *SA*).

Table 4: Overall Result Quality (All HITs completed)

Dataset	*FS*	*SA*	*ER*	*PSA*	*NSA*
Baseline	86.40%	72.20%	71.07%	80.85%	74.73%
CDAS	90.20%	73.80%	73.75%	81.58%	75.68%
AskIt!	87.90%	72.20%	71.78%	81.95%	73.16%
QASCA	**98.30%**	**84.60%**	**85.96%**	**95.70%**	**86.65%**
MaxMargin	88.00%	73.30%	72.02%	83.92%	75.96%
ExpLoss	87.30%	72.90%	71.36%	82.43%	73.38%

System Comparison Results. We next show the main results, i.e., the real result quality compared with other systems on all applications in Figure 5(a)-(e). We collect the completed HITs by time and calculate the corresponding result quality based on the derived results of different systems. Since we have shown that the quality improves a lot by selecting the optimal result vector R^* for F-score* both in simulated datasets (Figure 3(d)) and real datasets (Table 3). To make a fair comparison, we apply this optimization (i.e., selecting R^*) to all systems when the evaluation metric is F-score.

From Figure 5(a)-(e), we can observe that in the beginning, when the number of completed HITs is small, all systems have similar performance, as they all do not know much information about questions or workers. However, QASCA dominates other systems as time goes by. This is because QASCA assigns the best k questions for each coming worker to maximize the evaluation metric value (Accuracy* or F-score*), while other systems do not explicitly consider the impact of evaluation metrics on result quality in their task assignment process. For a clear comparison, Table 4 shows the final result quality value when all HITs are completed, and QASCA leads other systems over 8% for all applications. To be specific, QASCA leads the second best system by 8.1%, 10.8%, 12.21%, 11.78% and 10.69% on five real-world datasets (*FS*, *SA*, *ER*, *PSA* and *NSA*), respectively. We can also observe that MaxMargin outperforms ExpLoss, as for the inherently ambiguous questions, they will have high expected loss (ExpLoss will continuously assign them); while the marginal benefit of assigning these questions will be much lower as more answers are collected (MaxMargin can save the assignments for more beneficial questions).

We compare the efficiency of different systems in Figure 6(a). To make a fair comparison, for an application in each system, we record the worst case assignment time during the assignment process for all HITs. It is shown that all systems are efficient, and the worst case assignment of all systems can be finished within 0.06s, which is fairly acceptable in real applications. Even though QASCA is less efficient than other systems due to its complexity in assignments, it can significantly improve the result quality (over 8%). The reason why *ER* runs slower is that it contains 2000 questions while other applications contain 1000 questions.

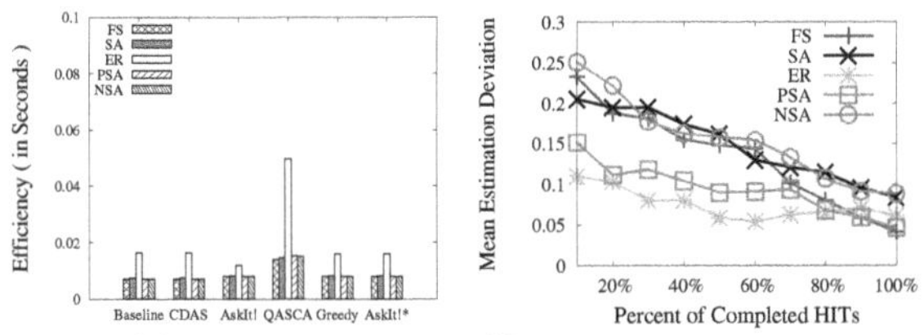

(a) Efficiency (b) Mean Estimation Deviation

Figure 6: Efficiency and Mean Estimation Deviation

Estimation of Worker Quality. We next examine how the estimated quality of workers is different from the real quality of workers[10] by ranging the percentage of completed HITs. Let us denote the real CM as $\widetilde{M}^w$ and the estimated CM as M^w. For a worker w, we further define the *estimation deviation* of worker quality as the absolute difference of estimated quality and real quality, i.e., $\frac{1}{\ell \times \ell} \cdot \sum_{j=1}^{\ell} \sum_{j'=1}^{\ell} |M^w_{j,j'} - \widetilde{M}^w_{j,j'}|$. Then we calculate the *mean estimation deviation* by averaging the calculated estimation deviation among all workers. The smaller the mean estimation deviation is, the closer the estimated worker quality (M^w) is to the real one ($\widetilde{M}^w$). We report the mean estimation deviation by ranging the percentage of completed HITs for all datasets in Figure 6(b). It shows that as more HITs are completed, the estimated worker quality gets closer to the real one, which may explain why QASCA performs much better compared with other systems as time goes by. That is, as more HITs are completed, the worker's quality is more accurately estimated, then QASCA takes the desired quality metric into consideration and can better leverage the estimated worker's quality to judge how the worker's answers might affect the quality metric if questions are assigned. Then it selects the assignment that could maximize the quality metric.

7. RELATED WORK

Crowdsourcing Systems: Nowadays, crowdsourcing has been widely used to address challenging problems that are hard for machines. Crowdsourced query processing systems, such as CrowdDB [14], Deco [41] and Qurk [35] are built to incorporate the crowd into query processing. Many studies investigate how to implement crowd-based operators, e.g., Join [34,56,59], Sort [5,34], Max [16,54], Group-by [9,33], and Enumeration [50]. Some recent work [57] uses sampling to reduce operators' costs. We explore how to devise online task assignment approaches to improve the result quality of generated questions. Our work can be extended to some of them. For example, in [59], the authors iteratively publish a batch of questions on the crowdsourcing platform and can benefit by publishing questions using our system in each iteration.

Evaluation Metrics: Accuracy [8,21,22,30,44] and F-score [25, 31,42,56,59,60,63] are two widely used evaluation metrics for crowdsourcing applications, where Accuracy evaluates the overall quality and F-score focuses on the quality of a specific label. Note that there are other metrics defined based on different purposes. In entity resolution, there are also several cluster-based metrics, such as K-measure [27], GMD measure [36] and Rand-index [49]. For strings, similarity-based metrics including Jaccard, Dice, Cosine and Edit Distances are defined and used [11,55,58]. We focus on studying the question-based metrics and propose solutions to estimate the result quality based on distribution matrices.

Parameter Computation: There are also some approaches addressing how to compute worker model and prior parameters. Two typical worker models are worker probability (WP) [16,26,30,62] and confusion matrix (CM) [1,22,61]. To compute them, Raykar et al. [43] leveraged empirical Bayesian analysis to estimate the parameters; Ipeirotis et al. [22] applied EM algorithm to iteratively update the parameters; Venanzi et al. [52] used Community Detection methods to compute parameters, which works well for workers with limited answers. There are also some works [8,26,61] addressing more general worker models and discussing how to infer the parameters. Other works [21,48] make a comparison among different inference methods. Different from them (*offline inference problem*), we study an *online task assignment problem*, and their parameter computation methods can be adapted to our framework.

Task Assignment: CDAS [30] and AskIt! [3] are the two systems that are most similar to QASCA. CDAS [30] adopts a quality-sensitive answering model along with an early termination scheme, and AskIt! [3] utilizes entropy-like methods to measure each question's uncertainty. Compared with these systems, QASCA takes into account different evaluation metrics in the assignment scheme, and achieved better result quality. There are some other works about online task assignment in crowdsourcing, but they focus on different perspectives. Parameswaran et al. [40] develop algorithms to filter items based on a set of properties; Gao et al. [15] introduce a cost sensitive method to determine whether questions can be better solved by crowdsourcing or machine-based methods; Xi et al. [6] address the budget allocation problem using the proposed extended Markov Decision Process framework; Mo et al. [38] study how to optimize the plurality of a HIT; Sheng et al. [47] investigate how much repeated labeling helps in achieving better results; Ho et al. [18,19] and Mo et al. [37] explore how to assign heterogeneous tasks (tasks of multiple types) to workers.

8. CONCLUSIONS AND FUTURE WORK

In this paper, we have studied the online task assignment problem. We proposed a novel assignment framework by incorporating evaluation metrics into assignment strategies. We generalized the widely used existing evaluation metrics (Accuracy and F-score) to be able to quantify the result quality w.r.t a distribution matrix. We designed optimal result vector selection algorithms and two respective efficient online assignment algorithms for Accuracy and F-score. We built the QASCA system by integrating our novel assignment framework with AMT, and evaluated our system on five real applications. The experimental results showed that QASCA achieved much better result quality than existing approaches.

In the future, we plan to extend our work in five aspects: (1) As QASCA maintains the worker history and expects them to come back to answer another set of questions, it might be interesting to construct certain scope of active advertisers and actively recruit them to answer questions; (2) We will further investigate the method of dealing with continuous values and more complicated question types (e.g., cluster-based question [56] and transcription question [23]); (3) More evaluation metrics will be incorporated in the assignment framework; (4) We focus on question assignments over a specific (or homogeneous) task, then how to incorporate heterogeneous tasks into the assignment framework is another direction; (5) We also plan to consider if a requester has multiple metrics in her mind (say both Accuracy and F-score), then how can we wisely assign questions to a coming worker.

Acknowledgement

We thank the reviewers for their insightful comments. Guoliang Li and Jianhua Feng were supported by the 973 Program of China (2015CB358700), the NSFC project (61422205, 61472198), the Chinese Special Project of Science and Technology (2013zx01039-002-002), Tencent, Huawei, SAP, YETP0105, the "NExT Research Center" (WBS: R-252-300-001-490), and the FDCT/106/2012/A3. Reynold Cheng and Yudian Zheng were supported by HKU (Projects 201311159095 and 201411159171).

[10] The real quality of each worker is calculated by leveraging the ground truth T and the answer set D. We can follow Section 6.2.2 (Equation 20) to compute the real CM.

9. REFERENCES

[1] A.P.Dawid and A.M.Skene. Maximum likelihood estimation of observer error-rates using em algorithm. *Appl.Statist.*, 28(1):20–28, 1979.

[2] M. Blum, R. W. Floyd, V. R. Pratt, R. L. Rivest, and R. E. Time bounds for selection. *Journal of Computer and System Sciences*, 7(4):448–461, 1973.

[3] R. Boim, O. Greenshpan, T. Milo, S. Novgorodov, N. Polyzotis, and W. C. Tan. Asking the right questions in crowd data sourcing. In *ICDE*, 2012.

[4] C.G.Small. *Expansions and asymptotics for statistics*. CRC Press, 2010.

[5] X. Chen, P. N. Bennett, K. Collins-Thompson, and E. Horvitz. Pairwise ranking aggregation in a crowdsourced setting. In *WSDM*, pages 193–202, 2013.

[6] X. Chen, Q. Lin, and D. Zhou. Optimistic knowledge gradient policy for optimal budget allocation in crowdsourcing. In *ICML*, pages 64–72, 2013.

[7] J. Costa, C. Silva, M. Antunes, and B. Ribeiro. On using crowdsourcing and active learning to improve classification performance. In *ISDA*, 2011.

[8] P. Dai, C. H. Lin, Mausam, and D. S. Weld. Pomdp-based control of workflows for crowdsourcing. *Artif. Intell.*, 202:52–85, 2013.

[9] S. B. Davidson, S. Khanna, T. Milo, and S. Roy. Using the crowd for top-k and group-by queries. In *ICDT*, pages 225–236, 2013.

[10] A. P. Dempster, N. M. Laird, and D. B. Rubin. Maximum likelihood from incomplete data via the em algorithm. *J.R.Statist.Soc.B*, 30(1):1–38, 1977.

[11] D. Deng, G. Li, S. Hao, J. Wang, and J. Feng. Massjoin: A mapreduce-based method for scalable string similarity joins. In *ICDE*, pages 340–351, 2014.

[12] W. Dinkelbach. On nonlinear fractional programming. *Management Science*, 13(7):492–498, March,1967.

[13] P. Efraimidis and P. G. Spirakis. Weighted random sampling with a reservoir. *Inf. Process. Lett.*, 97(5):181–185, 2006.

[14] M. J. Franklin, D. Kossmann, T. Kraska, S. Ramesh, and R. Xin. Crowddb: answering queries with crowdsourcing. In *SIGMOD Conference*, 2011.

[15] J. Gao, X. Liu, B. C. Ooi, H. Wang, and G. Chen. An online cost sensitive decision-making method in crowdsourcing systems. In *SIGMOD*, 2013.

[16] S. Guo, A. G. Parameswaran, and H. Garcia-Molina. So who won?: dynamic max discovery with the crowd. In *SIGMOD Conference*, pages 385–396, 2012.

[17] K. Hara, V. Le, and J. Froehlich. Combining crowdsourcing and google street view to identify street-level accessibility problems. In *CHI*, 2013.

[18] C.-J. Ho, S. Jabbari, and J. W. Vaughan. Adaptive task assignment for crowdsourced classification. In *ICML (1)*, pages 534–542, 2013.

[19] C.-J. Ho and J. W. Vaughan. Online task assignment in crowdsourcing markets. In *AAAI*, 2012.

[20] J. J. Horton and L. B. Chilton. The labor economics of paid crowdsourcing. In *ACM Conference on Electronic Commerce*, pages 209–218, 2010.

[21] N. Q. V. Hung, N. T. Tam, L. N. Tran, and K. Aberer. An evaluation of aggregation techniques in crowdsourcing. In *WISE*, pages 1–15. Springer, 2013.

[22] P. Ipeirotis, F. Provost, and J. Wang. Quality management on amazon mechanical turk. In *SIGKDD workshop*, pages 64–67, 2010.

[23] P. G. Ipeirotis. Analyzing the amazon mechanical turk marketplace. *ACM Crossroads*, 17(2):16–21, 2010.

[24] M. Jansche. A maximum expected utility framework for binary sequence labeling. In *ACL*, 2007.

[25] S. R. Jeffery, M. J. Franklin, and A. Y. Halevy. Pay-as-you-go user feedback for dataspace systems. In *SIGMOD*, pages 847–860, 2008.

[26] D. R. Karger, S. Oh, and D. Shah. Iterative learning for reliable crowdsourcing systems. In *NIPS*, pages 1953–1961, 2011.

[27] A. H. Laender, M. A. Gonçalves, R. G. Cota, A. A. Ferreira, R. L. T. Santos, and A. J. Silva. Keeping a digital library clean: New solutions to old problems. In *DocEng*, pages 257–262. ACM, 2008.

[28] D. D. Lewis. Evaluating and optimizing autonomous text classification systems. In *SIGIR*, pages 246–254, 1995.

[29] X. Li, X. L. Dong, K. Lyons, W. Meng, and D. Srivastava. Truth finding on the deep web: Is the problem solved? *PVLDB*, 6(2):97–108, 2012.

[30] X. Liu, M. Lu, B. C. Ooi, Y. Shen, S. Wu, and M. Zhang. Cdas: A crowdsourcing data analytics system. *PVLDB*, 5(10):1040–1051, 2012.

[31] C. D. Manning, P. Raghavan, and H. Schütze. *Introduction to information retrieval*. Cambridge University Press, 2008.

[32] C. D. Manning and H. Schütze. *Foundations of statistical natural language processing*. MIT Press, 2001.

[33] A. Marcus, D. R. Karger, S. Madden, R. Miller, and S. Oh. Counting with the crowd. *PVLDB*, 6(2):109–120, 2012.

[34] A. Marcus, E. Wu, D. R. Karger, S. Madden, and R. C. Miller. Human-powered sorts and joins. *PVLDB*, 5(1):13–24, 2011.

[35] A. Marcus, E. Wu, S. Madden, and R. C. Miller. Crowdsourced databases: Query processing with people. In *CIDR*, pages 211–214, 2011.

[36] D. Menestrina, S. E. Whang, and H. Garcia-Molina. Evaluating entity resolution results. *PVLDB*, 3(1-2):208–219, 2010.

[37] K. Mo, E. Zhong, and Q. Yang. Cross-task crowdsourcing. In *KDD*, 2013.

[38] L. Mo, R. Cheng, B. Kao, X. S. Yang, C. Ren, S. Lei, D. W. Cheung, and E. Lo. Optimizing plurality for human intelligence tasks. In *CIKM*, 2013.

[39] S. Nowozin. Optimal decisions from probabilistic models: the intersection-over-union case. In *CVPR*, 2014.

[40] A. G. Parameswaran, H. Garcia-Molina, H. Park, N. Polyzotis, A. Ramesh, and J. Widom. Crowdscreen: algorithms for filtering data with humans. In *SIGMOD Conference*, pages 361–372, 2012.

[41] H. Park, R. Pang, A. G. Parameswaran, H. Garcia-Molina, N. Polyzotis, and J. Widom. Deco: A system for declarative crowdsourcing. *PVLDB*, 5(12), 2012.

[42] R. Pochampally, A. D. Sarma, X. L. Dong, A. Meliou, and D. Srivastava. Fusing data with correlations. In *SIGMOD*, pages 433–444, 2014.

[43] V. C. Raykar and S. Yu. Ranking annotators for crowdsourced labeling tasks. In *NIPS*, pages 1809–1817, 2011.

[44] V. C. Raykar, S. Yu, L. H. Zhao, G. H. Valadez, C. Florin, L. Bogoni, and L. Moy. Learning from crowds. *Journal of Machine Learning Research*, 2010.

[45] S. H. Rice. A stochastic version of the price equation reveals the interplay of deterministic and stochastic processes in evolution. *BMC evolutionary biology*, 8:262, 2008.

[46] A. B. Sayeed, T. J. Meyer, H. C. Nguyen, O. Buzek, and A. Weinberg. Crowdsourcing the evaluation of a domain-adapted named entity recognition system. In *HLT-NAACL*, pages 345–348, 2010.

[47] V. S. Sheng, F. J. Provost, and P. G. Ipeirotis. Get another label? improving data quality and data mining using multiple, noisy labelers. In *KDD*, 2008.

[48] A. Sheshadri and M. Lease. SQUARE: A Benchmark for Research on Computing Crowd Consensus. In *Proceedings of the 1st AAAI Conference on Human Computation (HCOMP)*, pages 156–164, 2013.

[49] J. R. Talburt. *Entity Resolution and Information Quality*. Morgan Kaufmann Publishers Inc., San Francisco, CA, USA, 2010.

[50] B. Trushkowsky, T. Kraska, M. J. Franklin, and P. Sarkar. Crowdsourced enumeration queries. In *ICDE*, pages 673–684, 2013.

[51] C. Van Rijsbergen. *Information retrieval*. Butterworths, 1979.

[52] M. Venanzi, J. Guiver, G. Kazai, P. Kohli, and M. Shokouhi. Community-based bayesian aggregation models for crowdsourcing. In *WWW*, 2014.

[53] P. Venetis and H. Garcia-Molina. Quality control for comparison microtasks. In *Proceedings of the First International Workshop on Crowdsourcing and Data Mining*, pages 15–21. ACM, 2012.

[54] P. Venetis, H. Garcia-Molina, K. Huang, and N. Polyzotis. Max algorithms in crowdsourcing environments. In *WWW*, pages 989–998, 2012.

[55] R. Vernica, M. J. Carey, and C. Li. Efficient parallel set-similarity joins using mapreduce. In *SIGMOD*, pages 495–506. ACM, 2010.

[56] J. Wang, T. Kraska, M. J. Franklin, and J. Feng. CrowdER: crowdsourcing entity resolution. *PVLDB*, 5(11):1483–1494, 2012.

[57] J. Wang, S. Krishnan, M. J. Franklin, K. Goldberg, T. Kraska, and T. Milo. A sample-and-clean framework for fast and accurate query processing on dirty data. In *SIGMOD*, pages 469–480. ACM, 2014.

[58] J. Wang, G. Li, and J. Feng. Can we beat the prefix filtering?: an adaptive framework for similarity join and search. In *SIGMOD*, pages 85–96, 2012.

[59] J. Wang, G. Li, T. Kraska, M. J. Franklin, and J. Feng. Leveraging transitive relations for crowdsourced joins. In *SIGMOD*, 2013.

[60] S. E. Whang, P. Lofgren, and H. Garcia-Molina. Question selection for crowd entity resolution. *PVLDB*, 6(6):349–360, 2013.

[61] J. Whitehill, P. Ruvolo, T. Wu, J. Bergsma, and J. R. Movellan. Whose vote should count more: Optimal integration of labels from labelers of unknown expertise. In *NIPS*, pages 2035–2043, 2009.

[62] C. J. Zhang, L. Chen, H. V. Jagadish, and C. C. Cao. Reducing uncertainty of schema matching via crowdsourcing. *PVLDB*, 6(9):757–768, 2013.

[63] B. Zhao, B. I. Rubinstein, J. Gemmell, and J. Han. A bayesian approach to discovering truth from conflicting sources for data integration. *PVLDB*, 2012.

APPENDIX

A. QASCA ARCHITECTURE

QASCA contains four components, namely APP Manager, Web Server, Task Assignment and Database component in all. To deploy an application, a requester has to configure the three files in APP Manager. We first introduce the four components, and then show how to deploy an entity resolution application in QASCA.

APP Manager: To deploy n questions in QASCA, the requester first needs to create an application folder in APP Manager, which consists of three files: (1) Question File is a JSON-format file which stores the set of n questions and their possible labels; (2) UI Template File is used to render k questions as a user understandable HIT in HTML templates; (3) Configuration File contains all required information about the application, including the number of questions in each HIT (k), the amount of money paid for each HIT (b), the total budget (B), and the evaluation metric.

Web Server: Web Server processes the requests from workers in crowdsourcing platform (AMT). If a worker requests a HIT, Web Server calls Task Assignment, which dynamically generates a HIT and assigns it to the worker; if a worker completes a HIT, Web Server updates the answer set D and parameters (including prior and worker model) in Database.

Table 5: Table of Notations

Symbol	Description
	Question Model
q_i	The i-th question ($1 \le i \le n$)
L_j	The j-th label ($1 \le j \le \ell$)
t_i	The index of true label for q_i ($1 \le i \le n$), $1 \le t_i \le \ell$
D_i	Answer set for question q_i ($1 \le i \le n$)
S	Questions set: $S = \{q_1, q_2, \ldots, q_n\}$
D	Answer set for all questions: $D = \{D_1, D_2, \ldots, D_n\}$
Q^c	Current distribution matrix (size $n \times \ell$ matrix)
	Task Assignment
k	The number of questions per HIT
S^w	Candidate questions set for worker w
Q^w	Estimated distribution matrix for worker w (size $n \times \ell$ matrix)
X	Assignment vector ($1 \times n$), where each element $x_i = \{0, 1\}$
Q^X	Assignment distribution matrix for X (size $n \times \ell$ matrix)
R	Result vector ($1 \times n$), where each element $1 \le r_i \le \ell$
a_i^w	The index of answered label by worker w for q_i
	Parameters
m^w	Worker Probability (WP) for worker w
M^w	Confusion Matrix (CM) for worker w (size $\ell \times \ell$ matrix)
p_j	Prior probability for label L_j ($1 \le j \le \ell$)

Task Assignment: Task Assignment is the core component in QASCA. When a worker requests a HIT through Web Server, based on the question model and the worker model stored in Database, Task Assignment identifies k questions for the worker by considering the evaluation metric specified in APP Manager. Then it dynamically creates a HIT consisting of the identified k questions, and assigns the HIT to the worker via Web Server. The online task assignment problem is formally defined in Section 2.

Database: Database is the component that stores tables containing question and worker model. When a worker requests a HIT through Web Server, tables are queried by Task Assignment; when a worker completes a HIT, tables are updated by Web Server. After all HITs are completed, Database returns the result of each question based on the question model and the evaluation metric.

Suppose a requester wants to deploy an entity resolution application on QASCA and the application has generated $n = 1000$ questions where each question has the labels L_1 ="equal" and L_2 ="non-equal". The requester first creates an application folder in the APP Manager component. In the created folder, the requester (1) deploys the questions as JSON-format in the Questions File, (2) specifies the HTML template in the UI Template File, (3) indicates in the Configuration File that each HIT contains $k = 10$ questions and is paid $b = \$0.02$, and the total invested budget is $B = \$7$, and the evaluation metric is set as F-score for "equal" with α=0.5.

When a worker requests a HIT, Web Server acquires worker-id from AMT and passes it to Task Assignment, which identifies $k = 10$ questions based on the specified evaluation metric (F-score for "equal" with α=0.5) in APP Manager, and returns a HIT containing the identified questions to the worker. When a worker completes a HIT, Web Server updates the answer set and parameters.

The total number of HITs is denoted as $m = B/b = 350$. After obtaining the answers of all $m = 350$ HITs, QASCA terminates and returns the derived result for each question based on considering the question model (stored in Database) and the evaluation metric (F-score for "equal" with $\alpha = 0.5$).

B. SUMMARY OF NOTATIONS

We present the summary of notations in Table 5.

C. PROOF FOR THEOREM 1

Theorem 1: For Accuracy, the optimal result r_i^* ($1 \le i \le n$) of a question q_i is the label with the highest probability, i.e., $r_i^* = \arg\max_j Q_{i,j}$.*

PROOF. We prove the theorem by proof of contradiction. Suppose the theorem does not hold. Then in the optimal result vector $R^* = [r_1^*, r_2^*, \ldots, r_n^*]$, there exists an index t ($1 \le t \le n$), such that $r_t^* \ne \arg\max_j Q_{t,j}$. So we can construct a result vector $R' = [r_1', r_2', \ldots, r_n']$ where $r_t' = \arg\max_j Q_{t,j}$ and $r_i' = r_i^*$ for $i \ne t$. Then we have Accuracy$^*(Q, R')$ − Accuracy$^*(Q, R^*)$ = $(Q_{t,r_t'} - Q_{t,r_t^*})/n > 0$, which contradicts that R^* is the optimal result vector. Thus the theorem is correct. □

D. PROOF FOR THEOREM 2

Theorem 2: Given Q and α, for F-score, the optimal result r_i^* ($1 \le i \le n$) of a question q_i can be derived by comparing $Q_{i,1}$ with the threshold $\theta = \lambda^* \cdot \alpha$, i.e., $r_i^* = 1$ if $Q_{i,1} \ge \theta$ and $r_i^* = 2$ if $Q_{i,1} < \theta$.*

PROOF. In the proof for Theorem 2, we assume that λ^* is known, and we try to exploit how the optimal result vector R^* can be constructed with the known λ^*. As $\lambda^* = \max_R$ F-score$^*(Q, R, \alpha)$, which means that for any $R \in \{1,2\}^n$, the inequality $\lambda^* \ge$ F-score$^*(Q, R, \alpha)$ holds, i.e., we have $\lambda^* \ge \frac{\sum_{i=1}^n Q_{i,1} \cdot \mathbb{1}_{\{r_i=1\}}}{\alpha \cdot \sum_{i=1}^n \mathbb{1}_{\{r_i=1\}} + (1-\alpha)\cdot\sum_{i=1}^n Q_{i,1}}$, then we can further derive

$$\sum_{i=1}^{n} (Q_{i,1} - \lambda^* \cdot \alpha) \cdot \mathbb{1}_{\{r_i=1\}} \le \lambda^* \cdot (1-\alpha) \cdot \sum_{i=1}^{n} Q_{i,1}. \quad (22)$$

From another perspective, the optimal result vector R^* satisfies $\lambda^* =$ F-score$^*(Q, R^*, \alpha)$, thus similarly we can derive

$$\sum_{i=1}^{n} (Q_{i,1} - \lambda^* \cdot \alpha) \cdot \mathbb{1}_{\{r_i^*=1\}} = \lambda^* \cdot (1-\alpha) \cdot \sum_{i=1}^{n} Q_{i,1}. \quad (23)$$

As λ^*, Q, and α are known, for ease of representation let us denote a fixed constant A and a function $h(R)$ as follows

$$\begin{cases} A = \lambda^* \cdot (1-\alpha) \cdot \sum_{i=1}^n Q_{i,1}, \\ h(R) = \sum_{i=1}^n (Q_{i,1} - \lambda^* \cdot \alpha) \cdot \mathbb{1}_{\{r_i=1\}}. \end{cases}$$

Then Equation 22 and 23 can be represented as: (1) for any $R \in \{1,2\}^2$, $h(R) \le A$; and (2) the optimal R^* satisfies $h(R^*) = A$. Next we prove that if we can derive $R' = \arg\max_R \{\, h(R) \,\}$, then $R' = [r_1', r_2', \ldots, r_n']$ is the optimal result vector (i.e., $R' = R^*$). From Equation 22, since $R' \in \{1,2\}^2$, we can derive $h(R') \le A$. From $R' = \arg\max_R \{\, h(R) \,\}$, we know that $\max_R\{\, h(R) \,\} = h(R')$ and from Equation 23, we know that $\max_R\{\, h(R) \,\} \ge h(R^*) = A$. So we have $h(R') \ge A$. As $h(R') \le A$, we have $h(R') = A$, or $\sum_{i=1}^n (Q_{i,1} - \lambda^* \cdot \alpha) \cdot \mathbb{1}_{\{r_i'=1\}} = \lambda^* \cdot (1-\alpha) \cdot \sum_{i=1}^n Q_{i,1}$, and finally we can derive λ^* from the above Equation: $\lambda^* = \frac{\sum_{i=1}^n Q_{i,1} \cdot \mathbb{1}_{\{r_i'=1\}}}{\alpha \cdot \sum_{i=1}^n \mathbb{1}_{\{r_i'=1\}} + (1-\alpha)\cdot \sum_{i=1}^n Q_{i,1}}$.

As $\lambda^* =$ F-score$^*(Q, R', \alpha)$, i.e., R' derives the optimal λ^*, we know $R' = R^*$. Then $R^* = \arg\max_R\{\, h(R) \,\}$, i.e., $R^* = \arg\max_R \left\{ \sum_{i=1}^n (Q_{i,1} - \lambda^* \cdot \alpha) \cdot \mathbb{1}_{\{r_i=1\}} \right\}$. In order to maximize $h(R)$, we can set $\mathbb{1}_{\{r_i=1\}} = 1$ (or $r_i = 1$) if $Q_{i,1} \ge \lambda^* \cdot \alpha$ and $\mathbb{1}_{\{r_i=1\}} = 0$ (or $r_i = 2$) if $Q_{i,1} < \lambda^* \cdot \alpha$. Then we get

$$r_i^* = \begin{cases} 1 & \text{if } Q_{i,1} \ge \lambda^* \cdot \alpha, \\ 2 & \text{if } Q_{i,2} < \lambda^* \cdot \alpha. \end{cases}$$

Thus we have proved that there exists a threshold $\theta = \lambda^* \cdot \alpha$, such that $R^* = [\, r_1^*, r_2^*, \ldots, r_n^* \,]$ can be constructed as $r_i^* = 1$ if $Q_{i,1} \ge \lambda^* \cdot \alpha$ and $r_i^* = 2$ if otherwise. □

E. COMPUTING THE QUALITY OF Q FOR F-SCORE (ALGORITHM 1)

For a given Q, In order to derive the optimal λ^* such that $\lambda^* = \max_R$ F-score$^*(Q, R, \alpha)$, following the discussions in Section 3.2.3, we design Algorithm 1. It iteratively updates λ until convergence. Let λ_t denote the λ for the t-th iteration, so initially $\lambda_1 = \lambda_{init} = 0$. In the t-th iteration (λ_t is known), it first constructs a new result vector R' using the known λ_t (lines 5-7) and

Algorithm 1 *Measure the Quality of Q for F-score*

Input: Q, α
Output: λ

1: $\lambda = 0$; // initialized as 0 ($\lambda_{init} = 0$)
2: $R' = [\,]$;
3: **while** True **do**
4: $\quad\lambda_{pre} = \lambda$; // record λ for this iteration
5: $\quad$// construct new $R' = [r'_1, r'_2 \cdots r'_n]$
6: $\quad$**for** $i = 1$ to n **do**
7: $\quad\quad$**if** $Q_{i,1} \geq \lambda \cdot \alpha$ **then** $r'_i = 1$ **else** $r'_i = 2$
8: $\quad\lambda = \frac{\sum_{i=1}^{n} Q_{i,1} \cdot \mathbb{1}_{\{r'_i=1\}}}{\sum_{i=1}^{n} [\,\alpha \cdot \mathbb{1}_{\{r'_i=1\}} + (1-\alpha)\cdot Q_{i,1}\,]}$; // F-score*$(Q, R', \alpha)$
9: $\quad$**if** $\lambda_{pre} == \lambda$ **then**
10: $\quad\quad$**break**
11: $\quad$**else**
12: $\quad\quad\lambda_{pre} = \lambda$
13: **return** λ

Algorithm 2 *F-score Online Assignment*

Input: Q^c, Q^w, α, k, S^w
Output: HIT

1: $\delta = 0$; // initialized as 0 ($\delta_{init} = 0$)
2: **while** True **do**
3: $\quad\delta_{pre} = \delta$
4: $\quad$// get the updated δ_{t+1} and its corresponding X
5: $\quad X, \delta =$ *Update*$(Q^c, Q^w, \alpha, k, S^w, \delta)$
6: $\quad$**if** $\delta_{pre} == \delta$ **then**
7: $\quad\quad$**break**
8: $\quad$**else**
9: $\quad\quad\delta_{pre} = \delta$
10: // construct HIT based on the returned X
11: **for** $i = 1$ to n **do**
12: $\quad$**if** $x_i == 1$ **then**
13: $\quad\quad$HIT = HIT $\cup \{q_i\}$
14: **return** HIT

then update λ_t to $\lambda_{t+1} =$ F-score*(Q, R', α) (line 8) for the next iteration. The way to construct each r'_i ($1 \leq i \leq n$) in R' is based on comparing $Q_{i,1}$ with the threshold $\lambda_t \cdot \alpha$, i.e., $r'_i = 1$ if $Q_{i,1} \geq \lambda_t \cdot \alpha$ and $r_i = 2$ if otherwise. Finally it decides whether it converges (i.e., $\lambda_{t+1} = \lambda_t$) or not (lines 9-12).

F. PROOF FOR THEOREM 3

Theorem 3: The defined δ_{t+1} (in Definition 2) satisfies Property 1 and Property 2.

PROOF. As mentioned before, in the definition of computing δ_{t+1} (Definition 2), the construction of R^X (Equation 15) is similar to the construction of R' in choosing the optimal result vector for a given Q (Algorithm 1). Thus the basic idea of the proof is to make a comparison with Algorithm 1.

Before making the comparison, we present some theoretical results proved in [12] for the Dinkelbach framework (which applies to Algorithm 1). It has proved that starting from the initial $\lambda_{init} \leq \lambda^*$, the λ_{init} will be iteratively *increased* to λ^* until convergence. It means that the update from λ_t to λ_{t+1} in Algorithm 1 also conforms to our two properties, i.e., (1) if $\lambda_t < \lambda^*$, then $\lambda_t < \lambda_{t+1} \leq \lambda^*$ and (2) if $\lambda_t = \lambda^*$, then $\lambda_t = \lambda_{t+1} = \lambda^*$.

Recall that δ^* and X^* respectively denote the optimal value and the optimal assignment vector, and we can derive $\delta^* = \max_R$ F-score*(Q^{X^*}, R, α). Thus, if Algorithm 1 takes Q^{X^*} and α as the input, then $\lambda^* = \max_R$ F-score*(Q^{X^*}, R, α), which is exactly δ^*, i.e., $\lambda^* = \delta^*$.

The comparison is conducted based on comparing our online assignment algorithm with Algorithm 1, which takes Q^{X^*} and α as the input. As derived above, the optimal value for both algorithms are the same (i.e., δ^*).

To prove Property 1, suppose both algorithms start with $\delta_t < \delta^*$, and they update their respective values (denoted as δ_{t+1} and λ_{t+1} respectively) for the next iteration as follows

$$\begin{cases} \delta_{t+1} = \max_X \text{ F-score}^*(Q^X, \widehat{R}^X, \alpha), \\ \lambda_{t+1} = \text{F-score}^*(Q^{X^*}, R', \alpha). \end{cases} \tag{24}$$

Note that for a feasible X, $\widehat{R}^X$ is constructed by comparing each $Q^X_{i,1}$ ($1 \leq i \leq n$) with the threshold $\delta_t \cdot \alpha$. And R' is similarly constructed by comparing each $Q^{X^*}_{i,1}$ ($1 \leq i \leq n$) with the same threshold $\delta_t \cdot \alpha$. As X^* is also a feasible assignment, we have $(Q^{X^*}, R') \in \{(Q^X, \widehat{R}^X) \mid X \text{ is feasible }\}$. Then by considering Equation 24, we derive $\delta_{t+1} \geq \lambda_{t+1}$. As mentioned above, since $\delta_t < \delta^*$, the properties in [12] guarantee that $\lambda_{t+1} > \delta_t$, then we derive $\delta_{t+1} > \delta_t$. As δ^* is the optimal objective value, we can finally derive $\delta_t < \delta_{t+1} \leq \delta^*$, which proves Property 1.

To prove Property 2, we apply the same comparison. Suppose both algorithms start with $\delta_t = \delta^*$, then they are updated by Equation 24. Similarly we have $\delta_{t+1} \geq \lambda_{t+1}$. As $\delta_t = \delta^*$, following the properties in [12], we have $\lambda_{t+1} = \delta_t = \delta^*$. Since $\delta_{t+1} \leq \delta^*$, we derive $\delta_t = \delta_{t+1} = \delta^*$, which proves Property 2. ☐

G. PROOF FOR THEOREM 4

Theorem 4: The problem of computing δ_{t+1} (Definition 2) can be reduced to a 0-1 FP problem.

PROOF. Given Q^c, Q^w and a feasible X, from Equation 1 we know that Q^X can be expressed by X, Q^c and Q^w, then we have

$$Q^X_{i,1} = x_i \cdot Q^w_{i,1} + (1 - x_i) \cdot Q^c_{i,1}.$$

Given Q^X and δ_t, we know that $\widehat{R}^X$ is constructed by setting $\widehat{r}^X_i = 1$ if $Q^X_{i,1} \geq \delta_t \cdot \alpha$ and $\widehat{r}^X_i = 2$ if $Q^X_{i,1} < \delta_t \cdot \alpha$. It means that if we construct $\widehat{R}^c$ ($\widehat{R}^w$) by setting $\widehat{r}^c_i = 1$ ($\widehat{r}^w_i = 1$) if $Q^c_{i,1} \geq \delta_t \cdot \alpha$ ($Q^w_{i,1} \geq \delta_t \cdot \alpha$) and $\widehat{r}^c_i = 2$ ($\widehat{r}^w_i = 2$) if $Q^c_{i,1} < \delta_t \cdot \alpha$ ($Q^w_{i,1} < \delta_t \cdot \alpha$), then $\widehat{R}^X$ can be expressed with the given $\widehat{R}^c$ and $\widehat{R}^w$ as follows:

$$\mathbb{1}_{\{\widehat{r}^X_i=1\}} = x_i \cdot \mathbb{1}_{\{\widehat{r}^w_i=1\}} + (1 - x_i) \cdot \mathbb{1}_{\{\widehat{r}^c_i=1\}}.$$

As $x_i = \{0, 1\}$, if we plug the above derived $Q^X_{i,1}$ and $\mathbb{1}_{\{\widehat{r}^X_i=1\}}$ into F-score*$(Q^X, \widehat{R}^X, \alpha) = \frac{\sum_{i=1}^{n} Q^X_{i,1} \cdot \mathbb{1}_{\{\widehat{r}^X_i=1\}}}{\sum_{i=1}^{n} [\,\alpha \cdot \mathbb{1}_{\{\widehat{r}^X_i=1\}} + (1-\alpha)\cdot Q^X_{i,1}\,]}$, and set the parameters b_i, d_i ($1 \leq i \leq n$), β and γ following
(1) $b_i = d_i = 0$ for $q_i \notin S^w$, and
(2) b_i, d_i ($q_i \in S^w$), β and γ are set as:

$$\begin{cases} b_i = Q^w_{i,1} \cdot \mathbb{1}_{\{\widehat{r}^w_i=1\}} - Q^c_{i,1} \cdot \mathbb{1}_{\{\widehat{r}^c_i=1\}} \\ d_i = \alpha \cdot (\mathbb{1}_{\{\widehat{r}^w_i=1\}} - \mathbb{1}_{\{\widehat{r}^c_i=1\}}) + (1-\alpha) \cdot (Q^w_{i,1} - Q^c_{i,1}) \\ \beta = \sum_{i=1}^{n} Q^c_{i,1} \cdot \mathbb{1}_{\{\widehat{r}^c_i=1\}} \\ \gamma = \sum_{i=1}^{n} [\,\alpha \cdot \mathbb{1}_{\{\widehat{r}^c_i=1\}} + (1-\alpha) \cdot Q^c_{i,1}\,], \end{cases}$$

then the problem is to maximize

$$\text{F-score}^*(Q^X, \widehat{R}^X, \alpha) = \frac{\sum_{i=1}^{n} (x_i \cdot b_i) + \beta}{\sum_{i=1}^{n} (x_i \cdot d_i) + \gamma}. \tag{25}$$

s.t. X is a feasible assignment vector. As Q^c, Q^w, $\widehat{R}^c$, $\widehat{R}^w$, S^w, α, and δ_t are known, then x_i ($1 \leq i \leq n$) are the only unknown variables. Let all the feasible assignment vectors form the subspace $\Omega \subseteq \{0,1\}^n$ where $|\Omega| = \binom{|S^w|}{k}$. If we set $z_i = x_i$ ($1 \leq i \leq n$), then each $\mathbf{z} \in \Omega$ corresponds to a feasible assignment vector X. So the problem is to maximize $\frac{\sum_{i=1}^{n}(z_i \cdot b_i)+\beta}{\sum_{i=1}^{n}(z_i \cdot d_i)+\gamma}$ s.t. $\mathbf{z} \in \Omega \subseteq \{0,1\}^n$, which is a 0-1 FP problem. ☐

H. F-SCORE ONLINE ASSIGNMENT ALGORITHMS (ALGORITHM 2 AND 3)

Algorithm 2 is the *F-score Online Assignment Algorithm*, which iteratively updates δ_{init} until convergence. In each iteration (lines

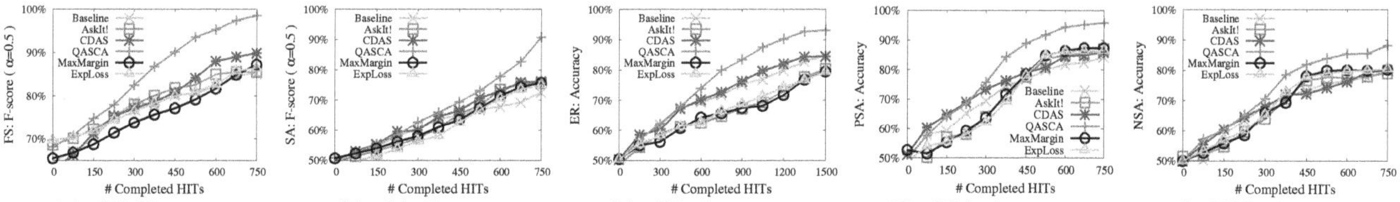

(a) *FS*: F-score (b) *SA*: F-score (c) *ER*: Accuracy (d) *PSA*: Accuracy (e) *NSA*: Accuracy

Figure 7: Additional Results on Real Datasets by Varying # Completed HITs

Algorithm 3 *Update*

Input: Q^c, Q^w, α, k, S^w, δ
Output: X, λ

1: $\lambda = 0$; // initialized as 0 ($\lambda_{init} = 0$)
2: $X = [\,]$;
3: $\widehat{R}^c = [\,]$; $\widehat{R}^w = [\,]$;
4: $b = d = [0, 0, \ldots, 0]$; $\beta = 0$; $\gamma = 0$;
5: // construct $\widehat{R}^c$ ($\widehat{R}^w$) by comparing Q^c (Q^w) with $\delta \cdot \alpha$; (lines 6-9)
6: **for** $i = 1$ to n **do**
7: **if** $Q^c_{i,1} \geq \delta \cdot \alpha$ **then** $\widehat{r}^c_i = 1$ **else** $\widehat{r}^c_i = 2$
8: **for** $q_i \in S^w$ **do**
9: **if** $Q^w_{i,1} \geq \delta \cdot \alpha$ **then** $\widehat{r}^w_i = 1$ **else** $\widehat{r}^w_i = 2$
10: Compute b_i, d_i ($1 \leq i \leq n$) and β, γ following the proof in Theorem 4;
11: // Update λ from λ_{init} until convergence; (line 12-21)
12: **while** True **do**
13: $\lambda_{pre} = \lambda$
14: compute TOP, a set which contains k questions in S^w that correspond to the highest value of $b_i - \lambda \cdot d_i$;
15: **for** $i = 1$ to n **do**
16: **if** $q_i \in TOP$ **then** $x_i = 1$ **else** $x_i = 0$
17: $\lambda = \frac{\sum_{i=1}^{n}(x_i \cdot b_i) + \beta}{\sum_{i=1}^{n}(x_i \cdot d_i) + \gamma}$;
18: **if** $\lambda_{pre} == \lambda$ **then**
19: **break**
20: **else**
21: $\lambda_{pre} = \lambda$
22: **return** X, λ

3-9), it first calls the *Update Algorithm* (the details are introduced in the following two paragraphs) to update δ (line 5), and then decide whether it converges or not (lines 6-9). Finally, it uses the assignment vector X corresponding to the converging δ to construct a HIT (lines 10-14). The converging δ and its corresponding assignment vector X are both optimal (i.e., respectively δ^* and X^*).

As we have proved that that the problem of computing λ_{t+1} can be reduced to a 0-1 FP problem (Theorem 4), following the Dinkelbach framework [12] as discussed in Section 3.2.3, the key is to solve the sub-problem $\mathbf{z}' = argmax_{\mathbf{z}} \sum_{i=1}^{n}(b_i - \lambda \cdot d_i) \cdot z_i$. In Theorem 4, in order to get $\mathbf{z}'$, due to the constraint of Ω (containing all feasible assignments), we should select k questions in S^w ($q_i \in S^w$) with the largest values of $(b_i - \lambda \cdot d_i)$.

We present the detailed *Update Algorithm* in Algorithm 3, which leverages Dinkelbach framework [12] to efficiently compute δ_{t+1} based on δ_t. For efficiency's sake it first constructs $\widehat{R}^c$, $\widehat{R}^w$ (lines 5-9), and b_i, d_i ($b_i \in S^w$), β, γ (line 10) following the details in Theorem 4 . Then it iteratively updates λ_{init} until convergence (lines 11-21). In each iteration (lines 13-21), with known λ, it selects k questions in S^w ($q_i \in S^w$) with the largest values of $(b_i - \lambda \cdot d_i)$ (line 14), which needs $\mathcal{O}(n)$ time by PICK algorithm [2]. Then it updates λ following Equation 25 (line 17). Finally it decides whether it converges or not (lines 18-21).

I. ADDITIONAL RESULTS

In order to show both Accuracy and F-score on all datasets, we add five additional experiments, and the evaluation metrics are respectively F-score for datasets *FS* and *SA*, and Accuracy for datasets *ER*, *PSA* and *NSA*. To be precise, for *FS*, we set the evaluation metric as F-score for label "$\geq$" with $\alpha = 0.5$; and for *SA*, we set the evaluation metric as F-score for label "positive" with $\alpha = 0.5$. Apart from the change of evaluation metrics, we apply the same experimental settings to the new experiments as our original ones (Table 1). We calculate the result quality for different systems with the number of completed HITs in Figure 7. The new experiments have similar results with our original ones and QASCA outperforms other systems on all datasets.

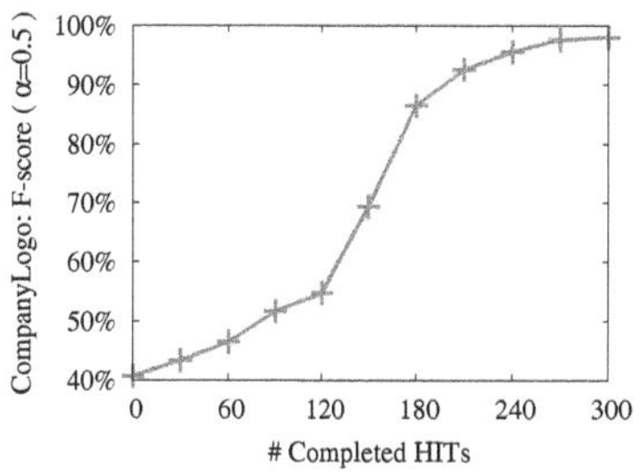

Figure 8: F-Score on CompanyLogo Dataset with 214 Labels

J. EXPERIMENT ON MULTIPLE LABELS

We evaluate the efficiency and effectiveness of our model for F-score on a real-world dataset with a large number of labels. The dataset was constructed using the logos of Fortune 500 companies[11], denoted by the "CompanyLogo" dataset. It had 500 questions in total, where each question contained a company logo, and we asked workers to decide in which country the company was founded. There were 214 labels (i.e., categories) in a question, where each label corresponded to a country. Each question was assigned to 3 workers on average and each HIT contained 5 questions. So there were $\frac{500 \times 3}{5} = 300$ HITs. We deployed the application on our system QASCA and set the evaluation metric as F-score for label "USA" with $\alpha = 0.5$. There were 128 out of 500 questions whose true labels corresponded to "USA". We recorded the result quality with different numbers of completed HITs and the maximal assignment time among all HITs.

The experimental results (see Figure 8) showed that QASCA achieved 90% F-score by completing only two thirds of the HITs. That is, each question got only 2 answers on average from the crowd. This result validated the effectiveness of our assignment model for a large number of categories. Moreover, the maximal assignment time was 0.005s, and thus our method was also fairly efficient. This is because F-score focuses on the quality of a specific label (or a certain group of labels), and we can optimize its calculation by reducing a large number of labels into two categories, where one category (called "*target label*") contains the focused label and the other category (called "*non-target label*") includes the remaining labels. In our example, the "target label" was "USA", and all the other labels formed the "non-target label". Therefore, the calculation of F-score was actually independent of the number of categories. If requesters focus on the quality of multiple labels, they can use Accuracy instead of F-score.

[11] http://en.wikipedia.org/wiki/Fortune_Global_500

tDP: An Optimal-Latency Budget Allocation Strategy for Crowdsourced MAXIMUM Operations

Vasilis Verroios
Stanford University
verroios@stanford.edu

Peter Lofgren
Stanford University
plofgren@stanford.edu

Hector Garcia-Molina
Stanford University
hector@cs.stanford.edu

ABSTRACT

Latency is a critical factor when using a crowdsourcing platform to solve a problem like entity resolution or sorting. In practice, most frameworks attempt to reduce latency by heuristically splitting a budget of questions into rounds, so that after each round the answers are analyzed and new questions are selected. We focus on one of the most extensively studied crowdsourcing operations, the MAX operation (finding the best element in a collection under human criteria), and we study the problem of budget allocation into rounds for this operation. We provide a polynomial-time dynamic-programming budget allocation algorithm that minimizes the latency when questions form tournaments in each round. Furthermore, we study the general case where questions can be asked in any arbitrary way in each round. Our theoretical results for the general case indicate that our approach is also optimal under certain worst and average-case scenarios. We compare our approach to alternatives on Amazon Mechanical Turk, where many of our theory assumptions do not necessarily hold. We find that our approach is also optimal in practice and achieves a notable improvement over alternatives in most cases.

1. INTRODUCTION

Crowdsourced operators like sort [15] or filtering [17] have been well studied over the last years by the database community. The two main dimensions explored are *cost* and *accuracy*. Therefore, in most cases, a budget of maximum questions to ask is given and the objective is to maximize accuracy. In other cases, a threshold for accuracy is given and the objective is to reach this threshold spending the least number of questions possible.

In this paper, we focus on a third dimension: *latency*. While humans can answer questions that machine algorithms cannot yet handle, they usually need a substantial amount of time to answer each question. For many crowdsourcing applications, latency is a critical factor: for example, consider monitoring the passengers in an airport against a database with images of known terrorists or choosing the next move in time-controlled chess.

The most typical approach of using a crowdsourcing platform, is to send questions in successive rounds. That is, a crowdsourced operator sends some questions in the first round, receives the answers on these questions, uses the answers to select the questions for the second round, and so on, until the budget of questions is spent or until the attained accuracy is above the given threshold. Given this mode of operation, an interesting cost–latency tradeoff appears; or an accuracy–latency tradeoff, depending on the problem setting.

For example, consider trying to find the best political-campaign response to an opponent's attack one day before the elections, over a collection of 1000 responses, using pairwise comparisons. In one extreme, we first pick two random responses, ask a question between them, get back the answer, and find the best out of the two. (Let us assume for now that we need a single comparison to get the best out of two responses, i.e., workers are not malicious and are always right.) Next, we compare the winner of the first comparison with a third random response from the collection. We continue like this until only one response is left; the one that didn't lose any comparisons. This strategy needs $1000 - 1$ questions to reach to the best response. In the other extreme, we ask all $\binom{1000}{2}$ questions in one round, and we reach to the best response when the answers we get back indicate that a single response has won over all the others. Clearly, asking one question at a time will save a huge number of questions. However, if we can afford the cost of $\binom{1000}{2}$ questions and if there is a large number of workers interested in our task, asking all questions in one round may prove beneficial in terms of latency. For instance, if there are more than $\binom{1000}{2}$ platform workers interested in the task, and each worker needs exactly one minute to answer a question, the first strategy would require $1000-1$ minutes (i.e., around 17 hours), while the second one would require only 1 minute; assuming the time to process the answers is negligible and no other delays take place. On the other hand, if there was just a single worker interested in our task, the first strategy would, again, require $1000-1$ minutes, while the second one could go on for $\frac{1000*999}{2}$ minutes; assuming that for almost one year this dedicated worker is answering our questions on this collection, day and night.

The same cost–latency tradeoff also appears in many other crowdsourcing operations, e.g., Entity Resolution [27] or Graph Search [16]. When we started our work on latency and budget allocation, we faced a choice: either focus on

SIGMOD'15, May 31–June 4, 2015, Melbourne, Victoria, Australia.

http://dx.doi.org/10.1145/2723372.2749440.

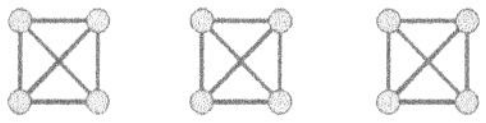

Figure 1: Example of three 4-element tournaments.

a specific crowdsourcing operator or study a general framework. We chose to focus on one specific operator because knowledge of the task at hand can impact the way questions are best allocated (more on this later). Thus, we felt it was important to fully understand latency and quantify potential improvements in a specific scenario before trying to generalize. The operator we focus on is finding the MAX element of a collection using pairwise comparisons. This problem is relatively simple, yet there are many opportunities for allocating questions wisely and for reducing latency.

In its most common setting, the MAX operator receives as input a vector of integers indicating how many questions should be posted in each round. The selection of the specific questions in each round, is done by a *question selection* algorithm that takes into account the answers to all the questions issued in rounds previous to the current one. At some point (before or after the end of the last round), the MAX operator decides that the answers retrieved, identify the MAX element in the collection.

Our focus in this paper is the computation of a good input vector for the MAX operator. That is, given an overall budget of questions that we can afford, we are interested in finding an allocation of this budget into rounds such that the overall latency until reaching to the MAX is minimized. For instance, in the debate-response example, when we were asking all $\binom{1000}{2}$ questions in one round, we were implicitly allocating our whole budget into a single round. Another possible allocation would be, for example, to split the budget of $\binom{1000}{2}$ questions into 10 batches, by allocating the same number of questions into each round. We call the algorithms that compute such allocations, *budget allocation* algorithms.

In addition to the overall budget of questions, we assume that *budget allocation* algorithms are also given as input a latency function $\mathcal{L}(q)$. This function gives an estimate of the time required to get back the answers when q pairwise comparisons are asked in one round. (Such a function can be estimated by the crowdsourcing platform based on statistics about the workers in the platform, their availability in different times during the day, and the type of the task. In Section 6.1, we run experiments to estimate $\mathcal{L}(q)$ for a specific task on Amazon Mechanical Turk.)

Our study focuses mostly on the latency and cost dimensions, assuming that humans do not make errors, or in other words, we need a single comparison to get the best out of two elements. There are several effective approaches for dealing with human errors [10, 12, 13, 14, 17, 22] and, thus, we choose to leave out this aspect of the problem, treating it as an orthogonal issue. Nevertheless, we also study an accuracy aspect of the problem: even when humans are always correct, some approaches may still not achieve a *singleton termination*, i.e., they may end up with more than one elements as candidates for the MAX after all questions are answered, as we will discuss later in the paper.

Most related to our work is the work of [23] that also studies the MAX operation in multiple rounds. However, the main focus of [23] is the accuracy and cost dimensions, with a simplified definition of latency: the total number of rounds. Moreover, there is no optimality guarantee for the hill-climb based heuristics proposed in [23]. Other papers (like [2, 10]), focus on finding the MAX after all (possibly erroneous) answers are retrieved, or focus on selecting which questions to ask in the next round using all previous answers as evidence.

One of the main contributions of this paper is tDP: a dynamic programming *budget allocation* algorithm that computes the optimal allocation of questions into rounds in polynomial time. This algorithm assumes the use of a very specific *question selection* algorithm that forms *tournaments*, in each round. For example, if the allocation for a round is 18 questions and there are 12 candidate elements, the tournament-formation algorithm forms three *tournaments* (cliques), each involving four elements; Figure 1 depicts the three *tournaments* using nodes to represent each element and edges to represent the questions between elements.

At first glance, the *tournament*-like formation of questions may seem a very restrictive way of asking questions in each round. Nevertheless, in Section 4, we present a number of interesting theoretical results showing that our dynamic programming algorithm, together with the tournament-formation question selection, is optimal under certain worst and average case scenarios, compared to any other combination of *budget allocation* and *question selection* algorithms. We also run experiments in Amazon Mechanical Turk, to test the effectiveness of our approach when some of the theory assumptions do not hold or when we have access only to a rough estimate of the latency function $\mathcal{L}(q)$. We compare our approach with several other approaches and we conclude that in all cases the dynamic programming algorithm gives the best outcome and in most cases outperforms the other approaches by a huge margin.

To summarize, our contributions are as follows:

- We formally define the problem of the optimal budget allocation for the MAX operator, in Section 2.
- We propose a dynamic-programming *budget allocation* algorithm, in Section 3.
- We analyze our approach, consisting of the *budget allocation* and *tournament question selection* algorithms, and we prove strong optimality guarantees in the average and worst-case scenarios, in Section 4.
- We present 4 alternative *budget allocation* heuristics that have a low computational cost, in Section 5.
- We experimentally compare our approach with the alternatives on Amazon Mechanical Turk, in Section 6.

2. PROBLEM DEFINITION

In this section, we give a formal definition to the problem of finding the MAX element of a collection, while minimizing the latency. In our problem definition, we assume that questions are selected by a specific *question selection* algorithm that forms *tournaments* between elements in each round. In Section 4, we discuss a generalized version of the problem, where questions can be selected by any *question selection* algorithm in each round, and we prove that the approach we propose is also optimal in that case.

2.1 Preliminaries

Our input is a set of elements, C, with $|C| = c_0$ elements, and a budget threshold, b, expressing the maximum number of questions we can ask, over all rounds. We are interested in finding the MAX element of C, by asking pairwise comparisons in each round. There is a true unknown permutation

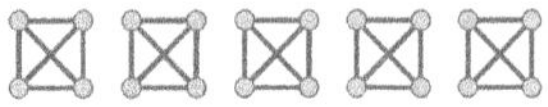

Figure 2: Tournament graph $G_T(20,5)$.

for the elements of C, that gives the order of the elements; we assume a strict order without equalities between elements. The first element in this order is the MAX element.

We assume that for 2 elements a and b, a single comparison is sufficient for resolving their true relation, based on the unknown true permutation of C. In practice, to handle this error-free assumption a *reliable worker layer* (RWL) can sit between our algorithms and the crowdsourcing platform. Such an RWL can harness techniques proposed in recent studies [10, 12, 13, 14, 17, 22], to handle human errors (or subjectiveness). The input to RWL, in each round, is a set of questions and the output is a conflict-free set of correct answers; with one answer per question. For example, if we ask questions $\{(a,b), (b,c), (c,a)\}$, RWL may issue multiple comparison tasks for each question on the platform and, based on the worker responses, RWL will infer 3 answers such that there is no cycle between elements a, b, and c (e.g., by applying the algorithms proposed in [10]). When we get an answer from RWL indicating that an element a is greater than an element b, we say that *a won* over b.

In each round the questions form tournaments (in Section 4 we relax this assumption) with each tournament giving a single element as a *winner* for the next round; the *winner* is the element that is greater than all other elements in the tournament. We denote this tournament structure by the graph $G_T(c_{i-1}, c_i)$:

DEFINITION 1. ***Tournament Graph,*** $G_T(c_{i-1}, c_i)$: *A graph consisting of c_{i-1} nodes that form c_i cliques(tournaments). (As our notation suggests, the c_i winners of $G(c_{i-1}, c_i)$ will be the input for graph $G(c_i, c_{i+1})$.)*

For example, consider $G_T(20,5)$, depicted in Figure 2. The graph nodes refer to elements and an edge between two nodes represents a comparison between the two respective elements. $G_T(20,5)$ consists of 20 nodes forming five 4-cliques. After receiving the answers on the 6 questions in each clique-tournament, there will be a single element in the tournament that will have won in all 3 comparisons it was involved in. Note that since we ask all questions between elements in a tournament, and all answers provided by RWL are correct and conflict-free (based on the single underlying permutation for C), there will be exactly one element that wins all the comparisons it is involved in the tournament.

In the example of Figure 2, the 5 winners from the tournaments advance to the next round, where they are, once more, organized in tournaments, e.g., a single tournament of 5 elements, or two tournaments, one with 3 elements and one with 2 elements. Furthermore, we assume a random assignment of the advancing elements to the tournaments of the next round (see Section 5 for the full description of the Tournament-formation algorithm).

Note that the tournaments formed in a round may not be all of the same size. For instance, if instead of 20 we had 24 elements and we still wanted to organize them in 5 tournaments, we would form 4 tournaments of 5 elements and one tournament of 4 elements, as depicted in Figure 3. In the general case, when we have c_{i-1} elements and we want to form c_i tournaments, $c_{i-1} \bmod c_i$ tournaments will involve $\lceil \frac{c_{i-1}}{c_i} \rceil$ elements, and the rest of the tournaments will involve $\lfloor \frac{c_{i-1}}{c_i} \rfloor$ elements.

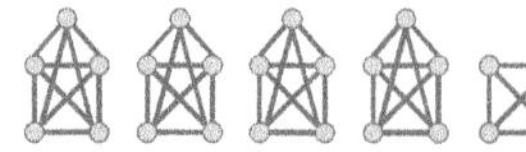

Figure 3: Tournament graph $G_T(24,5)$.

The number of questions that a tournament graph "spends" in one round is given by function $Q(c_{i-1}, c_i)$:

DEFINITION 2. ***Questions function*** $Q(c_{i-1}, c_i)$: *Function giving the number of edges-questions in $G_T(c_{i-1}, c_i)$.*

For example, $G_T(20,5)$ in Figure 2, uses $\binom{20/5}{2} * 5 = 30$ questions. In general, when c_{i-1} is a multiple of c_i, $Q(c_{i-1}, c_i)$ is given by:

$$Q(c_{i-1}, c_i) = \binom{c_{i-1}/c_i}{2} * c_i \tag{1}$$

However, c_{i-1} will not always be a multiple of c_i. For instance, consider $G_T(24,5)$ in Figure 3. The first 4 tournaments (from the left), involve 5 elements, while the last one involves just 4. The number of questions in this case is $\binom{\lceil 24/5 \rceil}{2} * (24 \bmod 5) + \binom{\lfloor 24/5 \rfloor}{2} * (5 - 24 \bmod 5) = \binom{5}{2} * 4 + \binom{4}{2} * 1 = 46$. Overall, $Q(c_{i-1}, c_i)$ is given by:

$$\binom{\lceil c_{i-1}/c_i \rceil}{2} \quad * \quad (c_{i-1} \bmod c_i) +$$
$$\binom{\lfloor c_{i-1}/c_i \rfloor}{2} \quad * \quad [c_i - (c_{i-1} \bmod c_i)] \tag{2}$$

Note that when c_{i-1} is a multiple of c_i, i.e, $c_{i-1} \bmod c_i = 0$, equation (2) is equivalent to equation (1).

The latency for getting all answers back in each round is a function of the number of questions we ask. We denote this function by $\mathcal{L}(q)$:

DEFINITION 3. ***Latency function,*** $\mathcal{L}(q)$: *Function that expresses the amount of time we have to wait for getting back the answers, when we ask q questions in a single round.*

For example, consider function $\mathcal{L}(q) = 60 + q$ seconds. When we form $G_T(24,5)$ in one round, we have to wait for $\mathcal{L}(Q(24,5)) = \mathcal{L}(46) = 106$ seconds to get back the 46 answers. Here, the constant term of 60 seconds in $\mathcal{L}(q)$, expresses an overhead of initiating a new round. The latency function can be based on statistics for a specific crowdsourcing platform and a specific type of task and it models the delays of the RWL. In addition, we assume that latency is an increasing function of q. Note that this assumption does not affect the optimality of our solution to Problem 1, defined in the next section. We only use this assumption to prove optimality for the, more general, Problem 2, in Section 4.1.

2.2 MinLatency Problem

Our objective is to decide on a sequence of tournament graphs, $G_T(c_0, c_1)$, $G_T(c_1, c_2)$, ..., $G_T(c_{r-1}, c_r)$, such that the aggregate number of edges-questions is less than or equal to the budget b and the overall latency is minimized. Note that we do not impose any constraint on the number of rounds r that the sequence must extend to.

For instance, consider a budget of $b = 108$ questions for finding the MAX of $c_0 = 40$ elements and the sequence

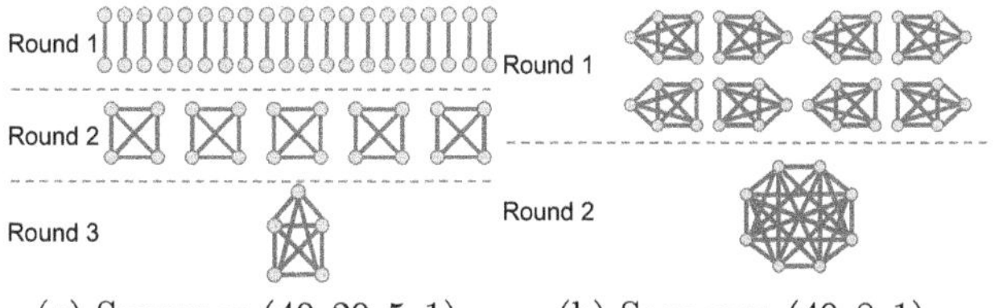

(a) Sequence $(40, 20, 5, 1)$ (b) Sequence $(40, 8, 1)$

Figure 4: Two tournament graph sequences.

$(c_i)_{i=0}^r = (40, 20, 5, 1)$, depicted in Figure 4(a) by $G_T(40, 20)$ in the first round, $G_T(20, 5)$ in the second round, and $G_T(5, 1)$ in the last round. The aggregate number of edges is $20 + 30 + 10 = 60$, that is, less than b. If we consider a latency function $\mathcal{L}(q) = 100 + q$ seconds, the overall latency to reach to the MAX is $\mathcal{L}(20) + \mathcal{L}(30) + \mathcal{L}(10) = 120 + 130 + 110 = 360$ seconds. Another sequence $(c'_i)_{i=0}^r = (40, 8, 1)$, depicted in Figure 4(b), achieves a lower overall latency without violating the budget constraint. In fact, $(c'_i)_{i=0}^r = (40, 8, 1)$ requires $80 + 28 = 108$ questions and gives an overall latency of $\mathcal{L}(80) + \mathcal{L}(28) = 180 + 128 = 308$ seconds.

The general formulation is given by the *MinLatency* optimization problem below:

PROBLEM 1 **(*MinLatency*)** . Given a set of c_0 initial elements, a budget constraint of b questions, and a latency function $\mathcal{L}(q)$, find the sequence $(c_i)_{i=0}^r$ solving:

$$\min_{(c_i)_{i=0}^r} \quad \sum_{i=1}^{r} \mathcal{L}(Q(c_{i-1}, c_i)) \quad (3)$$

$$\text{s.t.} \quad \sum_{i=1}^{r} Q(c_{i-1}, c_i) \leq b \quad (4)$$

$$c_r = 1, \forall i \; c_i \in \mathbb{N} \quad (5)$$

Equation (3) expresses the objective function over all sequences $\{c_i\}$, equation (4) expresses the budget constraint, and equation (5) expresses the obvious constraints, i.e., the last number in the sequence must be 1 (the MAX element), and all numbers in the sequence must be positive integers. (Note that a sequence $(c_i)_{i=0}^{r_1}$ consuming fewer overall questions than a sequence $(c'_i)_{i=0}^{r_2}$, does not necessarily give a lower overall latency. For example, if $r_1 > r_2$, c_i may give a much higher overall latency than c'_i, if the cost of initiating a new round in $\mathcal{L}(q)$ is high.)

Note that the optimization problem in Equations (3) to (5) will always have a solution, as long as the budget is greater than or equal to the number of initial elements (minus one). This property is formally stated in the following theorem.

THEOREM 1. *The* MinLatency *problem in Equations (3) to (5) has a solution if and only if* $b \geq c_0 - 1$.

PROOF.
We consider the following two cases:

- $b < c_0 - 1$: Let us assume that the problem of (3) to (5) has a solution. Each element needs to lose at least one comparison to stop being a candidate for the MAX. Since only one element must remain at the end of all rounds, we need to spend at least one comparison for all the other $c_0 - 1$ elements. Hence, we need a budget of at least $c_0 - 1$ questions and the problem of (3) to (5) cannot have a solution since constraint (4) cannot be satisfied in this case.
- $b \geq c_0 - 1$: Consider the sequence $(c_i)_{i=0}^{c_0-1}$ such that $c_{i+1} = c_i - 1$, i.e., in each round we ask a single question between two arbitrarily chosen elements and the winner advances to the next round. This sequence involves $c_0 - 1$ questions and ends with $c_r = 1$. Therefore, this sequence satisfies constraints (4) and (5) and constitutes a solution to the optimization problem.

□

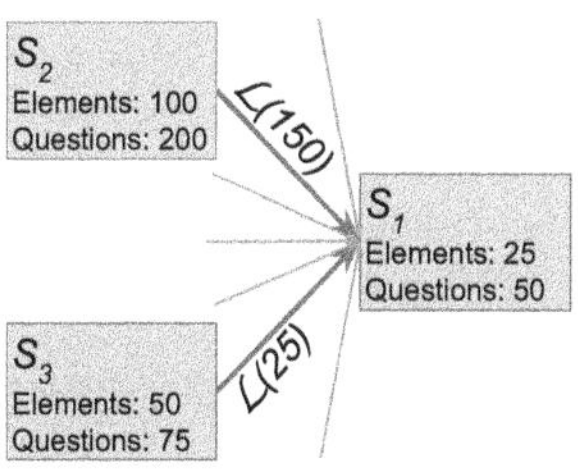

Figure 5: Insight for dynamic programming.

In the rest of the paper, we assume that we are always given a sufficient budget, i.e., $b \geq c_0 - 1$.

It is worth pointing out here that, in Section 4.1, we extend Problem 1 to the more general Problem 2, where questions do not necessarily form tournaments. Interestingly, the algorithm we describe in the next section gives the optimal solution to both problems, as we prove in Section 4.

3. DYNAMIC PROGRAMMING ALGORITHM

The *MinLatency* problem can be solved using dynamic programming. The insight for applying dynamic programming is based on the following observation: the sequence of tournament graphs that minimizes the latency when we are left with c_i elements and q remaining questions, does not depend on the sequence of graphs we followed in the previous rounds until reaching that state. That is, the lowest-latency sequence for reaching from the c_i elements and the q remaining questions, to the MAX element, is the same irrespectively of the sequence we used for reaching from the initial, c_0, elements and b questions to the remaining c_i elements and q questions.

In Figure 5 we use a box to represent a state where, after a number of rounds, we are left with c_i elements (not having lost any comparisons) and q questions (that we haven't used from our initial budget). The arrows express the cost of the transition from one state to another in a single round, i.e., the latency for that round. For instance, in Figure 5, we have a target state S_1 with 25 remaining elements and 50 remaining questions. We can reach S_1 in one round, from many other possible states. For example, we can reach S_1 from S_2 by asking 150 questions, i.e., we form $G_T(100, 25)$ and we reach from 100 elements to 25 elements by spending $Q(100, 25) = 6 * 25 = 150$ questions. A second state from which S_1 can be reached, is S_3. In order to reach S_1 from S_3, we need to form $G_T(50, 25)$, i.e., 25 tournaments with 2 elements each. The observation for dynamic programming is that the lowest-latency sequence from S_1 to the MAX element, does not depend on how we reach to S_1, i.e., through S_2, S_3 or any other possible state with a transition to S_1.

The above observation is formalized by the recursive function $OL(q, c_i)$:

DEFINITION 4. ***Optimal solution's latency,*** $OL(q, c_i)$: *The overall latency for the optimal solution to the* MinLatency *problem, given by equation (3), with input* c_i *elements and* q *remaining questions.*

For example, if we assume that the sequence $(c'_i)_{i=0}^r = \{40, 8, 1\}$ (depicted in Figure 4(b)) is the optimal solution to the *MinLatency* problem with input 40 elements and 108 remaining questions, then
$OL(108, 40) = \mathcal{L}(Q(40, 8)) + \mathcal{L}(Q(8, 1)) = \mathcal{L}(80) + \mathcal{L}(28)$

The following recursive equation expresses our dynamic programming insight for $OL(q, c_i)$:

$$OL(q,c_i) = \min_{c_{i+1} \in [1,c_i)} \{\mathcal{L}(Q(c_i,c_{i+1})) + OL(q - Q(c_i,c_{i+1}),c_{i+1})\} \quad (6)$$

$$OL(q,1) = 0 \quad (7)$$

Equation (6) refers to all possibilities for the next round. That is, in the next round a tournament graph $G_T(c_i, c_{i+1})$ will be formed, for $c_{i+1} \in [1, c_i)$. For example, if $c_i = 40$ and $c_{i+1} = 20$, the overall latency until finding the MAX will be: *a)* $\mathcal{L}(Q(40, 20))$ for the next round plus *b)* the latency of the optimal solution for an input of 20 elements and a budget of $q - Q(40, 20)$ questions, i.e., $OL(q - Q(40, 20), 20)$. The optimal solution's latency for an input of c_i elements and a budget of q questions (i.e, $OL(q, c_i)$) is the one minimizing the overall latency over all possible next rounds (i.e., $\forall c_{i+1} \in [1, c_i)$).

Equation (7) states that once we reach at a single element (i.e., the MAX), we do not have to "pay" for any additional latency no matter how many questions are left unasked.

Algorithm 1 is the top-down dynamic programming algorithm for solving the *MinLatency* problem. The recursive function, $OL(q, c_i)$ in lines 13-32, implements Equations (6) and (7). In lines 19-21, we examine if the remaining budget after a transition from c_i to c_{i+1} elements, is enough to reach from c_{i+1} to the MAX , based on Theorem 1. In line 1, we allocate a memoization array to avoid re-computing the value of $OL(q, c_i)$, for the same input.

The time complexity of the algorithm is $O(c_0^2 * b)$, while the space complexity is $O(c_0 * b)$. Taking into account that $b \in [c_0 - 1, \binom{c_0}{2})]$, the time complexity ranges from $O(c_0^3)$ to $O(c_0^4)$ and the space complexity ranges from $O(c_0^2)$ to $O(c_0^3)$.

Algorithm 1 DP tournaments (tDP)

```
Input: b: Initial budget of questions
Input: c_0: Initial number of elements
Input: L(q): Platform's latency function
Output: (c_i)_{i=0}^r: optimal solution's sequence
1: statesReached = allocate b × c_0 array
2: statesNext = allocate b × c_0 array
3: run OL(b, c_0)
4: append c_0 to (c_i)_{i=0}^r
5: c_i = c_0
6: while c_i > 1 do
7:     c_{i+1} = statesNext[b][c_i]
8:     append c_{i+1} to (c_i)_{i=0}^r
9:     b = b − Q(c_i, c_{i+1}); c_i = c_{i+1}
10: end while
11: return (c_i)_{i=0}^r
12:
13: Function OL(q, c_i)  #implements Equations (6) and (7)
14: if c_i is 1 then
15:     return 0
16: end if
17: l = ∞
18: for c_{i+1} in [1, c_i] with step 1 do
19:     if q − Q(c_i, c_{i+1}) < c_{i+1} − 1 then
20:         continue to line 18
21:     end if
22:     if statesReached[q − Q(c_i, c_{i+1})][c_{i+1}] is NULL then
23:         l' = OL(q − Q(c_i, c_{i+1}), c_{i+1})
24:     else
25:         l' = statesReached[q − Q(c_i, c_{i+1})][c_{i+1}]
26:     end if
27:     if L(Q(c_i, c_{i+1})) + l' < l then
28:         l = L(Q(c_i, c_{i+1})) + l'; next = c_{i+1}
29:     end if
30: end for
31: statesReached[q][c_i] = l; statesNext[q][c_i] = next
32: return l
```

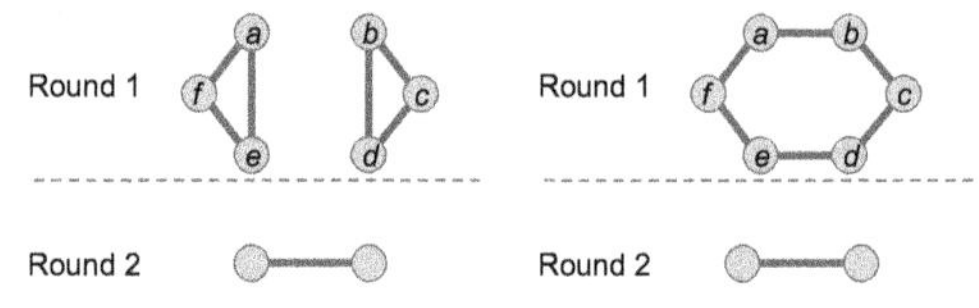

(a) Tournament (b) Cycle

Figure 6: Allocation $(6, 1)$ under two different *question selection* algorithms.

4. THEORETICAL RESULTS

The *MinLatency* optimization problem given by equations (3) to (5), assumes questions are formed in tournaments in each round. Here, we compare the tournament approach with a more general approach: questions are still asked in rounds, but they can be selected in each round by any *question selection* algorithm. That is, in each round questions do not have to form a tournament graph, but can instead form any graph. The elements that win in all of the comparisons they are involved in, advance to the next round; just like in the tournament graphs where the winners of the tournaments are the only elements not having lost any comparison.

An example of the general approach is given in Figures 6(a) and 6(b). In this example, the number of initial elements, c_0, is 6, while the budget, b, is 7. Consider the allocation $(6, 1)$ for the budget of 7 questions, i.e., 6 questions in the first round, and 1 question in the second round. Figure 6(a) shows the question selection by the tournament *question selection* algorithm we have discussed so far. That is, $G_T(6, 2)$ is formed in the first round and $G_T(2, 1)$ in the second round. A different *question selection* algorithm could have selected questions as shown by Figure 6(b), i.e., form a cycle-graph in the first round and then ask a single question between two elements that advance to the second round; if more than one elements advance.

While in the tournament approach we know exactly how many elements advance from one round to the next, this is not the case with other *question selection* algorithms. For instance, in Figure 6(b), 1 to 3 elements may advance from the first round to the second round. (An example where 3 elements advance is when the answers we receive in the first round are $\{(a > b), (a > f), (c > b), (c > d), (e > d), (e > f)\}$, while an example where just 1 element advances is when the answers are $\{(a > f), (a > b), (b > c), (c > d), (d > e), (e > f)\}$.) In case just 1 element advances (the MAX), we will have a reduced latency compared to the tournament approach, since there will be no reason to run round 2. However, if 3 elements advance, then the single question will not be enough to find the MAX in the second round: 2 elements will remain after the second round and 1 of them will have to be selected as the MAX. We call the event of being left with exactly one element after (or even before) all questions are asked, *singleton termination*. In our experimental evaluation, we study the probability of *singleton termination* for different *question selection* algorithms.

(a) DAG (b) Undirected

Figure 7: Example of DAG answer-represention.

The scenario where 3 elements advance in the second round, in Figure 6(b), is the worst case scenario for this example. (Note that we cannot have more than 3 elements not losing any comparisons in the first round.) In the worst case analysis we perform in this section, we assume that the worst case scenario happens in each round. In Appendix A, we also perform an average case analysis, where we focus on the expected number of elements that advance from one round to the next.

Our theoretical results consist of:
(1) A proof of optimality over multiple rounds in the worst-case scenario, for tDP combined with the tournament *question selection* algorithm. That is, tDP combined with the tournament-formation algorithm is guaranteed to give a latency lower than the latency achieved by any other combination of a *budget allocation* and a *question selection* algorithm, in the worst-case scenario (details in Section 4.1).
(2) A proof of optimality over a single round in the average-case scenario, for the tournament *question selection* algorithm. That is, the tournament-formation algorithm minimizes the expected number of elements that advance from a single round to the next one, under certain assumptions. In Appendix A, we discuss the details, including the assumptions and how tDP is related to those assumptions. Note that tDP combined with the tournament-formation algorithm is not necessarily optimal for the average-case scenario. Nevertheless, in our experimental evaluation where we examine what happens in the average case, tDP with the tournament-formation algorithm is substantially better than any other alternative we tried.

In the discussion of our theoretical results, we use a Directed Acyclic Graph (DAG) representation for the answers we get back from humans. A directed edge from node b to node a, expresses the answer $(a > b)$ to the comparison question asked between the two nodes. For example, in Figure 7(a), we ask the questions $\{(a,b),(b,c),(c,d),(d,a),(b,d)\}$ and we get back the answers $\{(a>b),(c>b),(d>c),(d>a),(d>b)\}$. Note that the answers we get back cannot form a cycle in the directed graph, since our answers are always correct and are based on the true unknown permutation of the initial elements that defines a strict element order. In practice, RWL resolves any formed cycles using methods like the ones proposed in [10].

4.1 Worst Case Analysis

Before discussing our main result in Theorem 4, we give some definitions and results that will simplify the discussion for the main result.

DEFINITION 5. ***Remaining Candidates*** (RC) ***set of a DAG*** : *The set of nodes that do not have any outgoing edges in the DAG.*

The set RC in our context, gives the elements that advance from one round to the next one, and remain as candidates for the MAX. For example, in Figure 7(a), $RC = \{d\}$ because d is the only element that has not lost any comparison; and since there are no other candidates remaining, d is the MAX element.

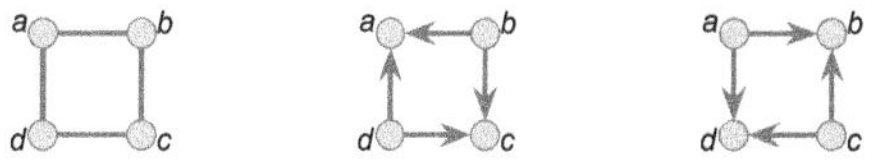

(a) Undirected (b) DAG 1 (c) DAG 2

Figure 8: Example of ***maxRC*** **sets of a graph.**

DEFINITION 6. ***Maximum Remaining Candidates*** ($maxRC$) ***set of an undirected graph*** G : *The largest RC set, for any DAG that can be formed by giving directions to the edges of G.*

For example, consider the undirected graph G in Figure 8(a). One $maxRC$ for G is given by the DAG of Figure 8(b) and consists of $\{a,c\}$. Note that, in this case, the $maxRC$ is not unique: the DAG of Figure 8(c) also gives an RC of 2 elements, consisting of $\{b,d\}$. On the contrary, the $maxRC$ of the graph in round 1 in Figure 9(a), is unique and consists of $\{a,c,e,g,i,k\}$.

The $maxRC$ of a graph G, expresses the worst case scenario when we ask the questions on G. That is, $maxRC$ gives the maximum possible number of remaining candidates for the MAX element, after asking the questions on G.

DEFINITION 7. ***Maximum Independent*** ($maxIND$) ***set of an undirected graph*** G : *An independent set of a graph $G=(V,E)$ is a subset of V such that there is no edge in E connecting two nodes of this subset. The maxIND set is the independent set of G with the most nodes.*

Consider the undirected graph G, for the DAG of Figure 7(a), depicted in Figure 7(b). Set $\{d\}$ is an independent set of G. However, the $maxIND$ of G, is set $\{a,c\}$.

Next, we prove a theorem that will enable us to use a graph theory result from [4]. This graph theory result will be our main building block for Theorem 4.

THEOREM 2. *For any undirected graph G, a set of nodes is a maxIND set if and only if it is a maxRC set.*

PROOF. The proof of Theorem 2 will be based on the Lemmas 1 and 2:

LEMMA 1. *For any undirected graph G, the maxRC set is an independent set of G.*

PROOF. We prove the contrapositive. Suppose that the $maxRC$ set, R, of an undirected graph G, is not an independent set of G. Then, there must be an edge e between two nodes a and b of R. Consider the DAG of G, for which R is an RC set. We give a direction to edge e, such that no cycle is formed in this DAG. By giving a direction to e, one of a or b acquires an outgoing edge and is no longer a remaining candidate. Hence, R cannot be an RC set.

LEMMA 2. *For any undirected graph G, the maxIND set is an RC set for a DAG of G.*

PROOF. We prove the contrapositive. Suppose that the $maxIND$ set is not an RC set. We can construct a DAG for G using the following process: *a)* pick a permutation p for the nodes of G, such that the top-$|maxIND|$ elements in the permutation are the nodes of the $maxIND$ set (order others arbitrarily) and *b)* for each edge e, give e a direction based on p, i.e., from the first endpoint, a, to the second, b, if b is greater than a in p and from b to a otherwise. Based on this process, no one of the nodes in the $maxIND$ set will have an outgoing edge: there are no edges between nodes in the $maxIND$ set (by the independent set definition), and for an edge between a node $a \in maxIND$ and a node $b \notin maxIND$, the direction can only be from b to a, because in p the top-

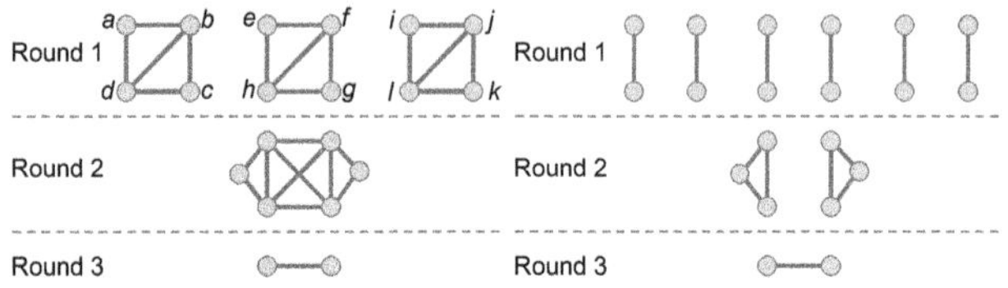

(a) non-tournament graphs (b) tournament graphs

Figure 9: Examples of graph sequences for the *Generalized Worst MinLatency* problem.

$|maxIND|$ elements are the nodes of $maxIND$. Hence, we found a DAG for which the $maxIND$ set is an RC set.

Based on Lemmas 1 and 2, for any undirected graph G, a $maxRC$ set is an independent set and a $maxIND$ set is also an RC set. Therefore, a set of nodes is a $maxIND$ set if and only if it is a $maxRC$ set.

□

Our optimality guarantees for the worst case scenario are based on a known graph theory result found in [4], summarized by the following theorem.

THEOREM 3. *For any positive integers c_{i-1} and c_i, any undirected graph $G = (V, E)$ that has $|V| = c_{i-1}$ and a $|maxIND| = c_i$, must have $|E| \geq Q(c_{i-1}, c_i)$, i.e., at least as many edges as the tournament graph $G_T(c_{i-1}, c_i)$.*

Theorem 3 suggests that we can reduce the number of questions we ask in each round, by replacing an arbitrary graph with a tournament graph. Figure 9(b), gives an example of replacing the graph sequence of Figure 9(a) with tournament graphs: $G_T(12, 6)$ in the first round, $G_T(6, 2)$ in the second round, and $G_T(2, 1)$ in the last round. (Note that, in Figure 9(a), the $maxRC$ of the graph in Round 1, i.e., set $\{a, c, e, g, i, k\}$, has a size of 6, while the $maxRC$ of the graph in Round 2 has a size of 2.) The number of questions in the first round drops from 15 to 6 and in the second round from 10 to 6. Thus, the new graph sequence allows us to find the MAX element with fewer questions. We formally state this implication of Theorem 3 in Lemma 3.

Now, let us define a generalized version of the *MinLatency* problem, where in each round questions can form any arbitrary graph. Using Theorems 2 and 3, we will prove that the Algorithm 1 optimally solves the general problem.

Our domain in the general problem consists of any sequence of graphs $(G_i = (V_i, E_i))_{i=0}^{r}$, such that $|V_{i+1}| = |maxRC(G_i)|$, i.e., the number of vertices for the graph in round $i + 1$ must be equal to the size of the $maxRC$ set of the graph in the previous round. In other words, after each round, we examine the worst possible scenario, i.e., being left with the maximum number of candidates possible; given by the $maxRC$ of the graph in that round. For example, in Figure 9(a), in the first round the graph of questions has a $maxRC$ set of 6 elements, $\{a, c, e, g, i, k\}$, in the second round the graph of the 6 nodes has a $maxRC$ set of 2 elements, which is the number of nodes in the graph of the third round.

As opposed to the *MinLatency* problem, where the graph in each round must be a tournament graph, here the domain is broader by allowing any graph of questions in each round. Still, the budget constraint and the objective function remain the same:

PROBLEM 2 (***Generalized Worst MinLatency***). Given a set of c_0 initial elements, a budget constraint of b questions, and a latency function $\mathcal{L}(q)$, find the sequence of graphs $(G_i = (V_i, E_i))_{i=0}^{r}$ solving:

$$\min_{(G_i=(V_i,E_i))_{i=0}^{r}} \quad \sum_{i=0}^{r} \mathcal{L}(|E_i|) \tag{8}$$

$$\text{s.t.} \quad \sum_{i=0}^{r} |E_i| \leq b \tag{9}$$

$$|V_0| = c_0, |maxRC(G_r)| = 1, \quad \forall i \ |V_{i+1}| = |maxRC(G_i)| \tag{10}$$

Note that in equation (10) the constraint $|maxRC(G_r)| = 1$ indicates that the $maxRC$ set of the last round graph must have a size of 1, i.e., even in the worst case we will be left with a single element (the MAX element).

We will prove that Algorithm 1 optimally solves the *Generalized Worst MinLatency* problem using the following lemma:

LEMMA 3. *Consider a graph sequence $\{(G_i = (V_i, E_i))_{i=0}^{r}$ satisfying equations (9) and (10). We can replace each graph $G_i = (V_i, E_i)$ in the sequence with the tournament graph $G_T(|V_i|, maxRC(G_i))$ and reduce the overall cost given by equation (8).*

PROOF. Based on Theorem 3, $G_i = (V_i, E_i)$ cannot have fewer edges than $G_T(|V_i|, |maxIND(G_i)|)$. Based on Theorem 2, the $maxIND$ and $maxRC$ sets are equivalent, therefore, $G_T(|V_i|, |maxIND(G_i)|) \equiv G_T(|V_i|, |maxRC(G_i)|)$. Thus, the number of questions we ask in each round will be reduced or remain the same. Taking into account the fact that $\mathcal{L}(q)$ is an increasing function, we conclude that the overall cost given by equation (8) will be reduced (or remain the same).

□

Taking into account Lemma 3 and the fact that Algorithm 1 optimally solves the *MinLatency* problem we reach to the following theorem:

THEOREM 4. *Algorithm 1 optimally solves the* Generalized Worst MinLatency *problem.*

PROOF. Based on Lemma 3, any graph sequence satisfying the constraints (equations (9) and (10)) can have a lower cost if we replace the graphs with tournament graphs. Therefore, the optimal solution to the *Generalized Worst MinLatency* problem consists of a sequence of tournament graphs. Since Algorithm 1 finds the optimal sequence of tournament graphs using dynamic programming, it is also optimal for the *Generalized Worst MinLatency* problem.

□

5. ALTERNATIVE APPROACHES

In this section, we present some simple alternative *budget allocation* and *question selection* algorithms that we will later compare against the combination of tDP with the tournament formation algorithm. In particular, we discuss four heuristics for budget allocation and two *question selection* strategies. The two *question selection* strategies are the tournament-formation algorithm we discussed so far, and the combination of two algorithms proposed in [10]. Besides those two strategies, we also ran experiments (not reported in this paper) with a number of other *question selection* algorithms, proposed in [10], as we briefly discuss in the end of Section 5.2. The two strategies we present here are the ones that worked best in terms of latency and *singleton termination* probability.

(a) HE (b) HF

Figure 10: Examples of HE and HF allocations.

5.1 Budget Allocation Algorithms

We present two simple heuristics along with their uniform versions. In the description of the heuristics (Figures 10(a) and 10(b)) we assume the tournament-formation algorithm is applied in each round, however, the heuristics can also be combined with any other *question selection* algorithm.

Heavy End (HE): The HE heuristic allocates the budget "conservatively" in the first rounds, until it detects that the MAX can be found in a single round; this round becomes the last round and the remaining budget gets allocated there. "Conservative" here means that no question can be "redundant" in the rounds before the last one. Consider the simple example of Figure 10(a) and assume a budget, b, of 51 questions for finding the MAX out of the $c_0 = 24$ initial elements. In the first and second round, HE allocates the budget so that exactly one question is allocated per element. This "conservative" allocation halves the number of candidates in each round; from 24 to 12 and from 12 to 6. In the third round, the remaining budget is enough to form a single tournament with all the remaining candidates. Hence, HE computes allocation $(12, 6, 33)$ in this example; note that in the last round HE allocates all of the remaining budget and not just 15 questions that would be enough for $G_T(6, 1)$.

Heavy Front (HF): The HF heuristic applies the same process with HE, in reverse order. We use the same example to illustrate, depicted in Figure 10(b). HF starts from the last round and assumes that in previous rounds there was exactly one question per element, i.e., the allocation halves the number of candidates in each of the last rounds. At some point, the remaining budget is enough to reach from the initial number of elements to the current number of elements: this point in our example takes place in Round 2 where the remaining budget is enough to reach from the 24 initial elements to the 8 elements in Round 2 through $G_T(24, 8)$. Thus, HF generates allocation $(44, 4, 2, 1)$; note that in the first round we do not just allocate 24 questions, but all of the remaining budget.

uniform Heavy End (uHE): uHE first applies HE to compute the number of rounds that HE would involve. As opposed to HE, uHE will then uniformly distribute the budget into this number of rounds. In the example used in this section, uHE first applies HE to compute the $(12, 6, 33)$ allocation and then divides the budget of 51 questions into three rounds, which results to the allocation: $(17, 17, 17)$.

uniform Heavy Front (uHF): Like uHE, uHF first applies HF to compute the number of rounds and then performs a uniform budget distribution. In the example here, uHF divides the budget of 51 questions into four rounds, which results to the allocation: $(13, 13, 13, 12)$.

It is important to clarify at this point that uHE and uHF combined with the tournament-formation *question selection* algorithm, are two adaptations of the multiprocessor MAX algorithm described in [21] to our setting. As we discuss in detail in the related work section, in settings studied for multiprocessor systems there is no budget constraint. Algorithms uHE and uHF use the same number of questions (which corresponds to the number of processors in a multiprocessor system) in each round, without violating the constraint on the total number of questions that can be asked.

5.2 Question Selection Algorithms

Each *question selection* algorithm uses as input in a given round j:

1. b_j: the available budget for round j; as given by the allocation generated by the budget allocation algorithm.
2. $\mathcal{C}_j$: the set of elements that have not lost any comparison in previous rounds, i.e., rounds 0 to $j - 1$.

Tournament-formation: The tournament-formation algorithm is the mechanism we discussed so far for selecting questions in each round. Here we give the general description of the algorithm. In each round the algorithm finds the lowest possible integer c_{j+1}, such that $Q(|\mathcal{C}_j|, c_{j+1}) \leq b_j$. That is, the algorithm tries to form the least number of tournaments possible, such that the questions required to form the tournaments is less than the budget available for this round. (Note that the fewer tournaments formed, the more questions required.) In case $b_j - Q(|\mathcal{C}_j|, c_{j+1}) > 0$, the remaining questions are randomly selected between elements of different tournaments. As stated earlier, the assignment of elements to tournaments is random, hence, the score of each element is not taken into account by the tournament-formation algorithm.

CT25: CT25 combines two *question selection* algorithms: *a)* SPREAD that randomly selects pairs of elements, as long as each element is involved in the same number of questions, and *b)* COMPLETE that spends part of the budget b_j on a single tournament between the "strongest" candidates and the rest of the budget to ask questions between the rest of the elements and the elements of the tournament; so that each element is involved in at least one question. (We describe the two algorithms in detail, in our technical report [25].)

Since COMPLETE needs to distinguish between "strong" and "weak" candidates, we need to rank each element in $\mathcal{C}_j$ based on all the answers from previous rounds. One option is to use the probability of an element being the MAX, to define the element's rank. However, as we prove in Appendix B.1, computing the probability of being the MAX is a #P-hard problem. Hence, we use instead a PageRank-like function that we discuss in detail in Appendix B.2.

CT25 applies SPREAD in the first 25% of all rounds and COMPLETE in the last 75% of all rounds. For example, if an allocation of 4 rounds is used, SPREAD will select the questions in the first round and COMPLETE will select the questions in the last 3 rounds. In experiments that we do not present here, we also tried CT50 and CT75, i.e., applying SPREAD in the first 50% and 75% of the allocation, respectively. In the same experiments, we tried a second *question selection* strategy that combines SPREAD with the GREEDY algorithm proposed in [10]. We give our main observations from those experiments in the experimental evaluation, in Section 6.8.

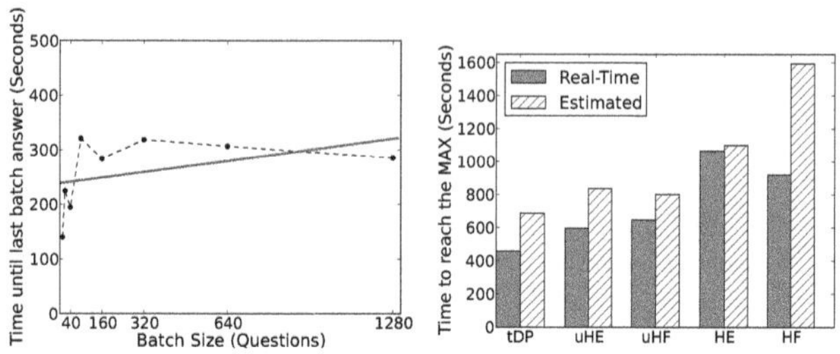

(a) Estimation of $\mathcal{L}(q)$ (b) Alternatives Comparison

Figure 11: Experiments in MTurk.

6. EXPERIMENTAL EVALUATION

Outline: In Section 6.1, we estimate $\mathcal{L}(q)$ for a specific comparison task and crowdsourcing platform. In Section 6.2, we use the estimated $\mathcal{L}(q)$ as an input to our algorithm and we issue the questions to the crowdsourcing platform to measure the real latency until finding the MAX: our objective is to verify that even when we are not fully aware of the real latency function and we just have a rough estimation for $\mathcal{L}(q)$, our approach shows significant gains compared to the alternatives. In Section 6.3, we compare different *question selection* algorithms and in Sections 6.4 to 6.6 we compare different *budget allocation* algorithms as we vary different parameters of the input. In Section 6.7, we study the running time of tDP.

Setup: We use a collection of 500 car photos. In each pairwise comparison, we present two car photos to a worker in Amazon Mechanical Turk (MTurk), and we ask the following question: "Which of the two cars is the most expensive?". The compensation for each answer is \$0.01. All of our experiments were performed during weekdays, in the same 8-hour window every day. We simulate error-free workers by ignoring their answers and replacing them with correct answers, i.e., answers consistent with the true ordering of the 500 cars. As discussed in Section 2, handling human errors requires an RWL that harnesses techniques like question repetition and cycle resolution in the directed graph of answers: these techniques are thoroughly studied in related work [10, 12, 13, 14, 17, 22].

6.1 Estimation of $\mathcal{L}(q)$ in MTurk

In this section, we estimate the latency function, $\mathcal{L}(q)$, when posting car-comparison questions on MTurk. The latency function $\mathcal{L}(q)$ is required by our tDP algorithm to compute the budget allocation. In the next section, we apply tDP using this estimate of $\mathcal{L}(q)$, and we compare it to HE, HF, uHE, and uHF by posting real-time car-comparison questions on MTurk.

To estimate $\mathcal{L}(q)$, we publish batches of different sizes and for each batch size we measure the time from publishing the first question of the batch until receiving the last answer back. For each batch size we publish a batch 20 times and we compute the average over the 20 runs.

In Figure 11(a), the dashed line shows the time until the last answer is returned (y-axis) for the different batch sizes (x-axis). As the dashed line shows, the time needed to receive all answers back is considerably lower for batches up to 40 questions and then increases; for 80 questions or more. Note also the slight decrease in the time needed to receive the answers as the batch size increases from 320 to 1280 questions. The reason for this decrease is that more workers are attracted as the batch size increases in this range, and the increased parallelism compensates for the increased number of questions. Nevertheless, even in cases where the task is very popular to workers (as it is the case with the task used here), there is a point where the batch size becomes much greater than the number of workers interested in the task (we did not reach that point in Figure 11(a)). After that point, there will inevitably be a significant increase in the time to get additional answers back.

The solid line in Figure 11(a) is our estimation for $\mathcal{L}(q)$, fitted using least-squares linear regression. As we discussed earlier, our objective is not to accurately predict $\mathcal{L}(q)$, but to roughly estimate it. Therefore, we just use a linear function of the following form: $\mathcal{L}(q) = \delta + \alpha * q$ seconds. We estimate a δ of 239 and an α of 0.06.

6.2 Real-Time Experiments in MTurk

Using the linear-regression estimation for $\mathcal{L}(q)$, we apply tDP and we decide upon the allocation of $b = 4000$ questions to find the MAX in the collection of 500 cars. We also apply each of the other four allocation algorithms, HF, HE, uHF, uHE, to compute four additional allocations. For each allocation, we post questions in successive rounds on MTurk. The questions are selected by the tournament-formation algorithm. We analyze the answers after the end of each round, and we stop asking questions if just a single element (MAX) not having lost any comparison remains. We repeat the experiment five times for each allocation.

The y-axis of Figure 11(b) depicts the time from posting the first question of the first round in MTurk until reaching at the MAX element. The solid bars depict the time until reaching the MAX for each allocation. We also use stripped bars to plot the time until reaching the MAX based on the estimated $\mathcal{L}(q)$, i.e., for each round instead of actually posting the questions on MTurk, we compute the time it would take to get back all answers, if latency were exactly as predicted by $\mathcal{L}(q)$.

The stripped bars roughly approximate the solid ones. In spite of the coarseness of estimation, tDP is also more effective in the real-time experiments, giving a substantial 30% improvement over the second-best uHE. Furthermore, compared to HE and HF the improvement is more than 2x. Thus, even when the $\mathcal{L}(q)$ function is only a course approximation to the actual latency, it provides enough guidance for tDP to make a very good budget allocation.

In the rest of the experiments, we use the estimated $\mathcal{L}(q)$ from Section 6.1, to compute the latency in each round. The reason is twofold. First, by using the same deterministic latency function for all approaches we avoid any variations on latency, induced by using a real-world crowdsourcing platform. (As our experiment in this section showed, the estimated latency follows the same trend with the real-time latency.) Second, from now on, in order to accurately measure the latency and *singleton termination* probability for each approach we increase the number of runs per experiment from 5 to 100: this number of runs induces a prohibitive cost for running the experiment on MTurk.

6.3 Comparison of the Question Selection Algorithms

We compare the two question selection strategies, tournament formation and CT25, when we vary the available budget from 500 questions to 8000 questions. In Figure 12(a), we plot the time until reaching the MAX (y-axis) for the different values of available budget (x-axis). Each curve refers

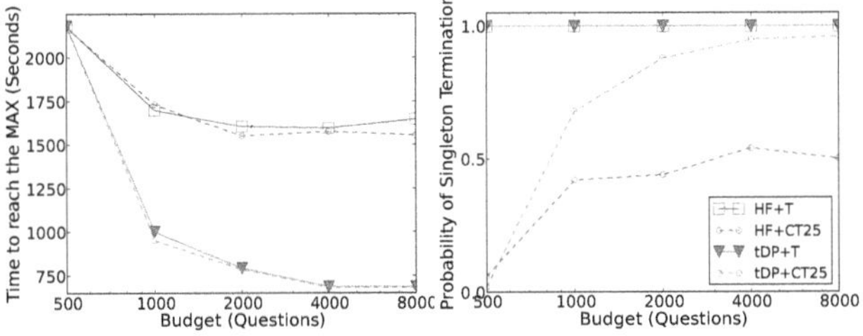

(a) Latency (b) *Singleton termination*

Figure 12: *Question selection* algorithms.

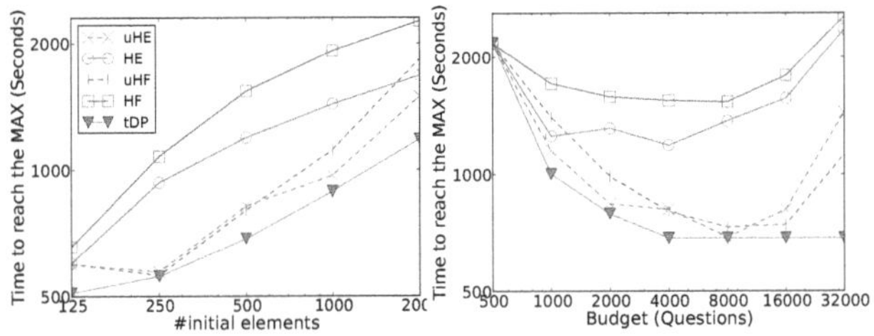

(a) $b = 4000$ questions (b) $c_0 = 500$ elements

Figure 13: Latency for a fixed b or c_0.

to a combination of a *budget allocation* with a *question selection* algorithm. To avoid clutter, we plot only four curves here. Nevertheless, our findings (discussed next) also hold for the other combinations of *budget allocation* and *question selection* algorithms. As Figure 12(a) shows, there is a slight improvement in most cases when CT25 is used instead of the tournament algorithm, under both HF and tDP. However, this slight improvement comes with a significant cost as the *singleton termination* plot of Figure 12(b) points out.

In particular, in Figure 12(b) we plot the percentage of runs with a *singleton termination* for each approach (y-axis). The cost of the slight improvement in latency for the approaches under CT25, is the high probability of being left with more than a single element after all questions are asked, especially when the budget is low. In other words, in some runs the approaches under CT25 finish faster compared to the approaches under Tournament-formation, but in other runs the CT25 approaches are left with more than one element. Moreover, our tDP allocation under CT25 gives a much higher probability of *singleton termination* compared to HF + CT25, when the budget is more than 500 questions. On the other hand, the Tournament-formation is more likely to achieve a *singleton termination*: here, *singleton termination* is achieved in every run, for all budget values, under both HF and tDP.

In the experiments that follow we always combine tDP with the Tournament-formation algorithm and all the other *budget allocation* algorithms with CT25. Our goal is to explore whether our approach gives significant gains in latency compared to the alternatives, even if the alternatives have a low probability of *singleton termination*.

6.4 Different sizes for the collection of initial elements

The next direction we explore is to keep the budget, b, of 4000 questions fixed and use different collections of initial elements. Specifically, we use collections of 125, 250, 500, 1000, and 2000 elements. As in Figure 12(a), latency is measured using the estimated $\mathcal{L}(q)$ instead of actually publishing the questions on MTurk and waiting for the answers.

As Figure 13(a) points out, tDP gives a significant improvement over alternatives for certain sizes of the initial-element collection (x-axis). For example, for $c_0 = 2000$ elements, the increase in latency when using the second-best uHE instead of tDP is over 25%, while the increase in latency when using HF is over 90%. Note that for some number of initial elements, the uniform allocation algorithms (uHF and uHE) reach very close to the latency achieved by tDP. The reason is that, coincidentally, the allocations generated by uHF and uHE in those cases are "similar" to the one tDP generates. For instance, for 250 elements, uHF generates allocation $(1000, 1000, 1000, 1000)$, while tDP generates allocation $(884, 465)$. Since, in this example, uHF always reaches to the MAX element without having to initiate the third round, the latency for the tDP and uHF is almost the same. Overall, tDP always achieves the best latency and in cases uHF and uHE are "unlucky", the improvement over the second-best is quite substantial.

6.5 Different sizes for the available budget

In Figure 13(b), we compare tDP with the other alternatives when we vary the available budget (x-axis) for finding the MAX in a collection of 500 initial elements. tDP constantly improves the overall latency as the budget is increased from 500 to 4000 questions, however, the improvement stops after 4000 questions and the latency remains the same for the increased budget. Surprisingly, this is not the case with all the other allocation algorithms: after a point, latency increases steeply and becomes two to four times the latency of tDP for 32000 questions.

The trend in Figure 13(b) can be explained by the fact that tDP, taking into account the $\mathcal{L}(q)$, chooses after a point (4000 questions in this case) not to spend any more of the available budget. In fact, tDP produces the same allocation, $(2250, 1225)$, for any budget available, after 4000 questions, i.e., tDP only uses 3475 questions from that point on. On the contrary, the other *budget allocation* algorithms, which do not take into account the latency function, always use the whole budget. As Figure 13(b) points out, using more questions can vastly increase latency instead of reducing it.

To illustrate this point further, consider the following example: finding the MAX in a collection of 500 elements using a budget of $b = \binom{500}{2} = 124750$ question. Forming the complete tournament $G_T(500, 1)$ in one round is feasible given the budget, however, workers may end up answering questions that are largely redundant and waste a lot of time, instead of focusing on a few remaining comparisons that reveal the MAX element. On the other hand, a strategy where a smaller number of questions is split into multiple rounds can be much more time-effective given the number of workers available and other parameters captured by the latency function $\mathcal{L}(q)$. Hence, our tDP approach doesn't just provide a near-optimal allocation of the available budget, but it also finds if the available budget should be limited in order to improve the overall latency, taking into account the latency function $\mathcal{L}(q)$. We study further how tDP limits the budget used in the next section, where we run experiments using different latency functions $\mathcal{L}(q)$.

6.6 Experiments using other Latency Functions

In platforms like MTurk, workers find the tasks they are interested in through a browse/search interface. Once the number of questions in the batch becomes greater than the

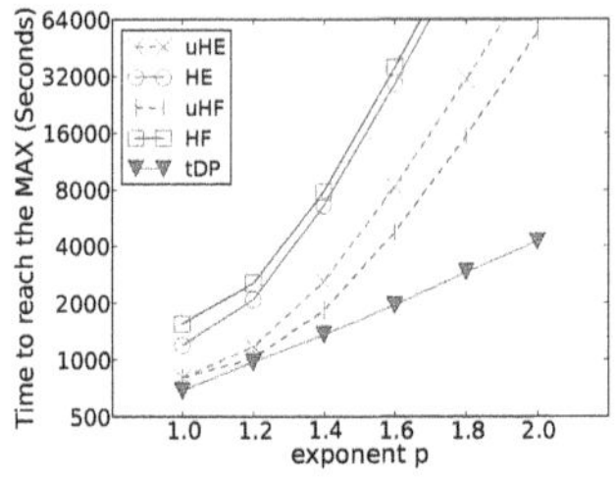

(a) Latency

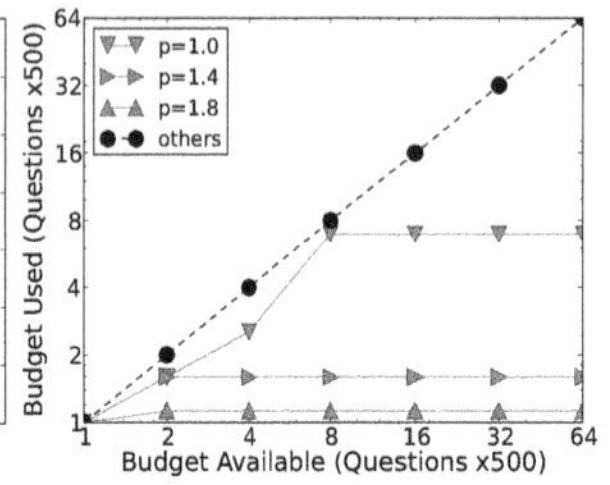

(b) Budget used

Figure 14: Comparison over different $\mathcal{L}(q)$ functions.

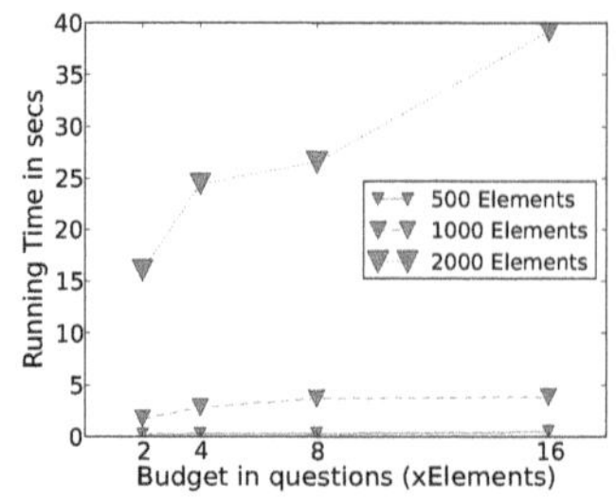

Figure 15: Running time of tDP.

number of interested workers, the latency increases rapidly; although, as it appears in Figure 11(a), we did not reach that point with our car-images task. In addition, the entries in the browse/search display usually appear in chronological order, i.e., the latest the batch was posted, the higher it appears in the entry list. In such cases, as a large batch starts going down in the entry list over time, the number of interested workers drops; since workers often switch from one task to another even if there are still unanswered questions in the batch. Such factors affect the latency function $\mathcal{L}(q)$, which may become super-linear after a given batch size, q.

In this section, we study how the different approaches perform on a variety of latency functions. In particular, we try a more general $\mathcal{L}(q)$ (with respect to the linear one we used so far) of the form: $\mathcal{L}(q) = \delta + \alpha * q^p$ seconds. We keep a δ of 239 and an α of 0.06, and we vary p.

Figure 14(a) depicts the latency until reaching the MAX for each approach, for the different values of p (x-axis). The budget is 4000 questions for 500 initial elements. As p increases, the gap between tDP and the other approaches increases exponentially. For $p = 2.0$, tDP gives a 12x improvement over the second-best uHF. This improvement is a consequence of tDP limiting the budget used based on the $\mathcal{L}(q)$, as we discussed in Figure 13(b).

To illustrate further the budget-limiting behavior of tDP, we plot the budget used by tDP for different values of p, in Figure 14(b). The x-axis shows the budget available, while the y-axis shows how many of these questions are actually used by tDP. For example, if the available budget is 3000 questions and tDP generates allocation (1000, 1000), then it uses 2000 questions out of the 3000 questions. Each curve refers to applying tDP under a specific p value, except for the "others" curve that refers to all the other allocation algorithms; the value of p does not matter for the other algorithms, since they do not take into account $\mathcal{L}(q)$.

The larger the value of p, the sooner tDP limits the budget used: for $p = 1.0$ the budget is limited at around 3500 questions, for $p = 1.4$ the budget is limited at around 800 questions, and for $p = 1.8$ the budget is limited at around 600 questions. Note also that even before the point where the curves become flat, tDP may decide to use less questions than the available budget. On the other hand, the other allocation algorithms use all of the available budget, until the available budget becomes more than the budget required to form a complete tournament with all of the 500 initial elements in one round, i.e., $\binom{500}{2} = 124750$ questions (not shown in Figure 14(b)). Effectively limiting the budget used, based on $\mathcal{L}(q)$, is the reason why tDP attains the substantial improvement over other alternatives, in Figure 14(a).

6.7 Cost of computing a tDP allocation

Algorithm tDP generates allocations that substantially improve the overall latency compared to heuristics. Nevertheless, there is a cost for computing a tDP allocation. In Figure 15, we measure the running time of tDP on a 1.8 GHz Intel Core i5 processor with 4 GB of RAM. Each curve refers to a different number of initial elements, the y-axis shows the running time in seconds, and the x-axis gives the budget of overall questions; as a multiple of the initial elements. For example, for $x = 8$ on the curve for $c_0 = 1000$ elements, the budget is $b = 8 * 1000 = 8000$ questions and the running time of tDP is around 4 seconds.

Surprisingly, as Figure 15 shows, the running time for each curve slightly increases as we increase the budget. Since the time complexity of tDP is $O(c_0^2 * b)$, one would expect the running time to double when the budget b is doubled (x-axis). However, our top-down implementation of tDP effectively prunes the set of states (out of the overall $c_0 * b$ states) that we have to visit, as we double b. On the other hand, when we double the number of initial elements c_0 (from one curve to another), the running time does increase by a factor of 4; as one would expect based on the $O(c_0^2 * b)$ time complexity. In that case, tDP needs to examine more states (compared to when we double the budget), to find the optimal sequence to the MAX.

It is worth pointing out here that the running time of tDP is not critical, if we consider the time it takes for humans to answer all these questions. For instance, as we saw in Figure 13(a), it takes more than 1000 seconds to find the MAX for $c_0 = 2000$ elements and a budget, b, of 4000 questions. For such an input of $c_0 = 2000$ elements and $b = 4000$ questions, the running time of tDP is around 15 seconds as Figure 15 shows, which is two orders of magnitude lower than the 1000 seconds to find the MAX. In addition, one should take into account that the car-images task is one of the easiest tasks we could use and the average time to answer a question is around 3 seconds. For more difficult tasks where the number of interested workers decreases, the time to answer each question increases, and $\mathcal{L}(q)$ scales up, the computational cost of tDP starts to become even more negligible. In addition, in many cases, the same budget allocation is used multiple times by crowdsourcing workflows in different runs for the same type of task, with the same budget and number of initial elements. For the corner-cases where the running time of tDP cannot be considered trivial, there are various approaches proposed for implementing parallel dynamic programming algorithms (e.g. [20]) that can achieve a significant speedup.

6.8 Summary of our findings

We conclude the experimental section by summarizing our main findings from the experiments we presented here and other experiments that we did not include in this paper:
(1) Algorithm tDP always achieves the lowest latency. In addition, when combined with the tournament formation

algorithm it always achieves *singleton termination*. Combining tDP with other *question selection* strategies may, in some cases, give a slight improvement in latency, however, it may also cause a significant decrease in the probability of *singleton termination*. Hence, our experimental results are consistent with our theoretical optimality guarantees for our approach in the worst and average case scenarios.

(2) By batching multiple questions in one round, we seek to increase parallelism at the cost of redundancy. The tDP algorithm takes into account $\mathcal{L}(q)$ to estimate this cost of redundancy, and produces allocations that are not wasteful and may consume less than the available budget. Even when $\mathcal{L}(q)$ is just a rough estimation to the actual latency, the gains from effectively allocating and/or restricting the budget can be quite substantial.

(3) The uniform allocation algorithms, uHF and uHE, achieve lower latency compared to HF and HE, for any *question selection* strategy they are combined with.

(4) The uniform *budget allocation* algorithms achieve a higher probability of *singleton termination* compared to HF and HE, for any *question selection* strategy. The only exception is when the budget, b, is near the lower limit, i.e., the number of initial elements, c_0: in this case, HF and HE are usually more likely to achieve *singleton termination*.

(5) The Tournament-formation algorithm achieves a higher probability of *singleton termination* under any *budget allocation* algorithm, compared to the other *question selection* strategies, in almost all of the cases we studied. In some cases, the increased *singleton termination* probability comes with a very small cost in latency.

(6) While non-trivial, the running time of tDP is orders of magnitude lower than the time spent on the crowdsourcing platform due to the human factor.

7. RELATED WORK

The main focus in crowdsourcing research the last years has been on the accuracy and cost dimensions. Nevertheless, part of the study in a number of papers (e.g., [19, 16, 27, 24, 15, 23, 9]) is related to the latency dimension, as well. In paper [19] the problem of finding k elements satisfying a human-decidable property in a larger collection of elements is studied. Latency is defined by the number of rounds (in each round a batch of questions is issued) and the overall objective is to find the skyline of solutions on the latency-cost axes. Paper [16] also considers the latency dimension: questions for finding the target node in a graph (e.g., classifying an object given a hierarchy of classes) are issued in batches and latency is measured by the number of rounds. The number of rounds is also the metric defining latency in crowd entity resolution papers [27, 24].

MAX and sorting algorithms have been studied in the field of parallel computation (e.g., papers [5, 11, 21]): given a number of processors minimize the number of steps (in each step all processors run in parallel) until finding the MAX or sorting all elements. In such settings, all processors are synchronized and take the exact same time to process a comparison. Therefore, the number of steps becomes a very accurate proxy for latency. On the other hand, in a crowdsourcing platform, humans are not "synchronized" and the number of workers can vary in each round. Hence, latency depends on how many questions we ask, in each round. A second important difference is the budget constraint, which is necessary in crowdsourcing settings because of factors like the workers' monetary compensation, but is missing in the parallel computation studies. In particular, in multiprocessor systems, the number of processors is fixed and each processor runs one comparison in each step, without any restriction on the total number of comparisons processed.

Sorting [15], top-k [7], and MAX [10, 23] have also been studied extensively in the crowdsourcing literature. Finding the MAX while taking into account the graph of possibly erroneous human answers is the subject of paper [10]. This work also proposes question selection algorithms that we have used in our experimental evaluation. Closer to the scope of our paper is paper [23], where hill-climb techniques are proposed for finding the MAX in successive rounds. Once more, the metric for latency is the number of rounds. Nevertheless, in real-world crowdsourcing platforms, latency is not always a constant-time function (as implicitly assumed when the metric is the number of rounds), but greatly varies depending on factors like the task, the worker requirements, and the compensation [8]. Hence, our approach does not assume a specific latency function but is applicable for any function while providing strong optimality guarantees.

Another problem related to the one we study here, is the leader election problem in distributed systems [1, 3, 18, 26]. The main difference with our setting, is the lack of a central processing unit: in our case, there is a central unit that keeps track of all the comparisons taking place. On the contrary, in leader election algorithms, each node only knows a subset of the nodes that are still candidates for becoming a leader, based on exchanged messages. Without having a central unit to keep track of all "nodes" (elements) being eliminated, leader election algorithms focus on minimizing the number of messages (or rounds) until the leader is elected and every node is aware of that leader.

8. CONCLUSION

We studied the problem of allocating a budget of questions into rounds in crowdsourcing platforms. We focused on the MAX operator and we derived a polynomial dynamic-programming algorithm that computes the optimal allocation in terms of latency when questions form tournaments in each round. We also compared our approach to any other combination of budget allocation and question selection algorithms, and through our theoretical results we proved optimality in the worst-case scenario and we gave optimality guarantees for the average case scenario under certain assumptions. Our experiments show that our approach is always better than any other alternative we tried, offering important gains in latency, even when we have access only to a rough estimate of a platform's latency behavior on a specific task. Especially, in case the crowdsourcing platform is governed by non-linear (convex/concave) latency functions, the improvement over alternatives can be vast.

In this paper, we focused on the widely studied MAX operator to quantify the gains on latency when the operator is well-understood. The same cost-latency tradeoff arises in other crowdsourcing problems, but the question selection strategy must be adapted to those problems in order to maximize performance gains. Nevertheless, we believe that our dynamic programming approach can be adapted to other scenarios. Furthermore, we believe that having a latency function available, even if coarse, will make it possible to make good budget allocations.

9. ACKNOWLEDGEMENTS

We would like to thank Peter Shor for helping us derive our main results in the average case analysis. We would also like to thank Akash Das Sarma for the fruitful discussions we shared. This research was supported by the National Science Foundation under grant no. 1009916.

10. REFERENCES

[1] Y. Afek and E. Gafni. Time and message bounds for election in synchronous and asynchronous complete networks. In *PODC*, 1985.
[2] M. Ajtai, V. Feldman, A. Hassidim, and J. Nelson. Sorting and selection with imprecise comparisons. In *Automata, Languages and Programming (ICALP)*, 2009.
[3] B. Awerbuch. Optimal distributed algorithms for minimum weight spanning tree, counting, leader election, and related problems. In *STOC*, 1987.
[4] C. Berge. *Graphs and Hypergraphs*. North-Holland, Amsterdam, 1973.
[5] B. Bollobás and A. Thomason. Parallel sorting. *Discrete Applied Mathematics*, 1983.
[6] G. Brightwell and P. Winkler. Counting linear extensions is #p-complete. In *STOC*, 1991.
[7] S. B. Davidson, S. Khanna, T. Milo, and S. Roy. Using the crowd for top-k and group-by queries. In *ICDT*, 2013.
[8] S. Faradani, B. Hartmann, and P. G. Ipeirotis. What's the right price? pricing tasks for finishing on time. In *HCOMP*, 2011.
[9] R. Gomes, P. Welinder, A. Krause, and P. Perona. Crowdclustering. In *NIPS*, 2011.
[10] S. Guo, A. Parameswaran, and H. Garcia-Molina. So who won?: Dynamic max discovery with the crowd. In *SIGMOD*, 2012.
[11] R. Häggkvist and P. Hell. Sorting and merging in rounds. *SIAM J. Algebraic Discrete Methods*, 1982.
[12] P. G. Ipeirotis, F. Provost, and J. Wang. Quality management on amazon mechanical turk. In *HCOMP*, 2010.
[13] D. R. Karger, S. Oh, and D. Shah. Iterative learning for reliable crowdsourcing systems. In *NIPS*, 2011.
[14] X. Liu, M. Lu, B. C. Ooi, Y. Shen, S. Wu, and M. Zhang. Cdas: A crowdsourcing data analytics system. *PVLDB*, 2012.
[15] A. Marcus, E. Wu, D. Karger, S. Madden, and R. Miller. Human-powered sorts and joins. *PVLDB*, 2011.
[16] A. Parameswaran, A. D. Sarma, H. Garcia-Molina, N. Polyzotis, and J. Widom. Human-assisted graph search: It's okay to ask questions. *PVLDB*, 2011.
[17] A. G. Parameswaran, H. Garcia-Molina, H. Park, N. Polyzotis, A. Ramesh, and J. Widom. Crowdscreen: algorithms for filtering data with humans. In *SIGMOD*, 2012.
[18] D. Peleg. Time-optimal leader election in general networks. *J. Parallel and Distributed Computing*, 1990.
[19] A. D. Sarma, A. G. Parameswaran, H. Garcia-Molina, and A. Y. Halevy. Crowd-powered find algorithms. In *ICDE*, 2014.
[20] A. Stivala, P. J. Stuckey, M. G. de la Banda, M. Hermenegildo, and A. Wirth. Lock-free parallel dynamic programming. *J. Parallel and Distributed Computing*, 2010.
[21] L. G. Valiant. Parallelism in comparison problems. *SIAM J. Comput.*, 1975.
[22] P. Venetis and H. Garcia-Molina. Quality control for comparison microtasks. In *Int. Workshop on Crowdsourcing and Data Mining (CrowdKDD)*, 2012.
[23] P. Venetis, H. Garcia-Molina, K. Huang, and N. Polyzotis. Max algorithms in crowdsourcing environments. In *WWW*, 2012.
[24] V. Verroios and H. Garcia-Molina. Entity resolution with crowd errors. In *ICDE*, 2015.
[25] V. Verroios, P. Lofgren, and H. Garcia-Molina. tdp: An optimal-latency budget allocation strategy for crowdsourced maximum operations. *Technical report, Stanford University, available at* `http://ilpubs.stanford.edu:8090/1129/`.
[26] J. Villadangos, A. Cordoba, F. Farina, and M. Prieto. Efficient leader election in complete networks. In *Parallel, Distributed and Network-Based Processing (PDP)*, 2005.
[27] J. Wang, G. Li, T. Kraska, M. J. Franklin, and J. Feng. Leveraging transitive relations for crowdsourced joins. In *SIGMOD*, 2013.

APPENDIX

A. AVERAGE CASE ANALYSIS

In the worst case analysis of Section 4.1, we examined the scenario where after asking a set of questions, the answers we get back leave us with the maximum number of candidate elements remaining. In this section, we examine what happens in the average case, i.e., we focus on the expected number of candidates that will remain, when we ask a set of questions. In addition, to simplify the analysis, we focus on a single round (as opposed to the worst-case analysis), i.e., we study when the expected number of candidates that will remain after a single round, is minimized. The analysis for multiple rounds is beyond the scope of this paper, however, in the end of this section we have a brief discussion related to this topic.

We start with the definition for the expected number of remaining candidates:

DEFINITION 8. ***Expected size of the Remaining Candidates set*** $(\mathbb{E}[\mathcal{R}])$ ***of an undirected graph*** G **:** *The expected size of the RC set, over all possible DAGs that can be formed by giving directions to the edges of G. (Note that the probability of each DAG may be different.)*

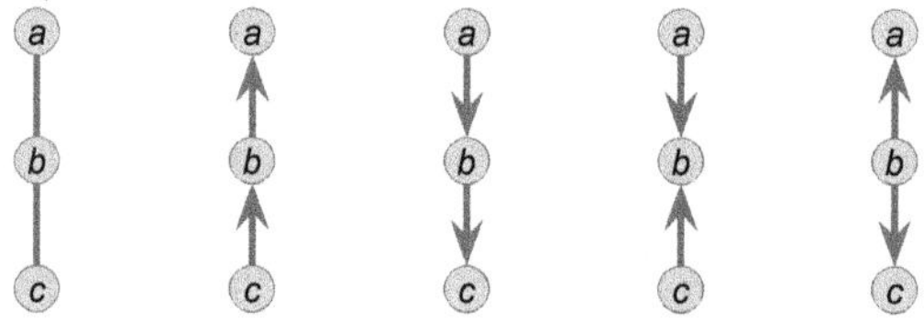

(a) undirected (b) DAG_1 (c) DAG_2 (d) DAG_3 (e) DAG_4

Figure 16: Example for the expected size of the *RC* set of an undirected graph.

For example, consider the undirected graph in Figure 16(a), involving three elements and two edges-questions. There are four possible DAGs that can be formed, depicted in Figures 16(b) to 16(e). Each of these four DAGs refer to a possible set of answers that we may get back when we ask questions $\{(a, b), (b, c)\}$. Consequently, each of the four DAGs has a probability of being formed: the probability of getting back the answers forming this DAG. Let us assume that each of the $3! = 6$ possible permutations of elements a, b, c have the same likelihood of being the true underlying permutation. Thus, the probability of DAG_1 in Figure 16(b) is $\frac{1}{6}$, since only permutation $\{a > b > c\}$ is consistent with answers $\{(a > b), (b > c)\}$. Likewise, the probability of DAG_2 is also $\frac{1}{6}$, since only permutation $\{c > b > a\}$ is consistent with answers $\{(a < b), (b < c)\}$, while the probability of DAG_3 and DAG_4 is $\frac{2}{6}$ (permutations $\{b > a > c\}$ and $\{b > c > a\}$ are consistent with the answers in DAG_3 and permutations $\{a > c > b\}$ and $\{c > a > b\}$ are consistent with the answers in DAG_4). Moreover, the RC set of DAG_1 is $\{a\}$, the RC set of DAG_2 is $\{c\}$, the RC set of DAG_3 is $\{b\}$, and the RC set of DAG_4 is $\{a, c\}$.

Let us denote by $\mathcal{R}$ the random variable for the size of the RC set. The expected size of the RC set, $\mathbb{E}[\mathcal{R}]$, is $\frac{1}{6} * 1 + \frac{1}{6} * 1 + \frac{2}{6} * 1 + \frac{2}{6} * 2 \approx 1.33$. (Note that the size of the $maxRC$ set is 2, based on the RC set of DAG_4.)

In the example of Figures 16(a) to 16(e), we assumed that all 6 possible permutations have the same likelihood. In the results that follow, we assume that for the elements that remain after a number of rounds, all permutations of those elements have the same likelihood of being the true unknown permutation; consistent with the true unknown permutation of the initial elements. We call this state a *uniform history*:

DEFINITION 9. ***uniform history*** : *When after a number of rounds, all permutations of the elements that have not lost any comparison yet have the same likelihood, we say that the* history *is* uniform.

To illustrate, consider a toy example of 3 initial elements, a, b, and c. Before the first round all 6 permutations have the same likelihood; no questions are asked yet and we don't assume any prior information. Hence, we have a *uniform history* before the first round. In the first round we ask question (a, b) and we get the answer $a > b$. This answer lets us know that the true underlying permutation is $\{c > a > b\}$, $\{a > c > b\}$, or $\{a > b > c\}$. Thus, permutation $\{c > a\}$ happens only in case of $\{c > a > b\}$ being the true permutation, while permutation $\{a > c\}$ happens in the other two cases. In other words, after round 1 the permutations of the two remaining candidates, a and c, do not have the same likelihood and, hence, the *history* is *non-uniform*.

Note that when questions form tournament graphs in each round and when all the tournament graphs in one round have the same size, a *uniform history* is preserved after any number of rounds. For example, in Figure 9(b), all tournaments in the first round have a size of 2 elements, and all tournaments in the second round have a size of 3 elements. Therefore, there is a *uniform history* after round 1 and after round 2. In the end of the section, where we comment on the multiple-round analysis, we also discuss some of the *non-uniform history* effects.

Next we prove our main theoretical result for the average case analysis: $\mathbb{E}[\mathcal{R}]$ is minimized when G is a tournament graph, under the *uniform history* assumption, as we discuss in Theorem 5.

LEMMA 4. *When the* history *is* uniform, $\mathbb{E}[\mathcal{R}] = \sum_{v \in V} \frac{1}{d_v+1}$, *where $G = (V, E)$ is the graph that the questions form and d_v is the degree of element v in this graph.*

PROOF. Let us denote by S_v the indicator random variable for element v winning all of the d_v comparisons it is involved in. In particular, variable S_v is 1 when v wins all of the comparisons and 0 when v loses one or more comparisons. The expected size of the RC set, $\mathbb{E}[\mathcal{R}]$, is given by the expectation over all S_v, i.e., $\mathbb{E}[\sum_{v \in V} S_v]$. Because of the linearity of expectation, $\mathbb{E}[\sum_{v \in V} S_v] = \sum_{v \in V} \mathbb{E}[S_v]$ (even if S_v variables are not independent). Since we assume a *uniform history*, the ratio of permutations where an element, v, is greater than all of the elements being compared with, to all the possible permutations, is $\frac{1}{d_v+1}$. For instance, if a candidate a is being compared to two other candidates b and c, this ratio will be $\frac{1}{3}$, i.e., in one third of all the possible permutations a is greater than both b and c; given the *uniform history*. Therefore, $\mathbb{E}[S_v] = \frac{1}{d_v+1}$ and $\mathbb{E}[\mathcal{R}] = \sum_{v \in V} \frac{1}{d_v+1}$. □

LEMMA 5. *Given a* uniform history, *$\mathbb{E}[\mathcal{R}]$ is minimized when $\forall v \in V$, $d_v \in [\lfloor\frac{2|E|}{|V|}\rfloor, \lceil\frac{2|E|}{|V|}\rceil]$, where $G = (V, E)$ is the graph that the questions form.*

PROOF. In other words, the statement of Lemma 5 is that $\mathbb{E}[\mathcal{R}]$ is minimized when G is a regular graph, i.e., when all elements have the same degree, i.e., $\frac{2|E|}{|V|}$. In case $\frac{2|E|}{|V|}$ is not an integer, not all of the elements can have the same degree. In that case, $\mathbb{E}[\mathcal{R}]$ is minimized when the difference of the maximum degree with the minimum degree in G, is not more than one, i.e., $\lceil\frac{2|E|}{|V|}\rceil - \lfloor\frac{2|E|}{|V|}\rfloor$.

To prove this statement we consider the case where questions form a graph $G = (V, E)$ with at least two elements, a and b, with $d_a < \lfloor\frac{2|E|}{|V|}\rfloor$ and $d_b > \lfloor\frac{2|E|}{|V|}\rfloor$, i.e., the difference between the degrees of a and b is at least two. Now, let us change an edge, between b and a third element c, into a question between a and c. After this change, d_a is increased by 1, d_b is decreased by 1, while d_c remains the same. Hence, $\mathbb{E}[\mathcal{R}]$, which is equal to $\sum_{v \in V} \frac{1}{d_v+1}$ based on Lemma 4, decreases if $\frac{1}{d_a+2} + \frac{1}{d_b} < \frac{1}{d_a+1} + \frac{1}{d_b+1}$. Indeed,

$$\frac{1}{d_a+2} + \frac{1}{d_b} < \frac{1}{d_a+1} + \frac{1}{d_b+1} \Rightarrow$$
$$\frac{d_a+2+d_b}{(d_a+2)d_b} < \frac{d_a+1+d_b+1}{(d_a+1)(d_b+1)} \Rightarrow$$
$$d_a d_b + d_a + d_b + 1 < d_a d_b + 2d_b \Rightarrow$$
$$d_a + 1 < d_b$$

The last relation is true since we assume $d_a < \lfloor\frac{2|E|}{|V|}\rfloor < d_b$.

What we just proved is that the more equal the element degrees in G are, the lower $\mathbb{E}[\mathcal{R}]$ is. Therefore, $\mathbb{E}[\mathcal{R}]$ is minimized when $\forall v \in V$, $d_v \in [\lfloor\frac{2|E|}{|V|}\rfloor, \lceil\frac{2|E|}{|V|}\rceil]$. □

THEOREM 5. *When the* history *is* uniform, *the tournament graph minimizes $\mathbb{E}[\mathcal{R}]$.*

PROOF. Note that in any tournament graph $G = (V, E)$, the degree of each element is either $\lfloor\frac{2|E|}{|V|}\rfloor$ or $\lceil\frac{2|E|}{|V|}\rceil$ when $\frac{2|E|}{|V|}$ is not an integer, otherwise, the degree is the same for all elements, i.e., equal to $\frac{2|E|}{|V|}$. Therefore, based on Lemma 5, $\mathbb{E}[\mathcal{R}]$ is minimized.

□

In our average-case analysis, we focused on the expected number of remaining candidates in a single round. Over multiple rounds, the analysis becomes much more complex. Let us assume that in each round tournaments of the same size are formed; just like in the example of Figure. 9(b).

Taking into account that *a)* the *uniform history* is preserved after each round (as we noted earlier), *b)* tournament graphs minimize $\mathbb{E}[\mathcal{R}]$ under a *uniform history* (as Theorem 5 states), and *c)* tDP finds the optimal allocation (under tournament graph formation), one may think that tDP under tournament-formation is also optimal over multiple rounds in the average-case scenario. Nevertheless, this is not necessarily the case. The reason is that tDP under tournament-formation is "greedy" in a sense: it tries to eliminate as many candidates as possible in every round (based on Theorem 5). A different approach would be to spend the "first" rounds trying to build a *non-uniform history* that would be exploited in subsequent rounds to "massively" eliminate candidates and reach to the MAX element. In other words, such an "exploration-exploitation" approach would first try to find "strong" and "weak" candidates in the "first" rounds, and then try to reach to the MAX element, in a "few" rounds, by spending most of the questions on "strong" candidates and the rest on "weak" candidates. In the experimental evaluation, we compare such an approach with our tournament-graph approach.

B. RANKING THE ELEMENTS IN EACH ROUND

As we discussed in Section 5.2, the remaining candidates after each round are ranked using a scoring function; the computed scores can be then used by the *question selection* algorithm that picks the questions for the next round. The most straightforward option is to rank each element based on the likelihood of the element for being the MAX, however, computing the MAX likelihood is a #P-hard problem. In this section, we give the #P-hardness proof and we describe the PageRank-like function we used in our experiments, to rank each element.

B.1 Computing the likelihood of being the MAX

The #P-hardness proof for computing the likelihood of an element being the MAX is based on a reduction from the problem of counting the number of linear extensions of a partially ordered set (LE-Count) [6]. Note that #P-hard problems are at least as difficult as NP-hard problems.

Suppose we have n elements, and after a number of rounds we want the probability that element i is the MAX. We represent all previous answers with a DAG $G = (V, E)$, where an edge $(j, k) \in E$ means element k won over j (i.e., we use the same DAG representation we used in our theoretical results).

DEFINITION 10. ***Respecting a set of answers*:** *Given a permutation σ and a DAG $G = (V, E)$, we say σ* respects *E if $\forall (j, k) \in E, \sigma(j) < \sigma(k)$.*

Then we can formalize the problem of computing the probability of an element being the MAX as

$$\text{P-Max}(i, n, E \subset [n] \times [n]) = \Pr[\sigma(i) = n | \sigma \text{ respects } E]$$

where $[n] = \{1, \dots, n\}$ and random variable σ is a permutation chosen from a uniform random prior. Equivalently,

$$\text{P-Max}(i, n, E \subset [n]\times[n]) = \frac{\#\{\sigma : \sigma(i) = n \text{ and } \sigma \text{ respects } E\}}{\#\{\sigma : \sigma \text{ respects } E\}}.$$

Also define

$$\text{LE-Count}(n, E) = \#\{\text{permutations } \sigma : \sigma \text{ respects } E\}$$

We now show that if we could compute P-Max in polynomial time, then we could also compute LE-Count in polynomial time. Since LE-Count is #P-complete [6], this shows that P-Max is #P-hard.

THEOREM 6. *Computing* P-Max *is #P-hard.*

PROOF. Let $(n, E \subset [n]\times[n])$ be a given input to LE-Count, so $G = ([n], E)$ is a DAG. Let τ be any fixed permutation consistent with E. This can be found in polynomial time using the topological sort algorithm. If we could find the probability of τ conditioned on E, we could find the number of linear extensions σ of E, since

$$\#\{\sigma : \sigma \text{ respects } E\} = \frac{1}{\Pr[\sigma = \tau | \sigma \text{ respects } E]}. \quad (11)$$

When we write probabilities in this section, the only random variable is the permutation σ and it has a uniform prior. Now we can re-write this probability as a product of conditional probabilities. To clarify notation, we first write it for the case $n = 3$:

$$\begin{aligned}&\Pr[\sigma{=}\tau|\sigma \text{ respects } E]{=}\\&\Pr[\sigma(\tau^{-1}(1)){=}1|\sigma(\tau^{-1}(2)){=}2,\sigma(\tau^{-1}(3)){=}3,\sigma \text{ respects } E]\\&\cdot\Pr[\sigma(\tau^{-1}(2)){=}2|\sigma(\tau^{-1}(3)){=}3,\sigma \text{ respects } E]\\&\cdot\Pr[\sigma(\tau^{-1}(3)){=}3|\sigma \text{ respects } E].\end{aligned}$$

This can be seen by simply applying the definition $\Pr[A|B] = \frac{\Pr[A,B]}{\Pr[B]}$ to each probability and canceling common terms.

For general n,

$$\begin{aligned}&\Pr[\sigma{=}\tau|\sigma \text{ respects } E]{=}\\&\prod_{j=1}^{n}\Pr[\sigma(\tau^{-1}(j)){=}j|\forall k{>}j\ (\sigma(\tau^{-1}(k)){=}k),\sigma \text{ respects } E]\end{aligned} \quad (12)$$

Finally, we note that each probability on the right-hand side of (12) is actually an instance of P-Max on a different graph. Given j,

$$\begin{aligned}\Pr[\sigma(\tau^{-1}(j)){=}j|\forall k{>}j\ (\sigma(\tau^{-1}(k)){=}k),\sigma \text{ respects } E]{=}\\\Pr[\sigma'(\tau^{-1}(j)){=}j|\sigma' \text{ respects } E']\end{aligned}$$

where σ' is a random permutation on $n' = j$ elements and E' is the set of answers in E only involving elements l such that $\tau(l) \leq j$. This equality follows from the fact that there is a one-to-one correspondence between permutations σ on n elements respecting E and permutations σ' on n' elements respecting E'. Thus, given an oracle for P-Max, we can compute each of the n terms on the right side of (12). Then applying equation (11), we have computed the given instance of LE-Count. Since LE-Count is #P-complete, we conclude that P-Max is #P-hard.

□

B.2 Scoring Algorithm

From a random-walks perspective, the element scores that our algorithm computes, express the following probability: consider a walker that chooses a starting point uniformly at random and at each element choses one of the outgoing edges uniformly at random. When she reaches an element with no outgoing edges, she is trapped there. The score of each element is the probability that the walker will be trapped at that specific element.

Algorithm 2 Scoring Function

Input: C: Collection of initial elements
Input: G: Directed graph of answers in previous rounds (0 to $j-1$)
Output: $\mathcal{C}_j$: Scores of elements that have not lost any comparisons
1: $\forall e \in C$: $e[energy] = \frac{1}{|C|}$
2: **while** there are elements with non-zero *energy* and at least one outgoing edge in G **do**
3: e = element with the least number of won comparisons (implicitly or explicitly) that has a non-zero *energy*.
4: O = endpoints of the outgoing edges of e.
5: $\forall e' \in O$: $e'[energy] = e'[energy] + \frac{e[energy]}{|O|}$
6: **if** $|O| > 0$ **then**
7: $e[energy] = 0$
8: **end if**
9: **end while**
10: $\mathcal{C}_j$ = set of elements with non-zero *energy*, along with their *energies*.

To compute the random-walk probabilities, our scoring algorithm transfers the *energy* of the elements that lost at least one comparison in previous rounds, to those that have not lost any comparisons yet. The full description is given by Algorithm 2. Initially, all elements have the same *energy*, $\frac{1}{c_0}$ (line 1). We start from the elements that have not won any comparisons in previous rounds (line 3) and we "pass" their *energy* to the elements that have won a comparison over them (if any). For instance, if an element a has not won any comparison but instead has lost to two elements b and c, a will transfer half of its *energy* to b and half of its *energy* to c. The *energy* of b and c then becomes $\frac{1}{c_0} + \frac{1}{2c_0}$, i.e., we add the received *energy* to the pre-existing *energy* of an element (line 5). (The energy of a becomes 0 after the transfer.) In the next steps (line 2), we transfer the *energy* of the elements that won exactly one comparison, to the elements that won a comparison over them (if any) and so on. At the end of the loop (lines 2 to 9), all the initial *energy* (which sums up to one) will accumulate to the elements that have not lost any comparisons.

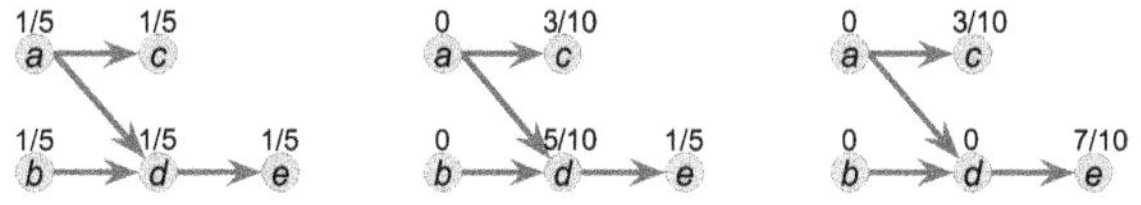

(a) Step 0 (b) Step 3 (c) Step 4

Figure 17: Example run of the Scoring Function.

An example run of the algorithm is given in Figures 17(a) to 17(c). Initially, all elements have an *energy* of $\frac{1}{5}$, as depicted in Figure 17(a). In steps 1 and 2, a and b, which have not won any comparisons, transfer their energy through their outgoing edges. The energy of the elements after the first step becomes, 0 for a and b, $\frac{1}{5}+\frac{1}{10}=\frac{3}{10}$ for c, $\frac{1}{5}+\frac{1}{5}+\frac{1}{10}=\frac{5}{10}$ for d, and remains the same ($\frac{1}{5}$) for e (Figure 17(b)). In step 3, only element c has won exactly one comparison, but it does not have any outgoing edges, so all energies remain unchanged. (Note that element e has won over three elements; implicitly or explicitly.) In step 4, element d, which has won two comparisons, transfers its energy to e, which now becomes $\frac{1}{5}+\frac{5}{10}=\frac{7}{10}$ (Figure 17(c)). The loop ends in step 4 since there are no more elements with outgoing edges that have a non-zero energy.

Thrifty: Offering Parallel Database as a Service using the Shared-Process Approach

Petrie Wong[†‡*] Zhian He[‡] Ziqiang Feng[‡] Wenjian Xu[‡] Eric Lo[‡]
[†]Department of Computer Science, The University of Hong Kong
[‡]Department of Computing, The Hong Kong Polytechnic University
kfwong2@cs.hku.hk {cszahe, cszqfeng, cswxu, ericlo}@comp.polyu.edu.hk

ABSTRACT

Recently, Amazon has announced Redshift, a Parallel-Database-as-a-Service (PDaaS). Redshift adopts the "virtual cluster" approach to implement multi-tenancy, which has the merit of *hard isolation* among tenants (i.e., tenants do not interfere even when sharing resources). However, that benefit comes with *poor resource utilization* due to the significant redundancy incurred in the resources.

In this demonstration, we present *Thrifty*, a Parallel-Database-as-a-Service operated using the "shared-process" approach. Compared with Redshift, each tenant in Thrifty does not occupy an exclusive amount of resource but share the database processes together, leading to *better resource utilization.* To avoid contention among tenants, Thrifty uses a proper cluster design, a tenant placement scheme, and a query routing mechanism to achieve *soft isolation.*

In the demonstration, an attendee will be invited to register with Thrifty as a tenant to rent a parallel database instance. Then the attendee will be allowed to view the dashboard of a Thrifty's administrator. Next, the attendee will be invited to control (e.g., increase) the workload of the tenant so as to see how Thrifty carries out online re-consolidation and elastic scaling.

1. INTRODUCTION

In this demonstration, we present *Thrifty* [11], a prototype Parallel-Database-as-a-Service (PDaaS) operated using the shared-process approach. The shared-process approach advocates the sharing of database installation and process among tenants [4]. Thrifty adopts the shared-process approach and utilizes the fact that real multi-tenancy environments have active tenant ratios as low as 10% [8], so that it can consolidate tenants that are active in different periods on to the set of machine nodes running a single parallel database process. Thrifty aims to deal with a general and realistic setting of providing a high availability PDaaS to thousands of tenants. Each tenant requests a multi-node parallel database that serves multiple users. Queries might be submitted by a report generating application in a batch, or submitted by a user sequentially in an interactive analysis session. The query sets may be known or unknown beforehand. For report generating applications, the query templates are known and could be found in the applications' stored procedures. For interactive analysis, however, a data analyst may craft and submit an arbitrary/ad-hoc query at any time. Thrifty is able to deal with that general setting using a simple methodology called *Tenant-Driven Design* (TDD), which consists of three parts: (a) [Cluster Design] arrange the machine nodes in the cluster into *groups* and create a parallel database for each group of nodes, (b) [Tenant Placement] assign each tenant to several parallel databases (for replication), and (c) [Query Routing] route a tenant's query to a parallel database containing that tenant's data at run-time.

Our preliminary results [11] show that in a setting of 5000 PDaaS tenants, where each tenant requests 2 to 32 nodes parallel database to query against 200GB to 3.2TB of data, Thrifty can serve all the tenants with a 99.9% performance SLA guarantee and a high availability replication factor of 3, using only 18.7% of the nodes requested by the tenants. The full technical details of Thrifty can be found in [11].

*This work was done while affiliated with ‡; This work is partly supported by the Research Grants Council of Hong Kong (GRF PolyU 520413 and 521012) and a research gift from Microsoft Hong Kong.

SIGMOD'15, May 31–June 4, 2015, Melbourne, Victoria, Australia.

http://dx.doi.org/10.1145/2723372.2735352.

2. THRIFTY OVERVIEW

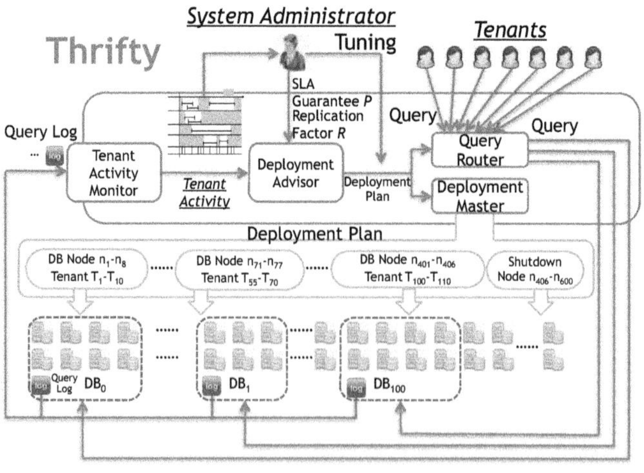

Figure 1: The architecture of the Thrifty system.

Thrifty adopts a pricing model that charges a tenant based on the number of nodes (the degree of parallelism) requested and its active usage. It begins with a set of independent parallel database tenants running analytical workloads, where each tenant runs a parallel database on a disjoint set of machine nodes. Figure 1 shows the architecture of Thrifty. The components of Thrifty are:

(a) *Tenant Activity Monitor*: The Tenant Activity Monitor automatically collects the query logs of the deployed parallel databases, derives the tenant activities, and summarizes the query characteristics of individual tenants. For example, it continuously monitors the active tenant ratio of all tenants in the past 30 days. This information is passed to the *Deployment Advisor* for further processing, and is available to the system administrator for advanced system tuning.

(b) *Deployment Advisor*: The Deployment Advisor takes as inputs the tenant activity statistics, the individual tenant information (e.g., number of nodes requested), a replication factor R (specified by a system administrator for high availability), and a performance SLA guarantee P (also specified by the system administrator which ensures that, after consolidation, the tenants can still meet their SLA for a P%, e.g., 99.9%, of time). It returns as output a *deployment plan*. The deployment plan consists of two parts: *cluster design* and *tenant placement*. The cluster design details how the machine nodes in the cluster are arranged into groups. Each group of nodes then runs a single parallel database instance. The tenant placement specifies which created parallel database instances a tenant should be deployed on; and a tenant is deployed on R parallel database instances. At runtime, the Deployment Advisor may fine-tune the cluster-design according to the live-updated tenant activities supplied by the Tenant Activity Monitor. Currently, Thrifty assumes all nodes in the cluster are identical in configurations (e.g., CPU, RAM).

(c) *Deployment Master*: The Deployment Master follows the deployment plan devised by the Deployment Advisor to start the parallel database instances and deploy the tenants onto them. It also switches off/hibernates nodes that are not listed in the deployment plan. The deployment is supposed to be static for days. A (re)-consolidation process is expected to be executed periodically, because it is expected that there are new tenants register with and existing tenants de-register with the service.

(d) *Query Router*: The Query Router accepts queries from tenants and routes the queries to the proper parallel database instance according to the tenant placement.

The crux of Thrifty is to devise a good deployment plan to serve thousands of tenants using few machine nodes. Thrifty targets on tenants with temporal skew [7] analytical workloads, i.e., tenants that mostly submit queries within a certain period (e.g., 9am to 5pm) but not in a 24×7 fashion. That type of temporal skew workload is not uncommon in today's data analytical market [2]. The target tenants are supposed to have up to only some tens terabytes of data but hope to enjoy the parallel speedup offered by the expensive parallel database products. These are what enable consolidation (and business opportunities!). Tenants that are always active and/or with more than terabytes of data could be detected by Thrifty and they will be excluded from consolidation.

Tenant	T_1	T_2	T_3	T_4	T_5	T_6	T_7	T_8	T_9	T_{10}
n_i	6	6	5	5	5	4	4	3	2	2

(a) Tenant Characteristics (42 nodes requested)

Group	G_0	G_1	G_2
Parallel Database	DB_0	DB_1	DB_2
Parallelism	6-node	6-node	6-node

(b) Cluster Design (18 nodes)

Parallel Database	DB_0	DB_1	DB_2
Hosting	$T_1 - T_{10}$	$T_1 - T_{10}$	$T_1 - T_{10}$

(c) Tenant Placement

Figure 2: A Toy Example

3. TENANT-DRIVEN DESIGN (TDD)

The principle of Tenant-Driven Design (TDD) is to exploit the low active tenant ratio found in real multi-tenant cloud environments to design a deployment plan (a cluster design plus a tenant placement) that let each active tenant exclusively use a parallel database that just fits (or, over-fits) its parallelism requirement. By following that principle, tenants' SLA can be met easily.

The whole Tenant-Driven Design consists of three parts: (1) Cluster Design (Section 3.1), which governs how many parallel databases should be created and the parallelism of each parallel database; (2) Tenant Placement (Section 3.2), which governs the assignments of tenants to the created parallel databases; and (3) Query Routing (Section 3.3), which governs the query routing mechanism based on the cluster design and tenant placement.

3.1 Cluster Design

The cluster design of TDD is to divide a set of machine nodes into A groups (we will discuss how to set the value of A later). Then, each group of nodes form a separate parallel database. Let T be the number of tenants, n_i be the number of nodes requested by tenant T_i, and N be the total number of nodes requested by all T tenants (i.e., $N = \sum_1^T n_i$). Without loss of generality, we assume $n_i \leq n_j$ if $i > j$. Then, our tenant-driven design assigns n_1 nodes to groups $G_1, G_2, ..., G_{A-1}$. Group G_0 is a special group. Our tenant-driven design assigns a variable of U nodes to G_0, where $n_1 \leq U \leq (N - (A-1)n_1)$. We call the parallel database created from group G_0 as the "tuning parallel database", which is used for system tuning. The choice of U is very tricky and would be explained during the demonstration. In this paper, let us assume $U = n_1$.

As a toy example, assume that there are $T = 10$ tenants and the number of nodes requested by each tenant is listed in Figure 2a. In this toy example, the service provider requires a total of $N = 42$ nodes to host these tenants before consolidation. So, assume that $A = 3$, there are three groups and TDD results in an 18-node cluster design as listed in Figure 2b.

3.2 Tenant Placement

The tenant placement of TDD is very simple. Specifically, each parallel database is assigned to host all tenants. Figure

2c illustrates the tenant placement for the example. From the above discussion, we observe the Property 1.

PROPERTY 1. *The tenant-driven design enforces a replication factor of A for each tenant.*

Replication is a standard way to ensure high availability and load balancing. Usually, the replication factor is around two to four.

3.3 Query Routing

Algorithm 1 presents the query routing algorithm based on our tenant-driven design. The idea is to "route an active tenant" (compare with the concept of "route a query") to a parallel database and let that parallel database exclusively process all that tenant's (concurrent) queries until that tenant becomes inactive. Here, we use a strong notion of *inactive* — as long as a tenant does not have any queries being executed by any parallel database, that tenant is inactive at that moment.

Algorithm 1: TDD Query Routing

```
Input: Tenant T_i, Query Q
if T_i has queries running on DB_x then
    route Q to DB_x;
else
    if DB_0 currently is free then
        route Q to DB_0;
    else
        if there is any free parallel database then
            route Q to a free DB_j;
        else
            route Q to DB_0 for concurrent processing;
```

3.4 SLA Guarantee and Load Balancing

GUARANTEE 1. *No matter a tenant's queries are* linear-scale-out, non-linear-scale-out, *submitted* sequentially and possibly in an ad-hoc manner *(interactive analysis), or* submitted in a batch for concurrent execution (report generation) at any multi-programming-level (MPL). *Tenant-Driven Design ensures the SLAs of a maximum of A concurrent active tenants are met.*

Although simple, the tenant-driven design can obtain a strong performance SLA guarantee under a very general and practical parallel-database-as-a-service setting because tenants' queries are always *served by dedicated parallel databases with exact or higher degree of parallelism.*

The tenant-driven design achieves load balancing among tenants implicitly. That is because TDD uses a strong notion of inactive and it applies replication on the tenant data, therefore the tenants can be quickly served by an available parallel database. We remark that load balancing *within* a tenant is not TDD's but the tenant's own issue. The pricing model of Thrifty is to charge a tenant based on the number of nodes it requested. Therefore, if a tenant rents only a 2-node parallel database instance to serve many concurrent users (e.g., MPL=100), the possibly slow down of the tenant's performance due to the high load is brought by the tenant's own node-choice — TDD is just honestly offering what the tenant should get.

Node failure is handled directly by the parallel database. All parallel database products we know can still stay online even with (some) node failure. Thrifty will replace a failure node by starting a new node upon receiving node failure notification from the underlying parallel database. Node failure, or having more than A active tenants at run-time may cause performance delay and thus SLA violations. That is an important issue of Thrifty. Section 4 contains more details.

3.5 Tenant Grouping

In the above, we only consider a small number of tenants and the total cluster size (i.e., the total number of nodes involved) is small. Practically, if there are a lot of tenants, say $T = 5000$, and if the (average) active tenant ratio is 10%, the average number of active tenants at a certain point may reach 500 and the maximum number of active tenants could be even larger. According to Guarantee 1, in order to ensure all that 500+ active tenants can meet their SLAs together, we need to set $A > 500$. That would enforce each tenant's data get replicated more than 500 times, according to Property 1. We approach this problem by grouping the tenants into *tenant-groups* so that there are only some tens tenants in each tenant-group.

There are two considerations when grouping the tenants. First, of course, we want to group the tenants in a way that can minimize the total number of nodes used after consolidation. Second, we want to ensure the active tenant ratio in each tenant-group is low enough to meet the replication factor R. For example, if we put 30 tenants that are always active together into the same tenant-group, we still need to set $A = 30$ for that tenant-group in order to meet all tenants' SLA. Finding an optimal tenant-group formation that can address the two considerations above, unfortunately, has been proven by us to be a generalization of the classical single-dimensional bin packing problem, which is clearly $\mathcal{NP}$-hard. We have developed a two-step heuristic algorithm to approach the problem. The algorithm works by solving the two considerations separately. Specifically, we first look at *what kind of grouping can generate a cluster design that can save more nodes?* Recall that for T tenants, our tenant-driven design uses at least $A \cdot n_1$ nodes. So, we can see that the total number of nodes used by a cluster design is dictated by the largest tenant that requests the most number of nodes. For the example in Figure 2, T_1 is the largest tenant and it requests six nodes, so a cluster design that requires $A \cdot n_1 = 3 * 6 = 18$ nodes is generated. That cluster design could save $42 - 18 = 24$ nodes. If we group ten tenants of equal size, each requests six nodes, the resulting cluster design would still be the same because the size of the largest tenant remains the same, but that could save a total of $6 \times 10 - 18 = 42$ nodes. Therefore, the first step of the algorithm is based on the intuition that *we should put tenants of the same size (i.e., requesting the same number of nodes) into the same tenant-group.*

Next, we look at the second consideration, i.e., *how to ensure a low active tenant ratio within each tenant-group?* A natural intuition is that *we should analyze the tenants' activities, and put a tenant into a tenant-group that (a) minimizes the increase in the maximum number of active tenants of that tenant-group and (b) ensures that the maximum number of active tenants in the resulting tenant-group does not exceed R.* The second step of the algorithm is based on this intuition.

After tenant-grouping, the suggested cluster design and

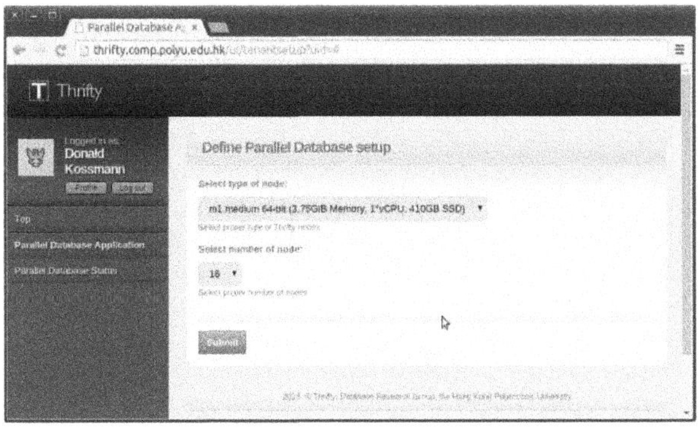

Figure 3: Tenant View: Requesting parallel database instance

tenant-placement are presented to system administrator and she can instruct the Deployment Master to carry out the consolidation, with $A = R$.

4. LIGHTWEIGHT ELASTIC SCALING

At run-time, if Thrifty detects that some tenants in a tenant group become more active than what the past tenant activities have indicated, Thrifty will carry out elastic scaling.

Unlike traditional cloud computing where elastic scaling can be done in a lightweight manner (e.g., adjusting RAM in virtual machines), elastic scaling in PDaaS could be very heavyweight. Take Vertica as an example, it takes about 14.5 hours to start a new 10-node instance and bulk load 1TB of tenant data. Therefore, Thrifty uses a lightweight approach to deal with the case of having over-active tenants in a tenant group. Specifically, it runs an over-active-tenant-identification algorithm to identify the tenant(s) that are more active than the history indicated, and create a new parallel database to serve them. As loading only the data of the over-active tenant(s) is much faster than loading all tenant data, the scaling operation is much more efficient. When the new parallel database is ready, the Deployment Advisor will notify the Query Router to route queries from the over-active tenant(s) to the new parallel database.

For any tenant-group that has ever gone through the above elastic scaling process, Thrifty will add tenants in those tenant-groups to a re-consolidation list. Those tenants, together with new tenants, over-active tenants, and tenants in tenant-groups with de-registered tenants, will get re-consolidated in the next (re)-consolidation cycle.

5. DEMONSTRATION

This demonstration would be the first public demonstration of Thrifty to our community. An attendee will experience Thrifty from both the perspectives of a tenant (who rents a parallel database instance from Thrifty) and a Thrifty's administrator. The whole demonstration requires two laptops, one for the tenant, one for the administrator. The detail of the demonstration is illustrated as follows.

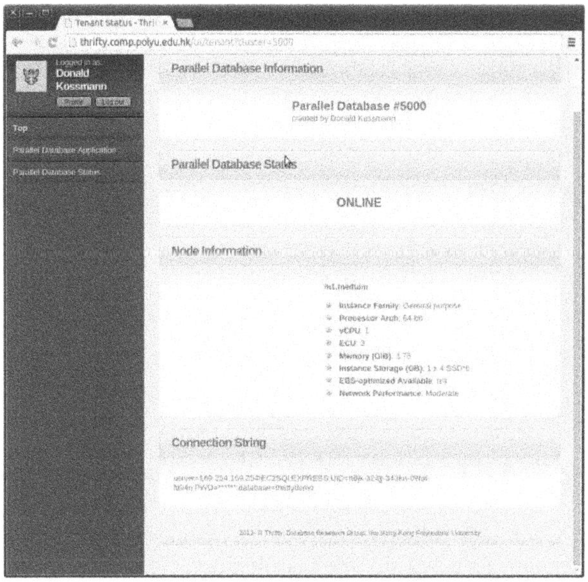

Figure 4: Tenant View: Front page

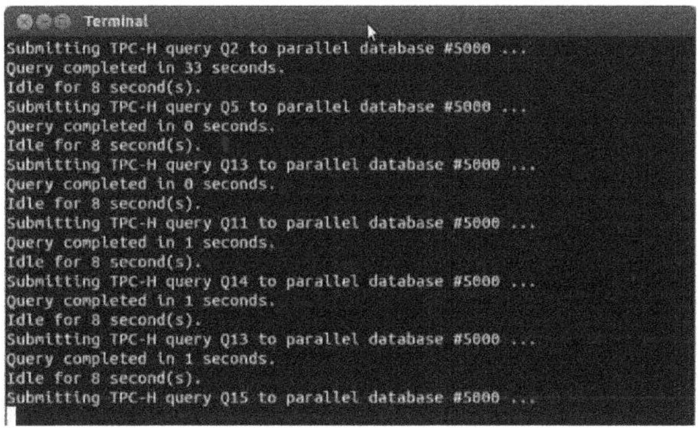

Figure 5: Tenant View: Submitting queries

1. An attendee registers to Thrifty as a tenant, starts a parallel database instance, and poses a workload of queries

In the beginning, an attendee will be invited to register to Thrifty as a tenant. During the registration, she will be allowed to choose the degree of parallelism of the parallel database instance to be created and the type of each node (Figure 3).

After registration, the attendee will see the page shown in Figure 4. The page shows the details of the parallel database instance that she has requested and the connection string to access that instance. Next, we will guide the attendee to connect to the created parallel database through a console, run a script to load a TPC-H database, and submit a loop of TPC-H queries to the created parallel database instance (Figure 5).

2. The attendee logs into Thrifty as an administrator

Next, the attendee will be invited to another laptop who has been logged in as a Thrifty's administrator. The front page of the administrator's account is a dashboard of all created tenant groups, like Figure 6.

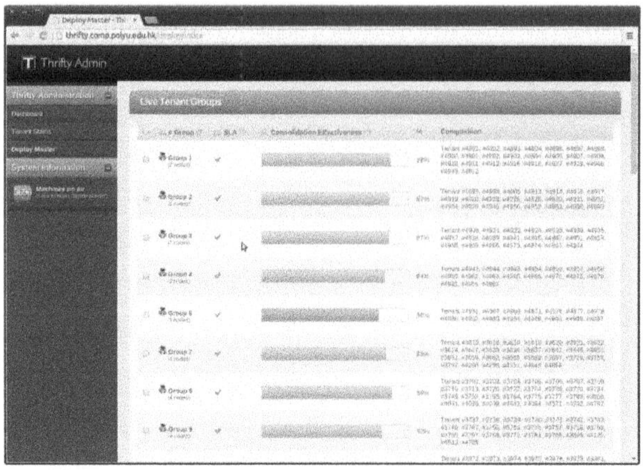

Figure 6: Administrator View: Dashboard

We will then explain to the attendee the meaning of tenant groups and the current consolidation effectiveness in the cluster. Next, the attendee will be invited to view the activity of her parallel database instance (which has TPC-H queries being issued; on the other laptop) from the system administrator's point of view (Figure 7).

From that view (Figure 7), the attendee shall see that her parallel database actually falls into tenant group #180.

3. The attendee is invited to increase the workload of the tenant group and observe how Thrifty reacts

Next, the attendee will be invited to be back to the tenant's laptop, but this time, we will open up three more terminals (Figure 8). The three terminals represent three other tenants of Thrifty. We will deliberately select three tenants falling into the same tenant group as with the attendee (i.e., tenant group #180) and control those three tenants to submit queries to Thrifty. Thrifty by default set $R = 3$, so our objective here is to create a setting of $A = 4 > R$ for that tenant group.

Finally, the attendee will be invited to observe what is happening inside Thrifty (Figure 9). The attendee shall see that the query performance of the tenant group #180. In the performance chart (the upper plot in Figure 9), a performance of 1.0 means the average query response time of tenants in that tenant group is the same as a tenant executes her queries on a dedicated owned virtual cluster. A performance of 2.0 means the average query response time of tenants in that tenant group is two times slower than what the tenant should get.

The RT-TTP chart (the lower plot in Figure 9) shows the violations of SLA guarantee of that tenant-group [11]. RT-TTP stands for the Total Time Percentage that the number of active tenants is smaller than or equal to R in a tenant-group for the past, say, 24 hours. Recall that P is the performance SLA guarantee of Thrifty, set by the system administrator. So Thrifty shall ensure that RT-TTP $> P\%$ in each tenant group. In the demonstration, as we deliberately make four tenants of the same tenant group active, the attendee shall see that the RT-TTP drops below $P = 99.9\%$ like what Figure 9 shown. However, after a while, Thrifty shall select some tenants in that tenant group to carry out elastic scaling. Consequently, the attendee shall eventually see the performance and RT-TTP of that tenant group return to normal status (Figure 10).

6. RELATED WORK

To the best of our knowledge, this is the first paper to discuss PDaaS and provide a real implementation to support the very stringent query-latency SLA for analytical workloads. There are several approaches to achieve database multi-tenancy [6]. The VM approach is to pack each individual tenant's database instance into a virtual machine (VM) and multiple VMs on a single physical machine [10]. This approach can consolidate only a few tenants onto one server because of the significant redundancy among the tenants (e.g., multiple copies of the OS and DBMS). Therefore, it is appropriate only when hard isolation between databases is more important than cost or performance [3]. The Shared Table approach is to share a single database instance and a set of tables among all tenants. In this approach, the tenants' data schemas are mostly identical or similar, which is common in database application as a service (e.g., Salesforce.com). The Shared Table approach can largely reduce the overhead and thus thousands of small (data size) and mostly inactive tenants can be packed onto a single server [1, 9, 5]. This approach is orthogonal to our work, as our tenants are autonomous and tenants' schemas are typically different.

7. REFERENCES

[1] S. Aulbach, T. Grust, D. Jacobs, A. Kemper, and J. Rittinger. Multi-tenant databases for software as a service: schema-mapping techniques. In *SIGMOD*, pages 1195–1206, 2008.

[2] Y. Chen, S. Alspaugh, and R. H. Katz. Interactive analytical processing in big data systems: A cross-industry study of mapreduce workloads. *PVLDB*, 5(12):1802–1813, 2012.

[3] C. Curino, E. P. C. Jones, S. Madden, and H. Balakrishnan. Workload-aware database monitoring and consolidation. In *SIGMOD*, pages 313–324, 2011.

[4] C. Curino, E. P. C. Jones, R. A. Popa, N. Malviya, E. Wu, S. Madden, H. Balakrishnan, and N. Zeldovich. Relational cloud: a database service for the cloud. In *CIDR*, pages 235–240, 2011.

[5] M. Hui, D. Jiang, G. Li, and Y. Zhou. Supporting database applications as a service. In *ICDE*, pages 832 –843, 2009.

[6] D. Jacobs and S. Aulbach. Ruminations on multi-tenant databases. In *BTW Proceedings*, pages 514–521, 2007.

[7] A. Pavlo, C. Curino, and S. Zdonik. Skew-aware automatic database partitioning in shared-nothing, parallel OLTP systems. In *SIGMOD*, pages 61–72, 2012.

[8] B. Reinwald. Multitenancy. *University of Washington and Microsoft Research Summer Institute*, 2010.

[9] O. Schiller, B. Schiller, A. Brodt, and B. Mitschang. Native support of multi-tenancy in RDBMS for software as a service. In *EDBT*, pages 117–128, 2011.

[10] A. A. Soror, U. F. Minhas, A. Aboulnaga, K. Salem, P. Kokosielis, and S. Kamath. Automatic virtual machine configuration for database workloads. *ACM TODS*, 35(1), 2010.

[11] P. Wong, Z. He, and E. Lo. Parallel analytics as a service. In *SIGMOD*, 2013.

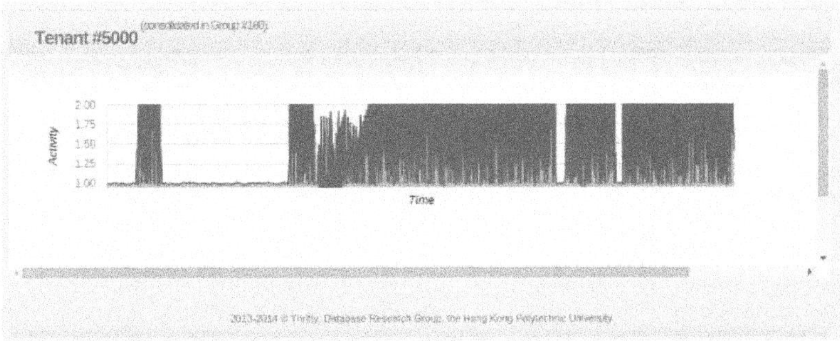

Figure 7: Administrator View: The activity of the attendee's created instance

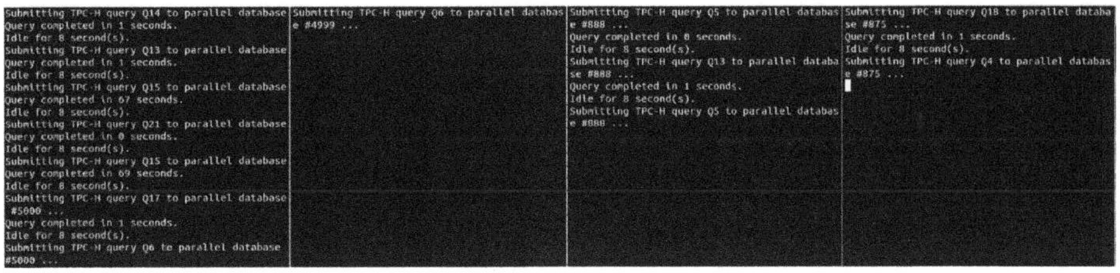

Figure 8: Having four active tenants

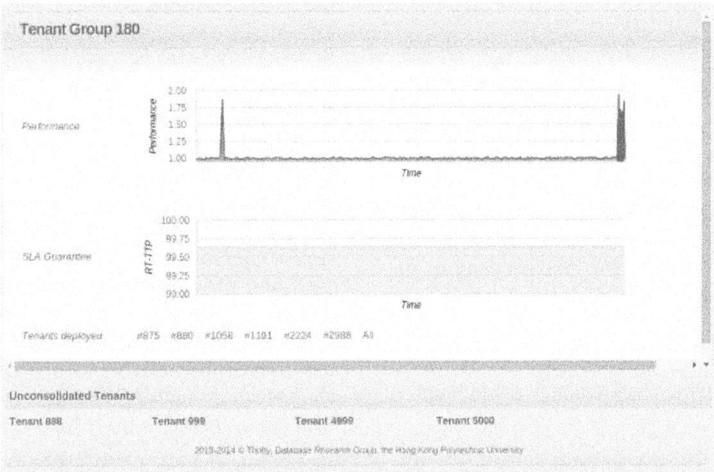

Figure 9: Administrator View: Detailed activity within a tenant group (before elastic scaling)

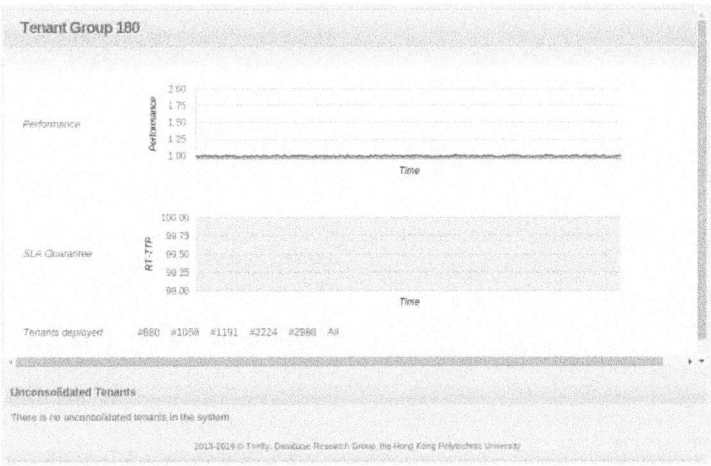

Figure 10: Administrator View: Detailed activity within a tenant group (after elastic Scaling)

BenchPress: Dynamic Workload Control in the OLTP-Bench Testbed

Dana Van Aken
Carnegie Mellon University
dvanaken@cs.cmu.edu

Djellel E. Difallah
University of Fribourg
djelleleddine.difallah@unifr.ch

Andrew Pavlo
Carnegie Mellon University
pavlo@cs.cmu.edu

Carlo Curino
Microsoft Corporation
ccurino@microsoft.com

Philippe Cudré-Mauroux
University of Fribourg
philippe.cudre-mauroux@unifr.ch

ABSTRACT

Benchmarking is an essential activity when choosing database products, tuning systems, and understanding the trade-offs of the underlying engines. But the workloads available for this effort are often restrictive and non-representative of the ever changing requirements of the modern database applications. We recently introduced OLTP-Bench, an extensible testbed for benchmarking relational databases that is bundled with 15 workloads. The key features that set this framework apart is its ability to tightly control the request rate and dynamically change the transaction mixture. This allows an administrator to compose complex execution targets that recreate real system loads, and opens the doors to new research directions involving tuning for special execution patterns and multi-tenancy. In this demonstration, we highlight OLTP-Bench's important features through the BenchPress game. It allows users to control the benchmark behavior in real time for multiple database management systems.

Categories and Subject Descriptors

H.3.4 [**Systems and Software**]: Performance evaluation

General Terms

Experimentation, Performance

Keywords

Benchmarking, Configuration, Tuning

1. INTRODUCTION

New database initiatives are motivated by either emerging use-cases or the need to improve existing deployments. For these efforts to be successful, it is important to use precise and flexible measurement tools for comparing database management systems (DBMSs) and stressing them under different circumstances. One such way is to use benchmarks, as it allows one to understand and compare the performance of these systems. Over the years, benchmarking has evolved from a set of simple routines that generate a single performance number to become what is now often a complex effort involving different workloads, parameters, system configurations, and other variables [4].

Database administrators and researchers test DBMSs using either common industry standard benchmarks or, if need be, custom workloads [2, 5]. In the latter case, the code and the data sets (if any) for these workloads are not always available or are not well maintained. Thus, this makes it difficult for others to verify results from previous projects, or to port the benchmarks to additional DBMSs. In addition to this, although a number of prominent benchmarks have been proposed in the past, to the best of our knowledge an extensive and adaptable testbed was previously not available. Researchers and practitioners often "reinvent the wheel" for each new project, and repeatedly spend time gathering data, constructing real or synthetic workloads, deploying database systems, building software that drives their systems, and finally creating tools to gather and analyze the results. Over the years, we noticed that many of the software components that we and others built for evaluating DBMSs are reusable.

Aside from the redundant work, the lack of an existing tool significantly limits the opportunities to compare related systems and approaches, since setting up testing conditions for heterogeneous deployments is time-consuming. Making this software available to the database community fosters and encourages experimental repeatability.

For these reasons, we developed the OLTP-Bench benchmarking testbed that is aimed at making it easier to reliably and repeatedly evaluate DBMSs [3]. OLTP-Bench is capable of dynamically controlling the transaction rate, mixture, and workload skew during the execution of an experiment. This allows one to simulate a multitude of practical scenarios that are typically hard to test (e.g., time-evolving access skew). Our framework provides an easy way to monitor the performance and resource consumption of the database system under test. It currently supports over 15 benchmarks, including synthetic micro-benchmarks, OLTP benchmarks, and real-world Web applications. These were ported by the authors of this work and as well as from several contributors in the community.

One challenging aspect that we focused on while building OLTP-Bench is the ability to control the rate of requests

SIGMOD'15, May 31–June 4, 2015, Melbourne, Victoria, Australia.

http://dx.doi.org/10.1145/2723372.2735354 .

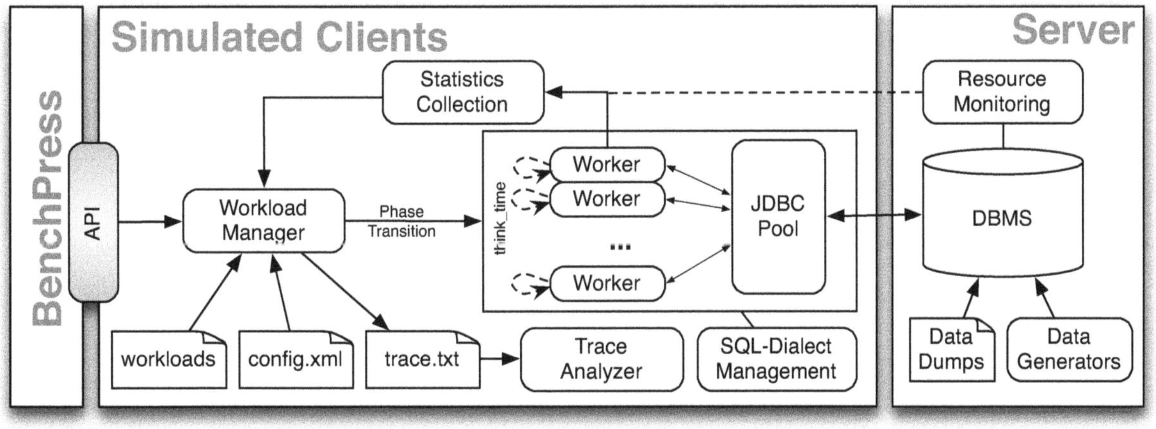

Figure 1: OLTP-Bench Architecture – The client-side handles workers and generates the transaction workload according to a configuration provided by the user, or via the real-time control API. On the left side, BenchPress utilizes the API to send the commands and to track the execution in real time. The framework also employs monitoring tools to gather server-side resource utilization statistics.

with great precision. As we describe in Section 2, this is hard to achieve for multiple DBMSs in a single codebase. Moreover, OLTP-Bench also supports changing transaction request rates dynamically during execution based on user-defined workloads. With these two features, one is able to design complex execution scenarios in OLTP-Bench. For example, one can run multiple workloads in parallel to test a DBMS's ability to support multi-tenant deployments.

In this demonstration, we showcase the dynamic and flexible control features of OLTP-Bench through **BenchPress**. BenchPress is a graphical interface that allows users to control OLTP-Bench's behavior in real-time. It supports the dynamic modification of a benchmark's transaction workload mixture and throughput rates, as well as the execution of additional benchmarks on-the-fly. The demonstration also allows users to compare different DBMSs within the same framework.

We next provide an overview of the key technical contributions of OLTP-Bench in Section 2, and discuss the datasets and benchmarks available in our demo in Section 3. Finally, we discuss in Section 4 how BenchPress allows the user to play with these various aspects in our testbed for the demo.

2. OVERVIEW

OLTP-Bench is an extensible, "batteries included" database benchmarking testbed [3]. It works with a number of single-node DBMSs, distributed DBMSs, and DBaaS systems that supports SQL through JDBC. As shown in Fig. 1, the architecture of our framework is comprised of two main components: (1) the client-side benchmark driver and (2) a server-side module. OLTP-Bench is written entirely in Java, including all of the built-in benchmarks. The client-side portion is small and portable (less than 5MB). The framework has been tested and deployed on a variety of Unix-like platforms.

2.1 Architecture

OLTP-Bench's client-side component contains a centralized *Workload Manager* that is responsible for tightly controlling the characteristics of the workload via a centralized request queue. It takes as input a configuration file describing a predefined workload with multiple execution phases, where a phase is defined as (1) a target transaction rate, (2) a transaction mixture, and (3) a time duration in seconds.

The Workload Manager spawns multiple client *Worker* threads that each connect to the target DBMS using JDBC and iteratively pull tasks from the request queue. For each new transaction request, a Worker invokes the corresponding transaction's control code (i.e., program logic with parameterized queries) and either commits or aborts the transaction. The Worker thread then returns to the queue to retrieve its next task.

To handle portability across multiple DBMS SQL dialects, we decided to use support human-written dialect translation instead of automatic tools. In that way, we allow experts for individual systems to contribute specific SQL variants—both for DML and DDL queries and operations—for different systems.

On the server side, we use standard server monitoring tools [7] that are launched in parallel to OLTP-Bench and provide system performance metrics in real time as they are collected on the host.

2.2 Features

In [3], we introduced the requirements that motivated the design decisions behind OLTP-Bench. We provide below an overview of these key features that we implemented.

2.2.1 Rate Control

The ability to control request rates with great precision in a DBMS is important for understanding performance anomalies. Even small oscillations in the throughput can make the interpretation of results difficult. OLTP-Bench can either execute transactions in an open loop fashion or with a throttled transaction per second rate for predefined periods of time [6]. This allows one to evaluate how well a DBMS can sustain long periods of continuous load.

As described above, the runtime throughput is controlled through the Workload Manager's request queue. At runtime, the manager generates new requests and adds them to this queue. The Workers pull a request from the queue, execute it, sleep for an optional "think time" period, and then return the queue for a new request. Using a centralized queue allows us to control the throughput from one location without needing to coordinate the multiple Worker threads. The exact number of requests configured is added to the queue each second, and each arrival is interleaved with a uniform or exponential arrival time. When the workers cannot keep up with all requests, the remainder is postponed in such a way that the framework never exceeds the target rate. In case an unlimited throughput is requested, the arrival is set to a large configurable constant.

2.2.2 *Mixture Control*

While the Workload Manager inserts work requests into the queue, the workers choose the benchmark's specific transactions to execute by sampling from a predefined distribution (or mixture). In OLTP-Bench, we added the ability to change the mixture of transactions used in a given benchmark in every phase, or on demand via the new control API (cf. Section 2.2.4). This allows the user to experiment with different combinations [3], for example by transitioning from read-heavy to write-heavy workloads.

2.2.3 *Multi-tenancy*

OLTP-Bench can be configured to run multiple workloads and benchmarks in parallel. A novel feature that we introduce allows the users to perform multi-tenancy tests that isolate different workloads within the same instance.

2.2.4 *Application Programming Interface*

For the purpose of this demo and in response to user feedback, we created a RESTful application programming interface (API) for OLTP-Bench that exposes the ability to programmatically control its execution at the runtime. This includes changing the current phase parameters (cf. Section 2.1) by throttling the throughput or changing the workload mixture. In addition, this API also provides instantaneous feedback about the current execution throughput and average latency per transaction type. As we discuss in Section 4, this API enables us to turn our benchmark system into the BenchPress interactive game. As users control their character in the game, their input is are converted into API commands that adjust the current benchmark running in OLTP-Bench. The game then receives status updates from the API and then modifies the games' visuals accordingly.

Beyond BenchPress, this API for controlling the execution load facilitates the integration of OLTP-Bench in the context of broader test infrastructures. This could be useful to dynamically create new workload mixtures in response to application-level observations.

3. BENCHMARK DATA & WORKLOADS

The recent growth in Web and mobile-based applications requiring transactional support pushed the boundaries of traditional benchmarks. Instead of trying to be exhaustive, we chose an initial set of benchmarks that covers a number of currently popular applications. Table 1 gives an overview of the 15 benchmarks currently ported to OLTP-Bench, along with their application domain. We believe that each benchmark in that table is useful in modeling a specific application domain. We note that the size of the database corresponding to each benchmark is configurable by the administrator and that the working set size can be automatically scaled.

Class	Benchmark	Application Domain
Transactional	**AuctionMark**	On-line Auctions
	CH-benCHmark	Mixture of OLTP and OLAP
	SEATS	On-line Airline Ticketing
	SmallBank	Banking System
	TATP	Caller Location App
	TPC-C	Order Processing
	Voter	Talent Show Voting
Web-Oriented	**Epinions**	Social Networking
	LinkBench	Social Networking
	Twitter	Social Networking
	Wikipedia	On-line Encyclopedia
Feature Testing	**ResourceStresser**	Isolated Resource Stresser
	YCSB	Scalable Key-value Store
	JPAB	Object-Relational Mapping
	SIBench	Transactional Isolation

Table 1: The set of benchmarks supported in OLTP-Bench.

More detailed information, including descriptions of the individual transactions in each benchmark and their source code, is available on our website [1].

4. DEMONSTRATION DESCRIPTION

BenchPress is a game that allows users to control the behavior of OLTP-Bench through its API. The objective is to be able to navigate a game character throughout a horizontally scrolling obstacle course. The vertical height of the character at a given point in time is based on the current throughput (transactions per second) of the target DBMS. The user controls their character by increasing or decreasing the target throughput using the keyboard or the controller. The character, however, only responds to the actual throughput delivered by the DBMS as measured by OLTP-Bench. The boundaries of obstacles correspond to different target throughput rates. If the DBMS cannot deliver the requested transaction rate, then the character will crash into an obstacle.

BenchPress is a JavaScript application that runs in a browser. It connects to a Web-based application server that connects to OLTP-Bench. The benchmark framework is deployed on a machine that contains several target DBMSs.

Our system features many tests to challenge the user, for example by linearly increasing or decreasing the execution patterns using higher and lower obstacles. This demonstration allows users to (1) gain insight about the benchmarks included in OLTP-Bench, (2) become familiar with the functionalities offered by OLTP-Bench, and (3) stir a discussion on how a specific execution pattern might influence the performance of a DBMS and potentially expose hidden weaknesses. We now describe the different components of the BenchPress demonstration.

4.1 Gameplay

Our demo is a side-scrolling game where the character is indirectly controlled using a keyboard or an external input device. As shown in Fig. 2a, the user starts the game by picking the desired benchmark. Each benchmark corresponds to a different character in the game. They then select the target DBMS (Fig. 2b). Each DBMS corresponds to a different stage with varying environment conditions. For example, the screenshot in Fig. 2c shows that MySQL is the forest level.

The character has to progress through a series of *obstacles* by either *jumping* over them or letting the character *fall* due

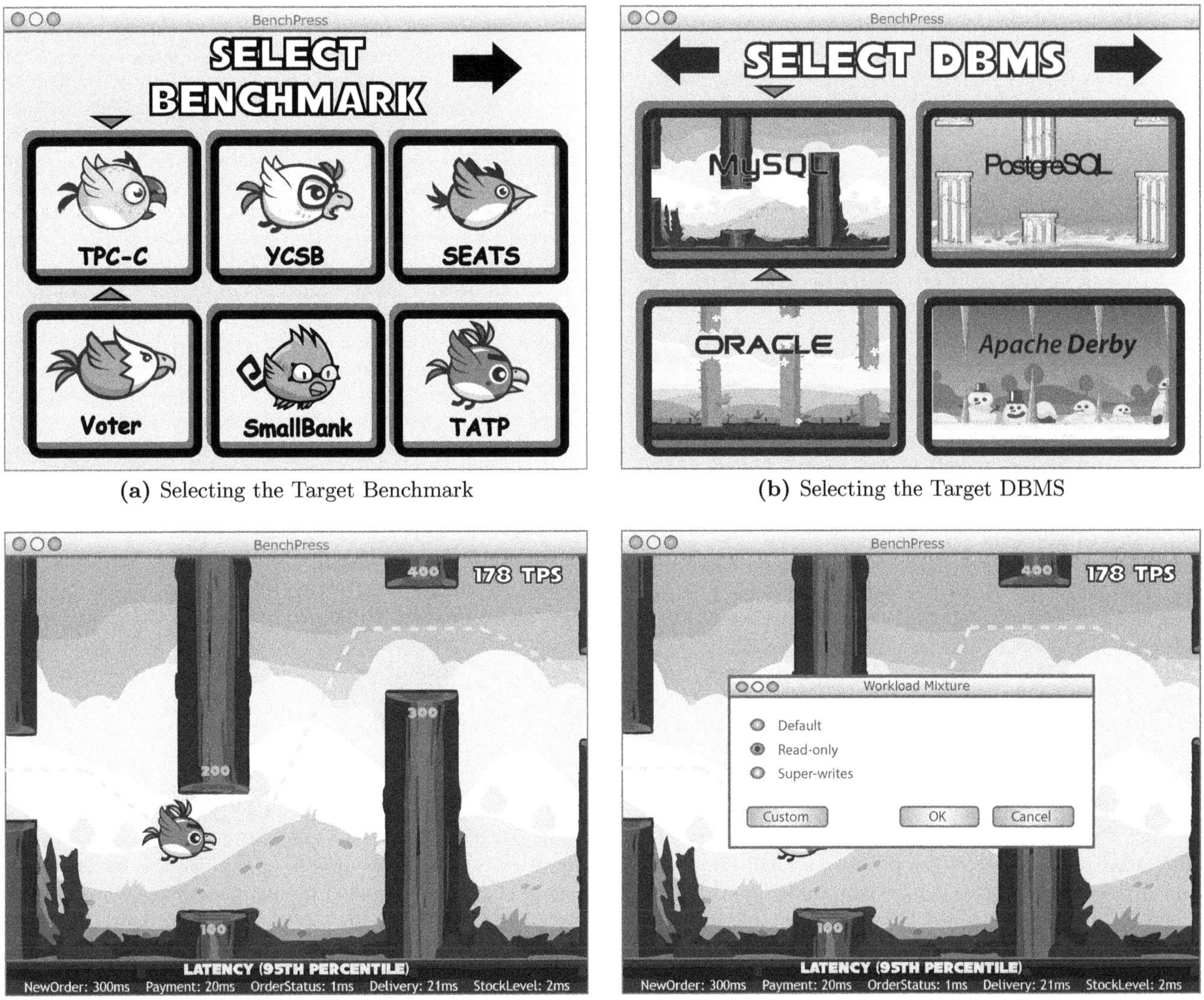

(a) Selecting the Target Benchmark

(b) Selecting the Target DBMS

(c) Main Game Screen

(d) Dynamically Change the Workload Mixture

Figure 2: The BenchPress game screenshots.

to the simulated gravity. We now describe these concepts in the context of database benchmarking in further detail:

- An *obstacle* is a set of vertical "pipes" that limits the character's movement within a defined range. This range is given by the height of the pipes and represents the expected throughput at which the challenge is preset for a given period of time. If the user fails to navigate their character past these obstacles, then the game is over. This will cause BenchPress to halt the benchmark and reset the database.
- A *jump* requests a higher throughput rate and makes the game character move upwards. The movement of the character however only reflects the actual throughput delivered by the DBMS rather than the requested one. This measures the ability of the DBMS to changes in the OLTP-Bench's requested load, thereby allowing the user to easily perceive the different system' responsiveness.
- A *fall* makes the game character go down following some simulated gravity, in the sense that the throughput automatically decreases linearly until reaching 0 transactions per second, at which point the character falls on the floor. A different setup would allow the user to manually decrease the throughput using the commands.

4.1.1 Mixture Control

In addition to the basic controls described above, the user can alter the benchmark mixture on-the-fly. That is, the user can pause BenchPress at any moment in time to change the workload parameters order to avoid an obstacle. This will cause OLTP-Bench to temporarily block any Worker thread from executing a transaction request. Beside the ability to fully customize a workload by manually assigning new probability distributions for the transactions, BenchPress includes preset mixtures. As shown in Fig. 2d, these include "read-heavy" and "write-heavy" workload mixtures. Modifying the workload mixture allows players to have a tighter control of the character (effectively on the throughput) when the DBMS struggles at maintaining the rate required to pass some difficult obstacle. For example, switching the workload mixture to a "read-heavy" workload will boost the DBMS's throughput due to reduced lock contention.

4.1.2 Challenges

Our goal is to create a simulated load that the DBMS must respond to. To that end, the challenges represent the throughput to achieve during the game at any given point in time. In BenchPress, challenges take the form of pairs of vertical obstacles with a narrow opening between them. This opening serves as a visual representation of the expected throughput range to achieve.

Other challenges in the game are *auto-pilot zones*, where the user has to identify the right throughput and mixture that allows the character to pass through the obstacles successfully without any external input. That is, users are not able to control the throughput as their game character moves through these zones. In that case, the obstacle is a target throughput that must be achieved for a given period of time. This challenge will make the user reflect on the different parameters that can be used to reach a given target execution.

For this demo, we created challenges following four different shapes (although this list is not exhaustive, and new challenges can be created using a configuration file):

Steps: The character has to go through a set of increasing or decreasing throughput levels. This simulates an increasing load on the database; at some point the DBMS will become saturated and be unable to process any more transactions. In the worst case, the performance may actually get worse depending on the workload.

Sinusoidal: The character has to move up and down in a recurring pattern. This demonstrates a fluctuating load and tests the ability of the DBMS to gracefully respond without much jitter.

Peak: After a period of low throughput simulating some steady-state workload, a peak in throughput is created for a short period before going back to normal. Again, this will show the ability of a DBMS to respond to some sporadic and sudden increase in load.

Tunnels: The auto pilot zones are long tunnels where the target execution is fixed to a constant range of high (or low) target throughput. This challenge expects the DBMS to deliver a constant tight throughput for a long period of time.

4.2 Performance Visualization

The BenchPress interface provides a visual overview about the DBMS's performance in terms of throughput and latency. To complement this information, the OLTP-Bench monitoring tool will display in real time the metrics collected from the system on which the DBMS is running. This information can be useful for the user to predict potential drops in performance (e.g., when getting close to being CPU-bound). Hence, the user can take the necessary actions to prevent an eventual crash into an obstacle by tuning down the transaction rate and potentially causing a performance drop (see Section 4.1.1). For example, the user could in that context lower the percentage of write-intensive transactions if the disk IO activity seems to saturate.

4.3 Demo Takeways

The goals of this demo are threefold. First, we aim at engaging the audience with an interactive demonstration that goes beyond the typical back-end demonstrations of DBMSs. Second, we seek to showcase OLTP-Bench's ability to control a multiplicity of database benchmarking parameters dynamically. Lastly, we hope that the game provides users with a number of key insights about DBMSs and transactional workloads. Examples of this include understanding a DBMS weaknesses and the idiosyncrasies of the various workloads that are built into OLTP-Bench (cf. Table 1). The player will learn that certain types of transactions are more difficult to sustain than others, that some cannot be used to achieve high throughput, or that certain DBMSs (and tuning combinations) cannot pass the tunnel tests, since they produce oscillating throughputs. Moreover, the two-player version of the game allows the players to experience in real-time the effects of multi-tenancy, with one player affecting the other.

5. ACKNOWLEDGEMENTS

This research was funded (in part) by the U.S. National Science Foundation (III-1423210), and the Swiss National Science Foundation (PP00P2_128459). We also give props to Peter Bailis, whose database and trapping skills are slaying it. All doubters will be blown out when his mixtape drops.

6. CONCLUSION

BenchPress is a new approach in benchmarking DBMSs that is based on defining execution expectations (i.e., challenges), and dynamically controlling the workload through a game interface. In this demonstration, we propose an initial set of predefined challenges that leverage the set of benchmarks that are supported by our underlying OLTP-Bench framework. This allows a user to explore their properties through stress testing various DBMSs.

7. REFERENCES

[1] OLTPBenchmark.com. http://oltpbenchmark.com.

[2] C. Curino, E. Jones, R. A. Popa, N. Malviya, E. Wu, S. Madden, H. Balakrishnan, and N. Zeldovich. Relational Cloud: A Database Service for the Cloud. In *CIDR*, pages 235–240, 2011.

[3] D. E. Difallah, A. Pavlo, C. Curino, and P. Cudré-Mauroux. OLTP-Bench: An Extensible Testbed for Benchmarking Relational Databases. *PVLDB*, 7(4):277–288, 2013.

[4] J. Gray. *Benchmark Handbook: For Database and Transaction Processing Systems*. Morgan Kaufmann Publishers Inc., 1992.

[5] A. Pavlo, E. P. Jones, and S. Zdonik. On predictive modeling for optimizing transaction execution in parallel OLTP systems. *Proc. VLDB Endow.*, 5:85–96, October 2011.

[6] B. Schroeder, A. Wierman, and M. Harchol-Balter. Open versus closed: a cautionary tale. NSDI, pages 18–18, 2006.

[7] D. Wieers. Dstat: Versatile resource statistics tool. http://dag.wiee.rs/home-made/dstat.

Demonstrating "Data Near Here": Scientific Data Search

V.M. Megler
Portland State University
Department of Computer Science
Portland, Oregon
vmegler@cs.pdx.edu

David Maier
Portland State University
Department of Computer Science
Portland, Oregon
maier@pdx.edu

ABSTRACT

Prior work proposed "Data Near Here" (DNH), a data search engine for scientific archives that is modeled on Internet search engines. DNH performs a periodic, asynchronous scan of each dataset in an archive, extracting lightweight features that are combined to form a dataset summary. During a search, DNH assesses the similarity of the search terms to the summary features and returns to the user, at interactive timescales, a ranked list of datasets for further exploration and analysis. We will demonstrate the search capabilities and ancillary metadata-browsing features for an archive of observational oceanographic data. While comparing search terms to complete datasets might seem ideal, interactive search speed would be impossible with archives of realistic size. We include an analysis showing that our summary-based approach gives a reasonable approximation of such a "complete dataset" similarity measure.

Categories and Subject Descriptors

H.3.1 [**Information Storage and Retrieval**]: Content Analysis and Indexing – *abstracting methods.* H.3.3 [**Information Storage and Retrieval**]: Information Search and Retrieval – *retrieval models, search process.* H.3.4 [**Information Storage and Retrieval**]: Systems and Software – *performance evaluation (efficiency and effectiveness).* H.2.8 [**Information Systems**]: Database Applications – *scientific databases, spatial databases & GIS.*

Keywords

Scientific data, ranked data search.

1. INTRODUCTION

With the dramatic growth in available scientific data, methods scientists used in the past to locate data relevant to their research interests are no longer effective [8, 24]. The challenge is exacerbated by the push to move scientific data into shared archives; scientists are often searching for data that has been collected, categorized and stored by other people [16]. The scientist may not be intimately familiar with every archive that caters to his specialization, making navigating some archives a frustrating experience and creating a risk that relevant data is not found and therefore not used – undermining the value of data collection and of the archives themselves [12]. Prior archive search methods exclude results that do not exactly match the scientist's search terms, but may in fact be very close to the desired data. The search engines may provide "near" results for textual metadata, but sufficiently descriptive textual metadata rarely exists [2, 10, 11], and much of the desired and collected observational data is numeric. Even in genomic research, gene expression test results are often reported as numeric ranges [25].

We demonstrate a solution to this problem: "Data Near Here" (DNH), an Internet-search inspired engine that provides ranked search of datasets with interactive response times (a geospatial and temporal-search only version of which was previously described [17]). We search over dataset summaries, diverging from text-search approaches that include all individual terms (or numbers) as features. DNH has been deployed over an existing archive of oceanographic observational data at an NSF-funded center for science and technology, CMOP[1]. The scientists using this archive complained about the problem described above, despite having available to them a variety of state-of-the-art visualization and analysis tools. Figure 1 shows the search interface (further discussed below) for the most recent version.

We will demonstrate Data Near Here using a test platform consisting of the search engine and a recent copy of the live metadata catalog of CMOP's observational data archive.[2] We allow the demo attendee to issue ad-hoc searches using two versions of the search engine: one version that operates over the same metadata repository but returns the results that would be found if searches only returned exact matches (as do other data search engines), and the other using the ranked search proposed and implemented in DNH. Although DNH is currently used by CMOP scientists, it has not been previously demonstrated to wider audiences. A proof-of-concept is also being developed with genomics data, and may be included in the demo.

DNH has the following characteristics: demonstrated usability and effectiveness; flexibility; extensibility; scalability.

DNH usability and effectiveness was shown in two user studies. Megler and Maier [15] initially evaluated the appropriateness of a proposed similarity measure, based in cognitive science, via a user study that tested whether a population of scientists had a relatively consistent mental model of what it meant for a collection of numeric data to be "close" to a numeric search term. They found that the population of scientists surveyed provided markedly similar responses, and concluded that it might be possible to replicate the scientists' assessments. They also showed that a candidate similarity measure sufficiently replicated user assessments to warrant further study. A second user study, using a prototype implementation of DNH over an observational archive, asked users of that archive to evaluate the results of a set of self-selected searches. Under both qualitative and quantitative

SIGMOD'15, May 31 - June 04, 2015, Melbourne, VIC, Australia

ACM 978-1-4503-2758-9/15/05 $15.00
http://dx.doi.org/10.1145/2723372.2735360

[1] Center for Coastal Margin Observation and Management, http://www.stccmop.org

[2] While DNH also has a metadata-collection component, the lack of visual or interaction elements makes for a boring demo.

measures commonly used in evaluating Information Retrieval systems, DNH received high scores (precision at 10 of 0.96 across all search types, with 0.55 for highly relevant results only; Mean Reciprocal Rank of 0.95, with 0.72 for highly relevant results only).

We exhibit flexibility through the variety of data that we can search. DNH incorporates in a seamless fashion data with widely different geospatial, temporal and environmental-variable characteristics. A single search is issued over data collected from static and mobile observation platforms ranging from autonomic underwater vehicles to satellite-collected data, and including both observed phenomena and modeled phenomena. The source data is stored in many different locations and formats. In addition, the ability to "segment" a dataset in multiple ways to reflect different scientist perspectives and needs provides additional flexibility for the archive, by providing a layer of separation between how the data is stored and how it is retrieved, and for the scientist by allowing her to retrieve the most useful segment.

The extensibility and scalability of DNH comes from the loosely-coupled architecture (briefly described below, and in more detail along with the abstract model by Megler [14]).

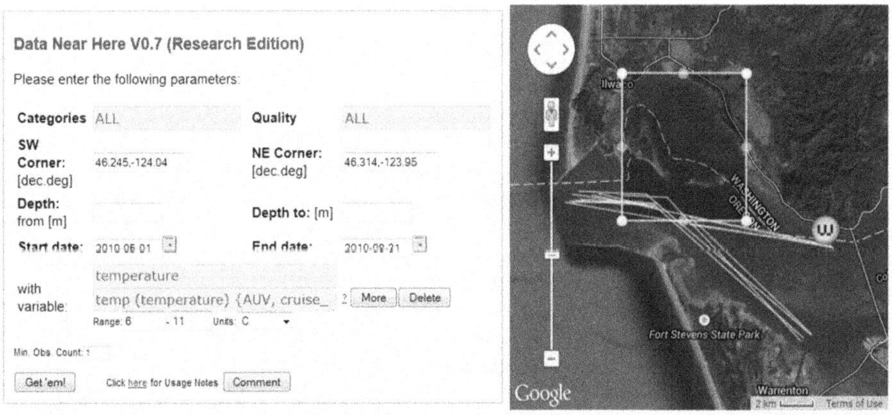

Display	Type	Collection	Quality	Start Time	End Time	From Depth	To Depth	temp	Observations	Data Location	Score	DNH
1	cruise_flothru	April 2010, Wecoma, 2010-04-17, Segment 4	preliminary_data	2010-04-17 04:06 PDT	2010-04-17 04:26 PDT	-5	-5	10.60:10.85 C	21	Download	98	DNH
2	cruise_flothru	May-June 2010, Wecoma, 2010-07-16, Segment 3	preliminary_data	2010-07-16 05:18 PDT	2010-07-16 05:29 PDT	-5	-5	9.89:12.14 C	14	Download	98	DNH
3	cruise_flothru	April 2010, Wecoma, 2010-04-17, Segment 11	preliminary_data	2010-04-17 18:52 PDT	2010-04-17 23:59 PDT	-5	-5	10.88:11.21 C	244	Download	97	DNH
4	cruise_flothru	April 2010, Wecoma, 2010-04-17, Segment 5	preliminary_data	2010-04-17 04:26 PDT	2010-04-17 05:26 PDT	-5	-5	10.65:10.86 C	61	Download	97	DNH

Figure 1. Search interface for "Data Near Here", showing a sample search for a geographic region (shown as a rectangle on the map) and date range, with temperature data in the range 6:11C. Result datasets (or subsets) are shown by markers and lines in the output pane, together with their relationship to the search region. In the ranked list of answers, no complete matches for the search conditions were found; four partial matches appear in the text panel segment shown here, and they are also shown on the map.

2. RELATED WORK

Many researchers propose novel visualizations as a method for scientists to deal with the volume of data [20, 22]. However, these methods assume that the data being visualized is of a consistent type and is stored in a consistent format; that the data can be accessed, loaded and visualized in a reasonable amount of time; and that the scientist can recognize a visual signal within a large amount of displayed data. While these assumptions may hold in some single-instrument archives (such as an astronomy archive storing data from the Hubble telescope), they do not hold for multi-instrument and multi-discipline archives such as CMOP's.

Some data archives [19, 21] provide search capabilities over textual metadata that is contributed by the original data source. However, scientists are often vitally interested in the data values within a dataset rather than a textual description. Further, manual metadata annotation is considered burdensome and is rarely provided [2, 10, 11]. One group noted that the users wanted more metadata than was provided and that providers stopped sharing data when more metadata was requested [4].

Much collected sensor data has geospatial and temporal components, and geospatially enabled databases are a common storage choice. Many geographic search systems [7, 9] score items based on word matches against metadata without considering the temporal span or geographic content of the items returned. More recent geospatial portals [6] allow searches using both geographic and temporal criteria; generally, three spatial tests are supported (the map view intersects, mostly contains, or completely contains the dataset), and temporal searches appear to be simple contains tests. Items that are very close but do not meet these tests are not returned.

Much collected scientific data is numeric in nature. Venetis et al. extract and search numbers in HTML tables [23] but their work focuses on extracting additional semantics. Agrawal and Srikant [1] also search numeric data. However, both of these approaches assume each "document" is small by our standards (for example, a single web page, say containing a product specification). Cafarella et al. also search over a large number of tables extracted from HTML, with a goal of returning ranked search responses based on table content [3]; they match on contained values or on synonyms of search terms, and appear to treat a number as a text term.

To our knowledge, Data Near Here is the first application of these Information Retrieval ideas to archives of large, heterogeneous datasets. The work perhaps most similar to DNH in scope and spirit is by D'Ulizia et al. [5]. They are interested in providing approximate results ranked in similarity across a combination of geospatial and non-geospatial attributes. Their approach differs from DNH in that each attribute is assumed to have a single value, and the attribute and the values are matched via known ontologies and taxonomies. They match individual data items, whereas DNH works with summaries of large datasets where the datasets may be (and most likely are) stored elsewhere. Please refer to Megler [14] for additional related work.

3. SYSTEM OVERVIEW

Our high-level architecture is shown in Figure 2. It follows and adapts the generic search architecture used by most Internet search engines today. It has two largely independent components, Asynchronous Indexing and Interactive Search, each of which communicates with a Metadata Catalog.

The primary processes in *Asynchronous Indexing* are:

- The Crawl process is given one or more starting points (for example, a link to a THREDDS[3] catalog) and navigates from there, creating a list of datasets to be cataloged.
- The Read process takes each dataset identified by the crawl process and attempts to read it. It may apply rules to identify the correct reader, based on clues such as file type.
- Extract Features summarizes each dataset it reads into a set of features and stores the summary in the Metadata Catalog. This process encapsulates additional functions such as dataset partitioning and hierarchy creation [17].

The primary processes in *Interactive Search* are:

- A scientist (or user) specifies her search criteria in the Search Interface (shown in Figure 1). The Search Interface passes the search criteria to the Scoring-and-Ranking component, and displays the results returned.
- The Scoring-and-Ranking component accesses the metadata catalog, identifies the highest-ranked datasets for the given search criteria, and returns summary information (similar to the "document snippets" shown in web search results) to the Search Interface.

The *Metadata Catalog* provides the linkage between the two sections: it stores the features, dataset summaries and hierarchy relationships resulting from the indexing process, and makes them available for use by the search processes. As soon as a feature or summary appears in the catalog, it is available for searching.

The components are decoupled from each other and communicate via APIs. This general architecture ensures separation and independence between the compute-intensive, asynchronous indexing functions of the system, and interactive search, which aims to provide fast response times to searchers. The loosely coupled nature of the components allows flexibility in altering a component without affecting the remaining components.

4. DEMONSTRATION SCENARIO

Our demonstration focuses on the Interactive-Search and Metadata Catalog components of Data Near Here. The demonstration consists of three elements: the current (browse-oriented) method for accessing CMOP's observational archive; an instance of our ranked search engine; and a second instance customized to only return "perfect matches" to a search. The second version of DNH will return the same subset of data that a Boolean search or scan of the data would find; that is, only data that completely matches the search criteria are returned. The Asynchronous Indexing component will not be demonstrated.

The demo user, emulating a research scientist, can search for data in the archive using any of the three elements. The user will be able to create and issue her own searches. We will provide sample scientific information needs, such as "dataset from near Newport, OR, containing salinity between 10 and 20 psu," or, "find whether data was collected that would allow me to place some physical context around this interesting water sample." The contrast between the results returned from the Boolean search and results from ranked search will allow the user to explore the uneven distribution of archive data, and the value of seeing whether there is data that might be interesting, even if not exactly meeting the initial search criteria.

[3] Thematic Realtime Environmental Distributed Data Services, http://www.unidata.ucar.edu/software/thredds/current/tds/

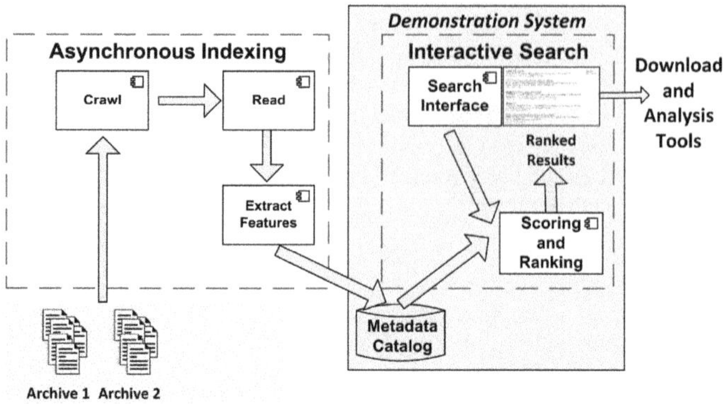

Figure 2. High-level dataset search architecture. The demonstration system is highlighted via a greyed box.

The user can also choose to view and explore the metadata we capture and store for individual datasets (Section 4.2), and summary information for each environmental variable showing what data is available in the archive (Section 4.3).

4.1 Search

The demo user will begin by entering a search into DNH's search interface (see the top section of Figure 1; the bottom section shows the results of a search) using a set of search-entry fields and optionally a Google map to position the geospatial component of

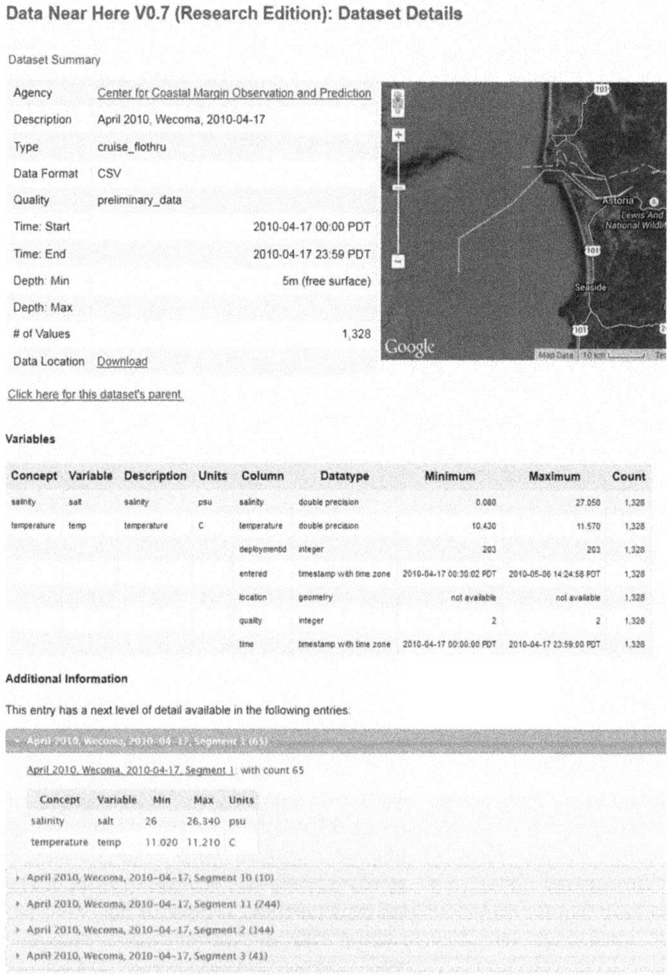

Figure 3. Dataset details page for a middle hierarchy level (single day) of a multi-week science cruise.

his search. He will enter some combination of search terms that may include time, geospatial location, depth and one or more environmental variables [13, 17]. For each variable search term, he can select one of the available variables found in CMOP datasets using a drop-down box. He can request that the variable has values within a specified range, or he can select a variable without specifying a range (called an "existence" search). He can limit the results returned to one or more categories of data (for example, water samples, stations, or cruises), and he can choose the desired data quality. He does not need to specify all search terms; for example, he can search on a single variable, or only on time, leaving all other search terms unspecified.

In the latest version of DNH we have added a second level of grouping to the environmental variables: concepts. This addition is an interim solution to organizing the long list of such variables, covering multiple disciplines and research areas, that can be searched [18]. Using a two-level hierarchy of "concept" and then "variable", the demo user can search to see what data exists in his desired concept, then further refine his search with that knowledge (see Figure 4, further described in Section 4.3). Some of these variables represent different levels or ways of measuring the same environmental phenomenon (e.g. "oxygen", vs. "oxygen_saturation"), or variations in context ("temperature" may mean "air temperature" or "water temperature", depending on the context of the source) [18].

DNH returns results within normal interactive response times (a few seconds). Results form a ranked list with the highest scoring datasets first. For the "Perfect Match" version, only perfect matches (highest possible score) will be shown. The geospatial extent of any dataset containing geospatial data is also shown on the map. The user can access the data directly from this results page via a data download. We also provide tool invocation directly wherever we can build a link to the tool and specify command-line parameters that identify the subset of data.

4.2 Dataset Details View

The user can explore a dataset summary, as stored in the metadata catalog, for any dataset in her search results, to confirm whether she wishes to download and further explore this data. She can access the summary directly from her search results (see the link in the "Collection" column in Figure 1). Figure 3 shows the dataset summary for some data captured by a mobile platform. A table at the top left of the page displays general information for the dataset, such as source agency, dataset name and format. A map displays the track of the mobile device, as calculated from the individual observations. The page also displays summary information about each environmental variable stored in the dataset, including its data type and its value range. This summary in essence describes the dataset's features, over which we search [17]. Summary creation is described by Megler [14].

The user can download the dataset this entry describes directly from this page (using the "download" link), or invoke any linked tools (e.g. Matlab, Excel) or visualizations on the search results. Where possible, DNH provides a link to a plot for each variable using CMOP's plotting service.

Data Near Here V0.7 (Research Edition): Variable Summary for 'oxygen'

	Context	Units	Datatype	Minimum	Maximum	Instances	Observations	Concept
+	APL	ml/l	double precision	0.00000e+0	5.791	10	21,078	oxygen
+	CMOP	mg/l	double precision	0.039	10.000	3,022	37,305,655	oxygen
-	CMOP	ml/l	double precision	0.00000e+0	9.995	3,170	86,413,340	oxygen

Some examples of datasets of this kind are:

Agency	Collection	Units	Datatype	Minimum	Maximum
CMOP	Baseline Feb 2013 1, Forerunner, bakerbay_inlet	ml/l	double precision	7.106	8.447
CMOP	Baseline Feb 2013 1, Forerunner, NC5	ml/l	double precision	6.596	8.093
CMOP	Baseline Feb 2013 1, Forerunner, RM10	ml/l	double precision	7.389	8.688
CMOP	Baseline Feb 2013 1, Forerunner, RM12	ml/l	double precision	7.676	8.918
CMOP	Baseline Feb 2013 1, Forerunner, RM14	ml/l	double precision	8.023	16.140
CMOP	Baseline Feb 2013 1, Forerunner, RM16	ml/l	double precision	8.742	9.037
CMOP	Baseline Feb 2013 1, Forerunner, RM18	ml/l	double precision	9.107	9.197
CMOP	Baseline Feb 2013 1, Forerunner, saturn01_profile	ml/l	double precision	7.047	9.258
CMOP	Baseline Feb 2013 1, Forerunner, saturn01_profile_2	ml/l	double precision	-102.914	10.278
CMOP	Baseline Feb 2013 1, Forerunner, saturn03	ml/l	double precision	7.478	8.485

	Context	Units	Datatype	Minimum	Maximum	Instances	Observations	Concept
+	CMOP	V	double precision	0.00000e+0	5	1,216	20,207,414	oxygen
+	OrCOOS	ml/l	double precision	1.237	7.247	17	6,984	oxygen
+	WDoE	ml/l	double precision	-0.086	9.943	79	458,337	oxygen

Figure 4. Variable summary page for "oxygen"

This example illustrates another feature the demo user may choose to explore: the "dataset" shown in Figure 3 is, in fact, a segment (in this case, one day's observations) of a larger dataset (with several weeks' observations). She can navigate to a superset of this data via links ("Click here for this dataset's parent"), and to subsets of data (shorter segments) via links under "Additional information". In this way, she can directly browse the metadata catalog and identify the most relevant subset of data, without directly using the search engine. User feedback tells us that this information and the subsets exposed allow the scientists to quickly and efficiently identifying the most relevant subset of data to analyze. The user can explore the different segments of datasets found during her searches.

4.3 Environmental Variable Summary

A demonstration user can explore what data exists in the archive for a particular environmental variable, to enable him to better formulate his searches. Figure 4 shows the Variable Summary page for the variable Oxygen, which supports this exploration by summarizing the data that the search engine has indexed for this variable. The user accesses this page (after selecting the desired variable in the search interface) via the small "?" link beside the variable search box. The page presents a table showing the variety of ways that oxygen is captured, such as the different units, the number of observations and the range of values measured for the variable in each unit. He can further explore some examples of datasets containing data in those units; these links are exposed by expanding a row in the table (in the figure, we show an expansion of the main table's third row). The "Collection" column gives a short dataset description and a link to the Dataset Details page for that dataset – from which the scientist can download, visualize or otherwise further explore the data.

5. SUMMARIZING DATA BY ITS BOUNDS

If datasets were as small as documents, it might be possible to evaluate search similarity over the complete contents of each. However, given the size of datasets such as in our example archive (some of which run to millions of observations), full-content search is infeasible at interactive speeds. Thus, we search against feature summaries, and our similarity function implicitly assumes uniform distribution of data within the summary bounds. One concern is how much such summarization might distort search results.

During interactive search, the search engine uses a similarity function to estimate the similarity between the given set of search terms and each dataset summary [14]. The result is a list of dataset summaries, ranked by similarity [14, 15]. Where the search contains multiple search terms, a similarity score is calculated for each search term separately, and the per-term scores are averaged into a final score. The per-term similarity function treats the bounds of a data field as a lightweight summary of the contained data distribution. The per-term similarity function we use is a range-based distance function, where the measure is also scaled by the range of the search term, and overlapping ranges of the search term and data bounds decrease the estimated distance; the distance function is not symmetric.

Conceptually, using the bounds as a summary of a dataset assumes that the data varies uniformly between those bounds. A potential concern with this assumption is whether it significantly distorts the resulting ranked list. That is, can the position of an item in the list, when using the bounds to score it, differ greatly from the placement it would receive had the score been calculated directly from the underlying data? With complete data, each point would be evaluated individually against the search terms, and the results aggregated over the dataset.

To test the validity of the assumption, we compared the scores calculated from a dataset summary and scores calculated from scoring that considered all observations in the dataset (and runs much more slowly). We separately tested search terms of each type (geospatial, temporal, and environmental variable), using user-generated searches from a prior study [15]. We applied our measure point-wise to the dataset contents to the 2,999 datasets that were assessed in that study. We show the results for three of these search types in Figure 5: in each case we graph the score calculated from the point-wise calculation (on the vertical axis) against the score calculated from the dataset summary (on the horizontal axis). The scores for temporal search terms shown in Figure 5a, for geospatial search terms in Figure 5b, and for variables search terms in Figure 5c. (The results for depth search terms have a similar strong correlation. Finally, we combined the scores from the individual search terms for each search, and show the results in Figure 5d. The strong orientation of the results around the diagonal axis shows that in most cases, the results from the two calculations are similar.

We evaluated the correspondence between the two applications of the measure by computing the coefficient of determination for each type of term, and also for the combined scores. These results are reported in Table 1. With correlation coefficients of close to 1.0 for each type of search term tested, we conclude that the uniformity assumption is reasonably valid for this archive's data, and would provide a similar ranking. We further conclude that the simple approximation of using a column's bounds to quickly estimate a dataset distance is reasonable.

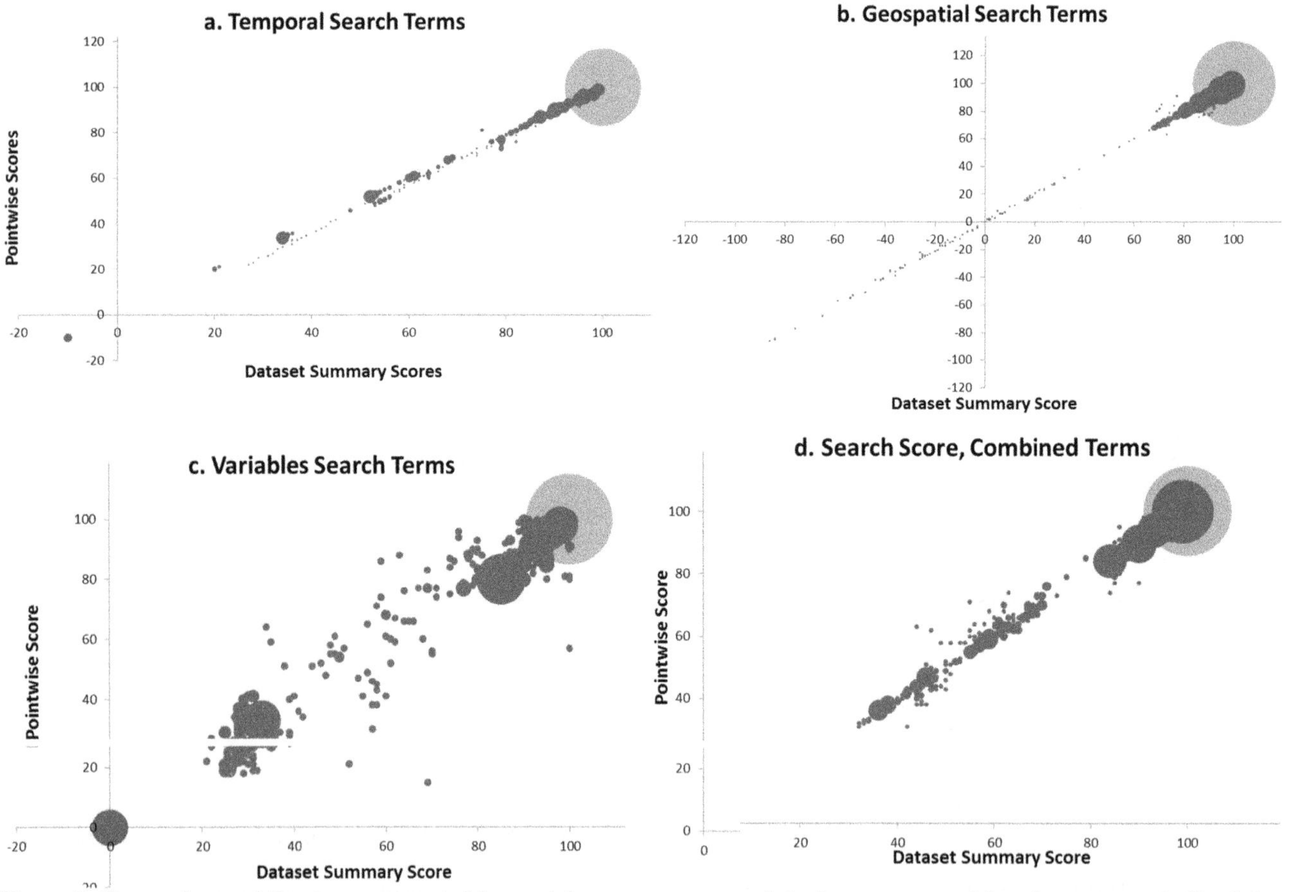

Figure 5. Comparisons of the scores generated by applying our measure point-wise, versus applying the measure to the dataset summary. Multiple scores at a single point are represented by bubbles, with the area of the bubble representing the number of scores with the same values. The bubble at (100,100), representing "complete matches" in both scoring approaches, is colored in grey and placed behind the other bubbles due to its size, in order to show the structure for other high-scoring values.

TABLE 1. COEFFICIENT OF DETERMINATION FOR COMPARISON OF POINT-WISE SCORING VERSUS DATASET SUMMARY SCORING

Search Term Type	r-squared
Temporal	0.998
Geospatial	0.996
Variables	0.961
Depth	0.872
Combined	0.991

Our results are clearly dependent on the nature of the data in this data archive; however, we expect many observational data collections to exhibit similar characteristics. CMOP's archive contains observations of natural phenomena of riverine, coastal and oceanographic processes and microbiology, and related context of atmospheric processes. We generally expect observations in a dataset to be evenly distributed along the temporal dimension, as the sensors aim to collect data continuously. However, there can be gaps due to instrument malfunction, data removed during quality control, and instrument relocation, which affect temporal uniformity. Geospatially, many of the datasets are either from a stationary device (in which case the result will be the same from both methods), or from a track from a mobile device. For mobile devices, the similarity measure is based on the closest and farthest points of a simplified line representing the locations of the observations [14], so it is less obvious that the scores would be close for these datasets. The environmental variables themselves generally shift relatively slowly, within some kind of limits or in a pattern. The scatterplot for environmental variables shows more variance under the two calculations. A number of the items furthest from the diagonal axis result from differences in applying the measure when the search term and dataset both had several instances of the same variable, but in different units.

6. CONCLUSION

This demonstration presents Data Near Here, a web-search-inspired search engine for scientific data archives with interactive response times. Unlike portals aimed at providing easier access to data or systems for data visualization, DNH addresses the problem scientists have in initially locating and identifying data they wish to access or visualize. The demo focuses on the system's interactive search component, and showcases the advantages of ranked dataset search over Boolean methods. The user will experience the ease of interacting with data that this approach enables, and the resulting heightened understanding of the available data in the archive. These characteristics translate to heightened productivity for scientists and value extracted from the archives and data collection efforts.

7. ACKNOWLEDGMENTS

This work is supported by NSF award OCE-0424602. We thank the staff of CMOP and OHSU for their support.

8. REFERENCES

[1] Agrawal, R. and Srikant, R. 2003. Searching with numbers. *IEEE TKDE* 15, 4 (Aug. 2003), 855 – 870.

[2] Batcheller, J.K. 2008. Automating geospatial metadata generation – An integrated data management and documentation approach. *Computers & Geosciences*. 34, 4 (2008), 387–398.

[3] Cafarella, M.J. et al. 2008. Webtables: exploring the power of tables on the web. *Proc. of VLDB*. 1, 1 (2008), 538–549.

[4] Cornillon, P. et al. 2003. OPeNDAP: Accessing data in a distributed, heterogeneous environment. *Data Science Journal*. 2, 0 (2003), 164–174.

[5] D'Ulizia, A. et al. 2009. Approximating geographical queries. *Journal of Computer Science and Technology*. 24, 6 (2009), 1109–1124.

[6] Geospatial One Stop (GOS): *http://gos2.geodata.gov/wps/portal/gos*. Accessed: 2011-01-19.

[7] Goodchild, M.F. and Zhou, J. 2003. Finding geographic information: Collection-level metadata. *GeoInformatica*. 7, 2 (2003), 95–112.

[8] Gray, J. et al. 2005. Scientific data management in the coming decade. *ACM SIGMOD Recd*. 34, 4 (2005), 34–41.

[9] Grossner, K.E. et al. 2008. Defining a digital earth system. *Transactions in GIS*. 12, 1 (2008), 145–160.

[10] Hey, T. and Trefethen, A. 2003. E-Science and its implications. *Philosophical Transactions of the Royal Society of London. Series A: Mathematical, Physical and Engineering Sciences*. 361, 1809 (2003), 1809.

[11] Lord, P. and Macdonald, A. 2003. E-Science curation report: Data curation for e-Science in the UK: an audit to establish requirements for future curation and provision.

[12] Maier, D. et al. 2014. Challenges for Dataset Search (keynote). (2014), 1–15.

[13] Maier, D. et al. 2012. Navigating oceans of data. *Scientific and Statistical Database Management* (2012), 1–19.

[14] Megler, V.M. 2014. *Ranked Similarity Search of Scientific Datasets: An Information Retrieval Approach (PhD Dissertation)*. Portland State University.

[15] Megler, V.M. and Maier, D. 2015. Are Datasets Like Documents?: Evaluating Similarity-Based Ranked Search Over Scientific Data. *IEEE Transactions on Knowledge and Data Engineering*. 27, 1 (Jan. 2015), 32–45.

[16] Megler, V.M. and Maier, D. 2013. Data Near Here: Bringing relevant data closer to scientists. *Computing in Science and Engineering*. 15, 3 (2013), 44–53.

[17] Megler, V.M. and Maier, D. 2011. Finding haystacks with needles: Ranked search for data using geospatial and temporal characteristics. *Scientific and Statistical Database Management* (2011), 55–72.

[18] Megler, V.M. and Maier, D. 2013. Taming the metadata mess. *2013 IEEE 29th International Conference on Data Engineering Workshops (ICDEW)* (2013), 286–289.

[19] Pallickara, S.L. et al. 2010. Efficient metadata generation to enable interactive data discovery over large-scale scientific data collections. *2nd IEEE Intnl. Conf. on Cloud Computing, Technology and Science* (2010), 573–580.

[20] Perlman, E. et al. 2007. Data exploration of turbulence simulations using a database cluster. *Proceedings of the ACM/IEEE Conference on Supercomputing* (2007), 1–11.

[21] Rajasekar, A. and Moore, R. 2010. Data and metadata collections for scientific applications. *High-Performance Computing and Networking* (2010), 72–80.

[22] Stolte, E. and Alonso, G. 2002. Efficient exploration of large scientific databases. *Proc. of VLDB* (2002), 633.

[23] Venetis, P. et al. 2011. Recovering semantics of tables on the web. *Proceedings of VLDB*. 4, 9 (2011), 528–538.

[24] Weidman, S. and Arrison, T. 2009. *Steps toward large-scale data integration in the sciences: Summary of a workshop*. Natnl. Res. Council of the National Academies.

[25] Zheng, C. Personal Communication, September 26, 2014.

Slider: an Efficient Incremental Reasoner

Jules Chevalier, Julien Subercaze, Christophe Gravier, Frédérique Laforest
Université de Lyon, F-42023, Saint-Etienne, France,
CNRS, UMR5516, Laboratoire Hubert Curien, F-42000, Saint-Etienne, France,
Université de Saint-Etienne, Jean Monnet, F-42000, Saint-Etienne, France.
firstname.name@univ-st-etienne.fr

ABSTRACT

The Semantic Web has gained substantial momentum over the last decade. It contributes to the manifestation of knowledge from data, and leverages implicit knowledge through reasoning algorithms. The main drawbacks of current reasoning methods over ontologies are two-fold: first they struggle to provide scalability for large datasets, and second, the batch processing reasoners who provide the best scalability so far are unable to infer knowledge from evolving data. We contribute to solving these problems by introducing Slider, an efficient incremental reasoner. Slider goes a significant step beyond existing system, including i) performance, by more than a 70% improvement in average compared to the fastest reasoner available to the best of our knowledge, and ii) inferences on streams of semantic data, by using intrinsic features that are themselves streams-oriented. Slider is fragment agnostic and conceived to handle expanding data with a growing background knowledge base. It natively supports ρdf and RDFS, and its architecture allows to extend it to more complex fragments with a minimal effort. In this demo a web-based interface allows the users to visualize the internal behaviour of Slider during the inference, to better understand its design and principles.

Keywords

Incremental Reasoning; Streamed Reasoning; Web of Data

1. INTRODUCTION

Data available on the Web can be represented through diverse range of formats. The Semantic Web movement enriches the available information by providing a stack of technologies – the core of which is the Resource Description Framework (RDF) for publishing data in machine-readable format. RDF data is represented as a set of triples of the form $<subject, predicate, object>$. Apart from the explicit data mapping, the integration of assertional data (i.e., instance data) with terminological data (i.e., structural data) described in ontologies permits deductive reasoning – i.e., inferring implicit knowledge. Although, various reasoning techniques has been described in literature but most popular of them is the rule-based reasoning – where each rule consist of i) an 'antecedent': a clause that allows the rule to be executed and ii) a 'consequent': the statements that can be inferred from the data that matched the antecedent clause. For instance,
`If` $<X, subClassOf, Y>$ `and` $<Y, subClassOf, Z>$
`Then` $<X, subClassOf, Z>$.
Reasoning can be described using a subsets of RDFS [5] and OWL standards [14] – also described as fragments. These fragments are set of rules with time complexity ranging from P to NEXTPTIME, and even undecideable for OWL2 Full [20].

Reasoning is inherently a complex process, and while there exists a large body of work in the area of reasoning algorithms and systems that work and scale well in confined environment [10, 19]; the distributed and dynamic nature of Web create new challenges for reasoning. This calls for new techniques to replace batch processing – where the arrival of new data initiate the reasoning process form the start – to incremental reasoning [2]. Thus to handle new data as soon as it arrive, without re-inferring the previously inferred knowledge.

The two main approaches for reasoning as discussed in literature includes, backward-chaining and forward-chaining. The first approach only uses the rules defined in the query to reason incoming triples at query time, while the second approach implements the materialisation process on the entire triple store. Both of these techniques have their pros and cons, in particular – backward-chaining suffers from more complex query evaluation that adversely affects performance and scalability but is suitable for more frequently changing knowledge bases, while forward-chaining enables scalability and very efficient responses at query time, but at the cost of an expensive up front closure computation. We choose forward-chaining (materialisation) to avoid high query response times and high resource usage that incurs in query-rewriting for backward-chaining – in order to conform to the dynamic and real-time nature of Web data.

Several solutions have been proposed to optimise incremental materialisation of ontologies. [8] proposed technique maintains classification of ontologies as they evolve, and provides encouraging results. However, its not a viable solution in case of static hierarchy of ontologies- i.e., if hierarchy is not affected by modification. Moreover, it is not adapted for ontologies with a high number of nominal. [12] handles both

SIGMOD'15, May 31–June 4, 2015, Melbourne, Victoria, Australia.

http://dx.doi.org/10.1145/2723372.2735363.

addition and deletion in the setting of incremental classification. It is however limited to the classification on the TBox, and dedicated to a specific ruleset.

The major drawbacks that state-of-the art approaches suffer from is the inability to deal with complex ontologies and are not tailored to deal with large amount of dynamic RDF data and particularly large A-Boxes.

To overcome these drawbacks, we introduce Slider, an efficient reasoner to perform forward-chaining incremental reasoning and strikes a balance between large pre-processing cost of materialization and complexity of pure backward-chaining reasoning. Its core features that stands it apart from the previous approaches are as following.

Parallel and Scalable Execution: We implement a parallel and scalable method to perform incremental reasoning. Each inference rule is mapped to an independent module. These modules receive indented triples according to defined rules and later distribute triples to other modules for further processing. Additionally, we refine our algorithm to avoid bottlenecks and capitalise on scalability by allowing multiple instances of same rule to run in parallel – in order to further enhance the performance of the reasoner. Moreover, we implement efficient techniques for synchronized access of triple store and use buffers (blocking queues) to handle the explosion of inferred statements and incoming triples. This avoids any overheads and certifies the completeness of the reasoning process.

Duplicates Limitation: Reasoning on equivalent statements could result in a massive amount of duplicated data that causes decrease in performance. Thus, to avoid such situation we use the vertical partitioning approach along-with multiple indexing (on predicates, subjects and objects) technique. This limits the production of duplicates and avoids any unnecessary computation.

Data Stream Support: The dynamic nature of Web data results in data streams [9], which requires incremental execution of reasoning process. Due to the parallel nature of our architecture, Slider can handle both dynamic triple streams and static triples set. This, further allows the parallelisation of parsing and reasoning process on multiple data sources at the same time – processing data as soon as it is published.

Fragment's Customization: Reasoning is usually considered as once-off rule processing task, where rules are known a-priori. However, the dynamicity of data requires to migrate from task-specific systems. Slider natively supports both RDF and ρdf [16] fragments, and its architecture allows it to be further extended to any other fragments.

Slider outperforms existing implementations by 70% on average. We use OWLIM-SE (used in industry and the fastest available reasoner to the best of our knowledge) as a baseline system for comparative measurements. Our experimental evaluations prove that Slider outperforms OWLIM-SE by 106.86% on ρdf and 36.08% on RDFS. The source code of Slider is publicly available here: `https://github.com/juleschevalier/slider`.

Our demo system presents the reasoning process of Slider through a web-based interface and covers three main areas: i) Tuning reasoning process through various parameters including buffer size, buffer timeouts and rulesets. ii) Visualisation of each module behaviour and inputs. iii) Visualisation of synthetic inferred data and retrieval of original ontology.

2. SYSTEM ARCHITECTURE

In this section, we provide an overall description of the architecture of Slider. Our decentralised system consists of a set of autonomous modules – where each rule is mapped on a distinct module. A single triple store is shared by various concurrent modules in a synchronised manner and to ensure fast data access, triples are stored in memory.

Figure 1 shows the high-level architecture of the system with three inference rules R_1, R_2 and R_3. Incoming triples are send to both triple store and buffer of certain module – where each module accepts the triples according to configured rules' predicates. Once the buffer exceeds the configured size or timeouts, it initiates a new instance of a module that applies rules on buffered triples and relevant triples stored in the triple store. These newly created instances are managed by the thread pool for load distribution and scalability of the system. The distributor collects the resulted inferred data to be used as an input, and identifies the modules that would require the resulted data for their inference process – thus ensuring the completeness. For instance, the result of R_1 is used by R_2, R_3 and R_1 itself. Distributors and buffers play an important role in the architecture, specifically buffer orchestrates the load distribution of triples and instance creation of rule modules – as new instance for each triple can exhaust CPU resources. The core functionality of the system's components is as following.

Input Manager: It receives new triples and register them into a dictionary that maps the expensive URIs (as they introduce overheads during comparison computation) to `Longs`. Mapped triples are finally pushed into the triple store. Multiple instances of input manager allows to retrieve data from various sources.

Buffers: Each rule module is assigned with a buffer that is in-charge of collecting triples from input manager – by comparing the predicate values of configured rules. Once the buffer is full or in-case of timeouts, it triggers a new instance of rule module that applies rules on buffered triples.

Rule Modules: Rule modules are configured with a set of rules to be executed on incoming triples. It implements the forward-chaining reasoning by employing the input triples and relevant triples from the triple store.

Thread Pool: This component is responsible for: i) Receiving a new instance of rule module and implement pooling techniques for efficient resource usage, ii) Passing the inferred result to distributor. It pools and runs each instance of rule module on available resource for load balancing and allows asynchronous execution of instances to avoid overheads. Thus, ensuring the scalability of the system.

Distributors: It involves in three main tasks: i) Collecting inferred triples from rule modules ii) Adding inferred triples to triple store iii) Dispatching relevant inferred triples to relevant set of rules. Each distributor has a list of buffers that should receive newly inferred triples. This list is dynamically generated during reasoner initialisation by employing a rules dependency graph, as discussed later.

2.1 Rules Inference

The forward-chaining incremental reasoning is reported in pseudocode in Algorithm 1. It specifies how a rule, e.g. `CAX-SCO` (table 7 from [15]), effectively runs.

The algorithm searches for $<c_1$,`subClassOf`, $c_2>$ in the triple store and for $<x$,`type`, $c_1>$ from incoming triples, and vice versa. For each couple (<c_1 ,**subClassOf**, c_2>, <x ,**type**, c_1>) found, it creates a new one <x ,**type**, c_2>.

Slider implements the rules from both ρdf and RDFS fragments and also support the addition of any new custom rules through Java interfaces.

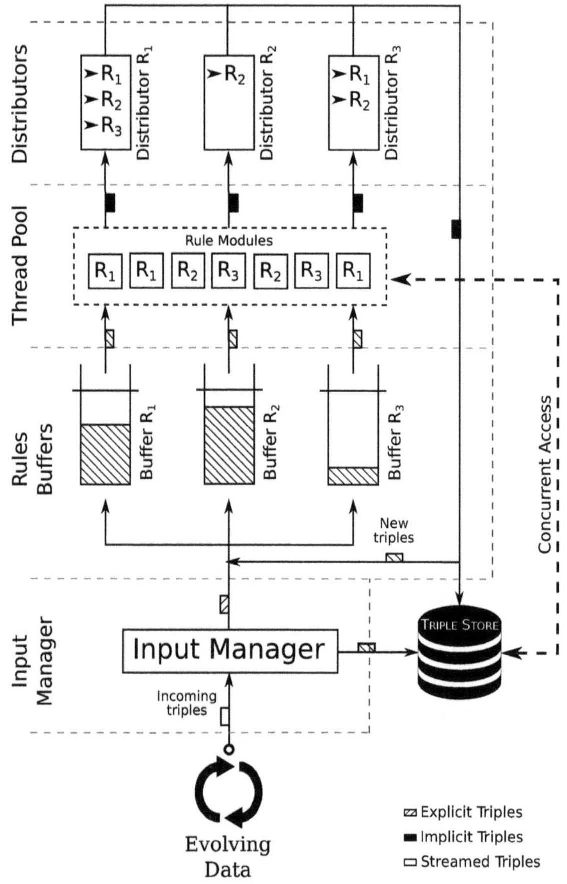

Figure 1: Global architecture of Slider

Algorithm 1 cax-sco

Require: tripleStore, newTriples, outputTriples

for all triple1 **in** TripleStore with predicate `subClassOf` **do**
  for all triple2 **in** `newTriples` with predicate `type` **do**
    if triple1.subject = triple2.object **then**
      output ← (triple2.subject,`type`,triple1.object)
      outputTriples ← outputTriples ∪ {output}
    end if
  end for
end for

for all triple1 **in** `newTriples` with predicate `subClassOf` **do**
  for all triple2 **in** TripleStore with predicate `type` **do**
    if triple1.subject = triple2.object **then**
      output ← (triple2.subject,`type`,triple1.object)
      outputTriples ← outputTriples ∪ {output}
    end if
  end for
end for

2.2 Triple Store

Triple store is another core component of the reasoning process – as good performance of the system relies on its ability to quickly retrieve a given pattern. In order to achieve high performance Slider uses a vertical partitioning approach as discussed in [1] – where triples are first indexed by predicates, later by subjects and finally by objects. We use **HashMaps** of **MulitMaps** from Guava library[1] to implement triples' indexing. The concurrency of the triple store is handled by using **ReentrantReadWriteLock**, which provides both read and write (during addition of new triples) locks. This two-layered locking mechanism not only ensures concurrency, but also allows parallel access to the triple store. The **HashMap** structure of indexing scheme ensures the duplicate management in triple store. Distributors in-charge of dispatching new triples to the buffers use this feature to exclude duplicates. Furthermore, after adding inferred triples in the triple store only distinct triples are send to the buffers.

If we consider the entire ruleset for OWL [15] (especially tables 4–8 and 9), all the associated rules processing require either to walk the entire set of triples (example **eq-ref** from Table 4 in [15]); or to access the triples by predicate first (example: **eq-sym** from the same table). For this reason, triples are firstly indexed by predicate, then by subject and finally by object. This provides the best trade-off for near-optimal indexing for nearly all rules even in the most expressive OWL fragment.

2.3 Rules Dependency Graph

During the initialization process, Slider creates a list of dependent buffers for each rule – that is later utilise by the distributor to send the inferred triples to the corresponding buffers. To implement such functionality, Slider builds a *rules dependency graph.* It is a a directed graph, where edges represent the links (dependency) between the rules (vertices). For instance, if there is a directed edge between rule A and B then the output of rule A can be used by rule B. Figure 2 depicts the dependency graph for ρdf fragment. The rules (**PRP-SPO**, **PRP-RNG**, **PRP-DOM**) with universal input accept all kinds of triples. As according to the Figure 2, the directed edge from rule **SCM-SCO** to **CAX-SCO** depicts that output of first rule, a **subclassOf** relation can be used as an input for second rule. This dependency graph is used to create a list of dependency buffers for each distributor.

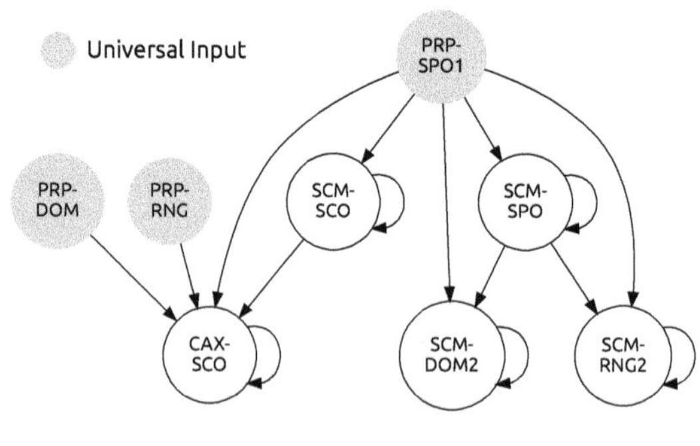

Figure 2: Rules dependency graph for ρdf

[1]https://github.com/google/guava

3. EXPERIMENTATIONS

In this section we describe the experimental details and comparison analysis of Slider with OWLIM-SE.

OWLIM-SE (Standard Edition) [3] is a semantic repository with reasoning features. It was setup to use the default ρdf and RDFS rulesets along-with the custom rule configuration available in OWLIM-SE for ρdf. Therefore, we use the same ruleset for inference process and it is strictly the same. As OWLIM-SE does not allows to separately compute the parsing and inference time, thus in our experiments, for both systems, the running times include both parsing and inferencing times.

Our experimental settings use a set of 13 ontologies divided in three categories. The first one contains generated ontologies, where we use Berlin SPARQL Benchmark (BSBM) [4] to generate five ontologies from 100,000 to 5 million triples. These ontologies shows Slider ability to handle high rates of data by producing smaller set of inferred triples during reasoning process.

The second category of ontologies only contains `subClassOf` relations, where Equation 1 details how a `subClassOf`n ontology is generated.

$$\begin{array}{ll} < 1, type, Class > & \\ < i, type, Class > & i \in \{2, 3, \ldots, n\} \\ < i, subClassOf, (i-1) > & \end{array} \qquad (1)$$

These ontologies are easy to generate but provide the utmost practical interest due to their complexity. The chain of n rules produce $O(n^2)$ unique triples, however commonly used iterative rules schemes produce $O(n^3)$ triples [19]. These ontologies are used to test and compare the Slider ability to handle duplicates.

The last category of ontologies contains the real-world ontologies: a Wikipedia based ontology, and the other based on WordNet [18].

These ontologies are representative of synthetic data (issued from BSBM benchmark generator tool), extensive closure computation[11] (chained subsomptions), and ontologies of practical interest (Wordnet and Wikipedia). This dataset contains more ontologies and of higher diversity than previous studies in the field [13, 17], and is publicly available on the Web using the link provided in this demo.

We ran our benchmark on on a standalone machine under Linux Ubuntu 12.04, with an AMD processor with 4 1.4GHz cores, and 16GB RAM.

Table 1 enumerates the ontologies, with the results of the benchmark. Figure 3 shows the comparison of inference time between OWLIM-SE and Slider, for both ρdf and RDFS. The results on `BSBM_5M` ontology have been omitted in Figure 3 for the sake of clarity.

These experiments show that Slider on average is 71.47% faster than OWLIM-SE, with a throughput up to 36,000 Triples/sec. It exhibits an interesting speed-up of 106.86% for ρdf and 36.08% for RDFS.

We believe that the outcome of our evaluation is very significant: Slider outperforms OWLIM-SE, a commercial product that itself outperforms Jena [7] and Sesame [6] native reasoners.

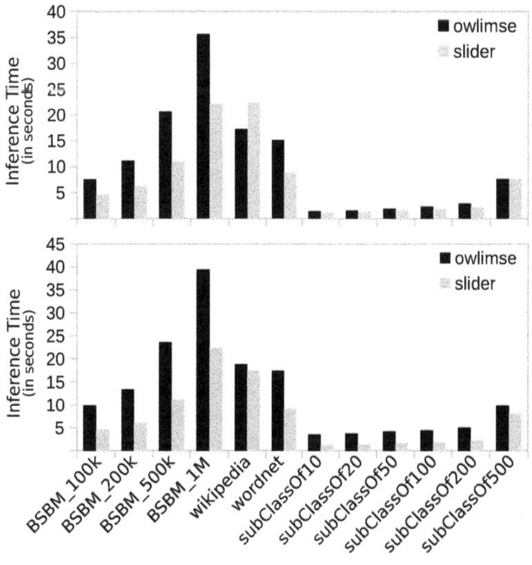

Figure 3: Inference time comparison between Slider and OWLIM-SE, on ρdf and RDFS(Lower is better)

		ρdf reasoning				RDFS reasoning			
Ontology	**Input**	**Inferred**	**OWLIM**	**Slider**	**Gain**	**Inferred**	**OWLIM**	**Slider**	**Gain**
BSBM_100k	99914	544	9.907s	**4.636s**	113.69%	33752	7.487s	**4.558s**	64.25%
BSBM_200k	200007	1102	13.338s	**6.059s**	120.12%	64492	11.064s	**6.198s**	78.52%
BSBM_500k	500037	4347	23.595s	**11.133s**	111.93%	157831	20.580s	**10.984s**	87.36%
BSBM_1M	1000000	8664	39.364s	**22.357s**	76.07%	304065	35.602s	**22.192s**	60.43%
BSBM_5M	5000000	43212	170.151s	**126.292s**	34.73%	1449107	160.699s	**127.037s**	26.50%
wikipedia	458369	191574	18.802s	**17.422s**	7.92%	555653	**17.186s**	22.443s	-23.42%
wordnet	473589	0	-	-	-	321888	15.075s	**8.828**s	70.77%
subClassOf10	20	36	3.507s	**1.209s**	190.05%	50	1.423s	**1.216s**	16.99%
subClassOf20	40	171	3.730s	**1.316s**	183.41%	195	1.536s	**1.330s**	15.53%
subClassOf50	100	1176	4.159s	**1.615s**	157.49%	1230	1.865s	**1.583s**	17.78%
subClassOf100	200	4851	4.397s	**1.827s**	140.60%	4955	2.242s	**1.805s**	24.21%
subClassOf200	400	19701	4.962s	**2.210s**	124.56%	19905	2.837s	**2.170s**	30.69%
subClassOf500	1000	124251	9.862s	**8.102s**	21.72%	124755	**7.584s**	7.625s	-0.54%
				Average	**106.86%**			Average	**36.08%**

Table 1: Benchmark results for Slider and OWLIM-SE inference on ρdf and RDFS

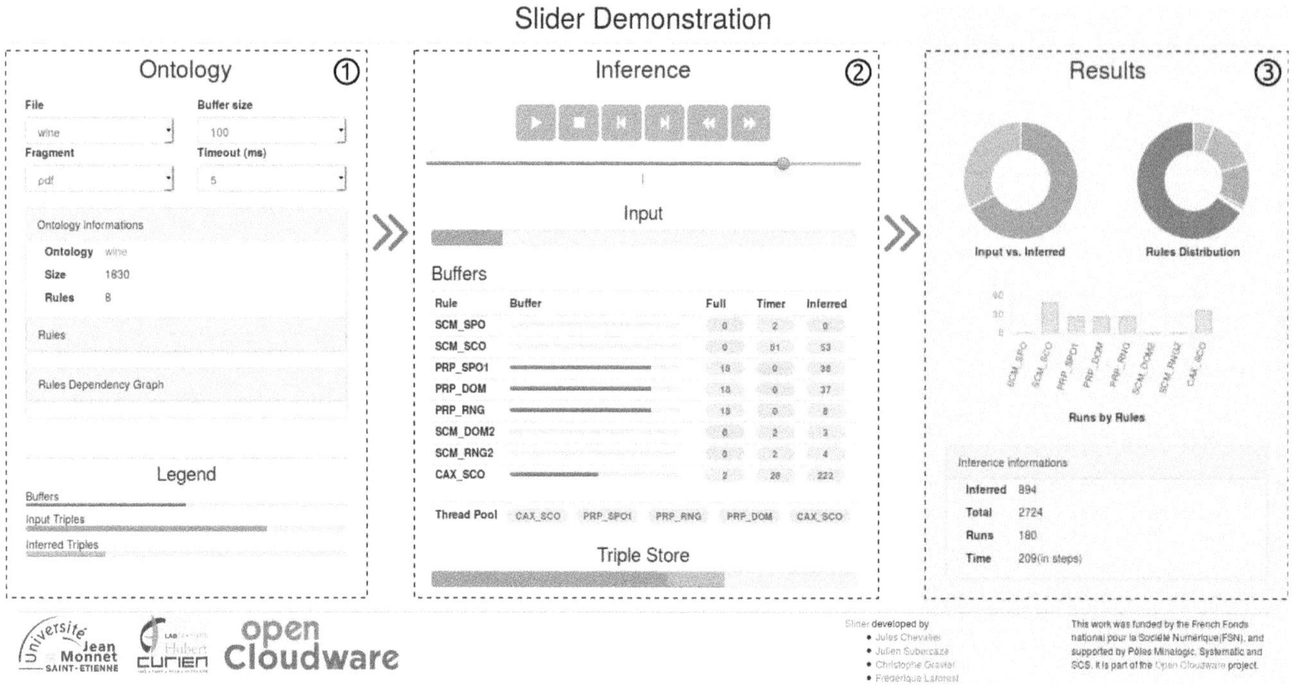

Figure 4: Demonstration Web Interface

4. DEMONSTRATION

The demonstration will allow attendees to visualize the internal behaviour of Slider during the inference. A comprehensive web GUI will enable users to edit Slider's parameters, to choose from a set of 11 ontologies, to interact with the inference process and to experience how the system actually performs. It allows the user to edit 24 configurations of the reasoner, and implement 264 different scenarios. For each one, we ran the reasoner and logged the state of all the modules of Slider at each step of the process. This allows the user, through an *inference player*, to pause the inference, to go backwards, and to replay any part of the inference. All the information on the inference process is presented to the users, and to provide them with the opportunity to appreciate the effect of each parameter.

Figure 4 is a screenshot of the demonstration. It is fully accessible at this link:
`http://demo-satin.telecom-st-etienne.fr/slider/`

The interface of the demonstration is composed of three sections, corresponding to the three following steps of the demonstration.

① **Setup**: To begin, the users can tune the parameters of the reasoner. They can choose the ontology among the 11 available ones. Then three additional parameters can be adjusted. The fragment (ρdf or RDFS), which defines the set of rules applied during the inference; the size of the buffers, which determines how many triples are needed to fire a new rule execution; and the timeout, which defines after how long a inactive buffer is forced to flush and throw a rule execution. The table *Informations*, located on the right of the panel, summarizes essential informations about the ontology. The ontologies can be downloaded following the links provided in this table. The definition of each rule of the chosen fragment is available on the bottom of the panel ①. The rules dependency graph follows this.

② **Run**: Once the configuration of the parameters is finished, users will be able to lunch the inference process. They will observe the internal modules behaviour during the reasoning process. The state of the input parsed, as well as the buffers and the triple store, are represented by progress bars. The input is progressively emptied, while the triples go through the buffers. For each buffer, three counters represent: i) the number of times it has been full (and so a new thread has been created), ii) the number of times the buffer has been forced to flush because of the timeout and iii) the amount of triples the rule associated to the buffer has inferred. Under the buffers, the thread pool is represented by the last five executed rules. Finally, on the bottom of the panel, the triple store is represented with a two-coloured progress bar, the green part representing the input triples, coming from the ontology, while the orange part represents the inferred triples.

To let the user see exactly what happened at every step, the entire process can be played, paused, accelerated and slowed down, played step by step, and a slider bar allow to scroll through each step.

③ **Summarize**: The last panel summarizes the informations about the inference: proportion of triples from the ontology compared with the triples inferred, distribution by rule of the triples inferred, and number of time each rule has run are presented in three charts. Miscellaneous informations on the *quality* of the inference and the impact of the parameters on it are shown in the table below. Number of rules executions, inferred triples, inference time, all these measures, coupled with the animation, help the user to evaluate the impact of the different parameters on the performance and on the behaviour of the reasoner.

5. CONCLUSION AND FUTURE WORK

In the frame of reasoning on evolving data, few proposals enable to continuously infer new knowledge as new explicit triple are sent to the reasoner. Most of the solutions limit the amount of data in the knowledge base by eliminating former triples.

Instead of firing a full inference at regular interval of time, we propose Slider, a reasoner that handles triples flows as the very core of its architecture. The triple store, built with the vertical partitioning, ensures fast triples retrieval and a minimal space occupation. To be fragment agnostic, Slider builds a rules dependency graph of the fragment it reasons over at initialization time. It then uses this information to plug the rules together, creating the route of the triples in the reasoner. This provides a high flexibility in its architecture. This design is strongly original towards traditional reasoning scheme like the famous RETE algorithm.

We evaluate Slider against 3 sets of ontologies : a first set containing generated ontologies, issued by BSBM benchmark tools, a second set specific to the worst-case reasoning on subsumption relationship, and finally real field ontologies. On all kinds of ontologies Slider significantly outperforms OWLIM-SE, an industrial-strength reasoner, by a factor of 71,47%.

For our future endeavours, we would like to focus on two main aspects of Slider. First, we will implement more complex inference rules, in order to implement reasoning over a more complex fragments. Second, we will implement a just-in-time optimisation of the rules execution's scheduling. Therefore, migrating from 'static' plans produced by traditional optimizers to the run-time dynamic plans will improves the Slider ability to adapt and be more reactive – i.e., learning from ontologies structures and previously executed runs.

6. ACKNOWLEDGMENTS

This work is supported by the OpenCloudware project. OpenCloudware is funded by the French FSN (Fond national pour la Socièté Numérique), and is supported by Pôles Minalogic, Systematic and SCS. We would also like to thank Syed Gillani for his careful help in proofreading this paper.

7. REFERENCES

[1] D. J. Abadi, A. Marcus, S. R. Madden, and K. Hollenbach. Scalable Semantic Web Data Management Using Vertical Partitioning. In *PVLDB*, 2007.

[2] D. Barbieri, D. Braga, S. Ceri, E. Valle, and M. Grossniklaus. Incremental Reasoning on Streams and Rich Background Knowledge. In *The Semantic Web: Research and Applications*. 2010.

[3] B. Bishop, A. Kiryakov, D. Ognyanoff, I. Peikov, Z. Tashev, and R. Velkov. OWLIM: A Family of Scalable Semantic Repositories. *Semantic Web*, 2011.

[4] C. Bizer and A. Schultz. The berlin sparql benchmark. *International Journal on Semantic Web and Information Systems*, 2009.

[5] D. Brickley and R. V. Guha. RDF vocabulary description language 1.0: RDF schema. 2004.

[6] J. Broekstra, A. Kampman, and F. van Harmelen. Sesame: A Generic Architecture for Storing and Querying RDF and RDF Schema. In *ISWC*. 2002.

[7] J. J. Carroll, I. Dickinson, C. Dollin, D. Reynolds, A. Seaborne, and K. Wilkinson. Jena: Implementing the Semantic Web Recommendations. In *WWW*, 2004.

[8] B. Cuenca Grau, C. Halaschek-Wiener, and Y. Kazakov. History Matters: Incremental Ontology Reasoning Using Modules. In *The Semantic Web*. 2007.

[9] M. M. Gaber, A. Zaslavsky, and S. Krishnaswamy. Mining data streams: a review. *SIGMOD*, 2005.

[10] J. Hoeksema and S. Kotoulas. High-performance distributed stream reasoning using s4. In *ISWC*, 2011.

[11] H. Jagadish, R. Agrawal, and L. Ness. A study of transitive closure as a recursion mechanism. In *SIGMOD*, 1987.

[12] Y. Kazakov and P. Klinov. Incremental Reasoning in OWL EL without Bookkeeping. In *ISWC*. 2013.

[13] J. Liagouris and M. Terrovitis. Efficient Identification of Implicit Facts in Incomplete OWL2-EL Knowledge Bases. *PVLDB*, 2014.

[14] D. L. McGuinness, F. Van Harmelen, et al. OWL web ontology language overview. *W3C Recommendation*, 2004.

[15] B. Motik, B. C. Grau, I. Horrocks, Z. Wu, A. Fokoue, and C. Lutz. Owl 2 web ontology language: Profiles. `http://www.w3.org/TR/owl2-profiles/`, 2009.

[16] S. Munoz, J. Pérez, and C. Gutierrez. Minimal deductive systems for RDF. In *The Semantic Web: Research and Applications*. 2007.

[17] T. Neumann and G. Weikum. The RDF-3X engine for scalable management of RDF data. *VLDB*.

[18] V. Snasel, P. Moravec, and J. Pokorny. WordNet ontology based model for web retrieval. In *Web Information Retrieval and Integration*, 2005.

[19] J. Urbani, S. Kotoulas, J. Maassen, F. Van Harmelen, and H. Bal. OWL reasoning with WebPIE: calculating the closure of 100 billion triples. In *The Semantic Web: Research and Applications*. 2010.

[20] W3C. OWL 2 Language Primer. `http://www.w3.org/TR/owl2-primer/`, 2012.

WANalytics: Geo-Distributed Analytics for a Data Intensive World

Ashish Vulimiri
UIUC
vulimir1@illinois.edu

Carlo Curino
Microsoft CISL
ccurino@microsoft.com

P. Brighten Godfrey
UIUC
pbg@illinois.edu

Thomas Jungblut
Microsoft
thjungbl@microsoft.com

Konstantinos Karanasos
Microsoft CISL
kokarana@microsoft.com

Jitu Padhye
Microsoft Research
padhye@microsoft.com

George Varghese
Microsoft Research
varghese@microsoft.com

ABSTRACT

Many large organizations collect massive volumes of data each day in a geographically distributed fashion, at data centers around the globe. Despite their geographically diverse origin the data must be processed and analyzed as a whole to extract insight. We call the problem of supporting large-scale geo-distributed analytics *Wide-Area Big Data (WABD)*. To the best of our knowledge, WABD is currently addressed by copying all the data to a central data center where the analytics are run. This approach consumes expensive cross-data center bandwidth and is incompatible with data sovereignty restrictions that are starting to take shape. We instead propose *WANalytics*, a system that solves the WABD problem by orchestrating distributed query execution and adjusting data replication across data centers in order to minimize bandwidth usage, while respecting sovereignty requirements. WANalytics achieves an up to 360× reduction in data transfer cost when compared to the centralized approach on both real Microsoft production workloads and standard synthetic benchmarks, including TPC-CH and Berkeley Big-Data. In this demonstration, attendees will interact with a live geo-scale multi-data center deployment of WANalytics, allowing them to experience the data transfer reduction our system achieves, and to explore how it dynamically adapts execution strategy in response to changes in the workload and environment.

1. INTRODUCTION

Large-scale organizations process massive volumes of data each day. The total volume of data from activities such as logging user interactions and monitoring compute infrastructures can be on the order of 10s or 100s of TBs each day. The data are collected in a geo-distributed fashion across multiple data centers to ensure low latency for end-users, regulatory compliance, and availability. Analyzing all these geographically dispersed data as a whole is necessary to expose valuable insight. We call the problem of supporting analytics on large volumes of geographically distributed data *Wide-Area Big Data* or *WABD*.

WABD is typically addressed today by retrieving all the data to a single data center where the analytics are run. This *centralized approach* is problematic at large scales because it uses a substantial amount of cross-data center bandwidth, which is growing increasingly expensive and scarce [10, 7]. Moreover, this approach may soon be rendered impossible by sovereignty regulations governing data movement.

In previous work we proposed an alternative geo-distributed execution approach which pushes part of the computation to each data center whenever this is beneficial, avoiding moving data between data centers and thus reducing bandwidth costs [17, 16]. Our system, WANalytics, automatically optimizes query execution and data replication strategies to minimize bandwidth cost, while respecting given regulatory and fault-tolerance constraints. It employs several novel techniques, including a *pseudo-distributed execution* mechanism to collect precise measures of data transfer costs (used during query optimization), and aggressive *caching* of intermediate results, which further reduce data transfers. In our experiments, WANalytics achieved a reduction in data transfer costs of up to 360× compared to the centralized baseline both on a Microsoft production workload and several standard synthetic benchmarks.

We have designed two versions of the system: one that focuses exclusively on SQL computation [17], as well as a more general-purpose version that supports arbitrary DAGs of computational tasks [16]. This demonstration will showcase the more mature SQL branch of WANalytics.

During the demonstration, attendees will interact with a live deployment of WANalytics spanning data centers spread across multiple continents. They will be able to submit queries, obtain results, visualize in real-time the data transfer reduction WANalytics achieves over the centralized baseline, and examine how it adapts its execution strategy due to changes in the workload and environment. We will provide pre-defined example workflows that attendees can follow to expose the interesting features of our system. Demo

SIGMOD'15, May 31–June 4, 2015, Melbourne, Victoria, Australia.

ACM 978-1-4503-2758-9/15/05 ...$15.00.
http://dx.doi.org/10.1145/2723372.2735365.

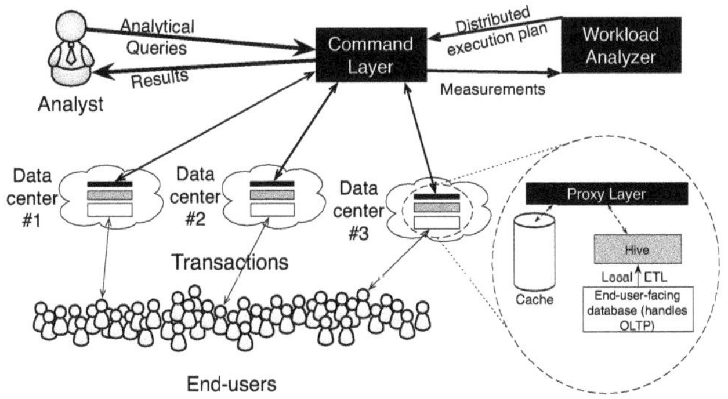

Figure 1: WANalytics architecture

attendees will also be able to write and execute their own arbitrary SQL queries.

We next provide a brief overview of WANalytics' design and capabilities (§2). We then describe the demonstration setup (§3) and provide an overview of related work (§5) before concluding (§5).

2. WANalytics OVERVIEW

Figure 1 shows an overview of WANalytics' architecture.

WANalytics manages data that are partitioned and/or replicated across several data centers. Data are generated externally by end-users processing transactions. WANalytics has no control over which data centers individual tuples are initially logged to — the data partitioning scheme is dictated by external considerations, such as the latency observed by end-users — but may replicate data to other data centers for performance and/or fault-tolerance.

The system presents an abstract, logically-centralized view over the distributed data. Analysts write and submit SQL queries against this logically centralized database. The WANalytics command layer receives queries, partitions them to create a distributed execution plan, and orchestrates distributed execution. At each data center the command layer interacts with a thin proxy layer managing a single-data center analytics stack (Apache Hive in our current implementation). The proxy layer provides support for transferring data between data centers and manages a cache used for the data transfer optimization in §2.3.

A workload analyzer (§2.1) analyzes measurements collected at runtime, potentially using pseudo-distributed execution (§2.2), to identify if changes to the query execution and data replication strategies would reduce data transfer costs. During normal WANalytics execution the workload analyzer would run periodically and occasionally, say once a day, but for the purposes of this demonstration we will reanalyze the workload each time an attendee submits a query.

2.1 Workload Analyzer

WANalytics is targeted towards applications with a slowly evolving core of recurrent queries. This matches our experience with Microsoft production workloads and is consistent with reports on data processing pipelines at other organizations. The workload optimizer jointly optimizes the combination of base data replication strategy, logical execution plan for each query, and the choice of which data center each task in the execution plan for each query is scheduled to run on.

WANalytics makes these decisions using a split, two-level optimization approach, in which (1) some choices, such as join order, are initially locked down by a centralized SQL query planner (a customized version we built of Apache Calcite[1]) using simple column-level statistics, and then (2) the remaining choices, such as distributed execution and data replication, are jointly optimized by an Integer Program formulation, based on measurements collected at runtime during query execution. [17] motivates this choice of architecture, and argues that it is an attractive point in the tradeoff between the complexity of the optimization process and the quality of the solution it generates.

In some cases collecting the measurements needed for phase (2) may require modifying query execution, using a mode we call *pseudo-distributed execution*.

2.2 Pseudo-distributed execution

Consider a single-table database with a workload consisting of one query performing an aggregation on the table. Suppose the system currently operates in a centralized configuration, in which all the data are copied to a single central data center where the aggregation query is then run. Now suppose we wish to evaluate the effect of moving to a distributed deployment in which data are left partitioned across data centers, and the query is executed by obtaining partial aggregation results from each data center which are then combined centrally.

To estimate the cost of distributed execution we would need to know the size of the partially aggregated output that would result at each data center. When the query is run centralized this information is unavailable, since all data are combined during operator execution.

To measure data sizes (and thus determine the most beneficial distributed execution plan), WANalytics instead simulates a virtual data center topology in which each partition is housed in a separate logical data center. This is accomplished by rewriting queries and pushing down `WHERE` clauses to restrict their operation to specific partitions/data centers. Details are discussed in [17]. This approach is both completely general, capable of rewriting arbitrary SQL queries to trace their execution on any given database, and very precise, since it directly measures each data transfer instead of relying on heuristic estimation.

Pseudo-distributed execution can end up slowing down query execution (by up to 20% in our experiments), but it never increases the volume of data transferred between data centers, which is the sole metric we are concerned with.

2.3 Data transfer optimization

Consider a query on a sales-log table, asking for the average number of orders from each country over the past week. Suppose the query is run once every day. Unoptimized WANalytics would recompute the query from scratch each day, but this transfers 7× more data than necessary since only the past day's worth of data would have changed each day.

To reduce data transfers, WANalytics aggressively caches all intermediate results produced during query execution. Before the results for any sub-query are transferred between

[1] http://optiq.incubator.apache.org/

two data centers, the system first checks to see if the sub-query results are cached. If they are, WANalytics only computes and sends the diff between the old and the new results.

Interestingly, caching helps not only when the same query is run repeatedly, but also when two different queries share the same sub-operation. For instance, the TPC-CH benchmark, one of the several synthetic benchmarks we evaluated [17], contains 6 different queries, all computing slightly different aggregates on top of the same data-intensive join, and caching reduces the cumulative data transfer for all these queries by 5.99×.

3. DEMONSTRATION

During the demonstration attendees will interact with a live geo-distributed deployment of WANalytics, with data stored across three data centers in North America, Europe and South-East Asia[2]. Attendees will be able to run SQL queries, visualize the reduction in data transfer costs from using geo-distributed execution, and explore how WANalytics' optimizer can adapt query plans in response to changing conditions.

The demonstration will proceed in two phases. In the first phase we will demonstrate example workflows (sets of queries) that showcase interesting features of our system. In the second phase attendees will be invited to interact with the system directly by writing and evaluating arbitrary SQL queries against the database.

3.1 Setup

The deployment will host a copy of the CH benchmark database [3]. The database will be populated with some initial data; attendees will also be able to have the system simulate OLTP transactions that update the database (increasing its total size) over the course of the demonstration.

Figure 2 shows the user interface that attendees will interact with. The interface provides three options:

- *Reset* the system to its initial state.
- *Update* the database by simulating a specified volume of OLTP transactions.
- *Run SQL queries* analyzing the data.

Whenever a query is submitted, WANalytics first generates an initial query plan using simple column-level histogram statistics. After the query is run once, the system will have collected enough detailed information (§2.2) to be able to produce an updated, optimized query plan, which will be used on subsequent runs of the query[3]. The log at the bottom of the UI provides a visualization of both plans. Note that WANalytics jointly optimizes the plans for all queries in the workload, and thus the optimal plan identified for a given query may change as the workload evolves and expands.

The dashboard on the top-right provides visualizations of both the current, real-time data transfer volumes along each network link, as well as a comparison of cumulative cost over time against the centralized baseline.

[2]We will also provide a simulated 3-data center setup, hosted locally on the demonstration machine, as a fallback in case of e.g. network connectivity problems at the conference site.

[3]Recall (§2) that WANalytics targets applications with a recurrent workload, consisting of queries that arrive repeatedly. Using a potentially sub-optimal plan for the very first run of any query is reasonable in this context.

3.2 Demo phase 1: Example workflows

In the first phase of the demonstration we will run through example workflows to showcase the interesting features of our system. Some candidate examples:

1. Intra-query caching

Consider a query asking for the total sales volume on each day:

```
Q: SELECT date, SUM(sales_price) AS total_sales
   FROM orders
   GROUP BY date
```

The first time Q is run, the system will need to retrieve daily sales volumes over all historical data from each data partition. But subsequent reruns of Q, after OLTP updates logging new orders, will be much less data-intensive — the caching mechanism WANalytics uses (§2.3) will ensure that only the new information since the last run is retrieved.

2. Inter-query caching

Consider the following two queries, run one after the other:

```
Q1: SELECT supplier_country,
           SUM(sales_price) AS total_sales
    FROM orders JOIN suppliers
    USING supplier_no
    GROUP BY supplier_country

Q2: SELECT supplier_category,
           SUM(sales_price) AS total_sales
    FROM orders JOIN suppliers
    USING supplier_no
    GROUP BY supplier_category
```

Both queries compute slightly different projections on top of the same (data-intensive) join. Since WANalytics caches all intermediate results produced during query computation (§2.3), it reduces data transfer volume almost by half by avoiding processing the join from scratch twice.

3. Single-query optimization

Consider the query

```
Q: SELECT customer_name, SUM(order_value)
   FROM customers JOIN orders
   USING customer_id
   WHERE orders.order_date BETWEEN
         '2001-01-01' AND '2001-12-31'
   GROUP BY customer_name
```

asking for historical sales volumes. Since the `customers` table keeps growing over time, as new customers keep being added, only a fairly small fraction of the `customers` table will have any matching entries in the orders table for the specified date range. A semi-join strategy, starting out by shipping out the list of distinct `customer_ids` who placed an order in the date range, turns out to be optimal in this scenario. However, the simple histogram heuristics that WANalytics' initial query planner uses [17] can cause it to overestimate the join cardinality and suggest a hash join instead. However, once statistics are collected after an initial run using this strategy (§2.2), the optimizer would notice and switch to the optimal query plan.

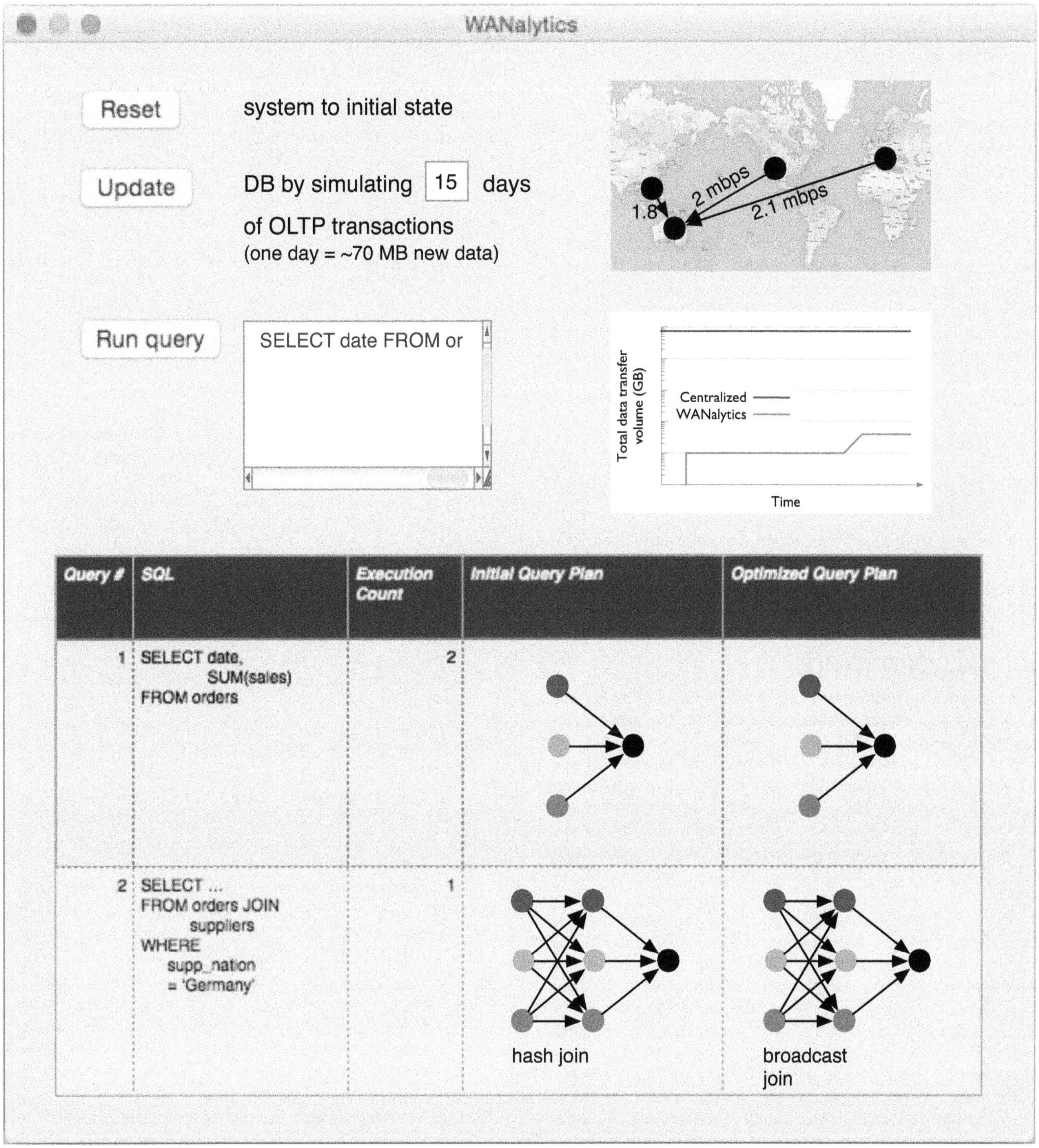

Figure 2: Demonstration GUI

4. Multi-query optimization

Consider the following two queries

```
Q1: SELECT item_id, COUNT(supplier_id)
    FROM stock JOIN suppliers
    USING (item_id)
    WHERE stock.country = 'USA'
    GROUP BY item_id

Q2: SELECT supplier_country, item_id, SUM(sale_price)
    FROM lineitems JOIN suppliers
    USING (supplier_id, item_id)
    GROUP BY supplier_country, item_id
```

The (filtered) `stock` table is much smaller than the `suppliers` table, which is in turn much smaller than the `lineitems` table. If `Q1` is the only query in the workload, WANalytics would process the join in `Q1` by filtering the `stock` table and broadcasting the results to each of the larger `suppliers` table's partitions. But once `Q2` is added to the workload, WANalytics notices that broadcasting the `suppliers` table instead for `Q1` would allow it to take advantange of cross-query caching, as in example 2, and amends the query plan for `Q1` accordingly.

3.3 Demo phase 2: Arbitrary user-provided workflows

In the second phase of the demonstration attendees will be invited to interact directly with the system, and explore how WANalytics processes and optimizes arbitrary SQL workloads they construct.

4. RELATED WORK

We now briefly discuss some directly relevant contributions from past work; we survey related work in greater detail in [16] and [17].

The WABD problem is closely related to literature in distributed and parallel databases [9, 13, 6], but our focus on analytics instead of transactions, the scale of the problem we target, our attention to bandwidth, and our exploration of more general computational models (with workflows of arbitrary tasks [16]) all render our problem significantly different.

Hive [15], Pig [12], Impala [1], Shark [18] and similar scale-out systems support analytics on continuously updated data, but are designed for single-cluster operation. PNUTS/Sherpa [4] does support geographically dispersed data but lays out data to reduce latency and not to minimize analytics cost. Spanner [5] supports OLTP workloads on geo-distributed data. Mesa [8] and Riak [2] replicate data across data centers for fault-tolerance but do not address distributed analytics execution.

Sensor networks [11] share a similar problem of minimizing the use of expensive network bandwidth, but not our massive scale or the breadth of our computational model. Stream-processing databases process long-standing queries on dispersed data, but the focus of work in this area has been on relatively simple computational models. A representative recent example, JetStream [14], targets a limited computational model centered around aggregation queries and does not, for instance, support joins.

5. CONCLUSION

Persistent growth in data volumes and rising interest in sovereignty regulation are rendering the current centralized approaches to geo-scale analytics increasingly untenable. We propose an alternative geo-distributed execution approach that is much better adapted to these requirements. Our system, WANalytics, incorporates several novel techniques inspired by revisiting classical database problems from a networking perspective. This demonstration showcases WANalytics' capabilities by allowing attendees to interactively construct and submit arbitrary SQL workloads on a live geo-scale multi-data center WANalytics deployment.

Acknowledgements

We gratefully acknowledge the support of an Alfred P. Sloan Research Fellowship.

6. REFERENCES

[1] Cloudera Impala. `http://bit.ly/1eRUDeA`.

[2] Greenplum. `http://basho.com/riak/`.

[3] R. Cole et al. The mixed workload CH-benCHmark. In *DBTest '11*, DBTest '11, pages 8:1–8:6, New York, NY, USA, 2011. ACM.

[4] B. F. Cooper, R. Ramakrishnan, U. Srivastava, A. Silberstein, P. Bohannon, H.-A. Jacobsen, N. Puz, D. Weaver, and R. Yerneni. Pnuts: Yahoo!'s hosted data serving platform. *Proc. VLDB Endow.*, 1(2):1277–1288, Aug. 2008.

[5] J. C. Corbett, J. Dean, M. Epstein, A. Fikes, C. Frost, J. Furman, S. Ghemawat, A. Gubarev, C. Heiser, P. Hochschild, W. Hsieh, S. Kanthak, E. Kogan, H. Li, A. Lloyd, S. Melnik, D. Mwaura, D. Nagle, S. Quinlan, R. Rao, L. Rolig, Y. Saito, M. Szymaniak, C. Taylor, R. Wang, and D. Woodford. Spanner: Google's globally-distributed database. In *10th USENIX Symposium on Operating Systems Design and Implementation (OSDI 12)*, pages 261–264, Hollywood, CA, Oct. 2012. USENIX Association.

[6] D. DeWitt and J. Gray. Parallel database systems: The future of high performance database systems. *Communications of the ACM*, 35(6):85–98, June 1992.

[7] A. Greenberg, J. Hamilton, D. A. Maltz, and P. Patel. The cost of a Cloud: Research problems in data center networks. *ACM CCR*, 39(1), 2008.

[8] A. Gupta, F. Yang, J. Govig, A. Kirsch, K. Chan, K. Lai, S. Wu, S. Dhoot, A. Kumar, A. Agiwal, S. Bhansali, M. Hong, J. Cameron, M. Siddiqi, D. Jones, J. Shute, A. Gubarev, S. Venkataraman, and D. Agrawal. Mesa: Geo-replicated, near real-time, scalable data warehousing. In *VLDB*, 2014.

[9] D. Kossmann. The state of the art in distributed query processing. *ACM Computing Surveys*, 32(4):422–469, Dec. 2000.

[10] N. Laoutaris, M. Sirivianos, X. Yang, and P. Rodriguez. Inter-datacenter bulk transfers with Netstitcher. In *SIGCOMM 2011*.

[11] S. Madden. Database abstractions for managing sensor network data. *Proc. of the IEEE*, 98(11):1879–1886, 2010.

[12] C. Olston, B. Reed, U. Srivastava, R. Kumar, and A. Tomkins. Pig Latin: a not-so-foreign language for data processing. In *SIGMOD 2008*.

[13] M. T. Özsu and P. Valduriez. *Principles of distributed database systems*. Springer, 2011.

[14] A. Rabkin, M. Arye, S. Sen, V. S. Pai, and M. J. Freedman. Aggregation and degradation in jetstream: Streaming analytics in the wide area. In *11th USENIX Symposium on Networked Systems Design and Implementation (NSDI 14)*, pages 275–288, Seattle, WA, Apr. 2014. USENIX Association.

[15] A. Thusoo, J. S. Sarma, N. Jain, Z. Shao, P. Chakka, N. Zhang, S. Antony, H. Liu, and R. Murthy. Hive - a petabyte scale data warehouse using hadoop. In *ICDE 2010*.

[16] A. Vulimiri, C. Curino, B. Godfrey, K. Karanasos, and G. Varghese. WANalytics: Analytics for a geo-distributed data-intensive world. *CIDR*, 2015.

[17] A. Vulimiri, C. Curino, B. Godfrey, J. Padhye, and G. Varghese. Global analytics in the face of bandwidth and regulatory constraints. In *12th USENIX Symposium on Networked Systems Design and Implementation (NSDI 15)*, Oakland, CA, May 2015. USENIX Association.

[18] R. S. Xin, J. Rosen, M. Zaharia, M. J. Franklin, S. Shenker, and I. Stoica. Shark: Sql and rich analytics at scale. In *Proceedings of the 2013 ACM SIGMOD International Conference on Management of Data*, SIGMOD '13, pages 13–24, New York, NY, USA, 2013. ACM.

FTT: A System for Finding and Tracking Tourists in Public Transport Services

Huayu Wu
Institute for Infocomm Research
A*STAR, Singapore
huwu@i2r.a-star.edu.sg

Jo-Anne Tan
Institute for Infocomm Research
A*STAR, Singapore
joanne-tan@i2r.a-star.edu.sg

Wee Siong Ng
Institute for Infocomm Research
A*STAR, Singapore
wsng@i2r.a-star.edu.sg

Mingqiang Xue
Institute for Infocomm Research
A*STAR, Singapore
xuem@i2r.a-star.edu.sg

Wei Chen
Institute for Infocomm Research
A*STAR, Singapore
chenwei@i2r.a-star.edu.sg

ABSTRACT

The tourism industry is a key economic driver for many cities. To understand tourists' traveling patterns can help both public and private relevant sectors design and improve their services to serve tourists better and get additional values from it. The existing approaches to discover tourists' traveling pattern focus on small sets of known tourists extracted from social media or other channels. The accuracy of the mining result cannot be guaranteed due to the small and bias set of samples.

In this paper, we present our system FTT (Finding and Tracking Tourists) to identify tourists from public transport commuters in a city, and to further track their movements from one place to another. Our target is a large set of tourists and their trajectories extracted from public transport riding records, which more accurately represent the movements of general tourists. In particular, we design an iterative learning algorithm to f nd the tourists among public transport commuters, and provide interface to answer user queries on tourists' traveling patterns. The result will be visualized on top of a city map.

Categories and Subject Descriptors

K.4.2 [**Computers and Society**]: Social Issues; H.4.0 [**Information Systems Applications**]: General

Keywords

Public transport; tourist f nding; travel pattern; data analytics

1. INTRODUCTION

The tourism industry is a key economic driver for many cities. Take Singapore, a famous tourist city in Southeast Asia as an example. In 2013, Singapore attracted more than 15.6 million foreign visitors, contributing 23.5 billion Singapore dollar (18.8 billion US dollar) tourism receipts [8].

To track the short-term stays of tourists and further understand their moving patterns is rather important for the public and private tourism-related sectors to design and improve their services. For example, if we know there are many tourists traveling from one place to another, the public sectors can introduce additional transport services between the two places during holiday seasons, and the private sectors can offer special tour or ticket packages that include the both places of interest.

Traditionally, tourists' travel information was mainly collected by surveys. In recently years, with the rapid development of ICT, many researchers try to identify tourists' traveling pattern from their GPS data [1] or social media posts [3, 5]. However, there is gap between those research results and their adoption in practice, because the small sample size considered may lead high variance and bias to the real insight. Although most mobile devices are GPS enabled now and many people are active in different online social networks, it is still diff cult for any entity to convince a large group of travelers to positively contribute their location data to help to understand the crowd behaviors of tourists. Also, many tourists, e.g., elder people, may not use GPS or Social network. The analysis result cannot be generalized to the whole population of tourists.

What data are richer to ref ect the travel patterns of general tourists? Our answer is the public transport data. Public transport is the f rst choice for most tourists in the cities with mature public transport systems. To know how tourists take buses or subways to travel around the city, we will surely get insight on the representative traveling patterns of tourists. On the other hand, due to the popularity of electric fare payment systems, in most modern cities public transport traveler's riding records are trackable. This motivates our work on leveraging public transport data to track tourists and understand their moving patterns.

We developed a system, which is named FTT, standing for **F**inding and **T**racking **T**ourists. The FTT system aims to identify tourists from public transport commuters, and then to support user queries to visualize how the tourist crowds travel from one place to another. The core technique for tourist identif cation was reported in our previous paper [9]. The key idea is to iteratively learn the

SIGMOD'15, May 31–June 4, 2015, Melbourne, Victoria, Australia.

http://dx.doi.org/10.1145/2723372.2735367.

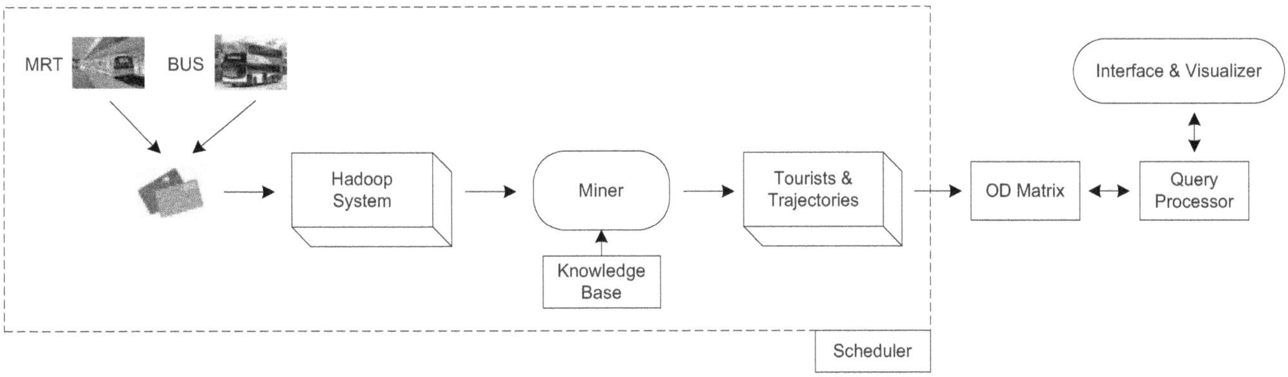

Figure 1: Architecture of the FTT system

quantified contribution of each MRT[1] station for tourist identification and the probability of each traveler to be a tourist, starting with some prior knowledge and a small set labeled data. According to the identified result, we build OD (Origin-Destination) matrices of tourists' public transport riding records, to support interactive location-based queries and visualize query results, which are helpful to understand the traveling behaviors of tourists.

In this demonstration, we first present the architecture of the FTT system. Then we showcase how the system can help to reveal some interesting traveling patterns of tourists in Singapore. Although our demonstration is based on the public transport data and use cases in Singapore, it can be generalized for the similar public transport data in any other city.

The rest of the paper is organized as follows. In Section 2, we briefly revisit related work. In Section 3 we introduce the architecture of the FTT system. In Section 4, we demonstrate how the system works and what the interface looks like, and also showcase some interesting insights we discovered using the system. Finally, we conclude this demo paper in Section 5.

2. RELATED WORK

Analyzing tourists' traveling patterns has been extensively studied in the community of tourism research. Generally, tourist data were collected from known sources, such as hotel registrations and other POI ticketing or registration systems. The analyses are often statistics based, but useful for tourism planning. In computer science, especially in the database and data mining communities, identifying tourists does not attract much research attention. Some works have been done on top of social media data. For example, [7] tries to mine the information such as what places are often visited by tourists and how long time they spend on there from geo-tagged images in Flickr. Similarly, [10, 6] identifies tourist POIs from Flickr data based on clustering. Those works did not really identify tourists from the crowd, but rather use the pre-assumed tourist data to find POIs, though the assumption based on Flickr images is reasonable and accurate to some extent. However, such data set can hardly represent the majority of tourists, and lack of rich information for deeper moving pattern discovery.

[1]MRT is a subway system in Singapore. Another subway system is called LRT, which uses light rails and smaller trains and acts as a feeder service to MRT to serve short distance transport in neighborhoods. To simplify the explanation, we do not distinguish between the two, and only use MRT to represent the whole subway system in Singapore.

On the other hand, plenty of work has been done on analyzing moving patterns based on GPS data, e.g. [2, 11, 4], etc. Intuitively, such works can be applied to tourists' trajectories to find interesting moving patterns. However, again, the problem is that how one can collect trajectory data of a large group of tourists.

Our work is from a new and useful angle to study tourists' behaviors, i.e., from public transport data. We did not identify any similar existing work to find tourists from public transport data and study their traveling patterns.

3. SYSTEM

3.1 Overview

The general architecture of the FTT system is shown in Figure 1. There are three main modules in the FTT system. The first module is the feature engineering module. Due to the large size of the public transport data (around 50GB per month), we use a Hadoop cluster for data storing and feature engineering. By training a small set of tourists and non-tourists, we identify a set of features that will be used for tourist identification. The features mainly contains the MRT stations and bus stops visited by each commuters, and the frequencies they were visited. We program MapReduce tasks to operate on the public transport data, and return the features for each commuter. The feature data will be pipelined to the main mining algorithm.

The second module is to mine the public transport riders with corresponding features to find out tourists. This process is controlled by a scheduler, which determines how often the mining process will be re-executed on the most recent riding records. The mining result will be stored in a database, and OD matrices will be constructed on top of the tourist and trajectory database. This module is the main module of the system, and will be described in detail below.

In the last module, a query processor will accept a location-based query issued by a user, and search the corresponding OD matrix to return the result. The result will be weighted destinations that are traveled by tourists from the neighborhood bus stops and MRT stations of the input location, and also the destinations that would be co-visited with the input location. Finally, the result will be visualized on top of a map.

3.2 Tourist Identification

Identifying tourists from all public transport commuters is the key component of the FTT system. We design a two-phase algorithm for tourist identification. The first phase is the initialization phase. In this phase, each MRT station is assigned an initial score to indicate whether it is more likely to be a destination for tourists or a destination for locals. Note that we could not simply use the attractiveness of each place to tourists, which can be found in, e.g., TripAdvisor, as the initial score. This is because one place that is popular to tourists may also be popular to locals. For example, most tourists will visit Orchard, the main shopping street in Singapore. But given a people who has visited Orchard, we cannot tell whether she is more likely to be a tourist or a local, as many local people also visit there. As a result, in our approach, we consider the popularity of a place to both tourists and locals, in order to assign a score to it.

In the second phase, we use a small set of manually labeled tourists to infer the tourists from the general public transport riders. We iteratively update the scores of MRT stations and the conf dence on each traveler to be a tourist, and f nally conclude the decisions.

3.2.1 Phase 1: Initialization

We def ne the initial score of each MRT station to be the probability that a commuter is a tourist given that she has visited this station, i.e., $\Pr(t|m_i)$ in which t denotes that a commuter is a tourist and m_i denotes the event that a commuter has visited the station m_i. Instead of directly estimating $\Pr(t|m_i)$ for each station, which is not feasible with our data, we re-write it based on Bayes Rule and estimate the relevant probabilities:

$$\Pr(t|m_i) = \Pr(t) \cdot \frac{\Pr(m_i|t)}{\Pr(m_i)} \quad (1)$$

In the above equation, $\Pr(m_i|t)$ is the probability for a tourist t to visit a station m_i, $\Pr(m_i)$ is the prior probability for anyone to visit m_i and $\Pr(t)$ is the prior probability for one to be a tourist.

To estimate all these probabilities, we make use of both the EZ-Link card records and Standard Ticket records in the public transport data of Singapore. EZ-Link card is the pre-paid fare payment card used for public transport riding in Singapore. Almost all local people have EZ-Link cards for long-term uses, and their public transport ridings are trackable due to the unique EZ-Link IDs for each card. On the other hand, Standard Ticket is a one-time ticket to take MRT. From our background knowledge, many Standard Ticket users are tourists. However, there are also many tourists tend to purchase EZ-Link cards when they stay in Singapore for a couple of days, as EZ-Link card is more convenient and the fare per ride is cheaper than Standard Ticket.

Local commuters may also use Standard Ticket occasionally. One of the main reasons that a local commuter purchases a Standard Ticket is that she forgets to bring her EZ-Link card or her EZ-Link card has insuff cient fund but she is not able to top it up. We assume that local people should have the same probability to use Standard Ticket rather than EZ-Link card at different MRT stations. For example, people from one station should have the same probability as those from another station to leave their EZ-Link cards at home, and thus have to purchase Standard Tickets. Based on this assumption, without the effect of tourists, the ratio between Standard Ticket local users to EZ-Link local users should be consistent across all MRT stations. This ratio, named θ, is the key parameter needs to be estimated in order to estimate other probabilities.

Since tourists are much more likely to use Standard Tickets than locals, the ratio between Standard Ticket users and EZ-Link users will be higher in those stations that attract more tourists. However, there are more than 100 MRT stations in Singapore, and most of them are not often visited by tourists. Thus, this ratio will have a long-tail effect, i.e., tend to be consistent for a big number of MRT stations that are not popular to tourists. This point was validated by analyzing the data. Finally, we can use the smallest ratio value in the long tail as an estimation of θ.

Table 1: Top ranked stations based on initial scores

Name	s_{m_i}
Changi Airport	0.213668
Marina Bay	0.145012
Clarke Quay	0.144702
Bayfront	0.128008
Little India	0.118879
Chinatown	0.113837
HarbourFront	0.106443
Bras Basah	0.104787
Esplanade	0.099637
Orchard	0.098623
Lavender	0.093104
Farrer Park	0.081844
Promenade	0.079080
Bugis	0.070973
City Hall	0.064815

Once we have the θ value, we can easily estimate the number of tourists in each MRT station, and then further estimate the probabilities in the equation above. The details can be found in [9]. The top MRT stations after the initial scoring and ranking are shown in Table 1. We see that all the stations are famous tourist POIs in Singapore, and the ranking is reasonable. For example, Changi Airport has the highest score, which means visiting Changi Airport gives more conf dence than visiting other POIs to infer a commuter as a tourist. However, although City Hall is another must-see place for tourists, its rank is not very high because many local residents also visit there.

3.2.2 Phase 2: Label Inference

In this phase, the task is to use the MRT stations with initialized scores and a set of labeled tourists with their riding records, to identify other tourists among the public transport commuters based on the riding records. We f rst model the problem as a label inference problem on a graph. In particular, we build a tripartite graph with three groups of entities, i.e., MRT stations *M*, labeled tourists *C* and other commuters *X*. The MRT stations sit in the middle, and connect to the other two groups. Figure 2(a) shows an example graph. Since we only require a small set of labeled data, the size of *C* is much smaller than the size of *X*. There is a class (tourist/non-tourist) probability distribution for each node in *C* and *X*. For the nodes in labeled set *C*, the distributions are initialized as either [1,0] or [1,0], depending on whether the corresponding node is a tourist node or not. For the nodes in *X*, the distributions are initialized as $[\hat{\Pr}(t), 1 - \hat{\Pr}(t)]$, where $\hat{\Pr}(t)$ is an estimation of Pr(t) in Equation (1). Alternatively, we can also set the initial distribution as [0.5,0.5]. Each MRT station *m* in *M* is also associated with a probability distribution $[p_m$, 1-$p_m]$, where p_m indicates the probability for one to be tourist if she visits *m*, under the current state. The weighted edge between each commuter in $C \cup X$ and a station in *M* indicates that the commuter has visited the corresponding station, and the weight indicates the frequency.

In our problem, we design an iterative learning algorithm to update the class probability distribution of all nodes in *X*, and f nally assign a class label to each of them based on the probability distribution.

In each iteration of the learning process, there are two tasks:

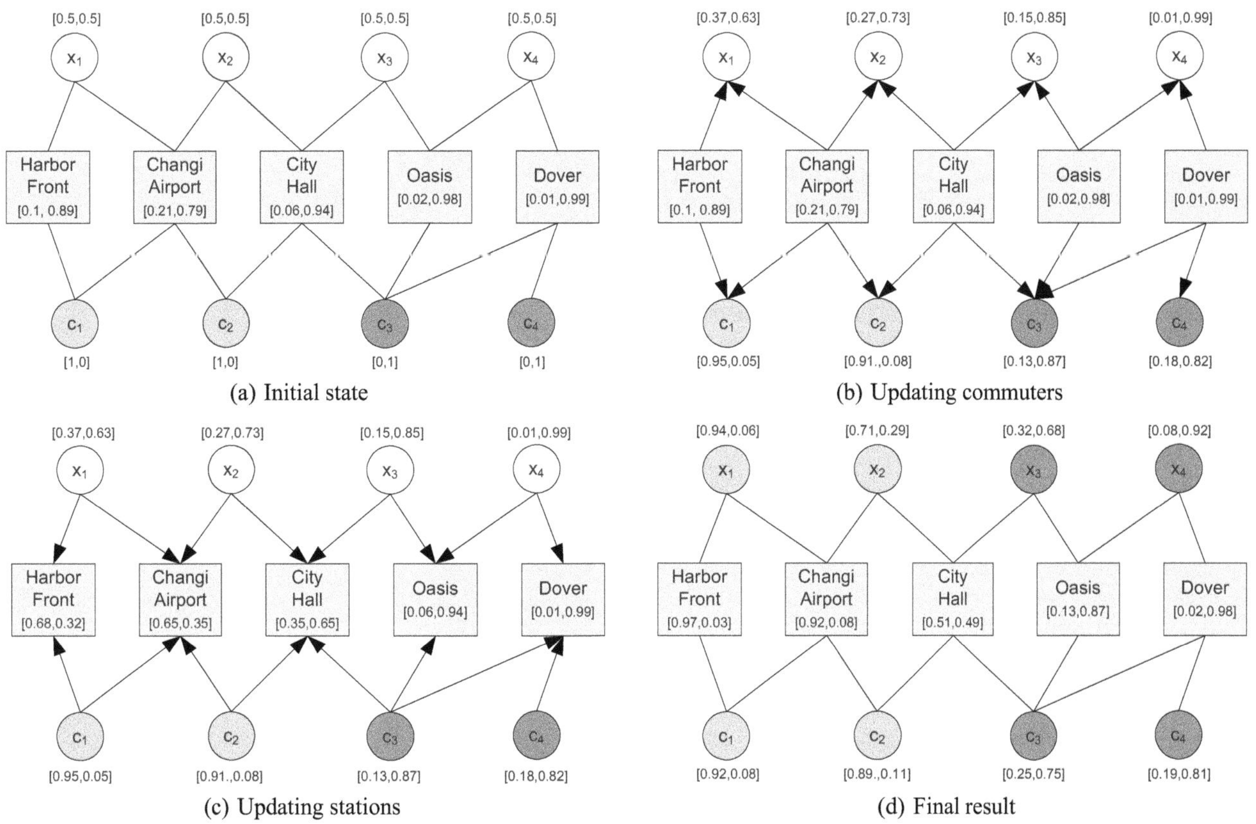

Figure 2: Example for label propagation

- T1: Update the class probability distribution of the commuters in *C* and *X*, based on the probability distribution of the MRT stations in *M* that they have visited.
- T2: Update the class probability distribution of the MRT stations in *M*, based on the class probability distribution of the commuters in *C* and *X*.

The iterative learning process will end when the number of iterations reach a predefined threshold, which is set to 150 in our practical test. The formula to update each node x_i in *X* at the *k*-th iteration is:

$$\phi_{x_i}^{k} \leftarrow \alpha \cdot \phi_{x_i}^{k-1} + (1-\alpha) \cdot \frac{\sum_{m \in N(x_i)} w_{x_i m} \cdot \phi_m^{k-1}}{\sum_{m \in N(x_i)} w_{x_i m}} \quad (2)$$

In the above formula, $w_{x_i m}$ is the edge weight between x_i and m, i.e., the number of times x_i visited m. $N(x_i)$ returns the neighbor stations of x_i in the graph, and ϕ_m^{k-1} stands for the probability distribution of m at the *(k-1)*-th iteration. The formulas to update *C* and *M* are similar, and omitted in this demo paper.

Finally, after the learning process ends, each commuter x_i in X is assigned a class label *l* to indicate whether she is a tourist or not, such that:

$$\hat{l} = \underset{l}{argmax} \frac{P(x_i|l)}{P(x_i)} = \underset{c}{argmax} \frac{P(l|x_i)}{P(l)} \quad (3)$$

A running example is shown in Figure 3.2.1. Figure 2(a) shows the initial state of labeled commuters, unlabeled commuters, and MRT stations with initial scores. In Figure 2(b), the probability distributions of the both labeled and unlabeled commuter are updated. As the second step of the first iteration, the updated distributions of *X* and *C* will be used to update the probability distributions of the stations in *M*, as shown in Figure 2(c). After a certain number of iterations, the final state is shown in Figure 2(d). Then we can calculate to find the label of, e.g., x_2 as $\hat{l} = argmax(0.71/(0.94 + 0.71 + 0.32 + 0.08), 0.29/(0.6 + 0.29 + 0.68 + 0.92))$. Then x_2 will be labeled as a tourist. Similarly, x_3 will be labeled as a non-tourist.

The details of the iterative algorithm can be found in [9].

3.3 Query Support

After identifying a group of tourists, their detailed public transport trajectories will be extracted and stored in a database. Then an offline algorithm will be triggered to search the tourists' trajectories and construct two OD matrices to support queries on next destinations and co-visited locations. Since there are more than 6 thousand MRT stations and bus stops in Singapore, and this number may be larger in other bigger cities and countries, the OD matrices may be large in size. We provide two solutions to maintain the OD matrices, i.e., disk based and memory based. In our current deployment and the online demonstration, we use the memory-based solution.

User queries are in terms of geo-locations on the map. The multiple input coordinates (we support multiple locations as input) will be mapped to location ID and searched against the corresponding OD matrix. The answers will be aggregated and returned to the frontend, and finally mapped to geo-locations and displayed on the map.

4. SYSTEM DEMO AND INSIGHTS

4.1 Demonstration Setup

We will use Singapore's public transport (including MRT and bus) data to demonstrate our system. The period of the data is from December 2012 to January 2013. There are totally 5.1 million unique commuter card numbers (excluding concession card for senior citizens, children and students), which contributed 0.5 billion MRT and bus riding records during the three months.

After applying our learning algorithm, we have identif ed 1.4 million tourists. We aggregate the visits of these identif ed tourists to the 6 thousand MRT stations and bus stops in Singapore, based on which, we deploy the interactive system frontend to support user queries[2].

4.2 System Functions

The system provides two main functions to help users understand tourists' traveling patterns. In the f rst function, the system accepts users' input locations and visualize the top destinations from those input places. The second function reveals what other places are often visited by tourists together with an input place.

The system offers two ways for users to input query locations. A user can select popular MRT stations and/or bus stops from a drop-down list from the left panel. Alternatively, a user can directly pick any location on the map as input. The system also provides options for users to change parameters. For example, for the input selected from the map, a user may specify the area of the input region. Also, a user can change the threshold of heat map visualization.

4.3 Demo and Insights

Figure 3 show the initial main page of the system, without accepting any queries. The heat map on the main page visualizes the distribution of tourist's favorite destinations in Singapore. This distribution is consistent with the common understanding on the tourist POIs in Singapore. We can see the places like Changi Airport, Zoo, Sentosa, city center, etc. are all very highlighted. Also, some MRT stations near to tourist POIs are also highlighted, e.g., the Boon Lay MRT station which is near to the Jurong Bird Park. It is worth mentioning that there are a couple of bus stops in the north of the island being highlighted. That is because there are direct bus services between those bus stops to the bus terminal in Johor Bahru of Malaysia. Many Malaysian visit Singapore by taking those buses and alight in the north of Singapore.

A user can use the dropdown MRT or bus stop list on the left panel to add in a single location to query. Besides, a user can also click on anywhere of the map to select a region to query. The area of the region can be changed in the Parameter panel. Once a region is selected, all the MRT stations and bus stops in the region will be treated as input locations. The system allows multiple locations as the input of one query. Figure 4 shows the query specif cation. After specifying the query locations, there are two options on the bottom of the left panel, prompting the user to either show the next destinations from the input locations or the places co-visited by tourists with the input locations.

Figure 5 showcases an example to use the next destination search to f gure out where the tourists stay in Singapore. By searching for the region of Changi Airport (including 5 bus stops and 1 MRT station), we can see the heat map of the next destinations of tourists coming from the airport, i.e., probably the places they stay in Singapore. On the left panel, we can see the bar chart of the top 10

[2]An online demonstration web site can be accessed from: http://datam.i2r.a-star.edu.sg/tourist-demo/

Figure 3: Interface of FTT system

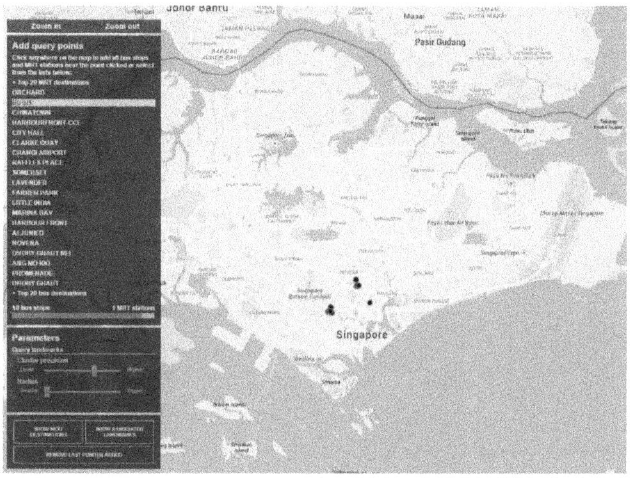

Figure 4: Query Specif cation

destinations. By putting the cursor on each bar, the corresponding destination will be highlighted with the percentage and the name label on the map. All the top 10 destinations are circled out. From the result in Figure 5, we know that most tourists prefer staying in the city center, which is quite reasonable.

One interesting observation is that the Ang Mo Kio station in Figure 3 (the big circle in the middle of the map) was visited by a lot of tourists, though it is only a local residence place. To f gure out why, we issue a query on Ang Mo Kio (1 MRT station and 4 bus stops are automatically detected), and f nd that most tourists are actually going to Singapore zoo from Ang Mo Kio, as shown in Figure 6. This may not be the best way to visit the zoo, but it was the recommended route on the zoo's website in 2011-2012. Thus Ang Mo Kio became a "POI". If this kind of information can be found, potential tourist-related activities can be carried out in those tourist transfer sites.

Finally, we demonstrate the association between the POIs. As shown in Figure 7, if we would like to know what other places the tourists would like to visit given that they have visited the Jurong Bird Park, we can issue such a query on the map. When we search for the top 5 answers, we can see three of them are actually the bus stops around the nearest MRT station to the Jurong Bird Park. It is easy to understand, because most tourists will take bus to the nearest MRT station for further transfer. Also, we can see the other two co-visited places are Sentosa (a famous tourist island, with Uni-

Figure 5: Next destinations from Changi Airport

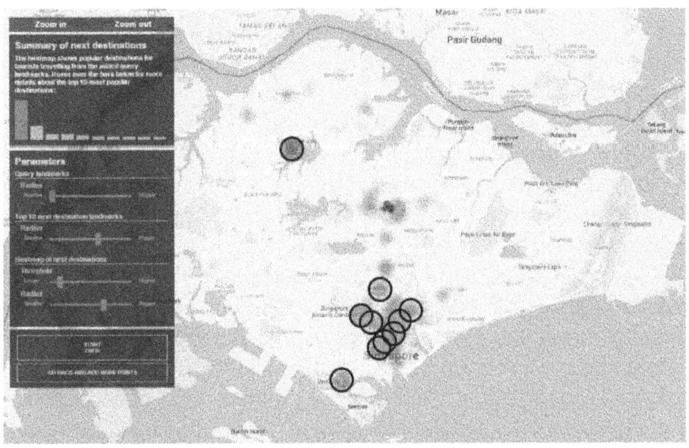

Figure 6: Next destinations from Ang Mo Kio

versal Studio and Casino inside) and Orchard (the main shopping street in Singapore). That means there are convenient bus services among these POIs, on which tourists tend to follow. However, there is no bus service from Jurong Bird Park to Singapore Zoo, though these two places are often co-visited.

5. CONCLUSION

In this paper, we demonstrate our FTT system for tourist f nding and tracking. The FTT system contains a backend module to discover tourists from all public transport commuters, and a frontend module to support user queries for understanding tourists' traveling patterns. At the backend, we devise an iterative learning algorithm for tourist identif cation. The algorithm takes prior scores of the MRT stations and a small set of labeled data, to propagate the knowledge to other commuters so that f nal decisions can be made. Based on the tourists and their riding records found at the backend, we support location-based user queries to search and visualize where the tourists travel from any given places, and how different places are co-visited by the tourists. We also elaborate some insights on tourists' traveling patterns gained through system demonstration.

Acknowledgement

This work was partially supported by the A*STAR Science and Engineering Research Council (SERC) Grant No. 1224200004 and 1224604057.

Figure 7: Co-visited places

6. REFERENCES

[1] O. Bernadó, A. Bigorra, Y. Pérez, A. P. Russo, and S. A. Clave. Analysis of tourist behavior based on tracking data collected by gps. *Discovery of Geospatial Resources: Methodologies, Technologies, and Emergent Applications*, page 241, 2012.

[2] Z. Chen, H. T. Shen, and X. Zhou. Discovering popular routes from trajectories. In *Data Engineering (ICDE), 2011 IEEE 27th International Conference on*, pages 900–911, 2011.

[3] B. Kádár. Measuring tourist activities in cities using geotagged photography. *Tourism Geographies*, 16(1):88–104, 2014.

[4] S. Khetarpaul, R. Chauhan, S. Gupta, L. V. Subramaniam, and U. Nambiar. Mining gps data to determine interesting locations. In *Proceedings of the 8th International Workshop on Information Integration on the Web: in conjunction with WWW 2011*, page 8, 2011.

[5] X. Y. Leung, F. Wang, B. Wu, B. Bai, K. A. Stahura, and Z. Xie. A social network analysis of overseas tourist movement patterns in beijing: The impact of the olympic games. *International Journal of Tourism Research*, 14(5):469–484, 2012.

[6] A. Majid, L. Chen, H. T. Mirza, I. Hussain, and G. Chen. A system for mining interesting tourist locations and travel sequences from public geo-tagged photos. *Data & Knowledge Engineering*, 2014.

[7] A. Popescu, G. Grefenstette, and P.-A. Moëllic. Mining tourist information from user-supplied collections. In *CIKM*, pages 1713–1716, 2009.

[8] Singapore Tourism Board. http://www.stb.gov.sg.

[9] M. Xue, H. Wu, W. Chen, W. S. Ng, and G. H. Goh. Identifying tourists from public transport commuters. In *The 20th ACM SIGKDD International Conference on Knowledge Discovery and Data Mining*, pages 1779–1788, 2014.

[10] Y. Yang, Z. Gong, and L. H. U. Identifying points of interest by self-tuning clustering. In *Proceedings of the 34th International ACM SIGIR Conference on Research and Development in Information Retrieval*, SIGIR '11, pages 883–892, 2011.

[11] Y. Zheng, L. Zhang, X. Xie, and W.-Y. Ma. Mining interesting locations and travel sequences from gps trajectories. In *WWW*, pages 791–800, 2009.

SharkDB:An In-Memory Storage System for Massive Trajectory Data

Haozhou Wang, Kai Zheng, Xiaofang Zhou, Shazia Sadiq
The University of Queensland, Australia
{h.wang16,kevinz,zxf,shazia}@uq.edu.au

ABSTRACT

An increasing amount of motion history data, which is called trajectory, is being collected from different sources such as GPS-enabled mobile devices, surveillance cameras and social networks. However it is hard to store and manage trajectory data in traditional database systems, since its variable lengths and asynchronous sampling rates do not fit disk-based and tuple-oriented structures, which are the fundamental structures of traditional database systems. We implement a novel trajectory storage system that is motivated by the success of column store and recent development of in-memory based databases. In this storage design, we try to explore the potential opportunities, which can boost the performance of query processing for trajectory data. To achieve this, we partition the trajectories into frames as column-oriented storage in order to store the sample points of a moving object, which are aligned by the time interval, within the main memory. Furthermore, the frames can be highly compressed and well structured to increase the memory utilization ratio and reduce the CPU-cache missing. It is also easier for parallelizing data processing on the multi-core server since the frames are mutually independent.

Categories and Subject Descriptors

H.2.8 [**Database Management**]: Database Applications—*Spatial databases and GIS*

General Terms

Algorithms, Performance

Keywords

Trajectory, in-memory, column-oriented data structure

1. INTRODUCTION

The trajectory of a moving object is typically modelled as a time-stamped sequence of consecutive locations in a multidimensional (generally three dimensional) space. Thanks to major advances in sensor technology, trajectories are currently generated from GPS-enabled mobile devices and wireless communications at an increasing rate. Trajectory data offers unprecedented amount of information to help understand the behaviour of moving objects. Effective and efficient technologies to manage large scale trajectory data is highly demanded as the foundation to serve a variety of application domains such as geographical information systems, location-based services, vehicle navigation and so on.

Currently, many commercial relational database management systems (RMDBS) have started to offer additional components or extensions to support spatial types and operators. However, only a few simple spatial data types such as points, lines and polygons are considered and supported in these RDBMS. On the other hand, more complex data types are needed to store trajectories. Because it contains continuous time information and the length of each trajectory is variable (i.e., the number of sample point of each trajectory is different). Traditionally, to solve this problem, it is easy to consider the trajectory of a moving object as one database object. While this approach has a clear semantic meaning for each trajectory record, it has several obvious drawbacks. Firstly, most RDBMS cannot handle records of variable lengths well. Secondly, many trajectory processing operations deal with, explicitly or implicitly, some segments of a trajectory only. For example, to find a point of interest (POI) closest to a trajectory, ideally only one part of the trajectory (that contributes to the identification of the resultant POI) needs to be used should that part be identified (using some indexing and filtering strategies). Treating a trajectory as whole cannot support this type of operations efficiently, as it needs to access the whole trajectory and then discard all but the relevant segments.

Recently, there is growing interest on column-oriented data structure such as MonetDB [5], Positional Delta Tree (PDT) [10], and so on. However they did not consider the trajectory data, which is a natural multi-dimensional data structure with complex data format. Meanwhile, the in-memory data management also receives lots of attention such as memory-based indexing techniques [9, 7, 3] and in-memory database systems [8, 6, 1, 4, 2]. However, these work mainly focus on relational data, which means processing spatial-temporal data (i.e., trajectory data) in memory system cannot be well supported. To address this problem, we introduce SharkDB, an in-memory column-oriented storage system for storing massive trajectory data. We propose a novel read-optimized storage structure, which combines the advantages of in-memory computing and column-oriented data structure for analytical tasks. Aligned with common in-memory database designs, where data compression is a key factor of consideration, SharkDB also supports compressing trajectory data effectively and allows processing analytical query

SIGMOD'15, May 31–June 4, 2015, Melbourne, Victoria, Australia.
Copyright © 2015 ACM 978-1-4503-2758-9/15/05 ...$15.00.
http://dx.doi.org/10.1145/2723372.2735368.

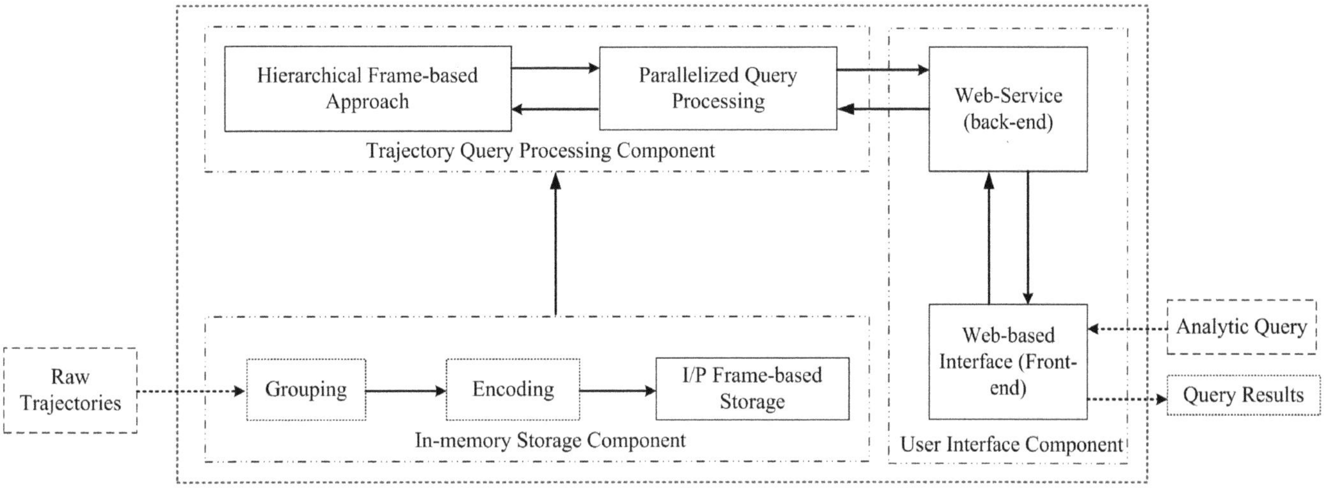

Figure 1: System Architecture

on the compressed data directly without the need to decompress the whole dataset.

2. SYSTEM OVERVIEW

SharkDB includes three components, the user interface component, the in-memory storage component and the trajectory query processing component. As shown in Fig. 1, the duty of the in-memory data storage component is to encode and compress the raw trajectories, and then to store them in the column-oriented data structure. The trajectory query processing component is responsible for processing trajectory data and answer trajectory-related queries in real time. The user interface component contains a front end (GUI) and a back end. The front end receives queries and communicate with the back end. Meanwhile, the back end is connected with the trajectory query processing component. We give a brief overview of these components in the following:

In-memory Storage System: In this component, we propose a frame-based and column-oriented data structure to store the trajectory data. We partition the whole trajectory dataset and align them into fixed time frame. Each time frame is treated as a virtual column, i.e., all trajectory samples within the same time frame will be stored consecutively in the main memory. We also borrow the idea of video compression techniques and use I/P frame encoding scheme to further reduce the footprint of data in the memory. We will discuss this part in the technical background section.

Trajectory Query Processing System: We propose a hierarchical frame based approach, whereas a multi-level frame data structure has been built, to support efficient trajectory query processing with flexible time granularity. To take full advantage of multi-core computing architecture, we also extend this approach to support parallel processing. We will elaborate this part in technical background section.

User Interface: We use web-based interface as the front end such that it can be accessed from most devices, including PC, tablets and smart phones. Our interface has a control panel to allow users to specify a trajectory-related query and set different parameters. Our back end is implemented as web service, which offers the flexibility to incorporate different storage structures and query processing algorithms for comparison purpose. We will discuss this part in demonstration section.

3. TECHNICAL BACKGROUND

In this section, we first discuss our frame-based data structure as well as its encoding algorithm, which is used to store the raw trajectory data in the column-oriented data structure. Then we briefly discuss the query processing on frame-based structure with parallel processing.

3.1 Frame-based In-memory Storage

Most trajectory-related queries such as window queries, nearest neighbour queries and similarity queries only care about the relevant trajectory segment, instead of the whole trajectory. Apparently keeping each single trajectory as one record is not good storage design for this type of queries, since we need to scan the whole table to get the query answers. Therefore, we implement a frame based data structure in the main memory, by leveraging the column-oriented data structure and the in-memory techniques. To implement this frame based structure, we first build a sequence of frames from trajectory data directly. Then each trajectory sample point is allocated to the related frame based on its timestamp. In this frame based structure, all trajectory sample points that belong to the same time interval are put into the same frame. We name such time interval as frame rate and a sample point in a frame is named as a frame point. For instance, as Fig. 2 shows, if we set the time interval to be 1 minute (i.e. the frame rate is 60 seconds), the time period from 9:01 to 9:05 can be split into 4 frames. Hence, the sample points in the trajectory $T_1 = p'_1, p'_2, p'_3, p'_4$ and $T_2 = p_1, p_2, p_3, p_4$ will be aligned to the related frame. In this example, p'_1, p_1 and p'_2, p_2 are assigned into $Frame1$ and $Frame2$ respectively. However, there are two challenges in our frame-based data structure. The first one is how to reconstruct the raw trajectory from time frames efficiently. The other one is how to reduce the footprint of trajectory data in the memory. We propose I/P frame data structure to tackle these challenges.

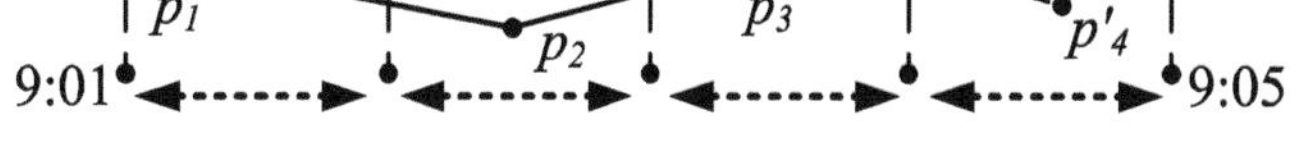

Figure 2: Trajectory Snapshot

There are two steps for building the I/P frame data structure, namely grouping step and encoding step. In the grouping step, the whole sequence of frames are split into small groups, called frame group, and each frame group contains n consecutive frames. Based on the example in Fig. 2 , if we set $n = 4$, then the $Frame1$ to $Frame4$ are allocated in one group. For each group, we set the first frame as I-frame, and the subsequent frames as P-frames. In the encoding process we use the delta encoding scheme to encode the P-frame points by calculating the difference between each P-frame point and its closest prior I-frame point. To increase the reconstruction performance, we set the length of each P-frame column the same as the length of I-frame column. To deal with variable lengths of trajectories, a place-holder Nil will be used once a trajectory segment does not fill a frame group. As shown in Table 1, if a trajectory segment has one I-frame point and one P-frame point in a $n = 4$ frame group, we put Nil codes in the rest of P-frame columns. As a result, the P-frame points now have the same offset (and thus the index) as its related I-frame point if they are belonging to the same trajectory. By this means, the P-frame points can be accessed directly with the index of the related I-frame point without the need to scan the whole P-frame columns. This encoding scheme also enables the delta encoding to compress the P-frame points.

Table 1: Example of I/P Frame-based Structure

9:01-9:02	9:02-9:03	9:03-9:04	9:04-9:05
(1,p)	(1,Δp)	(1,Δp)	(1,Δp)
(2,p)	(2,Δp)	Nil	Nil
(3,p)	(3,Δp)	(3,Δp)	Nil
(4,p)	(4,Δp)	(4,Δp)	(4,Δp)

CPU cache optimization is a key factor of consideration for in-memory based storage system. We implement a hybrid data structure to optimize the CPU cache utilization. A two dimensional array $array[x][y]$ is created for each frame group, where x equals to the number of I-frame points in this frame group, and y equals to the number of P-frame columns in this frame group. The value of x in the array is the index of an I-frame point; the value of y indicates the column number of a P-frame group; the object at $array[x][y]$ is the P-frame point. When CPU requests to fetch an I-frame point, its related P-frame points will be also put into the same cache line. Later when CPU tries to access the P-frame points, it can retrieve them directly from its cache that is much faster than memory access. Our experiments have already verified that, this mechanism can increase the trajectory reconstruction speed as well as the whole performance of query processing. Assuming a memory access reads 3 codes vertically from a P-frame array. As Fig. 3(a) shows, it will take 3 memory accesses in order to decode a trajectory segment in a frame group without cache line optimization , since the other codes in the cache line is not related to this segment. To the contrary, as Fig. 3(b) shows, it only takes 1 memory access after cache optimization .

3.2 Trajectory Query Processing

In the frame based data structure, sequential scan for I-frame columns and trajectory reconstruction are the most time consuming operations in the whole query processing. Therefore, reducing the number of sequential scan and trajectory reconstruction can significantly increase the system performance. In order to prune the unnecessary frame groups as much as possible during the sequential scan for I-frame columns, we propose a hierarchical frame based structure, as is shown in Fig. 4.

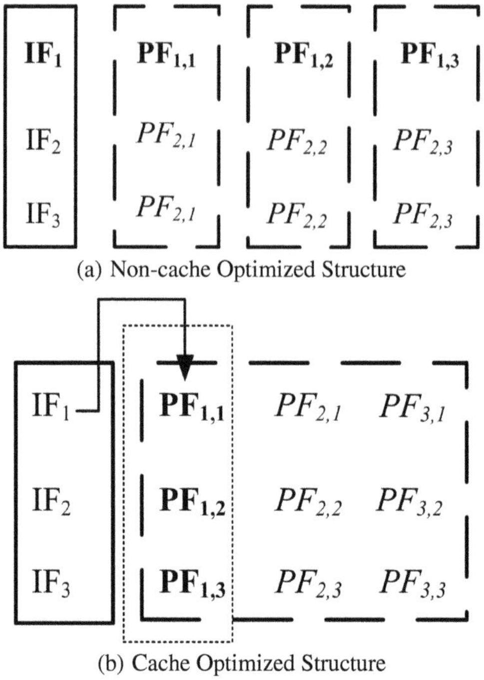

Figure 3: Example of Cache-aware I/P-frame Structure

First of all, we build hierarchical frame structure in bottom-up style, where the first level (bottom) of the hierarchical frame structure is the normal I/P frame data structure that contains all the frames. Then we only use the I-frame columns from current top level that form the new top level. Afterwards, we split every n I-frame columns and put them into a frame group, where n is the number of frames in a frame group. An advantage of this structure is that we can use the same encoding methods that are proposed before to encode the I-frame columns in the new frame groups. In Fig. 4, an example is provided to illustrate the process. If there are more levels created in this hierarchical structure, the time interval of each frame in the top level will increase and may become greater than the average duration of a trajectory. Therefore if the time duration of frame group is larger than the average time duration of trajectories at the top level, the construction process can terminate.

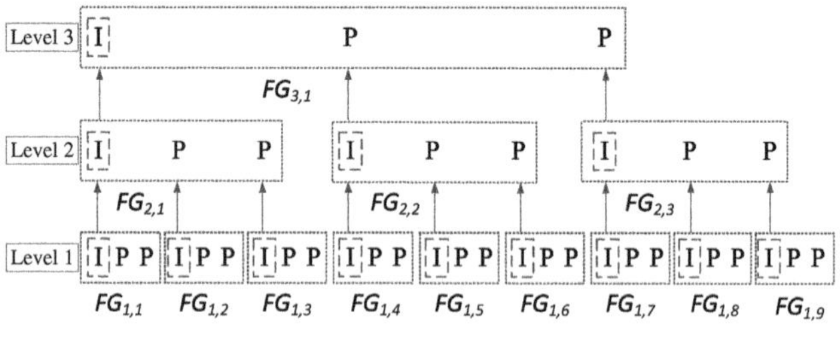

Figure 4: Hierarchical I/P-frame Data Structure

A best-first search paradigm is adopted to traverse the hierarchical frame structure. We first initialize a min-heap and push the top-level frame groups into the heap, of which the time interval of frame groups are in query time range. The entries in the heap are ordered by the MINDIST between their MBRs and query location. Then, for each frame group that is needed to check, we check its MBR first. If the MBR is out of query range, we can prune this frame group and remove it from the heap; otherwise we re-insert

Figure 5: Web Interface

it child frames in the hierarchy back into the heap. When an entry at the bottom level is retrieved from the heap, we decode it to get the raw trajectory segment and calculate the exact distance to the query.

As multi-CPU/core is the standard computing architecture nowadays, supporting parallel processing becomes necessary. One advantage of the frame-based data structure is that each frame group is completely independent and "share nothing" with each others. This allows us to divide a query into a series of sub-queries and assign them to different CPUs/cores for processing. Finally, the results returned from each CPU/cores are merged to get the final answer.

4. DEMONSTRATION

Currently, we implement three storage structures in this demo system, the segmented trajectory structure, the I/P frame structure and I/P frame structure with parallel processing. The last two storage structures are our proposed approaches. The segmented trajectory structure is to simulate a traditional storage, where it considers a trajectory as an object. To increase the performance of the segmented trajectory structure , we split each trajectory into small segments, where a segment contains a fixed number of sample points. Meanwhile, each segment contains its MBR information as well as the starting time and ending time. The aim is to provide an objective time cost comparison among all these structures. These structures can be either deployed on commercial in-memory database (e.g., SAP HANA) or by our own implementation. Two types of trajectory analytic queries are supported at this stage. The first query is window query, which finds all trajectories in the data set that are active during a given period and pass a given spatial region. The other one is kNN query, which finds top-k trajectories in the trajectory data set that are closest to a given point and active during a given period of time. The real datasets used for this demo system is the same as [11]. In this demonstration, we provide a web-based interface as the front end and web service based back end to bridge web interface and the query processing component as a middleware.

The web interface is shown in Fig. 5. The left-hand side is the control panel that allows user to select the storage structure and the type of query from the drop-down list. The right-hand side is the trajectory visualization panel based on Google map, which allows users to input a query intuitively. A user can either draw a query circle (for window query) or pin a reference point (for kNN query) on the map directly. Since our query has the time duration as a parameter, a user can also adjust the query time interval by sliding the time bar in the bottom of panel.

We start the demonstration by briefly explaining the work-flow of our system. Then a user can select the type of queries as well as the type of storage structures from the left panel. As Fig. 6 shows, if the window query is selected, then she can use mouse to draw a circle on the map to specify the query range and adjust the size and location of that circle. The audience can also adjust the time bar to select the day and using drop down list to specify the hour and minute. Upon completion of query input, she can press the "Show Trajectories" button to issue the query and the results should be displayed on the Google Map in real time. The system uses different colors to help users distinguish the trajectories in the result set. Fig. 7 demonstrates an example of the window query in previous example.

After results being shown on the map, the audiences can view the detail of trajectories by switching the control panel tab to "trajectories". Fig. 8 shows an instance of kNN query. In the "trajectories" view, a table is showing the detail of each trajectory in the results, which includes the length of trajectory with its start time and end time. The ID is the rank of the trajectories based on its minimum distance to the query point. If the user would like to investigate the individual trajectory, she can simply click the trajectory in the result table, and the selected trajectory will be highlighted on the map. For example, in Fig. 9 , if we select the first trajectory that listed in the table, then the nearest trajectory will be highlighted in the Map.

Figure 6: Example of Window Query Input

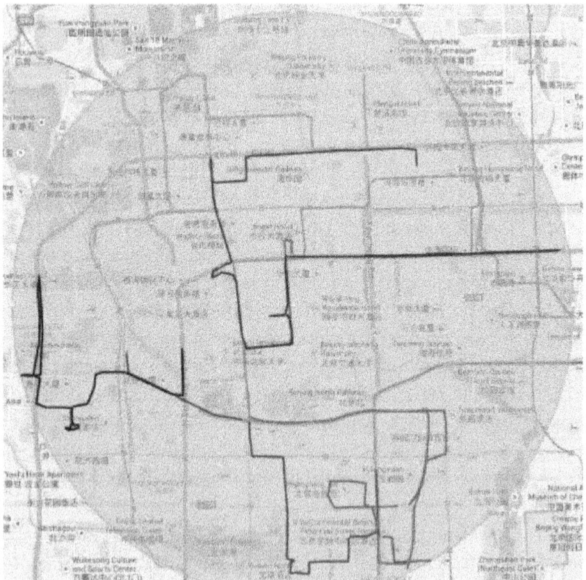

Figure 7: Example of Window Query Results

In addition to showing the results in Google Map, users may be interested in comparing the performances between these storage structures. To do this, they can click the "Compare" button, and the query processing time based on each storage structure will be reported and displayed. An example is shown in Fig. 10, the

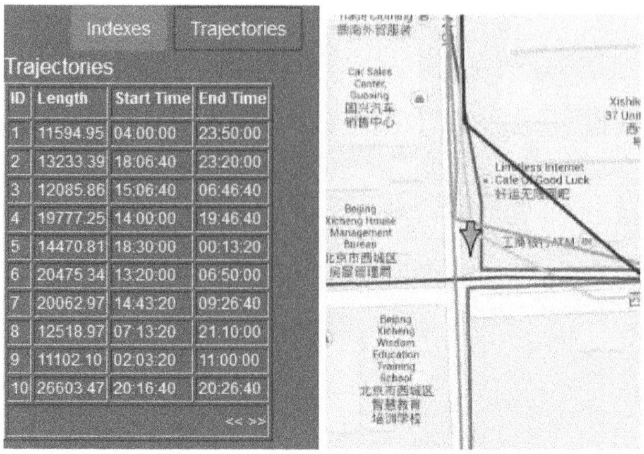

ID	Length	Start Time	End Time
1	11594.95	04:00:00	23:50:00
2	13233.39	18:06:40	23:20:00
3	12085.86	15:06:40	06:46:40
4	19777.25	14:00:00	19:46:40
5	14470.81	18:30:00	00:13:20
6	20475.34	13:20:00	06:50:00
7	20062.97	14:43:20	09:26:40
8	12518.97	07:13:20	21:10:00
9	11102.10	02:03:20	11:00:00
10	26603.47	20:16:40	20:26:40

(a) Table (b) Map

Figure 8: Example of kNN Query

segmented trajectory storage, the I/P frame structure and I/P frame structure with parallel processing are denoted as STD, I/P and I/P-P respectively. The y-axis is showing the query processing time of each storage structure in milliseconds.

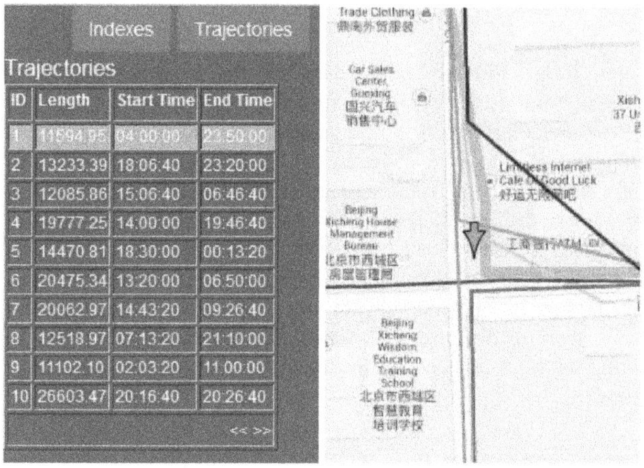

ID	Length	Start Time	End Time
1	11594.95	04:00:00	23:50:00
2	13233.39	18:06:40	23:20:00
3	12085.86	15:06:40	06:46:40
4	19777.25	14:00:00	19:46:40
5	14470.81	18:30:00	00:13:20
6	20475.34	13:20:00	06:50:00
7	20062.97	14:43:20	09:26:40
8	12518.97	07:13:20	21:10:00
9	11102.10	02:03:20	11:00:00
10	26603.47	20:16:40	20:26:40

(a) Table (b) Map

Figure 9: Example of Trajectory Selection on Map

Finally, to make more sense for result visualization, our web interface supports the playback function to visualize the motion of moving objects on the map directly. This function is naturally supported by the frame-based data structure, since all trajectories are synchronized and aligned by time. When a user checks the playback checkbox and issues the query, the back end will turn into playback mode. In this mode, it will send the query to our I/P frame based storage system with playback signal. Then, the system will get the result trajectories and cache the trajectory id, starting time and ending time of these trajectories.

When user presses the play button as shown in Fig. 5, the system searches the frame column by result trajectories' IDs, where the timestamp of this frame group matches the beginning of this query time interval. Then it decodes the frame points to sample points and sends these them back. After receiving such information, the front end displays these sample points on the map. The front end continues to request the sample points in the next frame column based on the result trajectories' IDs, and the points on the map

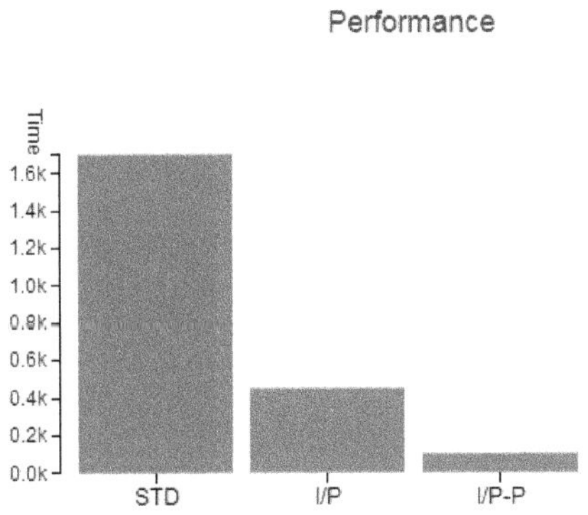

Figure 10: Performance Comparison

will keep moving and represent the motion of the result trajectory. Users can also jump to the time they are more interested directly. Moreover, in the playback mode, there is no need to transfer the whole results set to the client side, so not only the query latency but also the required memory for client devices are reduced.

5. CONCLUSION

In this demonstration proposal, we propose SharkDB, an in-memory frame-based storage design for massive trajectory data. Its novel time-oriented structure is more suitable for processing analytical queries and can make better use of main memory as the permanent storage medium. It also greatly benefits from convenient data compression and parallel processing. We have shown by several demonstration scenarios that SharkDB can process a variant of queries over large-scale trajectory data efficiently and accurately.

6. ACKNOWLEDGEMENTS

This research is partially supported by the Australian Research Council (LP130100164, DP120102829 and DE140100215).

7. REFERENCES

[1] A. C. Ammann, M. Hanrahan, and R. Krishnamurthy. Design of a memory resident DBMS. In *COMPCON*, pages 54–58, 1985.

[2] J. Baulier, P. Bohannon, S. Gogate, C. Gupta, and S. Haldar. DataBlitz storage manager: main-memory database performance for critical applications. In *SIGMOD*, pages 519–520, 1999.

[3] C. Binnig, S. Hildenbrand, and F. Farber. Dictionary-based order-preserving string compression for main memory column stores. In *SIGMOD*, pages 283–296, 2009.

[4] D. Bitton, M. Hanrahan, and C. Turbyfill. Performance of complex queries in main memory database systems. In *ICDE*, pages 72–81, 1987.

[5] P. A. Boncz, M. Zukowski, and N. Nes. Monetdb/x100: Hyper-pipelining query execution. In *CIDR*, pages 225–237, 2005.

[6] D. Gawlick and D. Kinkade. Varieties of concurrency control in IMS/VS fast path. *DEB*, 8(2):3–10, 1985.

[7] S. Manegold, P. Boncz, and M. L. Kersten. Generic database cost models for hierarchical memory systems. In *PVLDB*, pages 191–202, 2002.

[8] H. Plattner. A common database approach for OLTP and OLAP using an in-memory column database. In *SIGMOD*, pages 1–2, 2009.

[9] J. Rao and K. A. Ross. Making B+- trees cache conscious in main memory. In *SIGMOD*, pages 475–486, 2000.

[10] M. Stonebraker, D. J. Abadi, A. Batkin, X. Chen, M. Cherniack, M. Ferreira, E. Lau, A. Lin, S. Madden, E. O'Neil, P. O'Neil, A. Rasin, N. Tran, and S. Zdonik. C-store: a column-oriented DBMS. In *PVLDB*, pages 553–564, 2005.

[11] H. Wang, K. Zheng, J. Xu, B. Zheng, X. Zhou, and S. Sadiq. SharkDB: An in-memory column-oriented trajectory storage. In *CIKM*, pages 1409–1418, 2014.

Ringo: Interactive Graph Analytics on Big-Memory Machines

Yonathan Perez, Rok Sosič, Arijit Banerjee, Rohan Puttagunta, Martin Raison,
Pararth Shah, Jure Leskovec
Stanford University
{yperez, rok, arijitb, rohanp, mraison, pararth, jure}@cs.stanford.edu

ABSTRACT

We present Ringo, a system for analysis of large graphs. Graphs provide a way to represent and analyze systems of interacting objects (people, proteins, webpages) with edges between the objects denoting interactions (friendships, physical interactions, links). Mining graphs provides valuable insights about individual objects as well as the relationships among them.

In building Ringo, we take advantage of the fact that machines with large memory and many cores are widely available and also relatively affordable. This allows us to build an easy-to-use interactive high-performance graph analytics system. Graphs also need to be built from input data, which often resides in the form of relational tables. Thus, Ringo provides rich functionality for manipulating raw input data tables into various kinds of graphs. Furthermore, Ringo also provides over 200 graph analytics functions that can then be applied to constructed graphs.

We show that a single big-memory machine provides a very attractive platform for performing analytics on all but the largest graphs as it offers excellent performance and ease of use as compared to alternative approaches. With Ringo, we also demonstrate how to integrate graph analytics with an iterative process of trial-and-error data exploration and rapid experimentation, common in data mining workloads.

Categories and Subject Descriptors: H.2.4 [**Information Systems**]: Database Management—*Systems*
General Terms: Algorithms, Performance
Keywords: Graphs, networks, graph processing, graph analytics

1. INTRODUCTION

Detecting expert users in a question-answering forum, tracing the propagation of information in a social network, or reconstructing the Internet network topology from a set of traceroutes are examples of tasks faced by today's data scientists. A common theme to all these examples is that they involve input data manipulation as well as graph analytics, where graphs are analyzed using various graph algorithms. To solve such problems and extract valuable insights, data scientists must be able to quickly construct graphs from input data, and analyze the graphs using various graph algorithms.

SIGMOD'15, May 31–June 4, 2015, Melbourne, Victoria, Australia.

http://dx.doi.org/10.1145/2723372.2735369.

Thus, in order to support the work of data scientists, one requires a system that offers a rich set of *graph manipulation and analysis algorithms*. As graphs are rarely given as input, but have to be *constructed* from input data, a modern graph analytics system has to support easy manipulation of input data in order to build a desired graph. Arguably the most common form of input data are *relational tables* and while in principle tables can be used to represent graphs, dedicated graph structures where the neighbors of each node are easily accessible are more efficient for most graph computations. Thus, the system also needs to provide a way to *convert* between graphical and tabular data structures and data representations.

And last, the system also needs to provide *fast execution times* suitable for *interactive* use.

In summary, the desiderata for a modern data science oriented graph analytics system are:

(1) Ability to process large graphs, on the order of hundreds of millions of nodes and billions of edges,
(2) Fast execution times that allow for interactive, exploratory use (as opposed to batch-mode use),
(3) Easy to use front-end that provides many graph algorithms in a commonly used high-level programming language,
(4) Large number of efficient ready-to-use graph algorithms,
(5) Rich support for transformations of input data to graphs.

There are many challenges in building such systems. For example, what underlying hardware infrastructure shall one use? A cluster or a big server? How does one design data structures for tables and graphs that are efficient, flexible and fast? What operations are needed for building graphs from input data tables? What are the considerations for end-to-end graph analytics systems?

Ringo: Graph analytics on a big-memory machine. We present Ringo, an in-memory interactive graph analytics system that scales to large graphs. Ringo combines an easy-to-use Python front-end and a scalable parallel C++ back-end, which is responsible for rapid data handling and manipulation. Ringo provides functionality for efficiently building graphs from input data tables, for converting the tables to an efficient graph data structure, and for analyzing graphs using over 200 different graph functions through its core graph analytics package SNAP[1]. Ringo source code is open[2].

Recent research in graph analytics systems has been focused on distributed computing environments [8, 9, 10, 18, 21, 23, 24] or single-machine systems utilizing secondary storage [11, 13, 14]. Such systems offer scalability in the number of cores or in available throughput and size of the secondary storage, but these benefits

[1]SNAP is currently downloaded about a thousand times per month and actively used in our research group, as well as by over 500 students in Stanford University courses.
[2]`http://snap.stanford.edu/ringo`

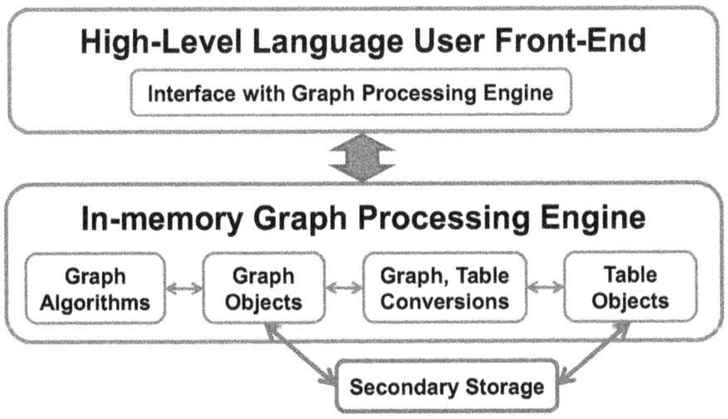

Figure 1: Ringo system overview.

come at a high price of increased communication cost, increased system complexity, and challenges when programming non-trivial graph algorithms. On the other hand, big-memory, multi-core machines are becoming affordable and widely available; a machine with 1TB of main memory and 80 cores costs around $35K.

We observe that most graphs being analyzed today comfortably fit in the memory of one such "big-memory" machine. Graph based computations require random data access patterns and exhibit notoriously poor data locality, so a single big-memory machine seems a natural hardware choice for analytics of all-but-largest graphs.

Ringo is built on the assumption that graphs being analyzed fit in memory of a single machine. This approach has significant benefits in that there is no network communication overhead, no need for managing the secondary storage, and that the programming model and the system use are straightforward. Even though the raw input data might not fit into the main memory initially, data cleaning and manipulation often result in significant data size reduction, so that the "interesting" part of the data nicely fits into the main memory.

Ringo showcases that a single multi-core machine offers a suitable platform for interactive graph analytics, while matching the performance of the fastest distributed graph processing systems (Section 3). Figure 1 illustrates Ringo.

The key features of Ringo are as follows:

- A system for interactive and exploratory analysis of large graphs with hundreds of millions or even billions of edges,
- Tight integration between graph and table processing and efficient conversions between graphs and tables,
- Powerful operations to construct various types of graphs,
- Ringo runs on a single machine with a large main memory, simplifying programming significantly and out performing distributed systems on all but the largest graphs.

The rest of the paper is organized as follows. Section 2 provides a system overview. System evaluation and benchmarks are presented in Section 3. Usage scenarios are described in Section 4. Finally, we conclude in Section 5.

2. SYSTEM OVERVIEW

2.1 Design Choices

In designing Ringo for interactive graph analytics, we were informed by two insights. The first insight is that all but the largest graphs being analyzed today fit comfortably in memory of a big-memory machine. The second insight is that graphs are not analyzed in isolation, but are part of a larger data mining workflow, which requires that, in addition to graph operations, table analytics operations are integrated in the system as well. We discuss those insights and design choices in more detail next.

Number of Edges	Number of Graphs
<0.1M	16
0.1M – 1M	25
1M – 10M	17
10M – 100M	7
100M – 1B	5
>1B	1

Table 1: Graph size statistics of 71 graphs publicly available in the Stanford Large Network Collection. 90% of graphs have less than 100M edges. Only one graph has more than 1B edges.

Graph sizes. Our goal is to provide fast execution time for commonly analyzed, average size graphs rather than provide a scalable solution for extremely large (and rare) graphs.

Classifying graphs from a widely used repository [4] of publicly available real-world networks (covering a wide range of areas, such as the Internet, social networks, road networks, Web networks) according to the number of edges shows that 90% out of 71 graphs have less than 100 million edges and only one graph has more than 1 billion edges (Table 1). Most graphs fit in a few GB of RAM, and the largest graph requires only about 30GB of RAM. Furthermore, very few real-world, non-synthetic graphs with more than one billion edges are discussed regularly in present research literature, Twitter2010 with 1.5B edges and Yahoo Web graph with 6.6B edges being the most common. Assuming 20 bytes of storage per edge, even the Yahoo Web graph requires only about 135GB and fits easily in a 1TB RAM machine. Other studies confirm our observation that most analytics datasets are limited in size [5, 22].

Based on this evidence we conclude that big-memory machines allow for storing and processing large graphs in-memory. As we show later in the experimental section, such machines also have sufficient compute power to execute graph analytics at speeds comparable to the fastest distributed graph processing systems.

Graph analytics workflow. Graph analytics often follow the workflow presented in Figure 2. Raw data is stored in a big data repository and handled by a system like Hadoop to extract the initial data for analysis. The extracted data is organized in a set of relational tables and a major part of the graph analytics workflow is then to construct many different graphs from the tables. Once graphs are built, we require graph specific operations, such as PageRank, connected components, shortest paths. Although graphs can be represented as relational tables and graph operations can be implemented using relational operations, we find it is more efficient (in terms of memory as well as speed) to have optimized graph-specific data structures. Thus, given graphs represented as tables, the next step is to convert these tables to a graph representation. We then execute graph operations and integrate the results back to tables. The result is an iterative process, where data can be rapidly converted from tables to graphs and vice versa.

To provide fast execution speed in Ringo, we implemented table processing as part of the system, which allows us to tightly integrate table and graph processing and to rapidly convert large datasets from one representation to another.

2.2 Graphs in Ringo

Ringo graph representation. A critical operation for fast execution of graph algorithms is quick access to neighboring nodes and edges. Additionally, we require that our graph representation is dynamic, so in existing graphs nodes and edges can be quickly added or removed. A challenge is thus to strike a balance between opposing requirements for fast access to a node's neighborhood and having a dynamic graph structure.

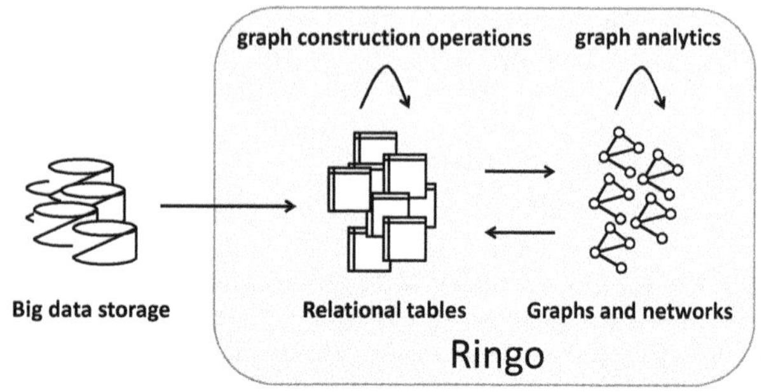

Figure 2: Graph analytics workflow. Using a system like Hadoop, data of interest is extracted from a big data storage into a set of relational tables. Graphs are built using graph construction operations on tables; the results are converted to graphs. Graph analytic operations are then applied to the graphs. Results of graph operations are added back to tables.

One possible approach for efficient graph representation would be to use the Compressed Sparse Row format [3]. This format uses two vectors, a vector for nodes and a vector for edges. The edge vector is sorted by source nodes and indexed by the node vector for fast access. While this approach offers high performance for traversal operations, it does not perform well for dynamic graphs, since graph updates cause prohibitive maintenance costs of the single big edge vector (e.g., deleting a single edge requires time linear in the total number of edges in the graph).

Ringo supports dynamic graphs by representing a graph as a hash table of nodes. Each node maintains sorted adjacency vector of neighboring nodes. Space requirements for this representation are similar to those of the Compressed Sparse Row format. However, we found that representing graphs as a hash table of nodes and the associated adjacency vectors does not dramatically impact the performance of graph algorithms (e.g., deleting a single edge only requires time linear in the node degree).

Ringo graph operations. To provide a rich set of graph constructs and algorithms, Ringo builds on the publicly available Stanford Network Analysis Platform (SNAP) [2]. SNAP provides more than two hundred out-of-the-box graph constructs and algorithms that are available for use on Ringo in-memory graph data structure.

2.3 Tables in Ringo

Table representation. In addition to graph objects, Ringo implements its own native relational table objects to allow for efficient and flexible parallel implementations of operations important for graph construction, to support fast conversions into graph objects, and to avoid any performance overheads related to frequent transitions to and from external systems during the iterative data analysis process. Tables in Ringo have a schema, which defines table columns and their types (integer, floating point, or string). Since tables have been studied extensively [25], we only describe some Ringo specific details here.

As most tabular operations in Ringo are graph related and primarily use iterations over columns, Ringo table representation optimizes this use by implementing tables with a column based store. In Ringo each row has a persistent unique identifier. This allows for fast in-place grouping, filtering and selection. Moreover, identifiers allow for fine-grained data tracking, so the user can identify data records even after they undergo a complex set of operations.

Ringo provides basic relational operations on table objects, such as select, join, project, group & aggregate, set operations, order (sort), and similar. In addition, Ringo also provides a number of advanced graph construction operations, described next.

Graph construction. In order to construct a graph, we first manipulate input data tables into an *edge table* that has two columns, a column with edge source nodes and a column with edge destination nodes. Once the edge table is constructed we transform it into a Ringo graph in-memory data structure.

In some cases, the edge table can be constructed using basic relational operations, such as join and select. However, often graph construction requires advanced operations unique to Ringo. Ringo allows for creating edges based on node similarity or temporal order of nodes. Ringo implements *SimJoin*, which joins two records if their distance is smaller than a given threshold, and *NextK*, which joins predecessor-successor records.

2.4 Converting Between Tables and Graphs

Fast conversions between graph and table objects are essential for data exploration tasks involving graphs. Without the loss of generality we limit our discussion to conversions of directed graphs.

Conversion of tables to graphs. The goal is to generate a directed graph $G = (V, E)$ from table T, with edge source column S and edge destination column D. Nodes V in the graph are defined by unique values in columns S and D. And each row $r \in T$ defines an edge $e \in E$ with the source node provided in column S and the destination node provided in column D, $e = (r_S, r_D)$.

A directed graph in Ringo is represented as a node hash table, where each node contains two sorted adjacency vectors providing its in-neighbors and out-neighbors. The problem of converting a table to a graph is how to transform an edge list given by two columns in a table to a node hash table with sorted neighbor vectors. The challenge is to transform tables with hundreds of millions of rows at speeds that make the system suitable for interactive use.

We experimented with several approaches and found that a "sort-first" algorithm works the best. The algorithm builds a graph representation from a table by first making copies of the source and destinations columns, then sorting the column copies, computing the number of neighbors for each node, and then copying the neighbor vectors to the graph hash table. Advantages of our method are that sorting can be done in parallel and that it does not require any thread-safe operations on vectors and hash tables. While concurrent access is still performed, there is no contention among the threads, which minimizes locking and allows fast execution on multi-core machines. Since the number of neighbors is calculated explicitly, there is also no need to estimate the size of the hash table or neighbor vectors in advance.

Conversion of graphs to tables. The conversion from a graph to a table involves building a node table or an edge table. This conversion can be easily preformed in parallel by partitioning the graph's nodes or edges among worker threads, pre-allocating the output table, and assigning a corresponding partition in the output table to each thread. The threads iterate over nodes or edges in their graph partitions and write the output to their assigned partitions in the output table.

2.5 Ringo Implementation

We highlight aspects of Ringo implementation that allow for high-performance graph processing in an interactive environment.

High-level language front-end. The user interacts with Ringo through a Python module. Ringo front-end utilizes our graph processing engine to execute time critical parts. We use SWIG [1] to connect the Python front-end with the parallel C++ table and graph processing back-end engine.

High-performance graph processing engine. Ringo graph processing engine is based on SNAP [2], a highly efficient C++ graph analysis library that implements complex graph classes and a rich

Graph Name	LiveJournal [7]	Twitter2010 [15]
Nodes	4.8M	42M
Edges	69M	1.5B
Text File Size	1.1GB	26.2GB
In-memory Graph Size	0.7GB	13.2GB
In-memory Table Size	1.1GB	23.5GB

Table 2: Experiment graphs. *Text Size* is the size of the input text file, *Graph Size* is the size of the corresponding Ringo graph object, and *Table Size* is the size of the Ringo table object.

Operation	LiveJournal	Twitter2010
PageRank	2.76s	60.5s
Triangle Counting	6.13s	263.6s

Table 3: Performance of parallel graph algorithms for PageRank and Triangle Counting on a single big-memory machine with 80 cores. For PageRank, ten iterations were timed.

set of graph constructs and algorithms. For Ringo, we have expanded SNAP with several new components, including table processing, conversions between tables and graphs, and parallel graph algorithms. OpenMP was used to parallelize critical loops in the code for full utilization of our target multi-core platforms.

Concurrent hash tables and vectors. The OpenMP layer relies on fast, thread-safe operations on concurrent hash tables and vectors, which are critical for achieving high performance of graph operations. We implemented an open addressing hash table with linear probing [16]. To support fast graph construction, we extended the node hash table with thread-safe insertions to a node's adjacency vector. Concurrent insertions to a vector are implemented by using an atomic increment instruction to claim an index of a cell to which a new value is inserted.

3. SYSTEM PERFORMANCE

In this section, we show Ringo performance on a single, big-memory, multi-core machine. Experiments demonstrate that such machines are able to execute critical operations at speeds that are needed for interactive graph analysis.

Experimental datasets and setup. For our benchmarks, we use two popular graphs, *LiveJournal* and the larger *Twitter2010* (Table 2), that have been widely used for benchmarks of other large-scale graph processing systems [6, 8, 11, 12, 14, 17, 18]. In many cases, graphs used for analyses are of sizes similar to *LiveJournal*. However, larger graphs do exist and can be easily processed on machines with 1TB RAM. For example, the *Twitter2010* graph takes only about 13GB of main memory in Ringo (Table 2), which means that the system could easily process graphs that are an order of magnitude larger.

Our measurements were performed on a machine with 1TB RAM and 4x Intel CPU E7-4870 at 2.40GHz, each CPU has 10 cores and supports 20 hyperthreads for a total of 80 hyperthreads, running CentOS 6.4. A similar machine costs $35K as of Nov 2014.

Parallel graph algorithms. We demonstrate graph analysis capabilities of big-memory machines by using PageRank [20] and undirected triangle counting—two key graph algorithms that are often used for benchmarking purposes. PageRank is an example of an iterative message-passing-like computation. We measured the runtime of 10 iterations. Triangle counting is directly related to relational joins, one of the central problems in database systems [19]. We ran each experiment 5 times, and report the average runtimes. Table 3 shows the results. It is worth comparing the performance of Ringo to the recently published results on the *Twitter2010* graph.

Dataset	LiveJournal	Twitter2010
Select 10K, in place	<0.2s	1.6s
Rows/s	405.9M	935.3M
Select all-10K, in place	<0.1s	1.6s
Rows/s	575.0M	917.7M
Join 10K	0.6s	4.2s
Rows/s	109.5M	348.8M
Join all-10K	3.1s	29.7s
Rows/s	44.5M	98.8M

Table 4: Ringo performance of Select and Join operations on tables. Numbers give measured times on our test datasets. The *Rows/s* gives the processing rate in millions of table rows processed per second. The processing rate for *Join* takes the sizes of both input tables into account.

For triangle counting, a recently published method [13] took 469s using 1 machine with 6 cores and SSD based secondary storage, while a different, distributed approach took 564s on a cluster of 200 processors [6]. Ringo takes 263s on 1 machine with 80 hyperthreads. The implementation of the algorithm in Ringo was simple, using a straightforward approach, similar to [6] and parallelizing the execution with a few OpenMP statements.

PowerGraph [8] is one of the highest performing graph processing systems. Using 64 machines with 512 cores, PowerGraph took 3.6s per iteration of the PageRank algorithm. On the other hand, Ringo takes around 6s per iteration, while using 6x fewer cores, only one machine and 13GB RAM. Similarly to the implementation of triangle counting, PageRank implementation in Ringo is based on a straightforward, sequential algorithm with a few OpenMP statements for parallel execution. Even though the purpose of Ringo is not to be the fastest graph engine, comparisons show the viability of big-memory machines for processing all-but-the-largest graphs.

In addition to fast execution times, Ringo graph processing also keeps a low memory footprint. The computation of 10 iterations of PageRank on the *Twitter2010* graph had a memory footprint of 18.3GB, and triangle counting on that same graph had a memory footprint of 22.6GB. In both cases the memory footprint was less than twice the size of the graph object itself.

Table operations. While the focus of Ringo is on graph analytics, table operations are necessary for processing the data prior to graph construction and are a fundamental part of the analysis process. To support interactive data exploration the table operations have to execute quickly and at speeds comparable to graph operations.

We benchmark Ringo on two essential table operations, *select* and *join* (Table 4). For select benchmarks, rows are chosen based on a comparison with a constant value. The value is determined so that it either selects 10,000 elements from the table or all elements except 10,000. The purpose of two measurements is to show performance when the output is either very small or similar in size to the input table. We show results for the select in-place operation, where the current table is modified.

For join benchmarks, the input table is joined with a second, single column table. The values in the second table are chosen so that the output table has either 10,000 elements or all elements from the input table except 10,000. Ringo join operation always produces a new table object. Overall, results in Table 4 demonstrate that Ringo offers robust performance over a range of scenarios.

Conversions between tables and graphs. Next we present performance of Ringo algorithms when converting tables to graphs and vice versa (discussed in Section 2.4).

Table 5 gives Ringo execution times for conversions of *LiveJournal* and *Twitter2010* datasets between table and graph representa-

Graph Name	LiveJournal	Twitter2010
Table to graph	8.5s	81.0s
Edges/s	13.0M	18.0M
Graph to table	1.5s	29.2s
Edges/s	46.0M	50.4M

Table 5: Execution times for converting tables to graphs and vice versa. The *Edges/s* row gives the processing rate in millions of edges processed per second.

Algorithm	Runtime
3-core	31.0s
SSSP	7.4s
SCC	18.0s

Table 6: Runtime of single-threaded implementations of commonly used graph algorithms on the *LiveJournal* graph: 3-core, single source shortest path (SSSP), and strongly connected component decomposition (SCC).

tions. For example, in the specific case of the *Twitter2010* graph, the conversion of the table containing a single large edge vector to a graph means that a table with 1.5B rows must be traversed, and 1.5B pairs of node identifiers are extracted. Each element of a pair is inserted to the node hash table in the graph and elements are added to the two corresponding adjacency vectors, which must be sorted. This results in a graph representation with a total of 42M nodes, and 84M vectors containing adjacent nodes.

Overall, the conversion from a table to a graph is performed at a rate of over 10M table rows or graph edges per second and about 50M edges per second in the opposite direction, so graphs with tens of millions of edges can be processed in seconds. The conversion scales well as the processing rate does not degrade for large graphs.

Sequential performance. For moderately large real-world graphs such as *LiveJournal*, even sequential implementations of graph algorithms are fast enough for interactive analysis. We measured the runtime of sequential implementations of 3 commonly used graph algorithms on the *LiveJournal* graph: *3-core* of the graph, *single source shortest path* (runtime averaged over 10 random sources), and finding *strongly connected components* (Table 6). All algorithms executed in about 30 seconds or less. For larger graphs, parallel implementations of graph algorithms are needed, and we are currently expanding the set of parallel algorithm implementations available through Ringo.

4. RINGO SCENARIOS

We demonstrate Ringo on real-world graph analytic scenarios, illustrating its applicability, ease of use, and performance.

4.1 End-to-end Graph Analytics

Our demo will showcase Ringo capabilities in an end-to-end graph analytics scenario. SIGMOD attendees will be able to interact with Ringo and observe ease of use and integration of table and graph operations.

Finding Java experts on StackOverflow. We will show a realistic and representative use case where the goal is to identify top Java experts in the StackOverflow user community. For demonstration we will use complete data from StackOverflow, which is the world's largest question-answering website, where users post questions, then others answer them. As the answers are given, the person posting the question has the option of picking the best answer by "accepting" it. In order to identify top experts our demo will start with complete StackOverflow data (8M questions, 14M answers, 34M comments). The demo will then follow these steps: manipulate tables to build a graph which connects users providing Java related questions and answers, and use a graph algorithm to identify top Java experts.

Demonstrantion scenario. The SIGMOD attendee will first load complete StackOverflow data[3] in a form of relational tables. The attendee will then manipulate the input tables in order to build a graph representing the interactions in the forum's social network. For example, one way to build a graph is to connect users who answered the same question. A different way is to connect StackOverflow users that answered each other's questions. Ringo provides rich functionality for the SIGMOD attendee to build various kinds of graphs based on the StackOverflow data. Once the graph is built, the attendee will identify important nodes in the graph. Ringo implements over 200 different graph analytics algorithms (e.g., PageRank, Hits, and various other node centrality measures) that the attendee may try out to find Java experts.

Below, we show Ringo Python commands for the above demo[4]. The attendee will load the StackOverflow posts table `P`, extract all the Java posts `JP`, and build two new tables: questions table `Q` and answers table `A`:

```
P = ringo.LoadTableTSV(schema,'posts.tsv')
JP = ringo.Select(P,'Tag=Java')
Q = ringo.Select(JP,'Type=question')
A = ringo.Select(JP,'Type=answer')
```

Next, the attendee will build a graph and apply the PageRank algorithm on it. Ringo primitives for this task are:

```
QA = ringoJoin(Q,A,'AnswerId','PostId')
G = ringo.ToGraph(QA,'UserId-1','UserId-2')
PR = ringo.GetPageRank(G)
S = ringo.TableFromHashMap(PR,'User','Scr')
```

The *Answers* table on column *PostId* is joined with the *Questions* table on column *AnswerId*. The resulting *QA* table has two *UserId* columns, corresponding to the users that asked questions and the users whose answers were accepted. Using these user columns in *QA*, `ToGraph()` transforms the *QA* table into an optimized graph data structure *G*, where each node represents a user and an edge indicates that an answer by the destination node was accepted by the source node. `GetPageRank()` calculates the PageRank scores of all the nodes in *G*. The remaining line builds the final table *S* with the users' PageRank scores.

The above example clearly demonstrates that a system cannot treat graph analytics in isolation, but that graph analytics needs to be integrated with table operations. With Ringo we will demonstrate a system, where graph and table operations are tightly integrated. Besides implementing table operations as part of the system, in Ringo this integration involves fast conversions between table and graph data structures as well as customized table operations, suitable for graph analytics.

Ringo ease of use. We will also demonstrate several factors that contribute to ease of use of Ringo: integrated processing of graphs and tables, Python front-end, and execution on a single machine.

What the attendees will see and do. The attendees will be able to load the StackOverflow dataset in Ringo and perform graph analytics on the dataset. First, an attendee will be able to execute operations that identify the top Java experts on StackOverflow. Second,

[3]Freely available at `http://data.stackexchange.com`.
[4]For complete code for the demo, see `http://snap.stanford.edu/ringo`

the attendee will be able to vary the parameters to identify top experts on StackOverflow in other programming languages and topics of interest, or change the operations to explore alternative measures of expertise. Third, the attendee will be invited to an open exploration of the StackOverflow dataset by applying Ringo graph analytics capabilities.

4.2 Performance Demonstration

This part of our demo will center around Ringo performance. Attendees will be able to observe system performance and resource utilization on a range of input datasets and hardware platforms.

Graph analytics operations. Several types of operations are critical for graph analytics: graph operations, table operations, conversions between tables and graphs, and data input/output. For the demo, we will show performance of a range of Ringo operations on the LiveJournal and the Twitter2010 datasets. LiveJournal is a typical representative of a graph dataset, while the Twitter2010 dataset is one of the largest publicly available real-world graph datasets.

Hardware used for demonstration. Big-memory machines provide a viable platform for interactive graph analytics. Large RAM on such machines can deliver fast random access, required by graph algorithms. In our demo, we will show how Ringo performs on a wide range of operations on a big-memory machine. For our demo, we will use a machine with 1TB RAM and 4x Intel CPU E7-4870 at 2.40GHz, running CentOS 6.5. Each CPU has 10 cores and supports 20 hyperthreads for a total of 80 hyperthreads.

Ringo also works well on standard personal computers, provided that the datasets fit in the RAM available. As discussed before, 90% of graphs in SNAP require only a few GB of RAM (see Table 1), so they can fit in memory of a typical desktop or laptop. We will demo Ringo also on a laptop with 8GB RAM and an Intel Core i5-4258U CPU at 2.40GHz with 2 cores, costing around $1,500.

What the attendees will see and do. The attendees will be able to use Ringo on a big-memory machine and on a personal computer. Initially, the attendee will choose either a big-memory machine or a laptop environment and load one of the datasets, LiveJournal or Twitter2010. (Only LiveJournal will be available on the laptop due to RAM limitations.) Next, the attendees will be able to execute a wide range of graph algorithms and observe their performance and the hardware utilization.

5. CONCLUSION

We presented Ringo—a system for interactive and exploratory analysis of large graphs with hundreds of millions of nodes and edges. Ringo exposes its functionality through high-level Python programming language, the language of choice of today's data scientists. Tight integration between graph and table processing and efficient conversions between graphs and tables allow for powerful operations that make it easy to perform complex analytic tasks.

Overall, we demonstrate that big-memory machines are suitable for performing interactive analyses of all, but the very largest graphs. In many real-world scenarios graph sizes are well below a terabyte and in such cases big-memory machines have significant benefit over large distributed clusters. Single machines are easier and more efficient to program, while the cost and complexity of cross-machine communication and scheduling are eliminated.

Acknowledgments. We thank Vikesh Khanna, Chantat Eksombatchai, Sheila Ramaswamy, Nicholas Shelly, Nikhil Khadke, and Jason Jong for their assistance with Ringo implementation, and Andrej Krevl for his help with the experimental setup. Yonathan Perez is supported by P. Michael Farmwald Stanford Graduate Fellowship. This research has been supported in part by NSF IIS-1016909, IIS-1149837, IIS-1159679, CNS-1010921, DARPA XDATA, DARPA GRAPHS, DARPA SIMPLEX, Boeing, Facebook, Volkswagen, Yahoo, and SDSI.

6. REFERENCES

[1] Simplified wrapper and interface generator SWIG. http://www.swig.org.

[2] SNAP: Stanford Network Analysis Platform. http://snap.stanford.edu.

[3] D. Gregor, J. Willcock, and A. Lumsdaine. Compressed Sparse Row Graph. http://www.boost.org/doc/libs/1_57_0/libs/graph/doc/compressed_sparse_row.html

[4] J. Leskovec, and A. Krevl. SNAP Datasets: Stanford Large Network Dataset Collection http://snap.stanford.edu/data

[5] R. Appuswamy, C. Gkantsidis, D. Narayanan, O. Hodson, and A. Rowstron. Scale-up vs scale-out for hadoop: Time to rethink? In *SoCC*, 2013.

[6] S. Arifuzzaman, M. Khan, and M. Marathe. Patric: A parallel algorithm for counting triangles in massive networks. In *CIKM*, 2013.

[7] L. Backstrom, D. Huttenlocher, J. Kleinberg, and X. Lan. Group formation in large social networks: membership, growth, and evolution. In *KDD*, 2006.

[8] J. Gonzalez, Y. Low, H. Gu, , D. Bickson, and C. Guestrin. Powergraph: Distributed graph-parallel computation on natural graphs. In *OSDI*, 2012.

[9] J. E. Gonzalez, R. S. Xin, A. Dave, D. Crankshaw, M. J. Franklin, and I. Stoica. Graphx: graph processing in a distributed dataflow framework. In *OSDI*, 2014.

[10] M. Han, K. Daudjee, K. Ammar, M. T. Ozsu, X. Wang, and T. Jin. An experimental comparison of pregel-like graph processing systems. In *VLDB*, 2014.

[11] W. Han, S. Lee, K. Park, J. Lee, M. Kim, J. Kim, and H. Yu. Turbograph: A fast parallel graph engine handling billion-scale graphs in a single pc. In *KDD*, 2013.

[12] S. Hong, H. Chafi, E. Sedlar, and K. Olukotun. Green-marl: A dsl for easy and efficient graph analysis. In *ASPLOS '12*,2012.

[13] J. Kim, W.-S. Han, S. Lee, K. Park, and H. Yu. Opt: a new framework for overlapped and parallel triangulation in large-scale graphs. In *SIGMOD*, 2014.

[14] A. Kryola, G. Blelloch, and C. Guestrin. Graphchi: Large-scale graph computation on just a pc. In *OSDI*, 2012.

[15] H. Kwak, C. Lee, H. Park, and S. Moon. What is twitter, a social network or a news media? In *WWW*, 2010.

[16] H. Lang, V. Leis, M.-C. Albutiu, T. Neumann, and A. Kemper. Massively parallel numa-aware hash joins. In *VLDB IMDM*, 2013.

[17] Y. Low, J. Gonzalez, A. Kryola, D. Bickson, C. Guestrin, and J. Hellerstein. Distributed graphlab: A framework for machine learning and data mining in the cloud. In *VLDB*, 2012.

[18] G. Malewicz, M. Austern, A. Bik, D. J., I. Horn, N. Leiser, and G. Czajkowski. Pregel: A system for large-scale graph processing. In *SIGMOD*, 2010.

[19] H. Q. Ngo, C. Ré, and A. Rudra. Skew strikes back: new developments in the theory of join algorithms. *SIGMOD Record*, 2013.

[20] L. Page, S. Brin, R. Motwani, and T. Winograd. The pagerank citation ranking: Bringing order to the web. Technical report, Stanford InfoLab, 1999.

[21] L. Qin, J. X. Yu, L. Chang, H. Cheng, C. Zhang, and X. Lin. Scalable big graph processing in mapreduce. In *SIGMOD*, 2014.

[22] A. Rowstron, D. Narayanan, A. Donnelly, G. O'Shea, and A. Douglas. Nobody ever got fired for using hadoop on a cluster. In *HotCDP*, 2012.

[23] N. Satish, N. Sundaram, M. M. A. Patwary, J. Seo, J. Park, M. A. Hassaan, S. Sengupta, Z. Yin, and P. Dubey. Navigating the maze of graph analytics frameworks using massive graph datasets. In *SIGMOD*, 2014.

[24] B. Shao, H. Wang, and Y. Li. Trinity: A distributed graph engine on a memory cloud. In *SIGMOD*, 2013.

[25] H. Garcia-Molina, J. Ullman, and J. Widom. Database Systems: The Complete Book. Prentice Hall Press 2nd edition, 2008.

STORM: Spatio-Temporal Online Reasoning and Management of Large Spatio-Temporal Data

Robert Christensen[1], Lu Wang[2], Feifei Li[1], Ke Yi[2], Jun Tang[1], Natalee Villa[1]
[1]University of Utah [2]Hong Kong University of Science and Technology
{robertc, lifeifei, jtang, villa}@cs.utah.edu {luwang, yike}@cse.ust.hk

ABSTRACT

We present the STORM system to enable spatio-temporal online reasoning and management of large spatio-temporal data. STORM supports *interactive* spatio-temporal analytics through novel spatial online sampling techniques. Online spatio-temporal aggregation and analytics are then derived based on the online samples, where approximate answers with approximation quality guarantees can be provided immediately from the start of query execution. The quality of these online approximations improve over time. This demonstration proposal describes key ideas in the design of the STORM system, and presents the demonstration plan.

Categories and Subject Descriptors

H.2.4 [**Information Systems**]: Database Management – *Systems*

Keywords

Spatial online sampling, spatial online analytics, STORM

1. INTRODUCTION

The increasing presence of smart phones and various sensing devices has led to humongous amounts of spatio-temporal data, and the imperative needs for rich data anlytics over such data. Many data from a measurement network and social media data sources are inherently spatial and temporal. As a result, numerous analytical tasks based on such data have a spatial and/or temporal extent.

Even though various forms of spatial and spatio-temporal analytics have been extensively studied, the ever-increasing size of spatio-temporal data introduces new challenges. In particular, when the underlying data set is large, reporting all points that satisfy a query condition can be expensive, since there could be simply too many points that satisfy a query. The CPU cost of performing an analytical task or computing an aggregation using all these points adds additional overhead, and may not scale well with increasing number of points. Hence, waiting for the exact analytical or aggregation results may take a long time.

SIGMOD'15, May 31–June 4, 2015, Melbourne, Victoria, Australia.
Copyright © 2015 ACM 978-1-4503-2758-9/15/05 ...$15.00.
http://dx.doi.org/10.1145/2723372.2735373.

An important observation is that approximate results are often good enough, especially when approximation guarantees are provided. It is even more attractive if the quality of an approximation improves continuously over time until the exact result is obtained in the end. We dub such an approach *online aggregation and analytics*. Online aggregation and analytics enables *interactive analytics and exploration* over large scale spatio-temporal data. A user may terminate a query whenever s/he is satisfied with the approximation quality provided by the system. The system can also be asked to terminate a query whenever the approximation quality for a query has met a query-specific (user specified) quality requirement. Alternatively, the system can also operate in the "best-effort" mode where user specifies the amount of time s/he is willing to spend on a given task, and the system will provide a result with the best possible approximation quality within the amount of time given.

Consider the following example. A user wants to understand the electricity usage in NYC over the first quarter. But s/he wants to explore different area and time range combinations. So s/he could zoom in to a particular area from NYC on a map and specify between January 5 to March 5, and ask for the average electricity usage per unit for units in this area and measurements in this time period. In interactive exploration, or formally interactive analytics, user can change his/her query condition without the need of waiting for the current query to complete. In other words, in the above example, user may change to a different area in NYC and/or adjust the time range to between January 15 and March 12, while the first query is still being executed.

On big spatial and spatio-temporal data sets, waiting for exact results may take a while. The user faces a *dilemma*: *either* waits for the current query to complete *or* terminates the current query and issue the new query. And the number of possible combinations a user wants to investigate in order to find interesting patterns, even for a small region like NYC and first quarter, can be daunting.

The STORM system solves this dilemma. STORM uses spatio-temporal online reasoning and management to achieve online aggregation and analytics on large spatio-temporal data. In the above example, assume that after 1 second into the execution of the first query, system reports that the average electricity usage is 973 kWh with a standard deviation of 25 kWh and 95% confidence, if the user is happy with the quality of this estimation, s/he can immediately change the query condition to stop the first query and start the second query. S/he could also wait a bit longer for better quality, say, using 1.5 seconds, system now reports the average electricity usage for the 1st query as 982 kWh with a standard deviation of 5 kWh and 98% confidence.

STORM uses *spatial online sampling* to achieve its objectives. In particular, spatial online sampling continuously returns randomly sampled points from a user specified spatio-temporal query region, until user terminates the process or enough samples have been obtained to meet an accuracy requirement. An unbiased estimator, tailored towards a given analytical query, is built using the spatial online samples, and its approximation quality improves in an online fashion while more samples are being returned.

To make it easy for users and different applications to enjoy the benefit of spatio-temporal online analytics and aggregation, STORM also implements a data connector, so that it can easily import data in different formats and schemas, and enable spatio-temporal online analytics over such data without much efforts. Lastly, it features a number of built-in analytical modules so that a set of common analytical tasks can be executed without further engineering efforts once data have been imported. More complex and other analytical tasks can be built in a customized fashion.

Demonstration proposal. This demonstration proposal describes the design of STORM, and explains its key technical ideas. It also presents a detailed demonstration plan, and some evaluations to illustrate the advantage of STORM.

- We formalize spatial online sampling and online analytics in Section 2.
- We describe the design of the STORM system in details, and explain its key technical ideas in Section 3
- We present a small set of performance evaluations to illustrate the superiority of the STORM design over a few baselines, and a detailed plan for the demonstration of the STORM system in Section 4.

Lastly, we review related works in Section 5.

2. OVERVIEW

Random sampling is a fundamental and effective approach for dealing with large data sets, with a strong theoretical foundation in statistics supporting its wide usage in a variety of applications that do not require completely accurate answers. The use of random sampling for approximate query processing in the database community also has a long history, notably with line of work on *online aggregation* [7].

In online aggregation, instead of evaluating a potentially expensive query until the very end, we repeatedly take samples from all tuples that satisfy the query condition, and continuously compute the required aggregate based on the sampled tuples returned so far. The accuracy of the computed aggregate gradually improves as we get more and more samples, which is measured by *confidence intervals*, and the user may stop the query processing as soon as the accuracy has reached a satisfying level. Recently, online aggregation has received revived attention [11, 18], as an effective tool for answering "big queries" that touch a huge number of tuples but the user can often be satisfied with just an accurate enough estimate.

However, past work on online aggregation has focused on relational aggregates, group-by, and join queries [5, 7, 11, 18], on relational data. Motivated by the needs for *interactive spatio-temporal exploration and analytics* as explained in Section 1, we build the STORM system to achieve spatial online analytics and aggregation over spatial and spatio-temporal data. Since the statistical side of online aggregation is relatively well understood [5, 7, 11, 13, 18], which we will discuss briefly in Section 3, the key challenge essentially reduces to that of *spatial online sampling*, i.e., how to repeatedly sample a tuple from a spatio-temporal query until the user says "stop". This is formally defined as follows.

Definition 1 (Spatial online sampling) Given a set of N points P in a d-dimensional space, store them in an index such that, for a given range query Q, return sampled points from $Q \cap P$ (with or without replacement) until the user terminates the query.

Spatial online aggregation is a direct product of spatial online sampling, where online estimators for different types of spatial and spatio-temporal aggregates, like sum or average, are built using spatial online samples. A spatial online estimator ideally should be an *unbiased estimator*, and its estimation quality, characterized by confidence intervals, improves over time in an online fashion while more spatial samples are obtained. This concept can be further generalized beyond simple aggregates to *spatio-temporal online analytics* that covers a wide range of analytical tasks, like spatial clustering, spatial kernel density estimate (KDE). More details on this topic are provided in Section 3.

The proposed STORM system (spatio-temporal online reasoning and management) uses spatial online sampling to build spatio-temporal online estimators. STORM builds on a cluster of commodity machines to achieve its scalability. It uses a DFS (distributed file system) as its storage engine. As a result, it integrates with many existing distributed data management systems seamlessly, such as Hadoop and Spark. In particular, we have based the development of STORM on top of a distributed installation of MongoDB, which uses a DFS and the JSON format for its record structures.

The STORM system provides a *query interface* that supports a number of commonly encountered analytical queries on spatio-temporal data sets, such as basic spatio-temporal aggregations. It also includes a few more complex, advanced analytical queries such as kernel density estimate, trajectory reconstruction, semantics analysis (on short-text data) to illustrate the wide applicability of spatio-temporal online analytics by building a customized online estimator.

It also uses a *data connector* to connect to different data sources in order to import or index data from different storage engines such as excel spreadsheets, relational databases, a key value store such as Cassandra or HBase.

Lastly, it exposes a set of library and APIs, and a query language to enable users to build customized spatio-temporal online analytical tasks. An overview of the STORM system is shown in Figure 1.

Demonstration overview. The demonstration consists of four different components, namely, basic analytics, data import, updates, and customized analytics.

In *basic analytics*, we will showcase spatio-temporal online analytics in STORM using a number of data sets that are already imported and indexed by STORM. Our data sets include a massive national atmospheric measurement network data from nearly 40,000 weather stations from the MesoWest project, and data from various social media data sources (in particular, a growing subset of twitter data from July, 2013 to present). Users are able to interactive with the system by issuing basic analytical queries in a map-based query and analytical interface such as spatio-temporal aggregations on MesoWest data (e.g, the average temperature reading from

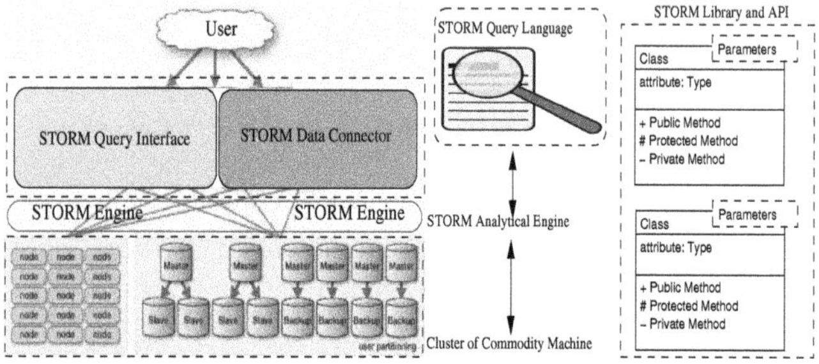

Figure 1: The STORM system overview.

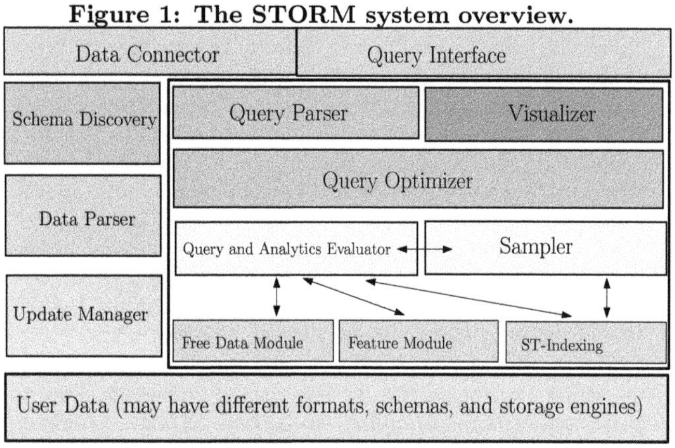

Figure 2: The STORM engine architecture.

a spatio-temporal region), population density estimate for a spatio-temporal region using KDEs over twitter data.

In *data import*, a user may import a data set from an external data source during the demo. Through its data connector module, STORM supports the import and indexing of data from a number of different storage engines, such as excel spreadsheets, MySQL, Cassandra, MongoDB. Users have the option of either importing the data into the STORM storage engine which is based on JSON format in a distributed MongoDB installation, or simply indexing the data through the data connector (without importing the data into the STORM storage engine).

In *updates*, we will demonstrate how STORM supports ad-hoc data updates efficiently. Its novel spatial online sampling module is able to update its indexing structure to reflect the latest state of the underlying data sets, so that a correct set of online spatio-temporal samples can always be returned with respect to the latest records in a data set.

Finally, in *customized analytics*, we will show how to construct a customized online analytical estimator for a spatio-temporal analytical query.

3. THE STORM SYSTEM

The design of the STORM engine is shown in Figure 2. In what follows, we explain the key technical ideas behind the *sampler* and the *ST-indexing* in details, and only briefly introduce the other modules.

3.1 The Sampler and ST-Indexing

The key objective of the *sampler* is to return spatial online samples as defined in Definition 1. Specifically, under the request of query and analytics evaluator, the *sampler* continuously returns independent random samples, one at a time, from a user specified spatio-temporal query region. In most

P	The raw data set in $\mathbb{R}^d$.
k	The number of samples to report.
N	$\|P\|$, the size of the raw data set.
Q	A range query in $\mathbb{R}^d$.
P_Q	$P \cap Q$, elements in the query range.
q	$\|P_Q\|$, the number of elements in the query range.
$u, v, \cdots$	Tree nodes.
$T(u)$	The subtree rooted at node u.
$P(u)$	The set of all data points covered by $T(u)$.
R_Q	The canonical set for Q.
$r(N)$	The size of a canonical set in a R-tree of size N.
B	The size of a disk block.

Table 1: Notation used in the paper.

cases, we need a relatively small sample whose size increases over time, i.e., k samples where $k \ll N$. Queries are *online and continuous*. The evaluator may keep asking for samples until satisfied with those returned (to meet an accuracy or time requirement). This means that k is *unknown* until the query is terminated by the system, somewhat like data stream algorithms. In fact k is never given to the sampler as a parameter, and we will design methods that efficiently extract *one* sample at a time. Hence, this problem can also be interpreted as asking the *sampler* to return k samples for an *arbitrary* (integer) value of k, from the set of $P \cap Q$.

The notation listed in table 1 will be used to describe the sampling procedures. The two most straightforward methods for this problem would be QueryFirst and SampleFirst:

QueryFirst Calculate $P \cap Q$ first, then repeatedly extract a sample from the pre-calculated set upon request.

SampleFirst Upon request, pick a point randomly from P and test if it is within Q. Return the sample if so, otherwise dispose it and repeat.

The running time of QueryFirst is $O(r(N) + q)$, the same as a full range reporting query. For SampleFirst, because a randomly picked point falls inside Q with probability q/N, we expect to draw $O(N/q)$ samples in order to see one inside. Thus, the expected cost of SampleFirst is $O(kN/q)$. This could be good for very large q, say, a query that covers a large constant fraction of P. However, for most queries, this cost can be extremely large. If $q = 0$, it never terminates.

A better solution is to adapt the random sampling method of Olken [15] to R-trees. His method takes a sample from P_Q by walking along a random path from the root down to the leaf level. When deciding which branch to take, the subtree sizes $|P(u)|$ are considered so that the probabilities can be set appropriately. This way, a sample can be obtained in $O(\log N)$ time. Over k samples, the total time is $O(k \log N)$. We call this method RandomPath. It is reasonably good, but only in internal memory. When the R-tree resides on disk, each random path may involve a traversal in a completely different part of the R-tree, resulting in at least $\Omega(k)$ I/Os in total, which is very expensive.

To further improve the efficiency and achieve better scalability, STORM uses a *ST-indexing* module (spatio-temporal indexing) to facilitate the *sampler* to retrieve spatial online samples. Two different indexing schemes are introduced.

The first index structure, LS-tree, is based on the "level sampling" idea. We independently sample elements from P_i with probability $1/2$ to create P_{i+1}, and stop when the last P_ℓ is small enough, in expectation $\ell = O(\log N)$. Then we build R-tree T_i for each P_i. We set $P_0 = P$. Since their sizes form a geometric series, the total size is still $O(N)$.

Upon a query Q, we simply execute an ordinary range reporting query on the R-trees in turn $T_\ell, T_{\ell-1}, \ldots, T_0$. Note that from T_i, each reported point is sampled with probability $1/2^i$ independently, and all must fall inside Q. Thus, they form a probability-$(1/2^i)$ coin-flip sample of P_Q. To turn this into a sample without replacement, we perform a random permutation, and start to report the points to the user one by one, until the user terminates the query, or all samples are exhausted. In the latter case, we move on to the next R-tree T_{i-1}. Since $P_j \subseteq P_i$ if $j > i$, we need to make sure no sample is reported twice, by maintaining a set of all the samples that have been reported for the running query Q.

Suppose the user terminates the query after receiving k samples. Then in expectation, we have reached tree T_j such that $q/2^j \approx k$, i.e., $j = \log(q/k)$. Thus, the total query cost (in expectation) is $O(k) + \sum_{j=\log(q/k)}^{\ell} r\left(\frac{N}{2^j}\right)$. This solution works well in external memory, since the query on each R-tree is just a normal R-tree range query. As a result, the term $O(k)$ does not lead to $O(k)$ IOs for disk-based data sets; rather we expect $O(k/B)$ IOs where B is the block size.

Note that distributed R-trees are used when applying the above idea in a distributed cluster setting.

But LS-tree needs to maintain multiple trees, which can be a challenge especially in distributed settings and/or with many updates. We can further improve this method by maintaining only one R-tree. The key idea is to associate a set of samples within each R-tree node, and visit as few nodes as possible. To ensure correctness and scalability, a number of effective ideas are employed:

Sample Buffering: We associate a set $S(u)$ of samples for each R-tree node u. $S(u)$ is obtained from the canonical cover of u. The size of $S(u)$ is properly calculated.

Lazy Exploration: We also maintain a count for each node u which is the number of data elements covered by u from the leaf level. Then, we can use a carefully constructed weighted sampling technique to save unnecessary exploration of nodes.

Acceptance/Rejection Sampling: Subtrees rooted at nodes in R_Q (the canonical set of Q) vary in size. The acceptance/rejection sampling is used to quickly locate large subtrees in R_Q. Observe that if we take a small set of random samples from $P \cap Q$, the larger subtree it is, the more likely we will take samples from it. The smaller subtree it is, the more time is necessary to locate it. So we want to avoid exploring small subtrees in R_Q which are expensive yet relatively useless.

Integrating the above ideas in a single R-tree leads to the design of the second indexing structure in the ST-indexing module, namely, the RS-tree. In particular, we develop RS-tree based on a single Hilbert R-tree over P. A distributed Hilbert R-tree is used to work with the underlying distributed cluster. For brevity, we omit the technical details for the construction and analysis of the RS-tree.

Lastly, since both LS-tree and RS-tree leverage on R-tree as its main data structure, supporting ad-hoc updates is easy, as long as we properly update the associated samples in the process. These technical details are also omitted for brevity.

3.2 Other Modules

The other modules in STORM are more or less similar to common modules found in a data management system. Its query interface supports a keyword based query language with a query parser, where predefined keywords are used to specify an aggregation or an analytical task that are already supported in the system. A temporal range and a spatial region (on a map) are used to define a spatio-temporal query range. A set of online estimators for common spatio-temporal aggregations and analytics are included in the *feature module*, which builds these estimators using spatial online samples.

Note that the statistical side is relatively well understood [5, 7, 11, 13, 18]. Essentially, any aggregate of the whole population can be estimated from a sample set, and the accuracy improves as more samples are obtained and the sample size increases. Suppose each point e in our data set is associated with an attribute $e.x$ of interest. Then for example, it is well known that the sample mean is an unbiased estimator of the real mean, i.e., letting S be the set of k samples returned and P_Q the set of all points in the query range, we have $E[\bar{X}] = E\left[\frac{1}{k}\sum_{e\in S} e.x\right] = \mu = \frac{1}{q}\sum_{e\in P_Q} e.x$.

Furthermore, by the central limit theorem, $X - \mu$ approaches $Normal(0, \sigma^2/k)$, where σ is the population standard deviation. This means sample variance is inversely proportional to sample size, and we expect to have a quality estimate with even when k is small. We can also estimate σ^2 from the sample, and further compute the confidence intervals, as in standard online aggregation [7].

In the spatial setting, there are more complicated statistics than simple aggregates like sum or mean. A widely used one is the *kernel density estimation (KDE)*, which construct a continuous spatial distribution from discrete points. Specifically, the distribution density at some point p is computed as $f(p) = \frac{1}{q}\sum_{e\in P_Q} \kappa(d(e,p))$, where $d(\cdot,\cdot)$ is the distance between two points, and $\kappa(\cdot)$ is the *kernel function* that models the "influence" of e at p, usually a decreasing function of distance. Then we can compute $f(p)$ at regularly spaced points (say, all grid points), and construct a density map of the underlying spatial distribution. We observe the distribution density at each point, $f(p)$, is still an average, so we can compute an approximated density map by drawing a sample from P_Q, and derive the confidence interval (for each point p).

Other spatial analytics tasks, such as clustering, can also be performed on a sample of points. Intuitively, the clustering quality also improves as the sample size increases. The STORM APIs allow a user to access the sampler and feature module directly to build complex, advanced, customized online estimators, with user-derived, operator-specific guarantees for confidence interval and approximation quality.

The data connector uses schema discovery and data parser for a number of data sources that are supported in STORM in order to import and index a data source from a specified storage engine. Additional storage engines can be added by extending the code-base for the data connector.

The query optimizer implements a set of basic query optimization rules for deciding which method (as we have discussed in Section 3.1) the sampler should use when generating spatial online samples for a given query. The visualizer implements a number of basic visualization tools to enable visualizing the results from an online estimator, such as visualizing density estimate from KDE. The update manager handles data updates for data sets currently indexed by STORM. Lastly, the free data module is used to convert between different record formats and JSON format, as used by the storage engine of STORM.

4. EVALUATION AND DEMONSTRATION

4.1 The performance of STORM

We carried out extensive experiments to evaluate the performance of STORM. In particular, the performance of STORM is compared against competing baselines for generating spatial online samples and executing spatio-temporal online analytics. A detailed report of these results is beyond the scope of this demonstration proposal.

We only report two results, concerning the query efficiency and the estimation accuracy respectively, both in an online fashion, using the full open street map (OSM) data set.

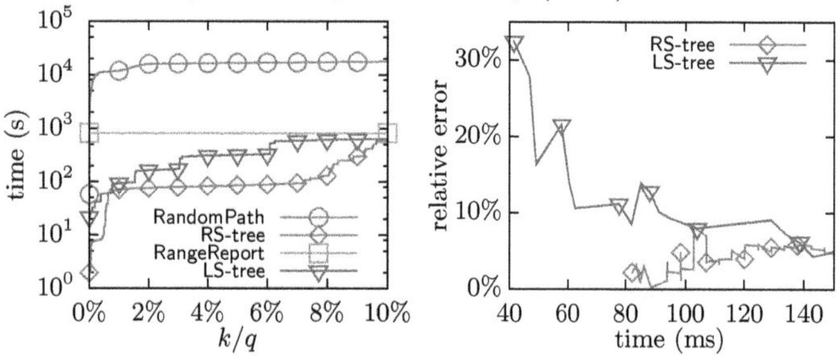

(a) query efficiency: vary k. (b) query accuracy: relative error on avg(altitude).

Figure 3: Query performance in STORM.

Figure 3(a) shows the time taken for different methods (as discussed in Section 3.1) to produce spatial online samples of increasing size, where we fixed a spatio-temporal range query Q with $q = 1$ billion ($q = |P_Q|$). Clearly, LS-tree and RS-tree perform much better than competing baselines.

Figure 3(b) shows how the relative error improves with respect to the increase in query execution time for a spatio-temporal aggregate query where it estimates the avg(altitude) for all points in a user-specified spatio-temporal query range. It clearly indicates that STORM is able to produce online estimations whose approximation quality improves over time.

4.2 The demonstration of STORM

The STORM system is available at `http://www.estorm.org` with username *guest* and password *guest@storm*.

Figure 4 shows the user interface of STORM. As introduced in Section 2, the demonstration of STORM consists of four components. In *basic analytics*, users may select different built-in analytical queries and data sources that are already indexed by STORM, to experience the benefits of spatio-temporal online analytics. For example, using the twitter data set and the online KDE estimator, we can estimate population density over an arbitrary spatio-temporal regions based on the location and timestamp of the underlying tweets *interactively in real time in an online fashion*, as shown in Figure 5 when user zooms out from Salt Lake City to the entire United States for tweets in last 30 days. The density estimate improves its accuracy with better visualization results as query time increases.

The user is also able to interact with the MesoWest data to issue spatio-temporal online aggregations over the MesoWest data (`http://mesowest.utah.edu/`).

In *data import*, we allow a user to import data from an external data source. Currently, STORM supports importing and indexing data from excel spreadsheets, text files, Cassandra, MySQL, and MongoDB. In particular, we will walk through the steps for importing a new data source from a plain text file and a MySQL database respectively. Once

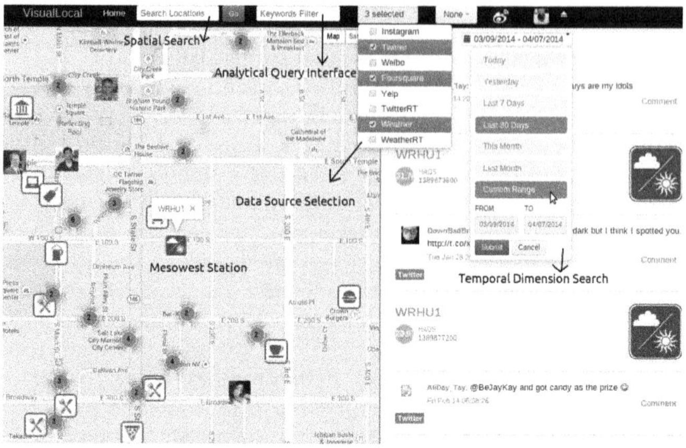

Figure 4: Overall query interface in STORM.

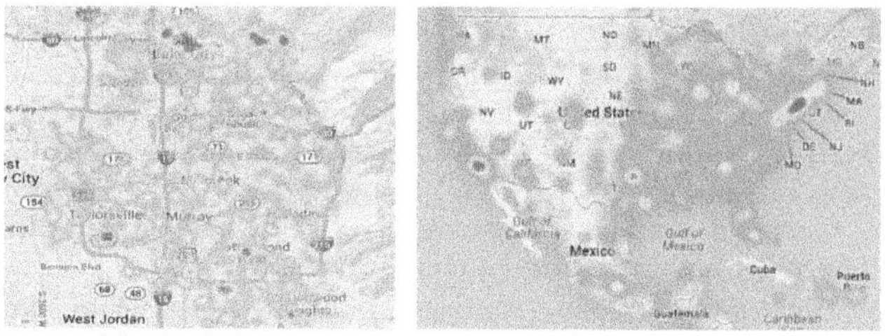

(a) SLC KDE. (b) USA KDE.

Figure 5: Interactive, online analytics.

imported, users are able to interact with the new data sets with the basic analytical queries supported in the system.

In *update*, we will make updates to an existing data set (e.g., the twitter data set in STORM is constantly updated with new tweets using the twitter API), and illustrate that STORM has successfully incorporated their impacts to analytical results by issuing analytical queries with time range that narrows down to the most recent time history.

Lastly, in *customized analytics*, we will showcase how to build advanced and more complex online analytics in STORM by accessing its *feature module* and *sampler* directly. We will use two examples for this purpose.

In the first example, we show how to build an online, approximate trajectory using spatial online samples for a given twitter user for a specified time range, using location and timestamp information from his/her tweets. The end result is shown in Figure 6(a). In the second example, we show how to perform online short-text understanding using online samples of tweets for an arbitrary spatio-temporal query range. There was a highly anomalous heavy snow in the Atlanta area in the days between February 10 and February 13, 2014. To see how the citizens of Atlanta reacted, we used a spatio-temporal window on downtown Atlanta during that period, and used our short-text understanding online estimator for twitter data in STORM; shown in Figure 6(b). We can quickly observe that the population was quite unhappy and frustrated, particularly considering the highlighted terms snow, ice, outage, shit, hell, why. Another interesting observation from this example is that STORM enables integrated online data analytics from multiple data sources; in this case, user can interactively explore both MesoWest data (to confirm the heavy snow) and the twitter data.

In both examples, we will show how to program a customized analytical task using the built-in feature module and spatial online samples returned from the sampler. Users

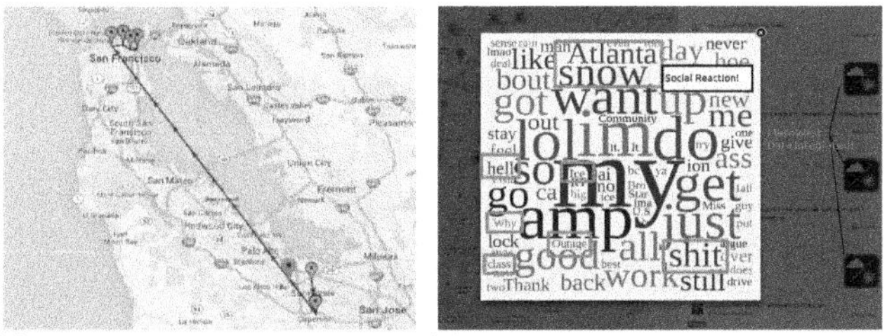

(a) online approximate trajectory construction. (b) spatio-temporal short-text understanding.

Figure 6: Advanced, customized online analytics.

may also import third party libraries to facilitate the implementation of a customized analytical task.

5. RELATED WORK

The concept of online aggregation was first proposed by Hellerstein et al. in [7], and has been revisited for different operators (e.g., join [5], group-by [19]) for relational data models, and computation models (e.g., MapReduce [18]). The standard approach is to produce online samples and build estimators that improve accuracy gradually over time using more and more samples [5–7, 18]. The connection from query accuracy (especially for standard aggregations) and estimation confidence to sample size is mostly well understood, see [5–7, 13, 18, 20] and many other work in the literature on building various kinds of estimators using random samples. Nevertheless, to the best of our knowledge, a comprehensive system such as STORM that supports spatio-temporal online analytics has not been investigated before.

Our work is closely related to online sampling and sampling from a database in general. Olken proposed the idea of taking a random sample from P_Q by walking along a random path from the root down to the leaf level in his PhD thesis [15]. This idea works for both B-tree in one dimension and R-tree in higher dimensions [15–17]. However, as explained in Section 3 and confirmed by experiments in Section 4.1, this method is too expensive for generating online samples in large spatial databases.

Hu et al. [8] recently showed how to produce samples for range queries with a new constraint that samples must be independent with respect to both intra-query and inter-queries. Their result is purely theoretical, and is too complicated to be implemented or used in practice. It holds only for one-dimensional data and their external memory data structure is static and does not support dynamic updates.

There is an increasing interest in integrating sampling as an operator in a database management system; see recent efforts in [1, 2, 9, 10, 12, 14, 21, 22]. Nevertheless, none have investigated spatial and spatio-temporal databases.

Finding samples from a set of geographic points for better map visualizations is described in [3]. Samples are taken from the data set such that the samples will be evenly distributed when the sampled data is drawn on a map. This differs from STORM, as their definition of *spatial sampling* has a different objective, which is to produce better visual representation of the underlying data.

The most closely related work is SpatialHadoop [4], which is a comprehensive system for building spatial and spatio-temporal analytical tasks on large spatio-temporal data, using the MapReduce computation framework. However, a fundamental difference between STORM and SpatialHadoop is *online* versus *batched offline* analytics. As a result, STORM and SpatialHadoop nicely complement each other and satisfy different application scenarios and user needs.

6. ACKNOWLEDGMENT

Robert Christensen, Feifei Li, Jun Tang, and Natalee Villa are supported in part by NSF grants 1443046 and 1251019. Feifei Li is also supported in part by NSFC grant 61428204 and a Google research award. Lu Wang and Ke Yi are supported by HKRGC under grants GRF-621413 and GRF-16211614, and by a Microsoft grant MRA14EG05.

7. REFERENCES

[1] S. Agarwal, B. Mozafari, A. Panda, H. Milner, S. Madden, and I. Stoica. BlinkDB: queries with bounded errors and bounded response times on very large data. In *EuroSys*, 2013.

[2] S. Agarwal, A. Panda, B. Mozafari, A. P. Iyer, S. Madden, and I. Stoica. Blink and it's done: Interactive queries on very large data. In *PVLDB*, 2012.

[3] A. Das Sarma, H. Lee, H. Gonzalez, J. Madhavan, and A. Halevy. Efficient spatial sampling of large geographical tables. In *SIGMOD*, 2012.

[4] A. Eldawy and M. F. Mokbel. A demonstration of SpatialHadoop: An efficient mapreduce framework for spatial data. *PVLDB*, 2013.

[5] P. Haas and J. Hellerstein. Ripple joins for online aggregation. In *SIGMOD*, pages 287–298, 1999.

[6] P. J. Haas. Large-sample and deterministic confidence intervals for online aggregation. In *SSDBM*, 1997.

[7] J. Hellerstein, P. Haas, and H. Wang. Online aggregation. In *SIGMOD*, 1997.

[8] X. Hu, M. Qiao, and Y. Tao. Independent range sampling. In *PODS*, 2014.

[9] R. Jampani, F. Xu, M. Wu, L. L. Perez, C. Jermaine, and P. J. Haas. The monte carlo database system: Stochastic analysis close to the data. *ACM TODS*, 36(3):18, 2011.

[10] P. Jayachandran, K. Tunga, N. Kamat, and A. Nandi. Combining user interaction, speculative query execution and sampling in the DICE system. *PVLDB*, 2014.

[11] C. Jermaine, S. Arumugam, A. Pol, and A. Dobra. Scalable approximate query processing with the dbo engine. *ACM Transactions on Database Systems*, 33(4), Article 23, 2008.

[12] A. Klein, R. Gemulla, P. Rösch, and W. Lehner. Derby/s: a DBMS for sample-based query answering. In *SIGMOD*, 2006.

[13] R. Motwani and P. Raghavan. *Randomized Algorithms*. Cambridge University Press, 1995.

[14] S. Nirkhiwale, A. Dobra, and C. M. Jermaine. A sampling algebra for aggregate estimation. *PVLDB*, 2013.

[15] F. Olken. *Random Sampling from Databases*. PhD thesis, University of California at Berkeley, 1993.

[16] F. Olken and D. Rotem. Random sampling from B+ trees. In *VLDB*, 1989.

[17] F. Olken and D. Rotem. Sampling from spatial databases. In *ICDE*, 1993.

[18] N. Pansare, V. R. Borkar, C. Jermaine, and T. Condie. Online aggregation for large mapreduce jobs. In *PVLDB*, 2011.

[19] F. Xu, C. M. Jermaine, and A. Dobra. Confidence bounds for sampling-based group by estimates. *ACM TODS*, 33(3), 2008.

[20] Y. Yan, L. J. Chen, and Z. Zhang. Error-bounded sampling for analytics on big sparse data. *PVLDB*, 7(13), 2014.

[21] K. Zeng, S. Gao, J. Gu, B. Mozafari, and C. Zaniolo. ABS: a system for scalable approximate queries with accuracy guarantees. In *SIGMOD*, 2014.

[22] K. Zeng, S. Gao, B. Mozafari, and C. Zaniolo. The analytical bootstrap: a new method for fast error estimation in approximate query processing. In *SIGMOD*, 2014.

PAXQuery: Parallel Analytical XML Processing

Jesús Camacho-Rodríguez*
Hortonworks Inc.
USA
jcamachorodriguez@hortonworks.com

Dario Colazzo*
Université Paris-Dauphine
France
dario.colazzo@dauphine.fr

Ioana Manolescu
Juan A. M. Naranjo
INRIA & Université Paris-Sud
France
ioana.manolescu@inria.fr
juan-alvaro.munoz-naranjo@inria.fr

ABSTRACT

XQuery is a general-purpose programming language for processing semi-structured data, and as such, it is very expressive. As a consequence, optimizing and parallelizing complex analytics XQuery queries is still an open, challenging problem.

We demonstrate PAXQuery, a novel system that parallelizes the execution of XQuery queries over large collections of XML documents. PAXQuery compiles a rich subset of XQuery into plans expressed in the PArallelization ConTracts (PACT) programming model. Thanks to this translation, the resulting plans are optimized and executed in a massively parallel fashion by the Apache Flink system. The result is a scalable system capable of querying massive amounts of XML data very efficiently, as proved by the experimental results we outline.

1. INTRODUCTION

Over the last years, the Hadoop Distributed File System (HDFS) has gained popularity as an inexpensive solution to store huge volumes of heterogenous data. MapReduce [8] is arguably the most widely adopted model to analyze data stored in HDFS; its main advantage is that data processing is distributed across many sites without the application having to explicitly handle data fragmentation, fragment placement, etc.

While the simplicity of MapReduce is an advantage, it is also a limitation, since large data processing tasks are represented by complex programs consisting of many *Map* and *Reduce* tasks. In particular, since these tasks are conceptually very simple, one often needs to write programs comprising many successive tasks, which limits parallelism. To overcome this problem, recent efforts have focused on proposing more expressive dataflow abstractions for massively parallel analytics data processing [10, 22].

The *PArallelization ConTracts* programming model [3] (**PACT**, in short) is one of the proposals that pushes the idea of MapReduce further. In a nutshell, PACT generalizes MapReduce by (*i*) manipulating records with any number of fields, instead of (key, value) pairs, (*ii*) enabling the *definition of custom parallel operators* by means of second-order functions, and (*iii*) allowing one parallel operator to receive as input the outputs of *several* other such operators. Due to its declarative nature, a PACT program can have multiple physical execution plans with varying performance. At compile time, the compiler choses an optimal strategy (plan) that maximizes parallelisation opportunities, and thus efficiency. The PACT model is implemented within the open-source Apache Flink data processing engine[1] [10].

*Part of this work was performed while the authors were with Université Paris-Sud and INRIA. The work was partially supported by the KIC EIT ICT Labs Europa activity 12115.

SIGMOD'15, May 31–June 4, 2015, Melbourne, Victoria, Australia.

ACM 978-1-4503-2758-9/15/05 ...$15.00.
http://dx.doi.org/10.1145/2723372.2735374

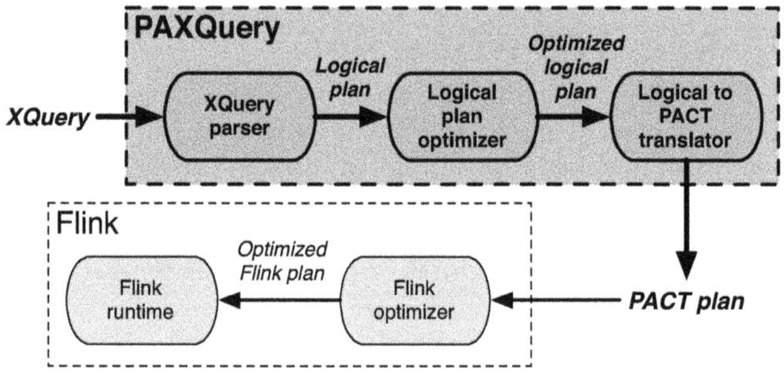

Figure 1: PAXQuery architecture overview.

Optimizing and parallelizing complex analytics queries on semi-structured data is extremely challenging and still a widely under-explored topic. For instance, given a very large collection of XML documents, evaluating a query that *navigates over these documents and also joins results from different documents* raises performance challenges, which may be addressed by parallelism.

Our demonstration features the PAXQuery system [6], a massively parallel processor of XML queries. Inspired by other high-level data analytics languages that are compiled to MapReduce and other dataflow abstractions (e.g. Pig [17] or Hive [23]), PAXQuery proposes a layered architecture to efficiently translate XQuery [24] into PACT plans. The main advantage of this approach is *implicit parallelism*: neither the application nor the user need to partition the XML input or the query across nodes. This contrasts with prior work [4, 7, 13]. Thus, we can rely on the Flink platform for the optimization of the PACT plan and its automatic transformation into a dataflow that is evaluated in parallel on top of HDFS; these steps are explained in [3].

In the sequel, Section 2 describes the PAXQuery architecture, and provides a beginning-to-end query translation example. Section 3 presents experimental results confirming the interest of PAXQuery' parallel XQuery processing approach. Section 4 describes the demonstration scenario and Section 5 concludes.

[1]Flink was known as Stratosphere prior to becoming an Apache incubator project in July 2014.

2. PAXQUERY ARCHITECTURE

Our approach for implicit parallel evaluation of XML queries is to *translate* them into PACT plans as depicted in Figure 1. Then, PAXQuery sends the PACT plan to the Flink platform, which optimizes it, and turns it into a data flow that is evaluated in parallel, as explained in [3].

The experiments we present in this work demonstrate not only that PAXQuery (unlike competitor systems [4, 7, 13]) parallelizes XQuery evaluation without any user intervention, but it is also more efficient than comparable implementations based on single-site processors running in parallel. This is because of its reliance on a highly parallel back-end (Flink), which is enabled by our algebraic translation methodology.

Below, we describe the steps taken by PAXQuery to translate an input XQuery query into an efficient PACT plan.

2.1 XQuery parser

Query language PAXQuery supports a representative fragment of XQuery [24], the W3C's standard query language for XML data, which has been recently enhanced with strongly requested features geared towards XML analytics. In particular, our goal was to cover (*i*) the main navigational mechanisms of XQuery, and (*ii*) its key constructs to express analytical style queries e.g. aggregation, explicit grouping, and rich comparison predicates. The grammar of the covered XQuery fragment can be found in [6].

Example. The following XQuery (over collections of documents extracted from an XMark [21] document) *lists the maximum price per postal code of any item bought or sold in France*:

```
let $pc := collection('people'),
    $cc := collection('auctions')
for $p in $pc//person[//country/text()='FR'],
    $i in $p/@id, $z in $p/zipcode/text()
let $r :=
  for $c in $cc//closed_auction, $b in $c/buyer/@person,
      $s in $c/seller/@person, $pr in $c/price
  where $i = $b or $i = $s
  return $pr
group by $z
return <res zip={$z}>{max($r)}</res>
```

The above query shows some of the main features of our XQuery fragment. It includes FLWR expressions, which are powerful enough to express complex operations like *iterating over sequences, joining multiple documents, and performing grouping*. XPath paths start from the root of each document in a *collection* of XML documents, or from the bindings of a previously introduced *variable*; the XPath fragment we support corresponds to $\text{XPath}^{\{/,//,[]\}}$ [15]. Our fragment supports rich predicates expressed in disjunctive normal form (DNF), including value- and node identity-based comparisons. Other XQuery constructs such as *if* or *switch* expressions can be integrated into our proposal in a straightforward manner.

From XQuery to logical plans In a first step, PAXQuery represents the XQuery query as an *equivalent algebraic expression* [6]. XQuery translation into algebraic formalisms has been extensively studied [1, 5, 9, 14, 20].

A significant source of XQuery complexity comes from *nesting*: an XQuery expression can be nested in almost any position within another. In particular, nested queries challenge the processor, as straightforward translation into nested plans leads to poor performance. Effective translation techniques represent nested XQuery as *unnested plans relying on joining and grouping*. Depending on the query shape, such *decorrelating* joins may be *nested* and/or *outer* joins.

We introduce our algebraic representation of XQuery by means of our running example, relying on the algebra of [14].

Example (*continuation*). The algebraic plan corresponding to the XQuery introduced previously is shown in Figure 2.a.

The XML *scan* operators take as input the `'people'` (respectively `'auctions'`) collection of XML documents and create a tuple out of each document in the collection.

XQuery may perform *navigation*, which, in a nutshell, *binds variables to the result of path traversals*. Navigation is commonly represented through *tree patterns*, whose nodes carry the labels appearing in the paths, and where some *target nodes* are also annotated with names of variables to be bound, e.g. `$pc`, `$i`, etc. Our algebra uses a *navigation* operator parameterized by an *extended tree pattern* (ETP) supporting multiple returning nodes, child and descendant axis, and nested and optional edges [6]. This allows *consolidating as many navigation operations as possible in a query, within a single navigation tree pattern*; in particular in a *navigation performed outside of the* `for` *clauses*, which leads to more efficient matching against XML documents [1].

The operator *navigation*(e_1) concatenates each input tuple successively with all @id attributes (variable `$i`), and text values of `country` (`$x1`) and `zipcode` (`$z`) elements resulting from the embeddings of e_1 in the value bound to `$pc`. Observe that the variable `$x1` did not appear in the original query; in fact, it is created by PAXQuery to hold the value needed for the *selection* operator above it. The operator *navigation*(e_2) is generated in a similar fashion.

Above the previous operators, we find a *nested left outer join* on a disjunctive predicate, which brings together people and the auctions they participated in, either as buyers *or* sellers. Observe that the join is *outer*, i.e., all people are kept in the output, even if they did not participate in any auction.

Then, we *group* the tuples coming from the previous operator by the value of their `zipcode`, and the result of the *aggregation* function *max* is calculated and concatenated to each of these tuples.

Finally, the XML construction operator is responsible for transforming a collection of tuples to XML. *For each tuple* in its input, *construct*(L) builds *one XML tree for each construction tree pattern* in the list L; more details can be found in [6].

2.2 Logical plan optimizer

After building a logical plan, PAXQuery optimizes it by using rewriting rules that create semantically equivalent alternative plans. The goal of these transformations is preparing the plan for the translation into a more efficient PACT plan. PAXQuery implements well-studied plan transformation rules [19], e.g. *push down projections, push down selections*, etc. We illustrate some of them next.

Example (*continuation*). The plan obtained after applying our transformation rules is shown in Figure 2.b (for readability reasons, *projection* operators have been omitted). First, observe that the *navigation* is integrated within the *scan* operator (*NavScan*), so the tuples resulting from the embeddings of the ETPs can be extracted as we read the XML documents. Further, note that the selection on the people whose `country` is France has been pushed into the ETP e_1. Finally, the *group-by* and *aggregation* operators have been rewritten into a single one that represents both operations.

2.3 Logical to PACT translator

The PACT model [3] is a generalization of MapReduce. A PACT plan is a DAGs of *implicitly parallel operators*, that are optimized and translated into *explicit parallel data flows* by Flink.

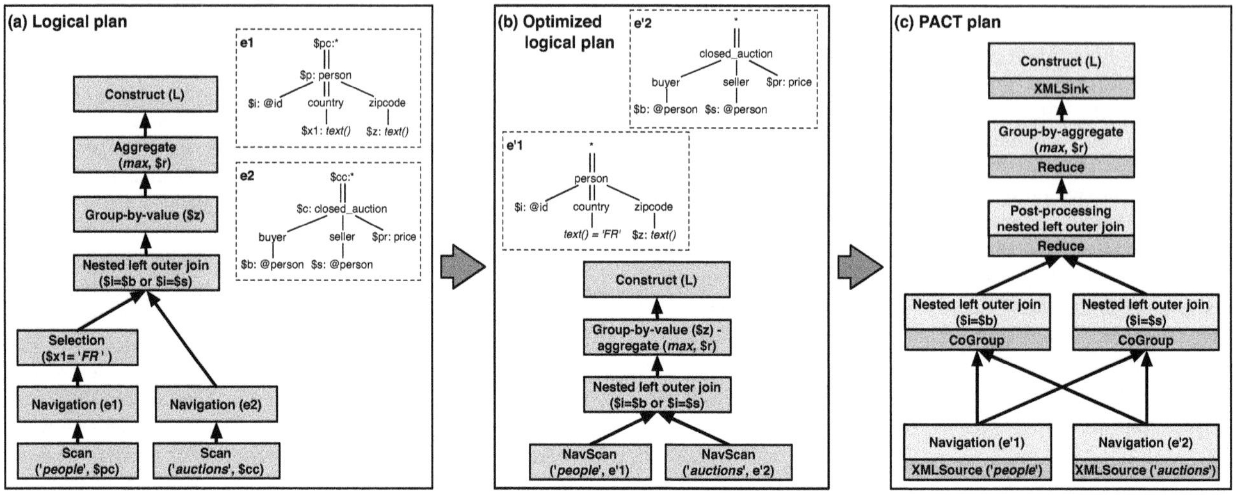

Figure 2: Sample translation from a logical plan to PACT.

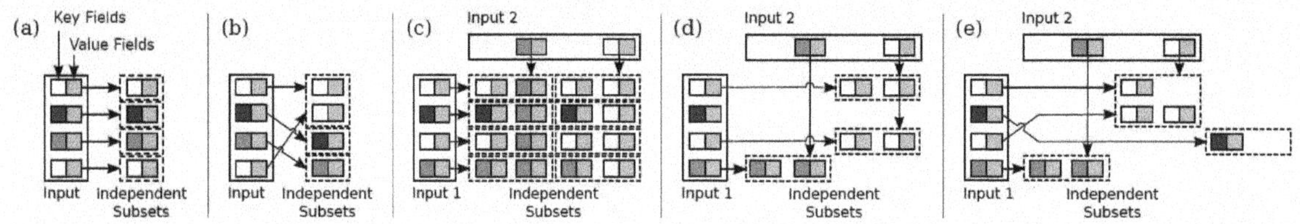

Figure 3: (a) Map, (b) Reduce, (c) Cross, (d) Match, and (e) CoGroup parallelization contracts.[2]

Data model. PACT plans manipulate *records* of the form $r = ((f_1, f_2, \ldots, f_n), (i_1, i_2, \ldots, i_k))$ where $1 \leq k \leq n$. The first component $(f_1, f_2, \ldots, f_n)$ is an ordered sequence of *fields* f_i; in turn, a field f_i is either an atomic value (string) or a ordered sequence $(r'_1, \ldots, r'_m)$ of records. On the other hand, the second component $(i_1, i_2, \ldots, i_k)$ is an ordered, possibly empty, sequence of record positions in $[1 \ldots n]$ indicating the *key* fields for the record. The *key of a record* r, denoted by $r.key$, is the list of all the key fields $(f_{i_1}, f_{i_2}, \ldots, f_{i_k})$.

Processing model. *Data sources and sinks* are, respectively, the starting and terminal nodes of a PACT plan. The input data is stored in files, e.g. in HDFS; a function parameterizing data source operators specifies how to structure the data into records. In turn, results can be output to files, with the destination and format similarly controlled by an output function.

The rest of data processing nodes in a PACT plan are *operators*. An operator manipulates bags of records. Its semantics is defined by (i) a *parallelization contract*, which determines how input records are organized into *groups*; (ii) a *user function* (or UF) that is executed independently over each bag (group) of records created by the parallelization contract (these executions can take place in parallel); and (iii) optional *annotations* that may enable further optimizations by Flink.

A set of the most common parallelization contracts is built in Flink: Map, Reduce, Cross, Match, and CoGroup (see Figure 3). The Map contract forms an individual group for every input record. The Reduce contract forms a group for every unique value of the key attribute in the input data set, and the group contains all records with that particular key value. The Cross contract builds the Cartesian product of the two input bags. The Match contract forms a group from every pair of records in its two inputs, only if the records have the same value for the key attribute. Finally, the CoGroup contract forms a group for every value of the key attribute (from the domains of both inputs), and places each record in the appropriate group.

Table 1: Algebra to PACT overview.

Algebra operators		PACT operators (#)
Scan / NavScan		Source (1)
Construct		Sink (1)
Navigation		Map (1)
Group-by / Group-by-aggregate		Reduce (1)
Flatten		Map (1)
Selection		Map (1)
Projection		Map (1)
Aggregation (on nested field)		Map (1)
Aggregation (on top-level field)		Reduce (1)
Duplicate elimination		Reduce (1)
Cartesian product		Cross (1)
Conjunctive equi-join	Inner	Match (1)
	Outer	CoGroup (1)
	Nested outer / Nested outer-aggr.	CoGroup (1)
Disjunctive equi-join (n conjunctions)	Inner	Match (n)
	Outer	CoGroup (n) & Reduce (1)
	Nested outer / Nested outer-aggr.	CoGroup (n) & Reduce (1)
Inequi-join	Inner	Cross (1)
	Outer	Cross (1) & Reduce (1)
	Nested outer Nested outer-aggr.	Cross (1) & Reduce (1)

[2]Figure reproduced from [12] with authorization.

From logical plans to PACT plans XQuery algebraic plans are translated into PACT plans recursively, operator by operator; for each XQuery operator, the translation outputs one or several PACT operators for which we need to choose the *parallelization contract* (and possibly its corresponding *key fields*), and the *user function*, which together determine the PACT behavior. Further, we annotate the PACT operators to take fully advantage of Flink's optimizer. More details about these steps can be found in [6].

Table 1 provides an overview on the algebra operators and the contracts used by the PACT operators resulting from our translation. Observe that the translation of the binary operators is the most complex, as it has to deal efficiently with the *nested* and/or *outer* nature of some joins, which may result in multiple operators at the PACT level. We illustrate PAXQuery translation to PACT with the following example.

Example (*continuation*). For the algebra plan in Figure 2.b, PAXQuery generates the PACT program shown in Figure 2.c; the key fields for each operator are omitted for readability. The XML source operators scan (in parallel) the respective collections and apply the *navigation* UF over each document to create records. The nested outer join is translated into two CoGroup operators and a post-processing Reduce. The core difficulty to address by our translation is to correctly express (i) the *disjunction* in the where clause of the query, and (ii) the *outerjoin* semantics (recall that in this example a `<res>` element must be output even for people with no auctions). The main feature of the *nested left outer join* UF associated to each CoGroup is to guarantee that no erroneous duplicates are generated when the parallel evaluation of more than one conjunctive predicate is true for a certain record. The Reduce operator groups all the results of the previous CoGroup operators having the same left hand-side record, and then the *post-processing* UF associated to it is applied to produce the final result for the join. The following Reduce groups together the records with the same `zipcode` and calculates the *aggregation* function over the `price` in each of them. Finally, the XML sink builds and returns XML results.

3. PAXQUERY SCALABILITY AND ALTERNATIVES

PAXQuery is implemented in Java 1.6, and runs on top of the Flink platform [10] supporting PACT. We describe an extended experimental evaluation in [6]; below, we borrow from that article the two most significant experiments, related on one hand to the platform scalability, and on the other to the comparison between PAXQuery and alternative massively parallel XQuery architectures.

Experimental setup. The experiments run in a cluster of 8 nodes on an 1GB Ethernet. Each node has 2 × 2.93GHz Quad Core Xeon CPUs, 16GB RAM and two 600GB SATA hard disks and runs Linux CentOS 6.4. PAXQuery is built on top of Flink 0.2.1; it stores the XML data in HDFS 1.1.2.

XML data. We used XMark [21] data; to study queries joining several documents, we used the `split` option of the XMark generator to create four collections of XML documents, each containing a specific type of XMark subtrees: *users* (10% of the dataset size), *items* (50%), *open auctions* (25%) and *closed auctions* (15%). We used datasets of up to **272GB** as detailed below. All documents are stored into HDFS, which replicates them three times and distributes them across the nodes.

XML queries. We used a subset of XMark queries from our XQuery fragment, and added queries with features from our dialect but absent from the original XMark, e.g. joins on disjunctive predicates.

Table 2 outlines the queries: the collection(s) that each query carries over, the corresponding XML algebraic operators and their numbers of occurrences, and the parallelization contracts used in the plan generated by our translation framework. *Queries q_9-q_{14} all involve value joins, which carry over thousands of documents arbitrarily distributed across the HDFS nodes.*

Table 2: Query details.

Query	Collections	Algebra operators (#)	Parallelization contracts (#)
q_1	*users*	Navigation (1)	Map (1)
q_2	*items*	Navigation (1)	Map (1)
q_3	*items*	Navigation (1)	Map (1)
q_4	*closed auctions*	Navigation (1)	Map (1)
q_5	*closed auctions*	Navigation (1)	Map (1)
q_6	*users*	Navigation (1)	Map (1)
q_7	*closed auctions*	Navigation (1) Aggregation (2)	Map (2) Reduce (1)
q_8	*items*	Navigation (1) Aggregation (2)	Map (2) Reduce (1)
q_9	*users* *closed auctions*	Navigation (2) Projection (1) Group-by/aggregation (1) Conjunctive equi-join (1)	Map (3) Reduce (1) Match (1)
q_{10}	*users* *items* *closed auctions*	Navigation (3) Projection (2) NLO conjunctive equi-join (2)	Map (5) CoGroup (2)
q_{11}	*users*	Navigation (2) Projection (1) Dup. elim. (1) NLO conjunctive equi-join (1)	Map (3) Reduce (1) CoGroup (1)
q_{12}	*users* *closed auctions*	Navigation (2) Projection (1) NLO conjunctive equi-join/ aggregation (1)	Map (3) CoGroup (1)
q_{13}	*users* *closed auctions*	Navigation (2) Projection (1) NLO disjunctive equi-join (1)	Map (3) Reduce (2) CoGroup (2)
q_{14}	*users* *open auctions*	Navigation (2) Projection (1) NLO inequi-join (1)	Map (3) Reduce (2) Cross (1)

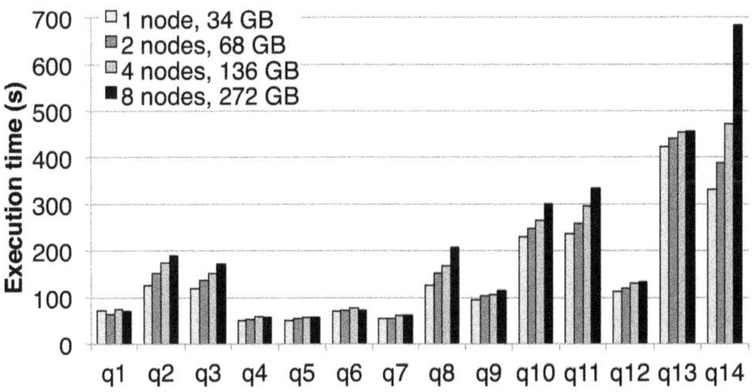

Figure 4: PAXQuery scalability evaluation.

3.1 PAXQuery scalability

Our first goal is to check that PAXQuery brings to XQuery evaluation the desired benefits of implicit parallelism. For this, we fixed a set of queries, generated 11,000 documents (**34GB**) per node, and varied the number of nodes from **1** to **2**, **4**, **8** respectively; the total dataset size increases accordingly in a linear fashion, up to **272GB**.

Figure 4 shows the response times for each query. Queries q_1-q_6 navigate in the input document according to a given navigation pattern of 5 to 14 nodes. The response time of these queries follows the size of the input, as each of them translates into a Map PACT. In Figure 4 we can see that these queries scale up well, with a moderate overhead as the data volume and number of nodes increases.

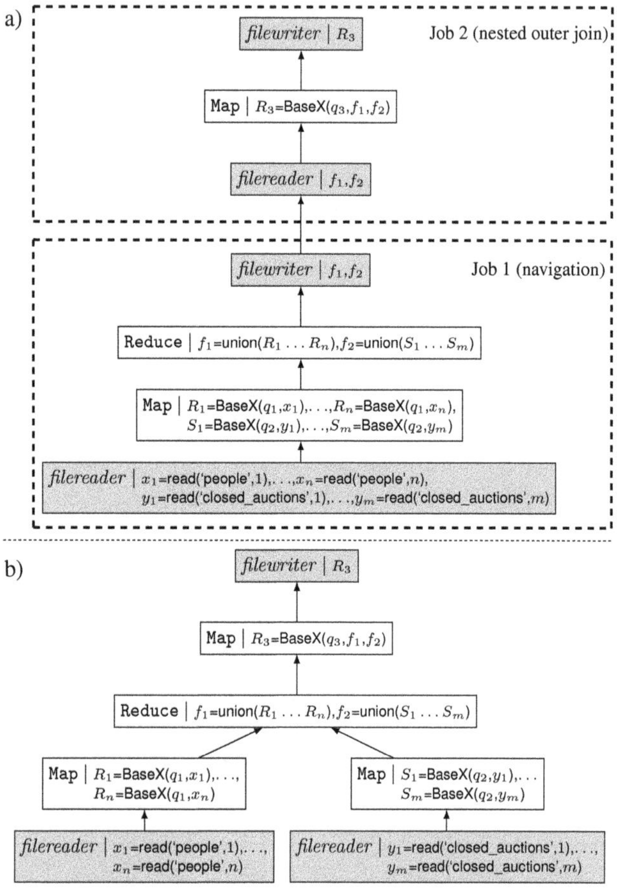

Figure 5: Execution of XQuery using alternative architectures based on MapReduce (a) and PACT (b) for comparison with PAXQuery.

Queries q_7 and q_8 apply an aggregation over all the records generated by a navigation. For both queries, the navigation generates nested records and the aggregation consists on two steps. The first step goes over the nested fields in each input record, and thus it uses a Map contract. The second step is executed over the results of the first. Therefore, a Reduce contract that groups together all records coming from the previous operator is used. Since the running time is dominated by the Map PACTs which parallelize very well, q_7 and q_8 also scale up well.

Queries q_9-q_{12} involve conjunctive equi-joins over the collections. Query q_{13} executes a NLO disjunctive equi-join, while q_{14} applies a NLO inequi-join. We notice a very good scaleup for q_9-q_{13}, whose joins are translated in many PACTs (recall Table 1). In contrast, q_{14}, which translates into a Cross PACT, scales noticeably less well. *This validates the interest of translating disjunctive equi-joins into many PACTs* (as our rules do), *rather than into a single Cross*, since, despite parallelization, it fundamentally does not scale.

3.2 Comparison against other alternatives

We next compare our system with other *alternatives for implicitly parallel evaluation of XQuery*. As explained in the Introduction, no comparable system is available yet. Therefore, for our comparison, we picked the BaseX 7.7 [2] centralized processor and used Hadoop-MapReduce on one hand, and Flink-PACT on the other hand, to parallelize its execution.

Table 3: Query evaluation time (8 nodes, 272GB).

Query	Evaluation time (seconds)		
	BaseX Hadoop-MR	BaseX Flink-PACT	PAXQuery
q_1	465	**66**	70
q_2	773	282	**189**
q_3	762	243	**172**
q_4	244	72	**58**
q_5	237	72	**57**
q_6	488	**70**	73
q_7	245	74	**62**
q_8	576	237	**206**
q_9	OOM	OOM	**114**
q_{10}	OOM	OOM	**299**
q_{11}	OOM	OOM	**334**
q_{12}	OOM	OOM	**132**
q_{13}	OOM	OOM	**456**
q_{14}	OOM	OOM	**683**

We compare PAXQuery, relying on the XML algebra-to-PACT translation we described, with the following alternative architecture. We deployed BaseX on each node, and parallelized XQuery execution as follows:

1. Manually decompose each query into a set of leaf subqueries performing just tree pattern navigation, followed by a recomposition subquery which applies (possibly nested, outer) joins over the results of the leaf subqueries;
2. Parallelize the evaluation of the leaf subqueries through one Map over all the documents, followed by one Reduce to union all the results. Moreover, if the recomposition query is not empty, start a new MapReduce job running the recomposition XQuery query over all the results thus obtained, in order to compute complete query results.

This alternative architecture is in-between ChuQL [13], where the query writer *explicitly* controls the choice of Map and Reduce keys, i.e., MapReduce is *visible at the query level*, and PAXQuery where parallelism is completely hidden. In this architecture, q_1-q_8 translate to one Map and one Reduce, whereas q_9-q_{14} feature joins which translates into a recomposition query and thus a second job. As we will illustrate with the following example, the manual decomposition takes a considerable effort.

Example (*continuation*). The MapReduce and PACT plans that execute the XQuery introduced in our example are depicted in Figure 5.

Observe that the MapReduce workflow contains two jobs. The *first job* creates a key/value pair out of each document in each collection, which contains the document's content. The pairs are correspondingly labeled so that they can be identified in the following steps. The Map user function uses BaseX to execute a navigation query on the content of each input pair; q_1 is equivalent to the tree pattern e'_1 in Figure 2.b, while q_2 is equivalent to e'_2. In turn, the Reduce gathers the pairs that originated from the same collection in a group, and applies a user function that unions the results for each of these collections, thus creating files f_1 and f_2 for collections 'people' and 'closed_auctions', respectively. Note that the `Reduce` operation is necessary because we execute a nested outer join between the results from both collections in the subsequent step. In the absence of our parallelization algorithms, BaseX needs a global view over the results from each collection.

The second job is Map-only. It reads the inputs from the first job, and then it uses BaseX to execute the nested outer join between the inputs. The result is then written to disk.

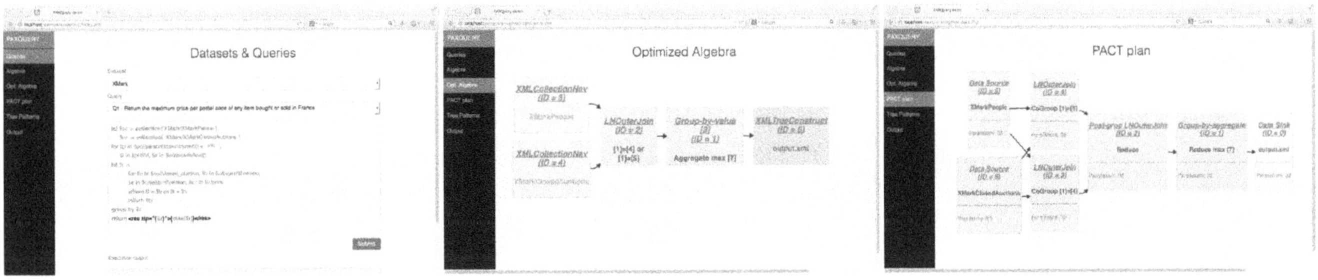

Figure 6: PAXQuery demonstration GUI.

The PACT plan is similar to the previous one, except for the fact that instead of being a linear workflow, it is a DAG of operators.

Table 3 shows the response times when running the query on the 8 nodes and 272GB; the shortest time is shown in bold, while OOM stands for *out of memory*. First, we notice that BaseX runs 2 to 5 times faster on Flink than on Hadoop. This is due to Hadoop's checkpoints (writing intermediary results to disk) while Flink currently does not, trading reliability for speed. For queries without joins (q_1-q_8), PAXQuery is faster for most queries than BaseX on Hadoop or Flink; this simply points out that our in-house tree pattern matching operator (physical implementation of nav) is more efficient than the one of BaseX. Queries with joins (q_9-q_{14}) fail in the competitor architecture. The reason is that intermediary join results grow too large and this leads to an out-of-memory error. PAXQuery evaluates such queries well, based on its massively parallel (outer) joins.

Our experiments demonstrate the efficiency of an XQuery processor built on top of PACT. First, our scalability evaluation has shown that the translation to PACT allows PAXQuery to parallelize every query execution step with no effort required to partition, redistribute data etc., and thus to scale out with the number of machines in a cluster. The only case where scale-up was not so good is q_{14} where we used a Cross (cartesian product) to translate an inequality join; an orthogonal optimization here would be to use a smarter dedicated join operator for such predicates, e.g. [16].

Second, PAXQuery outperformed an alternative architecture in which an XQuery processor runs on each node and Hadoop or Flink/Pact are used to parallelize *XPath navigation only* across the input. In such an architecture, the queries with joins across documents on the data volumes we considered could not complete, highlighting the need for parallel platforms supporting all XQuery processing steps, through an algebraic translation, such as PAXQuery.

4. DEMONSTRATION SCENARIO

For our demonstration, we upload multiple collections of XML datasets [11, 18] to our cluster, and we provide a selection of analytical queries that cover the most important aspects of the translation, e.g. rich tree pattern navigation, nested queries, aggregation, complex joins. The audience may also formulate their own queries.

Then, we showcase the different steps that PAXQuery takes to transform any input XQuery query into a PACT plan. Thus, for a given query, attendees are shown (*i*) the initial algebraic plan resulting from query parsing, (*ii*) an optimized algebraic plan as a result of applying rule-based optimization to the initial plan, (*iii*) the equivalent PACT plan, including the annotations over each PACT operator, and (*iv*) the final XML output. We have implemented a Web client for PAXQuery that visualizes all this information (see Figure 6). Further, we use the Flink monitoring tools to provide real-time information about the parallel execution in the cluster.

5. CONCLUSION

We demonstrate PAXQuery, a system that enables the parallelization of the execution of XML queries over large collections of XML documents. PAXQuery transforms an input XQuery query into an efficient PACT plan whose execution can be easily parallelized by the Flink platform; the feasability and performance improvements of this approach are proven by the experimental results provided. While PAXQuery's implementation is specific to XQuery, the concepts shown in this demonstration are applicable to other programming languages for semi-structured data, e.g. Jaql or JSONiq.

6. REFERENCES

[1] A. Arion, V. Benzaken, I. Manolescu, Y. Papakonstantinou, and R. Vijay. Algebra-Based identification of tree patterns in XQuery. In *FQAS*, 2006.

[2] BaseX. http://basex.org/products/xquery/.

[3] D. Battré, S. Ewen, F. Hueske, O. Kao, V. Markl, and D. Warneke. Nephele/PACTs: a programming model and execution framework for web-scale analytical processing. In *SoCC*, 2010.

[4] N. Bidoit, D. Colazzo, N. Malla, F. Ulliana, M. Nolè, and C. Sartiani. Processing XML queries and updates on map/reduce clusters. In *EDBT*, 2013.

[5] P. Boncz, T. Grust, M. van Keulen, S. Manegold, J. Rittinger, and J. Teubner. MonetDB/XQuery: a fast XQuery processor powered by a relational engine. In *SIGMOD*, 2006.

[6] J. Camacho-Rodríguez, D. Colazzo, and I. Manolescu. PAXQuery: Efficient Parallel Processing of Complex XQuery. *IEEE TKDE*, 2015.

[7] H. Choi, K.-H. Lee, S.-H. Kim, Y.-J. Lee, and B. Moon. HadoopXML: A suite for parallel processing of massive XML data with multiple twig pattern queries. In *CIKM*, 2012.

[8] J. Dean and S. Ghemawat. MapReduce: Simplified Data Processing on Large Clusters. In *OSDI*, 2004.

[9] A. Deutsch, Y. Papakonstantinou, and Y. Xu. The NEXT Logical Framework for XQuery. In *VLDB*, 2004.

[10] Apache Flink. http://flink.incubator.apache.org/.

[11] GeoNames. http://www.geonames.org/.

[12] F. Hueske, M. Peters, M. J. Sax, A. Rheinländer, R. Bergmann, A. Krettek, and K. Tzoumas. Opening the Black Boxes in Data Flow Optimization. *PVLDB*, 2012.

[13] S. Khatchadourian, M. P. Consens, and J. Siméon. Having a ChuQL at XML on the cloud. In *AMW*, 2011.

[14] I. Manolescu, Y. Papakonstantinou, and V. Vassalos. XML Tuple Algebra. In *Encyclopedia of Database Systems*. 2009.

[15] G. Miklau and D. Suciu. Containment and equivalence for an XPath fragment. In *PODS*, 2002.

[16] A. Okcan and M. Riedewald. Processing theta-joins using MapReduce. In *SIGMOD*, 2011.

[17] C. Olston, B. Reed, U. Srivastava, R. Kumar, and A. Tomkins. Pig Latin: A Not-So-Foreign Language for Data Processing. In *SIGMOD*, 2008.

[18] Open Weather Map. http://openweathermap.org/.

[19] R. Ramakrishnan and J. Gehrke. *Database Management Systems*. McGraw-Hill, Inc., New York, NY, USA, 3 edition, 2003.

[20] C. Re, J. Siméon, and M. F. Fernández. A Complete and Efficient Algebraic Compiler for XQuery. In *ICDE*, 2006.

[21] A. Schmidt, F. Waas, M. L. Kersten, M. J. Carey, I. Manolescu, and R. Busse. XMark: A benchmark for XML data management. In *VLDB*, 2002.

[22] Apache Tez. http://tez.apache.org/.

[23] A. Thusoo, J. S. Sarma, N. Jain, Z. Shao, P. Chakka, N. Zhang, S. Anthony, H. Liu, and R. Murthy. Hive - a PB scale data warehouse using Hadoop. In *ICDE*, 2010.

[24] XQuery 3.0: An XML Query Language, April 2014.

Cache-Efficient Aggregation: Hashing *Is* Sorting

Ingo Müller[1†‡], Peter Sanders[2†], Arnaud Lacurie[3‡]
Wolfgang Lehner[4*], Franz Färber[5‡]

[†]Karlsruhe Institute of Technology, [‡]SAP SE, [*]Dresden University of Technology

[1]ingo.mueller@kit.edu, [2]sanders@kit.edu, [3]arnaud.lacurie@sap.com,
[4]wolfgang.lehner@tu-dresden.de, [5]franz.faerber@sap.com

ABSTRACT

For decades researchers have studied the duality of hashing and sorting for the implementation of the relational operators, especially for efficient aggregation. Depending on the underlying hardware and software architecture, the specifically implemented algorithms, and the data sets used in the experiments, different authors came to different conclusions about which is the better approach. In this paper we argue that in terms of cache efficiency, the two paradigms are actually the same. We support our claim by showing that the complexity of hashing is the same as the complexity of sorting in the external memory model. Furthermore we make the similarity of the two approaches obvious by designing an algorithmic framework that allows to switch seamlessly between hashing and sorting during execution. The fact that we mix hashing and sorting routines in the same algorithmic framework allows us to leverage the advantages of both approaches and makes their similarity obvious. On a more practical note, we also show how to achieve very low constant factors by tuning both the hashing and the sorting routines to modern hardware. Since we observe a complementary dependency of the constant factors of the two routines to the locality of the input, we exploit our framework to switch to the faster routine where appropriate. The result is a novel relational aggregation algorithm that is cache-efficient—independently and without prior knowledge of input skew and output cardinality—, highly parallelizable on modern multi-core systems, and operating at a speed close to the memory bandwidth, thus outperforming the state-of-the-art by up to 3.7×.

Categories and Subject Descriptors

H.2.4 [**Database Management**]: Systems—*Query processing*; H.2.4 [**Database Management**]: Systems—*Parallel databases*

Keywords

Hashing, sorting, aggregation, grouping, cache-efficient, shared-memory, robust performance, "group by", adaptive algorithm

1. INTRODUCTION

GROUPING with AGGREGATION is one of the most expensive relational database operators, maybe the most expensive one after the JOIN. It occurs in many analytical queries, e.g., in queries with a `GROUP BY` clause in SQL. The dominant cost of AGGREGATION is, as with most relational operators, the movement of the data. In the days of disk-based database systems, relational operators were designed to reduce the number of I/Os needed to access the disk whereas access to main memory was considered free. In today's in-memory database systems, the challenge stays more or less the same but moves one level up in the memory hierarchy [32]: How should an aggregation operator be designed such that it uses the CPU caches efficiently to overcome the bottleneck to the much slower main memory?

Traditionally, there are two opposite approaches to implement this operator: hashing and sorting. HASHAGGREGATION inserts the input rows into a hash table, using the grouping attributes as key and aggregating the remaining attributes in-place. SORTAGGREGATION first sorts the rows by the grouping attributes and then aggregates the consecutive rows of each group. The question about which approach is better has been debated for a long time and different authors came to different conclusions about which is the better approach in which context [3, 7, 19, 26]. The consensus is that HASHAGGREGATION is better if the number of groups is small enough such that the output fits into the cache, and SORTAGGREGATION is better if the number of groups is very large. Many systems implement both operators and decide a priori which one to use. In this paper we argue that in terms of data movement, the two paradigms are actually the same. By recognizing the fact that hashing *is* sorting, we can construct a single AGGREGATION operator with the advantages of both worlds.

As a first argument for our claim, we compare the number of cache line transfers of HASHAGGREGATION and SORTAGGREGATION. We reason in a general external memory model [1], which holds in the cache setting as well as in the disk-based setting. We confirm that if implemented naively, the two algorithms indeed exhibit a certain duality with respect to the number of groups. However with two simple, commonly known optimizations, the respective drawbacks of both algorithms can be removed. The two approaches have then exactly the same costs in terms of cache line transfers, matching the lower bound of MULTISETSORTING in the common case.

As a second argument for the similarity of the two approaches, we design an algorithmic framework that allows seamless switching between hashing and sorting during execution. It is based on the observation that hashing is in fact equivalent to *sorting by hash value*. Since hashing is a special form of sorting, intermediate results of a hashing routine can be further processed by a sorting routine and vice versa. This allows us to apply state-of-the-art optimizations to both routines separately, but still combine them to benefit from their respective advantages. Furthermore is sorting by hash value an *easy* instance of sorting, since hashing makes the key domain

SIGMOD'15, May 31–June 4, 2015, Melbourne, Victoria, Australia.

ACM 978-1-4503-2758-9/15/05 ...$15.00.
http://dx.doi.org/10.1145/2723372.2747644.

dense and eliminates value skew. We also discuss how to apply this framework in the context of column-store database systems and just-in-time compiled query plans, which are two most commonly used architectures for analytical workloads.

Furthermore we show how to achieve very low constant factors for both the hashing and the sorting routine by tuning them to modern hardware, thus making our analysis in the external memory model meaningful. The main techniques are wait-free parallelization, enabling super scalar instruction execution, and careful cache management. This is more important on modern in-memory database systems than on traditional disk-based systems, since much fewer CPU instructions can be executed in the time of a cache line transfer than in the time needed for loading a page from disk. With our careful tuning, however, we are able to leave the memory access costs as the main remaining performance bottleneck.

Despite all tuning, there is an intrinsic reason why hashing and sorting have complementary performance vis-à-vis the locality of keys in the input: Hashing allows for *early aggregation* while sorting does not. If several rows of the same group occur close to each other, hashing aggregates them immediately to a single row. By reducing very early and possibly by large factors the amount of subsequent work, hashing is much faster than sorting in this case. In the other case however, i.e., in case of an input with few repeating keys, the additional effort of *trying* to aggregate is in vain, so regular sorting without early aggregation is faster here. Our framework can exploit this complementarity by effectively detecting locality during execution and switching to the faster routine when appropriate, thus putting the insights of the theoretical analysis into practice.

Putting everything together, we obtain a novel relational aggregation algorithm that is optimal in terms of memory access complexity—independently and without prior knowledge of input skew and output cardinality—and has very low constant factors on modern hardware. It is cache-efficient, highly parallelizable on modern multi-core systems, and operating at a speed close to the memory bandwidth. With our single, robust aggregation operator, the possibly error-prone decision of the optimizer before the query execution is eliminated. We present extensive experiments on a variety of data sets comparing our implementation to the state-of-the-art, which we are able to outperform by up to factor 3.7.

The rest of the paper is organized as follows: In Section 2 we discuss the complexity of textbook algorithms for external aggregation, followed by a presentation of our algorithmic framework in Section 3. We continue with tuning our routines to modern hardware in Section 4 and show how their advantages can be combined in Section 5. The resulting AGGREGATION operator is evaluated in Section 6. Finally, we compare our contributions to prior work in Section 7, and make some concluding remarks in Section 8.

2. ANALYSIS OF EXTERNAL AGGREGATION

In this section we analyse the text book aggregation algorithms briefly mentioned in Section 1 in terms of the number of cache line transfers they incur. We show that with two simple optimizations, SORTAGGREGATION and HASHAGGREGATION have in fact the same costs. This insight will guide the design of our algorithm in the later sections.

2.1 Analysis of Sort-Based Aggregation

We do the analysis in the *external memory* model [1] because this model yields very general results that are applicable for both cache line transfers and I/Os. The external memory model has the following parameters for the input data and the cache:

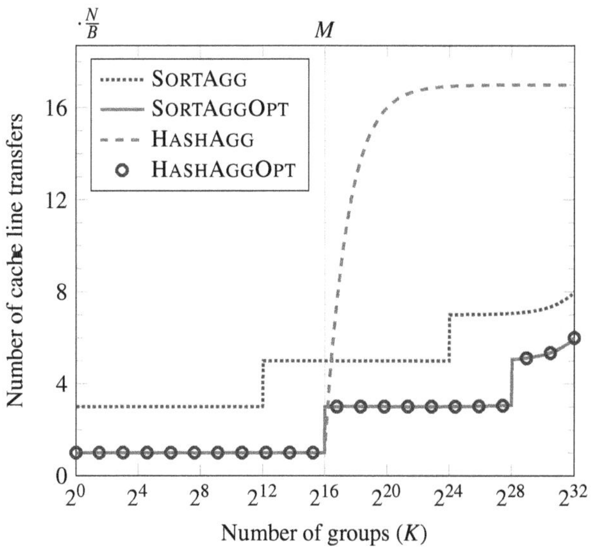

Figure 1: Comparison of aggregation algorithms in the External Memory model for $N = 2^{32}$, $M = 2^{16}$, and $B = 16$.

N = number of input rows

K = number of groups in the input

M = number of rows fitting into cache

B = number of rows per single cache line

Note that the output will be of size K. The costs of an algorithm are the number of cache line transfers in the worst case—computations and access to the cache are free.

When applied to CPU caches, the external memory model does not allow to make as precise performance predictions as it does for the disk-based setup, for which it was originally conceived. It is still widely adopted [18, 15, 6, 41, 5] as a formal method to understand and minimize memory access costs of algorithms and data structures. In this case the implicit assumption holds that CPU costs can be reduced or hidden in large parts, for example by making out-of-cache memory access sequential, eliminating branches, and using out-of-order execution or vectorization. We will show in Section 4 how to achieve this with the algorithms we propose.

We start with the analysis of SORTAGGREGATION. We use bucket sort because the analysis is simple, the result is valid for any other cache-efficient sort algorithm and because it can be easily turned into a state-of-the-art radix sort, the fastest known type of sort algorithms for dense domains [45, 25, 36]. Bucket sort recursively partitions the input into buckets until the data is sorted. Then a final pass over the data aggregates the rows of the same group, which reside in consecutive memory locations in the sorted input.

We use the tree representing the recursive calls of the algorithm for the analysis of SORTAGGREGATION, which we develop in three iterations. The first, simple iteration of the analysis works as follows: Since we can sort each cache line for free before we write it, the recursion stops when all partitions have size B, so there are as many leaves in the call tree as there are cache lines in the input: $\frac{N}{B}$. Furthermore the tree has degree $\frac{M}{B}$ since the number of partitions is limited by the number of buffers that fit into cache. This means that if we assume that the tree is somewhat balanced, it has a height of $\left\lceil \log_{\frac{M}{B}} \frac{N}{B} \right\rceil$. Since the input is read and written once per level of the tree and the subsequent aggregation pass reads the input ($\frac{N}{B}$) and writes the output once ($\frac{K}{B}$), the overall costs of SORTAGGREGATION are roughly:

$$\text{SORTAGGSTAT}(N,K) = 2 \cdot \frac{N}{B} \cdot \left\lceil \log_{\frac{M}{B}} \frac{N}{B} \right\rceil + \frac{N}{B} + \frac{K}{B}$$

The analysis is slightly simplified because it assumes a static depth of the call tree independently of K. In a second iteration, we can make the analysis more precise by taking into account the fact that the keys form a multiset in the cases where $K < N$. In this case the recursion actually stops earlier than for the case where $K = N$. In fact, the call tree only has $\min(\frac{N}{B}, K)$ leaves, at most one for each partition, so SORTAGGREGATION needs the following number of cache line transfers:

$$\text{SORTAGG}(N,K) = 2 \cdot \frac{N}{B} \cdot \left\lceil \log_{\frac{M}{B}} \left(\min \left(\frac{N}{B}, K \right) \right) \right\rceil + \frac{N}{B} + \frac{K}{B}$$

It is known that this is a lower bound for multiset sorting [33], i.e., no sort algorithm can do asymptotically less cache line transfers in the general case. Other than bucket sort, also distribution sort, sample sort, quicksort, and radix sort achieve this bound, with an analysis very similar to the above, first shown by Aggarwal and Vitter [1], as well as variants of heap sort [43] and sorting with buffer trees [4].

Figure 1 plots the number of cache line transfers as function of K for $N = 2^{32}$, $M = 2^{16}$, and $B = 16$, which are typical values for modern CPU caches. For small K, SORTAGGREGATION needs one pass for sorting and one pass for aggregating. For larger K, the number of passes only increases logarithmically. Due to the large base and the rounding, the logarithm has only values $\in \{1,2,3\}$ in our plot (corresponding to the steps) and is never larger than four in most realistic settings. Only for very large K, where K gets close to N, the $\frac{K}{B}$ cache line transfers for writing the output become noticeable.

In the third iteration of the analysis, we make a small modification to SORTAGGREGATION: we merge the last bucket sort pass with the final aggregation pass, i.e., instead of writing a cache-line to memory when the buffer of a partition runs full, we aggregate the elements of this cache-line to make space. Since there are few enough groups left in the last pass, this produces the final result of the current bucket in cache and thus completely eliminates one pass over the entire data. Furthermore it allows us to hold a factor B more partitions (M instead of $\frac{M}{B}$), so there are now only $\frac{K}{B}$ leaves in the call tree of the algorithm. This optimization requires that intermediate results are of size $O(1)$, which is true for *distributive* and *algebraic* aggregation functions [22], including the most common ones like `COUNT`, `SUM`, `MIN`, `MAX`, and `AVG`, but not for `MEDIAN`. With this analysis and a small reorganization of the formula, the number of cache line transfers made by SORTAGGREGATIONOPTIMIZED is the following:

$$\text{SORTAGGOPT}(N,K) = \frac{N}{B} + 2 \cdot \frac{N}{B} \left(\left\lceil \log_{\frac{M}{B}} \frac{K}{B} \right\rceil - 1 \right) + \frac{K}{B}$$

The first and the last term correspond to reading the input and writing the output respectively. The second term corresponds to writing intermediate results and reading them again in the next level of recursion.

Figure 1 plots the costs of SORTAGGREGATIONOPTIMIZED. It shows that the optimization eliminates an entire pass and slightly delays the necessity of an additional pass due to better cache usage in the last pass. In particular, for $K < M$, the algorithm just reads the data once and calculates the result in cache.

2.2 Analysis of Hash-Based Aggregation

We now analyze the number of cache line transfers that HASHAGGREGATION needs. Apart from the $\frac{K}{B}$ cache lines for writing the result, the algorithm just needs the $\frac{N}{B}$ cache line transfers for reading the input—as long as the resulting hash table fits into the cache, i.e., $K < M$, and assuming that intermediate aggregates can be saved in a state of size $O(1)$ like above. In the other case, if $K > M$, even with a perfect cache and without hash collisions, only a fraction of $\frac{M}{K}$ rows can be in the cache at the same time, so every access to one of the other rows produces a cache miss (= 1 write + 1 read). The overall number of cache line transfers is therefore:

$$\text{HASHAGG}(N,K) = \frac{N}{B} + \begin{cases} \frac{K}{B} & \text{if } K < M \\ 2 \cdot \left(1 - \frac{M}{K}\right) \cdot N & \text{otherwise} \end{cases}$$

Figure 1 shows the costs of HASHAGGREGATION: As long as the output K is small enough to fit into the cache, HASHAGGREGATION is really fast. However as soon as the cache cannot hold the output anymore, HASHAGGREGATION triggers a cache miss for almost every input row, so the number of cache line transfers explodes.

A common optimization to overcome this problem is to (recursively) partition the input by hash value and to apply HASHAGGREGATION on each partition separately. Since each partition contains only a part of the groups, i.e., since K is reduced, this makes the algorithm work in cache. However the partitioning also entails costs, which are the same as the partitioning of bucket sort. Consequently the analysis works the same way as the one for SORTAGGREGATIONOPTIMIZED: $\left\lceil \log_{\frac{M}{B}} \frac{K}{B} \right\rceil - 1$ partitioning passes plus the reading ($\frac{N}{B}$) and writing ($\frac{K}{B}$) of the HASHAGGREGATION pass of the partitions. In total HASHAGGREGATIONOPTIMIZED needs the following number of cache line transfers:

$$\text{HASHAGGOPT}(N,K) = 2 \cdot \frac{N}{B} \left(\left\lceil \log_{\frac{M}{B}} \frac{K}{B} \right\rceil - 1 \right) + \frac{N}{B} + \frac{K}{B}$$

Figure 1 shows that HASHAGGREGATIONOPTIMIZED has the same cost in terms of number of cache line transfers as the optimized sort-based aggregation above.

2.3 Conclusions from the Analysis

Our analysis shows that SORTAGGREGATION and HASHAGGREGATION have indeed a complementary behavior if implemented naively: HASHAGGREGATION performs better when the number of groups is small, while SORTAGGREGATION is more efficient in the other case. However the respective drawback of both algorithms can be removed if each of them includes a simple, well-known optimization: doing the aggregation pass together with the last sorting pass and recursive partitioning as preprocessing respectively. This suggests that—at least on this level of abstraction—there is no such thing as a duality between hashing and sorting. In terms of cache line transfers, the two approaches are actually the same. Note that since bucket sort matches the lower bound for sorting in the common case, this reasoning is valid for any other optimal sort algorithm as well.

Since no algorithm is known to date that requires fewer cache line transfers than the algorithms presented above, one might even wonder whether this is an intrinsic property of aggregation itself rather than being a property of specific algorithms, i.e., whether there is a lower bound on the cache line transfers needed to compute an aggregation query. We conjecture that there is indeed such a bound and that it matches the bound of multiset sorting for the most interesting parameter ranges, but leave the proof open for future research.

Algorithm 1 Algorithmic Building Blocks

```
 1: func PARTITIONING(run: Seq. of Row, level)
 2:     for each row in run do
 3:         R_h ← R_h ∪ row with h = HASH(row.key, level)
 4:     return (R_1, ..., R_F)
 5: func HASHING(run: Seq. of Row, level)
 6:     for each row in run do
 7:         table.INSERTORAGGREGATE(row.key, row, level)
 8:         if table.ISFULL() then
 9:             tables ← tables ∪ table ; table.RESET(())
10:     return (R_1, ..., R_F) with R_i ← ⋃_{t∈tables} GETRANGE(t,i)
```

Algorithm 2 Aggregation Framework

```
1: AGGREGATE(SPLITINTORUNS(input), 0)            ▷ initial call
2: func AGGREGATE(input: Seq. of Seq. of Row, level)
3:     if |input| == 1 and ISAGGREGATED(input[0]) then
4:         return input[0]
5:     for each run at index j in input do
6:         PRODUCERUNS ← HASHINGORPARTITIONING()
7:         R_{j,1}, ..., R_{j,F} ← PRODUCERUNS(run, level)
8:     return ⋃_{i=1}^{F} AGGREGATE(⋃_j R_{j,i}, level + 1)
```

The insights of this analysis shall be the design principles of the following sections. We show how to engineer a single aggregation algorithm similar to the optimized versions of both SORTAGGREGATION and HASHAGGREGATION that has excellent practical performance characteristics independently of the value of K.

3. ALGORITHMIC FRAMEWORK

In this section we present an algorithmic framework for an AGGREGATION operator putting the theoretical insights of the previous section into practice. The main idea is to design the algorithm like an integer sort algorithm on the dense hash values with hashing as a special case used for early aggregation. Furthermore we show how to achieve wait-free parallelization of the algorithm. Finally we also discuss how to fit the framework into popular processing models of modern database systems.

3.1 Mixing Hashing and Sorting

As presented in the previous section, sort-based and hash-based aggregation have the same complexity in the external memory model. This is very intuitive considering the fact that the two algorithms have the same high-level structure: they recursively partition the input—either by the keys of the groups or by their hash values—until there are few enough groups left to process each partition in cache. However the two approaches are even more similar: the process of building up a hash table also partitions the input by hash value.

Consequently we can define the following two partitioning routines, which will be the main building blocks of our framework and which are shown in Algorithm 1: plain partitioning by hash value called PARTITIONING (Line 1) and a partitioning routine based on the creation of hash tables called HASHING (Line 5). Both routines produce partitions in form of "runs"[1]: PARTITIONING produces one run per partition by moving every row to its respective run. HASHING starts with a first hash table of the size of the cache and replaces its current hash table with a new one whenever it is full. Every full hash table is split into one run per partition—merely a logical operation since the hash values of one hash partition are stored in a consecutive range in the hash table.

Note that the working set of both HASHING and PARTITIONING is strictly limited to the CPU cache. The working set of PARTITIONING is limited through its partitioning fan-out, while HASHING has a limited working set because the hash table size is fixed to the size of the cache.

We can now combine these two building blocks into a recursive algorithm similar to both SORTAGGREGATIONOPTIMIZED and HASHAGGREGATIONOPTIMIZED. The algorithm is shown in Algorithm 2: The input is first split into runs. Then each run of the input is processed by one of the two routines selected by HASHINGORPARTITIONING (line 6), which produces runs for the different buckets. Once the entire input has been processed, the algorithm treats all runs of the same partition as a single bucket and recurses into the buckets one after each other. With every step of the recursive partitioning, more and more hash digits are in common within a bucket, thus reducing the number of groups per bucket more and more. The recursion stops when there is a single run left for each bucket and in that run, all rows with of same group have been aggregated to a single output row.

Using the hash values as partition criterion has the advantage that it solves the problem of balancing the number of groups in the buckets, which was an assumption of the analysis in Section 2. The hash function distributes the groups uniformly—it makes the key domain dense and hence the partitioning easier.

The way we use HASHING has also the advantage that it enables *early aggregation* [19, 27]. In contrast to the two illustrative algorithms from the previous section, we can now aggregate in *all* passes, not just the last. Since HASHING can aggregate rows from the same group, the resulting hash tables and hence the output runs are potentially much smaller than the input run, thus reducing the amount of data for subsequent passes by possibly large factors. It is important to understand that this does not change the number of cache lines needed in the worst case, but it is very beneficial in case of locality of the groups. So one might even wonder why we do not used HASHING all the time, similarly to recent work on disk-based systems [23]. As we show in the next section, on modern hardware, PARTITIONING can be tuned to a 4 times higher throughput than HASHING, which makes it the better routine in cases where early aggregation is not helpful.

The fact that our framework supports HASHING and PARTITIONING interchangeably not only makes the similarity between the two approaches obvious but also gives it the power to switch to the better routine where appropriate: In presence of locality or clusters, our framework can use HASHING, whose early aggregation reduces the amount of work for later passes. In absence of locality, we can switch to the faster PARTITIONING instead. The switching can happen spontaneously during runtime, without loosing work accomplished so far, and without coordination or planning. Algorithm 2 still uses HASHINGORPARTITIONING as a black box, but in Section 5, we discuss several switching strategies.

We argue that the design of our framework resembles that of a sort algorithm. While the similarity to bucket sort from the previous section is obvious, our framework has similarities with other sort algorithms as well: Since the bucket of an element is determined by some bits of a hash function, our algorithm is in fact a radix sort rather than a bucket sort. Thus hashing turns AGGREGATION into an instance of *integer sorting*, which is easier than sorting in general [45, 25, 36]. Furthermore it repeatedly merges intermediate

[1] We consciously use the term "run" from the disk-based era, which was commonly used to denote temporary files for intermediate processing results on disk [19].

runs from different parts of the input, so in a way the algorithm is also similar to merge sort. Finally, hashing can be seen as a variant of insertion sort, which is commonly used for the leaves of recursive sort algorithms [14].

An interesting interpretation is the following: The concatenation of the final runs of our algorithm is a hash table like HASHAGGREGATION would produce but it is built with a sorting algorithm—which is actually much faster. This suggests that the optimal way to do hashing *is* sorting.

Finally the fact that we mix hashing and sorting requires some technical attention: The buckets may contain rows that were just copied from the input, but also rows that are already aggregates of several rows from the input. In order to aggregate two aggregated values, one needs to use the so-called super-aggregate function [22], which is not always the same as the function that aggregates two values from the input. For example the super-aggregate function of `COUNT` is `SUM`. However it is easy to keep some meta-information associated with the intermediate runs indicating which aggregation function should be used.

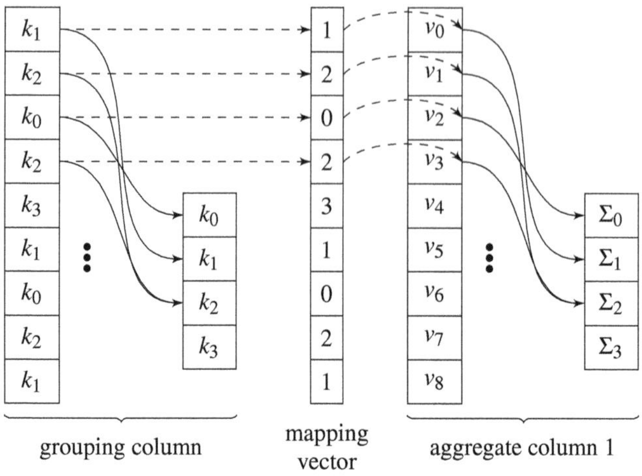

Figure 2: Column-wise processing.

3.2 Parallelization

Apart from cache-efficiency, the design of our framework is also influenced by the requirement for intra-operator parallelism of large analytical systems. It allows for full parallelization of all phases of the algorithm: First, the main loop that partitions the input in Line 5 of Algorithm 2 can be executed in parallel without further synchronization since neither input nor output are shared among the threads. Second, the recursive calls on the different buckets in Line 8 can also be done in parallel. Only the management of the runs between the recursive calls (the $\bigcup$-operations in our pseudocode) require synchronization, but this happens infrequently enough to be negligible.

We use user level scheduling to balance the two axes of parallelism as follows: we always create parallel tasks for the recursive calls, which are completely independent of each other, while we use work-stealing to parallelize the loop over the input. It is important to see that the latter form of parallelization implies that several runs per bucket are produced (at least one per thread), which in turn implies another level of recursion. By using work-stealing, our framework limits the creation of additional work to situations where no other form of parallelism is available. In particular, parallelizing the main loop is needed in the following two cases: First it is the only way to parallelize the initial call of the algorithm and second it allows for full parallelization even in presence of heavy skew: the buckets after the first call can be of arbitrarily different sizes because even an ideal hash function only distributes the *groups* evenly over the buckets, but does not affect the distribution of *rows* into these groups (which is given by the input). With work-stealing in the main loop however, our framework can schedule the threads to help with the large buckets once they have finished their own recursive call.

3.3 System Integration

We now want to discuss how to integrate our operator into the two prevailing processing models of analytical in-memory database systems, column-wise processing and just-in-time compiled (JiT) query plans.

Column-wise processing is the traditional processing model of column store database systems. It imposes some specific requirements for the implementation of aggregation operators. While our framework fulfills these requirements, this is not true for all aggregation algorithms proposed in the past. In the column store architecture, the question arises *when* and *how* the aggregate columns should be processed with respect to the grouping columns. The question has been discussed in the literature for the column store architecture in general [10, 11, 31], but there are some additional aspects specific to aggregation.

One possibility for column-wise processing is to process all columns at the same time, similarly to a row store. An aggregation operator would read the values of a single row from one column after another, compute the aggregates, and then store them in their respective result columns one after each other. This approach is known to have the disadvantage that the data is not processed in tight loops [11], which results in considerable performance deterioration on modern hardware. Furthermore it effectively decreases the size of the cache during aggregation: Since all relevant attributes of a row together are larger than than just a single attribute, less elements fit into cache, so an aggregation operator needs more passes for cache-efficient processing.

Another possibility is to do the processing one column at a time, like it is done for example in MonetDB [10, 31]. With this approach, aggregation is split into two operators as illustrated by Figure 2: The first operator processes the grouping column and produces a vector with identifiers of the groups and a mapping vector, which maps every input row to the index of its group. The second operator applies this mapping vector by aggregating every input value with the current aggregate of the group as indicated by the mapping vector and is executed once for each aggregate column. This approach is known to have the disadvantage to require additional memory access to write and read the mapping vector. Furthermore it ignores the insights of our analysis for cache-efficient aggregation: if we aggregate the input values directly to their group in the output column, we get the same sub-optimal memory access pattern as HASHAGGREGATION, producing close to a cache miss for every input row for large outputs. Since there are often many more aggregate columns than grouping columns, this would even have a worse impact on performance than inefficient processing of the keys.

The state-of-the-art column-wise processing model was introduced in MonetDB/X100 [11] and combines the advantages of the above two possibilities by interleaving the processing of the different columns in blocks of the size of the cache. Applied to aggregation, this allows to process the columns in tight loops without materialization of the mapping vector to memory. However we also need to adopt this model *inside* the aggregation operator to make it compatible with our recursive run production. Consequently our framework operates as follows if used for column-wise processing:

While producing a run of the grouping column, both HASHING and PARTITIONING produce a mapping vector as depicted in Figure 2, but *only for this run*. This mapping is then applied to the corresponding parts of the aggregate columns. When the corresponding runs of all columns have been produced, the framework continues with the processing of the rest of the input.

One important aspect of this discussion is that not all techniques for aggregation proposed in prior work are compatible with column-wise processing. Our two routines, hashing and partitioning, move every input element directly to its final location, so it is easy to create the required mapping vector. However it is unclear how to fit some other routines into this scheme, for example vectorized sorting networks recently used for joins [7] or software-caching used for cache-efficient aggregation in row stores [13].

Recent work [35, 17, 34] promises to replace column-wise processing by a processing model based on just-in-time compilation (JiT). In this model, each pipeline of the execution plan of a query is compiled into a fragment of machine code just before execution, thus enabling processing in tight loops without decoupling the processing of different columns. It is straightforward to fit our framework into this model: The main part of the operator, i.e., the initial call to the AGGREGATE function of Algorithm 2, is compiled into the pipeline fragment including (and ending with) the aggregation operator. When this pipeline ends, all data resides in intermediate runs in the first level of the buckets. For the recursive function calls, a second code fragment is compiled, which only contains the code to process the buckets further. Both fragments contain the code path of both the PARTITIONING and the HASHING routine from Algorithm 1. Since the runtime decision between the two paths is the same for the entire run, it is easy to predict by the hardware and does hence not hurt performance.

4. MINIMIZING COMPUTATIONS

In this section we study the details of the two routines used in our algorithm: hashing and partitioning. The goal is to bring the behaviour of our implementation on real hardware as close as possible to the idealized external memory machine model. Our analysis and the algorithmic framework built upon it are only relevant if we turn the movement of the data into the dominant part of the execution time by reducing the computational overhead to a minimum (i.e., ideally by making it "free"). We show that this is much more difficult in the cache setting of modern hardware than it used to be in the disk setting, since the gap between fast and slow memory is much narrower and small differences in the implementation can change the performance by factors.

The microbenchmarks that we run in this section are run in the same experimental setup as the experiments in Section 6.

4.1 Minimizing CPU Costs of Hashing

We conducted a performance comparison of several hash table implementations. It turned out that the simplest approach has the lowest CPU overhead: a single level hash table with linear probing, similar to the state-of-the-art **dense_hash_map** of Google[2]. We fix the hash table to the size of the L3 cache and consider it full at a very low fill rate of 25%. With this configuration, collisions are very rare or even non-existing with high probability if the number of groups is more than two orders of magnitude smaller than the cache, so no CPU cycles are lost for collision resolution. The apparent waste of memory is in fact negligible because it is limited to one or very few hash tables per thread in our final algorithm presented in the next section. Interestingly this is the opposite of what Barber et

[2]https://code.google.com/p/sparsehash/

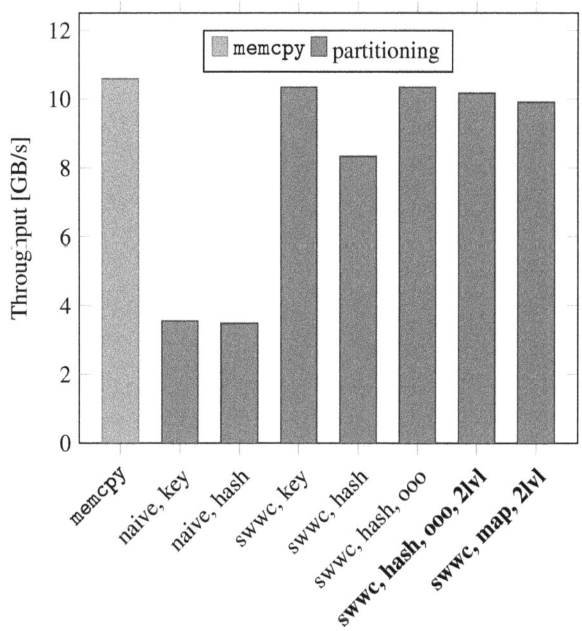

Figure 3: Microbenchmark of degenerated partitioning routines.

al. [8] recently proposed for JOINs, where denser storage increased performance. We tried out many different hash functions that are popular among practitioners and found that for small elements, MurmurHash2[3] is the fastest. On a technical note, we adapted the linear probing to work within blocks, such that we can cleanly split a table into ranges for the recursive calls. The final insertion costs of our implementation are below 6 ns per element. This is roughly 4 times more than an L1 cache access, but more than an order of magnitude faster than out-of-cache insertion, where CPU costs are dwarfed by the costs of cache misses and our reasoning in the external memory model is meaningful.

4.2 Minimizing CPU Costs of Partitioning

To minimize the CPU costs of the partitioning routine, we use a technique known from integer sorting for dense domains. A large body of prior work suggests that this kind of sort algorithms is faster than comparison based sorting [45, 25, 36], except special cases such as sorting almost sorted data [12]. With partitioning, integer sorting is made branch- and even comparison-free, which eliminates most CPU costs of comparison-based sort algorithm.

The key idea is to use a technique called "software write-combining", first described by Intel [24] and used by various other authors [7, 38, 42]. Software write-combining is designed to avoid the *read-before-write* overhead and to reduce the number of TLB misses inherent in partitioning [30], which writes to a high number of memory pages. It consists in buffering one cache line per partition, which is flushed when it runs full using a non-temporal store instruction that by-passes the cache. This scheme works best with 256 partitions, so we use this number to split runs into ranges in our framework. Since the final size of the partitions is unknown before processing, most authors start with a counting pass to determine output positions. Wassenberg et al. [42] eliminate this pass using a trick with virtual memory to over-allocate every partition so that it can hold the entire input. This is not possible with the memory

[3]https://code.google.com/p/smhasher/

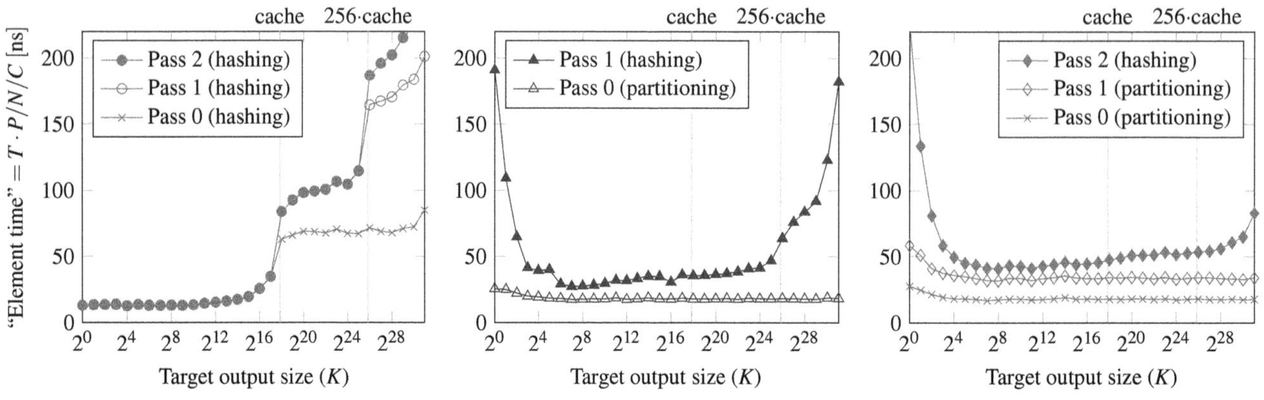

(a) HASHINGONLY (b) PARTITIONALWAYS (2 passes) (c) PARTITIONALWAYS (3 passes)

Figure 4: Breakdown of passes of illustrative aggregation strategies using $P = 20$ threads.

management of industry-grade database systems, but using a two-level data structure, a list of arrays, has the same benefit and only very low overhead, as we show below. We use this technique for processing not only for the grouping column but also for the aggregate columns as discussed in Section 3.3, since their memory access pattern is equivalent.

We conducted a series of microbenchmarks to measure the impact of our optimizations. Figure 3 shows the (payload) bandwidth of different versions of the partitioning routine on uniformly distributed random data. The first bar shows the bandwidth of a self-implemented `memcpy` using non-temporal store instructions as a reference. The next two bars show the throughput of a naive partitioning scheme, once partitioning according to some bits of the keys themselves (called *key*) once partitioning according to bits of the hash function (called *hash*). The difference between the two is only small as the throughput is mainly limited by the inherent TLB misses mentioned before. The next two bars show how software write-combining considerably improves performance (called *swwc*): The *key*-variant is 2.9 times faster than the naive counterpart. The variant partitioning by hash value seems to suffer from the computational overhead though. However we can benefit from out-of-order execution by manually unrolling the main loop into blocks of 16 elements, which are first all hashed and then all put into their partition buffers. The next bar (denoted *ooo*) shows that we gain 24% throughput with this optimization, thus achieving a 3.0 times higher throughput than the naive partitioning routine. Finally we replace over-allocated output partitions by the two-level data structure, which lowers performance by roughly 2%. This final routine runs at 97% of the bandwidth of our `memcpy`. The last bar shows the bandwidth of applying the mapping vector to an aggregate column using software write-combining and our two-level data structure (denoted *map*). Since reading the mapping vector adds memory traffic that we do not count as application bandwidth, the bandwidth here is slightly lower than that of the previous variant, namely 93% of our measured memory bandwidth.

To sum things up, like in the case of hashing, partitioning of both grouping and aggregate columns can be tuned to modern hardware such that the inevitable movement of the data remains the dominant part of the processing time.

5. ADAPTATION TO LOCALITY

In the previous sections, we describe an algorithmic framework for designing an aggregation operator similar to a sort algorithm and how to reduce the CPU costs of two possible subroutines. In this section, we answer the remaining question of when to select which of the two.

To that aim we present a series of experiments with naive strategies for selection of one of the two routines that illustrate their respective performance characteristics. Figure 4 shows the results. In HASHINGONLY the only subroutine used is HASHING (Figure 4(a)), whereas with PARTITIONALWAYS, the input is always preprocessed by one or two passes of PARTITIONING before a final HASHING pass (Figure 4(b) and 4(c)). To keep our implementation simple, we only allow a single HASHING pass by exceptionally letting its hash tables grow larger than the cache. This prevents full parallelization for very small K and cache misses for very large K, but these effects do not occur in our final algorithm. The experiments are run on uniformly distributed data.

The first observation that can be made in this experiment is the fact that HASHINGONLY automatically does the right number of passes: If $K <$ cache, it computes the result in cache. The subsequent merging of the runs of the different threads is insignificant due to their small size and thus not visible in the plot. Once $K >$ cache, HASHING recursively partitions the input until the result is computed in cache and the recursion stops automatically. For PARTITIONALWAYS this is not the case. Since it does not aggregate during partitioning, it can only be used as preprocessing and external knowledge is necessary to find the right depth of recursion before the final HASHING pass.

The second observation is that PARTITIONING is *much* faster than HASHING if $K >$ cache, i.e., if the latter produces more than one run (by more than factor 4 in our experiments). In this case HASHING suffers from its non-sequential memory access and wasted space and hence wasted memory transfers intrinsic to hash tables. Furthermore, as discussed in Section 2, as soon as there are only slightly more groups than fit into one hash table, chances are very low to find two elements with the same key, so the amount of data is not reduced significantly. In contrast PARTITIONING achieves a high throughput independently of K thanks to the tuning from the previous section.

In the case of uniformly distributed data, the best strategy is obvious: use PARTITIONING until the number of groups per partition is small enough such that HASHING can do the rest of the work in cache. However it is not clear how to find out when this is the case if K is not known. Furthermore the best strategy is less obvious with other distributions: consider a clustered distribution with a high locality where each key mostly occurs in one narrow region of the input. HASHING is then able to reduce the amount of data significantly *although* the entire partition has more groups than fit into cache. Hence HASHING can be the better choice even before the last pass if the ratio of input data size to output data size high enough.

This leads us to defining an ADAPTIVE strategy. The algorithm starts with HASHING. When a hash table gets full, the algorithm determines the factor $\alpha := \frac{n_{in}}{n_{out}}$ by which the input (run) has been reduced, where n_{in} is the number of processed rows and n_{out} the size of the hash table. If $\alpha > \alpha_0$ for some threshold α_0, HASHING was the better choice as the input was reduced significantly, so the algorithm continues with HASHING. Otherwise it switches to PARTITIONING. The parameter α_0 balances the performance penalty of HASHING compared to PARTITIONING with its benefit of reducing the work of later passes. We show how we determine this machine constant in Appendix A.1. When enough data was processed with the faster PARTITIONING routine such that the overhead of the (inadequate) HASHING is amortized, i.e., when $n_{in} = c \cdot \text{cache}$ for some c, the algorithm switches back to its initial mode in case the distribution has changed. In experiments shown in Appendix A.2, we found $c = 10$ to be a good compromise between amortization effect and reactivity to distribution changes.

Figure 5 shows the performance of ADAPTIVE compared to the illustrative strategies from Figure 4. It shows that ADAPTIVE automatically partitions the input using PARTITIONING until HASHING can process each partition in cache—without knowing K in advance. Consequently its performance corresponds piecewise to the best of the other strategies. If $K <$ cache (or $K/256^i <$ cache for pass i), each thread only works with a single hash table, which never runs full. If however the input does not fit into one hash table, input is partitioned with the faster PARTITIONING routine first. The fact that PARTITIONING is interleaved with occasional HASHING to check whether the distribution has changed has only low overhead and is barely noticeable for $K < 256 \cdot \text{cache}$. In the following section, we show that ADAPTIVE not only works well on uniform data, but has a robust performance on many distributions.

We see the main advantage of our approach in the fact that it combines the respective advantages of two complementary routines by switching between them based on a simple, local criterion. No completed work is ever thrown away; no extra work or preprocessing is necessary; no potentially unprecise information from the optimizer is needed; no synchronization is needed among the threads. In fact the different threads do not even need to take the same decision: they can benefit from changing locality or clusteredness in the input by aggregating where the locality is high and partitioning first where it is low.

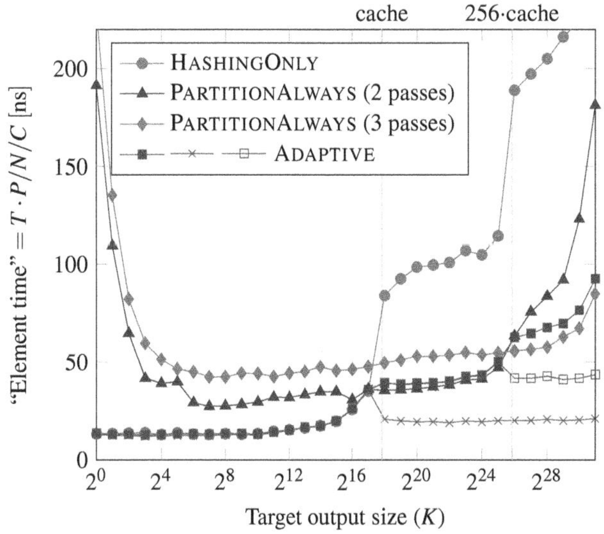

Figure 5: ADAPTIVE strategy in comparison with HASHINGONLY and PARTITIONALWAYS (2 and 3 passes) using $P = 20$ threads.

6. EVALUATION

In this section we evaluate the effectiveness of our algorithm design, assess the quality of our implementation, and compare the performance of our operator with previous work.

We implemented our algorithm for column-wise processing, but argue that the experiments have a certain validity for the JiT processing model as well: Where not otherwise mentioned, the experiments are run just on the grouping column, so the inner loops of both processing models are exactly equivalent.

6.1 Test Setup

We run the experiments on two Intel Xeon E7-8870 CPU[4] with 256 GB of main memory. They run at 2.4 GHz and have 10 cores each. Each core has 64 kB of private L1 cache, 256 kB of private L2 cache, and access to a shared 30 MB on-chip L3 cache (3 MB per core). The TLB of the CPUs have two levels, the first of which have 64 entries for data and 128 for instructions and the second 512 entries for both combined. The operating system is SLES 11.3 with Linux kernel 3.0.101 for x86_64. We use GCC 4.8.3 as compiler using `-O3 -march=native` optimizations.

Our data sets consist of $N = 2^{31}$ rows where all columns are 64-bit integers. If not otherwise mentioned we report run times as "Element Time" $= T \cdot P/N/C$, where T is the total run time, P the number of cores, and C the number of columns (grouping and aggregate columns combined). This metric represents the time each core spends to process one element and makes numbers of different configurations easily comparable—among themselves and to known machine constants such as the time of a cache miss.

All presented numbers are the median of 10 runs.

6.2 Scalability with the Number of Cores

We first assess the parallelization mechanisms of Section 3.2 and the quality of our implementation in terms of scalability with the number of cores. Figure 6 shows the speedup of ADAPTIVE for different numbers of groups K compared to its respective performance on a single core. As the plot shows, the speedup is around 16 on our 20 CPU cores no matter K, which is as close to optimal speedup as practical implementations usually get. Section 6.5 also shows the experiments with other distributions, where we found our algorithm to perform just as well. Finally we also ran this experiment with concurrent dummy threads on the idle cores in order to simulate a real system under load: If the dummy threads loop over their respective 3 MB of cache to keep the cache warm, the performance of our algorithm is not influenced since its threads only rely on their respective part of the cache. However if the dummy threads run an out-of-cache `memcpy`, the performance of our algorithm deteriorates by up to factor two, confirming that memory bandwidth is the main bottleneck our algorithm faces. The good scalability in all situations does not come to a surprise, since the threads of our algorithm do not share any resources and synchronize only at a very coarse granularity.

[4] http://ark.intel.com/products/53580

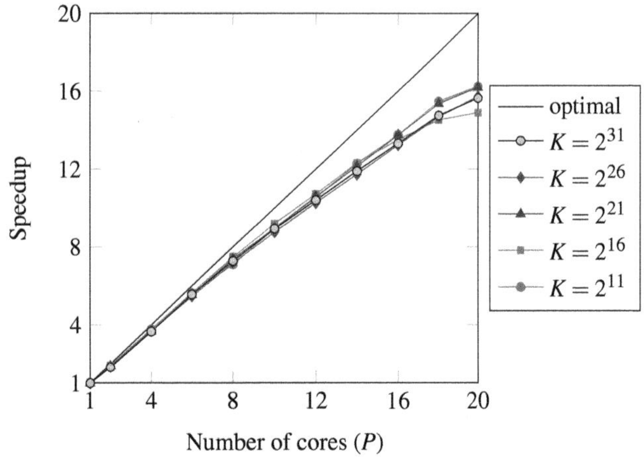

Figure 6: Speedup of ADAPTIVE compared to single core performance.

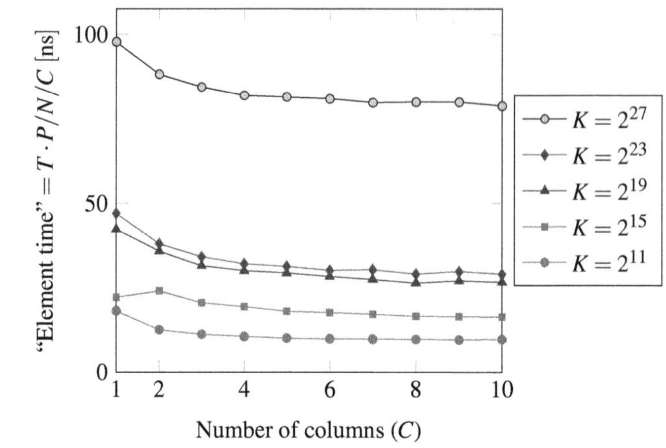

Figure 7: Scalability of ADAPTIVE with the number of columns using $P = 20$ threads.

6.3 Scalability with the Number of Columns

Figure 7 shows how the number of aggregate columns affects the performance of ADAPTIVE for different output cardinalities K. Just for this plot, we use $N = 2^{28}$ input elements to compensate the memory increase due to the additional columns. The experiment evaluates the effectiveness of the column-wise processing presented in Section 3.3, which is designed to process the different columns independently. Indeed the plot indicates that the run time per element is almost the same for any number of columns. As discussed in Section 4, the processing of the grouping column is a bit more expensive as the processing of the other columns because of the hashing and collision resolution, which explains the slightly higher costs per element with lower number of aggregates.

We also confirmed the scalability of our operator with the number of columns in experiments with other data distributions omitted here due to space constraints. Since the number of columns does not affect the processing cost per element, we run all other experiments only with a grouping column, i.e., without aggregate columns or $C = 1$.

6.4 Comparison with Prior Work

We now show an experimental analysis of several state of the art algorithms for in-memory aggregation from the work of Cieslewicz and Ross [13] and Ye et al. [46] and compare them to ADAPTIVE. Since their work targets the row store architecture (implicitly assuming JiT query compilation) while our implementation targets the column store architecture, we use a `DISTINCT` query with no aggregate columns ($C = 1$) for the comparison. In this type of query, the input and output data structure are equivalent in both architectures, and our algorithm does not need to produce a mapping vector for column-wise processing, so the experiments abstracts from all architectural differences.

We used the original implementations, but made the following modifications to tune them to this experiment: First we changed the minimal output data structure size to the size of the L3 cache, which effectively eliminates collision resolution for small K and consequently reduces the run time in these cases by up to 25%. Second we removed padding and redundant fields in the intermediate and output data structures, in order to reduce tuple size and hence memory traffic. This reduces the run time by roughly 20% for large K and even up by to 50% where the reduction in size makes the output just fit into cache. The padding originally improved the collision resolution in the high-throughput cases of small K, but our first modification improves theses cases even more. Third we replaced system mutexes by much smaller spin locks, again to reduce memory traffic, which also reduces the time by roughly 20% for the variants using them. Finally we replaced the multiplicative hashing by MurmurHash2, which we use in our algorithms as well. This has the same effect on the algorithms from prior work than on ours: a more predictable performance with up to 20% run time reduction due to less collisions, but noticeable overhead for small K. Furthermore we exceptionally provide ADAPTIVE with the output size, which is an information that all algorithms from the shown competitors rely on and which makes our algorithms somewhat faster due to implementation details (the benefit is only noticeable for large output cardinalities, i.e., if $K \approx N$, and always less than 10%).

Figure 8 shows a comparison of run times on data with uniform distribution. As we analyze in the following, all algorithms from prior work have an intrinsic limit in terms of K. They all consist of a fixed number of passes (either one or two) over the data, which means that they work well until a certain number of groups, but are penalized by a high number of cache misses beyond this limit. This is in line with our analysis of Section 2.

We describe the different algorithms and analyze their performance in more detail:

HYBRID (1 pass): Each thread aggregates its part of the input into a private hash table with a size fixed to its part of the shared L3 cache. When this table is full, old entries are evicted similarly to an LRU cache and inserted into a global, shared hash table. This becomes inefficient as soon as most of the output does not fit into the private tables, which happens for $K > 2^{16}$ (marked with L3 in Figure 8).

ATOMIC (1 pass): All threads work on a single, shared hash table protected by atomic instructions. This approach can suffer from contention due to concurrent updates as discussed by the original authors [13], but in the present `DISTINCT` query without aggregate columns, virtually no updates occur, so the problem is inexistent. It reaches its cache efficiency limit when the shared hash table exceeds the cache size, namely at around $K = 2^{19}$ (marked with ΣL3). This gives ATOMIC an advantage over all other algorithms for numbers of groups where it can fit its output into the *combined* cache while the shared-nothing approaches cannot.

INDEPENDENT (2 passes): In a first pass, every thread produces a hash table of his part of the input. In a second pass, the hash tables

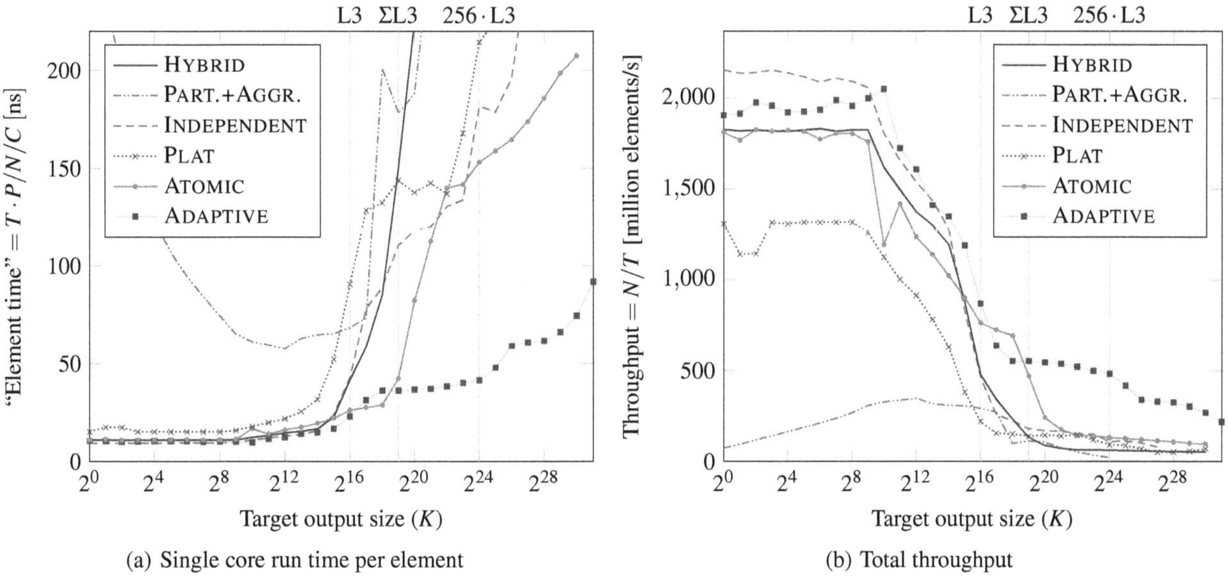

(a) Single core run time per element

(b) Total throughput

Figure 8: Comparison with prior work of Cieslewicz and Ross [13] and Ye et al. [46] using $P = 20$ threads.

are split and merged in parallel[5]. This makes the algorithm similar to HASHINGONLY with two passes, but since the hash tables of the first pass can be larger than the cache, both passes can trigger close to a cache miss per row. This limit is reached when the working set exceeds the L3 cache fraction *corresponding to each thread*, namely roughly at $K = 2^{16}$ for the first pass (marked with L3) and $K = 2^{24}$ for the second (marked with $256 \cdot$ L3).

PARTITION-AND-AGGREGATE (2 passes): Similarly to PARTITIONALWAYS with two passes, this algorithm first partitions the entire input by hash value and then merges each partition into its part of a hash table. Like our algorithm if limited to two passes as shown in Figure 4(b), this algorithm cannot do the merging in a cache-efficient manner if $K > 256 \cdot \text{cache} = 2^{24}$ ($256 \cdot$ L3 in the plot). Furthermore its partitioning uses the naive implementation as presented in Section 4 and is therefore slower than ours.

PLAT (Partition with Local Aggregation Table, 2 passes): Similarly to HYBRID, in this algorithm each thread aggregates into a private, fixed-size hash table. When it is full, new entries are overflown into hash partitions, which are merged in a subsequent pass like in the previous algorithm. This entails the same limit: the merging becomes inefficient if $K > 256 \cdot \text{cache} = 2^{24}$ (marked with $256 \cdot$ L3 in the plot). The partitioning in itself is also less efficient than ours, but in contrary to the previous algorithm, our optimization could not be applied here, since the private hash tables would destroy the explicit L1 cache management of software write-combining.

ADAPTIVE (variable number of passes): Our algorithm is the only algorithm that gracefully degrades with larger K thanks to the efficient additional passes. Compared to the fastest of the other algorithms, it achieves a speedup of at least factor 2.7 for all $K \leq 2^{21}$. The peak speedup factor of 3.7 is achieved at $K = 2^{24}$ where ADAPTIVE needs only 41 ns/element while ATOMIC needs 153 ns/element. Note that this speedup is higher than one usually hopes for for such a fundamental operator like aggregation, where improvements of several tens of percent are already worth some effort.

It is also worth noting that the second best algorithm for large values of K is actually the simplest in terms of cache management: While the cache-efficiency mechanisms of the other algorithms take extra time even though they do not work outside the range of K they were designed for, ATOMIC "just" pays single cache miss per row.

As Figure 8(b) shows, ADAPTIVE is also as least as fast as almost all other algorithm for other values of K[6]. The similarity of all algorithms for small K does not come as a surprise, since all hash-based algorithms do effectively exactly the same in these scenarios. It is interesting to see however that the throughput starts dropping slightly later for ADAPTIVE than for the other algorithms. The reason is that the linear probing scheme our algorithms use can store more elements in the same amount of space than the chaining scheme used by the other algorithms, which need to store an additional pointer[7]. Only for $K = 2^{18}$, ATOMIC can fit the output just into its shared L3 cache, and is therefore slightly faster than ADAPTIVE, which already needs a partitioning pass. Since the partitioning is so fast though, the difference is only very small.

6.5 Skew Resistence

We now extend the experiments on uniform data to other data sets in order to test the skew resistance of our ADAPTIVE operator. We use the synthetic data generators of Cieslewicz et al. [13], which generate input data for any combination of N and K for a series of distributions with different characteristics (since data cannot have $K = N$ groups *and* be skewed at the same time, K is only approximated). The distributions are namely heavy-hitter, moving-cluster, self-similar, sorted, uniform, and zipf[8]. In short, in heavy-hitter, 50% of all records have the key 1, the others are distributed uniformly between 2 and K. In moving-cluster, the keys are chosen uniformly from a sliding window of size 1024. Self-similar is the Pareto distribution with an 80–20 proportion (also known as 80–20 rule) and zipf is the Zipfian distribution with exponent 0.5.

[5]Note that the time of the second pass was not taken into account in the original paper [13].

[6]We leave the narrow gap to INDEPENDENT as small open problem.

[7]This is also the reason why the cache sizes indicated in Figure 8 are off by factor two for ADAPTIVE.

[8]We omit the distribution sequence because of its similarity to uniform.

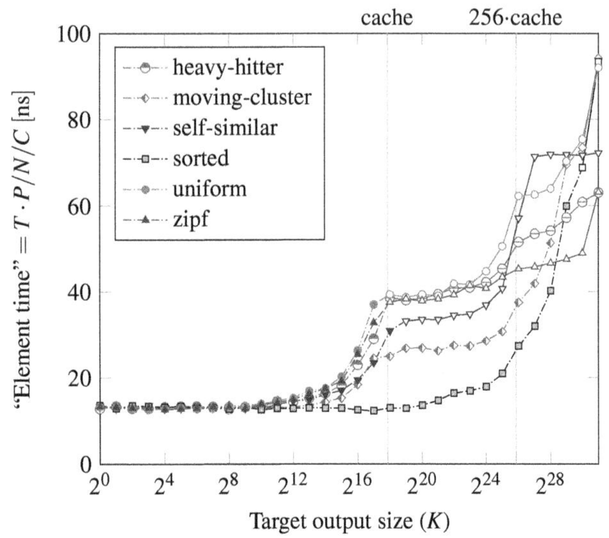

Figure 9: ADAPTIVE on different data sets using $P = 20$ threads.

Figure 9 shows the performance of ADAPTIVE on all data sets. The first and most important observation is that ADAPTIVE is not slower on the other distribution than uniform. In this sense, uniform is the hardest distribution for our operator and skew only improves its performance. Since skew means that some keys occur more often than others, our operator can benefit from skew by using hashing for early aggregation of these values.

To show the mechanics of *how* our algorithm adapts to the skew, we plot those cases of each distribution with solid markers where our algorithm uses only hashing in the first phase, while we plot with hollow markers the cases where it switches to partitioning in the first phase at least once. This way we can see that on the sorted data set, ADAPTIVE switches to partitioning only where $K \geq N/2$. Before that point every values is repeated at least 4 times, so every run of hashing reduces the data by factor $\alpha = 4 \geq \alpha_0$ or more, so our algorithm uses hashing for the next run as well. Since all hash tables are produced in cache and there are only very few of them except for the largest K, the second pass remains negligible and makes the run time only grow slowly with larger K. The behaviour with moving-cluster is very similar, except that the hashing is more costly due to inferior locality. Since self-similar only exhibits relatively mild skew, the same effect is less pronounced on this data set: the reduction factor α is only high enough where there are just more groups that would fit into cache. The run time is consequently very similar to that of uniform data, except that our algorithm switches to partitioning slightly later, namely for $K \geq 2^{19}$. Heavy-hitter even switches to partitioning at the same point as uniform, so for our algorithm this distribution does not have noticeable skew. In particular it does not cause contention since there are no shared data structures in our algorithm. It rather seems like the non-hitter keys are the hard part of this distribution. The zipf data set is so little skewed that it is processed just like uniform data. The fact that it takes less time for the largest K is an artifact intrinsic to the generation of skewed data as discussed above.

As discussed and shown experimentally in the original papers, some of the algorithms of Cieslewicz and Ross [13] and Ye et al. [46] also adapt to skew, but to a lesser degree than ours. All of them are based on hashing and therefore profit from locality. However only HYBRID can adapt to changes in locality as occurring in data sets like sorted or moving-cluster since it maintains a set of "hot" groups similarly to an LRU cache. Furthermore HYBRID can be complemented with ATOMIC, which has the best performance of the algorithms known at the time for larger K, as shown by Cieslewicz and Ross [13]. By using sampling during execution, they can choose the best of the two algorithms, which is quite robust but has considerably higher constants than our ADAPTIVE. All other shown competitors have no mechanism to adapt to changing locality.

Maybe even more importantly, the authors of above algorithms do not give mechanisms to adapt to unknown K and rely on a prediction of the optimizer instead. This could be fixed by growing the data structures on demand, but would be highly non-trivial (if at all possible efficiently) for the shared data structure of ATOMIC, which would decrease the performance of their best algorithm for large K. In contrast, our recursive, run-based algorithm handles any K transparently.

7. RELATED WORK

We now give a brief overview about other work on AGGREGATION. The problem has been studied extensively in the disk-based setting. Many of the algorithms presented in the last decades were built with an analysis in mind that is similar to ours, thus often consisting of recursive processing with some optimization for the case of small output. Examples of early work include a merge-sort with early aggregation by Bitton and DeWitt [9] and a hybrid aggregation by DeWitt et al. [16], which does as much hash aggregation as possible during recursive partitioning of the input. Shatdal and Jeffrey [39] propose to use an algorithm similar to INDEPENDENT for small results and an algorithm similar to PARTITIONALWAYS for large results. They either sample to decide on the algorithm beforehand or switch from hashing to partitioning when the first hash table is full. This is similar to our switching criterion, but somewhat more naive and without mechanism to switch back. Helmer et al. [23] maintain a cache with LRU replacement with "hot" groups for early aggregation and partition the rest recursively similarly to PLAT. Finally Graefe [20] designed a sort-based aggregation algorithm through clever scheduling of disk pages such that it behaves like hash-based aggregation for small cardinalities while keeping its advantage of recursive processing for large cardinalities. The algorithm was later implemented by Albutiu et al. [2, 3]. Other techniques can be found in surveys on the topic [19, 21, 44].

As argued throughout the paper, not all of the techniques from the disk-based world can be applied directly in the in-memory setting because computations are relatively more expensive in the latter scenario. However we think that the basic ideas to reduce data movement are still relevant, so it comes to a surprise that none of the in-memory algorithms we found is recursive. As dissected in detail in Section 6, Cieslewicz and Ross [13] and Ye et al. [46] studied many algorithms in the in-memory setting, but all of them with a fixed number of passes and the consequent short-comings. DB2 BLU [37] and HyPer [28] both implement algorithms similar to PLAT, where aggregation is done in private hash tables if possible and additional data is overflown to partitions for later merging, but both of them do not mention recursive processing, so they are most likely limited as well in the number of groups they can process efficiently.

Finally it is interesting to note that the Reduce phase of MapReduce is very similar to aggregation. It is therefore not surprising that Vernica et al. [40] study cache-efficiency and adaptation mechanisms for the MapReduce framework remotely similar to ours.

8. CONCLUSION

In summary, our work starts with the assumption that even in the in-memory setting, the movement of data is the hard part of relational operators such as aggregation. We use an external memory model to show that HASHAGGREGATION and SORTAGGREGATION are equivalent in terms of the number of cache lines transfers they incur. Consequently we design an algorithmic framework based on sorting by hash value that allows to combine hashing for early aggregation and state of the art integer sorting routines depending on the locality of the data. We tune both the hashing and the sorting routine to modern hardware and devise a simple, yet effective criterion of locality to switch between the two. We show extensive experiments on different data sets and a comparison with several algorithms from prior work. Thanks to the combination of optimal high-level design guided by our theoretical analysis and low-level tuning to modern hardware, we are able to outperform all our competitors by up to factor 3.7. We expect work like ours to become of increasing importance in the near future, since memory bandwidth is developing at a lower rate than processing speed of multi-core CPUs. In particular we believe that other cache-efficient sort algorithms can be augmented with early aggregation similar to what we do with bucket sort, so we invite more work on the duality of hashing and sorting.

Acknowledgments

We would like to thank SAP, the SAP HANA development team, and the students from the SAP HANA Campus for the fruitful work environment and helpful discussions and feedback. We would also like to express our gratitude to Cieslewicz and Ross [13] and Ye et al. [46] for providing the code of their work.

9. REFERENCES

[1] A. Aggarwal and J. S. Vitter. The Input/Output Complexity of Sorting and Related Problems. *Commun. ACM*, 31(9):1116–1127, 1988.

[2] M.-c. Albutiu. *Scalable Analytical Query Processing*. PhD thesis, 2013.

[3] M.-C. Albutiu, A. Kemper, and T. Neumann. Massively Parallel Sort-Merge Joins in Main Memory Multi-Core Database Systems. In *PVLDB*, volume 5, pages 1064–1075, 2012.

[4] L. Arge. The Buffer Tree: A New Technique for Optimal I/O-Algorithms. *BRICS*, pages 334–345, 1996.

[5] L. Arge, G. S. l. Brodal, and R. Fagerberg. Cache-Oblivious Data Structures. In *Handbook of Data Structures and Applications*, pages 38/1–38/28. 2005.

[6] L. Arge, M. T. Goodrich, M. Nelson, and N. Sitchinava. Fundamental parallel algorithms for private-cache chip multiprocessors. In *SPAA*, page 197, 2008.

[7] C. Balkesen, G. Alonso, J. Teubner, and M. T. Özsu. Multi-core, main-memory joins: Sort vs. hash revisited. In *PVLDB*, volume 7, pages 85–96, 2013.

[8] R. Barber, G. Lohman, I. Pandis, G. Attaluri, N. Chainani, S. Lightstone, V. Raman, R. Sidle, and D. Sharpe. Memory-Efficient Hash Joins. In *PVLDB*, pages 353–364, 2015.

[9] D. Bitton and D. J. DeWitt. Duplicate record elimination in large data files. *TODS*, 8(2):255–265, 1983.

[10] P. A. Boncz and M. L. Kersten. MIL primitives for querying a fragmented world. *The VLDB Journal*, 8(2):101–119, 1999.

[11] P. A. Boncz, M. Zukowski, and N. Nes. MonetDB/X100: Hyper-Pipelining Query Execution. In *CIDR*, pages 225–237, 2005.

[12] B. Chandramouli and J. Goldstein. Patience is a Virtue: Revisiting Merge and Sort on Modern Processors. In *SIGMOD*, pages 731–742, 2014.

[13] J. Cieslewicz and K. Ross. Adaptive Aggregation on Chip Multiprocessors. In *PVLDB*, pages 339–350, 2007.

[14] T. H. Cormen, C. E. Leiserson, R. L. Rivest, and C. Stein. *Introduction To Algorithms*. MIT Press, 2001.

[15] E. D. Demaine. Cache-Oblivious Algorithms and Data Structures. *BRICS*, page 29, 2002.

[16] D. J. DeWitt, R. H. Katz, et al. Implementation Techniques for Main Memory Database Systems. In *SIGMOD*, pages 1–8, 1984.

[17] C. Freedman, E. Ismert, and P.-A. k. Larson. Compilation in the Microsoft SQL Server Hekaton Engine. *IEEE Data Eng. Bull.*, 37(1):22–30, 2014.

[18] M. Frigo, C. Leiserson, H. Prokop, and S. Ramachandran. Cache-oblivious algorithms. In *FOCS*, pages 285–297, 1999.

[19] G. Graefe. Query evaluation techniques for large databases. *ACM Computing Surveys*, 25(2):73–169, 1993.

[20] G. Graefe. New algorithms for join and grouping operations. *Computer Science – R&D*, 27(1):3–27, 2011.

[21] G. Graefe, R. Bunker, and S. Cooper. Hash Joins and Hash Teams in Microsoft SQL Server. In *PVLDB*, pages 86–97, 1998.

[22] J. Gray, A. Bosworth, A. Lyaman, and H. Pirahesh. Data cube: a relational aggregation operator generalizing GROUP-BY, CROSS-TAB, and SUB-TOTALS. In *ICDE*, pages 152–159, 1996.

[23] S. Helmer, T. Neumann, and G. Moerkotte. Early Grouping Gets the Skew. Technical report, 2011.

[24] Intel Corporation. *Intel® 64 and IA-32 Architectures Optimization Reference Manual*. 2009.

[25] D. Jimenez-Gonzalez, J. Navarro, and J.-L. Larriba-Pey. CC-Radix: a cache conscious sorting based on Radix sort. In *PDP*, pages 101–108. IEEE, 2003.

[26] C. Kim, T. Kaldewey, V. W. Lee, E. Sedlar, et al. Sort vs. Hash Revisited: Fast Join Implementation on Modern Multi-Core CPUs. *PVLDB*, 2(2):1378–1389, 2009.

[27] P.-k. Larson. Grouping and duplicate elimination: Benefits of early aggregation. Technical report, 1997.

[28] V. Leis, P. Boncz, A. Kemper, and T. Neumann. Morsel-driven parallelism. In *SIGMOD*, pages 743–754, 2014.

[29] C. Lemke, K.-U. Sattler, F. Faerber, and A. Zeier. Speeding Up Queries in Column Stores – A Case for Compression. In *DaWaK*, pages 117–129, 2010.

[30] S. Manegold, P. Boncz, and M. Kersten. Optimizing main-memory join on modern hardware. *TKDE*, 14(4):709–730, 2002.

[31] S. Manegold, P. Boncz, N. Nes, and M. Kersten. Cache-conscious radix-decluster projections. In *PVLDB*, volume 30, pages 684–695, 2004.

[32] S. Manegold, P. A. Boncz, and M. L. Kersten. Optimizing database architecture for the new bottleneck: memory access. *The VLDB Journal*, 9(3):231–246, 2000.

[33] Y. Matias, E. Segal, and J. S. Vitter. Efficient Bundle Sorting. *SIAM Journal on Computing*, 36(2):394, 2006.

[34] F. Nagel, G. Bierman, and S. D. Viglas. Code generation for

efficient query processing in managed runtimes. In *PVLDB*, pages 1095–1106, 2014.
[35] T. Neumann. Efficiently compiling efficient query plans for modern hardware. volume 4, pages 539–550, 2011.
[36] O. Polychroniou and K. A. Ross. A comprehensive study of main-memory partitioning and its application to large-scale comparison- and radix-sort. In *SIGMOD*, pages 755–766, 2014.
[37] V. Raman, G. Attaluri, R. Barber, N. Chainani, et al. DB2 with BLU Acceleration: So Much More than Just a Column Store. In *PVLDB*, page 773, 2013.
[38] N. Satish, C. Kim, J. Chhugani, A. D. Nguyen, V. W. Lee, D. Kim, and P. Dubey. Fast sort on CPUs and GPUs. In *SIGMOD*, page 351, 2010.
[39] A. Shatdal and J. F. Naughton. Adaptive Parallel Aggregation Algorithms. In *SIGMOD*, pages 104–114, 1995.
[40] R. Vernica, A. Balmin, K. S. Beyer, and V. Ercegovac. Adaptive MapReduce using situation-aware mappers. In *EDBT*, page 420, 2012.
[41] J. S. Vitter. External memory algorithms and data structures: dealing with massive data. *ACM Computing Surveys*, 33(2):209–271, 2001.
[42] J. Wassenberg and P. Sanders. Engineering a multi-core radix sort. In *Euro-Par*, pages 160–169, 2011.
[43] L. Wegner and J. Teuhola. The External Heapsort. *TSE*, 15(7):917–925, 1989.
[44] J. Wen. *Revisiting aggregation techniques for data intensive applications*. PhD thesis, 2013.
[45] Wikipedia. Integer sorting — Wikipedia, the free encyclopedia, 2015. [Online; accessed 22-January-2015].
[46] Y. Ye, K. A. Ross, and N. Vesdapunt. Scalable Aggregation on Multicore Processors. In *DaMoN*, pages 1–9, 2011.

APPENDIX

A. TUNING OF ALGORITHM CONSTANTS

In this section we show how we empirically determine the constants of the ADAPTIVE algorithm described in Section 5.

A.1 Switching Threshold α_0

The parameter α_0 balances the performance penalty of HASHING compared to PARTITIONING with its benefit of reducing the work of later passes. In order to determine its value for our system, we run both HASHINGONLY and PARTITIONALWAYS on data sets with varying skew using our parameterized data generators from Section 6.5. For every data set, we observe the value of $\alpha = \frac{n_{in}}{n_{out}}$ in the traces of HASHINGONLY. For unclustered distributions like uniform, the transition from $\alpha = \infty$, where all elements fit into the a single hash table, to the other extreme, $\alpha = 1$, where all keys are distinct, is very sharp and only small values of α occur at all. Almost any value of α_0 works in these cases.

However the three distributions moving-cluster, self-similar, and heavy-hitter can be parameterized to a large range of degrees of spatial locality. In Figure 10, we plot the run times of HASHINGONLY and PARTITIONALWAYS on different data sets with these distributions as function of the observed values of α. As expected, for high values of α and any distribution, HASHINGONLY outperforms PARTITIONALWAYS. In these cases the input of the first pass can be reduced by large factors, so it exhibits enough spatial locality for the HASHING routine to be beneficial. For values of α approaching 1, the order of the routines is inverted: it is better to ignore low locality and use PARTITIONING instead. The desired threshold α_0

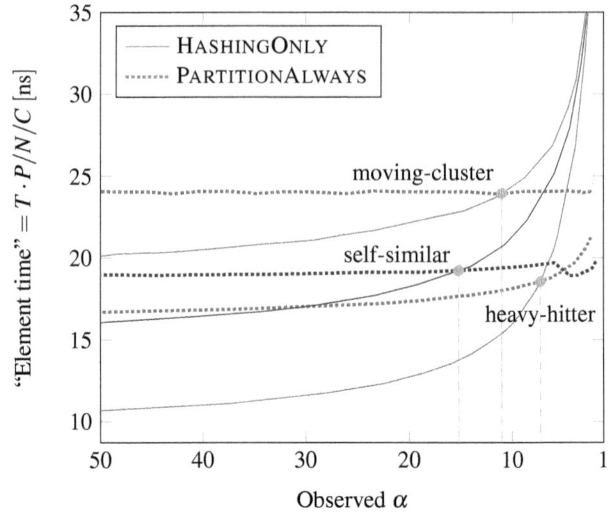

Figure 10: Determining the cross-over of HASHINGONLY and PARTITIONONLY.

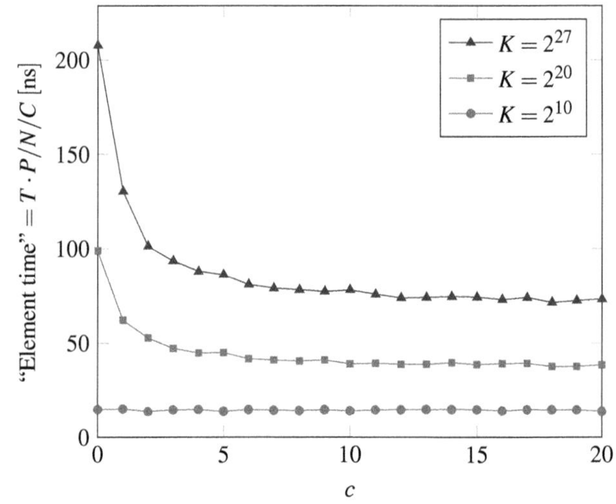

Figure 11: Impact of tuning constant c on the run time of ADAPTIVE.

should separate the first case from the latter. We observe that the respective lines of a particular distribution all intersect in the range of $\alpha \in [7, 16]$ and use the α with the smallest overall error as value for α_0 in our system, which is roughly 11.

A.2 Ratio of HASHING VS PARTITIONING (c)

The constant c in the ADAPTIVE algorithm controls how long the PARTITIONING routine is run before the algorithm switches back to HASHING, which happens after $c \cdot$ cache processed rows. Figure 11 shows the impact of c on the run time of ADAPTIVE for different K and the uniform data set. For $K <$ cache, such as $K = 2^{10}$ in the plot, the algorithm never switches to PARTITIONING in the first place, so c does not have any impact. In the extreme case of $c = 0$, the algorithm degenerates into HASHINGALWAYS, which is quite slow for $K >$ cache (cf. Figure 5). The larger c gets, the more data is processed with the faster PARTITIONING in the non-leaf recursive calls, so the more the performance of ADAPTIVE approaches that of PartitionAlways. This suggests that $c = \infty$ is the best choice, i.e., never to switch back.

However, smaller c have the benefit to be able to adapt to changing distributions, which are likely to occur after `UNION ALL` operators or as an artifact of reordering of rows for compression purposes [29]. This benefit is hard to quantify because it depends on the database system and typical workloads. Because with growing c the benefit diminishes, a smaller c seems affordable anyway: For $c = 5$, the difference to PartitionAlways is 17% for $K = 2^{20}$ (19% for $K = 2^{27}$), while it is 5% (11%) for $c = 10$ and still 4% (5%) for $c = 20$.

In summary c allows to choose a trade-off between robustness to changing distributions and maximum throughput. We choose a rather performance oriented value of $c = 10$ for the experiments of this paper, which are all done on data sets of a single distribution, but suggest a slightly lower value for productive systems.

Efficient Similarity Join and Search on Multi-Attribute Data

Guoliang Li[†] Jian He[†] Dong Deng[†] Jian Li[‡]

[†]Department of Computer Science, Tsinghua University, Beijing, China

[‡]Institute for Interdisciplinary Information Sciences, Tsinghua University, Beijing, China

{liguoliang, lijian83}@tsinghua.edu.cn; {hejian13, dd11}@mails.tsinghua.edu.cn

ABSTRACT

In this paper we study similarity join and search on multi-attribute data. Traditional methods on single-attribute data have pruning power only on single attributes and cannot efficiently support multi-attribute data. To address this problem, we propose a prefix tree index which has holistic pruning ability on multiple attributes. We propose a cost model to quantify the prefix tree which can guide the prefix tree construction. Based on the prefix tree, we devise a filter-verification framework to support similarity search and join on multi-attribute data. The filter step prunes a large number of dissimilar results and identifies some candidates using the prefix tree and the verification step verifies the candidates to generate the final answer. For similarity join, we prove that constructing an optimal prefix tree is NP-complete and develop a greedy algorithm to achieve high performance. For similarity search, since one prefix tree cannot support all possible search queries, we extend the cost model to support similarity search and devise a budget-based algorithm to construct multiple high-quality prefix trees. We also devise a hybrid verification algorithm to improve the verification step. Experimental results show our method significantly outperforms baseline approaches.

Categories and Subject Descriptors

H.2 [Database Management]: Database applications;
H.3.3 [Information Search and Retrieval]: Search process

Keywords

Similarity Search; Similarity Join; Multi-Attribute Data

1. INTRODUCTION

Real-world data is rather dirty due to typographical errors and different representations of the same entity [11]. Traditional exact-matching join and search operations cannot tolerate the dirty data and thus similarity join and search are recently proposed to tolerate the dirty data. Given two multi-attribute tables (e.g., products and movies), similarity join finds all *similar* pairs from the two tables, where the similarity can be quantified by similarity functions, e.g., edit distance and Jaccard. Given a table with multiple attributes and a query, similarity search finds the records from the table that are similar to the query. Similarity join and search are two important operations in data cleaning and integration and have many real-world applications, e.g., duplicate detection, data fusion, and spell checking [11]. For example, in the event of plane crash like Malaysia airlines flight MH17, there are many data sources about passengers on MH17, e.g., tables from Malaysia airlines, departure country, destination county, and passengers' countries. We require to integrate them to generate high-quality data. As another example, a user wants to search movies directed by "`James Cameron`" and acted by "`Arnold Schwarzenegger`" from a movie database with actors, directors, and movie names. However the user does not know the exact spelling of "`Arnold Schwarzenegger`" and inputs a query with typos. Obviously exact-matching search cannot find any results while similarity search can alleviate this problem and help the user to find the relevant answers.

Existing algorithms on string similarity join [20,26,28,29] and search [9,14,15,22,30] have pruning power only on single attributes. For similarity join and search with constraints on multiple attributes, they have to first use a single attribute to identify candidates and then check whether the candidates satisfy the constraints on other attributes. Obviously these algorithms are rather expensive because they have no pruning power on other attributes and generate many intermediate results. It calls for effective methods to support holistic similarity join and search on multi-attribute data.

To address this problem, we propose a prefix tree index which has holistic pruning power on multiple attributes. Based on the prefix tree, we devise a filter-verification framework. The filter step prunes a large number of dissimilar results and identifies some candidates using the prefix tree and the verification step verifies the candidates to generate the final answer. For similarity join, we propose a cost model to quantify the prefix tree. We prove that constructing an optimal prefix tree is NP-complete and we develop a greedy algorithm to achieve high performance. Different from similarity join, one prefix tree cannot support all possible search queries with different similarity functions and thresholds. To address this issue, we extend the cost model to support similarity search. We develop a budge-based algorithm to build high-quality prefix trees to achieve high search performance. Since the similarity join and search queries contain multiple attributes, the verification order on attributes has a significant effect on the verification performance. In addition, many filtering algorithms can be used

SIGMOD'15, May 31–June 4, 2015, Melbourne, Victoria, Australia.

http://dx.doi.org/10.1145/2723372.2723733.

to verify the candidates which also have a great effect on the performance. To this end, we devise a hybrid algorithm to improve the verification performance. To summarize, we make the following contributions. (1) We propose a prefix tree index which has holistic pruning power on multiple attributes and can be utilized to support both similarity join and search queries. (2) For similarity join, we develop a cost model to quantify the prefix tree. We prove that constructing an optimal prefix tree is NP-complete and we develop a greedy algorithm to construct a high-quality prefix tree (see Section 3). (3) For similarity search, we devise a budget-based method to construct multiple high-quality prefix trees to support similarity search queries (see Section 4). (4) We propose a hybrid verification algorithm to improve the verification performance (see Section 5). (5) Experimental results on real-world datasets show our method significantly outperforms baseline approaches (see Section 6).

2. PRELIMINARIES

We first formally define the problem in Section 2.1 and then briefly introduce a well-known technique – prefix filter in Section 2.2. Lastly, we review related works in Section 2.3.

2.1 Problem Definition

Consider two multi-attribute tables $\mathcal{R}$ and $\mathcal{S}$. Table $\mathcal{R}$ has x attributes $\mathcal{R}^1, \mathcal{R}^2, \cdots, \mathcal{R}^x$ and m rows $r_1, r_2, \cdots, r_m$. Table $\mathcal{S}$ has y attributes $\mathcal{S}^1, \mathcal{S}^2, \cdots, \mathcal{S}^y$ and n rows $s_1, s_2, \cdots, s_n$. Let $r_p = [r_p^1, r_p^2, \cdots, r_p^x]$ where r_p^i denotes the value of r_p on attribute $\mathcal{R}^i$, and $s_q = [s_q^1, s_q^2, \cdots, s_q^y]$ where s_q^j denotes the value of s_q on attribute $\mathcal{S}^j$.

An atomic similarity join operation $\mathcal{R}^i \sim \mathcal{S}^j$ returns all similar pairs $\{(r_p \in \mathcal{R}, s_q \in \mathcal{S})\}$ such that $r_p^i \sim s_q^j$, where $\sim$ is a similarity operator which will be defined later.

A complex similarity join operation is composed by more than one atomic similarity join operation, e.g., $\Phi = \mathcal{R}^{i_1} \sim \mathcal{S}^{j_1} \wedge \mathcal{R}^{i_2} \sim \mathcal{S}^{j_2} \wedge \cdots \wedge \mathcal{R}^{i_k} \sim \mathcal{S}^{j_k}$, which finds all similar pairs $\{(r_p{\in}\mathcal{R}, s_q{\in}\mathcal{S})\}$ such that $r_p^{i_1} \sim s_q^{j_1} \wedge r_p^{i_2} \sim s_q^{j_2} \wedge \cdots \wedge r_p^{i_k} \sim s_q^{j_k}$ where $\forall t{\in}[1,k]$, $i_t{\in}[1,x]$ and $j_t{\in}[1,y]$. We call $\Phi_t{=}\mathcal{R}^{i_t}{\sim}\mathcal{S}^{j_t}$ a predicate or attribute if the context is clear.

We utilize similarity measures to define the similarity operator $\sim$, which can be broadly classified into two categories, character-based similarity and token-based similarity.

Character-based Similarity. It defines the similarity between two strings based on character transformations. The well-known character-based similarity is edit distance. Consider two string values r_p^i and s_q^j. The edit distance $\mathsf{ED}(r_p^i, s_q^j)$ is the minimum number of single-character edit operations (including insertion, deletion and substitution) needed to transform r_p^i to s_q^j. The edit similarity extends edit distance by taking into account the string length, which is defined as $\mathsf{ES}(r_p^i, s_q^j) = 1 - \frac{\mathsf{ED}(r_p^i, s_q^j)}{\max(|r_p^i|, |s_q^j|)}$, where $|r_p^i|$ is the length of r_p^i. Two strings r_p^i and s_q^j are similar with respect to edit similarity if their similarity exceeds a given threshold τ, i.e.,

$$r_p^i \overset{\mathsf{ES},\tau}{\sim} s_q^j \text{ iff. } \mathsf{ES}(r_p^i, s_q^j) \geq \tau.$$

For example, given the Name attribute of table $\mathcal{R}$ in Figure 1, r_1^1 = '**Jeffery Ullman**', r_4^1='**Jeffer Ullman**'. We have $\mathsf{ED}(r_1^1, r_4^1) = 1$ and $\mathsf{ES}(r_1^1, r_4^1) = 1 - \frac{1}{14} = \frac{13}{14}$.

Token-based Similarity. It first splits each string into a set of tokens by white spaces and then utilizes the set-based similarity functions to quantify the similarity. The well-known similarity functions include Overlap and Jaccard, defined as below (see Appendix B for more functions).

$\mathcal{R}$: **Customer records of BOA**

Id	Name ($\mathcal{R}^1$)	Address ($\mathcal{R}^2$)	Country ($\mathcal{R}^3$)
r_1	Jeffery Ullman	EE UCLA	USA
r_2	Jennifer Widom	CS Stanford CA	USA
r_3	Jerry Wang	CS Berkeley	ENG
r_4	Jeffer Ullman	CS Stanford CA	USA
r_5	Don Antenio	CS Stanford CA	USA

$\mathcal{S}$: **Customer records of Wells Fargo**

Id	Name ($\mathcal{S}^1$)	Address ($\mathcal{S}^2$)	Country ($\mathcal{S}^3$)
s_1	Jeffery Ullman	Stanford CA	USA
s_2	Herry Wang	Berkeley CA	ENG
s_3	Don Ertenio	CS Berkeley	ENG

Figure 1: Two example tables: $\mathcal{R}$ and $\mathcal{S}$.

- Overlap similarity: $\mathsf{OLP}(r_p^i, s_q^j) = |r_p^i \cap s_q^j|$
- Jaccard similarity: $\mathsf{JAC}(r_p^i, s_q^j) = \frac{|r_p^i \cap s_q^j|}{|r_p^i \cup s_q^j|}$

where $|r_p^i|$ denotes the size of set r_p^i.

r_p^i and s_q^j are similar with respect to the token-based similarity if their similarity exceeds a threshold τ, e.g.,

$$r_p^i \overset{\mathsf{JAC},\tau}{\sim} s_q^j \text{ iff. } \mathsf{JAC}(r_p^i, s_q^j) \geq \tau.$$

For example, given the Address attribute of table $\mathcal{R}$ in Figure 1, r_3^2 ='**CS Berkeley**' and r_4^2 ='**CS Stanford CA**'. $\mathsf{OLP}(r_3^2, r_4^2) = 1$ and $\mathsf{JAC}(r_3^2, r_4^2) = \frac{1}{4}$.

Traditional similarity join and search methods focus on atomic operations, while in this paper we emphasize on complex operations. Next, we formalize the problems of string similarly join and search on multi-attribute data.

DEFINITION 1. (SIMILARITY JOIN ON MULTI-ATTRIBUTE DATA) *Given two multi-attribute tables $\mathcal{R}$ and $\mathcal{S}$ and a complex similarity operation $\Phi = \mathcal{R}^{i_1} \sim \mathcal{S}^{j_1} \wedge \mathcal{R}^{i_2} \sim \mathcal{S}^{j_2} \wedge \cdots \wedge \mathcal{R}^{i_k} \sim \mathcal{S}^{j_k}$, it finds all similar pairs $\{(r_p \in \mathcal{R}, s_q \in \mathcal{S})\}$ such that $r_p^{i_1} \sim s_q^{j_1} \wedge r_p^{i_2} \sim s_q^{j_2} \wedge \cdots \wedge r_p^{i_k} \sim s_q^{j_k}$.*

DEFINITION 2. (SIMILARITY SEARCH ON MULTI-ATTRIBUTE DATA) *Given a multi-attribute table $\mathcal{R}$ and a query $\mathcal{Q} = (\mathcal{R}^{i_1} \sim \mathcal{Q}^{i_1}, \mathcal{R}^{i_2} \sim \mathcal{Q}^{i_2}, \cdots, \mathcal{R}^{i_k} \sim \mathcal{Q}^{i_k})$, where $\mathcal{Q}^{i_t}$ denotes the query value on attribute $\mathcal{R}^{i_t}$ for $t \in [1,k]$, it finds similar strings $r_p \in \mathcal{R}$ such that $r_p^{i_1}{\sim}\mathcal{Q}^{i_1} \wedge r_p^{i_2}{\sim}\mathcal{Q}^{i_2} \wedge \cdots \wedge r_p^{i_k}{\sim}\mathcal{Q}^{i_k}$.*

For example, given two multi-attribute tables $\mathcal{R}$ and $\mathcal{S}$ in Figure 1 and a complex operation $\mathcal{R}^1 \overset{\mathsf{ES},0.8}{\sim} \mathcal{S}^1 \wedge \mathcal{R}^2 \overset{\mathsf{JAC},0.5}{\sim} \mathcal{S}^2$. The first predicate is $\mathsf{ES}(r_p^1, s_q^1) \geq 0.8$ and the second is $\mathsf{JAC}(r_p^2, s_q^2) \geq 0.5$. Similarity join on multi-attribute data returns $\{(r_4, s_1)\}$ as $\mathsf{ES}(r_4^1, s_1^1) = 0.93 \geq 0.8$ and $\mathsf{JAC}(r_4^2, s_1^2) = 0.67 \geq 0.5$. Although $r_1^1 = s_1^1$, (r_1, s_1) is not a similar pair, as their **Address** values are not similar ($\mathsf{JAC}(r_1^2, s_1^2){=}0{\leq}0.5$).

Given a multi-attribute table $\mathcal{R}$ in Figure 1 and a query $\mathcal{Q} = (\mathcal{R}^1 \overset{\mathsf{ES},0.8}{\sim}$ '**Jenifer Widom**', $\mathcal{R}^2 \overset{\mathsf{OLP},2}{\sim}$ '**CS Stanford**'). The first predicate is $\mathsf{ES}(r_p^1, \mathcal{Q}^1) \geq 0.8$ and the second is $\mathsf{OLP}(r_p^2, \mathcal{Q}^2) \geq 2$. Similarity search on multi-attribute data returns $\{r_2\}$ as $\mathsf{ES}(r_2^1, \mathcal{Q}^1){=}0.93{\geq}0.8$ and $\mathsf{OLP}(r_2^2, \mathcal{Q}^2){=}2{\geq}2$.

2.2 Prefix Filter

We briefly introduce the prefix filter [1,2]. It first transforms each string to a set. For edit distance, the set contains all q-grams of the string where a q-gram is a substring with length q. For token-based similarity, the set contains all tokens in the string. Then it converts character-based and token-based similarities to the overlap similarity: if string s is similar to string r, the overlap of their corresponding sets must exceed o, where o can be deduced as below.

- If $\mathsf{OLP}(r, s) \geq \tau$ then $o = \tau$.

Name

e^1_1	e^1_2	e^1_3	e^1_4	e^1_5	e^1_6	...
an	do	ef	en	er	fe	...

Country

e^3_1	e^3_2
ENG	USA

Address

e^2_1	e^2_2	e^2_3	e^2_4	e^2_5	e^2_6
Berkeley	CA	CS	EE	Stanford	UCLA

Prefix Table for $\mathcal{R}$ and $\mathcal{S}$

	Name	Address	Country
r_1	$\{e^1_1, e^1_3, e^1_5\}$	$\{e^2_4, e^2_6\}$	$\{e^3_2\}$
r_2	$\{e^1_2, e^1_4, e^1_5\}$	$\{e^2_2, e^2_3, e^2_5\}$	$\{e^3_2\}$
r_3	$\{e^1_1, e^1_5, e^1_{11}\}$	$\{e^2_1, e^2_3\}$	$\{e^3_1\}$
r_4	$\{e^1_1, e^1_3, e^1_5\}$	$\{e^2_2, e^2_3, e^2_5\}$	$\{e^3_2\}$
r_5	$\{e^1_1, e^1_2, e^1_4\}$	$\{e^2_2, e^2_3, e^2_5\}$	$\{e^3_2\}$
s_1	$\{e^1_1, e^1_3, e^1_5\}$	$\{e^2_5, e^2_2\}$	$\{e^3_2\}$
s_2	$\{e^1_1, e^1_5, e^1_{10}\}$	$\{e^2_1, e^2_2\}$	$\{e^3_1\}$
s_3	$\{e^1_2, e^1_4, e^1_5\}$	$\{e^2_1, e^2_3\}$	$\{e^3_1\}$

Figure 2: Prefix Tokens for $\mathcal{R}$ and $\mathcal{S}$ in Figure 1 (Use Dictionary Order).

- If $\mathsf{JAC}(r,s) \geq \tau$ then $o = \lceil \tau |r| \rceil$.
- If $\mathsf{ED}(r,s) \leq \tau$ then $o = |r| - q\tau$.
- If $\mathsf{ES}(r,s) \geq \tau$, then $o = \lceil |r| - (|r| + q - 1)\frac{(1-\tau)}{\tau}|r|) \rceil$.

where $|r|$ is the size of r(for ED/ES, r is the q-gram set).

For simplicity, we use string and set interchangeably if the context is clear and each element in the set is called a token. The prefix filter fixes a global order for the tokens and sorts tokens of each set by this global order. Finally for each set r, it selects the first $|r| - o + 1$ tokens as its prefix, denoted as $\mathtt{pre}(r)$. It is easy to prove that if two strings r and s are similar, $\mathtt{pre}(r) \cap \mathtt{pre}(s) \neq \phi$ [29].

For example, given two multi-attribute tables $\mathcal{R}$ and $\mathcal{S}$ in Figure 1 and a complex similarity operation $\mathcal{R}^1 \overset{\mathsf{ED},1}{\sim} \mathcal{S}^1 \wedge \mathcal{R}^2 \overset{\mathsf{JAC},0.3}{\sim} \mathcal{S}^2 \wedge \mathcal{R}^3 \overset{\mathsf{OLP},1}{\sim} \mathcal{S}^3$. For attributes $\mathcal{R}^1$ and $\mathcal{S}^1$, we generate 2-gram set. For simplicity, we use the dictionary order as a global order. For each attribute of each record, we compute its prefix and generate a table of prefixes as shown in Figure 2. We use $\mathcal{R}^2 \overset{\mathsf{JAC},0.3}{\sim} \mathcal{S}^2$ to demonstrate how to compute the prefix. The prefix length for $\mathsf{JAC}(r^2_p, s^2_q) \geq 0.3$ is $|\mathtt{pre}(r^2_p)| = |r^2_p| - \lceil |r^2_p|\tau \rceil + 1$. So for r_2, $|\mathtt{pre}(r^2_1)| = 2$ and $\mathtt{pre}(r^2_1) = \{\mathtt{EE}, \mathtt{UCLA}\} = \{\mathtt{e}^2_4, \mathtt{e}^2_6\}$.

2.3 Related Works

Similarity Join on Single Attribute. Since the prefix filter is effective, many methods are proposed to optimize it for different similarity operators [6,16,20,24,26,28,29]. ED-join [12,28] proposed a location-based mismatch filter to reduce prefix length and a content-based mismatch filter to reduce the number of candidates for ED. Pivotal prefix filter [4] reduced the prefix length for ED. PassJoin [17] proposed segment filter to improve pruning power. PPJoin [29] used the positions of prefix and suffix to improve pruning power for token-based similarities. Length filter was proposed to prune dissimilar answers based on length difference [8]. TrieJoin [23] used a different framework that directly computed real similarity using the trie structure.

Similarity Search on Single Attribute. Li et al. [14] proposed a list-merge framework that converts other similarities to overlap, builds inverted index, and merges inverted lists of the query tokens to identify answers. Li et al. [15] proposed variable length q-grams (VGram) to improve the pruning power. Zhang et al. [30] proposed B^{ed}-tree which uses q-grams as signatures and indexes the q-grams using the B-tree. Deng et al. [5] addressed the top-k similarity search problem with the trie structure. Hadjieleftheriou et

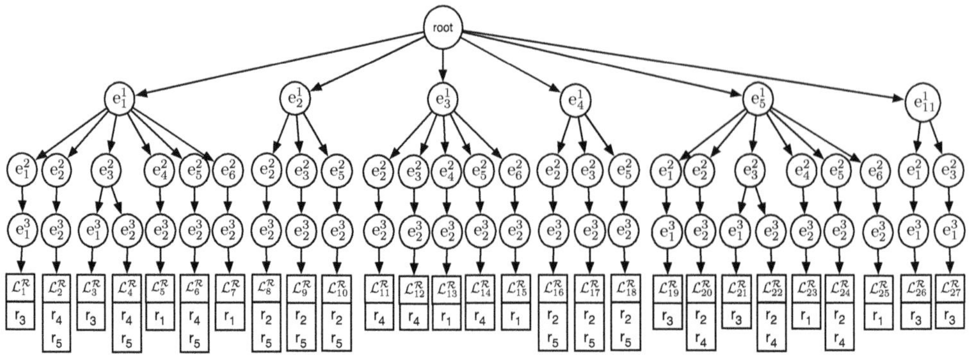

Figure 3: Complete Prefix Tree for $\mathcal{R}$ in Figure 2.

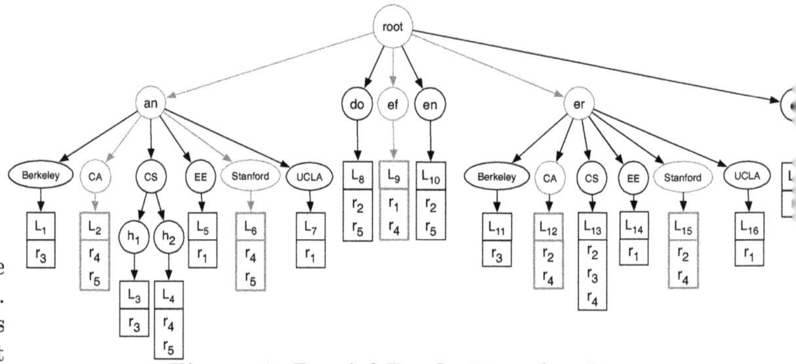

Figure 4: Partial Prefix Tree for $\mathcal{R}$.

al. [9] devised a technique to support data updates in similarity search. Wang et al. [25] proposed a dynamic prefix length scheme for effective filtering in similarity search.

Blocking-based Join Algorithm. There are many blocking-based join algorithms on entity resolution [11,13,19,27]. To link the records, they defined some rules (e.g., the same zip code leads to the same entity), utilized the rules to generate blocks (e.g., records with the same zip code will be in the same block), and took records in the same block as candidates. Different from the blocking-based algorithms [3,18] that focused on learning blocking schemes to improve the recall, our paper emphasizes on devising effective indexes and efficient algorithms to improve the performance for given fuzzy-matching rules. Sarma et al. [21] proposed a blocking-tree structure and devised a bottom-up algorithm to improve the recall. Our method on similarity joins has the following differences. First, the objectives are different. They merged blocks by enumerating every pair of leaf nodes to improve the recall while we merged leaf nodes with the same parent to reduce the candidate sizes to improve the efficiency. The high enumeration overhead is not acceptable in our problem. Second, the strategies of building tree structures are different. The inverted lists on our tree have overlaps while their blocks are disjoint. Third, the bottom-up algorithm is still expensive for our problem, because it checks many tree nodes to determine whether to combine. To further improve the performance, we devise a greedy top-down algorithm.

3. SIMILARITY JOIN WITH PREFIX TREE

Given a complex similarity operation $\Phi = \mathcal{R}^{i_1} \sim \mathcal{S}^{j_1} \wedge \mathcal{R}^{i_2} \sim \mathcal{S}^{j_2} \wedge \cdots \wedge \mathcal{R}^{i_k} \sim \mathcal{S}^{j_k}$, we devise a filter-verification framework to answer the join query. The filter step identifies the candidate pairs $\langle r, s \rangle$ such that $\mathtt{pre}(r^{i_t}) \cap \mathtt{pre}(s^{j_t}) \neq \phi$ for every $t \in [1,k]$ and the verification step verifies the candidate paris by computing the real similarity on each attribute $\mathcal{R}^{i_t}$ and $\mathcal{S}^{j_t}$. We study the filter step in this section and the verification algorithm will be discussed in Section 5.

Algorithm 1: PREFIXTREE-JOIN ($\mathcal{R}$, $\mathcal{S}$, Φ)

Input: $\mathcal{R}$, $\mathcal{S}$: Two multi-attribute tables
Φ: A complex similarity operation
Output: $\mathcal{A}$: Answer

```
1 Build one prefix tree with two tables R and S;
2 for each leaf node do
3   if there are two inverted lists L^R and L^S then
4     for each (r, s) ∈ L^R × L^S do
5       VERIFY(r, s);
6       if r is similar to s then
7         Add ⟨r, s⟩ to A;
```

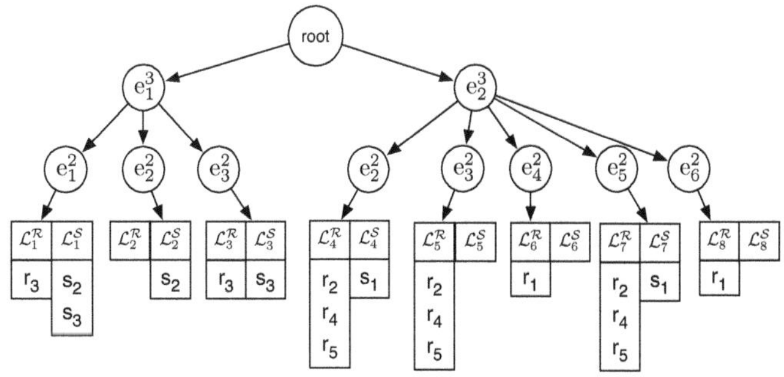

Figure 5: Prefix Tree for Tables $\mathcal{R}$ and $\mathcal{S}$ in Figure 2 ($\mathcal{L}^\mathcal{R}(\mathcal{L}^\mathcal{S})$: inverted list for $\mathcal{R}$ ($\mathcal{S}$)).

3.1 Prefix Tree

To efficiently identify the candidates, we build a *complete prefix tree*. Given a similarity operation Φ, we first sort the predicates in Φ. Suppose the sorted predicates are $\mathcal{R}^{i_1} \sim \mathcal{S}^{j_1} \wedge \mathcal{R}^{i_2} \sim \mathcal{S}^{j_2} \wedge \cdots \wedge \mathcal{R}^{i_k} \sim \mathcal{S}^{j_k}$ (the details on sorting the attributes will be discussed in Section 3.2.3). For simplicity, we first discuss how to construct a complete prefix tree for $\mathcal{R}$ with the attribute order $\mathcal{R}^{i_1}, \mathcal{R}^{i_2}, \cdots, \mathcal{R}^{i_k}$ as follows. For each record $r \in \mathcal{R}$, each prefix token combination $\langle e^1, e^2, \cdots, e^k\rangle$ where $e^t \in \texttt{pre}(r^{i_t})$ corresponds to a path from the root to a leaf node, and each token e^t corresponds to a tree node. At the leaf node, we keep an inverted list of records that contain this token combination. For example, Figure 3 shows the complete prefix tree for $\mathcal{R}$ in Figure 2.

Next we discuss how to utilize the complete prefix tree to support similarity joins. We extend the complete prefix tree to support two tables, where two inverted lists on each leaf node l are maintained, $\mathcal{L}_l^\mathcal{R}$ for $\mathcal{R}$ and $\mathcal{L}_l^\mathcal{S}$ for $\mathcal{S}$. For each record $r \in \mathcal{R}$, we append it to the inverted list $\mathcal{L}^\mathcal{R}$ of the corresponding leaf node, and for each record $s \in \mathcal{S}$, we append it to inverted list $\mathcal{L}^\mathcal{S}$. Obviously, for each leaf node l, the pair $(r, s) \in \mathcal{L}_l^\mathcal{R} \times \mathcal{L}_l^\mathcal{S}$ must be a candidate because r and s share a prefix token on every predicate. On the other hand, if (r, s) is a candidate, they must appear on the inverted lists of the same leaf node, because the complete prefix tree contains all prefix token combinations.

Algorithm 1 shows the pseudo-code. PREFIXTREE-JOIN first constructs one prefix tree for tables $\mathcal{R}$ and $\mathcal{S}$, and a given predicate order of the complex similarity operation Φ (line 1). On each leaf node, it maintains two inverted lists: $\mathcal{L}^\mathcal{R}$ for $\mathcal{R}$ and $\mathcal{L}^\mathcal{S}$ for $\mathcal{S}$. Then it identifies all leaf nodes, and for each leaf node, if there are two inverted lists (line 3), it enumerates the candidate pairs in these two lists (line 4). Next it verifies them (line 5), and if they are actually similar, it adds this pair to the result set (line 7).

For example, given two tables $\mathcal{R}$ and $\mathcal{S}$ with a complex similarity operation $\mathcal{R}^3 \overset{\mathsf{OLP},1}{\sim} \mathcal{S}^3 \wedge \mathcal{R}^2 \overset{\mathsf{JAC},0.3}{\sim} \mathcal{S}^2$. We first construct a complete prefix tree as shown in Figure 5. Then we enumerate all leaf nodes to generate candidate pairs. Take the leaf node e_1^2 as an example. We add the pairs from its two inverted lists $\mathcal{L}_1^\mathcal{R} \times \mathcal{L}_1^\mathcal{S}$, i.e., $\{(r_3, s_2), (r_3, s_3)\}$, to the candidate set. Finally, there are 9 candidate pairs. If we use the brute-force enumeration, there are $3 \cdot 5 = 15$ candidate pairs. After verification, the results are $\{(r_4, s_1), (r_3, s_2)\}$.

However the complete prefix tree has a rather large index size (see space complexity in Appendix D), because it requires to enumerate every token combination for each record, especially for records with long prefixes. To address this issue, we propose a *partial prefix tree* which is a shrunk complete prefix tree. Different from complete prefix tree, we do not maintain every path. Instead, we select some subtrees and for each subtree, we shrink it as a leaf node, and merge the inverted lists of its leaf descendants as the inverted list of the new leaf node.

For example, Figure 4 shows a partial prefix tree for $\mathcal{R}$ in Figure 2. Compared to the complete prefix tree in Figure 3, the partial prefix tree shrinks the subtrees rooted at $\{e_2^1, e_3^1, e_4^1, e_{11}^1\}$ and removes many unnecessary branches. Obviously the partial prefix tree is much smaller than the complete prefix tree since the partial prefix tree does not maintain every token combination. However there may be many possible partial prefix trees and next we discuss how to construct an optimal partial tree.

3.2 Optimal Prefix Tree

For simplicity, we use prefix tree and partial prefix interchangeably if the context is clear. To construct an optimal prefix tree, we first define a cost model to evaluate a prefix tree in Section 3.2.1. Then we discuss how to construct an optimal prefix tree with a specific predicate order in Section 3.2.2. Next, we prove that the problem of selecting the optimal predicate order is NP complete and propose a greedy algorithm in Section 3.2.3.

3.2.1 Join Cost Model with Prefix Tree

Since the join algorithm enumerates all pairs in the two inverted lists, our goal is to minimize the Cartesian product of the inverted lists. Next we define the cost model.

DEFINITION 3 (PREFIX TREE JOIN COST). *Given a prefix tree $\mathcal{T}$ built with two tables $\mathcal{R}$ and $\mathcal{S}$, the join cost is*

$$\Theta(\mathcal{T}) = \sum_{l \in \mathrm{LEAF}(\mathcal{T})} |\mathcal{L}_l^\mathcal{R}||\mathcal{L}_l^\mathcal{S}|cost_v \quad (1)$$

where $\mathrm{LEAF}(\mathcal{T})$ is the leaf node set of the prefix tree, $\mathcal{L}_l^\mathcal{R}$ and $\mathcal{L}_l^\mathcal{S}$ are respectively the inverted lists of $\mathcal{R}$ and $\mathcal{S}$ on the leaf node l and $cost_v$ is the average cost of verifying a candidate.

For example, consider the prefix tree built with tables $\mathcal{R}$ and $\mathcal{S}$ in Figure 5. The join cost of prefix tree $\Theta(\mathcal{T}) = \sum_{i=1}^{8} |\mathcal{L}_i^\mathcal{R}||\mathcal{L}_i^\mathcal{S}|cost_v = 9 * cost_v$. [1]
Then we define the optimal prefix tree.

DEFINITION 4. (OPTIMAL PREFIX TREE WITH A PREDICATE ORDER) *Given a similarity operation with a predicate order and two tables $\mathcal{R}$ and $\mathcal{S}$, a partial prefix tree is an optimal prefix tree with the predicate order if it has the minimum join cost among all prefix trees with this predicate order.*

For example, Figure 6 shows an optimal prefix tree of the complete prefix tree in Figure 5.

[1]Our cost model does not consider the duplicate candidate pairs in different leaf nodes. For example, (r_4, s_1) will be counted 2 times under different leaves in Figure 5. In practice, we only verify a candidate pair once by utilizing a hash table to avoid the duplicate verification.

Algorithm 2: OPTIMAL-BOTTOMUP ($\mathcal{R}$, $\mathcal{S}$, Φ, π)

Input: $\mathcal{R}$, $\mathcal{S}$: Two multi-attribute data tables
Φ: A sorted complex similarity operation
Output: $\mathcal{T}$: Optimal prefix tree

1 Construct a complete prefix tree $\mathcal{T}$ with $\mathcal{R}$,$\mathcal{S}$ and Φ;
2 **for** *each node* $v \in \mathcal{T}$ *from bottom to top* **do**
3   **if** v *is a leaf* **then** $\Theta(v) = |\mathcal{L}_v^{\mathcal{R}}||\mathcal{L}_v^{\mathcal{S}}|$ **else**
4     $\mathcal{L}_v^{\mathcal{R}} = \cup_{c \in \text{CHILD}(v)} \mathcal{L}_c^{\mathcal{R}}$;
5     $\mathcal{L}_v^{\mathcal{S}} = \cup_{c \in \text{CHILD}(v)} \mathcal{L}_c^{\mathcal{S}}$;
6   **if** $\sum_{c \in \text{CHILD}(v)} \Theta(c) < |\mathcal{L}_v^{\mathcal{R}}||\mathcal{L}_v^{\mathcal{S}}|$ **then**
7       $\Theta(v) = \sum_{c \in \text{CHILD}(v)} \Theta(c)$;
8   **else**
9       $\Theta(v) = |\mathcal{L}_v^{\mathcal{R}}||\mathcal{L}_v^{\mathcal{S}}|$;
10   Mark v as leaf and remove its children;
11 **return** $\mathcal{T}$;

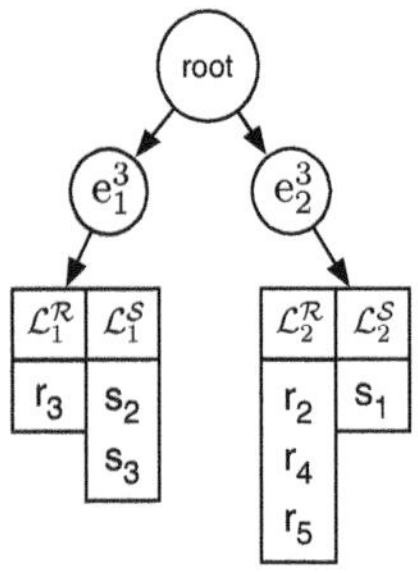

Figure 6: Optimal Prefix Tree for Tables $\mathcal{R}$ and $\mathcal{S}$.

3.2.2 Optimal Prefix Tree with A Predicate Order

Given a complex similarity operation with a specified order of predicates, we show how to construct an optimal prefix tree with the minimum join cost. The basic idea is that we first build a complete prefix tree and then determine if we combine some paths in the complete prefix tree in a bottom-up manner based on the join cost model. We devise a two-step algorithm to construct the optimal prefix tree as shown in Algorithm 2. In the first step, it constructs a complete prefix tree given a specific predicate order (line 1). In the second step, it revisits nodes from bottom to top to prune subtrees (line 3). When checking each node, it compares the cost of the subtree ($|\mathcal{L}_v^{\mathcal{R}}||\mathcal{L}_v^{\mathcal{S}}|$) and the cost of merging its children ($\sum_{c \in \text{CHILD}(v)} \Theta(c))^2$. If the latter is smaller, we keep its children (line 7); otherwise we merge its children(lines 9-10). As it visits nodes in a bottom-up manner, it guarantees the subtree rooted at each node is optimal.

For example, given two tables $\mathcal{R}$ and $\mathcal{S}$ in Figure 1, and a complex similarity operation with an order $\mathcal{R}^3 \overset{\text{OLP},1}{\sim} \mathcal{S}^3 \wedge \mathcal{R}^2 \overset{\text{JAC},0.3}{\sim} \mathcal{S}^2$. We first construct the complete tree as shown in Figure 5. Then we enumerate all the nodes from bottom to top to prune branches. Taking node e_1^3 as an example, the cost of its subtree is $|\mathcal{L}_1^{\mathcal{R}}||\mathcal{L}_1^{\mathcal{S}}|+|\mathcal{L}_2^{\mathcal{R}}||\mathcal{L}_2^{\mathcal{S}}|+|\mathcal{L}_3^{\mathcal{R}}||\mathcal{L}_3^{\mathcal{S}}| = 3$, which is larger than the merging cost $|\mathcal{L}_1^{\mathcal{R}} \cup \mathcal{L}_2^{\mathcal{R}} \cup \mathcal{L}_3^{\mathcal{R}}||\mathcal{L}_1^{\mathcal{S}} \cup \mathcal{L}_2^{\mathcal{S}} \cup \mathcal{L}_3^{\mathcal{S}}| = 2$. Thus we remove the children of e_1^3 and mark e_1^3 as a leaf node. Similarly, we prune the subtree of node e_2^3 and all nodes with an empty list and construct an optimal prefix tree as shown in Figure 6. The join cost with the optimal prefix tree is 5 while that of the complete tree is 9.

The OPTIMAL-BOTTOMUP algorithm can find the optimal tree correctly as shown in Lemma 1.

LEMMA 1. *The partial tree built by* OPTIMAL-BOTTOMUP *is an optimal prefix tree with the given predicate order.*

[2]For ease of presentation we omit the same coefficient $cost_v$

Algorithm 3: GREEDY-TOPDOWN ($\mathcal{R}$, $\mathcal{S}$, Φ)

Input: $\mathcal{R}$, $\mathcal{S}$: Two multi-attribute tables
Φ: A sorted complex similarity operation
Output: $\mathcal{T}$: A prefix tree

1 Initialize $\mathcal{F}$ with (root, Φ_1); /* Φ_1: the 1st operation*/
2 **for** *each* $(v, \Phi_i) \in \mathcal{F}$ **do**
3   Split v to generate children CHILD(v) with Φ_{i+1};
4   **if** $\sum_{c \in \text{CHILD}(v)} |\mathcal{L}_c^{\mathcal{R}}||\mathcal{L}_c^{\mathcal{S}}| < |\mathcal{L}_v^{\mathcal{R}}||\mathcal{L}_v^{\mathcal{S}}|$ **then**
5   Add all (c, Φ_{i+1}) to $\mathcal{F}$ for each $c \in$ CHILD(v);
6   **else**
7   Mark v as a leaf;
8 **return** $\mathcal{T}$;

Though Algorithm 2 can build the optimal prefix tree with a specified ordered complex similarity operation, its construction cost is expensive (see the complexity in Appendix D). To address this issue we propose a greedy algorithm to construct a partial prefix tree. Different from the optimal solution which directly builds the complete prefix tree, we construct a prefix tree in a top-down manner. For each node, we compare the cost of splitting the subtree rooted at it and that of not splitting the subtree. If the former is better, we split the node; otherwise we take it as a leaf node. The pseudo-code is shown in Algorithm 3. Given a complex operation Φ, it first initializes a queue $\mathcal{F}$ with the root and the first similarity predicate Φ_1 (line 1). Then for each record in the queue $\mathcal{F}$, it splits the node and generates its children (line 3). If $\sum_{c \in \text{CHILD}(v)} |\mathcal{L}_c^{\mathcal{R}}||\mathcal{L}_c^{\mathcal{S}}| < |\mathcal{L}_v^{\mathcal{R}}||\mathcal{L}_v^{\mathcal{S}}|$, it splits the node and adds its children into $\mathcal{F}$ (line 5); otherwise, it takes this node as a leaf node (line 7).

For example, consider the prefix tree in Figure 5. Given node e_3^1, the cost of splitting node e_3^1 is $|\mathcal{L}_1^{\mathcal{R}}||\mathcal{L}_1^{\mathcal{S}}|+|\mathcal{L}_2^{\mathcal{R}}||\mathcal{L}_2^{\mathcal{S}}| = 3$, and the cost of not splitting node e_3^1 is $|\mathcal{L}_1^{\mathcal{R}} \cup \mathcal{L}_2^{\mathcal{R}}||\mathcal{L}_1^{\mathcal{S}} \cup \mathcal{L}_2^{\mathcal{S}}| = 2$. Thus we do not split e_3^1.

3.2.3 Optimal Prefix Tree without A Predicate Order

Given a similarity operation with $|\Phi|$ atomic predicates, there are $|\Phi|!$ predicate order, and for each order, there is an optimal prefix tree. We would like to find the optimal prefix tree among these prefix trees.

DEFINITION 5. (OPTIMAL PREFIX TREE) *Given a similarity operation and two tables $\mathcal{R}$ and $\mathcal{S}$, a partial prefix tree is an optimal prefix tree if it has the minimum join cost among all partial prefix trees.*

However, the problem of finding the optimal prefix tree is NP-Hard as formalized in Lemma 2.

LEMMA 2. *Given two tables $\mathcal{R}$ and $\mathcal{S}$, a complex similarity operation Φ, finding the optimal prefix tree is NP-Hard.*

Since find the optimal prefix tree is NP-Hard, we propose an approximation algorithm. We first evaluate the cost of each predicate on the whole table as follows

$$\text{COST}(\Phi_i) = \sum_{c \in \text{CHILD}(root)} |\mathcal{L}_c^{\mathcal{R}}||\mathcal{L}_c^{\mathcal{S}}| \quad (2)$$

where Φ_i is the ith operation of Φ. Then it sorts the predicates by COST(Φ_i) and constructs a prefix tree based on the sorted order. For example, given tables in Figure 1 and a complex operation $\mathcal{R}^1 \overset{\text{ED},1}{\sim} \mathcal{S}^1 \wedge \mathcal{R}^2 \overset{\text{JAC},0.3}{\sim} \mathcal{S}^2 \wedge \mathcal{R}^3 \overset{\text{OLP},1}{\sim} \mathcal{S}^3$. We first evaluate the cost of each predicate. The size of the inverted list built with Φ_3 is $|\mathcal{L}_1^{\mathcal{R}}| = 1, |\mathcal{L}_1^{\mathcal{S}}| = 2, |\mathcal{L}_2^{\mathcal{R}}| = 4, |\mathcal{L}_2^{\mathcal{S}}| = 1$. $\text{COST}(\Phi_3) = \sum_{c=1}^{2} |\mathcal{L}_c^{\mathcal{R}}||\mathcal{L}_c^{\mathcal{S}}| = 6$. Similarly, we compute $\text{COST}(\Phi_2) = 15$ and $\text{COST}(\Phi_1) = 26$. As $\text{COST}(\Phi_3) < \text{COST}(\Phi_2) < \text{COST}(\Phi_1)$, the predicate order is $\langle \Phi_3, \Phi_2, \Phi_1 \rangle$.

4. SIMILARITY SEARCH WITH PREFIX TREE

We extend the prefix tree to support similarity search on multi-attribute data. We first give an overview in Section 4.1. Then we discuss how to utilize the prefix tree to answer a search query in Section 4.2. Finally we propose to build the prefix trees for similarity search in Section 4.3.

4.1 Overview

For a similarity join query, the cost of constructing a prefix tree is less than the join cost. However for a similarity search query, the construction cost is much more expensive than the cost of answering a search query. Thus for a similarity search query, we want to construct the prefix tree offline so as to utilize it to answer online search queries. To utilize prefix trees to support similarity search queries, we need to answer the following questions.

First, different search queries have various similarity functions and thresholds. For example, given the table in Figure 1, a user is familiar with the address but is not sure how to spell the name, and issues a query (NAME $\overset{\text{ES},0.6}{\sim}$ '**Jenifer Ullman**', ADDRESS $\overset{\text{JAC},0.8}{\sim}$ '**CS Stanford**'). Another user knows the name but is not familiar with the address, and issues a query (NAME $\overset{\text{ES},0.9}{\sim}$ '**Jeffery Ullman**', ADDRESS $\overset{\text{JAC},0.7}{\sim}$ '**EE Stanford**'). Obviously the two queries involve different functions and thresholds. Since the prefixes depend on the similarity functions and thresholds, can we still use prefix trees to support similarity search? The answer is yes. A common technique is to set a smallest possible similarity threshold that a system can tolerate, e.g., 0.6, and we utilize this threshold to construct prefix trees. An alternative is to build delta prefix trees. That is we build a prefix tree for each threshold range, e.g., $[1, 0.9], (0.9, 0.8], (0.8, 0.7], (0.7, 0.6]$. Given a query threshold 0.8, we use the first two prefix trees to answer the query. For simplicity, we take the first method as an example. To support various functions, we transform them to the overlap similarity and use the smallest threshold o to generate the prefix (see Section 2.2).

Second, since there are many search queries and different queries involve different attribute combinations, a single prefix tree cannot efficiently answer all search queries and we have to construct multiple prefix trees to answer search queries. There are two issues we need to address. The first is how to construct multiple high-quality prefix trees to answer search queries? Since search queries are not given and different queries have different similarity functions and thresholds, the cost model for similarity joins cannot support search queries. To address this issue, we propose a new model to support similarity search in Section 4.3. The second is that given multiple prefix trees, how to efficiently utilize them to answer a search query? We propose efficient algorithms to address this issue in Section 4.2.

Based on these questions, we devise a framework to support similarity search queries on multi-attribute data. First we construct multiple prefix trees offline (see Section 4.3). Then given an online query, we devise efficient algorithms to answer the query using these prefix trees (see Section 4.2).

4.2 Prefix-Tree-Based Search Algorithms

Using A Single Prefix Tree $\mathcal{T}$ to Answer A Query $\mathcal{Q}$. If the first-level attribute of $\mathcal{T}$ appears in $\mathcal{Q}$, we can use $\mathcal{T}$ to answer $\mathcal{Q}$. The basic idea is to find the leaf nodes of $\mathcal{T}$ such that the tokens on the path from the root to

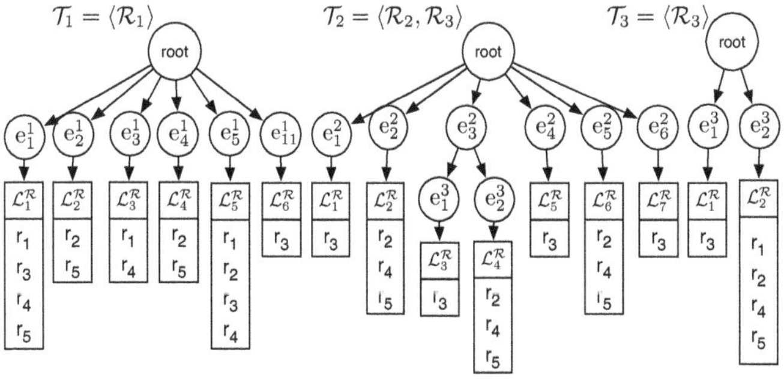

Figure 7: Mutiple Prefix Trees for Table $\mathcal{R}$.

each leaf also appear in the prefix tokens of $\mathcal{Q}$. The records on the inverted lists of leaf nodes are candidates. To this end, we first find the longest sequence of attributes from $\mathcal{T}$, i.e., $\mathcal{R}^{i_1}, \mathcal{R}^{i_2}, \cdots, \mathcal{R}^{i_t}$, where each attribute also appears in the query attributes. Then from the root, we identify its children with labels of prefix tokens in $\mathcal{Q}^{i_1}$. For each identified child, if it is a leaf, the records on inverted lists are candidates; otherwise we identify its children with labels of prefix tokens in $\mathcal{Q}^{i_2}$. Iteratively, we can find all leaf nodes.

Algorithm 4 shows the pseudo-code for using a prefix tree to answer $\mathcal{Q}$. Given a query $\mathcal{Q}$, SINGLEPREFIXTREESEARCH first recursively searches the prefix tree to get a set of leaves where each token on the path is also a prefix token of $\mathcal{Q}$ (line 1-9): it first identifies the longest sequence (line 1) and adds the root to the candidate node list (line 2); Then for each node, it checks whether its child contains a prefix token in $\mathcal{Q}$; If yes, this child will be added into the node list (line 4); Iteratively it finds all leaf nodes (line 9). Next it retrieves the inverted list of each identified leaf (line 11) and verifies each candidate based on the other similarity predicates (line 13). If a record is similar to the query, it is added into the result set (line 14).

For example, consider a prefix tree of $\mathcal{R}$ in Figure 4 and taking $s_1 \in \mathcal{S}$ as a search query $\mathcal{Q}$ with $\texttt{pre}(\mathcal{Q}^1) = \{e^1_1, e^1_3, e^1_5\}$, $\texttt{pre}(\mathcal{Q}^2) = \{e^2_2, e^2_5\}$, $\texttt{pre}(\mathcal{Q}^3) = \{e^3_2\}$. From the root, we find its children $\{e^1_1, e^1_3, e^1_5\}$ which contain a prefix token in $\texttt{pre}(\mathcal{Q}^1)$. e^1_3 is a leaf node and we get an inverted list $\mathcal{L}^{\mathcal{R}}_9$. Then we check whether e^1_1 and e^1_5 have children with labels e^2_5, e^2_2, and we find 4 leaf nodes whose inverted lists are $\{\mathcal{L}^{\mathcal{R}}_2, \mathcal{L}^{\mathcal{R}}_6, \mathcal{L}^{\mathcal{R}}_{11}, \mathcal{L}^{\mathcal{R}}_{15}\}$ (surrounded by red rectangles in Figure 3). From these five lists, we get 4 candidates $\{r_1, r_2, r_4, r_5\}$. Finally we verify candidates and get a result $\{r_4\}$.

Thus given a prefix tree $\mathcal{T}_i$, the time cost of using $\mathcal{T}_i$ to answer $\mathcal{Q}$, denoted by $\text{COST}(\mathcal{T}_i, \mathcal{Q})$, includes two parts. The first part is to identify the leaves and the second part is to verify the candidates, which can be computed as below.

$$\text{COST}(\mathcal{T}_i, \mathcal{Q}) = \Big(\prod_{\mathcal{R}^{j_k} \in \Psi(\mathcal{T}_i \cap \mathcal{Q})} |\texttt{pre}(\mathcal{Q}^{j_k})| \Big) + |\mathcal{C}_i| cost_v \quad (3)$$

where $\Psi(\mathcal{T}_i \cap \mathcal{Q})$ is the longest sequence of attributes in $\mathcal{T}_i$ and $\mathcal{Q}$, and $\mathcal{C}_i$ is the candidate set by searching $\mathcal{Q}$ in $\mathcal{T}_i$. $|\mathcal{C}_i|$ can be estimated by adding the size of all identified inverted lists which is very efficient.

Using Multiple Prefix Trees to Answer A Query. Next we study how to utilize multiple prefix trees to answer a search query. First we identify the candidate prefix trees that can answer the query $\mathcal{Q}$, by checking whether the attribute in the first level appears in $\mathcal{Q}$. Second, we rank these candidate prefix trees based on the cost of using the prefix tree to answer $\mathcal{Q}$, i.e., $\mathcal{T}_1, \mathcal{T}_2, \cdots$, where $\text{COST}(\mathcal{T}_1, \mathcal{Q}) \leq \text{COST}(\mathcal{T}_2, \mathcal{Q}) \leq \cdots$.

Algorithm 4: SINGLEPREFIXTREE-SEARCH ($\mathcal{T}$, $\mathcal{Q}$, Φ)

Input: $\mathcal{T}$: Prefix tree
$\mathcal{Q}$: Search query
Φ: A complex similarity operation
Output: $\mathcal{A}$: Answer set

Identify the longest sequence of attributes $\mathcal{R}^{i_1}, \mathcal{R}^{i_2}, \cdots, \mathcal{R}^{i_t}$ of $\mathcal{T}$ that also appear in $\mathcal{Q}$;
NodeSet = {root};
for $j = 1$ *to* t **do**
  for *node in NodeSet* **do**
    NodeSet′ = ϕ;
    for e^j *in prefix of* $\mathcal{Q}^{i_j}$ **do**
      if *node has a child* n_j *with label* e^j **then**
        if n_j *is a leaf* **then** LeafSet $\leftarrow n_j$ **else**
        NodeSet′ $\leftarrow n_j$
    NodeSet = NodeSet′;
for *each leaf* $l \in$ *LeafSet* **do**
  Retrive its inverted list $\mathcal{L}(l)$;
  for *each candidate* $c \in \mathcal{L}(l)$ **do**
    VERIFY (c, $\mathcal{Q}$);
    if *c is simlar to* $\mathcal{Q}$ **then** Add c to $\mathcal{A}$;

Then we have two strategies to answer the query. The first one is that we use the prefix tree $\mathcal{T}_1$ with the minimum cost to generate a candidate set $\mathcal{C}_1$ and verify the candidates using other attributes. The second one is that we utilize another tree $\mathcal{T}_i$ to identify another candidate set $\mathcal{C}_i$ and intersect $\mathcal{C}_1$ and $\mathcal{C}_i$. Based on the new candidate set $\mathcal{C}_1 \cap \mathcal{C}_i$, we can still utilize these two strategies to compute the answer. Iteratively, we can find all the results.

Next we define a cost model to select a better strategy. The cost of the first strategy is

$$\text{COST}_1 = \text{COST}(\mathcal{T}_1, \mathcal{Q}). \tag{4}$$

The cost of the second strategy is

$$\text{COST}_2 = \prod_{\mathcal{R}^{j_k} \in \Psi(\mathcal{T}_1 \cap \mathcal{Q})} |\texttt{pre}(\mathcal{Q}^{j_k})| + \prod_{\mathcal{R}^{j_k} \in \Psi(\mathcal{T}_i \cap \mathcal{Q})} |\texttt{pre}(\mathcal{Q}^{j_k})| + |\mathcal{C}_1| + |\mathcal{C}_i| + |\mathcal{C}_1 \cap \mathcal{C}_i| cost_v. \tag{5}$$

where $|\mathcal{C}_1 \cap \mathcal{C}_i|$ can be obtained through sampling.

If $\text{COST}_1 \leq \text{COST}_2$, we select the first strategy; otherwise we select the second strategy.

The pseudo code is shown in Algorithm 5. It first retrieves prefix trees that can answer $\mathcal{Q}$ from $\mathcal{W}$ (line 1). Then it estimates $\text{COST}(\mathcal{T}_i, \mathcal{Q})$ and sorts $\mathcal{T}_i$ (line 2). It estimates the cost of the two methods (line 4-7). If the intersection-based method is better, it intersects the two candidates and iteratively decides to verify or intersect two candidate sets (line 9-11). Otherwise, it verifies the candidates (line 12).

4.3 Multiple Prefix-Trees Construction

The cost of searching prefix trees depends on two factors. The first is the query distribution, e.g. which attributes or attribute combinations are frequently searched. The second is data distribution, e.g. some attributes have more unique values than other attributes. Since we do not know the distribution of search queries, in this paper we only consider the data distribution.

As there are at least x prefix trees, we first build x trees using each attribute at the first level. We can use these trees to answer any query. If there is more space, we optimize

Algorithm 5: MULTITREESEARCH ($\mathcal{R}$, $\mathcal{Q}$, Φ, $\mathcal{W}$)

Input: $\mathcal{R}$: Multi-attribute data table
$\mathcal{Q}$: Search query
$\mathcal{W}$: Multiple prefix trees $\mathcal{T}_1, \mathcal{T}_2..\mathcal{T}_m$
Output: $\mathcal{A}$: Answer set

1 $\mathcal{W}_\mathcal{Q} \leftarrow \{\mathcal{T}_i | \mathcal{T}_i \in \mathcal{W}, \mathcal{R}^{i_1} \in \mathcal{Q}\}$;
2 Sort $\mathcal{T}_i \in \mathcal{W}_\mathcal{Q}$ by $\text{COST}(\mathcal{T}_i, \mathcal{Q})$;
3 $\mathcal{A} \leftarrow$ Candidates using $\mathcal{T}_1$;
4 $\text{COST}_1 = \text{COST}(\mathcal{T}_1, \mathcal{Q}) + |\mathcal{C}_1| cost_v$;
5 **for** *each* $\mathcal{T}_i \in \mathcal{W}_\mathcal{Q}$ **do**
6   Estimate $\text{COST}_2(\mathcal{T}_i)$ by Equation(5) ;
7 Choose $\mathcal{T}_p$ with smallest $\text{COST}_2(\mathcal{T}_p)$;
8 **if** $\text{COST}_2(\mathcal{T}_p) < \text{COST}_1$ **then**
9   $\mathcal{C}_p \leftarrow$ Candidates using $\mathcal{T}_p$;
10   $\mathcal{A} = \mathcal{A} \cap \mathcal{C}_p$;
11   Decide to verify $\mathcal{A}$ or further intersect;
12 **else** Verify all records in $\mathcal{A}$;
13 **return** $\mathcal{A}$;

these prefix trees and propose a cost-based method. Next we define the cost and benefit of adding an attribute $\mathcal{R}^j$ to current tree $\mathcal{T}_i$. The cost is the space increase by adding $\mathcal{R}^j$ to $\mathcal{T}_i$ and the benefit is query performance improvement.

As the new prefix tree shares many tree nodes with $\mathcal{T}_i$, we only consider the cost of new inverted lists by adding $\mathcal{R}^j$ to $\mathcal{T}_i$. As each record in $\mathcal{T}$ appears $|\texttt{pre}(r^{\mathcal{R}_j})|$ times in the new tree and thus the space cost can be computed as below.

$$\text{COST}_{\text{SPACE}}(\mathcal{T}_i, \mathcal{R}^j) = \sum_{l \in \text{LEAF}(\mathcal{T}_i)} \sum_{r \in \mathcal{L}_l^\mathcal{R}} (|\texttt{pre}(r^{\mathcal{R}_j})|) \tag{6}$$

The benefit is hard to measure and different queries have different benefits. Here our objective is to avoid slow queries, i.e., there are no rather long inverted lists on the prefix tree. Thus we want to make inverted lists evenly distributed after adding $\mathcal{R}^j$. To achieve this goal, we use a modified Shannon entropy to capture this information.

DEFINITION 6. *The entropy of prefix tree $\mathcal{T}$ in search is*

$$\mathcal{H}(\mathcal{T}) = \sum_{l \in \text{LEAF}(\mathcal{T})} -\mathcal{P}(l) \log \mathcal{P}(l) \tag{7}$$

where $\text{LEAF}(\mathcal{T})$ *is the leaf set of* $\mathcal{T}$ *and* $\mathcal{P}(l)$ *is the ratio of inverted-list size of node* l *to the sum of inverted-list sizes,*

$$\mathcal{P}(l) = \frac{|\mathcal{L}_l^\mathcal{R}|}{\sum_{l' \in \text{LEAF}(\mathcal{T}_i)} |\mathcal{L}_{l'}^\mathcal{R}|}. \tag{8}$$

Obviously, the larger entropy, the smaller average search cost of using prefix tree to answer a query. With this entropy cost model, we can define the benefit of adding $\mathcal{R}^j$,

$$\text{BENEFIT}(\mathcal{T}_i, \mathcal{R}^j) = \mathcal{H}(\mathcal{T}_i, \mathcal{R}^j) - \mathcal{H}(\mathcal{T}_i) \tag{9}$$

where $\mathcal{H}(\mathcal{T}_i, \mathcal{R}^j)$ denotes the entropy of the new tree by adding $\mathcal{R}^j$ to $\mathcal{T}_i$.

Using the cost and benefit, our goal is to achieve the maximum benefit with a given space budget $\mathcal{B}$. However, this generalizes the classical knapsack problem, which is NP-Hard. To this end, we devise a greedy algorithm to build the prefix trees. We select the attribute $\mathcal{R}^j$ and $\mathcal{T}_i$ with the largest value $\frac{\text{BENEFIT}(\mathcal{T}_i, \mathcal{R}^j)}{\text{COST}_{\text{SPACE}}(\mathcal{T}_i, \mathcal{R}^j)}$, and insert the new tree into the tree set. The algorithm terminates until there is no space to accommodate any prefix tree. Algorithm 6 shows pseudo code. It first creates one-level prefix trees for each attribute (lines 1-2). Then it greedily adds a new prefix tree (lines 6-9). It terminates when meeting the space budget (line 6).

Algorithm 6: BUILDMULTIPLETREES ($\mathcal{R}$, $\mathcal{B}$)

Input: $\mathcal{R}$: Multi-attribute table
$\mathcal{B}$: Space budget
Output: $\mathcal{W}$: A set of prefix trees

for *each attribute* $\mathcal{R}^i$ **do**
  Construct $\mathcal{T}_i$ with $\mathcal{R}^i$ and add $\mathcal{T}_i$ to $\mathcal{W}$;
while $\mathcal{B} > 0$ **do**
  for *each* $\mathcal{T}_i \in \mathcal{W}$ **do**
    for *each* $\mathcal{R}^j$ **do**
      Compute $\text{COST}_{\text{SPACE}}(\mathcal{T}_i, \mathcal{R}^j)$ with Equation 6;
      Compute $\text{BENEFIT}(\mathcal{T}_i, \mathcal{R}^j)$ with Equation 9;
  Expand $\mathcal{T}_i$ using $\mathcal{R}^j$ with largest $\frac{\text{BENEFIT}(\mathcal{T}_i,\mathcal{R}^j)}{\text{COST}_{\text{SPACE}}(\mathcal{T}_i,\mathcal{R}^j)}$;
  $\mathcal{W} \leftarrow \mathcal{T}(\mathcal{T}_i, \mathcal{R}^j)$;
  $\mathcal{B} \leftarrow \mathcal{B} - \text{COST}_{\text{SPACE}}(\mathcal{T}_i, \mathcal{R}^j)$;
return $\mathcal{W}$;

For example, consider adding an attribute to $\mathcal{T}_1$ in Figure 7. If we add attribute $\mathcal{R}^3$, the benifit $\text{BENEFIT}(\mathcal{T}_1, \mathcal{R}^3) = 0.298$ and the cost $\text{COST}_{\text{SPACE}}(\mathcal{T}_1, \mathcal{R}^3) = 4$. Similarly we can estimate $\text{BENEFIT}(\mathcal{T}_1, \mathcal{R}^2) = 1.057$ and $\text{COST}_{\text{SPACE}}(\mathcal{T}_1, \mathcal{R}^2) = 39$. $\frac{\text{BENEFIT}(\mathcal{T}_1,\mathcal{R}^3)}{\text{COST}_{\text{SPACE}}(\mathcal{T}_1,\mathcal{R}^3)} = 0.0745$ and $\frac{\text{BENEFIT}(\mathcal{T}_1,\mathcal{R}^2)}{\text{COST}_{\text{SPACE}}(\mathcal{T}_1,\mathcal{R}^2)} = 0.0271$, As $\frac{\text{BENEFIT}(\mathcal{T}_1,\mathcal{R}^3)}{\text{COST}_{\text{SPACE}}(\mathcal{T}_1,\mathcal{R}^3)} > \frac{\text{BENEFIT}(\mathcal{T}_1,\mathcal{R}^2)}{\text{COST}_{\text{SPACE}}(\mathcal{T}_1,\mathcal{R}^2)}$, we expend $\mathcal{T}_1$ with $\mathcal{R}^3$.

5. HYBRID VERIFICATION

In this section, we study how to efficiently verify a candidate pair. There are two challenges in verifying a pair. The first is to determine the order of verifying different predicates. The second is to decide the order of using different filtering algorithms. To address these challenges, we propose a hybrid verification framework and prove its optimality.

5.1 Hybrid-based Verification Framework

Given a complex similarity operation Φ and a candidate pair $\langle r, s\rangle$, we check whether $\langle r, s\rangle$ satisfies each predicate in Φ. A straightforward way is to examine each predicate one by one through computing the real similarity. However this method has two weaknesses. First, directly computing the similarity is expensive. For example, the cost to verify $\langle r, s\rangle$ on the token-based function is $|r| + |s|$ while the cost on the character-based function is $(2\tau + 1) \cdot \min(|r|, |s|)$. Second, the pruning power of each predicate is also different and it is important to select an appropriate order of predicates to verify candidates. For example, given a candidate pair $\langle r_1, s_1\rangle$ and a complex similarity operation $\mathcal{R}^1 \overset{\text{ED},1}{\sim} \mathcal{S}^1 \wedge \mathcal{R}^2 \overset{\text{JAC},0.3}{\sim} \mathcal{S}^2 \wedge \mathcal{R}^3 \overset{\text{OLP},1}{\sim} \mathcal{S}^3$, if we verify them with the order $\langle \Phi_1, \Phi_3, \Phi_2\rangle$. The cost is $(3 \cdot 14) + (1 + 1) + (2 + 2) = 48$. However, if we use the order $\langle \Phi_2, \Phi_1, \Phi_3\rangle$, then the pair fails in predicate Φ_2, and thus the cost is only $2 + 2 = 4$.

To reduce the verification cost, we can use lightweight filters instead of computing the actual similarity. If the pair cannot pass the filter, we prune it; otherwise we use other filters or compute the actual similarity. For example, the length filter can prune those pairs with length difference larger than τ for edit distance. However different filters have different cost and pruning power and it is also important to select an appropriate order for using filtering algorithms.

Formally, suppose a similarity operation Φ has k similarity predicates $\Phi_1, \Phi_2, \cdots, \Phi_k$, v filters $\Gamma_1, \Gamma_2, \cdots, \Gamma_v$, and each predicate Φ_i also has a best verification algorithm Λ_i. There are many possible ways to verify the pair. A naive way that does not use any filter is $\langle \Phi_1, \Lambda_1\rangle, \langle \Phi_2, \Lambda_2\rangle, \cdots, \langle \Phi_k, \Lambda_k\rangle$.

Algorithm 7: HYBRIDVERIFICATION ($\mathcal{C}$, $\mathcal{Q}$, Φ, $\mathcal{F}$)

Input: $\mathcal{C}$: Candidate after prefix tree; $\mathcal{Q}$: Search query
Φ: A complex similarity operation,
$\mathcal{F}$: A set of filters and verification algorithms
Output: $\mathcal{A}$: Answer

1 Compute and sort verification methods by $\frac{\Theta(\langle\Phi,\Gamma\rangle)}{\mathcal{P}(\langle\Phi,\Gamma\rangle)}$;
2 **for** *each* $\langle r, s\rangle \in \mathcal{C}$ **do**
3   **for** *each* $\langle \Phi, \Gamma\rangle$ **do**
4   **if** (r, s) *does not pass* $\langle \Phi, \Gamma\rangle$ **then**
5   break;
6   Add $\langle r, s\rangle$ to $\mathcal{A}$;
7   Update $\frac{\Theta(\langle\Phi,\Gamma\rangle)}{\mathcal{P}(\langle\Phi,\Gamma\rangle)}$;
8 **return** $\mathcal{A}$;

Another solution that uses all possible filters is $\langle \Phi_1, \Gamma_{11}\rangle$, $\langle \Phi_1, \Gamma_{12}\rangle, \cdots, \langle \Phi_1, \Lambda_1\rangle, \langle \Phi_2, \Gamma_{21}\rangle, \langle \Phi_2, \Gamma_{22}\rangle, \cdots, \langle \Phi_2, \Lambda_2\rangle$, $\langle \Phi_k, \Gamma_{k1}\rangle, \langle \Phi_k, \Gamma_{k2}\rangle, \cdots, \langle \Phi_k, \Lambda_k\rangle$. We require to find an order with the minimum cost to verify the pair. Suppose each filter $\langle \Phi_i, \Gamma_j\rangle$ (or each verification algorithm $\langle \Phi_i, \Lambda_i\rangle$) has a time cost Θ to preform the filter (or the algorithm) and a pruning probability $\mathcal{P}$ to prune the pair. We discuss how to compute the time cost and pruning ability in Section 5.2.

Given a verification sequence $\Psi = \{\langle \Phi_1, \Gamma_1\rangle, \langle \Phi_2, \Gamma_2\rangle, \cdots\}$, we compute its expected verification cost as follows.

$$\text{COST}(\Psi) = \sum_{\langle\Phi,\Gamma\rangle\in\Psi} \Theta(\langle\Phi,\Gamma\rangle) \cdot \mathcal{P}_\Psi(\langle\Phi,\Gamma\rangle), \quad (10)$$

where $\Theta(\langle\Phi,\Gamma\rangle)$ is the cost to use the filter Γ to verify predicate Φ and $\mathcal{P}_\Psi(\langle\Phi,\Gamma\rangle)$ is the probability that $\langle\Phi,\Gamma\rangle$ is used to verify the pair given the sequence Ψ, that is the probability the verification methods before $\langle\Phi,\Gamma\rangle$ in Ψ cannot prune the pair, which can be computed as

$$\mathcal{P}_\Psi(\langle\Phi,\Gamma\rangle) = \prod_{\langle\Phi',\Gamma'\rangle \text{ is before } \langle\Phi,\Gamma\rangle} 1 - \mathcal{P}(\langle\Phi',\Gamma'\rangle), \quad (11)$$

where $\mathcal{P}(\langle\Phi',\Gamma'\rangle)$ is the probability that the filter Γ' on Φ' can prune a pair.

We design a hybrid verification algorithm to address this problem. Algorithm 7 gives the pseudo code of the algorithm. It first computes $\frac{\Theta(\langle\Phi,\Gamma\rangle)}{\mathcal{P}(\langle\Phi,\Gamma\rangle)}$ for each pair of filter and attribute, and sorts them in an ascending order (line 1). Then it utilizes this order to verify each candidate pair. If the candidate passes the filter, it selects the next filter or verification algorithm; otherwise terminates (lines 2 - 5). Finally it adds the pair which passes all verification algorithms to the answer set (line 6). Then it updates the expected cost for other verification methods based on Equation 11 (line 7). Iteratively, the algorithm can find a verification order.

Note that the above greedy algorithm is known to be optimal (see e.g., [10]), and for the sake of completeness, we provide a simple proof of this fact in Appendix C.

For example, given a filter Γ_1, a verification algorithm Λ_2 and two similarity predicates Φ_1, Φ_2 with the following expected cost $\frac{\Theta(\langle\Phi,\Gamma\rangle)}{\mathcal{P}(\langle\Phi,\Gamma\rangle)}$. $\langle\Phi_1,\Gamma_1\rangle$: $\frac{1.0}{0.4} = 2.5$, $\langle\Phi_1,\Lambda_2\rangle$:$\frac{8.3}{0.9} = 9.2$, $\langle\Phi_2,\Gamma_1\rangle$: $\frac{1.0}{0.25} = 4.0$, $\langle\Phi_2,\Lambda_2\rangle$:$\frac{2.2}{0.6} = 3.7$. We sort verification methods by $\frac{\Theta(\langle\Phi,\Gamma\rangle)}{\mathcal{P}(\langle\Phi,\Gamma\rangle)}$ and get an order $\langle\Phi_1,\Gamma_1\rangle, \langle\Phi_2,\Lambda_2\rangle$, $\langle\Phi_2,\Gamma_1\rangle, \langle\Phi_1,\Lambda_2\rangle$. Then we compute $\mathcal{P}(\langle\Phi,\Gamma\rangle|\Psi)$ iteratively by Equation (11) and get a sequence $\mathcal{P}(\langle\Phi_1,\Gamma_1\rangle|\Psi) = 1$, $\mathcal{P}(\langle\Phi_2,\Lambda_2\rangle|\Psi) = 0.6, \mathcal{P}(\langle\Phi_2,\Gamma_1\rangle|\Psi) = 0.24, \mathcal{P}(\langle\Phi_1,\Lambda_2\rangle|\Psi) = 0.18$. Thus $\text{COST}(\Psi) = \sum_{\langle\Phi_i,\Gamma_j\rangle\in\Psi} \Theta(\langle\Phi_i,\Gamma_j\rangle)\cdot\mathcal{P}(\langle\Phi_i,\Gamma_j\rangle|\Psi) = 2.5 \cdot 1 + 2.2 \cdot 0.6 + 4.0 \cdot 0.24 + 8.3 \cdot 0.18 = 6.274$. If we choose order $\langle\Phi_1,\Lambda_2\rangle, \langle\Phi_2,\Gamma_1\rangle, \langle\Phi_2,\Lambda_2\rangle, \langle\Phi_1,\Gamma_1\rangle$, $\text{COST}(\Psi) = 8.64$.

5.2 Verification Cost and Pruning Probability

We first discuss the verification cost of various filters. Here we only take important filters as examples. It is worth noting that our method is orthogonal to the filtering techniques and our method can be easily extended to support any filter.

Length Filter. It prunes $\langle r, s\rangle$ if their length difference is larger than τ for ED and $|r|\frac{1-\tau}{\tau}$ for JAC. The time cost Θ is $\mathcal{O}(1)$ for the search problem, since the length/size can be materialized; but for the join problem, the cost is $\mathcal{O}(1)$ for the attribute in the similarity operation as we can get the length when computing the prefixes; $\mathcal{O}(|r| + |s|)$ otherwise.

Prefix Filter. It prunes $\langle r, s\rangle$ if their prefixes have no common token. The time cost Θ is $\mathcal{O}(\texttt{pre}(r) + \texttt{pre}(s))$. (If the prefix filter is used in the filtering step for this attribute, we will not use it again and set its pruning probability as 0.)

Count Filter. It is useful only for character-based functions. If two strings are similar, they must share $\max(|r|, |s|) - q + 1 - \tau q$ common q grams. The time cost Θ is $\mathcal{O}(|r| + |s|)$.

Content Filter. It is useful only for character-based similarity functions. For example, for ED, it computes the sum of the number of character difference and if the difference is larger than 2τ, it prunes the pair. The cost is $\mathcal{O}(|r| + |s|)$.

The well-known verification algorithm for ED is the dynamic-programming algorithm with time cost of $\mathcal{O}(2\tau \min(|r|, |s|))$. The verification algorithm for JAC is $\mathcal{O}(|r| + |s|)$.

Next we analyze the filtering probability. Initially, we can utilize a sampling-based method to compute the pruning probability of each filter. Then, after verifying each record, we update the pruning probability of each filter. However it is not free to get the pruning probability and it is expensive to compute an appropriate order for every pair. Instead, we periodically update the order. For similarity join, we group the candidates based on a record in $\mathcal{R}$ and use the same order for candidates in the same group; for similarity search, we can use the same order for all candidates.

6. EXPERIMENT

We have implemented our techniques to support similarity join and search on multi-attribute data and our goal is to evaluate the efficiency. We used two real datasets DBLP and IMDB in the experiments, as shown in Table 1.

DBLP: It is a publication dataset (dblp.uni-trier.de/xml/). We ran self-join on DBLP with 4 attributes {title, journal, author, year}. The similarity operation was $\texttt{title} \overset{\mathsf{COS},\tau}{\sim} \texttt{title} \wedge \texttt{journal} \overset{\mathsf{JAC},\tau}{\sim} \texttt{journal} \wedge \texttt{author} \overset{\mathsf{ES},\tau}{\sim} \texttt{author} \wedge \texttt{year} \overset{\mathsf{ES},\tau}{\sim} \texttt{year}$ by varying τ in [0.75, 0.95].

IMDB: It is a movie database (imdb.com). We ran self-join on IMDB with 4 attributes {title, genres, director, writer}. The similarity operation was $\texttt{title} \overset{\mathsf{ES},\tau}{\sim} \texttt{title} \wedge \texttt{genres} \overset{\mathsf{JAC},\tau}{\sim} \texttt{genres} \wedge \texttt{director} \overset{\mathsf{ES},\tau}{\sim} \texttt{director} \wedge \texttt{writer} \overset{\mathsf{ES},\tau}{\sim} \texttt{writer}$ by varying τ in [0.75, 0.95].

All the algorithms were implemented in C++ and compiled using GCC 4.7 with the -O3 flag. All the experiments were conducted on a machine running 64bit Ubuntu 14.04 with Intel Xeon E2650 2.0GHz processor and 16GB RAM.

6.1 Evaluation on Prefix Trees for Join

In this section, we evaluated our prefix trees for similarity join. We first compared our optimal prefix tree and the greedy prefix tree with CBlockTree [21], which was used to merge blocks to improve the recall of the blocking-based scheme (see Appendix C for details). Figure 8 shows the

Table 1: Datasets.

Datasets	# Records	# Attributes	Size
DBLP	1M	4	174MB
IMDB	400K	4	159MB

candidate numbers and join time, where the bars from bottom to top respectively denote the time of building trees, filtering time and verification time. We had the following observations. First, CBlockTree reduced the number of candidates, because it enumerated every two leaves and merged the leaves with the join cost on the merged node smaller than the cost on two individual leaves, while our method only checked whether to combine the leaf nodes with the same parent. However, enumerating every pair of leaf nodes had expensive overhead, and thus CBlockTree had worse performance than our method. Second, our greedy prefix tree nearly had the same number of candidates with the optimal prefix tree, because if merging a subtree had a large benefit, our greedy prefix tree would not split the subtree and our cost model can effectively decide whether to split a node or not. Third, our greedy prefix tree had much better join performance than the optimal prefix tree. The reason is obvious that it took less time to construct the greedy prefix tree, and the optimal tree generated a large complete prefix tree and then merged many subtrees, which was rather time consuming, especially for large datasets. Another reason was that the greedy tree had similar pruning power with the optimal tree and thus it did not loss much performance.

Then, we compared different orders of predicates in constructing the prefix trees. We compared the random order with our greedy order. Figure 9 shows the results. We can see that our greedy order significantly outperformed the random order, even by 1-2 orders of magnitude. This is because if we used predicates with large cost in top levels, then both indexing and filtering took much time. Our greedy algorithm selected an appropriate order of predicates and made inverted lists on leaf nodes much shorter. For example, on DBLP, for $\tau = 0.8$, the random order took nearly 1000 seconds while our greedy order took less than 80 seconds.

6.2 Evaluation on Prefix Trees on Search

We generated 100K search queries based on the same similarity operations, varied the thresholds, and reported the average search time. To build prefix index, we set a threshold bound (0.7) for each predicate and built our multiple prefix trees with the bound. We first evaluated our techniques by using multiple prefix trees to answer a query (proposed in Section 4.2). Suppose the size of the multiple prefix tree with the first level was 1. We set $\mathcal{B} = 2$ in this experiment. We implemented three methods. (1) Intersection-based Method: It computed the candidates using each predicate and then intersected them. (2) Pipeline-based Method: It selected the best predicate and utilized this predicate to generate candidates. (3) Cost-based Method: It used our cost model to generate the candidates. Figure 10 shows the results (bottom/top bars denote filtering/verification time).

We had the following observations. First, on DBLP, the pipeline-based method was better than the intersection-based method, because the pipeline-based method first used a highly selective attribute to identify less candidates and then verified the candidates, and thus achieved rather high performance. However, the intersection-based method used each predicate to identify many candidates and thus was expensive. For example, consider a query (AUTHOR $\overset{\mathsf{ES},0.8}{\sim}$ 'Dieter Baum, Vladimir V. Kalashnikov', JOURNAL $\overset{\mathsf{JAC},0.8}{\sim}$

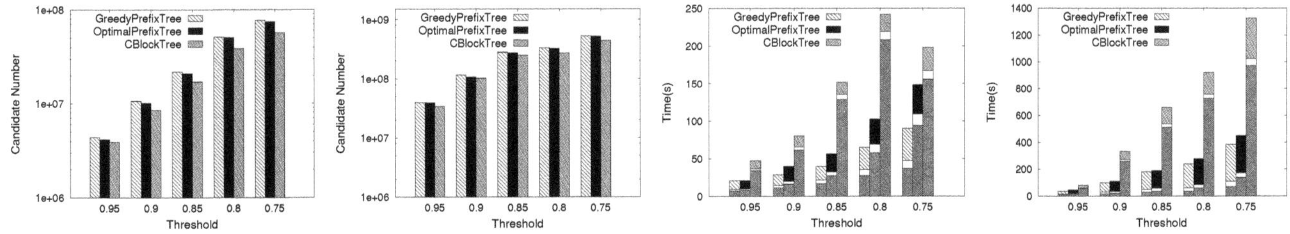

(a) Candidate Number (DBLP) (b) Candidate Number (IMDB) (c) Efficiency (DBLP) (d) Efficiency (IMDB)

Figure 8: Evaluation on Prefix Trees for Similarity Join: Optimal vs Greedy vs CBlockTree

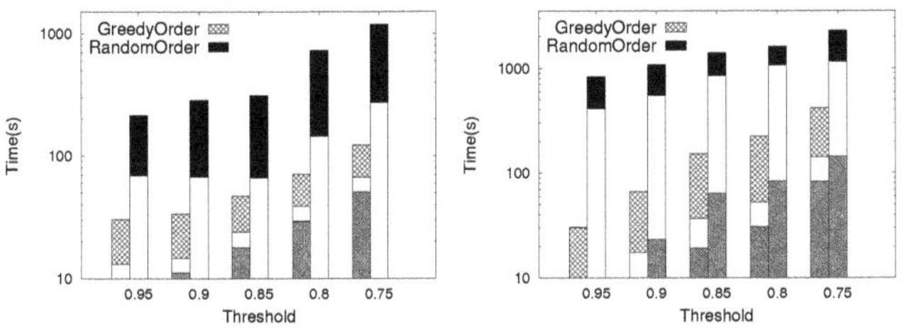

(a) Efficiency (DBLP) (b) Efficiency (IMDB)

Figure 9: Evaluation on Predicate Order for Join

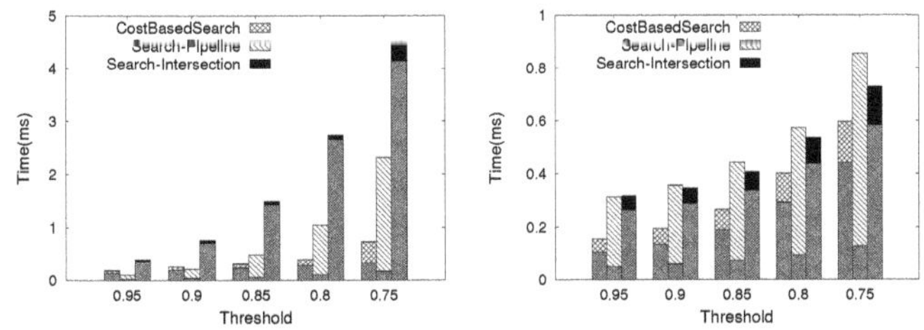

(a) Efficiency (DBLP) (b) Efficiency (IMDB)

Figure 10: Evaluation on Prefix Trees for Search.

'University Trier, Mathematik/Informatik'). Attribute JOURNAL only generated 300 candidates (by prefix filtering), while attribute AUTHOR generated over 10K candidates. The intersection-based method identified 10K candidates from attribute AUTHOR and 300 candidates from JOURNAL while the pipeline-based method only identified 300 candidates and then verified them. Obviously, the latter was faster. Second, on IMDB, the intersection-based method was better than the pipeline-based method because every predicate generated nearly the same number of answers and the intersection-based method can further reduce the candidate number by intersecting them, which had lower cost than directly verifying each candidate. For example, a query generated 1000 candidates on attribute TITLE and 1000 candidates on attribute DIRECTOR, and there were 100 results. The pipeline-based method identified 1000 candidates and verified 1000 candidates while the intersection-based method identified 2000 candidates and verified 150 candidates (there were 150 candidates after the intersection). As the verification cost was much more expensive than the filtering cost, the intersection-based method was better. Third, our cost-based method always achieved the best performance because it judiciously selected appropriate predicates to generate the candidates. If the best predicate generated a small number of candidates, it directly verified the candidates; otherwise it selected another predicate to further reduce the number of candidates. For example, on DBLP, for $\tau = 0.75$, the intersection-based method took 4.6 milliseconds for each query, and the pipeline-based method took 2.3 milliseconds, while our cost-based method improved it to 0.4 milliseconds.

Then we evaluated the performance by varying the given budget $\mathcal{B}$. Suppose the size of all the 1-level prefix trees was 1. We varied $\mathcal{B}$ in 1.0, 1.5, 2.0, 2.5, and 3.0, and evaluated

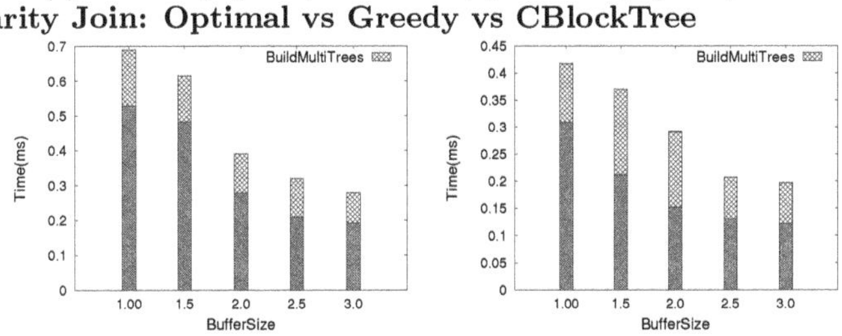

(a) Efficiency (DBLP) (b) Efficiency (IMDB)

Figure 11: Evaluation on Search by Varying Budgets

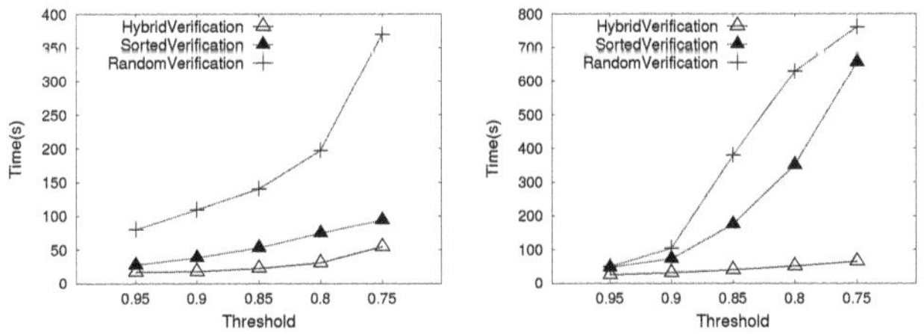

(a) Efficiency (DBLP) (b) Efficiency (IMDB)

Figure 12: Evaluation on Verification Algorithms.

the average search performance. Figure 11 shows the results. We can see with the increase of $\mathcal{B}$, our method achieved higher performance, this is because we can use more prefix trees to answer search queries, which obviously can improve the performance. Especially, if each query attribute was contained by a prefix tree, then the prefix tree can significantly improve the performance than the 1-level prefix tree.

6.3 Evaluation on Verification Techniques

We evaluated our verification techniques. We compared three methods. (1) Random Verification: we randomly verified a candidate. (2) Sorted Verification: we sorted the predicates based on our techniques in Section 5.1. (3) Hybrid Verification: we used our cost model in Section 5.1 to verify a candidate. We used the length filter, prefix filter, count filter, and content filter in the experiment. Figure 12 shows the results. We can see that the hybrid verification outperformed the other two methods. This is because our hybrid verification method always judiciously selected appropriate orders of predicates to verify a candidate and used the appropriate filtering algorithms to prune dissimilar pairs. Our hybrid verification algorithm was better than the sorted verification method, especially for a small threshold. This is because selecting a predicate order was not enough to achieve high performance and our hybrid verification method can also utilize lightweight filters to prune many candidates. For example, our method can utilize the length filter and count filter on some attributes to prune many candidate with little cost. The improvement of our hybrid method over the sorted-based method on IMDB was significant because there were many candidates in IMDB and our hybrid can utilize different filters to effectively prune these candidates. However, on DBLP, there were few candidates using an appropriate predicate and thus the improvement was not significant.

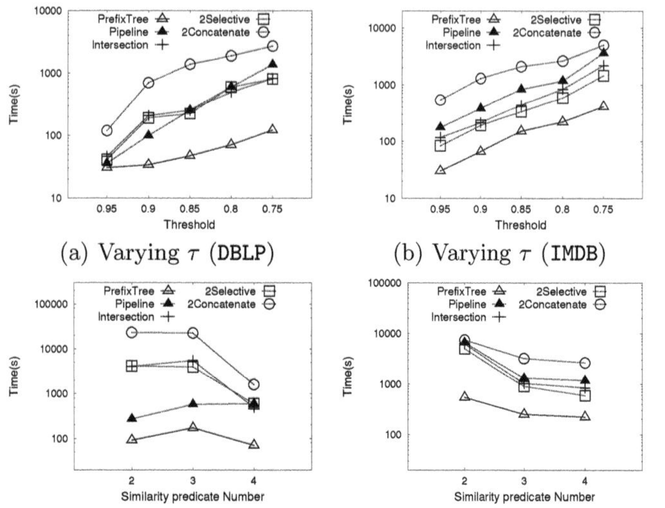

(a) Varying τ (DBLP) (b) Varying τ (IMDB)

(c) Varying # Predicates(DBLP) (d) Varying # Predicates(IMDB)

Figure 13: Comparison on Similarity Joins.

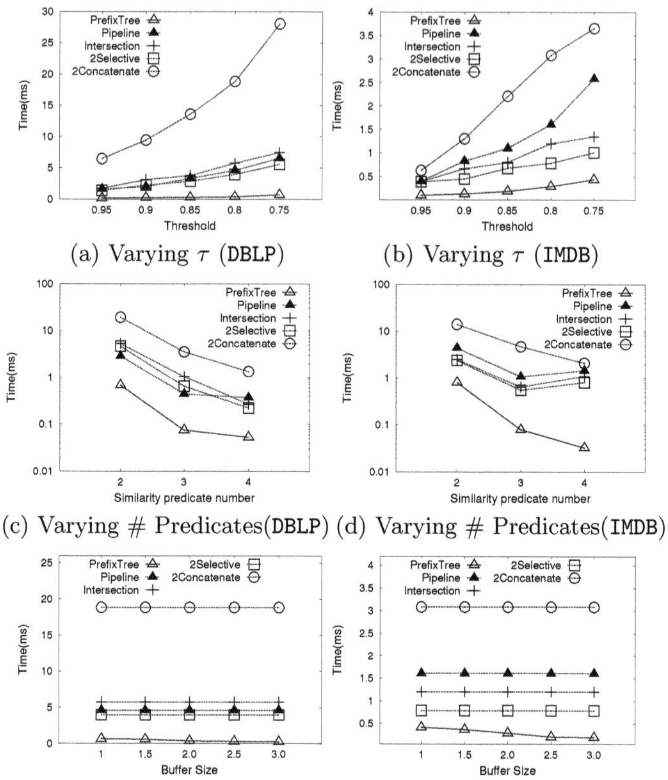

(a) Varying τ (DBLP) (b) Varying τ (IMDB)

(c) Varying # Predicates(DBLP) (d) Varying # Predicates(IMDB)

(e) DBLP (f) IMDB

Figure 14: Comparison on Similarity Search with Baselines (Including filtering&verification)

6.4 Comparison with Baselines

We compared our method with state-of-the-art q-gram-based methods, PPJoin [29] for token-based similarity and ED-join [28] for character-based similarity. For fair comparison, we used the same filters with these two algorithms, including length filter, count filter, content filter, and prefix filter. We extended them and took them as baseline approaches (see Appendix C for details): (1) INTERSECTION: It used PPJoin or ED-join to identify the candidates on every predicate, intersected the candidates, and verified the intersected candidates. (2) PIPELINE: It selected the best predicate using our model and used PPJoin or ED-join to identify the candidates, and then verified the candidates. (3) 2SELECTIVE: It first identified candidates for two most selective attributes and then intersected them. (4) 2CONCATENATE: It concatenated two selective attributes as a single attribute and then used PPJoin or ED-join to identify the candidates. We also extended them to support search by using the threshold 0.7 (which was the same as our method).

6.4.1 Comparison on Similarity Joins

We compared the performance by varying the thresholds and the number of similarity predicates, and the result is shown in Figure 13. We had the following observations. First, with the decrease of τ, the performance of all the methods become worse because a small threshold will generate more results and thus all the algorithms generated more candidates and involved more verification time. Second, the query with more predicate numbers may not have worse performance, because a "lightweight" attribute will improve the performance. For example, on DBLP, answering the query with attributes **title**, **journal**, **author** was easier than answering query with attributes **title**, **author**, because the attribute **journal** can prune many dissimilar pairs. Third, the intersection-based method was always worse because it was very expensive to identify candidates for every predicate. Fourth, 2CONCATENATE achieved the lowest performance because it generated many more candidates than INTERSECTION. Actually, the candidate set obtained by concatenating two attributes is a super set of the candidate set obtained by intersecting two attributes, because if r is a candidate of intersecting two attributes, then the concatenated attribute of r must satisfy the combined constraint and thus r is a candidate of concatenating two attributes (see Appendix C for more details). Fifth, alghouth 2SELECTIVE was better than INTERSECTION, it was still worse than our method, because it only used two attributes and cannot adaptively select a better strategy for queries with more than two attributes. Sixth, our method always outperformed the baseline approaches. This was attributed to the pruning power of our prefix tree and the effectiveness of our hybrid verification algorithm. The first technique can prune a large number of dissimilar results and the second technique can efficiently verify each candidate pair.

6.4.2 Comparison on Similarity Search

We compared the search performance by varying the thresholds, the number of similarity predicates, and the budge $\mathcal{B}$. The result is shown in Figure 14. We had the following observations. First, our method was still much better than the four baselines for different buffer sizes, even the same buffer size with existing methods. This is because our algorithm selected a better search strategy to reduce the number of candidates and utilized a cost-based verification algorithm to improve the verification performance. Second, similar to similarity join, with the decrease of thresholds, the performance was also decreased because there will be more candidates and answers. Third, with the increase of the buffer $\mathcal{B}$, the baseline kept the same performance and our method became better, because our method can utilize the budget to generate more prefix trees. Fourth, the search time actually decreased when we used more similarity predicates. This is because the last two similarity predicates actually had very high pruning power and cheap filtering cost.

6.5 Scalability

We evaluated the scalability of different methods by varying the dataset sizes. Figure 15 shows the scalability on join and Figure 16 shows the scalability on search. We can see that with the increase of the dataset sizes, our method

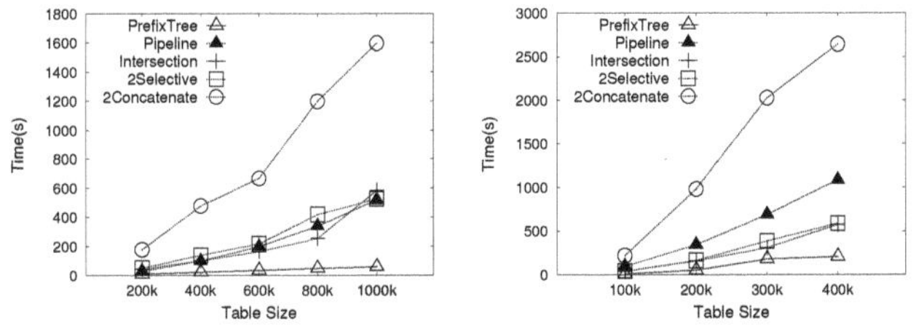

(a) Scalability (DBLP) (b) Scalability (IMDB)

Figure 15: Scalability on Joins.

Table 2: Scalability of index size

# of records (DBLP)	400k	600k	800k	1M
Index Size	39MB	52MB	81MB	95MB
# of records (IMDB)	100k	200k	300k	400k
Index Size	100MB	150MB	230MB	309MB

scaled well and always outperformed the baselines. On similarity joins, with the increase of dataset sizes, our method increased linearly. For example, on DBLP, our method took 10 seconds to join 200K records, and 50 seconds for 1M records. On similarity search, our method also increased linearly with the increase of dataset sizes on both of the two datasets. This is attributed to the high pruning power of our prefix trees which can prune a large number of dissimilar results and the efficient verification algorithms which can efficiently verify each candidate pair.

We also evaluated the index size, which included two parts: prefix tree nodes and inverted lists. Since the index size can be controlled by $\mathcal{B}$ for search, here we reported the index size of similarity joins on the DBLP dataset in Table 2, where we indexed all the four attributes with $\tau = 0.8$. We can see the index size scaled well as the dataset sizes increased.

7. CONCLUSION

We have studied similarity search and join on multi-attribute data. We devised a prefix tree index structure and utilized it to support similarity search and join. For similarity join, we proposed a cost model to quantify the prefix tree and proved that finding the optimal prefix tree is NP-complete and we devised a greedy algorithm to construct a high-quality prefix tree. We extended the prefix tree to support similarity search and constructed multiple prefix trees to answer search queries. We devised a hybrid verification algorithm by finding an appropriate order of predicates and filtering algorithms to improve the verification performance. Experimental results on two real datasets show that our method significantly outperformed baseline approaches.

Acknowledgement. This work was partly supported by the 973 Program of China (2015CB358700 and 2011CB302206), and the NSFC project (61373024, 61422205, 61472198), Tencent, Huawei, SAP, YETP0105, the "NExT Research Center" (WBS: R-252-300-001-490), and the FDCT/106/2012/A3.

8. REFERENCES

[1] R. J. Bayardo, Y. Ma, and R. Srikant. Scaling up all pairs similarity search. In *WWW*, pages 131–140, 2007.

[2] S. Chaudhuri, V. Ganti, and R. Kaushik. A primitive operator for similarity joins in data cleaning. In *ICDE*, pages 5–16, 2006.

[3] N. N. Dalvi, V. Rastogi, A. Dasgupta, A. D. Sarma, and T. Sarlós. Optimal hashing schemes for entity matching. In *WWW*, pages 295–306, 2013.

[4] D. Deng, G. Li, and J. Feng. A pivotal prefix based filtering algorithm for string similarity search. In *SIGMOD Conference*, pages 673–684, 2014.

[5] D. Deng, G. Li, J. Feng, and W.-S. Li. Top-k string similarity search with edit-distance constraints. In *ICDE*, pages 925–936, 2013.

[6] D. Deng, G. Li, S. Hao, J. Wang, and J. Feng. Massjoin: A mapreduce-based method for scalable string similarity joins. In *ICDE*, pages 340–351, 2014.

[7] M. Garey and D. Johnson. *A guide to the theory of NP-completeness.* WH Freeman and Company, 1979.

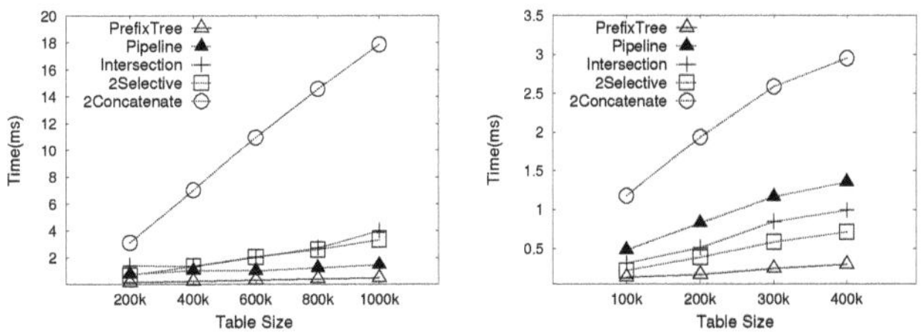

(a) Scalability (DBLP) (b) Scalability (IMDB)

Figure 16: Scalability on Search.

[8] L. Gravano, P. G. Ipeirotis, H. V. Jagadish, N. Koudas, S. Muthukrishnan, and D. Srivastava. Approximate string joins in a database (almost) for free. In *VLDB*, pages 491–500, 2001.

[9] M. Hadjieleftheriou, N. Koudas, and D. Srivastava. Incremental maintenance of length normalized indexes for approximate string matching. In *SIGMOD Conference*, pages 429–440, 2009.

[10] J. M. Hellerstein and M. Stonebraker. Predicate migration: Optimizing queries with expensive predicates. In *SIGMOD Conference*, pages 267–276, 1993.

[11] M. A. Hernández and S. J. Stolfo. Real-world data is dirty: Data cleansing and the merge/purge problem. *Data Min. Knowl. Discov.*, 2(1):9–37, 1998.

[12] Y. Jiang, G. Li, J. Feng, and W. Li. String similarity joins: An experimental evaluation. *PVLDB*, 7(8):625–636, 2014.

[13] N. Koudas, S. Sarawagi, and D. Srivastava. Record linkage: similarity measures and algorithms. In *SIGMOD Conference*, pages 802–803, 2006.

[14] C. Li, J. Lu, and Y. Lu. Efficient merging and filtering algorithms for approximate string searches. In *ICDE*, pages 257–266, 2008.

[15] C. Li, B. Wang, and X. Yang. Vgram: Improving performance of approximate queries on string collections using variable-length grams. In *VLDB*, pages 303–314, 2007.

[16] G. Li, D. Deng, and J. Feng. A partition-based method for string similarity joins with edit-distance constraints. *ACM Trans. Database Syst.*, 38(2):9, 2013.

[17] G. Li, D. Deng, J. Wang, and J. Feng. Pass-join: A partition-based method for similarity joins. *PVLDB*, 5(3):253–264, 2011.

[18] A. McCallum, K. Nigam, and L. H. Ungar. Efficient clustering of high-dimensional data sets with application to reference matching. In *SIGKDD*, pages 169–178, 2000.

[19] M. Michelson and C. A. Knoblock. Learning blocking schemes for record linkage. In *AAAI*, pages 440–445, 2006.

[20] J. Qin, W. Wang, Y. Lu, C. Xiao, and X. Lin. Efficient exact edit similarity query processing with the asymmetric signature scheme. In *SIGMOD Conference*, pages 1033–1044, 2011.

[21] A. D. Sarma, A. Jain, A. Machanavajjhala, and P. Bohannon. An automatic blocking mechanism for large-scale de-duplication tasks. In *CIKM*, pages 1055–1064, 2012.

[22] J. Wang, G. Li, D. Deng, Y. Zhang, and J. Feng. Two birds with one stone: An efficient hierarchical framework for top-k and threshold-based string similarity search. In *ICDE*, 2015.

[23] J. Wang, G. Li, and J. Feng. Trie-join: Efficient trie-based string similarity joins with edit-distance constraints. *PVLDB*, 3(1):1219–1230, 2010.

[24] J. Wang, G. Li, and J. Feng. Fast-join: An efficient method for fuzzy token matching based string similarity join. In *ICDE*, pages 458–469, 2011.

[25] J. Wang, G. Li, and J. Feng. Can we beat the prefix filtering?: an adaptive framework for similarity join and search. In *SIGMOD Conference*, pages 85–96, 2012.

[26] W. Wang, J. Qin, C. Xiao, X. Lin, and H. T. Shen. Vchunkjoin: An efficient algorithm for edit similarity joins. *IEEE Trans. Knowl. Data Eng.*, 25(8):1916–1929, 2013.

[27] S. E. Whang, D. Menestrina, G. Koutrika, M. Theobald, and H. Garcia-Molina. Entity resolution with iterative blocking. In *SIGMOD Conference*, pages 219–232, 2009.

[28] C. Xiao, W. Wang, and X. Lin. Ed-join: an efficient algorithm for similarity joins with edit distance constraints. *PVLDB*, 1(1):933–944, 2008.

[29] C. Xiao, W. Wang, X. Lin, and J. X. Yu. Efficient similarity joins for near duplicate detection. In *WWW*, pages 131–140, 2008.

[30] Z. Zhang, M. Hadjieleftheriou, B. C. Ooi, and D. Srivastava. Bed-tree: an all-purpose index structure for string similarity search based on edit distance. In *SIGMOD*, pages 915–926, 2010.

APPENDIX

A. PROOF

A.1 Proof of Lemma 1

LEMMA 1. *The partial tree built by the* OPTIMAL-BOTTOMUP *is optimal.*

PROOF. Given any two tables $\mathcal{R}$ and $\mathcal{S}$, a complex similarity operation Φ with i atomic operations and a specified attribute order, we want to prove that the partial tree built by the OPTIMAL-BOTTOMUP is optimal. We prove it by reduction. For $i = 1$, there is only one atomic operation in Φ. There are only two prefix trees for this situation, one contains only one root node and the other one is a complete prefix tree. The OPTIMAL-BOTTOMUP selects the optimal one from these two prefix trees by comparing their costs. Thus the partial tree built by OPTIMAL-BOTTOMUP is optimal. Suppose for $i = n - 1$ the OPTIMAL-BOTTOMUP can find the optimal prefix tree. For $i = n$, for any prefix tree with depth larger than 0, the optimal one must be the one that all the subtrees rooted at the first level nodes are gotten by the OPTIMAL-BOTTOMUP method (when $i = n - 1$). Then the OPTIMAL-BOTTOMUP will compare the cost of this prefix tree with that of the prefix tree with only one root node and select the optimal one. As there is only one prefix tree with depth equal to 0 that is the one only contains a root node, the OPTIMAL-BOTTOMUP can find the optimal prefix tree when $i = n$. □

A.2 Proof of Lemma 2

To prove Lemma 2, we first introduce the problem of exact set cover as follows.

DEFINITION 1 (EXACT-COVER). *We are given a set $\mathcal{U}$ and a collection $\mathcal{C}$ of subsets of $\mathcal{U}$. Each set $S_i \in \mathcal{C}$ contains exactly 3 elements of $\mathcal{U}$. The* EXACT-COVER *problem asks if there exist $\frac{|\mathcal{U}|}{3}$ subsets in $\mathcal{C}$ which exactly covers the set $\mathcal{U}$ (i.e., each element of $\mathcal{U}$ is covered exactly once).*

The EXACT-COVER problem is a well known NP-Complete problem [7].

DEFINITION 2. (OPTIMAL PARTIAL PREFIX TREE PROBLEM (PARTIAL)). *Given two tables $\mathcal{R}$ and $\mathcal{S}$ and a complex similarity operation Φ, the* PARTIAL *problem is to find the optimal prefix tree with the minimum join cost.*

LEMMA 2. *The* PARTIAL *problem is NP-hard.*

PROOF. We present a reduction from the EXACT-COVER problem, which is NP-Complete. In our reduction, the two tables are the same, i.e., $\mathcal{R} = \mathcal{S}$. Given an instance ($\mathcal{U} = \{1, \ldots, n\}, \mathcal{C} = \{S_1, \ldots, S_m\}$) of EXACT-COVER, we construct a PARTIAL instance $(\Phi, \mathcal{R})$ as follows. The complex similarity operation Φ contains m atomic operations $\Phi_1, \Phi_2, \ldots, \Phi_m$ and the table R contains $n{+}1$ records $r_0, r_1, \ldots, r_n$. Each Φ_i corresponds to subset $S_i \in \mathcal{C}$ and record r_i corresponds to element $i \in \mathcal{U}$ for $1 \leq i \leq n$. r_0 is a *special record*. For each 3-size subset $S_i = \{x, y, z\}(1 \leq i \leq m, 1 \leq x, y, z \leq n)$, let $\texttt{pre}(r^i_x) = \{e_x\}$, $\texttt{pre}(r^i_y) = \{e_y\}$, $\texttt{pre}(r^i_z) = \{e_z\}$ and $\texttt{pre}(r^i_w) = \{e\}$ where $w \notin S_i$. Note e_x, e_y, e_z and e are all different tokens. For the special record r_0, let $\texttt{pre}(r^i_0) = \{e, e^i_0\}$ where e^i_0 is another different token. See Table 1 for an example.

R	$\texttt{pre}(R^1)$	$\texttt{pre}(R^2)$	$\texttt{pre}(R^3)$	$\texttt{pre}(R^4)$
r_0	$\{e^1_0, e\}$	$\{e^2_0, e\}$	$\{e^3_0, e\}$	$\{e^4_0, e\}$
r_1	$\{e_1\}$	$\{e\}$	$\{e\}$	$\{e\}$
r_2	$\{e_2\}$	$\{e_2\}$	$\{e\}$	$\{e\}$
r_3	$\{e_3\}$	$\{e_3\}$	$\{e_3\}$	$\{e\}$
r_4	$\{e\}$	$\{e_4\}$	$\{e_4\}$	$\{e_4\}$
r_5	$\{e\}$	$\{e\}$	$\{e_5\}$	$\{e_5\}$
r_6	$\{e\}$	$\{e\}$	$\{e\}$	$\{e_6\}$

Table 1: The table $\mathcal{R}$ ($\mathcal{R} = \mathcal{S}$) constructed from Exact-Cover instance ($\mathcal{U} = \{1, \ldots, 6\}$), $\mathcal{C} = \{S_1, \ldots, S_4\}$, where $S_1 = \{1, 2, 3\}$, $S_2 = \{2, 3, 4\}$, $S_3 = \{3, 4, 5\}$, $S_4 = \{4, 5, 6\}$.

Next we show that the EXACT-COVER instance has an exact cover if and only if there is a partial prefix tree for the corresponding PARTIAL instance with cost $n + \frac{n}{3} + 1$. Suppose we can find $\frac{n}{3}$ subsets $T_1, T_2, \ldots, T_{\frac{n}{3}}$ from $\mathcal{C}$ which can exactly cover U, we build a prefix tree with $\frac{n}{3} + 1$ levels. Each internal node (including the root) corresponding to a chosen subset T_i and each leaf corresponds to an element. Level 1 is the root node, which corresponds to T_1. The internal node at level i corresponds to T_i. For each $i \in [1, \frac{n}{3}]$, suppose $T_i = \{x, y, z\}$. Then, we can see T_i has five child nodes e, e_x, e_y, e_z, e^i_0. For ease of exposition, we always arrange e as the leftmost child of any internal node. Hence, all nodes on leftmost path (except the root) are labeled with token e and the rests are leaves. Moreover, each leaf node corresponds to a record in R (namely, e_x corresponds to r_x, ..., e^i_0 corresponds to r_0). We say a leaf corresponding to r_0 a *special leaf*. Therefore each leaf is associated with two same inverted lists (since $\mathcal{R} = \mathcal{S}$) with exactly one (the same) record. Each r_i for $1 \leq i \leq n$ appears exactly once and the special record r_0 appears $\frac{n}{3} + 1$ times as special leaves (each internal node has a special leaf, except that the last level has two special leaves, see Figure 1). This tree has a cost of $n + \frac{n}{3} + 1$.

Now we show the other direction: If there is a prefix tree with cost $n + \frac{n}{3} + 1$, the corresponding EXACT-COVER instance has an exact cover. Consider an arbitrary prefix tree. Suppose the set of internal nodes corresponds to a collection Q of subsets of $\mathcal{C}$. Suppose k elements are covered by Q. We can see the cost of the tree is $|Q|$ (each internal node has a special leaf r_0) $+k$ (each non-special leaf)$+$ $(n-k+1)^2$ (all uncovered elements and r_0 are all in the leftmost leaf). We know that $|Q| \geq k/3$. There are three cases:

1. If $k \leq n-1$, the above quantity is larger than $4n/3+1$, which does not satisfy the assumption.
2. If $k = n$ and $|Q| > n/3$, the above quantity is larger than $4n/3 + 1$, which does not satisfy the assumption.
3. If $k = n$ and $|Q| = n/3$, the above quantity is equal to $4n/3 + 1$ and the $n/3$ subsets in Q is an exact cover of $\mathcal{U}$.

This concludes that PARTIAL is NP-hard. □

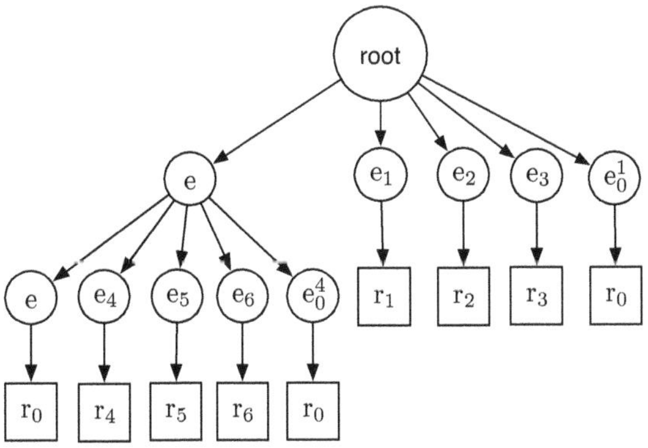

Figure 1: The optimal prefix tree built based on an exact cover $T_1 = S_1$ and $T_2 = S_4$ of the Exact-Cover instance in Table 1.

B. OTHER SIMILARITY FUNCTIONS

We give the definitions of COS and DICE.

- Cosine similarity: $\text{COS}(r_p^i, s_q^j) = \frac{|r_p^i \cap s_q^j|}{\sqrt{|r_p^i| \cdot |s_q^j|}}$.
- Dice similarity: $\text{DICE}(r_p^i, s_q^j) = \frac{2|r_p^i \cap s_q^j|}{|r_p^i| + |s_q^j|}$.

We compute the threshold o for COS and DICE.

- If $\text{COS}(r, s) \geq \tau$ then $o = \lceil \tau^2 |r| \rceil$.
- If $\text{DICE}(r, s) \geq \tau$ then $o = \lceil \frac{\tau}{2-\tau} |r| \rceil$.

C. BASELINE APPROACHES

Given an atomic similarity operation $\mathcal{R}^i \sim \mathcal{S}^j$, the prefix filter identifies the pairs of records whose prefixes on the two attributes overlap as the candidates. To efficiently compute the candidate, we can build an inverted index on top of the tokens. Each token is associated with an inverted list of records whose prefixes on the attribute contain the token. Then we can utilize the inverted lists to identify candidates.

Baseline Approaches. We extend prefix filtering to support complex similarity operations and give the following baselines.

(1) Intersection-based Method. For each predicate, we use existing algorithms to identify the similar answers on this predicate, and then intersect them to compute the final answers. This method has two weaknesses. First, it is rather expensive to compute the similar results for every predicate, especially there are many predicates. Second, there may be large numbers of candidates for each predicate and it is time- and space-consuming to maintain and intersect the intermediate results.

(2) Pipeline-based Method. It first computes the results for a predicate and then verifies these candidates using other similarity predicates. Since the candidates are record pairs, we cannot utilize existing indexes to do further pruning and have to verify them by computing their similarities on other predicates. This method has the following disadvantages. First, a single attribute has low pruning power and it will generate a large number of candidates. Second, it is important to determine an appropriate order of predicates as different orders have different pruning power. It is challenging to select the best order.

(3) 2Concatenate Method. It concatenates two selective attributes as a single attribute. However it is nontrivial to concatenate two attributes, because different attributes may use different similarity functions, e.g., edit distance and Jaccard. To address this issue, we first transform them to the overlap similarity. Then given the two most selective attributes, we calculate the overlap thresholds o^1 and o^2 for the two attributes. Next we concatenate tokens of the two attributes, use $o = o^1 + o^2$ as the new overlap threshold, and generate the signatures for the concatenated attribute. This method would generate large numbers of candidates. Actually the candidate set obtained by the concatenate-based method is a super set of the candidate set obtained by the intersection-based method.[3]

(4) 2Selective Method. Given a simlarity operation, it first selectes two most selective attributes, identifies the candidates of the two attributes, and then intersects them.

(5) Extending The Roll-up Algorithm [21] to Generate CBlockTree. We extended the roll up algorithm [21] to construct a CBlockTree so as to reduce the join cost of our prefix tree. Figure 2 illustrates a CBlockTree. It first builds a complete prefix tree, then enumerates every pair of leaf nodes and merges any two leaves with the join cost on the merged node smaller than the join cost on the two individual leaves. Although this method can reduce the candidate size, it has a large overhead to enumerate every pair of leaves. Since a prefix has many leaves, checking every pair of leaves is rather expensive. Moreover, our problem focuses on improving the performance, and thus this method is not efficient to address our problem.

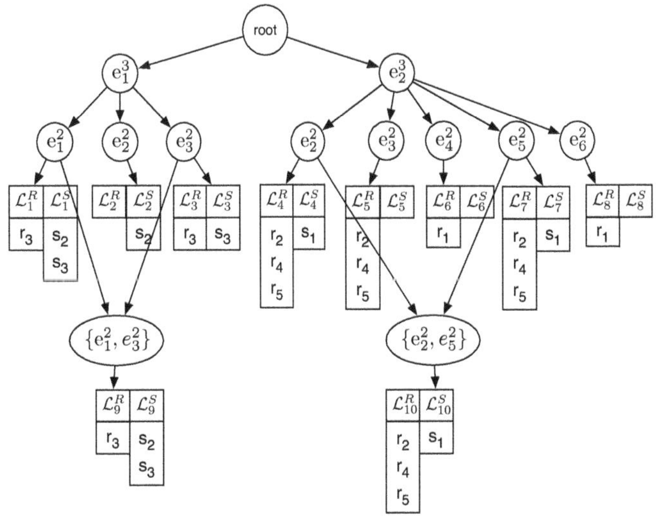

Figure 2: Merge leaves in Prefix Tree to further reduce cost. (Tables $\mathcal{R}$ and $\mathcal{S}$ from Figure 2)

[3]Consider a record with two attributes, $\{a, b, c, d\}$ and $\{\alpha, \beta, \gamma, \delta\}$, where the token orders are $a < b < c < d$ and $\alpha < \beta < \gamma < \delta$ respectively. Suppose $o_1 = 2$ and $o_2 = 1$. The prefixes of the two attributes are $\{a, b\}$ and $\{\alpha\}$. The intersection-based method takes $(\mathcal{L}(a) \cup \mathcal{L}(b)) \cap \mathcal{L}(\alpha)$ as candidates, where $\mathcal{L}(a)$ is the inverted list of a. The pipeline-based method takes $\mathcal{L}(a) \cup \mathcal{L}(b)$ or $\mathcal{L}(\alpha)$ as candidates. The concatenated attribute is $\{a, b, c, d, \alpha, \beta, \gamma, \delta\}$. Then the prefix filtering selects 3 signatures from $\{a, b, c, d, \alpha, \beta, \gamma, \delta\}$ in order. Based on the order, there are 4 possible cases: $\{a, b, c\}$, $\{a, b, \alpha\}$, $\{a, \alpha, \beta\}$, $\{\alpha, \beta, \gamma\}$. The candidates are respectively $\mathcal{L}(a) \cup \mathcal{L}(b) \cup \mathcal{L}(c)$, $\mathcal{L}(a) \cup \mathcal{L}(b) \cup \mathcal{L}(\alpha)$, $\mathcal{L}(a) \cup \mathcal{L}(\alpha) \cup \mathcal{L}(\beta)$, $\mathcal{L}(\alpha) \cup \mathcal{L}(\beta) \cup \mathcal{L}(\gamma)$. In any case, the result is a super set of the candidates obtained by the intersection-based method. In addition, in most cases, the concatenate-based method is even worse than the pipeline-based method.

D. COMPLEXITY

D.1 Time Complexity of Constructing The Optimal Prefix Tree

Time Complexity: Given two tables $\mathcal{R}$ and $\mathcal{S}$ and a complex similarity operation $\Phi = \mathcal{R}^{i_1} \sim \mathcal{S}^{j_1} \wedge \mathcal{R}^{i_2} \sim \mathcal{S}^{j_2} \wedge \cdots \wedge \mathcal{R}^{i_k} \sim \mathcal{S}^{j_k}$. The OPTIMAL-BOTTOMUP builds the optimal prefix tree by two steps. The first step of building the complete prefix tree has a time complexity of $\mathcal{O}\Big((|\mathcal{R}| + |\mathcal{S}|)|\hat{\texttt{pre}}|^k\Big)$, where $|\hat{\texttt{pre}}|$ is the maximal prefix length of an attribute. (It is worth noting that $|\hat{\texttt{pre}}|$ is not large, which is not larger than the size of the corresponding token set). The second step of generating the optimal tree has a time complexity of $\mathcal{O}\Big(k(|\mathcal{R}| + |\mathcal{S}|)|\hat{\texttt{pre}}|^k\Big)$, where k is the number of predicates in the complex similarity operation. This is because there are at most $(|\mathcal{R}| + |\mathcal{S}|)|\hat{\texttt{pre}}|^k$ records in inverted lists of all leaves, and each record will be checked at most k times to build the optimal tree.

D.2 Time Complexity of Constructing The Greedy Prefix Tree

Time Complexity: In the worst case, the greedy prefix tree is exactly the same as the complete prefix tree, and thus the time complexity of building the greedy prefix tree is $\mathcal{O}\Big((|\mathcal{R}| + |\mathcal{S}|)|\hat{\texttt{pre}}|^k\Big)$. In practice, many internal nodes will not split and the greedy algorithm can be very efficient.

D.3 Space Complexity of Prefix Tree

Space Complexity: In the worst case, the optimal prefix tree is exactly the same as the complete prefix tree. The size of the prefix tree consists two parts. The first part is the number of records on inverted lists of leaf nodes, i.e., $\mathcal{O}\Big((|\mathcal{R}| + |\mathcal{S}|)|\hat{\texttt{pre}}|^k\Big)$, where $|\hat{\texttt{pre}}|$ is the maximal prefix length of an attribute. The second part is the number of tree nodes, which is $\mathcal{O}\Big(|\texttt{pre}(\mathcal{R})|^k + |\texttt{pre}(\mathcal{S})|^k\Big)$, where $|\texttt{pre}(\mathcal{R})|$ is the number of unique prefix tokens in an attribute. Thus the total space cost is $\mathcal{O}\Big((|\mathcal{R}| + |\mathcal{S}|)|\hat{\texttt{pre}}|^k + |\texttt{pre}(\mathcal{R})|^k + |\texttt{pre}(\mathcal{S})|^k\Big)$. In practice, the size of the optimal prefix tree is much smaller than the size of the complete prefix tree, because many internal nodes will not split.

E. OPTIMALITY OF THE GREEDY VERIFICATION ALGORITHM

For simplicity, we use c_i to denote $\Theta(\langle\Phi_i, \Gamma_i\rangle)$ and p_i to denote $\mathcal{P}(\langle\Phi_i, \Gamma_i\rangle)$. Our goal is to find an order π such that $\textsc{Cost}(\pi) = \sum_i c_{\pi(i)} \cdot \prod_{j=1}^{i-1}(1 - p_{\pi(j)})$ is minimized. We need to prove the optimal order is the increasing order of c_i/p_i. We prove by contradiction. Suppose π is an optimal order but $c_{\pi(k)}/p_{\pi(k)} > c_{\pi(k+1)}/p_{\pi(k+1)}$ for some k. Consider the order π' obtained by swapping $\pi(k)$ and $\pi(k+1)$. We can see that

$$\textsc{Cost}(\pi) - \textsc{Cost}(\pi') = \prod_{j=1}^{k-1}(1 - p_{\pi(j)})\times$$

$$\big(c_{\pi(k)} + c_{\pi(k+1)}(1 - p_k) - (c_{\pi(k+1)} + c_{\pi(k)} \cdot (1 - p_{\pi(k+1)})\big)$$

$$= \prod_{j=1}^{k-1}(1 - p_{\pi(j)})\,\big(c_{\pi(k)}p_{\pi(k+1)} - c_{\pi(k+1)}p_{\pi(k)}\big) > 0.$$

This contradicts that π is the optimal order. Thus our greedy verification algorithm is optimal.

Holistic Indexing in Main-memory Column-stores

Eleni Petraki
CWI Amsterdam
petraki@cwi.nl

Stratos Idreos
Harvard University
stratos@seas.harvard.edu

Stefan Manegold
CWI Amsterdam
manegold@cwi.nl

ABSTRACT

Great database systems performance relies heavily on index tuning, i.e., creating and utilizing the best indices depending on the workload. However, the complexity of the index tuning process has dramatically increased in recent years due to ad-hoc workloads and shortage of time and system resources to invest in tuning.

This paper introduces *holistic indexing*, a new approach to automated index tuning in dynamic environments. Holistic indexing requires zero set-up and tuning effort, relying on adaptive index creation as a side-effect of query processing. Indices are created incrementally and partially; they are continuously refined as we process more and more queries. Holistic indexing takes the state-of-the-art adaptive indexing ideas a big step further by introducing the notion of a system which never stops refining the index space, taking educated decisions about which index we should incrementally refine next based on continuous knowledge acquisition about the running workload and resource utilization. When the system detects idle CPU cycles, it utilizes those extra cycles by refining the adaptive indices which are most likely to bring a benefit for future queries. Such idle CPU cycles occur when the system cannot exploit all available cores up to 100%, i.e., either because the workload is not enough to saturate the CPUs or because the current tasks performed for query processing are not easy to parallelize to the point where all available CPU power is exploited.

In this paper, we present the design of holistic indexing for column-oriented database architectures and we discuss a detailed analysis against parallel versions of state-of-the-art indexing and adaptive indexing approaches. Holistic indexing is implemented in an open-source column-store DBMS. Our detailed experiments on both synthetic and standard benchmarks (TPC-H) and workloads (SkyServer) demonstrate that holistic indexing brings significant performance gains by being able to continuously refine the physical design in parallel to query processing, exploiting any idle CPU resources.

Categories and Subject Descriptors

H.2.2 [**Database Management**]: Physical Design

Keywords

Holistic Indexing, Self-organization

SIGMOD'15, May 31–June 4, 2015, Melbourne, Victoria, Australia.

http://dx.doi.org/10.1145/2723372.2723719.

1. INTRODUCTION

The big data era is causing the research community to rethink fundamental issues in the design of database systems towards more usable systems [32] that can access data better and faster [36, 37, 39, 40], that can better exploit modern hardware and opportunities for massive parallelization [15] that can support efficient processing of OLTP and/or OLAP queries [6, 34, 35, 41].

The Physical Design Problem. Physical design, and in particular proper index selection, is a predominant factor for the performance of database systems and has only become more crucial in the big data era. With new dynamic and exploratory environments, physical design becomes especially hard given the instability of workloads and the continuous stream of big data; a single physical design choice is not necessarily correct or useful for long stretches of time, while at the same time workload knowledge is scarce given the exploratory user behavior.

State-of-the-Art. In database applications, where "the future is known", physical design is assigned to database administrators who may also be assisted by auto-tuning tools [5, 14, 50]. Still though, a significant amount of human intervention is necessary and everything needs to happen offline. Thus, offline indexing can be applied with good results only on applications where there is enough workload knowledge and idle time to prepare the physical design appropriately before queries arrive.

Unfortunately, for many modern applications "the future is unknown", e.g., in scientific databases, social networks, web logs, etc. In particular, the query processing patterns follow an exploratory behavior, which changes so arbitrarily that it cannot be predicted. Such environments cannot be handled by offline indexing. Online indexing [10, 47] and adaptive indexing [27] are two approaches to automatic physical design in such dynamic environments, but none of them in isolation handles the problem sufficiently. Online indexing periodically refines the physical design but it may negatively affect running queries every time it needs to use resources for reconsidering the physical design and it may not be quick to follow the workload changes as it reacts only periodically. Adaptive indexing does not have this problem as it introduces continuous, incremental and partial index refinement but it adjusts the physical design only during query processing based on queries.

Always Indexing. In this paper, we make the observation that in real systems there are plenty of resources that remain under-utilized and we propose to exploit those resources to be able to better address dynamic and ad-hoc environments. In particular, we focus on exploiting CPU cycles to the maximum by continuously detecting idle CPU cycles and using them to refine the physical design (in parallel with query processing). Such idle CPU cycles occur when the system does not exploit all available cores up to 100%. We distinguish between "*idle time*" as in "*there is no user-driven work-*

Indexing	Statistical analysis	Exploitation of idle resources *before* query processing	Exploitation of idle resources *during* query processing	Index materialization	Updates, projection cost	Workload
Offline	√	√	×	full	high	static
Online	√	×	√	full	high	dynamic
Adaptive	×	×	×	partial	low	dynamic
Holistic	√	√	√	partial	low	dynamic

Table 1: Qualitative difference among offline, online, adaptive and holistic indexing.

load at all and the entire CPU (all its hardware contexts) is idle (except possible occasional operating system background activity)" and "*idle CPU resources*" as in "*the active user-driven workload does / can not use all physically available CPU hardware contexts.*" Intuitively, there are two options when resources are under-utilized but still there are active queries in the system. The first option is to introduce more parallel query processing algorithms to maximize utilization for the existing workload. The second one is to exploit the extra resources towards a different goal (extra indexing actions in our case). We investigate and compare both directions.

Holistic Indexing. In this paper, we introduce a new indexing approach, called *holistic indexing*. Holistic indexing addresses the automatic physical design problem in modern applications with dynamic and exploratory workloads. It continuously monitors the workload and the CPU utilization; when idle CPU cycles are detected, holistic indexing exploits them in order to partially and incrementally adjust the physical design based on the collected statistical information. Each index refinement step may take only a few microseconds to complete and the system will typically perform several such steps in one go depending on available system resources. Everything happens in parallel to query processing but without disturbing running queries. The net effect is that holistic indexing refines the physical design, improving performance and robustness by enabling better data access patterns for future queries. Table 1 summarizes the qualitative difference between holistic indexing and current state-of-the-art indexing approaches. Compared to past approaches, holistic indexing manages to minimize both initialization and maintenance costs, as it relies on partial indexing, and to exploit all possible CPU resources in order to provide a more complete physical design.

Contributions. Our contributions are as follows:

- We introduce the idea of exploiting idle CPU resources towards continuously adapting the physical design to ad-hoc and dynamic workloads.
- We discuss in detail the design of holistic indexing on top of modern column-store architectures, i.e., how to detect and exploit idle CPU resources during query processing.
- We implemented holistic indexing in an open-source column-store, MonetDB [26, 52]. Through a detailed experimental analysis both with microbenchmarks and with TPC-H we demonstrate that we can exploit idle CPU resources to prepare the physical design better, leading to significant improvements over past indexing approaches in dynamic environments.

Paper Structure. The rest of the paper is structured as follows: Section 2 provides an overview of related work. In Section 3, we shortly recap the basics of column-store architectures and the basics of adaptive indexing. Then, Section 4 introduces holistic indexing, while Section 5 presents a detailed experimental analysis. Finally, Section 6 discusses future work and concludes the paper.

2. RELATED WORK

In this section we briefly discuss previous approaches to automated physical design, i.e., offline, online and adaptive indexing.

Offline Indexing. Offline indexing is the earliest approach on self-tuning database systems. Nowadays, all major database products offer auto-tuning tools [5, 14, 50] to automate the database physical design. Auto-tuning tools mainly rely on a "what-if analysis" [12] and close interaction with the optimizer [11] to decide which indices are potentially more useful for a given workload.

Offline indexing requires heavy involvement of a database administrator (DBA). Specifically, a DBA invokes the tool and provides its input, i.e., a representative workload. The tool analyzes the given workload and recommends an appropriate physical design. However, the DBA is the one that decides which of the changes in the physical design should be applied. The main limitation of offline indexing appears when the workload cannot be predicted and/or there is not enough idle time to invest in the offline analysis and the physical design implementation.

Online Indexing. Online indexing addresses the limitation of offline indexing. Instead of making all decisions a priori, the system continuously monitors the workload and the physical design is periodically reevaluated. System COLT [47] was one of the first online indexing approaches. COLT continuously monitors the workload and periodically in specific epochs, i.e., every N queries, it reconsiders the physical design. The recommended physical design might demand creation of new indices or dropping of old ones. COLT requires many calls to the optimizer to obtain cost estimations. A "lighter" approach, i.e., requiring less calls to the optimizer, was proposed later [10]. Soft indices [43] extended the previous online approaches by building full indices on-the-fly concurrently with queries on the same data, sharing the scan operator.

The main limitation of online indexing is that reorganization of the physical design can be a costly action that a) requires a significant amount of time to complete and b) requires a lot of resources. This means that online indexing is appropriate mainly for moderately dynamic workloads where the query patterns do not change very frequently. Otherwise, it may be that by the time we finish adapting the physical design, the workload has changed again leading to a suboptimal performance.

Adaptive Indexing. Adaptive indexing is the latest and the most lightweight approach in self-tuning databases. Adaptive indexing addresses the limitations of offline and online indexing for dynamic workloads; it instantly adjusts to workload changes by building or refining indices partially and incrementally as part of query processing. By reacting to every single query with lightweight actions, adaptive indexing manages to instantly adapt to a changing workload. As more queries arrive, the more the indices are refined and the more performance improves. Adaptive indexing has been studied in the context of main-memory column-stores [27, 48], Hadoop [46] as well as for improving more traditional disk-based settings [20]. It has been shown to work for many core database architecture issues such as updates [28], multi-attribute queries [29], concurrency control [8, 16, 17], partition-merge-like logic [20, 31]. In addition, [18] shows how to benchmark adaptive indexing techniques, while stochastic database cracking [21] shows how to be robust on various workloads and [19] shows how adaptive indexing can apply to key columns. Finally, recent work on parallel adaptive indexing studies CPU-efficient implementations and proposes algorithms to exploit multi-cores [8, 44]. Recently, adaptive indexing concepts have been extended to provide adaptive indexes for time series data [51] as well as using incoming queries for more broad storage layout decisions, i.e., reorganizing base data (columns/rows) according to incoming query requests [7], or even about which data should be loaded [25]. In addition, adaptive indexing ideas have been used to design new generation data exploration tools such as touch-based data systems [30, 42].

The main limitation of adaptive indexing is that it works only during query processing. In this way, the only opportunity to improve the physical design is only when queries arrive.

Database Systems for the Multi-core Era. Modern hardware offers opportunities for high parallelism; a single machine may be equipped with chip multiprocessors, which contain multiple cores with support for multiple context threads. Recent research focuses on exploiting parallelism opportunities by a) processing multiple queries concurrently, and b) by parallelizing tasks in the critical path during query processing [22, 23, 24, 33]. Sorting is one of the most important database tasks (and a core component of adaptive indexing in column-stores) that can be highly-parallelized using modern hardware advances [9, 38, 45, 49].

Holistic Indexing. Contrary to past indexing approaches, holistic indexing results in an always-on self-tuning database system. Holistic indexing is inspired by all past approaches and it maintains the design points which are useful for dynamic workloads. For example, it uses adaptive indices as in adaptive indexing and it monitors the workload as in online indexing. Contrary to other approaches though, holistic indexing is always active, always trying to improve the physical design with every opportunity that occurs when it detects under-utilized CPU cores. Compared to recent research that tries to adapt modern database systems to the multi-core era by parallelizing core database operators, holistic indexing provides an additional way to exploit those resources when either the workload is not enough to saturate the CPUs or when simply we cannot fully parallelize all database actions.

3. BACKGROUND

Holistic indexing is designed for column-oriented database architectures and it exploits the main design points of adaptive indexing. In this section, we provide the necessary technical background about column-store database architectures [4] and we discuss the basics of adaptive indexing.

3.1 Column-oriented DBMS

Column-oriented DBMS are inspired by the Decomposition Storage Model [13]. Data is stored one column at a time instead of one row at a time as in traditional row-oriented DBMS. Every relational table is vertically fragmented into a set of columns (one for each attribute). Each value of a single tuple is stored in the same position across all columns. Full vertical fragmentation significantly reduces the I/O and memory footprint of queries that require only part of a table's attributes; only the attributes that are relevant to a query are loaded from disk to memory. Moreover, the alignment across all base columns allows for efficient late tuple reconstruction with tuple order-preserving operators. For instance, assume the following query.

select B from R where A>10 and A<20

A column-store DBMS performs two main steps to answer this query. First, a select operator searches column *A* for attribute values between 10 and 20. The intermediate result is a new column which contains the positions of the qualifying attribute values in the relation. Second, a project operator fetches the values residing in attribute *B* at the positions specified by the intermediate result. Thus, column-oriented architectures allow for independent manipulation of the columns that are relevant to the query, which allows for operator implementations that exploit CPU and cache friendly patterns with tight for loops in an array-processing style.

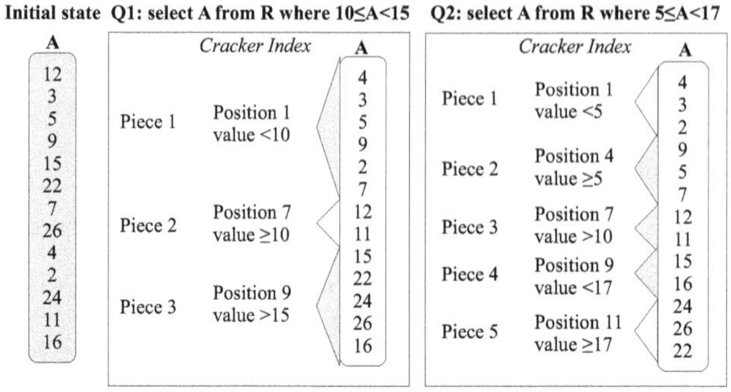

Figure 1: Adaptive indexing.

With no indexing support, a column-store select operator has to completely scan a column in order to identify the qualifying tuples. The cost of scanning a column with N tuples is expressed in data accesses, i.e., how many of the column values are "touched", and thus it is $O(N)$. The search for the qualifying tuples can be accelerated by orders of magnitude with a full indexing strategy. That is, we can first sort a column and then we may use binary search actions to find the qualifying tuples. The average cost of a binary search is $O(log(N))$, while the average cost of sorting an entire column in memory, e.g., using quicksort, is $O(N * log(N))$.

3.2 Adaptive Indexing

The cost of the sorting phase is a considerable overhead. Adaptive indexing is a significantly more lightweight approach that spreads the sorting cost across many queries in the workload. This helps when there is not enough idle time to create the full index upfront and the system has to answer queries. In addition, it is helpful when we do not know which columns are relevant for the workload a priori so we can sort them. This is especially important as today, as applications and schemas get more complex, we may have hundreds of columns in a database.

In adaptive indexing, the first time an attribute *A* is required by a query, a copy of the base column A is created, called *the cracker column* A_{CRK} of *A*. Each selection operator on A triggers the physical reorganization of A_{CRK} based on the requested range of the query. The query predicates are used as a hint on how the data should be stored, i.e., values that are less than the lower bound are moved before the lower bound while values that are greater than the upper bound are moved after the upper bound in the respective column. Thus, the column is partitioned on-the-fly, i.e., during query processing, based on the query predicates. The partitioning information for each cracker column is maintained in an AVL-tree, called *cracker index* of A. Index refinement is integrated with the query processing, since it is part of the select operator. Future queries on column *A* search the cracker index for the partition where the requested range falls. If the requested values already exist in the index, i.e., if past queries have cracked on exactly those ranges, then the select operator can return the result immediately. Otherwise, the select operator refines on-the-fly the column further, i.e., only the partitions/pieces of the column where the predicates fall will be reorganized.

For instance, Figure 1 shows an example of two queries cracking a single column, one after the other. The first query creates three partitions, while the second query refines only the first partition, where its lower bound falls, and the third partition, where its upper bound falls. The more queries arrive, the more partitions/pieces are created. Thus, future queries have to refine smaller and smaller pieces, which results in a performance improvement as smaller pieces means that queries need to access less data.

The cost of the first cracking query in terms of data accesses is $O(N)$, since it has to analyze every tuple in the column. Assuming for simplicity that every query cracks a single piece in half, then the second query will touch N/2 tuples and so on. Thus, the cost of the i-th query becomes $N/2^{floor(log_2(i))}$. The i-th query pays also the cost of searching the values in the cracker index. This cost is at most log(i), i.e., the depth of the AVL-tree.

The overall cost depends on the workload. However, the tendency is always the same; as more queries arrive, more partitions are created and, and each query has to touch less and less data during the select operator. In this way, adaptive indexing provides a lightweight alternative to full indexing; it can instantly adjust to a workload change and keep improving as the workload patterns persist, eventually reaching similar performance to full indexing but without requiring big initialization costs and workload knowledge.

Holistic Indexing vs. Adaptive Indexing. Holistic indexing maintains the design points of adaptive indexing, i.e., lightweight indexing with partial and incremental indices integrated with query processing. It extends adaptive indexing in that with holistic indexing the adaptive indices are continuously refined and improved; holistic indexing is always active; it continuously monitors the workload and the CPU utilization and reorganizes the physical design concurrently with query processing as soon as there are under-utilized CPU resources.

4. HOLISTIC INDEXING

In this section we discuss the fundamentals of holistic indexing. We designed holistic indexing on top of column-store architectures inspired by their flexibility on manipulating some attributes without affecting the rest. During query processing indices are built and optimized incrementally by adapting to query predicates, as in adaptive indexing. However, in contrast to adaptive indexing, index refinement actions are not triggered only as a side-effect of query processing; in holistic indexing incremental index optimization actions take place continuously in order to exploit under-utilized CPU cores. Thus, concurrently with user queries, system queries also refine the index space. Holistic indexing monitors the workload and CPU resources utilization and every time it detects that the system is under-utilized it exploits statistical information to decide which indices to refine and by how much.

Thus, with holistic indexing we achieve an always active self-organizing DBMS by continuously adjusting the physical design to workload demands.

Problem Definition: *Given a set of adaptive indices, statistical information about the past workload, storage constraints and the CPU utilization, continuously select indices from the index space and incrementally refine them, while the materialized index space size does not exceed the storage budget.*

In the rest of this section, we discuss in detail how we fit holistic indexing in a modern DBMS architecture.

4.1 Preliminary Definitions

First, we give a series of definitions.

Workload. A workload W consists of a sequence of user queries, inserts and deletes. Updates are translated into a deletion that is followed by an insertion.

CPU Utilization. CPU utilization in a time interval dt describes how much of the available CPU power is used in dt. Specifically, it expresses the percentage of total CPU time, i.e., the amount of time for which the CPU is used for processing user or kernel processes instead of being idle. CPU utilization is calculated using (operating system) kernel statistics.

Configuration. A configuration is defined as a set of adaptive indices that can be used in the physical design. There are three kinds of configurations. The *actual configuration*, C_{actual}, contains indices on attributes that have already been accessed by user queries in the workload. Indices are inserted in C_{actual} when they are created during query processing. For instance, assume a query Q enters the system and contains a selection on an attribute A. If the adaptive index on A does not exist, it is created on-the-fly and it is inserted in C_{actual}.

Besides C_{actual}, holistic indexing also maintains the *potential configuration*. $C_{potential}$, which contains indices on attributes that have not been queried yet. Indices are inserted in $C_{potential}$ either automatically by the system or manually by the user. Finally, the *optimal configuration*, $C_{optimal}$, contains indices that have reached the optimal status (the next paragraph describes when an index is considered optimal). The union of C_{actual} and $C_{potential}$ constitutes the index space *IS*, i.e., the indices which are candidates for incremental optimization when the system is under-utilized. Later, in Section 4.2, we describe how the system is educated to pick an index from *IS*. Indices from $C_{optimal}$ are not considered for further refinement during the physical design reorganization.

Optimal Index. Holistic indexing exploits adaptive indices. As seen in Section 3.2, an adaptive index is refined during query processing by physically reorganizing pieces of the cracker column based on query predicates. As more queries arrive, more pieces are created, and thus, the pieces become smaller. We have found that when the size of the pieces becomes equal to L_1 cache size ($|L_1|$), further refinements are not necessary; a smaller size increases administration costs to maintain the extra pieces and it does not bring any significant extra benefit as scanning inside L_1 is fast anyway (no cache misses). Pieces of size smaller than L_1 cache can either be sorted or queries simply need to scan them (a range select operator has to scan at most two L_1 pieces). An index I on an attribute A is considered optimal (I_{opt}), when the average size of pieces ($|p|$) in A_{CRK} is equal to the size of L_1 cache. Equation (1) describes the distance between I and I_{opt}.

$$d(I, I_{opt}) = |p| - |L_1| = \frac{N_A}{p_A} - |L_1| \quad (1)$$

N_A is the total number of tuples in A_{CRK} while p_A is the total number of pieces in A_{CRK}. This information is readily available and thus we can easily calculate the average piece size in a cracker column and in turn we can calculate the distance of the respective cracker index from its optimal status.

Statistical Information. During query processing holistic indexing continuously monitors the workload and the CPU utilization. For each column in the schema it collects information regarding how many times it has been accessed by user queries, how many pieces the relevant cracker column contains, how many queries did not need to further refine the index because there was an exact hit. Besides the statistical information about the workload, kernel statistics are used in order to monitor the CPU utilization.

4.2 System Design

Holistic indexing is always active. It continuously monitors the workload and the CPU utilization. When under-utilized CPU cores are detected, holistic indexing exploits them in order to adjust the physical design based on the collected statistical information. The system performs several index refinement steps simultaneously depending on available CPU resources. Everything happens in parallel to query processing, but without disturbing running queries.

We discuss in detail the continuous tuning process and how to exploit under-utilized CPU cycles. We also discuss how existing adaptive indexing solutions on core database architectures issues-such as updates and concurrency control can be directly adapted to work with holistic indexing.

Statistics per Column/Index. Statistics per column are collected during query processing. This is the job of the select operator as it is within the select operator that all (user query) adaptive indexing actions take place. Every time an attribute is accessed for a selection of a user query, the select operator updates a data structure, which contains all statistics for the respective index. Given that the select operator performs adaptive indexing actions anyway, it already has access to critical information such as how many new pieces were created during new cracking actions for this query, whether the select was an exact match, etc. All information is stored in a heap structure (one node per index) which allows us to easily put new indices in the configuration or drop old ones. The structure is protected with read/write latches as multiple queries or holistic workers (discussed later on) may be cracking in parallel.

Tuning Cycle. At all times there is an active *holistic indexing thread* which runs in parallel to user queries. The responsibility of the holistic indexing thread is to monitor the CPU utilization and to activate *holistic worker threads* to perform auxiliary index refinement actions whenever idle CPU cycles are detected. The tuning process is shown in Figure 2. The holistic indexing thread continuously monitors the CPU load at intervals of 1 second at a time. In case holistic worker threads are activated, the holistic indexing thread waits for all worker threads to finish and measures the CPU utilization within the next 1 second. In our analysis, we found that 1 second is the time limit that gives proper kernel statistics. When n idle CPU cores are detected, n holistic worker threads are activated. Each worker thread executes an instance of the IdleFunction, which picks an index from the Index Space IS and performs x partial index refinement actions on it. Every time an index is refined, the respective statistics, e.g., distance from the optimal index, are updated. When an index reaches the optimal status, it is moved into the optimal configuration $C_{optimal}$.

A side-effect of the tuning process is that some of the holistic worker threads might remain idle while the holistic indexing thread waits for all workers to finish. However, as we show later in Section 5.1 (Figure 6(d)), this happens only for very short periods of time and as the system adapts to the workload this phenomenon disappears (as the pieces queried in the adaptive indices become smaller and smaller the holistic indexing workers end up doing tasks of similar weight as none is going to touch a very big piece).

Index Refinement. Every time a worker thread wakes up, it performs x index refinements on a single column. x is a tuning parameter. In our analysis in Section 5.5 (Figure 15) we found that a good value for our hardware set-up is $x = 16$. The index refinements are performed by picking x random values in the domain of the respective attribute and cracking the column based on these values. In this way, each time a worker thread cracks a single piece of a column it splits this piece into two new pieces based on the pivot.

There are numerous choices on how to choose a pivot. We found that picking a random pivot is the most cost efficient choice. Other options include to crack the biggest piece of the column, i.e., with the rationale that this takes more work out of future queries. Another option is to crack the smallest piece, i.e., with the rationale that this piece is small because it is hot (because many queries access it for cracking). However, such options are hard to achieve

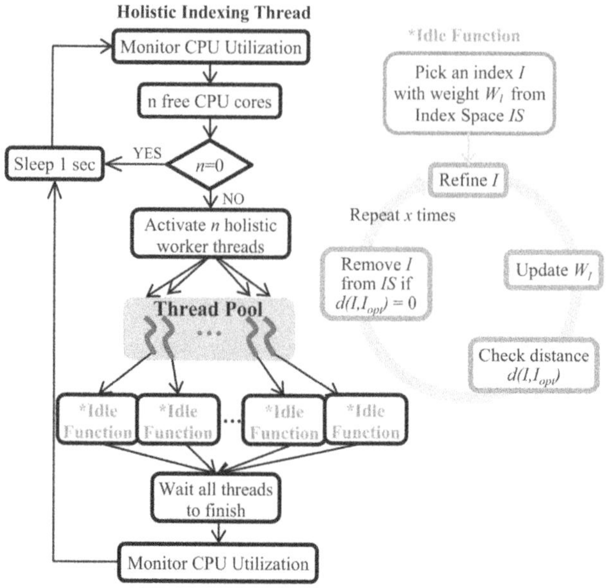

Figure 2: Tuning actions.

in a lightweight way as we need to maintain a structure such as a priority queue to know which piece is the biggest or smallest every time. Since every cracking action costs a few microseconds or milliseconds it is not worth the extra storage and CPU cost to maintain auxiliary structures. Random pivots converge quickly to cracking the whole domain, providing a column which is balanced in terms of which pieces are cracked and requiring no extra costs in deciding which pivot to choose.

Index Decision Strategies. Another decision we have to make is which index to refine out of the pool of candidate indices. Here, we describe four different strategies we can follow in order to pick an index from the index space. The notion behind the first three strategies is that, since the only information we have is the past workload, we can exploit this information in order to prepare the physical design for a similar future workload. On the contrary, the fourth strategy makes random choices.

For all strategies, a weight W_I is assigned to each index I in the index space. When an index I is added in the candidate indices, its weight is initialized to the distance between I and I_{opt}, which is given by Equation (1). For each index I, initially, there is only one partition ($p_I = 1$) in I, i.e., the entire column. Thus, the initial weight $W_{I_{init}}$ is equal to $N_I - L_{1_s}$, where N_I is the cardinality of the respective attribute (with type T) and L_{1_s} is the number of elements of type T that can fit into L_1 cache. The weight is used as a priority number in the first three strategies. The index with the highest priority, i.e., the maximum weight, in C_{actual} is refined first. When W_I becomes equal to zero, I is transferred from C_{actual} to $C_{optimal}$ and it is not considered for further refinement in the future. If C_{actual} is empty, an index is randomly picked from $C_{potential}$. The weight of each index is constantly updated after every index refinement regardless of whether it is caused by a user query or by holistic indexing. Below we describe the four strategies.

- **W1:** $W_I = d_I = d(I, I_{opt})$. Using this strategy, we give a priority to indices with large partitions.
- **W2:** $W_I = f_I * d_I$. Priority is given to indices that have large partitions and at the same time are accessed frequently in the workload. f_I is the number of user queries that access I.
- **W3:** $W_I = (f_I - f_{I_h}) * d_I$. In this strategy we try to identify indices that are accessed frequently in the workload and at the same time have large partitions, because they have a high

Example of latching actions in holistic indexing. It depicts latching actions during concurrent processing of two user queries and a holistic worker thread (HW). HW cracks a random piece. Red box indicates a write latch. Green box indicates a read latch. Grey boxes indicate pieces that are free to be refined by holistic worker threads.

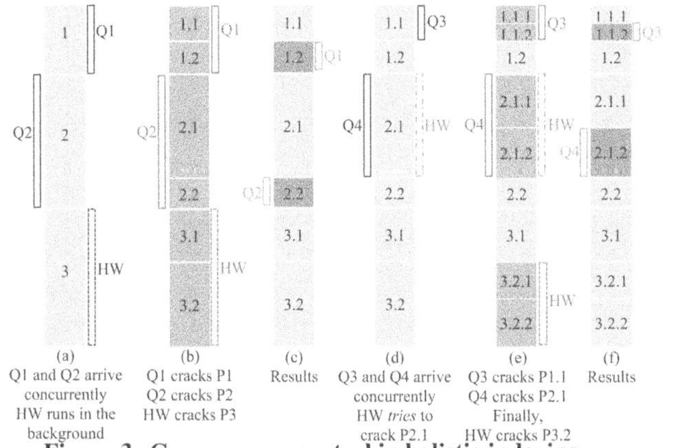

Figure 3: Concurrency control in holistic indexing.

hit rate. These indices have a smaller priority compared to indices with large partitions that are accessed less frequently. f_I is the number of user queries that access I, while f_{I_h} is the number of user queries that do not trigger a refinement of I because the requested value bound already exists in I.

- **W4:** Make a random choice.

Overall, our analysis, which is described later in Section 5.4 (Figure 13), with numerous workloads showed that even though small improvements can be achieved when picking the perfect strategy for each workload, the random strategy gives a good and robust overall solution that is always close to the best for all workloads.

Concurrency Control. An index refinement due to holistic indexing happens in parallel with user queries. Since user queries may also cause refinement of adaptive indices, we need to properly control these changes. In addition, as more than one holistic thread may be active at any time, they may be trying to refine the same index. The study of concurrency control for adaptive indexing [16, 17] showed that it is possible to allow multiple concurrent index refinements in adaptive indices via lightweight concurrency control, i.e., relying only on latches of individual pieces in an adaptive index. The point is that an index refinement only changes the structure of the index and not its contents (contrary to an actual update). In this case, an index refinement only rearranges values in a single piece of a column at a time. Thus it is sufficient to allow other queries to work on different pieces in parallel by taking read/write latches on individual pieces, called piece latches in [16, 17]. We exploit these techniques here in order to allow user queries and holistic workers to work concurrently over a single column, but we also identify extra opportunities to increase parallelism for holistic workers.

Figure 3 shows an example of an adaptive index where two queries are actively cracking it. Each query is interested in its own value range and needs to crack one piece, i.e., at the value of its selection. The idea is that *all* other pieces of the column are available for index refinement by holistic worker threads. One direction would be that each holistic worker decides which piece of an index to refine by picking from a list of pieces that currently have no locks. However, such information is expensive to maintain similarly to our discussion in the "Index Refinement" paragraph. Thus, holistic workers make random choices regarding which value to use as pivot and thus which piece to crack. However, when a holistic worker requests a write latch to crack a piece and it happens that the piece is locked at the moment, then if the latch is not given immediately, the worker picks another random pivot and repeats the procedure

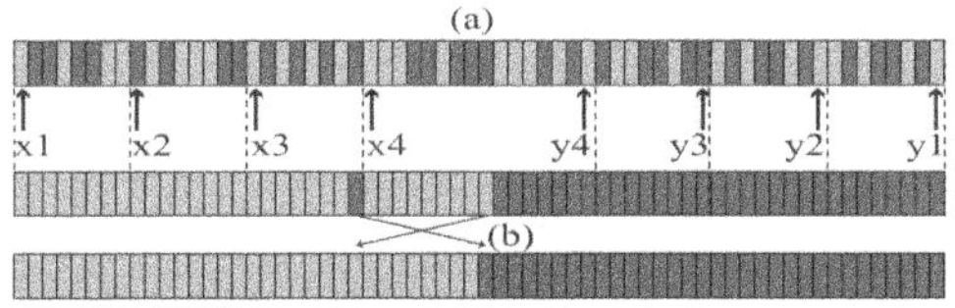

Figure 4: Refined Partition & Merge (multi-threaded) [44].

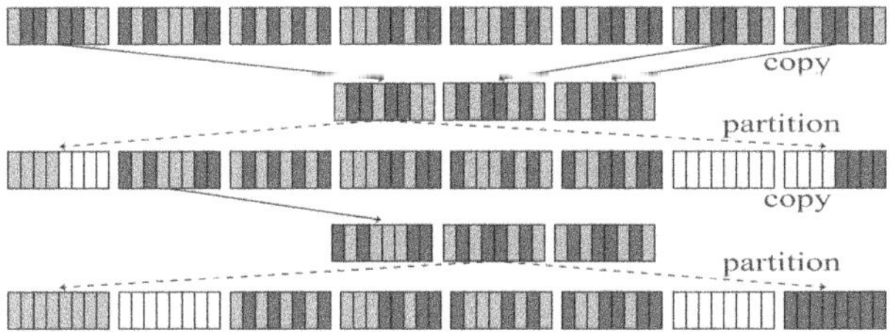

Figure 5: Vectorized Cracking [44].

until it finds a free piece to crack. In contrast, user queries need to always block in such cases and wait for the piece to be unlocked. For instance, in Figure 3(d) the holistic worker thread tries to lock piece 2.1, which is already locked by Q4. Instead of waiting for the lock to be released, the worker chooses another pivot. The new pivot falls in piece 3.2, which is not locked and it is reorganized finally by the worker (Figure 3(e)). As we process more queries and as we perform more holistic indexing, the number of pieces in an index grows; as a side-effect the waiting time for taking a latch decreases as there are more candidate pieces to pick from.

Updates. Updates for adaptive indexing have been studied in [29]. The design in [29] is that updates remain as pending updates and are merged during query processing, i.e., if a query requests a value range that contains one or more pending updates, then only those updates are merged on-the-fly and without destroying any of the information on the adaptive index. Each query needs to lock at most one column piece at a time for cracking and can update this piece at the same time if pending updates for this piece exist [16, 17]. Multiple queries may work in parallel updating and cracking separate pieces (value ranges) of the same column.

The difference here is that with holistic indexing, holistic workers not only perform auxiliary index refinement actions but also merge pending updates. That is, if a holistic worker picks a pivot which falls within a piece of the respective column and the value range, for which this piece holds values, has pending updates, then all those pending updates are merged by the holistic worker. In this way, holistic worker threads not only refine the adaptive indices in the background but also bring them more up to date which removes further load from future queries.

Storage Constraints. Holistic indexing works within a limited storage budget. Adaptive indices may be dropped or recreated at any time. They consist auxiliary information and thus dropping an index does not lead to any loss of data. In case the storage budget does not allow adding a new index triggered by a user query, then indices are removed with a least frequently used (LFU) policy from the index space at an index-level granularity or at a fine-grained granularity that allows for creating and dropping individual ranges dynamically, as partial cracking suggested in [29].

Multi-core Adaptive Indexing. The goal of holistic indexing is to improve the physical design by fully utilizing the available CPU resources. An alternative approach to achieve maximum CPU utilization is to parallelize the index refinement actions triggered by user queries. This problem was studied in [44], which introduced a multi-core, CPU efficient cracking algorithm shown in Figure 4. In this algorithm, the to-be-cracked piece is partitioned initially into as many slices as the number of threads, e.g., n (Figure 4(a)). The

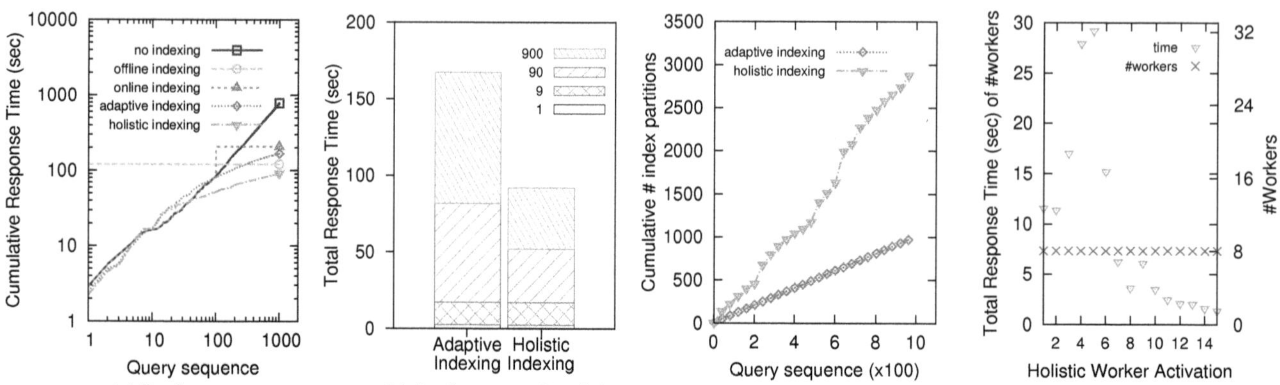

(a) Performance (b) Performance Breakdown (c) Index Partitions (d) Idle CPU Utilization

Figure 6: Improving performance with holistic indexing.

center slice is contiguous, while the remaining $n-1$ slices consist of two disjoint halves, each, that are arranged concentrically around the center slice (x_i and y_i indicate the first and the last element of piece i respectively). n threads crack the n slices independently applying a vectorized, out-of-place cracking algorithm (Figure 5), which was proven in [44] to be the most CPU efficient single-threaded cracking implementation reported so far. Finally, the local data are merged into a big cracked piece (Figure 4(b)). We found that devoting all resources to perform adaptive indexing for user queries in parallel does not lead to the absolute best performance. Specifically, we found that we can improve performance even more by assigning part of the resources to holistic indexing. In this way, some of the CPU resources are assigned to parallel cracking for user queries but the rest of the CPU resources are distributed across several holistic workers for additional index refinements. In the experimental section we show why this approach is better than assigning all available resources to user queries.

5. EXPERIMENTAL ANALYSIS

In this section, we demonstrate that holistic indexing leads to a self-organizing always-on DBMS with substantial benefits in terms of response time; with zero administration or set-up effort holistic indexing improves performance adaptively by exploiting all available CPU resources to the maximum. We present a detailed experimental analysis using both standard benchmarks such as TPC-H and real-life workloads such as SkyServer as well as synthetic microbenchmarks for a fine-grained analysis.

We use a dual-socket machine equipped with two 2.00 GHz Intel(R) Xeon(R) CPU E5-2650 processors and with 256 GB RAM. Each processor has 8 hyper-threading cores resulting in 32 hardware threads in total. The operating system is Fedora 20 (kernel version 3.12.10). All experiments we report are based on an implementation of holistic indexing in MonetDB and assume a main-memory environment.

5.1 Improving over State-of-the-Art Indexing

In our first experiment we demonstrate that holistic indexing has the potential to bring substantial performance improvements over existing state-of-the-art indexing approaches. We test holistic indexing against parallel versions of adaptive indexing (database cracking), offline indexing, online indexing and plain scans.

For plain scans (no indexing), we use a parallel select operator implemented in MonetDB. For offline and online indexing we sort the columns using a highly parallel NUMA-aware sorting algorithm that was introduced in [9] (m-way, 16-byte keys) and is publicly available in [1]. Specifically, in offline indexing we pre-sort all the columns before query processing, while in online indexing we assume that after processing a few queries we understand the workload patterns and then we sort the relevant columns. MonetDB automatically detects that a column is sorted and can use efficient binary search actions during select operations. For adaptive indexing we use the parallel vectorized database cracking algorithm that was introduced in [44] (see Section 4.2).

Here we use a synthetic benchmark. The query workload consists of 10^3 range select queries over a table of 10 attributes; each query touches a single attribute (we will see more complex queries later on). Each attribute consists of 2^{30} uniformly distributed integers, while the value range requested by each query (and thus the selectivity) is random. All queries are of the following form.

$$select\ A\ from\ R\ where\ A < v$$

The tested scenario assumes a dynamic and ad-hoc environment with zero workload knowledge and zero idle time to pre-index the data. Figure 6(a) shows the results. On the x-axis queries are ranked in execution order. The y-axis represents the cumulative response time as the query sequence evolves, i.e., each point (x, y) represents the sum of the execution time y for the first x queries. In this way, the graph shows how the response times evolve as we process more and more queries.

If there is no indexing support (plain scans), the entire column is scanned in parallel by 32 threads for every query. Because of this stable access pattern, the cumulative response time of the query sequence grows linearly as every query has similar cost. With offline indexing, on the other hand, it takes 12 seconds to completely sort each column, assuming a priori workload knowledge. This leads to a 120 seconds initialization overhead to sort all 10 columns. Since there is no idle time before the first query, the sorting cost is added to the execution time of the first query in Figure 6(a). After the first query, all queries are answered with fast binary search actions which results in a rather flat cumulative curve. With online indexing, the first 100 queries are answered without any index support and thus the cost grows linearly. After the 100th query, assuming enough workload knowledge has been obtained via monitoring, we proceed to sort all 10 columns. The sorting cost is added to the execution cost of the 101st query, since there is no idle time between the 100th and the 101st query. As with offline indexing, all subsequent queries are answered very fast with binary search over the sorted column. Thus, both in offline and in online indexing, the whole query sequence is affected by the sorting costs. On the other hand, adaptive indexing continuously improves performance requiring no workload knowledge and without penalizing individual queries. This improvement is due to the fact that adaptive indexing builds only partial indices which it incrementally refines as queries arrive. However, there is still room for big improvements.

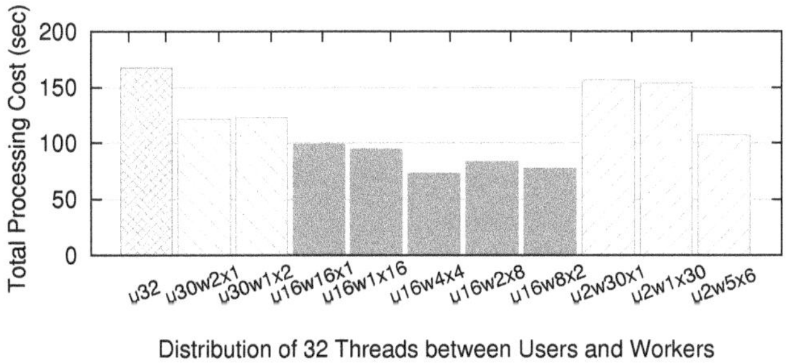

Figure 7: Performance improves if we distribute the threads equally between user queries and holistic workers.

Holistic indexing manages to further improve the performance of the workload by about 50%. Contrary to the other indexing approaches, MonetDB with holistic indexing enabled monitors the CPU utilization and constantly tries to maximize it. When holistic indexing detects idle CPU resources, it triggers index refinement actions on existing adaptive indices. In this experiment, an index is inserted in the index set, and specifically in C_{actual}, when a user query creates it. For holistic indexing the actual user queries behave in exactly the same way as in adaptive indexing, i.e., the first query will create an adaptive index and subsequent queries refine it using the very efficient and almost linearly scaling parallel vectorized cracking implementation from [44]. The difference is that with holistic indexing enabled idle CPU resources are exploited towards further refining the adaptive indices in a way which does not hurt running queries. Since parallel vectorized cracking [44] is designed to be CPU efficient, encountering only very little resource stalls, we generated kind of a worst-case scenario for holistic indexing: we limited the maximal number of hardware context assigned to user queries to 16 (equal to number of physical cores), leaving at least 16 (otherwise not effectively usable by the prime user query workload) hardware contexts ("hyper-threads") available for holistic indexing. Constantly, our load-checker usually detects 16 idle hardware contexts, and consequently starts 8 holistic indexing workers (each using two threads) as shown in Figure 6(d). Figure 7 shows that the combination of using maximal 16 (out of 32) hardware contexts for user queries (performing parallel vectorized adaptive indexing [44]), while devoting any remaining idle hardware context to holistic indexing, improved the overall performance by a factor 2 over using all 32 hardware contexts for user queries (and thus none for holistic indexing).

Figure 6(b) is a breakdown of the performance of holistic indexing and adaptive indexing. The y-axis represents the total response time of the first query, the next 9 queries, etc. The total height of each bar represents the total response time to run the entire workload of 10^3 queries. The first few queries do not see any improvement because holistic indexing cannot concurrently refine a column if there are user queries cracking it. This is because initially columns have not been cracked at all and thus the first few user queries will lock big pieces for cracking. However, as each column is cracked into smaller pieces, holistic indexing may invoke actions to refine a column even if concurrent queries are cracking it. Essentially, each user query needs to lock at most one piece of an adaptive index at a time, i.e., the piece it is about to crack, and thus holistic indexing may choose any of the remaining pieces to perform further index refinements.

Holistic indexing outperforms adaptive indexing by a factor 2 by injecting additional index refinements on top of those that adaptive indexing does anyway. Figure 6(c) shows the amount of pieces which have been created in all 10 adaptive indices; holistic indexing creates more pieces than adaptive indexing. As a result, future user queries need to touch less data as they find a fine-grained index, and thus performance improves for holistic indexing. As Figure 8 shows, the first queries that access the same index run slower, because they reorganize big partitions. Thus, additional pieces have to be inserted in the index as early as possible in the query sequence.

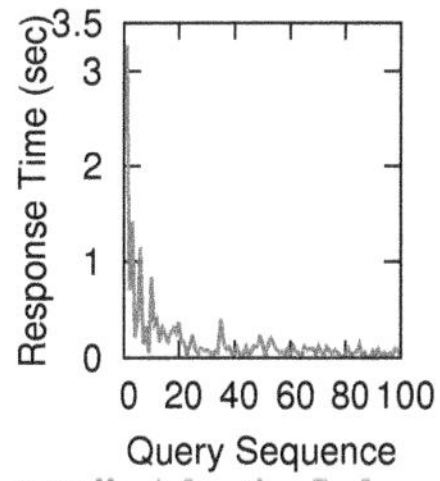

Figure 8: Adaptive Ind.

As discussed in Section 4.2, on some occasions the main holistic indexing thread waits for all workers to finish before assigning new tasks, leaving under-utilized CPU resources for some brief periods. Figure 6(d) shows how the total response time of all workers in every tuning cycle changes over time and as the query sequence evolves. The right y-axis shows the number of holistic worker threads the holistic indexing thread activates whenever it detects idle CPU resources. The maximum number of workers that holistic indexing can activate is 8. The left y-axis represents the total response time of all workers during a single tuning cycle. The x-axis represents the activations of holistic indexing. A single activation of holistic indexing triggers the activation of multiple holistic workers. The total response time of the workload is 90 seconds. Within this amount of time, holistic indexing is activated only 15 times, because of the waiting time (1 second) between two CPU load measurements and because of the waiting time until all workers finish in every tuning cycle. We observe that the response time of the workers is high only for the first few activations and reduces very fast as the index becomes fine-grained. In this way, the system adapts on its own and eventually no worker is a bottleneck.

Holistic indexing sees even bigger performance benefits when there is idle time before query processing. When there is idle time and no workload knowledge, holistic indexing chooses random indexes to insert in $C_{potential}$ and refines them until the first query arrives. Here using the same set-up as in the previous experiment, we manually induce idle time and holistic indexing adds 10 random indices in $C_{potential}$. Figure 9 shows the results. Compared to adaptive indexing, which does not exploit the a priori idle time (22 seconds), holistic indexing exploits this time to spread tuning actions over 10 indices. Thus, when user queries are processed they reorganize smaller partitions and the benefit is already obvious in the beginning of the workload compared to Figure 6(b), where the benefit in the workload appears after the 10th query when all indices have been inserted in the index set automatically by the system.

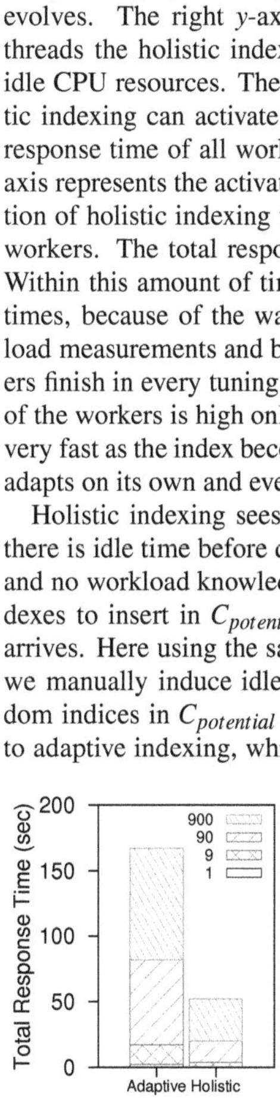

Figure 9: Indexing.

By being able to completely automatically utilize available CPU resources and direct them towards lightweight actions that may improve future requests, holistic indexing can bring significant performance gains on top of existing indexing approaches. It outperforms adaptive indexing by a factor 2 in terms of individual query performance. At the same time it outperforms offline and online indexing, especially in the beginning of the workload, when offline indexing penalizes the first queries with the index building cost and online indexing does not provide any indexing support until the 100th query. Besides the difference in performance, the qualitative difference described in Table 1, makes holistic indexing a very appealing indexing approach in modern dynamic environments.

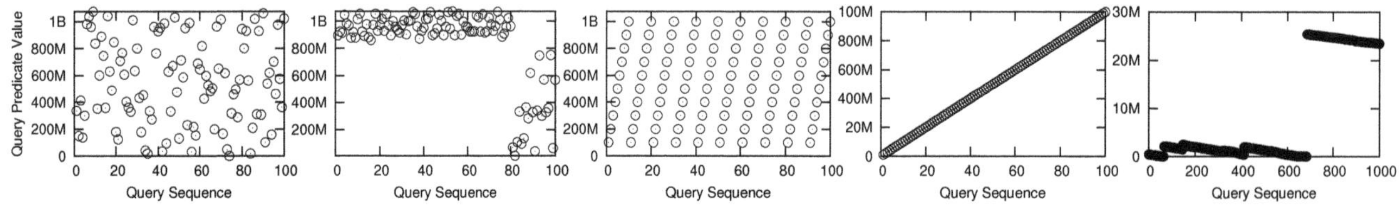

(a) Random (b) Skewed (c) Periodic (d) Sequential (e) SkyServer

Figure 10: Various workload patterns.

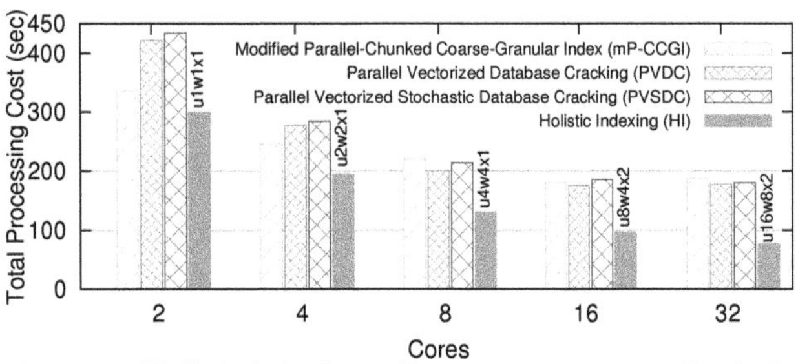

Figure 11: Holistic indexing utilizes resources more effectively than multi-core state-of-the-art adaptive indexing baselines.

5.2 Holistic Vs. Multi-core Adaptive Indexing

Assuming there are several CPU cores available in a modern system, in holistic indexing we utilize them by spreading auxiliary tuning actions across multiple indices. An alternative way to "keep the CPU busy", is to parallelize the existing adaptive indexing algorithms. In this experiment we study how state-of-the-art adaptive indexing baselines compare to holistic indexing. In particular, we study parallel vectorized database cracking (PVDC), parallel vectorized stochastic database cracking (PVSDC) [44] and a modified version of parallel chunked coarse granular index (P-CCGI) [8] that we name mP-CCGI.

Stochastic cracking aims to provide robustness by performing auxiliary stochastic indexing actions. Although stochastic cracking studied the option of collecting statistics to target the proper value ranges to index, it was shown in [21] that reacting immediately to workload changes by auxiliary stochastic cracking actions has a better effect (i.e., more robust). This is because in stochastic cracking a running query performs auxiliary random cracking only within the piece that is already about to be cracked within a given column and as a result any action brings a benefit as it imposes more order. Holistic indexing considers a much more broad space of statistics keeping track of column-statistics to decide which columns to fine tune.

Both stochastic cracking and plain database cracking in this experiment utilize multi-cores as described in the last paragraph of Section 4. The original P-CCGI algorithm partitions the data into as many chunks as the available number of threads and the first query cracks each chunk in parallel having a separate cracking index for each chunk. Subsequent queries crack the chunks in parallel, while they benefit from the initial range partitioning. However, this way, data that belongs in a single value range is physically stored in separate chunks/arrays and feeding from there other relational operators is not compatible with a column-store such as MonetDB that relies on bulk processing; it does not allow to exploit tight for loops without intermediate if statements to detect when we should skip from one chunk to the next during an operator. To address this we extended the original P-CCGI algorithm [8] with the ability to consolidate selection results in a single array using the same techniques that were used for hybrid adaptive indexing which also operates on multiple chunks (but not in parallel) [31]; each query consolidates only the qualifying value ranges and each value range needs to be written to the contiguous array by a single query only, i.e., subsequent queries will only have to do consolidation if they need a new value range never consolidated before. In a vectorized column-store this could be done without consolidation, potentially improving performance further as has been indicated by partial sideways cracking [29]; vectorized processing for adaptive indexing is an open topic, though, orthogonal to this work.

The workload in this experiment consists of 10^3 select-project queries (as in the previous experiment) on 10 integer attributes. Each attribute consists of 2^{30} uniformly distributed integers. The value range requested by each query is random while we vary the number of available CPU cores from 2 to 32, i.e., the maximum number of cores in our system. For holistic indexing we give half of the cores to user queries and the rest of the cores are used by the workers (after testing all possible configurations, we found that this is the one that performs best in all cases). The labels on top of the bars that represent the performance of holistic indexing indicate the distribution of the threads between user queries and workers in every case (similar to Figure 7).

Figure 11 shows the results. In all cases, the performance improves as we invoke more cores into query processing. For multi-core database cracking and stochastic cracking the performance improves because many threads crack in parallel for one query at a time while for holistic indexing performance improves because many threads work in the background in parallel with query processing to further refine the various indices with auxiliary indexing actions. Holistic indexing sees a bigger improvement, because it is active all the time, i.e., maximizing CPU usage.On the contrary, multi-core vectorized database cracking and multi-core stochastic cracking improve the performance only during user queries and only during the cracking actions. Another subtle difference but one with a major performance impact is that while stochastic cracking and database cracking target all their adaptive indexing actions on specific pieces as they are driven by individual queries, holistic indexing spreads its actions across the whole range of the domain and thus across the whole range of an adaptive index (stochastic cracking does random actions but only within a single piece). This creates a nicely balanced index which has more potential to benefit future queries. The modified version of P-CCGI initially range partitions the data, which can be seen as a pre-index step. However, this is a cost that penalizes the first set of queries.

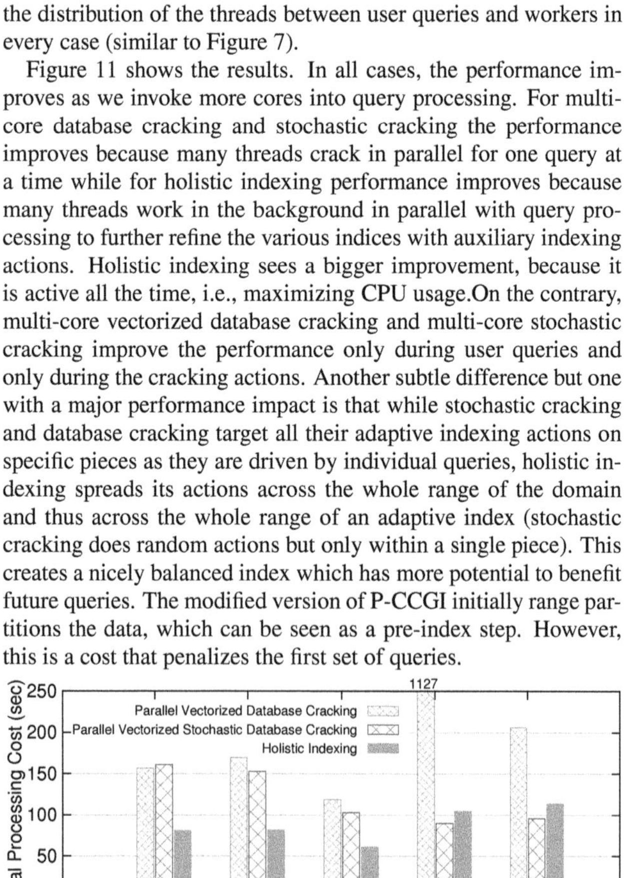

Figure 12: Holistic indexing is robust.

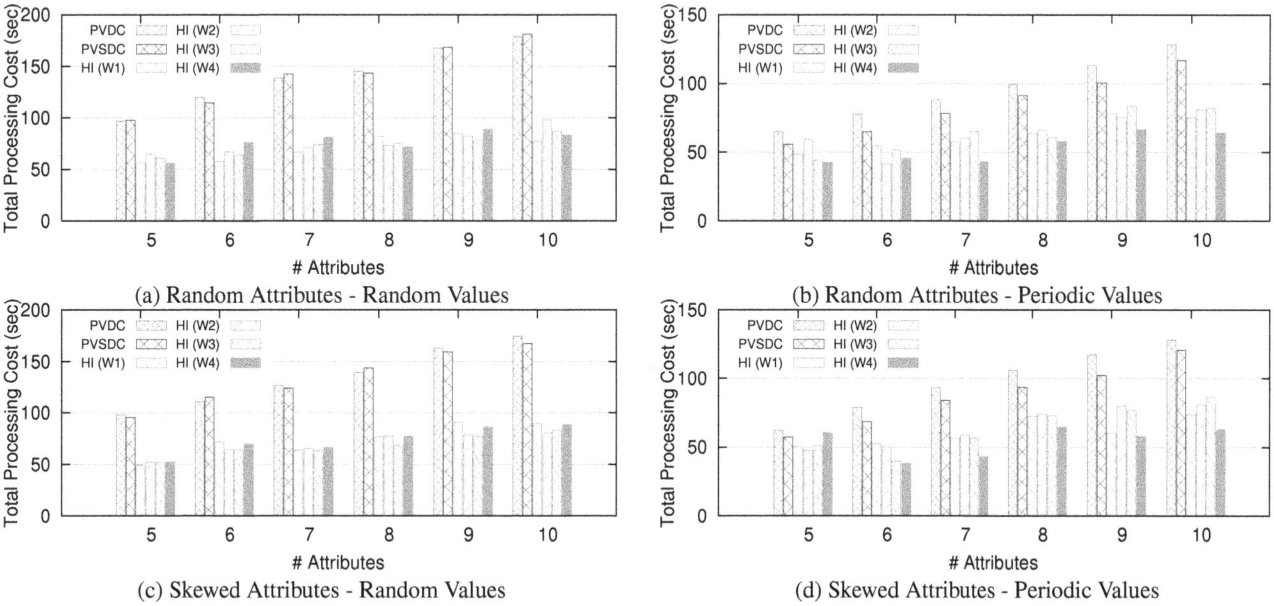

Figure 13: More performance gains for holistic indexing as more attributes exist in a schema. All strategies have similar performance.

5.3 Robustness

In our next experiment we study how holistic indexing compares to parallel database cracking and parallel stochastic cracking in terms of robustness. We show that holistic indexing maintains the good properties of adaptive indexing by utilizing the available CPU resources more effectively. Both holistic indexing and the parallel variants of adaptive indexing utilize all the available CPU cores.

We test four synthetic workloads. Each workload consists of 10^3 queries on 10 attributes ($\sim$100 queries/attribute). Each attribute consists of 2^{30} uniformly distributed integers. The queries follow a different pattern in each workload. The first four subfigures in Figure 10 depict those workload patterns. For each workload, the respective figure illustrates graphically how a sequence of queries touches the value domain of a single attribute.

Furthermore, we test holistic indexing in a real-life workload using data and queries from SkyServer [2]. SkyServer collects astronomical data and the database can be accessed publicly by individual users and institutions. We pose 10^4 real user queries that have been logged by the project servers on the "Photoobjall" table. The "Photoobjall" table consists of 1.2 Billion tuples. All queries access the "Ascension" attribute and are posed in exactly the same chronological order they were logged. The pattern the SkyServer queries follow is shown in Figure 10(e).

Figure 12 shows the results. For each indexing method we report the total time needed to process all queries for each workload.

Synthetic Workloads. In all synthetic workloads holistic indexing outperforms multi-core database cracking by a factor 2-10 depending on the workload. Multi-core database cracking is strictly driven by query predicates, and thus, can leave large unindexed pieces to be reorganized by future queries. For instance, in the sequential workload in Figure 10(d), each query cracks a column in a small piece and in a big piece, and then, a future query needs to crack the big piece again, resulting in a high cost. Multi-core stochastic cracking solves these robustness issues by injecting one extra random cracking action for each user query in order to distribute cracking more evenly. However, holistic indexing can materialize an even bigger advantage. This is because it is not restricted to perform auxiliary index refinement actions only during user queries but it can exploit all possible CPU cycles to refine the indices, resulting in many more actions taking place in parallel with user queries. Moreover, holistic indexing spreads the auxiliary index refinements across the entire value domain (by choosing random pivots) without leaving big unindexed pieces. For example, in the skewed workload in Figure 10(b), both multi-core database cracking and multi-core stochastic cracking show a similar performance, because they restrict the index refinements to a small region of the domain according to user query predicates, i.e, from 800 million to 2^{30}. Future queries have to reorganize a big unindexed area, i.e., from 0 to 800 million; this area is already indexed in holistic indexing before the 800th query arrives. Thus, holistic indexing prepares the physical design better for (ad-hoc) future queries.

SkyServer. The SkyServer workload in Figure 10(e) shows the pattern logged in SkyServer for queries using the "right ascension" attribute of the "Photoobjall" table. We observe that the queries follow non-random patterns, i.e., they focus on a specific part of the sky before moving to a different part. Figure 12 shows that holistic indexing manages to significantly outperform multi-core database cracking by inducing auxiliary index refinement actions in parallel with query processing without penalizing individual user queries.

Overall, in all workloads tested, holistic indexing not only maintains the nice properties of the parallel variants of database cracking and stochastic cracking, but it also enhances the behavior further by being able to exploit all available CPU resources effectively for a better prepared physical design.

5.4 More Benefits with Complex Schemas

In this experiment, we show that as the database schema becomes more complex by containing more attributes, this brings more opportunities for holistic indexing to gain in performance; more attributes make the indexing space bigger and thus any a priori decisions are even more prone to be wrong. In addition, we test the various strategies for choosing among the candidate indices and we show that indeed making random decisions is a robust approach.

Here, we assume a gradually bigger database table which consists of 5-10 attributes. Each attribute consists of 2^{30} uniformly distributed integers. We fire select-project queries as in the previous experiments but this time we may query up to X attributes in every run. Each query touches a single attribute and we vary the frequency with which each attribute is accessed, i.e., we run both a random workload where every attribute is evenly queried as well

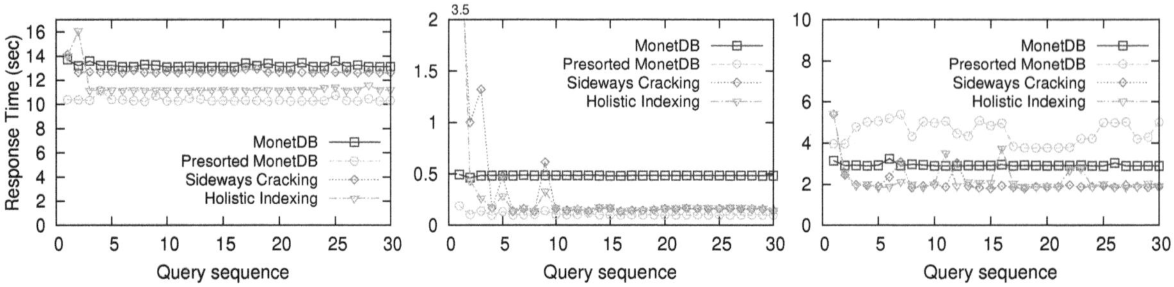

(a) TPC-H Query 1 (b) TPC-H Query 6 (c) TPC-H Query 12

Figure 14: TPC-H results (Scale Factor 10, "pre-sorted" times exclude pre-sorting costs; Q1,6,12: 8 sec).

as a skewed workload where some attributes are queried more than others. For each workload we vary also the workload pattern followed by the queries. Here, we present the results for random and periodic workload patterns. For each case, we perform 10^3 queries.

We compare holistic indexing using one of the four strategies described in Section 4.2 against multi-core variants of database cracking and stochastic cracking. Figure 13 shows the results; for all cases, holistic indexing materializes a big benefit. As the number of attributes in the database table grows, the performance benefit for holistic indexing increases. What happens is that holistic indexing makes sure to evenly spread auxiliary index refinement actions across all attributes in parallel with user queries whenever free CPU cycles are available. Then, future queries on those attributes can exploit this refined indexing. Compared to the case where we have a few attributes, having more attributes means that more heavy indexing actions have to be performed overall in order to crack the columns into small pieces. This allows holistic indexing to materialize a bigger benefit as it performs those actions in the background as opposed to only during user queries as in multi-core database cracking and multi-core stochastic cracking.

In addition, all index choosing strategies have similar performance on workloads where attributes are queried on random values (Figures 13(a) and (c)), because indices are already fine-grained in such cases (even when some indices are refined more than others in a skewed workload). However, in case of queries on periodic values (Figures 13(b) and (d)) the random choice ($W4$) shows a clear performance benefit compared to the rest of the strategies, because it refines indices with big unindexed partitions, and proves to be a robust design decision.

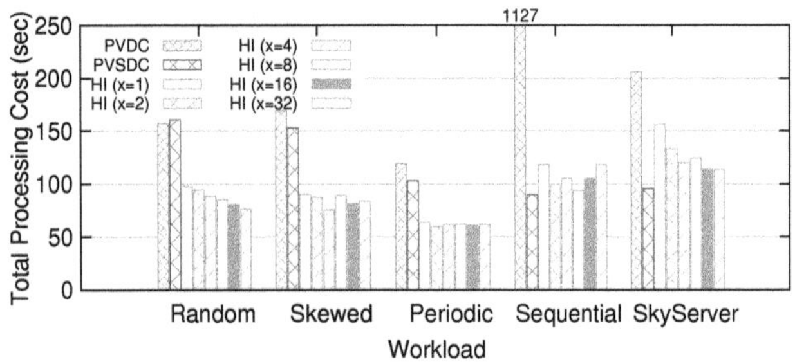

Figure 15: Performance of holistic indexing improves while the number of index refinements x increases.

5.5 Design Decisions

Holistic Worker Thread Refinements. In this experiment we demonstrate how the tuning parameter x, i.e., the number of index refinements per worker (Figure 2), affects the workload performance. We test five workloads that consist of 10^3 queries on a relation with 10 attributes as in Section 5.3 (Figure 12). We vary the number of index refinements each holistic worker thread does from 1 to 32 and we compare holistic indexing with multi-core variants of database cracking and stochastic cracking. Figure 15 shows the results. The more index refinements each thread does, the bigger the benefit for holistic indexing because more pieces are created and thus future queries need to refine smaller pieces, touching less data. However, when we increase the number of index refinements from 16 to 32, performance does not improve significantly, because in both cases indices converge very fast to optimal ones. Thus, we use 16 as the number of index refinements that each holistic worker thread does in all our experiments.

5.6 TPC-H

In our next experiment, we evaluate holistic indexing on the standard database benchmark, TPC-H [3]. We compare against offline indexing and plain scans. We use scale factor 10 and we test with Queries 1, 6, and 12. For each query type, we created a sequence of 30 variations using the random query generator distributed with the benchmark. For offline indexing, we created the proper column-store projections by pre-sorting the data depending on each query individually, i.e., we created the perfect projection for each query. Specifically, for Queries 1 and 6 we created a copy of the Lineitem table sorted on the l_shipdate attribute. For Query 12 we created a copy of the Lineitem table sorted on the l_receiptdate attribute.

Figure 14 depicts the results. For all cases, holistic indexing brings a significant advantage, resulting in a robust and stable performance across all queries. The first query is slower as it creates the first adaptive indices which implies extra data copying but after that all queries perform significantly better than plain MonetDB. Holistic indexing matches offline indexing without having to incur the high offline indexing cost and without requiring any workload knowledge. The pre-sorting cost for all queries is 8 seconds. For Query 12, it turns out that pre-sorting does not help. This happens because even though we may improve the selection by pre-sorting the Lineitem table, it turns out we hurt the join between the Lineitem and the Orders table. This is because in the base data, the Lineitem table contains the order date ordered and this can be exploited during the join. With holistic indexing we do not face this problem, because the initial order changes only partially.

5.7 Updates

So far we tested read-only workloads. In this experiment we demonstrate that holistic indexing maintains its nice properties in workloads where read-only queries interleave with write queries. We test two scenarios. In the first scenario (High Frequency Low Volume - HFLV), 10 inserts arrive every 10 queries. In the second scenario (Low Frequency High Volume - LFHV), 100 inserts arrive every 100 queries. In both scenarios the workload consists of 500 select project range queries on a single attribute A and 500 insertions in total on a single attribute A. While all queries are processed sequentially one after the other, the 11th query arrives 20 seconds after the 10th query resulting in idle time of 20 seconds in the system. Attribute A consists of 10^9 uniformly distributed integers.

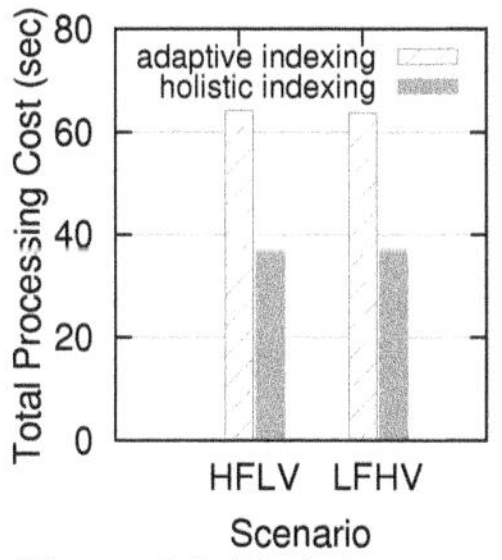

Figure 16: Updates.

Updates are temporarily stored in a pending insertions column. We use the Ripple algorithm [28] in order to apply the updates; a pending inserted value is merged with the original data if and only if the index partition, where the specific value belongs, is refined. Thus, the merging process happens on-the-fly and maintains the information of the index. In this experiment we test single-threaded adaptive indexing against holistic indexing with a single worker that refines the index only during idle time. In holistic indexing, auxiliary index refinement actions also cause insertions to be merged. In this way, holistic indexing not only refines the indices but also consumes pending insertions, which speeds up future queries even more and all that by exploiting idle CPU resources in parallel with query processing. Figure 16 shows the results. In both scenarios, holistic indexing maintains its advantage over adaptive indexing; it is not affected by updates and still provides roughly a 50% improvement.

5.8 Varying Number of Clients

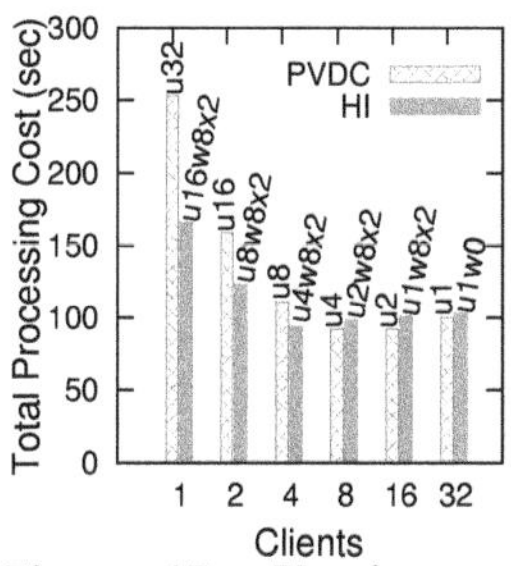

Figure 17: Varying number of clients.

In this experiment we test the performance of holistic indexing with varying number of concurrent clients in the system. Our workload consists of 1024 queries on a relation with 10 attributes. We vary the number of concurrent clients between 1 and 32, where 32 is the number of CPU cores in our machine. Figure 17 shows that holistic indexing brings a big benefit in case of a few clients. The labels on top of the bars indicate the distribution of the available threads across user queries and holistic workers (similar to Figure 7). When the number of clients increases, holistic indexing does not bring significant benefits, because it easily detects these cases as it monitors the CPU load continuously and so it is triggered only if the load is below a threshold.

6. CONCLUSIONS

Ad-hoc environments become more and more common in the big data era, where we have little workload knowledge and time to properly tune a database system. In this paper, we present holistic indexing; it continuously adapts to workload changes and makes maximum use of available CPU resources, requiring zero human administration. Holistic indexing continuously monitors the workload and refines the physical design with lightweight actions whenever spare CPU cycles are detected. We implemented holistic indexing in an open-source column-store DBMS and we demonstrate that even though holistic indexing runs in the background and on-the-fly, i.e., while processing user queries, it does not affect the running queries negatively; instead by continuously refining the physical design based on the workload and by exploiting spare CPU cycles it brings substantial improvements. A detailed experimental analysis shows that holistic indexing maintains all the good benefits and properties of adaptive indexing, while it brings an additional performance gain which is typically a factor of 2.

Holistic indexing opens a promising research path. Studying holistic indexing for traditional row stores or emerging hybrid systems is an interesting topic. While major database vendors support hybrid storage layouts, auto-tuning tools may take into account holistic indexing and depending on the workload decide which indices to build up front and which indices to assign to holistic indexing. In addition, even though we considered primarily indices for improving selections in this paper there is room to consider other indices that may be improved by holistic indexing such as join indices. Furthermore, this work and most recent work on adaptive indexing has focused on column-stores that work under the bulk processing model with the data stored in fixed width and dense arrays which allows for efficient tight for loops. However, work on partial sideways cracking [29] and more recently chunked coarse granular indexing [8] shows that even more benefits for adaptive indexing are possible if we drop the dense arrays restriction, especially since this enables effective parallelization [8]. This has side-effects of course to the whole architecture of a database system as it affects the design and access patterns of all relational operators. Thus, it is very interesting to investigate whether it is beneficial to drop certain restrictions and reconsider the whole architecture and data flow in column-stores to accommodate further adaptive indexing benefits. Finally, in this paper we focused on improving the overall response time of a workload but further interesting directions may rise once we consider energy consumption, targeting systems with the maximum performance but within specific energy bounds.

Acknowledgments We would like to thank Victor Alvarez, Felix Martin Schuhknecht, Jens Dittrich and Stefan Richter for kindly providing the source code of the chunked coarse granular adaptive indexing algorithm. We would also like to thank the anonymous reviewers for their truly insightful remarks.

7. REFERENCES

[1] Sort-Merge Joins. http://www.systems.ethz.ch/projects/paralleljoins.

[2] Sloan Digital Sky Survey (SkyServer). http://cas.sdss.org/.

[3] TPC Benchmark H. http://www.tpc.org/tpch/.

[4] D. Abadi, P. A. Boncz, S. Harizopoulos, S. Idreos, and S. Madden. The Design and Implementation of Modern Column-Oriented Database Systems. *Foundations and Trends in Databases*, 5(3):197–280, 2013.

[5] S. Agrawal, S. Chaudhuri, L. Kollár, A. P. Marathe, V. R. Narasayya, and M. Syamala. Database Tuning Advisor for Microsoft SQL Server 2005. In *Proceedings of the 30th International Conference on Very Large Data Bases (VLDB)*, pages 1110–1121, 2004.

[6] I. Alagiannis, R. Borovica, M. Branco, S. Idreos, and A. Ailamaki. NoDB: Efficient Query Execution on Raw Data Files. In *Proceedings of the ACM SIGMOD International Conference on Management of Data*, pages 241–252, 2012.

[7] I. Alagiannis, S. Idreos, and A. Ailamaki. H2O: A Hands-free Adaptive Store. In *Proceedings of the ACM SIGMOD International Conference on Management of Data*, pages 1103–1114, 2014.

[8] V. Alvarez, F. M. Schuhknecht, J. Dittrich, and S. Richter. Main Memory Adaptive Indexing for Multi-core Systems. In *Proceedings of the 10th International Workshop on Data Management on New Hardware (DaMoN)*, 2014.

[9] C. Balkesen, G. Alonso, J. Teubner, and M. T. Özsu. Multi-Core, Main-Memory Joins: Sort vs. Hash Revisited. *Proceedings of the Very Large Data Bases Endowment (PVLDB)*, 7(1):85–96, 2013.

[10] N. Bruno and S. Chaudhuri. An Online Approach to Physical Design Tuning. In *Proceedings of the IEEE 23rd International Conference on Data Engineering (ICDE)*, pages 826–835, 2007.

[11] S. Chaudhuri and V. R. Narasayya. An Efficient Cost-Driven Index Selection Tool for Microsoft SQL Server. In *Proceedings of the 23rd International Conference on Very Large Data Bases (VLDB)*, pages 146–155, 1997.

[12] S. Chaudhuri and V. R. Narasayya. AutoAdmin "What-if" Index Analysis Utility. In *Proceedings of the ACM SIGMOD International Conference on Management of Data*, pages 367–378, 1998.

[13] G. P. Copeland and S. N. Khoshafian. A Decomposition Storage Model. In *Proceedings of the ACM SIGMOD International Conference on Management of Data*, pages 268–279, 1985.

[14] B. Dageville, D. Das, K. Dias, K. Yagoub, M. Zaït, and M. Ziauddin. Automatic SQL Tuning in Oracle 10g. In *Proceedings of the 30th International Conference on Very Large Data Bases (VLDB)*, pages 1098–1109, 2004.

[15] J. Dittrich, J.-A. Quiané-Ruiz, A. Jindal, Y. Kargin, V. Setty, and J. Schad. Hadoop++: Making a Yellow Elephant Run Like a Cheetah (Without It Even Noticing). *Proceedings of the Very Large Data Bases Endowment (PVLDB)*, 3(1):518–529, 2010.

[16] G. Graefe, F. Halim, S. Idreos, H. A. Kuno, and S. Manegold. Concurrency Control for Adaptive Indexing. *Proceedings of the Very Large Data Bases Endowment (PVLDB)*, 5(7):656–667, 2012.

[17] G. Graefe, F. Halim, S. Idreos, H. A. Kuno, S. Manegold, and B. Seeger. Transactional Support for Adaptive Indexing. *The Very Large Data Bases Journal (VLDB J.)*, 23(2):303–328, 2014.

[18] G. Graefe, S. Idreos, H. A. Kuno, and S. Manegold. Benchmarking Adaptive Indexing. In *Proceedings of the 2nd Technology Conference on Performance Evaluation and Benchmarking (TPCTC)*, pages 169–184, 2010.

[19] G. Graefe and H. Kuno. Adaptive Indexing for Relational Keys. In *Workshops Proceedings of the IEEE 26th International Conference on Data Engineering (ICDE)*, pages 69–74, 2010.

[20] G. Graefe and H. A. Kuno. Self-Selecting, Self-Tuning, Incrementally Optimized Indexes. In *Proceedings of the 13th International Conference on Extending Database Technology (EDBT)*, pages 371–381, 2010.

[21] F. Halim, S. Idreos, P. Karras, and R. H. C. Yap. Stochastic Database Cracking: Towards Robust Adaptive Indexing in Main-Memory Column-Stores. *Proceedings of the Very Large Data Bases Endowment (PVLDB)*, 5(6):502–513, 2012.

[22] N. Hardavellas, M. Ferdman, B. Falsafi, and A. Ailamaki. Near-Optimal Cache Block Placement with Reactive Nonuniform Cache Architectures. In *IEEE Micro*, page 29, 2010.

[23] S. Harizopoulos and A. Ailamaki. A Case for Staged Database Systems. In *Proceedings of the Conference on Innovative Data Systems Research (CIDR)*, 2003.

[24] S. Harizopoulos, V. Shkapenyuk, and A. Ailamaki. QPipe: A Simultaneously Pipelined Relational Query Engine. In *Proceedings of the ACM SIGMOD International Conference on Management of Data*, pages 383–394, 2005.

[25] S. Idreos, I. Alagiannis, R. Johnson, and A. Ailamaki. Here are my Data Files. Here are my Queries. Where are my Results? In *Proceedings of the 5th Biennial Conference on Innovative Data Systems Research (CIDR)*, pages 57–68, 2011.

[26] S. Idreos, F. Groffen, N. Nes, S. Manegold, K. S. Mullender, and M. L. Kersten. MonetDB: Two Decades of Research in Column-oriented Database Architectures. *IEEE Data Engineering Bulletin*, 35(1):40–45, 2012.

[27] S. Idreos, M. L. Kersten, and S. Manegold. Database Cracking. In *Proceedings of the 3rd Biennial Conference on Innovative Data Systems Research (CIDR)*, pages 68–78, 2007.

[28] S. Idreos, M. L. Kersten, and S. Manegold. Updating a Cracked Database. In *Proceedings of the ACM SIGMOD International Conference on Management of Data*, pages 413–424, 2007.

[29] S. Idreos, M. L. Kersten, and S. Manegold. Self-Organizing Tuple Reconstruction in Column-Stores. In *Proceedings of the ACM SIGMOD International Conference on Management of Data*, pages 297–308, 2009.

[30] S. Idreos and E. Liarou. dbTouch: Analytics at your Fingertips. In *Proceedings of the 6th Biennial Conference on Innovative Data Systems Research (CIDR)*, 2013.

[31] S. Idreos, S. Manegold, H. A. Kuno, and G. Graefe. Merging What's Cracked, Cracking What's Merged: Adaptive Indexing in Main-Memory Column-Stores. *Proceedings of the Very Large Data Bases Endowment (PVLDB)*, 4(9):585–597, 2011.

[32] H. V. Jagadish, A. Chapman, A. Elkiss, M. Jayapandian, Y. Li, A. Nandi, and C. Yu. Making Database Systems Usable. In *Proceedings of the ACM SIGMOD International Conference on Management of Data*, pages 13–24, 2007.

[33] R. Johnson, I. Pandis, N. Hardavellas, A. Ailamaki, and B. Falsafi. Shore-MT: A Scalable Storage Manager for the Multicore Era. In *Proceedings of the 12th International Conference on Extending Database Technology (EDBT)*, pages 24–35, 2009.

[34] R. Kallman, H. Kimura, J. Natkins, A. Pavlo, A. Rasin, S. B. Zdonik, E. P. C. Jones, S. Madden, M. Stonebraker, Y. Zhang, J. Hugg, and D. J. Abadi. H-store: A High-Performance, Distributed Main Memory Transaction Processing System. *Proceedings of the Very Large Data Bases Endowment (PVLDB)*, 1(2):1496–1499, 2008.

[35] A. Kemper and T. Neumann. HyPer: A Hybrid OLTP&OLAP Main Memory Database System Based on Virtual Memory Snapshots. In *Proceedings of the IEEE 27th International Conference on Data Engineering (ICDE)*, pages 195–206, 2011.

[36] M. L. Kersten, S. Idreos, S. Manegold, and E. Liarou. The Researcher's Guide to the Data Deluge: Querying a Scientific Database in Just a Few Seconds. *Proceedings of the Very Large Data Bases Endowment (PVLDB)*, 4(12):1474–1477, 2011.

[37] U. Khurana and A. Deshpande. HiNGE: Enabling Temporal Network Analytics at Scale. In *Proceedings of the ACM SIGMOD International Conference on Management of Data*, pages 1089–1092, 2013.

[38] C. Kim, E. Sedlar, J. Chhugani, T. Kaldewey, A. D. Nguyen, A. D. Blas, V. W. Lee, N. Satish, and P. Dubey. Sort vs. Hash Revisited: Fast Join Implementation on Modern Multi-Core CPUs. *Proceedings of the Very Large Data Bases Endowment (PVLDB)*, 2(2):1378–1389, 2009.

[39] A. Kumar, F. Niu, and C. Ré. Hazy: Making it Easier to Build and Maintain Big-Data Analytics. *Communications of the ACM*, 56(3):40–49, 2013.

[40] N. Laptev, K. Zeng, and C. Zaniolo. Very Fast Estimation for Result and Accuracy of Big Data Analytics: The EARL System. In *Proceedings of the IEEE 29th International Conference on Data Engineering (ICDE)*, pages 1296–1299, 2013.

[41] Y. Li and J. M. Patel. BitWeaving: Fast Scans for Main Memory Data Processing. In *Proceedings of the ACM SIGMOD International Conference on Management of Data*, pages 289–300, 2013.

[42] E. Liarou and S. Idreos. dbTouch in Action Database Kernels for Touch-based Data Exploration. In *Proceedings of the IEEE 30th International Conference on Data Engineering (ICDE)*, pages 1262–1265, 2014.

[43] M. Lühring, K.-U. Sattler, K. Schmidt, and E. Schallehn. Autonomous Management of Soft Indexes. In *Proceedings of the 2nd International Workshop on Self-Managing Data Bases (SMDB)*, pages 450–458, 2007.

[44] H. Pirk, E. Petraki, S. Idreos, S. Manegold, and M. L. Kersten. Database Cracking: Fancy Scan, not Poor Man's Sort! In *Proceedings of the 10th International Workshop on Data Management on New Hardware (DaMoN)*, 2014.

[45] O. Polychroniou and K. A. Ross. A Comprehensive Study of Main-memory Partitioning and Its Application to Large-scale Comparison- and Radix-sort. In *Proceedings of the ACM SIGMOD International Conference on Management of Data*, pages 755–766, 2014.

[46] S. Richter, J.-A. QuianÃľ-Ruiz, S. Schuh, and J. Dittrich. Towards Zero-Overhead Static and Adaptive Indexing in Hadoop. *The Very Large Data Bases Journal (VLDB J.)*, 23(3):469–494, 2013.

[47] K. Schnaitter, S. Abiteboul, T. Milo, and N. Polyzotis. COLT: Continuous On-Line Tuning. In *Proceedings of the ACM SIGMOD International Conference on Management of Data*, pages 793–795, 2006.

[48] F. M. Schuhknecht, A. Jindal, and J. Dittrich. The Uncracked Pieces in Database Cracking. *Proceedings of the Very Large Data Bases Endowment (PVLDB)*, 7(2):97–108, 2013.

[49] J. Zhou and K. A. Ross. Implementing Database Operations Using SIMD Instructions. In *Proceedings of the ACM SIGMOD International Conference on Management of Data*, pages 145–156, 2002.

[50] D. C. Zilio, J. Rao, S. Lightstone, G. M. Lohman, A. J. Storm, C. Garcia-Arellano, and S. Fadden. DB2 Design Advisor: Integrated Automatic Physical Database Design. In *Proceedings of the 30th International Conference on Very Large Data Bases (VLDB)*, pages 1087–1097, 2004.

[51] K. Zoumpatianos, S. Idreos, and T. Palpanas. Indexing for Interactive Exploration of Big Data Series. In *Proceedings of the ACM SIGMOD International Conference on Management of Data*, pages 1555–1566, 2014.

[52] *MonetDB*. `www.monetdb.org`.

CliffGuard: A Principled Framework for Finding Robust Database Designs

Barzan Mozafari   Eugene Zhen Ye Goh   Dong Young Yoon
University of Michigan, Ann Arbor
{mozafari,vanblaze,dyoon}@umich.edu

ABSTRACT

A fundamental problem in database systems is choosing *the best physical design*, i.e., a small set of auxiliary structures that enable the fastest execution of future queries. Almost all commercial databases come with designer tools that create a number of indices or materialized views (together comprising the *physical design*) that they exploit during query processing. Existing designers are what we call *nominal*; that is, they assume that their input parameters are precisely known and equal to some nominal values. For instance, since future workload is often not known *a priori*, it is common for these tools to optimize for past workloads in hopes that future queries and data will be similar. In practice, however, these parameters are often noisy or missing. Since nominal designers do not take the influence of such uncertainties into account, they find designs that are sub-optimal and remarkably brittle. Often, as soon as the future workload deviates from the past, their overall performance falls off a cliff. Thus, we propose a new type of database designer that is *robust* against parameter uncertainties, so that overall performance degrades more gracefully when future workloads deviate from the past. Users express their risk tolerance by deciding on how much nominal optimality they are willing to trade for attaining their desired level of robustness against uncertain situations. To the best of our knowledge, this paper is the first to adopt the recent breakthroughs in *robust optimization theory* to build a practical framework for solving one of the most fundamental problems in databases, replacing today's brittle designs with robust designs that guarantee a predictable and consistent performance.

Categories and Subject Descriptors

H.2.2 [**Database Management**]: [Physical Design]

Keywords

Physical Design; Robust Optimization; Workload Resilience

1. INTRODUCTION

Database management systems are among the most critical software components in our world today. Many important applications across enterprise, science, and government depend on database technology to derive insight from their data and make timely decisions.

SIGMOD'15, May 31–June 4, 2015, Melbourne, Victoria, Australia.
Copyright © 2015 ACM 978-1-4503-2758-9/15/05 ...$15.00.
http://dx.doi.org/10.1145/2723372.2749454.

To fulfill this crucial role, a database (or its administrator) must make many important decisions on how to provision and tune the system in order to deliver the best performance possible, such as which materialized views, indices, or samples to build. While these auxiliary structures can significantly improve performance, they also incur storage and maintenance overheads. In fact, most practical budgets only allow for building a handful of indices and a dozen materialized views out of an exponential number of possible structures. For instance, for a data-warehouse with 100 columns, there are at least $\Omega(3^{100})$ sorted projections to choose from (each column can be either absent, or in ascending/ descending order). Thus, a fundamental database problem is finding the best *physical design*; that is, finding a set of indices and/or materialized views that optimizes the performance of future queries.

Modern databases come with designer tools (a.k.a. auto-tuning tools) that take certain parameters of a target workload (e.g., queries, data distribution, and various cost estimates) as input, and then use different heuristics to search the design space and find an optimal design (e.g., a set of indices or materialized views) within their time and storage budgets. However, these designs are only optimal for the input parameters provided to the designer. Unfortunately, in practice, these parameters are subject to many sources of uncertainty, such as noisy environments, approximation errors (e.g., in the query optimizer's cost or cardinality estimates [11]), and missing or time-varying parameters. Most notably, since future queries are unknown, these tools usually optimize for past queries in *hopes* that future ones will be similar.

Existing designer tools (e.g., Index Tuning Wizard [7] and Tuning Advisor in Microsoft SQL Server [26], Teradata's Index Wizard [20], IBM DB2's Design Advisor [76], Oracle's SQL Tuning Adviser [31], Vertica's DBD [47, 71], and Parinda for Postgres [54]) do not take into account the *influence of such uncertainties* on the optimality of their design, and therefore, produce designs that are *sub-optimal* and *remarkably brittle*. We call all these existing designers ***nominal***. That is, all these tools assume that their input parameters are precisely known and equal to some nominal values. As a result, overall performance often plummets as soon as future workload deviates from the past (say, due to the arrival of new data or a shift in day-to-day queries). These dramatic performance decays are severely disruptive for time-critical applications. They also waste critical human and computational resources, as dissatisfied customers request vendor inspections, often resulting in re-tuning/re-designing the database to restore the required level of performance.

Our Goal — To overcome the shortcomings of nominal designers, we propose a new type of designers that are immune to parameter uncertainties as much as desired; that is, they are ***robust***. Our robust designer gives database administrators a *knob* to decide exactly how much nominal optimality to trade for a desired level of robustness. For instance, users may demand a set of optimal materialized views with an assurance that they must remain robust against change in their workload of up to 30%. A more conservative user may demand a higher degree of robustness, say 60%, at the expense of less nominal optimality. Robust designs are highly superior to nominal ones, as:

(a) Nominal designs are inherently brittle and subject to performance cliffs, while the performance of a robust design will degrade *more gracefully.*

(b) By taking uncertainties into account, robust designs can guard against worst-case scenarios, delivering a more consistent and predictable performance to time-sensitive applications.

(c) Given the highly non-linear and complex (and possibly non-convex) nature of database systems, a workload may have more than one optimal design. Thus, it is completely conceivable that a robust design may be nominally optimal as well (see [15, 16] for such examples in other domains).

(d) A robust design can significantly reduce operational costs by requiring less frequent database re-designs.

Previous Approaches — There has been some pioneering work on incorporating parameter uncertainties in databases [11, 25, 30, 35, 56, 63]. These techniques are specific to run-time query optimization and do not easily extend to physical designs. Other heuristics have been proposed for improving physical designs through workload compression (i.e., omitting workload details) [24, 45] or modifying the query optimizer to return richer statistics [36]. Unfortunately, these approaches are not principled and thus do not necessarily guarantee robustness. (In Section 6.4, we compare against commercial databases that use such heuristics.)

To avoid these limitations, adaptive indexing schemes such as Database Cracking [39, 43] take the other extreme by completely ignoring the past workload in deciding which indices to build; instead of an *offline* design, they incrementally create and refine indices as queries arrive, *on demand.* However, even these techniques need to decide which subsets of columns to build an incremental index on.[1] Instead of completely relying on past workloads or abandoning the offline physical design, in this paper we present a principled framework for directly maximizing robustness, which enables users to decide on the extent to which they want to rely on past information, and the extent of uncertainty they want to be robust against. (We discuss the merits of previous work in Section 7.)

Our Approach — Recent breakthroughs in Operations Research on robust optimization (RO) theory have created new hopes for achieving robustness and optimality in a principled and tractable fashion [15, 16, 29, 75]. In this paper, we present the first attempt at applying RO theory to building a practical framework for solving one of the most fundamental problems in databases, namely finding the best physical design. In particular, we study the effects of workload changes on query latency. Since OLTP workloads tend to be more predictable (e.g., transactions are often instances of a few templates [57, 58]), we focus on OLAP workloads where exploratory and ad-hoc queries are quite common. Developing this robust framework is a departure from the traditional way of designing and tuning databases: from today's brittle designs to a principled world of robust designs that guarantee a predictable and consistent performance.

[1]Moreover, on-demand and continuous physical re-organizations are not acceptable in many applications, which is why nearly all commercial databases still rely on their offline designers.

RO Theory — The field of RO has taken many strides over the past decade [15]. In particular, the seminal work of Bertsimas et al. [16] has been successfully applied to a number of drastically different domains, from nano-photonic design of telescopes [16] to thin-film manufacturing [18] and system-on-chip architectures [60]. To the best of our knowledge, developing a principled framework for applying RO theory to physical design problems is the first application of these techniques in a database context, which involves a number of unique challenges not previously faced in any of these other applications of RO theory (discussed in Section 4.2).

A common misconception about the RO framework is that it requires knowledge of the extent of uncertainty, e.g., in our case, an upper bound on how much the future workload will deviate from the past one.[2] To the contrary, the power of the RO formulation is that it allows users to freely request any degree of robustness that they wish, say Γ, *purely* based on their own risk tolerance and preferences [13, 17]. Regardless of whether the actual amount of uncertainty exceeds or stays lower than Γ, the RO framework guarantees will remain valid; that is, the delivered design is promised to remain optimal as long as the uncertainty remains below the user-requested threshold Γ, and beyond that (i.e., if uncertainty exceeds Γ) is in accordance to user's accepted degree of risk [17]. In other words, the beauty of RO theory is that it provides a framework for expressing and delivering reliability guarantees by decoupling them from the actual uncertainty in the environment (here, the future workload).

Contributions — In this paper, we make these contributions:

- We formulate the problem of robust physical design using RO theory (Section 3).
- We design a principled algorithm, called `CliffGuard`, by adapting the state-of-the-art framework for solving non-convex RO problems. `CliffGuard`'s design is generic and can potentially work with any existing designers and databases without modifying their internals (Section 4).
- We implement and evaluate `CliffGuard` using two major commercial databases (HP Vertica and DBMS-X[3]) on two synthetic workloads as well as a real workload of 430+K OLAP queries issued by one of Vertica's major customers over a 1-year period (Section 6).

In summary, compared to Vertica's state-of-the-art commercial designer [47, 71], our robust designer reduces the average and maximum latency of queries on average by 7× and 18× (and up to 14× and 40×), respectively. Similarly, `CliffGuard` improves over DBMS-X by 3–5×. CliffGuard is currently available as an open-source, third-party tool [1].

2. SYSTEM OVERVIEW

Physical Database Designs — A physical design in a database is a set of auxiliary structures, often built *offline*, which are used to speed up future queries as they arrive. The type of auxiliary structures used often depend on the specific database architecture. Most

[2]This misconception is caused by differing terminology used in other disciplines, such as mechanical engineering (ME) where "robust optimization" refers to a different type of optimization which requires some knowledge of the uncertainty of the physical environment [32]. The Operations Research notion of RO used in this paper is called *reliability optimization* in the ME literature [68].

[3]DBMS-X is a major database system, which we cannot reveal due to the vendor's restrictions on publishing performance results.

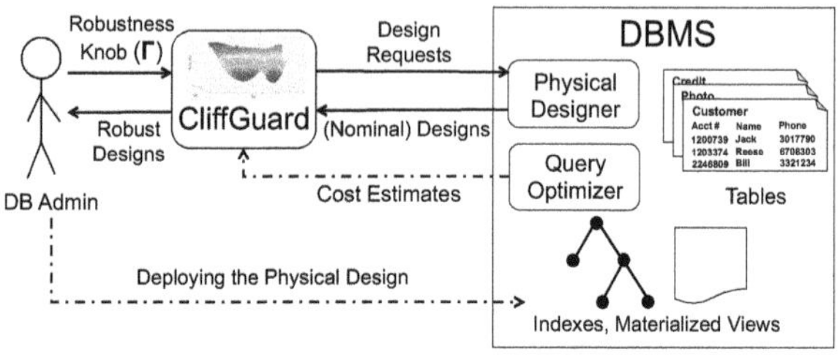

Figure 1: The `CliffGuard` architecture.

databases use both materialized views and indices in their physical designs. Materialized views are typically more common in analytical workloads. Approximate databases use small samples of the data (rather than its entirety) to speed up query processing at the cost of accuracy [2, 3, 4, 23, 73, 74]. Physical designs in these systems consist of different types of samples (e.g., stratified on different columns [5, 23]). Some modern columnar databases, such as Vertica [71], build a number of column *projections*, each sorted differently. Instead of traditional indices, Vertica chooses a projection with the appropriate sort order (depending on the columns in the query) in order to locate relevant tuples quickly. In all these examples, the space of these auxiliary structures is extremely large if not infinite, e.g., there are $O(2^N \cdot N!)$ possible projections or indices for a table of N columns (i.e., different subsets and orders of columns). Thus, the physical design problem is choosing a small number of these structures using a fixed budget (in terms of time, space, or maintenance overhead) such that the overall performance is optimized for a target workload.

Design Principles — A major goal in the design of our `CliffGuard` algorithm is compatibility with almost any existing database in order to facilitate its adoption in the commercial world. Thus, we have made two key decisions in our design. First, `CliffGuard` should operate alongside an existing (nominal) designer rather than replacing it. Despite their lack of robustness, existing designers are highly sophisticated tools hand-tuned over the years to find the best physical designs efficiently, given their input parameters. Because of this heavy investment, most vendors are reluctant to abandon these tools completely. However, some vendors have expressed interest in `CliffGuard` as long as it can operate alongside their existing designer and *improve* its output. Second, `CliffGuard` is designed to treat existing designers as a *black-box* (i.e., without modifying their internal implementations). This is to conform to the proprietary nature of commercial designers and also to widen the applicability of `CliffGuard` to different databases. By delegating the nominal designs to existing designers, `CliffGuard` remains a genetic framework agnostic to the specific details of the design objects (e.g., they can be materialized views, samples, indices, or projections).

These design principles have already allowed us to evaluate `CliffGuard` for two database products with drastically different design problems (i.e., Vertica and DBMS-X). Without requiring any changes to their internal implementations, `CliffGuard` significantly improves on the sophisticated designers of these leading databases (see Section 6). Thus, we believe that `CliffGuard` can be easily used to speed up other database systems as well.

Architecture — Figure 1 depicts the high-level workflow of how `CliffGuard` is to be used alongside a database system. The database administrator states her desired degree of robustness Γ to `CliffGuard`, which is located outside the DBMS. `CliffGuard` in turn invokes the existing physical designer via its public API. After evaluating the output (nominal) design sent back from the existing designer, `CliffGuard` may decide to manipulate the existing designer's output by merely modifying some of its input parameters (in a principled manner) and invoking its API again. `CliffGuard` repeats this process, until it is satisfied with the robustness of the design produced by the nominal designer. The final (robust) design is then sent back to the administrator, who may decide to deploy it in the DBMS.

3. PROBLEM FORMULATION

In this section, we present a simple but powerful formulation of robustness in the context of physical database design. This formulation will allow us to employ recently proposed ideas in the theory of robust optimization (RO) and develop a principled and effective algorithm for finding robust database designs, which will be presented in Section 4. First, we define some notations.

Notations — For a given database, the **design space** $\mathcal{S}$ is the set of all possible structures of interest, such as indices on different subsets of columns, materialized views, different samples of the data, or a combination of these. For example, Vertica's designer [71] materializes a number of *projections*, each sorted differently:

```
CREATE PROJECTION   projection_name
  AS SELECT   col1, col2, ..., colN
  FROM   anchor_table
  ORDER BY   col1', col2', ..., colK';
```

Here, $\mathcal{S}$ is extremely large due to the exponential number of possible projections. Similarly, for decisions about building materialized views or (secondary) indices, $\mathcal{S}$ will contain all such possible structures. Existing database designers solve the following optimization problem (or aim to[4]):

$$D^{nom} = \mathbb{D}(W_0, B) = \underset{D \subseteq \mathcal{S},\ price(D) \leq B}{ArgMin} f(W_0, D) \quad (1)$$

where W_0 is the target **workload** (e.g., the set of user queries), B is a given **budget** (in terms of storage or maintenance overhead), $\mathbb{D}$ is a **nominal designer** that takes a workload and budget as input parameters, $price(D)$ is the **price** of choosing D (e.g., the total size of the projections in D), and $f(W_0, D)$ is our **cost function** for executing workload W_0 using design D (e.g., f can be the query latency). We call such designs **nominal** as they are optimal for the nominal value of the given parameters (e.g., the target workload). All existing designers [7, 31, 54, 71, 76] are *nominal*: they either minimize the expression above directly, or follow other heuristics aimed at approximate minimization. Despite several heuristics to avoid over-fitting a given workload (e.g., omitting query details [24, 45]), nominal designers suffer from many shortcomings in practice; see Sections 1 and 6.4.

Robust Designs — This paper's goal is finding designs that are robust against *worst-case* scenarios that can arise from uncertain situations. This concept of *robustness* can be illustrated using the toy example of Figure 2, which features a design space with only three possible designs and a toy workload that is represented by a single real-value parameter μ. When our current estimate of μ is μ_0, a nominal designer will pick design D_1 since it minimizes the cost at μ_0. But if we want a design that remains optimal even if our parameter changes by up to Γ, then a robust designer will pick design D_2 instead of D_1, even though the latter has a lower cost at μ_0. This is because the *worst-case* cost of D_2 over the $[\mu_0 - \Gamma, \mu_0 + \Gamma]$ is lower than that of D_1; that is, D_2 is robust against uncertainty of up to Γ. Similarly, if we decide to guard against a still greater degree of uncertainty, say for an estimation error as high as $\Gamma' > \Gamma$, a robust designer would this time pick D_3 instead of D_2, as the former has a lower worst-case cost in $[\mu_0 - \Gamma', \mu_0 + \Gamma']$ than the other designs.

[4]Existing designers often use heuristics or greedy strategies [55], which lead to *approximations* of the nominal optima.

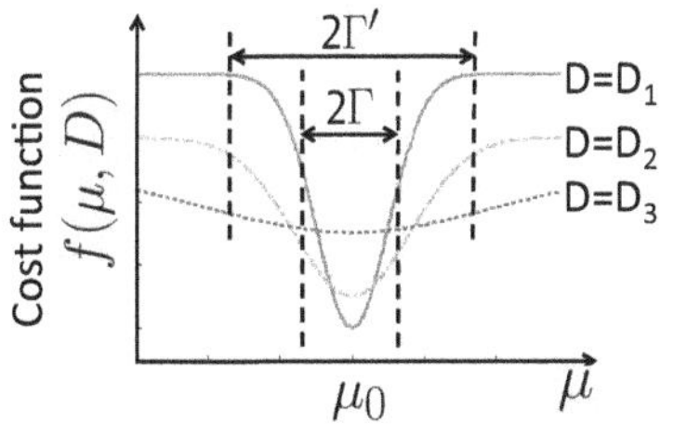

Figure 2: Design D_1 is nominally optimal at μ_0 while designs D_2 and D_3 are robust against an uncertainty of $\pm\Gamma$ and $\pm\Gamma'$ in our parameter μ_0, respectively.

Formally, a robust design D^{rob} can be defined as:

$$D^{rob} = \tilde{\mathbb{D}}(W_0, B, \mathcal{U}) = \underset{D \subseteq \mathcal{S},\ price(D) \leq B}{ArgMin} \quad \underset{W \in \mathcal{U}(W_0)}{Max} \ f(W, D)$$

where $\mathcal{U}(W_0)$ defines an uncertainty region around our target workload W_0. Here, $\tilde{\mathbb{D}}$ is a robust designer that will search for a design that minimizes the cost function regardless of where the target workload lands in this uncertainty region. In other words, this MiniMax formulation of robustness defines a robust design as one with the **best worst-case performance**.

Although the uncertainty region $\mathcal{U}(W_0)$ does not have to be circular, for ease of presentation in this paper we always define $\mathcal{U}(W_0)$ as a circular region of radius $\Gamma \geq 0$ centered at W_0, which we call the **Γ-neighborhood** of W_0. For instance, the Γ-neighborhood will be an interval when $W_0 \in \mathbb{R}$ (see Figure 2) and a circle when $\Gamma \in \mathbb{R}^2$. Since database workloads are not easily represented as real numbers, we need to use a distance function to define the Γ-neighborhood of a database workload W_0, namely:

$$D^{rob} = \tilde{\mathbb{D}}(W_0, B, \Gamma) = \underset{D \subseteq \mathcal{S},\ price(D) \leq B}{ArgMin} \quad \underset{\delta(W, W_0) \leq \Gamma}{Max} \ f(W, D) \tag{2}$$

Here, $\delta(.)$ is a user-defined distance function that takes a pair of workloads and returns a non-negative real number as their distance. Formulation (2) allows users to express their desired level of robustness by choosing the value of $\Gamma \geq 0$, where the larger the Γ, the more robust their design is. Note that a nominal design is a special case of a robust design where $\Gamma = 0$. In the rest of this paper, we will not explicitly mention the $price(D) \leq B$ constraint in our notations, but it will always be implied in both nominal and robust designs. (Appropriate choices of Γ and δ are discussed later in this section and in Section 5, respectively.)

We have chosen this formulation of robustness for several reasons. First, (2) is the standard notion of *robust optimization* in Operations Research [15], which enables us to adopt recently proposed RO algorithms that are highly tractable and effective (see Section 4). Second, formulation (2) requires no knowledge of the uncertainty distribution. (We will discuss the role of Γ shortly.) This is in contrast to an alternative formulation seeking to minimize the *expected* or 99%-quantile latency (rather than its worst-case). However, such a formulation would be a different type of optimization, called *stochastic optimization* [29], requiring a probability distribution on every possible workload (which is impossible to obtain in most real-world scenarios). Finally, despite their MiniMax (i.e., worst-case) formulation, the RO solutions may not be overly conservative; surprisingly, they are often similar to those produced by stochastic optimization, which is substantially less tractable (see [15]). In fact, in our database context, RO solutions are also nominally superior, thanks to databases' non-convex cost functions and complex design spaces (see Section 6.4).

A Knob for Robustness — As mentioned in Section 1, the role of Γ in RO formulation (2) is sometimes misunderstood to be an upper bound on the degree of uncertainty, i.e., Γ should be chosen such that the future workload W will lie in W_0's Γ-neighborhood. To the contrary, the beauty of formulation (2) is that it allows users to choose any Γ value based purely on their own business needs and risk tolerance, regardless of the actual amount of uncertainty in the future. In other words, Γ is *not* an upper bound on the actual uncertainty in the environment, but rather the amount of actual uncertainty that the user decides to guard against. This is a subtle but important distinction, because robustness comes at the price of reduced nominal optimality. In the example of Figure 2, D_2 is robust against a greater degree of uncertainty than D_2 but is nominally more expensive at $\mu = \mu_0$. Therefore, it is important to interpret Γ as a *robustness knob* and not a prediction of future uncertainty.

The choice of Γ depends completely on the end users' risk tolerance and is not the focus of this paper. Our paper's contribution is a framework that will deliver a design that guarantees the requested level of robustness for any value of Γ chosen by the user. For instance, a user may take the simplest approach and use the sequence of workload changes over the past N windows of queries, say

$$\delta(W_0, W_1), \delta(W_1, W_2), \cdots, \delta(W_{N-1}, W_N)$$

and take their average, max, or $k \times$max (for some constant $k > 1$) as a reasonable choice of Γ when finding a robust design for W_{N+1} using W_N. Alternatively, a user may employ more sophisticated techniques (e.g., timeseries forecasting [22]) to obtain a more accurate prediction for $\delta(W_N, W_N + 1)$. Regardless of the strategy, the actual uncertainty can always exceed a user's predictions. However, this problem is no different from any other provisioning problem. For instance, many customers provision their database resources according to, say, 3× their current peak load. This means that according to their business needs, they accept the risk of their future workload suddenly increasing by 4×. This is analogous to the user's choice of Γ here. Also, note that even if users magically knew the exact value of $\delta(W_N, W_{N+1})$ in advance, the existing nominal designers' performance would remain the same since they have no mechanism for incorporating a bounded uncertainty into their analysis. (A nominal designer would only perform better if we knew the actual W_{N+1} and not just its distance from W_N.) As previously explained, while our proposed designer does not *require* any prior knowledge of the uncertainty in order to deliver the user's robustness requirements, it can naturally incorporate additional of the future workload if made available by the user.

In Section 6.5, we study the effects of different Γ choices and show that, in practice, our algorithm performs no worse than the nominal designer even when presented with poor (i.e., extremely low or extremely high) Γ choices.

4. OUR ALGORITHM

In the previous section, we provided the RO formulation of the physical design for databases. Over the past decade, there have been many advances in the theory of RO for solving problems with similar formulations as (2), for many different classes of cost functions and uncertainty sets (see [15] for a recent survey). Here, the most relevant to our problem is the seminal work of Bertsimas et al. [16], hereon referred to as the BNT algorithm. Unlike most RO algorithms, BNT does not require the cost function to have a closed-form. This makes BNT an ideal match for our database context: our cost function is often the query latency, which does not have an explicit closed-form, i.e., latency can only be *measured* by executing the query itself or *approximated* using the query optimizer's cost estimates. BNT's second strength is that it does not re-

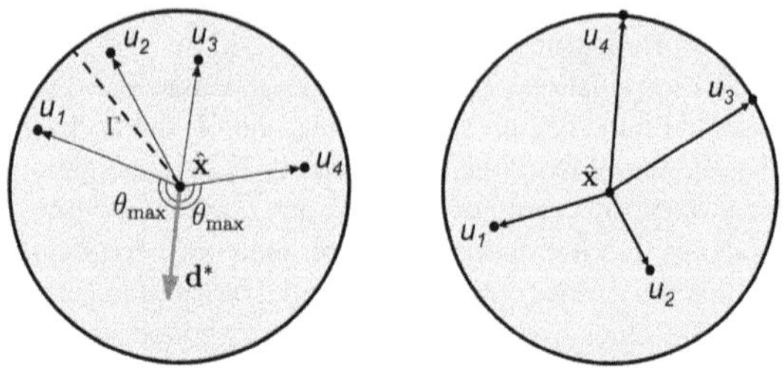

Figure 3: (a) A descent direction d^* is one that moves away from *all* the worst-neighbors ($\theta_{max} \geq 90°$); (b) here, due to the location of the worst-neighbors, no descent direction exists.

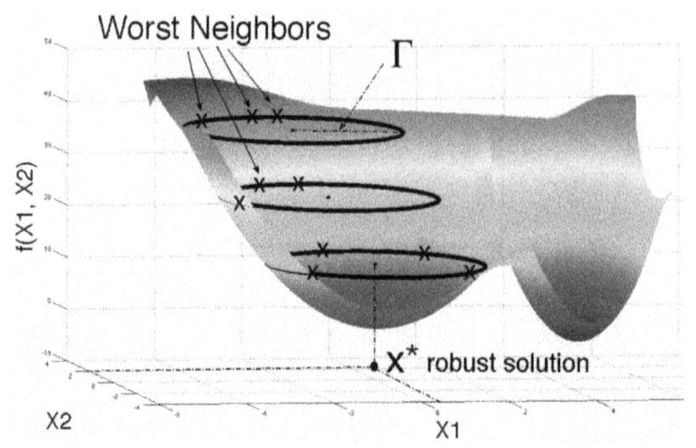

Figure 4: Geometric interpretation of the iterations in BNT.

quire convexity: BNT guarantees a global robust solution when the cost function is convex, and convergence to a local robust solution even when it is not convex. Given the complex nature of modern databases, establishing convexity for query latencies can be difficult (e.g., in some situations, additional load can reduce latency by improving the cache hit rate [57]).[5]

First, we provide background on the BNT framework in Section 4.1. Then, in Section 4.2, we identify the unique challenges that arise in applying BNT to database problems. Finally, in Section 4.3, we propose our BNT-based `CliffGuard` algorithm, which overcomes these challenges.

4.1 The BNT Algorithm

In this section, we offer a geometric interpretation of the BNT algorithm for an easier understanding of the main ideas behind the algorithm. (Interested readers can find a more formal discussion of the algorithm in the Operations Research literature [16].)

We use Figure 3(a) to illustrate how the BNT algorithm works. Here, imagine a simplified world in which each decision is a 2-dimensional point in Euclidean space. Since the environment is noisy or unpredictable, the user demands a decision x^* that comes with some *reliability* guarantees. For example, instead of asking for a decision x^* that simply minimizes $f(x)$, the user requires an x^* whose worst-case cost is minimized for arbitrary noise vectors Δx within a radius of Γ, namely:

$$x^* = \underset{x}{ArgMin} \underset{||\Delta x||_2 \leq \Gamma}{Max} \quad f(x + \Delta x) \tag{3}$$

Here, $||\Delta x||_2$ is the length (L_2-norm) of the noise vectors. This means that the user expresses his/her reliability requirement as an uncertainty region, here a circle of radius Γ, and demands that our $f(x^* + \Delta x)$ still be minimized no matter where the noisy environment moves our initial decision within this region. This uncertainty region (i.e., the Γ-neighborhood) is shown as a shaded disc in Figure 3(a).

To meet the user's reliability requirement, the BNT algorithm takes a starting point, say $\hat{x}$, and performs a number of iterations as follows. In each iteration, BNT first identifies all the points within the Γ-neighborhood of $\hat{x}$ that have the highest cost, called the *worst-neighbors* of $\hat{x}$. In Figure 3(a), there are four worst-neighbors, shown as $u_1, \cdots, u_4$. Let $\Delta x_1, \cdots, \Delta x_4$ be the vectors that connect $\hat{x}$ to each of these worst-neighbors, namely $u_i = \hat{x} + \Delta x_i$ for i=1, 2, 3, 4.

Once the worst-neighbors of $\hat{x}$ are identified, the BNT algorithm finds a direction that moves away from all of them. This direction is called the *descent direction.* In our geometric interpretation, a descent direction $\vec{\mathbf{d}}^*$ is one that maximizes the angle θ in Figure 3(a) by halving the reflex angle between the vectors connecting $\hat{x}$ to u_1 and u_4. The BNT algorithm then takes a small step along this descent direction to reach a new decision point, say $\hat{x}'$, which will be at a greater distance from all of the worst-neighbors of $\hat{x}$. The algorithm repeats this process by looking for the new worst-neighbors in the Γ-neighborhood of $\hat{x}'$. (Bertsimas et al. prove that taking an appropriately-sized step along the descent direction reduces the worst-case cost at each iteration [16].) The algorithm ends (i.e., a robust solution is found) when no descent direction can be found. Figure 3(b) illustrates this situation, as any direction of movement within the Γ-neighborhood will bring the solution closer to at least one of the worst-neighbors. (Bertsimas et al. prove that this situation can only happen when we reach a local robust minimum, which will also be a global robust minimum when the cost function is convex.)

To visually demonstrate this convergence, we again use a geometric interpretation of the algorithm, as depicted in Figure 4.1. In this figure, the decision space consists of two-dimensional real vectors $(x_1, x_2) \in \mathbb{R}^2$ and the $f(x_1, x_2)$ surface corresponds to the cost of different points in this decision space. Here, the Γ-neighborhood in each iteration of BNT is shown as a transparent disc of radius Γ. Geometrically, to move away from the worst-neighbors at each step is equivalent to sliding down this disc along the steepest direction such that the disc always remains within the cost surface and parallel to the (x_1, x_2) plane. The algorithm ends when this disc's boundary touches the cost surface and cannot be sliced down any further without breaking through the cost surface—this is the case with the bottom-most disc in Figure 4.1; when this condition is met, the center of this disc represents a locally robust solution of the problem (marked as x^*) and its worst-neighbors lie on the boundary of its disc (marked as $\times$). The goal of BNT is to quickly find such discs and converge to the locally robust optimum.

The pseudocode of BNT is presented in Algorithm 1. Here, x_k is the current decision at the k'th iteration. As explained above, each iteration consists of two main steps: finding the worst-neighbors (neighborhood exploration, Line 5) and moving away from those neighbors if possible (local robust move, Lines 7–16). In Section 4.2, we discuss some of the challenges posed by these steps when applied to physical design problems in databases.

Theoretical Guarantees — When $f(x)$ is continuously differentiable with a bounded set of minimum points, Bertsimas et al. [16] show that their algorithm converges to the local optimum of the robust optimization problem (3), as long as the steps sizes t_k (Line 14 in Algorithm 1) are chosen such that $t_k > 0$, $\lim_{k \to \infty} t_k = 0$, and $\sum_{k=1}^{\infty} t_k = \infty$. For convex cost surfaces, this solution is also the global optimum. (With non-convex surfaces, BNT needs to be

[5]When the cost function is non-convex, the output of existing nominal designers is also only *locally* optimal. Thus, even in these cases, finding a local robust optimum is still a worthwhile endeavor.

Algorithm 1: Generic robust optimization via gradient descent.

Inputs: Γ: the radius of the uncertainty region,
$f(x)$: the cost of design x
Output: x^*: a robust design, i.e.,
$x^* = \underset{x}{ArgMin} \underset{||\Delta x||_2 \leq \Gamma}{Max} f(x + \Delta x)$

1 $x_1 \leftarrow$ pick an arbitrary vector **// the initial decision**
2 $k \leftarrow 1$ **// k is the number of iterations so far**
3 **while** *true* **do**
    // Neighborhood Exploration:
5     $U \leftarrow$ Find the set of worst-neighbors of x_k within its Γ-neighborhood
    // Robust Local Move:
7     $\vec{\mathbf{d}}^* \leftarrow$ FindDescentDirection(x_k, U)
    // See Fig 3(a) for FindDescentDirection**'s geometric intuition (formally defined in [59])**
9   **if** there is no such direction $\vec{\mathbf{d}}^*$ pointing away from all $u \in U$ **then**
11         $x^* \leftarrow x_k$ **// found a local robust solution**
12   **return** x^*
    else
14         $t_k \leftarrow$ choose an appropriate step size
15         $x_{k+1} \leftarrow x_k + t_k \cdot \vec{\mathbf{d}}^*$ **// move along the descent direction**
16         $k \leftarrow k + 1$ **// go to next iteration**
    end
end

repeated from different starting points to find multiple local optima and choose one that is more globally optimal.[6])

4.2 Challenges of Applying BNT to Database Problems

As mentioned earlier, since BNT does not require a closed-form cost function (or even convexity), it presents itself as the most appropriate technique in the RO literature for solving our physical design problems, especially since we want to avoid modifying the internals of the existing designers (due to their proprietary nature, see Section 2). However, BNT still hinges on certain key assumptions that prevent it from being directly applicable to our design problem. Next, we discuss each of these requirements and the unique challenges that they pose in a database context.

Proper distance metric — BNT requires a *proper* distance metric over the decision space, i.e., one that is symmetric and satisfies the triangle property. E.g., the L2-norm $||x||_2$ is a proper distance over the m-dimensional Euclidean space, since $||x_1 - x_2||_2 + ||x_2 - x_3||_2 \geq ||x_1 - x_3||_2 = ||x_3 - x_1||_2$ for any $x_1, x_2, x_3 \in \mathbb{R}^m$.

Challenge C1. To define an analogous notion of uncertainty in a database context, we need to have a distance metric $\delta(W_1, W_2)$ for any two sets of SQL queries, say W_1 and W_2, in order to express the uncertainty set of an existing workload W_0 as $\{W \mid \delta(W_0, W) \leq \Gamma\}$. Note that δ must be symmetric, triangular, and also capable of capturing the user's notion of a *workload change*. To the best of our knowledge, such a distance metric does not currently exist for database workloads.[7]

[6]When $f(x)$ is non-convex, the output of existing designers is also a local optimum. Thus, even in this case, finding local robust optima is still preferable (to a local nominal optimum).

[7]While workload drift is well-observed in the database community [40, 64], quantifying it has received surprisingly little attention.

Finding the worst-neighbors — BNT relies on our ability to find the worst-neighbors U (Algorithm 1, Line 5) in each iteration, which equates to finding *all* global maxima of the following optimization problem:

$$\underset{||\Delta x||_2 \leq \Gamma}{ArgMax} \; f(x_k + \Delta x) \tag{4}$$

In other words, the worst-neighbors are defined as:

$$U = \{x_k + \Delta x \mid f(x_k + \Delta x) = g(x_k), \; ||\Delta x||_2 \leq \Gamma\}$$

where $g(x)$ represents our worst-case cost function, defined as:

$$g(x) = \underset{||\Delta x||_2 \leq \Gamma}{Max} \; f(x + \Delta x)$$

When $g(x)$ is differentiable, finding its global maxima is straightforward, as one can simply take its derivative and solve the following equation:

$$g'(x) = 0 \tag{5}$$

All previous applications of the BNT framework have either involved a closed form cost function $f(x)$ with a differentiable worst-case cost function $g(x)$, where the worst-neighbors can be found by solving (5) (e.g., in industrial engineering [15] or chip design [60]), or a black-box cost function guaranteed to be continuously differentiable (e.g., in designing nano-photonic telescopes [16]).

Challenge C2. Unfortunately, most cost functions of interest in databases are not closed-form, differentiable, or even continuous. For instance, when f is the query latency, it does not have a closed-form; it is measured either via actual execution or by consulting the query optimizer's cost estimates. Also, even a small modification in the design or the query can cause a drastically different latency, e.g., when a query references a column that is omitted from a materialized view.

Finding a descent direction — BNT relies on our ability to efficiently find the (steepest) descent direction via a second-order cone program (SOCP) [16]. SOCPs require a continuous domain and can be solved via interior point methods [19].

Challenge C3. We cannot use the same SOCP formulation because the space of physical designs is not continuous. A physical design, say a set of projections, can be easily encoded as a binary vector. For instance, each projection can be represented as a vector in $\{0, 1\}^m$ where the i'th coordinate represents the presence or absence of the i'th column in the database. Different column-orders and a set of such structures can also be encoded using more dimensions. However, this and other possible encodings of a database design are inherently discrete. For instance, one cannot construct a conventional projection with only 0.3 of a column—a column is either included in the projection or not.

Moving along a descent direction — BNT assumes that the decision space (i.e., the domain of x) is continuous and hence, moving along a descent direction is trivial (Algorithm 1, Line 15). In other words, if x_k is a valid decision, then $x_k + t_k \cdot \vec{\mathbf{d}}^*$ is also a valid decision for any given $\mathbf{d}^*$ and $t_k > 0$.

Challenge C4. Even when a descent direction is found in the database design space, moving along that direction does not have any database equivalence. In other words, even when our vectors x_k and $\vec{\mathbf{d}}^*$ correspond to legitimate physical designs, $x_k + t_k \cdot \vec{\mathbf{d}}^*$ may no longer be meaningful since it may not correspond to any legitimate design, e.g., it may involve fractional coordinates for some of the columns depending on the value of t_k. Thus, we need to establish a different notion of *moving along a descent direction* for database designs.

In summary, in order to use BNT's principled framework, we need to develop analogous techniques in our database context for expressing distance and finding the worst-neighbors; we also need to define equivalent notions for finding and moving along a descent direction. Next, we explain how our `CliffGuard` algorithm overcomes challenges C1–C4 and uses BNT's framework to find robust physical database designs.

4.3 Our Algorithm: CliffGuard

In this section, we propose our novel algorithm, called `CliffGuard`, which builds upon BNT's principled framework by tailoring it to the problem of physical database design.

Before presenting our algorithm, we need to clarify a few notional differences. Unlike BNT, where the cost function $f(x)$ takes a single parameter x, the cost in `CliffGuard` is denoted as a two-parameter function $f(W, D)$ where W is a given workload and D is a given physical design. In other words, each point x in our space is a pair of elements (W, D). However, unlike BNT where vector x can be updated in its entirety, in `CliffGuard` (or any database designer) we only update the design element D; this is because the database designer can propose a new physical design to the user, but cannot impose a new workload on her as a means to improve robustness.

Algorithm 2 presents the pseudocode for `CliffGuard`. Like Algorithm 1, Algorithm 2 iteratively explores a neighborhood to find the worst-neighbors, then moves farther away from these neighbors in each iteration using an appropriate direction and step size. However, to apply these ideas in a database context (i.e., addressing challenges C1–C4 from Section 4.2), Algorithm 2 differs from Algorithm 1 in the following important ways.

Initialization (Algorithm 2, Lines 1–2) — `CliffGuard` starts by invoking the existing designer $\mathbb{D}$ to find a nominal design D for the initial workload W_0. (Later, D will be repeatedly replaced by designs that are more robust.) `CliffGuard` also creates a finite set of perturbed workloads $P = \{W_1, \cdots, W_n\}$ by sampling the workload space in the Γ-neighborhood of W_0. In other words, given a distance metric δ, we find n workloads $W_1, \cdots, W_n$ such that $\delta(W_i, W_0) \leq \Gamma$ for $i = 1, 2, \cdots, n$. (Section 5 discusses how to define δ for database workloads, how to choose n, and how to sample the workload space efficiently.) Next, as in BNT, `CliffGuard` starts an iterative search with a neighborhood exploration and a robust local move in each iteration.

Neighborhood Exploration (Algorithm 2, Line 6) — To find the worst-neighbors, in `CliffGuard` we need to also take the current design D into account (i.e., the set of worst-case neighbors of W_0 will depend on the physical design that we choose). Given that we cannot rely on the differentiability (or even continuity) of our worst-case cost function (Challenge C2), we use the worst-case costs on our sampled workloads P a proxy; instead of solving

$$\underset{\delta(W,W_0)\leq\Gamma}{Max} f(W, D) \tag{6}$$

we solve

$$\underset{W\in P}{Max} f(W, D) \tag{7}$$

Note that (7) cannot provide an unbiased approximation for (6) simply because P is a finite sample, and finite samples lead to biased estimates for extreme statistics such as min and max [70]. Thus, we do not rely on the nominal value of (7) to evaluate the quality of our design. Rather, we use the solutions to (7) as a proxy to guide our search in moving away from highly (though not necessarily the most) expensive neighbors. In our implementation, we further mitigate this sampling bias by loosening our selection criterion to include all neighbors that have a high-enough cost (e.g., top-K or top 20%) instead of only those that have the maximum cost. To implement this step, we simply enumerate each workload in P and measure its latency on the given design.

Robust Local Move (Algorithm 2, Lines 8–15) — To find equivalent database notions for finding and moving along a descent direction (C3 and C4), we use the following idea. The ultimate goal of finding and moving along a descent direction is to reduce the worst-case cost of the current design. In `CliffGuard`, we can achieve this goal directly by *manipulating* the existing designer by feeding it a mixture of the existing workload and its worst-neighbors as a single workload.[8] The intuition is that since nominal designers (by definition) produce designs that minimize the cost of their input workload, the cost of our previous worst-neighbors will no longer be as high, which is equivalent to moving our design farther away from those worst-neighbors. The questions then are (i) how do we mix these workloads, and (ii) what if the designer's output leads to a higher worst-case cost?

The answer to question (i) is a weighted union, where we take the union of all the queries in the original workload as well as those in the worst-neighbors, after weighting the latter queries according to a scaling factor α, their individual frequencies of occurrence in their workload, and their latencies against the current design. Taking latencies and frequencies into account encourages the nominal designer to seek designs that reduce the cost of more expensive and/or popular queries. Scaling factor α, which serves the same purpose as step-size in BNT, allows `CliffGuard` to control the distance of movement away from the worst-neighbors.

We also need to address question (ii) because unlike BNT, where the step size t_k could be computed to ensure a reduction in the worst cost, here our α factor may in fact lead to a worse design (e.g., by moving too far from the original workload). To solve this problem, `CliffGuard` dynamically adjusts the step-size using a common technique called *backtracking line search* [19], similar to a binary-search. Each time the algorithm succeeds in moving away from the worst-neighbors, we consider a larger step size (by a factor $\lambda_{success} > 1$) to speed up the search towards the robust solution, and each time we fail, we reduce the step size (by a factor $0 < \lambda_{failure} < 1$) as we may have moved past the robust solution (hence observing a higher worst-case cost).

Termination (Algorithm 2, Lines 17–20) — We repeat this process until we find a local robust optimum (or reach the maximum number of steps, when under a time constraint).

5. EXPRESSING ROBUSTNESS GUARANTEES

In this section, we define a database-specific distance metric δ so that users can express their robustness requirements by specifying a Γ-neighborhood (as an uncertainty set, described in Section 3) around a given workload W_0, and demanding that their design must be robust for any future workload W as long as $\delta(W_0, W) \leq \Gamma$. Thus, users can demand arbitrary degrees of robustness according to their performance requirements. For mission-critical applications more sensitive to sudden performance drops, users can be more conservative (specifying a larger Γ). At the other extreme, users expecting no change (or less sensitive to it) can fall back to the nominal case ($\Gamma = 0$).

[8]Remember that existing designers only take a single workload as their input parameter.

Algorithm 2: The `CliffGuard` algorithm.

Inputs: Γ: the desired degree of robustness,
δ: a distance metric defined over pairs of workloads,
W_0: initial workload,
$\mathbb{D}$: an existing (nominal) designer,
f: the cost function (or its estimate),

Output: D^*: a robust design, i.e., $D^* = \underset{D}{ArgMin} \underset{\delta(W-W_0)\leq\Gamma}{Max} f(W, D)$

$D \leftarrow \mathbb{D}(W_0)$ **// Invoke the existing designer to find a nominal design for W_0**
$P \leftarrow \{W_i \mid 1 \leq i \leq n,\ \delta(W_i, W) \leq \Gamma\}$ **// Sample some perturbed workloads in the Γ-neighbor of W_0**
Pick some $\alpha > 0$ **// some initial size for the descending steps**

while *true* **do**
    // Neighborhood Exploration:
    $U \leftarrow \{\tilde{W}_1, \cdots, \tilde{W}_m\}$ where $\tilde{W}_i \in P$ and $f(\tilde{W}_i, D) = \underset{W\in P}{Max} f(W, D)$ **// Pick perturbed workloads with the worst performance on D**
    // Robust Local Move:
    $W_{moved} \leftarrow$ MoveWorkload($W_0, \{\tilde{W}_1, \cdots, \tilde{W}_m\}, f, D, \alpha$) **//Build a new workload by moving closer to W_0's worst-neighbors (see Alg. 3)**
    $D' \leftarrow \mathbb{D}(W_{moved})$ **// consider the nominal design for W_{moved} as an alternative design**
    if $\underset{W\in P}{Max} f(W, D') < \underset{W\in P}{Max} f(W, D)$ ***// Does D' improve on the existing design in terms of the worst-case performance?***
    then
        $D \leftarrow D'$ **// Take D' as your new design**
        $\alpha \leftarrow \alpha * \lambda_{success}$ (for some $\lambda_{success} > 1$) **// increase the step size for the next move along the descent direction**
    else
        $\alpha \leftarrow \alpha * \lambda_{failure}$ (for some $\lambda_{failure} < 1$) **// consider a smaller step next time**
    end
    if your time budget is exhausted or many iterations have gone with no improvements
    then
        $D^* \leftarrow D$ **// the current design is robust**
        return D^*
    end
end

A distance metric δ must satisfy the following criteria to be effectively used in our BNT-based framework (the intuition behind these requirements can be found in our technical report [59]):

R1. *Soundness*, which requires that the smaller the distance $\delta(W_1, W_2)$, the better the performance of W_2 on W_1's nominally optimal design. Formally, we call a distance metric *sound* if it satisfies:

$$\delta(W_1, W_2) \leq \delta(W_1, W_3) \Rightarrow f(W_2, \mathbb{D}(W_1)) \leq f(W_3, \mathbb{D}(W_1)) \quad (8)$$

R2. δ should account for intra-query similarities; that is, if $r_i^1 > r_i^2$ and $r_j^1 < r_j^2$, the distance $\delta(W_1, W_2)$ should become smaller based on the similarity of the queries q_i and q_j, assuming the same frequencies for the other queries.

R3. δ should be symmetric; that is, $\delta(W_1, W_2) = \delta(W_2, W_1)$ for any W_1 and W_2. (This is needed for the theoretical guarantees of the BNT framework.)

R4. δ must satisfy the *triangular property*; that is, $\delta(W_1, W_2) \leq \delta(W_1, W_3) + \delta(W_3, W_2)$ for any W_1, W_2, W_3. (This is an implicit assumption in almost all gradient-based optimization techniques, including BNT.)

Before introducing a distance metric fulfilling these criteria, we need to introduce some notations. Let us represent each query as the union of all the columns that appear in it (e.g., unioning all the columns in the `select`, `where`, `group by`, and `order by` clauses). With this over-simplification, two queries will be considered identical as long as they reference the same set of columns, even if their SQL expressions, query plans, or latencies are substantially different. Using this representation, there will be only $2^n - 1$ possible queries where n is the total number of columns in the database (including all the tables). (Here, we ignore queries that do not reference any columns.) Thus, we can represent a workload W with a $(2^n - 1)$-dimensional vector $V_W = \langle r_1, \cdots, r_{2^n-1}\rangle$ where r_i represents the normalized frequency of queries that are represented by the i'th subset of the columns for $i = 1, \cdots, 2^n - 1$. With this notation, we can now introduce our Euclidean distance for database workloads as:

$$\delta_{euclidean}(W_1, W_2) = |V_{W_1} - V_{W_2}| \times S \times |V_{W_1} - V_{W_2}|^T \quad (9)$$

Here, S is a $(2^n - 1) \times (2^n - 1)$ similarity matrix, and thus $\delta_{euclidean}$ is always a real-valued number (i.e., 1×1 matrix). Each $S_{i,j}$ entry is defined as the total number of columns that are present only in q_i or q_j (but not in both), divided by $2 \cdot n$. In other words, $S_{i,j}$ is the Hamming distance between the binary representations of i and j, divided by $2 \cdot n$. Hamming distances are divided by $2 \cdot n$ to ensure a normalized distance, i.e., $0 \leq \delta_{euclidean}(W_1, W_2) \leq 1$.

One can easily verify that $\delta_{euclidean}$ satisfies criteria (b), (c), and (d). In Section 6.3, we empirically show that this distance metric also satisfies criterion (a) quite well. Finally, even though V_W is exponential in the number of columns n, it is merely a conceptual model; since V_W is an extremely sparse matrix, most of the computation in (9) can be avoided. In fact, $\delta_{euclidean}$ can be computed in $O(T^2 \cdot n)$ time and memory complexity, where T is the number of input queries (e.g., in a given query log).

Limitations — $\delta_{euclidean}$ has a few limitations. First, it does not factor in the clause in which a column appears. For instance, for fast filtering, it is more important for a materialized view to cover a column appearing in the `where` clause than one appearing only in the *select* clause. This limitation, however, can be easily resolved by representing each query as a 4-tuple $\langle v_1, v_2, v_3, v_4 \rangle$ where v_1 is the set of columns in the `select` clause and so on. We refer to this distance as $\delta_{separate}$, as we keep columns appearing in different clauses separate. $\delta_{separate}$ differs from $\delta_{euclidean}$ only in that it creates 4-tuple vectors, but it is still computed using Equation (9).

The second (and more important) limitation is that $\delta_{euclidean}$ may ignore important aspects of the SQL expression if they do not change the column sets. For example, presence of a `join` operator or using a different query plan can heavily impact the execution time, but are not captured by $\delta_{euclidean}$. In fact, as a stricter version of requirement (8), a better distance metric will be one that for all workloads W_1, W_2, W_3 and *arbitrary* design D satisfies:

$$\delta(W_1, W_2) \leq \delta(W_1, W_3) \Rightarrow \quad (10)$$
$$|f(W_2, D) - f(W_1, D)| \leq |f(W_3, D) - f(W_1, D)|$$

In other words, the distance functions should directly match the performance characteristics of the workloads (the lower their distance, the more similar their performance). In Appendix C, we introduce a more advanced metric that aims to satisfy (11). However, in our experiments, we still use $\delta_{euclidean}$ for three reasons.

First, requirement (11) is unnecessary for our purposes. `CliffGuard` only relies on this distance metric during the neighborhood exploration and feeds *actual* SQL queries (and not just their column sets) into the existing designer. Internally, the existing designer compares the actual latency of different SQL queries, accounting for their different plans, joins, and all other details of every input query. For example, the designer ignores the less expensive queries to spend its budget on the more expensive ones.

Second, we must be able to efficiently sample the Γ-neighborhood of a given workload (see Algorithm 2, Line 2), which we can do when our cost function is $\delta_{euclidean}$. The sampling algorithm (which can be found in Appendix B) becomes computationally prohibitive when our distance metric involves computing the latency of different queries. In Section 6, we thoroughly evaluate our `CliffGuard` algorithm overall, and our distance function in particular.

The third, and final, reason is that the sole goal of our distance metric is to provide users a means to express and receive their desired degree of robustness. We show that despite its simplistic nature, $\delta_{euclidean}$ is still quite effective in satisfying (8) (see Section 6.3), and most importantly in enabling `CliffGuard` to achieve decisive superiority over existing designers (see Section 6.4).

In the end, we note that *quantifying* the amount of change in SQL workloads is a research direction that will likely find many other applications beyond robust physical designs, e.g., in workload monitoring [40, 64], auto-tuning [31], or simply studying database usage patterns. We believe that $\delta_{euclidean}$ is merely a starting point in the development of more advanced and application-specific distance metrics for database workloads.

6. EXPERIMENTAL RESULTS

The purpose of our experiments in this section is to demonstrate that (i) real world workloads can vary over time and be subject to a great deal of uncertainty (Section 6.2), (ii) despite its simplicity, our distance metric $\delta_{euclidean}$ can reasonably capture the performance implications of a changing workload (Section 6.3), and most importantly (iii) our robust design formulation and algorithm improve the performance of the state-of-the-art industrial designers by up to an order of magnitude, without having to modify the internal implementations of these commercial tools (Section 6.4). We also study different degrees of robustness (Section 6.5). Additional experiments are deferred to Appendix A, where we evaluate the effects of different distance functions and other parameters on `CliffGuard`'s performance, and show that `CliffGuard`'s processing overhead is negligible compared to that of the deployment phase.

Algorithm 3: The subroutine for moving a workload.

Inputs: W_0: an initial workload,
$\{\tilde{W}_1, \cdots, \tilde{W}_m\}$: workloads to merge with W_0,
f: the cost function (or its estimate),
D: a given design,
α: a scaling factor for the weight ($\alpha > 0$)
Output: W_{moved}: a new (merged) workload which is closer to $\{\tilde{W}_1, \cdots, \tilde{W}_N\}$ than W_0, i.e., $\Sigma_i \delta(\tilde{W}_i, W_{moved}) < \Sigma_i \delta(\tilde{W}_i, W_0)$

Subroutine `MoveWorkload` $(W_0, \{\tilde{W}_1, \cdots, \tilde{W}_m\}, f, D, \alpha)$
    $W_{moved} \leftarrow \{\}$
    $Q \leftarrow$ the set of all queries in W_0 and $\tilde{W}_1, \cdots, \tilde{W}_m$ workloads
    foreach query $q \in Q$ **do**
        $f_q \leftarrow f(\{q\}, D)$ **// the cost of query q using design D**
        $\omega_q \leftarrow (f_q \cdot \sum_{i=1}^{m} \text{weight}(q, \tilde{W}_i))^\alpha + \text{weight}(q, W_0)$
        $W_{moved} \leftarrow W_{moved} \cup \{(q, \omega_q)\}$
    end
    return W_{moved}
end

6.1 Experimental Setup

We have implemented `CliffGuard` in Java. We tested our algorithm against Vertica's database designer (called DBD [71]) and DBMS-X's designer as two of the most heavily-used state-of-the-art commercial designers, as well as two other baseline algorithms (introduced later in this section). For Vertica experiments, we used its community edition and invoked its DBD and query optimizer via a JDBC driver. Similarly, we used DBMS-X's latest API. We ran each experiment on two machines: a server and a client. The server ran a copy of the database and was used for testing different designs. The client was used for invoking the designer and sending queries to the server. We ran the Vertica experiments on two Dell machines running Red Hat Enterprise Linux 6.5, each with two quad-core Intel Xeon 2.10GHz processors. One of the machines had 128GB memory and $8 \times$ 4TB 7.2K RPM disks (used as server) and the other had 64GB memory and $4 \times$ 4TB 7.2K RPM disks. For DBMS-X experiments, we used two Azure Standard Tier A3 instances, each with a quad-core AMD Opteron 4171 HE 2.10GHz processor, 7GB memory, and 126GB virtual disks. In this section, when not specified, we refer to our Vertica experiments.

Workloads[9] — We conducted our experiments on a real-world (R1) workload and two synthetic ones (S1 and S2). R1 belongs to one of the largest customers of the Vertica database, composed of 310 tables and $430{+}K$ time-stamped queries issued between March 2011 and April 2012 out of which $15.5K$ queries conform to their latest schema (i.e., can be parsed). We did not have access to their original dataset but we did have access to their data distribution, which we used to generate a 151GB dataset for our Vertica

[9]Common benchmarks (e.g., TPC-H) are not applicable here as they only contain a few queries, and do not change over time.

Work-load	Min $\delta(W_i,W_{i+1})$	Max $\delta(W_i,W_{i+1})$	Avg $\delta(W_i,W_{i+1})$	Std $\delta(W_i,W_{i+1})$
R1	m=0.00016	M=0.00311	0.00120	0.00122
S1	0.1m	m	0.00006	0.00003
S2	m	M	0.00178	0.00063

Table 1: Summary of our real-world and synthetic workloads.

experiments. Since we did not have access to any real workloads from DBMS-X's customers, we used the same query log but on a smaller dataset (20GB) given the smaller memory capacity of our Azure instances (compared to our Dell servers). We also created two synthetic workloads, called S1 and S2, as follows. We used the same schema and dataset as R1, but chose different subsets and relative ordering of R1 queries to artificially cause different degrees of workload change. Table 1 reports basic statistics on the amount workload changes (in terms of $\delta_{euclidean}$) between consecutive windows of queries where each window was 28 days (different window sizes are studied in Section 6.2). S1 queries were chosen to mimic a workload with minimal change over time (between $0.1m$ and m, where m is the minimum change observed in R1). S2 queries were chosen to exhibit the same range of $\delta_{euclidean}$ as R1 but more uniformly. More detailed analysis of these workloads will be presented in the subsequent sections.

Algorithms Compared — We divided the queries according to their timestamps into 4-week windows, $W_0, W_1, \cdots$. We re-designed the database at the end of each month to simulate a tuning frequency of a month (a common practice, based on our oral conversations). In other words, we fed W_i queries into each of the following designers and used the produced design to process W_{i+1} (except for `FutureKnowingDesigner`; see below).

1. `NoDesign`: A dummy designer that returns an empty design (i.e., no projections). Using `NoDesign` all queries simply scan the default super-projections (which contain all the columns), providing an upper limit on each query's latency.

2. `ExistingDesigner`: The nominal designer shipped with commercial databases. For instance, Vertica's DBD [71] recommends a set of projections while DBMS-X's designer finds various types of indices and materialized views. We used these state-of-the-art designers as our main baselines.

3. `FutureKnowingDesigner`: The same designer as `ExistingDesigner`, except that instead of feeding queries from W_i and testing on W_{i+1}, we both feed and test it on W_{i+1}. This designer signifies the best performance achievable where the designer knows exactly which queries to expect in the future and optimize for.

4. `MajorityVoteDesigner`: A designer that uses sensitivity analysis to identify elements of the nominal design that are *brittle* against changes of workload. This designer uses the same technique as `CliffGuard` to explore the local neighborhood of the current W_i, and generate a set of perturbed workloads $W_i^1, \cdots, W_i^n$. Then, it invokes the `ExistingDesigner` to suggest an optimal design for each W_i^j. Finally, for each structure (e.g., index, materialized view, projection) s, `MajorityVoteDesigner` counts the number of times that s has appeared in the nominal design of the neighbors, and selects those structures that have appeared in different designs most frequently. The idea behind this heuristic is that structures that appear in the optimal design of fewer neighbors (have fewer votes) are less likely to remain beneficial when the future workload changes.

5. `OptimalLocalSearchDesigner`: Similar to `MajorityVoteDesigner`, this designer starts by searching the local neighborhood of the given workload and generating perturbed workloads. However, instead of selecting structures that have been voted for by the most number of neighbors, this designer takes the union of the queries in the neighboring workloads as the *expectation* (i.e., representative) of the future workload, say $\bar{W}$. This algorithm then solves an Integer Linear Program to find an optimal set of structures that fit in the budget and minimize the cost of $\bar{W}$.[10]

7. `CliffGuard`: Our robust database designer from Section 4.

Note that DBD and DBMS-X's designer (`ExistingDesigner`) are our goal standards as the state-of-the-art designers currently used in the industry. However, we also aim to answer the following question. How much of `CliffGuard`'s overall improvement over nominal designers is due to its exploration of the initial workload's local neighborhood, and how much is due to its carefully selected descent direction and step sizes in moving away from the worst neighbors? Since `MajorityVoteDesigner` and `OptimalLocalSearchDesigner` use the same neighborhood sampling strategy as `CliffGuard` but employ greedy and local search heuristics, we will be able to break down the contribution of `CliffGuard`'s various components to its overall performance.

Since Vertica automatically decides on the storage budget (50GB in our case), we used the same budget for the other algorithms too. For DBMS-X experiments, we used a maximum budget of 10GB (since the dataset was smaller). Also, unless otherwise specified, we used n=20 samples in all algorithms involving sampling, and 5 iterations, $\lambda_{success} = 5$, and $\lambda_{success} = 0.5$ in `CliffGuard`.

6.2 Workloads Change Over Time

First, we studied if and how much our real workload has changed over time. While OLTP and *reporting* queries tend to be more repetitive (often instantiated from a few templates with different parameters), analytical and exploratory workloads tend to be less predictable (e.g., Hive queries at Facebook are reported to access over 200–450 different subsets of columns [5]). Likewise, in our analytical workload R1, we observed that queries issued by users have constantly drifted over time, perhaps due to the changing nature of their company's business needs.

Figure 6.1 shows the percentage of queries that belonged to templates that were shared among each pair of windows as the time lag grew between the two windows. Here, we have defined templates by stripping away the query details except for the sets of columns used in the `select`, `where`, `group by`, and `order by` clauses. This is an overly optimistic analysis assuming that queries with the same column sets in their respective clauses will exhibit a similar performance. However, even with this optimistic assumption, we observed that for a window size of one week, on average only 51% of the queries had a similar counterpart between consecutive weeks. This percentage was only 35% when our window was 4 weeks. Regardless of the window size, this commonality drops quickly as the time lag increases, e.g., after 2.5 months less than 10% of the

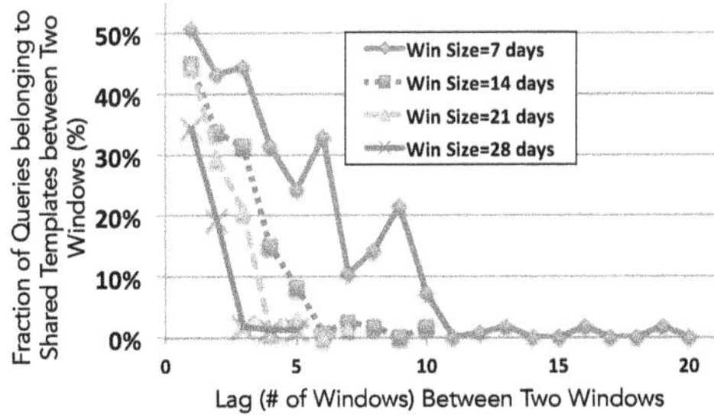

Figure 5: Many workloads drift over time ($15.5K$ queries, 6 months).

[10]A greedy version of this algorithm and a detailed description of the other baselines can be found in our technical report [59].

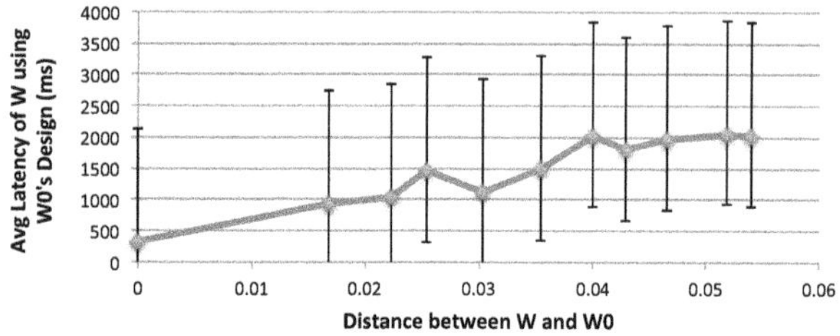

Figure 6: Performance decay of a window W on a design made for another window W_O is highly correlated with their distance.

queries had similar templates appearing in the past. The unpredictability of analytical workloads underlines the important role of a robust designer. We show in Section 6.4 that failing to take into account this potential change (i.e., uncertainty) in our target workload has a severe impact on the performance of existing physical designers — one that we aim to overcome via our robust designs.

6.3 Our Distance Metric Is Sound

In Section 5, we introduced our distance metric $\delta_{euclidean}$ to concisely quantify the dissimilarity of two SQL workloads. While we do not claim that $\delta_{euclidean}$ is an ideal one (see Section 5), here we show that it is sound. That is, in general:

$$\delta(W_O, W) \leq \delta(W_O, W') \Rightarrow f(W, \mathbb{D}(W_O)) \leq f(W', \mathbb{D}(W_O))$$

which means that a design made for W_O is more suitable for W than it is for W', i.e., W will experience a lower latency than W'. Figure 6 reports an experiment where we chose 10 different starting windows as our W_O and created a number of windows with different distances from W_O. The curve (error bar) shows the average (range) of the latencies of these different windows for each distance. This plot indicates a strong correlation and monotonic relationship between performance decay and $\delta_{euclidean}$. Later, in Section 6.4, we show that even with this simplistic distance metric, our CliffGuard algorithm can consistently improve on Vertica's latest designer by severalfold.

6.4 Quality of Robust vs. Nominal Designs

In this section, we turn to the most important questions of this paper: is our robust designer superior to state-of-the-art designers? And, if so, by what measure? We compared these designers using all 3 workloads. In R1, out of the 15.5K queries, only 515 could benefit from a physical design, i.e., the remaining queries were either trivial (e.g., `select version()`) or returned an entire table (e.g., '`select * from T`' queries with no filtering used for backup purposes) in which case they always took the same time as they only used the super-projections in Vertica and table-scans in DBMS-X. Thus, we only considered queries for which there existed an *ideal* design (no matter how expensive) that could improve on their bare table-scan latency by at least a factor of 3×.

Figure 7 summarizes the results of our performance comparison on Vertica, showing the average and maximum latencies (both averaged over all windows) for all three workloads. On average, MajorityVoteDesigner improved on the existing designer by 13%, while OptimalLocalSearchDesigner's performance was slightly worse than Vertica's DBD. However, CliffGuard was superior to the existing designer by an astonishing margin: on average, it cut down the maximum latency of each window by 39.7× and 13.7× for R1 and S2, respectively. Interestingly, for these workloads, even CliffGuard's average-case performance was 14.3× and 5.3× faster than ExistingDesigner. The last result is surprising because our CliffGuard is designed to protect against worst-case scenarios and ensure a predictable performance. However, improvement even on the average case indicates that the design space of a database is highly non-convex — and as such can easily delude a designer into a local optimum. Thus, by avoiding the proximity of bad neighbors, CliffGuard seems to find designs that are also more globally optimal. In fact, for S2, Figure 7(c) shows that CliffGuard is only 30% worse than a hypothetical, ideal world where future queries are precisely known in advance (i.e., the FutureKnowingDesigner). For S1, however, CliffGuard's improvement over ExistingDesigner is more modest: 1.5× improvement for worst-case latency and 1.2× for average latency. This is completely expected since S1 is designed to exhibit no or little change between different windows (refer to Table 1). This is the ideal case for a nominal designer since the amount of uncertainty across workloads is so negligible that even our hypothetical FutureKnowingDesigner cannot improve much on the nominal designer. Thus, averaging over all three workloads, compared to ExistingDesigner, CliffGuard improves the average and worst-case latencies by 6.9× and 18.3×, respectively.

Figure 10 reports a similar experiment for workload R1 but for DBMS-X. (DBMS-X experiments on workloads S1 and S2 can be found in Appendix A.3.) Even though DBMS-X's designer has been fine-tuned and optimized over the years, CliffGuard still improves its worst-case and average-case performances by 2.5–5.2× and 2–3.2×, respectively. This is quite encouraging given that CliffGuard is still in its infancy stage of development and treats the database as a black-box. While still significant, the improvements here are smaller than those observed with Vertica. This is due to several heuristics used in DBMS-X's designer (such as omitting workload details) that prevent it from overfitting its input workload. However, this also shows that dealing with such uncertainties in a principled framework can be much more effective.

These experiments confirm our hypothesis that failing to account for workload uncertainty can have significant consequences. For example, for R1 on Vertica, ExistingDesigner is on average only 25% better than NoDesign (with no advantage for the worst-case). Note that here the database was re-designed every month, which means even this slight advantage of ExistingDesigner over NoDesign would quickly fade away if the database were to be re-designed less frequently (as the distance between windows often increases with time; see Figure 6.1). These experiments show the ample importance of re-thinking and re-architecting the existing designers currently shipped and used in our database systems.

6.5 Effect of Robustness Knob on Performance

To study the effect of different levels of robustness, we varied the Γ parameter in our algorithm and measured the average and worst-case performances in each case. The results of this experiment for workloads R1 and S2 are shown in Figures 8 and 9, respectively. (As reported in Section 6.4, workload S1 contains minimal uncertainty and thus is ruled out from this experiment, i.e., the performance difference between ExistingDesigner and CliffGuard remains small for S1). Here, experiments on both workloads confirm that requesting a large level of robustness will force CliffGuard to be overly conservative, eliminating its margin of improvement over ExistingDesigner. Note that in either case CliffGuard still performs no worse than ExistingDesigner, which is due to two reasons. First, ExistingDesigner is only marginally better than NoDesign (refer to Section 6.4) and as Γ increases, its relevance for the actual workload (which has a much lower $\delta_{euclidean}$) degrades. As a result, both designers approach NoDesign's performance, which serves an upper bound on latency (i.e., unlike theory, latencies are always bounded in practice, due to the finite cost of the worst query plan). The second reason is that, during each iteration of CliffGuard (unlike BNT), our new workload always contains the original workload which ensures that even when Γ is large, the

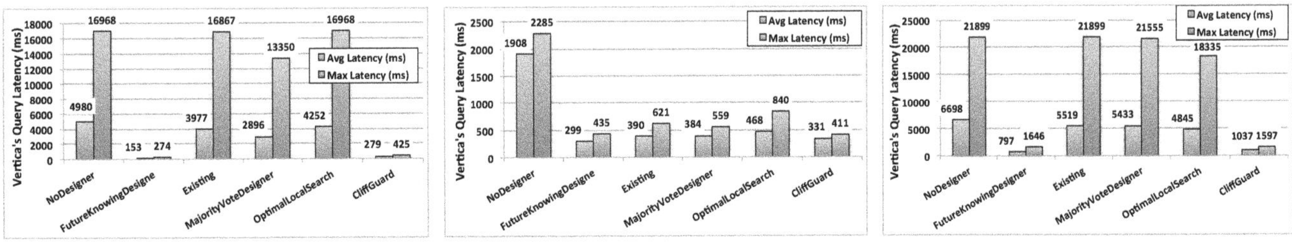

(a) Real-world workload R1 on Vertica.

(b) Synthetic static workload S1 on Vertica.

(c) Synthetic drifting workload S2 on Vertica.

Figure 7: Average and worst-case performances of designers for Vertica, averaged over all windows, for workloads R1, S1, and S2.

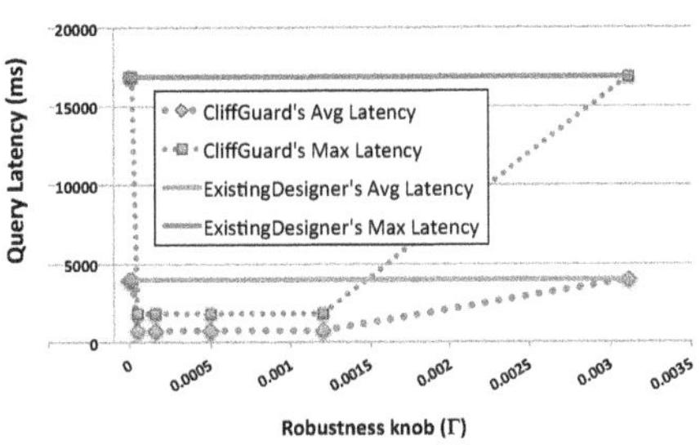

Figure 8: Different degrees of robustness for Workload R1.

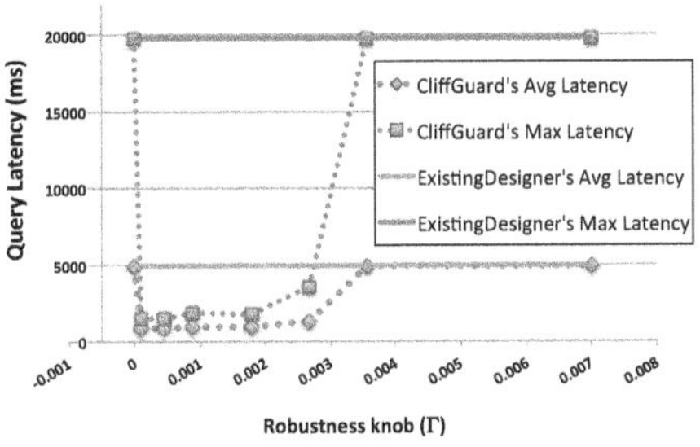

Figure 9: Different degrees of robustness for Workload S2.

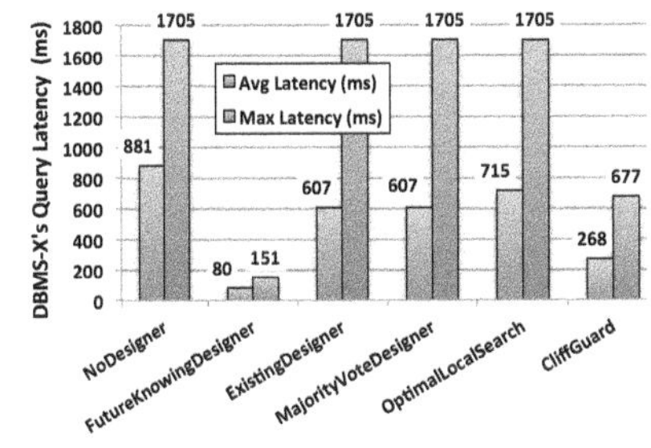

Figure 10: Performance of different designers for DBMS-X on workload R1.

designer will not completely ignore the original workload (see Algorithm 3). Also, as expected, as Γ approaches zero, CliffGuard's performance again approaches that of a nominal designer.

7. RELATED WORK

There has been much research on physical database design problems, such as the automatic selection of materialized views [42, 51, 65, 72], indices [27, 54, 61, 69], or both [7, 31, 46, 76]. Also, most modern databases come with designer tools, e.g., Tuning Wizard in Microsoft SQL Server [7], IBM DB2's Design Advisor [76], Teradata's Index Wizard [20], and Oracle's SQL Tuning Adviser [31]. Other types of design problems include project selection in columnar databases [33, 47, 71], stratified sample selection in approximate databases [3, 5, 12, 23], and optimizing different replicas for different workloads in a replicated databases [67]. All these designers are nominal and assume that their target workload is precisely known. Since future queries are often not known in advance, these tools optimize for past queries as approximations of future ones. By failing to take into account the fact that a portion of those queries will be different in the future, they produce designs that are sub-optimal and brittle in practice. To mitigate some of these problems, a few heuristics [28] have been proposed to compress and summarize the workload [24, 45] or modify the query optimizer to produce richer statistics [36]. However, these approaches are not principled and thus, do not necessarily guarantee robustness. In contract, CliffGuard takes the possible changes of workload into account in a principled manner, and directly maximizes the robustness of the physical design.

To avoid these limitations, adaptive indexing schemes [37, 38, 39, 44, 64]) take the other extreme by avoiding the offline physical design, and instead, creating and adjusting indices incrementally, *on demand*. Despite their many merits, these schemes do not have a mechanism to incorporate prior knowledge under a bounded amount of uncertainty. Also, one still needs to decide which subsets of columns to build an adaptive index on. For these reasons, most commercial databases still rely on their offline designers. In contrast, CliffGuard uses RO theory to directly minimize the effect of uncertainty on optimality, and guarantee robustness.

The effect of uncertainty (caused by cost and cardinality estimates) has also been studied in the context of query optimization [11, 25, 30, 35, 56, 63] and choosing query plans with a bounded worst-case [10]. None of these studies have addressed uncertainties caused by workload changes, or their impact on physical designs. Also, while these approaches produce plans that are more predictable, they are not principled in that they do not directly maximize robustness, i.e., they do not guarantee robustness even in the context of query optimization. Finally, most of these heuristics are specific to a particular problem and do not generalize to others.

Theory of robust optimization has taken many strides in recent years [15, 16, 17, 29, 34, 48, 75] and has been applied to many other disciplines, e.g., supply chain management [15], circuit [62] and antenna [53] design, power control [41], control theory [14], thin-film manufacturing [18], and microchip architecture [60]. However, to the best of our knowledge, this paper is the first application of RO theory in a database context (see Section 4.2).

8. CONCLUSION AND FUTURE WORK

The state-of-the-art database designers rely on heuristics that do not account for uncertainty, and hence produce sub-optimal and brittle designs. On the other hand, the principled framework of robust optimization theory, which has witnessed remarkable advances over the past few years, has largely dealt with problems that are quite different in nature than those faced in databases. In this paper, we presented CliffGuard to exploit these techniques in the context of physical design problems in a columnar database. We compared our algorithm to a state-of-the-art commercial designer using several real-world and synthetic workloads. In summary, compared to Vertica's state-of-the-art designer, our robust designer reduces the average and maximum latency of queries by up to 5× and 11×, respectively. Similarly, CliffGuard improves upon DBMS-X's designer by 3–5×. Since CliffGuard treats the existing designer as a block-box, with no modifications to the database internals, an interesting future direction is to extend CliffGuard to other major DBMSs with other types of design problems.

Acknowledgements

This work is in part supported by Amazon AWS and Microsoft Azure. The authors are grateful to the anonymous reviewers for their insightful feedback, Michael Stonebraker and Samuel Madden for their early contributions, Stephen Tu for his SQL parser, Shiyong Hu and Ruizhi Deng for implementing our distance metrics, Yingying Zhu for plotting Figure 4, Andrew Lamb and Vivek Bharathan for helping with Vertica experiments, and Alice Tsay and Suchee Shah for their comments on this manuscript.

9. REFERENCES

[1] CliffGuard: A General Framework for Robust and Efficient Database Optimization. `http://www.cliffguard.org`.

[2] S. Acharya, P. B. Gibbons, and V. Poosala. Aqua: A fast decision support system using approximate query answers. In *VLDB*, 1999.

[3] S. Acharya, P. B. Gibbons, and V. Poosala. Congressional samples for approximate answering of group-by queries. In *SIGMOD*, May 2000.

[4] S. Agarwal, H. Milner, A. Kleiner, A. Talwalkar, M. Jordan, S. Madden, B. Mozafari, and I. Stoica. Knowing when you're wrong: Building fast and reliable approximate query processing systems. In *SIGMOD*, 2014.

[5] S. Agarwal, B. Mozafari, A. Panda, H. Milner, S. Madden, and I. Stoica. Blinkdb: queries with bounded errors and bounded response times on very large data. In *EuroSys*, 2013.

[6] S. Agarwal, A. Panda, B. Mozafari, A. P. Iyer, S. Madden, and I. Stoica. Blink and it's done: Interactive queries on very large data. *PVLDB*, 2012.

[7] S. Agrawal, S. Chaudhuri, and V. Narasayya. Materialized view and index selection tool for microsoft sql server 2000. 2001.

[8] I. Alagiannis, D. Dash, K. Schnaitter, A. Ailamaki, and N. Polyzotis. An automated, yet interactive and portable db designer. In *SIGMOD*, 2010.

[9] I. Alagiannis, S. Idreos, and A. Ailamaki. H2o: a hands-free adaptive store. In *SIGMOD*, 2014.

[10] M. Armbrust and et. al. Piql: Success-tolerant query processing in the cloud. *PVLDB*, 5, 2011.

[11] B. Babcock and S. Chaudhuri. Towards a robust query optimizer: A principled and practical approach. In *SIGMOD*, 2005.

[12] B. Babcock, S. Chaudhuri, and G. Das. Dynamic sample selection for approximate query processing. In *VLDB*, 2003.

[13] A. Ben-Tal, L. El Ghaoui, and A. Nemirovski. *Robust optimization*. Princeton University Press, 2009.

[14] D. Bertsimas and D. B. Brown. Constrained stochastic lqc: a tractable approach. *Automatic Control, IEEE Transactions on*, 52(10), 2007.

[15] D. Bertsimas and et. al. Theory and applications of robust optimization. *SIAM*, 53, 2011.

[16] D. Bertsimas, O. Nohadani, and K. M. Teo. Robust nonconvex optimization for simulation-based problems. *Operations Research*, 2007.

[17] D. Bertsimas and M. Sim. The price of robustness. *Operations research*, 52(1), 2004.

[18] J. R. Birge and et. al. Improving thin-film manufacturing yield with robust optimization. *Applied optics*, 50, 2011.

[19] S. P. Boyd and L. Vandenberghe. *Convex optimization*. Cambridge university press, 2004.

[20] D. P. Brown, J. Chaware, and M. Koppuravuri. Index selection in a database system, Mar. 3 2009. US Patent 7,499,907.

[21] N. Bruno, S. Chaudhuri, A. C. König, V. R. Narasayya, R. Ramamurthy, and M. Syamala. Autoadmin project at microsoft research: Lessons learned. *IEEE Data Eng. Bull.*, 34(4), 2011.

[22] C. Chatfield. *Time-series forecasting*. CRC Press, 2002.

[23] S. Chaudhuri, G. Das, and V. Narasayya. Optimized stratified sampling for approximate query processing. *TODS*, 2007.

[24] S. Chaudhuri, A. K. Gupta, and V. Narasayya. Compressing sql workloads. In *SIGMOD*, 2002.

[25] S. Chaudhuri, H. Lee, and V. R. Narasayya. Variance aware optimization of parameterized queries. In *SIGMOD*, 2010.

[26] S. Chaudhuri and V. Narasayya. Self-tuning database systems: A decade of progress. In *VLDB*, 2007.

[27] S. Chaudhuri, V. Narasayya, M. Datar, et al. Linear programming approach to assigning benefit to database physical design structures, Nov. 21 2006. US Patent 7,139,778.

[28] A. N. K. Chen and et. al. Heuristics for selecting robust database structures with dynamic query patterns. *EJOR*, 168, 2006.

[29] X. Chen, M. Sim, and P. Sun. A robust optimization perspective on stochastic programming. *Operations Research*, 55, 2007.

[30] F. Chu, J. Y. Halpern, and P. Seshadri. Least expected cost query optimization: An exercise in utility. In *PODS*, 1999.

[31] B. e. Dageville. Automatic sql tuning in oracle 10g. In *VLDB*, 2004.

[32] K. Deb. Geneas: A robust optimal design technique for mechanical component design. 1997.

[33] X. Ding and J. Le. Adaptive projection in column-stores. In *FSKD*, 2011.

[34] I. Doltsinis and et. al. Robust design of non-linear structures using optimization methods. *Computer methods in applied mechanics and engineering*, 194, 2005.

[35] D. Donjerkovic and R. Ramakrishnan. Probabilistic optimization of top n queries. In *VLDB*, 1999.

[36] K. E. Gebaly and A. Aboulnaga. Robustness in automatic physical database design. In *Advances in database technology*, 2008.

[37] G. Graefe and H. Kuno. Adaptive indexing for relational keys. In *ICDEW*, 2010.

[38] G. Graefe and H. Kuno. Self-selecting, self-tuning, incrementally optimized indexes. In *ICEDT*, 2010.

[39] F. Halim and et. al. Stochastic database cracking: Towards robust adaptive indexing in main-memory column-stores. *PVLDB*, 5, 2012.

[40] M. Holze, A. Haschimi, and N. Ritter. Towards workload-aware self-management: Predicting significant workload shifts. In *CDEW*, 2010.

[41] K.-L. Hsiung, S.-J. Kim, and S. Boyd. Power control in lognormal fading wireless channels with uptime probability specifications via robust geometric programming. In *American Control Conference*, 2005.

[42] R. Huang, R. Chirkova, and Y. Fathi. Two-stage stochastic view selection for data-analysis queries. In *Advances in Databases and Information Systems*, 2013.

[43] S. Idreos, M. L. Kersten, and S. Manegold. Database cracking. In *CIDR*, 2007.

[44] S. Idreos, M. L. Kersten, and S. Manegold. Self-organizing tuple reconstruction in column-stores. In *SIGMOD*, 2009.

[45] A. C. Konig and S. U. Nabar. Scalable exploration of physical database design. In *ICDE*, 2006.

[46] M. Kormilitsin, R. Chirkova, Y. Fathi, and M. Stallmann. View and index selection for query-performance improvement: quality-centered algorithms and heuristics. In *CIKM*, 2008.

[47] A. Lamb, M. Fuller, R. Varadarajan, N. Tran, B. Vandiver, L. Doshi, and C. Bear. The vertica analytic database: C-store 7 years later. *PVLDB*, 5(12), 2012.

[48] K.-H. Lee and G.-J. Park. A global robust optimization using kriging based approximation model. *JSME*, 49, 2006.

[49] J. LeFevre, J. Sankaranarayanan, H. Hacigumus, J. Tatemura, N. Polyzotis, and M. J. Carey. Opportunistic physical design for big data analytics. In *SIGMOD*, 2014.

[50] J. Li, A. C. König, V. Narasayya, and S. Chaudhuri. Robust estimation of resource consumption for sql queries using statistical techniques. *PVLDB*, 5(11), 2012.

[51] W. Liang, H. Wang, and M. E. Orlowska. Materialized view selection under the maintenance time constraint. *Data & Knowledge Engineering*, 37(2), 2001.

[52] S. S. Lightstone, G. Lohman, and D. Zilio. Toward autonomic computing with db2 universal database. *SIGMOD Record*, 31(3), 2002.

[53] R. G. Lorenz and S. P. Boyd. Robust minimum variance beamforming. *Signal Processing, IEEE Transactions on*, 53(5), 2005.

[54] C. Maier and et. al. Parinda: an interactive physical designer for postgresql. In *ICEDT*, 2010.

[55] I. Mami and Z. Bellahsene. A survey of view selection methods. *SIGMOD*, 41(1), 2012.
[56] V. Markl and et. al. Robust query processing through progressive optimization. In *SIGMOD*, 2004.
[57] B. Mozafari, C. Curino, A. Jindal, and S. Madden. Performance and resource modeling in highly-concurrent OLTP workloads. In *SIGMOD*, 2013.
[58] B. Mozafari, C. Curino, and S. Madden. Dbseer: Resource and performance prediction for building a next generation database cloud. In *CIDR*, 2013.
[59] B. Mozafari, E. Z. Y. Goh, and D. Y. Yoon. Cliffguard: An extended report. Technical report, University of Michigan, Ann Arbor, 2015.
[60] G. Palermo, C. Silvano, and V. Zaccaria. Robust optimization of soc architectures: A multi-scenario approach. In *Embedded Systems for Real-Time Multimedia*, 2008.
[61] S. Papadomanolakis and A. Ailamaki. An integer linear programming approach to database design. In *ICDE Workshop*, 2007.
[62] D. Patil, S. Yun, S.-J. Kim, A. Cheung, M. Horowitz, and S. Boyd. A new method for design of robust digital circuits. In *ISQED*, 2005.
[63] V. Raman and et. al. Constant-time query processing. In *ICDE*, 2008.
[64] K. Schnaitter, S. Abiteboul, T. Milo, and N. Polyzotis. On-line index selection for shifting workloads. In *ICDE Workshop*, 2007.
[65] A. Shukla, P. Deshpande, J. F. Naughton, et al. Materialized view selection for multidimensional datasets. In *VLDB*, volume 98, 1998.
[66] Z. A. Talebi, R. Chirkova, and Y. Fathi. An integer programming approach for the view and index selection problem. *Data & Knowledge Engineering*, 83, 2013.
[67] Q. T. Tran, I. Jimenez, R. Wang, N. Polyzotis, and A. Ailamaki. Rita: An index-tuning advisor for replicated databases. *arXiv preprint arXiv:1304.1411*, 2013.
[68] J. Tu, K. K. Choi, and Y. H. Park. A new study on reliability-based design optimization. *Journal of Mechanical Design*, 121(4), 1999.
[69] G. Valentin and et. al. Db2 advisor: An optimizer smart enough to recommend its own indexes. In *ICDE*, 2000.
[70] A. van der Vaart. *Asymptotic statistics*, volume 3. Cambridge university press, 2000.
[71] R. Varadarajan, V. Bharathan, A. Cary, J. Dave, and S. Bodagala. Dbdesigner: A customizable physical design tool for vertica analytic database. In *ICDE*, 2014.
[72] J. X. Yu, X. Yao, C.-H. Choi, and G. Gou. Materialized view selection as constrained evolutionary optimization. *Systems, Man, and Cybernetics, Part C: Applications and Reviews, IEEE Transactions on*, 33(4), 2003.
[73] K. Zeng, S. Gao, J. Gu, B. Mozafari, and C. Zaniolo. Abs: a system for scalable approximate queries with accuracy guarantees. In *SIGMOD*, 2014.
[74] K. Zeng, S. Gao, B. Mozafari, and C. Zaniolo. The analytical bootstrap: a new method for fast error estimation in approximate query processing. In *SIGMOD*, 2014.
[75] Y. Zhang. General robust-optimization formulation for nonlinear programming. *JOTA*, 132, 2007.
[76] D. C. Zilio and et. al. Recommending materialized views and indexes with the ibm db2 design advisor. In *ICAC*, 2004.

APPENDIX

Appendix A provides additional experiments. Appendix B provides the detailed sampling strategy used in `CliffGuard`, when the Γ-neighborhood is expressed using distance $\delta_{euclidean}$ (introduced in Section 5). Appendix C discusses an alternative distance metric for database workloads. Finally, Appendix D provides additional references.

A. ADDITIONAL EXPERIMENTS

Sections A.1 and A.2 study the effects of different distance metrics and other parameters on `CliffGuard`'s performance. Section A.3 provides additional experiments on DBMS-X, while Section A.4 reports the offline times for various design algorithms.

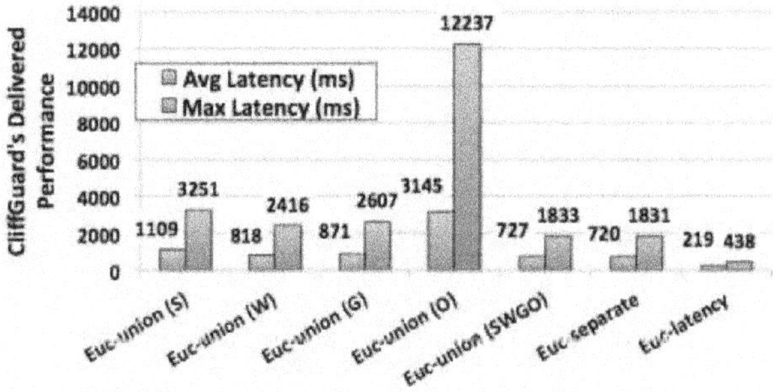

Figure 11: The effect of different distance functions on `CliffGuard`'s effectiveness (on workload R1).

A.1 The Distance Metric's Effect on CliffGuard

To study the implications of our choice of distance function on `CliffGuard`'s effectiveness, we have repeated our experiments on R1 using various distance metrics. The results are shown in Figure 11. Here, Euc-union is our $\delta_{euclidean}$ metric defined in Section 5, annotated by the clauses used in its binary vector. For instance, in Euc-union (S), we only consider the set of columns appearing in the `select` clause while in Euc-union (SWGO) represents our default choice where we take the union of all columns appearing in the `select`, `where`, `group by`, and `order by` clauses. Euc-separate is our extension of $\delta_{euclidean}$, called $\delta_{separate}$, which was defined in Section 5. Finally, Euc-latency is another extension of our Euclidean distance that besides the intra-column similarities, it also accounts for the actual latency of the queries to differentiate queries that share the same set of columns but differ in their latencies significantly. (The latency-aware metric is formally defined as $\delta_{latency}$ in Appendix C.)

As expected, `CliffGuard`'s reaches its best performance when using Euc-latency since it can quantify the changes of the workload more accurately. Interestingly, despite using more bits, the difference between Euc-separate and Euc-union (SWGO) is quite negligible. When constrained to only consider the columns in one of the clauses, the `where` and `group by` clauses seem to be the most informative ones to the `CliffGuard`, as they inform the underlying nominal designer which sets of columns will be filtered on or grouped. Columns in the `order by` clause are only involved in post-processing of the queries and hence, do not prove as useful. The `select` clauses, however, seem suprisingly informative. Upon closer examination, we have discovered that this is because the majority of the columns referenced in the `where` and `group by` clauses of our queries also appear in the `select` clause. Thus, the `select` clause indirectly informs the designer about the filtering and group columns. In summary, while Euc-latency appears to the be the most effective in capturing the workload uncertainty, `CliffGuard`'s default choice is still Euc-union (SWGO) since the former cannot be efficiently computed and hence, is impractical. However, we can Êcompute $\delta_{euclidean}$ much more efficiently; see Section 5 and Appendix C).

A.2 Studying various Parameters in CliffGuard

Besides Γ, which is a user-provided parameter, there are two other important parameters in `CliffGuard`. Figure 12 studies the effect of varying the number of sampled workloads (i.e., n in Line 2 of Algorithm 2) on both average and worst-case performances, indicating that with as few as 10 sampled workloads, `CliffGuard` is able to infer a general direction of descent which will make it farther from its worst-neighbors. We also varied the number of iterations, shown in Figure 13. Surprisingly, `CliffGuard` is capable of moving away from its worst-neighbors and quickly reaching a local robust optimum within a few iterations. We believe this is

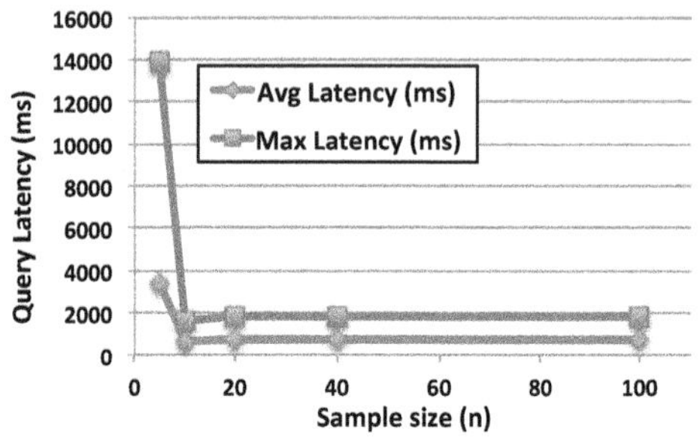

Figure 12: The effect of sample size on `CliffGuard`'s performance.

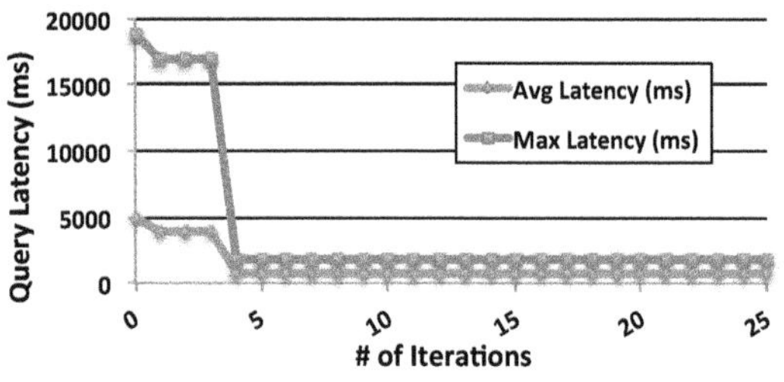

Figure 13: The effect of number of iterations on `CliffGuard`'s performance.

due to BNT's principled framework, which by moving along the (steepest) descent direction guarantees fast convergence in practice. For this reason, the default number of iterations in `CliffGuard` is currently 5, as we rarely observe any improvement after that (i.e., we reach a robust solution earlier).

A.3 Additional Comparisons for DBMS-X

We have compared our various baselines for DBMS-X on all three workloads. In Section 6.4, we reported the results for the real workload R1. The results for workloads S1 and S2 can be found in Figure 15.

A.4 Offline Processing Time

The last question that we study is how expensive a robust designer is compared a nominal one, and also compared to the deployment phase (i.e., the actual creation of the selected projections). Figure 14 shows that our robust designer, `CliffGuard`, takes 2.3 hours to finish while `ExistingDesigner` takes about 30 minutes. This is of course expected since `CliffGuard` is an iterative algorithm that invokes `ExistingDesigner` in each iteration (refer to our design principles in Section 2). As noted earlier, the maximum number of iterations is `CliffGuard` is currently 5. The fastest baseline is `MajorityVoteDesigner`, which only performs counting after the initial design.

Note that while finding a robust design takes 5× longer than finding a nominal one, this is still an attractive price to pay for robustness due to the following reasons. First, the superiority of `CliffGuard` over `ExistingDesigner` is *not* due to the longer time that the former takes, but rather the different type of design that it produces. In other words, we cannot provide `ExistingDesigner` with more time to find a better design as it has already found the *nominal* optimum after 30 minutes and will not search for a robust design since it is not a robust designer (remember than `ExistingDesigner` does not take a time budget and finishes when it has completed its search). Second, finding a physical design is an *offline* process that only occurs monthly or a few times a year. The reason why databases are not re-designed more frequently is not because of the cost of finding a new design, but rather due to the prohibitive cost of *creating and deploying* a new design. For instance, our database

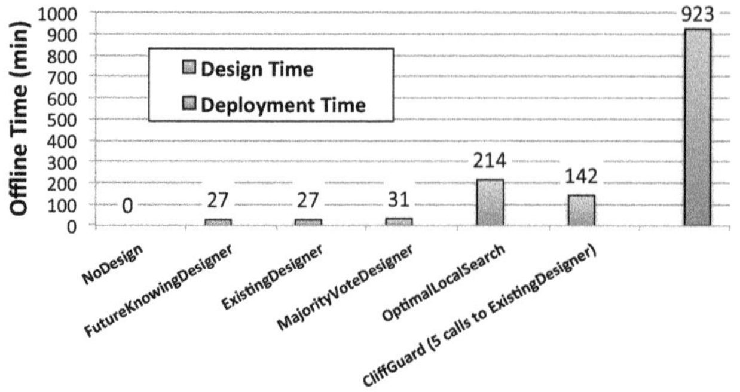

Figure 14: Offline-time taken by each designer compared to the deployment time.

takes more than 15 hours to completely deploy a new design, i.e., the design time is negligible compared to the actual deployment time. (Also, as a database grows in size, design time remains the same but deployment cost grows linearly). Finally, many users will be willing to pay a 5× penalty in offline processing time to win a 5–10× improvement in their online query processing latency (see Section 6.4 for our latency comparison).

B. SAMPLING THE WORKLOAD SPACE

To implement `CliffGuard` we must be able to efficiently sample the workload space (Algorithm 2, Line 2). In other words, given a workload W_0 and a certain distance Γ we must find $n > 1$ neighbors $W_1, \cdots, W_n$ such that $\delta(W_0, W_i) \leq \Gamma$ for $i = 1, \cdots, n$. To solve this problem, it suffices to solve the following sub-probem. Given a workload W_0 and a certain distance α, find a workload W_1 such that $\delta(W_0, W_1) = \alpha$. Assuming we have a randomized algorithm to solve the latter problem, we can achieve the former goal by simply repeating this procedure n times, each time randomly picking a new $\alpha \in [0, \Gamma]$.

We can perform this problem efficiently when our distance metric is $\delta_{euclidean}$ defined in Section 5. The pseudocode for this procedure is presented in Algorithm 4. Here, to implement Line 2, one can construct different query sets Q by restricting oneself to only pick queries that are not already contained in W_0. One can start with $k = 1$ and if unsuccessful, continue to increase k until such a Q is found. Note that finding such a Q is much easier than the original problem; it suffices to find a Q that is sufficiently different from Q. Once such a Q is found, Algorithm 4 is guaranteed to find a workload W_1 where $\delta_{euclidean}(W_0, W_1){=}\alpha$ (see [59] for proof). In our experiments, we have typically found such Q with a few trials for $k \leq 5$.

C. LATENCY-AWARE DISTANCE METRICS

In Section 6, we showed that $\delta_{euclidean}$ can sufficiently capture workload changes for our physical design purposes. However, we have also explored the natural question of whether incorporating performance-specific characteristics into the distance of two SQL workloads would improve our distance metric. Specifically, we have sought a more sophisticated distance metric that can satisfy the stricter requirement (11), introduced in Section 5. In other words, the distance functions should directly match the performance characteristics of the workloads (the lower their distance, the more similar their performance). To meet this strict requirement, we can define a latency-aware distance metric, as follows:

$$\delta_{latency}(W_1, W_2) = (1-\omega)\cdot\delta_{euclidean}(W_1, W_2) + \omega\cdot\mathcal{R}(W_1, W_2) \quad (11)$$

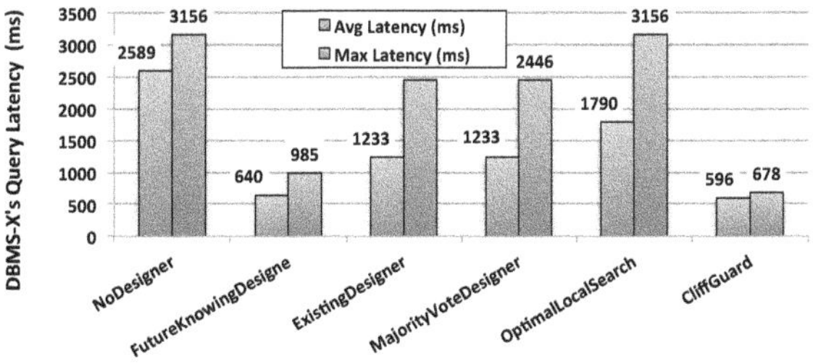

(a) Synthetic static workload S1 on DBMS-X.

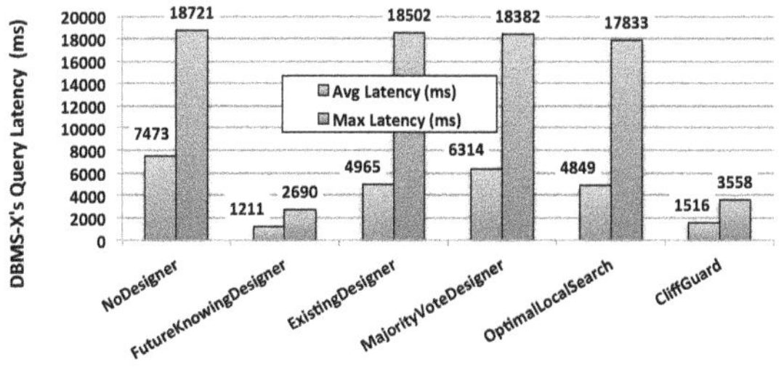

(b) Synthetic drifting workload S2 on DBMS-X.

Figure 15: Avg. and worst-case performances of designers for DBMS-X, averaged over all windows.

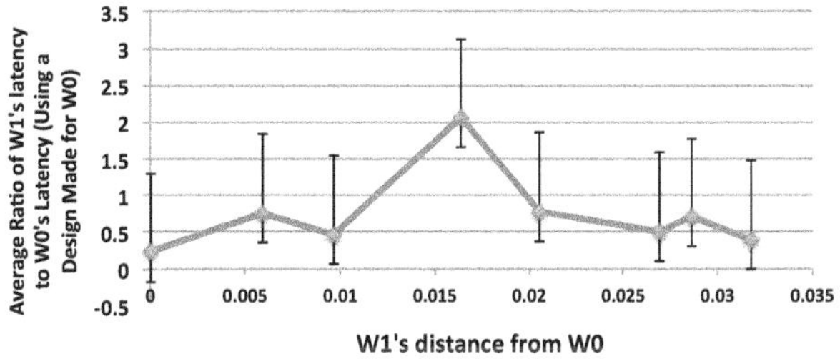

(a) The correlation of $\delta_{latency}$ with actual performance, when ω=0.1.

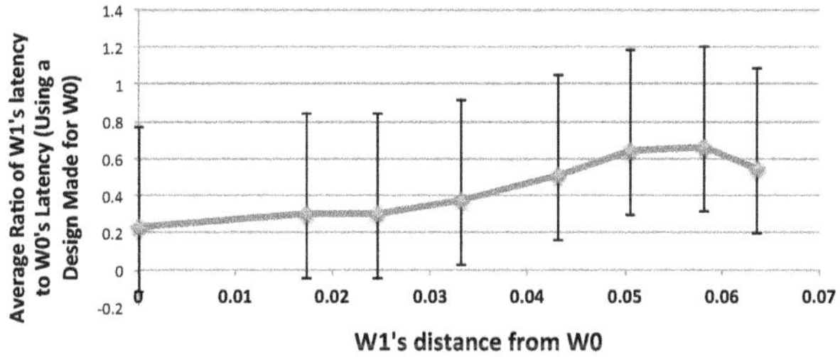

(b) The correlation of $\delta_{latency}$ with actual performance, when ω=0.2.

Figure 16: Empirical evaluation of our latency-aware distance metric (compare to $\delta_{euclidean}$ in Figure 6).

Algorithm 4: The subroutine for sampling the workload space based on a given value of $\delta_{euclidean}$ distance.

Inputs: W_0: the initial workload,
α: the required distance
Output: W_1: a new workload satisfying
$\delta_{euclidean}(W_0, W_1) = \alpha$

// Find a set of queries not contained in W_0
Find $Q = \{q_1, \cdots, q_k\}$ such that
$Q \cap W_0 = \emptyset$ and $\delta_{euclidean}(W_0, Q) > \alpha$
$\beta \leftarrow \delta_{euclidean}(W_0, Q)$
$\lambda \leftarrow \sqrt{\frac{\alpha}{\beta}}$
$n \leftarrow |W_0|$ **// n is the number of queries in W_0 (including duplicate queries)**
$c \leftarrow \frac{n \cdot \lambda}{k \cdot (1-\lambda)}$ **// k is the number of iterations so far**
$W1 \leftarrow W_0 \biguplus_{i=1}^{\lfloor c \rfloor} Q$ **// take the original queries in W_0 plus $\lfloor c \rfloor$ instances of every $q \in Q$ without removing duplicates**
return W_1

---

where $0 \leq \omega \leq 1$ is a constant and $\mathcal{R}(W_1, W_2)$ is a term capturing the difference of latency between W_1 and W_2, defined as:

$$\mathcal{R}(W_1, W_2) = \frac{|f(W_1, \emptyset) - f(W_2, \emptyset)|}{|f(W_1, \emptyset) + f(W_2, \emptyset)|} \quad (12)$$

Remember that $f(W, D)$ is the sum of the latencies of all queries in W. However, since the distance metric should be independent of a specific design, in this definition we use $D = \emptyset$, i.e., we take their baseline latencies (using no designs). In the two extreme cases, when the cost of either W_1 or W_2 is zero, $\mathcal{R}(W_1, W_2) = 1$ and when the two windows exhibit identical latencies, we have $\mathcal{R}(W_1, W_2) = 0$. The constant ω acts as a penalty factor to tune the behavior of $\delta_{latency}$, i.e., when latency difference is less important than structural similarities, one can choose a smaller value of ω (With $\omega = 0$, this distance degenerates to $\delta_{euclidean}$).

Using the same testing scenario as Section 6.3, we have empirically evaluated $\delta_{latency}$, as shown in Figure 16. Here, instead of showing the absolute latency, we have reported the ratio of the latencies of the two windows. Ideally, this ratio should be monotonic with the value of $\delta_{latency}$. This is not the case in Figure 16(a) where the penalty factor is $\omega = 0.1$. However, increasing this value to $\omega = 0.2$ yields a relatively monotonic trend, as shown in Figure 16(b). This underlines the importance of choosing an appropriate value of ω for obtaining desirable results. Our simpler distance metric $\delta_{euclidean}$, which provides a comparably reasonable accuracy in capturing the performance requirements of SQL workloads (as demonstrated in Section 6.3), does not need parameter tuning. For this and several other reasons discussed in Section 5, we currently use $\delta_{euclidean}$ in `CliffGuard`.

D. ADDITIONAL RELATED WORK

While most commercial designers are based on greedy search algorithms, several academic solutions have proposed integer programming for finding the best set of views/indices. By observing and characterizing various properties of the views and indices that appear in an optimal solution, Talebi et al. [66] prune the space of potentially beneficial views and indices while keeping at least one globally optimal solution in the search space. Integer programming has also been used for finding an optimal set of stratified samples in approximate databases [5, 6] and indices in PostgreSQL [54].

Autonomic Computing [52] and AutoAdmin [21, 25] projects have motivated self-tuning systems. Li et al. [50] address lack of robustness in resource estimation of SQL queries. LeFevre et al. [49] introduce the concept of opportunistic physical design, whereby materializing intermediate results in a MapReduce environment can lead significant opportunities for speeding up revised instances of the same query. Alagiannis et al. [8] allow the DBA to simulate various physical design features and get immediate feedback on their effectiveness. The H2O system [9] dynamically adapts its data storage layout based on the incoming query workload.

Exploiting Correlations for Expensive Predicate Evaluation

Manas Joglekar
Stanford University
Stanford, California 94305
manasrj@stanford.edu

Hector Garcia-Molina
Stanford University
Stanford, California 94305
hector@cs.stanford.edu

Aditya Parameswaran
University of Illinois at Urbana
Champaign
Champaign, Illinois 61801
adityagp@illinois.edu

Christopher Re
Stanford University
Stanford, California, 94305
chrismre@cs.stanford.edu

ABSTRACT

User Defined Function(UDFs) are used increasingly to augment query languages with extra, application dependent functionality. Selection queries involving UDF predicates tend to be expensive, either in terms of monetary cost or latency. In this paper, we study ways to efficiently evaluate selection queries with UDF predicates. We provide a family of techniques for processing queries at low cost while satisfying user-specified precision and recall constraints. Our techniques are applicable to a variety of scenarios including when selection probabilities of tuples are available beforehand, when this information is available but noisy, or when no such prior information is available. We also generalize our techniques to more complex queries. Finally, we test our techniques on real datasets, and show that they achieve significant savings in UDF evaluations of up to 80%, while incurring only a small reduction in accuracy.

Categories and Subject Descriptors

H.2.4 [**Database Management**]: Systems—*Query Processing*

Keywords

Approximate Query Processing; User defined functions

1. INTRODUCTION

User defined functions (UDFs) provide query languages with extra, application-dependent functionality. UDFs are especially important in data science, enabling data scientists to augment their workflows with complex computation, including calls to machine learning algorithms or external APIs. Overall, UDFs come in many flavors: they could invoke external services (e.g., calls to an up-to-date weather monitoring service, or a credit check service), expensive algorithms (e.g., image, video or text analysis algorithms), or even crowdsourced workers (e.g., workers on Mechanical Turk in CrowdDB or Deco [18, 34]). UDFs have become even more common in the past few years, due to the increasing use of crowdsourcing [18, 34], large scale machine learning [23, 33], and scientific procedures [11] in conjunction with traditional database systems. In all of these cases, UDFs are costly to evaluate, either (i) in terms of time, for instance in the expensive algorithm scenario, or (ii) in terms of monetary cost, for instance in the crowdsourcing or external service call scenario.

In this paper we study techniques for reducing the number of UDF invocations during execution of a select query with a UDF predicate, provided the user tolerates some reduction in accuracy. In our case we define accuracy in information retrieval terms (and not in terms of errors of individual values). That is, say C (a set of tuples) is the correct result of a query (performing all UDF calls), and R is the approximate result. Then the precision is $|R \cap C|/|R|$ and the recall is $|R \cap C|/|C|$. The user specifies bounds on precision and recall to indicate what accuracy is acceptable.

EXAMPLE 1.1. *To motivate our approach, consider the following simple example. A user wants to contact customers with a very good credit rating to offer a special promotion. The following query describes his needs:*

$$\texttt{Q : SELECT * FROM R(A, ID) WHERE f(ID)} = 1.$$

Here `f` *involves a call to a UDF, say a credit check service, and returns 1 (for "good") or 0 ("bad") depending on whether or not the credit score is above a threshold.*

If the user requires perfect precision and recall, then the system must retrieve every `R` *record and check if its* `f(ID)` *value is* `1`*. The cost, either in terms of time taken or money paid to the credit bureau, will be high. Instead say the user is willing to tolerate a slightly lower value of precision and/or recall, say 90% for each. (The precise meaning of this bound will be discussed later.) In other words, the user is willing to pitch the promotion to a few customers with a bad credit rating, and to miss a few good customers, in order to get the query results significantly faster or cheaper.*

Then, one straightforward query execution strategy is to simply evaluate `f` *on as many tuples as necessary in sequence until the recall and precision constraints are met. Thus, we will end up making close to* $90\% \times 3000 = 2700$ *calls to the credit check* `f` *function.*

Another approach, which we will explore in depth in this paper, is to estimate and then exploit correlations. In our example, let us assume there is an attribute `A` *of* `R` *that is correlated to the output of* `f`*. For instance,* `A` *could be an income attribute or a housing status that could indicate a higher likelihood for having a good credit score. (We discuss later how we can discover one or more attributes that may be correlated to the UDF.)*

Step 1: Estimating Correlations. *One way to estimate correlations is by sampling some* `R` *tuples. For example, after reading*

SIGMOD'15, May 31–June 4, 2015, Melbourne, Victoria, Australia.

http://dx.doi.org/10.1145/2723372.2723715.

5% of the tuples with each `A` *value, the system has the following estimates:*

- *If* `A=1, f(ID) = 1` *with probability 0.9*
- *If* `A=2, f(ID) = 1` *with probability 0.5*
- *If* `A=3, f(ID) = 1` *with probability 0.1.*

(As we discuss later, sampling is not the only way to obtain the statistics needed by our next step.) The system also knows that there are 1000 tuples with each of the possible `A` *values, for a total of 3000* `R` *records.*

Step 2: Executing Query. *Then, a better query execution strategy is to handle tuples with each* `A` *value differently: Tuples with* `A=1` *are very likely to satisfy the predicate, so we can add them to the result without evaluating* `f`*. Tuples with* `A = 3` *are unlikely to match, so we can simply discard them. Tuples with* `A = 2` *can go either way, so we evaluate* `f` *on each tuple with* `A = 2` *and only add the tuples that match to the result. With this strategy we only need to evaluate* `f` *1000 times (plus the evaluations needed for sampling), not the 2700 calls of the straightforward approach, and we still get an expected precision and recall of (approximately) 90%.*

Note that the execution strategy illustrated above is one of many: for every group of tuples that shares the same `A` *value, we can choose to (a) directly add all of them to the result without evaluating* `f`*, (b) discard all of them, or (c) evaluate all of them and then decide whether to add it to the result or not. Thus, if* n *is the number of distinct values of* `A`*, we have* 3^n *possible execution strategies. We could also employ probabilistic execution strategies, where we toss a biased coin for each tuple in a group of tuples sharing the same* `A` *value, and decide what to do based on the outcome. Overall, it is not immediately obvious which of these strategies we should use in order to meet our precision and recall guarantees. Indeed, as we will see in the following, designing optimized execution strategies is NP-Hard.*

Our approach avoids UDF evaluations by exploiting *correlations* between the results of boolean UDF calls and values of other categorical attributes. In our example we have swept a number of details and possible generalizations "under the rug" in order to present the essence of our approach. The details will be formalized in the sections that follow, but we make a few clarifications:

- The attribute `A` in our example could be several attributes or even a virtual attribute representing the output of a machine learning algorithm that predicts the value of `f` based on values in a tuple. That is, with appropriate training data we may develop a less expensive function `f'` that predicts `f` (and also provides confidences for its predictions). With such a function we can skip Step 1, and in Step 2 use the `f'` values to decide whether to discard a tuple, output it immediately, or evaluate the expensive `f` function. We will focus on the sampling approach because it makes it easier to account for the cost of obtaining correlations.
  That said, our techniques for step 2 are agnostic to the source of the confidences values. As a result, we can use confidences generated by say, logistic regression or least squares estimation, or any other statistical techniques. We experimentally evaluate the impact of where the confidences come from (including sampling and logistic regression) in Section 6.
- We assume that `f` values have not been cached in advance. If the values are available, then the expense of evaluating `f` on every tuple has been paid in advance, and conventional query processing strategies can be used. Our techniques can be applied even if some of the values are available in advance. Note that in many cases `f` outputs vary with time and should not be cached. For example, weather predictions or credit ratings change over time.

We reiterate that our approach hinges on two assumptions: (a) that the user is willing to accept imperfect precision and/or recall, and (b) that there is an attribute (possibly virtual, possibly multiple attributes) that is correlated to the UDF output. For (a), we believe that users are familiar with document retrieval models where it is not practical to get the complete and exact answer to a query. Often, the output of the UDF itself is subjective or approximate (e.g., whether a patient is prone to a particular illness, or an image is inappropriate), so errors cannot be ruled out no matter what we do. For (b), if correlated attributes are not known in advance, there are well known techniques for learning what attributes are good predictors, and for combining these attributes into a virtual attribute that can be used by our solution.

When these assumptions hold, we will show (with real data sets) that queries can be evaluated very efficiently. These savings will grow in importance as data sets grow in size and UDFs become more and more popular. In our experiments we will also study various performance related questions: For example, how much sampling should one do in Step 1? As we sample more, our statistics improve, but our cost savings decrease. How sensitive is our approach to the number of `A` values? As the number of values grows, the number of tuples with a given value shrinks, possibly making it harder to get estimates.

Prior work has addressed optimal placement of UDF evaluation in query plans [14, 15, 21, 24], assuming users provide hints for UDF costs; in our work, we aim to avoid UDF evaluations entirely by exploiting correlations. Our work is also similar to the work on reducing evaluations in sensor networks [16], however, the scenario is very different, necessitating different approaches. There has been significant work on Approximate Query Processing [13, 19, 20, 22, 28]. However, these papers only approximate numerical aggregate quantities, while we focus on set-valued queries. Finally, there is some recent work on finding correlations between attributes of a relation [12, 26, 29], which can then be used to better estimate costs of intermediate results for query optimization. Our work, on the other hand, exploits correlations between attributes in a relation and an external UDF. Related work is surveyed in more detail in Section 7.

Contributions: We propose a novel approach to optimize expensive UDFs by exploiting correlation information. Specifically,

- In Section 2, we introduce the relevant notation for the setup of the problems we consider.
- In Section 3, we study the case where correlations are known. We consider three scenarios where we can exploit existing correlations, and we show NP-Hardness for the first scenario and describe asymptotically optimal algorithms for the other two scenarios.
- In Section 4, we study the case where correlations are not known in advance, and we must jointly estimate correlations, and exploit them. We describe a method of obtaining correlation information, how to use this information adaptively, and provide a rule of thumb to use in practice.
- In Section 6, we experimentally evaluate the performance of our algorithms on four real datasets, and also demonstrate the correctness of the algorithms.

In Section 5, we extend our methods to more advanced SQL queries that involve more than one table and/or UDF predicate.

2. PRELIMINARIES

We begin by considering queries like our example query `Q` in Section 1. We reproduce the query here:

Tuple No.	A	ID	f(ID)
1	1	999-999-999	1
2	1	913-418-777	1
3	1	719-334-111	1
4	1	999-999-999	1
5	2	913-418-737	0
6	2	719-334-113	1
7	2	999-999-299	0
8	3	913-418-737	0
9	3	719-334-121	0
10	3	999-999-959	0
11	3	913-418-727	0
12	3	719-334-311	1

Table 1: Example Data for R

$\texttt{Q : SELECT} * \texttt{ FROM R(A, ID) WHERE f(ID)} = 1$

The relation R contains an attribute A, the values of which are correlated with the output of f(ID) across tuples. It is straightforward to generalize to queries with more correlated attributes, with joins or projects, or with categorical predicates for f with operators other than equality. (We discuss generalizations in Section 5.)

In practical applications, the value of the correlated column A may not be known in advance. In Section 4.4, we describe a general procedure for finding the best correlated column in any table.

To assist the description of our terminology, we provide example data for R in Table 1. Naturally, f(ID) is not known in advance (and instead must be computed using UDF evaluations), but is also shown along with the table. The tuples in R that satisfy the predicate (i.e., f(ID) equals 1) are called *correct*, while those that do not are called *incorrect*. Thus, in Table 1, tuples 1-4, 6, and 12 are correct, while the rest are incorrect.

Groups of Tuples: We use A to denote both the correlated attribute, as well as the set of distinct values that appear in R.A. Therefore, we use $a \in$ A to denote a value that attribute A can take. In Table 1, a can be $1, 2$, or 3. The set of tuples that share the same value of A is called a *group*. We let t_a be the number of tuples in the group that has A=a. Thus, $t_1 = 4, t_2 = 3$, and $t_3 = 5$ in our example. In a group corresponding to A=a, we let c_a denote the number of correct tuples (i.e., tuples satisfying the predicate), and w_a be the number of incorrect tuples. Thus, for $a = 2$, $c_2 = 1$, while $w_2 = 2$. While we assume c_a, w_a to be known in our example (and also in our initial setting in Section 3.1), typically these values are not known, and are treated as random variables. In such cases, we use upper case C_a and W_a to denote the random variables. We assume t_a for all $a \in$ A is always known.

Actions and Costs: For our simple query Q, we must decide if each tuple in R is in the result. We have three alternative *actions* we could take:

- First, we could *discard* the tuple, i.e., no action is taken on the tuple, and the tuple does not contribute to the output. In this case, we are predicting that the tuple is not correct.
- Next, we could *retrieve but not evaluate* the tuple, i.e., retrieve the tuple from R, and add it to the result without actually evaluating the UDF. In this case, we are predicting that the tuple is correct.
- Last, we could *retrieve and evaluate* the tuple, i.e., retrieve the tuple from R, evaluate the UDF on the tuple, and add the tuple to the result if it satisfies the condition f(ID)=1. Then we are certain to be accurate in our assessment of the tuple.

Say we incur a cost of o_e for every tuple evaluated, and a cost of o_r for every tuple retrieved from storage. Since UDFs are expensive, o_e is likely to be much greater than o_r. Thus, the cost of discarding a tuple is 0, the cost of retrieving and not evaluating is o_r, and the cost of retrieving and evaluating is $o_r + o_e$. Note that this cost model implies we have some type of index on A so we can reach the examined tuples with constant cost independent of the discarded tuples.

We now present expressions denoting costs across tuples. We first define the following terms for convenience:

- R_a^+ denotes the total number of correct tuples that we retrieved from group a, while R_a^- denotes the total number of incorrect tuples that we retrieved from group a.
- E_a^+ denotes the total number of correct tuples that we evaluated from group a. E_a^- denotes the total number of incorrect tuples we evaluated from group a.

Then, our overall cost, which we will aim to minimize, is:

$$\mathcal{O} = \sum_{a \in A} o_r(R_a^+ + R_a^-) + o_e(E_a^+ + E_a^-) \quad (1)$$

Metrics and Constraints: Our output must meet a user-specified *precision* and *recall* constraint. As defined earlier, precision is the fraction of tuples in the output that are correct. Using our notation, $\sum_{a \in A} R_a^+$ is the number of correct tuples that we return, whereas $\sum_{a \in A} R_a^+ + R_a^- - E_a^-$ is the total number of tuples we return (incorrect tuples that are retrieved and evaluated get discarded). Hence,

$$\mathcal{P} = \frac{\sum_{a \in A} R_a^+}{\sum_{a \in A} R_a^+ + R_a^- - E_a^-}$$

Analogously, recall is the fraction of the correct tuples that are present in the output, i.e.,

$$\mathcal{R} = \frac{\sum_{a \in A} R_a^+}{\sum_{a \in A} C_a}$$

The user specifies a precision lower-bound $\alpha \in [0, 1]$, and a recall lower-bound $\beta \in [0, 1]$. Our output must then satisfy:

$$\mathcal{P} \geq \alpha; \quad \mathcal{R} \geq \beta$$

A special case of interest is the *browsing* scenario, where 100% precision is required, and thus we have to evaluate every tuple we retrieve, and our objective is to minimize expected cost while satisfying the recall constraint.

Probabilistic Constraints: The above bounds are strict, but if we are making discard and evaluate decisions based on imprecise statistics, there is a (hopefully small) chance that the output will violate the bounds. Thus, we also allow the user to define a *satisfaction probability* ρ (which we expect to be very close to 1). The system should then guarantee that with probability ρ the precision and recall constraints are met.

3. EXPLOITING CORRELATIONS

In the example of Section 1 we described the two steps of our approach: Step 1 obtains correlations, and Step 2 takes this correlation information as input to process the query efficiently. We consider three forms of such correlations.

- Perfect Information: In this case, Step 2 receives both W_a and C_a (the exact number of wrong and correct tuples, respectively) for all a. This case is only included as a baseline, so we can compare the other more realistic cases against it.
- Perfect Selectivities: in this case, we know the probability of each tuple in a group being correct, i.e., s_a for each group a. If we take a random tuple from group a, then f(ID)=1 for that tuple with probability s_a independent of other tuples. Thus the number of tuples in group a with f(ID)=1 follow a binomial distribution.

- Estimated Selectivities: in this case we do not know the selectivity s_a precisely. That is, we have a random variable S_a that represents the selectivity of group a. Selectivity s_a is now the mean of S_a and v_a is the variance of S_a.

Exploiting these different types of correlations is the technical focus of this section.

3.1 Warm-up: Perfect Information

We begin by considering the *perfect information* case, i.e., we know, in advance, the precise number of correct and incorrect tuples in each group. That is, for each $a \in A$, we know the values of C_a, i.e., the number of correct tuples, and W_a, the number of incorrect tuples. Thus, in this section, these values are constants.

While these assumptions are not completely realistic (we will rarely have such information available in advance), this section will demonstrate that even when perfect information is available, the problem of selecting which groups to retrieve and evaluate, which groups to retrieve but not evaluate, and which groups to discard is already intractable. Furthermore, the section will act as an introduction to the more complex schemes in subsequent sections. In later sections, we will show that allowing our algorithm to provide weaker (probabilistic) guarantees makes the problem tractable.

Optimization Problem: Given the values of C_a and W_a for each a, our goal is to optimally determine boolean decision variables R_a and E_a to satisfy recall and precision constraints while minimizing cost. The boolean variable R_a is set to 1 if the tuples in that group with $A = a$ are to be retrieved during query execution (and 0 if the tuples are to be discarded), and the boolean variable E_a is set to 1 if the tuples in that group with $A = a$ are to be evaluated during query execution (and 0 if they are not). Note that $R_a \geq E_a$ for each $a \in A$ since we may only evaluate the UDF on a tuple if it is retrieved first.

We now rewrite the constraints in the previous section in terms of the new boolean variables R_a, E_a. The recall constraint becomes:

$$\sum_{a \in A} C_a R_a \geq \beta \sum_{a \in A} C_a \qquad (2)$$

Note that given C_a values, the right hand side of the inequality is a constant. The precision constraint becomes:

$$\frac{\sum_{a \in A} C_a R_a}{\sum_{a \in A} C_a R_a + W_a(R_a - E_a)} \geq \alpha$$

$$\Leftrightarrow \sum_{a \in A} ((\frac{1}{\alpha} - 1)C_a - W_a)R_a + W_a E_a \geq 0 \qquad (3)$$

Then, the optimization problem can be restated as:

PROBLEM 1 (PERFECT-INFORMATION). *Given $C_a, W_a, t_a \forall a$, identify $R_a, E_a \in \{0, 1\}$; $R_a \geq E_a$ to minimize $\mathcal{O} = \sum_{a \in A}(W_a + C_a)(R_a o_r + E_a o_e)$, such that Constraints 2 and 3 are satisfied.*

We demonstrate that Problem 1 is NP-hard, which motivates the more relaxed semantics throughout this section.

Hardness of Special Case. We can show that Problem 1 is NP-hard even when there is no precision constraint. Since Problem 1 can be cast as an Integer Linear Program (ILP), overall, the problem is NP-Complete.

THEOREM 3.1. *Problem 1 is NP-Complete in $|A|$ (i.e., the number of distinct values of A).*

Unless otherwise noted, complete proofs of our results (like Theorem 3.1) can be found in our extended technical report [1]. In some selected cases, the proofs are included in the appendix of this paper.

3.2 Perfect Selectivity Information

In the previous section, we demonstrated that the optimization problem to generate deterministic execution schemes meeting precision and recall guarantees exactly, was NP-Hard. We will now show that the problem can be solved efficiently by relaxing it to allow probabilistic execution schemes, along with probabilistic guarantees. In this section we make the following modifications to the problem in the previous section:

- **Selectivities:** We now assume that $W_a, C_a, \forall a \subset A$ are not provided to us. Instead, we assume that we know the selectivity s_a of each group $a \in A$, i.e., for a tuple with $A = a$, the probability of it being correct is independently true with probability s_a. These selectivities could be learned using historical data. We assume that the selectivity values are *perfect.* (In the next section, we consider selectivity values that may be *imperfect.*)
- **Satisfaction Probability:** Since we are dealing with selectivities which are probabilities, rather than deterministic W_a, C_a values, there are always adversarial inputs on which any query execution strategy would perform poorly. Thus, in this section (and subsequent ones) we assume that the user has given us a probability value ρ such that our precision and recall constraints must be met with probability ρ.

In addition, since we are dealing with probabilities for both the quantities mentioned previously, it is more natural to consider probabilistic execution strategies rather than deterministic ones. Accepting fractional solutions to our linear problem, and consequently providing only probabilistic guarantees to error bounds, makes our new optimization problem tractable.

We now present the problem formally.

Query Optimization and Execution: As before, our processing proceeds in two steps:

- **Optimization:** We determine, for each group, whether to (a) retrieve and evaluate, (b) retrieve but not evaluate, or (c) directly discard the tuples in that group. We do this by generating probabilities $0 \leq E_a \leq R_a \leq 1, \forall a \in A$. The objective of this step is to choose R_as and E_as such that the results after execution (described next) satisfy the precision and recall constraints with probability at least ρ, while minimizing expected cost $\mathcal{O}$. No query execution happens at this point.
- **Execution:** We then execute the query by retrieving each of the tuples in group a with probability R_a, independent of all other tuples, and evaluate each of the retrieved tuples from group a with probability $\frac{E_a}{R_a}$, again independently of all other tuples. (Note that these two probabilities when multiplied together give E_a, which is precisely the probability we evaluate a tuple from group a.) Tuples that are retrieved but not evaluated are returned in the output (that is, we assume those tuples are correct).

Optimization Problem: For each $a \in A$, we are given the selectivity s_a of group a, i.e., each tuple in group a is correct with probability s_a independent of other tuples.

Our constraints can be expressed as follows: We have the basic constraint $0 \leq E_a \leq R_a \leq 1$. Recall that R_a^+ denotes the random variable corresponding to the number of correct tuples retrieved from group a (similarly for R_a^-, E_a^+, E_a^-.) The precision constraint, which must be satisfied with probability ρ, can be expressed as:

$$\sum_{a \in A} R_a^+ - \alpha \sum_{a \in A} (R_a^+ + R_a^- - E_a^-) \geq 0 \qquad (4)$$

The recall constraint, which again must be satisfied with probability ρ, can be expressed as:

$$\sum_{a \in A} R_a^+ - \beta \sum_{a \in A} C_a \geq 0 \quad (5)$$

Since our solution is now probabilistic, we try to minimize the expected value of the objective.

$$\mathcal{O} = E\left[\sum_{a \in A} o_r(R_a^+ + R_a^-) + o_e(E_a^+ + E_a^-)\right]$$
$$= \sum_{a \in A}(W_a + C_a)(o_r R_a + o_e E_a) = \sum_{a \in A} t_a(o_r R_a + o_e E_a)$$

PROBLEM 2 (PERFECT-SELECTIVITIES). *Given $s_a, t_a \forall a$, identify $0 \leq E_a \leq R_a \leq 1$ to minimize $\mathcal{O} = \sum_{a \in A} t_a(o_r R_a + o_e E_a)$, such that Constraints 4 and 5 are satisfied with probability greater than ρ.*

In the next few subsections, we will (a) describe a LP-based solution for Problem 2 (b) demonstrate that the LP-based solution is asymptotically optimal (c) describe how we may speed up the computation of the LP, by leveraging the special structure of the LP.

We later study the performance of this LP-based solution, referred to as 'Optimal', in the Experiments section.

3.2.1 LP-Based Solution

First, notice that the expected value of the LHS of Constraint 4 can be rewritten as follows:

$$G^p = \sum_{a \in A} t_a s_a (1-\alpha) R_a + t_a(1 - s_a)\alpha(E_a - R_a) \quad (6)$$

We get the above equation by substituting $E[R_a^+] = s_a t_a R_a$, $E[R_a^-] = (1 - s_a)t_a R_a$ (the E_a equations are similar). Similarly, the expected value of the LHS of Constraint 5 can be rewritten as follows:

$$G^r = \sum_{a \in A} t_a s_a R_a - \sum_{a \in A} \beta t_a s_a \quad (7)$$

Our approach will be to ensure that G^p and G^r, i.e., the expected values of quantities closely related to precision and recall, are greater than some carefully chosen thresholds h_ρ^p and h_ρ^r respectively, to ensure that the corresponding constraints 4 and 5 are satisfied with probability ρ.

We define h_ρ^p, h_ρ^r as follows:

$$h_\rho^p = \sqrt{\frac{\log(1-\rho)\sum_{a \in A} t_a}{2}} \quad (8)$$

$$h_\rho^r = \sqrt{\frac{\log(1-\rho)\sum_{a \in A} t_a(1-\beta)}{2}} \quad (9)$$

The key observation is that the LHS of constraint 4 can be written as a sum of independent random variables, with one random variable per tuple of the table. Thus, Hoeffding's inequality applies [36], and we choose h_ρ^p such that the LHS is within h_ρ^p of its expected value with probability $\geq \rho$ as needed by constraint 4. h_ρ^r is defined similarly for constraint 5.

Then, consider the following linear program:

LINEAR PROG. 3.2 (PERFECT-SELECTIVITIES). *Minimize $\sum_{a \in A} t_a(R_a o_r + E_a o_e)$ subject to:*

$$\sum_{a \in A} t_a s_a (1-\alpha) R_a + t_a(1 - s_a)\alpha(E_a - R_a) \geq h_\rho^p \quad (10)$$

$$\sum_{a \in A} t_a s_a R_a - \sum_{a \in A} \beta t_a s_a \geq h_\rho^r \quad (11)$$

$$\forall a \in A; 1 \geq R_a \geq E_a \geq 0$$

It can be shown that solving the linear program above gives us R_a and E_a that satisfy the precision and recall constraints with probability at least ρ. Our proof uses repeated applications of Hoeffding's inequality, union bounds [36], as well as other standard results in probability. As stated earlier, unless otherwise noted see our extended technical report [1] for proofs.

THEOREM 3.3. *Solving Linear-Prog. 3.2 provides a feasible solution for Problem 2.*

The theorem above only states that the solution will be feasible, but not how close the resulting cost $\mathcal{O}$ is to the optimal cost. Thankfully, as we will show below, our solution is close to optimal.

Tightness. We state the tightness bound on our result below, and prove it in the appendix.

THEOREM 3.4. *Let s_a^{min} be the smallest non-zero value of s_a. Then, the difference between the cost of the optimal solution to Linear-Prog. 3.2, and the cost of the optimal solution to Problem 2, is at most*

$$(o_e + o_r)\frac{1}{s_a^{min}} \max(h_\rho^r + h_{1-\rho}^r, \frac{h_\rho^p + h_{1-\rho}^p}{1-\alpha})$$

The idea behind this result is as follows: The LHS of constraint 4 in the optimal solution must be greater than $-h_{1-\rho}^p$, because if it is not, then Hoeffding's inequality would imply that the constraint is violated with probability $\geq 1 - \rho$. We can make a similar claim about the recall constraint. Then we can show that by increasing the R_a, E_a values of the optimal solution, we can make it satisfy constraints of Linear Program 3.2, while increasing expected cost by at most $(o_e + o_r)\frac{1}{s_a^{min}}\max(h_\rho^r + h_{1-\rho}^r, \frac{h_\rho^p + h_{1-\rho}^p}{1-\alpha})$. The resulting cost must be greater than of equal to the cost of our solution, which was optimal for Linear Program 3.2. This gives us a bound on the cost difference between our solution and the optimal solution to Problem 2.

This cost difference described in the previous theorem is $O(\sqrt{n})$ where n is number of tuples, because the h^p, h^r values are $O(\sqrt{n})$. Now consider what happens as $n \to \infty$ for fixed s_a's, α, β. This means we have the same constraints, and groups with the same selectivities, but the group sizes are scaled up. As $n \to \infty$, the ratio of our cost to optimal cost $\to 1$, as indicated by the theorem below:

THEOREM 3.5. *As $n \to \infty$, the ratio of the cost of the optimal solution to Linear-Prog. 3.2, to the cost of the optimal solution to Problem 2 approaches 1.*

Thus, our solution for Problem 2 is asymptotically optimal.

3.2.2 BiGreedy Solution for the linear problem

In this section, we describe an efficient way to solve Linear-Prog. 3.2 without even using a linear solver, in $O(|A| \log |A|)$ time:

THEOREM 3.6. *If the following constraints hold:*

$$h_\rho^p < \sum_{a \in A} \max(t_a(s_a - \alpha), 0)$$

$$h_\rho^r < \sum_{a \in A}(1-\beta)t_a s_a$$

then the solution to Linear-Prog 3.2 can be found in $O(|A| \log |A|)$

The first constraint simply states that the variance term h_ρ^p is not too large (the constraint is trivially satisfied if the term is 0). It ensures that the precision constraint can be satisfied without evaluating any tuple with selectivity $\geq \alpha$, while the second constraint simply ensures that the problem has a solution.

Our improved algorithm for solving the Linear Program is:

Algorithm BIGREEDY-LP

- Initialize all R_a and E_a to 0. Sort the a's based on s_a.
- Then start increasing the values of R_a in a greedy fashion. That is, increase R_a for the highest selectivity a until it becomes 1, then increase R_a for the next highest selectivity a, and so on. Keep repeating this step until the recall constraint Equation 11 is satisfied.
- After that, keep the R_as fixed, and start increasing the E_as in a greedy fashion, but in reverse order. That is, start by increasing E_a for the a with lowest selectivity and non-zero R_a, until it reaches R_a, then move to the a with next lowest selectivity, and so on. Keep repeating this step until the precision constraint Equation 10 is satisfied.

Thus the approach is to round up the values of the R_a in the order of decreasing s_a, and then round up the values of the values of the E_a in the order of increasing s_a. The intuition is simple; we want to retrieve all the groups where the selectivity is high, in order to meet our recall constraint. Once we know we're retrieving enough groups to meet our recall constraint, we then ensure that we're evaluating enough groups to meet the precision constraint. Naturally, we'd rather evaluate UDFs for the *most incorrect groups among those we're already retrieving* — i.e., those with the lowest s_a first, so that we can have the maximum impact on precision. The proof that Algorithm BIGREEDY-LP provides the solution to Linear-Prog. 3.2 can be found in the technical report [1].

3.3 Estimated Selectivity Information

In the previous section, we developed probabilistic execution strategies when the selectivity of each group is precisely known in advance. In reality, however, we are unlikely to know the precise selectivity of each group, and must instead rely on *estimates of selectivity* (found using sampling or some other method). We now consider the case where we only have an estimate of the selectivity.

As in the previous section, we focus on probabilistic execution strategies that ensure that the precision and recall constraints are met with satisfaction probability ρ. Further, as in the previous section, our query processing proceeds in two steps, one, that solves an optimization problem, and second, that actually executes the query using the solution to the optimization problem.

Optimization Problem: Suppose the tuple selectivity for each value $a \in A$ is a value s'_a unknown to us. What is known instead is an estimate s_a of s'_a, which is an instance of a random variable S_a. Let $E[S_a] = s'_a$ and $\mathrm{Var}(S_a) \approx v_a$, where v_a is our estimate of the variance of S_a. Note that in this section s_a is an estimate of S_a, and not the actual selectivity like in the previous section.

We are given α, β, ρ, and we want to choose probabilities $1 \geq R_a \geq E_a \geq 0, \forall a \in A$, such that when execution strategy retrieves and evaluates tuples probabilistically as described in Section 3.2, the eventual result satisfies the precision and recall constraints with probability at least ρ, while minimizing cost:

PROBLEM 3 (ESTIMATED-SELECTIVITIES). *Given s_a, v_a, identify $0 \leq E_a \leq R_a \leq 1$ to minimize $\mathcal{O} = \sum_{a \in A} t_a(o_r R_a + o_e E_a)$, such that Constraints 4 and 5 are satisfied with probability greater than ρ.*

3.3.1 Convex Optimization-Based Solution

Until now, we have not specified the correlations between S_as for different as. We solve the problem for two cases, one where the correlations are unknown (and hence we assume the worst case of maximum correlation between S_as) and the other case where S_as for different a's are independent of each other. Let $e_\rho = \frac{1}{\sqrt{1-\rho}}$. Then our solutions for the two cases are:

CONVEX PROG. 3.7 (UNKNOWN CORRELATIONS). *Minimize $\sum_{a \in A} t_a(R_a o_r + E_a o_e)$ such that*

$$\sum_{a \in A}(1-\alpha)t_a R_a s_a - t_a \alpha(R_a - E_a)(1 - s_a) \geq X$$

$$\sum_{a \in A} t_a R_a s_a - \beta t_a s_a \geq Y$$

$$e_\rho \sum_{a \in A} \sqrt{v_a} t_a (R_a - \alpha E_a) + 0.5\sqrt{t_a} = X$$

$$e_\rho \sum_{a \in A} \sqrt{v_a} t_a |R_a - \beta| + 0.5\sqrt{t_a} = Y$$

$$R_a, E_a \in \{0, 1\}; R_a \geq E_a$$

Notice that the first two constraints and the objective of the problem above are identical to those in Linear-Prog. 3.2. However, the next two constraints (regarding X, Y) are highly non-linear, forcing the problem to be a convex problem. Solving this problem gives a solution which has precision $\geq \alpha$ and recall $\geq \beta$ with probability at least ρ each.

CONVEX PROG. 3.8 (INDEPENDENT GROUPS). *Minimize $\sum_{a \in A} t_a(R_a o_r + E_a o_e)$ such that*

$$\sum_{a \in A}(1-\alpha)t_a R_a s_a - t_a \alpha(R_a - E_a)(1 - s_a) \geq X$$

$$\sum_{a \in A} t_a R_a s_a - \beta t_a s_a \geq Y$$

$$e_\rho \sqrt{\sum_{a \in A} t_a^2 v_a (R_a - \alpha E_a)^2 + 0.25 t_a} = X$$

$$e_\rho \sqrt{\sum_{a \in A} t_a^2 v_a (R_a - \beta)^2 + 0.25 t_a} = Y$$

$$R_a, E_a \in \{0, 1\}; R_a \geq E_a$$

Once again, the first two constraints and the objective of the problem above are identical to those in Linear-Prog. 3.2, while the next two constraints make it highly non-linear.

Solving this problem gives a solution which has precision $\geq \alpha$ and recall $\geq \beta$ with probability at least ρ each. Later in the experiments section, we study the performance of the above solution, referred to as 'Intel-Sample'.

THEOREM 3.9. *Solving Convex-Prog. 3.7 provides a feasible solution for Problem 3 when correlations between S_as are unknown.*

THEOREM 3.10. *Solving Convex-Prog. 3.8 provides a feasible solution for Problem 3 when S_as are independent.*

Let Q_p be the LHS of constraint 4. Using Chebyshev's inequality [36], we argue that in order to satisfy the constraint $Q_p \geq 0$ with probability $\geq \rho$, it is sufficient to satisfy $E[Q_p] \geq \frac{\mathrm{Dev}(Q_p)}{\sqrt{1-\rho}} = e_\rho \mathrm{Dev}(Q_p)$. The variable X in our convex program is an upper bound on $e_\rho \mathrm{Dev}(Q_p)$, and the LHS of the first convex program constraint is $E[Q_p]$. The other two constraints of the convex program similarly correspond to recall. Complete proofs of the above theorems can be found in Appendix A.2.

The above theorems show that our solution is correct, but not how close it is to optimal. However, if we obtain our selectivity estimates by sampling (as described in Section 4), then our method is asymptotically optimal:

THEOREM 3.11. *Let n be the total number of tuples in the table. Suppose we increase n, scaling up group sizes while keeping group selectivities fixed. Let the sample size used to obtain selectivity estimates be given by any function that is in $o(n)$. Also let $\mathcal{O}_n^{ind}$ denote the cost of the optimal solution to Convex-Prog. 3.8, $\mathcal{O}_n^{unk}$ the cost of the optimal solution to Convex-Prog. 3.7, and $\mathcal{O}_n^{opt}$ the cost of the optimal solution to Problem 2. Then as $n \to \infty$, $\frac{\mathcal{O}_n^{ind}}{\mathcal{O}_n^{opt}} \to 1$ and $\frac{\mathcal{O}_n^{unk}}{\mathcal{O}_n^{opt}} \to 1$.*

Thus the ratio of cost of our algorithm to the cost of the optimal algorithm tends to 1 as n tends to infinity.

4. JOINT ESTIMATION & EXPLOITATION

In the previous section, we developed probabilistic execution strategies when selectivity estimates are already available. But in many cases, selectivity estimates are not usually available beforehand and need to be gathered on-the-fly. In this section, we focus on the problem of jointly estimating and exploiting selectivity information. We will estimate selectivities using sampling (i.e., retrieving and evaluating a small fraction of the tuples).

Our key idea will be to adapt the technique from Section 3.3 to work with sampling-based estimates of selectivities. We first examine how we can map knowledge from samples to the setting from Section 3.3 in Section 4.1. We then describe our extension of the solution from Section 3.3 to this new scenario, assuming samples are given, in Section 4.2. Lastly, we consider the problem of deciding how much to sample from each group in Section 4.3.

4.1 Sampling-based Estimates

For the purposes of this subsection, we assume that some number of tuples per group have been sampled, i.e., for each of those tuples, we have retrieved and evaluated them. We now describe how the sampled UDF evaluations lead to selectivity estimates.

For each $a \in A$, we use random variable S_a to represent the distribution of selectivity estimates we may obtain for tuples from group a. We assume that the S_as themselves are independent of each other for different as, so evaluating a tuple for $a = a_1 \in A$ tells us nothing about the selectivity S_{a_2}, for $a_2 \neq a_1$.

Suppose for each $a \in A$, we have evaluated the UDF on F_a tuples, and found F_a^+ of them to satisfy the predicate, and F_a^- that don't (thus $F_a = F_a^+ + F_a^-$). Then at that point, the probability density function of our estimate at any value x will be given by us a Beta distribution [36]: Beta$(F_a^+ + 1, F_a^- + 1)(x)$. Therefore

$$s_a = E\left[\text{Beta}(F_a^+ + 1, F_a^- + 1)\right] = \frac{F_a^+ + 1}{F_a + 2};$$

$$v_a = \text{Var}(\text{Beta}(F_a^+ + 1, F_a^- + 1)) = \frac{s_a(1 - s_a)}{F_a + 3}$$

where s_a and v_a are defined as per Section 3.3.

4.2 Solution given Sampling-based Estimates

As described above, we can use sampling to obtain selectivity estimates. The estimates can then be used to solve the problem in a way similar to Section 3.3.

However, there is a small wrinkle that needs to be dealt with: in addition to giving us selectivity estimates, the sampled tuples will themselves have been evaluated already. So, among these tuples, those that are correct (based on the UDF invocation on that tuple) can be simply returned as part of the query result without re-evaluating them.

Expressing the mean and variance of selectivities in terms of F_a^+, F_a^- and F_a, and taking into account the tuples that have already been sampled (and hence retrieved and evaluated), we can rephrase the optimization problem from Section 3.3 as below:

CONVEX PROG. 4.1 (SAMPLING SELECTIVITIES). *Minimize* $\sum_{a \in A}(t_a - F_a)(R_a o_r + E_a o_e) + F_a(o_e + o_r)$ *such that*

$$\sum_{a \in A} F_a^+(1-\alpha) + (1-\alpha)(t_a - F_a)R_a s_a - (t_a - F_a)\alpha(R_a - E_a)(1 - s_a) \geq X$$

$$\sum_{a \in A} F_a^+ + (t_a - F_a)R_a s_a - \beta(t_a - F_a)s_a\beta F_a^+ \geq Y$$

$$e_\rho\sqrt{\sum_{a \in A}(t_a - F_a)^2 v_a(R_a - \alpha E_a)^2 + 0.25(t_a - F_a)} = X$$

$$e_\rho\sqrt{\sum_{a \in A}(t_a - F_a)^2 v_a(R_a - \beta)^2 + 0.25(t_a - F_a)} = Y$$

$$R_a, E_a \in \{0, 1\}; R_a \geq E_a$$

where $e_\rho = \frac{1}{\sqrt{1-\rho}}$. And we have:

THEOREM 4.2. *When S_as are been obtained by sampling F_a tuples from group a for each $a \in A$, of which F_a^+ tuples turn out to be correct (based on UDF evaluations for each of the F_a tuples), solving Convex-Prog. 4.1 provides a feasible solution for Problem 3.*

Note that nothing prevents us from going back-and-forth between estimating selectivities and exploiting them: that is, we may continuously update our selectivity estimates as we evaluate more tuples. We can start off with certain selectivity estimates, apply CONVEXPROG 4.1, decide whether to retrieve and/or evaluate for each group, and as we evaluate more tuples per group, we can go back to Section 4.1, derive new estimates for selectivities, and then apply CONVEXPROG 4.1 again: Thus, our algorithms can be used multiple times in an adaptive fashion.

4.3 Deciding how much to Sample

We now consider the question of how many tuples F_a to sample from each group a. One simple baseline, is to fix a constant c and then sample c tuples from each group. However, since we know the sizes of the different groups, we can use that to significantly reduce overall cost.

We first state a property, and then use that to derive a rule of thumb for how many tuples to sample per group. Let n be the total number of tuples in the table. Then, if the precision and recall thresholds are fixed, it can be shown that a desirable F_a should be

$$O(t_a n^{-\frac{1}{3}})$$

The justification for this statement can be found in the appendix of the technical report. Therefore, our rule of thumb is:

> For a suitably chosen parameter *num*, F_a, the number of tuples sampled from group a for each $a \in A$ should be
> $$F_a = num \times t_a n^{-\frac{1}{3}}$$

We can use this rule of thumb in conjunction with the previous sections to decide how much to sample from each group. Naturally, the rule of thumb (as stated) cannot be applied if the value of the parameter *num* is not known to us. As we will see in the experimental section, the rule of thumb is not very sensitive to the value of *num*, and will work even for values of *num* in a fairly large range in a variety of experimental scenarios.

As it turns out (as we will see in the experimental section), the optimal value of *num* is proportional to α, the desired precision threshold. In fact, we find that a value $num = z\alpha$, with $2 \leq z \leq 5$ usually works well. But even if it doesn't, we can guess the optimal value of *num* using adaptive sampling as follows: We start with a small value of *num*, and keep increasing it. We also keep solving the convex optimization problem (CONVEXPROG. 4.1) for each value of *num* and keep estimating the cost of the solution as we increase *num*. The cost will initially fall as *num* increases, and will later start to rise as *num* crosses its optimal value. When cost starts to rise, we can stop further sampling and proceed to solve the problem using our technique from Section 4.2.

4.4 Finding a correlated column

Until now, we have assumed that a correlated column `A` is known to us. In practical settings, we may not know such a column in advance, and hence we need an efficient way to figure out which column to use. We propose two ways of doing this below.

In both methods, we sample a small fraction, say 1%, of the tuples and obtain the `f` value for those tuples. We then use these 'labeled tuples' to decide which column to use, in one of two ways:

- We consider every column x of the table, and use the labeled tuples to estimate selectivities for each value of x. To avoid overfitting selectivities, we restrict our attention to columns which have $\leq \sqrt{t}$ distinct values if t is the number of sampled tuples. If there are no such columns, we keep increasing t (sampling more tuples) until do get such a column. We then run our algorithm from Section 3.2 for each of the columns, using the estimated selectivities, to get an estimate of the cost. We can then choose the column that gives the minimum cost to be our 'correlated column.' This approach is used to find the correlated column in all of our experiments except the one in Section 6.3.2.
- The 'correlated column' does not need to be a single column from the table. It can be a virtual column created using available data. In this case, we use the labeled data to learn a logistic regression model from the available columns of the table to the UDF `f`. We then apply the regressor to get a probability score for each unlabeled tuple of the table, and split the tuples into buckets based on their probability scores. The bucket number can then be treated as our correlated virtual column. This approach is used in the experiment in Section 6.3.2.

We observe in the experiments that this procedure adds a negligible runtime cost to our algorithm. The amount of sampling we need later to estimate selectivities is larger than 1%. Also, the 1% labeled tuples can be re-used for both selectivity estimation and as part of the output. These procedures may not select a column with the highest correlation; in this case, this algorithm is still correct but may run more slowly than with the most correlated column.

5. EXTENSIONS

We mention some variations of the above problems that can be handled using small extensions to the techniques discussed so far. Further details on the extensions are given in the technical report [1].

Alternate Objective Functions. There may be scenarios where the user has a fixed cost budget, and wishes to maximize the number of tuples returned while ensuring a lower bound on precision.

Multiple Predicates. Another variation of the problem is where the query might have multiple chained UDF selects on a table (which is equivalent to a conjunction of multiple UDF predicates). Since precision and recall constraint are specified by the user for the final output, for this variation it may be possible to trade-off accuracy in one predicate for higher accuracy in the other at the same cost. This problem can be handled by introducing one decision variable per mapping of UDF to decisions. For example, there may be one decision variable which is true if and only if we retrieve for the first predicate and retrieve and evaluate the second predicate.

Single Predicate with Join. We also consider a situation in which the table T being selected on is later joined with another table T'. Each tuple of the table T may match with a different number of tuples of T', possibly making it worthwhile for us to evaluate a tuple with low correctness-probability that matches with a large number of tuples from T', over a tuple with higher correctness probability that joins with fewer tuples from T'.

6. EXPERIMENTS

Our experimental evaluation studies three items: In Experiment 1, we discuss the performance of 'Intel-Sample', our query evaluation algorithm, on a variety of datasets with different selectivities, versus baseline algorithms and algorithms that have perfect knowledge. We show that our algorithm can achieve upto 80% reduction in evaluations compared to baseline approaches, and is in fact competitive with (unrealistic) approaches that have perfect knowledge of selectivities up front. We then study the relationship between the selectivity of the UDF predicate and the cost savings attained by our algorithm. We also verify that our approaches meet the specified precision and recall constraints. In Experiment 1 evaluation we sample a fixed fraction of tuples. In Experiment 2, we discuss the sensitivity of our approach to the choice of sampling procedure and its parameters. We also demonstrate that our method can be used with more sophisticated sampling models, such as a logistic regressor. In Experiment 3, we discuss the sensitivity of the performance of our approach to the precision, recall, and probability constraints in the query.

6.1 Experimental Setup

We use four datasets for our experiments, described below. The selectivities of our datasets are presented in the first column of Table 2. Additional information on the groups of tuples in the datasets is shown in a table in Appendix A.3.

Lending Club: The first dataset, denoted LC, consists of loan data from the peer-to-peer lending website, the Lending Club [2]. The data consists of two csv files, which together contain about 53000 labeled tuples. Each tuple corresponds to a single loan application, and includes attributes like applicant's id, loan amount, term, applicant's grade (a grade assigned by the lending club to reflect borrower quality), employment title, housing status, annual income, purpose of loan. One of the columns is Loan Status, which is the current status of the loan. Values for this column include 'Current', 'Charged Off' (which means that the loan is considered unlikely to be repaid), 'Fully Paid', 'Default' and 'Late'. We assign a value of 'good' to 'Fully Paid' and a value of 'bad' to 'Charged Off', 'Late', and 'Defaulted'.

Marketing: The second dataset is related to direct marketing campaigns of a Portuguese banking institution [10, 32]. The campaign was based on phone calls used to get clients to subscribe to a term deposit. The data consists of a csv file containing about 41000 tuples. Each tuple corresponds to a person called during the campaign, and has attributes of the person such as age, job, marital status, and also some social and economic context indicators such as employment variation rate and consumer price index. The last column has value 'y' or 'n', which corresponds to whether the client did or did not subscribe to the term deposit. We consider the value 'y' 'good' and 'n' 'bad'.

Census: The third dataset is from the Census Bureau Database [10]. It has about 45000 tuples, each tuple describing one person. The tuple has demographic information such as age, work class, sex and country. The last column says whether or not the person's income is above 50000 per year. We consider > 50000 'good' and ≤ 50000 'bad'. This UDF could again be relevant for marketing, since a company might want to preferentially pitch their product to people having higher income.

Prosper: The fourth dataset is similar to LC, and consists of loan data from the website Prosper [3]. It consists of about 30000 tuples, each tuple corresponds to an individual loan application. It has columns such as amount borrowed, debt to income ratio, and grade. The Loan Status column has values which we classify as 'good' and 'bad'. 'good' values correspond to loans which were paid back on time, while 'bad' ones are for loans which were either paid late or not repaid at all.

Protocol. For each dataset, we have a *designated* attribute for which we specified 'good' and 'bad' values. We assume that the UDF f on each tuple returns the value 'good'/'bad', which is the value of this attribute for that tuple. We consider the query that selects all tuples from the table that have a 'good' value for the designated attribute.

The value of the UDF `f` for all tuples is known precisely to us for the purposes of evaluation, but assumed to be unknown to any of the query evaluation algorithms initially. We can then simulate 'sampling' by revealing the value of `f` for any tuple requested by the query evaluation algorithm. Moreover, we can check the precision and recall obtained by any query evaluation algorithm using our knowledge of `f`. Unless otherwise specified, we set the default value for the query constraints to be $\alpha = 0.8$ (precision), $\beta = 0.8$ (recall), $\rho = 0.8$ (satisfaction probability). We experimented with different costs for evaluation versus retrieval, but found our results were not significantly sensitive to these parameters. Hence we set $o_e = 3$ and $o_r = 1$, which implies that evaluating the UDF is a factor of three more expensive than retrieving the tuple.

6.2 Experiment 1 : Performance Comparison

We compare five different query evaluation algorithms. The first two are our algorithms from Section 3 of this paper. The three algorithms after that are baselines:

- Intel-Sample: This is our main algorithm, from Section 3.3. We first use the procedure described in Section 4.4 to decide which correlated column to use. Then we form groups based on that correlated column, sample to get selectivity estimates, and then solve convex problem 3.8 from Section 3.3 to decide what to retrieve and evaluate. For this experiment, we keep the sample size fixed at 5% of the data.
- Optimal: Here we use the technique from Section 3.2. The technique is unrealistic as it requires that selectivities be known exactly, so we use our knowledge of all values of `f` to compute the selectivities and provide them as input to the technique. This algorithm has perfect knowledge of selectivities and is a cost lower bound to Intel-Sample.
- Naive: In this baseline algorithm, we randomly retrieve β fraction of the tuples (where β is the recall constraint) and evaluate all of them. This approach only satisfies the recall constraint in expectation, and not with a given probability.
- Learning (Semi-supervised Learning) : This is a baseline algorithm that uses semi-supervised learning. Here, we evaluate some tuples, and then use semi-supervised learning to infer the predicate value of the remaining tuples. We then return the tuples that originally evaluated to true as well as those estimated to be true by the semi-supervised classifier. The number of tuples we initially evaluated (labeled training data) is varied until the precision and recall constraints are met. Note that this gives an unfair advantage to the Learning baseline (and also to Multiple), since in practice we do not know how many tuples to evaluate in advance to get the required precision and recall. In spite of this, we will see that our algorithm performs much better than these two baselines.
- Multiple (Multiple Imputations): This is another baseline using semi-supervised learning. However in this case, we use multiple imputations based on class probabilities estimated by the semi-supervised learning algorithm. Once again, we choose the number of tuples to initially evaluate so as to satisfy precision and recall constraints on average across the imputed datasets.

Our method, Intel-Sample, obtains selectivity information via sampling. The cost of sampling tuples to estimate the selectivity is included in its cost. The cost of labelling the training data used by Learning and Multiple is included in their cost.

6.2.1 Comparison of Costs

Summary: *Intel-Sample provides up to 80% savings over the naive algorithm, and at the same time, is not much worse than an optimal algorithm that knows all selectivities in advance.*

We estimate the average number of tuples evaluated by Naive, Intel-Sample and Optimal over 50 iterations, and plot them in the bar chart in Figure 1(a). We see that our algorithm (Intel-Sample) performs far better than the Naive baseline in all datasets, with over 80% savings on the LC dataset, while still being not too much worse than Optimal. Since theorem 3.11 implies asymptotically optimality of Intel-Sample, the fact that its cost is not too far from the Optimal algorithm is not surprising.

Summary: *Intel-Sample outperforms two machine learning baselines by up to 60%; the gains reduce as the selectivity reduces.*

Figure 1(b) compares Intel-Sample to the two Machine Learning baselines. For both the baselines (Learning and Multiple), we choose the smallest number of tuples to evaluate that lets us satisfy the precision and recall constraints. Note that these two baselines also satisfy the constraints in expectation and not necessarily with high probability. Yet, Intel-Sample outperforms the baselines by about 60% on LC, about 20% on Prosper and Census, and very slightly on Marketing.

We notice that our savings in general seem to be highest on LC, and lowest on Marketing. This is because of the selectivities of the UDF predicates in the two datasets. Intel-Sample performs better when the selectivity is higher. Table 2 shows the selectivities and savings (relative to Naive and Learning) for each dataset. We note that while savings for very low selectivities are smaller, Intel-Sample still performs marginally better than other algorithms in this worst case, while still giving large savings for moderate and high selectivities.

Intel Sample does not add much in terms of computation cost. We measure the computation time taken by our method, including time for finding the best correlated column to use, sampling tuples, learning selectivities, and running the convex optimization—this

Dataset	Selectivity	Savings vs. Naive	Savings vs. ML
LC	0.72	81%	62%
Prosper	0.45	43%	21%
Census	0.24	51%	22%
Marketing	0.11	24%	3%

Table 2: Selectivities and Savings for different Datasets

value is less than 1 second on each of the datasets. This time is insignificant compared to the reduction in UDF evaluations.

In the above experiment, we chose the best correlated column using the scheme in Section 4.4. Sometimes, our scheme may end up choosing a non-optimal column, or we may have a UDF that does not have a strongly correlated column. In order to study the effect of having a weakly correlated column on the performance of our algorithm, we conducted an experiment using different columns (instead of just the "best" column) on the LC dataset. We tried out all columns in the table that had between 1 and 50 distinct values. Column number 8 was the most correlated column. In addition to column 8, we tried using 35 different columns as the correlated column. The number of UDF evaluations required ranges from 9000 for the best column, to 17000 for the worst column. If we had a perfect column which exactly equals the UDF, the cost would have been close to 0. Thus our algorithm seems to perform reasonably well on arbitrary columns, and its cost in our experiments while using column 8 is somewhere in between its cost on the worst column (17000), and its cost on a perfect column ($\approx$ 0). Moreover, the cost for even the worst column is much lower than the cost on using the Naive baseline algorithm (45000). In addition, we note the following:

- If a UDF is very hard to learn, that will reduce the savings of our method, but will also correspondingly reduce the savings of machine learning baselines. Since a machine learning algorithm that guesses the UDF using other columns can be plugged into our algorithm to create a 'virtual' column, our algorithm's savings will only be low in cases that are already hard for other baselines.
- Even in the worst case with all columns being completely uncorrelated with the UDF, our algorithm still provides a 'correct' set of tuples (satisfying the precision and recall constraints), only without as significant a saving in evaluations. Thus, the downside of using our algorithm is bounded by the small computational overhead of running it, while the upside is potentially huge when we do find a column (real or virtual) that is somewhat correlated with the UDF.

6.2.2 *Satisfaction of Precision and Recall Constraints*

While our algorithms avoid several evaluations, they do so at the cost of slightly lower precision and recall. In this experiment, we show that the precision and recall guarantees are met by our algorithm. Our algorithms are supposed to guarantee that the precision and recall constraints will be satisfied with probability at least ρ. We now test if this guarantee is being met.

We first fix a value of ρ. For that ρ value, we execute the Sampling algorithm 100 times (all the way from sampling, to retrieving and evaluating and returning tuples), and for each execution, we note whether the precision and recall constraints were satisfied or not. Then we compute the accuracy i.e. the fraction of times the constraints were satisfied for this ρ, and repeat this procedure for different values of ρ. The accuracy is plotted vs. ρ, in Figures 2(a) (Precision Accuracy) and 2(b) (Recall Accuracy). The $x = y$ line in the figures is the minimum level of accuracy required to satisfy our guarantee. As the figures show, our accuracy is consistently above the line, which means our algorithms do satisfy the precision and recall constraints more than ρ fraction of the time, as desired.

In addition, the average precision and recall values of our algorithm are slightly higher than the constraint values (about 0.82). This is because our algorithm aims for a higher expected precision and recall so as to satisfy the constraints with high probability. For the machine learning baselines from Section 6.2, one of the values is around 0.8 while the other ranges from $0.8 - 0.9$.

6.3 Experiment 2: Robustness of Estimation

As we saw in the previous section, the Intel-Sample algorithm does not involve any unrealistic assumptions like knowing exact selectivities, and still performs far better than the baselines. However, the Intel-Sample algorithm contains free parameters such as the number of tuples to be sampled to obtain from each group to obtain selectivity estimates. In this section, we will attempt to explore how the parameters may be chosen so as to obtain good results.

Sampling Algorithms. We compare two different sampling algorithms. Each sampling algorithm tells us how many tuples to sample from each group, before finalizing the selectivity estimates. The output of the sampling algorithm is then used by our algorithm Intel-Sample as input. The sampling algorithms are:

- Constant(c): This algorithm samples c tuples from each group.
- Two-Third-Power(*num*): This algorithm uses our result from Section 4 which says that if a table has n tuples, and group a has t_a tuples, then the optimal number of tuples to sample from group a is proportional to $t_a n^{-\frac{1}{3}}$. Hence this algorithm samples *num* $\times$ $t_a n^{-\frac{1}{3}}$ tuples from group a.

6.3.1 *Sampling Schemes and Sample Sizes*

We now explore the question of how many tuples to sample per group. When we have formed groups but not sampled any tuples, the only information we have is the sizes of the groups.

The schemes of Section 6.3 tell us the proportion in which to sample tuples from each group. Each scheme has an additional free parameter (c or *num*), which we use to determine the exact number of tuples to sample from each group. We study the average cost of evaluating tuples as a function of this parameter, for each scheme.

We first fix the value of the parameter (c or *num*) and use the parameter value to compute the number of tuples to sample from each group. Then we randomly sample and evaluate the corresponding number of tuples from the groups, and form estimates about the selectivity of each group. We then solve the convex optimization problem in Section 3.3 to decide how many tuples to retrieve and evaluate from each group, and compute the expected number of tuples we needed to evaluate to determine cost (the number of tuples retrieved does not vary much for different sampling schemes or sizes). We do this for 100 iterations, and take the average the number of evaluations across iterations. We find average evaluations for several different values of the parameter, and using different correlated columns, and plot the results. The correlated columns chosen and used by our algorithm are Grade for LC and Prosper, Employment Variation Rate for Marketing, and Marital Status for Census. The evaluations vs. parameter c for the **Constant** Sampling scheme is plotted in Figure 3(a), while evaluations vs. parameter *num* for the **Two-Third-Power** scheme is in Figure 3(b).

We make three observations about Figures 3(a) and 3(b). The first observation is that sampling too little or too much leads to higher cost; too little because our selectivity estimates are bad, and too much because of the cost of sampling itself. There is a region in between that gives low cost. The second observation is that the **Two-Third-Power** scheme generally leads to lower optimal costs than the **Constant** scheme. For instance, the optimal cost for LC is about 10500 for the **Constant** scheme, while it is about 9400

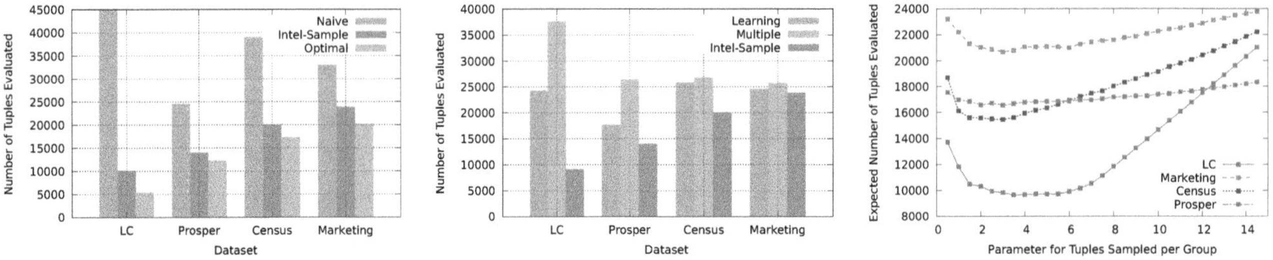

Figure 1: (a) Number of evaluations for our algorithms compared to baselines (b) Number of evaluations for our algorithms compared with Machine Learning Baselines (c) Expected number of evaluations for different levels of sampling, using logistic regression

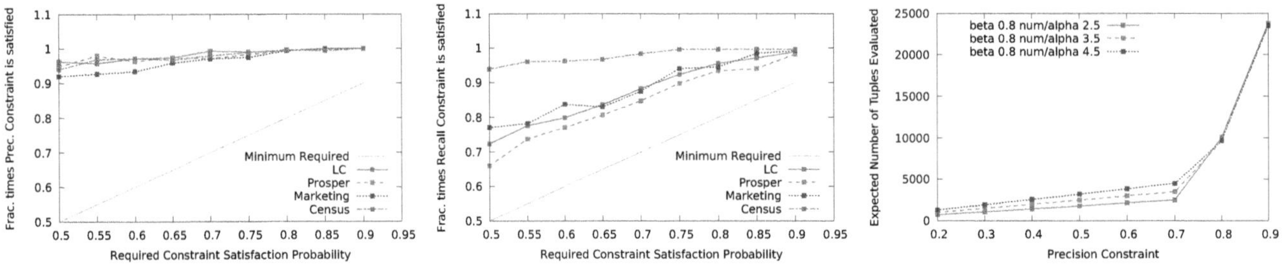

Figure 2: (a) Fraction of times precision constraint was satisfied, for different values of ρ (b) Fraction of times recall constraint was satisfied, for different values of ρ (c) Expected number of tuples evaluated for different levels of alpha

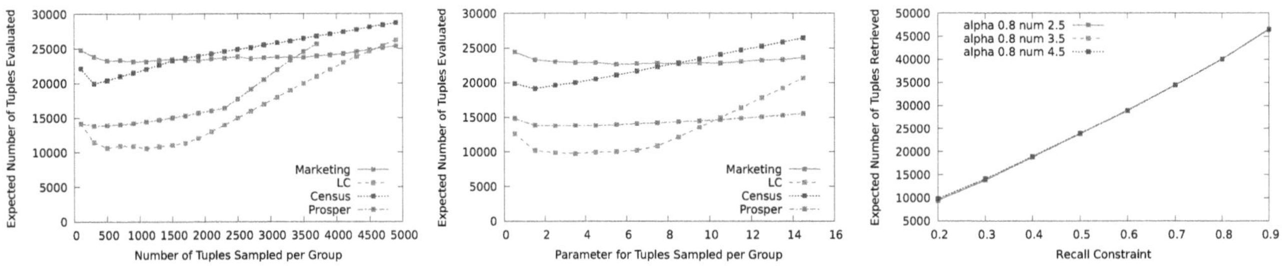

Figure 3: (a) Expected number of tuples evaluated for different levels if sampling per group for the ***Constant*** *sampling scheme (b) Expected number of tuples evaluated for different levels of sampling per group for the* ***Two-Third-Power*** *sampling scheme (c) Expected number of tuples retrieved for different levels of beta*

for the **Two-Third-Power** scheme. Similarly, for Census, the optimal cost for scheme **Constant** is about 20000, while for scheme **Two-Third-Power**, the optimal cost is about 19000. The third observation is that a value of *num* between 2α and 5α (where α is the precision constraint) leads to near optimal cost for all four datasets, while for the **Constant** scheme, the optimal number of tuples to sample varies quite a bit for different datasets (We discuss further the dependence of optimal *num* on α in Section 6.4). Thus the **Two-Third-Power** scheme is also robust to small changes in the parameter values, or changes in the predictor or dataset.

While a *num* parameter value between 2α and 5α works fine for the current datasets, it may not necessarily be optimal on other datasets. We do not need to know the optimal value of the parameter up front by running our adaptive algorithm in Section 4.

6.3.2 Using logistic regression to estimate selectivity

In Section 4.4, we described a technique that uses logistic regression to create a 'virtual column' that can act as a correlated column. We first randomly sample and evaluate the UDF `f` on 1% of the rows of the table. The resulting set of rows is used as training data to learn a logistic regressor from available columns to the predicate `f`. To avoid overfitting, we only use columns that are either numeric or nominal with < 50 different values.

After learning the regressor, we apply it to the table to get a probability score for each tuple (The training tuples are included in the table as well, and the cost of evaluating them before training is taken into account in our cost graphs). Then we split the tuples into 10 buckets (groups) based on the probability score. The bucket ranges are chosen so as to get equal sized buckets. For example, if 10% of the training data tuples got a probability score between 0 and 0.55, and the remaining probability scores were uniformly distributed between 0.55 and 1, then we may create one bucket for tuples with score in $[0, 0.55)$, one for $[0.55, 0.6)$ and so on. Then, we proceed as earlier for these buckets, sampling from them to estimate their selectivities. We do not directly use the selectivity estimates output by the logistic regressor, because we do not have guarantees on the correlation between probability scores of different tuples. (Sampling seems to confirm this lack of correlation; e.g., the fraction of tuples having probability score ≈ 0.5 which actually satisfy predicate `f` is not close to 0.5). Thus we make buckets and treat them as groups instead, sample from them to estimate selectivities, and apply the convex optimization from Section 3.3. Contrast this with the machine learning baselines from Section 6.2, where we directly use machine learned scores to determine which tuples to pick. Learning simply applies a threshold on the score, while Multiple picks probabilistically using the score.

In Figure 1(c), we use the **Two-Third-Power** scheme to decide how many tuples to sample per group, and plot the average number of evaluations across 100 iterations, versus the sampling parameter. The number of tuples evaluated as shown in the plot includes the tuples evaluated to generate training data for the logistic regressor. Note that in spite of this, the number of evaluations required by our algorithm is far lower than that required by the Naive algorithm baseline. On LC, we evaluate about 10000 tuples, which is similar to the cost when using a single predictor column. On Census and Marketing, we do noticeably better than when using a single column, while on Prosper, we do slightly worse. But more importantly, using logistic regression to create the correlated column obviates needing to know which column to use.

6.4 Experiment 3: Query Parameters

We study the effect of precision and recall constraints (α and β) on the cost of Intel-Sample and demonstrate that some approximation can result in a large cost saving. We consider LC with Grade as the predictor, we vary α and β and plot average retrieval and evaluation costs over 50 iterations for each combination of α and β. We keep ρ fixed at 0.8 and use the **Two-Third-Power** sampling scheme. The results are similar for other predictors, other ρ values, and other datasets. Figure 2(c) compares the number of evaluations vs α for $\beta = 0.8$, and Figure 3(c) compares the number of retrieves vs β for $\alpha = 0.8$. The graph of number of evaluations vs. β for $\alpha = 0.8$ is very similar to that in Figure 2(c), while the number of retrieves is nearly independent of α.

When α and β equal 1, we must necessarily retrieve and evaluate every tuple, whereas when they're 0, we don't need to retrieve or evaluate any tuple. But when they are both 0.8 we don't need to evaluate 80% of the tuples, but much fewer. The figures show that cost as a function of either α or β is a convex function. This tells us why approximating results can be a performance win: a small loss in accuracy can lead to a much larger saving in cost.

As we vary α and β, we observe that the optimal value of the *num* parameter is approximately proportional to α. So we set the value of *num* to 2.5α, 3.5α, and so on for the plots. The plots show that *num* $= 2.5\alpha$ performs slightly better than other values of *num*consistently (for all values of α), which reflects our observation that the optimal value of *num* is proportional to α.

7. RELATED WORK

Related work can be divided into a few categories. We describe each one in turn below:

Sensor Networks: There has been a lot of work on data processing on sensor networks (see [7] for a survey). We could regard taking additional sensor readings as an expensive operation (which only must be done as needed, say to answer a user query), much like the expensive UDFs we consider in this paper. There has been some work on query processing for sensor networks while minimizing power consumption for data acquisition [31]. This paper uses techniques such as batching of sensor readings, and improved predicate ordering. In addition, there is some work on using correlated attributes to avoid acquiring data [16]. This work focuses on queries with a conjunction of multiple expensive predicates, and uses correlations to determine the optimal predicate order to minimize the expected number of predicate evaluations. The above works still attempt to solve the query exactly, rather than obtain an approximation at a reduced cost. Finally, there is some work on approximate query processing for sensor networks [17] that treats sensor outputs as a UDF. Since the UDF type is known beforehand, the work relies on pre-training a model reflecting relationships between different sensor outputs and other variables. In contrast, our work involves a UDF specified in the query itself, requiring us to learn correlations on the fly, while taking learning cost into account. Additionally, the sensor UDF occurs in the query output rather than in the predicate, so the uncertainty is measured as numerical error in output values, rather than as precision or recall in the set of displayed tuples.

Approximate Query Processing: Over the past decade, there has been a lot of work on approximate query processing; see [13, 20, 22, 28]. Garofalakis et al. [19] provides a good survey of the area. There are multiple systems that support approximate query processing, including BlinkDB [6] and Aqua [5], allowing users to trade-off accuracy for performance. Often, these schemes achieved the desired level of accuracy by running the query on a sample of the database. There has also been work on deciding how to choose appropriate samples for query processing [4, 9]. All of these systems and algorithmic papers focus only on approximating numerical aggregate quantities, having operators such as `SUM`, `AVG`, `VAR`, as well as frequency moments [8]. On the other hand, our paper focuses on approximating selection (i.e., set-valued) queries. Ioannidis et al. [27] use histograms to approximate set-valued queries, but their notion of approximation involves approximating values within tuples not with respect to precision and recall constraints.

Query Processing with UDFs: UDFs occur often in database queries. The work on optimizing queries with UDFs has focused mainly on identifying optimal placement of UDFs in query plans [15,25], and not on using correlations to avoid UDF evaluations in the first place. Recently, crowd-powered database systems, such as CrowdDB [18] and Deco [35] have been treating calls to human workers for data processing and data gathering on-the-fly, as expensive UDFs that should be used sparingly. Our optimization techniques could easily be applied to these systems.

Correlation-aware Query Processing: There has been some recent work on finding correlations between attributes of a relation [12, 26, 29] — these papers could be used to identify the correlated attributes to bootstrap our techniques for estimating and exploiting correlations. Correlations have also been used for traditional query optimization, allowing for more accurate estimates of intermediate result sizes, and therefore of query-plan costs. Recent work has also looked at appropriately choosing which indexes and materialized views to maintain taking correlations into account [30]. While these papers mainly focus on correlations between attributes within a relation (and therefore there is no cost to acquiring data since it is already provided), our paper exploits correlations between attributes in a relation and an external UDF.

8. CONCLUSION

We introduced techniques for efficiently approximating select queries with expensive UDF predicates. We found that even though the basic problem for even the simplest scenario is NP-Hard, there are efficient techniques that allow us to achieve near-optimality. Our techniques apply to a variety of different scenarios, based on what information is available to us, and allow us to reduce cost while satisfying precision and recall constraints specified by the user. As UDFs become increasingly ubiquitous and datasets get larger, the cost savings can become quite significant. Moreover, our methods integrate well with machine learning techniques such as logistic regression, allowing us to leverage these techniques to reduce cost even further. Our techniques can also be generalized to other classes of queries, such as selects followed by joins, or multiple selection conditions. Finally, our experiments on real data show that we can obtain cost savings up to 80%, which are quite large relative to the small loss in accuracy. As future work, we plan to explore generalizing our techniques to complete select-from-where queries, as well as queries involving nesting and aggregation.

9. REFERENCES

[1] https://dl.dropboxusercontent.com/u/1617347/Technical%20Report.pdf.

[2] http://www.lendingclub.com.

[3] http://www.prosper.com.

[4] S. Acharya, P. B. Gibbons, and V. Poosala. Congressional samples for approximate answering of group-by queries. In *Proc. 2000 ACM SIGMOD*, SIGMOD '00, pages 487–498, New York, NY, USA, 2000. ACM.

[5] S. Acharya, P. B. Gibbons, V. Poosala, and S. Ramaswamy. The aqua approximate query answering system. In *Proc. 1999 ACM SIGMOD*, SIGMOD '99, pages 574–576, New York, NY, USA, 1999. ACM.

[6] S. Agarwal, B. Mozafari, A. Panda, H. Milner, S. Madden, and I. Stoica. Blinkdb: queries with bounded errors and bounded response times on very large data. In *EuroSys*, pages 29–42, 2013.

[7] I. F. Akyildiz, W. Su, Y. Sankarasubramaniam, and E. Cayirci. Wireless sensor networks: a survey. *Computer networks*, 38(4):393–422, 2002.

[8] N. Alon, Y. Matias, and M. Szegedy. The space complexity of approximating the frequency moments. In *STOC*, pages 20–29, 1996.

[9] B. Babcock, S. Chaudhuri, and G. Das. Dynamic sample selection for approximate query processing. In *Proc. 2003 ACM SIGMOD*, SIGMOD '03, pages 539–550, New York, NY, USA, 2003. ACM.

[10] K. Bache and M. Lichman. UCI machine learning repository, 2013.

[11] P. G. Brown. Overview of scidb: Large scale array storage, processing and analysis. In *Proc. 2010 ACM SIGMOD*, SIGMOD '10, pages 963–968, New York, NY, USA, 2010. ACM.

[12] P. G. Brown and P. J. Hass. Bhunt: Automatic discovery of fuzzy algebraic constraints in relational data. In *Proc. 29th VLDB - Volume 29*, VLDB '03, pages 668–679, 2003.

[13] K. Chakrabarti et al. Approximate query processing using wavelets. In *VLDB*, pages 111–122, 2000.

[14] S. Chaudhuri and K. Shim. Query optimization in the presence of foreign functions. In *VLDB*, pages 529–542, 1993.

[15] S. Chaudhuri and K. Shim. Optimization of queries with user-defined predicates. *ACM Trans. Database Syst.*, 24(2):177–228, 1999.

[16] A. Deshpande, C. Guestrin, W. Hong, and S. Madden. Exploiting correlated attributes in acquisitional query processing. In *ICDE*, pages 143–154, 2005.

[17] A. Deshpande, C. Guestrin, S. R. Madden, J. M. Hellerstein, and W. Hong. Model-driven data acquisition in sensor networks. In *Proc. VLDB - Volume 30*, VLDB '04, pages 588–599, 2004.

[18] M. J. Franklin, D. Kossmann, T. Kraska, S. Ramesh, and R. Xin. Crowddb: answering queries with crowdsourcing. In *SIGMOD*, 2011.

[19] M. N. Garofalakis and P. B. Gibbon. Approximate query processing: Taming the terabytes. In *Proc. 27th VLDB*, VLDB '01, pages 725–, San Francisco, CA, USA, 2001. Morgan Kaufmann Publishers Inc.

[20] P. B. Gibbons. Distinct sampling for highly-accurate answers to distinct values queries and event reports. In *VLDB*, pages 541–550, 2001.

[21] J. M. Hellerstein. Practical predicate placement. In *SIGMOD Conference*, pages 325–335, 1994.

[22] J. M. Hellerstein, P. J. Haas, and H. J. Wang. Online aggregation. In J. Peckham, editor, *SIGMOD 1997*, pages 171–182. ACM Press, 1997.

[23] J. M. Hellerstein, C. Ré, F. Schoppmann, D. Z. Wang, E. Fratkin, A. Gorajek, K. S. Ng, C. Welton, X. Feng, K. Li, and A. Kumar. The madlib analytics library: Or mad skills, the sql. *Proc. VLDB Endow.*, 5(12):1700–1711, Aug. 2012.

[24] J. M. Hellerstein and M. Stonebraker. Predicate migration: Optimizing queries with expensive predicates. In *SIGMOD Conference*, pages 267–276, 1993.

[25] J. M. Hellerstein and M. Stonebraker. Predicate migration: Optimizing queries with expensive predicates. In *Proc. 1993 ACM SIGMOD*, SIGMOD '93, pages 267–276, New York, NY, USA, 1993. ACM.

[26] I. F. Ilyas, V. Markl, P. Haas, P. Brown, and A. Aboulnaga. Cords: Automatic discovery of correlations and soft functional dependencies. In *Proc. 2004 ACM SIGMOD*, SIGMOD '04, pages 647–658, New York, NY, USA, 2004. ACM.

[27] Y. E. Ioannidis and V. Poosala. Histogram-based approximation of set-valued query-answers. In *Proc. 25th VLDB*, VLDB '99, pages 174–185, San Francisco, CA, USA, 1999. Morgan Kaufmann Publishers Inc.

[28] C. Jermaine et al. Scalable approximate query processing with the dbo engine. *ACM Trans. Database Syst.*, 33(4), 2008.

[29] H. Kimura, G. Huo, A. Rasin, S. Madden, and S. B. Zdonik. Correlation maps: A compressed access method for exploiting soft functional dependencies. *Proc. VLDB Endow.*, 2(1):1222–1233, Aug. 2009.

[30] H. Kimura, G. Huo, A. Rasin, S. Madden, and S. B. Zdonik. Coradd: Correlation aware database designer for materialized views and indexes. *Proc. VLDB Endow.*, 3(1-2):1103–1113, Sept. 2010.

[31] S. Madden, M. Franklin, J. Hellerstein, and W. Hong. The design of an acquisitional query processor for sensor networks. In *Proc. 2003 ACM SIGMOD*, SIGMOD '03, pages 491–502, New York, NY, USA, 2003. ACM.

[32] S. Moro, P. Cortez, and P. Rita. A data-driven approach to predict the success of bank telemarketing. *Decision Support Systems*, 62:22–31, 2014.

[33] F. Niu, C. Zhang, C. Ré, and J. Shavlik. Elementary: Large-scale knowledge-base construction via machine learning and statistical inference. *IJSWIS Special Issue on Web-Scale Knowledge Extraction*, 2012.

[34] A. Parameswaran, H. Park, H. Garcia-Molina, N. Polyzotis, and J. Widom. Deco: Declarative crowdsourcing. Technical report, Stanford University, 2012.

[35] H. Park, H. Garcia-Molina, R. Pang, N. Polyzotis, A. Parameswaran, and J. Widom. Deco: A system for declarative crowdsourcing. *Proc. VLDB Endow.*, 5(12):1990–1993, Aug. 2012.

[36] L. Wasserman. *All of Statistics*. Springer, 2003.

APPENDIX

A. APPENDIX

A.1 Proof of Tightness Bound for solution to Perfect Selectivities Case

In Section 3.2, we stated the tightness result of our LP-baaed solution as follows:

THEOREM A.1. *Let s_a^{min} be the smallest non-zero value of s_a. Then, the difference between the cost of the optimal solution to Linear-Prog. 3.2, and the cost of the optimal solution to Problem 2, is at most*

$$(o_e + o_r)\frac{1}{s_a^{min}} \max\left(h_\rho^r + h_{1-\rho}^r, \frac{h_\rho^p + h_{1-\rho}^p}{1-\alpha}\right)$$

We now prove this theorem.

An optimal solution consists of a pair (R_a^o, E_a^o) for each $a \in A$ such that precision and recall constraints are satisfied with probability ρ and expected cost is minimized. The expected cost for this solution is $\sum_{a \in A} t_a(R_a^o o_r + E_a^o o_e)$. Consider the expected values of LHS of their precision and recall constraints. For precision, it is given by:

$$P^o = \sum_{a \in A} t_a s_a(1-\alpha)R_a^o + t_a(1-s_a)\alpha(E_a^o - R_a^o)$$

and for recall, it is given by:

$$R^o = \sum_{a \in A} t_a s_a R_a^o - \beta t_a s_a$$

Let the solution produced by our algorithm be denoted by R_a', E_a' for each $a \in A$. And let:

$$P' = \sum_{a \in A} t_a s_a(1-\alpha)R_a' + t_a(1-s_a)\alpha(E_a' - R_a')$$

and for recall, it is given by:

$$R' = \sum_{a \in A} t_a s_a R_a' - \beta t_a s_a$$

Hence $P' \geq h_\rho^p$, $R' \geq h_\rho^r$. Moreover, we must have $P^o \geq -h_{1-\rho}^p$, since if the expected value of the LHS of precision constraint for the optimal solution is less than $-h_{1-\rho}^p$, then by the chernoff bound, the LHS of the precision constraint will be ≤ 0 with probability $\geq 1-\rho$, and hence the precision constraint will be satisfied with probability $\leq \rho$. Similarly, we must have $R^o \geq -h_{1-\rho}^r$.

The expected cost of a solution (R_a, E_a) is given by

$$\sum_{a \in A}(t_a s_a + t_a(1-s_a))(R_a o_r + E_a o_e)$$

We know that

$$\sum_{a \in A} R_a^o t_a s_a - \sum_{a \in A} \beta t_a s_a \geq -h_{1-\rho}^r$$

$$\text{and} \quad \sum_{a \in A}(1-\alpha)t_a s_a R_a^o + t_a(1-s_a)\alpha(E_a^o - R_a^o) \geq -h_{1-\rho}^p$$

We will increase some values of R_a, and increase the corresponding values of E_a by the same amount, so as to get the resulting R_a and E_a values to satisfy $\sum_{a \in A} R_a^{o2} t_a s_a \geq h_\rho^r + \sum_{a \in A} \beta t_a s_a$ and $\sum_{a \in A}(1-\alpha)t_a s_a R_a^o + t_a(1-s_a)\alpha(E_a^o - R_a^o) \geq h_\rho^p$.

We choose which R_as value to raise in a greedy manner: We choose the a with highest value of selectivity ($\frac{t_a s_a}{t_a s_a + t_a(1-s_a)}$) for which $R_a < 1$, and keep increasing that R_a (and E_a) till R_a becomes 1 (or both the constraints are satisfied), then move on to the next highest a, and so on. When a R_a and E_a are increased by d, the value of $\sum_{a \in A} R_a t_a s_a$ increases by $d t_a s_a$, the value of $\sum_{a \in A}(1-\alpha)t_a s_a R_a + t_a(1-s_a)\alpha(E_a - R_a)$ increases by $d(1-\alpha)t_a s_a$ while cost goes up by $(o_r + o_e)d(t_a s_a + t_a(1-s_a))$. If we keep raising the values until both constraints $\sum_{a \in A} R_a^{o2} t_a s_a \geq h_\rho^r + \sum_{a \in A} \beta t_a s_a$ and $\sum_{a \in A}(1-\alpha)t_a s_a R_a^o + t_a(1-s_a)\alpha(E_a^o - R_a^o) \geq h_\rho^p$ are satisfied, then the cost increase will be at most

$$(o_e + o_r)\frac{1}{s_a} Max(h_\rho^r + h_{1-\rho}^r, \frac{h_\rho^p + h_{1-\rho}^p}{1-\alpha})$$

where s_a is the smallest value of selectivity from among the as whose R_a, E_a we raised. Now since the resulting R_a and E_a values satisfy these constraints, the total cost $\sum_{a \in A}(t_a s_a + t_a(1-s_a))(R_a o_r + E_a o_e)$ has to be more than the cost of our solution (R_a', E_a') (which was optimal for the linear problem with the given constraints). Thus the difference between the cost of our solution, and the cost of the optimal solution to the original problem, is at most

$$(o_e + o_r)\frac{1}{s_a} Max(h_\rho^r + h_{1-\rho}^r, \frac{h_\rho^p + h_{1-\rho}^p}{1-\alpha})$$

which proves our tightness bound.

We note that our solution is asymptotically optimal in the following sense: If table size is n, and the minimum s_a is constant as n grows, the cost difference between our solution and the optimal is $O(\sqrt{n})$ because the t^p, t^r values are $O(\sqrt{n})$. Since the cost of the solution is expected to be linear in n, the ratio of our cost to the optimal cost must tend to 1 as $n \rightarrow \infty$.

A.2 Correctness Proof for our solution to the Estimated Selectivities Case

We now prove that Convex-Prog. 3.7 and Convex-Prog. 3.8 provide a feasible solution for Problem 3 when correlations between S_as are unknown, and zero respectively. For each $a \in A$, we define the following random variables:

1. R_a^+ is the number of correct tuples ($f(B) = 1$) that we end up retrieving for $A = a$.
2. R_a^- is the number of incorrect tuples that we end up retrieving for $A = a$.
3. E_a^+ is the number of correct tuples we end up evaluating (and hence accepting) for $A = a$.
4. E_a^- is the number of incorrect tuples we end up evaluating (and hence rejecting) for $A = a$.

In addition, we have

1. C_a is the number of tuples satisfying the predicate for $A = a$.
2. W_a is the number of tuples not satisfying the predicate for $A = a$.

Then we must satisfy constraints:

$$\sum_{a \in A} R_a^+ - \alpha \sum_{a \in A}(R_a^+ + R_a^- - E_a^-) \geq 0$$

$$\sum_{a \in A} R_a^+ - \beta C_a \geq 0$$

with probability ρ. We will now prove that the R_a and E_a values obtained by solving our convex problem satisfy these constraints. Let $P = \sum_{a \in A} R_a^+ - \alpha \sum_{a \in A}(R_a^+ + R_a^- - E_a^-)$ and $R = \sum_{a \in A} R_a^+ - \beta C_a$ Now we use Chebyshev's inequality to transform the probabilistic constraints of the problem into deterministic constraints.

Dataset	Number of Groups	Size Standard Deviation	Selectivity Standard Deviation	Correlation Coefficient
LC	7	5233	0.13	0.84
Prosper	8	1521	0.20	0.20
Census	7	8183	0.15	0.36
Marketing	10	5070	0.20	−0.65

Table 3: Size, Selectivity statistics for Dataset Groups

Specifically, for $e_\rho = \frac{1}{\sqrt{1-\rho}}$, the problem requires us to satisfy the constraints $P \geq 0$ and $R \geq 0$ with probability ρ each. For this, due to Chebyshev's inequality, it is sufficient if we satisfy

$$E\left(P\right] \geq e_\rho \text{Dev}(P) \text{ and } E\left(R\right] \geq e_\rho \text{Dev}(R)$$

Next, we want to find the expectation and variances of P and R in terms of R_a, E_a, and fixed quantities. For any random variable U (from among R_a^+, R_a^-, E_a^+, E_a^-, C_a, W_a), and a tuple number i, let $I_{U,i}$ denote the indicator variable that is 1 if the ith tuple adds one to U, and 0 otherwise. For example, $I_{R_a^+,2}$ is 1 if tuple number 2 for $A = a$ is retrieved and satisfies the predicate, and 0 otherwise. Thus $U = \sum_{i=1}^{t_a} I_{U,i}$. The I's are all Bernoulli random variables. Both P and R can be expressed as weighted sums of these Bernoulli random variables. We will first try to find the expectation, variance, and covariances of the I variables. Each tuple with $A = a$ is retrieved with probability R_a, and evaluated with probability E_a. Moreover, it satisfies the predicate with probability S_a. Thus this tuple contributes 1 to R_a^+ with probability $R_a S_a$. So for each i,

$$E\left[I_{R_a^+,i}\right] = R_a S_a$$

Similarly,

$$E\left[I_{R_a^- - E_a^-,i}\right] = (R_a - E_a)(1 - S_a)$$

$$E\left[I_{C_a,i}\right] = S_a$$

$$\forall U, i: \text{Var}(I_{U,i}) = E\left[I_{U,i}\right](1 - E\left[I_{U,i}\right])$$

To find covariances, we note that

$$E\left[S_a^2\right] = E\left[(1 - S_a)^2\right] = s_a^2 + v_a$$

$$\text{and } E\left[(1 - S_a)S_a\right] = s_a(1 - s_a) - v_a$$

Thus for $i \neq j$

$$\text{Cov}(I_{R_a^+,i}, I_{R_a^+,j}) = R_a^2 v_a$$

$$\text{Cov}(I_{R_a^- - E_a^-,i}, I_{R_a^- - E_a^-,j}) = (R_a - E_a)^2 v_a$$

$$\text{and } \text{Cov}(I_{C_a,i}, I_{C_a,j}) = v_a$$

Moreover,

$$\text{Cov}(I_{R_a^+,i}, I_{R_a^- - E_a^-,j}) = -R_a(R_a - E_a)v_a$$

$$\text{Cov}(I_{R_a^+,i}, I_{C_a,j}) = R_a v_a$$

Finally,

$$\text{Cov}(I_{R_a^+,i}, I_{R_a^- - E_a^-,i}) = -R_a(R_a - E_a)s_a(1 - s_a)$$

$$\text{and } \text{Cov}(I_{R_a^+,i}, I_{C_a,i}) = R_a s_a(1 - s_a)$$

Now that we know the relevant expectations, variances and covariances, we can compute the expectation and variance of P and R.

$$P = \sum_{a \in A} \sum_{i=1}^{t_a} (1 - \alpha) I_{R_a^+,i} - \alpha I_{R_a^- - E_a^-,i}$$

and

$$R = \sum_{a \in A} \sum_{i=1}^{t_a} I_{R_a^+,i} - \beta I_{C_a,i}$$

Hence,

$$E\left[P\right] = \sum_{a \in A} t_a((1 - \alpha)R_a s_a - \alpha(R_a - E_a)(1 - s_a))$$

$$E\left[R\right] = \sum_{a \in A} t_a(R_a s_a - \beta s_a)$$

Let $P^a = (1 - \alpha)R_a^+ - \alpha(R_a^- - E_a^-)$ and $R_a = R_a^+ - \beta C_a$. Thus $P = \sum_{a \in A} P^a$ and $R = \sum_{a \in A} R^a$

$$\begin{aligned}\text{Var}(P^a) =& t_a((1 - \alpha)^2 R_a s_a(1 - R_a s_a) + \\ & \alpha^2(R_a - E_a)(1 - s_a)(1 - (R_a - E_a)(1 - s_a)) \\ & + 2\alpha(1 - \alpha)R_a s_a(R_a - E_a)(1 - s_a)) \\ & + t_a(t_a - 1)v_a(R_a - \alpha E_a)^2\end{aligned}$$

Furthermore, we have:

$$\begin{aligned}\text{Var}(R^a) =& t_a(R_a s_a(1 - R_a s_a) + \beta^2 s_a(1 - s_a) - 2\beta R_a s_a(1 - s_a)) \\ & + t_a(t_a - 1)v_a(R_a - \beta)^2\end{aligned}$$

Until now, we have not used any assumptions regarding the correlation between S_as for different as. We now consider two cases.

Unknown Correlations Case:

For the case where correlations are unknown, we prove that solving Convex Problem 3.7 gives us a feasible solution. If we know nothing about the correlations between S_as, the best bounds we can place on the deviations of P and R are $\text{Dev}(P) \leq \sum_{a \in A} \text{Dev}(P^a)$ and $\text{Dev}(R) \sum_{a \in A} \text{Dev}(R^a)$ respectively.

When we write the constraints $E\left[P\right] \leq e_\rho \text{Dev}(P)$ and $E\left[P\right] \leq e_\rho \text{Dev}(R)$, we want the resulting optimization problem to be easy to solve. To achieve this, we determine a best linear upper bound on the deviations on the RHS. Expectations of P and R are already linear in decision variables R_a and E_a, and so is the objective function. The RHS of both constraints are going to be a sum of standard deviations over $a \in A$. The standard deviation is a square root of the variance, which consists of a t_a factor and a $t_a(t_a - 1)$ factor. The key observation is that t_a is the only large quantity in the expression, where large means that is scales with the size of the table. The other terms, like R_a, E_a, s_a, α, β are all between 0 and 1. Thus only the $t_a(t_a - 1)$ factor under the square root can contribute an $O(n)$ factor to the RHS (where $n = \sum_{a \in A} t_a$ is the size of the table), while the t_a factor can contribute at most $O(\sqrt{n})$. Moreover, since the cost of our final solution is likely to be $O(n)$, we can be asymptotically optimal as long as we add a factor that is at most $O(\sqrt{n})$ to the RHS. Specifically, we have:

$$\begin{aligned}
&(1-\alpha)^2 R_a s_a(1-R_a s_a)\\
&\quad+\alpha^2(R_a-E_a)(1-s_a)(1-(R_a-E_a)(1-s_a))\\
&\quad+2\alpha(1-\alpha)R_a s_a(R_a-E_a)(1-s_a)\\
&\leq 0.25(1-\alpha)^2+0.25\alpha^2+0.25*2\alpha(1-\alpha)\\
&=0.25
\end{aligned}$$

We can similarly show that

$$R_a s_a(1-R_a s_a)+\beta^2 s_a(1-s_a)-2\beta R_a s_a(1-s_a)\leq 0.25$$

And hence

$$\text{Var}(P^a)\leq t_a^2 v_a(R_a-\alpha E_a)^2+0.25t_a$$

We can then use

$$\sqrt{x^2+y^2}\leq |x|+|y|$$

to get

$$\begin{aligned}
\text{Dev}(P^a)=&\sqrt{\text{Var}(P^a}\\
\leq&\sqrt{v_a}t_a(R_a-\alpha E_a)+0.5\sqrt{t_a}
\end{aligned}$$

Hence

$$\text{Dev}(P)\leq\sum_{a\in A}\sqrt{v_a}t_a(R_a-\alpha E_a)+0.5\sqrt{t_a}$$

giving us a linear upper bound on the RHS of the constraint as needed. Similarly, we can get

$$\text{Dev}(R)\leq\sum_{a\in A}\sqrt{v_a}t_a|R_a-\beta|+0.5\sqrt{t_a}$$

Thus we get the convex optimization problem:

$$\begin{aligned}
&\text{minimize}\sum_{a\in A}t_a(R_a o_r+E_a o_e)\text{ such that}\\
&\sum_{a\in A}(1-\alpha)t_a R_a s_a-t_a\alpha(R_a-E_a)(1-s_a)\\
&\geq e_\rho\sum_{a\in A}\sqrt{v_a}t_a(R_a-\alpha E_a)+0.5\sqrt{t_a}\\
&\sum_{a\in A}t_a R_a s_a-\beta t_a s_a\geq e_\rho\sum_{a\in A}\sqrt{v_a}t_a|R_a-\beta|+0.5\sqrt{t_a}\\
&R_a,E_a\in\{0,1\};R_a\geq E_a
\end{aligned}$$

And solving this problem gives a solution which has precision $\geq\alpha$ and recall $\geq\beta$ with probability at least ρ each.

Independent S_a's case:
Now we move to the case where S_as are independent of each other. This case is especially worth considering for the following reason: If we groups tuples by their value in a column, and evaluate a sample of tuples from each group, then we get independent selectivity estimates for each group, as tuple evaluations from one group don't give us information about selectivity of other groups. Thus in case of sampling, we have independent random variables S_a for each $a\in A$. Due to independence, we have:

$$\text{Var}(P)=\sum_{a\in A}\text{Var}(P^a)\text{ and Var}(R)=\sum_{a\in A}\text{Var}(R^a)$$

Thus in the optimization problem constraints are

$$E[P]\leq e_\rho\sqrt{\sum_{a\in A}\text{Var}(P^a)}$$

$$E[R]\leq e_\rho\sqrt{\sum_{a\in A}\text{Var}(R^a)}$$

Again, the objective function as well as LHS of both constraints are linear in decision variables R_a and E_a. The RHS has a square root. Like we did before, we would like to upper bound the RHS so as to make the optimization problem linear or convex. In this case, there does not seem to be a way to make the RHS linear without increasing it significantly. But it is possible to make the problem convex instead, with a slight increase in the RHS.

As in the last section, we note that

$$\text{Var}(P^a)\leq t_a^2 v_a(R_a-\alpha E_a)^2+0.25t_a$$

Thus

$$\text{Dev}(P)\leq\sqrt{\sum_{a\in A}t_a^2 v_a(R_a-\alpha E_a)^2+0.25t_a}$$

The RHS is a square root of a sum of squares and a positive constant. Suppose we have a $|A|+1$ dimensional vector $\vec{R}$ whose components are the $R_a\sqrt{t_a^2 v_a}$ for each $a\in A$ and the constant $\sqrt{\sum_{a\in A}0.25t_a}$ and a $|A|+1$ dimensional vector $\vec{E}$ whose components are $\alpha E_a\sqrt{t_a^2 v_a}$ for each $a\in A$ and 0. Then the RHS is given by $\left\|\vec{R}-\vec{E}\right\|_2$. For vectors $\vec{R_1}$, $\vec{E_1}$, $\vec{R_2}$, $\vec{E_2}$, by the triangle inequality, we have

$$\begin{aligned}
\left\|\vec{R_1}-\vec{E_1}\right\|_2+\left\|\vec{R_2}-\vec{E_2}\right\|_2&\geq 2\left\|\frac{\vec{R_1}-\vec{E_1}}{2}+\frac{\vec{R_2}-\vec{E_2}}{2}\right\|_2\\
&=2\left\|\frac{\vec{R_1}+\vec{R_2}}{2}-\frac{\vec{E_1}+\vec{E_2}}{2}\right\|_2
\end{aligned}$$

Thus the function $\left\|\vec{R}-\vec{E}\right\|_2$ is convex over the R_as and E_as.

Now consider the precision constraint

$$E[P]\geq e_\rho\left\|\vec{R}-\vec{E}\right\|_2$$

Since the LHS is linear in R_as and E_as, while the RHS is convex, the constraint is convex. Similarly, we can show that upper bounding $\text{Dev}(R)$ by $\sqrt{\sum_{a\in A}t_a^2 v_a(R_a-\beta)^2+0.25t_a}$ makes the recall constraint convex. Thus we reduce our problem to the following convex optimization problem

$$\begin{aligned}
&\text{minimize}\sum_{a\in A}t_a(R_a o_r+E_a o_e)\text{ such that}\\
&\sum_{a\in A}(1-\alpha)t_a R_a s_a-t_a\alpha(R_a-E_a)(1-s_a)\\
&\geq e_\rho\sqrt{\sum_{a\in A}t_a^2 v_a(R_a-\alpha E_a)^2+0.25t_a}\\
&\sum_{a\in A}t_a R_a s_a-\beta t_a s_a\geq e_\rho\sqrt{\sum_{a\in A}t_a^2 v_a(R_a-\beta)^2+0.25t_a}\\
&R_a,E_a\in\{0,1\};R_a\geq E_a
\end{aligned}$$

This proves our claim that Convex-Prog. 3.7 and Convex-Prog. 3.8 provide a feasible solution for Problem 3 when correlations between S_as are unknown and the S_as are independent, respectively.

A.3 Additional statistics on our datasets

Table 3 further describes our datasets and the groups formed using the correlated column chosen by our scheme described in Section 4.4.

Query-Oriented Data Cleaning with Oracles

Moria Bergman [1] Tova Milo [1] Slava Novgorodov [1] Wang-Chiew Tan [2]
[1]Tel-Aviv University [2]UC Santa Cruz
[1] {moriaben, milo, slavanov}@post.tau.ac.il [2] tan@cs.ucsc.edu

ABSTRACT

As key decisions are often made based on information contained in a database, it is important for the database to be as complete and correct as possible. For this reason, many data cleaning tools have been developed to automatically resolve inconsistencies in databases. However, data cleaning tools provide only best-effort results and usually cannot eradicate all errors that may exist in a database. Even more importantly, existing data cleaning tools do not typically address the problem of determining what information is missing from a database.

To overcome the limitations of existing data cleaning techniques, we present QOCO, a novel *query-oriented* system for cleaning data with oracles. Under this framework, incorrect (resp. missing) tuples are removed from (added to) the result of a query through edits that are applied to the underlying database, where the edits are derived by interacting with domain experts which we model as oracle crowds. We show that the problem of determining minimal interactions with oracle crowds to derive database edits for removing (adding) incorrect (missing) tuples to the result of a query is NP-hard in general and present heuristic algorithms that interact with oracle crowds. Finally, we implement our algorithms in our prototype system QOCO and show that it is effective and efficient through a comprehensive suite of experiments.

1. INTRODUCTION

Databases are accessed for the information they contain and key decisions are often made based on the results that are returned. Regardless of the query interface that is provided for accessing information (e.g., free-text search in an internet bookstore or form-based filters for choosing travel destinations in travel agency website), users naturally expect to obtain correct and complete results to a query that is posed against the database. In practice, however, the expectation of always obtaining correct and complete results is difficult to realize since many of the databases are constructed by (semi-)automatically aggregated data from different sources and are likely to contain some inaccuracies and inconsistencies even if individual sources are free of errors.

Even though data cleaning is a long standing problem that has attracted significant research efforts (e.g., see [20, 28, 52]) for a number of years, the state-of-the-art data cleaning techniques that have been developed cannot usually eradicate all errors in a database. YAGO [57] ontology is one such example of a database that was built by automatically extracted data from Wikipedia and other sources. Data cleaning techniques have been applied to the YAGO dataset and achieved an accuracy of about 95%, namely leaving 5% still erroneous [57]. Even highly curated databases [7] (i.e., databases that were constructed through extensive human effort of verifying and aggregating existing sources) such as Uniprot [60] and the CIA world fact book [13] are unlikely to be completely void of errors. At the same time, the sheer volume of such databases also makes it impossible to manually examine each piece of data for its correctness. Even more importantly, existing data cleaning tools do not usually address the problem of determining what information is missing from a database.

To complement the efforts and overcome the limitations of existing data cleaning techniques, we propose a novel *query-oriented* data cleaning approach with oracle crowds. In our framework, materialized views (i.e., views which are defined through user queries) are used as a trigger for identifying incorrect or missing information. Our premise is that users' queries (and their corresponding materialized views) provide relevant and focussed perspectives of the underlying database and hence, facilitates the discovery of errors. If an error (i.e., a wrong tuple or missing tuple) in the materialized view is detected, our system will interact minimally with a crowd of oracles by asking only pertinent questions. Given a view, we assume the crowd are relevant domain experts (hence, the name "oracle crowds[1]") who are likely to answer questions posed by our system correctly. The answers to the questions will help to identify how to clean the underlying database in order to correct the error in the materialized view. More precisely, the answers to a question will help to identify the next pertinent questions to ask and ultimately, a sequence of edits is derived and applied to the underlying database. The edits will bring the database closer to the state of the ground truth and, at the same time, correct the error in the materialized view. As we will describe, our algorithms effectively prune the search space and minimize the amount of interaction with the crowd while, at the same time, maximize the potential "cleaning benefit" derived from the oracles' answers.

Our algorithms are implemented in QOCO system. We emphasize that even though QOCO can be used as a standalone system for data cleaning, it can also be used to complement existing data cleaning techniques. Specifically, after the data is cleaned with traditional techniques, QOCO can be activated to monitor the views that are served to users/applications. Whenever an error is reported

SIGMOD'15, May 31–June 4, 2015, Melbourne, Victoria, Australia.

http://dx.doi.org/10.1145/2723372.2737786.

[1]Even though there may not always be oracle crowds for every dataset, it is reasonable to assume that every important or curated dataset will have some domain experts who will be the oracles.

Games

Date	Winner	Runner-up	Stage	Result
13.07.14	GER	ARG	Final	1:0
11.07.10	ESP	NED	Final	1:0
09.07.06	ITA	FRA	Final	5:3
30.06.02	BRA	GER	Final	2:0
12.07.98	ESP	NED	Final	4:2
17.07.94	ESP	NED	Final	3:1
08.07.90	GER	ARG	Final	1:0
11.07.82	ITA	GER	Final	4:1
25.06.78	ESP	NED	Final	1:0

Teams

Country	Continent
GER	EU
ESP	EU
BRA	EU
NED	SA
ITA	EU

Players

Name	Team	Birth year	Birth place
Mario Götze	GER	1992	GER
Andrea Pirlo	ITA	1979	ITA
Francesco Totti	ITA	1976	ITA

Goals

Name	Date
Mario Götze	13.07.14
Andrea Pirlo	09.06.06
Francesco Totti	09.06.06

Figure 1: World Cup Games database

in a view, QOCO can take over to clean the underlying database by interacting with the crowd.

An overview example Next, we illustrate the key ideas behind QOCO with an example database of World Cup Games. Assume that the data was extracted from some sport websites (e.g., [64, 63] and is therefore partially incorrect and incomplete due to errors in the automatic website scraping tools. Although one could argue that some of the errors in the data could be cleaned with previous automatic techniques (e.g., by comparing to FIFA official data [24]), the choice of this dataset for our running examples is deliberate. The true facts about World Cup Games are well-known, and it makes it easy for us to illustrate our key ideas without the need to delve heavily into the data. This choice also makes it easy for the reader to play the role of the crowd and/or user of QOCO.

We use D to denote the given dirty database and D_G to denote the correct ground truth database. A small sample of the World Cup Games dataset is depicted in Figure 1, which shows portions of four relations: Games lists the World Cup Games and stores the date, playing teams, stage of the tournament and the final score of each game. Teams records the teams' names and continents for teams that participated in various World Cup Games. Players records players who participated in the World Cup Games, including their team's name, birth year and birth place. Finally, Goals shows each player's name and a date of a game in which this player scored a goal. In the figure, the dark gray tuples are the wrong tuples in D (i.e., tuples that do not belong to the ground truth database D_G). The light gray tuples are the tuples that are missing from D (i.e., tuples that are in D_G but do not appear in D). All other tuples (marked in white) are correct (i.e., they belong to both D and D_G).

Consider a user query Q_1, defined below, which searches for European teams that won the World Cup at least twice.

$$(x) \text{ :- } \text{Games}(d_1, x, y, Final, u_1), \text{Games}(d_2, x, z, Final, u_2), \text{Teams}(x, EU), d_1 \neq d_2.$$

When Q_1 is evaluated against the database D, the query result $Q_1(D)$ (i.e., materialized view of Q_1) consists of two tuples $\{(GER), (ESP)\}$. This output contains wrong answers such as Spain as well as missing ones such as Italy.

Note that in the absence of any knowledge about the ground truth (D_G), there are multiple ways to update D so that the wrong answers will no longer be part of the result. For example, to remove (ESP) from $Q_1(D)$, one can remove (ESP, EU) from Teams, or two of the four facts in Teams that represent a winning game of Spain. To add the missing tuple (ITA) to the result, one can add the tuple $(Italy, Europe)$ to Teams.

QOCO could ask the crowd whether Spain is in Europe, or if the tuples representing the World Cup finals in 1978, 1994, 1998, or 2010 are correct. Similarly, QOCO could ask the crowd whether there are tuples missing from the query result. Their replies would help QOCO correct the database.

In this simple example, it happens that there is a small number of tuples to verify for its correctness and hence, one or two questions would suffice. However, in general, the space of potential fixes may be large, and hence examining all of them may be prohibitively expensive. Our system employs an efficient novel algorithm to effectively prune the search space by carefully considering the order in which tuples should be examined. This way, the cleaning process is accelerated and the number of crowd questions is minimized.

Contributions. This paper makes the following contributions:

1. We formulate and present a novel query-oriented framework for data cleaning with oracle crowds. Under this framework, an incorrect (resp. missing) answer is removed from (added to) the result of a query through edits that are derived and applied to the underlying database. These edits are derived by minimally interacting with crowd oracles.

2. To assess the difficulty of the problem we first study two important special cases; determine the minimal interactions needed to derive a set of database edits to remove a tuple from a view, and resp. to add a tuple to the view. We show that these problems are NP-hard to solve even in these special settings.

3. We present heuristic algorithms for these special cases and show how these algorithms can be combined to arrive at a solution for the general query-oriented approach to data cleaning. Our algorithm for answer removal uses a greedy approach that is repeatedly applied until the right sequence of database edits can be completely determined. Our algorithm for answer addition exploits the fact that typically most relevant data does reside in the database. It greedily splits the query to identify, with the help of the crowd, where data is missing. To highlight the key ingredients of our solution we first consider a simplified setting using a single oracle who always answers correctly, then adapt the algorithm to support scenarios where there may be multiple crowd members who may not always provide correct answers.

4. We have implemented our solution in the QOCO prototype system and applied it on real use cases, demonstrating the efficiency of our query-oriented, oracle-based approach. We performed experimental evaluations on real datasets with both real and simulated crowd, that showed how our algorithms consistently outperformed alternative baseline algorithms, and effectively cleaned the data while asking fewer questions.

Outline of paper. Section 2 contains our preliminaries. We formalize and present our model and basic architecture in Section 3. Sections 4 and 5 examine two special cases of the query-oriented data cleaning problem, where hardness results along with heuristic algorithms are presented. The general algorithms is then presented in Section 6. The implementation of QOCO prototype system, as well as experimental results, are described in Section 7. Related work is in Section 8, and we conclude in Section 9.

2. PRELIMINARIES

Database and Queries We assume a relational schema **S** to be a finite set $\{R_1, \ldots, R_m\}$ of relational symbols, each with a fixed arity. A database instance D of **S** is a set $\{R_1^D, \ldots, R_m^D\}$, where R_i^D is a finite relation of the same arity as R_i. We use R_i to denote both the relation symbol and the relation R_i^D that interprets it. We refer to a tuple t of a relation R or a fact $R(t)$ interchangeably.

Let $\mathcal{V}$ be a fixed set of variables and $\mathcal{C}$ be a fixed set of constants called the underlying vocabulary. A query Q over a relational schema $\mathbf{S}$ is an expression of the form

$Ans(\bar{u}_0)$:- $R_1(\bar{u}_1), ..., R_n(\bar{u}_n), E_1, ..., E_m$

where

- $R_1, ..., R_n$ are relation symbols in $\mathbf{S}$, Ans is a relation symbol not in $\mathbf{S}$.
- $\bar{u}_i$ is a vector $(l_1, ..., l_k)$, where $\forall j \in \{1, ..., k\}$, we have $l_j \in \mathcal{V} \cup \mathcal{C}$ and k is the arity of R_i.
- E_i is an expression of the form $l_j \neq l_k$, where $l_j \in \mathcal{V}$ and $l_k \in \mathcal{V} \cup \mathcal{C}$, and l_j (resp. l_k) occurs in some $R_i(\bar{u}_i)$.
- for every $l \in \bar{u}_0$, there exists some $0 < i$ such that $l \in \bar{u}_i$.

In other words, Q is a conjunctive query with inequalities. Ans $(\bar{u}_0)$ is the head of Q, denoted by *head*(Q). The set $R_1(\bar{u}_1), \ldots, R_n(\bar{u}_n), E_1, ..., E_m$ is the body of Q, denoted by *body*(Q). We will omit Ans and simply write $(\bar{u}_0)$ for *head*(Q). The variables and constants in *body*(Q) are denoted by $Var(Q)$ and $Const(Q)$, respectively. Our results in this paper extend to unions of conjunctive queries with inequalities. However, for simplicity, we will only describe our results for conjunctive queries with inequalities.

EXAMPLE 2.1. *Consider again query Q_1 that finds the European teams that won the World Cup at least twice; i.e.,* (x) :- $\text{Games}(d_1, x, y, Final, u_1), \text{Games}(d_2, x, z, Final, u_2), \text{Teams}$ (x, EU)*;* $d_1 \neq d_2$*. Notice that* $Var(Q_1) = \{d_1, d_2, x, y, u_1, u_2\}$ *and* $Const(Q_1) = \{Final, EU\}$*. The result,* $Q_1(D)$*, contains two answers* $\{(GER), (ESP)\}$*.*

Assignments and Results An *assignment* $\alpha : Var(Q) \to \mathcal{C}$ for a query Q is a mapping from the variables of Q to constants. An assignment for Q is *valid* w.r.t. database D if for every relational atom $R(\bar{u})$ in *body*(Q), it is the case that $R(\alpha(\bar{u}))$ is a fact in D and for every inequality atom E in *body*(Q), $\alpha(E)$ is true.

A *partial assignment* for Q is an assignment which may not be total. We say a partial assignment α for Q is *satisfiable* w.r.t. D if there is an extension of α to a total assignment α' for Q that is valid w.r.t. D.

Given a (partial) assignment α, the notation $\alpha(head(Q))$ refers to the tuple obtained from *head*(Q) by replacing each occurrence of a variable l in *head*(Q) by $\alpha(l)$. We denote by $\alpha(body(Q))$ the set of tuples and inequalities that are obtained by replacing every variable l in *body*(Q) with $\alpha(l)$.

Witness Let α be an assignment for Q that is valid w.r.t. database D. A *witness* for α consists of all facts in $\alpha(body(Q))$.

The set of all valid assignments for a query Q w.r.t. database D is denoted by $A(Q, D)$, and the result of evaluating a query Q on D, denoted by $Q(D)$, is the set $\cup_{\alpha \in A(Q,D)} \alpha(head(Q))$. Given a tuple $t \in Q(D)$, we write $A(t, Q, D)$ to denote the set of all valid assignments of Q w.r.t. D that yields t, $\{\alpha \in A(Q, D) \mid t = \alpha(head(Q))\}$. We refer to the witnesses for the assignments in $A(t, Q, D)$ as witnesses for t. Observe that a witness can in fact be extracted from a semiring of polynomials [30]. However, we use the term witness and witness set since we do not require the full generality of a provenance semiring.

Note that each tuple $t \in Q(D)$ induces a unique (partial) assignment that maps the variables in $head(Q)$ to the respective constants of t. With abuse of notation we refer to t also as a partial assignment, which is by definition satisfiable for D.

EXAMPLE 2.2. *Using the same query and notations from Example 2.1, recall that* $Q_1(D) = \{(GER), (ESP)\}$*. Answer* t = (GER) *has two assignments,* $\{\alpha_1, \alpha_2\}$*, where* $\alpha_1 = \{x \mapsto GER, y, z \mapsto ARG, d_1 \mapsto 13.7.14, d_2 \mapsto 8.7.90, u_1 \mapsto 1{:}0, u_2 \mapsto 1{:}0\}$*, and* α_2 *is similar except that* d_1 *and* d_2 *switches. Answer* t *uniquely defines the partial assignment* $t = \{x \mapsto GER\}$ *and* t *can be extended into all valid assignments in* $A(t, Q_1, D)$*. The assignment* $\{x \mapsto GER, y \mapsto ARG, d_1 = d_2 \mapsto 13.7.14, u_1 \mapsto 1{:}0, u_2 \mapsto 1{:}0\}$ *is invalid only because it does not satisfy the inequality* $d_1 \neq d_2$*. Partial assignment* $\beta = \{x \mapsto ITA, y \mapsto FRA\}$ *is non-satisfiable because it cannot be extended into a valid assignment w.r.t.* D*.*

3. PROBLEM DEFINITION

We now present the formal model and problem statements behind our framework for query-driven interactive data cleaning.

3.1 Model and Problem

Let D be our underlying database. Under the open world assumption, a fact that is in D is true and a fact that is not in D can be true or false. To model real-world data, we adopt the *truly open world assumption* where a fact that is in D can also be true or false, in addition to the assumption that a fact that is not in D can be true or false. In other words, we assume that a given database can contain mistakes, in addition to being incomplete. The truth of a tuple is given by the ground truth database D_G that contains all true tuples and only them. Hence, a database D is *dirty* w.r.t. D_G if $D \neq D_G$. The database D_G determines the *true answers* and *true result* of any query. The two databases D and D_G together determine the set of missing/wrong answers w.r.t. a given query.

DEFINITION 3.1. *Types of answers:*

- *(True Answer, True Result) A tuple t is a* true answer *to a query Q and database D if* $t \in Q(D)$ *and* $t \in Q(D_G)$*. We call* $Q(D_G)$ *the* true result *of* Q*.*
- *(Missing Answer) A tuple t is a* missing answer *to a query Q and database D if* $t \in (Q(D_G) - Q(D))$*.*
- *(Wrong Answer) A tuple t is a* wrong answer *to a query Q and database D if* $t \in (Q(D) - Q(D_G))$*.*

As in interactive systems such as data cleaning systems (e.g., [53, 21]) and mapping-design systems (e.g., [45]), we assume that a (domain expert) member has at least some knowledge about the ground truth. Hence, in our context, the crowd member could point out missing answers or wrong answers. Whenever a crowd member determines that a set of tuples is missing or wrong, the database D will be cleaned, with the help of the crowd, only as much as needed to obtain D' so that the missing answers occur in $Q(D')$ and the wrong answers no longer occur in $Q(D')$.

In our framework, the database D' is achieved through a sequence of updates that are generated through answers to questions posed to the crowd. Each question-and-answer is an *interaction* with the crowd and each update is called an *edit*. An *insertion edit* $R(\bar{a})^+$ inserts the tuple $\bar{a}$ into relation R in the database, while a *deletion edit* $R(\bar{a})^-$ removes the tuple $\bar{a}$ from R. An update to an existing tuple can be modeled by a deletion followed by an insertion. The result of updating D with an edit e is denoted by $D \oplus e$. We assume idempotent edits, that is, if $R(\bar{a})$ exists in D then $D \oplus R(\bar{a})^+ = D$ and the same for deletion, if $R(\bar{a})$ is missing from D then $D \oplus R(\bar{a})^- = D$. The minimization problem that we wish to solve is the following.

PROBLEM 3.2. (EDIT GENERATION PROBLEM) *Given a database instance D, a ground truth database D_G, and a query Q,* *interact with the crowd minimally to derive a sequence $e_1, \ldots, e_k$ of edits such that $Q(D') = Q(D_G)$, where $D' = D \oplus e_1 \oplus \ldots \oplus e_k$.*

Observe that we may have $Q(D') = Q(D_G)$ even though $D' \neq D_G$. In other words, the database D' may produce the same query result as $Q(D_G)$ even when D' is still incomplete and/or dirty.

As we shall describe more precisely in subsequent sections under the special cases where a tuple in the output is to be removed or inserted, an interaction can be a boolean question with YES/NO answer. In general, however, the number of edits that is derived may not correspond to the number of interactions with the crowd as multiple edits may be derived with one, or even no questions. Our results show that even in these special cases, Problem 3.2 is intractable. Furthermore, the hardness holds under the assumption that a crowd member has full knowledge of the ground truth DB and every question yields exactly one correct edit on the dirty DB.

3.2 Basic Architecture

As mentioned above, we start by examining two special cases of Problem 3.2. The first case is when there is a single wrong answer. The goal here is to find a list of deletion edits to apply on D so that the resulting database D' will not yield the wrong answer under Q. The second case deals with a single missing answer. The goal here is to find a list of insertion edits so that the resulting database D' will yield the missing answer. We start by considering the following simple architecture (to be extended later).

Target actions There are two possible target actions that a user can specify: *(1)* remove a wrong answer from $Q(D)$ or, *(2)* add a missing answer to $Q(D)$.

Crowd In what follows, we assume there is a single crowd member who is a *perfect oracle*. A perfect oracle always speaks the truth and knows about D_G. Our techniques will be extended to multiple crowd members who may provide incorrect answers in Section 6.2.

Questions to crowd members We first consider a boolean question where we solicit YES or NO answers from the crowd to determine whether or not a tuple in D should be inserted or deleted. In the next sections, we will consider interactions with the crowd members through other types of questions. For now, every question posed to the crowd is of the form $\text{TRUE}(R(\bar{a}))$?, which means "Is $R(\bar{a})$ true?". A YES answer will generate an insertion edit $R(\bar{a})^+$ and a NO answer will generate a deletion edit $R(\bar{a})^-$. The result of updating D according to the answer for question q is denoted by $D \oplus \textit{ans}(q)$, where $\textit{ans}(q)$ is the edit that is generated respectively to the answer for q. Note that in general one may infer further edits based on the given answers and we will see some important examples for this later. But let us first assume for simplicity that no such inference is done and thus the length of the generated edit sequence equals to the number of questions asked. Hence, under these assumptions, minimizing the number of asked questions is the same as minimizing the number of edits.

Workflow The workflow that our system, called QOCO, follows can be intuitively described as follows. For now we assume that QOCO starts by receiving a target action on $Q(D_0)$, where D_0 is the initial database instance. QOCO will then generate a question and pose it to the crowd, and generate an edit based on the answer it receives from the crowd. The edit is then applied on D_0 to obtain a new database D_1. The question-answer-edit generation is repeated until QOCO determines that the desired target action can be achieved. The final database D_k, for some $k > 0$, is such that the target action is achieved with $Q(D_k)$.

At this point, a natural question is whether a strategy for generating questions to achieve a desired target action always exists. We first show that every edit on a database D tends to bring D "closer" to D_G. Formally, the *distance between two database instances D and D'*, denoted by $|D - D'|$, is defined to be the size of the symmetric difference between D and D' ($|D - D'| = |D' - D|$). Since the ground truth database is finite, and the perfect oracle provides only correct answers, there exists a naïve strategy that guarantees that the workflow described above always converges for a specific target action, as long as questions are never repeated and values of the domain can be systematically enumerated. The following two propositions can then be easily proved (see Appendix).

PROPOSITION 3.3. *Let e be an edit that is generated based on the oracle's answer to a question. We have $|(D \oplus e) - D_G| \leq |D - D_G|$.*

PROPOSITION 3.4. *Let D_G be a finite database instance that represents the ground truth, D be a database instance, Q be a query, and t be a target action. If the domain is ordered, then there is a finite number of questions $q_1, \ldots, q_k$ s.t. $Q(D \oplus \text{ans}(q_1) \oplus \ldots \oplus \text{ans}(q_k))$ achieves the desired target action.*

A naïve strategy that systematically enumerates all possible tuples in the domain, is of course too expensive to be practical. Hence, a more efficient solution is required. To illustrate the main principle of our algorithm, let us assume first, for simplicity, that there is just one wrong answer in the query result, and then that there is just one missing answer. We next describe our solutions to two sub-problems that correspond to the target actions of removing a wrong answer or adding a missing answer. These will form the essence of our solution to the general problem.

4. REMOVING A WRONG ANSWER

The first sub-problem of Problem 3.2 corresponds to the target action of removing a wrong answer (i.e., delete a tuple $t \in Q(D)$ and $t \notin Q(D_G)$). The problem of identifying a set of k corrective updates that need to be performed for removing a wrong tuple from the query result can be formalized as follows.

PROBLEM 4.1. *(Deletion Question Search Problem) Given D, D_G, Q, $t \in (Q(D) - Q(D_G))$, generate at most k questions $q_1, \ldots, q_k$ of the type $\text{TRUE}(R(\bar{a}))$? s.t. $t \notin Q(D \oplus \text{ans}(q_1) \oplus \ldots \oplus \text{ans}(q_k))$.*

THEOREM 4.2. *Problem 4.1 is NP-hard.*

We prove the theorem by showing that the corresponding decision problem is NP-hard. For that we use reduction from a well known NP-hard problem, called the Hitting Set Problem [40] (See Appendix). The above result suggests that, in general, heuristics are needed in the design of an efficient algorithm for generating the right questions for removing a wrong answer from the output.

Before presenting our algorithm, we give some intuition for the solution. Recall that we have a wrong answer $t \in (Q(D) - Q(D_G))$, which we wish to delete. This answer is supported by a set of witnesses in D, $\{w_1, w_2, \ldots w_n\}$, each w_i is the set of facts in $\alpha_i(\textit{body}(Q))$ where α_i is a valid assignment in $A(t, Q, D)$). Since t is a wrong answer, at least one tuple in each w_i must be false. We will use the crowd oracles to identify these false tuples. The challenge is thus to identify those false tuples with the fewest possible crowd questions. A minimal set of false tuples that covers all the witnesses is a *minimal hitting set*, defined below.

DEFINITION 4.3 (HITTING SET). *Consider the pair (U, S) where U is a universe of elements and S is a set of subsets of U. A set $H \subseteq U$ is a hitting set if H hits every set in S. In particular, $H \cap S' \neq \emptyset$ for every $S' \in S$. A minimal hitting set H, is s.t. $\forall e \in H$. $H \setminus \{e\}$ is not a hitting set.*

Algorithm 1: CrowdRemoveWrongAnswer

Input: A query Q, a database D and a wrong tuple t.
Output: A list of deletion edits.
Init: DeletionEdits = $\emptyset$, $S = wit(A(t, Q, D))$

1: **while** $S \neq \emptyset$ **do**
2: **foreach** *Singleton* $s = \{R'(\bar{a}')\}$ *in S* **do**
3: DeletionEdits $\leftarrow R'(\bar{a}')^-$
4: Remove from S all sets that contain $R'(\bar{a}')$
5: **if** $S \neq \emptyset$ **then**
6: $R(\bar{a})$ = MostFrequentTuple(S)
7: **if** *CrowdVerify*($R(\bar{a})$) **then**
8: $S = \{s \setminus \{R(\bar{a})\} \mid s \in S\}$
9: **else**
10: Remove from S all sets that contain $R(\bar{a})$
11: DeletionEdits $\leftarrow R(\bar{a})^-$
12: **return** *DeletionEdits*

Consider a minimal hitting set where the universe U is exactly the facts in D and the sets in S are the witnesses for answer t. In general cases, there may exist more than one minimal hitting set for the witness set. Finding those hitting sets that contain only false tuples is not trivial, nor is identifying the smallest one among them (see the proof of Theorem 4.2). However, in certain cases, when there exists just one unique minimal hitting set, things become simpler: if there exist a unique minimal hitting set, all other hitting sets contain this set. Hence, it must be a set of false tuples which is safe to remove and no crowd questions are needed.

EXAMPLE 4.4. *Consider two witnesses $\{t_1\}$ and $\{t_1, t_2\}$ for some false answer. $\{t_1\}$ is a unique minimal hitting set, and thus it must be the case that t_1 is false. In contrast, the witnesses $\{t_1, t_2\}$ and $\{t_1, t_3\}$ have two minimal hitting sets; $\{t_1\}$ and $\{t_2, t_3\}$. Hence, no unique minimal hitting set exists, and to determine which are the false tuples the crowd must be consulted.*

The following theorem proves that it is not hard to identify when a unique minimal hitting set exists, and it shows how to find it. (The proof is given in the Appendix.) Our algorithm will use this technique to reduce the number of crowd questions.

THEOREM 4.5. *Given a pair (U, S), as described in Definition 4.3, a unique minimal hitting set exists if and only if the elements of the singleton sets of S forms a hitting set for S.*

Greedy deletion algorithm Our algorithm employs a greedy heuristic, asking the crowd first about tuples that occurs in the highest number of witnesses. This heuristic could be replaced by others, such as asking the crowd first about influential tuples [38] or, tuples with high causality/responsibility [44], or tuples which are least trustworthy (assuming that they have trust scores).

Out algorithm asks the crowd first about tuples that hit the largest number of witnesses. Intuitively, if a frequent tuple is indeed incorrect, deleting it from the database will eliminate all the witnesses in which it appears at once, whereas if found to be correct, it will provide a negative indication about the other tuples in those witnesses. This heuristic is repeatedly applied until either a unique minimal hitting set exists (and hence false tuples can be determined automatically), or all witnesses has been destroyed. This approach is described in Algorithm 1.

At the beginning of each iteration (lines 2-4), all tuples in the singleton sets are added to the deletion list. Then, all sets in S that contain these singleton tuples are eliminated from S. This routine (lines 2-4) guarantees, according to Theorem 4.5, that our algorithm will not pose questions to the crowd once there exists a unique minimal hitting set. Then, our algorithm greedily searches for tuples that, if found false, can eliminate the largest number of witnesses (lines 5-11). If the most frequent tuple is identified as correct, the algorithm removes it from all sets in S (line 8), otherwise it is added to the deletion list (line 11) and all sets in S containing this tuple are removed (line 10). Finally, the algorithm returns the list of deletion edits.

EXAMPLE 4.6. *To exemplify, consider the same query Q_1 that finds the European teams that won the World Cup at least twice. Assume that our expert crowd member examines the answers for the query and finds the answer (ESP) to be wrong. Note that this answer is supported by six witnesses, $w_1, w_2, \ldots, w_6$, in D.*

	Tuples of the witness
w_1	t_1 = Games(11.7.10, $ESP, NED, Final$, 1:0) t_2 = Games(12.7.98, $ESP, NED, Final$, 4:2) t_3 = Teams(ESP, EU)
w_2	t_2 = Games(12.7.98, $ESP, NED, Final$, 4:2) t_4 = Games(11.7.94, $ESP, NED, Final$, 3:1) t_3 = Teams(ESP, EU)
w_3	t_4 = Games(11.7.94, $ESP, NED, Final$, 3:1) t_1 = Games(11.7.10, $ESP, NED, Final$, 1:0) t_3 = Teams(ESP, EU)
w_4	t_1 = Games(11.7.10, $ESP, NED, Final$, 1:0) t_5 = Games(25.06.78, $ESP, NED, Final$, 1:0) t_3 = Teams(ESP, EU)
w_5	t_2 = Games(12.7.98, $ESP, NED, Final$, 4:2) t_5 = Games(25.06.78, $ESP, NED, Final$, 1:0) t_3 = Teams(ESP, EU)
w_6	t_4 = Games(11.7.94, $ESP, NED, Final$, 3:1) t_5 = Games(25.06.78, $ESP, NED, Final$, 1:0) t_3 = Teams(ESP, EU)

No singletons exist in the witness set and hence we jump to lines 6-11. Tuple t_3 is most frequent, appearing in all witnesses, and so the algorithm poses the question TRUE(t_3)? *to the crowd (line 7). Since t_3 is correct ($t_3 \in D_G$), the expert answers YES. True tuple t_3 =* Teams(ESP, EU) *is removed from each set (line 8). The remaining tuples in the witness set are now, respectively,*

$\{t_1, t_2\}$, $\{t_2, t_4\}$, $\{t_4, t_1\}$, $\{t_1, t_5\}$, $\{t_2, t_5\}$, $\{t_4, t_5\}$

As all tuples occur equally often in the witnesses, QOCO *will choose randomly between them. Suppose* QOCO *first poses the question* TRUE(t_5)? *(line 7). Since t_5 is a false tuple ($t_5 \notin D_G$), the expert answers NO. Consequently, all witnesses that contain tuple t_5 are removed from the witness set, and t_5 is added to the deletion list (lines 10-11). The remaining witnesses and candidate tuples are now, respectively,*

$\{t_1, t_2\}$, $\{t_2, t_4\}$, $\{t_4, t_1\}$

All tuples are again equally frequent, so suppose that QOCO *now chooses to pose the question* TRUE(t_1)? *(line 7), and hence our expert answers YES. At this point, the sets in S are reduced to:*

$\{t_2\}$, $\{t_2, t_4\}$, $\{t_4\}$

and there exists a unique minimal hitting set $\{t_2, t_4\}$. The remaining deletions can be automatically determined, without posing further questions to the crowd. Indeed, QOCO *adds the tuples in the singletons to the deletion list and removes all sets that contain these tuples (lines 2-4). This step eliminates all remaining sets, and the algorithm terminates and the deletion list of false tuples is returned.*

The list of deletion edits consists of false tuples that form a hitting set for the set of witnesses. In this example it is also a minimal hitting set, but generally, due to the greedy nature of the algorithm, this is not guaranteed. Note however that even when the set is not minimal the extra work is not wasted - the elimination of the redundant tuples does improve the correctness of the database, even if not essential to the removal of the given wrong answer. More generally, observe that the set of questions being asked may not be minimal. For example, we asked the expert here about tuple t_3, that turned out to be correct and thus not added to the deletion list. Any algorithm that can be devised for this problem would confront the same issue (i.e., that a tuple picked by the algorithm as a candidate for deletion may be verified by the crowd to be correct), as the optimal strategy depends on D_G which is unknown.

5. ADDING A MISSING ANSWER

The second sub-problem of Problem 3.2 corresponds to the target action of inserting a missing answer to the output. Analogously, we formalize the problem of identifying a set of k corrective updates to be performed for adding a missing tuple to a query result as follows.

PROBLEM 5.1. *(Insertion Question Search Problem) Given D, D_G, Q, $t \in (Q(D_G) - Q(D))$, generate at most k questions $q_1, ..., q_k$ of the type* TRUE$(R(\bar{a}))$? *s.t.* $t \in Q(D \oplus \text{ans}(q_1) \oplus ... \oplus \text{ans}(q_k))$.

THEOREM 5.2. *Problem 5.1 NP-hard.*

To prove this we use reduction from another known NP-hard problem named One-3SAT [40], see Appendix. Similarly to the case of removing a wrong answer, the above result suggests that, even if we had access to the ground truth database D_G, heuristics are needed in the design of an efficient algorithm for generating the right questions to insert the relevant tuples to the database. To address this we will leverage the crowd's knowledge of D_G and ask them more general questions than the simple boolean ones we have used so far. We approach crowd oracles to directly identify some of the true tuples that should be inserted to the database to add a missing answer to the output.

A naïve approach could be asking an oracle to provide the facts in a witness of the missing answer. Recall that given a missing answer t we abuse the notation and t is also the induced partial assignment which maps the variables in $head(Q)$ to t. So, simply presenting to the crowd member $t(body(Q))$, and asking her to complete it into a witness for t, seems a possible solution. This way, the facts in this new witness can be inserted to D, and t becomes an answer in the output $Q(D)$.

For that, we define another crowd question[2], additional to the crowd question defined in Section 3.2. Given a partial assignment α for query Q, QOCO may ask the crowd COMPL(α, Q), which means: if α is satisfiable, complete $\alpha(body(Q))$ into a witness through a total valid assignment α' that extends α. Otherwise, do nothing. If an extended assignment α' is found, QOCO will interpret the facts in $\alpha'(body(Q))$ that are not in D as insertion candidates, and QOCO will create the compatible edit list of insertions.

In general, given a missing answer t, the number of tuples in $t(body(Q))$ which we ask the crowd member to complete (i.e., map the variables in those tuples), may be large. Note however that if the underlying database D is nearly clean and complete, most tuples in $t(body(Q))$ may exist in D, and hence only minor changes and small amount of mappings are in fact needed so that t will appear in the output. Hence, the crowd may be asked to do more work than needed in terms of the number of new tuples generated in the task. To avoid this we pursue the following approach.

5.1 Query split

It is well-known that crowdsourcing works best when tasks can be broken down into simpler pieces. An entire witness generation may be a too large task for the crowd. Hence, we suggest an approach that exploits both the crowd and the underlying database D which is likely to work well if the underlying database is mostly correct and complete w.r.t. the query Q. The goal is to help the crowd members by directing them with facts existing in the underlying database D. For that we present the notion of *splitting a query*. Before continuing we define a subquery for a given query.

DEFINITION 5.3 (SUBQUERY). *Let Q' be the following query $ans(u_0')$:- $R_1'(u_1), ..., R_k'(u_k), E_1', ..., E_f'$ and Q be the query $ans(u_0)$:- $R_1(u_1), ..., R_n(u_n), E_1, ..., E_m$. We say that Q' is a* subquery *of Q, denoted by $Q' \leq Q$, if the following hold.*

- $R_1'(u_1), ..., R_k'(u_k) \subseteq R_1(u_1), ..., R_n(u_n)$
- $E_1', ..., E_f' \subseteq E_1, ..., E_m$

Splitting a query means decomposing the query into two or more subqueries where every relational atom in the body of the original query appears in the body of at least one subquery. We assume that the head of each subquery contains all the variables that appears in its body (i.e., no projection).

The intuition behind splitting a query into subqueries is to seek partial assignments for Q using assignments of its subqueries. These partial assignments are good candidates for being extended into a valid assignment (if satisfiable), and can be used to reduce the number of tuples we ask the crowd to complete. We next illustrate with an example, how splitting queries can be used to potentially reduce the required crowd work.

Before that, we define how we embed a given missing answer into the query Q, and thus obtain a new query. Given a query Q and a missing answer t, we denote by $Q|_t$ the query whose body is $t(body(Q))$ and its head consists of all the variables that appear in $t(body(Q))$. Our goal is to complete $t(body(Q))$, which amounts to finding a valid assignment for Q

EXAMPLE 5.4. *Consider the query Q_2, that finds all European players who scored a goal in a World Cup final game; formally it is* (x) :- Players (x, y, z, w), Goals(x, d), Games$(d, y, v, Final, u)$, Teams(y, EU). *Notice that tuple (ITA, EU) is missing from D (but is in D_G), and hence all Italian players are missing from the output. For our discussion we look at missing answer t = $(Pirlo)$ which defines the partial assignment $\{x \mapsto Pirlo\}$. Consider query $Q_2|_t$ that is* (z, w, d, v, u) :- Players$(Pirlo, y, z, w)$, Goals$(Pirlo, d)$, Games$(d, y, v, Final, u)$, Teams(y, EU). *We split $Q_2|_t$ into two subqueries*

Subquery	*Head*	*Body*
Q'	(y, z, w, d, u, v)	Players$(Pirlo, y, z, w)$ Goals$(Pirlo, d)$ Games$(d, y, v, Final, u)$
Q''	(y)	Teams(y, EU)

Notice there is one valid assignment for Q' w.r.t. D:
$\alpha_1 = \{y = w \mapsto$ ITA, $z \mapsto$ 1979, $d \mapsto$ 9.6.06, $v \mapsto$ FRA, $u \mapsto$ *5:3* $\}$, *and 3 valid assignment for Q'' w.r.t. D:*
$\alpha_2 = \{y \mapsto \text{GER}\}$, $\alpha_3 = \{y \mapsto \text{ESP}\}$, $\alpha_4 = \{y \mapsto \text{BRA}\}$.
Evaluating $body(Q_2|_t)$ under assignment α_1, induces four tuples: Players$(Pirlo, ITA, 1979, ITA)$, Goals$(Pirlo, 9.6.06)$ Games$(9.6.06, ITA, FRA, Final, 5:3)$, Teams$(ITA, EU)$.

Notice that α_1 is a total assignment for $Q_2|_t$ (and not just for Q'). QOCO *system presents to the crowd members $\alpha_1(body(Q_2|_t))$, and the crowd members affirm that α_1 is a valid assignment w.r.t. D_G. Hence,* QOCO *concludes that the tuples in $\alpha_1(body(Q_2|_t))$ need to exist in D to make $(Pirlo)$ an answer. On the other hand, $\alpha_2, \alpha_3, \alpha_4$ are non satisfiable partial assignments for $Q_2|_t$ w.r.t. D. Hence, when* QOCO *system presents to the crowd $\alpha_i(body(Q_2|_t))$*

[2]Although strictly speaking, this is not a question but a task.

for $i = 1, 2, 3$, *they answer that these assignments are non-satisfiable. This is due to tuples such as* Players($Pirlo, GER, z, w$) *which occurs in* $\alpha_2(body(Q_2|_t))$ *or* Players($Pirlo, ESP, z, w$) *which occurs in* $\alpha_3(body(Q_2|_t))$, *that cannot be completed into a fact of* D_G.

If we consider the naïve approach a user would have to complete all 4 tuples in query Q_2 through binding 6 variables. On the other hand, Example 5.4 showed that the crowd task can be reduced to a question whether a given assignment is valid or satisfiable, and ask for its completion, if possible. Consequently, in this example, the tuples in $\alpha_1(body(Q|_t))$ are verified as true tuples, and QOCO can automatically conclude that Teams(ITA, EU) should be inserted to D in order to add ($Pirlo$) to the output $Q_2(D)$.

In this example we showed how a specific query split helped to reduce the amount of work done by the crowd and helped them to provide a witness for the missing answer. However, it can be tricky in general to decide how to split the query, and how to evaluate the subqueries to obtain a partial satisfiable assignment. Ideally, we should consider all subqueries of the query, but the number of subqueries is exponential, and so the amount of work required from the crowd is infeasible. We propose a greedy approach for splitting the query, which splits the query into two subqueries (see Subsection 5.2), evaluate each one of them and present to the crowd their partial assignments. The crowd is asked to verify if the partial assignment is also a valid total assignment, or complete the assignment if possible. We continue to split those subqueries recursively until a witness for the missing answer is found. If a valid assignment is not found through this process, we fall back to the naïve approach that asks the crowd to provide all tuples in the witness.

The assignments for subqueries of $Q|_t$ w.r.t. D can result in one of the cases: *(Case 1) A total valid assignment* (e.g., α_1 Example 5.4) or *a total invalid assignment*. In this case, the crowd needs to answer a simple true and false questions whether it is valid or not w.r.t. $Q|_t$ and D_G. *(Case 2) A partial unsatisfiable assignment* (e.g., α_2 Example 5.4). Such assignments can never be completed into one that "fits" D_G and hence, effectively useless. *(Case 3) A partial satisfiable assignment.* In this case, the crowd will be asked to complete the partial assignment into a valid assignment.

As we will show in Section 7, under our assumptions that D is mostly clean and complete, this heuristic is effective in helping the crowd to provide a valid assignment for the missing answer.

Greedy insertion algorithm We are now ready to describe our algorithm that uses the crowd as oracles to access D_G for the goal of adding a missing answer to the output.

Algorithm 2 uses two helper methods. CrowdVerify(X) is a crowdsourcing function that takes as input a set of tuples and inequalities. It verifies against crowd members whether facts (i.e., tuples with no variables) are true or false. It returns false if at least one of the tuples in the input is false, or if one of the inequalities is incorrect. CrowdComplete(α, Q) is another crowdsourcing function that takes as input a query Q and a partial assignment α for Q w.r.t. D. This method asks the crowd COMPL(α, Q). If α is satisfiable w.r.t. Q and D_G, the crowd member completes $\alpha(body(Q))$ to a valid assignment α', and then, CrowdComplete() method returns the corresponding list of insertion edits according to the witness $\alpha'(body(Q))$. Otherwise, it returns null.

The algorithm starts by splitting the input query and adding the subqueries to a queue (line 3). The main loop continues until a valid assignment for the missing answer is found, or if the subqueries queue is empty (line 4). At each iteration we pop a subquery from the queue (line 5). We evaluate the current subquery (line 6) and verify against the crowd whether it is a valid total assignment for the input query Q (lines 8-10) or a partial assignment that should

Algorithm 2: CrowdAddMissingAnswer

Input: A query Q, a database D and a missing tuple t.
Output: void
Init: Queries = $\emptyset$, InsertionActions = $\emptyset$

1: TrueTuples = $\{R(\bar{a})^+ \mid R(\bar{a}) \in body(Q|_t) \wedge \bar{a}$ consists of only constants$\}$
2: D = D $\oplus$ TrueTuples
3: Queries $\leftarrow$ Split($Q|_t$)
4: **while** $Q|_t(D) = \emptyset$ *&&* *Queries* $\neq \emptyset$ **do**
5: $\quad CurrQ$ = pop(Queries)
6: $\quad$ **foreach** *Assignment* α *in* $A(CurrQ, D)$ **do**
7: $\quad\quad$ **if** *CrowdVerify*($\alpha(body(Q|_t))$) **then**
8: $\quad\quad\quad$ **if** α *is a total assignment of* $Q|_t$ **then**
9: $\quad\quad\quad\quad$ D $\oplus$ $\{R(\bar{a})^+ \mid R(\bar{a}) \in \alpha(body(Q|_t))\}$
10: $\quad\quad\quad\quad$ **return**
11: $\quad\quad\quad$ **else**
12: $\quad\quad\quad\quad$ InsertionActions = CrowdComplete($\alpha, Q|_t$)
13: $\quad\quad\quad\quad$ **if** *InsertionActions* $\neq \emptyset$ **then**
14: $\quad\quad\quad\quad\quad$ D $\oplus$ InsertionActions
15: $\quad\quad\quad\quad\quad$ **return**
16: $\quad$ **if** *body(CurrQ) has more than 1 tuple* **then**
17: $\quad\quad$ Queries $\leftarrow$ Split($CurrQ$)
18: InsertionActions = CrowdComplete($Q|_t$, id)
19: D $\oplus$ InsertionActions
20: **return**

be completed with the crowd (lines 12-15). If not, we split the current query (lines 16-17) and continue to the next iteration. If the algorithm fails to find a partial assignment that can be extended into a valid assignment for Q it posts to the crowd a question to provide a witness for the missing answer (line 18). In line 19 the algorithm executes the insertions of the true missing tuples.

5.2 Implementations of Split()

The Split() method, which appears in lines 3 and 17, is the heart of our algorithm. This is the heuristic discussed before, which breaks the input query into two subqueries.

Split() method can be implemented in different ways and we next describe two approaches that we examined and experimented on.

Data-directed approach This approach exploits provenance metadata [12], when available, to split the query. If we have database provenance for the query result, we can instrument methods similar to the WhyNot? system in [58]. In that work, they try to provide explanations to missing answers by identifying the manipulation operation(s) in the query plan that are responsible for excluding the missing answers. As opposed to WhyNot? we are not interested in explaining why an answer is missing, or describing the possible ways in which it potentially could be added but we wish to identify the *correct* edits to the underlying database that will add the answer to the result. Nevertheless, we can still exploit the output of WhyNot? system to wisely split a query. Our input to WhyNot? system is a query with no projection and no answers (i.e., $Q|_t$ or one of its subqueries), and we ask "Why no answers?". When we get the manipulation operation(s) that are responsible for excluding the missing answer, we split accordingly. We omit here the details for lack of space, but illustrate in Figure 2 (right) such a split. In this example the WhyNot? mechanism outputs a join operation, and QOCO splits the query atoms accordingly, further adding to each subquery all the inequality involving its variables.

Query-directed approach In the absence of provenance information that points to the missing data items, one can try to use the

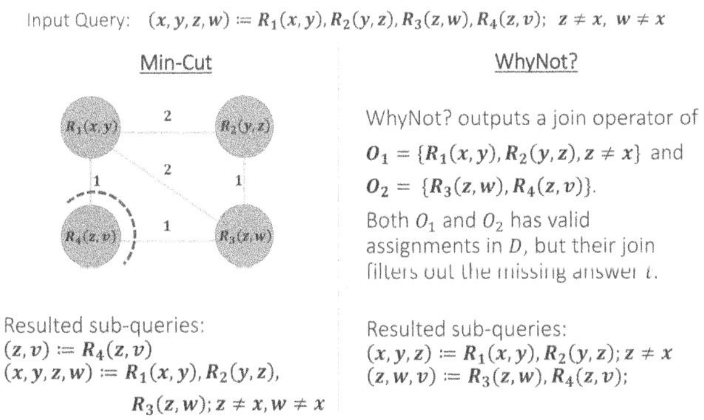

Figure 2: Example of split using different methods

structure of the query to guide the split. For example consider the query as a weighted graph, described shortly. We may use this graph to split the query in a manner that will produce two subqueries that their graphs are connected (up to certain limitations). This way we are more likely to avoid situations where the same variable appears in both subqueries, and avoid the loss of inequalities (as happens in the WhyNot?-based split in Figure 2 (right), where the inequality $w \neq x$ does not appear in the subqueries because variables w and x are divided into different subqueries).

In our graph, vertices represent tuples in the query's body and edges occur between vertices that represent tuples with joint variables, or tuples with variables that share an inequality. Moreover, the edges of the graph are weighted with the number of variables that appear in both relations represented by its adjacent nodes, plus the number of inequalities that are relevant to the variables of those same two nodes. On this graph we can look for a Min-Cut [18] that will define how to split the query. Figure 2 (left) illustrates a split of the query after finding a Min-Cut of the query graph.

As one can see in Figure 2, different split methods may result with different subqueries. In the provenance approach we are more likely to obtain subqueries that their evaluated results on the database are not empty. In this example (right), we assumed a join operation was returned from WhyNot? (recall that we ask "Why no answers?" for $Q|_t$), which means that both subqueries has results when evaluated on the database. In the query-directed split we are more likely to have a small number of variables that appear in both subqueries and a larger number of inequalities that are captured within the subqueries. In the same example (left), the inequality $w \neq x$ appears in the second subquery, while it is meaningless for both subqueries in the other split. This way, we can satisfy more constraints in each subquery. One could also apply heuristic to keep relational atoms with key-foreign key relationship together.

Interestingly, as shown in the experiments, since the ideal split depends in practice on what data is missing, rather than on the query structure, sophisticated structure-based analysis as the one above often does not perform better than a simple random split.

6. THE GENERAL ALGORITHM

The principles described above extend naturally to handle multiple wrong/missing answers and multiple imperfect experts. We detail these two extensions next.

6.1 Iterative Cleaning

In the general case our systems first needs to identify the set of wrong answers (resp., multiple missing answers). Then it can continue to process the actions of deleting (resp., inserting) an answer

Algorithm 3: Main Algorithm

```
    Input: A query Q, and an underlying database D
    Output: A clean and complete database D w.r.t. Q and D_G
    Init: VerifiedResults = ∅, FirstIter = true
    1: while FirstIter || Q(D) \ VerifiedResults ≠ ∅ do
Del 2:   foreach Tuple t in Q(D) \ VerifiedResults do
    3:     if CrowdVerify(Q(D), t) then
    4:       VerifiedResults ← t
    5:     else
    6:       D ⊕ CrowdRemoveWrongAnswer(Q, D, t)
Ins 7:   foreach Tuple t in CrowdComplete(Q(D)) do
    8:     CrowdAddMissingAnswer(Q, D, t)
    9:     VerifiedResults ← t
   10:   FirstIter = false
   11: return
```

using the suggested solutions of Problems 4.1 and 5.1. For that we define two more crowd questions:

- TRUE(Q,t)?: Is the result tuple $t \in Q(D_G)$?
- COMPL$(Q(D))$: Complete $Q(D)$ into $Q(D_G)$.

A perfect oracle will answer YES to a question TRUE(Q,t)? if and only if $t \in Q(D_G)$. An answer to a question COMPL$(Q(t))$ is a missing answer $t \in Q(D_G)$, or null if $Q(D) \subseteq Q(D_G)$.

Note however that when both types of errors exist, fixing one type (e.g., a wrong answer) may lead to the occurrence of new errors of the second type (e.g., missing answers), and vice versa. For example, the deletion of false tuples that were the cause of an incorrect answer in the output, may cause the deletion of correct answers (that were previously there due some false tuples). Adding correct witnesses for these answers may in turn generate other incorrect answers (due to newly formed incorrect witness sets), and so on.

EXAMPLE 6.1. *Consider again query Q_2 in Example 5.4, and the missing answer $(Pirlo) \notin Q_2(D)$.* QOCO *needs to execute the insertion edit of [*$\text{Teams}(ITA, EU)^+$*] on database D to add $(Pirlo)$ to $Q_2(D)$. Note that D contains the false tuple* $\text{Goals}(Totti, 9.6.06)$. *Thus, if we add true tuple* $\text{Teams}(ITA, EU)$, *the wrong answer $(Totti)$ will be added to the output of Q_2, as a side effect.*

A key observation which goes back to Proposition 3.3, is that each step in this tuple addition/deleting sequence brings the database closer to the ground truth database, and thus our algorithm, that iteratively handles these newly generated wrong/missing answers, is guaranteed to converge to the correct query result.

The algorithm enters the outer loop (line 1) in one of two cases; *(1)* during the first iteration, to cover the case when $Q(D)$ is empty but $Q(D_G)$ is not. (2) when $Q(D) \setminus$ VerifiedResults $\neq \emptyset$, which means that there are unverified answers in $Q(D)$ that must be verified against the crowd. This algorithm is iterative. It first handles wrong answers in the deletion part (lines 2-6). It identifies incorrect tuples in $Q(D)$ by asking TRUE(Q,t)? (line 3) and then calls CrowdRemoveWrongAnswer from Section 4 (line 6) to execute the deletion algorithm on wrong answers. Afterwards, it continues to the insertion part (lines 7-9). It uses the crowd to find tuples that should be added to $Q(D)$ using the method CrowdComplete$(Q(D))$ (line 7) that poses questions of the type COMPL$(Q(D))$ to the crowd. Then it calls CrowdAddMissingAnswer from Section 5 (line 8) to execute the needed insertion edits.

The helper method CrowdComplete$(Q(D))$ (line 7), that poses questions of the type COMPL$(Q(D))$, needs to know when to stop posting these questions (i.e., when $Q(D)$ is complete). In [59] the authors developed statistical tools to enable developers to reason about query completeness. We use their technique as a black-box, called enumeration black-box, to decide when the query result is complete. This black-box notifies QOCO once posing additional crowd questions asking to add missing answers is no longer necessary, because the query result is complete with high probability.

6.2 Multiple Imperfect Experts

For simplicity, up to this point, we assumed a single perfect oracle. We next extend our framework to support multiple crowd (imperfect) experts working in parallel. This extension has two different aspects; parallelism, and dealing with the fact that humans, even if experts, are imperfect and may make mistakes.

Imperfect experts Recall that QOCO system has four types of questions. Two boolean questions that verify tuples and answers, and two open questions (tasks) that ask to complete partial assignments of queries to complete the result sets of queries. To deal with potential errors in boolean questions, we use below a simple estimation method where each question is posed to a fixed-size sample of the crowd members and the answers are averaged. More generally one could use any black-box (e.g., of [2, 47]) to determine the number of users to be asked and how to aggregate their answers (e.g., using majority vote). Regarding open questions, once a single expert provides an answer, the system poses an additional set of boolean questions to verify that the obtained answer is correct (using the black-box aggregator). More precisely, if tuple t is an answer to $\text{COMPL}(Q(D))$, the system will ask several experts the closed question $\text{TRUE}(Q, t)$?. If a set of tuples S is the answer to some question $\text{COMPL}(\alpha, Q)$, the system poses the question $\text{TRUE}(R(\bar{a}))$? for each tuple $R(\bar{a}) \in S$. Note that the iterative nature of our algorithm provides further protection against wrong insterions/deletions: If some wrong (resp. correct) tuple was mistakenly inserted (deleted), it may be removed (added) in the next iterations, if it caused for a new wrong/missing answer.

Parallelism Recall that Algorithm 3 consists of two components: deletion (lines 2-6), and insertion (lines 7-9). It also has the outer loop (lines 1-10) that iteratively runs deletion and insertion components over and over again until termination. We would like to be able to maximize the use of all available crowd members at any point, to speed up the computation. Thus, we run the deletion and insertion parts in parallel. To allow that, we need a dedicated variable $Res_{complete}$ to hold the set of tuples in $Q(D)$ at the time when the insertion loop is done according to enumeration black-box (line 7). We use this variable to add another condition $Q(D) \neq Res_{complete}$ to the outer loop (line 7). It is necessary because the deletion part, which is now executed simultaneously with the insertion part, might delete correct answers. We further use parallel foreach loops, in both deletion and insertion components. We verify the correctness of all tuples in $Q(D)$ at the same time (line 3), or post together multiple completion questions (line 7). For a summarized list of the modifications to Algorithms 1, 2 and 3, previously discussed, see Appendix.

7. IMPLEMENTATION

We have implemented all the techniques described in the previous sections in QOCO. QOCO is implemented in PHP (backend), JavaScript (front-end) and uses MySQL as the database engine. The system architecture is detailed in the Appendix.

Crowd members in popular crowdsourcing platforms such as Amazon Mechanical Turk or CrowdFlower are not always experts for the domains we use in our experiments. These platforms also do not allow to dynamically compute the questions to the crowd based on previously collected answers. We have thus implemented our own system and recruited our crowd through the relevant social networks to ensure that they have the necessary expertise for judging the truthfulness and completeness of the query results.

Our experiments are based on two different real-world datasets. A smaller database used as a showcase for the usefulness of our approach, and a larger dataset for comparing the performance to alternative baseline algorithms w.r.t. varying parameters. In our experiments we measured the efficiency of the algorithms in terms of number of questions posed the crowd. We also measured the running time required to select to next question. For our datasets this was always not more than one or two seconds and negligible for the user interaction, and we thus omit the exact measures here.

7.1 DBGroup database

The first database is our real-life DB group database (DBGroup), recording information on our group members, their research activities, publications, academic events, achievements etc. This dataset was created about 10 years ago and continuously maintained by various group members since, and currently contains around 2000 tuples. The DBGroup database is used to generate reports about the group's research projects and achievements for various purposes, e.g., to be included in periodic grant reports. Thus, each item in the database has attributes that relate it to relevant grants and topics.

To showcase how QOCO can be used to effectively clean the database we have launched it with queries used to generate past reports, and were (positively) surprised by the results. Even though we expected the database, being maintained and curated by past and present members and extensively used for reports, to be correct, QOCO helped to discover several unnoticed mistakes.

To illustrate we present four queries from the last grant report.

- *Q1:* Find all keynotes and tutorials on topics related to ERC.
- *Q2:* Find all current group members financed by ERC.
- *Q3:* Find all students who participated in conferences in the past 30 months, where the travel was sponsored by ERC.
- *Q4:* Find all publications with the topic "crowdsourcing" published in the last 30 months.

With QOCO, we ran the above queries and our group members played the role of crowd experts. The black-box used for a decision mechanism was simple: three users were required for determining the correctness of an answer and the majority vote was taken. The whole experiment for this report took less then one hour from the posting of the call for participation in the group's social network. During the process, we discovered 5 wrong answers (1 wrong keynote and 4 wrong group members) and 7 missing answers (1 missing keynote, 1 missing member, and 5 missing conferences). Consequently, QOCO cleaned the DBGroup database and removed 6 wrong tuples and added 8 missing tuples, which we have later manually verified to be all indeed correct edits.

7.2 Soccer database

The second database we experimented on is about Soccer games, including in particular the World Cup games. The Soccer database contains data about the games, goals, players, teams (national), clubs, etc. and consists of around 5000 tuples. This is a real-life database derived using automatic website scraping tools from sites [63, 64]. We first cleaned the Soccer database by comparing the data with reference data from FIFA official data [24] and used this as our ground truth, then added to the dataset some controlled noise (to be explained in Section 7.2). Our experiments were carried out with 3 different notions of crowd; *(1)* a simulated perfect

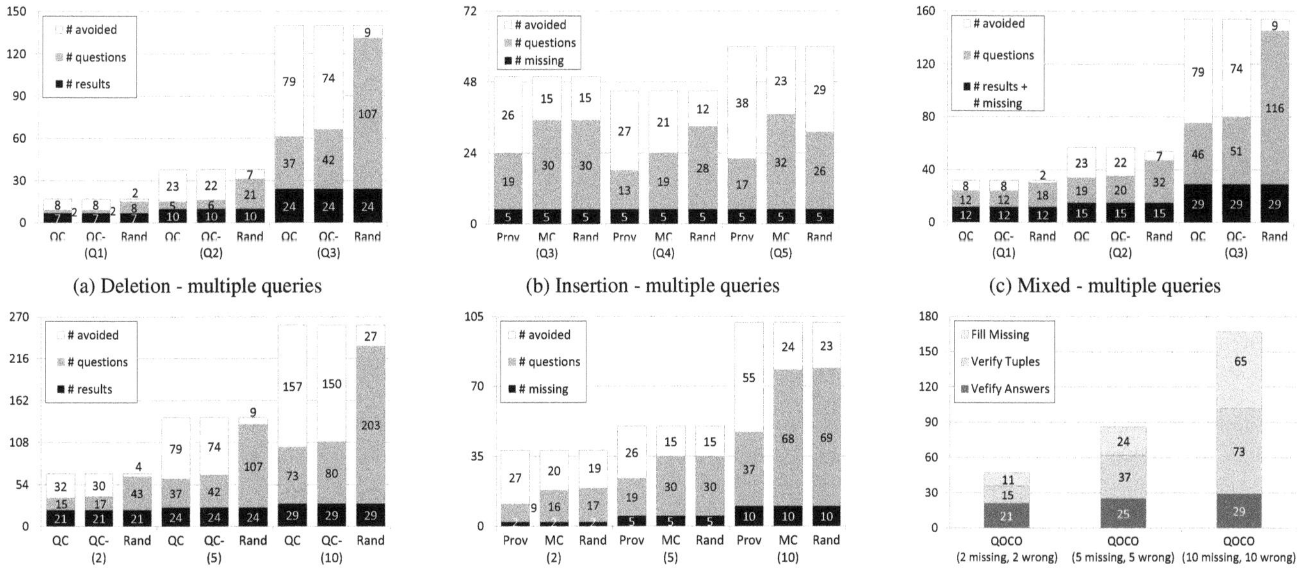

(a) Deletion - multiple queries (b) Insertion - multiple queries (c) Mixed - multiple queries

(d) Deletion - varying # of wrong answers ($Q3$) (e) Insertion - varying # of missing answers ($Q3$) (f) Mixed - Types of questions ($Q3$)

Figure 3: Results with a simulated oracle. Notation: QOCO (QC), QOCO^- (QC-), Random (Rand), Provenance (Prov), Min-Cut (MC).

oracle, namely an implemented oracle that consults with the ground truth Soccer database, (*2*) a real person who is a perfect expert; in fact, to make sure the results that we obtain are consistent, we repeated the experiments with three distinct people whom we know to be true Soccer experts, and (*3*) real crowd of imperfect experts consisting of soccer fans. Surprisingly, in all our experiments the perfect experts provided the exact same results as the simulated perfect oracle. First, the Soccer games database is at a reasonable scale and it was not difficult to find ardent fans who are extremely knowledgeable about the World Cup and soccer games in general. Second, these fans are usually competitive and will do all it takes (e.g., searching the answers on Google) for being the "master" of FIFA. As we shall explain, our results with imperfect experts are somewhat different.

The parameters we considered in our experiments are below.

Degree of data cleanliness refers to the ratio of number of true tuples in the dataset (i.e., $|D \cap D_G|$) to the total number of tuples in the dataset plus the tuples missing from the dataset (namely $|D| + |D_G - D|$). For example, if the *data cleanliness* is 50%, then the number of true tuples in the dataset is exactly the same as the total number of false and missing tuples. To simulate a dirty database which contains wrong and missing tuples, we add false tuples and remove true tuples to the cleaned Soccer data. We vary the cleanliness of our datasets from 60% to 95%. The default value is 80%.

Noise skewness refers to the ratio of the number of false tuples in the dataset (i.e., $|D - D_G|$) to the number of these false tuples plus the number of the missing true tuples (namely $|D - D_G| + |D_G - D|$)) . We vary it from 100% where we have only false tuples and no true missing tuples, through 50% where the number of false and missing true tuples are equal, to 0% where we have only missing tuples and no false tuples. For our experiments with the deletion algorithm (Algorithm 1), the default value is 100% and for experiments with our insertion algorithm (Algorithm 2), the default value is 0%. For experiments in the general case (Algorithm 3), the default value is 50%.

Degree of result cleanliness is similar to the *Data Cleanliness* parameter, but considers the cleanliness of the *query result*, and thus refers to the ratio between $|Q(D) \cap Q(D_G)|$ and $|Q(D)| + |Q(D_G) - Q(D)|$.

We illustrate our findings with the following five representative queries that are inspired by World Cup trivia quizzes from various websites e.g., [26, 25]. These queries have varying result sizes, from the smallest to largest:

- *Q1:* Find all European teams who lost at least two finals.
- *Q2:* Find all teams from the same continent that played at least twice against each other.
- *Q3:* Find all non-Asian teams that reached the World Cup knockout phase and won at least once.
- *Q4:* Find all teams that lost two games with the same score.
- *Q5:* Find all teams that won at least two games, while one of the opponents was a South American team.

Next, we describe the alternative baseline algorithms that we compared to our solution. Specifically, we compared the number of different crowd actions (i.e., boolean questions and open questions) posed by our solution (Algorithms 1, 2, and 3) to that posed by the competing algorithms running on the same input.

Deletion baseline algorithms For the case of deletions, we have two baseline algorithms (*Random* and QOCO^-) that decide which tuples among the witnesses to verify against the crowd. In our experimental setup, QOCO executes in a loop and iteratively asks the crowd whether a given answer in $Q(D)$ is correct. If the crowd deems that an answer in $Q(D)$ is incorrect, then one of these baseline algorithms is used to determine which tuples in the witnesses of the wrong tuple should be verified against the crowd.

- *Random* - a naïve algorithm that randomly picks a tuple, among the tuples in the witnesses of the wrong answer, to verify next.
- QOCO^- - a simplified version of our deletion algorithm that greedily picks the most frequent tuple among the tuples in the witnesses of the wrong answer, but does not identify when a unique minimal hitting set exists. Consequently, it continues posing further questions to verify the remaining tuples.

Insertion baseline algorithms Recall that the core of Algorithm 2 is the Split() method. Hence, we would like to study the effect of using different methods for splitting a query on the performance of Algorithm 2. We consider the following alternatives.

- *Naïve* - the naïve approach does not split the query.
- *Random* - randomly splits the given query into two subqueries.
- *Min-Cut* - splits the given query according to structure-based process presented in Subsection 5.2.
- *Provenance* - uses data provenance and the WhyNot? algorithm from [58], as discussed in Subsection 5.2.

Results for Perfect Oracle. Figure 3 shows the results of simulated perfect oracle (and thus also for a real perfect expert), for insertion, deletion, and the mixed general case algorithms with varying parameters. We refer to the version of Algorithm 3, that uses a combination of our deletion algorithm (i.e., Algorithms 1) with the Provenance-based insertion algorithm (i.e., Algorithms 2), as the "Mixed" algorithm. Each graph is the result of an experiment for an algorithm with a change in one of the parameters (mentioned in parenthesis), while the remaining parameters are assigned default values. For graphs 3a,...,3e the bottom part of each bar (in black) represents the lower bound count, i.e., the number of query answers that must be verified - for deletion algorithms , the number of missing answers - for insertion algorithms, and respectively, the number of query answers and missing answers for the mixed case. The middle part of each bar (in red) represents the actual number of verification questions (i.e., deletion questions) or the number of filled variables (i.e., insertion questions) or their sum when relevant. The top portion of each bar (in white) represents the number of questions saved or avoided relative to the upper bound. For example, for deletion, the total number of questions that one would ask with the naïve algorithm corresponds to the number of distinct tuples in the witness set of the answer that is to be deleted. Hence the total is always constant for a given query. Figure 3a shows that the total number of possible questions is 17 for Q1, 38 for Q2, and 140 for Q3. For insertion, the total number of questions is what would be asked by the naïve algorithm that does not split the query (that is, the highest number of unique variables that the expert needs to provide, in the worst case). We next detail the results.

Deletion algorithms. In all our experiments, QOCO had better performance results than its competitors. We present only a few representative graphs in the figure. We show only the graphs of queries Q1, Q2, and Q3 since the trends in queries Q4 and Q5 are similar. Figure 3a shows how the performance varies across queries Q1, Q2, and Q3. The difference between QOCO and QOCO$^-$ due QOCO's ability to identify unique hitting sets becomes more apparent as the size of the query grows (i.e., both number of results and number of tuples). In all cases, the two perform better than the Random algorithm that verifies all tuples of all witnesses. Figure 3d demonstrates how different levels of noise (i.e., varying degree of data cleanliness and result cleanliness) affects the performance. The numbers mentioned at the bottom of the graph, i.e., (2), (5), (10) represent the number of wrong answers among the answers in the result $Q(D)$. The gap between the performance of QOCO and the Random algorithm increases with the noise level.

Insertion algorithms. In all our experiments the split-based algorithms performed better than the Naive (the upper bound in the graphs), and the provenance-based split performed best. Interestingly however, there was no clear winner between the Min-Cut approach and the Random split. To illustrate Figure 3b shows the results for queries Q3, Q4 and Q5 (Queries Q1 and Q2 show similar trends to Q3 and are thus omitted). As we can see, the provenance based algorithm always performs best, whereas for Min-Cut and Random, in Q3 the two perform the same, in Q4 Min-Cut is better than Random, and in Q5 the opposite holds. This confirms our intuition that the ideal split depends in practice on what data is missing, rather than on the structure of the query.

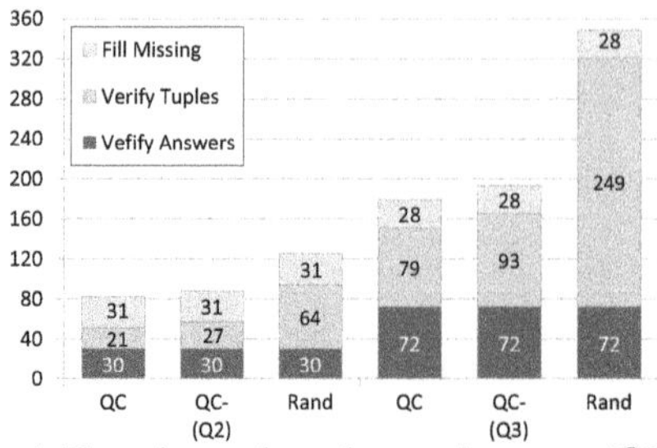

Figure 4: Experimental results - real experts ($Q2$ and $Q3$)

Figure 3e illustrates the performance of the algorithms for increasing degrees of noise for a specific query (Q3). Here again, for all setups of parameters, the provenance based algorithm performed better than both Min-Cut and Random algorithms, and among the these two, Min-cut was marginally better than Random for this query, but overall there was no clear winner.

Mixed algorithms. As mentioned before, we consider here an implementation of Algorithm 3 that uses QOCO deletion algorithm (as opposed to the weaker QOCO$^-$ or Random) and the Provenance-based insertion algorithm. Results with other insertion algorithms are not presented for space constraints because they yield weaker results than the provenance based algorithm. As shown in Figure 3c, QOCO performed better than its competitors. In figure 3f we use the Mixed algorithm, and the same query (Q3), but vary the number of missing and wrong answers. We demonstrate the distribution of different types of question presented to the crowd: verification of a result answer, verification of a tuple (a tuple contained in a false answer's witness), and filling blanks that refer to both adding a missing answer and completing a missing tuple. As expected, the graph shows that the number of tuples and answers that are verified increases as the number of errors increases.

Results for Real Experts Crowd. Figure 4 illustrates that QOCO is also effective with the real crowd (imperfect experts for a certain domain). The trends we observed are similar to the set of experiments with a simulated oracle (or a perfect expert). We aggregated the results from 3 experts using majority vote rule for all the answers from the crowd (our chosen implementation for the black-box aggregator). Recall that for each answer to an open question, QOCO poses to the crowd 2 additional closed verification questions (see Section 6.2). The way we count crowd answers is slightly different for boolean (closed) questions and open ones. Answers to closed questions increase the counter by one, while answers to open questions increase the counter by the number of (unique) variables that the expert provided their values. In addition, since the decisions are made by majority vote, once two experts give the same answer, a decision can be made and a third answer is no longer needed. Hence the total number of crowd answers in Figure 4 may be smaller than 3 times the number presented in the matching graph for the single perfect expert experiment. The results of the two illustrated queries contained 5 missing and 5 wrong answers (but the computation of Q3 involves more tuples hence the corresponding larger number of crowd questions). 60% of the errors in each query (the more popular and well-known answers) were identified and corrected within an hour from the time the queries were posted on the social network. 90% was fixed within another hour, and the whole experiment completed within 3.5 hours, identifying all errors. Observe that the "fill missing" numbers are identical across different algorithms of Q2 (resp. Q3). This is because we use the same provenance-based insertion algorithm and hence, the same (number of) questions are posed to the experts.

8. RELATED WORK

Data cleaning As mentioned in the Introduction, numerous data cleaning techniques have been proposed in the past. Cleaning problems can be classified between single-source and multi-source problems and between schema and instance related problems [52]. Existing tools address problems such as deduplication [17], entity resolution [1, 4], and schema matching [46]. Common technical approaches are, inter alia, clustering and similarity measures [4]. Data mining tools for outlier detection [22] or association rules [55] are also used to improve data, to complete missing values, correct illegal values and identify duplicate records. [66] used query aware approach in a different context of determining uncertain objects in probalistic data. The goal there is to generate a deterministic representation that optimize the quality of answers to queries/triggers that execute over the determinized data. In the context of data cleaning [62] introduced the idea of cleaning only a sample of data to obtain unbiased query results with confidence intervals. Experimental results have indicated that only a small sample needs to be cleaned to obtain accurate results. QOCO is similar in spirit to [62] in that it uses the crowd to correct query results, but unlike QOCO, [62] does not propagate the updates back to the underlying database. Another critical difference from [62], as well as from prior work on data cleaning, is that the open world assumption that we support allows to add missing true tuples to the database.

Crowdsourcing Crowdsourcing, or human computation, is a model where humans perform small tasks to help solve challenging problems. Incentives can range from small payments to public recognition and social reputation to the desire to help scientific progress [51]. It is a powerful tool that has been employed for database cleaning tasks such as entity/conflict resolution [61, 65], duplicate detection [6, 11], schema matching [67, 35, 43], and filling up missing data [50, 49, 27]. These complimentary techniques can be used for the initial data cleaning and then refined by our approach. As previously mentioned, extensive research has also been devoted to develop algorithms to ensure the quality of answers, both for individual answers (e.g., outlier detection [42, 59, 16]) and aggregated answers (e.g., using error probability, or an average weighted by trust [48, 47, 54]). In addition, previous works propose different methods for evaluating crowd workers' quality, e.g., to filter spammers and identify domain experts [42, 39, 36, 29, 37]. These methods too are complementary to our work and can be used here as a preliminary step to select our experts. Depending on the task, crowdsourced solutions may require a massive work force and may be expensive and time consuming. For instance, verifying that an ontology corresponds to an experts model of the scientific domain requires checking every relationship in the ontology [19]. As mentioned, we propose our query-oriented approach as means to focus resources to the most relevant portions of the underlying data.

View updates The problem of translating updates on the view into source updates so that the updates on the view are effectively captured is called the *view update problem*. Some of the works (e.g., [14, 9, 41]) compute the necessary updates on the source that will remove or insert the desired output tuple and, at the same time, minimizes the changes to the output. Our work follows more closely to the idea of automatically identifying "minimal updates" on the *source* that will correct one or more tuples in the query result [9]. However, a minimal source update does not always reflect the actual ground truth D_G. In fact, even though a minimal update to the source database will fix the query result, it may not correct the *database*. Even worse, it may actually further corrupt the database. Our algorithm in QOCO interactively leverages oracle crowds to identify a correct sequence of updates which may not always be "minimal" in the sense [9], to be performed. Such updates correct tuples in the underlying database in addition to fixing the errors in the query result.

Provenance The topic of data provenance (i.e., the origins or source of data) has been extensively studied in the past. Various notions of data provenance, such as lineage [15], why and where provenance [8], provenance semirings [30], have been proposed. Related to data provenance is the topic on explaining the reason(s) a tuple is in the result. Naturally, the data provenance of an output tuple can be used to explain the existence of the tuple in the output. In addition, other works, such as [3, 56], have considered how to explain the result or differences in aggregates in the result. More recently, there has been a number of research on deriving the changes that are needed to the underlying databases [34, 33, 32] or query [5, 10, 58, 31] so that a missing tuple appears in the output. The focus of our work, however, is neither to compute the data provenance nor to provide (all) explanations to the why or why-not questions but rather, to identify correct updates to apply to the underlying database to rectify the error in the output. Even if the explanations from prior work can be translated into corrective updates, their results do not suggest which corrective updates to apply.

9. CONCLUSIONS

We present QOCO, a novel query-oriented system for cleaning data with crowd oracles. An incorrect (resp. missing) tuple is removed from (resp. added to) the result of a query through updates on the underlying database, where the updates are derived by interacting with crowd oracles. The system uses a set of novel algorithms for minimizing the required interaction. Our experimental results on real-world datasets demonstrate the promise that QOCO is an effective and efficient tool for data cleaning.

There are several challenging directions for future work. Specifically, we plan to extend QOCO by supporting richer view languages, such as queries with aggregates and negation. Aggregates introduce significant complications as there are potentially numerous ways to achieve the same aggregate (e.g., to SUM to 100) and pruning the search space to identify the correct updates is challenging. On a related direction, we plan to investigate how constraints such as key and foreign key constraints can be incorporated into our framework. The presence of such constraints will require a more nuanced calculation of the (potential) interactions with the crowd, that take into account the dependencies among tuples and possible constraints violation. In addition, we plan to consider richer crowd interactions by allowing composite crowd questions where, for example, the correctness of several tuples is posed in a single question. Composite questions can potentially reduce the number of questions posed in general. We plan to investigate how to decide what kind of composite questions to ask and when to ask such questions. The crowd incentive and rewards model can also be improved. Currently we compute a user's effort based on the number of tuples and variables she adds. The model can be enhanced to account for the frequency and novelty of a particular answer (e.g., rare facts are harder to find), and motivate users to provide less-trivial answers in general. Another extension is to consider a richer crowd interaction paradigm that allows for attributes modification or tuples merge, in addition to deletions and insertions. Finally, an intriguing question is how to incrementally maintain the cleaned data when the underlying ground truth changes.

Acknowledgements We are grateful to the anonymous reviewers for their insightful comments. This work has been partially funded by the European Research Council under the FP7, ERC grant MoDaS, agreement 291071 and by the Israel Ministry of Science. Tan is partially supported by NSF grant IIS-1450560.

10. REFERENCES

[1] Y. Altowim, D. V. Kalashnikov, and S. Mehrotra. Progressive approach to relational entity resolution. *Proceedings of the VLDB Endowment*, 7(11), 2014.

[2] Y. Amsterdamer, Y. Grossman, T. Milo, and P. Senellart. Crowd mining. In *SIGMOD*, pages 241–252, 2013.

[3] T. Arora, R. Ramakrishnan, W. G. Roth, P. Seshadri, and D. Srivastava. Explaining program execution in deductive systems. In *DOOD*, pages 101–119, 1993.

[4] I. Bhattacharya and L. Getoor. Collective entity resolution in relational data. *ACM Transactions on Knowledge Discovery from Data (TKDD)*, 1(1):5, 2007.

[5] N. Bidoit, M. Herschel, and K. Tzompanaki. Query-based why-not provenance with nedexplain. In *EDBT*, pages 145–156, 2014.

[6] M. Bilenko and R. J. Mooney. Adaptive duplicate detection using learnable string similarity measures. *KDD*, pages 39–48, 2003.

[7] P. Buneman, J. Cheney, W. C. Tan, and S. Vansummeren. Curated databases. In *ACM PODS*, pages 1–12, 2008.

[8] P. Buneman, S. Khanna, and W. C. Tan. Why and where: A characterization of data provenance. In *ICDT*, pages 316–330, 2001.

[9] P. Buneman, S. Khanna, and W. C. Tan. On propagation of deletions and annotations through views. In *PODS*, pages 150–158, 2002.

[10] A. Chapman and H. V. Jagadish. Why not? In *SIGMOD*, pages 523–534, 2009.

[11] M. Charika, S. Chaudhuri, R. Motwani, and V. R. Narasayya. Towards estimation error guarantees for distinct values. *PODS*, pages 268–279, 2000.

[12] J. Cheney, L. Chiticariu, and W. C. Tan. Provenance in databases: Why, how, and where. *Foundations and Trends in Databases*, 1(4):379–474, 2009.

[13] Cia world fact book. https://www.cia.gov/library/publications/the-world-factbook/.

[14] Y. Cui and J. Widom. Run-time translation of view tuple deletions using data lineage. Technical Report 2001-24, Stanford InfoLab, 2001.

[15] Y. Cui, J. Widom, and J. L. Wiener. Tracing the lineage of view data in a warehousing environment. *ACM TODS*, 25(2):179–227, 2000.

[16] T. Dasu and T. Johnson. Exploratory data mining and data cleaning. In *Wiley*, 2003.

[17] P. Domingos. Multi-relational record linkage. In *In Proceedings of the KDD-2004 Workshop on Multi-Relational Data Mining*. Citeseer, 2004.

[18] J. Edmonds and R. M. Karp. Theoretical improvements in algorithmic efficiency for network flow problems. *JACM*, 19(2):284–264, 1972.

[19] J. Evermanna and J. Fangb. Evaluating ontologies: Towards a cognitive measure of quality. *Information Systems*, 35(4):391–403, 2010.

[20] W. Fan and F. Geerts. *Foundations of Data Quality Management*. Synthesis Lectures on Data Management. 2012.

[21] W. Fan, J. Li, S. Ma, N. Tang, and W. Yu. Cerfix: A system for cleaning data with certain fixes. In *PVLDB*, pages 1375–1378, 2011.

[22] U. M. Fayyad. Mining databases: Towards algorithms for knowledge discovery. *IEEE Data Eng. Bull.*, 21(1):39–48, 1998.

[23] U. Feige, M. Langberg, and K. Nissim. On the hardness of approximating NP witnesses. In K. Jansen and S. Khuller, editors, *Approximation Algorithms for Combinatorial Optimization*, volume 1913 of *LNCS*, pages 120–131. Springer, 2000.

[24] Fifa official site. http://www.fifa.com/.

[25] Fifa trivia quizzes and games. http://www.sporcle.com/games/g/fifaworldcup.

[26] Fifa world cup trivia. http://en.trivia.fifa.com/.

[27] M. J. Franklin, D. Kossmann, T. Kraska, S. Ramesh, and R. Xin. Crowddb: Answering queries with crowdsourcing. In *SIGMOD*, pages 61–72, 2011.

[28] V. Ganti and A. D. Sarma. *Data Cleaning: A Practical Perspective*. Synthesis Lectures on Data Management. Morgan & Claypool Publishers, 2013.

[29] S. Ghosh, N. Sharma, F. Benevenuto, N. Ganguly, and K. Gummadi. Cognos: crowdsourcing search for topic experts in microblogs. *SIGIR*, pages 575–590, 2012.

[30] T. J. Green, G. Karvounarakis, and V. Tannen. Provenance semirings. In *ACM PODS*, pages 31–40, 2007.

[31] Z. He and E. Lo. Answering why-not questions on top-k queries. In *ICDE*, pages 750–761, 2012.

[32] M. Herschel and M. A. Hernández. Explaining missing answers to SPJUA queries. *PVLDB*, 3(1):185–196, 2010.

[33] M. Herschel, M. A. Hernández, and W. C. Tan. Artemis: A system for analyzing missing answers. *PVLDB*, 2(2):1550–1553, 2009.

[34] J. Huang, T. Chen, A. Doan, and J. F. Naughton. On the provenance of non-answers to queries over extracted data. *PVLDB*, 1(1):736–747, 2008.

[35] N. Q. V. Hung, N. T. Tam, Z. Mikló, K. Aberer, A. Gal, and M. Weidlich. Pay-as-you-go reconciliation in schema matching networks. In *ICDE*, pages 220–231, 2014.

[36] P. G. Ipeirotis, F. Provost, and J. Wang. Quality management on amazon mechanical turk. *HCOMP*, pages 64–67, 2010.

[37] J. Jiao, J. Yan, H. Zhao, and W. Fan. Expertrank: An expert user ranking algorithm in online communities. *NISS*, pages 674–679, 2009.

[38] B. Kanagal, J. Li, and A. Deshpande. Sensitivity analysis and explanations for robust query evaluation in probabilistic databases. In *ACM SIGMOD*, pages 841–852. ACM, 2011.

[39] D. R. Karger, S. Oh, and D. Shah. Iterative learning for reliable crowdsourcing systems. *NIPS*, pages 1953–1961, 2011.

[40] R. M. Karp. Reducibility among combinatorial problems. In R. E. Miller and J. W. Thatcher, editors, *Complexity of Computer Computations*, pages 85–103, Plenum Press, New York, 1972.

[41] B. Kimelfeld, J. Vondrák, and R. Williams. Maximizing conjunctive views in deletion propagation. In *ACM PODS*, pages 187–198, 2011.

[42] A. Marcus, D. Karger, S. Madden, R. Miller, and S. Oh. Counting with the crowd. *PVLDB*, 6(2):109–120, 2012.

[43] R. Mccann, W. Shen, and A. Doan. Matching schemas in online communities: A web 2.0 approach. In *ICDE*, pages 110–119, 2008.

[44] A. Meliou, W. Gatterbauer, K. F. Moore, and D. Suciu. The complexity of causality and responsibility for query answers and non-answers. *PVLDB*, 4(1):34–45, 2010.

[45] R. J. Miller, L. M. Haas, and M. A. Hernández. Schema mapping as query discovery. In *VLDB*, pages 77–88, 2000.

[46] T. Milo and S. Zohar. Using schema matching to simplify heterogeneous data translation. In *VLDB*, volume 98, pages 24–27. Citeseer, 1998.

[47] A. Parameswaran, H. Garcia-Molina, H. Park, N. Polyzotis, A. Ramesh, and J. Widom. Crowdscreen: Algorithms for filtering data with humans. In *SIGMOD*, pages 361–372, 2012.

[48] A. G. Parameswaran, S. Boyd, H. Garcia-Molina, A. Gupta, N. Polyzotis, and J. Widom. Optimal crowd-powered rating and filtering algorithms. *VLDB*, 7(9):685–696, 2014.

[49] H. Park, R. Pang, A. Parameswaran, H. Garcia-Molina, N. Polyzotis, and J. Widom. An overview of the deco system: data model and query language; query processing and optimization. In *SIGMOD*, pages 22–27, 2012.

[50] H. Park and J. Widom. Crowdfill: collecting structured data from the crowd. In *SIGMOD*, pages 577–588, 2014.

[51] M. J. Raddick, G. Bracey, P. L. Gay, C. J. Lintott, P. Murray, K. Schawinski, A. S. Szalay, and J. Vandenberg. Galaxy zoo: exploring the motivations of citizen science volunteers. *Astronomy Education Review*, 9(1), 2010.

[52] E. Rahm and H. H. Do. Data cleaning: Problems and current approaches. *IEEE Data Eng. Bull.*, 23(4):3–13, 2000.

[53] V. Raman and J. M. Hellerstein. Potter's wheel: An interactive data cleaning system. In *VLDB*, pages 381–390, 2001.

[54] V. C. Raykar, S. Yu, L. H. Zhao, A. Jerebko, C. Florin, G. H. Valadez, L. Bogoni, and L. Moy. Supervised learning from multiple experts: whom to trust when everyone lies a bit. *ICML*, 2009.

[55] C. Sapia, G. Höfling, M. Müller, C. Hausdorf, H. Stoyan, and U. Grimmer. On supporting the data warehouse design by data mining techniques. In *Proc. GI-Workshop Data Mining and Data Warehousing*, page 63. Citeseer, 1999.

[56] S. Sarawagi. Explaining differences in multidimensional aggregates. In *VLDB*, pages 42–53, 1999.

[57] F. M. Suchanek, G. Kasneci, and G. Weikum. Yago: a core of semantic knowledge unifying wordnet and wikipedia. In *WWW*, pages 697–706, 2007.

[58] Q. T. Tran and C.-Y. Chan. How to conquer why-not questions. In *SIGMOD Conference*, pages 15–26, 2010.

[59] B. Trushkowsky, T. Kraska, M. J. Franklin, and P. Sarkar. Crowdsourced enumeration queries. In *ICDE*, pages 673–684, 2013.

[60] Uniprot. http://www.uniprot.org/.

[61] J. Wang, T. Kraska, M. J. Franklin, and J. Feng. Crowder: Crowdsourcing entity resolution. *PVLDB*, 5(10):1483–1494, 2012.

[62] J. Wang, S. Krishnan, M. J. Franklin, K. Goldberg, T. Kraska, and T. Milo. A sample-and-clean framework for fast and accurate query processing on dirty data. In *SIGMOD*, pages 469–480, 2014.

[63] Open football. https://github.com/openfootball/.

[64] World cup history. http://www.worldcup-history.com/.

[65] S. E. Whang, H. Garcia-Molina, and P. Lofgren. Question selection for crowd entity resolution. *PVLDB*, 6(6):349–360, 2013.

[66] J. Xu, D. V. Kalashnikov, and S. Mehrotra. Query aware determinization of uncertain objects. *IEEE Trans. Knowl. Data Eng.*, 27(1):207–221, 2015.

[67] C. J. Zhang, Z. Zhao, L. Chen, H. V. Jagadish, and C. C. Cao. Crowdmatcher: crowd-assisted schema matching. In *SIGMOD*, pages 721–724, 2014.

APPENDIX

A. PROOFS

We provide below the proofs for the theorems and propositions presented in the paper.

PROPOSITION 3.3. *Let e be an edit that is generated based on the oracle's answer to a question. We have* $|(D \oplus e) - D_G| \leq |D - D_G|$.

PROOF. The edit e is either $R(\bar{a})^+$ or $R(\bar{a})^-$. Since $D \oplus e$ either removes a false tuple from D, or adds a true tuple to D, or leaves D unchanged, the above inequality holds. □

PROPOSITION 3.4. *Let D_G be a finite database instance that represents the ground truth, D be a database instance, Q be a query, and t be a target action. If the domain is ordered, then there is a finite number of questions $q_1, \ldots, q_k$ s.t. $Q(D \oplus \text{ans}(q_1) \oplus \ldots \oplus \text{ans}(q_k))$ achieves the desired target action.*

PROOF. Since the domain consists of values with an order, one can systematically enumerate all possible facts. For every fact f, we ask the question TRUE(f)? to the crowd and apply the corresponding edits to the database until the target action t is achieved. It is easy to see that all facts in $(D - D_G) \cup (D_G - D)$ will be asked after a finite number of steps and hence, the desired target action must be achieved after a finite number of steps. □

THEOREM 4.2. *Problem 4.1 is NP-hard.*

PROOF. We prove the theorem by showing that the corresponding decision problem is NP-hard. The deletion question decision problem asks: Given D, D_G, Q, $t \in (Q(D) - Q(D_G))$, does there exist at most k questions $q_1, ..., q_k$ of the type TRUE($R(\bar{a})$)? s.t. $t \notin Q(D \oplus ans(q_1) \oplus ... \oplus ans(q_k))$? Clearly, the deletion question search problem is at least as hard as the deletion question decision problem.

Our reduction makes use of the Hitting Set Problem which asks: Given an instance (U, S) where U is a universe of elements and S is a set of subsets of U, and a positive number k, does there exists a hitting set H for (U, S) such that $|H| \leq k$?

We will reduce an instance of the decision version of the Hitting Set Problem with (U, S) and k to the deletion question decision problem as follows: The underlying vocabulary is $\{u_1, \ldots, u_{|U|}, S_1, \ldots, S_{|S|}, d\}$, for each $u_i \in U$, $S_i \in S$ and d stands for a constant that is different from the rest of the values. The instance D consists of $|U| + 1$ relations. For each element $u_i \in U$, $1 \leq i \leq |U|$, there is a unary relation schema $R_i(X_i)$ where the relation R_i has two facts $R_i(u_i)$ and $R_i(d)$. In addition, we have the relation schema $R(Z, A, X_1, \ldots, X_{|U|})$. For every set $S_i \in S$, we record in R the characteristic vector of S_i that describes the elements which occur in S_i. The instance D_G consists of the facts $\{R_1(d), ..., R_{|U|}(d)\}$. We define the query Q to be (z) :- $R(z, y, w_1, \ldots, w_{|U|}), R_1(w_1), ..., R_{|U|}(w_{|U|})$.

Notice that $Q(D)$ consists of a single tuple (d), while $Q(D_G) = \emptyset$. The input target action is to delete tuple $(d) \in Q(D)$. Recall that given an assignment α for a result tuple t, we call the set of tuples in $\alpha(body(Q))$ the witness for α, (or simply, a witness for t). Notice that every witness for (d) w.r.t. D contains a characteristic vector of a different $S_i \in S$.

For example, if (U, S) is such that $U = \{u_1, u_2, ..., u_4\}$ $S = \{S_1 = \{u_2, u_3, u_4\},\ S_2 = \{u_1, u_2\}\}$, then D consists of the following facts $R_1(u_1)$, $R_1(d)$, $R_2(u_2)$, $R_2(d)$, $R_3(u_3)$, $R_3(d)$, $R_4(u_4)$, $R_4(d)$, and 2 facts of the relation R, one for each $S_i \in S$. The set S_1 corresponds to the fact $R(d, S_1, d, u_2, u_3, u_4)$, and the set S_2 corresponds to the fact $R(d, S_2, u_1, u_2, d, d)$. The instance D_G consists of the facts $\{R_1(d), R_2(d), R_3(d), R_4(d)\}$, and the query Q is (z) :- $R(z, y, w_1, w_2, w_3, w_4), R_1(w_1), R_2(w_2), R_3(w_3), R_4(w_4)$. In this example tuple (d) has 2 different assignments and 2 witnesses (one for each $S_i \in S$):

$w_1 = R(d, S_1, d, u_2, u_3, u_4), R_1(d), R_2(u_2), R_3(u_3), R_4(u_4)$
$w_2 = R(d, S_2, u_1, u_2, d, d), R_1(u_1), R_2(u_2), R_3(d), R_4(d)$

It is easy to verify that the input to the deletion question decision problem can be constructed in polynomial time in the size of (U, S) and k.

We now show that there is a hitting set of size at most k if and only if there exists at most k questions $q_1, ..., q_k$ such that $t \notin Q(D \oplus ans(q_1) \oplus ... \oplus ans(q_k))$.

Suppose H is a hitting set of size at most k. It is straightforward to verify that one can pose the questions TRUE$(R_i(u_i))$? for every $u_i \in H$ in any order. Recall that D_G doesn't contain facts of type $R_i(u_i)$, for all i. Thus, the answer to every question TRUE$(R_i(u_i))$? for every $u_i \in H$ is NO, and a deletion edit $R_i(u_i)^-$ is generated. Since H is a hitting set, its elements hit every set in S, and hence their respective relations of the form $R_i(u_i)$ hit every witness of the tuple (d). The result of applying all such deletion edits to D is a database D' such that $(d) \notin Q(D')$.

For the converse, suppose there exists at most k questions $q_1, ...,$ q_k such that $t \notin Q(D \oplus ans(q_1) \oplus ... \oplus ans(q_k))$. We can assume wlog that each q_i, $1 \leq i \leq k$, must be a question on facts of D since questions regarding facts not in D are unnecessary towards the removal of (d) from the output. Similarly, we can assume wlog that these questions will not be about facts of D_G, because they are unnecessary towards the removal of the wrong answer (d) as well.

Furthermore, we can assume wlog that each question is of the form TRUE$(R_i(u_i))$? where $1 \leq i \leq |U|$. If the question is of the form TRUE$(R(\bar{t}_i))$?, where $\bar{t}_i$ is a tuple of relation R, we can always replace this question with the question TRUE$(R_j(u_j))$? for some element u_j contained in the set represented by $R(t_i)$ in order to destroy the same witness. Since the deletion edits consists of facts of relations of type R_j and $t \notin Q(D \oplus ans(q_1) \oplus ... \oplus ans(q_k))$, it must be that the set of all subsets that correspond to the deletion edits forms a hitting set for U and this hitting set has size at most k. □

THEOREM 4.5. *Given a pair (U, S), as described in Definition 4.3, a unique minimal hitting set exists if and only if the elements of the singleton sets of S forms a hitting set for S.*

PROOF. Let M denote the elements that occur in all singleton sets of S. Clearly, any hitting set must contain M. If M itself is a hitting set, then M is also a unique minimal hitting set because none of the elements of M can be removed. We show next that if a unique minimal hitting set exists, then M must be a hitting for S. Assume by contradiction that the hitting set must include, in addition to the elements in M, some other element that hits a set $s' \in S$. Then, s' must contain at least 2 elements and the elements of s' do not occur among M. If this is the case, different elements of s' will constitute to different minimal hitting sets. □

THEOREM 5.2. *Problem 5.1 NP-hard.*

PROOF. We prove the theorem by describing a reduction from the following NP-hard problem, which we call One-3SAT. An instance of the One-3SAT problem is a satisfiable 3CNF formula Φ where each clause in Φ has three literals. The problem of constructing a satisfying assignment for a satisfiable formula Φ is NP-hard [23]. We will show that if there is a polynomial time algorithm for generating at most k questions such that $t \in Q(D \oplus ans(q_1) \oplus ... \oplus ans(q_k))$, then one can construct a satisfying assignment for Φ in polynomial time.

Suppose there is a polynomial time algorithm P for the output insertion question search problem. Given a 3SAT formula Φ, we construct an input instance for the output insertion question search problem as follows: The database instance D is the empty database. Construct a relation for every clause in Φ as follows. For every clause $\varphi_i \in \Phi$, where $1 \leq i \leq |\Phi|$, construct a relation $R_i(A, X_{i1}, X_{i2}, X_{i3})$ where X_{ij} denotes the jth literal in φ_i and A is a fresh attribute that does not occur among the literals of Φ. In database D_G, every relation R_i, $1 \leq i \leq |\Phi|$, consists of facts that represent the satisfying assignments of the corresponding clause φ_i. For example, given $\varphi_1 = (X_1 + X_2 + X_4)$, there are 7 facts (all of $R_1(d, 1, 1, 1)$ to $R_1(d, 0, 0, 1)$ except $R_1(d, 0, 0, 0)$) in D_G. For the clause $\varphi_2 = (X_1 + X_2 + \neg X_3)$, there are 7 facts in D_G, all except for the tuple $R_2(d, 0, 0, 1)$. The value d is a fresh constant that is different from 0 or 1. Recall that the crowd member must answer YES to questions of the form TRUE$(R_i(\bar{a}))$?, if $R_i(\bar{a}) \in D_G$. Now, define the query Q to be (x) :- $R_1(x, x_{1,1}, x_{1,2}, x_{1,3}), \ldots, R_{|\Phi|}(x, x_{|\varphi|,1}, x_{|\varphi|,2}, x_{|\varphi|,3}))$, where the variables $x_{i,1}, x_{i,2}, x_{i,3}$ correspond to the literals in clause $\varphi_i \in \Phi$ for $1 \leq i \leq |\Phi|$. For example, the corresponding query for φ_1 and φ_2 is (x) :- $R_1(x, X_1, X_2, X_4), R_2(x, X_1, X_2, X_3)$ and $Var(Q) = \{x, X_1, X_2, X_3, X_4\}$. The output $Q(D)$ is $\emptyset$ since D is empty. The wanted target action is to insert tuple (d), because $(d) \in Q(D_G)$ and $t \notin Q(D)$. It is straightforward to verify that the input to the output insertion question search problem can be constructed in polynomial time in the size of Φ.

We now execute our polynomial time algorithm P on D, D_G, Q, and (d) with $k = |\Phi|$. We show that a solution to $P(D, D_G, Q, (d),$ $k)$ leads to a satisfying assignment for Φ. For (d) to appear in the output, there must be at least one tuple per relation R_i, where $1 \leq i \leq |\Phi|$, such that the tuples from different relations join according to Q. Since we are only allowed $|\Phi|$ questions, a solution to $P(D, D_G, Q, (d), k)$ must contain exactly one question TRUE$(R_i(t_j))$? for a tuple in each relation and the answer to the question must be YES. Furthermore, since these tuples must join together to produce (d), we can conclude that the satisfying assignment for each clause together form a satisfying assignment for Φ. □

B. THE GENERAL ALGORITHM

The list of modifications to Algorithms 1, 2 and 3, designed to support multiple imperfect experts in parallel, described in Section 6.2, are:

1. Post all closed questions multiple times according to the aggregator black-box. These questions are in Algorithm 1 in line 7, Algorithm 2 line 7, and Algorithm 3 line 3.
2. Verify an answer to each opened question with closed verification questions posted to the crowd. These questions appear in Algorithm 2 lines 12, 18, and Algorithm 3 line 7.
3. Run both deletion and insertion parts in parallel. To allow that, we add another condition $Q(D) \neq Res_{complete}$ to the outer "while' loop in Algorithm 3 line 1.

4. Use parallel foreach loops, in both deletion part (Algorithm 3 lines 2-6) and insertion part (Algorithm 3 lines 7-9).

C. SYSTEM ARCHITECTURE

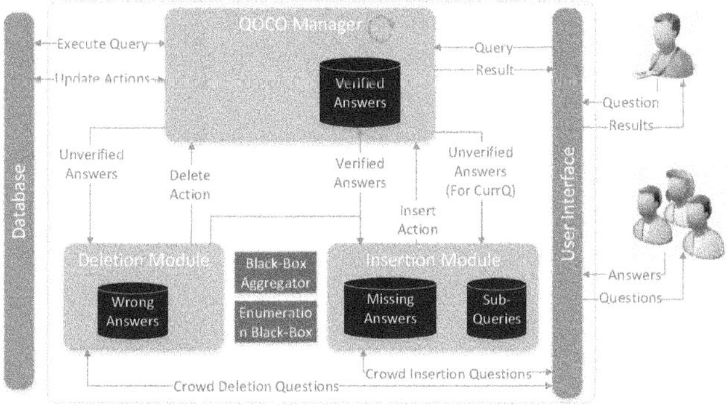

Figure 5: QOCO architecture

Figure 5 illustrates QOCO's system architecture. We describe the major components next. The crowd, who are answering questions, and the user (requester) who is running the query over the DB, interact with QOCO through the *User Interface*. In our experiments with simulated oracle, the *User Interface* was replaced with a simulator (called the *ground truth*) that returned answers to queries from the ground truth database). There are three core modules. *QOCO Manager* is responsible for interacting with the *Database*, and managing iterations and deletions as described in Algorithm 3. It receives the query from the requester and executes it on the *Database*. It performs the needed insert and delete actions identified by the *Deletion module* (Algorithm 1) and *Insertion* module (Algorithm 2).

BigDansing: A System for Big Data Cleansing

Zuhair Khayyat[†*] Ihab F. Ilyas[‡*] Alekh Jindal[♯] Samuel Madden[♯]
Mourad Ouzzani[§] Paolo Papotti[§] Jorge-Arnulfo Quiané-Ruiz[§] Nan Tang[§] Si Yin[§]
[§]Qatar Computing Research Institute [♯]CSAIL, MIT
[†]King Abdullah University of Science and Technology (KAUST) [‡]University of Waterloo
zuhair.khayyat@kaust.edu.sa ilyas@uwaterloo.ca {alekh,madden}@csail.mit.edu
{mouzzani,ppapotti,jquianeruiz,ntang,siyin}@qf.org.qa

ABSTRACT

Data cleansing approaches have usually focused on detecting and fixing errors with little attention to scaling to big datasets. This presents a serious impediment since data cleansing often involves costly computations such as enumerating pairs of tuples, handling inequality joins, and dealing with user-defined functions. In this paper, we present BIGDANSING, a Big Data Cleansing system to tackle efficiency, scalability, and ease-of-use issues in data cleansing. The system can run on top of most common general purpose data processing platforms, ranging from DBMSs to MapReduce-like frameworks. A user-friendly programming interface allows users to express data quality rules both declaratively and procedurally, with no requirement of being aware of the underlying distributed platform. BIGDANSING takes these rules into a series of transformations that enable distributed computations and several optimizations, such as shared scans and specialized joins operators. Experimental results on both synthetic and real datasets show that BIGDANSING outperforms existing baseline systems up to more than two orders of magnitude without sacrificing the quality provided by the repair algorithms.

1. INTRODUCTION

Data quality is a major concern in terms of its scale as more than 25% of critical data in the world's top companies is flawed [31]. In fact, cleansing dirty data is a critical challenge that has been studied for decades [10]. However, data cleansing is hard, since data errors arise in different forms, such as typos, duplicates, non compliance with business rules, outdated data, and missing values.

Example 1: Table 1 shows a sample tax data D in which each record represents an individual's information. Suppose that the following three data quality rules need to hold on D: ($r1$) a zipcode uniquely determines a city; ($r2$) given two distinct individuals, the one earning a lower salary should have a lower tax rate; and ($r3$) two tuples refer to the same individual if they have similar names, and their cities are inside the same county. We define these rules as follows:

	name	zipcode	city	state	salary	rate
t_1	Annie	10001	NY	NY	24000	15
t_2	Laure	90210	LA	CA	25000	10
t_3	John	60601	CH	IL	40000	25
t_4	Mark	90210	SF	CA	88000	28
t_5	Robert	60827	CH	IL	15000	15
t_6	Mary	90210	LA	CA	81000	28

Table 1: Dataset D with tax data records

($r1$) $\phi_F : D(\text{zipcode} \rightarrow \text{city})$
($r2$) $\phi_D : \forall t_1, t_2 \in D, \neg(t_1.\text{rate} > t_2.\text{rate} \wedge t_1.\text{salary} < t_2.\text{salary})$
($r3$) $\phi_U : \forall t_1, t_2 \in D, \neg(\text{simF}(t_1.\text{name}, t_2.\text{name}) \wedge \text{getCounty}(t_1.city) = \text{getCounty}(t_2.city))$

ϕ_F, ϕ_D, and ϕ_U can respectively be expressed as a functional dependency (FD), a denial constraint (DC), and a user-defined function (UDF) by using a procedural language. ϕ_U requires an ad-hoc similarity function and access to a mapping table to get the county information. Tuples t_2 and t_4 form an error *w.r.t.* ϕ_F, so do t_4 and t_6, because they have the same zipcode but different city values. Tuples t_1 and t_2 violate ϕ_D, because t_1 has a lower salary than t_2 but pays a higher tax; so do t_2 and t_5. Rule ϕ_U does not have data errors, *i.e.*, no duplicates in D *w.r.t.* ϕ_U. □

Cleansing the above dataset typically consists of three steps: (1) specifying quality rules; (2) detecting data errors *w.r.t.* the specified rules; and (3) repairing detected errors. Generally speaking, after step (1), the data cleansing process *iteratively* runs steps (2) and (3) until obtaining an instance of the data (*a.k.a.* a repair) that satisfies the specified rules. These three steps have been extensively studied in single-node settings [6, 7, 11, 16–18, 23, 34]. However, the main focus has been on how to more effectively detect and repair errors, without addressing the issue of scalability.

Dealing with large datasets faces two main issues. First, none of the existing systems can scale to large datasets for the rules in the example. One main reason is that detecting errors, *e.g.*, with ϕ_F and ϕ_D, or duplicates, *e.g.*, with ϕ_U, is a combinatorial problem that quickly becomes very expensive with large sizes. More specifically, if $|D|$ is the number of tuples in a dataset D and n is the number of tuples a given rule is defined on (*e.g.*, $n = 2$ for the above rules), the time complexity of detecting errors is $O(|D|^n)$. This high complexity leads to intractable computations over large datasets, limiting the applicability of data cleansing systems. For instance, memory-based approaches [6, 7] report performance numbers up to 100K tuples while a disk-based approach [17] reports numbers up to 1M records only. Apart from the scale

*Partially done while at QCRI.

SIGMOD'15, May 31–June 4, 2015, Melbourne, Victoria, Australia.

http://dx.doi.org/10.1145/2723372.2747646.

problem, implementing such rules in a distributed processing platform requires expertise both in the understanding of the quality rules and in the tuning of their implementation over this platform. Some research efforts have targeted the usability of a data cleansing system (*e.g.,* NADEEF [7]), but at the expense of performance and scalability.

Therefore, designing a distributed data cleansing system to deal with big data faces two main challenges:

(1) *Scalability.* Quality rules are varied and complex: they might compare multiple tuples, use similarity comparisons, or contain inequality comparisons. Detecting errors in a distributed setting may lead to shuffling large amounts of data through the network, with negative effects on the performance. Moreover, existing repair algorithms were not designed for distributed settings. For example, they often represent detected errors as a graph, where each node represents a data value and an edge indicates a data error. Devising algorithms on such a graph in distributed settings is not well addressed in the literature.

(2) *Abstraction.* In addition to supporting traditional quality rules (*e.g.,* ϕ_F and ϕ_D), users also need the flexibility to define rules using procedural programs (UDFs), such as ϕ_U. However, effective parallelization is hard to achieve with UDFs, since they are handled as black boxes. To enable scalability, finer granular constructs for specifying the rules are needed. An abstraction for this specification is challenging as it would normally come at the expense of generality of rule specification.

To address these challenges, we present BIGDANSING, a Big Data Cleansing system that is easy-to-use and highly scalable. It provides a rule specification abstraction that consists of five operators that allow users to specify data flows for error detection, which was not possible before. The internal rewriting of the rules enables effective optimizations. In summary, we make the following contributions:

(1) BIGDANSING abstracts the rule specification process into a logical plan composed of five operators, which it optimizes for efficient execution. Users focus on the logic of their rules, rather than on the details of efficiently implementing them on top of a parallel data processing platform. More importantly, this abstraction allows to detect errors and find possible fixes *w.r.t.* a large variety of rules that cannot be expressed in declarative languages (Section 3).

(2) BIGDANSING abstraction enables a number of optimizations. We present techniques to translate a logical plan into an optimized physical plan, including: (i) removing data redundancy in input rules and reducing the number of operator calls; (ii) specialized operators to speed up the cleansing process; and (iii) a new join algorithm, based on partitioning and sorting data, to efficiently perform distributed inequality self joins (which are common in quality rules);

(3) We present two approaches to implement existing repair algorithms in distributed settings. First, we show how to run a centralized data repair algorithm in parallel, without changing the algorithm (Section 5.1). Second, we design a distributed version of the seminal *equivalence class* algorithm [5] (Section 5.2).

(4) We use both real-world and synthetic datasets to extensively validate our system. BIGDANSING outperforms baseline systems by up to more than two orders of magnitude. The results also show that BIGDANSING is more scalable than baseline systems without sacrificing the quality provided by the repair algorithms (Section 6).

2. FUNDAMENTALS AND AN OVERVIEW

We discuss the data cleansing semantics expressed by BIGDANSING and then give an overview of the system.

2.1 Data Cleansing Semantics

In BIGDANSING, the input data is defined as a set of data units, where each *data unit* is the smallest unit of input datasets. Each unit can have multiple associated *elements* that are identified by model-specific functions. For example, tuples are the data units for the relational model and attributes identify their elements, while triples are the data units for RDF data (see Appendix C). BIGDANSING provides a set of parsers for producing such data units and elements from input datasets.

BIGDANSING adopts UDFs as the basis to define quality rules. Each rule has two fundamental abstract functions, namely Detect and GenFix. Detect takes one or multiple data units as input and outputs a *violation*, *i.e.,* elements in the input units that together are considered as erroneous *w.r.t.* the rule:

$$\text{Detect(data\_units)} \rightarrow \text{violation}$$

GenFix takes a violation as input and computes alternative, possible updates to resolve this violation:

$$\text{GenFix(violation)} \rightarrow \text{possible\_fixes}$$

The language of the possible fixes is determined by the capabilities of the repair algorithm. With the supported algorithms, a *possible fix* in BIGDANSING is an expression of the form x op y, where x is an element, op is in $\{=, \neq, <, >, \geq, \leq\}$, and y is either an element or a constant. In addition, BIGDANSING has new functions to enable distributed and scalable execution of the entire cleansing process. We defer the details to Section 3.

Consider Example 1, the Detect function of ϕ_F takes two tuples (*i.e.,* two data units) as input and identifies a violation whenever the same zipcode value appears in the two tuples but with a different city. Thus, $t_2(90210, LA)$ and $t_4(90210, SF)$ are a violation. The GenFix function could enforce either t_2[city] and t_4[city] to be the same, or at least one element between t_2[zipcode] and t_4[zipcode] to be different from 90210. Rule ϕ_U is more general as it requires special processing. Detect takes two tuples as input and outputs a violation whenever it finds similar name values and obtains the same county values from a mapping table. GenFix could propose to assign the same values to both tuples so that one of them is removed in set semantics.

By using a UDF-based approach, we can support a large variety of traditional quality rules with a parser that automatically implements the abstract functions, *e.g.,* CFDs [11] and DCs [6], but also more procedural rules that are provided by the user. These latter rules can implement any detection and repair method expressible with procedural code, such as Java, as long as they implement the signatures of the two above functions, as demonstrated in systems such as NADEEF [7]. Note that one known limitation of UDF-based systems is that, when treating UDFs as black-boxes, it is hard to do static analysis, such as consistency and implication, for the given rules.

BIGDANSING targets the following *data cleansing problem*: given a dirty data D and a set of rules Σ, compute a *repair*

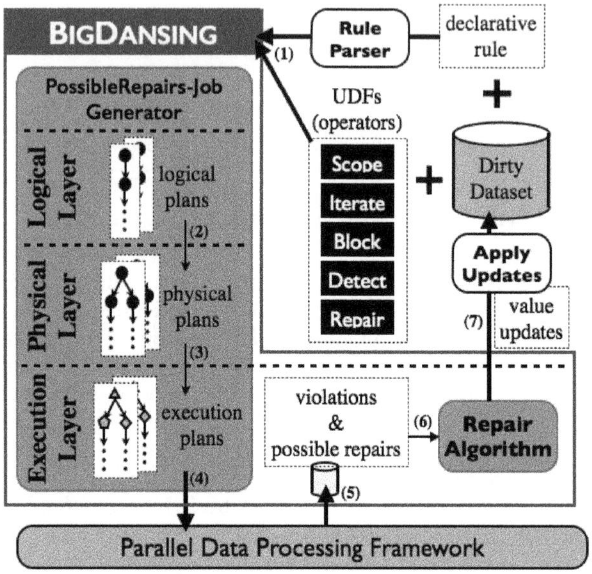

Figure 1: BigDansing architecture

which is an updated instance D' such that there are no violations, or there are only violations with no possible fixes.

Among the many possible solutions to the cleansing problem, it is common to define a notion of minimality based on the cost of a repair. A popular *cost* function [5] for relational data is the following: $\sum_{t \in D, t' \in D_r, A \in A^R} dis_A(D(t[A]), D(t'[A]))$, where t' is the fix for a specific tuple t and $dis_A(D(t[A]), D(t'[A]))$ is a distance between their values for attribute A (an exact match returns 0). This models the intuition that the higher is the sum of the distances between the original values and their fixes, the more expensive is the repair. Computing such *minimum* repairs is NP-hard, even with FDs only [5, 23]. Thus, data repair algorithms are mostly heuristics (see Section 5).

2.2 Architecture

We architected BIGDANSING as illustrated in Figure 1. BIGDANSING receives a data quality rule together with a dirty dataset from users (1) and outputs a clean dataset (7). BIGDANSING consists of two main components: the RuleEngine and the RepairAlgorithm.

The RuleEngine receives a quality rule either in a UDF-based form (a BIGDANSING *job*) or in a declarative form (a declarative rule). A job (*i.e.,* a script) defines users operations as well as the sequence in which users want to run their operations (see Appendix A). A declarative rule is written using traditional integrity constraints such as FDs and DCs. In the latter case, the RuleEngine automatically translates the declarative rule into a job to be executed on a parallel data processing framework. This job outputs the set of violations and possible fixes for each violation. The RuleEngine has three layers: the *logical*, *physical*, and *execution* layers. This architecture allows BIGDANSING to (i) support a large variety of data quality rules by abstracting the rule specification process, (ii) achieve high efficiency when cleansing datasets by performing a number of physical optimizations, and (iii) scale to big datasets by fully leveraging the scalability of existing parallel data processing frameworks. Notice that, unlike a DBMS, the RuleEngine also has an execution abstraction, which allows BIGDANSING to run on top of general purpose data processing frameworks ranging from MapReduce-like systems to databases.

(1) *Logical layer.* A major goal of BIGDANSING is to allow users to express a variety of data quality rules in a simple way. This means that users should only care about the logic of their quality rules, without worrying about how to make the code distributed. To this end, BIGDANSING provides five logical operators, namely Scope, Block, Iterate, Detect, and GenFix, to express a data quality rule: Scope defines the relevant data for the rule; Block defines the group of data units among which a violation may occur; Iterate enumerates the candidate violations; Detect determines whether a candidate violation is indeed a violation; and GenFix generates a set of possible fixes for each violation. Users define these logical operators, as well as the sequence in which BIGDANSING has to run them, in their jobs. Alternatively, users provide a declarative rule and BIGDANSING translates it into a job having these five logical operators. Notice that a job represents the logical plan of a given input quality rule.

(2) *Physical layer.* In this layer, BIGDANSING receives a logical plan and transforms it into an optimized physical plan of physical operators. Like in DBMSs, a physical plan specifies how a logical plan is implemented. For example, Block could be implemented by either hash-based or range-based methods. A physical operator in BIGDANSING also contains extra information, such as the input dataset and the degree of parallelism. Overall, BIGDANSING processes a logical plan through two main optimization steps, namely the *plan consolidation* and the *data access optimization*, through the use of specialized join and data access operators.

(3) *Execution layer.* In this layer, BIGDANSING determines how a physical plan will be actually executed on the underlying parallel data processing framework. It transforms a physical plan into an execution plan which consists of a set of system-dependent operations, *e.g.,* a Spark or MapReduce job. BIGDANSING runs the generated execution plan on the underlying system. Then, it collects all the violations and possible fixes produced by this execution. As a result, users get the benefits of parallel data processing frameworks by just providing few lines of code for the logical operators.

Once BIGDANSING has collected the set of violations and possible fixes, it proceeds to repair (*cleanse*) the input dirty dataset. At this point, the repair process is independent from the number of rules and their semantics, as the repair algorithm considers only the set of violations and their possible fixes. The way the final fixes are chosen among all the possible ones strongly depends on the repair algorithm itself. Instead of proposing a new repair algorithm, we present in Section 5 two different approaches to implement existing algorithms in a distributed setting. Correctness and termination properties of the original algorithms are preserved in our extensions. Alternatively, expert users can plug in their own repair algorithms. In the algorithms that we extend, each repair step greedily eliminates violations with possible fixes while minimizing the cost function in Section 2.1. An iterative process, *i.e.,* detection and repair, terminates if there are no more violations or there are only violations with no corresponding possible fixes. The repair step may introduce new violations on previously fixed data units and a new step may decide to again update these units. To ensure termination, the algorithm put a special variable on such units after a fixed number of iterations (which is a user defined parameter), thus eliminating the possibility of future violations on the same data.

3. RULE SPECIFICATION

BIGDANSING abstraction consists of five logical operators: Scope, Block, Iterate, Detect, and GenFix, which are powerful enough to express a large spectrum of cleansing tasks. While Detect and GenFix are the two general operators that model the data cleansing process, Scope, Block, and Iterate enable the efficient and scalable execution of that process. Generally speaking, Scope reduces the amount of data that has to be treated, Block reduces the search space for the candidate violation generation, and Iterate efficiently traverses the reduced search space to generate all candidate violations. It is worth noting that these five operators do not model the repair process itself (*i.e.*, a repair algorithm). The system translates these operators along with a, generated or user-provided, BIGDANSING job into a *logical plan*.

3.1 Logical Operators

As mentioned earlier, BIGDANSING defines the input data through *data units* Us on which the logical operators operate. While such a fine-granular model might seem to incur a high cost as BIGDANSING calls an operator for each U, it in fact allows to apply an operator in a highly parallel fashion.

In the following, we define the five operators provided by BIGDANSING and illustrate them in Figure 2 using the dataset and rule FD ϕ_F (zipcode $\rightarrow$ city) of Example 1. Notice that the following listings are automatically generated by the system for declarative rules. Users can either modify this code or provide their own for the UDFs case.

(1) Scope removes irrelevant data units from a dataset. For each data unit U, Scope outputs a set of filtered data units, which can be an empty set.

$$\mathsf{Scope}(U) \rightarrow \mathsf{list}\langle U' \rangle$$

Notice that Scope outputs a list of Us as it allows data units to be replicated. This operator is important as it allows BIGDANSING to focus only on data units that are relevant to a given rule. For instance, in Figure 2, Scope projects on attributes zipcode and city. Listing 4 (Appendix B) shows the lines of code for Scope in rule ϕ_F.

(2) Block groups data units sharing the same blocking key. For each data unit U, Block outputs a blocking key.

$$\mathsf{Block}(U) \rightarrow \mathsf{key}$$

The Block operator is crucial for BIGDANSING's scalability as it narrows down the number of data units on which a violation might occur. For example, in Figure 2, Block groups tuples on attribute zipcode, resulting in three blocks, with each block having a distinct zipcode. Violations might occur inside these blocks only and not across blocks. See Listing 5 (Appendix B) for the single line of code required by this operator fro rule ϕ_F.

(3) Iterate defines how to combine data units Us to generate candidate violations. This operator takes as input a list of lists of data units Us (because it might take the output of several previous operators) and outputs a single U, a pair of Us, or a list of Us.

$$\mathsf{Iterate}(\mathsf{list}\langle\mathsf{list}\langle U\rangle\rangle) \rightarrow U' \mid \langle U_i, U_j\rangle \mid \mathsf{list}\langle U''\rangle$$

This operator allows to avoid the quadratic complexity for generating candidate violations. For instance, in Figure 2,

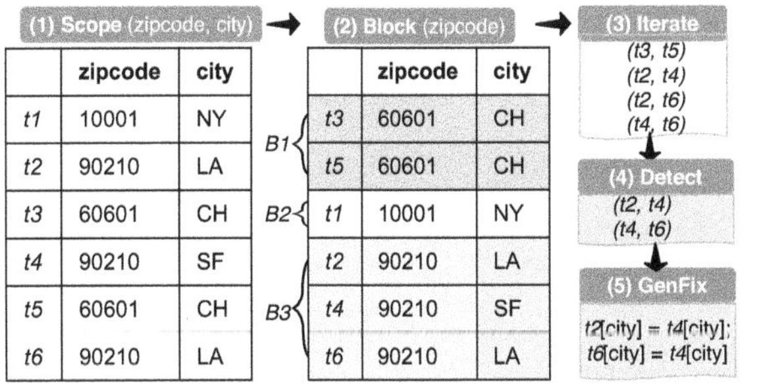

Figure 2: Logical operators execution for rule FD ϕ_F

Iterate passes each unique combination of two tuples inside each block, producing four pairs only (instead of 13 pairs): (t_3, t_5) from B_1, (t_2, t_4), (t_2, t_6), and (t_4, t_6) from B_3. Listing 6 (Appendix B) shows the code required by this Iterate operator for rule ϕ_F.

(4) Detect takes a single U, *a pair-U*, or a *list o Us*, as input and outputs a list of violations, possibly empty.

$$\mathsf{Detect}(U \mid \langle U_i, U_j\rangle \mid \mathsf{list}\langle U'\rangle) \rightarrow \{\mathsf{list}\langle\mathsf{violation}\rangle\}$$

Considering three types of inputs for Detect allows us to achieve better parallelization by distinguishing between different granularities of the input. For example, having 1K Us as input, rather than a single list of Us, would allow us to run 1K parallel instances of Detect (instead of a single Detect instance). In Figure 2, Detect outputs two violations, $v_1 = (t_2, t_4)$ and $v_2 = (t_6, t_4)$, as they have different values for city; and it requires the lines of code in Listing 1.

```
public ArrayList<Violation> detect(TuplePair in) {
    ArrayList<Violation> lst = new ArrayList<Violation>();
    if (!in.getLeft().getCellValue(1).equals(
    in.getRight().getCellValue(1))) {
        Violation v = new Violation("zipcode => City");
        v.addTuple(in.getLeft());
        v.addTuple(in.getRight());
        lst.add(v); }
    return lst; }
```

Listing 1: Code example for the Detect operator.

(5) GenFix computes a set of possible fixes for a given violation.

$$\mathsf{GenFix}(\mathsf{violation}) \rightarrow \{\mathsf{list}\langle\mathsf{PossibleFixes}\rangle\}$$

For instance, assuming that only right-hand side values can be modified, GenFix produces one possible repair for each detected violation (Figure 2): $t_2[\mathsf{city}] = t_4[\mathsf{city}]$ and $t_6[\mathsf{city}] = t_4[\mathsf{city}]$. Listing 2 shows the code for this GenFix.

```
public ArrayList<Fix> GenFix(Violation v) {
    ArrayList<Fix> result = new ArrayList<Fix>();
    Tuple t1 = v.getLeft();
    Tuple t2 = v.getRight();
    Cell c1 = new Cell(t1.getID(),"City",t1.getCellValue(1));
    Cell c2 = new Cell(t2.getID(),"City",t2.getCellValue(1));
    result.add(new Fix(c1,"=",c2));
    return result; }
```

Listing 2: Code example for the GenFix operator.

Additionally, to better specify the data flow among the different operators, we introduce a *label* to stamp a data item and track how it is being processed.

In contrast to DBMS operators, BIGDANSING's operators are UDFs, which allow users to plug in any logic. As a result, we are not restricted to a specific data model. However, for

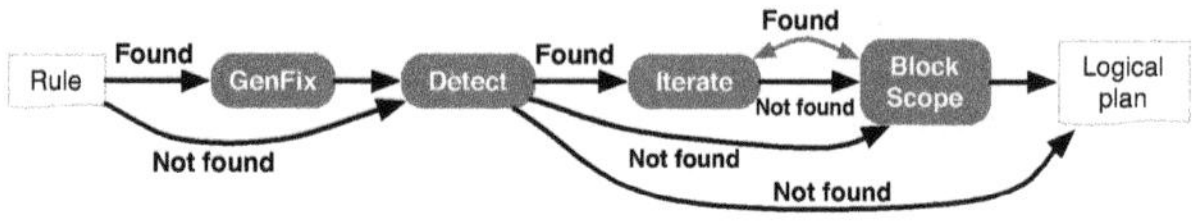

Figure 3: Planner execution flow

ease of explanations all of our examples assume relational data. We report an RDF data cleansing example in Appendix C. We also report in Appendix D the code required to write the same rule in a distributed environment, such as Spark. The proposed templates for the operators allow users to get distributed detection without any expertise on Spark, only by providing from 3 to 16 lines of Java code. The benefit of the abstraction should be apparent at this point: (i) ease-of-use for non-expert users and (ii) better scalability thanks to its abstraction.

3.2 The Planning Process

The logical layer of BIGDANSING takes as input a set of labeled logical operators together with a job and outputs a logical plan. The system starts by validating whether the provided job is correct by checking that all referenced logical operators are defined and at least one Detect is specified. Recall that for declarative rules, such as CFDs and DCs, users do not need to provide any job, as BIGDANSING automatically generates a job along with the logical operators.

After validating the provided job, BIGDANSING generates a logical plan (Figure 3) that: (i) *must* have at least one input dataset D_i; (ii) *may* have one or more Scope operators; (iii) *may* have one Block operator or more linked to an Iterate operator; (iv) *must* have at least one Detect operator to possibly produce a set of violations; and (v) *may* have one GenFix operator for each Detect operator to generate possible fixes for each violation.

BIGDANSING looks for a corresponding Iterate operator for each Detect. If Iterate is not specified, BIGDANSING generates one according to the input required by the Detect operator. Then, it looks for Block and Scope operators that match the input label of the Detect operator. If an Iterate operator is specified, BIGDANSING identifies all Block operators whose input label match the input label of the Iterate. Then, it uses the input labels of the Iterate operator to find other possible Iterate operators in reverse order. Each new detected Iterate operator is added to the plan with the Block operators related to its input labels. Once it has processed all Iterate operators, it finally looks for Scope operators.

In case the Scope or Block operators are missing, BIGDANSING pushes the input dataset to the next operator in the logical plan. If no GenFix operator is provided, the output of the Detect operator is written to disk. For example, assume the logical plan in Figure 4, which is generated by BIGDANSING when a user provides the job in Appendix A. We observe that dataset $D1$ is sent directly to a Scope and a Block operator. Similarly, dataset $D2$ is sent directly to an Iterate operator. We also observe that one can also iterate over the output of previous Iterate operators (*e.g.,* over output D_M). This flexibility allows users to express complex data quality rules, such as in the form of "bushy" plans as shown in Appendix E.

4. BUILDING PHYSICAL PLANS

When translating a logical plan, BIGDANSING exploits two main opportunities to derive an optimized physical plan: (i) static analysis of the logical plan and (ii) alternative

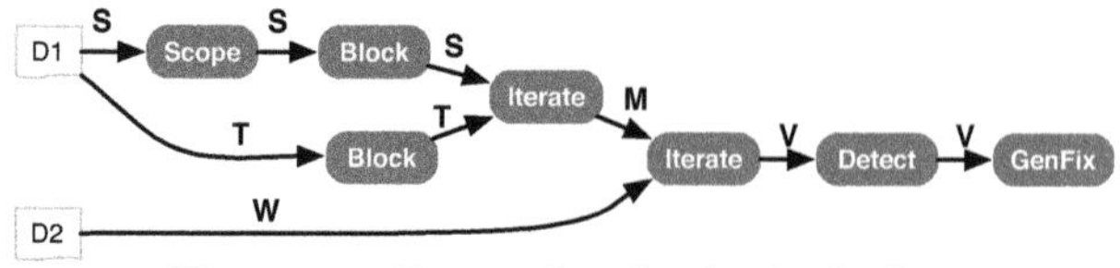

Figure 4: Example of a logical plan

translations for each logical operator. Since quality rules may involve joins over ordering comparisons, we also introduce an efficient algorithm for these cases. We discuss these aspects in this section. In addition, we discuss data storage and access issues in Appendix F.

4.1 Physical Operators

There are two kinds of physical operators: *wrappers* and *enhancers*. A wrapper simply invokes a logical operator. Enhancers replace wrappers to take advantage of different optimization opportunities.

A wrapper invokes a logical operator together with the corresponding physical details, *e.g.,* input dataset and schema details (if available). For clarity, we discard such physical details in all the definitions below. In contrast to the logical layer, BIGDANSING invokes a physical operator for a set D of data units, rather than for a single unit. This enables the processing of multiple units in a single function call. For each logical operator, we define a corresponding wrapper.

(1) PScope applies a user-defined selection and projection over a set of data units D and outputs a dataset $D' \subset D$.

$$\mathsf{PScope}(D) \rightarrow \{D'\}$$

(2) PBlock takes a dataset D as input and outputs a list of key-value pairs defined by users.

$$\mathsf{PBlock}(D) \rightarrow \mathsf{map}\langle\mathsf{key}, \mathsf{list}\langle U\rangle\rangle$$

(3) PIterate takes a list of lists of Us as input and outputs their cross product or a user-defined combination.

$$\mathsf{PIterate}(\mathsf{list}\langle\mathsf{list}\langle U\rangle\rangle) \rightarrow \mathsf{list}\langle U\rangle \mid \mathsf{list}\langle\mathsf{Pair}\langle U\rangle\rangle$$

(4) PDetect receives either a list of data units Us or a list of data unit pairs U-pairs and produces a list of violations.

$$\mathsf{PDetect}(\mathsf{list}\langle U\rangle \mid \mathsf{list}\langle\mathsf{Pair}\langle U\rangle\rangle) \rightarrow \mathsf{list}\langle Violation\rangle$$

(5) PGenFix receives a list of violations as input and outputs a list of a set of possible fixes, where each set of fixes belongs to a different input violation.

$$\mathsf{PGenFix}(\mathsf{list}\langle Violation\rangle) \rightarrow \mathsf{list}\langle\{PossibleFixes\}\rangle$$

With declarative rules, the operations over a dataset are known, which enables algorithmic opportunities to improve performance. Notice that one could also discover such operations with code analysis over the UDFs [20]. However, we leave this extension to future work. BIGDANSING exploits such optimization opportunities via three new enhancers operators: *CoBlock*, *UCrossProduct*, and *OCJoin*. CoBlock is a physical operator that allows to group multiple datasets by a given key. UCrossProduct and OCJoin are basically two additional different implementations for the PIterate operator. We further explain these three enhancers operators in the next section.

Algorithm 1: Logical plan consolidation

input : LogicalPlan lp
output: LogicalPlan clp
1 PlanBuilder lpb = new PlanBuilder();
2 **for** *logical operator* $lop_i \in lp$ **do**
3 $\quad lop_j \leftarrow$ findMatchingLO(lop_i, lp);
4 $\quad$ DS$_1 \leftarrow$ getSourceDS(lop_i);
5 $\quad$ DS$_2 \leftarrow$ getSourceDS(lop_j);
6 $\quad$ **if** $DS_1 == DS_2$ **then**
7 $\quad\quad$ lop$_c \leftarrow$ getLabelsFuncs(lop_i, lop_j);
8 $\quad\quad$ lop$_c$.setInput(DS_1, DS_2);
9 $\quad\quad$ lpb.add(lop_c);
10 $\quad\quad$ lp.remove(lop_i, lop_j);
11 **if** *lpb.hasConsolidatedOps* **then**
12 $\quad$ lpb.add(lp.getOperators());
13 $\quad$ return lpb.generateConsolidatedLP();
14 **else**
15 $\quad$ return lp;

4.2 From Logical to Physical Plan

As we mentioned earlier, optimizing a logical plan is performed by static analysis (plan consolidation) and by plugging enhancers (operators translation) whenever possible.

Plan Consolidation. Whenever logical operators use a different label for the same dataset, BigDansing translates them into distinct physical operators. BigDansing has to create multiple copies of the same dataset, which it might broadcast to multiple nodes. Thus, both the memory footprint at compute nodes and the network traffic are increased. To address this problem, BigDansing consolidates redundant logical operators into a single logical operator. Hence, by applying the same logical operator several times on the same set of data units using shared scans, BigDansing is able to increase data locality and reduce I/O overhead.

Algorithm 1 details the consolidation process for an input logical plan lp. For each operator lop_i, the algorithm looks for a matching operator lop_j (Lines 2-3). If lop_j has the same input dataset as lop_i, BigDansing consolidates them into lop_c (Lines 4-6). The newly consolidated operator lop_c takes the labels, functions, and datasets from lop_i and lop_j (Lines 7-8). Next, BigDansing adds lop_c into a logical plan builder lpb and removes lop_i and lop_j from lp (Lines 9-10). At last, if any operator was consolidated, it adds the non-consolidated operators to lpb and returns the consolidated logical plan (Lines 11-13). Otherwise, it returns lp (Line 15).

Let us now illustrate the consolidation process with an example. Consider a DC on the TPC-H database stating that if a customer and a supplier have the same name and phone they must be in the same city. Formally,

$$DC : \forall t_1, t_2 \in D1, \neg(t_1.c\_name = t_2.s\_name \wedge t_1.c\_phone = t_2.s\_phone \wedge t_1.c\_city \neq t_2.s\_city) \quad (1)$$

For this DC, BigDansing generates the logical plan in Figure 5(a) with operators Scope and Block applied twice over the same input dataset. It then consolidates redundant logical operators into a single one (Figure 5(b)) thereby reducing the overhead of reading an input dataset multiple times. The logical plan consolidation is only applied when it does not affect the original labeling of the operators.

Operators Translation. Once a logical plan have been consolidated, BigDansing translates the consolidated logical plan into a physical plan. It maps each logical operator to its corresponding wrapper, which in turn maps to one or more physical operators. For example, it produces the physical plan in Figure 5(c) for the consolidated logical plan in Figure 5(b). For enhancers, BigDansing exploits some particular information from the data cleansing process. Below, we detail these three enhancers operators as well as in which cases they are used by our system.

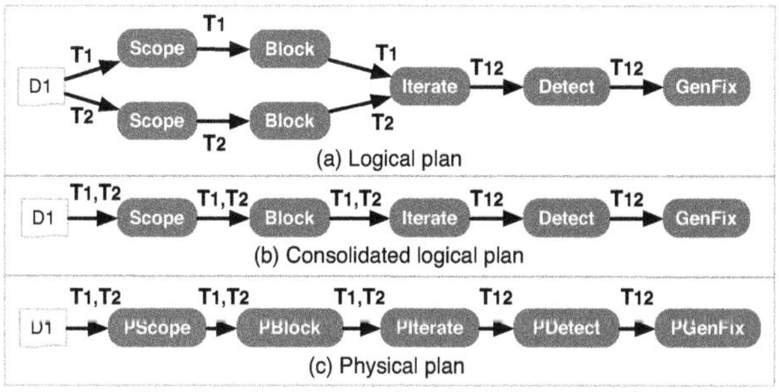

Figure 5: Plans for DC in rule 1

- *CoBlock* takes multiple input datasets $\mathbb{D}$ and applies a group-by on a given key. This would limit the comparisons required by the rule to only blocks with the same key from the different datasets. An example is shown in Figure 16 (Appendix E). Similar to the CoGroup defined in [28], in the output of CoBlock, all keys from both inputs are collected into bags. The output of this operator is a map from a key value to the list of data units sharing that key value. We formally define this operator as:

$$\mathsf{CoBlock}\ (\mathbb{D}) \rightarrow \mathsf{map}\langle \mathsf{key}, \mathsf{list}\langle \mathsf{list}\langle U\rangle\rangle\rangle$$

If two non-consolidated Block operators' outputs go to the same Iterate and then to a single PDetect, BigDansing translates them into a single CoBlock. Using CoBlock allows us to reduce the number of candidate violations for the Detect. This is because Iterate generates candidates only inside and not across CoBlocks (see Figure 6).

- *UCrossProduct* receives a single input dataset D and applies a self cross product over it. This operation is usually performed in cleansing processes that would output the same violations irrespective of the order of the input of Detect. UCrossProduct avoids redundant comparisons, reducing the number of comparisons from n^2 to $\frac{n\times(n-1)}{2}$, with n being the number of units Us in the input. For example, the output of the logical operator Iterate in Figure 2 is the result of UCrossProduct within each block; there are four pairs instead of thirteen, since the operator avoids three comparisons for the elements in block B1 and six for the ones in B3 of Figure 2. Formally:

$$\mathsf{UCrossProduct}(D) \rightarrow \mathsf{list}\langle \mathsf{Pair}\langle U\rangle\rangle$$

If, for a single dataset, the declarative rules contain only symmetric comparisons, *e.g.*, $=$ and $\neq$, then the order in which the tuples are passed to PDetect (or to the next logical operator if any) does not matter. In this case, BigDansing uses UCrossProduct to avoid materializing many unnecessary pairs of data units, such as for the Iterate operator in Figure 2. It also uses UCrossProduct when: (i) users do not provide a matching Block operator for the Iterate operator; or (ii) users do not provide any Iterate or Block operator.

- *OCJoins* performs a self join on one or more ordering comparisons (*i.e.*, $<, >, \geq, \leq$). This is a very common operation

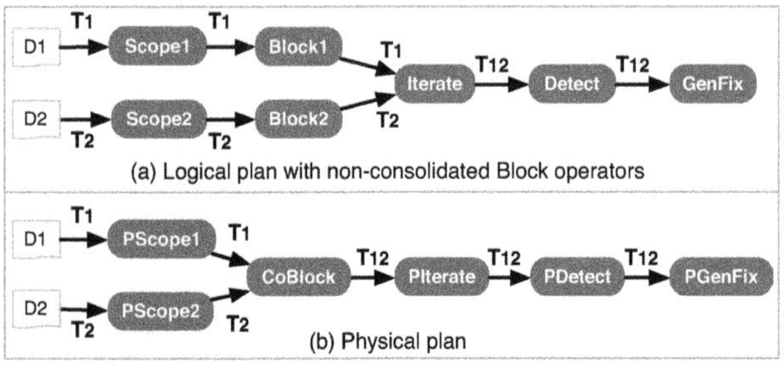

Figure 6: Example plans with CoBlock

in rules such as DCs. Thus, BigDansing provides OCJoin, which is an efficient operator to deal with join ordering comparisons. It takes input dataset D and applies a number of join conditions, returning a list of joining U-pairs. We formally define this operator as follows:

$$\mathsf{OCJoin}(D) \rightarrow \mathsf{list}\langle\mathsf{Pair}\langle U\rangle\rangle$$

Every time BigDansing recognizes joins conditions defined with ordering comparisons in PDetect, *e.g.*, ϕ_D, it translates Iterate into a OCJoin implementation. Then, it passes OCJoin output to a PDetect operator (or to the next logical operator if any). We discuss this operator in detail in Section 4.3.

We report details for the transformation of the physical operators to two distributed platforms in Appendix G.

4.3 Fast Joins with Ordering Comparisons

Existing systems handle joins over ordering comparisons using a cross product and a post-selection predicate, leading to poor performance. BigDansing provides an efficient ad-hoc join operator, referred to as OCJoin, to handle these cases. The main goal of OCJoin is to increase the ability to process joins over ordering comparisons in parallel and to reduce its complexity by reducing the algorithm's search space. In a nutshell, OCJoin first range partitions a set of data units and sorts each of the resulting partitions in order to validate the inequality join conditions in a distributed fashion. OCJoin works in four main phases: *partitioning*, *sorting*, *pruning*, and *joining* (see Algorithm 2).

Partitioning. OCJoin first selects the attribute, *PartAtt*, on which to partition the input D (line 1). We assume that all join conditions have the same output cardinality. This can be improved using cardinality estimation techniques [9,27], but it is beyond the scope of the paper. OCJoin chooses the first attribute involved in the first condition. For instance, consider again ϕ_D (Example 1), OCJoin sets *PartAtt* to rate attribute. Then, OCJoin partitions the input dataset D into *nbParts* range partitions based on *PartAtt* (line 2). As part of this partitioning, OCJoin distributes the resulting partitions across all available computing nodes. Notice that OCJoin runs the range partitioning in parallel. Next, OCJoin forks a parallel process for each range partition k_i to run the three remaining phases (lines 3-14).

Sorting. For each partition, OCJoin creates as many sorting lists (*Sorts*) as inequality conditions are in a rule (lines 4-5). For example, OCJoin creates two sorted lists for ϕ_D: one sorted on rate and the other sorted on salary. Each list contains the attribute values on which the sort order is and the tuple identifiers. Note that OCJoin only performs a local sorting in this phase and hence it does not require any data transfer across nodes. Since multiple copies of a

Algorithm 2: OCJoin

```
   input : Dataset D, Condition conds[], Integer nbParts
   output: List Tuples⟨Tuple⟩
   // PARTITIONING PHASE
1  PartAtt ← getPrimaryAtt(conds[].getAttribute());
2  K ← RangePartition(D, PartAtt, nbParts);
3  for each k_i ∈ K do
4      for each c_j ∈ conds[] do // SORTING
5          Sorts[j] ← sort(k_i, c_j.getAttribute());
6      for each k_l ∈ {k_{i+1}...k_{|K|}} do
7          if overlap(k_i, k_l, PartAtt) then // PRUNING
8              tuples = ∅;
9              for each c_j ∈ conds[] do // JOINING
10                 tuples ← join(k_i, k_l, Sorts[j], tuples);
11                 if tuples == ∅ then
12                     break;
13             if tuples != ∅ then
14                 Tuples.add(tuples);
```

partition may exist in multiple computing nodes, we apply *sorting* before *pruning* and *joining* phases to ensure that each partition is sorted at most once.

Pruning. Once all partitions $k_i \in K$ are internally sorted, OCJoin can start joining each of these partitions based on the inequality join conditions. However, this would require transferring large amounts of data from one node to another. To circumvent such an overhead, OCJoin inspects the *min* and *max* values of each partition to avoid joining partitions that do not overlap in their *min* and *max* range (the *pruning* phase, line 7). Non-overlapping partitions do not produce any join result. If the selectivity values for the different inequality conditions are known, OCJoin can order the different joins accordingly.

Joining. OCJoin finally proceeds to join the overlapping partitions and outputs the join results (lines 9-14). For this, it applies a distributed sort merge join over the sorted lists, where some partitions are broadcast to other machines while keeping the rest locally. Through pruning, OCJoin tells the underlying distributed processing platform which partitions to join. It is up to that platform to select the best approach to minimize the number of broadcast partitions.

5. DISTRIBUTED REPAIR ALGORITHMS

Most of the existing repair techniques [5–7,11,17,23,34] are centralized. We present two approaches to implement a repair algorithm in BigDansing. First, we show how our system can run a centralized data repair algorithm in parallel, without changing the algorithm. In other words, BigDansing treats that algorithm as a black box (Section 5.1). Second, we design a distributed version of the widely used *equivalence class* algorithm [5,7,11,17] (Section 5.2).

5.1 Scaling Data Repair as a Black Box

Overall, we divide a repair task into independent smaller repair tasks. For this, we represent the violation graph as a hypergraph containing the violations and their possible fixes. The nodes represent the elements and each hyperedge covers a set of elements that together violate a rule, along with possible repairs. We then divide the hypergraph into smaller independent subgraphs, *i.e.*, *connected components*,

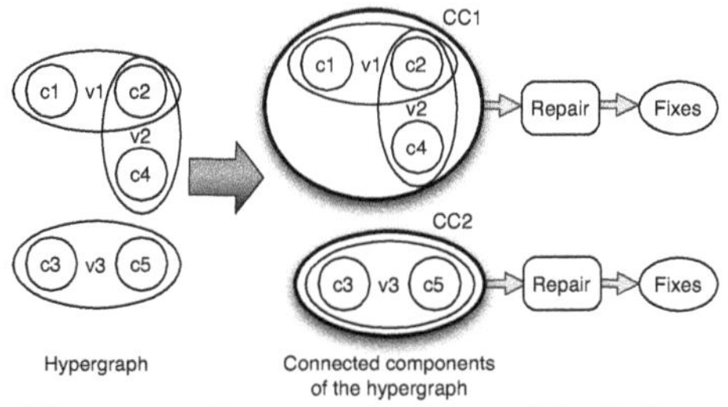

Figure 7: Data repair as a black box.

and we pass each connected component to an *independent data repair instance.*

Connected components. Given an input set of violations, form at least one rule, BIGDANSING first creates their hypergraph representation of such possible fixes in a distributed manner. It then uses GraphX [37] to find all connected components in the hypergraph. GraphX, in turn, uses the Bulk Synchronous Parallel (BSP) graph processing model [25] to process the hypergraph in parallel. As a result, BIGDANSING gets a connected component ID for each hyperedge. It then groups hyperedges by the connected component ID. Figure 7 shows an example of connected components in a hypergraph containing three violations $v1$, $v2$, and $v3$. Note that violations $v1$ and $v2$ can be caused by different rules. Violations $v1$ and $v2$ are grouped in a single connected component $CC1$, because they share element $c2$. In contrast, $v3$ is assigned to a different connected component $CC2$, because it does not share any element with $v1$ or $v2$.

Independent data repair instance. Once all connected components are computed, BIGDANSING assigns each of them to an independent data repair instance and runs such repair instances in a distributed manner (right-side of Figure 7). When all data repair instances generate the required fixes, BIGDANSING updates the input dataset and pass it again to the RuleEngine to detect potential violations introduced by the RepairAlgorithm. The number of iterations required to fix all violations depends on the input rules, the dataset, and the repair algorithm.

Dealing with big connected components. If a connected component does not fit in memory, BIGDANSING uses a k-way multilevel hypergraph partitioning algorithm [22] to divide it into k equal parts and run them on distinct machines. Unfortunately, naively performing this process can lead to inconsistencies and contradictory choices in the repair. Moreover, it can fix the same violation independently in two machines, thus introducing unnecessary changes to the repair. We illustrate this problem with an example.

Example 2: Consider a relational schema D with 3 attributes A, B, C and 2 FDs $A \rightarrow B$ and $C \rightarrow B$. Given the instance $[t_1]$(a1, b1, c1), $[t_2]$(a1, b2, c1), all data values are in violation: $t_1.A$, $t_1.B$, $t_2.A$, $t_2.B$ for the first FD and $t_1.B$, $t_1.C$, $t_2.B$, $t_2.C$ for the second one. Assuming the compute nodes have enough memory only for five values, we need to solve the violations by executing two instances of the algorithm on two different nodes. Regardless of the selected tuple, suppose the first compute node repairs a value on attribute A, and the second one a value on attribute C. When we put the two repairs together and check their consistency, the updated instance is a valid solution, but the repair is not minimal because a single update on attribute B would have solved both violations. However, if the first node fixes $t_1.B$ by assigning value "b2" and the second one fixes $t_2.B$ with "b1", not only there are two changes, but the final instance is also inconsistent. □

We tackle the above problem by assigning the role of *master* to one machine and the role of *slave* to the rest. Every machine applies a repair in isolation, but we introduce an extra test in the union of the results. For the violations that are solved by the master, we mark its changes as immutable, which prevents us to change an element more than once. If a change proposed by a slave contradicts a possible repair that involve a master's change, the slave repair is undone and a new iteration is triggered. As a result, the algorithm always reaches a fix point to produce a clean dataset, because an updated value cannot change in the following iterations.

BIGDANSING currently provides two repair algorithms using this approach: the equivalence class algorithm and a general hypergraph-based algorithm [6, 23]. Users can also implement their own repair algorithm if it is compatible with BIGDANSING's repair interface.

5.2 Scalable Equivalence Class Algorithm

The idea of the equivalence class based algorithm [5] is to first group all elements that should be equivalent together, and to then decide how to assign values to each group. An *equivalence class* consists of pairs of the form (t, A), where t is a data unit and A is an element. In a dataset D, each unit t and each element A in t have an associated equivalence class, denoted by $\mathsf{eq}(t, A)$. In a repair, a unique *target value* is assigned to each equivalence class E, denoted by $\mathsf{targ}(E)$. That is, for all $(t, A) \in E$, $t[A]$ has the same value $\mathsf{targ}(E)$. The algorithm selects the target value for each equivalence class to obtain a repair with the minimum overall cost.

We extend the equivalence class algorithm to a distributed setting by modeling it as a distributed word counting algorithm based on map and reduce functions. However, in contrast to a standard word count algorithm, we use two map-reduce sequences. The first map function maps the violations' possible fixes for each connected component into key-value pairs of the form ⟨⟨ccID,value⟩,count⟩. The key ⟨ccID,value⟩ is a composite key that contains the connected component ID and the element value for each possible fix. The value *count* represents the frequency of the element value, which we initialize to 1. The first *reduce* function counts the occurrences of the key-value pairs that share the same connected component ID and element value. It outputs key-value pairs of the form ⟨⟨ccID,value⟩,count⟩. Note that if an element exists in multiple fixes, we only count its value once. After this first map-reduce sequence, another map function takes the output of the reduce function to create new key-value pairs of the form ⟨ccID,⟨value,count⟩⟩. The key is the connected component ID and the value is the frequency of each element value. The last reduce selects the element value with the highest frequency to be assigned to all the elements in the connected component $ccID$.

6. EXPERIMENTAL STUDY

We evaluate BIGDANSING using both real and synthetic datasets with various rules (Section 6.1). We consider a variety of scenarios to evaluate the system and answer the following questions: (i) how well does it perform compared with baseline systems in a single node setting (Section 6.2)? (ii) how well does it scale to different dataset sizes compared to the state-of-the-art distributed systems (Section 6.3)? (iii) how well does it scale in terms of the number of nodes

Dataset	Rows	Dataset	Rows
$TaxA_1$–$TaxA_5$	100K – 40M	customer2	32M
$TaxB_1$–$TaxB_3$	100K – 3M	NCVoter	9M
$TPCH_1$–$TPCH_{10}$	100K – 1907M	HAI	166k
customer1	19M		

Table 2: Statistics of the datasets

Identifier	Rule
φ_1 (FD):	Zipcode → City
φ_2 (DC):	$\forall t_1, t_2 \in TaxB, \neg(t_1.\mathsf{Salary} > t2.\mathsf{Salary}$ $\wedge t_1.\mathsf{Rate} < t_2.\mathsf{Rate})$
φ_3 (FD):	o_custkey → c_address
φ_4 (UDF):	Two rows in Customer are duplicates
φ_5 (UDF):	Two rows in NCVoter are duplicates
φ_6 (FD):	Zipcode → State
φ_7 (FD):	PhoneNumber → Zipcode
φ_8 (FD):	ProviderID → City, PhoneNumber

Table 3: Integrity constraints used for testing

(Section 6.4)? (iv) how well does its abstraction support a variety of data cleansing tasks, e.g., for deduplication (Section 6.5)? and (v) how do its different techniques improve performance and what is its repair accuracy (Section 6.6)?

6.1 Setup

Table 2 summarizes the datasets and Table 3 shows the rules we use for our experiments.

(1) TaxA. Represents personal tax information in the US [11]. Each row contains a person's name, contact information, and tax information. For this dataset, we use the FD rule φ_1 in Table 3. We introduced errors by adding random text to attributes City and State at a 10% rate.

(2) TaxB. We generate TaxB by adding 10% numerical random errors on the Rate attribute of TaxA. Our goal is to validate the efficiency with rules that have inequality conditions only, such as DC φ_2 in Table 3.

(3) TPCH. From the TPC-H benchmark data [2], we joined the lineitem and customer tables and applied 10% random errors on the address. We use this dataset to test FD rule φ_3.

(4) Customer. In our deduplication experiment, we use TPC-H customer with 4.5 million rows to generate tables customer1 with 3x exact duplicates and customer2 with 5x exact duplicates. Then, we randomly select 20% of the total number of tuples, in both relations, and duplicate them with random edits on attributes name and phone.

(5) NCVoter. This is a real dataset that contains North Carolina voter information. We added 20% random duplicate rows with random edits in name and phone attributes.

(6) Healthcare Associated Infections (HAI) (http://www.hospitalcompare.hhs.gov). This real dataset contains hospital information and statistics measurements for infections developed during treatment. We added 10% random errors on the attributes covered by the FDs and tested four combinations of rules (φ_6 – φ_8 from Table 3). Each rule combination has its own dirty dataset.

To our knowledge, there exists only one full-fledged data cleansing system that can support all the rules in Table 3:

(1) NADEEF [7]: An open-source single-node platform supporting both declarative and user defined quality rules.

(2) PostgreSQL v9.3: Since declarative quality rules can be represented as SQL queries, we also compare to PostgreSQL for violation detection. To maximize benefits from large main memory, we configured it using pgtune [30].

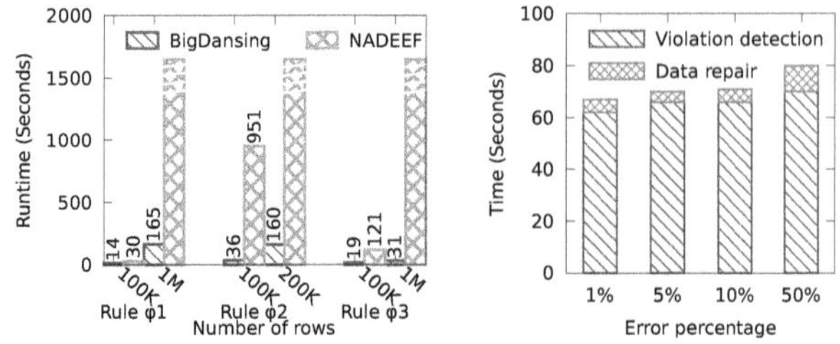

(a) Rules φ_1, φ_2, and φ_3. (b) Rule φ_1.

Figure 8: Data cleansing times.

The two declarative constraints, DC φ_2 and FD φ_3 in Table 3, are translated to SQL as shown below.

φ_2:	SELECT a.Salary, b.Salary, a.Rate, b.Rate FROM TaxB a JOIN TaxB b WHERE a.Salary > b.Salary AND a.Rate < b.Rate;
φ_3:	SELECT a.o_custkey, a.c_address, b.c_address FROM TPCH a JOIN TPCH b ON a.custkey = b.custkey WHERE a.c_address ≠ b.c_address;

We also consider two parallel data processing frameworks:

(3) Shark 0.8.0 [38]: This is a scalable data processing engine for fast data analysis. We selected Shark due to its scalability advantage over existing distributed SQL engines.

(4) Spark SQL v1.0.2:It is an experimental extension of Spark v1.0 that allows users run relational queries natively on Spark using SQL or HiveQL. We selected this system as, like BigDansing, it runs natively on top of Spark.

We ran our experiments in two different settings: (i) a single-node setting using a Dell Precision T7500 with two 64-bit quad-core Intel Xeon X5550 (8 physical cores and 16 CPU threads) and 58GB RAM and (ii) a multi-node setting using a compute cluster of 17 Shuttle SH55J2 machines (1 master with 16 workers) equipped with Intel i5 processors with 16GB RAM constructed as a star network.

6.2 Single-Node Experiments

For these experiments, we start comparing BigDansing with NADEEF in the execution times of the whole cleansing process (*i.e.,* detection and repair). Figure 8(a) shows the performance of both systems using the TaxA and TPCH datasets with 100K and 1M (200K for φ_2) rows. We observe that BigDansing is more than three orders of magnitude faster than NADEEF in rules φ_1 (1M) and φ_2 (200K), and φ_3 (1M). In fact, NADEEF is only "competitive" in rule φ_1 (100K), where BigDansing is only twice faster. The high superiority of BigDansing comes from two main reasons: (i) In contrast to NADEEF, it provides a finer granular abstraction allowing users to specify rules more efficiently; and (ii) It performs rules with inequality conditions in an efficient way (using OCJoin). In addition, NADEEF issues thousands of SQL queries to the underlying DBMS. for detecting violations. We do not report results for larger datasets because NADEEF was not able to run the *repair* process for more than 1M rows (300K for φ_2).

We also observed that violation detection was dominating the entire data cleansing process. Thus, we ran an experiment for rule φ_1 in TaxA with 1M rows by varying the error rate. Violation detection takes more than 90% of the time, regardless of the error rate (Figure 8(b)). In particular, we observe that even for a very high error rate (50%), the violation detection phase still dominates the cleansing process. Notice that for more complex rules, such as rule φ_2, the dominance of the violation detection is even ampli-

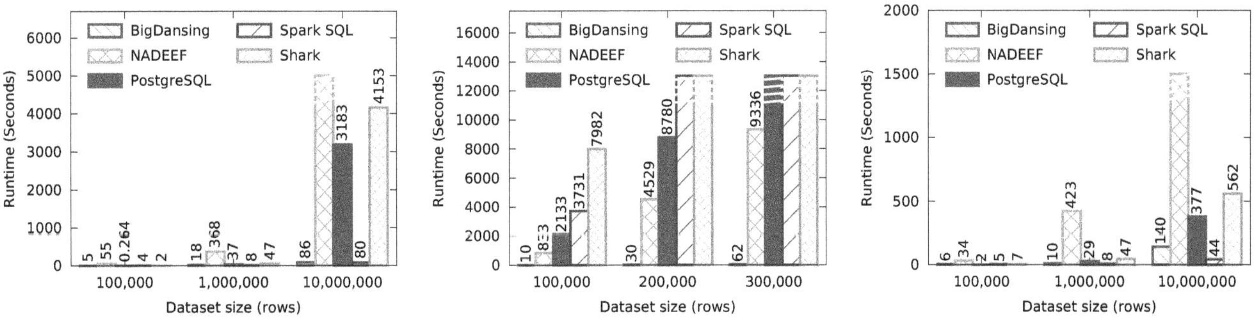

(a) TaxA data with φ_1 (b) TaxB data with φ_2 (c) TPCH data with φ_3

Figure 9: Single-node experiments with φ_1, φ_2, and φ_1

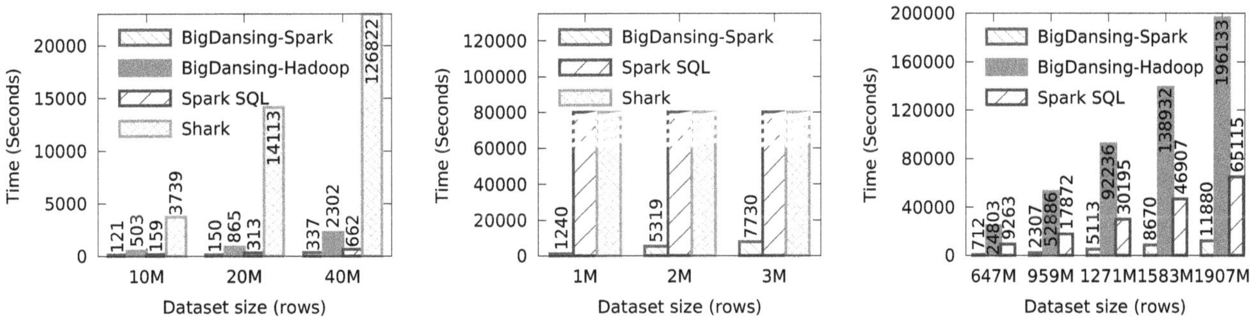

(a) TaxA data with φ_1 (b) TaxB data with φ_2 (c) Large TPCH on φ_3

Figure 10: Multi-nodes experiments with φ_1, φ_2 and φ_3

fied. Therefore, to be able to extensively evaluate BIGDANSING, we continue our experiments focusing on the violation detection phase only, except if stated otherwise.

Figures 9(a), Figure 9(b), and 9(c) show the violation detection performance of all systems for TaxA, TaxB, and TPCH datasets. TaxA and TPCH datasets have 100K, 1M, and 10M rows and TaxB has 100K, 200K, and 300K rows. With equality-based rules φ_1 and φ_3, we observe that PostgreSQL is always faster than all other systems on the small datasets (100K rows). However, once we increase the size by one order of magnitude (1M rows), we notice the advantage of BIGDANSING: it is at least twice faster than PostgreSQL and more than one order of magnitude faster than NADEEF. For the largest dataset (10M rows), BIGDANSING is almost two orders of magnitude faster than PostgreSQL for the FD in TaxA and one order of magnitude faster than PostgreSQL for the DC in TaxA. For the FD in TPCH, BIGDANSING is twice faster than PostgreSQL. It is more than three orders of magnitude faster than NADEEF for all rules. Overall, we observe that BIGDANSING performs similarly to Spark SQL. The small difference is that Spark SQL uses multithreading better than BIGDANSING. We can explain the superiority of BIGDANSING compared to the other systems along two reasons: (i) BIGDANSING reads the input dataset only once, while PostgreSQL and Shark read it twice because of the self joins; and (ii) BIGDANSING does not generate duplicate violations, while SQL engines do when comparing tuples using self-joins, such as for TaxA and TPCH's FD. Concerning the inequality-based rule φ_2, we limited the runtime to four hours for all systems. BIGDANSING is one order of magnitude faster than all other systems for 100K rows. For 200K and 300K rows, it is at least two orders of magnitude faster than all baseline systems. Such performance superiority is achieved by leveraging the inequality join optimization that is not supported by the baseline systems.

6.3 Multi-Node Experiments

We now compare BIGDANSING with Spark SQL and Shark in the multi-node setting. We also implemented a lighter version of BIGDANSING on top of Hadoop MapReduce to show BIGDANSING independence *w.r.t.* the underlying framework. We set the size of TaxA to 10M, 20M, and 40M rows. Moreover, we tested the inequality DC φ_2 on TaxB dataset with sizes of 1M, 2M, and 3M rows. We limited the runtime to 40 hours for all systems.

BIGDANSING-Spark is slightly faster than Spark SQL for the equality rules in Figure 10(a). Even though BIGDANSING-Spark and Shark are both implemented on top of Spark, BIGDANSING-Spark is up to three orders of magnitude faster than Shark. Even BIGDANSING-Hadoop is doing better than Shark (Figure 10(a)). This is because Shark does not process joins efficiently. The performance of BIGDANSING over baseline systems is magnified when dealing with inequalities. We observe that BIGDANSING-Spark is at least two orders of magnitude faster than both Spark SQL and Shark (Figure 10(b)). We had to stop Spark SQL and Shark executions after 40 hours of runtime; both Spark SQL and Shark are unable to process the inequality DC efficiently.

We also included a testing for large TPCH datasets of sizes 150GB, 200GB, 250GB, and 300GB (959M, 1271M, 1583M, and 1907M rows resp.) producing between 6.9B and 13B violations. We excluded Shark as it could not run on these larger datasets. BIGDANSING-Spark is 16 to 22 times faster than BIGDANSING-Hadoop and 6 to 8 times faster than Spark SQL (Figure 10(c)). BIGDANSING-Spark significantly outperforms Spark SQL since it has a lower I/O complexity and an optimized data cleansing physical execution plan. Moreover, the performance difference between BIGDANSING-Spark and BIGDANSING-Hadoop stems from Spark being generally faster than Hadoop; Spark is an in-memory data processing system while Hadoop is disk-based.

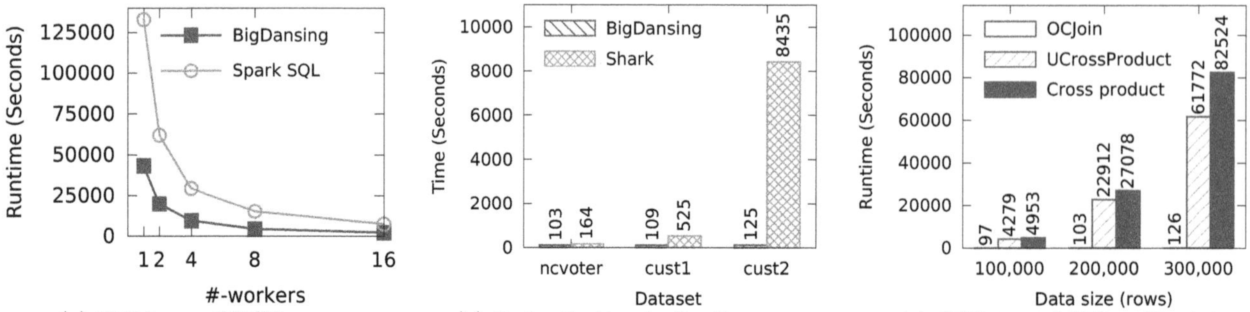

(a) 500M rows TPCH on φ_3 (b) Deduplication in BigDansing (c) OCJoin and UCrossProdut

Figure 11: Results for the experiments on (a) scale-out, (b) deduplication, and (c) physical optimizations.

6.4 Scaling BigDansing Out

We compared the speedup of BigDansing-Spark to Spark SQL when increasing the number of workers on a dataset size of 500M rows. We observe that BigDansing-Spark is at least 3 times faster than Spark SQL starting from one single worker and up to 16 (Figure 11(a)). We also notice that BigDansing-Spark is about 1.5 times faster than Spark SQL while using only half the number of workers used by Spark SQL. Although both BigDansing-Spark and Spark SQL generally have a good scalability, BigDansing-Spark performs better than Spark SQL on large input datasets since it does not copy the input data twice.

6.5 Deduplication in BigDansing

We show that one can run a deduplication task with BigDansing. We use *cust1*, *cust2*, and *NCVoters* datasets on our compute cluster. We implemented a Java version of Levenshtein distance and use it as a UDF in both BigDansing and Shark. Note that we do not consider Spark SQL in this experiment since UDFs cannot be implemented directly within Spark SQL. That is, to implement a UDF in Spark SQL the user has to either use a Hive interface or apply a post processing step on the query result. Figure 11(b) shows the results. We observe that BigDansing outperforms Shark for both small datasets as well as large datasets. In particular, we see that for cust2 BigDansing outperforms Shark up to an improvement factor of 67. These results not only show the generality of BigDansing supporting a deduplication task, but also the high efficiency of our system.

6.6 BigDansing In-Depth

Physical optimizations. We first focus on showing the benefits in performance of the UCrossProduct and OCJoin operators. We use the second inequality DC in Table 3 with TaxB dataset on our multi-node cluster. Figure 11(c) reports the results of this experiment. We notice that the UCrossProduct operator has a slight performance advantage compared to the CrossProduct operator. This performance difference increases with the dataset size. However, by using the OCJoin operator, BigDansing becomes more than two orders of magnitudes faster compared to both cross product operators (up to an improvement factor of 655).

Abstraction advantage. We now study the benefits of BigDansing's abstraction. We consider the deduplication scenario in previous section with the smallest TaxA dataset on our single-node machine. We compare the performance difference between BigDansing using its full API and BigDansing using only the Detect operator. We see in Figure 12(a) that running a UDF using the full BigDansing API makes BigDansing three orders of magnitudes faster compared to using *Detect* only. This clearly shows the benefits of the five logical operators, even for single-node settings.

Scalable data repair. We study the runtime efficiency of the repair algorithms used by BigDansing. We ran an experiment for rule φ_1 in TaxA with 1M rows by varying the error rate and considering two versions of BigDansing: the one with the parallel data repair and a baseline with a centralized data repair, such as in NADEEF. Figure 12(b) shows the results. The parallel version outperforms the centralized one, except when the error rate is very small (1%). For higher rates, BigDansing is clearly faster, since the number of connected components to deal with in the repair process increases with the number of violations and thus the parallelization provides a stronger boost. Naturally, our system scales much better with the number of violations.

Repair accuracy. We evaluate the accuracy of BigDansing using the traditional *precision* and *recall* measure: *precision* is the ratio of correctly updated attributes (exact matches) to the total number of updates; *recall* is the ratio of correctly updated attributes to the total number of errors.

We test BigDansing with the equivalence class algorithm using HAI on the following rule combinations: (a) FD φ_6; (b) FD φ_6 and FD φ_7; (c) FD φ_6, FD φ_7, and FD φ_8. Notice that BigDansing runs (a)-combination alone while it runs (b)-combination and (c)-combination concurrently.

Table 4 shows the results for the equivalence class algorithm in BigDansing and NADEEF. We observe that BigDansing achieves similar accuracy and recall as the one obtained in a centralized system, *i.e.,* NADEEF. In particular, BigDansing requires the same number of iterations as NADEEF even to repair all data violations when running multiple rules concurrently. Notice that both BigDansing and NADEEF might require more than a single iterations when running multiple rules because repairing some violations might cause new violations. We also tested the equivalence class in BigDansing using both the black box and scalable repair implementation, and both implementations achieved similar results.

We also test BigDansing with the hypergraph algorithm using DC rule ϕ_D on a TaxB dataset. As the search space of the possible solutions in ϕ_D is huge, the hypergraph algorithm uses quadratic programming to approximates the repairs in ϕ_D [6]. Thus, we use the euclidean distance to measure the repairs accuracy on the repaired data attributes compared to the attributes of the ground truth.

Rule(s)	NADEEF precision	NADEEF recall	BigDansing precision	BigDansing recall	Iterations
φ_6	0.713	0.776	0.714	0.777	1
φ_6&φ_7	0.861	0.875	0.861	0.875	2
φ_6–φ_8	0.923	0.928	0.924	0.929	3
	|R,G|/e	**|R,G|**	**|R,G|/e**	**|R,G|**	**Iter.**
ϕ_D	17.1	8183	17.1	8221	5

Table 4: Repair quality using HAI and TaxB datasets.

Table 4 shows the results for the hypergraph algorithm in BigDansing and NADEEF. Overall, we observe that BigDansing achieves the same average distance ($|R, G|/e$) and similar total distance ($|R, G|$) between the repaired data R and the ground truth G. Again, BigDansing requires the same number of iterations as NADEEF to completely repair the input dataset. These results confirm that BigDansing achieves the same data repair quality as in a single node setting. This by providing better data cleansing runtimes and scalability than baselines systems.

7. RELATED WORK

Data cleansing, also called data cleaning, has been a topic of research in both academia and industry for decades, *e.g.,* [6, 7, 11–15, 17–19, 23, 29, 34, 36]. Given some "dirty" dataset, the goal is to find the most likely errors and a possible way to repair these errors to obtain a "clean" dataset. In this paper, we are interested in settings where the detection of likely errors and the generation of possible fixes is expressed through UDFs. As mentioned earlier, traditional constraints, *e.g.,* FDs, CFDs, and DCs, are easily expressed in BigDansing and hence any errors detected by these constraints will be detected in our framework. However, our goal is not to propose a new data cleansing algorithm but rather to provide a framework where data cleansing, including detection and repair, can be performed at scale using a flexible UDF-based abstraction.

Work in industry, *e.g.,* IBM QualityStage, SAP BusinessObjects, Oracle Enterprise Data Quality, and Google Refine has mainly focused on the use of low-level ETL rules [3]. These systems do not support UDF-based quality rules in a scalable fashion as in BigDansing.

Examples of recent work in data repair include cleaning algorithms for DCs [6,17] and other fragments, such as FDs and CFDs [4,5,7,11,17]. These proposals focus on specific logical constraints in a centralized setting, without much regards to scalability and flexibility as in BigDansing. As shown in Section 5, we adapted two of these repair algorithms to our distributed platform.

Another class of repair algorithms use machine learning tools to clean the data. Examples include SCARE [39] and ERACER [26]. There are also several efforts to include users (experts or crowd) in the cleaning process [33,40]. Both lines of research are orthogonal to BigDansing.

Closer to our work is NADEEF [7], which is a generalized data cleansing system that detects violations of various data quality rules in a unified programming interface. In contrast to NADEEF, BigDansing: (i) provides a richer programming interface to enable efficient and scalable violation detection, *i.e., block*(), *scope*(), and *iterate*(), (ii) enables several optimizations through its plans, (iii) introduces the first distributed approaches to data repairing.

SampleClean [35] aims at improving the accuracy of aggregate queries by performing cleansing over small samples of the source data. SampleClean focuses on obtaining unbiased query results with confidence intervals, while BigDansing focuses on providing a scalable framework for data cleansing. In fact, one cannot use SampleClean in traditional query processing where the entire input dataset is required.

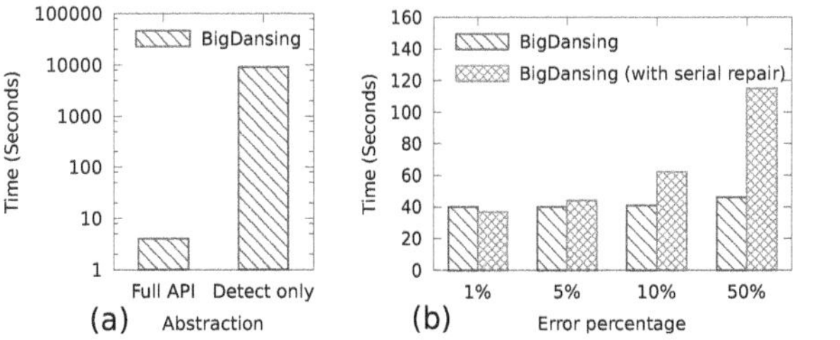

Figure 12: (a) Abstraction and (b) scalable repair.

As shown in the experiment section, scalable data processing platform, such as MapReduce [8] or Spark [41], can implement the violation detection process. However, coding the violation detection process on top of these platforms is a tedious task and requires technical expertise. We also showed that one could use a declarative system (*e.g.,* Hive [32], Pig [28], or Shark [1]) on top of one of these platforms and re-implement the data quality rules using its query language. However, many common rules, such as rule ϕ_U, go beyond declarative formalisms. Finally, these frameworks do not natively support inequality joins.

Implementing efficient theta-joins in general has been largely studied in the database community [9, 27]. Studies vary from low-level techniques, such as minimizing disk accesses for band-joins by choosing partitioning elements using sampling [9], to how to map arbitrary join conditions to Map and Reduce functions [27]. These proposals are orthogonal to our OCJoin algorithm. In fact, in our system, they rely at the executor level: if they are available in the underlying data processing platform, they can be exploited when translating the OCJoin operator at the physical level.

Dedoop [24] detects duplicates in relational data using Hadoop. It exploits data blocking and parallel execution to improve performance. Unlike BigDansing, this service-based system maintains its own data partitioning and distribution across workers. Dedoop does not provide support for scalable validation of UDFs, nor repair algorithms.

8. CONCLUSION

BigDansing, a system for fast and scalable big data cleansing, enables ease-of-use through a user-friendly programming interface. Users use logical operators to define rules which are transformed into a physical execution plan while performing several optimizations. Experiments demonstrated the superiority of BigDansing over baseline systems for different rules on both real and synthetic data with up to two order of magnitudes improvement in execution time without sacrificing the repair quality. Moreover, BigDansing is scalable, *i.e.,* it can detect violation on 300GB data (1907M rows) and produce 1.2TB (13 billion) violations in a few hours.

There are several future directions. One relates to abstracting the repairing process through logical operators, similar to violation detection. This is challenging because most of the existing repair algorithms use different heuristics to find an "optimal" repair. Another direction is to exploit opportunities for multiple data quality rule optimization.

9. REFERENCES

[1] Shark (Hive on Spark). https://github.com/amplab/shark.

[2] TPC-H benchmark version 2.14.4. http://www.tpc.org/tpch/.

[3] C. Batini and M. Scannapieco. *Data Quality: Concepts, Methodologies and Techniques*. Springer, 2006.

[4] G. Beskales, I. F. Ilyas, and L. Golab. Sampling the repairs of functional dependency violations under hard constraints. *PVLDB*, 3:197–207, 2010.

[5] P. Bohannon, M. Flaster, W. Fan, and R. Rastogi. A cost-based model and effective heuristic for repairing constraints by value modification. In *SIGMOD*, 2005.

[6] X. Chu, I. F. Ilyas, and P. Papotti. Holistic Data Cleaning: Putting Violations into Context. In *ICDE*, 2013.

[7] M. Dallachiesa, A. Ebaid, A. Eldawy, A. Elmagarmid, I. F. Ilyas, M. Ouzzani, and N. Tang. NADEEF: A Commodity Data Cleaning System. In *SIGMOD*, 2013.

[8] J. Dean and S. Ghemawat. MapReduce: Simplified Data Processing on Large Clusters. *Communications of the ACM*, 51(1):107–113, 2008.

[9] D. J. DeWitt, J. F. Naughton, and D. A. Schneider. An evaluation of non-equijoin algorithms. In *VLDB*, 1991.

[10] W. Fan and F. Geerts. *Foundations of Data Quality Management*. Morgan & Claypool, 2012.

[11] W. Fan, F. Geerts, X. Jia, and A. Kementsietsidis. Conditional Functional Dependencies for Capturing Data Inconsistencies. *ACM Transactions on Database Systems (TODS)*, 33(2):6:1–6:48, 2008.

[12] W. Fan, F. Geerts, N. Tang, and W. Yu. Conflict resolution with data currency and consistency. *J. Data and Information Quality*, 5(1-2):6, 2014.

[13] W. Fan, J. Li, S. Ma, N. Tang, and W. Yu. Interaction between record matching and data repairing. In *SIGMOD*, 2011.

[14] W. Fan, J. Li, N. Tang, and W. Yu. Incremental Detection of Inconsistencies in Distributed Data. In *ICDE*, 2012.

[15] I. Fellegi and D. Holt. A systematic approach to automatic edit and imputation. *J. American Statistical Association*, 71(353), 1976.

[16] T. Friedman. Magic quadrant for data quality tools. http://www.gartner.com/, 2013.

[17] F. Geerts, G. Mecca, P. Papotti, and D. Santoro. The LLUNATIC Data-Cleaning Framework. *PVLDB*, 6(9):625–636, 2013.

[18] F. Geerts, G. Mecca, P. Papotti, and D. Santoro. Mapping and Cleaning. In *ICDE*, 2014.

[19] M. Interlandi and N. Tang. Proof positive and negative in data cleaning. In *ICDE*, 2015.

[20] E. Jahani, M. J. Cafarella, and C. Ré. Automatic optimization for mapreduce programs. *PVLDB*, 4(6):385–396, 2011.

[21] A. Jindal, J.-A. Quiané-Ruiz, and S. Madden. Cartilage: Adding Flexibility to the Hadoop Skeleton. In *SIGMOD*, 2013.

[22] G. Karypis and V. Kumar. Multilevel K-way Hypergraph Partitioning. In *Proceedings of the 36th Annual ACM/IEEE Design Automation Conference*, DAC. ACM, 1999.

[23] S. Kolahi and L. V. S. Lakshmanan. On Approximating Optimum Repairs for Functional Dependency Violations. In *ICDT*, 2009.

[24] L. Kolb, A. Thor, and E. Rahm. Dedoop: Efficient Deduplication with Hadoop. *PVLDB*, 2012.

[25] G. Malewicz, M. H. Austern, A. J. Bik, J. C. Dehnert, I. Horn, N. Leiser, and G. Czajkowski. Pregel: A System for Large-scale Graph Processing. In *SIGMOD*, 2010.

[26] C. Mayfield, J. Neville, and S. Prabhakar. ERACER: a database approach for statistical inference and data cleaning. In *SIGMOD*, 2010.

[27] A. Okcan and M. Riedewald. Processing theta-joins using mapreduce. In *SIGMOD*, 2011.

[28] C. Olston, B. Reed, U. Srivastava, R. Kumar, and A. Tomkins. Pig Latin: A Not-so-foreign Language for Data Processing. In *SIGMOD*, 2008.

[29] E. Rahm and H. H. Do. Data cleaning: Problems and current approaches. *IEEE Data Eng. Bull.*, 23(4):3–13, 2000.

[30] G. Smith. *PostgreSQL 9.0 High Performance: Accelerate your PostgreSQL System and Avoid the Common Pitfalls that Can Slow it Down*. Packt Publishing, 2010.

[31] N. Swartz. Gartner warns firms of 'dirty data'. *Information Management Journal*, 41(3), 2007.

[32] A. Thusoo, J. S. Sarma, N. Jain, Z. Shao, P. Chakka, S. Anthony, H. Liu, P. Wyckoff, and R. Murthy. Hive: A Warehousing Solution over a Map-reduce Framework. *PVLDB*, 2(2):1626–1629, 2009.

[33] Y. Tong, C. C. Cao, C. J. Zhang, Y. Li, and L. Chen. CrowdCleaner: Data cleaning for multi-version data on the web via crowdsourcing. In *ICDE*, 2014.

[34] M. Volkovs, F. Chiang, J. Szlichta, and R. J. Miller. Continuous data cleaning. In *ICDE*, 2014.

[35] J. Wang, S. Krishnan, M. J. Franklin, K. Goldberg, T. Kraska, and T. Milo. A Sample-and-Clean Framework for Fast and Accurate Query Processing on Dirty Data. In *SIGMOD*, 2014.

[36] J. Wang and N. Tang. Towards dependable data repairing with fixing rules. In *SIGMOD*, 2014.

[37] R. S. Xin, J. E. Gonzalez, M. J. Franklin, and I. Stoica. GraphX: A Resilient Distributed Graph System on Spark. In *First International Workshop on Graph Data Management Experiences and Systems*, GRADES. ACM, 2013.

[38] R. S. Xin, J. Rosen, M. Zaharia, M. J. Franklin, S. Shenker, and I. Stoica. Shark: SQL and Rich Analytics at Scale. In *SIGMOD*, 2013.

[39] M. Yakout, L. Berti-Equille, and A. K. Elmagarmid. Don't be SCAREd: use SCalable Automatic REpairing with maximal likelihood and bounded changes. In *SIGMOD*, 2013.

[40] M. Yakout, A. K. Elmagarmid, J. Neville, M. Ouzzani, and I. F. Ilyas. Guided data repair. *PVLDB*, 2011.

[41] M. Zaharia, M. Chowdhury, M. J. Franklin, S. Shenker, and I. Stoica. Spark: Cluster computing with working sets. In *HotCloud*, 2010.

APPENDIX

A. JOB EXAMPLE

```
1  BigDansing job = new BigDansing("Example Job" );
2  String schema = "name,zipcode,city, state , salary , rate";
3  job.addInputPath(schema,"D1", "S", "T");
4  job.addInputPath(schema,"D2", "W");
5  job.addScope(Scope, "S");
6  job.addBlock(Block1, "S");
7  job.addBlock(Block2, "T");
8  job. addIterate("M", Iterate1 , "S", "T");
9  job. addIterate("V", Iterate2 , "W", "M");
10 job.addDetect(Detect, "V");
11 job.addGenFix(GenFix,"V");
12 job.run();
}
```

Listing 3: Example of a user's BigDansing job.

Let us explain with a BigDansing job example how users can specify to BigDansing in which sequence to run their logical operators. Users can fully control the execution flow of their logical operators via *data labels*, which in other words represent the data flow of a specific input dataset. For example, users would write the BigDansing job in Listing 3 to generate the logical plan in Section 3.2. First of all, users create a job instance to specify BigDansing their requirements (Line 1). Users specify the input datasets they want to process by optionally providing their schema (Line 2) and their path (D1 and D2 in Lines 3 & 4). Additionally, users label input datasets to defines the number data flows they desire to have (S and T for D1 and W for D2). Notice that, in this example, the job creates a copy of D1. Then, users specify the sequence of logical operations they want to perform to each data flow (Lines 5-11). BIGDANSING respect the order in which users specify their logical operators, e.g., BIGDANSING will first perform Scope and then Block1. Users can also specify arbitrary number of inputs and outputs. For instance, in Iterate1 get data flows S and T as input and outputs a signal data flow M. As last step, users run their job as in Line 12.

B. LOGICAL OPERATORS LISTINGS

We show in Listing 4 the code for Scope, Listing 5 the code for Block and in Listing 6 the code for Iterate in rule ϕ_F.

```
public Tuple scope(Tuple in) {
    Tuple t = new Tuple(in.getID());
    t.addCell(in.getCellValue(1));// zipcode
    t.addCell(in.getCellValue(2));// city
    return t;  }
```

Listing 4: Code example for the Scope operator.

```
public String block(Tuple t) {
    return t.getCellValue(0);// zipcode  }
```

Listing 5: Code example for the Block operator.

```
public Iterable<TuplePair> iterator( ListTupleList<String> in) {
    ArrayList<TuplePair> tp = new ArrayList<TuplePair>();
    List<Tuple> inList = in.getIterator().next().getValue();
    for (int i = 0; i < inList.size(); i++) {
        for (int j = i + 1; j < inList.size(); j++) {
            tp.add(new TuplePair(inList.get(i), inList.get(j)));
        }
    }
    return tp;  }
```

Listing 6: Code example for the Iterate operator.

C. RDF DATA REPAIR

Let us explain how BIGDANSING works for RDF data cleansing with an example. Consider an RDF dataset containing students, professors, and universities, where each student is enrolled in one university and has one professor as advisor. The top-left side of Figure 13 shows this RDF dataset as set of triples (RDF input) and Figure 14 shows the graph representation of such an RDF dataset. Let's assume that there cannot exist two graduate students in two different universities and have the same professor as advisor. According to this rule, there are two violations in this RDF dataset: (Paul, John) and (Paul, Sally).

Figure 15 illustrates the logical plan generated by BIGDANSING to clean this RDF dataset while the rest of Figure 14 explains the role of each logical operator on the RDF data. The plan starts with the Scope operator where it removes unwanted RDF projects on attributes Subject and Object and passes only those triples with *advised_by* and *study_in* predicates to the next operator. After that, we apply the first Block to group triples based on student name (*i.e.,* Paul) followed by Iterate operator to join the triples

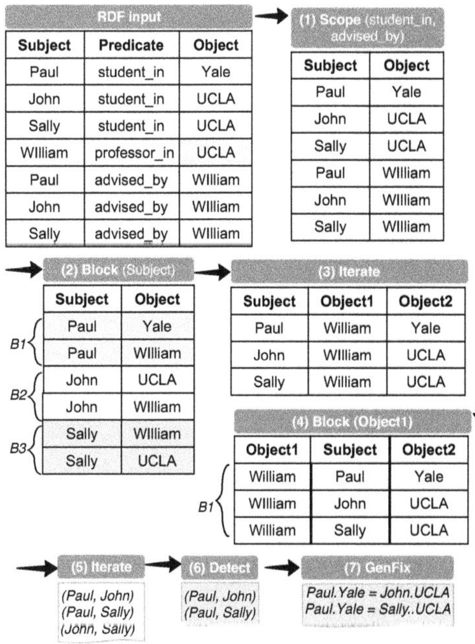

Figure 13: Logical operators execution for the RDF rule example.

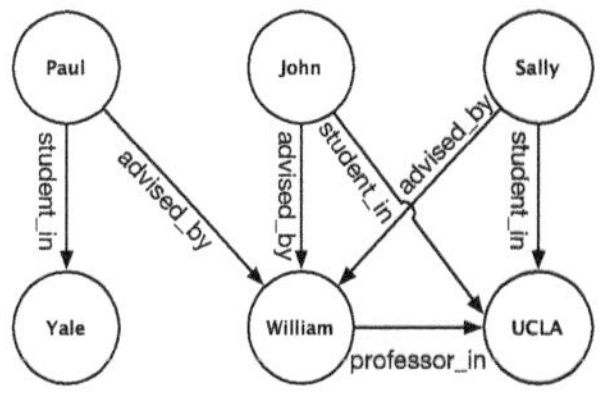

Figure 14: Example of an RDF graph.

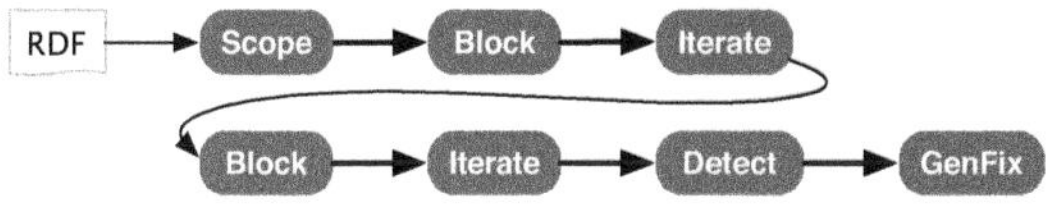

Figure 15: An RDF logical plan in BigDansing.

in each group. The output of this Iterate is passed to the second Block and Iterate operators to group incoming triples based on advisor name (*i.e.,* William). The Detect operator generates violations based on incoming triples with different university names. Finally, the GenFix operator suggests fixing the university names in incoming violations.

D. SPARK CODE FOR ϕ_F IN EXAMPLE 1

We show in Listing 7 an example of the physical translation of the logical plan for rule ϕ_F in Spark. Lines 3 to 7 in Listing 7 handles the processing of the UDF operators in Listings 4, 5, 6, 1 and 2. Lines 8 to 16 implement the repair algorithm in Section 5.2. The repair algorithm invokes Listing 8 in line 9 to build the graph of possible fixes and finds the graph's connected components through GraphX. Finally, lines 17 to 19 in Listing 7 applies the selected candidate fixes to the input dataset. Note that the Spark plan translation in Listing 7 is specific to rule ϕ_F, where lines 3 to 16 changes according the the input rule or UDF. The repair algorithm in Listing 7 seems far complex than the rule engine. However, as the number of violations in a dataset does not usually exceeds 10% of the input dataset size, the rule engine dominates the execution runtime because it has

```
//Input
JavaPairRDD<LongWritable,Text> inputData =
    sc.hadoopFile(InputPath,
    org.apache.hadoop.mapred.TextInputFormat.class,
    LongWritable.class, Text.class, minPartitions);
JavaRDD<Tuple> tupleData = tmpLogData.map(new
    StringToTuples());
//----Rule Engine----
JavaRDD<Tuple> scopeData = tupleData.map(new fdScope());
JavaPairRDD<Key,Iterable<Tupke>> blockData =
    scopedData.groupByKey(new
    fdBlock());
JavaRDD<TuplePair> iterateData = blockingData.map(new
    fdIterate());
JavaRDD<Violation> detectData = iterateData.map(new fdDetect());
JavaRDD<Fix> genFixData = detectData.map(new fdGenFix());
//----Repair Algorithm----
JavaRDD<Edge<Fix>> edges = genFixData.map(new extractEdges());
JavaRDD<EdgeTriplet<Object, Fix>> ccRDD = new
    RDDGraphBuilder(edges.rdd()).buildGraphRDD();
JavaPairRDD<Integer, Fix> groupedFix = ccRDD.mapToPair(new
    extractCC());
JavaPairRDD<Integer, Tuple4<Integer, Integer, String, String>>
    stringFixUniqueKeys = groupedFix.flatMapToPair(new
    extractStringFixUniqueKey());
JavaPairRDD<Integer, Tuple4<Integer, Integer, String, String>>
    countStringFixes = stringFixUniqueKeys.reduceByKey(new
        countFixes());
JavaPairRDD<Integer, Tuple4<Integer, Integer, String, String>>
    newUniqueKeysStringFix = countStringFixes.mapToPair(new
    extractReducedCellValuesKey());
JavaPairRDD<Integer, Tuple4<Integer, Integer, String, String>>
    reducedStringFixes = newUniqueKeysStringFix.reduceByKey(new
    reduceStringFixes());
JavaPairRDD<Integer,Fix> uniqueKeysFix =
    groupedFix.flatMapToPair(new
    extractFixUniqueKey());
JavaRDD<Fix> candidateFixes candidateFixes =
    uniqueKeysFix.join(reducedStringFixes).values().flatMap(new
        getFixValues());
//----Apply results to input----
JavaPairRDD<Long, Iterable<Fix>> fixRDD = candidateFixes.keyBy(
    new getFixTupleID()).groupByKey();
JavaPairRDD<Long, Tuple> dataRDD = tupleData.keyBy(new
    getTupleID());
JavaRDD<Tuple> newtupleData =
    dataRDD.leftOuterJoin(fixRDD).map(
    new ApplyFixes());
```

Listing 7: Spark code for rule ϕ_F

more data to process compared to the repair algorithm.

```
class RDDGraphBuilder(var edgeRDD: RDD[Edge[Fix]]) {
  def buildGraphRDD:JavaRDD[EdgeTriplet[VertexId, Fix]] = {
    var g: Graph[Integer, Fix] = Graph.fromEdges(edgeRDD, 0)
    new JavaRDD[EdgeTriplet[VertexId,Fix]](
      g.connectedComponents().triplets)
  }
}
```

Listing 8: Scala code for GraphX to find connected components of fixes

E. BUSHY PLAN EXAMPLE

We show a bushy plan example in Figure 16 based on the following two tables and DC rules from [6]:

Table Global (G): GID, FN, LN, Role, City, AC, ST, SAL

Table Local (L): LID, FN, LN, RNK, DO, Y, City, MID, SAL

$(c1) : \forall t_1, t_2 \in G, \neg(t_1.\mathsf{City} = t_2.\mathsf{City} \wedge t_1.\mathsf{ST} \neq t_2.\mathsf{ST})$

$(c2) : \forall t_1, t_2 \in G, \neg(t_1.\mathsf{Role} = t_2.\mathsf{Role} \wedge t_1.\mathsf{City} = "NYC" \wedge t_2.\mathsf{City} \neq "NYC" \wedge t_2.\mathsf{SAL} > t_1.\mathsf{SAL})$

$(c3) : \forall t_1, t_2 \in L, t_3 \in G, \neg(t_1.\mathsf{LID} \neq t_2.\mathsf{LID} \wedge t_1.\mathsf{LID} = t_2.\mathsf{MID} \wedge t_1.\mathsf{FN} \approx t_3.\mathsf{FN} \wedge t_1.\mathsf{LN} \approx t_3.\mathsf{LN} \wedge t_1.\mathsf{City} = t_3.\mathsf{City} \wedge t_3.\mathsf{Role} \neq "M")$

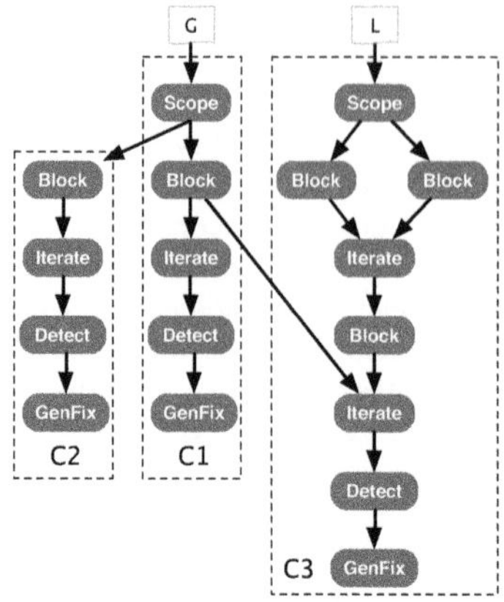

Figure 16: Example of bushy plan

The plan starts with applying the Scope operator. Instead of calling Scope for each rule, we only invoke Scope for each relation. Next we apply the Block operator as follows: block on "City" for c1, on "Role" for c2, and on "LID" and "MID" for c3. Thereafter, for c1 and c2, we proceed to iterate candidate tuples with violations (Iterate) and feed them to Detect and GenFix operators respectively. For c3, we iterate over all employees who are managers combine them with data units from the global table G and then finally feed them to the Detect and GenFix operators.

The key thing to note in the above bushy data cleaning plan is that while each rule has its own Detect/GenFix operator, the plan shares many of the other operators in order to reduce: (1) the number of times data is read from the base relations, and (2) the number of duplicate data units generated and processed in the dataflow.

F. DATA STORAGE MANAGER

BigDansing applies three different data storage optimizations: (i) data *partitioning* to avoid shuffling large amounts of data; (ii) data *replication* to efficiently support a large variety of data quality rules; and (iii) data *layouts* to improve I/O operations. We describe them below.

(1) Partitioning. Typically, distributed data storage systems split data files into smaller chunks based on size. In contrast, BigDansing partitions a dataset based on its content, *i.e.,* based on attribute values. Such a logical partitioning allows to co-locate data based on a given blocking key. As a result, BigDansing can push down the Block operator to the storage manager. This allows avoiding to co-locate datasets while detecting violations and hence to significantly reduce the network costs.

(2) Replication. A single data partitioning, however, might not be useful for mutliple data cleansing tasks. In practice, we may need to run several data cleansing jobs as data cleansing tasks do not share the same blocking key. To handle such a case, we replicate a dataset in a heterogenous manner. In other words, BigDansing logically partitions (*i.e.,* based on values) each replica on a different attribute. As a result, we can again push down the Block operator for multiple data cleansing tasks.

(3) Layout. BigDansing converts a dataset to binary format when storing it in the underlying data storage framework. This helps avoid expensive string parsing operations.

Also, in most cases, binary format ends up reducing the file size and hence I/Os. Additionally, we store a dataset in a column-oriented fashion. This enables pushing down the Scope operator to the storage manager and hence reduces I/O costs significantly.

As underlying data storage layer, we use Cartilage [21] to store data to and access data from HDFS. Cartilage works both with Hadoop and Spark and uses HDFS as the underlying distributed file system. Using Cartilage, the storage manager essentially translates BigDansing data access operations (including the operator pushdowns) to three basic HDFS data access operations: (i) *Path Filter*, to filter the input file paths; (ii) *Input Format*, to assign input files to workers; and (iii) *Record Reader*, to parse the files into tuples. In Spark, this means that we specify these three UDFs when creating RDDs. As a result, we can manipulate the data access right from HDFS so that this data access is invisible and completely non-invasive to Spark. To leverage all the data storage optimizations done by BigDansing, we indeed need to know how the data was uploaded in the first place, e.g., in which layout and sort order the data is stored. To allow BigDansing to know so, in addition to datasets, we store the *upload plan* of each uploaded dataset, which is essentially the upload metadata. At query time, BigDansing uses this metadata to decide how to access an input dataset, *e.g.,* if it performs a full scan or an index scan, using the right UDF (path filter, input format, record reader) implementation.

G. EXECUTION LAYER

G.1 Translation to Spark Execution Plans

Spark represents datasets as a set of *Resilient Distributed Datasets* (RDDs), where each RDD stores all Us of an input dataset in sequence. Thus, the Executor represents each physical operator as a RDD data transformation.

Spark-PScope. The Executor receives a set of RDDs as well as a set of PScope operators. It links each RDD with one or more PScope operators, according to their labels. Then, it simply translates each PScope to a map() Spark operation over its RDD. Spark, in turn, takes care of automatically parallelizing the map() operation over all input Us. As a PScope might output a null or empty U, the Executor applies a *filter*() Spark operation to remove null and empty Us before passing them to the next operator.

Spark-PBlock. The Executor applies one Spark groupBy() operation for each PBlock operator over a single RDD. BigDansing automatically extracts the key from each U in parallel and passes it to Spark, which in turn uses the extracted key for its groupBy operation. As a result, Spark generates a RDDPair (a key-value pair data structure) containing each a grouping key (the key in the RDDPair) together with the list of all Us sharing the same key (the value in the RDDPair).

Spark-CoBlock. The Executor receives a set of RDDs and a set of PBlock operators with matching labels. Similar to the Spark-PBlock, the Spark-CoBlock groups each input RDD (with groupBy()) using its corresponding PBlock. In addition, it performs a *join*() Spark operation on the keys of the output produced by groupBy(). Spark-CoBlock also outputs an RDDPair, but in contrast to Spark-PBlock, the produced value is a set of lists of Us from all input RDDs sharing the same extracted key.

Spark-CrossProduct & -UCrossProduct. The Executor receives two input RDDs and outputs an RDDPair of the resulting cross product. Notice that we extended Spark's Scala code with a new function $selfCartesian()$ in order to efficiently support the UCrossProduct operator. Basically, $selfCartesian()$ computes all the possible combinations of pair-tuples in the input RDDs.

Spark-OCJoin. The Executor receives two RDDs and a set of inequality join conditions as input. The Executor applies the OCJoin operator on top of Spark as follows. First, it extracts PartAtt (the attribute on which it has to partition the two input RDDs) from both RDDs by using the $keyBy()$ Spark function. Then, the Executor uses the $sortByKey()$ Spark function to perform a range partitioning of both RDDs. As a result, the Executor produces a single RDD containing several data blocks using the $mapPartitions()$ Spark function. Each data block provides as many lists as inequality join conditions; each containing all Us sorted on a different attribute involved in the join conditions. Finally, the Executor uses the $selfCartesian()$ Spark function to generate unique sets of paired data blocks.

Spark-PDetect. This operator receives a PIterate operator, a PDetect operator, and a single RDD as input. The Executor first applies the PIterate operator and then the PDetect operator on the output. The Executor implements this operator using the *map*() Spark function.

Spark-PGenFix The Executor applies a PGenFix on each input RDD using spark's *map*() function. When processing multiple rules on the same input dataset, the Executor generates an independent RDD of fixes for each rule. After that it combines all RDDs of possible repairs into a single RDD and pass it to BigDansing's repair algorithm. This operator is also implemented by the Executor inside the Detect operator for performance optimization purposes.

G.2 Translation to MR Execution Plans

We now briefly describe how the Executor runs the four wrapper physical operators on MapReduce.

MR-PScope. The Executor translates the PScope operator into a Map task whose *map* function applies the received PScope. Null and empty U are discarded within the same Map task before passing them to the next operator.

MR-PBlock. The Executor translates the PBlock operator into a Map task whose *partitioner* function applies the received PBlock to set the intermediate key. The MapReduce framework automatically groups all Us that share the same key. The Executor does the same for the CoBlock operator, but it also labels each intermediate key-value pair with the input dataset label for identification at Reduce tasks.

MR-PIterate. The Executor translates PIterate into a Reduce task whose *reduce* function applies the received PIterate.

MR-PDetect. The Executor translates the PDetect operator into a Reduce task whose *reduce* function applies the received PDetect. The Executor might also apply the received PDetect in the *reduce* function of a Combine task.

MR-PGenFix. The Executor translates the PGenFix operator into a Map task whose *map* function applies the received PRepair. The Executor might also apply the received PGenFix at the *reduce* function of PDetect.

Data X-Ray: A Diagnostic Tool for Data Errors

Xiaolan Wang
University of Massachusetts
Amherst, MA, USA
xlwang@cs.umass.edu

Xin Luna Dong
Google Inc.
Mountain View, CA, USA
lunadong@google.com

Alexandra Meliou
University of Massachusetts
Amherst, MA, USA
ameli@cs.umass.edu

ABSTRACT

A lot of systems and applications are data-driven, and the correctness of their operation relies heavily on the correctness of their data. While existing data cleaning techniques can be quite effective at purging datasets of errors, they disregard the fact that a lot of errors are *systematic*, inherent to the process that produces the data, and thus will keep occurring unless the problem is corrected at its source. In contrast to traditional data cleaning, in this paper we focus on *data diagnosis*: explaining where and how the errors happen in a data generative process.

We develop a large-scale diagnostic framework called DATAXRAY. Our contributions are three-fold. First, we transform the diagnosis problem to the problem of finding common properties among erroneous elements, with minimal domain-specific assumptions. Second, we use Bayesian analysis to derive a cost model that implements three intuitive principles of good diagnoses. Third, we design an efficient, highly-parallelizable algorithm for performing data diagnosis on large-scale data. We evaluate our cost model and algorithm using both real-world and synthetic data, and show that our diagnostic framework produces better diagnoses and is orders of magnitude more efficient than existing techniques.

1. INTRODUCTION

Systems and applications rely heavily on data, which makes data quality a detrimental factor for their function. Data management research has long recognized the importance of data quality, and has developed an extensive arsenal of data cleaning approaches based on rules, statistics, analyses, and interactive tools [1,25,37,53,54]. While existing data cleaning techniques can be quite effective at purging datasets of errors, they disregard the fact that a lot of errors are *systematic*, inherent to the process that produces the data, and thus will keep occurring unless the problems are corrected at their source. For example, a faulty sensor will keep producing wrong measurements, a program bug will keep generating re-occurring mistakes in simulation results, and a bad extraction pattern will continue to derive incorrect relations from web documents.

In this paper, we propose a data diagnostic tool that helps data producers identify the possible systematic causes of errors in the data. This is in contrast to traditional data cleaning methods, which treat the symptom (the errors in a dataset) rather than the underlying condition (the cause of the errors). Since finding particular causes is often domain specific, we instead aim to provide a generic approach that finds groupings of errors that may be due to the same cause; such groupings give clues for discerning the underlying problems. We call our tool DATAXRAY: just as a medical X-ray can facilitate (but not in itself give) the diagnosis of medical conditions, our tool shows the inherent relationship between errors and helps diagnose their causes. We use examples from three different domains to illustrate how DATAXRAY achieves this goal.

EXAMPLE 1 (KNOWLEDGE EXTRACTION). *Web-scale knowledge bases [20,24,36] often contain a large number of errors, resulting both from mistakes, omissions, or oversights in the knowledge extraction process, and from erroneous, out-of-date information from the web sources. Existing knowledge curation techniques focus on finding correct knowledge in the form of* (subject, predicate, object) *triples by analyzing extractions from multiple knowledge extractors [20,21]; however, they do not offer any insight on why such errors occur and how they can be prevented in the future.*

We applied DATAXRAY *on 2 billion knowledge triples from Knowledge Vault [20], a web-scale probabilistic knowledge base that continuously augments its content through extraction of web information, such as text, tables, page structure, and human annotations. Our tool returns groupings of erroneous triples that may be caused by the same systematic error. Among the many different types of errors that* DATAXRAY *reports, we give three examples.*

Annotation errors: DATAXRAY *reports a grouping of about 600 knowledge triples from besoccer.com with object "Feb 18, 1986", which were extracted from webmaster annotations according to schema.org; among them the error rate is 100% (all triples conflict with the real world). A manual examination of three to five instances quickly revealed that the webmaster used* "2/18/1986" *to annotate the date of birth for all soccer players, possibly by copying HTML segments.*

Reconciliation errors: DATAXRAY *reports a grouping of about 700,000 triples, extracted by a particular extractor from various websites, with object "baseball coach"; among them the error rate is 90%. Manual investigation showed that the mistakes resulted from reconciliation errors:* all coaches *were reconciled to* baseball coaches.

Extraction errors: DATAXRAY *reports a grouping of about 2 million triples, extracted by a particular extractor from various websites, with predicates containing "olympics"; among them the error rate is 95%. Manual investigation showed that the mistakes resulted from an over-generalized extraction pattern that extracts all sports games as olympic games.*

SIGMOD'15, May 31–June 4, 2015, Melbourne, Victoria, Australia.

ACM 978-1-4503-2758-9/15/05 ...$15.00.
http://dx.doi.org/10.1145/2723372.2750549.

These three examples illustrate that the errors exposed by our tool cover a variety of problems, from data errors to extraction errors. Some of these problems can be very hard to detect; for example, web annotations are typically not visible from webpages. Even though DATAXRAY *does not report the causes directly, it guides diagnosis by reporting sets of errors that are likely due to the same cause.*

EXAMPLE 2 (WIRELESS PACKET LOSS). *A wireless sensor network experiences significant packet loss.* DATAXRAY *reports a grouping of messages containing the range of node IDs 10–15 as destinations, where the message drop rate is very high. Manual investigation unveils that nodes 10–15 are all located on a side of the building with poor connectivity due to interference.*

EXAMPLE 3 (TRAFFIC INCIDENTS). *We use* DATAXRAY *to analyze traffic incident and weather data collected by the US department of Transportation on multiple freeways in Portland, OR, over two months [59]. Our algorithm uses the reported traffic incidents as "error" labels, and automatically derives that surface water level of more than 2cm is likely a cause of accidents.*

Diagnosing errors in big data environments raises three major challenges that make existing techniques, such as provenance analysis, feature selection, and causal analysis, not applicable.

Massive scale. Many applications, such as knowledge extraction and sensing, continuously produce huge volumes of data. A sampling that results in a manageable data size often loses statistical strength. Algorithms working with data of this size require linear time complexity and the ability to process data in parallel. Existing techniques such as feature selection [48, 57] cannot handle this increased scale, because they are not easy to implement in shared-nothing architectures [42].

System complexity. Data generative processes, such as knowledge extractors, often implement a large number of algorithms, invoke external tools, set different parameters, and so on. As a result, it is not feasible to analyze them and reason with them directly. Existing provenance techniques [15, 19] are not well-suited for this level of complexity, and most existing tools on data auditing focus on much simpler, relational settings [31, 55].

High error rates. In some applications such as knowledge extraction from the web, the error rate can be as high as 70% [21]. This disqualifies causal analysis techniques [44, 45], whose premise relies on the assumption that errors, and generally observations that require explanation, are rare.

DATAXRAY addresses these challenges by analyzing the relationship between erroneous instances in an efficient and scalable manner. More concretely, we make the following contributions.

- We abstract the processes that derive data using a hierarchical structure of *features*. Each feature corresponds to a subset of data properties and each cause of errors can be considered to be associated with a feature. We then transform the problem of error diagnosis to the problem of finding the features that best represent erroneous elements. This transformation enforces minimal assumptions, can model a large range of application scenarios, and allows for efficient exploration of possible diagnoses (Section 2).
- We apply Bayesian analysis to estimate the *causal likelihood* of a set of features being associated with the causes of the errors, and use that to determine the most likely diagnosis for a given set of errors. We identify three intuitive principles for good diagnoses: conciseness (simpler diagnoses are preferable), specificity (each diagnosis should be closely associated with the real cause), and consistency (diagnoses should not be contradicted by a lot of correct data). We design a cost model that captures these principles and can be evaluated efficiently (Section 3).
- We exploit the hierarchical structure of features and propose a top-down iterative algorithm with linear time complexity that evaluates possible diagnoses from broader to more concise using our cost model. We then extend our algorithm to a parallel, MapReduce-based version (Section 4).
- Our evaluation includes three phases of experiments. First, we evaluate our cost model on real-world extraction data and demonstrate that it is significantly more effective at deriving diagnoses than other feature selection methods, including logistic regression. Second, we show that our algorithm is orders of magnitude more efficient than other feature selection methods. Third, we present experiments on synthetic data demonstrating that our approach can scale effectively to very large data sizes (Section 5).

2. DATA MODEL ABSTRACTIONS

In this section, we introduce a running example motivated by knowledge extraction, and describe a model abstraction to formalize the problem of diagnosing errors in this setting. Although we focus on knowledge extraction as the driving application for our framework, our approach can easily adapt to general settings.

EXAMPLE 4. *Figure 1a depicts two example web tables that reside on the same wiki page, containing information about musicians. Figure 1b depicts the knowledge triples extracted from these web tables using an extraction system. For example, the triple (*P. Fontaine, DoB, c.1380*) represents the information that the date of birth of P. Fontaine is c. 1380.*

Some of the extracted triples are incorrect, and are highlighted in the table of Figure 1b (t_5, t_9, and t_{12}). While traditional cleaning techniques may simply remove these triples from the knowledge base, or further provide a list of such triples as feedback, our objective is to help diagnose *the problem and understand the reasons for these errors. In this case, the reason for the incorrect results is that the extractors assign a default value ("01/01/1900") to unknown dates.*

In this work, we assume that we know which extracted triples are incorrect. Such labels can be obtained by existing cleaning and classification techniques [21, 25, 26]. They may also occur naturally in the data, such as extraction confidence from the extraction systems, or the occurrence of accidents in Example 3. *Our goal is not to identify the errors, but to reveal common properties of the errors that may be helpful in diagnosing the underlying causes.*

2.1 The element-feature model

We observe that a *cause* of errors is often associated with some *properties* of the erroneous instances and causes a high error rate for data with these properties. In Example 4, the three erroneous triples are caused by using *01/01/1900* as the default value when a date is unknown. Indeed, they share a common property that their objects are all *01/01/1900*. By highlighting the observation that the error rate is high (1.0 in our example) for triples with "object value: 01/01/1900", we can help users diagnose this possible cause. As another example, imagine a high error rate for triples extracted from *Tbl #1* (Figure 1b) where the objects are of the *Date* type. It suggests that the date format in that table may not be captured properly by the extractors. Surfacing such observation for triples with "source tableID: Tbl # 1" and "object type: date" can help the diagnosis.

Based on this intuition, we define the *element-feature model*, where we consider each data instance as an *element*, and capture its properties by a set of *property* values. We then use a subset of property values, which we call a *feature*, to capture a possible cause of errors. Features can be derived from data using their schema, types, and values, as well as from provenance metadata. Features form a

Musicians – Table 1

Name	Date of Birth	Date of Death
P. Fontaine	c.1380	c.1450
J. Vide	unknown	1433

Composers – Table 2

Name	Date of Birth	Date of Death
G. Legrant	fl.1405	N/A
H. Lantins	fl.c.1420	unknown

(a) Two web tables with information about musicians, that appear on the same wiki page.

Extracted triples		Triple properties							
ID	**knowledge triple**	***source*** **URL**	**tableID**	***subject*** **type**	**instance**	***predicate*** **type**	**instance**	***object*** **type**	**instance**
t_1	{P. Fontaine, Profession, Musician}	wiki	tbl #1	People	P. Fontaine	Bio	Profession	Profession	Musician
t_2	{P. Fontaine, DoB, c.1380}	wiki	tbl #1	People	P. Fontaine	Bio	DoB	Date	c.1380
t_3	{P. Fontaine, DoD,c.1450}	wiki	tbl #1	People	P. Fontaine	Bio	DoD	Date	c.1450
t_4	{J. Vide, Profession, Musician}	wiki	tbl #1	People	J. Vide	Bio	Profession	Profession	Musician
t_5	{J. Vide, DoB, 01/01/1900}	wiki	tbl #1	People	J. Vide	Bio	DoB	Date	01/01/1900
t_6	{J. Vide, DoD, 1433}	wiki	tbl #1	People	J. Vide	Bio	DoD	Date	1433
t_7	{G. Legrant, Profession, Composer}	wiki	tbl #2	People	G. Legrant	Bio	Profession	Profession	Composer
t_8	{G. Legrant, DoB, fl.1405}	wiki	tbl #2	People	G. Legrant	Bio	DoB	Date	fl.1405
t_9	{G. Legrant, DoD, 01/01/1900}	wiki	tbl #2	People	G. Legrant	Bio	DoD	Date	01/01/1900
t_{10}	{H. Lantins, Profession, Composer}	wiki	tbl #2	People	H. Lantins	Bio	Profession	Profession	Composer
t_{11}	{H. Lantins, DoB, fl.c.1420}	wiki	tbl #2	People	H. Lantins	Bio	DoB	Date	fl.c.1420
t_{12}	{H. Lantins, DoD, 01/01/1900}	wiki	tbl #2	People	H. Lantins	Bio	DoD	Date	01/01/1900

(b) Knowledge triples extracted from the web tables in (a) and values of their properties in all dimensions. Incorrect triples are highlighted.

Figure 1: Error diagnosis in information extraction motivated by Example 1. An extraction pipeline processes the web tables in (a) and derives 12 knowledge triples (elements). Each element has four property dimensions with different granularity levels. The extractors assign a default value to dates that are unknown ("01/01/1900"), leading to three highlighted incorrect triples (t_5, t_9, and t_{12}).

natural hierarchy based on containment relationships; for example, the feature with object_type=Date contains, and thus is an ancestor of, the feature with object_type=Date ∧ object_instance=01/01/1900. The problem of error diagnosis then reduces to the problem of finding a set of features that best summarizes all erroneous data elements. We next define the terms used in this model.

Property dimension: A property dimension describes one aspect of a data instance. For our example dataset, there can be four dimensions: source, subject, predicate, and object. Without losing generality, we consider a certain ordering of the dimensions.

Property hierarchy: Recall that features in each dimension form a hierarchy. In our example, the source dimension has three levels in the hierarchy: Root, source_URL, source_tableID. Each other dimension also has three levels; taking subject as an example, the hierarchy is Root, subject_type, subject_instance.

Accordingly, we define the property hierarchy as follows. The root of the hierarchy represents the coarsest granularity and each dimension has value ALL for the root level (Root). Descendant properties are finer-granularity representations of their ancestors; we say property A is a child of property B if one of the features of A is a child of the corresponding feature of B. For example, property {ALL, ALL, ALL, (object_instance, 01/01/1900)} is a child of property {ALL, ALL, ALL, (object_type, Date)}. As we show later, the hierarchy will allow us to solve the problem efficiently, using an algorithm that explores it in a top-down fashion (Section 4).

Property vector: With property dimensions and hierarchies, we can use a property vector to represent a data instance or a set of instances that share common properties. The vector contains one (property, value) pair for each dimension, where the property is in the hierarchy of that dimension, and the value is for the particular property. The root-level property corresponds to the pair (Root, ALL), but we write just ALL for short. For example:

- {ALL, ALL, ALL, (object_instance, 01/01/1900)} represents all triples with object 01/01/1900.
- {(source_tableID, Tbl#1), ALL, ALL, (object_type, Date)} represents all triples from *Tbl#1* of the particular *wiki* page with objects of the *Date* type.

Element: For each data instance (triple) we define an element to capture its truthfulness and property vector; the vector should contain a value for the leaf-level property for every dimension.

DEFINITION 5 (ELEMENT). *Consider a dataset with m property dimensions. A data instance is an element $e = (V, P)$, where*

- *V is* `true` *if the instance is correct and* `false` *otherwise;*
- *$P = \{d_1, \ldots, d_m\}$ is a property vector, where $d_i, i \in [1, m]$, is a (property, value) pair for the leaf property of the i-th dimension.*

Figure 2a presents a subset of the elements that correspond to the triples in Figure 1b.

Feature: Each property vector defines a set of triples that share a set of properties; we call it a *feature*.

DEFINITION 6 (FEATURE). *Consider a dataset with m property dimensions. A Feature f is a pair $f = (P, \mathbf{E})$, where*

- *$P = \{d_1, \ldots, d_m\}$ is a property vector, where $d_i, i \in [1, m]$, is a (property, value) pair for a property in the hierarchy of the i-th dimension.*
- *$\mathbf{E}$ is the set of elements with the properties represented by P.*

Figure 2b shows some example features for Example 4. As an example, feature f_6 represents all triples whose object is *01/01/1900*; elements e_5, e_9, and e_{12} carry this feature.

Problem definition.

We now formalize the problem of deriving diagnoses for data errors using the element-feature model. Each feature identifies a possible cause of error, and a diagnosis is a set of features that collectively explain the causes of the observed errors.

Element	V	Property Vector			
e_1	`true`	{(source_tableID, tbl #1),	(subj_instance, P. Fontaine),	(pred_instance, Profession),	(obj_instance, Musician)}
e_2	`true`	{(source_tableID, tbl #1),	(subj_instance, P. Fontaine),	(pred_instance, DoB),	(obj_instance, c.1380)}
e_3	`true`	{(source_tableID, tbl #1),	(subj_instance, P. Fontaine),	(pred_instance, DoD),	(obj_instance, c.1450)}
e_4	`true`	{(source_tableID, tbl #1),	(subj_instance, J. Vide),	(pred_instance, Profession),	(obj_instance, Musician)}
e_5	`false`	{(source_tableID, tbl #1),	(subj_instance, J. Vide),	(pred_instance, DoB),	(obj_instance, 01/01/1900)}
...	...	...	...	...	...

(a) List of Elements: The triples of Figure 1b, represented in the element format. The truthfulness value (V) of incorrect elements is `false`.

	Feature	Property vector	Structure vector	List of elements
Level 0	f_0	{ALL, ALL, ALL, ALL}	{0, 0, 0, 0}	$\{e_1, e_2, e_3, e_4, e_5, e_6, e_7, e_8, e_9, e_{10}, e_{11}, e_{12}\}$
Level 1	f_1	{(source_URL, *wiki*), ALL, ALL, ALL}	{1, 0, 0, 0}	$\{e_1, e_2, e_3, e_4, e_5, e_6, e_7, e_8, e_9, e_{10}, e_{11}, e_{12}\}$
	f_2	{ALL, (subj_type, *People*), ALL,ALL}	{0, 1, 0, 0}	$\{e_1, e_2, e_3, e_4, e_5, e_6, e_7, e_8, e_9, e_{10}, e_{11}, e_{12}\}$
	f_3	{ALL, ALL, (pred_type, *Bio*), ALL}	{0, 0, 1, 0}	$\{e_1, e_2, e_3, e_4, e_5, e_6, e_7, e_8, e_9, e_{10}, e_{11}, e_{12}\}$
	f_4	{ALL, ALL, ALL, (obj_type, *Profession*)}	{0, 0, 0, 1}	$\{e_1, e_4, e_7, e_{10}\}$
	f_5	{ALL, ALL, ALL, (obj_type, *Date*)}	{0, 0, 0, 1}	$\{e_2, e_3, e_5, e_6, e_8, e_9, e_{11}, e_{12}\}$
Level 2	f_6	{ALL, ALL, ALL, (obj_instance, *01/01/1900*)}	{0, 0, 0, 2}	$\{e_5, e_9, e_{12}\}$
	f_7	{ALL, ALL, ALL, (obj_instance, *c.1380*)}	{0, 0, 0, 2}	$\{e_2\}$
...	...	...	...	...
Level 4	f_8	{(source_tableID, *tbl #1*), ALL, (pred_instance, *DoB*), ALL }	{2, 0, 2, 0}	$\{e_2, e_5\}$
	f_9	{(source_tableID, *tbl #2*), ALL, (pred_instance, *DoD*), ALL }	{2, 0, 2, 0}	$\{e_9, e_{12}\}$
...	...	...	...	...

(b) List of Features: Candidate reasons of extraction errors in the feature format. The incorrect elements in each feature are marked as red. *Structure vector* and *feature level* are defined in Section 4.

Figure 2: The Element-Feature model is a more efficient representation of the data instance and the possible error causes that takes advantage of the hierarchical relationship of the extraction properties.

DEFINITION 7 (OPTIMAL DIAGNOSIS). *Given a dataset of elements $\mathcal{E} = \{e_1, ..., e_n\}$ and a cost function c, the optimal diagnosis is the set of features, $\mathcal{F} = \{f_1, ..., f_k\}$, such that*

- *$\forall e_i \in \mathcal{E}$ with $e_i.V =$*`false`*, $\exists f_j \in \mathcal{F}$ such that $e_i \in f_j.\mathbf{E}$;*
- *$c(\mathcal{F})$ is minimized.*

The first condition of the definition requires that the diagnosis explains *all* errors, while the second condition requires that the diagnosis is optimal with respect to a cost function c. Note again that the output is a set of features that are associated with the causes, instead of the causes themselves.

In the rest of the paper we tackle two challenges: (1) how to derive an appropriate cost function, and (2) how to solve the optimal diagnosis problem efficiently.

Overview: cost model (Section 3).

We start by using Bayesian analysis to derive the set of features with the highest probability of being associated with the causes for the mistakes in the dataset. We derive our cost function from the Bayesian estimate: the lowest cost corresponds to the highest *a posteriori* probability that the selected features are the real causes for the errors. The resulting cost function contains three types of penalties, which capture the following three intuitions:

Conciseness: Simpler diagnoses with fewer features are preferable.
Specificity: Each feature should have a high error rate.
Consistency: Diagnoses should not include many correct elements.

We propose an additive cost function based on these three penalties that approximates the Bayesian estimate and is efficient to compute.

Overview: diagnostic algorithm (Section 4).

We can prove that finding the set of features with the minimal cost is NP-complete. We design a top-down, iterative algorithm with linear-time complexity. Our algorithm traverses the feature hierarchy from coarser to finer granularity features. It uses local stopping conditions to decide whether to accept the current feature or explore deeper. We extend our algorithm to a parallel, MapReduce-based version that is effective at large-scale diagnosis tasks.

3. DIAGNOSTIC FRAMEWORK

The core of our diagnostic framework is the cost model used to determine the optimal diagnosis (Definition 7). In this section, we focus on deriving a cost function that is effective in identifying good diagnoses and that can be computed efficiently. We start by using Bayesian analysis to compute the probability that a set of features is the cause of the mistakes in the dataset (Section 3.1). Then, we propose a cost function that approximates the Bayesian analysis efficiently, through simple, additive penalty functions (Section 3.2). Finally, we show that deriving the optimal diagnosis is NP-complete, which further motivates the need for efficient algorithms with parallelization potential (Section 3.3).

3.1 Bayesian estimate of causal likelihood

Given a set of elements $\mathcal{E} = \{e_1, \ldots, e_n\}$ and their correctness, we wish to estimate the probability $\Pr(\mathcal{F}|\mathcal{E})$ that a set of features $\mathcal{F} = \{f_1, \ldots, f_k\}$ is the cause for the incorrect data instances in $\mathcal{E}$. From Bayesian inference, the *a posteriori* probability $\Pr(\mathcal{F}|\mathcal{E})$ is proportional to the likelihood $\Pr(\mathcal{E}|\mathcal{F})$ times the prior $\Pr(\mathcal{F})$:

$$\Pr(\mathcal{F}|\mathcal{E}) \propto \Pr(\mathcal{E}|\mathcal{F}) \Pr(\mathcal{F}) \quad (1)$$

We assume that mistakes represented by features are independent. This assumption is reasonable because even for related features, the associated causes can still be independent. For example, feature $f_6 = \{\text{ALL}, \text{ALL}, \text{ALL}, (\textit{obj\_instance}, 01/01/1900)\}$ is subsumed by feature $f_5 = \{\text{ALL}, \text{ALL}, \text{ALL}, (\textit{obj\_type}, \textit{Date})\}$; however, f_6 can be associated with the cause of incorrectly assigning the default value *01/01/1900*, while f_5 can be associated with the cause of inability of an extractor to parse dates, and the two causes are independent. Using this independence assumption, we can express the prior $\Pr(\mathcal{F})$ as follows.

$$\Pr(\mathcal{F}) = \prod_{f_i \in \mathcal{F}} \Pr(f_i) \quad (2)$$

We further use α to denote the *a priori* probability that a feature is a cause ($\Pr(f_i) = \alpha$).[1] Then, $\Pr(\mathcal{F}) = \alpha^k$.

Now consider $\Pr(\mathcal{E}|\mathcal{F})$: We assume the elements in $\mathcal{E}$ are independent conditioned on $\mathcal{F}$. For an element $e_j \in \mathcal{E}$, we denote by $F(e_j) \subseteq \mathcal{F}$ the features that contain e_j; only errors associated with features in $F(e_j)$ can affect the correctness of e_j. Thus, we have the following.

$$\Pr(\mathcal{E}|\mathcal{F}) = \prod_{e_j \in \mathcal{E}} \Pr(e_j|\mathcal{F}) = \prod_{e_j \in \mathcal{E}} \Pr(e_j|F(e_j)) \quad (3)$$

We assume that for each cause of errors, there is an error rate between 0 and 1. For example, assigning a default date *01/01/1900* often has an error rate close to 1 (if not 1), date format parsing error from a particular webpage can also have a high error rate, whereas a webtable providing erroneous data often has a lower error rate. We denote by ϵ_i the error rate of the cause associated with feature f_i. The error rate ϵ_i can be derived directly from $f_i.\mathbf{E}$ and denotes the probability that an element represented by feature f_i is incorrect when f_i is associated with a cause of error.

Then, the probability of an element e_j being correct is the probability that none of the causes associated with the features it belongs to affects its correctness. Similarly, we can compute the probability of an element being incorrect.

$$\Pr(e_j.V = \texttt{true}|F(e_j)) = \Pi_{f_i \in F(e_j)}(1 - \epsilon_i) \quad (4)$$

$$\Pr(e_j.V = \texttt{false}|F(e_j)) = 1 - \Pi_{f_i \in F(e_j)}(1 - \epsilon_i) \quad (5)$$

As special cases, we define $Pr(e_j.V = \texttt{true}|\varnothing) = 1$, rewarding not including correct elements in the returned features, and define $Pr(e_j.V = \texttt{false}|\varnothing) = 0$, penalizing not including incorrect elements in the returned features. Since Definition 7 requires covering all incorrect elements, we assume in the rest of the paper that $F(e_i) \neq \varnothing$ for every $e_i \in \mathcal{E}, e_i.V = \texttt{false}$.

Equations (1–5) together compute the probability that the features in set $\mathcal{F}$ are the causes of the errors in data instances of $\mathcal{E}$. Our goal is to find the set $\mathcal{F}$ with the highest probability $\Pr(\mathcal{F}|\mathcal{E})$.

EXAMPLE 8. *We consider two sets of features, $\mathcal{F}_1 = \{f_6\}$ and $\mathcal{F}_2 = \{f_8, f_9\}$, as possible causes for the errors in the set of elements $\mathcal{E} = \{e_1, \dots, e_{12}\}$ in Figure 2a. Semantically, the former means that the errors are caused by the wrong default value "01/01/1900"; the latter means that the errors are caused by two mistakes: wrongly parsing the dates of birth in Table 1 and wrongly parsing the dates of death in Table 2.*

Feature f_6 has 3 incorrect elements and no correct elements; its error rate is $\epsilon_6 = 1$. Using $\alpha = 0.5$, we get that $Pr(\mathcal{F}_1) = 0.5$, $Pr(\mathcal{E}|\mathcal{F}_1) = 1 - (1 - 1) = 1$, so $Pr(\mathcal{F}_1|\mathcal{E}) \propto 0.5$.

On the other hand, f_8 has one incorrect element, and one correct element ($\epsilon_8 = 0.5$), and f_9 has two incorrect elements and no correct elements ($\epsilon_9 = 1$). Thus, $Pr(\mathcal{F}_2) = 0.5^2$, $Pr(e_2|\mathcal{F}_2) = Pr(e_2|f_8) = (1 - 0.5) = 0.5$, $Pr(e_5|\mathcal{F}_2) = Pr(e_5|f_8) = 1 - (1-0.5) = 0.5$, $Pr(e_9|\mathcal{F}_2) = Pr(e_{12}|\mathcal{F}_2) = 1-(1-1) = 1$, so $Pr(\mathcal{F}_2|\mathcal{E}) \propto 0.5^2 \cdot 0.5 \cdot 0.5 \cdot 1 \cdot 1 = 0.0625$. This result indicates that $\mathcal{F}_1$ is more likely to be the cause of the errors than $\mathcal{F}_2$.

[1]For simplicity, we assume that all features have the same *a priori* probability of failure. However, this is not imperative in our model, and different probabilities can be used.

3.2 The diagnostic cost model

The Bayesian analysis described previously represents the probability that a set of features $\mathcal{F}$ are the causes of the errors in $\mathcal{E}$. It requires probability computation for each element. Since our goal is to find the set of features that best diagnose the errors, it would be much more intuitive to transform the *a posteriori* probability to a cost function that computes a cost for each feature, and sums up the cost for all selected features.

Note that both $\Pr(\mathcal{F})$ and $\Pr(e_j.V = \texttt{true}|F(e_j))$ can be written as the product of a set of terms, each associated with a feature. If we can transform $\Pr(e_j.V = \texttt{false}|F(e_j))$ to such a form, we can then define a cost function for each feature and take an aggregation. For this purpose, we estimate $\Pr(e_j.V = \texttt{false}|F(e_j))$ as follows.

$$\Pr(e_j.V = \texttt{false}|F(e_j)) = \Pi_{f_i \in F(e_j)}\epsilon_i \quad (6)$$

In general, this estimate can be arbitrarily bad (consider the extreme case $|F(e_j)| \to \infty$). However, in practice, an erroneous element is usually due to one or two reasons instead of many. Therefore, ideally, $|F(e_j)|$ should be small in the diagnosis (i.e., little overlap between returned features). Our estimate is precise when $|F(e_j)| = 1$. Furthermore, when $|F(e_j)| > 1$, Equation (6) computes a lower probability than (5), penalizing overlapping features even hasher, which is consistent with our intuition. Our experimental results verify that this estimate leads to good diagnosis results.

We combine Equations (1–4) and (6) to get the following expression for the probability $\Pr(\mathcal{F}|\mathcal{E})$.

$$\Pr(\mathcal{F}|\mathcal{E}) \propto \prod_{f_i \in \mathcal{F}} \Pr(f_i) \prod_{e_j \in \mathcal{E}} \Pr(e_j|F(e_j))$$
$$= \prod_{f_i \in \mathcal{F}} \alpha \epsilon_i^{|f_i.\mathbf{E}_i^-|}(1 - \epsilon_i)^{|f_i.\mathbf{E}_i^+|} \quad (7)$$

where $f_i.\mathbf{E}^-$ and $f_i.\mathbf{E}^+$ are the sets of `false` and `true` elements of f_i, respectively. Equation (7) contains three distinct components that comprise the probability $\Pr(\mathcal{F}|\mathcal{E})$: a fixed factor ($\alpha$), a factor that corresponds to `false` elements of the feature, and a factor that corresponds to `true` elements. Accordingly, we define a cost function for each feature.

DEFINITION 9 (FEATURE COST). *The cost $c(f_i)$ of a feature f_i is the sum of the* fixed cost, false cost, *and* true cost, *defined as:*

$$c_{fixed}(f_i) = \log \frac{1}{\alpha}$$
$$c_{false}(f_i) = |f_i.\mathbf{E}^-| \log \frac{1}{\epsilon_i}$$
$$c_{true}(f_i) = |f_i.\mathbf{E}^+| \log \frac{1}{1 - \epsilon_i}$$

The use of logarithms[2] allows our cost function to be additive. Then, the diagnosis cost, which we define below, is logarithmically proportional to the *a posteriori* probability $\Pr(\mathcal{F}|\mathcal{E})$ in Equation (7).

DEFINITION 10 (DIAGNOSIS COST). *The cost $c(\mathcal{F})$ of a diagnosis $\mathcal{F} = \{F_1, ..., F_k\}$ is the sum of the costs of all its features:*

$$c(\mathcal{F}) = \sum_{f_i \in \mathcal{F}} c(f_i)$$

EXAMPLE 11. *We revisit the candidate diagnoses of Example 8: $\mathcal{F}_1 = \{f_6\}$ and $\mathcal{F}_2 = \{f_8, f_9\}$. The costs of the relevant features*

[2]Without loss of generality, we assume logarithms of base 2.

are: $c(f_6) = c_{fixed}(f_6) + c_{false}(f_6) + c_{true}(f_6) = 1 + 1 \cdot 0 + 0 = 1$*,* $c(f_8) = 1 + 1 \cdot 1 + 1 \cdot 1 = 3$*, and* $c(f_9) = 1 + 2 \cdot 0 + 0 = 1$*. Therefore,* $c(\mathcal{F}_1) = 1$ *and* $c(\mathcal{F}_2) = 3 + 1 = 4$*. Since* $\mathcal{F}_1$ *has a lower cost, it is a better diagnosis than* $\mathcal{F}_2$*.*

Note also that both $\mathcal{F}_1$ *and* $\mathcal{F}_2$ *contain only disjoint features, so their costs estimate the corresponding probabilities precisely:* $\Pr(\mathcal{F}_1|\mathcal{E}) = 2^{-c(\mathcal{F}_1)} = 0.5$ *and* $\Pr(\mathcal{F}_2|\mathcal{E}) = 2^{-c(\mathcal{F}_2)} = 0.0625$*.*

Interestingly, the three penalties considered for the feature cost capture the three important properties for the returned diagnosis.

Conciseness: Penalty $c_{fixed}(f_i) > 0$ represents the *a priori* probability. This means that the diagnosis cost increases as the size of $\mathcal{F}$ increases, so this factor prioritizes smaller feature sets (i.e., concise explanations).

Specificity: Penalty $c_{false}(f_i)$ prioritizes the choice of features with higher error rate to cover the same wrong element. If two features cover the same wrong elements, the one with higher error rate will result in a lower cost.

Consistency: Penalty $c_{true}(f_i)$ prioritizes the choice of features that contain fewer correct elements. Feature sets that cover a lot of correct elements will result in a high cost.

Adding these cost penalties balances conciseness, specificity, and consistency. For example, the diagnosis with a single feature that contains all elements is obviously the most concise diagnosis, but its error rate is presumably low and it involves a lot of correct elements, so there is a high true cost and false cost. On the other hand, returning each element as a single-element feature in the diagnosis is obviously the most specific and consistent diagnosis, but the number of features is high, resulting in a high fixed cost.

3.3 Complexity

For a given dataset of elements $\mathcal{E}$, our cost model assigns a constant cost to each feature. This transforms the problem of deriving optimal diagnoses (Definition 7) to a weighted set cover problem [29]. There is a straightforward reduction from weighted set cover to the problem of optimal diagnosis, which means that our problem is NP-complete.

THEOREM 12 (NP-COMPLETENESS). *Given a dataset of elements* $\mathcal{E} = \{e_1, ..., e_n\}$*, the cost function c of Definition 10, and a maximum cost K, determining whether there exists a diagnosis* $\mathcal{F}$*, such that* $c(\mathcal{F}) \leq K$*, is NP-complete.*

Weighted set cover is a well established problem, with extensive related work. Specifically, there are several approximation algorithms for this problem [13, 16, 27], but typically, they do not come near to addressing the scale of problems that are relevant to our motivating application domain. These algorithms typically have high-degree polynomial complexity (e.g., quadratic in the number of features [27]), and they are not amenable to parallelism.

In the next section, we introduce a powerful, sort-free, top-down iterative algorithm for the optimal diagnosis problem, with *linear time complexity* and great parallelization potential. We extend our algorithm to a MapReduce-based implementation, and show that it is both effective and efficient.

4. DERIVING A DIAGNOSIS

In this section, we propose an algorithm that can derive diagnoses efficiently, by exploiting the hierarchical structure of features. We start with a description of the feature hierarchy (Section 4.1). We then propose an algorithm that constructs a diagnosis by traversing the hierarchy in a top-down fashion (Section 4.2). Finally, we present a MapReduce version of our algorithm that makes causal diagnosis practical for large-scale datasets (Section 4.3).

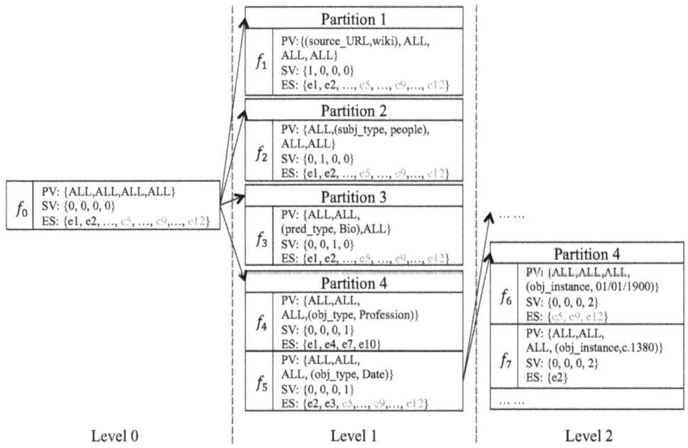

Figure 3: The hierarchy structure of the features of Figure 2b.

4.1 The feature hierarchy

Features form a natural hierarchy due to the property hierarchy (Section 2.1). For example, the feature {(source_URL, wiki), ALL, ALL, ALL} contains the feature {(source_tableID, tbl #1), ALL, ALL, ALL}; semantically, the table is a subset of the wiki page. This hierarchy is embedded in the features' property vectors, and we model it explicitly by deriving a feature's *structure vector* and its hierarchy *level*.

Structure vector (SV): A SV is an integer vector $\{s_1, \ldots, s_m\}$, where the i-th element represents the granularity of the feature in the i-th property dimension. Lower numbers represent coarser granularity, with 0 mapping to Root. For example, in the source dimension, we have the granularity levels Root, source_URL, and source_tableID, which are represented in the structure vector with 0, 1, and 2, respectively. Therefore, the structure vector of feature f_1 in Figure 2b is $\{1, 0, 0, 0\}$, because *wiki* is a value at the granularity level of source_URL. The structure vector is derived from a feature's property vector, and provides an intuitive representation of the feature's relationship with other features.

Feature level: The feature level is an integer that denotes the distance of a feature from the root of the feature hierarchy. It can be computed directly from the structure vector, as the sum of all its dimensions ($\sum_i s_i$). For example, feature f_1 has level 1.

Feature hierarchy: We define the parent-child relationships in the feature hierarchy using the list of feature elements ($f.\mathbf{E}$), the feature structure vector (SV_f) and the feature level (L_f).

DEFINITION 13 (PARENT-CHILD FEATURES). *A feature* f_p *is the parent of feature* f_c *(equivalently,* f_c *is a child of* f_p*) when the following conditions hold:*

(a) $e \in f_c.\mathbf{E} \Rightarrow e \in f_p.\mathbf{E}$

(b) $L_{f_p} = L_{f_c} - 1$

(c) $\forall i \in [1, m]$, $SV_{f_p}(i) \geq SV_{f_c}(i)$

The conditions of the definition ensure that (a) the elements of a parent feature are a superset of the elements of the child feature, (b) the parent feature is one level closer to the root of the hierarchy, and (c) each dimension of the child feature has equal or finer granularity than the parent.

A feature can have multiple parents. For example, the features {(source_URL, wiki), ALL, (pred_instance, DoB), ALL} and {(source_tableID, tbl #1), ALL, (pred_type, Bio), ALL} are both parents of feature {(source_tableID, tbl #1), ALL, (pred_instance, DoB),

Algorithm 1 DATAXRAY

Require: A set of elements $\mathcal{E}$;
Ensure: A set of problematic features **R**;
1: $parentList \leftarrow$ InitialFeature($elementList$);
2: $R \leftarrow \varnothing$;
3: **while** $parentList! = \varnothing$ **do**
4: $\quad S, U, childList, nextLevel \leftarrow \varnothing$;
5: $\quad$ **for** each $parentF \in parentList$ **do**
6: $\quad\quad$ SPLITFEATURE($parentF, childList$);
7: $\quad$ **end for**
8: $\quad partitionList \leftarrow$ getPartition($parentList, childList$);
9: $\quad$ **for** each $partition \in partitionList$ **do**
10: $\quad\quad$ COMPAREFEATURE($partition, S, U$);
11: $\quad$ **end for**
12: $\quad$ MERGEFEATURE($parentList, nextLevel, S, U, R$);
13: $\quad parentList \leftarrow nextLevel$;
14: **end while**
15: **return** R

ALL}. The hierarchy defined by the parent-child feature relationships is a directed acyclic graph (DAG). The root of the hierarchy is feature {ALL, ALL, ALL, ALL}, and each leaf is a feature that maps to a unique element. For example, the feature {(source_tableID, tbl #1), (subj_instance, J. Vide), (pred_instance, DoB), (obj_instance, 01/01/1900)}, at level 8, represents element e_5 in Figure 2a, and equivalently, triple t_5 in Figure 1b.

Feature partitions: Features at the same hierarchy level generally have overlapping sets of elements. For example, f_1 and f_4 have four elements in common. This can be a problem for an algorithm that explores the hierarchy, because it is harder to compare features that overlap in an arbitrary way. To address this problem, we organize the child features of a parent feature f_p into m *partitions*, where m is the number of property dimensions.

DEFINITION 14 (PARTITION). *A partition $\mathcal{P}_i^{f_p}$ contains every feature f that is a child feature of f_p and $SV_{f_p}(i) = SV_f(i) - 1$.*

For example, f_4 and f_5 form partition $\mathcal{P}_4^{f_0}$ in level 1: they share the same parent, f_0, and $SV_{f_4}(4) = SV_{f_5}(4) = SV_{f_0}(4) + 1$. Overall, level 1 has four partitions: $\mathcal{P}_1^{f_0} = \{f_1\}$, $\mathcal{P}_2^{f_0} = \{f_2\}$, $\mathcal{P}_3^{f_0} = \{f_3\}$, and $\mathcal{P}_4^{f_0} = \{f_4, f_5\}$. By construction, partitions ensure that their features do not overlap (e.g., $f_4.\mathbf{E} \cap f_5.\mathbf{E} = \varnothing$), and the union of all their features cover all the parent elements (e.g., $f_4.\mathbf{E} \cup f_5.\mathbf{E} = f_0.\mathbf{E}$).

4.2 Top-down iterative diagnosis

Our diagnostic algorithm traverses the hierarchy in a top-down fashion (breadth-first), exploring coarse-granularity features first, and drilling down to finer-granularity features while improving the cost estimate at every step. The algorithm maintains three sets of features in the traversal.

- *Unlikely causes* **U**: features that are not likely to be causes.
- *Suspect causes* **S**: features that are possibly the causes.
- *Result diagnosis* **R**: features that are decided to be associated with the causes.

Our algorithm, DATAXRAY, is described in Algorithm 1. At a high level, every iteration of the algorithm considers features at a particular level (Line 5–Line 7), compares each parent feature with its child features, and populates the list of suspect causes **S** and the list of unlikely causes **U** (Line 8–Line 11). At the end of the iteration, the sets **S** and **U** are consolidated (Line 12): parent features that occur only in **S** are added to the result diagnosis **R**, and all elements that **R** contains are marked as "covered"; child features that occur only in **S** are kept for traversal in the next iteration. The traversal completes once all incorrect elements are marked as being covered by some feature in **R**.

We next describe the major components of the algorithm.

SPLITFEATURE: Given a feature and its elements, this component derives the corresponding child features and partitions. It uses the structure vector of the parent feature to derive the structure vectors of the children and the partition of the parent. It then generates the property vectors of each child feature by examining the elements in the parent. Finally, if the parent feature is marked as "covered", all the elements of the feature are already covered by ancestor features selected to **R**. To avoid producing redundant diagnoses, the child features of the current feature are also marked as "covered". Features marked as "covered" will not be added to **R**.

COMPAREFEATURE: Given a parent node and a partition, this component compares the feature set containing only the parent, and the feature set containing all child features in the partition, to determine which is a better solution. The winner features are added to **S** and the loser features are added to **U**. The comparison is based on the cost model of Definition 10. In Section 4.2.1 we describe two additional criteria that simplify this computation.

MERGEFEATURE: In the previous step, each partition populates the sets **S** and **U** independently. This component consolidates the results. Parent features only in **S** and not in **U** transfer to the result diagnosis **R**, and their child features are marked as "covered". Parent features in **U** are discarded, since it means there exists some partition where the child features form a better solution. Child features in **S** are sent to the next iteration for further traversal.

THEOREM 15 (COMPLEXITY AND BOUNDS). *Algorithm 1 has complexity $O(|\mathcal{F}|)$, and provides an $O(n)$-approximation of the minimum cost diagnosis, where n is the number of elements in $\mathcal{E}$ and $\mathcal{F}$ is the set of features that can be derived from $\mathcal{E}$.*

DATAXRAY provides an $O(n)$-approximation of the optimal diagnosis, which is worse than the greedy approximation bound for set cover ($O(\log n)$). However, this worst case setting requires that errors are uniformly distributed among the child nodes of a feature, *across all dimensions*. This is extremely unusual in practice, and in most cases DATAXRAY significantly outperforms approximations for set cover.

In Section 5, we show that DATAXRAY outperforms greedy set cover by an order of magnitude. Our algorithm exploits the hierarchy of the features, leading to better worst-case complexity (linear in the number of features) than other approximations for set cover. We note that the number of features can be huge: $O(l^m|\mathcal{E}|)$, where m is the number of dimensions and l the maximum number of levels in the property hierarchy for each dimension. However, in practice, m is usually small. Moreover, DATAXRAY is by design highly-parallelizable and we show how to implement it in the MapReduce framework (Section 4.3).

4.2.1 Optimizations

Line 10 of Algorithm 1 compares two sets of features using the cost model of Definition 10. This computation requires enumerating each element in the feature sets. We use two heuristic criteria that simplify computation and prune features faster.

Variance pruning: The *variance* of a feature describes how the errors are distributed among the child features. We compute the variance in each partition $\mathcal{P}_i^f$ of a feature f as:

$$Var_i^f = \sum_{f_c \in \mathcal{P}_i^f} \frac{(\epsilon_{f_c} - \epsilon_f)^2}{|\mathcal{P}_i^f|}$$

Intuitively, if a feature is associated with a cause of errors, it is likely to result in uniform mistakes across its child features, resulting in low variance of error rates among its children. A feature with high variance indicates that the actual culprit is deeper in the feature hierarchy; we thus add a parent feature f to $\mathbf{U}$ if $Var_i^f \geq \theta_{max}$. Based on empirical testing, we chose $\theta_{max} = 0.1$ for our experiments. For example, feature f_5 in Figure 2b has 6 child features in partition $\mathcal{P}_4^{f_5}$; five with zero error rate, and one with $\epsilon = 1$. Then, the variance in that partition is $Var_4^{f_6} = 0.14 > \theta_{max}$, so f_6 is added to $\mathbf{U}$.

Error rate pruning. When a feature is associated with a cause of errors, typically its error rate would not be too low. Accordingly, we add a parent feature f to $\mathbf{U}$ if $\epsilon_f \leq \delta_{min}$. Again, empirically, we chose $\delta_{min} = 0.6$.

4.2.2 Greedy refinement

Our diagnostic framework does not consider correlations among features. If correlations exist, they can result in diagnoses that contain redundant features (i.e., features with a lot of overlap). DataXRay detects redundancies across features of different levels, but is unaware of overlap in features selected from the same hierarchy level. To eliminate such redundancies in the resulting diagnosis, we post-process it with a greedy set-cover step. This greedy step looks for a minimal set of features among those chosen by DataXRay. Since the number of features in the DataXRay result is typically small, this step is very efficient. In Section 5, we show that with negligible overhead, DataXRay with greedy refinement results in significant improvements in accuracy.

4.3 Parallel diagnosis in MapReduce

We design our algorithm with parallelization in mind: the split, compare, and merge steps can each execute in parallel, as the computation always focuses on a specific partition or feature. In this section, we describe how our algorithm works in a MapReduce framework, creating a separate map-reduce stage for each of the split, compare, and merge functions.

Stage I parallelizes the generation of child features. The *Map* phase maps each element in the parent feature to relevant child features; in other words, for each element in a parent feature, it generates pairs where the element is the value and a child property vector is the key. The *Reduce* phase generates each child feature according to the set of elements, and computes its error rate and cost.

Stage II parallelizes the comparison of each parent feature and a partition of child features. The *Map* phase generates, for each child feature, the partitions it belongs to; in other words, for each partition that contains the child feature, it generates a pair where the child is the value and the parent-partition pair is the key. The *Reduce* phase compares the parent feature with each partition of its child features.

Stage III parallelizes the decision of whether to discard a feature, or to return a feature in the diagnosis, or to keep it for further traversal. The *Map* phase populates $\mathbf{S}$ and $\mathbf{U}$; in other words, for each feature in the comparison, it generates a pair where the feature is the key and the decision for adding it to $\mathbf{S}$ or $\mathbf{U}$ is the value. The *Reduce* phase makes a final decision for each feature.

5. EXPERIMENTAL EVALUATION

This section describes a thorough evaluation of our diagnostic framework on real-world knowledge extraction data, as well as large-scale synthetic data. Our results show that (1) our cost function models the quality of diagnoses effectively; (2) our algorithm is both more effective and more efficient than other existing techniques; and (3) our MapReduce implementation of the algorithm is effective at handling datasets of large scale.

Extraction	false triples	true triples	error rate
$reverb$	304	315	0.49
$reverbnolex$	338	290	0.54
$textrunner$	478	203	0.70
woe^{pos}	535	218	0.71
woe^{parse}	557	324	0.63

Figure 4: Real-world datasets from 5 different knowledge extraction systems of the ReVerb ClueWeb Extraction dataset [24].

Datasets

We first describe the real-world data used in our evaluation; we describe our synthetic data experiments in Section 5.2.

Knowledge triple extraction systems. We demonstrate the effectiveness of our diagnosis framework in practice, using five real-world knowledge extraction systems of the ReVerb ClueWeb Extraction dataset [24]. Figure 4 provides high-level characteristics about each of these 5 extractors. The dataset samples 500 sentences from the web, using Yahoo!'s random link service. The dataset contains labeled knowledge triples: each triple has a `true` or `false` label indicating whether it is correct or incorrect, respectively.

We proceed to describe how we model the knowledge extraction datasets in our feature-based framework. In our model, each knowledge triple is an element with a 5-dimensional property vector, with the following property hierarchies:

1. Source (Root, sentenceID) describes which sentence the triple is extracted from.

2–4. Subject, Predicate, Object (Root, structure, content). Each of these dimensions describes the structure of the sentence, and the content value. The structure is composed by the *Pos Tags* [58] (e.g., *none, verb*). The content is the actual content value of the triple.

5. Confidence (Root, confidence bucket). Extraction systems annotate the extracted knowledge with confidence values as an assessment of their quality. We capture the confidence bucket as part of the property dimensions.

In our experiments, we focused on these 5 dimensions, because of limited knowledge of each systems' inner workings. In practice, domain experts are likely to include more dimensions (e.g., specific extraction patterns) to derive more accurate diagnoses.

Silver standard. The dataset does not provide a "gold standard" of diagnoses for the erroneous triples. We manually derived a "silver standard" against which we evaluate our methods. In particular, we considered every feature returned by each alternative technique we implemented, and manually investigated if it is very likely to be associated with a particular error. To the best of our knowledge, there is no freely available dataset with labeled diagnoses; our manually derived silver standard is the best-effort approach to evaluating our techniques while grounded to real-world data.

Comparisons

We compare two versions of our algorithms, DataXRay and DataXRay+Greedy with several alternative algorithms and state-of-the-art methods designed for similar problem settings: a greedy algorithm for set cover, Greedy, and a variant with different optimization objective, REDBLUE; a data quality exploration tool, DATAAUDITOR; and two classification algorithms, FEATURESELECTION and DECISIONTREE.

DATAXRAY (Section 4): Derives diagnoses by identifying "bad" features using the DATAXRAY algorithm proposed in this paper. We set $\alpha = 0.1$, used in the fixed cost, and $\theta_{max} = 0.1$ and $\delta_{min} = 0.6$, used in the pruning and filtering heuristics.

DATAXRAY+GREEDY (Section 4.2.2): This algorithm applies a greedy set-cover refinement step on the result of DATAXRAY to eliminate redundancies.

GREEDY [13]: We apply the greedy approximation for weighted set cover to select the set of features of minimum cost that cover all of the `false` elements, according to our cost model (Section 3.2). Our cost model allows set cover to penalize features that cover `true` elements, which it does not do in its default objective.

REDBLUE [10,50]: Given a collection of sets with "blue" and "red" elements, the red-blue set cover problem looks for a sub-collection of sets that covers all "blue" elements and minimum number of "red" elements. In contrast to regular set-cover, red-blue set cover can model both correct and incorrect element coverage. We map `false` elements to "blue" elements, and `true` elements to "red" elements, while features are sets. We use a greedy approximation algorithm [50] to find the cover.

DATAAUDITOR [31,32]: We use Data Auditor, a data quality exploration tool that uses rules and integrity constraints to construct *pattern tableaux*. We annotate `false` elements as a consequent (dependent) value in a FD, and use Data Auditor to learn a pattern for this rule, which we treat as a diagnosis. We set support $\hat{s} = 1$ to diagnose all `false` elements; the confidence $\hat{c}$ corresponds to the error rate pruning in DATAXRAY, so we set $\hat{c} = \delta_{min} = 0.6$.

FEATURESELECTION [48,57]: We use logistic regression to derive a set of features that is a good classifier between `true` and `false` elements. For each feature the algorithm learns a weight between -1 and 1: a positive weight indicates that the feature is positive proportional to the class (in our context the feature is a cause), and a negative weight indicates the opposite. We use our labeled data as the training dataset, excluding features with only `true` elements to speed up learning, and return features with positive weights. We apply L_1-regularization, which favors fewer features for the purpose of avoiding over-fitting. We use 0.01 as the regularization parameter (a higher parameter applies a higher penalty for including more features), as we empirically found that it gives the best results.

DECISIONTREE [51]: We use decision trees with pruning as an alternative classification method. Pruning avoids overfitting, which would lead decision trees to always select features at the lowest hierarchy levels. We set low confidence (0.25) to promote pruning, and restrict the minimum number of instances to two (each selected feature should have at least two elements). We found empirically that these parameters provide the best results.

We use the SLEP package implementation for logistic regression [40] and WEKA [35] for decision trees, and we implemented the rest of the algorithms in Java. In addition, the MapReduce version of DATAXRAY uses Hadoop APIs.

Metrics

We evaluate the effectiveness and efficiency of the methods.

Precision/Recall/F-measure: We measure the correctness of the derived diagnoses using three measures: *Precision* measures the portion of features that are correctly identified as part of the optimal diagnosis; *Recall* measures the portion of features associated with causes of errors that appear in the derived diagnosis; *F-measure* computes their harmonic mean ($\frac{2 \cdot precision \cdot recall}{precision + recall}$). Note that we do not know all causes for the errors, so recall is evaluated against the union of all features marked as correct diagnoses in our silver standard.

Execution time: We report the execution time for each method, broken down into preprocessing time (prep.), computation time (comp.), and total execution time (total time). The preprocessing time for GREEDY, REDBLUE, and FEATURESELECTION accounts for the time to find all eligible features and compute their costs if necessary. The other methods (DATAXRAY, DATAXRAY+GREEDY, DATAAUDITOR, and DECISIONTREE) only need to compose the initial root feature at level 0 during preprocessing. Computation time is the time that each method takes on average, after the preprocessing step. The total time is the sum of preprocessing and computation time.

We ran experiments comparing all of the methods on an iMac with 3.2 GHz Intel Core i5 processor, 8GB RAM. We also conducted experiments on the scalability of our MapReduce implementation. The experiments were conducted on a Hadoop 2.2.0 cluster with 15 slave nodes. The head node has 2.4 GHz processor and 24GB RAM. The slave nodes have 2.66 GHz processor and 16GB RAM.

5.1 Real-world data

In our first round of experiments, we test our diagnostic framework using real-world knowledge extraction data. Figures 5a–5e report the quality of the diagnoses produced by each method on the data extracted by five real-world extraction systems. Figure 5f reports the average execution time for each method. Our results in Figure 5 demonstrate that our framework derives better diagnoses than the other approaches, and does so more efficiently.

Our first goal is to evaluate the effectiveness of our cost function. The results in Figures 5a–5e demonstrate that the methods that apply our cost function (DATAXRAY, DATAXRAY+GREEDY, and GREEDY) result in diagnoses of significantly better quality. REDBLUE generally has high recall, but lower precision. This is because REDBLUE favors finer-granularity features: its objective function depends on the number of red elements (i.e., `true` elements) that are included in the diagnosis, but does not consider the number of returned features (size of the diagnosis). DATAAUDITOR also uses a different objective and prioritizes coarse features, leading to bad performance across all extractors. The logistic regression method (FEATURESELECTION) shows low quality in all datasets. The goal of FEATURESELECTION is to build a good prediction model, which is different from our diagnosis goal. Even with L_1-regularization, it may still select small features for the purpose of optimizing classification. We found that the FEATURESELECTION results often contained redundancy and features with low error rates, resulting in both low precision and low recall. DECISIONTREE performs the worst, with F-measure values below 0.015. Compared to FEATURESELECTION, DECISIONTREE is restricted to non-overlapping rules; this reduces the search space, but ignores many of the features, leading to bad performance. These results show that our cost model is successful at producing good diagnoses, and the quality of the diagnoses is significantly better than those produced by methods with alternative objectives.

Our second goal is to evaluate the effectiveness of our approximation algorithms in solving the optimization problem. All of the methods that use our cost model (DATAXRAY, DATAXRAY+GREEDY, and GREEDY) achieve high recall scores in all five datasets. We observe that typically DATAXRAY has a higher recall, whereas GREEDY has a higher precision, especially for the *textrunner*, woe^{pos}, and woe^{parse} datasets. One weakness of DATAXRAY is that it does not detect overlap across features that are selected at the same level of the hierarchy. When that occurs, the resulting diagnoses contain redundancies (multiple features that explain the

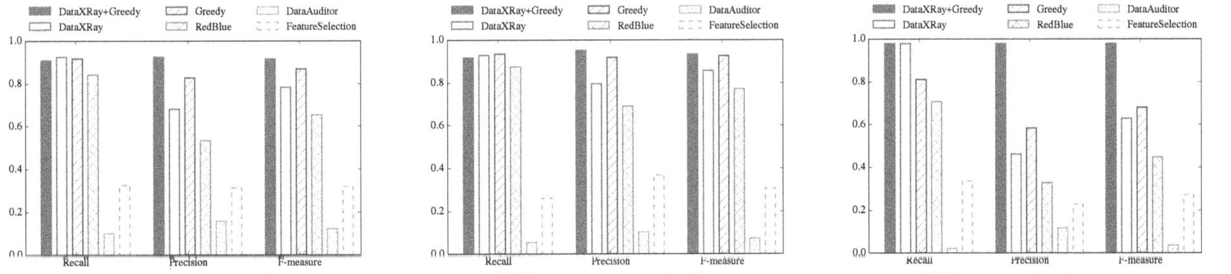

(a) Extractor: *reverb* (b) Extractor: *reverbnolex* (c) Extractor: *textrunner*

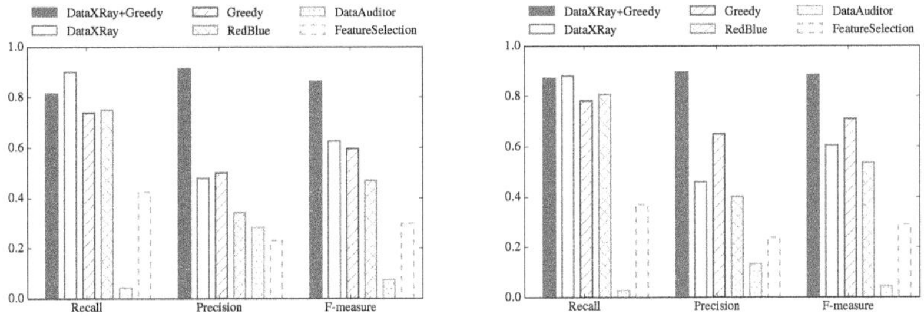

(d) Extractor: woe^{pos} (e) Extractor: woe^{parse}

Method	Prep.	Comp.	Total
DATAXRAY+GREEDY	0.02	0.41	0.43
DATAXRAY	0.01	0.40	0.41
GREEDY	0.7	2.3	3.0
REDBLUE	0.7	3.5	4.2
DATAAUDITOR	0.03	0.17	0.2
FEATURESELECTION	0.9	4.6	5.5
DECISIONTREE	0.03	0.1	0.13

(f) Average execution time (sec)

Figure 5: The quality of the derived diagnoses for all of the methods, across five knowledge extraction systems; the maximum F-measure value achieved by DECISIONTREE was 0.0148, which was too low to display in the graphs. Our approach that combines DATAXRAY with a greedy set-cover step outperforms all other approaches, in some cases significantly. It is also faster than other methods except DATAAUDITOR and DECISIONTREE, but the latter two produce results of very low quality for our problem.

same errors), leading to low precision. DATAXRAY+GREEDY overcomes this weakness by applying the greedy set-cover method over the result of DATAXRAY. This eliminates the redundancy from the DATAXRAY diagnoses, leading to big improvements in precision, and usually with a very small drop on recall. Overall, our DATAXRAY+GREEDY method maintains excellent performance, with F-measure above 0.85 across all five of our datasets.

Our final goal is to evaluate the efficiency of the different algorithms. Figure 5f reports the average execution time for each method. DATAAUDITOR and DECISIONTREE are a bit faster that DATAXRAY on this dataset, but they are not viable for this problem given their terrible F-measure performance. DATAXRAY is an order of magnitude faster than the remaining methods. The greedy refinement is only slightly slower than DATAXRAY: since it executes greedy set cover on the solution of DATAXRAY, the problem space is significantly reduced and thus the greedy step is very efficient.

Interesting diagnoses: Our diagnostic framework identified several interesting problems in these real-world extraction systems. In one case, we found that on the *reverb* dataset our system produced the feature {ALL, ALL, ALL, (obj_structure, ECC), ALL} as part of a diagnosis, where ECC stands for objects ending with coordinating conjunction such as *and, but, for,* and *nor* (e.g., "newspapers and"). This feature corresponds to elements whose objects are extracted from coordinating conjunctions. This indicates a clear problem with the extraction process, as it does not make sense to have a coordinating conjunction as an object in a knowledge triple.

As another example, our method identified {ALL, (subj_structure, CD), ALL, ALL, ALL} as a problem feature in the *textrunner* dataset, where CD stands for cardinal numbers. This feature corresponds to the use of cardinal numbers as subject. This, again, provides a clear pointer to a specific mistake with the extraction process.

5.2 Scaling with synthetic data

We built a synthetic data generator to test our diagnostic framework across varied data sizes and error rates. We have three goals for these experiments: (1) evaluate how the different methods perform in terms of diagnostic accuracy across datasets of varied size and varied error rates, (2) evaluate how the different methods scale, and (3) evaluate the accuracy and scalability of DATAXRAY in a parallel setting across a large range of data sizes. All figures presented in this section display averages across 50 executions.

In the first round of our synthetic data experiments, we test all methods against datasets that range from 100 to 10,000 elements. In this experiment, each feature fails (becomes a cause of error) with probability 0.3, and the error rate of failed features is 0.95. We present the performance results in Figure 6. We note that DATAXRAY and DATAXRAY+GREEDY have almost identical performance in the synthetic data experiments (other than a negligible difference in execution time), so we omit the DATAXRAY+GREEDY line to make the plots less crowded. This is because our synthetic data generator avoids feature overlap at the same hierarchy levels, which makes the greedy refinement unnecessary. Therefore, from here on we do not include results for the greedy refinement.

DATAXRAY is extremely effective across different data sizes, showing superior performance in both effectiveness and efficiency. As the size of the dataset increases, the F-measure of the competing methods steadily declines, falling below 0.6 for GREEDY and below 0.4 for the other methods at 10,000 elements. In contrast, our techniques maintain F-measure above 0.8 for all data sizes. DATAXRAY is also the fastest of the diagnostic methods across all data sizes, in several cases by multiple orders of magnitude (Figure 6b). Figure 6c evaluates the conciseness of the produced diagnoses. It is interesting that FEATURESELECTION derives diagnoses of very similar size to DATAXRAY, yet its F-measure is much lower, indicating that its objective is not suitable for the problem that we tackle in this work. DATAAUDITOR heavily favors features at higher levels of the hierarchy, which results in diagnoses with fewer features, but leads to low F-measure. We include additional results on the granularity of features chosen by different methods in the Appendix.

In our second round of experiments, we generate datasets of 10,000 elements but vary the probability that a feature is incorrect (Figure 7a) and the error rate among the elements of an incorrect feature (Figure 7b). As both these probabilities increase, they increase

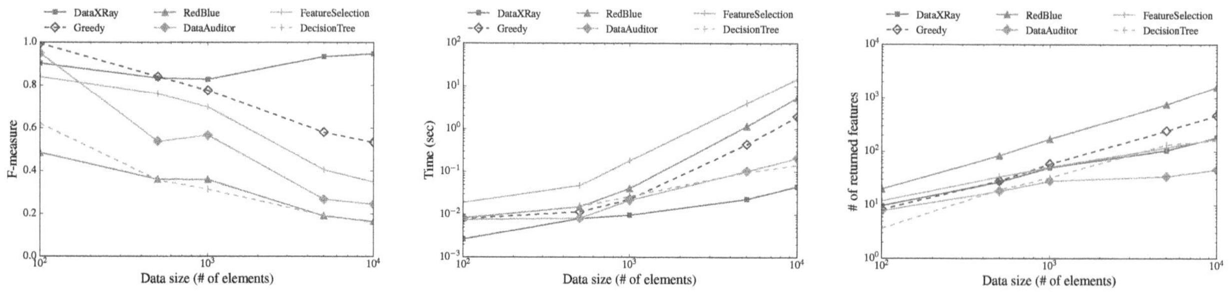

(a) F-measure

(b) Execution time

(c) Number of returned features

Figure 6: Performance of different methods on synthetic data when we vary the size of the data. DATAXRAY maintains consistently good performance, while the effectiveness of the other methods drops dramatically as the size increases.

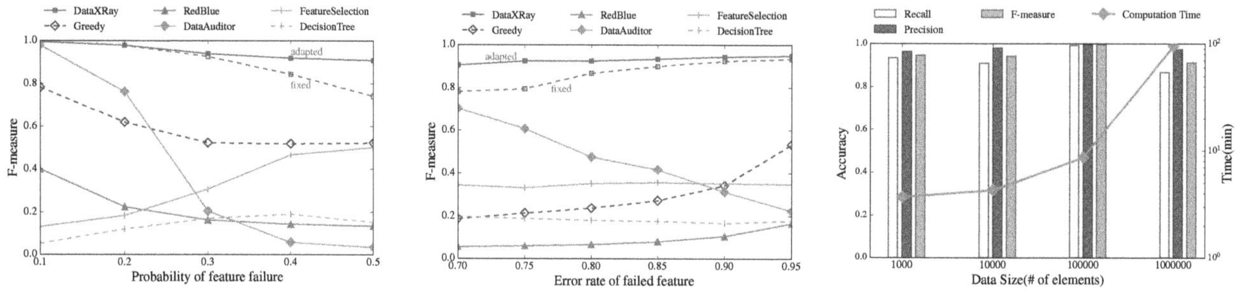

(a) F-measure

(b) F-measure

(c) Accuracy & execution time

Figure 7: Performance of different methods when we vary the parameters of our synthetic data generator. (a) and (b) show the robustness of DATAXRAY whereas (c) shows the scalability of our parallel implementation of DATAXRAY.

the overall error rate of the dataset, which leads us to consider adjustments to the error pruning parameter (δ_{min}). Figures 7a and 7b display the performance for two versions of DATAXRAY: *fixed* uses fixed $\delta_{min} = 0.6$, while *adapted* adapts this parameter according to the overall error rate $\delta_{min} = \max(0.6, \epsilon_{\mathcal{E}})$.

Both versions of DATAXRAY maintain F-measure well above the other methods under this range of configurations, with DATAXRAY-adapted having a natural advantage. The performance of GREEDY decreases as the probability of feature failure increases (Figure 7a). The greedy approximation is prone to mistakenly rejecting large features from the diagnosis since they frequently contain `true` elements, which translates to higher feature weight. This occurrence is more common at high feature failure probability, where such features are more likely to be incorrect. On the other hand, FEATURESELECTION improves because the algorithm is better at selecting the larger incorrect features under the classification objective. When the error rate of an incorrect feature decreases, the performance of GREEDY drops (Figure 7b). This is also expected: with lower error rates, incorrect features include more correct elements, which leads the greedy approximation to a lot of mistakes. For DATAAUDITOR, increases in the overall error rate exacerbate its innate tendency to select features at higher hierarchy levels, leading to sharp drops in its performance. In contrast, the consistently high F-measure of DATAXRAY shows the robustness of our algorithm.

5.2.1 *Parallel evaluation*

We evaluated our framework with even larger data sizes using our MapReduce implementation of DATAXRAY (Section 4.3). Figure 7c presents results on our MapReduce DATAXRAY algorithm. We do not include data for the competing techniques, as we were not able to scale them beyond 10,000 elements, and we were not able to find comparable parallel implementations of these methods.[3]

We ran our parallel implementation of DATAXRAY on a Hadoop cluster with 15 slave nodes, ranging the data size from 1,000 to 1 million elements. Our results in Figure 7c show that the quality of our diagnoses does not degrade as the problem size grows larger. In addition, using a parallel framework allows us to derive diagnoses efficiently, even for large data sizes: our algorithm processes the 1 million elements in about 100 minutes and the execution time grows linearly with the data size. This execution time is very reasonable for this type of problem, as data diagnosis, similarly to data cleaning, is an offline process.

6. RELATED WORK

DATAXRAY targets the problem of data diagnosis: explaining where and how the errors happen in a data generative process. This is in contrast to traditional data cleaning [53], which focuses on identifying and repairing incorrect data. Identifying and correcting data errors is an important and well studied problem. Data management research has supplied a variety of tools to deal with errors originating from integrating data from multiple sources [1,5,49,52], identifying data items that refer to the same entity [34,39], resolving conflicts [22,62,63], and providing language extensions for cleaning [28]. The ultimate goal for all of these techniques is to identify which items in a dataset are correct, and which are incorrect. These techniques are complementary to our work; they can be used to label the truthfulness of elements in our diagnostic framework. Consequently, our work focuses on identifying mistakes in the process that produced the data, rather than finding errors in the dataset itself.

A major research thrust in the domain of data cleaning is to automatically generate repairs for the recovered errors [12]. Again, there is a large arsenal of tools in this category that use rules [7, 14] and functional dependencies [12, 26], while there is also work that focuses on generating repairs in an interactive fashion, using user

[3]To the best of our knowledge, existing parallel implementations of logistic regression target shared-memory architectures, so they are limited to shared-memory, multi-core systems [42].

feedback [54,61]. DATAXRAY is a diagnostic tool, rather than a cure. It can offer insight on the likely causes of error, but it does not suggest specific repairs for these errors.

Data Auditor [31,32] is a data quality exploration tool that uses rules and integrity constraints to construct *pattern tableaux*. These tableaux summarize the subsets of elements that fail to satisfy a constraint, with some flexibility to avoid over-fitting. The tableaux outputs resemble diagnoses with a list of features, and Data Auditor also uses a top down algorithm to derive them. However, there are several distinctions to DATAXRAY. First, users need to select the attributes and constraints that will be in the tableaux. Second, the objective function that it applies focuses only on the number of returned attributes (features), and the coverage of satisfying and non-satisfying elements is specified as confidence constraints. In our evaluation, we showed that Data Auditor has much lower F-measure than our methods. We also observed that its performance is extremely sensitive to the confidence constraint, but the optimal setting of this parameter was not consistent across data sizes and other experimental settings (Section 5).

As DATAXRAY traces errors in the processes that produce data, it has connections to the field of *data and workflow provenance*. Data provenance studies formalisms that express why a particular data item appears in a query result, or how that query result was produced in relation to input data [9, 11, 15, 33]. However, since we often do not know the details of each data generator (e.g., knowledge extractors), we cannot easily apply these approaches. In comparison, DATAXRAY describes how collections of data items were produced in relation to high-level characteristics of the data generative process. Roughly, features in our framework are a form of provenance annotations, but these are much simpler than the complex process steps and interactions that workflow provence [2, 19] typically captures and maintains. Work on interactive investigation of information extraction [18] uses provenance-based techniques and discusses a concept of diagnosis under a similar application setting. The focus of that work however, is on interactive exploration and repair tools, which is different from the scope of our work.

The work on database causality [43, 44, 46] refines the notions of provenance, and describes the dependencies that a query result has on the input data. Similar to DATAXRAY, causality offers a diagnostic method that identifies data items that are more likely to be causes of particular query outputs. This leads to a form of post-factum data cleaning, where errors in the output can be traced and corrected at their source [45]. There are four significant differences between causality and DATAXRAY. First, causal reasoning can only be applied to simple data generative processes, such as queries and boolean formulas, whereas DATAXRAY works with arbitrarily complex processes by relying on feature annotations. Second, existing algorithms for causality do not scale to the data sizes that we tackle with DATAXRAY. Third, existing work on causality in databases has focused on identifying fine-grained causes in the input data, which would correspond to individual elements in our setting, and no higher level features. Fourth, the premise of causality techniques relies on the assumption that errors, and generally observations that require explanation, are rare. This assumption does not hold in many practical settings that our diagnostic algorithms target.

Existing work on explanations is also limited in its applicability, as it is tied to simple queries or specific applications. The Scorpion system [60] finds predicates on the input data as explanations for a labeled set of outlier points in *an aggregate query over a single relation*. Roy and Suciu [55] extended explanations with a formal framework that handles complex SQL queries and database schemas involving multiple relations and functional dependencies. Predicate explanations are related to features, but these approaches are again limited to relational queries, rather than general processes. Finally, application-specific explanations study this problem within a particular domain: performance of MapReduce jobs [38], item rating [17,56], auditing and security [6,23]. Recent work [30] introduced sampling techniques (Flashlight and Laserlight) to derive explanation summaries. The objective of these methods is to find features that maximize the information gain. We evaluated Flashlight and Laserlight experimentally, but they faired very poorly when applied to our diagnostic problems (maximum F-measure below 0.1).

A natural step in the problem of data diagnosis is to use feature selection [48,57] to identify the features that can distinguish between the `true` and the `false` elements. There are different methods for performing feature selection, and logistic regression [8,40] is one of the most popular. In our experiments, we used logistic regression with L_1 regularization to minimize the number of returned features. However, as our evaluation showed, it is not well suited for deriving good diagnoses. Moreover, machine learning methods such as logistic regression are hard to parallelize. Existing shared-memory implementations [42] offer significant speedups, but they cannot benefit from the MapReduce design that DATAXRAY uses. Efforts to implement feature selection in a MapReduce framework showed that this paradigm is not as effective as the shared-memory designs [41].

Other techniques like clustering [3, 4, 47] can be used to create groups of `false` elements as explanations of errors. However, most of the clustering work assumes non-overlapping clusters. This assumption makes these techniques ill-suited for our context as a `false` element may be caused by several reasons and it may be involved in multiple returned features.

Finally, the problem of finding an optimal diagnosis is related to different versions of the set cover problem [27]. Weighted set cover [16] seeks the set of features of minimum weight that covers all the `false` elements. By assigning feature weights using our cost model, we get an alternative algorithm for computing the optimal diagnoses. We use the greedy heuristic approximation for weighted set cover [13], but our evaluation showed that this algorithm is not as effective as DATAXRAY. Red-blue set cover [10,50] is a variant of set cover; it seeks the set of features that cover all blue (`false`) elements, and tries to minimize the number of covered red (`true`) elements. Our experiments showed that the objective of red-blue set cover produces diagnoses of lower accuracy compared to DATAXRAY.

7. CONCLUSIONS

In this paper, we presented DATAXRAY, a large-scale, highly-parallelizable framework for error diagnosis. Diagnosis is a problem complementary to data cleaning. While traditional data cleaning focuses on identifying errors in a dataset, diagnosis focuses on tracing the errors in the systems that derive the data. We showed how to model the optimal diagnosis problem using feature hierarchies, and used Bayesian analysis to derive a cost model that implements intuitive properties for good diagnoses. Our experiments on real-world and synthetic datasets showed that our cost model is extremely effective at identifying causes of errors in data, and outperforms alternative approaches such as feature selection. By using the feature hierarchy effectively, DATAXRAY is also much faster than the other techniques, while our parallel MapReduce implementation allows us to scale to data sizes beyond the capabilities of the other methods.

Acknowledgements: We thank Evgeniy Gabrilovich, Ramanathan Guha, and Wei Zhang for inspiring discussions and use-case examples on Knowledge Vault. This work was partially supported by NSF CCF-1349784, IIS-1421322, and a Google faculty research award.

8. REFERENCES

[1] S. Abiteboul, S. Cluet, T. Milo, P. Mogilevsky, J. Siméon, and S. Zohar. Tools for data translation and integration. *IEEE Data Engineering Bulletin*, 22(1):3–8, 1999.

[2] Y. Amsterdamer, S. B. Davidson, D. Deutch, T. Milo, J. Stoyanovich, and V. Tannen. Putting lipstick on pig: Enabling database-style workflow provenance. *PVLDB*, 5(4):346–357, Dec. 2011.

[3] P. Arabie, J. D. Carroll, W. S. DeSarbo, and J. Wind. Overlapping clustering: A new method for product positioning. *Journal of Marketing Research*, 18:310–317, 1981.

[4] A. Banerjee, C. Krumpelman, J. Ghosh, S. Basu, and R. J. Mooney. Model-based overlapping clustering. In *Proceedings of the Eleventh ACM SIGKDD International Conference on Knowledge Discovery in Data Mining*, KDD, pages 532–537, New York, NY, USA, 2005. ACM.

[5] C. Batini, M. Lenzerini, and S. B. Navathe. A comparative analysis of methodologies for database schema integration. *ACM Comput. Surv.*, 18(4):323–364, Dec. 1986.

[6] G. Bender, L. Kot, and J. Gehrke. Explainable security for relational databases. In *Proceedings of the 2014 ACM SIGMOD International Conference on Management of Data*, SIGMOD, pages 1411–1422, New York, NY, USA, 2014. ACM.

[7] G. Beskales, I. F. Ilyas, and L. Golab. Sampling the repairs of functional dependency violations under hard constraints. *PVLDB*, 3(1-2):197–207, Sept. 2010.

[8] J. K. Bradley, A. Kyrola, D. Bickson, and C. Guestrin. Parallel coordinate descent for l1-regularized loss minimization. In *International Conference on Machine Learning (ICML)*, Bellevue, Washington, June 2011.

[9] P. Buneman, S. Khanna, and W. C. Tan. Why and where: A characterization of data provenance. In *ICDT*, pages 316–330, 2001.

[10] R. D. Carr, S. Doddi, G. Konjevod, and M. Marathe. On the red-blue set cover problem. In *In Proceedings of the 11th Annual ACM-SIAM Symposium on Discrete Algorithms*, pages 345–353, 2000.

[11] J. Cheney, L. Chiticariu, and W. C. Tan. Provenance in databases: Why, how, and where. *Foundations and Trends in Databases*, 1(4):379–474, 2009.

[12] X. Chu, I. F. Ilyas, and P. Papotti. Holistic data cleaning: Putting violations into context. In *ICDE*, pages 458–469. IEEE Computer Society, 2013.

[13] V. Chvatal. A greedy heuristic for the set-covering problem. *Mathematics of Operations Research*, 4(3):233–235, 1979.

[14] G. Cong, W. Fan, F. Geerts, X. Jia, and S. Ma. Improving data quality: Consistency and accuracy. In *Proceedings of the 33rd International Conference on Very Large Data Bases*, VLDB '07, pages 315–326. VLDB Endowment, 2007.

[15] Y. Cui, J. Widom, and J. L. Wiener. Tracing the lineage of view data in a warehousing environment. *ACM Transactions on Database Systems*, 25(2):179–227, 2000.

[16] M. Cygan, L. Kowalik, and M. Wykurz. Exponential-time approximation of weighted set cover. *Information Processing Letters*, 109(16):957–961, July 2009.

[17] M. Das, S. Amer-Yahia, G. Das, and C. Yu. Mri: Meaningful interpretations of collaborative ratings. *PVLDB*, 4(11):1063–1074, 2011.

[18] A. Das Sarma, A. Jain, and D. Srivastava. I4e: Interactive investigation of iterative information extraction. In *Proceedings of the 2010 ACM SIGMOD International Conference on Management of Data*, SIGMOD, pages 795–806, New York, NY, USA, 2010. ACM.

[19] S. B. Davidson and J. Freire. Provenance and scientific workflows: Challenges and opportunities. In *Proceedings of the 2008 ACM SIGMOD International Conference on Management of Data*, SIGMOD, pages 1345–1350, New York, NY, USA, 2008. ACM.

[20] X. L. Dong, E. Gabrilovich, G. Heitz, W. Horn, N. Lao, K. Murphy, T. Strohmann, S. Sun, and W. Zhang. Knowledge vault: A web-scale approach to probabilistic knowledge fusion. In *20th ACM SIGKDD Conference on Knowledge Discovery and Data Mining*, 2014.

[21] X. L. Dong, E. Gabrilovich, G. Heitz, W. Horn, K. Murphy, S. Sun, and W. Zhang. From data fusion to knowledge fusion. *PVLDB*, 2014.

[22] X. L. Dong and F. Naumann. Data fusion–resolving data conflicts for integration. *PVLDB*, 2009.

[23] D. Fabbri and K. LeFevre. Explanation-based auditing. *PVLDB*, 5(1):1–12, Sept. 2011.

[24] A. Fader, S. Soderland, and O. Etzioni. Identifying relations for open information extraction. In *EMNLP*, 2011.

[25] W. Fan, F. Geerts, and X. Jia. A revival of integrity constraints for data cleaning. *Proc. VLDB Endow.*, 1(2):1522–1523, Aug. 2008.

[26] W. Fan, F. Geerts, X. Jia, and A. Kementsietsidis. Conditional functional dependencies for capturing data inconsistencies. *ACM Transactions on Database Systems*, 33(2):6:1–6:48, June 2008.

[27] T. A. Feo and M. G. C. Resende. A probabilistic heuristic for a computationally difficult set covering problem. *Operations Research Letters*, 8(2):67–71, Apr. 1989.

[28] H. Galhardas, D. Florescu, D. Shasha, and E. Simon. Ajax: An extensible data cleaning tool. In *Proceedings of the 2000 ACM SIGMOD International Conference on Management of Data*, SIGMOD, page 590, New York, NY, USA, 2000. ACM.

[29] M. R. Garey and D. S. Johnson. *Computers and Intractability: A Guide to the Theory of NP-Completeness*. W. H. Freeman & Co., New York, NY, USA, 1979.

[30] K. E. Gebaly, P. Agrawal, L. Golab, F. Korn, and D. Srivastava. Interpretable and informative explanations of outcomes. *PVLDB*, 8(1):61–72, 2014.

[31] L. Golab, H. Karloff, F. Korn, D. Srivastava, and B. Yu. On generating near-optimal tableaux for conditional functional dependencies. *PVLDB*, 1(1):376–390, Aug. 2008.

[32] L. Golab, H. J. Karloff, F. Korn, and D. Srivastava. Data auditor: Exploring data quality and semantics using pattern tableaux. *PVLDB*, 3(2):1641–1644, 2010.

[33] T. J. Green, G. Karvounarakis, and V. Tannen. Provenance semirings. In *PODS*, pages 31–40, 2007.

[34] A. Gruenheid, X. L. Dong, and D. Srivastava. Incremental record linkage. *PVLDB*, 7(9):697–708, 2014.

[35] M. Hall, E. Frank, G. Holmes, B. Pfahringer, P. Reutemann, and I. H. Witten. The weka data mining software: An update. *SIGKDD Explor. Newsl.*, 11(1):10–18, Nov. 2009.

[36] J. Hoffart, F. M. Suchanek, K. Berberich, and G. Weikum. YAGO2: A Spatially and Temporally Enhanced Knowledge Base from Wikipedia. 2012.

[37] D. V. Kalashnikov and S. Mehrotra. Domain-independent data cleaning via analysis of entity-relationship graph. *ACM*

Transactions on Database Systems, 31(2):716–767, June 2006.

[38] N. Khoussainova, M. Balazinska, and D. Suciu. Perfxplain: debugging mapreduce job performance. *Proc. VLDB Endow.*, 5(7):598–609, Mar. 2012.

[39] N. Koudas, S. Sarawagi, and D. Srivastava. Record linkage: Similarity measures and algorithms. In *Proceedings of the 2006 ACM SIGMOD International Conference on Management of Data*, SIGMOD '06, pages 802–803, New York, NY, USA, 2006. ACM.

[40] J. Liu, S. Ji, and J. Ye. *SLEP: Sparse Learning with Efficient Projections*. Arizona State University, 2009.

[41] Y. Low, D. Bickson, J. Gonzalez, C. Guestrin, A. Kyrola, and J. M. Hellerstein. Distributed graphlab: A framework for machine learning and data mining in the cloud. *PVLDB*, 5(8):716–727, Apr. 2012.

[42] Y. Low, J. Gonzalez, A. Kyrola, D. Bickson, C. Guestrin, and J. M. Hellerstein. Graphlab: A new parallel framework for machine learning. In *Conference on Uncertainty in Artificial Intelligence (UAI)*, Catalina Island, California, July 2010.

[43] A. Meliou, W. Gatterbauer, J. Halpern, C. Koch, K. F. Moore, and D. Suciu. Causality in databases. *IEEE Data Engineering Bulletin*, Sept. 2010.

[44] A. Meliou, W. Gatterbauer, K. F. Moore, and D. Suciu. The complexity of causality and responsibility for query answers and non-answers. *PVLDB*, 4(1):34–45, 2010.

[45] A. Meliou, W. Gatterbauer, S. Nath, and D. Suciu. Tracing data errors with view-conditioned causality. In *SIGMOD Conference*, pages 505–516, 2011.

[46] A. Meliou, S. Roy, and D. Suciu. Causality and explanations in databases. *PVLDB*, 7(13):1715–1716, 2014.

[47] K. P. Murphy. *Machine Learning: A Probabilistic Perspective*. The MIT Press, 2012.

[48] A. Y. Ng. Feature selection, l1 vs. l2 regularization, and rotational invariance. In *In ICML*, 2004.

[49] C. Parent and S. Spaccapietra. Issues and approaches of database integration. *Commununications of the ACM*, 41(5):166–178, 1998.

[50] D. Peleg. Approximation algorithms for the label-cover< sub> max</sub> and red-blue set cover problems. *Journal of Discrete Algorithms*, (1):55–64, March 2007.

[51] J. R. Quinlan. Induction of decision trees. *Machine Learning*, 1(1):81–106, Mar. 1986.

[52] E. Rahm and P. A. Bernstein. A survey of approaches to automatic schema matching. *The VLDB Journal*, 10(4):334–350, Dec. 2001.

[53] E. Rahm and H. H. Do. Data cleaning: Problems and current approaches. *IEEE Data Engineering Bulletin*, 23(4):3–13, 2000.

[54] V. Raman and J. M. Hellerstein. Potter's wheel: An interactive data cleaning system. In *Proceedings of the 27th International Conference on Very Large Data Bases*, VLDB '01, pages 381–390, San Francisco, CA, USA, 2001. Morgan Kaufmann Publishers Inc.

[55] S. Roy and D. Suciu. A formal approach to finding explanations for database queries. In *Proceedings of the 2014 ACM SIGMOD International Conference on Management of Data*, SIGMOD, pages 1579–1590, New York, NY, USA, 2014. ACM.

[56] S. Thirumuruganathan, M. Das, S. Desai, S. Amer-Yahia, G. Das, and C. Yu. Maprat: meaningful explanation, interactive exploration and geo-visualization of collaborative ratings. *PVLDB*, 5(12):1986–1989, Aug. 2012.

[57] R. Tibshirani. Regression shrinkage and selection via the lasso. *Journal of the Royal Statistical Society, Series B*, 58(1):267–288, 1996.

[58] K. Toutanova, D. Klein, C. D. Manning, and Y. Singer. Feature-rich part-of-speech tagging with a cyclic dependency network. In *Proceedings of the 2003 Conference of the North American Chapter of the Association for Computational Linguistics on Human Language Technology*, NAACL, pages 173–180, Stroudsburg, PA, USA, 2003. Association for Computational Linguistics.

[59] US Department of Transportation, Federal Highway Administration. Freeway incident and weather data. `http://portal.its.pdx.edu/Portal/index.php/fhwa`.

[60] E. Wu and S. Madden. Scorpion: Explaining away outliers in aggregate queries. *PVLDB*, 6(8):553–564, June 2013.

[61] M. Yakout, A. K. Elmagarmid, J. Neville, M. Ouzzani, and I. F. Ilyas. Guided data repair. *PVLDB*, 4(5):279–289, Feb. 2011.

[62] X. Yin, J. Han, and P. S. Yu. Truth discovery with multiple conflicting information providers on the web. In *KDD*, pages 1048–1052, New York, NY, USA, 2007. ACM.

[63] B. Zhao, B. I. P. Rubinstein, J. Gemmell, and J. Han. A Bayesian approach to discovering truth from conflicting sources for data integration. *PVLDB*, 5(6):550–561, 2012.

APPENDIX

A. SUMMARY OF NOTATIONS

Notation	Description
$e(V, P)$	Element with truthfulness V and property vector P
$f(P, \mathbf{E})$	Feature with property vector P and set of elements $\mathbf{E}$
$\mathcal{E}$	Dataset of elements $\mathcal{E} = \{e_1, \dots, e_n\}$
$\mathcal{F}$	Set of features $\mathcal{F} = \{f_1, \dots, f_k\}$; candidate diagnosis
$\Pr(\mathcal{F}\|\mathcal{E})$	Causal likelihood: probability that $\mathcal{F}$ caused the errors in $\mathcal{E}$
$f.\mathbf{E}^-$	The `false` elements in f: $\{e \mid (e \in f.\mathbf{E}) \wedge (\neg e.V)\}$
$f.\mathbf{E}^+$	The `true` elements in f: $\{e \mid (e \in f.\mathbf{E}) \wedge e.V\}$
ϵ_i	The error rate of feature f_i: $\epsilon_i = \frac{\|f_i.\mathbf{E}^-\|}{\|f_i.\mathbf{E}\|}$
α	The *a priori* probability that a feature is a cause of error
SV_f	The structure vector of feature f
L_f	The level of feature f
$\mathcal{P}_i^{f_p}$	Partition i of the child features of f_p
Var_i^f	The variance of error rates of features in partition $\mathcal{P}_i^{f_p}$

Figure 8: Summary of notations used in the paper.

B. THEORETICAL RESULTS

THEOREM 15 (COMPLEXITY AND BOUNDS). *Algorithm 1 has complexity $O(|\mathcal{F}|)$, and provides an $O(n)$-approximation of the minimum cost diagnosis, where n is the number of elements in $\mathcal{E}$ and $\mathcal{F}$ is the set of features that can be derived from $\mathcal{E}$.*

PROOF. Let D be the diagnosis produced by Algorithm 1, and let D_{OPT} be the diagnosis of minimum cost that covers all the elements. Algorithm 1 compares the cost of a parent feature with that of its children, and decides to proceed if the cost decreases. That means that for every $F \in D$, $Ancestors(F) \cap D_{OPT} = \varnothing$: If F', ancestor of F, was in D_{OPT}, we could produce a diagnosis of lower cost than D_{OPT} by replacing F' with its children.

Therefore, D_{OPT} contains no ancestors of $F \in D$, but it could contain its descendants instead of F. Let n_F be the total number of elements under feature F, and let ϵ be the error rate of the feature. The cost of feature F is the sum of the three cost types in Definition 9:

$$C_F = \log\frac{1}{\alpha} + n_F \log\frac{1}{\epsilon^{\epsilon}(1-\epsilon)^{(1-\epsilon)}}$$

In the worst case, F can be replaced by a single descendant feature F'' with error rate 1. This means that the false and true costs of F'' are 0, and therefore, its overall cost is $C_{F''} = \log\frac{1}{\alpha}$. Since $\log\frac{1}{\epsilon^{\epsilon}(1-\epsilon)^{(1-\epsilon)}} \leq 1$, the cost of F is at most $O(n_F)$ worse than the cost of the optimal descendant set of F. Adding these worst-case costs for all features in the diagnosis D, we get overall worst-case approximation bound $O(n)$, where n is the total number of elements.

Finally, Algorithm 1 accesses each feature at most once. Therefore, its time complexity is $O(|\mathcal{F}|)$. □

THEOREM 16 (TIGHTNESS). *The $O(n)$ approximation bound is tight.*

PROOF. Let F_0 be a feature that is the root of a subtree in the hierarchy. Let also F_0 have exactly two child nodes, F_1 and F_2, each containing n elements. Therefore, F_0 contains $2n$ elements. We assume that the error rates of features F_1 and F_2 are $\epsilon_1 = \epsilon_2 = \epsilon$. Therefore, the cost of F_0 is $C_0 = \log\frac{1}{\alpha} + 2n\log\frac{1}{\epsilon^{\epsilon}(1-\epsilon)^{(1-\epsilon)}}$, and the cost of F_1 and F_2 is $C_1 + C_2 = 2\log\frac{1}{\alpha} + 2n\log\frac{1}{\epsilon^{\epsilon}(1-\epsilon)^{(1-\epsilon)}}$. Therefore, DATAXRAY will select F_0 instead of its children and will terminate the descent to that part of the hierarchy. However, the optimal diagnosis can be F_1' and F_2', descendants of F_1 and F_2 respectively, with total cost $2\log\frac{1}{\alpha}$. This means that the cost C_0 is $O(n)$ worse than OPT. □

The worst-case analysis of the approximation bound only occurs when the errors are distributed uniformly across the children of a node, across all dimensions. If this is not true for some dimension, then the algorithm will descent into the corresponding partition to approach the optimal solution. It is in fact very unusual for this to happen in practice, which is why DATAXRAY performs much better than GREEDY in our experimental evaluation.

C. ADDITIONAL RESULTS

Figure 9 shows how the produced diagnoses compare with the ground truth at different granularities. For each level of the hierarchy, we depict the total incorrect features in a diagnosis (total false positive and false negative) for each method, normalized by the total number of features at that level. The plot presents an average of 50 executions over randomly generated datasets with 10,000 tuples and feature hierarchies of 5 levels.

DATAXRAY is the method closest to the ground truth, with only a few mistakes among features of average granularity (middle of the hierarchy). DATAAUDITOR tends to select more features at higher hierarchy levels, and this is where most of its mistakes are concentrated. REDBLUE and GREEDY make mistakes that are more evenly distributed across the hierarchy levels. In contrast, the classification techniques (FEATURESELECTION and DECISIONTREE) tend to make the most mistakes in the middle of the hierarchy, with almost 60% of the features at that level being incorrectly included to or excluded from the diagnosis.

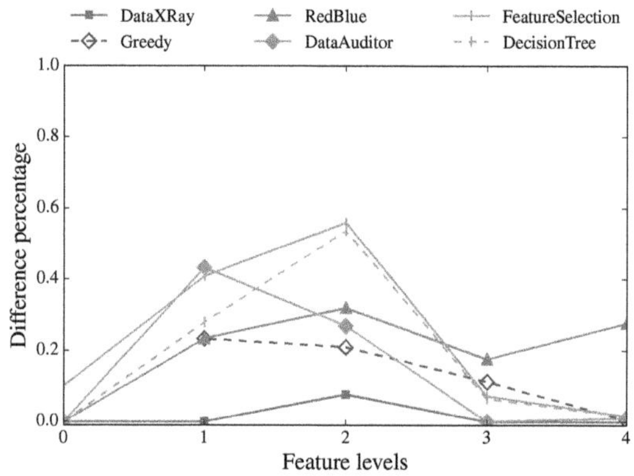

Figure 9: We evaluate how much the selected features at each hierarchy level deviate from the ground truth for each technique, over datasets of 10,000 elements. Level 0 is the root of the hierarchy, and level 4 contains the leaves (individual elements). DATAXRAY has the smallest difference from the ground truth.

KATARA: A Data Cleaning System Powered by Knowledge Bases and Crowdsourcing

Xu Chu[1*] John Morcos[1*] Ihab F. Ilyas[1*]
Mourad Ouzzani[2] Paolo Papotti[2] Nan Tang[2] Yin Ye[2]
[1]University of Waterloo [2]Qatar Computing Research Institute
{x4chu,jmorcos,ilyas}@uwaterloo.ca {mouzzani,ppapotti,ntang,yye}@qf.org.qa

ABSTRACT

Classical approaches to clean data have relied on using integrity constraints, statistics, or machine learning. These approaches are known to be limited in the cleaning accuracy, which can usually be improved by consulting master data and involving experts to resolve ambiguity. The advent of knowledge bases (KBs), both general-purpose and within enterprises, and crowdsourcing marketplaces are providing yet more opportunities to achieve higher accuracy at a larger scale. We propose KATARA, a knowledge base and crowd powered data cleaning system that, given a table, a KB, and a crowd, interprets table semantics to align it with the KB, identifies correct and incorrect data, and generates top-k possible repairs for incorrect data. Experiments show that KATARA can be applied to various datasets and KBs, and can efficiently annotate data and suggest possible repairs.

1. INTRODUCTION

A plethora of data cleaning approaches that are based on integrity constraints [2,7,9,20,36], statistics [30], or machine learning [43], have been proposed in the past. Unfortunately, despite their applicability and generality, they are best-effort approaches that cannot ensure the accuracy of the repaired data. Due to their very nature, these methods do not have enough evidence to precisely identify and update errors. For example, consider the table of soccer players in Fig. 1 and a functional dependency $B \rightarrow C$, which states that B (country) uniquely determines C (capital). This would identify a problem for the four values in tuple t_1 and t_3 over the attributes B and C. A repair algorithm would have to guess which value to change so as to "clean" the data.

To increase the accuracy of such methods, a natural approach is to use external information in tabular master data [19] and domain experts [19,35,40,44]. However, these resources may be scarce and are usually expensive to employ. Fortunately, we are witnessing an increased availability of both general purpose knowledge bases (KBs) such as

	A	B	C	D	E	F	G
t_1	Rossi	Italy	Rome	Verona	Italian	Proto	1.78
t_2	Klate	S. Africa	Pretoria	Pirates	Afrikaans	P. Eliz.	1.69
t_3	Pirlo	Italy	Madrid	Juve	Italian	Flero	1.77

Figure 1: A table $\mathcal{T}$ for soccer players

Yago [21], DBpedia [31], and Freebase, as well as special-purpose KBs such as RxNorm[1]. There is also a sustained effort in the industry to build KBs [14]. These KBs are usually well curated and cover a large portion of the data at hand. In addition, while access to an expert may be limited and expensive, crowdsourcing has been proven to be a viable and cost-effective alternative solution.

Challenges. Effectively exploring KBs and crowd in data cleaning raises several new challenges.

(*i*) Matching (dirty) tables to KBs is a hard problem. Tables may lack reliable, comprehensible labels, thus requiring the matching to be executed on the data values. This may lead to ambiguity; more than one mapping may be possible. For example, Rome could be either city, capital, or club in the KB. Moreover, tables usually contain errors. This would trigger problems such as erroneous matching, which will add uncertainty to or even mislead the matching process.

(*ii*) KBs are usually incomplete in terms of the coverage of values in the table, making it hard to find correct table patterns and associate KB values. Since we consider data that could be dirty, it is often unclear, in the case of failing to find a match, whether the database values are erroneous or the KB does not cover these values.

(*iii*) Human involvement is needed to validate matchings and to verify data when the KBs do not have enough coverage. Effectively involving the crowd requires dealing with traditional crowdsourcing issues such as forming easy-to-answer questions for the new data cleaning tasks and optimizing the order of issuing questions to reduce monetary cost.

Despite several approaches for understanding tables with KBs [13,28,39], to the best of our knowledge, they do not explicitly assume the presence of dirty data. Moreover, previous work exploiting reference information for repair has only considered full matches between the tables and the master data [19]. On the contrary, with KBs, partial matches are common due to the incompleteness of the reference.

To this end, we present KATARA, the first data cleaning system that leverages prevalent trustworthy KBs and crowdsourcing for data cleaning. Given a dirty table and a KB,

*Work partially done while interning/working at QCRI.

[1]`https://www.nlm.nih.gov/research/umls/rxnorm/`

SIGMOD'15, May 31–June 4, 2015, Melbourne, Victoria, Australia.

http://dx.doi.org/10.1145/2723372.2749431.

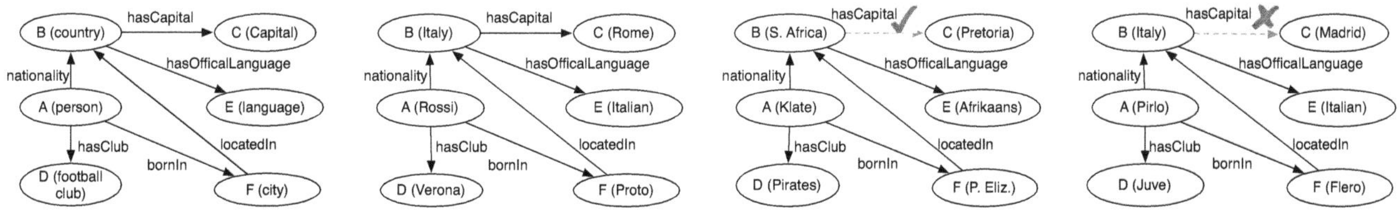

(a) A table pattern φ_s (b) t_1: KB validated (c) t_2: KB & crowd validated (d) t_3: erroneous tuple

Figure 2: Sample solution overview

KATARA first discovers *table patterns* to map the table to the KB. For instance, consider the table of soccer players in Fig. 1 and the KB Yago. Our table patterns state that the types for columns A, B, and C in the KB are person, country, and capital, respectively, and that two relationships between these columns hold, *i.e.,* A is related to B via nationality and B is related to C via hasCapital. With table patterns, KATARA annotates tuples as either correct or incorrect by interleaving KBs and crowdsourcing. For incorrect tuples, KATARA will extract top-k mappings from the KB as possible repairs. In addition, a by-product of KATARA is that data annotated by the crowd as being valid, and which is not found in the KB, provides new facts to enrich the KB. KATARA actively and efficiently involve crowd workers, who are assumed to be experts in the KBs, when automatic approaches cannot capture or face ambiguity, for example, to involve humans to validate patterns discovered, and to involve humans to select from the top-k possible repairs.

Contributions. We built KATARA for annotating and repairing data using KBs and crowd, with the following contributions.

1. *Table pattern definition and discovery.* We propose a new class of table patterns to explain table semantics using KBs (Section 3). Each table pattern is a directed graph, where a node represents a type of a column and a directed edge represents a binary relationship between two columns. We present a new rank-join based algorithm to efficiently discover table patterns with high scores. (Section 4).
2. *Table pattern validation via crowdsourcing.* We devise an efficient algorithm to validate the best table pattern via crowdsourcing (Section 5). To minimize the number of questions, we use an entropy-based scheduling algorithm to maximize the uncertainty reduction of candidate table patterns.
3. *Data annotation.* Given a table pattern, we annotate data with different categories (Section 6): (*i*) correct data validated by the KB; (*ii*) correct data jointly validated by the KB and the crowd; and (*iii*) erroneous data jointly identified by the KB and the crowd. We also devise an efficient algorithm to generate top-k possible repairs for those erroneous data identified in (*iii*).
4. We conducted extensive experiments to demonstrate the effectiveness and efficiency of KATARA using real-world datasets and KBs (Section 7).

2. AN OVERVIEW OF KATARA

KATARA consists of three modules (see Fig. 9 in Appendix): pattern discovery, pattern validation, and data annotation. The *pattern discovery* module discovers table patterns between a table and a KB. The *pattern validation* module uses crowdsourcing to select one table pattern. Using the selected table pattern, the *data annotation* module interacts with the KB and the crowd to annotate data. It also generates possible repairs for erroneous tuples. Moreover, new facts verified by crowd will be used to enrich KBs.

Example 1: Consider a table $\mathcal{T}$ for soccer players (Fig. 1). $\mathcal{T}$ has opaque values for the attributes' labels, thus its semantics is completely unknown. We assume that we have access to a KB $\mathcal{K}$ (*e.g.,* Yago) containing information related to $\mathcal{T}$. KATARA works in the following steps.

(1) Pattern discovery. KATARA first discovers table patterns that contain the types of the columns and the relationships between them. A table pattern is represented as a labelled graph (Fig. 2(a)) where a node represents an attribute and its associated type, *e.g.,* "C (capital)" means that the type of attribute C in KB $\mathcal{K}$ is capital. A directed edge between two nodes represents the relationship between two attributes, *e.g.,* "B hasCapital C" means that the relationship from B to C in $\mathcal{K}$ is hasCapital. A column could have multiple candidate types, *e.g.,* C could also be of type city. However, knowing that the relationship from B to C is hasCapital indicates that capital is a better choice. Since KBs are often incomplete, the discovered patterns may not cover all attributes of a table, *e.g.,* attribute G of table $\mathcal{T}$ is not captured by the pattern in Fig. 2(a).

(2) Pattern validation. Consider a case where pattern discovery finds two similar patterns: the one in Fig. 2(a), and its variant with type location for column C. To select the best table pattern, we send the crowd the question "*Which type (*capital *or* location*) is more accurate for values (*Rome, Pretoria *and* Madrid*)?*". Crowd answers will help choose the right pattern.

(3) Data annotation. Given the pattern in Fig. 2(a), KATARA annotates a tuple with the following three labels:

(i) *Validated by the* KB. By mapping tuple t_1 in table $\mathcal{T}$ to $\mathcal{K}$, KATARA finds a full match, shown in Fig. 2(b) indicating that Rossi (resp. Italy) is in $\mathcal{K}$ as a person (resp. country), and the relationship from Rossi to Italy is nationality. Similarly, all other values in t_1 *w.r.t.* attributes A-F are found in $\mathcal{K}$. We consider t_1 to be correct *w.r.t.* the pattern in Fig. 2(a) and only to attributes A-F.

(ii) *Jointly validated by the* KB *and the crowd.* Consider t_2 about Klate, whose explanation is depicted in Fig. 2(c). In $\mathcal{K}$, KATARA finds that S. Africa is a country, and Pretoria is a capital. However, the relationship from S. Africa to Pretoria is missing. A positive answer from the crowd to the question "*Does* S. Africa hasCapital Pretoria*?*" completes the missing mapping. We consider t_2 correct and generate a new fact "S. Africa hasCapital Pretoria".

(iii) *Erroneous tuple.* For tuple t_3, there is also no link from Italy to Madrid in $\mathcal{K}$ (Fig. 2(d)). A negative answer from the crowd to the question "*Does* Italy hasCapital Madrid*?*" confirms that there is an error in t_3, At this point, however, we cannot decide which value in t_3 is wrong, Italy or Madrid. KATARA will then extract related evidences from $\mathcal{K}$, such as Italy hasCapital Rome and Spain hasCapital Madrid, and use these evidences to generate a set of possible repairs for this tuple. □

The pattern discovery module can be used to select the more relevant KB for a given dataset. If the module cannot find patterns for a table and a KB, KATARA will terminate.

3. PRELIMINARIES

3.1 Knowledge Bases

We consider knowledge bases (KBs) as RDF-based data consisting of *resources*, whose schema is defined using the Resource Description Framework Schema (RDFS). A *resource* is a unique identifier for a real-word entity. For instance, Rossi, the soccer player, and Rossi, the motorcycle racer, are two different resources. Resources are represented using URIs (Uniform Resource Identifiers) in Yago and DBPedia, and mids (machine-generated ids) in Freebase. A *literal* is a string, date, or number, *e.g.,* 1.78. A *property* (*a.k.a. relationship*) is a binary predicate that represents a relationship between two resources or between a resource and a literal. We denote the property between resource x and resource (or literal) y by $P(x, y)$. For instance, locatedIn(Milan, Italy) indicates that Milan is in Italy.

An RDFS ontology distinguishes between classes and instances. A *class* is a resource that represents a set of objects, *e.g.,* the class of countries. A resource that is a member of a class is called an *instance* of that class. The type relationship associates an instance to a class *e.g.,* type(Italy) = country.

A more specific class c can be specified as a *subclass* of a more general class d by using the statement subclassOf(c, d). This means that all instances of c are also instances of d, *e.g.,* subclassOf(capital, location). Similarly, a property P_1 can be a sub-property of a property P_2 by the statement subpropertyOf(P_1, P_2). Moreover, we assume that the property between an entity and its readable name is labeled with "label", according to the RDFS schema.

Note that an RDF ontology naturally covers the case of a KB without a class hierarchy such as IMDB. Also, a more expressive languages, such as OWL (Web Ontology Language), can offer more reasoning opportunities at a higher computational cost. However, KBs in industry [14] as well as popular ones, such as Yago, Freebase, and DBpedia, use RDFS.

3.2 Table Patterns

Consider a table $\mathcal{T}$ with attributes denoted by A_i. There are two basic semantic annotations on a relational table.

(1) *Type of an attribute* A_i. The type of an attribute is an annotation that represents the class of attribute values in A_i. For example, the type of attribute B in Fig. 1 is country.

(2) *Relationship from attribute* A_i *to attribute* A_j. The relationship between two attributes is an annotation that represents how A_i and A_j are related through a directed binary relationship. A_i is called the *subject* of the relationship, and A_j is called the *object* of the relationship. For example, the relationship from attribute B to C in Fig. 1 is hasCapital.

Table pattern. A *table pattern* (*pattern* for short) φ of a table $\mathcal{T}$ is a labelled directed graph $G(V, E)$ with nodes V and edges E. Each node $u \in V$ corresponds to an attribute in $\mathcal{T}$, possibly typed, and each edge $(u, v) \in E$ from u to v has a label P, denoting the relationship between two attributes that u and v represent. For a pattern φ, we denote by φ_u a node u in φ, $\varphi_{(u,v)}$ an edge in φ, φ_V all nodes in φ, and φ_E all edges in φ.

We assume that a table pattern is a connected graph. When there exist multiple disconnected patterns, *i.e.,* two table patterns that do not share any common node, we treat them independently. Hence, in the following, we focus on discussing the case of a single table pattern.

Semantics. A tuple t of $\mathcal{T}$ *matches* a table pattern φ containing m nodes $\{v_1, \ldots, v_m\}$ *w.r.t.* a KB $\mathcal{K}$, denoted by $t \models \varphi$, if there exist m distinct attributes $\{A_1, \ldots, A_m\}$ in $\mathcal{T}$ and m resources $\{x_1, \ldots, x_m\}$ in $\mathcal{K}$ such that:

1. there is a one-to-one mapping from A_i (and x_i) to v_i for $i \in [1, m]$;
2. $t[A_i] \approx x_i$ and either $\mathsf{type}(x_i) = \mathsf{type}(v_i)$ or $\mathsf{subclassOf}(\mathsf{type}(x_i), \mathsf{type}(v_i))$;
3. for each edge (v_i, v_j) in φ_E with property P, there exists a property P' for the corresponding resources x_i and x_j in $\mathcal{K}$ such that $P' = P$ or subpropertyOf(P', P).

Intuitively, if t matches φ, each corresponding attribute value of t maps to a resource r in $\mathcal{K}$ under a domain-specific similarity function ($\approx$), and r is a (sub-)type of the type given in φ (conditions 1 and 2). Moreover, for each property P in a pattern, the property between the two corresponding resources must be P or its sub-properties (condition 3).

Example 2: Consider tuple t_1 in Fig. 1 and pattern φ_s in Fig. 2(a). Tuple t_1 matches φ_s, as in Fig. 2(b), since for each attribute value (*e.g.,* $t_1[A]$ = Rossi and $t_1[B]$ = Italy) there is a resource in $\mathcal{K}$ that has a similar value with corresponding type (person for Rossi and country for Italy) for conditions 1 and 2, and the property nationality holds from Rossi to Italy in $\mathcal{K}$ (condition 3). Similarly, conditions 1–3 hold for other attribute values in t_1. Hence, $t_1 \models \varphi_s$. □

We say that a tuple t of $\mathcal{T}$ *partially matches* a table pattern φ *w.r.t.* $\mathcal{K}$, if at least one of condition 2 and condition 3 holds.

Example 3: Consider t_2 in Fig. 1 and φ_s in Fig. 2(a). We say that t_2 partially matches φ_s, since the property hasCapital from $t_2[B]$ = S. Africa to $t_2[C]$ = Pretoria does not exist in $\mathcal{K}$, *i.e.,* condition 3 does not hold. □

Given a table $\mathcal{T}$, a KB $\mathcal{K}$, and a pattern φ, Fig. 3 shows how KATARA works on $\mathcal{T}$.

(1) *Attributes covered* by $\mathcal{K}$. Attributes A–F in Fig. 1 are covered by the pattern in Fig. 2(a). We consider two cases for the tuples.

(a) *Fully covered by* $\mathcal{K}$. We annotate such tuples as semantically correct relative to φ and $\mathcal{K}$ (Fig. 2(b)).
(b) *Partially covered by* $\mathcal{K}$. We use crowdsourcing to verify whether the non-covered data is caused by the incompleteness of $\mathcal{K}$ (Fig. 2(c)) or by actual errors (Fig. 2(d)).

(2) *Attributes not covered* by $\mathcal{K}$. Attribute G in Fig. 1 is not

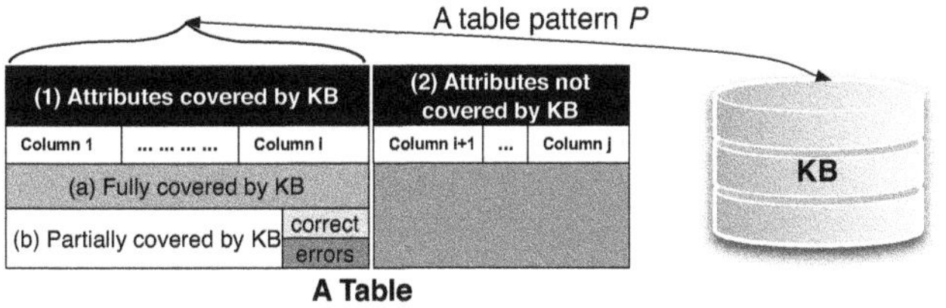

Figure 3: Coverage of a table pattern

covered by the pattern in Fig. 2(a). In this case, KATARA cannot annotate G due to the missing information in $\mathcal{K}$.

For non-covered attributes, we could ask the crowd open-ended questions, such as "*What are the possible relationships between* Rossi *and* 1.78*?*". While approaches have been proposed for open-ended questions to the crowd [38], we leave the problem of extending the structure of the KBs to future work, as discussed in Section 9.

4. TABLE PATTERN DISCOVERY

We first describe candidate types and candidate relationships generation (Section 4.1). We then discuss the scoring to rank table patterns (Section 4.2). We also present a rank-join algorithm to efficiently compute top-k table patterns (Section 4.3) from the candidate types and relationships.

4.1 Candidate Type/Relationship Discovery

We focus on cleaning tabular data for which the schema is either unavailable or unusable. This is especially true for most Web tables and in many enterprise settings where cryptic naming conventions are used. Thus, for table-KB mapping, we use a more general instance based approach that does not require the availability of meaningful column labels. For each column A_i of table $\mathcal{T}$ and for each value $t[A_i]$ of a tuple t, we map this value to several resources in the KB $\mathcal{K}$ whose type can then be extracted. To this end, we issue the following SPARQL query which returns the types and supertypes of entities whose label (*i.e.*, value) is $t[A_i]$.

Q_{types}	**select** $?c_i$ **where** $\{?x_i$ rdfs:label $t[A_i]$, $?x_i$ rdfs:type/rdfs:subClassOf$*$ $?c_i\}$

Similarly, the relationship between two values $t[A_i]$ and $t[A_j]$ from a KB $\mathcal{K}$ can be retrieved via the two following SPARQL queries.

Q^1_{rels}	**select** $?P_{ij}$ **where** $\{?x_i$ rdfs:label $t[A_i]$, $?x_j$ rdfs:label $t[A_j]$, $?x_i$ $?P_{ij}$/rdfs:subPropertyOf$*$ $?x_j\}$
Q^2_{rels}	**select** $?P_{ij}$ **where** $\{?x_i$ rdfs:label $t[A_i]$, $?x_i$ $?P_{ij}$/rdfs:subPropertyOf$*$ $t[A_j]\}$

Query Q^1_{rels} retrieves relationships where the second attribute is a resource in KBs and Q^2_{rels} retrieves relationships where the second attribute is a literal value, *i.e.*, untyped.

Example 4: In Fig. 1, both Italy and Rome are stored as resources in K, thus their relationship hasCapital would be discovered by Q^1_{rels}; while numerical values such as 1.78 are stored as literals in the KBs, thus the relationship between Rossi and 1.78 would be discovered by query Q^2_{rels}. □

In addition, for two values $t[A_i]$ and $t[A_j]$, we consider them as an ordered pair, thus in total four queries are issued.

Ranking Candidates. We use a normalized version of tf-idf (term frequency-inverse document frequency) [29] to rank the candidate types of a column A_i. We simply consider each cell $t[A_i], \forall t \in \mathcal{T}$, as a query term, and each candidate type T_i as a document whose terms are the entities of T_i in $\mathcal{K}$. The tf-idf score of assigning T_i as the type for A_i is the sum of all tf-idf scores of all cells in A_i:

$$\text{tf-idf}(T_i, A_i) = \sum_{t \in \mathcal{T}} \text{tf-idf}(T_i, t[A_i])$$

where $\text{tf-idf}(T_i, t[A_i]) = \text{tf}(T_i, t[A_i]) \cdot \text{idf}(T_i, t[A_i])$.

The term frequency $\text{tf}(T_i, t[A_i])$ measures how frequently $t[A_i]$ appears in document T_i. Since every type has a different number of entities, the term frequency is normalized by the total number of entities of a type.

$$\text{tf}(T_i, t[A_i]) = \begin{cases} 0 & \text{if } t[A_i] \text{ is not of Type } T_i \\ \frac{1}{\log(\text{Number of Entities of Type } T_i)} & \text{otherwise} \end{cases}$$

For example, consider a column with a single cell Italy that has both type Country and type Place. Since there is a smaller number of entities of type Country than that of Place, Country is more likely to be the type of that column.

The inverse document frequency $\text{idf}(T_i, t[A_i])$ measures how important $t[A_i]$ is. Under local completeness assumption of KBs [15], if the KB knows about one possible type of $t[A_i]$, the KB should have all possible types of $t[A_i]$. Thus, we define $\text{idf}(T_i, t[A_i])$ as follows:

$$\text{idf}(T_i, t[A_i]) = \begin{cases} 0 & \text{if } t[A_i] \text{ has no type} \\ \log \frac{\text{Number of Types in } \mathcal{K}}{\text{Number of Types of } t[A_i]} & \text{otherwise} \end{cases}$$

Intuitively, the less the number of types $t[A_i]$ has, the more contribution $t[A_i]$ makes. For example, consider a column that has two cells "Apple" and "Microsoft". Both have Type Company, however, "Apple" has also Type Fruit. Therefore, "Microsoft" being of Type Company says more about the column being of Type Company than "Apple" says about the column being of Type Company.

The tf-idf scores of all candidate types for A_i are normalized to $[0, 1]$ by dividing them by the largest tf-idf score of the candidate type for A_i. The tf-idf score $\text{tf-idf}(P_{ij}, A_i, A_j)$ of candidate relationship P_{ij} assigned to column pairs A_i and A_j are defined similarly.

4.2 Scoring Model for Table Patterns

A table pattern contains types of attributes and properties between attributes. The space of all candidate patterns is very large (up to the Cartesian product of all possible types and relationships), making it expensive for human verification. Since not all candidate patterns make sense in practice, we need a meaningful scoring function to rank them and consider only the top-k ones for human validation.

A naive scoring model for a candidate table pattern φ, consisting of type T_i for column A_i and relationship P_{ij} for column pair A_i and A_j, is to simply add up all tf-idf scores of the candidate types and relationships in φ:

$$\text{naiveScore}(\varphi) = \Sigma_{i=0}^{m} \text{tf-idf}(T_i, A_i) + \Sigma_{ij} \text{tf-idf}(P_{ij}, A_i, A_j)$$

However, columns are not independent of each other. The choice of the type for a column A_i affects the choice of the relationship for column pair A_i and A_j, and vice versa.

Example 5: Consider the two columns B and C in Fig. 1. B has candidate types economy, country, and state, C has candidate types city and capital, and B and C have a candidate relationship hasCapital. Intuitively, country as a candi-

Algorithm 1 PDISCOVERY

Input: a table $\mathcal{T}$, a KB $\mathcal{K}$, and a number k.
Output: top-k table patterns based on their scores

```
1: types(A_i) ← get a ranked list of candidate types for A_i
2: properties(A_i, A_j) ← get a ranked list of candidate relationships for A_i and A_j
3: Let P be the top-k table patterns, initialized empty
4: for all T_i ∈ types(A_i), and P_ij ∈ properties(A_i, A_j) in descending order of tf-idf scores do
5:     if |P| > k and TYPEPRUNING(T_i) then
6:         continue
7:     generate all table patterns P' involving T_i or P_ij
8:     compute the score for each table pattern P in P'
9:     update P using P'
10:    compute the upper bound score B of all unseen patterns, and let φ_k ∈ P be the table pattern with lowest score
11:    halt when score(φ_k) > B
12: return P
```

date type for column B is more compatible with hasCapital than economy since capitals are associated with countries, not economies. In addition, capital is also more compatible with hasCapital than city since not all cities are capitals. □

Based on the above observation, to quantify the "compatibility" between a type T and relationship P, where T serves as the type for the resources appearing as *subjects* of the relationship P, we introduce a coherence score $\mathsf{subSC}(T,P)$. Similarly, to quantify the "compatibility" between a type T and relationship P, where T serves as the type for the entities appearing as *objects* of the relationship P, we introduce a coherence scores $\mathsf{objSC}(T,P)$. $\mathsf{subSC}(T,P)$ (resp. $\mathsf{objSC}(T,P)$) measures how likely an entity of Type T appears as a subject (resp. object) of the relationship P.

We use pointwise mutual information (PMI) [10] as a proxy for computing $\mathsf{subSC}(T,P)$ and $\mathsf{objSC}(T,P)$. We use the following notations: $\mathsf{ENT}(T)$ - the set of entities in $\mathcal{K}$ of type T, $\mathsf{subENT}(P)$ - the set of entities in $\mathcal{K}$ that appear in the subject of P, $\mathsf{objENT}(P)$ - the set of entities in $\mathcal{K}$ that appear in the object of P, and $\mathcal{N}$ - the total number of entities in $\mathcal{K}$. We then consider the following probabilities: $\mathsf{Pr}(T) = \frac{|\mathsf{ENT}(T)|}{\mathcal{N}}$, the probability of an entity belonging to T, $\mathsf{Pr_{sub}}(P) = \frac{|\mathsf{subENT}(P)|}{\mathcal{N}}$, the probability of an entity appearing in the subject of P, $\mathsf{Pr_{obj}}(P) = \frac{|\mathsf{objENT}(P)|}{\mathcal{N}}$, the probability of an entity appearing in the object of P, $\mathsf{Pr_{sub}}(P \cap T) = \frac{|\mathsf{ENT}(T) \cap \mathsf{subENT}(P)|}{\mathcal{N}}$, the probability of an entity belonging to type T and appearing in the subject of P, and $\mathsf{Pr_{obj}}(P \cap T) = \frac{|\mathsf{ENT}(T) \cap \mathsf{objENT}(P)|}{\mathcal{N}}$, the probability of an entity belonging to type T and appearing in the object of P. Finally, we can define $\mathsf{PMI_{sub}}(T,P)$:

$$\mathsf{PMI_{sub}}(T,P) = \log \frac{\mathsf{Pr_{sub}}(P \cap T)}{\mathsf{Pr_{sub}}(P)\mathsf{Pr}(T)}$$

The PMI can be normalized into $[-1,1]$ as follows [3]:

$$\mathsf{NPMI_{sub}}(T,P) = \frac{\mathsf{PMI_{sub}}(T,P)}{-\mathsf{Pr_{sub}}(P \cap T)}$$

To ensure that the coherence score is in $[0,1]$, we define the *subject semantic coherence* of T for P as

$$\mathsf{subSC}(T,P) = \frac{\mathsf{NPMI_{sub}}(T,P) + 1}{2}$$

The *object semantic coherence* of T for P can be defined similarly.

Example 6: Below are sample coherence scores computed from Yago.

Algorithm 2 TYPEPRUNING

Input: current top-k table patterns $\mathcal{P}$, candidate type T_i.
Output: a **boolean** value, true/false means T_i can/cannot be pruned

```
curMinCohSum(A_i) ← minimum sum of all coherence scores involving column A_i in current top-k P
maxCohSum(A_i, T_i) ← maximum sum of all coherence scores if the type of column A_i is T_i
if maxCohSum(A_i, T_i) < curMinCohSum(A_i) then
    return true
else
    return false
```

$\mathsf{subSC}(\mathsf{economy}, \mathsf{hasCapital}) = 0.84$
$\mathsf{subSC}(\mathsf{country}, \mathsf{hasCapital}) = 0.86$
$\mathsf{objSC}(\mathsf{city}, \mathsf{hasCapital}) = 0.69$
$\mathsf{objSC}(\mathsf{capital}, \mathsf{hasCapital}) = 0.83$

These scores reflect our intuition in Example 5: country is more suitable than economy to act as a type for the subject resources of hasCapital; and capital is more suitable than city to act as a type for the object resources of hasCapital. □

We now define the *score* of a pattern φ as follows:

$$\mathsf{score}(\varphi) = \Sigma_{i=0}^{m}\mathsf{tf\text{-}idf}(T_i, A_i) + \Sigma_{ij}\mathsf{tf\text{-}idf}(P_{ij}, A_i, A_j) + \Sigma_{ij}(\mathsf{subSC}(T_i, P_{ij}) + \mathsf{objSC}(T_j, P_{ij}))$$

4.3 Top-k Table Pattern Generation

Given the scoring model of table patterns, we describe how to retrieve the top-k table patterns with the highest scores without having to enumerate all candidates. We formulate this as a rank-join problem [22]: given a set of sorted lists and join conditions of those lists, the rank-join algorithm produces the top-k join results based on some score function for early termination without consuming all the inputs.

Algorithm. The algorithm, referred as PDISCOVERY, is given in Algorithm 1. Given a table $\mathcal{T}$, a KB $\mathcal{K}$, and a number k, it produces top-k table patterns. To start, each input list, *i.e.*, candidate types for a column, and candidate relationships for a column pair, is ordered according to the respective tf-idf scores (lines 1-2). When two candidate types (resp. relationships) have the same tf-idf scores, the more discriminative type (resp. relationship) is ranked higher, *i.e.*, the one with less number of instances in $\mathcal{K}$.

Two lists are joined if they agree on one column, *e.g.*, the list of candidate types for A_i is joined with the list of candidate relationships for A_i and A_j. A join result is a candidate pattern φ, and the scoring function is *score*(φ). The rank-join algorithm scans the ranked input lists in descending order of their tf-idf scores (lines 3-4), table patterns are generated incrementally as we move down the input lists. Table patterns that cannot be used to produce top-k patterns will be pruned (lines 5-6). For each join result, *i.e.*, each table pattern φ, the score $\mathsf{score}(\varphi)$ is computed (lines 7-8). We also maintain an upper bound $\mathcal{B}$ of the scores of all unseen join results, *i.e.*, table patterns (line 10). Since each list is ranked, $\mathcal{B}$ can be computed by adding up the support scores of the current positions in the ranked lists, plus the maximum coherence scores a candidate relationship can have with any types. We terminate the join process if either we have exhaustively scanned every input list, or we have obtained top-k table patterns and the score of the kth table pattern is greater than or equal to $\mathcal{B}$ (line 11).

Lines 5-6 in Algorithm 1 check whether a candidate type T_i for column A_i can be pruned without generating table patterns involving T_i by calling Algorithm 2. The intuition behind type pruning (Algorithm 2) is that a candidate type T_i is useful if it is more coherent with any relationship P_{ix} than previously examined types for A_i. We first calculate the current minimum sum of coherence scores involving column A_i in the current top-k patterns, *i.e.*, $\mathsf{curMinCohSum}(A_i)$ (line 1). We then calculate the maximum possible sum of coherence scores involving type T_i, *i.e.*, $\mathsf{maxCohSum}(A_i, T_i)$ (line 2). T_i can be pruned if $\mathsf{maxCohSum}(A_i, T_i) < \mathsf{curMinCohSum}(A_i)$ since any table pattern having T_i as the type for A_i will have a lower score than the scores of the current top-k patterns (lines 3-6).

Example 7: Consider the rank-join graph in Fig. 4 ($k = 2$) for a table with just two columns B and C as in Fig. 1. The tf-idf scores for each candidate type and relationship are shown in the parentheses. The top-2 table patterns φ_1, φ_2 are shown on the top. $score(\varphi_1) = \mathsf{sup}(\mathsf{country}, B) + \mathsf{sup}(\mathsf{capital}, C) + \mathsf{sup}(\mathsf{hasCapital}, B, C) + 5 \times (\mathsf{subSC}(\mathsf{country}, \mathsf{hasCapital}) + \mathsf{objSC}(\mathsf{capital}, \mathsf{hasCapital})) = 1.0 + 0.9 + 0.9 + 0.86 + 0.83 = 4.49$. Similarly, we have $score(\varphi_2) = 4.47$.

Suppose we are currently examining type state for column B. We do not need to generate table patterns involving state since the maximum coherence between state and hasCapital or isLocatedIn is less than the the current minimum coherence score between type of column B and relationship between B and C in the current top-2 patterns.

Suppose we are examining type whole for column C, and we have reached type state for B and hasCapital for relationship B, C. The bound score for all unseen patterns is $\mathcal{B} = 0.7 + 0.5 + 0.9 + 0.86 + 0.83 = 3.78$, where 0.7, 0.9 and 0.5 are the tf-idf scores for state, whole and hasCapital respectively, and 0.86 (resp. 0.83) is the maximum coherence score between any type in $\mathsf{types}(B)$ (resp. $\mathsf{types}(C)$) and any relationship in $\mathsf{properties}(B, C)$. Since $\mathcal{B}$ is smaller than $score(\varphi_2) = 4.47$, we terminate the rank join process. □

Correctness. Algorithm 1 is guaranteed to produce the top-k table patterns since we keep the current top-k patterns in $\mathcal{P}$, and we terminate when we are sure that it will not produce any new table pattern with a higher score. In the worst case, we still have to exhaustively go through all the ranked lists to produce the top-k table patterns. However, in most cases the top ranked table patterns involve only candidate types/relationships with high tf-idf scores, which are at the top of the lists.

Computing coherence scores for a type and a relationship is an expensive operation that requires set intersection. Therefore, for a given $\mathcal{K}$, we compute offline the coherence score for every type and every relationship. For each relationship, we also keep the maximum coherence score it can achieve with any type, to efficiently compute the bound $\mathcal{B}$.

5. PATTERN VALIDATION VIA CROWD

We now study how to use the crowd to validate the discovered table patterns. Specifically, given a set $\mathcal{P}$ of candidate patterns, a table $\mathcal{T}$, a KB $\mathcal{K}$, and a crowdsourcing framework, we need to identify the most appropriate pattern for $\mathcal{T}$ *w.r.t.* $\mathcal{K}$, with the objective of minimizing the number of crowdsourcing questions. We assume that the crowd workers are experts in the semantics of the reference KBs, *i.e.*, they can verify if values in the tables fit into the KBs.

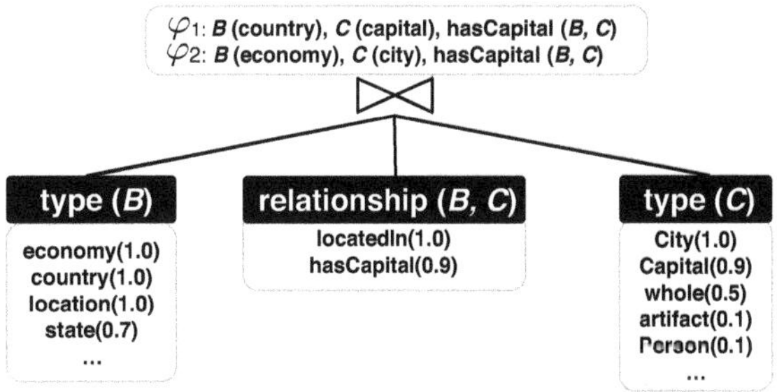

Figure 4: Encoding top-k as a rank-join

5.1 Creating Questions for the Crowd

A naive approach to generate crowdsourcing questions is to express each candidate table pattern as a whole in a single question to the crowd who would then select the best one. However, table pattern graphs can be hard for crowd users to understand (*e.g.*, Fig. 2(a)). Also, crowd workers are known to be good at answering simple questions [41]. A practical solution is to decompose table patterns into simple tasks: (1) type validation, *i.e.*, to validate the type of a column in the table pattern; and (2) binary relationship validation, *i.e.*, to validate the relationship between two columns.

Column type validation. Given a set of candidate types $\mathsf{candT}(A_i)$ for column A_i, one type $T_i \in \mathsf{candT}(A_i)$ needs to be selected. We formulate the following question to the crowd about the type of a column: *What is the most accurate type of the highlighted column?*; along with k_t randomly chosen tuples from $\mathcal{T}$ and all candidate types from $\mathsf{candT}(A_i)$. A sample question is given as follows.

> Q_1 : *What is the most accurate type of the highlighted column?*
> (A, B, C, D, E, F, ...)
> (Rossi, Italy, Rome, Verona, Italian, Proto, ...)
> (Pirlo, Italy, Madrid, Juve, Italian, Flero,, ...)
> ◯ country ◯ economy
> ◯ state ◯ none of the above

After q questions are answered by the crowd workers, the type with the highest support from the workers is chosen.

Crowd workers, even if experts in the reference KB, are prone to mistakes when $t[A_i]$ in tuple t is ambiguous, *i.e.*, $t[A_i]$ belongs to multiple types in $\mathsf{candT}(A_i)$. However, this is mitigated by two observations: (i) it is unlikely that all values are ambiguous and (ii) the probability of providing only ambiguous values diminishes quickly with respect to the number of values. Consider two types T_1 and T_2 in $\mathsf{candT}(A_i)$, the probability that randomly selected entities belong to both types is $p = \frac{|ENT(T_1) \cap ENT(T_2)|}{|ENT(T_1) \cup ENT(T_2)|}$. After q questions are answered, the probability that all $q \cdot k_t$ values are ambiguous is $p^{q \cdot k_t}$. Suppose $p = 0.8$, a very high for two types in K, and five questions are asked with each question containing five tuples, *i.e.*, $q = 5, k_t = 5$, the probability $p^{q \cdot k_t}$ becomes as low as 0.0038.

For each question, we also expose some contextual attribute values that help workers better understand the question. For example, we expose the values for A, C, D, E in question Q_1 when validating the type of B. If the the number of attributes is small, we show them all; otherwise, we use off-the-shelf technology to identify attributes that are related to the ones in the question [23]. To mitigate the risk of workers making mistakes, each question is asked three times, and the majority answer is taken. Indeed, our empirical study in Section 7.2 shows that five questions are enough to pick the correct type in all the datasets we experimented.

Relationship validation. We validate the relationship for column pairs in a similar fashion, with an example below.

Q_2 : *What is the most accurate relationship for*
highlighted columns (A, B, C , D, E, F, ...)
(Rossi, Italy, Rome , Verona, Italian, Proto, ...)
(Pirlo, Italy, Madrid , Juve, Italian, Flero, ...)
○ B hasCapital C ○ C locatedIn B ○ none of the above

Candidate types and candidate relationships are stored as URIs in KBs; thus not directly consumable by the crowd workers. For example, the type capital is stored as http://yago-knowledge.org/resource/wordnet_capital_10851850, and the relationship hasCapital is stored as http://yago-knowledge.org/resource/hasCapital. We look up type and relationship descriptions, *e.g.*, capital and hasCapital, by querying the KB for the labels of the corresponding URIs. If no label exists, we process the URI itself by removing the text before the last slash and punctuation symbols.

5.2 Question Scheduling

We now turn our attention to how to minimize the total number of questions to obtain the correct table pattern by scheduling which column and relationship to validate first.

Note that once a type (resp. relationship) is validated, we can prune from $\mathcal{P}$ all table patterns that have a different type (resp. relationship) for that column (resp. column pair). Therefore, a natural choice is to choose those columns (resp. column pairs) with the maximum uncertainty reduction [45].

Consider φ as a variable, which takes values from $\mathcal{P} = \{\varphi_1, \varphi_2, \ldots, \varphi_k\}$. We translate the score associated with each table pattern to a probability by normalizing the scores, *i.e.*, $Pr(\varphi = \varphi_i) = \frac{score(\varphi_i)}{\Sigma_{\varphi_j \in \mathcal{P}} score(\varphi_j)}$. Our translation from scores to probabilities follows the general framework of interpreting scores in [25]. Specifically, our translation is rank-stable, *i.e.*, for two patterns φ_1 and φ_2, if $score(\varphi_1) > score(\varphi_2)$, then $Pr(\varphi = \varphi_1) > Pr(\varphi = \varphi_2)$.

We define the uncertainty of φ *w.r.t.* $\mathcal{P}$ as the entropy.

$$H_{\mathcal{P}}(\varphi) = -\Sigma_{\varphi_i \in \mathcal{P}} Pr(\varphi = \varphi_i) \log_2 Pr(\varphi = \varphi_i)$$

Example 8: Consider an input list of five table patterns $\mathcal{P} = \{\varphi_1, \ldots, \varphi_5\}$ as follows with the normalized probability of each table pattern shown in the last column.

	type (B)	type (C)	$P(B, C)$	score	prob
φ_1	country	capital	hasCapital	2.8	0.35
φ_2	economy	capital	hasCapital	2	0.25
φ_3	country	city	locatedIn	2	0.25
φ_4	country	capital	locatedIn	0.8	0.1
φ_5	state	capital	hasCapital	0.4	0.05

□

We use variables v_{A_i} and $v_{A_iA_j}$ to denote the type of the column A_i and the relationship between A_i and A_j respectively. The set of all variables is denoted as V. In Example 8, $V = \{v_B, v_C, v_{BC}\}$, $v_B \in \{\text{country}, \text{economy}, \text{state}\}$, $v_C \in \{\text{capital}, \text{city}\}$ and $v_{BC} \in \{\text{hasCapital}, \text{isLocatedIn}\}$. The probability of an assignment of a variable v to a is obtained by aggregating the probability of those table patterns that have that assignment for v. For example, $Pr(v_B = \text{country}) = Pr(\varphi_1) + Pr(\varphi_3) + Pr(\varphi_4) = 0.35 + 0.25 + 0.1 = 0.7$, $Pr(v_B = \text{economy}) = 0.25$, and $Pr(v_B = \text{state}) = 0.05$.

Algorithm 3 PatternValidation

Input: a set of table patterns $\mathcal{P}$
Output: one table pattern $\varphi \in \mathcal{P}$
1: $\mathcal{P}_{re}$ be the remaining table patterns, initialized $\mathcal{P}$
2: initialize all variables V, representing column or column pairs, and calculate their probability distributions.
3: **while** $|\mathcal{P}_{re}| > 1$ **do**
4: $\quad E_{best} \leftarrow 0$
5: $\quad v_{best} \leftarrow null$
6: $\quad$**for all** $v \in V$ **do**
7: $\quad\quad$compute the entropy $H(v)$.
8: $\quad\quad$**if** $H(v) > E_{best}$ **then**
9: $\quad\quad\quad v_{best} \leftarrow v$
10: $\quad\quad\quad E_{best} \leftarrow H(v)$
11: $\quad$validate the variable v, suppose the result is a, let $\mathcal{P}_{v=a}$ to be the set of table patterns with $v = a$
12: $\quad \mathcal{P}_{re} = \mathcal{P}_{v=a}$
13: $\quad$normalize the probability distribution of patterns in $\mathcal{P}_{re}$.
14: **return** the only table pattern φ in $\mathcal{P}_{re}$

After validating a variable v to have value a, we remove from $\mathcal{P}$ those patterns that have different assignment for v. The remaining patterns are denoted as $\mathcal{P}_{v=a}$. Suppose column B is validated to be of type country, then $\mathcal{P}_{v_B=\text{country}} = \{\varphi_1, \varphi_3, \varphi_4\}$. Since we do not know what value a variable can take, we measure the expected reduction of uncertainty of variable φ after validating variable v, formally defined as:

$$E(\Delta H(\varphi))(v) = \Sigma_a Pr(v = a) H_{\mathcal{P}_{v=a}}(\varphi) - H_{\mathcal{P}}(\varphi)$$

In each iteration, we choose the variable v (column or column pair) with the maximum uncertainty reduction, *i.e.*, $E(\Delta H(\varphi))(v)$. Each iteration has a complexity of $O(|V||\mathcal{P}|^2)$ because we need to examine all $|V|$ variables, each variable could take $|\mathcal{P}|$ values, and calculating $H_{\mathcal{P}_{v=a}}(\varphi)$ for each value also takes $O(|\mathcal{P}|)$ time. The following theorem simplifies the calculation for $E(\Delta H(v))$ with a complexity of $O(|V||\mathcal{P}|)$.

Theorem 1. *The expected uncertainty reduction after validating a column (column pair) v is the same as the entropy of the variable. $E(\Delta H(\varphi))(v) = H(v)$, where $H(v) = -\Sigma_a Pr(v = a) \log_2 Pr(v = a)$.*

The proof of Theorem 1 can be found in Appendix A. Algorithm 3 describes the overall procedure for pattern validation. At each iteration: (1) we choose the best variable v_{best} to validate next based on the expected reduction of uncertainty of φ (lines 4-10); (2) we remove from $\mathcal{P}_{re}$ those table patterns that have a different assignment for variable v than the validated value a (lines 11-12); and (3) we renormalize the probability distribution of the remaining table patterns in $\mathcal{P}_{re}$ (line 13). We terminate when we are left with only one table pattern (line 3).

Example 9: To validate the five patterns in Example 8, we first calculate the entropy of every variable. $H(v_B) = -0.7 \log_2 0.7 - 0.25 log_2 0.25 - 0.05 log_2 0.05 = 1.07$, $H(v_C) = 0.81$, and $H(v_{BC}) = 0.93$. Thus column B is validated first, say the answer is country. The remaining set of table patterns, and their normalized probabilities are:

	type (B)	type (C)	$P(B, C)$	prob
φ_1	country	capital	hasCapital	0.5
φ_3	country	city	locatedIn	0.35
φ_4	country	capital	locatedIn	0.15

Now $\mathcal{P}_{re} = \{\varphi_1, \varphi_3, \varphi_4\}$. The new entropies are: $H(v_B) = 0$, $H(v_C) = 0.93$ and $H(v_{BC}) = 1$. Therefore, column pair

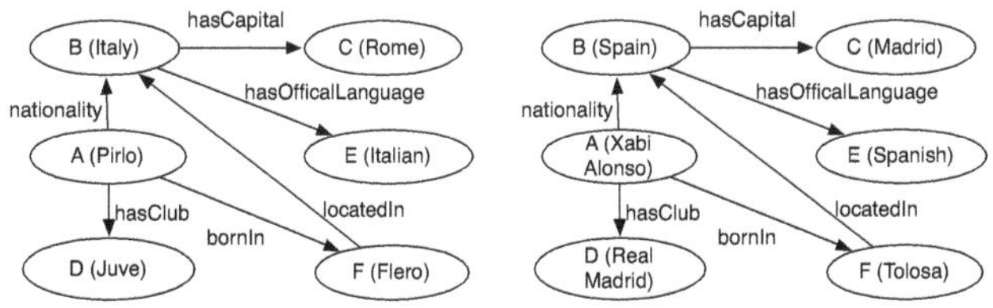

(a) Possible repair G_1 (b) Possible repair G_2

Figure 5: Sample instance graphs

B, C is chosen, say the answer is hasCapital. We are now left with only one pattern φ_1, thus we return it. □

In Example 9, we do not need to validate v_C following our scheduling strategy. Furthermore, after validating certain variables, other variables may become less uncertain, thus requiring a smaller number of questions to validate.

6. DATA ANNOTATION

In this section, we describe how KATARA annotates data (Section 6.1). We also discuss how to generate possible repairs for identified errors (Section 6.2).

6.1 Annotating Data

KATARA annotates tuples as correct data validated by KBs, correct data jointly validated by KBs and the crowd, or data errors detected by the crowd, using the following two steps.

Step 1: Validation by KBs. For each tuple t and pattern φ, KATARA issues a SPARQL query to check whether t is fully covered by a KB $\mathcal{K}$. If it is fully covered, KATARA annotates it as a correct tuple validated by KB (case (*i*)). Otherwise, it goes to step 2.

Step 2: Validation by KBs *and Crowd.* For each node (*i.e.*, type) and edge (*i.e.*, relationship) that is missing from $\mathcal{K}$, KATARA asks the crowd whether the relationship holds between the given two values. If the crowd says yes, KATARA annotates it as a correct tuple, jointly validated by KB and crowd (case (*ii*)). Otherwise, it is certain that there exist errors in this tuple (case (*iii*)).

Example 10: Consider tuple t_2 (resp. t_3) in Fig. 1 and the table pattern in Fig. 2(a). The information about whether Pretoria (resp. Madrid) is a capital of S. Africa (resp. Italy) is not in KB. To verify this information, we issue a boolean question Q_{t_2} (resp. Q_{t_3}) to the crowd as:

Q_{t_2} :*Does* S. Africa hasCapital Pretoria*?*   ○ Yes ○ No
Q_{t_3} :*Does* Italy hasCapital Madrid*?*   ○ Yes ○ No

In such case, the crowd will answer **yes** (resp. **no**) to question Q_{t_2} (resp. Q_{t_3}). □

Knowledge base enrichment. Note that, in step 2, for each affirmative answer from the crowd (*e.g.*, Q_{t_2} above), a new fact that is not in the current KB is created. KATARA collects such facts and uses them to enrich the KB.

6.2 Generating Top-k Possible Repairs

We start by introducing two notions that are necessary to explain our approach for generating possible repairs.

Instance graphs. Given a KB $\mathcal{K}$ and a pattern $G(V, E)$, an *instance graph* $G_I(V_I, E_I)$ is a graph with nodes V_I and edges E_I, such that (i) each node $v_i \in V_I$ is a resource in $\mathcal{K}$; (ii) each edge $e_i \in E_I$ is a property in $\mathcal{K}$; (iii) there is a one-to-one correspondence f from each node $v \in V$ to a node $v_i \in V_I$, *i.e.*, $f(v) = v_i$; and (iv) for each edge $(u, v) \in E$, there is an edge $(f(u), f(v)) \in E_I$ with the same property. Intuitively, an instance graph is an instantiation of a pattern in a given KB.

Example 11: Figures 5(a) and 5(b) are two instance graphs of the table pattern of Fig. 2(a) in Yago for two players. □

Repair cost. Given an instance graph G, a tuple t, and a table pattern φ, the *repair cost* of aligning t to G *w.r.t.* φ, denoted by $\mathsf{cost}(t, \varphi, G) = \sum_{i=1}^{n} c_i$, is the cost of changing values in t to align it with G, where c_i is the cost of the i-th change and n the number of changes in t. Intuitively, the less a repair cost is, the closer the updated tuple is to the original tuple, hence more likely to be correct. By default, we set $c_i = 1$. The cost can also be weighted with confidences on data values [18]. In such case, the higher the confidence value is, the more costly the change is.

Example 12: Consider tuple t_3 in Fig. 1, the table pattern φ_s in Fig. 2(a), and two instance graphs G_1 and G_2 in Fig. 5. The repair cost to update t_3 to G_1 is 1, *i.e.*, $\mathsf{cost}(t_3, \varphi_s, G_1) = 1$, by updating $t_3[C]$ from Madrid to Rome. Similarly, the repair cost from t_3 to G_2 is 5, *i.e.*, $\mathsf{cost}(t_3, \varphi_s, G_2) = 5$. □

Note that the possible repairs are ranked based on repair cost in ascending order. We provide top-k possible repairs and we leave it to the users (or crowd) to pick the most appropriate repair. In the following, we describe algorithms to generate top-k repairs for each identified erroneous tuple.

Given a KB $\mathcal{K}$ and a pattern φ, we compute all instance graphs $\mathcal{G}$ in $\mathcal{K}$ *w.r.t.* φ. For each tuple t, a naive solution is to compute the distance between t and each graph G in $\mathcal{G}$. The k graphs with smallest repair cost are returned as top-k possible repairs. Unfortunately, this is too slow in practice.

A natural way to improve the naive solution for top-k possible repair generation is to retrieve only instance graphs that can possibly be repairs, *i.e.*, the instance graphs whose values have an overlap with a given erroneous tuple. We leverage inverted lists to achieve this goal.

Inverted lists. Each inverted list is a mapping from a key to a posting list. A *key* is a pair (A, a) where A is an attribute and a is a constant value. A *posting* list is a set $\mathcal{G}$ of graph instances, where each $G \in \mathcal{G}$ has value a on attribute A.

For example, an inverted list *w.r.t.* G_1 in Fig. 5(a) is:

country, Italy $\rightarrow$ G_1

Algorithm. The optimized algorithm for a tuple t is given in Algorithm 4. All possible repairs are initialized (line 1) and instantiated by using inverted lists (lines 2-3). For each

Algorithm 4 TOP-k repairs

Input: a tuple t, a table pattern φ, and inverted lists $\mathcal{L}$
Output: top-k repairs for t
1: $\mathcal{G}_t = \emptyset$
2: **for each** attribute A in φ **do**
3: $\quad\mathcal{G}_t = \mathcal{G}_t \cup \mathcal{L}(A, t[A])$
4: **for each** G in $\mathcal{G}_t$ **do**
5: $\quad$compute $\mathsf{cost}(t, \varphi, G)$
6: **return** top-k repairs in $\mathcal{G}_t$ with least cost values

possible repair, its repair cost *w.r.t.* t is computed (lines 4-5), and top-k repairs are returned (line 6).

Example 13: Consider t_3 in Fig. 1 and pattern φ_s in Fig. 2(a). The inverted lists retrieved are given below.

A, Pirlo	→ G_1	D, Juve	→ G_1
B, Italy	→ G_1	E, Italian	→ G_1
C, Madrid	→ G_2	F, Flero	→ G_1

It is easy to see that the occurrences of instance graphs G_1 and G_2 are 5 and 1, respectively. In other words, the cost of repairing t_3 *w.r.t.* G_1 is $6 - 5 = 1$ and *w.r.t.* G_2 is $6 - 1 = 5$. Hence, the top-1 possible repair for t_3 is G_1. □

The practicability of possible repairs of KATARA depends on the coverage of KBs, while existing automatic data repairing techniques usually require certain redundancy in the data to perform well. KATARA and existing techniques complement each other, as demonstrated in Section 7.4.

7. EXPERIMENTAL STUDY

We evaluated KATARA using real-life data along four dimensions: (*i*) the effectiveness and efficiency of table pattern discovery (Section 7.1); (*ii*) the efficiency of pattern validation via the expert crowd (Section 7.2); (*iii*) the effectiveness and efficiency of data annotation (Section 7.3); and (*iv*) the effectiveness of possible repairs (Section 7.4).

Knowledge bases. We used Yago [21] and DBpedia [27] as the underlying KBs. Both were transformed to Jena format (`jena.apache.org/`) with LARQ (a combination of ARQ and Lucene) support for string similarity. We set the threshold to 0.7 in Lucene to check whether two strings match.

Datasets. We used three datasets: WikiTables and WebTables contains tables from the Web[2] with relatively small numbers of tuples and columns, and RelationalTables contains tables with larger numbers of tuples and columns.

- WikiTables contains 28 tables from Wikipedia pages. The average number of tuples is 32.
- WebTables contains 30 tables from Web pages. The average number of tuples is 67.
- RelationalTables has three tables: Person has personal information joined on the attribute country from two sources: a biographic table extracted from wikipedia [32], and a country table obtained from a wikipedia page[3] resulting in 316K tuples. Soccer has 1625 tuples about soccer players and their clubs scraped from the Web[4]. University has 1357 tuples about US universities with their addresses[5].

All the tables were manually annotated using types and relationships in Yago as well as DBPedia, which we considered as the *ground truth.* Table 1 shows the number of columns that have types, and the number of column pairs that have relationships, using Yago and DBPedia, respectively.

All experiments were conducted on Win 7 with an Intel i7 CPU@3.4Ghz, 20GB of memory, and an SSD 500GB hard disk. All algorithms were implemented in JAVA.

[2] `http://www.it.iitb.ac.in/~sunita/wwt/`

[3] `http://tinyurl.com/qhhty3p`

[4] `www.premierleague.com/en-gb.html`, `www.legaseriea.it/en/`, `www.premierleague.com/en-gb.html`

[5] `ope.ed.gov/accreditation/GetDownLoadFile.aspx`

	Yago		DBPedia	
	#-type	#-relationship	#-type	#-relationship
WikiTables	54	15	57	18
WebTables	71	33	73	35
RelationalTables	14	7	14	16

Table 1: Datasets and KBs characteristics

7.1 Pattern Discovery

Algorithms. We compared four discovery algorithms.

(i) RankJoin - our proposed approach (Section 4).

(ii) Support - a baseline approach that ranks the candidate types and relationships solely on their support scores, *i.e.*, the number of tuples that are of the candidate's types and relationships.

(iii) MaxLike [39] - infers the type of a column and the relationship between a column pair separately using maximum likelihood estimation.

(iv) PGM [28] - infers the type of a column, the relationship between column pairs, and the entities of cells by building a probabilistic graphic model to make holistic decisions.

Evaluation Metrics. A type (relationship) gets a score of 1 if it matches the ground truth, and a partial score $\frac{1}{s+1}$ if it is the super type (relationship) of the ground truth, where s is the number of steps in the hierarchy to reach the ground truth. For example, a label Film for a column, whose actual type is IndianFilm, will get a score of 0.5, since Film is the super type of IndianFilm with $s = 1$. The precision P of a pattern φ is defined as the sum of scores for all types and relationships in φ over the total number of types and relationships in φ. The recall R of φ is defined as the sum of scores for all types and relationships in φ over the total number of types and relationships in the ground truth.

Effectiveness. Table 2 shows the precision and recall of the top pattern chosen by four pattern discovery algorithms for three datasets using Yago and DBPedia. We first discuss Yago. (1) Support has the lowest precision and recall in all scenarios, since it selects the types/relationships that cover the most number of tuples, which are usually the general types, such as Thing or Object. (2) MaxLike uses maximum likelihood estimation to select the best type/relationship that maximizes the probability of values given the type/relationship. It performs better than Support, but still chooses types and relationships independently. (3) PGM is a supervised learning approach that requires training and tuning of a number of weights. PGM shows mixed effectiveness results: it performs better than MaxLike on WebTables, but worse on WikiTables and RelationalTables. (4) RankJoin achieves the highest precision and recall due to its tf-idf style ranking, as well as for considering the coherence between types and relationships. For example, consider a table with two columns `actors` and `films` that have a relationship `actedIn`. If most of the values in the `films` column also happen to be `books`, MaxLike will use `books` as the type, since there are fewer instances of `books` than `films` in Yago. However, RankJoin would correctly identify `films` as the type, since it is more coherent with `actedIn` than `books`.

The result from DBPedia, also shown in Table 2, confirms that RankJoin performs best among the four methods. Notice that the precision and recall of all methods are consistently better using DBPedia than Yago. This is because the

	Support		MaxLike		PGM		RankJoin	
	P	**R**	**P**	**R**	**P**	**R**	**P**	**R**
WikiTables	.54	.59	.62	.68	.60	.67	.78	.86
WebTables	.65	.64	.63	.62	.77	.77	.86	.84
RelationalTables	.51	.51	.71	.71	.53	.53	.77	.77
Yago								
	P	**R**	**P**	**R**	**P**	**R**	**P**	**R**
WikiTables	.56	.70	.71	.89	.61	.77	.71	.89
WebTables	.65	.69	.80	.84	.76	.80	.82	.87
RelationalTables	.64	.67	.81	.86	.74	.77	.81	.86
DBPedia								

Table 2: Pattern discovery precision and recall

	Support	MaxLike	PGM	RankJoin
WikiTables	153	155	286	153
WebTables	160	177	1105	162
RelationalTables/Person	130	140	13842	127
Person	252	258	N.A.	257
Yago				
WikiTables	50	54	90	51
WebTables	103	104	189	107
RelationalTables/Person	400	574	11047	409
Person	368	431	N.A.	410
DBPedia				

Table 3: Pattern discovery efficiency (seconds)

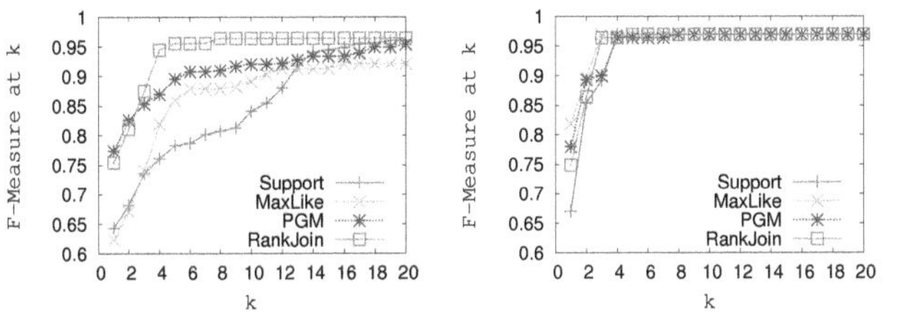

(a) Yago (b) DBPedia

Figure 6: Top-k F-measure (WebTables)

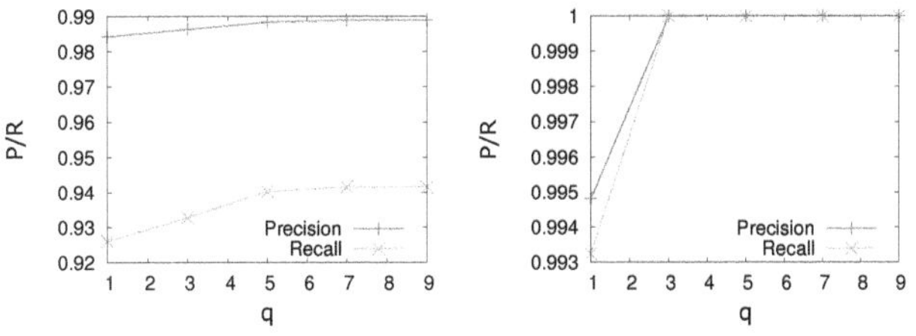

(a) Yago (b) DBPedia

Figure 7: Pattern validation P/R (WebTables)

	Yago		DBPedia	
	MUVF	AVI	MUVF	AVI
WikiTables	64	79	88	102
WebTables	81	105	90	118
RelationalTables	24	28	28	36

Table 4: #-variables to validate

number of types in DBPedia (865) is much smaller than that of Yago (374K), hence, the number of candidate types for a column using DBPedia is much smaller, causing less stress for all algorithms to rank them.

To further verify the effectiveness of our ranking function, we report the F-measure F of the top-k patterns chosen by every algorithm. The F value of the top-k patterns is defined as the best value of F from one of the top-k patterns. Figure 6 shows F values of the top-k patterns varying k on WebTables. RankJoin converges faster than other methods on Yago, while all methods converge quickly on DBPedia due to its small number of types. Top-k F-measure results for the other two datasets show similar behavior, and are reported in Appendix B.

Efficiency. Table 3 shows the running time in seconds for all datasets. We ran each test 5 times and report the average time. We separate the discussion of Person from RelationalTables due to its large number of tuples. For Person, we implemented a distributed version of candidate types/relationships generation by distributing the 316K tuples over 30 machines, and all candidates are collected into one machine to complete the pattern discovery. Support, MaxLike, and RankJoin have similar performance in all datasets, because their most expensive operation is the disk I/Os for KBs lookups in generating candidate types and relationships, which is linear *w.r.t.* the number of tuples. PGM is the most expensive due to the message passing algorithms used for the inference of probabilistic graphical model. PGM takes hours on tables with around 1K tuples, and cannot finish within one day for Person.

7.2 Pattern Validation

Given the top-k patterns from the pattern discovery, we need to identify the most appropriate one. We validated the patterns of all datasets using an expert crowd with 10 students. Each question contains five tuples, *i.e.*, $k_t = 5$.

We first evaluated the effect of the number of questions used to validate each variable, which is a type or a relationship, on the quality of the chosen pattern. We measure the precision and recall of the final chosen validation *w.r.t.* the ground truth in the same way as in Section 7.1. Figure 7 shows the average precision and recall of the validated pattern of WebTables while varying the number of questions q per variable. It can be seen that, even with $q = 1$, the precision and recall of the validated pattern is already high. In addition, the precision and recall converge quickly, with $q = 5$ on Yago, and $q = 3$ on DBPedia. Pattern validation results on WikiTables and RelationalTables show a similar behavior, and are reported in Appendix C.

To evaluate the savings in crowd pattern validation that are achieved by our scheduling algorithm, we compared our method (denoted MUVF, short for most-uncertain-variable-first) with a baseline algorithm (denoted AVI for all-variables-independent) that validates every variable independently. For each dataset, we compared the number of variables needed to be validated until there is only one table pattern left. Table 4 shows that MUVF performs consistently better than AVI in terms of the number of variables to validate, because MUVF may spare validating certain variables due to scheduling, *i.e.*, some variables become certain after validating some other variables.

The validated table patterns of RelationalTables for both Yago and DBPedia are depicted in Fig. 10 in the Appendix. All validated patterns are also used in the following experimental study.

7.3 Data Annotation

Given the table patterns obtained from Section 7.2, data values are annotated *w.r.t.* types and relationships in the validated table patterns, using KBs and the crowd. The result of data annotation is shown in Table 5. Note that

	type			relationship		
	KB	crowd	error	KB	crowd	error
WikiTables	0.60	0.39	0.01	0.56	0.42	0.02
WebTables	0.69	0.28	0.03	0.56	0.39	0.05
RelationalTables	0.83	0.17	0	0.89	0.11	0
Yago						
	KB	crowd	error	KB	crowd	error
WikiTables	0.73	0.25	0.02	0.60	0.36	0.04
WebTables	0.74	0.24	0.02	0.56	0.39	0.05
RelationalTables	0.90	0.10	0	0.91	0.09	0
DBPedia						

Table 5: Data annotation by KBs and crowd

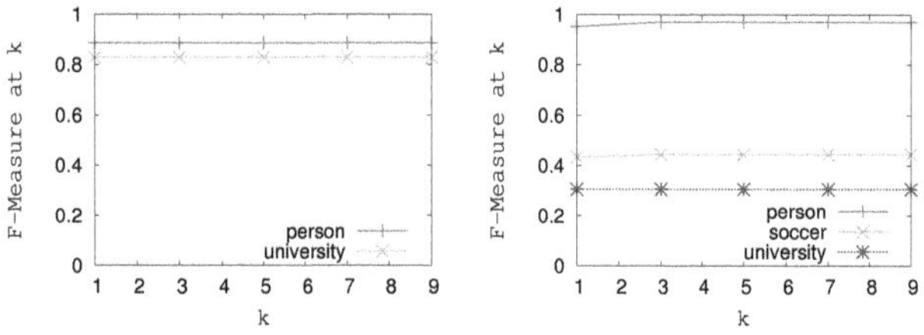

(a) Yago (b) DBPedia

Figure 8: Top-k repair F-measure (RelationalTables)

KATARA annotates data in three categories (cf. Section 6.1): when KB has coverage for a value, the value is said to be validated by the KB (KB column in Table 5), when the KB has no coverage, the value is either validated by the crowd (crowd column in Table 5), or the value is erroneous (error column in Table 5). Table 5 shows the breakdown of the percentage of values in each category. Data values validated by the crowd can be used to enrich the KBs. For example, a column in one of the table in WebTables is discovered to be the type `state capitals in the United States`. Surprisingly, there are only five instances of that type in Yago[6], we can add the rest of 45 state capitals using values from the table to enrich Yago. Note that the percentage of KB validated data is much higher for RelationalTables than it is for WikiTables and WebTables. This is because data in RelationalTables is more redundant (*e.g.,* Italy appears in many tuples in Person table), when a value is validated by the crowd, it will be added to the KB, thus future occurrences of the same value will be automatically validated by the KB.

7.4 Effectiveness of Possible Repairs

In these experiments, we evaluate the effectiveness of our possible repairs generation by (1) varying the number k of possible repairs; and (2) comparing with other state of the art automatic data cleaning techniques.

Metrics. We use standard precision, recall, and F-measure for the evaluation, which are defined as follows.

precision = (#-corrected changed values)/(#-all changes)
recall = (#-corrected changed values)/(#-all errors)
F-measure= 2 × (precision × recall)/(precision + recall)

For comparison with automatic data cleaning approaches, we used an equivalence-class [2] (*i.e.,* EQ) based approach provided by an open-source data cleaning tool NADEEF [12], and a ML-based approach SCARE [43]. When KATARA provides nonempty top-k possible repairs for a tuple, we count it as correct if the ground truth falls in the possible repairs, otherwise incorrect.

[6]http://tinyurl.com/q65yrba

	KATARA (Yago)		KATARA (DBPedia)		EQ		SCARE	
	P	R	P	R	P	R	P	R
Person	1.0	0.80	1.0	0.94	1.0	0.96	0.78	0.48
Soccer	N.A.		0.97	0.29	0.66	0.29	0.66	0.37
University	0.95	0.74	1.0	0.18	0.63	0.04	0.85	0.21

Table 6: Data repairing precision and recall (RelationalTables)

Since the average number of tuples in WikiTables and WebTables is 32 and 67, respectively, both datasets are not suitable since both EQ and SCARE require reasonable data redundancy to compute repairs. Hence, we use RelationalTables for comparison. We learn from Table 5 that tables in RelationalTables are clean, and thus are treated as ground truth. Thus, for each table in RelationalTables, we injected 10% random errors into columns that are covered by the patterns to obtain a corresponding dirty instance, that is, each tuple has a 10% chance of being modified to contain errors. Moreover, in order to set up a fair comparison, we used FDs for EQ that cover the same columns as the crowd validated table patterns (see Appendix D). SCARE requires that some columns to be correct. To enable SCARE to run, we only injected errors to the right hand side attributes of the FDs, and treated the left hand side attributes as correct attributes (*a.k.a.* reliable attributes in [43]).

Effectiveness of k. We examined the effect of using top-k repairs in terms of F-measure. The results for both Yago and DBPedia are shown in Fig. 8. The result for soccer using Yago is missing since the discovered table pattern does not contain any relationship (cf. Fig. 10 in Appendix). Thus, KATARA cannot be used to compute possible repairs *w.r.t.* Yago. We can see the F-measure stabilizes at $k = 1$ using Yago, and stabilizes at $k = 3$ using DBPedia. The result tells us that in general the correct repairs fall into the top ones, which justifies our ranking of possible repairs. Next, we report the quality of possible repairs generated by KATARA, fixing $k = 3$.

Results of RelationalTables. The precision/recall of KATARA, EQ and SCARE on RelationalTables, are reported in Table 6. The result shows that KATARA always has a high precision in cases where KBs have enough coverage of the input data. It also indicates that if KATARA can provide top-k repairs, it has a good chance that the ground truth will fall in them. The recall of KATARA depends on the coverage of the KBs of the input dataset. For example, DBPedia has a lot of information for Person, but relatively less for Soccer and University. Yago cannot be used to repair Soccer because it does not have relationships for Soccer.

Both EQ and SCARE have precision that is generally lower than KATARA, because EQ targets at computing a consistent database with the minimum number of changes, which are not necessarily the correct changes, and the result of SCARE depends on many factors, such as the quality of the training data in terms of its redundancy, and a threshold ML parameter that is hard to set precisely. The recall for both EQ and SCARE is highly dependent on data redundancy, because they both require repetition of data to either detect errors.

Results of WikiTables *and* WebTables. Table 7 shows the result of data repairing for WikiTables and WebTables. Both EQ and SCARE are not applicable on WikiTables and WebTables, because there is almost no redundancy in them.

	KATARA (Yago)		KATARA (DBPedia)		EQ	SCARE
	P	R	P	R	P/R	P/R
WikiTables	1.0	0.11	1.0	0.30	N.A.	
WebTables	1.0	0.40	1.0	0.46	N.A.	

Table 7: Data repairing precision and recall (WikiTables and WebTables)

Since there is no ground truth available for WikiTables and WebTables, we manually examine the top-3 possible repairs returned by KATARA. As we can see, KATARA achieves high precision on WikiTables and WebTables as well. In total, KATARA fixed 60 errors out of 204 errors, which is 29%. In fact, most of remaining errors in these tables are null values whose ground truth values are not covered by given KBs.

Summary. It can be seen that KATARA complements existing automatic repairing techniques: (1) EQ and SCARE cannot be applied to WebTables and WikiTables since there is not enough redundancy, while KATARA can, given KBs and the crowd; (2) KATARA cannot be applied when there is no coverage in the KBs, such as the case of Soccer with Yago; and (3) when both KATARA and automatic techniques can be applied, KATARA usually achieves higher precision due to its use of KBs and experts, while automatic techniques usually make heuristic changes. The recall of KATARA depends on the coverage of the KBs, while the recall of automatic techniques depends on the level of redundancy in the data.

8. RELATED WORK

The traditional problems of matching relational tables and aligning ontologies have been largely studied in the database community. A matching approach where the user is also aware of the target schema has been recently proposed [34]. Given a source and a target single relation, the user populates the empty target relation with samples of the desired output until a unique mapping is identified by the system. A recent approach that looks for isomorphisms between ontologies is PARIS [37], which exploits the rich information in the ontologies in a holistic approach to the alignment. Unfortunately, our source is a relational table and our target is a non-empty labeled graph, which make these proposals hard to apply directly. On one hand, the first approach requires to project all the entities and relationships in the target KB as binary relations, which leads to a number of target relations to test that is quadratic *w.r.t.* the number of entities, and only few instances in the target would match with the source data. On the other hand, the second approach requires to test 2^n combinations of source attributes, given a relation with n attributes. The reason is that PARIS relies on structural information, thus all possible attributes should be tested together to get optimal results. If we tested only binary relations, structural information would not be used and inconsistent matches may arise. For example, attributes A, B can be matched with X, Y in the KB, while at the same time, attributes B, C may match Z, W, resulting in inconsistency (Attribute B matches two different classes X and Z). KATARA actually solves this problem by first retrieving top-k types and relationships, and then using a rank-join based approach to obtain the most coherent pattern.

Another line of related work is known as *Web tables semantics understanding*, which identifies the type of a column and the relationship between two columns *w.r.t.* a given KB, for the purpose of serving Web tables to search applications [13,28,39]. Our pattern discovery module shares the same goal. Compared with the state of the art [28,39], our rank join algorithm shows superiority in both effectiveness and efficiency, as demonstrated in the experiments.

Several attempts have been made to do repairing based on integrity constraints (ICs) [1,9,11,17,20]; they try to find a consistent database that satisfies given ICs in a minimum cost. It is known that the above heuristic solutions do not ensure the accuracy of data repairing [19]. To improve the accuracy of data repairing, experts have been involved as first-class citizen of data cleaning systems [19,35,44], high quality reference data has been leveraged [19,24,42], and confidence values have been placed by the users [18]. KATARA differs from them in that KATARA leverages KBs as reference data. As remarked earlier, KATARA and IC based approaches complement each other.

Numerous studies have attempted to discover data quality rules, *e.g.,* for CFDs [6] and for DCs [8]. Automatically discovered rules are error-prone, thus cannot be directly fed into data cleaning systems without verification by domain experts. However, and as noted earlier, they can exploit the output of KATARA, as rules are easier to discover from clean samples of the data [8].

Another line of work studies the problem of combining ontological reasoning with databases [5,33]. Although their operation could also be used to enforce data validation, our work differs in that we do not assume knowledge over the constraints defined on the ontology. Moreover, constraints are usually expressed with FO logic fragments that restrict the expressive power to enable polynomial complexity in the query answering. Since we limit our queries to instance-checking over RDFS, we do not face these complexity issues.

One concern with regards to the applicability of KATARA is the accuracy and coverage of the KBs and the quality of crowdsourcing: neither the KBs nor the crowdsourcing is ensured to be completely accurate. There are several efforts that aim at improving the quality and coverage of both KBs [14–16] and crowdsourcing [4,26]. With more accurate and big KBs, KATARA can discover the semantics of more long tail tables, and further alleviate the involvement of experts. A full discussion of the above topics lies beyond the scope of this work. Nevertheless, KBs and experts are usually more reliable than the data at hand, thus can be treated as relatively trusted resources to pivot on.

9. CONCLUSION AND FUTURE WORK

We proposed KATARA, the first *end-to-end* system that bridges knowledge bases and crowdsourcing for high quality data cleaning. KATARA first establishes the correspondence between the possibly dirty database and the available KBs by discovering and validating the table patterns. Then each tuple in the database is verified using a table pattern against a KB with possible crowd involvement when the KB lacks coverage. Experimental results have demonstrated both the effectiveness and efficiency of KATARA.

One important future work is to cold-start KATARA when there is no available KBs to cover the data, *i.e.,* bootstrapping and extending the KBs at the intensional level by soliciting structural knowledge from the crowd. It would be also interesting to assess the effects of using multiple KBs together to repair one dataset. Another line of work is to extend our current definition of tables patterns, such as a person column A_1 is related to a country column A_2 via two relationships: A_1 wasBornIn city, and city isLocatedIn A_2.

10. REFERENCES

[1] S. Abiteboul, R. Hull, and V. Vianu. *Foundations of Databases.* Addison-Wesley, 1995.

[2] P. Bohannon, W. Fan, M. Flaster, and R. Rastogi. A cost-based model and effective heuristic for repairing constraints by value modification. In *SIGMOD*, 2005.

[3] G. Bouma. Normalized (pointwise) mutual information in collocation extraction. *Proceedings of GSCL*, pages 31–40, 2009.

[4] S. Buchholz and J. Latorre. Crowdsourcing preference tests, and how to detect cheating. 2011.

[5] A. Calì, G. Gottlob, and A. Pieris. Advanced processing for ontological queries. *PVLDB*, 2010.

[6] F. Chiang and R. J. Miller. Discovering data quality rules. *PVLDB*, 2008.

[7] F. Chiang and R. J. Miller. A unified model for data and constraint repair. In *ICDE*, 2011.

[8] X. Chu, I. F. Ilyas, and P. Papotti. Discovering denial constraints. *PVLDB*, 2013.

[9] X. Chu, I. F. Ilyas, and P. Papotti. Holistic data cleaning: Putting violations into context. In *ICDE*, 2013.

[10] K. W. Church and P. Hanks. Word association norms, mutual information, and lexicography. *Comput. Linguist.*, 16(1):22–29, Mar. 1990.

[11] G. Cong, W. Fan, F. Geerts, X. Jia, and S. Ma. Improving data quality: Consistency and accuracy. In *VLDB*, 2007.

[12] M. Dallachiesa, A. Ebaid, A. Eldawy, A. K. Elmagarmid, I. F. Ilyas, M. Ouzzani, and N. Tang. NADEEF: a commodity data cleaning system. In *SIGMOD*, 2013.

[13] D. Deng, Y. Jiang, G. Li, J. Li, and C. Yu. Scalable column concept determination for web tables using large knowledge bases. *PVLDB*, 2013.

[14] O. Deshpande, D. S. Lamba, M. Tourn, S. Das, S. Subramaniam, A. Rajaraman, V. Harinarayan, and A. Doan. Building, maintaining, and using knowledge bases: a report from the trenches. In *SIGMOD Conference*, 2013.

[15] X. Dong, E. Gabrilovich, G. Heitz, W. Horn, N. Lao, K. Murphy, T. Strohmann, S. Sun, and W. Zhang. Knowledge vault: A web-scale approach to probabilistic knowledge fusion. In *SIGKDD*, 2014.

[16] X. L. Dong, E. Gabrilovich, G. Heitz, W. Horn, K. Murphy, S. Sun, and W. Zhang. From data fusion to knowledge fusion. *PVLDB*, 2014.

[17] W. Fan. Dependencies revisited for improving data quality. In *PODS*, 2008.

[18] W. Fan, J. Li, S. Ma, N. Tang, and W. Yu. Interaction between record matching and data repairing. In *SIGMOD*, 2011.

[19] W. Fan, J. Li, S. Ma, N. Tang, and W. Yu. Towards certain fixes with editing rules and master data. *VLDB J.*, 21(2), 2012.

[20] F. Geerts, G. Mecca, P. Papotti, and D. Santoro. The LLUNATIC Data-Cleaning Framework. *PVLDB*, 2013.

[21] J. Hoffart, F. M. Suchanek, K. Berberich, and G. Weikum. YAGO2: A spatially and temporally enhanced knowledge base from wikipedia. *Artif. Intell.*, 194, 2013.

[22] I. F. Ilyas, W. G. Aref, and A. K. Elmagarmid. Supporting top-*k* join queries in relational databases. *VLDB J.*, 13(3), 2004.

[23] I. F. Ilyas, V. Markl, P. J. Haas, P. Brown, and A. Aboulnaga. Cords: Automatic discovery of correlations and soft functional dependencies. In *SIGMOD*, 2004.

[24] M. Interlandi and N. Tang. Proof positive and negative data cleaning. In *ICDE*, 2015.

[25] H.-P. Kriegel, P. Kröger, E. Schubert, and A. Zimek. Interpreting and unifying outlier scores. In *SDM*, pages 13–24, 2011.

[26] R. Lange and X. Lange. Quality control in crowdsourcing: An objective measurement approach to identifying and correcting rater effects in the social evaluation of products and services. In *AAAI*, 2012.

[27] J. Lehmann, R. Isele, M. Jakob, A. Jentzsch, D. Kontokostas, P. N. Mendes, S. Hellmann, M. Morsey, P. van Kleef, S. Auer, and C. Bizer. DBpedia - a large-scale, multilingual knowledge base extracted from wikipedia. *Semantic Web Journal*, 6(2):167–195, 2015.

[28] G. Limaye, S. Sarawagi, and S. Chakrabarti. Annotating and searching web tables using entities, types and relationships. *PVLDB*, 3(1), 2010.

[29] C. D. Manning, P. Raghavan, and H. Schütze. Scoring, term weighting and the vector space model. *Introduction to Information Retrieval*, 100, 2008.

[30] C. Mayfield, J. Neville, and S. Prabhakar. ERACER: a database approach for statistical inference and data cleaning. In *SIGMOD*, 2010.

[31] M. Morsey, J. Lehmann, S. Auer, and A. N. Ngomo. Dbpedia SPARQL benchmark - performance assessment with real queries on real data. In *ISWC*, 2011.

[32] J. Pasternack and D. Roth. Knowing what to believe (when you already know something). In *COLING*, 2010.

[33] A. Poggi, D. Lembo, D. Calvanese, G. D. Giacomo, M. Lenzerini, and R. Rosati. Linking data to ontologies. *J. Data Semantics*, 10, 2008.

[34] L. Qian, M. J. Cafarella, and H. V. Jagadish. Sample-driven schema mapping. In *SIGMOD*, 2012.

[35] V. Raman and J. M. Hellerstein. Potter's Wheel: An interactive data cleaning system. In *VLDB*, 2001.

[36] S. Song, H. Cheng, J. X. Yu, and L. Chen. Repairing vertex labels under neighborhood constraints. *PVLDB*, 7(11), 2014.

[37] F. M. Suchanek, S. Abiteboul, and P. Senellart. Paris: Probabilistic alignment of relations, instances, and schema. *PVLDB*, 2011.

[38] B. Trushkowsky, T. Kraska, M. J. Franklin, and P. Sarkar. Crowdsourced enumeration queries. In *ICDE*, 2013.

[39] P. Venetis, A. Y. Halevy, J. Madhavan, M. Pasca, W. Shen, F. Wu, G. Miao, and C. Wu. Recovering semantics of tables on the web. *PVLDB*, 2011.

[40] M. Volkovs, F. Chiang, J. Szlichta, and R. J. Miller. Continuous data cleaning. In *ICDE*, 2014.

[41] J. Wang, T. Kraska, M. J. Franklin, and J. Feng. Crowder: Crowdsourcing entity resolution. *PVLDB*, 2012.

[42] J. Wang and N. Tang. Towards dependable data repairing with fixing rules. In *SIGMOD*, 2014.

[43] M. Yakout, L. Berti-Equille, and A. K. Elmagarmid. Don't be SCAREd: use SCalable Automatic REpairing with maximal likelihood and bounded changes. In *SIGMOD*, 2013.

[44] M. Yakout, A. K. Elmagarmid, J. Neville, M. Ouzzani, and I. F. Ilyas. Guided data repair. *PVLDB*, 2011.

[45] C. J. Zhang, L. Chen, H. V. Jagadish, and C. C. Cao. Reducing uncertainty of schema matching via crowdsourcing. *PVLDB*, 6, 2013.

APPENDIX

A. PROOF OF THEOREM 1

The expected uncertainty reduction is computed as the difference between the current entropy and the expected one.

$$E(\Delta H(\varphi))(v) = -H_{\mathcal{P}}(\varphi) + \sum_a Pr(v=a) H_{\varphi_i \in \mathcal{P}_{v=a}}(\varphi_i)$$

The uncertainty of the conditional distribution of patterns given $v = a$, $H_{\varphi_i \in \mathcal{P}_{v=a}}(\varphi_i)$ can be computed as follows:

$$H_{\varphi_i \in \mathcal{P}_{v=a}}(\varphi_i)$$
$$= \sum_{\varphi_i \in \mathcal{P}_{v=a}} \frac{Pr(\varphi_i)}{\sum_{\varphi_i \in \mathcal{P}_{v=a}} Pr(\varphi_i)} \log_2 \frac{Pr(\varphi_i)}{\sum_{\varphi_i \in \mathcal{P}_{v=a}} Pr(\varphi_i)}$$

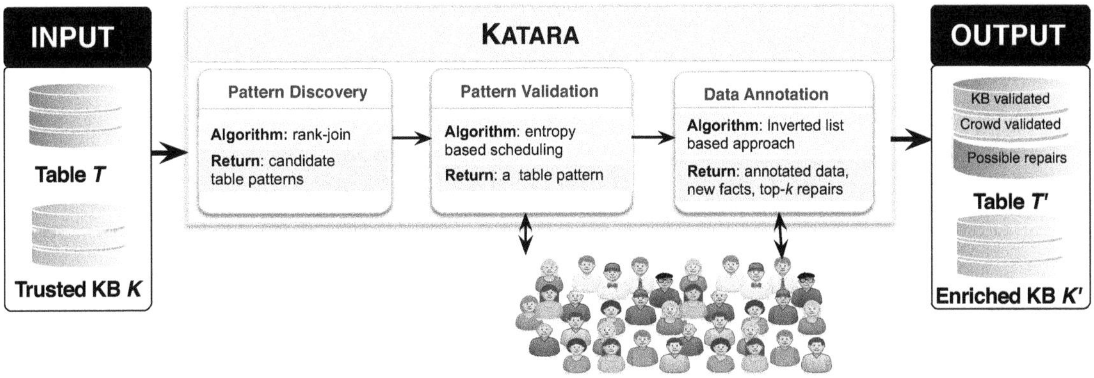

Figure 9: Workflow of KATARA

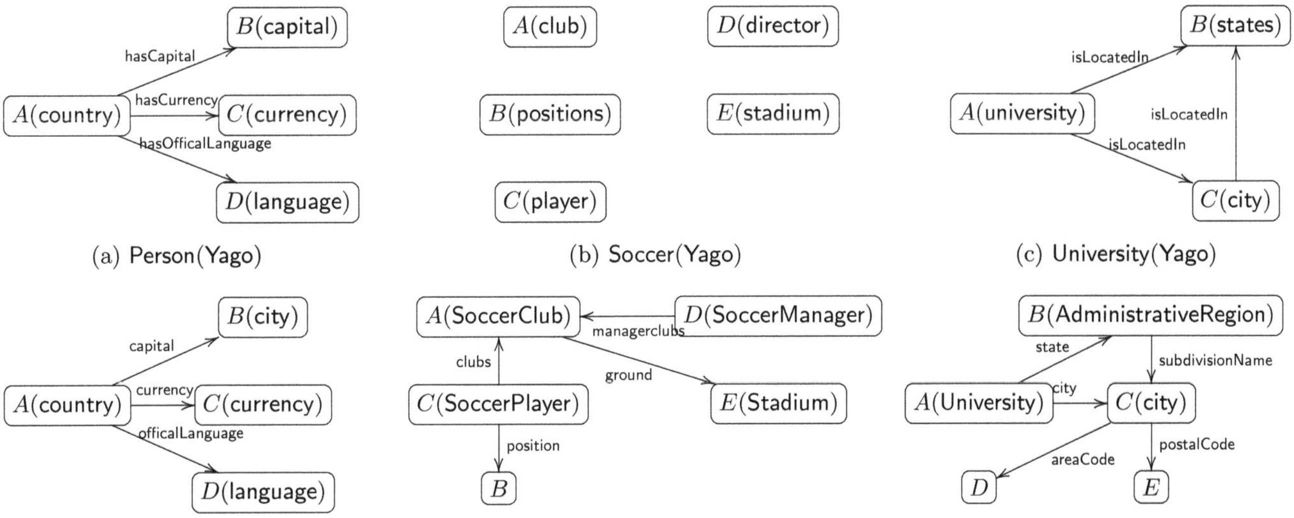

(a) Person(Yago) (b) Soccer(Yago) (c) University(Yago)

(d) Person(DBPedia) (e) Soccer(DBPedia) (f) University(DBPedia)

Figure 10: Validated table patterns

However, $\sum_{\varphi_i \in \mathcal{P}_{v=a}} Pr(\varphi_i)$ is exactly $Pr(v = a)$. Thus, we can replace for $H_{\varphi_i \in \mathcal{P}_{v=a}}(\varphi_i)$.

$E(\Delta H(\varphi))(v)$

$$= -H_{\mathcal{P}}(\varphi) + \sum_a Pr(v = a) \sum_{\varphi_i \in \mathcal{P}_{v=a}} \frac{Pr(\varphi_i)}{Pr(v=a)} \log_2 \frac{Pr(\varphi_i)}{Pr(v=a)}$$

$$= -H_{\mathcal{P}}(\varphi) + \sum_a \sum_{\varphi_i \in \mathcal{P}_{v=a}} Pr(\varphi_i)(\log_2 Pr(\varphi_i) - \log_2 Pr(v = a))$$

$$= -H_{\mathcal{P}}(\varphi) + \sum_a \sum_{\varphi_i \in \mathcal{P}_{v=a}} Pr(\varphi_i) \log_2 Pr(\varphi_i)$$

$$- \sum_a \sum_{\mathcal{P}_{v=a}} Pr(\varphi_i) \log_2 Pr(v = a)$$

The first double summation is exactly the summation over all the current patterns, ordering them by the value of v. Thus, we have the following:

$E(\Delta H(\varphi))(v)$

$$= -H_{\mathcal{P}}(\varphi) + \sum Pr(\varphi) \log_2 Pr(\varphi)$$

$$- \sum_a \log_2 Pr(v = a) \sum_{\varphi_i \in \mathcal{P}_{v=a}} Pr(\varphi_i)$$

$$= -H_{\mathcal{P}}(\varphi) + H_{\mathcal{P}}(\varphi) - \sum_a \log_2 Pr(v = a) \times Pr(v = a)$$

$$= - \sum_a Pr(v = a) \log_2 Pr(v = a)$$

$$= H(v)$$

The above result proves Theorem 1.

B. TOP-K PATTERNS ANALYSIS

Figure 11 shows the F-measure of the top-k patterns varying k on WikiTables and RelationalTables. It tells us that RankJoin converges much quicker than other methods on Yago, while all methods converge quickly on DBPedia due to its small number of types.

C. PATTERN VALIDATION

Figure 12 shows the quality of the validated pattern, varying the number of questions per variable q, on WikiTables and RelationalTables. Notice that RelationalTables only require one question per variable to achieve 1.0 precision and recall. This is because RelationalTables are less ambiguous compared with WikiTables and WebTables. Experts can correctly validate every variable with only one question.

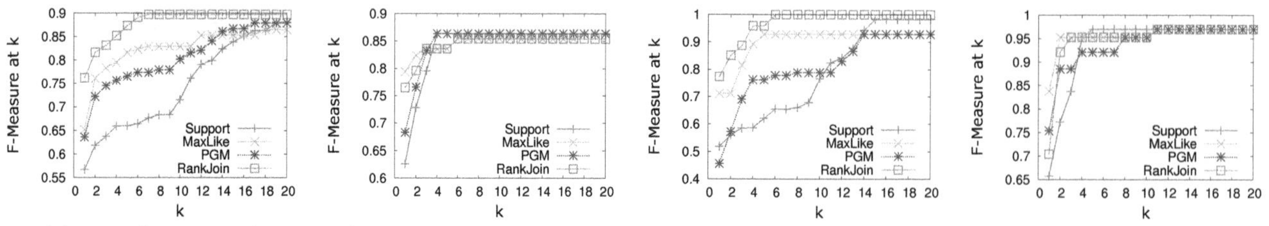

(a) Yago (WikiTables) (b) DBPedia (WikiTables) (c) Yago (RelationalTables) (d) DBPedia (RelationalTables)

Figure 11: Top-k F-measure

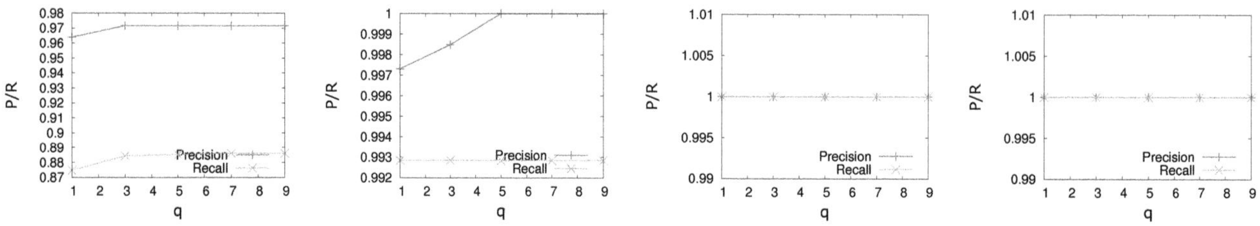

(a) Yago (WikiTables) (b) DBPedia (WikiTables) (c) Yago (RelationalTables) (d) DBPedia (RelationalTables)

Figure 12: Pattern validation P/R

D. DATA REPAIRING

We use the following FDs for algorithm EQ, referring to Fig. 10.

(1) Person, we used $A \to B, C, D$.

(2) Soccer, we used $C \to A, B$, $A \to E$, and $D \to A$.

(3) University, we used $A \to B, C$ and $C \to B$.

Crowd-Based Deduplication: An Adaptive Approach

Sibo Wang Xiaokui Xiao Chun-Hee Lee
School of Computer Engineering
Nanyang Technological University
Singapore
{wang0759, xkxiao, lee.ch}@ntu.edu.sg

ABSTRACT

Data deduplication stands as a building block for data integration and data cleaning. The state-of-the-art techniques focus on how to exploit crowdsourcing to improve the accuracy of deduplication. However, they either incur significant overheads on the crowd or offer inferior accuracy.

This paper presents *ACD*, a new crowd-based algorithm for data deduplication. The basic idea of *ACD* is to adopt *correlation clustering* (which is a classic machine-based algorithm for data deduplication) under a crowd-based setting. We propose non-trivial techniques to reduce the time required in performing correlation clustering with the crowd, and devise methods to postprocess the results of correlation clustering for better accuracy of deduplication. With extensive experiments on the Amazon Mechanical Turk, we demonstrate that *ACD* outperforms the states of the art by offering a high precision of deduplication while incurring moderate crowdsourcing overheads.

Categories and Subject Descriptors

H.2 [**Database Management**]: Systems

Keywords

Crowdsourcing; Data Deduplication; Correlating Clustering

1. INTRODUCTION

Given a set of records from heterogenous sources, the *data deduplication* problem aims to cluster the records into several groups, such that records in the same group correspond to the same entity in the real world. This problem finds important applications in data integration [28], data cleaning [13, 40], and web searching [21], etc. The problem is easy to address when the records to be clustered share some common identifiers; but in many practical scenarios, such common identifiers either do not exist or are rather noisy, which makes it challenging to deduplicate records accurately.

Numerous techniques have been proposed for automatic data deduplication based on pre-defined rules, similarity metrics, supervised learning, etc. (see [17] for a recent survey). Such *machine-based* techniques, however, often face difficulties when processing records that represent different entities but look highly similar. For example, consider three records about commercial brands: Chevrolet, Chevy, and Chevron. All of these records resemble each other, due to which they might be identified as the same entity by machine-based techniques; nevertheless, only Chevrolet and Chevy represent the same brand. To remedy the deficiency of machine-based techniques, recent works [46–48] propose to utilize crowdsourcing to improve the accuracy of data deduplication. The rationale is that humans are often better than machines in tackling complex tasks. In particular, given the three brand records above, humans can easily determine that Chevron is a different brand from Chevrolet and Chevy.

Given a set R of records, a naive approach to deduplicate R via crowdsourcing is to generate all possible pairs of records from R, and then ask the crowd to examine each pair to see if it contains duplicate records. Nevertheless, this approach incurs a prohibitive cost due to the enormous number of record pairs that need to be processed by the crowd. To address this problem, Wang et al. [46] propose a hybrid approach that utilizes both the crowd and machines. Specifically, Wang et al.'s approach runs in three steps. First, it evaluates the similarity between each pair of records in R using a machine-based algorithm. After that, it eliminates the pairs whose similarity scores are below a pre-defined threshold τ. Finally, it invokes the crowd to process the remaining pairs of records, and then derives the final deduplication results accordingly.

The above hybrid approach is shown to be much more accurate than conventional machine-based methods [46]. However, it still entails a large crowdsourcing overhead when there exist a large number of record pairs whose similarity scores are above the threshold τ. To improve, Wang et al. [47] present a more advanced approach (referred to as *TransM*) that reduces crowdsourcing costs by exploring the transitive relationship among records. In particular, for any three records x, y, z, if the crowd has decided that $x = y$ and $y = z$, then *TransM* determines that $x = z$, without issuing the pair (x, z) to the crowd. On the other hand, if the crowd suggests that $x = y$ and $y \neq z$, then *TransM* infers that $x \neq z$. As such, *TransM* considerably reduces the number of record pairs that requires human efforts.

The reduced crowdsourcing overhead of *TransM*, however, comes with a cost of deduplication accuracy, as demonstrated in the experiments in [47]. The reason is that *TransM* implicitly assumes that the crowd always returns correct results, which is not always the case in practice. When human errors occur in the processing of crowdsourced record pairs, *TransM*'s transitivity mechanism tends to amplify errors, leading to less accurate deduplication results. For example, consider the scenario in Figure 1, where we have two groups of records $\{a_i\}$ and $\{b_j\}$, each of which corre-

SIGMOD'15, May 31–June 4, 2015, Melbourne, Victoria, Australia.

ACM 978-1-4503-2758-9/15/05 ...$15.00.
http://dx.doi.org/10.1145/2723372.2723739 .

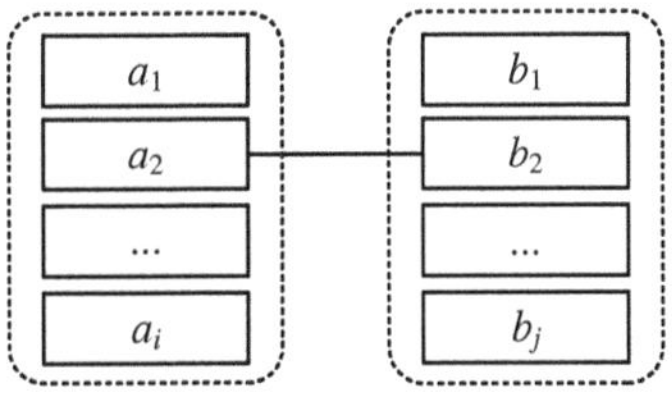

Figure 1: Illustration of the deficiency of *TransM*.

sponds to one entity. Assume that *TransM* correctly clusters all a_i into one group and all b_j into another, and then issues a pair (a_2, b_2) to the crowd. If the crowd mistakenly marks $a_2 = b_2$, then by transitivity, *TransM* would put all a_i and b_j into one group, resulting in significant errors.

Contributions. To address the deficiency of existing solutions, this paper presents *ACD (Adaptive Crowd-based Deduplication)*, a new deduplication technique that utilizes both human and machine power. *ACD* consists of three phases: a pruning phase, a cluster generation phase, and a cluster refinement phase. The pruning phase applies a machine-based algorithm to eliminate record pairs with low similarities. After that, the cluster generation phase collects the remaining record pairs, and produces an initial clustering of the records using a small number of *Human Intelligent Tasks (HITs)*. The initial clustering is then passed over to the cluster refinement phase, which refines the clustering using additional HITs and then returns the final deduplication results. Compared with *TransM*, *ACD* is much less sensitive to human errors, as it does not overly rely on the transitivity relationship among records. Instead, *ACD* adopts a more robust approach that is able to reconcile inconsistent results from the crowd, by borrowing idea from *correlation clustering* [9]. Furthermore, *ACD* incorporates a parallelization method that enables it to issue HITs in a batch manner in both the cluster generation and refinement phases, which significantly improves the efficiency of crowdsourcing. We experimentally evaluate *ACD* with real-world datasets, and we demonstrate the superiority of *ACD* against existing state-of-the-art crowd-based deduplication solutions.

In summary, the main contributions of this paper are as follows:

- We present *ACD*, a crowd-based data deduplication algorithm that overcomes the deficiencies of *TransM* and strikes a better balance between deduplication accuracy and crowdsourcing overheads.
- We devise a novel crowd-based approach for refining the clusters generated by *ACD*, yielding further improved deduplication results.
- We propose mechanisms to process HITs in *ACD* in a batch manner, which significantly improves the efficiency of crowdsourcing.
- We experimentally compare *ACD* with the states of the art on the Amazon Mechanical Turk (AMT). Our results show that *ACD* outperforms competitors by offering a high precision of deduplication while incurring moderate crowdsourcing overheads.

2. PRELIMINARIES

In this section, we formally define the data deduplication problem, and revisit the existing crowd-based deduplication approaches. Table 1 lists the notations that we will frequently use in the paper.

Notation	Description
$R = \{r_1, r_2, \cdots, r_n\}$	a set of records
S	a candidate set of record pairs (see Section 3)
$G = (V_R, E_S)$	an undirected graph where each vertex represents a record in R and each edge represents a record pair in S
$f(r_i, r_j)$	similarity score between r_i and r_j
$f_c(r_i, r_j)$	crowd's confidence that $r_i = r_j$
$\Lambda'(R)$	the optimization goal of *ACD* (see Equation 2)
$b(o)$	benefit of operation o
$b^*(o)$	estimated benefit of operation o
$c(o)$	crowdsourcing cost of performing operation o

Table 1: Table of notations.

2.1 Problem Definition

Let $R = \{r_1, r_2, \ldots, r_n\}$ be a set of records and g be a function that maps each r_i to the real world entity that r_i represents. Given R, the data deduplication problem aims to divide the records in R into a set of disjoint clusters $\mathcal{C} = \{C_1, C_2, \ldots, C_k\}$, such that for any two records $r_i, r_j \in R$, if $g(r_i) = g(r_j)$ then r_i and r_j appear in the same cluster, and vice versa.

In practice, however, the function g is either unknown or difficult to obtain in many scenarios. In that case, it is often assumed that there exists a similarity score function $f : R \times R \rightarrow [0, 1]$, such that $f(r_i, r_j)$ equals the likelihood that r_i and r_j represent the same entity. (Such a function can be constructed using either machine-based or crowd-based algorithms.) Under this setting, the objective of data deduplication is to construct the clustering $\mathcal{C} = \{C_1, C_2, \ldots, C_k\}$ in a manner that minimizes a certain error metric based on f. In this paper, we use a cost metric $\Lambda(R)$ that has been widely adopted in previous work [8, 11, 27, 41] on machine-based deduplication. In particular,

$$\Lambda(R) = \sum_{r_i, r_j \in R, i<j} x_{i,j} \cdot (1 - f(r_i, r_j)) + \sum_{r_i, r_j \in R, i<j} (1 - x_{i,j}) \cdot f(r_i, r_j), \qquad (1)$$

where $x_{i,j} = 1$ if r_i and r_j are in the same cluster and $x_{i,j} = 0$ otherwise. In other words, for any record pair (r_i, r_j), if r_i and r_j are put into the same cluster, then $\Lambda(R)$ assigns a penalty of $1 - f(r_i, r_j)$ on the pair; otherwise, the penalty assigned is $f(r_i, r_j)$. As such, the minimization of $\Lambda(R)$ tends to put similar (resp. different) records into the same (resp. different) clusters. Example 1 shows an example of the data deduplication problem with $\Lambda(R)$ as the optimization goal.

EXAMPLE 1. Suppose that we have a set of six records $R = \{a, b, c, d, e, f\}$. Table 2 shows the similarity score of each pair of records, omitting those pairs with low similarity scores. It can be verified that $\Lambda(R)$ is minimized when the records in R are divided into two clusters, $\{a, b, c\}$ and $\{d, e, f\}$. □

In general, minimizing $\Lambda(R)$ is an NP-hard problem [9]. Motivated by this, a number of approximation or heuristic algorithms [5, 9, 14, 36, 41] have been proposed for machine-based data deduplication. All these algorithms formulate similarity score function f (used in $\Lambda(R)$) with machine-based approaches, such as character-based metrics [32], token-based metrics [12], and phonetic similarity metrics [39], etc. However, these algorithms tend to struggle when handling "difficult" pairs of records that have similar

Record Pair	Similarity Score	Record Pair	Similarity Score
(a, b)	0.81	(e, f)	0.69
(b, c)	0.75	(c, d)	0.45
(a, c)	0.73	(a, d)	0.43
(d, e)	0.72	(a, e)	0.37
(d, f)	0.70	$\cdots$	≤ 0.3

Table 2: Similarity scores for the record pairs in Example 1.

representations but differ inherently. This motivates the utilization of crowdsourcing to improve the accuracy of data deduplication, as we explain in Section 2.2.

2.2 Crowd-based Deduplication

Crowdsourcing. There exist a number of crowdsourcing platforms, such as Amazon Mechanical Turk, CrowdFlower, and MobileWorks. In such platforms, we can request human "workers" to complete *micro-tasks*, e.g., we may ask them to answer questions like "do r_i and r_j refer to the same entity?". Each micro-task is referred to as a *human intelligent task (HIT)*. The completion of a HIT by a worker is rewarded with a certain amount of money based on the difficulty of the HIT, i.e., invoking the crowd for data deduplication comes with a monetary cost. In addition, a human worker may not always produce a correct answer for a HIT. A standard practice to mitigate such human errors is to issue a HIT to multiple workers, and then take a majority vote. As we will show in Section 6, however, even when majority votes are used, we may still get incorrect answers from the crowd. As a consequence, it is crucial to take human errors into account when designing a crowd-based algorithm.

Existing Crowd-based Deduplication Algorithms. There exist five crowd-based deduplication algorithms in the literature, namely, *Crowdclustering* [25], *CrowdER* [46], *GCER* [48], *TransM* [47], and a very recent approach by Vesdapunt et al. [44] (referred to as *TransNode*). As we have explained *CrowdER* and *TransM* in Section 1, we focus on the other three approaches in the following.

Given a set R of records, *Crowdclustering* first creates a number of small subsets of R, and then ask the crowd workers to perform clustering on each subset individually. After that, *Crowdclustering* inspects the clustering results produced by the crowd workers on each subset, and applies a machine learning approach to generalize the clustering results to the original dataset R. In other words, *Crowdclustering* assumes that the clustering results on a small subset of records can be representative of the results on R. This, however, does not always hold. In particular, if there do not exist too many records in R corresponding to the same entity (as is often the case in practice), then a small subset of R may not even contain two records that are duplicates. In that case, the clustering results on the subset would not give a machine learning algorithm any useful information about when two records should be regarded as duplicates; as a consequence, the deduplication accuracy of *Crowdclustering* would be poor. In general, *Crowdclustering* is more suitable for *data categorization*, which asks whether different records belong to the same category (i.e., whether *Chevrolet* and *Chevron* are both car brands) instead of whether they are duplicates. The reason is that, in data categorization, it is common that a large number of records belong to the same category, in which case even a small subset of the records could provide representative information about the whole dataset.

GCER shares the same spirit as *Crowdclustering* in that it first asks the crowd to process a subset of the data, and then generalizes the crowd's results to the entire data. In particular, it first constructs a machine-based similarity score function f. After that, it iteratively issues record pairs to the crowd, and utilizes the crowd's answers to refine f for better deduplication accuracy. As with *TransM*, however, *GCER* is also susceptible to mistakes made by the crowd, in the sense if the crowd gives an incorrect answer regarding whether two records are duplicate, then *GCER* would adjust f based on the incorrect answer, which degrades the precision of deduplication.

TransNode performs data deduplication in a way that is similar to *TransM*. In particular, they both discard dissimilar record pairs based on a machine-based similarity score function, and then exploit the crowd to process the remaining record pairs (referred to as *candidate pairs*), using transitive relations to improve efficiency and reduce crowdsourcing costs. The main difference between *TransM* and *TransNode* lies in the order which they inspect candidate pairs. In *TransM*, candidate pairs are issued in decreasing order of their machine-based similarity scores. In contrast, *TransNode* adopts a more advanced approach to order record pairs, which leads to a non-trivial worst-case guarantee on the number of record pairs that need to be crowdsourced to complete the clustering task. However, as *TransNode* also relies on transitive relations, it suffers from the same deficiency as *TransM*.

3. SOLUTION OVERVIEW

At a high level, our *ACD* algorithm for crowd-based deduplication consists of three phases:

1. *Pruning Phase:* This phase invokes a machine-based algorithm to construct the similarity score function f, and then generates a candidate set S from the set R of the input records, using a similarity threshold τ. In particular, S consists of all record pairs (r_i, r_j) such that $f(r_i, r_j) > \tau$.
2. *Cluster Generation Phase:* This phase issues a selected subset of the pairs in S to the crowd. After that, based on the crowd answers, it divides the records in R into a set of disjoint clusters $\mathcal{C} = \{C_1, C_2, \cdots, C_k\}$.
3. *Cluster Refinement Phase:* This phase issues some pairs in S that are previously not processed by the crowd, and then refines $\mathcal{C}$ based on the crowd answers.

Note that the pruning phase utilizes only machine-based algorithms, which have been well studied in the literature. Therefore, we will focus only on the cluster generation and refinement phases of *ACD*, assuming that a machine-based algorithm for the pruning phase is given.

Cluster Generation Phase. Let $f_c : R \times R \to [0, 1]$ be a crowd-based similarity score function, such that $f_c(r_i, r_j)$ equals the crowd's confidence that $r_i = r_j$. Without loss of generality, we assume that $f_c(r_i, r_j)$ equals the fraction of crowd workers (among those who inspect the record pair (r_i, r_j)) that mark r_i and r_j as duplicates. In addition, we set $f_c(r_i, r_j) = 0$ if (r_i, r_j) is eliminated in the pruning phase. The cluster generation phase of *ACD* aims to minimize the following metric $\Lambda'(R)$:

$$\Lambda'(R) = \sum_{r_i, r_j \in R, i<j} x_{i,j} \cdot (1 - f_c(r_i, r_j)) + \sum_{r_i, r_j \in R, i<j} (1 - x_{i,j}) \cdot f_c(r_i, r_j), \quad (2)$$

where $x_{i,j} = 1$ if r_i and r_j are in the same cluster and $x_{i,j} = 0$ otherwise. The minimization of $\Lambda'(R)$ is an instance of the *correlation clustering* problem [9], which is NP-hard. The classic approximate solution for the problem is *Pivot* [5], which is a randomized algorithm that yields a 5-approximation in expectation. Accordingly, we adopt *Pivot* in the cluster generation phase of *ACD*.

The adoption of *Pivot* under the crowd-based setting is non-trivial, since *Pivot* is a *sequential* algorithm. In particular, *Pivot* constructs clusters one by one, such that the formation of the i-th ($i > 1$) cluster depends on those of the first $i-1$ clusters. Therefore, if we are to translate *Pivot* directly into a crowd-based algorithm, we need to crowdsource the generation of clusters one at a time, i.e., we cannot construct the i-th cluster until we get the crowd's answer to the HITs pertinent to the first $i-1$ clusters. Such sequential processing of clusters leads to a large total overhead in terms of processing time. In contrast, if we can simultaneously crowdsource the construction of multiple clusters, then the total time required to complete the clustering procedure could be significantly reduced, due to the concurrent generation of clusters by the crowd.

To parallelize the construction of clusters, one may attempt to post a large number of HITs in one batch, and *dynamically* adjust the content of HITs according to the crowd workers' answers. For example, we may issue a number n of HITs to the crowd, such that the first n' HITs are pertinent to the generation of the first cluster, while the remaining HITs are left as blank initially. Then, whenever a crowd worker (say, Alice) finishes answering the first n' HITs, we inspect her answers to decide the formation of the first cluster; based on that, we dynamically generate the HITs required for the construction of the second cluster, and show them to Alice by utilizing some of the $n - n'$ blank HITs previously "reserved". (Such dynamic adjustment can be implemented on Amazon Mechanic Turk using the *iFrame* technique.) This approach, albeit intuitive, assumes that the HITs required for the i-th cluster can be chosen based only on Alice's answers to the HITs for the first $i-1$ clusters. In practice, however, we usually need to take answers from multiple workers on each HIT, as a means to mitigate human errors. Therefore, Alice's answers for the first $i-1$ clusters are insufficient to decide the HITs for the i-th cluster; instead, we need to incorporate multiple users' responses to HITs for the first $i-1$ clusters, before we can decide HITs to be shown next. This requires us to synchronize the efforts of multiple workers, which is highly challenging and not supported by the standard interface of the existing crowdsourcing platforms.

To remedy the drawbacks of the above approach, we propose a method to parallelize the *Pivot* algorithm under the crowd-based setting, while retaining its approximation guarantee. The basic idea of our method is to predict the HITs required by *Pivot* in constructing clusters, and then issue them to the crowd in one batch, at the minor cost of posting some HITs that are unnecessary in the sequential version of *Pivot*. In Section 4, we provide the details of our parallel method.

Cluster Refinement Phase. Although *Pivot* returns a 5-approximation in the expected case, its performance in a single run may be rather inferior, due to the fact that it is a randomized algorithm. To circumvent this drawback of *Pivot*, a standard under the machine-based setting is to repeat *Pivot* a large number of times, and then choose the result from the run that minimizes the cost metric. This approach, however, does not work under the crowd-based setting. First, repeating *Pivot* for a large number of times would incur a significant crowdsourcing overhead. Second, if we are to evaluate the output of a run of *Pivot* according to the cost metric $\Lambda'(R)$ in Equation 2, we would have to first obtain the crowd-based similarity score function f_c, in which case we need to issue all record pairs in the candidate set S to the crowd. This also leads to a tremendous crowdsourcing cost.

To tackle the above problem, we propose a crowd-based algorithm to refine the initial clustering result returned by the cluster generation phase. The basic idea of the algorithm is to issue selected record pairs to the crowd, and check if the crowd answers are consistent with the initial clustering; if many of crowd answers contradict the initial clustering, then we adjust the clustering to alleviate its contradiction with the crowd. As such, we mitigate the deficiency of *Pivot* and obtain higher accuracy in deduplication. As with the case of cluster generation phase, we also devise a parallel version of our cluster refinement algorithm, so as to reduce the total time required in crowdsourcing. We provide details of our refinement algorithms in Section 5.

Algorithm 1: *Crowd-Pivot*

input : The set R of records and the candidate set S generated by the pruning phase
output: A set $\mathcal{C}$ of clusters }

1 initialize $\mathcal{C}$ as an empty set;
2 construct an undirected graph $G = (V_R, E_S)$, where each vertex in V_R represents a record in R, and each edge $(r_i, r_j) \in E_S$ corresponds to a record pair in S;
3 **while** $V_R \neq \emptyset$ **do**
4   randomly pick a vertex r from V_R as a pivot;
5   initialize an empty set P;
6   **for** *each neighbor* r' *of* r *in* G **do**
7   add the record pair (r, r') into P;
8   issue all record pairs in P to the crowd;
9   initialize a set $C = \{r\}$;
10   **for** *each record pair* (r, r') *in* P **do**
11   **if** *the crowd decides that* $f_c(r, r') > 0.5$ **then**
12   add r' into C;
13   add C into $\mathcal{C}$;
14   remove from G all vertices that appear in C;
15 **return** $\mathcal{C}$;

4. CLUSTER GENERATION

This section details the algorithms used in the cluster generation phase of *ACD*. We first present a crowd-based version of the *Pivot* algorithm in Section 4.1, and then describe its parallelization in Sections 4.2 and 4.3.

4.1 Crowd-Pivot Algorithm

Algorithm 1 shows the pseudo-code of *Crowd-Pivot*, a simple adoption of the *Pivot* algorithm [9] under the crowd-based setting. The input of *Crowd-Pivot* includes the set R of records to be deduplicated, and the candidate set S of record pairs generated by the pruning phase of our solution (see Section 3). Its output is a set of disjoint clusters $\mathcal{C} = \{C_1, C_2, \ldots, C_k\}$ whose union equals R.

Crowd-Pivot first initializes $\mathcal{C} = \emptyset$, and constructs an undirected graph $G = (V_R, E_S)$, such that each vertex in V_R is a record in R, and each edge $(r_i, r_j) \in E_S$ corresponds to a record pair in S (Lines 1-2). The subsequent part of *Crowd-Pivot* runs in several iterations (Lines 3-14). In the i-th iteration, *Crowd-Pivot* randomly selects a vertex r from V_R as a *pivot*, and creates a set P that contains all record pairs (r, r') that correspond to the edges incident to r in G (Lines 4-7). After that, it posts all record pairs in P to the crowd (Line 8). Each record pair (r, r') will be evaluated by multiple crowd workers, and we set the crowd-based similarity score between r and r' (denoted as $f_c(r, r')$) to the percentage of crowd workers who believe that r and r' correspond to the same entity.

Once all record pairs in P are processed by the crowd, *Crowd-Pivot* forms a cluster C that includes r, as well as any record r' such that $(r, r') \in W$ and $f_c(r, r') > 0.5$ (Lines 9-12). Then, *Crowd-Pivot* removes from G all vertices that appear in C, and proceeds to the next iteration (Line 13). This iterative process terminates when all vertices in G are removed.

Crowd-Pivot is almost identical to the standard *Pivot* algorithm [9]. The only difference is that *Pivot* assumes that the similarity score for each edge in G is predefined, whereas *Crowd-Pivot* decides the similarity scores on the fly with the crowd. By the existing results on *Pivot* [5], we have the following lemma:

LEMMA 1. *Algorithm 1 returns a 5-approximation for the minimization of $\Lambda'(R)$ (in Equation 2), in expectation to its random choices made.* □

We omit the proof of Lemma 1 and refer interested readers to [5].

4.2 Parallel Crowd-Pivot: Rationale

Recall that, in each iteration of *Crowd-Pivot*, we issue a set of candidate pairs to the crowd and wait for the crowd to answer, before we can proceed to the next iteration. As a consequence, the running time of *Crowd-Pivot* mainly depends on the number of iterations. To reduce the running time of *Crowd-Pivot*, we aim to reduce the number of iterations in *Crowd-Pivot*, by selecting multiple pivots in each iteration and constructing multiple clusters simultaneously. Although similar ideas have been studied under a machine-based setting [34], the algorithm thus proposed does not retain the approximation guarantee of *Pivot*. In contrast, we propose a parallel version of *Crowd-Pivot* that constructs multiple clusters at the same time, without compromising the worst-case guarantee on the clustering results.

Let $\mathcal{M}$ be a random permutation of the records in R. For any record $r \in R$, if r is the i-th record in $\mathcal{M}$, then we say that the *permutation rank* of r in $\mathcal{M}$ equals i. Recall that, in each iteration of *Crowd-Pivot*, we randomly pick a record r from the un-clustered ones as a *pivot*, and then construct a cluster centering at r. Equivalently, we can first select a random permutation $\mathcal{M}$ before *Crowd-Pivot* starts, and then in each iteration of *Crowd-Pivot*, we can choose r as the record that has the smallest permutation rank among the un-clustered ones.

Our idea to parallelize *Crowd-Pivot* is that, in each iteration of the algorithm, we choose multiple pivots with the smallest permutation ranks among the un-clustered vertices, instead of selecting only one pivot. Given the chosen pivots, we issue to the crowd all record pairs pertinent to the pivots, and we construct clusters based on the crowd workers' answers, in such a way that the clustering results produced are identical to the case when we run the sequential version of *Crowd-Pivot* given the same permutation order $\mathcal{M}$. This ensures that the parallelization of *Crowd-Pivot* retains its approximation guarantee. In the following, we first consider a simple setting where we choose, in each iteration, 2 pivots with the smallest permutation ranks among the un-clustered vertices. (We will soon extend our discussions to the case when k pivots are chosen simultaneously.)

Consider the graph G constructed in Line 2 of *Crowd-Pivot*. Let G_i be the version of G at the beginning of *Crowd-Pivot*'s i-th iteration, i.e., each vertex in G_i represents a record that is not clustered in the first $i-1$ iterations. Assume that, in the i-th iteration of *Crowd-Pivot*, we choose two pivots r_1 and r_2 that have the smallest and second smallest permutation ranks, respectively, among the vertices in G_i. Let $d_i(r_1, r_2)$ be the number of hops between r_1 and r_2 in G_i, e.g., $d_i(r_1, r_2) = 1$ if they are neighbors in G_i. We differentiate three cases: (i) $d_i(r_1, r_2) > 2$, (ii) $d_i(r_1, r_2) = 2$, and

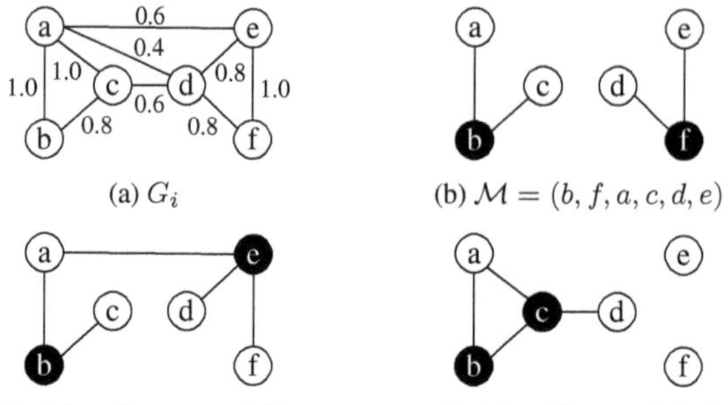

(a) G_i (b) $\mathcal{M} = (b, f, a, c, d, e)$

(c) $\mathcal{M} = (b, e, a, c, d, f)$ (d) $\mathcal{M} = (b, c, a, f, d, e)$

Figure 2: Different cases for the pivot choice.

(iii) $d_i(r_1, r_2) = 1$. We will demonstrate each case, assuming that G_i is as illustrated in Figure 2a, where the number on each edge (x, y) indicates the similarity score $f_c(x, y)$ that we would obtain if we issue (x, y) to the crowd.

Case 1: $d_i(r_1, r_2) > 2$. Consider a permutation $\mathcal{M} = (b, f, a, c, d, e)$ on the vertices in G_i in Figure 2a. Given $\mathcal{M}$, we would choose $r_1 = b$ and $r_2 = f$ as pivots, and then issue to the crowd all edges incident to r_1 and r_2, namely, (b, a), (b, c), (f, d), and (f, e), as shown in Figure 2b. Observe that, for each of these four edges, the crowd-based similarity score for the two records in the edge is above 0.5. Accordingly, we construct a cluster C_1 that contains $r_1 = b$ and its two neighbors a and c, as well as a cluster C_2 consisting of $r_2 = f$ and all of its neighbors d and e. Notice that this parallel clustering result is identical to the case when we run the sequential version *Crowd-Pivot* on G_i, using $r_1 = b$ as a pivot, followed by $r_2 = b$. In addition, the number of edges crowdsourced are also identical in both cases. □

Case 2: $d_i(r_1, r_2) = 2$. Consider a permutation $\mathcal{M} = (b, e, a, c, d, f)$ on the vertices in G_i in Figure 2a. In that case, we set $r_1 = b$ and $r_2 = e$, and crowdsource all edges incident to b and e, i.e., (b, a), (b, c), (e, a), (e, d), and (e, f), as shown in Figure 2c. Each of these edges has a crowd-based similarity score above 0.5. Given the crowd answer on each edge, we first generate a cluster C_1 that includes $r_1 = b$ and its neighbors a and c. After that, we construct a cluster C_2 that consists of $r_2 = e$ and two of its neighbors, namely, d and f. Notice that C_2 does not include a, as it has been contained in C_1. Observe that this result is the same as the case when we apply *Crowd-Pivot* on G_i with $r_1 = b$ as a pivot, followed by $r_2 = e$. However, *Crowd-Pivot* would not issue the edge (e, a) to the crowd, because once C_1 is formed, it removes all records in C_1 from G_i, after which (e, a) is no longer under consideration. In other words, our parallel construction of C_1 and C_2 incurs a small additional overhead, in that it crowdsources one "useless" edge (e, a) that has no effect on the clustering result. □

Case 3: $d_i(r_1, r_2) = 1$. Consider a permutation $\mathcal{M} = (b, c, a, f, d, e)$ on the vertices in G_i in Figure 2a. With this permutation, we select $r_1 = b$ and $r_2 = c$ and post all edges of b and c to the crowd. Figure 2d shows all edges posted, i.e., (b, a), (b, c), (c, a), and (c, d), all of which have crowd-based similarity scores above 0.5. In that case, we first form a cluster C_1 with $r_1 = b$ and its neighbors a and c. Then, we are unable to form a second cluster using c as a pivot, since c is already included in C_1. This result is identical to the case when we run *Crowd-Pivot* on G_i with $r_1 = b$ as a pivot. In other words, although we crowdsource all edges incident to $r_1 = b$ and $r_2 = c$, we end up with one cluster C_1 only. Furthermore, compared with *Crowd-Pivot*, we pay extra cost in crowdsourcing the edge (c, d) (which is not considered in *Crowd-Pivot*). □

As we can observe from the above discussions, it is possible to parallelize the construction of clusters in *Crowd-Pivot*, at the potential cost of having some *wasted pairs*, e.g., the edge (e, a) in Case 2 and the edge (c, d) in Case 3. In particular, we define a candidate pair as a wasted pair, if it is crowdsourced by our parallelized version of *Crowd-Pivot* but not in the sequential version. We now extend our discussions to the case when we choose k pivots simultaneously.

Given G_i, we first identify the k records $r_1, r_2, \ldots, r_k$ with the smallest permutation ranks in G_i. After that, we crowdsource all edges in G_i that are adjacent to r_j ($j \in [1, k]$). Let P' be the subset of those edges whose crowd-based similarity scores are above 0.5, and H_i be the subgraph of G_i induced by the edges in P'. Then, we generate a cluster that consists of r_1 and all of its neighbors in H_i, and remove all records in the cluster from H_i. Subsequently, we inspect each r_j ($j \in [2, k]$) in ascending order of j. For each r_j, if r_j has not been removed from H_i, we create a cluster that contains r_j and its remaining neighbors in H_i (i.e., we exclude the neighbors of r_j that have been eliminated in the processing of $r_1, \ldots, r_{j-1}$). In other words, we simultaneously crowdsource all record pairs pertinent to $r_1, \ldots, r_k$, and we construct multiple clusters from $r_1, \ldots, r_k$ in one batch based on the crowd workers' answers. Algorithm 2 shows the pseudo-code of this parallel method (referred to as *Partial-Pivot*). Lemma 2 establishes the correctness of the algorithm.

LEMMA 2. *Let G_i be the version of G in the beginning of Crowd-Pivot's i-iteration, and $\mathcal{M}$ be the permutation of records implicitly used by Crowd-Pivot. Let r_k be the record with the k-th smallest permutation rank in G_i, and $\mathcal{C}'_i$ be the set of clusters generated by Crowd-Pivot from its i-th iteration until it chooses a pivot with a larger permutation rank than r_k. Then, given G_i, k, and $\mathcal{M}$, Partial-Pivot outputs $\mathcal{C}_i = \mathcal{C}'_i$.* □

In Section 4.3, we will use *Partial-Pivot* to develop a parallelized version of *Crowd-Pivot*. Before that, we first introduce a method for deriving the maximum number of wasted pairs incurred by *Partial-Pivot*. Let $r_1, r_2, \ldots, r_k$ be as defined in Line 2 of *Partial-Pivot*, and w_j be defined as follows:

$$w_j = \begin{cases} \text{the number of vertices (in } G_i) \text{ adjacent to} \\ r_j, \text{ except } r_1, \ldots, r_{j-1}, \\ \qquad\qquad \text{if } d(r_j, r_x) = 1 \text{ for some } x < j; \\ \text{the number of vertices (in } G_i) \text{ adjacent to} \\ \text{both } r_j \text{ and some } r_l \ (l < j), \\ \qquad\qquad\qquad\qquad \text{otherwise.} \end{cases} \quad (3)$$

We have the following lemma:

LEMMA 3. *The number of wasted pairs incurred by Partial-Pivot equals $\sum_{j=1}^{k} w_j$ in the worst case.* □

4.3 Parallel Crowd-Pivot: Algorithm

Observe that, if we set $G_i = G$ and $k = |R|$ in the input to *Partial-Pivot*, then it would cluster all records in R with a single-batch of HITs, and its output would be identical with the output of *Crowd-Pivot* given G and the same permutation $\mathcal{M}$. This leads to a maximum degree of parallelization, but at a tremendous cost: It requires issuing all edges in G to the crowd, which incurs a significant amount of wasted pairs. On the other hand, if we set $k = 1$, then *Partial-Pivot* can only generate one cluster, in which case it avoids wasted pairs but fails to achieve any parallelism. A natural idea here is to choose k in a way that strike a balance between the number of wasted pairs and the degree of parallelism. Towards that end, we introduce a constant ε, and consider the following optimization problem: Given G_i and $\mathcal{M}$, we aim to select the maximum k under the constraint that

$$\textstyle\sum_{j=1}^{k} w_j \quad \leq \quad \varepsilon \cdot |P_j|, \qquad (4)$$

where P_j is the set of edges in G_i that are incident to $r_1, r_2, \ldots, r_j$. In other words, we maximize k while ensuring that, among the record pairs issued by *Partial-Pivot* to the crowd, at most a ε fraction is wasted. Observe that such k can be easily derived using a linear scan of all w_j and P_j.

Based on the above method for deciding k, we propose a parallel version of *Crowd-Pivot* (referred to as *PC-Pivot*), as shown in Algorithm 3. The input to *PC-Pivot* is identical to that of *Crowd-Pivot*, which includes a set S of records to be clustered and a candidate set S of record pairs produced by the pruning phase of our solution. As with *Crowd-Pivot*, *PC-Pivot* also begins by initializing an empty set $\mathcal{C}$ and constructing a graph G that represents the records in R as vertices and the record pairs in S as edges (Lines 1-2). After that, it selects a random permutation $\mathcal{M}$ of the records in R, and generates clusters in an iterative manner (Lines 3-7). In particular, in the first iteration, *PC-Pivot* inspects G, and derives the maximum k that satisfies Equation 4. Then, it invokes *Partial-Pivot* with $G_i = G$, k, and $\mathcal{M}$ as input, and obtains as output a set of clusters $\mathcal{C}'$ and a modified version of G (where some vertices are removed). After that, *PC-Pivot* inserts the clusters in $\mathcal{C}'$ into $\mathcal{C}$. Each subsequent iteration of *PC-Pivot* is performed in the same manner: *PC-Pivot* first decides k based on the current version of G, and applies *Partial-Pivot* to construct clusters. This iterative proce-

Algorithm 2: *Partial-Pivot*

input : G_i, k, and $\mathcal{M}$
output: A set $\mathcal{C}_i$ of clusters and G_{i+1} (a subgraph of G_i)

1 initialize $\mathcal{C}_i$ as an empty set;
2 identify the record r_j ($j \in [1, k]$) with the j-th smallest permutation rank in G_i;
3 let P be a set that contains all edges in G_i that are adjacent to $r_1, r_2, \ldots, r_k$;
4 issue all edges in P to the crowd;
5 let P' be the set of edges $(r, r') \in W$ with $f_c(r, r') > 0.5$;
6 let H_i be the subgraph of G_i induced by the edges in P';
7 **for** $j = 1$ *to* k **do**
8   **if** r_j *remains in* H_i **then**
9   create a cluster C that contains r_j and all of its neighbors in H_i;
10   insert C into $\mathcal{C}_i$;
11   remove all vertices in C from both H_i and G_i;
12 **return** $\mathcal{C}_i$ and $G_{i+1} = G_i$;

Algorithm 3: *PC-Pivot*

input : The set R of records and the candidate set S generated by the pruning phase
output: A set $\mathcal{C}$ of clusters

1 initialize $\mathcal{C}$ as an empty set;
2 construct an undirected graph $G = (V_R, E_S)$, where each vertex in V_R represents a record in R, and each edge $(r_i, r_j) \in E_S$ corresponds to a record pair in S;
3 select a random permutation $\mathcal{M}$ of the records in R;
4 **while** $V_R \neq \emptyset$ **do**
5   derive the maximum k that satisfies Equation 4;
6     $(\mathcal{C}', G)$ = *Partial-Pivot*(G, k, $\mathcal{M}$);
7     $\mathcal{C} = \mathcal{C} \cup \mathcal{C}'$;
8 **return** $\mathcal{C}$;

dure terminates when all vertices in G are removed, in which case *PC-Pivot* returns $\mathcal{C}$ as output.

The following lemma shows the performance guarantees of *PC-Pivot*.

LEMMA 4. *PC-Pivot returns a 5-approximation for the minimization of $\Lambda'(R)$ (in Equation 2), in expectation to its random choices made. In addition, among the record pairs crowdsourced by PC-Pivot, at most a fraction ε is wasted.* □

5. CLUSTER REFINEMENT

Although our cluster generation phase returns a 5-approximation in expectation (for the minimization of $\Lambda'(R)$), its performance in a particular run could be rather inferior, because of its randomized nature. To address this issue, the cluster refinement phase of our solution *post-processes* the results produced by the cluster generation phase, by using additional HITs to fine-tune the clusters, so as to reduce $\Lambda'(R)$. In what follows, we will introduce postprocessing operations in Section 5.1, analyze the cost and benefit of postprocessing operations in Section 5.2, present crowd-based postprocessing algorithm in Section 5.3, and demonstrate parallelized postprocessing algorithms in Section 5.4.

5.1 Rationale and Basic Operations

There exist several machine-based algorithms (e.g., [5, 23]) for postprocessing the results generated by a randomized correlation clustering algorithm. These algorithms, however, require as input the similarity scores of all record pairs, which incur significant monetary costs under a crowd-based setting. For example, consider the *BOEM* algorithm [5]. It runs in several iterations, each of which moves one record from one cluster to another. To determine the record to be moved in an iteration, *BOEM* first identifies a set R of candidate records, and then examines the similarity scores of all record pairs involving at least one record in R, based on which it selects a record whose move leads to the largest reduction in the cost function of correlation clustering (see Equation 1). If we directly adopt *BOEM* in a crowd-based setting, then in each iteration, we need to crowdsource a large number of record pairs to obtain their crowd-based similarity scores, which results in significant overheads.

To address the above problem, we propose to adjust clusters with a sequence of operations that are economical in terms of the number of additional record pairs that need to be crowdsourced. In particular, we consider two basic operations, *split* and *merger*. A split operation removes a vertex v from a cluster, and uses v to constructs a singleton cluster. A merger operation combines two clusters C_1 and C_2 into a new cluster $C_1 \cup C_2$. Our objective is to develop a crowd-based algorithm that takes as input a set of clusters, and identifies a split or merger operation that will reduce $\Lambda'(R)$ without substantial crowsourcing costs. Given such an algorithm, we can then recursively apply it on the clustering results produced by our cluster generation phase, so as to improve the quality of clustering. As a first step, we will analyze the cost and benefit of performing a split or merger operation on a set of clusters.

5.2 Cost-Benefit Analysis

Suppose that we split a record r from a cluster C. Let o_s denote this split operation, and $C' = C \setminus \{r\}$. According to Equation 2, after the split, $\Lambda'(R)$ decreases by:

$$b(o_s) = \sum_{r' \in C \setminus \{r\}} (1 - 2f_c(r, r')). \quad (5)$$

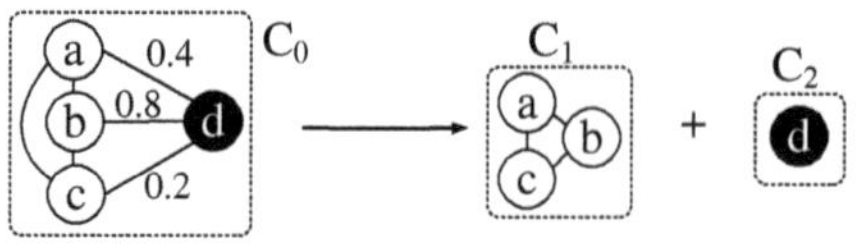

Figure 3: illustration of a split operation.

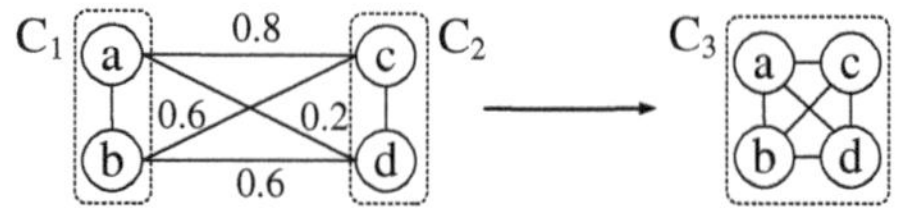

Figure 4: illustration of a merger operation.

We define $b(o_s)$ as the *benefit* of o_s. On the other hand, if we merge two clusters C_1 and C_2, then the merger operation (denoted as o_m) would reduce $\Lambda'(R)$ by:

$$b(o_m) = \sum_{r_1 \in C_1, r_2 \in C_2} (2f_c(r_1, r_2) - 1). \quad (6)$$

We refer to $b(o_m)$ as the benefit of o_m. We illustrate $b(o_s)$ and $b(o_m)$ with an example.

EXAMPLE 2. Figure 3 demonstrates a split operation o_s to split record d from a cluster $C_0 = \{a, b, c, d\}$. The number on each edge (x, y) indicates the similarity score $f_c(x, y)$ that we would obtain if we issue (x, y) to the crowd. We omit the similarity score if the edge is irrelevant to the operation. Based on Equation 5, the benefit of this operation is 0.2. That is, by applying this split operation, $\Lambda'(R)$ can be reduced by 0.2. After the split operation, we obtain two clusters $C_1 = \{a, b, c\}$ and $C_2 = \{d\}$. Figure 4 illustrates a merger operation o_m to merge cluster $C_1 = \{a, b\}$ and $C_2 = \{c, d\}$. With Equation 6, it can be calculated that the benefit of this merger operation is 0.4. After the merger operation, we obtain a new cluster $C_3 = \{a, b, c, d\}$. □

Intuitively, if we are to fine-tune a set $\mathcal{C}$ of clusters, we should identify the operation o with the largest positive benefit $b(o)$, and then apply o on $\mathcal{C}$. However, the computation of $b(o)$ requires the crowd-based similarity scores of various record pairs, which may not be readily available. In particular, if a record pair (r, r') has not been crowdsourced during the cluster generation phase, then $f_c(r, r')$ remains unknown in the cluster refinement phase, unless we post (r, r') to the crowd. That is, the derivation of $b(o)$ incurs crowdsourcing overheads. Therefore, we cannot solely rely on $b(o)$ to identify the best operation for cluster refinement. Instead, we adopt a more economical approach as follows:

1. Let O be the set of all possible (split and merger) operations on a given set $\mathcal{C}$ of clusters, and O^+ be the set of operations in O whose benefits are known and are larger than zero. If $O^+ \neq \emptyset$, then we choose the operation in O^+ with the largest benefit, and apply it on $\mathcal{C}$.
2. If $O^+ = \emptyset$, then we estimate the benefit of each operation in O, and choose an operation o. After that, we compute the exact benefit $b(o)$ of o (by crowdsourcing the relevant record pairs with unknown similarity scores), to check if $b(o) > 0$. If $b(o) > 0$, then we perform o on $\mathcal{C}$; otherwise, we ignore o.

We now clarify how we estimate $b(o)$ when it is unknown. For simplicity, we assume that o is a split operation that removes a record r from a cluster C; our discussions can be easily extended to the case of merger operations. By Equation 5, the computation of $b(o)$ requires the crowd-based similarity scores $f_c(r, r')$ of all record pairs (r, r') with $r' \in C \setminus \{r\}$. Let P be the set of record pairs (among those required by the computation of $b(o)$) that are unknown. Our idea is to (i) estimate the crowd-based similarity score $f_c(r, r')$ of each record pair $(r, r') \in P$ based on its machine-based similarity score $f(r, r')$, and then (ii) compute an estimated value of $b(o)$ accordingly. Towards this end, a straightforward solution is to set directly use $f(r, r')$ as an estimation of $f_c(r, r')$ [46,47]. However, this solution is often inaccurate due to the limitations of machine based algorithms. As an improved solution, previous work [48] proposes to (i) crowdsource a number of record pairs and then (ii) utilize the crowd workers' answers to construct a histogram, which maps each $f(r, r')$ into a more accurate estimation of $f_c(r, r')$. We adopt a similar solution as follows.

First, we collect the set A of record pairs whose crowd-based similarity scores are known from the cluster generation phase. Then, we inspect the machine-based similarity scores of those record pairs, and construct an equi-depth histogram H with m buckets on the machine-based scores. (Following [48], we set $m = 20$.) After that, for each bucket B in H, we examine the record pairs whose machine-based similarity scores fall in B, and compute the average crowd-based similarity score of those record pairs. Subsequently, if we have any record pair (r, r') whose crowd-based similarity score $f_c(r, r')$ is unknown, we first identify the bucket that covers $f(r, r')$, and then we estimate $f_c(r, r')$ as the average crowd-based similarity score associated with the bucket. In addition, whenever we crowdsource additional record pairs in the cluster refinement phase, we also insert the record pairs into A and reconstruct the histogram H, for more accurate estimation.

Next, we explain how we choose the operation to be performed on $\mathcal{C}$, given a benefit estimation of each operation of interest. As we aim to minimize $\Lambda'(R)$, an intuitive choice is to select the operation o with the maximum estimated benefit. However, this choice may incur a large crowdsourcing cost, since we need to first compute the exact value of $b(o)$ (to confirm o's benefit) before we apply o on $\mathcal{C}$. That is, if the computation of $b(o)$ requires crowsourcing a large number of record pairs, then o may not be an ideal choice of operation. Motivated by this, we select operations based on a metric that takes into account both the estimated benefit of an operation and the crowdsourcing overhead incurred. In particular, we choose the operation o that maximizes $b^*(o)/c(o)$, where $b^*(o)$ is the estimated value of $b(o)$, and $c(o)$ is the *cost* of o defined as follows. If o splits a vertex v from a cluster C,

$$c(o) = \left|\left\{r' \;\middle|\; r' \in C \setminus \{r\} \wedge f_c(r, r') \notin A\right\}\right|, \quad (7)$$

where A denotes the set of record pairs that have been crowdsourced. In other words, $c(o)$ equals the number of record pairs that need to be posted to the crowd, if we are to compute $b(o)$ exactly. Similarly, if o merges two clusters C_1 and C_2, then

$$c(o) = \left|\left\{(r_1, r_2) \;\middle|\; r_1 \in C_1 \wedge r_2 \in C_2 \wedge f_c(r_1, r_2) \notin A\right\}\right|. \quad (8)$$

Intuitively, by selecting an operation o with the maximum $b^*(o)/c(o)$, we strike a better balance between the minimization of $\Lambda'(R)$ and the overhead of crowdsourcing. For convenience, we refer to $b^*(o)/c(o)$ as the *benefit-cost ratio* of o.

5.3 Crowd-Based Postprocessing

Based on the discussions in Sections 5.1 and 5.2, Algorithm 4 illustrates a (sequential) crowd-based method for cluster refinement, referred to as *Crowd-Refine*. The algorithm takes as input the set $\mathcal{C}$ of clusters produced by the cluster generation phase, as well as the set A of record pairs that have been crowdsourced. It first constructs, based on A, a histogram H that maps machine-based similarity scores to estimated crowd-based similarity scores (Line 1), using the method described in Section 5.2. The subsequent execution of *Crowd-Refine* consists of a number of iterations (Lines 2-16). In each iteration, it first identifies the set O of all (split and merger) operations on $\mathcal{C}$, and the set O^+ of operations in O whose benefits are known and positive (Lines 3-4). If $O^+ \neq \emptyset$, then there exists at least one operation that can reduce $\Lambda'(R)$ without incurring any crowdsourcing overhead; accordingly, *Crowd-Refine* pinpoints the operation in O^+ with the maximum benefit, and applies it on $\mathcal{C}$ (Lines 5-7). On the other hand, if $O^+ = \emptyset$, then *Crowd-Refine* proceeds to derive the operation $o' \in O$ with the largest benefit-cost ratio $b^*(o')/c(o')$ (Line 9). If this ratio is larger than 0, then *Crowd-Refine* computes the exact value of $b(o)$ to check if the benefit of o' is indeed positive (Line 12), and the record pairs crowdsourced during the derivation of $b(o)$ are added into A and used to update the histogram H (Lines 15-16). In case that $b(o') > 0$ holds, *Crowd-Refine* performs o' on $\mathcal{C}$ (Line 13-14). However, if the benefit-cost ratio of o' is non-positive in the first place, then all operations in O should have non-positive estimated benefits. In that case, *Crowd-Refine* terminates by returning $\mathcal{C}$ (Lines 10-11).

Algorithm 4: *Crowd-Refine*

input : A set $\mathcal{C}$ of clusters and a set A of crowdsourced record pairs, both obtained from the cluster generation phase
output: A set $\mathcal{C}$ of improved clusters

1 construct a histogram H that maps machine-based similarity scores to estimated crowd-based similarity scores;
2 **while** *true* **do**
3   let O be the set of all operations on $\mathcal{C}$;
4   let O^+ be the set of operations (in O) whose benefits are known and larger than zero;
5   **if** $O^+ \neq \emptyset$ **then**
6   let o be the operation in O^+ with the largest benefit;
7   apply o on $\mathcal{C}$;
8   **else**
9   let o' be the operation in O with the largest benefit-cost ratio $b^*(o')/c(o')$;
10   **if** $b^*(o')/c(o') \leq 0$ **then**
11   **return** $\mathcal{C}$;
12   compute $b(o')$ by crowdsourcing relevant record pairs with unknown crowd-based similarity scores;
13   **if** $b(o') > 0$ **then**
14   apply o' on $\mathcal{C}$;
15   insert all newly crowdsourced record pairs into A;
16   update H;

Let n be the total number of records in R. Observe that, on any set $\mathcal{C}$ of clusters on R, there are $O(n)$ split operations and $O(n^2)$ merger operations. Therefore, in each iteration of *Crowd-Refine*, we consider $O(n^2)$ operations, which is a reasonable number given that we need to process $O(n^2)$ record pairs in our clustering tasks. We refer the reader to Appendix B for an example that demosntrates the execution of *Crowd-Refine*.

5.4 Parallel Postprocessing

Notice that *Crowd-Refine* is a sequential algorithm, in that it adjusts clusters using one operation at a time, and each operation may require posting some record pairs to the crowd and wait for the answers. Such sequential processing leads to significant processing time, as we point out in Section 3. To remedy this deficiency, we aim to parallelize *Crowd-Refine*, in a manner similar to the parallelization of *Crowd-Pivot*. To that end, we first introduce the concept of *independence* between different operations on $\mathcal{C}$.

Specifically, we say that two operations o_1 and o_2 are *independent*, if the clusters adjusted by o_1 are completely different from those adjusted by o_2. For instance, if o_1 splits a vertex from a cluster C_0, and o_2 merges two other clusters C_1 and C_2, then o_1 and o_2 are independent of each other. In contrast, o_1 is not independent of an operation that merges C_0 with another cluster, or one that splits another vertex from C_0. Observe that if two operations are independent, then we can apply them simultaneously on $\mathcal{C}$ without any side effect. Therefore, if we are to parallelize *Crowd-Refine*, a natural idea is to first identify a large number of independent operations, and then process them concurrently by crowdsourcing all relevant record pairs in one batch.

Based on the above idea, we propose to refine a given set $\mathcal{C}$ of clusters with a two-step approach as follows:

1. Let O^+ be the set of operations on $\mathcal{C}$ whose benefits are known and are larger than zero. We recursively choose the operation in O^+ with the largest benefit and apply it on $\mathcal{C}$, until O^+ becomes empty. Note that this step can be conducted without the crowd.

2. Whenever $O^+ = \emptyset$, we identify a set O^i of independent operations on $\mathcal{C}$, and process the operations in O^i concurrently with the crowd. After that, if O^+ becomes non-empty, we go back to Step 1; otherwise, we repeat this step.

The key issue in the above approach is the choice of O^i. Intuitively, O^i should contain operations o with large estimated benefits $b^*(o)$ but small crowdsourcing costs $c(o)$. Motivated by this, we select O^i as the set with the maximum *overall benefit-cost ratio*, which is defined as:

$$\Psi(O^i) = \frac{\sum_{o \in O^i} b^*(o)}{\sum_{o \in O^i} c(o)}. \tag{9}$$

Unfortunately, deriving such a set of independent operations is NP-hard, as shown in the following lemma.

LEMMA 5. *Given a set $\mathcal{C}$ of clusters, it is NP-hard to identify a set O^i of independent operations that maximizes $\Psi(O^i)$.* □

Given Lemma 5, we resort to a greedy heuristic for constructing O^i. In particular, we first set $O^i = \emptyset$, and then linearly scan all operations in O in descending order of their benefit-cost ratios. For each operation inspected, if its benefit-cost ratio is positive and it is independent of all operations in O^i, then we insert it into O^i; otherwise, we ignore the operation. This linear scan terminates when $\sum_{o \in O^i} c(o)$ (i.e., the total crowdsourcing cost of the operations in O^i) reaches a predefined threshold T. After that, the construction of O^i is completed. The reason that we impose a threshold τ on the total crowdsourcing cost of O^i is to avoid packing O^i with an excessive number of operations, since the operations examined in the later stage of the linear scan tend to have small benefits.

Based on the above heuristic, Algorithm 5 shows our parallel method for crowd-based cluster refinement, referred to as *PC-Refine*. *PC-Refine* is similar to *Crowd-Refine* (Algorithm 4), but differs in the handling of the case when $O^+ = \emptyset$, i.e., when there does not exist any operation whose benefit is known and positive. Specifically, when $O^+ = \emptyset$, *PC-Refine* adopts the heuristic approach previously discussed to construct a set O^i of independent operations (Lines 9-14), and then computes the exact benefits of all operations in O^i by crowdsourcing all relevant record pairs in one batch (Line 15), instead of processing one operation at a time with the crowd. After that, for each operation in O^i with positive benefit,

Algorithm 5: *PC-Refine*

```
input : A set C of clusters and a set A of crowdsourced record pairs,
        both obtained from the cluster generation phase
output: A set C of improved clusters
1  construct a histogram H that maps machine-based similarity scores to
   estimated crowd-based similarity scores;
2  while true do
3      let O be the set of all operations on C;
4      let O+ be the set of operations (in O) whose benefits are known
       and larger than zero;
5      if O+ ≠ ∅ then
6          let o be the operation in O+ with the largest benefit;
7          apply o on C;
8      else
9          set O^i = ∅;
10         for each o' ∈ O in descending order of b*(o')/c(o') do
11             if b*(o')/c(o') <= 0 or Σ_{o∈O^i} c(o) ≥ T then
12                 break;
13             if o' is independent of all operations in O^i then
14                 insert o' into O^i;
15         compute b(o) for all o ∈ O^i by crowdsourcing all relevant
           record pairs in one batch;
16         for each o ∈ O^i do
17             if b(o) > 0 then
18                 apply o on C;
19         if none of the operation in O^i is applied on C then
20             return C;
21         insert all newly crowdsourced record pairs into A;
22         update H;
```

PC-Refine applies the operation on $\mathcal{C}$ to reduce $\Lambda'(R)$. However, if none of the operation in O^i has a positive benefit, then it is unlikely that we can further decrease $\Lambda'(R)$, in which case *PC-Refine* terminates and returns $\mathcal{C}$ (Lines 19-20).

It remains to clarify how we set the threshold T on the total cost of the operations in O^i. Intuitively, T controls the tradeoff between *PC-Refine*'s processing time and crowdsourcing cost. When T is large, *PC-Refine* issues fewer batches of questions to the crowd, which leads to smaller processing time. However, a large T also makes *PC-Refine* pack more operations into O^i, which results in higher crowdsourcing overheads. To strike a balance between processing time and crowdsourcing cost, we set T as follows. First, given a set $\mathcal{C}$ of clusters, we first compute $\frac{|R|^2}{2\cdot|\mathcal{C}|}$, which is the maximum number of record pairs that we need to crowdsource, if we are to perform all operations on $\mathcal{C}$ in one batch. (This maximum number is achieved when each cluster contains $|R|/|\mathcal{C}|$ records, and we conduct $|\mathcal{C}|/2$ merger operations simultaneously.) After that, we retrieve the number N_u of record pairs whose crowd-based similarity scores are currently unknown. Let N_m be the smaller one between $\frac{|R|^2}{2\cdot|\mathcal{C}|}$ and N_u. We set $T = N_m/x$, where x is a pre-defined constant. In Section 6, we will decide x with experiments.

6. EXPERIMENTS

This section experimentally evaluates *ACD* against the states of the art in terms of deduplication accuracy, the number of record pairs crowdsourced, and the number of crowd iterations required.

6.1 Experimental Setup

Datasets and Baselines: We use three benchmark datasets in the literature of crowd-based data deduplication [46–48], namely, *Pa-*

datasets	# of records	# of entities	# of candidate pairs	crowd error rate (3w)	crowd error rate (5w)
Paper	997	191	29,581	23%	21%
Restaurant	858	752	4,788	0.8%	0.2%
Product	3,073	1,076	3,154	9%	5%

Table 3: Characteristics of datasets and crowd answers.

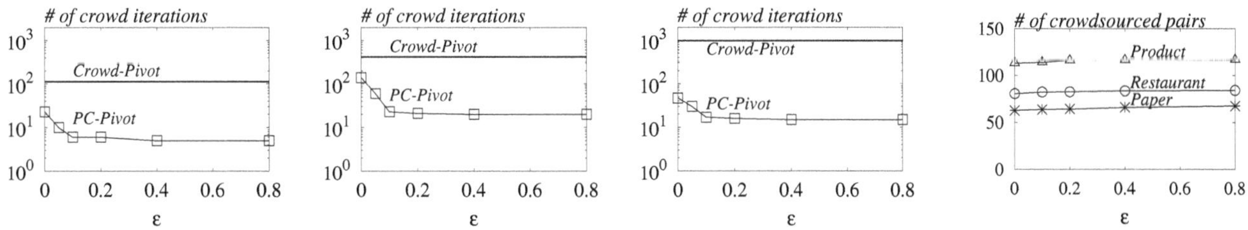

(a) # of iterations on *Paper*. (b) # of iterations on *Restaurant*. (c) # of iterations on *Product*. (d) # of crowdsourced record pairs

Figure 5: Impacts of ε.

per [1], *Restaurant* [2], and *Product* [3]. Table 3 shows the number of records and entities in each dataset.

We compare our *ACD* method against existing four state-of-the-art algorithms: *TransNode* [44], *TransM* [47], *CrowdER* [46], and *GCER* [48]. Note that *CrowdER* does not specify the algorithm for clustering crowdsourced record pairs. In our implementation, we use the *sorted neighborhood* algorithm [48] to produce clusters from crowd answers for *CrowdER*, following previous work [48]. We denote this implementation as *CrowdER+*. Meanwhile, *GCER* requires a user-specified parameter on the number of record pairs to be issued to the crowd. We set this parameter for *GCER*, so that it crowdsources the same number of record pairs as *ACD* does. This enables us to compare the deduplication accuracy of *ACD* and *GCER* under the same crowdsourcing budget. In addition, we also evaluate *ACD* against *PC-Pivot*, i.e., a "crippled" version of *ACD* that incorporates the pruning phase and cluster generation phase of *ACD* but omits the cluster refinement phase.

Following previous work [47], we use the F1-measure to gauge the deduplication accuracy of each method, and we evaluate the crowdsourcing overhead of each method in terms of the number of record pairs crowdsourced, as well as the number of crowd iterations (i.e., the number of batches of HITs that are issued to the crowd). For *ACD* and *PC-Pivot*, we repeat each of them 5 times in each experiment and report the average measurements, since they are both randomized algorithms. Note that *TransNode* [44] does not incorporate any parallel mechanism to issue HITs in a batch manner. Therefore, we omit *TransNode* from the experiments on the number of crowd iterations.

Pruning Phase Setting: All methods that we test require a machine-based approach in their pruning phases to generate a set S of candidate pairs. Following previous work [47], we compute the machine-based similarity score for each record pair using the *Jaccard* similarity metric, and we set the threshold value for machined-based similarity scores as $\tau = 0.3$. That is, only the record pairs with Jaccard similarity above 0.3 are retained in the candidate set S. Table 3 shows the size of S on each dataset.

AMT Setting: We use the Amazon Mechanical Turk (AMT) as our crowdsourcing platform. For each dataset, we post all record pairs in the candidate set S to AMT, and record the crowd's answers in local file F. Then, during our experiments, whenever a method requests to crowdsource a record pair (r, r'), we retrieve the answers for (r, r') from F instead of posting (r, r') to AMT. This ensures that all methods utilize the same set of crowdsourced results, for fairness of comparison.

Note that the above evaluation approach is adopted in previous work [46, 47]. We obtain, from the authors of [46, 47], the crowd answers used in their experiments, and reuse them in our evaluation. The AMT setting pertinent to those results are as follows. Each HIT contains 20 record pairs, and each record pair requires inputs from three workers. Each worker must pass a qualification test before she can work on the HITs, and she is paid 2 cents for completing each HIT.

In addition to reusing data from [46, 47], we also obtain an additional set of crowd answers from AMT under a more stringent setting[1]. In particular, we require each worker to not only pass a qualification test, but also has completed 100 approved HITs and has an approval rate at least 95%. (Previous work [24] adopts the same setting.) This setting is intended to ensure that all workers provide reasonably accurate answers to the HITs. To further reduce the impact of human errors, we require inputs from 5 workers for each record pair, and we only pack 10 record pairs into each HIT. The monetary reward for each HIT is set to 2 cents. For each dataset D, we denote the crowd answers obtained from this 5-worker setting as $D(5w)$, and those from the previous 3-worker setting as $D(3w)$.

Table 3 shows, for each dataset, the percentages of crowd answers that are incorrect under the 3-worker and 5-worker settings. Evidently, the 5-worker setting results in more accurate outputs from the crowd, at a higher monetary cost. Furthermore, the crowd's error rate for *Paper* is above 20% under both settings, which indicate that the records in *Paper* are more difficult to deduplicate.

6.2 Tuning Parameters for *ACD*

Recall from Section 4.3 that, in the cluster generation phase of *ACD*, the *PC-Pivot* algorithm requires a parameter ε that decides the maximum allowed amount of wasted pairs. In the first set of experiments, we study the effect of ε on the efficiency and crowdsourcing cost of *PC-Pivot*. We only show results obtained from the 3-worker setting, but the results from the 5-worker setting are similar.

Figure 5(a), 5(b), and 5(c) show the number of crowd iterations required by *PC-Pivot*, when ε varies. For comparison, we also show the number of crowd iterations required by *Crowd-Pivot*, i.e., the sequential version of *PC-Pivot*. Observe that *PC-Pivot* incurs a

[1]We make this set of crowd answers available at [4].

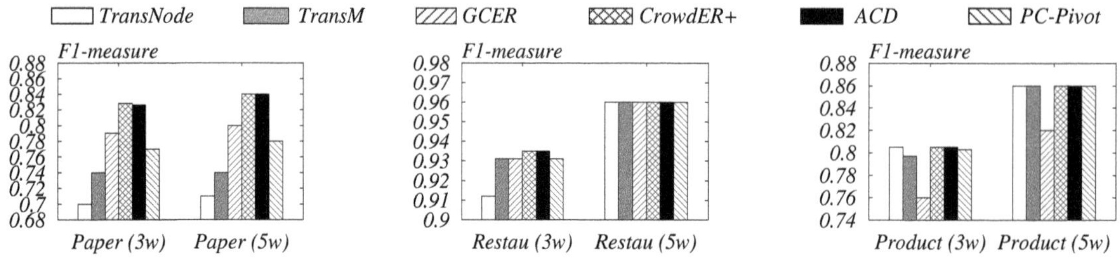

(a) *Paper* dataset (b) *Restaurant* dataset (c) *Product* dataset

Figure 6: Comparison of deduplication accuracy.

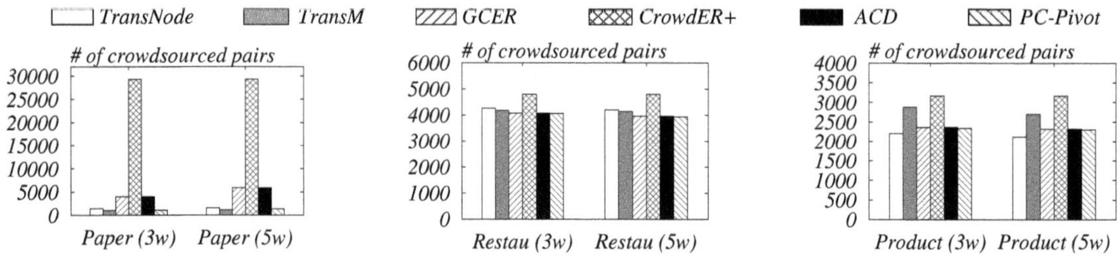

(a) *Paper* dataset (b) *Restaurant* dataset (c) *Product* dataset

Figure 7: Comparison of crowdsourcing costs.

much smaller number of crowd iterations than *Crowd-Pivot* does. For example, even when we set ϵ as small as 0.1, *PC-Pivot*'s number of crowd iterations is 20 times smaller than that of *Crowd-Pivot* on the *Restaurant* dataset.

When ε increases, the number of crowd iterations decreases. This is because, with a larger ε, *PC-Pivot* can choose more pivots in each iteration, and hence, the clustering process can be accelerated. However, the decrement of crowd iterations is more significant when ε increases from 0.0 to 0.1, comparing to the case from 0.1 to 0.8. The reason is that the larger ε is, the more pivots are selected, in which case there is a higher chance that the remaining pairs are predicted as wasted pairs by the *PC-Pivot* algorithm.

Meanwhile, a larger ε leads to higher crowdsourcing costs, as shown in Figure 5(d). In particular, when ε increases, the number of HITs required by *PC-Pivot* also increases. In the following experiments, we set ε to 0.1 since it strikes a good balance between efficiency and crowdsourcing cost.

In addition to the ε, we have also conducted an experiment to evaluate the effect of T, i.e., which is a threshold used in the cluster refinement phase of *ACD* to restrict the total crowdsourcing cost of the independent operations to be performed in each iteration (see Algorithm 5). In particular, we vary T from $N_m/16$ to $N_m/2$, where N_m is as defined in Section 5.4. We observe that $T = N_m/8$ nicely balances the efficiency and cost of cluster refinement. Interested readers are referred to Appendix C for the experimental results on T. In the rest of our experiments, we set $T = N_m/8$.

6.3 Comparison of All Methods

In our next set of experiments, we evaluate all methods on their deduplication accuracy (in terms of F1-measure), crowdsourcing costs (in terms of the number of record pairs crowdsourced), and crowdsourcing efficiency (in terms of the number of crowd iterations). Figure 6 (resp. Figure 7) shows the F1-measures (resp. numbers of crowdsourced record pairs) of each method on each dataset under both the 3-worker and 5-worker settings. *CrowdER+* consistently provides the highest accuracy, but incurs significant crowdsourcing costs (especially on *Paper*, since it requires issuing all record pairs in the candidate set S to the crowd). In contrast, *ACD* provides an accuracy that is highly comparable to that of *CrowdER+*, but incurs considerably lower crowdsourcing costs. In particular, on *paper*, the number of record pairs crowdsourced by *ACD* is less than $1/7$ (resp. $1/5$) the number by *CrowdER+* under the 3-worker (resp. 5-worker) setting. Meanwhile, *PC-Pivot* is much less accurate than *ACD* on *Paper*, which demonstrates the effectiveness of the cluster refinement phase of our solution. On the other hand, on *Restaurant* and *Product*, *PC-Pivot* provides similar accuracy to *ACD*. The reason is that, on those two datasets, the crowd workers make a relatively smaller number mistakes in processing record pairs. As a consequence, *PC-Pivot* alone can produce high-quality clustering results, which leaves little room for the cluster refinement phase to improve.

GCER's accuracy is lower than *ACD* in all cases, except for *Restaurant* under the 5-worker setting. This indicates that *GCER* provides lower-quality clustering results than *ACD* does, when both of them crowdsource the same number of record pairs. Both *TransNode* and *TransM* provide inferior deduplication accuracy on *Paper*, since they are susceptible to errors made by the crowd workers, as we analyzed in Sections 1 and 2.2. Their performance are much better on *Restaurant* and *Product*, due to the smaller amount of errors made by crowd workers on those datasets. However, on *Restaurant* and *Product*, the numbers of record pairs crowdsourced by *TransNode* and *TransM* are almost the same as that by *ACD*, i.e., they do not provide any advantage over *ACD* on those two datasets.

Overall, all methods yield higher accuracy in the 5-worker setting than the 3-worker setting, which shows that all methods benefit from more accurate results from the crowd. However, we observe that the performance of *TransNode* and *TransM* degrades more significantly than other methods in the 3-worker setting. This, again, is consistent with our analysis that *TransNode* and *TransM* are vulnerable to human errors.

Figure 8 illustrates the number of crowd iterations incurred by each method. The results of all methods are roughly comparable in all cases, except that *CrowdER+* requires only one crowd iterations, as it issues all record pairs in S in one batch. This shows that

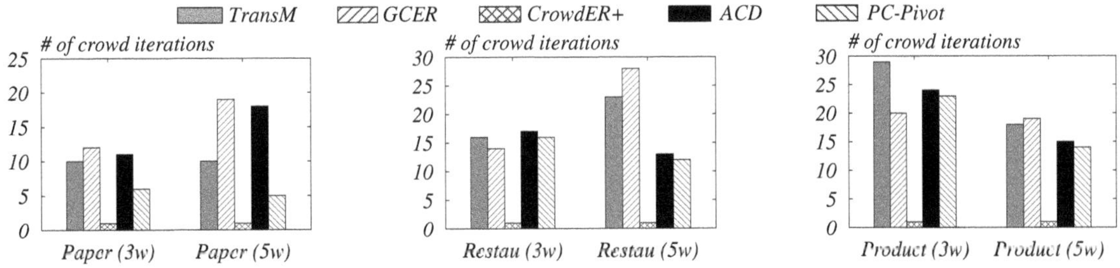

(a) *Paper* dataset (b) *Restaurant* dataset (c) *Product* dataset

Figure 8: Comparison of crowdsourcing efficiency

crowdsourcing efficiency of *ACD* is comparable to that of *TransM* and *GCER*.

In summary, our experimental results show that *ACD* provides high deduplication accuracy at moderate costs of crowdsourcing, and its crowdsourcing efficiency is comparable to the states of the art. In contrast, the existing methods for crowd-based deduplication either provide inferior clustering results, or incur significant crowdsourcing overheads. Therefore, *ACD* is a favorable method for crowd-based data deduplication.

7. RELATED WORK

Correlation clustering is a classic method used in large scale data deduplication [8,27]. Optimal correlation clustering is shown to be NP-hard [9], which motivates a line of research [5, 10, 22] to seek good approximation algorithms. In particular, Ailon et al. [5] propose the *Pivot* algorithm, which returns a 5-approximation when the similarity score of each record pair is a fractional number in $[0, 1]$. Meanwhile, if the similarity scores are either in $\{0, 1\}$, the algorithm yields a 3-approximation. This 3-approximation result is improved to a 2.5-approximation [5] with a linear programming approach, which, however, incurs a larger computational overhead than *Pivot*. [42] proposes a deterministic version of *Pivot* that provides the same approximation guarantee, but it also relies on linear programming. Gionis et al. [22] propose the *BOEM* algorithm for postprocessing the results of correlation clustering to improve accuracy. As we point out in Section 5.1, however, *BOEM* is unsuitable under the crowd-based setting, as it would incur a significant overhead in crowdsourcing. Besides correlation clustering, there exists a large body of literature on machine-based data deduplication algorithms (see [17] for a survey).

As we review in Section 2.2, there exist five crowd-based solutions [25,44,46–48] for data deduplication. Among them, *Crowdclustering* [25] is designed for data categorization, which is a variant of data deduplication that aims to identify records belonging to the same category, instead of identifying duplicates. Meanwhile, *CrowdER* [46] provides a high precision of deduplication, but incurs a significant crowdsourcing overhead. The other three methods, namely, *GCER* [48], *TransM* [47], and *TransNode* [44], reduce the costs of crowdsourcing but compromise deuplication accuracy, as shown in our experiments. In contrast, our *ACD* approach yields as accurate results as *CrowdER* does, only at moderate costs of crowsourcing.

Besides data deduplication, there also exist many research works that incorporate crowdsourcing into record linkage, which targets to link records representing the same entity across databases. However, in such tasks, it is usually assumed that, given three records r_1, r_2, and r_3, if $r_1 = r_2$, then r_3 cannot represent the same entity as r_1 or r_2 does. Nonetheless, if r_1 does not represent the same entity as r_2 does, then r_3 can represent the same entity as r_1 or r_2 does but not both. Existing work on record linkage uses this assumption to prune a plenty of record pairs. Nevertheless, such an assumption does not hold for data deduplication scenario, which makes them inapplicable under data deduplication scenarios. Arasu et al. [7] mainly use human power to build up the classifier for the dataset, while as shown in previous work [46], these techniques often face difficulties when processing records that represent different entities but look highly similar. On the contrary, our solution can still work in such scenarios. Demartini et al. [16] propose *ZenCrowd* to do record linkage for large collections of online pages with the crowd. Gokhale et al. [24] study how to do hands-off crowdsourcing record linkage which requires no involvement of developers.

In addition, recent work has developed several crowdsourcing platforms for various tasks. Franklin et al. [19, 20] propose a *CrowdSQL* query language, and develop the *CrowdDB* database. Marcus et al. [35] propose *Qurk*, a query processing system for allowing crowd-powered processing of relational databases. Parameswaran et al. [38] develop *Deco*, a database system that answers, with crowd assistance, declarative queries posted over relational data. Jeffery et al. [30, 31] construct a hybrid crowd-machine data integration system. Furthermore, several database operations are also studied under the crowd setting, such as JOIN [35], MAX [26], TOP-K, and GROUP BY queries [15]. Others have also investigated crowd-based techniques for data mining [6], web table matching [18], and data analysis [33]. Finally, previous work [29, 37, 43, 45] have studied how one can extract high-quality answers from crowdsourcing platforms.

8. CONCLUSION

This paper presents *ACD*, a crowd-based algorithm for data deduplication. Compared with the existing solutions, *ACD* distinguishes itself in that it is more robust to errors made by the crowd in identifying duplicates. In addition, *ACD* incorporates several advanced techniques to improve efficiency without compromising deduplication accuracy. We experimentally evaluate *ACD* on the Amazon Mechanical Turk, and show that *ACD* outperforms the states of the art by providing high-precision deduplication with moderate crowdsourcing overheads. For future work, we plan to further improve the performance of *ACD*, by investigating techniques for adaptively assigning more crowd workers to more *difficult* record pairs in data deduplication.

9. ACKNOWLEDGMENTS

This work was supported by AcRF Tier 2 Grant ARC19/14 from the Ministry of Education, Singapore, an SUG Grant from the Nanyang Technological University, and a gift from the Microsoft Research Asia. The authors would like to thank the anonymous reviewers for their constructive and insightful comments.

10. REFERENCES

[1] http://www.cs.umass.edu/~mccallum/data/cora-refs.tar.gz.

[2] http://www.cs.utexas.edu/users/ml/riddle/data/restaurant.tar.gz.

[3] http://dbs.uni-leipzig.de/Abt-Buy.zip.

[4] https://sourceforge.net/p/acd2015/.

[5] N. Ailon, M. Charikar, and A. Newman. Aggregating inconsistent information: ranking and clustering. *Journal of the ACM (JACM)*, 55(5):23, 2008.

[6] Y. Amsterdamer, Y. Grossman, T. Milo, and P. Senellart. Crowd mining. In *Proceedings of the 2013 ACM SIGMOD International Conference on Management of Data*, pages 241–252. ACM, 2013.

[7] A. Arasu, M. Götz, and R. Kaushik. On active learning of record matching packages. In *Proceedings of the 2010 ACM SIGMOD International Conference on Management of Data*, pages 783–794, 2010.

[8] A. Arasu, C. Ré, and D. Suciu. Large-scale deduplication with constraints using dedupalog. In *Data Engineering, 2009. ICDE'09. IEEE 25th International Conference on*, pages 952–963. IEEE, 2009.

[9] N. Bansal, A. Blum, and S. Chawla. Correlation clustering. In *FOCS*, pages 238–, 2002.

[10] M. Charikar, V. Guruswami, and A. Wirth. Clustering with qualitative information. In *Foundations of Computer Science, 2003. Proceedings. 44th Annual IEEE Symposium on*, pages 524–533. IEEE, 2003.

[11] Z. Chen, D. V. Kalashnikov, and S. Mehrotra. Exploiting context analysis for combining multiple entity resolution systems. In *Proceedings of the 2009 ACM SIGMOD International Conference on Management of data*, pages 207–218. ACM, 2009.

[12] W. W. Cohen. Integration of heterogeneous databases without common domains using queries based on textual similarity. In *ACM SIGMOD Record*, volume 27, pages 201–212. ACM, 1998.

[13] W. W. Cohen, H. Kautz, and D. McAllester. Hardening soft information sources. In *Proceedings of the sixth ACM SIGKDD international conference on Knowledge discovery and data mining*, pages 255–259. ACM, 2000.

[14] W. W. Cohen and J. Richman. Learning to match and cluster large high-dimensional data sets for data integration. In *Proceedings of the eighth ACM SIGKDD international conference on Knowledge discovery and data mining*, pages 475–480. ACM, 2002.

[15] S. B. Davidson, S. Khanna, T. Milo, and S. Roy. Using the crowd for top-k and group-by queries. In *Proceedings of the 16th International Conference on Database Theory*, pages 225–236. ACM, 2013.

[16] G. Demartini, D. E. Difallah, and P. Cudré-Mauroux. Zencrowd: leveraging probabilistic reasoning and crowdsourcing techniques for large-scale entity linking. In *WWW*, pages 469–478, 2012.

[17] A. K. Elmagarmid, P. G. Ipeirotis, and V. S. Verykios. Duplicate record detection: A survey. *Knowledge and Data Engineering, IEEE Transactions on*, 19(1):1–16, 2007.

[18] J. Fan, M. Lu, B. C. Ooi, W.-C. Tan, and M. Zhang. A hybrid machine-crowdsourcing system for matching web tables. Technical report, Technical report, National University of Singapore, 2013.

[19] A. Feng, M. Franklin, D. Kossmann, T. Kraska, S. Madden, S. Ramesh, A. Wang, and R. Xin. Crowddb: Query processing with the vldb crowd. *Proceedings of the VLDB Endowment*, 4(12), 2011.

[20] M. J. Franklin, D. Kossmann, T. Kraska, S. Ramesh, and R. Xin. Crowddb: answering queries with crowdsourcing. In *Proceedings of the 2011 ACM SIGMOD International Conference on Management of data*, pages 61–72. ACM, 2011.

[21] J. Gemmell, B. I. Rubinstein, and A. K. Chandra. Improving entity resolution with global constraints. *arXiv preprint arXiv:1108.6016*, 2011.

[22] A. Gionis, H. Mannila, and P. Tsaparas. Clustering aggregation. *ACM Transactions on Knowledge Discovery from Data (TKDD)*, 1(1):4, 2007.

[23] A. Goder and V. Filkov. Consensus clustering algorithms: Comparison and refinement. In *Proceedings of the Tenth Workshop on Algorithm Engineering and Experiments, ALENEX 2008, San Francisco, California, USA, January 19, 2008*, 2008.

[24] C. Gokhale, S. Das, A. Doan, J. F. Naughton, N. Rampalli, J. W. Shavlik, and X. Zhu. Corleone: hands-off crowdsourcing for entity matching. In *Proceedings of the 2014 ACM SIGMOD International Conference on Management of Data*, 2014.

[25] R. Gomes, P. Welinder, A. Krause, and P. Perona. Crowdclustering. In *NIPS*, pages 558–566, 2011.

[26] S. Guo, A. Parameswaran, and H. Garcia-Molina. So who won?: dynamic max discovery with the crowd. In *Proceedings of the 2012 ACM SIGMOD International Conference on Management of Data*, pages 385–396. ACM, 2012.

[27] O. Hassanzadeh, F. Chiang, H. C. Lee, and R. J. Miller. Framework for evaluating clustering algorithms in duplicate detection. *Proceedings of the VLDB Endowment*, 2(1):1282–1293, 2009.

[28] M. A. Hernández and S. J. Stolfo. The merge/purge problem for large databases. In *ACM SIGMOD Record*, volume 24, pages 127–138. ACM, 1995.

[29] P. G. Ipeirotis, F. Provost, and J. Wang. Quality management on amazon mechanical turk. In *Proceedings of the ACM SIGKDD workshop on human computation*, pages 64–67. ACM, 2010.

[30] S. R. Jeffery, M. J. Franklin, and A. Y. Halevy. Pay-as-you-go user feedback for dataspace systems. In *Proceedings of the 2008 ACM SIGMOD international conference on Management of data*, pages 847–860. ACM, 2008.

[31] S. R. Jeffery, L. Sun, M. DeLand, N. Pendar, R. Barber, and A. Galdi. Arnold: Declarative crowd-machine data integration. In *CIDR*, 2013.

[32] V. I. Levenshtein. Binary codes capable of correcting deletions, insertions and reversals. In *Soviet physics doklady*, volume 10, page 707, 1966.

[33] X. Liu, M. Lu, B. C. Ooi, Y. Shen, S. Wu, and M. Zhang. Cdas: a crowdsourcing data analytics system. *Proceedings of the VLDB Endowment*, 5(10):1040–1051, 2012.

[34] M. Luby. A simple parallel algorithm for the maximal independent set problem. *SIAM journal on computing*, 15(4):1036–1053, 1986.

[35] A. Marcus, E. Wu, D. Karger, S. Madden, and R. Miller. Human-powered sorts and joins. *Proceedings of the VLDB Endowment*, 5(1):13–24, 2011.

[36] A. McCallum and B. Wellner. Conditional models of identity uncertainty with application to noun coreference. In *NIPS*, 2004.

[37] A. G. Parameswaran, H. Garcia-Molina, H. Park, N. Polyzotis, A. Ramesh, and J. Widom. Crowdscreen: Algorithms for filtering data with humans. In *Proceedings of the 2012 ACM SIGMOD International Conference on Management of Data*, pages 361–372. ACM, 2012.

[38] A. G. Parameswaran, H. Park, H. Garcia-Molina, N. Polyzotis, and J. Widom. Deco: declarative crowdsourcing. In *Proceedings of the 21st ACM international conference on Information and knowledge management*, pages 1203–1212. ACM, 2012.

[39] L. Philips. Hanging on the metaphone. *Computer Language*, 7(12 (December)), 1990.

[40] E. Rahm and H. H. Do. Data cleaning: Problems and current approaches. *IEEE Data Eng. Bull.*, 23(4):3–13, 2000.

[41] W. M. Soon, H. T. Ng, and D. C. Y. Lim. A machine learning approach to coreference resolution of noun phrases. *Computational linguistics*, 27(4):521–544, 2001.

[42] A. Van Zuylen and D. P. Williamson. Deterministic pivoting algorithms for constrained ranking and clustering problems. *Mathematics of Operations Research*, 34(3):594–620, 2009.

[43] P. Venetis and H. Garcia-Molina. Quality control for comparison microtasks. In *Proceedings of the First International Workshop on Crowdsourcing and Data Mining*, pages 15–21. ACM, 2012.

[44] N. Vesdapunt, K. Bellare, and N. Dalvi. Crowdsourcing algorithms for entity resolution. *Proceedings of the VLDB Endowment*, 7(12), 2014.

[45] P. Wais, S. Lingamneni, D. Cook, J. Fennell, B. Goldenberg, D. Lubarov, D. Marin, and H. Simons. Towards building a high-quality workforce with mechanical turk. *Proceedings of computational social science and the wisdom of crowds (NIPS)*, pages 1–5, 2010.

[46] J. Wang, T. Kraska, M. J. Franklin, and J. Feng. Crowder: Crowdsourcing entity resolution. *Proceedings of the VLDB Endowment*, 5(11):1483–1494, 2012.

[47] J. Wang, G. Li, T. Kraska, M. J. Franklin, and J. Feng. Leveraging transitive relations for crowdsourced joins. In *Proceedings of the 2013 international conference on Management of data*, pages 229–240. ACM, 2013.

[48] S. E. Whang, P. Lofgren, and H. Garcia-Molina. Question selection for crowd entity resolution. *Proceedings of the VLDB Endowment*, 6(6):349–360, 2013.

APPENDIX

A. PROOFS

Proof of Lemma 2. We prove this lemma by induction. Observe that in the first iteration, $G_1 = G$, and r_k is exactly the record who ranks k-th in $\mathcal{M}$. In *Crowd-Pivot* algorithm, assume that r_i is clustered into C_j where $j \leq i$ and r_j is the record first added into the cluster, then it can be concluded that if there exist incident edges between r_i and records with permutation ranks smaller than r_j, then the crowd infers them as non-deduplicates. Otherwise, it will be clustered into a cluster $C_{j'}$ with $\mathcal{M}(r_{j'}) < \mathcal{M}(r_j)$. With the constraints in our Algorithm 2 (Lines 7-11), r_i will be also clustered to C_j. So for all records with permutation rank no higher than r_k, *Crowd-Pivot* and *Partial-Pivot* will output the same cluster.

Then, assume that Lemma 2 still holds in the m-th iteration, and let r_w be the record with k-th smallest permutation rank in G_m, in the $(m+1)$-th iteration, G_{m+1} will be the same as the input graph of *Crowd-Pivot* after removing $r_1, r_2, \cdots, r_w$. Given the same input graph, and the same permutation order for the records, it can be similarly proved that *Crowd-Pivot* and *Partial-Pivot* will provide the same cluster result. So for all iterations, we guarantee that, given G_i, k, and $\mathcal{M}$, *Partial-Pivot* outputs $\mathcal{C}_i = \mathcal{C}'_i$. □

Proof of Lemma 3. Recall that a wasted pair is a pair of records that is issued in *Partial-Pivot* algorithm but not issued in *Crowd-Pivot* algorithm. The reason why we may issue wasted pairs in *Partial-Pivot* algorithm is that *Crowd-Pivot* algorithm removes records that have been clustered by $r_1, \cdots, r_{k-1}$ before issuing pairs incident to r_k, while *Partial-Pivot* algorithm will issue all the incident pairs to $r_1, r_2, \cdots, r_k$ in a batch.

If there exists an $x < j$, such that $d(r_j, r_x) = 1$, then r_j can be clustered by r_x. As a result, for all vertices r' incident to r_j, it can be a wasted pair. The exception is that if r' is a vertex in $\{r_1, r_2, \cdots, r_{j-1}\}$, then the pair is not a wasted pair for r_j. The reason is that, if pair (r', r_j) is not estimated as a wasted pair before, then it means that r' is the vertex with the smallest permutation rank that is incident to r_j and r' is not incident to pivots chosen earlier than it. So (r', r_j) will be issued in the *Crowd-Pivot* algorithm as well, which indicates that (r', r_j) is not a wasted pair. However, if (r', r_j) is estimated as a wasted pair before, then recounting this pair will overestimate the wasted pair, which will not guarantee tight bound.

If there does not exist such an $x < j$ such that $d(r_j, r_x) = 1$, then r_j will not be clustered by $r_1, r_2, \cdots, r_{j-1}$. As a result, for any records that are incident to r_j but not to any records in $r_1, r_2, \cdots, r_{j-1}$, then it is not a wasted pair, since in *Crowd-Pivot* algorithm, this record pair will also be issued. At the meantime, if it is incident to a record in $r_1, r_2, \cdots, r_{j-1}$, then it can be a wasted pair and we estimate it as a wasted pair.

By summing up all the wasted pairs incurred by $r_1, ..., r_k$, we get the upper bound of the total number of wasted pairs as $\sum_{j=1}^{k} w_j$. We next show that this upper bound is tight. If there exists an $x < j$, such that $d(r_j, r_x) = 1$, then if r_x and r_j are inferred as duplicates, then all the record pairs that incident to r_j become wasted pairs except the case in which the adjacent record is from $r_1, r_2, \cdots r_{j-1}$, which is exactly the value defined in Equation 3 with the first case. If there does not exist such an $x < j$ such that $d(r_j, r_x) = 1$, the worst case is that all the records adjacent to some records r_i with $i < j$ are clustered. Then all such pairs are wasted pairs, which is exactly the value defined in Equation 3 with the second case. Thus the total number of wasted pairs is exactly $\sum_{j=1}^{k} w_j$ in the worst case and the upper bound is tight. □

Proof of Lemma 4. We first prove that *PC-Pivot* returns a 5-approximation for the minimization of $\Lambda'(R)$ in expected case. Based on Lemma 2, it can be concluded that given a permutation $\mathcal{M}$, *PC-Pivot* and *Crowd-Pivot* return the same clustering result, which means both algorithms will have the same $\Lambda'(R)$ value. As a result, *Crowd-Pivot* and *PC-Pivot* have the same expected value of $\Lambda'(R)$ from all possible permutations, which means *PC-Pivot* returns a 5-approximation for the minimization of $\Lambda'(R)$ in expected case.

Next we prove that *PC-Pivot* has the following guarantee: among the record pairs crowdsourced by *PC-Pivot*, at most a fraction of ϵ is wasted. Given a random permutation $\mathcal{M}$, we let I^i_W be the number of issued wasted pairs in the i-th iteration of *PC-Pivot*, and I^i_{PCP} be the number of pairs issued by *PC-Pivot* in the i-th iteration. Then,

$$\epsilon \cdot I^i_W \leq I^i_{PCP}.$$

By summing the pairs in all iterations, we have $\epsilon \cdot I_W \leq I_{PCP}$ for the given permutation $\mathcal{M}$, where I_W and I_{PCP} denote the number of wasted pairs and issued pairs of *PC-Pivot* algorithm, respectively. By summing for all possible permutations, we have:

$$\epsilon \cdot E(I_W) \leq E(I_{PCP}).$$

This finishes the proof. □

Proof of Lemma 5. We prove it by reduction from the maximal independent set problem [34]. A maximal independent set in an undirected graph is a maximal collection of vertices I subject to the restriction that no pair of vertices in I are adjacent. To reduce this problem to our problem of finding a set O^i of independent operations that maximizes $\Psi(O^i)$, we take each vertex of the graph as an operation. If there is an edge between two vertices, we regard the operation corresponding to the two vertices as a dependent operation. For each operation o corresponding to the vertex in the graph, we assume the $b(o)$, $c(o)$ are all the same and N is larger than the cost of all operations.

Now assume that we can obtain such a set O^i of the independent operation maximizing $\Psi(O^i)$ in polynomial time. Then by solving the above constructed problem, we can find a maximal independent set in polynomial time as well. This contradicts the fact that the maximal independent set problem is NP-hard. So by contradiction, we prove that finding a set O^i of independent operations that maximizes $\Psi(O^i)$ is NP-hard. □

B. ADDITIONAL EXAMPLE

EXAMPLE 3. Given a set of six records $R = \{a, b, c, d, e, f\}$, assume that after the pruning phase, the candidate pairs are as shown in Figure 9a. The number on each edge (x, y) indicates the similarity score $f_c(x, y)$ that we would obtain if we issue (x, y) to the crowd. At the meantime, $b^*(o)$ is identical to $b(o)$. Then given a random permutation $P = \{c, e, b, d, a, f\}$ with $\epsilon = 0.4$, in cluster generation phase, *PC-Pivot* selects incident edges to c and e to the crowd in a batch, since the fraction of wasted pairs would not exceed 0.4. The issued pairs are (a, c), (b, c), (c, d), (e, a), (e, d) and (e, f). With the crowd answers, two clusters $\{a, b, c, d\}$ and $\{e, f\}$

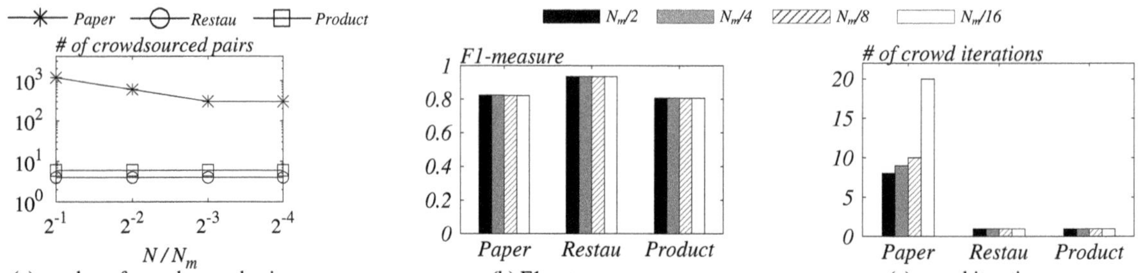

(a) number of crowdsourced pairs (b) F1-measure (c) crowd iterations

Figure 10: *PC-Refine*: impact of T on crowdsourced pairs, F1-measure, and crowd iterations on three datasets.

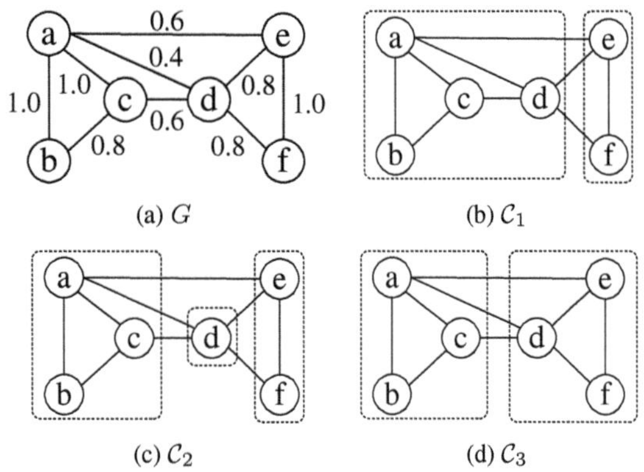

(a) G (b) $\mathcal{C}_1$ (c) $\mathcal{C}_2$ (d) $\mathcal{C}_3$

Figure 9: Example of cluster refinement phase.

are generated in one iteration. As the records are clustered after one iteration, *PC-Pivot* finishes. The clustering result after cluster generation phase is as shown in Figure 9b, where each dashed box corresponds to a cluster. Afterwards, in the postprocessing phase, *Crowd-Refine* algorithm first inspects each operation and calculates the benefit-cost ratio correspondingly. It can be verified that the operation o_s to split vertex d from cluster $\{a, b, c, d\}$ has the highest benefit-cost ratio. Then *Crowd-Refine* issues pair (a, d) to the crowd and obtains $f_c(a, d)$. As $f_c(a, d) = 0.4$, $f_c(b, d) = 0$, and $f_c(c, d) = 0.6$, $b(o_s)$ can be calculated with Equation 5 and equals 1. So o_s will be proceeded. After operation o_s proceeded, the clustering result is as shown in Figure 9c. Next, *Crowd-Refine* recomputes the benefit-cost ratio, and the merger operation o_m to merge $\{d\}$ and $\{e, f\}$ incurs the highest benefit-cost ratio. Only pair (d, f) is required to be issued to the crowd since (d, e) was issued in the cluster generation phase. After issuing pair (d, f) to the crowd, we obtain the crowd similarity $f_c(d, f) = 0.8$. The benefit of o_m can be calculated with Equation 6 and equals 1.2. The operation hence is proceeded. The clustering result is as shown in Figure 9d. After the two operations, $b^*(o)$ for all operations are no larger than zero. Hence *Crowd-Refine* stops and returns the clustering result. □

C. ADDITIONAL EXPERIMENTS

Recall that in the cluster refinement phase of *ACD*, *PC-Refine* algorithm requires a parameter T to specify the number of record pairs to issue in a crowd iteration. In this set of experiments, we study the impact of T to our *ACD* algorithm in terms of the crowdsourcing cost, accuracy, and efficiency.

Figure 10(a) demonstrates the impact of T in terms of the number of crowdsourced pairs. For the *Restaurant* and *Product* datasets, as the clustering result provided by the cluster generation phase is already of high quality, there are very few operations with expected benefit greater than zero to reduce $\Lambda'(R)$. Hence, the issued crowdsourced pairs can be less than the pre-defined threshold T in the first crowd-iteration. On *Paper* dataset, the number of crowdsourced pairs is reduced as T decreases. When T is small enough (e.g, $N_m/8$), it decreases smoothly or shows the same value. This is because for a large T, our algorithm packs many unnecessary operations with low benefit-cost ratio; in contrast, for a small enough T, it does not pack such operations further.

Figure 10(b) shows the impact of parameter T in terms of the accuracy to the deduplication result. Observe that the F1-measure value for each dataset is insensitive to T. The reason is that our algorithm stops when optimization goal $\Lambda'(R)$ cannot be further reduced, and this stopping condition is not significantly affected by the choice of T.

Figure 10(c) demonstrates the impact of T in terms of the number of crowd iterations. Notice that for the *Restaurant* and *Product* datasets, the result of the cluster generation phase is already of high quality. Therefore, the algorithm stops after one crowd iteration, regardless how we change N. On the other hand, on the *Paper* dataset, the number of crowd iterations increases with T. However, when T changes from $N_m/2$ to $N_m/8$, the increase of the number of crowd iterations is not significant. The main reason is that the number of crowd iterations is effected only by the postprocessing operations that can reduce $\Lambda'(R)$; when T is large, *PC-Refine* algorithm packs many operations with low benefit-cost ratio, which have low probability of reducing $\Lambda'(R)$. However, when we further decrease the size of T from $N_m/8$ to $N_m/16$, we can observe that the number of crowd iterations is doubled. The reason is that when T is small enough, the packed operations are mainly the operations that can reduce $\Lambda'(R)$. Therefore, the number of iterations in $N_m/16$ is 2 times more than that in $N_m/8$.

So in *ACD*, we set $T = N_m/8$, as it is the setting under which the *PC-Refine* algorithm provides good clustering accuracy while uses only a small number of crowdsourced pairs and crowd iterations.

Minimizing Commit Latency of Transactions in Geo-Replicated Data Stores

Faisal Nawab Vaibhav Arora Divyakant Agrawal Amr El Abbadi

Department of Computer Science
University of California, Santa Barbara
Santa Barbara, CA 93106
{nawab,vaibhavarora,agrawal,amr}@cs.ucsb.edu

ABSTRACT

Cross datacenter replication is increasingly being deployed to bring data closer to the user and to overcome datacenter outages. The extent of the influence of wide-area communication on serializable transactions is not yet clear. In this work, we derive a lower-bound on commit latency. The *sum* of the commit latency of any two datacenters is at least the Round-Trip Time (RTT) between them. We use the insights and lessons learned while deriving the lower-bound to develop a commit protocol, called Helios, that achieves low commit latencies. Helios actively exchanges transaction logs (history) between datacenters. The received logs are used to decide whether a transaction can commit or not. The *earliest* point in the received logs that is needed to commit a transaction is decided by Helios to ensure a low commit latency. As we show in the paper, Helios is theoretically able to achieve the lower-bound commit latency. Also, in a real-world deployment on five datacenters, Helios has a commit latency that is close to the optimal.

Categories and Subject Descriptors

H.2.4 [**Database Management**]: Systems—*Transaction processing; Distributed databases*

Keywords

Cloud computing; geo-replication; multi-datacenter

1. INTRODUCTION

A key requirement for today's Internet services is availability. Complete outages of datacenters have been a major cause of disruption to availability. These outages can be due to technical problems [1], unforeseen natural disasters [39], or due to a sudden surge in traffic [2]. Datacenter outages can be overcome with the aid of geo-replication. However, replicating data at such large distances accentuates the trade-off between consistency and performance. Many solutions in the last decade investigated sacrificing consistency to deliver better performance [5, 15, 19, 48, 52]. However, in the last few years, interest in providing transactional guarantees has been increasing in both industry [9, 16] and research [27, 44, 47, 54] communities. This interest is due to the need for transactional guarantees for many applications, such as e-commerce. Furthermore, developing applications on top of an eventually consistent data store is complex [42]. Pushing the problem of handling consistency to the application developer is error-prone and debugging these problems for eventually consistent data stores is a complex task.

SIGMOD'15, May 31–June 4, 2015, Melbourne, Victoria, Australia.

http://dx.doi.org/10.1145/2723372.2723729.

We focus on systems that provide serializable transactions. Committing arbitrary transactions requires coordination between datacenters mainly for detecting conflicts [6]. This coordination leads to higher commit latencies. Communication latency between datacenters can be in the order of hundreds of milliseconds. Studies show that a response time of more than 200ms can drive customers away [46]. This has motivated a plethora of research work that focuses on designing protocols that provide serializable transactions with the objective of achieving better commit latency [27, 38, 40, 54].

We develop a lower-bound on transaction *commit latency* that is due to the coordination needed to detect conflicts. The commit latency is defined as the time it takes the datacenter to decide whether a transaction executing can be committed or not. A transaction t cannot commit unless the datacenter is certain that there can be no other concurrent transactions that conflict with t, which leads to the need of coordination between datacenters. As we will demonstrate, *for any two datacenters to maintain serializability, the summation of their commit latencies cannot, in any case, be lower than the RTT between them.* The lower-bound result is applicable to a group of datacenters each maintaining a full replica of the data. Any pair of datacenters must satisfy the lower-bound commit latency.

We also propose Helios, an optimistic commit protocol influenced by the lower-bound study. It allows manual tuning of commit latency as long as the commit latency does not violate the lower bound. Each transaction is timestamped by a local loosely synchronized clock. The transaction commits by waiting for transaction information from other datacenters. The amount of received information needed to commit a transaction depends on the transaction's timestamp. Datacenters exchange their *preparing transactions* (transactions trying to commit) and *finished transactions* (committed or aborted transactions) using an ordered shared log. As logs arrive, the datacenter decides which local preparing transactions can be committed given the new information. Helios judiciously decides the earliest point in the received logs that will enable committing a transaction. Recognizing the *earliest* point in the received logs to commit a transaction will lead to lower commit latency. We focus in this paper on achieving the lowest *average* commit latency. However, Helios allows tuning the commit latencies of individual datacenters to achieve other objectives.

Helios cleanly separates the protocol to guarantee serializability from the mechanism to ensure liveness in the presence of failures. This design is followed by other geo-replicated protocols such as Spanner [16] and Scatter [23] that use Two-Phase Commit (2PC) to guarantee consistency and Paxos [30, 31] to perform state replication. Helios leverages a separate synchronous replication component and augments it with the Helios commit protocol. This clear separation allows the flexible use of any replication protocol such as Paxos. Paxos, however, requires two rounds of communication. Also, it replicates to a majority of datacenters and does not provide any flexibility in setting the number of tolerated datacenter outages. We design a state replication protocol that utilizes the replicated log used for the commit protocol to ensure liveness in the presence of failures while allowing the flexibility of setting the number of tolerated datacenter outages.

Related work is presented in Section 2. Section 3 derives a lower bound on transactions running on replicated data. The Helios commit protocol and replication are described in Section 4. Then, evaluation results are presented in Section 5. The paper concludes in Section 6.

2. RELATED WORK

There is a large body of work on the management of replicated data [26]. Here we focus on work that targets or is related to wide-area replication.

Geo-replication. Early solutions for geo-replication proposed weakening consistency guarantees in favor of performance [5, 15, 19]. At one end of the spectrum are systems that provide eventual consistency [7] like Cassandra [5] and Dynamo [19]. Other systems provide different forms of consistency that are stronger than eventual consistency. Causal consistency, inspired by the causal ordering concept [29], preserves causal relations between transactions in a replicated data environment [8, 28, 36, 37]. COPS/Eiger, for example, define Causal+ consistency, which adds a data convergence guarantee to causal consistency. However, they do not provide general transactions. Snapshot Isolation [11, 26] is another notion of consistency. It prevents concurrent write-write conflicts and ensures that a transaction always reads a consistent snapshot of the data. Solutions in this category often rely on exchanging write-sets of transactions to decide whether to commit or abort [18, 33, 34, 47].

Relaxed consistency guarantees, however, are unsuitable for a wide-range of applications that require strong consistency. Also, developing applications on top of data stores that provide relaxed consistency guarantees is complex [42] and debugging consistency problems of these applications is error-prone.

Serializability. The need for stronger guarantees inspired the design of systems such as Megastore [9] and Paxos-CP [44] that use Paxos [30, 31] to serialize a replicated log of transactions. The use of Paxos, however, leads to higher commit latency due to the multi-round nature of the protocol. This also applies to distributed transaction managers that provide cross-datacenter replication via a Paxos replication of storage, such as Calvin [50]. Other systems use traditional commit protocols to manage transactions. Spanner [16] and Scatter [24] use Two-Phase Commit to manage transaction consistency and underneath it Paxos is used to ensure storage durability. The use of 2PC and Paxos incur multiple cross-datacenter messages making the commit latency high. Recent works identified this trade-off between latency and consistency and designed systems that will adapt accordingly to manage this trade-off. Pileus [48] allows developers to prioritize the level of consistency and latency requirements. SPANStore [52], on the other hand, optimizes for cost function given an application's consistency, latency, and fault tolerance requirements along with its workload characteristics. However these systems still incur a latency penalty similar to other systems when providing strong consistency. Bailis et al. [6] propose invariant confluence analysis, which determines whether a coordination-free execution is safe, thus allowing committing a transaction with no wide-area latency. Safety is determined according to application-level invariants provided by the programmer. The wide-area latency is still observed by transactions that are not invariant confluent.

Low latency. Large wide-area communication latency affects the cost of coordination and thus dramatically increases the commit latency of transactions. This resulted in a large body of research work that focuses on achieving lower commit latencies for serializable transactions. Transaction Chains [54] leverages *a priori* knowledge of transactions to perform a static analysis of conflicts in order to structure commitment plans that result in low latency. Not having this *a priori* static analysis will limit the benefits of Transaction Chains. MDCC [27] uses Fast Paxos [32] to enable committing transactions in one round of communication to a single, but larger than a majority, quorum. Replicated Commit [38] uses Paxos to drive inter-datacenter communication and 2PC and 2PL to manage transactions within a datacenter with the objective of minimizing commit latency. Message Futures [40] reserves commit points for future transactions to achieve low commit latency. Message Futures and Replicated Commit are part of the evaluation study in Section 5. More information on Message Futures and Replicated Commit are provided in Section 5.2.

Clock synchronization for conflict detection. The use of loosely synchronized clocks has been proposed for conflict detection [3, 4, 16, 21, 35]. The Thor project proposes using loosely synchronized clocks for conflict detection [3, 4]. Clients execute transactions optimistically and transactions are assigned a commit timestamp from a physical clock that will translate into a serial order. Other systems use a similar approach for different consistency guarantees like Clock-SI [21] for snapshot isolation, and Orbe [20] and GentleRain [22] for causal consistency. Spanner [16] uses synchronized clocks with bounded uncertainty by TrueTime to achieve external consistency. Spanner, unlike Helios and the aforementioned systems, *requires* high-precision clocks for the correctness of external consistency.

Log-structured data stores. Building a distributed data store using a shared log has been investigated in the literature [12, 40, 41, 43, 51]. Hyder [12] builds a multi-version log-structured database over a distributed shared log storage. A transaction executes optimistically on a snapshot of the database and broadcasts the record of changes to *all* servers and appends a record of changes to the distributed shared log. The servers then commit the transaction by detecting conflicts in the shared log. LogBase [51] and RAMCloud [43] are also multi-version log-structured databases built over a shared log. Helios, like these systems, is also an optimistic concurrency control manager that leverages a shared log for validation. However, Hyder, LogBase and RAMCloud are not designed for a geo-replicated environment. Message Futures [40], mentioned above, uses a geo-replicated shared log. Like Helios, Message Futures uses Replicated Dictionary [53] for validating transactions. Replicated Dictionary is a causally ordered shared log for single atomic events. It has several features that distinguish it from other log replication techniques that maintain causal order [10, 28, 45, 49]. Replicated Dictionary maintains a timetable representing the extent of each replica's knowledge. This timetable is used for various tasks like garbage collection and transitive propagation between replicas. It does not, however, provide transactional support. Helios extends the basic data structures of Replicated Dictionary to achieve transactional geo-replication with minimal commit latencies. Chariots [41] is a design of a scalable geo-replicated shared log, influenced by Replicated Dictionary [53]. Chariots might provide a more efficient log replication framework for Helios.

Helios is a system that supports **serializable transactions** on **geo-replicated** data stores with the objective of achieving **low latency** by leveraging **loosely synchronized clocks** and **log replication**. Helios starts with a clear understanding of the true limits of achievable commit latencies, which leads to a design that is theoretically able to achieve the optimal commit latency and that is practically able to achieve latency close to the optimal. Helios allows tuning the commit latency of individual datacenters and allows the flexibility to set the desired fault-tolerance level in terms of the number of datacenter outages to be tolerated.

3. COMMIT LATENCY LOWER-BOUND

The objective of this section is to develop a lower-bound on commit latency of transactions on replicated data stores *while maintaining serializability* [13]. Maintaining serializability requires coordination between replicas (datacenters in our case). The communication latency necessary for this coordination imposes a limit on *commit latency*, which is the time duration to decide whether a transaction commits or aborts. Achieving low commit latency is the focus of this study. Consider two datacenters A and B with unique commit latencies L_A and L_B, respectively. We show in this section that the *summation* of L_A and L_B must be at least the Round-Trip Time (RTT) between A and B. Note that this is a summation which means that the commit latency of a datacenter can be lower than RTT.

The lower-bound result extends to larger groups of datacenters by applying the lower-bound to all pairs in the group. This will allow us to judge whether the group of datacenters can commit with a certain set of commit latency values. We are particularly interested in minimizing the average commit latency of all datacenters. We call the minimum average latency a *Minimum Average Optimal* (MAO) latency or optimal latency for short.

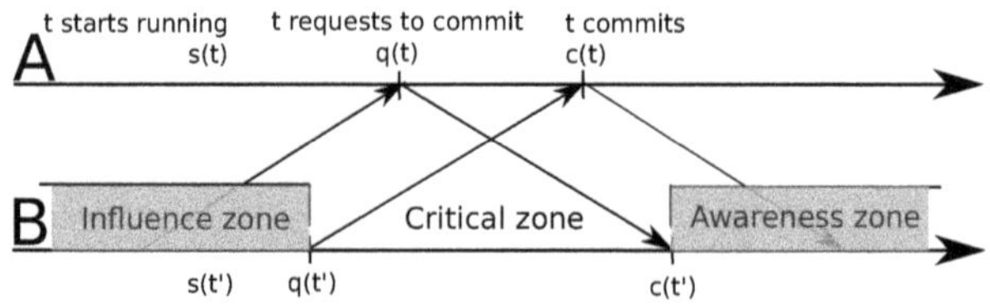

Figure 1: Two transactions, t and t', executing in a scenario with two datacenters

3.1 Theoretical model and assumptions

We consider a theoretical model that consists of datacenters with communication links connecting them. Each transaction undergoes two phases. First, the transaction is issued and it becomes visible to the datacenter. At that stage it is called a *preparing* transaction. Then, at a later time the datacenter decides whether it commits or aborts and it becomes a *finished* transaction. The time spent as a preparing transaction is the *commit latency.*

The following are the assumptions on communication and computation for this model. *These assumptions are made for the theoretical development of this section only and are not part of the Helios system design in Section 4.*

- *Compute power:* Infinite compute power is assumed in the model. The datacenter does not experience any overhead in processing and storing transactions. We make this assumption to focus our attention on communication overhead.
- *Communication links:* Sending a message through a link takes a specific latency to be delivered to the other end. Links are symmetric and take the same amount of time in both directions. Note that different links could have different latencies. However, triangle inequality must hold.
- *Arbitrary read-write transactions:* All datacenters have no restrictions on their choice or order of objects to be read or written in a transaction. Additionally, each transaction must have at least a single write operation. Thus, the model does not apply to optimizations for read-only transactions and disjoint data manipulation techniques. Also, transactions must try to commit, hence aborting all transactions is not allowed.
- *Knowledge:* Each datacenter A knows precisely every preparing and finished transaction that exists at another datacenter B up to the current time minus half the RTT between them, *i.e.*, *now* - $\frac{RTT(A,B)}{2}$. This reflects the fastest time a datacenter knows about any event in another datacenter. In a realistic setting this is a lower bound of such knowledge.
- *Commit latency:* We assume that the commit latency at each datacenter is fixed. This assumption simplifies the presentation. The discussions can be extended to the general case by taking each point in time in isolation.

3.2 Lower-bound proof

Intuition. For any two concurrent conflicting transactions, at least one of them must be able to detect the other before committing. Otherwise, both transactions will commit, which could result in incorrect executions. Here, we show that there is a lower-bound on commit latency. If the commit latency is lower than the lower-bound, then two conflicting transactions could commit without detecting each other, thus possibly violating correctness.

Formulation. Consider two datacenters A and B and a transaction t executing at datacenter A and transaction t' executing at datacenter B that could be conflicting with t. Figure 1 shows these transactions. In the figure, $s(t)$ is the transaction's start time, $q(t)$ is the commit request time, and $c(t)$ is the commit time. Transaction t's read and write-set are visible at the commit request time. Given the knowledge assumption, B knows about t starting from time $q(t) + \frac{RTT(A/B)}{2}$. Transaction t is preparing from time $q(t)$ until time $c(t)$ when it is committed. Three *zones* are defined at datacenter B with respect to t: (1) The *awareness zone* where B can possibly know about t, (2) The *influence zone* where B's transactions can be known to t, and (3) the *critical zone* where B is neither in the awareness nor influence zone.

LEMMA 1. *The sum of the commit latencies of two datacenters is greater than or equal to the RTT between them,* i.e., $L_A+L_B \geq RTT(A,B)$*, where L_X is the commit latency at datacenter X.*

Proof: Let the time when t requests to commit be $q(t)$ and the time it commits be $c(t)$, *i.e.*, $c(t) - q(t) = L(t)$. These times are illustrated in Figure 1. The earliest time that B can be aware of the commit request made by t is at time $q(t) + \frac{RTT(A,B)}{2}$, since half the RTT is needed to get a message from A to B. Thus, t can affect B only at the *awareness zone* which is at any time greater than or equal to $q(t) + \frac{RTT(A,B)}{2}$. Likewise, t cannot be affected by events at B that happened after time $c(t) - \frac{RTT(A,B)}{2}$ since they cannot be received at A before the commit decision is made. We denote the times when an event at B can affect the outcome of t as the *influence zone* which is any time less than or equal to $c(t) - \frac{RTT(A,B)}{2}$.

Now consider the time duration that is neither in the awareness zone nor in the influence zone. Call this time duration the *critical zone*. Consider a transaction t' at B that requests to commit and commits in the critical zone. Transaction t' will not affect the outcome of t, since t' is not in the influence zone. Also, t will not affect t', since t' is not in the awareness zone. Assume that t' can successfully commit. However, t' can conflict with t. Since t' is not aware of t and t is, likewise, not aware of t', both transactions successfully commit. This potentially results in an inconsistency, a contradiction to the assumption that t' can successfully commit. This means that a transaction that starts at the beginning of the critical zone at B cannot commit with a commit latency smaller than the duration of the critical zone. This duration is equal to $RTT(A,B) - L(t)$.

Repeating the same steps above for each point in time at datacenter A will yield that the commit latency at A, L_A, is equal to $L(T)$ and the commit latency at any point in B, L_B, is larger than or equal to $RTT(A,B) - L_A$. Thus, the sum of L_A and L_B must be greater than or equal to $RTT(A,B)$. ■

Protocol	L_A	L_B	L_C	Average
Master/Slave (A master)	0	30	20	16.67
Master/Slave (C master)	20	40	0	20
Majority	20	30	20	23.33
Optimal (MAO)	5	25	15	15

Table 1: Possible commit latencies, L_A, L_B and L_C, for three datacenters with Round-Trip Times $RTT(A,B) = 30$, $RTT(A,C) = 20$, and $RTT(B,C) = 40$.

The previous lemma shows that there is a direct trade-off between the commit latencies of two datacenters. Given this lemma we are now able to judge whether a set of commit latencies are *achievable* or violates the lower-bound for scenarios with more than two datacenters by applying the lower-bound to each pair of datacenters.

Example. Consider an example of three datacenters, A, B, and C. The RTTs between the datacenters are: $RTT(A,B) = 30$, $RTT(A,C) = 20$, and $RTT(B,C) = 40$. Table 1 shows four achievable commit latencies and the average commit latency of the datacenters. The first two represent a master-slave replication approach, where a single master is responsible for committing transactions. In this approach, the master commits immediately, and the other datacenters commit latencies are the RTT to the master. Note how each pair of datacenters satisfies the lower-bound, *e.g.*, when A is the master $L_A+L_B = 30 = RTT(A,B)$. The third row represents a majority replication approach. For the case of three datacenters, the commit latency of a datacenter is the RTT to the nearest datacenter. These replication protocols experience different average commit latencies: 16.67, 20, and 23.33. However, the minimum average commit latency (MAO) that is achievable for this scenario is 15. The fourth row in the figure show the commit latencies, L_A, L_B, and L_C, that achieve an average commit latency of 15 while not violating the lower-bound.

Deriving the achievable minimum average commit latency for a given set of datacenters is outlined next.

3.3 Minimum average optimality

A MAO set of commit latency values minimizes the average commit latency of all datacenters without violating the lower-bound condition (Lemma 1) for any pair of datacenters. The MAO solution can be derived using the following linear programming formulation:

PROBLEM 1. ***(Minimum Average Optimal)*** *The Minimum Average Optimal commit latencies for n datacenters is derived using a linear program with the following objective and constraints:*

Minimize	$\sum_{A \in R}$	L_A
subject to	$\forall_{A,B \in R}$	$L_A + L_B \geq RTT(A,B)$
and	$\forall_{A \in R}$	$L_A \geq 0$

where R is the set of datacenters. This formulation follows directly from Lemma 1. Minimizing the latency is our objective and the constraints are the correctness conditions that commit latencies are not negative and Lemma 1 is satisfied. We will use this methodology to derive the commit latency values used with the Helios commit protocol. This linear program can be adapted to other objectives. In Section A.2, we discuss optimizing for throughput.

4. HELIOS COMMIT PROTOCOL

In this section we propose Helios. The protocol design and operation are developed followed by a discussion on handling datacenter outages.

4.1 Helios architecture

System model. We consider a multi-datacenter system consisting of datacenters and clients. Each datacenter contains a *full copy of the data* and runs an instance of Helios, which is an optimistic concurrency control manager. Read operations are performed by clients first, and write operations are buffered. When the client is ready to commit, it sends a commit request containing its read and write-sets to the closest Helios instance. Helios replies to read requests with the current version and version timestamp of the requested data object. The version timestamp is the timestamp of the most recent write operation that wrote the data object. Blind writes are allowed, meaning that an object can exist in the write-set without being read. The commit request contains the read-set with the read version timestamps and the buffered write-set. Helios upon receiving the commit request will start the commit protocol to commit the transaction and propagate all updates to other datacenters. After committing the transaction, the commit decision is sent back to the client. *The time spent by the client from sending the commit request to receiving the commit decision is called the* ***commit latency***.

Communication. Helios uses a *log replication protocol* to exchange transaction information between datacenters. The log is continuously being propagated between datacenters. Each record in the log contains the information of either a *preparing transaction* that is trying to commit or a *finished transaction* that is either committed or aborted. Each transaction has two records in the log, one added when it starts as a preparing transaction and one record when it becomes a finished transaction. The transaction information includes the read and write sets. Each transaction is timestamped. The log is ordered according to transaction timestamps. Furthermore, *records are received by other datacenters according to their order in the log.* This means that receiving a record of a transaction with timestamp τ will follow all transactions with lower timestamps. Timestamps reflect the local clock of the datacenter. Clocks are loosely synchronized.

Helios conducts this replication using a replication protocol that is similar to Replicated Dictionary (RDict) [53]. RDict is an efficient protocol to replicate logs while maintaining their order. A $N \times N$ timetable, T_A, is maintained at each datacenter A where N is the number of datacenters. Each entry in the timetable is a timestamp representing a bound on how much a datacenter knows about another datacenter's records. For example, entry $\mathbf{T_A[B, C]} = \tau$ means that datacenter A knows that datacenter B is aware of all events at datacenter C up to timestamp τ. This notation will be used while describing Helios.

4.2 Helios overview

4.2.1 *Intuition*

To provide an intuition of the Helios commit protocol, consider the scenario in Figure 1. The figure shows the timeline of two datacenters, A and B. At A, a transaction t is issued at time $q(t)$ and committed at time $c(t)$. Transaction t commits immediately after receiving a log from B that is shown as an arrow going from B to A. This log carries transactions that were issued up to the time of sending the log, including transaction t' (assume t' is issued at the time of log transmission). The time the log was sent from B is $q(t')$. $q(t')$ is also the commit request time of t'. Helios receives the log in order, meaning that all transactions, preparing or finished, at B prior to or at time $q(t')$ are known to A at time $c(t)$.

Detecting conflicts. Transactions at B must not conflict with t. The approach to avoid conflicts is influenced by the way the lower-bound latency was developed in Section 3. However, here we do not make any assumptions regarding clock synchronization or communication. Rather, we rely on the exchanged logs and received transaction timestamps.

A transaction, t', at B is either issued during the influence zone, critical zone, or awareness zone. If t' starts during the influence zone, then transaction t will detect it because the log will contain a record of t'. If t' starts in the awareness zone, then it will detect t. Thus, for these two cases, conflicts will be detected. An undetected conflict can arise only if t' starts *and* commits within the critical zone. Thus, if t' is issued in the critical zone, Helios must ensure that it does not commit until it is in the awareness zone, which means that B will detect the conflict between t and t'.

Commit offsets. A *commit offset* is a time duration that represents the extent of knowledge needed by a transaction from other datacenters prior to committing. This duration ensures that a transaction t' that is issued in the critical zone will commit in the awareness zone (more on how to optimally assign these commit offsets in Section 4.5). Each datacenter maintains a commit offset for all "other" datacenters. For example, in the figure, A has a commit offset for B, denoted co_A^B, and B has a commit offset for A, denoted co_B^A.

Committing. When a transaction, t, requests to commit, it is assigned a timestamp, $q(t)$. Helios uses $q(t)$ and co_A^B to calculate a timestamp called the *knowledge timestamp* (*kts*). There is a *kts* value for every other datacenter B:

$$kts_t^B = q(t) + co_A^B \tag{1}$$

The commit condition for t is the following: *t can commit if its datacenter, A, knows about the transactions at every other datacenter B that were issued up to time kts_t^B at B.*

Consider Figure 1. When t is issued, Helios records that $kts_t^B = q(t)+co_A^B$. Assume that kts_t^B is equal to $q(t')$. Thus, A waits until it receives the log sent at $q(t')$ to commit. In the figure, t receives that log at time $c(t)$ and is then able to commit.

4.2.2 *Condition on commit offset*

In order to guarantee that a transaction t' that is issued in the critical zone will commit in the awareness zone, Helios needs to enforce a condition on the assignment of commit offsets.

Consider the scenario in Figure 1. Assume that the commit request time of t', $q(t')$, is in the beginning of the critical zone, as is shown in the figure. Transaction t', similar to t, is assigned a knowledge timestamp when it requests to commit. This value for t' is: $kts_{t'}^A = q(t') + co_B^A$. Thus, t' will know about all transactions at A up to time $kts_{t'}^A$ at A. For t' to be aware of t before committing, the value $kts_{t'}^A$ must be greater than or equal to the time t was issued, *i.e.*, $q(t)$. By expanding the value of $kts_{t'}^A$, the inequality to guarantee

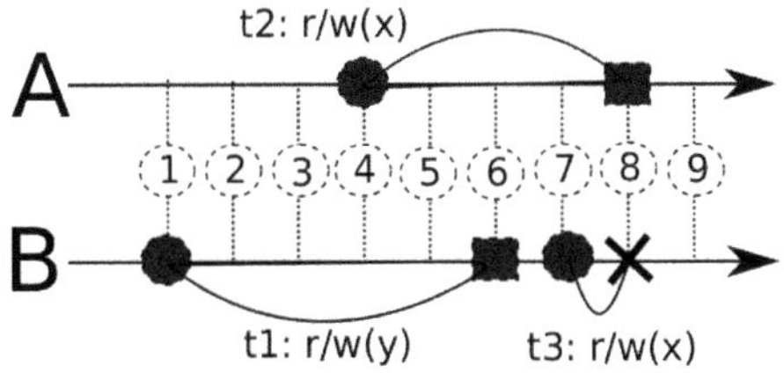

Figure 2: A scenario of Helios. Commit latencies are 3 and 5 for A and B. RTT is 8. A circle is a commit request, the square is a commit, and an X sign is an abort.

detecting conflicts is: $q(t') + co_B^A \geq q(t)$. $q(t)$ is equal to $q(t') - co_A^B$. Substituting this into the inequality and rearranging, the inequality becomes: $(co_A^B + co_B^A) \geq 0$. This is summarized by the following rule:

RULE 1. *For the Helios commit protocol to be able to detect conflicts, the sum of any two symmetric commit offsets* (e.g., $co_A^B + co_B^A$) *must be greater than or equal to 0.*

The requirement above specifies what is necessary to ensure correctness. However, a range of possible commit offset assignments might be used. We show later in Section 4.5 how Helios assigns commit offsets to minimize commit latencies. This assignment by Helios can theoretically achieve the lower-bound commit latency. Note that although timestamps are used, time synchronization is *not* required for correctness. Nonetheless, better synchronization will yield better performance as we demonstrate in Section A.

4.2.3 Example scenarios

To better illustrate how Helios works, consider the example in Figure 2 with two datacenters A and B. Time is denoted by the number between A and B's timelines. A commit request is denoted by a black circle and is connected to commit or abort time represented as a black square for a commit or an X sign for an abort. Transaction information is displayed as the read and write-sets. For example, transaction t_1 reads and writes y. Assume that the read version is the latest available version prior to requesting the commit. Log transmissions are omitted from the timeline, but assume for this example that they are being propagated at each tick of the clock. The RTT between A and B, $RTT(A,B)$, is equal to 8 time units. To simplify the presentation of the example, assume that the log takes exactly 4 time units to be delivered. Thus, at time 5, B knows about all events at A up to time 1.

For this example we pick the commit offset values to be -1 for co_A^B and +1 for co_B^A, hence $co_A^B + co_B^A$ is greater than or equal to 0. Now, follow the example scenario. Transaction t_1 reads and writes y and requests to commit at time 1, hence $q(t_1) = 1$. The knowledge timestamp for t_1 is given by: $kts_{t_1}^A = q(t_1) + co_B^A$ which is equal to 2. The transaction waits until B receives the log sent from A at time 2, which is the value for $kts_{t_1}^A$. At time 6, t_1 successfully commits after receiving the log from A that was sent at time 2 (the log takes 4 time units to be received). t_2, which reads and writes x, requests to commit at A at time 4. The knowledge timestamp for t_2 is given by: $kts_{t_2}^B = q(t_2) + co_A^B$ which is equal to 3. Assume that the log transmission from B at time 3 took more time than usual and was received at A at time 8, one time unit late. For this reason, t_2 commits at time 8 when the history of datacenter B is received up to time 3, which is the value of $kts_{t_2}^B$. Now consider t_3. It requests to commit at B at time 7. The knowledge timestamp value is given by: $kts_{t_3}^A = q(t_3) + co_B^A$, which is equal to 8. However, one time unit after its request, it receives t_2's information that was sent at time 4 from A. A conflict is detected and t_3 aborts immediately.

Algorithm 1: Processing commit requests at A

1: t := local transaction requesting to commit at A
2: **if** t conflicts with any $t' \in$ PTPool $\cup$ EPTPool **then**
3:     Abort t; exit
4: **for each** object o in $t.readset$ **do**
5:     **if** o is overwritten **then**
6:         abort t; exit
7: $t.timestamp = get\_time()$
8: **for each** datacenter $X \in datacenters$ **do**
9:     $t.kts^X = t.timestamp + co_A^X$
10: PTPool.$append(t)$; $Log_A.append(t)$

Algorithm 2: Processing transactions in the log at A

for each transaction t *in* Log_A **do**
    if t is local **then**
        skip to next
    if t conflicts with any t' $\in$ PTPool **then**
        abort t'; $t'.timestamp = get\_time()$
        $Log_A.append(t')$
    if $t.type ==$ preparing **then**
        EPTPool.$append(t)$
    else // $t.type ==$ finished
        if t.committed==true **then**
            for each object o in $t.writeset$ **do**
                Apply o to data store
        Remove t from EPTPool
    $T_A[A, host(t)] = t.timestamp$

4.3 Concurrency control protocol

In this section we discuss the design of Helios. The main tasks performed are: (1) process commit requests (Algorithm 1), (2) process remote transactions received in the shared log (Algorithm 2), and (3) commit preparing transactions (Algorithm 3). We also briefly discuss read-only transactions in Section B.

4.3.1 Commit requests

When Helios receives a commit request for a transaction t at datacenter A, it checks whether it conflicts with preparing transactions (Lines 2-3). Preparing transactions are maintained in the *Preparing Transactions Pool* (PTPool) for local transactions and the *External Preparing Transactions Pool* (EPTPool) for remote transactions. Transaction t aborts if a conflict exists, which is an intersection between the read or write-set of t with the write-set of any preparing transaction. Then, the read-set of t is verified to have not been overwritten (Lines 4-6). If no conflicts are detected and the read-set is not overwritten, the knowledge timestamps are calculated as defined in Equation 1 (Lines 7-9). A preparing record of t is appended to both the PTPool and the local log, Log_A (Line 10). Appending to the log includes adding the record and updating the timetable so that $T_A[A, A]$ equals to t's timestamp.

4.3.2 Log processing

Helios processes transactions in the log in order (Algorithm 2). Local transaction records are not processed

Algorithm 3: Committing preparing transactions at A

```
1: for each transaction t in PTPool do
2:     for each datacenter X ∈ datacenters do
3:         if T_A[A, X] < t.kts^X then
4:             skip to next transaction
5:     Apply t.write-set to local data store at A
6:     commit t; t.timestamp = get_time();
7:     Log_A.append(t)
```

(Lines 2-3). For a coming transaction t, conflicts are detected with local preparing transactions in PTPool. A conflict exists if the read or write set of a local preparing transaction, t', intersects with the write-set of t (Lines 4-6). A conflicting transaction in PTPool is aborted by changing its state to aborted and updating its timestamp. An abort record is added to the log (Lines 5-6). Remember that adding to the log includes updating the timetable to reflect the addition of a new transaction record.

Remote transactions are either preparing or finished. When a preparing transaction is received from another datacenter, it is added to EPTPool (Lines 7-8). A finished transaction contains a flag to indicate whether it has committed or aborted. If it is committed, then the write operations in the write-set are applied to the local data store (Lines 11-12). However, whether a finished transaction is committed or aborted, it is removed from the EPTPool (Line 13). Finally, the timetable is updated to reflect that t is processed (Line 14).

4.3.3 Committing preparing transactions.

A preparing transaction, t, can successfully commit by satisfying two conditions: (1) *External knowledge:* Helios must have processed transactions from other datacenters up to the *knowledge timestamp* (*kts*) calculated according to Equation 1. (2) *Conflict freedom:* no conflicts were observed with t up to the point when the first condition is satisfied. Algorithm 3 checks whether the external knowledge condition is satisfied for transactions in PTPool (Lines 2-4). If the condition is satisfied for a transaction t, then it can successfully commit. The write-set of t is applied and a record is added to the log (Lines 5-7). Conflicts are already detected when the transaction requested to commit (Algorithm 1) and while the log is being processed (Algorithm 2). Thus, there is no need to detect conflicts at this point.

Commit condition. The commit condition can be summarized as the following:

RULE 2. *A transaction t in A commits if no conflicts are detected, and*

$$T_A[A, B] \geq kts_t^B, \quad \forall_B (B \in R)$$

where R is the set of other datacenters and *kts* is the knowledge timestamp defined in Equation 1.

4.4 Liveness

Intuition. Helios needs information from other datacenters to be able to commit its preparing transactions (see Rule 2). An outage of a datacenter will cause other datacenters to block waiting for its transaction log. The blocking will continue until the datacenter is back up again and Helios is recovered. This is similar to blocking scenarios in 2PC. State machine replication (SMR) is used to overcome these blocking scenarios. Here, we present the way Helios achieves liveness while enabling the flexibility to set the number of tolerated datacenter outages. Thus, Helios enables controlling the trade-off between liveness and performance.

The main idea is to ensure that a transaction, t, at datacenter A does not commit before its information exists at f other datacenters, where f is the number of datacenter outages to be tolerated. Verifying that t's information exists at another datacenter, B, can be done by waiting for an acknowledgment of the receipt of t. B should keep the information about t until it is completed and its information are propagated to other datacenters. This is important to enable B to propagate the information about t in case A experiences an outage.

Committing. A datacenter can know whether another datacenter received the record of a transaction by examining the transaction's timestamp and comparing it to the extent of the other datacenter's knowledge using RDict (see Section 4.1). If the number of datacenter outages that are to be tolerated is f out of n total datacenters, then the transaction waits for its information to be received by f other datacenters.

Failure case. When a datacenter B fails, a datacenter A might have to delay the commitment of a transaction until it can ascertain the identity of all previously finished transactions at the failed datacenter B by communicating with other datacenters, C, where backup information for B exists. However, it is not always possible to conclude that a datacenter has failed since a network partition might render the messages sent from B undelivered. Consider the following scenario: a datacenter A is waiting for information from B. A network partition makes information from B unable to be delivered to other datacenters. Given that no information is received at A from B, datacenter A consults C for information about B's finished transactions. Datacenter A can commit transactions since it knows that B cannot commit any transactions without getting an acknowledgment of its receipt from either B or C.

Grace time. The subtlety here is about knowing when a datacenter C can be certain about the state of another datacenter (B). Helios adopts a *time-based invalidation* technique to enable a datacenter to ascertain the state of a failed datacenter. Helios makes the commitment of a transaction dependent on the reception time at the other datacenters. We call this time the *Grace Time* (GT). A datacenter C will acknowledge the receipt of transaction t from B if and only if the transaction information is received at C at time τ that is smaller than the commit request timestamp of t plus GT, *i.e.*, $\tau \leq (q(t) + GT)$. Otherwise, C will not acknowledge the reception of t.

The implication of this bounded acknowledgment is that at time τ at datacenter C, we have a guarantee that no transactions with a request timestamp less than (τ-GT) will be able to synchronously replicate to C. Thus, B and C will be able to infer information about A. Specifically, B and C will be confident that no transactions (unknown to them) will commit at A with a timestamp less than $min\{now_B, now_C\} - GT$, where now_X is the current time at datacenter X. This is because even if a transaction with an earlier timestamp existed at A it will be invalidated since it was not acknowledged by B and C. This is very useful information for Helios because it allows transactions at B and C to commit even if A fails or cannot communicate with other datacenters.

Integration. This acknowledgment mechanism can be easily incorporated in Helios by extending commitment Rule 2 to reflect the acknowledgment requirement and invalidation. First, the extent of A's knowledge of B's events, $T_A[A, B]$, can be inferred by other participants. Thus, when $T_A[A, B]$ is used in Rule 2 it can be substituted by:

$$\hat{T}_A[A, B] = max\{T_A[A, B], \eta\} \quad (2)$$

where η is the extent of knowledge of A about B that can be inferred using a set of any $n - f$ other datacenters called κ. η is calculated as the following:

$$\eta = min\{T_A[C, C]\} \forall_{C \in \kappa} - GT \quad (3)$$

The other needed extension to Rule 2 is to restrict the commitment of a transaction until it has been successfully acknowledged by a number of datacenters equal to the number of outages to be overcome. A transaction t at A is considered acknowledged by B if $T_A[B, A]$ is greater than or equal to t's timestamp: $q(t)$. Thus, what is needed is to ensure that the transaction was acknowledged by a set of $f+1$ total datacenters. However, remember that for a transaction to be successfully acknowledged it needs to be received by the other datacenter in a bounded time, hence $q(t)+GT$. This is ensured by examining $ts_C(t)$, which is the time the transaction record of t was received at C. Given the aforementioned extensions, the commitment rule can now be written as the following:

RULE 3. *A pending transaction t in A commits if no conflicts are detected, and*
(1) $\hat{T}_A[A, B] \geq kts_t^B, \ \forall_B(B \in R)$
(2) $T_A[C, A] \geq q(t), \quad \forall_C(\ C \in \kappa')$
(3) $ts_C(t) < q(t) + GT, \quad \forall_C(\ C \in \kappa')$

where κ' is a set of any $n-f$ datacenters where n is the number of datacenters and f is the number of tolerated outages.

Grace time. The choice of the value of GT is controlled by the trade-off between minimizing the effect of datacenter outages on progress and minimizing the number of aborted transactions due to delays in the acknowledgment process. A datacenter outage increases the latency because rather than waiting for the knowledge timestamp (Equation 1) from the failed datacenter, a datacenter has to wait for an additional duration of GT, to accumulate knowledge of the transactions in the failed datacenter from all the running ones. Also, having a small GT might lead to some transactions unnecessarily aborting due to message delays or drops while waiting for the acknowledgment.

4.5 Commit offsets assignment

The assignment of commit offsets directly influences the commit latency of each datacenter. It is not straightforward to assign commit offsets to minimize commit latencies. However, it is possible to estimate commit latencies given the assigned commit offsets. To simplify this estimation we assume that clocks are synchronized and that messages take exactly $\frac{RTT(A,B)}{2}$ time to be sent from A to B. This is of course not true of real systems and will introduce an estimation error of the commit latency.

Estimating commit latency. A transaction t at A waits for information from other datacenters. For every other datacenter B, t can commit only after receiving information from B up to time $(q(t) + co_A^B)$. This information is received at A at time $(q(t) + co_A^B + \frac{RTT(A,B)}{2})$. Since, t commits after receiving information from all datacenters, the commit latency of t is delayed until the time it receives the information from the last datacenter; if that datacenter is C, then the commit latency of transactions at datacenter A is

$$L_A = co_A^C + \frac{RTT(A, C)}{2} \quad (4)$$

Setting commit offsets. Helios can assign arbitrary values to commit offsets, thus targeting the desired commit latency as long as they do not violate the commit offset correctness requirement (Rule 1). The linear program in Section 3.3 can be used to derive the commit latency values that will minimize the commit latency. Thus, we can set the commit offsets by the following rearrangement of Equation 4

$$co_A^C = L_A - \frac{RTT(A, C)}{2} \quad (5)$$

where L_A is the target commit latency calculated using the linear program in Section 3.3 and $RTT(A, C)$ is an estimation of the RTT.

Correctness. The optimal assignment is guaranteed to satisfy the correctness requirement of commit offsets shown in Rule 1. This can be verified by substituting Equation 5 into the sum requirement (Rule 1) that $(co_A^C + co_C^A)$ must be greater than or equal to 0. This will yield to the requirement that ($L_A + L_C$ - $RTT(A, C)$) must be greater than 0. Since the linear program of Section 3.3 has a constraint that the sum of two commit latencies must be greater than the RTT between them, this yields that ($L_A + L_C$ - $RTT(A, C)$) is always greater than 0. Thus, the assignment guarantees detection of conflicts.

Estimation vs. reality. In a real deployment the assignment in equation 5 will not yield the exact lower-bound commit latency because of communication links variability and lack of perfect synchronization. We quantify some of these effects in Section A and show in the evaluation (Section 5) that a real-life deployment is able to achieve a commit latency close to the optimal.

	V	O	C	I	S
V	-	66 (11)	78 (10)	84 (9)	268 (7)
O	66 (10)	-	19 (1)	175 (7)	210 (4.4)
C	78 (9)	19 (1)	-	175 (7)	182 (6)
I	84 (8)	175 (7)	175 (6)	-	194 (4)
S	268 (6)	210 (4)	182 (6)	194 (4)	-

Table 2: RTT latencies between different datacenters in milliseconds and the standard deviation inside parentheses.

5. EVALUATION

5.1 Evaluation framework

The evaluation of Helios is performed using Amazon's AWS. Helios is evaluated for three different liveness levels: Helios-0 tolerating no datacenter outages, Helios-1 tolerating a single outage, and Helios-2 tolerating two outages. We compare the performance of Helios with Message Futures [40], Replicated Commit [38], and an implementation of Two-Phase Commit (2PC) over Paxos (2PC/Paxos) that is inspired from Spanner [16]. The calculated lower-bound commit latency is also shown for reference.

Objective. The evaluation focuses on quantifying and testing the performance of Helios in addition to its resilience to a lack of strict clock synchronization and RTT estimation errors. The performance metrics we report are commit latency and throughput. These are calculated for transactions that successfully commit. Helios resiliency is tested by artificially reducing the level of synchronization and accuracy of RTT estimation.

Highlights. The highlights of the results of this evaluation are the following:

- Helios-0 achieves a commit latency that is within 54ms from the calculated lower-bound commit latency. This overhead increases as the level of liveness increases (Figure 3).
- All variants of Helios achieve lower commit latency and higher throughput compared to Message Futures and 2PC/Paxos. Replicated Commit achieves a lower throughput when compared to Helios but it experiences a commit latency within what Helios-0 and Helios-2 achieve (Figures 3 and 4).
- Inaccurate synchronization and RTT estimation lead to a higher commit latency (Figure 5). The overhead recorded for this set of experiments is up to 52% higher average commit latency.

Setup. Amazon Elastic Compute Cloud (EC2) machines used are High-CPU Extra Large (c3.x2large) which have eight CPU cores and 7GB of RAM memory. Five datacenters were used in the following locations: California (C), Virginia (V), Oregon (O), Ireland (I), and Singapore (S). The average RTT latencies observed are shown in Table 2. These RTT numbers are sampled over 24 hours. The standard deviations of the samples are shown inside parentheses. Each datacenter hosts a full replica of the data. One machine in each datacenter runs Helios, serving transactions issued by clients. Helios uses HBase [25] as the underlying data store. Clock synchronization is achieved by running the command "ntpdate ntp.ubuntu.com" before each experiment run.

Workload. Dedicated machines in each datacenter are used to simulate clients and evaluate Helios. We use Transactional YCSB (T-YCSB) [17], a multi-record transactional benchmarking framework, for our evaluations. T-YCSB, an extended version of YCSB [14], generates transactional workloads. It issues transactions that consist of a set of read and write operations, where each operation accesses a different record of the data store. Each client can have one outstanding transaction at a time. Clients issue transactions as fast as they can unless mentioned otherwise. An operation is either a read or a write to a key from a pool of 50000 keys. The key is chosen using a Zipfian distribution. Each transaction contains five operations. Half of these operations are reads and the other half are writes. Each experiment runs for a duration of 10 minutes.

Configuration. Helios assigns the commit offsets to target achieving the lower-bound commit latency. The RTT average values in Table 2 are used to derive the optimal commit latencies using the method shown in Section 3.3. The calculated optimal commit latencies are: 69ms, 10ms, 10ms, 166ms, and 200ms for V, O, C, I, and S, respectively. These are then used to derive commit offsets to be used to commit transactions in Helios using Equation 5. As a baseline, we also display results of Helios without performing RTT estimations and optimal latency calculations by setting all the commit offsets to 0. This baseline is called **Helios-B**.

5.2 Systems for comparison

We report Helios results compared with results obtained from Message Futures [40], Replicated Commit [38], and a Two-Phase Commit over Paxos protocol (2PC/Paxos) that is inspired by Spanner [16].

Message Futures, like Helios, uses replicated logs that are causally ordered to exchange transactions information and detect conflicts. In Message Futures, partial logs are continuously being propagated between datacenters [53]. Transactions, t^i, which request to commit at A between the transmissions of partial log i and $i+1$ are assigned a reservation number i. Partial log transmissions are acknowledged by other datacenters. The acknowledgment contains a log of all transactions (not known to A) up to the time, τ, of the transmission of the acknowledgment. Transactions t^i can commit when log i is acknowledged by all other datacenters and no conflicts are detected. Helios follows a different approach where a transaction commits by waiting for partial logs from other datacenters up to calculated timestamps that minimizes the commit latency while preserving correctness.

Replicated Commit uses Paxos for cross datacenter replication and Two-Phase Locking (2PL) to avoid conflicts. Clients first perform read operations by trying to lock the read object in a majority of datacenters. Write operations are buffered. Then, committing the transaction is done by replicating it using Paxos to all datacenters. As the transaction is received by datacenters, locks are acquired for buffered write operations and read locks are validated. If the locks were acquired and validated at a majority of datacenters, then the client will commit the transaction. Thus, its commit latency should be in the order of a single RTT to the closest majority, which is the time required by Helios-2 to commit. However, Replicated Commit performs poorly in terms of throughput due to the read strategy. The client spends more time reading before the commit request is issued.

2PC/Paxos uses 2PC to avoid conflicts and Paxos for replication. In this evaluation the datacenter in Virginia (V) is assigned to be the 2PC coordinator. Clients, scattered across all five datacenters issue reads to the coordinator. The coordinator maintains a lock table. When a read is received, a read lock is placed on the corresponding key. Write operations are buffered. When a transaction is ready, a request to commit is sent to the coordinator with information of all operations. Once the coordinator receives the commit request it tries to acquire the write locks and verifies that the read locks are still held. If successful, the transaction commits. Then, the coordinator replicates the log to a majority of datacenters using Paxos [30]. The coordinator is assumed to have a lease so that it will not need to go through the leader election phase, hence reducing the required time to replicate the log by one RTT. After replicating the log, the output of the transaction is sent to the client. Transactions that are detected to be involved in a deadlock are immediately aborted.

Replicated Commit and 2PC/Paxos replicate to a majority before committing a transaction. Thus, in the setup used for the following experiments with five datacenters, they tolerate two datacenter failures. Thus, they tolerate the same number of failures as Helios-2. Message Futures does not inherently overcome datacenter outages, thus its liveness guarantee is equivalent to Helios-0.

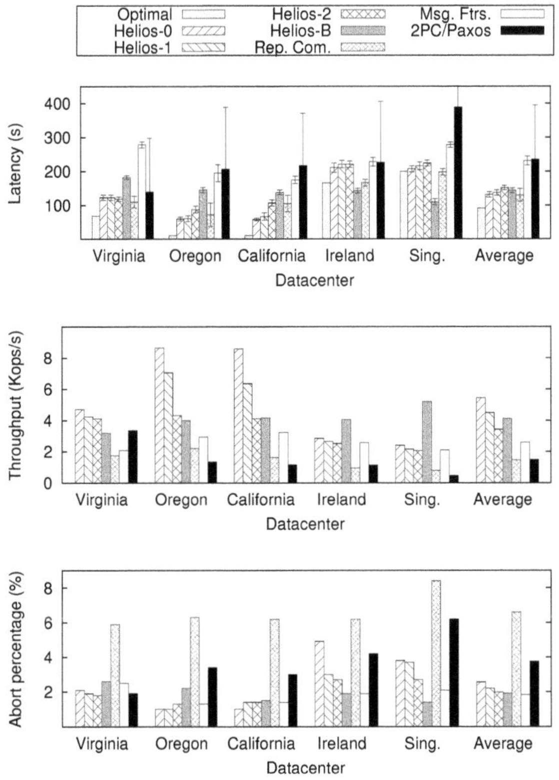

Figure 3: The commit latency, throughput, and abort rate of a scenario with 60 clients and 5 datacenters.

5.3 Helios performance

In the following experiments, 60 clients scattered across all datacenters issue back-to-back transactions to Helios instances. We report the results for each datacenter separately in addition to confidence intervals for the commit latency numbers.

Latency. The commit latency results are shown in Figure 3(a) for Helios with varying liveness levels. We also show the commit latency of the baseline systems. In the figure, the average latency of clients that are running at each datacenter is shown. Helios-0 has the closest latencies to the optimal since it does not need to synchronously replicate any transactions before committing them. The overhead of Helios-0 over the optimal commit latency is within 7 to 54ms. This overhead is caused by different factors such as execution time, I/O access, network variability, and the network latency between the client and server. Some of these factors are analyzed in Section A.

Increasing the level of fault-tolerance results in an increase in commit latency (see Section A.2 for more details). This increase is caused by the difference between the commit latency needed to commit consistently and the required time to get the acknowledgment of the transaction's reception by the number of tolerated datacenter failures. This difference can vary, which explains why the overhead of tolerating one datacenter failure by using Helios-1 to Helios-0 ranges from 0-1ms for Virginia and Oregon while the overhead is 9-10ms for the remaining datacenters. Virginia and Oregon do not experience a significant overhead because their commit latencies are equal to or greater than the RTT to the closest datacenter, thus receiving the acknowledgment of the replication happens while waiting for transaction commitment. Similar behavior is observed when increasing the number of tolerated datacenter failures from 1 to 2, which results in an increase of commit latency ranging from no observed overhead for Virginia, Ireland, and Singapore to 27ms and 40ms overhead for Oregon and California. The average commit latency for Helios-2 at Virginia is actually 4ms lower than the latency of Helios-1. This does not mean that less time is required to commit for Helios-2, rather it is due to the variability of the compute and network conditions.

Replicated Commit commits transactions with a latency equal to the closest RTT majority. The achieved average latency is 20ms lower than the one achieved by Helios-2. This is because Helios experiences more compute overhead to process and send the log, while Replicated Commit's communication process is lightweight. The average commit latency of Replicated Commit is also close to Helios-0. The evaluation topology and RTT values for this set of experiments make the overhead for tolerating two datacenter outages not so large. Coupled with the higher compute overhead of Helios, this results in observing similar commit latency for Helios-0 and Replicated Commit. However, in topologies where the overhead to tolerate two datacenter outages is higher, Helios-0 should show a more significant advantage over Replicated Commit.

Message Futures requires roughly a RTT to all other datacenters to commit transactions. This causes an overhead compared to Helios-0 that ranges from 17ms for Ireland to 181ms for Singapore. The average overhead is 99ms. 2PC/Paxos requires more time to commit when compared to Helios-2, which has the same degree of fault tolerance. The difference in commit latency between 2PC/Paxos and Helios-2 ranges from 15-17ms for Virginia, Ireland, and Singapore to 146-159ms for Oregon and California. In 2PC/Paxos, a transaction experiences a latency equal to the time required to send the transaction to Virginia in addition to a RTT to a majority from Virginia. This gives an advantage to Virginia and datacenters close to it. Helios-B, which is Helios-0 but without assigning optimal commit latencies, has an average overhead of 12.2ms compared to Helios-0.

Helios and Message Futures are stable with standard deviation values that are less than 10. Replicated Commit and 2PC/Paxos on the other hand show unstable performance with standard deviation values of up to 35 for Replicated Commit and values ranging from 154 to 278 for 2PC/Paxos. The stability observed for Helios and Message Futures is due to the use of a log to exchange transactions between datacenters. If a transmission i was affected by the variability of the communication network, the next transmission, $i+1$, will include i because it is part of the log that was not acknowledged [53].

Throughput. The throughput results are presented in Figure 3(b). Helios-2 achieves a throughput 37% lower than what is achieved by Helios-0. The throughput achieved by Replicated Commit, Message Futures, and 2PC/Paxos is lower than what is achieved by Helios. The commit latency causes this lower throughput for Message Futures. Replicated Commit and 2PC/Paxos have a larger overhead due to their read strategy. Replicated Commit reads from a majority and 2PC/Paxos directs reads to Virginia which increases the amount of time spent by a client prior to requesting to commit. Remember that the commit latency is the time from the client's commit request till a decision is received and does not include the read latency incurred prior to the commit request. Replicated Commit and 2PC/Paxos achieve an average throughput that is 56-57% lower than Helios-2. Note that Virginia in 2PC/Paxos achieves the closest throughput to Helios-2 although it was not the closest to Helios in terms of commit latency. This illustrates the advantage of 2PC/Paxos clients at the master datacenter ridding them from the overhead of wide-area reads. Message Futures's throughput is 52% lower than the throughput of Helios-0. For Message Futures, the achieved throughput by each datacenter compared to Helios is directly correlated to the overhead in commit latency. This is because Message Futures, like Helios, reads from the closest datacenter. Helios-B achieves a throughput that is 24% lower than Helios-0. Like Message Futures, the throughput overhead correlates directly with the latency overhead.

Contention. The abort rates are shown in Figure 3(c). The abort rate is a product of many factors, such as the amount of contention, the number of concurrent transactions, the lifetime of the transaction, among others. However, we can observe a pattern in the average abort rates of different systems. Increasing the liveness level of Helios causes the abort rate to decrease, which is a sign of less contention that results from the decrease in throughput. Message Futures has the lowest abort rate although it has a higher commit latency compared to Helios. Replicated commit and 2PC/Paxos on the other hand achieve worse abort rates. 2PC/Paxos has the highest commit latency and additionally holds locks for an extended period of time, beginning from the read operations prior to the commit request until releasing locks after the commit phase. This increases contention and is a factor causing this high abort rate. Replicated Commit locks data object in lock tables scattered across datacenters which increases the chance of experiencing deadlocks. Abort rates of individual datacenters illuminate how having a larger commit latency is a disadvantage causing more transactions to be aborted; Singapore experiences larger abort rates when compared to other datacenters.

Peak throughput. Now, we measure the peak achievable throughput and the number of clients required to converge to that throughput for Helios. We increase the load on the system by gradually increasing the number of clients issuing transactions. In Figure 4(a), the cumulative achievable throughput is plotted with the number of clients in the system increasing from 15 clients to up to 285 clients in 30-clients increments. Note how the Helios protocols converge to a throughput between 6000 and 7000 operations per second. Helios-0 and Helios-1 are the fastest to converge as soon as the number of clients is 195. Helios-2 and Helios-B converge with 255 clients. Message Futures takes a slower pace than Helios. This is mainly due to its higher commit latency values. 2PC/Paxos is not able to achieve a throughput that is larger than 1700 operations per second. The demand placed on the coordinator causes thrashing as soon as the number of clients reaches 195 clients. Replicated Commit experiences a similar throughput to 2PC/Paxos but does not thrash.

Converging to the peak throughput signals an I/O bottleneck. Increasing the demand (number of clients) past the convergence point stresses the bottleneck, causing a gradual degradation of the performance of individual transactions. Figure 4(b) shows the effect of increasing the number of clients on the commit latency. Helios variants maintain their commit latency up to the convergence point between 195 and 255 clients. Message Futures and Replicated Commit maintain their commit latency because they need more clients than what is shown for them to converge. 2PC/Paxos starts a gradual increase in commit latency from the beginning signaling a stress on the system even with a small number of clients. Placing a large demand on a single coordinator causes resources to be exhausted rapidly, leading to this observation on 2PC/Paxos.

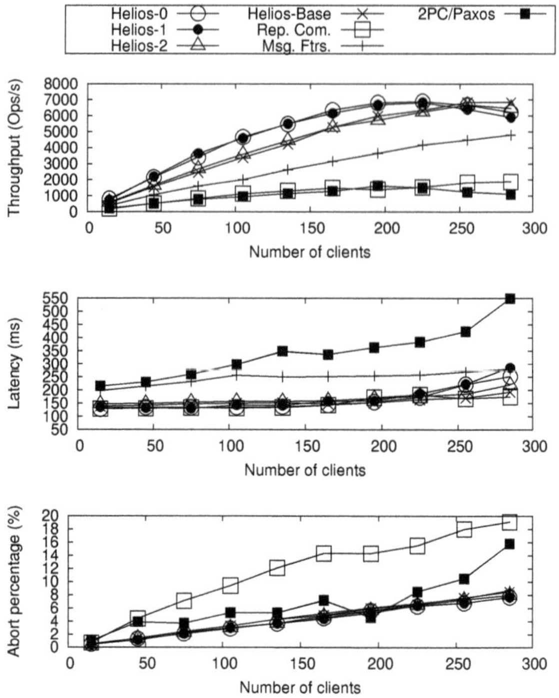

Figure 4: The throughput, average latency, and abort rate as the number of clients is increased.

Increasing the number of clients increases the contention and leads to more aborts. Figure 4(c) shows this effect. All protocols except Replicated Commit and 2PC/Paxos have similar abort rates that are increasing around 0.7% for every 30 clients added. 2PC/Paxos abort rate increases significantly for 258 clients to have 15.8% aborts, while Replicated Commit experiences close to 20% aborts for 258 clients.

5.4 Synchronization and estimation errors

Synchronization. The performance of the Helios protocols relies heavily on the level of synchronization. Using the readily available NTP clients provided by Ubuntu for the previous experiments shows that the available synchronization tools enable Helios to achieve good performance. However, we would like to get an insight on Helios performance with more hostile environments with clocks that are not synchronized. Now we will show results from a set of experiments while changing the clock readings of machines to emulate a lack of synchronization. In these experiments Helios-0 is used. The results are shown in the leftmost four groups of results in Figure 5(a). In the figure we display

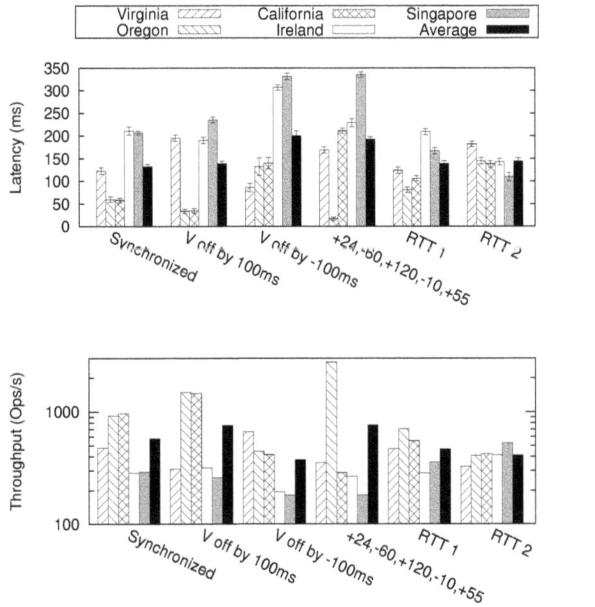

Figure 5: The effect of the lack of synchronization on the performance of Helios-0 in the leftmost four groups of results and the effect of erroneous RTT estimation in the rightmost two groups of results.

three experiments and compare them with the results from a synchronized run using NTP. The first non-synchronized scenario is to set the clock at Virginia ahead of the others by 100ms. Note how this resulted in its commit latency to increase by 62ms. Other datacenters commit latencies improved except for Singapore. This improvement is caused by setting Virginia's clock ahead in time, it puts it in a disadvantage compared to other datacenters which leads to a better commit latency for others. The second scenario has Virginia's clock 100ms behind other clocks. This change puts Virginia in an advantage that is shown by a decrease in commit latency of 37ms. However, other datacenters consequently achieve a higher commit latency and cause an increase in the average commit latency by 64ms compared to the synchronized case. In the final scenario we introduce random errors to all datacenters. The errors are presented by a sequence of numbers denoting the shift in time for the ordered set of datacenters in milliseconds: V, O, C, I, and S. Consider the case {+24,-60,+120,-10,+55}. We find that for this case the average commit latency is 60ms higher than the synchronized case. However, for some individual datacenters, this caused a significant improvement of the commit latency; California, for example, achieves a commit latency 23ms lower than California in the synchronized case.

The results demonstrate that small to medium clock skews introduce tolerable increases in the average commit latency of up to 64ms for the scenarios we considered. These increases are correlated with the level of synchronization.

RTT estimation errors. A vital part of Helios is the assignment of optimal commit latencies to datacenters. However, deriving these values requires estimating the RTT between datacenters. RTTs can be variable and change occasionally. Thus, the calculated assigned commit latencies suffer from the potential of being inaccurate. Here we perform tests to quantify the effect of non-accurate estimations of the RTT on the commit latency of Helios. Helios-0 will also be used for these experiments. We will experiment with two cases where high margins of error are introduced to our RTT estimations. The results are shown in Figure 5(a) labeled RTT estimation 1 and 2. The first RTT estimation is calculated by introducing an error to the correct estimates by increasing one fifth of the RTTs by 25ms, another fifth by 75ms, decrease a fifth of RTTs by 25ms, and decrease yet another fifth by 75ms, and the remaining RTTs are not changed. This scenario leads to the average latency being 4.5% higher that the one achieved by the original estimate. The second RTT estimate is of an erroneous estimation of no latency between datacenters. This will lead to assigning all datacenters a commit latency of 0. With this input, Helios-0 observes the following commit latencies for V, O, C, I, and S: 182ms, 145ms, 138ms, 143ms, 110ms, averaging to 144ms. This average is 9% higher than the average commit latency achieved by the original estimate.

These results illustrate that even with highly erroneous RTT estimations, Helios-0 observes a slight increase in the achieved commit latencies by 4.5% and 9% for the introduced errors. Helios shows the same stability observed in previous experiments where standard deviation values are less than 10.

Throughput. When errors are introduced to clock synchronization and RTT estimation, the commit latency is affected for different datacenters. Some datacenters have their commit latency increase while for others their commit latency decrease. The commit latency of a datacenter is a major factor of the observed throughput. Thus, we expect different datacenter throughputs to be affected in correlation with the commit latency. We present the achieved throughput results in Figure 5(b). For the scenario when Virginia's clock is 100ms ahead of others, notice how the throughput of Oregon and California increase as a result of the decrease in their commit latency. Likewise, the throughput of Virginia decreases in correlation to the commit latency's increase. This effect is observed throughout the set of experiments. However, an interesting observation is that for some scenarios, this leads to the average throughput to become larger than the synchronized case. For the *+24,-60,+120,-10,+55* case, for example, throughput is 31% higher than the synchronized case. This is even though the average commit latency of *+24,-60,+120,-10,+55* is higher than the original case. The increase in throughput is due to the extremely low resulting latency of Oregon allowing it to achieve a throughput of 2764 operations/s that caused the average throughput to exceed that of the synchronized case. We provide more discussion on this trade-off in Section A.2.

6. CONCLUSION

In this paper we have formulated a lower-bound on commit latency of transactions running on replicated data stores. We also designed an optimistic commit protocol, called Helios, using insights from the lower-bound. Helios allows tunable performance for individual datacenters. In the paper we demonstrate tuning Helios to minimize the average commit latency. Helios separates consistency from liveness guarantees. This allows the flexibility of setting the number of tolerated datacenter outages. Helios is compared experimentally to three systems: Replicated Commit, Message Futures, and 2PC/Paxos.

7. ACKNOWLEDGEMENTS

This work is supported by NSF grant IIS 1018637 and is partially funded by a gift grant from NEC Labs America. Faisal Nawab is partially funded by a scholarship from King Fahd University of Petroleum and Minerals. We would also like to thank Amaozn for access to Amazon EC2.

8. REFERENCES

[1] Summary of the Amazon EC2 and Amazon RDS service disruption in the US East Region. `http://aws.amazon.com/message/65648/`, 2011. [Online; acc. 5-Oct-2011].

[2] Summary of the December 24, 2012 Amazon ELB Service Event in the US-East Region. `http://aws.amazon.com/message/680587/`, 2012. [Online; acc. 10-May-2013].

[3] A. Adya, R. Gruber, B. Liskov, and U. Maheshwari. Efficient optimistic concurrency control using loosely synchronized clocks. *ACM SIGMOD Record*, 24(2):23–34, 1995.

[4] A. Adya and B. Liskov. Lazy consistency using loosely synchronized clocks. In *Proceedings of the sixteenth annual ACM symposium on Principles of distributed computing*, pages 73–82. ACM, 1997.

[5] Apache Cassandra, 2011. [Online; acc. 5-Oct-2011].

[6] P. Bailis, A. Fekete, M. J. Franklin, A. Ghodsi, J. M. Hellerstein, and I. Stoica. Coordination avoidance in database systems. *Proceedings of the VLDB Endowment*, 8(3), 2014.

[7] P. Bailis and A. Ghodsi. Eventual Consistency today: Limitations, extensions, and beyond. *ACM Queue*, 11(3):20:20–20:32, Mar. 2013.

[8] P. Bailis, A. Ghodsi, J. M. Hellerstein, and I. Stoica. Bolt-on causal consistency. In *SIGMOD*, 2013.

[9] J. Baker, C. Bond, J. Corbett, J. Furman, A. Khorlin, J. Larson, J.-M. Leon, Y. Li, A. Lloyd, and V. Yushprakh. Megastore: Providing scalable, highly available storage for interactive services. In *Conf. Innovative Data Systems Research*, pages 223–234, 2011.

[10] N. M. Belaramani, M. Dahlin, L. Gao, A. Nayate, A. Venkataramani, P. Yalagandula, and J. Zheng. Practi replication. In *NSDI*, volume 6, pages 5–5, 2006.

[11] H. Berenson, P. Bernstein, J. Gray, J. Melton, E. O'Neil, and P. O'Neil. A critique of ansi sql isolation levels. *ACM SIGMOD Record*, 24(2):1–10, 1995.

[12] P. Bernstein, C. Reid, and S. Das. Hyder-a transactional record manager for shared flash. In *Proc. of CIDR*, pages 9–20, 2011.

[13] P. A. Bernstein, V. Hadzilacos, and N. Goodman. *Concurrency Control and Recovery in Database Systems*. Addison-Wesley, 1987.

[14] B. Cooper, A. Silberstein, E. Tam, R. Ramakrishnan, and R. Sears. Benchmarking cloud serving systems with ycsb. In *Proc. 1st ACM Symp. Cloud Computing*, pages 143–154. ACM, 2010.

[15] B. F. Cooper, R. Ramakrishnan, U. Srivastava, A. Silberstein, P. Bohannon, H.-A. Jacobsen, N. Puz, D. Weaver, and R. Yerneni. Pnuts: Yahoo!'s hosted data serving platform. *Proc. VLDB Endow.*, 1(2):1277–1288, Aug. 2008.

[16] J. Corbett, J. Dean, M. Epstein, A. Fikes, C. Frost, J. Furman, S. Ghemawat, A. Gubarev, C. Heiser, P. Hochschild, et al. Spanner: Google's globally-distributed database. *in Proceedings of OSDI*, page 1, 2012.

[17] S. Das, S. Nishimura, D. Agrawal, and A. El Abbadi. Albatross: lightweight elasticity in shared storage databases for the cloud using live data migration. *Proc. VLDB Endowment*, 4(8):494–505, 2011.

[18] K. Daudjee and K. Salem. Lazy database replication with snapshot isolation. In *Proceedings of the 32nd international conference on Very large data bases*, pages 715–726. VLDB Endowment, 2006.

[19] G. DeCandia, D. Hastorun, M. Jampani, G. Kakulapati, A. Lakshman, A. Pilchin, S. Sivasubramanian, P. Vosshall, and W. Vogels. Dynamo: Amazon's highly available key-value store. In *Proc. 21st ACM Symp. Operating Systems Principles*, pages 205–220, 2007.

[20] J. Du, S. Elnikety, A. Roy, and W. Zwaenepoel. Orbe: scalable causal consistency using dependency matrices and physical clocks. In *Proceedings of the 4th annual Symposium on Cloud Computing*, page 11. ACM, 2013.

[21] J. Du, S. Elnikety, and W. Zwaenepoel. Clock-si: Snapshot isolation for partitioned data stores using loosely synchronized clocks. In *Reliable Distributed Systems (SRDS), 2013 IEEE 32nd International Symposium on*, pages 173–184. IEEE, 2013.

[22] J. Du, C. Iorgulescu, A. Roy, and W. Zwaenepoel. Gentlerain: Cheap and scalable causal consistency with physical clocks. In *Proceedings of the ACM Symposium on Cloud Computing*, pages 1–13. ACM, 2014.

[23] L. Glendenning, I. Beschastnikh, A. Krishnamurthy, and T. Anderson. Scalable consistency in scatter. In *Proceedings of the Twenty-Third ACM Symposium on Operating Systems Principles*, SOSP '11, pages 15–28, New York, NY, USA, 2011. ACM.

[24] L. Glendenning, I. Beschastnikh, A. Krishnamurthy, and T. Anderson. Scalable consistency in scatter. In *Proceedings of the Twenty-Third ACM Symposium on Operating Systems Principles*, pages 15–28. ACM, 2011.

[25] HBase. `http://hbase.apache.org`, 2011. [Online; acc. 18-Jul-2011].

[26] B. Kemme, R. Jimenez-Peris, and M. Patino-Martinez. Database replication. *Synthesis Lectures on Data Management*, 2(1):1–153, 2010.

[27] T. Kraska, G. Pang, M. J. Franklin, S. Madden, and A. Fekete. Mdcc: Multi-data center consistency. In *Proceedings of the 8th ACM European Conference on Computer Systems*, pages 113–126. ACM, 2013.

[28] R. Ladin, B. Liskov, L. Shrira, and S. Ghemawat. Providing high availability using lazy replication. *ACM Transactions on Computer Systems (TOCS)*, 10(4):360–391, 1992.

[29] L. Lamport. Time, clocks, and the ordering of events in a distributed system. *Commun. ACM*, 21(7):558–565, July 1978.

[30] L. Lamport. The part-time parliament. *ACM Trans. Computer Systems*, 16(2):133–169, May 1998.

[31] L. Lamport. Paxos made simple. *ACM SIGACT News*, 32(4):18–25, December 2001.

[32] L. Lamport. Fast paxos. *Distributed Computing*, 19(2):79–103, 2006.

[33] Y. Lin, B. Kemme, M. Patiño-Martínez, and R. Jiménez-Peris. Middleware based data replication providing snapshot isolation. In *Proceedings of the 2005 ACM SIGMOD international conference on Management of data*, pages 419–430. ACM, 2005.

[34] Y. Lin, B. Kemme, M. Patino-Martinez, and R. Jimenez-Peris. Enhancing edge computing with database replication. In *Reliable Distributed Systems, 2007. SRDS 2007. 26th IEEE International Symposium on*, pages 45–54. IEEE, 2007.

[35] B. Liskov. Practical uses of synchronized clocks in distributed systems. *Distributed Computing*, 6(4):211–219, 1993.

[36] W. Lloyd, M. J. Freedman, M. Kaminsky, and D. G. Andersen. Don't settle for eventual: scalable causal consistency for wide-area storage with cops. In *Proceedings of the Twenty-Third ACM Symposium on Operating Systems Principles*, pages 401–416. ACM, 2011.

[37] W. Lloyd, M. J. Freedman, M. Kaminsky, and D. G. Andersen. Stronger semantics for low-latency geo-replicated storage. In *Symposium on Networked Systems Design and Implementation*, 2013.

[38] H. Mahmoud, F. Nawab, A. Pucher, D. Agrawal, and A. El Abbadi. Low-latency multi-datacenter databases using replicated commits. *Proceedings of the VLDB Endowment*, 6(9), 2013.

[39] R. Miller. Massive Flooding Damages Several NYC Data Centers. `http://www.datacenterknowledge.com/archives/2012/10/30/major-flooding-nyc-data-centers/`, 10 2012. [Online; acc. 10-May-2013].

[40] F. Nawab, D. Agrawal, and A. El Abbadi. Message futures: Fast commitment of transactions in multi-datacenter environments. In *Conf. Innovative Data Systems Research*, 2013.

[41] F. Nawab, V. Arora, D. Agrawal, and A. E. Abbadi. Chariots : A scalable shared log for data management in multi-datacenter cloud environments. In *EDBT*, 2015.

[42] D. Obasanjo. When databases lie: Consistency vs. availability in distributed systems, 2009.

[43] D. Ongaro, S. M. Rumble, R. Stutsman, J. Ousterhout, and M. Rosenblum. Fast crash recovery in ramcloud. In *Proceedings of the Twenty-Third ACM Symposium on Operating Systems Principles*, pages 29–41. ACM, 2011.

[44] S. Patterson, A. J. Elmore, F. Nawab, D. Agrawal, and A. E. Abbadi. Serializability, not serial: Concurrency control and availability in multi-datacenter datastores. *PVLDB*, 5(11):1459–1470, 2012.

[45] K. Petersen, M. J. Spreitzer, D. B. Terry, M. M. Theimer, and A. J. Demers. *Flexible update propagation for weakly consistent replication*, volume 31. ACM, 1997.

[46] E. Schurman and J. Brutlag. Performance related changes and their user impact. In *velocity web performance and operations conference*, 2009.

[47] Y. Sovran, R. Power, M. K. Aguilera, and J. Li. Transactional storage for geo-replicated systems. In *Proceedings of the Twenty-Third ACM Symposium on Operating Systems Principles*, pages 385–400. ACM, 2011.

[48] D. B. Terry, V. Prabhakaran, R. Kotla, M. Balakrishnan, M. K. Aguilera, and H. Abu-Libdeh. Consistency-based service level agreements for cloud storage. In *Proceedings of the Twenty-Fourth ACM Symposium on Operating Systems Principles*, pages 309–324. ACM, 2013.

[49] D. B. Terry, M. M. Theimer, K. Petersen, A. J. Demers, M. J. Spreitzer, and C. H. Hauser. *Managing update conflicts in Bayou, a weakly connected replicated storage system*, volume 29. ACM, 1995.

[50] A. Thomson, T. Diamond, S.-C. Weng, K. Ren, P. Shao, and D. J. Abadi. Calvin: fast distributed transactions for partitioned database systems. In *Proceedings of the 2012 international conference on Management of Data*, pages 1–12. ACM, 2012.

[51] H. T. Vo, S. Wang, D. Agrawal, G. Chen, and B. C. Ooi. Logbase: a scalable log-structured database system in the cloud. *Proceedings of the VLDB Endowment*, 5(10):1004–1015, 2012.

[52] Z. Wu, M. Butkiewicz, D. Perkins, E. Katz-Bassett, and H. V. Madhyastha. Spanstore: cost-effective geo-replicated storage spanning multiple cloud services. In *Proceedings of the Twenty-Fourth ACM Symposium on Operating Systems Principles*, pages 292–308. ACM, 2013.

[53] G. T. Wuu and A. J. Bernstein. Efficient solutions to the replicated log and dictionary problems. In *Proceedings of the third annual ACM symposium on Principles of distributed computing*, PODC '84, pages 233–242, New York, NY, USA, 1984. ACM.

[54] Y. Zhang, R. Power, S. Zhou, Y. Sovran, M. K. Aguilera, and J. Li. Transaction chains: achieving serializability with low latency in geo-distributed storage systems. In *Proceedings of the Twenty-Fourth ACM Symposium on Operating Systems Principles*, pages 276–291. ACM, 2013.

APPENDIX

A. ANALYSIS AND TRADE-OFFS

In this section, we provide an analysis of the factors affecting the commit latency and the trade-off between commit latency on one hand and liveness or throughput on the other hand.

A.1 Commit latency analysis

This analysis shows how loose synchronization, communication links and compute variability affect the observable commit latency of Helios. We assume that Helios is assigned the *correct* commit offsets, which would lead to the exact lower-bound commit latency in perfect conditions.

Synchronization. Helios does not require clock synchronization for its correctness. However, the degree of synchronization affects the achieved commit latency. In particular, a low level of synchronization or the lack of synchronization will lead to degraded performance. Better clock synchronization will lead to commit latency values that are

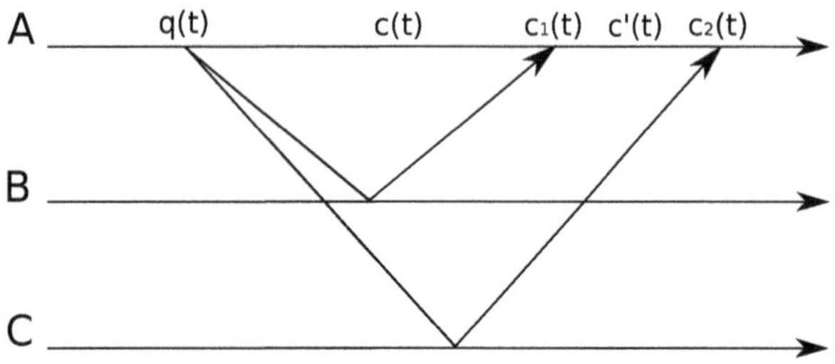

Figure 6: A transaction t executing at A demonstrating the trade-off between liveness and commit latency

closer to the optimal. Recall that the commit condition in Rule 2 states that a transaction must wait for every datacenter to send a message with a timestamp calculated by using the commit offsets. Using this protocol will result in the transaction committing with the commit latency estimated in Equation 4. However, with a clock skew between datacenters, the observed commit latency will be affected. Clock skew between two datacenters, A and B, will cause one of them to receive the expected message later than intended and the other will receive it earlier than intended. Thus, the actual time that a datacenter A waits until it receives the expected message from B for a transaction t is $L_A + \theta(A, B)$, where $\theta(A, B)$ is the time difference between A and B. $\theta(A, B)$ has a positive value if A's clock is ahead of B's clock. It is possible that A receives the message prior to requesting the commit; this is the case when $\theta < -L_A$. With the presence of clock skew the actual observed commit latency at A, $\bar{L_A}$, is given by

$$\bar{L_A} = L_A + Max_{B \in R}\{\theta(A, B)\} \tag{6}$$

RTT estimate accuracy. RTT estimation also plays a role in determining the achieved commit latency. To analyze the effect of RTT estimation errors, assume that the difference between the real RTT and the estimated RTT for A and B is given by $\rho_{A,B}$, a positive value if the real RTT is larger than the estimate. For a transaction waiting for a log of events (history) from other datacenters with a certain time, the one way latency is affected by a magnitude equal to half the error in the estimation. Thus, the average achieved latency when the effect of the propagation rate and RTT estimation error are factored becomes

$$\bar{L_A} = L_A + Max_{B \in R}\{\theta(A, B) + \frac{\rho_{A,B}}{2}\} \tag{7}$$

Communication link variability. The observable commit latency of individual transactions differ due to the variability of the communication latency. Thus, the RTT between two datacenters is best represented as a statistical random variable. In this case, Equation 7 will observe $\rho_{A,B}$, the error in RTT estimation, as a random variable, $\varrho_{A,B}$, rather than a fixed value, which means that $\bar{L_A}$ is also itself best represented as a random variable.

Compute overhead. The overhead of processing the log and requests in addition to various I/O and interface overheads increase the observed latency. For brevity we call the cumulative effect of all of these overheads, *compute overhead.* Measuring the compute overhead is intractable. However, it effects the observable commit latency in two ways: First, it is the overhead factors of the host of the transaction that we are observing. This can be accounted for in our expression by a random variable, call it $\boldsymbol{C}_{local}$, that affects the observable commit latency directly. Second, it determines the overhead factors that are taking place at other datacenters. These are observed in the commit latency of a transaction as a delay in receiving the needed information. This delay is represented with $\boldsymbol{C}^B_{remote}$, where B is the remote datacenter experiencing the overhead. This will make the observable commit latency be

$$\bar{L_A} = L_A + \boldsymbol{C}^A_{local} + Max_{B \in R}\{\theta(A, B) + \frac{\rho_{A,B}}{2} + \boldsymbol{C}^B_{remote}\} \tag{8}$$

Bounding observable commit latency. The observable commit latency depends on random variables that are unbounded. This results in the possibility of observing commit latencies that ranges from 0 to an infinitely large number, regardless of the assigned commit latency. Although Equation 8 can help us learn the distribution of observable commit latency values, it does not enable us to place an upper-bound or a lower-bound greater than zero on an individual transaction's commit latency. However, since it is a random variable, it will allow us to calculate a probability that a transaction's latency is greater than or equal to a certain value. This, indeed, remains an arduous task, since estimating the compute overhead and link variability random variables is still an area of research.

A.2 Trade-off with liveness and throughput

Liveness trade-off. There is a trade-off between the observable commit latency and liveness. As the number of tolerated datacenter failures increases, the commit latency is likely to increase as well. To illustrate this consider the scenario in Figure 6. A transaction t at A is trying to commit in a scenario with three datacenters. It requests to commit at time $q(t)$. Assume that there are no conflicts and that the knowledge required to commit t is accumulated by time $c(t)$. This means that if we did not want to tolerate failures, and thus use Helios-0, t is able to commit at time $c(t)$. However, if we want to tolerate a single datacenter failure and use Helios-1, t would need to wait until the record of the transaction is acknowledged by another datacenter, which happens to be at time $c_1(t)$. This means that the cost of increasing the level of liveness on t was increasing its commit latency by $(c_1(t) - c(t))$. Likewise, if two datacenter outages are to be tolerated, transaction t commits at time $c_2(t)$ causing an additional penalty on commit latency.

It is not always the case that increasing the number of tolerated datacenter failures will lead to an increase in commit latency. It is possible that the commit latency will remain the same. In Figure 6 assume that transaction t receives the sufficient information necessary to commit it at time $c'(t)$. Thus, Helios-0, without tolerating any failures, will commit t at time $c'(t)$. Now, Helios-1, tolerating a single datacenter failure will still commit t at time $c'(t)$. This is because t is already acknowledged by B at time $c'(t)$.

Throughput trade-off. In the paper we have focused on minimizing the average commit latency. However, there is an interesting trade-off between average commit latency and throughput. Assigning the optimal commit latency values to Helios will not necessarily result in the best overall throughput. Consider the topology and latency assignment in Table 1 of three datacenters with the following RTTs: $RTT(A, B) = 30$, $RTT(A, C) = 20$, and $RTT(B, C) = 40$. The optimal commit latency assignment to minimize the average commit latency is 5 for A, 25 for B, and 15 for C.

Assume that there are no aborts and that transactions complete in exactly the duration of the commit latency. Also, assume that the commit latency values are in ms. For N clients per datacenter, the cumulative throughput when the optimal commit latencies are assigned is: $1000 * N * (\frac{1}{5} + \frac{1}{25} + \frac{1}{15})$, which is $(N * 306.66)$ transactions per second. However, another correct assignment which is 1 for A, 29 for B, and 19 for C results in a cumulative throughput of $(N * 1087.11)$ transactions per second, which is larger than the throughput achieved by the optimal commit latency assignment.

Optimizing for higher throughput can be performed by utilizing the linear programming method in Section 3.3. The minimization condition can be changed to be a maximization condition to optimize for the sum of the rate of execution (inverse of commit latency) to be: $\sum_{A \in R} \frac{1}{L_A + c}$, where c is a constant value estimating the execution overhead of a transaction. Introducing c is necessary because otherwise the linear program would assign one of the datacenters a commit latency of 0, which erroneously yields an infinite throughput in the optimization problem. However, in a realistic environment execution takes time and therefore must be accounted for in this case.

More details can be introduced for this optimization to make it more accurate, hence higher throughput. One important factor is contention and the possibility of aborts. The maximization above assumes that all running transactions will commit successfully. However, it is likely that some transactions can abort, and a commit latency assignment that maximizes the expression above for throughput might lead to more contention than other assignments, one of which might have a higher throughput of *committed* transactions.

B. READ-ONLY TRANSACTIONS

Read-only transactions in Helios do not contend with other read-write transactions and are performed at the local datacenter. When a Helios instance receives a read-only transaction it chooses a log position to serve as the *snapshot point*. Thus, the read-only transaction will read the state of the data store as of the snapshot point. Every read request, r, will read the data object version that is written by a transaction t, where t is the most recent transaction that writes the data object, r, prior to the snapshot point. This approach is proposed by various log-structured systems such as Hyder [12] and LogBase [51] and is similar to read-only transactions in multi-version databases.

Optimizing Optimistic Concurrency Control for Tree-Structured, Log-Structured Databases

Philip A. Bernstein
Microsoft Research
philbe@microsoft.com

Sudipto Das
Microsoft Research
sudiptod@microsoft.com

Bailu Ding†
Cornell University
blding@cs.cornell.edu

Markus Pilman†
ETH Zurich
mpilman@inf.ethz.ch

ABSTRACT

Scaling-out a database system typically requires partitioning the database across multiple servers. If applications do not partition perfectly, then transactions accessing multiple partitions end up being distributed, which has well-known scalability challenges. To address them, we describe a high-performance transaction mechanism that uses optimistic concurrency control on a multi-versioned tree-structured database stored in a shared log. The system scales out by adding servers, without partitioning the database.

Our solution is modeled on the Hyder architecture, published by Bernstein, Reid, and Das at CIDR 2011. We present the design and evaluation of the first full implementation of that architecture. The core of the system is a log roll-forward algorithm, called meld, that does optimistic concurrency control. Meld is inherently sequential and is therefore the main bottleneck. Our main algorithmic contributions are optimizations to meld that significantly increase transaction throughput. They use a pipelined design that parallelizes meld onto multiple threads. The slowest pipeline stage is much faster than the original meld algorithm, yielding a 3x improvement of system throughput over the original meld algorithm.

Categories and Subject Descriptors

H.2.4 [Database Management]: Systems—*Concurrency, Distributed databases, Transaction processing*

General Terms

Algorithms, Design, Experimentation, Performance

Keywords

Scale-out transaction processing; optimistic concurrency control.

1. INTRODUCTION

Most approaches to scaling out a distributed transaction processing system beyond a few servers require some degree of database partitioning. However, not all databases are partitionable such that most transactions refer to only one partition. For example, if there is a frequently-accessed many-to-many relationship that is equally likely to be traversed in both directions, then no partitioning of the relationship instances will ensure that most transactions are single-partition. A good example is a friend-status relation of users in a social network application. If the relation is partitioned by user, then each user U's status must appear in the partition of all of U's friends. Therefore, when U's status changes, it must be updated in many partitions (unless U has at most one friend).

Recently a technique that scales out without partitioning the database was introduced in a system called Hyder. It uses a network-attached log as the database, which is accessible by all servers [7]. The only point of arbitration between servers is when they append records to the totally-ordered log that they share. That is why the system can scale out without partitioning.

In this technique, the database is organized as a tree-structured index. Each server executes each transaction against a locally-cached partial-copy of its latest database snapshot (Figure 1, step (1)). The snapshot is defined by a log position *S* and hence is immutable. It is the state produced by all transactions up to *S* that committed.

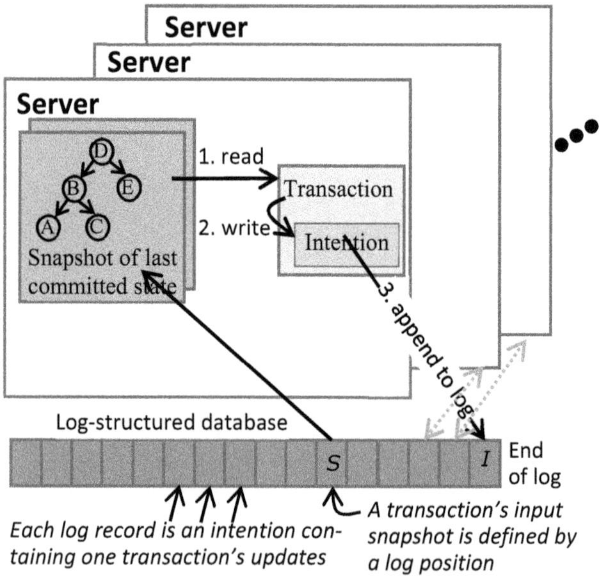

Figure 1: System architecture

Each transaction *T* executes optimistically with no synchronization. While *T* executes, it accumulates its updates in an **intention record** (Figure 1, step (2)). Conceptually, the intention contains new versions of the data that *T* updated and a logical pointer to a log position that defines the database snapshot that *T* read. Physically, an intention is quite different than this and is described later.

† Work performed while employed at Microsoft Research.

SIGMOD'15, May 31–June 4, 2015, Melbourne, Victoria, Australia.
Copyright 2015 ACM 978-1-4503-2758-9/15/05…$15.00
http://dx.doi.org/10.1145/2723372.2737788

When T finishes executing, the system appends T's intention to the log (Figure 1, step (3)). In general, other transactions' intentions are appended to the log while T was executing. Therefore, there are usually many intentions in the log that follow the position of T's snapshot S and precede T's intention I, as shown in Figure 1.

Every server runs an algorithm called **meld** that rolls forward the log against the latest version of its locally-cached copy of the database. Meld analyzes each intention for conflicts using an optimistic concurrency control algorithm. If the intention did not experience a conflict (with respect to a given isolation level), then the transaction commits and meld merges the updated values in the intention into the server's locally-cached database. If the intention did experience a conflict, then it is discarded and has no effect.

The complete persistent database is in the log. The database at each server is only a partial cached copy. All servers have data that was updated by recently executed transactions, since that data was needed by meld. But different servers also have different data, if they read data that is not needed for conflict detection at weak isolation levels and hence is not logged. That data comes from executing read-only, read-committed, or snapshot-isolated transactions.

If a transaction accesses data not in its server's cache, then the server must do a random access to the log to get the data. Therefore, for good performance, the log should be stored on solid state disks.

To avoid synchronization between servers, meld is designed to be deterministic. All servers execute the same meld algorithm. Since the log is shared by all servers, they execute meld on the same sequence of intentions. Thus, for every intention they all make the same commit or abort decision, and they apply the committed intentions to their cached database copies in the same order. In effect, the system operates as a replicated database where each server has a cached subset of the database.

A natural implementation of meld processes intentions sequentially in log order, as in [8]. Since meld is sequential and the sequential processing speed of today's processors is not increasing very fast, meld is obviously a potential bottleneck. Other potential bottlenecks are the rate at which the log can be written and read, the network that connects servers to the log, and the abort rate due to conflicts between transactions. However, in our system, which uses a state-of-the-art network and servers, meld has been the bottleneck that limits transaction throughput.

Since queries execute against snapshots, they are not logged or melded. Hence, they scale out linearly until the log's read bandwidth or the network bandwidth is saturated.

One goal of this paper is to speed up meld. One approach is to speed up the sequential meld algorithm that analyzes intentions one-by-one to detect conflicts. However, the meld algorithm described in [8] is already heavily optimized, and we have been unable to improve it. If speed-ups are possible, we predict they will be small.

The second approach is to parallelize meld, which is the main subject of this paper. We do it by using other threads to preprocess intentions in ways that reduce the amount of work required by meld. The speed of that **final meld** step is what ultimately determines transaction throughput.

There are three preprocessing steps. The first is **deserialization**, which transforms each intention from its log format into an object structure. The original meld algorithm in [8] used several deserialization threads to reduce meld's execution time by up to 45%.

In this paper, we introduce two new preprocessing steps that execute after deserialization and before final meld. Each step executes on a deserialized intention I that final meld has not yet processed. The speed of meld is largely determined by the size of each intention and the fraction of each intention that meld has to process. Group meld reduces the former and premeld reduces the latter.

The first optimization, called **premeld**, does a trial meld of I that looks for conflicts with committed transactions in the part of the log that the final meld processing step has already processed. It also "refreshes" I by replacing stale data in I by committed updates from that earlier part of the log. This reduces the fraction of I that the final meld step has to process.

The second optimization, called **group meld**, combines adjacent intentions. As we will see, intentions usually have overlapping information, which collapses into one copy in the grouped intention. This speeds up final meld, which has to process that overlapping information only once instead of twice.

Implementing premeld and group meld presents two technical challenges. First, since every server runs premeld and group meld, they both need to be deterministic. Otherwise, different servers will end up in different database states, leading to database corruption. Second, since the meld algorithm is quite complicated, it is important to factor out meld's core behavior that can be used in premeld, group meld, and final meld, to ensure that all three algorithms have consistent semantics. We were able to accomplish this with a relatively small number of modifications of the original meld algorithm. The resulting algorithm can be abstracted as a generic operator, which could be used in other contexts.

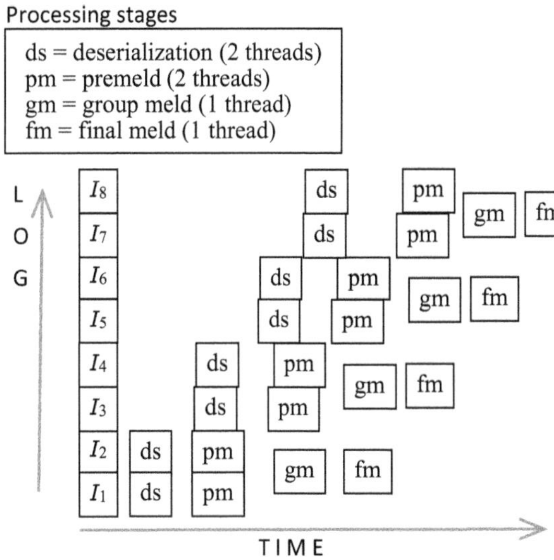

Figure 2: Pipeline parallelism of meld using four stages

In essence, our use of three preprocessing steps is a pipeline parallelism strategy (see Figure 2). We split the meld task for each intention into a pipeline of preprocessing stages (labelled ds, pm and gm), followed by final meld processing (labelled fm). The earlier stages execute in parallel with final meld processing, on intentions that the final meld step has not yet reached. For example, in Figure 2, in the first time unit, we see two parallel threads executing the deserialization (ds) stage on log entries I_1 and I_2. In the second time unit, two parallel threads execute the premeld (pm) stage on I_1 and I_2, and two parallel threads execute the ds stage on log entries I_3 and I_4. Next, we see two parallel threads execute ds on log entries

I_5 and I_6, two threads execute pm on I_3 and I_4, and one thread executes group meld (gm) on the combination of I_1 and I_2.

To show the benefit of these optimizations, we developed **Hyder II**, a distributed implementation of this architecture on a shared network-attached log. The performance measurements reported in this paper are the first ones for a complete end-to-end implementation of meld on a cluster of machines connected to a shared persistent log. By contrast, the implementation described in [8] was entirely in main memory on one server, and the one in [7] was a simulation. Moreover, our implementation uses a log based on solid-state disks (SSDs) [4], rather than the custom hardware proposed in [7].

In our experiments, five premeld threads give a 3x throughput improvement, and one group meld thread gives a 1.6x improvement. We found little benefit in running both premeld and group meld, compared to running premeld alone. Therefore, although we exercised the complete pipeline shown in Figure 2, for the workloads we tried, if enough processor cores are available to run several premeld threads, then premeld should be used. Otherwise, group meld can give a significant speedup with only one core.

In summary the main contributions of this paper are the following:

1. Two new optimizations for optimistic concurrency control validation of transactions on a multi-versioned tree-structured index and incorporating them into the meld algorithm.
2. A modified meld algorithm that can be reusable as an operator for premeld, group meld, and meld itself.
3. A comprehensive performance evaluation of meld in an end-to-end distributed implementation. We show the new optimizations give a 3x speedup over the best published meld technique. When executing a mix of 5% read-write and 95% read-only transactions with serializable isolation, Hyder II scales almost linearly, reaching peak throughput of 670K transactions per second (**tps**) for transactions with ten operations.

The paper is organized as follows. As background, Section 2 describes the basic meld algorithm. Sections 3 and 4 present our new optimizations. Section 5 describes our implementation, and Section 6 reports on experiments that evaluate its performance. Section 7 summarizes related work, and Section 8 is the conclusion. Three appendices expand on certain aspects of the meld algorithm.

2. MELD

The meld algorithm operates on a database organized as a tree-structured index, such as a binary search tree or B-tree. Since it operates on main memory structures and is serialized to a sequential log (rather than written out in fixed-size pages), a binary tree consumes less storage per record than a B-tree [7]. So we use binary trees in our examples and in our implementation. Each node has a key and value, i.e., a payload.

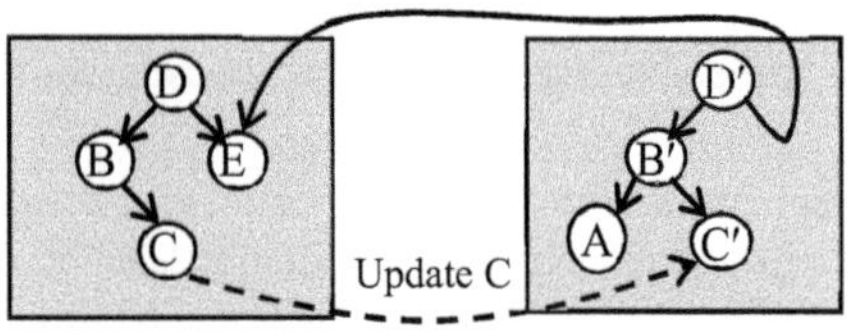

Figure 3: Inserting node A and updating node C

Since a transaction operates on an immutable database snapshot, updates must use **copy-on-write**. That is, an update must create a new version rather than modify data in place. For example, consider Figure 3. The left side shows a database snapshot. A transaction inserts a new node A and updates node C, resulting in an intention shown on the right. The update of C must create a new version C′, which requires updating B's pointer to C, which requires creating a new version B′, and so on up the tree.

Conceptually, the intention I for a transaction T contains T's updates. Physically, I defines the entire database state that T produced. That is, if T executed stand-alone on its input snapshot, then the resulting database state would be I. Given the use of copy-on-write, for every node n that T modified, I contains every node on a path from the root to n, including n itself. For example, in Figure 3 the transaction's updates are "insert A" and "update C". But its intention, in the right box, defines the state that the transaction produced, which includes B′ and D′.

If a transaction's isolation level is serializable, then its intention also contains the nodes in its readset. Such nodes are annotated to identify them as having been read but not written.

The meld algorithm operates on an intention I and the **last committed state** (or **LCS**), which is the database state produced by the last transaction that preceded I in the log and committed (e.g., in Figure 4, state S_1 produced by intention I_1). Its goal is to determine whether the transaction that generated I, T(I), experienced a conflict. If so, it discards I. If not, then T(I) commits so meld merges I's updated nodes into the last committed state. In effect, meld produces the intention that T(I) would have produced if it had executed against snapshot I_1 instead of I_0 (see Figure 4).

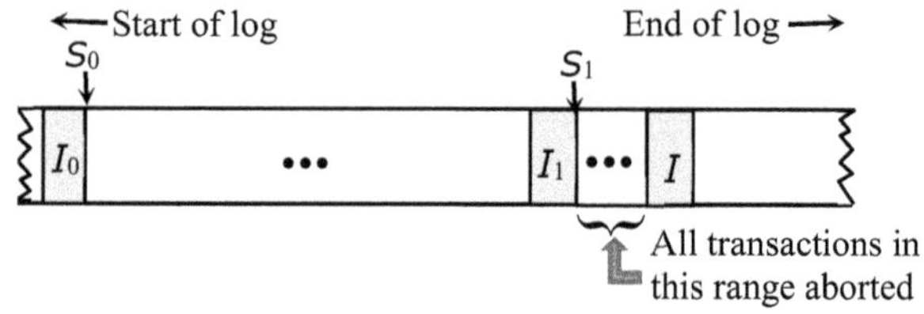

S_0 – state that intention I read (T(I)'s snapshot)
S_1 – last committed state to meld with I

Figure 4: Log positions relevant to meld

Every database state S includes metadata that tells how S relates to the previous database state, Prev(S), from which it was generated. For an intention I, the metadata tells how I relates to T(I)'s snapshot. For a state S produced by meld, it tells how S relates to meld's input state, e.g., S_1 in Figure 4.

The metadata is attached to each node n in a state S. Examples of that metadata are the following:

- A reference to the node n_{prev} in Prev(S) that has the same key as n (if n_{prev} exists).
- A flag indicating that n's payload differs from n_{prev}'s payload, e.g., because S is an intention and T(S) updated n.
- The identity of the first version of n that produced n's payload.
- If S is an intention, a flag indicating that T(S) read n.

With the exception of the flag that indicates T(S) read n, the metadata is redundant, in that it could be computed from the log. However, it would be quite expensive to do so, leading to an inefficient meld implementation. Part of the beauty of the meld algorithm is that it can compute this metadata incrementally and efficiently.

Meld uses this metadata to help it detect conflicts and merge its input intention and database state. Most details of how it does this are not important for understanding the optimizations in this paper. Still, to give the reader a sense of how conflicts are detected, we sketch a basic version of the meld algorithm in Appendix A.

There is one detail of the meld algorithm that is relevant to the optimizations in this paper, namely, the generation of **ephemeral nodes**. To understand ephemeral nodes and how they arise, suppose meld executes on state S and intention I, and determines that node n was updated by T(I) and was unchanged by any other transaction concurrent with T(I). This implies that the subtree under n in I was unchanged, since if it were then n would have changed too (as in Figure 3). Therefore, meld can simply replace n in S (denoted n_S) by n in I, which also replaces n_S's subtree by n's subtree. (This merging of subtrees is why the algorithm is called "meld.") If n_S is not the root of S (as is usually the case), then n_S's parent p must be replaced in S by a new node p', due to copy-on-write. Notice that p' is produced by meld, not by a transaction. Therefore p' is not written to an intention that is stored in the log—it only exists in main memory. In this sense, it is ephemeral. As in Figure 3, ephemeral nodes are generated for all of the ancestors of p' too.

An ephemeral node e might be read or overwritten by a later transaction T. T's intention will have a node with the same key as e and that node will refer to e. Since meld is deterministic and every server will meld T's intention, all servers must generate e with the same identity so that T's intention is interpreted the same way on every server. As we will see, this complicates premeld.

3. PREMELD

3.1 Premeld Overview

For a given intention I, the intentions in the log between I and the snapshot that T(I) read are called I's **conflict zone** (see Figure 5). The process of melding I with its input LCS involves combining I's updates with parts of the database that were updated by committed transactions in I's conflict zone. One way to parallelize meld is to use a parallel thread to do a preliminary meld of I with a state that is earlier than its input LCS, such as S_1 in Figure 5. This preliminary meld is called **premeld**. The LCS S_1 that it merges with I is called I's **premeld input** and the log region between I's snapshot and its premeld input is called I's **premeld conflict zone**.

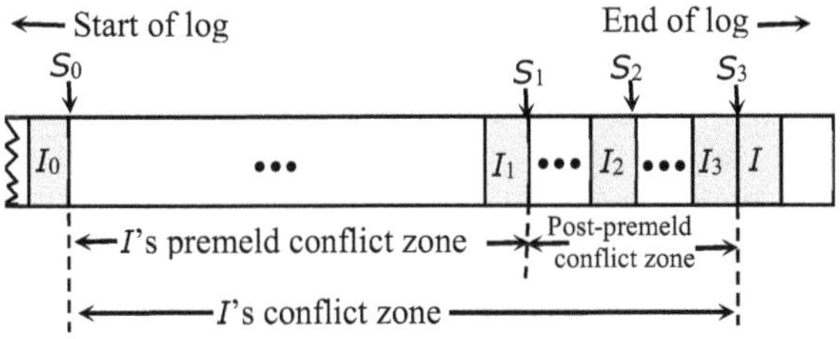

S_0 - state that intention I read (I's snapshot)
S_1 – state to minimeld with I (I's premeld input)
S_2 – state when I arrived at the meld log
S_3 – state to meld with I (I's input LCS)

Figure 5: Log Positions Relevant to Premeld

Premeld serves two purposes. First, it checks for conflicts in a prefix of I's conflict zone, that is, its premeld conflict zone. If it discovers a conflict, then final meld can skip processing I, since it knows that I will abort.

Second, if premeld finds no conflicts, then it produces an updated intention I_m that appears to have executed against I's premeld input. Later, final meld will meld I_m (instead of I) into I's input LCS. This requires less work than melding I, because there is less conflict checking to do. So the effect is to speed up final meld.

Surprisingly, the premeld algorithm is almost exactly the same as meld, but with different inputs. We will explain that later. First, let us look at why the optimization is effective and how it works.

3.2 Premeld Details

Meld's throughput is a function of the number of nodes it has to traverse. *This depends on the number of nodes in each intention I with descendants that were changed by committed transactions in I's conflict zone.*

For example, consider the states in Figure 6, which correspond to Figure 5. Intention I executed on snapshot S_0 and updated leaf E, producing E″. Since T(I) did not read or write node C, C is outside of I. While T(I) was executing, another transaction T_1 updated node C, producing C′. Since T_1's intention was appended to the log before I and it committed, its updated node C′ appears in I's input LCS. When melding I with its input LCS, an ephemeral node D^e is generated, which connects to C′ and E″. This generates a new ephemeral parent for D^e, and so on up the tree. If this were a tree with a million nodes, the root-to-leaf path would have 20 nodes, so 19 ephemeral nodes would be generated.

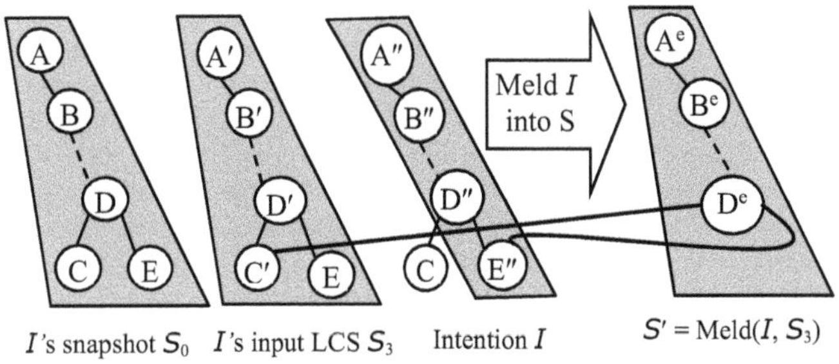

Figure 6: Detailed example of premeld

Suppose that node C was the left child of node A instead of the left child of node D. In this case, melding I with its input LCS would generate only one ephemeral node, namely A^e, connecting to C′ and B″. That is, it would graft I's subtree rooted at B″ into the LCS. Comparing these two cases, we see that in the first case 19 nodes in I had a descendant that changed in I's conflict zone, while in the second case, only one node (i.e., node A) in I has such a descendent.

Now, suppose that the state in Figure 6 that is labelled "I's input LCS S_3" is instead I's premeld input, that is, state S_1 in Figure 5. Since premeld performs the same computation as meld, its output is still S'. However, as we describe in the next section, S' is interpreted as an intention, not as an LCS, and substitutes for I as input to meld. So final meld will meld S' into the LCS, which is S_3.

To produce S', premeld paid the cost of generating the ephemeral nodes on the path from C′ to the root. When melding S' into S_3, that work will be repeated only for nodes on that path that have a descendant that is updated in the post-premeld conflict zone. That conflict zone is usually much smaller than I's original conflict zone, and hence is unlikely to have many updated descendants of nodes on that root-to-C′ path. Therefore, few if any nodes on that path will be traversed during final meld. Thus, as a result of I's premeld, which executed on a separate hardware thread in parallel with the final meld thread, the final meld of S', which substitutes for I, will be faster than if it had been had it executed on I's entire conflict zone. Since final meld is performed on a separate thread, the speedup of final meld increases overall transaction throughput.

Premeld is beneficial mostly because I's post-premeld conflict zone is much smaller than its premeld conflict zone. This ensures that most of the work of meld is done by premeld, rather than final meld. The post-premeld conflict zone size is governed by the distance in the log between I and its premeld input. By design, this is kept quite small. In our experiments, it is just a few hundred transactions. By contrast, when throughput is ~50K tps, the conflict zone is typically 10K-30K transactions, and the premeld conflict zone is just a few hundred less. Thus, we see a ratio of 100:1 between the sizes of premeld and post-premeld conflict zones.

We considered running premeld on an intention I immediately after T(I) terminated and before I was appended to the log. This would merge in updates applied by meld at T(I)'s server during T(I)'s execution. However, since a transaction executes in tens of microseconds, the benefit would be much smaller than running premeld after the log append, which takes milliseconds. Running premeld after the log append makes it useless to also run it before.

3.3 Meld Implements Premeld Semantics

We now explain why meld, with a small modification, implements the semantics required for premeld. It is based on two observations: (i) each transaction is represented as a pair of states, and (ii) the output of meld is a pair of states and hence is a transaction.

First, consider the representation of a transaction. In the database field, we normally think of a transaction either as a program or as a sequence of operations on shared data that is generated by an execution of a program. From a transaction processing standpoint, it is a little unusual to think of a transaction execution as a pair of states $<S_{in}, S_{out}>$. However, from a programming language standpoint, it is a natural representation. In our case, it is how a transaction's semantics is physically represented.

The execution of a transaction T generates an intention I, which represents the database state produced by T executing against its input snapshot. I includes the identity of the snapshot against which it executed. That identity is represented as metadata attached to each node in I. Taken together, that per-node metadata defines an input database state. Therefore, we can abstract its semantics as simply $<S_{in}, S_{out}>$, where S_{in} is its snapshot and S_{out} is its intention.

Second, to see why meld's output is a transaction, remember that its goal is to merge the updates of an intention I with I's input state S_{in}, producing an output state S_{out}. This is equivalent to saying that S_{out} is the result of running T(I) on S_{in}. In this sense, we can regard its output as a transaction $<S_{in}, S_{out}>$. In fact, its output is physically represented that way, since the metadata attached to each node of S_{out} describes how it relates to its previous version.

There is one omission in this explanation: readsets. Since meld's output is interpreted as a transaction that undergoes an optimistic concurrency control check, it is not enough to represent each transaction by a pair of states, $<S_{in}, S_{out}>$. It must also include its readset, to enable conflict detection for serializable isolation. An intention generated by executing a transaction includes this information. However, an intention generated by meld in [8] does not. This is correct in [8] because meld's result is interpreted only as a database state, not as a transaction. Thus, that output need not retain readset information for further optimistic concurrency control checks.

However, when we use meld to implement premeld, its output will be interpreted as a transaction that will be melded at least one more time by final meld. Therefore, it needs to include readset information. Since meld's output transaction represents the execution of the same program as the one that produced meld's input intention, the output transaction's readset should remain unchanged. Therefore, meld should copy the transaction's readset to its output. This requires changing only one line of the algorithm in [8]: When meld determines that a read-only subtree of an intention I is the same as the corresponding subtree L of the LCS, it should return I's subtree as the output, rather L's subtree, because I's subtree has the readset metadata while L's subtree does not. That is, line 7 of meld in Appendix C of [8] should read "*rtree* = *itree*; **return false**;" instead of "*rtree* = *lcstree*; **return false**;"

3.4 Determinism of Premeld

Meld runs independently on all servers that share the log, producing a sequence of database snapshots. We want the system to behave as if it has one shared database. Hence, all servers should generate an identical sequence of snapshots. Thus, meld must be deterministic.

It is not enough that the snapshots on different servers contain the same set of [key, payload] pairs. They must be physically identical. To see why, recall that the intention generated by each transaction may include ephemeral nodes. When the intention is melded, some of those ephemeral nodes may become part of the database. A later transaction T may refer to such an ephemeral node, e, in its intention. For example, T may have read e or updated a node whose root-to-leaf path refers to e. T's intention I will be broadcast to all servers. To meld that intention, other servers may need to follow I's reference to e. Therefore, the reference must point to the same node on all servers. This requires meld to produce physically identical trees with the same node identities on all servers.

To understand whether trees on all servers will use the same node identities, consider the two ways that a node identity can be generated. First, the node can be inserted by a transaction T and stored in T's intention. Since the intention is broadcast to all servers, the node has the same identity at all servers. Second, it can be an ephemeral node created by meld. Ephemeral node identities are allocated sequentially in the order they are generated. Therefore, ephemeral nodes must be generated in the same order on all servers to ensure they have the same identity on all servers. This property holds if meld is deterministic, such as the algorithm described in [8]. In this case meld will produce physically identical trees on all servers.

However, when premeld is used, ephemeral nodes might no longer be generated in the same order on all servers, for two reasons. First, for a given intention, premeld might execute against different database states on different servers. For example, suppose the log contains a sequence of intentions I_1, I_2, I_3, I_4. One server might run premeld for I_4 on the state produced by I_1, while another server runs premeld for I_4 on the state produced by I_2. These premeld executions might generate different sequences of ephemeral nodes. Thus, an ephemeral node with a given identity, e, might contain a different [key, value] pair at different servers. From then on, their servers' database states will diverge, which causes the system to malfunction. For example, an intention I that was generated at server S_x and that points to e will later arrive at another server S_y, where I will point to e, but the content of e is different at the two servers. A detailed example is in Appendix C.

To solve this problem, we ensure each server runs the same number of premeld threads, and each premeld thread executes on the same sequence of [intention, database state] pairs. We do this by means of index calculations. If there are t premeld threads, then each intention is assigned to the thread identified by its intention id modulo t. Each intention is premelded against the state created by the $(t \times d)^{th}$ intention that precedes it, where d is a fixed, global parameter, called the **premeld distance**. If that state precedes I's snapshot, then premeld does nothing. If that state is not yet available because final meld is slow, then the premeld thread waits until final meld creates the state. Note that the system must retain each state until the intention that premelds against it has executed.

The second reason that different ephemeral node identities might differ on different servers is that premeld executes in parallel with final meld. If these threads generate ephemeral nodes in different orders on different servers, then a node may have different identities on different servers. To avoid this, the final meld thread and each premeld thread generate thread-local sequence numbers. We use a two-part identity for each ephemeral node, consisting of the id of the thread that generated it plus the sequence number of the ephemeral node in that thread. Combined with the previous technique of premelding each intention to the same state at all servers, this ensures premeld generates the same ephemeral node identities at all servers. Premeld is shown in Algorithm 1 below.

Algorithm 1: PREMELD.

Input: Intention I_v at position v in the log; a sequence of database states corresponding to log positions: S_1 after I_1, S_2 after I_2, etc.; an integer premeld distance d; an integer number of threads t; and the most recent database state, S_r

Output: Abort, I_v, or the result of running meld on I_v and $S_{v-(t \times d)-1}$

```
m ← v – (t × d) – 1 // the database version to meld against
snap ← ReadVersion(I_v) // the snapshot on which T(I_v) executed
if snap ≥ m then
    return I_v // S_m is older than S_snap. So there's no need to meld.
else if m ≥ r then // Final meld hasn't produced S_m yet
    wait for S_m to become available
S_out ← Meld(I_v, S_m)
if S_out says T(I_v) experienced a conflict then return Abort
else return S_out
```

To maximize the benefit of meld, we want to minimize the size of the post-premeld conflict zone. We therefore want a small value of d. But it should be large enough to give premeld enough time to finish before final meld is ready for premeld's output. Otherwise, final meld will stall, reducing throughput. In our experiments, five premeld threads with d=10 resulted in the best throughput.

4. GROUP MELD

A second way to speed up meld is to combine a pair of adjacent intentions in the log into a single intention, called a **group intention**. Later, final meld evaluates the group intention as one intention. This is beneficial because the group intention is generally smaller than the concatenation of its two input intentions, because the input intentions contain overlapping sets of nodes. So it takes less time to meld it. Two overlapping nodes collapse into a single node in the group intention. Thus, the more nodes the two input intentions have in common, the smaller the group intention.

For example, Figure 7 shows a database tree comprising six nodes. Intention I_1 updated A′, so it includes B′ and D′, and I_2 updated C″, so it includes B″ and D″. I_1 and I_2 have overlapping nodes D and B, each of which collapses to a single node when I_1 and I_2 are melded into a group intention I_3 (which includes new ancestors D‴ and B‴, due to copy-on-write). Together, I_1 and I_2 have six nodes, but the group intention that combines them has only four nodes.

Like premeld, group meld uses the standard meld algorithm, as modified in Section 3.3 to include readsets. However, group meld requires special logic in one case: Suppose nodes n_1 and n_2 in I_1 and I_2 (respectively) have the same key (e.g., A′ and A″), and I_1 precedes I_2. Suppose n_1 is in T(I_1)'s readset and n_2 is in T(I_2)'s readset or writeset. Then the readset metadata for the melded node n_{12} must refer to the maximum of n_1's and n_2's conflict zones. That is, if T(I_1)'s snapshot precedes T(I_2)'s snapshot, then n_{12}'s readset must refer to T(I_1)'s snapshot, so that meld checks for conflicting updates in between the two snapshots. Thus, meld must replace n_2 by an ephemeral node, so it can update n_2's readset metadata. This arises in the meld algorithm in several spots, which requires special-case logic for group meld. Note that if T(I_2)'s snapshot precedes T(I_1)'s, then no action is needed because n_2's existing metadata dominates.

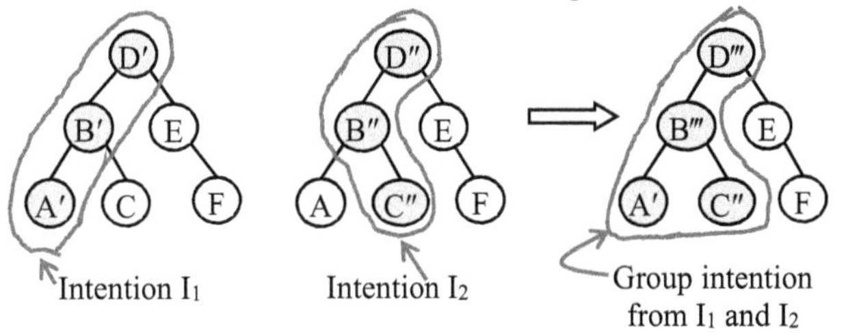

Figure 7: Combining two intentions into a group intention

The **group meld** optimization melds every adjacent pair of intentions, thereby halving the number of intentions in final meld. Like premeld, it has to be deterministic. A way to ensure this is to have each group intention be an odd-numbered intention in the log followed by the next one, which is even. Thus, intentions 1 and 2 form a group intention, then intentions 3 and 4, and so forth.

A disadvantage of group meld is that the group intention commits if and only if both intentions commit. Thus, it ties the commit/abort decision of each intention with that of another. This effect, called **fate sharing**, could increase the abort rate by up to a factor of two.

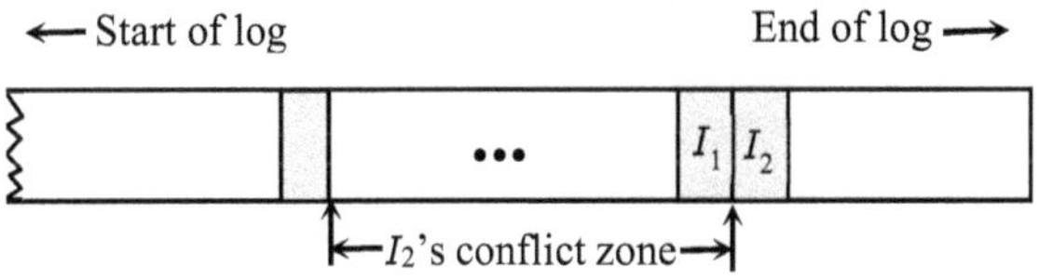

Figure 8: I₁ and I₂ meld into a group intention

However, there is one case where fate sharing does not occur. When melding two intentions into a group intention, if the first intention I_1 includes an update that conflicts with the second intention I_2, then group meld aborts I_2, because I_1 is in I_2's conflict zone (see Figure 8). Therefore, I_1 becomes the group intention and can still commit.

When premeld and group meld are combined in a pipeline, they can execute in either order. In our experiments, we ran premeld first, since it is more likely to find aborted transactions than group meld. The sooner in the pipeline that aborted transactions are identified, the better, since it reduces the amount of downstream work.

5. IMPLEMENTATION DETAILS

Our Hyder II implementation runs Hyder's meld algorithm [8] on a shared log manager. The core design comprises a cluster of **transaction servers** that execute transactions and the meld algorithm, and **log servers** that store the database. Our implementation allows for a single machine to run both a transaction server and log server. However, in our experiments, they run on different machines. The database is an immutable balanced binary search tree (a red-black tree [17]). As argued in [7], a binary tree is preferable to a B-tree, because it leads to smaller intentions.

5.1 Log Service

The log ensures persistence and enforces a total order on transactions. We used CORFU [4] as the log service, due to its good performance and feasibility compared to the custom hardware proposed in [7]. CORFU runs on a set of log servers on the same local area network as the transaction servers running transactions and meld. However, the transaction servers see it as a single shared log service, not as a set of log servers. Each log entry is a fixed-sized page, called an **intention block**. An **append** operation adds a given block to the end of the log and returns the position in the log where the block was stored. Given a log position, a **read** operation returns the block stored at that position. To ensure good append and read bandwidth, the log is striped across a set of storage units that are directly attached to the log servers. As we show in the next section, the log manager is much faster than meld and hence is never a bottleneck.

There are nontrivial error cases when read or append operations fail or fail to reply at all [4]. As these problems are not unique to Hyder II and this paper is about optimizing throughput and not fault tolerance, we regard them as out of scope.

Hyder II stores intentions in intention blocks. Depending on the size of the intentions, many intentions might fit in one block or an intention might span many blocks. In the latter case, the blocks of an intention need not be contiguous; the position of the intention in the log is identified by the position of its last intention block.

5.2 Transaction Servers

Hyder II is implemented in C#. Our implementation comprises the multi-versioned index structure storing the database tree, the transaction executer, and the meld pipeline that rolls forward the log. Bernstein et al. [8] presented an optimized and detailed design of the meld algorithm for the in-memory setting. Our meld implementation uses that algorithm, with the modification described at the end of Section 3.3. However, we re-implemented it in C# to efficiently use the new implementation of the database backed by our network-attached log.

A transaction executor dispatches transactions and processes their termination. Each transaction *T* executes on the current last-committed state (**LCS**) reported by the final meld thread at the time *T* starts. Due to copy-on-write, *T*'s first write generates a new intention and all of *T*'s subsequent writes add to it. After the transaction finishes executing, the executor serializes the intention into one or more blocks, appends it to the log, and then broadcasts it to the other transaction servers. *T*'s outcome will become known to *T*'s executor only after meld on the same server processes the intention. Until then, *T* is blocked. However, the executer is non-blocking and moves on to execute the next transaction while awaiting the commit decision from meld. The executer stops processing transactions if the number of transactions awaiting their outcome exceeds a configurable threshold which is determined empirically. Ideally, the threshold for the number of concurrent transactions allowed should be dynamically determined by admission control logic, which is future work. Such admission control is essential to avoid thrashing when the offered load exceeds capacity.

An intention tree is serialized into an intention block via a post-order tree traversal. Post-order ensures that each node points to children that are either in the log or already serialized. Once the block fills, serialization continues with a new block. The intention block containing the root of the database tree is appended last.

Each transaction server has a log reader that transforms the sequence of intention blocks in the log into an in-memory representation of the intentions that feeds the meld pipeline. For each intention block, it spins off a deserialization task, which generates a tree of objects. A configurable number of threads run the deserialization tasks. They transform each node pointer in an intention into an object pointer if the object is in memory. Otherwise, the node pointer is left as a log position; if dereferenced later, the log position is used to fetch the corresponding intention block from the log.

The pipeline of premeld, group meld, and final meld processes the deserialized intentions in log order. Configuration parameters are used to turn-off premeld and/or group meld, and to control the number of threads for premeld and group meld.

Meld is inherently sequential and ideally CPU-bound. Any stalls during meld significantly reduce its throughput. Since meld does not need synchronization, the only sources of stalls are late-arriving intentions and cache misses. If meld is ready to process the next intention *I* but has not yet received *I*, it stalls until *I* is read from the log. Similarly, if meld accesses a block that is not cached, it must read the block from the log. The latency to read a log block is on the order of milliseconds while the latency to meld an intention is typically tens to a few hundred microseconds. Therefore, it is important to avoid intention block misses in the final meld thread. Pipelined parallelism helps mask log access latencies, since premeld and group meld fetch blocks well before final meld needs them. To ensure that final meld does not stall on a cache miss, additional threads can be used to pre-fetch blocks not accessed in the earlier phases of the meld pipeline.

For optimal meld performance, it is also critical to avoid context switches. Therefore, meld spins if the next intention is not available to process. Each premeld, group meld, and final meld thread is also affinitized to a core to prevent inter-core thread migration.

5.3 Optimizations

Implementing Hyder II in managed code had advantages as well as challenges. It improved productivity and reduced the time to complete the first implementation. However, we had to iterate over the implementation to make its performance competitive with the optimized native in-memory implementation reported in Bernstein et al. [8]. A performance comparison with [8] is in Section 6.4.

Our first challenge was memory management and garbage collection (GC) overhead. Much progress has been made to minimize the overhead of GC. Even so, we found GC to be detrimental to performance. Therefore, each thread in Hyder II, such as the transaction executer, deserializer, and meld, has its own local memory pool to reuse objects whenever possible. Pre-allocated thread-local memory pools significantly reduced GC overhead and stalls. Careful profiling revealed that GC was also triggered by some language constructs, such as lambda expressions and library functions that do not allow reusing objects, and asynchronous API calls that automatically generate a callback on call completion. Eliminating these poor memory users was a tedious and iterative process, but we were rewarded with significant performance improvement. As described in Section 2, meld generates ephemeral nodes. Since the pipelined design has more instances of meld, it can generate more ephemeral nodes. Therefore, ephemeral nodes must be carefully managed to avoid unnecessary demand for memory.

The second problem was serialization and deserialization of the intention blocks and manipulation of byte arrays, which is CPU-intensive. This needed careful optimization.

The third problem was network errors. After an intention is appended to the log, it is broadcast to all servers. Our initial implementation simulated this broadcast over UDP. However, as the network utilization and contention increased, significant packet loss resulted in many out-of-order intention deliveries, which degraded performance. Even though simulating the broadcast using TCP was more expensive than using UDP, the switch to TCP resulted in another significant performance boost.

6. EXPERIMENTS

We present an experimental study of our Hyder II implementation. We start by analyzing the performance of the log service to ensure it is not a bottleneck. We then evaluate Hyder II for various configurations and demonstrate the benefits of the premeld and group meld optimizations for a variety of workload mixes and isolation levels. We also compare Hyder II's throughput with that reported for Hyder [8] and Tango [5], whose designs are similar to Hyder II's. Hyder's performance studies have been limited to simulations [7] or a single-node implementation with an in-memory log designed to test the limits of the meld operator [8]. This paper presents the first detailed experimental evaluation of Hyder's architecture.

6.1 Experimental Setup and Workload

We ran our experiments on a cluster of twenty servers. Each server has a two-socket Intel Xeon E5-2650L 1.8 GHz processor (16 physical cores, 32 logical processors, two NUMA nodes), 192 GB RAM, a commodity Intel SATA SSD, and a dual-port Intel 10 Gbps network adapter. Servers in the rack are connected through a 64 port 10 Gbps top-of-rack switch to provide a high speed private network interconnect within the cluster.

The CORFU log service consists of a token server, a sequencer for log entries, and six disk servers, which store the log on direct-attached SSDs. The installation has a number of Hyder II transaction servers, which use CORFU's client API to append and read intention blocks. A Hyder II server generates two types of network traffic: unicast traffic with the log servers for appends and reads, and broadcast traffic among the transaction servers after an intention is appended to the log. To avoid interference, each type of traffic uses a different port of the dual-port network adapter.

We use a workload generator adapted from the Yahoo! Cloud Serving Benchmark (YCSB), adding support for multi-operation transactions [10]. The workload generator allows us to vary the number of operations in a transaction, the distribution of reads and writes within a transaction, the fraction of range vs. point lookups, the database size, and the distribution from which the keys are selected.

Unless otherwise specified, we use a database with 10M items, each with a 4 byte key and 1K payload. In most experiments, we vary the number of transaction servers generating and executing the workload. Each server has 20 update threads. Each thread allows up to 80 in-flight transactions, that is, transactions that have been appended to the log but not yet received a commit decision. This limit simulates coarse-grained admission control to avoid overload and thrashing due to high resource contention. Each transaction has 8 reads and 2 writes. The keys read and written are selected uniformly from the keys in the database. For experiments that vary one of these default parameters, the number of servers is fixed at 6.

The uniform distribution of reads and writes is adversarial for any transaction or data partitioning scheme, since a transaction's accesses do not naturally cluster. We select this workload to demonstrate Hyder II's ability to scale-out without partitioning.

As discussed earlier, Hyder II has four critical resources: log appends, network bandwidth, meld, and data contention. An update transaction stresses all of them. So most of our analyses involve a write-only workload to help us identify resource bottlenecks.

All of our measurements are the average result of three runs. We do not report the standard deviation, since it is low in all cases except under heavy contention, a well-known phenomenon. We observed a standard deviation in the range of 2-5% of the averages.

6.2 Summary of Results

The key takeaways from our experimental results are:

- The optimizations proposed to parallelize meld result in significant throughput improvements. Group meld improves throughput by 1.6x with only one thread. Premeld improves throughput by 3x with five threads across a variety of workloads and isolation levels.
- When premeld and group meld are combined in a pipeline, they do not improve throughput beyond that of premeld.
- For transactions with 8 reads and 2 writes, snapshot isolation (SI) improves throughput by 3x compared to serializable. With SI, premeld results in an additional 2x improvement, while group meld's improvements are not significant.
- Read-only workloads scale almost linearly. With a workload of 5% read-write and 95% read-only transactions, we achieve about 670K transactions per second with ten servers and serializable isolation executing a non-partitionable workload.

6.3 Performance of the Log Service

This section analyzes the throughput and latency of our shared log implementation. Our goal is to ensure that log appends are not a bottleneck that limit Hyder II's throughput.

The log service uses six disk servers. Clients append and read blocks of data. In Hyder II, log "clients" are transaction servers. The log service has a pre-configured block size; we use 8K blocks for Hyder II and for these experiments.

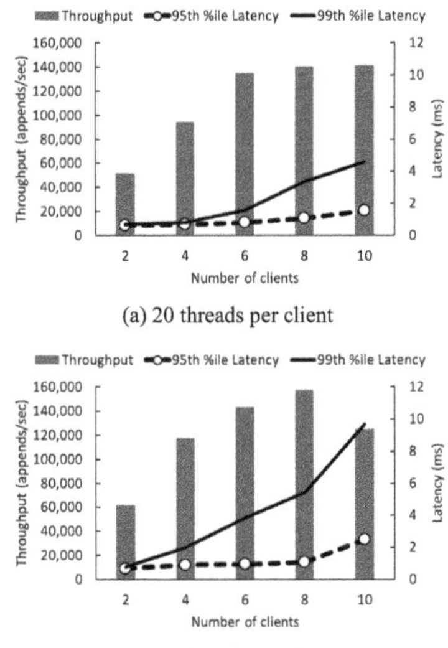

(a) 20 threads per client

(b) 30 threads per client

Figure 9: Throughput and latency of append operations to a shared log.

Figure 9 plots the throughput and latency of appends as we vary the number of clients appending to the log and the number of concurrent threads per server. Figure 9(a) and Figure 9(b) report results for 20 and 30 threads per server, respectively. As we increase the number of concurrent appends, the 95th and 99th percentile latencies increase, plotted on the right vertical axis. However, even the 99th percentile latencies are under 10 milliseconds. The peak throughput is more than 140K appends/sec. In our later experiments, Hyder II's transaction load generates at most 110K append/sec using a log configuration identical to these experiments. Hence, the log is not a bottleneck.

6.4 Performance of Hyder II

We first analyze Hyder II's performance using a workload executing all write transactions with serializable isolation to compare the benefits of premeld and group meld in isolation and in combination. Subsequently, we experiment with workloads with varying fractions of read-only transactions, with different isolation levels, and varying other workload parameters such as data access distribution, and transaction size. In all experiments, "throughput" means the number of *committed* transactions per second.

6.4.1 Workload with all Write Transactions

A write transaction stresses all the critical resources. Hence, a workload comprising all write transactions helps identify the architecture's performance limits. In this experiment, we use the default workload parameters described in Section 6.1. Figure 10 reports Hyder II's throughput in transactions per second (tps) as we vary the number of servers. The first bar corresponds to Hyder II with only final meld. The second bar (**Hyder II-Grp**) corresponds to Hyder II with group meld applied before final meld. The third (**Hyder II-Pre**) corresponds to Hyder II with premeld applied before final meld. The fourth (**Hyder II-Opt**) corresponds to applying both group meld and premeld. For experiments with premeld, there are 5 premeld threads with a premeld distance of 10. For experiments with group meld, there is one group meld thread grouping two intentions into one.

In Figure 10, Hyder II's peak throughput with no optimizations is 15K tps, which is achieved with 2 transaction servers. By contrast, peak throughput of Hyder II-Grp is 23.5K tps, Hyder II-Pre is 45.3K tps, and Hyder II-Opt is 44.8K tps. Thus, group meld improves throughput by 1.6x and premeld improves it by 3x. However, combining the optimizations does not improve throughput beyond that of premeld. Therefore, when enough cores are available to run many premeld threads, premeld should be used alone. Otherwise, group meld should be used to give a significant improvement with just one core.

The improvement with premeld is more significant as we increase the concurrency. For instance, with 10 servers, each with 20 threads and 80 in-flight transactions, there are up to 16K concurrent transactions, i.e., transactions that started executing but have not yet been melded. At such high degrees of concurrency, Hyder II-Pre has 3.5x the throughput of Hyder II.

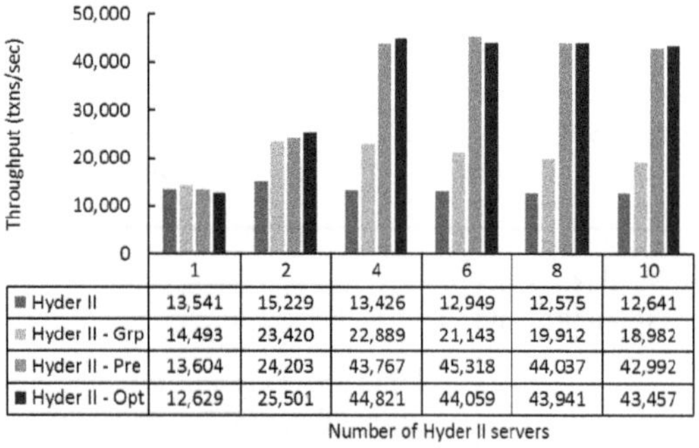

	1	2	4	6	8	10
Hyder II	13,541	15,229	13,426	12,949	12,575	12,641
Hyder II - Grp	14,493	23,420	22,889	21,143	19,912	18,982
Hyder II - Pre	13,604	24,203	43,767	45,318	44,037	42,992
Hyder II - Opt	12,629	25,501	44,821	44,059	43,941	43,457

Number of Hyder II servers

Figure 10: Throughput (committed transactions/sec) for Hyder II and the impact of premeld and group meld optimizations.

As concurrency increases beyond six transaction servers, there is some reduction in throughput of Hyder II-Pre. This is due to more contention and queuing delays for resources, such as log appends (see Figure 9) and network broadcast, which increases transaction processing latency and in turn throttles the executers when they reach their in-flight-transaction limit. That is, the small reduction in throughput is primarily due to the "back-pressure" on the executers due to higher resource contention.

Premeld and group meld help reduce the work done by final meld by reducing the number of tree nodes that final meld visits. Figure 11 reports the number of nodes visited per transaction by final meld for each optimization technique. As is evident, group meld reduces the number of nodes by 2x and premeld reduces them by 8-10x.

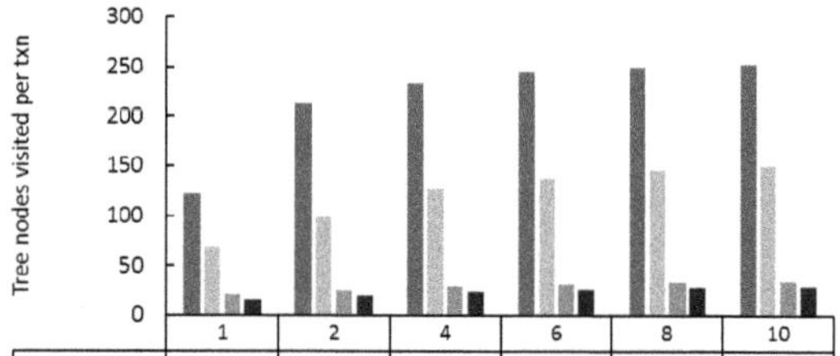

	1	2	4	6	8	10
Hyder II	122	212	234	245	250	253
Hyder II - Grp	70	100	127	138	146	151
Hyder II - Pre	21	25	29	31	33	34
Hyder II - Opt	17	20	24	26	28	29

Number of Hyder II servers

Figure 11: Group meld and premeld reduce the number of nodes visited in the final meld thread.

Premeld merges the intention with a recent LCS, eliminating a large fraction of the conflict zone that final meld has to process. Most of the readset and writeset validations that require traversing deep into the database tree are processed by premeld. Final meld mostly terminates high up in the tree, merging the updates into the LCS and creating ephemeral nodes as needed. As a result, even though the number of nodes is reduced by 8-10x, the throughput improvement is only in the range of 3-3.5x.

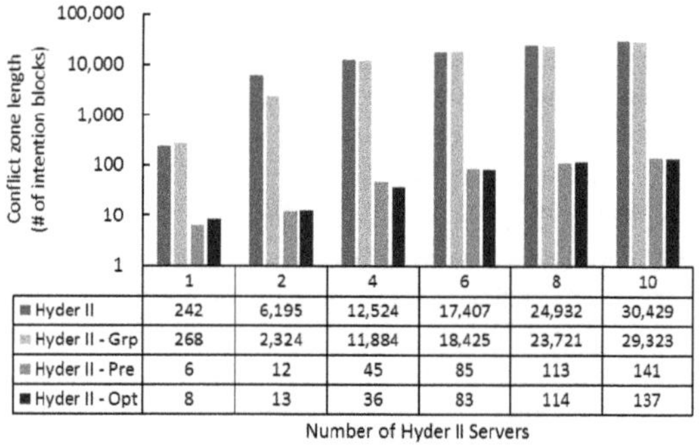

	1	2	4	6	8	10
Hyder II	242	6,195	12,524	17,407	24,932	30,429
Hyder II - Grp	268	2,324	11,884	18,425	23,721	29,323
Hyder II - Pre	6	12	45	85	113	141
Hyder II - Opt	8	13	36	83	114	137

Number of Hyder II Servers

Figure 12: Impact of group meld and premeld on the effective conflict zone observed by the final meld thread.

Figure 12 reports the number of intention blocks in the conflict zone observed by final meld. In our configuration, one intention spans two intention blocks on average. Thus, the number of intentions in the conflict zone is about half of the intention-block numbers reported. As the figure shows, premeld shrinks the conflict zone by 40x-500x by melding the intention with an updated LCS very late in the intention's conflict zone. However, the conflict zone size is unchanged by group meld. Its benefit stems from overlapping nodes and paths in the two intentions—final meld needs to process only one of these overlapped nodes, which reduces the number of nodes processed by final meld. Combining premeld and group meld does not significantly change the number of nodes visited or the conflict zone length, which explains why the two optimizations together do not result in any improvement beyond that of premeld.

While both premeld and group meld reduce the work done by the final meld thread, they perform redundant work in parallel threads. Figure 13 reports on the total number of tree nodes visited per transaction by each optimization. The work done in the critical path of final meld (the pattern-filled bar) decreases with every optimization, while the work done in parallel threads (solid bars) is often higher in aggregate than the sequential final meld thread without any optimizations.

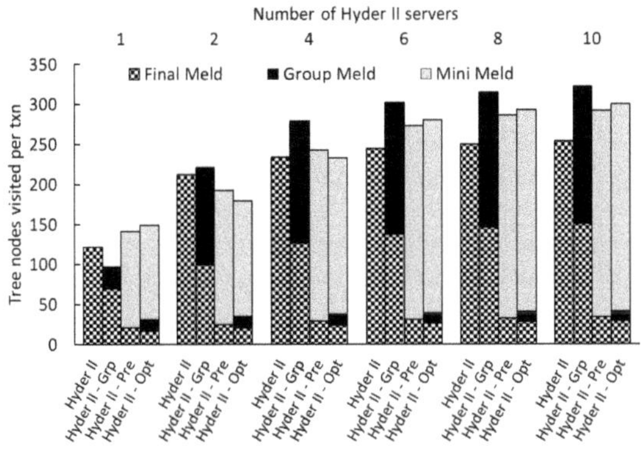

Figure 13: Number of tree nodes visited in different stages of the meld pipeline. The hatched bar corresponds to final meld. The solid bars correspond to group meld and premeld.

6.4.2 Comparison with Hyder and Tango

Tango is the system whose architecture is the closest to Hyder II. In this section, we compare them, along with the in-memory setup of Hyder [8]. Tango and Hyder reported throughput for a database of 100K items. To compare them with Hyder II, we repeated the experiment of Section 6.4.1 for a database of 100K items running a workload similar to that used in Hyder and Tango. In this experiment Hyder-II's peak throughput was ~20K tps (compared to 15K tps in Figure 10). Tango reported throughput of 15-25K tps on similar hardware [5]. Thus, Hyder II's performance is comparable to Tango's, in spite of its tree index, which is more expensive to maintain than Tango's hash index. With the premeld optimization, Hyder II's performance is significantly better than Tango's.

The throughput of Hyder's in-memory implementation, using a workload with ~10 operations per transaction was 50-60K tps [8]. The lower throughput of Hyder II's meld operator can be attributed to multiple factors. Experiments for in-memory Hyder involved only one server, and the workload generator limited the conflict zone length to 256. Hyder II needs to operate at much higher degrees of concurrency with tens of thousands of concurrent transactions (as in Figure 12) to mask the latency of serializing and deserializing intentions, appending to the log, and broadcasting intentions. Premeld reduces the conflict zone length for final meld to the same range as the in-memory implementation, which results in a throughput of 50-60K tps for a 100K item database. Other factors contributing to Hyder-II's lower throughput are that Hyder-II's experiments use a slower processor and a distributed shared log, and Hyder II is implemented in C# while Hyder is written in C++.

6.4.3 Workload with Read-Write Transaction Mix

Read-only transactions in Hyder II run on a database snapshot (the LCS when the transaction starts) and commit locally, without stressing any of Hyder II's critical resources. Therefore, read-only transaction throughput should scale linearly as we increase the number of servers and the number of read-only transactions. To demonstrate this, we run an experiment that executes an increasing number of read-only transactions with a fixed load of write transactions using the setup of Section 6.4.1.

Both read-only and write transactions execute ten operations; write transactions have two updates and eight reads, as in Section 6.4.1. We use separate executers for read-only transactions. This ensures adding more read-only transactions does not reduce the number of write transactions admitted to the system. We gradually increase the number of read-only transaction executors while keeping the write workload fixed with six dedicated executors per server.

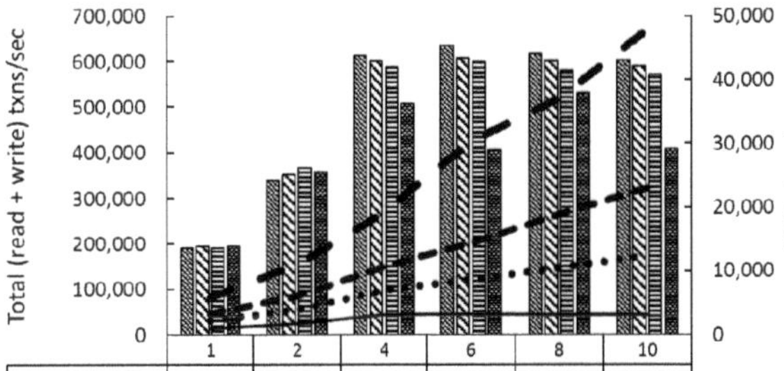

	1	2	4	6	8	10
6W-0R-Write	13,604	24,203	43,767	45,318	44,037	42,992
6W-1R-Write	13,838	25,214	42,811	43,399	42,839	42,056
6W-2R-Write	13,528	26,136	42,013	42,699	41,389	40,699
6W-4R-Write	13,828	25,504	36,290	28,904	37,822	29,189
6W-0R-Total	13,604	24,203	43,767	45,318	44,037	42,992
6W-1R-Total	31,132	54,423	97,670	119,756	146,416	173,182
6W-2R-Total	45,461	84,497	150,007	200,790	264,083	322,024
6W-4R-Total	82,104	153,130	268,024	423,834	517,495	670,313

Number of Hyder II servers

Figure 14: Linear scaling of transaction throughput with a mix of read-only and read-write transactions.

Figure 14 plots the throughput of write transactions and of read and write combined ("total"). As we increase the number of servers, the offered load increases. We vary the number of read-only executers from 0 to 4, denoted by 0R, 1R, 2R, and 4R in the figure. With 6W-0R, there are no read-only transactions, re-creating the setup in Section 6.4.1. For brevity, we only report numbers using premeld.

First consider the lines, which plot total throughput (i.e., of read and write transactions) on the left vertical axis (labeled total txns/sec). They correspond to the last four rows of the table. As we increase the number of read-only executors (from 0R to 4R) and servers (from 1 to 10), total throughput scales almost linearly. With 10 transaction servers, total throughput for 6W-4R peaks at ~670K. This linear scalability demonstrates that Hyder II's architecture scales out without partitioning.

The bars in the graph plot the throughput of write transactions on the right vertical axis (labeled write txns/sec). They correspond to the first four rows of the table. As in Section 6.4.1, write throughput peaks at 45K tps with 6 servers (6W-0R). For a given number of servers, as the number of read-only executors increases from 0 to 1 to 2, there is a small decrease in write throughput. This is due to higher CPU contention since more cores are processing transactions (10 in 6W-4R vs. 6 in 6W-0R), thereby reducing the number of cores available to broadcast and deserialize intentions.

With four read-only executors, no cores are dedicated to broadcast and deserialization. Both activities slow down and meld throughput decreases, causing a corresponding drop in write throughput (the right bars for 6, 8 and 10 servers). This shows the importance of reserving enough cores for basic system functions, such as meld, broadcast, and deserialization.

6.4.4 *Snapshot Isolation*

In this experiment, we compare Hyder II's performance when transactions execute with serializable isolation (**SR**) versus snapshot isolation (**SI**). With SI, meld does not need to validate the readset, so the readset is not included in the intention. This considerably reduces the intention sizes and hence the load on many critical resources, such as the log, network, and meld. In this experiment, each transaction performs 8 reads and 2 writes. Therefore, eliminating the readset results in almost a 4x reduction in intention sizes. This results in about a 2.5x improvement in throughput, as shown in Figure 15, which plots the result of running Hyder II with no optimizations. The reduction (3x-4x) in the work done by meld is also evident from the number of tree nodes visited by meld, shown by the lines plotted on the right vertical axis.

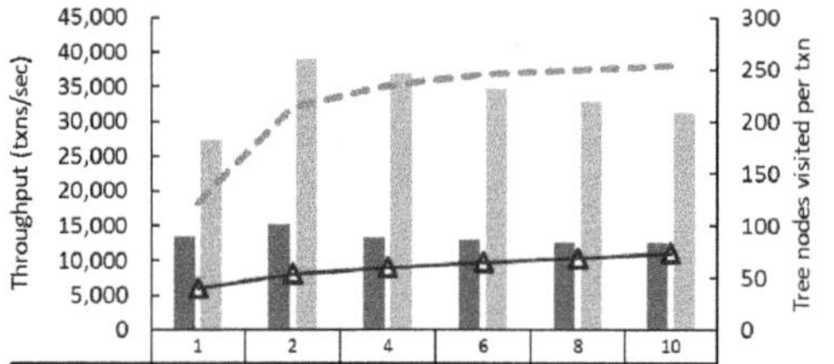

	1	2	4	6	8	10
TPS-SR	13,541	15,229	13,426	12,949	12,575	12,641
TPS-SI	27,356	38,970	36,941	34,701	32,978	31,213
Nodes-SR	122	213	234	245	250	254
Nodes-SI	40	54	60	65	69	74

Number of Hyder II servers

Figure 15: Serializable (SR) vs. snapshot isolation (SI).

The reason why a 4x reduction in the number of nodes yields only a 2.5x increase in throughput is that SI eliminates only readset nodes and reads are cheaper to meld than writes. Reads only require conflict testing while writes require creating ephemeral nodes.

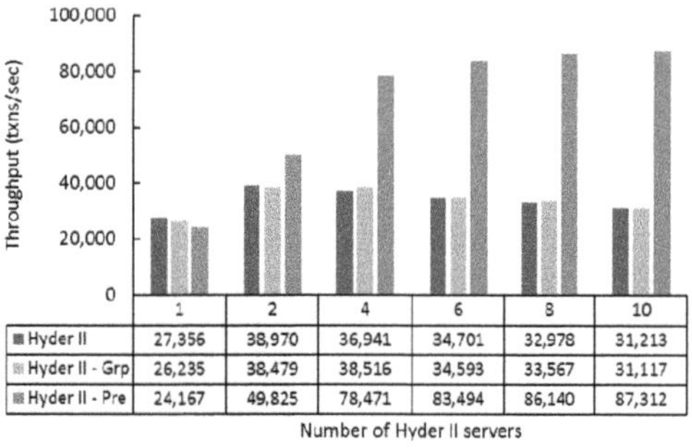

	1	2	4	6	8	10
Hyder II	27,356	38,970	36,941	34,701	32,978	31,213
Hyder II - Grp	26,235	38,479	38,516	34,593	33,567	31,117
Hyder II - Pre	24,167	49,825	78,471	83,494	86,140	87,312

Number of Hyder II servers

Figure 16: Impact of the premeld and group meld optimizations with snapshot isolation.

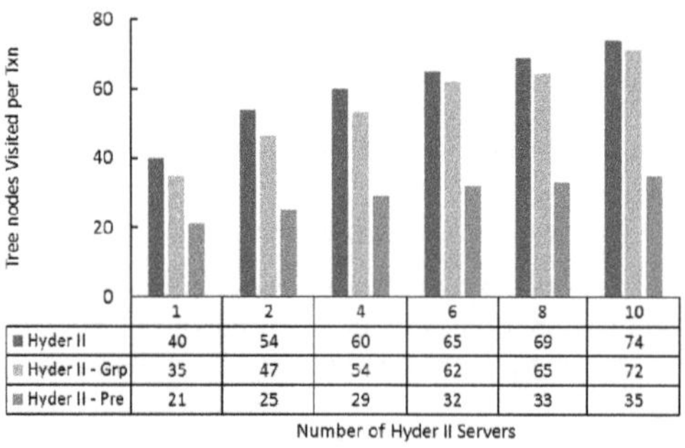

	1	2	4	6	8	10
Hyder II	40	54	60	65	69	74
Hyder II - Grp	35	47	54	62	65	72
Hyder II - Pre	21	25	29	32	33	35

Number of Hyder II Servers

Figure 17: Only premeld results in a reduction in number of tree nodes visited by final meld with SI.

In Figure 16 we report the benefits of group meld and premeld for transactions executing with SI. Hyder II with premeld continues to demonstrate 2x-3x higher throughput than without the optimization. This benefit arises from premeld's ability to reduce the number of nodes visited by final meld (see Figure 17). Group meld's 10% reduction does not significantly improve performance, because in SI each intention only has two writes. Therefore, there are fewer overlapping nodes in two consecutive intentions.

6.4.5 *Varying Workload Parameters*

Our workload generator is able to vary different parameters, such as the distribution used to select data items accessed by a transaction, number of operations per transaction, database size, and number of read and write operations per transaction. We evaluated Hyder II's performance for a variety of these workloads and observed similar benefits with premeld providing 3x-3.5x improvement in throughput. We present the results varying the access distribution here; more results are included in Appendix B.

The goal of this experiment is to evaluate the impact of data access distribution on the premeld and group meld optimizations. The workload creates a hotspot where fraction x of data items is accessed by fraction $(1.0 - x)$ of operations. We vary x from 0.05 to 1.0; $x = 1$ results in the uniform access distribution used earlier.

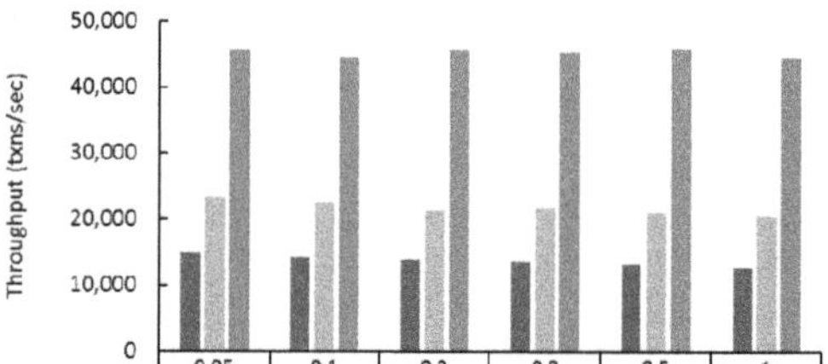

	0.05	0.1	0.2	0.3	0.5	1
Hyder II	14,888	14,232	13,832	13,565	13,281	12,706
Hyder II - Grp	23,263	22,590	21,347	21,555	21,050	20,600
Hyder II - Pre	45,686	44,456	45,665	45,415	45,830	44,557

Size of the hotspot (fraction of data items)

Figure 18: Premeld is effective with skewed data accesses.

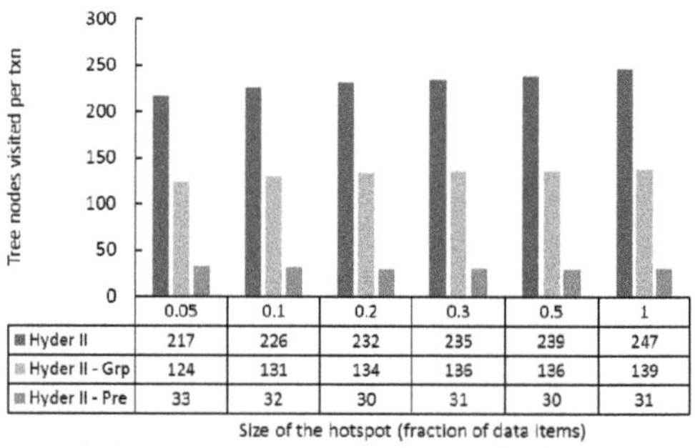

	0.05	0.1	0.2	0.3	0.5	1
Hyder II	217	226	232	235	239	247
Hyder II - Grp	124	131	134	136	136	139
Hyder II - Pre	33	32	30	31	30	31

Size of the hotspot (fraction of data items)

Figure 19: Number of tree nodes visited as a function of skew.

Figure 18 plots the throughput and Figure 19 plots the number of tree nodes visited by the final meld. As the skew increases, the probability of a conflict increases, which would increase the abort rates. Interestingly, without any optimizations, Hyder II's throughput increases with increase in skew. With skew of 0.05, the abort rate is slightly higher, about 0.14% compared to 0.02% with uniform. However, with increasing skew, the work done by final meld decreases, since transactions access similar data, thus allowing meld to terminate higher in the tree. Since final meld is the bottleneck, speeding it up results in higher throughput. Notice that skew has negligible impact on the work done by final meld when premeld is turned on, and hence negligible effect on throughput. However, the benefit of premeld still prevails with Hyder II-Pre's throughput being 3.5x that of Hyder II.

6.4.6 Analyzing Premeld

Recall that with t premeld threads, an intention is premelded against the state created by the $(t \times d)^{th}$ intention that precedes it. Therefore, for a fixed t, the smaller the value of the premeld distance d, the smaller the conflict zone length for the final meld thread, which in turn increases throughput. In this experiment, we evaluate the impact on d by setting $t=5$. Figure 20 reports transaction throughput as a function of premeld distance with five premeld threads, which empirically validates the expected behavior. Since $d=10$ results in best throughput, we used this setting in all our experiments.

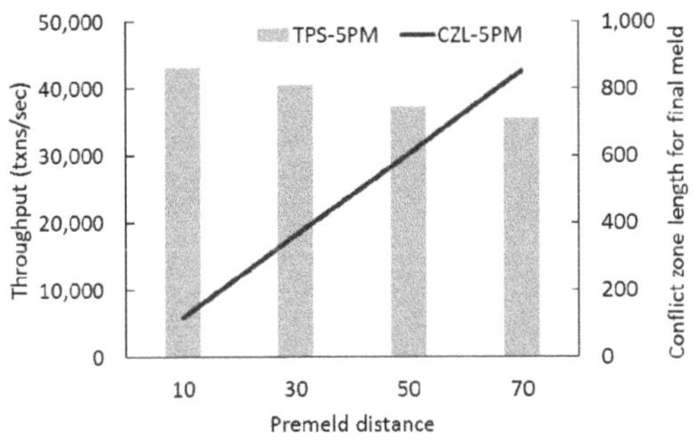

Figure 20: Analyzing the behavior of premeld by varying the premeld distance.

7. RELATED WORK

Hyder II is based on optimistic concurrency control and log-structured storage. We discuss each in turn, followed by systems that have some similarity with Hyder II.

Optimistic concurrency control (OCC) was introduced in [19], and its performance studied in [1][2][16][21][26][30]. It was initially unpopular due to lower throughput than locking, but has attracted interest recently as its non-blocking behavior is highly desirable for parallel hardware. Tashkent uses a centralized OCC validator over distributed data [11]. A distributed B-tree implementation with OCC is in [3], but it uses distributed transactions, single-version data, and simple version ids for conflict detection. OCC for an in-memory database is described in [20]. Hybrid schemes have also been proposed to combine the benefits of locking and OCC [21][26][29]. None of these systems are similar to Hyder II.

Log-structured storage has been widely studied in file systems [3] [12][24][27] and database systems [5][7][8][15][22][25][28][32] [33]. It was initially proposed for write-once media [12], and then used to improve disk I/O performance [27]. It has regained popularity due to the recent adoption of flash-based storage [1][5][7][22], which inherently does copy-on-write.

The main performance benefit of log-structured storage is from batching updates and from using sequential rather than random I/O [27]. Some implementations batch updates into larger sequential writes [15][22][33]. Others merge update batches into a hierarchical snapshot of the data, such as bLSM [28]. However, none of these systems supports a server cluster with shared-storage and ACID transactions, like Hyder II. Tokutek [32] uses a log-structured multi-versioned index, but with locking, not OCC.

Amoeba [24] is a log-structured distributed file system that uses OCC. Like Hyder II, it uses copy-on-write for file updates, and uses OCC to check update conflicts. Unlike Hyder II, it serializes conflict checks across servers and does not consider replication.

The system closest to Hyder II is Tango [5], which implements a distributed object store on the CORFU log manager [3]. CORFU provides the interface of a distributed SSD and takes care of distributed wear-leveling, data distribution, fault tolerance, and scalability. Its concurrency control protocol is inspired by Hyder [7]. But it uses a hashed access method and hence does not require optimized validation over trees or merging of trees, i.e., meld. Since it uses hashing, it suffers the usual weakness of failing to handle range predicates, especially over continuous domains.

OXenstored [14] is another system that uses a similar log-based strategy for OCC conflict detection. It works over multi-version tries [13] and does very coarse-grain conflict detection, and hence has much lower throughput than Hyder II.

Eve [17] uses a similar copy-on-write tree as Hyder II, but a very different technique for ensuring all replicas reach the same state. It batches requests that are not conflicting and executes requests within a batch in parallel. Operations that require creating a new tree node are postponed until the end of the batch to achieve determinism. It uses state machine replication to check if enough replicas reached the same state. If not, it reruns the batch sequentially.

Calvin [31] is a transaction system that scales out to multiple servers. As in Hyder II, determinism plays a prominent role in Calvin; both approaches rely on determinism to avoid synchronization across servers. Calvin replicates requests to run transactions and executes them deterministically in a pre-determined order. By contrast, Hyder II replicates the result of executing transactions, totally orders them in a shared log, and then melds them deterministically.

8. CONCLUSION

We presented an optimized version of the optimistic concurrency control algorithm in [8], for a log-structured, multi-versioned, tree-structured database. The algorithm, called meld, performs deterministic roll-forward of the log, analyzing each successive transaction in the log for conflicts. Our optimized version of meld uses pipeline parallelism to preprocess the log and thereby speed up the algorithm by 3x or more. We showed that the system scales out over multiple servers without partitioning the database.

A follow-on paper by two of the authors [6] leverages an approximate partitioning of the workload to parallelize meld into multiple threads, where each thread executes over a different partition of the transactions. Transactions that span partitions execute on a separate multi-partition thread, which is synchronized with each of the single-partition threads with which the transactions might conflict. To minimize this synchronization, some static analysis of transactions would likely be beneficial, such as that proposed in [9][23].

Acknowledgements

The authors are heavily indebted to Mahesh Balakrishnan for providing us with the CORFU log service and extending it for our experimental environment. We also thank Colin Reid and Soner Terek for input on premeld, the .Net runtime team for help with tooling and techniques to optimize performance, Ming Wu for help with the original Hyder implementation, and Andy Pavlo for many excellent suggestions that helped us improve the paper.

9. REFERENCES

[1] Adya, A., R. Gruber, B. Liskov, U.Maheshwari. Efficient optimistic concurrency control using loosely synchronized clocks. SIGMOD 1995, pp. 23-34.

[2] Agrawal, D., A. Bernstein, P. Gupta, S. Sengupta. Distributed optimistic concurrency control with reduced rollback. Distributed Computing 2, 1 (1987), pp. 45-59.
[3] Aguilera, M.K., W.M. Golab, and M.A. Shah: A practical scalable distributed B-tree. PVLDB 1(1): 598-609, 2008.
[4] Balakrishnan, M., D. Malkhi, J.D. Davis, V. Prabhakaran, M. Wei, T. Wobber: CORFU: A distributed shared log. ACM Trans. Comput. Syst. 31(4): 10 (2013).
[5] Balakrishnan, M., D. Malkhi, T. Wobber, M. Wu, V. Prabhakaran, M. Wei, J.D. Davis, S. Rao, T. Zou, A. Zuck: Tango: distributed data structures over a shared log. SOSP 2013, pp. 325-340
[6] Bernstein, P.A. and S. Das. Scaling optimistic concurrency control by approximately partitioning the certifier and log. IEEE Data Eng. Bull 38, 1 (March 2015).
[7] Bernstein, P.A., C.W. Reid, S. Das: Hyder - A transactional record manager for shared flash. CIDR 2011, pp. 9-20
[8] Bernstein, P.A., C.W. Reid, M. Wu, X. Yuan: Optimistic concurrency control by melding trees. PVLDB 4(11): 944-955 (2011).
[9] Bernstein, P.A., D.W. Shipman, J.B. Rothnie Jr.: Concurrency Control in a System for Distributed Databases (SDD-1). ACM TODS 5(1): 18-51 (1980).
[10] Cooper, B.F, A. Silberstein, E. Tam, R. Ramakrishnan, R. Sears: Benchmarking cloud serving systems with YCSB. SoCC 2010, pp. 143-154.
[11] Elnikety, S., S. Dropsho, and F. Pedone. Tashkent: Uniting durability with transaction ordering for high-performance scalable database replication. EuroSys 2006, pp. 117-130.
[12] Finlayson, R., and D. Cheriton. Log Files: An extended file service exploiting write-once storage. SOSP 1987, pp. 139-148.
[13] Fredkin, E.: Trie memory. CACM, 3(9):490–499, 1960.
[14] Gazagnairem, T. and V. Hanquez: OXenstored—An efficient hierarchical and transactional database using functional programming with reference cell comparisons. ICFP 2009, pp. 203-214.
[15] Graefe, G. Write-optimized B-trees. VLDB 2004, pp. 672-683.
[16] Gruber, R. E. Optimistic concurrency control for nested distributed transactions, 1989.
[17] Guibas, L.J., and R. Sedgewick: A Dichromatic Framework for Balanced Trees. FOCS 1978, pp. 8-21.
[18] Kapritsos, M., Y. Wang, V. Quema, A. Clement, L. Alvisi, M. Dahlin. All about Eve: Execute-verify replication for multi-core servers. OSDI 2012, pp. 237-250.
[19] Kung, H. T., and J.T. Robinson. On optimistic methods for concurrency control. ACM TODS 6, 2 (June 1981), 213-226.
[20] Larson, P.-A., S. Blanas, C. Diaconu, C. Freedman, J.M. Patel, M. Zwilling. High-performance concurrency control mechanisms for main-memory databases. PVLDB 5, 4 (2011): 298-309.
[21] Lausen, G. Concurrency control in database systems: A step towards the integration of optimistic methods and locking. ACM 1982, pp. 64-68.
[22] Lee, S.-W., and B. Moon. Design of flash-based DBMS: An in-page logging approach. SIGMOD 2007, pp. 55-66.
[23] Mu, S., Y. Cui, Y. Zhang, W. Lloyd, J. Li. Extracting more concurrency from distributed transactions. OSDI 2014, pp. 479-494.
[24] Mullender, S. J., and A.S. Tanenbaum. A distributed file service based on optimistic concurrency control. SOSP 1985, pp. 51-62.
[25] O'Neil, P.E., E. Cheng, D. Gawlick, E.J. O'Neil. The log-structured merge-tree (LSM-tree). Acta Inf. 33, 4 (June 1996): 351-385.
[26] Phatak, S. and B.R. Badrinath, Bounded locking for optimistic concurrency control. Rutgers Univ., Dept. of Computer Science, Tech. Report #DCS-TR-380.
[27] Rosenblum, M., and J.K. Ousterhout. The design and implementation of a log-structured file system. SOSP 1991, pp. 1-15.
[28] Sears, R., and R. Ramakrishnan. blsm: A general purpose log structured merge tree. SIGMOD 2012, pp. 217-228.
[29] Sheth, A. P., and M.T. Liu. Integrating locking and optimistic concurrency control in distributed database systems. ICDCS 1986, pp. 89-99.
[30] Thomasian, A., and E. Rahm. A new distributed optimistic concurrency control method and a comparison of its performance with two-phase locking. ICSCS 1990, pp. 294-301.
[31] Thomson, A., T. Diamond, S-C Weng, K. Ren, P. Shao, D.J. Abadi: Calvin: fast distributed transactions for partitioned database systems. SIGMOD 2012, pp. 1-12
[32] Tokutek. http://www.tokutek.com/.
[33] Wu, C.-H., L.-P Chang, T.-W. Kuo. An efficient R-tree implementation over flash-memory storage systems. GIS 2003, pp. 1724.

APPENDIX

A. SKETCH OF MELD

We present a simplified version of meld, to give the reader a deeper understanding of the algorithm. However, none of it is required background for the rest of this paper.

Each node is identified by a version number (abbr. VN), which is calculated from its log address. Thus, each new version of a node has a new VN. For example, in Figure 3, D′, B′, and C′, have different VN's than D, B, and C, respectively.

Each node also has some metadata that is used by meld to determine whether the intention that wrote the node experienced a conflict. The metadata includes an **Altered flag, Depends-On flag, source structure version** (**SSV**), and **source content version** (**SCV**). This is simplified metadata; a complete description is in [8].

For a node *n* in an intention *I*, Altered(*n*) is TRUE if T(*I*) updated *n*'s payload. The flag DependsOn(*n*) is TRUE if *I* depends on *n*'s payload not having changed during T(*I*)'s execution, that is, T(*I*) read *n* and ran with repeatable read or serializable isolation level. Additional metadata is needed for phantom avoidance; see [8].

For a node *n* in an intention *I*, SSV(*n*) is the VN of the node in *I*'s snapshot that has the same key value as *n*. For example, in Figure 3, SSV(C′) = VN(C), SSV(B′) = VN(B), and SSV(D′) = VN(D). If *n* is a new node inserted by *I*, then SSV(*n*) = null, such as SSV(A) in Figure 3.

For a node *n* in an intention *I*, SCV(*n*) is the VN of the node that first generated the payload of SSV(*n*). If SCV(*n*) = SSV(*n*) in *I*, then the transaction that produced the node whose VN is SSV(*n*) also updated *n*'s payload. If SCV(*n*) < SSV(*n*), then a node in SCV(*n*)'s subtree was updated after the transaction that produced SCV(*n*)'s payload. This caused a copy-on-write of SCV(*n*)'s node, which led directly or indirectly (though subsequent updates to that subtree) to a node whose VN is SSV(n).

Meld works by a recursive preorder traversal of I, starting at I's root and comparing each node n in I with the corresponding node n_L in LCS. There are two cases. In case one, n_L has the same key as n and meld works as follows:

- If n is NULL or outside of I, then return n
- If SSV(n) = VN(n_L), then n and its subtree were not changed after T(I) read them. Therefore, meld can simply replace n_L by n, which also replaces n_L's subtree by n's subtree. Otherwise, SSV(n) ≠ VN(n_L), so something in n's subtree changed and we have to determine if that change implies a conflict.
- If Altered(n) = TRUE and either

  (Altered(n_L) = TRUE and SCV(n) ≠ VN(n_L)) or
  (Altered(n_L) = FALSE and SCV(n) ≠ SCV(n_L)),

  then T(I)'s update of n conflicts with a write in its conflict zone, so I aborts.
- Otherwise, if DependsOn(n) = TRUE and either

  (Altered(n_L) = TRUE and SCV(n) ≠ VN(n_L)) or
  (Altered(n_L) = FALSE and SCV(n) ≠ SCV(n_L)),

  then T(I)'s read of n conflicts with a write in its conflict zone, so I aborts.
- Otherwise, copy n into an ephemeral node n_e.
  - Set the left child of n_e to be the result of melding n's and n_L's left children
  - Set the right child of n_e to be the result of melding n's and n_L's right children.

In case two, there is no n_L that has the same key as n. This complicates the recursion and is described in detail in [8].

B. ADDITIONAL EXPERIMENTS

We now present more experiments analyzing Hyder II's performance by varying various workload parameters such as the number of operations per transaction (or transaction size) and the fraction of update operations in a ten-operation write transaction. Other workload parameters are set to the default values described in Section 6.1. The number of transaction servers is set to 6.

As the number of operations per transaction increases, the number of tree nodes included in an intention increases. This increases the load on each of Hyder II's critical resources. In this workload, we fix the fraction of update operations in a transaction to 0.2, with at least one update operation in the transaction. Therefore, as the transaction size increases, the number of update operations in the transaction also increases. This results in more work for the meld pipeline, since meld has to create ephemeral nodes for the updated nodes for parts of the tree that were updated concurrently. Thus, as the transaction size increases, we expect the transaction throughput to decrease proportionately, as is observed in Figure 21. The increase in work done by final meld is evident in Figure 22. However, premeld continues to be as effective, with a 3x performance improvement and ~7x reduction in the number of nodes visited. The other contributor to the cost of final meld, the number of ephemeral nodes created, shows a similar pattern. With four operations per transaction, the meld pipeline in Hyder II-Pre creates an average of 23 ephemeral nodes per transaction. With transaction size of 32, it grows to 171 ephemeral nodes per transaction.

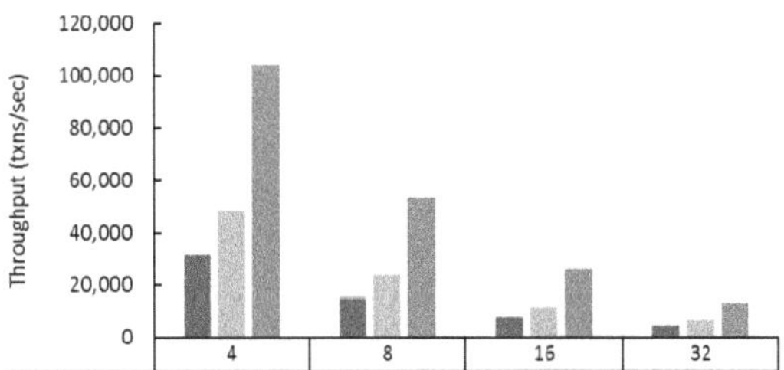

	4	8	16	32
Hyder II	31,412	15,359	7,460	4,195
Hyder II - Grp	48,656	23,851	11,357	6,275
Hyder II - Pre	103,993	53,408	25,977	12,979

Number of operations per transaction

Figure 21: Varying the number of operations in a transaction. Every transaction has at least one write operation.

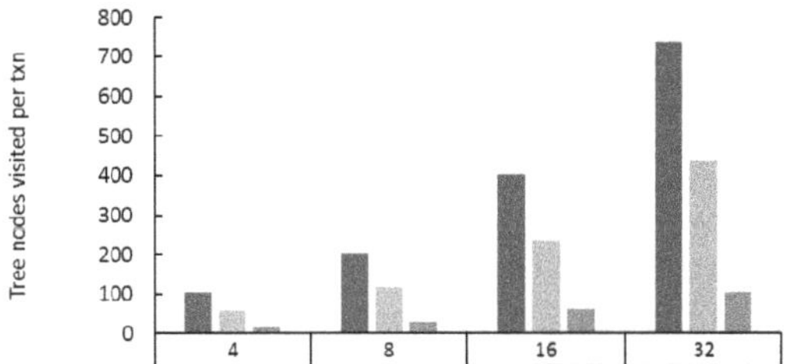

	4	8	16	32
Hyder II	104	203	402	737
Hyder II - Grp	60	117	237	438
Hyder II - Pre	17	31	61	104

Number of operations per transaction

Figure 22: Premeld significantly reduces the number of tree nodes visited by final meld even as we vary the number of operations in a transaction.

A similar increase in the number of ephemeral nodes created by the meld pipeline is observed as we increase the number of update operations in a transaction. In this experiment, we fix the number of operations per transaction at 10 and vary the fraction of update operations from 0.1 to 1.0. As the fraction of update operations decreases, the throughput increases (see Figure 23). Figure 24 plots the number of ephemeral nodes created by the meld pipeline. It shows that a higher update fraction results in the creation of more ephemeral nodes, because updates lead to the creation of ephemeral ancestor nodes. As expected, premeld and group meld result in slightly more ephemeral nodes being created.

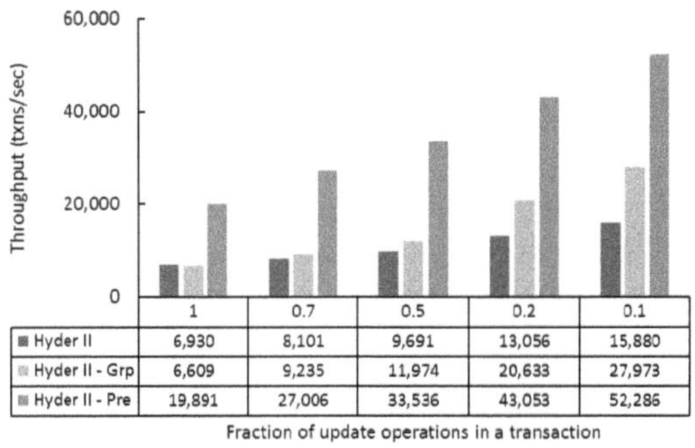

	1	0.7	0.5	0.2	0.1
Hyder II	6,930	8,101	9,691	13,056	15,880
Hyder II - Grp	6,609	9,235	11,974	20,633	27,973
Hyder II - Pre	19,891	27,006	33,536	43,053	52,286

Fraction of update operations in a transaction

Figure 23: Impact of varying the fraction of update operations per transaction on the throughput.

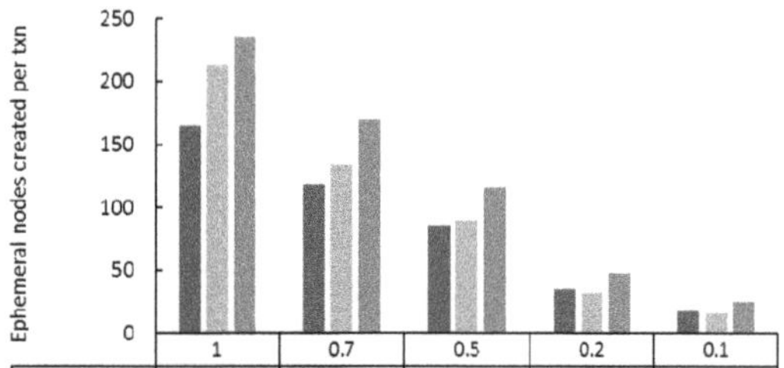

	1	0.7	0.5	0.2	0.1
Hyder II	165	118	86	35	18
Hyder II - Grp	213	134	90	32	16
Hyder II - Pre	235	169	116	48	25

Fraction of update operations in a transaction

Figure 24: As the number of update operations per transaction increases, so does the number of ephemeral nodes created.

C. DETERMINISM OF PREMELD WITH EPHEMERAL NODES

We present an example of an intention that is premelded with different database states at two different servers, leading to an ephemeral node identity that has different content at the two servers. The example is shown in Figure 25.

The initial database state, S_0, is shown in row 1. It is a tree whose root is A with children B and D. The number "0" in parentheses after each node indicates that it was written by transaction T_0 (not shown), which initialized the database.

The log is shown in row 2. It contains intentions written by a sequence of transactions $T_1 \ldots T_4$, all of which executed against state S_0. A dashed line indicates a pointer to a node (shown in gray) outside of the transaction's intention. The number in parentheses after each node identifies the transaction that wrote it. The transactions performed the following actions:

- T_1 updated the content of B, which generated a new version of node A due to copy-on-write.
- T_2 updated the content of D, which generated a new version of node A due to copy-on-write.
- T_3 inserted node C, which generated new versions of nodes B and A due to copy-on-write.
- T_4 inserted node E, which generated new versions of nodes D and A due to copy-on-write.

The sequence of states in the third row shows the result of applying meld to each transaction, in turn. None of the transactions conflict with each other, so they all commit. Since all transactions ran against S_0, for each transaction after T_1 meld produces ephemeral nodes, denoted by $e_1 \ldots e_5$.

In row 4, premeld at server X processes T_4 against state S_1, producing T_{4x}. Since it runs on a separate thread, the ephemeral node that it generates has a compound identifier [1,1], comprised of its premeld thread id followed by a sequence number. The final meld thread melds T_1, T_2, and T_3 as before. However, instead of melding T_4, it melds the result of premeld, T_{4x}, producing S_{4x}. Notice that meld recognizes that $B(e_2)$ is the immediate successor of state B(1) and therefore retains it in the meld result. However, since it merges the subtree $B(e_2)$ in S_3 with the updated D subtree that melds D(2) in S_3 and D(4) in T_{4x}, it produces a new ephemeral root, $A(e_4)$.

In row 5, at a different server Y, premeld processes T_4 against state S_2, unlike X which processed premeld against S_1. It produces T_{4y}.

Like at server X, server Y's final meld thread melds T_1, T_2, and T_3 and then melds the result of premeld, T_{4y}, producing S_{4y}.

Notice that servers X and Y both generate a node identified by $e_{1,1}$. However, they are entirely different nodes. Suppose a transaction executes at server Y and produces an intention that references node $D(e_{1,1})$. When that intention is melded at server X, the reference will be incorrectly interpreted as pointing to the root $A(e_{1,1})$, which is the wrong node and is from an earlier state. From this point on, the system at node X will go haywire.

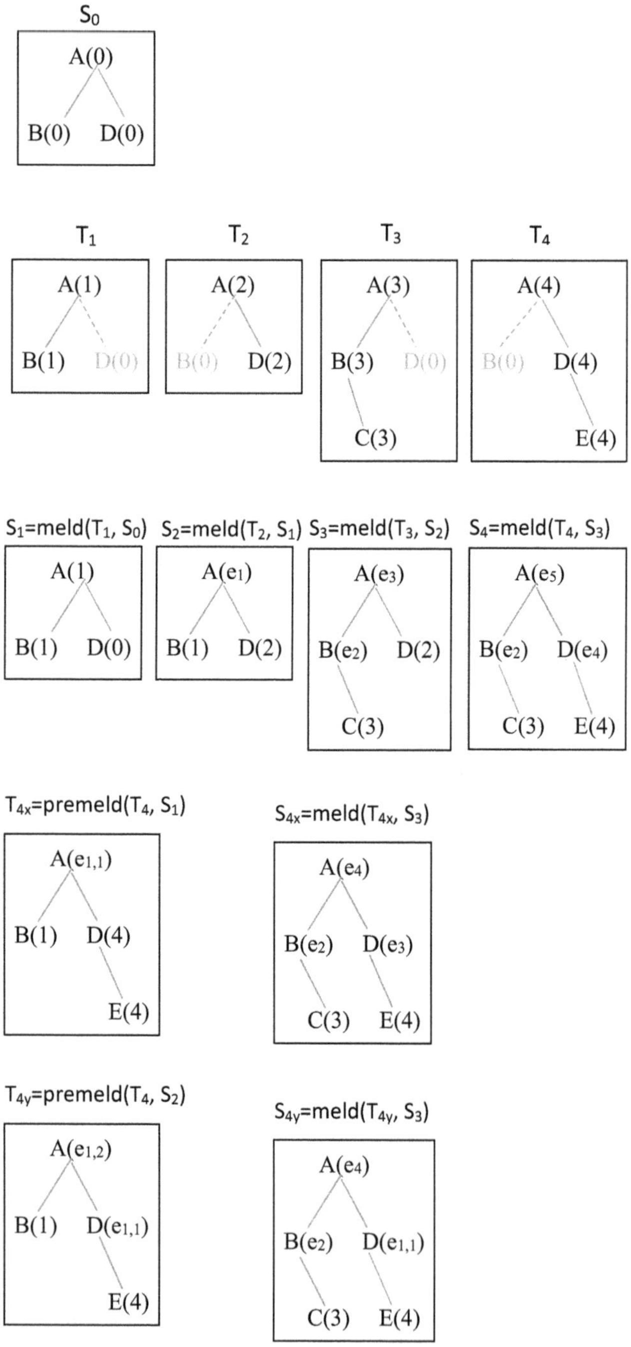

Figure 25: Running premeld against different database states

The Homeostasis Protocol: Avoiding Transaction Coordination Through Program Analysis

Sudip Roy[1,2*], Lucja Kot[2], Gabriel Bender[2], Bailu Ding[2], Hossein Hojjat[2], Christoph Koch[3], Nate Foster[2], Johannes Gehrke[2,4*]

[1]Google Research [2]Cornell University [3]EPFL [4]Microsoft Corp.

{sudip, lucja, gbender, blding, hojjat}@cs.cornell.edu, christoph.koch@epfl.ch, {jnfoster, johannes}@cs.cornell.edu

ABSTRACT

Datastores today rely on distribution and replication to achieve improved performance and fault-tolerance. But correctness of many applications depends on strong consistency properties—something that can impose substantial overheads, since it requires coordinating the behavior of multiple nodes. This paper describes a new approach to achieving strong consistency in distributed systems while minimizing communication between nodes. The key insight is to allow the state of the system to be inconsistent during execution, as long as this inconsistency is bounded and does not affect transaction correctness. In contrast to previous work, our approach uses program analysis to extract semantic information about permissible levels of inconsistency and is fully automated. We then employ a novel *homeostasis protocol* to allow sites to operate independently, without communicating, as long as any inconsistency is governed by appropriate *treaties* between the nodes. We discuss mechanisms for optimizing treaties based on workload characteristics to minimize communication, as well as a prototype implementation and experiments that demonstrate the benefits of our approach on common transactional benchmarks.

1. INTRODUCTION

Modern datastores are huge systems that exploit distribution and replication to achieve high availability and enhanced fault tolerance at scale. In many applications, it is important for the datastore to maintain global consistency to guarantee correctness. For example, in systems with replicated data, the various replicas must be kept in sync to provide correct answers to queries. More generally, distributed systems may have global consistency requirements that span multiple nodes. However, maintaining consistency requires coordinating the nodes, and the resulting communication costs can increase transaction latency by an order of magnitude or more [41].

Today, most systems deal with this tradeoff in one of two ways. A popular option is to bias toward high availability and low latency, and propagate updates asynchronously. Unfortunately this approach only provides eventual consistency guarantees, so applications must use additional mechanisms such as compensations or custom conflict resolution strategies [36, 13], or they must restrict the programming model to eliminate the possibility of conflicts [2]. Another option is to insist on strong consistency, as in Spanner [11], Mesa [17] or PNUTS [10], and accept slower response times due to the use of heavyweight concurrency control protocols.

This paper argues for a different approach. Instead of accepting a trade-off between responsiveness and consistency, we demonstrate that by carefully analyzing applications, it is possible to achieve the best of both worlds: strong consistency and low latency in the common case. The key idea is to exploit the semantics of the transactions involved in the execution of an application in a way that is safe and completely transparent to programmers.

It is well known that strong consistency is not always required to execute transactions correctly [20, 41], and this insight has been exploited in protocols that allow transactions to operate on slightly stale replicas as long as the staleness is "not enough to affect correctness" [5, 41]. This paper takes this basic idea much further, and develops mechanisms for automatically extracting safety predicates from application source code. Our *homeostasis protocol* uses these predicates to allow sites to operate without communicating, as long as any inconsistency is appropriately governed. Unlike prior work, our approach is fully automated and does not require programmers to provide any information about the semantics of transactions.

Example: top-k query. To illustrate the key ideas behind our approach in further detail, consider a top-k query over a distributed datastore, as illustrated in Figure 1. For simplicity we will consider the case where $k = 2$. This system consists of a number of *item sites* that each maintain a collection of (*key*, *value*) pairs that could represent data such as airline reservations or customer purchases. An *aggregator site* maintains a list of top-k items sorted in descending order by *value*. Each item site periodically receives new insertions, and the aggregator site updates the top-k list as needed.

A simple algorithm that implements the top-k query is to have each item site communicate new insertions to the aggregator site, which inserts them into the current top-k list in order, and removes the smallest element of the list. However, every insertion requires a communication round with the aggregator site, even if most of the inserts are for objects not in the top-k. A better idea is to only communicate with the aggregator node if the new *value* is greater than the minimal value of the current top-k list. Each site can maintain a cached value of the smallest value in the top-k and only notify the

*Work done while at Cornell University.

SIGMOD'15, May 31–June 4, 2015, Melbourne, Victoria, Australia.

http://dx.doi.org/10.1145/2723372.2723720.

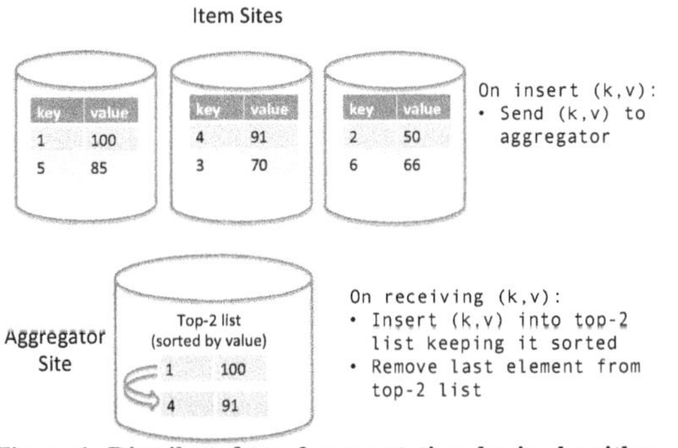

Figure 1: Distributed top-2 computation, basic algorithm.

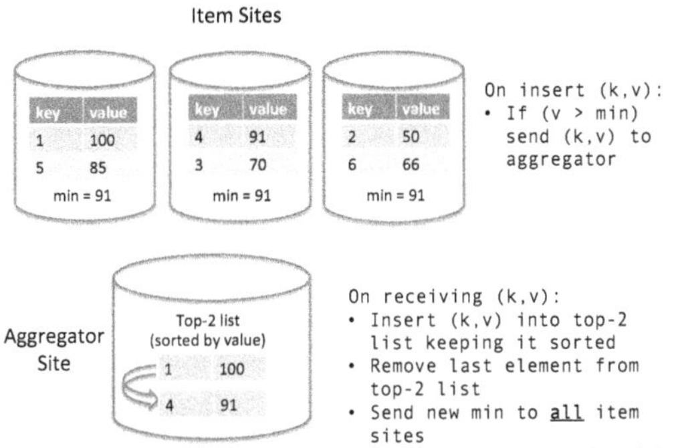

Figure 2: Distributed top-2 computation, improved algorithm.

aggregator site if an item with a larger value is inserted into its local state. This algorithm is illustrated in Figure 2, where each item site has a variable *min* with the current lowest top-k value. In expectation, most item inserts do not affect the aggregator's behavior, and consequently, it is safe for them to remain unobserved by the aggregator site.

This improved top-k algorithm is essentially a simplified distributed version of the well-known *threshold algorithm* for top-k computation [14]. However, note that this algorithm can be extracted *automatically* by analyzing the code for the aggregator site.

Our solution and contributions. This paper presents a new semantics-based method for guaranteeing correct execution of transactions over an inconsistent datastore. Our method is geared towards improving performance in OLTP settings, where the semantics of transactions typically involve a shared global quantity (such as product stock level), most transactions make small incremental changes to this quantity, and transaction behavior is not sensitive to small variations in this quantity except in boundary cases (e.g. the stock level dips below zero). However, our method will still work correctly with workloads that do not satisfy these properties.

We make contributions at two levels. First, we introduce our solution as a high-level framework and protocol. Second, we give concrete instantiations and implementations for each component in the framework, thus providing one particular end-to-end, proof-of-concept system that implements our solution. We stress that the design choices we made in the implementation are not the only possible ones, and that the internals of each component within the overall framework can be refined and/or modified if desired.

The first step in our approach is to analyze the transaction code used in the application (we assume all such code is known up front) to compute a global predicate that tracks its "sensitivity" to different input databases. We then "factorize" the global predicate into a set of local predicates that can be enforced on each node. In the example above, the analysis would determine that the code for the aggregator site leaves the current top-k list unchanged if each newly inserted item is smaller than every current top-k element.

Analyzing transaction code is challenging. It is not obvious what the analysis should compute, although it should be some representation of the transaction semantics that explains how inputs affects outputs. Also, we need to design general analysis algorithms that are not restricted in the same ways as the demarcation protocol [5] or conit-based consistency [41], which are either limited to specific datatypes or require human input.

Our first contribution (Section 2) is an analysis technique that describes transaction semantics using *symbolic tables*. Given a transaction, a symbolic table is a set of pairs in which the first component is a logical predicate on database states and the second component concisely represents the transaction's execution on databases that satisfy the predicate. We show how to compute symbolic tables from transaction code in a simple yet expressive language.

Our second contribution (Section 3) is to use symbolic tables to execute transactions while avoiding inter-node communication. Intuitively, we exploit the fact that if the database state does not diverge from the current entry in the symbolic table, then it is safe to make local updates without synchronizing, but if the state diverges then synchronization is needed. In our top-k example in Figures 1 and 2, as long as no site receives an item whose value exceeds the minimal top-k value, no communication is required. On the other hand, if a value greater than the minimal value is inserted at a site then we would need to notify the aggregator, compute the new top-k list, and communicate the new minimal value to all the sites in the system (including sites that have not received any inserts).

Our *homeostasis protocol* generalizes the example just described and allows disconnected execution while guaranteeing correctness. To reason about transaction behavior in a setting where transactions are deliberately executed on inconsistent data, we introduce a notion of execution correctness based on *observational equivalence* to a serial execution on consistent data. Our protocol is provably correct under the above definition, and subsumes the demarcation protocol and related approaches. It relies on the enforcement of *global treaties*; these are logical predicates that must hold over the global state of the system. In our example, the global treaty is the statement "the current minimal value in the top-k is 91". If an update to the system state violates the treaty, communication is needed to establish a new treaty.

In general, the global treaty can be a complex formula, and checking whether it has been violated may itself require inter-site communication. To avoid this, it is desirable to split the global treaty into a set of *local treaties* that can be checked at each site and that together imply the global treaty. This splitting can be done in a number of ways, which presents an opportunity for optimization to tune the system to specific workloads. Our third contribution (Section 4) is an algorithm for generating local treaties that are chosen based on known workload statistics.

Implementing the homeostasis protocol is nontrivial and raises many systems challenges. Our fourth contribution is a prototype implementation and experimental evaluation (Sections 5 and 6).

2. ANALYZING TRANSACTIONS

This section introduces our program analysis techniques that capture the abstract semantics of a transaction in *symbolic tables*. We first introduce our formal model of transactions (Sections 2.1) and symbolic tables (Section 2.2). We then present a simple yet expressive language $\mathcal{L}$ and explain how to compute symbolic tables for that language (Sections 2.3). Finally, we discuss a higher-level language $\mathcal{L}$++ (Section 2.4) that builds on $\mathcal{L}$ without adding expressiveness and is more suitable for use in practice.

2.1 Databases and transactions

We begin by assuming the existence of a countably infinite set *Obj* of *objects* that can appear in the database, denoted $x, y, z, \ldots$. A database can be thought of as a finite set of objects, each of which has an associated integer value. Objects not in the database are associated with a null default value. More formally, a database D is a map from objects to integers that has finite support.

A *transaction* T is an ordered sequence of atomic *operations*, which can be `read`s, `write`s, computations, or `print` statements. A `read` retrieves a value from the database, while a `write` evaluates an expression and stores the resulting value in a specific object in the database. A computation neither reads from nor writes to the database, but may update temporary variables. Finally, `print` statements allow transactions to generate user-visible output. We define transaction evaluation as follows:

Definition 2.1 (Transaction evaluation). *The result of evaluating a transaction T on a database D, denoted* $\mathrm{Eval}(T, D)$, *is a pair $\langle D', G' \rangle$ where D' is an updated database and G' is a log containing the list of values that the transaction printed during its execution. The order of values in the log is determined by the order in which the print statements were originally executed.*

We assume that transactions are *deterministic*, meaning that D' and G' are uniquely determined by T and D.

2.2 Symbolic tables

We next introduce *symbolic tables*, which allow us to capture the relationship between a transaction's input and its output. The symbolic table for a transaction T can be thought of a map from databases to *partially evaluated transactions*. For any database D, evaluating T on D is equivalent to first finding the transaction associated with D in the symbolic table (which will generally be much simpler than T itself; hence the term "partially evaluated") and then evaluating this transaction on D.

More formally, a symbolic table for a transaction T is a binary relation Q_T containing pairs of the form $\langle \varphi_{\mathcal{D}}, \phi \rangle$ where $\varphi_{\mathcal{D}}$ is a formula in a suitably expressive first-order logic and ϕ is a transaction that produces the same log and final database state as T on databases satisfying $\varphi_{\mathcal{D}}$. The symbolic tables for transactions T_1 and T_2 from Figure 3a and 3b are shown in Figure 4a and Figure 4b. For example, the transaction T_1 behaves identically to the simpler transaction $\texttt{write}(x = \texttt{read}(x) + 1)$ on all databases which satisfy $x + y < 10$, so the symbolic table contains the tuple

$$\langle x + y < 10, \texttt{write}(x = \texttt{read}(x) + 1) \rangle$$

Typically, each execution path through the transaction code corresponds to a unique partially evaluated transaction, although this is not always true if, for example, a transaction executes identical code on both branches of a conditional statement.

We can extend the notion of symbolic tables to work with a set of transactions $\{T_1, T_2, \cdots T_k\}$. A symbolic table for a set of K transactions is a $K + 1$-ary relation. Each tuple in this relation is now of the form $\langle \varphi_{\mathcal{D}}, \phi_1, ..., \phi_N \rangle$ where ϕ_i produces the same final database and log as T_i when evaluated on any database satisfying $\varphi_{\mathcal{D}}$. Such a relation can be constructed from the symbolic tables of individual transactions as follows. For each tuple $\langle \varphi_1, \phi_1, ..., \varphi_N, \phi_N \rangle$ in the cross-product of the symbolic tables of all transactions we add a tuple $\langle \varphi_1 \wedge \varphi_2 \wedge ... \wedge \varphi_K, \phi_1, ..., \phi_N \rangle$ to the symbolic table for $\{T_1, T_2, \ldots, T_k\}$. Figure 4c shows a symbolic table for $\{T_1, T_2\}$.

2.3 Computing symbolic tables

We now explain how to use program analysis to compute symbolic tables automatically from transaction code. Our analysis is specific to a custom language we call $\mathcal{L}$. This language is not Turing-complete – in particular, it has no loops – but it is powerful enough to encode a wide range of realistic transactions. For instance, it allows us to encode all five TPC-C transactions [1], which are representative of many realistic OLTP workloads. We describe how to express a large class of relational database queries in $\mathcal{L}$ in the Appendix, Section A.

```
T1 ::= {x̂ := read(x);
        ŷ := read(y);
        if (x̂ + ŷ < 10) then
          write(x = x̂ + 1)
        else
          write(x = x̂ − 1) }
```

(a) **Transaction T_1**

```
T2 ::= {x̂ := read(x);
        ŷ := read(y);
        if (x̂ + ŷ < 20) then
          write(y = ŷ + 1)
        else
          write(y = ŷ − 1) }
```

(b) **Transaction T_2**

Figure 3: Example transactions for symbolic tables. x and y are database objects, $\hat{x}$ and $\hat{y}$ are temporary program variables.

$\varphi_{\mathcal{D}}$	ϕ
$x + y < 10$	$\texttt{w}(x = \texttt{r}(x) + 1)$
$x + y \geq 10$	$\texttt{w}(x = \texttt{r}(x) - 1)$

(a) **Symbolic table for T_1.**

$\varphi_{\mathcal{D}}$	ϕ
$x + y < 20$	$\texttt{w}(y = \texttt{r}(y) + 1)$
$x + y \geq 20$	$\texttt{w}(y = \texttt{r}(y) - 1)$

(b) **Symbolic table for T_2.**

$\varphi_{\mathcal{D}}$	ϕ_1	ϕ_2
$x + y < 10$	$\texttt{w}(x = \texttt{r}(x) + 1)$	$\texttt{w}(y = \texttt{r}(y) + 1)$
$10 \leq x + y < 20$	$\texttt{w}(x = \texttt{r}(x) - 1]$	$\texttt{w}(y = \texttt{r}(y) + 1)$
$x + y \geq 20$	$\texttt{w}(x = \texttt{r}(x) - 1)$	$\texttt{w}(y = \texttt{r}(y) - 1)$

(c) **Symbolic table for the transaction set $\{T_1, T_2\}$**

Figure 4: Symbolic tables for T_1 and T_2. The `read` and `write` commands are abbreviated as `r` and `w` respectively.

Let $\widehat{Var}$ be a countably infinite set of temporary variables used in the transactions (and not stored in the database). Metavariables $\hat{x}, \hat{y}, \hat{i}, \hat{j}$... range over temporary variables. There are four types of statements in $\mathcal{L}$:

- arithmetic expressions *AExp* (elements are denoted $e, e_0, e_1, ...$)
- boolean expressions *BExp* (elements are denoted $b, b_0, b_1, ...$)
- commands *Com* (elements are denoted $c, c_0, c_1, ...$)
- transactions *Trans* (elements are denoted $T, T_0, T_1, ..$). Each transaction takes a list *Params* of zero or more integer parameters $p, p_0, p_1, \ldots$.

The syntax for the language is shown in Figure 5. The expression $\texttt{read}(x)$, when evaluated, will return the current value of the database object x, while the command $\texttt{write}(x = e)$ will evaluate the expression e and store the resulting value in database object x. There is also a `print` command that evaluates an expression e and appends the resulting value to the end of a log. Unlike other commands, `print` produces output that is visible to external observers.

Given a transaction T in $\mathcal{L}$, we can construct a symbolic table for T inductively using the rules shown in Figure 6. $\varphi\{\frac{e}{x}\}$ denotes the formula obtained from φ by substituting expression e for all occurrences of x.

Algorithmically, we can compute the symbolic table by working backwards from the final statement in each possible execution path. Each such path generates one tuple in the symbolic table. We give an example of how to compute the symbolic table for transaction T_1 from Figure 3a. The left side of Figure 7 shows the code and the right side the computation.

$$
\begin{aligned}
(AExp)\ e &::= n \mid p \mid \hat{x} \mid e_0 \oplus e_1 \mid -e \mid \texttt{read}(x) \\
(BExp)\ b &::= \texttt{true} \mid \texttt{false} \mid e_0 \odot e_1 \mid b_0 \wedge b_1 \mid \neg b \\
(Com)\ c &::= \texttt{skip} \mid \hat{x} := e \mid c_0; c_1 \mid \texttt{if}\ b\ \texttt{then}\ c_1\ \texttt{else}\ c_2 \mid \\
&\quad\ \texttt{write}(x = e) \mid \texttt{print}(e) \\
(Trans)\ T &::= \{c\}\ (P) \\
(Params)\ P &:= \texttt{nil} \mid p, P \\
\oplus &::= + \mid * \qquad \odot ::= \ < \mid = \mid \leq
\end{aligned}
$$

Figure 5: Syntax for the language $\mathcal{L}$

$$[\![T, \{\}]\!] \to [\![c, \{\langle \texttt{true}, \texttt{skip}\rangle\}]\!] \quad \text{where } T = \{c\} \tag{1}$$

$$[\![c_1; c_2, Q]\!] \to [\![c_1, [\![c_2, Q]\!]]\!] \tag{2}$$

$$\left[\!\!\left[\begin{array}{l}\texttt{if}\ b\ \texttt{then}\ c_1 \\ \texttt{else}\ c_2\end{array}, Q\right]\!\!\right] \to \left\{\begin{array}{l}\{\langle b \wedge \varphi, \phi\rangle \mid \langle \varphi, \phi\rangle \in [\![c_1, Q]\!]\} \cup \\ \{\langle \neg b \wedge \varphi, \phi\rangle \mid \langle \varphi, \phi\rangle \in [\![c_2, Q]\!]\}\end{array}\right\} \tag{3}$$

$$[\![(\hat{x} := e), Q]\!] \to \left\{\langle \varphi\{\frac{e}{\hat{x}}\}, (\hat{x} := e; \phi)\rangle \mid \langle \varphi, \phi\rangle \in Q\right\} \tag{4}$$

$$[\![\texttt{skip}, Q]\!] \to Q \tag{5}$$

$$[\![\texttt{write}(x = e), Q]\!] \to \left\{\langle \varphi\{\frac{e}{x}\}, (\texttt{write}(x = e); \phi)\rangle \mid \langle \varphi, \phi\rangle \in Q\right\} \tag{6}$$

$$[\![\texttt{print}(e), Q]\!] \to \left\{\langle \varphi, (\texttt{print}(e); \phi)\rangle \mid \langle \varphi, \phi\rangle \in Q\right\} \tag{7}$$

Figure 6: Rules for constructing a symbolic table for transaction T; Q is the running symbolic table.

First, Rule (1) initializes the symbolic table with a *true* formula representing all database states and a trivial transaction consisting of a single `skip` command. Next, the symbolic table is constructed by working backwards through the code as suggested by Rule (2).

Because the last command is an `if` statement, we apply Rule (3) to create a copy of our running symbolic table; we use one copy for processing the "true" branch and the other for processing the "false" branch. On each branch, we encounter a write to the variable x and apply Rule (6). The statement immediately preceding the `if` is an assignment of a temporary variable. We apply Rule (4), performing a variable substitution on each formula and prepending a variable assignment to each partially evaluated transaction. We apply the same rule again to process the command $\hat{x} := \texttt{read}(x)$.

Note that each tuple in the symbolic table corresponds to a unique execution path in the transaction, and thus a given database instance D may only satisfy a single formula φ in Q_T.

2.4 From $\mathcal{L}$ to $\mathcal{L}$++

$\mathcal{L}$ is a low-level language that serves to set up the foundation for our analysis; we do not expect that end users will specify transactional code in $\mathcal{L}$ directly. In particular, although it is possible to encode many SQL `SELECT` and `UPDATE` statements in $\mathcal{L}$ as described in the Appendix Section A, the direct translation would lead to a large $\mathcal{L}$ program and an associated large symbolic table. Fortunately, we do not need to work with this $\mathcal{L}$ program directly. Because it was generated from a higher-level language, it will have a very regular structure which will translate into regularity in the symbolic table and enable compression.

Therefore, we have created a higher-level language we call $\mathcal{L}$++ which does not add any mathematical expressiveness to $\mathcal{L}$, but directly supports bounded arrays/relations with associated read, update, insert and delete operations. Our algorithm for computing symbolic tables for $\mathcal{L}$ programs can be extended in a straightforward way to compute symbolic tables for programs in $\mathcal{L}$++.

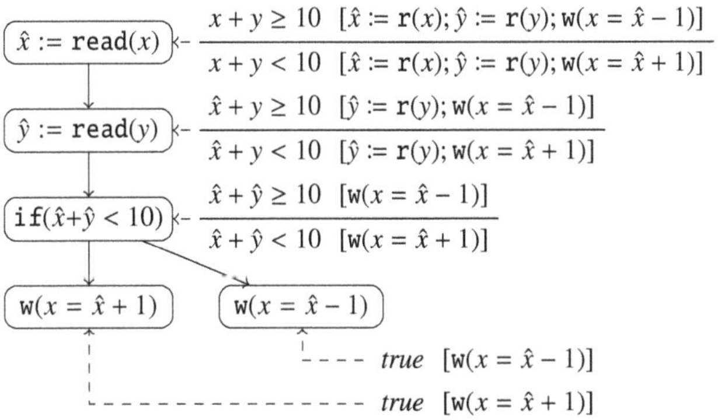

Figure 7: Example of symbolic table construction for T_1 from Figure 3a. Table construction occurs from bottom to top, and `read` and `write` are abbreviated as `r` and `w` respectively.

3. THE HOMEOSTASIS PROTOCOL

This section gives the formal foundation for our homeostasis protocol that uses semantic information to guarantee correct disconnected execution in a distributed and/or replicated system. We introduce a simplified system model (3.1) and several preliminary concepts (3.2) and present the protocol (3.3). The material in this section applies to transactions in any language, not just $\mathcal{L}$ or $\mathcal{L}$++ from Section 2.

3.1 Distributed system model

Assume the system has K sites, each database object is stored on a single site, and transactions run across several sites. Formally, a distributed database is a pair $\langle D, Loc\rangle$, where D is as before and $Loc : Obj \to \{1, \ldots, K\}$ is a mapping from variables to the site identifiers where the variable values are located. Each transaction T_j runs on a particular site i. Formally, there is a *transaction location function* ℓ that maps transactions T_j to site identifiers $\ell(T_j)$.

For ease of exposition, the discussion in Sections 3.2 and 3.3 will focus on systems where the following assumption holds.

Assumption 3.1 (All Writes Are Local). *If T_j runs on site i, it only performs writes on variables x such that* $\mathrm{Loc}(x) = i$. *In other words, all writes are local to the site on which the transaction runs.*

This assumption can be lifted and we can apply the homeostasis protocol in systems and workloads with remote writes. We explain how and under what circumstances this can be done in the Appendix, Section B.

3.2 LR-slices and treaties

As explained in the introduction, the idea behind the homeostasis protocol is to allow transactions to operate *disconnected*, i.e. without inter-site communication, and over a database state that may be inconsistent, as long as appropriate *treaties* are in place to bound the inconsistency and guarantee correct execution. Our protocol relies on the crucial assumption that all transaction code is known in advance. This assumption is standard for OLTP workloads.

In our model of disconnected execution, a transaction is guaranteed to read up-to-date values for variables that are local to the site on which it runs. For values resident at other sites, the transaction conceptually reads a locally available older – and possibly stale – *snapshot* of these values. The actual implementation of how that snapshot is maintained can vary. If we are concerned about space overhead and do not wish to store an actual snapshot, we can simply transform the transaction code by inlining the snapshot value where it is needed. However, we will have to repeat this inlining

```
                          T4 ::= {x̂ := read(x);
T3 ::= {x̂ := read(x);             ŷ := read(y);
        if (x̂ > 0) then           if (ŷ = 1) then
          write(y = 1)              write(z = (x̂ > 10))
        else                      else
          write(y = −1) }           write(z = (x̂ > 100)) }
```

(a) **Transaction T_3** *(b)* **Transaction T_4**

Figure 8: Example transactions for protocol. x is remote for both transactions, while y and z are local.

at the start of each protocol round when the snapshots are synchronized with the actual remote values.

As a concrete example, consider transaction T_3 from Figure 8a. Suppose that T_3 runs on the site where y resides, but that x resides on another site. We can avoid the remote read of x by setting $\hat{x}$ to a locally cached old value of x, say 10. The transaction would still produce the correct writes on y even if the value of x should change on the remote site, as long as that site never allows x to go negative. Thus, if we can set up a *treaty* whereby the system commits to keeping x positive, we can safely run instances of the transaction on stale data that is locally available.

To formalize the intuition provided by the above example, we explore how the local and remote reads of a transaction affect its behavior. Consider transaction T_4 from Figure 8b. Assume that y and z are local and x is remote. The behavior of T_4 depends on both local and global state. Specifically, *if the local value y is* 1 then it matters whether x is greater than 10, and *if the local value y is not* 1, then it matters whether x is greater than 100.

The next few definitions capture this behavior precisely.

Definition 3.2 (Local-remote partition). *Given a database D, a* local-remote partition *is a boolean function p on database objects in D. If $p(x)$ = true we say x is* local *under p; otherwise, it is* remote.

Given a local-remote partition p, we can express any database D as a pair (l, r) where l is a vector containing the values of local database objects and r is a vector containing the values of remote objects. Any transaction T has an associated local-remote partition that marks exactly the objects on site $\ell(T)$ as local.

We next formalize what it means for transactions to behave *equivalently* on different databases. Our notion of equivalence is based on the *observable execution* of transactions: we assume that an external observer can see the final database produced by a transaction as well as any logs it has produced (using `print` statements), but not the intermediate database state(s). Informally, the executions of two (sequences of) transactions are indistinguishable to an external observer if (i) both executions produce the same final database state and (ii) each transaction in the first sequence has a counterpart in the second sequence that produces exactly the same logs.

Alternative notions of observational equivalence are possible: for example, we could assume that an external observer can also see the intermediate database states as the transactions run. Although it is possible to define a variant of the homeostasis protocol that uses this stronger assumption, the protocol will allow fewer interleavings and less concurrency. We therefore use the weaker assumption that only the final database state and logs are externally observable; we believe this is well-justified in practice.

To formally define observational equivalence under Assumption 3.1, we do not need to worry about transactions' effect on the remote part of the database, because remote variables will not be written. This leads to the following definition.

Definition 3.3 (Observational equivalence ($\equiv$)). *Fix some local-remote partition. Let l, l' be vectors of values to be assigned to local objects, let r, r' be vectors of values to be assigned to remote objects, and let G and G' be logs. Then $\langle (l, r), G\rangle \equiv \langle (l', r'), G'\rangle$ if $l = l'$ and $G = G'$.*

The notion of equivalence defined above is reflexive, transitive, and symmetric. We can use it to formalize the assurances that our protocol provides when reading stale data.

Definition 3.4 (Local-remote slice). *Let T be a transaction with an associated local-remote partition. Consider a pair L, R, where each $l \in L$ is a vector of values to be assigned to local objects and each $r \in R$ is a vector of values to be assigned to remote objects. Then $\{(l, r) \mid l \in L, r \in R\}$ defines a set of databases. Suppose* $\mathrm{Eval}(T, (l, r)) \equiv \mathrm{Eval}(T, (l, r'))$ *for every $l \in L$ and $r, r' \in R$. Then (L, R) is a* local-remote slice *(or LR-slice for short) for T.*

For any database in the LR-slice we know that as long as the remote values stay in R, the writes performed and the log produced by the transaction are determined *only* by the local values.

Example 3.5. *Consider our transaction T_4 from above, with y being local and x remote. For notational clarity, we omit z and list the permitted values for y first, then those for x. One LR-slice for T_4 is $(\{1\}, \{11, 12, 13\})$, another is $(\{1\}, \{11, 12, 13, 14\})$, and yet another is $(\{2, 3, 4\}, \{0, 1, 2, 3\})$.*

There is no maximality requirement in our definition of *LR*-slices, as the above example shows. Next, we define global treaties.

Definition 3.6 (Global Treaty). *A* global treaty *Γ is a subset of the possible database states $\mathcal{D}$ for the entire system. The system* maintains *a treaty by requiring synchronization before allowing a transaction to commit with a database state that is not in Γ.*

For our purposes, it will be useful to have treaties that require the system to remain in the same *LR*-slice as the original database. Under such a treaty, by Definition 3.4, it will be correct to run transactions that read old (and potentially out-of-date) values for remote variables. We formalize the treaty property we need as follows.

Definition 3.7 (Valid Global Treaty). *Let $\{T_1, T_2, \ldots, T_n\}$ be a finite set of transactions. We say that Γ is a* valid global treaty *if the following is true. For each transaction T_j with associated site $\ell(T_j)$ and associated local-remote partition, let $L = \{l \mid (l, r) \in \Gamma\}$ and $R = \{r \mid (l, r) \in \Gamma\}$. Then (L, R) must be a LR-slice for T_j.*

3.3 Homeostasis protocol

We next present our protocol to guarantee correct execution of transactions executed on inconsistent data.

The protocol proceeds in rounds. Each round has three phases: treaty generation, normal execution and cleanup. Ideally, the system would spend most of its time in the normal execution phase of the protocol, where sites can execute transactions locally without the need for any synchronization. However, if a client issues a transaction T' that would leave the database in a state that violates the current treaty, the system must end the current round of the protocol, negotiate a new treaty, and move on to the next round.

Treaty generation: In this phase, the system uses the current database D to generate a valid global treaty Γ such that $D \in \Gamma$.

Normal execution: In this phase, each site runs incoming transactions in a disconnected fashion, using local snapshots in reads of remote values as previously explained. Transactions running on a single site may interleave, as long as two invariants are enforced.

First, for each site i there must exist a serial schedule $T_1, \ldots, T_m$ of the committed transactions at that site that produces the same log for each transaction and the same final database state as the interleaved schedule. This is a relaxation of view-serializability and can be enforced conservatively by any classical algorithm that guarantees view-serializability. Second, executing any prefix $T_1, T_2, \ldots, T_j$ of the transactions in this sequence (with $j \leq m$) must yield a final database in Γ. This can be enforced by directly checking whether Γ holds before committing each transaction. The details of how this check can be performed are discussed extensively in Section 4.

If a pre-commit check ever determines that a running transaction T' will terminate in a database state not in Γ, the transaction is aborted and the *cleanup* phase begins.

Cleanup: First, the sites synchronize: each site i broadcasts the value of every local object x that has been updated since the start of the round. Next, we determine the transaction T' that triggered the cleanup phase and was aborted, and we run T' to completion at every site. Finally, we start a new round of the protocol.

In a multi-site system, several transactions may try to make treaty-violating writes at the same time; we rely on a suitable voting algorithm to choose one "winner" T' among them. We abort any "loser" transactions that also tried to violate the treaty and wait for all transactions other than T' to terminate. (If, due to the local concurrency control algorithm used, some transactions are blocking/waiting for T', they are aborted as well.). At the start of the next round, we rerun any remaining "loser" transactions.

We now argue that the protocol above is correct. It is not trivial to capture a good notion of "correctness;" we are after all reasoning about transactions that execute on *inconsistent data*, which is not a common setting in classical concurrency theory.

Our notion of correctness is based on observational equivalence as introduced in Section 3.2. Even though transactions are permitted to operate on inconsistent data, it should be impossible for an external observer to distinguish between the execution of the transactions $T_1, T_2, \ldots, T_n$ using the homeostasis protocol and a serial execution of those same transactions that started on a consistent database. In particular, this means that (i) every transaction executed by the protocol must produce the "right" log, and (ii) we must end up with the "right" final database at the end of each round.

The following theorem captures the correctness of our protocol following the above intuition. In the theorem statement, we use the fact that the transactions executed at any given site can be totally ordered without altering the final database or logs that are produced – this is guaranteed by the invariants that the protocol enforces during the *normal execution* phase (discussed above).

THEOREM 3.8. *Suppose that Γ is a valid global treaty, and let $T_1, T_2, \ldots, T_n$ be a total order on the transactions executed during a single round of the homeostasis protocol such that if T_j is executed before T_k on some site i then $j < k$. If we execute the transactions $T_1, T_2, \ldots, T_n$ in sequence then (i) each T_j produces the same logs as it did in the homeostasis protocol, and (ii) the final database state is the same as the one produced by the homeostasis protocol.*

The proof is in the technical report version of our paper [32].

4. GENERATING TREATIES

Having laid the theoretical groundwork for the homeostasis protocol, we move to the two most important practical considerations: how the global treaty is generated and how it is enforced. Our approach uses symbolic tables as described in Section 2; however, it does not depend on the way that symbolic tables are computed, or even on the language of the transactions. It can be applied to any workloads for which we can compute symbolic tables.

As a running example, we use transactions T_1 and T_2 from Figure 3. Assume that x and y are on different sites, T_1 runs on the site where x resides, and T_2 runs on the site where y resides.

For ease of exposition, we temporarily assume that we are working with transactions whose "output" (writes and logs) are functions of local database objects only; formally:

ASSUMPTION 4.1. *For each transaction T, each partially evaluated transaction ϕ_T in the symbolic table for T, and each database variable x that is read by ϕ_T we assume that $Loc(x) = \ell(T)$.*

This assumption holds for T_1 and T_2 from our previous example; we explain how to lift it in the Appendix, Section C.

4.1 Global and local treaties

In the homeostasis protocol, the first step in every round is to generate a valid global treaty (per Definition 3.7). A naïve but valid global treaty would restrict the database state to the initial D, i.e. require renegotiation on every write. This reduces the homeostasis protocol to a distributed locking protocol; of course, we hope to do better. Intuitively, a good global treaty is one that maximizes the expected length of a protocol round—i.e. one that has a low probability of being violated.

To find a good global treaty, we use the symbolic tables we computed for our transaction workload. At the start of a protocol round, we know the current database D, the set $\mathcal{T}$ of all transactions that may run in the system, and the symbolic table $Q_{\mathcal{T}}$ for $\mathcal{T}$, as shown in Figure 4c for our example set $\{T_1, T_2\}$.

We then pick the unique formula ψ in $Q_{\mathcal{T}}$ that is satisfied by D. For T_1 and T_2, assume that the initial database state is $x = 10$ and $y = 13$. Then ψ is $x + y \geq 20$ (third row of $Q_{\mathcal{T}}$ in Figure 4c). Note that the symbolic table can be precomputed once and reused at each treaty computation, so finding ψ can be done very quickly.

Unfortunately, ψ is not guaranteed to be a valid global treaty under Definition 3.7. In addition, even if it were, it would not be very useful to us as is, since it may be an arbitrarily complex formula and checking whether the database state satisfies ψ may itself require inter-site communication.

For these two reasons, our next step is to factorize ψ into a collection of *local treaties* $\langle \varphi_{\Gamma_1}, \varphi_{\Gamma_2}, \ldots, \varphi_{\Gamma_K} \rangle$. Each local treaty φ_{Γ_i} is a first-order logic formula associated with the site i and uses as free variables only the database objects on site i. The conjunction of all the local treaties should imply ψ:

$$\forall D'. \bigwedge_{1 \leq i \leq K} \varphi_{\Gamma_i}(D') \rightarrow \psi(D') \tag{H1}$$

We also require each local treaty to hold on the original database D; this excludes trivial factorizations such as setting all local treaties to *false*. Formally, for each i ($1 \leq i \leq K$) we require the following:

$$\varphi_{\Gamma_i}(D) \tag{H2}$$

Finally, we take the conjunction of all the local treaties to obtain a global treaty:

$$\varphi_{\Gamma} = \bigwedge_{1 \leq i \leq K} \varphi_{\Gamma_i}(D')$$

Due to the way the global treaty is constructed, all sites can enforce only their respective local treaties and still have the assurance that the global treaty is preserved.

LEMMA 4.2. *Let Γ be the set of all databases satisfying φ_Γ. Under Assumption 4.1, Γ is a valid global treaty.*

The proof is in the technical report version of our paper [32].

From now on, we will blur the distinction between Γ and φ_Γ, and work with an intensional notion of a treaty as a first-order logic formula that represents a set of possible database states.

4.2 Computing good local treaties

The crux to computing φ_Γ is finding local treaties, which is difficult in the general case. The requirements in H1 and H2 create a set of Horn clause constraints $\mathcal{H}$. For an undecidable fragment of first-order logic (such as non-linear arithmetic over integers) finding the solution to $\mathcal{H}$ is undecidable, so the local treaties may not exist. For some first-order theories such as the theory of arrays, solving $\mathcal{H}$ is decidable but the local treaties are not necessarily quantifier-free. However, for certain theories such as linear integer arithmetic, the existence of solutions to $\mathcal{H}$ is decidable, solutions can be effectively computed and the solutions are guaranteed to be quantifier-free. These fragments of first-order logic are the theories that have the quantifier-free Craig's interpolation property. For a more elaborate discussion of solving Horn clause systems, see [33].

We present a method for computing local treaties that is not precise – i.e. it may not find the "optimal" local treaties that maximize protocol round length. However, it always works; in the worst case it degenerates to requiring synchronization on every write. It also allows us to optimize the local treaties based on a model of the expected future transaction workload. Such a model could be generated dynamically by gathering workload data as the system runs, or in other ways. The length of time spent in the optimization is a tunable knob so we can trade off treaty quality versus treaty computation time. This is important because local treaties need to be computed at the start of every protocol round; we do not want the cost of treaty computation to wipe out the savings from reduced communication during the protocol round itself.

There are three steps in our algorithm; preprocessing the global treaty, generating *templates* for the local treaties, and running an optimization to instantiate the templates into actual local treaties.

We begin by preprocessing the formula ψ to obtain a stronger but simpler formula that is a conjunction of *linear constraints*. A linear constraint is an expression of the form

$$\left(\sum_i d_i x_i\right) \odot n$$

where the d_i and n are integers, the x_i are variables and $\odot$ is either $=$, $<$ or $\leq$. The preprocessing causes a loss of precision in that we are now enforcing a stronger property than ψ. However, linear constraints and their variants arise frequently as global treaties in OLTP workloads and feature prominently in related work [5, 20, 41]; thus, we expect to handle most real-world global treaties with minimal precision loss. The preprocessing itself is straightforward and described in the Appendix, Section C.

The next step is to create *local treaty templates*; these contain fresh *configuration variables* that are instantiated later. We generate a template for each site k using the following method. Start with ψ and proceed clause by clause. Given a clause of the form

$$\left(\sum_i d_i x_i\right) \odot n,$$

we replace it by

$$\left(\sum_{Loc(x_i)=k} d_i x_i + c_k\right) \odot n$$

where c_k is a fresh configuration variable.

With our running example transactions T_1 and T_2, initial database state $x = 10$ and $y = 13$ and $\psi : x+y \geq 20$, this process would yield the local treaty templates $\varphi_{\Gamma_1} : (x+c_y \geq 20)$ and $\varphi_{\Gamma_2} : (c_x+y \geq 20)$, where c_x and c_y are configuration variables.

The following theorem states there is always at least one assignment of values to configuration variables that yields actual local treaties. We call any such assignment a *valid treaty configuration*.

THEOREM 4.3. *Given a starting formula ψ and database D, and a set of local treaty templates generated using the above process, there always exists at least one way to assign values to the configuration variables that satisfies H1 and H2.*

The proof is in the technical report version of our paper [32].

In general, many valid treaty configurations may exist. Our final step is to run an optimization to find a configuration that yields local treaties with a low probability of being violated. As mentioned, we assume we have a model that describes expected future workloads; the details of this model and how it is generated are independent of our algorithm. All that we need is a way to use the model to sample (generate) a number of possible future system executions. Once these are available, we create a MaxSAT instance and use a solver to generate the optimal treaty configuration for these future executions. The number and length of future executions we consider are tunable parameters that allow us to trade off quality of treaties versus time spent in the solver. The details of how we generate the MaxSAT instance are in the Appendix, Section C.

4.3 Discussion and scope of our solution

We have presented our approach for supporting disconnected yet correct transaction execution. The homeostasis protocol allows for provably correct disconnected execution as long as a *global treaty* is maintained. The global treaty is enforced using *local treaties* at each site. We compute the treaties automatically, by analyzing transaction code semantics to generate symbolic tables; treaty computation also takes into account expected workload characteristics.

Our key contributions are, first, a fully general homeostasis protocol, and second, a concrete instantiation and implementation of the protocol. Our instantiation uses the language $\mathcal{L}$++ for specifying transactions and performing analysis, and it uses the algorithm described in Section 4.2 for computing local treaties. However, it is possible to use the homeostasis protocol with another language and/or local treaty computation algorithm.

We now discuss the scope of the homeostasis protocol versus that of the most similar existing approaches such as the demarcation protocol [5] and conit-based consistency [41]. Our current algorithm for local treaty computation only generates treaties which are conjunctions of linear constraints; the protocols in the above related work are able to enforce any such constraints if they are specified manually. However, generating linear constraints manually is tedious and error prone, and an automatic approach is preferable.

Consider the problem of maintaining a more complex aggregate than top-k, such as a top-k of minimums. This might arise in a weather monitoring scenario, where an application records temperature observations and displays the k record daily low temperatures for a date, the k *highest* daily low temperatures, and so on. The constraints for correct disconnected computation of the top-k daily low temperatures are linear and in principle derivable manually, but nontrivial. Suppose we now make the program more complex and also request the top-k days with the highest temperature difference (between the daily low and high temperatures). The treaties required remain linear but become quite difficult to infer manually. We discuss both these examples in the Appendix, Section D.

Moreover, there may be applications where the treaties cannot be expressed as linear constraints unless they are trivial (i.e., force synchronization on every write). In such cases, our algorithm from Section 4.2 will generate trivial treaties; however, our protocol is compatible with more powerful local treaty generation algorithms which are not so restricted, whereas the demarcation protocol is fundamentally limited to handle only linear constraints.

In summary, our automated approach removes the error-prone task of manually inferring constraints. Also, our protocol is fully independent of the language used for the transactions and for the treaties. Thus, our solution is open to handling more expressive treaties with suitable algorithmic extensions, which are future work.

5. HOMEOSTASIS IN PRACTICE

In this section, we highlight some of the practical challenges in implementing the homeostasis protocol and discuss specific design decisions we made in our prototype implementation.

5.1 System design

Our system has two main components – an offline component which analyzes application transaction code, and an online server which receives transaction execution requests from clients and coordinates with other servers to establish and maintain treaties. We discuss each of these components next.

Offline preprocessing As shown in Figure 9, there are two main offline components: the analyzer and the protocol initializer.

The analyzer accepts as input transactions in $\mathcal{L}$++ (Section 2.4) and computes (joint) symbolic tables. In doing so, it applies a number of compression techniques to exploit independence properties and keep the size of the symbolic tables small.

Often transaction code operates on multiple database objects independently; for example, the TPC-C New Order transaction orders several different items. The stock level of each item affects the transaction behavior, but each item affects a different portion of the code. Using a read-write dependency analysis like the one in SDD-1 [31], we identify such points of independence and use them to encode symbolic tables more concisely in a factorized manner.

Moreover, transactions may take integer parameters, and the behavior of the transaction obviously depends on the concrete parameter values. Rather than instantiate parameters now, we push the parameterization into the symbolic tables for further compression.

The protocol initializer sets up the *treaty table* – a data structure that at any given time contains the current global treaty and the current local treaty configuration. The treaty table is thus dependent on the current database state; it is initialized offline based on the database state before the system starts accepting transaction requests. Subsequently, it is updated at each treaty negotiation in the online component.

The protocol initializer also performs some further setup for the online component. For every partially evaluated transaction in the symbolic tables produced by the analyzer, it creates and registers a stored procedure which executes this partially evaluated transaction. The stored procedure also includes checks for the satisfaction of the corresponding treaty as maintained in the treaty table. The stored procedure returns a boolean flag indicating whether the local treaty is violated after execution. The protocol initializer also creates a catalog that maps transactions to corresponding stored procedures in the treaty table.

Online execution The online component accepts and executes transactions using the homeostasis protocol. When a transaction execution request arrives from the clients, the system identifies the appropriate stored procedure in the catalog created during offline preprocessing. The server executes the stored procedure within the

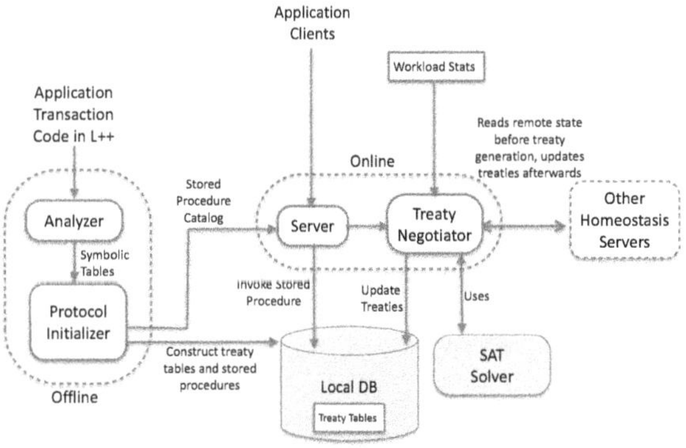

Figure 9: Homeostasis System Architecture.

scope of a transaction. If the local treaty associated with the stored procedure is satisfied, then the transaction commits locally. Otherwise, the server invokes the treaty negotiator to synchronize with other servers and renegotiate a set of treaties. The negotiator uses an optimizer such as a SAT solver to determine local treaties. It then updates the treaty table and propagates the new treaties to all the other nodes. Therefore, every treaty negotiation requires two rounds of global communication—one for synchronizing database state across nodes and one for communicating the new treaties. However, it is possible to eliminate the second round of communication if the solver is deterministic and therefore arrives at the same configuration at each of the replicas independently.

Our implementation uses an underlying 2PC-like protocol for negotiation, and relies on the concurrency control mechanism of the transaction processing engine to ensure serializable execution locally. However, it would be easy to port it to any infrastructure which supports strongly consistent transaction execution.

5.2 Implementation details

Our system is implemented in Java as middleware built on top of the MySQL InnoDB Engine. Each system instance has a similar setup and communicates with the other instances through network channels. When handling failures, we currently rely on the recovery mechanisms of the underlying database. All in-memory state can be recomputed after failure recovery. In the offline component, we use ANTLR-4 to generate a parser for transactions in $\mathcal{L}$++. For finding optimal treaty configurations, we use the Fu-Malik Max SAT procedure [15] in the Microsoft Z3 SMT solver [12].

6. EVALUATION

We now show an experimental evaluation of a prototype implementation of the homeostasis protocol. We run a number of microbenchmarks (Section 6.1), as well as a set of experiments based on TPC-C [1](Section 6.2) to evaluate our implementation in a realistic setting. All experiments run in a replicated system, using the transformations described in the Appendix, Section B.

6.1 Microbenchmarks

With our microbenchmark, we wanted to understand how the homeostasis protocol behaves in our intended use case – an OLTP system where treaty violations and negotiations are rare. In particular, we were interested in the following questions:

- Since our protocol reduces communication, will it yield more performance benefits as the network round trip time (RTT) between replicas increases?

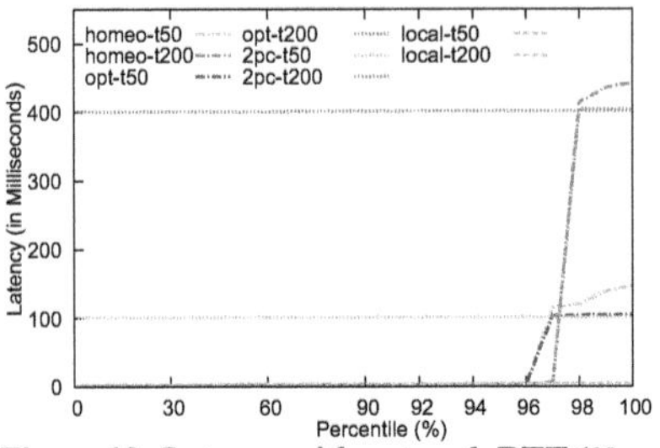

Figure 10: Latency with network RTT ($N_r = 2, N_c = 16$)

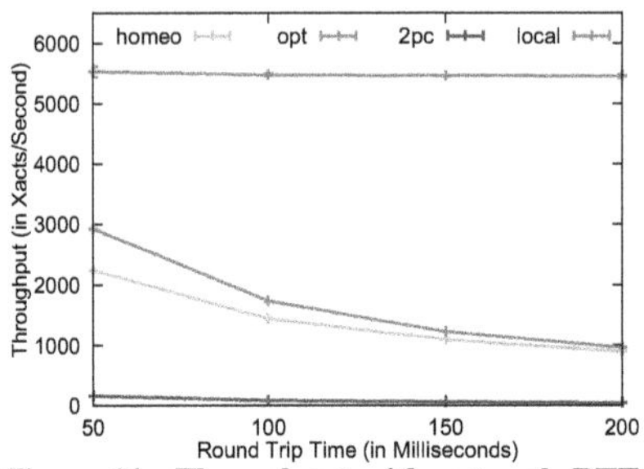

Figure 11: Throughput with network RTT ($N_r = 2, N_c = 16$)

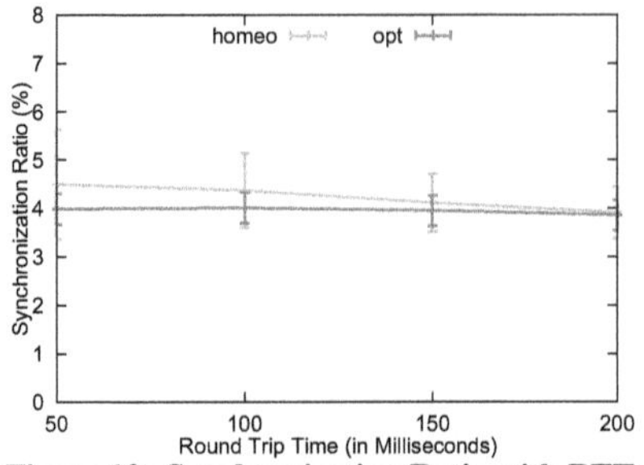

Figure 12: Synchronization Ratio with RTT ($N_r = 2, N_c = 16$)

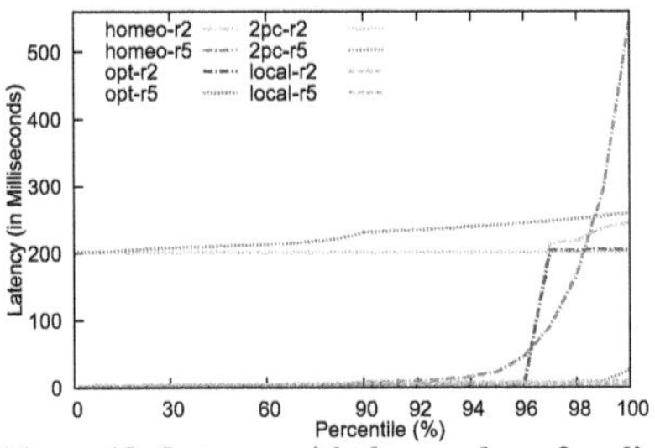

Figure 13: Latency with the number of replicas ($RTT = 100ms, N_c = 16$)

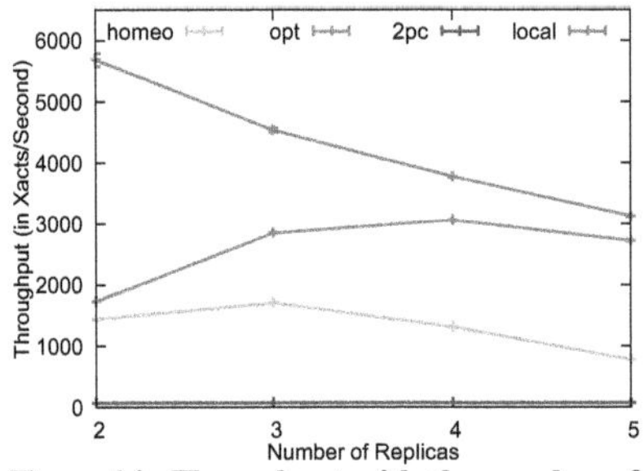

Figure 14: Throughput with the number of replicas ($RTT = 100ms, N_c = 16$)

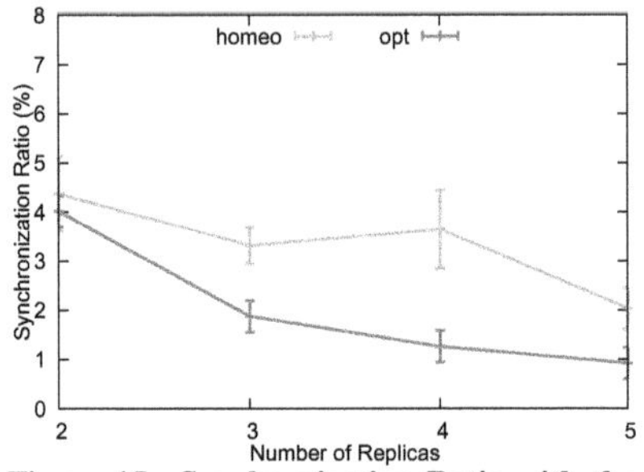

Figure 15: Synchronization Ratio with the number of replicas ($RTT = 100ms, N_c = 16$)

- As the number of replicas increases, treaty negotiations will become more frequent, because each replica must be assigned a "smaller" treaty that is more likely to be violated. How does the performance change with the degree of replication?
- Each replica/server runs multiple clients that issue transactions. How does the performance change when the number of clients per server (i.e., the degree of concurrency) increases?
- How much benefit can we gain from the protocol as compared to three baselines — two-phase commit (2PC), running all transactions locally without synchronizing, and a hand-crafted variant of the demarcation protocol [5]?

To answer these questions, we designed a configurable workload inspired by an e-commerce application. We use a database with a single table `Stock` with just two attributes: item ID (`itemid` INT) and quantity (`qty` INT). The item ID is the primary key. The workload consists of a single parameterized transaction which reads an item specified by `itemid` and updates the quantity as though placing an order. If the quantity is initially greater than one, it decreases the quantity; otherwise, it refills it. SQL pseudocode for the transaction template is shown below.

Listing 1: The microbenchmark transaction; @itemid is an input parameter, while REFILL is a constant.

```
SELECT qty FROM stock WHERE itemid=@itemid;
if (qty>1) then
    new_qty=qty-1
else
    new_qty=REFILL-1
UPDATE stock SET qty=new_qty WHERE itemid=@itemid;
```

We implemented two baseline transaction execution solutions: *local* and *two phase commit (2PC)*. In *local* mode, each replica executes the transactions locally without any communication; thus, database consistency across replicas is not guaranteed. Whereas the local mode provides a bare-bones performance baseline for how fast our transactions run locally, the 2PC mode provides a baseline of the performance of a geo-replicated system implemented in a classical way. In addition to these baselines, we also compare against a hand-crafted solution (OPT) which exploits the transaction semantics in the same way as the demarcation protocol [5]. At each synchronization point, this solution splits and allocates the remaining stock level of each item equally among the replicas. For uniform workloads, it is therefore the optimal solution.

Our workload has several configurable parameters: network RTT, number of replicas (N_r), number of clients per replica (N_c), and the REFILL value. By default, we set RTT to 100 ms, the number of replicas to two, the number of clients per replica to 16 and REFILL to 100. The database is populated with ten thousand items.

All the experiments are run on a single Amazon EC2 c3.8xlarge instance, with 32 vCPUs, 60GB memory, and 2x320GB SSDs, running Ubuntu 14.04 and MySQL Version 5.5.38 as the local database system. We run all replicas on the same instance, and we simulate different RTTs. For each run, we start the system for 5 seconds as a warm-up phase to allow the system to reach a steady state, and then measure the performance for the next 300 seconds. All data points are averages over three runs, and error bars are given in the figures to account for the differences between runs.

Varying RTT Our first experiment varies the network RTT from 50 ms to 200 ms, using the default values for all other parameters. Figure 10 shows the transaction latency by percentile. When using the homeostasis protocol, 97% of the transactions execute locally, with latency less than 4 ms. When a transaction requires treaty negotiation, the latency goes up to around 2RTT plus an additional overhead of less than 50 ms to find new treaties using the solver. This solver overhead manifests at the far right of Figure 10 where the latency for the homeostasis protocol is higher than for OPT for the same RTT setting. Under 2PC, each transaction requires two RTTs, and thus the transaction latency is consistently twice the RTT. In local mode, all the transactions complete in about 2 ms.

Figure 11 shows the throughput per second for each replica. In 2PC mode, it is less than 10 transactions per second due to the network communication cost. The homeostasis protocol allows 100x-1000x more throughput than 2PC, depending on the RTT setting. The difference between the throughput for the homeostasis protocol and local mode can be attributed to the small fraction of trans-

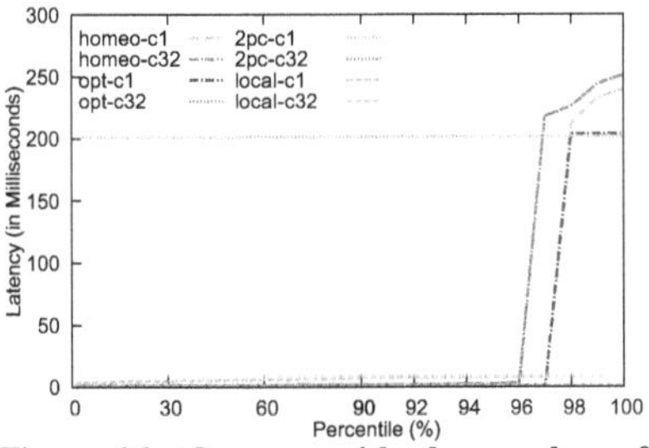

Figure 16: Latency with the number of clients ($N_r = 2, RTT = 100ms$)

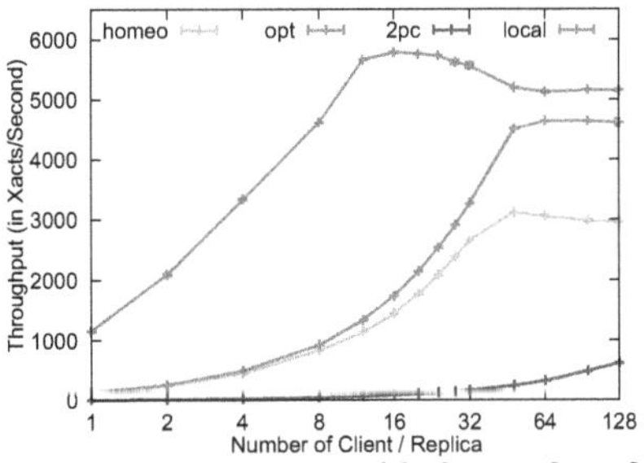

Figure 17: Throughput with the number of clients ($N_r = 2, RTT = 100ms$)

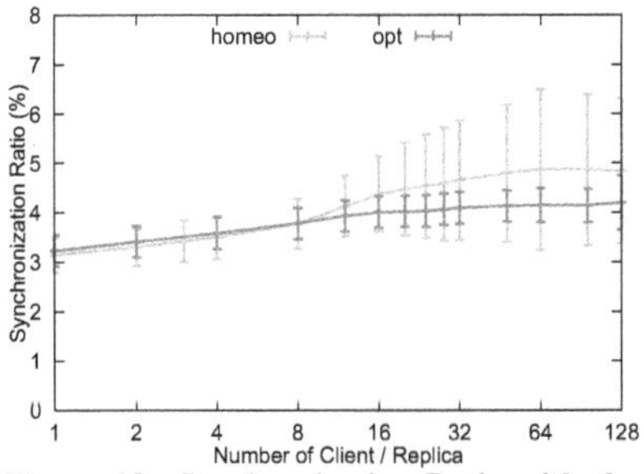

Figure 18: Synchronization Ratio with the number of clients ($N_r = 2, RTT = 100ms$)

actions which require synchronization; for example, if only 2% of transactions require treaty negotiation and the RTT is 100ms, this leads to an average latency of 4*0.98+200*0.02=7.92ms. Finally, Figure 12 shows the synchronization ratio, i.e., the percentage of transactions which require synchronization under the homeostasis protocol and under OPT. The ratio is almost identical, showing that we achieve near optimal performance for this workload.

Varying number of replicas Next, we vary the number of replicas from 2 to 5, while setting the other parameters to their default values. Figure 13 shows the transaction latency profile. With a higher number of replicas, the local treaties are expected to be more conservative and therefore lead to more frequent violations; this leads to an increase in latency. The transaction latency also increases for the local and 2PC modes. In the local case, this is due to the increased resource contention since our experimental setup requires us to run all the replicas on the same server. In 2PC, each transaction stays in the system longer since it has to wait for communication with more replicas; this causes an increase in conflict rates which further increases transaction latency. Figure 14 shows the throughput per second for each replica. As expected, the throughput decreases for all modes as the degree of replication increases. The synchronization ratio shown in Figure 15 also decreases with the decrease in the overall throughput of the system.

Varying number of clients Finally, we vary the number of clients per replica from 1 to 128, while setting the other parameters to their default values. Figure 16 shows the transaction latency profile. In all modes, the transaction latency increases with the number of clients due to higher data and resource contention but is mostly dominated by network latency. Figure 17 shows the throughput per replica. When using the homeostasis protocol with 16 clients, the throughput per client reaches 80% of the throughput per client we observe for 4 clients, indicating good scalability with the number of clients. The curve for the local mode shows a plateau or even exhibits a drop in throughput as the number of clients per replica approaches 16; with a 32-core instance, we reach a point where all cores are in use and the system is overloaded. When running the homeostasis protocol or OPT in the same case, transactions in the treaty negotiation phase free up the CPU and therefore exhibit a plateau at a higher number of clients per replica.

We discuss additional experiments that explore the behavior of the system when we vary other parameters in Appendix Section F.

6.2 TPC-C

To evaluate the performance of the homeostasis protocol over more realistic workloads with multiple transactions, larger databases, and non-uniform workload characteristics, we created a set of experiments based on the TPC-C benchmark.

Data The benchmark describes an order-entry and fulfillment environment. The database contains the following tables: `Warehouse`, `District`, `Orders`, `NewOrder`, `Customers`, `Items`, `Stock` and `Orderline` with attributes as specified in the TPC-C benchmark. The initial database is populated with 10,000 customers, 10 warehouses, 10 districts per warehouse and 1000 items per district for a total of 100,000 entries in the `Stock` table. Initial stock levels are set to a random value between 0 and 100.

Workload We use three transactions based on the three most frequent transactions in TPC-C. The `New Order` transaction places a new order for some quantity (chosen uniformly at random between 1 to 5) of a particular item from a particular district and at a particular warehouse. The `Payment` transaction updates the customer, district and warehouse balances as though processing a payment; we assume that the customer is specified based on customer number. The `Delivery` transaction fulfills the oldest order at a particular warehouse and district. We explain how we encode the transactions in $\mathcal{L}$++ and what treaties are produced in the Appendix, Section E.

For all experiments, we issue a mix of 45% `New Order`, 45% `Payment` and 10% `Delivery` transactions. To simulate a skew in the workload, we mark 1% of the items as "hot" and vary the percentage of `New Order` transactions that order hot items. We denote this percentage as H. For example, a value of $H = 10$ indicates that 10% of all `New Order` transactions order the 1% hot items.

Setup We run all our experiments on c3.4xlarge Amazon EC2 instances (16 cores, 30GB memory, 2x160GB SSDs) deployed at the Virginia (UE), Oregon (UW), Ireland (IE), Singapore (SG) and Sao Paolo (BR) datacenters. The average round trip latencies between these datacenters are shown in Table 1. For all the experiments, we use a single c3.4xlarge node per datacenter. All two-replica experiments use instances from the UE and UW datacenters. There are eight clients per replica issuing transactions. All measurements are performed over a period of 500s after a warmup period of 100s. We only report measurements for the `New Order` transactions, following the TPC-C specification. For comparison, we run the same workload against an implementation of the two-phase commit protocol and a version of the homeostasis protocol with hand crafted treaties (OPT) which minimize the expected number of treaty violations for uniform workloads. All reported values are averages of at least three runs with a standard deviation of less than 6% in all experiments.

	UE	UW	IE	SG	BR
UE	< 1	64	80	243	164
UW	-	< 1	170	210	227
IE	-	-	< 1	285	235
SG	-	-	-	< 1	372
BR	-	-	-	-	< 1

Table 1: Average RTTs between Amazon datacenters (in milliseconds)

Varying Workload Skew For this experiment we vary H, i.e., the percentage of transactions that involve hot items, from 1 to 50. The latency profile for different values of H is shown in Figure 19. As the value of H increases, the treaties for the hot items are vio-

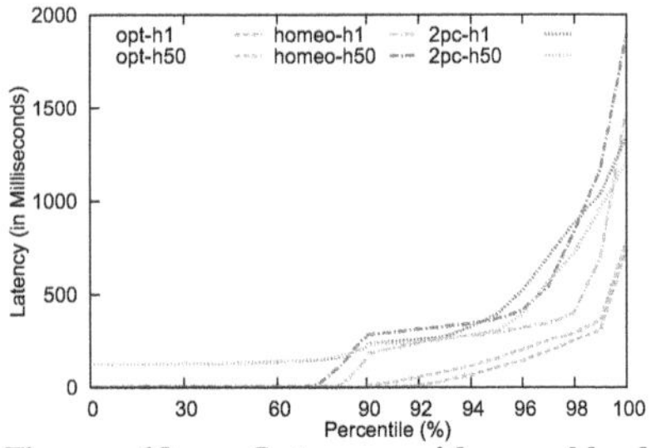

Figure 19: Latency with workload skew(N_r = 2, N_c = 8)

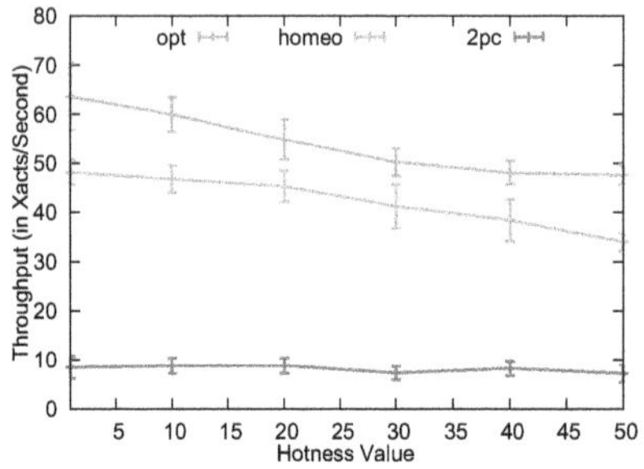

Figure 20: Throughput with workload skew(N_r = 2, N_c = 8)

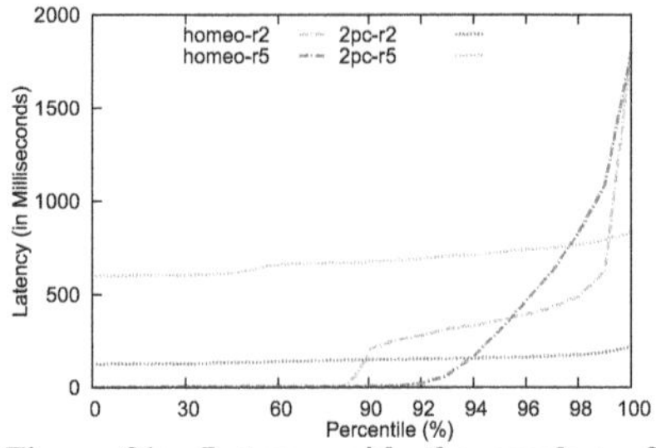

Figure 21: Latency with the number of replicas(N_c = 8, H = 10)

lated more often, so a higher fraction of transactions takes a latency hit. In comparison, the latency profile for two-phase commit (2PC) is relatively unaffected as it always incurs a two RTT latency hit. As shown in Figure 20, the throughput for 2PC drops with increased H due to an increased rate of conflicts. The throughput for the homeostasis protocol drops as well, but the throughput per replica is still significantly higher than that for 2PC. Note that we only show throughput numbers for the `New Order` transaction, which constitutes 45% of the workload. The actual number of successful transactions committed by the system per second is more than twice this value. We can increase throughput by running more clients per replica; we omit these results due to space constraints.

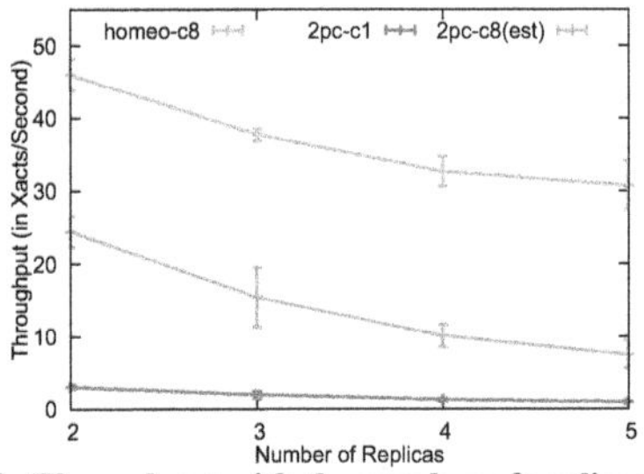

Figure 22: Throughput with the number of replicas(H = 10)

Varying the number of replicas For this experiment, we set the value of H to 10 and measure the latency and throughput of the `New Order` transactions as we increase the number of replicas. The replicas are added in the order UE, UW, IE, SG and BR. The latency profile and the throughput per replica are shown in Figures 21 and 22. As we add replicas, the maximum RTT between any two replicas increases. This manifests itself towards the 98th percentile as an upward shift in the latency profiles. With five replicas, the treaties become more expensive to compute, which also contributes to the upwards latency shift. On the other hand, with fewer replicas, the throughput is significantly higher, which means that with more replicas, a higher fraction of transactions cause treaty violations. This explains the leftward shift of the inflection point on the curves as the number of replicas decreases. In all cases, the `New Order` throughput values for the homeostasis protocol are substantially higher than the 2PC baseline. In our 2PC implementation, we only use a single client per replica: with a larger number of clients, conflicts caused frequent transaction aborts. Figure 22 also shows a very conservative upper bound on maximum throughput for 2PC that is obtained by multiplying the measured throughput for a single client by a factor of 8. Clearly, even this estimate still has a significantly lower throughput than the homeostasis protocol. Thus, the homeostasis protocol clearly outperforms 2PC in all situations.

The long tail for latencies is due to the fact that the minimum allowable value of MySQL's lock wait time-out is 1 second. In high-contention environments, more transactions time out, giving long tail latencies for high values of H or high numbers of replicas.

Distributed Deployment The goal of this experiment is to study the feasibility of deploying the homeostasis protocol in a realistic setting where each database replica is distributed across a number of machines. We distribute our database so that each machine handles all requests pertaining to one TPC-C warehouse. This distributed database is replicated across the UE and UW datacenters. We use 10 warehouses (and therefore 10 machines per datacenter), 100 districts per warehouse, 1M customers and a total of 1M entries in the stock relation. We use a transaction mix of 49% New Order, 49% Payment and 2% Delivery transactions. Due to space limitations we only highlight our results here and present them more fully in the Appendix, Section F.2.

Using the homeostasis protocol, we achieve an overall system throughput of nearly 9000 transactions per second, or around 80% of what is achievable under OPT. As expected, the fraction of transactions requiring synchronization under homeostasis is higher than under OPT and increases as we increase the skew in the workload. Unsurprisingly, given the average latency between the two datacenters, the maximum possible throughput achievable using 2PC is around an order of magnitude smaller than with OPT.

7. RELATED WORK

Exploiting application semantics to improve performance in concurrent settings has been explored extensively, from thirty years ago [16] up to today [3]. We refer the reader to [39] for a more complete survey, and only highlight the approaches most similar to ours.

The demarcation protocol [5, 21] and distributed divergence control protocols [40, 29] based on epsilon serializability [30] exploit semantics to allow non-serializable interleavings of database operations. The demarcation protocol allows asynchronous execution of transactions in a replicated system by maintaining an integrity constraint. The distributed divergence control protocol allows some inconsistency but bounds it to ensure that the schedules produced are within epsilon of serializability. More recently, Yu and Vahdat proposed a continuous consistency model for replicated services [41] which allows bounded inconsistency and uses anti-entropy algorithms [27, 28] to keep it at an acceptable level. As discussed in Section 4.3, the distinguishing feature of our work is the use of program analysis techniques to automatically infer the constraints to be maintained, and the fact that the homeostasis protocol is independent both of the transaction language and the constraint language.

The Calvin [37] and Lynx [42] systems also perform static analysis of transactions to improve performance; however, they ensure that all transactions operate on consistent data, whereas we allow them to see inconsistent data if the inconsistency is "irrelevant."

There is extensive research on identifying cases where transactions or operations commute and allowing interleavings which are non-serializable yet correct [22, 23, 19, 34, 2, 24]. Our solution extends this work, as the use of LR-slices allows transactions to commute in special cases where they may not commute in general. The approach in [9] allows for state-dependent commutativity, but at the interface level rather than the read/write level. $\mathcal{I}$-confluence invariants [3] and warranties [25] both have similarities to our treaties, but neither is inferred automatically from code.

Some systems allow inconsistency that does impact transaction semantics when deemed acceptable cost-wise for the application [20, 4]. Including the cost of inconsistency into our treaty optimization metric is future work.

There is more general distributed systems work that explains how to detect whether global properties hold [7, 26], and how to enforce them using local assertions [6]. However, this work does not address how the local assertions may be computed.

There is a large body of work on using synthesis to develop concurrent programs [8, 38, 35, 18]. Our applications are database transactions rather than general-purpose code, and we deal with extra challenges such as the need to optimize based on workload.

8. CONCLUSION

We have presented the homeostasis protocol, which allows transactions to execute correctly in a multi-node system while minimizing communication. We extract consistency requirements from transaction code *automatically via program analysis* rather than requiring human input, which enables a fully automated adaptive consistency management protocol. We have presented the method as a general framework and provided concrete implementations for each component in the framework.

9. ACKNOWLEDGMENTS

We would like to thank Peter Bailis and the anonymous SIGMOD reviewers for their insightful comments.

This research has been supported by the NSF under Grants CNS-1413972, CCF-1253165, CNS-1012593 and IIS-0911036, by the European Research Council under grant ERC Grant 279804, by the iAd Project funded by the Research Council of Norway and by a Google Research Award. Any opinions, findings, conclusions or recommendations expressed in this paper are those of the authors and do not necessarily reflect the views of the sponsors.

10. REFERENCES

[1] http://tpc.org/tpcc.

[2] P. Alvaro, N. Conway, J. M. Hellerstein, and W. R. Marczak. Consistency analysis in Bloom: a CALM and collected approach. In *CIDR*, pages 249–260, 2011.

[3] P. Bailis, A. Fekete, M. J. Franklin, A. Ghodsi, J. M. Hellerstein, and I. Stoica. Coordination avoidance in database systems. In *VLDB*, 2015.

[4] P. Bailis, S. Venkataraman, M. J. Franklin, J. M. Hellerstein, and I. Stoica. Probabilistically bounded staleness for practical partial quorums. *Proc. VLDB Endow.*, 5(8):776–787, Apr. 2012.

[5] D. Barbará-Millá and H. Garcia-Molina. The demarcation protocol: a technique for maintaining constraints in distributed database systems. *The VLDB Journal*, 3(3):325–353, July 1994.

[6] O. S. Carvalho and G. Roucairol. On the distribution of an assertion. In *PODC '82*, pages 121–131, 1982.

[7] K. M. Chandy and L. Lamport. Distributed snapshots: Determining global states of distributed systems. *ACM Trans. Comput. Syst.*, 3(1):63–75, Feb. 1985.

[8] S. Cherem, T. Chilimbi, and S. Gulwani. Inferring locks for atomic sections. In *PLDI*, 2008.

[9] A. T. Clements et al. The scalable commutativity rule: Designing scalable software for multicore processors. In *SOSP*, pages 1–17, 2013.

[10] B. F. Cooper et al. PNUTS: Yahoo!'s hosted data serving platform. *Proc. VLDB Endow.*, 1(2):1277–1288, Aug. 2008.

[11] J. C. Corbett et al. Spanner: Google's globally-distributed database. In *OSDI*, pages 251–264, 2012.

[12] L. De Moura and N. Bjørner. Z3: An efficient smt solver. TACAS'08/ETAPS'08, 2008.

[13] G. DeCandia et al. Dynamo: Amazon's highly available key-value store. In *SOSP*, pages 205–220, 2007.

[14] R. Fagin, A. Lotem, and M. Naor. Optimal aggregation algorithms for middleware. In *PODS*, pages 102–113, 2001.

[15] Z. Fu and S. Malik. On solving the partial max-sat problem. SAT'06.

[16] H. Garcia-Molina. Using semantic knowledge for transaction processing in a distributed database. *ACM TODS*, June 1983.

[17] A. Gupta et al. Mesa: Geo-replicated, near real-time, scalable data warehousing. In *VLDB*, 2014.

[18] P. Hawkins, A. Aiken, K. Fisher, M. Rinard, and M. Sagiv. Concurrent data representation synthesis. In *PLDI*, 2012.

[19] M. Herlihy and E. Koskinen. Transactional boosting: a methodology for highly-concurrent transactional objects. In *PPOPP*, 2008.

[20] T. Kraska, M. Hentschel, G. Alonso, and D. Kossmann. Consistency rationing in the cloud: pay only when it matters. *Proc. VLDB Endow.*, 2(1):253–264, Aug. 2009.

[21] T. Kraska, G. Pang, M. J. Franklin, S. Madden, and A. Fekete. MDCC: multi-data center consistency. In *EuroSys*, 2013.

[22] A. Kumar and M. Stonebraker. Semantics based transaction management techniques for replicated data. In *SIGMOD*, 1988.

[23] C. Li, D. Porto, A. Clement, J. Gehrke, N. Preguica, and R. Rodrigues. Making geo-replicated systems fast as possible, consistent when necessary. In *OSDI*, pages 265–278, 2012.

[24] C. Li et al. Automating the choice of consistency levels in replicated systems. In *USENIX ATC 14*, pages 281–292, June 2014.

[25] J. Liu, T. Magrino, O. Arden, M. D. George, and A. C. Myers. Warranties for faster strong consistency. NSDI'14, pages 503–517.

[26] K. Marzullo and G. Neiger. Detection of global state predicates. In *In WDAG '91*, pages 254–272. Springer-Verlag, 1991.

[27] C. Olston, B. T. Loo, and J. Widom. Adaptive precision setting for cached approximate values. In *SIGMOD*, 2001.

[28] C. Olston and J. Widom. Offering a precision-performance tradeoff for aggregation queries over replicated data. In *VLDB*, 2000.

[29] C. Pu and A. Leff. Replica control in distributed systems: as asynchronous approach. In *SIGMOD*, pages 377–386, 1991.

[30] K. Ramamritham and C. Pu. A formal characterization of epsilon serializability. *IEEE TKDE.*, 7(6):997–1007, Dec. 1995.

[31] J. Rothnie,Jr. et al. Introduction to a system for distributed databases (sdd-1). *ACM TODS*, 1980.

[32] S. Roy, L. Kot, N. Foster, J. Gehrke, H. Hojjat, and C. Koch. Writes that fall in the forest and make no sound: Semantics-based adaptive data consistency. *CoRR*, abs/1403.2307, 2014.

[33] P. Rümmer, H. Hojjat, and V. Kuncak. Disjunctive interpolants for horn-clause verification. In *CAV*, pages 347–363, 2013.

[34] M. Shapiro, N. Preguica, C. Baquero, and M. Zawirski. A comprehensive study of convergent and commutative replicated data types. Technical report, INRIA, Rocquencourt, France, 2011.

[35] A. Solar-Lezama, C. G. Jones, and R. Bodik. Sketching concurrent data structures. In *PLDI*, volume 43, pages 136–148, 2008.

[36] D. B. Terry, M. M. Theimer, K. Petersen, A. J. Demers, M. J. Spreitzer, and C. H. Hauser. Managing update conflicts in Bayou, a weakly connected replicated storage system. In *SOSP*, 1995.

[37] A. Thomson, T. Diamond, S.-C. Weng, K. Ren, P. Shao, and D. J. Abadi. Calvin: Fast distributed transactions for partitioned database systems. In *SIGMOD*, pages 1–12, 2012.

[38] M. Vechev, E. Yahav, and G. Yorsh. Abstraction-guided synthesis of synchronization. In *POPL*, volume 45, pages 327–338, 2010.

[39] G. Weikum and G. Vossen. *Transactional Information Systems*. Morgan Kaufmann, 2002.

[40] K.-L. Wu, P. S. Yu, and C. Pu. Divergence control for epsilon-serializability. In *ICDE*, pages 506–515, 1992.

[41] H. Yu and A. Vahdat. Design and evaluation of a continuous consistency model for replicated services. In *OSDI*, 2000.

[42] Y. Zhang, R. Power, S. Zhou, Y. Sovran, M. K. Aguilera, and J. Li. Transaction chains: Achieving serializability with low latency in geo-distributed storage systems. In *SOSP*, pages 276–291, 2013.

APPENDIX

A. EXPRESSING TRANSACTIONS IN $\mathcal{L}$

In this section, we explain how to translate programs in a higher-level language such as SQL or $\mathcal{L}$++ to $\mathcal{L}$. The translation lets us formalize the intuition that adding native support for bounded relations to $\mathcal{L}$ does not alter the expressive power of the language.

$\mathcal{L}$ does not have built-in support for relations or arrays. However, these data structures and read/write accesses to them can be simulated using nested if-then-else statements. An array a of length n is stored in the database as a set of objects $\{a_0, a_1, \ldots, a_{n-1}\}$. The following code reads the $\hat{\imath}$th element of the array a into a temporary variable $\hat{x}$:

$$\texttt{if } \hat{\imath} = 0 \texttt{ then } \hat{x} := \texttt{read}(a_0)$$
$$\texttt{else if } \hat{\imath} = 1 \texttt{ then } \hat{x} := \texttt{read}(a_1)$$
$$\texttt{else if ... else skip}$$

We use the command $\hat{x} := \texttt{read}(a(\hat{\imath}))$ as syntactic sugar for the code above. Analogously, we use the command $\texttt{write}(a(\hat{\imath}) := \hat{x})$ as syntactic sugar for a sequence of if-then-else statements that writes the value of the temporary variable $\hat{x}$ into the $\hat{\imath}$th element of a.

Once we have one-dimensional arrays, we can extend them to two-dimensional arrays in the standard manner, by storing a two-dimensional array in row-major order inside a single-dimensional array and accessing elements by offset computation. Thus $a(\hat{\imath})(\hat{\jmath})$ (accessing the i, jth element in the two dimensional array a) is syntactic sugar for $a(\hat{\imath} * D + \hat{\jmath})$, where D is the size of the array along the first dimension.

Two-dimensional arrays allow us to represent relations (tables). If we assume a bound on the maximum number of tuples in any relation, we can encode bounded (foreach) iteration over relations and express `SELECT-FROM-WHERE` clauses as a sequential scan over the entire relation. In the sequential scan, for each tuple in the array we check whether it matches the selection condition using if-then-else statements.

For SQL `UPDATE` statements, database insertions and deletes are modeled by "preallocating" extra space in the array and keeping track of used vs. unused space with suitable placeholder values for unused portions of the array.

The above encoding is very straightforward and can easily be performed automatically by a compiler. Encoding more expressive language constructs than `SELECT-FROM-WHERE` will require more elaborate compilation techniques. Depending on the source language, the process may run into the theoretical expressiveness limits of $\mathcal{L}$; however, we have determined (through manual inspection) that $\mathcal{L}$ is expressive enough to encode all five TPC-C transactions, which are representative of many realistic OLTP workloads.

It is possible to add extensions to $\mathcal{L}$ and make it more expressive so it provides support for unbounded iteration or complex data structures. These extensions are compatible with our analysis, as long as we add appropriate rules for symbolic table computation and understand that the symbolic table formulas φ may need a more expressive logical language.

B. HANDLING REMOTE WRITES

In this section, we explain how to adapt the homeostasis protocol to handle non-local writes, removing the need for Assumption 3.1. The most common use case for remote writes is replicated systems, where – conceptually – a write to an object requires a remote write on each site which keeps a replica of the object.

The basic idea is to add extra logic to the existing protocol that transforms arbitrary transactions into transactions containing only local writes prior to execution. The transformations are conceptually simple and are easily applied automatically, without human intervention. We first explain in detail how to do this for programs in our language $\mathcal{L}$ from Section 2.3, and then discuss how the transformation would apply to programs in other and/or richer languages.

(a) Original transaction	(b) Transformed for Site 1
$\hat{x} := \texttt{r}(x)$	$\hat{x} := \texttt{r}(x) + \texttt{r}(dx_1)$
$\texttt{if } 0 < \hat{x} \texttt{ then}$	$\texttt{if } 0 < \hat{x} \texttt{ then}$
$\quad \texttt{w}(x = \hat{x} - 1)$	$\quad \texttt{w}(dx_1 = \hat{x} - 1 - \texttt{r}(x))$
$\texttt{else}$	$\texttt{else}$
$\quad \texttt{w}(x = 10)$	$\quad \texttt{w}(dx_1 = 10 - \texttt{r}(x))$

$$\texttt{if } 0 < \texttt{r}(x) + \texttt{r}(dx_1) \texttt{ then}$$
$$\quad \texttt{w}(dx_1 = \texttt{r}(dx_1) - 1)$$
$$\texttt{else}$$
$$\quad \texttt{w}(dx_1 = 10 - \texttt{r}(x))$$

(c) **Transformed and simplified**

Figure 23: Transforming transactions to eliminate non-local writes. The `read` and `write` commands are abbreviated as `r` and `w` respectively.

Given a set of transactions in $\mathcal{L}$, we proceed as follows. For each database object x we introduce a set of fresh database objects $\{dx_1, dx_2, \ldots, dx_M\}$ – one for each site that runs transactions that perform remote writes on x. Each dx_i is local to site i and is initialized to 0. We modify any transaction executed on site i so it writes to dx_i instead of x.

An example of this transformation is shown in Figure 23. We assume that the original transaction (Figure 23a) runs on site 1, but x resides on some other site. To keep the example simple, we also assume that this transaction is the *only* transaction in the system that reads or writes to x.

The transformed transaction (Figure 23b) writes to the local dx_1 instead of the remote x; however, it maintains the invariant that $x + dx_1$ will always be equal to the "real" value of x. Thus every remote write is replaced with a local one. However, synchronization may still be required because of remote reads. For example, the transaction from Figure 23b must always perform a remote read to determine the value of x.

If we had other transactions in the system that read x, they would need to be transformed to read both x and dx_1 each time, and to work with the sum of these two values instead of just the value of x. If we had transactions running on sites other than i that *write* to x, we would need to introduce additional dx_i objects and apply appropriate transformations. In the common case where x is a replicated object that is read and written on each of K sites, we would introduce a dx_i for every site. Every statement of the form $\texttt{read}(x)$ would be translated to

$$\texttt{read}(x) + \sum_{j=1 \text{ to } K} \texttt{read}(dx_j)$$

Every $\texttt{write}(x = \hat{x})$ for a transaction running on site i would be translated to

$$\texttt{write}(dx_i) = \hat{x} - \texttt{read}(x) - \sum_{j=1 \text{ to } K,\, j \neq i} \texttt{read}(dx_j)$$

The next step is to eliminate as many remote reads as possible using semantics-preserving program transformations. In our running example, the resulting transaction for Site 1 is shown in Figure 23c. This transaction replaces the expression $\hat{x} - 1 - \texttt{r}(x)$, which references the remote variable x, with the equivalent expression

$$(\mathtt{r}(x) + \mathtt{r}(dx_1)) - 1 - \mathtt{r}(x) \quad = \quad \mathtt{r}(dx_1) - 1$$

which does not. This simplified transaction can avoid remote reads much of the time: if we can generate a treaty which ensures that $0 < x + dx_1$ then the transaction can be executed on Site 1 using only locally available information about the value of dx_1.

All the transformations described above are easy to perform automatically. Once we have applied the transformations to all transaction code, we can run the system using the homeostasis protocol as described previously, because Assumption 3.1 now holds. In practice, we might initialize the dx objects to 0 and reset them to 0 at the end of each protocol round, but this is not required for correctness. The protocol still yields provably correct execution; however, to complete the proof we now need to show that the above transformations preserve the observable behavior of transactions. A full treatment of the issue requires us to define formal evaluation semantics for $\mathcal{L}$, and is beyond the scope of this paper.

For transactions in a language that is richer than $\mathcal{L}$ and may support data types other than integers, it is still possible to perform the above transformation if each data type comes with a suitable *merge function* that is the equivalent of addition in the integer case. Under this merge function, elements of the data type must form an Abelian group. For example, we can apply the transformation to multisets (bags) of integers, using bag union as the merge function.

If the data type we wish to use does not come with a suitable merge function, the above transformations cannot be used and it is necessary to synchronize on every update to a replicated object of this type. However, existing research has shown that there are numerous commutative replicated data types which do come with the merge functions we need [34]. Thus we expect our transformation technique to be broadly applicable in practice.

C. TREATY COMPUTATION DETAILS

C.1 Preprocessing the formula ψ

The preprocessing of ψ involves identifying all subexpressions θ that prevent it from being a conjunction of linear constraints, for example θ may be a negated boolean expression $\neg b$. For each such expression, we replace it within ψ by the actual value of θ on D. In addition, if the variables in θ are $x_1, x_2, \cdots x_n$, we transform ψ to $\psi \wedge \bigwedge_i (x_i = D(x_i))$. Intuitively, any variables involved in the subexpression have their values fixed to the current ones. It is clear that the transformed ψ implies the original one so we can use it in what follows without sacrificing correctness.

C.2 Finding a good treaty configuration

Algorithm 1 computes valid treaty configurations. It has two tunable parameters: a lookahead interval L and a cost factor f. We examine f possible future system executions, where each execution is a sequence of L transactions and is constructed using our workload model. We search for a configuration that minimizes the number of treaty violations in our f executions. For larger f and L, the probability of a future treaty violation decreases, but the search for an optimal configuration takes more time to run.

The configuration search is performed by a suitable MaxSAT solver. We assume that we have an efficient solver that takes as input a first-order logic formula, finds the largest satisfiable subset of constraints that includes all the *hard constraints* and also produces a model (a concrete assignment of values to configuration variables) which satisfies this subset of constraints.

We now discuss the algorithm in more detail. The algorithm first generates θ_h—this is a formula that says the local treaties must enforce the global treaty. This must always be true for a valid treaty configuration, so we will have θ_h as a hard constraint (Line 4). Next (Lines 6-12) the algorithm generates f sequences of transactions of length L using the workload model. For each sequence, it simulates the execution of transactions in the sequence to produce a sequence of databases, one per transactional write (Line 8). The desired behavior is that none of the databases in the sequence violate the local treaties. We therefore add an appropriate constraint for each database in the sequence (Line 10). This process yields a set Θ_s of soft constraints, which are fed to the MaxSAT solver together with the hard constraints in θ_h (Line 13).

Algorithm 1 Finding a valid treaty configuration that reduces the probability of future violation.

1: Let L be the lookahead interval.
2: Let f be the cost factor.
3: Let $\varphi = \bigwedge_{i \in [1,K]} \varphi_{\Gamma_i}$ {Conjunction of local treaty templates.}
4: $\theta_h = \{\forall\, Vars(\varphi_\Gamma),\ \bigwedge_{\{i \in [1:K]\}}(\varphi_{\Gamma_i}) \Rightarrow \varphi_\Gamma\}$ {Local treaties enforce global treaty.}
5: $\Theta_s = \emptyset$
6: **for** $i = 1$ to f **do**
7:    Generate a sequence S of L transactions using model
8:    Let $[D_0, D_1, ..., D_L]$ be the sequence of databases obtained by executing S on D (we have $D_0 = D$).
9:    **for** $j = 1$ to L **do**
10:       $\Theta_s = \Theta_s \cup \{\varphi(D_j)\}$ {Treaty holds on D_j.}
11:    **end for**
12: **end for**
13: $C = MaxSAT(\{\theta_h\} \cup \Theta_s)$ {Hard constraints θ_h, soft Θ_s}

We illustrate an execution of Algorithm 1 by continuing with our example and our local treaty templates $\varphi_{\Gamma_1} : (x + c_y \geq 20)$ and $\varphi_{\Gamma_2} : (c_x + y \geq 20)$. We have $\theta_h = (\forall[x, y], \varphi_{\Gamma_1} \wedge \varphi_{\Gamma_2} \Rightarrow \varphi_\Gamma)$.

Suppose that $L = 3$ and $f = 3$ and transaction T_1 is twice as likely as T_2. We construct 3 possible transaction sequences of length L drawn from this distribution. Suppose these are $S_1 = [T_1; T_1; T_2]$, $S_2 = [T_1; T_1; T_1]$ and $S_3 = [T_1; T_2; T_1]$. If we execute S_1 on the initial database we obtain the sequence of states $[(10, 13); (9, 13); (8, 13); (8, 12)]$ where each element represents an ordered pair of x and y values. This sequence can be computed by looking up in the symbolic table the partially evaluated transaction for each transaction in S_1 and applying it.

The desired behavior is that no database in the above sequence violates a local treaty. Thus $\varphi_{\Gamma_1} \wedge \varphi_{\Gamma_2}$ must hold on each of the four databases. Plugging in the x and y values from each database into $\varphi_{\Gamma_1} \wedge \varphi_{\Gamma_2}$, taking the conjunction and performing some simplification yields the soft constraints $\{(c_y \geq 12), (c_x \geq 8)\}$. Repeating the procedure for S_2 and S_3, we get soft constraints $\{(c_y \geq 13), (c_x \geq 7)\}$ and $\{(c_y \geq 12), (c_x \geq 8)\}$.

By passing all these constraints to a MaxSAT solver, we find that not all of the soft constraints can be satisfied in addition to θ_h. However, for $c_y = 12$ and $c_x = 8$, we can satisfy both the first and third set of soft constraints. The algorithm therefore chooses $C = \{(c_y = 12, c_x = 8)\}$. Note that this configuration allows more flexibility to the site at which T_1 runs, since it is more frequent. As desired, we have minimized the probability of a treaty violation subject to the computational constraints f and L.

C.3 Lifting Assumption 4.1

We now explain how to handle transactions that violate Assumption 4.1. An example of such a transaction would be one that reads the value of remote object y and copies it into the local object x. Intuitively, if we wish to avoid the remote read of y yet guarantee correct execution, we need a global treaty that guarantees the value of y will never change. We can achieve this by adding a constraint to the local treaty *on the site where y resides*. To do this, we need to perform a post-processing step on the local treaty templates. Specifically, for every transaction T executing at site i, we consider the partially evaluated transaction ϕ_T found in the relevant row of the symbolic table. For every variable x such that read(x) appears in ϕ_T but $Loc(x) \neq i$, we substitute it with a new local variable c_x and modify $\varphi_{\Gamma_{Loc(x)}}$ to $\varphi_{\Gamma_{Loc(x)}} \wedge (x = c_x)$. Once this postprocessing step is complete, we can run Algorithm 1 as before.

D. EXAMPLES BEYOND TOP-K

In this section, we elaborate on the examples from in Section 4.3.

The first example is the "maximum of minimums" case, which we encode as a program which maintains a list of lists in a two-dimensional array. In our weather scenario, each list represents a day and contains the temperature measurements for that day. The program adds a value to a specific list, finds the minimum value in each list, finds the top k values among these minimums and prints them to the screen.

The output of the program changes if the inserted value is a minimum in its own list and is one of the k highest minimum values among the other lists. Thus, there are $k + 2$ high-level cases to handle: one where the new value is not a minimum in its own list and the remaining $k + 1$ for the case where it is, and has a particular relative ordering with respect to the current top-k minimums. For each of these cases, the program will print a different result.

The actual local treaties required for correct disconnected execution at each site depend on the above information as well on what (portions of the) lists are stored on each site. For instance, if each list is stored on a different site, it is necessary to synchronize when a new minimum value is added to the local list, and this value is higher than the lowest value in the current top-k. If multiple lists are stored on one site or a list is distributed (or indeed replicated) across multiple sites, the treaties will be more complex. The treaties can be expressed as conjunctions of linear constraints and can in principle be derived manually, although the derivation process will require some care if the lists are stored on the various sites according to one of the more complex schemes we described.

Our second example looks for the top-k days with the highest temperature difference, where the temperature difference is the daily high temperature minus the daily low temperature. It can be implemented like the previous example, but now upon inserting a value we find and print the indexes of the top k lists which have the highest difference between max and min.

There are two high-level cases that affect how this program behaves – either the list that was updated enters the top-k after the update or it does not. If it does not, there are three possible reasons and subcases. Either the the new value that is inserted is neither a new min nor a new max in its list, or it is a new max but the resulting new min-max difference for that list is not greater than the current top-k, or it is a new min but the resulting new min-max difference is not greater than the current top-k. If the updated list does enter the top-k, we need $k+1$ subcases for each relative ordering. As before, the actual treaties required for correct disconnected execution will depend on what is stored where.

Like the first example, this too can in principle be handled manually by a careful and motivated human treaty generator. However, it is unclear how much more complexity can be added without overwhelming the human and introducing errors. On the other hand, our analysis can compute correct symbolic tables and local treaties for both examples automatically.

E. ANALYZING TPC-C TRANSACTIONS

In this section, we explain how to express the TPC-C transactions `New Order`, `Delivery` and `Payment` in $\mathcal{L}$++, and we explain what treaties the homeostasis protocol produces for them.

E.1 Encoding the TPC-C transactions

Recall that the `New Order` transaction places a new order for some quantity (between 1 to 5) of a particular item from a particular district and at a particular warehouse. The `Payment` transaction updates the customer, district and warehouse balances as though processing a payment, and the `Delivery` transaction fulfills orders at a particular warehouse and district.

Expressing these three transactions in $\mathcal{L}$++ is largely straightforward, since they consist primarily of a sequence of SQL `SELECT`, `UPDATE`, `INSERT` and `DELETE` statements, and map directly to relation read and write statements in $\mathcal{L}$++ that are syntactic sugar for $\mathcal{L}$ code, as discussed in the Appendix Section A.

`New Order` and `Delivery` both write to the `NEW-ORDER` table; the TPC-C specification requires an ordering where `New Order` creates orders with monotonically increasing order ids for a given warehouse and district, whereas `Delivery` fulfills the oldest order (i.e. the one with the smallest id) for a given warehouse and district each time. However, the specification does not describe how this ordering should function in a replicated version of TPC-C and what constraints it needs to obey.

For our implementation, we assume that the ordering must exist and that `Delivery` must fulfill the lowest-numbered order each time, but that the assignment of new order ids does not need to be monotonic across all sites. That is, each site generates monotonically increasing order ids (for each district and warehouse) and no two sites can ever generate the same order id. Thus we ensure the existence of a global ordering, but no synchronization is required when `New Order` executes.

Finally, to make our code suitable for a replicated setting, we apply transformations as described in Appendix Section B.

E.2 Treaties for TPC-C

We now explain in more detail what treaties were generated from our $\mathcal{L}$++ implementation described above.

The `Payment` transaction with customer specified by number updates several balance amounts. These amounts are never read by any transaction, including other instances of `Payment`. As explained in Appendix Section B, incrementing a balance by a given amount can be done without reading the amount itself if we use auxiliary local objects to store the local "deltas" of the balance. Thus, no treaties are required on the balance values for the homeostasis protocol, and instances of `Payment` run without ever needing to synchronize.

The `New Order` transaction requires treaties on the stock values for each item and for each warehouse, i.e. on the `S_QUANTITY` for each row of the `STOCK` table in the TPC-C schema. The global treaty for each such quantity q ensures that q may never be negative, i.e. $q >= 0$. The local treaties generated by our protocol constrain q further and have the form $dq_i > c$, where dq_i is the auxiliary local object corresponding to q on site i (see Appendix Section B) and c is chosen through optimization as explained in Section 4.

The `Delivery` transaction, as explained above, needs to delete a tuple from the `NEW-ORDER` table which has the lowest order id for a given district and warehouse. This does require synchronization. In our $\mathcal{L}$++ code, we keep a database object for each warehouse and district that stores the current lowest order id in `NEW-ORDER` for that warehouse and district. Each such object has an associated global treaty that fixes it to its current value in the database. Be-

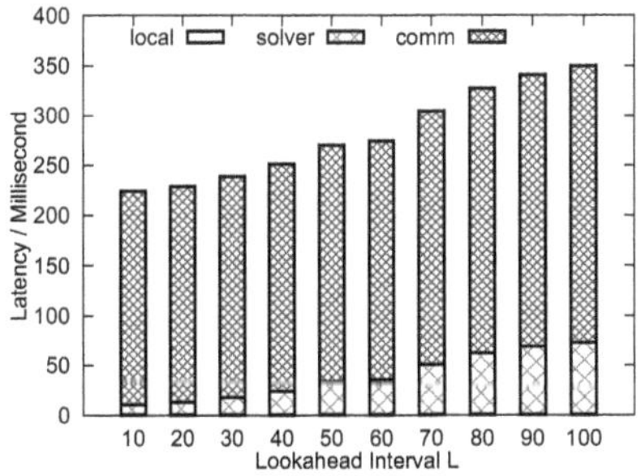

Figure 24: Transaction Latency Breakdown with Lookahead Interval L ($RTT = 100ms, N_c = 16, REFILL = 100$)

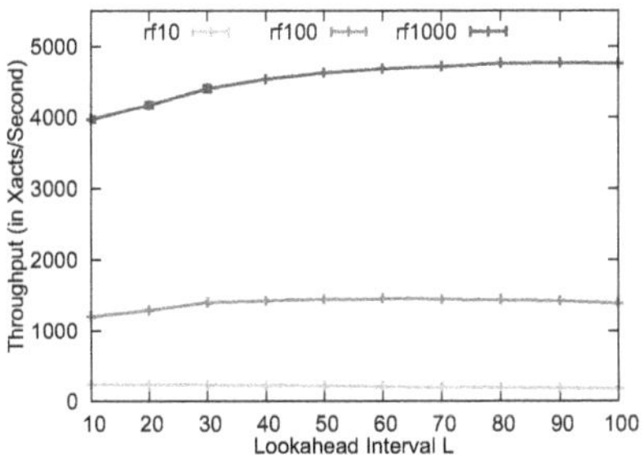

Figure 25: Throughput with Lookahead Interval L for different REFILL values ($RTT = 100ms, N_c = 16$)

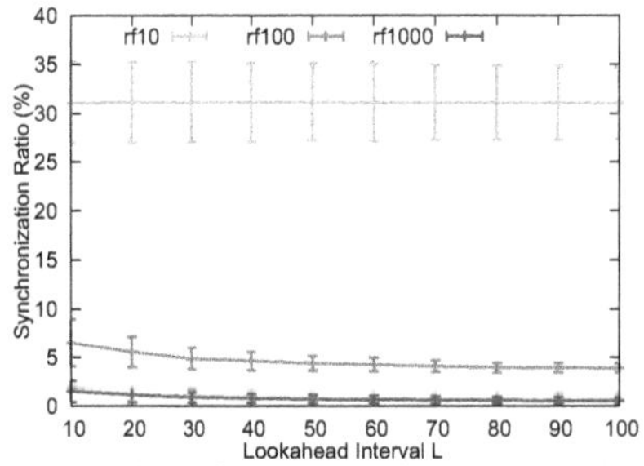

Figure 26: Synchronization Ratio with Lookahead Interval L for different REFILL values ($N_r = 2, RTT = 100ms, N_c = 16$)

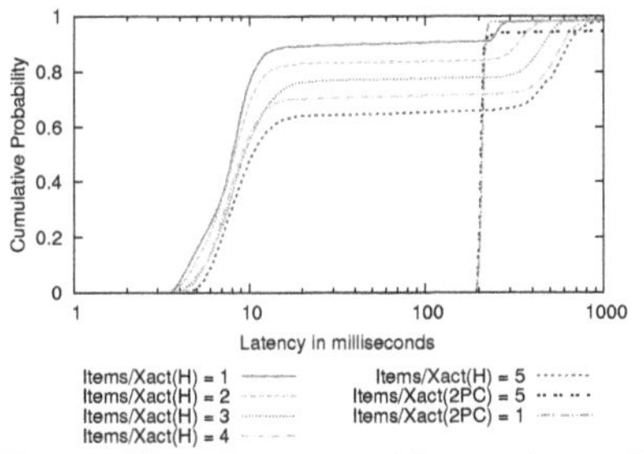

Figure 27: Latency with number of items accessed per transaction ($RTT = 100, REFILL = 100, N_c = 20, L = 20$)

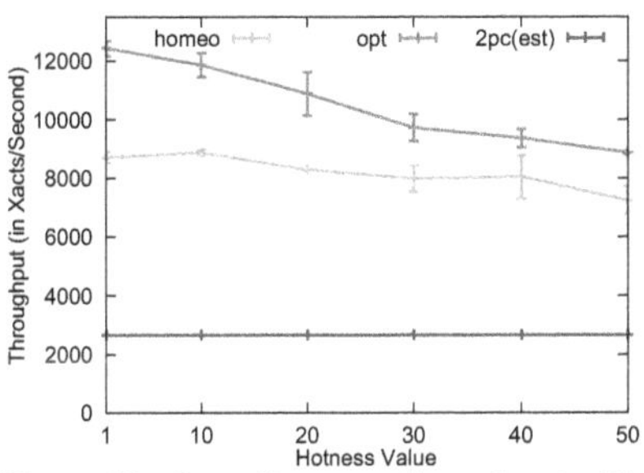

Figure 28: Overall system throughput with H ($REFILL = 100, N_c = 16$)

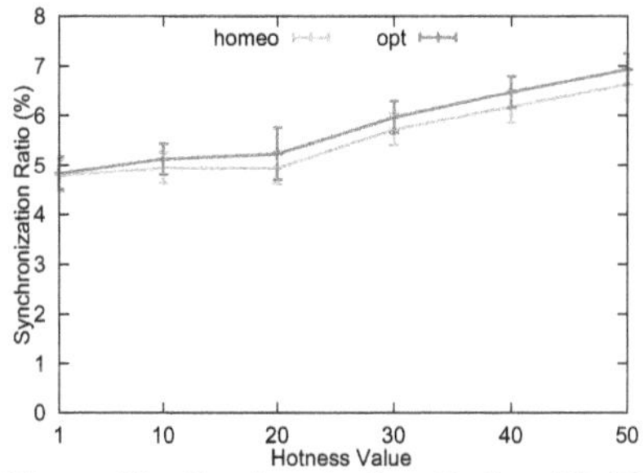

Figure 29: Synchronization Ratio with H ($REFILL = 100, N_c = 16$)

cause `Delivery` also updates (increments) that object, executing it causes a treaty violation and forces a synchronization. The only transaction reading or writing to that object is `Delivery`, and so synchronization occurs every time that transaction runs.

In addition, we need to ensure that the `Delivery` transaction never sees an empty `NEW-ORDER` table unless the table is truly empty (rather than containing inserts which have not been propagated to the site running `Delivery`). To achieve this, we maintain a treaty for each warehouse and district that requires the number of unfulfilled orders to remain above zero. If a `Delivery` transaction processes the order with the *highest* order id that it is "aware of," this will cause a violation of the treaty and synchronization will occur.

In summary, for the TPC-C transactions we use, there is a global treaty of the form $q > 0$ for every quantity q in the `STOCK` table. There is also a treaty for the current lowest unprocessed order id in the `NEW-ORDER` table for each warehouse and district, which fixes that order id to its current value. Finally, there is a treaty for each warehouse and district stating that the highest unprocessed order id is greater than the lowest unprocessed order id.

F. ADDITIONAL EXPERIMENTS

In this section, we present a number of additional experiments.

F.1 Microbenchmark setting

Varying the lookahead interval Within the microbenchmark setting from Section 6.1, we experiment with using the homeostasis protocol and varying the lookahead interval L used in Algorithm 1 from Appendix Section C. Varying this parameter trades off the time overhead of treaty generation versus the quality of the generated treaties, where a better treaty is one that requires less frequent synchronization. We also vary the value of REFILL, since a larger REFILL value allows for more flexible treaties. The REFILL values we used were 10, 100 and 1000.

Figure 24 gives the time breakdown for transaction latencies of transactions which caused a treaty violation as we vary L, showing time spent in actual transaction execution (*local*), in communication with other replicas(*comm*), treaty computation and in generating treaties using Algorithm 1 (*solver*). The values for *local* are negligibly small as compared to *comm* and *solver* and therefore do not appear in Figure 24. As L increases, the time spent in finding new treaties also increases. However, since the algorithm is able to find better treaties with larger values of L, the percentage of transactions which actually cause a treaty violation decreases as shown in Figure 26. As expected, using a larger value for REFILL leads to a significantly lower synchronization ratio and higher throughput as shown in Figures 25 and 26.

Varying the number of items accessed For this experiment, we modify our microbenchmark transaction to order more than one item at a time. We vary the number of items purchased in a single transaction from 1 to 5. The latency CDF for the experiment is shown in Figure 27. As expected, as the transactions purchase more items, the probability of synchronization increases since it is more likely that the treaty governing any one of the purchased items is violated. This manifests itself in the downward shift of the inflection point in the CDF. This inflection point differentiates between locally executed transactions and those which cause a treaty violation. Under 2PC, the system behavior is unaffected by increasing the number of items ordered per transaction.

F.2 TPC-C setting

Finally, we give detailed results for the distributed TPC-C experiment introduced in Section 6.2. Figure 28 shows how increasing the value of H (the percentage of transactions ordering "hot" items) affects transaction throughput. As the value of H increases, the treaties corresponding to hot items are violated more often, thus throughput falls. This increase in treaty violations is also apparent in Figure 29 where the synchronization ratio increases with increasing values of H. In summary, in a realistic workload and deployment scenario, the homeostasis protocol far outperforms 2PC and achieves near optimal throughput without sacrificing consistency.

Feral Concurrency Control: An Empirical Investigation of Modern Application Integrity

Peter Bailis, Alan Fekete[†], Michael J. Franklin, Ali Ghodsi, Joseph M. Hellerstein, Ion Stoica
UC Berkeley and [†]University of Sydney

ABSTRACT

The rise of data-intensive "Web 2.0" Internet services has led to a range of popular new programming frameworks that collectively embody the latest incarnation of the vision of Object-Relational Mapping (ORM) systems, albeit at unprecedented scale. In this work, we empirically investigate modern ORM-backed applications' use and disuse of database concurrency control mechanisms. Specifically, we focus our study on the common use of *feral*, or application-level, mechanisms for maintaining database integrity, which, across a range of ORM systems, often take the form of declarative correctness criteria, or invariants. We quantitatively analyze the use of these mechanisms in a range of open source applications written using the Ruby on Rails ORM and find that feral invariants are the most popular means of ensuring integrity (and, by usage, are over 37 times more popular than transactions). We evaluate which of these feral invariants actually ensure integrity (by usage, up to 86.9%) and which—due to concurrency errors and lack of database support—may lead to data corruption (the remainder), which we experimentally quantify. In light of these findings, we present recommendations for database system designers for better supporting these modern ORM programming patterns, thus eliminating their adverse effects on application integrity.

1. INTRODUCTION

The rise of "Web 2.0" Internet applications delivering dynamic, highly interactive user experiences has been accompanied by a new generation of programming frameworks [80]. These frameworks simplify common tasks such as content templating and presentation, request handling, and, notably, data storage, allowing developers to focus on "agile" development of their applications. This trend embodies the most recent realization of the larger vision of object-relational mapping (ORM) systems [29], albeit at a unprecedented scale of deployment and programmer adoption.

As a lens for understanding this modern ORM behavior, we study Ruby on Rails (or, simply, "Rails") [50, 74], a central player among modern frameworks powering sites including (at one point) Twitter [35], Airbnb [9], GitHub [70], Hulu [31], Shopify [40], Groupon [67], SoundCloud [28], Twitch [71], Goodreads [2], and Zendesk [83]. From the perspective of database systems research, Rails is interesting for at least two reasons. First, it continues to be a popular means of developing responsive web application front-end and business logic, with an active open source community and user base. Rails recently celebrated its tenth anniversary and enjoys considerable commercial interest, both in terms of deployment and the availability of hosted "cloud" environments such as Heroku. Thus, Rails programmers represent a large class of consumers of database technology. Second, and perhaps more importantly, Rails is "opinionated software" [41]. That is, Rails embodies the strong personal convictions of its developer community, and, in particular, David Heinemeier Hansson (known as DHH), its creator. Rails is particularly opinionated towards the database systems that it tasks with data storage. To quote DHH:

> "I don't *want* my database to be clever! ... I consider stored procedures and constraints vile and reckless destroyers of coherence. No, Mr. Database, you can not have my business logic. Your procedural ambitions will bear no fruit and you'll have to pry that logic from my dead, cold object-oriented hands ... I want a single layer of cleverness: My domain model." [55]

Thus, this wildly successful software framework bears an actively antagonistic relationship to database management systems, echoing a familiar refrain of the "NoSQL" movement: get the database out of the way and let the application do the work.

In this paper, we examine the implications of this impedance mismatch between databases and modern ORM frameworks in the context of application integrity. By shunning decades of work on native database concurrency control solutions, Rails has developed a set of primitives for handling application integrity in the application tier—building, from the underlying database system's perspective, a *feral* concurrency control system. We examine the design and use of these feral mechanisms and evaluate their effectiveness in practice by analyzing them and experimentally quantifying data integrity violations in practice. Our goal is to understand how this growing class of applications currently interacts with database systems and how we, as a database systems community, we can positively engage with these criticisms to better serve the needs of these developers.

We begin by surveying the state of Rails' application-tier concurrency control primitives and examining their use in 67 open source applications representing a variety of use cases from e-Commerce to Customer Relationship Management and social networking. We find that, these applications overwhelmingly use Rails' built-in support for declarative invariants—*validations* and *associations*—to protect data integrity—instead of application-defined transactions, which are used more than 37 times less frequently. Across the survey, we find over 9950 uses of application-level validations designed to ensure correctness criteria including referential integrity, uniqueness, and adherence to common data formats.

SIGMOD'15, May 31–June 4, 2015, Melbourne, Victoria, Australia.

ACM 978-1-4503-2758-9/15/05 ...$15.00.
http://dx.doi.org/10.1145/2723372.2737784.

Given this corpus, we subsequently ask: are these feral invariants correctly enforced? Do they work in practice? Rails will execute validation checks concurrently, so we study the potential for data corruption due to races if validation and update activity does not run within a serializable transaction in the database. This is a real concern, as many DBMS platforms use non-serializable isolation by default and in many cases (despite labeling otherwise) do not provide serializable isolation as an option at all. Accordingly, we apply invariant confluence analysis [17] and show that, in fact, up to 86.9% of Rails validation usage by volume is actually safe under concurrent execution. However, the remainder—which include uniqueness violations under insertion and foreign key constraint violations under deletion—are not. Therefore, we quantify the impact of concurrency on data corruption for Rails uniqueness and foreign key constraints under both worst-case analysis and via actual Rails deployment. We demonstrate that, for pathological workloads, validations reduce the severity of data corruption by orders of magnitude but nevertheless still permit serious integrity violations.

Given these results, we return to our goal of improving the underlying data management systems that power these applications and present recommendations for the database research community. We expand our study to survey several additional web frameworks and demonstrate that many also provide a notion of feral validations, suggesting an industry-wide trend. While the success of Rails and its ilk—despite (or perhaps due to) their aversion to database technology—are firm evidence of the continued impedance mismatch between object-oriented programming and the relational model, we see considerable opportunity in improving database systems to better serve these communities—via more programmer- and ORM-friendly interfaces that ensure correctness while minimizing impacts on performance and portability.

In summary, this paper makes the following contributions:

- We analyze 67 open source Ruby on Rails applications to determine their use of both database-backed and feral concurrency control mechanisms. This provides a quantitative picture of how mainstream web developers interact with database systems, and, more specifically, concurrency control.
- We study these applications' feral mechanisms potential for application integrity violations. We analytically and experimentally quantify the incidence and degree of inconsistency allowed by Rails's uniqueness and association validations.
- We survey six additional frameworks for similarly unsafe validations. Based on these results and those above, we present a set of recommendations for database systems designers, including increasing database support for application invariants while avoiding coordination and maintaining portability.

In all, this paper is an attempt to understand how a large and growing class of programmers and framework authors interact with the data management systems that this community builds. We hope to raise awareness about prevalent and under-supported application programming patterns and their impact on the integrity of real-world, end-user database-backed applications. Our contributions do not include a new system for database concurrency control; rather, our goal is to inform designers and architects of next-generation data management systems and provide quantitative evidence of the practical shortcomings and pitfalls in real-world database concurrency control today. We view this work as an early example of the promising opportunity in empirical analysis of open source database-backed software as written and deployed in practice.

The remainder of this paper proceeds as follows. Section 2 briefly provides background on Rails MVC and deployment, while Section 3 surveys Rails's supported concurrency control mechanisms. Section 4 presents analysis of mechanism usage in open source applications as well as safety under weak isolation. Section 5 experimentally quantifies the integrity violations allowed in a Rails deployment. Section 6 describes support for feral validations in additional frameworks, and Section 7 presents recommendations for better supporting these framework demands. Section 8 presents related work, and Section 9 concludes with a reflection on the potential of empirical methods in database systems research.

2. BACKGROUND

As a primary focus of our study, we investigate the operational model, database use, and application primitives provided in Rails. In this section, we provide a brief overview of the Rails programming model and describe standard Rails deployment architectures.

2.1 Rails Tenets and MVC

Rails was developed in order to maximize developer programmability. This focus is captured by two core architectural principles [74]. First, Rails adopts a "Don't Repeat Yourself" (DRY) philosophy: "every piece of knowledge should be expressed in just one place" in the code. Data modeling and schema descriptions are relegated to one portion of the system, while presentation and business logic are relegated to two others. Rails attempts to minimize the amount of boilerplate code required to achieve this functionality. Second, Rails adopts a philosophy of "Convention over Configuration," aiming for sensible defaults and allowing easy deployment without much—if any—modifications to configuration.

A natural corollary to the above principles is that Rails encourages an idiomatic style of programming. The Rails framework authors claim that "somehow, [this style] just seems right" for quickly building responsive web applications [74]. The framework's success hints that its idioms are, in fact, natural to web developers.

More concretely, Rails divides application code into a three-component architecture called Model-View-Controller [49, 60]:

- The **Model** acts as a basic ORM and is responsible for managing business objects, including schemas, querying, and persistence functionality. For example, in a banking application, an account's state could be represented by a model with a numeric owner ID field and a numeric balance field.
- The **View** acts as a presentation layer for application objects, including rendering into browser-ingestible HTML and/or other formats such as JSON. In our banking application, the View would be responsible for rendering the page displaying a user's account balance.
- The **Controller** encapsulates the remainder of application's business logic, including actual generation of queries and transformations on the Active Record models. In our banking application, we would write logic for orchestrating withdrawal and deposit operations within the Controller.

Actually building a Rails application is a matter of instantiating a collection of models and writing appropriate controller and presentation logic for each.

As we are concerned with how Rails utilizes database backends, we largely focus on how Rails applications interact with the Model layer. Rails natively supports a Model implementation called `Active Record`. Rails's Active Record module is an instantiation of the Active Record pattern originally proposed by Martin Fowler, a prominent software design consultant [48]. Per Fowler, an Active Record is "an object that wraps a row in a database or view, encapsulates the database access, and adds domain logic on that data" (further references to Active Record will correspond to Rails's implementation). The first two tasks—persistence and database encapsulation—fit squarely in the realm of standard ORM design, and Rails adopts Fowler's recommendation of a one-to-one correlation between object fields and database columns (thus, each declared Active Record class is stored in a separate table in the database). The third component, domain logic, is more complicated. Each Rails model may contain a number of attributes (and must include a special primary-key-backed `id` field) as well as associated logic including data validation, associations, and other constraints. Fowler suggests that "domain logic that isn't too complex" is well-suited for encapsulation in an Active Record class. We will discuss these in greater depth in the next section.

2.2 Databases and Deployment

This otherwise benign separation of data and logic becomes interesting when we consider how Rails servers process concurrent requests. In this section, we describe how, in standard Rails deployments, application logic may be executed concurrently and without synchronization within separate threads or processes.

In Rails, the database is—at least for basic usages—simply a place to store model state and is otherwise divorced from the application logic. All application code is run within the Ruby virtual machine (VM), and Active Record makes appropriate calls to the database in order to materialize collections of models in the VM memory as needed (as well as to persist model state). However, from the database's perspective (and per DHH's passionate declaration in Section 1), logic remains in the application layer. Active Record natively provides support for PostgreSQL, MySQL, and SQLite, with extensions for databases including Oracle and is otherwise agnostic to database choice.

Rails deployments typically resemble traditional multi-tier web architectures [10] and consist of an HTTP server such as Apache or Nginx that acts as a proxy for a pool of Ruby VMs running the Rails application stack. Depending on the Ruby VM and Rails implementation, the Rails application may or may not be multi-threaded.[1] Thus, when an end-user makes a HTTP request on a Rails-powered web site, the request is first accepted by a web server and passed to a Rails worker process (or thread within the process). Based on the HTTP headers and destination, Rails subsequently determines the appropriate Controller logic and runs it, including any database calls via Active Record, and renders a response via the View, which is returned to the HTTP server.

Thus, in a Rails application, the *only* coordination between individual application requests occurs within the database system. Controller execution—whether in separate threads or across Ruby VMs (which may be active on different physical servers)—is entirely independent, save for the rendezvous of queries and modifications within the database tier, as triggered by Active Record operations.

The independent execution of concurrent business logic should give serious pause to disciples of transaction processing systems. Is this execution strategy actually safe? Thus far, we have yet to discuss any mechanisms for maintaining correct application data, such as the use of transactions. In fact, as we will discuss in the next section, Rails has, over its lifetime, introduced several mechanisms for maintaining consistency of application data. In keeping with Rails' focus on keeping application logic within Rails (and not in the database), this has led to several different proposals. In the remainder of this paper, we examine their use and whether, in fact, they correctly maintain application data.

[1]Ruby was not traditionally designed for highly concurrent operations: its standard reference VM—Ruby MRI—contains (like Python's CPython) a "Global VM Lock" that prevents multiple OS threads from executing at a given time. While alternative VM implementations provide more concurrent behavior, until Rails 2.2 (released in November 2008), Rails embraced this behavior and was unable to process more than one request at a time (due to state shared state including database connections and logging state) [69]. In practice today, the choice of multi-process, multi-threaded, or multi-process and multi-threaded deployment depends on the actual application server architecture. For example, three popular servers—Phusion Passenger, Puma, and Unicorn —each provide a different configuration.

3. FERAL MECHANISMS IN RAILS

As we discussed in Section 2.2, Rails services user requests independently, with the database acting as a point of rendezvous for concurrent operations. Given Rails's design goals of maintaining application logic at the user level, this appears—on its face—a somewhat cavalier proposition with respect to application integrity. In response, Rails has developed a range of concurrency control strategies, two of which operate external to the database, at the application level, which we term *feral concurrency control* mechanisms.

In this section, we outline four major mechanisms for guarding against integrity violations under concurrent execution in Rails. We subsequently begin our study of 67 open source applications to determine which of these mechanisms are used in practice. In the following section, we will determine which are sufficient to maintain correct data—and when they are not.

3.1 Rails Concurrency Control Mechanisms

Rails contains four main mechanisms for concurrency control.

1. Rails provides support for **transactions**. By wrapping a sequence of operations within a special `transaction` block, Rails operations will execute transactionally, backed by an actual database transaction. The database transaction either runs at the database's configured default isolation level or, as of Rails 4.0.0, can be configured on a per-transaction basis [64].
2. Rails provides support for both optimistic and pessimistic per-record **locking**. Applications invoke pessimistic locks on an Active Record object by calling its `lock` method, which invokes a `SELECT FOR UPDATE` statement in the database. Optimistic locking is invoked by declaring a special `lock_version` field in an Active Record model. When a Rails process performs an update to an optimistically locked model, Active Record atomically checks whether the corresponding record's `lock_version` field has changed since the process last read the object; if it has not changed, Rails transactionally increments `lock_version` and updates the database record.
3. Rails provides support for application-level **validations**. Each Active Record model has a set of zero or more validations, or boolean-valued functions, and a model instance many only be saved to the database if all of its declared validations return true. These validations ensure, for example, that particular fields within a record are not null or, alternatively, are unique within the database. Rails provides a number of built-in validations but also allows arbitrary user-defined validations (we discuss actual validations further in subsequent sections). The framework runs each declared validation sequentially and, if all succeed, the model state is updated in the database; this happens within a database-backed transaction.[2] The validations supported by Rails today include ones that are natively supported by many commercial databases today, as well as others.

[2]The practice of wrapping validations in a transaction dates to the earliest public Rails commit (albeit, in 2004, transactions were only supported via a per-Ruby VM global lock [54]). However, as late as 2010, updates were only partially protected by transactions [75].

4. Rails provides support for application-level **associations**. As the name suggests, "an association is a connection between two Active Record models," effectively acting like a foreign key in an RDBMS. Associations can be declared on one or both sides of a one-to-one or one-to-many relationship, including transitive dependencies (via a `:through` annotation). Declaring an association (e.g., `:belongs_to dept`) produces a special field for the associated record ID within the model (e.g., `dept_id`). Coupling an association with an appropriate validation (e.g., `:presence`) ensures that the association is indeed valid (and is, via the validation, backed by a database transaction). Until the release of Rails 4.2 in December 2014, Rails did not provide native support for database-backed foreign key constraints. In Rails 4.2, foreign keys are supported via manual schema annotations declared separately from each model; declaring an association does not declare a corresponding foreign key constraint and vice-versa.

Overall, these four mechanisms provide a range of options for developers. The first is squarely in the realm of traditional concurrency control. The second is, in effect, a coarse-grained user-level implementation of single-record transactions via database-level "compare-and-swap" primitives (implemented via `SELECT FOR UPDATE`). However, the latter two—validations and associations—operate, in effect, at the application level. Although some validations like uniqueness validations have analogs in an RDBMS, the semantics of these validations are entirely contained within the Rails code. In effect, from the database's perspective, these validations exist external to the system and are *feral* concurrency control mechanisms.

Rails's feral mechanisms—validations and associations—are a prominent feature of the Active Record model. In contrast, neither transactions nor locks are actually discussed in the official "Rails Guides," and, generally, are not promoted as a means of ensuring data integrity. Instead, the Rails documentation [7] prefers validations as they are "are database agnostic, cannot be bypassed by end users, and are convenient to test and maintain." Moreover, the Rails documentation opines that "database constraints and/or stored procedures make the validation mechanisms database-dependent and can make testing and maintenance more difficult." As we will show shortly, these feral mechanisms accordingly dominate in terms of developer popularity in real applications.

3.2 Adoption in Practice

To understand exactly how users interact with these concurrency control mechanisms and determine which deserved more study, we examined their usage in a portfolio of publicly available open source applications. We find that validations and associations are overwhelmingly the most popular forms of concurrency control.

Application corpus. We selected 67 open source applications built using Ruby on Rails and Active Record, representing a variety of application domains, including eCommerce, customer relationship management, retail point of sale, conference management, content management, build management, project management, personal task tracking, community management and forums, commenting, calendaring, file sharing, Git hosting, link aggregation, crowdfunding, social networking, and blogging. We sought projects with substantial code-bases (average: 26,809 lines of Ruby) multiple contributors (average: 69.1), and relative popularity (measured according to GitHub stars) on the site. Table 2 (in the Appendix) provides a detailed overview.

While several of these applications are projects undertaken by hobbyists, many are either commercially supported (e.g., Canvas LMS, Discourse, Spree, GitLab) and/or have a large open source community (e.g., Radiant, Comfortable Mexican Sofa, Diaspora). A larger-scale commercial, closed-source Rails application such as Twitter, GitHub, or Airbnb might exhibit different trends than those we observe here. However, in the open source domain, we believe these applications represent a diverse selection of Rails use cases and are a good-faith effort to obtain a representative sample of popular open source Rails applications as hosted on GitHub.

Mechanism usage. We performed a simple analysis of the applications to determine how each of the concurrency control mechanisms were used (see Appendix A for more methodological details).

Overwhelmingly, applications did not use transactions or locks (Figure 1 and Table 2). On average, applications used 0.13 transactions, 0.01 locks, 1.80 validations, and 3.19 associations per model (with an average of 29.1 models per application). While 46 (68.7%) of applications used transactions, all used some validations or associations. Only six applications used locks. Use of pessimistic locks was over twice as common as the use of optimistic locks.

Perhaps most notable among these general trends, we find that validations and associations are, respectively, 13.6 and 24.2 times more common than transactions and orders of magnitude more common than locking. These feral mechanisms are—in keeping with the Rails philosophy—favored by these application developers. That is, rather than adopting the use of traditional transactional programming primitives, Rails application writers chose to instead specify correctness criteria and have the ORM system enforce the criteria on their behalf. It is unclear and even unlikely that these declarative criteria are a complete specification of program correctness: undoubtedly, some of these programs contain errors. However, given that these criteria are nevertheless being declared by application writers and represent a departure from traditional, transaction-oriented programming, we devote much of the remainder of this work to examining exactly what they are attempting to preserve (and whether they are actually sufficient to do so).

Understanding specific applications. Over the course of our investigation, we found that application use of mechanisms varied. While our focus is largely on aggregate behavior, studying individual applications is also interesting. For example, consider Spree, a popular eCommerce application:

Spree uses only six transactions, one for each of 1.) canceling an order, 2.) approving an order (atomically setting the user ID and timestamp), 3.) transferring shipments between fulfillment locations (e.g., warehouses), 4.) transferring items between shipments, 5.) transferring stock between fulfillment locations, and 6.) updating an order's specific inventory status. While this is a reasonable set of locations for transactions, in an eCommerce application, one might expect a larger number of scenarios to require transactions, including order placement and stock adjustment.

In the case of Spree stock adjustment, the inventory count for each item to is indeed a potential hotspot for concurrency issues. Manual adjustments of available stock (`adjust_count_on_hand(value)`) is indeed protected via a pessimistic lock, but simply setting the available stock (`set_count_on_hand(value)`) is not. It is unclear why one operation necessitates a lock but the other does not, given that both are ostensibly sensitive to concurrent accesses. Meanwhile, the stock level field is wrapped in a validation ensuring non-negative balances, preventing negative balances but not necessarily classic Lost Update anomalies [8].

At one point, Spree's inventory count was protected by an optimistic lock; it was removed due to optimistic lock failure during customer checkouts. On relevant GitHub issue pertaining to this lock removal, a committer notes that "I think we should get rid of the [optimistic lock] if there's no documentation about why it's there...I think we can look at this issue again in a month's time

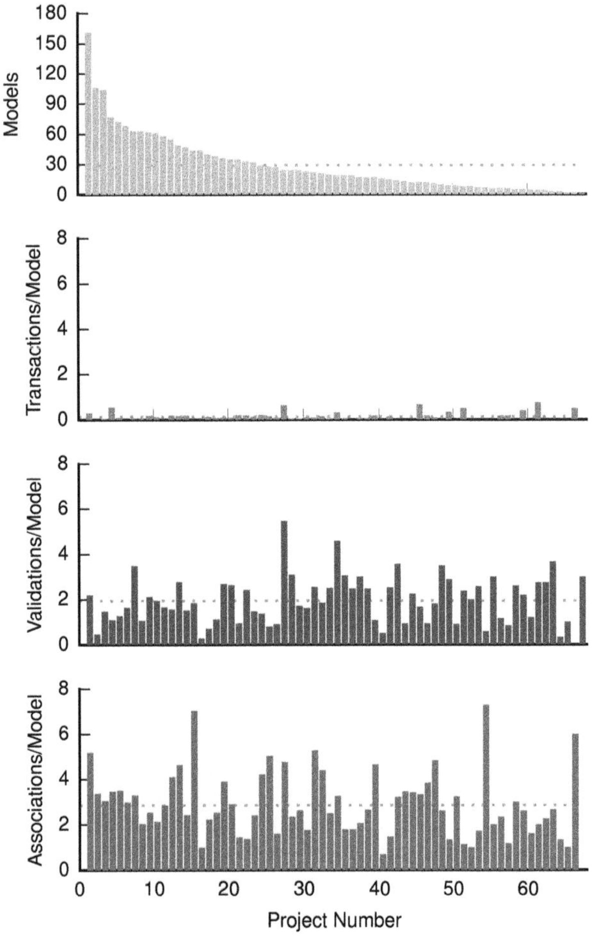

Figure 1: Use of concurrency control mechanisms in Rails applications. We maintain the same ordering of applications for each plot (i.e., same x-axis values; identical to Table 2) and show the average for each plot using the dotted line.

and see if there's been any problems since you turned it off" [38]. This removal has, to our knowledge, not been revisited, despite the potential dangers of removing this point of synchronization.

The remainder of the application corpus contains a number of such fascinating examples, illustrating the often ad-hoc process of deciding upon a concurrency control mechanism. Broadly, the use of each style of concurrency control varies across repositories, but our results demonstrate a clear trend towards feral mechanisms within Rails rather than traditional use of transactions.

Additional metrics. To better understand how programmers used each of these mechanisms, we performed two additional analyses.

First, we analyzed the number of models, transactions, validations, and associations over each project's lifetime. Using each project's Git history, we repeated the above analysis at a fixed set of intervals through the project's lifespan (measured by commits). Figure 6 (see Appendix) plots the median number of occurrences across all projects. The results show that concurrency control mechanisms (of all forms) tend to be introduced after models are introduced. That is, additions to the data model precede (often by a considerable amount) additional uses of transactions, validations, and associations. It is unclear whether the bulk of concurrency control usage additions are intended to correct concurrency issues or are instead due to natural growth in Controller code and business logic. However, the gap between models and concurrency control usage shrinks over time; thus, the data model appears to stabilize faster than the controller logic, but both eventually stabilize. We view additional longitudinal analysis along these lines as worthwhile future work.

Second, we analyze the distribution of authors to commits compared to the distribution of authors to validations and associations authored.[3] As Figure 7 (see Appendix, page) demonstrates, 95% of all commits are authored by 42.4% of authors. However, 95% of invariants (validations plus associations) are authored by only 20.3% of authors. This is reminiscent of traditional database schema authorship, where a smaller number of authors (e.g., DBAs) modify the schema than contribute to the actual application code.

3.3 Summary and Discussion

Returning to the Rails design philosophy, the applications we have encountered do indeed express their logic at the application layer. There is little actual communication of correctness criteria to the database layer. Part of this is due to limitations within Rails. As we have mentioned, there is no way to actually declare a foreign key constraint in Rails without importing additional third-party modules. Insofar as Rails is an "opinionated" framework encouraging an idiomatic programming style, if our application corpus is any indication, DHH and his co-authors advocating application-level data management appear to have succeeded en masse.

Having observed the relative popularity of these mechanisms, we turn our attention to the question of their correctness. Specifically, do these application-level criteria actually enforce the constraints that they claim to enforce? We restrict ourself to studying declared validations and associations for three reasons. First, as we have seen, these constructs are more widely used in the codebases we have studied. Second, these constructs represent a deviation from standard concurrency control techniques and are therefore perhaps more likely to contain errors. Third, while analyzing latent constraints (i.e., those that might be determined via more sophisticated techniques such as pre- and post-condition invariant mining [65, 73] and/or by interviewing each developer on each project) would be instructive, this is difficult to scale. We view these forms of analysis as highly promising avenues for future research.

4. ISOLATION AND INTEGRITY

We now turn our attention to understanding which of Rails' feral validations and associations are actually correct under concurrent execution as described in Section 2.2 and which require stronger forms of isolation or synchronization for correct enforcement.

4.1 Understanding Validation Behavior

To begin, recall that each sequence of validations (and model update as well, if validations pass) is wrapped within a database-backed transaction, the validation's intended integrity will be preserved provided the database is using serializable isolation. However, relational database engines often default to non-serializable isolation [16]; notably for Rails, PostgreSQL and MySQL actually default to, respectively, the weaker Read Committed and Repeatable Read isolation levels.

We did not encounter evidence that applications changed the isolation level. Rails does not configure the database isolation level for validations, and none of the application code or configurations we encountered change the default isolation level, either (or mention doing so in documentation). Thus, although we cannot prove that

[3]We chose to analyze commits authored rather than lines of code written because git tracks large-scale code refactoring commits as an often large set of deletions and insertions. Nevertheless, we observed a close correlation between lines of code and commits authored.

this is indeed the case, this data suggests that validations are likely to run at default database isolation in production environments.

Validations with weak isolation. Given that validations are not likely to be perfectly isolated, does this lack of serializable isolation actually affect these invariants? Just because validations effectively run concurrently does not mean that they are necessarily incorrect. To determine exactly which of these invariants are correct under concurrent execution, we draw on the recently developed theory of invariant confluence [17].

Invariant confluence (I-confluence) provides a necessary and sufficient condition for whether or not invariants can be preserved under coordination-free, concurrent execution of transactions. Informally, the condition ensures that, if transactions maintain database states that are correct with respect to an invariant when run in isolation, the transactions can be run simultaneously and their results combined ("merged") to produce another correct state. In the case of Rails, we wish to determine whether, in the event of concurrent validations and model saves, the result of concurrent model saves will not violate the validation for either model. In the event that two concurrent controllers save the same model (backed by the same database record), only one will be persisted (a some-write-wins "merge"). In the event that two concurrent controllers save different models (i.e., backed by different database records), both will be persisted (a set-based "merge"). In both cases, we must ensure that validations hold after merge.

Our I-confluence analysis currently relies on a combination of manual proofs and simple static analysis: given a set of invariant and operation pairs classified as providing the I-confluence property, we can iterate through all operations and declared invariants and check whether or not they appear in the set of I-confluent pairs. If so, we label the pair as I-confluent. If not, we can either conservatively label the pair as unsafe under concurrent execution or prove the pair as I-confluent or not. (To prove a pair is I-confluent, we must show that the set of database states reachable by executing operations preserves the invariant under merge, as described above.)

Returning to our task of classifying Rails validations and associations as safe or not, we applied this I-confluence analysis to the invariants[4] in the corpus. In our analysis, we found that only 60 out of 3505 validations were expressed as user-defined functions. The remainder were drawn from the standard set of validations supported by Rails core.[5] Accordingly, we begin by considering built-in validations, then examine each of the custom validations.

4.2 Built-In Validations

We now discuss common, built-in validations and their I-confluence. Many are I-confluent and are therefore safe to execute concurrently.

Table 1 presents the ten most common built-in validations by usage and their occurences in our application corpus. The exact coordination requirements depended on their usage.

The most popular invariant, `presence`, serves multiple purposes. Its basic behavior is to simply check for empty values in a model before saving. This is I-confluent as, in our model, concurrent model saves cannot result in non-null values suddenly becoming null. However, `presence` can also be used to enforce that the opposite end of an association is, in fact, present in the database (i.e., referential integrity). Under insertions, foreign key constraints are I-confluent [17], but, under deletions, they are not.

[4]We focus on validations here as, while associations *do* represent an invariant, it is only when they are coupled with validations that they are enforced.

[5]It is unclear exactly why this is the case. It is possible that, because these invariants are standardized, they are more accessible to users. It is also possible that Rails developers have simply done a good job of codifying common patterns that programmers tend to use.

Name	Occurrences	I-Confluent?
`validates_presence_of`	1762	Depends
`validates_uniqueness_of`	440	No
`validates_length_of`	438	Yes
`validates_inclusion_of`	201	Yes
`validates_numericality_of`	133	Yes
`validates_associated`	39	Depends
`validates_email`	34	Yes
`validates_attachment_content_type`	29	Yes
`validates_attachment_size`	29	Yes
`validates_confirmation_of`	19	Yes
Other	321	

Table 1: Use of and invariant confluence of built-in validations.

The second most popular invariant, concerning record uniqueness, is *not* I-confluent [17]. That is, if two users concurrently insert or modify records, they can introduce duplicates.

Eight of the next nine invariants are largely concerned with data formatting and are I-confluent. For example, `numericality` ensures that the field contains a number rather than an alphanumeric string. These invariants are indeed I-confluent under concurrent update.

Finally, the safety of `associated` (like `presence`) is contingent on whether or not the current updates are both insertions (I-confluent) or mixed insertions and deletions (not I-confluent). Thus, correctness depends on the operation.

Overall, a large number of built-in validations are safe under concurrent operation. Under insertions, 86.9% of built-in validation occurrences as I-confluent. Under deletions, only 36.6% of occurrences are I-confluent. However, associations and multi-record uniqueness are—depending on the workload—not I-confluent and are therefore likely to cause problems. In the next section, we examine these validations in greater detail.

4.3 Custom Validations

We also manually inspected the coordination requirements of the 60 (1.71%) validations (from 17 projects) that were declared as UDFs. 52 of these custom validations were declared inline via Rails's `validates_each` syntax, while 8 were custom classes that implemented Rails's validation interface. 42 of 60 validations were I-confluent, while the remaining 18 were not. Due to space constraints, we omit a discussion of each validation but discuss several trends and notable examples of custom validations below.

Among the custom validations that were I-confluent, many consisted of simple format checks or other domain-specific validations, including credit card formatting and static username blacklisting.

The validations that were not I-confluent took on a range of forms. Three validations performed the equivalent of foreign key checking, which, as we have discussed, is unsafe under deletion. Three validations checked database-backed configuration options including the maximum allowed file upload size and default tax rate; while configuration updates are ostensibly rare, the outcome of each validation could be affected under a configuration change. Two validations were especially interesting. Spree's `AvailabilityValidator` checks whether an eCommerce inventory has sufficient stock available to fulfill an order; concurrent order placement might result in negative stock. Discourse's `PostValidator` checks whether a user has been spamming the forum; while not necessarily critical, a spammer could technically foil this validation by attempting to simultaneously author many posts.

In summary, again, a large proportion of validations appear safe. Nevertheless, the few non-I-confluent validations should be cause for concern under concurrent execution.

5. QUANTIFYING FERAL ANOMALIES

While many of the validations we encountered were I-confluent, not all were. In this section, we specifically investigate the effect of concurrent execution on two of the most popular non-I-confluent validations: uniqueness and foreign key validations.

5.1 Uniqueness Constraints and Isolation

To begin, we consider Rails's uniqueness validations: 12.7% of the built-in validation uses we encountered. In this section, we discuss how Rails implements uniqueness and show that this is—at least theoretically—unsafe.

When a model field is declared with a `:validates_uniqueness` annotation, any instance of that model is compared against all other corresponding records in the database to ensure that the field is indeed unique. ActiveRecord accomplishes this by issuing a "`SELECT`" query in SQL and, if no such record is found, Rails updates the instance state in the database (Appendix B.1).

While this user-level uniqueness validation runs within a transaction, the isolation level of the transaction affects its correctness. For correct execution, the `SELECT` query must effectively attain a predicate lock on the validated column for the duration of the transaction. This behavior *is* supported under serializable isolation. However, under Read Committed or Repeatable Read isolation, no such mutual exclusion will be performed, leading to potential inconsistency.[6] Moreover, under Snapshot Isolation, may similarly result in inconsistency.[7] Thus, unless the database is configured for serializable isolation, integrity violations may result.

As we have discussed, MySQL and PostgreSQL each support serializable isolation but default to weaker isolation. Moreover, in our investigation, we discovered a bug in PostgreSQL's implementation of Serializable Snapshot Isolation that allowed duplicate records to be created under serializable isolation when running a set of transactions derived from the Rails primary key validator. We have confirmed this anomalous behavior with the core PostgreSQL developers[8] and, as of March 2015, the behavior persists. Thus, any discussion of weak isolation levels aside, PostgreSQL's implementation of serializability is non-serializable and is insufficient to provide correct behavior for Rails' uniqueness validations. So-called "serializable" databases such as Oracle 12c that actually provide Snapshot Isolation will similarly fall prey to duplicate validations.

The Rails documentation warns that uniqueness validations may fail and admit duplicate records [7]. Yet, despite the availability patches that remedy this behavior by the use of an in-database constraint and/or index, Rails provides this incorrect behavior by default. (One patch was rejected; a developer reports "[t]he reasons for it not being incorporated...are lost in the mists of time but I suspect it's to do with backwards compatibility, cross database compatibility and applications varying on how they want/need to handle these kind of errors." [27]).

[6]Using `SELECT FOR UPDATE` under these weaker models would be safe, but Rails does not implement its predicate-based lookups as such (i.e., it instead opts for a simple `SELECT` statement).

[7]The first reference to the potential integrity violations resulting from this implementation in the Rails code that we are aware of dates to December 2007, in Rails v.2.0.0 [59]. In September 2008, another user added additional discussion within the code comments, noting that "this could even happen if you use transactions with the 'serializable' isolation level" [62]. Without reading too closely, the use of "'serializable'" possibly suggests familiarity with the common, erroneous labeling of Snapshot Isolation as "serializable" (as in Oracle 12c documentation and PostgreSQL documentation prior to the introduction of SSI in version 9.1.1 in September 2011).

[8]"BUG #11732: Non-serializable outcomes under serializable isolation" at `http://www.postgresql.org/message-id/20141021071458.2678.9080@wrigleys.postgresql.org`

In another bug report complaining of duplicates due to concurrent uniqueness validation, a commenter asserts "this is not a bug but documented and inherent behavior of validates_uniqueness_of" [72]. A Rails committer follows up, noting that "the only way to handle [uniqueness] properly is at the database layer with a unique constraint on the column," and subsequently closes the issue. The original bug reporter protests that "the problem extends beyond unique constraints and into validations that are unique to a Rails application that can't [sic?!] be enforced on the DB level"; the Rails committer responds that "with the possible exception of [associations,] all of the other validations are constrained by the attribute values currently in memory, so aren't susceptible to similar flaws." This final statement is correct for many of the built-in validations but is not correct for arbitrary user-defined validations. We discuss the user-defined validation issue further in Section 7.

Understanding validation behavior. Given that entirely feral mechanisms can introduce duplicates, how many duplicates can be introduced? Once a record is written, any later validations will observe it via `SELECT` calls. However, *while* a record is being validated, any number of concurrent validations can unsafely proceed. In practice, the number of concurrent validations is dependent on the Rails environment. In a Rails deployment permitting P concurrent validations (e.g., a single-threaded, multi-process environment with P processes), each value in the domain of the model field/database column can be inserted no more than P times. Thus, validations—at least theoretically—bound the worst-case number of duplicate records for each unique value in the database table.

5.2 Quantifying Uniqueness Anomalies

Given that feral uniqueness validations are acknowledged to be unsafe under non-serializable isolation yet are widely used, we sought to understand exactly how often uniqueness anomalies occur in an experimental deployment. In this section, we demonstrate that uniqueness validations in Rails are indeed unsafe under non-serializable isolation. While they prevent some data integrity errors, we observe—depending on the workload—many duplicate records.

Experimental setup. We developed a Rails 4.1.5 application that performed insertions to a non-indexed string column and compared the incidence of violations both with and without a uniqueness validator (see also Appendix C.1).[9] We deployed this application on two Amazon EC2 `m2.4xlarge` instances, offering 68.4 GB RAM, 8 CPU cores, and 1680GB local storage, running Ubuntu 14.04 LTS. On one instance, we deployed our application, using Nginx 1.6.2 as a web frontend proxied to a set of Unicorn 4.8.3 (Ruby VM pool) workers. Nginx acts as a HTTP frontend and forwards incoming requests to a variably sized pool of Rails VMs (managed by Unicorn, in a multi-process, single-threaded server) that `epoll` on a shared Linux file descriptor. On the other EC2 instance, we deployed PostgreSQL 9.3.5 and configured it to run on the instance local storage. We used a third EC2 instance to direct traffic to the front-end instance and drive load. We plot the average and standard deviation of three runs per experiment.

Stress test. We began our study by issuing a simple stress test that executed a number of concurrent insertion requests against a

[9]In our experimental evaluation, we use the custom applications described below (and in Appendix C) for two reasons. First, these test cases allow us to isolate ActiveRecord behavior to the relevant set of validations as they are deployed by default, independent of any specialized controller logic. Second, this reduces the complexity of automated testing. Many of the applications in our corpus indeed use the same code paths within ActiveRecord, but evaluating these custom applications simplifies programmatic triggering of validation logic.

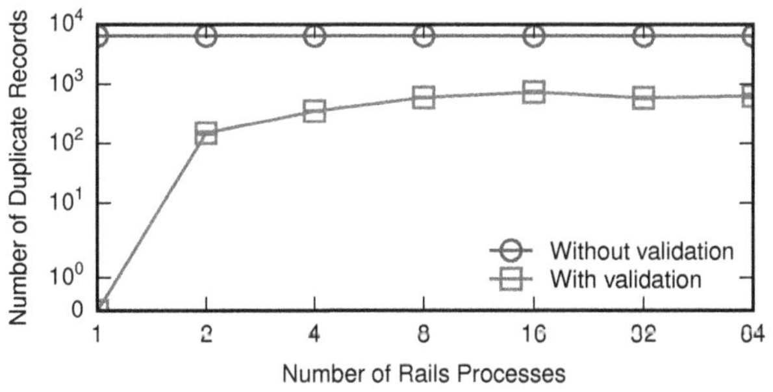

Figure 2: Uniqueness stress test integrity violations.

variable number of Unicorn workers. We repeatedly issued a set of 64 concurrent model creation (SQL insertion) requests, each with the same validated key (e.g., all with field key set to value 1) against the Rails application. Across an increasing number of Unicorn workers, we repeated this set of requests 100 times (blocking in-between rounds to ensure that each round is, in fact, a concurrent set of requests), changing the validated key each round (Appendix C.2).

Figure 2 shows the results. With no validation, all concurrent requests succeed, resulting in 6300 duplicate records (100 rounds of 64-1 duplicate keys). With validations enabled, the number of violations depends on the degree of concurrency allowed by Unicorn. With only one process, Unicorn performs the validations serially, creating no duplicates. However, with two processes, Unicorn processes race, resulting in 70 duplicate records spread across 70 keys. With three processes, Unicorn produces 249 duplicate records across all 100 keys. The number of duplicates increases with the number of processes, peaking at 16 workers. With additional workers, duplicate counts decrease slightly, which we attribute to thrashing between workers and within PostgreSQL (recall that each instance has only 8 cores). Nevertheless, using validations, the microbenchmark duplicate count remains below 700—nearly an order-of-magnitude fewer duplicates than without using validations. Therefore, even though these validations are incorrectly implemented, they still result in fewer anomalies. However, when we added in in-database unique index on the `key` column[10] and repeated the experiment, we observed no duplicates, as expected.

Actual workloads. The preceding experiment stressed a particularly high-contention workload—in effect, a worst case workload for uniqueness validations. In practice, such a workload is likely rare.[11] Accordingly, we set up another workload meant to capture a less pathological access pattern. We ran another insert-only workload, with key choice distributed among a fixed set of keys. By varying the distribution and number of keys, we were able to both capture more realistic workloads and also control the amount of contention in the workload. As a basis for comparison, we ran four different distributions. First, we considered uniform key access. Second, we used YCSB's Zipfian-distributed accesses from `workloada` [36]. Third and fourth, we used the item distribution access from Facebook's LinkBench workload, which captures MySQL record access when serving Facebook's social graph [14]. Specifically, we used—separately—the insert and update traffic from this benchmark.

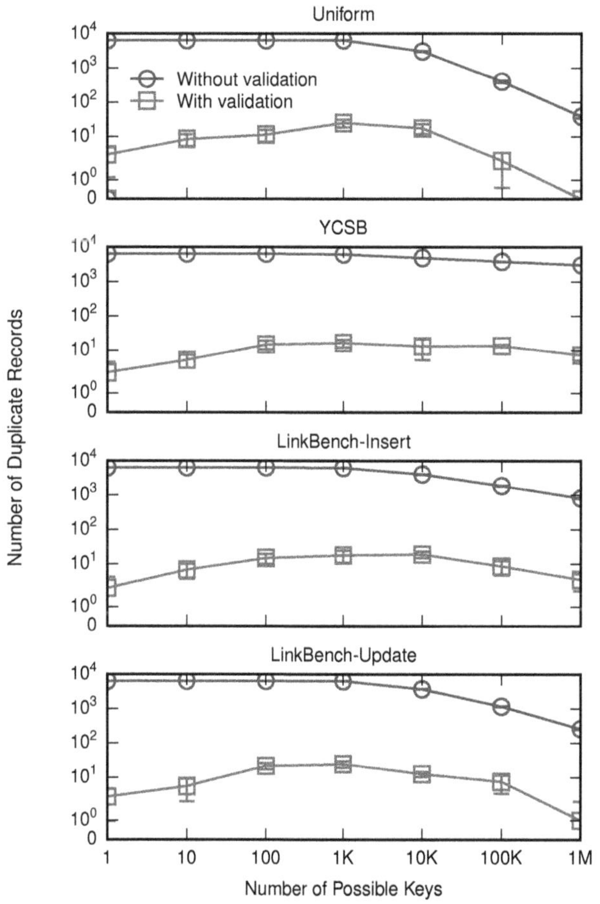

Figure 3: Uniqueness workload integrity violations.

For each trial in this workload, we used 64 concurrent clients independently issuing a set of 100 requests each, with a fixed number of 64 Unicorn workers per process (Appendix C.3).

Figure 3 illustrates the number of duplicate records observed under each of these workloads. As we increase the number of possible keys, there are two opposing effects. With more keys, the probability of any two operations colliding decreases. However, recall that, once a key is written, all subsequent validators can read it. While the uniform workload observes an average of 2.33 duplicate records with only one possible key, it observes an average of 26 duplicate keys with 1000 possible keys. Nevertheless, with 1 million possible keys, we do not observe any duplicate records.

The actual "production" workloads exhibit different trends. In general, YCSB is an extremely high contention workload, with a Zipfian constant of 0.99, resulting in one very hot key. This decreases the beneficial effect of increasing the number of keys in the database. However, LinkBench has less contention and anomalies decrease more rapidly with increased numbers of keys.

5.3 Association Validations and Isolation

Having investigated uniqueness constraints, we turn our attention to association validations. We first, again, discuss how Rails enforces these validations and describe how—at least theoretically—validations might result in integrity errors.

When a model field is declared with an association (e.g., it `:belongs_to` another model) *and* a `:validates_presence` validation, Rails will attempt to ensure that the declared validation is

[10] In this case, we added a unique index to the model using Active Record's *database migration*, or manual schema change functionality. Migrations are written separately from the Active Record model declarations. Adding the index was not difficult, but, nevertheless, the index addition logic is separate from the domain model. Without using third-party models, we are unaware of a way to enforce uniqueness within Rails without first declaring an index that is *also* annotated with a special `unique: true` attribute.

[11] In fact, it was in the above workload that we encountered the non-serializable PostgreSQL behavior under serializable isolation. Under serializable isolation, the number of anomalies is reduced compared to the number under Read Committed isolation (as we report here), but we still detected duplicate records.

valid before saving the model. Rails accomplishes this by issuing a "SELECT WHERE" query in SQL to find an associated record (e.g., to ensure the "one" end of a one-to-many relationship exists) and, if a matching association is found, Rails updates the instance state in the database (Appendix B.2). On deletion, any models with associations marked with :dependent => destroy (or :dependent => delete) will have any associated models destroyed (i.e., removed by instantiating in Rails and calling destroy on the model) or deleted (i.e., removed by simply calling the database's DELETE method).

This feral association validation runs within a transaction, but, again the exact isolation level of the transaction affects its correctness. For correct execution, the SELECT query must also attain a predicate lock on the specific value of the validated column for the duration of the transaction. Similar to the uniqueness validator, concurrent deletions and insertions are unsafe under Read Committed, Repeatable Read, and Snapshot Isolation. Thus, unless the database is configured for serializable isolation, inconsistency may result and the feral validation will fail to prevent data corruption.

Unlike uniqueness validations, there is no discussion of associations and concurrency anomalies in the Rails documentation. Moreover, in Rails 4.1, there is no way to natively declare a foreign key constraint;[12] it must be done via a third-party library such as foreigner [57] or schema_plus [1]. Only two applications (canvaslms and diaspora) used foreigner, and only one application (juvia) used schema_plus. One application (jobsworth) used a custom schema annotation and constraint generator.

Understanding association behavior. Given that entirely feral mechanisms can introduce broken associations, how many dangling records can be introduced? Once a record is deleted, any later validations will observe it via SELECT calls. However, in the worst case, the feral cascading deletion on the one side of a one-to-many relation can stall indefinitely, allowing an unlimited number of concurrent insertions to the many side of the relation. Thus, validations—at least theoretically—only reduce the worst-case number of dangling records that were inserted prior to deletion; any number of concurrent insertions may occur during validation, leading to unbounded numbers of dangling records.

5.4 Quantifying Association Anomalies

Given this potential for errors, we again set out to quantify integrity errors. We demonstrate that weak isolation can indeed lead to data integrity errors in Rails' implementation of associations.

We performed another set of experiments to test association validation behavior under concurrent insertions and deletions. Using the same Unicorn and PostgreSQL deployment as above, we configured another application to test whether or not Rails validations would correctly enforce association-based integrity constraints. We consider an application with two models: Users and Departments. We configure a one-to-many relationship: each user belongs_to a department, and each department has_many user (Appendix C.4).

As a basic stress test, we initialize the database by creating 100 departments with no users. Subsequently, for each department in the database, we issue a single request to delete the department along with 64 concurrent requests to insert users in that department. To correctly preserve the one-to-many relationship, the database should either reject the deletion operation or perform a cascading deletion of the department and any users (while rejecting any future user creation requests for that department). We can quantify the degree of inconsistency by counting the number of users left in the database who have no corresponding department (Appendix C.5).

[12]Rails 4.2 added support for foreign keys via migration annotation (separate from models; similarly to adding a unique index) in December 2014.

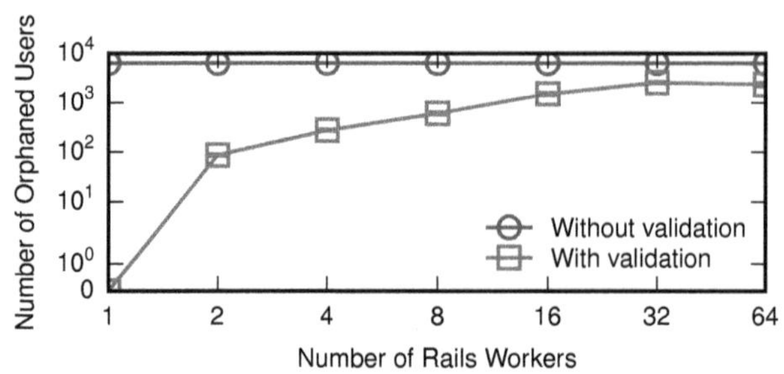

Figure 4: Foreign key stress association anomalies.

With associations declared in Rails, the Rails process performing the deletion will attempt a cascading delete of users upon department deletion. However, this cascade is performed, again, ferally—at the application level. Thus, under non-serializable isolation, any user creation events that are processed while the search for Users to delete is underway will result in Users without departments.

Figure 4 shows the number of "orphaned" Users (i.e., Users without a matching Department) as a function of Rails worker processes. With no constraints declared to Rails or to the database, all User creations succeed, resulting in 6400 dangling Users. With constraints declared in Rails (via a mix of validation and association), the degree of inconsistency depends on the degree of parallelism. Under the worst case, with 64 concurrent processes, the validations are almost worthless in preventing integrity errors. In contrast, when we declare a foreign key constraint within the database[13] and run the workload again, we observe no inconsistency.

The above stress test shows that inconsistency due to feral concurrency control occurs only during times of contention—parallel deletions and insertions. We subsequently varied the degree of contention within the workload. We configured the same application and performed a set of insertions and deletions, but spread across a greater number of keys and at random. A set of 64 processes concurrently each issued 100 User creation and Department deletion requests (at a ratio of 10 to 1) to a set of randomly-selected keys (again at a ratio of 10 Users to each Department). By varying the number of Users and Departments, we were able to control the amount of contention within the workload. Under this workload, inconsistency resulted only when a Department deletion proceeded concurrently with a User creation event and the feral cascading deletion "missed" the User creation (Appendix C.6).

Figure 5 shows the results. As the number of Departments increases, we observe two trends. First, with only one Department, there is again less chance of inconsistency: all operations contend on the same data item, so the total number of inconsistent, orphaned users is limited by the number of potentially racing. However, as the number of Departments increases, the chance of concurrent deletions and insertions drops.

5.5 Takeaways and Discussion

The preceding experiments demonstrate that, indeed, Active Record is unsafe as deployed by default. Validations are susceptible to data corruption due to sensitivity to weak isolation anomalies.

This raises the question: why declare validations at all? As we observe, validations protect against *some* data corruption. First, they correctly guard against non-concurrency-related anomalies such as data entry or input errors. For example, if a user attempts to reserve a username that was previously chosen, a validation would succeed.

[13]In this case, we introduced the constraint via SQL using a direct connection to the database. This change was straightforward but—like the unique index addition—was not reflected in the base Active Record models.

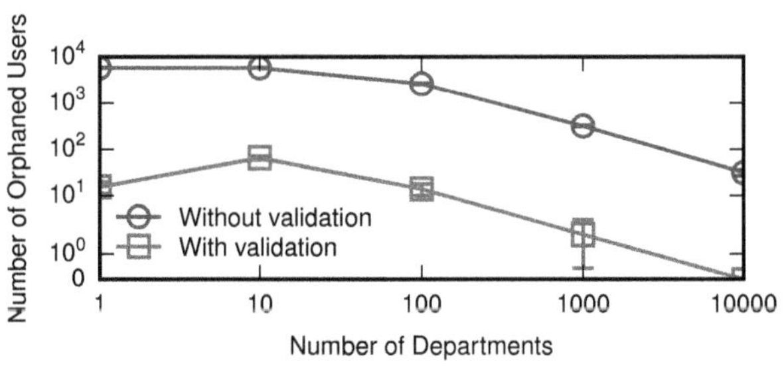

Figure 5: Foreign key workload association anomalies.

The failures we observe here are solely due to concurrent execution. Without concurrent execution, validations are correct. Second, validations *do* reduce the incidence of inconsistency. Empirically, even under worst-case workloads, these validations result in order-of-magnitude reductions in inconsistency. Under less pathological workloads, they may eliminate it. It is possible that, in fact, the degree of concurrency and data contention within Rails-backed applications simply does not lead to these concurrency races—that, in some sense, validations are "good enough" for many applications.

Nevertheless, in both cases, Rails's feral mechanisms are a poor substitute for their respective database counterparts—at least in terms of integrity. We re-examine the Rails community's reluctance to embrace these mechanisms in Section 7.

6. OTHER FRAMEWORKS

While our primary focus in this paper is Rails, we briefly investigated support for uniqueness, foreign key, and custom validations in several other ORM frameworks. We find widespread support for validations and varying susceptibility to integrity errors.

Java Persistence API (JPA; version EE 7) [3] is a standard Java Object persistence interface and supports both uniqueness and primary key constraints in the database via specialized object annotations. Thus, when JPA is used to create a table, it will use the database to enforce these constraints. In 2009, JPA introduced support for UDF validations via a JavaBean interface [23]. Interestingly, both the original (and current) Bean validation specifications specifically address the use of uniqueness validations in their notes:

> "Question: should we add @Unique that would map to @Column(unique=true)? @Unique cannot be tested at the Java level reliably but could generate a database unique constraint generation. @Unique is not part of the [Bean Validation] spec today." [21]

An author of a portion of the code specification notes separately:

> "The reason @Unique is not part of the built-in constraints is the fact that accessing the [database] during a valiation [sic] is opening yourself up for potenital [sic] phantom reads. Think twice before you go for [an application-level] approach." [46]

By default, JPA Validations are run upon model save and run in a transaction at the default isolation level, and therefore, as the developers above hint, are susceptible to the same kinds of integrity violations we study here.

Hibernate (version 4.3.7) [56], a Java ORM based on JPA, does *not* automatically enforce declared foreign key relationships: if a foreign key constraint is declared; a corresponding column is added, but that column is *not* backed by a database foreign key. Instead, for both uniqueness and foreign key constraints, Hibernate relies on JPA schema annotations for correctness. Therefore, without appropriate schema annotations, Hibernate's basic associations may contain dangling references. Hibernate also has an extensive user-level validation framework implementing the JPA Validation Bean specification [47] and is sensitive to weak isolation anomalies, similar to Rails validations.

CakePHP (version 2.5.5) [4], a PHP-based web framework, supports uniqueness, foreign key, and UDF validations. CakePHP does *not* back any of its validation checking with a database transaction and relies on the user to correctly specify any corresponding foreign keys or uniqueness constraints within the database the schema. Thus, while users can declare each of these validations, there is no guarantee that they are actually enforced by the database. Thus, unless users are careful to specify constraints in both their schema and in their validations, validations may lead to integrity violations.

Laravel (version 4.2) [6], another PHP-based web framework, supports the same set of functionality as CakePHP, including application-level uniqueness, foreign key, and UDF validations in the application. Any database-backed constraints must be specified manually in the schema. Per one set of community documentation [43], "database-level validations can efficiently handle some things (such as uniqueness of a column in heavily-used tables) that can be difficult to implement otherwise" but "testing and maintenance is more difficult...[and] your validations would be database- and schema-specific, which makes migrations or switching to another database backend more difficult in the future." In contrast, model-level validations are "the recommended way to ensure that only valid data is saved into your database. They are database agnostic, cannot be bypassed by end users, and are convenient to test and maintain."

Django (version 1.7) [5], a popular Python-based framework, backs declared uniqueness and foreign key constraints with database-level constraints. It also supports custom validations, but these validations are not wrapped in a transaction [15]. Thus, Django also appears problematic, but only for custom validations.

Waterline (version 0.10) [20], the default ORM for Sails.js (a popular MVC framework for Node.js [19]), provides support for in-DB foreign key and uniqueness constraints (when supported by the database) as well as custom validations (that are *not* supported via transactions; e.g., "TO-DO: This should all be wrapped in a transaction. That's coming next but for the meantime just hope we don't get in a nasty state where the operation fails!" [78]).

Summary. In all, we observe common cross-framework support for feral validation/invariants, with inconsistent use of mechanisms for enforcing them, ranging from the use of in-database constraints to transactions to no ostensible use of concurrency control in either application or database.

7. IMPLICATIONS FOR DATABASES

In light of this empirical evidence of the continued mismatch between ORM applications and databases, in this section, we reflect on the core database limitations for application writers today and suggest a set of directions for alleviating them.

7.1 Summary: Shortcomings Today

The use of feral invariants is not well-supported by today's databases. At a high level, today's databases effectively offer two primary options for ORM framework developers and users:

1. **Use ACID transactions.** Serializable transactions are sufficient to correctly enforce arbitrary application invariants, including transaction-backed feral validations. This is core to the transaction concept: isolation is a means towards preserving integrity.

Unfortunately, in practice, for application developers, transactions are problematic. Given serializability's performance and availability overheads [26], developers at scale have largely eschewed the use of serializable transactions (which are anyway not required for correct enforcement of approximately 75% of the invariants we encountered in the Rails corpus). Moreover, many databases offering "ACID" semantics do not provide serializability by default and often, even among industry-standard enterprise offerings, do not offer it as an option at all [16] (to say nothing of implementation difficulties, as in Footnote 8). Instead, developers using these systems today must manually reason about a host of highly technical, often obscure, and poorly understood weak isolation models expressed in terms of low-level read/write anomalies such as Write Skew and Lost Update [8, 13]. We have observed (e.g., Footnote 7) that ORM and expert application developers are familiar with the prevalence of weak isolation, which may also help explain the relative unpopularity of transactions within the web programming community.

2. **Custom, feral enforcement.** Building user-level concurrency control solutions on a per-framework or, worse, per-application basis is an expensive, error-prone, and difficult process that neglects decades of contributions from the database community. While this solution is sufficient to maintain correctness in the approximately 87% (I-confluent) invariants in our corpus, the remainder can—in many modern ORM implementations—lead to data corruption on behalf of applications.

   However, and perhaps most importantly, this feral approach preserves a key tenet of the Rails philosophy: a recurring insistence on expressing domain logic in the application. This also enables the declaration of invariants that are not among the few natively supported by databases today (e.g., uniqueness constraints).

In summary, application writers today lack a solution that guarantees correctness while maintaining high performance *and* programmability. Serializability is too expensive for some applications, is not widely supported, and is not necessary for many application invariants. Feral concurrency control is often less expensive, is trivially portable, but is not sufficient for many other application invariants. In neither case does the database respect and assist with application programmer desires for a clean, idiomatic means of expressing correctness criteria in domain logic. We believe there is an opportunity and pressing need to build systems that provide all three criteria: performance, correctness, and programmability.

7.2 Domesticating Feral Mechanisms

Constructively, to properly provide database support and thereby "domesticate" these feral mechanisms, we believe application users and framework authors need a new database interface that will enable them to:

1. *Express correctness criteria in the language of their domain model, with minimal friction, while permitting their automatic enforcement.* Per Section 2, a core factor behind the success of ORMs like Rails appears to be their promulgation of an idiomatic programming style that "seems right" for web programming. Rails' disregard for advanced database functionality is evidence of a continued impedance mismatch between application domain logic and current database primitives: databases today do not understand the semantics of feral validations.

   We believe any solution to domestication must respect ORM application patterns and programming style, including the ability to specify invariants in each framework's native language. Ideally, database systems could enforce applications' existing feral invariants without modification. This is already feasible for a subset of invariants—like uniqueness and foreign key constraints—but not all. An ideal solution to domestication would provide universal support with no additional overhead for application writers.

2. *Only pay the price of coordination when necessary.* Per Section 4, many invariants can be safely executed without coordination, while others cannot. The many that do not need coordination should not be unnecessarily penalized.

   An ideal solution to domestication would enable applications to avoid coordination whenever possible, thus maximizing both performance and operation availability. The database should facilitate this avoidance, thus evading common complaints (especially within the Internet community) about serializable transactions.

3. *Easily deploy to multiple database backends.* ORM frameworks today are deployed across a range of database implementations, and, when deciding which database features to exercise, framework authors often choose the least common denominator for compatibility purposes.

   An ideal solution to domestication would preserve this compatibility, possibly by providing a "bolt on" compatibility layer between ORM systems and databases lacking advanced functionality (effectively, a "blessed" set of mechanisms beneath the application/ORM that correctly enforce feral mechanisms).

Fulfilling these design requirements would enable high performance, correct execution, and programmability. However, doing so represents a considerable challenge.

Promise in the literature. The actual vehicle for implementing this interface is an open question, but the literature lends several clues. On the one hand, we do not believe the answer lies in exposing additional read/write isolation or consistency guarantees like Read Committed; these fail our requirement for an abstraction operating the level of domain logic and, as we have noted, are challenging for developers (and researchers) to reason about. On the other hand, more recent proposals for invariant-based concurrency control [17, 65] and a litany of work from prior decades on rule-based [82] and, broadly, semantics-based concurrency control [79] appear immediately applicable and worth (re-)considering. Recent advances in program analysis for extracting invariants [73] and subroutines from imperative code [33] may allow us to programatically suggest new invariants, perform correspondence checking for existing applications, and apply a range of automated optimizations to legacy code [34, 76]. Finally, clean-slate language design and program analysis obviate the need for explicit invariant declaration (thus alleviating concerns of specification completeness) [11, 12, 84]; while adoption within the ORM community is a challenge, we view this exploration as worthwhile.

Summary. In all, the wide gap between research and current practice is both a pressing concern and an exciting opportunity to revisit many decades of research on alternatives to serializability with an eye towards current operating conditions, application demands, and programmer practices. Our proposal here is demanding, but so are the framework and application writers our databases serve. Given the correct primitives, database systems may yet have a role to play in ensuring application integrity.

8. RELATED WORK

There is a large body of related work that we consider in four categories: object relational mapping systems, the study of weak isolation and application requirements, the quantification of isolation behavior, and empirical open source software analysis.

ORMs. Database systems and application programming frameworks have a long history [24, 30, 63]. The "impedance mismatch" between object-oriented programming and the relational model is a perennial problem in data management systems. Ruby on Rails is no exception, and the concurrency control issues we study here are endemic to this mismatch—namely, the disuse of common concurrency control mechanisms like database-backed constraints. Bridging this gap remains an active area of research [66].

The latest wave of web programming frameworks has inspired diverse research spanning databases, verification, and security. StatusQuo uses program analysis and synthesis to transform imperative ORM code into SQL, leveraging the efficiency of database-backed web applications written in the Spring framework [33]. Rails has been the subject of study in the verification of cross-site scripting attacks [32], errors in data modeling of associations [68], and arbitrary, user-specified (non-validation) invariants [25]. Rails-style ORM validations have been used to improve systems security via client-side execution [58, 76]. Our focus here is on the concurrency control requirements and usages of applications written in Rails.

Applications and weak isolation. The issues we examine here are fundamental to the use of weak isolation in data management systems. Non-serializable isolation dates to the mid-1970s [52] and has a colorful history [8]; today, by volume, many database management systems are non-serializable by default [16]. The isolation anomalies surfaced by the stores we study here are directly responsible for violating the integrity of the validations we consider.

However, serializable isolation is not strictly necessary for maintaining application integrity. Semantic-based concurrency control criteria has almost as long a lineage as serializability [44, 53] and suggests that, with additional, non-syntactic knowledge about applications (e.g., integrity constraints) [61], correctness is achievable without serializability. This use of invariants has enjoyed recent popularity in work by Li et al. [65], Roy et al. [73], and Bailis et al. [17]. We use the concept of invariant confluence from [17] to determine whether Rails's built-in validators and applications written in Rails are indeed safe under any coordination-free execution. Our methodology is closest in spirit to [17], but, here, we examine real applications instead of standardized benchmarks.

Quantifying anomalies. A range of research similarly quantifies the effect of non-serializable isolation in a variety of ways.

Perhaps closest to our work is a study by Fekete et al., which quantitatively analyzed data inconsistencies arising from non-serializable schedules [45]. This study used a hand-crafted benchmark for analysis but is nevertheless one of the only studies of actual application inconsistencies. Here, we focus on open source applications from the Rails community.

A larger body of work examines isolation anomalies at the read-write interface (that is, measures deviations from properties such as serializability or linearizability but *not* the end effect of these deviations on actual application behavior). Wada et al. evaluated the staleness of Amazon's SimpleDB using end-user request tracing [81], while Bermbach and Tai evaluated Amazon S3 [22], each quantifying various forms of non-serializable behavior. Golab et al. provide algorithms for verifying the linearizability of and sequential consistency arbitrary data stores [51] and Zellag and Kemme provide algorithms for verifying their serializability [85] and other cycle-based isolation anomalies [86]. Probabilistically Bounded Staleness provides time- and version-based staleness predictions for eventually consistent data stores [18]. Our focus here is on anomalies as observed by application logic rather than read-write anomalies observed under weak isolation.

Empirical software analysis. Empirical software analysis of open source software is a topic of active interest in the software engineering research community [77]. In the parlance of that community, in this work, we perform a mixed-methods analysis, combining quantitative survey techniques with a confirmatory case study of Rails's susceptibility to validation errors [42]. In our survey, we attempt to minimize sampling bias towards validation-heavy projects by focusing our attention on popular projects, as measured by GitHub stars. Our use of quantitative data followed by supporting qualitative data from documentation and issue tracking—as well as the chronology of methodologies we employed to attain the results presented here—can be considered an instance of the sequential exploration strategy [37]. We specifically use these techniques in service of better understanding use of database concurrency control.

9. CONCLUSIONS

In this work, we examined the use of concurrency control mechanisms in a set of 67 open source Ruby on Rails applications and, to a less thorough extent, concurrency control support in a range of other web-oriented ORM frameworks. We found that, in contrast with traditional transaction processing, these applications overwhelmingly prefer to leverage application-level *feral* support for data integrity, typically in the form of declarative (sometimes user-defined) validation and association logic. Despite the popularity of these invariants, we find limited use of in-database support to correctly implement them, leading to a range of quantifiable inconsistencies for Rails' built-in uniqueness and association validations. While many validations are invariant confluent and therefore correct under concurrent execution given standard RDBMS weak isolation and concurrent update semantics, we see considerable opportunity to better support these users and their feral invariants in the future.

Coda: A Call for Empiricism

This work is a first step towards better understanding how users in the wild actually interact with the database systems that this community builds. Given the ascendancy of open source, there is unprecedented opportunity to empirically and quantitatively study how our systems are and are not serving the needs of application programmers. Lightweight program analysis has never been easier, and the corpus of readily-accessible code—especially in an academic context—has never been larger.

These open source applications are undoubtedly dwarfed by many other commercial and enterprise-grade codebases in terms of size, quality, and complexity. However, compared to alternatives such as TPC-C, which today is almost 23 years old and is still the preferred standard for transaction processing evaluation, open source corpuses are far better proxies for modern applications. Recent efforts like the OLTPBenchmark suite [39] are promising but are nevertheless (and perhaps necessarily) not a substitute for real applications. The opportunity to perform both quantitative surveys across a large set of applications as well as longitudinal studies over the history of each application repository (and the behavior of a given programmer over time and across repositories) are particularly compelling. While these studies are inherently imprecise (due to limitations of the corpuses), the resulting quantitative trends are invaluable.

In summary, in this era of "Big Data" analytics, we see great promise in turning these analyses inwards, towards an empirical understanding of the usage of data management systems today, in service of better problem selection and a more quantitatively informed community dialogue.

Acknowledgments. The authors would like to thank Peter Alvaro, Michael R. Bernstein, Colin Jones, Xavier Shay, and the SIGMOD reviewers for their insightful commentary and feedback on this work. This research is supported in part by NSF CISE Expeditions Award CCF-1139158, LBNL Award 7076018, DARPA XData Award FA8750-12-2-0331, the NSF Graduate Research Fellowship (grant DGE-1106400), and gifts from Amazon Web Services, Google, SAP, The Thomas and Stacey Siebel Foundation, Adatao, Adobe, Apple, Inc., Blue Goji, Bosch, C3Energy, Cisco, Cray, Cloudera, EMC, Ericsson, Facebook, Guavus, Huawei, Informatica, Intel, Microsoft, NetApp, Pivotal, Samsung, Splunk, Virdata, VMware, and Yahoo!.

10. REFERENCES

[1] SchemaPlus. https://github.com/SchemaPlus/schema_plus.

[2] How a quiet developer built Goodreads.com into book community of 2.6+ million members – with Otis Chandler, November 2009. http://mixergy.com/interviews/goodreads-otis-chandler/.

[3] Java EE 7 API: Package javax.persistence, 2013. http://docs.oracle.com/javaee/7/api/javax/persistence/package-summary.html.

[4] CakePHP, 2014. http://cakephp.org/ and http://book.cakephp.org/2.0/en/index.html.

[5] Django: The Web framework for perfectionists with deadlines, 2014. https://www.djangoproject.com/ and https://github.com/django/django.

[6] Laravel: The PHP Framework for Web Artisans, 2014. http://laravel.com/ and https://github.com/laravel/laravel.

[7] RailsGuide: Active Record Validations, 2014. http://guides.rubyonrails.org/active_record_validations.html.

[8] A. Adya. *Weak consistency: a generalized theory and optimistic implementations for distributed transactions*. PhD thesis, MIT, 1999.

[9] R. Allen. Airbnb Engineering Blog: "Upgrading Airbnb from Rails 2.3 to Rails 3.0", October 2012. http://nerds.airbnb.com/upgrading-airbnb-from-rails-23-to-rails-30/.

[10] G. Alonso, F. Casati, H. Kuno, and V. Machiraju. *Web services*. Springer, 2004.

[11] P. Alvaro, N. Conway, J. M. Hellerstein, and D. Maier. Blazes: Coordination analysis for distributed programs. In *ICDE 2014*.

[12] P. Alvaro, N. Conway, J. M. Hellerstein, and W. Marczak. Consistency analysis in Bloom: a CALM and collected approach. In *CIDR 2011*.

[13] P. Alvaro et al. Consistency without borders. In *SoCC 2013*.

[14] T. G. Armstrong, V. Ponnekanti, D. Borthakur, and M. Callaghan. Linkbench: a database benchmark based on the Facebook social graph. In *SIGMOD 2013*.

[15] J. Aylett. django-database-constraints, 2013. https://github.com/jaylett/django-database-constraints.

[16] P. Bailis, A. Davidson, A. Fekete, A. Ghodsi, J. M. Hellerstein, and I. Stoica. Highly Available Transactions: Virtues and limitations. In *VLDB 2014*.

[17] P. Bailis, A. Fekete, M. J. Franklin, J. M. Hellerstein, A. Ghodsi, and I. Stoica. Coordination avoidance in database systems. In *VLDB 2015*.

[18] P. Bailis, S. Venkataraman, M. J. Franklin, et al. Probabilistically Bounded Staleness for practical partial quorums. In *VLDB 2012*.

[19] Balderdash. Sails.js: Realtime MVC Framework for Node.js, 2014. https://github.com/balderdashy/sails.

[20] Balderdash. Waterline: An adapter-based ORM for Node.js with support for mysql, mongo, postgres, redis, [sic] and more, 2014. https://github.com/balderdashy/waterline.

[21] Bean Validation Expert Group. Jsr-000303 bean validation 1.0 final release specification, 2009. http://download.oracle.com/otndocs/jcp/bean_validation-1.0-fr-oth-JSpec/.

[22] D. Bermbach and S. Tai. Eventual consistency: How soon is eventual? An evaluation of Amazon S3's consistency behavior. In *MW4SOC*, 2011.

[23] E. Bernard. Java Specification Request 349: Bean Validation 1.1, 2013. https://jcp.org/en/jsr/detail?id=349.

[24] P. A. Bernstein, A. Y. Halevy, and R. A. Pottinger. A vision for management of complex models. *ACM Sigmod Record*, 29(4):55–63, 2000.

[25] I. Bocić and T. Bultan. Inductive verification of data model invariants for web applications. In *ICSE*, ICSE 2014, pages 620–631, New York, NY, USA, 2014. ACM.

[26] E. Brewer. CAP twelve years later: How the "rules" have changed. *Computer*, 45(2):23–29, 2012.

[27] J. Brough. #645: Alternative to validates_uniqueness_of using db constraints, 2011. rails/rails at https://github.com/rails/rails/issues/645.

[28] P. Calcado. Building products at SoundCloud – Part I: Dealing with the monolith, June 2014. https://developers.soundcloud.com/blog/building-products-at-soundcloud-part-1-dealing-with-the-monolith.

[29] M. J. Carey and D. J. DeWitt. Of objects and databases: A decade of turmoil. In *VLDB*, 1996.

[30] M. J. Carey et al. Shoring up persistent applications. In *SIGMOD 1994*.

[31] A. Carter. Hulu Tech Blog: "At a glance: Hulu hits Rails Conf 2012", May 2012. http://tech.hulu.com/blog/2012/05/14/347/.

[32] A. Chaudhuri and J. S. Foster. Symbolic security analysis of Ruby-on-Rails web applications. In *CCS*, 2010.

[33] A. Cheung, O. Arden, S. Madden, A. Solar-Lezama, and A. C. Myers. StatusQuo: Making familiar abstractions perform using program analysis. In *CIDR 2013*.

[34] A. Cheung, S. Madden, O. Arden, and A. C. Myers. Automatic partitioning of database applications. In *VLDB 2012*.

[35] B. Cook. Scaling Twitter, SDForum Silicon Valley Ruby Conference, 2007. http://www.slideshare.net/Blaine/scaling-twitter.

[36] B. F. Cooper, A. Silberstein, E. Tam, R. Ramakrishnan, and R. Sears. Benchmarking cloud serving systems with YCSB. In *ACM SoCC 2010*.

[37] J. W. Creswell. *Research design: Qualitative, quantitative, and mixed methods approaches*. Sage, 2013.

[38] K. Crum. #3238: Activerecord::staleobjecterror in checkout, 2013. spree/spree at https://github.com/spree/spree/issues/3238.

[39] D. E. Difallah, A. Pavlo, C. Curino, and P. Cudre-Mauroux. OLTP-Bench: An extensible testbed for benchmarking relational databases. In *VLDB 2014*.

[40] J. Duff. How Shopify scales Rails, Big Ruby 2013, April 2013. http://www.slideshare.net/jduff/how-shopify-scales-rails-20443485.

[41] E. Dumbill. O'Reilly: "Ruby on Rails: An interview with David Heinemeier Hansson", August 2005. http://www.oreillynet.com/pub/a/network/2005/08/30/ruby-rails-david-heinemeier-hansson.html.

[42] S. Easterbrook et al. Selecting empirical methods for software engineering research. In *Guide to advanced empirical software engineering*, pages 285–311. Springer, 2008.

[43] M. Ehsan. Input validation with Laravel, 2014. http://laravelbook.com/laravel-input-validation/.

[44] K. P. Eswaran et al. The notions of consistency and predicate locks in a database system. *Commun. ACM*, 19(11):624–633, 1976.

[45] A. Fekete, S. N. Goldrei, and J. P. Asenjo. Quantifying isolation anomalies. In *VLDB 2009*.

[46] H. Ferentschik. Accessing the Hibernate Session within a ConstraintValidator, May 2010. https://developer.jboss.org/wiki/AccessingtheHibernateSessionwithinaConstraintValidator.

[47] H. Ferentschik and G. Morling. Hibernate validator JSR 349 reference implementation 5.1.3.final, 2014. https://docs.jboss.org/hibernate/stable/validator/reference/en-US/html/.

[48] M. Fowler. *Patterns of enterprise application architecture*. Addison-Wesley Longman Publishing Co., Inc., 2002.

[49] E. Gamma, R. Helm, R. Johnson, and J. Vlissides. *Design patterns: elements of reusable object-oriented software*. Pearson Education, 1994.

[50] D. Geer. Will software developers ride Ruby on Rails to success? *Computer*, 39(2):18–20, 2006.

[51] W. Golab, X. Li, and M. A. Shah. Analyzing consistency properties for fun and profit. In *PODC 2011*.

[52] J. Gray, R. Lorie, G. Putzolu, and I. Traiger. Granularity of locks and degrees of consistency in a shared data base. Technical report, IBM, 1976.

[53] P. W. Grefen and P. M. Apers. Integrity control in relational database systems–an overview. *Data & Knowledge Engineering*, 10(2):187–223, 1993.

[54] D. H. Hansson. active_record/transactions.rb, 2004. rails/rails githash db045db at https://github.com/rails/rails/blob/db045dbb.

[55] D. H. Hansson. Choose a single layer of cleverness, September 2005. http://david.heinemeierhansson.com/arc/2005_09.html.

[56] Hibernate Team and JBoss Visual Design Team. Hibernate reference documentation 4.3.7.final, 2014. http://docs.jboss.org/hibernate/orm/4.3/manual/en-US/html/.

[57] M. Higgins. Foreigner. https://github.com/matthuhiggins/foreigner.

[58] T. Hinrichs et al. Caveat: Facilitating interactive and secure client-side validators for ruby on rails applications. In *SECURWARE 2013*.

[59] M. Koziarski. Warn users about the race condition in validates_uniqueness_of. [koz], 2007. rails/rails githash c01c28c at https://github.com/rails/rails/commit/c01c28c.

[60] G. E. Krasner, S. T. Pope, et al. A description of the model-view-controller user interface paradigm in the smalltalk-80 system. *Journal of object oriented programming*, 1(3):26–49, 1988.

[61] H.-T. Kung and C. H. Papadimitriou. An optimality theory of concurrency control for databases. In *SIGMOD*, 1979.

[62] H. Lai. Document concurrency issues in validates_uniqueness_of., 2008. rails/rails githash adacd94 at https://github.com/rails/rails/commit/adacd94.

[63] C. Lamb, G. Landis, J. Orenstein, and D. Weinreb. The ObjectStore database system. *Communications of the ACM*, 34(10):50–63, 1991.

[64] J. Leighton. Support for specifying transaction isolation level, 2012. rails/rails githash 392eeec at https://github.com/rails/rails/commit/392eeec.

[65] C. Li, J. Leitao, A. Clement, N. Preguiça, R. Rodrigues, et al. Automating the choice of consistency levels in replicated systems. In *USENIX ATC 2014*.

[66] A. Malpani et al. Reverse engineering models from databases to bootstrap application development. In *ICDE*, 2010.
[67] S. McCullough. Groupon Engineering Blog: "Geekon: I-Tier", October 2013. https://engineering.groupon.com/2013/node-js/geekon-i-tier/.
[68] J. Nijjar and T. Bultan. Bounded verification of ruby on rails data models. In *ACM ISSTA*, 2011.
[69] C. Nutter. Q/a: What thread-safe Rails means, August 2008. http://blog.headius.com/2008/08/qa-what-thread-safe-rails-means.html.
[70] T. Preston-Werner. How we made GitHub fast, October 2009. https://github.com/blog/530-how-we-made-github-fast.
[71] J. Rizzo. Twitch: The official blog "Technically Speaking – Group Chat and General Chat Engineering", April 2014. http://blog.twitch.tv/2014/04/technically-speaking-group-chat-and-general-chat-engineering/.
[72] D. Roberts. #13234: Rails concurrency bug on save, 2013. rails/rails at https://github.com/rails/rails/issues/13234.
[73] S. Roy, L. Kot, et al. The homeostasis protocol: Avoiding transaction coordination through program analysis. In *SIGMOD*, 2015.
[74] S. Ruby, D. Thomas, D. H. Hansson, et al. *Agile web development with Rails 4*. The Pragmatic Bookshelf, Dallas, Texas, 2013.
[75] N. Singh. update_attributes and update_attributes! are now wrapped in a transaction, 2010. rails/rails githash f4fbc2c at https://github.com/rails/rails/commit/f4fbc2c.
[76] N. Skrupsky et al. Waves: Automatic synthesis of client-side validation code for web applications. In *IEEE CyberSecurity 2012*.
[77] K.-J. Stol et al. The use of empirical methods in open source software research: Facts, trends and future directions. In *FLOSS*, 2009.
[78] C. Stoltman. initial stab at creating has_many relationships, 2013. balderdashy/waterline githash b05fb1c at https://github.com/balderdashy/waterline/commit/b05fb1c. As of November 2014, this code has been moved but is still non-transactional and the comment remains unchanged.
[79] M. Tamer Özsu and P. Valduriez. *Principles of distributed database systems*. Springer, 2011.
[80] Tim O'Reilly. What is web 2.0: Design patterns and business models for the next generation of software. *Communications and Strategies*, 65(1):17–37, 2007.
[81] H. Wada, A. Fekete, L. Zhao, K. Lee, and A. Liu. Data consistency properties and the trade-offs in commercial cloud storage: the consumers' perspective. In *CIDR 2011*.
[82] J. Widom and S. Ceri. *Active database systems: Triggers and rules for advanced database processing*. Morgan Kaufmann, 1996.
[83] A. Williams. Techcrunch: Zendesk launches a help center that combines self-service with design themes reminiscent of Tumblr, August 2013. http://techcrunch.com/2013/08/21/zendesk-launches-a-help-center-that-combines-self-service-with-design-themes-reminiscent-of-tumblr/.
[84] F. Yang et al. Hilda: A high-level language for data-drivenweb applications. In *ICDE*, 2006.
[85] K. Zellag and B. Kemme. How consistent is your cloud application? In *SoCC 2012*.
[86] K. Zellag and B. Kemme. Real-time quantification and classification of consistency anomalies in multi-tier architectures. In *ICDE 2011*.

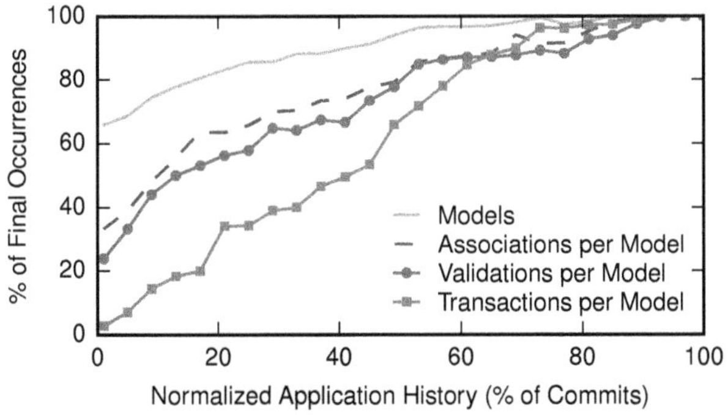

Figure 6: Use of mechanisms over each project's history. We plot the median value of each metric across projects and, for each mechanism, omit projects that do not contain any uses of the mechanism (e.g., if a project lacks transactions, the project is omitted from the median calculation for transactions).

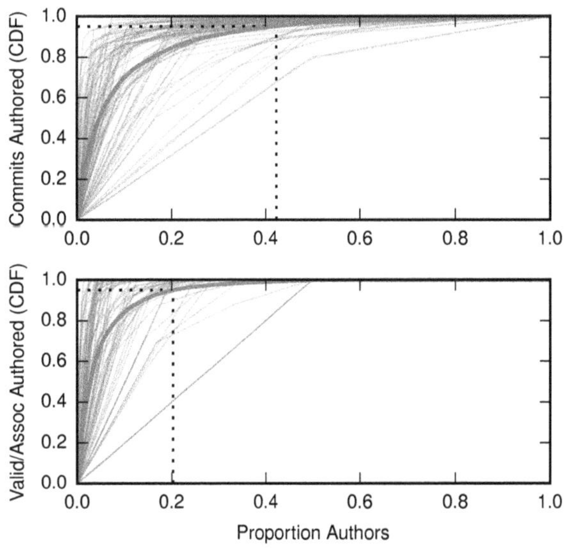

Figure 7: CDFs of authorship of invariants (validations plus associations) and commits. Bolded line shows the average CDF across projects, while faint lines show CDFs for individual projects. The dotted line shows the 95th percentile CDF value.

APPENDIX

A. ANALYSIS METHODOLOGY

To determine the occurrences and number of models, transactions, locks, validations, and associations in Rails, we wrote a set of analysis scripts that performed a very rudimentary syntactic static analysis . We do not consider the analysis techniques here a contribution; rather, our interest is in the output of the analysis. The syntactic approach proved portable between the many versions of Rails against which each application is linked; otherwise, porting between non-backwards-compatible Rails versions was difficult and, in fact, unsupported by several of the Rails code analysis tools we considered using as alternatives The choice to use syntax as a means of distinguishing code constructs led to some ambiguity. To compensate, we introduced custom logic to handle esoteric syntaxes that arose in particular projects (e.g., some projects extend `ActiveRecord::Base` with a separate, project-specific base class, while some validation usages vary between constructs like `:validates_presence` and `:validates_presence_of`).

To determine code authorship, we used the output of git `log` and `blame` and did not attempt any sophisticated entity resolution.

B. DETAILED VALIDATION BEHAVIOR

B.1 Uniqueness Validation

When a controller attempts to save an ActiveRecord model instance i of type M, if M has a declared `:validates_uniqueness` annotation on attribute a, the following actions will be performed:

1. Assuming that instances of M are stored in database table T_M (with attribute a stored in column C_a), Active Record will perform the equivalent of

   `SELECT 1 FROM` T_M `where` C_a `=` $i.a$ `LIMIT ONE;`

   (`SELECT COUNT(*)` would be sufficient here as well, but this is not how the query is actually implemented).
2. If this result set is empty, the validation succeeds.
3. If this result set is not empty, the validation fails. If the validation was called during `save`, it returns `false`. If the validation was called during `save!`, it raises an `ActiveRecord::RecordInvalid` exception.

This is a classic example of the phantom problem. Changing this `SELECT` call to `SELECT FOR UPDATE` would be sufficient. However, Rails is not implemented this way.

Name	Description	Authors	LoC Ruby	Commits	M	T	PL	OL	V	A	Stars	Githash	Last commit
Canvas LMS	Education	132	309,580	12,853	161	46	12	1	354	837	1,251	3fb8e69	10/16/14
OpenCongress	Congress data	15	30,867	1,884	106	1	0	0	48	357	124	850b602	02/11/13
Fedena	Education management	4	49,297	1,471	104	5	0	0	153	317	262	40cafe3	01/23/13
Discourse	Community discussion	440	72,225	11,480	77	41	0	0	83	266	12,233	1cf4a0d	10/20/14
Spree	eCommerce	677	47,268	14,096	72	6	0	0	92	252	5,582	aa34b3a	10/16/14
Sharetribe	Content management	35	31,164	7,140	68	0	0	0	112	202	127	8e0d382	10/21/14
ROR Ecommerce	eCommerce	19	16,808	1,604	63	2	3	0	219	207	857	c60a675	10/09/14
Diaspora	Social network	388	31,726	14,640	63	2	0	0	66	128	9,571	1913397	10/03/14
Redmine	Project management	10	81,536	11,042	62	11	0	1	131	157	2,264	e23d4d9	10/19/14
ChiliProject	Project management	53	66,683	5,532	61	7	0	1	118	130	623	984c9ff	08/13/13
Spot.us	Community reporting	46	94,705	9,280	58	0	0	0	96	165	343	61b65b6	12/02/13
Jobsworth	Project management	46	24,731	7,890	55	10	0	0	86	225	478	3a1f8e1	09/12/14
OpenProject	Project management	63	84,374	11,185	49	8	1	3	136	227	371	c1e66af	11/21/13
Danbooru	Image board	25	27,857	3,738	47	9	0	0	71	114	238	c082ed1	10/17/14
Salor Retail	Point of Sale	26	18,404	2,259	44	0	0	0	81	309	24	00e1839	10/07/14
Zena	Content management	7	56,430	2,514	44	1	0	0	12	43	172	79576ac	08/18/14
Skyline CMS	Content management	7	10,404	894	40	5	0	0	28	89	127	64b0932	12/09/13
Opal	Project management	6	10,707	474	38	3	0	0	42	96	45	11edf34	01/09/13
OneBody	Church portal	33	20,398	3,973	36	3	0	0	97	140	1,041	2dfbd4d	10/19/14
CommunityEngine	Social networking	67	13,967	1,613	35	3	0	0	92	101	1,073	a4d3ea2	10/16/14
Publify	Blogging	93	16,763	5,067	35	7	0	0	33	50	1,274	4acf86e	10/20/14
Comas	Conference management	5	5,879	435	33	6	0	0	80	45	21	81c25a4	09/09/14
BrowserCMS	Content management	56	21,259	2,503	32	4	0	0	47	77	1,183	d654557	09/30/14
RailsCollab	Project managment	25	8,849	865	29	6	0	0	40	122	262	9f6c8c1	02/16/12
OpenGovernment	Government data	15	9,383	2,231	28	4	0	0	22	141	160	fa80204	11/21/13
Tracks	Personal productivity	89	17,419	3,121	27	2	0	0	24	43	639	eb2650c	10/02/14
GitLab	Code management	671	39,094	12,266	24	15	0	0	131	114	14,129	72abe9f	10/20/14
Brevidy	Video sharing	2	7,608	6	24	1	0	0	74	56	167	d0ddb1a	01/18/14
Insoshi	Social network	16	121,552	1,321	24	1	0	0	41	63	1,583	9976cfe	02/24/10
Alchemy	Content management	34	19,329	4,222	23	2	0	0	37	40	240	91d9d08	10/20/14
Teambox	Project management	48	32,844	3,155	22	2	0	0	56	116	1,864	62a8b02	09/20/11
Fat Free CRM	Customer relationship	99	21,284	4,144	21	3	0	0	39	92	2,384	3dd2c62	10/17/14
linuxfr.org	FLOSS community	29	8,123	2,271	20	1	0	0	50	50	86	5d4d6df	10/14/14
Squash	Bug reporting	28	15,776	231	19	6	0	0	87	62	879	c217ac1	09/15/14
Shoppe	eCommerce	14	3,172	349	19	1	0	0	58	34	208	19e60c8	10/18/14
nimbleShop	eCommerce	12	8,041	1,805	19	0	0	0	47	34	47	4254806	02/18/13
Piggybak	eCommerce	16	2,235	383	17	1	0	0	51	35	166	2bed094	09/10/14
wallgig	Wallpaper sharing	6	5,543	350	17	1	0	0	42	45	18	4424d44	03/23/14
Rucksack	Collaboration	7	5,346	445	17	3	0	0	18	79	169	59703d3	10/05/13
Calagator	Online calendar	48	9,061	1,766	16	0	0	0	8	11	196	6e5df08	10/19/14
Amahi Platform	Home media sharing	15	6,244	577	15	2	0	0	38	22	65	5101c8b	08/20/14
Sprint	Project management	5	3,056	71	14	0	0	0	50	45	247	584d887	09/17/14
Citizenry	Community directory	17	8,197	512	13	0	0	0	12	45	138	e314fe4	04/01/14
LovdByLess	Social network	17	30,718	150	12	0	0	0	27	41	568	26e79a7	10/09/09
lobste.rs	Link sharing	24	4,963	624	12	8	0	0	20	40	646	b0b9654	10/18/14
BucketWise	Personal finance	10	4,644	258	12	2	0	0	11	46	484	5c73f2b	06/10/12
Sugar	Forum	13	7,703	1,316	11	1	0	0	20	53	89	49ca79f	10/21/14
Comf. Mexican Sofa	Content management	106	8,881	1,746	10	0	0	0	35	26	1,523	fecef0c	10/09/14
Radiant	Content management	100	15,923	2,385	9	3	0	1	26	12	1,554	0c9ef9b	10/01/14
Forem	Forum	100	4,676	1,383	9	0	0	0	8	29	1,302	519f2de	08/14/14
Saasy	eCommerce	2	163,170	21	8	4	0	0	19	9	520	4fe610f	08/03/09
Refinery CMS	Content management	438	10,847	9,107	8	0	0	0	16	8	2,979	f4e24ef	10/20/14
BostonRB	Ruby community	40	2,135	889	7	0	0	0	18	12	199	05fc100	10/21/14
Inkwell	Social networking	6	6,764	156	7	0	0	0	4	51	327	d1938d3	07/15/14
Boxroom	File sharing	9	1,956	368	6	0	0	0	18	12	218	1e74e06	10/18/14
Copycopter	Copy writing	9	2,347	46	6	1	0	0	7	14	652	d3607c4	06/28/12
Enki	Blogging	29	4,678	562	6	1	0	0	5	7	835	b793d48	12/01/13
Fulcrum	Project planning	46	3,190	637	5	0	0	0	13	15	1,335	8397de2	08/20/14
GitLab CI	Continuous integration	80	3,700	870	5	2	0	0	11	13	1,188	7d51134	10/17/14
Kandan	Persistent chat	56	1,694	808	5	0	0	0	6	8	2,249	15a8aab	10/06/14
Juvia	Commenting	8	2,302	202	4	3	0	0	11	8	937	43a1c48	05/09/14
Go vs Go	Go board game	2	2,378	302	4	0	0	0	11	9	145	c8d739d	02/21/13
Adopt-a-Hydrant	Civics	14	14,165	1,242	3	0	0	0	11	8	182	5b7ea0e	10/21/14
Selfstarter	Crowdfunding	23	577	127	3	0	0	0	1	4	2,688	740075f	05/16/14
Heaven	Code deployment	19	2,090	387	2	0	0	0	2	2	163	2d4162e	10/21/14
Carter	eCommerce	3	1,093	70	2	1	0	0	0	12	22	60ad49d	07/22/14
Obtvse	Blogging	27	455	393	1	0	0	0	3	0	1,516	1542856	03/21/13
Average:		**69.10**	**26,809.51**	**2,950.85**	**29.07**	**3.84**	**0.24**	**0.10**	**52.31**	**92.87**	**1,272.42**		**02/06/14**

Table 2: Corpus of applications used in analysis (M: Models, T: Transactions, PL: Pessimistic Locking, OL: Optimistic Locking, V: Validations, A: Associations). Stars record number of GitHub Stars as of October 2014.

B.2 Association Validation

When a controller attempts to save an ActiveRecord model instance i of type M, if M has a declared `:belongs_to` annotation on attribute a pointing to attribute b of model N *and* M has a declared `:validates_presence` annotation on attribute a, the following actions will be performed:

1. Assuming that instances of N are stored in database table T_N (with attribute b stored in column C_b), Active Record will perform the equivalent of

   SELECT 1 FROM T_N where C_b = $i.a$ LIMIT ONE;

2. If this result set is not empty, the validation succeeds.
3. If this result set is empty, the validation fails. If the validation was called during `save`, it returns `false`. If the validation was called during `save!`, it raises an `ActiveRecord::RecordInvalid` exception.

C. EXPERIMENTAL DESCRIPTION

We describe our applications from Section 5 in greater detail.

C.1 Uniqueness Validation Schema

We declare two models, each containing two attributes: `key`, a string, and `value`, also a string. The generated schema for each of the models, which we call `SimpleKeyValue` and `ValidatedKeyValue`, is the same. The schema for `SimpleKeyValue` is as follows:

```
create_table "validated_key_values", force: true do |t|
  t.string "key"
  t.string "value"
  t.datetime "created_at"
  t.datetime "updated_at"
end
```

For the non-uniqueness-validated model, we simply require that the `key` and `value` fields are not null via a `presence: true` annotation. For the ferally validated model, we add an additional `uniqueness: true` validation to the `key` field in the Active Record model. The remainder of the application consists of a simple View and Controller logic to allow us to `POST`, `GET`, and `DELETE` each kind of model instance programatically via HTTP.

C.2 Uniqueness Stress Test

For the uniqueness stress test (Figure 2), we repeatedly attempt to create duplicate records. We issue a set of 64 concurrent requests to create instances with the key field set to an increasing sequence number (k, below) and repeat 100 times. At the end of the run, we count the number of duplicate records in the table:

```
for model m ∈ {SimpleKeyValue, ValidatedKeyValue} do
    for k ← 1 to 100 do
        parfor 1 to 64 do
            via HTTP: create new m with key=k
    dups ←execute(SELECT key, COUNT(key)-1 FROM T_M
                  GROUP BY key HAVING COUNT(key) > 1;)
```

Under correct validation, for each choice of k (i.e., for each key k), all but one of the model creation requests should fail.

C.3 Uniqueness Workload Test

For the uniqueness workload test (Figure 3), a set of 64 workers sequentially issues a set of 100 operations each. Each operation attempts to create a new model instance with the key field set to a random item generated according to the distributions described in Section 5:

```
for model m ∈ {SimpleKeyValue, ValidatedKeyValue} do
    parfor 1 to 64 do
        for 1 to 100 do
            k ← pick new key according to distribution
            via HTTP: create new m with key=k
    dups ←execute(SELECT key, COUNT(key)-1 FROM T_M
                  GROUP BY key HAVING COUNT(key) > 1;)
```

C.4 Association Validation Schema

We declare two sets of models, each containing two models each: a `User` model and a `Departments` model. Each `User` has a(n implicit) `id` (as generated by Rails ActiveRecord) and an integer corresponding `department_i`. Each `Department` has an `id`. Both models have a timestamp of the last updated and creation time, as is auto-generated by Rails. Aside from the table names, both schemas are equivalent. Below is the schema for the non-validated users and departments:

```
create_table "simple_users", force: true do |t|
    t.integer "simple_department_id"
    t.datetime "created_at"
    t.datetime "updated_at"
end

create_table "simple_departments", force: true do |t|
    t.datetime "created_at"
    t.datetime "updated_at"
end
```

The two pairs of models vary in their validations. One pair of models has no validations or associations. The other pair of models contain validations, including rules for cascading deletions. Specifically, we place an association `has_many :users, :dependent => :destroy` on the department, and, on the user, an association `belongs_to :department` and validation `validates :department, :presence => true` (note that we only delete from Departments in our workload, below). Thus, on deletion of a model of type `ValidatedDepartment`, ActiveRecord will attempt to call `destroy` on each matching `ValidatedUser`.

C.5 Association Stress Test

For the association stress test (Figure 4), we repeatedly attempt to create orphan users. We issue a set of 64 concurrent requests to create Users belonging to a particular department, while simultaneously deleting that department and repeat 100 times. At the end of the run, we count the number of users with a department that does not exist:

```
for model m ∈ {Simple, Validated} do
    for i ← 1 to 100 do
        via HTTP: create mDepartment with id=i
    for i ← 1 to 100 do
        parfor w ∈ 1 to 65 do
            if w = 1 then
                via HTTP: delete mDepartment with id=i
            else
                via HTTP: create new mUser department_id=i
    orphaned ←execute("SELECT m_department_id,
                       COUNT(*) FROM m_users AS U
                       LEFT OUTER JOIN m_departments AS D
                       ON U.m_department_id = D.id
                       WHERE D.id IS NULL
                       GROUP BY m_department_id
                       HAVING COUNT(*) > 0;")
```

C.6 Association Workload Test

For the association workload test (Figure 5), we begin by creating a variable number of departments (Figure 5 x-axis; D). We next have 64 concurrent clients simultaneously attempt to create users belonging to a random department and delete random departments (in a 10:1 ratio of creations to deletions, for 100 operations each). We end by counting the number of orphaned users, as above.

```
for model m ∈ {Simple, Validated} do
    for d ← 1 to D do
        via HTTP: create mDepartment with id=i
    parfor w ∈ 1 to 64 do
        d ← uniformRandomInt([1, D])
        if uniformRandomDouble([0, 1]) < 1/11 then
            via HTTP: delete mDepartment with id=d
        else
            via HTTP: create new mUser department_id=d
    orphaned ← as above, in stress test
```

REEF: Retainable Evaluator Execution Framework

Markus Weimer[a], Yingda Chen[a], Byung-Gon Chun[c], Tyson Condie[b], Carlo Curino[a], Chris Douglas[a], Yunseong Lee[c], Tony Majestro[a], Dahlia Malkhi[f], Sergiy Matusevych[a], Brandon Myers[e], Shravan Narayanamurthy[a], Raghu Ramakrishnan[a], Sriram Rao[a], Russell Sears[d], Beysim Sezgin[a], Julia Wang[a]
[a]: Microsoft, [b]: UCLA, [c]: Seoul National University, [d]: Pure Storage, [e]: University of Washington, [f]: VMware

ABSTRACT

Resource Managers like Apache YARN have emerged as a critical layer in the cloud computing system stack, but the developer abstractions for leasing cluster resources and instantiating application logic are very low-level. This flexibility comes at a high cost in terms of developer effort, as each application must repeatedly tackle the same challenges (e.g., fault-tolerance, task scheduling and coordination) and re-implement common mechanisms (e.g., caching, bulk-data transfers). This paper presents REEF, a development framework that provides a control-plane for scheduling and coordinating task-level (data-plane) work on cluster resources obtained from a Resource Manager. REEF provides mechanisms that facilitate resource re-use for data caching, and state management abstractions that greatly ease the development of elastic data processing work-flows on cloud platforms that support a Resource Manager service. REEF is being used to develop several commercial offerings such as the Azure Stream Analytics service. Furthermore, we demonstrate REEF development of a distributed shell application, a machine learning algorithm, and a port of the CORFU [4] system. REEF is also currently an Apache Incubator project that has attracted contributors from several instititutions.[1]

Categories and Subject Descriptors

H.0 [**Information Systems**]: General

General Terms

Design, Experimentation, Performance

Keywords

Big Data; Distributed Systems; Database; High Performance Computing; Machine Learning

1. INTRODUCTION

Apache Hadoop has become a key building block in the new generation of scale-out systems. Early versions of analytic tools over Hadoop, such as Hive [44] and Pig [30] for SQL-like queries, were implemented by translation into MapReduce computations. This approach has inherent limitations, and the emergence of resource managers such as Apache YARN [46], Apache Mesos [15] and Google Omega [34] have opened the door for newer analytic tools to bypass the MapReduce layer. This trend is especially significant for iterative computations such as graph analytics and machine learning, for which MapReduce is widely recognized to be a poor fit. In fact, the website of the machine learning toolkit Apache Mahout [40] explicitly warns about the slow performance of some of its algorithms when run on Hadoop MapReduce.

Resource Managers are a first step in re-factoring the early implementations of MapReduce into a common scale-out computational fabric that can support a variety of analytic tools and programming paradigms. These systems expose cluster resources—in the form of machine slices—to higher-level applications. Exactly how those resources are exposed depends on the chosen Resource Manager. Nevertheless, in all cases, higher-level applications define a single *application master* that elastically acquires resources and executes computations on them. Resource Managers provide facilities for staging and bootstrapping these computations, as well as coarse-grained process monitoring. However, runtime management—such as runtime status and progress, and dynamic parameters—is left to the application programmer to implement.

This paper presents the Retainable Evaluator Execution Framework (REEF), which provides runtime management support for task monitoring and restart, data movement and communications, and distributed state management. REEF is devoid of a specific programming model (e.g., MapReduce), and instead provides an application framework on which new analytic toolkits can be rapidly developed and executed in a resource managed cluster. The toolkit author encodes their logic in a Job `Driver`—a centralized work scheduler—and a set of `Task` computations that perform the work. The core of REEF facilitates the acquisition of resources in the form of `Evaluator` runtimes, the execution of `Task` instances on `Evaluators`, and the communication between the `Driver` and its `Tasks`. However, additional power of REEF resides in its ability to facilitate the development of reusable data management services that greatly ease the burden of authoring the `Driver` and `Task` components in a large-scale data processing application.

REEF is, to the best of our knowledge, the first framework that provides a re-usable control-plane that enables systematic reuse of resources and retention of state across arbitrary tasks, possibly from different types of computations. This common optimization yields significant performance improvements by reducing I/O, and enables resource and state sharing across different frameworks or computation stages. Important use cases include pipelining data between different operators in a relational pipeline and retaining

[1]`http://reef.incubator.apache.org`

SIGMOD'15, May 31–June 4, 2015, Melbourne, Victoria, Australia.

ACM 978-1-4503-2758-9/15/05 ...$15.00.
http://dx.doi.org/10.1145/2723372.2742793.

state across iterations in iterative or recursive distributed programs. REEF is an (open source) Apache Incubator project to increase contributions of artifacts that will greatly reduce the development effort in building analytical toolkits on Resource Managers.

The remainder of this paper is organized as follows. Section 2 provides background on Resource Manager architectures. Section 3 gives a general overview of the REEF abstractions and key design decisions. Section 4 describes some of the applications developed using REEF, one being the Azure Stream Analytics Service offered commercially in the Azure Cloud. Section 5 analyzes REEF's runtime performance and showcases its benefits for advanced applications. Section 6 investigates the relationship of REEF with related systems, and Section 7 concludes the paper with future directions.

2. RISE OF THE RESOURCE MANAGERS

The first generation of Hadoop systems divided each machine in a cluster into a fixed number of slots for hosting map and reduce tasks. Higher-level abstractions such as SQL queries or ML algorithms are handled by translating them into MapReduce programs. Two main problems arise in this design. First, Hadoop clusters often exhibited extremely poor utilization (on the order of $5-10\%$ CPU utilization at Yahoo! [17]) due to resource allocations being too coarse-grained.[2] Second, the MapReduce programming model is not an ideal fit for some applications, and a common workaround on Hadoop clusters is to schedule a "map-only" job that internally instantiates a distributed program for running the desired algorithm (e.g., machine learning, graph-based analytics) [38, 1, 2].

These issues motivated the design of a second generation Hadoop system, which includes an explicit resource management layer called YARN.[3] Additional examples of resource managers include Google Omega [34] and Apache Mesos [15]. While structurally different, the common goal is to directly lease cluster resources to higher-level computations, or jobs. REEF is designed to be agnostic to the particular choice of resource manager, while providing support for obtaining resources and orchestrating them on behalf of a higher-level computation. In this sense, REEF provides a logical/physical separation between applications and the resource management layer. For the sake of exposition, we focus on obtaining resources from YARN in this paper.[4]

Figure 1 shows a high-level view of the YARN architecture, and Figure 2 contains a table of components that we describe here. A typical YARN setup would include a single Resource Manager (RM) and several Node Manager (NM) installations; each NM typically manages the resources of a single machine, and periodically reports to the RM, which collects all NM reports and formulates a global view of the cluster resources. The periodic NM reports also provides a basis for monitoring the overall cluster health at the RM, which notifies relevant applications when failures occur.

A YARN job is represented by an Application Master (AM), which is responsible for orchestrating the job's work on allocated *containers* i.e., a slice of machine resources (some amount of CPU, RAM, disk, etc.). A client submits an AM package—that includes a shell command and any files (i.e., binary executables, configurations) needed to execute the command—to the RM, which then selects a single NM to host the AM. The chosen NM creates a shell environment that includes the file resources, and then executes the

[2]Hadoop MapReduce tasks are often either CPU or I/O bound, and slots represent a fixed ratio of CPU and memory resources.

[3]YARN: Yet Another Resource Negotiator

[4]Comparing the merits of different resource management layers is out of scope for this paper. REEF is primarily relevant to what happens with allocated resource, and not how resources are requested.

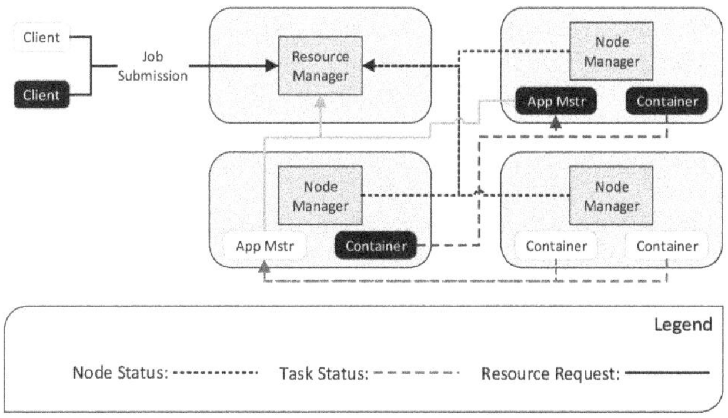

Figure 1: Example YARN Architecture showing two clients submitting jobs to the Resource Manager (RM), which launches two client Application Master (AM) instances on two Node Managers (NM). Each AM requests containers from the RM, which allocates the containers based on available resources reported from its NMs. If supported by the application, tasks running on containers report status to the respective AM.

Component (abbr.)	Description
Resource Manager (RM)	A service that leases cluster resources to applications.
Node Manager (NM)	Manages the resources of a single compute entity (e.g., machine). Reports the status of managed machine resources to the RM
Application Master (AM)	Implements the application control-flow and resource allocation logic.
Container	A single unit of resource allocation e.g., some amount of CPU/RAM/Disk.

Figure 2: Glossary of components (and abbreviations) described in this section, and used throughout the paper.

given shell command. The NM monitors the AM for resource usage and exit status, which the NM includes in its periodic reports to the RM. At runtime, the AM uses an RPC interface to request containers from the RM, and to ask the NMs that host its containers to launch a desired program. Returning to Figure 1, we see two AM instances running, each with allocated containers executing a job-specific task.

2.1 Example: Distributed Shell on YARN

To further set the stage, we briefly explain how to write an application directly on YARN i.e., without REEF. The YARN source code contains a simple example implementation of a distributed shell (DS) application. Within that example is code for submitting an AM package to the RM, which proceeds to launch a distributed shell AM. After starting, the AM establishes a periodic heartbeat channel with the RM using a YARN provided client library. The AM uses this channel to submit requests for containers in the form of resource specifications: such as container count and location (rack/machine address), and hardware requirements (amount of memory/disk/cpu). For each allocated container, the AM sets up a launch context—i.e., file resources required by the executable (e.g., shell script), the environment to be setup for the executable, and a command-line to execute—and submits this information to the NM hosting the container using a YARN provided client library. The AM can obtain the process-level status of its containers from the RM or more directly with the host NM, again using a YARN provided client library. Once the job completes (i.e., all containers complete/exit), the AM sends a completion message to the RM, and exits itself.

The YARN distribution includes this distributed shell program as an exercise for interacting with its protocols. It is around 1300 lines of code. A more complete distributed shell application might include the following features:

- Provide the result of the shell command to the client.
- More detailed error information at the AM and client.
- Reports of execution progress at the AM and client.

Supporting this minimal feature set requires a runtime at each NM that executes the given shell command, monitors the progress, and sends the result (output or error) to the AM, which aggregates all results and sends the final output to the client. REEF is our attempt to capture such control-flow code, that we believe will be common to many YARN applications, in a general framework. In Section 4.1 we will describe a more feature complete version of this example developed on REEF in about half (530) the lines of code.

3. REEF

Resource managed applications leverage leased resources to execute massively distributed computations; here, we focus on data analytics jobs that instantiate compute tasks, which process data partitions in parallel. We surveyed the literature [53, 16, 8, 5, 11, 52] for common mechanisms and design patterns, leading to the following common components within these architectures.

- A centralized per-job scheduler that observes the runtime state and assigns tasks to resources e.g., MapReduce task slots [11].
- A runtime for executing compute tasks and retaining state in an organized fashion i.e., contexts that group related object state.
- Communication channels for monitoring status and sending control messages.
- Configuration management for passing parameters and binding application interfaces to runtime implementations.

REEF captures these commonalities in a framework that allows application-level logic to provide appropriate implementations of higher-level semantics e.g., deciding which resources should be requested, what state should be retained within each resource, and what task-level computations should be scheduled on resources. The REEF framework is defined by the following key abstractions.

- `Driver:` application code that implements the resource allocation and `Task` scheduling logic.
- `Evaluator:` a runtime environment on a container that can retain state within `Contexts` and execute `Tasks` (one at a time).
- `Context:` a state management environment within an Evaluator, that is accessible to any `Task` hosted on that `Evaluator`.
- `Task:` the work to be executed in an `Evaluator`.

Figure 3 further describes REEF in terms of its runtime infrastructure and application framework. The figure shows an application `Driver` with a set of allocated `Evaluators`, some of which are executing application `Task` instances. The `Driver Runtime` manages events that inform the `Driver` of the current runtime state.

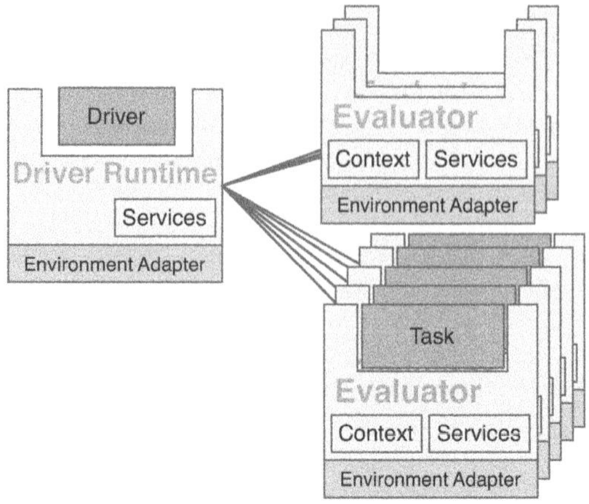

Figure 3: An instance of REEF in terms of its application framework (`Driver` and `Task`) and runtime infrastructure components (`Evaluator`, `Driver Runtime`, `Environment Adapter`).

Each `Evaluator` is equipped with a `Context` for capturing application state (that can live across `Task` executions) and `Services` that provide library solutions to general problems e.g., state checkpointing, group communication among a set of participating `Task` instances. An `Environment Adapter` insulates the REEF runtime from the underlying Resource Manager layer.[5] Lastly, REEF provides messaging channels between the `Driver` and `Task` instances—supported by a highly optimized event management toolkit (Section 3.1.2)—for communicating runtime status and state, and a configuration management tool (Section 3.1.3) for binding application logic and runtime parameters. The remainder of this section provides further details on the runtime infrastructure components (Section 3.1) and on the application framework (Section 3.2).

3.1 Runtime Infrastructure

The `Driver Runtime` hosts the application control-flow logic implemented in the `Driver` module, which is based on a set of asynchronous event-handlers that react to runtime events e.g., resource allocations, task executions and failures. The `Evaluator` executes application tasks implemented in the `Task` module, and manages application state in the form of `Contexts`. The `Environment Adapter` deals with the specifics of the utilized resource management service. Lastly, `Services` add extensibility to the REEF framework by allowing isolated mechanisms to be developed and incorporated into an application's logic. This section further describes these runtime infrastructure components.

3.1.1 Environment Adapter

REEF is organized in a way that factors out many of the environment specific details into an `Environment Adapter` layer (see Figure 3), making the code base easy to port to different resource managers. The primary role of the `Environment Adapter` is to translate `Driver` actions (e.g., requests for resources) to the underlying resource manager protocol. We have implemented three such adapters:

1. **Local Processes:** This adapter leverages the host operating system to provide process isolation between the `Driver` and `Evaluators`. The adapter limits the number of processes active at a given time and the resources dedicated to a given process. This environment is useful for debugging applica-

[5]REEF is able to expose Resource Manager specific interfaces (e.g., for requesting resources) to application `Driver` modules.

tions and examining the resource management aspects of a given application or service on a single node.
2. **Apache YARN:** This adapter executes the `Driver Runtime` as a YARN Application Master [46]. Resource requests are translated into the appropriate YARN protocol, and YARN containers are used to host `Evaluators`.
3. **Apache Mesos:** This adapter executes the `Driver Runtime` as a "framework" in Apache Mesos [15]. Resource requests are translated into the appropriate Mesos protocol, and Mesos executors are used to host `Evaluators`.

Creating an `Environment Adapter` involves implementing a couple of interfaces. In practice, most `Environment Adapters` require additional configuration parameters from the application (e.g. credentials). Furthermore, `Environment Adapters` expose the underlying Resource Manager interfaces, which differ in the way that resources are requested and monitored. REEF provides a generic abstraction to these low-level interfaces, but also allows applications to bind directly to them for allocating resources and dealing with other subtle nuances e.g., resource preemption.

3.1.2 Event Handling

We built an asynchronous event processing framework called Wake, which is based on ideas from SEDA [49], Rx [26] and the Click modular router [19]. As we will describe in Section 3.2.1, the `Driver` interface is comprised of handlers that contain application code that react to events. Wake allows the `Driver Runtime` to trade-off between cooperative *thread sharing* that synchronously invokes these event handlers in the same thread, and asynchronous *stages*, where events are queued for execution inside of an independent thread pool. Using Wake, the `Driver Runtime` has been designed to prevent blocking from long-running network requests and application code. In addition to handling local event processing, Wake also provides remote messaging facilities built on top of Netty [43]. We use this for a variety of purposes, including full-duplex control-plane messaging and a range of scalable data movement and group communication primitives. The latter are used every day to process millions of events in the Azure Streaming Service (see Section 4.4). Lastly, we needed to guarantee message delivery to a logical `Task` that could physically execute on different `Evaluators` e.g., due to a prior failure. Wake provides the needed level of indirection by addressing `Tasks` with a logical identifier, which applications bind to when communicating among `Tasks`.

3.1.3 Tang Configuration

Configuring distributed applications is well-known to be a difficult and error prone task [48, 31]. In REEF, configuration is handled through dependency injection, which is a software design pattern that binds dependencies (e.g., interfaces, parameter values, etc.) to dependent objects (e.g., class implementations, instance variables, constructor arguments, etc.). Google's Guice [13] is an example of a dependency injection toolkit that we used in an early version of REEF. The Guice API is based on binding patterns that link dependencies (e.g., application `Driver` implementations) to dependents (e.g., the REEF `Driver` interface), and code annotations that identify injection targets (e.g., which class constructors to use for parameter injection). The dependency injection design pattern has a number of advantages: client implementation independence, reduction of boilerplate code, more modular code, easier to unit test. However, it alone did not solve the problem of mis-configurations, which often occurred when instantiating application `Driver`, `Context`, or `Task` implementations on some remote container resources, where it was very difficult to debug.

This motivated us to develop our own dependency injection system called Tang, which restricts dynamic bind patterns.[6] This restriction allows Tang configurations to be strongly typed and easily verified for correctness through static analysis of bindings; prior to instantiating client modules on remote resources, thus allowing Tang to catch mis-configuration issues early and provide more guidance into the problem source. More specifically, a Tang specification consists of binding patterns that resolve REEF dependencies (e.g., the interfaces of a `Driver` and `Task`) to client implementations. These binding patterns are expressed using the host language (e.g., Java, C#) type system and annotations, allowing unmodified IDEs such as Eclipse or Visual Studio to provide configuration information in tooltips, auto-completion of configuration parameters, and to detect a wide range of configuration problems (e.g., type checking, missing parameters) as you edit your code. Since such functionality is expressed in the host language, there is no need to install additional development software to get started with Tang. The Tang configuration language semantics were inspired by recent work in the distributed systems community on CRDTs (Commutative Replicated Data Types) [35] and the CALM (Consistency As Logical Monotonicity) conjecture [3]. Due to space issues, we refer the reader to the online documentation for further details (see `http://reef.incubator.apache.org/tang.html`).

3.1.4 Contexts

Retaining state across task executions is central to the REEF design, and to the support for iterative data flows that cache loop invariant data or facilitate delta-based computations e.g., Naiad [27] and Datalog. Moreover, we also needed the option to clean up state from prior task executions, which prompted the design of stackable contexts in the `Evaluator` runtime. `Contexts` add structure to `Evaluator` state, and provide the `Driver` with control over what state gets passed from one task to the next, which could cross a computational stage boundary. For example, assume we have a hash-join operator that consists of a build stage, followed by a probe stage. The tasks of the build stage construct a hash-table—on the join column(s) of dataset `A`—and stores it in the root context that will be shared with the tasks of the probe stage, which performs the join with dataset `B` by looking up matching `A` tuples in the hash-table. Let us further assume that the build stage tasks require some scratch space, which is placed in a (child) scratch context. When the build stage completes, the scratch context is discarded, leaving the root context, and the hash-table state, for the probe stage tasks. For REEF applications, `Contexts` add fine-grained (task-level) mutable state management, which could be leveraged for building a DAG scheduler (like Dryad [16], Tez [33], Hyracks [8]), where vertices (computational stages) are given a "localized" context for scratch space, and use the "root" context for passing state.

3.1.5 Services

The central design principle of REEF is in factoring out core functionalities that can be re-used across a broad range of applications. To this end, we allow users to deploy services as part of the `Context` definition. This facilitates the deployment of distributed functionalities that can be referenced by the application's `Driver` and `Tasks`, which in turn eases the development burden of these modules. For example, we provide a name-based communication service that allows developers to be agnostic about re-establishing communication with a `Task` that was re-spawned on a separate `Evaluator`; this service works in concert with Wake's logi-

[6]Injection of dependencies via runtime code, or what Guice calls "provider methods."

cal Task addressing. Services are configured through Tang, making them easy to compose with application logic.

3.2 Application Framework

We now describe the framework used to capture application logic i.e., the code written by the application developer. Figure 4 presents a high-level control-flow diagram of a REEF application. The control channels are labeled with a number and a description of the interaction that occurs between two entities in the diagram. We will refer to this figure in our discussion by referencing the control-flow channel number. For instance, the client (top left) initiates a job by submitting an Application Master to the Resource Manager (**control-flow 1**). In REEF, an Application Master is configured through a Tang specification, which requires (among other things) bindings for the Driver implementation. When the Resource Manager launches the Application Master (**control-flow 2**), the REEF provided Driver Runtime will start and use the Tang specification to instantiate the Driver components i.e., event-handlers described below. The Driver can optionally be given a channel to the client (**control-flow 7**) for communicating status and receiving commands e.g., via an interactive application.

3.2.1 Driver

The Driver is responsible for scheduling the task-level work of an application. For instance, a Driver that schedules a DAG of data-processing elements—common to many data-parallel runtimes [52, 16, 39, 8, 5, 53]—would launch (per-partition) tasks that execute the work of individual processing elements in the order of data dependencies. However, unlike most data-parallel runtimes[7], resources for executing such tasks must first be allocated from the Resource Manager. This added dimension increases the scheduler complexity, which motivated the design of the REEF Driver to adopt an Reactive Extensions (Rx) [26] API[8] that consists of asynchronous handlers that react to events triggered by the runtime. We categorize the events, that a Driver reacts to, along the following three dimensions:

1. **Runtime Events:** When the Driver Runtime starts, it passes a start event to the Driver, which must react by either requesting resources (**control-flow 3**)—using a REEF provided request module that mimics the underlying resource management protocol—or by setting an alarm with a callback method and future time. Failure to do one of these two steps will result in the automatic shutdown of the Driver. In general, an automatic shutdown will occur when, at any point in time, the Driver does not have any resource allocations, nor any outstanding resource requests or alarms. Lastly, the Driver may optionally listen for the stop event, which occurs when the Driver Runtime initiates its shutdown procedure.
2. **Evaluator Events:** The Driver receives events for Evaluator allocation, launch, shutdown and failure. An *allocation* event occurs when the resource manager has granted a resource, from an outstanding request, to the Driver. The Evaluator allocation event API contains methods for configuring the initial Context state (e.g., files, services, object state, etc.), and methods to launch the Evaluator on the assigned resource (via **control-flow 4**), or release it (deallocate) back to the Resource Manager, triggering a *shutdown* event. Furthermore, Evaluator allocation events contain resource descriptions that provide the Driver with information needed to constrain state and assign tasks e.g., based on data-locality. A *launch* event is trigged when confirmation of the Evaluator bootstrap is received at the Driver. The launch event includes a reference to the initial Context, which can be used to add further sub-Context state (described in Section 3.1.4), and to launch a sequence of Task executions (one at a time) (via **control-flow 5**). A failure at the Evaluator granularity is assumed not to be recoverable (e.g., due to misconfiguration or hardware faults), and as a result, the relevant resource is automatically deallocated, and a *failure* event—containing the exception state—is passed to the Driver. On the other hand, Task events (discussed below) are assumed to be recoverable, and do not result in an Evaluator deallocation, allowing the Driver to recover from the issue; for example, an out-of-memory exception might prompt the Driver to configure the Task differently e.g., with a smaller buffer.
3. **Task Events:** All Evaluators periodically send status updates that include information about its Context state, running Services and the current Task execution status to the Driver Runtime (**control flow 6**). The Task execution status is surfaced to the Driver in the form of events: launch, message, failed, and completion. The *launch* event API contains methods for terminating or suspending the Task execution, and a method for sending messages—in the form of opaque byte arrays—to the running Task (via **control-flow 6**). Messages sent by the Driver are immediately pushed to the relevant Task to minimize latency. Task implementations are also able to send messages (opaque byte arrays) back to the Driver, which are piggy-backed on the (periodic) Evaluator status updates. Furthermore, when a Task completes, the Driver is passed a *completion* event that includes a byte array "return value" of the Task main method (described below). We further note that REEF can be configured to limit the size of these messages in order to avoid memory pressure. Lastly, Task failures result in an event that contains the exception information, but (as previously stated) do not result in the deallocation of the Evaluator hosting the Task failure.

3.2.2 Task

A Task is a piece of application code that contains a main method, which will be invoked by the Evaluator. The application-supplied Task implementation has access to its configuration parameters and the Evaluator state, which is exposed as Contexts. The Task also has access to any services that the Driver may have started on the given Evaluator; for example, a Task could deposit its intermediate data in a buffer manager service so that it can be processed by a subsequent Task running on the same Evaluator.

A Task ends when its main method returns with an optional return value, which REEF presents to the Driver. The Evaluator catches any exceptions thrown by the Task and includes the exception state in the failure event passed to the Driver. A Task can optionally implement a handle for receiving messages sent by the Driver. These message channels can be used to instruct the Task to suspend or terminate its execution in a graceful way. For instance, a suspended Task could return its checkpoint state that can be used to resume it on another Evaluator. To minimize latency, all messages asynchronously sent by the Driver are immediately scheduled by Wake to be delivered to the appropriate Task i.e., REEF does not wait for the next Evaluator "heartbeat" interval to transfer and deliver messages. Wake could be configured to impose a rate limitation, but we have not explored that approach in this initial version, nor have we encountered such a bottleneck in our applications.

[7]Today, exceptions include Tez [33] and Spark [52].

[8]Supported by Wake, which was described in Section 3.1.2.

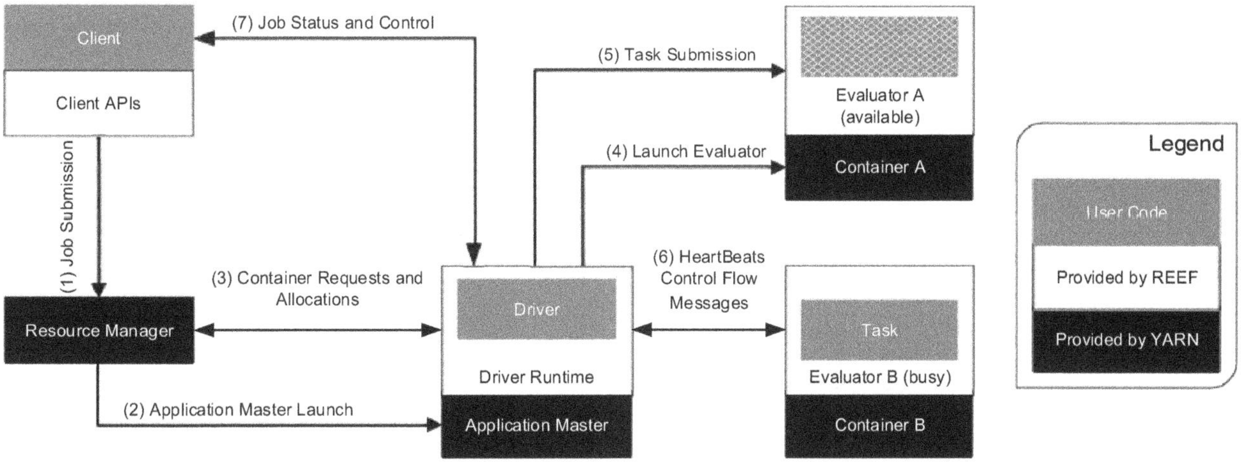

Figure 4: High-level REEF control-flow diagram—running within an example YARN environment—that captures an application with two `Evaluator` instances, one of which is running a `Task`. Each control channel is labeled with a number and description of the interaction that occurs between the two entities.

	C#	Java	CPP	Total
Tang	10,567	6,976	0	17,543
Wake	7,749	4,681	0	12,430
REEF	13,136	15,118	1,854	30,108
Services	0	5,319	0	5,319
Total	31,452	32,094	1854	65,400

Figure 5: Lines of code by component and language

3.3 Implementation

REEF's design supports applications in multiple languages; it currently supports Java and C#. Both share the core `Driver Runtime` Java implementation via a native (C++) bridge, therefore sharing advancements of this crucial runtime component. The bridge forwards events between Java and C# application `Driver` implementations. The `Evaluator` is implemented once per language to avoid any overhead in the performance-critical data path.

Applications are free to mix and match `Driver` side event handlers in Java and C# with any number of Java and C# `Evaluators`. To establish communications between Java and C# processes, Wake is implemented in both languages. Tang is also implemented in both languages, and supports configuration validation across the boundary; it can serialize the configuration data and dependency graph into a neutral form, which is understood by Tang in both environments. This is crucial for the early error detection in a cross-language applications. For instance, a Java `Driver` receives a Java exception when trying to submit an ill-configured C# `Task` *before* attempting to launch the `Task` on a remote `Evaluator`.

To the best of our knowledge, REEF is the only distributed control flow framework that provides this deep integration across such language boundaries. Figure 5 gives an overview of the effort involved in the development of REEF, including its cross-language support.[9] About half of the code is in Wake and Tang, while the other half is in the REEF core runtime. Interestingly, both Tang and Wake are bigger in C# than in Java. In the case of Wake, this is largely due to the extensive use of the Netty Java library, which is not available in C#. For Tang, its Java implementation relies heavily on reflection and leverages the runtime leniency of the Java type system; a luxury that a more rigid and expressive type system like the C# runtime does not permit.

[9]All numbers where computed on the Apache REEF git repository found at **http://git.apache.org**, commit `fa353fdabc8912695ce883380fa962baea2a20fb`

3.4 Discussion

REEF is an active open-source project that started in late 2012. Over the past two years, we have refined our design based on feedback from many communities. The initial prototype of REEF's application interface were based on the Java Concurrency Library. When the `Driver` made a request for containers, it was given a list of objects representing allocated evaluators wrapped in Java Futures. This design required us to support a pull-based API, whereby the client could request the underlying object, even though the container for that object was not yet allocated, turning it into blocking method call. Extending the Future interface to include callbacks somewhat mitigated this issue. Nevertheless, writing distributed applications, like a MapReduce runtime, against this pull-based API was brittle; especially in the case of error handling e.g., exceptions thrown in arbitrary code interrupted the control-flow in a manner that was not always obvious, instead of being pushed to a specific (e.g., `Task`) error event-handler that has more context. As a result, we rewrote the REEF interfaces around an asynchronous event processing (push-based) model implemented by Wake, which greatly simplified both the REEF runtime and application-level code. For example, under the current event processing model, we have less of a need for maintaining bookkeeping state e.g., lists of Future objects representing outstanding resource requests. Wake also simplified performance tuning by allowing us to dedicate Wake thread pools to heavily loaded event handlers, without changes to the underlying application (handler) code.

4. APPLICATIONS

This section describes several applications built on REEF, ranging from basic applications to production level services. We start with an interactive distributed shell to further illustrate the life-cycle of a (basic) REEF application. Next, we highlight the benefits of developing on REEF with a novel class of machine learning research enabled by the REEF abstractions. We then conclude with a description of two real-world applications that leverage REEF to deploy on YARN, emphasizing the ease of development on REEF. The first is a Java version of CORFU [4], which is a distributed log service. The second is Azure Streaming Analytics, which is a publicly available service deployed on the Azure Cloud Platform. Additional REEF applications and tutorials can be found at `http://reef.incubator.apache.org`.

4.1 Distributed Shell

We illustrate the life-cycle of a REEF application with a simple interactive distributed shell, modeled after the YARN example described in Section 2.1. Figure 6 depicts an execution of this application on two `Evaluators` (i.e., on two machines) that execute `Tasks` running a desired shell command. During the course of this execution, the `Evaluators` enter different states defined by time-steps t_1, t_2, t_3, t_4 e.g., in time-step t_2, both `Evaluators` are executing `Task 1`. The lines in the figure represent control flow interactions and are labeled with a numbering scheme (e.g., `i1 for interaction 1`) that we refer to in our description below.

The application starts at the Client, which submits the Distributed Shell Driver (DSD) to the Resource Manager (RM) for execution; this interaction is labeled (i1). The RM then launches the `Driver Runtime` as an Application Master. The `Driver Runtime` bootstrap process establishes a bidirectional communication channel with the Client (i3) and sends a start event to the DSD, which requests two containers (on two separate machines) with the RM (i2). The RM will eventually send container allocation notifications to the `Driver Runtime`, which sends allocation events to the DSD. The DSD uses those events to submit a root `Context`—defining the initial state on each `Evaluator`—to the `Driver Runtime`, which uses the root `Context` configuration to launch the `Evaluators` in containers started by the Node Managers.

The `Evaluator` bootstrap process establishes a bidirectional connection to the `Driver Runtime` (i4). At time t_1, the `Evaluator` informs the `Driver Runtime` that it has started and that the root `Context` is active. The `Driver Runtime` then sends two active context events to the DSD, which relays this information to the Client via (i3). The Client is then prompted for a shell command. An entered command is sent via (i3) and eventually received by the DSD in the form of a client message event. The DSD uses the shell command in that message to configure `Task 1`, which is submitted to the `Driver Runtime` for execution on both `Evaluators`. The `Driver Runtime` forwards the `Task 1` configuration via (i4) to the `Evaluators`, which execute an instance of `Task 1` in time-step t_2. Note that `Task 1` may change the state in the root `Context`. When `Task 1` completes in time-step t_3, the `Evaluator` informs the `Driver Runtime` via (i4). The DSD is then passed a completed task event containing the shell command output, which is sent to the client via (i3). After receiving the output of `Task 1` on both `Evaluators`, the Client is prompted for another shell command, which would be executed in a similar manner by `Task 2` in time-step t_4.

Compared to the YARN distributed shell example described in Section 2.1, our implementation provides cross-language support (we implemented it in Java and C#), is runnable in all runtimes that REEF supports, and presents the client with an *interactive* terminal that submits subsequent commands to retained Evaluators, avoiding the latency of spawning new containers. Further, the REEF distributed shell exposes a RESTful API for `Evaluator` management and `Task` submission implemented using a REEF HTTP `Service`, which takes care of tedious issues like finding an available port and registering it with the Resource Manager for discovery.

Even though the core distributed shell example on REEF is much more feature rich, it comes in at less than half the code (530 lines) compared to the YARN version (1330 lines).

4.2 Distributed Machine Learning

Many state-of-the-art approaches to distributed machine learning target abstractions like Hadoop MapReduce [10, 40]. Part of the attraction of this approach is the transparent handling of failures and other elasticity events. This effectively shields the algorithm developers from the inherently chaotic nature of a distributed system. However, it became apparent that many of the policy choices and abstractions offered by Hadoop are not a great fit for the iterative nature of machine learning algorithms [50, 1, 47]. This lead to proposals of new distributed computing abstractions specifically for machine learning [7, 52, 23, 24, 22]. Yet, policies for resource allocation, bootstrapping, and fault-handling remain abstracted way through a high-level domain specific language (DSL) [7, 52] or programming model [23, 24, 22].

In contrast, REEF offers a lower-level programming abstraction that can be used to take advantage of algorithmic optimizations. This added flexibility sparked a line of ongoing research that integrates the handling of failures, resource starvation and other elasticity challenges directly into the machine learning algorithm. We have found a broad range of algorithms can benefit from this approach, including linear models [28], principal component analysis [21] and Bayesian matrix factorization [6]. Here, we highlight the advantages that a lower-level abstraction like REEF offers for learning linear models, which are part of a bigger class of Statistical Query Model algorithms [18].

4.2.1 Linear Models

The input to our learning method is a dataset D of examples (x_i, y_i) where $x_i \in R^d$ denotes the features and $y_i \in R$ denotes the label of example i. The goal is to find a linear function $f_w(x_j) = \langle x_j, w \rangle$ with $w \in R^d$ that predicts the label for a previously unseen example. This goal can be cast as finding the minimizer $\hat{w}$ for the following optimization problem:[10]

$$\hat{w} = \operatorname*{argmin}_{w} \sum_{x,y \in D} l(f_w(x), y) = \operatorname*{argmin}_{w} \sum_{x,y \in D} l(\langle x, w \rangle, y) \quad (1)$$

Here, $l(f, y)$ is the loss function the model $\hat{w}$ is to minimize, e.g. the squared error $l(f, y) = \frac{1}{2}(f - y)^2$. This function is typically convex and differentiable in f and therefore the optimization problem (1) is convex and differentiable in w, and therefore can be minimized with a simple gradient-based algorithm.

The core gradient computation of the algorithm decomposes per example. This allows us to partition the dataset D into k partitions $D_1, D_2, \ldots, D_k$ and compute the gradient as the sum of the per-partition gradients. This property gives rise to a simple parallelization strategy: assign each `Evaluator` a partition D_i and launch a `Task` to compute the gradient on a per-partition basis. The per-partition gradients are aggregated (i.e., summed up) to a global gradient, which is used to update the model w. The new model is then broadcast to all `Evaluator` instances, and the cycle repeats.

4.2.2 Elastic Group Communications

In parallel work, we designed an elastic group communications library as a REEF `Service` that exposes Broadcast and Reduce operators familiar to Message Passing Interface (MPI) [14] programmers. It can be used to establish a communication topology among a set of leaf `Task` participants and a root `Task`. The leaf `Tasks` are given a Reduce operator to send messages to the root `Task`, which can aggregate those messages and use a Broadcast operator to send a message to all leaf `Tasks`. If the Reduce operation is associative,

[10]Note that we omit the regularizer which, despite its statistical importance, does not affect the distribution strategy.

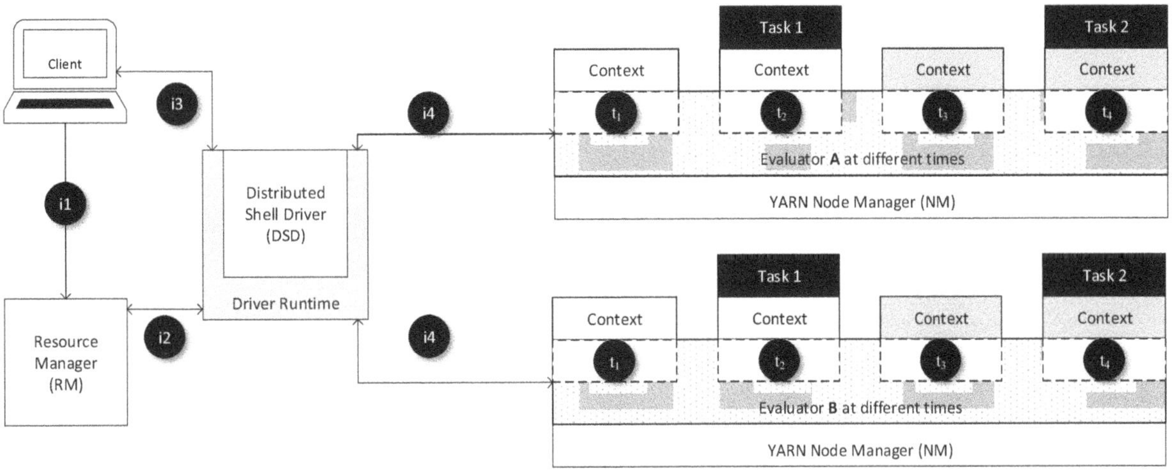

Figure 6: A Client executing the distributed shell job on two `Evaluators` **A** and **B**. The `Evaluators` execute shell commands—submitted by the Client—in `Task 1` and `Task 2` at time instances t_2 and t_4.

then a tree topology is established, with internal nodes performing the pre-aggregation steps. The `Service` also offers synchronization primitives that can be used to coordinate bulk-synchronous processing (BSP) [45] rounds. Crucially, the `Service` delegates topology changes to the application `Driver`, which can decide how to react to the change, and instruct the `Service` accordingly. For example, the loss of a leaf `Task` can be simply ignored, or repaired synchronously or asynchronously.[11] And the loss of the root `Task` can be repaired synchronously or asynchronously. The application is notified when asynchronous repairs have been made.

In an elastic learning algorithm, the loss of leaf `Tasks` can be understood as the loss of partitions D_i in the dataset. We can interpret these faults as being a sub-sample of the data, in the absence of any statistical bias that this approach could introduce. This allows us to tolerate faults algorithmically, and avoid pessimistic fault-tolerance policies enforced by other systems e.g., [52, 1, 11, 23, 24]. The performance implications are further elaborated in Section 5.2, and in greater detail in [28].

4.3 CORFU on REEF

CORFU [4] is a distributed logging tool providing applications with consistency and transactional services at extremely high throughput. There are a number of important use cases which a shared, global log enables:

- It may be used for driving remote checkpoint and recovery.
- It exposes a log interface with strict total-ordering and can drive replication and distributed locking.
- It may be leveraged for transaction management.

Importantly, all of these services are driven with no I/O bottlenecks using a novel paradigm that separates control from the standard leader-IO, which prevails in Paxos-based systems. In a nutshell, internally a CORFU log is striped over a collection of *logging units*. Each unit accepts a stream of logging requests at wire-speed and sequentializes their IO. In aggregate, data can be streamed in parallel to/from logging-units at full cluster bisection bandwidth. There are three operational modes, in-memory, non-atomic persist, and atomic-persist. The first logs data only in memory (replicated across redundant units for "soft" fault tolerance). The second logs data opportunistically to stable storage, with optional explicit sync barriers. The third persists data immediately before acknowledging appends. A soft-state *sequencer* process regulates appends in a circular fashion across the collection of stripes. A CORFU *master* controls the configuration, growing and shrinking the stripe-set. Configuration changes are utilized both for failure recovery and for load-rebalancing.

The CORFU architecture perfectly matches the REEF template. CORFU components are implemented as task modules, one for the sequencer, and one for each logging-unit. The CORFU master is deployed in a REEF `Driver`, which provides precisely the control and monitoring capabilities that the CORFU master requires. For example, when a logging unit experience a failure, the `Driver` is informed, and the CORFU master can react by deploying a replacement logging unit and reconfiguring the log. In the same manner, the CORFU master interacts with the log to handle sequencer failures, to react when a storage unit becomes full, and for load-rebalancing.

An important special failure case is the CORFU master itself. For applications like CORFU, it is important that a master does not become a single point of failure. REEF provides `Service` utilities for triggering checkpointing and for restarting a `Driver` from a checkpoint. The CORFU master uses these hooks to backup the configuration-state it holds onto the logging units themselves. Should the master fail, a recovery CORFU `Driver` is deployed by the logging units.

In this way, REEF provides a framework that decouples CORFU's resource deployment from its state, allowing CORFU to be completely elastic for fault tolerance and load-management.

Using CORFU from REEF: A CORFU log may be used from other REEF jobs by linking with a CORFU client-side library. A CORFU client finds (via CORFULib) the CORFU master over a publicized URL. The master informs the client about direct ports for interacting with the sequencer and the logging-units. Then, CORFULib interacts with the units to drive operations like log-append and log-read directly over the interconnect.

CORFU as a REEF service: Besides running as its own application, CORFU can also be deployed as a REEF `Service`. The `Driver` side of this `Service` subscribes to the events as described above, but now in addition to the other event handlers of the application. The CORFU and application event handlers compose to form the `Driver` and jointly implement the control-flow of the application, each responsible for a subset of the `Evaluators`. This greatly simplifies the deployment of such an application, as CORFU

[11]The loss of an internal node in a tree topology can be modeled as the loss of a set of leaf `Task` nodes.

then shares the event life-cycle with it and does not need external coordination.

4.4 Azure Stream Analytics

Azure Stream Analytics (ASA) is a fully managed stream processing service offered in the Microsoft Azure Cloud. It allows users to setup resilient, scalable queries over data streams that could be produced in "real-time." The service hides many of the technical challenges from its users, including machine faults and scaling to millions of events per second. While a description of the service as a whole is beyond the scope here, we highlight how ASA uses REEF to achieve its goals.

ASA implements a REEF `Driver` to compile and optimize–taking user budgets into consideration–a query into a data-flow of processing stages, similar to [30, 44, 33, 16, 53, 8, 5, 52]. Each stage is parallelized over a set of partitions i.e., an instance of a stage is assigned to process each partition in the overall stage input. Partitioned data is pipelined from producer stages to consumer stages according to the (compiled) data-flow. All stages must be started before query processing can begin on input data streams. The `Driver` uses the stage data-flow to formulate a request for resources; specifically, an `Evaluator` is requested per-stage instance. A `Task` is then launched on each `Evaluator` to execute the stage instance work on an assigned partition. It is highly desirable that this bootstrap process happens quickly to aid experimentation.

At runtime, an ASA `Task` is supported by two REEF `Services`, which aided in shortening the development cycle. The first is a communications `Service` built on Wake for allowing `Tasks` to send messages to other `Tasks` based on a logical identifier, which is independent to the `Evaluator` on which they execute, making `Task` restart possible on alternate `Evaluator` locations. The communication `Service` is highly optimized for low-latency message exchange, which ASA uses to communicate streaming partitions between `Tasks`. The second is the checkpointing `Service` that provides each `Task` with an API for storing intermediate state to stable storage, and an API to fetch that state e.g., on `Task` restart.

ASA is a production-level service that has had very positive influence on recent REEF developments. Most notably, REEF now provides mechanisms for capturing the `Task`-level log files—on the containers where the `Task` instances executed—to a location that can be viewed (postmortem) locally. Another recent development is an embedded HTTP server as a REEF `Service` that can be used to examine log files and execution status at runtime. These artifacts were motivated during the development and initial deployment phases of ASA. Further extensions and improvements are expected as more production-level services (already underway at Microsoft) are developed on REEF.

4.5 Summary

The applications described in this section underscore our original vision of REEF as being:

1. A flexible framework for developing distributed applications on Resource Manager services.
2. A standard library of reusable system components that can be easily composed (via Tang) into application logic.

Stonebraker and Cetintemel argued that the "one size fits all model" is no longer applicable to the database market [36]. We believe this argument naturally extends to "Big Data" applications. Yet, we also believe that there exists standard mechanisms common to many such applications. REEF is our attempt to provide a foundation for the development of that common ground in open source.

	Wake Event	REEF Task	YARN Container
Time(ns)	1	30,000	1.2E7

Figure 7: Startup times for core REEF primitives

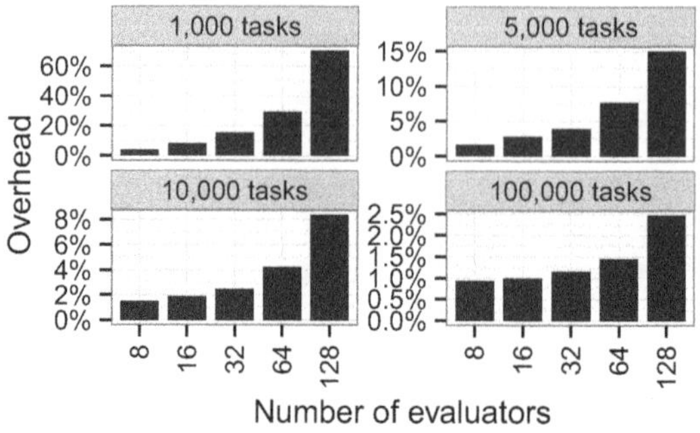

Figure 8: Combined (REEF + YARN) overheads for jobs with short-lived (1 second) tasks

5. EVALUATION

Our evaluation focuses on microbenchmarks (Section 5.1) that examine the overheads of REEF for allocating resources, bootstrapping `Evaluator` runtimes, and launching `Task` instances; we then report on a task launch overhead comparison with Apache Spark. Section 5.2 then showcases the benefits of the REEF abstractions with the elastic learning algorithm (from Section 4).

Experimental setup: We report experiments in three environments. The first is using the local process runtime. The second is based on YARN version 2.6 running on a cluster of 35 machines equipped with 128GB of RAM and 32 cores; each machine runs Linux and Java 1.7. We submit one job at a time to an empty cluster to avoid job scheduling queuing effects. Third, we leveraged Microsoft Azure to allocate 25 D4 instances (8 cores, 28 GB of RAM and 400 GB of SSD disk each) in an experiment that compares the overheads of REEF to Apache Spark [52].

5.1 Microbenchmark

Key primitive measurements: Figure 7 shows the time it takes to dispatch a local Wake Event, bootstrap an `Evaluator`, and launch a `Task`. There are roughly three orders of magnitude difference in time between these three actions. This supports our intuition that there is a high cost to reacquiring resources for different `Task` executions. Further, Wake is able to leverage multi-core systems in its processing of fine-grained events, achieving a throughput rate that ranges from 20-50 million events per second per machine.

Overheads with short-lived Tasks: In this experiment, the `Driver` is configured to allocate a fixed number of `Evaluators` and launch `Tasks` that sleep for one second, and then exit. This setup provides a baseline (ideal) job time interval (i.e., #`Tasks` $*$ one second) that we can use to assess the combined overhead of allocating and bootstrapping `Evaluators`, and launching `Tasks`. Figure 8 evaluates this setup on jobs configured with various numbers of `Evaluators` and `Tasks`. The combined overhead is computed from $\frac{actual\ runtime}{ideal\ runtime} - 1$, where:

$$ideal\ runtime = \frac{\#\texttt{Tasks} * task\ execution\ time}{\#\texttt{Evaluators}}.$$

The figure shows that as we run more `Tasks` per `Evaluator`, we amortize the cost of communicating with YARN and launching `Evaluators`, and the overall job overhead decreases. This is consistent with the earlier synthetic measurements that suggest spawning tasks is orders of magnitudes faster than launching `Evaluators`.

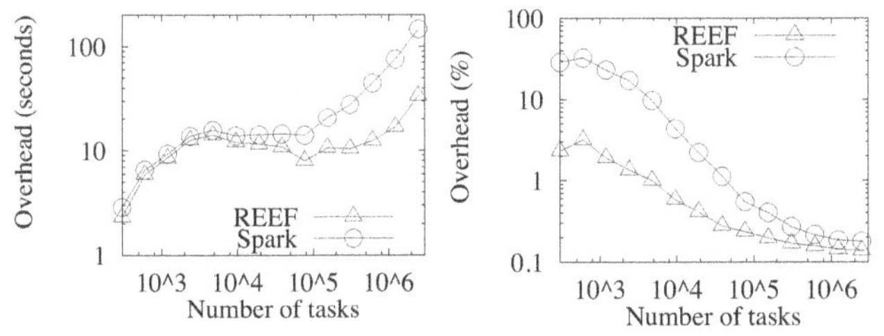

(a) Absolute running time (y-axis) of jobs with varying numbers of tasks (x-axis).

(b) Computed overheads (y-axis) of jobs with varying numbers of tasks (x-axis).

Figure 9: Overheads of REEF and Apache Spark for jobs with short-lived (100ms) tasks.

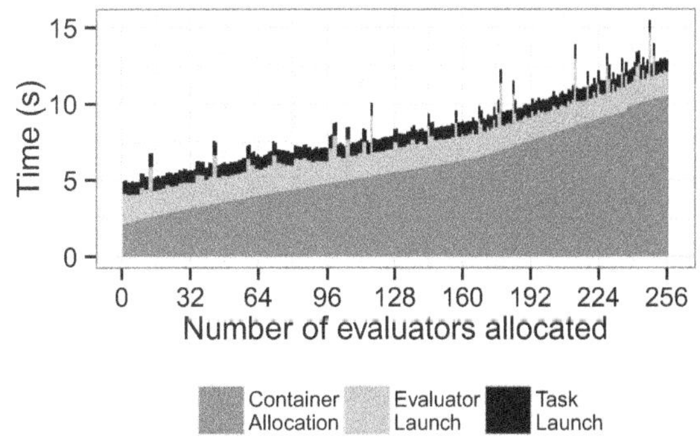

Figure 10: `Evaluator/Task` allocation and launch time breakdown

Since job parallelism is limited to the number of `Evaluators`, jobs with more `Evaluators` suffer higher overheads but finish faster.

Comparison with Apache Spark: Next, we leveraged 25 D4 Microsoft Azure instances (the third experimental setup) to run a similar experiment comparing to Apache Spark. Out of the total 200 cores available, we allocated 300 YARN containers, each with 1GB of available memory. In addition, each application master was allocated 4GB of RAM. The experiment begins by instantiating a task runtime (an `Evaluator` in the REEF case, and an `Executor` in the Spark case) on each container. The respective application masters then begin to launch a series of tasks, up to a prescribed number. The combined overhead is computed as above.

Before reporting results for this experiment, we first describe the differences in the overheads for launching tasks. In Spark, launching a task requires transferring a serialized closure object with all of its library dependencies to the Spark `Executor`, which caches this information for running subsequent tasks of the same type i.e., stage. In REEF, library dependencies are transferred upfront i.e., when the `Evaluator` is launched. This highlights a key difference in the REEF design, which assumes complete visibility into what tasks will run on an `Evaluator`. Thus, the overhead cost of launching a `Task` in REEF boils down to the time it takes to package and transfer its Tang configuration.

Figure 9 reports on the overheads of REEF and Apache Spark for jobs that execute a fixed number of tasks configured to sleep for 100ms before exiting. The total running time is reported in Figure 9a and the percentage of time spent on overhead work (i.e., total running time normalized to ideal running time) is in Figure 9b. In all cases, the overhead in REEF is less than Spark. In both systems, the overheads diminish as the job size (i.e., number of tasks) increases. On the lower end of the job size spectrum, Spark overheads for transferring task information (e.g., serialized closure and library dependencies) are much more pronounced; larger jobs benefit from the caching this information on the `Executor`. At larger job sizes, both system overheads converge to about the same (percentage) amount.

Evaluator/Task allocation and launch time breakdown: Here we dive deeper into the time it takes to allocate resources from YARN, spawn `Evaluators`, and launching `Tasks`. Figure 10 shows these times (as a stacked graph) for a job that allocates 256 `Evaluators`. The red and green portions are very pessimistic estimates of the REEF overhead in starting an `Evaluator` on a Node Manager and launching a `Task` on a running `Evaluator`, respectively. The majority of the time is spent in container allocation (blue portion) i.e., the time from container request submission to the time the allocation response is received by the `Driver`; this further underscores the need to minimize such interactions with YARN by retaining `Evaluators` for recurring `Task` executions.

The time to launch an `Evaluator` on an allocated container is shown by the red portion, which varies between different `Evaluators`. YARN recognizes when a set of processes (from its perspective) share files (e.g., code libraries), and only copies such files once from the Application Master to the Node Manager. This induces higher launch times for the first wave of `Evaluators`. Later scheduled `Evaluators` launch faster, since the shared files are already on the Node Manager from earlier `Evaluator` executions; recall, we are scheduling 256 `Evaluators` on 35 Node Managers. Beyond that, starting a JVM and reporting back to the `Driver` adds about 1-2 seconds to the launch time for all `Evaluators`. The time to launch a `Task` (green porition) is fairly consistent (about 0.5 seconds) across all `Evaluators`.

5.2 Resource Elastic Machine Learning

In this section, we evaluate the elastic group communications based machine learning algorithm described in Section 4.2. The learning task is to learn a a linear logistic regression mode using a Batch Gradient Descent (BGD) optimizer. We use two datasets for the experiments, both derived from the `splice` dataset described in [1]. The raw data consists of strings of length 141 with 4 alphabets (A, T, G and C).

Dataset A contains a subset of 4 million examples sampled from `splice` was used to derive binary features that denote the presence or absence of n-grams at specific locations of the string with $n = [1,4]$. The dimensionality of the feature space is $47,028$. This dataset consists of 14GB of data.

Dataset B contains the entire dataset of 50 million examples was used to derive the first $100,000$ features per the above process. This dataset consists of 254GB of data.

Algorithm: We implemented the BGD algorithm described in Section 4.2.1 on top of the elastic group communications `Service` described in Section 4.2.2. The `Driver` assigns a worker `Task` to cache and process each data partition. Each worker `Task` produces a gradient value that is reduced to a global gradient on the root `Task` using the `Reduce` operator. The root `Task` produces a new model that is `Broadcast` to the worker `Tasks`. The job executes in iterations until convergence is achieved.

Developing on REEF: REEF applications can be easily moved between `Environment Adapters` (3.1.1). We used this to first develop and debug BGD using the Local Process adapter. We then moved the application to YARN with only a single configuration change. Figure 11 shows the convergence rate of the algorithm running on Dataset A on the same hardware in these two modes: "Local" denotes a single cluster machine. In the YARN mode, 14 compute `Tasks` are launched to process the dataset. The first thing

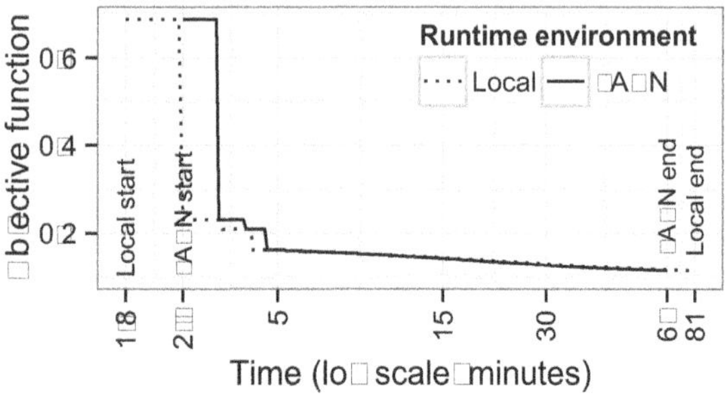

Figure 11: Objective function over time for Dataset A when executing locally and on a YARN cluster

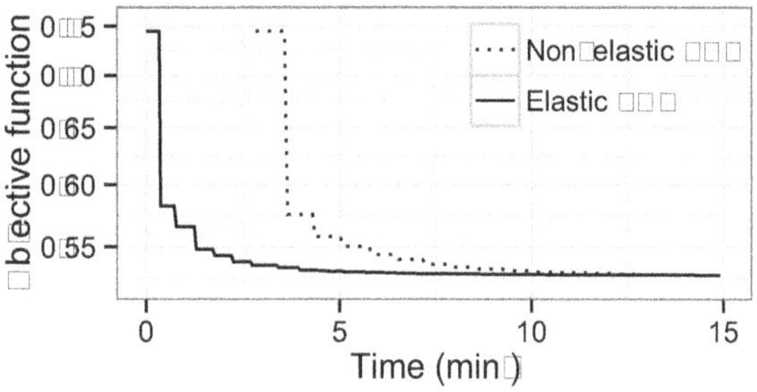

Figure 12: Ramp-up experiment on Dataset B

to note is that the algorithm performs similarly in both environments. That is, in each iteration, the algorithm makes equivalent progress towards convergence. The main difference between these two environments is in the start-up cost and the response time of each iteration. YARN suffers from a higher start-up cost due to the need to distribute the program, but makes up for this delay during execution, and converges about 14 minutes earlier than the local version. Considering the 14x increased hardware, this is a small speedup that suggests to execute the program on a single machine which REEF's `Environment Adapters` made it easy to discover.

Elastic BGD: Resource Managers typically allocate resources as they become available. Traditional MPI-style implementations wait for all resources to come online before they start computing. In this experiment, we leverage the Elastic Group Communications `Service` to start computing as soon as the first `Evaluator` is ready. We then add additional `Evaluators` to the computation as they become available. Figure 12 plots the progress in terms of the objective function measured on the full dataset over time for both elastic and non-elastic versions of the BGD job. The line labeled *Non-elastic BGD* waits for *all* `Evaluators` to come online before executing the first iteration of the learning algorithm. The line labeled *Elastic BGD* starts the execution as soon as the first `Evaluator` is ready, which occurs after the data partition is cached. New `Evaluators` are incorporated into the computation at iteration boundaries.

We executed these two strategies on an idle YARN cluster, which means that resource requests at the Resource Manager were immediately granted. Therefore, the time taken for an `Evaluator` to become ready was in (1) the time to bootstrap it, and (2) the time to execute a `Task` that loaded and cached data in the root `Context`. As the Figure shows, the elastic approach is vastly preferable in an on-demand resource managed setting. In effect, elastic BGD (almost) finishes by the time the non-elastic version starts.

While this application-level elasticity is not always possible, it is often available in machine learning where each machine represents a partition of the data. Fewer partitions therefore represent a

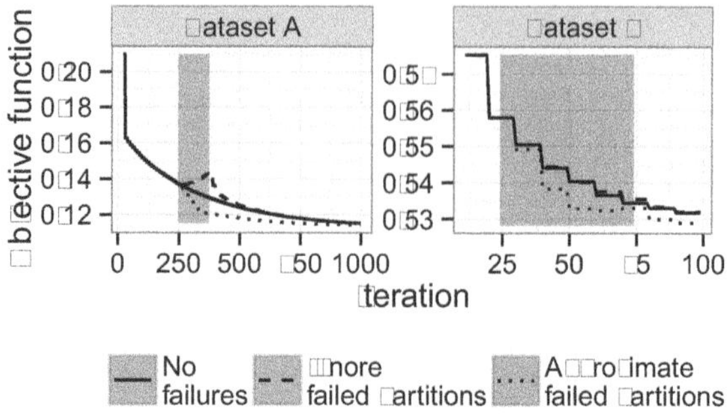

Figure 13: Learning progress over iterations with faulty partitions. Grey areas between iterations 250..375 for Dataset A and 25..75 for Dataset B indicate the period of induced failure.

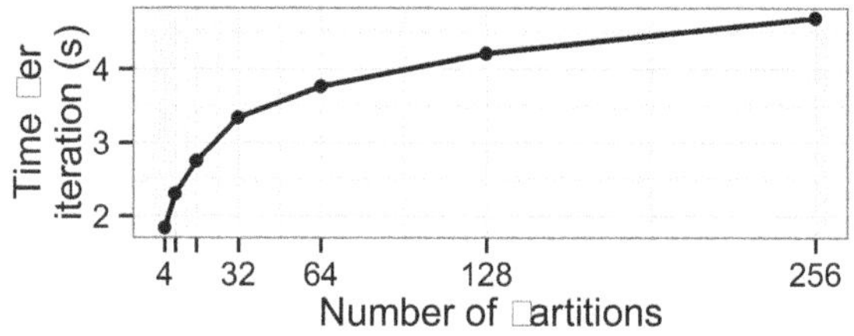

Figure 14: Scale-out iteration time with partitions of 1GB.

smaller sample of the data set. And models obtained on small samples of the data can provide good starting points [9] for subsequent iterations on the full data.

Algorithmic fault handling: We consider machine failure during the execution. We compare three variants: (1) No failure; (2) ignoring the failure and continuing with the remaining data and (3) our proposal: use a first-order Taylor approximation of the missing partitions' input until the partitions come back online. Figure 13 shows the objective function over iterations. Our method shows considerable improvement over the baselines. Surprisingly, we even do better than the no failure case. This can be explained by the fact that the use of the past gradient has similarities to adding a momentum term which is well-known to have a beneficial effect [32].

Scale-out: Figure 14 shows the iteration time for varying scale-up factors. It grows logarithmically as the the data scales linearly (each partition adds approximately 1GB of data). This is positive and expected, as our `Reduce` implementation uses a binary aggregation tree; doubling the `Evaluator` count adds a layer to the tree.

6. RELATED WORK

REEF provides a simple and efficient framework for building distributed systems on Resource Managers like YARN [46] and Mesos [15]. REEF replaces software components common across many system architectures [39, 33, 52, 5, 8, 16, 53] with a general framework for developing the specific semantics and mechanisms in a given system e.g., data-parallel operators, an explicit programming model, or domain-specific language (DSL). Moreover, REEF is designed to be extensible through its `Service` modules, offering applications with library solutions to common mechanisms e.g., group communication, data shuffle, or a more general RDD [52]-like abstraction, which could then be exposed to other higher-level programming models (e.g., MPI).

With its support for state caching and group communication, REEF greatly simplifies the implementation of iterative data processing models such as those found in GraphLab [23], Twister [12], Giraph [38], and VW [1]. REEF can also be leveraged to support stream processing systems such as Storm [25] and S4 [29] on managed resources, as demonstrated with Azure Streaming Analytics (Section 4.4). Finally, REEF has been designed to facilitate hand-over of data across frameworks, short-circuiting many of the HDFS based communications and parsing overheads incurred by state-of-the-art systems.

The Twill project [42] and REEF both aim to simplify application development on top of resource managers. However, REEF and Twill go about this in different ways. Twill simplifies programming by exposing a developer abstraction based on Java Threads that specifically targets YARN, and exposes an API to an external messaging service (e.g., Kafka [20]) for its control-plane support. On the other hand, REEF provides a set of common building blocks (e.g., job coordination, state passing, cluster membership) for building distributed applications, virtualizes the underlying Resource Manager layer, and has a custom built control-plane that scales with the allocated resources.

Slider [41] is a framework that makes it easy to deploy and manage long-running static applications in a YARN cluster. The focus is to adapt existing applications such as HBase and Accumulo [37] to run on YARN with little modification. Therefore, the goals of Slider and REEF are different.

Tez [33] is a project to develop a generic DAG processing framework with a reusable set of data processing primitives. The focus is to provide improved data processing capabilities for projects like Hive, Pig, and Cascading. In contrast, REEF provides a generic layer on which diverse computation models, like Tez, can be built.

7. SUMMARY AND FUTURE WORK

We embrace the industry-wide architectural shift towards decoupling resource management from higher-level applications stacks. In this paper, we propose a natural next step in this direction, and present REEF as a scale-out computing fabric for resource managed applications. We started by analyzing popular distributed data-processing systems, and in the process we isolated recurring themes, which seeded the design of REEF. We validated these design choices by building several applications, and hardened our implementation to support a commercial service in the Microsoft Azure Cloud.

REEF is an ongoing project and our next commitment is towards providing further building-blocks for data processing applications. Specifically, we are actively working on a checkpoint service for fault-tolerance, a bulk-data transfer implementation that can "shuffle" massive amounts of data, an improved low-latency group communication library, and an abstraction akin to RDDs [51], but agnostic to the higher-level programming model. Our intention with these efforts is to seed a community of developers that contribute further libraries (e.g., relational operators, machine learning toolkits, etc.) that integrate with one another on a common runtime. In support of this goal, we have set up REEF as an Apache Incubator project. Code and documentation can be found at `http://reef.incubator.apache.org`. The level of engagement both within Microsoft and from the research community reinforces our hunch that REEF addresses fundamental pain-points in distributed system development.

Acknowledgements

We would like to thank our many partners in the Microsoft Big Data product groups and the SNU CMSLab group for their feedback and guidance in the development of REEF. This work is supported at SNU by a Microsoft Research Faculty Fellowship. Additionally, REEF is supported in academia at UCLA through grants NSF IIS-1302698 and CNS-1351047, and U54EB020404 awarded by the National Institute of Biomedical Imaging and Bioengineering (NIBIB) through funds provided by the trans-NIH Big Data to Knowledge (BD2K) initiative (`www.bd2k.nih.gov`). Lastly, we would like to thank Matteo Interlandi for running the experiments that compare the overheads of REEF versus Apache Spark.

8. REFERENCES

[1] A. Agarwal, O. Chapelle, M. Dudík, and J. Langford. A reliable effective terascale linear learning system. *CoRR*, abs/1110.4198, 2011.

[2] A. Ahmed, M. Aly, J. Gonzalez, S. Narayanamurthy, and A. J. Smola. Scalable inference in latent variable models. In *WSDM '12*, 2012.

[3] P. Alvaro, N. Conway, J. Hellerstein, and W. R. Marczak. Consistency analysis in bloom: a calm and collected approach. In *CIDR*, pages 249–260, 2011.

[4] M. Balakrishnan, D. Malkhi, J. D. Davis, V. Prabhakaran, M. Wei, and T. Wobber. Corfu: A distributed shared log. *ACM Transactions on Computer Systems (TOCS)*, 31(4):10, 2013.

[5] D. Battré, S. Ewen, F. Hueske, O. Kao, V. Markl, and D. Warneke. Nephele/PACTs: A programming model and execution framework for web-scale analytical processing. In *SOCC*, 2010.

[6] A. Beutel, M. Weimer, V. Narayanan, and Y. Z. Tom Minka. Elastic distributed bayesian collaborative filtering. In *NIPS workshop on Distributed Machine Learning and Matrix Computations*, 2014.

[7] V. Borkar, Y. Bu, M. J. Carey, J. Rosen, N. Polyzotis, T. Condie, M. Weimer, and R. Ramakrishnan. Declarative systems for large-scale machine learning. *TCDE*, 35(2), 2012.

[8] V. Borkar, M. Carey, R. Grover, N. Onose, and R. Vernica. Hyracks: A flexible and extensible foundation for data-intensive computing. In *ICDE*, 2011.

[9] O. Bousquet and L. Bottou. The tradeoffs of large scale learning. In *Advances in Neural Information Processing Systems*, pages 161–168, 2007.

[10] C.-T. Chu, S. K. Kim, Y.-A. Lin, Y. Yu, G. R. Bradski, A. Y. Ng, and K. Olukotun. Map-reduce for machine learning on multicore. In *Advances in Neural Information Processing Systems*, 2006.

[11] J. Dean and S. Ghemawat. MapReduce: simplified data processing on large clusters. *Commun. ACM*, 51, 2008.

[12] J. Ekanayake, H. Li, B. Zhang, T. Gunarathne, S.-H. Bae, J. Qiu, and G. Fox. Twister: a runtime for iterative mapreduce. In *HPDC*, 2010.

[13] Google. Guice. `https://github.com/google/guice`.

[14] W. Gropp, S. Huss-Lederman, A. Lumsdaine, E. Lusk, B. Nitzberg, W. Saphir, and M. Snir. *MPI - The Complete Reference: Volume 2, The MPI-2 Extensions*. MIT Press, Cambridge, MA, USA, 1998.

[15] B. Hindman, A. Konwinski, M. Zaharia, A. Ghodsi, A. D. Joseph, R. Katz, S. Shenker, and I. Stoica. Mesos: A platform for fine-grained resource sharing in the data center. In *NSDI*, pages 22–22. USENIX Association, 2011.

[16] M. Isard, M. Budiu, Y. Yu, A. Birrell, and D. Fetterly. Dryad: distributed data-parallel programs from sequential building blocks. In *Eurosys*, 2007.

[17] S. Kavulya, J. Tan, R. Gandhi, and P. Narasimhan. An analysis of traces from a production mapreduce cluster. In *Proceedings of the 10th IEEE/ACM International Conference on Cluster, Cloud and Grid Computing*, CCGRID '10, pages 94–103, Washington, DC, USA, 2010. IEEE Computer Society.

[18] M. Kearns. Efficient noise-tolerant learning from statistical queries. *J. ACM*, 45(6):983–1006, 1998.

[19] E. Kohler, R. Morris, B. Chen, J. Jannotti, and M. F. Kaashoek. The click modular router. *ACM Transactions on Computer Systems (TOCS)*, 18(3):263–297, 2000.

[20] J. Kreps, N. Narkhede, and J. Rao. Kafka: A distributed messaging system for log processing. In *NetDB*, 2011.

[21] A. Kumar, N. Karampatziakis, P. Mineiro, M. Weimer, and V. Narayanan. Distributed and scalable pca in the cloud. In *BigLearn NIPS Workshop*, 2013.

[22] M. Li, D. G. Andersen, J. W. Park, A. J. Smola, A. Ahmed, V. Josifovski, J. Long, E. J. Shekita, and B.-Y. Su. Scaling distributed machine learning with the parameter server. In *Proc. OSDI*, pages 583–598, 2014.

[23] Y. Low, J. Gonzalez, A. Kyrola, D. Bickson, C. Guestrin, and J. M. Hellerstein. GraphLab: A New Parallel Framework for Machine Learning. In *Conference on Uncertainty in Artificial Intelligence (UAI)*, Catalina Island, California, 2010.

[24] G. Malewicz, M. H. Austern, A. J. Bik, J. C. Dehnert, I. Horn, N. Leiser, and G. Czajkowski. Pregel: a system for large-scale graph processing. In *Proceedings of the ACM SIGMOD International Conference on Management of data*, SIGMOD '10, pages 135–146, New York, NY, USA, 2010. ACM.

[25] N. Marz. Storm: Distributed and fault-tolerant realtime computation. `http://storm.apache.org`.

[26] E. Meijer. Your mouse is a database. *Commun. ACM*, 55(5):66–73, 2012.

[27] D. G. Murray, F. McSherry, R. Isaacs, M. Isard, P. Barham, and M. Abadi. Naiad: A timely dataflow system. In *Proceedings of the Twenty-Fourth ACM Symposium on Operating Systems Principles*, SOSP '13, pages 439–455, New York, NY, USA, 2013. ACM.

[28] S. Narayanamurthy, M. Weimer, D. Mahajan, T. Condie, S. Sellamanickam, and S. S. Keerthi. Towards resource-elastic machine learning. In *BigLearn NIPS Workshop*, 2013.

[29] L. Neumeyer, B. Robbins, A. Nair, and A. Kesari. S4: Distributed stream computing platform. In *ICDMW*, 2010.

[30] C. Olston, B. Reed, U. Srivastava, R. Kumar, and A. Tomkins. Pig latin: a not-so-foreign language for data processing. In *Proceedings of the ACM SIGMOD international conference on Management of data*, SIGMOD '08, pages 1099–1110, New York, NY, USA, 2008. ACM.

[31] A. Rabkin. Using program analysis to reduce misconfiguration in open source systems software. *Ph.D. Dissertation, UC Berkeley*, 2012.

[32] D. E. Rumelhart, G. E. Hinton, and R. J. Williams. Learning internal representations by error propagation. Technical report, DTIC Document, 1985.

[33] B. Saha, H. Shah, S. Seth, G. Vijayaraghavan, A. Murthy, and C. Curino. Apache tez: A unifying framework for modeling and building data processing applications. In *SIGMOD 2015*, 2015.

[34] M. Schwarzkopf, A. Konwinski, M. Abd-El-Malek, and J. Wilkes. Omega: flexible, scalable schedulers for large compute clusters. In *EuroSys*, pages 351–364, 2013.

[35] M. Shapiro and N. M. Preguiça. Designing a commutative replicated data type. *CoRR*, abs/0710.1784, 2007.

[36] M. Stonebraker and U. Cetintemel. One size fits all: An idea whose time has come and gone. In *Proceedings of the 21st International Conference on Data Engineering*, ICDE '05, pages 2–11, Washington, DC, USA, 2005. IEEE Computer Society.

[37] The Apache Software Foundation. Apache Accumulo. `http://accumulo.apache.org/`.

[38] The Apache Software Foundation. Apache Giraph. `http://giraph.apache.org/`.

[39] The Apache Software Foundation. Apache Hadoop. `http://hadoop.apache.org`.

[40] The Apache Software Foundation. Apache Mahout. `http://mahout.apache.org`.

[41] The Apache Software Foundation. Apache Slider. `http://slider.incubator.apache.org/`.

[42] The Apache Software Foundation. Apache Twill. `http://twill.incubator.apache.org/`.

[43] The Netty project. Netty. `http://netty.io`.

[44] A. Thusoo, J. S. Sarma, N. Jain, Z. Shao, P. Chakka, S. Anthony, H. Liu, P. Wyckoff, and R. Murthy. Hive – a warehousing solution over a map-reduce framework. In *PVLDB*, 2009.

[45] L. G. Valiant. A bridging model for parallel computation. *Commun. ACM*, 33(8):103–111, 1990.

[46] V. K. Vavilapalli, A. C. Murthy, C. Douglas, S. Agarwal, M. Konar, R. Evans, T. Graves, J. Lowe, H. Shah, S. Seth, B. Saha, C. Curino, O. O'Malley, S. Radia, B. Reed, and E. Baldeschwieler. Apache hadoop yarn: Yet another resource negotiator. In *SOCC*, 2013.

[47] M. Weimer, S. Rao, and M. Zinkevich. A convenient framework for efficient parallel multipass algorithms. In *LCCC*, 2010.

[48] M. Welsh. What I wish systems researchers would work on. `http://matt-welsh.blogspot.com/2013/05/what-i-wish-systems-researchers-would.html`.

[49] M. Welsh, D. Culler, and E. Brewer. Seda: an architecture for well-conditioned, scalable internet services. In *SIGOPS*, volume 35, pages 230–243. ACM, 2001.

[50] J. Ye, J.-H. Chow, J. Chen, and Z. Zheng. Stochastic gradient boosted distributed decision trees. In *Proceedings of the 18th ACM Conference on Information and Knowledge Management*, CIKM '09, pages 2061–2064, New York, NY, USA, 2009. ACM.

[51] M. Zaharia, M. Chowdhury, T. Das, A. Dave, J. Ma, M. McCauley, M. Franklin, S. Shenker, and I. Stoica. Resilient distributed datasets: A fault-tolerant abstraction for in-memory cluster computing. In *NSDI*, 2012.

[52] M. Zaharia, M. Chowdhury, M. J. Franklin, S. Shenker, and I. Stoica. Spark: cluster computing with working sets. In *HotCloud*, 2010.

[53] J. Zhou, N. Bruno, M.-C. Wu, P.-A. Larson, R. Chaiken, and D. Shakib. Scope: Parallel databases meet mapreduce. *VLDB Journal*, 21(5), 2012.

Apache Tez: A Unifying Framework for Modeling and Building Data Processing Applications

Bikas Saha[h], Hitesh Shah[h], Siddharth Seth[h],
Gopal Vijayaraghavan[h], Arun Murthy[h], Carlo Curino[m]
[h]Hortonworks, [m]Microsoft
[h]{bikas, hitesh, sseth, gopal, acm}@hortonworks.com, [m]ccurino@microsoft.com

ABSTRACT

The broad success of Hadoop has led to a fast-evolving and diverse ecosystem of application engines that are building upon the YARN resource management layer. The open-source implementation of MapReduce is being slowly replaced by a collection of engines dedicated to specific verticals. This has led to growing fragmentation and repeated efforts—with each new vertical engine re-implementing fundamental features (e.g. fault-tolerance, security, stragglers mitigation, etc.) from scratch.

In this paper, we introduce Apache Tez, an *open-source framework designed to build data-flow driven processing runtimes*. Tez provides a scaffolding and library components that can be used to quickly build scalable and efficient data-flow centric engines. Central to our design is fostering *component re-use, without hindering customizability* of the performance-critical data plane. This is in fact the key differentiator with respect to the previous generation of systems (e.g. Dryad, MapReduce) and even emerging ones (e.g. Spark), that provided an d mandated a fixed data plane implementation. Furthermore, Tez provides native support to build runtime optimizations, such as dynamic partition pruning for Hive.

Tez is deployed at Yahoo!, Microsoft Azure, LinkedIn and numerous Hortonworks customer sites, and a growing number of engines are being integrated with it. This confirms our intuition that most of the popular vertical engines can leverage a core set of building blocks. We complement qualitative accounts of real-world adoption with quantitative experimental evidence that Tez-based implementations of Hive, Pig, Spark, and Cascading on YARN outperform their original YARN implementation on popular benchmarks (TPC-DS, TPC-H) and production workloads.

1. INTRODUCTION

Large scale data analytics, once an exotic technology leveraged exclusively by large web-companies, is nowadays available and indispensable for most modern organizations. This broader user base has fostered an explosion of interest in this area, and led to a flourishing BigData industry. In this paper, we use the lens of the Hadoop ecosystem to describe industry-wide trends, as this provides the ideal context for introducing our system: Apache Tez. We postpone to Section 8 a broader comparison with the related projects like Dryad, Nephele, Hyracks[24, 14, 15] etc., which undeniably served as an inspiration and sometimes the blueprint for the design of Tez.

SIGMOD'15, May 31–June 4, 2015, Melbourne, Victoria, Australia.

ACM 978-1-4503-2758-9/15/05 ...$15.00.
http://dx.doi.org/10.1145/2723372.2742790

Hadoop, which was initially designed as a single-purpose system (to run MapReduce jobs to build a web index), has evolved into a catch-all data analytics platform. The first phase of this journey consisted of several efforts proposing *higher level abstractions* atop MapReduce[21], examples of which are Hive [30], Pig [28], and Cascading [4]. This sped-up the adoption of Hadoop, but led to inefficiencies and poor performance [29]. These limitations and the pressure towards more flexibility and efficiency led to the refactoring of Hadoop into a general purpose, OS-like resource management layer, namely YARN [32], and an application framework layer allowing for arbitrary execution engines. This enabled different applications to share a cluster, and made MapReduce *just another application* in the Hadoop ecosystem. Important examples of applications that break-free of the MapReduce model (and runtime) are Spark [38], Impala [25] and Flink [5]. This has accelerated innovation, but also led to a less efficient ecosystem, where common functionalities were being replicated across frameworks. For example, MapReduce and Spark independently developed mechanisms to implement delay scheduling[36].

In this paper, we introduce Tez, a project that embraces the architectural shift to YARN, and pushes it further, by proposing a reusable, flexible and extensible scaffolding that can support arbitrary data-flow oriented frameworks, while avoiding replicated functionalities. Tez APIs allow frameworks to clearly model the logical and physical semantics of their data flow graphs, with minimal code. It is important to clarify that Tez is a library to build data-flow based runtimes/engines and not an engine by itself—for example, the Hive runtime engine for Hadoop has been rewritten in version 0.13 to use Tez libraries.

Tez makes the following key contributions:

1. Allows users to model computation as a DAG (Directed-Acyclic-Graph) — akin to Dryad/Nephele/Hyracks. The novelty lies in a finer grained decomposition of the classical notions of vertex and edge, that delivers greater control and customization of the data plane.

2. Exposes APIs to dynamically evolve the (finer grained) DAG definition. This enables sophisticated runtime query optimizations, such as pruning data partitions, based on online information.

3. Provides a scalable and efficient implementation of state-of-the-art features, e.g., YARN-compatible security, data-locality awareness, resource-reuse, fault-tolerance and speculation.

4. Provides the opportunity for framework writers and researchers to innovate quickly and create real-world impact by providing experimentation support via pluggable APIs, and an open-source community to learn about the project and contribute back to it.

What sets Tez aside from many alternative proposals of 'unification frameworks' is: 1) proven flexibility and dynamic adaptation, 2) attention to operational concerns (production readiness), and 3) a community-driven effort to embed Tez in multiple existing domain-specific engines.

This is proven by the Tez support of MapReduce, Hive, Pig, Spark, Flink, Cascading, and Scalding, and its adoption in production data-processing clusters at Yahoo, Microsoft Azure, LinkedIn as well as several other organizations using the Hortonworks Data Platform. Beyond discussing the broad practical adoption of Tez, we demonstrate its competence to support Hive, Pig, and Spark, by running standard benchmarks such as TPC-H and TPC-DS, and production workloads from Yahoo!.

The rest of this paper is organized as follows: Section 2 provides some more historical context, and rationale for the design of Tez, while Section 3 introduces the architecture of Tez. Section 4 discusses the implementation of Tez, and highlights pragmatic considerations on efficiency and production-readiness. Section 5 and 6 are devoted to prove its practical relevance, by presenting real-world applications, and a broad experimental evaluation. We conclude by discussing future and related work in Sections 7 and 8, and conclude in Section 9

2. BACKGROUND AND RATIONALE

To understand the motivation and rationale behind Tez, we must first start by providing some background on terminology, and a historical context of distributed computation in Hadoop. The reader not interested in this historical and motivational perspective is invited to continue to Section 3, where we dive into the technical aspects of the Tez architecture.

Terminology. We have used graph terminology so far, appealing to the reader's intuitions. We now introduce our terminology more precisely:

DAG: Directed Acyclic Graph representing the structure of a data processing workflow. Data flows in the direction of the edges.

Vertex: Represents a logical step of processing. A processing step transforms data by applying application-supplied code to filter, or modify the data.

Logical DAG: A logical DAG is comprised of a set of vertices, where each vertex represents a specific step of the computation.

Task: Represents a unit of work in a vertex. In distributed processing, the logical work represented by a single vertex is physically executed as a set of tasks running on potentially multiple machines of the cluster. Each task is an instantiation of the vertex, that processes a subset (or partition) of the input data for that vertex.

Physical DAG: A physical DAG comprises of the set of tasks that are produced by expanding the vertices of a logical DAG into their constituent tasks.

Edge: Represents movement of data between producers and consumers. An edge between vertices of a logical DAG represents the logical data dependency between them. An edge between tasks in the physical DAG represents data transfers between the tasks.

This applies to problems in which different steps can be partitioned into smaller pieces that can be processed in parallel. Typically, the partitioning aligns with distributed shards of data and tries to co-locate processing with its data, thus reducing the cost of computation [21].

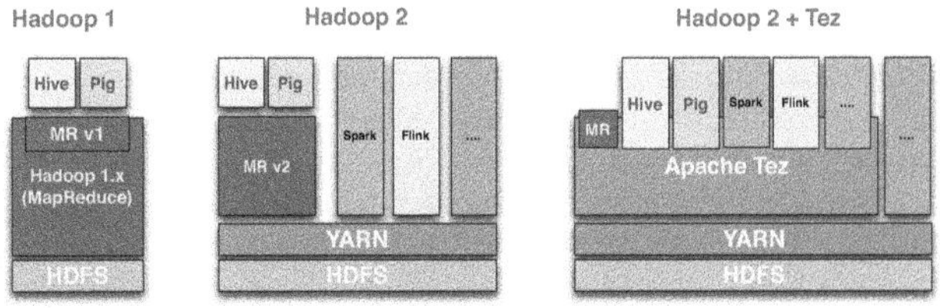

Figure 1: Evolution of Hadoop

Hadoop 1 and Hadoop 2 (YARN). Hadoop started off as a single monolithic software stack where MapReduce was the only execution engine [32]. All manners of data processing had to translate their logic into a single MapReduce job or a series of MapReduce jobs. MapReduce was also responsible for cluster resource management and resource allocation. Hadoop 2 is the current generation of Hadoop which separates these responsibilities by creating a general purpose resource management layer named YARN [32]. This de-couples applications from the core Hadoop platform and allows multiple application types to execute in a Hadoop cluster in addition to MapReduce. There are many domain-specific applications like Apache Hive for SQL-like data processing, Apache Pig for ETL scripting or Cascading for writing data processing applications in Java, which were earlier restricted to relying on MapReduce to execute their custom logic. These applications can now have a more customized implementation of their logic by running natively on YARN.

While specialization can deliver performance advantages, there is a substantial opportunity to create a common set of building blocks that can be used by these applications for their customized implementation on YARN. We try to seize that opportunity with Tez, as discussed next. An analysis of popular Hadoop ecosystem applications like Apache Hive, Pig, Spark etc. suggests that there are shared features that all of them need. These include negotiating resources from YARN to run application's tasks, handling security within the clusters, recovering from hardware failures, publishing metrics and statistics etc. A lot of this is highly specialized, hard to develop infrastructure that everyone has to replicate when building from scratch. A common implementation makes it easier to write applications because it removes that burden from the application writers and lets them focus on the unique logic of their application.

Henceforth, unless otherwise specified, when we mention Hadoop we imply the Hadoop 2 compute stack with YARN as the underlying resource allocation layer; and by Hadoop ecosystem we imply the compute ecosystem consisting of open source and commercial projects running on YARN such as Apache Hive, Pig etc.

An effort to provide these common features requires the creation of a framework to express and model these workloads optimally. Then this model can be applied and executed on the YARN application framework via a shared substrate library. This rationalizes the following requirements for such a shared library, which we have high-lighted by comparisons with MapReduce — a general purpose engine that has been forced to act as shared substrate until now.

Expressiveness. MapReduce has a simple modeling API for describing the computation by requiring all application algorithms to be translated into *map* and *reduce* functions. As observed by others before in [24, 14, 15], this is too constraining, and a DAG-oriented model can more naturally capture a broader set of computations. Thus we define Tez's central model around DAGs of execution as well. Moreover, MapReduce also provides built-in semantics to the logic running in map/reduce steps and imposed a *sorted & partitioned* movement of data between map and reduce steps [21]. These built-in semantics, ideal in some core use cases, could be pure overhead in many other scenarios and even undesirable in some. The observation here is the need for an API to describe the structure of arbitrary DAGs without adding unrelated semantics to that DAG structure.

Data-plane Customizability. Once the structure of distributed computation has been defined, there can be a variety of alternative implementations of the actual logic that executes in that structure. These could be algorithmic, e.g. different ways of partitioning the data or these could be related to using different hardware, e.g. using remote memory access (RDMA) where available. In the context of MapReduce, the built-in semantics of the engine makes such customizations difficult because they intrude in the implementation of the engine itself. Secondly, the monolithic structure of the tasks executing the MapReduce job on the cluster makes plugging in alternative implementations difficult. This motivates that data transformations and data movements that define the data plane need to be completely customizable. There is a need to be able to model different aspects of task execution in a manner that allows individual aspects of the execution, e.g. reading input, processing data etc. to be customized easily. Interviewing several members of the Hadoop community we confirmed that evolving existing engines (e.g., changing the shuffle behavior in MapReduce) is far from trivial.

While other frameworks such as [24, 15, 38], already support a more general notion of DAGs, they share the same limitation of MapReduce, built-in semantics and implementations of the data-plane. With Tez we provide a lower level abstraction, that enables such semantics and specialized implementations to be added on top of a basic shared scaffolding.

Late-binding Runtime Optimizations. Applications need to make late-binding decisions on their data processing logic for performance [13]. The algorithm, e.g. join strategies and scan mechanisms, could change based on dynamically observing data being read. Partition cardinality and work division could change as the application gets a better understanding of its data and environment. Hadoop clusters can be very dynamic in their usage and load characteristics. Users and jobs enter and exit the cluster continuously and have varying resource utilization. This makes it important for an application to determine its execution characteristics based on the current state of the cluster. We designed Tez to make this late-binding and on-line decision-making easier to implement, by enabling updates to key abstractions at runtime.

This concludes our overview of historical context and rationale for building Tez. We now turn to describing the high level architecture of Tez, and provide some insight into the key building blocks.

3. ARCHITECTURE

Apache Tez is designed and implemented with a focus on the issues discussed above, in summary: 1) expressiveness of the underlying model, 2) customizability of the data plane, and 3) facilitate runtime optimizations. Instead of building a general purpose execution engine, we realize the need for Tez to provide a *unifying framework for creating purpose-built engines that customize data processing for their specific needs.* Tez solves the common, yet hard problem of orchestrating and running a distributed data processing application on Hadoop and enables the application to focus on providing specific semantics and optimizations. There is a clear separation of concerns between the application layer and the Tez library layer. Apache Tez provides cluster resource negotiation, fault tolerance, resource elasticity, security, built-in performance optimizations and a shared library of ready to use components. The application provides custom application logic, custom data plane and specialized optimizations.

This leads to three key benefits: 1) amortized development costs (Hive and Pig completely rewrote their engines using the Tez libraries in about 6 months), 2) improved performance (we show in Section 6 up to 10× performance improvement while using Tez), and 3) enabling future pipelines that leverage multiple engines, to be run more efficiently because of a shared substrate.

Tez is composed of a set of core APIs that define the data processing and an orchestration framework to launch that on the cluster. Applications are expected to implement these APIs to provide the execution context to the orchestration framework. Its useful to think of Tez as a library to create a scaffolding representing the structure of the data flow, into which the application injects its custom logic (say operators) and data transfer code (say reading from remote machine disks). This design is both tactical and strategic. Long-term, this makes Tez remain application agnostic while in the short term, allows existing applications like Hive or Pig to leverage Tez without significant changes in their core operator pipelines. We will begin with describing the DAG API and Runtime API. These are the primary application facing interfaces used to describe the DAG structure of the application and the code to be executed at runtime. Next we explain support for applying runtime optimizations to the DAG via an event based control plane using VertexManagers and DataSourceInitializers. Finally, in Section 4 we describe the YARN based orchestration framework to execute the all of this on a Hadoop cluster. In particular, we will focus on the performance and production-readiness aspects of the implementation.

3.1 DAG API

The Tez DAG API is exposed to runtime engine builders as an expressive way to capture the structure of their computation in a concise way. The class of data processing application we focus on, are naturally represented as DAGs, where data proceeds from data sources towards data sinks, while being transformed in intermediate vertices. Tez focuses on acyclic graphs, and by assuming deterministic computation on the vertex and data routing on the edges, we enable re-execution based fault tolerance, akin to [24] and is further explained in Section 4.3. Modeling computations as a DAG is not new but hitherto most systems have typically designed DAG APIs in the context of supporting a higher level engine. Tez is designed to model this data flow graph as the main focus. Using well-known concepts of vertices and edges the DAG API enables a clear and concise description of the structure of the computation.

Vertex. A vertex in the DAG API represents transformation of data and is one of the steps in processing the data. This is where the core application logic gets applied to the data. Hence a vertex must be configured with a user-provided *processor* class that defines the logic to be executed in each task. One 'vertex' in the DAG is often executed in parallel across a (possibly massive) number of parallel tasks. The definition of a vertex controls such parallelism. Parallelism is usually determined by the need to process data that is distributed across machines or by the need to divide a large operation into smaller pieces. The task parallelism of a vertex may be defined statically during DAG definition but is typically determined dynamically at runtime.

Edge. An edge in the graph represents the logical and physical aspects of data movement between producer and consumer vertices.

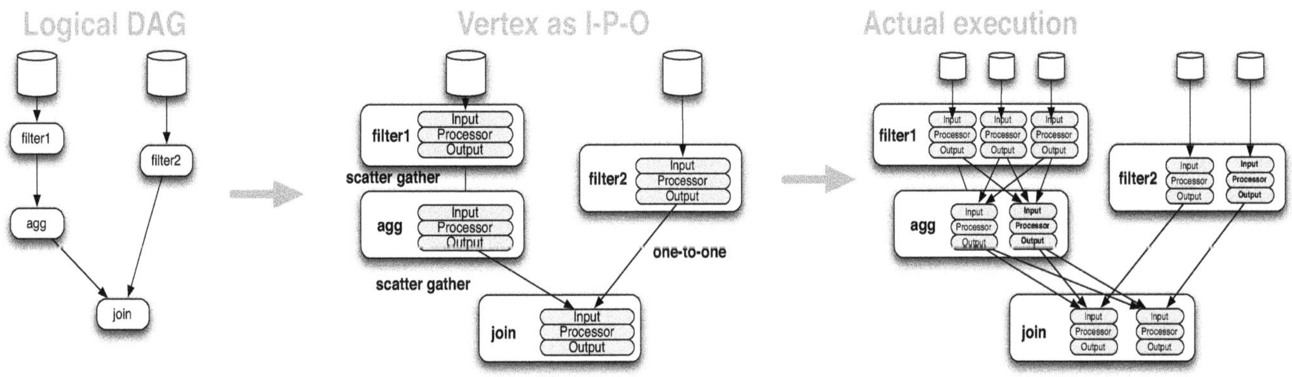

Figure 2: Expansion of the logical vertex DAG to a physical task DAG based on vertex parallelism and edge definition

- *Connection Pattern:* The logical aspect of an edge is the connection pattern between producer and consumer vertex tasks and their scheduling dependency. This enables the orchestration framework to route data from the output of the producer task to the correct input of the consumer task. This routing table must be specified by implementing a pluggable EdgeManagerPlugin API. Figure 3 shows 3 common connection patterns (one-to-one, broadcast, scatter-gather), that can be used to express most DAG connections and come built-in with the project. For cases where custom routing is needed, applications are allowed to define their own routing by providing their own implementation (we give a concrete example in Section 5.2).
- *Transport Mechanism:* The physical aspect of an edge is the storage or transport mechanism employed to move the data. This could be local-disk, or local/remote main-memory, etc. The actual data transfer operation of the edge is performed by a compatible pair of input and output classes that are specified for the edge. Compatibility is based on using the same data format and physical transport mechanisms. E.g. both operate on key-value pairs and operate on disks, or both operate on byte streams and use main memory. Tez comes with built-in inputs and outputs for common use cases as described in Section 4.1

Vertex parallelism and the edge properties can be used by Tez to expand the logical DAG to the real physical task execution DAG during execution as shown in Figure 2

Data Sources and Sinks. The DAG can be defined by creating vertices and connecting them via edges using the DAG API. Typically, the data flow will read initial input from some data sources and write final output to some data sinks. Data sources may be associated with a DataSourceInitializer that can be invoked at runtime to determine the optimal reading pattern for the initial input. E.g. in MapReduce parlance, this corresponds to 'split' calculation [27] where a split is a shard of distributed data that is read by a map task. The initial split calculation for map tasks can be performed using an initializer that considers the data distribution, data locality and available compute capacity to determine the number of splits and the optimal size of each split. Similarly, data sinks may be associated with a DataSinkCommitter that is invoked at runtime to commit the final output. The definition of commit may vary with the output type but is guaranteed to be done once, and typically involves making the output visible to external observers after successful completion.

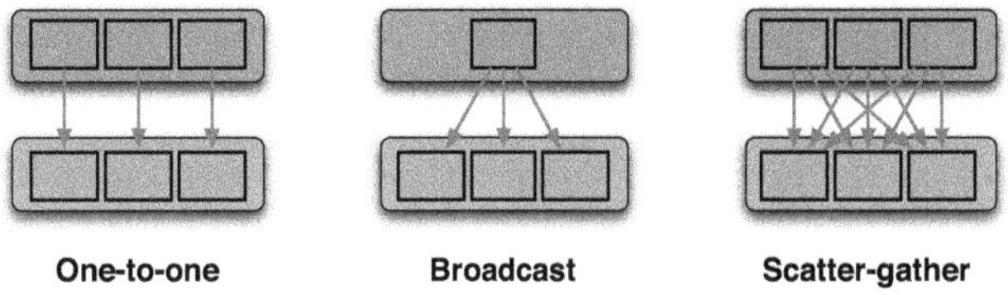

Figure 3: Edge properties: define movement of data between producers and consumers

```
1: DAG dag = DAG.create("WordCount");

2: Vertex tokenizerVertex = Vertex.create("Tokenizer", TokenProcessor.class)
                          .addDataSource("Input", HdfsInitializer.class);

3: Vertex summationVertex = Vertex.create("Summation", SumProcessor.class)
                          .addDataSink("Output", HdfsCommitter.class);

4: EdgeProperty edgeProperty = EdgeProperty.create(scatter_gather,
                          KeyValueShuffleWriter.class, KeyValueShuffleReader.class);

5: dag.addVertex(tokenizerVertex).addVertex(summationVertex)
      .addEdge(Edge.create(tokenizerVertex, summationVertex, edgeProperty);
```

Figure 4: Essence of the Tez API shown via pseudo-code for the canonical WordCount example

This manner of DAG assembly allows for pluggable and re-usable components. A common shared library of inputs and outputs can be re-used by different applications, thus only needing to supply the processor logic in a vertex. Conversely, the same DAG structure may be executed more optimally in a different hardware environment by replacing the inputs/outputs on the edges. Tez comes with an input/output library for data services built into Hadoop - HDFS and the YARN Shuffle Service. This enables Hadoop eco-system applications like Hive and Pig to quickly leverage Tez by implementing only their custom processors. Figure 4 shows a condensed view of describing a logical DAG using the API.

3.2 Runtime API

The DAG API defines the scaffolding structure of the data processing. The Runtime API is used to inject the actual application code that fills the scaffolding. Concretely, the Runtime API defines the interfaces to be implemented to create processor, input and output classes that are specified in the DAG above.

Inputs, Processor, Outputs. A vertex is a logical representation of a transformation step in the DAG. The actual transformations are applied by running tasks, for that vertex, on machines in the cluster. Tez defines each task as a composition of a set of inputs, a processor and a set of outputs (IPO). The processor is defined by the vertex for that task. The inputs are defined by the output classes of the incoming edges to that vertex. The outputs by the input classes of the outgoing edges from that vertex. This enables the processor to have a logical view of the processing, thus retaining the simplified programming model popularized in MapReduce. The inputs and outputs hide details like the data transport, partitioning of data and/or aggregation of distributed shards. The Runtime API is a thin wrapper to instantiate and interact with inputs, processors and outputs. After the IPO objects have been created, they are configured.

IPO Configuration. The framework configures IPOs via an opaque binary payload specified during DAG creation. This manner of binary payload configuration is a common theme to configure any application specific entity in Tez. This allows applications to instantiate their code using any mechanism of their choice. Not only can this be used for simple configuration but also for code injection (as exemplified in Section 5.4). After configuration, the processor is presented with all its inputs and outputs and asked to run. Thereafter, it's up to the processor, inputs and outputs to cooperate with each other to complete the task. The framework interacts with them via a context object to send and receive events about completion, update progress, report errors etc.

Data Plane Agnostic. Tez specifies no data format and in fact, is not part of the data plane during DAG execution. The actual data transfer is performed by the inputs and outputs with Tez only routing connection information between producers and consumers. When a producer task output generates data then it can send metadata about it, say its access URL and size, via Tez, to the consumer task input. Tez routes this metadata using the connection pattern encoded in the edge connecting the producer and consumer. Thus Tez adds minimal overhead on the data plane. This also makes Tez data format agnostic. The inputs, processor and outputs can choose their own data formats (e.g. bytes, records or key-value pairs etc.) as suited for the application, exemplified in Section 5.5

This novel IPO based approach to task composition allows for separation of concerns and makes the system pluggable. The same DAG structure can be instantiated with environment dependent IOs. E.g. different cloud environments can plug in IOs that are optimized for their storage subsystems. We will see in the next sections, how the IPOs can be dynamically configured during execution for even further runtime customizations.

3.3 Event Based Control Plane

The open architecture of the Tez orchestration framework requires a de-coupled control plane that allows a variety of entities to communicate control information with each other. In order to achieve this Tez has an event based control plane that is also exposed to the application. Software components generate events that get routed to receivers. By design, this is an asynchronous, non-blocking, push-based method of communication. Events are used for all communications, be it framework to framework, application to framework and vice versa, or application to application. As shown in Figure 5, a DataEvent is generated by the output of a producer task and contains output metadata (say a URL) for the consumer task to read the data. This event is received by the framework and routed to the input of the consumer task by utilizing the connection information specified by the edge. If a task input has

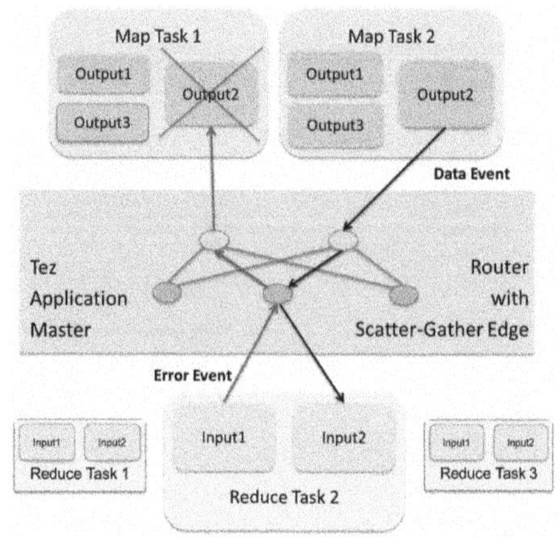

Figure 5: Events used to route metadata between application IOs and error notifications from applications to the framework

an error while reading its data then it can send an ErrorEvent to the framework. Based on such error events, Tez could re-execute the producer task to re-generate the data. Other events could be used to send statistics, progress etc. Event based communication also provides the flexibility to add more entities and communication channels without changing the interaction model or APIs. Tez only routes the events. Each event has an opaque binary payload that is interpreted by the sender and receiver to exchange control metadata. Events flow to and from tasks to the orchestrator on every task heartbeat. Event transfer latency depends on the heartbeat latency and processing latency at the orchestrator. These latencies increase in proportion to the size of the job as they depend on the number of concurrent connections and event load supported by the orchestrator. If control plane events lie on the data plane critical path then they would negatively affect application latency but if they are used only for data plane setup then Tez would not introduce any additional latency on the data plane for low latency applications.

3.4 Vertex Manager: dynamically adapting the execution

As motivated earlier, data processing clusters have variability in compute capacity or data distribution (where data is stored on physical nodes) that applications may consider to plan their work. Data dependent actions like sample based range partitioning or optimizations like partition pruning need the ability to change the DAG on the fly. It is not possible to encode all such current and future graph re-configurations statically, nor can this be done by Tez itself (as it requires too much domain knowledge). Thus Tez needs to allow the application to make such decisions at runtime and coordinate with Tez to dynamically adapt the DAG and its execution. This is enabled via the VertexManager abstraction, similar to [24].

Runtime Graph Re-configuration. When constructing the DAG, each vertex can be associated with a VertexManager. The VertexManager is responsible for vertex re-configuration during DAG execution. The orchestration framework contains various state machines that control the life-cycle of vertices, tasks etc. and the vertex state machine is designed to interact with the VertexManager during state transitions. The VertexManager is provided a context object that notifies it about state changes like task completions etc. Using the context object, the VertexManager can make changes to its own vertex's state. Among other things, the VertexManager can

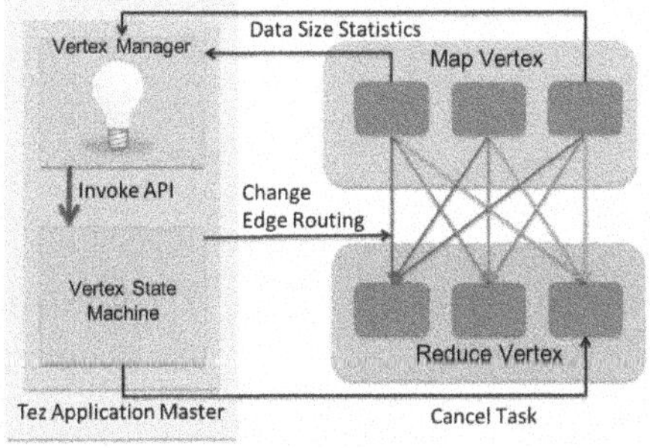

Figure 6: DAG reconfiguration by VertexManager to apply partition cardinality estimated at runtime

control the vertex parallelism, the configuration payloads of the inputs, processors and outputs, the edge properties and scheduling of tasks. As with other entities there is a VertexManager API that can be implemented by applications to customize the vertex execution. Using the same API, Tez comes with some built-in VertexManagers. If a VertexManager is not specified in the DAG, then Tez will pick one of these built-in implementations based on the vertex characteristics.

Automatic Partition Cardinality Estimation. As an example of a runtime optimization, we present a solution to a well-known problem in MapReduce about determining the correct number of tasks in the reduce phase. This number typically depends on the size of the data being shuffled from the mappers to the reducers and is accurately available only at runtime. Shuffle is the term used to describe the cross-network read and aggregation of partitioned input done prior to invoking the reduce operation. In Tez, the ShuffleVertexManager can be used to control the vertices that are reading shuffled data. The tasks producing the data to be shuffled, send data statistics to the ShuffleVertexManager using VertexManager events. As visualized in Figure 6, the ShuffleVertexManager gathers these statistics to calculate the total data size and estimate the correct number of reducers to read that data using a per-reducer desired data size heuristic. Since the number of reducers essentially represents the partition cardinality, this solution can be generalized to estimating the optimal number of partitions at runtime (e.g. partitions participating in a distributed join operation).

Scheduling Optimizations. VertexManagers also control the scheduling of tasks in their vertex. Typically, tasks should be started after their input data is ready. However, if the tasks can proceed meaningfully with partial input then they could be started out of order and use any free compute capacity. The shuffle operation mentioned above is an example of a case where partial inputs can be read by tasks pro-actively. This is an expensive data transfer across the network and starting early can help hide its latency by overlapping it with the completion of tasks that will produce the remaining input. Out of order scheduling can result in scheduling deadlocks in a resource constrained cluster where an out of order task ends up blocking one of its input tasks because it has occupied resources in the cluster. Tez has built-in deadlock detection and preemption to take care of such situations. It will use the DAG dependency to detect tasks running out of order and preempt them to resolve the deadlock.

3.5 Data Source Initializer

In Tez we have modeled data sources as first class entities in our design. The first step in a DAG usually involves reading initial input from data sources like distributed file systems, and typically is the largest in terms of resource consumption. Hence, a good or bad decision at this step can significantly improve or degrade performance. A data source in a DAG can be associated with a DataSourceInitializer that is invoked by the framework before running tasks for the vertex reading that data source. The initializer has the opportunity to use accurate information available at runtime to determine how to optimally read the input. Like the VertexManager, the initializer can also send and receive events from other entities. It also has access to cluster information via its framework context object. Based on these and other sources of information, the initializer can configure the task inputs or notify the vertex manager about vertex re-configurations (E.g. the optimal parallelism needed to process the input).

As an example, we will present a Hive dynamic partition pruning use case. It often happens that a data source will be read and subsequently joined on some key. If the join key space is known then we could only read a subset of the data that is relevant to the join. Sometimes this metadata is only available at runtime after inspecting the data in a different sub-graph of the DAG. Hive uses InputInitializer events to send this metadata from tasks in the other vertices to the initializer of the data source. The initializer uses that metadata to decide the relevant subset of data to read. This can lead to large performance gains depending on the join selectivity.

The above discussion has been a broad overview of the architecture and features in Tez. More details about the semantics around the API's and user defined entities is available in the API documentation on the project website [2]

4. IMPLEMENTATION AND PRACTICAL CONSIDERATIONS

We now turn to describing how the architecture of the previous section is instantiated in YARN, and discuss in more details efficiency and production-readiness aspects of Tez. From an engineering perspective this is where much of our effort was devoted, and what makes Tez a useful building block for data-processing engines.

4.1 Implementation in YARN

The Apache Tez project consists of 3 main parts:

- API library: This provides the DAG and Runtime APIs and other client side libraries to build applications
- Orchestration framework: This has been implemented as a YARN Application Master [32] (hereafter referred to as AM) to execute the DAG in a Hadoop cluster via YARN
- Runtime library: This provides implementations of various inputs and outputs that can be used out of the box.

Typical Tez Application Lifecycle. A Tez based application is written using the API library by constructing the DAG representing the application logic. Typically, higher level applications like Apache Pig construct DAGs on the fly by encoding their native language constructs into Tez DAGs. Since Tez is designed to operate in Hadoop clusters we have provided implementations of inputs and outputs to standard storage services present in all Hadoop clusters - HDFS [16] for reliable data storage and YARN Shuffle Service

[32] for temporary data storage. Applications that use only these services, need to implement just their processors to get up and running. Typically applications create a generic processor host that can be configured to execute DAG dependent operators. Tez inputs and outputs are based on the key-value data format for ease of use within the key-value dominated Hadoop ecosystem of projects like Apache Hive, Pig etc., and can be extended to other data formats. The DAG is then submitted to a YARN cluster using the Tez client library. YARN launches the Tez Application Master (AM - a per-application controller) to orchestrate the DAG execution. The DAG executed by the AM is typically a logical DAG that describes the data flow graph. The AM expands this graph to incorporate task parallelism per vertex. It does this using the input initializers and vertex managers specified in the DAG. The AM then requests YARN for resources to run the tasks from different vertices. YARN responds in the form of containers. A container is a unit of resource allocation on a cluster node. The AM launches tasks on these containers and routes control events. Tasks are typically executed in their dependency order and the DAG completes when all its tasks complete. The AM logs tracing and metadata information for monitoring and debugging.

By leveraging existing libraries and services from YARN and MapReduce, we have been able to quickly build on top of several man-years of production ready code for security and high volume network data shuffling; and integrate with the proven resource sharing and multi-tenancy model in YARN. Thus, applications built using Tez will benefit from all these without expending further effort.

4.2 Execution Efficiency

The YARN implementation of the orchestration framework is built with execution efficiency and performance in mind and incorporates well known ideas learned over the years in various distributed data processing systems.

Locality Aware Scheduling. Scheduling processing close to the data location is important for large-scale data-processing [21, 32]. Tez tries to run tasks close to their input data location. Location may be specified statically during DAG creation but is typically determined at runtime. The tasks that read from initial input data sources typically get locality information from their data sources while intermediate task locality is inferred from their source tasks and edge connections. E.g. tasks with scatter-gather inputs have no specific locality but may prefer to run close to the larger input data shards. 1-1 edges specify strict locality relationships between their source and destination tasks. Since getting perfect locality may not be guaranteed in a busy cluster, the framework automatically relaxes locality from node to rack and so on with delay scheduling [36] used to add a wait period before each relaxation.

Speculation. Large clusters can have heterogeneous hardware and varying loads and hardware-aging. This can lead to environment induced task slowdowns. Such slow tasks are termed stragglers and launching a clone of such tasks is typically used to mitigate their effects on latency [21]. Tez monitors task progress and tries to detect straggler tasks that may be running much slower than other tasks in the same vertex. Upon detecting such a task, a speculative attempt may be launched that runs in parallel with the original task and races it to completion. If the speculative attempt finishes first then it is successful in improving the completion time.

Container Reuse. Recall that the Tez AM runs tasks in containers allocated to it by YARN. When a task completes, the AM has an option to return the container to YARN and ask for another container with different capabilities or locality. However, each container allocation cycle has overheads associated with resource negotiation from YARN as well as launching the container process. This overhead can be minimized by re-using the container to run other pending tasks that match the resource allocation and locality of that container. When there are no such matching tasks, the Tez AM releases the idle containers back to YARN in return for new resources with different capabilities. In the Java world, this reuse has the additional benefit of giving the JVM optimizer a longer time to observe and optimize the hot code paths leading to further performance benefits [1].

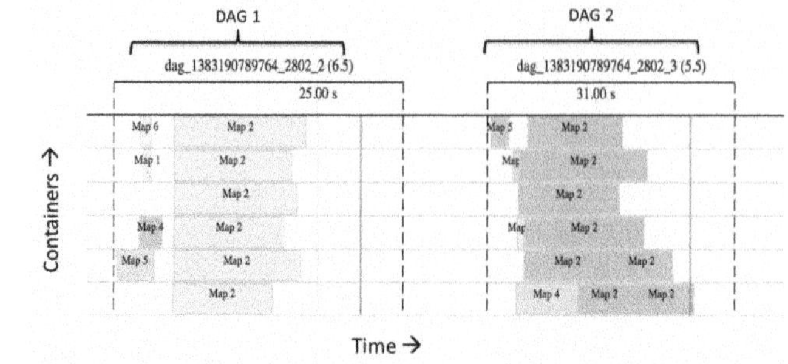

Figure 7: Execution trace of 2 DAGs executed in the same Tez Session. Containers are re-used by tasks within a DAG and across DAGs. Cross DAG re-use happens only in session mode.

Session. A session takes the concept of container reuse one step further. A Tez AM can be run in session mode in which it can run a sequence of DAGs submitted to it by the client. This allows tasks from multiple DAGs to reuse containers and leads to further efficiencies and performance gains. In addition, a session can be pre-warmed by requesting the AM to launch containers before the first DAG is ready to execute. These pre-warmed containers can execute some pre-determined code to allow JVM optimizations to kick in. This extends the benefits of container reuse to the first DAG that gets submitted to the session. E.g. Apache Hive and Pig use the session mode to run multiple drill-down queries in the same session for performance benefits. Tez sessions also enable iterative processing to be performed efficiently. Each iteration can be represented as a new DAG and submitted to a shared session for efficient execution using pre-warmed session resources. Figure 7 shows the trace of a Tez session with containers shared across tasks of multiple DAGs.

Shared Object Registry. Tez extends the benefits of container reuse to the application by providing an in-memory cache of objects that can be populated by a task and then re-used by subsequent tasks. The lifecycle of objects in the cache can be limited to a vertex, a DAG or the session and is managed by the framework. It can be used to avoid re-computing results when possible. E.g. Apache Hive populates the hash table for the smaller side of a map join in Hive parlance (broadcast join). Once a hash table has been constructed by a join task, other join tasks don't need to re-compute it and improve their performance.

4.3 Production Readiness

While performance and efficiency are important for a framework such as Tez, we cannot ignore the standard abilities that are prerequisites for a production ready and dependable framework for large scale data processing. A plethora of entities use technologies like Apache Hive, Pig and other commercial software like Cascading to run mission critical operations. If they are to confidently build using Apache Tez, then items like fault tolerance, security and multi-tenancy become necessary requirements. Fortunately, Tez has been able to build on top of proven and tested platforms like Hadoop YARN and MapReduce and draws from their strengths for achieving some of these abilities. The YARN integration exemplifies the specialized code implemented in Tez that can be leveraged by higher-level engines using Tez.

Multi-Tenancy. Data processing clusters are becoming increasingly large and sharing their capital expenditure among multiple applications and users is essential from a capex point of view [32]. Applications must be written with such sharing and cooperative behavior in mind. The discrete task based processing model in Tez lends itself nicely to such cooperative behavior. Short lived ephemeral tasks allow resources to be periodically released by Tez applications so that they can be allocated to other users and applications as deemed appropriate by the cluster resource allocation policy. This also enables higher resource utilization by transferring resources from applications that don't need them to applications that do.

This is where engines that effectively deploy services daemons suffer from a drawback. Typically, the service daemons have to pre-allocate a large share of resources that cannot be shared with other applications. For better utilization, these daemons try to run multiple 'tasks' concurrently but that is not useful when there isn't enough load on the system, besides introducing the possibility of interference between concurrent tasks. With Tez, since each task runs in its own container process, the resource allocations are much finer grained. This improves utilization (by reducing allocated resources that are idle) and also provides process-based resource isolation (for CPU/memory etc.). This also provides resource elasticity to Tez applications in that they can scale up to utilize as much resources as the cluster can spare to speed up job execution time while gracefully degrading performance but still completing the job when resources are scarce. To be clear, this discussion about daemon based designs is in the specific context of ephemeral data processing jobs. There are many contexts like data storage, web services, PAAS applications etc. where a long running shared service provided by a daemon based engine is suitable.

Security. Security is real concern with the variety and volume of data stored in modern data processing clusters. Hadoop has built-in Kerberos and token based authentication and access control [32] and Tez natively integrates with the Hadoop security framework to provide the application with secure access. In addition to that, the inputs and outputs provided with Tez support encryption for data read across the network. Security is a real concern with the variety of data stored and concurrent access from multiple users. Being outside the data plane reduces the contribution of Tez in the threat surface of the application. The only interaction between Tez and the app is control metadata routed via events by Tez. This metadata is presented to Tez as an opaque binary payload and thus can be protected by the app by encryption or other techniques as deemed necessary. In the control plane, secure Hadoop provides Kerberos and token based authentication for applications to access storage or compute resources and Tez integrates with the secure API's exposed by Hadoop. Tez has some built-in input and output libraries for HDFS and local storage. In a secure Hadoop cluster, these libraries use HDFS token based authentication to access the data. In a secure cluster local data is written in the OS security content of the user and read via secure SSL channel provided by the YARN Shuffle Service.

Another aspect of security is isolation between tasks running on the same machine but belonging to different users. YARN provides this security isolation between containers by running the containers in the security context of the application user. Due to its fine-grained, ephemeral task model, Tez can leverage this container security by running tasks for single user in the containers of an application, thus guaranteeing user level isolation. This is much harder to achieve when using application engines that deploy service daemons. The daemons need to run tasks from different users in the same daemon process, making security isolation difficult or impossible. To work around this, multiple instances of the service daemons need to be launched (one per user) and that may reduce resource utilization, as described above. We believe that the fine-grained, ephemeral task model of Tez makes it more suitable for secure and multi-tenant YARN clusters.

Fault Tolerance. Failures are a norm in clusters of commodity hardware. Failures can be on the compute nodes or the network. Tez provides robust fault tolerance against failures using task re-execution as a means of recovering from errors. When a task fails due to machine errors, it is re-executed on a different machine. Task re-execution based fault tolerance depends on deterministic and side-effect free task execution. Being side-effect free allows a task to be executed multiple times. Being deterministic, guarantees that if identical code is executed on identical input data then it will produce identical output data for each execution. These enable the system to safely re-execute tasks to recover from failures and data loss. Since the outputs are identical, the already completed consumer tasks of that output do not need to be re-executed. This limits the amount of re-execution and reduces the cost of failures.

Since Tez is not on the data plane, it exposes an InputReadError event that task inputs can use to notify Tez about loss of intermediate data. Using the DAG dependency information Tez can determine which task outputs produced the missing data and re-execute that task to regenerate the data. It may happen that the re-executed task also reports an input error. This would cause Tez to go up one more step in the DAG dependency and so on, until it has found stable intermediate data. The edge API allows for the specification of intermediate data resiliency such that Tez can be informed that a given edge data has been reliably stored, thus creating an barrier to cascading failures. Tez built-in input/output libraries leverage heuristics inherited from MapReduce for mitigating and recovering from network errors and cascading failures when shuffling large volumes of data. E.g. temporary network errors are retried with back-off before reporting an error event. Partially fetched data is cached and the consumer task stays alive until the remaining missing data is regenerated. The Tez AM periodically checkpoints its state. If the node, that is running the Tez AM, has a failure then YARN will restart the AM on another node and the AM can recover its state from the checkpoint data.

Tez tightly integrates with YARN to handle planned and unplanned cluster outages. It listens to notifications about machine loss or decommissioning and pro-actively re-executes the tasks that were completed on such machines. This decreases the chance that consumers of those task outputs will fail. Tez also understands actions taken by YARN such as preempting containers for capacity re-balancing or terminating badly behaving containers and responds to those actions appropriately.

Limitations. The current implementation of Tez is Java based and thus we are limited to JVM based applications right now. The Tez based MapReduce implementation has successfully executed non-JVM user code using MapReduce's approach of forking off non-Java code. However, a more native Tez support would need non-Java APIs for writing IPOs and executors to support them.

Work is in progress to have a portable text based representation of the DAG API to enable non-Java compilers that target Tez. Tez can only be used in a YARN based Hadoop cluster because the current scheduling implementation has been written for YARN. Our recent work to enable developer debugging capability has abstracted out the dependence on a cluster. Extensions of that work could enable Tez to utilize other systems for execution. The current fault tolerance model depends on the assumption that intermediate task outputs are localized to the machine on which the task ran. Thus intermediate data loss causes re-execution of the task on a different machine. This may not be true of all IOs. e.g. if data is being streamed directly over the network. Also, such network streaming may result in collapse of the connected streaming sub-graph, which would need extensions of the fault tolerance model to handle such correlated failures.

5. APPLICATIONS & ADOPTION

In this section we will outline projects that have been updated or prototyped to use the Tez framework to run on YARN. These projects represent a significant variety of application types and help show the applicability of the Tez APIs for modeling and building high-performance data processing applications.

5.1 Apache MapReduce

MapReduce is a simple yet powerful means of scalable data processing that can be credited with ushering in the era of inexpensive hyper-scale data processing. At its core, it is a simple 2 vertex connected graph. In Tez, it can be represented with a map vertex and a reduce vertex that are connected using a scatter-gather edge. Tez has a built-in MapProcessor and a ReduceProcessor that run in the respective Map and Reduce vertices and provide the MapReduce interface functionality. Thus MapReduce can be easily written as a Tez based application and, in fact, the Tez project comes with a built-in implementation of MapReduce. Any MapReduce based application can be executed without change using the Tez version of MapReduce by simply changing a MapReduce configuration on a YARN cluster.

5.2 Apache Hive

Apache Hive is one of the most popular SQL-based declarative query engines in the Hadoop ecosystem. It used to translate queries written in HiveQL (a SQL-like dialect) to MapReduce jobs and run them on a Hadoop cluster. Like other SQL engines, Hive translates the queries into optimized query trees. Often these translations to MapReduce were inefficient due to the restricted expressiveness of MapReduce. These trees translate directly to DAGs specified using the Tez DAG API. Thus they can be represented efficiently in Tez. In addition, Hive uses custom edges (written to the Tez API) to perform sophisticated joins that were hitherto very difficult to do. E.g. In a join variant called Dynamically Partitioned Hash Join; Hive uses a custom vertex manager to determine which subsets of data shards to join with each other and creates a custom edge that routes the appropriate shards to their consumer tasks. While these query planning improvements provide algorithmic performance gains, Hive benefits from the execution efficiencies (Section 4.2) to get significant performance benefits out of the box. This integration has been implemented by the Apache Hive community with Hive 0.13 being the first release of Hive to have Tez integration[7]. Further Tez-based optimizations (like dynamic partition pruning) have been released in Hive 0.14 with more work planned in future releases.

5.3 Apache Pig

Apache Pig provides a procedural scripting language (named PigLatin) that is designed to write complex batch processing ETL pipelines. The procedural nature of PigLatin allows the creation of complex DAGs with vertices having multiple outputs. In MapReduce, applications could write only 1 output and thus were forced to use creative workarounds like tagging the data or writing side-effect outputs. Being able to model multiple outputs explicitly via the Tez APIs allows the planning and execution code in Pig to be clean and maintainable. Pig supports joins with data-skew detection and this was earlier done by running different MapReduce jobs to read and sample the data, then create histograms based on the samples on the client machine and finally run another job that uses the histogram to read and partition the data. This complex workflow of jobs can now be represented as a sub-graph of any Pig DAG when using Tez. The samples are collected in a histogram vertex that calculates the histogram. The histogram is sent via an event to a custom vertex manager that re-configures the partition vertex to perform the optimal partitioning. Pig developers from Yahoo, Netflix, LinkedIn, Twitter and Hortonworks came together to implement this integration. Pig 0.14 is the first release of Pig to support Tez based execution in addition to MapReduce[8].

5.4 Apache Spark

Apache Spark [38] is a new compute engine that provides an elegant language integrated Scala API for distributed data processing. It specializes in machine learning but the API lends itself to mixed workloads and pipeline processing. Data distribution metadata is captured at the language layer in a concept called Resilient Distributed Dataset (RDD) [37] and this metadata is used during compilation to construct a DAG of tasks that perform the distributed computation. Spark comes with its own processing engine service to execute these tasks. We were able to encode the post-compilation Spark DAG into a Tez DAG and run it successfully in a YARN cluster that was not running the Spark engine service. User defined Spark code is serialized into a Tez processor payload and injected into a generic Spark processor that deserializes and executes the user code. This allows unmodified Spark programs to run on YARN using Spark's own runtime operators. Apache Hive and Pig were already designed to translate to MapReduce and the translation to Tez is an evolutionary step. Modeling a net new engine like Spark on YARN using Tez presents a strong proof of the generality and modeling power of the Tez framework. Tez sessions also enable Spark machine learning iterations to run efficiently by submitting the per-iteration DAGs to a shared Tez session. This work is an experimental prototype and not part of the Spark project[22].

5.5 Apache Flink

Apache Flink [5] is a new project in the Apache community with roots in the Stratosphere research project of the TU Berlin data management community. It is a parallel processing engine that provides programming APIs in Java and Scala, a cost-based optimizer for these APIs, as well as its own execution engine. Flink is another example of a new platform that could be integrated with YARN using the Tez framework instead of running it as a standalone service. The post-optimization DAG is translated to a Tez DAG for this integration. While Apache Hive and Pig work on key-value data formats and could use the built-in Tez inputs and outputs, Flink keeps intermediate data in a custom binary format. This format can be used to perform operations like group by etc. without much deserialization overhead. The pluggable and composable Tez task model allowed Flink to incorporate its runtime operators and binary format inside Tez tasks, thus allowing unmodified programs to run on

YARN using Flink's native runtime model. This work is currently in progress in the Apache Flink developer community[6].

5.6 Commercial Adoption

The customizability and performance focused design of Tez has resulted in rapid uptake from commercial software projects. Concurrent Inc. supports an open source language integrated API in Java, called Cascading, for distributed data processing. Cascading has been updated to run on YARN using the Tez framework with promising performance results. Scalding is a Scala dialect over Cascading that automatically gets the benefits of Tez via Cascading. Cascading 3.0 is currently available as a developer preview and integrates with Tez [3]. Datameer provides a visual analytics platform that uses Tez to run optimized analytics queries on YARN. It also uses Tez sessions to maintain a query service pool for fast response times in a secure, multi-tenant environment. Datameer 5.0 is the first release that uses Tez [33]. Release 8 of Syncsort's Hadoop product, DMX-h, shipped with an intelligent execution layer to enable transparent targeting of execution frameworks other than Mapreduce. Following this, they are in the process of integrating with Tez as one of their supported execution frameworks [11].

5.7 Deployments

Apache Tez has been deployed across multiple organizations and on a variety of cluster configurations. Most prominently, Yahoo! has deployed Tez on multiple clusters ranging from 100s to 1000s of nodes to run Hive and Pig with Tez [35]. LinkedIn has completed migration of all their Hadoop clusters to YARN and is running Hive and Pig with Tez. Microsoft Azure has deployed Hive with Tez as part of its cloud Hadoop offering [10]. Hortonworks has provided Tez as a part of its Hadoop distribution since April 2014 and is seeing rapid adoption of Tez by its install base. At the time of publication, nearly 100 Hortonworks customers have explored the capabilities of Tez.

The growing adoption of Tez we described in this section provides a qualitative metric of the project success. In the next section, we turn to the experiment results obtained as a result of these applications being integrated with Tez.

6. EXPERIMENTAL RESULTS

We devote this section to present several experiments, showcasing how Tez-based implementations of Hive, Pig and Spark on YARN outperform their original implementation on YARN. The experiments are derived from both standard benchmarks, and production workloads.

6.1 Hive 0.14 Performance Tests

Hive utilizes various features available in Tez, such as broadcast edges, runtime re-configuration and custom vertex managers, to achieve a better overall execution of the user's processing goals. In conjunction with Hive 0.14's Cost Based Optimizer, Tez enables the execution of bushy join plans which can take advantage of intermediate broadcast joins. The pluggable task model of Tez allows Hive to use custom vectorized operators throughout the processing. Custom edges are used to perform efficient Hive sort-merge-bucket joins. In Figure 8 we show the impact of these optimizations on a TPC-DS derived Hive workload, run at 30 terabytes scale on a 20 node cluster with 16 cores, 256Gb RAM and 6 x 4Tb drives per node. The Tez-based implementation substantially outperforms the traditional MapReduce based one.

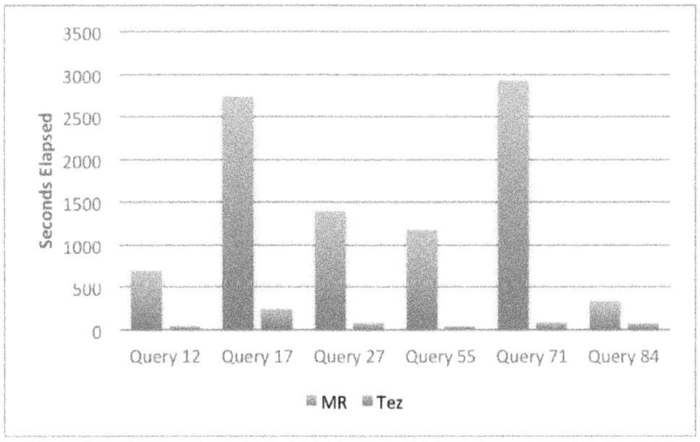

Figure 8: Hive: TPC-DS derived workload (30TB scale)

6.2 Yahoo Hive Scale Tests

In Figure 9 we show a comparative scale test of Hive on Tez, with a TPC-H derived Hive workload [35], at 10 terabytes scale on a 350 node research cluster with 16 cores, 24Gb RAM and 6 x 2Tb drives per node. This was presented at Hadoop Summit 2014, San Jose. This shows that Tez based implementation outperforms the MapReduce based implementation at large cluster scale.

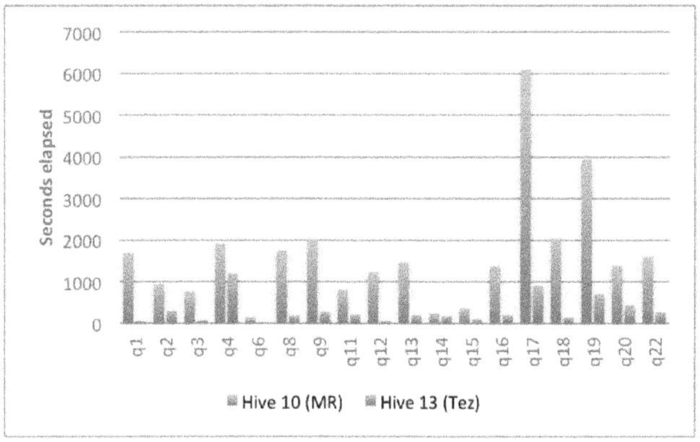

Figure 9: Hive: TPC-H derived workload at Yahoo (10TB scale)

6.3 Yahoo Pig Production Tests

At Yahoo!, Pig on Tez was tested on large production ETL pig jobs that run in the order of minutes to hours. To test different aspects of scale and features of the implementation, the pig scripts run had varying characteristics like terabytes of input, 100K+ tasks, complex DAGs with 20 to 50 vertices and doing a combination of various operations like group by, union, distinct, join, order by, etc. The tests were run on different production clusters where data resided and already running regular jobs with average utilization of 60-70%. The cluster had 4,200 servers, 46 PB HDFS storage and 90TB aggregate memory. Most data nodes were with 12/24G RAM, 2 x Xeon 2.40GHz, 6 x 2TB SATA on Hadoop 2.5, RHEL 6.5, JDK 1.7 There were performance improvements of 1.5 to 2x compared to MapReduce keeping all the configuration (memory, shuffle configuration, etc.) same as MapReduce. Figure 10 shows the results of these tests.

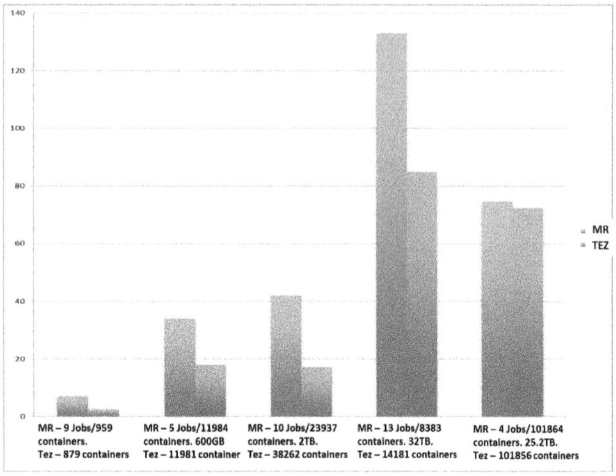

Figure 10: Pig workloads at Yahoo

6.4 Pig KMeans Iteration Tests

As noted in Section 4.2, Tez session and container-reuse features work in favor of fast iterative workloads, which require consecutive DAGs to execute over the same data-set. In Figure 11 we show performance improvements for a K-means iterative PIG script [20], run for 10, 50 and 100 iterations against a 10,000 row input dataset on a single node. This was presented at the Hadoop Summit 2014, San Jose.

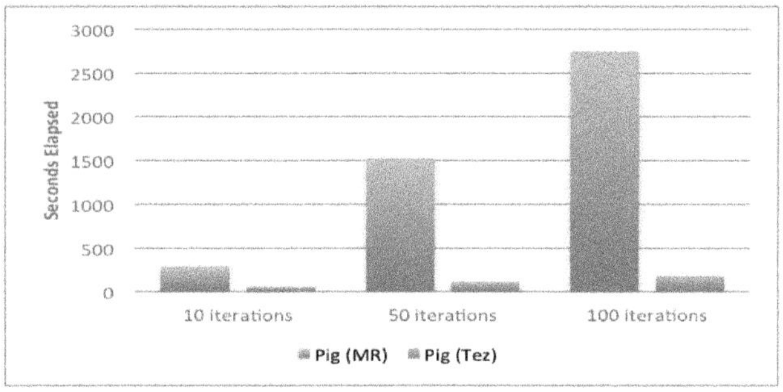

Figure 11: Pig iteration workload (k-means)

6.5 Spark Multi-Tenancy on YARN Tests

As explained in Section 4.3, Tez's ephemeral task based model is better for multi-tenancy and resource-sharing. This is demonstrated in Figure 12 by comparing service-based vs Tez-based implementations of Spark on YARN. The Tez based implementation releases idle resources that get assigned to other jobs that need them, thus speeding them up, as shown in Figure 13, while the service-based implementation holds on to resources for the life of the service. For the experiment, we have a 5-user concurrency test [22] of partitioning a TPC-H lineitem data-set along the L SHIPDATE column, on a 20 node cluster. The tests were run across data sets which correspond to 100 GB, 200 GB, 500 Gb and 1 TB warehouse scale factors. The cluster used to run this workload was identical to the Hive 0.14 benchmarks, having 16 cores, 256Gb of RAM and 6 x 4Tb disks per node.

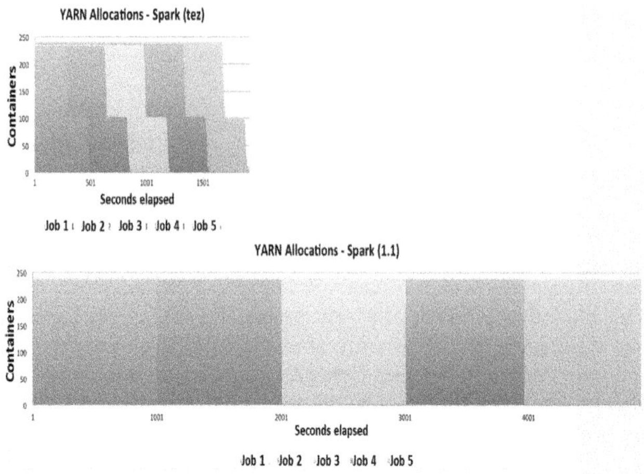

Figure 12: Sharing a cluster across 5 concurrent Spark jobs with Tez (identical x-axis time scales)

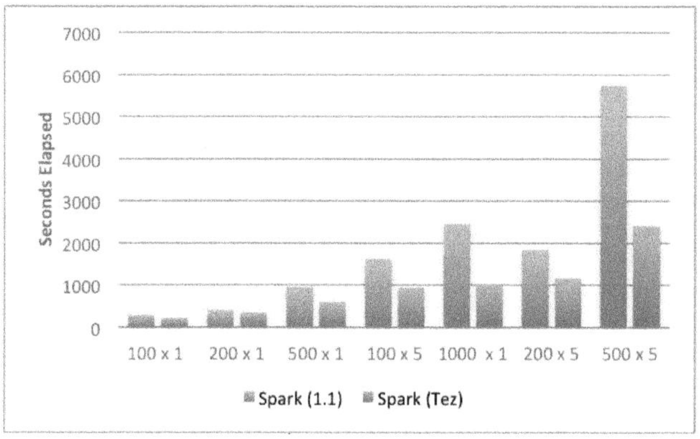

Figure 13: Spark Multi-Tenancy on YARN Latency Results

7. OPEN SOURCE AND FUTURE WORK

Apache Tez has been developed as an open source project under the Apache Software Foundation. It's a community driven project with contributors from Microsoft, Yahoo, Hortonworks, LinkedIn among others as well as individual enthusiasts. The source code for the project is available at http://git.apache.org/tez.git and the project website is at [2]

The open architecture of Tez and its fundamentally customizable design lends it to becoming a platform for experimentation and innovation. We believe that the current use cases built on Tez are only the initial steps of a longer journey. There is considerable interest in a variety of areas to improve and leverage Tez. Progressive query optimization which allows a complex and large query to be executed partially and optimized incrementally as the query proceeds. Apache Hive [30] and Apache Calcite [17] are working together on materialized views for speeding up common sub-queries. We want to provide deep integration with in-memory storage capabilities being added to HDFS [12] so that Tez applications can benefit from in-memory computing. Tez currently supports Java applications and extending it to support other languages would widen the scope of applications built using Tez. Another area of interest is tooling for debugging failure and performance performance bottlenecks. Increasingly, geographical distribution and legal/privacy requirements are making cross data-center job execution important [34]. Improving the Tez orchestration and API to model such jobs may help in executing them efficiently. The above are only a few of the many possibilities in which Tez may be evolved or used by academic and commercial communities. Many runtime optimizations are also in the works. E.g. automatically choosing optimal data transport mechanisms like in-memory data for machine co-located tasks or using a reliable store for outputs of extremely long tasks so that their outputs are safeguarded against loss. An tactical idea is to create tooling that enables a full MapReduce workflow to be stitched into a single Tez DAG. This would enable legacy MapReduce workflows to easily use the MapReduce im

8. RELATED WORK

Apache Tez has been fortunate to learn from the development and experiences of similar systems such as Dryad, Hyracks and Nephele [24, 15, 14]. All of them share the concept of modeling data processing as DAGs with vertices representing application logic and edges or channels representing data transfer. Tez makes this more fine-grained by adding the concepts of inputs, processor and outputs to formally define the tasks executing the DAGs, leading to clear separation of concerns and allowing pluggable task composition. All of them participate to varied extents in the data plane and define some form of data format, which allows applications to define custom formats that derive from the base definition. All of them define on-disk, over-network and in-memory communication channels. Tez, on the other hand, does not define any data format and is not part of the data plane at all. On a similar note, Hyracks defines an operator model for execution that allows it to understand the data flow better for scheduling. Tez treats processors as black boxes so that the application logic can be completely decoupled from the framework. Nephele is optimized for cloud environments where it can elastically increase or decrease resources and choose appropriate virtual machines. Tez also enables resource elasticity by acquiring and releasing resources in YARN. Dryad and Tez share the concept of vertex managers for dynamic graph re-configurations. Tez takes this concept a step further by formalizing an API that allows the managers to be written without knowing the internals of the framework and also defining an event based communication mechanism that enables application code in tasks to communicate with application code in vertex managers in order to actuate the re-configurations. In addition, Tez adds the concept of input initializers to formally model primary data sources and apply runtime optimizations while reading them. Dryad schedules tasks when all the inputs of the tasks are ready to be consumed, to prevent scheduling deadlocks. Tez allows out of order execution for performance reasons and has built-in preemption to resolve scheduling deadlocks. Overall, Tez differs from these systems in its modeling capabilities and the design goal of being a library to build engines rather than being an engine by itself. MapReduce is, of course, the incumbent engine in the Hadoop ecosystem. Tez subsumes the MapReduce APIs such that it is possible to write a fully functional MapReduce application using Tez.

Dremel [26] is a processing framework for interactive analysis of large data sets based on multi-level execution trees that is optimized for aggregation queries and has motivated systems like Presto [9] and Apache Drill [23]. These, and other SQL query engines like Impala [25] or Apache Tajo [18], differ from Tez by being engines optimized for specific processing domains whereas Tez is a library to build data processing applications. Spark [38] is a new general purpose data processing engine. It exposes a Resilient Distributed Dataset (RDD) [37] based computation model that eventually gets executed on an in-memory storage and compute engine. Tez, again differs being a library and not a general purpose engine. Tez does not provide any storage service but applications can use existing in-memory stores, e.g. HDFS memory storage [12], to get the advantage of in-memory computing. The Spark notion of using RDDs as a means of implicitly capturing lineage dependency between steps of processing can be related to capturing that same dependency explicitly via defining the DAG using Tez APIs.

An important category of systems to compare against are other frameworks to build YARN-applications. The two most relevant in this space are Apache REEF [19] and Apache Twill [31]. These systems focus on a much broader class of applications (including services), than Tez, and thus provide a lower-level API. Tez focuses on supporting data-flow driven applications, and thus consciously chooses to provide a structured DAG-based control-flow.

9. CONCLUSIONS

Today, Hadoop is a booming ecosystem for large-scale data processing, blessed with an ever growing set of application frameworks, providing diverse abstractions to process data. We recognize that this is invaluable, yet we highlight substantial concerns of fragmentation and repeated work, as each application framework solves similar fundamental problems over and over again.

To address this issue we present Apache Tez, an *open-source framework designed to build data-flow driven processing engines.* Tez provides a scaffolding and libraries to facilitate the design and implementation of DAG-centric data processing applications, and focuses on re-use, while balancing customizability of the performance critical data plane. Tez makes a conscious effort to enable dynamic optimizations, such as partition pruning. Besides these key architectural choices, what sets Tez apart from other attempts of unifying frameworks is a sizeable open-source community, that is pushing Tez towards becoming the framework of choice for building DAG-orientied data processing engines. As of today, the most popular projects (Hive, Pig and Cascading) have integrated with Tez. We demonstrated experimentally that the Tez-based incarnations of these systems deliver substantial performance benefits beyond the qualitative argument of leveraging common functionalities.

We argue that the standardization we are promoting can foster even faster innovation, and enable integration plays that would be otherwise cumbersome (e.g., pipelines made up of multiple application frameworks). Tez's customizability and open-source community makes it an ideal playground for research, as novel ideas can be tested, integrated, and gain real-world impact with minimal overhead.

Acknowledgements

Apache Tez is an open source community driven project with contributions gratefully accepted from numerous individuals and organizations. In particular we would like to call out Rajesh Balamohan for keeping a watchful eye on performance and Tassapol Athiapinya and Yesha Vora for testing and system validation. We would like to thank members of other project communities who have helped in adopting and demonstrating the value of Tez. Notably, Gunther Hagleitner and Vikram Dixit for Apache Hive; Rohini Palaniswamy, Cheolsoo Park, Daniel Dai, Olga Natkovich, Mark Wagner and Alex Bain for Apache Pig; Chris Wensel for Cascading; Oleg Zhurakousky for Apache Spark; Kostas Tzoumas and Stephan Ewen for Apache Flink. We are also grateful to Yahoo and Hortonworks for providing experimentation infrastructure. We hope that the innovation platform provided by Tez will lead to further contributions from many more.

10. REFERENCES

[1] Understanding just-in-time compilation and optimization. https://docs.oracle.com/cd/E15289_01/doc.40/e15058/underst_jit.htm.

[2] Apache tez project website, 2014. http://tez.apache.org.

[3] Cascading integration with tez project, 2014. http://www.cascading.org/2014/09/17/cascading-3-0-wip-now-supports-apache-tez.

[4] Cascading: Project website, 2014. http://www.cascading.org.

[5] Flink: apache incubator project (formerly stratosphere), 2014. http://flink.incubator.apache.org/.

[6] Flink integration with tez project jira, 2014. http://issues.apache.org/jira/browse/FLINK-972.

[7] Hive integration with tez project jira, 2014. http://issues.apache.org/jira/browse/HIVE-4660.

[8] Pig integration with tez project jira, 2014. http://issues.apache.org/jira/browse/PIG-3446.

[9] Presto: Distributed sql query engine for big data, 2014. http:/prestodb.io.

[10] What's new in the hadoop cluster versions provided by hdinsight?, 2014. http://azure.microsoft.com/en-us/documentation/articles/hdinsight-component-versioning/.

[11] New syncsort big data software removes major barriers to mainstream apache hadoop adoption, 2015. http://www.syncsort.com/en/About/News-Center/Press-Release/New-Syncsort-Big-Data-Software.

[12] A. Agarwal. https://issues.apache.org/jira/browse/hdfs-5851, 2014. https://issues.apache.org/jira/browse/HDFS-5851.

[13] S. Babu. Towards automatic optimization of mapreduce programs. In *Proceedings of the 1st ACM Symposium on Cloud Computing*, SoCC '10, pages 137–142, New York, NY, USA, 2010. ACM.

[14] D. Battré, S. Ewen, F. Hueske, O. Kao, V. Markl, and D. Warneke. Nephele/PACTs: A programming model and execution framework for web-scale analytical processing. In *SOCC*, 2010.

[15] V. Borkar, M. Carey, R. Grover, N. Onose, and R. Vernica. Hyracks: A flexible and extensible foundation for data-intensive computing. In *ICDE*, 2011.

[16] D. Borthakur. Hdfs architecture guide. *HADOOP APACHE PROJECT http://hadoop. apache. org/common/docs/current/hdfs design. pdf*, 2008.

[17] Calcite developer community (formerly Optiq). Calcite: Apache incubator project, 2014. https://github.com/apache/incubator-calcite.

[18] H. Choi, J. Son, H. Yang, H. Ryu, B. Lim, S. Kim, and Y. D. Chung. Tajo: A distributed data warehouse system on large clusters. In *Data Engineering (ICDE), 2013 IEEE 29th International Conference on*, pages 1320–1323. IEEE, 2013.

[19] B.-G. Chun, T. Condie, C. Curino, C. Douglas, S. Matusevych, B. Myers, S. Narayanamurthy, R. Ramakrishnan, S. Rao, J. Rosen, et al. Reef: Retainable evaluator execution framework. *Proceedings of the VLDB Endowment*, 6(12):1370–1373, 2013.

[20] Daniel Dai and Rohini Palaniswamy. Pig on Tez: Low latency ETL, 2014. http://www.slideshare.net/Hadoop_Summit/pig-on-tez-low-latency-etl-with-big-data/25.

[21] J. Dean and S. Ghemawat. MapReduce: simplified data processing on large clusters. *Commun. ACM*, 51, 2008.

[22] Gopal Vijayaraghavan and Oleg Zhurakousky. Improving Spark for Data Pipelines with Native YARN Integration, 2014. http://bit.ly/1IkZVvP.

[23] M. Hausenblas and J. Nadeau. Apache drill: interactive ad-hoc analysis at scale. *Big Data*, 1(2):100–104, 2013.

[24] M. Isard, M. Budiu, Y. Yu, A. Birrell, and D. Fetterly. Dryad: distributed data-parallel programs from sequential building blocks. *SIGOPS*, 2007.

[25] M. Kornacker, A. Behm, V. Bittorf, and et al. Impala: A modern, open-source sql engine for hadoop. In *CIDR*, 2015.

[26] S. Melnik, A. Gubarev, J. J. Long, G. Romer, S. Shivakumar, M. Tolton, and T. Vassilakis. Dremel: Interactive analysis of web-scale datasets. *Proc. VLDB Endow.*, 3(1-2):330–339, Sept. 2010.

[27] A. C. Murthy, C. Douglas, M. Konar, O. O'Malley, S. Radia, S. Agarwal, and V. KV. Architecture of next generation apache hadoop mapreduce framework. Technical report, Tech. rep., Apache Hadoop, 2011.

[28] C. Olston, B. Reed, U. Srivastava, R. Kumar, and A. Tomkins. Pig latin: a not-so-foreign language for data processing. In *Proceedings of the 2008 ACM SIGMOD international conference on Management of data*, SIGMOD '08, pages 1099–1110, New York, NY, USA, 2008. ACM.

[29] M. Stonebraker, D. Abadi, D. J. DeWitt, S. Madden, E. Paulson, A. Pavlo, and A. Rasin. Mapreduce and parallel dbmss: Friends or foes? *Commun. ACM*, 53(1):64–71, Jan. 2010.

[30] A. Thusoo, J. S. Sarma, N. Jain, Z. Shao, P. Chakka, S. Anthony, H. Liu, P. Wyckoff, and R. Murthy. Hive – a warehousing solution over a map-reduce framework. In *PVLDB*, 2009.

[31] Twill developer community. Twill: Apache incubator project, 2014. http://twill.incubator.apache.org/.

[32] V. K. Vavilapalli, A. C. Murthy, C. Douglas, S. Agarwal, M. Konar, R. Evans, T. Graves, J. Lowe, H. Shah, S. Seth, B. Saha, C. Curino, O. O'Malley, S. Radia, B. Reed, and E. Baldeschwieler. Apache hadoop yarn: Yet another resource negotiator. In *SOCC*, 2013.

[33] P. Voss. The challenge to choosing the "right" execution engine, 2014. http://bit.ly/1wXP9Wp.

[34] A. Vulimiri, C. Curino, B. Godfrey, K. Karanasos, and G. Varghese. Wanalytics: Analytics for a geo-distributed data-intensive world. In *CIDR*, 2015.

[35] Yahoo Hadoop Platforms Team. Yahoo Betting on Apache Hive, Tez, and YARN, 2014. http://yahoodevelopers.tumblr.com/post/85930551108/yahoo-betting-on-apache-hive-tez-and-yarn.

[36] M. Zaharia, D. Borthakur, J. Sen Sarma, K. Elmeleegy, S. Shenker, and I. Stoica. Delay scheduling: a simple technique for achieving locality and fairness in cluster scheduling. In *Proceedings of the 5th European conference on Computer systems*, pages 265–278. ACM, 2010.

[37] M. Zaharia, M. Chowdhury, T. Das, A. Dave, J. Ma, M. McCauley, M. J. Franklin, S. Shenker, and I. Stoica. Resilient distributed datasets: A fault-tolerant abstraction for in-memory cluster computing. In *Proceedings of the 9th USENIX conference on Networked Systems Design and Implementation*, pages 2–2. USENIX Association, 2012.

[38] M. Zaharia, M. Chowdhury, M. J. Franklin, S. Shenker, and I. Stoica. Spark: Cluster computing with working sets. In *Proceedings of the 2Nd USENIX Conference on Hot Topics in Cloud Computing*, HotCloud'10, pages 10–10, Berkeley, CA, USA, 2010. USENIX Association.

Design and Implementation of the LogicBlox System

Molham Aref Balder ten Cate Todd J. Green Benny Kimelfeld Dan Olteanu
Emir Pasalic Todd L. Veldhuizen Geoffrey Washburn
LogicBlox, Inc. *
firstname.lastname@logicblox.com

ABSTRACT

The LogicBlox system aims to reduce the complexity of software development for modern applications which enhance and automate decision-making and enable their users to evolve their capabilities via a "self-service" model. Our perspective in this area is informed by over twenty years of experience building dozens of mission-critical enterprise applications that are in use by hundreds of large enterprises across industries such as retail, telecommunications, banking, and government. We designed and built LogicBlox to be the system we wished we had when developing those applications.

In this paper, we discuss the design considerations behind the LogicBlox system and give an overview of its implementation, highlighting innovative aspects. These include: LogiQL, a unified and declarative language based on Datalog; the use of purely functional data structures; novel join processing strategies; advanced incremental maintenance and live programming facilities; a novel concurrency control scheme; and built-in support for prescriptive and predictive analytics.

Categories and Subject Descriptors

H.2 [**Database Management**]

General Terms

Algorithms, Design, Languages

Keywords

LogicBlox; LogiQL; Datalog; Leapfrog Triejoin; Incremental Maintenance; Transaction Repair; Live Programming; Predictive Analytics

*We wish to acknowledge the many people at LogicBlox who contributed to the development of the LogicBlox 4.X platform and its various components described in this paper. These include Thiago Bartolomei, Martin Bravenboer, Eelco Dolstra, Mihai Gavrilescu, Shan Shan Huang, Wes Hunter, Eugene Kamarchik, Grigoris Karvounarakis, Yannis Kassios, George Kollias, Patrick Lee, Ruy Ley Wild, Rafael Lotufo, Laurent Oget, Søren Olesen, Trevor Paddock, Wael Sinno, Kurt Stirewalt, Zografoula Vagena, Nikolaos Vasiloglou, Rob Vermaas, Daniel Zinn. We also wish to acknowledge the support of our enterprise clients, our partners, our academic collaborators, and DARPA.

SIGMOD'15, May 31–June 4, 2015, Melbourne, Victoria, Australia.

ACM 978-1-4503-2758-9/15/05 ...$15.00.
http://dx.doi.org/10.1145/2723372.2742796.

1. INTRODUCTION

Recently there has been a trend towards specializing database system architectures to particular use cases, such as transactions, analytics, graphs, arrays, documents, or streams [39]. The driving argument behind this trend is performance: specialized transactional or analytical systems, for example, have demonstrated 10-100X speedups over the traditional "OldSQL" database architectures first developed over three decades ago.

At the same time, we are witnessing a trend towards sophisticated applications for enhancing and automating decision making, where application requirements combine aspects of several of these use cases. Moreover, these applications typically have to *evolve* frequently, making *developer productivity* a key concern. In our experience, developing and operating such applications using a "hairball" of specialized databases and programming languages is prohibitively expensive, and end-user maintenance of such applications is impossible.

This observation motivates us to re-examine the argument for specialization in database systems. Are the performance differences observed to date between specialized and general-purpose architectures due to reasons that are fundamentally significant? Or do traditional database architectures simply not embody the best approach to building a general-purpose system?

We believe the latter is the case. To validate our hypothesis, we have built a database system that demonstrates that it is possible to meet the requirements for such applications without unacceptable compromises in performance or scalability. In our experience, the operational and developmental efficiencies gained by using such a system provide a significant reduction in cost and time and overall improvement in the utility, usability, and continued relevance of the application.

1.1 Design Principles

In order to support sophisticated analytical applications, we have expanded our notion of "database system" to include features and capabilities commonly found in programming languages, spreadsheets, statistical systems, and mathematical optimization systems. We also have taken a fresh look at a number of the basic architectural building blocks of a general-purpose database system, challenging some deeply-held beliefs and sacred cows.

A useful analogy to what we are aiming to achieve is that of the smartphone: less than a decade ago, the iPhone redefined what it means to be a phone and subsumed a variety of specialized consumer devices such as cameras, music players, gaming devices, and GPS devices. A smartphone is not the highest resolution camera, the highest fidelity music player, the most accurate GPS device, the most entertaining gaming device, or even the best phone. However, by providing so many capabilities in one device with a unified user experience, the smartphone has made the specialized devices irrelevant for most use cases. Moreover, smartphones have made it possible to build new kinds of applications integrating several of these capabilities in useful and interesting ways.

LogicBlox is a "smart" database system in the same sense that the iPhone was the prototypical "smart" phone. Our aim is not to beat the performance of, say, specialized column stores or in-memory transactional systems; such systems make extreme trade-offs that render them useless outside of their comfort zones. Rather, we aim to come close enough (say, within a factor of 5) to the performance of specialized systems, such that we can satisfy applications needs without sacrificing the flexibility required to cope with mixed workloads and the desire to support application evolution via self-service.

In order to achieve this, we follow a philosophy of "brains before brawn" where we prefer to achieve high performance with better algorithms and data structures before resorting to the use of brute force techniques based on throwing money and hardware at the problem (e.g., by partitioning an application across thousands of cores or loading all application data in memory). We also follow a philosophy of aggressive simplification and consolidation: we aim for a relatively small set of language and system features that compose elegantly in ways that cover a broad range of use cases. This is in contrast to competing systems,which from our point of view do not address the complexity hairball, but simply move it inside the database (e.g., by including separate column-store and row-store sub-engines or requiring the use of several disparate query and scripting languages for application development).

The interplay between a number of key themes characterizes our system architecture:

T1: Simple, declarative, and uniform language. A major goal of our system is to unify the programming model for applications that automate and enhance decision making by using a single, expressive, *declarative* language that can be used by domain experts to understand and evolve the application. To achieve this goal, we have developed *LogiQL*, an extended form of Datalog [29, 2, 19] that is expressive enough to allow coding of entire applications (including queries and views; stored procedures; reactive rules and triggers; and statistical and mathematical modeling).

LogiQL is based on Datalog much in the same way that functional languages are based on the lambda calculus. Datalog is highly declarative, and we believe it strikes the right balance between usability, expressive power, safety, and performance. The resurgence of Datalog in academic circles has been well documented [34, 1, 23]. Other recent industrial systems based on Datalog include Google's Yedalog [13], Datomic[1], and the nascent EVE project[2], funded by Andreessen Horowitz.

As a relatively simple language with a transparent semantics, LogiQL also lends itself well to presentation via alternative "surface syntaxes" which can be more appropriate for a given user community and task at hand. Like SQL and the formula languages found in spreadsheets, LogiQL is first-order and first normal form, making it easier to understand by less technical end-users, who we have previously observed to struggle with higher-order concepts such as passing functions to functions or building list-based data structures.

LogiQL is both expressive and "safe," with natural syntactic fragments capturing important complexity classes such as PTIME. The ability to control the expressive power of the language has useful practical benefits. On the one hand, we can effectively control how much power to put in the hands of end users who would otherwise be able to write non-terminating or otherwise harmful programs, which are especially unpleasant in a shared server environment. On the other hand, the ability to "dial up" the expressive power of the language (all the way to Turing-complete, if need be) makes us confident that we ultimately will not need to have support for imperative and other programming paradigms to handle unanticipated use cases.

The semantics of a LogiQL program is largely independent of the order in which elements of the program appear, and is not deeply tied to a particular physical evaluation strategy. This is a rare property among programming languages: even LogiQL's closest cousin, Prolog, relies on a fixed, top-to-bottom and left-to-write reading of the program. This "disorderliness" of the language (to borrow an apt phrase from the Bloom project [4]) allows great flexibility in optimization and evaluation, and makes LogiQL amenable to high-performance implementations based on memory-hierarchy friendly, set-at-a-time, bottom-up methods, as well as automatic parallelization of queries and views. Moreover, we are able to draw on a rich literature for automatic optimizations and incremental evaluation strategies.

T2: Clear and easy to understand semantics. The semantics of LogiQL is based on ordinary two-valued logic and sets, with fully serializable transactions. Historically, this kind of commitment to simplicity and correctness had to come at the expense of application performance and scalability. We will demonstrate below how we avoid such compromises.

LogiQL encourages a high level of schema normalization, namely sixth normal form (6NF) [11][3]. By encouraging the use of relations with at most one non-key variable, we derive a number of benefits:

1. We avoid the use of nulls, eliminating many hard-to-spot mistakes. The treatment of null values in databases, and the three-valued logic that it carries with it, has long been a source of conceptual problems and awkwardness [27].
2. We improve semantic stability by making the addition or removal of schema information easier as the application evolves. The more changes a user is forced to make to a model or query to cope with an application change, the less stable it is. Adding and removing new entities and relationships to the LogiQL application requires far less surgery and database downtime than is the case when using tables in lower normal forms (i.e., the wide tables used in SQL row stores).
3. We improve the performance of queries that involve a smaller number of attributes than would normally exist in a wide table. The low information entropy of normalized tables allows compression schemes and efficiency approaching that of column stores.
4. We make it easier to support temporal features like transaction time and valid time for each piece of information in the database.
5. We make it easier to support alternative syntaxes. For example, there is a direct mapping between LogiQL and conceptual modeling languages like ORM [22]. It is also straightforward to support function- and array-based language syntax since this highly normalized schema does not require naming of relation variables (i.e., table columns).

Conventional wisdom favors wide relations, motivated by a compulsion to avoid joins whenever possible. Naturally, embracing

[1] `www.datomic.com`

[2] `www.incidentalcomplexity.com`

[3] For example, to store (supplier-name, status, city) data in 6NF, one uses separate supplier-name, status, and city tables, which map identifiers to attribute values.

6NF introduces the challenge that queries often involve a much larger number of relations. Selection conditions in queries typically apply to multiple relations, and simultaneously considering all the conditions that narrow down the result becomes important. These concerns require new kinds of join algorithms. *Leapfrog trie-join* [40], the workhorse join algorithm in our system, lets us support a clean semantics without unacceptable compromises in performance or scalability.

Similarly, traditional SQL-based relational database systems adhere to a bag (multiset) semantics, in order to avoid the cost of frequent sorting and deduplication. This design choice drastically reduces the opportunity for query optimization, since it often happens that queries that are logically equivalent under set semantics are not under the bag-semantics. In our experience, it also makes queries harder for the end users to write and to reason about. LogiQL, in constrast, adheres to the set semantics, which enables us to implement a wider array of query rewriting and optimization techniques.

T3: Incrementality. LogicBlox supports efficient incremental materialized view maintenance. Our incremental maintenance algorithm is inspired by work done in the programming languages community. It improves significantly on the classical `count` and `DRed` algorithms [20] by guaranteeing that the work done is proportional to the trace edit distance between the before and after computations.

We have observed that although commercial database systems typically offer some degree of support for materialized views, the quality of this feature is usually rather poor: views are restricted to some subset of SQL queries and often perform very poorly in mixed OLTP and OLAP use cases (such that OLAP views must be refreshed manually at periodic offline intervals due to the inefficiency of existing view maintenance algorithms in the context of OLTP workloads). Difficulties in providing high-quality materialized view implementations have motivated some systems, such as HANA [16], to dispense with them altogether, and instead require that analytical queries always be computed on the fly. Besides sometimes being obviously wasteful in terms of computational resources, this approach also strikes us as problematic for truly computation-intensive applications. No matter how fast query evaluation can be made via parallelization, specialized storage schemes, and so forth, data sets and queries will be encountered that simply cannot be processed in this manner at interactive speed.

We will describe below how we used efficient view maintenance (along with purely functional data structures and efficient joins) as a key building block for our concurrency control scheme, *transaction repair*.

Finally, LogicBlox is designed to support efficient incremental changes to LogiQL programs. This capability makes it possible for us to support "live programming" use cases that allow end users to evolve their applications using a spreadsheet metaphor. This problem is quite different from traditional view maintenance, and requires a new set of techniques as outlined below.

T4: Immutability. The LogicBlox runtime makes pervasive use of *purely functional data structures* [35] (a form of *immutable* data structures) at all levels of the architecture. These data structures, originally motivated by purely functional programming languages, have a number of significant virtues in the context of database systems engineering:

1. Sharing of immutable substructures means that multiple versions of a relation or database can be represented together compactly, and changes between versions can be enumerated efficiently.
2. There is no need to maintain either read or write database locks. Each transaction starts by branching a version of the database in $O(1)$ time (a few nanoseconds—we have measured 80,000 branches per core per second). Changes in one branch (one transaction) have no visibility outside the transaction and are therefore perfectly isolated. Read-only transactions are perfectly scalable and do not need to be concerned about other changes occurring in other branches (i.e., throughput = # cores $\times$ single core transactions per second). Read-write transactions keep track of what they have read and written, and can be incrementally repaired with our efficient view maintenance machinery at commit time to achieve full serializability.
3. With purely functional data structures, a pointer or object-identifier uniquely identifies the state of an object. In the distributed setting, this avoids the need for cache coherence protocols.
4. We get useful temporal features such as time-travel essentially for free. We can branch any past version of the database, and the version graph can be an arbitrary directed acyclic graph.
5. There is no need for a transaction log for rollback and recovery purposes. Aborting a transaction means simply dropping all references to it; committing a transaction is, conceptually at least, just a pointer swap to the new head version of the database.

1.2 Outline

In the rest of the paper, we focus in more detail on several novel aspects of the LogicBlox system. Further aspects, including parallel and distributed computation, data compression, write-optimized data structures to support large transactional loads, and sampling-based query optimization are not discussed in this paper due to lack of space.

Section 2 presents the LogiQL language, and illustrates, by means of an example application, the way it is used. In Section 3, we highlight several innovative aspects of the LogicBlox system implementation. Section 3.1 discusses the use of persistent data structures and branching, which pervade the architecture. Section 3.2 overviews our workhorse join algorithm, leapfrog triejoin, and its associated view maintenance algorithm. Section 3.3 describes the meta-engine, which is the core architectural component enabling live programming. Section 3.4 presents our approach to concurrency control via transaction repair. We finally conclude in Section 4.

2. APPLICATION DEVELOPMENT IN LOGIQL

We illustrate the use of the LogicBlox system by means of a small example that highlights the need to support a variety of use cases in one application. After that, we give an overview of the LogiQL language itself.

2.1 Example Application

A user community made up of several hundred merchants, planners, supply chain personnel, and store managers at a large retailer wants to analyze historical sales and promotions data in order to assess the effectiveness of their product assortments, plan future promotions, predict future sales, and optimize the fulfillment of the demand generated by those assortments and promotions. The data in this scenario are several terabytes in size, and the model of the business is made up of a few thousand metrics.

There are multiple users concurrently using the application. Some are analyzing historical sales data via pivot tables, some are editing the data to specify different future promotional strategies

Figure 1: Screenshots of a retail planning application.

and generating new predictions of the demand created by those promotions, some are editing and overriding previously generated sales projections based on new information that is not available to the system yet, and some are asking the system for a recommended plan for fulfilling the demand generated by the promotions. All reads and writes occur at various levels of resolution, e.g., SKU/-Store/Day or Dept/Region/Month. These levels are not known a priori by the application developers.

Furthermore, as the competitive landscape and the macroeconomic picture changes, some of the privileged users of the system (i.e., power users or approved managers) would like to evolve the application to refine the financial, statistical, or mathematical models used within the application in order to enhance the groups' effectiveness and to increase the profits of the enterprise.

Figure 1 shows the environment in which users can visualize their data and their model, both of which can be evolved in order to reflect new knowledge about their business.

Through the notion of *workbooks*, we enable users to create branches of (subsets of) the database that can be modified independently. These workbooks allow us to support a variety of long-running transaction use cases. For example, workbooks can be created to allow a business person to analyze a variety of scenarios that model certain decisions that can be made to shape or fulfill client demand. Workbooks can also be created to support long running predictive and prescriptive analytics that will take several hours of machine time to run. Multiple users and processes may be working concurrently on different workbooks. It is important that the users of the system not be impacted negatively as hundreds of these long running transactions are taking place along with millions of smaller ones.

2.2 The LogiQL Language

In this section, we give an overview of the LogiQL language. Our overview is high-level and omits many details. See [21] for more details.[4]

[4]Visit `https://developer.logicblox.com` for a LogiQL tutorial and an online REPL for interactive tryout programming.

2.2.1 *Basic Syntactic Elements*

In this section we describe the core elements of a LogiQL program, namely *predicates*, *derivation rules*, *integrity constraints*, and *reactive rules*.

Predicates. LogicBlox supports predicates (relations) of the form $R(x_1,...,x_n)$ or $R[x_1,...,x_{n-1}] = x_n$ where each attribute x_i has either a primitive type (e.g., int, float, decimal, string, or date) or a user-defined *entity type*. As noted in T2 in Section 1, this type of schema encourages a strong form of normalization, corresponding to 6NF.

Each predicate may be declared as being either a *base predicate* (a.k.a. *extensional* or *EDB* predicate or relation), or a *derived predicate* (a.k.a. *intensional* or *IDB* predicate). If left unspecified, the predicate kind (base or derived), as well as the attribute types, are inferred from usage within the program. Base predicates contain input data and derived predicates are *views* over the base data. Derived predicates default to being materialized. However, if the derivion rule does not use aggregation or recursion, they can be left unmaterialized.

Derivation Rules. Derivation rules are used to specify view definitions. LogiQL admits two types of derivation rules.

A *basic derivation rule* is an expression of one of the two forms

$$R(t_1,\ldots,t_n) \leftarrow F$$
$$R[t_1,\ldots,t_{n-1}] = t_n \leftarrow F$$

where R is a derived predicate, $t_1,\ldots,t_n$ are variables and/or constants, and F is a formula containing all variables occurring in $t_1,\ldots,t_n$. The *formula*, here, may be a conjunction of atoms and/or negated atoms. The atoms involve base predicates, derived predicates, and/or built-in predicates such as equality, arithmetic addition, etc. An example of a basic derivation rule is

$$\begin{aligned}\text{profit}[sku] = z \leftarrow\ & \text{sellingPrice}[sku] = x,\\ & \text{buyingPrice}[sku] = y,\ z = x - y.\end{aligned}$$

which, using abbreviated syntax, may also be written as the expression

$$\text{profit}[sku] = \text{sellingPrice}[sku] - \text{buyingPrice}[sku].$$

Besides basic derivation rules, LogiQL also supports derivation rules that perform, for instance, aggregation. This is supported in an extensible way via the general construct of a higher order *Predicate-to-Predicate Rule* (*P2P rule*). For example, the P2P rule

$$\begin{aligned}\text{totalShelf}[\,] = u \leftarrow\ & \text{agg}\ll u = \text{sum}(z)\gg \text{Stock}[p] = x,\\ & \text{spacePerProd}[p] = y,\ z = x * y.\end{aligned}$$

performs a simple weighted sum-aggregation to compute the total amount of required shelf space, which, using abbreviated syntax, can also be written as:

$$\text{totalShelf}[] += \text{Stock}[p] * \text{spacePerProd}[p].$$

It is worth noting that every view definition definable in the relational algebra can be encoded by means of derivation rules (by introducing auxiliary predicates for intermediate results if necessary).[5] A collection of derivation predicates may be defined by rules with a cyclic dependency graph, in which case the rules in question can be viewed as *recursive* view definitions.

Integrity Constraints. An *integrity constraint* is an expression of the form $F \rightarrow G$ (note the use of a rightward arrow instead of a

[5]Indeed, it follows from the Immerman-Vardi theorem [25] that every PTIME-computable view definition is expressible.

$$
\begin{aligned}
&\text{// Base predicates:}\\
&\quad \text{spacePerProd}[p] = v \rightarrow \text{Product}(p), \text{float}(v).\\
&\quad \text{profitPerProd}[p] = v \rightarrow \text{Product}(p), \text{float}(v).\\
&\quad \text{minStock}[p] = v \rightarrow \text{Product}(p), \text{float}(v).\\
&\quad \text{maxStock}[p] = v \rightarrow \text{Product}(p), \text{float}(v).\\
&\quad \text{maxShelf}[\,] = v \rightarrow \text{float}[64](v).\\
&\text{// Derived predicates and rules:}\\
&\quad \text{Stock}[p] = v \rightarrow \text{Product}(p), \text{float}(v).\\
&\quad \text{totalShelf}[\,] = v \rightarrow \text{float}(v).\\
&\quad \text{totalProfit}[\,] = v \rightarrow \text{float}(v).\\
&\quad \text{totalShelf}[\,] = u \leftarrow \text{agg}\ll u = \text{sum}(z)\gg \text{Stock}[p] = x,\\
&\qquad\qquad \text{spacePerProd}[p] = y,\ z = x * y.\\
&\quad \text{totalProfit}[\,] = u \leftarrow \text{agg}\ll u = \text{sum}(z)\gg \text{Stock}[p] = x,\\
&\qquad\qquad \text{profitPerProd}[p] = y,\ z = x * y.\\
&\text{// Integrity constraints:}\\
&\quad \text{Product}(p) \rightarrow \text{Stock}[p] \geq \text{minStock}[p].\\
&\quad \text{Product}(p) \rightarrow \text{Stock}[p] \leq \text{maxStock}[p].\\
&\quad \text{totalShelf}[\,] = u,\\
&\quad \text{maxShelf}[\,] = v \rightarrow u \leq v.
\end{aligned}
$$

Figure 2: Example constraints and rules.

leftward arrow), where F and G are formulas. Both inclusion dependencies and functional dependencies can be naturally expressed by such expressions. Examples of integrity constraints are:

$$
\begin{aligned}
\text{Stock}[p] = v &\rightarrow \text{Product}(p), \text{float}(v).\\
\text{Product}(p) &\rightarrow \text{Stock}[p] = \_.\\
\text{totalShelf}[\,] = u, \text{maxShelf}[\,] = v &\rightarrow u \leq v.
\end{aligned}
$$

The first constraint can in fact be viewed as a type declaration: it expresses that the key-attribute of the Stock predicate consists of products (Product is a user defined type here), and that the value-attribute is a float. The second constraint is an inclusion dependency that expresses that every product has a stock value. The third constraint expresses that the value of totalShelf[ ] is bounded by the value of maxShelf[ ].

Whereas derivation rules define views, integrity constraints specify the set of legal database states. Traditionally, integrity constraints are used to determine if a transaction succeeds. As we will see below, we also use integrity constraints to encode mathematical optimization problems.

Figure 2 shows an example that involves predicates, derivation rules, and integrity constraints. The program is intended to model a simple retail assortment-planning scenario where the products picked for an assortment cannot take up more space than is available on the shelf.

Reactive Rules. Reactive rules are used to make and detect changes to the database state. They are a special form of derivation rules that refer to versioned predicates and delta predicates [28]. A simple example of a reactive rule is:

$$+\text{sales}[\text{“Popsicle”}, 2015\text{-}01] = 122.$$

which inserts a new fact into the sales predicate. A more interesting example is the following.

$$
\begin{aligned}
\hat{}\text{price}[\text{“Popsicle”}] = 0.8 * x \leftarrow\\
&\text{price}@start[\text{“Popsicle”}] = x,\\
&\text{sales}@start[\text{“Popsicle”}, 2015\text{-}01] < 50,\\
&+promo(\text{“}Popsicle\text{''}, 2015-01).
\end{aligned}
$$

This code discounts the price of popsicles if the sales in January 2015 are lower than 50 units, and there is a promotion being created for popsicles.

As we can see from the above examples, reactive rules are derivation rules that may refer to system-provided *versioned predicates* and *delta-predicates* such as $R@start$ (the content of R at the start of the transaction), $+R$ (the set of tuples being inserted into R in the current transaction), $-R$ (the set of tuples being deleted from R in the current transaction). $\hat{}R$ is a shorthand notation for a combination of $+R$ and $-R$. If R is a base predicate, the content of R after the transaction is determined by means of the following system-provided *frame rules*:

$$
\begin{aligned}
R(x_1,\ldots,x_n) &\leftarrow R@start(x_1,\ldots,x_n), !(-R(x_1,\ldots,x_n)).\\
R(x_1,\ldots,x_n) &\leftarrow +R(x_1,\ldots,x_n).
\end{aligned}
$$

The above presentation is much simplified. For more details see [21].

2.2.2 *Workspaces and Transactions*

A *workspace* consists of (i) a collection of declared predicates, derivation rules, and constraints (collectively called *logic*) and (ii) contents of the base predicates. One can think of a workspace as an instance of the database, at a particular moment in time, including both data and logic. In order to facilitate workspace management, the logic in a workspace is organized in modules that are called *blocks*. Each block is a separate collection of predicate declarations, derivation rules and constraints. The derivation rules and integrity constraints of one block may refer to predicates declared in another block. In order to support programming in the large, LogiQL also supports a more refined module system, involving abstractions and hiding, which we will not explain for lack of space. We will only describe some types of transactions supported by the system.

Query transactions. These transactions are used for querying the workspace state. A query is specified by means of a program that has a designated answer predicate, for example,

$$
\begin{aligned}
&\text{query}\{\\
&\quad \_(icecream, week, sales, revenue, profit) \leftarrow\\
&\qquad \text{week\_sales}[icecream, week] = sales,\\
&\qquad \text{week\_revenue}[icecream, week] = revenue,\\
&\qquad \text{week\_profit}[icecream, week] = profit.\}
\end{aligned}
$$

where _ is the designated answer predicate.

Exec transactions. These are used to modify the workspace state by changing the content of base predicates (which may subsequently trigger changes in the content of derived predicates). Exec transactions are specified using reactive logic as described above.

Addblock and Removeblock. These transactions are used to add or remove named collections of rules to the workspace program.

For example,

addblock *–name salesAgg1*{

$\text{Sales\_yr}[sku, store, yr] = z \leftarrow$

$\text{agg} \ll z = \text{sum}(s) \gg \text{Sales}[sku, store, wk] = s, year[wk] = yr.$}

installs a new view into the workspace, and

removeblock salesAgg1

removes it again, thereby restoring the workspace to its prior state. Addblock transactions do not effectuate any changes to existing base predicates. Instead, they may create new base predicates and/or derived predicates, add derivation rules for new or existing derived predicates, and/or add new integrity constraints.

Addblock and removeblock transactions can be viewed as supporting a form of *live programming* (see Section 3.3). In addition, they are central to the workflow of many applications developed using LogiQL, cf. Section 2.1.

Branch and Delete-branch. These transactions create and delete branches of the workspace, that is, copies of the workspace that can be manipulated independently. Branching can be used for creating checkpoints, as well as for supporting speculative what-if analyses. These are crucial in the context of modeling and prediction. As discussed in Section 3.1, the use of purely functional data structures in our implementation makes it possible to support the creation of a new branch as an instantaneous operation, as no actual (deep) copying of data takes place when a new branch is created.

2.3 Prescriptive and Predictive Analytics

The subset of LogiQL presented so far (namely derivation rules, integrity constraints, and reactive rules) allows us to define application logic that traditionally would have to be defined using SQL, SQL triggers, an imperative stored-procedure language such as PL/SQL, and an imperative object-oriented language such as Java or C#.

We now illustrate how LogiQL supports prescriptive and predictive analytics, providing functionality that is not traditionally offered by SQL databases and traditional application servers and is usually supported by the addition of specialized analytic systems to the application architecture.

2.3.1 Prescriptive analytics

By adding one more language feature, LogiQL can be extended to gracefully supports mathematical optimization and prescriptive analytics [8]. The idea is that a predicate $R[x_1, \ldots, x_n] = y$ can be declared to be a *free second-order variable*, which means that the system is responsible for populating it with tuples, in such a way that the integrity constraints are satisfied. Furthermore, a derived predicate of the form $R[\,] = y$ can be declared to be an objective function that should be minimized or maximized.

Continuing the example program in Figure 2, suppose that we would like to automatically compute stock amounts so as to maximize profit. Then, it suffices to add to the program the following lines of code:

```
lang:solve:variable(`Stock).
lang:solve:max(`totalProfit).
```

The first line is shorthand for an second order existential quantifier and it states that the predicate Stock should be treated as a free second-order variable that we are solving for, while the second line states that the predicate totalProfit is an objective function that needs to be maximized (subject to the integrity constraints).

Under the hood, the program is translated into a Linear Programming (LP) problem and passed on to the appropriate solver, e.g., [36, 3]. LogicBlox grounds (i.e., eliminates the quantifiers in) the problem instance in a manner similar to [33] via automatic synthesis of another LogiQL program that translates the constraints over variable predicates into a representation that can be consumed by the solver. This improves the scalability of the grounding by taking advantage of all the query evaluation machinery in the LogicBlox system (e.g. query optimization, query parallelization, etc). The system then invokes the appropriate solver and populates the value of existentially quantified predicates with the results (turning unknown values into known ones). Furthermore, the grounding logic incrementally maintains the input to the solver, making it possible for the system to incrementally (re)solve only those parts of the problem that are impacted by changes to the input.

If the sample application is changed such that the stock predicate is now defined to be a mapping from products to integers, LogicBlox will detect the change and reformulate the problem so that a different solver is invoked, one that supports Mixed Integer Programming (MIP).

Examples of research in this area include [12, 18, 38, 30]. As far as we know, LogicBlox is the first commercial database system that provides native support for prescriptive analytics.

2.3.2 Predictive analytics

Predictive analytics in LogicBlox was initially supported by means of a collection of built-in machine learning algorithms. This is done via special "predict" P2P rules that come in two modes: the *learning* mode (where a model is being learned) and the *evaluation* mode (where a model is being applied to make predictions). We do not give here the formal syntax and semantics for these rules; rather, we give an illustrative example.

Suppose that we wish to predict the monthly sales of products in branches. We have the predicate $\text{Sales}[sku, store, wk] = amount$ as well as a predicate $\text{Feature}[sku, store, name] = value$ that associates with every sku, store and feature name a corresponding feature value. The following learning rule learns a logistic-regression model for each *sku* and *branch*, and stores the resulting *model object* (which is a handle to a representation of the model) in the predicate $\text{SM}[sku, store] = model$.

$$\text{SM}[sku, store] = m \leftarrow \text{predict} \ll m = \text{logist}(v|f) \gg \text{Sales}[sku, store, wk] = v, \text{Feature}[sku, store, n] = f.$$

The following rule evaluates the model to get specific predictions.

$$\text{Sales\_pred}[sku, store] = v \leftarrow \text{predict} \ll v = \text{eval}(m|f) \gg \text{SM}[sku, store] = m, \text{Feature}[sku, store, n] = f.$$

The above rules are evaluated using a built-in machine learning library, which implements a variety of state-of-the-art, scalable machine learning algorithms to support regression, clustering, density estimation, classification, and dimensionality reduction.

2.3.3 Towards Declarative Probabilistic Modeling

The above approach to statistical model building and predictive analytics is not fully satisfying as it is imperative and requires the user to be well-versed in statistical modeling. We briefly discuss some extensions to LogiQL that we are currently developing to make statistical and probabilistic model building more natural by using the native modeling constructs of the language.

Statistical Relational Models. Markov Logic Networks (MLN) [15] and Probabilistic Soft Logic (PSL) [9] are two examples of languages that combine logical and statistical modeling. This is accomplished through the use of *soft constraints*, i.e., weighted constraints that are not required to always hold, but whose violations carry a specified penalty.

As an example, suppose that we wish to predict whether customer c will purchase product p. Further assume that we have base predicates that specify similarity among products, $\mathsf{Similar}(p_1, p_2)$; friendship among customers, $\mathsf{Friends}(c_1, c_2)$; and products under promotion, $\mathsf{Promoted}(p)$. Consider the following soft constraints.

$$\begin{aligned}
w_1 &: \text{Customer}(c), \text{Promoted}(p) \rightarrow \text{Purchase}(c,p) \\
w_2 &: \text{Customer}(c), \text{Promoted}(q), \text{Similar}(p,q) \rightarrow !\text{Purchase}(c,p) \\
w_3 &: \text{Purchase}(d,p), \text{Friends}(c,d) \rightarrow \text{Purchase}(c,p) \\
w_4 &: !\text{Purchase}(d,p), \text{Friends}(c,d) \rightarrow !\text{Purchase}(c,p)
\end{aligned}$$

Here, w_1, w_2, w_3 and w_4 are numerical weights. While ordinary (hard) constraints in a LogiQL program specify the set of legal database states, soft constraints assign to each state a score indicating whether it is more or less "likely" compared to other database states. For example, in the case of MLNs, the likelihood of a possible world is proportional to the product of the factors, where a *factor* is defined for each satisfying grounding a rule (in the possible extension) and constitutes (a function of) the weight of that rule. As an example, if the weight of the first rule, w_1, is 2.0, then the likelihood of a possible world is multiplied by $e^{2.0}$ for every product p and customer c that satisfy $\mathsf{Promoted}(p) \rightarrow \mathsf{Purchase}(c,p)$.

In these formalisms, *Maximum-A-Priori* (*MAP*) inference finds the most likely possible world, such as the most likely purchases given partial knowledge about real purchases. This can be formulated as a mathematical optimization problem, which can be solved using the machinery described in Section 2.3.1.

Probabilistic-Programming Datalog. Formalisms for specifying general statistical models, such as probabilistic-programming languages [17], typically consist of two components: a specification of a stochastic process (the prior), and a specification of observations that restrict the probability space to a conditional subspace (the posterior). We plan to enhance LogiQL with capabilities for probabilistic programming, in order to facilitate the design and engineering of machine-learning solutions. Towards that, we have initiated a theoretical exploration of such an extension. In a recent paper [5], we considered the LogiQL fragment of conjunctive derivation rules (i.e., traditional Datalog) and arbitrary integrity constraints. We proposed an extension that provides convenient mechanisms to include common numerical probability functions; in particular, conclusions of rules may contain values drawn from such functions.

As an example, we will consider a case where we wish to detect that a product is being promoted, which leads to a significant increase in sales. We have a relation $\mathsf{Promotion}[p] = b$, determining whether product p is likewise promoted (where $b = 1$ or $b = 0$), where we do not know the value of b. We also have the relation $\mathsf{BuyRate}[p,b] = r$ that determines the probability r that a product p is sold without a promotion ($b = 0$) and with a promotion ($b = 1$). Finally, we have a relation $\mathsf{Customer}(c)$ of customers and a relation $\mathsf{Buys}[c,p] = b$ that determines whether client c purchased product p. The following program models a random behavior of customers ($\text{Flip}[r]$ defines a Bernoulli distribution with parameter r).

$$\begin{aligned}
\text{Promotion}[p] = \text{Flip}[0.01] &\leftarrow . \\
\text{Buys}[c,p] = \text{Flip}[r] &\leftarrow \text{BuyRate}[p,b] = r, \\
&\qquad \text{Promotion}[p] = b.
\end{aligned}$$

To determine whether or not a promotion is in place, we use the (say, daily) purchase data to condition the probability space.

$$\text{Visited}(c), \text{Bought}[c,p] = b \rightarrow \text{Buys}[c,p] = b.$$

Here, Visited and Bought are base predicates with known values. The resulting probability space is the one defined by the two derivation rules, conditioned on the following integrity constraint (observations). Inference on the program is supported: for example, one can ask for the most likely value b such that $\mathsf{Promotion}[p] = b$.

Defining the precise semantics of such a program is not at all straightforward, and we refer the interested reader to [5] for the formal framework underlying our proposal.

3. FACETS OF THE IMPLEMENTATION

In this section, we highlight several innovative aspects of the LogicBlox system implementation.

3.1 Branching and persistent data structures

One of the core design choices in the implementation of the LogicBlox engine is the use of persistent data structures. Our structures have *"mutable until shared"* objects that sit at a useful tradeoff point between imperative and purely functional. The objects are mutable when created and while local to a thread, and become immutable at synchronization and branching points (e.g., when the data structure is communicated to another thread, committed, or branched). This allows the efficiency benefits of the imperative RAM model while doing thread-local manipulations, but preserves the *"pointer value uniquely determines extensional state"* property of purely functional data structures when objects are shared, which simplifies the programming model for incremental maintenance, concurrent transactions, and live programming. In addition, our internal framework transparently persists, restores, and garbage-collects these objects as needed, which greatly simplifies the engineering of many aspects of the runtime internals.

Persistent data structures are used for both paged relational data and meta-data, which are C++ objects representing for instance LogiQL programs and workspaces. For paged data, we use a family of persistent B-tree-like data structures. Collections of meta-data objects such as sets, vectors, and maps are implemented as treaps. These are randomized binary search trees that offer efficient search, insertion, and deletion [37]. Treaps have the unique representation property: the structure of the tree depends only on its contents, not on the operation history. With memoization, this permits extensional equality testing in $O(1)$ time, using pointer comparison. The treaps are purely functional [35], i.e., the treap nodes cannot be modified once constructed and all mutating (insert/erase) operations are performed by duplicating a path from the root to where the change occurs. Set intersection, union, and difference are also efficient [7].

Recall that the *branch* transaction command of LogiQL creates a new branch of a workspace. Since both data and the meta-data are stored using persistent data structures, this is an $O(1)$ operation. Moreover, the branching functionality, coupled with functional-style techniques, enables versioned data structures that provide efficient search and set operations such as the difference between versions of objects. Efficient diffing is crucial for incremental maintenance, while efficient branching is used by our lock-free concurrent transactions to execute in parallel on different branches of the current version of the database.

3.2 Queries and incremental maintenance

Leapfrog Triejoin (LFTJ) [42] is a join algorithm developed at LogicBlox and can be seen as an improved version of the classical sort-merge join algorithm. It is used to compute the derived predicates (more specifically, it enumerates the satisfying assignments for bodies of derivation rules). We next give an overview of the algorithm and its properties. To simplify the presentation, we focus on equi-joins. As the details of this algorithm are needed for describing various important aspects of our system (e.g., indices, concurrency and incremental maintenance), the description here is more elaborate than that of the other components we consider in this paper.

LFTJ for unary predicates. We first describe how LFTJ works for the special case of joining unary predicates $A_1(x),\dots,A_k(x)$. This case is of no particular novelty (see, e.g., [24, 14]), but it serves as the basic building block towards the general case.

The input predicates A_i are assumed to be given in sorted order, and accessible though a *linear iterator* interface that supports the following methods:

- next() proceeds to the next value (i.e., tuple of the unary A_i).
- seek(v) proceeds to the least upper bound for v; that is, it positions the iterator at the smallest value u satisfying $u \geq v$, or the end if no such u exists. The given v must be greater or equal to the value at the current position.

These methods are required to take $O(\log N)$ time, where N is the cardinality of the predicate. Moreover, if m values are visited in ascending order, the amortized complexity is required to be $O(1+\log(N/m))$, which can be accomplished using standard data structures such as B-trees. Initially, the linear iterator method is located at the first value in the predicate.

The unary LFTJ algorithm itself implements the same *linear iterator* interface: it provides an iterator for the join of A_1 to A_k, i.e., for the intersection $A_1 \cap \cdots \cap A_k$, that efficiently supports next() and seek(). The algorithm maintains a priority queue of pointers to input iterators, one for each predicate being joined, where the priority reflects the value at which the iterator is currently positioned. The algorithm repeatedly takes an iterator with the smallest value and performs a seek for the largest value, "leapfrogging" the iterators until they are all positioned at the same value.

Figure 3 illustrates a join of three unary predicates, A, B, and C, with $A = \{0,1,3,4,5,6,7,8,9,11\}$, $B = \{0,2,6,7,8,9\}$, and $C = \{2,4,5,8,10\}$. Initially, the iterators for A, B, and C are positioned at the first elements 0, 0, and respectively 2. Since 2 is the largest from these three values, the iterator for A performs a seek(2) which positions the iterator for A at 3. The iterator for B then performs a seek(3), which lands at 6. The iterator for C does seek(6), which lands at 8, and so on. LFTJ ends when the iterator for B, while performing seek(11), reaches the end.

Sensitivity intervals. As LFTJ calls the next() and seek() methods of the participating iterators, there is a natural notion of a *sensitivity interval*: an interval where changes may actually affect the result of the LFTJ computation. For instance, in the example in Figure 3, inserting the fact $C(3)$ or deleting the fact $C(4)$ would not affect the computation, given that the seek(6) instruction skips over these values anyway. The sensitivity intervals, i.e., intervals where changes *do* affect the LFTJ computation, for the example in Figure 3 are as follows:

$$A: [-\infty,0],[2,3],[8,8],[10,11]$$
$$B: [-\infty,0],[3,6],[8,8],[11,+\infty]$$
$$C: [-\infty,2],[6,8],[8,10]$$

The sensitivity indices can, in this example, also be viewed as representing an execution trace of the LFTJ algorithm. In the LogicBlox runtime, sensitivity intervals play an important role for both incremental maintenance and concurrent transactions.

Predicate $A(x,y,z)$ Trie presentation

(1,3,4)
(1,3,5)
(1,4,6)
(1,4,8)
(1,4,9)
(1,5,2)
(3,5,2)

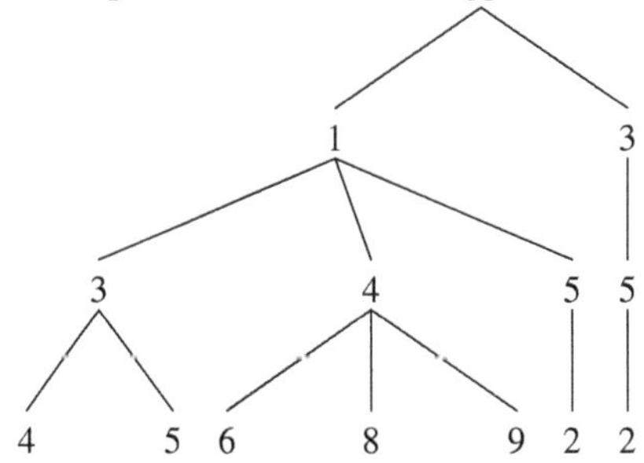

Figure 4: Example: Trie presentation of a ternary predicate.

Arbitrary arity. Non-unary input predicates, such as $A(x,y,z)$, are (logically) presented as *tries*, that is, trees in which each level corresponds to a different argument position, and each tuple $(a,b,c) \in A$ corresponds to a unique root-to-leaf path. The linear iterator interface is augmented with two methods for vertical trie navigation:

- open() for proceeding to the first value at the next depth (i.e., the first child of the current node in the trie).
- up() for returning to the parent of the current node in the trie.

These methods can also be supported in $O(\log N)$ time for the input predicates. The next() and seek() methods perform horizontal navigation between siblings in the trie, as before.

We now describe the LFTJ algorithm for equi-joins of predicates of arbitrary arity. We assume that each variable appears at most once in each atom. For example, $R(x,x)$ can be rewritten to $R(x,y), x=y$ to satisfy this requirement. Likewise, we may assume that constants may not appear in the query: a subformula such as $A(x,2)$ is rewritten to $A(x,y)$, $\mathsf{Const}_2(y)$, where $\mathsf{Const}_2 = \{2\}$. Here, the equality (=) and Const_2 are virtual (i.e., non-materialized) predicates that allow for efficient access through the same trie-iterator interface.

The algorithm requires a *variable ordering* that is consistent with the order in which variables occur in the atoms in the query. For instance, in the join $R(a,b), S(b,c), T(a,c)$ we might choose the variable ordering $[a,b,c]$. In cases where no consistent variable order exists, such as for the join $R(a,b,c), S(c,b)$, a secondary index is required on one of the two predicates. For example, if the chosen variable ordering is $[a,b,c]$, a secondary index on S is needed that efficiently supports access to $S'(c,b) = S(b,c)$ via the trie-iterator interface.

Once a variable order is chosen, the algorithm proceeds by performing a unary LFTJ for each variable. Consider the example $R(a,b)$, $S(b,c)$, $T(a,c)$ with the variable ordering $[a,b,c]$. We first apply the unary LFTJ algorithm to enumerate the values for a that are in both the projections $R(a,\_)$ and $T(a,\_)$. For each successful binding for a, we proceed to the next variable in the chosen order. Again, a unary LFTJ is performed to enumerate bindings for b that satisfy both $R(a,b)$ and $S(b,\_)$ (for the current value of a). Finally, for each successful binding of b, we proceed to the variable c, and perform a unary LFTJ to enumerate values for c satisfying both $S(b,c)$ and $T(a,c)$ (for the current values of a and b). Each time a unary LFTJ run finishes, having exhausted its list of possible bindings, we retreat to the previous level and seek another binding for the corresponding variable. Thus, conceptually, we can regard the entire LFTJ run as a backtracking search through a trie of potential variable bindings.

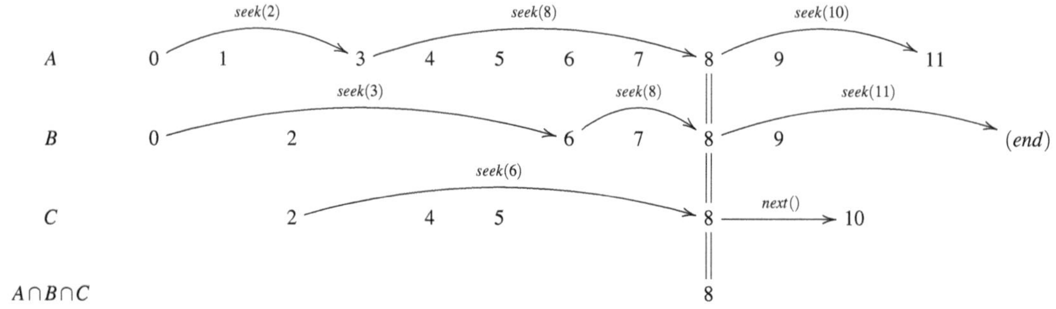

Figure 3: Example of a LFTJ run with unary predicates.

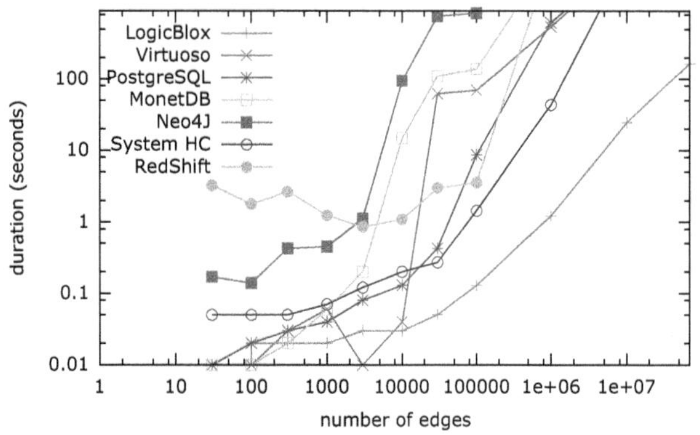

Figure 5: Running time of the 3-clique query on (increasingly larger subsets of) the LiveJournal graph dataset [26] using LogicBlox 4.1.4, Virtuoso 7, PostgreSQL 9.3.4, Neo4j 2.1.5, MonetDB 1.7 (Jan2014-SP3), a commercial in-memory column store (System HC), and RedShift. See [32] for full details and more experiments.

LFTJ is a *worst-case optimal join algorithm* for any equi-join query, in the following sense (cf. [31]): the running time of the algorithm is bounded by the worst-case cardinality of the query result (modulo logarithmic factors) [42].

Scenarios where LFTJ excels particularly compared to other join algorithms are multi-way joins such as the join returning all 3-cliques on the LiveJournal graph dataset, cf. Figure 5.

Optimization and parallelism. When joins are evaluated using LFTJ, query optimization essentially boils down to choosing a good variable order. Recall that, depending on the chosen variable order, secondary indices may need to be created and maintained for some predicates. The LogicBlox query optimizer uses sampling-based techniques: small representative samples of predicates are maintained. These samples are used to compare candidate variable orderings for LFTJ evaluation, and, consequently, also for automatic index creation. Furthermore, the samples are used to determine domain decompositions for automatic parallelization.

Incremental maintenance. As we explained in the introduction, incremental maintenance is of central importance in LogicBlox applications. We support incremental maintenance of derived predicates efficiently by means of an extension of the LFTJ algorithm. The basic setup is as follows. We have a derivation rule such as

$$T(x) \leftarrow A_1(x,y), A_2(y,z), A_3(x,z)$$

and, for each input predicate A_i, we are given an *old* version A_i^{old}, a *new* version A_i^{new}, and a *delta* predicate A_i^{Δ}, where A_i^{Δ} is a set of insertions and deletions that, when applied to A_i^{old}, yields A_i^{new}. We are also given T^{old}, and the task is to compute T^{new} as well as T^{Δ} which is then propagated forward to other rules. Recall that our versioned data structures allow us to compute differences between two versions of a predicate efficiently.

The derivation rule maintenance problem is, conceptually, split into two parts: *maintaining the set of satisfying assignments for the rule body under changes to the input predicates* ("rule body maintenance") and *maintaining the rule head predicate under changes to the set of satisfying assignments for the rule body* ("rule head maintenance"). For recursive LogiQL programs, additional machinery is used to maintain the results of fixpoint computations.

Rule head maintenance is implemented using a variety of data structures for different derivation rules. In the case of the above example, a count predicate is maintained, indicating, for each value a, the number of different ways in which it is derived (i.e,. the number of satisfying assignments of the rule body that support the derivation of that value). For P2P rules performing operations such as aggregation, different data structures are used. Support for efficient *rule body maintenance* is provided by the LFTJ algorithm through the use of *sensitivity indices*. These sensitivity indices maintain sensitivity intervals for a LFTJ run at various levels in the trie and in various contexts (where the context of a sensitivity interval consists of the values for earlier-chosen variables under which the sensitivity occurs). The maintenance algorithm is designed to be optimal in the sense that the cost of maintenance under changes to the input predicates is proportional to the trace-edit distance of the corresponding runs of the LFTJ algorithm [41].

3.3 Live programming and self service

In order to support end-user driven application evolution, we have added support for live programming in LogicBlox, where the traditional edit-compile-run cycle is abandoned in favor of a more interactive user experience with live feedback on a program's runtime behavior [10]. For instance, in our retail planning applications, we enable users to define and change schemas and formulas on the fly. These changes trigger updates to the application code in the database server and the challenge is to quickly update the user views in response to these changes. Section 2.1 describes such a scenario.

From a technical perspective, live programming is far from trivial—especially when working with programs and data of the scale encountered in the real world (e.g., a typical application has about 5k LogiQL rules and several TBs of data). To achieve interactive response times in those scenarios, changes to application

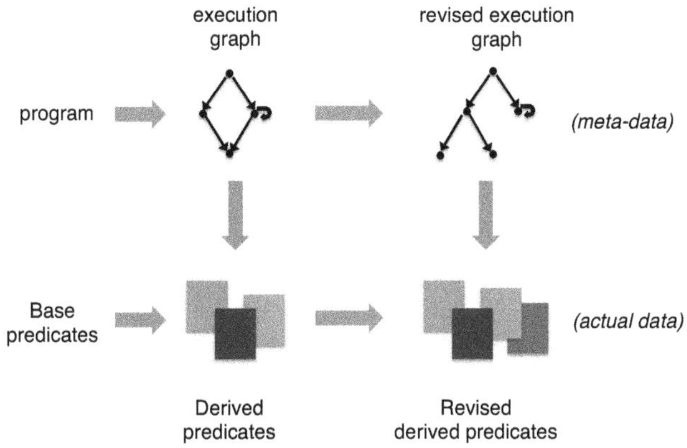

Figure 6: While the engine proper deals with maintenance of the derived predicates (materialized views) for a given program (left half), the meta-engine maintains the program under code updates and informs the engine proper which derived predicates should be revised (right half).

code must be quickly compiled and "hot-swapped in" to the running program, and the effects of those changes must be efficiently computed in an incremental fashion.

Live programming is supported in the LogicBlox system via the meta-engine, which is a *higher-level lightweight engine* that manages metadata representing LogiQL application code. The meta-engine maintains the program state declaratively and incrementally. Figure 6 depicts schematically how the meta-engine differs from the engine proper and how the two engines work together. The LogiQL program is compiled into an execution graph, where the predicates are the nodes and the edges between nodes represent rules. The engine proper evaluates the execution graph bottom-up on the input database and materializes the derived predicates. The meta-engine is activated when the program changes: it incrementally maintains the execution graph (depicted by a revised execution graph) and informs the engine proper which derived predicates have to be maintained as result of the program change. To achieve this, the meta-engine uses *meta-rules* to declaratively describe the LogiQL code as collections of meta-facts and their relationships. These collections are implemented using persistent data structures, cf. Section 3.1. There are currently about 200 meta-rules that support the incremental code maintenance mechanism and various code invariants and optimizations, such as rule inlining and on-the-fly creation of sampling rules to support LFTJ optimization. The meta-rules are expressed in non-recursive Datalog with negation, and additional functionality is available via an extensible set of primitive built-ins and computed meta-predicates.

Compared with an imperative specification of the complicated state transitions involved in live programming, the declarative approach is simpler, uses less code, is more robust, and is easily extensible.

We next give two examples of actual meta-rules. The first example meta-rule is used to determine whether a given predicate is a base predicate (recall from Section 2 that the user is not required to specify if a given predicate is a base predicate or a derived predicate, and that, when not specified explicitly, the information in question is derived from the way the predicate is used):

$$\text{lang\_edb}(\textit{name}) \leftarrow \text{lang\_predname}(\textit{name}), !\text{lang\_idb}(\textit{name}).$$

The meta-predicate `lang_edb` denotes the set of all base predicates, whereas the meta-predicate `lang_idb` denotes the set of all derived predicates. The above meta-rule states that every predicate that is not implied (by other meta-rules) to be an derived predicate is a base predicate (the ! symbol is used for negation). In a live programming application, any of the two body meta-predicates may change, i.e., new predicates are declared or existing ones are removed, and the meta-engine updates the `lang_edb` meta-predicate (i.e., the set of base predicates) after each such change.

As a second example, we give (a simplified version of) the meta-rule that determines whether frame rules are needed for a specific base predicate. Recall from Section 2 that frame rules are used to compute the new extension of an base predicate Foo based on the previous version Foo@*start* together with the extension of the corresponding delta-predicates +Foo and −Foo. The system needs to maintain the following logical invariant: *if +Foo or −Foo appears in the head of a rule, then we need a frame rule for Foo.* The following meta-rule maintains this invariant:

$$\begin{aligned}&\text{need\_frame\_rule}(\textit{predName}) \leftarrow \text{user\_rule}(\_, \textit{rule}),\\&\quad \text{rule\_head}[\textit{rule}] = \textit{head}, \text{head\_predicate}(\textit{head}, \textit{predName}),\\&\quad \text{is\_delta\_predicate}(\textit{predName}).\end{aligned}$$

Here, the meta-predicate `needs_frame_rule` denotes the set of delta predicates for which a frame rule needs to be generated. The above meta-rule inspects the head of each user rule and checks whether it contains a delta predicate.

3.4 Transaction Repair

In this section we describe our ongoing effort to support *concurrent write-transactions.* Recall that the LogicBlox engine aims to provide a unified platform for mixed workload data processing. As such, efficient and transparent support for concurrent transactions is of crucial importance.

Traditional approaches to concurrent transactions either settle for lower levels of isolation, such as Snapshot Isolation, or employ costly locking mechanisms that reduce the potential for parallel speedup. Instead, our approach, which we call *transaction repair* [43], provides full serializability (the highest level of correctness and semantic transparency) while avoiding the use of locks. Unlike other concurrency mechanisms that support full serializability through the use of versioned data structures, transaction repair is able to accommodate large-footprint write-transactions efficiently, which are common in planning scenarios. To do so, we take advantage not only of our purely functional and versioned data structures, but also of the fact that our system supports efficient incremental maintenance:

1. Branching an entire workspace is an $O(1)$ operation due to the use of persistent data structures, cf. Section 3.1. This means that we can run transactions simultaneously, with no locking, each in a separate branch of the database. This immediately supports a "multiple reader, single writer" form of concurrency.

2. As explained in Section 3.2, sensitivity indices can be used to track which changes in the underlying data may affect the evaluation of derivation rules. In the same way, sensitivity indices can be used to track what changes to a workspace may affect the execution of a transaction. In particular, we can use sensitivity indices to detect conflicts between concurrent transactions.

3. In case of conflicts, our incremental maintenance machinery can be used to maintain the result of the second transaction under relevant changes resulting from the first transaction, i.e., to *repair transactions.* This is what allows us to support concurrent transactions with full serializability without using locks.

(a) A single transaction

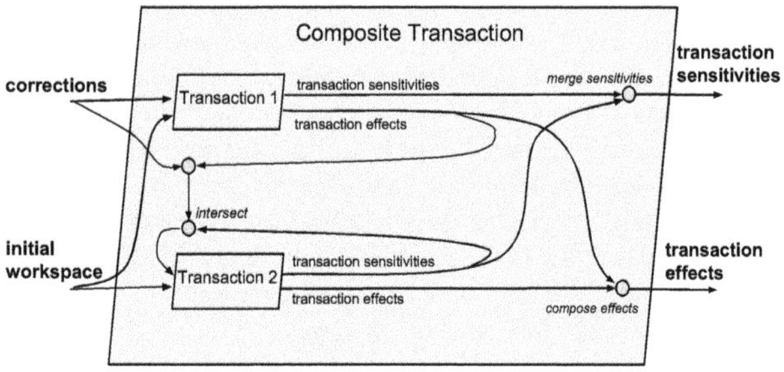

(b) Composition of two transactions

Figure 7: The transaction-repair framework

4. Once all conflicts for the group of transactions in flight (or an initial segment) have been repaired, they can be committed together.

Below, we describe the transaction-repair framework in somewhat more detail.

Transaction Maintenance In the transaction-repair framework, a transaction takes as input a workspace and any number of corrections (which may be supplied over time) and provides as output *transaction effects* and *transaction sensitivities*. Moreover, these output effects and sensitivities are kept up-to-date as corrections are received. This is depicted graphically in Figure 7(a).

The transaction sensitivities are not the intervals where changes could affect the output workspace, but rather intervals where changes could affect the *transaction effects*, i.e.,, the changes that, when applied to the corrected input workspace, yield the output workspace.

For example, suppose the workspace contains base predicates inventory and auto_order, and a derived predicate place_order defined by the derivation rule

$$\text{place\_order}(x) \leftarrow \text{inventory}[x] = 0, \text{auto\_order}(x).$$

Consider the transaction

$$\begin{aligned}&\text{exec}\{\\ &\quad \hat{}\text{inventory}[\text{“Popsicle”}] = x \leftarrow\\ &\qquad\quad \text{inventory}@start[\text{“Popsicle”}] = y, x = y - 1.\}\end{aligned}$$

(Assume in the discussion below that l stands for "Popsicle".) If the input workspace contains a record $\text{inventory}[l] = 2$, then the transaction effects will include

$$-\text{inventory}[l] = 2 \text{ and } +\text{inventory}[l] = 1,$$

while the transaction sensitivities for the predicate inventory will contain the (singleton) interval $[l,l]$. Now, suppose the transaction receives the above two side effects on inventory as incoming corrections. Then, the updated transaction effects will include

$$-\text{inventory}[l] = 1, +\text{inventory}[l] = 0, \text{ and } +\text{place\_order}(l),$$

and the sensitivities for auto_order will include the singleton interval $[l,l]$. Note that the precise set of sensitivity indices recorded depends on the execution of the LFTJ algorithm, and, more specifically, the order in which the iterators are visited.

Transaction Circuits Two transactions performed concurrently can be composed into a single object that implements the same interface described above, cf. Figure 7(b).

Observe that, in the case where transaction effects of the first transaction do not intersect with the transaction sensitivities of the second transaction (and no incoming corrections are received), each transaction is executed exactly once, and no incremental maintenance is needed. In general, however, the second transaction may need to be incrementally repaired multiple times.

By repeated application we can treat an entire sequence of transactions as a single composite transaction, implemented through a binary tree-shaped circuit whose nodes correspond to different processes that are run in parallel. This is a simplified picture, and further details can be found in [43].

Illustration: Transaction Repair vs Row-Level Locking. Consider the following variation of the above example, involving a large number of transactions. Each transaction adjusts a number of items in the `inventory` predicate. Suppose there are n items in total, and each transaction modifies the `inventory` value for any given item with independent probability $\alpha n^{-1/2}$, for some fixed parameter $\alpha > 0$. That is, each transaction has the form

$$\begin{aligned}&\text{exec}\{\\ &\quad \hat{}\text{inventory}[S_1] = x \leftarrow \text{inventory}@start[S_1] = y, x = y - 1.\\ &\quad \vdots\\ &\quad \hat{}\text{inventory}[S_k] = x \leftarrow \text{inventory}@start[S_k] = y, x = y - 1.\}\end{aligned}$$

where $S_1, \ldots, S_k$ are items chosen independently and at random with probability $\alpha n^{-1/2}$. Most pairs of transactions will conflict when $\alpha \gg 1$: the expected number of items common to two transactions is $E[\cdot] = n \cdot (\alpha n^{-1/2})^2 = \alpha^2$, an instance of the Birthday Paradox. Row-level locking [6] is a bottleneck when $\alpha \gg 1$: since most transactions have items in common, they quickly encounter lock conflicts and are put to sleep. Even with an efficient implementation of row-level locking, on a multi-core machine, only a limited parallel speedup can be obtained unless the expected number of conflicts is very small (say, $\alpha = 0.1$). Even for $\alpha = 1$, parallel speedup is sharply limited; and for $\alpha = 10$ almost no parallel speedup is possible. Transaction repair allows us to achieve near-linear parallel speedup in the number of cores, even for high values of α such as $\alpha = 10$ [43].

4. CONCLUSION

We presented the design considerations behind the LogicBlox system architecture, and gave an overview of the implementation of the system. We highlighted several innovative aspects, which include: LogiQL, a unified and declarative language based on Datalog; the use of purely functional data structures; novel join processing strategies; advanced incremental maintenance and live programming facilities; and built-in support for prescriptive and predictive analytics.

Our program for the LogicBlox system is admittedly an ambitious one, and replacing the enterprise hairball requires a pragmatic and incremental approach. But already today, the LogicBlox platform has matured to the point that it is being used daily in dozens of mission-critical applications in some of the largest enterprises in the world, whose aggregate revenues exceed \$300B.

5. REFERENCES

[1] `http://www.datalog20.org/programme.html`.

[2] Serge Abiteboul, Richard Hull, and Victor Vianu. *Foundations of Databases*. Addison-Wesley, 1995.

[3] Tobias Achterberg. SCIP: Solving constraint integer programs. *Math. Programming Computation*, 1(1):1–41, 2009.

[4] Peter Alvaro, Neil Conway, Joseph M. Hellerstein, and William R. Marczak. Consistency analysis in Bloom: a calm and collected approach. In *CIDR*, 2011.

[5] Vince Barany, Balder ten Cate, Benny Kimelfeld, Dan Olteanu, and Zografoula Vagena. Declarative statistical modeling with Datalog. *arXiv:1412.2221*, 2014.

[6] Philip A. Bernstein and Nathan Goodman. Concurrency control in distributed database systems. *ACM Comput. Surv.*, 13(2):185–221, 1981.

[7] Guy E. Blelloch and Margaret Reid-Miller. Fast set operations using treaps. In *SPAA*, pages 16–26, 1998.

[8] C. Borraz-Sánchez, J. Ma, D. Klabjan, R. Fourer, E. Pasalic, and M. Aref. Algebraic modeling in Datalog. `http://dynresmanagement.com/uploads/3/3/2/9/3329212/datalog_modeling.pdf`.

[9] Matthias Bröcheler, Lilyana Mihalkova, and Lise Getoor. Probabilistic similarity logic. In *UAI*, pages 73–82, 2010.

[10] Brian Burg, Adrian Kuhn, and Chris Parnin. First Int. Workshop on Live Programming (LIVE). In *ICSE*, pages 1529–1530, 2013.

[11] S. Swaminathan C. J. Date, A. Kannan. *An Introduction to Database Systems*. Pearson Education, eighth edition, 2008.

[12] Marco Cadoli, Giovambattista Ianni, Luigi Palopoli, Andrea Schaerf, and Domenico Vasile. Np-spec: an executable specification language for solving all problems in np. *Computer Languages*, 26(2):165–195, 2000.

[13] B. Chin, D. von Dincklage, V. Ercegovak, P. Hawkins, M. S. Miller, F. Och, C. Olston, and F. Pereira. Yedalog: Exploring knowledge at scale. In *SNAPL*, 2015. To appear.

[14] Erik D. Demaine, Alejandro López-Ortiz, and J. Ian Munro. Adaptive set intersections, unions, and differences. In *SODA*, pages 743–752, 2000.

[15] Pedro Domingos and Daniel Lowd. *Markov Logic: An Interface Layer for Artificial Intelligence*. Synthesis Lectures on AI and Machine Learning. 2009.

[16] Franz Färber, Sang Kyun Cha, Jürgen Primsch, Christof Bornhövd, Stefan Sigg, and Wolfgang Lehner. SAP HANA database: Data management for modern business applications. *SIGMOD Rec.*, 40(4):45–51, 2012.

[17] Noah D. Goodman. The principles and practice of probabilistic programming. In *POPL*, pages 399–402, 2013.

[18] Sergio Greco, Cristian Molinaro, Irina Trubitsyna, and Ester Zumpano. NP datalog: A logic language for expressing search and optimization problems. *TPLP*, 10(2):125–166, 2010.

[19] Todd J. Green, Shan Shan Huang, Boon Thau Loo, and Wenchao Zhou. Datalog and recursive query processing. *Foundations and Trends in Databases*, 5(2):105–195, 2013.

[20] A. Gupta, I. S. Mumick, and V. S. Subrahmanian. Maintaining views incrementally (extended abstract). In *Proc. of the 1993 ACM SIGMOD International Conference on Management of Data SIGMOD'93*, pages 157–166, Washington, DC, 1993.

[21] Terry Halpin and Spencer Rugaber. *LogiQL: A Query Language for Smart Databases*. CRC Press, 2014.

[22] Terry A. Halpin, Matthew Curland, Kurt Stirewalt, Navin Viswanath, Matthew J. McGill, and Steven Beck. Mapping ORM to datalog: An overview. In *OTM Workshops'10*, pages 504–513, 2010.

[23] Shan Shan Huang, Todd Jeffrey Green, and Boon Thau Loo. Datalog and emerging applications: An interactive tutorial. In *SIGMOD*, pages 1213–1216, 2011.

[24] Frank K. Hwang and Shen Lin. A simple algorithm for merging two disjoint linearly-ordered sets. *SIAM J. Comput.*, 1(1):31–39, 1972.

[25] N. Immerman. *Descriptive Complexity*. Springer, 1999.

[26] Jure Leskovec and Andrej Krevl. SNAP Datasets: Stanford large network dataset collection. `http://snap.stanford.edu/data`, June 2014.

[27] Leonid Libkin. SQL's three-valued logic and certain answers. In *ICDT*, 2015. To appear.

[28] Bertram Ludäscher. *Integration of Active and Deductive Database Rules*, volume 45 of *DISDBIS*. Infix Verlag, St. Augustin, Germany, 1998.

[29] David Maier and David S. Warren. *Computing With Logic: Logic Programming With Prolog*. Addison-Wesley, 1988.

[30] Alexandra Meliou and Dan Suciu. Tiresias: The database oracle for how-to queries. In *SIGMOD*, pages 337–348, 2012.

[31] Hung Q. Ngo, Ely Porat, Christopher Ré, and Atri Rudra. Worst-case optimal join algorithms: [extended abstract]. In *PODS*, pages 37–48, 2012.

[32] Dung Nguyen, Molham Aref, Martin Bravenboer, George Kollias, Hung Q. Ngo, Christopher Ré, and Atri Rudra. Join processing for graph patterns: An old dog with new tricks. arXiv:1503.04169, 2015.

[33] Feng Niu, Christopher Ré, AnHai Doan, and Jude W. Shavlik. Tuffy: Scaling up statistical inference in markov logic networks using an rdbms. *PVLDB*, 4(6):373–384, 2011.

[34] Tim Furche Andrew Sellers Oege de Moor, Georg Gottlob, editor. *Datalog Reloaded: Proceedings of the First International Datalog 2.0 Workshop*. Springer, 2011.

[35] Chris Okasaki. *Purely Functional Data Structures*. Cambridge University Press, Cambridge, UK, 1999.

[36] Gurobi Optimization. Gurobi optimizer reference manual, 2015.

[37] Raimund Seidel and Cecilia R. Aragon. Randomized search trees. *Algorithmica*, 16(4/5):464–497, 1996.

[38] Timothy E. Sheard. Painless programming combining reduction and search: Design principles for embedding decision procedures in high-level languages. In *ICFP*, pages 89–102, 2012.

[39] Michael Stonebraker and Ugur Cetintemel. "One size fits all": An idea whose time has come and gone. In *ICDE*, pages 2–11, 2005.

[40] Todd L. Veldhuizen. Incremental maintenance for leapfrog triejoin. *CoRR*, abs/1303.5313, 2013.

[41] Todd L. Veldhuizen. Incremental maintenance for leapfrog triejoin. Technical Report LB1202, LogicBlox Inc., 2013. arXiv:1303.5313.

[42] Todd L. Veldhuizen. Leapfrog triejoin: A simple, worst-case optimal join algorithm. In *ICDT*, pages 96–106, 2014.

[43] Todd L. Veldhuizen. Transaction repair: Full serializability without locks. *CoRR*, abs/1403.5645, 2014.

Spark SQL: Relational Data Processing in Spark

Michael Armbrust[†], Reynold S. Xin[†], Cheng Lian[†], Yin Huai[†], Davies Liu[†], Joseph K. Bradley[†], Xiangrui Meng[†], Tomer Kaftan[‡], Michael J. Franklin[†‡], Ali Ghodsi[†], Matei Zaharia[†*]

[†]Databricks Inc. [*]MIT CSAIL [‡]AMPLab, UC Berkeley

ABSTRACT

Spark SQL is a new module in Apache Spark that integrates relational processing with Spark's functional programming API. Built on our experience with Shark, Spark SQL lets Spark programmers leverage the benefits of relational processing (*e.g.,* declarative queries and optimized storage), and lets SQL users call complex analytics libraries in Spark (*e.g.,* machine learning). Compared to previous systems, Spark SQL makes two main additions. First, it offers much tighter integration between relational and procedural processing, through a declarative DataFrame API that integrates with procedural Spark code. Second, it includes a highly extensible optimizer, Catalyst, built using features of the Scala programming language, that makes it easy to add composable rules, control code generation, and define extension points. Using Catalyst, we have built a variety of features (*e.g.,* schema inference for JSON, machine learning types, and query federation to external databases) tailored for the complex needs of modern data analysis. We see Spark SQL as an evolution of both SQL-on-Spark and of Spark itself, offering richer APIs and optimizations while keeping the benefits of the Spark programming model.

Categories and Subject Descriptors

H.2 [**Database Management**]: Systems

Keywords

Databases; Data Warehouse; Machine Learning; Spark; Hadoop

1 Introduction

Big data applications require a mix of processing techniques, data sources and storage formats. The earliest systems designed for these workloads, such as MapReduce, gave users a powerful, but low-level, procedural programming interface. Programming such systems was onerous and required manual optimization by the user to achieve high performance. As a result, multiple new systems sought to provide a more productive user experience by offering relational interfaces to big data. Systems like Pig, Hive, Dremel and Shark [29, 36, 25, 38] all take advantage of declarative queries to provide richer automatic optimizations.

SIGMOD'15, May 31–June 4, 2015, Melbourne, Victoria, Australia.

ACM 978-1-4503-2758-9/15/05 ...$15.00.
http://dx.doi.org/10.1145/2723372.2742797.

While the popularity of relational systems shows that users often prefer writing declarative queries, the relational approach is insufficient for many big data applications. First, users want to perform ETL to and from various data sources that might be semi- or unstructured, requiring custom code. Second, users want to perform advanced analytics, such as machine learning and graph processing, that are challenging to express in relational systems. In practice, we have observed that most data pipelines would ideally be expressed with a combination of both relational queries and complex procedural algorithms. Unfortunately, these two classes of systems—relational and procedural—have until now remained largely disjoint, forcing users to choose one paradigm or the other.

This paper describes our effort to combine both models in Spark SQL, a major new component in Apache Spark [39]. Spark SQL builds on our earlier SQL-on-Spark effort, called Shark. Rather than forcing users to pick between a relational or a procedural API, however, Spark SQL lets users seamlessly intermix the two.

Spark SQL bridges the gap between the two models through two contributions. First, Spark SQL provides a *DataFrame API* that can perform relational operations on both external data sources and Spark's built-in distributed collections. This API is similar to the widely used data frame concept in R [32], but evaluates operations lazily so that it can perform relational optimizations. Second, to support the wide range of data sources and algorithms in big data, Spark SQL introduces a novel extensible optimizer called *Catalyst.* Catalyst makes it easy to add data sources, optimization rules, and data types for domains such as machine learning.

The DataFrame API offers rich relational/procedural integration within Spark programs. DataFrames are collections of structured records that can be manipulated using Spark's procedural API, or using new relational APIs that allow richer optimizations. They can be created directly from Spark's built-in distributed collections of Java/Python objects, enabling relational processing in existing Spark programs. Other Spark components, such as the machine learning library, take and produce DataFrames as well. DataFrames are more convenient and more efficient than Spark's procedural API in many common situations. For example, they make it easy to compute multiple aggregates in one pass using a SQL statement, something that is difficult to express in traditional functional APIs. They also automatically store data in a columnar format that is significantly more compact than Java/Python objects. Finally, unlike existing data frame APIs in R and Python, DataFrame operations in Spark SQL go through a relational optimizer, Catalyst.

To support a wide variety of data sources and analytics workloads in Spark SQL, we designed an extensible query optimizer called Catalyst. Catalyst uses features of the Scala programming language, such as pattern-matching, to express composable rules in a Turing-complete language. It offers a general framework for transforming trees, which we use to perform analysis, planning, and runtime code generation. Through this framework, Catalyst can also be extended with new data sources, including semi-structured data such as JSON and "smart" data stores to which one can push filters (*e.g.*, HBase); with user-defined functions; and with user-defined types for domains such as machine learning. Functional languages are known to be well-suited for building compilers [37], so it is perhaps no surprise that they made it easy to build an extensible optimizer. We indeed have found Catalyst effective in enabling us to quickly add capabilities to Spark SQL, and since its release we have seen external contributors easily add them as well.

Spark SQL was released in May 2014, and is now one of the most actively developed components in Spark. As of this writing, Apache Spark is the most active open source project for big data processing, with over 400 contributors in the past year. Spark SQL has already been deployed in very large scale environments. For example, a large Internet company uses Spark SQL to build data pipelines and run queries on an 8000-node cluster with over 100 PB of data. Each individual query regularly operates on tens of terabytes. In addition, many users adopt Spark SQL not just for SQL queries, but in programs that combine it with procedural processing. For example, 2/3 of customers of Databricks Cloud, a hosted service running Spark, use Spark SQL within other programming languages. Performance-wise, we find that Spark SQL is competitive with SQL-only systems on Hadoop for relational queries. It is also up to 10× faster and more memory-efficient than naive Spark code in computations expressible in SQL.

More generally, we see Spark SQL as an important evolution of the core Spark API. While Spark's original functional programming API was quite general, it offered only limited opportunities for automatic optimization. Spark SQL simultaneously makes Spark accessible to more users and improves optimizations for existing ones. Within Spark, the community is now incorporating Spark SQL into more APIs: DataFrames are the standard data representation in a new "ML pipeline" API for machine learning, and we hope to expand this to other components, such as GraphX and streaming.

We start this paper with a background on Spark and the goals of Spark SQL (§2). We then describe the DataFrame API (§3), the Catalyst optimizer (§4), and advanced features we have built on Catalyst (§5). We evaluate Spark SQL in §6. We describe external research built on Catalyst in §7. Finally, §8 covers related work.

2 Background and Goals

2.1 Spark Overview

Apache Spark is a general-purpose cluster computing engine with APIs in Scala, Java and Python and libraries for streaming, graph processing and machine learning [6]. Released in 2010, it is to our knowledge one of the most widely-used systems with a "language-integrated" API similar to DryadLINQ [20], and the most active open source project for big data processing. Spark had over 400 contributors in 2014, and is packaged by multiple vendors.

Spark offers a functional programming API similar to other recent systems [20, 11], where users manipulate distributed collections called Resilient Distributed Datasets (RDDs) [39]. Each RDD is a collection of Java or Python objects partitioned across a cluster. RDDs can be manipulated through operations like `map`, `filter`, and `reduce`, which take functions in the programming language and ship them to nodes on the cluster. For example, the Scala code below counts lines starting with "ERROR" in a text file:

```
lines = spark.textFile("hdfs://...")
errors = lines.filter(s => s.contains("ERROR"))
println(errors.count())
```

This code creates an RDD of strings called `lines` by reading an HDFS file, then transforms it using `filter` to obtain another RDD, `errors`. It then performs a `count` on this data.

RDDs are fault-tolerant, in that the system can recover lost data using the lineage graph of the RDDs (by rerunning operations such as the `filter` above to rebuild missing partitions). They can also explicitly be cached in memory or on disk to support iteration [39].

One final note about the API is that RDDs are evaluated *lazily*. Each RDD represents a "logical plan" to compute a dataset, but Spark waits until certain output operations, such as `count`, to launch a computation. This allows the engine to do some simple query optimization, such as pipelining operations. For instance, in the example above, Spark will pipeline reading lines from the HDFS file with applying the filter and computing a running count, so that it never needs to materialize the intermediate `lines` and `errors` results. While such optimization is extremely useful, it is also limited because the engine does not understand the structure of the data in RDDs (which is arbitrary Java/Python objects) or the semantics of user functions (which contain arbitrary code).

2.2 Previous Relational Systems on Spark

Our first effort to build a relational interface on Spark was Shark [38], which modified the Apache Hive system to run on Spark and implemented traditional RDBMS optimizations, such as columnar processing, over the Spark engine. While Shark showed good performance and good opportunities for integration with Spark programs, it had three important challenges. First, Shark could only be used to query external data stored in the Hive catalog, and was thus not useful for relational queries on data *inside* a Spark program (*e.g.*, on the `errors` RDD created manually above). Second, the only way to call Shark from Spark programs was to put together a SQL string, which is inconvenient and error-prone to work with in a modular program. Finally, the Hive optimizer was tailored for MapReduce and difficult to extend, making it hard to build new features such as data types for machine learning or support for new data sources.

2.3 Goals for Spark SQL

With the experience from Shark, we wanted to extend relational processing to cover native RDDs in Spark and a much wider range of data sources. We set the following goals for Spark SQL:

1. Support relational processing both within Spark programs (on native RDDs) and on external data sources using a programmer-friendly API.
2. Provide high performance using established DBMS techniques.
3. Easily support new data sources, including semi-structured data and external databases amenable to query federation.
4. Enable extension with advanced analytics algorithms such as graph processing and machine learning.

3 Programming Interface

Spark SQL runs as a library on top of Spark, as shown in Figure 1. It exposes SQL interfaces, which can be accessed through JDBC/ODBC or through a command-line console, as well as the DataFrame API integrated into Spark's supported programming languages. We start by covering the DataFrame API, which lets users intermix procedural and relational code. However, advanced functions can also be exposed in SQL through UDFs, allowing them to be invoked, for example, by business intelligence tools. We discuss UDFs in Section 3.7.

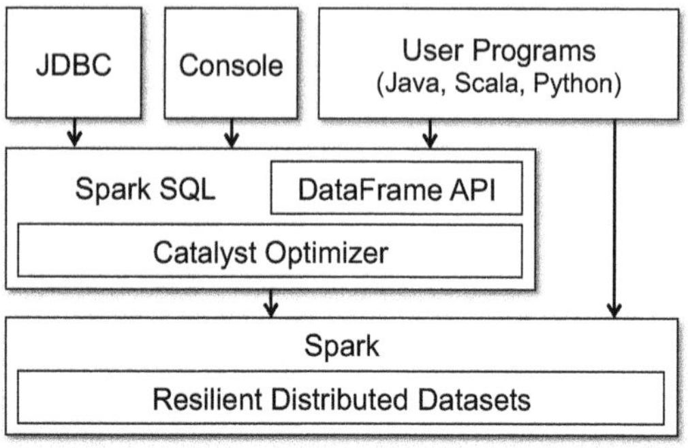

Figure 1: Interfaces to Spark SQL, and interaction with Spark.

3.1 DataFrame API

The main abstraction in Spark SQL's API is a DataFrame, a distributed collection of rows with the same schema. A DataFrame is equivalent to a table in a relational database, and can also be manipulated in similar ways to the "native" distributed collections in Spark (RDDs).[1] Unlike RDDs, DataFrames keep track of their schema and support various relational operations that lead to more optimized execution.

DataFrames can be constructed from tables in a system catalog (based on external data sources) or from existing RDDs of native Java/Python objects (Section 3.5). Once constructed, they can be manipulated with various relational operators, such as `where` and `groupBy`, which take expressions in a domain-specific language (DSL) similar to data frames in R and Python [32, 30]. Each DataFrame can also be viewed as an RDD of Row objects, allowing users to call procedural Spark APIs such as `map`.[2]

Finally, unlike traditional data frame APIs, Spark DataFrames are lazy, in that each DataFrame object represents a *logical plan* to compute a dataset, but no execution occurs until the user calls a special "output operation" such as `save`. This enables rich optimization across all operations that were used to build the DataFrame.

To illustrate, the Scala code below defines a DataFrame from a table in Hive, derives another based on it, and prints a result:

```
ctx = new HiveContext()
users = ctx.table("users")
young = users.where(users("age") < 21)
println(young.count())
```

In this code, `users` and `young` are DataFrames. The snippet `users("age") < 21` is an *expression* in the data frame DSL, which is captured as an abstract syntax tree rather than representing a Scala function as in the traditional Spark API. Finally, each DataFrame simply represents a logical plan (*i.e.*, read the users table and filter for age < 21). When the user calls `count`, which is an output operation, Spark SQL builds a physical plan to compute the final result. This might include optimizations such as only scanning the "age" column of the data if its storage format is columnar, or even using an index in the data source to count the matching rows.

We next cover the details of the DataFrame API.

3.2 Data Model

Spark SQL uses a nested data model based on Hive [19] for tables and DataFrames. It supports all major SQL data types, including boolean, integer, double, decimal, string, date, and timestamp, as well as complex (i.e., non-atomic) data types: structs, arrays, maps and unions. Complex data types can also be nested together to create more powerful types. Unlike many traditional DBMSes, Spark SQL provides first-class support for complex data types in the query language and the API. In addition, Spark SQL also supports user-defined types, as described in Section 4.4.2.

Using this type system, we have been able to accurately model data from a variety of sources and formats, including Hive, relational databases, JSON, and native objects in Java/Scala/Python.

3.3 DataFrame Operations

Users can perform relational operations on DataFrames using a domain-specific language (DSL) similar to R data frames [32] and Python Pandas [30]. DataFrames support all common relational operators, including projection (`select`), filter (`where`), `join`, and aggregations (`groupBy`). These operators all take *expression* objects in a limited DSL that lets Spark capture the structure of the expression. For example, the following code computes the number of female employees in each department.

```
employees
  .join(dept, employees("deptId") === dept("id"))
  .where(employees("gender") === "female")
  .groupBy(dept("id"), dept("name"))
  .agg(count("name"))
```

Here, `employees` is a DataFrame, and `employees("deptId")` is an expression representing the `deptId` column. Expression objects have many operators that return new expressions, including the usual comparison operators (*e.g.*, === for equality test, > for greater than) and arithmetic ones (+, -, etc). They also support aggregates, such as `count("name")`. All of these operators build up an abstract syntax tree (AST) of the expression, which is then passed to Catalyst for optimization. This is unlike the native Spark API that takes functions containing arbitrary Scala/Java/Python code, which are then opaque to the runtime engine. For a detailed listing of the API, we refer readers to Spark's official documentation [6].

Apart from the relational DSL, DataFrames can be registered as temporary tables in the system catalog and queried using SQL. The code below shows an example:

```
users.where(users("age") < 21)
     .registerTempTable("young")
ctx.sql("SELECT count(*), avg(age) FROM young")
```

SQL is sometimes convenient for computing multiple aggregates concisely, and also allows programs to expose datasets through JDBC/ODBC. The DataFrames registered in the catalog are still unmaterialized views, so that optimizations can happen *across* SQL and the original DataFrame expressions. However, DataFrames can also be materialized, as we discuss in Section 3.6.

3.4 DataFrames versus Relational Query Languages

While on the surface, DataFrames provide the same operations as relational query languages like SQL and Pig [29], we found that they can be significantly easier for users to work with thanks to their integration in a full programming language. For example, users can break up their code into Scala, Java or Python functions that pass DataFrames between them to build a logical plan, and will still benefit from optimizations across the *whole* plan when they run an output operation. Likewise, developers can use control structures like if statements and loops to structure their work. One user said that the DataFrame API is "concise and declarative like SQL, except I can name intermediate results," referring to how it is easier to structure computations and debug intermediate steps.

To simplify programming in DataFrames, we also made API analyze logical plans *eagerly* (*i.e.*, to identify whether the column

[1]We chose the name DataFrame because it is similar to structured data libraries in R and Python, and designed our API to resemble those.

[2]These Row objects are constructed on the fly and do not necessarily represent the internal storage format of the data, which is typically columnar.

names used in expressions exist in the underlying tables, and whether their data types are appropriate), even though query results are computed lazily. Thus, Spark SQL reports an error as soon as user types an invalid line of code instead of waiting until execution. This is again easier to work with than a large SQL statement.

3.5 Querying Native Datasets

Real-world pipelines often extract data from heterogeneous sources and run a wide variety of algorithms from different programming libraries. To interoperate with procedural Spark code, Spark SQL allows users to construct DataFrames directly against RDDs of objects native to the programming language. Spark SQL can automatically infer the schema of these objects using reflection. In Scala and Java, the type information is extracted from the language's type system (from JavaBeans and Scala case classes). In Python, Spark SQL samples the dataset to perform schema inference due to the dynamic type system.

For example, the Scala code below defines a DataFrame from an RDD of `User` objects. Spark SQL automatically detects the names ("name" and "age") and data types (string and int) of the columns.

```
case class User(name: String, age: Int)

// Create an RDD of User objects
usersRDD = spark.parallelize(
  List(User("Alice", 22), User("Bob", 19)))

// View the RDD as a DataFrame
usersDF = usersRDD.toDF
```

Internally, Spark SQL creates a logical data scan operator that points to the RDD. This is compiled into a physical operator that accesses fields of the native objects. It is important to note that this is very different from traditional object-relational mapping (ORM). ORMs often incur expensive conversions that translate an entire object into a different format. In contrast, Spark SQL accesses the native objects in-place, extracting only the fields used in each query.

The ability to query native datasets lets users run optimized relational operations within existing Spark programs. In addition, it makes it simple to combine RDDs with external structured data. For example, we could join the `users` RDD with a table in Hive:

```
views = ctx.table("pageviews")
usersDF.join(views, usersDF("name") === views("user"))
```

3.6 In-Memory Caching

Like Shark before it, Spark SQL can materialize (often referred to as "cache") hot data in memory using columnar storage. Compared with Spark's native cache, which simply stores data as JVM objects, the columnar cache can reduce memory footprint by an order of magnitude because it applies columnar compression schemes such as dictionary encoding and run-length encoding. Caching is particularly useful for interactive queries and for the iterative algorithms common in machine learning. It can be invoked by calling `cache()` on a DataFrame.

3.7 User-Defined Functions

User-defined functions (UDFs) have been an important extension point for database systems. For example, MySQL relies on UDFs to provide basic support for JSON data. A more advanced example is MADLib's use of UDFs to implement machine learning algorithms for Postgres and other database systems [12]. However, database systems often require UDFs to be defined in a separate programming environment that is different from the primary query interfaces. Spark SQL's DataFrame API supports inline definition of UDFs, without the complicated packaging and registration process found in other database systems. This feature has proven crucial for the adoption of the API.

In Spark SQL, UDFs can be registered inline by passing Scala, Java or Python functions, which may use the full Spark API internally. For example, given a `model` object for a machine learning model, we could register its prediction function as a UDF:

```
val model: LogisticRegressionModel = ...

ctx.udf.register("predict",
  (x: Float, y: Float) => model.predict(Vector(x, y)))

ctx.sql("SELECT predict(age, weight) FROM users")
```

Once registered, the UDF can also be used via the JDBC/ODBC interface by business intelligence tools. In addition to UDFs that operate on scalar values like the one here, one can define UDFs that operate on an entire table by taking its name, as in MADLib [12], and use the distributed Spark API within them, thus exposing advanced analytics functions to SQL users. Finally, because UDF definitions and query execution are expressed using the same general-purpose language (*e.g.,* Scala or Python), users can debug or profile the entire program using standard tools.

The example above demonstrates a common use case in many pipelines, *i.e.,* one that employs both relational operators and advanced analytics methods that are cumbersome to express in SQL. The DataFrame API lets developers seamlessly mix these methods.

4 Catalyst Optimizer

To implement Spark SQL, we designed a new extensible optimizer, Catalyst, based on functional programming constructs in Scala. Catalyst's extensible design had two purposes. First, we wanted to make it easy to add new optimization techniques and features to Spark SQL, especially to tackle various problems we were seeing specifically with "big data" (*e.g.,* semistructured data and advanced analytics). Second, we wanted to enable external developers to extend the optimizer—for example, by adding data source specific rules that can push filtering or aggregation into external storage systems, or support for new data types. Catalyst supports both rule-based and cost-based optimization.

While extensible optimizers have been proposed in the past, they have typically required a complex domain specific language to specify rules, and an "optimizer compiler" to translate the rules into executable code [17, 16]. This leads to a significant learning curve and maintenance burden. In contrast, Catalyst uses standard features of the Scala programming language, such as pattern-matching [14], to let developers use the full programming language while still making rules easy to specify. Functional languages were designed in part to build compilers, so we found Scala well-suited to this task. Nonetheless, Catalyst is, to our knowledge, the first production-quality query optimizer built on such a language.

At its core, Catalyst contains a general library for representing *trees* and applying *rules* to manipulate them.[3] On top of this framework, we have built libraries specific to relational query processing (*e.g.,* expressions, logical query plans), and several sets of rules that handle different phases of query execution: analysis, logical optimization, physical planning, and code generation to compile parts of queries to Java bytecode. For the latter, we use another Scala feature, quasiquotes [34], that makes it easy to generate code at runtime from composable expressions. Finally, Catalyst offers several public extension points, including external data sources and user-defined types.

[3] Cost-based optimization is performed by generating multiple plans using rules, and then computing their costs.

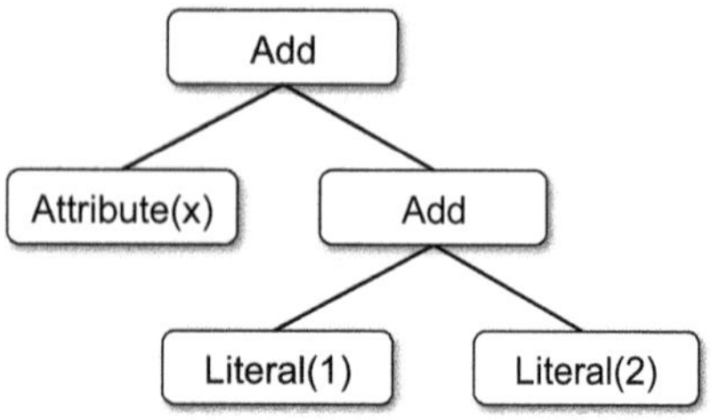

Figure 2: Catalyst tree for the expression `x+(1+2)`.

4.1 Trees

The main data type in Catalyst is a *tree* composed of *node* objects. Each node has a node type and zero or more children. New node types are defined in Scala as subclasses of the `TreeNode` class. These objects are immutable and can be manipulated using functional transformations, as discussed in the next subsection.

As a simple example, suppose we have the following three node classes for a very simple expression language:[4]

- `Literal(value: Int)`: a constant value
- `Attribute(name: String)`: an attribute from an input row, *e.g.,* "x"
- `Add(left: TreeNode, right: TreeNode)`: sum of two expressions.

These classes can be used to build up trees; for example, the tree for the expression `x+(1+2)`, shown in Figure 2, would be represented in Scala code as follows:

```
Add(Attribute(x), Add(Literal(1), Literal(2)))
```

4.2 Rules

Trees can be manipulated using *rules*, which are functions from a tree to another tree. While a rule can run arbitrary code on its input tree (given that this tree is just a Scala object), the most common approach is to use a set of *pattern matching* functions that find and replace subtrees with a specific structure.

Pattern matching is a feature of many functional languages that allows extracting values from potentially nested structures of algebraic data types. In Catalyst, trees offer a `transform` method that applies a pattern matching function recursively on all nodes of the tree, transforming the ones that match each pattern to a result. For example, we could implement a rule that folds Add operations between constants as follows:

```
tree.transform {
  case Add(Literal(c1), Literal(c2)) => Literal(c1+c2)
}
```

Applying this to the tree for `x+(1+2)`, in Figure 2, would yield the new tree `x+3`. The `case` keyword here is Scala's standard pattern matching syntax [14], and can be used to match on the type of an object as well as give names to extracted values (`c1` and `c2` here).

The pattern matching expression that is passed to `transform` is a *partial function*, meaning that it only needs to match to a subset of all possible input trees. Catalyst will tests which parts of a tree a given rule applies to, automatically skipping over and descending into subtrees that do not match. This ability means that rules only need to reason about the trees where a given optimization applies and not those that do not match. Thus, rules do not need to be modified as new types of operators are added to the system.

[4]We use Scala syntax for classes here, where each class's fields are defined in parentheses, with their types given using a colon.

Rules (and Scala pattern matching in general) can match multiple patterns in the same `transform` call, making it very concise to implement multiple transformations at once:

```
tree.transform {
  case Add(Literal(c1), Literal(c2)) => Literal(c1+c2)
  case Add(left, Literal(0)) => left
  case Add(Literal(0), right) => right
}
```

In practice, rules may need to execute multiple times to fully transform a tree. Catalyst groups rules into *batches*, and executes each batch until it reaches a *fixed point*, that is, until the tree stops changing after applying its rules. Running rules to fixed point means that each rule can be simple and self-contained, and yet still eventually have larger global effects on a tree. In the example above, repeated application would constant-fold larger trees, such as `(x+0)+(3+3)`. As another example, a first batch might analyze an expression to assign types to all of the attributes, while a second batch might use these types to do constant folding. After each batch, developers can also run sanity checks on the new tree (*e.g.,* to see that all attributes were assigned types), often also written via recursive matching.

Finally, rule conditions and their bodies can contain arbitrary Scala code. This gives Catalyst more power than domain specific languages for optimizers, while keeping it concise for simple rules.

In our experience, functional transformations on immutable trees make the whole optimizer very easy to reason about and debug. They also enable parallelization in the optimizer, although we do not yet exploit this.

4.3 Using Catalyst in Spark SQL

We use Catalyst's general tree transformation framework in four phases, shown in Figure 3: (1) analyzing a logical plan to resolve references, (2) logical plan optimization, (3) physical planning, and (4) code generation to compile parts of the query to Java bytecode. In the physical planning phase, Catalyst may generate multiple plans and compare them based on cost. All other phases are purely rule-based. Each phase uses different types of tree nodes; Catalyst includes libraries of nodes for expressions, data types, and logical and physical operators. We now describe each of these phases.

4.3.1 Analysis

Spark SQL begins with a relation to be computed, either from an abstract syntax tree (AST) returned by a SQL parser, or from a DataFrame object constructed using the API. In both cases, the relation may contain unresolved attribute references or relations: for example, in the SQL query `SELECT col FROM sales`, the type of `col`, or even whether it is a valid column name, is not known until we look up the table `sales`. An attribute is called unresolved if we do not know its type or have not matched it to an input table (or an alias). Spark SQL uses Catalyst rules and a Catalog object that tracks the tables in all data sources to resolve these attributes. It starts by building an "unresolved logical plan" tree with unbound attributes and data types, then applies rules that do the following:

- Looking up relations by name from the catalog.
- Mapping named attributes, such as `col`, to the input provided given operator's children.
- Determining which attributes refer to the same value to give them a unique ID (which later allows optimization of expressions such as `col = col`).
- Propagating and coercing types through expressions: for example, we cannot know the type of `1 + col` until we have resolved `col` and possibly cast its subexpressions to compatible types.

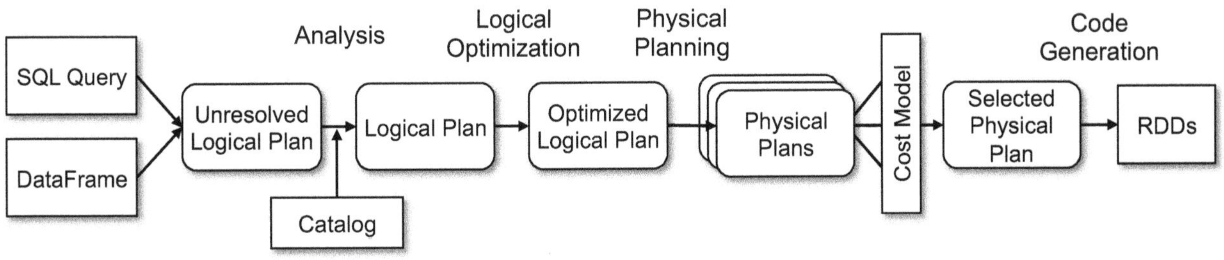

Figure 3: Phases of query planning in Spark SQL. Rounded rectangles represent Catalyst trees.

In total, the rules for the analyzer are about 1000 lines of code.

4.3.2 Logical Optimization

The logical optimization phase applies standard rule-based optimizations to the logical plan. These include constant folding, predicate pushdown, projection pruning, null propagation, Boolean expression simplification, and other rules. In general, we have found it extremely simple to add rules for a wide variety of situations. For example, when we added the fixed-precision `DECIMAL` type to Spark SQL, we wanted to optimize aggregations such as sums and averages on `DECIMAL`s with small precisions; it took 12 lines of code to write a rule that finds such decimals in `SUM` and `AVG` expressions, and casts them to unscaled 64-bit `LONG`s, does the aggregation on that, then converts the result back. A simplified version of this rule that only optimizes SUM expressions is reproduced below:

```
object DecimalAggregates extends Rule[LogicalPlan] {
  /** Maximum number of decimal digits in a Long */
  val MAX_LONG_DIGITS = 18

  def apply(plan: LogicalPlan): LogicalPlan = {
    plan transformAllExpressions {
      case Sum(e @ DecimalType.Expression(prec, scale))
              if prec + 10 <= MAX_LONG_DIGITS =>
        MakeDecimal(Sum(LongValue(e)), prec + 10, scale)
    }
}
```

As another example, a 12-line rule optimizes `LIKE` expressions with simple regular expressions into `String.startsWith` or `String.contains` calls. The freedom to use arbitrary Scala code in rules made these kinds of optimizations, which go beyond pattern-matching the structure of a subtree, easy to express. In total, the logical optimization rules are 800 lines of code.

4.3.3 Physical Planning

In the physical planning phase, Spark SQL takes a logical plan and generates one or more physical plans, using physical operators that match the Spark execution engine. It then selects a plan using a cost model. At the moment, cost-based optimization is only used to select join algorithms: for relations that are known to be small, Spark SQL uses a broadcast join, using a peer-to-peer broadcast facility available in Spark.[5] The framework supports broader use of cost-based optimization, however, as costs can be estimated recursively for a whole tree using a rule. We thus intend to implement richer cost-based optimization in the future.

The physical planner also performs rule-based physical optimizations, such as pipelining projections or filters into one Spark `map` operation. In addition, it can push operations from the logical plan into data sources that support predicate or projection pushdown. We will describe the API for these data sources in Section 4.4.1.

In total, the physical planning rules are about 500 lines of code.

[5] Table sizes are estimated if the table is cached in memory or comes from an external file, or if it is the result of a subquery with a `LIMIT`.

4.3.4 Code Generation

The final phase of query optimization involves generating Java bytecode to run on each machine. Because Spark SQL often operates on in-memory datasets, where processing is CPU-bound, we wanted to support code generation to speed up execution. Nonetheless, code generation engines are often complicated to build, amounting essentially to a compiler. Catalyst relies on a special feature of the Scala language, quasiquotes [34], to make code generation simpler. Quasiquotes allow the programmatic construction of abstract syntax trees (ASTs) in the Scala language, which can then be fed to the Scala compiler at runtime to generate bytecode. We use Catalyst to transform a tree representing an expression in SQL to an AST for Scala code to evaluate that expression, and then compile and run the generated code.

As a simple example, consider the Add, Attribute and Literal tree nodes introduced in Section 4.2, which allowed us to write expressions such as `(x+y)+1`. Without code generation, such expressions would have to be interpreted for each row of data, by walking down a tree of Add, Attribute and Literal nodes. This introduces large amounts of branches and virtual function calls that slow down execution. With code generation, we can write a function to translate a specific expression tree to a Scala AST as follows:

```
def compile(node: Node): AST = node match {
  case Literal(value) => q"$value"
  case Attribute(name) => q"row.get($name)"
  case Add(left, right) =>
    q"${compile(left)} + ${compile(right)}"
}
```

The strings beginning with `q` are quasiquotes, meaning that although they look like strings, they are parsed by the Scala compiler at compile time and represent ASTs for the code within. Quasiquotes can have variables or other ASTs spliced into them, indicated using `$` notation. For example, `Literal(1)` would become the Scala AST for 1, while `Attribute("x")` becomes `row.get("x")`. In the end, a tree like `Add(Literal(1), Attribute("x"))` becomes an AST for a Scala expression like `1+row.get("x")`.

Quasiquotes are type-checked at compile time to ensure that only appropriate ASTs or literals are substituted in, making them significantly more useable than string concatenation, and they result directly in a Scala AST instead of running the Scala parser at runtime. Moreover, they are highly composable, as the code generation rule for each node does not need to know how the trees returned by its children were built. Finally, the resulting code is further optimized by the Scala compiler in case there are expression-level optimizations that Catalyst missed. Figure 4 shows that quasiquotes let us generate code with performance similar to hand-tuned programs.

We have found quasiquotes very straightforward to use for code generation, and we observed that even new contributors to Spark SQL could quickly add rules for new types of expressions. Quasiquotes also work well with our goal of running on native Java

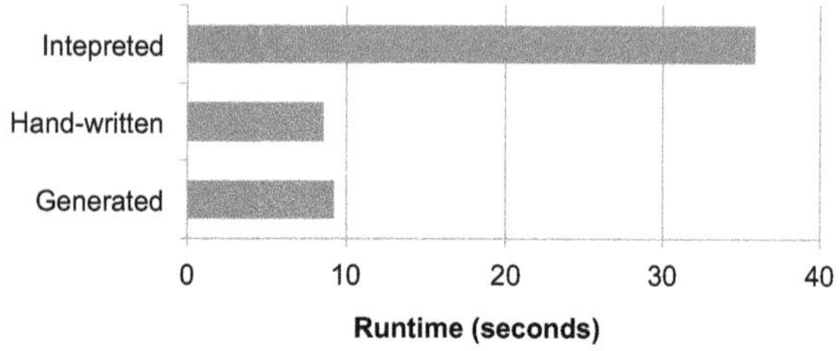

Figure 4: A comparision of the performance evaluating the expresion `x+x+x`, where `x` is an integer, 1 billion times.

objects: when accessing fields from these objects, we can code-generate a direct access to the required field, instead of having to copy the object into a Spark SQL Row and use the Row's accessor methods. Finally, it was straightforward to combine code-generated evaluation with interpreted evaluation for expressions we do not yet generate code for, since the Scala code we compile can directly call into our expression interpreter.

In total, Catalyst's code generator is about 700 lines of code.

4.4 Extension Points

Catalyst's design around composable rules makes it easy for users and third-party libraries to extend. Developers can add batches of rules to each phase of query optimization at runtime, as long as they adhere to the contract of each phase (*e.g.,* ensuring that analysis resolves all attributes). However, to make it even simpler to add some types of extensions without understanding Catalyst rules, we have also defined two narrower public extension points: data sources and user-defined types. These still rely on facilities in the core engine to interact with the rest of the rest of the optimizer.

4.4.1 Data Sources

Developers can define a new data source for Spark SQL using several APIs, which expose varying degrees of possible optimization. All data sources must implement a `createRelation` function that takes a set of key-value parameters and returns a `BaseRelation` object for that relation, if one can be successfully loaded. Each `BaseRelation` contains a schema and an optional estimated size in bytes.[6] For instance, a data source representing MySQL may take a table name as a parameter, and ask MySQL for an estimate of the table size.

To let Spark SQL read the data, a `BaseRelation` can implement one of several interfaces that let them expose varying degrees of sophistication. The simplest, `TableScan`, requires the relation to return an RDD of `Row` objects for all of the data in the table. A more advanced `PrunedScan` takes an array of column names to read, and should return Rows containing only those columns. A third interface, `PrunedFilteredScan`, takes both desired column names and an array of Filter objects, which are a subset of Catalyst's expression syntax, allowing predicate pushdown.[7] The filters are advisory, *i.e.,* the data source should attempt to return only rows passing each filter, but it is allowed to return false positives in the case of filters that it cannot evaluate. Finally, a CatalystScan interface is given a complete sequence of Catalyst expression trees to use in predicate pushdown, though they are again advisory.

These interfaces allow data sources to implement various degrees of optimization, while still making it easy for developers to add simple data sources of virtually any type. We and others have used the interface to implement the following data sources:

- CSV files, which simply scan the whole file, but allow users to specify a schema.
- Avro [4], a self-describing binary format for nested data.
- Parquet [5], a columnar file format for which we support column pruning as well as filters.
- A JDBC data source that scans ranges of a table from an RDBMS in parallel and pushes filters into the RDBMS to minimize communication.

To use these data sources, programmers specify their package names in SQL statements, passing key-value pairs for configuration options. For example, the Avro data source takes a path to the file:

```
CREATE TEMPORARY TABLE messages
USING com.databricks.spark.avro
OPTIONS (path "messages.avro")
```

All data sources can also expose network locality information, *i.e.,* which machines each partition of the data is most efficient to read from. This is exposed through the RDD objects they return, as RDDs have a built-in API for data locality [39].

Finally, similar interfaces exist for writing data to an existing or new table. These are simpler because Spark SQL just provides an RDD of Row objects to be written.

4.4.2 User-Defined Types (UDTs)

One feature we wanted to allow advanced analytics in Spark SQL was user-defined types. For example, machine learning applications may need a vector type, and graph algorithms may need types for representing a graph, which is possible over relational tables [15]. Adding new types can be challenging, however, as data types pervade all aspects of the execution engine. For example, in Spark SQL, the built-in data types are stored in a columnar, compressed format for in-memory caching (Section 3.6), and in the data source API from the previous section, we need to expose all possible data types to data source authors.

In Catalyst, we solve this issue by mapping user-defined types to structures composed of Catalyst's built-in types, described in Section 3.2. To register a Scala type as a UDT, users provide a mapping from an object of their class to a Catalyst Row of built-in types, and an inverse mapping back. In user code, they can now use the Scala type in objects that they query with Spark SQL, and it will be converted to built-in types under the hood. Likewise, they can register UDFs (see Section 3.7) that operate directly on their type.

As a short example, suppose we want to register two-dimensional points (x, y) as a UDT. We can represent such vectors as two `DOUBLE` values. To register the UDT, we write the following:

```
class PointUDT extends UserDefinedType[Point] {
  def dataType = StructType(Seq( // Our native structure
    StructField("x", DoubleType),
    StructField("y", DoubleType)
  ))
  def serialize(p: Point) = Row(p.x, p.y)
  def deserialize(r: Row) =
    Point(r.getDouble(0), r.getDouble(1))
}
```

After registering this type, Points will be recognized within native objects that Spark SQL is asked to convert to DataFrames, and will be passed to UDFs defined on Points. In addition, Spark SQL will store Points in a columnar format when caching data (compressing `x` and `y` as separate columns), and Points will be writable to all of Spark SQL's data sources, which will see them as pairs of `DOUBLE`s. We use this capability in Spark's machine learning library, as we describe in Section 5.2.

[6]Unstructured data sources can also take a desired schema as a parameter; for example, there is a CSV file data source that lets users specify column names and types.

[7]At the moment, Filters include equality, comparisons against a constant, and `IN` clauses, each on one attribute.

```
{
  "text": "This is a tweet about #Spark",
  "tags": ["#Spark"],
  "loc": {"lat": 45.1, "long": 90}
}

{
  "text": "This is another tweet",
  "tags": [],
  "loc": {"lat": 39, "long": 88.5}
}

{
  "text": "A #tweet without #location",
  "tags": ["#tweet", "#location"]
}
```

Figure 5: A sample set of JSON records, representing tweets.

```
text STRING NOT NULL,
tags ARRAY<STRING NOT NULL> NOT NULL,
loc STRUCT<lat FLOAT NOT NULL, long FLOAT NOT NULL>
```

Figure 6: Schema inferred for the tweets in Figure 5.

5 Advanced Analytics Features

In this section, we describe three features we added to Spark SQL specifically to handle challenges in "big data" environments. First, in these environments, data is often unstructured or semistructured. While parsing such data procedurally is possible, it leads to lengthy boilerplate code. To let users query the data right away, Spark SQL includes a schema inference algorithm for JSON and other semistructured data. Second, large-scale processing often goes beyond aggregation and joins to machine learning on the data. We describe how Spark SQL is being incorporated into a new high-level API for Spark's machine learning library [26]. Last, data pipelines often combine data from disparate storage systems. Building on the data sources API in Section 4.4.1, Spark SQL supports query federation, allowing a single program to efficiently query disparate sources. These features all build on the Catalyst framework.

5.1 Schema Inference for Semistructured Data

Semistructured data is common in large-scale environments because it is easy to produce and to add fields to over time. Among Spark users, we have seen very high usage of JSON for input data. Unfortunately, JSON is cumbersome to work with in a procedural environment like Spark or MapReduce: most users resorted to ORM-like libraries (*e.g.,* Jackson [21]) to map JSON structures to Java objects, or some tried parsing each input record directly with lower-level libraries.

In Spark SQL, we added a JSON data source that automatically infers a schema from a set of records. For example, given the JSON objects in Figure 5, the library infers the schema shown in Figure 6. Users can simply register a JSON file as a table and query it with syntax that accesses fields by their path, such as:

```
SELECT loc.lat, loc.long FROM tweets
WHERE text LIKE '%Spark%' AND tags IS NOT NULL
```

Our schema inference algorithm works in one pass over the data, and can also be run on a sample of the data if desired. It is related to prior work on schema inference for XML and object databases [9, 18, 27], but simpler because it only infers a static tree structure, without allowing recursive nesting of elements at arbitrary depths.

Specifically, the algorithm attempts to infer a tree of `STRUCT` types, each of which may contain atoms, arrays, or other `STRUCT`s. For each field defined by a distinct path from the root JSON object (*e.g.,* `tweet.loc.latitude`), the algorithm finds the most specific Spark SQL data type that matches observed instances of the field. For example, if all occurrences of that field are integers that fit into 32 bits, it will infer `INT`; if they are larger, it will use `LONG` (64-bit) or `DECIMAL` (arbitrary precision); if there are also fractional values, it will use `FLOAT`. For fields that display multiple types, Spark SQL uses `STRING` as the most generic type, preserving the original JSON representation. And for fields that contain arrays, it uses the same "most specific supertype" logic to determine an element type from all the observed elements. We implement this algorithm using a single `reduce` operation over the data, which starts with schemata (*i.e.,* trees of types) from each individual record and merges them using an associative "most specific supertype" function that generalizes the types of each field. This makes the algorithm both single-pass and communication-efficient, as a high degree of reduction happens locally on each node.

As a short example, note how in Figures 5 and 6, the algorithm generalized the types of `loc.lat` and `loc.long`. Each field appears as an integer in one record and a floating-point number in another, so the algorithm returns `FLOAT`. Note also how for the `tags` field, the algorithm inferred an array of strings that cannot be null.

In practice, we have found this algorithm to work well with real-world JSON datasets. For example, it correctly identifies a usable schema for JSON tweets from Twitter's firehose, which contain around 100 distinct fields and a high degree of nesting. Multiple Databricks customers have also successfully applied it to their internal JSON formats.

In Spark SQL, we also use the same algorithm for inferring schemas of RDDs of Python objects (see Section 3), as Python is not statically typed so an RDD can contain multiple object types. In the future, we plan to add similar inference for CSV files and XML. Developers have found the ability to view these types of datasets as tables and immediately query them or join them with other data extremely valuable for their productivity.

5.2 Integration with Spark's Machine Learning Library

As an example of Spark SQL's utility in other Spark modules, MLlib, Spark's machine learning library, introduced a new high-level API that uses DataFrames [26]. This new API is based on the concept of machine learning *pipelines*, an abstraction in other high-level ML libraries like SciKit-Learn [33]. A pipeline is a graph of transformations on data, such as feature extraction, normalization, dimensionality reduction, and model training, each of which exchange *datasets*. Pipelines are a useful abstraction because ML workflows have many steps; representing these steps as composable elements makes it easy to change parts of the pipeline or to search for tuning parameters at the level of the whole workflow.

To exchange data between pipeline stages, MLlib's developers needed a format that was compact (as datasets can be large) yet flexible, allowing multiple types of fields to be stored for each record. For example, a user may start with records that contain text fields as well as numeric ones, then run a featurization algorithm such as TF-IDF on the text to turn it into a vector, normalize one of the other fields, perform dimensionality reduction on the whole set of features, etc. To represent datasets, the new API uses DataFrames, where each column represents a feature of the data. All algorithms that can be called in pipelines take a name for the input column(s) and output column(s), and can thus be called on any subset of the fields and produce new ones. This makes it easy for developers to build complex pipelines while retaining the original data for each record. To illustrate the API, Figure 7 shows a short pipeline and the schemas of DataFrames created.

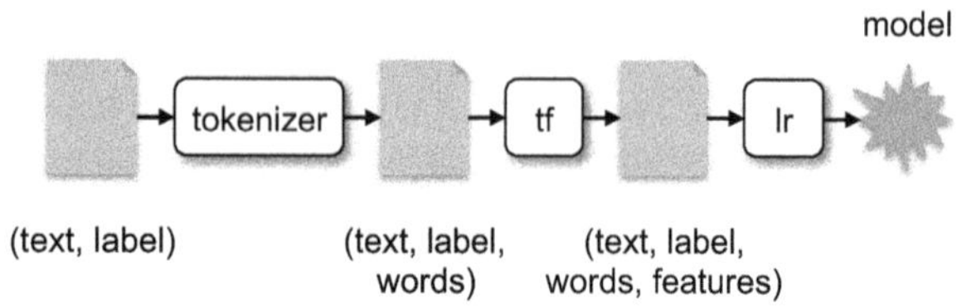


```
data = <DataFrame of (text, label) records>

tokenizer = Tokenizer()
  .setInputCol("text").setOutputCol("words")
tf = HashingTF()
  .setInputCol("words").setOutputCol("features")
lr = LogisticRegression()
  .setInputCol("features")

pipeline = Pipeline().setStages([tokenizer, tf, lr])
model = pipeline.fit(data)
```

Figure 7: A short MLlib pipeline and the Python code to run it. We start with a DataFrame of (text, label) records, tokenize the text into words, run a term frequency featurizer (`HashingTF`) to get a feature vector, then train logistic regression.

The main piece of work MLlib had to do to use Spark SQL was to create a user-defined type for vectors. This vector UDT can store both sparse and dense vectors, and represents them as four primitive fields: a boolean for the type (dense or sparse), a size for the vector, an array of indices (for sparse coordinates), and an array of double values (either the non-zero coordinates for sparse vectors or all coordinates otherwise). Apart from DataFrames' utility for tracking and manipulating columns, we also found them useful for another reason: they made it much easier to expose MLlib's new API in all of Spark's supported programming languages. Previously, each algorithm in MLlib took objects for domain-specific concepts (*e.g.,* a labeled point for classification, or a (user, product) rating for recommendation), and each of these classes had to be implemented in the various languages (*e.g.,* copied from Scala to Python). Using DataFrames everywhere made it much simpler to expose all algorithms in all languages, as we only need data conversions in Spark SQL, where they already exist. This is especially important as Spark adds bindings for new programming languages.

Finally, using DataFrames for storage in MLlib also makes it very easy to expose all its algorithms in SQL. We can simply define a MADlib-style UDF, as described in Section 3.7, which will internally call the algorithm on a table. We are also exploring APIs to expose pipeline construction in SQL.

5.3 Query Federation to External Databases

Data pipelines often combine data from heterogeneous sources. For example, a recommendation pipeline might combine traffic logs with a user profile database and users' social media streams. As these data sources often reside in different machines or geographic locations, naively querying them can be prohibitively expensive. Spark SQL data sources leverage Catalyst to push predicates down into the data sources whenever possible.

For example, the following uses the JDBC data source and the JSON data source to join two tables together to find the traffic log for the most recently registered users. Conveniently, both data sources can automatically infer the schema without users having to define it. The JDBC data source will also push the filter predicate down into MySQL to reduce the amount of data transferred.

```
CREATE TEMPORARY TABLE users USING jdbc
OPTIONS(driver "mysql" url "jdbc:mysql://userDB/users")

CREATE TEMPORARY TABLE logs
USING json OPTIONS (path "logs.json")

SELECT users.id, users.name, logs.message
FROM users JOIN logs WHERE users.id = logs.userId
AND users.registrationDate > "2015-01-01"
```

Under the hood, the JDBC data source uses the PrunedFilteredScan interface in Section 4.4.1, which gives it both the names of the columns requested and simple predicates (equality, comparison and `IN` clauses) on these columns. In this case, the JDBC data source will run the following query on MySQL:[8]

```
SELECT users.id, users.name FROM users
WHERE users.registrationDate > "2015-01-01"
```

In future Spark SQL releases, we are also looking to add predicate pushdown for key-value stores such as HBase and Cassandra, which support limited forms of filtering.

6 Evaluation

We evaluate the performance of Spark SQL on two dimensions: SQL query processing performance and Spark program performance. In particular, we demonstrate that Spark SQL's extensible architecture not only enables a richer set of functionalities, but brings substantial performance improvements over previous Spark-based SQL engines. In addition, for Spark application developers, the DataFrame API can bring substantial speedups over the native Spark API while making Spark programs more concise and easier to understand. Finally, applications that combine relational and procedural queries run faster on the integrated Spark SQL engine than by running SQL and procedural code as separate parallel jobs.

6.1 SQL Performance

We compared the performance of Spark SQL against Shark and Impala [23] using the AMPLab big data benchmark [3], which uses a web analytics workload developed by Pavlo et al. [31]. The benchmark contains four types of queries with different parameters performing scans, aggregation, joins and a UDF-based MapReduce job. We used a cluster of six EC2 `i2.xlarge` machines (one master, five workers) each with 4 cores, 30 GB memory and an 800 GB SSD, running HDFS 2.4, Spark 1.3, Shark 0.9.1 and Impala 2.1.1. The dataset was 110 GB of data after compression using the columnar Parquet format [5].

Figure 8 shows the results for each query, grouping by the query type. Queries 1–3 have different parameters varying their selectivity, with 1a, 2a, etc being the most selective and 1c, 2c, etc being the least selective and processing more data. Query 4 uses a Python-based Hive UDF that was not directly supported in Impala, but was largely bound by the CPU cost of the UDF.

We see that in all queries, Spark SQL is substantially faster than Shark and generally competitive with Impala. The main reason for the difference with Shark is code generation in Catalyst (Section 4.3.4), which reduces CPU overhead. This feature makes Spark SQL competitive with the C++ and LLVM based Impala engine in many of these queries. The largest gap from Impala is in query 3a where Impala chooses a better join plan because the selectivity of the queries makes one of the tables very small.

6.2 DataFrames vs. Native Spark Code

In addition to running SQL queries, Spark SQL can also help non-SQL developers write simpler and more efficient Spark code through the DataFrame API. Catalyst can perform optimizations on

[8]The JDBC data source also supports "sharding" a source table by a particular column and reading different ranges of it in parallel.

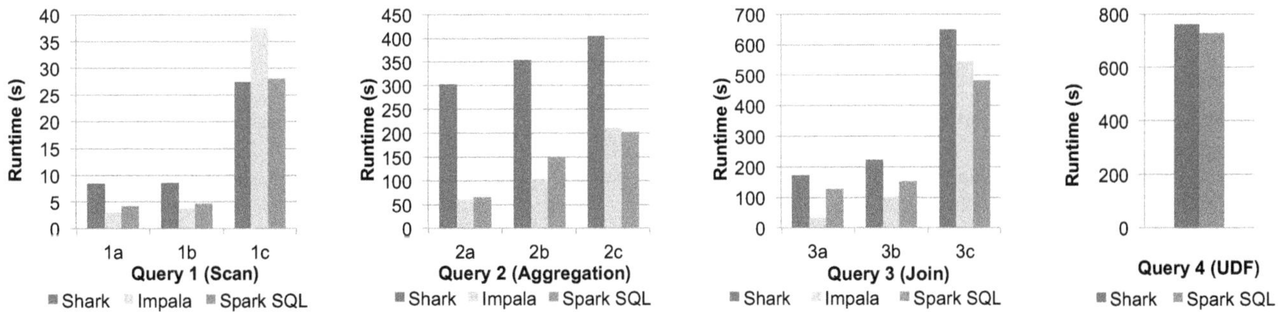

Figure 8: Performance of Shark, Impala and Spark SQL on the big data benchmark queries [31].

DataFrame operations that are hard to do with hand written code, such as predicate pushdown, pipelining, and automatic join selection. Even without these optimizations, the DataFrame API can result in more efficient execution due to code generation. This is especially true for Python applications, as Python is typically slower than the JVM.

For this evaluation, we compared two implementations of a Spark program that does a distributed aggregation. The dataset consists of 1 billion integer pairs, `(a, b)` with 100,000 distinct values of `a`, on the same five-worker `i2.xlarge` cluster as in the previous section. We measure the time taken to compute the average of `b` for each value of `a`. First, we look at a version that computes the average using the `map` and `reduce` functions in the Python API for Spark:

```
sum_and_count = \
  data.map(lambda x: (x.a, (x.b, 1))) \
      .reduceByKey(lambda x, y: (x[0]+y[0], x[1]+y[1])) \
      .collect()
[(x[0], x[1][0] / x[1][1]) for x in sum_and_count]
```

In contrast, the same program can written as a simple manipulation using the DataFrame API:

```
df.groupBy("a").avg("b")
```

Figure 9, shows that the DataFrame version of the code outperforms the hand written Python version by 12×, in addition to being much more concise. This is because in the DataFrame API, only the logical plan is constructed in Python, and all physical execution is compiled down into native Spark code as JVM bytecode, resulting in more efficient execution. In fact, the DataFrame version also outperforms a Scala version of the Spark code above by 2×. This is mainly due to code generation: the code in the DataFrame version avoids expensive allocation of key-value pairs that occurs in hand-written Scala code.

6.3 Pipeline Performance

The DataFrame API can also improve performance in applications that combine relational and procedural processing, by letting developers write all operations in a single program and pipelining computation across relational and procedural code. As a simple example, we consider a two-stage pipeline that selects a subset of text messages from a corpus and computes the most frequent words. Although very simple, this can model some real-world pipelines, *e.g.,* computing the most popular words used in tweets by a specific demographic.

In this experiment, we generated a synthetic dataset of 10 billion messages in HDFS. Each message contained on average 10 words drawn from an English dictionary. The first stage of the pipeline uses a relational filter to select roughly 90% of the messages. The second stage computes the word count.

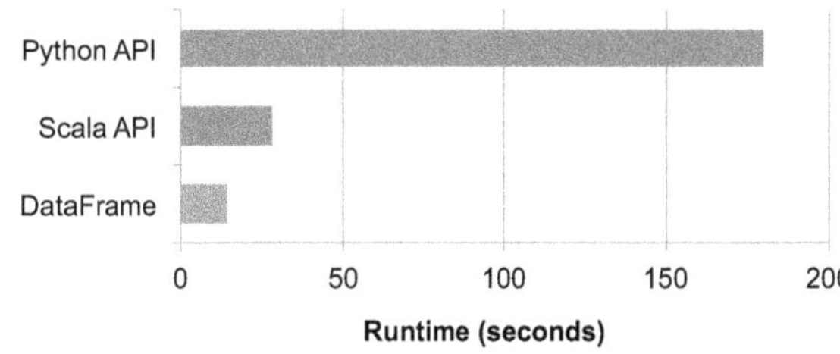

Figure 9: Performance of an aggregation written using the native Spark Python and Scala APIs versus the DataFrame API.

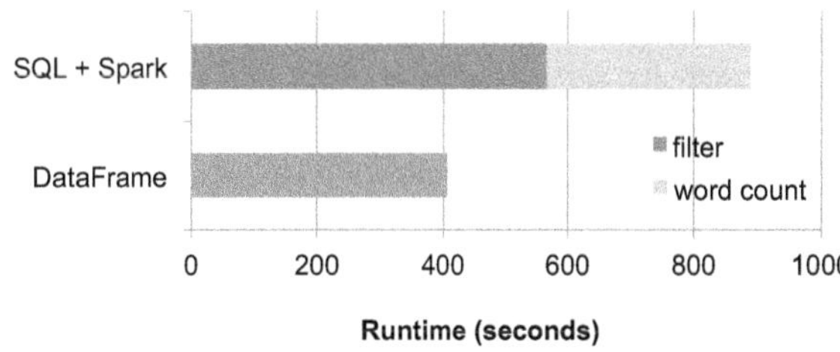

Figure 10: Performance of a two-stage pipeline written as a separate Spark SQL query and Spark job (above) and an integrated DataFrame job (below).

First, we implemented the pipeline using a separate SQL query followed by a Scala-based Spark job, as might occur in environments that run separate relational and procedural engines (*e.g.,* Hive and Spark). We then implemented a combined pipeline using the DataFrame API, *i.e.,* using DataFrame's relational operators to perform the filter, and using the RDD API to perform a word count on the result. Compared with the first pipeline, the second pipeline avoids the cost of saving the whole result of the SQL query to an HDFS file as an intermediate dataset before passing it into the Spark job, because SparkSQL pipelines the `map` for the word count with the relational operators for the filtering. Figure 10 compares the runtime performance of the two approaches. In addition to being easier to understand and operate, the DataFrame-based pipeline also improves performance by 2×.

7 Research Applications

In addition to the immediately practical production use cases of Spark SQL, we have also seen significant interest from researchers working on more experimental projects. We outline two research projects that leverage the extensibility of Catalyst: one in approximate query processing and one in genomics.

7.1 Generalized Online Aggregation

Zeng et al. have used Catalyst in their work on improving the generality of online aggregation [40]. This work generalizes the execution of online aggregation to support arbitrarily nested aggregate queries. It allows users to view the progress of executing queries by seeing results computed over a fraction of the total data. These partial results also include accuracy measures, letting the user stop the query when sufficient accuracy has been reached.

In order to implement this system inside of Spark SQL, the authors add a new operator to represent a relation that has been broken up into sampled batches. During query planning a call to `transform` is used to replace the original full query with several queries, each of which operates on a successive sample of the data.

However, simply replacing the full dataset with samples is not sufficient to compute the correct answer in an online fashion. Operations such as standard aggregation must be replaced with stateful counterparts that take into account both the current sample and the results of previous batches. Furthermore, operations that might filter out tuples based on approximate answers must be replaced with versions that can take into account the current estimated errors.

Each of these transformations can be expressed as Catalyst rules that modify the operator tree until it produces correct online answers. Tree fragments that are not based on sampled data are ignored by these rules and can execute using the standard code path. By using Spark SQL as a basis, the authors were able to implement a fairly complete prototype in approximately 2000 lines of code.

7.2 Computational Genomics

A common operation in computational genomics involves inspecting overlapping regions based on a numerical offsets. This problem can be represented as a join with inequality predicates. Consider two datasets, `a` and `b`, with a schema of `(start LONG, end LONG)`. The range join operation can be expressed in SQL as follows:

```
SELECT * FROM a JOIN b
WHERE a.start < a.end
  AND b.start < b.end
  AND a.start < b.start
  AND b.start < a.end
```

Without special optimization, the preceding query would be executed by many systems using an inefficient algorithm such as a nested loop join. In contrast, a specialized system could compute the answer to this join using an interval tree. Researchers in the ADAM project [28] were able to build a special planning rule into a version of Spark SQL to perform such computations efficiently, allowing them to leverage the standard data manipulation abilities alongside specialized processing code. The changes required were approximately 100 lines of code.

8 Related Work

Programming Model Several systems have sought to combine relational processing with the procedural processing engines initially used for large clusters. Of these, Shark [38] is the closest to Spark SQL, running on the same engine and offering the same combination of relational queries and advanced analytics. Spark SQL improves on Shark through a richer and more programmer-friendly API, DataFrames, where queries can be combined in a modular way using constructs in the host programming language (see Section 3.4). It also allows running relational queries directly on native RDDs, and supports a wide range of data sources beyond Hive.

One system that inspired Spark SQL's design was DryadLINQ [20], which compiles language-integrated queries in C# to a distributed DAG execution engine. LINQ queries are also relational but can operate directly on C# objects. Spark SQL goes beyond DryadLINQ by also providing a DataFrame interface similar to common data science libraries [32, 30], an API for data sources and types, and support for iterative algorithms through execution on Spark.

Other systems use only a relational data model internally and relegate procedural code to UDFs. For example, Hive and Pig [36, 29] offer relational query languages but have widely used UDF interfaces. ASTERIX [8] has a semi-structured data model internally. Stratosphere [2] also has a semi-structured model, but offers APIs in Scala and Java that let users easily call UDFs. PIQL [7] likewise provides a Scala DSL. Compared to these systems, Spark SQL integrates more closely with native Spark applications by being able to directly query data in user-defined classes (native Java/Python objects), and lets developers mix procedural and relational APIs in the same language. In addition, through the Catalyst optimizer, Spark SQL implements both optimizations (*e.g.,* code generation) and other functionality (*e.g.,* schema inference for JSON and machine learning data types) that are not present in most large-scale computing frameworks. We believe that these features are essential to offering an integrated, easy-to-use environment for big data.

Finally, data frame APIs have been built both for single machines [32, 30] and clusters [13, 10]. Unlike previous APIs, Spark SQL optimizes DataFrame computations with a relational optimizer.

Extensible Optimizers The Catalyst optimizer shares similar goals with extensible optimizer frameworks such as EXODUS [17] and Cascades [16]. Traditionally, however, optimizer frameworks have required a domain-specific language to write rules in, as well as an "optimizer compiler" to translate them to runnable code. Our major improvement here is to build our optimizer using standard features of a functional programming language, which provide the same (and often greater) expressivity while decreasing the maintenance burden and learning curve. Advanced language features helped with many areas of Catalyst—for example, our approach to code generation using quasiquotes (Section 4.3.4) is one of the simplest and most composable approaches to this task that we know. While extensibility is hard to measure quantitatively, one promising indication is that Spark SQL had over 50 external contributors in the first 8 months after its release.

For code generation, LegoBase [22] recently proposed an approach using generative programming in Scala, which would be possible to use instead of quasiquotes in Catalyst.

Advanced Analytics Spark SQL builds on recent work to run advanced analytics algorithms on large clusters, including platforms for iterative algorithms [39] and graph analytics [15, 24]. The desire to expose analytics functions is also shared with MADlib [12], though the approach there is different, as MADlib had to use the limited interface of Postgres UDFs, while Spark SQL's UDFs can be full-fledged Spark programs. Finally, techniques including Sinew and Invisible Loading [35, 1] have sought to provide and optimize queries over semi-structured data such as JSON. We hope to apply some of these techniques in our JSON data source.

9 Conclusion

We have presented Spark SQL, a new module in Apache Spark providing rich integration with relational processing. Spark SQL extends Spark with a declarative DataFrame API to allow relational processing, offering benefits such as automatic optimization, and letting users write complex pipelines that mix relational and complex analytics. It supports a wide range of features tailored to large-scale data analysis, including semi-structured data, query federation, and data types for machine learning. To enable these features, Spark SQL is based on an extensible optimizer called Catalyst that makes it easy to add optimization rules, data sources and data types by embedding into the Scala programming language. User feedback and benchmarks show that Spark SQL makes it significantly simpler and more efficient to write data pipelines that mix relational and procedural processing, while offering substantial speedups over previous SQL on Spark engines.

Spark SQL is open source at `http://spark.apache.org`.

10 Acknowledgments

We would like to thank Cheng Hao, Tayuka Ueshin, Tor Myklebust, Daoyuan Wang, and the rest of the Spark SQL contributors so far. We would also like to thank John Cieslewicz and the other members of the F1 team at Google for early discussions on the Catalyst optimizer. The work of authors Franklin and Kaftan was supported in part by: NSF CISE Expeditions Award CCF-1139158, LBNL Award 7076018, and DARPA XData Award FA8750-12-2-0331, and gifts from Amazon Web Services, Google, SAP, The Thomas and Stacey Siebel Foundation, Adatao, Adobe, Apple, Inc., Blue Goji, Bosch, C3Energy, Cisco, Cray, Cloudera, EMC2, Ericsson, Facebook, Guavus, Huawei, Informatica, Intel, Microsoft, NetApp, Pivotal, Samsung, Schlumberger, Splunk, Virdata and VMware.

11 References

[1] A. Abouzied, D. J. Abadi, and A. Silberschatz. Invisible loading: Access-driven data transfer from raw files into database systems. In *EDBT*, 2013.

[2] A. Alexandrov et al. The Stratosphere platform for big data analytics. *The VLDB Journal*, 23(6):939–964, Dec. 2014.

[3] AMPLab big data benchmark. https://amplab.cs.berkeley.edu/benchmark.

[4] Apache Avro project. http://avro.apache.org.

[5] Apache Parquet project. http://parquet.incubator.apache.org.

[6] Apache Spark project. http://spark.apache.org.

[7] M. Armbrust, N. Lanham, S. Tu, A. Fox, M. J. Franklin, and D. A. Patterson. The case for PIQL: a performance insightful query language. In *SOCC*, 2010.

[8] A. Behm et al. Asterix: towards a scalable, semistructured data platform for evolving-world models. *Distributed and Parallel Databases*, 29(3):185–216, 2011.

[9] G. J. Bex, F. Neven, and S. Vansummeren. Inferring XML schema definitions from XML data. In *VLDB*, 2007.

[10] BigDF project. https://github.com/AyasdiOpenSource/bigdf.

[11] C. Chambers, A. Raniwala, F. Perry, S. Adams, R. R. Henry, R. Bradshaw, and N. Weizenbaum. FlumeJava: Easy, efficient data-parallel pipelines. In *PLDI*, 2010.

[12] J. Cohen, B. Dolan, M. Dunlap, J. Hellerstein, and C. Welton. MAD skills: new analysis practices for big data. *VLDB*, 2009.

[13] DDF project. http://ddf.io.

[14] B. Emir, M. Odersky, and J. Williams. Matching objects with patterns. In *ECOOP 2007 – Object-Oriented Programming, volume 4609 of LNCS*, pages 273–298. Springer, 2007.

[15] J. E. Gonzalez, R. S. Xin, A. Dave, D. Crankshaw, M. J. Franklin, and I. Stoica. GraphX: Graph processing in a distributed dataflow framework. In *OSDI*, 2014.

[16] G. Graefe. The Cascades framework for query optimization. *IEEE Data Engineering Bulletin*, 18(3), 1995.

[17] G. Graefe and D. DeWitt. The EXODUS optimizer generator. In *SIGMOD*, 1987.

[18] J. Hegewald, F. Naumann, and M. Weis. XStruct: efficient schema extraction from multiple and large XML documents. In *ICDE Workshops*, 2006.

[19] Hive data definition language. https://cwiki.apache.org/confluence/display/Hive/LanguageManual+DDL.

[20] M. Isard and Y. Yu. Distributed data-parallel computing using a high-level programming language. In *SIGMOD*, 2009.

[21] Jackson JSON processor. http://jackson.codehaus.org.

[22] Y. Klonatos, C. Koch, T. Rompf, and H. Chafi. Building efficient query engines in a high-level language. *PVLDB*, 7(10):853–864, 2014.

[23] M. Kornacker et al. Impala: A modern, open-source SQL engine for Hadoop. In *CIDR*, 2015.

[24] Y. Low et al. Distributed GraphLab: a framework for machine learning and data mining in the cloud. *VLDB*, 2012.

[25] S. Melnik et al. Dremel: interactive analysis of web-scale datasets. *Proc. VLDB Endow.*, 3:330–339, Sept 2010.

[26] X. Meng, J. Bradley, E. Sparks, and S. Venkataraman. ML pipelines: a new high-level API for MLlib. https://databricks.com/blog/2015/01/07/ml-pipelines-a-new-high-level-api-for-mllib.html.

[27] S. Nestorov, S. Abiteboul, and R. Motwani. Extracting schema from semistructured data. In *ICDM*, 1998.

[28] F. A. Nothaft, M. Massie, T. Danford, Z. Zhang, U. Laserson, C. Yeksigian, J. Kottalam, A. Ahuja, J. Hammerbacher, M. Linderman, M. J. Franklin, A. D. Joseph, and D. A. Patterson. Rethinking data-intensive science using scalable analytics systems. In *SIGMOD*, 2015.

[29] C. Olston, B. Reed, U. Srivastava, R. Kumar, and A. Tomkins. Pig Latin: a not-so-foreign language for data processing. In *SIGMOD*, 2008.

[30] `pandas` Python data analysis library. http://pandas.pydata.org.

[31] A. Pavlo et al. A comparison of approaches to large-scale data analysis. In *SIGMOD*, 2009.

[32] R project for statistical computing. http://www.r-project.org.

[33] scikit-learn: machine learning in Python. http://scikit-learn.org.

[34] D. Shabalin, E. Burmako, and M. Odersky. Quasiquotes for Scala, a technical report. Technical Report 185242, École Polytechnique Fédérale de Lausanne, 2013.

[35] D. Tahara, T. Diamond, and D. J. Abadi. Sinew: A SQL system for multi-structured data. In *SIGMOD*, 2014.

[36] A. Thusoo et al. Hive–a petabyte scale data warehouse using Hadoop. In *ICDE*, 2010.

[37] P. Wadler. Monads for functional programming. In *Advanced Functional Programming*, pages 24–52. Springer, 1995.

[38] R. S. Xin, J. Rosen, M. Zaharia, M. J. Franklin, S. Shenker, and I. Stoica. Shark: SQL and rich analytics at scale. In *SIGMOD*, 2013.

[39] M. Zaharia et al. Resilient distributed datasets: a fault-tolerant abstraction for in-memory cluster computing. In *NSDI*, 2012.

[40] K. Zeng et al. G-OLA: Generalized online aggregation for interactive analysis on big data. In *SIGMOD*, 2015.

Author Index

www.ingramcontent.com/pod-product-compliance
Ingram Content Group UK Ltd.
Pitfield, Milton Keynes, MK11 3LW, UK
UKHW051419290926
15471UKWH00009B/1677

9 781450 338639